DICTIONARY OF

MEDIEVAL LATIN

FROM BRITISH SOURCES

FASCICULE I

A—B

DICTIONARY OF MEDIEVAL LATIN FROM BRITISH SOURCES

Fascicule I A–B

PREPARED BY R. E. LATHAM, M.A.

UNDER THE DIRECTION OF A COMMITTEE
APPOINTED BY THE BRITISH ACADEMY

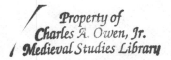

LONDON · *Published for* THE BRITISH ACADEMY
by OXFORD UNIVERSITY PRESS
1975

Oxford University Press, Ely House, London W. 1

GLASGOW NEW YORK TORONTO MELBOURNE WELLINGTON
CAPE TOWN IBADAN NAIROBI DAR ES SALAAM LUSAKA ADDIS ABABA
DELHI BOMBAY CALCUTTA MADRAS KARACHI LAHORE DACCA
KUALA LUMPUR SINGAPORE HONG KONG TOKYO

ISBN 0 19 725948 0

Printed in Great Britain
at the University Press, Oxford
by Vivian Ridler
Printer to the University

FORMER MEMBERS OF COMMITTEES

BRITISH COMMITTEE

Rev. Prof. J. H. Baxter (*Vice-Chairman* 1946–63)
Prof. H. E. Butler
The Very Rev. David Callus, O.P.
G. C. Coulton, F.B.A.
Sir David Evans, O.B.E.
Sir Cyril Flower, C.B., F.B.A.
Prof. V. H. Galbraith, F.B.A.
Sir Stephen Gaselee, K.C.M.G., C.B.E.
J. P. Gilson
Sir Israel Gollancz, F.B.A.
R. W. Hunt, F.B.A.
M. R. James, O.M., F.B.A.
Rev. Prof. C. Jenkins
Sir Hilary Jenkinson, C.B.E.
C. Johnson, C.B.E., F.B.A. (*Secretary* 1924–34)
H. C. Johnson, C.B., C.B.E. (*Secretary* 1934–70)
Sir Frederic Kenyon, G.B.E., K.C.B., F.B.A.
Prof. R. Klibansky
Prof. M. L. W. Laistner
Prof. W. M. Lindsay, F.B.A.
Prof. A. G. Little, F.B.A.
Prof. E. A. Lowe
Sir Henry Maxwell-Lyte, K.C.B., F.B.A. (*Chairman* 1924–41)
Prof. Sir Roger Mynors, F.B.A. (*Chairman* 1967–73)
C. T. Onions, C.B.E., F.B.A.
W. Page
Rev. C. Plummer, F.B.A.
Prof. Sir Maurice Powicke, F.B.A.
F. J. E. Raby, C.B., F.B.A. (*Chairman* 1963–6)
Prof. C. Singer
A. E. Stamp, C.B.
Sir Frank Stenton, F.B.A. (*Chairman* 1946–63)
Prof. A. Hamilton Thompson, F.B.A.
Prof. T. F. Tout, F.B.A.
E. Ashworth Underwood
Prof. Sir Paul Vinogradoff, F.B.A.
Rev. Prof. E. W. Watson
C. C. J. Webb, F.B.A.
Sir Mortimer Wheeler, C.H., C.I.E., F.R.S., F.B.A. (*Secretary of the British Academy* 1949–68)
Rev. Dom A. Wilmart, O.S.B.

SCOTTISH COMMITTEE

J. T. T. Brown
Rev. Prof. J. H. Baxter
W. R. Cunningham (*Secretary*)
J. Edwards
Prof. C. J. Fordyce
Prof. V. H. Galbraith, F.B.A.
Prof. J. D. Mackie
David Murray (*Chairman*)
Prof. J. S. Phillimore
D. Baird Smith, C.B.E.

IRISH COMMITTEE

E. Alton, M.R.I.A.
Prof. L. Bieler (*Secretary*)
Rev. Prof. T. Corcoran, S.J., M.R.I.A.
Rev. Prof. J. D'Alton
Rev. J. Fahey
Rev. A. Gwynn, S.J., M.R.I.A. (*Secretary*)
Prof. R. M. Henry, M.R.I.A.
Prof. J. Hogan, M.R.I.A.
Prof. E. MacNeill, M.R.I.A. (*Chairman*)
Prof. L. C. Purser, F.B.A., M.R.I.A.

AMERICAN COMMITTEE

Prof. C. A. Beeson (*Secretary*)
Rev. Prof. F. S. Betten, S.J.
Prof. H. Caplan
Prof. G. R. Coffman
Prof. R. J. Deferrari
Prof. G. H. Gerould
L. R. Lind (*Secretary*)
Prof. W. E. Lunt
Prof. M. R. P. McGuire
Prof. W. A. Morris
Prof. N. Neilson
Prof. J. S. P. Tatlock
Prof. J. F. Willard (*Chairman and Acting Secretary*)
Prof. G. E. Woodbine

PREFACE

THIS Dictionary is the result of a cumulative effort, whose origins can be traced back to 1913. In February of that year Mr. R. J. Whitwell made proposals to the British Academy for a new Dictionary of Medieval Latin to replace the great *Glossarium Mediae et Infimae Latinitatis* of Charles Dufresne, Seigneur du Cange, first issued in 1678 and supplemented by the learned Benedictines in 1733 and again by Dom Carpentier in 1766. Although this was twice reprinted in the nineteenth century, no effective revision was undertaken. The latest improvement, Didot's Paris edition by Henschel 1840–50, consisted mainly in the fusion of the six volumes of the *Glossarium* with the four volumes of Carpentier's supplement, adding little, if anything. No philological backbone was given to the work, examples were not consistently dated, and the printed texts were uncritical. Need was, therefore, felt for a new Dictionary edited to meet the requirements of modern scholarship.

Mr. Whitwell's proposals were formulated in a memorial signed by many distinguished scholars and addressed to the Council of the British Academy. The Council received the memorial with most favourable consideration and suggested that Mr. Whitwell should make a statement on the subject at the International Congress of Historical Studies, which was to meet in April 1913, so that the opinion of foreign scholars on the subject should be elicited. The project was duly presented to the Congress in a paper read by Mr. Whitwell, and a resolution was carried inviting the British Academy to consider and, if it thought fit, to propose in due course to the Union Académique Internationale a scheme for a new Medieval Latin Dictionary on lines and conditions to be determined. The Council of the Academy thereupon appointed a committee to discuss the project and report its findings. The committee held several meetings and received many offers of assistance; but with the outbreak of war in 1914 its proceedings were suspended.

In 1920 a new project for a Dictionary of Medieval Latin was launched through the U.A.I. with the co-operation of the British Academy. This envisaged an international dictionary covering a limited period (eventually defined as A.D. 800–1200), based on material supplied by each country, and also a series of national dictionaries covering the whole Middle Ages. In spite of setbacks due to the 1939 war and its aftermath, it became possible in 1957 for the U.A.I., with the financial help of UNESCO, to issue a preliminary fascicule of the international *Novum Glossarium Mediae Latinitatis* covering the letter L under the editorship of Professor Franz Blatt of Aarhus. This has since been followed by further fascicules covering M, N, and O. The production of the *Novum Glossarium* is supervised by the U.A.I. through an International Committee, which latterly worked for many years under the chairmanship of Professor J. H. Baxter of St. Andrews. It has also maintained contact with national committees responsible for launching national or regional dictionaries covering most of the area once comprised in Latin Christendom.

In Britain two committees were appointed by the British Academy in 1924 to collect excerpts (mainly by recruiting unpaid volunteer labour) from British and Irish sources, one with the primary object of providing material for the international dictionary, the other drawing upon later sources with a view to the eventual production of a Dictionary of British Medieval Latin. As a convenient date for British purposes, the dividing line was fixed at the compilation of Domesday Book (1086). In 1930 the two committees were amalgamated under the chairmanship of Sir Henry Maxwell-Lyte, Deputy Keeper of the Public Records, who was succeeded after his death in 1941 by Sir Frank Stenton. From the beginning the committee concerned with the later period had the assistance of an American committee, whose chairman, Professor J. F. Willard, organized the services of a great number of voluntary readers of texts in the United States. Similar committees were formed for Scotland in 1927 and for Ireland in 1931, with responsibility for work on Scottish and Irish sources respectively. Substantial contributions continued to be received from these three committees up to the outbreak of war in 1939 and for some years after. But by 1950 the American and Scottish Committees had ceased to function, and in 1968 a reconstructed Irish Committee decided to embark on a separate project of an Irish (or Insular Celtic) Dictionary for the period before 1200, while continuing to work with the British Committee in so far as the two projects might overlap.

One of the first tasks of the British Committee had been to prepare a preliminary list of potential sources for the projected international and national dictionaries within their area. This resulted in the *Index of British and Irish Writers* A.D. *400–1520*, compiled by Professor Baxter, Professor Willard, and Mr. Charles Johnson of the Public Record Office, published in 1932 in Volume VII of the *Bulletin du Cange* (*ALMA*). Concurrently with this work, proposals were adopted in 1928 for the publication of a preliminary Word-List, with the primary aim of 'interesting students in the progress of the future Dictionary and enlisting their help in the collection of further material, and in the elucidation of individual words'. In 1934 this was published by the Oxford University Press as a *Medieval Latin Word-list from British and Irish Sources*, edited by Professor Baxter, responsible for the pre-Domesday period, and Mr. Johnson (with the assistance of Dr. Phyllis Abrahams), responsible for the later period. Apart from its main object, this work was found to meet a widely felt need and was reissued five times.

After the publication of the *Word-List* the work of collecting and sorting slips continued; but, so far as practicable, it was concentrated on making good the more remediable defects in the range of sources used, particularly in writings on technical subjects. Readers were instructed to omit words and usages marked in the *Word-List* with an asterisk, indicating that sufficient examples had been received for the given meaning and period. And, as before, they were told to make slips only for words obviously non-Classical or Classical words used in a non-Classical manner. This formula lent itself to a considerable variety of interpretation, perhaps to the ultimate benefit of the Dictionary. By 1950 enough new material had been collected, especially for the later period, to justify the preparation of a revised and enlarged edition of the *Word-List*. This, edited by Mr. R. E. Latham, was published in 1965 as the *Revised Word-List of Medieval Latin from British and Irish Sources*.

With this publication in the press, the Committee regarded its immediate task as accomplished and in 1963 submitted proposals to the British Academy for the appointment of a new committee to undertake a full-scale National Dictionary of Medieval Latin, covering the whole period from the sixth century to the sixteenth. These proposals were accepted by the Academy, which has adopted the Dictionary as an official project. Dr. F. J. E. Raby was appointed chairman of the new committee, its other members being Dr. R. W. Hunt, Mr. H. C. Johnson, Sir Roger Mynors, and Mr. Latham. Subsequent additions to the Committee have been Professor C. N. L. Brooke, Professor C. R. Cheney, Mr. J. R. Ede, Mr. A. B. E. Hood, Dr. J. D. Latham, Dr. F. Taylor, Dr. M. Winterbottom, and the late Professor F. Wormald. Mr. D. F. Allen and Dr. N. J. Williams, successively secretaries to the British Academy, have taken part in its discussions. After Dr. Raby's death in 1966, the chair was occupied by Sir Roger Mynors and on the latter's resignation in 1973 by Mr. Johnson.

Mr. Latham was appointed full-time editor of the Dictionary from the date of his retirement from the Public Record Office in 1967, with Mrs. H. K. Thomson as assistant editor. Later Mrs. A. H. Powell has been appointed junior assistant editor, and valuable service has been rendered by three successive part-time assistants, Miss V. Elsley, Mr. I. W. Rowlands, and Miss J. Batty. The editor and his staff have maintained contact with the editor of the *Novum Glossarium*, supplying copies of their slips for the period A.D. 800–1200, and contributing to the correction of the proofs.

This first fascicule of the Dictionary, covering the letters A and B, represents approximately one-eighth of the entire work. It is based on material used for the *Revised Word-List*, supplemented by some further reading, particularly in order to provide a framework of examples of continuing Classical usage (see Note on Editorial Method). The pre-Conquest material, in view of the many new texts and editions published in the past forty years, has been largely revised by the editorial staff, with some help from members of the Committee and others. Mr. Latham has been responsible for the selection and arrangement of the entries and has written the Note on Editorial Method. Mrs. Thomson has been primarily responsible for the Bibliography.

The publication has been made possible by the continued financial support of the British Academy and by the hospitality of successive heads of the Public Record Office, first extended to the post-Conquest committee by its chairman, Sir Henry Maxwell-Lyte, in providing a meeting place for the committee, storage room for its growing accumulation of slips, access to a library and repository of manuscript sources, and a centre for its activities, not to speak of the help freely given by various members of the Office staff. The Committee is no less indebted to the army of voluntary readers, whose often arduous labours over a period of fifty years have assembled the basic material of the Dictionary from a wide range of sources, many of them as yet unprinted. It is impossible here to render more than a collective tribute to these workers and to the many scholars who have helped in the solution of particular problems. But among those who are happily still active in this field special acknowledgement is due to Dom Frederick Hockey and Mr. J. H. Ward for their conscientious excerpting of texts and to Mr. John Harvey for his help in bringing to notice and elucidating sources relating to architecture.

Finally the present Committee is very conscious of its debt to its own former members and the members of its associated committees who have not lived to see the work enter on its final phase.

H. C. JOHNSON

On 19 December 1973, soon after the writing of the above preface, the Committee suffered a grave loss in the death of Mr. H. C. Johnson. During his forty-three years of active membership he had made a unique contribution to every aspect of its work, not least by his labours as a diligent and perspicacious excerptor of texts on a wide range of subjects. His place as Chairman has been taken by Dr. R. W. Hunt, F.B.A.

A NOTE ON EDITORIAL METHOD

Scope of the work

This dictionary is designed to present a comprehensive picture of the Latin language current in Britain from the sixth century to the sixteenth. The earliest literary source listed in the bibliography is Gildas *De Excidio Britanniae* (c550); the latest is Camden's *Britannia* (1586), included mainly for its antiquarian interest. Sources later than 1550 are normally excluded, though some use has been made of Latin records in the Medieval tradition as late as the seventeenth century (*cf. accomputare, adurere 3 b, archipresbyter c*). In view of the project launched by the Royal Irish Academy for a Dictionary of Insular Celtic Latin, most Irish sources prior to 1200, together with certain Welsh sources, have been excluded. Some Anglo-Irish sources of later date have been included, together with such documents as the Norman Rolls and Gascon Rolls, regarded as records (mostly preserved in England) of the administration of estates held by an English ruler. The scope of the work embraces letters from abroad contained in such series as Rymer's *Foedera* and Theiner's *Monumenta Hiberniae et Scotiae*, besides the writings of Britons resident overseas, from Boniface to Duns, and of foreigners resident in Britain, from Theodore of Tarsus to Polydore Vergil. John Beleth figures on the strength of his appearance, on somewhat tenuous grounds, in the *Dictionary of National Biography*; William of Poitiers and Guy of Amiens because their writings are directly concerned with English affairs; an *Anatomia* of uncertain provenance ('Pseudo-Galen') because it was at one time mistakenly attributed to Ricardus Anglicus (cited here as Ricardus Medicus); one work of a ninth-century Irishman (Eriugena *Periphyseon*) in recognition of its significance in the general development of ML during a period poorly represented by English sources.

Within such widely drawn limits it has obviously been impracticable to cover the ground exhaustively. Users of the Dictionary will soon discover that some of the authors named in the bibliography have been drawn upon much less extensively than their work deserves and that some important names are missing. But it is hoped that no significant class or period of writing has been wholly disregarded.

The field has been appreciably narrowed by the exclusion of vernacular words (English, Anglo-Norman, Welsh, or Gaelic) that appear undisguisedly in Latin writings, though examples of these may be cited to supplement the evidence of Latinized forms (*cf. e.g. Atrebatensis, bordmannus*). Where such vernacular words occur in quotations, they are commonly printed here in italics. Names of persons, historical or mythical, have been excluded unless they carry some special connotation (*Apella, Bellona*). So have names of places, apart from one or two countries presenting points of special interest (*Anglia, Britannia*). But national appellatives (*Angligena, Basculus*) have been included, together with some derivatives of proper names (*Albigensis, Benedictinus*).

General Principles

The material dealt with falls roughly into three categories, which have been accorded somewhat different treatment:

(*a*) The use by British authors of CL words in approximately their basic classical meanings (*e.g. accipere, auctor, bonus*) is illustrated by two or three examples of each, drawn in the main from a narrow range of sources (mostly Aldhelm, Bede, Domesday Book, and a selection of twelfth-century writings); here no attempt has been made to distinguish and exemplify every shade of the semantic spectrum, but the examples chosen, wherever possible, have been such as to illustrate the use of the word in an original Medieval context, in preference to mere echoes of earlier writers.

(*b*) Words and usages that belong to the post-classical development of Latin as a whole are dealt with more fully; but, since this category consists in large part of the technical terms of Christian thought (*angelus, anima, benedicere*) and church organization (*abbas, apostolicus, beneficium*) and of various arts and sciences (*alchimia, ars, braciare*), whose evolution cannot be adequately documented from British sources alone, its presentation is inevitably sketchy.

(*c*) The fullest treatment is reserved for what is distinctively British, either because of its links with Anglo-Saxon, Anglo-Norman, or some other vernacular (*acra, amobragium, betagius, boscus, botha*), or because it reflects the growth of institutions with specifically British features, sometimes distinguishable as English, Scots, Welsh, or Anglo-Irish (*advocare, assisa, baillivus, baro, brevis, burgus*, and their derivatives).

The layout of the entries is based on the same general plan as the *Oxford Latin Dictionary* with certain modifications. Since the sources quoted are generally far less accessible than those of CL and the interpretations of words are less well established, resting in many cases simply on inference from the contexts under reference, it has often seemed advisable to quote at greater length than would be requisite in a CL Dictionary. Sometimes, by the use of cross-references, one quotation has been made to do duty for several different words.

Space has been saved by the omission of most particulars relating to grammar. Unless otherwise indicated, it may be assumed that CL words retain their classical inflexions and that new formations follow regular CL models. There are no specific entries for suffixes, as new (post-classical) ones scarcely occur; an exception is *-agium* (OF *-age* < *-aticum*), which is sometimes added to a Latin stem (*e.g. capitagium* = OF *chevage* < *capaticum*). New prefixes are likewise rare, except that certain Latin adverbs (*foris, infra, subtus*) are sometimes joined to a following verb, and Greek prefixes may be added to Latin words (*anticardinalis, archisacerdos*).

Etymology

Derivation, where it is self-evident, is not normally indicated. Against words of non-Latin origin the presumed source (Greek, Old French, Middle English, etc.) is shown in square brackets; but as a general rule there is no discussion of etymological problems, except in cases where the ML examples appear to afford independent evidence (*e.g. averus, bederna, berefellarius, billa, binghaia*).

This restriction does not apply to those words of Arabic provenance that have made such a mark on the scientific and technical vocabulary of ML. The etymologies assigned to most of these in the first fascicule (A–B) have been supplied, many of them on the basis of original research, by the generous co-operation of Dr. J. D. Latham, which it is hoped will continue to be available. They are set out by him with more detailed explanation in *Journal of Semitic Studies* (Manchester U.P.) xvii (1972), 30–64, where he also discusses the bewildering processes of corruption involved in transliteration and translation through the distorting media of various Semitic, Romance, and sometimes other dialects.

Grouping under Key-words

Key-words that are CL or Greek in form, or directly derived from a classical origin, are spelt according to standard CL practice (*abundare, acmasticus, aetas, harena*) even though this spelling may be seldom or never found in Medieval manuscripts. It has been thought better, however, to write J and V rather than I and U where their Medieval value was probably that of consonants. Vowel quantity is not indicated, except to distinguish homonyms (*ānus, ănus*), and to show the conjugation of a verb (*appendēre, appendĕre*; *assīdēre, assīdĕre*). Where the key-word is followed by an alternative spelling in round brackets, *e.g. abundare* (*hab-*), this indicates that the second spelling is commonly found in our sources. For words of non-classical origin, the spelling selected for the key-word is normally one that shows its relation to the presumed vernacular original and to other cognate words in ML (*bacinus, billettare, bracium*). Variant spellings are not separately indicated at the beginning of an entry; but examples of all significant variants are included in the illustrative quotations and indicated where necessary by cross-references. Variants have not necessarily been noted if they result from normal features of ML spelling (*acomodus, apocrifus, asingnacio, authumpnus, equevus*).

Variants, however diverse, that appear to represent the same vernacular original have normally been grouped under one key-word (*affrus, averus*; *albergagia, herbergagium*; *bahudum, barura*). Forms that differ merely in gender without apparent semantic significance (*e.g. bala, balum, balus*) have not been treated as distinct words, since they would often be indistinguishable in oblique cases and in the suspended forms common in manuscripts. Where possible, forms that can be regarded as directly derived from a Latin source are distinguished from those obviously derived through a vernacular intermediary (*aurifragium, aurifrixium* etc., as against *orfresium* < OF *orfreis*, ultimately from the same source, probably *aurum Phrygium*). The distinction, however, is often somewhat arbitrary, and where the recorded forms present a continuous series (*e.g. advocare, avocare, advoare, avoare*) it may be more satisfactory to abandon it. Thus *arura* (< OF *areure* < *aratura*) has been grouped with *aratura* (thus linking it with *aratrum* etc.); but in a closely parallel case *armura* has been separated from *armatura* in order to emphasize its connexion with such derivative words as *armurarius*.

Words that are identical in form but presumably different in origin are treated separately and distinguished by preceding numbers. But in cases of uncertain or composite derivation (*cf. abscissio, actionarius*) some inconsistency in practice may be inescapable.

Form and content of quotations

In quotations the spelling is that of the original (or a near-contemporary) manuscript, so far as this is readily ascertainable. In passages cited from texts such as those in the Rolls Series, the classicized forms employed by the editors have been brought more nearly into line with other texts by adopting a spelling more consistent with Medieval usage (thus it is assumed that between about 1100 and 1500 the diphthongs *ae* and *oe* are likely to have been written *e* and that in the course of the thirteenth century intervocalic -ti- was normally replaced by -ci-). In the interests of clarity some degree of standardization has also been applied to such matters as punctuation, the use of capitals, and the form of numerals. Except in cases of serious doubt, contracted and suspended forms have usually been expanded.

The context of a quotation is sometimes elucidated by the insertion of a word or two in square brackets. The omission of one or more words, other than mere connecting words or the like, is indicated by a pair of dots.

Quotations from sources to which a single date is assigned in the bibliography are normally undated. Others usually bear a precise date (**1250**) or an approximate one (*a*[*nte*], *c*[*irca*], or *p*[*ost*] **1250**, or **12 . .** indicating an undetermined date in the thirteenth century). To quotations from pre-Conquest charters and other documents purporting to be of much earlier date than that of the earliest extant manuscript, it has sometimes been thought helpful to assign a double date, e.g. †**947** (14c) [i.e. fourteenth century], where the obelus indicates a doubt (or denial) of the authenticity of the ostensible date. In some cases the date forms an essential part of the reference (see paragraph six of the Introductory Note to the Bibliography).

The date prefixed to certain entries, especially from chronicles, takes a form such as *s*[*ub*] **1250**, denoting the date assigned to the incident under reference; this may enable readers to identify the incident, if it is one of historical importance, and also help them to trace a passage reproduced, with or without variations, by successive chroniclers. In annals compiled over a long period, this date may correspond to the date of the writing. Where the chronicler wrote long after the event (as shown in the Bibliography), the phrase quoted may either originate with him or be derived from an unidentified source (not necessarily a British one). Incidents that cannot be dated precisely may be dated approximately, e.g. by mention of a ruler.

Quotations included in a single subsection have usually been arranged in chronological order. But this practice may be varied for special reasons, e.g. to emphasize a similarity or contrast between particular quotations.

The quotations have been selected with a view to illustrating the range of occurrence of the reference-word not only in time but, where appropriate, over different districts and different types of source (technical, documentary, literary) as well as different forms and different grammatical and semantic contexts. In the case of a non-classical word or usage, the first quotation given usually represents its earliest recorded occurrence in our source material. But no special point has been made (as in the *Revised Word-List*) of noting in every case the latest recorded occurrence.

The reference-word is commonly quoted in an abbreviated form consisting of a tilde (~) followed by the termination. This practice is not, however, adopted unless the tilde would replace at least three letters (thus *acus* does not appear as ~us). In passages of verse the reference-word is always written in full to facilitate scanning, and in special instances the scansion is also shown (brāvĭum < βρᾰβεῖον).

Treatment of phrases

A special problem is posed by the importance in ML of set phrases, some of them functioning as quasi-compounds, composed wholly or in part of CL words but quite new in effect. The adjective *altus*, for instance, underwent no general change of meaning between Classical and Medieval times; its interest for the student of ML lies in the set phrases in which it is combined with such nouns as *dies*, *filum*, *justitia*, *manus*, *missa*, *proditio*, and *via*. These phrases are here exemplified *s.v. altus*, but most of them are more fully treated under the noun concerned. On the other hand, a phrase such as *molendinum blaereticum* receives fuller treatment under the adjective, which is not used in any other context; but for *molendinum ad bladum* the student should turn first to *molendinum*, though he will find the phrase noted and exemplified (not necessarily by the same quotations) under *bladum* and under *ad*.

Classification and Interpretation

The classification of the various uses of a particular word rests in part on fairly objective criteria, e.g. whether a verb (*accipere, arripere, allocare, attornare*) is used transitively or intransitively and whether its object, or its subject, is a person or a thing; in part on much more subjective ones. The uses of the preposition *ad*, for instance, might have been classified in countless different ways, and even within the chosen system of classification certain phrases whose meaning is not in doubt might reasonably have been assigned to two or three alternative positions. Where there is any doubt about the precise meaning, the subjective element becomes proportionately greater. In quotations drawn from texts so varied and for the most part so imperfectly explored as those of British Medieval Latin, such doubt is a factor that cannot be overlooked. Where practicable, the objective criteria have been preferred. But in dealing with difficult passages it has often been necessary to choose one explanation out of several possible ones, or to explain away the difficulty by conjectural emendation. Even where explanation is kept to a minimum, the mere process of selecting, classifying, and grouping quotations is a more arbitrary one than the reader may realize.

As a matter of practical convenience quotations are grouped in numbered sections, which may be divided into lettered subsections. In order to save space, the number 1 is omitted, except in those rare instances (e.g. the prepositions *a* and *ad*) in which some general information is given before the first section. Where the first subsection of a particular section covers a usage that can be regarded as primary or general, the letter **a** is also omitted; where all the subsections are treated as on the same level, **a** is prefixed (like **b**, **c** etc.) to the relevant definition and also to the first of the corresponding quotations.

It has seldom been possible to set out the different meanings or usages of a particular word in sections and subsections with any confidence that this classification represents an actual process of historical evolution. Wherever possible, CL usage has been taken as the foundation. But the superstructure is designed primarily to provide a coherent framework within which a place can be found for any semantic and grammatical distinctions clearly recognizable in the material to hand. In some cases, rather than create a new subsection, the editor has found it convenient to clarify the meaning of a word in a special context by appending his own translation in square brackets (instances will be found under the preposition *a, ab*). Other minor differences in meaning, shown by a contemporary gloss or an *Anglice* or implied by the context, have been left to speak for themselves, in the belief that quotation can be more informative than exposition or commentary and is much less likely to mislead.

BIBLIOGRAPHY

THIS bibliography is intended to include all sources used (or intended to be used) in the Dictionary, except a few that have been cited so rarely that it has seemed simpler to make the citations bibliographically adequate in themselves. A few sources that have been drawn upon very frequently are cited in a highly abbreviated form (*e.g. BBC, CS, DB, GAS*). In other cases the abbreviation adopted is designed to be recognizable by anyone familiar with the source.

Unless otherwise indicated, passages from published prose works are cited by reference to the pages of the edition specified in the bibliography. In some cases, however, if this edition indicates the foliation of the manuscript or the pagination of a previous edition (e.g. in *Patrologia Latina*), it has been judged preferable to take this as the basis of reference. Alternatively, if the text consists of numbered items, sections, or chapters, these may provide the most satisfactory basis, supplemented where desirable by page references. Passages of verse are cited where practicable by reference to the line, but in the case of lengthy metrical texts without numbered lines reference is by page or folio. In citations direct from manuscript, some other means of reference may be appropriate. Where any doubt may arise, the method of reference is indicated in square brackets at the end of the entry in the bibliography (e.g. by book and chapter, by column of *PL*, by folio, by membrane, by rotulet).

Occasionally a passage taken direct from an unpublished manuscript is cited by reference to the page of a printed calendar in which it appears only in extract or translation.

Citations from glossaries etc., in which items are listed or indexed alphabetically, usually omit any page reference.

Citations from sources of diverse content (*e.g.* Rymer's *Foedera*, *Archaeologia*, the *English Historical Review*) usually include indications of at least the general nature of the document cited, and letters or other documents included in chronicles are distinguished where practicable from the actual writing of the chroniclers.

Where appropriate, each source noted in the Bibliography bears at least an approximate indication of date, even if only the obit of the author. Citations from sources not so dated bear individual dates, which in some cases form an essential part of the reference (thus '**1263** assummatis omnibus particulis solucionis *Cl* 295' refers to p. 295 of the published volume of Close Rolls covering the years 1261–64; '**1423** eisdem viciis . . assuetos, . . que quidem assuefactio ex ipsa iteracione decernatur *Reg. Cant.* III 518' refers to the published Register of Henry Chichele, archbishop of Canterbury 1414–43, Vol. III p. 518).

A few passages cited are based on material supplied by readers working on manuscripts to which the editorial staff have not had access. In such cases it is not always certain that the particulars given are adequate for precise identification of the source.

In general the information given in the Bibliography is reduced to the minimum necessary to enable the user to identify the source of a citation, besides forming at least an approximate notion of its date and (where relevant) its local provenance. Thus, little space has been allotted to bibliographical details of internationally famous publications such as *Analecta Bollandiana* or *Monumenta Germaniae Historica.* In listing readily traceable works, especially editions of the writings of named authors, it has not always been thought necessary to name the editor. The place of publication is sometimes omitted (especially when it is London). The fact that a particular volume is noted as published by a county record society or the like is taken to be sufficient evidence of its local connexions. For the purposes of the Bibliography italics have been used for Latin titles whether modern (*Monumenta Germaniae* etc.) or medieval.

Those seeking further particulars of certain items may consult *inter alia* the following works of reference:

Cambridge Bibliography of English Literature vol. I (600–1660), (1940). Supplement (600–1900) (Cambridge, 1957).

A Bibliography of English History to 1485, by C. Gross. Revised and expanded by E. B. Graves (OUP, 1974).

Guide to the Public Records, 2 vols. (HMSO, 1963).

Publications of the Royal Commission on Historical Manuscripts, sectional list of government publications no. 17, HMSO [revised periodically].

British National Archives, sectional list of government publications no. 24, HMSO [revised periodically].

Texts and Calendars, an analytical Guide to serial publications, RHS (1958) [supplement (1958–68) in prep.].

Guide to the Historical and Archaeological publications of Societies in England and Wales, 1901–33 (Institute of Historical Research, London, 1968).

Medieval Cartularies of Great Britain, ed. G. R. C. Davis (1958).

Anglo-Saxon charters: an annotated list and bibliography, by P. H. Sawyer, RHS (1968).

History of Anglo-Latin literature 597–1066, ed. W. F. Bolton, vol. I 597–740 (Princeton U.P., 1967–)

Writers of 13th century England (Bull. IHR, 1936).

Eng. Hist. Lit. 15c. *v. infra.*

Ancient Libraries of Canterbury and Dover, by M. R. James (Cambridge, 1903).

Medieval Libraries of Great Britain, ed. N. R. Ker, 2nd ed. RHS (1964).

The medical practitioners in medieval England: a biographical register, ed. C. H. Talbot & E. A. Hammond, Wellcome Hist. Med. Libr. (1965).

A. MEAUX Susanna Alan de Melsa [*fl. c*1212]: Poem on Susanna, Studi Medievali, NS III (1950) 41–50.

A. TEWK. Alan of Tewkesbury [*ob.* 1202]: **Ep.** *Epistolae*, in *Scripta*, Caxton Soc. (1846) 33–58 [by no.]; **Prol. Thom.** Prologue to *V. S.Thomae* by John of Salisbury, Becket Mat. II 299–301; **Add. Thom.** Additions to above, *ib.* 322–52 [by cap.].

ALMA *Archivum Latinitatis medii aevi* (Bulletin du Cange) I– (Brussels, 1924–).

ANQuellen Liebermann, F.: Ungedruckte Anglo-Normanische Geschichtsquellen (Strasbourg, 1879).

APScot. Acts of the Parliaments of Scotland, RC, vol. I (1124–1423), vol. II (1424–1567), (1814) (1844) [N.B. pag. not contin.]; *v. et. Iter Cam., Iter Cam. Artic., Leg. IV Burg., Quon. Attach., RegiamM., Stat. Gild. Berw.*

AS Chr. Anglo-Saxon Chronicle [cited only as source of Latin chroniclers; by date].

Abbat. Abingd. *v.* Chr. Abingd.

ABBO Abbo of Fleury [*ob.* 1004]: **Edm.** *Vita S.Edmundi*, ed. M. Winterbottom in Three Lives of English Saints, Toronto Med. Latin Texts (Toronto, 1972); 67–87 also printed as *Passio S.Eadmundi*, Mem. S.Edm. I 1–25 [by cap.]; **QG** *Quaestiones grammaticales*, ed. A. Mai, in *Classicorum Auctorum e Vaticanis Codicibus Editorum Liber V* (1833) 329–49; **QG Pref.** Prose preface *ib.* 329; **QG Prol.** Verse prologue in *Chr. Rams.* xxviii; [**for** corrections to ch. XII of **QG** *v.* Bradley, H., Proc. Brit. Acad. X (1922) 174–5].

Abbotsford Club publications (Edinburgh, 1883–66).

Abbr. Orig. *Rotulorum originalium in curia scaccarii abbreviatio*, 2 vols., RC (1805, 1810).

Abbr. Plac. *Placitorum abbreviatio*, RC (1811).

Ac. Almon. Peterb. The book of William Morton [*ob. a*1471], almoner of Peterborough monastery 1448–67, Northants Rec. Soc. XVI (1954).

Ac. Beaulieu Accounts of Beaulieu Abbey, Hants (*c*1276), BM Add. MS 48978; **Ac. Beaulieu (Faringdon)** Accounts of the manor of Faringdon [Berks], Bodley MS Barlow 49 [both by f.; in prep. Camd.].

Ac. Bridge Masters Bridge Masters' account rolls (1381–1405), MS Guildhall RO, London.

Ac. Build. Hen. III Building accounts of King Henry III, ed. H. M. Colvin (Oxford, 1971).

Ac. Chamb. Cant. Chamberlains' accounts of the city of Canterbury, HMC Rep. IX App. 1. (1883) 131–9.

Ac. Chamb. Chesh Accounts of the chamberlains..of the county of Chester 1301–60, Lancs & Chesh Rec. Soc. LIX (1910) [*v. et.* Pipe Chesh.].

Ac. Chamb. Winchester Chamberlains' accounts, Winchester City, MS Winchester City RO.

Ac. Churchw. Bath Churchwardens' accounts of the church.. of St. Michael without the North Gate, Bath, 1349–1575, ed. C. B. Pearson, Arch. Soc. Som supplements to vols. XXIII–XXVI (1877–80) [contin. pag.].

Ac. Churchw. Glast. Churchwardens' accounts of St. John's, Glastonbury (1366–1574), Som & Dors N. & Q. IV (1894–5), (1584–1610), *ib.* V (1896–7).

Ac. Churchw. Sal. Churchwardens' accounts of S.Edmund and S.Thomas, Salisbury (1443–1702), Wilts Rec. Soc. I (1896).

Ac. Churchw. Som Churchwardens' accounts of Somerset parishes..1349–1560, Som Rec. Soc. IV (1890).

Ac. Coll. Wint. Account rolls, MS Winchester College.

Ac. Cornw Ministers' accounts of the Earldom of Cornwall, 1296–7, Camd. 3rd S. LXVI, LXVIII (1942, 1945).

Ac. Dom. Ep. Wint. Roll of Bishop Wykeham's household expenses, 1393, MS Winchester College.

Ac. Durh. Extracts from the account rolls of the Abbey of Durham (1278–1580), Surtees Soc. XCIX (1–284), C (285–576), CIII (577–989) (1898–1901).

Ac. Ep. Bath. Household roll (1337–8) of Ralph of Shrewsbury, Bishop of Bath and Wells [*ob.* 1363], Som Rec. Soc. XXXIX (1924) 72–174.

Ac. Esch. *v.* LTR.

Ac. Exec. Ep. Exon. Account..of the executors of Thomas, Bishop of Exeter, 1310, Camd. Soc. NS X (1874) 1–45.

Ac. Exec. Ep. Lond. Account of the executors of Richard, Bishop of London, 1303, Camd. Soc. NS X (1874) 47–116.

Ac. Exec. W. Merton Accounts of the executors of Walter de Merton (1277–8) in Rolls Merton 90–169.

Ac. Foreign Exchequer Rolls of foreign accounts (Pipe Office), MS PRO (E. 364).

Ac. Galley Newcastle The 'Newcastle' galley A.D. 1294, *Arch. Aeliana* 4th S. II (1926) 142–193.

Ac. H. Derby Expeditions..made by Henry, Earl of Derby.. 1390–1 and 1392–3, ..accounts kept by his Treasurer, Camd. Soc. NS LII (1894).

Ac. Havener Cornw Haveners' Accounts, Duchy of Cornwall, MS PRO (E. 306).

Ac. LChamb. Lord Chamberlain's Accounts, MS PRO (L.C. 9).

Ac. Lenton Lenton Priory (Notts), estate accounts 1296–8, Thoroton Soc. XIX (1959).

Ac. Linlithgow Account of work done at the Peel of Linlithgow (*c*1302), in Ac. Palaces Scot. lxiii–lxviii.

Ac. Man. Cant. Manorial accounts, Christchurch, Canterbury, MS Canterbury Cathedral Library [*v. et.* DCCant].

Ac. Man. Coll. Wint. Manorial accounts, MS Winchester College.

Ac. Man. Westm. Manorial accounts, MS Westminster Abbey.

Ac. Man. Wint. Manorial accounts, MS Winchester Cathedral Library.

Ac. Mayor Winchester Accounts of the Mayor of Winchester, MS Winchester City RO.

Ac. Obed. Abingd. Accounts of the Obedientiars of Abingdon Abbey (1322–1532), Camd. Soc. NS LI (1892).

Ac. Palaces Scot. Accounts of the Masters of Works for building ..royal palaces..Scotland, I (1529–1615), Scot. RO (1957).

Ac. Sheriffs Sheriffs' Accounts, MS PRO (E. 199).

Ac. Stratton Accounts and surveys of the Wiltshire lands of Adam de Stratton (1271–89), Wilts Rec. Soc. XIV (1959).

Ac. Swinfield Household expenses (1289–90) of Richard de Swinfield, Bishop of Hereford, Camd. Soc. LIX, LXII (1854/5).

Ac. Trin. Dublin Account roll of the Priory of the Holy Trinity, Dublin (1337–46), Royal Soc. of Antiquaries of Ireland, extra vol. (1891).

Ac. W. Wales Ministers' accounts for West Wales, 1277–1306, Y Cymmrodorion Rec. S., XIII (1936).

Ac. Wardr. MS., incl. in Chanc. Misc., KRAc, or TR Bk. (PRO).

Ac. Wardr. (1300) *Liber quotidianus contrarotulatoris garderobae* ..1299–1300, Soc. of Antiquaries of London (1787) [by p.].

Ac. Wardr. (4 Ed. II) Wardrobe account 1310–11, MS BM Cotton Nero CVII.

Ac. Wellingb. Wellingborough manorial accounts, 1258–1323, from account rolls of Crowland Abbey, Northants Rec. Soc. VIII (1936).

Act. Hen. II Recueil des actes de Henri II..concernant les provinces françaises..1138–89, Acad. des Inscriptions, etc., Chartes et Diplômes III, 2 vols. of text (1916, 1920) [by p.].

Act. PC Proceedings and ordinances of the Privy Council of England, 1386–1542, 7 vols. RC (1834–7).

Act. PC Ir. Acts of the Privy Council in Ireland, 1556–71, HMC Rep. XV App. Pt. III (1897) 1–256.

Act. Cant. *Acta Stephani Langton*, 1207–28, Cant & York Soc. (1950).

Acta SS Ben. *Acta sanctorum ordinis S.Benedicti..coll. d'Achery*, ed...J. Mabillon et Th. Ruinart, 9 vols. (Paris, 1668–1701).

Acta SS Boll. *Acta sanctorum..coll. J. Bollandus* (Venice, etc, 1734–).

Acta Wulf. et Ruff. *v. V. Wulf. et Ruff.*

AD. EYNS. Hug. Adam of Eynsham [*ob. p*1233]: *Magna vita S.Hugonis* [*ob.* 1200], 2 vols., Med. Texts (1961–2) [by bk. & cap.].

AD. MARSH Ep. Adam Marsh (de Marisco) [*ob.* 1257]: *Epistolae* (mainly *c*1250), in *Mon. Francisc.* I 77–489 [by no.].

AD. MUR. Adam Murimouth [*ob.* 1347]: Chronicle (*Continuatio Chronicarum*) (1303–47), RS (1889) 1–219; **App.** Appendix, text of BM Cotton MS Nero D. X (1340–4), *ib.* 220–53; **Cont. A** *Continuatio* (1337–77), Eng. Hist. Soc. (1846) 171–227; **Cont. B** *Continuatio continuationis* (1377–80), *ib.* 228–43.

AD. SCOT Adam Scot [*fl. c*1180]: **OP** *De ordine..canonicorum Ordinis Praemonstratensis*, in *PL* CXCVIII (1855) 439–610; **Serm.** *Sermones*, *ib.* 97–440; **Sol.** *Soliloquiorum de instructione animae libri duo*, *ib.* 843–72; **TGC** *De triplici genere contemplationis*, *ib.* 795–842; **TT** *De tripartito tabernaculo*, *ib.* 609–792 [*v. et.* Chr. Witham].

AD. USK Adam of Usk [*ob.* 1430]: *Chronicon* (1377–1421) ed. E. M. Thompson, 2nd ed. (1904).

ADEL. Adelard of Bath [*a*1150]: **Alch.** *Libri ysagogarum alchorismi* bks. I–III, in Abhandlungen zur Gesch. der Mathematik VIII (1898) 3–27 [here pub. anon.; attrib. to ADEL. in Med. Sci. (1927) 24]; **Astr.** Extr. from *De opere astrolapsus* (*c*1142–6), Med. Sci. (1927) 25, 28–9; **CA** *De cura accipitrum*, Allard Pierson Stichting, Afdeling voor mod. lit. wetenschap (1937); **ED** *De eodem et diverso*, Beitr. zur Gesch. der Philos. des Mittelalters IV, i (1903) 3–34; **Euclid** Extr. from transl. of Euclid, Abhandlungen zur Gesch. der Mathematik III (1880) 143–66; **QN** *Quaestiones naturales*, Beitr. zur Gesch. der Philos. des Mittelalters XXX (1934) [by cap.]; **QN prol.** Prologue to above, *ib.* 1–5 [by p.].

ADEL. BLANDIN. Adelard of Blandinium [*fl. a*1011]: **Dunst.** *Epistola..de vita S. Dunstani* Mem. Dunst. 53–68.

ÆLF. Ælfric, abbot of Eynsham [*ob. c*1025]: **Æthelwold** *V. S. Æthelwoldi*, ed. M. Winterbottom in Three lives of English Saints, Toronto Med. Latin Texts (Toronto, 1972) 17–29; also in *Chr. Abingd.* II App. I, 253–66; **Coll.** Colloquy, WW 89–163 [for authorship see Ælfric's Colloquy, ed. G. N. Garmonsway (1939) 5–11] [by p. of WW]: **EC** *De ecclesiastica consuetudine*, Die Hirtenbriefe Ælfrics, ed. B. Fehr (Hamburg, 1914) 234–49 [by cap.]; **Ep.** *Epistolae*, *ib.* 35–57 (*Ep.* 2), 222–7 (*Ep.* 2a), 58–67 (*Ep.* 3) [by section]; **Gl.** Glossary or vocabulary, WW 104–67; **Sup.** Supplement to above, *ib.* 168–91.

ÆLNOTH Cnut Ælnoth [*fl. c*1085–1109]: *Historia..S.Canuti*, *Acta SS Boll.* July III 127–42.

Aen. Laur. *Aenigmata Laureshamensia* (or *Anglica*), in *Corpus Christianorum, S. Lat.* CXXXIII (1968) 345–58 [by no. & line].

ÆTHELW. Æthelweard [*ob. c*998]: Chronicle (Creation–975), Med. Texts (1962) [by bk. & cap.].

ÆTHELWALD, King of Mercia [*ob.* 757], *v. Carm. Aldh.*

ÆTHELWOLD, Saint [*ob.* 984], *v. RegulC.*

ÆTHELWULF Abb. Æthelwulf [*fl. c*810): *Carmen de abbatibus cellae suae* ed. A. Campbell (Oxford, 1967); also in S. DURH. I 263–94.

Aids Inquisitions and Assessments relating to feudal aids, etc. (1284–1431), 6 vols. HMSO (1899–1920).

AILR. Ailred (Ethelred) of Rievaulx [*ob.* 1166]: **Anima** *De anima*, Med. & Renaiss. Stud. sup. I (1952) [by f.]; also ed. C. H. Talbot in *Corpus Christianorum, continuatio mediaevalis* I (Turnholt, 1971) 683–754; **Comp. Spec. Car.** *Compendium speculi caritatis*, ed. R. Vander Plaetse, *ib.* 171–240; **Dilect. Dei** *Sermo de dilectione Dei*, ed. A. Hoste, *ib.* 241–4; **Ed. Conf.** Vita S. Edwardi regis in *PL* CXCV (1855) 739–90; **Gen. Regum** *De genealogia regum Anglorum*, ed. R. Twysden, in *Hist. Angl. Script. X* 347–70; **Inst. Inclus.** *De institutione inclusarum*, as *Anima* 1971, 635–82; **Jes.** *De Jesu puero duodenni* [sermon on Luke ii 42] in *PL* CLXXXIV (1854) 849–70; also as *Dilect. Dei* above 245–78; **Nin.** *Vita Niniani*, Historians of Scotland V (1874) 137–57 [by cap.]; **OP** *Oratio pastoralis*, ed. A. Wilmart in *Corpus Christianorum, contin. mediaevalis* I 755–63; **Serm.** *Sermones*, in *PL* CXCV 209–500; **Spec. char.** *Speculum charitatis*, *ib.* 501–620; also as *Anima* above, 2–161; **Spir. Amicit.** *De spiritali amicitia ib.* as *Dilect. Dei* above, 279–350; **Spir. Amicit. Abbr.** *Abbreviationes de spiritali amicitia*, ib. as *Dilect. Dei* above, 351–63; **SS Hex.** *De sanctis ecclesiae Haugustaldensis* (634–1154), Surtees Soc. XLIV, vol I (1864) 173–203 [by cap.]; **Stand.** *Relatio de standardo* Chr. Steph. III 181–99 [by f.; *v. et. V. Ed. Conf. metr.*].

ALCUIN Alcuin (Albinus) [735–804]: **Carm**: *Carmina* in PLAC I (1881) 169–351; **CR** *Carmina rhythmica*, *ib.* IV pt. 3 (1923) 903–10; **Ep.** *Epistolae*, ed. E. Duemmler, *MGH, Ep. Carol. Aevi* II (1895) 1–481 [by no.; *v. et. Ep. Alcuin.*]; **Orth**: *Orthographia*, ed. H. Keil, *Grammatici Latini* VII (1878) 295–312 [ref. by pp. of ed. Putschius 2327–50]; **Rhet.** *De rhetorica*, ed. C. Halm, *Rhetores Latini minores* (1863) 525–50 [by section]; **SS Ebor** *Versus de pontificibus et sanctis Eboracensis ecclesiae*, in *PLAC* I 169–206 [by line]; **Vedast.** *Vita Vedasti episcopi Atrebatensis* [*ob.* 539], *MGH Script. rer. Merov.* III (Hanover, 1896) 414–27; **Will. P.** *Vita S. Willibrordi* (prose), *Mon. Alcuiniana* (1873) 39–64 [by cap.]; **Will. V.** *Vita S. Willibrordi* (verse) in *PLAC* I (1881) 207–20 [by line]; other works, including some of doubtful attribution, cited from *PL* C and CI: **Didasc.** *Op. didascalica* CI 847–1002; **Dogm.** *Op. dogmatica ib.* 9–304; **Dub.** *Op. dubia ib.* 1001–1170; **Exeg.** *Op. exegetica* C 515–1156; **Hag.** *Op. hagiographica* CI 655–724; **Liturg.** *Op. liturgica ib.* 439–614; **Moral.** *Op. moralia ib.* 613–56; **Suppos.** *Op. supposita ib.* 1169–1514.

ALDH. Aldhelm [*ob.* 709]: **Aen.** *Enigmata*, *MGH Auct. Antiq.* XV (1919) 97–149 [by no. and line]; **CE** *Carmina ecclesiastica*, *ib.* 3–32 [by no. and line]; *v. et. Carm. Aldh.*; **Ep.** *Epistulae*, *ib.* 475–503 [by no.] [letters to Aldhelm cited as *Ep. Aldh.*]; **Met.** *De metris etc.*, *ib.* 59–96 [by cap.]; **PR** *De..pedum regulis*, *ib.* 150–204 [by cap.]; **VirgP** *De virginitate* (prose), *ib.* 226–323 [by cap.]; **VirgV** *De virginitate* (verse), *ib.* 350–471 [by line].

ALEX. CANT. Alexander of Canterbury [12c.]: **V. Anselmi** *Brevis vita Anselmi*, extr. in EADMER **HN** cxx–cxxvii.

ALEXANDER OF HALES *v.* HALES.

ALF. ANGL. Alfredus Anglicus (of Shareshull) [*fl. c*1200]: **Cor** *De motu cordis*, Beitr. zur Gesch. der Philos. des Mittelalters XXIII, pts. 1–2 (1923) [by cap.]; **Min.** *Mineralia* or *De congelatione et conglutinatione lapidum* [transl. of Avicenna], in *Theatrum chem.* IV 883–7; also ed. E. J. Holmyard and D. C. Mandeville (1927) 45–55; **Plant.** *De plantis* [transl. of Nic. Damasc. *via* Arabic] (Leipzig, 1841).

Alph. *Alphita*: a medico-botanical glossary (14c.), ed. J. L. G. Mowat, *Anecdota Oxoniensia* (1887) [Eng. recension of *Alphita* **(Alph. I)**, ed. S. de Renzi, *Collect. Salern.* III (1854) 272–322].

Ambrosden Parochial antiquities..in the history of Ambrosden (Oxon), ed. White Kennett, 2 vols. (Oxford, 1818).

AMUND. John Amundesham [*c*1425]: *Annales monasterii S.Albani* (1421–40), 2 vols. *Chr. Mon. S.Alb.* V.

Anal. Boll. *Analecta Bollandiana*, vol. I– (Brussels, 1882–).

Anal. Cisterc. *Analecta Sacri Ordinis Cisterciensis*, vol. I– (Rome, 1945–).

Anal. Etheldr. *v.* RIC. ELY.

Anal. Hymn. *Analecta hymnica medii aevi*, ed. G. M. Dreves and C. Blume. 55 vols. (Leipzig, 1886–1922) [vols. cited: XL, XLVIII, XLIX, L, LI, pt. 1; by vol. and no.].

Analog. Cant. Pilg. Analogues of Chaucer's Canterbury pilgrimage (15c. docs.), ed. F. J. Furnivall and R. E. G. Kirk (1903).

AncC Ancient Correspondence, MS PRO (S.C. 1).

AncCh. Ancient Charters royal and private prior to A.D. 1200, Pipe R. Soc. X (1888) [by no.].

AncD Ancient Deeds, MS PRO (Var.).

AncExt Ancient Extents, MS PRO (E. 142).

AncIndict Ancient Indictments, MS PRO (K.B. 9).

AncPet Ancient Petitions, MS PRO (S.C. 8).

AncrR The Latin text of the Ancrene Riwle [early 14c. transl. of Eng. work attrib. to Simon of Ghent (*ob.* 1315)], EETS CCXVI (1944) [Eng. text cited from EETS CCXXV].

ANDRÉ Hen. VII Bernard André of Toulouse [*ob. p*1520]: *De vita atque gestis Henrici septimi..historia*, in Mem. Hen. VII 1–130; (*Vita* [1497] 1–75; *Annales* [1504–8] 77–130).

Anecd. Poet. *Anecdota quaedam poetica*, Surtees Soc. LXX (1878) 72–89 [by no. and line].

Anglia Sacra *Anglia sacra, sive collectio historiarum..de archiepiscopis et episcopis Angliae* (to 1540), ed. H. Wharton, 2 vols. (1691).

Anglo-Scot. Rel. Anglo-Scottish relations, 1174–1328, ed. E. L. G. Stones, Med. Texts (1965).

Ann. Ang. & Scot. *Annales Angliae et Scotiae* (1292–1300), *Chr. Mon. S.Alb.* II 369–408.

Ann. Berm. *Annales monasterii de Bermundeseia* [Bermondsey, Surrey] (1042–1432), *Ann. Mon.* III 423–87.

Ann. Burton *Annales de Burton* [Staffs] (1004–1263), *Ann. Mon.* I 183–500.

Ann. Cambr. *Annales Cambriae* (444–1288), RS (1860).

Ann. Cestr. *Annales Cestrienses*, or chronicle of the Abbey of S.Werburgh at Chester (Creation–1297), Lancs and Chesh Rec. Soc. XIV (1887).

Ann. Dunstable *Annales prioratus de Dunstaplia* [Beds] (1–1297), *Ann. Mon.* III 1–420; also ed. T. Hearne as *Chronicon seu annales de prioratus de Dunstaple*, 2 vols. (Oxford, 1733) [to 1241 attrib. R. de Morins].

Ann. Durh. Durham annals (1207–86) and documents (13c.) (pp. 85–202), Surtees Soc. CLV (1940).

Ann. Ed. I *Annales Regis Edwardi Primi* (3 frags., 1285–1307), *Chr. Mon. S.Alb.* II 435–99.

Ann. Hen. IV *Annales Henrici Quarti Regis Angliae* (1399–1406), *Chr. Mon. S.Alb.* III 280–420.

Ann. Lond. *Annales Londonienses* (1195–1311), Chr. Ed. I and II, I 3–251.

Ann. Margan *Annales de Margan* [Margam, Glam] (1066–1232), *Ann. Mon.* I 1–40.

Ann. Midi *Annales du Midi* I– (Toulouse, 1899–).

Ann. Mon. *Annales Monastici*, RS, 5 vols. (1864–9).

Ann. Osney *Annales monasterii de Oseneia* [Oxon] (1016–1347), *Ann. Mon.* IV 3–352; *v. et.* WYKES.

Ann. Paul. *Annales Paulini* (St. Paul's, London) (1307–41), Chr. Ed. I and II, I 253–370.

Ann. Regni Scot. *Annales regni Scotiae* (1291–2), *Chr. Mon. S.Alb.* II 231–368.

Ann. Ric. II *Annales Ricardi Secundi, Regis Angliae* (1392–9), *Chr. Mon. S.Alb.* III 153–280.

Ann. S.Edm. *Annales S.Edmundi* (1032–1212), Mem. S.Edm. II 1–25.

Ann. Tewk. *Annales monasterii de Theokesberia* [Tewkesbury, Glos] (1066–1263), *Ann. Mon.* I 41–180.

Ann. Wav. *Annales monasterii de Waverleia* [Waverley, Surrey] (1–1291), *Ann. Mon.* II 127–411.

Ann. Wint. *Annales monasterii de Wintonia* (519–1277), *Ann. Mon.* II 3–125.

Ann. Worc. *Annales prioratus de Wigornia* (1–1377), *Ann. Mon.* IV 365–564.

ANSELM Anselm Archb. of Canterbury [*ob.* 1109], *Opera omnia*, ed. F. S. Schmitt, 6 vols. (1946–61): **Azym.** *Epistola de sacrificio azimi et fermentati* II 221–32; **Casus Diab.** *De casu diaboli* I 227–76; **CurD** *Cur Deus homo* II 37–133; **Ep.** *Epistolae* III 93–294, IV, V [letters to Anselm cited as *Ep. Anselm.*]; **Gram.** *De grammatico* I 141–68; **Incarn.** *Epistola de incarnatione Verbi* **A** I 277–90, **B** II 1–35; **Lib. Arb.** *De libertate arbitrii* I 201–26; **Med.** *Meditationes* III 76–91; **Mon.** *Monologion* I 1–87; **Or.** *Orationes* III 1–75; **Orig. Pecc.** *De conceptu virginali et de originali peccato* II 135–73; **Praesc.** *De concordia praescientiae* (2 recensions) II 243–88; **Proc. Sp.** *De processione spiritus sancti* II 175–219; **Prosl.** *Proslogion* I 89–122; **Resp. Ed.** *Ad proslogion responsio editoris* I 131–9; **Resp. Insip.** *Ad proslogion responsio Gaunilonis pro insipiente* I 125–9; **Sacr.** *Epistola de sacramentis ecclesiae* II 239–42; **Ver.** *De veritate* I 169–99 [*v. et. Simil. Anselmi*].

Antiq. Antiquity, a quarterly journal of archaeology, vol. I– (1927–).

Antiq. Cant. Somner, W.: Antiquities of Canterbury, 2nd ed. (1703).

Antiq. J. Society of Antiquaries of London, journal, vol. I– (1921–).

Antiq. Salop Eyton, R. W.: Antiquities of Shropshire, 12 vols. (1854).

Antiq. Warw Dugdale, W.: Antiquities of Warwickshire (Coventry, 1765).

Arch. *Archaeologia*, Soc. of Antiquaries of London, vol. I– (1775–)

Arch. Aeliana, Society of Antiquaries of Newcastle-upon-Tyne, publications, I– (1822–).

Arch. Bridgw. Bridgwater borough archives, 1200–1377, Som Rec. Soc. XLVIII (1933).

Arch. Cambr. *Archaeologia Cambrensis*, Cambrian Archaeol. Assoc., NS vol. 1– (1850–).

Arch. Cant. *Archaeologia Cantiana*, transactions of Kent Arch. Soc., vol. I– (1858–).

Arch. Gironde Archives historiques du départment de la Gironde, I–XLIX (Paris and Bordeaux, 1859–1914).

Arch. Hist. Camb. Willis, R. The architectural history of the University of Cambridge..w. additions..by J. Willis Clark, 4 vols. (Cambridge, 1886).

Arch. J. Archaeological journal, Royal Archaeological Inst. of G.B. and Ireland, vol. I– (1844–).

Arch. Mun. Bordeaux Archives municipales de Bordeaux, I– (1867–).

Arch. Ox. Mediaeval archives of the University of Oxford (*c*1179–*c*1571), OHS LXX, LXXIII (1917, 1919).

Arch. Soc. Derb Derbyshire Archaeological..Society, journal, vol. I– (1879–).

Arch. Soc. Essex Essex Archaeological Society, transactions, I– (Colchester, 1858–); **Occ. Pubs.** Occasional publications, I– (*ib.* 1946–).

Arch. Soc. Norf Norfolk archaeology, I– (1846–).

Arch. Soc. Salop Shropshire Archaeological Society, transactions, vol. I– (1878–).

Arch. Soc. Som Somersetshire Archaeological Society, proceedings, I– (Taunton, 1851–).

Arch. Soc. Suss *v. Collect. Suss.*

Arch. Soc. Yorks Yorkshire Archaeological Association: **J** Journal I– (1870–); **Rec. S.** Record Series I– (1885–).

Archiv für Gesch. der Medizin ed. K. Sudhoff, Leipzig Univ. I– (Leipzig, 1908–).

Arthur and Gorlagon (13c.), ed. G. L. Kittredge (Harvard, 1903).

Artic. Cam. *v. Iter Cam. Artic.*

ASCHAM Ep. Roger Ascham [1515–68]: *Epistolarum libri IV* (1703).

ASSER Asser [*ob. c*909] [attrib.]: **Alf.** *De rebus gestis Ælfridi*

(Oxford, 1904, repr. 1959) [by cap.]; **Chr. S.Neoti** *Chronicon fani S.Neoti sive annales* (44–914), *ib.* 117–45.

AssessR. Cornw Duchy of Cornwall Assession Rolls, MS PRO (E. 306).

AssizeR. Durh The assize roll[s] for Co. Durham (1235–6, 1242), Surtees Soc. CXXVII (1916) 1–105.

AssizeR. Northants The earliest Northamptonshire assize rolls (1202 & 1203), Northants Rec. Soc. V (1930).

AssizeR. Northumb Three early assize rolls for the county of Northumberland (1256, 1269, 1279), Surtees Soc. LXXXVIII (1891).

Augm. Bk. Exchequer, Augmentation Office, Miscellaneous Books, MS PRO (E. 315).

AVESB. Robert of Avesbury [*ob. a*1360]: *De gestis mirabilibus regis Edwardi Tertii*, RS (1889) 279–471 [by f.].

AYLWARD Thomas Aylward [*ob.* 1413]: Life of William of Wykeham, in Moberley, G. H.: Life of W. W. 2nd ed. (1893), app. D, 287–92.

B. COTTON Bartholomew Cotton (*ob. c*1298]: *Historia Anglicana* (449–1298), RS (1859) 1–344; *Liber de archiepiscopis et episcopis Angliae* (582–1228), *ib.* 345–418.

BBAdm. *Monumenta juridica* or the black book of the Admiralty (14c.–15c.), 4 vols. RS (1871–6).

BBC British borough charters (1042–1660), ed. A. Ballard, J. Tait, and M. Weinbaum, 3 vols. (Cambridge): I 1042–1216 (1913); II 1216–1307 (1923); III 1307–1660 (1943) [ref. by p. and date, omitting vol. no.].

BBExch. *Liber niger Scaccarii* Little black book of the Exchequer (E. 164/12) ed. T. Hearne, 2nd ed. 2 vols. (1774).

BBHouseh. *Liber niger domus Regis Angliae, etc.*, in Myers, A. R.: The household of Edward IV (1959) 76–197.

BB Lismore The black book of Lismore, frags. in Ware, James: Antiquities of Ireland (1704–5).

BB S.Aug. *v. Reg. S.Aug.*

BB St. Davids The black book of St. Davids: an extent of lands etc. in 1326, Cymmrodorion Rec. Series V (1902).

BB Winchester The black book of Winchester [Corporation] (Winchester, 1925).

BM Ch. Facsimiles of royal and other charters in the British Museum vol. I (1070–98) (1903) [no more pub.].

BNB Bracton's note book, extr. from *Curia Regis* Rolls, *temp.* Hen. III, made for Henry de Bracton [*ob.* 1268], 3 vols. (1887) [by p.].

BR Will. I *Anonymi auctoris brevis relatio de origine Willelmi Conquestoris* (*a*1135), *Scriptores rerum gestarum Willelmi Conquestoris*, ed. J. A. Giles (1845) 1–26.

Babio *De Babione*: poème comique du XIIe siècle (? *c*1180), ed. E. Faral, (Paris 1948) [by line].

BACON Roger Bacon [*ob.* 1294]: **CSPhil.** *Compendium studii philosophiae*, RS (1859) 393–519; **CSTheol.** *Compendium studii theologiae*, Brit. Soc. Franciscan Studies III (1911); **Maj.** *Opus majus* (1267), 3 vols. (Oxford, 1897–1900), *corrigenda* in vol. III; **Min.** *Opus minus* (1267), RS 313–89; **Mor. Phil.** *Moralis philosophia*, ed. E. Massa, *Thesaurus mundi* (Zürich, 1953) [part VII of *Maj.*; supersedes ed. of 1897–1900 II 223–404 and III 144–151]; **NM** *De..nullitate magiae*, RS XV 523–51; **Tert.** *Opus tertium* (1267), RS 3–310; **Tert. Sup.** [additional portions of *Tert.*], Brit. Soc. Franciscan Studies IV (1912); other works cited only by vol. and p. from *Opera hactenus inedita*, ed. R. Steele *et al.*, 16 vols. (1905–40): I *Metaphysica de viciis contractis in studio theologie*; II–IV *Communia naturalia*; V *Secretum secretorum*; VI 2–198 *Compotus*; 199–211 *Kalendarium*; 212–67 *Compotus v.* GROS; VII *Questiones supra undecimum prime philosophie Aristotelis*; VIII *Questiones supra libros IV physicorum Aristotelis*; IX 1–83 *De retardatione accidentium senectutis* (attrib.), 84–9 *Summaria expositio epistole predicte*; 90–5 *De universali regimine senum*; 96–7 *De balneis senum*; 98–102 *De compositione..medicinarum*; 103–19 *Antidotarius*; 120–43 *De conservatione iuventutis*; 144–9 *De graduatione medicinarum* 150–79 *De erroribus medicorum*; 181–6 Extr. from *Liber sex scientiarum*; 186–208 *De diebus creticis*; X *Questiones supra libros prime philosophie Aristotelis*; XI 1–170 *Questiones altere supra libros prime philosophie Aristotelis*; 171–252 *Questiones supra De plantis*; 253–312 *Metaphysica vetus Aristotelis*; XII 1–158 *Questiones supra librum de causis*; 159–87 *Liber de causis*; XIII *Questiones supra libros octo physicorum Aristotelis*; XIV 1–134 *Liber de sensu et sensato*; 135–208 *Summa de sophismatibus et distinctionibus*; XV 1–190 *Summa gramatica*; 191–359 *Sumule dialectices*; XVI *Communia mathematica.*

BACONTHORPE John Baconthorpe [*ob.* 1346]: **Quaest. Sent.** *Quaestiones in iv libros sententiarum*, vols. I and II to p. 582, (Cremona, 1618; facsim. ed. Farnborough, Hants 1969); **Quodl.** *Quodlibetorum libri IV*, *ib.* II, 583–779; **Sent.** *Opus super iv sententiarum libris*, (Paris, 1484).

BAD. AUR. Johannes de Bado Aureo (? of Guildford) [*fl. c*1400]: *Tractatus de armis* [2 versions], in Mediaeval Heraldry, ed. J. Jones (Cardiff, 1943) 95–212.

Baga Secr. *Baga de secretis*, MS PRO (K.B. 8).

BAKER Geoffrey le Baker (*alias* Walter of Swinbroke): *Chronicon* (1303–56) [incl. extr. printed in Chr. Ed. I and II, II 297–319] (Oxford, 1889) [by f.].

BALD. CANT. Baldwin, Archb. of Canterbury (*ob.* 1190]: **Commend. Fid.** *De commendatione fidei*, in *PL* CCIV (1855) 571–640; **Sacr. Alt.** *De sacramento altaris*, *ib.* 641–774; **Tract.** *Tractatus*, *ib.* 403–572 [by no. and col.].

BALSH. Adam of Balsham (*alias* de Parvo Ponte) [*ob.* 1181]: **AD** *Ars disserendi* (*Dialectica Alexandri*) (1132), in Twelfth century logic, texts and studies, I, ed. L. Minio-Paluello (Rome, 1956) 1–68; **AD rec. 2** [second recension, possibly by NECKHAM], *ib.* footnotes and 69–111 [both by cap.]; **Ut.** *De utensilibus*, in N. & E. XXXIV pt. 1, ed. J. B. Hauréau (1891) 33–59 [*vv. ll.* checked with variants in A. Scheler, Jahrbuch für romanische und eng. Lit. VIII (1867) 75–93.

Bannatyne Club publications (Edinburgh, 1823–48).

Bannatyne Misc. Miscellany..of original papers..relating to the history..of Scotland, 3 vols. Bannatyne Club (1827–55).

Banstead History of Banstead in Surrey (selected docs. 1086–), ed. H. C. M. Lambert, 2 vols. (Oxford, 1912, 1931).

Baronial Reform Jacob, E. F.: Studies in the period of Baronial reform (Oxford, 1925).

BART. ANGL. Bartholomaeus Anglicus (*alias* de Glanville) [*fl.* 1230–50]: *De proprietatibus rerum* [mainly from ed. Cologne, 1472, by bk. and cap.].

BART. EXON. Pen. Bartholomew of Exeter [*ob.* 1184]: *Liber poenitentialis*, ed. A. Morey: Bartholomew of Exeter (Cambridge, 1937) 175–300 [by cap.].

Bec Morgan, M.: The English lands of the Abbey of Bec (Oxford, 1946).

BECKET Thomas Becket, Archb. of Canterbury [1162–70]: **Ep.** *Epistolae*, Becket Mat. V–VII [by no.]; **Sim.** Satire against the Symoniacs, in: Poésies Pop. 175–7.

Becket Mat. Materials for the history of Thomas Becket, Archb. of Canterbury, 7 vols. RS (1875–85) [mainly cited under authors; *v. et. V. Thom* A and B].

Becket to Langton Cheney, C. R.: From Becket to Langton (Manchester, 1956).

BEDE Bede (Baeda) [673–735]: **AM** *De arte metrica*, ed. H. Keil, in *Grammatici Latini* VII (1878) 227–60 [ref. by pp. of ed. Putschius 2349–2382]; **Cuthb.** Prose life of S. Cuthbert [c.721], in Colgrave, B.: Two lives of S. Cuthbert (1940) 141–306 [by cap.]; **Egb.** *Epistola ad Ecgbertum episcopum* (734) in *Op. Hist.* I 405–23 [by cap.]; **Ezra** *In Ezram et Neemiam*, in *Corpus Christianorum, S. Lat.* CXIXA (1969) 235–392 [by col. of *PL* XCI; Bks. I and II are commentaries on Ezra, Bk. III on Nehemiah (sometimes known as Ezra II)]; **Gen.** *Libri quatuor in principium Genesis* (*p*721) *ib.* CXVIIIA (1967) [by col. of *PL* XCI 9–190]; **HA** *Historia abbatum* [Benedict, Ceolfrid, Eosterwin, Sigfrid Hwaetbehrt (*p*716)], in *Op. Hist.* I 364–87 [by cap.]; **HE** *Historia ecclesiastica gentis Anglorum* (731), ed. C. Plummer, *Op. Hist.* I (Oxford, 1896) 5–360 [by bk. and cap.] also ed. B. Colgrave and R. A. B. Mynors in Med. Texts (Oxford, 1969); **HE Cont.** *ib.* 361–3;

Hom. Homilies, as Ezra above, CXXII (1955) 1–143; [this vol. contains all the genuine homilies of Bede; cited by col. of *PL* XCIV]; **Hymn.** *Liber hymnorum, etc., ib.* 405–73 [by no. and line]; **Kings** *In Regum librum XXX quaestiones, ib.* CXIX (1962) 289–322 [by col. of *PL* XCI]; **Luke** *In Lucae evangelium expositio, ib.* CXX (1960) 1–425 [by col. of *PL* XCII]; **Mark** *In Marci evangelium expositio, ib.* 427–648 [ref. as above]; **Mart.** Martyrology (prose, attrib.) *PL* XCIV 797–1148; **Nom. Loc.** *Nomina locorum ex beati Hieronimi presbiteri et Flavi Josephi collecta opusculis* in *Corpus Christianorum, S. Lat.* CXIX 273–87; **Orth.** *De orthographia*, as *AM* above 261–94 [ref. as above, 2775–2804]; **Pleg.** *Epistola ad Pleguinam* (708), as *TR* below, 305–15 [by cap.]; **ST** *De schematibus et tropis*, ed. C. Halm, in *Rhetores Latini minores* (1863) 607–18 [by p.]; **Sam.** *In primam partem Samuhelis libri* IIII, as Ezra above, CXIX 1–272 [by col. of *PL* XCI]; **TR** *De temporum ratione*, in *Opera de temporibus*, ed. C. W. Jones, Med. Acad. of America XLI (1943) 175–291 [by cap.]; **Tab.** *De tabernaculo* (*a*729), as Ezra above CXIXA 1–139 [by col. of *PL* XCI]; **Temp.** *De temporibus* (703), as *TR* above, 293–303 [by cap.]; **Templ.** *De templo*, as Ezra above, CXIXA 141–234 [by col. of *PL* XCI]; **Wict.** *Epistola ad Wicthedum* (708), as *TR* above, 317–25 [by cap.]; other works, including some of doubtful attribution, cited from *PL* XC–XCIV.

BEKINSAU John Bekinsau [*ob.* 1559]: *De supremo et absoluto regis imperio*, in *Monarchia* I 735–56.

BEKYNTON Thomas Bekynton [king's secretary etc., *ob.* 1465]: Official [diplomatic] correspondence, 2 vols. RS (1872); **App. 285** Dialogue in praise of William of Wykeham (incl. life of Bekynton) attrib. Chaundler, II 321–6.

BELETH RDO John Beleth [*fl. c*1182]: *Rationale divinorum officiorum* (*a*1190), in *PL* CCII (1855) 13–166 [by cap. and col.].

BEN. PET. Benedict of Peterborough [*ob.* 1193]: **Mir. Thom.** *Miracula S.Thomae Cantuariensis*, Becket Mat. II 21–298 [by cap.]; **Pass. Thom.** *Passio S.Thomae Cantuariensis, ib.* 1–19 [by frag.] [*v. et. G. Hen. II, G. Ric. I*].

Best. Bestiary..from MS I i. iv. 26 in the University Library, Cambridge (12c.), ed. M. R. James, Roxburghe Club (1928) [by serial no. (cf. pp. 28–34) and f.].

Best. Leningrad Ein engl. Bestiar des 12. Jahrhunderts in der Staatsbibl. zu Leningrad, ed. A. Konstantinova (Leningrad, 1929).

Bibl. Chem. *Bibliotheca chemica curiosa*, ed. J.-J. Manget, 2 vols. (Geneva, 1702).

Bibl. Vet. Pat. *Maxima bibliotheca veterum patrum et antiquorum scriptorum ecclesiasticorum* (–1600), ed. M. de La Bigne, 27 vols. (Lyon, 1677).

BIRCHINGTON Arch. Cant. Stephen Birchington [*fl.* 1382] [attrib.]: *Vitae archiepiscoporum Cantuariensium* (507–1369), in *Anglia Sacra* I 1–48.

BLAKMAN Hen. VI John Blakman [*ob. p*1457]: *De virtutibus et miraculis Henrici VI*, ed. M. R. James (Cambridge, 1919).

BLANEFORD Henry de Blaneford: Chronicle (1323–4), *Chr. Mon. S.Alb.* III 129–52.

BLUND An. *v.* J. Blund *An.*

BOECE Hector Boece (Boethius) [*ob.* 1536]: *Scotorum historiae a prima gentis origine..libri XIX* (to *c*1436) (Paris, 1526) [by f.].

Boldon Bk. Boldon Buke, survey of possessions of see of Durham (1183), Surtees Soc. XXV (1852) [by p.].

BONIF. Boniface (*alias* Winfrith] [*ob.* 755]: **AG** *Ars* [*grammaticalis*], in *Classicorum auctorum* VII, ed. A. Mai (1835) 475–548; **Aen.** *Aenigmata* (*Virt. and Vit.*) in *Collect. Aen. Meroving. Aet., Corpus Christianorum S. Lat.* CXXXIII (1968) 273–343 [by line]; also ed. E. Dümmler, in *PLAC* I; **Carm.** *Carmina*, in *PLAC* I (1881) 16–20 [by no. and line]; **Ep.** *Epistolae*, in Briefe des heiligen Bonifatius und Lullus, in *MGH, Ep. selectae* I (1916) [by no.; letters to Boniface from British correspondents cited as *Ep. Bonif.*]; **Met.** *De caesuris et metris*, in Gaisford, T: *Scriptores Latini rei metricae* (1837) 577–85 [here printed as anon., attrib. Bonif. by F. J. E. Raby].

Borough Cust. Borough customs, ed. M. Bateson, 2 vols. Selden Soc. XVIII, XXI (1904, 1906).

BOWER, W. *v.* Fordun *Cont.*

BRACTON Henry de Bracton (*alias* Bratton) [*ob.* 1268]: *De legibus et consuetudinibus Angliae* (*c*1258), ed. G. E. Woodbine, 4 vols. (New Haven, etc., 1915–42) [by f.; *v. et.* BNB].

BRADW. CD Thomas Bradwardine [*ob.* 1349]: *De causa Dei, contra Pelagium..lib. tres* (1344), ed. H. Savile (1618) [*v. et.* Sci. Mech.].

BRAKELOND Jocelin of Brakelond [*ob. p*1214]: *Cronica..de rebus gestis Samsonis Abbatis monasterii S.Edmundi* [Suff] (1173–1202), Med. Texts (1949) [by f.].

Brev. Aberd. *Breviarium Aberdonense* (first printed 1509–10), 2 vols. Bannatyne Club (1854).

BRIDFERTH [*fl. c*1000] *v. V. Dunst. B.*

BRINTON Serm. Thomas Brinton (*alias* Brunton), Bishop of Rochester [1373–89]: Sermons, Camd. 3rd S. LXXXV, LXXXVI (1954).

Brokage Bk. Southampt. The brokage book of Southampton I (1439–40), Southampt. Rec. Soc. XL (1941); II and III (1443–4), *ib.* Rec. S. IV, VI (1960, 1961).

BROMPTON John Brompton [*fl. c*1436] [attrib.]: *Chronicon* (588–1198), in *Hist. Angl. Script. X*, ed. R. Twysden (1652) 728–1284 [by col.].

BROMYARD Summa John of Bromyard [*fl. c*1390]: *Summa praedicantium*, 2 vols. (Venice, 1586).

Bronnen Bronnen tot de Geschiedenis van den Handel met Engeland Schotland en Ierland (1150–1585), ed. H. J. Smit, 4 vols. Commissie van advies voor's Rijks Geschiedkundige LXV, LXVI, LXXXVI, XCI (The Hague, 1928–50).

BRUNTON *v.* Brinton.

BRUSSIUS *v.* W. Bruce.

BRYGG Itin. Thomas Brygg: *Itinerarium in Terram Sanctam domini Thomae de Swynburne* (1392–3), Archives de l'Orient Latin II (Paris, 1884) 378–88.

Building in Eng. Salzman, L. F.: Building in England down to 1540, a documentary history (Oxford, 1952).

Bull. DuC. *v.* Alma.

BURLEY Comment. Pol. Walter Burley [*ob. c*1345]: Commentary on the Politics [of Aristotle], extr. in Wilkinson Essays 278–81; **Expos. Art. Vet.** *Expositio super artem veterem* [cited from GLA III].

Bury St. E. Lobel, M.D.: The borough of Bury St. Edmund's (Oxford, 1935), app. 1. Documents (*c*1190–1479) 171–95.

CBaron The Court Baron..w. select pleas from the Bishop of Ely's Court of Littleport (1285, 1316–27). Selden Soc. IV (1891).

CD *Codex diplomaticus aevi Saxonici* [604–1061], ed. J. M. Kemble. 6 vols. Eng. Hist. Soc. (1839–48) [by no.; used where not superseded by *CS*].

CS *Cartularium Saxonicum*..[604–975] ed. W. de G. Birch, 4 vols. (1885–99) [by no.; partly checked in light of Sawyer: *Anglo-Saxon Charters*, etc.].

CAIUS John Caius (*alias* Keyes) [1510–73]: **Anim.** *De rariorum animalium historia libellus* (1570), in Works, ed. E. S. Roberts (Cambridge, 1912); **Can.** *De canibus Britannicis libellus* (1570), *ib.*

Cal. Bart. *v.* Cart. Bart.

CalCh Calendar of Charter Rolls..1226–1516, 6 vols. HMSO (1903–27) [*v. et. ChartR, RChart.*].

Cal. Chanc. R. Var. Calendar of various Chancery Rolls (1277–1326), HMSO (1912).

CalCl Calendar of the Close Rolls (1272–), HMSO (1900–) [*v. et. Cl.*].

Cal. Co. CourtR Chester Calendar of County Court, City Court and Eyre rolls of Chester, 1259–97, w. inquest of military service, 1288, Chetham Soc. ns LXXXIV (1925).

Cal. Coron. R. Lond. Calendar of Coroners' rolls of the City of London (1300–78) (1913).

Cal. Deeds Ormond Calendar of Ormond deeds (1170–1603), 6 vols. IMC (Dublin, 1932–43).

Cal. Doc. France Documents preserved in France, illustrative of the history of Great Britain and Ireland (918–1206) ed. J. H. Round, HMSO (1899) [by no.].

Cal. Exch. The antient kalendars and inventories of the Treasury of H.M. Exchequer, 3 vols. RC (1836).

Cal. FineR Calendar of Fine Rolls 1272–1509, 22 vols. HMSO (1911–63) [*v. et.* FineR.].

CalIMisc Calendar of Inquisitions Miscellaneous (1219–), HMSO (1916–) [by no.].

Cal. IPM Calendar of inquisitions *post mortem* etc.: Ser. I, vol. I– (Hen. III–) (1904–); Ser. II, vol. I– (Hen. VII–) (1898–) [by no.].

Cal. Ir. Calendar of documents relating to Ireland (1171–1307), 5 vols. HMSO (1875–86).

Cal. LBLond. Calendar of letter books preserved..at the Guildhall [London], A–L (Ed. I–Hen. VII), 11 vols. (1899–1912).

Cal. Liberate Calendar of Liberate Rolls preserved in PRO (1226–72), 6 vols. HMSO (1916–64) [vol. VI by no.; others by p.].

Cal. Mayor's CourtR. Lond. Calendar of early Mayor's court rolls..at the Guildhall, London (1298–1307) (1924).

Cal. Mem. Calendar of Memoranda rolls (Exch.) (Michaelmas 1326–Michaelmas 1327), HMSO (1968).

Cal. Pat. Calendar of Patent Rolls 1232– , Vol. III– HMSO (1906–) [*v. et.* Pat.].

Cal. Pl. Mem. Lond. Calendar of Plea and Memoranda Rolls.. of the City of London (1323–81), 2 vols. (1926, 1929); also Calendar of Select Pleas and Memoranda (1381–1412) (1932).

Cal. Recog. R. Chester Calendar of Recognizance Rolls of Chester (13c.–1830), PRO DK's Reps. 36, 37, 39, app. II, sep. pub. (1875–8).

Cal. Scot. Calendar of documents relating to Scotland (1108–1509), 4 vols. Scot. RO (1881–8).

Cal. Scot. Mary Calendar of State Papers relating to Scotland and Mary, Queen of Scots (1547–1603) 13 vols. in 14, Scot. RO (1898–1969).

Cal. SP Scot. Calendar of State Papers relating to Scotland, Scot. S. (I 1509–89, II 1543–1602) (1858).

Camb. Antiq. Soc. Cambridge Antiquarian Society, publications, 4° S. I and II (1840–9); New 4° S. I– (1908–); 8° S. I– (1859–).

CAMD. Br. William Camden [1551–1623]: *Britannia* (1586) [by p. of ed. 1600].

Camd. Misc. The Camden miscellany, Vol. I– Camd. Soc. XXXIX– (1847–) *et alia.*

Camd. Soc. Camden Society, publications: Vols. I–CV (1808–70); NS New Series, vols. I–LXII (1871–99); **Camd. 3rd S.** vols. I–XCIV (1900–63); **Camd. 4th S.** vol. I– (1964–); 3rd and 4th S. pub. by R. Hist. Soc.

Canon. G. Sempr. Un procès de canonisation..(1201–2); le livre de Saint Gilbert de Sempringham [*ob.* 1189], ed. R. Foreville (? Lille 1943) [by f.].

Cant. Cath. Pri. Smith, R. A. L.: Canterbury Cathedral Priory (597–1540) (Cambridge, 1943).

Cant. Coll. Ox. Canterbury College, Oxford, ed. W. A. Pantin OHS VI, VII, VIII (1947–50).

Cant. & York Soc. Canterbury and York Society, publications I– (London, 1909–).

CANTLOW Orig. Canteb. Nicholas Cantlow [*ob.* 1441]: *Historiola de antiquitate et origine Universitatis Cantebrigiensis*, ed. T. Hearne in T. SPROTT *Chr.* 253–80.

CAPGR. John Capgrave [1393–1464]: **Dunst.** *Vita et miracula Dunstani*, in Mem. Dunst. 325–53 [by cap., *v. et. NLA*]; **Hen.** *Liber de illustribus Henricis*, RS (1858) w. app. of extr. from other works.

Capt. Seis. Cornub. *Captio seisinae Ducatus Cornubiae* (1337–8), MS PRO (E. 120).

Carm. Aldh. *Carmina rhythmica* 1–5, in *Aldhelmi Opera, MGH Auct. Antiq.* XV (1919) 523–37 (1 anon., 2–5 by Æthelwald) [by line].

Cart. Aberd. *Cartularium ecclesiae S.Nicholai Aberdonensis* (1328–), 2 vols. New Spalding Club (Aberdeen, 1888–92).

Cart. Antiq. *Cartae antiquae* (Ric. I–Ed. II), vol. I (rolls 1–10), Pipe Roll Soc. NS XVII (1939); vol. II (rolls 11–20), *ib.* XXXIII (1960) [by p.]; rolls 21–46, MS PRO (C. 52).

Cart. Bart. Cartulary of St. Bartholomew's hospital [London] (12c–), calendar, ed. N. J. M. Kerling (1973).

Cart. Bath Two chartularies of the Priory of St. Peter at Bath (9c.–), Som Rec. Soc. VII (1893).

Cart. Beaulieu Cartulary of the Abbey of Beaulieu (13c.–), MS BM Loan 29/330 [by f.].

Cart. Beauly Historical notices and charters of the Priory of Beauly, Ross-shire (13c.–), Trans. R. Hist. Soc. IV (1876) 1–74 [*v. et.* Ch. Beauly].

Cart. Bilsington The cartulary and terrier of the Priory of Bilsington [Kent], ed. N. Neilson (1928): Cartulary (mainly 13c.) 65–147; Terrier (1567) 148–218.

Cart. Boarstall The Boarstall [Bucks.] cartulary (1170–1498), OHS LXXXVIII (1930) [by no.].

Cart. Bonport Cartulaire de l'abbaye royale de Notre-Dame de Bonport [Norm.] (1190–1467) (Evreux, 1862).

Cart. Boxgrove The chartulary of Boxgrove Priory (13c.–) [transl. only] Sussex Rec. Soc. LIX (1960).

Cart. Brecon *Cartularium prioratus..de Brecon* (12c.–), *Arch. Cambr.* 4th S. XIII, XIV (1882–3).

Cart. Burton Abstract of Chartulary of Burton Abbey (1004–1437), Collect. Staffs V i (1884).

Cart. Canons Ashby Cartulary of the Priory of Canons Ashby, Northants (late 13c.), MS BM Egerton 3033.

Cart. Chester The chartulary..of the Abbey of St. Werburgh, Chester (10c.–early 14c.) w. addit. docs., Chetham Soc. NS LXXIX, LXXXII (1920–3).

Cart. Chich. The cartulary of the High Church of Chichester (*c*1250–), Sussex Rec. Soc. XLIV (1946) [by no.].

Cart. Ciren. The cartulary of Cirencester Abbey, Glos (12c.–), ed. C. D. Ross, 2 vols. (1964) [by no.].

Cart. Cockersand The chartulary of Cockersand Abbey [Lancs] (12c.–), 3 vols. in 7, Chetham Soc. NS XXXVIII–XL, XLIII, LVI, LVII, LXIV (1898–1909).

Cart. Colch. *Cartularium monasterii..de Colecestria* [Essex] (11c.–), 2 vols. Roxburghe Club (1897).

Cart. Coldstream Chartulary of the Cistercian Priory of Coldstream [Berw] (12c.–), Grampian Club (London, 1879).

Cart. Colne *Cartularium Prioratus de Colne* (12c.) Arch. Soc. Essex, occ. pub. I (1946) [by f.].

Cart. Dale The cartulary of Dale Abbey (13c.–) Arch. Soc. Derb Rec. S. II and HMC XI Joint Pub. (HMSO, 1967).

Cart. Darley The cartulary of Darley Abbey (late 12c.–), 2 vols., Arch. Soc. Derb (1945).

Cart. Dieul. Chartulary of Dieulacres Abbey (12 c.–), Collect. Staffs NS IX (1906) 291–362; **add.**, *ib.* 363–6.

Cart. Dublin Chartularies of St. Mary's Abbey, Dublin, etc. (12c.–), 2 vols. RS (1884).

Cart. Dunstable Digest of the cartulary of Dunstable (late 12c.–), Beds Hist. Rec. Soc. X (1926).

Cart. Eynsham The Eynsham cartulary (1005–1539), incl. Vision of the Monk of Eynsham (*c*1197), OHS XLIX, LI (1907–8).

Cart. Fount. Abstracts [in Eng.] from charters..contained in Chartulary of Fountains Abbey [Yorks] (12c.–), ed. W. T. Lancaster, 2 vols. (1915) [very little Lat.].

Cart. Glam. *Cartae et alia munimenta quae ad Dominium de Glamorgancia pertinent* (5c.–), revised ed. 1910, 6 vols. (–224/–712/–1176/–1632/–2096/ Index) [some docs. cited from fuller text in first ed. 1885].

Cart. Glast. The great chartulary of Glastonbury (12c.–), Som Rec. Soc. LIX [LXII, LXIV] (1947–56).

Cart. Glouc. *Historia et cartularium Monasterii S.Petri Gloucestriae* (7c.–), 3 vols. RS (1863–7); vol. I 3–125 = *Hist. Glouc.*

Cart. Harrold Records of Harrold Priory, incl. Cartulary (12c.–), Beds Hist. Rec. Soc. XVII (1935).

Cart. Healaugh Chartulary of the..Park of Healaugh (12c.–), Arch. Soc. Yorks, Rec. S. XCII (1936) [by f.].

Cart. Heming. Hemingus [*fl.* 1096]: *Chartularium ecclesiae*

Wigorniensis (8c.–11c.), ed. T. Hearne, 2 vols. (1723) [*v. et.* Cart. Worc.].

Cart. Holyrood *Liber cartarum S.Crucis, munimenta ecclesie S.Crucis de Edwinesburg* (12c.–), extr., Bannatyne Club LXX (1840).

Cart. Hosp. S.John Cartulary of the Hospital of St. John, Oxford (13c.–), OHS LXVI, LXVIII, LXIX (1914–16).

CartINorm. Cartulaire des Îles normandes (11c.–), Soc. jersiaise (1924).

Cart. Lindores Chartulary of the Abbey of Lindores [Fife] (12c.–), SHS XLII (1903).

Cart. Newent Cartulary of Newent [Glos] (13c.), MS BM Add. MS 15668 ff. 50–68 [by f.].

Cart. Newm. *Chartularium Abbathiae de Novo Monasterio* [Northumb] (12c.–), Surtees Soc. LXVI (1878).

Cart. Newnham The cartulary of Newnham Priory [Beds] (12c.–), Beds Hist. Rec. Soc. XLIII pts. 1 and 2 (1963–4).

Cart. Osney Cartulary of Oseney Abbey (12c.–), OHS LXXXIX–XCI, XCVII, XCVIII, CI (1929–36).

Cart. Pontefr. Chartulary of Pontefract (12c.–), Arch. Soc. Yorks Rec. S. XXV, XXX (1899, 1902).

Cart. Rams. *Cartularium monasterii de Rameseia* [Hunts] (11c.–), 3 vols. RS (1884–93).

Cart. Rievaulx *Cartularium Abbathiae de Rievalle* [Yorks] (12c.–), Surtees Soc. LXXXIII (1889).

Cart. Rufford The Rufford [Notts] cartulary (12c.) MS BM (Loans 41 ff. 1–16).

Cart. S.Denys Southampt. Cartulary of the priory of St. Denys, Portswood, Southampton (1157–), comp. *p*1342, MS BM Add. 15314.

Cart. S.Fridesw. Cartulary of the monastery of St. Frideswide at Oxford (11c.–), OHS XXVIII, XXXI (1895–9).

Cart. S.Greg. Cant. Cartulary of the Priory of St. Gregory, Canterbury (late 11c.–), Camd. 3rd S. LXXXVIII (1956) [by no.].

Cart. S.Neot. Cartulary of the Priory of St. Neots, Hunts (*c*1175–), MS BM Cotton Faustina A4).

Cart. S.Thom. Hosp. Chartulary of the Hospital of St. Thomas Martyr, Southwark (1213–1525), calendar ed. F. G. Parsons, private pub. (1932).

Cart. Sallay The chartulary..of Sallay in Craven (*c*1250–), Arch. Soc. Yorks Rec. S. LXXXVII, XC (1933–4) [by no.].

Cart. Staff. The Staffordshire chartulary (1072–1237), Collect. Staffs II pt. 1 (1881) 178–276.

Cart. Stoke by Clare Cartulary..of Stoke by Clare [Suff] (*p*1250), MS BM Cotton App. XXI.

Cart. Tutbury The cartulary of Tutbury Priory (*c*1145–), Collect. Staffs 4th S. IV (1962) [by no.].

Cart. Wardon Cartulary..of Old Wardon (12c.–), Beds Hist. Rec. Soc. XIII (1930) [by f.].

Cart. Whitby *Cartularium Abbathiae de Whiteby* (11c.–), Surtees Soc. LXIX, LXXII (1879, 1881).

Cart. Winchcombe *v.* Reg. Winchcombe.

Cart. Worc. The cartulary of Worcester Cathedral Priory, Register I (964–14c.), Pipe R. Soc. NS XXXVIII (1968) [by no.; *v. et.* Cart. Heming.].

Carte Nativ. *Carte nativorum*, a Peterborough Abbey cartulary of the 14c., Northants Rec. Soc. XX (1960) [by no.].

CatAncD A descriptive catalogue of Ancient Deeds in the Public Record Office (1213–1564), 6 vols. HMSO (1890–1915) [*v. et.* AncD.].

Catalog. Durh. Catalogues of the Library of Durham Cathedral ..from the Conquest to the Dissolution, Surtees Soc. VII (1838).

CathA *Catholicon Anglicum*, an English–Latin wordbook (1483) Camd. Soc. NS XXX (1882).

Cath. Rec. Soc. Catholic Record Society, pubs., vol. I– (1905–).

Ch. Beauly The charters of the Priory of Beauly [Ross-shire], ed. E. C. Batten, Grampian Club (1877) [*v. et.* Cart. Beauly].

Ch. Coupar Angus Charters of the Abbey of Coupar Angus, (I–1376, II–1608), SHS 3rd S. XL, XLI (1947).

Ch. Crispin *v.* G. CRISPIN

Ch. Danelaw *v.* Danelaw.

Ch. Derb. A descriptive catalogue of Derbyshire charters (*c*1130–1550) ed. J. H. Jeayes (London, 1906) [by no.].

Ch. Edinburgh Charters..relating to the City of Edinburgh, 1143–1540, ed. J. D. Marwick (Edinburgh, 1871).

Ch. Gilb. Transcripts of charters relating to Gilbertine houses (*c*1150–*c*1258), Linc. Rec. Soc. XVIII (1922).

Ch. Glouc. Earldom of Gloucester charters..to 1217, ed. R. B. Patterson (Oxford, 1973).

Ch. Heref. Charters of the Earldom of Hereford (1095–1201), Camd. Misc. XXII, Camd. 4th S. I (1964) 1–75.

Ch. & Rec. Heref. Charters and records of Hereford Cathedral (*c*840–1421) ed. W. W. Capes (Hereford, 1908).

Ch. Hib. *Chartae, privilegia et immunitates* (1171–1395), Irish RC (1889).

Ch. Mowbray Charters of the Honour of Mowbray, 1107–91, ed. D. E. Greenway (1972) [by no.].

Ch. Sal. Charters and documents illustrating the history of the cathedral, city and diocese of Salisbury (1109–1300), RS (1891).

Ch. Stirling Charters and documents relating to the Royal Burgh of Stirling (1124–1705), ed. R. Renwick (Glasgow, 1884).

Chain Bk. Dublin The Dublin chain book (1309), in *Doc. Ir.* 230–9.

Chanc. Forest Proc. Chancery Forest Proceedings (Hen. VIII–Chas. I), MS PRO (C. 99).

Chanc. Misc. Miscellanea of the Chancery (Hen. I–18c.), MS PRO (C. 47) [*v. et.* DipDocC].

Chanc. Orders Orders of the High Court of Chancery (1388–1743), ed. G. W. Sanders, I pt. 1 (1845).

Chanc. Proc. Chancery Proceedings, MS PRO (C. 2 and 3) [*v. et. E. Chanc. Proc.*].

Chanc. R. *v.* Pipe (Chanc.).

Chap. Ely *v.* Ord. Ely.

Chap. Linc. Chapter acts of the Cathedral Church..of Lincoln (1520–59), Linc. Rec. Soc. XII, XIII, XV (1915–20); also Act Bks. MS (1305–1520), DC Linc.

ChartR Charter Rolls (1199–1517), MS PRO (C. 53) [*v. et. RChart*, CalCh].

CHAUNCY Passio Maurice Chauncy [*ob.* 1581]: *Passio sanctorum patrum Carthusianorum Anglie* (1550) (London, 1935).

CHAUNDLER Laud. Thomas Chaundler [*ob.* 1490]: *Libellus de laudibus duarum civitatum et sedium episcopalium Welliae scilicet et Bathoniae* (*c*1460), Arch. Soc. Som. XIX pt. 2 (1874) 99–122 [*v. et.* BEKYNTON App. 285].

Chetham Soc. Chetham Society, Remains historical and literary connected with the Palatine Counties of Lancaster and Chester, I– (1844–).

CHONNOE *v.* CONWAY.

Chr. Abingd. *Chronicon monasterii de Abingdon* (12c.), 2 vols. RS (1858) [app. in vol. II incl. *Abbat. Abingd.* (12c.) and *Obed. Abingd.* (13c.)].

Chr. Angl. *Chronicon Angliae* (1328–88), *auct. monacho quodam S.Albani* [prob. T. Walsingham], RS (1874).

Chr. Angl. Peterb. *Chronicon Angliae Petriburgense* (654–1368), Caxton Soc. (1845) [supersedes *Hist. Angl. Script.* i 1–137; *cf. Chr. Peterb.*].

Chr. Barnwell *v.* W. COVENTRY.

Chr. Battle Chronicon monasterii de Bello [Battle, Sussex] 1066–1176, *Anglia Christiana* Soc. (1846); **Id. (1258–65)**, in *V. Montf.* 373–80.

Chr. Bury *Chronica Buriensis* The chronicle of Bury St. Edmund's [Suff] (1212–1301), Med. Texts (1964); (1212–65) 1–33 [*v.* TAXTER]; **Cont. A** (1266–96) 33–136; **Cont. B** (1296–1301) 136–63.

Chr. Cant. *Chronicon Anonymi Cantuariensis* (1436–67), in J. READING 187–227.

Chr. Clun. Notes on an English Cluniac chronicle (St. Andrew's Priory, Northampton, –1339), extr. in EHR XLIV (1929) 94–104.

Chr. Dale Chronicle of the Abbey of St. Mary de Parco Stanley *alias* Dale (mid 12c.–13c.), attrib. T. de Musca (*ob. p*1235], Arch. Soc. Derb. LXXXVII (1968) 18–38 [by cap.] [incomplete text also in *MonA* VI 892–5].

Chr. Dunstable *v.* Ann. Dunstable.

Chr. Ebor. Metr. *Chronicon Metricum Ecclesie Eboracensis*: **A** (*c*1390), Hist. Church York II 446–9; **B** (? *c*1370), *ib.* 469–87.

Chr. Ed. I & II Chronicles of the reigns of Edward I and Edward II, 2 vols. RS (1882–3) [*v. et. Ann. Lond.*, *Ann. Paul.*, BAKER, *G. Ed. II Bridl.*, *G. Ed. III Bridl.*, J. LOND. *Commend. Ed. I*, MORE Chr. Ed. II, *V. Ed. II*].

Chr. Evesham *Chronicon Abbatiae de Evesham* [Worcs], RS (1863): (*c*700–1086) attrib. Prior Dominic [*fl. c*1125] 1–29, 36–67; (*c*700–1214) attrib. Thomas of Marlborough [Abbot 1230–6] 69–257; (1214–1419) anon. 257–310; (1418–1539) anon.338–40; incl. also *Mir. Transl.*, and *V S.Ecgwini* (? wr. 12c.) 1–6, and *Mir. Odulph.*, *Mir. Wistan.*, *V. Wistan.*, *q.v.*

Chr. Hen. II & Ric. I Chronicles of the reigns of Henry II and Richard I, 2 vols. RS (1867) [contains *G. Hen. II* and *G. Ric. I*].

Chr. Hen. VI & Ed. IV Brief notes of occurrences under Hen. VI and Ed. IV, in Three fifteenth-century chronicles, Camd. Soc. NS XXVIII (1880) 148–63.

Chr. Holyrood *Chronicon Coenobii Sanctae Crucis Edinburgensis* (40 B.C.–1163), Bannatyne Club (1828).

Chr. Kirkstall The Kirkstall chronicle (1355–1400), J. R. L. Bull. XV (1931) 121–37.

Chr. Louth *Chronicon abbatiae de Parco Lude* w. app. of docs. (1066–1404), ed. E. Venables, Lincs Rec. Soc. I (1891).

Chr. Man. *Chronica regum Manniae et Insularum* (1000–1374), Manx Soc. XXII (text and transl.), XXIII (docs.) (1874).

Chr. Melrose *Chronica de Mailros* (731–1270), Bannatyne Club (1835).

Chr. Mon. S.Alb. *Chronica monasterii S.Albani*, 7 vols. in 12, RS (1863–70): I WALS. *HA*; II RISH.; III TROKELOWE and BLANEFORD; IV *G. S.Alb.*; V AMUND., *etc.*; VI *Reg. Whet.*; VII WALS. *YN.*

Chr. Peterb. *Chronicon Petroburgense* (1122–1289), Camd. Soc. XLVII (1849) 1–155; **App.** *Liber niger monasterii S.Petri de Burgo* (1125–8), *ib.* 157–83; *cf. Chr. Angl. Peterb.*, *Hist. Angl. Script.*

Chr. Pont. Ebor. *Chronica pontificum Ecclesiae Eboracensis* (601–1519), Hist. Church York II; **A** Anon. (601–1140, wr. *a*1150) 312–87; **B** 388–421, *v.* T. STUBBS; **C** Anon. (1374–1519) 422–45.

Chr. Rams. *Chronicon Abbatiae Rameseiensis* [Hunts], (10c.–*c*1200], RS (1886).

Chr. S.Alb. (1406–20) The St. Albans chronicle, ed. V. H. Galbraith (1937) [attrib. WALS.; supersedes WALS. *HA* pt. 2, 272–336].

Chr. S. Alb. (1422–31) *Chronicon rerum gestarum in monasterio S.Albani..a quodam auctore ignoto compilatum*, *Chr. Mon. S.Alb.* V 1–69.

Chr. S.Edm. The St. Edmundsbury chronicle 1296–1301, EHR LVIII (1943) 51–78.

Chr. S. Neoti *v.* ASSER.

Chr. Sprotti *v.* T. SPROTT *Chr.*

Chr. Steph. Chronicles of the reign of Stephen, Henry II and Richard I, 4 vols. RS (1884–9) [mainly cited under authors].

Chr. Wallingf. The chronicle attributed to John of Wallingford (449–1035, wr. *a*1258), Camd. Misc. XXI, Camd. 3rd S. XC (1958).

Chr. Westm. Chronicle (1381–94) [formerly attrib. John of Malvern] wr. late 14c. by a monk of Westminster, printed as app. in HIGD. IX 1–283; new ed. for Med. Texts in prep. [by p. of HIGD.].

Chr. Witham Witham Charterhouse chronicle, a fragment (13c.) *De vita et conversatione Magistri Cartusiensis* [prob. AD. SCOT, *c*1180], *secundum quod habetur in Cronica Domus de Witham*, J. R. L. Bull. XVI (1932) 482–506.

CIREN. Richard of Cirencester [*ob.* 1401]: *Speculum historiale* (447–1066), 2 vols. RS (1863, 1869).

Cl 1204–27 *Rotuli litterarum clausarum*, 2 vols. RC (1833, 1844) [by p. and col.]; 1227–72 Close Rolls, 14 vols. HMSO (1902–38) [by p.]; 1272– , MS PRO (C. 54) [by roll and m.; *v. et.* CalCl]; **Frag.** Close Roll fragments 1215–16, Pipe Roll Soc. NS XXXI 127–44.

Cl. Suppl. Close Rolls supplementary MS PRO (C. 55).

CLAPWELL, Richard, *v.* KNAPWELL, Richard.

Cloveshoe Various councils and synods held at Cloveshoe [unidentified] (716–825), *Conc.* HS III (1871).

COGGESH. Ralph de Coggeshall: *Chronicon Anglicanum* (1066–1224), RS (1875) 1–208 [by f.; *v. et. Expugn. Terrae Sanctae*].

COLET. John Colet, Dean of St. Paul's [*ob.* 1519]: **Corp. Myst.** *De compositione sancti corporis Christi mystici* in *Ep.* 183–95 [*v. infra*]; **Cel. Hier.** The celestial hierarchy, in Two treatises on the hierarchies of Dionysius [wr.? 1498] (1869) 163–96; **Eccl. Hier.** The ecclesiastical hierarchy *ib.* 197–272; **Ep.** Letters, in Letters to Radulphus (1876) 165–82; **In I Cor.** *Enarratio in primam epistolam S. Pauli ad Corinthios* [wr.? *a*1499] (1874); **In I Pet.** *Enarratio in primam B. Petri epistolam* [attrib.], in *Ep.* 283–303; **Rom. Enarr.** *Enarratio in epistolam B. Pauli and Romanos* [wr.? 1498–9] (1873); **Rom. Exp.** *Epistolae B. Pauli ad Romanos expositio* in *Ep.* 197–281; **Sacr. Eccl.** *De sacramentis ecclesiae* [wr. ? 1499] (1867) [all the above ed. J. H. Lupton]; **Stat.** Statutes *Reg. S. Paul.* 217–36 & 237–49; **Stat. Cantar.** *Excerpta..ex libro statutorum ea quae concernunt capellanos..ad cantarias suas admittendos*, ed. W. S. Simpson *Archaeologia*, LII; pt. 1 (1890) 161–7; [*v. et. Ep. Erasmi*].

Collect. Aen. Meroving. *Collectiones aenigmatum Merovingicae aetatis* (*Corpus Christianorum, S. Lat.*, CXXXIII) 2 vols. (1968) [mainly cited under authors].

Collect. Ox. *Collectanea*, 4 vols. OHS V, XVI, XXXII, XLVII (1885–1905).

Collect. Salern. *Collectio Salernitana*, 5 vols. (Naples, 1852–9) [*v. et. Alph.*].

Collect. Staffs Collections for a history of Staffordshire, William Salt Archaeol. Soc., since 1936 known as Staffs Rec. Soc., Vol. I– (1880–).

Collect. Suss Sussex archaeological collections, Arch. Soc. Suss, I– (1853–).

Comm. Lond. Round, J. H.: The commune of London and other studies (1899).

Comm. Sph. Commentary on The sphere of Sacrobosco, attrib. to Michael Scot [*ob.* 1234], ed. L. Thorndike: The Sphere of Sacrobosco (1949) 247–342.

Comp. Dom. Buck. *Compota domestica familiarum de Bukingham et d'Angoulême*, 1443, 1452, 1463; *annexae expensae cujusdam comitis* 1273, Abbotsford Club (1836).

Comp. Swith. Compotus rolls of the obedientiaries of St. Swithun's Priory, Winchester (14c.–16c.), Hants Rec. Soc. (1892).

Comp. Worc. I Early compotus rolls of the Priory of Worcester (1278–1352), Worcs Hist. Soc. (1908); **II** Compotus rolls of the Priory of Worcester (14c. and 15c.), *ib.* (1910).

Compilatio *Compilatio de gestis Britonum et Anglorum*, concluding portion (1422–7), Camd. Soc. NS XXVIII (1880) 164–85.

Conc. *Concilia Magnae Britanniae et Hiberniae* (446–1717), ed. D. Wilkins, 4 vols. (1737) [superseded in part by *Conc.* HS or *Conc. Syn.*].

Conc. HS Councils and ecclesiastical documents relating to Great Britain and Ireland (200–1295), ed. A. W. Haddan and W. Stubbs, vol. III (Eng., 595–1066) (Oxford, 1871).

Conc. Scot. *Concilia Scotiae, Ecclesiae Scoticae statuta..*, 1225–1559, ed. J. Robertson, 2 vols. Bannatyne Club (1866).

Conc. Syn. Councils and synods, vol. I not yet pub.; vol. II (1205–1313) ed. F. M. Powicke and C. R. Cheney (Oxford, 1964), 2 pts. (–723, –1393).

Const. Clar. The constitutions of Clarendon (1164), in GERV. CANT. I 178–80 [by cap.].

CONWAY Def. Mend. Roger Conway (*alias* Chonnoe) [*ob.* 1360]: *Defensio religionis mendicantium* (*c*1357), in *Monarchia* II 1410–44.

Cop. Pri. S.Andr. *Copiale Prioratus Sanctiandree,* the letter-book of James Haldenstone, Prior 1418–43, w. app. of docs. 1378–1450, St. Andrews Univ. pub. XXXI (1930).

CoramR *Coram Rege* Rolls 1272–1702, MS PRO (K.B. 27).

Correct. Alch. *Correctorium alchemiae* (? *a*1200), in *Theatrum chem.* II 385–406 [attrib. RIC. MED.].

COTTON *v.* B. COTTON, J. COTTON.

Couch. Furness The coucher book of Furness Abbey [Lancs], 2 vols. in 6, Chetham Soc. NS IX, XI, XIV (= vol. I, –260/–536/–706) LXXIV, LXXVI, LXXVIII (= vol. II, –288/–583/–880) (1886–1919).

Couch. Kirkstall The coucher book of the Cistercian Abbey of Kirkstall, Yorks, Thoresby Soc. VIII (1904).

Couch. Selby The coucher book of Selby, Arch. Soc. Yorks, Rec. S. X, XIII (1891–3).

Council in North Reid, R. R.: The King's council in the North (1921).

CourtR Court Rolls (13c.–), MS PRO (S.C. 2).

CourtR A. Stratton Wilts Rec. Soc. [in prep].

CourtR Banstead Court rolls of the manor of Banstead, MS Surrey RO [*v. et.* Banstead].

CourtR Carshalton Court rolls of the manor of Carshalton (Ed. III–Hen. VII), Surrey Rec. Soc. II (1916).

CourtR Castle Combe *v.* Hist. Castle Combe.

CourtR Chester *v.* Cal. Co. CourtR Chester.

CourtR Hales Court rolls of the manor of Hales (1270–1307), 3 pts. in 2 vols., Worcs Hist. Soc. (1912–33).

CourtR Lancs Some court rolls of the manors of Thomas, Earl of Lancaster (1323–4), Lancs and Chesh Rec. Soc. XLI (1901).

CourtR Lygh Court rolls of the manor of Lygh (Abbotsleigh, Som) (1461–1507), MS Univ. Bristol.

CourtR Nursling Court roll of the manor of Nursling (1413), MS Mun. Herriard Park [Hants].

CourtR Ottery St. M. Court roll of Ottery St. Mary [Devon] 1407–8), MS Exeter City Lib.

CourtR Ramsey Court rolls of the Abbey of Ramsey [Hunts] and of the Honor of Clare [Suff] (1255–1384), Yale Hist. Pubs., MSS and ed. texts IX (1928).

CourtR Ruthin Court rolls of the lordship of Ruthin [Denb].. (1294–6), Cymmrodorion Rec. Soc., II (1893).

CourtR Tooting Beck Court rolls of Tooting Beck manor (1246–1422), LCC (1909).

CourtR Wakefield Court rolls of the manor of Wakefield (1274–1331), Arch. Soc. Yorks, Rec. Series XXIX, XXXVI, LVII, LXXVIII, CIX (1901–45).

CourtR Wimbledon I, II Extracts from the Court Rolls of the Manor of Wimbledon..1 Ed. IV to 1864, ed. for use of Wimbledon Common Committee (1866); **III** Extracts from the Court Rolls of the Manor of Wimbledon (Ed. IV–Hen. VII) and..from miscellaneous MSS (1869).

CourtR Winchester Winchester city court rolls (1269–19c.), MS Winchester City Archives.

Crawley Gras, N. S. B. and E. C.: The economic and social history of an English village (Crawley, Hants) (909–1928), (Harvard, 1930) [incl. extr. from *Pipe Wint.*].

Croyl. Pseudo-Ingulf [14c.]: *Historia..monasterii Croyland* [Crowland, Lincs] (616–1089), *Rerum Anglicarum Scriptorum Veterum* I, ed. J. Fell and W. Fulman (Oxford, 1684) 1–107; **Cont. A** *Continuatio* (*temp.* Will. II–1117) [wrongly attrib. P. BLOIS], *ib.* 108–32; **Cont. B** (1149–1470), *ib.* 451–546; **Cont. C** (1459–86), *ib.* 549–78; **Cont. D** (Oct. 1485–Apr. 1486), *ib.* 581–93.

Cumb. & Westmor. Antiq. Soc. Cumberland and Westmorland Antiquarian Society, transactions I– (Kendal, 1886–).

CurR *Curia Regis* Rolls (1194–1272), HMSO vol. I– (1922–), in prog. [I–X by p.; XI– by no.]; later Rolls, MS PRO (K.B. 26), [by r.]; **CurR PR** 1194–5 Pipe R. Soc. XIV (1891), 1196–8 *ib.* XXXI 69–118 (1955); **CurR RC** (1194–1200), 2 vols. RC (1835).

Cust. Abingd. *De consuetudinibus Abbendoniae* [*c*1190], in *Chr. Abingd.* II *app.* III 296–334.

Cust. Battle Custumals of Battle Abbey [Sussex] 1283–1312, Camd. Soc. NS XLI (1887).

Cust. Bleadon The custumal of Bleadon, Som, 13c., Archaeol. Inst. G.B. and Ir., Memoirs..of Wilts and Salisbury (1851) 182–210.

Cust. Bury St. E. *v.* Kal. Samson.

Cust. Cant. Customary of..St. Augustine's, Canterbury (*c*1330–40) in Customary of Benedictine Monasteries, ed. E. M. Thompson, I; **Abbr.** Earlier customary (? *c*1245), *ib.* II 249–318, HBS XXIII, XXVIII (1902–4) [*v. et.* Cust. Westm.].

Cust. Fordwich *v.* Hist. Fordwich.

Cust. Glast. *Rentalia et custumalia..abbatum monasterii B. Mariae Glastoniae* (1235–61), Som Rec. Soc. V (1891).

Cust. Heacham The custumal of Heacham, Norfolk (13c.), MS Norfolk RO (L'Estrange pps., Q. 33).

Cust. Kent Manors Custumal of the Archbishop's manors in Kent (1285), MS DCCant. (E. 24. 1–91).

Cust. Loventon, Cust. Malling *v.* Cust. Suss II.

Cust. Norm. *Statuta et consuetudines Normannie* (*a*1200), ed. E.-J. Tardif (Rouen, 1881).

Cust. Rents Neilson, N.: Customary rents (12c.–15c.) (Oxford, 1910).

Cust. Roff. *Custumale Roffense* (? compiled *a*1320 by John de Westerham), ed. J. Thorpe (1788).

Cust. S.Malling, Cust. Slyndon *v.* Cust. Suss II.

Cust. Suss I–III Sussex custumals (13c.–14c.), Sussex Rec. Soc. XXXI, LVII, LX (1925, 1959, 1962) [incl. entries direct from MS]; II incl. custumals (1285) of Loventon, 16–21; Malling, 111–20; S. Malling, 30–47; Slyndon, 1–10; Tangmere, 11–16; Terring, 21–30.

Cust. Swith. A consuetudinary of the 14th cent...of the house of St. Swithin in Winchester, Winchester Cathedral Records I (1886).

Cust. Tangmere *v.* Cust. Suss II.

Cust. Taunton The medieval customs of the manors of Taunton and Bradford on Tone (13c.), Som Rec. Soc. LXVI (1962).

Cust. Terring *v.* Cust. Suss II.

Cust. Westm. Customary of..St. Peter's, Westminster (*c*1266), in Customary of Benedictine monasteries, ed. E. M. Thompson, II, HBS XXVIII (1904) 1–247 [*v. et.* Cust. Cant.; Cust. Cant. Abbr.].

Cust. York *v. Ord. Ebor.*

CUTCL. John Cutcliffe [*fl.* 1345]: **CL** *De confectione veri lapidis philosophorum, Bibl. Chem.* II 80–3; **LL** *Liber lucis, Theatrum Chem.* III 191–200 [by cap.].

CUTHB. Ob. Baedae Cuthbert, Abbot of Wearmouth and Jarrow [*ob. p*764]: *De obitu Baedae,* in BEDE *Op. Hist.,* I clx–clxiv [*v. et. Ep. Bonif.*].

Cymmrodor Y Cymmrodor, embodying transactions of the Cymmrodorion Soc. of London, vol. I– (1877–).

D. BEC. Daniel of Beccles [? *fl. c*1180]: *Urbanus magnus,* ed. J. G. Smyly (Dublin, 1939).

D. EDW. Anat. David Edwardes [*ob. c*1542]: *In anatomicen introductio* (1532), facsimile ed. (Oxford, 1961).

D. MORLEY Daniel of Morley (*alias* Merlai) [*fl.* 1170–1200]: *De naturis inferiorum et superiorum libri II,* ed. K. Sudhoff Archiv für die Gesch. der Naturwissenschaften und Technik VIII (1917) 6–40; *vv. ll., ib.* IX 50–1.

DB Domesday-book (1086), 2 vols (first ed. 1783, facsimile 1863) [by f.]; **Add.** *Additamenta,* 2 vols. (1861) [*v. Dom. Exon., Inq. Ely, Lib. Wint.*].

DB Exon. *v. Dom. Exon.*

DCCant. Muniments of Dean and Chapter of Canterbury, incl. some listed in HMC Var. Coll. I (1901) 205–81 [*v. et.* Ac. Man. Cant.].

DCChich. Muniments of Dean and Chapter of Chichester, incl. some listed in HMC Var. Coll. I (1901) 187–204.

DCDurh. Muniments of the Dean and Chapter of Durham, incl. miscellaneous charters MS.

DCEbor. Muniments of the Dean and Chapter of York, incl. *Registrum antiquum de..actis capitularibus,* 1335–42, (Reg.K) MS.

DCLichf. Muniments of the Dean and Chapter of Lichfield, incl. testimony (1252) transcr. in Arch. Soc. Derb V (1883) 150–6.

DCLinc. *v.* Chap. Linc.

DC S.Paul. Muniments of Dean and Chapter of St. Paul's incl. some listed in HMC Rep. IX app. I (1883) 1–72.

DCSal. Muniments of Dean and Chapter of Salisbury, incl. some listed in HMC Var. Coll. I (1901) 338–88.

DCWestm. Muniments of Dean and Chapter of Westminster Abbey, MS.

DCornw. Records in Duchy of Cornwall R.O. (London), MS.

DL Duchy of Lancaster: **Ac. Var.** Accounts various, MS PRO (D.L. 28); **Cart. Misc.** *Cartae Miscellaneae* (D.L. 36); **ChancR** Chancery Rolls (Ed. III–Hen. VII) (D.L. 37); **Coucher** Coucher Book (D.L. 42/1 and 2), incl. extr. in N. Riding Records NS II–IV (1895–7); **CourtR** Court Rolls (D.L. 30); **DeedsL** Deeds Series L (D.L. 25); **Forest Proc.** Forest Proceedings (D.L. 39); **MinAc** Ministers' Accounts (D.L. 29); **Misc. Bk.** Miscellaneous Books (D.L. 42); **Rent. & Surv.** Rentals and Surveys (D.L. 43).

Danelaw Documents illustrative of the social and economic history of the Danelaw, ed. F. M. Stenton (1920).

DASTIN John Dastin [*fl. c*1320]: **Ros.** *Rosarium, secretissimum philosophorum arcanum comprehendens* in *Bibl. chem.* II 309–24 [by cap.]; **Visio** *Visio super artem alchemicam, ib.* 324–6.

Davenports Highet, T. P. The early history of the Davenports of Davenport, Chetham Soc. 3rd S. IX (1960).

DEE Monas John Dee [*ob.* 1608]: *Monas Hieroglyphica* (1564), in *Theatrum Chem.* II 178–215.

Deeds, Ancient *v.* AncD.

Deeds Balliol The Oxford deeds of Balliol College, OHS LXIV (1913).

Deeds Mon. & Ep. Ir. Irish monastic and episcopal deeds (IMC Ormond Deeds Series) (Dublin, 1936).

Deeds Newcastle Early deeds relating to Newcastle-upon-Tyne, Surtees Soc. CXXXVII (1924).

Deeds Wards Deeds and Evidences, Court of Wards, MS PRO (Wards 2).

DEVIZES Richard of Devizes [*fl. c*1191–4]: *Chronicon..de tempore regis Richardi I*, Med. Texts (1963) [by f.; N.B. some rearrangement of ff. in this ed.]; also in Chr. Steph. III RS (1886) 381–454.

Dial. Scac. [attrib., Richard Fitzneal *ob.* 1198]: *De necessariis observantiis scaccarii dialogus* (*c*1178), Med. Texts (1950) [by bk. and cap., incl. serial letters given in earlier ed. (Oxford, 1902)].

DICETO Ralph de Diceto, dean of St. Paul's [*ob.* 1202]: **Abbr. Norm.** *Abbreviatio de gestis Normannorum*, RS (1876) II 241–65 [mainly abbr. from W. JUM.]; **Chr.** *Abbreviationes chronicorum* (Creation–1147), *ib.* I 3–263; **YH** *Ymagines historiarum* (1148–79), *ib.* I 289–440; (1180–1202) *ib.* II 3–174 [ref. to *Opuscula, ib.* II 175–285 by vol. and p. only].

Dieta Verses on diet (15c.), EETS XXXII pt. 2 (1868) 56–7.

Dietarium *Dietarium* (verses on diet *c*1460), EETS XXXII pt. 1 (1868) 55–9.

Dieul. Chronicle of Dieulacres Abbey [Staffs] (1381–1403, wr. *a*1413) J.R.L. Bull. XIV (1930) 164–81 [by f.].

Digby Plays The Digby plays (1480–90), EETS, Extra S. LXX (1896).

Dign. Peer Reports from the Lords Committees touching the dignity of a Peer of the Realm 5 vols. 3rd ed. (1829) [vols. III–V contain app. of docs.].

Dip. Corr. Ric. II Diplomatic correspondence of Richard II, Camd. 3rd S. XLVIII (1933).

DipDoc Diplomatic documents preserved in the Public Record Office (1101–), HMSO vol. I– (1964–).

DipDoc. C. Diplomatic Documents, Chancery Miscellanea bundles 27–32. MS PRO (C. 47) [*v. et.* Chanc. Misc.].

DipDoc. E Diplomatic Documents of the Exchequer, MS PRO (E. 30).

Ditchley Pps. Ditchley Papers, MS County Hall, Oxford.

Doc. Bec Select documents of the English lands of the Abbey of Bec [Norm.], Camd. 3rd S. LXXIII (1951).

Doc. Bev. Beverley town documents, Selden Soc. XIV (1900).

Doc. Bury Feudal documents from the abbey of Bury St. Edmunds [Suff], ed. D. C. Douglas (1932) [by no.].

DocCOx Oxford city documents, OHS XVIII (1891).

Doc. Coll. Wint. Winchester College muniments [*v. et. Ac. Dom. Ep. Wint., Ac. Man. Coll. Wint.*].

Doc. Eng. Black Monks Documents illustrating the activities.. of the English Black Monks, 1215–1540, ed. W. A. Pantin, Camd. 3rd S. XLV, XLVIII, LIV (1931–7).

DocExch Documents illustrative of English history in the 13th and 14th centuries, selected from the records..of the Queen's Remembrancer of the Exchequer, ed. H. Cole, RC (1844).

Doc. Francisc. Franciscan papers, lists and documents, ed. A. G. Little, Manchester (1943).

Doc. G. Chart Documents concerning land transfers (1570–1630) MS (copies) in Parish Reg. I, Great Chart, Kent, DCCant.

Doc. Interdict. Interdict documents (1207–13), ed. P. M. Barnes and W. R. Powell, PipeR. Soc. NS XXXIV (1960).

Doc. Ir. Historic and municipal documents of Ireland 1172–1320, RS (1870).

Doc. Leeds Documents relating to the manors and borough of Leeds, 1066–1400, Thoresby Soc. XLV (1957).

Doc. Robertsbr. Documents relating to Robertsbridge Abbey, Sussex (1160–1537), HMC Rep. LXXVII, DeLisle and Dudley MSS I (1925) 33–171.

Doc. S.Paul. Documents illustrating the history of St. Paul's Cathedral (1262–1798), Camd. Soc. NS XXVI (1880).

Doc. Scot. Documents illustrative of the history of Scotland.. 1286–1306, ed. J. Stevenson. 2 vols. Chr. and Mem. Scot. III, Scot. RO (1870).

Doc. W. Abb. Westm. Documents illustrating the rule of Walter de Wenlok, abbot of Westminster, 1283–1307, Camd. 4th S. II (1965).

DOCKING Thomas Docking [*ob. p*1269]: extr. from biblical commentaries, in *Doc. Francisc.* 98–121.

Doctus dicetur Verses on table manners (15c.) EETS XXXII p. 2 (1868) 26–9.

Dom. Cant. Domesday *monachorum* of Christ Church, Canterbury (12c.), ed. D. C. Douglas, RHS (1944) 75–110.

Dom. Chesh Cheshire Domesday roll (*temp.* Ric. I–1289), calendar and fragments printed in A memoir on the Cheshire Domesday roll, by G. Ormerod (1851), bound with his *Parentalia* (1851).

Dom. Exon. Exeter Domesday (1086) DB Add., I 1–493 [by f.].

Dom. S.Paul. The Domesday of St. Paul's (1181, 1222 etc.), Camd. Soc. LXIX (1858).

DOMERH : Glast. Adam de Domerham [*ob.* 1291]: *Historia de rebus gestis Glastoniensibus* (1126–1291), ed. T. Hearne (Oxford, 1727) pt. ii [for pt. i *v.* W. MALM. *Glast.*].

Domus Reg. *Constitutio domus Regis* (*c*1136], in *Dial. Scac.* (1950) 129–35.

Dryburgh *Liber S.Mariae de Dryburgh* [Berwickshire] (1153–), Bannatyne Club (1847).

DuC Du Cange, C. D.: *Glossarium mediae et infimae Latinitatis*, revised ed. 8 vols. (Paris, 1840–57).

Dugdale Soc. Dugdale Society, publications [on the history of Warwickshire], vol. I– (1921–).

DUMBLETON *v.* Sci. Mech.

DUNS John Duns Scotus [*ob. c*1308]: **PW** [Selections from] Philosophical writings, Med. Texts (1962) [by section and cap.]; other refs. to *Opera Omnia*, 26 vols. (Paris, 1891–5) as follows: **Gram.** *De modis significandi sive grammatica speculativa*, vol. I 1–50; **Metaph.** *Quaestiones..super libros metaphysicorum Aristotelis I–XII*, vol. VII; **Praedic.** *In librum praedicamentōrum quaestiones* (or *Super praedicamenta*), vol. I 437–538; **Prim. Princ.** *De primo rerum omnium principio*, vol. IV 722–99; **Sent.** *Quaestiones in primum et secundum librum sententiarum*, vols. VIII–XIII; **Sent. cont.** *Quaestiones in tertium et quartum librum sententiarum*, vols. XIV–XXI; **Univ.** *In universam logicam quaestiones* (or *Super universalia Porphyrii quaestiones acutissimae*), vol. I 51–435.

DUNST. Classbk. St. Dunstan's classbook from Glastonbury, ed. R. W. Hunt, *Umbrae Codicum Occidentalium* IV (Amsterdam, 1961).

E. FAVERSHAM Eustace of Faversham [*ob. p*1244]: Life of Edmund Rich, Archb. of Canterbury [*ob.* 1240], ed. C. H. Lawrence, in St. Edmund of Abingdon (Oxford, 1960) 203–21.

E. Ch. Chesh. Facsimiles of early Cheshire charters (*c*1146–*c*1237), Lancs. and Chesh. Rec. Soc. (1957) [by no.].

E. Ch. Ox. Facsimiles of early charters in Oxford muniment rooms (*c*1097–1251), ed. H. E. Salter (1929) [by no.].

E. Ch. S.Paul. Early charters of the Cathedral Church of St. Paul, London (9c.–13c.), Camd. 3rd S., LVIII (1939) [by p.].

E. Ch. Scot. Early Scottish charters prior to..1153, ed. A. C. Lawrie (Glasgow, 1905) [by no.].

E. Ch. Wessex The early charters of Wessex (7c.–11c.), ed. H. P. R. Finberg (Leicester, 1964).

E. Ch. Yorks Early Yorkshire charters, ed. W. Farrer, 3 vols. (Edinburgh, 1914–16); 10 vols. pub. Arch. Soc. Yorks, Rec. Soc., Extra Series (1935–65) [by vol. and no.].

E. Chanc. Proc. Early Chancery Proceedings to 1558, MS PRO (C. 1).

EE Text given by agreement of Epinal glossary (8c.) and first Erfurt glossary (? 8c.). *Cf. Corpus Glossariorum Latinorum* V (Leipzig, 1894) 337–401, and Lindsay, W.: The Corpus, Epinal, Erfurt and Leyden glossaries, Philol. Soc., pub. VIII (1921).

EEC Gras, N. S. B.: The early English customs system (13c.–16c.) (Harvard, 1918).

EE County Court Morris, W. A.: The early English County Court (13c.–14c.) (Univ. California, 1926).

EETS Early English Text Society, publications, I– (1864–).

EHR English Historical Review, I– (1886–).

ERO Essex Record Office (Chelmsford).

E. Schools Yorks Early Yorkshire schools, Arch. Soc. Yorks, Rec. S. XXVII, XXXIII (1899, 1903).

EADMER Eadmer [*ob. c*1124]: **Breg.** *Vita S.Bregwini* [*ob.* 765], *Acta SS Boll.* Aug. V 831–5; **HN** *Historia novorum in Anglia* (960–1122), RS (1884) [by p. of MS (in margin)]; **Mir. Anselmi** *Descriptio miraculorum..Anselmi*, in *V. Anselmi* 152–71; **Mir. Dunst.** *Quaedam de miraculis quae idem pater [Dunstanus]..fecit*, Mem. Dunst. 223–49 [by cap.]; **Mir. Osw.** *Miracula S.Oswaldi*, Hist. Church York II 41–59 [by cap.]; **Odo** *Vita S.Odonis* in *Anglia Sacra* II 78–87; **Rel. S.Audoeni** *De reliquiis S. Audoeni*, in GERV. CANT. I 7–9; **V. Anselmi** *Vita Anselmi*, Med. Texts (1962) 1–151 [by bk. and cap.]; **V. Dunst.** *Vita S.Dunstani Archiepiscopi Cantuariensis*, Mem. Dunst. 162–222 [by cap.]; **V. Osw.** *Vita S.Oswaldi Eboracensis archiepiscopi* Hist. Church York II 1–40 [by cap.]; **Wilf.** *Vita Wilfridi Episcopi Eboracensis*, *ib.* I 161–226 [by cap.]; **Wilf. Brev.** *Breviloquium vitae S.Wilfridi* (attrib.), *ib.* I 227–37.

Early Sci. Ox. Gunter, R. T.: Early science in Oxford OHS LXXVII, LXXVIII (1923) [*v. Nav. Ven.*, Turquet, WALLINGF.].

Eccl. Doc. Ecclesiastical documents (misc.), Camd. Soc. VIII (1840) [*v. et. Episc. Som.*].

ECCLESTON Adv. Min. Thomas Eccleston [*fl. c*1250]: *De adventu fratrum minorum in Angliam*, Collection d'études..sur l'histoire religieuse..du moyen-âge, VII (Paris, 1909) [supersedes *Mon. Francisc.* II 3–28], also ed. A. G. Little (Manchester, 1951).

Econ. Condit. Neilson, N.: Economic conditions on the manors of Ramsey Abbey [Hunts] (1898); app. (sep. pag.) contains Ministers' Accounts for Wistow [Hunts].

Econ. HR Economic History Review, I– (1927–).

EDDI Eddi (*alias* Stephanus) [*ob.* 731] Life of Bishop Wilfrid (*a*720) (Cambridge, 1927) [by cap.].

EDMUND Spec. Eccles. Edmund Rich, Archb. of Canterbury [*ob.* 1240]: *Speculum ecclesie*, ed. H. P. Forshaw in Edmund of Abingdon, *Speculum Religiosorum* and *Speculum ecclesie* (1973); **Spec. Relig.** *Speculum religiosorum, ib.* [both by cap.] [*Spec. Eccles.* also in *Bibl. Vet. Pat.* XXV (1677) 316–27].

Educ. Ch. Leach, A. F.: Educational charters and documents, 598–1909 (Cambridge, 1911).

EGB. Egbert, Archb. of York [*ob.* 766]: **Dial.** Dialogue, in *Conc.* HS III 403–13; **Pen.** Penitential, *ib.* 413–31 [by cap. and para.]; longer version (dub.) printed in *Conc.* I 113–44; **Pont.** *Pontificale Ecgberhti* (8c–10c.), Surtees Soc. XXVII (1853).

ELMER CANT. Ep. Elmer of Canterbury [*ob.* 1137]: *Epistolae*, in H. Los. *Ep.* 213–33 [by no.].

ELMH. Thomas Elmham [*ob. c*1427]: **Cant.** *Historia monasterii S.Augustini Cantuariensis*, RS (1858); **Hen. V** *Henrici V, Angliae Regis, gesta* (1413–16) (attrib.), ed. B. Williams, Eng. Hist. Soc. (1850) 1–108 [*v. et. G. Hen. V*]; **Hen. V Cont.** (1417–22), Continuation (anon.), *ib.* 109–63 [abbr. of Ps.-ELMH. Hen. V 90–338]; **Metr. Hen. V** *Liber metricus de Henrico V*, Mem. Hen. V 77–166 [by line]; [*v. et. Ps.-*ELMH.]

ELVEDEN Cal. Walter de Elveden: Calendar (1387), extr. in *SB* 5–7.

Enc. Emmae *Encomium Emmae Reginae* [*ob.* 1052] (wr. 1040–2), Camd. 3rd S. LXXII (1949) [by bk. and cap.].

Enf. Stat. Lab. Putnam, B. H.: The enforcement of the Statute of Labourers..1349–59 (Columbia Univ., N.Y., 1908).

Eng. Abbots to Cîteaux Letters from the English abbots to the Chapter at Cîteaux, 1442–1521, Camd. 4th S. IV (1967).

Eng. Aust. Fri. Roth, F.: English Austin Friars, 1249–1538, 2 vols. (N.Y., 1966).

Eng. Clergy Thompson, A. H.: The English clergy..in the later middle ages (Oxford, 1947).

Eng. Corn Market Gras, N. S. B.: The evolution of the English corn market from the 12th to the 18th cent. (Harvard, 1915).

Eng. Dip. Admin. Cuttino, G. P.: English diplomatic administration, 2nd ed. (Oxford, 1971).

Eng. Feudalism Stenton, F. M.: The first century of English Feudalism 1066–1166 (Oxford, 1932).

Eng. Friars Smalley, B.: English friars and antiquity in the early 14th cent. (Oxford, 1960).

Eng. Gilds The original ordinances of more than one hundred early English gilds, EETS XL (1870).

Eng. Handelspol. Englische Handelspolitik gegen Ende des Mittelalters, ed. G. Schanz, 2 vols. (Leipzig, 1881).

Eng. Hist. Lit. 15c. Kingsford, C. L.: English historical literature in the 15th cent. (Oxford, 1913).

Eng. Justice Stenton, D. M.: English justice..1066–1215 (Philadelphia, 1964).

Eng. Roy. Chap. Denton, J. H.: English royal free chapels (1100–1300) (Manchester, 1970).

Eng. Roy. Writs Facsimiles of English royal writs (1044–1100), pres. to V. H. Galbraith, ed. T. A. M. Bishop and P. Chaplais (1957) [by no.].

Eng. Sec. Cath. Edwards, K.: The English secular cathedrals in the middle ages..w. spec. ref. to the 14c. Revised ed. (Manchester, 1967).

Eng. Weights Select tracts..relating to English weights and measures (1100–1742), Camd. Misc. XV, Camd. 3rd S. XLI (1929).

Enr. Chester Palatinate of Chester, Enrolments, MS PRO (Chester 2).

Entries William Rastell [*ob.* 1565]: Collection of entries..etc. [by p. of ed. 1670, which contains additions to ed. 1564].

EpAcOx *Epistolae academicae Oxonienses* (*Registrum* F), a collection of letters..(1421–1509), OHS XXXV, XXXVI (1898) [by p.].

Ep. Aldh. *v.* ALDH. *Ep.*

Ep. Anselm. *v.* ANSELM *Ep.*

Ep. Bonif. *v.* BONIF. *Ep.*

Ep. Cant. *Epistolae Cantuarienses* (1185–1211) Mem. Ric. I, vol. II [by no.].

Ep. Erasm. *Opus epistolarum Des. Erasmi Roterdami*, letters to Erasmus (1484–1536) 12 vols. (1906–58) [by vol. and no.].

Ep. G. Foliot *v.* G. FOLIOT *Ep.*

Ep. Innoc. III Selected letters of Pope Innocent III (1198–1216) concerning England, Med. Texts (1953) [by no.].

Ep. J. Sal. *v.* J. SAL. *Ep.*
Ep. Lanfr. *v.* LANFR. *Ep.*
Epigr. Misc. *Epigrammata miscellanea* (12c.), Sat. Poets II 156–62.
Epinal Gl. *v. EE.*
Episc. Som. *Historiola de primordiis Episcopatus Somersetensis*, (–1175) [wr. *temp.* Hen. II], Camd. Soc. VIII (1840) 9–28; **Eccl. Doc.** Ecclesiastical documents (misc.), *ib.* 43–91.
Erf. 2 & 3 The second and third Erfurt glossaries as quoted in Lindsay, W. M.: The Corpus, Epinal, Erfurt and Leiden glossaries, Philol. Soc., publ VIII (1921); *v. et.* EE.
ERIUG. Per. John Scotus (*alias* Eriugena) [*fl. c*850]: *Periphyseon, de divisione naturae, lib. I and II*, ed. I. P. Sheldon-Williams, *Scriptores Latini Hiberniae* VII and IX (Dublin, 1968, 1972) [by col. of *PL* CXXII] [in prog.].
EschF Escheators' Files, MS PRO (E. 153).
Estates Crowland Page, F. M.: The estates of Crowland Abbey [Lincs] (*c*1258–1528) (Cambridge, 1934).
Eul. Hist. *Eulogium* (*historiarum sive temporis*), *chronicon ab orbe condito usque ad..1366, a monacho quodam Malmesburiensi exaratum*, 3 vols. RS (1858–63); **Annot.** *Id.* Annotations incorporated in parts of text, II and III **Chr. Brev.** *Chronicon brevius* (–1364), III 243–313; **Cont.** *Continuatio eulogii* (1361–1413), III 333–421.
Eur. Love lyric Dronke, E. P. M.: Medieval Latin and the rise of the European Love Lyric, 2 vols., 2nd ed. (Oxford, 1968).
EUSEBIUS *v.* WHÆTBERT.
Exc. Hist. Bentley, S.: *Excerpta historica* (13c.–16c.) (1833).
ExcRFin *Excerpta e rotulis finium*..1216–72, 2 vols. RC (1835–6); *cf.* FineR.
ExchScot *Rotuli Scaccarii Regum Scotorum*, The Exchequer Rolls of Scotland (1264–1579), 23 vols. Scot. RO, Record Pub. VI (Edinburgh, 1878–1908) [ref. by date and p.].
Expug. Terrae Sanctae *De expugnatione Terrae Sanctae per Saladinum libellus* (1186–8), in COGGESH. 209–62 [by f.].
Ext. Alien Pri. Extents of alien priories, MS PRO (E. 106).
Ext. Guern. The extentes of Guernsey 1248 and 1331, ed. H. de Sausmarez, Soc. Guernesiaise (1934).
Ext. Hadleigh *Extenta manerii de Hadleghe* (1305), Suff. Inst. of Archaeol. Proc. III (1863), app. A 229–52.
Extr. Chr. Scot. *Extracta e variis cronicis Scocie*, ed. W. B. D. D. Turnbull, Abbotsford Club (1842).
Extr. R Extract Rolls, or *extracta donationum*, MS PRO (C. 59).
Eyre Chester Pleas before Justices in Eyre in counties Chester and Flint, MS PRO (Chester 17).
Eyre Kent The Eyre of Kent, 1313–14, Selden Soc. XXIV, XXVII, XXIX (= Yr. Bk. of Ed. II, nos V, VII, VIII) (1909–13).
Eyre Lincs Rolls of Justices in Eyre..for Lincolnshire (1218–19) 1–440; **Eyre Worcs** (1221) *ib.* 441–655 Selden Soc. LIII (1934).
Eyre Lond. The Eyre of London (14 Ed. II) 2 vols. Selden Soc. LXXXV, LXXXVI (= Yr. bk. Ed. II, no. XXVI, pts. 1 and 2) (1968–9).
Eyre Worcs *v.* Eyre Lincs.
Eyre Yorks Rolls of Justices in Eyre..for Yorkshire (1218–19), Selden Soc. LVI (1937).

F. MALM. Fabricius of Malmesbury [*ob.* 1117]: **V. Aldh.** *Vita Aldhelmi* in *PL* LXXXIX (1863) 63–84.
Fabr. Westm. superseded by Ac. Build. Hen. III.
Fabr. York The fabric rolls of York Minster (14c.–17c.), Surtees Soc. XXXV (1859) 1–120; app. of docs. (12c.–18c.), *ib.* 121–334.
Fasti Sal. *Fasti ecclesiae Sarisburiensis* (634–19c), ed. W. H. Rich Jones (1879).
FAVENT Thomas Favent [*c*1390]: *Historia..de modo..mirabilis Parliamenti apud Westmonasterium* (1386–8), Camd. Misc. XIV Camd. 3rd S. XXXVII (1926).
Fees *Liber feodorum*, the book of fees (1198–1293), 3 vols. [I and II contin. pag.], (–636/, –1483/, index) HMSO (1920–31).
FELIX Guthl. Felix of Crowland [*c*730]: Life of S. Guthlac [*ob.* 716] (prob. wr. 730–40), ed. B. Colgrave (Cambridge, 1956) [by cap.].
Feod. Durh. *Feodarium Prioratus Dunelmensis* (15c.), w. other docs. (11c.–16c.), Surtees Soc. LVIII (1871).
FERR. Kinloss Johannes Ferrerius of Riva (Piedmont) [*ob. p*1574]: *Historia Abbatum de Kynlos* [Moray] (1150–1537), Bannatyne Club (1839).
Feudal Eng. Round, J. H.: Feudal England, historical studies on the 11th and 12th cents. (1895).
Finc. The Priory of Finchale [Durh.], charters..inventories, account rolls etc., Surtees Soc. VI (1837).
FineR Chancery Fine Rolls (1204–1641), MS PRO (C. 60) [*v. et.* CalFineR., *ExcRFin.*, *RFin.*].
Fines Feet of Fines, MS PRO (C.P. 25); **Fines P. Hen. II & Ric. I** Feet of Fines (1182–96), PipeR. Soc. XVII (1894); **Fines P. Ric. I** (1196–7), *ib.* XX (1896), (1197–8), XXIII (1898, repr. 1929), (1198–9), XXIV (1900, repr. 1929); **Fines P. Lincs** Feet of Fines for co. Lincoln..1196–1216, *ib.* NS XXIX (1954); **Fines P. Norf** Feet of Fines for..Norfolk.. 1198–1202, *ib.* NS XXVII (1950); **Fines P. Norf & Suff** Feet of Fines for..Norfolk..1201–15 and for..Suffolk..1199–1214, *ib.* NS XXXII (1958); **Fines RC** *Fines siue pedes finium siue finales concordiae in curia Domini Regis* (1195–1214), RC (1835, 1844): I Beds, Berks, Bucks, Cambs, Cornw; II Cumb, Derbs, Devon, Dorset; **Fines Warw** Warwickshire Feet of Fines (abstr.), Dugdale Soc. XI, XV, XVIII (1932–43): I (1195–1284), II (1284–1345), III (1345–1509).
Firma Burgi Madox, T.: *Firma Burgi* (1726).
FITZRALPH *v.* RIC. ARMAGH.
FITZTHEDMAR *v. Leg. Ant. Lond.*
FL. WORC. Florence of Worcester [*ob.* 1118]: Chronicle (450–1117), 2 vols. (1848–9) I–II 70; **Cont. A** (1118–41), *ib.* II 71–136 [mainly superseded by J. WORC.]; **Cont. B** (1152–1265), *ib.* II 136–96 [mainly superseded by TAXTER *Chr. Bur.* or B. COTTON 136–40]; **Cont. C** (1266–95), *ib.* II 196–279.
Fleta *Fleta seu commentarius juris Anglicani* (*c*1290), 6 bks.; bks. I–IV, Selden Soc. LXII (1955), LXXXIX (1972), ed. in prog. [ref. to all bks. by p. of ed. 1647].
FLETE Westm. John Flete [*ob.* 1469]: History of Westminster Abbey (to 1386) (Cambridge, 1909).
Flor. Hist. *Flores historiarum* (Creation–1327) [attrib. 'Matthew of Westminster' and to 1249 prob. wr. M. PAR., *q.v.*], 3 vols. RS (1890).
Foed. Rymer, Thomas: *Foedera, conventiones, literae et..acta publica..ab anno 1101 usque ad nostra tempora* (1654), 20 vols., 2nd ed. (1704–35) [addit. entries from 4th ed. (1066–1383), 4 vols. in 7, RC (1816–69)].
FOLC. J. Bev. Folcard: Life of St. John of Beverley [*ob.* 721, wr. *a*1070], Hist. Church York I 239–60 [by cap.].
FORDUN John Fordun [*ob. c*1385]: **Chr.** *Chronica gentis Scotorum* (*alias Scotichronicon*), bks. I–V (Creation–1153), in Historians of Scotland I, ed. W. F. Skene (1871) 1–253 [by bk. and cap.]; **GA** *Gesta annalia* (1153–1385), *ib.* 254–383 [by cap.]; **Cont.** *Scotichronicon, cum supplemento et continuatione Walteri Boweri* (Creation–1447), ed. W. Goodall, 2 vols. (1759) [bks. VI–XVI (1153–1447) by bk. and cap.; I–V superseded by ed. 1871].
FormA Madox T: *Formulare Anglicanum*, or a collection of ancient charters and instruments (1066–1547) (1702) [by p.].
Form. Hist. Doc. Hall, H.: Formula book of official historical documents, 2 vols. (Cambridge, 1908–9): vol. I Diplomatic docs.; vol. II Ministerial and judicial records.
FormMan Legal and manorial formularies, ed...in memory of J. P. Gilson (Oxford, 1933): I Text of BM Add. MS 41201 (*c*1300), 1–24; II Text of PRO Wards 2, box 56, 197/5 (*c*1300), 25–49.
FormMan. Shorwell Specimen accounts of the manor of Shorwell, I.o.W. (*c*1258), MS Caius Coll. Camb. (no. 205) pp. 367–91.
FormOx Formularies which bear on the history of Oxford *c*1204–1420, OHS NS IV (–255), V (–491) (1942).
Form. S.Andr. The St. Andrews formulare (1514–46), Stair Soc. VII, IX (Edinburgh, 1942–4).

FORTESCUE John Fortescue [*c*1394–1476]: **Def. Lanc.** *Defensio juris domus Lancastriae*, in Works I (1869) 503–10 [by cap.]: **LLA** *De laudibus legum Angliae* (Cambridge, 1942) [by cap.].

Found. Holyrood *Historia miraculose fundationis Monasterii Sancte Crucis prope Edinburgh* (1128), Bannatyne Misc. II, Bannatyne Club (1836) 9–31 (incl. app.).

Found. Waltham The foundation of Waltham Abbey [Essex], *De inventione Sanctae Crucis* (wr. *a*1200), ed. W. Stubbs (1861) [by cap.].

Fourteenth Cent. Stud. *v.* Stud. 14 cent.

Frag. Rit. Dunst. *Fragmenta ritualia de Dunstano* (11c.), Mem. Dunst. 440–57.

Free Peasantry Stenton, F. M.: The free peasantry of the Northern Danelaw, w. app. of charters (12c., 13c.) Bull. Soc. Royale des Lettres (Lund, 1926) 74–185.

FRIDUG. Fridugisus [*c*800]: *De substantia nihili et tenebrarum*, ed. C. Gennaro (Padua, 1963).

FRITH. Frithegode of Canterbury: *Breviloquium vitae beati Wilfridi* (*c*950), ed. A. Campbell, *Thesaurus Mundi* (1950) 1–62 [by line; for *var. ll. v. ALMA* XXV (1955) 71–98].

G. AMIENS Hast. Guy, Bishop of Amiens [*ob.* 1075]: *Carmen de Hastingae proelio* (1066), ed. C. Morton and H. Muntz, Med. Texts (1972) [by line].

G. COLD. Durh. Geoffrey de Coldingham: *Liber Gaufridi sacristae de Coldingham de statu ecclesiae Dunelmensis* (1152–1214), *Hist. Durh. Script.* Surtees Soc. IX (1939) 3–31 [by cap.; *v. et. V. Bart. Farn.*].

G. CORNW. Guy Warw. Girardus Cornubiensis [? *fl.* *c*1350]: *Historia Guidonis de Warwyke*, ed. T. Hearne in *Chr. Dunstable* II 825–30.

G. CRISPIN Gilbert Crispin, Abbot of Westminster [*ob.* 1117]: **Ep.** Correspondence, in Gilbert Crispin, ed. J. A. Robinson (1911) 77–84 [by no.]; **Herl.** *Vita Domini Herluini Abbatis Beccensis* [*ob.* 1078], *ib.* 85–110; **Simon.** *De simoniaciis*, *ib.* 111–24; **Ch. Crispin** Selected charters (1071–1122), *ib.* 125–57.

G. FOLIOT Ep. Gilbert Foliot, Bishop of Hereford and London [*ob.* 1178]: Letters and charters, ed. A. Morey and C. N. L. Brooke (Cambridge, 1967) [by no.; letters to G. Foliot cited as *Ep. G. Foliot.*

G. FONT. Geoffrey de Fontibus [12c.]: *Liber de infantia S.Eadmundi*, in Mem. S.Edm. I 93–103.

G. HOYLAND Gilbert of Hoyland (*alias* of Swineshead) [*ob.* 1172]: **Ascet.** *Tractatus ascetici*, in *PL* CLXXXIV (1854) 251–90; **Ep.** *Epistolae*, *ib.* 289–98; **Serm.** *Sermones*, *ib.* 11–252.

G. MON. Geoffrey of Monmouth [*ob.* 1154]: *Historia regum Britanniae* (1136) (1929) [by bk. and cap.; *v. et. V. Merl.*].

G. WINT. Godfrey of Winchester [*ob.* 1107]: **Epigr.** *Epigrammata* Sat. Poets II 103–47; **Epigr. Hist.** *Epigrammata historica*, *ib.* 148–55 [both by no.].

GAS Gesetze der Angelsachsen, ed. F. Liebermann, text vol. I (Halle, 1903), incl. the following: *Consiliatio Cnuti* (1130–5), [*Benedictio scuti et baculi ad*] *duellum* (1067–1130), *Instituta Cnuti*, (*c*1110) *Judicium Dei rituale* (*c*850–*c*1210), *Leges Edwardi Confessoris* (1130–5), *Leges Henrici primi* (1114–18), also ed. L.J Downer (Oxford, 1972), [*Legum*] *Willelmi articuli Londoniis retractati* (*c*1210), *Leis Willelme* [OF and Lat.] (*c*1200), *Libertas Londoniensis* (*c*1133–*c*1154), Pseudo-Cnut *Constitutiones de foresta* (? *c*1184), *Quadripartitus* (*c*1114, incl. *Argumentum* and *Rectitudines singularum personarum*) [Dates are those ascribed by Liebermann].

G. Cnut. Reg. *v. Enc. Emmae.*

G. Durh. *Gesta Dunelmensia* (1300), Camd. Misc. XIII, Camd. 3rd S. XXXIV (1924).

G. Ed. II Bridl. *Gesta Edwardi de Carnarvon auctore canonico Bridlingtoniensi* Chr. Ed. I and II, vol. II (1883) 25–92; **G. Ed. III Bridl.** *Gesta regis Edwardi tertii auctore* (?) *eodem* (to 1339, w. brief additions to 1377) *ib.* 93–151.

G. Hen. II *Gesta regis Henrici secundi* [wrongly attrib. to Benedict of Peterborough], Chr. Hen. II and Ric. I, I 1–361, II 1–71.

G. Hen. V *Gesta Henrici V* (1413–16) [anon., wr. 1416–17], ed. F. Taylor and J. S. Roskell [in prep.; also cited as ELMH. Hen. V].

G. Herw. *Gesta Herwardi, incliti exulis et militis* [*fl.* *c*1070] (wr. *c*1150) Lestorie des Engles I (1888) 339–404 [by f.].

GLA Prantl, Carl: Geschichte der Logik im Abendlande, vols. III and IV in 1 vol. (Leipzig, 1867–70).

G. Ric. I *Gesta Ricardi* [wrongly attrib. to Benedict of Peterborough] Chr. Hen. II and Ric. I, II (1867), *Ducis* (–1189) 71–9, *Regis* (1189–99) 79–252.

G. S. Alb. *Gesta abbatum monasterii S.Albani* [Herts.] (793–1396) IV Chr. Mon. S.Alb. in 3 parts (1867–9): I 1–324 (793–1255) mainly by Matthew Paris; I 325 to II 109 (1235–1308) anon.; II 111 to III 372 (1308–96) by Thomas Walsingham; III 373–535 (1349–1401) cont. anon.

G. Steph. *Gesta Stephani* (1135–54), Med. Texts (1955) [by cap.].

GAD. John of Gaddesden [*ob.* *a*1350]: *Rosa medicinae* or *Rosa Anglica* (Venice, 1502) [by f. and col.].

Gall. Christ. *Gallia Christiana in provincias ecclesiasticas* [*Franciae*] *distributa*, ed. D. Sammarthanus *et al.* 16 vols. (Paris, 1716–1865).

Gaol. Del. Gaol Delivery Rolls (1271–1476), MS PRO (Just. Itin. 3).

Gaol File Wales Gaol Files, Writs etc., MS formerly PRO (Wales 4) now in Nat. Library of Wales (Aberystwyth).

GARDINER Stephen Gardiner [*ob.* 1555]: **CC** *Confutatio Cavillationum* (1552) (ed. Louvain, 1554); **Bucher** Answer to Bucher (1541), in Obedience to Church and State, three political tracts. ed. P. Janelle (Cambridge, 1930) 174–211; **Legat.** Address to the Legates (1529) *ib.* 1–9; **Si sedes** Tract on Fisher's execution (1535) *ib.* 22–65; **VO** *De vera obedientia oratio* (1535) *ib.* 67–171 [supersedes *Monarchia* I 716–32].

GARL. John of Garland [*ob.* *p*1258]: **Aeq.** *Fragmentum ex libro de aequivocis* (attrib.), *PL* CL (1854) 1589–90; **Dict.** *Dictionarius* (*a*1230), ed. T. Wright, in Vocabularies. . 10c.–15c. I (1857) 120–38 [readings checked against A. Scheler's ed. in Jahrbuch für Romanische und Englische Literatur VI (1865) 142–62, 287–321, 370–9]; **GS** *Georgica spiritualia* (*c*1220) extr. in *Speculum* VIII (1933) 358–77; **Hon. Vit.** *Exempla honestae vitae* (1258), ed. E. Habel, in Romanische Forschungen XXIX pt. 1 (1911) 131–54 [by line]; **Mor. Scol.** *Morale scolarium* (1241), in Two medieval texts, ed. L. J. Paetow (Berkeley, 1927) 185–260 [by line]; **Mus.** *De musica mensurabili positio*, *Introductio musice*, *De musica mensurabili*, *Script. Mus.* I (1864) 97–117, 157–75, 175–82; **Myst. Eccl.** *De mysteriis ecclesiae* (1245) *Comm. Critici*, in *Codices Bibl. Acad. Gissensis* (Giessen, 1842) 131–48 [by line]; **Myst. Eccl. add.** Additional (alternative) lines to above, *ib.* 148–51 [by p.]; **SM** *Stella Maris* or *Miracula B.Marie Virginis* (1248–9), (Cambridge, Mass., 1946) [by line]; **Syn.** *Opus synonymorum* (attrib.), in *PL* CL (1854) 1578–90; **Tri. Eccl.** *De triumphis ecclesiae* ed. T. Wright Roxburghe Club (1856) [by p.].

GASCOIGNE Loci Thomas Gascoigne [*ob.* 1458]: *Loci e libro veritatum*, passages selected from Gascoigne's Theological Dictionary, illustr. the condition of Church and State, 1403–58, ed. J. E. T. Rogers (Oxford, 1881).

Gavelkind Somner, W.: A treatise of gavelkind (1660).

General Register House *v.* Scot. RO.

GEOFFREY DE VINSAUF *v.* VINSAUF.

GERV. CANT. Gervase of Canterbury [*ob.* *c*1210]: RS, 2 vols. (1879–80); I Chronicle (1135–99), II 3–106 *Gesta Regum* (abbr. of G. MON. cont. to 1207); **Cont.** Anon. cont. of *Gesta Regum* (1208–1328), *ib.* II 106–324; **AP** *Actus Pontificum* (582–1205), *ib.* 325–414; **MM** *Mappa Mundi*, *ib.* 419–49.

GERV. CIC. Gervase of Chichester [*fl.* *c*1170]. **Hom.** Homilies on martyrdom of T. Becket (incomplete) MS BM Royal 3BX ff. 113– , frag. printed in GERV. CANT. II app. I xlviii–ix; **Mal** Commentary on Malachi MS *ib.* ff. 2–112b; **Vers.** Verses prefacing Mal. in GERV. CANT. II app. I xlvii–viii.

GERV. MELKLEY Gervase of Melkley [*fl.* (?) *a*1220]: Verses on John Gray, Bishop of Norwich, extr. in GERV. CANT. I xxxvii.

GERV. TILB. Gervase of Tilbury [*fl.* *c*1211] *Otia imperialia* (1211) *Scriptores rerum Brunsvicensium* I (1707) 881–1004, II (1710)

751–84 [by bk. and cap.]. (extr. from bk. II, caps. 10, 16, 17, and 20 also in COGGESH. 419–49) [Med. Text in prep.].

Gesch. Stahlhofes Lappenberg, J. M. Urkundliche Geschichte des Hansischen Stahlhofes zu London 2 pts. in 1 vol.; app. of docs. w. sep. pag. 1–218 (Hamburg, 1851).

GILB. Gilbertus Anglicus [*ob. c*1250]: *Compendium medicinae* (Lyon, 1510) [by bk., f., and col.].

Gild. Camb. Cambridge gild records (14c.), ed. M. Bateson, Camb. Antiq. Soc., 8° ser., XXXIX (1903).

Gild Merch. Gross, C.: The gild merchant (1066–17c.), 2 vols. (Oxford, 1890).

GILDAS Gildas: **EB** *De excidio et conquestu Britanniae* (? *a*547), *MGH Chr. Min.* III (Berlin, 1898) 25–85 [by section]; **Ep.** *Epistularum..fragmenta, ib.* 86–8; **Pen.** *De poenitentia, ib.* 89–90.

GIR. Giraldus Cambrensis [*ob. c*1223]: **Inv.** *De invectionibus* (*c*1205), Y Cymmrodorion XXX (1920); other works cited from RS (8 vols. 1861–91) as follows: **Ad S.Langton** *Epistola ad Stephanum Langton* (1215), I 401–7; **Catal. Brevior** *Catalogus brevior librorum suorum,* I 421–3; **DK** *Descriptio Kambriae* (1194), VI 153–227; **David** *Vita S.Davidis* [? *ob.* 601], III 377–404; **EH** *Expugnatio Hibernica* (1187–1189), V 205–411; **Galf.** *De vita Galfridi* (*c*1193), IV 355–431; **GE** *Gemma Ecclesiastica* (1197), II; **Hug.** *Vita S.Hugonis* (*c*1214), VII 81–147; **IK** *Itinerarium Kambriae* (*c*1191), VI 1–152; **JS** *De Jure et Statu Menevensis Ecclesiae* (*c*1218), III 99–404; **LS** *De libris a se scriptis,* I 409–19; **Opusc.** minor works cited by vol. and p. of RS; **PI** *De Principis Instructione Liber* (*c*1217), VIII; **RG** *De rebus a se gestis* (*c*1205), I 1–122; **Rem.** *Vita S.Remigii* [2nd version *c*1214; incl. lives of various bishops], VII 3–80; **Retr.** *Retractationes,* I 425–7; **Spec.** *Speculum Ecclesiae* (*c*1220), IV 1–354; **Symb.** *Symbolum Electorum* (*c*1205), I 197–335; **Symb. Metr.** *Symbolum electorum* (metr.), I 337–87 [by no. and p.]; **TH** *Topographia Hibernica* (wr. (?) *a*1188), V 1–204 [1st recension, ed. J. J. O'Meara, Proc. RIA LII sec. C (1949) 113–78]; [most of above cited by cap.].

Gl. Arch. Spelman, H.: *Glossarium archaiologicum* (1664).

GlC An eighth-century Latin–Anglo-Saxon glossary (Cambridge, Corpus MS 144), ed. W. M. Lindsay (Cambridge, 1921); *cf.* Philol. Soc. pub. VIII (1921) [*v. et.* EE, Erf. 2 and 3, and Gl. Leid.].

Gl. Durh. The Durham Glossary of the names of worts (11c.), in Leechdoms III (1866) 297–305.

Gl. Leid. A late 8th century Latin–Anglo-Saxon glossary preserved in..Leiden Univ., ed. J. H. Hessels (Cambridge, 1906) [*v. et.* GlC].

GLANV : Ranulf Glanvill [*ob.* 1190]; [attrib.] *De legibus et consuetudinibus Regni Angliae* (*c*1185), ed. G. D. G. Hall, Nelson and Selden Soc. (1965); also ed. G. E. Woodbine (Yale, 1932) [both by bk. and cap.].

GOSC. Goscelin [? *ob. p*1107]: **Aug. Maj.** *Vita S.Augustini, historia major,* in *PL* LXXX (1850) 41–94; **Aug. Min.** *Historia minor, ib.* CL (1854) 743–63; **Edith** *Vita S.Eadgitae seu Edithae* [*ob.* 984] (*c*1080), in *Anal. Boll.* LVI (1938) 5–101, *Translatio ejusdem, ib.* 265–307; **Lib. Confort.** *Liber confortatorius* (*c*1081) in *Studia Anselmiana,* fasc. XXXVII (1955) 1–31; **Mellitus** *De adventu B.Melliti..in Britanniam,* extr. in FLETE Westm. 38–40; **Mir. Aug.** *Libellus de miraculis S.Augustini* (*c*1094), in *Acta SS Ben.* I (1668) 535–59; **Mir. Iv.** *Miracula S.Ivonis,* in *Chr. Rams.* app. II lix–lxxxiv; **Transl. Aug.** *Historia translationis S.Augustini* (*p*1099), in *PL* CLV (1880) 13–46; **V. Iv.** *Vita S.Ivonis episcopi, ib.* 81–90; **Wulfh.** *Vita S.Wulfhilde* [*ob. c*1000] (*p*1086), in *Anal. Boll.* XXXII (1913) 10–26 [by cap.]; **Wulsin** The life of St. Wulsin of Sherborne (*a*1080), Rev. Bénédict. LXIX (1959) 68–85 [by cap.; *cf. V. Ed. Conf.* app. C 91–111; *v. et. Ps.*-Gosc.].

GOWER John Gower [*ob.* 1408]: Complete works, ed. G. C. Macaulay, IV Latin works (1902): Minor poems 343–5 and 355–68 [by p. and line]; **CT** *Chronica tripartita* (*p*1399), 314–43; **VC** *Vox clamantis* (begun 1381, finished *a*1399), 3–313; **VP** *Carmen super..vitiroum pestilentia* (1396–7), 346–54 [all by line].

Grampian Club publications (London, 1869–80; Edinburgh, 1882–91).

GRAYSTANES Robert de Graystanes: *Historia de statu Ecclesiae Dunelmensis* (1214–1336), Hist. Durh. Script. Surtees Soc. IX (1889) 33–123 [by cap.].

Great Seal Maxwell Lyte, H. C.: Historical Notes on the use of the Great Seal of England (1926).

GREG. Mir. Rom. Gregory (Magister Gregorius) [*p*1200]: *De mirabilibus Urbis Romae,* ed. M. R. James, EHR XXXII (1917) 531–54 [by cap.]; also ed. G. M. Rushforth, JRS IX (1919) 14–48.

Grey Friars Ox. Little, A. G.: The grey friars in Oxford, OHS XX (1892).

GRIM Edward (or Everardus) Grim: **Thom.** *Vita S.Thomae* (*c*1175), in Becket Mat. II 353–450 [by cap.] (*cf.* BROMPTON 1052–5]; **App.** Appendix to above, *ib.* 451–8; **Pass.** *Passio S.Thomae,* ed. E. Martène and U. Durand, *Thes. Nov. Anecd.* III (1737–46).

GROS. Robert Grosseteste [Bishop of Lincoln 1235–53]: cited by page from Die philosophische Werke [incl. some works of doubtful attribution], ed. L. Baur, Beitr. zur Gesch. der Phil. des Mittelalters IX (1912) 1–274, except the following: **Comp.** *Compotus factus ad correctionem communis Kalendarii nostri,* in BACON VI 212–67; **Ep.** *Epistolae* (*a*1210–53), RS (1861) [by no.] [*Ep.* no. 1 = pp. 106–19 in Baur's ed.]; **Quaest. Theol.** *Quaestiones theologicae* [attrib.], ed. D. A. Callus, in Powicke Studies 194–209 [*v. et. Ps.*-GROS.].

Growth Eng. Indust. Cunningham, W.: The growth of English industry and commerce during the early and middle ages (Cambridge, 1896).

Guild Cert. Chancery Guild Certificates (1388–9), MS PRO (C. 47/38–46); *cf.* extr. in EETS XL (1870, repr. 1924).

GUISB. *v.* W. GUISB.

H. ALBUS Hugh Albus (*alias* Candidus), monk of Peterborough [*ob. a*1175]: Chronicle (656–1155), ed. W. T. Mellows (Oxford, 1949) [supersedes *Hist. Angl. Script.* ii 1–94].

H. AVR. Henry of Avranches [*ob.* 1260]: **CG** *Comoda gramatice* (? 1219), extr. ed. J. P. Heironimus and J. C. Russell, in Colorado Coll. pubs., Gen. S., CLVIII (1929) 3–27 [by f. and l.]; **Prol. & Epil.,** Prologue and Epilogue in Poems (Cambridge, Mass., 1935) 58–9; **Guthl.** *Vita Sancti Guthlaci* [*ob.* 714], MS Cambridge University Library (Dd. xi. 78); **Hugh** Metrical life of S.Hugh, Bishop of Lincoln [*ob.* 1200] (*c*1220) [attrib.], ed. J. F. Dimock (Lincoln, 1860); **Poems** The shorter Latin poems relating to England, ed. J. C. Russell and J. P. Heironimus, in Med. Acad. Am. Stud. and Doc. I (Cambridge, Mass., 1935) [complete poems by no. and line; extr. by no. and p.].

H. BOS. Herbert of Bosham [*ob. c*1186]: **CE** *Causa exsilii.. B.Thomae,* in *PL* CXC (1893) 1413–16; **Ep.** *Epistolae, ib.* 1415–74; **Hom.** *Homilia in festo S.Thomae, ib.* 1403–14; **LM** *Liber melorum, ib.* 1293–1404; **Thom.** *Vitae S.Thomae,* in Becket Mat. vol. III 155–534 [by bk. and cap.; this version differs somewhat from that in *PL* CXC 1073–1292].

H. CANDIDUS *v.* H. ALBUS.

H. CANTOR Hugh the Chantor (*alias* Sottovagina), Archdeacon of York [*ob. c*1139]: History of the Church of York, 1066–1127, ed. C. Johnson, Med. Texts (1961) [by f.]; **Cont.** Additions (to 1153), Hist. Church York II 220–7; **Vers.** *Versus,* Sat. Poets II 219–29 [by p.].

H. HARTLEPOOL Hugh of Hartlepool [*ob. c*1302]: Sermon (1291), OHS XCVI (1934) app. I 192–204.

H. HUNT. Henry (Archdeacon) of Huntingdon [*ob.* ? 1155]: **CM** *Epistola ad Walterum de contemptu mundi, HA* [*v. infra*] 297–320 [by cap.]; **Ep. ad Warinum** *Epistola ad Warinum de regibus Britonum,* in TORIGNI 65–75; **HA** *Historia Anglorum* I–VIII (55 B.C.–A.D. 1154), RS (1879) 1–292 [by bk. and cap.]; **HA IX** (*De miraculis*), extr. *ib.* xxv–xxx; **HA X** (*De summitatibus*) *v. supra CM, Ep. ad Warinum* [remainder not printed]; **HA XI** *Historiae liber undecimus*, Sat. Poets II 163–74 [by p.].

H. KIRKSTALL *v.* SERLO GRAM.

H. LOS. Herbert de Losinga, Bishop of Norwich [*ob.* 1119]: **Ep.** *Epistolae*, ed. R. Anstruther, Caxton Soc. (1846) 1–107 [by no.]; **Serm.** Sermons, in Life, letters, and sermons, ed. E. M. Goulburn and H. Symonds (1878) II.

H. READING (I) Hugh, Abbot of Reading [*ob.* 1164]: **Adjut.** *V.S. Adjutoris*, in *PL* CXCII (1855) 1345–52; **Dial.** *Dialogorum libri VII*, *ib.* 1141–1248 [by bk. and col.]; **Ep.** *Epistolae*, *ib.* 1131–8 [by no. and col.]; **Fid. Cath.** *Super fide catholica*, *ib.* 1323–46; **Haeret.** *Contra haereticos*, *ib.* 1255–98 [by bk. and col.]; **Hex.** *Tractatus in hexameron*, *ib.* 1247–56; **Mem.** *Tractatus de memoria*, *ib.* 1299–1324.

H. READING (II) Cel. Hugh, Abbot of Reading [*ob.* 1207]: Epistle to Celestine III (*c*1197), in Wilkinson Essays 29–31.

H. SALTREY Henry of Saltrey [Hunts.] [*fl. c*1150]: *Purgatorium S.Patricii*, in M. PAR. *Maj.* II 192–203.

H. SOTTOVAGINA *v.* H. CANTOR.

HBS Henry Bradshaw Society, pubs. I– (1891–).

HCA High Court of Admiralty: **Act Bk.** Instance and Prize courts, Acts, MS PRO (H.C.A. 3); **Crim.** Oyer and terminer records, criminal MS PRO (H.C.A. 1); **Libel.** Libels, etc., *ib.* (H.C.A. 24); **Warrant Bk.** Warrant books, *ib.* (H.C.A. 38).

HMC Rep. Reports of the Historical Manuscripts Commission, I– (1874–).

HMSO His [Her] Majesty's Stationery Office.

Hal. Durh. *Halmota Prioratus Dunelmensis*, extr. from Halmote Court or Manor Rolls (1296–1384), Surtees Soc. LXXXII, vol. I (1889) [vol. II not pub.].

HALES Alexander of Hales [*ob.* 1245]: **Qu.** *Quaestiones disputatae 'antequam esset frater'*, [sometimes wrongly referred to as *Summa Abendonensis*] *Bibliotheca Franciscana scholastica medii aevi* XIX–XXI (Florence, 1960); **Sent.** *Glossa in quatuor libros Sententiarum Petri Lombardi*, *ib.* XII–XV (1951–7); **Summa** *Summa theologica* 5 vols. (1924–48).

HANV. John de Hanville (*alias* Hauville, or de Alta Villa) [*fl. c*1184]: *Architrenius*, Sat. Poets vol. I 240–392 [by bk. and p.], also ed. P. G. Schmidt (München, 1974).

HAUBOYS John Hauboys (*alias* Hanboys) [*fl. c*1470]: *Summa super musicam continuam et discretam*, in *Script. Mus.* I 403–67.

HAUDLO Robert de Haudlo (*alias* Handlo) [*fl. c*1326]: *Regulae*, in *Script. Mus.* I 383–403.

HEETE Robert Heete [*ob. c*1432]: **Catalog. Coll. Wint.** *Libri B.Mariae prope Winton'* (*temp.* Hen. V, Hen. VI), in Arch. J. XV (1858) 59–74; **Wykeham** Life of William of Wykeham [1324–1404], in Moberly, G. H.: Life of William of Wykeham (1887) 293–308.

HENGHAM Ralph de Hengham [Chief Justice, *ob.* 1311]: **Magna** *Summa Magna* (*a*1275), in *Radulphi de Hengham Summae*, ed. W. H. Dunham, (Cambridge, 1932) 1–50 [by cap.]; **Parva** *Summa parva* (*p*1285), *ib.* 51–71 [by cap.].

HERM. ARCH. Herman, Archdeacon of Thetford [*ob. c*1095]: *Liber de miraculis S.Eadmundi*, Mem. S.Edm. I 26–92 [by cap.]; also ed. F. Liebermann, ANQuellen 202–81 [*v. et.* SAMSON].

HERRISON Abbr. Chr. John Herrison: *Abbreviata cronica* (1377–1469), Cambridge Antiq. Soc., 4° S., II (1840).

Hexham The Priory of Hexham, 2 vols., Surtees Soc. XLIV, XLVI (1863–4); *v. et.* J. HEX., RIC. HEX.

HEYTESBURY *v.* Sci. Mech.

HIGD. Ralph Higden [*ob.* 1364]: *Polychronicon* (Creation–1352), 9 vols. RS (1865–86) [by bk. and cap.]; **Cont. A** Continuation (–1381) [attrib. John of Malvern], *ib.* VIII 355–428; **Cont. B** (1381–94), *ib.* IX 1–283, *v.* Chr. Westm.

HIL. RONCE. Hilarius of Ronceray [*fl. c*1125: *Versus et ludi*, ed. J. B. Fuller (N.Y., 1929).

Hist. Abb. Jarrow *Historia abbatum, auctore anonymo* (*c*716), in BEDE *Op. Hist.* I 388–404 [by cap.].

Hist. Abingd. Stenton, F. M.: The early history of the Abbey of Abingdon [Berks] (Reading, 1913).

Hist. Angl. Script. *Historiae Anglicanae scriptores varii*, ed. J. Sparke (1723); *v. Chr. Angl. Peterb.*, H. ALBUS, SWAFHAM, WHITTLESEY.

Hist. Angl. Script. X. *Historiae Anglicanae Scriptores X*, ed. R. Twysden (1652); *v.* BROMPTON, THORNE, AILR.

Hist. Brit. Iron & Steel Ind. Schubert, H. R.: History of the British iron and steel industry (*c*450 B.C.–A.D. 1775) (1957).

Hist. Castle Combe Scrope, P. G.: History of the manor and.. barony of Castle Combe [Wilts] (1852).

Hist. Cath. Cant. Dart, J.: The history and antiquities of the Cathedral Church of Canterbury (1726).

Hist. Chester Ormerod, G.: The history of the County Palatinate and City of Chester, 2nd ed. (1882).

Hist. Church York The historians of the Church of York and its Archbishops, 3 vols. RS (1879–94) [mainly cited under authors]; *v. et. Chr. Ebor.*; *Chr. Pont. Ebor.*; *V. Osw.*; *Mir. J. Bev.*; *Mir. Will.*; *Misc. Scrope*; *V. Will.*

Hist. Crawley *v.* Crawley.

Hist. Cuthb. *Historia de S.Cuthberto* [*ob.* 687] (10c.), in S. DURH. *Auct.* I 196–214.

Hist. Durh. William de Chambre [? *fl. c*1356] *et al.*: *Continuatio historiae Dunelmensis* (1336–1571), in Hist. Durh. script. 127–56 [by cap.].

Hist. Durh. Script. *Historiae Dunelmensis scriptores tres*, Surtees Soc. IX (1889). **App.** appendixes to above [by p.; *v. et.* G. COLD., GRAYSTANES, Hist. Durh.

Hist. Eng. Bar Cohen, H.: History of the English Bar (–1450) (1929).

Hist. Exch. Madox, T.: History of the Exchequer (1066–1327) (1711).

Hist. Fordwich Woodruff, C. E.: A history of the town and port of Fordwich [Kent] (Canterbury, 1895).

Hist. Francisc. Eng. Little, A. G.: Studies in English Franciscan History (Manchester, 1917).

Hist. Glouc. *v.* Cart. Glouc.

Hist. Imbank. Dugdale, W.: The history of imbanking and drainage (1772).

Hist. Meriadoci *Historia Meriadoci* (*c*1250), ed. J. D. Bruce (Baltimore, 1900).

Hist. N. Durh. Raine, J.: The history..of North Durham (1852).

Hist. Norm. Script. *Historiae Normannorum scriptores antiqui*, ed. A. Duchesne (Paris, 1619).

Hist. Roff. *Historia Roffensis* (1314–50) [attrib. to William Dene], with supporting docs. [by folio MS BM Faust. B.V; some refs. may be to pp. of *Anglia Sacra* I 356–77].

Hist. S.Paul. Dugdale, W.: The history of St. Paul's Cathedral in London (1818).

Hist. Shrewsb. Owen, H. and Blakeway, J. B.: A history of Shrewsbury, 2 vols. (1825).

Hist. Staffs Shaw, S.: The history and antiquities of Staffordshire, 2 vols. (1798, 1801).

Hist. Tynemouth Gibson, W. S.: The history of the monastery founded at Tynemouth [Northumb], 2 vols. (1846–7).

Hist. Wells *Historia major* (704–1408) *et minor* (704–1367) *Wellenses*, in *Collectanea* I, Som Rec. Soc. XXXIX (1924) 48–71.

Holy Rood-Tree Latin Versions [12c.] ed. A. S. Napier in History of the Holy Rood-Tree, EETS CIII (1894) 41–62.

HORN Mir. Just. Andrew Horn [*ob.* 1328]: Mireur à justices (*c*1290), Selden Soc. VII (1895), prefatory verses (p. 1).

Hosp. in Eng. The Knights Hospitallers in England, report to Grand Master (1338), Camden Soc. LXV (1857).

HOTHBY John Hothby [*ob.* 1487]: **Cant. Fig.** *De cantu figurato*, in *Script. Mus.* III 330–2; **Contrap.** *Regulae super contrapunctum*, *ib.* 333–4; **Prop.** *Regulae super proportionem*, *ib.* 328–30.

Househ. Bk. Durh. Household Book (bursar's accounts) of the monastery of Durham 1530–4, Surtees Soc. XVIII (1844).

Hug. Soc. Proceedings of the Huguenot Society of London, I– (Lymington, 1887–).

Hund. *Rotuli hundredorum Hen. III et Ed. I*, 2 vols. RC (1812–18).

Hund. & Hund. R. Cam, Helen M.: The hundred and the hundred rolls (1930).

Hund. Highworth The rolls of Highworth hundred (1257–87), Wilts Arch. . Soc., Rec. Branch, XXI, XXII (Devizes, 1966–8).

Husb. Walter of Henley: Husbandry, ed. D. Oschinsky (Oxford, 1971) [cited as source of passages in *Fleta*; *v. et.* Senesch.].

IAQD Inquisitions *ad quod damnum*, MS PRO (C. 143).

ICrim Criminal Inquisitions, MS PRO (C. 144).

IMC Irish Manuscripts Commission, pubs. I– Irish SO (Dublin, 1931–).

IMisc Miscellaneous Inquisitions, MS PRO (C. 145).

IPM Inquisitions *post mortem*, MS PRO: Hen. III (C. 132); Ed. I (C. 133); Ed. II (C. 134); Ed. III (C. 135); Ric. II (C. 136); Hen. IV (C. 137); Hen. V (C. 138); Hen. VI (C. 139); Ed. IV (C. 140); Ric. III (C. 141); Hen. VII, Hen. VIII etc., (C. 142).

Illust. Scot. Illustrations of Scottish history, 12th to 16th century, ed. J. Stevenson, Maitland Club XXVIII (1834).

Inchaffray Charters. . relating to the Abbey of Inchaffray, Perth, SHS 1st S. LVI (1908) [by p.].

Indict. (Assizes) Indictments, S.E. Circuit (1559–), MS PRO (Assizes 35).

Inq. Cantab. *Inquisitio comitatus Cantabrigiensis* (1086), ed. N. E. S. Hamilton (1876).

Inq. Ely *Inquisitio Eliensis* (1086), *DB Add.* I 495–528; also ed. N. E. S. Hamilton in *Inq. Cantab.* 97–195 [differs from DB text].

Inq. Non. *Nonarum inquisitiones in Curia Scaccarii* (*temp.* Ed. III), ed. G. Vanderzee, RC (1807).

Inst. Sempr. *Institutiones B.Gilberti ordinis de Sempringham* (*c*1148), pp. *xix–*lix in *MonA* VI, between pp. 946 and 947; [roman pag. in ed. 1846 differs from that in ed. 1817].

Instr. Nov. *Instructio noviciorum secundum consuetudinem ecclesie Cantuariensis* (? 13c.), in Lanfr. Const. 133–49 [by marginal no.].

Invent. Ch. Ch. Inventories of Christchurch Canterbury, ed. J. W. Legg and W. H. St. J. Hope (1902).

Invent. Exch. Inventories of goods and chattels roll 1/1 (1207–8) in Pipe Roll Soc. NS XXXI 119–25; later rolls MS PRO (E. 154).

Invent. Norw. Archdeaconry of Norwich, inventory of church goods. . (1368), Norf Rec. Soc. XIX, 2 vols. (1947–8).

Invent. S.Paul. Two inventories of the cathedral church of St. Paul, London, . . 1245 and 1402, in *Arch.* L pt. 2, 439–524.

Invent. York *Inventarium. . librorum. . fratrum Heremitarum Sancti Augustini. .* 1372, N. & Q., S.1, I (1850) 83–4; also ed. M. R. James, *Fasciculus Joanni Willis Clark dicatus* (Cambridge, 1909), 2–96.

Isis Isis I– (Brussels and Cambridge, Mass., 1913–) (*v. et.* Wallingf.].

IssueR Issue Rolls of the Exchequer of Receipt, MS PRO (E. 403).

Iter Cam. *Modus procedendi in itinere camerarii infra regnum Scocie*, in APScot I app. 4, 329–38 [by cap.]; **Iter Cam. Artic.** *De articulis inquirendis. . in itinere camerarii. .*, *ib.* app. 3, 316–18 [by cap.].

Itin. Ric. *Itinerarium peregrinorum et gesta regis Ricardi* (*c*1200) [attrib. Richard de Templo, prior of Holy Trinity, London], Mem. Ric. I vol. I [by bk. and cap.; anon. source of Bk I. ed.H. E. Mayer, *MGH* Schriften XVIII (Stuttgart, 1962)].

J. ACTON Comment. John of Acton (*alias* Ayton) [*ob.* 1350]: *Commentaria in constitutiones legatinas D. Othonis et D. Othoboni*, pub. w. Lyndw. (1679).

J. BLUND. An. John Blund [*ob.* 1248]: *Tractatus de anima* (*c*1200), ed. D. A. Callus and R. W. Hunt (1970) [by section].

J. Burgh PO John de Burgh [*ob.* 1386]: *Pupilla oculi*, (Strasbourg, 1514) [by bk. and cap.].

J. BURY Glad. Sal. John of Bury: *Gladius Salomonis* (*c*1460), extr. in Pecock *Repressor* vol. II RS (1860) 566–613.

J. CORNW. John of Cornwall (*alias* de Sancto Germano) [*fl.* *c*1170]: **Canon.** *Libellus de canone mystici libaminis* [attrib.], in *PL* CLXXVII (1854) 455–70; **Eul.** *Eulogium ad Alexandrum III Papam* (*c*1180), in *PL* CXCIX (1855) 1043–86; **Verb.** *Apologia de Verbo incarnato* [attrib.], in *PL* CLXXVII (1854) 295–316.

J. COTTON John Cotton [12c.]: *Tractatus de musica*, in *PL* CL (1854) 1391–1430.

J. EXON. BT Joseph of Exeter: *De bello Trojano* (*c*1184), ed. R. J. Valpy (1825); Bk. I, ed. J. J. Jusserand (1877) [by bk. and line]; also ed. L. Gompf, Werke und Briefe, in Mittellateinische Studien und Texte (Leyden, 1910).

J. FURNESS Jocelin (*alias* Jordan) of Furness [*fl.* *c*1200]: **Kentig.** *Vita S. Kentigerni*, ed. A. P. Forbes, Lives of S.Ninian and S.Kentigern (Edinburgh, 1874) 159–242 [by cap.; *v. et. V. Walthevi*].

J. FORD Wulf. John of Ford [*ob.* *c*1220]: *Vita B.Wulfrici* [*ob.* 1154], Som. Rec. Soc. XLVII (1932) [by cap.].

J. GLAST. John of Glastonbury [*fl.* *c*1400]: *Historia de rebus Glastoniensibus* (foundation –1342), 2 vols. Contin. pag. w. app. etc. (Oxford, 1726); *cf.* W. Malm. Glast., Wych.

J. GODARD John Godard, Abbot of Newenham [*ob.* *p*1248]: **Ap.** *Apostropha in Virginem gloriosam*, *Anal. Cisterc.* X (1954) 246–67; **Ep.** *Epistola ad sororem*, *ib.* 220–45.

J. HERD Hist. IV Regum John Herd [*ob.* 1588]: *Historia Quatuor Regum Angliae* (Ed. IV, Ed. V, Ric. III, Hen. VII), Roxburghe Club (1868).

J. HEX. HR Cont. John of Hexham [*fl.* *c*1180]: Cont. (1130–53) of S. Durh. *HR* in S. Durh. II 284–332.

J. HOWD. John of Howden [*ob.* 1275]: **CA** *Canticum amoris*, Surtees Soc. CLIV (1939) 206–40; **Cant.** *Quinquaginta cantica, ib.* 8–117; **Cyth.** *Cythara, ib.* 118–75; **Gaudia** *Quindecim gaudia, ib.* 1–7; **Lira** *Lira, ib.* 203–5; **O Mira** *O mira creatura, ib.* 241–2; **Ph.** *Philomena*, Hymnologische Beiträge IV (Leipzig, 1930); **Sal.** *Quinquaginta salutaciones*, Surtees Soc. CLIV176–93; **Viola** *Viola, ib.* 194–202.

J. LOND. Commend. Ed. I John of London [*ob.* *c*1311]: *Commendatio. . in transitu. . Regis Edwardi* (1307), Chr. Ed. I and II, II 1–21.

J. MALVERN *v.* Chr. Westm.

J. MASON Ep. John Mason: A formulary of letters from St. Augustine's, Canterbury (1307–50), in Wilkinson Essays 192–219.

J. MIRFIELD John Mirfield [*fl.* *c*1393] *v. SB.*

J. READING John of Reading [*ob.* *c*1349]: *Chronica* (Manchester, 1914) [by f.].

J. ROUS Hist. Reg. Angl. John Rous (*alias* Ross) [*ob.* 1491]: *Historia Regum Angliae* (–1485), ed. T. Hearne, 2nd ed. (Oxford, 1745).

J. SAL. John of Salisbury [*ob.* 1180]: **Anselm.** Life of S.Anselm [abridged from Eadmer *V. et Mir. Anselmi*], *PL* CXCIX (1855) 1009–40; **Enth. Phil.** *Entheticus de dogmate philosophorum*, (Hamburg, 1843); **Enth. Pol.** *Entheticus in Policraticum*, in *Pol.* (ed. 1919) 1–11; **Ep.** *Epistolae*, in *PL* CXCIX (1855) 1–378, superseded for years 1153–61 by Med. Texts, vol. 1 (1955) [by no. of *PL*+no. of Med. Texts (in brackets) where available; letters addressed to John cited as *Ep. J. Sal.*]; **Hist. Pont.** *Historiae pontificalis quae supersunt* (1148–52) (Oxford, 1927); also Med. Texts (1956) [by cap.]; **Met.** *Metalogicon* (1159) (Oxford, 1929) [by col. of *PL* CXCIX]; **Pol.** *Policraticus* (1159), 2 vols. (Oxford, 1909) [by col. of *PL*]; **SS** *De septem septenis*, in *PL* CXCIX 845–964; **Thom.** *Vita S.Thomae*, Becket Mat. II 302–22 [by cap.; *v. et.* A. Tewk.].

J. SCAWBY John of Scawby (Schalby) [*c*1324]: *Vita episcoporum Lincolniensium*, in Gir. VII 193–216.

J. SHEPPEY Fab. John of Sheppey [*ob.* 1360]: *Fabulae*, ed. L. Hervieux, Les fabulistes latins IV (Paris, 1896) 417–50 [by no.].

J. TYNEMOUTH John of Tynemouth [*ob.* *c*1348] *v. NLA.*

J. WALEYS John Waleys (*Wallensis*) [*ob.* *c*1285]: **Schak.** *Comparatio mundi ad ludum schakarum*, in *Speculum* VI (1931) 463–5; other works cited from *Opera* (Lyon, 1511), as follows: **Brev. Sap.** *Breviloquium de sapientia sanctorum*, ff. 195–200b; **Brev. Virt.** *Breviloquium de quatuor virtutibus cardinalibus*, ff. 200–16; **Commun.** *Communiloquium*, ff. 1–139; **Compend.** *Floriloquium sive compendiloquium de vita et dictis..philosophorum*, ff. 140–94; **V. Relig.** *Ordinarium*, or *alphabetum vitae religiosae*, ff. 217–55 [by cap. and f.].

J. WORC. John of Worcester: Chronicle (1118–40) (Oxford, 1908) [largely supersedes FL. WORC. II 71–136].

J. YONGE Vis. Purg. Pat. James Yonge: *Memoriale super visitatione Laurentii Ratholdi ad Purgatorium S.Patricii* (c1411), *Anal. Boll.* XXVII (1908) 43–60.

JRL Bull. Bulletin of the John Rylands Library, I– (Manchester, 1903–).

JRS Journal of Roman Studies, I– (1911–).

Jacob Studies *v.* Baronial Reform.

Jahrb. rom. Lit. Jahrbuch für romanische und englische Literatur, I– (Berlin, 1859–).

Jenkinson Studies Essays in memory of Sir Hilary Jenkinson, ed. A. E. J. Hollaender (Chichester, 1962).

JEWEL Apol. John Jewel [*ob.* 1571]: *Apologia ecclesiae Anglicanae* (1562), S.P.C.K. (1948).

JOHN DE ALTA VILLA *v.* HANV.

JOHN DUNS SCOTUS *v.* DUNS.

JOHN LUTTERELL *v.* LUTTERELL.

JOHN PECKHAM (*alias* PECHAM or PATCHAM) *v.* PECKHAM.

JOHN DE S. GERMANO *v.* J. CORNW.

JOHN SCOTUS ERIUGENA *v.* ERIUG.

JOHN WYCLIF *v.* WYCL.

JustIt Assize Rolls etc. (1201–1482), MS PRO (Just. Itin. 1).

KR Records of the Exchequer, King's Remembrancer, MS PRO: **Ac** Accounts, Various (E. 101); **AcCust** Customs Accounts (E. 122); **Ext. & Inq.** Extents and Inquisitions (E. 143); **Forest Proc.** Forest Proceedings (E. 146); **Invent.** *v.* Invent. Exch.; **Mem.** Memoranda Rolls (E. 159); **Mem. PR** Memoranda Roll 1230–1, Pipe Roll Soc. NS XI (1933); **Misc.** *Miscellanea* (E. 163); **Spec. Comm.** Special Commissions (E. 178); **Writs** (E. 202).

Kal. Samson The kalendar of Abbot Samson of Bury St. Edmunds [Suff] [*ob.* 1212]: pp. 1–72 *Liber de consuetudinibus monasterii S.Edmundi* (c1186–91) [by f.]; pp. 73–170 charters (1182–1211) [by no.], Camd. 3rd S. LXXXIV (1954).

Kelso *Liber S.Mariae de Calchou*, 2 vols. Bannatyne Club (1846) [by no.].

KETEL J. Bev. William Ketel: Miracles of St. John of Beverley (c1150), Hist. Church York I 261–91.

KILLINGWORTH Alg. John Killingworth [*ob.* 1445]: *Algorismus*, extr. in EHR XXIX (1914) 707–17.

KILWARDBY Robert Kilwardby, Archbishop of Canterbury [*ob.* 1279]: **Injunc.** Injunctions for Merton College (1276), ed. H. W. Garrod (Oxford, 1929); **Jejun.** *Sermo in capite jejunii*, in Studies in the life of Robert Kilwardby, O.P., *Institutum Historicum Fratrum Praedicatorum Romae* (1937) 163–76; **Quomodo Deus** *Quomodo Deus sit homini philosopho cognitus*, extr. in N. & E. (Hauréau) V 116–30; [*v. et. Ps.*-GROS.].

King's Serjeants Round, J. H.: The King's Serjeants and Officers of State, with their Coronation Services (1911).

King's Works History of the King's works, ed. H. M. Colvin, vol. I– HMSO (1963–).

KNAPWELL Richard Knapwell (*alias* Clapwell) [*fl.* 1286]: **Not.** *Notabilia super primum sententiarum usque ad distinctionem XIX*, Archives d'Histoire Doctr. et Litt. III (Paris, 1928) 185–200; **Quodl.** *Quodlibet*, Zeitschr. Kath. Theol. LII (Innsbruck, 1928) 473–91.

KNIGHTON Henry Knighton [c1366]: *Chronicon* (939–1366), 2 vols. RS (1889, 1895) (I and II 1–123); **Cont.** anon. (1377–95) II 124–322.

KYMER Gilbert Kymer, Dean of Salisbury [*ob.* 1463]: *Diaetarium de sanitatis custodia* (1424), extr. in BBExch. 550–9.

L. DURH. Laurence, prior of Durham [*ob.* 1154]: **Brigida** *Vita S.Brigidae*, in *Acta SS Boll.* Feb. I 172–85, also in *Acta SS Hib.* 1–75; **Dial.** *Dialogi*, Surtees Soc. LXX (1880) 1–61; **Hypog.** *Hypognosticon*, extr. *ib.* 62–71.

LBLond Letter Books of the City of London, MS Corp. of London RO; extr. in *MGL* I 534–739 [by f.; *v. et.* CalLB Lond.].

LC *Lexicon Chymicum* (1652), ed. William Johnson in *Bibl. Chem.* I 217–90 [cited only to elucidate other passages].

L. & P. Hen. VIII Letters and papers..of the reign of Henry VIII, 21 vols.+2 vols. of *addenda*, HMSO (1884–1932).

L. & P. Ric. III–Hen. VII Letters and papers illustrative of the reigns of Richard III and Henry VII, 2 vols. RS (1861–3).

LTR Records of the Exchequer, Lord Treasurer's Remembrancer and Pipe Office, MS PRO: **Ac** Accounts Miscellaneous (E. 358); **Ac. Esch.** Escheators' Accounts (E. 357); **Ac. Wardr.** Wardrobe and Household Accounts (E. 361); **Enr. Estr.** Enrolled Estreats (E. 362); **Mem.** Memoranda Rolls (E. 368); **Mem. PR** Memoranda Rolls 1199–1200 and 1207–8, Pipe Roll Soc. NS XXI (1943) and XXXI (1957); **Misc. R** Miscellaneous Rolls (E. 370).

Lancs & Chesh Rec. Soc. Lancashire and Cheshire Record Society, publications, I– (n. p., 1879–).

Land-ch. Earle, J.: A handbook to the land-charters and other Saxonic documents (Oxford, 1888).

Lanercost *Chronicon de Lanercost* [Cumb] (1201–1346), 2 vols. Bannatyne Club (1839).

LANFR. Lanfranc, Archb. of Canterbury [*ob.* 1089]: **Annot. Cassian.** *Annotatiunculae in Cassiani collationes*, in *PL* CL (1854) 443–4; **Cel. Conf.** *De celanda confessione libellus*, *ib.* 625–32; **Comment. Paul.** *Commentaria in epistolas S.Pauli*, *ib.* 101–406 [partly checked w. ed. L. d'Achery (1648) which more clearly distinguishes Lanfranc's from earlier notes]; **Const.** Constitutions (*Decreta*), Med. Texts (1951) 1–132 [by marginal no.]; reprinted w. extra notes as *Corpus consuetudinum monasticarum*, vol. III (Siegburg, 1967); *v. et. Instr. Nov.*; **Corp. & Sang.** *De corpore et sanguine Domini*, in *PL* CL 407–42; **Ep.** *Epistolae*, *ib.* 516–51 [by no.] [*v. et. Ep. Lanfr.*]; **Sermo**, *ib.* 637–40.

LANTFR. Lantfred (attrib.) [*fl.* c980]: **Mir. et Transl. Swith A** *Historia translationis et miraculorum S. Swithuni* in *Acta SS Boll.* July I 328–37; **B** Another version, ed. E. P. Sauvage, in *Anal. Boll.* IV (1885) 367–410.

Latin Stories A selection of Latin Stories.., of the 13th and 14th cents., ed. T. Wright (1842).

Law & Cust. Sea Documents relating to the law and custom of the sea, 2 vols. Navy Rec. Soc. XLIX, L (1915–16); vol. I (1205–1648), vol. II (1649–1767).

Law Merch. Select cases concerning the law merchant A.D. 1270–1638, 3 vols. Selden Soc. XXIII, XLIV, XLIX (1908–32).

Laws Romney Marsh The charter..or laws and customs of Romney Marsh, ed. H. de Bathe (1686) pp. 55–7.

LEDEREDE Carm. Richard de Lederede, Bishop of Ossory [*ob.* c1361]: Latin poems [attrib.], HMC Rep. X, App. V 242–53; *v. et.* Proc. A. Kyteler.

Leechdoms Leechdoms, wortcunning and starcraft of early England, ed. O. Cockayne, 3 vols. RS (1864–6).

Leet Coventry The Coventry Leet Book (1420–1555), 4 parts, EETS CXXXIV, CXXXV, CXXXVIII, CXLVI (1907–13).

Leet Norw. Leet jurisdiction in the city of Norwich, Selden Soc. V (1891).

Leg. Angl. Lond. *Leges Anglorum..Londoniis collectae* (13c.), ed. F. Liebermann (Halle, 1894).

Leg. Ant. Lond. *De antiquis legibus liber* (London Chronicle of Arnold Fitzthedmar [*ob.* ? 1274], 1178–1274, w. app.), Camd. Soc. 1st S. XXXIV (1846).

Leg. Baronum *v. Quon Attach.*

Leg. Hen. *v.* GAS.

Leg. IV Burg. *Leges et consuetudines quatuor burgorum, Berewic, Rokisburg, Edinburg, et Strivelin* (c1270), *APScot* I 15–44 [by cap.].

LESLEY RGScot John Lesley (*alias* Leslie), Bishop of Ross [*ob.* 1596]: *De origine, moribus et rebus gestis Scotorum*, (Rome, 1578) [by p. of ed. of 1675].

Let. Ch. Ch. Letters relating to the..Priory of Christ Church Canterbury (14c.–16c.), Camd. Soc. NS XIX (1877).

Lib. Cust. Northampt. *Liber Custumarum*, the book of the ancient usages..of Northampton..to 1448, ed. C. A. Markham (Northampton, 1895).

Lib. Eli. *Liber Eliensis* (499–1171), Camd. 3rd S. XCII (1962) [by bk. and cap.]; *v. et.* Ric. Ely, T. Ely.

Lib. Evesham *Officium ecclesiasticum abbatum secundum usum Eveshamensis monasterii* (1282–1316), HBS VI (1893).

Lib. Exempl. *Liber exemplorum ad usum praedicantium* (13c.), Brit. Soc. for Franciscan Studies I (1908).

Lib. Hyda *Liber monasterii de Hyda* [Hants] (455–1023), RS (1866).

Lib. Kilken. *Liber primus Kilkenniensis* (1231–1586), IMC (Dublin, 1931).

Lib. Mem. Bernewelle *Liber memorandorum ecclesie de Bernewelle* [Cambs] (1092–1296; wr. 1295–6, w. later addit. to 1304), ed. J. W. Clark (Cambridge, 1907) [*v. et.* Obs. Barnwell].

Lib. Prot. *Liber protocollorum S.* [Cuthbert Simon]..*scribae capituli Glasguensis* (1499–1513), 2 vols. Grampian Club (Glasgow, 1875).

Lib. Regal. *Liber regalis seu ordo consecrandi regem etc.* (14c.), Roxburghe Club (1870), also in Rec. Coronation 81–112 [by f.].

Lib. Wint. *Liber Wintoniae* c1110 (ff. 1–12b) and 1148 (ff. 13b–33), DB *Add.* I 529–62 [by f.].

Liberate Liberate Rolls, Chancery (1200–1436) MS PRO (C. 62) [*v. et.* Cal. Liberate]; **Liberate (Exch.)** Liberate Rolls, Exchequer, *ib.* (E. 403); **Liberate RC** *Rotuli de Liberate* (1200–4) *etc.*, RC (1844).

LINACRE Emend. Lat. Thomas Linacre [*ob.* 1524]: *De emendata structura Latini sermonis* (1524) [by p. of ed. 1591].

Linc. Chapter Acts *v.* Chap. Linc.

Linc. Rec. Soc. Lincoln Record Society, publications, I– (1911–).

Lit. Cant. *Literae Cantuarienses* [14c.–16c.], 3 vols. RS (1887–9).

Little RB Bristol The little red book of Bristol (1331–1574), 2 vols. (Bristol, 1900).

LIV. Hen. V Titus Livius de Frulovisiis: *Vita Henrici V regis Angliae* (p1437) [by p. of ed. 1716].

Lives Ed. Conf. Lives of Edward the Confessor, RS (1858) [*v. et. V. Ed. Conf.*, *V. Ed. Conf. Metr.*].

Lond. Ed. I & II Weinbaum, M.: London unter Edward I und Edward II, 2 vols. (Stuttgart, 1933).

Loseley MSS. Manuscripts of W. M. Molyneux of Loseley Park [Surrey], HMC Rep. VII (1877) 596–681.

LUCIAN Chester *Liber Luciani de laude Cestrie* (c1195), Lancs and Chesh Rec. Soc. LXIV (1912) 1–78.

LUPSET Ep. Thomas Lupset [*ob.* 1530]: Letters, ed. J. Archer Gee, in Life and Works of T. L. (New Haven, Conn., 1928).

LUTTERELL John Lutterell [*ob.* 1335]: **Occam** *Libellus contra doctrinam Guilelmi Occam*, ed. F. Hoffmann, Erfurter Theologische Studien VI (Leipzig, 1959) 3–102 [by sec.]; **Vis. Beat.** *Epistula de visione beatifica*, ed. *Id. ib.* 103–19 [by f.].

LYNDW. William Lyndwood [*ob.* 1446]: *Provinciale* [by p. and serial letter of ed. 1679: *v. et.* J. Acton].

M. CRISPIN Lanfr. Miles Crispin [*ob.* c1150]: *Vita B. Lanfranci*, in *PL* CL (1854) 19–58.

M. PAR. Matthew Paris [*ob.* c1259]: **Abbr.** *Abbreviatio Chronicorum Angliae* (1000–1255), RS (1869) III 159–348; **Edm.** Life of Edmund Rich, Archb. of Canterbury [*ob.* 1240], in Wallace, W.: Life of St. Edmund of Canterbury (1893) 543–88 [here attrib. E. Faversham]; also in Lawrence, C. H.: Life of St. Edmund of Abingdon (Oxford, 1960) 222–89; **Maj.** *Chronica majora* (Creation–1259), 7 vols. RS (1872–83); **Min.** *Historia Anglorum..sive historia minor*, 3 vols. RS (1866–9) [*v. et. Flor. Hist.* (–1249) I and II 1–363 prob. wr. M. Par.].

M. SCOT Michael Scot [*ob.* c1235]: **Alch.** *De arte alchimiae* [attrib.], extr. in Med. Cult. cap. vii; **Intr.** *Liber Introductorius*, extr. in Med. Sci. cap. xiii; **Lumen** *Lumen luminum*, ed. J. Wood Brown, in Enquiry into the Life and Legend of Michael Scot (Edinburgh, 1897) 240–68; **Part.** *Liber Particularis*, extr. in Med. Cult. cap. vii; **Phys.** *Liber Physiognomiae* (Pavia, 1515) [by cap.]; **Sol** *Quaestio curiosa de natura solis et lunae* [attrib.; p1235], *Theatrum chem.* V 713–22; **Sphera** *v.* Comm. Sph.

MED Middle English Dictionary, ed. H. Kurath and S. H. Kuhn, vol. I– (Ann Arbor, Mich., and Oxford, 1956–).

MFG Medieval farming glossary of Latin and English words taken mainly from Essex records (1200–1600), ed. J. L. Fisher, National Council of Social Service (1968).

MGH *Monumenta Germaniae Historica.*

MGL *Munimenta Gildhallae Londoniensis*, 3 vols. in 4, RS (1859–62).

MLLM *Mediae Latinitatis lexicon minus*, ed. J. F. Niermeyer, Fasc. I– (Leyden, 1954–).

MLW Mittellateinisches Wörterbuch, I– (München, 1967–).

Magna Carta *Magna Carta* (1215), in SelCh 292–302; (1216), *ib.* 336–9 [by cap.].

MAIDSTONE Clement Maidstone (*alias* Maydeston) [*ob.* c1456]: Tracts, HBS VII (1894) 1–237.

Maitland Club publications, I–LXXV (Glasgow, 1829–59).

MAJOR John Major (*alias* Mair) [*ob.* 1550]: *Historia Majoris Britanniae* (1521), ed. 1740 [by bk. and cap.].

Man. Ebor. *Manuale et processionale ad usum insignis Ecclesie Eboracensis* (14c.), Surtees Soc. LXIII (1875) 1–207.

Man. Sal. *Manuale ad usum percelebris ecclesie Sarum* (prob. mainly 15c.; from ed. printed Rouen, 1543), ed. A. J. Collins HBS XCI (1960); also ed. W. G. Henderson in abbreviated form printed as app. to *Man. Ebor.* 1*–112*.

Mandeville Round, J. H.: Geoffrey de Mandeville, a study of the anarchy (1892).

Manners Manners and household expenses of England in the 13th and 15th centuries, Roxburghe Club LVII (1841); [3–115 Household roll of Eleanor, Countess of Leicester, 1265; 116–45 Accounts of the executors of Eleanor, Queen Consort, 1291].

MAP NC Walter Map [*ob.* c1210]: *De nugis curialium distinctiones quinque*, *Anecdota Oxoniensia* XIV (1914) [*v. et.* Ps.-Map].

March. SWales The marcher lordships of S. Wales (1415–1536), select doc., ed. T. B. Pugh (Cardiff, 1963).

Mayor's CourtR Lond. Mayor's Court Rolls (1298–1307), MS, Corp. of London RO [*v. et.* Cal. Mayor's CourtR. Lond.].

Meaux *Chronica monasterii de Melsa* [Yorks] (1150–1406), 3 vols. RS (1866–8).

Med. Admin. Hist. Tout, T. F.: Chapters in the administrative history of Medieval England, etc., 6 vols. (Manchester, 1920–33).

Med. Cult. Haskins, C. H.: Studies in mediaeval culture (Oxford, 1929).

Med. E. Anglia Douglas, D. C.: The social structure of medieval East Anglia (Oxford, 1927).

Med. Eng. Sheriff Morris, W. A.: The medieval English sheriff to 1300 (Manchester, 1927).

Med. Mason Knoop, D., and Jones, G. P.: The medieval mason (Manchester, 1933).

Med. & R. Stud. Mediaeval and Renaissance studies, I– Warburg Inst. (1941–).

Med. Sci. Haskins, C. H.: Studies in the history of mediaeval science (Cambridge, Mass., 1924, repr. 1927).

Med. Stage Chambers, E. K.: The medieval stage, 2 vols. (Oxford, 1903).

Med. Texts Medieval Texts, Oxford University Press, earlier pub. T. Nelson (1949–) [incl. earlier vols. called Medieval Classics].

Melrose *Liber Sancte Marie de Melros* [Roxb] (1124–1625), 2 vols. Bannatyne Club (1837) [by no.].

MELTON William Melton [*fl.* 1420–30] Sermon (preached 1431), in *Doc. Francisc.* 247–56.

Mem. Beverley Memorials of Beverley Minster [Yorks] (1286–1347), 2 vols. Surtees Soc. XCVIII, CVIII (1897, 1903).

Mem. Dunst. Memorials of Saint Dunstan, Archb. of Canterbury [*ob.* 988], RS (1874) [mainly cited under authors].

Mem. Fount. Memorials of the abbey of St. Mary of Fountains [Yorks], 3 vols. Surtees Soc. XLII, LXVII, CXXX (1863–1918) [*v. et.* SERLO. GRAM., SWYNTON *Mem.*].

Mem. Hen. V Memorials of Henry V, RS (1858) [*v. et.* ELMH., REDMAN, Vers. Hen. V].

Mem. Hen. VII Memorials of King Henry VII, RS (1858) [*v. et.* ANDRÉ Hen. VII].

Mem. Ir. Memoranda Rolls of Ireland, extr. (1312–16), in Doc. Ir. 312–58; MS PRO Dublin.

Mem. Parl. *Memoranda de Parliamento* (1305), ed. F. W. Maitland, RS (1893) [by no.].

Mem. Pri. East. Henry of Eastry, prior of Christ Church, Canterbury [*ob.* 1331]: *Memoriale,* MS BM Cotton Galba E. IV ff. 1–186.

MemR Memoranda Rolls 1231–3, HMSO (in prep.) [*v. et.* CalMem, KRMem, LTRMem.].

Mem. Ric. I Chronicles and memorials of the reign of Richard I, RS, vol. I *Itin. Ric.* (1864), vol. II *Ep. Cant.* (1865).

Mem. Ripon Memorials of the church of..Ripon [Yorks.], 4 vols. Surtees Soc., LXXIV, LXXVIII, LXXXI, CXV (1882–1908).

M. S.Edm. Memorials of St. Edmund's Abbey [Suff.], 3 vols. RS (1890–6) [mainly cited under authors].

Mem. York York memorandum book, 2 vols. Surtees Soc. CXX, CXXV (1912–15).

Midlothian *Registrum Domus de Soltre, necnon Ecclesie Collegiate S.Trinitatis prope Edinburgh, etc.*, Bannatyne Club (1861).

MILEMETE Nob. Walter de Milemete: *De nobilitatibus..regum* (*c*1327), ed. M. R. James, Roxb. Club (1913).

MinAc Ministers' and receivers' Accounts (Ser. I Hen. III–Ric. III) MS PRO (S.C. 6); **Essex** Ministers' Accounts, MS Essex RO [*v. et.* MFG]; **Hen. VII (Hen. VIII etc.)** Ministers' and receivers' Accounts (Ser. II, Hen. VII–Chas. II), MS PRO (S.C. 6); **Westm., Wint.** (*etc.*) *v.* Ac. Man. Westm. *etc.*; **W. Wales** Ministers' Accounts for West Wales 1277–1306 pt. 1, ed. M. Rhys, Cymmrodorion Rec. S. XIII (1936).

Mir. Crisp. *Miraculum quo B.Maria subvenit Willelmo Crispino seniori* (*a*1100), in *PL* CL (1854) 735–44.

Mir. Cuthb. *Capitula de Miraculis et translationibus S.Cuthberti* (*a*1130), capp. 1–7 in S. DURH. *Auct.* I 229–61, capp. 8–21, *ib.* II 333–62.

Mir. Ecgwini *v.* Chr. Evesham.

Mir. Fridesw. *Miracula S.Frideswide* [? *ob.* 735], ? *auctore Philippo priore* [1175–91], *Acta SS Boll.* Oct. VIII (Brussels, 1853) 568–89.

Mir. Furs. *Miracula S.Furse abbatis Latiniacensis* [*ob.* 650], *Acta SS Ben.* II 309–14.

Mir. J. Bev., A, B, C Miracles of St. John of Beverley, Hist. Church York I: **A** (*c*1175) 293–320; **B** (12c. or 13c.) 321–5; **C** (*c*1275) 327–47.

Mir. Montf. The miracles of Simon de Montfort (*c*1280), ed. J. O. Halliwell, Camd. Soc. XV (1840) 67–110.

Mir. Odulphi *Miracula S.Odulphi* [canon of Utrecht, *fl. c*830] [*et aliorum*] attrib. Dominic, Prior of Evesham [*fl. c*1125], Chr. Evesham 313–20 [*v. et. V. Odulphi*].

Mir. Will. *Miracula quaedam S.Willelmi* [*ob.* 1154] (? *c*1285), Hist. Church York II 531–43 [*v. et. V. Will.*].

Mir. Wist. *Miracula S.Wistani* [*ob. c*850] attrib. Thomas of Marlborough [Abbot of Evesham 1230–6], Chr. Evesham 332–7 [*v. et. V. Wist.*].

Mir. Wulfst. Miracles of St. Wulfstan [*ob.* 1095] (*c*1240), Camd. 3rd S. XL (1928) 115–88.

MIRK John Mirk, prior of Lilleshall, Salop (*c*1403): *Manuale sacerdotis,* MS BM Harley 5306 ff. 1–61b.

Misae 1209–10, in *Liberate* RC 109–71; 1212–13, in Doc. Exch. 231–69.

Misc. Bannatyne *v.* Bannatyne Misc.

Misc. Chester Miscellanea (1311–), PRO MS (Chester 38).

Misc. Scrope Miscellanea relating to Archb. Scrope (1399–1405), in Hist. Church York II 292–311.

Miss. R. Jum. The missal (1013–17) of Robert of Jumièges [Archb. of Canterbury 1051–2], HBS XI (1896).

Miss. Rosslyn The Rosslyn missal, HBS XV (1899).

Miss. Sarum The Sarum missal (? early 14c.), ed. J. Wickham Legg (Oxford, 1916).

Miss. Westm. *Missale ad usum ecclesie Westmonasteriensis* (1362–86), HBS I, V, XII (1891–7).

Mod. Comp. Brevia *Modus componendi brevia* (*p*1285), in Four 13th-cent. Law Tracts, ed. G. E. Woodbine, Yale Univ. thesis (1910) 143–62.

Mod. Ten. CBaron *Modus tenendi curiam baronum cum visu franci plegii* (1510), ed. C. Greenwood (1915).

Mod. Ten. Parl. *Modus tenendi parliamentum* (14c.), RC (1846); also ed. M. V. Clarke, Medieval representation and consent (1936) 373–92.

MonA *Monasticon Anglicanum*, ed. W. Dugdale, 6 vols. in 8 (1846) [also pub. 3 vols. (1661–82) and 6 vols. in 8 (1817–30); *v. et. Inst. Sempr.*].

Mon. Alcuiniana *Monumenta Alcuiniana*, ed. P. Jaffé, *Bibliotheca Rerum Germanicarum* VI (Berlin, 1873).

MonExon *Monasticon Diocesis Exoniensis*, ed. G. Oliver (1846).

Mon. Francisc. *Monumenta Franciscana*, 2 vols. RS (1858–82) [partly superseded by ECCLESTON *Adv. Min.* (1909); *v. et.* AD. MARSH].

Mon. Hib. & Scot. *Vetera monumenta Hibernorum et Scotorum historiam illustrantia* (1216–1547) [mainly papal letters], ed. A. Theiner (Rome, 1864).

Mon. Rit. *Monumenta ritualia Ecclesiae Anglicanae, etc.*, ed. W. Maskell, 3 vols. (Oxford, 1882).

Monarchia *Monarchia S.Romani Imperii*, ed. M. Goldast, 3 vols. (Hanover and Frankfurt, 1611–14) [cited under authors].

MORE Chr. Ed. II Thomas de la More [attrib.]: *Vita et Mors Edwardi II, Chr. Ed. I and II*, II 297–319 [copied w. minor variations from BAKER].

MORE Ut. Thomas More [*ob.* 1535]: *Utopia* (1518), ed. J. H. Lupton (Oxford, 1895).

MORTON, William *v.* Ac. Almon. Peterb.

MunAcOx *Munimenta academica* (Oxford, 1214–1549), 2 vols. (–366, –795) RS (1868).

MunCOx *Munimenta civitatis Oxonie* (1285–1545,) OHS LXI (1920).

Mun. K's Lynn King's Lynn muniments, in Norfolk RO.

Mun. Merton Merton [College] muniments (with facsimiles) (*c*1154–1519), ed. P. S. Allen and H. W. Garrod (Oxford, 1928).

Mun. Univ. Glasg. *Munimenta alme universitatis Glasguensis* (1453–1727), ed. C. Innes, Maitland Club (Glasgow, 1854).

Mus. Mens. (Anon. VI) *De musica mensurabili* (1391) in *Script. Mus.* III (1869) 398–403.

MUSCA *v.* Chr. Dale.

MYLN Dunkeld Alexander Myln [*ob. c*1548]: *Vitae Dunkeldensis ecclesiae Episcoporum* (1127–1515) Bannatyne Club (1831) [incl. app. of compotus rolls 1513–16].

Mythog. Lat. *Mythographi Latini*, ed. T. Muncker. 2 vols. (Amsterdam, 1681).

N. & E. Notices et extraits des MSS de la Bibliothèque Nationale, I– (1787–).

N. & E. (Hauréau) Notices et extraits de quelques manuscrits latins de la Bibliothèque Nationale, ed. B. Hauréau, vols. I–VI (Paris, 1890–3).

NGML *Novum Glossarium Mediae Latinitatis* (800–1200), ed. F. Blatt, L–O (Copenhagen, 1957–) (in prog.).

NLA *Nova legenda Anglie* collected by John of Tynemouth [*ob. c*1348], w. additions by John Capgrave (*ob.* 1464] *et al.*, 2 vols. (Oxford, 1901); **Prol.** Prologue, prob. wr. for ed. 1516.

N. & Q. Notes and Queries, I– (1849–).

N. Riding Rec. Soc. North Riding Record Society, publications I– (London, 1884–).

Nav. Ven. *Navicula de Venetiis* (*a*1400), Early Sci. Ox. II 375–9 (*cf. ib.* 38–41).

NECKAM Alexander Neckam (*melius* Nequam) [*ob.* 1217]:

Descriptio vernae pulchritudinis

Moribus esse feris prohibet me gratia veris,
Et formam mentis mihi mutuor ex elementis;
Ipsi naturae congratulor, ut puto, jure.
Distingunt flores diversi mille colores.
Gramineum vellus superinduit sibi tellus.
Fronde virere nemus et fructificare videmus.
Aviculi, merulae, graculi, pici, philomenae
Certant laude pari varios cantus modulari.
Nidus nonnullis stat in arbore, non sine pullis,
Et latet in dumis nova progenies sine plumis.
Egrediente rosa viridaria sunt speciosa.
Adjungas istis campum qui canet aristis,
Adjungas vites, uvas quoque, postmodo nuces.
Annumerare queas nuruum matrumque choreas,
Et ludos juvenum, festumque diemque serenum.
Qui tot pulchra videt, nisi flectitur, et nisi ridet,
Intractabilis est, et in ejus pectore lis est.
Qui speciem terrae non vult cum laude referre,
Invidet auctori, cujus subservit honori
Bruma rigens, aestas, autumnus, veris honestas.

PL 171, col. 1717

Now must I mend my manners
  And lay my gruffness by.
The earth is making merry,
  And so, I think, must I.
The flowers are out in thousands,
  Each in a different dress.
The woods are green and like to fruit,
  The earth has donned her grassy fleece,
And blackbirds, jackdaws, magpies, nightingales
Shouting each other down in equal praise.

There's a nest in the tree with young ones in it,
  And lurking in the branches are the unfledged birds.
The bearded grain is whitening to harvest,
  Lovely are the gardens with the half-blown rose;
Add to these the vines, and the grapes, and the hazel nuts,
The young girls dancing, and their mothers dancing too,
And the young men at play, and the good feast toward,
  And the quiet shining day.

So many lovely things, and if a man looks on them,
And his mood is not softened, nor a smile on his face,
An intractable clod is he, at odds with his heart is he,
For he who can behold earth's beauty without praising it
Has a grudge against earth's Maker, whose honour all these serve,
  Cold winter, summer, autumn, comely spring.

MARBOD OF RENNES *c.* 1035–1123

Son of a furrier, Marbod was born in Angers, educated there under Rainaldus, disciple of Fulbert of Chartres, and became successively master of the cathedral school of Angers in 1067, bishop of Rennes in 1096, and finally in his eighty-eighth year simple Benedictine monk of the monastery of St Aubin at Angers, where he died shortly afterwards. He was one of the most eminent literary men of the eleventh century. His renowned pupil Baudry of Bourgeuil addressed him as '*divine poeta*', while his friend Hildebert regarded him as 'the Orpheus of our age', a judgement posterity has reversed in Hildebert's own favour. H W translated the poems of both Marbod and Hildebert from PL 171, the only source then available. Research students of today would naturally turn also to Walther Bulst's edition of Marbod's *Liber Decem Capitulorum* (Heidelberg, 1947), and to the critical edition of Hildebert's *Carmina Minora* (Teubner, 1969), published by Dr A. Brian Scott of Queen's, Helen's own University of Belfast. The Bodleian has recently acquired a precious little volume of Marbod's poems printed in double columns in black letter in 1524. Its opening poem decorated with a handsome floriated initial is that in honour of St Mary Magdalen (p. 244).

Marbod is no Puritan. If a man can look out on a spring day, the nests with the unfeathered birds, and not be touched by it, and go unsmiling, he is intractable, and there is strife in his heart (p. 240). His reproof written to a censorious monk is annihilating (p. 246). Marbod's wisdom is the wisdom of open country: when the town wearied him, he took refuge on his uncle's farm (p. 250). Green grass and quiet trees, a soft little wind and gay, a spring well in the grass, these things give me back to myself... and dreaming under the trees, he watches the eager present slip back into the still grave of the past.

H W

MARBOD OF RENNES

MORE LATIN LYRICS

FROM VIRGIL TO MILTON

translated by

HELEN WADDELL

Edited & with an Introduction by
DAME FELICITAS CORRIGAN

W · W · NORTON & COMPANY · INC ·
NEW YORK

Corrog. *Corrogationes Promethei*, Bodley MS 550 [by f.]; also extr. in N. & E. XXXV pt. 2 (1897) 641–82; also in Med. Sci. 363–4; **DS** *De laudibus divinae sapientiae*, RS (1863) 355–503 [by bk. and line]; **Eccles.** *Commentarium in Ecclesiastem* III 1–11, MS Magdalen Coll. Ox. 139; **Fab.** *Fabulae*, ed. L. Hervieux, Fabulistes latins II (1894) 392–416 [by no. and line]; **NR** *De naturis rerum*, RS 1–354 [by bk. and cap.]; **Poem.** Poems (attrib.), ed. M. Esposito, EHR XXX (1915) 450–71; **Sac.** *Sacerdos ad altare* [attrib.], MS Caius Coll. Camb. 385, extr. in Med. Sci. 361–76; **Ut.** *De nominibus utensilium*, ed. T. Wright: Vocabularies I (1857) 96–119, also ed. A. Scheler, Jahrbuch für romanische u. engl. Lit. VII (1866) 58–74, 155–73 [by p. of ed. 1857]; **VM** *De vita monachorum* (attrib.), Sat. Poets II 175–200.

NEN. Nennius [*fl.* c800]: **HB** *Historia Brittonum cum additamentis Nennii*, in *MGH Auctores Antiqui* XIII (1898) 143–219; **Pref.** *Praefatio* (? 13c.), *ib.* 126–7.

NETTER DAF Thomas Netter of Walden [*ob.* 1430]: *Doctrinale antiquitatum fidei Ecclesiae Catholicae* (1426–7), 3 vols. (Venice, 1571) [Vol. I by p., II and III by f.; *v. et. Ziz.*].

New Liturg. Pfaff, R. W.: New liturgical feasts in later medieval England (Oxford, 1970).

New Spalding Club (formerly Spalding Club), publications (Aberdeen, 1877–).

Nicolas Controv. *v.* Scrope *v.* Grosvenor.

NIG. Nigel Wireker [*fl.* c1190]: **Cur.** *Tractatus contra curiales et officiales clericos*, Sat. Poets I 146–53 (verse), 153–230 (prose); **Ely** *Versus ad Episc. Eliensem* [*ob.* 1197], *ib.* 231–9; **Laur.** *Passio S.Laurencii*, MS BM Cotton Vesp. D. XIX ff. 28–45; **Mir. BVM** *Miracula S. ..Virginis Mariae*, *ib.* ff. 5–24; **Paul.** *Vita Pauli primi heremitae*, *ib.* ff. 45v–52; **Poems** Extr. from unprinted poems in Vesp. D. XIX ff. 1–53 (incl. *Laur.*, *Mir. BVM*, and *Paul.*), *Speculum* VII (1932), 398–423; **SS** *Speculum stultorum* Univ. of California Pubs., Engl. Studies XVIII (1960), also in Sat. Poets I 3–145 [by line].

Norf. Arch. *v.* Arch. Soc. Norf.

Norm. Inst. Haskins, C. H.: Norman institutions (Cambridge, Mass., 1918).

Northants Rec. Soc. Northamptonshire Record Society, publications, I– , (1924–).

O. CANT. Pref. Frith. Odo, Archb. of Canterbury [*ob.* 959]: *Praefatio Frithegodi* in FRITH 1–3 [by line].

O. CHERITON Odo of Cheriton [*ob.* 1247]: **Fab.** *Fabulae*, ed. L. Hervieux: Les fabulistes latins IV (Paris, 1896) 171–255; **Par.** *Parabolae*, *ib.* 265–343 [both by no.].

OED A new English dictionary on historical principles (Oxford, 1888–1928).

OHS Oxford Historical Society, publications, I– (1885–).

Oak Bk. Southampt. The Oak Book of Southampton (c1300), 3 vols. Southampton Rec. Soc. (1910–11).

Obed. Abingd. *v.* Chr. Abingd.

ObitR. Durh. The obituary roll of William Ebchester and John Burnby, priors of Durham, etc. (1233–15c.), Surtees Soc. XXXI (1856).

Obs. Barnwell The observances in use at the Augustinian Priory at Barnwell [Cambs] (1295–6), ed. J. W. Clark (Cambridge, 1897) [*v. et. Lib. Mem. Bernewelle*].

Obsess. Durh. *De obsessione Dunelmi* (c1090), in S. DURH. *Auct.* I 215–20 [by cap.].

OCKHAM William of Ockham [*ob.* 1349]: **Brev.** *Breviloquium de potestate Papae* (1341–2), ed. L. Baudry, Études de Philosophie médiévale XXIV (Paris, 1937); **Dial.** *Dialogus* (1333– ?) in *Monarchia* II 392–957; **Disp.** *Disputatio super potestate praelatis ecclesiae atque principibus terrarum commissa*, *ib.* I 13–18; **Err. Papae** *Compendium errorum Johannis papae XXII* (1338), *ib.* II 957–76; **I. & P.** *De imperatorum et pontificum potestate* (1346–7), ed. C. K. Brampton (Oxford, 1927); **I. & P. Suppl.** supplementary text in *Archivum Franciscanum Historicum* XVI 469–92, XVII 72–97 (Quaracchi, 1923–4); **Pol.** *Opera politica*, ed. J. G. Sikes *et al.* 3 vols. (Manchester, 1940–56), as follows: I 1–221 *Octo quaestiones de potestate Papae* (c1340); 223–71 *An Princeps, pro suo succursu scilicet guerrae, possit recipere bona ecclesiarum, etiam invito Papa* (c1338); 273–86 *Consultatio de causa matrimoniali* (c1342); 287–II 858 *Opus nonaginta dierum* (c1332); III 1–17 *Epistola ad Fratres Minores* (1334), also ed. C. K. Brampton (Oxford, 1929); 19–156 *Tractatus contra Joannem* [XXII] (1335); 157–322 *Tractatus contra Benedictum* [XII] (1337–8); **Sacr. Alt.** *De sacramento altaris* (? 1323) ed. T. Bruce Birch (Burlington, Iowa, 1930); **Sent.** *Quaestiones in quatuor libros sententiarum* (c1320) (Lyon, 1495); **Summa** *Summa logice* (repr. Oxford, 1675).

OCREATUS Helceph N. Ocreatus: *Prologus in Helceph ad Adelardum Batensem* (c1150).., Fragm. in Abhandlungen zur Gesch. der Mathematik III (Leipzig, 1880) 129–39.

ODINGTON Walter Odington, of Evesham [*fl.* c1320]: *De speculatione musice*, in *Script. Mus.* I 182–250.

Offic. Evesham *Officium ecclesiasticum abbatum secundum usum Eveshamensis monasterii* (1282–1316), HBS VI (1893).

Offic. R. Rolle *Officium de S.Ricardo heremita..et legenda de vita ejus*, EETS XX revised ed. (1920), xix–xlv.

Offic. S.Andr. *Liber officialis* [*curie consistorialis*] *S.Andree* (1513–88), Abbotsford Club (1845).

Offic. Sal. *De officiis ecclesiasticis tractatus* (p1215), *Reg. S.Osm.* I 1–185 [by cap.].

Op. Chr. *Opus Chronicorum* (1259–95), *Chr. Mon. S.Alb.* III 3–59.

Ord. Cartus. *Ordinarium Cartusiense* (c1500), Tracts on the mass, HBS XXVII (1904) 97–110.

Ord. Ebor. Ordinal and customary of St. Mary's abbey, York (c1400), HBS LXXIII, LXXV, LXXVI (for 1934, 1936, 1937).

Ord. Ely Ely chapter ordinances and visitation records (1241–1515), Camd. Misc. XVII, Camd. 3rd S. LXIV (1940) 1–3, 24–8, 36–43 [*v. et.* Vis. Ely].

ORD. VIT. Orderic Vitalis [*ob.* c1143]: *Historia ecclesiastica* (–1141), ed. A. Le Provost, 5 vols. (Paris, 1838–55), also in Med. Texts, ed. M. Chibnall (1969–) [by bk. and cap.].

Orthog. Gall. *Orthographica Gallica* (c1300), ed. J. Stürzinger, in Foerster, W.: Altfranzösische Bibliothek VIII (Heilbronn, 1884) [*cf. Medium Aevum* VI 193–209].

OSB. Osbern of Canterbury [*fl.* c1090]: **Mir. Dunst.** *Liber Miraculorum*, in Mem. Dunst. 129–61; **Transl. Elph.** *Historia de translatione corporis S.Elphegi*, in *Anglia Sacra* II 143–7; **V. Dunst.** *Vita Dunstani*, in Mem. Dunst. 69–128; **V. Elph.** *Vita S.Elphegi* (*alias* Ælfeah), *archiepiscopi Cantuariensis* [*ob.* 1012], in *Anglia Sacra* II 122–42.

OSB. BAWDSEY Osbert of Bawdsey [*fl.* c1149] (attrib.): *De expugnatione Lyxbonensi* (1147), in Mem. Ric. I, I cxlii–clxxxii.

OSB. CLAR. Osbert of Clare [*ob.* c1136]: **Anne** *Sermo et versus in honorem S.Anne*, Annales de Bretagne XXXVII 11–33 [by cap. or line]; **Ep.** *Epistolae* (Oxford, 1929) [by no.]; **V. Ed. Conf.** *Vita S.Edwardi Confessoris*, *Anal. Boll.* XLI (1923) 5–131.

OTTERB. Thomas Otterbourne: *Chronica Regum Angliae* (–1420), ed. T. Hearne, *Duo rerum Anglicarum scriptores veteres* I (1732) 1–283.

Ox. Essays Salter Oxford Essays in medieval history presented to H. E. Salter, ed. F. M. Powicke (Oxford, 1934).

OXNEAD John of Oxnead [*ob.* c1293]: **Chr.** *Chronica* (–1292), RS (1859); **Chr. Min.** *Chronica minor* (–1294, cont. to 1503) *ib.* 412–39; **S.Ben. Holme** Early history of the Abbey of St. Benet Holme [*alias* Hulme (Norf)], *ib. app.* I 289–300.

P. BLOIS Peter of Blois [*ob.* 1212]: **Caro et spir.** *Cantilena de lucta carnis et spiritus*, in *PL* CCVII (1855) 1127–30; **Cervisia** *Responsio..contra cervisiam*, *ib.* 1155–8; **Contra Clericos** *Contra clericos voluptati deditos*, *ib.* 1129–36; **Dict.** *De arte dictandi* [abridgement of work by Bernard of Meung], *ib.* 1127–8; **Ep.** *Epistolae*, *ib.* 1–560 [by no.]; **Euch.** *Tractatus de..eucharistiae mysteriis*, *ib.* 1138–54; **Euch. Prol.** Prologue to above, 1135–8; **Opusc.** *Opuscula* [incl. some of doubtful origin], *ib.* 777–1126; **Perf. Jud.** *Contra perfidiam Judaeorum*, *ib.* 825–70; **Poems** *Poemata*, *ib.* 1127–58; **Serm.**, *ib.* 559–776;

Sil. *De silentio servando, ib.* 1125–8; **Vinum** *Versus de commendatione vini, ib.* 1155–6; *v. et.* Croyl. Cont. A.

P. CORNW. Disp. Peter of Cornwall [*ob.* 1221]: *Liber disputationum..contra Symonem Judeum*, extr. in Powicke Studies 143–56.

P. VERG. Polydore Vergil [*ob.* 1555]: *Anglicae historiae libri* XXVII (–1538) (Basle, 1556) [by bk. and p.]; **Camd.** Bks. XXIV (XXVI) and XXV (XXVII), ed. D. Hay, Camd. 3rd S. LXXIV (1950) [supersedes ed. 1556 for these 2 bks.]; **Praef.** Preface to GILDAS *EB* (prob. Antwerp, 1525); **Vat.** Extr. from *Anglica Historia*, Vatican MSS I and II, in Hay, D.: Polydore Vergil (Oxford, 1952) 199–207.

PL *Patrologia Latina*, ed. J. P. Migne, 221 vols. (Paris, 1844–64); **Sup.** *Supplementum*, ed. A. Hamman, 4 vols. (*ib.*, 1958–71).

PLAC *Poetae Latini aevi Carolini*, ed. E. Duemmler, 4 vols. in *MGH* (Berlin, 1881–1923).

PN English Place-names, arr. by county, series published by the English Place-names Soc. II– (Cambridge, 1925–); **Elements** English place-name elements, ed. A. H. Smith, XXV, XXVI (1956); **Intro.** Introduction to the survey of English place-names; pt. 1 ed. A. Mawer and F. M. Stenton, pt. 2 ed. A. Mawer, I (1924).

PP *Promptorium parvulorum sive clericorum dictionarius Anglo-Latinus princeps, auctore fratre Galfrido Grammatico dicto..* 1440, ed. A. L. Mayhew, EETS Extra S. CII (1908).

PQW *Placita de Quo Warranto, temp. Edw. I–Edw. III*, RC (1818).

PRO Public Record Office, London.

PS Privy Seal Warrants, MS PRO [cited as providing OF equivalent of letters patent etc.].

PS Rec. Council and Privy Seal Records MS PRO (E. 28).

Parl. Ir. Parliaments and councils of mediaeval Ireland, ed. H. G. Richardson and G. O. Sayles, vol. I (1290–1420) IMC (Dublin, 1947).

Parl. Writs Parliamentary writs and writs of military summons etc. (1272–1327), 2 vols. in 4, RC (1827–34).

Paston Let. The Paston letters, 1422–1509, ed. J. Gairdner, 3 vols. (1895) [by no.], also ed. *Id.*, 6 vols. (1904).

Pat 1201–16 *Rotuli litterarum patentium*, RC (1835); 1216–32 Patent Rolls, 2 vols. HMSO (1901, 1903); 1232– MS PRO (C. 66) [by roll and m.; *v. et.* CalPat.].

Pat. Hib. Hen. V *Transcripta omnium litterarum patentium.. sub testimonio loca-tenentium Hiberniae..temp. R. Hen. V*, in *RSelecti* 39–80.

Pat. Sup. Patent Rolls Supplementary, MS PRO (C. 67).

PAUL ANGL. ASP Paul (*alias* Thomas) Anglicus, canonist [*fl.* c1404]: *Aureum speculum Papae*, in *Monarchia* II 1527–58.

Peasants' Rising The peasants' rising and the Lollards (documents 1381–99), ed. E. Powell and G. M. Trevelyan (1899).

PECKHAM John Peckham (*alias* Pecham or Patcham), Archb. of Canterbury [*ob.* 1292]: **Def. Mend.** *Defensio fratrum mendicantium*, Brit. Soc. of Franciscan Studies II (Aberdeen, 1910) 148–97; *Ep. Registrum epistolarum fratris J. P.*, 3 vols. RS (1882–5) [by no.]; **Exp. Thren.** *Expositio threnorum* (or *In lamentationes Jeremie*), in Bonaventura: *Opera* VII (Quaracchi, 1895) 607–51 [by bk. and cap.]; **Kilw.** *Tractatus contra fratrem Robertum Kilwardby*, Brit. Soc. Franciscan Studies II 91–147; **Paup.** *Tractatus pauperis*, extr., *ib.* 13–90; **Persp.** *Perspectiva communis* per L. Gavricum Neapolitanum emendata (Venice, 1504) [by bk. and cap.]; **Phil.** *Philomena*, in *Anal. Hymn.* L (1907) 602–16; **Puer. Obl.** *Quaestio de pueris oblatis*, in *Archivum. Francisc. Hist.* VIII (Quaracchi, 1915) 414–49; **QA** *Quaestiones tractantes de anima* (c1270), in Beitr. zur Gesch. Philos. des Mittelalters XIX pts. 5 and 6 (Münster, 1918); **QR** *Quodlibet Romanum*, ed. F. M. Delorme, *Spicileg. Pontif. Athen. Anton.* I (Rome, 1938) [*v. et. Reg. Cant.*].

PECOCK Abbr. Reynold (Reginald) Pecock, Bishop of Chichester [*ob.* c1460]: *Abbreviatio* (1447), in *Repressor*, RS (1860) II 615–19.

Peramb. Dartmoor Rowe, S.: A perambulation of the forest of Dartmoor and the Venville precincts, 3rd ed. (1896).

Pickering The honor and forest of Pickering [Yorks], ed. R. B. Turton, N. Riding Rec. Soc. I–IV (1894–7).

Pipe Exchequer Pipe Rolls (1130, 1155–8) 2 vols. RC (1833, 1844, repr. in facsimile HMSO, 1929–30); (1158–) pub. by Pipe Roll Soc. I– (1884–) [by p.]; later Rolls MS PRO (E. 372); **Pipe (Chanc.)** Chancellor's Roll (E. 352) [duplicate of Pipe; cited as *v.l.* or to supply deficiency].

Pipe Chesh Cheshire in the Pipe Rolls (1158–1301), Lancs and Chesh Rec. Soc. XCII (1938); **App.** Account of Chamberlain of Chester (1301), *ib.* 187–220 [*v. et.* Ac. Chamb. Chesh].

Pipe Cloyne *Rotulus Pipae Clonensis* (1364–1403) w. other docs. (Cork, 1859).

Pipe Ir. The Irish Pipe Roll of 14 John, 1211–12, Ulster J. of Arch. 3rd S. IV sup. (Belfast, 1941).

Pipe Wint. Pipe Roll of the Bishopric of Winchester (1208–9), ed. H. Hall (1903); (1210–11) ed. N. R. Holt (Manchester, 1964); later rolls, MS Hants RO [*v. et.* Crawley].

Pl. Anglo-Norm. *Placita Anglo-Normannica* Will. I–Ric. I, ed. M. M. Bigelow (1879).

PlCrGlouc. Pleas of the Crown for the county of Gloucester 1221, ed. F. W. Maitland (1884).

Pl. K. or J. Pleas before the King or his Justices (1198–1202), Selden Soc. LXVII, LXVIII, LXXXIII, LXXXIV (1932–67) [by no.].

Pl. Mem. Lond. Plea and Memoranda Rolls of the City of London (1323–1484), MS Guildhall RO; *v. et.* Cal. Pl. Mem. Lond.

PlRChester Plea Rolls, Palatinate of Chester, MS PRO (Chester 29).

PlRCP Plea Rolls (*Placita de Banco*), Court of Common Pleas, MS PRO (C.P. 40).

PlRExch Plea Rolls, Exchequer of Pleas, MS PRO (E. 13).

PlRJews Jewish Plea Rolls (1219–87), MS PRO (E. 9) [*v. et.* SelPlJews].

PlRMarshalsea Plea Rolls, *Aula Regis* or Marshalsea Court, MS PRO (E. 37).

Planct. Univ. Ox. *Planctus Universitatis Oxoniensis contra laicos..*(1354), OHS XXXII, *Collectanea* III (1896) 170–9.

Plant. & Tudor Chester Morris, R. H.: Chester in the Plantagenet and Tudor reigns (Chester, 1893).

Plusc. *Liber Pluscardensis* VI cap. 15–XI (1141–1445), Historians of Scotland VII (Edinburgh, 1877) [by bk. and cap; earlier portion omitted by ed. as adding nothing material to FORDUN].

Poem S.Greg. Poem on St. Gregory [Greg. I *ob.* 604] (10c. MS), Poésies Pop. 237–8; **Poem S.Thom.** Poem on St. Thomas Becket (*a*1200), *ib.* 70–93.

Poésies Pop. Poésies populaires latines du moyen âge, ed. E. du Méril (Paris, 1847).

Pol. Poems Political poems and songs..composed 1327–1483, 2 vols. RS (1859–61).

Pol. Songs Political songs of England (John–Edw. II), Camd. Soc. VI (1839).

Pont. Ebor. *Liber pontificalis Archiep. Ebor.* (12c.–), Surtees Soc. LXI (1875).

Pont. Exon. *Liber pontificalis Ep. Exon.* [Edmund Lacy, *ob.* 1455] (Exeter, 1847).

Pont. Sal. Pontifical of Salisbury (13c.–15c.), extr. in *Mon. Rit.* I 3–272.

Poole Essays Essays in history presented to R. L. Poole, ed. H. W. C. Davis (Oxford, 1927).

Port Bk. Port Books, MS PRO (E. 190).

Port Bk. Southampt. Port book of Southampton for 1439–40, Southampt. Rec. S. vol. V (1961); port books..of Southampton for the reign of Ed. IV vol. I– , *ib.* XXXVII– (1937–).

Powicke Studies Studies in medieval history presented to F. M. Powicke (Oxford, 1948).

Praest. *Rotulus de Praestito* 1205–6, in DocExch 270–6; 1210–11, in *Liberate* RC 173–253.

Praxis Francis Clarke: *Praxis in curiis ecclesiasticis* (1596), 2nd ed. (1684) [by cap.].

Prejudice & Promise Kingsford, C. L.: Prejudice and promise in 15th century England (Oxford, 1925).
Prests Book of prests of the king's wardrobe for 1294–5, presented to J. G. Edwards (Oxford, 1962).
Pri. Cold. Correspondence etc. of the Priory of Coldingham [Berwick] (1261–15c.), Surtees Soc. XII (1841).
Proc. A. Kyteler Proceedings against Dame Alice Kyteler 1324, by R. de Ledrede, Bishop of Ossory [*ob.* 1360], Camd. Soc. XXIV (1843).
Proc. Ant. Scot. Society of Antiquaries of Scotland, proceedings, I– (Edinburgh, 1855–).
Proc. J. P. Proceedings before Justices of the Peace in the 14th and 15th centuries, ed. B. H. Putnam, Harvard Univ., Ames Foundation (London, 1938).
Proc. PC *v.* Act. PC.
Proc. RC *v.* RC.
Proc. RIA Proceedings of the Royal Irish Academy, I– (Dublin, 1841–).
Proc. v. Crown Ehrlich, L.: Proceedings against the Crown (1216–1377) (Oxford, 1921).
Process. Sal. Ceremonies and processions of the Cathedral Church of Salisbury (wr. *c*1445), ed. C. Wordsworth (Cambridge, 1901).
Ps.-ELMH. Hen. V Pseudo-Elmham: *Vita et gesta Henrici V* (*c*1446), ed. T. Hearne (Oxford, 1727) [by cap.]; [*v. et* ELMH.
Ps.-GOSC. Pseudo-Goscelin: **Swith.** *Vita S.Swithuni* [*ob.* 862] (11c.), w. *appendix miraculorum*, in *PL* CLV (1880) 47–80 and 91–2; **Werb.** *Vita S.Werburge* [*ob. c*700] (11c.), *ib.* 93–110; also in EETS LXXXVIII (1887) xix–xxvi [*cf. V. Ed. Conf.*, app. C, 111].
Ps.-GROS. Pseudo-Grosseteste: **Summa** *Summa theologica* (*c*1270), in Beitr. zur Gesch. der Phil. des Mittelalters IX (1912) 275–643 [possibly by KILWARDBY].
Ps.-INGULF *v.* Croyl.
Ps.-MAP Latin poems commonly attrib. MAP (12c.–), Camd. Soc. XVI (1841).
Ps.-OCKHAM Pseudo-Ockham: **Princ. Theol.** *Tractatus de principiis theologiae* (*a*1550) attribué à G. d'Occam, ed. L. Baudry, Études de Philos. Médiévale XXIII (Paris, 1936).
Ps.-RIC. Anat. Pseudo-Galen: *Anatomia vivorum*, wrongly attrib. RIC. MED., ed. R. Töply (Vienna, 1902) [by cap.].
Pub. Works Public works in medieval law, Selden Soc. XXXII, XL (1915, 1923).
PULL. Sent. Robert Pullen (*alias* Pullus) [*ob. c*1147]: *Sententiarum theologicarum libri VIII* (*c*1133), *PL* CLXXXVI (1854) 639–1010.

Quaest. Ox. *Quaestiones disputatae*, in Oxford Theology and Theologians (*c*1282–1302), OHS XCVI (1934).
Qui majora cernitis.. Poem (*c*1225) addressed to John of Garland, ed. Guerri, D.: Studi Lit. et Ling. dedicati al Pio Rajna (Milan, 1911).
Quon. Attach. *Quoniam attachiamenta, sive leges Baronum* (? 14c.), ed. J. Skene, in *RegiamM* 105–31; also *ib.* Stair Soc. XI (1947) 305–81 [by cap.; preferred to text in APScot I app. II 283–95].

R. BOCKING Ric. Cic. Ralph Bocking [*ob.* 1270]: Life of S. Richard of Wych, Bishop of Chichester [*ob.* 1253], *Acta SS Boll.* Apr. I 282–318; 284–5 *Prol.*; 286–308 *V.*; 308–17; *Mir.*; 317–18 *Epil.*
R. BURY Richard of Bury [*ob.* 1345]: **Phil.** *Philobiblon*, ed. E. G. Thomas (1888) [by cap. and section of ed. 1888]; also ed. A. Altamura (Naples, 1954).
R. CANT. Reynold (Reginald) of Canterbury [*fl. c*1112]: **Malch.** *Vita S.Malchi* (Urbana, Ill., 1942) [by bk. and line]; **Poems**, in Sat. Poets II 259–67.
R. COLD. Reynold (Reginald) of Coldingham [*ob. c*1173]: **Cuthb.** *Libellus de admirandis B.Cuthberti* [*ob.* 687] *virtutibus*, Surtees Soc. I (1835) [by cap.]; **Godr.** *De vita* [1–315] *et miraculis* [316–615] *S.Godrici..de Finchale* [*ob.* 1170], *ib.* XX (1847) [by section]; **Osw.** *Vita S.Oswaldi regis et martyris* [*ob.* 642], in S. DURH. I app. III 326–85.
R. COURÇON Robert de Courçon [*ob.* 1219]: *Summa*, extr. in N. & E. XXXI pt. 2 (1884) 261–74; **Us.** Le traité *De usura*, extr. ed. G. Lefèvre (Lille, 1902).
R. DYMMOK Roger Dymmok [? *ob. c*1418]: *Liber contra XII errores et hereses Lollardorum* (? 1395), Wycl. Soc. (1923).
R. HOWD. Roger Howden (*alias* Hovedene) [? *ob.* 1201]: *Chronica* (732–1201), 4 vols. RS (1868–71).
R. de MONTE *v.* TORIGNI.
R. de MORINS *v.* Ann. Dunstable, RIC. ANGL.
R. NIGER Ralph Niger [*ob. p*1180]: **Chr. I** Chronicle [incl. cont.] (Creation–1199), Caxton Soc. (1851) 1–104; **Chr. II** (Creation–1162, w. cont. to 1178), *ib.* 105–91; **MR** *Moralia regum* (*a*1189), cap. 19 in Med. & R. Stud. I pt. 2 (1943) 249–52.
R. PARTES Robert Partes [*ob.* 1172]: Poems, *Speculum* XII (1937) 215–50 [by p.].
R. RICH Robert Rich [*fl. c*1240] *v.* RICH Edm.
R. de TEMPLO *v. Itin. Ric.*
R. WINCHELSEA Quest. Robert Winchelsea, Archb. of Canterbury [*ob.* 1313]: Two questions, OHS XCVI (1934) 137–45 [*v. et. Reg. Cant.*].
RBExch The Red Book of the Exchequer (12c.–16c.), 3 vols. (–445, –806, –1081) RS (1896).
RBHeref. The Red Book..of the Hereford bishopric estates (13c.), Camd. Misc. XV Camd. 3rd S. XLI (1929).
RBKildare The Red Book of the Earls of Kildare (1185–1519), IMC (Dublin, 1964).
RBOrmond The Red Book of Ormond (*c*1197–*c*1547), IMC (Dublin, 1932).
RBOssory The Red Book of Ossory (14c.–16c.), extr. in Carrigan, W.: History..of the Diocese of Ossory IV 363–93 (Dublin, 1905).
RBWorc. The Red Book of Worcester, surveys of Bishops' Manors (chiefly 12c.–13c.), ed. M. Hollings, 4 vols. Worcs. Hist. Soc. (1934–50).
RC Record Commission publications (1802–52); **Rep.** Reports and proceedings, various, I–IX (1719–1839).
RChart. *Rotuli chartarum* 1199–1216, RC (1835) [*v. et.* ChartR, CalCh.].
RCoron Coroners' Rolls, MS PRO (Just. Itin. 2).
RDomin *Rotuli de dominabus* (1185), Pipe Roll Soc. XXXV (1913).
RFin *Rotuli de Oblatis et Finibus* (1199–1216), RC (1835) 197–605 [*v. et.* CalFineR, *ExcRFin*, FineR].
RGasc Roles gascons, 3 vols. in 4, I (1242–54), I Sup. (1254–5), II (1272–90), III (1290–1307), Ministère de l'Instruction publique (Paris, 1885–1906) [by p.]; IV (1307–17), *ib.* (1962), also HMSO [by no.]; later rolls MS PRO (C. 61).
RHS Royal Historical Society: **Trans.** Transactions, I– (1873–).
RL Royal Letters 1216–72, 2 vols. RS (1862–6); 1399–1413, 2 vols. RS (1860, 1965).
RMS Scot. *Registrum magni sigilli regum Scotorum* (1306–1668), 11 vols. Scot. RO pub. (1882–1914, incl. vol. I, 2nd ed. 1912) [by date and no.].
RNorm *Rotuli Normanniae* 1200–5, 1417–18, RC (1835); 1203 Fragm. of Norman Roll of 5 John, Pipe Roll Soc. NS XXI (1943) 87–8.
ROblat *Rotuli de Oblatis et Finibus* (1199–1216), RC (1835) 1–196 [*v. et. RFin*].
RParl *Rotuli Parliamentorum* (1278–1552), 7 vols. (1767–83; index I–VI 1832); other rolls MS PRO (C. 65); **Exch.** Exchequer series, MS PRO (S.C. 9), nos. 3, 4, 14, 21, and 22 printed in DocExch 55–82, 129–38, 1–54, no. 8 in *RParl. Ined.* 30–45, no. 12 in *Mem. Parl.* 1–188, 232–314; **Ined.** *Rotuli parliamentorum Anglie hactenus inediti* (1279–1373), Camd. Soc. 3rd S. LI (1935).
RParl. Ir. Parliaments and councils of mediaeval Ireland (1296–1421), ed. H. G. Richardson and G. O. Sayles, I– IMC (Dublin, 1947–).
RR K's Lynn Red Registers of King's Lynn [Norf.] (*c*1307–*c*1395), ed. H. Ingleby, 2 vols. (King's Lynn, 1919, 1922).

RS Rolls Series, or Chronicles and Memorials of Great Britain and Ireland during the Middle Ages (1858–97).

RScacNorm *Magni rotuli scaccarii Normanniae* (1180–1201), 2 vols. Soc. of Antiquaries of London (1840–4).

RScot *Rotuli Scotiae*, 2 vols. RC (1814–19), I (1291–1377), II (1377–1509) [by date, p., and col.].

RSelecti *Rotuli selecti ad res Anglicas et Hibernicas spectantes* (1205–1431), RC (1834).

Rara Math. *Rara mathematica*, ed. J. O. Halliwell (1839).

Rec. Barts. Records of St. Bartholomew's, Smithfield [London] (12c.–), ed. E. A. Webb (Oxford, 1921).

Rec. Burford MSS of extinct corporation of Burford, Oxfordshire (1350–), HMC Var. Coll. I (1901) 29–64.

Rec. Caern. The Record of Caernarvon (1258–16c.), RC (1838).

Rec. Coronation English coronation records (9c.–), ed. L. G. W. Legg (1901) [*v. et. Lib. Regal.*].

Rec. Crondal Records..relating to the hundred and manors of Crondal (*c*880–17c.), pt. 1 Historical and manorial, Hants Rec. Soc. (1891).

Rec. Edinb. Extracts from the records of the burgh of Edinburgh, 1403–1571, 3 vols. Scottish Burgh Rec. Soc. (1869–75).

Rec. Elton Elton [Hunts and Northants] manorial records 1279–1351, Roxburghe Club (1946).

Rec. Eton Calendar of Eton College records (12c.–), ed. N. Blakiston, I– (1939–) [TS Copy at PRO].

Rec. Gild Camb. Cambridge Gild Records (14c.), Cambridge Antiq. Soc. 8° S. XXXIX (1903).

Rec. Leic. Records of the Borough of Leicester (1103–), ed. M. Bateson *et al.*, I–VI (London, 1899–1901; Cambridge, 1905–23, Leicester, 1965–7); NS I–II (1196–) (Leicester, 1927–33).

Rec. Lewes Records of the..Rape of Lewes (1265–15c.), Sussex Rec. Soc. XLIV (Lewes, 1939).

Rec. Lincoln's Inn Records of Lincoln's Inn (1420–), ed. W. P. Baildon *et al.*, 7 vols. (1896–1968).

Rec. Lostwithiel Records of the corporation of Lostwithiel [Cornw] (1190–), HMC Var. Coll. I (1901) 327–37.

Rec. Merton Records of Merton Priory [Surrey] (1114–1539), ed. A. Heales (1898).

Rec. Norw. Records of the City of Norwich (1086–), ed. W. Hudson and J. C. Tingey, 2 vols. (Norwich, 1906–10).

Rec. Nott. Records of the borough of Nottingham..(1155–), ed. J. Raine *et al.* 9 vols. (London and Nottingham, 1882–1956).

Rec. Prescot Selection from Prescot court leet and other records (1447–1600), Lancs and Chesh Rec. Soc. LXXXIX (1937).

Rec. Reading Records of the Borough of Reading (1431–1654), ed. J. M. Guilding 4 vols. (London, 1892–6).

Rec. Scot. Documents and records illustrating the history of Scotland (1236–1306), ed. F. Palgrave, RC (1837).

Rec. Stan. Records..relating to the Stannaries of Cornwall (*c*1197–) (appendix to The Case of Vice against Thomas), ed. E. Smirke (1843).

Rec. Templ. (Templars) Records of the Templars in England, Inquest (1185) 1–135, charters etc. 137–236, British Acad. IX (1935).

RecogR Chester *v.* Enr. Chester.

Rect. Adderbury Adderbury *rectoria* (14c.–15c.), Oxfordshire Rec. Soc. VIII (1926).

RecusantR Exchequer, Recusant Rolls (1592–), MS PRO (E. 376, E. 377) [*v.* Cath. Rec. Soc. XVIII, LVII, LXI].

REDMAN Hen. V Robert Redman [*ob.* 1540]: *Henrici quinti..historia* (1413–22) (wr. *a*1540) in Mem. Hen. V 1–59.

Reg. Aberbr. *Registrum Abbacie de Aberbrothoc* [Arbroath, Angus] (1178–1536), 2 vols. Bannatyne Club (1846–56).

Reg. Aberd. *Registrum episcopatus Aberdonensis* (12c.–), 2 vols. Spalding Club XIII, XIV (1845).

Reg. Ant. Linc. *Registrum antiquissimum* of the Cathedral Church of Lincoln (1061–), Linc. Rec. Soc. XXVII, XXVIII, XXIX, XXXII, XXXIV, XLI, XLVI, LI, LXII– (Hereford, 1931–).

Reg. Armagh The register of Primate John Swayne, Archb. of Armagh 1418–39, incl. earlier and later entries HMSO (Belfast, 1935).

Reg. Bath Registers of Bishops of Bath and Wells: 1407–24, Nicholas Bubwith, Som Rec. Soc. XXIX, XXX (1914); 1425–43, John Stafford, *ib.* XXXI, XXXII (1915, 1916) [by date, vol., and p.].

Reg. Black Pr. Register of Edward the Black Prince (1346–8, 1351–65), 4 vols. HMSO (1930–3).

Reg. Brechin. *Registrum Episcopatus Brechinensis* [Brechin, Angus] (1165–), 2 vols. Bannatyne Club (1856).

Reg. Brev. *Registrum brevium tam originalium quam judicialium* (mainly 15c.), 4th ed. (1687) pt. 1 (*Originalia*) 1–321; **Jud.**, *ib.* pt. 2 (*Judicialia*) 1–85.

Reg. Butley The register or chronicle of Butley Priory, Suffolk (1510–35), ed. A. G. Dickens (Winchester, 1951).

Reg. Cant. Registers of Archbishops of Canterbury, Cant. and York Soc. (1928–); 1279–92 John Peckham, LXIV, LXV (1968–9); 1294–1313 Robert Winchelsea, LI, LII (1956); 1366–8 Simon de Langham, LIII (1956); 1414–43 Henry Chichele, XLII, XLV–XLVII (1937–47); 1454–86 Thomas Bourgchier, LIV (1957); 1559–75 Matthew Parker, XXXV, XXXVI, XXXIX (1928–33) [by date, vol., and p.; *v. et. Act. Cant.*].

Reg. Carl. Registers of Bishops of Carlisle, Cant. and York Soc. (1913–): 1292–1324 John de Halton, XII, XIII (1913) [by date, vol., and p.].

Reg. Clogher Fragments of a lost register of the diocese of Clogher (wr. 1525), Arch. Soc. Louth IV (Dundalk, 1920) 226–7.

Reg. Coll. Exon. *Registrum Collegii Exoniensis* [Oxford] (1314–), OHS XXVII (1894).

Reg. Dunferm. *Registrum abbatie..de Dunfermelyn* [Fife], (12c.–) Bannatyne Club (1842) [by no.].

Reg. Durh. *Registrum Palatinum Dunelmense*: 1311–16 Richard de Kellawe, 4 vols. RS (1873–8); 1333–45 Richard d'Aungerville of Bury, extr. in Surtees Soc. CXIX (1910) 10–64; 1406–37 Thomas Langley, *ib.* CLXIV, CLXVI, CLXIX, CLXX, CLXXVII, CLXXXII (1956–70); 1494–1501 Richard Fox, *ib.* CXLVII (1932); 1530–59 Cuthbert Tunstall, *ib.* CLXI (1952) 1–131; 1561–76 James Pilkington, *ib.* 140–82 [by date, vol., and p.].

Reg. Ebor. Registers of the Archbishops of York, Surtees Soc.: 1215–55 Walter Gray, LVI (1872) [1215–24 are missing]; 1266–79 Walter Giffard, CIX (1904); 1279–85 William Wickwane, CXIV (1907); 1286–96 John le Romeyn, CXXIII, CXXVIII 1–203 (1913, 1916); 1296–9 Henry of Newark, CXXVIII 205–35; 1300–4 Thomas of Corbridge, CXXXVIII, CXLI (1925, 1928); 1305–6 John of Cracumbe, vicar-general, CXLV (1931) 1–2; 1306–15 William Greenfield, CXLV 3–288, CXLIX, CLI, CLII, CLV (1931–8) [by date, vol., and p.].

Reg. Ewell Register or memorial of Ewell [Surrey] (wr. 1408) w. notes on priors of Merton, ed. C. Deeds (1913) 1–135 [cont. also undated custumal 135–8 and other 15c. docs.].

Reg. Exon. Bishops' registers, Exeter, 10 vols.: 1138–55 Robert Chichester, I (1889) 2; 1194–1206 Henry Marshall, *ib.*; 1214–23 Simon de Apulia, *ib.* 2–4; 1224–44 William Briwere, *ib.* 5–7; 1245–57 Richard Blondy, *ib.* 7 [these five are frags.]; 1258–80 Walter Bronescombe, *ib.* 8–305; 1280–91 Peter Quivil, *ib.* 309–95; 1292–1307 Thomas de Bytton, *ib.* 399–437; 1307–26 Walter de Stapeldon, II (1892); 1327 James de Berkeley, III (1894) 1–33; 1327–69 John de Grandisson, *ib.* 37–603, IV (1897), V (1899); 1370–94 Thomas de Brantynhgam, VI, VII (1901, 1906); 1395–1419 Edmund Stafford, VIII (1886); 1420–55 Edmund Lacy, IX (1909), X (1915) [this last vol. superseded and cont. by Devon and Cornw Rec. Soc. pubs. NS VII, X, XIII, XVI (1963–71), which = Cant. and York Soc. LX–LXIII (1963–72)].

Reg. Glasg. *Registrum Episcopatus Glasguensis* (12c.–), 2 vols. Bannatyne Club (1843).

Reg. Godstow The English register of Godstow nunnery, near Oxford [mainly Eng. transl. (*c*1450) of Latin docs.], EETS CXXIX, CXXX, CXLII (1911) [*v. et.* Vis. Godstow].

Reg. Heref. Registers of the Bishops of Hereford, Cant. and York Soc.: 1275–82 Thomas de Cantilupo, II (1907); 1283–1317 Richard de Swinfield, VI (1909); 1317–27 Adam de Orleton, V (1908); 1327–44 Thomas de Charlton, IX (1913); 1344–61 John de Trillek, VIII (1912); 1361–70 Lewis de Charltone, XIV (1914); 1370–5 William de Courtenay, XV (1914); 1375–89 John Gilbert, XVIII (1915); 1389–1404 John Trefnant, XX (1916); 1404–16 Robert Mascall, XXI (1917); 1417–20 Edmund Lacy, XXII (1918) 1–128; 1120–2 Thomas Poltone, *ib.* [sep. pag.] 1–25; 1422–48 Thomas Spofford, XXIII (1919); 1449–50 Richard Beauchamp, XXV (1919) 1–17; 1451–3 Reginald Boulers, *ib.* [sep. pag.] 1–26; 1453–74 John Stanbury, *ib.* [sep. pag.] 1–203; 1474–92 Thomas Myllyng, XXVI (1920); 1504–16 Richard Mayew, XXVII (1921); 1516–35 Charles Bothe, XXVIII (1921) 1–360; 1535–8 Edward Foxe (abstr.), *ib.* 361–80; 1538–9 Hugh Coren (abstr.), *ib.* 381–2; 1539 Edmund Boner (abstr.), *ib.* 383–5 [all by date, vol., and p.]; index vol. 1275–1535 (Hereford, 1925).

Reg. Holm Cultram Register and records of Holm Cultram [Cumb] (12c.–), Antiq. Soc. Cumberland and Westmorland, Rec. S. VII (Kendal, 1929).

Reg. Linc. Rolls and registers of Bishops of Lincoln, Lincoln Rec. Soc.: 1209–35 Hugh de Welles, III, VI, IX (1912–14); 1235–53 Robert Grosseteste, XI (1914) 1–507; 1254–8 Henry de Lexington, *ib.* 509–14; 1258–79 Richard Gravesend, XX (1925) [all the above vols. also pub. w. same pag. by Cant. and York Soc. I (1909), III (1907), IV (1908), X (1913), XXXI (1925)]; 1280–99 Oliver Sutton, XXXIX, XLIII, XLVIII, LII, LX, LXIV– (1948–); 1405–19 Philip Repingdon, LVII, LVIII (1963) [by date, vol., and p.; some MS refs. by f.].

Reg. Lond. Registers of the Bishops of London, Cant. and York Soc.: 1304–13 Ralph Baldock, VII (1911) 1–168 and 174–6; 1313–16 Gilbert Segrave, *ib.* 169–73; 1317–18 Richard Newport, *ib.* 177–94; 1318–38 Stephen de Gravesend, *ib.* 195–320; 1362–75 Simon de Sudbury, XXXIV, XXXVIII (1927, 1938) [by date, vol., and p.].

Reg. Magdalen A register of members of St. Mary Magdalen College, Oxford, 1st. S. 8 vols. (1853–85); 2nd S. 8 vols. (15c.–) (1894–1915).

Reg. Malm. *Registrum Malmesburiense* (*c*685–14c.), 2 vols. RS (1879–80).

Reg. Merton *Registrum annalium Collegii Mertonensis* [Oxford] 1483–1521, OHS LXXVI (1921).

Reg. Moray *Registrum episcopatus Moraviensis* (1160–), Bannatyne Club (1837).

Reg. Newbattle *Registrum S.Marie de Neubotle* [Midloth] (1140–), Bannatyne Club (1849).

Reg. North. Historical papers and letters from the Northern Registers (1265–1413), RS (1873).

Reg. Paisley *Registrum monasterii de Passelet* [Renf] (1163–1529), Maitland Club (1832).

Reg. Pinchbeck Walter Pinchbeck [*fl.* *c*1333]: Pinchbeck register of the Abbey of Bury St. Edmunds (1286–7), ed. Lord F. Harvey, 2 vols. (Brighton, 1925).

Reg. Pri. Worc. *Registrum..Prioratus B.Mariae Wigorniensis* (1235–*c*1285) Camd. Soc. XCI (1865).

Reg. Richm. *Registrum Honoris de Richmond* [Yorks] etc. (1087–), app. w. sep. pag., ed. R. Gale (1722).

Reg. Roff. *Registrum Roffense*, records..of the Diocese and Cathedral Church of Rochester (600–17c.), ed. J. Thorpe (1769).

Reg. Roff. Cap. Capitular register of Rochester Cathedral (1142–8), MS BM Cotton Domitian A. X.

Reg. Roff. Ep. Register of Bishop of Rochester, Cant. and York Soc.: 1319–52 Hamo de Hethe [*alias* Hythe] (incl. 12c. and 13c. chs.), XLVIII, XLIX (1948) [by f.].

Reg. Rough Register of Daniel Rough, common clerk of Romney, 1353–80, Arch. Soc. Kent, Kent Recs. XVI (Ashford, 1945).

Reg. S.Andr. *Liber cartarum Prioratus S.Andree* [Fife] (12c.–), Bannatyne Club (1841) [by f.].

Reg. S.Aug. Register of St. Augustine's Abbey, Canterbury, ed. G. J. Turner and H. E. Salter, 2 vols. (1915–24).

Reg. S.Bees Register of the Priory of St. Bees [Cumb] (early 12c.), Surtees Soc. CXXVI (1915).

Reg. S.Ben. Holme Register of the Abbey of St. Benet of Holme [*alias* Hulme] 1020–1210, Rec. Soc. Norf II, III (1932).

Reg. S.Osm. *Vetus registrum Sarisberiense alias dictum registrum S.Osmundi Episcopi* (10c.–13c.), 2 vols. RS (1883–4) [*v. et. Offic. Sal.*].

Reg. S. Paul. *Registrum statutorum et consuetudinum Ecclesiae Cathedralis S.Pauli Londinensis* (674–), ed. W. Sparrow Simpson (1873).

Reg. S.Thom. Dublin Register of the Abbey of St. Thomas, Dublin (12c.–), RS (1889) [by no.].

Reg. Sal. Registers of Bishops of Salisbury, Cant. and York Soc.: 1297–1315 Symon de Gandavo, XL, XLI (1934); 1315–30 Roger Martival, LV, LVI, LVII, LVIII, LIX (1959–72) [by date, vol., and p.].

Reg. Stoneleigh Book or register of Stoneleigh Abbey [Warw] (12c.–14c.), Dugdale Soc. XXIV (1960).

Reg. Temp. *Registrum temporalium* (14c.) MS Kent RO (DRcR3 Rochester).

Reg. Whet. *Registrum..Johannis Whethamstede* [Abbot of St. Albans (1420–40, 1451–65)], Chr. Mon. S.Alb. VI, RS 2 vols. (1872–3).

Reg. Winchcombe *Landboc sive registrum monasterii..de Winchelcumba* [Glos] (798–1422), ed. D. Royce, 2 vols. (Exeter, 1892, 1903).

Reg. Wint. Registers of Bishops of Winchester, Cant. and York Soc. and Hants Rec. Soc.: 1282–1304 John de Pontissara, XIX, XXX (1915–24) [also pub. Surrey Rec. Soc. I, VI (1916–24)]; 1305–16 Henry Woodlock, XLIII, XLIV (1940–1); 1316–19 John de Sandale, Hants Rec. Soc. (1897) 3–264; 1320–3 Rigaud de Asserio, *ib.* 387–606; 1367–1404 William de Wykeham, 2 vols. *ib.* (1896–9); 1529–30 Thomas Wolsey, Cant. and York Soc. XXXII (1926); 1531–2, 1553–5 Stephen Gardiner, XXXVII (1930) 1–91; 1551–3 John Poynet, *ib.* 93–103; 1556–9 John Whyte, XVI (1914) [by date, vol., and p.].

Regesta *Regesta Regum Anglo-Normannorum*, ed. H. W. C. Davis *et. al.*: I (1066–1100); II (1100–35); III (1135–54) (Oxford, 1913, 1956, 1968) [by no. or p. (of appendix)].

Regesta PR *Regesta Pontificum Romanorum* (1198–1304), ed. A. Potthast, 2 vols. (Berlin, 1874–5).

Regesta Scot. *Regesta Regum Scottorum*, ed. G. W. S. Barrow: I (1153–65, w. earlier docs. not incl. in E. Ch. Scot.); II (1165–1214) (Edinburgh, 1960, 1971) [by no.].

RegiamM *Regiam Majestatem* (14c.), ed. J. Skene (Edinburgh, 1609) also in Stair Soc. XI (1947) 280–304 [by cap.; preferred to text in APScot I, app. I 231–77].

RegulC *Regularis concordia Anglicae nationis monachorum sanctimonialiumque* (*c*970) [? *auctore Æthelwold* (*ob.* 984)], Med. Texts (1953) [by sect.].

Reign of Hen. VII Pollard, A. F.: The reign of Henry VII, 3 vols. (1913–14).

Reliq. Antiq. *Reliquiae Antiquae*, scraps from ancient MSS, ed. T. Wright and J. O. Halliwell, 2 vols. (1841–3).

Rent. Glasgow Rental book of the diocese of Glasgow (1509–70) [bound w. *Lib. prot.*], 2 vols. Grampian Club (1875).

Rent. Glouc. Rental of all the houses in Gloucester (1455), ed. R. Cole (Gloucester, 1890).

Rent. Ottery St. M. Rental of Ottery St. Mary [Devon] (? 14c.), BM Add. MS 28838.

Rent. Pri. Nuneaton Nuneaton Priory rental MS BM Addit. R. 49466.

Rent. S.Andr. *Rentale S.Andree*, Chamberlain and Granitar accs. of the Archbishopric..1538–46, SHS, 2nd S. IV (1913).

RentSurv. P Rentals and Surveys, MS PRO, Portfolios (S.C. 12); **R,** *ib.* Rolls (S.C. 11).

Rep. PR Ir. Reports..respecting the Public Records of Ireland (1810–25), 3 vols. RC (1815–29).

RIC. ANGL. Summa Ricardus Anglicus [? = Richard de

Morins, prior of Dunstable (*ob.* 1242)]: *Summa de ordine judiciario* (*c*1196), ed. L. Wahrmund, Quellen zur Gesch. des romisch-kanonischen Processes im Mittelalter, II iii (Innsbruck, 1915) [by cap.].

RIC. ARMAGH Richard Fitzralph, Archb. of Armagh [*ob.* 1360]: **Def. Cur.** *Defensio curatorum*, in *Monarchia* II 1391–1410; **AP** Autobiographical prayer (= *Summa contra Armenos* XIX 35), in Hammerich, L. L.: The beginning of the strife between R. F. and the Mendicants (Copenhagen, 1938); **Serm.** Sermons, extr., *ib.* 30–42; **Unusq.** The proposition *Unusquisque*, *ib.* 53–84.

RIC. ELY Etheldr. Richard prior of Ely [*ob. c*1194]: *Analecta S.Etheldredae, Acta SS Boll.* June IV 577–82 [*v. et. Lib. Eli.* (attrib. in part)].

RIC. HEX. Richard prior of Hexham [*ob. p*1154]: **Hist. (Pri.) Hex.** History of the church of Hexham (*c*674–*c*1114), Surtees Soc. XLIV (1864) pt. 1, 1–62 [by cap.]; **Stand.** *De gestis Regis Stephani et de bello standardii* [sic] (1135–8), in Chr. Steph. III 139–78, also in Surtees Soc. XLIV pt. 1, 63–106 [by f.].

RIC. MED. Ricardus Medicus (*alias* Anglicus): **(Micr., Anat.** *Anatomia* (= *Micrologus*, section 3) (*a*1200), ed. K. Sudhoff, Archiv für Gesch. der Medizin XIX (Leipzig, 1927) 209–39; **Signa** *Signa pronostica infirmitatum* (= *Micrologus*, section 5), earlier part ed. H. E. Beusing, in Leben und Werke des Ricardus Anglicus (Leipzig, 1922) [*v. et. Ps.*-RIC].

RICH Edm. Life of Edmund Rich, Archb. of Canterbury [*ob.* 1240], Anon. B, formerly attrib. to Robert Rich, in Wallace, W.: Life of St. Edmund of Canterbury (1893) 614–24 [*v. et.* E. FAVERSHAM, M. PAR., *V. Edm. Rich*].

RICHARD KNAPWELL (*alias* CLAPWELL) *v.* KNAPWELL.

RISH. William of Rishanger [*ob. p*1312]: *Chronica* (1259–1307), Chr. Mon. S.Alb. II 1–230.

Rit. Durh. *Rituale ecclesiae Dunelmensis* [? *c*1000] Surtees Soc. X (1839).

ROB. ANGL : Robertus Anglicus (*alias* of Chester, Ketene, etc.) [translator from Arabic, *fl. c*1143]: **Alch.** *Liber de compositione alchemiae*, in *Bibl. Chem.* I 509–19; **Alg.** *Liber restaurationis et oppositionis numeri*, transl. of the Algebra of Al-Khowirasmi [*c*825], ed. L. C. Karpinski (Ann Arbor, 1915); **Chr. Mend.** *Chronica mendosa et ridiculosa Saracenorum* (Basle, 1550); **Jud.** *Judicia Alkindi*, extr. in EHR XXX (1915) 63; **Koran** Latin version of the Koran, bound w. *Chr. Mend.*

ROB. ANGL. II Robertus Anglicus [*fl. c*1272]: Commentary on the Sphere of Sacrobosco, in SACROB. *Sph.* 143–246.

ROB. BACON Psalt. Robert Bacon [*ob.* 1248]: *Tractatus super psalterium*, extr. in Trans. R. Hist. Soc. 4th S. XXX (1948) 1–19.

ROBERT GROSSETESTE *v.* GROS.

ROBERT KILWARDBY *v.* KILWARDBY.

ROBERT PULLEN *v.* PULL.

ROBYNS Com. John Robyns [*ob.* 1558]: *De Cometis*, extr. in *Rara Math.* 48–54.

Rois Thaumaturges Bloch, M.: Les rois thaumaturges (Strasbourg, 1924).

ROLLE IA Richard Rolle of Hampole [*ob.* 1349]: *Incendium amoris*, ed. M. Deanesly (Manchester, 1915).

Rolls Merton The early rolls of Merton College, Oxford (1274–1300) w. app. of charters, OHS, NS XVIII (1964).

RomR Roman Rolls (1306–58), MS PRO (C. 70).

Roxb. Club Roxburghe Club, publications (1814–).

Royal Writs Royal writs in England from the Conquest to Glanvill, Selden Soc. LXXVII (1959).

Rutland MSS Accounts of the estates of the Duke of Rutland (16c.), MS Belvoir Castle.

S. DURH. Simeon of Durham [*ob. c*1130]: *Opera* 2 vols. RS (1882–5); **Auct.** *Auctarium*, I 170–261, II 333–62, *v. Hist. Cuthb.*, *Mir. Cuthb.*, *Obsess. Durh.*, *Vex. Will.*; **Durh.** *Historia ecclesiae Dunelmensis* (635–1096), *ib.* I 3–135 [by bk. and cap.]; **Durh. Cont. A** (1096–1144), *ib.* 135–60; **Durh. Cont. B** (1141–54), *ib.* 616–19; **Ep. Hug.** *Epistola ad Hugonem decanum Ebor. de archiepiscopis Ebor.* (? *a*1110), *ib.* I 222–8 [by cap.]; **HR** *Historia Regum* (161–1129), *ib.* II 1–283 [by cap.]; **HR Cont.** *v.* J. HEX.

S. LANGTON Quaest. Stephen Langton, Archb. of Canterbury [*ob.* 1228]: *Quaestiones*, extr. in Franciscan Studies XIV (1954) pt. iv, 52–63 [by f.].

S. SIM. Itin. Simon Simeon: *Itinerarium ab Hybernia ad Terram Sanctam* (*c*1322–3), ed. M. Esposito (Dublin, 1960) [by cap.].

SB *Sinonoma Bartholomei* [a medico-botanical glossary (14c.) attrib. John Mirfield *c*1393], ed. J. L. G. Mowat, *Anecdota Oxoniensia* (1887) [*v. et.* ELVEDEN].

SHR Scottish Historical Review I–XXV (Edinburgh, 1904–28); XXVI— (1947–).

SHS Scottish History Society publications, I– (Edinburgh, 1887–).

S. Jers. Société jersiaise: **I** (1876) Extente de l'Île de Jersey, 1331, PRO (E. 101/89/15); **II** (1877) 1–13, Extente des Îles de Jersey etc., 1274, PRO (C. 47/10/5/1), *ib.* 14–48, Inquisitions dans les Îles de Jersey et Guernesey, 1274, *ib.* (10/1–3); **XVIII** (1903) Rolls of the Assizes held in the Channel Islands, etc., 1309, PRO (Just. Itin. 1/1160–1).

SP Dom. Eliz. State papers domestic, Eliz. I, MS PRO (S.P. 12 and 13) [calendared in 7 vols. (1856–71)].

SP Hen. VIII State papers, foreign and domestic, Henry VIII, MS PRO (S.P.I).

SPIr State papers Ireland (1509–1603), MS PRO (S.P. 60–3) calendared in 11 vols. (1860–1912).

Sacr. Ely Sacrist Rolls of Ely (1291–1360), ed. F. R. Chapman 2 vols. (Cambridge, 1907).

Sacr. Lichf. Sacrist's roll of Lichfield [Staffs.] Cathedral (1345), Arch. Soc. Derb. IV (1882) 107–17.

SACROB. Sph. John de Sacro Bosco (*alias* of Holywood) [*fl. c*1230]: *De Sphaera*, ed. L. Thorndike in The Sphere of Sacrobosco (Chicago, 1949) 76–117.

SAMSON Mir. Edm. Samson, abbot of S.Edmund's [Suff] [*ob.* 1212]: *Liber de miraculis S.Eadmundi*, Mem. S.Edm. I 107–208 [by bk. and cap.] [*v. et.* Kal. Samson].

Sanct. Bev. *Sanctuarium Dunelmense* (1464–1524) *et Sanctuarium Beverlacense* (*c*1478–1539), Surtees Soc. V (1837) 112–211; **Durh.** *ib.* 1–90 [both by no.].

Sat. Poets Anglo-Latin satirical poets and epigrammatists of the 12th c., 2 vols. RS (1872) [cited under poets].

Sci. Mech. Clagett, M.: The science of mechanics in the Middle Ages (Oxford, 1959), extr. from: Thomas Bradwardine: *De proportionibus* (1328) and *De continuo*; John Dumbleton [*ob. p*1348]: *Summa logicae et philosophiae naturalis*; William Heytesbury: *Regulae solvendi sophismata* (1335); Richard Swineshead: *Liber calculationum* (*c*1350).

Scone *Liber Ecclesie de Scon* Maitland Club (Edinburgh, 1843) [by no.].

Scot. Grey Friars The Scottish grey friars, ed. W. M. Bryce, 2 vols. (Edinburgh, 1909).

Scot. RO Scottish Record Office, General Register House, Edinburgh 2.

Scot. Saints Lives of the Scottish Saints, ed. J. Pinkerton, revised W. M. Metcalf, 2 vols. (Paisley, 1889).

Script. Mus. Coussemaker, E.: *Scriptorum de musica medii aevi novam seriem a Gerbertina alteram collegit nuncque primum edidit*, 4 vols. (1864–76) [mainly cited under authors: GARL.; HAUBOYS; HAUDLO; HOTHBY; **Mus. Mens. (Anon. VI)**, ODINGTON; TUNST.].

Scrope v. Grosvenor The Scrope and Grosvenor controversy (1385–90), ed. N. H. Nicolas, 2 vols. (1832).

Sea Terms Middle English sea terms, ed. B. Sandahl, I– (Upsala, 1951–).

Seals Sir Christopher Hatton's book of seals (12c.–13c.), ed. L. C. Lloyd and D. M. Stenton, Northants Rec. Soc. XV (1950) [by no.].

Seignorial Admin. Denholm-Young, N.: Seignorial administration in England (Oxford, 1937).

SelBEyre Select Bills in Eyre 1292–1333, Selden Soc. XXX (1914).

SelCChanc Select cases in Chancery (1346–1471), Selden Soc. X (1896).

SelCCoron Select cases from the coroners' rolls 1265–1413, Selden Soc. IX (1895).

SelCCouncil Select cases before the King's Council (1243–1482), Selden Soc. XXXV (1919).

SelCExchCh Select cases in the Exchequer Chamber before all the Justices of England 1377–1461, Selden Soc. LI (1933).

SelCExchPl Select cases in the Exchequer of Pleas (Hen. III and Ed. I), Selden Soc. XLVIII (1932).

SelCKB Select cases in the Court of King's Bench, 7 vols. Selden Soc. LV, LVII, LVIII, LXXIV, LXXVI, LXXXII, LXXXVIII (1936–71).

SelCReq Select cases in the Court of Requests 1497–1569, Selden Soc. XII (1898).

SelCWW Select cases of procedure without writ under Hen. III, Selden Soc. LX (1941).

SelCh Select charters and other illustrations of English constitutional history..to the reign of Ed. I, ed. W. Stubbs, 9th ed. (1913).

SelCivPl Select civil pleas I (1200–3), Selden Soc. III (1890) [no more pub.].

SelPlAdm Select pleas in the Court of Admiralty, 2 vols. Selden Soc. VI, XI (1892–7).

SelPlCrown Select pleas of the Crown I, Selden Soc. I (1887) [no more pub.].

SelPlForest Select pleas of the forest (1209–1334), Selden Soc. XIII (1901).

SelPlJews Select pleas, Starrs, and other records from the Rolls of the Exchequer of the Jews 1220–84, Selden Soc. XV (1902).

SelPlMan Select pleas in manorial and other seignorial courts, vol. I (Hen. III and Ed. I), Selden Soc. II (1889) [no more pub.].

SelPlStarCh Select pleas of the Court of Star Chamber (1477–1544), 2 vols. Selden Soc. XVI, XXV (1903–11). .

SelTracts *v.* Eng. Weights.

Selden Soc. Selden Society, pub. [of legal records or sim.], I– (1888–).

Senesch. The seneschaucy, printed w. Husb. (1971) [cited as source of passages in *Fleta*].

SERLO BAY. Serlo of Bayeux (*alias* Parisiacensis) [*ob. c*1122]: *Poemata*, Sat. Poets II 208–12, 233–58.

SERLO GRAM: Serlo Grammaticus [*ob. c*1207]: **Bell. Stand.** (attrib.) *De bello inter regem Scotie et barones Anglie* (1138), in SERLO WILT. 7–9; **Mon. Font.** *Narratio de fundatione Fontanis Monasterii* [dictated by S. G. to Hugh of Kirkstall], Mem. Fount. I 1–129.

SERLO WILT: Serlo of Wilton [*ob. c*1180]: Poèmes latins, *Studia Latina Stockholmiensia* XIV (1965) [*v. et.* Eur. Love Lyric II 510–12].

SessPCambs Some sessions of the peace in Cambridgeshire (1340, 1380–3), ed. M. M. Taylor, Camb. Antiq. Soc. 8° S. LV (1942).

SessPEssex Essex sessions of the peace, 1351, 1377–9, ed. E. C. Furber, Arch. Soc. Essex, occ. pub. III (1953).

SessPLincs Some sessions of the peace in Lincolnshire (1360–96), 2 vols. Linc. Rec. Soc. XXX, LVI (1936–62).

SessPNorthants Rolls of Northamptonshire sessions of the peace (1314–16, 1320), ed. M. Gollancz, Northants Rec. Soc. XI (1940).

SessPWarw Rolls of the Warwickshire and Coventry sessions of the peace, 1377–97, ed. E. G. Kimball, Dugdale Soc. XVI (1939).

Sess. Pps. H. of C. Sessional papers printed by order of the House of Commons, I– (1693–).

SHIRWOOD William Shirwood, treasurer of Lincoln [*fl.* 1260] *v.* GLA.

SILGRAVE Henry of Silgrave (*alias* Sulgrave) [*ob. a*1292]: *Chronicon* (–1274), Caxton Soc. (1849).

SIM. HENTON Simon of Henton (*alias* Hinton) [*fl. c*1250]: **Post. Mor.** *Postille morales in prophetas minores*, MS New Coll. Oxford 45.

Simil. Anselmi *Liber de S. Anselmi similitudinibus* in *PL* CLIX (1865) 605–708.

Simon. Her. *De Simoniaca haeresi carmen* (? *c*1091), *MGH Libelli de lite* III (Hanover, 1897), 615–17.

SKELTON John Skelton [*ob.* 1529]: Poetical works, 2 vols. (1843).

Som Rec. Soc. Somerset Record Society, publications, I– (1887–).

Spalding Club publications (Aberdeen, 1839–71) [cont. as New Spalding Club].

Spec. Alch. *Speculum Alchemiae* (? 13c.; attrib. to Roger Bacon), *Theatrum Chem.* II 377–85.

Speculum *Speculum*, a journal of Mediaeval Studies, I– (Boston, 1926–).

Spons. Mariae The spousells of the Princess Mary (1508), Camd. Misc. IX, Camd. NS LIII (1893).

Sports & Pastimes Strutt, Joseph: Sports and pastimes of the people of England, revised ed. (1903).

Stair Soc. Stair Society, publications I– (Edinburgh, 1936–).

STANBR. Vulg. John Stanbridge [*ob.* 1510]: *Vulgaria*, EETS CLXXXVII (1932) 1–30.

STANIHURST Hib. Richard Stanihurst of Dublin [*ob.* 1618]: *De rebus in Hibernia gestis* (Antwerp, 1584).

Stans Puer *Stans puer ad mensam*, verses on behaviour of page at table (15c.) EETS XXXII pt. 2 (1868) 30–3.

Starrs Starrs and Jewish charters (1182–1280) preserved in the British Museum, w. illustrative docs. etc., ed. I. Abrahams *et al.*, 3 vols. Jewish Hist. Soc. (1930–2).

Stat. CCOx Statutes of Corpus Christi College, Oxford, in Statutes of the Colleges of Oxford II, 3 vols. HMSO (Oxford, 1853).

StatCantab The original statutes of Cambridge University, ed. M. B. Hackett (Cambridge, 1970).

Stat. Durh. The statutes of the cathedral church of Durham, Surtees Soc. CXLIII (1929).

Stat. Gild. Berw. *Statuta gilde apud Berwicum facta* (*c*1250–94), APScot I app. 2, 89*–96*.

StatIr Early statutes of Ireland (1204–1482), 4 vols. PRO Ireland (Dublin, 1907–39).

Stat. Linc. Statutes of Lincoln Cathedral, ed. H. Bradshaw and C. Wordsworth, 2 vols. in 3 (Cambridge, 1892–7).

Stat. Ottery St. M. Dalton, J. N.: The collegiate church of Ottery St. Mary [Devon], being the *ordinacio et statuta*.. 1338, 1339 (Cambridge, 1917).

StatOx *Statuta antiqua Universitatis Oxoniensis*, ed. Strickland Gibson (Oxford, 1931).

Stat. Sal. Statutes and customs of the cathedral church..of Salisbury, ed. C. Wordsworth and D. Macleane (1915).

Stat. Wells *Ordinale et statuta ecclesie cathedralis S. Andree Wellensis* (*c*1150), ed. H. E. Reynolds in Wells Cathedral (1881) 1–113.

State Tri. Ed. I State Trials of the reign of Ed. I, 1289–93, Camd. 3rd S. IX (1906).

Stenton Misc. A medieval miscellany for D. M. Stenton, ed. P. M. Barnes and C. F. Slade, Pipe R. Soc. NS XXXVI (1962).

STEPH. ROUEN Stephen of Rouen [*ob. c*1170]: *Draco Normannicus* (1118–69), Chr. Steph. II 585–757; **Addit.** *Additamenta* 758–62; **App.** Appendix of miscellaneous verse 765–79.

Stewards' Bk. Southampt. The Stewards' Books of Southampton (1428–39), Southampt. Rec. Soc. XXXV, XXXIX (1935–9).

STONE Chr. John Stone, monk of Christ Church, Canterbury [*ob. c*1480]: Chronicle (1415–71), Camb. Antiq. Soc. 8° S. XXXIV (1902) 1–152.

Stonor Pps. The Stonor letters and papers (1290–1483), 2 vols. Camd. 3rd S. XXIX, XXX (1919); **Sup.** Camd. Misc. XIII, *ib.* XXXIV (1924).

StRealm Statutes of the Realm (1236–1713), 11 vols. in 12, RC (1810–28).

STRECCHE Hen. V John Strecche [*fl.* 15c.]: Chronicle of the reign of Hen. V, ed. F. Taylor JRL Bull. XVI (1932) 146–87.

Stud. 14 Cent. Clarke, M. V.: Fourteenth-century studies (Oxford, 1937).

Suff Hund. Powell, E.: A Suffolk hundred [Blackbourne] in 1283 (Cambridge, 1910).

SULCARD Sulcard of Westminster [*fl.* c1075]: *Libellus de fundatione Abbatiae Westmonasteriensis*, extr. in *PL* CLV (1880) 1635–8; **Prol.** *Prologus de constructione Westmonasterii*, ed. B. W. Scholz, *Trad.* XX (N.Y., 1964) 80–91.

SULGRAVE *v.* SILGRAVE.

Summa Abend. *v.* HALES.

Surtees Soc. Surtees Society, pub. [concerning Northumbria *sensu latiore*], I– (Durham, 1835–).

Surv. Denb. Survey of the honour of Denbigh, 1334, ed. P. Vinogradoff and F. Morgan (1914).

Surv. Devon Risdon, T.: The chorographical description, or survey of the County of Devon [printed from 17c. MS] (1811).

Surv. Durh. Hatf. Bishop Hatfield's Survey, a record of the possessions of the See of Durham (1345–81), Surtees Soc. XXXII (1857).

Surv. Linc. The Lincolnshire Domesday and the Lindsey survey (1115–18), Linc. Rec. Soc. (1924) 327–60.

Surv. Pembr. Survey of the lands of William, earl of Pembroke and Montgomery (1566–73) [w. earlier docs.], 2 vols. Roxb. Club (1909).

Surv. Wye A survey of the manor of Wye [Kent] (c1450), ed. H. E. Muhlfeld (N.Y., 1933).

SWAFHAM Robert Swafham: *Historia coenobii Burgensis* [Peterborough] (1177–1245), in *Hist. Angl. script.* 97–122.

SWINESHEAD, R. [*fl.* c1350] *v.* Sci. Mech.

SWYNTON Mem. Thomas Swynton, abbot of Fountains: Memorandum book (1446–58), Mem. Fount. III 93–255.

T. ELY Etheldr. Thomas of Ely [*ob.* 1175]: **Acta** *Acta S.Etheldredae*, in *Acta SS Boll.* June IV 497–538; **Prol.** Prologue to above, *ib.* 493–4; **Transl.** Second translation of S.Etheldreda [*ob.* 679], *Lib. Eli.* II capp. 143–4; **Mir.** Miracles of S.Etheldreda, *ib.* III capp. 27–138 (*passim*), also in *Acta SS Boll.* June IV 538–76 [*v. et.* RIC. ELY].

T. MON. Will. Thomas of Monmouth [*ob.* p1172]: Life and miracles of S.William of Norwich [*ob.* 1144], ed. A. Jessopp and M. R. James (Cambridge, 1896).

T. SPROTT Chr. Thomas Sprott (*alias* Spott) [? *fl.* c1270] [attrib.]: *Chronica*, ed. T. Hearne (Oxford, 1719) 3–164 [prob. wr. 1300.].

T. STUBBS (Chr. Pont. Ebor. B.) Thomas Stubbs [? *ob.* p1380]: *Continuatio chronicae de vitis Archiepiscoporum Eboracensium* (1147–1373), Hist. Church York II 388–421 [*cf. Chr. Pont. Ebor. A & C*].

T. SUTTON Thomas of Sutton (*alias* Anglicus) [*ob.* p1300]: **Quaest.** *Quaestiones de reali distinctione inter essentiam et esse*, ed. F. Pelster, Beitr. zur Gesch. der Philos. des Mittelalters (Münster, 1928); **Quodl.** *Quodlibeta* (1284–7), extr., ed. D. Sharp, Revue néoscolastique de philosophie, XXXVI, XXXVII (Louvain, 1934).

T. YORK Sap. Thomas of York [? *ob.* c1260]: *Sapientiale*, extr. and cap. headings in Longpré, P. E., Fr. Thomas d'York, O.F.M., La première somme métaphysique du XIIIe siècle in *Archivum Franciscanum Historicum* XIX (Quaracchi, 1926) 875–930.

TR Bk Exchequer, Treasury of the Receipt Books, MS PRO (E. 36); **Forest Proc.** Forest Proceedings, *ib.* (E. 32).

Tap. Bayeux The Bayeux Tapestry (a1080), ed. D. C. Douglas, English Historical Documents II (1953) [by panel].

TATWIN Tatwin, Archb. of Canterbury [*ob.* 734]: **Aen.** *Aenigmata*, in *Corpus Christianorum S.Latina* CXXXIII (Turnholt, 1968) 143–208; **Ars** *Ars* [*de partibus orationis*], *ib.* 1–141 [by sect.].

TAXTER Chr. Bury John Taxter (*alias* Tayster): *Chronica Buriensis* (to 1265), in Chr. Bury 1–33 [partly supersedes FL. WORC. *Cont.* B].

Terr. Fleet A terrier of Fleet, Lincs (1316) [w. other docs.], ed. N. Neilson, (1920).

Test. Ebor. *Testamenta Eboracensia* (c1300–1550), Surtees Soc. IV, XXX, XLV, LII, LXXIX, CVI (1836–1902).

Test. Ep. Heref. The will of Peter de Aqua Blanca, Bishop of Hereford (1268), Camd. Misc. XIV, Camd. 3rd S. XXXVII (1926).

Test. Karl. *Testamenta karleolensia* (1353–86), Cumb and Westmor Antiq. Soc., extra S. IX (1893).

Text. Roff. *Textus Roffensis* (attrib. to Ernulf, Bishop of Rochester [*ob.* 1124]), ed. P. Sawyer, Early Eng. MSS in facsimile vols. VII and XI (Copenhagen, 1957–62) [*cf. Archaeol. Cantiana* XXIII (1898) 94–112] [by folio; refs. to pp. are to T. Hearne's ed. 1720].

Theatrum Chem. *Theatrum chemicum*, ed. L. Zetzner, 6 vols. (Strasbourg, 1659–61).

THEOD. Pen. Theodore of Tarsus, Archb. of Canterbury [*ob.* 690]: *Paenitentiale*, in *Conc.* HS III 173–213 [by bk., cap., and para.], also ed. P. W. Finsterwalder: Die *Canones Theodori Cantuariensis* und ihre Ueberlieferungsformen (Weimar, 1929).

Theol. Ox. Little, A. G. and Pelster, F.: Oxford theology and theologians c1282–1302, OHS XCVI (1934).

Thes. Nov. Anecdot. *Thesaurus novus anecdotorum*, ed. E. Martène and U. Durand, 5 vols. (Paris, 1717).

Thingoe Gage, J.: The history and antiquities of Suffolk, Thingoe hundred (1838).

THOMAS ANGLICUS *v.* PAUL. ANGL.

THOMAS BRADWARDINE *v.* BRADW.

THOMAS DOCKING *v.* DOCKING.

Thoresby Soc. Thoresby Society, publications, I– (Leeds, 1891–).

THORNE William Thorne [*fl.* c1397]: *Chronica de rebus gestis abbatum S.Augustini Cantuariae* (578–1397), in *Hist. Angl. Script. X* 1753–2296.

Thoroton Soc. Thoroton Society, publications [mainly concerning Notts], I– (1903–).

TORIGNI Robert de Torigni (*alias* de Monte): **Access. Sig.** *Accessiones ad Sigebertum*, in Chr. Steph. IV 3–60; **Chr.** *Chronica* (1100–86), *ib.* 81–315; **Cont. Bec.** *Continuatio Beccensis* (1157–60), *ib.* 317–27 [*v. et.* H. HUNT., W. JUM.].

Tout Essays Essays in medieval history presented to T. F. Tout (Manchester, 1925).

Tract. Ebor. Gerard, Archb. of York [*ob.* 1108] (attrib.): *Tractatus Eboracenses*, ed. H. Böhmer, *Libelli de lite* III, *MGH* (Hanover, 1897) 645–87.

Tract. Ed. II *Tractatus pacis*, Edward II, the Lords Ordainers etc. (1312–13), Camd. Misc. XV, Camd. 3rd S. XLI (1929).

Transl. Ecgwini *v.* Chr. Evesham.

Trad. *Traditio* I– (N.Y. 1943–).

Treat. J.P. Early treatises on the practice of the Justices of the Peace in the 15c. and 16c., ed. B. H. Putnam (Oxford, 1924).

TreatyR Treaty Rolls I– (1234–1325), HMSO (1955–), [by vol. and no.]; later Rolls, MS PRO (C. 76).

TREVET Nicholas Trevet (*alias* Trivet) [*ob.* 1328]: *Annales sex regum Angliae*..1136–1306 (1854).

Tribal System Seebohm, F.: The tribal system in Wales (1895) [app. of docs. w. sep. pag.].

TROKELOWE John of Trokelowe (*ob.* p1330]: *Annales* (1307–24), *Chr. Mon. S.Alb.* III 61–127.

Trop. Wint. The Winchester troper (from MSS 10c. and 11c.), HBS VIII (1894).

TUNST. Simon Tunsted [*ob.* 1369]: *Quatuor principalia musicae*, in *Script. Mus.* IV 201–98.

TURNER William Turner [*ob.* 1568]: **Av.** *Avium..brevis historia* (1544) (Cambridge, 1823); **Herb.** *Libellus de re herbaria* (1538), facs. ed. (1877).

Turquet *De Turketo* (a1350), Early Sci. Ox. II 370–5.

UPTON Nicholas Upton [*ob.* 1457]: *De studio militari*, ed. E. Bysshe (1654).

V. Bart. Farn. *Vita Bartholomaei Farnensis* [*ob.* 1193] (attrib. G. COLD)., in S. DURH. *Auct.* I (1882) 295–325.

VCH Victoria History of the counties of England, ed. H. A Doubleday, W. Page *et al.* (1900–).

V. Cuthb. *Vita S.Cuthberti* [*ob.* 687] *auctore anonymo* (*a*705), in Two lives of S.Cuthbert, ed. B. Colgrave (Cambridge, 1940) 59–139 [by cap.].

V. Dunst. B. *S.Dunstani* [*ob.* 988] *vita, auctore B.* [? Bridferth] (*c*1000), in Mem. Dunst. 3–52 [by cap.].

V. Ecgwini *v.* Chr. Evesham.

V. Ed. Conf. *Vita Aedwardi regis* [*ob.* 1066]. .*S.Bertini monacho ascripta* (? wr. *c*1067), Med. Texts (1962), also in Lives Ed. Conf. 389–435 [by f.].

V. Ed. Conf. Metr. Metrical lives of Edward the Confessor: I 15c. abridgement of AILR. *Ed. Conf.* in Lives Ed. Conf. 359–77; II extr. from MS Caius Coll. Camb. no. 153, *ib.* 379–83 [both by line].

V. Ed. II *Vita Edwardi Secundi* [*ob.* 1307] (? wr. *c*1326), Med. Texts (1957) [by marginal pp. (from Chr. Ed. I and II, II 155–289); *v. et.* BAKER].

V. Edm. Rich Life of St. Edmund Rich, Archb. of Canterbury [*ob.* 1240] [attrib. Bertrand of Pontigny; wr. *a*1250], *Thes. Nov. Anecdot.* III 1775–1826 [*v. et.* RICH. Edm., E. FAVERSHAM, M. PAR.].

V. Furs. *Vita S.Fursei abbatis Latiniacensis* [*ob.* 650] [*auct. anon. coaev.*], *Acta SS Ben.* II 309–14.

V. Greg. *Vita S.Gregorii* [*ob.* 604], by a monk of Whitby (? *a*730), extr. in BEDE *Op. Hist.* II 389–91; fuller extr. in EHR III (1888) 305–10.

V. Har. *Vita Haroldi* [*ob.* 1066] (wr. *a*1216), ed. W. de G. Birch (1885) [by cap. and f.].

V. Hug. Metr. *v.* H. AVR. Hugh.

V. Merl. *Vita Merlini* [attrib. G. MON.] (wr. *c*1150), ed. J. J. Parry (Urbana, 1925) [by line].

V. Montf. Bémont, C.: Simon de Montfort. .sa vie (1208–65) (Paris, 1884) [Life 1–261; **App.** Appendix of docs. 263–380, incl. Chr. Battle, 1258–65, 373–80].

V. Odulphi *Vita S.Odulphi*, canon of Utrecht [*fl. c*830], *Acta SS Boll.* June II (1742) 592–5.

V. II Off. *Vitae duorum Offarum sive Offanorum Merciorum regum* [attrib. M. PAR.], ed. W. Wats (1639).

V. Osw. *Vita Oswaldi Archiep. Ebor.* [*ob.* 992] (wr. *c*1000], Hist. Church York I 399–475.

V. Ric. II *Historia vitae et regni Ricardi II* [*ob.* 1399] *monacho quodam de Evesham consignata* (*c*1404), ed. T. Hearne (Oxford, 1729).

V. Thom. A *Vita S.Thomae A* [attrib. Roger of Pontigny], in Becket Mat. IV 1–79; **B** *Vitae S.Thomae B* (? wr. *a*1175), *ib.* 80–144 [both by cap.].

V. Walth. *Vita S.Waltheofi* [*ob.* 1159] [attrib. Jocelin (*alias* Jordan), monk of Furness] (wr. *a*1215), *Acta SS Boll.* Aug. I (1867) 249–78.

V. Will. *Vita S. Willelmi* [ob. 1154] Hist. Church York II 270–91 [*v. et. Mir. Will.*].

V. Wist. *Vita S.Wistani* [*ob. c*850] attrib. Thomas of Marlborough, Abbot of Evesham 1230–6, Chr. Evesham 326–32 **Prol.** Prologue, *ib.* 325–6.

VAC. Vacarius [*ob. c* 1200] **Lib. paup.** *Liber pauperum*, ed. F. de Zulueta, Selden Soc. XLIV (1927); **Mat.** *De matrimonio*, ed. F. W. Maitland in Law Quarterly Review L and LI (1897) 133–43 and 270–87 [by sect.].

Val. Eccl. *Valor ecclesiasticus* (1535), 6 vols. RC (1810–24).

Val. Norw. The valuation of Norwich 1254, w. other docs. 1217–91, ed. W. E. Lunt (Oxford, 1926).

Vers. Ed. Conf. *v. V. Ed. Conf. Metr.*

Vers. Hen. V *Versus rhythmici de Henrico V* (? by a contemporary), Mem. Hen. V 63–74 [by l.]; *cf. Pref.* xxviii–xl.

Vex. Will. *De injusta vexatione Willelmi* [*de S.Carilevo*] *episcopi* [*Dunelm.*] (? *p*1125), in S. DURH. *Auct.* I 170–95 [*cf.* EHR LXVI (1951) 32–41].

Villainage in Eng. Vinogradoff, . P.: Villainage in England, essays in English medieval history (Oxford, 1892).

VINSAUF Geoffrey de Vinsauf [*ob. p*1200]: **AV** *Documentum de modo et arte dictandi et versificandi*, ed. E. Faral in Les arts poétiques du XIIe et du XIIIe siècle (Paris, 1924) 265–320 [by bk. and section]; **CR** *Summa de coloribus rhetoricis, ib.* 321–7; **Interdict.** [attrib.] Poèmes sur l'interdit de l'Angleterre, *ib.* 24–6; **PN** *Poetria nova, ib.* 197–262 [by line].

Vis. Derry Acta of Archb. Colton [*ob.* 1404] in his metropolitan visitation of the Diocese of Derry, 1397, w. a rental of the See estates at that time, Irish Archaeol. Soc. (Dublin, 1850).

Vis. Ely Ely. .visitation recs. in Ord. Ely 4–23, 29–35, 44–67.

Vis. Godstow Visitation of Godstow nunnery by William, Bishop of Lincoln (1432) in Reg. Godstow EETS CXXIX lxxxi–lxxxvii.

Vis. Linc. 1420–49 Visitations of Religious Houses in the diocese of Lincoln, 3 vols. Linc. Rec. Soc. VII, XIV, XXI (1914–23) (= Cant. and York Soc. XVII, XXIV, XXXIII); 1517–31, Linc. Rec. Soc. XXXIII, XXXV, XXXVII (1940–7).

Vis. Norw. Visitations of the diocese of Norwich 1492–1532, Camd. NS XLIII (1888).

Vis. S.Paul. 1249–52 Visitations of churches belonging to St. Paul's Cathedral, Camd. Misc. IX, Camd. NS LIII (1895); 1295 *Visitatio facta in thesaura* (sic) *S.Pauli*, in Hist. S.Paul 310–35 (also in *MonA*, ed. 1673, III 308–31).

Vis. Southwell Visitations and memorials of Southwell [Notts] Minster (1469–1553), Camd. Soc. NS XLVIII (1891).

Vis. Wells Visitation of religious houses and hospitals by Bishop's Vicar-general (Bath and Wells) (1526), Som Rec. Soc. XXXIX (1924) 207–25.

W. BRUCE William Bruce (Brussius) [*fl. c*1480]: **Tart.** *De Tartaris diarium* (Frankfurt, 1598); **Turc.** *De bello adversus Turcos gerendo* (Leipzig, 1595).

W. CANT. William of Canterbury [*fl. c*1170]: **Mir. Thom.** *Miracula S.Thomae*, Becket Mat. I 173–545; **V. Thom.** *Vita et passio S.Thomae, ib.* 1–135 [both by bk. and cap.].

W. de CHAMBRE *v.* Hist. Durh.

W. COVENTR. *Memoriale fratris Walteri de Coventria* (wr. *p*1293), 2 vols. RS (1872–3) [vols. I and II pp. 1–195 (–1201) are derived from known chroniclers; vol. II pp. 196–279 (1202–25) is Anon. Chron. (–1225), based for 1202–25 on anon. chron. of Barnwell (wr. *c*1227)].

W. DAN. Walter Daniel: **Ailred** *Vita Ailredi Abbatis Rievall'* [*ob.* 1167] (wr. *c*1170), Med. Texts (1950) [by cap.]; **Ep.** *Epistola ad Mauricium* (*c*1170), *ib.* 66–81 [by f.].

W. DROGHEDA SA William of Drogheda, canonist [*ob.* 1245]: *Summa Aurea continens modum advocandi* [*etc.*] (wr. *c*1239), ed. L. Wahrmund, Quellen zur Gesch. des römisch-kanonischen Processes im Mittelalter, II ii (Innsbruck, 1914) [by cap.].

W. FITZST. William Fitzstephen [*ob.* 1190]: **Thom.** *Vita S.Thomae*, Becket Mat. III 13–154; **prol.** *Prologus* (*Descriptio Londoniae*), *ib.* 1–13 [both by cap.].

W. GUISB. Walter of Guisborough (alias of Hemingford or Hemingburgh) [? *ob. c*1315]: Chronicle (1048–1315), Camd. 3rd S. LXXXIX (1957); **Cont.** *De gestis Regis Edwardi Tertii et caeteris eventibus* (1327–46), in *Chronicon Domini Walteri de Hemingburgh*, Soc. of Antiquaries of London (1849) II 297–426 [otherwise superseded by prec.].

W. JUM. William of Jumièges [? *ob.* 1087]: *Gesta Normannorum ducum* I–VII (–1087), ed. A. Duchesne in *Hist. Norm. Script.* 215–92; **Cont.** Continuation (–1137) by TORIGNI here printed as VIII, 292–317 [by bk. and cap.] [this ed. cont. many interpolations by ORD. VIT. and TORIGNI, subsequently excised by J. Marx in his ed. (Rouen and Paris, 1914)]; also printed in *PL* CXLIX 779–914.

W. LEIC. Sim. William of Leicester (*alias* de Montibus) [*ob.* 1213]: *Similitudinarius*, MS Ancaster 16/1 Lincs RO; Cambridge, Peterhouse 255.

W. MALM. William of Malmesbury [*ob. c*1143]: **Dunst.** *Vita S.Dunstani*, in Mem. Dunst. 251–324 [by bk. and cap.]; **GP** *De gestis pontificum Anglorum* (wr. *p*1125), RS (1870) [by bk. and cap.]; **GR** *De gestis regum Anglorum* (wr. *c*1125), 2 vols. RS (1887–9) [by bk. and cap.]; **Glast.** *De antiquitate Glastoniensis Ecclesiae* (–1126), in DOMERH. *Glast.* (1727) pt. i; **HN** *Historia novella* (1125–42) Med. Texts (1955) [by cap.]; **Wulfst.** *Vita Wulfstani* [*ob.* 1095], Camd. 3rd S. XL (1928) 1–67; **Wulfst Abbr.** Abbreviated versions *ib.* 68–114 [*v. et. Mir. Wulfst.*].

W. MERLE William Merle (*alias* Morley) [*ob.* 1347]: *Consideraciones temperiei pro 7 annis* (1337–44), ed. G. J. Symons (1891).

W. de MONTIBUS *v.* W. LEIC.

W. NEWB. William of Newburgh [*ob. c*1200]: *Historia rerum Anglicarum* (1066–1198), Chr. Steph. I 1–408, II 409–500 [by bk. and cap.]; **Cont.** *Continuatio..ad annum* 1298, *ib.* II 501–83 [by p.].

W. POIT. William of Poitiers, Dean of Lisieux [*ob. p*1087]: *Gesta Willelmi ducis Normannorum et..Regis Anglorum* (wr. *c*1075), ed. R. Foreville (Paris, 1952) [by bk. and cap.].

W. RAMSEY William of Ramsey [*c*1200]: **Cant.** *Distinctio super cantico* MS (Prague).

WW Anglo-Saxon and Old English Vocabularies, ed. T. Wright and R. P. Wülcker, 2 vols. (1884) [mainly 10c. (? 11c.) or 15c.; undated entries are 15c.; for refs. *v.* vol. II (Index); cols. 1–54 superseded by GlC; *v. et.* ÆLF. *Coll.* and ÆLF. *Gl.*]; earlier ed. T. Wright, 2 vols. (1857, 1873) [*v. et.* GARL. *Dict.*, NECKAM *Ut.*].

W. WORC. William of Worcester (*alias* Botonier) [*ob. c*1482]: **Anecd.** *Anecdota*, BBExch. II 522–41; **Ann.** *Annales rerum Anglicarum* (1324–1468; anon add. to 1491), Letters and papers illustrative of the wars of the English, RS (1864) vol. II 743–93; **Itin.** Itineraries (Oxford, 1969).

WALCHER Walcher, prior of Malvern [*ob.* 1135]: **Drac.** *De dracone* (1120), paraphr. of tract by Petrus Alphonsi, extr. in Med. Sci. 116–18; **Exp.** *De experientia scriptoris* (*p*1092), extr. *ib.* 114–15.

WALLINGF: Richard of Wallingford [*ob.* 1336]: **Alb.** Albion (1327), Early Sci. Ox. 349–70; **Rect.** *Rectangulus* (1326), *ib.* 337–48; **Quad.** *Quadripartitum de sinibus demonstratis*, Isis V (Brussels, 1923) 99–115, 359–63.

WALS. Thomas Walsingham of St. Albans [*ob. c*1422]: **HA** *Historia Anglicana* (1272–1422), 2 vols. Chr. Mon. S.Alb. I (1863); **YN** *Ypodigma neustriae* (–1419), *ib.* pt. vii (1876); [*v. et. Chr. Angl.*, *G.S. Alb.*].

WALT. ANGL. Fab. Walterus Anglicus [*fl. c*1200]: *Fabulae*, Univ. of Illinois Studies. V (1919) 49–214, also ed. L. Hervieux, Fabulistes latins II (1894) 317–91 [by no. and l.].

WALT. EVESHAM *v.* ODINGTON.

War. Issue Exchequer of Receipt, Writs and Warrants for Issues, MS PRO (E. 404).

War. PS *v.* PS.

WelshR Welsh Rolls, MS PRO (C. 77).

WEND. Roger of Wendover [*ob.* 1236]: *Flores Historiarum* (1154–1235), 3 vols. RS (1886–9) [earlier portion (447–1153), incl. in ed. H. O. Coxe, 4 vols. Eng. Hist. Soc. 1841–4, is cited only in so far as it is incorporated in M. PAR. *Maj.* I and II].

WEY Itin. William Wey (*alias* Way) [*ob.* 1476]: Itineraries.. to Jerusalem, 1458 and 1462; to S.James of Compostella, 1456, Roxb. Club (1857).

WHÆTBERT Whætbert (*alias* Eusebius), Abbot of Wearmouth and Jarrow [*ob. c*744]: *Aenigmata*, in *Corpus Christianorum, S.Lat.* CXXXIII (1968) 209–71 [by no. and line].

WHITTINGTON Vulg. Robert Whittington: *Vulgaria* (1520), EETS CLXXXVII (1932) 31–128.

WHITTLESEY Walter of Whittlesey [? *ob. c*1321]: *Historia coenobii Burgensis* [Peterborough] (1246–1321), *Hist. Angl. Script.* 125–216; **Cont.** *Continuatio* (1321–38), *ib.* 217–37.

Wilkinson Essays Essays in medieval history presented to B. Wilkinson, ed. T. A. Sandquist and M. R. Powicke (Toronto, 1969).

WILL. GLASG. Sum. William of Glasgow: *Carmen de Morte Sumerledi*, in S. DURH. *Auct. etc.* II 386–8.

WILLIAM of OCCAM *v.* OCKHAM.

Wills Dublin Register of wills and inventories in the diocese of Dublin..1457–83, R. Soc. Antiq. of Ireland, extra vol. (1898).

Wills N. Country North country wills..of York, Nottingham, Northumberland, Cumberland, Westmorland, etc. (1383–1604), Surtees Soc. CXVI, CXXI (1908–12).

Wills Richm. Wills and inventories from the registry of the Archdeaconry of Richmond, etc. (1442–1579), Surtees Soc. XXVI (1853).

Wills Wells Wells Wills (1528–36), ed. F. W. Weaver (1890).

Wilts Rec. Soc. Wiltshire Record Society, publications, XXIII– (1967–) [formerly Wiltshire Archaeological and Natural History Society, Records Branch, I–XXII (1939–66)].

Windsor Castle Hope, W. H. St.John: Windsor Castle, an architectural history (1086–), 2 vols. (1913).

WINFRITH *v.* BONIFACE.

WULF. Wulfstan of Winchester [*fl. c*1000]: **Æthelwold** Life of S.Æthelwold [*ob.* 984], ed. M. Winterbottom, in Three lives of English Saints, Toronto Med. Latin Texts (Toronto, 1972) 33–63 [by cap.]; also *Acta SS Ben.* V 608–24; **Poem** Poems in *Anal. Hymn.* LI 164–6, etc.; **Swith.** *Narratio metrica de S.Swithuno* [*ob.* 862], ed. A. Campbell (Zürich, 1951) [by bk. and line]; **Swith. pref.** Preface to above [by line].

WYCH William Wych [*fl. a*1500]: *Liber monasterii B.Mariae Glastoniae quem Willelmus Wych monachus scribi fecit* (1342–1493), in J. GLAST. I 272–83.

WYCL. John Wycliffe [*ob.* 1384] works pub. by Wyclif Soc. unless otherwise stated: **Act.** *v. Misc. Phil.*; **Chr. & Antichr.** *v.* Pol.; **Civ. Dom.** *De civili dominio* (1375–6), 4 vols. (1885–1904); **Compl.** The Latin text of Wycliffe's Complaint (1382), *Speculum* VII (1932), 87–94; **Compos. Hom.** *De compositione hominis* (*c*1360) (1884); **Concl.** *De Eucharistia Conclusiones* XV (1381), *Ziz.* 105–6; **Conf.** *De Eucharistia confessio* or *Tractatus minor de Eucharistia* (1381), *Ziz.* 115–32 [*v. et. Speculum* VIII (1933) 503–10]; **Dom. Div.** *De dominio divino* (*a*1377) (1890); **Eccl.** *De ecclesia* (1378) (1886); **Ente** [*Summae*] *De ente librorum duorum excerpta: Libri I. Tractatus tertius et quartus. Libri II. Tractatus primus et tertius et fragmentum de annihilatione* (*a*1367) (1909, repr. 1966); **Ente (Spec.)** A lost chapter of Wyclif's *Summa de Ente* (*a*1367), *Speculum* IV (1929) 339–46; **Ente (Sum.)** *Summa de ente, libri primi tractatus primus et secundus* (*c*1365) (Oxford, 1930); **Ente Praed.** *De ente praedicamentali* (*p*1360), w. *Quaest. Log.* (1891) 221–306; **Euch.** *De Eucharistia tractatus major* w. *Tractatus de Eucharistia et poenitentia sive de confessione* (1379) (1892); **Form.** *v. Misc. Phil.*; **Incarn.** *Tractatus de benedicta Incarnacione* (1371) (1886); **Innoc.** *Tractatus de statu innocencie* (*c*1375–6) *v. Mand. Div.* (1922); **Log.** *Tractatus de logica* (? 1361), 3 vols. (1893–9); **Mand. Div.** *Tractatus de mandatis divinis* (1375–6) w. *Innoc.* 475–524 and *Peccatum* 527–33 (1922); **Min.** *Opera minora* (1913); **Misc. Phil.** *Miscellanea philosophica*, 2 vols. (1902–5), incl *De actibus anime* **(Act.)** I, 1–127, and *De materia et forma* (? 1365) **(Form.)** I 163–242, besides works (unspec.) of dubious authorship; **Peccatum** *Differentia inter peccatum mortale et veniale*, *v. Mand. Div.*; **Pol.** Polemical works in Latin, 2 vols. (1883), incl. *De Christo et..Antichristo* (1383–4) **(Chr. & Antichr.)** II 653–92 besides minor works (unspec.); **Potest. Pape** *De potestate Papae* (1379) (1907); **Quaest. Log.** *Quaestiones XIII logicae et philosophicae* (1360–2) *v. Ente Praed.*; **Sim.** *De Simonia* (1379–80) (1898); **Trial.** *Trialogus cum supplemento Trialogi* (1382), ed. G. Lechler (Oxford, 1869); **Ver.** *De veritate sacrae scripturae* (1378–9), 3 vols. (1905–7, repr. in 1 vol. N.Y., 1966); **Versut.** *De versuciis anti-Christi*, in EHR XLVII (1932) 95–103 [cf. Bibliog. of Wyclif in Camb. Med. Hist. VII (1932) 900–7].

Wycl. & Ox. Robson, J. A.: Wyclif and the Oxford schools, the relation of the *Summa de Ente* to scholastic debates at medieval Oxford (Cambridge, 1961).

Wycl. Soc. The Wiclif (or Wyclif) Society [founded 1882, dissolved 1925], publications (1883–1924) [*v. et.* Note on Wyclif Soc. in Poole Essays 98–114].

WYKES Thomas Wykes (*alias* de Wyta): *Chronicon* (1066–1289) [attrib.], *Ann. Mon.* IV 6–319 [*cf.* Pol. Songs 132].

Year Bk. Year Books (20–22 and 30–35 Ed. I and 11–20 Ed. III), 20 vols. RS (1863–1900); Year Books of Ed. II etc., Selden Soc., Year Book S. I– (1903–).

Yorks Archaeol. Soc. *v.* Arch. Soc. Yorks.

Ziz. *Fasciculi Zizaniorum Magistri Johannis Wyclif cum tritico* [attrib. NETTER *q.v.*], incl. statements by or proc. against: ASTON, John (1382); CROMPE (Henry Crumpe) (1384, 1392); HERFORD (Nicholas Hereford) w. Philip Repyngdon (1382); KYN. (John Cunningham) (*c*1363); LANGTON, John (*c*1390); LAVENHAM, Richard (*c*1380); PURVEY, John (1401); SAUTRY, William (1399); STOKES, Peter (*ob.* 1399); SWYND, (William Swynderby) (1382); TYSS, (John Tyssyngton) (1382); WYCHE, Richard (*c*1401; *cf.* EHR V 531–44); WYNTERTON, Thomas (*c*1390); besides WYCL. *et al.*

If necessary, addenda to the Bibliography will be printed at the beginning of succeeding fascicules.

ABBREVIATIONS AND SIGNS

THIS list covers abbreviations used in the bibliography, as well as in the text of the dictionary, omitting some abbreviations in normal English use, such as the shortened forms of the names of counties. The books of the Bible are cited in the form familiar to English readers (*Kings*, *Chron.*, etc.), though the reference is normally to the Vulgate text (including the Vulgate numeration of the Psalms).

A.	*Anglice*
a	*ante*
AS	Anglo-Saxon
abbr.	abbreviated, -iation
abl.	ablative
absol.	absolute(ly)
abstr.	abstract(ion)
acad.	academic
acc.	according to, accusative
act.	active(ly)
ad.	adaptation of
add.	addenda, addition
adj.	adjective
adv.	adverb
agr.	agriculture, -ural
al. div.	*alias divisim*
alch.	alchemy, -ical
anal.	analogy
anat.	anatomy, -ical
ap.	*apud*
app.	apparently, appendix
appl.	applied (to)
approx.	approximate(ly)
Ar.	Arabic
arch.	architecture, -ural
assoc.	associated, -iation
astr.	astrology, -ical, -onomy, -ical
attrib.	attributed, -ive(ly)
B.	*Beat(us)*
BM	British Museum
BVM	*Beata Virgo Maria*
Beitr.	Beiträge
bibl.	biblical
bk.	book
bot.	botany, -ical
bus.	*bussell(us)*
Byz.	Byzantine
c (before a figure)	*circa*
c (after a figure)	century
C.I.	Channel Islands
CL	Classical Latin (to *c*200 A.D.)
cap. (capp.)	*capitulum(-a)*, chapter(s)
cf.	*confer*, compare
ch.	charter
chr.	chronicle
cl.	clause
col.	column
collect.	collective(ly)
com.	*comitat(us)*
comp.	compound, -position
compar.	comparative
compl.	complement
conf.	confused, -ion
conj.	conjugation, -junction
cont.	containing, continuation, -uator, -ued
contin.	continuous (of pagination)
contr.	contracted, -ion
corr.	corrected
d.	*dorso, denari(us)*
dat.	dative
decl.	declension, declined
def.	definite, -ition
dep.	deponent
deriv.	derivation, -ative
diff.	difference, -ent(ly)
dim.	*dimidi(us)*
dim.	diminutive
dir.	direct
dist.	distinguished
doc.	document
dub.	*dubi(us)*
dub.	dubious
eccl.	ecclesiastical
ed., edd.	edited by, edition(s), editor(s)
ellipt.	elliptical(ly)
emph.	emphasis, -atic
Eng.	England, English
ep.	*episcop(us)*, *epistol(a)*
epil.	epilogue
epith.	epithet
erron.	erroneous(ly)
esp.	especially
etym.	etymology
euphem.	euphemism, -istic(ally)
ex., exx.	example(s)
exc.	except
excl.	excluding, -sive(ly)
expl.	explained, explanatory
expr.	expressed, -ing, -ion
extr.	extract(s)
f.	feminine, folio
f.l.	*falsa lectio*
facet.	facetious(ly)
falc.	falconry
feud.	feudal(ly)
foll.	followed, -ing
Fr.	France, French
frag.	fragment
freq.	frequent(ly)
Frk.	Frankish (or sim.)
fut.	future
G.	*Gallice*
Gael.	Gaelic
Gall.	Gallic (Gaulish)
Gasc.	Gascon, -ony (or sim.)
gd., gdv.	gerund, -ive
gen.	genitive
geog.	geography, -ical

geom.	geometry, -ical
Germ.	German, -anic, -any
Gesch.	Geschichte
Gk.	Greek
gl.	gloss, -ary, -ed
gram.	grammar, -atical
Heb.	Hebrew
her.	heraldic, -ry
i.	*id est*
ib.	*ibidem*
id.	*idem*
imp.	imperative
imperf.	imperfect
impers.	impersonal
impl.	implied, -cation, -ying
inanim.	inanimate
incl.	including, -usive(ly)
ind.	indicative
indir.	indirect
inf.	infinitive
infl.	influence(d)
inscr.	inscription(s)
interj.	interjection
interl.	interlineated, -tion
interp.	interpreted, -ation
interr.	interrogative
intr.	intransitive(ly), introduction
Ir.	Ireland, Irish
iron.	ironical(ly), irony
irreg.	irregular(ly)
l., ll.	*lĕge, lectio, -ones*
LL	Late Latin (*c*200–*c*600 A.D.)
leg.	legal(ly)
li.	*libr(a)*
lit.	*litera*
lit.	literal(ly)
log.	logic(al)
Lomb.	Lombard
m.	*marc(a)* (= 13*s.* 4*d.*)
m.	masculine, membrane
ME	Middle English
ML	Medieval Latin (*c*600 A.D.–)
MS(S)	manuscript(s)
man.	manor(ial)
math.	mathematics, -ical
Med.	Medieval
med.	medical(ly)
metr.	metrical
mil.	military, -ily
misc.	miscellaneous
misinterp.	misinterpreted, -ation
misr.	misread, -ing
mon.	monastic
mun.	municipal, muniment(s)
mus.	music, -ical
myth.	mythology, -ical
n.	neuter, note
n.d.	no date
n. marg.	note in margin
NS	New Series
naut.	nautical(ly)
neg.	negative(ly)
nom.	nominative
OF	Old French
ON	Old Norse
ob.	*obol(us)*
obi(it),	*(-erunt)*
obj.	object(ive)
occ.	occasional(ly)
opp.	opposed, -ite
orig.	origin, -al(ly)
p	*post*
p., pp.	page(s)
p. ppl.	past participle
pag.	pagination
pass.	passive(ly)
perf.	perfect
perh.	perhaps
Pers.	Persian
pers.	person(al)
Pg.	Portuguese
phil.	philosophy, -ical
phr.	phrase
phys.	physics, -ical (science)
pl.	plural
poss.	possessive
ppl.	participle, -icipial
pps.	papers
pr. ppl.	present participle
prec.	preceded, -ing
pred.	predicate, -ive(ly)
pref.	preface
prep.	preparation, preposition
pres.	present
prob.	probable, -ly
proc.	proceeding(s)
prog.	progress
prol.	prologue
pron.	pronoun, -nominal
Prov.	Provençal
prov.	proverb, -ial(ly)
pub.	publication(s), published
qu.	question
quad.	*quadr(ans)*
quar.	*quarteri(um)* (or sim.)
r.	rotulet
r.c.	*reddit(-unt) compotum*
RO	Record Office
rec.	recension, record
ref.	reference
refl.	reflexive
reg.	register
rel.	relative
rep.	report
repr.	representing, reprinted
rhet.	rhetorical(ly)
Rom.	Romance
rub.	*rubrica*
S.	*Sanct(us)*
s.	*solid(us)*
s	*sub (data)*
S.	Series
s. act. (pass.)	*sensu activo (passivo)*
s. dub.	*sensu dubio*
s.v.	*sub verbo*
sb.	substantive
sc.	*scilicet*
Sc., Scot.	Scotland, Scottish
sched.	*schedul(a)*
sect.	section
sep.,	separate
sg.	singular
sim.	(something) similar
Soc.	Society

Sp. Spanish
spec. species, -ial, -ifically
sts. sometimes
sub. cl. subordinate clause
subj. subject(ive), -junctive
subst. substitute, -ion
sup. supplement
superl. superlative
syll. syllable(s)
syn. synonym(ous)
Syr. Syriac

TRE *tempore regis Edwardi* (*ob.* 1066)
tech. technical(ly)
temp. *tempore*
test. *testamentum, test*(*ibus*)
theol. theology, -ical(ly)
tit. *titulus*
topog. topography, -ical(ly)
trans. transitive
transf. transference, -red
transl. translated, -ating, -ation
Turk. Turkish

unspec. unspecified
usu. usually

v. *verso, vide*
v. et. *vide etiam*
v.l. *varia lectio*
var. variant, various
vb. verb
vers. *vers*(*us*)
vic. *vicecom*(*es*)
viz. *videlicet*
voc. vocative
vol. volume
vulg. vulgar(ly)

W. Wales, Welsh
w. with
wr. written

A query (?) indicates doubt, usually as to the meaning or date assigned to a word.

An obelisk (†) indicates a suspicion (sometimes amounting to certainty) that the form of a particular word is due to a misprint, a misreading, or a scribal error, or that a date is erroneous.

Square brackets [ ] are used to indicate explanatory insertions, usually by the editor of the Dictionary.

The signs < and > are used in etymologies to mean respectively 'derived from' and 'developing into'.

The signs ʒ and ℥ in medical texts represent respectively *drachma* and *uncia*.

A

1 A [CL], A (letter of alphabet). **b** (musical note).

addidit episcopus nomina litterarum: "dicito A"; dixit ille "A" BEDE *HE* V 2; accusativae praepositiones solae quae in A exeunt producuntur, ut 'intrā' *Id. AM* 2363; Ā ante F breviatur, ut 'colăfus' BACON *Tert.* 258. **b** cum.. inter ipsam A et B rotundam sit semitonium TUNST. 215A.

2 a, ah [CL], ah (interj.).

a Gisleberte, prudens pater, abba diserte R. CANT. *Poems* 259; in..interjectionibus indignandi 'vah', 'ah' BACON *CSPhil.* 510.

3 a, ab [*as in CL, but often replaced by* de *or* per; *for use w. adv.* v. et. abante, abhinc, abinde, abintus, abinvicem, abolim, abundique, adesuper, aforis, aliunde 2, amodo, aretro].

1 from (in space: expr. **a** position at a distance; **b** motion; **c** withdrawal, taking or sending away; **d** view-point; **e** starting-point or basis of reckoning; **f** place of origin, used in descriptive title).

a non longe ab Eburaco ad orientem BEDE *HE* II 13; ad flumen..a quo..remotus manserat duarum spatio leucarum J. SAL. *Ep.* 246. 289B; distantibus a se [*from one another*] virgis..pedis..spatio *Dial. Scac.* I 1A; ad urbem.. per milia passuum quasi xij a Banua distantem GIR. *EH* I 3; a longe sedit O. CHERITON *Fab.* 25. **b** superis tranavit ab astris ALDH. *VirgV* 1723; domum redire..a loco BEDE *HE* III 26; s**793** pagani ab aquilonali climate..Britanniam venientes S. DURH. *Durh.* II 5; quasi ab adverso pectentes J. SAL. *Met.* 877A; nonnulli qui..a Dermitio discesserant GIR. *EH* I 3; ab aliunde venisse comperiri non potuit *Id. GE* II 18; cum..illa [sc. aqua] super membrum cadit ab alto *SB* 19; a dicto castro suo..ad mare descendit ELMH. *Hen. V* 13. **c** quem Deus a nostri detrudat pectoris antro ALDH. *VirgV* 2865; si me..ejicere proponit a facie clementie sue AD. SCOT. *Serm.* 434 (v. et. facies); **1194** sanguinem a capite suo extraxerunt *CurR RC* I 66 (cf. *State Tri. Ed. I* 26); c**1238** mentis..ab inutilibus cogitationibus segregatio GROS. *Ep.* 57 p. 175; justiciarius.. transmissus a latere regis BRACTON 182; **1309** [confuge], dum in ea [sc. ecclesia]..consistunt, ab intra per potenciam laicalem subtrahuntur *Reg. Cant.* II 1023; **1319** J. abscondit se a cariagio domini *CBaron* 129; **1328** ..omnes.. ab undique locorum..convocare J. MASON *Ep.* 60; secreta temptatio quam emittit a longe *AncrR* 92. **d** ut [puppes] ..flammeae..viderentur a longe aspicientibus *Enc. Emmae* II 4; s**1333** ut ab extra [v.l. extraneis] adjutorium exspectarent AD. MUR. 67; aliquem quem video a remotis OCKHAM *Dial.* 434; arbores..fructum faciunt vel occultum vel manifestum, cum tamen ab homine sit celatum *Eul. Hist.* I 10. **e** **1241** unum capud [stabuli] sit a porta versus austrum *Liberate* 15 m. 8; **1285** homines..a civitate Caturci supra [*upstream*] *RGasc* II 262; **1477** pro nova construccione unius turris..a fundamentis *Ac. Durh.* III 646; a majore usque ad minorem mutua cede..totum regnum turbatum est *Plusc.* IX 29; armati penitus a vertice ad plantas [*cap à pie*] MAP *NC* I 29; novam a capite (quod dici solet) ad pedes..contexat historiam FERR. *Kinloss* 9. **f** Waleranius ab Effria miles erat illiteratus MAP *NC* V 5 (cf. ib. V 6: Adam a Gernemue sigillator); praetorio ducis a Norfolkia CHAUNCY *Passio* 118; cepi contexere historiam abbatum a Kynlos FERR. *Kinloss* 10.

2 from (in time: expr. **a** immediacy; **b** start of indeterminate period; **c** start of determinate period; **d** point from which a later date is reckoned; **e** start of period leading up to the present; **f** start of period extending into the future).

a celi dispositio fuit optima a principio BACON *Min.* 374; a**1380** quotidie a tempore [? = *betimes*] ingressus *Pri. Cold.* 54; ab ipsa ejus [Kenelmi] spelunca a repente [*of a sudden*] fons emersit CIREN. I 313. **b** **1456** a tempore in tempus (*Billa Parl.*) *Reg. Whet.* I 260. **c** a festivitate S. Michaelis usque ad festum S. Andree *DB* I 1; **1254** ab..instanti festo Omnium Sanctorum ad annum continuum *RGasc* I 548; **1272** debent..sectam ad curiam..a tribus septimanis in tres septimanas [*every 3 weeks*] *Cl* 510. **d** **1196** dies datus est eis a die Pasche in xv dies [*on the quinzaine of Easter*] *CurR* I 15; **1257** quod erit coram baronibus..a die S. Michaelis in unum mensem *Cl* 89. **e** a prima etate annisque pueritie GIR. *TH* III 48; **11..** a puero [= a puerili etate] in ipsa patria educati fuimus *Feod. Durh.* lxiii; **1202** ipse et antecessores sui illas [consuetudines] ceperunt a conquestu Anglie *SelPlCrown* 21; c**1250** domos in quibus scole esse consueverunt a decennio et infra nullus ad inhabitandum conducat *Stat. Cantab.* 213; **1265** cum.. predecessores sui ab antiquo [sc. tempore) percipere consueverint..j quadrantem *Cl* 75; **1276** a tempore a quo non extat memoria *Hund.* II 132; **1299** nesciunt a quo tempore *SelPlForest* 117; **1310** a xx annis citra [*for the last 20 years*] quolibet anno fuit in capitulo *Conc.* II 356; non videtur talis translatio fuisse facta a D annis et citra OCKHAM *Pol.* I 90; quod..scire a multis temporibus affectavi *Id. Dial.* 589; **1333** a jam diu, videlicet ab anno *LTRMem* 105 *rec.* r. 33; Scoti..ligancie regis Francie a diu astricti AD. MUR. *app.* 252; **1380** pro quibusdam..negociis inter nos et dictum consanguineum nostrum a diu est [cf. *il y a longtemps*] habitis (*TreatyR*) *Foed.* VII 254. **f** c**1250** quo die..ab hucusque in feriam secundam..prorogatum est negocium AD. MARSH *Ep.* 192; rex concessit..omnem servilem condicionem..de regno a cetero extirpari AD. USK 2.

3 from (of rank or condition: expr. **a** distance; **b** change).

a sit secundus ab episcopo, sc. major persona post episcopum in episcopatu *Feod. Durh.* 212. **b** s**1011** ab archiepiscopo..martyrem gloriosum efficiens M. PAR. *Maj.* I 483; quod alteretur vinum a suis naturalibus saporibus *Cust. Westm.* 216.

4 (apart) from, without (**a** w. word expr. deprivation, exemption, prohibition, etc.; **b** (?) absol.).

a terra vastata est a pecunia *DB* I 14; concessit iii hidas ex his quietas a geldo *Ib.* 170; liberi et quieti sunt ab omni exercitu (*Lib. Lond.*) *GAS* 675; a**1216** vendidi et dimisi et.. quietam clamavi a me et ab heredibus meis..quandam soppam *AncD* A 2722; **1267** cum contigerit..Johannem.. ab eadem terra abjudicari *Cl* 373; voluit predicta esse excipienda a potestate quam..indulsit Petro OCKHAM *Pol.* I 37; **1296** contra..proclamacionem a cariorando forum *Leet Norw.* 47. **b** c**1237** si quis ab infirmitatis causa.. murmurare presumpserit *Ann. Durh.* 100.

5 (different) from, (other) than (**a** w. word expr. distinction; **b** w. *alius*; **c** w. compar.; **d** absol. w. *re* = irrelevant [CL]).

a habet personas ratione..officiorum a se distinctas *Dial. Scac.* I 3A; nec pars a toto tanta generis diversitate distare consuevit GIR. *TH* I 26; eo quod a..civitate Gallie dicta Meldis nomine tenus differretur *Meaux* I 78. **b** **1233** tenementum aliud ab eo unde assisa arramiata est *BNB* II 599; in scripturis aliis a biblia OCKHAM *Dial.* 843. **c** femina que..paulo minor a regina habebatur AILR. *Ed. Conf.* 783B; sagum est undecimum, quod nimirum et a cortinis amplius est, quia ille non sunt nisi decem AD. SCOT. *TT* 648C. **d** nec ab re est unum..enarrare BEDE *HE* III 2.

6 (sought, received or derived) from (a source: w. ref. to **a** a personal donor, informant or sim.; **b** a feudal overlord; **c** an ancestor; **d** a word (etym.); **e** a material source; **f** a foregoing event, cause or originator; **g** a logical ground [? *sc. argumento; v. et. locus, posterior, prior*]).

a quamlibet a nullo solandi verba capessat ALDH. *VirgV* 2050; rex habet omne servitium ab eis *DB* I 4b; **1221** serviens cepit mercedem a quibusdam *SelPlCrown* 110; perquirens..a quodam eorum comite didicit..R. COLD. *Cuthb.* 38; s**1274** rex petiit licentiam a civibus..transfretandi *Leg. Ant. Lond.* 9. **b** civitas Cantuaria, quam Lanfrancus in beneficio a rege tenebat EADMER *HN* 43. **c** ex descendentibus secum ab eodem Philippo WALS. *HA* I 202. **d** dicitur apozima ab *apos* quod est 'decoccio' et *zeo* quod est 'ferveo' *SB* 11. **e** phenix..ingentes ab aromate jungit acervos *V. Merl.* 1348; epilencia est morbus caducus a cerebro *SB* 19. **f** episcopus..a constitutione antiquorum temporum habet omnes redditiones socharum *DB* I 172b; Pater a nullo habet essentiam nisi a seipso ANSELM (*Mon.* 45) I 61; in hiis que sunt a casu vel a nobis, non est voluntas Dei causa antecedens per intentionem, ut velit hoc esse vel illud a sua scilicet voluntate immediate, sed vult hoc a nostra voluntate vel a casu fieri GROS. 198; **1264** cum..per maris intemperiem a casu applicuerint apud E. *Cl* 81; s**1307** eum ab insolentiis, quibus nimis indulsit, facete corripuit TROKELOWE 63; ut hos laudes ab experientia cognitioneque multiplici, illos autem vituperes ab ignoratione FERR. *Kinloss* 8. **g** sponte manans ex myrrha sudor pretiosior est; ..a simili videtur quod disciplina spontanea pluris sit quam injuncta NECKAM *NR* II 69; reges xlviij.., e quibus a verisimili plures vi et armis quam sanguine successerunt OTTERB. 8; **1412** a probabili videtur quod.. *Conc.* III 349; **1413** quod ecclesie Dei est Cesari non debetur; ..a majori ergo..temporalibus viris tradenda non est Christi hereditas *Ib.* 361; potestas regis Francorum distincta est a potestate Pape; et per consequens a fortiori potestas Imperatoris OCKHAM *Dial.* 903.

7 by (**a** agent [replaced by *per* in common usage after *c.*1100]; **b** instrument).

a non tulit opprobrium judex a virgine factum ALDH. *VirgV* 2050; libentissime ab omnibus suscipiebatur BEDE *HE* IV 2; credo non a te sed †pro [v.l. per] te dicta esse quae scripseras: revera per os tuum locutus est Ille LANFR. *Ep.* 61 (cf. *Scala Cronica* 222); summa natura nullatenus est per aliud..; quare summa natura nec a se nec ab alio fieri potuit ANSELM (*Mon.* 6) I 19; ab eisdem [Danis] patria deturbatus W. MALM. *GR* I 96; cum ab officialibus.. extorquetur pecunia a subditis GIR. *GE* II 32; s**1310** archiepiscopus..a clero [*at the instance of the clergy*] sentenciam excommunicacionis..promulgavit TROKELOWE 67. **b** s**1174** Flandrenses a suorum interemptione deterriti DICETO *YH* I 393; rex..a W. Tyrel..a sagitta percussus *Flor. Hist.* II 33; **1207** pro habendo..bosco..a vento prostrato *Pipe* 177; corrosio dentium causatur ab humore putrido GAD. 119 v. 2; **1397** omne quod est natum stat ab hoc vitio vitiatum GOWER *VP* 126; vexati sunt a tribulacione malorum et dolore ELMH. *Cant.* 220.

8 at, on the side or in the direction of. **b** (w. ref. to an official w. specific duties).

sacrum scripture theologice tectum a superiori concludere et sic edificium..stabilire GIR. *RG* II 1; Hispaniam ab austro..collateralem habet *Id. TH* I 1; pomarium..juxta ecclesiam..a parte aquilonali *Chr. Battle* 19; **1240** quotiens ..vitreolas a toto vel a parte reparaverint *DC Chich.* (*HMC*) I 193; effracto a latere sepulcro M. PAR. *Maj.* I 303; **1311** habebat duos capellanos..sibi assidentes unum a dextris et alium a sinistris *Conc.* II 384; **1511** privilegia.. concessa civitati..ejusque territorio et maneriis ab extra *Ib.* III 653. **b** †**970** (12c) a secretis noster Athelwulfus *CS* 1266; [rex] ponit eum [Godwinum] sibi a secretis *V. Ed. Conf.* 38 v.; habebat..rex Henricus episcopum Salesbiriensem Rogerum a secretis W. MALM. *GR* V 408; ut ejus fieret assecretis *Becket Mat.* IV 84; *a cownselour*, ..consul, .. assecretis indecl. *CathA*; **1550** Christianissimi regis consiliarius et status regni a secretis (*DipDoc* E 1058) *Foed.* XV 231; abatis, *fætfellere* ÆLF. *Gl.* (*cf.* 3 batus 2); *buttelere*, pincerna, ..†acalis [? l. a calicibus] *PP*; *a butler*, †acalicus indecl., †acellarius [l. a cellariis], pincerna *CathA*; *a lawyour*, ..aresponsis indecl., ..*a pleter*, actor, advocatus, arisponsis *Ib.*; si a consiliis fueris..alicui principi MORE *Ut.* 37 (cf. ib. 38: quicunque regibus a consilio sunt); **1553** in re medica nobis intime a consiliis *CalPat* V 197; **1550** ordinis S. Michaelis ab actis seu grapharius (*DipDoc* E 1058) *Foed.* XV 231; his proximi fuere armigeri, qui..quia principibus et majoribus illis ab armis erant nomen traxerunt CAMD. *Br.* 140.

9 (in comp.) from, away (rare in new formations, *e.g. abaequare, abcariare, abexcommunicatus*; occ. conf. w. *ad*, as *abminiculum*, or *ob*, as *abaudire, abstuppare*).

aab [Heb.], a Jewish month.

quintus [Hebraeorum mensis] aab Augusto..comparatur BEDE *TR* 11 p. 203.

aaron v. arum. aatia v. atia. abacia v. abbatia.

abacista, calculator.

[Gerbertus] abacum..primus a Saracenis rapiens regulas dedit que a sudantibus ~is vix intelliguntur W. MALM. *GR* II 167 (cf. *Meaux* I 268).

abactio, removal.

[filius virginis] suorum..~one fidelium nulla intercapedine separatur H. LOS. *Ep.* 6 p. 12.

abactor, a cattle-thief. **b** drover.

a ne..~ores [*gl.*: fures pecorum]..subintrent curiam et armenta abducant NECKAM *Ut.* 111. **b** *a drywer of nawte*, ~or, armentarius *CathA*.

abacula, cloth for sideboard.

1551 una ~a de *dyaper* vocata *a cubberd cloth Pat* 840 m. 15.

abacus [CL < ἄβαξ], 'cupboard', clothes-press or sideboard.

cupborde, ~us *PP*; **1501** item ij †apocus, quorum unus altero et antiquior et minus prestancior est *Cant. Coll. Ox.* I 37; pro..vestibus..duos ~os—vulgo conservatoria nuncupantur FERR. *Kinloss* 76; **1551** de..uno veteri ~o bene juncto vocato *a cubberde*, ..uno stante ~o *Pat* 840 m. 14; **1553** de..uno conjuncto ~o, Anglice *one joyned cubborde Ib.* 852 m. 29.

2 reckoning-board, abacus. **b** (in word play) soulless calculator.

si quid in digitis et articulis ~i numeralibus ex multiplicatione creverit ADEL. *ED* 11; a manibus Grecorum ~us nondum excidit J. SAL. *Pol.* 399B; [Girbertus] docens astronomiam et ~um atque nigromantiam discipulos nobiles habuit R. NIGER II 154. **b** c**1200** abbas factus de monacho non erit ultra monachus; / assumitur pro monacho negociator abbacus (*Carmen contra avariciam abbatum* 64) *EHR* V 322.

abaequare, to make unequal.

alii..exercent fenebrem pecuniam, alternis vicibus inequalia rotundantes et adjectione multiplici quod rotundaverant ~antes J. SAL. *Met.* 831C.

abaia, ~um [cf. 2 baia], bay (of mill-pond).

1235 cum pratum esset superinundatum per aquam, ..[fecerunt] quandam abayam longitudinis xxxij pedum *CurR* XV 1437; **1283** molendinum..abbatis Westm' in Amwell' et stagnum et abbayum dicti molendini *Pat* 102 m. 4*d*.

abalienare, to alienate, part with.

milites..ejus vestimenta..sortitione ~arunt BELETH *RDO* 104. 109; **1281** procuratorem omnia..ad ecclesiam nostram..pertinencia, si qua..minus juste fuerint ~ata, repetendi *Reg. Heref.* 297; **14..** [reges Danorum] multa jura..a corona regni hujus ~averunt *MGL* II 633.

2 to estrange.

qui..matri [sc. ecclesie] satisfaciendo non auscultat, genitricis gremio obstinacie culpa se ~at PULL. *Sent.* 899B; **s1165** rex Anglorum..se ab Alexandro papa..~avit W. CANT. *V. Thom.* I 43; qua..~atos auditorum pedetemptim subiret animos T. MON. *Will.* II 14 p. 103.

abalienatio, estrangement.

s1165 ~io regis et imperatoris..ab Alexandro W. CANT. *V. Thom.* I 43 *rub.*

abalternatim v. subalternatim.

abamita, (paternal) great-great-great-aunt. **b** great-aunt.

~a mea, *minre fapan pridde moder* ÆLF. *Sup.*; fratres abavi vel abavie, qui dicuntur abpatruus magnus et ~a magna BRACTON 68b. **b** hec ~a, soror avi WW.

abandare, ~atio, v. abaud-.

abandonare [OF *abandoner*], to abandon, surrender.

1258 noverit universitas vestra me obligasse et ~asse.. Johanni..omnia bona mea..*Deeds Balliol* 325.

abante [cf. OF *avant*], before (adv.), formerly. **b** before (prep.).

1397 vertit et econtra quicquid ab ante tulit GOWER *VP* 160; hec et plura ferox rabies, que nullus ab ante / viderat, insolita fecit in urbe mala GOWER *VC* I 1355; **c1440** ea que..pro magnificatione ipsius ab ante fecimus BEKYNTON I 102; **1464** quem equum..dominus W. ~e namavit *Reg. Aberbr.* II 140. **b** comes ab ante diem armatus ierat Londoniam capere DEVIZES 36.

†abarath [Ar. *al-bārūq*], white lead.

~ath, i. cerusa *SB* 10.

abarnare [?], to reveal, denounce.

si homo furtivum aliquid in domo sua occultabit et ita fuerit ~atus [AS: *arasod*], rectum est ut habeat quod quesivit (*Quad.*) *GAS* 363; si Francigena qui parentes non habeat in murdro perimatur, habeat precium natalis ejus qui murdrum ~averit (*Leg. Hen.*) *Ib.* 592.

abaso [a basso; cf. bassus 1 b], ground floor. **b** (? by conf. due to *f.l.*) infirmary.

~o, infima domus *GlC* A 18. **b** †abaro [*Erf.* 2. 259. 2: ~o], infirma domus *Ib.* 31; ~o, infirmatorium, *seocera manna hus* ÆLF. *Sup.*

abastardare [cf. OF *abastardir*], to bastardize, declare illegitimate.

1199 pro habendo recordo loquele sue quam habuit versus Hamonem de Masci juniorem, qui ~atus est in curia Christianitatis *Pipe* 152; **1202** ei voluit malum, quia non potuit eum ~are *SelPlCrown* 25.

abastergere v. abstergere.

abatamentum, abatement, unlawful entry.

13.. in placito terre et tenementi quod placitetur in civitate..quasi ad modum nove disseisine per vim friscam recenter factam, ..ille qui hujusmodi hamsoken et abatiamentum fecit in hac parte attachietur ad respondendum querelanti (*Cust.* c. 17) *Rec. Norw.* I 153; **1365** pro falso clamore versus J. H. in quodam abatiamento *CourtRWinchester*; **1414** perdonavimus..omnimoda ingressus, intrusiones, ~a..in et de maneriis de Balythermot [etc.] (*Pat. Hib. Hen. V*) *RSelecti* 41.

abatare [OF *abatre*], to abate, annul.

1513 ~atur hic *BBWinchester* f. 48 (in margin).

2 to abate, enter unlawfully on a freehold (*cf.* OF *enbatre*).

1539 immediate post decessum predicti R. P. ..in predictum tenementum..abbatavit, intravit et intrusit super possessionem domini manerii predicti *Entries* 132b.

abatatio, abatement, annulment.

1413 pro abbatacione et cassacione brevis assise *BBWinchester* f. 20.

abathia, v. abbatia. abatiamentum v. abatamentum. abatissa v. abbatissa.

abaudare [cf. OF *baud* < baldus], to train (hounds).

1237 quod commodet canes suos ad currendum cum canibus regis quousque ipsi fuerint †abandati *Cl* 2; **1238** ad currendum..cum canibus regis ad brokettos et ad canes regis †abandandos *Ib.* 44.

abaudatio, encouragement, instigation.

1352 noluit deservire nisi ad voluntatem propriam per †abandacionem predicti Thome (*Anc. Indict. Suff.* 114) *Enf. Stat. Lab.* 410.

abaudire v. obaudire.

abavia [CL], great-great-grandmother. **b** great-grandmother.

~ia, *feowerþe moder* ÆLF. *Sup.*; tunc vocantur fratres abavi vel ~ie BRACTON 68b. **b** hec abava, *the secunde fro the modyr* WW

abavunculus, (maternal) great-great-great-'uncle'.

~us meus, *mines eames pridde fæder* ÆLF. *Sup.*; sic gradatim vocandi sunt ~us magnus et abmatertera magna BRACTON 68b.

abavus [CL], great-great-grandfather.

~us, id est avi avus *GlC* A 25; ~us, *feowerþe fæder* ÆLF. *Sup.*; **955** (12c) ~o meo rege, videlicet Aelfredo *CS* 906; **12..** Auketinus ~us meus *ChartR* 80 m. 6; BRACTON 68b (v. abavia).

abaya v. abaia. abbadissa v. abbatissa.

abbas, ~a [ἀββας < Heb.], abbot, head of monastery. **b** apt title for bishop.

a680 Aldelmus..~atis officio functus ALDH. *Ep.* 4 p. 481; reverentissimus ~a Ceolfrid BEDE *HE* V 21; eidem monasterio Segendi ~as et presbyter praefuit *Ib.* III 5; **747** ut episcopi in suis parochiis ~ates atque abbatissas moneant quatenus..ut praepositi praepositeque monasteriorum curam sibi injunctam..fideliter †dispensant [? l. dispensent] *Conc.* HS 364; decreverunt ut ~atum et abbatissarum electio cum regis consensu..sanctae regulae ageretur documento *RegulC proem.* 9; **10..** ~as, *abbod, oððe fæder* WW; abbas cum eligitur, omnes fratres, vel major et melior pars, in ejus electionem consentire debent LANFR. *Const.* 140; ex his habet..T. homo ~atis S. E[dmundi] j domum, ..~as de Eli j mansura[m] *DB* II 117; **1100** nec mortuo..episcopo sive ~ate aliquid accipiam de dominio ecclesie..donec successor in eam ingrediatur (*Ch. Hen. I*) *GAS* 521; **c1101** super animas, propter quas -as et dicitur et constituitur, nemo quemquam potest constituere nisi quibus Deus dedit potestatem ligandi atque solvendi ANSELM (*Ep.* 251) IV 162; **c1128** ita..ut ~as et monachi ejusdem ecclesie a quocunque episcopo voluerint..crisma suum et oleum et ordinationem ipsius ~atis et monachorum..accipiant (*Kelso*) *E. Ch. Scot.* 82; a Gisleberte, prudens pater, abba diserte R. CANT. *Poems* 259; quid amplius in monachum artioris regule dictasset ~as severus? J. SAL. *Pol.* 605C; lex ligat abbatis monachorum colla, sed ipsum / immunem legis lex jubet esse sue (R. PARTES) *Speculum* XII 237; hec ecclesia, sicut et alie per Hiberniam et Walliam plures, ~atem laicum habet GIR. *IK* II 4; **1206** ~as duobus capellanis monachis, uno advocato, uno notario et x servientibus preter pueros ad servicium ejus necessarios..sit contentus (*Vis. York*) *EHR* XLVI 450; **s1218** convenerunt primo ~ates nigri apud Oxoniam *Meaux* I 400; **s1235** primus erat in ~atem futurus electus post consilium Lateranense generale..in quo constitutum erat ut ~ates exempti ab ipso Papa confirmarentur *G. S. Alb.* I 307 (cf. M. PAR. *Maj.* III 308); **12..** ~ates induantur in superpelliciis et cappis, mitrati cum mitris *Conc. Scot.* II 4; ~as tenetur ex officio in festis principalibus ..vesperas..celebrare; et erit in hujusmodi vesperis solempniter revestitus, sc. in alba, capa, mitra, cirothecis et anulo, cum baculo pastorali *Cust. Cant.* 45; **s1379** comites [solverent] sex marcas, episcopi quoque et ~ates mitrati tantum, non obstante quod ~ates tenerentur solvere pro singulis capitibus monachorum suorum xl d. WALS. *HA* I 392; hic ~as, *a abotte* WW; verba minus Latina, longo usu.. jampridem in consuetudinem quotidiani sermonis venisse.. item ~as, prior, pro monachorum praefecto P. VERG. (*Camd.*) 336. **b** quamvis et ipsi antistites, si paternam curam..subjectis suis impendant, non absurde ~ates.. appellari queant LANFR. *Const.* 86.

2 abbot of misrule ('Mar-all', 'Mayfool' etc.) in Mayday revels.

1521 pro expensis factis super Ricardum Glasyer ~atem de Marham, pro honestate et jocunditate ville (*Acc.*) *Hist. Shrewsb.* I 332 (cf. ib.: ~as de Mayvole [**1542**], ~as de Marall [**1547**]).

abbatare, to hold the office of abbot.

c1198 cum sacerdotibus / depilant vertices / et in abbatibus / abbatant simplices (*Contra pontifices pilatisantes*) *EHR* V 323.

abbatatio v. abatatio.

abbatatus, abbacy, dignity or office of abbot.

†c700 praesul..ex apostolici pontificis auctoritate orationem ei ~us attribuat (*Priv. Pap.*, *CS* 105) W. MALM. *GP* V 221; **†705** ego Aldhelmus..proposui..ut monasteriis meis, quibus jamdudum in ~us gradu constitutus..praefui, ..abbatem..constituerem (*CS* 114) *Ib.* 225; singuli singulis possessionibus, ..archiepiscopatibus, episcopatibus, ~ibus [ab Arthuro] donantur *Eul. Hist.* II 329; **s1197** Thomas abbas, ..accito patre abbate de Fontibus, officium abbatiatus ei resignavit *Meaux* I 234.

abbatessa v. abbatissa. abbathanus v. abthanus.

abbatia, a abbacy, dignity or office of abbot w. its emoluments. **b** (collect.) body of abbots. **c** abbey, religious house under rule of abbot or abbess, w. its possessions. **d** (fig.). **e** 'abthain', abbey estate (Sc.) (*cf.* abthania).

a c1087 Baldewyno abbati ~iam suam..pleniter habere concedo (*Ch. Will. II*) *Regesta* 131; Stigandus,..publicas nundinas ex episcopatibus et ~iis faciens, multas ~ias solus ipse possidebat W. MALM. *GP* I 23; cum ambitiosus quidam monachus ad ~iam quam preemerat vocaretur et.. modestiam simulans..recusaret honorem J. SAL. *Pol.* 679C; dans sorori ~iam sanctimonialium, "esto" ait "abbatissa" R. NIGER II 159; **s1258** dominus W. de Pontisara resignavit abbaciam Cluniacensem (*Chr. Clun.*) *EHR* XLIV 100; **1265** Jacobum ut abbatem predictum in abbacia ejusdem per deliberationem biblie et clavium ecclesie dicti monasterii instituit *Inchaffray* 164; **s1283** vacavit ~ia..usque in xx diem Junii.., antequam [rex] liberaret temporalia fratri W...in abbatem..electo et consecrato FLETE *Westm.* 116. **b c748** tota ~ia cum omni congregationi (*sic*) servorum Dei in nostra provincia (ÆLBWALD) *Ep. Bonif.* 81. **c** ipse abbas tenet C.; T.R.E. tenuit ~ia *DB* I 17; Bucfestre est caput ~iae *Ib.* 104; **s1135** reliquie regalis cadaveris..sepulte sunt..apud ~iam Redinges quam rex Henricus fundaverat H. HUNT. *HA* VIII 2; **s1136** cum..revertens ad villas ~ie jam venisset, ..accesserunt ad eum barones, milites et liberi homines fere totius ~ie *Chr. Rams.* 328; **1153** nos dedisse..~iam de insula Lochlevene..ad canonicos regulares constituendum in ea (*Reg. S. Andr.*) *E. Ch. Scot.* 263; **c1177** rex..voverat quod..~iam quandam canonicorum regularium edificaret in remissionem peccatorum suorum *G. Hen. II* I 134; **1189** ut prefata ~ia [de Godestowe] in perpetuum libera et in capite de corona nostra sit, sicut ~ia S. Edmundi et alie ~ie regales que per Angliam sunt constitute (*Ch. Ric. I*) *MonA* IV 364; duas domos canonicas fecit, unam de canonicis nigris, ..altera[m] vero de canonicis albis..et ~ias ambas redditibus amplis tam in ecclesiis quam in terris, abunde dotavit GIR. *Spec.* III 19 p. 245; **a1240** acram quam..dedit abacie de Caldra *Reg. S. Bees* 280; perrexit per ~ias ad probandum statum monachorum ECCLESTON *Adv. Min.* 78; **c1262** Reynham appropriata abbathie de Lesnes *Val. Norw.* 334; **c1300** cum subeunt hospitium / cujusdam patriote / vel abbathie note, / quo potus et cibaria / et cuncta necessaria / eis dentur devote *Pol. Songs* 229; **1346** ad quandam abathiam (*Lit. Confessoris Regis*) AD. MUR. 213; **1349** minorisse ordinis abbacie minorissarum extra Algate London' *IPM* 106/17; **s1418** ~iam validissimam in montis S. Katerine fastigiis situatam..antesedit ELMH. *Hen. V Cont.* 124; hec abathia, *a nabbay* WW. **d** W. comes Pictavorum.., habitacula quedam quasi monasteriola construens, ~iam pellicum ibi se positurum delirabat, nuncupatim illam et illam..abbatissam vel priorissam..instituturum cantitans W. MALM. *GR* V 439. **e a1160** donum in abbacia de Rossim cum appenticiis suis *Regesta Scot.* 120; **c1200** totam terram illam de Madernin que antiquitus abbacia vocabatur *Inchaffray* 11 (cf. ib. 19: terra illa de Madernin que antiquitus *abbethen* vocabatur).

abbatialis, pertaining to an abbot (or abbess).

1349 eidem abbatesse, quam dicte relique moniales in dicto monasterio de Watrebech elegerunt, execucionem et administracionem ~is regiminis interdices *Reg. Heref.* 152; **1460** licet..Calistus Papa III..incorporaciones de quibusdam beneficiis ecclesiasticis quibusvis aliis beneficiis seu episcopalibus, capitularibus vel ~ibus mensis..annullasset *Mon. Hib. & Scot.* 427 (cf. *Conc. Scot.* II 94); **s1477** inter que [edificia] supereminent..ad..gloriam curie ~is camere ille solennes *Croyl. Cont. C* 560; **1525** (v. abbatissalis).

abbatiare v. abbatizare. abbatiatus v. abbatatus.

†abbaticia [? *for* abbacia], abbey.

1205 de placito ~ie fundate *CurR* III 142.

abbatissa, abbess. **b** girl 'abbess' (at Christmas festival).

c720 Eangyth indigna ancilla ancillarum Dei et nomine ~ae sine merito functa (EANGYTH) *Ep. Bonif.* 14; facta est ~a in monasterio BEDE *HE* IV 23; **786** sorori tuae Seleðryðe abbadisse *CS* 248; obiit Hild ~a famula Christi ÆTHELW. II 8; ~a de Ambresberie *DB* I 56; **s1160** Maria ~a de Rumesie nupsit comiti Matheo DICETO *YH* 303; moribus et gestis fuit abbatissa venustis NIG. *Mir. BVM* f. 22v; **c1240** abbates et ~e, ..postquam eorum electio canonice fuerit confirmata, extra cathedralem ecclesiam cui obedientiam..benedictionis tempore..tenentur repromittere, munus benedictionis decetero non accipiant *Conc. Syn.* 384; **1268** ~a et priorissa..monasteria non exeant nisi ex evidenti monasterii utilitate *Ib.* 791; **1349** eidem abbatesse (v. abbatialis); **1370** scriptum factum..~e Minorissarum extra Algate (*LBLond* G 255) *MGL* I 554; **1430** rex..~e et conventui de Berkyng (*Pat.*) *MonA* I 441; hec ~a, A. *a abatyse*, ..*a abeyse* WW. **b 1526** habent in festo Natalis Domini juniorem monialem in ~am assumptam †vocandi [? l. jocandi] gratia *Vis. Norw.* 209.

abbatissalis, pertaining to an abbess.

1525 nominibus ac dignitatibus abbatialibus et ~ibus seu aliarum dignitatum..suppressis et extinctis necnon.. monacorum sive monialium..personis ad alia..loca religiosa translatis (*Pat*) *Foed.* XIV 32 (cf. ib. 24).

abbatizare, to hold the office of abbot.

illuc ~ante Uvio sub monachili constitutione constituto primo HERM. ARCH. 17; **s1132** tresdecim monachi egressi sunt de cenobio B. Marie Eboraci, ..abbates septem; reliqui vero quinque monachi non †abbatiantes [v.l. abbatizantes] obierunt *Meaux* I 74 (= *MonA* V 390); **s1223** obiit Willelmus abbas Glastonie et successit ei prior Bathonie; iste Willelmus primus ~avit ibidem *Ann. Wav.* 299; jam ~ante Thoma [1349–96] *G. S. Alb.* III 101.

†abbatus [? *for* abbatatus], abbey.

c1243 sacci predicti fuerunt de ~u de Maunevic qui est in Anglia (*CurR* 125, *in sched.*) *Law Merch.* II p. lxxxvi; **14..** *Entries* 346.

abbayum v. abaia. abbestus v. asbestos. abbet- v. abet-.

†abbita [? *for* allica, cf. allec], a kind of fish.

14.. lucius et perca, saxacilus, abbita, truta (*Versus de Dieta*) *EETS* XXXII pt. ii, 56.

abblandiri, to flatter, be pleasing.

occultos cordis motus vanitate caliginosos sibi adblandiri super subtilitate sapientie AD. SCOT. *Serm.* 332A; usque adeo assentantes ei ut parasiti quoque ejus inventis, quae dominus per jocum non aspernabatur, adblandirentur MORE *Ut.* 78; mihi coeperunt adblandiri [versus mei] postquam eos video multis commendari (*Id. Ep.*) *Ep. Erasmi* IV 1096.

abbregiare, ~ere [OF *abreger* < abbreviare], to shorten, expedite. **b** to lessen, relieve.

1276 clericus coronatoris..cepit..pro negociis domini regis abbregendis x sol. *Hund.* II 104. **b a1309** lego..

communitati Lenne iiij li. ad abregiand' talliacionem pauperum Lenne *RR K's Lynn* I 4.

abbreviamentum, a diminution. **b** abridgement, epitome.

a 1581 ad extremum decasum mercatorum et ad magnum nocumentum et abreviamentum custume nostre (*Pat*) *Gild Merch.* II 281. **b 1499** ~um statutorum *Treat. J. P.* 44.

2 account, record of expenses (*cf. breviare* 2).

1391 ut patet per rotulos de ~o factos per dietas *Ac. H. Derby* 102

abbreviare, a to shorten (in space). **b** to shorten (in time), expedite. **c** to reduce (in amount). **d** to abridge (writings).

a sicut..res quarum usus est frequens modicam quantitatem et ~iatam recipiunt, ut eis aptius uti liceat, sic est de sermonibus Bacon XV 175; **c1520** crinibus decenter ~iatis *Conc. Scot.* I cclxx. **b 1215** ut assise de nova dissaisina et de morte antecessoris ~ientur (*Artic. Baronum* 13) *SelCh.* 287 (cf. *EHR* XXXV 401); **1230** propter lapsum vj mensium dies abreviandi sunt ex causa *BNB* II 352; **s1096** supplicat ut tutor Normannie..terminos non ~iaret M. Par. *Min.* I 76; **s1223** Deo vindice ~iati sunt dies ejus *Ib.* II 259; abbreviant magis arma brevem funebria vitam Garl. *Tri. Eccl.* 60; est..possibilis..magna prolongatio vite; sed nunc ~iata est ultra modum Bacon *Min.* 374; quod dilationes in placitis amputentur et ~ientur *Fleta* 215; si..conventus..tardius ad matutinas surrexerit, ita quod..aliquid de obsequio divino ob hanc causam abrevietur *Cust. Cant.* 117; **s1399** miserat..rex occulte..ut dies ejus [ducis Gloucestrie] sine sanguinis effusione ~iarent *V. Ric. II* 161; circiter octo dietas..abreviavimus iter nostrum Elmh. *Hen. V* 44. **c** consummatio ~iata †mandavit justitiam Lanfr. *Comment. Paul.* (*Rom.* ix 28) 138 (cf. *Is.* x 22); **1213** magna custodia debet invenire xij homines; sed per libitum vicecomitis ~iata est usque ad viij homines (*De excubiis*) *Comm. Lond.* 255; **1362** custumam xx s. ..usque ad j m. duximus abreviandam *RScot* 867a; **s1456** res regie..per..prodigam regis largicionem.. ~iate..ac diminute *Reg. Whet.* I 249; predicta A. ~iavit demandam suam *Entries* 233b. **d** ut genealogiam regum Danorum..seriatim [v.l. strictim] ~iem W. Malm. *GR* III 258; **1171** super hoc ipso †verbo [? l. verbum] ~iatum vobis duximus faciendum (*Lit. Ep. Meld.*) *Becket Mat.* VII 446; Justinianus libros legum Romanorum ~iavit in uno volumine M. Par. *Maj.* I 238 (cf. III 328); lectorem hujus libelli ~iati ad historiam transmitto prolixiorem *Id. Abbr.* 209; istam cronicam..pro nimia prolixitate ~iavi (*Chr. Brev.* 1) *Eul. Hist.* III 245; **s1259** rex Anglie litterarum suarum ~iavit titulum, ut neque ducem Normannie neque comitem Andegavie se deinceps vocaret Capgr. *Hen.* 93; **1413** doctoris de Lira super Bibliam [liber] ~iatus *StatOx* 224.

2 to record (particulars of) in writing.

c1166 sex talee sunt ibi que sunt adbreviate (*KRMisc* 1/1b) *EHR* XXVIII 227; **s1125** a quibus abbatia tota et ad eam pertinentia ~iata sunt *Chr. Battle* 60; **1214** nomina recognitorum abreviantur in dorso brevis *CurR* VII 82; **1231** petens nominabit sectam suam, sc. duos testes; et ~iabuntur (*Eyre*) *MGL* I 62; **1269** clericus curie debet omnia ~iare *CBaron* 72; **s1275** quedam libertas in Londoniis provisa, ut apprenticiorum nomina ~iarentur in papirio camere Gildaule *Ann. Lond.* 86; **s1297** mandante rege.. adbreviare..quot equitaturas quisque posset invenire *Flor. Hist.* III 101; **1302** qui quidem dies abreviati fuerunt in rotulis precedentibus *KRAc* 482/20 r. 4.

abbreviarium, epitome.

doctores videntes solum theologie abreviarium per theologos decurtatum Wycl. *Ver.* III 70.

abbreviate, in brief.

posset allegari autoritas Averrois..~e superius memorata Bradw. *CD* 223e.

abbreviatio, a shortening (in time). **b** reduction (in amount). **c** (?) payment by instalments. **d** shortening (of writings), epitomizing. **e** abridgement, epitome.

a causam hujus prolongationis et ~onis [vite] estimaverunt multi a parte celi Bacon *Min.* 374; **1350** priori et monachis..quod compareant..ad terminum nimis brevem et peremptorium, nulla hujusmodi abreviacionis aut peremptorie vocacionis causa expressa, ..mandastis *Reg. Heref.* 156; **1559** pro ~one processuum curiarum Consistorialium *Conc. Scot.* II 171. **b** consummationem..et ~onem ..Deus..faciet Lanfr. *Comment. Paul.* (*Rom.* ix 28) 138 (cf. *Is.* x 23); ad abreviationem materie vitanda sunt omnia illa que prolixitatem inducant, sc. descriptiones, circumlocutiones et cetera Vinsauf *AV* II 2. 30; **s1453** volumus..ut..vadat residuum pecunie..integraliter, absque defalcacione sive ~one, ad manus suas *Reg. Whet.* I 117. **c 1365** dicti cx s. dati fuerunt per preceptum thesaurarii.. et..ita fieri consuevit propter ~onem vadiorum eorundem *Cl* 203 m. 24. **d** lux apertionis ex ordinata ~one genita, perstrictis hujus libri summitatibus, lectori diligenter anteponenda est H. Hunt. *HA* V 31; multis rationibus, ..quas duxi ad presens ~onis gracia supprimendas Ockham *Pol.* I 63. **e** Elfricus..reliquit..~onem Passionis S. Edmundi W. Malm. *GP* V 254; **1172** quam obedientem..se curaverit exhibere, non est opus presenti ~one referre (*Litt. A. et T. cardinalium*) *Becket Mat.* VII 521; hec est~o compendiosa cronicorum Anglie M. Par. *Abbr.* 159; **s1235** composite sunt sub compendiosa ~one decretales Gregoriane *Flor. Hist.* II 216; **1451** ~o statutorum..edita..in conventu B. Marie *Mon. Francisc.* II 81.

abbreviator, a epitomist. **b** writer of drafts (in Papal Chancery).

a Justinus..Trogi Pompeii ~or Diceto *Abbr. Norm.* 20. **b 1406** literarum apostolicarum scriptor et ~or *Conc.* III 287; per vicecancellarium distribuuntur [littere apostolice] ~oribus Paul. Angl. *ASP* II 1552; **1543** advocatus consistorialis de majori presidentia ~or ac sacri palatii apostolici comes *Form. S. Andr.* II 253.

abbreviatura, abbreviation.

1543 supplendo et extendendo ~as ac clausulas *Form. S. Andr.* II 306.

abbrocator v. abrocator. abbuttare v. abuttare.

abcariare, to carry away, export (*cf. acariare*).

1491 licenciam dedimus..mercatoribus..quod ipsi.. eosdem lapides..extra idem regnum [nostrum] ad quascumque partes exteras in quacumque navi vel vase educere et ~iare, aut educi et ~iari facere, ..possint (*TreatyR*) *Foed.* XII 460; pro bladis suis..~iandis *Entries* 184.

abcariatio, carrying away, removal.

1471 pro ~one xv †carucarum fimi de schamellis *Ac. Chamb. Cant.* 142; **1566** pro ~one et asportatione *Entries* 410.

abcdarium v. abecedarium. abce-, abci-, v. absce-, absci-

abdecēre, to be unfitting.

~et, non decet *GlC* A 55.

abdellum v. bdellium.

abdere [CL], to hide.

~itis, *gehyddum GlC* A 87; **a690** [discipuli] oracula..in alveariis soñae..servanda condentes ~unt Aldh. *Ep.* 5 p. 491; emergentes de latibulis quibus ~iti fuerant Bede *HE* I 16; illa que ad evidentiam indicanda proponimus.. intricatis verborum involucris ~ere potius et velare Gir. *EH intr.*; Papa..contulit uni juveni transmarino eandem prebendam per viam reservacionis ~ite Wycl. *Civ. Dom.* III 334.

2 (p. ppl. as sb. n.) secrecy, hiding-place.

strofam in ~ito perpetratam Aldh. *VirgP* 37; repente juvenis ab ~ito..irruit Map *NC* III 3 p. 128; **s1329** sic longo tempore erat in ~itis quod estimabant eum omnes fore occisum *Ann. Paul.* 346; **s1385** [Scoti] de suis ~itis erumpebant *V. Ric. II* 62.

abdicabilis, able to be renounced.

dominium civile est dominium..incommunicabile singulis et ex equo multis dominis sed ~e servata justicia Wycl. *Civ. Dom.* I 126.

abdicamentum, refusal, rejection.

sin autem [haec precaria] invidis aemulorum ~is refutata tempnuntur, ignoratur utique quid satius inceptem quam ut..propriam messem..pro posse virium piare procedam *V. Dunst. B.* 1.

abdicare [CL], (intr., w. abl.) to withdraw (from).

non se posse absque suorum consensu..priscis ~are moribus Bede *HE* II 2.

2 (tr.) to repudiate, renounce, disavow. **b** (w. *a se*). **c** (w. *ab animo*) banish.

~avit, negavit vel †*discerede* [l. *biscerede*] *GlC* A 11; apocriforum deleramenta..penitus ~are Aldh. *VirgP* 24; ~ato conubio non legitimo Bede *HE* II 6; quos predicat hec ~at illa Gir. *TH* III 31; suam voluntatem ~at ut vestre satisfiat Map *NC* IV 15 p. 196. **b 1239** in electionis examine, quam a vobis penitus ~astis (*Lit. monachorum*) Gerv. Cant. *Cont.* 155; qui per..juramentum a se omnem principatum hujusmodi ~arent Ockham *Pol.* I 109; **1436** volens occupacionem spiritualium prioratus predicti a se penitus ~are *Cl* 286 m. 3. **c** terrenis aliis ~atis ab animo R. Bury *Phil. prol.* 11.

3 to deprive.

s1292 justiciarii..ipsos monachos proprio jure ~arunt *Flor. Hist.* III 82; **1549** jure collegii et academiae prorsus ~antur *StatOx* 358.

abdicatio, repudiation, renunciation. **b** negation.

10.. ~one, *bescyrednesse* WW; **c1250** per libidinum ~onem presentis vite jucunditatem penitus interimere Ad. Marsh *Ep.* 75; ~ones proprietatis omnium rerum Christus verbo docuit Ockham *Dial.* 706. **b** essentia est affirmatio; essentia non est ~o Eriug. *Per.* 462c.

abdicativus, renunciatory. **b** negative.

ut sit gule et omnium ejus specierum ~a exclusio J. Waleys *V Relig.* I 11 225k. **b** haec nomina..in pronuntiatione formam affirmativae, in intellectu vero virtutem ~ae obtineant Eriug. *Per.* 462c.

abdīcĕre [CL], to refuse.

abdixit, negavit *GlC* A 11 (cf. ib. 52, 212).

abditorium, hiding-place. **b** store-room, store-chest.

catulis in ~io repositis Neckam *Ut.* 102 (cf. 97). **b** *an hurde howse*, †abdicatorium [l. abditorium], repositorium *CathA*; hoc ~ium, *a cofyr* WW; **1519** item unum coffur et una pixis..; item tria ~ia et tria pixides de ebore ornate cum cupro deaurato (*Invent. York*) *MonA* VI 1205.

abditus v. abdere. abdom- v. et. hebdom-.

abdomen [CL], fat (of the belly).

arvina vel adeps..vel ~en, *hrysel* vel *gelend* vel *swind* vel *swines smere* Ælf. *Gl.*; omentum, zirbus, ~en, sagimen, arvina, auxungia idem sunt; quando simpliciter porcina intelligitur *SB* 32; **14..** adumen, *gres*.. WW.

abducere [CL], **a** to lead away (persons). **b** to abduct (women). **c** to drive off (beasts). **d** to export or transport (goods etc.).

a pueri..ad Chaldeos ~ti Aldh. *VirgP* 21; Britannia.. floridae juventutis alacritate spoliata, quae tyrannorum temeritate ~ta nusquam..rediit Bede *HE* I 12; sustinent ~i socios suos..in participium secuture redemptionis Neckam *NR* II 175; **1201** abstulerunt ei quendam nativum quem habuit in vinculis..et illum abduxerunt *SelPlCrown* 2; **1221** W. B. .., rettatus de morte P. de H., fugit in ecclesiam; ..et..venit abbas de Bordesle cum monachis suis et ipsum W. inductum capa unius monachi abduxit *Ib.* 86. **b 1221** Ricardus de P. et Iveta uxor ejusdem Ricardi queruntur quod..H. et R. ..fregerunt domum ipsius [Ricardi] et abduxerunt predictam Ivetam *Ib.* 102; de subtractione uxoris..si per parentes ~ta esset et detenta Bracton 203; **1296** appellavit W. C. et J. de H. de felonia et pace domini regis infracta de eo quod abduxerunt Caterinam uxorem R. G. domini sui *Eyre Kent* I 110. **c 1212** abduxerunt xiiij animalia tam boves quam vaccas *SelPlCrown* 80; **1221** abduxit equum ejus *PlCrGlouc* 21; **1293** oves non fuerunt ~te per aliquam maliciam *SelPlMan* 168; **1316** de xiiij martis ~tis per Scottos *Ac. Durh.* 11. **d 12..** de navibus que se oneraverunt super terram prioris ad ~endam mercandisam *Feod. Durh.* 270; **1313** [quia] illud frumentum ~eret ad molendinum et ibidem redigere faceret in farinam *Leet Norw.* 57 (cf. ib. 63: forstallavit diversa blada..et ea abduxit extra regnum); **s1364** miserunt [aurum]..ad ~endum in Franciam Knighton II 119; **1456** pro uno pari rotarum currus..ad ~endum bombardos de le T. ad L. *ExchScot* 204.

2 to seduce, mislead.

utinam..gentes ille Francorum..ab injusticiis et viis suis pessimis quibus ~te et involute dicuntur resileant Elmh. *Hen. V* 57.

abductio, a leading away (of persons). **b** abduction (of women). **c** driving off (of animals). **d** export (of goods).

a s1327 quibusdam burgensibus..qui ad ipsius [Edwardi] liberacionem et ~onem in partes transmarinas, quam optabat, se disponebant Baker 106b. **b** de raptu A. uxoris ejus et ~one cum bonis et catallis ejusdem R. *Reg. Brev. Or.* 278. **c 1229** queritur quod W. ..injuste cepit viij boves.. et eos abduxit..ad comitatum Buk'; ..et W. ..defendit injustam capcionem et..~onem extra comitatum *CurR* XIII 2113; **1344** item xvj vacce et non plures, quia..in morina viij et in ~one per latrones xvj *Ac. Durh.* 206. **d 1204** de ~one marcandiarum ab Anglia *Pat* 42b.

abductivus, seductive, misleading.

11.. ad ~a et multipliciter licentiosa illa..quibus creberrime falluntur verbis innitentes Balsh. *AD* (*rec.* 2) 44.

abductor, a remover. **b** abductor (of women).

a 1464 omnes et singulos hujusmodi quercuum, arborum et meremiorum succisores, projectores, ~ores *Reg. Heref.* 88. **b** de virginum et sanctimonialium et matronarum honeste vivencium raptoribus et ~oribus (*Capitula Corone* 8) *Fleta* 24.

abductorium, spinning-reel.

a rele, alabrum et alibrum, ~ium *CathA*.

abece, (?) ABC in the form of an ornament (e.g. necklace).

1255 unum firmaculum, unum ~e, unam nuscam *Pat* 69 m. 14 (*Cal* p. 400: †abete).

abecedarium, a alphabet. **b** spelling primer. **c** elementary lesson-book.

a incipit pontifex de sinistro ab oriente scribens per pavimentum..ABCdarium Egb. *Pont.* 33. **b** Lanfrancus ..intelligens quam prope nihil sciret, ~ium ipsi expediendum apposuit, ferociam hominis..eludens W. Malm. *GP* II 74 p. 150. **c** scripsit [S. Patricius] abegetoria trecenta sexaginta quinque et eo amplius Nen. *HB* 196 (= M. Par. *Maj.* I 223: abgetoria).

abectum v. abettum. abegatus v. abnegare 5.

abellana [CL], hazel-nut. **b** walnut.

abelena, *haeselhnutu GlC* A 2; avellanus, *haesl Ib.* 895; -ae, *hæsl* vel *hæselhnutu* Ælf. *Gl.*; **10..** ~us vel colurnus, *hæsl*; avilina, *hnutu* WW; nec avellanas in sylva gustavit Ord. Vit. V 19; tres pillulas ei fac in modum avellane, id est nucis corili Adel. *CA* 10; pulvis..testarum avellanarum Gilb. II 82 v. 2; dentur nuces cum ficubus vel avellane que vocantur †philolers [l. *philberts*] Gad. 69. 2; **1416** in vj^{ce} avalanarum *Ac. Durh.* 54; **1467** pro xij barellis avelanarum *EEC* 610. **b** avelana, A. *walnottre*, ..*bannenotte-tre* WW.

abellus, (?) hazel (less prob. abele, i.e. white poplar).

1279 omnes liberi et custumarii ville [*Belchamp, Essex*].. amputant omnibus horis tria genera arborum, sc. populum, salicem et ~um (*Tab. Reg. S. Paul* I 107) *Dom. S. Paul.* cxxvi.

aberrare [CL], to go astray (fig.), state erroneously.

numquid, cum numerus compositus sit, ipsam quoque animam compositam esse ~avit? Adel. *ED* 23; longe a via veritatis ~ant Gir. *GE* II 1.

abertivus v. abortivus. aberuncare v. averruncare.

abesse [CL; v. et. absens, absenturus], **a** to be distant. **b** to be absent, stay away. **c** to be lacking or non-existent.

a in insula Farne, quae duobus ferme milibus passuum

ab urbe procul abest BEDE *HE* III 16. **b** synodo..presbiter ipse existens abesse non poterat T. MON. *Will.* II 4; **1232** quod Dovorensis ibi prior abfuit, hoc nichil obstat,/ ..quia nec debebat adesse H. AVR. *Poems* 127 l. 65; **a1350** cancellarius ultra xv dies abfuturus neminem habeat vicarium *Stat. Cantab.* 315. **c** si Deus..accidentium est susceptivus, ut in Deo modo adsint modo absint PULL. *Sent.* I 4; omnibus diebus vite hujus regis [Alexandri III].. aruit vitium, abfuit dolus, cessavit injuria FORDUN *GA* 67.

2 (inf. as sb.) absence.

me tanto gravius ejus abesse gravat (R. PARTES) *Speculum* XII 234; vernas quos vovit adesse / unos post alios ducet serpens ad abesse D. BEC. 1933; hujus pueri nostri..adesse per abesse festinant tempora DEVIZES 40.

3 (*absit*) far be it! God forbid!

quod absit a catholica..fide! ALDH. *VirgP* 8; absit ut Johannem stultitiae reprehendamus! BEDE *HE* III 25; absit, absit e nobis hoc credere! ERIUG. *Per.* 571C; **10..** absit, *wana sie* WW; absit ut..studia..omissa pereant! GIR. *EH pref.*; **1239** si etiam haberet jus in re, quod absit, restitui non tenetur (*Lit. Fred. Imp.*) M. PAR. *Maj.* III 554.

†abestis [(?) a bestiis; cf. ab 8 b], haruspex or gelder.

~is intestina hostiarum aspiciens et A. *a gyller of bestys* WW; *a gelder of bestis*, ~is *CathA*.

abestrum, vine leaf.

vyny leefe, pampinus, ~um *PP*.

abete v. abece.

abettamentum, abetment, instigation.

1309 rectatus de ~o et consilio de morte Guillelmi B. feloniter interfecti (*JustIt*) *S. Jers.* XVIII 174; **1397** perdonavimus Ricardo..de eo quod ipse fuit de assensu, consilio, favore, abbettamento, covina, vi, retinencia seu adhesione predictorum ducis et comitum (*Pat*) *Foed.* VIII 26; **1415** non facient..excitaciones, procuramenta seu ~a alicui homini alteri de predictis villis..ad implacitandum, molestandum vel inquietandum dictos abbatem et conventum (*Forma Arbitrii*) *Croyl. Cont.* B 511.

abettare (abbettare) [OF *abeter* < Frk.], to abet, incite.

1288 J. arrettatus fuit de latrocinio, et pro tali traditus fuit predicto ballivo; et [? sc. ballivus] non maliciose eum ~avit *JustIt* 1280, r. 6; de placito quare ~averunt.. Willelmum indictari de..latrociniis *State Tri. Ed. I* 29; **1294** morti Nicholai..opem prebuit et assensum, et eundem R. ad committendam illam feloniam ~avit *Cl* 111 m. 8; **1393** consenciens et ~ans fuit Roberto M. ..de morte Ade *Pat* 338 m. 14; quod ipse ~asse et procurasse debuisset B., que fuit uxor E., F. et G. de morte predicti E. ..appellare *Reg. Brev.* 134; **1479** ipsi..presentes fuerunt, ~antes, confortantes et auxiliantes ad feloniam *Sanct. Durh.* 13.

abettatio, abetment.

1475 per †obettacionem, confortacionem, auxilium et consilium ejusdem P. *Proc. J. P.* 238; **1587** percusiones, ~ones, procuraciones, confortaciones *Pat* 1300 m. 9.

abettator, abetter.

1285 inquiratur per quorum abettum formatum fuerit hujusmodi appellum per maliciam..et, si inveniatur..quod aliquis sit ~or, per maliciam..puniatur (*St. 2 Westm.* c. 12) *StRealm* 81 (= *Reg. Malm.* I 86: †abettor); cum appellator non sufficiat, inquiratur de ~oribus ad instanciam appellati *Fleta* 53; **1315** sunt..de consensu et assensu dicte communitatis in omnibus maleficiis et contemptibus supradictis et eorum ~ores *RParl* 361b; **1354** delinquencium ~ores *RScot* 766a; manutentores, consiliarii, ~ores *Reg. Brev.* 180; **1575** auxiliatores et ~ores *Pat* 1131 m. 19.

abettum, abetment.

1247 dicunt quod ipse appellavit eos odio et atia per ~um Jacobi..et non per verum appellum *JustIt* 455 r. 3; **1258** idem appellator absque alicujus ~o appellavit eos (*JustIt* 873) *SelCWW* 86; indictati fuerunt de abbetto indictamenti facti super Willelmum *State Tri. Ed. I* 29; [inquisitores] sic jurent: ..“nec per alicujus ~um vel procuracionem omittam quin veritatem dicam” *Fleta* 21; **1293** quesitus quomodo se velit aquietare de abecto illo maliciose facto *RParl* 123a; **s1305** insurrexerunt iterum Scoti contra dominum regem Anglie per ~um Roberti Bruys *Ann. Worc.* 557; **1341** per procuracionem et abbettum quorundam emulorum suorum (*Pat*) *Foed.* V 247; ad procuracionem et abbettum predictorum B. et C. *Reg. Brev.* 134b.

abexcommunicatus, excommunicated.

1397 inhibitum est domino officiali curie Cantuariensis ne aliquid attemptaret contra J. F. ~um et pro sic excommunicato publice denunciatum (*Vis. Heref.*) *EHR* XLIV 447.

abfugare v. affugare. abgetorium v. abecedarium.

abhinc [al. div.], hence. **b** henceforth, thereafter. **c** ago.

in terra de Bueld non procul ~c [v.l. hinc] distante GIR. *IK* I 1 (cf. ib.: in provincia..que paucis ~c stadiis distat); **1391** ibidem eum detinuit et non ~c voluit eum abire *Leet Norw.* 71; **1508** pro cariagio vj signorum ab hinc usque Dunelm' *Ac. Durh.* 659. **b** siquis abhinc a laude Tonantis / clauserit ora WULF. *Swith.* I 1360; qui autem ~c a tali opere cessare..voluerit (*Inst. Cnut.*) *GAS* 291; omnes quas nominavi terras possident [Saraceni] usque hodie, annis ~c circiter quingentis W. MALM. *GR* IV 368. **c** abhinc aliquot annos..legi apud Bedam P. VERG. *Pref. ad Gildam.*

abhomin- v. abomin-.

abhorrēre [CL], to abhor, shrink from: **a** (w. acc.). **b** (w. *ab*). **c** (w. acc. and inf.). **d** (w. inf.).

a licet mulieres sint vitande, non tamen sunt ~ende O. CHERITON *Par.* 58; delicati qui ~ent medicinas GILB. I 35. v. 1. **b** ab omni crimine ~ebat W. MALM. *GR* IV 312. **c 1268** Dei filius..~ens in templo negotiationum commercia exerceri *Conc. Syn.* 781. **d** qui Deo famulatur, crimen incurrere mendacii..~ere solet AD. SCOT. *OP* 546; quam enormiter..vindictam exercuerit, noster explicare stilus ~uit GIR. *IK* I 10; **1240** quidam etiam..~ent hoc percipere sacramentum *Conc. Syn.* 306; **1301** vobis displicere.. ~entem *Reg. Cant.* II 740; rex..eos alloqui ~uit FAVENT 12.

2 to incur the hatred of.

non pungens ramnus, sed oliva nitens, sed adornans / ficus, sed blanda vitis abhorret eos [reprobos] GOWER *VC* I 1020n.

3 (impers.) to be abhorrent. **b** (pr. ppl. w. *ab*) abhorrent, offensive (to).

quod ~et fari ALDH. *Ep.* 3. **b** illud erat a natura ~ens, quod multi ancillas suas ex se gravidas..venditabant W. MALM. *GR* III 245.

abhort- v. abort-.

abicere [CL], to throw away, reject. **b** (fig.) to reject, renounce.

1246 abjecerunt saccum et fugerunt *SelPlForest* 84; scofe sunt grossa corpora, illa sc. que abjiciuntur ab hiis que colantur *SB* 38. **b** fidem quam olim..abjecerant..receperunt BEDE *HE* III 22; omnes..regnum ipsius abjicere [v.l. abjecere]..moliti sunt OSB. *V. Dunst.* 28; **1228** devotione populi Christiani abjecta (*Lit. Papae*) M. PAR. *Maj.* III 149.

2 (p. ppl.) abject, mean, squalid.

[Angli] parvis et abjectis domibus totos absumebant sumptus W. MALM. *GR.* III 245; **s1225** [Falcasius] vilis fuit, undique et abjectus, nec dignus ira Cesaris M. PAR. *Min.* II 272; scribe crucem, que transgressoribus / pena fuit abjectioribus J. HOWD. *Phil.* 764; vestimenta lanea et linea ..que nec nitida nimium nec abjecta plurimum erunt *Obs. Barnwell* 196.

abicies v. alyces. abiddare v. abundare 3.

abiegnus [CL], derived from fir.

exterit abjegnas Petri dignissime valvas FRITH. 737; ligna..abiegna salo madefacta NECKAM *DS* II 481.

abies [CL], fir. **b** (? by conf. of AS *æsp* and *sæp*) aspen.

~es, †*etspe GlC* A 5 (= EE 340. 5: *saepae*); ~es vel gallica, *gyrtreow* ÆLF. *Gl.*; **10..** ~es, *sæppe, gyr* WW; abundat et ~ete silvositas Hibernie, thuris et incensi matre GIR. *TH* III 10; subtus se nubes abies discurrere cernit NECKAM *DS* VIII 47; **1435** pro centum tabulis ~ietum, viz. *fyr ExchScot* 613; insula Lough Hakern..ibi crescunt arbores de †ebete vocate mastys pro navibus W. WORC. *Itin.* 134. **b 10..** ~es, *æps* WW.

abietinus, derived from fir.

[bernace] ex lignis..~is..quasi gummi nascuntur GIR. *TH* I 15 (cf. HIGD. I 32).

abigeatus [LL = cattle-lifting], (?) stolen.

abigiata, involata *GlC* A 60 (cf. ib. 8).

abigelus, ~ger v. abigeus.

1 abigere [CL], to drive away. **b** to drive, compel. **c** (fig.) to banish, avert. **d** (refl.) to withdraw.

abacta, involata vel exclusa *GlC* A 40 (cf. ib. 30); ea quae fraude abegerant sponte restituunt ALDH. *VirgP* 37; **10..** abegerunt, *from adreofan* WW; **s1138** virgines et viduas..sub jugo servitutis in Scottiam abegerunt J. HEX. *HR Cont.* 290; Erymanthus abacto / respiravit apro J. EXON. *BT* II 118; hi sunt musce..quas utinam Abraham cum flabello abegisset a sacrificiis GIR. *GE* II 33; **1507** abegit certa animalia, viz. xij boves et unam vaccam, et eos.. abegens (*sic*) ibidem dimisit *Sanct. Durh.* 47. **b** omnis *ceapscip*..pacem habeat que in portum veniet, ..si non sit abacta tempestatibus [AS: *gyf hit undrifen bið*] (*Quad.*) *GAS* 222. **c** coepit orando periculum..~ere BEDE *HE* II 7; timor [Domini] contemptus ~it caecitatem ERIUG. *Per.* 565B; meritis sibi funus abegit SERLO WILT. 38. 19. **d** ab ejus communione..se abegerunt OCKHAM *Err. Papae* 965.

2 (p. ppl.) enfeebled by age.

in abacte matris incidi amplexus [*gl.*: abactus dicitur quasi ab actu remotus] BALSH. *Ut.* 47.

2 abigere v. ambigere 1b.

1 abigeus [LL], cattle-lifter. **b** (fig.).

†abigelus, qui tollit servum aut pecus alienum *GlC* A 33; quantitas discernit furem ab ~eo, ..ut si quis suem surripuerit fur et si quis gregem ~eus erit BRACTON 105 (= *Fleta* 15: ~eo [v.l. †ambiguo]); *a thefe of bestis*, ~eus, abiges, abiger *CathA*. **b** istos, inquam, sentio graves abigeos, / qui de grege proprio mihi tollunt meos PECKHAM *Def. Mend.* 37.

2 Abigeus v. Albigensis. abigiatus v. abigeatus. abil- v. habil-.

abinde [al. div.], **a** thence. **b** thereafter. **c** therefrom (of origin).

a abbas..habens non longe ab inde monasterium BEDE *HE* IV 14; ab inde..ire praetendunt ÆTHELW IV 3; venenosos ~e vermes procul exterminant GIR. *TH* I 30; **1264** ad predictas partes..venerunt et ~e sine licencia nostra recesserunt *Cl* 405; **1380** pro predictis impedimentis..~e.. amovendis *FormOx* 255; quo plusquam centum removentur abinde clientum GOWER *CT* I 199. **b 1143** ista..condicione ut, illa possessione semel accepta, sibi ~e proprium haberet THORNE 1804 (= *Conc.* I 423); multis ~e diebus GIR. *TH* III 34; quod concessiones reddituum..a predicto festo vacue..existant, ad habendum..~e aliqua premissorum *Reg. Whet.* I 253; **1478** ~e et usque ad hos dies *Lit. Cant.* III 295. **c** dum virilis sexus extiterit, et hereditas ~e sit, femina non hereditetur (*Leg. Hen.*) *GAS* 589.

abinterponere, to impose.

1397 prior, ..violavit sequestrum ~positum in fructibus ..ecclesie per..episcopum (*Vis. Heref.*) *EHR* XLIV 288.

abintus, from within.

plagas..imposuerunt, ut ~us pulmo videretur W. CANT. *Mir. Thom.* IV 26; **1196** regum..hostilitas, ..possessiones ecclesie nostre deforis invadens, gloriam ejus ~us malicia civium denigratam ad enormem..confusionem..redegit (*Lit. Ep. Rotomag.*) DICETO *YH* II 144; locus idem ~us et a foris..amplissimi jubare luminis celitus illustrabatur *NLA* (*Edmund*) II 592; vix ego quod potui cognoscere si fuit extra / corpus quod vidi, seu quod abintus erat GOWER *VC* I 2056.

abinvicem [al. div.], mutually, from one another. **b** mutually (not impl. separation).

multum..generalitas et specialitas ab invicem differunt ALDH. *VirgP* 58; ab invicem discordabant BEDE *HE* III 6; monasteriis pro situ terrarum ab invicem sejunctis OSB. *V. Dunst.* 16; hae duae personae [Trinitatis] suis propriis vocibus aliae ab invicem..designantur ANSELM (*Incarn.*) I 285; quibus ab invicem digredientibus H. CANTOR 22; dies amara valde qua populus exul ~em discedit, in diversa iturus *Itin. Ric.* I 9; separare juratores ab invicem BRACTON 143b; **1423** ne vestra membra ~em discorditer separetis *Reg. Cant.* III 520. **b s1153** Stephanus..et Henricus ~em convenerunt in fedus sub vinculo pacis J. HEX. *HR Cont.* 331; **s1296** mutuo se cedebant et †~em corruerunt KNIGHTON I 303 (= W. GUISB. II 93: adinvicem).

abire [CL], to go away. **b** to pass. **c** to die. **d** to follow a course, behave.

ut cuneus votorum compos abiret ALDH. *VirgV* 1539; Romam abiens, ibi vitam finivit BEDE *HE* IV 12; **10..** abeuntem, *on weg farendan* WW; si abierit domum non apprehensus.., tamen minister regis eum sequetur *DB* I 1; amicis..retro abeuntibus et quasi in occulto disparentibus GIR. *EH* I 5; **s1243** in Alemannia multi retro abierunt et adversabantur ei M. PAR. *Min.* II 474. **b** tempus abit modicum WULF. *Swith.* II 226; nota tibi mundi sit nota: mundus abit SERLO WILT. 80. 1; cum labor a longo tempore cassus abit GOWER *VC* V 270. **c** si..abeat homo viam suam [AS: *forðfære*] (*Quad.*) *GAS* 105; **s1109** undecimo Kal. Maii in alterum seculum abiit W. MALM. *GP* I 66. **d** propterea quod..prorsus libidine atque arrogantia preceps abiret OSB. *V. Dunst.* 28.

2 to resort to or pass under feudal lordship or jurisdiction.

quidam liber homo hanc terram tenens et quo vellet abire valens summisit se in manu Walteri pro defensione sui *DB* I 36 (cf. II 96b); si quis foris faciens ibi calumpniatus fuisset, regi emendabat; si vero non calumpniatus abisset sub eo qui sacam et socam habuisset, ille emendam de reo haberet *Ib.* 32.

3 (*s. dub.*)

textor..cindulas habeat trabales, ..trabibus tenorem tele abientibus NECKAM *Ut.* 106.

abiss- v. abyss-. abit- v. habit-.

abjecte, abjectly, shamefully.

quam ~e ignavus es, qui non erubescis tantum fateri opprobrium MAP *NC* II 25; quanto sunt despicabiles ~ius *Ib.* V 5 p. 231.

abjectio, casting out, expulsion (from office), rejection. **b** rejection (fig.), renunciation.

s1191 gavisi sunt homines regni de ~one cancellari *G. Ric. I* 214; **c1250** legimus..de ~one nostri Adam de paradiso *Conc. Syn.* 321; **s434** cum calamitatem Britannie ~onemque Romanorum [*abandonment by the Romans*] intellexisset M. PAR. *Maj.* I 182. **b** est enim haeresis..~o gratiae Dei JEWEL *Apol.* 12.

2 something thrown away, scrap. **b** (fig.) outcast.

quid enim terra et cinis nisi ima quedam et levis ~o est? AD. SCOT. *OP* 522; **1323** de v quar. vescarum receptis de ~one avenarum *Ac. Wellingb.* 131. **b** ‘peripsema’ [scilicet] abjectio LANFR. *Comment. Paul.* (1 *Cor.* iv 13) 170; vir quondam celebris nunc est abjectio plebis NIG. *Mir. BVM* 16 v 2; **s1225** [Falcasius] exul fuit pauper..factus opprobrium hominum et ~o plebis M. PAR. *Min.* II 272; cibus vermium, derisio superstitum, ~o supernorum *Croyl. Cont.* A 125.

3 abject condition, meanness. **b** (fig., of style) crudeness.

longe quidem distant opulentia hec et ~o illa H. BOS. *Thom* III 15; sicut elatio, ita et ~o declinanda est J. SAL. *Pol.* 528A; [puella] quam sibi generis ~o prediorumque defectus negant MAP *NC* IV 12; quanquam..sui cognitionem ~one [*by his humble guise*] velaret GIR. *GE* I 23; **1228** ~onem [*sorry state*] corporis sui frivolis excusationibus ..gestiens palliare (*Lit. Papae*) M. PAR. *Maj.* III 149; victus austeritatem et vestium ~onem continue preferebat WYCL. *Ver.* I 360. **b** veniam..deposco..quod soloecismis et verborum ~one aures tuas vulnero T. MON. *Will. prol.* p. 6.

1 abjectivus, (?) degrading.

omnis natus in servitute ~a est nativus WYCL *Civ. Dom.* I 241.

2 abjectivus v. adjectivus.

abjector, rejector, thrower away.

prompte victorie crudelis ~or MAP *NC* V 5 p. 230.

1 abjectus (adj.) v. abicere.

2 abjectus, casting off, rejection.

~u veterum novisque virtutum incrementis..renovantur in melius GIR. *TH* I 18.

abjudicare [CL], **a** to take away. **b** to deprive. **c** to expel. **d** to deny. (All w. ref. to judicial decision).

a viri justi..~ant ei omne beneficium O. CHERITON *Fab.* 55; habebit tenens recuperare suum ubi in absentia sua.. ~ata fuerit ei seisina BRACTON 367; **1334** balliva..†adjudicata [? l. ~ata] fuit de se et de heredibus suis..in ultimo itinere *SelPlForest* 67. **b 1228** omnibus bonis..fuit ~atus *Pat* 211; quomodo rex..Johannes ~atus est a regno WEND. II 63; **1264** ballivam forestarie..de †quo idem R. ~atus fuit coram..justiciariis nostris *Cl* 338; **1286** ~atus est..prior..ab omni jure advocationis predicte domus *Lit. Cant.* III 378; **1341** justiciarii ~averunt eandem Amiam de quacumque responsione *SelCKB* VI 9. **c 1254** ~atus fuit a gilda *Rec. Leic.* I 69. **d** aldermannus..viros monastice professionis coram potestate seculari juramentum prestare debere ~ans *Chr. Rams.* 80.

abjudicatio, deprivation by judicial decision.

habere poterit tenens qui amisit si fraudulenta deceptio petentis intervenerit, ubi nulla..summonitio facta fuerit nec captio aliqua nec ~o per defaltam BRACTON 367; **c1419** ~ones, renunciaciones et adnullaciones (*Lib. Alb.*) *MGL* I 530; **1429** sic jus, titulus et possessio..illesa permanserunt..omni ~one hujusmodi..cessante (*Sentencia in Curia de Arcubus*) AMUND. I 247.

abjunctio, disconnection (gram.).

ex ~one, cum idem [dicitur] nunc ut de aliquo nunc ut abjunctum, ut cum dicitur 'negatio que fit in probabili responsione probabilis est', an in responsione probabili an responsione in probabili, dubitabit cui de majoribus dubitare rarum BALSH. *AD* 93.

abjunctus, disconnected, separate (gram.).

BALSH. *AD* 93 (v. abjunctio).

abjuramentum, abjurement (*v. abjurare* 4).

s1240 ~um regni: ..Rogerus..Joceum..occidit et fugit ad ecclesiam..; et ibi cognovit factum et abjuravit regnum *MGL* I 100.

abjurare [CL], to swear: **a** that one is innocent; **b** that one will not repeat an offence.

a si ad illum hominem pecunia vocetur qui prius ~averat vel ~are [AS: *oðswerian*] vult, perneget secundum modum wite et pecunie (*Quad.*) *GAS* 105. **b 1254** confessus est hoc verum esse et ~avit hujusmodi transgressionem *Rec. Leic.* I 69.

2 to repudiate: **a** kinsfolk; **b** wife or concubine.

a si quis..de parentela se velit tollere et eam forisjuraverit, ..si postea aliquis de parentibus suis ~atis moriatur, .. nichil ad eum de hereditate..pertineat (*Leg. Hen.*) *GAS* 604. **b s1102** habitum est..concilium: de..presbiteris in uxoribus ~andis (*Quad.*) *GAS* 545; **s1102** sacerdotes concubinarios excommunicavit nisi eas [sc. concubinas] ex tunc ~arent *Flor. Hist.* II 36; **12..** eas [sc. fornicarias] simpliciter ~are *Conc. Scot.* II 37.

3 to renounce: **a** right or claim; **b** possession or office; **c** (w. dat.).

a qui furem ceperit, habeat inde x sol., et rex ipsum furem; et parentes ejus [*sc.* furis] ~ent ei [sc. captori] factionem [AS: *swerian aðas unfæhða*] (*Quad.*) *GAS* 101; omnem ~at Sceve calumniam [*claim against S.*] MAP *NC* IV 16 p. 202. **b c1150** terram..reddidit..Deo..et ~avit a se et a suis heredibus *Reg. Malm.* I 455; **c1155** ~averunt totum honorem de Cerdestok' sicut rectum et hereditatem Gilberti *Ch. Sal.* 18; **c1175** acceptis ab ecclesia lxx m. argenti, ~arunt terras B. Andree *Episc. Som* 27; **1194** prior..reddidit prioratum in manum H. Coventr' episcopi et illi.. ~avit prioratum Coventr', ita quod promisit se numquam rediturum de cetero ad ecclesiam Coventr' *CurR RC* I 66; **1221** coram tota villata ~averunt illud [messuagium] secundum usagium ville [de Lichefeld] *BNB* III 716; **1301** [mensurator] qui contra officium venerit officium ~abit *MGL* I 86. **c c1150** tenuit de nobis in firma, cui firme.. tam ipse..quam heredes sui..~averunt coram liberis et legalibus hominibus *Reg. Malm.* I 454.

4 to abjure (swear to stay away from): **a** the realm or Islands (C.I.); **b** a town or liberty; **c** a court of law; **d** a market. **e** (p. ppl.) having abjured the realm, i.e. exiled.

a jam archipresul sacerdotem quemdam propter flagitium degradatum terram ~are compulerat H. Bos. *Thom.* III 23 (cf. ib. IV 13); **1195** fugerunt in ecclesiam et ~averunt terram *CurR RC* I 114 (cf. ib. 323); **1202** E...occidit R...et fugit in ecclesiam cognoscens mortem et ~avit regnum *SelPlCrown* 23; **1231** cujus catalla..quidam Hugo..homo suus furatus est.., propter que ~avit terram *Cl* 555; **s1260** quidam barones ~averunt regnum Anglie per unum annum et unum diem, ituri in exilium in Hiberniam *Leg. Ant. Lond.* 70; cum exire petat quis infra xl dies, accedant coronatores coram quibus..debet..petere ut regnum pro felonia sua valeat ~are *Fleta* 45; **1313** J...qui alias ~avit regnum..deviando de via versus portum Dovor', qui ei assignatus..fuerat, ..captus extra regiam viam *Eyre Kent* 102 (*cf.* 94); **1316** quandoque aliqui confugientes ad ecclesiam ~ant terram.. et prosequuntur laici eos..et a publica strata abstrahuntur et suspenduntur (*Artic. Cleri* 10) *StRealm* I 172; **1322** regnum Anglie ~avit et eodem die regiam stratam et warentum sancte ecclesie viz. crucem..reliquit *SelCCoron* 75; **1352** coram dicto coronatore ~avit regnum Anglie, et crux ei liberata fuit et via ei assignata de Waltham usque Dovorr' *SelCKB* VI 82; ubi fugiens ad ecclesiam pro aliquo crimine ~ans terram deducetur ad proximum portum, ut exeat terram, salva sibi vita et membris LYNDW. 256g; **1309** feloniam fecit pro qua Insulas domini regis ~avit *PQW* 825a. **b 1237** Ysobella cepit penitentiam suam et ~avit villam Bristollii *BNB* III 193; **1340** consueta est decipere gallinas; ideo ~et villam, et preceptum est quod nullus receptet illam *CBaron* 98; **14..** si..dictam libertatem †objurare voluerit, major ballivus et jurati ducent dictum felonem ad finem libertatis ville predicte et ibidem †facient [? l. faciet] †objuracionem secundum consuetudinem libertatis predicte *Reg. S. Aug.* 149 (cf. *Cust. Fordwich* 30 p. 273). **c 1347** idem [attornatus] tanquam convictus de falsitate.. ~et curiam domini regis; et amodo non audiatur pro aliquo in curia domini regis *SelCKB* VI 62. **d 1330** si tercia vice forstallaverit, ~are debet mercatum *PQW* 556. **e 1532** dixerunt sibi, pro eo quod ipse fuit homo ~atus, ideo omnes illi pejus expedirent si ipsum in consorcium eorum in naviculam..arriperent *CoramR* 1084 r. 7.

5 to renounce (obedience). **b** (w. dat. of person only).

s1095 qui..funditus ei quicquid prelato suo debebant se ~asse professi sunt EADMER *HN* II 74; **1168** imperator obedienciam vestram..~avit (*Lit. ad Papam*) DICETO I 331; **s1168** si nomen et obedientiam Alexandri pape ~aret participem se schismatis haberet W. CANT. *V. Thom.* I 44. **b 1207** qui non possunt recta fronte principi ~are, possunt tamen ipsum salubriter commonere (*Lit. arch. Cant.*) *Conc.* I 522.

6 to abjure, recant (a belief). **b** (refl. w. dat.).

1311 tradito sibi libro evangeliorum in manibus dictas hereses ~avit sub hac forma *Conc. Syn.* 1308; **1401** heresim ..per ipsum W. per antea in forma juris ~atam *Cl* 247 m. 6 (= *Foed* VIII 178: †~atum); **1457** quas hereses omnes et errores..in forma canonica judicialiter ~avi *Reg. Whet.* I 289. **b 1498** quousque..seipsum talibus nefandis sectis et opinionibus ~averit *Entries* 340.

7 (refl.) to perjure oneself.

†1222 (14c) simplex sacerdos non potest..absolvere.. falsos testes ~antes se super sacrosancta propter lucrum vel damnum aliorum (*Const. arch. Cant.*) *Conc.* I 597 (cf. *EHR* L 400).

8 (?) to take away by judicial decision (*cf. abjudicare* a).

s1078 jubet congregari v sciras ibique xxviij villas fecit eidem [abbati] ~ari et suo iniquo dominio usurpari *Chr. Evesham* II 97.

abjuratio, denial on oath.

inficiatio vel ~io, *borges andsæc* ÆLF. *Gl.*

2 renunciation of possession. **b** repudiation.

c1175 illis [terris]..renunciavit et..tam ipse W. quam.. heres ejus..eas abjuraverunt; nos vero propter hanc.. ~onem..promisimus.. *Reg. Malm.* I 457. **b c1258** ~ones fornicariarum..fieri prohibemus *Conc. Syn.* 598.

3 abjuration (of the realm etc.), promise to stay away.

1201 perdonavimus..Ricardo..~onem quam fecit de terra nostra Anglie postquam judicium aque subierat pro morte Osberti *Pat* 2b; **1218** fugam et ~onem regni nostri *Pat* 135; **1258** confugientes ab ecclesiis, cymiteriis, viis publicis post terre ~onem secundum regni consuetudines violenter extrahuntur *Conc. Syn.* 580; **1261** post ~onem patrie *Ib.* 679; **1316** seculares judices clericos..faciunt abjurare regnum et eorum ~ones admittunt (*Artic. Cleri* 15) *StRealm.* I 173; **1327** bona et catalla..que racione ~onis ipsius J. dicto regi..sunt forisfacta *KRMem* 103 r. 255*d*; **1309** perdonavit..Willelmo..tam feloniam quam fecit quam ~onem Insularum [*C.I.*] quam fecerat pro eadem *PQW* 825b; **14..** facient †objuracionem (v. abjurare 4b); **1330** usi sunt punire omnes forstallatores..per amerciamenta et nunquam per penam pillorii nec per ~onem mercati *PQW* 556a.

4 recantation of a belief.

sicut professio et juramentum, ita [fidei] juratio et ~o voluntatem supponunt firmatam OCKHAM *Dial.* 441 *bis*; **1428** ad ~onem hujusmodi faciendam debite requisitus, ..sic abjurare pertinaciter recusavit.., violentam suspicionem heresis et erroris..incurrendo *Reg. Cant.* III 200; **1489** lecta fuit suprascripta ~o *Lit. Cant.* III 314.

abjurator, abjurer of the realm (*cf. abjurare* 4a).

articuli visus franci plegii: ..item de utlagatis et ~oribus regni reversis *Fleta* 112; **1306** nec..imprisonentur dum possint..invenire plevinam, ..nisi..latro cum manuopere.. deprehensus, ..utlagatus patrie ~or.. *BBC* (*Swansea*) 192.

abjurgatio v. objurgatio.

ablactaneus, weaned.

s1168 abbates..pueros vix ~eos solebant ad monachilem habitum..suscipere THORNE 1815.

ablactare [LL], to wean: **a** children; **b** animals; **c** (fig.).

a 597 ad ejus concubitum vir suus accedere non debet quoadusque qui gignitur ~atur (*Lit. Papae*) BEDE *HE* I 27 p. 55; cibis eam postmodum ~atam competentibus educari precepit L. DURH. *Brigida* 173F; respondebat: "..nec.. magis delector quam puer in uberibus matris delectatur dum illis acerba amaritudine superlitis ~atur" EADMER *V. Anselm.* II 13; non secus quam amara superlinita uberibus ~andos avertunt a lactis suavitate AD. MARSH *Ep.* 247 c. 36. **b** †subruinos [l. subrumos] ~atos NECKAM *Ut.* 102; **c1250** ut vituli sui possint ~ari communiter in blado totius villate *Cart. Rams.* I 489; cum vitulus taurinus vituletur primo mense non ablectetur *Fleta* 166; **1304** vituli agni et porcelli a matribus separantur ~ati *Cant. Cath. Pri.* 215; **1345** pro vitulis suis †ablactriantibus in blado communitatis *Rec. Elton* 334; ~o, i. a lacte removere, A. *to awenye* WW. **c** quasi sacratioris philosophie lactatum uberibus ~atumque J. SAL. *Pol.* 386c; H. BOS. *Thom.* VII 1 (v. aspellere); **a1273** capitulum in cujus sinu suaviter ab inicio fuerat ~atus, nutritus et ad quandam perfectionem deductus *Ann. Durh.* 117; **1317** a lacte juvenilis etatis per adeptam scienciam ~atus *FormOx* 31; [J. Wyclif] quem nec verborum mollities nec minarum asperitas ab his conceptuum sceleratissimorum uberibus potuit ~are ELMH. *Hen. V* 2.

2 (?) to suckle.

s1300 ut providerent ei mulierem Anglicanam ut eum †abla[c]taret *Ann. Ed. I* 438.

ablactatio, weaning: **a** of children; **b** of animals; **c** (fig.).

a defertur ad avos suos..ut cum eis ~onis suae transigat infantiam *V. Ed. Conf.* 39 v.; ~onis ejus die, dum pater ejusdem..affines ad convivium evocatos festive pasceret T. MON. *Will.* I 12; **s1318** filium aurige..sumentes et pro filio regis supponentes usque ad ~onem nutriverunt *Ann. Osney* 345; **1433** natus infra territorium monasterii S. Albani ibique usque ad tempora ~onis enutritus (*Ch. Binham*) AMUND. I 349. **b 1233** de ix caseis factis ante plenam ~onem [sc. agnorum] *Crawley* 212; **1299** si vendatur vitulus tempore †ablactionis *Reg. Cant.* I 359 (cf. ib.: infra ~onem). **c 1410** dum talis..filius ab uberibus matris sue [sc. Universitatis] citra tempus ~onis eripitur *FormOx* 213. **1417** petimus quatinus..teneros nostre communitatis alumpnos adhuc in lacte matris sub spe ~onis vestri pastoralis baculi recubantes ablactare velitis (*Pet. Univ. Ox.*) *Reg. Cant.* III 48.

ablambere, to lick off. **b** (fig.) to appropriate.

aurum ab aliis oblatum exquisito furti genere deosculando ~ere solebat et ore reconditum asportare GIR. *IK.* I 2. **b** hodie unus est et cras alius, et sic de septimana in septimanam vices eorum episcopus abla[m]bit P. BLOIS *Ep.* 209. 491B.

ablaqueatio [CL], clearing tree-roots.

~o, *niderwart treowes delfing, bedelfing* ÆLF. *Gl.*

ablatarius, person deprived.

loquimur..de habere opposito ablacioni qua Deus aufert..: vel est ~ius contentatus de ablacione Dei vel remurmurat vel est neuter WYCL. *Eccl.* 254.

ablatio, taking away, removal. **b** carrying off, theft. **c** (?) refusal, withholding.

frequenti ~one pulveris sacri BEDE *HE* V 18; per ~onem unius contrarii..probat alterum, quia in religione Christiana immediata sunt bonum et malum LANFR. *Comment. Paul.* (*Rom.* vii 22) 128; per ~onem duarum syllabarum in fine BACON *CSPhil.* 455; ejusdem ~o imperfeccionis est declaracio HAUBOYS 427; **1542** solut'..pro ~one tumbe S. Cuthberti *Ac. Durh.* 741. **b 1187** que in eorum gravamen attentata sunt in invasione villarum..et..~one aliarum rerum, in statum pristinum..reducat (*Lit. Papae*) *Ep. Cant.* 129; **1201** de ~one catallorum *CurR* II 15; **1265** quod eisdem mercatoribus..~o aliqua vel distractio fieret [bonorum] *Cl* 46 (cf. ib. 113: victualium ~ones); **1433** de ~one temporalium ab ecclesia *Reg. Cant.* III 249; **1457** super ~one c li. de cista *MunAcOx* 669. **c** hanc peciit et in responso regio, etsi non ~onem, dilacionem audivit MAP *NC* V 4 p. 214.

2 stolen property.

[latro] ~one reddita provinciam forisjuret (*Leg. Ed.*) *GAS* 630.

ablative, in the ablative case.

nulla [persona] dicit alia ~e DUNS *Sent.* I 32. 2. 7; cum ~e dicitur 'rerum consumptibilium usu', semper iste ablativus 'usu' conjunctus cum verbo consumendi..accipitur pro.. actu quo res consumitur OCKHAM *Pol.* II 515.

2 by removal (robbery).

cum ymaginibus a dicto loco ~e spoliatis *Plusc.* IX 33.

ablativus [CL], ablative (case), or governing the ablative.

in obliquis casibus, id est genetivo et ~o ALDH. *PR* 113; praepositiones..~ae corripiuntur omnes BEDE *AM* 2363; 'ipsius enim sumus factura'..potest et 'factura' ~us esse LANFR. *Comment. Paul.* (*Eph.* ii 10) 292; compendia quedam / ablativus habet cum sit sine remige solus VINSAUF *PN* 696; ita hoc nomen 'natura' erit casus ~i BRACTON 3b; illi ~i possunt solum absoluti esse qui de se habent intellectum plene orationis BACON XV 116; **1342** cum ~orum absolutorum et gerundiorum multitudine scrupulosa *Conc.* II 691; aliquando solum participium in consequentiae ~o [*ablative absolute*] legitur..[e.g.] 'audito regem in Ciliciam tendere' LINACRE *Emend. Lat.* 297.

2 (usu. in word-play) apt to take away. **b** apt to be taken away (or rifled).

paupertas vitii declinativa, malorum / ablativa, virum genitiva, dativa bonorum HANV. VI 334; quoniam, ut liber artis grammatice docet.., ~us proprie Romanorum est, in sensum alium..quidam hoc retorquentes dicunt vere ~um proprie Romanorum esse, quia Romanorum est proprium aliis quecumque possunt auferre GIR. *Spec.* IV 14; est etiam vis ~a, ..cum aliquis scilicet fodiat in alieno vel falcet et sic perturbet ut auferat et asportet rem mobilem de re immobili BRACTON 162; philosophus..posuit in universo causas ~as aliquando cujuslibet imperfeccionis DUNS *PW* VI 155; **c1370** ast ablativus erit ipsi morte nocivus [*gl.*: i. auferens eum de vita] (J. BRIDL.) *Pol. Poems* I 178. **b 15..** vocativos oculos, ablativos loculos amant mulieres (*Versus adventicii*) *Reg. Whet.* II 297.

ablator, dispossessor.

1199 nunquam feffati fuerunt predecessores sui nisi per ~ores suos *CurR RC* I 362; **1201** si..alium habuerint ingressum in eandem ecclesiam nisi per predictum..comitem A., ~orem predicti Willelmi *CurR* I 417; **1309** si seisina ipsius R. injuriosa, qui R. fuit ~or ipsius E., ..debeat eis obstare *Year Bk. 2 Ed. II* 49.

ablatus v. auferre, offerre. ablectare v. ablactare. ablienigena v. alienigena.

abligurigo, waste, squandering.

wastynge, ~igo *CathA*.

abligurire [CL], to eat up. **b** to squander.

abligorrit, degustat *GlC* A 456. **b** *to waste*, ~ire *CathA*.

ablingere, to lick up.

oratio lingua vitulina est ~ens herbam campi GIR. *GE* I 5.

ablongare, to eloign, entice away.

1352 allocutus de eo quod ~avit..servientes domini de servicio domini (*CourtR Heref.*) *Enf. Stat. Lab.* 396.

abluere [CL], to wash off. **b** to wash away.

cataclismorum irruptio..scelestis vitae pervicaciam ultricibus undis ~ens ALDH. *Met.* 2 p. 63; decet..maculas sordium ~ere NECKAM *Ut.* 107. **b** fluvius..Thamesis..menia illa tractu temporis ~it W. FITZST. *Thom. prol.* 5.

2 to wash, cleanse; **b** (w. ref. to baptism).

oculos sibi cecus..~it de divino rivulo S. Ivonis GOSC. *Mir. Iv.* lx; fons cujus aquis si quis ~itur statim canus efficitur GIR. *TH* II 7; ~at manus et faciem cum aqua frigida in estate et cum calida in hyeme GAD. 92. 2. **b** episcopus..provinciae duces..sacrosancto fonte ~ebat BEDE *HE* IV 13; originalis mundus..non tantum est submersus quantum est ~tus et illis originalibus maculis nostri figura lavacri emersit baptizatus H. LOS. *Ep.* 6 p. 11.

abluibilis, removable by washing.

putans quod fuisset quedam macula in..carne per aquam ~is WYCL. *Act.* 45.

ablutarius v. alutarius.

ablutio, washing, cleansing; **b** (w. ref. to baptism).

vestimentorum ~o *RegulC* 64; frequenti oculorum ~one (GOSC. *Mir. Iv.*) *Chr. Rams.* lx; de aqua..quasi ad digitorum ~onem..in calicem fusa GIR. *GE* I 47; ~oni manuum sacerdotis aquam ministrare *Cust. Cant.* 118; **1382** in emendacione vestimentorum cum ~one eorundem *Cant. Coll. Ox.* II 131. **b** verus..baptismus constat non tam ~one corporis quam fide cordis LANFR. *Corp. & Sang.* 424D; in baptismo locio exterior significat ~onem anime interiorem *AncrR* 127.

2 water in which something has been washed.

si..super aliquem honestum pannum sanguis [Domini] ceciderit, ..pars illa panni in aliquo calice abluatur et prima ~o a fratribus absumatur, reliquae duae in sacrarium projiciantur LANFR. *Const.* 156; †**1214** si os interius abluerit sacerdos, non abjiciat ~onem sed deglutiat ipsam *Conc. Syn.* 28*n.*; **c1250** illam ~onem sacerdos sumat *Ib.* 642; si..corporalia..sanguine Dominico fuerint intincta, quod laventur tribus vicibus, semel videlicet vino et postea bis aqua, calice subterposito, et vini ~o a ministro sumatur, aque vero ~o in calice simpliciter recipiatur *Cust. Cant.* 288 (cf. *Cust. Westm.* 212).

ablutium, drain, sink.

sint etiam ibi [in coquina] †alucia [*gl.*: a *lavurs*; b *guteres*], ubi volatilium..et avium domesticarum entera et extremitates crebro a lixa proiciantur et purgentur NECKAM *Ut.* 97; *kychyn gotere*, †alucium *PP*; *a gutter*, alluvio, alluvies, †allucium, †allucia, †alluces *CathA*.

ablutor, cleanser.

~or peccaminum, Domine, qui animam..consolaris ALCUIN *Liturg.* 516B.

ablutorium, laundry.

a1300 ministri sartorii et ~ii de igne faciendo ministrabunt *Chr. Abingd.* II 386 (cf. ib. 390: magister ~ii).

ablutrix, laundress.

a1300 ~icem ornamentorum ecclesie remuneratione xx s. annua conducet *Chr. Abingd.* II 383.

abmatertera [CL], maternal great-great-great-aunt. **b** paternal great-aunt.

~a mea, *minre moddrian pridde moder* ÆLF. *Gl.*; sic gradatim vocandi sunt abavunculus magnus et ~a magna BRACTON 68b. **b** Eadgyfu..~a tua [*paternal great-aunt*] ÆTHELW. *Prol.* p. 2 (cf. p. xlvii).

abminiculum v. adminiculum.

abnegare [CL], **a** (w. acc. & inf.) to deny, refuse. **b** to deny guilt, reject a charge. **c** to repudiate. **d** (p. ppl. as sb. n.) denial.

a neque ~avit se etiam eandem subiturum esse religionem BEDE *HE* II 9. **b** qui de morte domini sui cogitabit ..sue ipsius vite culpabilis habeatur..vel secundum weram domini sui festinet ~are [AS: *getreowe*] (*Quad.*) *GAS* 51; si ~are [AS: *ætsacan*] velint et in triplici ordalio culpabiles inveniantur *Ib.* 155; Judei impositum sibi crimen ~ant T. MON. *Will.* I 16. **c** si ego confiteor nequitiam meam, tune ~abis benignitatem tuam? ANSELM (*Or.* 5) III 14; **s1460** si propositum [sc. matrimonium] hujusmodi non ~aret *Croyl. Cont. C* 572. **d** universale non est ~atum pluralitatis set quasi secundum rem multiplicatum est BACON XV 54.

2 to refuse, withhold: **a** something due; **b** submission etc.

a eo..pecuniam quam ejus fidei crediderat constanter ~ante GIR. *TH* II 44; **s1242** quod de jure debuit ~avit *Flor. Hist.* II 251. **b s1095** cum..mihi omnem subjectionem, fidem et amicitiam quam primati et patri vestro debetis ~atis, non recte proceditis EADMER *HN* 73; **s1138** rex..mandat episcopo..sue parti fidelitatem jurare..; ~at episcopus RIC. HEX. *Stand.* 42.

3 to deny, repudiate (Christ or Christian faith).

s1134 suadetur ~are Christianitatem J. WORC. 39; [rex Alapie] archiepiscopum [Edesse]..cum omni clero, quia Christum noluerunt ~are, ..decollari precepit *Meaux* I 114; **s1311** quod [Templarii] in recepcione sua..~abant Christum *Ann. Lond.* 180; **s1222** diaconus..Christiane religionis professionem ~avit W. COVENTR. II 251 (cf. *Conc. Syn.* 105); cum raro accidat quod aliquis appellando..Papam sibi imponat quod fidem ~averit Christianam OCKHAM *Dial.* 549.

4 (refl.) to deny oneself, subdue selfish desires.

c1238 non est ipse sibi presens, sed semet ipsum ~ans et proprie voluntati penitus renuncians GROS. *Ep.* 17 p. 174.

5 to poison (? misinterp. of Orosius *Hist.* V 14. 6: ~*ato cibo*).

†abegato, venenato *GlC* A 22.

abnegatio, denial (of guilt or intention).

fur, postquam est in vinculis regis, non habet hanc ~onem [AS: *swicne*] (*Quad.*) *GAS* 97; **s1460** consilium ~onis [sc. matrimonii] hujusmodi..clara..voce per omnia exequebatur *Croyl. Cont. C* 572.

2 refusal of submission or repudiation of overlord.

s1095 secuti sunt episcopi..penitentiam..agentes pro culpa sue ~onis quam..fecerant EADMER *HN* 82; per ~onem domini sui homagium et vinculum fidelitatis infringit BRACTON 81.

3 denial or repudiation of Christ or Christian faith.

s1311 tres [Templarii] deposuerunt se fore receptos cum ~one Christi et spuitione super crucem *Ann. Lond.* 181 (cf. *Conc. Syn.* 1318); vos [Judei] propter ejus [Christi] ~onem et occisionem fuistis et estis puniti graviter BRADW. *CD* 47D; fidei ~onem OCKHAM *Dial.* 448.

4 (w. *sui*) self-denial, self-abnegation.

c1238 monachalis in orando solitudo est..mentis..ab inutilibus cogitationibus segregatio, sui ipsius ~o et proprie voluntati renuntiatio et in solum Deum directa intentio GROS. *Ep.* 57 p. 175.

5 negation (log.).

inter justum et injustum..est aliquod medium, saltem per ~onem, quia actus aliarum virtutum et aliorum vitiorum..nec sunt justi nec injusti OCKHAM *Pol.* II 581; per ~onem extremorum R. BURY *Phil.* 15. 193; medium inter contraria duplex potest esse aut extremorum per participacionem vel per utriusque extremi ~onem HAUBOYS 427.

abnegativus, negative.

duabus principalibus theologiae partibus, ..affirmativa quidem..et ~a, quae ἀποφατική vocatur ERIUG. *Per.* 458A; diversa quesitu sunt 'quid fit' et 'quid est quod fit', nisi forte alterum excludatur initialiter prequirendi certificatione ~a BALSH. *AD* 145.

abnegator, denier (of God).

c1240 Dei ~or, diaboli proles GROS. *Ep.* 90 p. 280.

abnepos [CL], great-great-grandson.

~us, qui natus est de pronepote *GlC* A 24 (cf. ib. 612); ~os, *feowerþe sune* ÆLF. *Sup.*; erant [Hengestus et Hors] ~otes illius antiquissimi Woden W. MALM. *GR* I 5; filiorum Nemedi, nepotum ~umque successio GIR. *TH* III 3; dici poterunt remotiores respectu heredum remotorum, sicut pronepos, ~os, atnepos, trinepos et sic ulterius descendendo BRACTON 64b; **c1410** adolescens..cujus propagationis linea in me sui trinepotis ~em..est producta (J. SEWARD *Arpyilogus*) *Med. & R. Stud.* I 96*n.*

abneptis [CL], great-great-granddaughter. **b** great-great-niece.

~is, *feowrþe dohter* ÆLF. *Sup.* **b** erat illa [Mathildis]..regis Edwardi ex fratre Edmundo ~is W. MALM. *GR* V 393 (cf. AILR. *Ed. Conf.* 774A).

abnormis [CL], not conforming to rule.

withouten rewle, ~is, anormulus *CathA*.

abnuere [CL], to refuse. **b** (w. dat.).

amnuere, refugere *GlC* A 520 (cf. ib. 72); ut..pedum regulas propalare..non ~as ALDH. *PR* 112; fratres..qui prius ~erant..ipsi petere coeperunt BEDE *HE* III 11; utrumque [panem et caseum] ignorantes ~erunt GIR. *TH* III 26; ~o recipere munera tua *G. S. Alb.* I 127. **b** abnuit ille preci WULF. *Swith.* II 319.

abolēre [CL], **~ire,** to abolish, destroy, efface. **b** to forget (cf. Virg. *Aen.* I 720).

qui solus..pronepotum piacula proprii praerogativa meriti ~ere potuisset ALDH. *VirgP.* 53; ut nomen et memoria apostatarum de catalogo regum Christianorum prorsus ~eri deberet BEDE *HE* III 9; †**931** (13c) ne quamdiu Christianitas regnet aboletur (*sic*) unde mihi praefata possessio..donaretur *CS* 671; ~ita..foret estatis et hiemis distemperantia ADEL. *QN* 71; nec tamen omnino..poesis ~ita GIR. *TH Intr.* p. 4; **c1280** oblivionis pumice aboliri (*DCCant*) *HMC Rep. Var. Coll.* I 247; quod..mundentur segetes, quodque herbe dampnose penitus abole[a]ntur *Fleta* 170 (cf. ib. 165: necessarium est..hujusmodi pecora sapienter abolire); **1403** si..epitaphium insculptum lapide suo ~eri..contigerit *Cl* 251 m. 17*d*; **1588** pro mundificacione et ~endo macularum *Ac. L. Chamb.* 79 9v. **b** ~ere, neglegenter agere vel oblivisci *GlC* A 36 (cf. ib. 65, 85, 91).

abolescere [CL], to wane.

si aestate ~ente calor disjunctius accesserit ADEL. *QN* 64.

abolim [al. div.], from of old.

1278 super injuriis quoddam sequestrum ab olim in ecclesia de H. contingentibus *SelCKB* I 46; **1300** ~im siquidem inter prelatos..et fratres..gravis..discordia extitit *Reg. Carl.* I 125; **1356** ab olim necnon ab omni tempore, et presertim cujus contrarii memoria hominum non existit *Lit. Cant.* II 33; **1367** pia opera ibidem pro salute animarum..~im stabilita et ordinata *IMisc* 193/3 r. 1; **1446** ut, sicut ab olim et continue publicos..sermones dicturi..memoriale..agere obligati sunt, ita jam [etc.] *EpAcOx* 256.

abolire v. abolere.

abolitanus [< abolim], bygone.

668 sicut ~is temporibus fuerunt condonata in perpetuum, ita..immutilanda concedimus obtinenda (*Lit. Papae*) W. MALM. *GP* I 33.

abolitio, abolition, cancellation, effacement.

facit..scientia ignorantiae ~onem ERIUG. *Per.* 565B; [hypocrite] circumeunt ecclesias, ..~ones criminum portant J. SAL. *Pol.* 695C; **c1170** que mutatio et versibilitas nature diminutionem et ~onem facit J. CORNW. *Eul.* 1053; **1412** nulli librorum..per rasuras, ~onesve quaternorum seu foliorum dampnum..inferendo *StatOx* 218.

abominabilis (abhominabilis), abominable, hateful: **a** of persons; **b** of acts or objects.

a 'esca [sc. idolothytum] nos non commendat Deo', imo ~es facit LANFR. *Comment. Paul.* (1 *Cor.* viii 8) 182; confusi monachi [excommunicati] et omnibus quasi ~es effecti GERV. CANT. I 136. **b** quanto ~ior enormitas culpe H. BOS. *LM* 1304; hoc ~issimum et prorsus diabolicum..scelus AD. SCOT. *Sol.* 869; **1253** peccatum Domino Jhesu Christo ~issimum et humano generi perniciosissimum GROS. *Ep.* 128 p. 436; hostile est et ~e [in loca sancta] alias ingredi quam per portas BRACTON 8; **1395** imago usualis de Trinitate est maxime ~is (*Concl. Lollard.* 8) *Ziz.* 364.

2 offensive to the senses. **b** causing nausea. **c** wearisome.

s1226 musce quedam grosse..inter tentoria se stridore ~i ingerentes M. PAR. *Maj.* III 115; **1305** per feditates..aer..in tantum corrumpitur quod..ibidem conversantibus horror ~is incutitur *BBC* (*Oxford*) 374; delicatissimi quondam libri corrupti et ~es jam effecti murium..fetibus cooperti..jacebant R. BURY *Phil.* 8. 120; **1416** magnum et ~e sterquilinium *Fabr. York* 248. **b** dyasatirion aliquantulum ~e est et dyaforeticum GILB. VII 287 1; laxativis ~ibus BACON IX 49. **c** sint [que scribuntur] brevia moderate, quia superfluitas impedit multum ad cognitionem veritatis et reddit opus ~e *Id. Tert.* 57.

abominabiliter, abominably.

1233 sacra scriptura propter te, qui ore ~er polluti corporis eam doces, a pluribus abominabilis reputatur GROS. *Ep.* 10 p. 48; fuerat..episcopus..a Stowensibus monachis..jugi malediccione ~er execratus *Croyl. Cont. A* 127.

abominanter, abominably.

mulier ~er seducta serpenti credidit PULL. *Sent.* 747.

abominari (abhominari) [CL], to abominate, detest.

a680 Demetarum sacerdotes..nostram communionem magnopere ~antur ALDH. *Ep.* 4 p. 484; ~anda facinorum flagitia *Id. Met.* 2 p. 68; ejus quem toto corde ~aris habitum BEDE *HE* V 21; **931** ea..velud..nausiam ~ando *CS* 677; quod Deus usque quaque ~atur H. LOS. *Ep.* 6 p. 7; **s1138** Scotti..obscena et ~anda irreverenter perpetraverunt J. HEX. *HR Cont.* 290; aliter..lector..~aretur ejus formam WYCL. *Ver.* I 195.

abominatio (abhominatio), abomination, loathing. **b** nausea.

a706 respondete..utrum horrendae ~onis infamia sint exprobrandi qui..subjectionis frena ritu frenetico frangunt ALDH. *Ep.* 9; P. de Gavestone, qui fere omnes magnates Anglie habuit in ~onem et totaliter in despectum *Flor. Hist.* III 331; **13..** despeccione dignus habeatur et tam Dei quam hominum ~one *Reg. S. Andr.* 368. **b 1178** universa patiebantur spiritum vertiginis, spiritum ~onis et nausee P. BLOIS *Ep.* 52 158B; dolore capitis, siti, fastidio, ~one GILB. I 40. 2; (cf. ib. V 209 v. 2: ~ones acetosas, ructuationes..); que ~onem auferunt BACON IX 105; si..sit venenosum aut quod ~onem faciat *Cust. Westm.* 218.

2 object of loathing. **b** (object of) physical disgust, nuisance.

1188 ~o facti divitum, pauperes..elemosinis..vivimus pauperum *Ep. Cant.* 184; **s1320** in Matheo [xxiv 15] scriptum est 'cum videritis ~onem desolacionis sedentem in templo', ..ac si diceret 'cum videritis..illiteratum et fatuum in ecclesia Dei preminere' *V. Ed. II* 254; **s1417** [J. Oldcastelle] sacerdotes et ecclesias quasi ~ones odivit CAPGR. *Hen.* 122. **b** ~ones infirmorum, tam in vomitu quam in ceteris immundiciis, equo animo tolerabit *Obs. Barnwell* 204; **1391** habuit..equum..jacentem in regia via in magnam ~onem et corrupcionem *Leet Norw.* 75; **1403** inhumatus extitit..in populi nostri ~onem *Cl* 252 m. 21; **1409** propter fetoris ~onem ejusdem latrine *Fabr. York* 247.

3 abominable act or custom. **b** (play on *homo* and *abhominatio*) act of inhuman presumption.

s1178 de omnibus ~onibus suis [sc. Albigensium] malis *G. Hen. II* I 215; **s1217** milites..ultramarinos qui ~ones inauditas in comprovincialibus exercuerunt M. PAR. *Min.* II 202; **1288** hujusmodi..consuetudines, que proprie abusiones et ~ones dicuntur *FormOx* 358; **a1400** ~o magna est quod episcopi..sint ita magni domini in mundo (PURVEY) *Ziz.* 394. **b** [auguria etc.] ~ones sunt, dicente Domino [*Deut.* xviii 9]; et homo se supra hominem fieri opinatur cum istorum assecutus est disciplinam J. SAL. *Pol.* 475B.

abominator, detester.

Oxoniensium et aliorum abhominatorum [v.l. abhominancium] universalium..oppositum (WYCL. *Ente*) *Wycl. & Ox.* 153*n*.

aborigo, shoot, sucker or weed. **b** native animal.

weede or wyld herbe, ~o *PP*; hec ~o, abori[gin]es sunt superflue †faucies [l. frutices] WW; *a syon or a twige*, ~o et proprie est pluralis; ..*a wede*, †aborago *CathA*. **b** virgo Domini..hic suos advenas et ~ines..incluserat GOSC. *Edith* 65.

aboriri [CL], **abortus** (*p. ppl.*), born prematurely or still-born. **b** producing still-born young.

10.. ~us, *samboren* WW. **b** **1233** xvij matres [oves] fuerunt mortue ante partum et xxj stereles et xxiiij ~e *Crawley* 212.

2 (?) welling up.

set soror obstabat lacrimisque rogabat †abortis [v.l. obortis] / ut secum remaneret *V. Merl.* 349 (cf. ib. 54).

aborsus, abortion, miscarriage. **b** (fig.).

1211 iiij^{xx} oves fuerunt steriles et xj fecerunt ~um *Pipe Wint.* 136; **s1241** numquam ipsam Isabellam verberavit, unde puer de quo fecit ~um propinquior fuit morti *MGL* I 105; major est dolor in ~u quam in partu naturali GAD. 83. 2. **b** concilium totius Anglie cleri..propter contentionem inter archiepiscopos ibidem obortam..~um fecit GIR. *EH* II 31; **1422** pastor ac parens, in animo compatiens monstruosi ~us fetui [i.e. *a recalcitrant monk*] (*Lit. Abbatis*) AMUND. I 91.

abortire, ~iri, to miscarry. **b** (fig.).

eam imprisonavit..et verberavit ita quod ~ivit *CurR* II 295; causa ~iendi BART. ANGL. IV 4; mulieres male que nolunt impregnari accipiunt savinam et potant et ~iunt cum angustia GAD. 83. v. 1 (cf. ib. 83. 2: mulier que frequenter patitur in matrice de facile ~itur). **b** sic mater ecclesia pariendo filios ~iri compellitur R. BURY *Phil. prol.* 8.

abortive, by miscarriage (fig.).

s1457 illud horribile monstrum [sc. R. Pecok], quod regnum Anglie jam nuper ~e produxit †adesse [l. ad esse], in melius reformavit archipresularis auctoritas *Reg. Whet.* I 288.

abortivus, a still-born. **b** (alch., w. ref. to gold). **c** producing still-born young. **d** causing abortion.

a mulieres qui (*sic*) ~um faciunt antequam animam habeat, j annum..peniteant THEOD. *Pen.* I xiv 24; **s1241** verberavit eam..ita quod filium suum peperit ~um *MGL* I 103; **1449** xxj [matrices] projecerunt agnos suos ~os *Crawley* 483. **b** homines ante tempus fetus colligere cupientes abhortivos genuerunt M. SCOT. *Sol & Luna* 720. **c** **1306** cvij [ovium] fuerunt steriles et ~e *Crawley* 246. **d** ~am eam [molochiam] putant esse cum adipe anseris parti †genitale [l. genitali] subditam *Alph.* 120.

2 (fig.) **a** born out of time or misbegotten. **b** abortive, fruitless. **c** (sb. m. or n.) travesty, shadow.

a inter quos, auctore Domino, quasi ~us et eruditorum minimus discipulus qui scripsit hoc H. BOS. *Thom.* VII 1 p. 529. **b** non..est res perfecta cujus..~us labor tempus preveniat *FormOx* 445. **c** Cuthredus octo annis solo scilicet nomine regnavit; hinc regie dignitatis ~um Baldredus, postquam Cantiam octodecim annis obsedit..concessit W. MALM. *GR* I 15 (cf. *Eul. Hist. annot.* II 369: huic regie dignitatis ~o successit Aldredus).

3 'abortive', uterine vellum (made from skin of still-born animal).

1265 in xx duodenis parchameni ~i..ad portiforium xs. (*RHosp*) *Manners* 9; **1445** solut'..pro ~o viz. xxxv quaternis *DCCant. Reg. Var. Ac.* f. 43 (cf. ib. f. 93b [**1446**]: pro ij pellibus abertivi; f. 94: pro xx quaternis aburtivi).

4 (sb. f.) weed (*cf. aborigo*).

1410 ita quod spine, tribuli..et alie abhortive viam.. supercrescerent *IMisc.* 290/8.

1 abortus v. aboriri.

2 abortus [cf. aborsus], miscarriage.

~us, *misbyrd GlC* A 12; **1336** vj [oves] fecerunt ~um *Crawley* 275.

abpatruus [CL], great-great-great-uncle.

~us meus, *mines fæderan pridde fæder* ÆLF. *Sup.*; tunc vocantur fratres abavi vel abavie qui dicuntur ~us magnus et abamita magna BRACTON 68b.

abra [ἅβρα], handmaid (*cf. Judith* viii 32 *etc.*).

~a, ancella *GlC* A 10; ~a, i. ancilla, *pinen, wyln* ÆLF. *Gl.*; *wench*, ~a *PP*; hec -a, *a burwoman* WW; *an handemayden*, ~a, ancilla *CathA*.

abradere [CL], to shave, scrape bare. **b** (fig.).

[castores] notabiles..abrasa et attrita dorsorum depilatione GIR. *TH* I 26; quidam barbator dimidium barbe abrasit feneratori O. CHERITON *Par.* 151; **1258** si [clerici] sic [propter transgressionem foreste] capti malitiose tempore intermedio abrasi fuerint seu suspensi.. *Conc. Syn.* 578 (cf. LYNDW. 321 *z*). **b** nisi mox prelium diremisset, omnes mortis novacula abrasi fuissent W. JUM. VI 6; **s1098** exactionibus pessimis populos Anglorum non ~ens sed excorians H. HUNT. *HA* VII 20.

2 to scrape off, erase (writing or marks). **b** to erase (document). **c** to erase, blot out (fig.).

quicquid hac in editione contra orthographiae normam usurpatum repereris..~ere *V. Dunst.* B. *prol.* p. 4; **1166** x marce sunt abrase in cartis (*KRMisc* 1/16) *EHR* XXVIII 221; quod si forte..contigerit [scriptorem] errare in scriptura rotuli, non presumat ~ere set linea subtili subducta cancellet *Dial. Scac.* I 5V; scriptor habeat rasorium..ad ~endum sordes pergameni NECKAM *Ut.* 116; s **1208** rex ad omnia consensit, preter de spoliatorum restitutione facienda, et hoc petiit a cartis ~i *Eul. Hist.* III 95; **1427** si..litteras.. reperirimus sanas et integras non cancellatas nec abrasas, non abolitas, non viciatas *Reg. Cant.* III 147. **b** **1194** breve abrasum fuit *CurR RC* I 119; [breve] non abrasum in aliquo loco suspecto BRACTON 190. **c** **s1308** providit Dominus egregie militie Theotonicorum ut nomen acephali ..prudenter †abradarent, quod illorum in fronte..inpudenter impresserat torpedo confusa *Flor. Hist.* III 144.

3 to wipe out, destroy.

brutum illud homunculorum [sc. Albigensium]..genus magno fidelium sudore abrasum est AD. EYNS. *Hug.* IV 13; [Willelmus I], ducens exercitum in Northumbriam, universam patriam abrasit *Croyl.* 79; [Edmundus] v..civitates.. omni infidelitate abrasa Christiane fidei lumine illustravit *Plusc.*VI 16.

4 (p. ppl.) 'razed', levelled (of measure).

1298 exitus frumenti de mensura abrasa lxxij quart' frumenti *Doc. Bec* 175.

abradicare, to uproot: **a** plants; **b** buildings.

a **1308** habebit j garbam vocatam *topschef* quantum poterit ligare in quodam ligamine metato et non ~ato neque cum radicibus de terra extracto (*Ext.*) *Growth Eng. Indust.* 579; **1310** ~avit herbam in blado domini *CourtR Rams.* 257. **b** **1271** ad capellam episcopi que aradicata fuit cum magno vento *Pipe Wint.* (159299) r. 2*d.*; **1338** post adnullationem Templariorum omnes domus ~ate fuerunt et abducte per dominos feodorum *Hosp. in Eng.* 133; **1360** quandam domum..~avit et usque domum ipsius J.. duxit *Pat* 260 m. 21; **13..** si..tenens aliqua appenticia in domibus fecerit, et ad meremium..domus per clavos.. attachiata fuerint, non liceat tali tenenti hujusmodi appenticia..~are *MGL* I 432.

abramutium, abramounsey (a fabric).

1574 un' safgard de ~io ashcolor' miss' e regione Fraunci e *Ac. L. Chamb.* 65 f. 25.

abrasio, a shaving. **b** scraping off. **c** abrasion (of skin).

a ~o..capillorum et barbe, que ex superfluis stomachi nascuntur humoribus BELETH *RDO* 114. **b** [pellis] in lignis extensa suscipit ~onem pinguedinis WYCL. *Ver.* II 267. **c** mahemium dicitur ossis..fractio vel teste capitis per incisionem vel per ~onem attenuatio GLANV. XIV 1.

2 erasure in document.

si vero in scribendo liture occurrunt aut obliteratio, non cancelletur scriptura sed abradatur; opus est autem ut dente apri poliatur locus ~onis (NECKAM *Sac.*) *Med. Sci.* 361; si [in brevi] inveniatur ~o, tunc refert quo loco BRACTON 413b.

abrasor, extorter.

s1229 ~or pecuniarum, ..domini Pape capellanus M. PAR. *Maj.* III 189 (cf. ib. V 409: non pigri ~ores).

abreg- v. abbreg-.

abrenuntiare, (w. dat.) to renounce: **a** a way of life, practice, belief, or purpose; **b** a right, title, or office; **c** allegiance; **d** a promised wife; **e** the realm (*cf. abjurare* 4).

a cum..saeculo ~iare disponeret BEDE *HE* III 19; **1073** ~iandum eis [studiis] decrevimus LANFR. *Ep.* 33 (*cf. Conc.* I 362); temporalibus ~iavimus deliciis H. LOS. *Ep.* 14; ut studeret..~iare ecclesiastice confessioni J. SAL. *Pol.* 801A; **s1177** principes Teuthonici regni, ~iantes schismati,.. absolutionis beneficium meruerunt *G. Hen. II* I 185; in hac..curiosa languesco curia, meis ~ians voluntatibus ut placeam aliis MAP *NC* IV 13; **1232** ~iat..mundo vera religio GROS. *Ep.* 8 p. 44; **s1223** "~io legi nove et invente et commentis Jhesu pseudoprophete" M. PAR. *Min.* II 254; **1397** ~iando omni..supersticioni *Reg. Heref.* 144. **b** **s1095** ut Anselmus archiepiscopatui, reddito baculo et anulo, ~iaret EADMER *HN* 68; **1165** cognoscens quod ad regnum Cantuariensis ecclesie non valeat..redire, ipsi spontaneus ~iabit (*Lit. J. Card.*) *Becket Mat.* VI 382; **1219** juri suo et clamationi ejusdem predicte terre..~iavit *CurR* VIII 15; **12..** me..~iasse clamori quem clamabam *Cart. Holyrood* no. 72; **s1294** Papa..~iando honori et oneri..recusabat prolixius presulatum regere Romanorum *Flor. Hist.* III 276; nisi ~iaverit spontanea voluntate papatui OCKHAM *Dial.* 507 **s1339** nonnulli ipsorum novorum militum ordini milicie ~iarunt *Meaux* III 41. **c** **s1217** "vultisne ~iare obedientie quam Deo promittendo vovistis?" *G. S. Alb* I 257. **d** **s1188** Ricardus..puelle ~iavit *Eul. Hist.* III 90. **e** **1487** fatebatur feloniam, ibidem prestando juramentum corporale †abronunciandi regno Anglie *Sanct. Durh.* 70.

2 (w. abl.) to renounce (a right).

s1327 omni..jure regio sibi competente coram notariis ~iavit et a regni regimine se dimisit *Meaux* B 354.

3 (w. acc.) to renounce (a belief etc.).

~iatis idolis BEDE *HE* III 19; **s1177** imperator ~ians schisma..dextravit papam FL. WORC. *Cont. B* 154.

abrenuntiatio, renunciation: **a** of belief or way of life; **b** of a country; **c** of office.

a in peccati ~one non alterius detractione baptizamur LANFR. *Cel. Conf.* 627C; **c1400** fratres..debent..vivere..in omni sanctitate ac ~one seculi (*Concl. Loll.*) *EHR* XXVI 747; **s1427** errorum plenam ~onem *Chr. S. Alb.* 13. **b** erat [Wilfridus] timore Dei plenus, sicut..voluntaria regni ~one mundo probatum est W. MALM. *GP* III 107. **c** **a1170** quod ..significasti..Wintoniensem episcopum..episcopatui suo abrenuntiasse, ..~onem ipsam..nec possumus nec debemus ratam aut non ratam habere (*Lit. Papae*) *Becket Mat.* V 256.

abrepticius v. arrepticius. abrev- v. abbrev-.

abripere, to snatch away. **b** (refl.) to retire.

7.. erepta vel abrepta, i. sublata, *gened, pa genumenan* WW; puer abripit uvas / e manibus matris comedentis WULF. *Swith.* I 1055; oblationes accedentium vixdum apposite de manibus ~iebantur; abrepte in commessationes ..consumebantur W. MALM. *GR* II 201; qui consuli.. sponsam ~uit H. HUNT. *HA* VIII 15; sanctuaria..†abrepsit *G. Steph.* II 83; **s1298** cupientes denarios de manibus executorum defuncti ~ere *Chr. S. Edm.* 70 (cf. ib. 68: arepta costa sua). **b** ~it se in cameram G. CRISPIN *Herl.* 90.

abrizium v. obryzus.

abrocagium [cf. brocagium], brokerage.

1285 quod capiatur (*sic*) pro ~io dolii vini vj d. *Cal. LB Lond.* A 714 (cf. *MGL* I 706); **1291** de quadam convencione quam quidam mercator fecerat cum eis..nomine abroccagii pro pellibus suis bydencium vendendis (*St. Ives*) *Law Merch.* I 45.

abrocamentum, brokerage.

1306 mercimonia..libere vendantur et emantur absque aliquo forstallamento seu ~o *BBC* (*Yarmouth*) 294; **1320** ne qui forstallamenta, ~a aut alia hujusmodi..faciant *MunCOx* 33; **1355** pisces..emunt et ad domos dictorum forstallatorum, privatorum mercatorum et broggatorum ac aliorum, qui hujusmodi forstallamenta et abroggamenta per alios faciunt et fieri procurant, ad saliendum et extra terram nostram sine debita licencia transmittendum..ducunt *Stat. Ir.* I 400.

abrocarius, broker.

13.. de pena ~ii de foristalria convicti *MGL* I 250 (cf. ib. 269).

abrocatio, brokerage.

1300 (*convicted of forestalling and*) ~one carectarum *Cal. LBLond.* C 67.

abrocator [cf. brocator], broker.

1255 decetero non sint ~ores in predicta villa [*Dunwich*] per quos venditores vel emptores de vendicionibus vel empcionibus suis libere faciendis impediantur *ChartR.* 73 m. 12 (cf. *BBC* II 294); **1287** Johannes R., abrokcator predicti Reginaldi (*St. Ives*) *Law Merch.* I 25 (cf. ib. 54 [**1291**]: abroketor); **1319** quod abbrocatores aliquarum mercandisarum in civitate predicta decetero non existant, nisi per mercatores de mesteris in quibus ipsi ~ores habeant officia sua exercere ad hoc electi fuerint (*Ch. Ed. II*) *MGL* II 272; **1321** Johannem Molmer, ~orem de Bruges *CalCl* 21.

abrogabilis, revocable, due to be repealed.

primum locum..~is sui quaternarii NETTER *DAF* I 357C; **1433** illa clausula vitiosa est nimis, omnique jure ac ratione ~is (*Replicatio Abbatis*) AMUND. I 339.

abrogare [CL], to repeal, annul. **b** to renounce.

recuperatorem mundi..cirografum protoplastorum misericorditer ~antem ALDH. *Met.* 1; antiqua privilegia vel mutilare contendimus vel ~are GIR. *EH* II 36; orbem / confundit, leges abrogat NECKAM *DS* III 178; **s1377** in hoc Parliamento ~ata sunt statuta Parliamenti superioris WALS. *HA* I 324. **b** incolumem armis militem ~atis monachum fieri G. CRISPIN *Herl.* 87.

2 to depose.

s1386 licitum est..ipsum regem de regali solio ~are KNIGHTON II 219; [Ethelbertus] memoriter eruditus.. Lucium..regem..tres archiflamines ~ari [fecisse] et ad eorum sedes..tres archiepiscopos promoveri ELMH. *Cant.* 134.

abrogatio, prohibition.

s1382 Parliamentum..in quo plures articuli sunt.. decreti, videlicet..de ~one pellure et apparatus argenti in zonis WALS. *HA* II 48.

abroggamentum v. abrocamentum. abrenunciare v. abrenuntiare 1 e. abrostura v. abrustura. abrotanum v. habrotonum. abruere v. obruere.

abrumpere [CL], to break. **b** (fig.).

obvias fortiter ~unt acies MAP *NC* III 4. **b** inite transactionis fedus ~it W. CANT. *V. Thom.* II 8; dum vite abrumpit egestas / gaudia HANV. III 275.

2 (p. ppl.) abrupt, steep. **b** (sb. n.) steep place (also fig.). **c** (abl. or w. *ex*) abruptly, suddenly.

montem..in quo nihil repente arduum, nihil praeceps, nihil abruptum BEDE *HE* I 7. **b 1242** qui ad eam [ecclesiam] ambitiose per arupta intendat ascendere *RGasc* I 160; propter abrupta viarum ELMH. *Hen. V* 20 (cf. ib. 105: in abruptis rupium anchorare); viam morum elegistis optimam et viciorum respuistis abrupta CAPGR. *Hen.* 2 (cf. *Reg. Carl.* [1302] I 174: prelati..per †abruta viciorum incedere..presumentes). **c** ut nichil unquam in conventu abrupto aut importune fiat *Cust. Westm.* 136 (cf. *Cust. Cant.* I 222: ne aliquid unquam ex abrupto aut inconsulte agatur); **1297** cum Hibernici se dederunt ad guerrandum ex arrupto vel improviso *Stat. Ir.* I 206; volentes ex a[b]rupto vel ausu temerario..civitatem introire FAVENT 12; **1379** ad hujusmodi actum prosiliunt ex arrupto *StatOx* 178.

abrupte, abruptly, precipitately.

neque facile moveri loco neque ~e loqui OSB. *V. Dunst.* 8; Augustinus..non ita ~e ut tu dicis sacramentum sacrum esse signum definivit LANFR. *Corp. & Sang.* 422C; ne ecclesiarum possessiones tam ~e..pervaderent *G. Steph.* II 80; nolens aliquid ~e facere ne post factum peniteret *Chr. Wallingf.* 55.

abruptus, abruta v. abrumpere.

abrustura [cf. brustura], browsing (Norm.).

1157 concessisse..in parco..abrosturam boum *Act. Hen. II* I 136.

abrutio v. obruitio.

abscedere [CL], to depart. **b** (fig.) to disappear.

socii..procul abscedunt ALDH. *VirgV.* 2243; cum ad tempus abscessissem a te BEDE *HE* V 12; his dictis, abessit H. LOS. *Ep.* 28 p. 57; lupus, qui parumper abscesserat, iterum accessit GIR. *TH* V 19; portitorem ut abcederet.. inclamabant R. COLD. *Cuthb.* 39; ut unusquisque saltem panem dimidium accipiat, ne omnino vacui abcedant *G. S. Alb.* I 207. **b** resedit tumor, dolor omnis abcessit AILR. *Ed. Conf.* 762A.

abscessio, departure.

post tres ~ionis Wilfridi annos BEDE *HE* IV 12; his dictis, abessit [imago], suaque abessione meam absentiam presentibus reddidit H. LOS. *Ep.* 28 p. 57.

abscessus, departure. **b** withdrawal. **c** disposal, dispatch.

non multis annis post ~um ejus a Brittania transactis BEDE *HE* III 7; post abcessum Wilfridi GERV. CANT. II 340; ad hujus ~um..[fons] pristinos iterum redit in canales GIR. *TH* II 8. **b** ab ordine minatus ~um *Canon. G. Sempr.* 78. **c 1297** articulis arduis..de quibus..clero magna proveniret utilitas..necnon [qui] transitu et abcessu magnam celeritatem..desiderant *Reg. Cant.* I 179.

abscidere [CL], **a** to cut off, amputate, mutilate (part of body). **b** to cut down or lop (trees). **c** to cut off (cloth). **d** to cut (purses).

a abscisis nervorum nexibus ALDH. *VirgP.* 32 p. 273; quidam [tumorem] ~endum esse docebant BEDE *HE* IV 32; furtum facit exoculatos, / ..testes abscisos D. BEC. 1787; non debet quis membra pudoris realiter ~ere NECKAM *NR* II 140; **1202** ~it ei digitos suos, ita quod inde maimatus est *SelPlCrown* 35; **1209** unam damam habentem gorgiam abscisam *SelPlForest* 3; **1272** abciderunt caput unius dami *Ib.* 38. **b 1194** de placito bosci abscisi *CurR RC* I 67; **1291** forestam ..nec infeodari volumus nec ~i *RGasc* III 22; **c1340** ne quis..arbores alienas abcidat *FormOx* 160. **c** si palla altaris inde tincta fuerit, recidenda est illa particula et penitus ~enda *Cust. Cant.* 287. **d 1199** appellat R. ..quod..~it bursam suam et ostendit bursam †assisam [l. abscisam] *CurR RC* I 315; **1299** burse plurim[or]um hominum ad illas nundinas veniencium abscise fuerunt *SelCKB* III 87.

2 (p. ppl. m.) kind of gem (? *cf. Dan.* ii 34: *abscissus est lapis de monte*).

abscisus est gemma nigra ponderosa distincta venis rubentibus BART. ANGL. XVI 51.

abscindere [CL], to cut off (prob. conf. w. *abscidere*). **b** (geom.). **c** (fig.) to cut short, bring to a halt. **d** to rescind.

asseveravit quod linguam propriam, nisi dimitteretur, ~eret GIR. *GE* I 49; [naute] muniti sint..securi, ut malus ~i possit tempestate emergente NECKAM *Ut.* 114; **1221** nasus ei fuit abscissus et unum ex labris..et virilia ejus abscissa *PlCrGlouc.* 106; **14..** debet ~i una auris eorum per judicium datum *Cust. Fordwich* 30 p. 273. **b** ex utroque latere ~etur aliquid de diametro BACON *Maj.* I 159. **c** omne tedium prolixitatis ~o P. BLOIS *Ep.* 39 p. 119C; motus contrarii penes terminos quando veniunt ad eos ~untur per quietem BACON II 335. **d 1565** illa statuta que pertinent ad missas [etc.]..prorsus ~imus et amputamus *StatOx* 385.

abscincium v. apsinthium.

abscisio [CL; *conf. w.* abscissio, *which is treated here as a variant*], **a** cutting off of limbs etc., mutilation. **b** amputation (also fig.). **c** felling or lopping. **d** cutting off cloth. **e** cutting purses. **f** hewing stone.

a s795 Aegelberhtus..vita privatus est capitis ~one FL. WORC. I 63; minus est portentum si post patris [auricule] ~onem fuisset genitus MAP *NC* V 5 p. 222; s1312 [P. de Gaveston] abscissione capitis est peremptus *G. Ed. II Bridl.* 44. **b** [Gregorius VI] ferro abscissionis utendum judicans arma..conquisivit W. MALM. *GR* II 201; s1239 more prudentis medici, qui nunc fomentis nunc ferro ~onis..utitur M. PAR. *Maj.* III 532; esset utilis ~o GILB. VII 355 v. 1; s1430 quod unum os Lollardi esset causa abscissionis manus et brachii sui *Chr. S. Alb.* 50. **c 1143** bosculus..vendebatur per abscisionem ramorum (*Reg. Pipewell*) *MonA* V 436; s1235 exceptis irrestaurabilibus damnis de sylvarum abscissionibus *G. S. Alb.* I 297 (cf. *MonA* II 191n); **1384** in ~one ramusculorum pro clatibus faciendis *Ac. Obed. Abingd.* 46; **1467** propter ~onem..quercuum *ExchScot* 476. **d** si super..vestimentum [calix stillaverit], consimilis fiat ~o [sc. panni] *Cust. Cant.* 287. **e 1291** appellat S..de societate ~onis bursarum in nundinis *SelCCoron.* 131; **14..** si aliqui reperti fuerint cum ~one bursarum vel cum argento a loculo extracto *Cust. Fordwich* 30 p. 272. **f 1386** pro absesione lapidum et cariagio eorum *ExchScot* 683.

2 (point of) abscission (geom.).

a loco abscissionis diametri usque ad vas erunt duo spatia parva BACON *Maj.* I 159; **1326** abscicione linee *gc* ponatur nota *r* WALLINGF. *Albion* 356.

3 whittling away, cutting short, termination.

quedam [alteratio] est que est salus et receptio, et hec est in celo; alia est que est abscissio et corruptio BACON VII 48; motus..vadit per eandem inclinationem ad oriens et continue sine ~one motus *Id.* IV 335; suppono quod omne finitum per abscissionem vel diminutionem proportionabiliter aliquoties multiplicatam aliquando finitur et consumitur PECKHAM *Quaest.* II xiii A5.

abscondere [CL], to hide. **b** (refl.) to hide (from), evade.

si..errores pueritiae..bene faciendo a Dei oculis ~ere curasset BEDE *HE* V 13; qui..incomparabilem scientie thesaurum non ~unt GIR. *TH* III *intr.*; **1253** dixit quod invenit unam damam mortuam in parco et ~it eam *SelPl Forest* 106; **1275** ulnam illam fregit et ~idit quamcicius ballivi eam perceperunt esse contra assisam *SelPlMan* 155; **1268** fuerunt absconsi cum dicto W. in eadem brucia ad depredandum transeuntes *JustIt* 618 r.14*d*. **b** ne ~as te, domina, parum videnti animae te quaerenti ANSELM (*Or.* 7) III 21; **1319** J. le B. ~it se a cariagio domini *CBaron* 129; s1379 [garcio] in sentina, nullo sciente, se ~it *V. Ric. II* 12.

2 (p. ppl.) hidden. **b** (sb. n.) hiding-place, secrecy. **c** (sb. f.) screened light, sconce.

oppositio..galeari operimento fieri posset ~itior ADEL. *QN* 20; omnes thesauri sapientie et scientie ascunditi OCREATUS *Helceph. prol.* 132; thesauros habeo.. / sed tamen absconsos et tuta sede locatos NIG. *Laur.* 36b; prophetie spiritus / se toro jugali / subtrahit, †absonditus / operi carnali *Ps.*-MAP *Poems* 213; quibuscumque †abscyditi cancri fiunt, non curare melius est GILB. VII 329 v. 2. **b** ille sub absconso chlamydis canonicalis Christi et B. Benedicti monachum gerebat ~itum W. FITZST. *Thom.* 149 (cf. ib. 26); cum semper in ~ito secrecius nostri colloquantur principes MAP *NC* IV 13; [pastori incumbit gregem] introducere in arcanum firme credulitatis, ..in ~itum vivifice dilectionis AD. MARSH *Ep.* 1 p. 81; **c1320** tabernarii vina sua vendunt in ~ito et locis obscuris (*Eyre*) *Lond. Ed. I & II* II 184; Saraceni perfecti nunquam vinum bibunt nec casu publice, sed private et in absconso S. SIM. *Itin.* 37; s1333 jussit rex Anglie omnes captivos occidere; quod et factum est, nisi tantum qui in ~itis reservantur *Plusc.* IX 28. **c** debet prior cum absconsa accensa per chorum ire LANFR. *Const.* 89; sint ibi [in dispensa]..candelabrum, absconsa, laterna NECKAM *Ut.* 98; candelam..que in absconsa sive laterna.. portari solet *Cust. Westm.* 53; **1328** una absconsa vetus de latoun *Reg. Exon.* 563; absconsa, ..hic absconsus, A. *sconse* WW.

abscondite, secretly.

fingens se ad colloquium amici sui ~e ire DICETO *Chr.* 154.

absconditio, hiding.

persone existentes in sanctuario aut ~one *Entries* 665.

absconsa v. abscondere 2 c.

absconse, secretly.

angelus ~e tulit catinum O. CHERITON *Par.* 115; cum excommunicato..neque orare neque loqui, neque palam neque ~e [*ed. Twiss*: †absconditе] ..licet BRACTON 426b; Paulus ad Petrum ~e in..carcerem introivit *Eul. Hist.* I 163.

absconsio, hiding, concealment.

1153 hoc est..defodere idola Laban, si veteris..hominis imago fiat, in ~onem G. HOYLAND *Ascet.* 287B; advertit martyrem moleste ferentem reliquiarum suarum ~onem W. CANT. *Mir. Thom.* II 89; **1239** dilexerunt homines visitationem renuentes magis tenebras ~onis suorum operum quam lucem manifestationis eorum GROS. *Ep.* 127 p. 395; **1362** tegulatores..tegulas..vendicioni publice.. absque retencione sive ~one inde facienda exponant (*Procl.*) *G. S. Alb.* III 47; s1381 delitescebant miseri.., per fugam et ~onem vitam salvare cupientes WALS. *HA* I 466.

absconsus, abscyditus v. abscondere. absecundus v. obsecundus.

absens [CL; *pr. ppl. of* abesse], absent; **b** (as sb.) absent one.

c705 te..~entem..litteris exhortari non piget ALDH. *Ep.* 8; civitatem..in qua erat Putta episcopus, quamvis eo tempore ~ens BEDE *HE* IV 12; quia..adesse non poteram, literarum beneficio consilio quidem ~ens non fui GIR. *TH* II 19; **1220** quia idem F. ..~ens est, summoneatur *SelPlCrown* 138; **1257** [clerici] similiter condempnantur ~entes et ignorantes *SelPlForest* xc. **b 1237** quidam in ~entis beneficium oculos jacientes *Conc. Syn.* 249.

absentare, a to send away, (pass.) be absent. **b** (refl.) to absent onseself. **c** (intr.) to be absent.

a p754 quasi taedio ~ati patris familias (*Lit. Ep. Wigorn.*) *Ep. Bonif.* 111; s1134 jussu tiranni vermis ~atur J. WORC. 39; ne..suam ab eis..presentiam ~aret AD. EYNS. *Hug.* IV 7; s1259 comes..diutius ab eis ~atus *Flor. Hist.* II 422; **1363** nisi pro negociis..hospitalis..ipsum oporteat aliquociens ~ari *Lit. Cant.* II 438; **1472** si contigerit dictos W. et A. a..villa..~ari *Deeds Balliol* 126. **b** s1141 episcopus.. sese..conspectibus ejus ~avit FL. WORC. *Cont.* A 133; "tu scis..quoties me, cum quererer, ~averim" AILR. *Ed. Conf.* 780A; absentant sedi Jovis ad mortalia se dii SERLO WILT. 18. 47; a1164 illis absentibus, imo potius se contumaciter ~antibus J. SAL. *Ep.* 66; **1201** corruptus donis..~avit se *CurR* I 382; **1309** si vir ~averit se et noluerit jus uxoris sue defendere *Year Bk 2 Ed. II* 77n.; **1326** ~avit se in autumpno et noluit metere bladum domini *CBaron* 146; s1363 tenuit rex Parliamentum Londoniis a quo nullus magnus se potuit ~are WALS. *HA* I 299; **1552** a suis parochialibus missis.. sese ultro ~antes *ConcScot* II 131. **c** s1297 ~antibus.. sponte..comitibus *Flor. Hist.* III 295; c1350 si ex causa necessaria eos ~are contigerit *StatOx* 54; **1408** cum iisdem personis..de ~ando de beneficiis suis..dispensandum (*Reg. Ebor.*) *Eng. Clergy* 189; **1415** si contingat priorissam..ab eodem [hospitali] per unum diem ~are *Lit. Cant.* III 134.

absentatio, absenting oneself.

1337 ne per fraudulentas ~ones custodum eorum raciocinia indebite differantur *StatOx* 141; **1393** interdum..se poterit absentare..; causas tamen ~onis..patrono suo.. declaret *Lit. Cant.* III 23; **1415** pastorem [sc. Papam] oves linquentem audivimus; nec intelligere possumus quid sibi vult hec ~o (*Lit. Univ. Paris*) BEKYNTON II 137.

absentia [CL], absence.

quin..caritatis praecordia interdum plus ~ia pulsat quam praesentia pascat ALDH. *Met.* 4; non irrationalis diceretur [essentia] nisi ab habitu ~iae rationis ERIUG. *Per.* 466A; captata..Reimundi, qui adhuc Waterfordie moram fecerat, ~ia GIR. *EH* I 29; datur [exceptio]..mulieri.. petenti restitutionem contra dominum capitalem excipientem de ~ia viri BRACTON 203; in ~ia domini regis in partibus marinis agentis *State Tri. Ed. I* 49; a1350 nullus se absentare presumat quem ~ia racionabiliter non excusat *Stat. Cantab.* 316; **1549** si absunt, v s. pro singulis ~iis mulctentur *StatOx* 357.

absenturus (fut. ppl.), about to be absent.

1377 per certum tempus me ab abbathia mea ~um *FormOx* 383.

abserare v. obserare. absess- v. abscedere, abscessio. absida, ~ia, v. apsis.

absimilis [CL], unlike.

[Angli] Normannis ~es, qui amplis..edificiis modicas expensas agunt W. MALM. *GR* III 245.

absinth- v. apsinth-. absis v. apsis.

absistere [CL], **a** to retire. **b** to cease.

a ut procul, hoc vivo, .. / hosticus absistat terror et ira tumens *V. Ed. Conf.* 38. **b** furta..et latrocinia omnia radicitus ~ant (*Sin. Decr.*) *GAS* 255; inobedientia, que.. non ~et expugnare feminas MAP *NC* IV 3 p. 145; a1350 ut omnis timor subornacionis ~at *Stat. Cantab.* 324.

absit v. abesse. absolarium, absolere, absolescere, v. obsol-.

absolute [CL], absolutely: **a** completely, exhaustively; **b** unconditionally, without qualification; **c** (gram.).

a angulus unus..terrarum.., nec ille omnino intactus, nullius tamen hactenus stilo ~e comprehensus GIR. *TH intr.*; **1325** quod..appellationem..~e renunciaret *Mun AcOx* 115 (cf. 700); ~e necessario WYCL. *Ver.* III 161; **1430** ~e et integre quietam clamavit *Feod. Durh.* 36. **b** Deum esse dicentes, ..simpliciter et infinite et ~e in ipso dicimus ERIUG. *Per.* 482A; necesse est eam [summam essentiam] esse..quicquid..~e melius est quam non ipsum ANSELM (*Mon.* 15) I 29; hoc nomen 'pauca' ~e positum aliud significat quam cum ponitur respective NECKAM *NR* II 173; quedam autem vult fieri non ~e sed pro loco et tempore et ceteris conditionibus creaturarum GROS. *Quaest. Theol.* II 32; de hac..sapientia tam relate quam ~e scienda BACON *Maj.* III 1; nomen prune..dicitur ~e..de illo quod denigrat et locum inficit GAD. 29 v. 1. **c** verbum substantivum..aliquando intelligitur ~e, secundum quod absolutio transitioni verbali opponitur BACON XV 100.

absolutio [CL], loosening.

de anulorum lorice ~one J. FORD *Wulf.* 10; ad egestionem secedens, dum nimio impulsu naturalem ~onem acceleraret *Ib.* 64.

2 release, discharge from office. **b** release from attendance, dismissal (of chapter meeting).

s1093 ita sum astrictus ut..nec obedientiam pontificis †me subterfugere queam..absque ipsius ~one EADMER *HN* 39; ante ~onem fratris W. de N. ECCLESTON *Adv. Min.* 63; c1260 me..ob causas..oneris..quod in prioratu.. sustinui a capitulo Dunelm'..petisse ~onem *Ann. Durh.*

108; 1294 archiepiscopus..celerarium et camerarium ~onem petentes..absolvit DCCant Q 25b. b statim post ~onem capituli Cust. Cant. 2.

3 release: a from obligation or debt; b from oath.

a s1164 archiepiscopus..liber et absolutus ab omni ratiocinio.., cum..~onem factam hoc modo de voluntate regis..†probari [? l. probare] non posset Diceto YH I 314; nolunt..qui assident speciali debito per generalem ~onem derogari Dial. Scac. II 12c. b 1239 quatinus..~onem [juramenti] et inhibitionem [fidelitatis]..facias..publicari (Lit. Papae) M. Par. Maj. III 572; s1261 ne quis illam ~onem [de juramento] contradiceret Leg. Ant. Lond. 50; s1306 super ~one juramenti domini regis Anglie de foresta Ann. Lond. 146.

4 release from sentence, esp. of excommunication. b (w. ad cautelam) provisional release.

1204 Hugo propter multiplicem contumaciam excommunicationis sentencia innodatus..petat ~onem CurR III 147 (cf. BNB II 355); si querens excommunicatus fuerit, ..oportebit querentem docere de ~one Bracton 203; s1317 petiit ~onem et revocationem omnium sententiarum latarum per ipsum Hist. Roff. 357; a1350 omnium..delinquencium ~one cancellario..universitatis..reservata Stat. Cantab. 329. b 1330 copia tenoris littere ~onis ad cautelam quam procuratores vestri in Curia impetraverunt Lit. Cant. I 310.

5 absolution (eccl.), remission of sin. b (w. dies) Maundy Thursday (cf. absolvere 9e).

pro ~one animae ejus sepius missas facere curavit Bede HE IV 20; †878 (17c) pro remedio animae meae et criminum meorum ~one CS 545; in cibo et potu et aliis multis offendi..et inde peto ~onem vestram Lanfr. Const. 180; s1111 Romam..rex venit.., quem Papa..in imperatorem consecravit et ei suisque omnibus ~onem fecit Fl. Worc. II 64; festivam stationem ad sancti pontificis corpus..fieri decrevit, ad quam parrochianos pene omnes monitis et ~onibus atque benedictionibus invitavit Ord. Vit. V 4; similiter fiet [sc. consanguinei defuncti fratrum absolventur]..post sollempnem ~onem fratrum nostrorum.., in quibus ~onibus dicetur tantum: "requiescant in pace" (Inst. Sempr.) MonA VI 946 lv; s1213 venerunt ad eum [legatum]..burgenses quorum instinctu..duo clerici..suspensi fuerant, ~onem postulantes; quibus indicta penitentia..precepit ut..a presbyteris parochianis ~onis beneficium..impetrarent Wend. II 94; c1218 ~o talium in articulo mortis nulli est deneganda, saltem conditionalis Conc. Syn. 74; est enim ~o..perfecta quando absolvitur a culpa et pena.., imperfecta quando a culpa solum A. Hales Qu. 1071; p1381 sicut primum modum sequitur ~o pro deobligatione pene demerite, sic et isti ultimo modo confessionis necessaria est ~o quedam pro solvenda intricatione et seductione de mentibus simplicium (Wynt.) Ziz. 182; c1400 vadas ad talem sacerdotem petens ~onem pro me (Byland Ghost Stories) EHR XXXVII 415; recepit ~onem inscriptam in quadam cedula Ib. 416; ante assolucionem Ib. 418. b dies ille dies ~onis erat, quo totius episcopii catervatim penitentiales ad matrem ecclesiam Norwicensem convenire consueverant T. Mon. Will. I 25 (cf. ib. V 16: feria quinta ante Pascha que a Christianis dies ~onis dicitur); feria tertia ante Pascha, die videlicet ~onis Gir. IK II 11; 1207 die Jovis ~onis Cl 88b (cf. Doc. Bec 58).

6 absoluteness: a (gram.); b (log.).

a maxime nominativus inter omnes casus, cum non sit dependens et sine respectu, habet naturam ~onis Bacon XV 102 (v. et. absolute c). b ~o comparatio non sunt hujusmodi Duns Metaph. V 6.

absolutivus, perfective, final (gram.).

perfectivae vel absolutivae [sc. conjunctiones], quas alicui fini perfectionique praeponimus, sunt haec: ut, uti, ..ne Linacre Emend. Lat. 91.

absolutorius [CL], conveying release or acquittal. b (sb. f.) letter of acquittal.

1166 impetratis litteris dimissoriis et ~iis Canon. G. Sempr. 90; impetravit rex..litteram ~iam a domino papa super remissione sacramenti Gerv. Cant. II 210; 1311 ut super crimine..imposito..sentencie ~ie vel condempnatorie, prout justum fuerit, proferantur Conc. Syn. 1303; 1333 littera ~ia..monachorum..excommunicatorum Lit. Cant. II 19; 1357 sentenciam virtute clavium ecclesie ~iam Conway Def. Mend. 1412. b 1546 quum G. Benedictinus ..et J. Leich diu in rota Romana de..rectoria contendissent et Leich videret ~iam latam secundum G. Mon. Hib. & Scot. 620.

absolvere [CL], to loose, release, relieve. b (fig.).

exertis..absolvens vincula nodis Aldh. VirgV. 588; a1087 homines..quos Petrus..in capcione tenet..liberos et ~utos facite exire de capcione Regesta 41; s1409 qui cum comburi cepisset, clamavit dicens: "miseremini mei"; et quam cito potuerunt assolverunt eum, extrahentes ipsum de igne Eul. Hist. cont. III 417. b saeculi curis ~utus ad monasterium..pervenit Bede HE V 12; terrene conversationis excessibus ~utam animam H. Los. Ep. 11; s1087 "rex Anglie jacet Rotomagi more ~utarum partu feminarum cubile fovens" W. Malm. GR III 281.

2 to discharge (from office). b to dismiss (a chapter meeting).

completo..ministerio, ~utus in capitulo generali..ab omni fratrum officio Eccleston Adv. Min. 5; 1261 ~imus priorem provincialem Anglie et assignamus eum provincie Teutonie (Cap. Dominican.) EHR VIII 520; 1304 assumat sibi prior capellanum monachum..a gradu dyaconatus ~utum Ord. Ely 25; in quibusdam casibus generalia eorum [fratrum] capitula sunt superiora prelatis supremis, ita quod ipsos possunt ~ere Ockham Pol. I 86. b ~et presidens capitulum Cust. Cant. 2.

3 to release from obligation or debt.

†889 (11c) unam curtem..donamus..et totius debiti vel pene fiscalis vel publice rei..~uta persistat CS 561.

4 to release from sentence, esp. of excommunication. b (refl.) to vote.

rogo quatenus..clericos, quos a vobis excommunicatos didici, ~atis Lanfr. Ep. 19 525d; si aliquis excommunicatus ad emendationem ad episcopum venerit, ~utus eundo et redeundo pacem Dei habeat (Leg. Ed.) GAS 629; reos longe pronior ~ere quam condemnare Gir. TH III 49; 1204 excommunicacionis sentencia innodatus..et post, prestita juratoria caucione quod juri staret ~utus CurR III 147 (cf. ib. I 27). b 1370 ~entes se ad balatolas albas et nigras ..observata forma regularum communis Janue (DipDoc E 259) Foed. VI 674.

5 to absolve (from sin or penance), assoil. b (of the dead). c (of things) to cleanse of blood-guilt.

eos qui..sua peccata..confitebuntur, quantum possum.. ~o Anselm (Ep. 382) V 325; rege..~uto dataque ei benedictione, archiepiscopus..regressus est A. Tewk. Addit. Thom. 351; s1235 dicebant [Fratres Minores] se talem a domino papa suscepisse potestatem ut eis scilicet fideles que suo erubescunt sacerdoti confiteri..confiteantur, quibus injungant minores penitentias et ~ant M. Par. Maj. III 333; s1241 legatus missus ut sibi omnes obedientes ab omnibus peccatis suis ~eret Ib. IV 121; quando aliquis pro ..qualicumque transgressu ad gradum in capitulo ~itur Cust. Westm. 191; 1451 nullus..custos a penitentia quam imposuit vicarius ~at aliquem sine licentia imponentis Mon. Francisc. II 104; 1476 de..eligendo confessore in casibus reservatis qui eos ~at MunAcOx 350. b consanguinei defuncti fratrum nostri ordinis in annuo capitulo..debent ~i (Inst. Sempr.) MonA VI 946 lv (cf. ib.: ~atur defunctus in capitulo sic: anima ejus requiescat in pace, et omnes presentes..dicent pro eo vij psalmos penitentiales cum collectis 'absolve, fidelium'); c1250 cum dominus abbas obierit.., abbatis animam ebdomadarius ~et Lit. Cant. III 368; 14.. quidam ~unt sepulcra hominum prius per annos plurimos mortuorum Wycl. Versut. 102. c si quelibet arma..emundatori commissa sint ad purgandum..et.. arripiantur ad aliquid male agendum, justum est, cui ~uta commissa sunt, ~uta restituat (Leg. Hen.) GAS 601.

6 to resolve, interpret.

cum..regi que viderat enarrasset, miratus ille tali enodatione visionem ~it Osb. V. Dunst. 23.

7 to complete, conclude.

suspirio meditationem ~it altissimo Map NC III 2 p. 112; 1509 completorio ~uto omnes dormitorium adeant (Vis. Dorchester) EHR IV 311.

8 (w. super) to apply, extend (a name).

carbo et ignis Persicus, hec duo nomina fortasse ~uta sunt super omnem pustulam corrosivam; ..et quandoque ~itur nomen ignis Persici de isto super quod est pustula Gad. 29 v. 1;

9 (p. ppl. absolutus): a perfect, fully formed. b isolated. c absolute, unqualified. d absolute (gram.), intransitive (v. et. ablativus 1). e concerned w. absolution (cf. absolutio 5 b and OF jeudi absolu = Maundy Thursday).

a ~us pes est 'omnia' Aldh. Met. 10 p. 89; [liber] tam clare discretis et ~is litteris scriptus Bonif. Ep. 63. b nequaquam..intellectum standi ~um ab intellectu jacendi cogitabis Eriug. Per. 467a. c nonne hujus [summi spiritus] esse merito solum intelligitur simplex perfectumque et ~um? Anselm (Mon. 28) I 46; 1314 de potentia ~a etsi non de potentia ordinata MunAcOx 100; si..dominium [primorum parentum] fuit aliquid superadditum nature, constat quod fuit aliquid ~um; ..tale autem ~um supernaturale non fuit in illis Ockham Pol. II 434; si ~a coactione quis coactus fuerit actum hereticalem committere Id. Dial. 448. d qualecumque sit verbum, sive transitivum sive ~um Vinsauf AV II 2. 47; hec est expositio hujus verbi 'lego' secundum quod ~um est et non intransitivum Bacon XV 74. e s1177 [rex] in crastino summo mane diei Jovis ~i venit Cantuariam G. Hen. II I 158 (f. 96); 13.. cerei debent ministrari..usque ad diem Jovis ~i Cust. Swith. 17 (cf. ib. 21 etc.).

absonare, to be discordant.

to discorde, ~are.., dissonare CathA.

absonditus v. abscondere 2a.

absoniare [AS ascunian; (?) infl. by OF essoigner], to shun.

volo esse domino meo fidelis..et amare quod amet et ~iare quod ~iet [eal ascunian ðæt he ascunað] (Quad.) GAS 397.

absonus [CL], discordant, repugnant to reason.

ut.., quod ~um est, ex possibili impossibile..consentiam evenire J. Sal. Pol. 448c; ~um est si lugeat animus et lasciviat oculus Nig. Cur. 202; que prius abscidi, que normis absona vidi Garl. Mor. Scol. 366.

2 soundless, mute.

~us, homo sine sono GlC A 56; susceptivum coloris et soni..est non coloratum et ~um Bacon Maj. III 413.

absorbēre [CL], to engulf. b (fig.) to overwhelm, crush, quash.

ut [boa]..agricolas quoque..ad se tractos vi spiritus ~eat Aldh. VirgP. 29; praesul..absortus fuerat fluctibus Italici maris Bede HE II 20; s1100 mari tranquillo perierunt, undis absorti Gerv. Cant. I 92; non hic..terremotus ~ent Gir. TH I 38; filia..rapido meatu fluminis absorta Mir. Montf. 86; s1406 quattuor naves..inciderunt in Caribdim ..et..†abscorpte sunt Chr. S. Alb. 1406–20 9. b non Charibdim non Scyllam evasi, iisdem absorptus sed nondum ab iisdem evomitus H. Los. Ep. 12; divina pietas..ne [fideles] temptationibus ~eantur providet T. Mon. Will II 7; s1189 rex..in abyssum tristitie absortus maledixit diei in qua natus est Flor. Hist. II 102; 1365 nullo..ipsorum aliquod canonicum quod peticionem..religiosorum ~ere seu excludere poterat..proponente Lit. Cant. II 476; Ceolwlphus..rusticos..excoriavit, mercatores ~uit Croyl. 27; [Bonifacius VIII] dolore cordis absortus..diem cum luctu clausit extremum Thorne 2003.

†absorbitas, injury or calamity.

14.. plures ~ates et injurias his longe graviores velut.. excommunicacionis sentencias fulminando Chr. Pont. Ebor. III 424.

absorptio, engulfing, swallowing up.

maris attractio, ~o vicissim et ebullitio Gir. TH II 3; s1250 in Sabaudia civitatum..et multorum milium hominum ~o terribilis M. Par. Abbr. 319 (= Flor. Hist. II 374: absortio).

absorptus, engulfing.

s1294 per pelagus tantis..procellis quassatus est quod et videbatur ei absortibus maris incontinenter deperire Thorne 1962.

absort- v. absorbere, absorpt-. abspernere v. aspernere. absportare v. asportare.

absque [CL], without; b (w. gd. or gdve.); c (w. pr. ppl.); d (w. p. ppl.); e (w. inf.).

provincia..~e episcopo manens Bede HE V 23; c745 ~e ulla resipiscentia in peccatis suis perdurare praesumunt (Lit. Ep. Wint.) Ep. Bonif. 64. p. 133; hi tenent ~e voluntate presbiteri DB I 52; absque pari parit illa tibi J. Exon. BT II 288; nil agis absque bene Serlo Wilt. 26. 6; absque fame saties, absque labore quies Garl. Tri. Eccl. 129; nec debet evenire quod chorus..~e uno ad minus sit ordinis tutore Cust. Westm. 20; habebat usum rerum..~e proprietate Ockham Pol. I 300; 1377 clericus ~e libris piscis sine aqua FormOx 384; s1401 ejus determinationi..per omnia bene crederetur ~e pluri [without more ado] Meaux III 288. b 1278 ~e plus pacando Law Merch. II 21; 1362 ~e retentione sive absconsione inde facienda G. S. Alb. III 47. c serviebant preposito..~e firma donante DB I 86b. d ~e facta confessione personaliter proprio sacerdoti Conway Def. Mend. 1415. e mors absque mori, sitis absque sitire Hanv. VII 355; s1360 ~e juvare Scotos seu confederationes facere contra regem Anglie J. Reading Chr. 176b.

2 (w. pron., sts. omitted, and rel. cl.) on such terms that..not.

1285 cum duo vel plures teneant boscum..in communi, ~e hoc quod aliquis sciat suum separale Reg. Malm. I 90; quod..principes seculares, ~e hoc quod eis a papa aliquid committatur juris, dictiones temporales habeant exercere Ockham Pol. I 102; c1380 ordinavimus quod dictus redditus ..corone nostre..remaneat annexus..~e eo quod aliqua remissio..ejusdam..fiat Reg. Whet. I 85; 1426 infra domum illorum fratrum, receptus fuit..~e quod aliqui illorum dicto..fratri..aliquid de adventu suo notificassent Reg. Cant. III 176; 1449 ~e eo quod..augmentationem..exigent Lit. Cant. III 201; 1583 ~e hoc quod..intraverunt Pat 1236 m. 34.

3 besides, apart from.

jam quadringentis annorum cursibus absque / bis novem scribens aetatum lustra fuisse Aldh. VirgV 331; nil pecuniarum ~e pecoribus habebant Bede HE III 26; †878 (17c) ut ab omnium regalium tributorum et exactione operum.. ~e expeditione sola arcis et pontium structura..immunis ..permaneat CS 545 (cf. E. Ch. Wessex 123); Augustinus ..plusquam x millia Anglorum, ~e parvulorum et mulierum infinito numero, ..baptismatis lavacro regeneravit Birchington Arch. Cant. 1.

4 minus (math.).

postea rem cum re..multiplica, et fiet substantia rebus 40 ~e 4 substantiis equalis Rob. Angl. Alg. 104.

absquequaque v. usquequaque.

abstare [CL], to be distant. b to cease to exist.

~ans, distans GlC A 59. b nunc stat et abstat homo, flat et efflat, floret et aret Babio 417 (= Gower VC II 9).

abstemius [CL], abstemious, abstinent.

æbstemus, abstinens GlC 17 (cf. ib. 35); meminimus eum cuidam abbati ~io talia..dixisse: .."propter abstinentiam istam extraordinariam..peccabis." Ad. Eyns. Hug. V 16.

abstergere [CL], to wipe away. b (fig.).

cum manutergio †abastergatur Gilb. I 19 v. 2; mater.. amplexans..ejus oculos ~it [ME: wipeð] AncrR 84. b ut ..omnes palam quae gesserant confitendo proferrent..et confessa dignis..poenitentiae fructibus ~erent Bede (V. Cuthb.) HE IV 27; ut omnem ~eret dubietatem Gir. TH II 19.

absterrēre [CL], to deter.

libertas animi..nullo..absterrita monstro Hanv. IV 307; ut..istorum exemplo extere nationes ab ausu tam nefario imperpetuum ~eantur Gir. EH I 7.

abstersio, wiping, mopping.

talis abstercio faciem clarificat Bacon IX 47.

abstersivus, detergent.

medicina ~a Gilb. VII 318. 1; est [sal]..sicut accidit in cineribus ~um Ps.-Gros. 642; fiat clistere mundificativum et ~um GAD. 101. 1; mundificetur cum ~is fortibus, sc. cum lixivio, aqua maris aut salsa *Ib.* 125. 2.

abstersorius, for wiping. **b** (sb. n.) napkin (eccl.).

1295 due tualle ~ie; . . item j ~ium tuallum *Vis. S. Paul.* 331. **b** duo ~ia de panno lineo cum extremitatibus bordatis de serico ad extergendum digitos post perfusionem in majori altari *Ib.* 324.

abstinentia [CL], abstinence (esp. from food), austerity.

gastrimargiae draco . . frugalitatis ~ia explodatur ALDH. *VirgP.* 12; saluberrimum ~iae vel continentiae clericis exemplum reliquit BEDE *HE* III 5; ~ia, *syfernes* ÆLF. *Sup.*; a Quinquagesima . . quadragesimalem teneant ~iam *RegulC* 34; majorem coronam meretur simplex oboedientia quam praeter communem usum escarum ~ia ANSELM (*Ep.* 196) IV 86; ~ie et parcimonie ciborum non mediocriter indulgent GIR. *TH* III 27; non licet absolvi fratrem positum in ~ia . . absente . . abbate . . *Cust. Westm.* 192; potest facere seu dimittere prout vult, quantum ad cibum . . vestimentum et ~ias consimiles *AncrR* 6; **1382** sunt participes omnium missarum / et precum . . et abstinentiarum *Mon. Francisc. app.* I 596; **c1472** pro piscibus recentibus pro clxvij diebus ~ie *BBHouseh.* 109.

2 armistice.

1300 super sufferencia, ~ia sive treugis inter regem . . [Francorum] et . . regem Anglie *TreatyR* 140; **1385** super treugis et ~iis guerrarum hinc inde ineundis *RScot* 76a; **1409** contra formam treugarum et ~iarum intra nos et . . ducem Britannie *Cl* 258 m. 2.

abstinēre [CL], to abstain: **a** (refl.); **b** (intr.).

a ut . . ab illo se certamine funditus ~eat BEDE *HE* V 6; **1309** petitur quod . . rex se ~eat de rogando pro corrodiis *Reg. Cant.* II 1029. **b** si cum fidem Christi acceperitis mortui, id est separati, estis, ab abstinentia creaturarum mundi Judaico ritu ~ebatis LANFR. *Comment. Paul.* (*Col.* ii 20) 327; ~eat omnis homo a venariis meis (*Quad.*) *GAS* 367; non ~uit cubicularius quin . . cultellum . . abriperet W. MALM. *GR* II 169; monens . . quatinus ab expeditione crastina . . ~eret GIR. *EH* I 42; femoralibus . . sibi ~endum . . decreverunt *Id. Spec.* II 34; **s1400** per v dies . . a cibariis ~ens *Croyl. Cont. B* 495.

2 (pr. ppl.) abstinent, ascetic.

~ens, *syfer* ÆLF. *Sup.*; ciborum ~ens, somno temperans OSB. *V. Dunst.* 8; timeo ne, dum vis habere . . inanem intra cor tuum gloriam ~entis, incurras potius poenam inoboedientis ANSELM (*Ep.* 196) IV 86; ita est et ~ens qui perit in abstinentia sua H. BOS. *Thom.* IV 14.

abstracte, in abstraction.

dicentes quod . . ens nomen significat ~e ab esse actuali et cum communitate quadam ad ens et non ens actu BACON *CSTheol.* 56.

abstractibilis, susceptible of abstraction (log.).

si non est abstractum vel ~e, nec concretum *Ps.*-GROS. 322.

abstractio, dragging away. **b** extraction. **c** taking out (in tailoring).

1268 qui . . ad hujusmodi [ad ecclesias] confugarum ~onem . . de locis ipsis se conferunt impudenter *Conc. Syn.* 763; **1421** (v. abstractor). **b** **1509** pro ~one dentis, iiij d. *DCCant C* 11 f. 118b. **c** **1579** pro alteracione . . et ~one le fac[e] *Ac. L. Chamb.* 70 f. 4v.

2 abstraction (log.), abstractness.

non novit ratio esse actu universale nisi postquam a multis singularibus hanc fecerit ~onem et occurrit ei unum et idem in multis singularibus repertum (GROS. *Comm. Anal. Post.* I 18.1) *GLA* III 88; **a1250** quanto aliqua sunt majoris ~onis, tanto sunt majoris unionis (SIM. HINTON *Quaest.*) *Powicke Studies* 220n.; simplex non predicatur de compositis predicacione formali et inherencie et in ~one BACON II 53; habitus scientie fit per ~onem specierum rerum intelligibilium ab ipsis *Id.* VIII 2; duplex est ~o: una est a materia et suppositis, sicut homo abstrahitur ab illo homine et isto et a materia, ut ab homine albo et nigro; . . alia est ~o a suppositis sed non a materia, sicut homo albus abstrahitur ab illo homine et ab isto sed non a materia, quia album consequitur passiones materiales (DUNS *Quaest. Anal. Post.* I 37. 403A) *GLA* III 212 *n.* 120; tales predicaciones negantur de universalibus et de terminis ultimate ~onis WYCL. *Log.* III 2.

abstractive, in an abstract manner or sense.

hoc nomen 'vis' quandoque sumitur ~e, quandoque concretive J. BLUND *An.* 51; forme accidentales, ~e sumpte, nullum possunt actum exercere KNAPWELL *Not.* iii 7; ista perfectio data intellectui angelico, qua essentia divina esset ei presens distincte, licet ~e, potest dici naturalis DUNS *Sent.* II iii 9. 7; **c1301** veritas ~e abstrahitur a vero in intellectu et a vero in re (*Quest. Ox.*) *Ox. Hist. Soc.* XCVI 338; si aliquis . . tantum cognoscit Socratem et albedinem existentem in Socrate ~e, sicut aliquis potest imaginari in absentia eorum, non sciret evidenter quod Socrates esset albus OCKHAM *Sent. prol.* 1E; dicuntur justum et injustum . . ~e pro ipsis justicia et injusticia WYCL. *Ente Praed.* XII 109; **14..** licet rex non posset esse veritas ~e, ut Deus, potest tamen esse verax concretive *Cop. Pri. S. Andr.* 7.

abstractivus, abstractive, capable of forming abstractions (log.).

quod sensus sit ~us, sicut intellectus J. BLUND *An.* 232; intellectus est vis anime ~a, separans formas a rebus ipsis NECKAM *NR* II 173 p. 291; scientia naturalis non est abstrahens sed ~a; ergo ipsa non considerat formam BACON VIII 62; intellectione ~a tali quali cognoscitur universale DUNS *Sent.* II ix 2. 29; due noticie specie distincte, scilicet ~a et intuitiva *Ps.*-OCKHAM *Princ. Theol.* 132 (cf. *Ziz.* 11).

abstractor, one who drags away.

1421 qui ad ecclesiam . . fugientem inde abstraxerint violenter aut [? ad] abstraccionem hujusmodi ~oribus consilium prebuerint *Reg. Heref.* 10.

abstractus, removal.

computat . . in ~u mellis ad festum S. Petri . . viij [ruscas] *FormMan* 43.

abstrahere [CL], to drag away, pull out. **b** to subtract, deduct. **c** to appropriate, steal. **d** (fig.) to withdraw. **e** to mislead, seduce. **f** (p. ppl.) secluded.

Dunstanus . . lascivientem juvenculum violenter cubiculo abstraxit W. MALM. *GR* II 147; estus maris . . de divitiarum substantiis videbatur abtrahendo consumpsisse R. COLD. *Cuthb.* 33; si quis . . cutem hanc nitidam intellectualiter ~eret et intestina conspiceret GIR. *Spec.* II 28 p. 90; **1292** adjuvabit . . [linum] rakiare, abstraere, rippliare *Min. Ac. Essex* (*Wickham St. Paul's*); **1313** R. . . venit cum suis iij sociis . . ut . . Johannem a custodia illa ~eret *Eyre Kent* 98; **1316** a publica strata ~untur et suspenduntur (*Artic. Cleri* 10) *StRealm* I 172. **b** hujus summe radicem accipio, ex qua medietatem radicum ~o ROB. ANGL. *Alg.* 120; **1268** v solidi qui deberent ~i a parte . . Hugonis *Cl* 457. **c** in eadem villa sunt iiii hidae terrae quas injuste abstraxit Heraldus ab aecclesia Ambresberie *DB* 69. **d** homines ab amore scelerum ~ere . . curabat BEDE *HE* IV 24. **e** quatinus . . ad falsas . . videndum formas vi phantasmatis . . mirabiliter ~antur GIR. *TH* II 19. **f** **s1431** Eugenius IV . . fuit vir abstracte vite et bone fame *Eul. Hist. Cont.* I 289.

2 to abstract, summarize (writings). **b** (p. ppl. as sb. n.) abstract, summary.

c1290 vobis significo quendam tractatum, qui tabula juris appellatur, a jure canonico et civili esse abstractum et a quodam fratre minore esse compilatum *DCCant* (*HMC*) 278; **1412** errores ejusdam J. [Wyclif] abstracti de suo Dialogo *Conc.* III 346. **b** **1501** abstractum de vitis patrum *Cant. Coll. Ox.* I 41.

3 to abstract (log.); (p. ppl.) abstract (log.).

universalibus . ., que sic auctore Aristotele intelliguntur abstracta a singularibus ut tamen esse non habeant deductis singularibus J. SAL. *Met.* 888B; sunt qui more mathematicorum formas ~unt et ad illas quicquid de universalibus dicitur referunt *Id. Pol.* 665A; si ~entem tuleris intellectum, liberalium artium officina peribit *Ib.* 438A; illa natura univoca que est in genere generalissimo quantitatis . . ~itur a natura divisibilitatis BACON *Tert.* 198; alia [materia] per abstractionem intellectus mediante forma sensibili, que ab intellectu ~itur intelligibilis dicitur *Ps.*-GROS. 303; **a1400** dixisse memini quendam philosophum / quod abstrahencium non est mendacium; / iste sic abstrahit quod nullum medium / vel verum sapiat vel locum solidum (TRYVYTLAM *Laus Ox.* 469–72) *Collect. Ox.* III 209. **b** motus eorum est causa exitus ejus quod est in potentia in illis formis abstractis ad actum, scilicet ad formas materiales GROS. 95; [magnitudo] uno modo, in eo quod mathematica vel abstracta BACON VIII 148; **c1301** verum in abstracto est aliquid extra (*Quest. Ox.*) *Ox. Hist. Soc.* XCVI 338; quamlibet essenciam contingit sub racione propria intelligere et etiam significare, et tali modo intelligendi correspondet modus significandi abstractus (DUNS *Praedic.* 8. 3) *GLA* III 215 *n.* 128.

abstrahibilis, susceptible of abstraction (log.).

magnitudo . . quantum ad ejus [esse] primum in materia sua intelligibili sic est ~is BACON XIII 97; non cognoscitur anima a nobis . . nisi sub racione aliqua generali ~i a sensibilibus DUNS *Sent. prol.* 1. 11; cognicio abstractiva non est nisi cognicio alicujus universalis ~is a multis [singularibus] OCKHAM *Sent. prol.* 1 Z.

abstralogia v. astrologia.

1 abstringere, to cleanse, purge, keep clear.

ista pellicula ~it ipsum puerum [in utero] a sudore *Ps.*-RIC. *Anat.* 40; ut combibatur humiditas et abstergatur seu ~atur auris GILB. III 148. 2; gumma olivarum ~it oculum KILWARDBY *Jejun.* 173; agrifolium . . fastidium tollit, ventrem ~it *Alph.* 4.

2 abstringere v. astringere 2 a. abstructio, abstruere v. obstru-.

abstrusus [CL], abstruse. **b** (n. pl. as sb.) secrets.

quem prius abstrusus scaevis anfractibus error / trusit ALDH. *VirgV* 848; in [Anglorum] antiquis cartis est animadvertere quantum quibusdam verbis ~is et ex Greco petitis delectentur W. MALM. *GP* V 196; sed ubi, queso, in totis illis epistolis †obstrusior [? l. abstrusior] difficultas quam in materie hujus fossis BRADW. *CD pref.* b 3. **b** in ~a, in secreta *GlC* I 227 (cf. ib. O 98: obstrusa, occulta); ~a praecordiorum reserantes ALDH. *VirgP.* 27 p. 264.

abstuppare v. obstuppare.

absumere [CL], to remove. **b** to elide. **c** to consume. **d** to destroy.

quae singulatim ~pta quamlibet essentiam ad minus et minus esse deducunt, eadem ordinatim assumpta illam ad magis et magis esse perducunt ANSELM (*Mon.* 31) I 50; archidiaconi . . insperatis eventibus . . ab hac terra . . sunt ~pti GIR. *Spec.* III 3 p. 150. **b** priorem [vocalem] per synaliphum ~unt BEDE *AM* 2355. **c** LANFR. *Const.* 156 (v. ablutio 2). **d** monasterium . . flammis ~tum est BEDE *HE* IV 25; matrem meam ignis ~psit G. CRISPIN *Herl.* 94; corporis robur continue ~ebat edax incendium [febris] COGGESH. 107; nec tamen omnino vel poesis abolita vel ~pta est philosophia GIR. *TH intr.* p. 4.

absumptor, waster, destroyer.

religionis attritores et ~ores H. LOS. *Ep.* 52.

absurde [CL], absurdly.

ne limpidissimo Dei nutui ~e nitatur refragari O. CANT. *Pref. Frith.* 40; non ~e possumus dicere . . ANSELM (*Orig. Pecc.* III 13) II 287.

absurditas, discordance. **b** absurdity.

aliquis [sonus] propter ejus ~atem respuitur ab audiente J. BLUND *An.* 155. **b** **1300** super excessibus dictorum religiosorum, ~atibus et scandalis que obtentu dicte exempcionis indies patenter emergunt *Reg. Cant.* II 580; **1339** alioquin sequeretur et alia iniquitatis ~as, quod excluderetur collateralis convicinior [v.l. conjunccio] et remocior vocaretur (*Lit. Ed. III*) *Foed.*(ed. 1821) II 1086 (cf. *G. Ed. III Bridl.* 142); in ~ates hereticales . . incidere OCKHAM *Pol.* I 40; **1360** sequitur ~as . . quod . . *StatOx* 127.

absurdus [CL], absurd. **b** (?) contemptible.

~um arbitror . . per discolos philosophorum anfractus iter carpere ALDH. *Ep.* 3; quod quia consequenter non accidit, et antecedens ~um est ADEL. *QN* 8; **1175** ~um est et crudele ibi sanguinis judicium exerceri ubi et reis constituta est tutela refugii (*Decr. Westm.*) R. HOWD II 74 (= *G. Hen. II* I 86: †absurde); si mens humana singula cordetenus, quod ~um est, memorare valeret HENGHAM *Magna intr.*; **1287** ~um est clericis, ymmo probrosum, si forensium disceptationum executores existant *Conc. Syn.* 1023. **b** sit licet absurdum nomen meretricis GOWER *VC* V 315.

abthania [Gael. *abdhaine*; cf. abbatia d], 'abthain', abbey land (Sc.).

1291 me recepisse . . ad stipendia mea . . iiij li . . de firmis abthanye de Dul *DocScot* p. 248; **1310** M. de Monifuth dompnus abbathanie ejusdem *Reg. Aberbr.* I 278; **1358** de annuis redditibus shire de Kyngorne . . et de ~ia de Kyngorne *ExchScot* 564; **1370** totam terram de Estirfossache . . in ~ia de Dulle infra vicecomitatum de Perthe *RMSScot.* I 125.

abthanus, supposed title, based on false etym. of *abthania*.

Beatricem . . nuptam Crynyne ~o de Dul ac insularum senescallo, de quo quibusdam annalibus, vitio scriptoris, reperitur 'Crynyne abbas de Dul'; sed verius scripsisset '~us de Dul'; dirivatur autem ~us ab *abba*, quod est pater vel dominus, et *thana*, quod est respondens vel numerans, unde ~us quasi thanorum supremus FORDUN *Chr.* IV 39 p. 181 (cf. ib. *Vol.* II p. 413); viro nobilissimo Crinen nomine abbathano Insularum et Occidentalis Scotiae plagae BOECE 255.

abtinere v. obtinere. abtrahere v. abstrahere. abuctare v. abuttare. abunculus v. avunculus.

1 abunda [cf. bunda], boundary.

c1210 cum terris forinsecis . . per easdem metas et ~as *BBC* (*Kells*) 44; **1230** usque ad metas et ~as ibidem per me concessas et appositas (*Ch. Bicester*) *Ambrosden* I 294; **1287** removerunt abbundas per ballivum scitas *Hund. Highworth* 312; **1317** usque ad la Droveweye . . que est habunda inter terras domini regis . . et terras domini H. *Cart. Glast.* I 229.

2 †abunda, abundance.

1407 eo minus propter habundam casei maximam ubique in tota parochia hoc anno (*MinAc*) *Ambrosden* II 212.

abundanter (hab-) [CL], abundantly, copiously.

omnia quae necesse habebat ~er ipsi donabat BEDE *HE* V 19; donat abundanter nobis escas cereales P. BLOIS *Euch.* 17. 1148C; **1223** priori . . de N. et similiter priori . . de C. . . porciones assignentur, set amplius et ~ius priori . . de N. *Cl* 632a; **s1100** obstetricis consilio, que ligavit mammas ejus post partum effluentes lacte ~issime HIGD. VII 12 p. 424; **s1356** pater suus fuit . . satis dives et . . ~er sibi ministravit aurum AVESB. 134; multe naves omnibus mercimoniis onerate in regno hiis [sc. Alexandri III Scotiae] diebus sine periculo ~er et libenter veniebant *Plusc.* VII 33.

abundantia (hab-) [CL], abundance. **b** fulness (fig.; *cf. Matt.* xii 34). **c** (phr. w. *ex*) beyond what is necessary.

humidae naturae ~ia undique superfusa [terrae] ERIUG. *Per.* 548C; **10..** ~ia vel copia, *genihtsumnys* WW; Hagustaldensis [ecclesia], licet erat tempore posterior, non tamen in possessionum ~ia . . inferior habebatur RIC. HEX. *Pri. Hex. prol.*; **s1184** rex . . naves . . ~iis omnium omnis generis victualium . . oneravit DICETO *YH* II 28; abundant . . in ~ia . . aque GIR. *TH* II 7; preterfluentes mundi ~ias AD. MARSH *Ep.* 247; in faciem eorum [sc. a nuptiis redeuntium] frumentum projiciebant, clamantes "~ia! ~ia!", quod Gallice dicitur *plente Latin Stories* 111; **1324** desiderantes quod victualia ad eandem civitatem . . in magna †habuntia [l. habundantia] deferantur (*Breve Ed. II*) *MGL* II 307; **s1356** pluit in magna ~ia AVESB. 136. **b** pater [Leir] iratus . . ex ~ia cordis . . vehementer indignans G. MON. II 11.

1 abundare, to bound.

1346 sicut certis metis circulariter habundatur *AncD* B 9540.

2 abundare (hab-; cf. BACON *Tert.* 247) [CL], to abound, be well supplied: **a** (w. abl.); **b** (w. *in*). **c** (w. *in sensu*) to be fully persuaded (cf. *Rom.* xiv 5).

a flumina . . piscibus ~abant BEDE *HE* IV 13; anima . . inops harum divitiarum quibus sic opulenter ~as ANSELM

(*Or.* 12) III 45; eo quod [terra] optimo ~aret frumento *Chr. Battle* 56; **1220** inhabitantes qui..multis bonis ~averunt *Cl* 430b; **1237** latronum flagitia, quibus nimis ~at regio Anglicana *Conc. Syn.* 253. **b 1217** cum..ipsi in multis ~ent, episcopus eorum..egestate afflictus est *Pat* 111; in sputis †hadundare [l. habundare] signum est fleumatice complexionis BART. ANGL. V 22. **c** judices vel suo in sensu ~antes vel archiepiscopo..propitiantes GIR. *JS* iv 570; loquens de ~antibus in suo sensu et per consequens errantibus OCKHAM *Dial.* 444.

2 to be abundant, plentiful.

cum..eis victualia ~arent RIC. HEX. *Stand.* 41; cui et discrecio suppeciit et..eloquium ~avit W. DAN. *Ailred* 18; omnisque in vobis religio ~et modesta *Lib. Regal.* 28; **s1512** impossibile fuisset obtinere illam [civitatem] si victus †abiddaverit *Reg. Butley* 30.

3 (tr.) to make plentiful.

Phebus.. / omnia fecundat, nutrit, fovet, auget, habundat GOWER *VC* I 17.

4 (pr. ppl.) abundant, excessive. **b** (math.) less than the sum of its factors. **c** (phr. w. *ex*) beyond what is necessary.

cur negabis ~ans egenti..quod nulli est noxium? ANSELM (*Or.* 12) III 47; in sermone tuo nimis es diffusus, abundans / verbis non sensu NIG. *SS* 3081; multo munitus milite, castrorum et facultatis ~ans DEVIZES 33; **1337** ad cautelam ~antem *Lit. Cant.* II 170; **s1379** ~antioris frigoris causa WALS. *HA* I 425. **b** numerus..superfluus vel ~ans est cujus partes multiplicative reddunt summam majorem toto NECKAM *NR* II 173 p. 295. **c** licet..judicibus..respectare placitum ex abbundanti [v.l. competenti] (*Leg. Hen.*) *GAS* 563; femoralibus..sibi abstinendum..ex ~anti decreverunt GIR. *Spec.* II 34; **1230** abbas..dicit quod non debet hic respondere..; et dicit ex ~anti quod satisfecit executoribus *CurR* XIII 2482; **1268** huic convencioni..partes signa sua apposuerunt; et ex ~anti in curia regis irrotulari fecerunt *Cl* 489; **1272** ex habundanti ad cautelam (*CurR* 205) *EHR* XXXV 413; **1333** quatinus instare..velitis exhabundanti *Lit. Cant.* II 16; **1412** universitas..ex ~anti dispensavit *StatOx* 219.

abunde (hab-) [CL], plentifully.

~e, *genycthlice GlC* A 39; portiones comparatione fructuum ex eis ~e provenientium admodicas suscipiens *Chr. Battle* 130; abbatias..redditibus amplis..~e dotavit et ditavit GIR. *Spec.* III 19.

abundique [al. div.], from all sides.

omnes ab undique confluebant FELIX *Guthl.* 45.

abundus (hab-) [LL], **a** (w. abl.) abounding. **b** abundant.

a reddit honustus Gerbertus, ..liber et..muneribus ~us MAP *NC* IV 11 p. 179; est..Saxonia..mineriis ~a, auro..opulenta *Eul. Hist.* II 107; **s1377** transit annus iste..~us fruge sed fructibus arborum pene carens WALS. *HA* I 345. **b** quis facit ut tellus segetes producat habundas? NIG. *Laur.* 33b; **s1310** rex..consideravit..suam..paupertatem et suorum ~as divitias WALS. *HA* I 125; uvaque temporibus stabit habunda suis GOWER *VC* V 572.

abuntare v. abuttare. aburneus v. alburneus. aburtivus v. abortivus 3.

abusa, abuse, malpractice.

1573 perdonamus..omnes..contemptus, ~as, necgligencias..et alia mala et offensa *Pat* 1104 m. 6.

abuschiamentum [cf. OF *embuschement*], ambush.

1283 perceperunt ~um hominum armatorum..et pre timore eorundem..levaverunt hutesium *SelCKB* I 124.

abuschiari [cf. OF *embuschier*], to lie in ambush.

1223 juxta pontem illum ~iati fuerunt *CurR* XI 1079.

abusio [CL], misuse, wrongful or careless use.

si..primus homo..eo modo qui est per ~onem propriis potentiis non dejiceret ERIUG. *Per.* 537B; cum omni tempore literature sugillatrix logices ~o fuerit GIR. *GE* II 37 p. 355; **1253** hoc enim esset..sue..potestatis..vel defectio vel corruptio vel ~o GROS. *Ep.* 128; nec navis nec batellus [dat occasionem mortis] in salsa, licet in aqua dulci, et hoc per ~onem BRACTON 136b; **s1275** rex cupiens..leges languidas, que..per ~onem male utentium..dormitaverant, excitare WYKES 263; **1415** volumus ut de illis..inventor gaudeat sicut decet, dictis victualibus moderate utendo..sine destruccione seu ~one quacumque (*Stat. Hen. V. temp. guerre*) UPTON 140.

2 a abuse, malpractice, misconduct, or reprehensible fashion. **b** verbal abuse, insult. **c** sexual abuse.

a generalis abusio planctum / exigit L. DURH. *Dial.* I 49; **1191** propter superbiam et ~ones suas (*Lit. Ep. Coventr.*) *G. Ric. I* 217; est inter alias ~onum pestes prima in regno Anglorum tyrannidis forestariorum AD. EYNS. *Hug.* III 9; **s1164** que ~ones dici possunt potius quam consuetudines M. PAR. *Abbr.* 195; **c1300** [liber] de duodecim ~onibus (*Invent.*) *Chr. Rams.* xci (cf. abusivus 2); **s1319** exorta est discordia inter majorem, aldermannos et communitatem civitatis pro diversis querelis et ~onibus *Ann. Paul.* 285; **s1394** venerunt de Boemia in Angliam ~ones ille execrabiles, sotulares scilicet cum longis rostris *V. Ric. II* 126; **s1423** ut ..destruamus ~onum tribulos, si qui..silvescant in hortulo ecclesie Anglicane (*Lit. Ep. Linc.*) AMUND. I 78; **c1430** qualis ~o pejor quam ubi hii qui ideo de mundo recesserunt, ut tam otium quam ignaviam..devitarent, jam his vitiis vacant precipue? *Reg. Whet.* II 385. **b** in superbia et in ~one locutus est H. BOS. *Ep.* 1424; **s1238** janitor convitiando loquens in superbia et ~one introitum omnibus procaciter denegavit M. PAR. *Maj.* III 482; **s1417** cum summa superbia et ~one respondit WALS. *YN* 485. **c** oblationes..abrepte in commessationes et scortorum ~ones consumebantur W. MALM. *GR* II 201; usus formosorum ~o est J. SAL. *Pol.* 506A; ipsam..seducit et, cum ad libitum suum abutatur, illicita non satis ei placet ~o MAP *NC* IV 16.

abusitare, to misuse. **b** to abuse, insult. **c** (p. ppl.) untrained.

to misuse, †abutisare, abuti; ..*misusynge*, abutens, †abusitas [? l. abusitans] *CathA*. **b** quam stultum hominem †abusotare putabat Philippum GIR. *Symb. ep.* 31 p. 314. **c** ~atus, minus instructus in scientia *GlC* A 50.

abusive [CL], by abuse, wrongfully, wrongly.

s901 monasterium virginum..quarum..Ethelwoldus unam ~e rapiens eam sibi matrimonio copulavit M. PAR. *Maj.* I 435; **1298** a choro se nullatenus subtrahant sicut hactenus facere ~e solebant *Reg. Cant.* II 815; **c1350** lecciones cursorias, quas vocant audienciam ~e *StatOx* 23.

abusivus [LL], wrongful, wrong. **b** abusive, insulting.

s1138 incredibile..est que scelesta..et blasphema in Deum et ~a ipsius humanitatis exercitus ille Scottorum egerit J. HEX. *HRCont.* 290; **1303** ~is presumpcionibus et temerariis excessibus privilegii exempcionis *Reg. Cant.* II 640; **1332** in plures errores et ~os modos loquendi incidit OCKHAM *Pol.* II 523; **1375** consuetudo ~a et detestabilis [sc. quod bona que episcopi tempore sui obitus possidebant rex appropriare presumebat] *Mon. Hib. & Scot.* 353. **b s1250** archiepiscopus..in verba ~a et contumeliosa prorumpens, ipsos canonicos..indecenter nimis tractavit M. PAR. *Min.* III 79*n*.

2 (sb. f.), abuse, malpractice (w. ref. to treatise wrongly attributed to Augustine; cf. *abusio* 2 a).

11.. psalterium glosatum, cum xii ~is (*Invent.*) *Chr. Rams.* lxxxvi; de informatione dominorum bene in tractatu de duodecim ~is J. WALEYS I iii 12 f. 28.

abusor, abuser, misuser. **b** sexual abuser.

plebicitorum ~ores sive prevaricatores plebis statutorum NECKAM *Ut.* 105; **c1240** vasis pretiosissimi in Dei contemptum et offensam abominabilissimus ~or GROS. *Ep.* 90 p. 280; propter ~ores earum [scienciarum]..confutandos BRADW. *CD* 468B; lex vult quod juris abusor / amittat vicio quod sibi jura dabant GOWER *VC* III 1705. **b 12..** immundi sunt ~ores brutorum *Gl. in* D. BEC. 541.

abusus [CL], misuse. **b** (?) disuse.

bruta..non ad ~um sed ad usum creata GIR. *TH* II 23; nonnulli quorum damnat abusus opes GARL. *Tri. Eccl.* p. 27; **1301** si..privilegia..immutat, presertim propter ingratitudinem vel ~um illorum quibus..sunt concessa (*Lit. Papae*) *MGL* II 161. **b 1323** omnis libertas et libera consuetudo habet probari per usum earundem affirmative et non per ~um *MGL* I 442.

2 abuse, malpractice. **b** sexual abuse.

in dextra virgas quatiens castigat abusus GARL. *Epith.* VI 449; **1224** nolentes tante presumptionis et iniquitatis ~um [sc. ut nullus clericus de Hibernia ad aliquam dignitatem ecclesiasticam assumatur] sub dissimulatione transire (*Lit. Papae*) *RL* I 541; **1451** ad justificacionem..~uum et errorum suorum predictorum asserunt.. *Cl* 301 m. 6; **1549** ex his presertim duobus capitibus multi ~us oriuntur *Conc. Scot.* II 81. **b** cui [hirco] miserrima..se etiam ad ~um supponebat GIR. *TH* II 23.

abuti [CL], to abuse, misuse. **b** to maltreat, ravage. **c** to abuse sexually. **d** (refl.) to practice sexual abuse.

homo..naturali potentia..abusus est ERIUG. *Per.* 537A; inhumana sevitia abusi sunt fortuna GIR. *EH* I 13; **1313** inhibitum est..abbati..ne ulterius ~atur libertate illa *PQW* 312; **1356** asserendo..zonarios mestera sua..abusos esse (*Cl*) *RParl* II 456a. **b s1141** traditur comes..Willelmo Yprensi, qui Cantia ~ebatur GERV. CANT. I 121. **c s1138** postquam more brutorum animalium illis miserrimis ~i pertesi sunt, eas..sibi ancillas fecerunt RIC. HEX. *Stand.* 157; **s1307** interdicitur eis [Templariis] usus feminarum, ita quod, quando invaluerit temptatio carnis, ~antur licite sociis suis *Meaux* II 249. **d 1311** Robertus..~ebatur se cum quodam juvene *Conc.* II 384.

2 to make use of.

a690 Scotticos sciolos, quorum gemmato tua sagacitas dogmatum favo aliquantisper abusa est ALDH. *Ep.* 5 p. 493.

abutisare v. abusitare. abutissare, abutizare, v. abuttizare.

abuttamentum, abutment.

1251 faciet j caminum in garderoba..regis cum ~o extra caminum *Cl* 556; **c1290** habuttamenta de Neudich *Doc. Robertsbridge* 125.

abuttare [OF *aboter*], to abut (on), extend (to): **a** (w. *super*); **b** (w. other prep.); **c** (refl.).

a a1200 v acras prati que habuttant super Smalene *Kal. Samson* 169; **c1240** tres acras..terre..quarum una extremitas abbuttat super..rivulum molendini *Couch. Furness* II i 105; **12..** cujus unum capud abuttad (*sic*) super viam regalem *AncD* A 3487; **12..** sex acras terre..cujus unum caput habutat super pasturam meam *Cart. Eye* f. 106. **1255** terre sue arabiles..extendunt se et ~ant super dominicum boscum domini regis *SelPl Forest* 25; **1260** videri facias..strictos passus..et boscos passibus illis propinquos et super vias abutantes (*Breve regis*) *Flor. Hist.* III 355; **c1270** unam acram terre que ambuttat super S. *Cart. Sallay* 490; **1278** appropriavit sibi iij sulcos ad unam rodam suam de omnibus sell[ionibus] ~antibus super illam rodam *SelPlMan* 93; quarum [acrarum] unum capud abuctat super terram de P. *FormMan* 7; **1444** in quadam parcella more de Q. jacente sive ~ante versus orientem super quoddam clausum *Ac. Durh.* 144; **1583** omnes shopas, cellaria, sollaria [etc.] ~antia super tenementum Johannis *Pat* 1234 m. 18. **b 1219** x acras terre..que ~ant ex una parte a Beristret' et ex alia parte a Bromdun *CurR* VIII 124; **c1245** una acra que abottat in prato Wydonis *AncD* A 353; **12..** capud australe [acre] abbutat contra foreram Henrici *AncD* C 1868; **c1270** unum capud ambuttat ad terram Ade *Cart. Osney* IV 138; **1307** prout [cotagium]..abbuttat supra viam regiam *Kelso* I 42; **c1390** via regia..abbuttat versus villam de Patmer' (*Anc. Indict.*) *Pub. Works* I 102; **1415** iij dim. acras terre..~antes usque B. *CourtR Banstead*; **s1430** incluse sunt tres fenestreole..in uno tenemento †abuntante versus orientem in..hospitium abbatis *Chr. S. Alb.* 47; **1443** ~at secundum latitudinem ex parte occidentali ad tenementum Johannis *Deeds Balliol* 126; **14..** dimidia dola de R. est in marisco de Romeney..et ~at versus east cum heredibus Rogeri.., versus west cum Jacobo *Cart. Bilsington* 169*n*.; **1587** unam peciam terre..~antem in Ashbrooke *Pat* 1301 m. 19. **c 1270** selliones que..~ant se usque ad longam semitam *CourtR Hales* 20; **1278** quoddam mesuagium in Londonia quod se abutat super vicum de Colechurchstrete *SelPlJews* 105.

2 to delimit, demarcate.

1450 causa renovacionis cartarum ~ancium certas bundas in quarrera de H. *Fabr. York* 64.

abuttatio, demarcation.

1535 pro factura de lez stakes pro divisione et ~one prati domini vocati lez Yngez (*MinAc Norf* etc. 94) *Rutland MSS*.

abuttizare, to abut (on): **a** (w. *super*); **b** (w. dat.).

a a1200 croftum..abutizat super viam *Danelaw* 158; **a1224** unum sellionem..qui abutissat super Smidheseng *Reg. Ant. Linc.* IV no. 1121; **c1250** clausum..~ans versus austrum super communem viam *DL Cart. Misc.* II 230; **1316** placeam abbuttizantem super mercatum *Terr. Fleet* 31. **b** duas selliones illas que abutissant uno capite mesuagio G. filii E. et alio capite vie que dicitur Middilgat' *AncD* A 2997.

abyssalis, infernal.

1241 inter has ~es mundani principis obtenebrationes AD. MARSH *Ep.* 76 p. 188.

abyssus [ἄβυσσος; *sts. decl.* 4], deep pit or hollow, ocean depth.

~us, *deopnys* ÆLF. *Sup.*; **983** (12c) ~os gurgitum ante capturam locatos nemo retibus..piscari..audeat *CD* 640; statim ~us vallavit eum [cf. *Jon.* ii 6] AILR. *Ed. Conf.* 749C; **s1138** consulebant..laborem esse infructuosum ~um pelagi ..lapidum materia velle obstruere *G. Steph.* I 30; inter clitellarios..unus [in sabulum vivum] quasi in ~um descendit GIR. *IK* I 8 (cf. *Id. TH* II 14); **s1216** voragines ~us [i.e. *the Wash*] que absorbuerunt universa M. PAR. *Maj.* II 667; in fine..civitatis [London']..est castrum famosissimum..fossatis amplissimis, aquarum abissis ac aliis bellicis apparatibus circumdatum S. SIM. *Itin.* 14.

2 nether pit (Hell or sim.).

ascenderunt quidam spirituum obscurorum de ~o illa flammivoma BEDE *HE* V 12; **747** in profundum inferni et tartarum ~i demersi sunt BONIF. *Ep.* 73 p. 152; quasi ~o rupta et soluto Satana AD. MARSH *Ep.* 8 p. 88.

3 chaos, formlessness.

alii..~i..vocabulo invisibilis essentiae informitatem significari volunt ERIUG. *Per.* 548B (cf. 550C).

4 bottomless pit (fig.): **a** (of emptiness); **b** (of expenditure); **c** (of grief etc.); **d** (of wickedness); **e** (of obscurity); **f** (of divine wisdom; cf. *Ps.* xxxv 7).

a s1185 repperimus..angulum in rotundo, ~um in solido GERV. CANT. I 34. **b s1213** expressi quantum..nobis annuatim abstulit et quod hec omnia in suam ~um convertit *Chr. Evesham* 240. **c** tedii cujusdam ~o funditus absorberi AD EYNS. *Hug.* V 18; **s1213** rex Johannes..demersus in ~um desperationis M. PAR. *Abbr.* 227; **s1227** nullum in ~um terroribus aut minis satirice objurgantes demergant, sed potius in spem erigant spiritualem *Id. Maj.* III 136; **s1392** O fortuna fallax, que quos provehis ad tripudii momentum inopinate dejicis in meroris ~um! *Croyl. Cont.* B 491. **d** in ~um pravitatis heretice OCKHAM *Dial.* 683. **e** rudis et priscae legis patefecit abyssum ALDH. *VirgV* 1625; licet hec que ad presens inter nos agitatur questio abierit in ~um A. TEWK. *Ep.* 11; cui nuda est ~us humane conscientie AD. SCOT. *TT.* 754; qui capciosis exercitantur tota vita sermonibus, profunde rimatores abissus MAP *NC* I 31; in tantis ~is teterrimarum caliginum palpat.. zelus electorum AD. MARSH *Ep.* 14; **c1324** Edwardus [Confessor]..a profunda ~o eam [legem Edgari sopitam] extrahit et renovavit (*Lib. Cust.*) *MGL* II 645. **f** omnia disponens, ..cujus judicia ~us multa, ..impediebat AELNOTH *Cnut* II 29; O ~us multa judiciorum Dei! W. NEWB. IV 13; **a1290** ~um divine sciencie quam de nobis habet Deus (*Quest. Ox.*) *Ox. Hist. Soc.* XCVI 126.

ac v. atque. acabli- v. accabli-.

acacia [ἀκακία; CL = gum arabic], juice of plums or sloes.

galle, cortices mali granati, ..acatie temperentur cum aceto et inungantur GILB. II 83. 1; prunella nigra..ponantur loco acatie, que est succus prunellorum non maturorum GAD. 29. v. 2; ~ia, i. succus desiccatus prunellarum agrestium immaturarum *Alph.* 1 (cf. *SB* 9: achacia).

academia [Ἀκαδημία], Plato's Academy.

Achademici..dicti sunt ab Achademia, unde Plato extitit oriundus J. SAL. *Pol.* 641A.

2 university.

1421 querelas..~iarum Oxon' et Cantab' *Conc.* III 403a; **1511** in adventu Hispanii (*sic*) legatio videnti achademiam et collegium nostrum *Cant. Coll. Ox.* II 254; **1528** piorum operum per..~iam..fiendorum *StatOx* 335; **1545** in ~ia Oxoniae aut Cantabrigiae *Mem. Ripon* 246; **1549** in publicis gymnasiis et ~iis *Conc. Scot.* II 104; **1573** Achedemia Cantabrigiensis *Pat* 1106 m. 21.

academicus, a Platonic, Platonist. **b** (w. ref. to scholars at court of Charlemagne).

a ~ae disputationis sofisma ALDH. *VirgP* 27 p. 262; **804** Atheniensis Sophista ex ~a scola ALCUIN *Ep.* 307; si 'forte', 'fortasse' et 'forsitan' proferuntur, Achademico dicantur usi temperamento, eo quod temperatiores aliis Achademici fuerint J. SAL. *Pol.* 640D. **b 804** evangelicas quaestiones achademicis vestris a nobis enucleandas inquiritis ALCUIN *Ep.* 308.

2 (person) belonging to a university.

1578 ad magnum incommodum non solum oppidanorum sed etiam ~orum *StatOx* 412.

acalaber v. attelebus.

acalanthis [ἀκαλανθίς, *kind of song-bird*], nightingale.

achalantis vel luscinia..*nehtaegale GlC* A 121; arguta simul cantans luscinia ruscis, / quam lingua propria dicunt acalantida Graeci ALDH. *Aen.* 68. 8.

acalephe [ἀκαλήφη], nettle.

colofe, i. seminis urtice GILB. VII 286 v.l.; achalaphe, ..urtica pungens idem *Alph.* 1 (cf. ib. 4: alphe, urtica).

acalicus, acalis v. calix.

acanthus [ἄκανθος], bearsfoot or other prickly or stinging plant.

accintu, *denetle GlC* A 172; **10..** acantan, *beowirt* WW; anta, *eoforthrote Gl. Durh.*; armis muniris, asper achanthe, tuis NECKAM *DS* VII 368; ligna sethim esse dicuntur quedam arbores spinose..similes albe spine, que Grece †acharitis dicuntur BART. ANGL. XVII 149; arbor..similis spine quem †archeratum vel aromaticum dicunt *Ib.* 101; acantus, spina idem: inde acantus Egipciaca, inde acantus leuce, id est spina alba *Alph.* 1; acantum est semen urtice *SB* 9; **14..** acantus, A. *hoppyn* WW.

acap- v. accap-.

acariare [OF *acharier*; cf. abcariare], to carry, transport. **b** (?) to steal.

1215 in x doliis vini ~iatis a Suhamt' usque Corf' *Cl* 217b; **1331** debent invenire et ~iare meremium pro faciendo rotam..ejusdem molendini (*KRAc* 89/15) *S. Jers.* I 34. **b** *to steyle*, †acari, furari *CathA*.

acaristum v. acharistum.

†acaron [Sp. Ar. *zarcatôna* (*zarqaṭūnā*) < *bizr qaṭūnā*; (?) infl. by ἄκαρι or ἄκορον], fleabane (bot.).

zaitaron vel ~on, i. psillium *Alph.* 198(cf. ib. 16: archacon, respice in zacharon).

acarud, ~us, v. azarud.

acatalecticus [ἀκατάληκτος], acatalectic.

huiuscemodi versus [sc. qui dactilo terminantur] ~i nuncupantur ALDH. *Met.* 10 p. 90.

acatasticus v. apocatastaticus. acates v. achates. acatia v. acacia.

acation [ἀκάτιον], mainsail.

acateon, *se mæsta segl* ÆLF. *Sup.*

acatum v. accatum. acca v. haka.

accabliamentum, 'battery', knocking down (C.I.).

1309 rex habet omnimoda placita corone, tam de effusione sanguinis et clamore de harou et ~o (*JustIt*) *S. Jers.* XVIII 164; per acabliamentum quod fecit Helene..ipsa levavit clamorem de hareu *Ib.* 174; **1324** quilibet eorum alterum verberavit..cum plaga et sanguine et ~o *JustIt* 1164 r. 18.

accabliare [OF *achaabler*], to knock down (C.I.).

1300 vulneravit G. Malet et ad terram achabliavit *JustIt* 1158 r. 6; **1309** verberavit Helenam..et eam acabliavit ad terram (*JustIt*) *S. Jers.* XVIII 178.

accalvaster, bald in front.

14.. acalvaster, A. *ballyd byfore* WW.

accapere v. accipere 3.

accapitare [cf. achevare], to acknowledge feudal liability.

1226 habuit v heredes que ~are debent domino regi, et non ~ant nisi due earum *LTRMem* 8 r. 12d.; **1240** quelibet ipsarum [sororum] separatim debet ~are domino regi *BNB* III 288; cum..plures fuerint coheredes, ..omnes acapitabunt filie primogenite et maritus primogenite homagium faciet domino capitali de toto feodo BRACTON 78; omisso illo medio, [tenens medii tenentis] capitali domino acapitet et ei respondeat de eisdem serviciis *Fleta* 107 (cf. ib. 416).

2 to abut.

12.. dimidiam acram..que ~at super culturam dictarum sanctimonialium *Cart. Harrold* 11d.

accaptagium, ~ia, payment on change of feudal lord, relief (Gasc.).

1283 habebimus vj d. ..de acaptagio in mutacione domini *RGasc* II 209 (cf. ib. 314: obliarum et acaptagiarum); **1313** nobiles parochie de Gotbezio solvere tenentur..in mutacione cujuslibet regis Anglie et ducis Aquitanie ipsi duci nomine sporlarum seu acaptagii unum austurconem seu xxx s. Morlanorum *Ib.* IV 1019.

accaptamentum, payment on change of feudal lord, relief (Gasc.).

1289 cum uno aureo marbotino nobis..in mutacione domini solvendo pro acaptamento *RGasc* II 323; ad solvendum pro rata sporlam in mutacione domini ex utraque parte et eciam vendas seu ~a, si contingat vendi aliquam medietatem de rebus predictis *Ib.* 369 (cf. *Foed.* II 425).

accaptum, payment on change of feudal lord, relief (Gasc.).

1269 recepto homagio et fidelitatis juramento..et una lancea de ~o pro toto territorio de Brulhien (*Lib. B*) *Foed.* I 855; **1289** habebimus vj d. obliarum..et totidem de acapto in mutacione domini *RGasc* II 352 (cf. ib. 130: cum.. homagio et uno pari cirotecarum albarum in mutacione domini de acapte).

accasatus [cf. casatus], resident tenant, *chasé* (Gasc.).

1289 Hodinus nec sui debent..alii infeodare feodum.. nec ibi ponere ~um nec subaccasatum cum majori censu *RGasc* II 473.

accator [OF *achateor*], buyer.

1362 officia duorum pincernarum et duorum achatorum domus [de S. Edmundo] *Pat* 264 m. 5.

1 accatum, ~a [OF *achat* < accaptum], (property acquired by) purchase.

1130 R. filius G. debet x m. ut habeat rectum de achatis patris sui *Pipe* 137; **1156** quietantiam de theloneo et omni consuetudine de †cata venditione et ~o suo per totam Angliam et Normanniam *BBC* (*Hythe*) 182 (cf. *RChart* 153 [**1205**]: de tota venditione et ~o suo); **1180** in acato xv tonellorum vini *RScacNorm* I 68; **c1200** sciatis me concessisse..terram meam de Stanley..tanquam illam quam bene dare possum, que fuit de ~o meo et conquestu *MonA* VI 895; **1201** sciatis nos concessisse omnibus Judeis Anglie et Normannie..omnia illa que modo rationabiliter tenent in terris et vadiis et akatis suis (*Ch.*) *SelPlJews* 1; **1205** v dolia vini de ultimo achato nostro *Cl* 57b; **1215** concessimus ..burgensibus..quod liberé possint dare vel vendere purchatia et achata sua *BBC* (*Dunwich*) 68; **1278** quieti sint de..achato et rechato suo *BBC* (*Cinque Ports*) 260; **1406** cum..civibus..concessum sit..quod habeant omnia acata et vadia sua secundum consuetudinem civitatis *BB Winchester* 13; **1507** in divers' estuffur' et acchat' empt' pro expensis hospicii *MinAc Hen. VII* 1 r. 1d.

2 payment on change of feudal lord (Gasc.); *cf. accaptum.*

1242 facient eis servicium unius lancee de achata *RGasc* I 161.

2 accatum v. advocare 14. accaus- v. accus-. accearium v. aciarium.

accedenter, with full relevance or impact.

cum diutius in esse subsistant [superna], ~ius declarant Creatoris eternitatem NECKAM *NR* II *prol.*

accedere [CL], to go or come to, approach (a place). **b** to draw near (impers. pass.). **c** to come in, rise (of tide). **d** (trans.) to reach (a point in time).

ad hospitium, quo proposuerat, accessit BEDE *HE* III 9; ab ea sciscitans..cur..altari non accessisset T. MON. *Will.* VII 18; **1255** accesserunt ad prisonam et ipsum G. extraxerunt *SelPlForest* 13; nullus serviencium debet unquam.. ad sanctuaria..acedere *Cust. Cant.* 112; **s1416** accessit ad imperialem presenciam ELMH. *Hen. V* 103. **b** quanto ad euri partes magis ~itur GIR. *TH* I 3. **c** ~ente et recedente reumate BEDE *HE* III 3. **d 1220** termino treuge nondum accesso (*DipDoc* 67) *RL* I 140.

2 to go to, approach (a person, usu. for a specific purpose). **b** to resort to (a law-court). **c** to attain to (a dignity). **d** to perform, fulfil (an office).

~ens ad sacerdotem..confessus est reatum suum BEDE *HE* IV 25; **1221** consuluerunt eis ut ~erent ad dominum suum..et impetrarent amorem domini sui *SelPlCrown* 146; **1271** ita quod non oporteat ipsum de die in diem ad te ~ere pro eadem [pecunia] *Liberate* 48 m. 11. **b** accessit coram.. justiciariis et finem illum..calumpniabat *State Tri. Ed. I* 72; *cest briefe* quod vicecomes ~at in propria persona sua ad curiam etc. *Reg. Brev.* 9b. **c** qualiter ad sacros accessisset ordines *V. Ed. Conf.* 46v. **d 11..** archidiaconos..nunquam ad hoc officium accessisse, priore in quovis loco presente *Feod. Durh.* lxi.

3 a (of incidents) to come, occur (in addition). **b** to be added, accrue.

a ~ebat ad exercendos odiorum motus..quod terrae quaedam ducis contiguae erant *V. Ed. Conf.* 42; [accidentium] alia nullam omnino vel ~endo vel recedendo mutationem circa id de quo dicuntur efficere noscuntur ANSELM (*Mon.* 24) I 43; **a1162** gloria ~it, sed non superba; prosperitas venit, sed non effusa (*Lit. Abb. Cell.*) *Becket Mat.* V 4; **1236** ad aggravationem peccati..~it quod..GROS. *Ep.* 72* p. 230. **b 597** ut omni stipendio quod ~it quattuor debeant fieri portiones (*Lit. Papae*) BEDE *HE* I 27 p. 48; eadem *re* praepositio, si ad verba a vocalibus incipientia accesserit, *d* litteram crebro assumit ALDH. *PR* 140 p. 197; ut corporibus eorum robur ~at J. SAL. *Pol.* 594A; cedibus accedunt cedes HANV. VI 327; **s1386** accessit ejus [ducis] profeccioni favor papalis WALS. *HA* II 143.

4 to be near. **b** to be similar.

stelle que ~unt ad polum articum SACROB. *Sph.* 1 p. 82. **b** ora / accedunt candore nivi VINSAUF *PN* 1670.

5 to belong (as an accessory). **b** (pr. ppl.) pertinent, relevant.

advocatio..ecclesiarum juri spirituali..~it et innititur; unde cujus est de jure principali cognoscere, et de accessorio, cum unum de altero pendeat H. BOS. *Thom.* III 29. **b** ad artem..~entius est quid oporteat quam quid fieri possit considerare BALSH. *AD* 142.

6 (inf. as sb.) right of access.

1199 vicecomes returnavit breve suum ad ballivum abbatis.., in cujus libertatem [non] habet ~ere *CurR RC* II 86.

accedia v. acedia. accedula v. 1 acidula.

accelerare [CL], (trans.) to hasten, speed up.

strages ~antur crudeliores GILDAS *EB* 19; non conversionem peccatoris exspectans, sed mortem magis et eversionem ~ans GIR. *IK* I 2.

2 (intr.) to hasten. **b** (w. inf.).

adceleravit ocius ad legendum BEDE *HE* III 5; Griffinus ..accelerans tam equum quam ascensorem ejus lancea perforavit GIR. *EH* I 41; **1407** mandantes sibi ut illuc accelleret *Lit. Cant.* III 102. **b** ~avit venire Romam BEDE *HE* V 11; nisi..cultellum rejicere ~asset W. MALM. *GR* II 169; ~abo subsequi eum J. FORD *Wulf.* 92; hunc tractatum..~a exordiri OCKHAM *Dial.* 871.

3 (p. ppl.) speedy, prompt.

quanto nox hic contractior, tanto post galli cantum dies ~atior GIR. *TH* II 25; cursoris vestri..profectio ~atior AD. MARSH *Ep.* 52.

accelerate, speedily.

jus..per beneficium istius constitutionis commodius et ~ius expeditur GLANV. II 7.

acceleratim, speedily.

~im accessit ad regem H. BOS. *Thom III* 31 (cf. id. *LM* 1313).

acceleratio [CL], hastening, speeding up.

civitatem..sub omni ~one advenit *G. Steph.* I 62; regie opes que ad fabrice ~onem..cedebant *Chr. Battle* 8; **1214** propter ~onem adventus vestri in Angliam *Pat* 114b; eorum [accidentium senectutis] ~o potest retardari BACON IX 8; **1426** cum magna ~one recessit *Reg. Cant.* III 176; pro ~one et celeriori expedicione negociorum *Ib.* 194.

accendere [CL], to kindle. **b** to heat.

flagrans accenditur ignis ALDH. *VirgV* 1990; ut lucernam quae mihi ~sa erat extingueret BEDE *HE* IV 8; **11..** ascenso lumine (*Cap. Arrouas.*) *EHR* LII 275; candelis ~sis demonem illum excommunicavit GIR. *GE* I 53. **b** in loco ubi ferrum ~itur [ad judicium Dei] *Text. Roff.* 29.

2 (fig.) to inflame, incite. **b** (p. ppl.) eager. **c** (intr.) to burn with desire.

nititur accensam fraudis restingere flammam ALDH. *VirgV.* 1553; lector..sollertius ad exsequenda ea..~itur BEDE *HE pref.*; ut ~atur tepor meus ANSELM (*Or.* 2) III 7; quamplures..ad hoc perficiendum ipsius animum ~erunt RIC. HEX. *Pri. Hex.* 7; innatum illis [sc. animosis] ignem ~ens GIR. *TH pref.* p. 21. **b** solito erant acriores et ad regem perturbandum accensiores *G. Steph.* I 41. **c** ~ens ad communionem sacram, .."vere credo" inquit J. FORD *Wulf.* 17.

accendilia v. cicindela.

accensa [OF *acense*], lease, farm (Gasc.).

1255 hanc..assensam [de redditibus etc.] fecimus.. Brunoni pro m li. *RGasc* I *sup.* p. 36; **1280** (v. accensatio); **1289** de ascensa preposituree [Landarum]..solvatis..xx li. *Ib.* II 354; **1311** id quod ultra ascensam hujusmodi sibi defuerit *Ib.* IV 510 (= *Foed.* III 266).

accensamentum, lease, farm (Fr.). **b** leasehold tenement (Gasc.).

1259 qui ex parte regis Francie..tenent aliquid..per vendicionem vel per empcionem vel per ascensamentum *TreatyR* I 39. **b 1207** quod..burgenses nostri de Niort' juste habeant et possideant ~a et conquisita sua *Pat* 75b.

accensare [OF *acenser*], **a** to make (place or person) subject to rent. **b** to lease, farm out (Gasc.).

a non erat in censu Scottesam; R. Blondus adcensavit *DB* II 124; istos liberos homines addidit R. comes huic manerio, et in eodem sunt adcensati *Ib.* 133b. **b 1253** (v. accensatio); **1255** ascensavimus et ad firmam tradidimus Helie..salinum *RGasc* I *sup.* p. 7 (cf. ib. 49: assensavimus.. preposituram); **1313** volentes..effici cerciores quantum alta justicia in parochia de Samiaco valet per annum..et, si deberet ascensari, per quantum posset ad opus nostrum annuatim ascensari *Ib.* IV 1125.

†accensaria, (?) farm (Ir.); but *cf. accessorius* 2 b.

1298 perquisiciones hundredi una cum assensariis extenduntur per annum ad vj s *KRAc* 233/6.

accensatio, leasing, farming.

1253 si contingat ipsos..redditus nostros..impignorare vel acensare nomine nostro, ..hujusmodi impignoracionem vel acensacionem ratam..habebimus *RGasc* I 290; **1280** potestatem..tradendi ad firmam seu acensam..custumam ..Burdegale..usque ad unum annum..a tempore arrentacionis firme seu ascensacionis..numerandum *RGasc* II 112.

accensator, lessee, farmer (Gasc.).

1289 commisimus..Bernardo, Raymundo [etc.]..salinas ..Agennesii..sicut ascensatores earundem tenere consueverunt *RGasc* II 471.

accensibilis, inflammable (*v. et. accessibilis*).

radios multos concurrere in supremo aeris, quo elevantur fumi ~es, ibique per concursum radiorum fumum inflammari GROS. 41.

accensio, kindling. **b** inflammation (med.). **c** blaze (fig.). **d** (w. *lunae*) new moon.

s1099 accensis super altaria cereis, commissisque eorum singulis candelis extinctis, ut per ~onem indicium voluntatis divine panderetur M. PAR. *Min.* I 149; de ~one candelarum in Cena Domini ad matutinas *Offic. Sal.* 102; **s1243** in cereorum inestimabilium ~one *Flor. Hist.* II 265. **b** calorem naturalem mutatum in igneum ibi suscipere distemperantiam et ~onem GILB. I 3. 1. **c** ~one furoris incaluit *Eul. Hist.* I 150. **d** ~onem ejus [sc. lune] et plenilunium sequitur solis eclypsis et lune (WALCHER *Drac.*) *Med. Sci.* 117; vexationem suam non ~oni lune lunaticus ascribat W. CANT. *Mir. Thom.* II 8; in hoc anno MCCLXVII..non solum media conjunctio solis et lune..fuit sexto Kalendas Aprilis super B literam, sed prima ~o lune et visio prime lune BACON *Tert.* 289.

accensor, prompter, stimulator.

ut episcopus lateri adesset, qui ~or in prosperis..esset W. MALM. *GP* I 14.

accensorius, hortatory.

Honorius..papa misit ~ias Edwino regi litteras H. HUNT. *HA* III 29.

1 accensus v. accendere.

2 accensus [CL], attached, enrolled.

1546 scholares sparsim infra precinctum universitatis commorantes et nullius collegii aut aule numero ~i *StatOx* 392.

accentare, to accent, stress.

noviciorum magister tam de modo legendi et ~andi quam de modo naturaliter canendi suos novicios tenetur instruere *Cust. Westm.* 41; de modo legendi et ~andi et punctuandi *Cust. Cant.* 100.

accentuare, to accent, stress.

turbati sunt in dicendo et dicendi ordinem et etiam recte ~andi pronunciationem in nonnullis dictionibus perdiderunt H. BOS. *Thom.* IV 8; syllaba..non est aliter ~anda in metro quam extra metrum VINSAUF *AV* II 3. 175; **s1327** receptores literarum..sophisma commutaverunt, sc. ad sensum istum, "Edwardum occidere nolite timere", et tunc subjunxerunt legendo, "bonum est", malum dictamen.. male ~antes BAKER 107b; **1351** abusum quo certe dictiones contra regulas grammaticales..inter nos ~antur..tollere affectantes, statuimus ut 'Sidonis' penultima longa.. 'zizania' penultima †brevis [? l. brevi]..pronuncientur *G. S. Alb.* II 429; **1472** in ~ando, punctuando, legendo et cantando *Melrose* II 577.

accentus [CL], accent, stress or intonation.

~us, qui Graece *prosodia* nuncupatur ALDH. *PR* 140 p. 194; quodsi paenultima acuto aut circumflexo ~u pronuntiatur *Ib.* 112; ~us dictus quasi adcantus, quod ad cantilenam vocis nos faciat cognoscere syllabas BEDE *AM* 2358; est ~us regularis modulatio vocis ad significationem discernendam NECKAM *Corrog.* (*N. & E.*) 25; quelibet dictio habet naturaliter suum ~um proprium, et diverse dictiones habent distinctos ~us BACON *Tert.* 235 (v. et. accinere); sequitur de fallacia secundum ~um *Id.* XV 343; **s1327** hic vigebat sophistarum fallacia ~us [v.l. †accensa] per episcopum qui scripsit 'Edwardum occidere nolite timere bonum est' BAKER 107 (cf. accentuare) (cf. et. M. PAR. *Maj.* III 51).

acceptabilis, acceptable, welcome (*cf. acceptibilis*).

680 synodos beatorum et Deo ~ium patrum (*Syn. Hatfield*) BEDE *HE* IV 17; ut recipit monachus nimis acceptabile donum WALT. ANGL. *Fab.* 8; audiebat..quod ~is et carus esset Francorum regi MAP *NC* V 6 p. 243; fons.. aquas habens solis hominibus ~es GIR. *TH* II 7; mihi est valde ~e duras questiones audire (M. SCOT. *Part.*) *Med. Sci.* 294; **1245** sacrificium zeli, quo non est Deo ~ius GROS. *Ep.* 118 p. 340; **1268** stabulum ad equos nostros ~e *Reg. S. Thom. Dublin* 6; **1269** utrum ~is esset ad recipiendum in decena *CBaron* 87; **1423** omnibus melioribus..modis quibus eis videbitur expediens, ~e vel oportunum *RScot* 240b; **s1460** nec cedere [poterant fruges] in utilem ~emque usum hominum *Reg. Whet.* I 385.

acceptabiliter, acceptably.

1419 nisi ille aldermannus sit absens per racionabilem causam et..~er se poterit excusare (*Lib. Alb.*) *MGL* I 31.

acceptabulum v. acetabulum.

†acceptaculum [? *var. of* acetabulum], vessel for wine offering.

~um..dicitur vasculum in quo vinum Deo offerendum in sacrificio probari debuit an esset purum vel corruptum; vas autem ubi probabatur et acceptabatur acceptabulum dicebatur BART. ANGL. XIX 125.

acceptare [CL], to accept, admit. **b** to approve. **c** (w. inf.) to consent. **d** (w. *de*) to accept of. **e** (w. *personam*) to favour (*cf. accipere* 3c).

s1231 quem [episcopum] rex gratanter, quantum ad se pertinebat, ~ans M. PAR. *Maj.* III 207; **1292** nominationem hujusmodi vobis significamus, ut alterum eorum ~etis, gratificetis seu approbetis *DCCant* Q f. 1b; **1438** hoc indignum munusculum..dignemini ~are CAPGR. *Hen. app.* IV p. 231; **1467** receptus et ~atus..ad habitum monachalem *Invent. Ch. Ch.* 116; **1583** quamquidem sursumredditionem ~amus et allocamus *Pat* 1235 m. 19. **b** 1239 credendum est quod multum ~asset David si quis de pastoribus sibi subditis..arietem a leone vel urso captum de ore eorum eruisset GROS. *Ep.* 127 p. 386; papa [Adrianus IV] omnia [munera] ~avit, sed non accepit preter..sandalia *G. S. Alb.* I 127; quod audiens, abbas verbum non ~abat *Ib.* 256; **1274** eam [fidem] ~amus et..profitemur (*Lit. Imp. Graec.*) *Flor. Hist.* III 36; **s1307** scripsit papa regi, rogans eum ut collationem domus de Coldingham..nepoti suo ~aret GRAYSTANES 27. **c 1235** ~avimus ducere in uxorem ..Alyenoram *TreatyR* I 11; **s1396** abbas..comminabatur quod..singulos..in prisona faceret..detineri quousque ejus beneplacita admittere ~arent *Meaux* III 260. **d c1430** scripsit..ut ipsum libenter contentaret, saltem si in plenam solucionem ~are vellet de simili solucionis summa (*Lit. Ep. Lichf.*) *Reg. Whet.* II 370. **e 1268** ne..potius videatur ~asse personam quam justiciam dilexisse *Conc. Syn.* 777.

acceptatio, acceptance. **b** approval. **c** (w. *personarum etc.*) showing favour.

1220 si..finem illum acceptaveritis, mittatis nobis in testimonium ~onis vestre litteras vestras patentes *Cl* 414a; **1290** desicut predictus R. nichil profert quod ..dominus H. rex acceptavit donacionem, ..recordum domini regis nunc de †exceptacione [l. acceptacione] predicta ad warrantum vocare non potest *PQW* 696a; **1321** si..~o sua [sc. prebende] non sortiretur effectum *Reg. Heref.* 187; **1447** beneficium..quod tu..duxeris acceptandum..conferendum tibi post ~onem hujusmodi..reservamus *Mon. Hib. & Scot.* 379. **b 1274** presentes litteras de nostra recognitione, ~one et confessione [fidei]..signavimus (*Lit. Imp. Graec.*) *Flor. Hist.* III 37; **1366** contra consuetudinem, ~onem et approbacionem predictas *Reg. Brev.* 91b (cf. ib.: que quidem consuetudo in Parliamento nostro..accepta fuit et approbata); **s1378** post ~onem eleccionis [pape] a tota Christianitate *Eul. Hist. Cont.* III 342. **c** omnes cause.. discuciende sunt a judicibus et sine personarum ~one cum equalitate discernende (*Leg. Hen.*) *GAS* 547; **s1264** quod credat rex consiliariis suis sine personarum ~one in justicia exhibenda WALS. *YN app.* 532; **1426** ut ex pura et absoluta loquamur consciencia ac absque omni in ea parte ~one in persona *Reg. Whet.* II 366 (= *Conc.* III 476: acceptione).

2 acceptatio, acceptation, meaning.

de mense lunari et multiplici ~one ejus BACON VI 3.

acceptator, (?) author. **b** (w. *personarum*), respecter (*cf. acceptor* b).

~or, auctor *GlC* A 163. **b 1171** non acceptor munerum nec ~or esse dignatus est personarum P. BLOIS *Ep.* 27. 94B; tales sunt ~ores personarum OCKHAM *Dial.* 708.

accepte, cordially, w. affection.

illum..inter omnes curiae suae primates habuit ~issime G. CRISPIN *Herl.* 87.

acceptibilis, acceptable, admissible (*cf. acceptabilis*).

cuilibet singulari accepte vel ~i nulla singularis determinata accepta vel ~is repugnat DUNS *Sent.* II ii 9. 25.

acceptilatio [CL], notional payment.

igitur sua suffragio martyris receperunt; qui et marcas octo questionariis promissas ad trium ~onem moderatam perduxit W. CANT. *Mir. Thom.* IV 7; item [tollitur obligatio] per ~onem que dicitur imaginaria solutio BRACTON 101.

acceptio [CL], receipt, acceptance. **b** approval. **c** (w. *personarum etc.*) showing favour (cf. *Rom.* ii 11).

si datio non est sine ~one ANSELM (*Casus Diab.* 20) I 265; **1178** infra xx dies post ~onem litterarum nostrarum (*Lit. Papae*) ELMH. *Cant.* 428; munerum ~o multiplex est: sunt enim sex species GIR. *GE* II 30; **1450** donaciones, perquisiciones, ~ones..predictorum..toftorum *Mem. Ripon* 244. **b 1146** si est Dei voluntas et veniat tua nobilitas, in magnam ~onem erit hoc imperii mei (*Lit. Imp. Graec.*) DICETO *Chr.* 257. **c** 'secundum veritatem', id est, secundum justitiam sine ~one personarum LANFR. *Comment. Paul.* (*Rom.* ii 2) 111; tria sunt que..etiam prudentum..judicium subvertunt, amor munerum, ~o personarum, facilitas credendi J. SAL. *Pol.* 813C; capitulo..presidens..absque ~one persone justum exequatur examen *Cust. Westm.* 267; **12..** quatinus..unicuique sine †personaliter ~one..plenariam justiciam exhibeatis *Reg. S. Thom. Dublin* no. 380; **1254** habent..licenciam guerreandi Gastonem de B. ..et.. alios inimicos regis..sine ~one rerum vel personarum *RGasc* I 345 (cf. ib. 353); si terras suas..ambicionibus, ~onibus personarum..ac aliis viciis..neglexerint expurgare OCKHAM *Dial.* 505; **1426** (v. acceptatio 1c).

2 acceptio, acceptation, meaning.

in alia ~one accipitur dos secundum leges Romanas GLANV. VII 1; **a1228** secundum primam ~onem S. LANGTON *Quaest.* 208; adequatio animi et exterioris sui signi, secundum communem ~onem rem extra significatam significantis *Ps.*-GROS. 294; **1363** hujusmodi diversimode ~onis exemplum sumitur a B. Augustino: ..primo dicit eum [Eli] sacerdotis filium non esse, sc. naturalem..; set postea dicit eum fuisse ex filiis Aaron sacerdotis, i.e. ex posteris per successionem originis (KYN.) *Ziz.* 30.

acceptivus, receptive.

[Deus] movet ad se ipsum omnia amoris et dilectionis ~a ERIUG. *Per.* 520C; sensus est ~us specierum que sunt in materia preter materiam tantum BACON VII 13; patet quod Deus summe donativus sit proporcionabiliter maxime ~us; patet ex hoc quod, in quantum donat aliquid, in tantum illud accipit a se ipso WYCL. *Dom. Div.* 216.

1 acceptor [CL], accepter, receiver. **b** (w. *personarum*) respecter, favourer (*cf. Acts* x 34).

verecundus ~or, dator hilaris AILR. *Ed. Conf.* 745D; **c1236** et exactores et ~ores precii pro sepultura..grandem culpam incurrunt GROS. *Ep.* 72* p. 221; gratus ~or beneficii *Flor. Hist.* I 214; si Deo offerendorum venditoribus et ~oribus dictum est: 'vos fecistis domum Patris mei domum negociacionis' [*John* ii 16] PAUL. ANGL. *ASP* 1543. **b 1290** ex institutione Altissimi, qui non est ~or personarum (*Lit. regis*) *Chr. Rams.* 369; **1293** an decanus..sit ~or personarum *Reg. Cant.* II 1297; **s1340** justiciarios..tanquam..personarum et munerum ~ores diffamatos *Meaux* III 48; **1362** personarum nimis favorabiliter ~or *Conc.* III 55.

2 acceptor v. accipiter.

†acceptorium, (?) lectionary or alphabet (*cf. abecedarium*).

libellum quendam.., qui non est major ~io duarum septimanarum, legere cupio *Ep. Aldh.* I (6) p. 494.

acceptrix, receiver (f.).

c803 hujus precii [sc. salutis humanae] ~icem esse mortem ALCUIN *Ep.* 307, p. 466.

acceptus v. accipere. accerra v. acra 2 a. accerrus v. accessus 1 e. accersere, ~ire, v. arcessere. accerus v. acorus. accessarius v. accessorius.

†accessere, to enter.

domum..monachus..recens..in abbatem assumptus.. incontinenti jam ~ens..vitio..contaminavit GIR. *Spec.* III 2.

accessibilis, accessible, approachable; **b** (of a person) affable.

apparuit ignis tractabilis, id est palpabilis et †~is LANFR. *Comment. Paul.* 403 (cf. *Heb.* xii 18: ad tractabilem montem et accensibilem ignem); nostra etas..insulam [*Ely*] pedibus ~em fecit W. MALM. *GP* IV 184; Burch..est..per terram ~is preter ad orientalem plagam, per quam nisi navigio non venitur H. ALBUS 5; erat hoc [dolium in penitiori casule sue angulo] omnibus ignotum.., quia nulli domesticorum ejus..pervium sive ~e GIR. *GE* II 10 p. 215. **b** parvulis..lenem se et ~em prebebat AD. EYNS. *Hug.* III 14.

accessio [CL], (of time) coming. **b** (of fever) attack, bout.

deinde ~one temporum, cum herbas inde surgere videas, cui id..imponas? ADEL. *QN* 1. **b** ~o significat frigorem *GlC* A 161; puerulus..febrium incommodo..vexatus, qui, cum..sollicitus horam ~onis exspectaret.. BEDE *HE* III 12; **1201** appropinquante hora ~onis [tertiane febris], cum jam inciperet caro horrescere quasi ex frigore *Canon. G. Sempr.* 147; flobotomia in tertiana potest fieri, sed non ante tres vel quatuor ~ones GAD. 5. 1.

2 accessio, accession (leg.), addition, accrual. **b** accessory, adjunct, fitment.

acquiritur etiam jure gentium rerum dominium per ~onem discretam vel secretam, concretam seu continuam BRACTON 9; hec de ~one que fit tantum divina natura operante; est et alia que fit tantum humana natura operante, que fit per adjunctionem unius speciei ad aliam *Ib.* 9b. **b a1162** sic..per se..consistit [amicitia] ut in ipsa operum exhibitio non nisi vicem ~onis obtineat et sequele (*Lit. Ep. Lexov.*) *Becket Mat.* V 2; ecclesiam Cantuariensem cum omnibus terris et ~onibus ejus W. FITZST. *Thom.* 67; **1508** si ~ones hujus seculi veritatem Dei postponant, abdicande sunt *Reg. Merton.* 374; **1602** dicte navis..ac apparatuum, ~onum et tormentorum suorum *SelPlAdm* II 204.

accessor, accessory, accomplice.

1496 quod interfuit cum..fratre suo et ~or ei erat dum illud facinus perpetratum fuerat *Sanct. Durh.* 66 (cf. 76).

accessorie, as an accessory or adjunct.

1252 ipsos et omnes..simili modo principaliter vel ~ie obligatos ab hujusmodi obligationibus..quietos esse volumus *Cl* 219; **c1265** ne..indebitas exacciones exigatis, statuatis principaliter vel ~ie statuta exsequendo (*Forma appellationis*) *Ann. Durh.* 187; repugnat..liberalitati.. Regis Regum donare famulo suo tam egeno temporalia que Scriptura vocat stercora et pulverem nisi ~ie ad donum complecius WYCL. *Civ. Dom.* I 7.

accessorius, ~arius, accessory, subordinate.

eodem modo fiat execucio judicii in aliis brevibus ~oriis *Reg. Brev.* 152b.

2 (sb. n.) accessory, subordinate matter. **b** adjunct, appendage.

si bona omnia sapientie ~oria..sunt J. SAL. *Pol.* 653B; dixit.."[hospita nostra] parum butyri..sali imponit", cum ..~orium rei principali soleat apponi, subtili verborum trajectione..~orium principale constituens GIR. *DK* I 14; plus in accidenti quam substantiali, plus in ~ario quam principali confisus *Id. Invect.* I 4; concesso principali conceditur ~orium OCKHAM *Dial.* 711; **1389** sicut [mandatum] principale morte [concedentis] non perit, sic nec mandatum quod est ejus ~orium *Reg. Heref.* 77; omnes tituli ecclesiastici sunt ejusdem speciei, sed solum diversificantur penes ~ia PAUL. ANGL. *ASP* 1552. **b** naturali jure communia sunt..aer et mare et litora maris quasi mari ~oria

BRACTON 7b; **1331** visum franciplegii, ad quem hujusmodi mensure et pondera sunt ~oria *PQW* 70b.

3 (sb. n. or f.) complicity (as accessory to crime).

c1350 Ricardo principali prius deliberato, abbas..de ~orio..allocutus..non sine..expensarum effusione deliberatus est *Meaux* III 84; **1352** non est †juris [? l. juri] consonum quod hujusmodi de ~orio indictati occasionentur ex quo principales in hac parte convinci non possunt *SelCKB* VI 83; **1511** cum..pardonaverimus omnimodas felonias, ~arias et recepciones felonice transgressionis *Reg. Heref.* 101; **1573** pardonamus..omnes et omnimodas felonias, roborias et ~aria eorundem *Pat* 1106 m. 3.

4 (sb. m.) accessory (to crime), accomplice.

1507 Johannes..ut principalis..et..Robertus, ut ~arius, ..Willelmum percussit *Sanct. Durh.* 202.

accessus [CL], approach. **b** onset, beginning. **c** (of sea) flood tide. **d** hostile approach, attack. **e** attack (fig.).

rusticitate sua doctorum arcebant ~us BEDE (*V. Cuthb.*) *HE* IV 27; ad lucem inaccessibilem conceditur ~us per theofaniam ERIUG. *Per.* 557B; ut..sit per partes illis accessus ad artes SERLO WILT. *app.* 1A 4. 3; ubi..fuero.. absoluta..sacrati altaris promerebor ~um T. MON. *Will.* VII 18; **1311** est ibi frequens ~us et transitus ferarum ex utraque chacea usque in forestam *Cl* 129 m. 28; **1447** in primo ~u prioris ad dominum episcopum post eleccionem.. ejusdem prioris *Ac. Durh.* 631. **b** illa, quamvis ingratum quandoque sortiantur ~um, felici tamen semper exitu gloriantur (*Lit. Ep. Lexov.*) *Becket Mat.* V 3. **c** imitatur lunae cursum mare non solum communi ~u et recessu BEDE *TR* 29; avis marina que..~um maris sive refluxum predicere consuevit NECKAM *NR* II 36. **d** nec angues nec humanos ~us reformidant GIR. *TH* I 22; cum ~um prope mutuum utrimque fecissent armati ELMH. *Hen. V* 53. **e** cruciant me †accerrus [l. accessus] amoris ROLLE *IA* 245.

2 accession, addition, gain.

704 de vestrae..eximiae religionis ~ibus gaudemus (*Lit. Papae*) EDDI *Wilf.* 54 (cf. ib.: ut gaudium nostrum meliorum ~us amplificet); eorum..mores ingenuos ultro tam prudentie quam benignitatis nobilitavit ~us *Chr. Rams.* 12.

accet- v. acet-, 1 accire. acchatum v. accatum. acchiricus v. arthriticus. accidens v. accidere.

accidentalis, a casual, incidental. **b** accidental (log.), not forming part of substance or essence. **c** (of planetary house) ruling (astr.).

a **a1162** si vel de grege ~ium amicorum fuero, bene mecum fecisse dignationem vestram estimabo (*Lit. Abb. Cell.*) *Becket Mat.* V 4; confido..quod ad ~em occasionem.. anime mee desiderium..de personali visione..sanctitatis vestre opportunitate frequentiori replebitur AD. MARSH *Ep.* 247 c. 2; logica et grammatica sunt ~es scientie et non principales BACON *Tert.* 105 (cf. ib. 60 p. 241: declinatio ~is est accentui); **s1376** rex..decidit in languorem, non.. egritudinis senibus naturalis sed qui plerumque juvenibus ob inordinatum affectum Veneris dicitur ~is *Chr. Angl.* 104; **1390** honor transitorius aut status ~is *FormOx* 193. **b** sicut sumus idem in substantiali essentia, possumus esse in ~i LANFR. *Comment. Paul.* (*Gal.* iv 12) 277; harum duarum significationum illa, que per se est, ipsis vocibus significativis est substantialis, alia vero, que per aliud est, ~is ANSELM (*Gram.* 15) I 161; aqua naturaliter ut ex se frigida est, sed ~em ab aere contrahit humiditatem D. MORLEY *Inf. & Sup.* 20; nisi illo permittente qui facit omnes naturas substantiales et ~es, universales et individuas BRADW. *CD* 553A; quibus dantur octo regule, quarum quattuor dicuntur essenciales et quattuor ~es HOTHBY 333. **c** 5 planete ~es habent potestates in 5 signis residuis, ..unde hec sunt domicilia eorum ~ia BACON IX 192; **1387** deinde..describuntur domus ~es in figura celi et quis ibi gaudet planeta (ELVEDEN *Cal.*) *SB* 5.

2 (sb. n.) incident, accidental circumstance.

quod de facto dicitur, id de appellatis de forcia et de aliis ~ibus intelligatur *Fleta* 41; **1350** ut..queratur parti illi [orationis] quot accidunt et tunc per ordinem de ~ibus interrogetur *StatOx* 22; **c1370** ostendit auctor ~ia inter regnum Anglie et Scocie (J. BRIDL. *rub.*) *Pol. Poems* I 141.

accidentalitas, quality of an accident.

cum ista ~as non respiciat res secundum esse quidditativum DUNS *Metaph.* VI ii 76D; in trinitatibus prioribus tollitur omnis ~as unius ad aliud WYCL. *Log.* III 122.

accidentaliter, a by chance, casually. **b** accidentally (log.).

a **s1205** combusta est magna pars Rokesburch ~er *Chr. Melrose* 106; abbatum successiones, prout inter res gestas ~er incidere reperi, interponam ELMH. *Cant.* 1. **b** haec essentia, quam patuit omnimode sibi esse eandem substantialiter, nonne aliquando est a se diversa vel ~er? ANSELM (*Mon.* 25) I 43; quid unaqueque res sit, aut substantialiter definiendo aut ~er describendo demonstrat ADEL. *ED* 14; dum rerum quas natura substantialiter vel ~er assimilavit conformitatem percipit intellectus J. SAL. *Pol.* 439A; caliditas est ~er corruptiva BART. ANGL. IV 1; hoc dico essentialiter, quia ~er contingit in multis locis montuosis dominari frigiditatem GROS. 66; alio modo considerantur [res temporales], prout inter se sunt cause et effectus per accidens, prout una aliam perficit ~er PAUL. ANGL. *ASP* 1547.

accidentare, to qualify with accidents (log.).

consideret quod esse subjectum, esse quantum vel quomodolibet ~atum, presupponit ipsum esse quid proporcionaliter ad suscepcionem hujus accidentis (WYCL. *Incarn.*) *Speculum* VIII 201; panis sacramentalis rotundatur et figuratur vel taliter ~atur (*Id. Confess.*) *Ib.* 507; **1412** si albedo posset per se existere, tunc ipsius unio ad subjectum foret accidens, quo subjectum foret ~atum immediate formaliter, et non illa albedo (*Hereses J. Wycl.* 161) *Conc.* III 346.

accidentia, a circumstance, incident. **b** feudal incident (Scot.). **c** chance, 'accidency' (log.).

a hamsocna..fit pluribus modis, extrinsecis vel intrinsecis ~iis (*Leg. Hen.*) *GAS* 597; neque minoris glorie sunt que nativitas vel nature bonitas impressit quam que dignitatis ~ia concessit G. COLD. *Hist. Durh.* 7; hic declarat ..in quibus..mense et anno ista sibi ~ia, cujus tenor subsequitur, contingebat GOWER *VC* I i *rub.* **b** **c1200** respondebimus de omnibus serviciis et ~iis *Reg. Aberbr.* I 35; **1223** respondebimus de omnibus serviciis et ~iis que spectant vel spectare poterunt versus predictam terram *Reg. Newbattle* no. 130. **c** amodo ergo non contendam circa hujusmodi ~iam metaphysicam, nisi audivero novas argucias actenus inauditas WYCL. *Form.* 1 p. 170.

2 book of accidence or grammar.

1519 pro duobus primariis et pro duabus ~iis *DCCant* C 11 f. 131a.

accidere [CL], to happen. **b** (impers.).

exierat videre quid nobis ~eret BEDE *HE* V 1; [Deus] cui nullum ~it et ~it nulli ERIUG. *Per.* 468B; cum..in regione superlunari nihil renovetur preter situm et ea que ex situ renovato ~unt GROS. 36; **1248** intimavit toti villate que ~erant *SelPlForest* 83; **1228** de wrec dicit quod nunquam vidit hoc ~ere in terra prioris *Feod. Durh.* 226; **1321** in casibus predictis cum †ascidissent..in forma predicta disracionare consueverunt *PQW* 451; **1373** cum turnus suus ~erit *Hal. Durh.* 118. **b** ~it illi..quia..necesse habet.. BEDE *HE* V 14; ~it eam..fame..infestari J. FORD *Wulf.* 58; hinc ~it ut..senescant GIR. *TH intr.* p. 5; hinc ~it quod ecclesia..ipsum..elegit H. READING (II) 30; **1265** ~it quod..Johannes..inventus fuit submersus *SelCCoron* 41; **c1321** vobis..non ~it ut optastis J. MASON *Ep.* 64; **1573** et ita ~it quod predictus T. Griffen..prefatum H. Evanes cum gladio suo..percussit *Pat* 1104 m. 26.

2 to fall to (the share of), accrue. **b** (w. acc.). **c** to fall due.

1265 l m. de antiquis debitis Judeorum que nobis ~erunt *Cl* 169; **1315** habebit..amerciamenta de talibus ~encia *Reg. Aberbr.* I 294; **1363** taberna..que eidem..hereditarie ~it post mortem Idonie *Reg. Rough* 160; **1417** pro salvacione j pipe vini domino priori ~entis per wreccum maris *Ac. Durh.* 614. **b** 1267 maneria..que..Rogerum quocumque jure poterunt ~ere *Cl* 368. **c** **1279** debet scutagium quando ~it predicto Radulfo secundum scuti posicionem *Hund.* II 760.

3 (pr. ppl.) **a** casual, incidental. **b** accidental (log.), non-essential.

a **s1170** cum ipsi prius ardenti animo et quasi cum quodam ~enti tripudio ad sancti viri accelerarent occisionem H. BOS. *Thom.* VI 9. **b** si actus Deo ~entes quod sunt permaneant PULL. *Sent.* 681C.

4 (pr. ppl. as sb. n.) **a** accident, incident. **b** accident (log.), non-essential quality. **c** casual profit. **d** accident (gram.), inflexion.

a **s1077** [testa capitis] tantum rivum sudoris emisit quantum aliquis virorum quolibet ~enti de se emittere posset (*Mir. Wistani*) *Chr. Evesham app.* 337; per ~ens est quod collegium cardinalium habet jus eligendi summum pontificem OCKHAM *Dial.* 606; cedit ad gloriam Latinorum per ~ens hebetudo nativa, quoniam sicut fuerunt in studiis minus docti [quam Greci], sic in erroribus minus mali R. BURY *Phil.* 10. 164; sinthoma est pravum ~ens *SB* 39. **b** quot sunt ~entia pedum? ALDH. *PR* 112; prima..rerum omnium divisio est in essentias et ~entia ERIUG. *Per.* 508A; cum omne subjectum sine ~enti aut esse aut intelligi possit ANSELM (*Incarn.* 7) II 22; que inseparabilis ~entis est diffinitio separabili non convenit BALSH. *AD* 101; invariabilis Deus qualitatibus et ~entibus non est subjectus PULL. *Sent.* I 4; quatinus..non..transeuncium perturbent ~encia residenciam anime substancialem in Domino MAP *NC* IV 13; virtus anime aut est ~ens ejus aut substantia tota aut pars substantie GROS. *Ep.* 1 p. 10; quod species lucis in medio sit ~ens verum, et omnis species ~entis sit ~ens, et species substantie sit substantia BACON *Tert.* 115; cum videremus multos..in multis et maxime in ~entibus ipsius musice..errare HAUBOYS 403. **c** **1081** dedi..quandam terram Gersdunam nomine..cum omnibus sibi ~entibus *Reg. Malm.* I 327 (= *Regesta* 135); **1393** de acc' [? l. accidentibus] ut patet in extractis *Banstead* II 91. **d** ut secundum formam Donati sciat ~entia partium orationis BACON *CS Phil.* 434; **s1284** errores..contra regulas artis grammatice: ..verbum manens verbum potest privari omni ~enti *Ann. Osney* 298; **c1363** ut dicat non esse verbum aut ~ens verbi in Scriptura sacra positum absque notabili causa (KYN.) *Ziz.* 65.

accidi- v. acedi-. accidinetum v. acidinetum.

accinctus, circuit, compass. **b** curtain wall.

1262 extra libertatem Quinque Portuum et infra ascingtum comitatus *JustIt* 912 A r. 11d. **b** pontes castri et pons ~us turris debiles sunt *CalIMisc* I 252 (cf. ib.: plaunchiatura..turellorum in ~u meniarum).

2 girding (fig.), preparation, preliminary effort.

[Godwinus] assiduo laboris ~u incomparabilis *V. Ed. Conf.* 38v; in ipso religionis ~u, dum edificaret sibi cellulam antequam habitaret in ea J. FORD *Wulf.* 58; militem..jam in ~u [*gl.* vel procinctu] itineris expeditum R. COLD. *Cuthb.* 75.

accinere, to sing (in addition).

dum finem protrahimus et ei velut caudam ~imus BELETH *RDO* 38. 46; **c1267** accentus dicitur quasi 'accantus' de 'accino' BACON *Maj.* I 100; *to synge*, ~ere, calamizare, canere spiritu *CathA*.

accingere, to surround, girdle. **b** to bind in sheaves.

terram..que undique aquis accincta est *Chr. Rams.* 53; verres fulmineis accincti dentibus W. FITZST. *Thom. prol.* 17; brachii istius ora crebris hinc inde terris..~itur GIR. *TH* I 2; **s1333** Anglici exercitum suum fossato undique ~ebant *Meaux* II 368 (cf. ib. III 177: fossata..que.. clausum..~ebant). **b** **c1300** tassent bladum in grangia et ~ent in campis *DCCant J* 45.

2 to gird (w. belt or sword). **b** (in conferment of knighthood). **c** (fig.) to gird oneself, make ready. **d** (p. ppl.) ready for action.

accinctus gladio accepit lanceam in manu BEDE *HE* II 13; nec sit latus ense / accinctum D. BEC. 1450; tali accinctus funiculo, gravem pene vindictam subiit pro delicto R. COLD. *Cuthb.* 94. **b** **s1147** rex..filium suum..militie cingulo coram optimatibus honoranter accinxit *G. Steph.* II 109; gladio quo manu regis in militem fuerat accinctus DEVIZES 27v.; **s1191** non erant de militari ordine nec accincti gladio *Croyl. Cont. B* 458; **s1385** bene trecentos gladio militari [rex] accinxit *V. Ric. II* 62. **c** nunc accingamur sed nobiliore coturno *V. Ed. Conf.* 38v.; arripe clypeum obedientie, ~ere gladio patientie H. LOS. *Ep.* 13; ad exequendum..negotium ~itur pontifex T. MON. *Will.* VI 1; cum furor accinxit urbis utrumque latus GOWER *VC* I 920. **d** cum accinctissima militum cohorte *G. Steph.* I 65.

3 (p. ppl. as sb. f.) curtain wall (*cf. accinctus* 1b).

1252 ad faciendam quandam acinctam [*Cal.* †acinetam] circa novam turrim de Windesor' *Liberate* 28 m. 5.

accintus v. acanthus. accinus v. assassinus. accipenser v. acipenser.

accipere [CL], to take, get, seize, exact. **b** (absol.) to take payment. **c** (math.) to extract (a root). **d** (w. immaterial obj.). **e** (w. immaterial subj.).

accepit gladium in manu BEDE *HE* II 13; per nasum galeae, concitus, accipiens / vultum telluri..volvit G. AMIENS *Hast.* 492; inde prepositus regis ~iebat communem emendationem *DB* I 1; rex Danicus..loco contiguo Angliae ..~iens [*gaining*] litus HERM. ARCH. 3 p. 33; **1100** neque ego aliquid de suo pro hac licentia ~iam (*Ch. Hen. I*) *GAS* 521; si secundo venire noluerint, ~iatur unus bos et summoneantur tertio (*Artic. Will*) *Ib.* 488; non incongrue dicitur ~ere et qui concessa suscipit et qui illicita praesumit ANSELM (*Casus Diab.* 20) I 265; **1170** inquiratur si forestarii vel bailivi eorum aliquem acceperint vel attachaverint per vadium et per plegium (*Inq. Vic.* 7) GERV. CANT. I 218; accipiter dicitur ab ~iendo, id est rapiendo GIR. *GE* II 33; milvus cum rostro accepit unam [perdicem], cum alis duas O. CHERITON *Fab.* 38; **1269** vicecomes accepit securitatem de prosequendo *CBaron* 86; semen acceptum coleram ..deponit *Alph.* 185; **s1433** jussit eum..tria brevia regia.. a Cancellaria accipere AMUND. I 311. **b** aliorum equos vendunt..et frequenter ex utraque parte ~iunt *Latin Stories* 77. **c** hujus summe radicem..~ies ROB. ANGL. *Alg.* 72. **d** postquam materia informis formatas species.. accepit ALDH. *Met.* 2 p. 68; in monasterio quod juxta amnem Dacore constructum ab eo cognomen accepit BEDE *HE* IV 32; [universa natura] in quantum creatrix est nullam formam ~it in se ipsa ERIUG. *Per.* 525C; **c1180** controversia ..amicabili compositione finem accepit *Reg. Malm.* II 14. **e** accepit eum iliaca passio ECCLESTON *Adv. Min.* 95.

2 to accept (as offered): **a** a person; **b** a thing; **c** a promise, imposition, obligation, or sim. **d** to take upon oneself, undertake.

a puerulos quos..instruendos acceperat ALDH. *VirgP.* 33; accepta in conjugem..filia Aedilbercti BEDE *HE* II 19; ipsum sibi accepit in filium *Ib.* III 7; adjutores itineris.. accepit *Ib.* IV 18; has terras..habuit Ausfridus de Walterio ..cum ejus neptem accepit *DB* I 170; Ailricus accepit uxorem *Ib.* II 360b; si..diaconi..calumnietur..acceptis duobus diaconis secum purget se (*Inst. Cnut*) *GAS* 287. **b** salutarem calicem per pocula mortis / accipiunt ALDH. *VirgV.* 886; locum monasterii quem a..rege..acceperat BEDE *HE* III 19; accepto velamine sanctimonialis habitus *Ib.* IV 19; **s1171** injunctum est ei..quod..usque in triennium crucem ~eret [i.e. *become a crusader*] *Meaux* I 200; **1272** Abrahe licebit mutuo ~ere dictos denarios..ad usuram *SelPlJews* 65. **c** nolunt ~ere legem nisi regis E. *DB* I 44b; **s1086** ~iens hominium omnium terrariorum Anglie.., juramentum etiam fidelitatis recipere non distulit H. HUNT. *HA* VI 37; **s1066** homagiis a magnatibus cum fidelitatis juramento obsidibusque acceptis M. PAR. *Maj.* II 1; **12..** vidit sepe homines episcopi eciam, venientes ad curiam prioris, et deponere querelam, et ibi ~ere rectum de hominibus prioris *Feod. Durh.* 281; **a1350** debet rector.. a singulis bachellariis ~ere fidem *Stat. Cantab.* 313. **d** **1227** Gernemue [*Yarmouth*] habet diem ad reddendum firmam suam; ..prepositi acceperunt in manum *KRMem* 9 r. 18; **1500** custos accepit accionem contra eum *Reg. Merton* 243.

3 to receive (information), learn.

accape, audi *GlC* A 119 (cf. ib. 112); ab accolis acceperunt anguem istum galeam vocatum GIR. *TH* I 36; accepi a pluribus quod sermonum prolixitas dominos hic sepe accediat RIC. ARMAGH *Serm.* 80 p. 31.

4 to accept, approve. **b** (w. inf. or *quod*) to agree, maintain. **c** (w. *personam*) to favour (*cf. Deut.* x 17 *etc.*).

post accepta fidei rudimenta ALDH. *VirgP.* 25; fidem veritatis acceperant BEDE *HE* III 4. **b** qui verba vite accepit dare nobis AD. SCOT. *Serm.* 101A; **1294** acceptum est per inquisicionem quod W. non obiit seysitus de tenemento..*SelPlMan* 171; ad aliam..allegationem, ~ientem quod diffinicio generalis concilii tanquam diffinicio universalis ecclesie debet haberi, respondetur quod.. OCKHAM *Dial.* 830. **c 1268** dum ecclesie prospicere debet, personam hominis ~it *Conc. Syn.* 778.

5 a to take, react to (in a specified manner). **b** to take, construe (in a specified sense).

a quod nequaquam refellere valentes, episcopi humiliter deprecati sunt ne gravius ~eret H. CANTOR 3; **1334** vos rogamus quod non ~iatis pro malo quod tam distulimus.. solvere.. *Lit. Cant.* II 66; unum de peccatis quibus nomen Dei in vanum ~itur WYCL. *Mand. Div.* 17. **b 597** quod tamen aliter populus spiritalis intellegens sub eodem intellectu ~iet quo praefati sumus (*Lit. Papae*) BEDE *HE* I 27 p. 59; sillaba..adiaphoros est, id est indifferenter ~itur ALDH. *Met.* 10 p. 82; 'peccare in Deum' est peccare solo Deo sciente, et ita hic ~itur S. LANGTON *Quaest.* 202; hoc nomen 'usus' variis modis in scripturis ~itur OCKHAM *Pol.* I 301; 'gramen' est nomen cujuslibet herbe; tamen specialiter ~itur in medicina pro quadam herba.. *SB* 23.

6 (p. ppl. *acceptus*) **a** accepted, approved. **b** acceptable, welcome.

a 1466 [predicator] has perficiet determinaciones per media ~a, ex scriptis sacris [etc.] *MunAcOx* 716. **b** ad emulationem ejusdem Deo ~ae intentionis *V. Ed. Conf.* 49v.; ~issimus Deo martyr T. MON. *Will.* VI 1; ut..egroto ~ior sit medicina P. BLOIS *Ep.* 43 128A; ab ipso Rollone militie cingulum accipit, ut proinde sibi fiat ~ior MAP *NC* III 5.

accipitarius v. accipitrarius.

accipiter [CL], hawk, esp. sparrowhawk (*cf. 2 anceps*).

aves et animalia cetera, si in retibus strangulantur, non sunt comedenda hominibus, nec si ~er oppresserit THEOD. *Pen.* II xi 2; ~res pipant vel †plipiant ALDH. *PR* 131; **747** servis Dei..ut acceptores et uualcones non habeant prohibuimus BONIF. *Ep.* 78 p. 163; **c750** perpauci hujus generis ~res in nostris regionibus..repperiuntur (*Lit. Regis Cantiae*) *Ep. Bonif.* 105; decipio aves aliquando retibus, ..aliquando ~re [AS: *mid hafoce*] ÆLF. *Coll.* 95; ~er vel raptor, *spearhafoc Id. Gl.*; si essent ei canes vel ~res, presentabuntur regi *DB* I 56b (cf. ib. 172: ~rem Norrescum [*gerfalcon*]); **1130** reddit compotum de c ~ribus Norriscis.., ita quod iiij ex his ~ribus debent esse albi *Pipe* 111; **c1150** dedit..unam †aucipitrem [? l. ancipitrem] de gersuma *E. Ch. S. Paul.* 197; fit interdum ut aves regie regi..promittantur, ~res scilicet vel falcones; quod si promittens determinans dixerit '~rem instantis anni vel mutatum', vel locum etiam exprimat dicens 'Hibernensem [*peregrine*], Hispanensem [*saker*], Norrensem [*gerfalcon*] dabo', sic satisfaciat *Dial. Scac.* II 25; **1188** debet j ~rem sor Norreis *Pipe* 54; **1198** per custodiam j ancipitris regis *Fees* 7 (cf. 33); faciat custodiri..aprum et anticiptrum *CalCh* III 117; accipitris preda ditatur mensa potentum NECKAM *DS* II 283; assit ei..falco ascensorius, tardearius et gruarius et ancipiter [*gl. oustur*] *Id. Ut.* 100; GIR. *GE* II 33 (v. accipere 1a); **1242** omnes aves regis, tam gyrofalcones quam ancipitres et falcones ardearios, tempore opportuno volare faciat *Cl* 514; anticipiter magistri T... ejecit omnia alimenta *Mir. Montf.* 71; **1370** ad custodiendum ayerium anticepetrum in foresta de Inglewod' *IPM* 213/5 (cf. ib.: ayerium antiscipetrum); *a goshauke*, ancipiter vel ~er, falco, herodius, gruarius *CathA*; **1573** volucres pro cibo ancipitrum vocato *haukes meate Pat* 1105 m. 34.

2 (w. *pes*), (?) columbine (*Aquilegia*).

pes ancipitris i. columbina *SB* 33.

accipitrarius, keeper of hawks, falconer.

rex..artifices suos omnes et falconarios et ~ios..docere.. non desinebat ASSER *Alf.* 76 (cf. M. PAR. *Maj.* I 406); Willelmus ~ius *DB* I 14; Edrici accipitarii *Ib.* II 272; ipse erat quietus de aula, quia erat ancipitrarius comitis *Ib.* 125b; **1155** in donis..arcipitr' et falc' *Pipe* 40 (cf. ib. 54: in liberationibus ~iorum et falconariorum regis); omnis liberatio quorumcumque sive ~iorum sive falconariorum.. ad ejus [sc. constabularii] officium spectat *Dial. Scac.* I 5F; **1199** †aucipitrariis [? l. ancipitrariis] regis et hominibus eorum v m. ad expensas suas dum moram fecerunt in Devon' ad capiendos falcones regis *Pipe* 188.

1 accire [CL], to summon, invite.

accetum, *gefeotodne GlC* A 136; ~ito ad se..urbis Lundoniae..episcopo BEDE *HE* IV 11; abbates vicinos [ad synodum] ~iverat GIR. *TH* II 19; quosdam ~ivit de Majori Monasterio *Chr. Battle* 23.

2 accire v. 2 assisa.

†accitare, (?) to summon.

s1382 ut fideles regni ubicunque viderent rusticos vel communes ~are [v.l. excitare] suspecta consiliabula, ..eos capere eis foret licitum WALS. *HA* II 48.

2 (? *f.l.* for *actitare*) to do, act.

quidam post eum vadunt, quidam legationes mittunt..; et hoc ~abatur non clam..sed..publice *V. Ed. Conf.* 44; 'justus justificetur adhuc et sanctus sanctificetur adhuc' [*Apoc.* xxii 11]; quod in se per virum justum et sanctum ~ari unusquisque sentiebat AD. EYNS. *Hug.* IV 10 p. 51; **s1385** in mari tamen liceret eis nobisque predas agere, hostiliter ~are WALS. *HA* II 127.

accitor, summoner.

~or, advocator *GlC* A 126.

accitulium v. acidula.

†accitus, (*s. dub.*).

narrant Plinius et Albertus [*Animal.* xxiii] quod ~us avis paradisi tantam habet graciam pulcritudinis corporalis quod nulla avis ei possit..comparari BRINTON *Serm.* 12 p. 50.

acclamare [CL], to shout, cry aloud: **a** in welcome or approval; **b** in protest; **c** in appeal.

a ~ant illi omnes una voce prospere in adventu suo *V. Ed. Conf.* 44v.; populi..annuerunt cum principibus..et ~averunt, et non fuit qui reclamaret MAP *NC* V 6 p. 234. **b c1440** insultum fecit in ipsum innocentem, ..inermem et †acclamentem: "noli me percutere!" *FormOx* 466; **s1454** Henricus..instanter..magis pre aliis ~averat; frustra tamen *Reg. Whet.* I 138. **c 1452** dum habitatores Juda.. Holofernes invasisset, ~andum unanimiter ad Dominum decreverunt *Conc.* III 560.

2 (trans.) **a** to utter (a cry). **b** to hail (w. joy). **c** to denounce. **d** to proclaim. **e** to claim. **f** (w. *quietus*) to quitclaim.

a s1097 ~ate signo militari 'Deus vult!' W. MALM. *GR* IV 357. **b s1098** Christiani signum crucis ~antes H. HUNT. *HA* VII 11. **c** papa [Gregorius VI] ab omni populo homicida ~atur *Eul. Hist.* I 261. **d** erant quasi nundine cum rege, quocumque castra moveret, pro certitudine viarum suarum et aclamate perhendinacionis MAP *NC* V 5 p. 219; s **1202** rex fecit generaliter ~ari ut legalis assisa panis.. observaretur M. PAR. *Maj.* II 480; **s1225** libertates generales..sunt deceptorie ~ate *Ib.* III 92; **s1398** Henricum.. bannivit ac per universum regnum id ~ari fecit *Dieul.* 144. 2. **e** cum ipsa Elfleda esset comitissa..~avit ipsa jure hereditario has..terras S. DURH. *HR* III 8; **s1417** in novi abbatis institucione, archidiaconus Linc' alium palafridum, vel v m. pro ejus precio, solet ~are *Croyl. Cont.* B 513; **1479** per decidenciam..terrarum et tenementorum ~atorum per personas ecclesiasticas *ExchScot* 634; **1569** ~antes..sasinam (*Ch. Perth*) *Scot. Grey Friars* II 208. **f c1470** ut..relaxaret..annuum redditum ac quietum..in perpetuum ~aret *Reg. Whet.* I 428.

acclamatio, shouting. **b** acclamation, shout of approval. **c** (w. *quieta*) quit-claim.

742 adfirmant se vidisse..in Romana urbe.., quando Kalende Januarii intrant, ..adclamationes ritu gentilium et cantationes sacrilegas celebrare BONIF. *Ep.* 50 p. 84. **b** totius tam cleri quam populi unanimi voto et ~one GIR. *EH* II 26. **c** quietam ~onem *Reg. Whet.* I 428.

acclamatrix, informer (f.).

si quis in nemore multa ligna ceciderit.., solvat tria ligna ..nec amplius.., quia securis ~ix [AS: *melda*] potius est non fur (*Quad.*) *GAS* 109.

acclameum, claim.

1509 feci ~eum in nomine collegii *Reg. Merton.* 394.

acclaudere [cf. accludere], to close.

intrat et acclaudens ostia dixit ita NIG. *SS* 3484.

2 to enclose. **b** (p. ppl. as sb.) enclosure (C.I.).

c1140 pratum quod prestitum fuit Turgodo de dominio domini, quod adclausit (*Ch. Beadlow*) *MonA* III 276. **b 1274** quorum escaeta cum aclaus' valet iij quarteria frumenti (*Chanc. Misc.* 10/5/2) *S. Jers.* II 34.

acclaudicatus [cf. inclavare], 'accloyed', lamed (of a horse).

acloyd, aclaudicatus, †inclinatus *PP*.

acclibatus v. acclivatus.

acclinare [CL], to incline towards (trans.).

postulavit se..in modum orantium ad illud ~ari BEDE *HE* IV 9.

acclinis [CL], leaning towards. **b** favourably inclined. **c** subservient.

adclinis, *to-hald*, vel incumbens *GlC* A 203; [Naaman] Jordanis alveo ~is et cernuus incurvans ALDH. *Met.* 2. p. 70; cometae..portabant facem ignis contra Aquilonem, quasi ad accendendum adclinem BEDE *HE* V 23; remissis / acclines rogitant ancilibus ut benedicat FRITH. 797; mulierem ..inurvatam ac inclinatam humique ~em curavit *NLA* (*Wulfstan*) II 528; **s1389** feretrum quod equaliter utriusque humeris †~is [? l. ~e] erat WALS. *HA* II 186 (= *V. Ric. II* 111: †acclivis). **b** Coeddam / moribus acclinem, doctrinae robore fortem FRITH. 401; [Edredus] sanctorum pedibus ~is Deo et Dunstano vitam suam devoverat W. MALM. *GR* II 146; ubi..populus otio et securitati ~ior [v.l. acclivior] *G. Steph.* I 29; [Offa] virorum religiosorum precibus semper ~is *Croyl.* 6. **c** [Willelmus I] Britanniam sibi ~em fecerat H. HUNT. *HA* VI 39.

acclivatus, sloping, slanting.

adclibatum, oblicum *GlC* A 246.

acclivis [CL = *sloping upwards*], struggling uphill (fig.), contentious; *v. et acclinis.*

tu vero vacillas magis, dum quod discipuli forma addiscere deberes, ~is ita cum impudenter tum inefficaciter arguis ADEL *QN* 28.

accludere [cf. acclaudere; occludere], to shut to. **b** (fig.).

precipimus..ne ostium ~atis W. CANT. *V. Thom.* II 40; operculi..non perfectius et solidius acclusi..apertio R. COLD. *Cuthb.* 26; cui ~ebatur [porta] appulsa stipiti *NLA* (*Edmund*) II 628; intravimus januas ~entes *Latin Stories* 102. **b** clausis labiis ostiolum cordis acclusit W. CANT. *Mir. Thom.* V 32.

accoillare [OF *acoillir*], to overtake, overcome.

1218 Agnes..inventa fuit in bosco..; nullus malecreditur, quia ~ata fuit frigore *Eyre Yorks* 184.

accola [CL], inhabitant.

697 terminos..hujus terrulae ideo non ponimus quoniam ab ~is undique certi sunt *CS* 98; loci ~ae..timere..coeperunt BEDE *HE* IV 2; **780** materies auri.. / accula quem (*sic*) fessus profert de viscere terrae ALCUIN *Carm.* 4. 67; ab ~is acceperunt anguem istum galeam vocatum GIR. *TH* I. 36; **1560** pepigerunt cum..ejusdem littoris ~is *ActPCIr.* 103.

accolatus, residence.

squaloris carcerei tota vita ~um accepit W. MALM. *GR* V 398.

accolit- v. acolyt-. accolus v. acorus.

accommodare [CL], to accord, make available, lend (fig.). **b** to do as a (nominal) favour. **c** (of things) to accommodate, afford, provide.

dignus cui fidem narranti audientes ~arent BEDE *HE* IV 3; **s1191** rex Francorum eidem marchioni..favorem ~ans W. NEWB. IV 19; si..vel oculos ad hoc quandoque legendum vel saltem aures ad audiendum ~es GIR. *DK pref.* 2 p. 162; **1303** vacare nequivimus quin..tantis clamoribus ~aremus auditum (*Lit. Papae*) *Reg. Carl.* II 4; **1552** operam seu ministerium ~antes *Conc. Scot.* II 135. **b 12..** [debent] secare acram prati in qualibet ebdomada Augusti et, si necesse fuerit, ~are secationem sequentis ebdomade (*Cust. Otterton*) *Cust. Bleadon* 195. **c** versus districtus..in scansione pedum numquam orationem accomodat integram ALDH. *Met.* 10 p. 92; locus ille ab initio rupium maris..defensus erat hujusmodi lapidibus quos ~avit littus fluminis ELMH. *Hen.* V 15.

2 to lend, advance. **b** (w. *debitum*) to arrange, negotiate. **c** (w. *cum*) to bargain. **d** (w. *ab*) to receive on loan, borrow. **e** (p. ppl. as sb. n.) loan.

burgenses..~abant vicecomiti carrucas suas ter in anno *DB* I 189; abbas eum [manerium] ~avit Alfio et uxori suae tali conventione quod post obitium eorum rehaberet abbas suum manerium *Ib.* II 444b; perge illuc et dic, "~a mihi hoc", nominans quod volueris; et statim ~abitur, si terminum reddendi posueris (*Commendatio Britanniae*) DICETO I 15; **1204** ad reddendum..regi..xxxvij m. argenti quas accomodat fratri meo..ad quietandum se de carcere suo *Pat* 42; **s1255** ut..pecuniam inventam ad opus suum tollerent ministri sui, non quasi ablatam aut raptam sed ~atam M. PAR. *Abbr.* 347; **a1257** nullus eorum cogatur ~are ballivo suo ultra xij d. *BBC* (*Carmarthen*) 112; **1268** duo fratres..litigaverunt inter se..pro uno obulo, eo quod unus eorum alteri acomodaverit *SelCCoron* 11; **1324** ne aliqui possint arma sua familiaribus suis..accomodare (*Lib. Cust.*) *MGL* II 637; **1423** ut claustralibus exituris nec equum nec famulum..~are velint (*Ordinatio*) AMUND. I 111. **b 1155** de omnibus debitis suis que ~ata fuerint apud Londonias.., placita apud Londonias [teneantur] (*Ch. Hen. II*) *MGL* II 32; **1200** de debitis suis que accomodata fuerint apud Gippeswicum *Gild Merch.* II 115. **c** rex E. tenuit et ~avit eam Aluuino vicecomiti suo ut in vita sua haberet; non tamen dono dedit *DB* I 167. **d 1287** quidam.., cum sibi ecclesiastica deficiunt ornamenta, tempore visitacionis exhibent aliena pro suis, mendaciter asserentes illa sua esse que ab aliis ~arunt *Conc. Syn.* 1006. **e 1335** rogamus quatinus de uno palfredo..nobis ex ~ato subvenire velitis *Lit. Cant.* II 95.

3 to assign, apply. **b** (p. ppl.), adapted, fitted.

in ea [Trinitate] est quod veluti specialius singulis personis ~ari posse videtur ERIUG. *Per.* 568A. **b** [hec] demonstrandi modo demonstratis ~ato distinguemus BALSH. *AD* 67; munificentia tanto virtus antiquior quanto naturali justitie..~atior GIR. *PI* I. 8 p. 30; legem Anglie.. ~atiorem esse regno illi quam est lex civilis ambigere non sinimur FORTESCUE *LLA* 30.

accommodarius, (one) holding on loan, trustee.

Deus prestat hominibus quidquid habent; ..creatura ergo proprius accomodaria quam dominans debet dici WYCL. *Dom. Div.* I 3; omnes seculares vere divites sunt Dei †accomodotarii [v.l. accomodatores] et procuratores ecclesie matris sue *Id. Civ. Dom.* II 15.

accommodatio, loan. **b** extra boon-work (*cf. accommodare* 1b).

Ediet tenebat eum [manerium] per ~onem abbatis tali pacto quod post suum obitum rehaberet abbas *DB* II 286; **1201** si inter Christianum et Judeum fuerit dissensio de ~one alicujus pecunie *RChart* 93; **1204** xxiiij summas ordei quas..cepit in ~one *CurR* III 207; **1369** pro pecunia solvenda Anglicis pro acomodacione regi *ExchScot* 349; **1389** in accomodacione facta domino priori pro..utilitate domus, xx s. *Ac. Durh.* 266. **b 12..** debet metere sex ~ones domino in autumpno per totum diem, sc. iij ~ones cum ij hominibus et iij ~ones cum j homine *Cust. Bleadon* 203.

2 application.

exemplorum que posuimus..attenta consideratio et ad similia ~o BALSH. *AD* 83.

accommodator, lender (*v. et. accommodarius*).

1260 accomodatores poterunt adjuvare illos quibus suos denarios [accomodaverint] *Rec. Leic.* I 91.

accommodatorie, by way of loan.

omnis auctoritas partis ecclesie est principaliter Christi auctoritas communicata graciose et accomodatorie membro suo WYCL. *Civ. Dom.* II 8.

accommodus [CL], apt, suitable. **b** close, near.

fluvios balnearum calidarum omni aetati..~os BEDE *HE* I 1; 1197 DICETO *YH* II 157 (v. acquisitio 1a); instituit eis Dominicam orationem, compendiosam admodum et ~am et brevem GIR. *GE* I 49 p. 132; juris positivi..peritia dispensandis terrenis ~a R. BURY *Phil.* 11. 168. **b** momentanea est vita mortique ~a GIR. *TH* III *intr.* p. 139; **1309** edificia..in solo ~o..ecclesie..acquisito..constructa *Reg. Cant.* II 1057; **1313** in dicto ducatu et locis sibi acomodis *RGasc* 973.

accomparabilis, comparable.

quasi nec etiam modicum adcomparabile pulvículo a vobis incorrigibilibus accipiemus GIR. *GE* II 33.

accomplementum, accomplishment, fulfilment.

1545 in dicto manerio seisitus existens..in ~um et plenam execucionem cujusdam juncture *IPM* 12/92; **1574** in..~o convencionum predictarum *Entries* 257b; **1624** pro celeri ~o predicte proposite plantacionis *Rec. Virginia Co.* IV 310.

accomputare, to account.

1661 non assignavit..eidem cottagio..quatuor acras terre ad minus ~andas secundum statutum..de terris mensurandis *Quarter Sess. Surrey* 107.

acconcordare v. accordare.

accopa [cf. apocha], stock of tally.

de qualibet grossa recepcione fiat j tallia per se cissa et divisa in ~am et anticopam [i.e.] talliam et contratalliam; et nota quod ~a est major que datur solventi denarios et anticopa minor que datur recipienti, unde versus: 'accopa tradenti, anticopa recipienti' *FormMan* 14; †ancopa prebentem, anticopa suscipientem *Reg. Rough* 221; **1333** ad recipiendum fructus..necnon super receptis ~as de soluto sive refutaciones plenarie faciendum *Reg. Exon.* II 688; *a quytance, ..a tayle,* acopa, anticopa, apoca *CathA*.

accordare, to agree, conform. **b** (refl.).

s1155 elegerunt ex se xij seniores..qui eleccionem illam ..in secreto facerent, quoniam in multitudine non potuissent in id facile ~are [v.l. acconcordare] H. ALBUS 124; **1458** nos, ~antes dicte cure nostre, et ad complacendum Salvatori nostro, ..ponderavimus..controversias *Reg. Whet.* I 299. **b 1305** si..Arnaldus et relicta..Espanni in premissis se ~are non possint *RGasc* III 475; **s1292** nec..votum prelati contra privilegia ecclesie..valere poterit; ad hoc multa jura se ~ant *Plusc.* VIII 17.

accordum [OF *acord*], agreement.

1299 super quibusdam acordis, ordinacionibus et convencionibus dicte pacis negocium tangentibus (*DipDocE* 49) *Foed.* II 853.

accortinare, to decorate with curtains or hangings.

s1255 civitate Londoniarum nobilissime aturnata et acurtinata *Leg. Ant. Lond.* 22.

accorus v. acorus.

accostare [OF *acoster*], to adjoin.

c1200 unam cruftam versus orientem que acostat ad Netherhei, sicut fossatis includitur *AncD* C 5124.

accoupare v. acculpare. accrecensia v. accrescentia.

accredere [CL], to trust. **b** (refl.).

perfidie natis accredere si tenearis, / sit plegius pignus, ne fidus decipiaris D. BEC. 1761. **b** mihi te paulisper ~e et ipse ea que explicabo dijudica ADEL. *ED* 5.

2 to entrust, lend.

1166 de pecunia eorum ~ita et non reddita namium capiant *BBC* (*Truro*) 162; **c1202** pannos et..aliud mercatorium mihi ~ent per dies xl *Ib.* (*Egremont*) 88.

accreditare, to entrust, lend.

a1135 si burgenses villano vel alio aliquid ~arent infra burgum *BBC* (*Newcastle upon Tyne*) 143.

accredo v. acredo.

accredulitare, to clear oneself by oath.

qui in collegio fuerit, ubi aliquis occisus sit, ~et se [AS: *getriwe hine*] quod eum non percussit (*Quad.*) *GAS* 103.

accrementum, increase, addition.

1136 sciatis me concessisse..vj dies continuos de ~o ad feriam S. Egidii de Wintonia *CalCh* III 352; **c1144** preter hos dedi..predicte ecclesie..de acremento unam virgatam terre..in una essarta *MonA* VI 98; **c1190** preterea dedi eis in acrementum x acras propinquiores terre *Cart. Sallay* 124; **c1300** dedi..tantum de acramento de communa pasture quantum pertinet plenarie in pratis, paschuis et pasturis ad unam virgatam terre de dominico meo *MonA* IV 224; acrementum, A. *encres* WW; **1508** pro universe rei publice Christiane conservatione commodo et ~o *Spons. Mariae* 20.

accrescentia, increase.

a1190 viij s. vj d. de antiquo redditu in denariis et xviij de accrecensia *Kal. Samson* 107.

accrescere [CL], to increase (intr.), grow. **b** to grow to, attain.

virtutis imposterum vigor ~et GIR. *TH pref.*; **1239** ita quod occasione dictarum l m. predictus finis non ~at *KRMem* 18 r. 12d.; **1322** nempe Thome bonitas / ejus atque sanctitas / indies acressit (*Offic. T. Lanc.*) *Doc. S. Paul.* 14; **1375** emebat per forstallum iiij batellos plenos oyst'.., unde precium unius c acrescebat ad j d. ob. per j diem *Leet Norw.* 63. **b 1583** a..tempore quo predictus Walterus..accrevit plenam etatem suam xxj annorum *Pat* 1236 m. 7.

2 to accrue.

portiones sue ceteris que non forisfecerint ~ent GLANV. VII 12; **1236** si contingat quod alique terre ei ~ant processu temporis post hanc concessionem *KRMem* 15 r. 15; **1284** ita quod neutri vestrum aliquid ~at *BBC* (*Oxford*) 297; **1290** nullum jus sibi ~it in predicta virgata terre nec de jure secundum consuetudinem manerii ~ere debet *SelPlMan* 34; **1307** nec aliquid facti specialis..per quod liquere posset curie quod accio liberi tenementi accrevit in hac parte ostendunt *Year Bk. 1 Ed. II* 5; **1330** quicquid domino regi in geldabili possit †arrescere [l. acrescere]..ad ipsum abbatem debet pertinere *PQW* 554b; **s1377** ut aqua..descendendo.. bona que super terram †accruaverant [v.l. accreverant], puta, carbones, molares, lapides, ligna.., auferret suo impetu WALS. *HA* I 323; **1452** vult quod porcio illius recusantis ~at proximo consorciis suis *MunAcOx* 656; **1502** dedit dictum manerium..Ricardo..et Johanne uxori sue..et heredibus de corporibus eorundem legittime procreatis..; et Johanna ipsum [Ricardum] supervixit et se tenuit intus per jus ~endi *Cl* 362 m. 4.

3 a to increase (trans.), enlarge. **b** to add.

a 1201 Simon servicium de iiij virgatis terre.., unde.. non solebat reddere nisi j li. incensi, accrevit usque ad iiij s. et j li. incensi *FormA* 219; **1218** quelibet bovata.., que solebat reddere xxxij d. ..de annua firma, ~itur usque ad viij s. *Eyre Yorks* 391; **1220** episcopus..vestra negotia totis viribus in bonum promovet et ~it (*AncC* IV 157) *RL* I 124; **1236** accrevit feodum suum de quodam assarto *CurR* XV 1892; **1237** quod terminum suum acresceret et elongaret *BNB* III 189; **c1245** tenemur acrescere conventum nostrum de sex monachis sacerdotibus inperpetuum *Cart. Sallay* 34; **1250** Thomas..~it servicium de iiij s. per annum *Fees* 1202; poterit adicere et ~ere appellum et non minuere BRACTON 140b; **1335** petit quod justiciarii hic ~ant dampna *SelCKB* V 84. **b** huic manerio accrevit praepositus..duos bord[arios]..et iii molinos *DB* I 162b; **c1150** confirmavi ..donationem illius acre prati..; accrevi insuper..unam mansuram terre *Fabr. York* 147; **a1200** insuper accrevi eidem con[ventui] in puram..elemosinam j acram terre *Danelaw* 85; **c1356** brasiatrix non ~at quadrantem in gallonam *MunAcOx* 183.

4 (pr. ppl. as sb. n.) increase.

1180 de xx alnis scarlate de acrescenti *RScacNorm.* I 56; **1195** de c li. de ~enti pro molendin' *Ib.* 154.

5 (p. ppl. *accretus*) having accrued. **b** (as sb.) increase, addition.

1583 non obstante aliquo titulo..nobis..antehac ~o devoluto aut aliquo modo devento *Pat* 1235 m. 25. **b c1220** in defenso boscorum..nichil exigemus, salva nobis..communia.., et in ~is decimas garbarum et minutas decimas *Fabr. York* 145.

accresciamentum [OF *acroissement*], increase, addition.

1203 ibidem posuit pro timore inimicorum domini regis de acresciamento x milites *RNorm* 120.

accrescum, ~a [OF *acrois*], increase, addition.

1279 habet ibidem xij acras prati et habet ibidem v acras prati de nova acresc' *Hund.* II 660; **c1310** cum iiij carucatas terre, cum boscis, pratis..et aliis ad ea pertinentibus de ~o nostro corpori abbathie et successoribus..reliquerimus (*Const. Winchcombe*) *MonA* II 306.

accrestare, to fit w. cresting (arch.).

1265 murum juxta coquinam nostram castri nostri Wyndesor' acrestari [facias] *Liberate* 41 m. 3.

accriter v. acriter.

accrochiamentum, encroachment, appropriation.

1401 cum..vicarius..prosecutus fuisset quandam citacionem..versus ministrum ordinis Fratrum Minorum..et alios fratres de eo quod ipsi quandam domum..de novo construxerunt, acrochiando sibi diversa proficua et emolumenta ad..ecclesiam [parochialem] pertinencia..et..predicta acrochiamenta, injurias et usurpaciones..adhuc continuent (*Pat*) *Mon. Exon.* 151; **1412** abbas..accrociavit abbatie sue..fere totum cursum aque domini regis..qui deberet currere ad molendinum regis subtus castrum Oxonie.., occasione cujus ~i cursus aque..iiij molendina de novo sunt levata in abbatia *Cart. Osney* II 470; **1580** occasione acrochiamenti predicti *Ac. Esch.* 79 r. 2.

accrochiare, accrochare [OF *acrochier*], to encroach (upon), appropriate (by encroachment).

c1387 altam viam..artavit et sibi acrochavit ex parte de south' xx perticatas (*Anc. Indict.*) *Pub. Works* II 82; **1401, 1412** (v. accrochiamentum); **1475** super civitatem.. in divercionem aque illius a recto cursu suo..usurpavit et injuste ~iavit *Proc. J. P.* 243; **1573** ~iavit sibi de terris vicinorum suorum (*CourtR Nafferton*) *Yorks Arch. J.* X 81; **1583** que..premissa nuper ~iata fuerunt super vastum nostrum *Pat* 1247 m. 3.

accrocitare, to crow over.

quique nostro sepius ~arant funeri, carcerum tediis et miseria senuerunt (*Quad., argumentum*) *GAS* 534.

accruare v. accrescere 2. accrumina v. acrumen. accuatio v. acuatio.

accubare [CL], to recline (*v. et. accumbere*).

fontes lucidi per nitidos rivos..manantes pignus suavis soporis in ripis ~antibus irritant G. MON. I 2; ubi ~abant, ibi ventres purgabant W. CANT. *Mir. Thom.* III 19.

accubator, stone-layer.

1242 ad opus..carpentarii nostri et cujusdam ~oris *Liberate* (*Exch.*) 1205 m. 1.

accubitalis, for reclining on.

triclinia ~ia ORD. VIT. II 8 p. 310.

accubitare, to recline or (?) kneel. **b** to lean elbows. **c** (p. ppl.) submissive.

ubi vero cum suis sanctus ~abat, ibi nulla ruine suffusio fiebat OSB. *V. Dunst.* 36; natta qua orantes ~are solebant W. MALM. *GP* IV 149; Daci..per planitiem castri ~arunt atque scutis se cooperuerunt W. JUM. II 10; non jacet, non sedet, non ~at, non stat; totus in motu est MAP *NC* V 3 p. 208; nec alicubi ad sustentandum accumbere sive ~are prevaluit R. COLD. *Cuthb.* 102. **b** ad mensam conviva sedens non accubiteris; / accubitare tue poteris, sed non aliene D. BEC. 990–1. **c** tibi homines diversorum regnorum serviendo ~ati obedient W. JUM. II 5.

†accubitas, drooping, heaviness.

acubitas est gravitas palpebre de ventositate grossa GILB. III 142 v. 2.

accubitor, one who reclines.

[Johannes] sacer Dominici pectoris ~or ALDH. *Met.* 2 p. 65.

accubitus, lying down. **b** kneeling.

nec ~u fruebatur, ..sed impositus lectice baculoque innixus, nec stans nec jacens, dies et noctes transigebat W. CANT. *Mir Thom.* II 31. **b** ~us, *hnylung* ÆLF. *Gl.*

accuere v. acuere. accula v. accola.

acculpamentum, accusation.

1255 Gregorius..noluit facere legem quam invadiavit..sc. de accupamento diurnum russetorum que fuerunt Alexandri *Rec. Leic.* I 73; **1276** major aucupavit Adam..quod maledixit se et juratores ad dampnum gilde cuvate cervisie; et quia non defendidit (*sic*) verba aucupamenti vadiavit cuvatam cervisie *Ib.* 168; cum..in suo †accusamento [MS.: accupamento] dixisset.. *State Tri. Ed. I* 78.

acculpare, ~iare [cf. OF *acouper*], to accuse, arraign.

1246 Rogerus.., accupatus quod..deliquit contra communam gilde.., juravit quod decetero non delinquet *Rec. Leic.* I 68; **1257** acoupatus quod..brochiavit..duo rosseta *Ib.* 72; **1258** quia..R. ..insufficienter ~avit E., ideo per consideracionem curie E. sine die et R. in misericordia *SelPlMan* 56; **1270** acopiatus fuit in plena curia de pluralibus defaltis *CourtR Hales* 6 (cf. ib. 241 [**1293**]: acopati fuerunt; ib. 542 [**1306**]: acupatus est..de eo quod..prostravit..); **1276** (v. acculpamentum); **1286** Reginaldus.. ~atus coram majore..quod emit corea..contra statuta gilde *Rec. Leic.* I 201; **s1293** rex tenuit Parliamentum suum Londonie et ibi acoupiavit Eboracensem archiepiscopum de despectu sibi facto *Ann. Dunstable* 376; **s1329** coram justiciariis..super hoc allocutus sive accoupatus quod erat ..fautor malefactorum *Ann. Paul.* 346.

accumbere [CL], to lie down, recline (against). **b** to lie with (sexually). **c** to submit (to). *V. et. accubare.*

apposta ecclesiae, cui idem adcumbens obierat BEDE *HE* III 17; filii ~unt..in circuitu mensae suae Gosc. *Aug. Maj.* 92; pedibus ejus ~ens MAP *NC* III 3 p. 126; **s1238** accubuit ibidem graviter infirmatus..usque ad vite consummationem M. PAR. *Maj.* III 518. **b** cujusdam socii sui..uxorem seduxerat et accubueratW. FITZST. *Thom.* 11. **c** ecclesia, cui indubitata fide ~endum est J. GODARD *Ap.* 250.

accumina v. acumen.

accumulare [CL], to heap up, build up, amass. **b** (w. *ignem*) to spread conflagration. **c** (p. ppl.) abundant.

exemplorum copiam ~antes..congessimus ALDH. *Met.* 8; hujus numeri summam partim de Genesi partim de libro Judicum ~ans BEDE *Pleg.* 313; **10..** ~are, *heapian* WW; quatinus..paterna tibi gloria gloriam ~et GIR. *EH pref.*; laudibus accumulat laudes studiosa voluntas NECKAM *DS* II 73; **s1238** ut thesaurum ~aret et adaugeret M. PAR. *Maj.* III 518. **b** duxit exercitum per provincias Cunedagii ignemque †accumalare [v.l. ~are] incepit G. MON. II 15; Cassibellanus acceleravit provincias Androgei devastare, ignem ~are M. PAR. *Maj.* I 74. **c** opera virtutum..que in dies ~atoria accedebant PULL. *Sent.* 797A.

2 to load (fig.).

prophete animus ad iram commotus non est..gratia se sperans ~andum a Domino AD. SCOT. *Serm.* 380A.

accumulatio, accumulation, amassing.

edificacio ecclesie..non consistit in bonorum fortune appropriacione sed in virtutum ~one WYCL. *Civ. Dom.* I 39.

accumulative, cumulatively.

hec..~e ponuntur, institucio, collacio, recepcio in descripcione predicta [tituli ecclesiastici], quia, quamvis unum sepe recipitur pro alio, diversa tamen sunt..et quodlibet illorum dicit titulum ecclesiastici beneficii PAUL. ANGL. *ASP* 1529.

accup- v. acculp-.

accurare [CL], to take care of (iron.), finish off.

1214 hoc ei non suffecit, immo accessit ad eum et eum acuravit gladio suo *CurR* VI 253.

2 (p. ppl.) elaborate. **b** (?) burdened with cares.

delicatiori victu et ~atiori cultu W. MALM. *GP* I 44; cibi viliores et minus ~ati R. COLD. *Cuthb.* 118 (cf. ib. 63: ciborum ~atior indulgentia). **b 1509** quoniam..~ata nostra domus..se fassa est..apciorem neminem habituram eo qui maximis adventantibus..litigiis..plenarie queat obsistere *Reg. Merton* 375.

accurate [CL], carefully, attentively.

doctrinis ~e institutus FOLC. *J. Bev.* 1; quicquid injungebatur ~issime agens G. CRISPIN *Herl.* 93; qui vellent habitare cultius, amiciri elegantius, pasci ~ius W. MALM. *GR* V 400; archiepiscopus eum voluit ~e suscipere et honorifice procurare H. CANTOR *Hist.* 31; tam solicite, tam ~e, moniales..ignem..fovent GIR. *TH* II 34; panes azymos de purissima simila sacra sophie confectos ~issime paraverunt R. BURY *Phil.* 5. 76.

accurator, proctor.

a prokture, ~or, procurator *CathA.*

accurrere [CL], to run towards. **b** to flow in.

adcurrentes circumdederunt me BEDE *HE* V 12; ad parvulum suum..mater ocius ~it GIR. *TH* II 9. **b** est illud mare dulcius quam alia, propter flumina ~entia *Eul. Hist.* II 3.

accursus [CL], resort.

ferarum illuc multus erat ~us G. CRISPIN *Herl.* 94.

accurtare, to shorten. **b** to diminish.

uva..tangit..summitatem trachee, unde sepe..pectoris facit passiones quociens elongatur et ~atur RIC. MED. *Micr. Anat.* 221; ita acurtatur lingua quod vix vel nunquam potest extrahi BART. ANGL. V 24. **b** fecit empcionem et vendicionem in domo sua..et akortavit tolnetum et consuetudinem *Rec. Leic.* I 201.

accusabilis, reprehensible.

cum alias ~em presumptio faciat, hic excusabilem facit ipsa presumptio P. BLOIS *Ep.* 37 116C.

1 accusamentum v. acculpamentum.

2 accusamentum [cf. OF *acusement*], accusation.

1378 pro recordo et acusamento de stapula Wyntonie habendo apud Gloucestre *Ac. Mayor Winchester*; **1388** faciendo predictos..tenentes..per acusamenta et indictamenta..in curia sua..aparere *IMisc.* 243/9 r. 3.

accusare [CL], to accuse. **b** (p. ppl. as sb.) the accused. **c** to denounce, inform against. **d** to condemn (an act).

Christianae religionis titulo eas ~antes ALDH. *VirgP.* 52 p. 308; qui nuper Romam ~atus a suis atque ab apostolica sede judicandus advenerit BEDE *HE* V 19; qui domum incenderit et inde ~atus fuerit *DB* I 179; qui de occultis actionibus fuerit ~atus [AS: *betygen*], neget cxx hidis ipsum actum (*Quad.*) *GAS* 113; si inculpatio sit, et se purgare velit, eat ad ferrum calidum et allegiet manum †adcausatam [v.l. que inculpatur; AS: *mid ðe mon tyhð*] quod falsum fecerit *Ib.* 159; in hoc placito [homicidii] mulier auditur ~ans aliquem de morte viri sui si de visu loquatur GLANV. XIV 3; **c1300** qui non pacant gabulum suum..solebant acusari de gavelate *Reg. S. Aug.* 60; **s1341** omnes, etiam non indictati nec ~ati, excessive se redemerunt AD. MUR. 118. **b** ita ut ~atus perditurus sit propter delationem ~antis pecuniam aut vitam (*Inst. Cnut.*) *GAS* 321; in omnibus placitis de felonia solet ~atus per plegios dimitti preterquam in placito de homicidio GLANV. XIV 1; **1443** evidentie..que..Cancellario videantur sufficere ad indicandum ~atum melioris esse condicionis et verioris quam ipsum ~antes *MunAcOx* 538. **c s1260** ~ati sunt domino regi..quod se in..debitum nuper obligarunt pro..filio suo *Flor. Hist.* II 448; **1265** retulit domino S. de Monte Forti juniori..statum castri et acusavit homines domini R. de H. qui fuerunt in castro *IMisc.* 27/41; Galio proconsul.., cum Paulus sibi ~abatur a Judeis, ..accusacionem..audire nolebat OCKHAM *Dial.* 527. **d** non ~ando excessuum enormitates..sed excusando potius GIR. *PI* III 13.

2 to molest (*cf. occasionare*).

12.. si averia..monachorum evaserint.., non imparcabuntur nec accausabuntur *Cart. Newm.* 22.

accusatio [CL], accusation. **b** molestation.

retundens strofosae ~onis catapultas ALDH. *VirgP.* 44; sequuntur adversus ipsum ~ones malignorum, defensiones spirituum bonorum BEDE *HE* III 19; si *tyhtbisi* sit (id est ~onibus infamatus), ad triplex ordalium vadat (*Quad.*) *GAS* 217; si *anfeald tihla* [= simplex ~o] sit, immergatur manus ..usque ad *wriste*, et si triplex ~o sit usque ad cubitum *Ib.* 386; mulier in nullo placito de felonia ad ~onem admittitur nisi in quibusdam exceptis casibus GLANV. XIV 1; per ~onem factam in curia nostra de morte illa satis habetur suspectus (*Breve*) BRACTON 124. **b c1240** reducent illa [averia] ad..pasturam sine accausacione *Cart. Sallay* 392.

accusativus [CL], accusative (adj. or sb. m., *sc. casus*). **b** governing the accusative. **c** (in pun) accusatory.

'ob', praepositio ~i casus ALDH. *PR* 140 p. 196; quodsi 'vegeta' neutrale nomen esset ~o plurali *Ib.* 133; in Graecis ..breviatur..~us cum *a* vel *on*, ut 'Thesea', 'Delon'; alias longus est BEDE *AM* 2361. **b** ~ae praepositiones solae quae in *a* exeunt producuntur, ut 'intra' *Ib.* 2363. **c s1354** ast ablativus erit ipsi morte nocivus, / accusativus quia non fiet genitivus (J. BRIDL.) *Pol. Poems* I 176.

accusator [CL], accuser.

cum praesentibus ~oribus acciperet locum se defendendi BEDE *HE* V 19; ipse judex est ~or meus et ego sum manifestus peccator ejus ANSELM (*Or.* 10) III 34; ne fiam ~or causa mortis puero quem enutrivi MAP *NC* III 3; si nullus apparet certus ~or, sed fama solummodo accusat GLANV. XIV 1; si sit aliquis ordinarius qui..clerico ei liberato purgationem indicere sine ~ore coram eo de novo accusante noluerit BRACTON 124.

accusatrix, accuser (f.).

quod faceret contra quem staret ~ix cogitatio, testis conscientia W. CANT. *Mir. Thom.* II 91.

accustumabilis, customary.

redditum..debitum et accustomabilem *Entries* 134b.

accustumaliter, as a prostitute.

1541 prefatam (*sic*) Elizabethe..carnaliter et ~er usus fuit et ut concubinam suam custodivit *AncIndict.* 550/204.

accustumare, to levy custom.

1254 Willelmus.., quondam dominus loci, acostomavit seu subscriptas consuetudines burgo de Genzak imposui[t] *RGasc* I 545 (= *CalPat* p. 356).

2 (p. ppl.) accustomed, wonted.

1502 quolibet die legibili ~ato *StatOx* 303; **1550** operibus ..usitatis et accustomatis *Entries* 457.

acdenna [AS *āc*+*denn*], oak-dene (Kent).

c1170 abbatissa de Meallinges et moniales..seisinam duarum ~arum cum heittha ad quam naves applicant.. dirationaverunt *CalCh* V 62.

acecula v. acedula. acedere v. accedere.

acedia [ἀκηδία], accidy, boredom, spiritual sloth.

accidia, tedium vel anxietas, i. *sorg GlC* A 165 (= *EE* 343. 10: ~ium); **10..** accedia, *biternes* WW; tristitia et acidia suffocant intentionem H. LOS. *Ep.* 22; perseverantia ex spiritu fortitudinis, ~iam suffocans J. SAL. *SS* 954B; [Benedictus] regulam suam tanta discretionis arte depinxit ut monachorum moribus tolleret accidiam SERLO GRAM. *Mon. Font.* 14; soli sine solatio, pre accidia languidi et torpentes, neminem totis diebus videmus quem imitemur AD. EYNS. *Hug.* II 11; **c1204** nonne sic eam [ecclesiam] tam subito deserere..magis accedie vel etiam ignavie detestabilis quam bone prudentie..signum foret? GIR. *Ep.* (*ad S. Langton*) I p. 401; de tristitia vel accidia nascuntur malitia, rancor, mine, desperatio, negligentia erga Dei precepta, vagatio mentis extra illicita EDMUND *Spec.* 8; **1237** quartum peccatum est accidia, que appellatur tedium de bono, quod potest Anglice dici *ydelnesse* in servitio Dei *Conc. Syn.* 217; ~ia ex sua natura contraria est sapientie propter desidiam et tedium laboris in studio BACON *CSPhil.* II 409; videtur michi quod accidia..sit unum de peccatis maximis quibus nomen Dei in vanum accipitur, cum ociositas, torpor sive remissio, tristicia sive remurmuracio, maxime †indicent [v.l. indecent] servum Dei WYCL. *Mand. Div.* 17; **c1370** ~ia, septimum peccatum mortale (J. BRIDL. *gl.*) *Pol. Poems* I 174; **1429** litibus..sunt tria valde nociva / .. impetus, accidia, paupertas (WHETHAMSTEDE) AMUND. I 274.

acediare, to afflict with accidy, irk, bore.

~eatur, stomachatur *GlC* A 141; **1240** ut juxta concilium Sapientis [*Ecclus.* xxii 16] non accidiantur [v.l. accidientur] in eis, quos quasi vigiles oportet alios devenienti gladio premunire, precipimus ut discurrentes festinanter suscitent amicos *Conc. Syn.* 307; accepi a pluribus quod sermonum prolixitas dominos hic sepe accediat RIC. ARMAGH *Serm.* 80 p. 31; *hirkyn*, fastidio.., accidior *PP*; **1454** Deus..docet.. unumquemque..inicere pedes in compedibus nec accidiari in illis *Reg. Whet.* I 146.

acediose, with accidy, slothfully.

c1238 si ex vite hujus tedio et tristitia seculi que 'mortem operatur' [cf. 2 *Cor.* vii 10] accidiose mori desiderat, expedit magis ut vestro fruatur solatio..quam locum adeat ubi ..accidie magis inveniret fomentum GROS. *Ep.* 55; raro invenies mundo divitem, quin ex diviciarum affluencia reputet se magis dignum et sic injuriando fiat accidiose impius quoad Deum WYCL. *Civ. Dom.* I 22.

acediosus, afflicted with accidy, spiritually slothful.

accidiosus, mente inquietus *GlC* A 137 (cf. ib. 637: †anediosus, †tediasus); accidiosus vel tediosus, *asolcen* ÆLF. *Sup.*; scripta mea diriguntur gulosis, ebriosis, ..accidiosis H. LOS. *Ep.* 23; quid superest nisi ut ex occasione accidiose superstitionis fiat de monacho litigiosus, murmuriosus et invidus? SERLO GRAM. *Mon. Font.* 7; circuiendo incedere debent..ne forte inveniatur aliquis accidiosus aut scribens aut aliud quippiam faciens quod non licet *Cust. Westm.* 27; necessarium est ut humana fragilitas a curis..aliquando relaxet animum ad..recreationes corpori necessarias; nam aliter spiritus fit anxius et hebes et accidiosus et..cum tedio boni languens et querulus BACON *Maj.* II 362; **1284** vos horas canonicas..minime frequentatis, ..quod non solum accidiosi cordis est indicium..sed.. perverse indolis argumentum PECKHAM *Ep.* 589; accidiosus [ME: *þe slowe*] dormit in gremio diaboli *AncrR* 76; amplius accidia sibi qui fuit accidiosus / corporis ad placitum membra fovere negat GOWER *VC* VII 817.

acedo, sourness, acidity. **b** (fig.).

cineres a siccitate ignea ~inem contrahunt juxta Aristotelem [*Met.* II 2] *Ps.*-GROS. 624. **b 12..** homo vas stercorum, massa putredinis, / vas in quo latitat fervor libedinis, / fetor luxurie, calix acedinis (*Humana Miseria* 71) *EHR* XXXII 403.

acedula v. 1 acidula. acefalos v. acephalus.

acega, ~ia [cf. OF *acie*, It. *acceggia*], woodcock or snipe.

~a, *holthona GlC* A 125; ~ia, *snite Ib.* 138; aceta, *snite* vel *wudecocc* ÆLF. *Gl.*; **10..** de avibus: ..~a, *wuducoc*, ..~a, *holthana* WW; acete, que et cardioli dicuntur, tam majores et silvestres quam minores et palustres GIR. *TH* I 14.

acelaber v. attelebus.

acelga, ~as [OSp. *açelga* < Ar. *as-silq*; cf. σικελός], beet.

quedam herbe ad duas extremitates declinant ut..~a ALF. ANGL. *Plant.* I 12; clistere factum de herba que dicitur ~as GILB. VII 322. 2.

acella v. axilla, sella. acellarius v. cellarium. acemo v. essaimatio. acens- v. accens-, ascens-.

acephalare, to behead.

Flandrenses clipeis flammescunt, excutiuntque / Dovorie clipeos, ăcephalantque viros GARL. *Tri. Eccl.* 60; **c1322** proht dolor! acephalatur plebis pro juvamine (*Offic. T. Com. Lanc.*) *Pol. Songs* 270.

acephalus [ἀκέφαλος], headless.

~on, sine capite *GlC* A 140; *cephas*, caput; unde ~i, id est, sine capite LANFR. *Comment. Paul.* (1 *Cor.* i 12) 157; **s1191** unum..admiralium, truncato capite, neglexit ~um *Itin. Ric.* IV 29; Gothos ăcephalos reddidit ense malos GARL. *Tri. Eccl.* 90; **s1283** quatuor partes corporis ipsius azephali apud Bristolliam [etc.]..mittebantur *Flor. Hist.* III 59; *heedlesse*, asephalus, ..acepholus *PP*.

2 headless (fig.), leaderless. **b** without a feudal lord. **c** (w. ref. to a Monophysite sect) Acephalian.

s1066 Anglos jam ~os stupor depressit *Flor. Hist.* I 596; **1228** dolorem quem..sustinuimus..capite nostri destituti et auctoritate sedis apostolice ~i facti *Reg. S. Osm.* II 113; **s1251** [annus] Romanis..et Calabribus adhuc ~is minime securus M. PAR. *Min.* III 117; **1299** per ipsius regni [Scocie] proceres tunc velut †~es [? l. ~os] et ducis vel aurige suffragium non habentes (*Lit. Papae*) *Ann. Lond* 110 (cf. *Lanercost* [**s1289**] I 125: rex Anglie..susceptis..Scocie nunciis..petentibus ut ~is auxilium ferre dignaretur); si Christus sit caput ecclesie, tunc est pars ecclesie, quia aliter ecclesia foret corpus ~um WYCL. *Chr. & Antichr.* 661; **1427** [plebs] regnorum culmen regnandi despicit, omen / retrogradum, regimen optat et ăcephalum (WHETHAMSTEDE) AMUND. I 230. **b** sunt..quedam genera causarum ..in quarum emendacionibus rex particulariter communicat..super regios et ecclesiasticos et baronum homines et ~os [v.l. azephalos] et pauperes (*Leg. Hen.*) *GAS* 560. **c s463** apparuit heresis ~orum: ..ideo ~i, id est sine capite, nominantur quia qui prius illam heresim introduxit non invenitur; hi in Christo duarum substantiarum proprietatem negant M. PAR. *Maj.* I 190.

3 a without a heading. **b** lacking the initial syllable. **c** w. a short initial syllable, acephalic.

a 1285 infame folium ausus est..publicare.., cujus folii est ~um principium, malignum medium et finis fatuus..; ~um, inquam, quia tacito nomine..clam nisus est..pastorem percutere PECKHAM *Ep.* 645 p. 897 (= *Conc.* II 121). **b** si dixero 'papa Nocenti', / †ăcephatum nomen tribuam VINSAUF *PN* 2; sic differt Clemens nunc a clemente vocatus, / errat et ăcephalo nomine nomen habens [i.e. inclemens] GOWER *VC* III 956 (cf. ib. IV 715). **c** quid est acefalos? versus sine capite, cum prima sillaba contra naturam producitur ALDH. *Met.* 10 p. 94 (cf. W. MALM. *GP* V 195).

1 ăcer [CL], sharp, jagged. **b** (fig.) painful, disagreeable. **c** (?) constricted, narrow.

acria testularum fragmina ALDH. *VirgP.* 41. **b** acerrimae stimulo compunctionis instigatus *Ib.* 10; acri coepit dolore torqueri BEDE *HE* V 13; †acerrima palus ORD. VIT. II 15 (v. ater b); mos hiemis morti, mortis tamen acrior ira SERLO WILT. 4. 1. **c 1255** quia ille locus est in uno acriore loco totius foreste, ..si [iij acre ibi] essent assartate, bestie amitterent procursus suos ad transversum foreste (*Inq.*) *Ambrosden* I 353.

2 sour, acid. **b** (w. *vinum*) vinegar. **c** (sb.) kind of herb (? sorrel or ground ivy).

urgebantur ăcri furioso pectore bile FRITH. 813; electuarium Alexandrinum ad tussim, quando quod fluit acrum (*sic*) est GILB. IV 188 v. 2. **b 1265** vinum acrum, iiij d. (*RHosp.*) *Manners* 5; **1334** in..dimidia lagena vini acris *Ac. Durh.* 19; **1456** in..vino †atro *ExchScot* 134. **c** acer herba est; acer [v. **2** acer] etiam arbor est *SB* 9.

3 keen, vigorous.

acris erat ingenii BEDE *HE* V 19; **7..** acris, fortis vel *from* WW; ~er, i. vehemens, *strang* ÆLF. *Gl.*; [abbas] acris (*sic*) ingenio et..bellicosae artis non expers ASSER *Alf.* 97; turbinis ut ventus, sic irruit acra (*sic*) juventus GOWER *CT* II 27; qui magis impaciens verba per acra foret *Id. VC* III 1162.

2 ăcer [CL], maple.

acer, *mapulder* ÆLF. *Gl.*; dicitur arbor ăcer, vir fortis et improbus ăcer SERLO WILT. 2. 10; quanta sit utilitas ăceris privatior usus / novit et ars †torvi [l. torni] NECKAM *DS* VIII 67; acer arbor est, item acer herba *Alph.* 2; hec ascer, A. *mapulletre* WW.

3 acer [OF *acier* < aciarium; cf. acerum], steel.

1222 de ferro et ascere ad carucas meas (*AncC* VI 3) *RL* I 190; **1282** de qualibet garba aceris *Pat* 101 m. 14; **1308**

in ferro et assere *Ac. Durh.* 5; **1398** [faber] fabricat..j carucam per totum annum de ferro et acere domini *MinAc Wint.* (*Harmondsworth*) (cf. *Arch.* LVIII 350); **1419** billas de ferro et acere factas *Treat. JP* 71*n*.

acera v. acerum, 1 acus.

acerabulus [cf. 2 arabilis], maple.

†aerabulus [*EE* 340. 1: ~us], *mapuldur GlC* A 120.

1 acerare [cf. 3 acer], to tip with steel.

1223 cuneos bene ~atos *Cl* 564b; **1280** in stipendio fabri ferrantis et asserantis ferramenta carucarum de suo proprio ferro et assere (*Ac. Ruckinge*) *DCCant*; **1289** in pikos', securibus..et aliis utensilibus cementariis acuendis et ~andis *KRAc* 479/15 r. 3; **1325** pro iiij martellis asceratis de ascere regis *Ib.* 469/8 r. 1; **1359** mille garbas sagittarum bene ~atarum *Cl* 197 m. 9; **1378** in billis et weggis acuendis et asserandis (*Ac. Malthall*) *DCCant* X 1; **1412** in reparandis et †asselandis instrumentis cementariorum *Ch. & Rec. Heref.* 270.

2 acerare [cf. 1 acus], to cleanse (from chaff). **b** (p. ppl.) impure (mixed with chaff).

to clense, ~are, prod[ucitur] *ce*, p[er]acerare, colare.. *CathA*. **b** *foule*, ~atus, deformis.. *Ib.*

aceratio, tipping with steel.

1333 pro asceracione xv martellorum *KRAc* 469/12 r. 4; **1354** pro ~one et bateracione instrumentorum cementariorum *Ib.* 471/6 r. 4; **1413** solutum fabro pro..wellacione et ~one cuniorum et pykosarum *Rect. Adderbury* 7.

acerbare [CL], to distress.

nulla nox erat quibus sinistri..nuntii Saxonum animos non ~arent H. Hunt *HA* II 10; Alexander aurum, argentum ..et oleum obtulit; cui Dyndimus: "..ne te nimium ~em, oleum istud tantum sumo." Higd. III 29 p. 478.

acerbe [CL], harshly.

acerve, moleste *GlC* A 103; diras voces nimis ~e profudit R. Cold. *Cuthb.* 44; super eadem formidabili de Trinitate materia..nimis ~e disputavit Gir. *GE* I 51.

acerbitas [CL], harshness, ferocity.

acervitas, dolor, crudelitas *GlC* A 164; cum animadverteret Christianos ~atem poenarum libenter laturos Aldh. *VirgP* 35 p. 277; Walenses..probi..sunt..~ate inpugnandi et acredine resistendi Map *NC* II 20.

1 acerbus [CL], bitter. **b** cruel, grievous. **c** (sb. f.) crab apple.

acervus, malus vel immaturus *GlC* A 109; ponticum, i. ~um *SB* 35. **b** necem cernes moribundus acerbam Aldh. *VirgV*. 1562; ~a [v.l. acerva] clade diutius..desaeviens Bede *HE* III 27; ~e continueque pestilentie mucrone Gir. *TH* III 3. **c** **1501** iiij quart. j bus. ~arum *Ac. Durh.* 101.

2 acerbus v. 2 acervus. acerare v. acescere. acerinus v. acernus. acerium v. acerum.

†acerlus [cf. acra], plot of land (Norm.).

11.. ~os suos et terras suas claudere (*Ch. Caen*) *CalPat* 1327–30 392.

acernus [CL], of maple-wood.

~um, *mapuldern* Ælf. *Gl.*; robur †acervum [l. ~um] / pectine ferrato tacitos suspendit in usus J. Exon. *BT* I 481; sint ibi trabes ~e sive quercine Neckam *Ut.* 119; in ciphis acerinis auro et argento decenter ornatis Gir. *Spec.* III 13 p. 211.

aceronicus v. acheronicus.

acerra [CL], incense-box, incense-boat. **b** (fig.). **c** coffin.

nec doluit madidas subvertens augur acerras Frith. 974; **10..** ~a, *æte oððe gledfæte*, ..*rycelsbuce* WW; ~am cum thure deferente cantore Lanfr. *Const.* 101; **13..** turribulum magnum..et ~am ex onichino dedit *Cart. Bath* II no. 808; **s1386** reliquit omnia necessaria predicte capelle..ornamenta sacerdotalia, calices, thuribulum, ~am Flete *Westm.* 135; *schyp, vessel to put in rechellys*, ~a *PP*; hec aserra, A. *a shyppe* WW; **1493** duo thuribula argentea cum ~a argentea pro thure (*Invent.*) *Bannatyne Misc.* 25. **b** qualiter in cordis thesaurum condat acerra Aldh. *VirgV*. 2192. **c** in eodem plumbo in ~am refuso..corpusculum evectum est Gosc. *Edith* 92.

acertare [OF *acerter*], to make certain, assure. **b** (refl.).

si vero super hoc dubitaverint, ita quod non possint inde ~ari Glanv. VIII 8. **b** **1293** dominus rex debet in curia sua se ascertare de jure suo *PQW* 585.

acertum v. essartum.

acerum, ~ium, ~a [< aciarium; cf. 3 acer], steel.

c1160 viij esperduites de ferro et ~io *Dom. S. Paul.* 131; **1223** xx solidatas ~i *Cl* 564b; **1242** in ferro [et] ~o ad carrucas *Pipe* 119; **1257** in ferro et ascero emptis *Crawley* 216; **1271** ipsum percussit..de quodam ense de ferro et assera *SelCCoron* 21; **1283** de qualibet garba ~i venalis *Pat* 102 m. 6; **s1284** cum uno arcu de yf..unde sagitta fuit de ferro et assero *Ann. Dunstable* 309; **1285** quodam gladio de Colon' ferro et acerro fabricato (*JustIt*) *DocCOx* 222; garba aceri [consistit] ex xxx peciis *Fleta* 73; **c1300** pro j calo aceri sc. *stel MonA* III 229; **1304** pro una garba azeri empta pro utensilibus emendandis *KRAc* 486/15 m. 2; **1339** in acera empta pro officio fabri *Ib.* 462/15 m.3.

acervare [CL], to heap up (*v. et. acreare*).

districtis nostri gladiis insecuti magnas de inimicis strages ~ant W. Malm. *GR* IV 363.

acervatio, heaping.

fecerant..ex ~one cespitum super ripam..fluminis antemuralia et propugnacula *G. Herw.* 331b.

1 acervus, ~e, ~itas v. acerb-. 2 acervus v. acernus.

3 acervus [CL], heap, pile.

~us, *muha GlC* A 108 (cf. ib. 147); quales stragis acervos / a rege spreto pateretur Aldh. *VirgV* 85; **796** (12c) juxta uno acerbo lapidum quem nos Stancestil vocamus *CS* 282; in littore..maris ~us lapideus mediocriter magnus Gir. *TH* II 8; **s1332** [Scoti] a suis suffocati ~um valde mirabile[m] componebant *G. Ed. II Bridl.* 106.

acescere [CL], **~ari,** to turn sour. **b** (fig.).

10.. †acercatur, ..~atur, *asurige* WW; ollam plenam vino obturatam pone in aqua bullienti et statim ~et Gad. 135. 1. **b** non tamen arbitror quod acescant prorsus in aevum [pudicitiae botri] Aldh. *VirgV* 2794; ut dolor semper retractatione ~it W. Malm. *GR* IV 307; ira malum deforme viris quo pectus acescit Hanv. VI 326; mens ejus acescit / cujus mellifluum manat ab ore melos Walt. Angl. *Fab.* 45; virtutis alumpnus / nullius est pretii; quicquid commendat acessit D.Bec. 600.

aceta v. acega.

acetabulum [CL], cup (originally for vinegar, later esp. for oblations). **b** liquid measure. **c** hip socket. **d** sort of cymbal.

~um, *æcedfæt* Ælf. *Gl.*; offerebatur..in ~is acetum. sed, quia raro occurrit de oblatione aceti, quidam dicunt acceptabula, ubi scilicet previdebatur a sacerdotibus, que debebant offerri, utrum accepta essent, id est idonea, an non. postea subdividit acceptabula in tria: in phialas, in quibus vinum; in thuribula, in quibus thus..et sal; et cyathos, in quibus oleum Ad. Scot. *TT* 678b; Bart. Angl. XIX 125 (v. acceptaculum); **s1303** pixides, phialas, turribula, acceptabula, omnia ex auro puro, ..sacrilege asportarunt *Flor. Hist.* III 312; asitabulum, ..assitabulum, *a sauser, salere* WW; **1464** item..ij duodene discorum, ij duodene ~orum *Ac. Durh.* 640; **1501** iiij ~a de argento *Reg. Merton* 251. **b** accetabulus quarta pars est emine xij dragmas continens Bart. Angl. XIX 125. **c** ambitus ~i, quod armum excepit, pedum trium est Caius *Anim.* 14. **d** instrumenta..percussionalia, ut ~a et cymbala Bacon *Tert.* 230.

acetositas, sourness or astringency. **b** (fig.).

arbores que nascuntur in aqua acetosa faciunt fructum dulcem, quia ~as attrahit cum calore solis quod est sue qualitatis Alf. Angl. *Plant.* II 16; splen [continet].. sanguinem melancholicum, qui transmittitur ad superiorem partem stomachi, ut ex sua stipticitate et ~ate provocet appetitum *Ps.*-Ric. *Anat.* 34; allumen zucharinum..~atem mordacem.., allumen de rocco..~atem subtilem in se continens M. Scot. *Lumen* 256; fortis calor cum sit potius deberet introducere ~atem fortem Gilb. I 42 v. 2; quedam est de flegmate acetoso, ..cum..oris ~ate Gad. 11 v. 2. **b** Witclef mitigans ~atem doctrine sue Netter *DAF* I 354.

acetosus, sour or astringent.

panis acetosus assatus D. Bec. 2652 (= *EETS* 32 ii, p. 44, l. 132: †arcecosus); stiptica et ~a provocant appetitum *Ps.*-Ric. *Anat.* 34; potus acetosus et turbidus Vinsauf *PN* 1773; [caliditas] ~a et agrestia convertit in dulcia Bart. Angl. IV 1 (cf. ib. XIX 49: acetosior); **1279** [sacrista] pro altaris ministerio vinum non prebeat ~um Peckham *Ep.* 70 p. 83; nec acetum..nec aqua ~a debet poni Gad. 4 v. 1; ahoho, i. lac ~um de quo extractum est butirum *SB* 9; **1403** panem..purum, non ~um *Reg. Exon.* (*Stafford*) I f. 64*b*.

2 (sb. f.) sorrel (bot.).

una gutta vel due oculis instillentur, ut acetum album.. aut succus ~e..aut acetositatis citri Gad. 7. 2; acedula, ribes, herba ~a idem, G. *surelle*, A. *sourdocke Alph.* 2.

acetula v. 1 acidula.

acetum [CL], vinegar.

~um, *eced* Ælf. *Gl.*; conficiantur aceto / vel gelido latice si copia desit aceti D. Bec. 2660–1; utrum de..~o, quod vinum acre dicitur..[sanguis Domini] confici valeat, questio est Gir. *GE* I 8; magis esset tutum sacerdoti non celebrare quam cum vino putrido, aceto vel agreste ad celebrandum missam incaute se gerere *Obs. Barnwell* 70; si non sit ~um vini, capiatur ~um de pomis Gad. 5 v. 1; **1314** in asseto empto ij d. *E. Comp. Worc.* 37; ~um ex vino fit, A. et G. *vinegre Alph.* 2.

†acha, strength.

~a i. virtus, *strengð* Ælf. *Gl.*

acha- v. et aca-.

achaciare [OF *achacier*], to drive (beasts).

1252 ipsi ea ~iabunt in communem pasturam..sine dampno et inparchacione *Seals* no. 15.

†achaciteir [? misr. of Ar. *al-qanṭariya* < κενταυρίη], (?) knapweed.

~r, i. centaurea *SB* 10.

achalaphe v. acalephe.

†achalus, *f.l.* for *a* (or *in*) *Chaluz*; *cf.* M. Par. *Maj.* II 542.

acharis, ~us [ἄχαρις], thankless, graceless, or uncharitable.

cur igitur gracia et charitas non immediate denominat quenquam gratum et charum, maxime cum esse gratum et non esse gratum, seu esse non gratum sive ingratum, sicut charum et ~um, circa subjectum dispositum..sint immediate opposita privative? Bradw. *CD* 403A; quis tam ~is et ingratus ut pro augmento charitatis et gracie Deo non †referrat [l. referret] graciam, cum pro augmento bonorum temporalium hoc faceret prompto corde? *Ib.* 432B; *graceles*, ..*ongracyows*, ..*onkynd in herte*, ~is *PP*; *un happy*, ~is, infaustus, .. *CathA*.

acharistum [ἀχάριστον], a sort of antidote.

si dolor capitis fit cum reumate, acaristum vel dyaolibanum cum predictis opiatis detur Gilb. II 97 v. 1.

acharitis v. acanthus.

achates [ἀχάτης], agate. **b** Jew's stone (? marcasite). **c** lapis lazuli. **d** (?) grindstone.

visibus humanis subducere fertur achates / gestantem Neckam *DS* VI 171; gemma[m] que dicitur ~es reponit [aquila] in nido suo Bart. Angl. XII 2; non concipiet..si portet secum lapidem agatis Gad. 75. 2. **b** lapis Judaicus, i. agapis vel agatis *SB* 2; lapidis magnetis, ametisti, lapidis agapis Gilb. VII 358. 2. **c** lapis agapis sive lazuli blavii est †colore [l. coloris] satis bonus; idem fit azurium *Alph.* 90. **d** hec acates, A. *a grynstone* WW.

2 a kind of herb.

nullus lapis est pretiosus qui ad consequendam suam virtutem extrinsecum cum herba sui nominis aut cum sanguine avis aut bestie non consecretur..~es cum ~e herba facit virtutem Gerv. Tilb. III 28.

achathes v. aëtites. achator, ~um, v. accat-. achedemia v. academia. achellarium v. asshelarium.

acherium [OF *achier*], rush-bed.

1165 decimas de sylva..in porcis, in denariis, in ~iis, in annona *Act. Hen. II* I 551.

Acheron [Ἀχέρων], Hell.

aestivi ~ontis voragines Felix *Guthl.* 31; poenis Acherontis adusti Frith. 289; **965** sub horrida stagna tartarei sit projectus ~ontis *CS* 1165; quid seu ballivis dicam, qui sunt Acherontis / ut rapide furie? Gower *VC* VI 463.

†acheronicus [? *suggested by supposed etym. of* Acheron, quasi ἀχαίρων], sullen, ill-natured.

crabbyd, awk, or wraw, ceronicus, ..*soleyn of maners, or he þat lovyth no cumpany*, solitarius, aceronicus vel ~us *PP*.

Acheronticus, of Hell, infernal.

934 ~i ad ima Cociti *CS* 702 (= *MonA* I 59: acheuntici).

achersetus, a measure of grain (? acre-seed).

a1128 in corredio monachorum in singulis ebdomadis in pane xij ~os de frumento et viij ~os de brasio et iiij de grud et ij ~os de fabis *Chr. Peterb. app.* 168.

achesunare [OF *achoisoner* < occasionare], to molest.

1291 quod non debent amerciari neque ~ari (*CourtR*) *Estates Crowland* 335.

acheta v. excaeta. acheunticus v. acheronticus.

achevare, ~iare [OF *achever, achevir*; cf. accapitare], **a** to acknowledge feudal liability. **b** to complete, conclude.

a **1206** mandamus vobis quod..curam capiatis de tota foresta nostra in Lanc', quam custodiam inde vobis committimus, et inde ~etis Hugoni de Nevill' *Cl* 66b; **1214** non habet totum manerium; ..immo..medietas ei deforciatur, quam H. de M. tenet, qui non ~at ei nec de servicio nec de homagio *CurR* VII 263; **1220** dicit quod abbas..tenet xl acras terre in Sutton', qui in nullo ~iat ei de terra illa, immo illam tenet de Hamone *Ib.* VIII 250; **1232** recognovit quod ipse debet ~iare Jacobo..et heredibus suis de ix sol. annuis..pro tenementis quod..debet tenere de illo..per predictum servicium *KRMem* 11 r. 10*d.*; **1244** non dat hydagium nec facit sectam, quia ~iat ad heredes Marescalli *Cart. Rams.* I 441. **b** **1258** de querela sua..prelocuta fuit inde quedam pax et plene ~iata (*CurR*) *SelCWW* 37.

achia v. hachia. achile v. ancile. achillare v. asshelarium.

achillea [CL], milfoil (bot.).

10.. achillea, *colloncroh* WW; †achilles, i. millefolium *SB*.

Achilles, type of invincibility, conclusive argument.

per hoc frangitur eorum ~es, in quo pro demonstratione confidunt Bacon *Tert.* 126; istud etiam, quod habetur pro ~e, non videtur multum efficax argumentum Duns *Sent.* I iii 7. 31.

acholothus v. acolytus a. achonitum v. aconitum.

†achor [? cf. ἄχος], disturbance.

~or, i. conturbatio, *drefing* Ælf. *Gl.*

achora [ἄχωρ], scab.

si [tynea] humida et non saniosa fuerit, vocatur ~a Gilb. II 82 v. 1; acora est morbus capitis citra cutem, minuta habens foramina *Alph.* 1.

achrus v. acra 3. acia v. ascia, atia.

aciarium [< acies; cf. 3 acer, acerum], steel.

accearium, *steli GlC* A 129 (cf. ib. O 124: ocearium, *staeli*).

acicularius, for pins. **b** (sb.) pin-maker.

†acicuraria theca, *a pyncase* Stanbr. *Vulg.* 9. **b** ~ius, *pynner* Whittington *Vulg.* 66.

acidia v. acedia.

†acidinetum, (?) gorse-bush.

nomina arborum: . . accidinetum, *gost* ÆLF. *Gl.*; **10. .** ∼um, *gorst* WW.

aciditas, acidity.

∼as [vini] recessit propter calorem solis BACON IX 39.

1 acidula, ∼um, dock or sorrel (*Rumex*). **b** wood sorrel (*Oxalis*). **c** ramson (wild garlic).

nec tibi desunt olera si suppetit tibi facultas bete. . acedularum et malve NECKAM *NR* II 166; ăcīdule cedit ignis sacer *Id. DS* VII 131; acedula et verbena simul distemperatis potest fieri emplastrum fronti GAD. 6 1; acedula, ribes, herba acetosa idem, G. *surelle*, A. *sourdocke Alph.* 2 (cf. ib. 81: acedula); **1414** axsedule dim. lib. vj d. *Esch. F.* 1066/1; assedula, A. *surdokke* WW; *a sowredoke*, accedula *CathA.* **b** accitulium, *gaecessure GlC* A 131. **c** acitula, *hromsa Ib.* 129, acitelum, *hromsan crop Ib.* 130; acitellum vel acecula, *hramesun Gl. Durh.*; **10. .** acetula, *ramese*, **14. .** acticola, A. *ramsyn* WW.

2 †acidula [? cf. acredula], a kind of small bird.

cogitans quia, si de avicula comederet que lingua Francorum vocatur ∼a, salutem reciperet, . . abiit in ecclesiam. . . inter eundum contigit aviculam quam optabat nisum fugare eamque timidam fugere per tortuosos orbes W. CANT. *Mir. Thom.* V 23.

acidus [CL], acid, sour. **b** (fig.).

si forte quotidiani cibi satietatem ∼o sapore relevare te delectat BALSH. *Ut.* 44. **b** nosti quid sit amor? sic non desistis amare. / nescis? sic acidus. incipe, dulcis erit SERLO WILT. 19. 18.

acies [CL], blade or edge (of weapon). **b** sharpness (of sight or wits), attention.

1505 vir extraneus aciem *de le dagier* habuit in manu sua *Sanct. Durh.* 108. **b** non aciem cordis scabra rubigine perdunt ALDH. *VirgV* 2767; lepra. . corporis non aufert aciem mentis qua illum intelligimus ERIUG. *Per.* 531C; cum res ipsae. . acie cogitationis in mente conspiciuntur ANSELM (*Mon.* 10) I 24; in ipsos solaris corporis radios aciem defigunt oculorum GIR. *TH* I 13; cum voluntas convertat aciem animi ad illam que in memoria est J. BLUND *An.* 169; laboriosa giratio aciei intellectus LUTTERELL *Vis. Beatif.* 93v.

2 battle-line.

procedunt acies densa stipante caterva ALDH. *VirgV* 1547; cum hostibus qui ab aquilone ad aciem venerant BEDE *HE* I 15; acies, *geræwud feða* ÆLF. *Gl.*; aciebus statutis confligens H. HUNT. *HA* VII 35; s**1339** cum suis aciebus per ipsum in armis prudentissime ordinatis AVESB. 87; erat acies illa anterior acies pedestris ELMH. *Hen. V* 49; hec acies, *a scheltron* WW.

3 ladder.

vidit duas scalas sive acies, ut milites dicunt *Mir. Montf.* 86; s**1415** triplicatum gradatumque ascensum cum mira arte acierum cumque turribus et propugnaculis AD. USK 128.

acilium v. attillum.

acinaceum, (?) withered grape (cf. *Num.* vi 4) or refuse of wine press.

draf, segisterium, ∼ium, brasispurgium *CathA.*

acineta v. accingere 3.

acinus, ∼um [CL], berry (esp. grape) or pip. **b** malt wort.

∼um, *hindberiae* [*raspberry*] *GlC* A 132; **9. .** ∼os, *bergan* WW; ad ∼um, *ða grenan Ib.* (cf. *Num.* vi 4); ignea juniperus tendens in acinum NECKAM *DS* VIII 131; sicut vinum conficitur ex multis ∼is, sic corpus Christi ex multis membris GIR. *GE* I 8; †acimum est id quod de uva relinquitur extracto musto *Alph.* 2; *husk of frute or odyr lyke, . . pypyn of wyne or grape*, ∼us, ∼um *PP.* **b** ∼um, *mealtwurt* ÆLF. *Gl.*

acipenser [CL], (?) sturgeon.

qui se curare volunt molliter, accipenserem. . non querant, appositis que ibi inveniuntur deliciis W. FITZST. *Thom. prol.* 10.

acirma v. arcirma. acirologia v. acyrologia.

acisculus [CL], **∼um,** pickaxe.

∼um, quod habent instructores, quasi †mallioles [l. malleolus] ad cedendos lapides *GlC* A 168; ∼ium, *piic Ib.* 115; ∼um, *pic* ÆLF. *Gl.*; *a mason axe*, ascis, asciculus *CathA.*

acitellum, acitula, v. acidula. acl- v. et. accl-.

aclys [CL (?) < ἀγκυλίς], sort of javelin.

aclides, tela, arma, †gladia *GlC* A 154.

acmasticus [ἀκμαστικός, *infl. by* augmentum], (of fever) working up to a crisis. **b** (fig.). **c** (of age) approaching maturity, adolescent.

synochus. . dividitur in epaugmasticam, augmasticam et homotenam GILB. I 9 v. 1; species sinochi sunt tres, similiter sinoche: . . secunda est augmastica et est ut a principio augmentetur usque ad finem GAD. 18 v. 1; **b** febris ista [sc. libido] raro est omothona, rarius epaugmastica, sed frequenter augmastica NECKAM *NR* II 155. **c** contingit colicis juvenibus in estate regione calida circa †augmaticam etatem GILB. 91. 2; †angmastica [l. augmastica] etas, i. adolescencia *SB* 12.

acoco v. alcoto.

acoenonetus [ἀκοινώνητος], uncommunicative.

†acnonitus, qui nulli communicat *GlC* A 150.

acognitum v. aconitum.

acolytatus (acolitatus), office or degree of acolyte.

1220 . . a Sefrido quondam episcopo Cicestrensi. . ad ordinem ∼us fuit promotus *SelPlCrown* 121; **1258** item quod abbas potest conferre. . ordines ostiariatus et †occolitatus (*Summa privileg. Abb. Cant.*) *MonA* I 146; per subdiaconatum et ∼um. . consequitur quis graciam doni spiritualis OCKHAM *Pol.* I 167; adquisivit [abbas Johannes, ob. 1401] bullam perpetuam de ordine accolitatus debitis temporibus suis monachis solummodo †conferendis [l. conferendo] *G. S. Alb. Cont.* III 437; **1423** te. . accolitum pretensum in habitu accolitatus indutum. . ab ordine accolitatus degradamus *Reg. Cant.* III 172; **1467** abbas. . ordines Benedictinos et accolitatum per sacras manus suas in ipsos imposuit *Reg. Whet.* II 73.

acolytus (acolitus) [ἀκόλουθος], follower. **b** acolyte (holder of fourth degree in holy orders).

acholothus, sectator *GlC* A 107. **b** accolithus, ceroferarius *Ib.* 173; a primo sacramentorum ordine nominatim distincta per exorcistas et ∼os incrementa. . accipiunt ALDH. *Met.* 2 p. 70; accolitus cum ordinatur, primum ab episcopo doceatur qualiter in officio suo agere debeat; sed ab archidiacono accipiat ceroferarrium cum cera, ut sciat se ad accendenda aecclesiae luminaria mancipari EGB. *Pont.* 13; ∼us cum pulvillo sequatur *RegulC* 44; si forte quis hostiarius, ut irruentes clericos ab introitu repellat, virga percutit. . ; item si ∼us phonastro vel correptorio J. SAL. *Pont.* c. 3; in templo erant emunctores luminum qui candelas et accendebant et extinguebant; hi sunt in nostra ecclesia quos ∼os et ceroferarios dicimus BELETH *RDO* 13 27; nunc ∼i et amplius subdiaconi episcopale officium. . usurpare presumunt P. BLOIS *Ep.* 209. 490A; **1215** magistro R. †acolite [? l. acolito] domini Pape *Cl* 158b; **1229** nisi fuerit clericus et ad minus ordinatus in ∼um *Conc. Syn.* 177 (= *Conc.* I 626: †acoluthum); post exorcista venire / debet et ăcolytus GARL. *Myst. Eccl.* 374; hic acolitus, *a colyte*, . . hic acoletus *a colet* WW; ∼i, qui ignem et aquam templo amministrant, quod est factum in mundi templo a coelestibus ∼is longe alio et veriori modo COLET *Sacr. Eccl.* 47.

acomod- v. accommod-.

aconitum [ἀκόνιτον], aconite, (?) monkshood (bot.).

aconito, *pungas GlC* A 102 (cf. ib. 104: acognitum, genus herbae venenatae); nomina herbarum: . . ∼a, *pung* ÆLF. *Gl.*; illa [Livia] sponte miscuit aconiton MAP *NC* IV 3 p. 153; sic achonīta ferax herbarum gignit Achone NECKAM *DS* VII 371; tantum de aqua. . corrumperet animal statim quantum de psillio aut de †anconico BACON XIV 82.

acopa v. accopa. acopare, ∼iare, v. acculpare.

acopum [ἄκοπον], an anodyne or restorative.

∼um, i. mitigativum, et dicitur ab *a* quod est 'sine' et *copos* quod est 'labor' *Alph.* 1.

acora v. achora. acord- v. accord-.

†acoriare [? cf. accoillare], to overcome.

1242 Elyas. . ∼iatus fuit in campis. . per frigus *Assize R. Durh.* 24.

acorus [ἄκορον], water flag (*Iris*) or sedge.

succus ∼i et succus lactuce silvestris. . visum acuunt GAD. 112. 1; accorus est species yris *SB* 9; ∼us, i. radix gladioli; gladiolus juxta aquas crescit, cujus flos crocius est, radix rubea. . A. †*boure* [? l. *levre*] *uurt Alph.* 2; *gladon*, . . accorus, accolus, . . *segge of the fene or wyld gladone*, accerus *PP.*

acostare v. accostare. acostomare v. accustomare. acosus v. aquosus. acotimus, acoto, v. alcoto. acoup- v. acculp-.

acquaestus, ∼a, 'acquest', property acquired.

c**1148** quicquid de debitis redditibus. . aliisve justis acquestibus habere poterit (*Inst. Sempr.*) *MonA* VI 946* vii; **1283** jus. . quod dicebat se habere racione aquestarum in molendino ventricio *RGasc* III 570.

acquiescere [CL], to bring to rest, stop.

quia ullo modo fontem lacrimarum adquiescere non possum (BERTHGYTH) *Ep. Bonif.* 148.

2 to acquiesce, agree: **a** (w. dat.); **b** (w. *in*); **c** (w. inf.).

a cui cum ille libenter adquiesceret BEDE *HE* III 23; s**1180** rex. . petitioni eorum adquievit *G. Hen. II* I 245; **1309** ipse eis [suggestionibus] non adquievit *RScot* 64a. **b** s**1341** providemus quod, si in nostris consiliis adquiescere volueris, causa tua ad finem bonum perduceretur (*Lit. Imp.*) AVESB. 97b. **c** 11. . illi vitam pollicetur si. . proficisci adquieverit GOSC. *Mir. Iv.* lxxxii; **13. .** pensionem vicarie sue non acquievimus augmentare *Meaux* II 307.

acquietantia, quittance (of a liability or debt). **b** (w. *breve* or *litterae*). **c** document testifying quittance, receipt.

c**1160** duas domos cum ∼iis illarum domorum quas O.M. dedit *Act. Hen. II* I 328 (= *DuC*: †acquistantis); si plures dati fuerint plegii et. . aliqui eorum non habeant unde reddere possint, ipsum onus ∼ie ad ceteros. . spectabit GLANV. X 5; **1234** non permittit eum habere porcos suos quietos de pannagio, . . que aquietantia pertinet ad quandam firmam *CurR* XV 1260; **1287** quo ad adquietancias quas clamat habere in manerio suo *PQW* 1; *sake* [designat ∼iam de secta ad comitatum et hundredum; *tol* ∼iam theolonii ubique in regno; *them* ∼iam amerciamentorum sequele propriorum suorum *Fleta* 62; a**1300** ad aquitanciam reparacionis murorum *Chr. Peterb.* 52; **1310** in ∼ia operum fabri *MinAc* 992/8; **1333** recognovit se debere regi in ∼iam communitatis [ville]. . *LTRMem* 105 r. 31; **1503** habemus illius redditus perpetuam ∼iam *Cant. Coll. Ox.* II 238. **b 1214** mandamus quatinus. . omnes den. quos poteritis ad scaccarium. . mittatis, et vobis breve de adquietancia habere faciemus *Cl* 205a; **1278** habuit litteras aquitancie *Reg. Heref.* 67; **1334** recipientes ab eodem W. litteras suas ∼ie recepcionem pecunie illius testificantes *RScot* 264a; **1441** per litteras domine regine. . acquittancie sub signeto *ExchScot* 92. **c 1302** in ij aquietanciis partic[u]laribus et aquietancia totali facta super compoto loco omnium aliarum aquietanciarum particularium, iij s. *DCWestm.* 72/12, 335; s**1308** rex sub magno sigillo suo tunc fecit ∼iam dicto abbati. . de omnibus debitis *G. S. Alb.* II 32; **1318** si qui ∼ias coram vobis ostendant, prefigatis diem quod sint coram Baronibus de Scaccario. . ad recipiendum super ∼ias illas quod justicia suadebit *Reg. Carl.* II 194; **1333** ostendit unam ∼iam de c m. solutis eidem P. *LTRMem* 105 r. 159; **1373** in cera rubea empta pro ∼iis sigillandis *Ac. Durh.* 180; **1435** hec ∼ia indentata testatur quod. . AMUND. II 114; *a quytance*, acquitancia, accopa, apoca *CathA.*

acquietantialis, of quittance.

c**1284** deprecor. . quatinus michi quandam litteram adquietancialem de P.C. de x m. habere. . faciatis *AncC* XLVII 196; **1340** presentibus litteris ∼ibus sigillum meum apposui *SessPCambs* 35; **1423** restituent suas literas de soluto ∼es in ea parte necessarias *RScot* 242a.

acquietantiarius, of quittance.

1445 condicio istius scripti ∼ii talis sit quod, si [etc.]. , extunc presens scriptum ∼ium in suo robore permaneat *Lit. Cant.* III 193 (cf. ib. II 71 [**1334**]: litteras vestras †acquietancias).

acquietare, to settle (a vexed question).

[Henricus I] investituras ecclesiarum, . . que totam sanctam ecclesiam diutissime antea turbaverant, in perpetuum ∼avit *Croyl. Cont. A* 111.

2 to settle, discharge, pay: **a** obligations or debts; **b** price or costs; **c** rent; **d** money.

a nobis eum super fide sua adquietanda convenientibus convitiorum maledicta irrogat T. MON. *Will.* II 14 p. 102; **1192** omnia debita communiter ∼are *CurR RC* I cvi; **1232** aquietavit eidem H. omnia arreragia que ei debebantur *KRMem* 11 r. 10d.; **1464** pro debitis meis acquitandis *Reg. Aberbr.* II 135. **b** s**1193** episcopus. . dimidium pretii. . de thesauro suo adquietavit M. PAR. *Min.* II 44; **1218** custum suum. . aquietabit *Eyre Yorks* 7; **1267** ad expensas regine. . aquietandas *Cl* 287; s**1272** ad redemptionem civitatis versus dominum regem ∼andam *Leg. Ant. Lond.* 149. **c** haec terra nunquam reddidit aliquid consuetudinis vel scoti, quia xxiiii solini haec omnia adquietant *DB* I 2; p**1147** redditum . . warrantizabimus, ∼abimus et defendemus inperpetuum *Kelso* I 34; s**1233** ad firmam domini regis adquietandam *Leg. Ant. Lond.* 7. **d 1266** inde adquietantur [*are credited*] ei c li. quas recepit de arreragiis comitis de Dunbar *ExchScot* 11; s**1267** petitum est ut clerus adquietaret ix milia marcarum RISH. 52; p**1274** pro decima. . que pertinet ad fabricam ecclesie, unde sacrista tenetur ∼are ij m. *Val. Norw.* 482.

3 a to acquit, discharge (land etc.) of claims. **b** to quitclaim, release. **c** to redeem (a pledge). **d** to pay for, purchase. **e** to pay off (a ship).

a tenet. . per vim dim. virgam, . . quamvis monachi adquietant eam de geldo *DB* I 41b; c**1105** monachi. . ∼ent ecclesias suas de pecunia sua et habeant quiete amodo (*Ch. Wint.*) *EHR* XXXV 391; adquietet [AS: *werige*] *inland* domini sui. . de *sé wearde* (id est de custodia maris) (*Quad.*) *GAS* 446; si quis baronum. . comitatui. . interfuerit, totam terram. . ∼are poterit (*Leg. Hen.*) *Ib.* 553; qui terram adquietatam habet scyre. . testimonio, habeat sine querela (*Leg. Ed.*) *Ib.* 657; c**1117** tenet dim. hidam pro vj s., quam adquietat de gilda regis (*Cart. Burton*) *EHR* XX 276; a**1128** isti homines adquietant erga regem v hidas *Chr. Peterb. app.* 160. **b** a**1215** warantizabimus, aquietabimus et defendemus. . conventui. . de Dalmulin. . predictas terras . . contra omnes homines *Reg. Paisley* 23; **1292** domos et terras et. . tenementa predicta. . magistro W. . . contra omnes homines et feminas per servicia predicta ∼abimus et in perpetuum defendemus et warantizabimus *Deeds Balliol* no. 179 (cf. *Pri. Cold.* 100 [**1427**]). **c** s**1182** confessus est quod Peruna [*Péronne*]. . vadium suum erat; et concessit quod. . rex Francie eam ∼aret per lx milia librarum *G. Hen. II* I 286; **1482** ad foras ∼andum suos libros (*Indent.*) *Scot. Grey Friars* II 131. **d 1178** per hanc carrucatam terre quam eis dedi. . adquietavi ab eis unam carrucatam terre et dim. *Reg. Aberbr.* I 6; propter cartas quasdam quibus erga Aaron Judeum. . domus sua obligata fuerat, quas ipse [cellerarius] clam adquietatas diu penes se detinuerat et usuras currentes sub nomine Aaron. . in proprietatem convertens. . domum suam. . exhauserat GIR. *Symb.* I 1 p. 207; **1229** ad coria adquietanda que in Anglia vendidimus . . auxilium nobis. . fecerunt *Reg. Aberbr.* I 79; **1257** quilibet eorum adquietabit unam schopam *Rec. Leic.* I 77; **1259** equos quos regi emerit ibidem ∼et. . usque ad summam predictam *Cl* 440; **1265** unum dolium vini boni emi et ∼ari faciant *Cl* 70; c**1280** ad vina vel bona in mare sic projecta pro voluntate sua †acquietenda et restituenda (*De ejectione mercandisarum*) *MGL* I 491; **1280** discuciatur qui eundem calicem debeat ∼are *Reg. Heref.* I 238; ea [vestimenta] usque ad summam j m. per annum emere et ∼are *Obs. Barnwell* 198; **1313** tradidit ei vj d. ad ∼andum quoddam breve in cancellaria regis *SelCKB* IV 51. **e 1242** viginti buscia que parata sunt ad opus nostrum. . ∼ari faciatis et cariari usque Portesmue *Cl* 416.

4 to redeem, ransom (a captive).

1217 dedimus Falkesio de Breaute Rogerum. . prisonem, qui est in custodia vestra, ad adquietandum Willelmum de Breaute, fratrem suum, qui captus fuit in servicio nostro *Pat* 19.

5 to satisfy (a claimant).

ipsum super his adquietare..pepigerat GIR. *JS* III 7 p. 346.

6 a to release (debtor etc.) from obligation. **b** to acquit (accused person) of charge.

a **a1150** in omnibus quoad suas elemosinas dictum priorem aquietabunt *Cart. Glouc.* II 136; **c1150** ita quod.. heredes sui..Willelmum..de omni servitio quod ad manerium pertinebit debent adquietare versus..meos heredes *FormA* 1; semel prestitum relevium..utrumque, sc. tam maritum quam uxorem, ..de relevio ~abit GLANV. IX 4; precipe N. quod..~et R. de c m. unde eum applegiavit *Ib.* X 4; dominus..pro j d. adquietabit bordarios suos (*Leis Will.*) *GAS* 505; **1199** xx li. ..comodaverunt Willelmo ad ~andum eum versus Judeos *CurR* I 104; vos obtestor.. quatinus in his que..ad officium meum spectant me fideliter erga Deum adquietetis GIR. *Symb.* I 20; **1219** de illis vj s. aquietabunt..Willelmum..versus capitales dominos *CurR* VIII 93; carta..regis J. que eum aquitat de omnibus assisis *Ib.* 99; **1296** de quibus..arreragiis ~amus eos *Reg. Carl.* I 16. **b** **1218** Mauricius appellavit de vi Rogerum..; et Rogerus venit et non malecreditur, quia juratores aquietant eum; et ideo inde quietus *Eyre Yorks* 215; **1221** omnes isti preter R. .., quem prius aquietaverunt, sunt culpabiles de felonia illa *SelPlCrown* 179; **1255** inquisicio..aquietavit.. homines et leporarios *SelPlForest* 35; **1275** omnes isti prenominati sunt aquitati de murdro *Hund.* II 177.

7 (absol.) **a** to clear oneself of liability, make payment. **b** to clear oneself of a charge.

a **11..** licet..contra..monachorum voluntatem drengagium meum denariis adquietando tenuerim *Feod. Durh.* 142. **b** mittat in manum venditoris, qui vendidit ei, et roget ut mundificet et adquietet ei, si possit (*Quad.*) *GAS* 224; **c1258** si ille cui inponitur transgressio inde racionaliter adquietare non poterit *Reg. St. Bees* p. 349.

8 (refl.) **a** to clear oneself of liability, make payment. **b** to clear oneself of a charge.

a apud Ripam sunt c acrae quae se adquietant ubi T.R.E. se adquietabant *DB* I 2; manerium..post mortem R.E. non se adquietavit de gildo regis *Ib.* 132b; quando comitatus geldabat, pro xv hidis se civitas adquietabat *Ib.* 172; **a1128** hec villa adquietat se erga regem pro dim. hida *Chr. Peterb. app.* 160; **1130** regi se adquietavit in Normannia de xx m. argenti per breve regis *Pipe* 13; **a1185** ad aquitandum me de illis xx s. per singulos annos..do illas lxvj acras *Cart. Glouc.* II 230; **c1220** dominus A. ..bene se †addietavit [l. adquietavit] et liberationem facit pro nobis (*AncC* VI 8) *RL* I 167. **b** conscientie vel consensus in aliquo se ~et, si fuerit accusatus (*Leg. Hen.*) *GAS* 603; **1255** requisitus qualiter se velit aquietare de illa suspicione, dicit quod.. per iiij villatas propinquiores; qui (*sic*) dicunt super sacramentum suum quod non est culpabilis de aliquo malefacto *SelPlForest* 15; **1290** vadiavit legem; postea fecit legem et ~avit se sexta manu *SelPlMan* 37; **1315** ~avit se quod non est culpabilis; ..ideo inde quietus (*St. Ives*) *Law Merch.* I 94; **1321** potest se acquitare si velit per quamdam legem civitatis *PQW* 451b; **s1400** ut de objecto crimine legitime se ~aret *Croyl. Cont. B* 495.

acquietatio, quittance, settlement (of liability or debt). **b** document testifying quittance, receipt.

1198 breve ~onis quod idem B. mihi fecit *Pipe* 166; **1203** pro adquietatione decimi denarii redditum meorum *Reg. Paisley* 14; **1204** invadiacionem..quam..faciet de terris suis pro ~one redempcionis sue *Pat* 39a; **1226** in ~one debiti quod debemus..archiepiscopo *Pat* 49; **1258** in ~one seldagii *Rec. Leic.* I 78; **1321** in ~one firme sue *PQW* 449a; **1325** summa acquittacionis DCCCLIX li. *CartINorm.* 47; **s1485** recogniciones et ~ones per fines..conventui factas..allegant *Croyl. Cont. C* 576. **b** **1377** xlv s. ..per breve regis et ~onem ipsius R. *Banstead* 356.

2 quitclaim.

c1280 R. ..[se] obligavit ad acquietandum et defendendum ..[abbati] et conventui..boscum predictum; ..et pro hac ~one et defensione faciendis..concesserunt xij d. annui redditus *Reg. S. Aug.* I 83.

3 a release from liability. **b** release from charge, acquittal. **c** clearance (of self) from charge.

a **a1135** cum..omnibus..libertatibus et consuetudinibus et ~onibus ecclesie sue (*Ch. Hen. I*) *Reg. Heref.* (*1283–1317*) 50; **1439** in casu quod eedem litere..pro plena exoneratione et ~one..archiepiscopi..in hac parte erga nos..insufficientes..existant BEKYNTON I 46. **b** revocabitur judicium sue ~onis *Fleta* 56; **s1321** de..rege de suis..demeritis pardonacionis et ~onis beneficium petierunt *G. Ed. II Bridl.* 73; **s1381** si contingeret eos impeti..pro factis suis, ..idem abbas apponeret diligenciam suam pro adquietacione eorundem et gracia obtinenda WALS. *HA* II 31. **c** faciat homo suam ~onem contra dominum suum cum se duodecimo *Quon. Attach.* 24.

acquietatorius, of quittance.

a1300 quieti recesserunt portantes literas aquitatorias patentes domini regis *Chr. Peterb.* 25; **1362** ad..recipiendum dandumque litteras †acquitor' de receptis *Reg. Glasg.* 272.

acquirere [CL], to acquire, get, win. **b** (w. *ut*) to bring about.

acquisitorum..triumphorum felicitas ALDH. *VirgP.* 12; cum..non paucam Domino plebem adquisisset BEDE *HE* III 21; ut aliquod lucrum mihi adquiram [AS: *begyte*] ÆLF. *Coll.* 97; adquisivit Lavintone..per pecuniam suam *DB* I 376b; sic jurando adquirat triplex judicium (*Inst. Cnut.*) *GAS* 325; laus dum vitatur ~itur GIR. *EH* I 4; qualiter dominia rerum adquiruntur de jure naturali BRACTON 8b; **1314** quod ipse..retineat .omnia bona mobilia que super inimicos nostros..adquirere et occupare possit *RScot* 131b; **1345** reservata nobis libertate resumendi guerram per culpam..Philippi nobis..acquisita (*Lit. Regis*) AD. MUR. 167; adquirit domino, nil adquirit sibi servus GOWER *VC* VII 69; **1435** in vadio J. W. adquirentis, lucrantis et frangentis petras in quarera *Fabr. York* 55. **b** rex, ..Biscop Baducing inveniens, ..ut in suo comitatu [Wilfridus] esset adquisivit EDDI *Wilf.* 3.

2 (p. ppl. as sb. n.) acquisition, property acquired or purchased.

1225 ex dono Willelmi..vj li. de adquisito de Sandwico (*Ac. Treas.*) *DCCant.* I 70a; **1277** beneficia que de nostro adquisito dictis fratribus assignavimus *Reg. Malm.* II 228; **1324** [*land held*] de acquisito *CalIPM* VI p. 367.

acquiribilis, acquirable.

ut gracia, qua creatura racionalis est grata Deo, fundatur in virtute, a qua dependet; ideo est ~is et deperdibilis tanquam accidens temporale WYCL. *Ent. Praed.* 63.

acquisibilis, acquirable.

secundo modo est motus in locum propter aliquid existens in loco per applicationem ~e BACON VIII 183; capitur [hoc bonum] pro summo hominis bono humano simplici, ..essencialiter in presenti vita ab homine ~e WYCL. *Quaest. Log.* 251; magnitudinem..nullo humano ingenio ~em PAUL. ANGL. *ASP* 1544.

acquisitio [LL], acquisition, getting, winning, procurement: **a** of property; **b** of immaterial things; **c** of souls; **d** of wood, stones etc.; **e** of animals; **f** of agents or accomplices.

a **1197** per excambium domino regi ad tuitionem et adquisitionem terre sue accommodum (*Lit. Archiep. Rotom.*) DICETO *YH* II 157; in adquisitione tenementi BRACTON 165b; **1267** tenementa que..R. habuit de adquisitione sua *Cl* 391; **1268** nullum breve alicujus ~onis..eisdem viris religiosis..poterit valere *BBC* (*Bridgetown Pomeroy*) 89; **1286** terrarum..quas..Dei providencia loco prefato largitura est sive empcione sive donacione aut aliqua juxta [i.e. justa] adquisitione *PQW* 307a; **1314** tres carte adquisicionis *Rec. Leic.* I 287; **1343** in complementum solucionis c li. pro adquisicione castri de Edynburgh *ExchScot* 534; in ~one librorum R. BURY *Phil.* 8. 116; **s1379** fraudulenter agit in ~one sibi abbatie WALS. *HA* I 414 *rub.* **b** pietatis adquisitione OSB. *V. Dunst.* 34; **c1242** divine dilectionis adquisitio GROS. *Ep.* 100 p. 305; in omni genere virtutis est una naturalis et alia per adquisitionem BACON *Maj.* II 258; jure primo sibi retento absque ~one novi juris OCKHAM *Pol.* I 308. **c** **634** ut..vestra adquisitio..convalescendo amplius extendatur (*Lit. Papae*) BEDE *HE* II 18; **c693** vos..genus electum, populus adquisitionis [cf. *1 Peter* ii 9]..gaudete in Domino (*Lit. Papae*) W. MALM. *GP* I 34. **d** **1325** pro virgis et adquisicione virgarum *Ac. Durh.* 168; **1434** pro meliore adquisicione et lucracione petrarum *Fabr. York* 52; **1533** carbonariis operantibus in ~one carbonum *Househ. Bk. Durh.* 184. **e** **1479** pro adquisicione talparum *Ac. Durh.* 96. **f** **1194** quod ipsa consensit et instinctu et adquisicione ejus venerunt malefactores ad domum Willelmi *CurR RC* I 77.

2 acquisition, property acquired.

primum patris feodum primogenitus filius habeat; emptiones vero vel deinceps ~ones suas det [pater] cui magis velit (*Leg. Hen.*) *GAS* 589; **1198** totam terram..que fuit Radulfi..tanquam adquisitio sua quam..dedit ei pater suus *CurR* I 45; hanc firmam recepit Thomas; ..et recepit iiij li. ..de adquisitionibus *RDomin* 55; **s1191** dabo tibi medietatem totius ~onis mee, licet conventio facta fuerit.. de adquisitionibus nostris in terra Jerosolimitana tantummodo *G. Ric. I* 171; **s1192** constituerunt principem Christiane ~onis H. ..Campanie comitem W. NEWB. IV 28.

acquisitive, in a manner expressive of acquisition (or ownership).

aliquando..hoc verbum 'esse' non tenetur copulative set possessive vel adquisitive, ita quod construatur cum genitivo.., ut..'hoc est Platonis' BACON XV 132.

acquisitivus, acquisitive, involving gain.

alteratio est duplex, quedam ~a et quedam deperditiva *Ps.*-OCKHAM *Princ. Theol.* 93; nunquam penitet quis de tali peccato ~o rei talis quamdiu res illa tenetur RIC. ARMAGH *Unusq.* 267.

acquisitor, acquirer, purchaser. **b** collector.

947 iniquitatis adquisitores alienum lucrum sibi..vendicare satagunt *CS* 820; **s1307** [abbatem Westm.] ecclesie sue et fratribus multorum bonorum ~orem atque largitorem *Flor. Hist.* III 140; fortis inveccio contra adquisitores ROLLE *IA* (c. 30 *rub.*) 230. **b** fuit postea ~or eleemosynarum hospitali domui Beverlaci *Mir. J. Bev.* A 312.

acquisitrix, acquirer (f.).

humilitas virtutum omnium..~ix AD. SCOT. *Serm.* 406B.

acquisitum v. acquirere 2. acquistanta v. acquietantia a. acquit- v. acquiet-.

acra, ~us, ~um [AS *æcer*], strip of ploughland.

terra est v car[rucarum]; wasta est preter vii ~as seminatas *DB* I 267 (cf. ib. II 78b); si..comedant eorundem compascuales ~as [AS: *hiora gemænan æceras*] vel herbagium (*Quad.*) *GAS* 107; si quis hanc decimam dare nolit.., hoc est decima ~a [AS: *se teoða æcer*] sicut aratrum peragrabit *Ib.* 292; arabit..ad haec iij ~as precum [*æceras to bene*] et ij de herbagio (*Rect.*) *Ib.* 447; omnibus ehtemannis jure competit..*sulhæcer*, id est carruce ~a, ..in augmentum jure debiti recti *Ib.* 450; ipse abbas [Bernardus, ob. 1107] dedit x ~os de dominio ipsius ville *Chr. Rams.* 266; illos tres ~os terre *Text. Roff.* 215; unicuique [canonico] xv ~e assignate [sunt] que Northlande vocantur *Found. Waltham* 17; predia..fossatis clauduntur.., intra que habent [Cartusienses] ~a sua et pascua GIR. *Spec.* III 20 p. 250; **1234** prepositus..habebit j ~am frumenti de blado domini meliorem quam elegerit preter compostum et faldicium et preter capitales ~as *Cust. Glast.* 60; **1233** de vj d. de j parva ~a locata hoc anno *Crawley* 208; **c1268** ubi invenerunt terram unius loci et alterius equalis esse valoris, ~am pro ~a *Feod. Durh.* 189n.; **12..** dim. ~am que jacet juxta magnam ~am Mathei in eodem campo *Cart. Osney* IV 343; **1276** dimidia ~a forensis jacet apud P. *Ib.* 139; **1321** omnes custumarii debent cc acras terre..warectare, rebinare, arare, ..seminare, herciare, sarclare, metere, colligere, ligare et domi cariare (*Ext.*) WHITTLESEY 195; ~a, A. *an aker of land* WW; **1466** de firmis ~arum domini regis tam orientalium quam occidentalium *ExchScot* 402; **1586** pro j ~a terre jacente in communi campo vocato Myddelnorthefeild in Lytteldowne farlonge, et est prima ~a ibidem *Crawley* 528.

2 acre, determinate area of ploughland, usu. 40 rods by 4 (representing one day's ploughing); **b** (C.I.); **c** (Cornish, = virgate or larger area; cf. *Agric. Hist. Rev.* XVIII 2*n*); **d** (Flemish).

pertinent isti manerio xx ~ae terrae habentes x quar' in longitudine et ix in latitudine *DB* II 216b; ii ~ae in eodem pretio habent ix quar' in longitudine et iiii in latitudine *Ib.* 296b; **c1160** do eis et confirmo in elemosynam xl accerras terre de assartis de wasto forreste mee de Canod ad mensuram pertice regie (*Ch. Farewell*) *MonA* IV 111; **a1190** x ~as terre..secundum perticam xx pedum *Ch. Gilb.* 55; ~a habet in longitudine xl perticas et iiij in latitudine, quod si habuerit xx in longitudine habebit octo in latitudine *Chr. Battle* 11; **1222** in isto manerio [*Chingford*]..~a [constat] ex xl percatis in longitudine et iiij in latitudine, pertica autem ex xvj pedibus et dim. *Dom. S. Paul.* 92; **1278** iiij ~as terre per ~am baronum *FormA* 314 (*Hants*); **c1280** ~as ..mensuratas per perticam domini regis *Crawley* 238; **1295** ~as regales *CalIPM* III p. 203; (?) **1305** quando ~a terre continet x perticas in longitudine, tunc xvj in latitudine; ..quando lxxx longitudine, tunc latitudine ij perticas (*Horn. Bk. Lond.* 124) *StRealm* 206–7; **1306** caruca potest communiter †arari [l. arare] per diem j ~am terre ad minus *Ext. Hadleigh* 230. **b** **1331** nota quod xl perticate faciunt virgatam et iiij virgate ~um et v ~a bovatam *Ext. Guern.* 58. **c** **1201** si..seisitus fuit in dominico suo..de j ~a terre et de j ferling'..in Niweton' et in Polkiwas (*JustIt*) *Pl. K. or J.* II no. 469 (cf. ib. I p. 136); **1337** xxxij ~as vasti in dim. ~a Cornub' *Capt. Seis. Corn.* r. 22*d*; tenet..viij ~as terre Angl' in dim. ~a terre Cornub' *Ib.* r. 8 (cf. *MinAc* 816/11 [**1339**] r. 8*d.*: pro ij ~is terre Anglican' in bosco de Coyskentulys); **1355** qui tenet dim. ~am Cornub' arrabit dim. ~am Anglic' *AssessR Cornw.* 1 r. 20; **1567** xxj ~as terre Anglic' in dim. ~a terre Cornub' *MinAc Rillaton* (*DCornw.*). **d** **1211** duas ~as Flandrenses in novo marisco de Iclesham (*Ch. Bayham*) *MonA* VI 914.

3 area of uncultivated land.

una ~a prati *DB* I 30b; habet..v agros nemoris et x achros prati et xv achros pascue *DB Exon.* 481; **1159** tres ~as de prato *Regesta Scot.* no. 131; **1238** cum due sint magnitudines ~arum, sc. major ~a que est de wudeland' et de assartis et minor ~a et communis, que continet in longitudine xl rodas et iiij rodas in latitudine per perticam que continet xvj pedes et dim. *CurR* XVI 149B (*Hants*); **1251** quelibet ~a tam terre arabilis quam prati continebit xl perticatas in longitudine et iiij in latitudine, et perticata erit semper xvj pedum; et quicquid defecerit in uno loco supplebitur in alio *Cart. Harrold* no. 10; **1263** habeant in quolibet burgagio iij ~as terre sc. ij ~as arabiles et unam in burgo ad inedificandum *BBC* (*Agardsley*) 47; **1285** appropriavit..xl ~as pasture de dominico regis (*JustIt*) *Doc. COx* 206; **1308** in ix ~is subbosci succindendis *Comp. Swith.* 468; **1378** boscus..continet in se cdlix ~as per minus centum et non plus, quarum quelibet ~a continet in se xl perticatas *IMisc.* 215/4 r. 2; **1375** pro falcacione cujuslibet ~e prati per virgam xvj pedum mensurate *SessPLincs* 99.

4 judicial combat, *champ clos* (*cf. campus*).

s1237 ex abusu obtento de voluntate..regis Anglie et Scotie, non solum simplices clerici sed et abbates et priores in diocesi Karleoli, si appellati fuerint ab aliquo de regno Scotie de re aliqua, et e converso, compelluntur cum lanceis et gladiis, alias inermes, duellum quod dicitur ~am committere inter fores utriusque regni, ita videlicet quod abbas vel prior..vel duellum personale [sustinebit] vel ligatus in loco duelli habens pugilem [etc.] *Ann. Burton* 256.

acrahavedum [ME], acre-head, headland at end of acre-strip.

1202 x acras terre..cum ~is eisdem terris pertinentibus *Fines P. Lincs* 23; **c1300** [*a selion of arable land*] cum akrehevedo *Rec. Nott.* I 364.

acramentum v. accrementum.

†acreare, (?) *f.l.* for *acervare*, to heap up.

s1401 multa bona..abduxerunt, ut putaretur quasi impossibile tanta bona in tam modica plaga, principaliter bestiarum, ~ari *Dieul.* 146; **s1403** fitque grandis..strages, quoniam..nunquam putabatur..tanta multitudo ~ari pugna duarum horarum spacio *Ib.* 147.

acredo [< 1 ācer], acidity, sourness, harshness. **b** (fig.).

10.. ~inis, *surnesse* WW; ad expellendam ~inem rubee [colere] RIC. MED. *Micr. Anat.* 224; ~o sputi GILB. II 91. 1; trahit ad accredinem vel ponticitatem BART. ANGL. IV 11. **b** tergiversat ~inem passionum radicitus mitigans iniquorum motus animorum HERM. ARCH. 16; 'potaverunt me aceto' [*Ps.* lxviii 22], id est ~ine pravitatis sue GIR. *GE* I 50 p. 141; MAP *NC* II 20 (v. acerbitas); flagellorum cohereatur ~ine *Cust. Cant.* 392.

acredula [CL s. dub.], **a** small bird (*cf.* 2 *acidula*). **b** frog.

a hec agredula, *a tetmose* WW; *a golde finche*, ~a, carduelis *CathA*. **b** Grecia consuevit beta[m] rana[m] vocitare; / ..

et bene si numeras agredula jungitur isti GARL. *Syn.* 1582C; *a froske*, †agrecula, rana *CathA*.

acremanlanda, land held by 'acre-man'.

12.. Willelmus Acreman tenet acremanelandam.. Antonius habet iiij ~as in manu sua *Cart. Rams.* III 257.

acremannus [AS *æcerman*], 'acre-man', class of smallholder.

1222 terre akermannorum, quas dominus potest capere in manu sua cum vult sine injuriis hereditarie successionis: Randulfus Textor, v acras.. *Dom. S. Paul.* 52; **1251** x virgate et dim. virgata terre extra hydam, quas..persona, liberi ~i et cottarii tenent *Cart. Rams.* I 308; **1252** iiij akermanni tenent duas virgatas *Ib.* 360 (cf. 332); **1285** akermanni, qui tenent xv acras de akerlond, reddunt pro j virga et j ferling de virga cv opera; et vij cotmanni, qui tenent xviij acras, debent [etc.] *Cust. Suss.* II 29; **1297** de redditu iiij akirmannorum, dummodo non tenuerint caruc' domini *Ac. Cornw.* II 177; **1319** in acquietancia operum fabri de feodo, qui est akermannus *MinAc* (*Suff.*) 992/10; **1321** sunt ibidem [*Warmington*] ~i, quorum quilibet tenet j mesuagium et dim. virgatam terre; et reddunt per annum ..xl s., et nihil operantur (*Ext.*) WHITTLESEY 193; **1336** sunt apud Neuton' [*Hunts.*] ix custumarii vocati akermanni, qui reddunt inter se pro operibus et consuetudinibus suis xl s. *IPM* 48/2 r. 13; **1340** omnes ~i habent..unam peciam prati..et vocatur *acremannemede Rent. & Surv.* (*Wilts*) 700 m. 1d.; **1381** pro dim. virgata terre quondam Johannis in the Hirne in officio akirmanni *Econ. Condit. app.* 109.

acrementum v. accrementum. acremonia v. acrimonia. acresc- v. accresc-. acrestare v. accrestare.

†acresweda, (?) 'acre-swathe' (meadow appurtenant to acre-strip).

12.. iiij seliones terre arabilis cum hakereswedis dictis selionibus pertinentibus *AncD* A 9872.

acrewara, (?) acre of 'warland' (liable for geld).

1361 in stipend'..prepositi, ut in allocacione valoris reddituum, serviciorum et consuetudinum xv acrewar' terre, preter aruram gabuli, in precio operum suorum *MinAc* (*Eastwood, Essex*) 840/22 m. 3 (cf. 840/23 m. 3).

acrifolium, ~us, holly.

~us, *holegn GlC* A 123; nomina arborum: ..~ius, *holen* ÆLF. *Gl.*; **10..** acrivolus, *holen* WW; agrifolium arbor est ingens vel fortis, cujus semen similis (*sic*) est piperi et dulcis saporis *Alph.* 3; **1411** pars nonnullis..arborum generibus, sicut ~iis ceterisque spinosis arboribus obumbrata J. YONGE *Vis. Purg. Pat.* 48.

acriminia v. acrumen.

1 acrimonia [CL], **a** harshness, severity. **b** keenness, vehemence.

a acremonia, acumen vel saevitia *GlC* A 166; reditur.. ad minarum sevitias, ..ad objurgationum ~ias AD. MARSH *Ep.* 30 p. 127; **1295** homines variis penarum ~iis percellantur *Reg. Cant.* I 3; *sowre chere*, ~ia *PP*. **b** obtunsa mentis ~ia freti ALDH. *PR* 133 p. 184; primo impetu, ~ia, voce, vultu terribiles effecti GIR. *DK* II 3.

2 acrimonia v. agrimonia. acrimonium v. acruminum. acrimulatum v. agrimulatum. acris v. 1 acer. acrisia v. aorasia.

acriter [CL], harshly, severely. **b** fiercely, keenly.

acriter idcirco exarsit vindicta Tonantis ALDH. *VirgV* 1357; haec ăcrius torquenda foret cum luce sepulti WULF. *Swith.* II 1127; ut facerent laceras ulnarum acerrimĕ carnes *Ib.* 1134; **10..** incantatores..accriter oportet constringere (*Syn. Decr.*) *GAS* 249; [episcopi] ~er oppresserunt Cluniacenses ORD. VIT. XII 30; silphii radix..aures ~er calefaciens et vesicam ledens *Alph.* 173. **b** equites..~er irruentes GIR. *EH* I 4.

acritudo, sourness.

a crab of the wod, acroma, ab ~ine dictum *CathA*.

acrivolus v. acrifolium.

acroama [ἀκρόαμα], tune.

s938 regem et convivas musico acromate aliquantisper delinivit W. MALM. *GR* II 131; **s1367** omnibus in Roma sanctis sonet istud ăcrōma *Pol. Poems* I 118.

acroaticus [ἀκροατικός], esoteric.

familiares..admittebantur in agroatica [sc. studia], exotherica vero..extraneis..patebant J. SAL. *Pol.* 648A.

acroceraunium [Ἀκροκεραύνιον, a stormy headland], billow.

14.. acroceramen, A. *a wawe of the see* WW.

†acroceria [? cf. ἀκροχειρία *or* ἀκρωτήρια], (?) joint, ligament.

~ia, ligatura articulorum *GlC* A 143.

acrocerium v. acrocorium. acroch- v. et. accroch-.

acrochordon [ἀκροχορδών], kind of wart.

[verruce] quedam..fiunt ex sanguine et dicuntur †acrocornides GILB. III 169 v. 2; veruce sunt..multiplices dependentes, que vocantur acrocordines GAD. 29. 1; acrocordines sunt quedam dependencie..similes capitibus mamillarum *SB* 9.

acrocorium [v.l. ap. Plin. *NH* xix 30], dock (bot.).

nomina herbarum: ..dilla vel ~ium, *docce* ÆLF. *Gl.*; †acrocerium, *docca Gl. Durh.*

acroisia v. aorasia. acroma v. acroama, acrumen.

acromellarium, wort-vat.

a gilefatte, ~ium *CathA*.

acromellum, 'grout', wort (for brewing).

agromellum, A. *growte* WW; *growte*, idromellum, agromellum, ~um, granomellum *CathA*.

1 †acrum [? *for* rutrum], mattock.

de instrumentis agricolarum: ..~um, *sencen* ÆLF. *Gl.*; **10..** ~um, *scencel* WW.

2 acrum v. acra. acrumantia v. aërimantia.

acrumen [cf. OF *aigrun*], **a** crab apple. **b** piquant herb. **c** *hors d'œuvre* (fig.).

a *a crab of the wod*, acroma ab acritudine dictum *CathA*. **b** porros, cepe et alia hujusmodi acrimonia J. GODARD *Ep.* 223; post potionem oximellis comedunt salsa †acumina assata ad saturitatem GILB. II 112. 2 (cf. ib. III 131. 2: acruminibus); ex indigestione et rebus acutis, ut sunt accrumina BACON IX 28; his pultes ad legumina, / pro epulis acrumina, / ..hec sunt eorum fercula / que provocant ad pocula (*De Wallia*) HIGD. I 38; †acriminia appellamus allia, porros, cepas, sinapia et similia *SB* 9; †diamiffragia [l. drimifagia], id est †accumina *Alph.* 50. **c** [hujus operis] contexta sunt capitula summariam..noticiam continencia, ut cui.. plenam..cenam gustare non libuerit his saltem previis ~inibus delectetur HIGD. I 3.

1 acrus v. acra.

2 acrus [cf. ἄκρος], (?) outlying, remote.

ut Christi decus / conferret acris plebibus (WULFSTAN) *Anal. Hymn.* LI 141.

acrusticus v. paracrusticus. acsi v. atque.

1 acta [CL < ἀκτή], shore.

~a, ripa nemorosa vel continentes *GlC* A 149.

2 acta v. agere. actannare v. atterminare 1b. actare v. jactare. actatus v. attactus.

acte, ~is [ἀκτῆ], dwarf elder (bot.).

10.. nomina herbarum: ..~is, i. sambucus, *ellen* WW; †acus [v.l. ~is], sambucus, G. *seu*, A. *allertre Alph.* 2.

actenus, actinus v. hactenus. acticola v. 1 acidula c. actigenus v. 1 antigenus. actilium v. attillum.

actio [CL], action, activity. **b** sexual activity.

Gregorius, vir doctrina et ~one praecipuus BEDE *HE* I 23; considera num ~o passioque proprie de Deo praedicentur ERIUG. *Per.* 504A; est quippe ~o rationalis, ut dare elemosynam; et est irrationalis ~o, ut ~o ignis qui calefacit ANSELM (*Ver.*) I 181–2; si voluntas informat ~onem, et ipsa plerumque pro facto reputatur GIR. *IK* I 8; ex mutua ~one et passione quatuor qualitatum *SB* 16; dum mens egra fuit, dolet accio corporis GOWER *VC* I 1481. **b** tactus, / Cypridis excessus, deformis actio GARL. *Myst. Eccl.* 122; postquam puella ~onem presbitero concessisset *NLA* (*Wulfsige*) II 522.

2 doing, performance (w. obj. gen.). **b** action against, punishment. **c** (usu. w. *gratiarum*) thanksgiving, saying grace.

Dei pax super omnem pacis ~onem [*enforcement*]..propensius est observanda (*Quad.*) *GAS* 280; boni..malive ~o fidem recipit vel contempnit W. DAN. *Ep.* 61d. **b** parricidii ~o, *mægmorþres witnung* ÆLF. *Gl.* **c** dignis gratiarum ~onibus BEDE *HE* II 12; omnia manduco cum gratiarum ~one [AS: *þancung*] ÆLF. *Coll.* 102; **1244** quod ad perpetuas inde vobis teneamur ~ones (*AncC.* XLVII 26) *RL* II 38; pro eis graciarum ~ones omnipotenti Deo..agere propono *Plusc. pref.* p. 4; **1509** illo [jentaculo] cum graciarum ~one finito (*Vis. Dorchester*) *EHR* IV 310.

3 public function: **a** office; **b** session or proceeding of court; **c** record of proceedings.

a propinquis agrorum et prediorum hereditas relinquenda est, et ut plurimum ~onum J. SAL. *Pol.* 549C. **b** cujus synodicae ~onis hujusmodi textus est BEDE *HE* IV 5; **s747** hujus sinodi ~onem..Cuthbertus..Bonefatio.. misit W. MALM. *GP* I 6; [mercatores] homines quos secum ducunt ..ostendant regis preposito in publicis ~onibus [AS: *on folcgemote*] (*Quad.*) *GAS* 69. **c** si quae nomina tenent abbatum..per visitationum ~ones FERR. *Kinloss* 10.

4 legal action, lawsuit (esp. civil or canon law). **b** claim, right to institute legal action.

hucusque ubi personalem intendit ~onem; si vero in rem agere velit, libellum sic formare poterit RIC. ANGL. *Summa* 4; omnium ~onum sive placitorum..hec est prima divisio quod quedam sunt in rem, quedam in personam et quedam mixte BRACTON 101b; injurialium ~onum quedam ex delicto proveniunt et quedam ex contractu *Fleta* 63; hic ordo observatur in omnibus ~onibus et causis criminalibus, realibus et personalibus FORTESCUE *LLA* c. 26; **s1428** ~onem..contra..rectorem in ipsa curia [de Arcubus] intentans AMUND. I 235; **1500** custos accepit ~onem contra eum et fidejussores suos *Reg. Merton* 242. **b** **1229** remittit totum clamium et ~onem quam habuit versus eam *BNB* II 283; ~o nihil aliud est quam jus prosequendi in judicio quod alicui debetur BRACTON 98b; **12..** si velles unam de tuis civitatibus ponere infra ~onem [*to subject to a claim*, i.e. *to wager*] *Latin Stories* 2; **s1266** habeant plenam ~onem ad recuperandum catalla sua *Leg. Ant. Lond.* 93; **1275** reddendo inde annuatim..vj d. ..pro omni servicio, ~one et demanda *Reg. St. Bees* 324; **1286** jus, demandam, obligacionem, posse et calumpniam et quamcumque ~onem que predictus Judeus umquam habuit *Starrs* I 20; **1291** ratio loci occupationis de hiis nulli dat juris ~onem propter proprietatem petendi *Eyre Kent* 108; **1307** quod ~o liberi tenementi eis in camera..accrevit *Year Bk. 1 Ed. II* p. 5; **1384** ~onem de debito predicto versus eum habere non debet *PlRCP* 492 r. 520; **1409** nec aliquis eorum molestetur..per ~onem vasti *FormA* 204; **1463** cessit et dedit ~onem suam quam habuit contra T. *MunAcOx* 700.

5 canon of the mass.

canon..nuncupatur etiam ~o, quia tunc cum Deo nostra agitur causa BELETH *RDO* 46. 53.

6 (*s. dub.*) (?) action in ecclesiastical court (ed. *Ch. Sal.* p. 381 translates 'mystery plays'; but *cf.* Chambers: *Medieval Stage* II 394).

a1228 emolumentum ~onum si que competant in villa de Linham [canonici] inter se dividant *Ch. Sal.* 104 (cf. ib. 309: ~onem..remisit).

actionalis, behaving (in a specified manner),

ut..clericos male ~es de ecclesiis expelleret OSB. *V. Dunst.* 35.

actionare v. occasionare.

†actionari, (?) to accuse, *v. et. auctionari.*

~abatur, *scirde GlC* A 134.

actionarius, a public official, 'folk-reeve'. **b** agent, perpetrator. **c** broker (*cf. auctionarius*).

a ~iis *folcgeroebum GlC* A 114; **†747** (13c) praecipio.. praefectis, praepositis et ~iis..qui in illo portu habent.. aliquam potestatem ut haec mea donatio sit stabilis *CS* 173; **748** (15c) praecipio ac precor..patriciis, ducibus, comitibus, thelonearis, ~iis ac reliquis publicis dignitatibus ut haec inoffense donatio..percurrat *CS* 177; dux [Willelmus I].. immissis †auctionariis eum [locum] a ramis et sentibus purgavit W. JUM. III 7 (= WALS. *YN* 19: †ancionariis.. ramnis). **b** **1481** indictatus est..ut principalis actor et ~ius mortis cujusdam Johannis *Sanct. Durh.* 45. **c** qui aliorum equos vendunt, quos ~ios vel *corretiers* seu *cossors* Gallici dicunt, et frequenter ab utraque parte accipiunt et mendaciis multos a quibus recipiunt precium seducunt *Latin Stories* 77.

1 actionator, a 'folk-reeve'. **b** emperor.

a ~or, *folcgerefa* ÆLF. *Gl.* **b** *an emperour*, cesar ..imperator, ..~or *CathA*.

2 actionator v. auctionator. actis v. acte.

actitare [CL; v. et. accitare 2], to practise, perform, transact. **b** to make. **c** (p. ppl. as sb. n.) act, transaction.

Dunstanus, qui prius..vitam solitariam monachus ~arat W. MALM. *GP* II 191; **s1095** sensit in his Anselmus nimis implicitum negotium ~atum contra se EADMER *HN* 81; nisi [i.e. accipitris]..curam..solicitus ~abat GIR. *EH* I 4; **1238** quo..presente et consentiente hec omnia fuerant ~ata *Ch. Sal.* 247; **1285** coram me..acta seu †actita [? l. actitata] sunt infrascripta *RGasc* II 245; **1355** in actis ~atis et habitis coram nobis *MunCOx* 134; rogatus..quod..de bellis ..modo chronico aliquid ~arem *Eul. Hist. proem* I 2. **b** **†974** (13c) confestim truncatis lignis capellam ibi pulchro ~ari opere praecepit *CS* 1310 (cf. ib. 1311: †accitari). **c** recapitulando ejus [abbatis Thome, cessit 1399] ~ata, notifico quod tres magnas campanas..fecit *Meaux* III 273; **1425** salvis nobis registris, actis et ~is coram vobis durante vacacione predicta *Reg. Cant.* I 88.

2 to discuss. **b** (w. *secum*) to think over.

s1174 cujus esset preferendus assensus..diutius ~atum est DICETO *YH* I 388; de pace nostra fuerat ~atum H. Bos. *Ep.* 1242. **b** ut..me ad me colligens inciperem mecum aliquid utile ~are AILR. *Spec. Char.* 34 p. 542; si tecum super hiis ~averis, facile tibi valet occurrere *Dial. Scac.* II 2B.

3 to 'enact', bind by act of court (Scot.).

a1513 idem A. ~avit se in libro actorum curie consistorialis Glasguensis *Lib. Prot.* II no. 129; **1539** l li. pro quibus David H. ~atus existit quondam J. archiepiscopo *Rent. S. Andr.* 50.

1 †activare, to energize (*cf. actuare*).

quidam .autumati sunt..in auro virtutem nutritivam aliqualiter inserere, ut sic suo modo pullulet et germinet; hoc..nihil aliud est quam ipsas seminarias rationes ~are in virtutes radicis M. SCOT. *Sol & Luna* 715.

2 activare v. attingere 8c.

active, a actively. **b** in an active sense (gram.).

a Joseph velut ovis deducitur, qui vadit de virtute in virtutem, simplex, ~e, velut ovis de pascuis ad pascua AD. SCOT. *Serm.* VI 129D; **1305** auctoritatem..judicaturas et..alia..officia..administrandi ~e et passive *RGasc* III 446; ille qui..reddit se suspectum de crimine, scandalizat infirmos ~e OCKHAM *Dial.* 464; tam ~e quam passive symoniacus est capitalis hereticus WYCL. *Sim.* II 25; persone quarum requiritur consilium aut auxilium ~e seu cooperative ad aliquid faciendum PAUL. ANGL. *ASP* 1539. **b** intellectus predicatur ~e vel passive GILB. VI 243 v. 1; **1285** cum..verbum illud 'placitet'.. ~e interpretatur et passive *BBC* (*Yarmouth*) 154.

activitas, activity. **b** chemical action.

hec ~as intellectus a virtute immediate procedit; ..~as namque, que est in forma increata, idem ipsum et idem re et ratione quod virtus est *Ps.*-GROS. 381; perfeccius est communicare homini aliquam ~atem respectu sue perfeccionis consequende quam non communicare DUNS *Sent. prol.* i 18; [voluntas] cum sit determinate entitatis, videtur similiter determinate ~atis BRADW. *CD* 448B; en Jacob laboris, qui, moram faciens pro Rachele, Lye laboriosam ~atem non despexit *NLA* (*J. Bridl.*) II 77. **b** per ~atem illorum acetorum subtiliantur et depurantur omnes superfluitates partium (M. SCOT. *Alch.*) *Med. Cult.* 156.

activus [CL], active, devoted to action. **b** (sb. m.) man of action. **c** (sb. f.) active life.

in crescente ad homines luna vitae nobis activae, in reversa vero ad caelos speculativae, typus ostenditur BEDE *TR* 64 p. 289; videbatur abbas ~am vitam magis diligere quam contemplativam BRAKELOND 131V.; occupatio vite ~e sepe est occasio diminucionis actus diligendi Deum OCKHAM *Pol.* II 456. **b** recognovi..me esse miserum ~um WYCL. *Ver.* I 347; hic [Nicholaus VI 1447–55] fuit.. totus ~us *Eul. Hist. Cont. B* I 291. **c** contemplativa cum activa [v.l. contemplacio accione] gaudia sua miscet R. BURY *Phil.* 5. 75.

2 a active, generating action. **b** active (gram.). **c** dramatic.

a indolis activa placuit, passiva laborum / paupertas, vitii declinativa HANV. VI 334; resolvit eos virtus activa caloris NECKAM *DS* VI 97; dicuntur prime due [qualitates, sc. caliditas et frigiditas] principaliter ~e, non quia ille tantum agant, quia passive similiter agunt BART. ANGL. IV 1; principium ~um DUNS (v. actuabilis); nulla quantitas et per consequens nullum tempus est de genere ~orum WYCL. *Act.* II 1. **b** futuri temporis participia..venientia ..ab ~o..et neutro, ut 'fugiturus, ..habiturus' ALDH. *PR* 135; 'partio', 'populo'..~o genere non numquam proferuntur; ipsa communis generis verba saepius inveniuntur 'partior', 'populor' BEDE *Orth.* 2797; omnis ~a potest converti in passivam BACON XV 61; modus significandi ~us est modus sive proprietas vocis ab intellectu sibi concessa, qua mediante vox proprietatem rei significat (DUNS *Gram. Spec.* I 45A) *GLA* III 216 n. 130. **c** [poematos genus] dramaticon est vel ~um in quo persone loquentes introducuntur sine poetae interlocutione BEDE *Met.* 2381.

acto v. alcoto.

†actolicum, *f.l.* in corrupt passage (*Pri. Cold.* 200).

actomuus v. attonitus. actona v. alcoto.

actor [CL], agent, doer. **b** author (of book; *cf. auctor*).

si Deus..agens et ~or, faciens et factor, non jam proprie sed modo quodam translationis nominatur ERIUG. *Per.* 513A. **b** hoc..patet per ~orem Sex Principiorum BACON XIII 240; solum hoc dicit ~or [sc. Physicorum] *Ib.* 347; tota philosophia et ~ores clamant quod solum sunt decem predicamenta *Id.* III 292.

2 agent (on behalf of another): **a** town-reeve; **b** (eccl.).

a s912 obiit Aðulf in Norðhymbriis oris, qui tum praeerat ~ori oppidi Bebbanburgh condicto ÆTHELW. IV 4; villicus vel ~or vel curator, ..*tungerefa* ÆLF. *Gl.* **b** 1219 si non admittantur tanquam veri procuratores, ..eosdem admitti volumus ut ~ores *Pat* 197; c1250 quod nemo religiosus.. vel clerici..~ores vel administratores..in negociis secularibus fiant *Reg. Aberd.* II 13; 1445 nostros veros et legitimos procuratores, ~ores, factores, sindicos *Cart. Osney* IV 126.

3 plaintiff (esp. civil and canon law).

libellus iste ab ~ore judici tradatur RIC. ANGL. *Summa* 7; 1205 procurator episcopi, quum esset reus a re.., immo et a reatu.., ~or effectus est *Chr. Evesham* 151; c1250 in processibus causarum tam ~or quam reus..juramentum.. prestent corporale *Stat. Cantab.* 209; 12.. si canonice monitus non destiterit, ~or a jure siquid sibi competat cadat; reus, si consenciat, pro convicto habeatur *Conc. Scot.* II 20; 1253 controversia inter dominum T. ..~orem..ex una parte et..abbatem et conventum..ex altera ..coram justiciar' Scocie *Reg. Aberbr.* I 226; ne ipse rex per seipsum vel justiciarios suos sine paribus ~or sit et judex BRACTON 119b; 1259 officialis..prefatam mulierem ab impeticione prefati W. ~oris..diffinitive absolvit *Cl* 19; 1269 de querelis factis non poterit aliquid relaxari nisi ex consensu ~oris vel rei *CBaron* 79; rex [Willelmus II], causam este veram.. autumans, ~orem..tuebatur FORDUN V 22.

actornare v. attornare.

actrix, a agent, author (f.). **b** (w. *pars*) plaintiff.

a semper amans crimen fuit hec, actrixque ruine GOWER *VC* I 763. **b** cum ipse rex pars ~ix esse debeat in judicio BRACTON 119b; c1350 si pars ~ix contra hanc formam venerit, cadat a causa; ..si vero pars rea contra formam venerit, ..habebitur pro non defensata *StatOx* 91; 1392 processus cujusdam placiti..inter J. S. partem ~icem et J. C. partem ream *SelPlAdm* I 2; 1427 dominus W. ..pars ~ix pretensa ex parte una et magister J. ..pars rea pretensa ex altera *FormOx* 458.

actuabilis, able to be actualized.

principium activum, non in quantum est activum acti sed in quantum actu activum ~is DUNS *Metaph.* IX 4 p. 131D; omne quod est unius disposicionis et potest esse opposite, hoc potest per aliquam mutacionem, loquendo de potencia ~i et non penitus absoluta BRADW. *CD* 756D.

actualis, active, concerned with or involving action. **b** (of sin).

in practicae conversationis studio, quam ~em vocitamus ALDH. *VirgP.* 14; a690 ~em rigidae conversationis regulam *Id. Ep.* 4 481; contemplativam vitam in ~i agens *V. Cuthb.* III. 1; ~is nostra conversatio in duabus maxime virtutibus consistit, misericordia videlicet et innocentia BEDE *Tab.* I 6; ~is imaginatio, continuata per librum, actum intellectus super visas veritates non sustinet interrumpi R. BURY *Phil.* 2. 36; 1348 volentes dictos nuncios..ab injuriis.. ~ibus et verbalibus..preservare *RScot* 714b. **b** 640 homines cum peccato originali nascentes..etiam sine ~i peccato existentes (*Lit. Papae*) BEDE *HE* II 19; c1219 duplex est peccatum, originale quod absque consensu contrahitur et ~e quod committitur cum consensu *Conc. Syn.* 67.

2 actual (opp. to potential). **b** current, effective at the time. **c** (of possession).

sonus consonantis non habet esse in auditu et extra os nisi per sonum vocalis ~em GROS. 10; hoc verbum 'dividi'.. significat ~em divisionem corporis in puncta omnia, quod est impossibile BACON *Tert.* 132; de materia et forma.. contingit loqui..alio modo quantum ad esse ~e et quantum ad proximam potentiam *Id.* VII 14; vocant eum [Deum Patrem] memoriam ~issimam, semper gignentem actu sapienciam vel noticiam sibi parem; et illa est Filius WYCL. *Form.* 174; c1363 idem est esse ~e esse et esse ~e; ergo omne esse ~e absolute necessario est (KYN.) *Ziz.* 77. **b** 1321 post lectionum resumpcionem ~em *StatOx* 119. **c** 1479 servicium sive capellaniam in realem, ~em et corporalem possessionem ejusdem induximus *Reg. Dunferm.* 462 (cf. *Entries* 527).

actualitas, actuality (opp. to potentiality).

sua simplicitas non compatitur multitudinem ex ~ate proveniente[m] GROS. 122; sumitur actus ibi..pro ~ate, que opponitur potentie BACON *Tert.* 125; ad racionem generis requiritur quod multas habeat actu species..et quod actu habeant aptitudinem participiandi genus, quia talis ~as est illorum in quantum dicuntur species generis DUNS *Univ.* xviii 5; hoc verbum 'est' significat substanciam, id est ~atem substancie T. SUTTON *Quaest.* xxvi 35; ~as summa Dei per hoc specialiter demonstratur quod actus est melior et perfectior potentia BRADW. *CD* 4B; possibilitas rei non probat fundationem sed ~as J. BURY *Glad. Sal.* 594.

actualiter, in act, actually (opp. to potentially).

terra potentialiter in se sicca est, frigida vero ~er D. MORLEY 20; vapor est humidus ~er vel accidentaliter, in se virtutes minerales retinens M. SCOT. *Sol & Luna* 716; 1236 [Christus] actum..judicandi de temporalibus dumtaxat fugit.., monstrans in hoc principes ecclesie..non debere..temporalium judicia ~er exercere GROS. *Ep.* 23 p. 93; est humor quedam substancia ~er liquida BART. ANGL. IV 6; hec universalis 'omnis homo loquitur ~er' est possibilis et potest poni in esse BACON *Tert.* 133; concedit omne intuitum a Deo esse ~er, id est ~er et vere cognosci (KYN.) *Ziz.* 95; c1520 quamvis..merito poterat ad eorum deprivationes a suis beneficiis..ac ad alias pergraves penas ..procedere eosque ~er deprivare et punire (*Syn. S. Andr.*) *Conc. Scot.* I cclxxi.

2 currently, w. effect at the time. **b** (of possession).

1291 magister T. ..in decretis et magister J. ..in artibus apud Oxoniam ~er tunc regentes (*Reg. Linc.*) *EHR* XXVI 505; c1300 fratribus A. B. et C. ad studium generale Oxonie transmissis et in eodem ~er studentibus *Lit. Cant.* I 5; c1350 bachilarii cursorie legentes seu ~er determinantes *StatOx* 24; c1350 duo magistri arcium ~er regentes rectores ..eligantur *Stat. Cantab.* 316; 1424 in visitacione nostra.. per nos ~er exercita *Cart. Boarstall* no. 130. **b** 1458 ecclesias parrochiales..prefatis licenciato et bacallario.. assignatas et ab eisdem ~er possessas *Mon. Hib. & Scot.* 409b.

actuare [cf. activare], to actualize, bring from potentiality into actuality.

ista [potencia] summe ~ata, quare non ~atur alia? DUNS *Metaph.* V 7 p. 56D; omne de se potenciale, si debeat ~ari, hoc necessario erit per aliquem actum non immediate exterius sed omniquaque interius ~antem atque formantem BRADW. *CD* 162D; sicud materia prima non potest esse de Dei potencia, nisi ~ata fuerit vel formata WYCL. *Form.* 207.

actuarius [CL], (?) sort of ship. **b** amanuensis, registrar.

~ius, *wraec* [? sc. *scip*] *GlC* A 135. **b** †~iis [l. ~ius], acta qui facit *Ib.* 170; Origenes..cui velox adeo ingenium.. fuisse perhibent ut vix septem ~ii sibi invicem succedentes viro satis essent dictanti BOECE 89v; 1533 presens..instrumentum..per notarios, ..scribas et ~ios nostros [sc. archiepiscopi Cant.]..subscribi..jussimus *Conc.* III 760.

actuatio, actualization.

tunc est lepra actualis ~one materie vel forme GAD. 46. 1; privacio ~onis anime non repugnat formaliter risibilitati set vite hominis; verumptamen efficienter repugnat, cum facit privacionem risibilitatis WYCL. *Ente* 226.

actuativus, able to actualize.

racio hic posita, sc. transmutativum esse, non convenit proprie active potencie stricte sumpte; racio tamen metaphysica, sc. ~um esse, vere sibi convenit; nam actus secundus, secundum quod sic actuabile in actu per ipsum, vere est actus et perfectus, licet non talis quod sit proprie transmutacionis terminus DUNS *Metaph.* IX 4 p. 551.

actum v. agere 8.

actuosus, practical.

[genus vivendi] ex utroque temperatum, viz. ~o, quod exercet veram caritatem, et otioso AD. MARSH *Ep.* 77; scientie..~e, quarum finis principalis est non ut sciamus sed ut boni fiamus *Ps.*-GROS. 300.

actus [CL], **a** right of way (for driving). **b** cart road.

a tenenentum..in quo unus liberum tenementum habeat, et alius communiam pasture.., tertius iter et ~um *Fleta* 272. **b** ~us, *anes wænes gangweg* ÆLF. *Gl.*

2 act. **b** (qualified by gen.). **c** (pl.) Acts of the Apostles. **d** dramatic action.

peccata remittat / actibus aut dictis seu solo noxia sensu! ALDH. *VirgV.* 2826; rex..natu nobilis, quamlibet ~u ignobilis BEDE *HE* II 15; quae laude sunt digna in ejus ~ibus laudans *Ib.* III 17; differt etiam..siquid in ~u vel in sola tihla consistat (*Leg. Hen.*) *GAS* 555; s1183 mores antecessorum et ~us imitari non cessant DICETO *YH* II 17; s1318 constantem in omnibus suis ~ibus se habuit *Ann. Paul.* 284; in isto ~u intendo duo facere (KYN.) *Ziz.* 4; 1384 quociens cogniciones armorum in ~ibus bellicis.. ostendere voluerint *Pat* 317 m. 16. **b** genera et species.. in yle per potenciam fuerunt que postea ~u generationis prodierunt D. MORLEY 11 (cf. 3 infra); a1350 scrutatores.. jurent quod ~um eleccionis sine fraude exequentur *Stat. Cantab.* 314. **c** Praxapostolon, hoc est ~us Apostolorum ALDH. *Met.* 2 p. 70; fames..quae in ~ibus Apostolorum praedicta esse memoratur BEDE *HE* I 3; de quo ~uum octavo narratur R. BURY *Phil.* 15. 203. **d** contigit ut tempore quodam estivo intra septa polyandri ecclesie B. Johannis..larvatorum..et verbis et ~u fieret representacio Domini resurreccionis *Mir. J. Bev.* C 328.

3 official act: **a** process in court of law; **b** Parliamentary statute; **c** study or advancement at university, esp. inception.

a arbitrium est ~us legitimus personarum super civili questione et querela quasi in judicio contendentium *RegiamM* II 2; 1231 ei sicut excommunicato omnis ~us legitimus est interdictus *CurR* XIV 1358; 1321 debent recordare..consuetudines suas antiquas..quandocumque aliquid in ~u seu questione cadat coram quibuscumque justiciariis quod tangat consuetudines..predictas (*Eyre*) *MGL* II 313; 1426 ordinavit suum..procuratorem..ad.. testes..producendum..et ad quoscumque alios terminos sive ~us judiciales..procedendum *Reg. Cant.* I 238. **b** 1456 aliquo ~u sive ordinacione per Parliamentum..non obstante (*Billa Parl.*) *Reg. Whet.* I 252; 1457 prout in quodam ~u inde in dicto Parliamento facto plenius apparet *Lit. Cant.* III 226; quod rex [per] decretum parliamenti sui leges suas examinari faciat et cum ~ibus parliamenti per viros..juris peritos collacionari *Plusc.* VII 19. **c** 1269 contingit magistros et scolares..impediri, ita quod ~us scolasticos in quiete..nequeunt exercere *BBC* (*Cambridge*) 163; 1330 in ~ibus studialibus proficere J. MASON *Ep.* 78; 1327 ad omnem gradum et ~um scholasticum..inhabilis habeatur *StatOx* 130; 1379 in omni ~u qui non est incepcio *Ib.* 176; 1358 quod nunquam exerceret ~um doctoratus in universitate *MunAcOx* 209; effectus magister in artibus, cum laudabiliter ~us ipsi gradui incumbentes perfecisset *G. S. Alb.* II 299; scolastica dogmata cum ceteris ~ibus continue exercentur ad sciencie incrementum BLAKMAN *Hen. VI* 12; 1527 doctor in sacra theologia in ultimo ~u creatus (*Reg. Acad.*) *Grey Friars Ox.* 339.

4 actuality (opp. to potentiality). **b** (abl.) actually or currently. **c** form (ἐντελέχεια).

aliquid quod nec ~u nec intellectu dissolvi posset ANSELM (*Incarn.* A) II 18; cum id quod nihil in ~u rerum est se videre mentiantur ADEL. *ED* 7; cum in ~u rerum subsistentiam universalium querere exiguus fructus sit J. SAL. *Pol.* 438D; causa quare aliquid quod est in potentia nondum egreditur ad ~um est defectus alicujus conditionis ex parte agentis vel ex parte patientis GROS. 101; mediante calore nobilissime species et forme..de potencia ad ~um producuntur BART. ANGL. IV 1; ~us tripliciter accipitur: uno modo pro forma, secundum quod Aristoteles dicit secundo De Anima quod 'anima est ~us corporis', id est forma; ~us aliter sumitur pro operatione, ab hoc verbo 'agere' dictus, et sic vocatur ab A. '~us secundus' (nam forma est ~us primus..); tertio opponitur potentie, secundum quod dicit sepe quod ~us et potentia sunt opposita; et sic accipitur pro actualitate, secundum quod dicimus rem esse in ~u, id est actualitate, existendi BACON *Tert.* 125; terminata presencia in aere luminis facit ~um lucidum, absencia vero tenebrosum BAD. AUR. 105 (cf. BART. ANGL. XIX 7); ut sue feditatis corrupte intentum sub velamine sanctitatis in ~um produceret ELMH. *Hen. V* 6. **b** c1301 si potencia causaret, idem respectu ejusdem esset ~u et potencia (*Quaest. Ox.*) *Ox. Hist. Soc.* XCV 349; 1338 sacre theologie doctorem..~u regentem *FormOx* 102; 1425 omnes servientes mei ~u domestici et commensales *Reg. Cant.* II 351; 1460 qui..Bononie ~u studet de canonicatu *Mon. Hib. & Scot.* 454; 1471 cum muris..~u existentibus (*Instr. Sasine*) *Scot. Grey Friars* II 216. **c** Deus est ~us purus (PECKHAM) *Powicke Studies* 279; BACON (v. 3a supra); est duplex ~us, primus et secundus DUNS *Metaph.* I *prol.* 2B.

actutum [CL], immediately.

dum..gratatur sospite nato, / actutum scaevis reddunt direpta rapinis ALDH. *VirgV.* 1492; hujus magnificis actutum vultibus almus / offertur FRITH. 67; 10.. ~um, *sona* WW; pergat aliquis ~um et dicat domino regi quatinus sibi sine cunctatione provideat GIR. *PI* III 14.

acualis, needle-shaped (fig.), diminishing at the extremities.

pulsus tunc non erit sicut cauda soricina; sed erit ~is ad modum cultelli sutorum, parvus scilicet in extremitatibus et gracilis et in medio plus elevatus et grossior GAD. 22. 1.

1 acuare [cf. acuere], to whet. **b** to sour, make pungent.

c1357 pro stoneaxes..~andis *Ac. Durh.* 560. **b** cerotum resolutionis amoniaci aceto ~atum GILB. VI 264. 1; 1307 pro unguentis ~atis cum pulveribus castorii..et cum pulvere eufurbeo (*KRAc* 368/30) *EHR* LXVII 174.

2 acuare, ~ium, ~ia, needle-case.

habet in foro ista vendenda ante se: acus et ~ia (*gl. nedylcasys*) GARL. *Dict.* 123; ~ium, A. *an agulere*, ..hec aguaria, A. *nedylhows*, ..hoc ~e, *a nedylhows* WW.

acuarius, (?) needler.

a1200 in vico ~iorum *Cart. Worc.* 402; 12.. Godefridus ~ius *Cart. St. Thomas Hosp.* no. 150.

acuatio [cf. acuitio], whetting, sharpening.

1316 custus carucarum: . . in xxj ~onibus ferramentorum, vij d. *MinAc* 1132/13 B 9*d*.; **1327** pro ~one et *layng'* de *lez stoneaxez KRAc* 482/10 m. 3; **c1360** in emendacione et ~one securium *Fabr. York* 2; **1490** pro accuacione *lez pikkes* et *chesels Ac. Durh.* 99.

acub v. alzubd. acub- v. accub-.

†acucula [cf. acula (*Du. C.*)], exile, outlawry.

an exile, . . *an outelawry*, ~a, exilium *CathA*.

acuere [CL; cf. acuare], to whet, sharpen, make protuberant. **b** (fig.).

ungues falconum. . ad instar cavanorum ~untur Aldh. *VirgP.* 58 p. 318; ferrum cos acuit Neckam *DS* III 233; **1212** pro tribus molendinis ad ~endas secures *Pipe* 88; in ferris carucarum ~endis *FormMan* 32; superficies. . exterior non est omnino spherica, quia aliquantulum ~itur in anteriori parte Bacon *Maj.* II 22. **b** hoc argumento velut quibusdam cotibus ingenia ~untur Aldh. *Met.* 10 p. 82; spicula jaciant, non linguas accuant H. Los. *Ep.* 6 p. 7; ~at attendendi necessitas industriam Balsh. *AD* 29; oratores. . quibus. . ~enda precipue sunt arma facundie Gir. *TH intr.* p. 6.

2 to sharpen (taste), make pungent.

1220 pisces / post carnes acuunt gustum renovantque saporem H. Avr. *Poems* 2. 242; ~e medicinam Gilb. II 96 v. 2.

3 to accent.

peon primus et secundus. . ante paenultimam ~ere accentum. . compelluntur Aldh. *PR* 135; inde est quod differentia constituitur inter Vetus et Novum Testamentum: . . hujus etiam lectio in fine, in signum hujus rei, ~itur; illius vero lectio deprimitur Gir. *GE* II 25 (cf. ib. 36: penultimam ~endo); omnia Greca. . fere male accentuantur, unde. . sepe 'obelus'. . ~itur penultima, cum tamen debet gravari, quia in Greco scribitur per ε breve Bacon *Tert.* 236.

4 (p. ppl.) sharp, pointed. **b** acute (geom.). **c** pungent (acid or alkaline). **d** acute (accented) or treble (high-pitched). **e** acute, intense, painful (cf. 5 *infra*). **f** keen, shrewd (or requiring shrewdness).

semper acuta gero crudelis spicula belli Aldh. *Aen.* 20 (*Apis*) 4; rostra recurva et ~ta Gir. *TH* I 12; lappa. . cujus species duplex, ~ta et rotunda Bart. Angl. XVII 93; elleborus albus habet folia similia plantaginis, sed longiora et ~tiora *SB* 18; mirta agrestis. . folia habet. . ~ta in fine *Alph.* 119; **1303** pro. . bordis et petris ~tis [? *pointed stones or whetstones*; cf. acutorius] *EEC* 300. **b** de angulo ~to vel obtuso Gir. *GE* II 37. **c** de sapore ~to Bart. Angl. XIX 44; magis opponitur dulci ~tus quam amarus. ., quoniam amarus est extremum et ~tus est medium Bacon XIV 87; calcem. . aquis alkali et aliis aquis ~tis purifica *Id. N.M* 545. **d** si paenultima positione producitur, ~tum accentum habebit Aldh. *PR* 124; cum et musici cantores paucis caracteribus multas ~tarum et gravium differentias indicent vocum J. Sal. *Met.* 850D; 'pelicanus'. . habet penultimam ~tam Bacon *Tert.* 236 (cf. ib. 242: unus ~tus accentus non est alio ~tior); unisoni sunt quorum sonus unus est vel in gravi vel in ~to Tunst. 204b (cf. ib. 229b: modus ~tus); quando cantus planus sive tenor est gravis, contrapunctus sive discantus cantare debet ~tum Hothby 333. **e** s1119 ~ta passione subito percussus obmutuit Ord. Vit. XII 31; natura. . excitavit febrem ~tam H. Hunt. *HA* VII 43; sinantis interpretatur ~tissima prefocatio; inde quinancia ~ta prefocacio et squinancia minus ~ta *SB* 39; ungula caballina. . valet in febribus ~tis *Alph.* 193. **f** 10. . cautus, i. sagax, providus, ~tus *wær* WW; visu. . ~to W. Cant. *Mir. Thom.* II 79 (v. 2 acus 1a); gens ~ta minus sed robusta magis Gir. *TH* I 37; si sis subtilis rethor causis in acutis D. Bec. 1503.

5 (p. ppl. as sb. f.) acute fever, ague (cf. 4e *supra*).

prius passus in oculis, postea in ~tam incidi; tertiana successit ~te P. Blois *Ep.* 110 333C; nemo. . ulla trium generum specie febricitavit: sola vexantur ~ta Gir. *TH* I 33; cum calor resolvit spiritus et humores. ., ut in ethicis et ~tis et morti vicinantibus Gilb. II 106 v. 2; laborat in ~ta Bracton 150; etiam vulgus medicorum hoc percipit in regimine ~tarum Bacon IX 168.

acuitas, sharpness, pointedness. **b** pungency. **c** acuteness (of accent) or sharpness (of pitch). **d** acuteness, intensity.

consolidativa [oculi] non habet perfectam sphericitatem exterius. .; tendit enim in suo anteriori ad ~atem Bacon *Maj.* II 22. **b** si causarum efficientium mediocritas posset aptari, tunc ~as sequeretur dulcedinem, deinde ponticitas, et in punto medio stipticitas *Id.* XIV 97; dissolvatur in aqua acuta temperate ~atis *Id. NM* 546. **c** non auferetur aliquid de ~ate syllabe sequentis *Id. Tert.* 243; ars musice completur per adjunctionem sonorum secundum proportionem communicantem eos inter ~atem et gravitatem per circulos casuum temporum que sunt inter eorum percussiones *Ps.*-Ric. *Anat.* 24. **d** cum aliquis calor est major in ~ate alio calore J. Blund *An.* 175; si. . obviet tibi, cum ipsum tangis, caliditas multe ~atis Gad. 4. 1.

acuitio [v. et. acuatio], whetting, sharpening. **b** intensification.

1433 fabro pro ~one et fabricacione diversorum instrumentorum cementariorum *Fabr. York* 50. **b** spei et caritatis ex libertate ~o Wycl. *Ver.* III 133.

aculare, needle-case.

1288 agulare cum acu et filo *MinAc Essex* (*Little Dunmow*).

aculeare, to prick, goad (fig.). **b** (p. ppl.) armed with a sting or spine.

ventrem [Edgithe]. ., qui nulla sit ~eatus unquam libidine W. Malm. *GR* II 218. **b** s793 pagani ab aquilonali climate. . ut ~eati crab[r]ones venientes S. Durh. *HR* c. 56; [delphinum] ~eate sunt pinne dorsales Wals. *HA* II 204.

aculeosus, goading (fig.).

c1430 hic est ~us ille stimulus. . qui Antonium invasit in heremo *Reg. Whet.* II 460.

aculeus [CL], **~eum**, prick, sting, or sim. **b** hedgehog's prickle.

a690 dum acutis spinarum ~eis. . coronatur Aldh. *Ep.* 4 p. 483; de ~eis [? *tick-bites or ticks*] quos [accipiter] patitur, quod est cum uvariam explumat, quid disseres? carnem pulli cum pulvere satureie da ei, et morientur Adel. *CA* 12; exiguo scorpionis ~eo exagitatus occiditur Gir. *TH* I 27. **b** s1192 regis. . corpus circumquaque fuit obsitum pilis creberrimis infixis, sicut hericius ~eis *Itin. Ric.* VI 23.

2 goad, spike. **b** spike used as candlestick. **c** tip of shoe.

aquilium, *onga GlC* A 145; ~eus, *sticel* vel *gadisen Ælf. Gl.*; acus. . gutturi inhesit; . . quum nec evomere nec introrsus trahere impingentem ~eum valeret. . Gosc. *Mir. Iv.* lxii; **1191** ~eo pungebantur quem dominus pre manibus habebat (*Lit. Ep. Coventr.*) R. Howd. III 142; si agasonis. . officium explere velit, aculeo [*gl. agulyun*] fruatur Neckam *Ut.* 108; s1255 innumeris †eculeis pungentibus. . corpus ejus punxerunt *Meaux* II 134; hic aculius, *a brad* WW; **1546** pro duobus spiculis vel ~eis ferreis *Arch. Hist. Camb.* III 296*n*. **b** **1232** fieri faciat in capella. . unam albam perticam ex transverso capelle cum ~eis ligneis distantibus j pede adinvicem et similiter circum altare ejusdem capelle cum ~eis consimilibus ad figendum in eis cereos *Liberate* 10 m. 11. **c** tunc [temp. Willelmi II] usus calceorum cum arcuatis ~eis inventus W. Malm. *GR* IV 314.

3 prick, goad (fig.).

1253 erga nos cornua superbie et indignacionis ~ium crescebunt *RGasc* I 321; ~ei dolorum gementum (*sic*) viscera perfoduint Elmh. *Hen. V Cont.* 160.

1 acumen v. acrumen.

2 acumen, point. **b** pungency, intensity. **c** keenness of sight or intelligence.

venenosum spina sortitur ~en Gir. *TH* I 23; habent †spatula duo ~ina retro Bart. Angl. V 26; †mitammus, i. ~en spinarum habens *Alph.* 118. **b** causa intensionis et ~inis in sono J. Blund *An.* 173; **a1205** continuati incendii ~ine urebatur *Canon. G. Sempr.* 158; fuit substancia ejus [vesice] dura, ne ~ine urine. . lederetur Bart. Angl. V 44; [claretum] a vino contrahit fortitudinem et ~en *Ib.* XIX 54; caloris ~en. . temperatur *Ib.* V 3. **c** ingenii. . ~en Eriug. *Per.* 545C; cum. . credere non possent quod patentibus oculis ~en visionis inesset Osb. *Mir. Dunst.* 6; cum ad legendum. . utilia mentis intendit ~en J. Sal. *Pol.* 386A; ad superum lumen hinc erige mentis acumen Serlo Wilt. *App.* IV 1. 41; tanto visus ~ine Upton IV 172.

acuminatus, pointed. **b** ridged.

~is instar pyramidum tenebris lunam. . obscurari Bede *TR* 7. **b** tectum tabernaculi non ~um sed planum ad modum domorum Palestine fuit Ad. Scot *TT* 674A; ~as carinas, canabea vela reppererunt, omnia denique nostris similia More *Ut.* 31.

acupare v. acculpare.

acuperium, whetstone.

1393 [5 *dozen*] ~ia (*Ac. Cust.*) *Bronnen* 732B (16); hoc ~ium, *a wheston* WW.

acupictor, embroiderer.

~or, A. *a broderer* WW; **1562** Willelmo M. aucupictore *Ac. LChamb.* 55 f. 29; **1563** ~or (*SPDom* 48/47) *Huguenot Soc.* X 289.

acupictus [al. div.], embroidered. **b** (sb. f.) embroidered garment, 'jack' (sleeveless tunic).

erat. . velum. . opere plumario compositum, id est ~o: pluma enim lingua quadam acus dicitur Ad. Scot. *TT* 673B; s1422 solenne vestimentum operis ~i vocatum Jesse. . fecit operari *Croyl. Cont. B* 515. **b** acu picta vel frigia, *gediht* vel *gesiwed hrægel Ælf. Gl.*; **14..** hec ~a, *a jak of fens* WW.

acurare, acurtare, v. accur-. acurtinare v. accortinare. açurum v. azurum.

1 acus [CL], husk, chaff.

anseribus acera [*gl.*: *curayles*] substernat Neckam *Ut.* 101; quando. . frumentum nichil habebit acuris (*sic*)? W. Dan. *Ep.* 76; vendunt. . panes. . de avena, de acere et frequenter de furfure Garl. *Dict.* 127.

2 acus [CL], needle. **b** magnetic needle. **c** stylus. **d** pin or brooch. **e** obelisk. **f** (fig.) point, sharpness.

acus exilis Aldh. *Aen.* 29. 3; acus, *netl GlC* A 160; unde sutori subula sive sartori acus [AS: *nædl*]? Ælf. *Coll.* 99; visu. . in tantum acuto ut per foramen acus filum trahere posset W. Cant. *Mir. Thom.* II 79; ut non minus subtiliter quam alie mulieres acu suere consueverit Gir. *IK* II 11; s1192 culcitra acu variata operosa *Itin. Ric.* VI 3 (= Bromton 1245: acuvariata); **1410** pro filo et acubus *Ac. Durh.* 609. **b** habeat acum jaculo suppositam [v.l. superpositam]; rotabitur enim et circumvolvetur acus donec cuspis acus respiciat orientem [v.l. septentrionem], sicque comprehendunt quo tendere debeant naute cum cynosura latet Neckam *Ut.* 114; per calamitam scitur ubi est tramontana cum acu (M. Scot. *Part.*) *Med. Sci.* 294. **c** acum vero graphium, tabulas et cultellulum. . a. . vestiario. . recipiant monachi *Cust. Cant.* 401. **d** **1222** ne [moniales] in velo acus argenteas vel aureas audeant deportare *Conc. Syn.* 118; **1294** tres acus ad pallium de puro auro *Invent. Ch. Ch. Cant.* 5 (cf. ib. 7); **1461** unum tonellum de acubus capitis (*Chanc. Proc.*) *Prejudice & Promise* 186. **e** tale Rome visitur, in quo positi sunt cineres Julii Cesaris, vocaturque acus S. Petri Beleth *RDO* 159 157; in summitate columne solide quadrate, . . que quondam Julia vocata fuit, nunc acus B. Petri vulgo nuncupatur Gir. *PI* I 17; duo lapides quadri. ., quorum unus. . major est illo Rome erecto, qui a vulgaribus acus S. Petri nuncupatur S. Sim. *Itin.* 59. **f** nulloque retunditur ere / mentis acus cupide Hanv. V 317.

2 hornbeak or other fish.

acus, . . *gronuisc GlC* A 160; acus. . siccus piscis est et durus; . . *hornebeke* nostri dicunt Caius *Anim.* 26.

3 (bot.) **a** (w. *muscata*) musk storksbill (*Erodium*) conf. w. musk mallow. **b** (w. *palearis*) Christ's-thorn (*Paliurus*).

a si bruneta et acusmuscata ponantur. ., valebunt. . in omni ulcere sordido Gad. 125 v. 1; acus muscata minuta habet folia et fissa, florem indum vel subrufum. . acus muscata major, A. *pouclesnedele Alph.* 2; malva crispa, acus muscata idem, A. *poukelesnedele Ib.* 110. **b** paliurus ab aliis †actus [l. acus] paliaris vel cicer domesticum vocatur *Alph.* 136.

1 acusare, ~amentum, v. accus-.

2 acusare [cf. cusare], to stitch.

1328 item. . ij haketouns acusat' infra floryns (*Inq.*) *Proc. Rec. Comm. 1832–3* 395 (cf. ib. 399: aketons consut' infra de floreins).

†acusile, cobbler's knife (*cf. ansorium*).

14.. ~e, A. *a trenket* WW.

1 acutarius [cf. acuere 5], sufferer from ague.

dieta subtilis. . non competit sanis, sed egris ~iis Gad. 10. 2.

2 acutarius v. acutorius.

†acutatio, sharpening (*cf. acuatio*).

1409 in diversis instrumentis ferreis. . una cum emendacione et ~one eorundem (*Ac. Audit. Durh.*) *EHR* XIV 518.

acute [CL], **a** w. acute accent. **b** intensely, painfully. **c** keenly, shrewdly.

a hic *ma*, cum dicitur 'mater', longitudine sui circumflexus, tantum temporis bis occupat quantum *pa* semel cum ~e dicitur 'pater' Bede *AM* 2351. **b** ~ius perforat et vehementius incidit quia possit et sciat R. Niger *MR* 19; quid misericordie viscera penetrabit ~ius? R. Bury *Phil. prol.* 9. **c** ad ~ius intuendum Gir. *TH* II 39; artis arcana ~e discernentibus *Ib.* III 11.

acutella, (?) restharrow (*Ononis*).

ciminum Ethiopicum similis est ~e in foliis *Alph.* 40.

acuties, a sharpness. **b** acuteness (geom.). **c** point.

a aliud genus ferri magis est ad ~iem et scissionem, ut chalybs Bacon *Min.* 383; et nunc corpus est recisum / telorum acucie J. Howd. *Sal.* 31. 11; gladius. . cum sua ~ie, duricie et ceteris disponentibus ad scindendum Wycl. *Ente* 273; **1431** Christus sanguinem cordis effudit ut ~ies gladii tollatur (W. Melton *Serm.*) *Doc. Francisc.* 254. **b** propter ~iem. . angulorum Bradw. *CD* 367E; nec oportet nos sollicitari de ~ie anguli talis corporis Wycl. *Log.* III 92; **1444** capiatur. . lapis calculatorius cujus una superficies sit plana et altera superficies in altera parte sit declinans quomodo cum plana superficie causet ~iem que †~ie fiant Killingworth *Alg.* 714. **c** aquila. . in cujus rostr ~ie breve pendulum efficaciter extendit *NLA* (*J. Bridl.*) II 72.

acutorius, for whetting.

lapidem ~ium. . viro illi pernecessarium furtive abstulit R. Cold. *Cuthb.* 28; **1279** in una mola acutaria empta ad opus carpentariorum *KRAc* 467/7/7.

acutus v. acuere. acuvariatus v. 2 acus 1a.

acyrologia [ἀκυρολογία], misuse of language, catachresis.

reus acirologie Virgilius criminatur, dicens 'gramineo in campo', eo quod 'graminoso in campo' dici oportuit J. Sal. *Met.* 842D (cf. ib. 844A).

ad [*as in CL, but used more extensively, like Fr. à, esp. in place of dat. or abl.; its multiplicity of use is illustrated by the foll.*: **1395** ad inveniendum quoddam torticium ardens. . ad elevacionem corporis Christi ad omnimodas missas ad altare S. Petri *Pat* 342 m. 16. *For use w. adv.* v. et. adeo, adhuc, adinsimul, adinvicem, adstatim, adtunc, adusque].

1 (w. ref. to motion, change, or direction) **a** to (a place or object). **b** (w. other prep. or adv.). **c** to (a person). **d** to (an experience). **e** to (an office or privilege). **f** to (a rank). **g** to (the office, function, rank, or status of).

a sacellum / . . diruit ad fundum Aldh. *VirgV* 1326; ad sedes venit basterna relictas *Ib.* 1901; versis capitibus. . deorsum ad terram *V. Cuthb.* I 3; eum. . duxerunt ad locum Bede *HE* III 9; ad suam domum repedabat *Ib.* IV 24; sive ad superiora se semper intendat [angelica natura] ERIUG. *Per.* 485C; **s1117** repatriantes ad propria reversi sunt H. CANTOR 12; **s1242** acclamatum est..: 'ad arma, ad arma!' M. PAR. *Maj.* IV 213; **1313** ideo summonitor [sc. eat] ad prisonam *Eyre Kent* I 97; **1397** nulli mercenarii..portent ..mercandizas suas de ostio ad ostium, loco ad locum seu domo ad domum *Lib. Cust. Northampt.* 73 (cf. *Reg. Paisley* 11 [**1346**]: totum ipsius tenorem de verbo ad verbum transscripsi); **s1399** equitaverunt..primo ad Coventriam, .. deinde ad Dunstaple, deinde ad S. Albanum *V. Ric. II* 156; **1449** in introitu ad cellarium *Ac. Durh.* 87; **c1470** ad et in.. Domum Capitularem..accessimus *Reg. Whet.* I 11. **b** inclinacio ferri ad deorsum WYCL. *Log.* II 161; [abbas W., ob. 1396] turbariam..usque ad prope novum hospicium transferri..fecerat *Meaux* III 229; **1490** tunc navis venit ad circa placeam *Digby Plays* 126. **c** ad dominum tota conversus mente ALDH. *VirgV* 1864; ad famulum Christi scripsit *Ib.* 2154; in epistula ad regem missa BEDE *HE* II 18; dum sincere..humanus animus ad Deum perveniet ERIUG. *Per.* 534D; vertit se ad Alnod *DB* I 6; non reddunt censum ad Godric *Ib.* II 110b; **1208** nos inde ad vos capiemus sicut ad inimicos nostros *Pat* 85; **s1260** nihil vobis faciam; ite ad justiciarium *Flor. Hist.* II 451. **d** ad fidem catholicam conversus est ALDH. *VirgP* 48; ne forte properet paradisi ad gaudia *Id. VirgV* 1720; ciet ad pugnam mentes discordia fratrum *Ib.* 2627; cum ad mortem duceretur BEDE *HE* I 7; multi..ad crucis obsequium sunt allecti GIR. *TH* III 49; rupes..quam..totam ad facilem motum duxisti GERV. TILB. III 22; quicumque alium plegiaverit de stando ad rectum, ..si non habuerit eum ad rectum, ..incidet in misericordiam GLANV. X 5; ad missam audivit pulsare O. CHERITON *Fab. add.* A3; **1237** vicecomes non venit..; et ideo ad judicium *KRMem* 15 r 6*d.*; ut alterentur homines ad sanitatem BACON *Tert. Sup.* 15; **1296** adjudicati sunt ad juisam *SelPlMan* 45; **1311** filios suos..permiserunt ordinari ad primam tonsuram *Lit. Cant.* III 389; **1330** ponere filium suum ad studium (*Extent*) *Growth Eng. Indust.* 585; **1340** persequciones..que nos quasi ad interitum opprimunt *FormOx* II 303; **1392** nullo ad hoc cogente *SelCCoron* 126. **e** Waltero..electo ad episcopatum de Lincolnia BRAKELOND 133v; **1223** litteras de presentacione ad decanatum *Pat* 415; **1234** si Stephanus..presentavit ei [sc. episcopo] Willelmum ..ad ecclesiam de P. ..et ipse..ipsum admisit ad ecclesiam predictam *Cl* 536; **1309** clericum..ad competens beneficium promovere *Lit. Cant.* I 33; **s1279** coronator..usque festum SS. Innocencium..; quo die substituit loco suo ad coronam Johannem H. *MGL* II 239; **s1307** [episcopus] ad semigraciam regis recipitur TROKELOWE 64; **1390** quod possit ad dimidias communas..admitti *FormOx* 236. **f** discipulos.. ad sacerdotalem usque gradum..provexit BEDE *HE* III 5; **1440** quatinus dictum I. ad omnes sacros ordines quos nondum est assecutus..canonice ordinare velitis *FormOx* 465. **g** **796** (12c) manus Eadulf electi ad episcopum *CS* 279; revocant episcopum..ad protectorem *DB* I 1; **1221** eligatis tres viros..et nos unum ex illis tribus..vobis dabimus ad vicecomitem *Pat* 281; **1220** quod..†convincerat [l. convicerat]..Martinum ad villanum suum *CurR* VIII 216; disrationavit eum..ad nativum suum *Ib.* 322; **1232** cognoscit se ad villanum *Ib.* XIV 2349; **1235** si probatus fuerit ad nativum *Ib.* XV 1434; nullus est ad summum pontificem eligendus..OCKHAM *Dial.* 799; **1383** archiepiscopus preficiet quem voluerit ad custodem [collegii] *Lit. Cant.* II xxx.

2 (w. ref. to position) **a** at or near (a place or object). **b** (w. adj. or ppl.). **c** (w. adv.). **d** by or on (part of body). **e** within range of. **f** at (the house or church of). **g** at (an event). **h** on (a diet of). **i** at (work on). **j** in (a condition).

a in locum qui vocatur Ad Lapidem BEDE *HE* IV 16; in villam regiam quae vocatur Adgefrin [*Yeavering*] *Ib.* II 14; non habens scutum ad manum *Ib.* II 9; resederunt circa me, unus ad caput, et unus ad pedes *Ib.* V 13; ad hoc manerium erant..ii liberi homines *DB* II 24; si..in convivio sedere videatur ad calculum J. SAL. *Pol.* 726C; **1198** per libertatem sedendi ad scaccarium *Pipe* 167; **1227** mortuum boscum ad terram jacentem *Pat* 112; **1229** execucio judicii fiet..ad placeam et pillorium..episcopi *Feod. Durh.* 215; **12..** sedit ad mensam cum episcopo *Ib.* 250; **1269** dum sedebat ad prandium *SelCCoron* 13; **1279** omnes alii.. remanebunt ad domum *Hund.* II 461; **1282** nomina aldermannorum qui fuerunt ad hanc curiam (*Hustings Roll*) *Lond. Ed. I & II* II 244; abuctat ad unum capud super mesuagium *FormMan* 2; **1327** non habuit denarios ad manus..unde dictos sumptus..facere potuit *KRMem* 103 r. 268*d*; **1331** justiciarius decetero non concedat tuicionem pacis felonibus ad silvam existentibus *StatIr* I 324; **1345** tempore quo juratores fuerunt ad barram coram justiciariis *SelCKB* VI 42; **1432** personis..valentibus..expendere c li. ad universitatem *StatOx* 239. **b** **1255** si [ille tres acre] essent assartate, bestie amitterent procursus suos ad transversum foreste (*Inq.*) *Ambrosden* I 353; **1375** ubi ipse ad largum fuit et potuit se reddidisse vicecomiti *G. S. Alb.* III 207; **1325** tenemento quod R. ..inhabitat adoppositum ecclesie *FormA* 426; ad oppositum est Francho dicens.. HAUBOYS 432. **c** **1416** ita tamen quod crisma [et] oleum.. infra capellam regiam ad intra remaneant et non distribuantur ad extra *Reg. Cant.* IV 149; **1452** volumus sic vos regere quod nec retrocedet religio ad infra nec sollicitudo ad extra *Reg. Whet.* I 22; **1552** nulle omnino confirmationes ad intus et extra dentur *Conc. Scot.* II 130. **d** ad manum tractus, cum ad palatium pervenisset AILR. *Ed. Conf.* 762C; **1235** duos homines ad pedes ambulantes *CurR* XV 1359. **e** calefiant ad ignem *SB* 38; quod remanet desiccatur ad solem *Alph.* 74; [S. Germanus] jussit sculpi in pariete ad visum suum: 'V Kal. Maii' *Eul. Hist.* I 211; ad nostram non se offerunt visionem GERV. TILB. III 17; prout in pluribus monasteriis monialium..hodie vidimus ad oculum LYNDW. 212P. **f** **1229** ita quod sint apud London' ad regem *Pat* 263; **1266** sint ad nos cum equis et armis *Cl* 227; **s1216** perveniens Londonias, primo ad S. Paulum orans *Flor. Hist.* II 160. **g** **1221** fuerunt ad mortem illam et fugerunt *PlCr Glouc* 35 (cf. ib. 38: fuerunt ad occisionem illam); **1306** cum esset captus ad bellum de Rosslyn *RParl* I 193a. **h** **1219** debet falcare bis in anno..ad cibum suum proprium *CurR* VIII 150; **1264** sarclabit..per unum diem ad cibum domini *Reg. Whet.* II *app.* 324; esse debet..ad panem et aquam in quartis et sextis feriis *Cust. Westm.* 200; **1226** habebit palefridum suum ad fenum, forraginem et avenam *Reg. Linc.* II 297; **1234** quamdiu animalia fuerint ad herbam *Cust. Glast.* 103; **1290** in prebenda nichil, quia equi prius ponebantur ad herbam *Ac. Swinfield* 96; **1327** pro quolibet equo per diem et noctem per x dies quibus fuerunt ad herbam ob. quad. et per xiiij dies quibus fuerunt ad fenum j d. *LTRMem* 99 r. 120*d*. **i** **1272** tres dies operis ad fenum que valent j d. ob. *Cl* 509; **1450** operantibus ad molendinum *Ac. Durh.* 633. **j** **1242** quamdiu fuerit ad fidem et servicium *RGasc* I 46; **1254** non fuit ad fidelitatem nostram *Ib.* 350; **1262** Walensium.., qui non sunt ad fidem nec pacem regis *Pat* 77 m. 17*d*.; **1267** bene et fideliter..se habuit ad fidem nostram *Cl* 306; **1293** felo domini regis fuit et non ad pacem *RParl. Ir.* 41; **1297** cum Hybernicis ad guerram..existentibus *StatIr* I 204.

3 (w. ref. to time) **a** to, till. **b** for, during. **c** on, at, at the time of. **d** (w. adj., *sc. tempus?*). **e** (w. adv.).

a ad hanc diem curatio..celebrari non desinit BEDE *HE* I 7; a tempore matutinae laudis ad diem usque *Ib.* III 12; usque ad impletum tempus quod ipsi inter se constituerant *DB* I 172b; a festivitate S. Michaelis usque ad festum S. Andree *Ib.* I 1; ad festum S. Johannis fuit dimidius annus *Ib.* II 290; **c1217** cum [heres] ad etatem perveneri *Reg. Malm.* I 30; **1219** invadiavit..quandam partem dotis sue.. ad terminum x annorum *CurR* VIII 53; **1344** de tempore ad tempus AD. MUR. *app.* 237; **1486** continuavit..convocacionem..usque ad et in crastinum *Conc.* III 619. **b** cum ad tempus abscessissem a te BEDE *HE* V 12; ad breve tempus *Ib.* 13; ne..status ecclesiae..vel ad horam pastore destitutus vacillare inciperet *Ib.* II 4; dederunt xx naves regi una vice in anno ad xv dies *DB* I 1; **1164** excommunicati non debent dare vadium ad remanens (*Const. Clar.* 4) *Becket. Mat.* I 19; **c1250** [bedelli] vel ab officio perpetuo vel ad tempus ammoveantur *Stat. Cantab.* 209; **1269** inhibicionem..ne quid de..venacione caperetur..ad triennium *Cl* 171; **1308** percipiet per annum ad totam vitam suam x s. (*Anc. Ext.*) *DocExch* 208. **c** conveniant semper ad quatuor ebdomadas (*Quad.*) *GAS* 192; **1200** petiit eam [curiam] ad horam et terminum *CurR* I 337; **1219** ad diem illum venit abbas et petiit terram suam per plevinam ad horam *Ib.* VIII 12; **1256** capiat diem..ad quem eis inde plenarie possit satisfacere *Cl* 3; ad quatuor anni terminos, viz. ad festum S. Michaelis.., ad Nativitatem Domini.., ad Pascha, ..ad nativitatem S. Johannis Baptiste *FormMan* 27; **1327** ad gulam Augusti *LTRMem* 99 r. 40; **1511** ad xiij annos elapsos *Mem. Ripon* I 314; **1526** ad omne quasi verbum juras et membra Christi nominas irreverenter (*Vis. Thame*) *EHR* III 707. **d** venit ad extremum principes ALDH. *VirgV* 2264; ad ultimum..agonizarunt *Id. VirgP* 34; una vice.., una vice similiter.., et ad ultimum audivit *DB* II 177; ut nec ad modicum liceat nobis respirare GERV. CANT. I 51; **1271** cum molendina..reparacione..adpresens indigeant *Cl* 332; **1303** quinta die post festum nativitatis B. Virginis, qua die ad tardius camerario..debetis..vos offerre *Reg. Cant.* II 658; ad hoc relinquitur indeterminatum *Reg. Rough* 70. **e** **1194** die quo hoc malum ad sero factum fuit *CurR RC* I 58; ista ordinatio Christi..bene obligat ad semper, sed non pro semper OCKHAM *Dial.* 876; nescius ad mane que sibi sero foret GOWER *VC* I 1288; **1420** ad aretro.. recusaverunt *KRAc* 49/33.

4 (w. ref. to quantity) at (an amount or rate); **b** (w. adj.).

ad nihili te computabo GILDAS *Ep.* 3; **1225** amerc[i]atus fuit ad x m. *LTRMem* 7 r. 13; **1236** utlagaria nulla est et adjudicata ad nullam *BNB* III 161; **c1254** ecclesia..estimatur ad ij m. *Val. Norw.* 191; **1269** manerium..extenditur ad c..solidos *Cl* 67; **1270** de..cl li. ad quas dampnificatus fuit *Ib.* 207; [damna] taxantur ad xx m. *State. Tri. Ed. I* 11; **1356** assident damnum..abbatis..ad dim. m. (*PlRCP*) *G. S. Alb.* III 46. **b** **11..** dabunt..uxori mee ad carius bluet *MonA* V 490; **s1199** nisi vinum illud adeo bonum sit quod aliquis velit pro eo dare circa ij m. ad altius R. HOWD. IV 99; **1204** extendi faciatis manerium..ad plus quod poterit extendi *Cl* 4; **1227** amercietur ad dim. m. et non ad plus *LTRMem* 9 r. 6; **1233** qualitercunque scutagium currat, sive ad plus sive ad minus *Cart. Osney* IV 173; **a1240** ad melius quam poterit illam vendat *MGL* II 69; vir et uxor ad paria judicentur OCKHAM *Dial.* 772; **1374** repenedere vices non sufficimus ad condignum *Cant. Coll. Ox.* III 31.

5 (w. notion of addition) besides.

omnes..fures, sacrilegos, perjuros, ..adhec quicunque contra patriam conspirassent, ..relegavit exsilio OSB. *V. Dunst.* 34; **1214** hiis adicimus ut..ad hec precipimus ut.. ad hec prohibemus ne.. *Conc. Syn.* 29.

6 (w. notion of limit) **a** to, up to (a number or amount). **b** to the extent of. **c** at a distance of. **d** (w. *ultra*). **e** (w. adj. or adv.).

a **s1166** quod ad dc marcas summa inveniretur *G. S. Alb.* I 183; obtulit ei..episcopatum ampliare fundis ad equivalenciam archiepiscopatus predicti MAP *NC* V 6 p. 234; asportavit de..utensilibus ad valentiam iij m. *RDomin.* 5; **s1307** omnes terras suas..ad valentiam v milia marcarum W. GUISB. 383; candele ad sufficienciam debent exhiberi *Cust. Cant.* 103; **1373** ponent [averia] ad certum numerum, ita quod illum numerum nullus excedat *Hal. Durh.* 118; ad septem milia hominum Jerosolimam petentes..obsessi sunt M. PAR. *Maj.* II 4; Romani ad tres centum millia insurgunt AD. USK 99; **1459** pro factura murorum..ad iiij ulnas et dim. in altitudine *Ac. Durh.* 638; **1462** per decidenciam mensure, que minor est..nova ferlota..ad quantitatem unius bolle de celdra *ExchScot* 132; **1475** princeps.. ipsam..ad lx millia li. redditus annui..dotabit (*Conventio pacis*) *Foed.* XII 1475. **b** **s1217** subversionem ipsius.. modis omnibus ad posse procurarent M. PAR. *Maj.* III 30. **c** **1220** solitarii..manent ad xv leucas de Bertona *CurR* VIII 328. **d** **1514** cum nimio exercitu virorum armatorum ad ultra numerum..c millium *Ac. Durh.* 663. **e** sic mea turgescunt ad plenum viscera musto ALDH. *Aen.* 89 (*Cupa*) 5; id quod..non ad integrum promulgaveras *Id. Met.* 10 p. 85; **1257** cleyas ad †proprius [? l. propius] quod poterit versus G. ..cariari faciat *Cl* 45; **1263** de dicta pecunia vobis..satisfaciemus ad plenum *Cl* 282; **1192** si quis.. clericos duos ad minus..habuerit (*Stat. Resid. Canon.*) DICETO II lxxii; **1310** admittantur [scolares] pro mora v annorum ad majus *Reg. Whet.* II 315; **1362** ultra xxx dies ad magis *Lit. Cant.* II 429; **1389** habeat tres clericos ad magis hujusmodi condicionis *Chanc. Orders* I 1; **1448** nudato capite, zona sua abjecta seu pro tempore adminus dimissa (*Citatio heretici*) *Eng. Clergy* 225; **1505** iij vel iiij ad omne majus *Reg. Merton* 304; **1569** ad omne minus ante solutionem instantis termini *StatOx* 399; **1549** quaternis diebus in hebdomada ad minimum legat *Ib.* 343.

7 (w. notion of payment) **a** at (cost or expense). **b** at (a price). **c** in payment of or for. **d** in receipt of. **e** subject to (rent, service, or obligation).

a **s1177** moraturi..in partibus transmarinis ad custamentum eorum *G. Hen. II* 138; **1220** servientes non recipiatis ..ad sumptus vestros *Cl* 241; **1309** navem..salvaverunt ad magnos labores *PQW* (*C.I.*) 830a; cum conductor non teneatur domum..conservare ad expensas suas OCKHAM *Pol.* I 323; **14..** vivat in prisona nostra..ad custagium ipsius R. *Reg. Brev. Jud.* 8b. **b** **1268** c solidatas..panis, viz. iiij panes ad denarium *Cl* 11; per..suum [Edwardi II] tempus magna fames fuit in Anglia, ita ut aliquo tempore j quarterium frumenti ad xl s. venderetur *Meaux* II 392; **1366** in xv multonibus, pecia ad x d. *Ac. Durh.* 45. **c** dant de consuetudine..xvii s. ad pisces et viii s. ad sal *DB* I 180; inde exeunt lx d. ad victum monachorum *Ib.* II 372; **1253** habere faciat Galfrido..xv m...ad unum agnum *RGasc* I 364; **1282** lego..filio meo xx s. ad libros *Cart. Osney* I 411; **1283** debet ad stipendium prepositi..iiij d. *Cust. Battle* 4; **1334** carpentariis..ad potum, vj d. *Ac. Durh.* 116; **1430** subsacriste ad lumen in nocte Natalis Domini, vj d. *Ib.* 710. **d** **1225** precipimus quod navis illa cum.. marinellis sint (*sic*) ad denarios nostros *Pat* 546; fuit.. socius magistri A...et ad robas suas ECCLESTON *Adv. Min.* 22; **1283** illi soli de familia intelligantur existere qui..erunt ad victum et vestitum dominorum *RGasc* II 206. **e** valet lx sol. et tamen est ad firmam pro iiii li. *DB* I 8; Herbertus tenet ad firmam de rege Ringetone *Ib.* 11; non fuit positum ad firmam et ideo ignoratur quantum tunc valuit *Ib.* 179b; ii bovatae terrae ad geldum *Ib.* 343; qui ad expeditionem regis [AS: *to cynges utware*] v hidas teneret (*Inst. Cnut.*) *GAS* 457 (= *Quad. ib.*: ad utwaram regis); **c1120** in terra warlanda sunt xj bovate ad opus et xv ad malam *Cart. Burton* 18; **1234** abbas permisit eos [virgatarios] esse ad gabulum *Cust. Glast.* 149; **1433** recepit eosdem ad periculum suum proprium *Ac. Durh.* 232.

8 (w. notion of contact or connection) **a** to, at, on (of physical contact). **b** to (of belonging). **c** in resistance to. **d** to (of personal relation, incl. speech). **e** to (of logical relation). **f** in proportion to (of math. relation).

a **1202** in octabis S. Petri ad Vincula *CurR* II 97; **1255** venatorem..ligaverunt ad quandam quercum *SelPlForest* 32; **1277** ad pilam ludendo *CalIMisc* I 2209; **s1326** ad caudas equorum tractus usque ad furcas latronum AVESB. 77b; **1333** juro ad..Evangelia per me corporaliter tacta *Lit. Cant.* II 10. **b** episcopatus..ad Danihelem..pertinet BEDE *HE* V 23; **867** dabo..unam..villulam cum at (*sic*) eandem sedem recte pertinet *CS* 516; sunt ibi xxx et ii mansure et unum molendinum que tenent clerici S. Gregorii ad eorum ecclesiam *Dom. Monach.* 2v; **1213** clericis..ad hoc negotium contingentibus WEND. II 71; **1270** dotem meam que ad me contingebat *Cl* 251; **1285** predicte ville sunt guyldabiles cum hundredo ad regem *Aids* II 23; **1341** pagani non tenentur ad instituciones ecclesiasticas OCKHAM *Pol.* I 160. **c** fundavit..mentem.. / durior ut ferro foret ad tormenta ALDH. *VirgV* 1983. **d** taliter ad turmas infit cum voce procaci ALDH. *VirgV* 932; dicebant ad illos: "..quid hic sedetis?" BEDE *HE* V 14; adversum nos ad Deum suum clamant *Ib.* II 2; **1234** per sic quod intercederet pro eis ad dominum Robertum *CurR* XV 1115; cum dicimus "dixit ad Johannem", hic 'ad' acuitur BACON *Tert.* 238; **1268** orent ad Dominum *Conc. Syn.* 782; vir..tanti honoris ad terre principes quod quasi patrem venerarentur *Croyl.* 54; **1322** ob devocionem et dileccionem quas habuit ad beatum ..Thomam *Lit. Cant.* I 64; dileccio ad ipsum OCKHAM *Dial.* 648; communicacio heretici ad fidelem *Ib.* 579. **e** substantiam singulorum arbitrati sunt intuendam, quantitatem ad aliquid, qualitatem..J. SAL. *Pol.* 479C; 'ad aliquid' dicitur secundum plures modos HALES *Qu.* I 14; evum..erit ad eviterna sicut locus indivisibilis ad puncta BACON *Maj.* I 166; **c1300** habita consideracione..ad convenienciam illius *Lit. Cant.* I 28; **1325** ad diversitatem corporum sequitur diversitas voluntatum *Ib.* I 136; repugnanciam habere ad ordinem sacerdotalem OCKHAM *Pol.* I 20; actus exterior utendi re temporali..est indifferens ad actum licitum et illicitum *Ib.* II 551. **f** **s1136** danegeldum, id est duos solidos ad hidam H. HUNT. *HA* VIII 3; **1373** in contribucione facta..pro iij d. ad libram *Ac. Durh.* 186.

9 (w. notion of conformity) **a** to (of equality or likeness). **b** inclining towards (in appearance). **c** by, according to (a standard). **d** at, in response to. **e** at, (agreeably) to. **f** after (a model). **g** in (a manner), by way of (*v. et. admodum*). **h** (w. adj. esp. compar.).

a aequali..ad angelos ERIUG. *Per.* 535A (cf. ib.: per ipsam ad angelos aequalitatem); **c1301** veritas est adequacio rei ad intellectum (*Quaest. Ox.*) *Ox. Hist. Soc.*) XCVI 338; propter similitudinem ad principatum regalem OCKHAM *Dial.* 793; non invento simili ad Adam *Eul. Hist.* I 19. **b** **1388** ij materasses debiles, j blod[ium] ad album *EschF* 840/10. **c** reddit cxl li. ad ignem et ad pensam *DB* I 2b; reddit l li. ad arsuram et pensum *Ib.* 4; valuit xv li. ad numerum, modo xv li. ad pensum *Ib.* 30; denarios novem ad pensam (*Jud. Dei*) *GAS* 426; **1130** x peisas caseorum ad pensum Wiltone *Pipe* 39; ut firmam maneriorum non solum ad scalam sed ad pensum solverent *Dial. Scac.* I 7C; accenso ad ejus [mulieris] mensuram cereo AILR. *Ed. Conf.* 784B; ad novum standardum regis eadem vetus moneta dicebatur de totidem esse pejor (*Tract. Nov. Mon.*) *RBExch* III 994; lapides faciunt..ictus qui judicari non possunt ad plagam BRACTON 144b. **d** ad admonitionem apostolicae sedis..didicerunt BEDE *HE* III 3; si detur ad omnia verbi/condimenta fides HANV. IV 307; emollitur ille..ad gemituosa consilia circumflentium DEVIZES 36v; s**1195** ad pravam suggestionem quorundam DICETO *YH* II 129; facete satis et ad hominem magis quam ad orationem.. respondit GIR. *TH* I 13; **1220** ad sumonitionem et mandatum..majoris *Pat* 233; **1225** ad magnam..supplicationem ..fidelium *Pat* 1; **1236** ad incitamentum Hugonis *CurR* XV 1735; **12..** fuit institutus in ecclesia..ad presentacionem prioris *Feod. Durh.* 254; **1370** veniant..ad preceptum prepositi *Hal. Durh.* 103. **e** quidquid vis ad votum adest ANSELM (*Or.* 13) III 54; votis meis ad velle satisfeci (*Cnut*) *GAS* 277; potat ad affectum qui presto videt sibi lectum SERLO WILT. III a 17. 2; **1189** ad libitum suum et voluntatem *CalCh* III 394; **12..** proprio sacerdoti vel alteri ad ejus licentiam *Conc. Scot.* II 32; s**1236** liceret..regi..unam turrim erigere ad placitum munitissimam M. PAR. *Maj.* III 367; cibis et potibus..quos..invitans ad placitum suum poterit amovere OCKHAM *Pol.* I 304; sunt omnia bona sua ..ad voluntatem domini *FormMan* 27; quod de terra materiali ad literam adintellexit (KYN.) *Ziz.* 6; **1220** ad resignacionem..abbatis..regium adhibuimus assensum *Pat* 228; **1384** ad illum se aggreavit et assentivit *IMisc* 229/17; Henricus..ad hoc non consenciit *Dieul.* 146. 2; **1257** in clvj acris bladi sarclandis ad tascham, ..viz. iij acre j d. *Crawley* 217; s**1403** ad estimacionem v milia virorum cesi sunt *Croyl. Cont. B* 495; **1479** ad omnes acciones nostras.. implacitandum ad communem legem *Reg. Whet.* II 206; **15..** clamat tenere mesuagium..ad communem legem *Reg. Brev.* 11. **f** sulcos obliquat adinstar aratri ALDH. *Aen.* 32. 5; hominem ad imaginem et similitudinem suam [cf. *Gen.* i 26]..constituit BEDE *HE* II 10; puer..baptizatus ad nomen comitis Flandrie Philippus appellatus est GERV. CANT. I 198. **g** ad imitationem..apostolorum BEDE *HE* IV 28; v hidas..habuit ad eundem modum *DB* I 137; ad modum imaginis ornamentis decorata ELMH. *Hen. V* 67; circulum..intersecantem priorem circulum ad angulos rectos BACON *Maj.* I 289; **1200** quod nullus extraneus vendat pannos in civitate ad decisionem *RChart* 79; **1379** quod nullus alius..emat vel vendat..merchandisas.. ad retalliam *Gild Merch.* II 189. **h** **1228** parati sumus monstrare ad verum..attestaciones *Feod. Durh.* 219; licet ad cassum, in brevi reconsiliatus exstitit AD. USK 86; **1239** compareat coram baronibus..ad cicius quod fieri possit *KRMem* 17 r. 9*d.*; **1265** mandamus quod ad prudentius quod poteritis vos..subtrahatis *Cl* 51; id..ad cautius et diligentius quod poteritis..perquiratis *Ib.* 65; non intellexerunt ad purum seu plenum OCKHAM *Dial.* 746.

10 (w. notion of purpose) to, for, in aid or furtherance of (*v. et.* 11a). **b** (w. pron.). **c** (w. inf.).

si ferri vulnus minus ad mortem regis sufficeret BEDE *HE* II 9; hec [terra] deratiocinata est ad opus regis *DB* II 348b; **11..** domos..ad usum proprium habeant *Feod. Durh.* xli; **1538** mesuagium..habendum..Thome..ad opus tamen et usum mei..durante vita naturali mei *FormA* 415; **1220** ad majorem securitatem hujus rei..juraverunt.. *Pat* 245; **1244** ut sententias..relaxarent ad cautelam GROS. *Ep.* 110; s**1251** jussit ea [monilia] feretro indelebiliter ad memoriam sui..affirmari M. PAR. *Maj.* V 257; a**1350** ad augmentum ciste communis *StatOx* 68; **1391** ad honorem ..ecclesie..et majorem †decentiam [l. decentiam] ministrantium..ordinabat (*Stat. Archiep.*) *MonA* VI 1309; s**1396** ut essent adjuvantes..visitatori..ad finem quod.. libere posset officium..exercere *Meaux* III 233; **1450** ad effectum quod possit admitti *MunAcOx* 730; **1439** summe.. deposite ad custodiam *Ib.* 516. **b** cum quesissent ad quid eam..vexaret GIR. *GE* I 18; **1228** requisitus ad quid esset ibi *Feod. Durh.* 297; c**1230** est acolitus in..mantello serico ad hoc parato *Reg. S. Osm.* I 150; **1265** talliagium..assessum super Judaismum per Thomam..adhoc assignatum *Cl* 62; ad hoc quod pro catholicis habeantur, tenentur errorem suum..revocare OCKHAM *Dial.* 757. **c** s**1190** dum venire debebat ad capere, ..ova simul et obolum perdidit DEVIZES f. 29v; **1200** abbas..atturnavit W...ad esse senescallum suum *CurR* I 323; **1201** presentat fratrem R. B. ad esse baillivum eorum *Ib.* 464; **1219** summonitus fuit..ad esse [? l. adesse] in crastino S. Martini *Ib.* VIII 136; **1242** invenit plegios ad esse coram justiciariis *Assize R. Durh.* 10; **1270** attachementum sufficiens ad partes ligare *CartINorm* 179.

11 (w. gd. or gdv.) **a** for the purpose of. **b** (equivalent to inf. after vb. of commanding or sim.). **c** (in attrib. phr.).

a satellites ad impugnandam..aciem conspirati ALDH. *VirgP* 13; misit praefectum suum ad adducendum eum BEDE *HE* IV 1; silva magna ad venandum *DB* I 187; pueros ad confirmandos (*sic*) offerens W. MALM. *GP* III 100 p. 127; **1163** pro carretta locata ad conducendum obsides *Pipe* 45; **1226** duos magistros..ad ipsas galias nostras regendas ad eundum in servicium nostrum *Pat* 36; omnes aque in quibus capiuntur salmones ponuntur in defenso ad capiendum salmones *Quon. Attach.* 87. 1; **1333** quem rex assignavit ad eligendum iiij masones ad d petras pro ingeniis regis faciendum *LTRMem* 105 r. 174; quos duos filios Knutus rex ..misit in partibus transmarinis ad †educandos [? l. educandum] *Eul. Hist.* II 185. **b** **1310** ipsos..ad veniendum in Angliam..inducatis *RGasc.* 358; **1385** ipsos ad hoc faciendum..coegerunt et compulserunt *PIRCP* 494 r. 302 (*1d.*); si ..rogati fuerint ad publicandas dictas literas *Praxis* 21 (cf. ib.: eis stricte mandatur ad publicandum..dictas literas). **c** **1280** tenet manerium..per serjanciam ad inveniendum.. unum garcionem (*JustIt*) *SelPlForest* 137; **1417** pro informacione juvenum ad cantandum *Ac. Durh.* 226; **1458** ad effectum ad standum ipsorum regimini *Reg. Whet.* I 305; **1587** insultum fecit ea intencione ad ipsum J. ..interficiendum *Pat* 1301 m. 20.

12 (w. notion of use or means) **a** for use by. **b** for use at. **c** for use as. **d** for use in producing or dealing with. **e** for the exercise or conduct of. **f** (in attrib. phr.) designed or appointed for use as, or for dealing with or handling by.

a **1266** dedit..filio suo..xl fururas..ad milites suos *Cl* 272; **1325** pro iiij frokis ad iiij novicios *Ac. Durh.* 165; non minor sapiencia..requiritur ad principantem in spiritualibus ..quam ad regem OCKHAM *Dial.* 798. **b** est dominicum quod quis habet ad mensam suam et proprie, sicut sunt *bordlandes* Anglice BRACTON 263; **14..** collectanei..duo ad suffragia sanctorum, ..quartus..ad S. Michaelem, quintus qui est ad exequias defunctorum (*Cart. Reading*) *EHR* III 122. **c** habet..viii mansiones ad hospicia *DB* I 298; **1295** (*4 seams of wheat bought*) ad semen (*MinAc Cliffe*) *Cant. Cath. Pri.* 134. **d** [ibi] est nemus ad sepes, pastura ad pecuniam *DB* I 128; hi villani arant et seminant de proprio semine quater xx acras..ad avenas *Ib.* 179b; c**1230** debet arare dim. acram ad frumentum (*Cust. W. Preston*) *Bec* 85; **1265** faciant habere..monialibus..pannum ad..camisias *Cl* 73; **1278** in ij paribus rotarum ad carectas..emptis *Ac. Stratton* 93; **1281** invenient..xxix kariagia cum karectis suis, sc. medietatem ad fenum et medietatem ad bladum *IMisc.* 40/7; **1300** de croppis meremii prostrati ad cindulas venditis *MinAc* 925/2 m. 5. **e** **1264** justiciariis..itineraturis ad placita foreste *Cl* 5; ad gladios..et alia arma..sint jurati *Fleta* 36; **1466** non est juratus ad assisam domini regis *Mod. Ten. CBaron* 20; **1379** domino R. ad [*for playing*] organa, vj s. viij d. *Ac. Durh.* 212. **f** reddebat..vj canes ad ursum *DB* II 117; **1212** in expensis..vj canum ad porcos *Pipe* 169; c**1170** unum rete ad salmonem *Reg. Paisley* 6; **1210** pro una capa ad pluviam *Misae* 171; **1224** de molendino ad bladum *LTRMem* 7 r. 2 (1); **1265** v balistas..de quibus duo baliste sunt ad duos pedes et tres ad unum pedem *Cl* 149; **1264** coram justiciariis nostris ad placita foreste *Ib.* 2; **1297** generalem servientem hominum nostrorum ad arma *RGasc* III 372; **1297** non habent equos ad arma *StatIr* I 200; **1303** equus ad molendinum *Ac. Exec. Ep. Lond.* 94; **1299** molendinum ad equos *CatAncD* I A 1438; s**1355** habuit ..circiter duo millia sagittariorum ad equos AVESB. 125; s**1388** serjancius ad legem KNIGHTON II 295.

13 (made or fitted) with. **b** (in attrib. phr.).

1208 item j par bacinorum operatorum ad imagines et flores deauratorum *KR Invent.* 122; **1241** quandam turrim ..ad duas stagias fieri..faciatis *Liberate* 15 m. 11. **b** c**1158** reddendo michi annuatim nova calcaria ad aurum (*Ch.*) *VCHCumb* I 323; **1253** pannum sericum ad aurum *RGasc* I 364; **1261** balistas ad cornu *Cl* 502; pultes ad legumina (*De Wallia*) HIGD. I 38.

14 (in names of writs) **a** writ of inquiry as to damage that might result from a grant. **b** writ of entry after expiry of lease.

a **1385** in expensis bursarii..pro habendo 'ad quod dampnum' *Ac. Durh.* 595. **b** **1259** pro uno brevi 'ad terminum [qui preteriit]' *Cl* 379.

15 *Ad te levavi*, first Sunday in Advent (cf. *Psalm* xxiv).

12.. Dominicis, sc. Ad te levavi, Circumdederunt, Invocavit, Letare *Reg. Pri. Worc.* 127a.

16 (in comp.) denotes approach or direction (*addigitare, adherbare, adjornare, admallare*), addition (*adhabere, adinjungere*) or connection (*affeuatus, affilare, allottare, applegiare, attachiare*); for irreg. comp. v. *adjudex, advincula*; for pseudo-comp. v. *admannire, admirallus, advantagium, advunculus, coadservare*.

adacinum v. acinus.

adaequabilitas, potential correspondence.

hec autem veritas aut est adequatio duorum, id est rei et intellectus in actu aut in habitu aut in sola potentia, et tunc diceretur ~as.. *Ps.*-GROS. 292.

adaequare [CL], **a** to level, flatten. **b** to make equal or correspondent. **c** to make regular or rhythmical. **d** to equal, live up to.

a **1243** placeam..~ari..faciatis *RGasc* I 255. **b** decimarum mearum de residuo summam ~abo GIR. *IK* I 8; anima..habundat in aliquo quod facit animam non ~ari substantie J. BLUND *An.* 330; veritas secundum quam ~atur res ad intelleccionem vel intuicionem divinam WYCL. *Log.* II 233. **c** remigia ~are insistunt R. COLD. *Cuthb.* 28. **d** monachus..presbyteratus, quem bonis actibus ~abat, gradu praeminens BEDE *HE* V 12.

2 (p. ppl.) adequate, exactly corresponding.

consumpcio rei non est una significacio ~ata hujus nominis 'abusus' OCKHAM *Pol.* II 534; si significatum illius ~atum fuisset (KYN.) *Ziz.* 26; prima proposicio..non fuit dicta a Cristo pro ~ata mensura ascensionis WYCL. *Ver.* II 108.

adaequate, adequately, in the full sense.

Deus non determinatur ad sciendum Antichristum fore primo et ~e per totam suam scienciam infinitam BRADW. *CD* 222A; sic enim Deus wlt, intelligit vel intendit rem esse; sic res est ~e WYCL. *Log.* II 233; hec proposicio parcialis non significat ~e (KYN.) *Ziz.* 21.

adaequatio, a levelling. **b** equalization, bringing into balance. **c** correspondence.

a **1255** de dirutione murorum et ~one fossatorum *RGasc* I *sup.* 9; mediante ~one superficierum locantis et locati corpus locati continetur in loco BACON III 190. **b** calor dum est in gradu commensurationis et ~onis naturalis generat humores laudabiles GILB. VI 248 v. 1; sanitas causatur ex ~one humorum in aliquo puncto BACON XIII 309. **c** omnes soni..formati ab agentibus ejusdem speciei ..sunt ejusdem speciei; et in specie est ~o J. BLUND *An.* 160; veritas propositionis est ~o sermonis et rei GROS. 130; omnis propria racio intelligendi aliquod objectum per ~onem representat illud objectum DUNS *Sent.* II iii 9. 2; relacio ~onis signi ad suum signatum, que relacio est 'ipsum esse verum', cum sit ~o vel correspondencia ejus ad suum significatum WYCL. *Ente* 11.

†adagere [cf. adigere], (?) to accomplish in addition.

quid non ~eret virtus vigentior et circumspectior industria..? AD. MARSH *Ep.* 86.

adagium [CL], proverb.

ut fidem ~io facerent, crebro jactu jaci aliquando Venerem MORE *Ut.* 73.

adagonista, lawyer.

~a, A. *a man of lawe* WW: *a lawyour*, ~a, asecretis *CathA*.

adaliquitas [cf. ad 8e], relation (log.), relativity.

relacio, comparacio, habitudo, unicio vel annotacio, respectus, ~as, idem videntur significare DUNS *Metaph.* V 11 p. 269.

adamans v. adamas.

adamantinus [CL < ἀδαμάντινος], adamantine, of 'adamant'. **b** (fig.) adamantine, perdurable.

ut ~us scopulus..contra tormenta..induruit ALDH. *VirgP* 41; collisio tanta ut etsi ~a navis esset..putaretur elidi W. CANT. *Mir. Thom.* VI 145; lapides ~i..equali vi proportionis ferrum in medio collocatum sustinent NECKAM *NR* II 98; aliqua hujusmodi Greca: abyssus, adamas, †adamantius BACON *CSPhil* 441. **b** **1012** (12c) his testibus ..~o stilo firmantibus *CD* 719.

adamare [CL], **a** to love (sexually), make love to. **b** to mate with. **c** to love (a thing).

a **1220** in tantum locuta fuit cum eo et ita ~avit eum quod ipse duxit eam in uxorem *CurR* IX 66; filius..regis.. puellam ~averat et..eandem quam diu amaverat desponsavit O. CHERITON *Fab. add* B 14; s**1226** ob amorem regine.., quam carnaliter ~avit M. PAR. *Maj.* III 116. **b** hic [hircus] mulierem..bestialiter ~abat GIR. *TH* II 23. **c** s**1386** [rex Armenie] plus pecuniam ~avit quam plebem WALS. *HA* II 151.

adamas [ἀδάμας], 'adamant', lodestone (magnetic iron oxide) or diamond, or a substance supposed to combine the properties of both. **b** (fig.).

adamans, genus lapidis ferro durior *GlC* A 245; mox adamante Cypri praesente potentia fraudor ALDH. *Aen.* 25 (*Magnes*) 5; [gagates] levem materiam attrahit ut ~as ferrum GOSC. *Aug. Maj* 52; sed vincit victrix vis adamantis eum NECKAM *DS* VI 216; ~as est lapis Indicus; ..habet.. splendorem cristallinum; ..dissidet in hoc a magnete quia .. BART. ANGL. XVI 7; trahitur [trica] a stella illa sicut ferrum ab ~ante GROS. 38; magnes presente ~ante actionem hanc [attractivam] non exercet *Ps.*-GROS 613; **1346** item †en xij petris adamauntis vocatis *seilstones* *KRAc* 27/5; sicut inclinacio ferri ad deorsum suspenditur per attraccionem ~antis WYCL. *Log.* II 161; magnes lapis est qui et ~as dicitur et diamas, i. durissimus ille lapis *SB* 28; adamans, quidam lapis, G. et A. *aymant Alph.* 3. **b** adamante ligatur / janua HANV. II 259; cum..memoratis personis quasi quibusdam ~antibus attractivis librorum uteremur R. BURY *Phil.* 8. 144.

adamator, lover.

1180 salvationem..regis victoriosi, ~oris veridici verbi, ..soldani Sarracenorum (*Lit. Saladini*) GIR. *PI* III 18 (= *Itin. Ric.* I 18: †adunatoris).

adaperire [CL], to open wide.

quod in ipso ~erto vulnere trium pene latitudo digitorum ..infundi potuerit R. COLD. *Cuthb.* 94.

adaptare, a to fit. **b** to adapt. **c** to apply, direct. **d** to apply (a saying). **e** to compare. **f** to link (fig.), associate.

a ei [sc. dolio] operculum..ex asseribus ~avit GIR. *GE* II 10. **b** virtus immutativa ipsum [sanguinem] per coleram ~at ad membra colerica..nutrienda *Ps.*-GROS. 524; jura..debent ~ari ad ea que communiter accidunt PAUL. ANGL. *ASP* 1529. **c** s**1254** ad ea que Anglicam contingunt historiam calamum ~emus M. PAR. *Maj.* V 440. **d** sicut.. de Theutonicis legitur, sic et istis [sc. Kambris] ~ari potest GIR. *DK* II 2; illud Augustini in monachos..ironice.. dictum..et hic ~ari potest *Id. Symb.* 28 p. 301; ~atur [fabula] quibusdam militibus O. CHERITON *Fab.* 7. **e** nihil ..in omni vita mea expertus sum quod hujusmodi dulcedini valeam ~are SERLO GRAM. *Mon. Font.* 120. **f** cui..colori plumbeo ~atur..lapis crapodinus UPTON 118.

2 to train (hounds).

1256 cum..commiserit..vatletto suo canes suos ad sanguinem ~andos *Pat* 70 m. 16.

3 to turn to account, appropriate.

cenobium..de Ramesia, ..expulsis..monachis, ..castellum sibi ~avit *G. Steph.* II 83; rectius sunt ista possessionis meae quam est quod Adamus, diventitis caulibus sibi crediti horti, ~at in suos usus FERR. *Kinloss* 52.

adaptatio, application.

c**1230** ~io processionis hujus Dominice in ceteris Dominicis, cum earum exceptionibus *Offic. Sal.* 40 *rub.*; a**1250** ne ..videatur hec ~io in vanum quesita, attendamus quod dicit Augustinus in libello De Decem Plagis, unde hoc tractata est coaptatio (S. HINTON *Quest.*) *Powicke Studies* 216n.; in sensu litterali jacet tota philosophie potestas in naturis et proprietatibus rerum, ..ut per convenientes ~ones et similitudines elicientur sensus spirituales BACON *Tert.* 82.

2 training (of falcons).

1259 pro custodia et ~one falconum nostrorum *Liberate* 36 m. 10.

adaquare [CL], to water (animals). **b** (absol.). **c** (iron.) to drown.

debeo implere presepia boum feno et ~are [AS: *wæterian*] eos ÆLF. *Coll.* 91; **1171** pro j navicula ad oves ~andas *Pipe* 4; **1236** liberum ingressum et egressum ad averia sua fuganda usque ad aquam de Lyden' ad ea ibidem ~anda *Cl* 281; ut bene curetur sonipes, sitiens adaquetur GARL. *Mor. Scol.* 625; **1281** intravit in illud fossatum occasione †ad equandi equum suum *IMisc* 40/30; **1284** pro j freno empto pro quodam palefrido ~ando *KRAc* 97/3 m. 6; **1344** in uno freno empto pro palefridis..†adequandis *Ac. Durh.* 544; **c1380** pro licencia †adequandi animalia sua ad vivarium de Wydhop *Surv. Durh. Hatf.* 32. **b** audito quod ad cisternam equorum extra Jerusalem..fierent a paganis irrupciones in Christianos ~antes ibi MAP *NC* I 18. **c** Henrici nati pelago pereunt adaquati (*Versus de Hen. I*) *MGL* II 650.

2 to soak, steep. **b** (alch.) to heat (in water).

pluviis adaquetur amictus HANV. I 252; lixapericio dicitur a *lixa* quod est 'aqua' et *pir* quod est 'ignis', quasi adaquans ignem, i. minuens †colorem [l. calorem] *Alph.* 104. **b** philosophi..multa posuerunt artificia ad artis sue..occultacionem.., ut sunt commiscere, ..~are, putrefacere .., quorum tamen regimen est quod est coquere tantum DASTYN *Ros.* 6.

†adaquarium, ewer.

1398 cuppe, ciphi, ~ia [? l. ad aquaria] et vasa aurea (*Test. Ric. II*) *Foed* VIII 76.

adaquatio, (right of) watering (animals).

1239 cum concesserit eisdem circa eundem fontem plenaria eysiamenta necessaria ~oni *CurR* 120 r. 8*d*.; tenementum..in quo unus liberum tenementum habeat, et alius communiam pasture.., tertius iter et actum, et quartus ~onem in aliqua parte *Fleta* 272; **1411** de..xlvij frenis pro ~one *Ac. Foreign* 45D.

adar [Heb.], a Jewish month.

duodecimus [Hebraeorum mensis] adar Martio..comparatur BEDE *TR* 11.

†adarasca, white hellebore (*Veratrum*).

adarasta, i. elleborus albus *SB* 9; adarasia, adarasio, elebrus albus idem *Alph.* 3; (cf. ib. 52: adorasta).

adarce, ~es [ἀδάρκη, ~ης], salty efflorescence on water plants.

~is GILB. II 82 v. 1 (cf. ib. VII 330 v. 1: adarsis); ~is, i. †caro marina *Alph.* 2; alconnium, †adaras, †coro marina idem secundum nos *Ib.* 7; ~es res est in maritimis locis nascens..tanquam concreta salsilago..arundinibus ac herbis agglutinata *LC* 218.

adauctor, increaser.

rex David precipuus musicorum instrumentorum..cultor fuerat; multorum quidem auctor, omnium ~or GIR. *TH* III 14.

adauctus v. adaugēre, adigere.

adaugēre [CL], to increase, enhance. **b** to add.

exceptis..multiplicibus negotiis, que regis erarium quotidie ~ent ORD. VIT. IV 7; **s1143** materiam..belli suis.. nisibus ~ere *G. Steph.* II 75; paulatim in tantum hec [musice] disciplina adaucta est ut..turpe videretur musicam nescire GIR. *TH.* III 13. **b s1272** dixit episcopus quod ipse..adauserat [l. adauxerat] provisioni eorum vivarium de Ketton' *Ann. Durh.* 28.

adaugma [? *infl. by conf. of* augere *w.* ἀκμή; cf. acmasticus], increase.

c1310 de temporali ~ate quod nostris diebus..jam advenit (*Const. Winchcomb*) *MonA* II 306; *an ekynge*, ~a, augmentum, auccio, augmentacio *CathA*.

adauratus, wrought with gold thread.

a1386 pannis ~is de Nakta *Miss. Westm.* II 676; **1406** pannos..~os (*KRAc* 406/10) *Arch.* LXVII 176 (cf. ib. 174: unum gounum de panno †adauro [MS: adaur']); **1591** panni ~i viridis *branched*, xj virg' *KRAc* 432/10 r. 1*d*.

adavus v. atavus. adb- v. abb-. adc- v. et. acc-. adcantarii v. cantarium.

addecimare, to deduct tithe.

affirmant..quod nec de elemosynis panis..aut aliarum rerum hujusmodi modicarum teneantur donantes, in decimando lucra marcacionis ipsorum, ~are RIC. ARMAGH *Def. Cur.* 1394.

addere [CL], to add. **b** to grant in addition. **c** (w. *ad* or *in*) to contribute towards. **d** to enhance, exalt. **e** (w. *super*) to increase. **f** (w. inf.) to go on to.

~idit..lacrimas precibus BEDE *HE* V 5; laborant / erectis malis addere vela super G. AMIENS *Hast.* 83; huic manerio est ~ita dim. hida *DB* I 86b; si puncto punctum ~imus sine intervallo.., non fit nisi unum punctum ANSELM (*ProcSp* 16) II 218. **b** nam mihi versificum poterit Deus addere carmen ALDH. *Aen. praef.* 14. **c** videamus quid ~at quasi ad inconvenientiam repellendam ANSELM (*Incarn.* 5) II 18; res ~entes in putrefactionem GILB. I 6. 2. **d** ~ere et amplificare ALDH. *VirgP* 56; [ecclesia] in sedem pontificatus ~ita BEDE *HE* V 23. **e c1400** et super dolorem vulnerum meorum ~iderunt (*Lit. R. Wyche*) *EHR* V 531. **f** ~idit quasi per jocum inquirere BEDE *Cuthb.* 2; ~idit et ..verba dicenda illi proponere *Id. HE* V 2; Juno protinus ~idit effari, "vis tu..?" *Latin Stories* 162.

addibilis, able to be added.

homo..speculetur seipsum..et virtutes insitas in unoquoque membro ad servitium corporis, in quo nihil ~e vel mutabile est BRADW. *CD* 139C.

†addicare [? *for* addicere *or* addictare], **a** to assign. **b** to banish.

a s1139 filia regis Henrici, ..cui Anglia juramento ~ata fuerat, venit in Angliam H. HUNT. *HA* VIII 11. **b 1188** doleo ne qui patrem exulem adicaverunt..ab ipsius paternitatis sinu exulent et ipsi *Ep. Cant.* no. 268.

1 addicere [CL], to subject, sentence, condemn. **b** to appoint.

~tus, *forscrifen GlC* A 193; cuncti volentis naturae legibus ~ti ALDH. *VirgP* 20; inter plurimos gentis Anglorum.. servitio ~tos BEDE *HE* IV 26; quem fera multatrix lictoribus impietatis / addixit saevas mucronis pendere poenas FRITH. 194; **10**.. ~it, *fordemet*, ..~ti, damnati, ..adictus [? sc. morti] *forslægen* WW; **s1143** qui..introrsum confugerant ..ab altari abstractos..captivitati addixerunt *G. Steph.* II 74; dimidiam fere Angliam..legibus suis et preceptis ..~ere *Ib.* 75; sive trunculo per capitulum sit ~tus sive non *Cust. Westm.* 204; **s1364** milites..de morte ejus ~ti incarcerantur J. READING *Chr.* 162; **s1414** proposuit.. assultum fecisse in regem et suos et indifferenter omnes gladio et mortibus addixisse ELMH. *Hen. V* 4. **b s530** Justinianus..ne plures [canonici] ~erentur inhibuit R. NIGER 134.

2 (p. ppl.) addicted, devoted.

probitas, vires, audacia tuta / conveniunt bellis addictis atque duellis D. BEC. 1706; Martiis ille ludis ~tus, hic seriis GIR. *TH* III 51.

2 addicere v. edicere.

addictare, to sentence, condemn.

1291 istum..morti ~abant (H. HARTLEPOOL) *Ox. Hist. Soc.* XCVI 202; **s1387** justiciarius..~avit dominum T...de transgressionibus factis de feris..et multi alii cum illo ~ati sunt de patria KNIGHTON II 241.

1 addictio, sentence.

omnipotens sapientia contra..prepositos..exhorrendissimam sententie tonantis ~onem contorquet AD. MARSH *Ep.* 247 c. 18 p. 460.

2 addictio v. additio 2a.

addigitare, to point out (as).

si jacet in disco pinguis bolus ante sodalem, / illum non digites, ne rusticus addigiteris D. BEC. 1038.

addirare [OF *adirer* < addextrare], to lose, mislay (*cf.* W. S. Holdsworth *Hist. Eng. Law* II 366 *n.* 8).

1221 ostendit ballivis..quod stagnum fuit ei adiratum et peciit cerchiam *CurR* X 105; **1233** injuste detinuit ei tres porcos qui ei fuerunt addirati *Ib.* XV 905; poterit rem suam petere ut ~atam cum testimonio proborum hominum et sic consequi rem suam quamvis furatam BRACTON 150b; poterit rem suam petere civiliter ut ~atam [v.l. addisratam], quamvis furatam *Fleta* 55.

addiscere [CL], to learn, study.

Dominicam orationem ~endo GIR. *GE* I 13; dicebat quod partes transmarinas adiret et nigromantiam ~eret O. CHERITON *Fab. add.* A3; **s1248** ut introductiones militie initiales ~eret M. PAR. *Maj.* V 18; **1358** puerulos ad religionem attrahunt.., sed..tempus quo possint ~ere captandis favoribus..dominorum..sinunt consumere *MunAcOx* 207; **1370** in casu quod vult adissere, ..seneschallus concessit sibi licenciam pro duobus annis, ita quod bene adiscat *Hal. Durh.* 97; **s1384** dum..propriis damnis ~erent quanta mala pariat discordia WALS. *HA* II 115; te adjuro ut leges regni patris tui ~as FORTESCUE *LLA* 5.

addiscitio, learning, study.

c1210 si..in..psallendi ~one inventus fuerit idoneus *Reg. Linc.* I 19.

addisrare v. addirare.

additamentum [CL], addition, thing added, appendage. **b** addition, adding.

licet sinalipharum velut..explosa collisionis ~a..necessitate metri interponantur ALDH. *Met.* 9; hoc ~um valebat tunc xx li. *DB* II 22b; **1149** hoc ~um ad incrementum patris mei *Cart. Osney* IV 28; vocando ipsum [librum] Rosam Medicine propter quinque ~a que sunt in rosa quasi quinque digiti tenentes rosam GAD. 3. 1. **b** cur ex alterius ~o alter refrigeretur? ADEL. *QN* 34 p. 39; **1368** sine ~o cujuscumque candele gracilioris *Reg. Glasg.* 281.

additio [CL], addition, adding. **b** expansion (by adding).

'sal' Latine..~one T litere '*salt*' Anglice GIR. *IK* I 8; in illa unitione est aditio [v.l. adjectio] quanti cum quanto J. BLUND *An.* 52 (cf. ib. 54: non est ibi substractio materie.. sed adicio quedam); per ~onem sex lunationum embolismalium GROS. *Comp.* 249; **1283** summa cum ~one xvj denariorum *Cust. Battle* 105; **c1300** per ~onem multarum cifrarum WALLINGF. *Quad.* 103; **1444** tabula uniformis ~onis, ..tabula difformis ~onis KILLINGWORTH *Alg.* 716. **b 1458** articulorum prescriptorum interpretationem, reformationem, ~onem et declarationem *Mon. Hib. & Scot.* 411b.

2 addition, thing (clause) added. **b** epithet.

c1290 decretales..omnes ~ones plenissime continentes *Ann. Durh.* 130; **1293** unacum articulis corone cum omnibus ~onibus suis *PQW* 222; **1428** quamdam †addictionem ad ipsum libellum..proposuerat (*Sentencia*) AMUND. I 236. **b 1494** nuncupatus per nomen de M. tantum sine ~one *Entries* 47.

additionalis, additional.

poterit..quascunque..defensiones dare vel prius datis addere et eas declarare per viam positionum ~ium *Praxis* 148.

addocēre, to demonstrate.

1238 hoc vult ~ere vel per patriam vel per curiam Cristianitatis *BNB* III 244.

addretiare [OF *adrecier*], to redress, set right.

1170 exigent barones errantes..plegium ab omnibus vicecomitibus..quod erunt coram domino rege..ad rectum faciendum et ~iandum ei et hominibus suis quod ~iare debuerint (*Inq. Vic.*) GERV. CANT. I 217; **s1170** unusquisque vicecomitum et ballivi eorum plegios invenerunt..quod ad rectum starent ad adresciandum domino regi et hominibus regni quod eis adresciare deberent de prisis suis *G. Hen. II* I 5; si contra dominum suum [purpresturam fecerit].., tunc distringetur ipse occupator quod ad curiam domini sui veniat id adresciaturus GLANV. IX 11; **1198** juratores dicunt quod ita levavit fossatum. judicium: ..fossatum †adreciatur [? l. adrecietur] *CurR* I 53; **1200** priorissa queritur quod homines [regis colunt] in communi pastura que eas contingit..et petit ut dominus rex faciat ~iari *CurR RC* II 163; **1202** stagnum adrecietur sicut esse debet *SelCivPl* 95; **1207** quos attornavimus justiciarios nostros ad addresciandum et corrigendum ea que addresciari non possunt per justiciarios nostros quos prius attornaveramus *Pat* 72; **1221** domus..levata est..ad nocumentum [etc.]; et ideo purprestura; ..et adrecietur sicut debet et solet *SelPlCrown* 96; **1223** illud adretiari faciant ad plenum hominibus ipsius episcopi *LTRMem* 6 r. 1.

2 to put in place.

1320 in j ferro empto ad adressandum et fundendum simentum inter petras *KRAc* 469/1.

addubbare, to stud.

1245 feretrum..ligneum..coopertum platis argenteis.. et ~atum lapidibus contrafactis ad similitudinem carbunculorum (*Invent. S. Paul.*) *Arch.* L 470.

addubitare [CL], to doubt.

dum dicitur de quolibet 'non est sanus', ~at aliquis utrum insanus velit intelligi ABBO *QG* 21.

adducere [CL], to bring (a thing) to (a place or person). **b** to import. **c** (?) *f.l.* (*cf.* *adaugēre*).

lapillulos de..sablonibus ~tos ALDH. *VirgP* 23 p. 254; ut ne ad os quidem ~ere ipsum brachium..valeret BEDE *HE* III 2; quisquis ex alia scira carrum adducebat *DB* I 268; **c1090** in ~endis petris ad aquam *Regesta* 133; **1270** quos [canes]..cepit et adduxit domino regi *SelPlForest* 56. **b** emo res pretiosas..et ~o [AS: *togelæde*] vobis huc..super mare ÆLF. *Coll.* 96; **1347** de custuma..de qualibet clewa sive educta sive ~ta, quadrans *MinAc* 894/30. **c s1308** mores novellos seculo inauditos adinveniens, mirabili varietate vitam †adduxit [? l. adauxit] *Ann. Lond.* 156.

2 to bring (a person) to (a place or person). **b** (fig.). **c** to bring into court. **d** to bring forward, produce (as warrantor or witness).

in requiem.. / adduci merear ALDH. *VirgV* 2904; cum mitteretur Cantiam ob ~endam inde conjugem regi Osuio BEDE *HE* III 15; quod puella ei aliqua.., qua sibi remedium compararet, ..~eretur GIR. *GE* II 11; adduxit eam versus abbatiam *CurR* IX 66; **s1321** adduxerunt..tractui et suspendio barones inclitos *Flor. Hist.* III 207. **b** Deus.. hominem..de nihilo in essentiam adduxit ERIUG. *Per.* 585A. **c 1202** quia si ipse..interim posset inveniri ~eretur comitatui *SelPlCrown* 23; eum ceperunt cum toto blado et adduxerunt ad curiam episcopi *Ib.* 109. **d** postea non adduxit tutorem *DB* II 103 (v. et. adductio c).

3 to adduce (evidence or sim.), cite.

de hoc suum testimonium adduxit de melioribus.. hominibus totius comitatus *DB* I 44b; illud ad quod ~ebatur exemplum R. WINCHELSEA *Quest.* 144; ubi est ~ta ista instancia ad probandum DUNS *Sent.* II i 3. 17; sicut ~tum est prius OCKHAM *Pol.* I 317; scripture, raciones et jura superius ~ta meam..mentem ligant PAUL. ANGL. *ASP* 1541.

adductatio v. advocatio 6b.

adductio, a bringing in, importing (of goods). **b** conducting (a person) to (a place). **c** producing as warrantor or witness.

a 1204 de abductione marcandiarum ab Anglia capiatur xva, de ~one vero in Angliam capiantur salvi plegii *Pat* 42b; **1331** quietus..de custuma danda pro eisdem bonis in prima emcione, deportacione et ~one hujusmodi rerum et catallorum in civitatem predictam *PQW* 455. **b 1374** in expensis factis circa ~onem magistrorum J. ..et H. ..veniencium ad eleccionem *Ac. Durh.* 581. **c** volens..probare quod [etc.], adducit pro se Danielem dicentem [etc.]; hec ~o ejus [etc.] OCKHAM *Err. Papae* 968; **1443** fidejussores adducant.. Henricum ad Cancellarium..et..moneant magistrum collegii..de ~one ejusdem *MunAcOx* 535.

adductivus, adductive (productive in intention).

secundo modo producitur res..cum Deus intendit..rem illam..existere actualiter suo tempore..; et omnis talis producencia vel produccio, cum sit ~a, non operacio, .. facit.. WYCL. *Ente Praed.* 146.

adelingus [AS *æþeling*], prince.

Henricus..[Mathildem] desponsavit, ex qua Guillelmum Adelinum..genuit ORD. VIT. VIII 22 (cf. id. XII 18: Guillelmus Adelingus); Eadgarum..Eadwardus.., quia heredem putabat eum facere, nominavit *aþeling*, quod nos dicimus domicellum; sed nos de pluribus, quia filios baronum vocamus domicellos, Angli autem nullum preter filios regum..in quadam parte Saxoniae *ling* ymago dicebatur, *aþel* Anglice nobilis, quod conjunctum *a þeling*, id est nobilis imago, dicitur (*Leg. Ed.*) *GAS* 665; Margareta..cum fratre Eadgaro edelingo (*Leg. Ed. retr.*) *Ib.* 664; Edwardus filius Edmundi Irenside..fuit pater Edgari Atheling H. HUNT. *HA* VI 24; communiter Adelingi vocantur qui de regis sanguine descendunt HIGD. I 27 (cf. ib. VI 18).

adelphus [ἀδελφός], brother.

novit quid Petro, Petri quid solvis adelpho FRITH. 1255 (cf. 1117).

ademptio [CL], removal, withdrawal.

adimitio, ~io *GlC* A 265; per ~onem solis contra firmamentum in obliquitate zodiaci SACROB. *Sph.* 103.

ademptivus, tending to remove, eliminative.

cum talis concupiscencia esset eis nociva et perfecte beatitudinis ~a BRADW. *CD* 119B.

ademptorius, tending to remove, eliminative.

apparet ipsos tantum velle negare a libero voluntatis arbitrio necessitatem adversariam libertati seu ~iam libertatis BRADW. *CD* 686A.

1 adeo [CL], so, so much (that). **b** (w. neg.) not very (much).

exulat ~o ut..nequaquam..solis radio potiretur ALDH. *VirgP* 32 p. 274; ~o..erat barbarus ut ne sexui quidem muliebri parceret BEDE *HE* II 20; Greci..ipsos [Latinos] exosos habent, ~o quod ab ecclesie quoque Romane subjectione se subtraxerunt GIR. *PI* I 17 p. 75; **a1350** illis causis ..exceptis que..ad forum laicale usque ~o pertinere dinoscuntur quod per nullam..universitatis jurisdiccionem.. valeant expediri *Stat. Cantab.* 325; **a1350** quousque ~o profecerit ut sufficiens testimonium habuerit *StatOx* 30; **c1380** sordida..~o prope collegium..projecit..quod ex fetore..aier..inficitur *FormOx* 255; **s1380** cum pene per totum regnum Francie..illesi transissent, ~o ut nullum e suis..perdiderunt WALS. *HA* I 444. **b** sed non diu nec ~o bene [AS: *ne to wel*] ÆLF. *Coll* 98.

2 as, as much (as), equally.

nullius histrionis..scomata..~o placent mihi ut istius infantuli NECKAM *NR* II 157; sciens..non principium ~o ut finem attendi GIR. *GE* II 7; libentius quam aliis, ~o vel magis sibi propinquis *Ib.* 27; utinam ~o spiritualia sapiens sicut et secularia *Id. Retract.* 427; **1219** Robertus habet duos fratres, qui ~o magnum jus habent in terra..sicut et Robertus *CurR* VIII p. xi; **1232** navem reddet regi..in ~o bono statu ut eam recepit *Pat* 462; **c1283** clamant pasturam ..~o bene quando non faciunt servicium suum sicuti et quando faciunt *Cust. Battle* 51; multi..habent maximum dampnum.., ~o bene predicti H. et N. quam alii *State Tri. Ed. I* 44; **1364** in ~o bono statu quo ea recepit *Hal. Durh.* 34; **1379** reparabunt..messuagium..et ipsum in ~o bono statu vel melius dimittent *Deeds Balliol* 30.

3 thither.

1226 cum..ad eo venerint *Cl* 128b.

2 adeo v. adire.

adeps [CL], **a** fat (as part of body). **b** fat (as food or ointment). **c** (fig.). **d** cream. **e** fine flour (*cf. Psalm* lxxx 17).

a ÆLF. *Gl.* (v. abdomen); [carcannus] ventris adipe strictius insidebat R. COLD. *Cuthb.* 8; in ethica primo consumitur ~s recens circa membra solida, non in cute exterius, quia ibi est pinguedo GAD. 21. 1. **b** de adipe [suis]..calciamenta sua liniantes *V. Cuthb.* III 5; **786** votum obtulit de adipibus suis ALCUIN *Ep.* 3; Dominicis..adipem comedant LANFR. *Const.* 91; **1343** pro iij barellis adhipis *ExchScot* 527. **c** Francorum Dalvinus adeps FRITH. 106; ora ut caritatis adipe et pinguedine repleatur arida anima mea ANSELM (*Or.* 13) III 53; junctura illa solidissima est que ex adipe fidei et dilectionis procedit J. SAL. *Pol.* 555A; **c1198** ex cordis adipe prodit iniquitas (*Versus de W. de Longo Campo*) *EHR* V 317 (cf. *Psalm* lxxii 7); virginalis castimonia..domicilium mentis adipe virtutis illustrat R. COLD. *Cuthb.* 8. **d** mulier ..que in butiro et caseis de lactis adipe conficiendis ei.. famulatur *Ib.* 138. **e** **1342** pro v barellis adipis frumenti *ExchScot* 485; **1362** in j dim. bussello adipis frumenti, xij d. *MinAc* 1253/14.

1 adeptio, acquisition.

ecclesiarum possessiones devoverunt et omnimodas injustas ~ones MAP *NC* I 24; **c1205** puella, ..oculorum detersa caligine, pristine lucis gavisa est †adoptione [? ~one] *Canon. G. Sempr.* 160; **1232** nec artis / illi mundane sufficit adeptio H. AVR. *Poems* 127. 83; **1530** pro ccxl tonne petrarum una cum †adopcione *Fabr. York* 103.

2 adeptio v. adoptio. adeptus v. adipisci. adeq- v. et. adaeq-, adaq-. adequietatio v. quietatio.

adequitare, to ride beside.

decessit..cum regio lateri..~aret W. MALM. *GP* IV 177.

adespotus [ἀδέσποτος], anonymous.

praecipua quaeque ex..~is commentariolis libavi STANIHURST *Hib.* 59.

adesse [CL], to be present. **b** (of time). **c** (w. dat.) to be with. **d** (w. gen.) to be with. **e** to support, concur (with). **f** to be. **g** (w. inf.) to come to.

contigit et ipsum..in eadem tunc ecclesia ~e BEDE *HE* IV 32; ingrediens vias tuas benedixisti tuis, nec affui ANSELM (*Or.* 2) III 8; ut omnis populus credat te..in hoc judicio afuisse (*Jud. Dei*) *GAS* 416; nisi ego custos adsim [AS: *ætwese*] ÆLF. *Coll.* 98; de hoc manerio desunt xxv soc-[hemanni] qui aderant T. R. E. *DB* II 109; assunt quidam ..attoniti AD. EYNS. *Hug.* V 20; **c1225** nam quod / plus prodest ut adest, plus et obest ut abest H. AVR. *Poems.* 20. 108; **1327** mandata apostolica..in proximo affutura quandoque venerint recipiam reverenter *Lit. Cant.* I 234; **1313** quando major in eis adherit multitudo populorum *Reg. Carl.* II 95; partibus in cujus semper †adhēro manens GOWER *VC* VII 1296. **b** tempus adest sacras metris vulgare puellas ALDH. *VirgV* 1660; aderant..Quadragesimae venerabiles dies BEDE *HE* I 120; **1297** dum tempus affuerit *RGasc* III p. clxxxviii. **c** medicus..qui morienti illi..adfuit BEDE *HE* IV 17; homo, antequam in paradiso peccavit, carni sue ~e consuevit AD. SCOT. *Ord. Prem.* 561C. **d** **s893** post adest quorum rex Eðered Myrciorum ÆTHELW. IV 3. **e** adero, ausiliabor *GlC* A 285; huic sententie non adero W. FITZST. *Thom.* 33. **f** cantu gracili refugit contentus adesse ALDH. *VirgV* 70; contemplansque suam divino munere gazam / adfore servatam WULF. *Swith.* I 356; **1267** dum predicti heredes infra etatem affuerint *Cl* 381. **g** parentes accurrere et ejus delenire dolores..affuere R. COLD. *Cuthb.* 108.

2 a (pr. ppl.). **b** (gd.).

a jam eo spatio unius miliaris adessente, porta contra illum aperta est (*Purg. S. Pat.*) *Meaux* I 145; **1427** lego ad distribuendum pauperibus..ibidem adesssentibus..xl s. *Reg. Cant.* II 370. **b** **1339** manuceperunt villatam.. adessendi coram justiciariis *SelPlForest* 72 (cf. ib.: plegii.. adessendi).

adesuper, from above.

capella..discooperta et ..ymbrium infusionibus ~er patens et pervia R. COLD. *Cuthb.* 136.

adf- v. aff-. adg- v. et. agg-. adgist- v. agist-.

adhabēre [cf. adhibere], to receive in addition.

1296 a premissa denunciacione non cessantes quousque a nobis super hoc adhabueritis in mandatis *Reg. Carl.* I 76.

adhaec v. ad 5.

adhaerentia, adhesion, attachment. **b** adherence, support. **c** (collect.) company, faction.

ne habeat ex sua viscositate in villis stomachi et intestinorum ~iam GILB. II 95 v. 1; proprium nature unius est ~ia alterius, cum unum sine alio metallum generare non possit *Correct. Alch.* 9. **b** sicut ~ia [Deo] est bonum vie quo peregrini validius ambulent [cf. *Psalm* lxxii 28] H. Bos. *LM* 1397; **1291** persone capte vel propter ~iam alterius parcium punite revocabuntur (*Liber B*) *Foed.* II 503; **1302** pro ~ia partis nostre in guerra..exheredati sunt *RGasc* III 410; **s1306** ab ejus fide, dileccione et ~ia nuncquam recesserunt *Plusc.* IX 8; **1380** religiosus debet esse unus cum Deo per stabilitatem ~ie BRINTON *Serm.* xv p. 58; **1440** oportet reges..sanctitati vestre et Petri cathedre ~iam prestent BEKYNTON II 93. **c** **1336** quod..alii de eadem ~ia ad eadem castra redire..valeant *RScot* 397a.

adhaerēre [CL], to stick to, stay by. **b** (tr.) to adjoin. **c** (fig.) to conform or be devoted to (a belief or practice). **d** (pr. ppl.) concerned with.

tempore de primo noctis mihi nomen adhaesit ALDH. *Aen.* 58 (*Vesper*) 1; ibi reside et quietus manens ~e tumbae BEDE *HE* III 12; **10..** adhesit, *ætfealh and oncleofode* WW. **b** **s885** telluris in condenso, ~enti notheas fluvio partes Tamesi ÆTHELW. IV 3. **c** Veteris..Testamenti non medulle sed cortici ~entes GIR. *TH* III 19; injusticias.. quibus omnibus multitudo fratrum Minorum..favet et assentit et ~et OCKHAM *I. & P.* 3; nec diu in peccatis morabuntur, eciam si delectabilibus adheserunt ROLLE *IA* 42 p. 277. **d** **s1396** post multos tractatus concordie ~entes *V. Ric. II* 129.

2 to adhere, attach oneself to (a person or faction). **b** (refl.). **c** (pr. ppl. as sb.) adherent.

s1262 an vellent observare dictas ordinaciones..an pocius ~ere illis qui voluerunt illas infringere *Leg. Ant. Lond.* 54; Nicholao de S. ~endo *State Tri. Ed. I* 71; **1296** super dictum A. et alios sibi ~entes *SelPlMan* 43; **1341** quotquot inhabitabant Anglicis adheserunt *ExchScot* 472; **1558** non ~ebit nec confederabit cum inimicis..regis *Act. PCIr* 48. **b** **1286** Bertramus..~ebat se regi Francie *PQW* 484a (cf. ib. 485b: †adheredebat se regi Francie). **c** **1345** treuge..inter te ac regem ipsum et utriusque vestrum ~entes (*Lit. Papae*) AD. MUR. 178; **1435** pro se et suis singulis ~entibus *FormA* 364; **1491** pernoctans..cum suis ~entibus *Sanct. Durh.* 45.

adhaerescere [CL], to inhere.

nisi spiritus..castimonia..intrinsecus contubernali soliditate concorditer ~at ALDH. *VirgP* 27.

adhaesio, a appurtenance. **b** adherence (to a belief). **c** adherence (to a person or faction). **d** sexual union.

a **12..** dedi..ij carucatas terre in territorio ejusdem ville, ~onem predicte ecclesie et meam *Reg. S. Thom. Dublin* 244. **b** ~o presupponit apprehensionem DUNS *Metaph.* II 1 p. 23D; veritates..quibus..oportet ~one certissima consentire OCKHAM *Dial.* 413; BRADW. *CD* 221A (v. adhaesivus); duplex est eleccio ad propositum, sc. ~io per se bono secundum proheresim.. WYCL. *Sim.* IV p. 49; **1425** articulos..pertinaciam et heresim in ~one, sustentacione et defensacione ipsius dogmatizacionis erronee..concludentes *Reg. Cant.* III 127. **c** **1333** illos..de quibus suspicio de ~one Scotis..habeatur *RScot* 227a (cf. ib. 415b: literas de pardonacione dictarum ~onis et inimicicie); ex ~one ad personas hereticorum OCKHAM *Dial.* 650. **d** **1342** Rogerius ante omnem ~onem quam cum dicta Matilde illicite habuit..fuit in sacerdocio constitutus *Lit. Cant.* II 261.

adhaesitio, adherence, attachment.

habita plena noticia objecti beatifici..et plena ~one ac dilectacione in illo objecto WYCL. *Act.* 43.

adhaesivus, expressive of adherence or assent.

[sciencia divina] secunda vocetur complexa, compositiva vel divisiva, affirmativa aut negativa vel ~a, aut in abstracto composicio et divisio, affirmacio vel negacio, siv adhesio BRADW. *CD* 221A.

adher-, v. et. adhaer-, adesse.

adherbare, to put out to grass.

bubulco licet ~are [AS: *læswian*] duos boves..cum grege domini (*Rect.* 12; *Quad.*) *GAS* 450.

adhesia v. azeisa.

adhibēre [CL; cf. adhabere], **a** to apply, add (a thing). **b** to appoint (a person). **c** to apply, direct, devote (attention, thought, faith or sim.). **d** (?) to devote oneself (absol.).

a velut..chaos..~itis documentorum lanternis..illustrasti ALDH. *PR* 140; libanotidis folia..cathaplasmis ~ita ..emeroydas prohibent *Alph.* 102. **b** ~uit, *gelaðade* vel advocavit *GlC* A 287; **1228** episcopus ~uit custodes..qui observarent hostia *Feod. Durh.* 248. **c** **671** nisi frequens.. meditatio fuerit ~ita ALDH. *Ep.* 1 p. 478; sanandae scabredini capitis ejus curam ~ere BEDE *HE* V 2; **1166** quatinus.. aures benignas ~eatis..scriptis episcoporum *Canon. G. Sempr.* 93; singulis..fidem ~eo GIR. *TH* II *pref.*; **1230** rex ~uit assensum suum postulationi *Pat* 394; in nullo negocio debuerunt fideles..eis indubitatam credulitatem ~ere OCKHAM *Dial.* 591; **1348** vestram corporalem presenciam nobis..~ere non omittatis *Lit. Cant.* II 291; **13..** artem.. femine indagare mentem ~ui *Arthur & Gorlagon* 152; ~ita diligenti custodia ELMH. *Hen. V* 83. **d** **1217** vos rogamus quatinus..constanter nobis ~eatis *Pat* 22.

adhibitio, production (of witnesses). **b** appointment (of persons).

per secretam correccionem et ~onem testium OCKHAM *Dial.* 916. **b** aliquando per publice persone ~onem conceditur securitas UPTON 86.

adhicere v. adicere. adhimere v. adimere.

adhinnire [CL], to whinny.

equi feri ~iunt W. FITZST. *Thom. prol.* 14.

adhipis v. adeps.

adhorrēre, to shudder at.

1319 scelera, que eciam a scolaribus fieri ~ere auditus, ..jactitant se fecisse *FormOx* 52.

adhortari [CL], to exhort.

c625 ~antes quatinus..non differas (*Lit. Papae*) BEDE *HE* II 11.

adhortatio [CL], exhortation.

c625 divinae fidei calor ejus intelligentiam tuarum ~onum frequentatione succendat (*Lit. Papae*) BEDE *HE* II 11.

adhuc [CL], (of time) still, (continuously) till now. **b** now (as before). **c** (w. ref. to future) still (i.e. it is still possible that).

~c inattritam viam EDDI *Wilf.* 3; quo ~c superstite BEDE *HE* IV 5; informiter, id est ~c imperfecte ERIUG. *Per.* 546B; ~c tunc initium est, nondum disserendi ars BALSH. *AD* 3; dum ~c collibus incumbunt GIR. *TH* I 6; ego virgo Maria, / quam male lesisti, quam male ledis adhuc NIG. *MirBVM* (*Speculum* VII 412). **b** **1220** mandavimus vobis alias quod..redderetis; ~c autem..mandamus..ut.. liberetis *Pat* 250; **1278** ~c dicunt quod.. *SelPlMan* 89. **c** ecclesia B. Pauli..quondam fuit metropolitana et ~c futura creditur W. FITZST *Thom. prol.* 4; **1219** habuit bonas cartas; set tempore guerre fuit domus sua robata..et bene credit quod illas ~c recuperabit *CurR* VIII 14; **c1250** de terris quas..jam adquisivimus vel ~c adquiremus *Cart. Dieul.* 355; **s1311** spero quod..~c salvabunt me TROKELOWE 69.

2 (in headings) still (i.e. 'continued').

1214 ~c de octabis S. Hillarii *CurR* VII 77; **c1276** ~c termini redditus *Reg. S. Aug.* I 280; ~c in termino S. Johannis Baptiste *Ib.*; **1326** ~c in termino S. Mich.., ~c recorda *LTRMem.* 99 r. 18.

3 still, besides, in addition.

~c plus facio [AS: *þænne mare ic do*] ÆLF. *Coll.* 91; extra hanc [aecclesiam] sunt ~c ibi iii aecclesiolae *DB* I 2b; ~c apponens quia me generosum..cognoverat GIR. *Inv.* I 7.

adiantos [ἀδίαντος], maiden-hair fern (bot.).

adyantos, capillus Veneris GILB. I 18. 1; recipe..j partem capilli Vene[ris], adianthos, ceterach GAD. 12 v. 2; capillus Veneris, ~os idem, herba est in petris nascens *SB* 14.

adiaphoros [ἀδιάφορος], indifferent.

omnis sillaba in ultimo versu adiaforos est, id est indifferenter accipitur ALDH. *Met.* 10 p. 82; omnis syllaba novissima versus in quocumque metro adiaforos, id est indifferens, est BEDE *AM* 2355.

†adiascordion, (?) agrimony (bot.).

agrimonia, ferraria, lappa inversa idem, secundum Laurencium etiam vocatur ~ion, filantropos *Alph.* 6.

adicere [CL], **a** to impose. **b** to add, give in addition. **c** (absol.) to make an addition.

a 1234 petit..dim. m. nomine cujusdam pene adjecte in placito *CurR* XV 1165. **b** adjectis..embolismorum incrementis ALDH. *Met.* 2 p. 69; possessiones in usum eorum.. adjecit BEDE *HE* II 3; [Deus] discenderat ut omnia nostra.. desuper adjectis naturaliter insita faceret ERIUG. *Per.* 572A; **11..** concedo ij bovatas terre..et super hec omnia vj acras..aditio eidem ecclesie *Feod. Durh.* 134n; **1196** ~ient per annum..x li. *Pipe* 273. **c s1087** cum hostes suos adeo depresserint ut ~ere non possent H. HUNT. *HA* VI 38; ut nihil tam plenam cui non adjiciat GIR. *TH intr.* p. 6.

2 a (w. inf.) to continue. **b** to add, say in addition (that).

a s1024 dux Normannorum..vivere non adjecit H. HUNT. *HA* VI 16; **s1455** juratus..quod de cetero sic peccare non ~eret *Reg. Whet.* I 163. **b** adjecit..quia vellet ipsum.. audire BEDE *HE* II 13; **1200** ipsi idem concedunt et adhiciunt quod..rex precepit *CurR RC* II 232; **1201** adic[i]unt etiam quod..*CurR* I 467; **1290** adhycientes quod..illud ..parati sunt revocare (*Liber B*) *Foed.* II 469; **a1350** huic statuto ~imus quod..[magister] vocem suam amittat *Stat. Cantab.* 317.

3 (p. ppl. *adjectus*) attached, devoted. **b** (in abl. absol.) w. the addition (that).

s1327 ad unum aliquem familiarem ardenter ~us, quem.. pre ceteris honoraret *G. Ed. II Bridl.* 91. **b c1230** tenet eodem modo, hoc ~o quod solvet iij d. (*Cust.*) *Doc. Bec* 61; **1294** consimilis littera..eo ~o quod compelleret archidiaconum.. *Reg. Carl.* I 21.

4 (p. ppl. as sb. n.) addition. **b** adjective.

securus sum ex..animi virtute, non ex armorum ~o MAP *NC* III 2 p. 120. **b** ~um junctum cum sensu nominis hujus 'res' WHITTINGTON *Vulg.* 44.

adictio v. additio.

adigere [CL], to drive, thrust, impel (to or into). **b** to tack on. **c** to bind (fig.). **d** to extort. **e** to impose, administer (an oath).

ense..per utraque latera adacto ALDH. *VirgP* 52; turbas removeri jussit adactas FRITH. *Wilf.* 873; ferro visceribus ejus secretius adacto *Chr. Rams.* 141. **b** prologos aliquorum adactos inveniet DICETO *Chr. prol.* 19. **c** ut.. [Willelmus I] omnes liberos homines..sue fidelitati sacramento ~eret W. MALM. *GR* III 258. **d** quia verbum ab eis extorquere non potuerunt verbis, telis ~ere responsa parabant MAP *NC* IV 13. **e s1164** ne omnis controversia de fidei transgressione sit in foro ecclesiastico, sed tantum de fide adacta pro nuptiis..vel hujusmodi W. FITZST. *Thom.* 35; **s1194** licet ex parte regis..ad hoc observandum fuerit jusjurandum †adauctum [l. adactum] DICETO *YH* II 113.

†adilis [? conf. of Ar. *ad-dībī* (*adh-dhi'bī*) for *qātil adh-dhi'b*, wolf's-bane (*Aconitum*), w. Ar. *akhīh* for *qātil akhīh*, orchis], (?) kind of orchis.

cum decoccione feniculi aut rute aut herbe ~is: ..herba ~is est herba lupi interficiens eum, et est satirion GAD. III v. 2.

adimare, ~atio v. adun-. adimbreviare v. imbreviare.

adimere [CL], to take away. **b** (as euphem. for death).

ademto, †*gebinumini GlC* A 206 (cf. *EE* 341. 34: adempta, *binumni*); quo.. / redderet auditum misero miseratus ademptum WULF. *Swith.* II 487; **10..** ademptam, *genumene*, ..*oðbrogen* WW; **797** dies quae..lunari aetati adempta [v.l. adepta] est ALCUIN *Ep.* 126 p. 186; **s1035** majorem partem ademit illi tyrannice FL. WORC. I 190; [livor] admit virtutis odorem / nariculis fame HANV. VI 328; **1356** in xlviij acris dim. ..bladi metendis, ligandis et adhimendis *Crawley* 273; **s1399** ipsius [Ricardi] anulo..in signum deposicionis..adempto AD. USK 32. **b** fortuitis ademptam casibus [Eugeniam] ALDH. *VirgP* 44; fugit igitur rege adempto totus ejus exercitus H. HUNT. *HA* II 30.

adimitio v. ademptio.

adimmensus, immeasurable.

1303 vobis gracias referimus ~as *Reg. Cant.* II 653.

adimplēre [CL], **a** to fill up. **b** to complete (an amount or period). **c** to make good, fill (a role). **d** to fill the role of.

a 1253 dolia..vino ~eri faciat *RGasc* I 380; Deus..dat esse animabus ut ~eantur sedes intelligentiarum que ceciderunt BACON VII 61. **b** hec igitur 7 unam substantie radicem demonstrant, quam scilicet substantiam 49 ~ent ROB. ANGL. *Alg.* 74; manebunt 3 que unam partem numeri decem ~ent *Ib.* 108; sunt autem semper, quasi conventum ~entes, circa tredecim numero GIR. *TH* II 29; ~etus septimus annus erat NIG. *Mir. BVM.* f. 24. **c s1135** alium ..qui regis vices ~ens..regni periculis finem imponeret *G. Steph.* I 2; **s1301** abbas..fecit eis ministrari per suos monachos..absenciam predicti Petri [capellani] ~entes THORNE 1980. **d s1135** quam [copiam] si [archipresul] vivens distribuisset.., perfectum pastorem perfectius ~eret *G. Steph.* I 4.

2 to fulfil: **a** a task; **b** a desire or impulse; **c** a promise; **d** a prophecy; **e** a command or request.

a si possetis vel velletis opus vestrum per alios ~ere LANFR. *Ep.* 61 549D; **s1065** nequid tanto deesset edificio quod constructor pius..non ~esset *Chr. Rams.* 178; sic quod deerat ~etum AD. SCOT. *TT* 672C; **11..** libere officia sua semper ~eant *Feod. Durh.* xlix; **1237** didicimus.. quanto..vigore dispensationem ministerii vobis creditam ~etis GROS. *Ep.* 39 p. 131; **1340** preclare doctrine radiis auditores illuminans formam sue lecture ~evit *FormOx* 139; composicione et concordia per internuncios ~etis *Meaux* III 116; penitenciam..non potuit ~ere *V. Ric. II* 69. **b a675** desiderio..quod..cogitarem ~ens perficere ALDH. *Ep.* 2; velle suum facto ~ens EADMER *V. Osw.* 3; innuit.. illius malitiam irrefragabiliter ~endam J. SAL. *Pol.* 441B; **1218** sicut diligunt quod voluntates eorum ultime ~eantur *Conc. Syn.* 91; **1296** ob..desiderium nostrum ~endum (*Breve Regis*) *MGL* II 76; **1305** benivolenciam quam erga nos geritis et opere efficaciter ~etis *Reg. Cant.* II 671. **c** ea quae nunc promittis ~ere ne differas BEDE *HE* II 12; **1303** promissionem..~ere *MunCOx* 4; **s1454** sua promissa fideliter ~entes *Reg. Whet.* I 138. **d s1173** tunc ~etum est illud Merlini vaticinium *G. Hen. II* I 42; **s1174** ut ~eretur illud propheticum DICETO *YH* I 384; ut ~eatur quod dicitur ad litteram, 'lavamini et mundi estote' NECKAM *Ut.* 107; post obitum sancti viri [Dunstani] ceperunt dicte prophecie indies ~eri *Croyl.* 55. **e** alter alterius honera portate et sic ~bitis legem Scaccarii [cf. *Gal.* vi 2] *LTRMem PR* 32; **1203** omnes illas petitiones..parati eramus ~ere *Pat* 23b; omnia sua precepta jussit ~eri M. PAR. *Maj.* I 206; **1264** ea que per nos..sunt ordinata..volumus observari et in omnibus ~eri *Cl* 83; **1328** legem evangelicam pocius ~ere quam solvere *Lit. Cant.* I 265; illa que juberet ab aliis essent ~enda OCKHAM *Pol.* I 16.

adimpletio, fulfilment.

plaga occidentalis, que edificium tabernaculi consummat, recte ~onem sancte ecclesie, que in fine hujus mundi perficitur, designat AD. SCOT. *TT* 696C; quid hoc est nisi per ministros Dei..operande salutis salutaris ~o AD. MARSH *Ep.* 247 c. 9 p. 447; **1381** ~o..concordie *RScot* 38; **1440** pro pleniore observancia et ~one..premissorum *Reg. Dunferm.* p. 294.

adinducere, to induce.

1350 quod..suos subditos..instruant et ad informandum in lingua materna symbolum apostolorum moneant ipsos et ~ant *Conc.* III 11.

adinjungere, to add.

1433 fecit quendam actum solempnem, ..~endo quomodo censiendum esset et respondendum *Reg. Cant.* III 248.

†adinquirere [cf. acquirere], to acquire.

sicut..trigonus et tetragono..ita virtus animalis in acquisita et adinquisita in infusa continetur J. BURY *Glad. Sal.* 610.

adinsimul, together.

palmas ~ul percutiens, ..multos..convocavit GIR. *Hug.* II 6.

adinstar v. instar.

adinstare, to stand in place.

s1378 licet episcopi..in ordine suo ~antes..bene et rite celebrantes consecraverint *Eul. Hist. Cont.* III 341.

adintelligere, to understand.

quod de terra materiali ad literam adintellexit testatur (KYN.) *Ziz.* 6.

adinvenire [LL], to invent, devise. **b** to find.

~ientes tale praesidium GILDAS *EB* 23; novum solatii genus ~it magistra necessitas AILR. *Ed. Conf.* 775D; cibariorum diligendorum regulam luxuria ~it J. SAL. *Pol.* 733A; **c1177** edocti sunt..novum ~ire remedium DICETO *YH* I 423; **s1217** consuetudo est Romanis causas de levi ~ire M. PAR. *Maj.* III 23; **c1244** prefixo fine optimo viam ~it rectissimam GROS. *Ep.* 106; dicitur regale servitium quia specialiter pertinet ad regem..et secundum quod in conquestu fuit ~tum BRACTON 36; patriarche et prophete qui omnes sciencias ~erunt BACON *Tert.* 267; **s1274** quassabantur omnes ordines mendicantes, ..ita ut xxij varie religiones ~te cessarent W. NEWB. *cont.* 566; **s1308** (v. adducere 1c); **1350** nec ficcionem aliquam vel causam aliquam irracionabilem absencie ~ire *StatOx* 57; **1436** falsos rumores de se ipsis ~erunt *Cl* 286 m. 7d. **b s1268** quo rex..veniens resistentem neminem ~it *Flor. Hist.* III 16; **s1455** acceptior est regi..omnibus aliis..majoremque graciam ~it in oculis ipsius *Reg. Whet.* I 165.

adinventarium, inventory.

1310 quibus [expensis etc.] omnibus ab ~ii summa subtractis, remanent.. *Reg. Cant.* II 1078.

†adinventatio, inroad.

s946 unde Aquilonares partes Anglie..ab hostium incursu et adinventacione tueretur *Ann. Ed. I* 456 (= M. PAR. *Maj.* I 455: ab hostium adventantium incursione).

adinventio, (act or faculty of) invention. **b** (w. *falsa*) forging.

747 monasteria..quae..non divinae..legis ordinatione sed humanae ~onis praesumptione utcunque tenentur *Conc. HS* III 364; non hec tue ~oni sed mee promissioni ascribat AILR. *Ed. Conf.* 778A; nec quero gloriam de austeritate et ~one mandatorum H. LOS. *Ep.* 48; **s1192** cantavit et ipse nonnulla [pudenda] de ipsis, sed non plurimum laboravit in ~one, quia superabundans suppetebat materia *Itin. Ric.* VI 7; per ~onem humanam..est dominiorum divisio introducta OCKHAM *Pol.* II 669; hec regula fit ex preceptis Domini, non hominis ~one [ME: *fundleas*] *AncrR* 6; que antiqui anfractuosis ~onibus effoderunt R. BURY *Phil.* 9. 145; **1505** fecit ibi sermonem bone ~onis *Reg. Merton* 300. **b s1430** pro falsa ~one sigilli regii et patentis..suspensus fuit *Chr. S. Alb.* 48.

2 invention (i.e. thing invented), device. **b** invented story, lie.

†adventio, *sarwo GlC* A 281; propriis ~onibus..et libidinibus regis GILDAS *EB* 4; superfluis ~onum argumentis ALDH. *VirgP* 56; novis et inauditis ~onibus operam dare ÆLNOTH *Cnut* II 24; attende superfluas et vanas ~ones in edificiis, in vestibus, in cibariis NECKAM *NR* II 173; **s1207** floribus, cortinis..et cereis et quibusdam prodigialibus ~onibus resplenduit civitas M. PAR. *Min.* II 109; **c1236** nefandum est..locum Deo dicatum diabolicis ~onibus execrare GROS. *Ep.* 32; novarum harmoniarum curiositas et prosarum lubrica ~o BACON *Tert.* 297; **s1274** nec sufficere posset lingua..ad ornamenta civitatis..enumeranda, que..multifariis ~onibus pro regis magnificencia.. fuerant elaborata WYKES 259; in omnibus istis ~onibus humanis miscetur sepe iniquitas WYCL. *Ver.* III 48; pro salvacione nove ~onis humane stulte facte *Id. Sim.* VII 87. **b 1178** [heretici] sermonem sibi nequam callidis ~onibus firmaverunt (*Lit. Abb. Clarevall.*) *G. Hen. II* I 216; **1299** quibusdam malicie ~onibus *Reg. Cant.* I 304; **s1325** nescio quis ~onibus [MS: in adventionibus] eam instruxit *V. Ed. II* 287 (cf. WALS. *HA* I 373 [s1378]: asserens se in adventione [? l. adinventione] propria circumventum); **1341** cujus vexaciones..archiepiscopi..callidis; ~onibus ac reprobis consiliis sunt..ascribende (*Lit. Regis*) AVESB. 96b.

adinventiuncula, little trick.

semper novellas excogitare studet ~as effrons adulator NECKHAM *NR* II 180.

adinventor, inventor, deviser.

inmundae haereseos ~orem GILDAS *EB* 67; Willelmus cognomento Diabolus.., artifex subtilissimus et novarum rerum ~or peritissimus GERV. CANT. I 74; **1304** ~ores et auctores discordie *Reg. Cant.* II 667; **s1384** accusacionis ~or WALS. *YN* 339.

†adinventulare, to ventilate, discuss.

a1540 [placitum] in eadem curia ~atum *Entries* 496b.

adinvicem [al. div.], to one another, mutually. **b** (of seals) interchangeably (*cf. alternatim*). **c** together, side by side.

conferentes ad invicem BEDE *HE* II 2; junctis ad invicem manibus OSB. *Mir. Dunst.* 3; ad invicem animos..instigant ÆLNOTH *Cnut* III 38; **s1174** Franci..Flandrenses..damna suis illata conferebant ~em DICETO *YH* I 393; cum [amantes] vel ad invicem vel de invicem loquuntur AD. SCOT. *Serm.* 33 303A; **1200** inde placitant ~em *CurR* I 133; **1246** viderunt dictum cervum mortuum et quemdam alium cervum..pugnantes ~em *SelPlForest* 82; **1262** cum nos et vos ~em contigerit convenire *Cl* 170; se ad invicem decipere OCKHAM *Pol.* I 323; **1336** sic dileccionis vinculis colligantur quod nesciant ~em non amare *Lit. Cant.* II 138; rector ecclesie S. Augustini..et..rector..ecclesie S. Leonardi.. intendunt..ad invicem permutare *Ib.* 444. **b c1250** duplex instrumentum..sigillis..predictarum partium ~em confirmatum *Reg. Aberbr.* I 207; **1292** sigilla sua ~em alterius scripto ad modum cyrographi confecto apposuerunt *AncD* A 3683. **c** neque ad invicem sedebant nisi interente (*sic*) columna *Cust. Westm.* 162; **1300** cum ipsi..fuerant ~em in villa Hunt' (*St. Ives*) *Law Merch.* I 77; **1327** [selione terre] ~em [jacentes] *CalCh* IV 40; **1415** illi qui plura beneficia simul tenent, que absque dispensacione canonica nequeunt ~em simul retinere *Reg. Cant.* III 494; **1438** custodiam..diversarum terrarum..~em jacencium *FineR* 245 m. 9; **1451** infra mansum Johannis Broun..bibentes ~em et cantantes sedebant *Pat* 473 m. 8.

adipare [cf. adeps], to scald brose. **b** (p. ppl. as sb. n.) brose.

to scald browes, ~are *CathA*. **b** ~atum, A. *browys*, ..hoc adopatum, *brues* WW.

adipinus, adipose.

pinguedo..secundo modo accipitur pro carnositate aerea vel ~a, cum qua est adeps mixta totum remolliens GAD. 22. 1.

adipisci [CL], to get, attain, reach. **b** (?) (act. form).

qui..praeconia circensium ~untur ALDH. *VirgP* 3; hoc sibi glorie singularis desiderans ~i BEDE *HE* V 7; nec bene ~untur nec adeptis bene utuntur GIR. *GE* II 34 p. 339; potestatem..quam est..adepturus OCKHAM *Pol.* I 147. **b** ~it, adquirit *GlC* A 226; cum quis agere velit quod possessionem alicujus †~at *Fleta* 227; ubi non aberat quicquid bona voluntas †~eret [v.l. concupisceret] *Eul. Hist.* II 13.

2 (p. ppl. *adeptus*) **a** (s. act.); **b** (s. pass.). **c** (?) (w. *ad*) fit.

a virtutum culmen adeptis / virginibus ALDH. *VirgV* 1661; nullam..facultatem ~i sunt? BEDE *HE* II 10; martyrii coronam ~us GIR. *TH* III 32; qui rem sic adipiscitur ut eam incontinenti a se abdicare debeat, ~us proprie non dicatur OCKHAM *Pol.* I 351; **1391** quousque..assecutus fuerit et ~us liberum tenementum *ExchScot* 267; ~us est Angliam pridie quam spiritus exhalavit ELMH. *Hen. V* 99 (cf. ib. 103: cum ~us esset ejus aspectum). **b a690** adepto ..talento ALDH. *Ep.* 5 p. 492; pro ~a victoria BEDE *HE* III 24; **1070** ~i imperii..anno quarto *Regesta* p. 10; pacis ~e beneficio GIR. *TH* III 9; regis precepto, jugulo qui gaudet adepto GOWER *TC* II 98; ~o..triumpho ELMH. *Hen. V Cont.* 111. **c** ad quemlibet ecclesiasticum..convenientes et †~i [v.l. apti] gradum GILDAS *EB* 66.

adiposus, adipose.

adipis quoddam genus zirbus est, ex nervosis filis tenuique nervorum substantia ~a constans D. EDW. *Anat.* A 4.

adipsa [ἄδιψος], liquorice.

glicoriza aut squicia aut ~a..frutex est *Alph.* 76.

adirare v. addirare.

adire [CL], to go to, approach, visit: **a** (absol. or w. adv. or prep.); **b** (w. dat.); **c** (w. acc.); **d** (pass.).

a idem ire est adire et abire: abit enim de loco et adit ad locum Anselm (*Praesc.* I 4) II 253; **s1260** illuc jubetur adire *Flor. Hist.* II 459; Henricus imperator contra duos papas adiit *Eul. Hist.* I 260; **s1174** David..in Scociam..adivit *Plusc.* VI 26. **b 1201** adiit ballivis..et rogavit..*CurR* II 45; **c1380** vos deprecans..quod..mulieri adire dignemini, rogando eandem ex parte mea.. *FormOx* 320; Elle..Eboraco adiit *Eul. Hist.* III 4; **1458** jussus adire carceribus flevit *MunAcOx* 674. **c** cum sanctae limina valvae / vellet adire Aldh. *VirgV* 1042; Romam adiit, Brittaniam rediit Bede *HE* IV 13; ut omnis homo pacem habeat placitum adeundo et a placito redeundo (*Cons. Cnuti*) *GAS* 367; illud [phantasma] navicula remis ~e statuerunt Gir. *TH* II 12; **1269** adiit..regem, dicens..*SelPlForest* 45; **s1408** regem adiit exonerare de cancellaria *Chr. S. Alb.* 44. **d** Fons Sacer, Fons Clericorum, Fons S. Clementis..adeuntur celebriore accessu W. Fitzst. *Thom. prol.* 7; prior invitans adeatur D. Bec. 1371.

2 (?) (w. *bellum* and acc.) to attack.

cogitans plebs impiissima bella adire Occidentales Saxones Æthelw. IV 2.

3 to seek out.

primo causa potens est adeunda tibi Neckam *DS* IV 737.

adiscere, adissere, v. addiscere. 1 aditio v. additio. 2 aditio v. adicere 1b.

3 aditio [CL], entering (into an inheritance).

Ismaelem a paterne hereditatis ~one..cervix exclusit erecta Neckam *NR* II 155; omnia jura hereditaria transeunt ad heredes ex civili ~one Bracton 77; per ~onem hereditatis Upton 47.

aditum v. adytum.

aditus [CL], (way of) approach. **b** (fig.) approach, opening, occasion. **c** (w. *exercitūs*), military service, 'fyrd',

a per magis difficiles et inaccessibiles ~us ipsum ex industria circumduxit Gir. *IK* I 10; domum circuit ~uque reperto irruit Map *NC* II 12. **b** G. Mon. XII 7 (v. 2 burdo); J. Sal. *Met.* 870D (v. adviatio); non habes aliquem ~um castigando..ipsum corrigere Ockham *Dial.* 541; difficiles aditus impetus omnis habet Gower *VC* I 2030. **c 940** (12c) preter..tria, exercitus ~um, pontis edifitium, munitionis castellique auxilium *CS* 761 (cf. ib. 931).

adjacenter, attributively.

persuadere nitebatur res interdum pure, interdum ~er predicari J. Sal. *Met.* 893D; ubicumque predicatur aliquid esse verum, predicatur de eodem Deus, licet ~er et denominative et nuncupative Gros. 130; hoc verbum 'est'..~er significat, sc. per comparationem ad aliam substantiam Bacon XV 49.

adjacentia, proximity: **a** (of time); **b** (of quality). **c** range of meaning.

a nichil quod ex ~ia temporis relinquitur tempus est Bacon VIII 262; sequitur quod totalis etas sit continue eque magna; cum enim causatur ex ~ia temporis, patet quod causatur successive ex tempore Wycl. *Log.* III 198; ex ~ia temporis causata in re temporali Netter *DAF* I 28. **b** ut habituatus ad dandum quocumque gradu..posset sic circumstanciari quod habitus iste virtuose inclinaret, ut patet specialiter concomitante prudencia talem habitum et proporcionali ~ia facultatum Wycl. *Ente Praed.* XVIII 169. **c** si..ejus [adjectivi] ~ia terminetur per substantivum precedens, ut 'homo coloratus albus' Bacon XV 50.

2 a (pl.) neighbourhood. **b** appurtenance, adjunct.

a pertineat infractio pacis intra curiam vel adjacencias suas [AS: *binnan byrig oððon buton*] (*Quad.*) *GAS* 222. **b 1074** terram..quae dicitur Smedeton cum ~iis suis (*Ch. Odonis Archiep.*) Thorne 1789; **a1090** ecclesia [de Roffa]..teneat predicta maneria cum omnibus ~iis suis *CalCh* II 194; **1155** cum cunctis suis ~iis et in hominibus et ecclesiis et in terris..et in consuetudinibus omnibus *Ib.* 317; **s1256** appropriavit dictis monachis ecclesiam..de Ho cum pertinenciis et ecclesiam de Suttone cum ~iis *Flor. Hist.* II 415; spirituale ministerium quo ad Deum, et temporalium regni ~ia quo ad mundum Wycl. *Sim.* 32.

adjacentiari, to be adjacent.

1289 in terris..que sunt..inter feoda..regis, sicut superius ~iantur et confrontantur *RGasc* II 463.

adjacēre [CL], to lie near, be adjacent: **a** (absol. or w. prep.); **b** (w. dat.); **c** (w. abl.).

a excepta ecclesia sua et ~entibus agellis Bede *HE* III 17; **c1200** que terra ~et inter terram que fuit Maloisil et terram Willelmi *Cart. Osney* I 36; per decenas et villatas ~entes [v.l. ~ientes] *Fleta* 46 (cf. ib. 243: cum..hamelettis †adjicientibus); sicut sedens in navi videt terram ~entem moveri Lutterell *Occam* 128v. **b** sensit nescio quid frigidi suo lateri ~ere Bede *HE* III 2; Hibernia Britannie collateraliter ~et Gir. *TH* 1. 2. **c** tradidit ex praediis suis tria millia ~entia colle Æthelw. II 7.

2 to pertain, be attached to. **b** (pr. ppl. as sb. n. pl.) appurtenances, adjuncts.

de hoc monasterio sive ~entibus ei possessiunculis Bede *HE* IV 14; huic manerio ~ent vii hagae in Lewes *DB* I 16b; ista terra non ~et ulli suo manerio *Ib.* 48; ad hanc ecclesiam ~ent xx masurae bordariorum *Ib.* 52; haec duo maneria ~uerunt ad firmam Maurdine manerii regis *Ib.* 185b; volo ut sokna..tam pleniter monasterio S. Eadmundi modo ~eat sicut.. (*Ch. Will. II*) *EHR* XXIV 424 (cf. *Regesta* 138); **1091** ecclesias de Merleberga cum decimis ceterisque ibidem ~entibus *MonA* VI 1295; **c1220** homines eorum..quietos clamavi..de omnibus aliis sectis, nisi de hiis ubi vita et membrum ~et *Cart. Osney* IV 55; **s1231** de maneriis et rebus aliis ad archiepiscopatum ~entibus illum..investivit M. Par. *Maj.* III 207; **1315** de terra de Lincolnia eidem feodo ~ente *ChartR* 101 m. 11; de quocunque fortune bono quod ~et et non inheret datorio Wycl. *Civ. Dom.* I 27. **b** ecclesia de Bedeford cum ~entibus sibi valet c sol. *DB* I 210b.

3 (pr. ppl.) allied to, associated with (as attribute).

que..predicantur, suis applicantur subjectis..denominative si non prorsus eodem nec prorsus alio sed ~ente sibi vicinitate quadam intellectu verborum [predicantur]..; sic a bonitate bonus, a fortitudine fortis dicitur, ut ex ipsa verborum forma perpendatur quodammodo ~ens intellectus J. Sal. *Met.* 893A; tria sunt ~encia in proposicione, quamvis non in omni: primum ~ens est subjectum, secundum ~ens est copula et tercium ~ens est predicatum Wycl. *Log.* I 21.

adjectio [CL], throwing on or into. **b** adding, addition.

s1190 oppidani..prorumpunt et usque ad ~onem ignium de proximo papiliones invadunt *Itin. Ric.* I 40; **1236** in divisionem sui ab unitate corporis Christi..et perpetuam ~onem igni Gehenne Gros. *Ep.* 23 p. 90. **b** si..non intelligitur 'solus verus deus' sine ~one nominis alterius Anselm (*ProcSp* 3) II 190; quem [nodum] si cum ~one non inveneris..cum diminutione reperies Rob. Angl. *Alg.* 74; cito expediuntur horrea que assidua non fuerint ~one referta Gir. *EH pref.* 2 p. 223; **1246** dum modo..xl m. nobis..persolvant..juxta formam litterarum per quas nobis erant prius obligati et secundum ~onem obligationis quam postmodum..fecerunt *Reg. Paisley* 25.

2 addition, thing added. **b** additional clause. **c** epithet.

epactae Graeco vocabulo, id est '~ones', vocantur Bede *TR* 50. **b** ~onem illam, viz. 'salvo ordine', promisit se mutaturum H. Bos. *Thom.* III *intr.* p. 179; ~ones hujusmodi, 'si Deus voluerit', 'si vixerimus,' singulis de futuro promissionibus faciendas ostendit Gir. *IK* I 2; **s1222** concilium provinciale..ubi quedam instituta concilii generalis..cum quibusdam ~onibus..sunt recitata W. Coventr. II 25. **c 1309** dicit quod non est aliqua villa in comitatu isto [*Devon*] que vocatur Sutton' sine ~one; et dicit quod tenementa in visu posita sunt in Sutton Prioris et non in Sutton' *JustIt* 1349 r. 10; nullo (*sic*) scienti papam esse hereticum licet papam vocare nisi racione alicujus ~onis vel modi loquendi Ockham *Dial.* 721; **1387** de tenementis..Johannis Brounyng' de Heriettesham de com. Kanc' [qui] sub nomine Johannis Brounyng' absque ~one aliqua nomini illi..utlagatus fuit *PlRCP* 503 r. 324.

adjectivare, a to throw on. **b** to qualify (gram.).

a 14.. ~o, A. *to cast to* WW. **b** subvertisti sensum evangelii [*Luke* xiv 13] quando tres tantum posueris invitandos et ~ari tantum eos per ly 'pauperes' cum iiij sint Netter *DAF* I 503C.

adjectivatio, adjectival function, use as an epithet.

statim post convocari quatuor jubet copulative eosdem 'pauperes et debiles, cecos et claudos' [*Luke* xiv 21].., ubi satis notanter discernit vocabula; interposicio enim copule ~onem precedentis [sc. 'pauperes'] interimit Netter *DAF* I 504A.

adjective, adjectivally, as an epithet.

si illud adjectivum cui fiat appositio sit pure adjectivum ~e retentum Bacon XV 50; 'pater' potest sumi ~e vel substantive Duns *Sent.* I v 1. 10.

adjectivus, added, additional. **b** (sb.) (?) adjunct, appurtenance.

cum..unitates que cum nodis pronunciantur omnes ~e sive omnes diminutive fuerint Rob. Angl. *Alg.* 90. **b** 955 (12c) villam..cum omnibus suis †abjectivis [? l. ~is] *CS* 906.

2 adjectival. **b** (sb. n.) adjective. **c** (sb. n.) qualifying clause.

~e virtutis explet officium, que substantivorum determinat qualitatem J. Sal. *Met.* 842B; unumquodque verbum ~um significat esse sue rei Bacon XV 148. **b** qui secunde impositionis ~a prime institutionis substantivis applicant J. Sal. *Met.* 842C; O quam eleganter ~um depingit substantivum cum honesti mores naturalia ornant! Neckam *NR* II 173 p. 284; illa substancia ad quam qualitas significata per nomen ~um inclinatur non significatur per ~um purum, set solum intelligitur Bacon XV 6; **1293** cum..secta Phariseica ex interpretacione ipsius ~i sonet in divisionem *Reg. Cant.* II 1286. **c s1397** in principio suo responscionis imponebat sibi silencium, cum hoc ~o quod tempore futuro non sufficeret ad †abicienda [l. obicienda] contra se plenarie respondere *Chr. Kirkstall* 130.

adjectus v. adicere. adjestiamentum v. agistamentum 1.

adjocari, to play with.

talibus [parvulis] spirituali quadam suavitate dulcius ~abatur Ad. Eyns. *Hug.* III 14.

adjornamentum [OF *ajornement*], adjournment.

et hoc quolibet ~o usque ad finem placiti *State Tri. Ed. I* 19; sic evanescit ~um usque ad iter justiciariorum *Fleta* 377; **s1361** omnia placita adjornata fuerunt per commune ~um hic usque ad octabas S. Mich. *G. S. Alb.* III 46.

adjornare [OF *ajorner*], **a** to fix a day for appearance of (litigants etc.). **b** to appoint (a day). **c** to fix a day for, adjourn (proceedings). **d** to adjourn (Parliament).

a 1260 pro diversis negociorum generibus..pro quibus eciam ~ati estis coram prefato rege *Cl* 220; **1270** ipsum [comitem] ~avimus coram..nunciis nostris quod die predicto..sit ibidem *Cl* 235; **1284** [partes] adjournentur ad breves dies *Reg. Malm.* I 240; juratores ~ati fuerunt *State Tri. Ed. I* 15; **1307** partes..coram nobis ajornare curetis ad primam diem judicialem *RGasc.* III 465; **1327** ~antur usque ad proximum parliamentum..ad faciendum ibidem quod juris fuerit *ExchScot* 72; **1433** idem prior ~atur ulterius..usque ad octabas S. Michaelis (*Breve*) Amund. I 326. **b 1306** ad diem partibus illis per justiciarios..~atum (*Breve*) *MGL* II 211. **c 1262** appellum illud..ajornari facias coram justiciariis *Cl* 75; **1271** placita..adjurnetis ad aliquem certum terminum *Cl* 348; **1285** justiciarii itinerantes..reliquam partem [comitatus] apud W. adjornarunt in octabis Pasche (*Breve*) *Ann. Dunstable* 323; **1287** loquele de comitatu isto..~ate sunt ulterius *PQW* 9a; assisa..~ata ad alium diem legitimum (? *Stat. Dav. II* 21) *APScot app.* 275; **1415** justiciarii..sessionem ~arunt *March S. Wales* 56; **14..** que..recordum et processus..~ata sunt *Reg. Brev.* 3. **d s1468** Parliamentum ~atur W. Worc. *Ann.* 775; **1546** per quendam actum Parliamenti nostri..apud London' inchoati et deinde usque Westmonasterium ~ati (*Pat* 783) *Mon. Exon.* 421.

adjornatio, adjournment.

post ~onem..inventus fuit in curia *State Tri. Ed. I* 14; **1313** ~o Parliamenti per breve *Cal LB. Lond.* E f. 6b; **1522** absque ~one *Entries* 22b.

†adjudex [? f.l.], judge (*cf. Deut.* xvii 9: *venies ad sacerdotes..et ad judicem*).

c1236 quod si dicat quis non fuisse unum et eundem sacerdotem Levitici generis et adjudicem Gros. *Ep.* 72 p. 221.

adjudicare [CL], **a** to adjudge, impose (verdict, procedure, or penalty) by judgement. **b** to decide or decree judicially. **c** to judge or interpret in a specified manner.

a 1194 lex ~ata fuit illi et dies datus fuit illi de lege sua perficienda in Banco *CurR RC* I 71; **1229** cum duellum fuerit ~atum in curia prioris *Feod. Durh.* 215; **1259** murdrum decetero non ~etur coram justiciariis ubi infortunium tantummodo ~atum est (*Prov. Westm.* 25) *Cl* 150; si quis fuerit excommunicatus in non solvendo..sortem principalem, hoc est rem ~atam, utpote decimas ~atas *Praxis* 194. **b s870** rex Eadmundus..jussit a militibus de curia sua ~ari et legis peritis quid de homicida foret agendum M. Par. *Maj.* I 395; **1266** ~atum fuit in curia nostra quod..*Cl* 260; ~averunt..dampna..eis restitui *State Tri. Ed. I* 37; ~arunt quod..probaret *Ib.* 98; **s1399** rex eum ~avit decapitari W. Worc. *Ann.* 756. **c 1433** utrum eedem reclamacio, contradiccio et dissensio de jure ecclesiastico ~ari debeant valide..necne (*Plac. in Scac.*) Amund. I 323; **s1456** permulta..~are solent, presumentes aliquotiens id quod sit bonum malum dicere.. *Reg. Whet.* I 245; **1687** hec pardonacio..interpretetur et ~etur in beneficentissimo sensu (*Pat*) *N&Q* V 496.

2 a to adjudge (the accused) to (a procedure). **b** to condemn (to a punishment). **c** (w. *quietus*) to acquit.

a judicio aque ~atus est W. Cant. *Mir. Thom.* II 3; **1221** ~atus fuit ad legem quandam faciendam *PlCrGlouc* 6. **b** ad levis culpae satisfactionem ~atus frater a communi mensa separatur Lanfr. *Const.* 163; **1217** ~atus est E. ut reddat debitum *KRMem* 2 r. 1; **1229** cum aliquis..~atus fuerit ad pillorium *Feod. Durh.* 215; **s1251** ideo fuit morti ~atus *Leg. Ant. Lond.* 18 (cf. ib. 161: capta fuerunt retia piscatorum..et ibi ~ata); ~ati fuerunt prisone *State Tri. Ed. I* 32; **1390** proditores et banniti seu ~ati extra regnum *RScot* 106b; **1391** pro aliquibus amerciamentis in quibus ~ati fuerunt *ExchScot* 265. **c 1203** ipse et alii appellati de vi ~ati fuerunt quieti inde *SelPlCrown* 33.

adjudicatio, judgement.

12.. quedam averia..nobis pro ~one xx m. predictarum..tradita fuerunt *Meaux* II 19; **1433** ad habendum..~onem suam, secundum quod jus suum ecclesiasticum adjudicaverit in hac parte, per eum distincte..factam (*Plac. in Scac.*) Amund. I 323; **1499** in ~one ejusdem brevis *Entries* 291.

adjudicator, doomster (Scot.).

1539 ~ori curie de Roscoby *Rent. S. Andr.* 58.

†adjudicatorius, (?) judicial.

quod credit ejus adversarium nolle..obtinere sententiam †~ium [? l. †~iam *or* adjudicatorum] pro muliere..ab alio cognita *Praxis* 199.

adjumentum [CL], (means of) aid.

mei..laboris fiat fulcimentum vestrae intercessionis ~um Aldh. *VirgP* 60 p. 322; **10..** fomenta, i. ~a, adjutoria, medicamenta..vel *swæsunga* WW; quod dicitur esse per aliquid videtur esse aut per efficiens aut per materiam aut per aliquod aliud ~um, velut per instrumentum Anselm (*Mon.* 6) I 19 (cf. ib. 22: omnis causa necesse est aliquod ad essentiam effecti prebeat ~um); vite..subsidium et nichilominus anime sue protectionis ~um R. Cold. *Cuthb.* 47.

adjunctio [CL], combination. **b** marital union.

de causis rerum et ~one earum vel repugnantia J. Sal. *Pol.* 640C; ars musice conpletur per ~onem sonorum secundum proportionem.. *Ps.*-Ric. *Anat.* 24. **b** de legali ~one parentum ejus Felix *Guthl.* 3 *rub.*

2 drafting (of farm animals) into next age-group.

1277 de juvencis: idem respondet de ij juvencis de remanenti et de xij adjunctis [? de] juniori stauro; summa xiiij; exinde in ~one, ij *Ac. Stratton* 206; de vitulis:.. summa xlvij; exinde in ~one cum boviculis viij; in ~one cum juvenculis xij *Ib.*; **1281** de iiij bovettis.., de quibus in ~one cum bobus j *Ac. Wellingb.* 24; **1417** de v^xx xvij multonibus ex †admiccione [l. ~one] hoggestr' *Ac. Durh.* 316 (cf. ib. 317: de ~one agnorum).

adjunctura, drafting (*cf. adjunctio* 2).

in ~a [boviculorum] cum tauris *FormMan* 40; item reddit compotum..de iiij hurtardis receptis de ~a ut patet inferius *Ib.* 41 (cf. ib. 42: de [hogastris] in adjunccione..ut superius cum hurtardis, iiij); **c1380** reddit compotum de.. iij [jumentis de] adju[n]ctura *Reg. Rough* 221.

adjungere [CL], **a** to yoke, attach. **b** to attach (fig.), combine, associate. **c** to add (in speech). **d** (p. ppl. as sb. n.) zeugma.

a **1268** boves tercie caruce erant adjuncti aliis carucis (*Pipe Wint.*) *EconHR ser.* 2 XII 373. **b** adjuncta secum Brittanorum manu BEDE *HE* I 12; quid si creaturam creatori adjunxeris? ERIUG. *Per.* 528A; huic manerio Cliftone sunt adjunctae iii hidae *DB* I 80; hunc comes E. adjunxit suae terrae *Ib.* II 5b; praepositus adjunxit hunc liberum hominem ad firmam regis de B. *Ib.* II 446; Ingelric accepit eum ~ens isti terrae *Ib.* II 30b; viri sancti..se.. sibique adjunctos..a vitiorum tinea purgant GIR. *TH* I 18; [G. abbas, ob. **1321**] dedit..unum frontale magnum cum mappa adjunctum WHITTLESEY 167; **1359** compotum Rogeri..redditum pro se et pro Michaele..quondam adjuncto sibi custumario *ExchScot* 603. **c** cum..explanaret dictum.., adjunxit.. ALDH. *VirgP* 55; eis mox plura.. verba..adjunxit BEDE *HE* IV 22. **d** quando unum verbum respondet pluribus nominativis, ..si [verbum] preponitur vel postponitur, est color qui appellatur adjunctum; et figura appellatur zeuma a superiori quando preponitur, zeuma ab inferiori quando postponitur VINSAUF *AV* II 3. 60; ~um verbo posito in principio: 'assunt pontifices..' ~um verbo posito in fine: '..sed nos virgo, Dei mater, ad astra vehit' GARL. *Hon. Vit.* 127, 130.

2 to draft (farm animals) into next age-group. **b** (p. ppl. as sb. n.) draft (of such animals).

1209 idem reddunt compotum..de iij vaccis adjunctis de instauro *Pipe Wint.* 51; **c1258** boveti et jenicie..in anno quarto debent ~i bobus et vaccis *FormMan. Shorwell*; **1271** iij porci de adjunctis *MinAc* 1087/6 r. 4; **1284** de xxvj [ovibus] adjunctis de hogastris anno preterito remanentibus, qui debuerunt ~i cum ovibus matricibus *Ac. Wellingb.* 40; **1312** pulcini de remanenti qui ~untur gallinis ut supra (*Ac. Bocking*) *DCCant.*; **1417** de ccxxx jercis..; et omnes ~untur ad oves matrices *Ac. Durh.* 317. **b** **1273** de adjuncto ut inferius xxj multones *Ac. Stratton* 45; **1279** agni: ..summa ccccx; inde in adjuncto cum hogastris lxx et cum jerciis iiij^xx vj *Ib.* 225.

3 (intr. w. *super*) to adjoin.

1588 omnes illas..terras nostras submersas vocatas..lez Fleetes..~entes ex una parte super le Beache *Pat* 1319 m. 3.

1 adjurare [CL], to swear. **b** to adjure, entreat (esp. w. invocation of divine power). **c** to conjure (an animal or inanimate object). **d** to conjure (a demon or demoniac), exorcize. **e** to bind by oath.

~ant per Dominum BEDE *HE* IV 28; postulat, adjurat, hortatur et omnia spondet NIG. *SS* 1047; nomina sepe Jhesu; ..~a [ME: *halse him*] per penas ejus *AncrR* 110. **b** **671** quos obsecro et ~o per clementiam Christi ut pro me preces fundant ALDH. *Ep.* 1; ~o vos N. ..per S. Trinitatem ..et per istas sanctas reliquias..ut non presumatis..accedere ad altare si hoc fecistis (*Jud. Dei*) *GAS* 401; cum rex Dunstanum ~aret ut princeps fieret sacerdotum OSB. *V. Dunst.* 32; ~o per rubrificatum salvifico cruore patibulum quatenus..vani pavoris ineptias..exterminetis AD. MARSH *Ep.* 59; [regem] per S. Paulum ~ans, ..impetrat quod optat *Croyl.* 31; Joseph mortuus in Egipto [cf. *Gen.* l 24] ~avit ossa sua in locum patrum adduci RIC. ARMAGH *Unusq.* 66. **c** ~o te, creatura aquae, in nomine Dei.., ut nullo modo suscipias hos homines..si in aliquo sunt culpabiles (*Jud. Dei*) *GAS* 404; ~o te, aqua, per Deum omnipotentem atque preclara regis et martyris Edmundi merita ..ne hunc circulum intrare presumas (*Mir. Reg. Edm.*) CIREN. I p. 373; [lupus] ~atus per Deum omnipotentem.. ne eis noceret GIR. *TH* II 19. **d** exorcistae ex Greco in Latino ~antes vocantur EGB. *Pont.* 10; ~at Lanfrancus diabolum ut loquentem non impediat OSB. *Mir. Dunst.* 19; [demoniacus] interrogatus et ~atus utrum Christianos diligeret GIR. *GE* I 18; ~avit eum [mortuum] in nomine Domini ut requiesceret *Eul. Hist. annot.* III 22; spiritus immunde, ..procul inde fugias, ~atus per nomen..Dei.. *Pont. Exon.* 223; *to conjure*, ~o, con-, exorcizare *CathA*. **e** adeo in amorem alterutrum (*sic*) sunt adunati ut fratres ~ati Romam simul tenderent (*Obs. Durh.*) S. DURH. *Auct.* I 219; **s1191** cum ipse dominus meus sit et socius ~atus in illa peregrinatione R. HOWD. III 98; jussu regis [Henrici I] omnes Anglie et Normannie optimates illi [regis filie] ~ati sunt *Flor. Hist.* II 52.

2 to assign: **a** by oath; **b** by sentence of court.

a **s1115** rex..fecit omnes..potentes Anglicani regni ~are terram et regnum Willelmo filio suo GERV. CANT. I 92; **s1272** statim post mortem Henrici regis domino Edwardo primogenito ejus..Anglia ~ata est SILGRAVE 106. **b** **1199** captionem venationis in boscis illis, que fuit illi ~ata per legales milites in curia nostra *CalCh* I 180; quedam ecclesia sua....capitulo fuit ~ata, sed tamen..ad usus communes reversura GIR. *RG* II 7.

2 adjurare v. adjuvare a.

adjuratio, a oath, adjuration, entreaty (w. invocation of divine power). **b** conjuration of water or iron before ordeal. **c** conjuration of demons, exorcism.

a antequam communicent, interroget eos sacerdos cum ~one et dicat: adjuro vos..(*Jud. Dei*) *GAS* 401 (cf. adjurare 1b); tremenda eum ~one constringens ne..visionem ipsam ediceret EADMER *Wilf.* 747A; viro cuidam..eadem qua se rex obligaverat ~one constricto reserat..sermonem AILR. *Ed. Conf.* 761A; **s1185** rex..omnes suos fideles..~onibus multis astrinxit ut quod..crederent expedire proferrent in medium DICETO *YH* II 33; **1299** hujuscemodi ~one profunda vobis interdicimus *Reg. Cant.* II 849; **s1264** barones.. contra omnium opinionem et ~onem campum..adepti sunt WALS. *YN app.* 529. **b** incipit ~o aquae (*Jud. Dei*) *GAS* 404 (cf. adjurare 1c); incipit ~o ferri vel aquae ferventis *Ib.* 406. **c** magna..est ~o et major consecratio quae demonia eiciunt..quoties infans baptizatur aut corpus Domini consecratur (*Inst. Cnut.*) *GAS* 285; *a conjuryson*, ~o, con-, exorcismus *CathA*.

adjurative, by way of entreaty.

'suscipe illum sicut me'..~e LANFR. *Comment. Paul.* (*Philem.* 17) 374.

adjurator, exorcist.

in tempore veteris legis exorciste, id est ~ores, ex doctrina Salomonis demones ab hominibus abigebant BELETH *RDO* 13. 27; *a conjurer*, ~or, con-, exorcista *CathA*.

adjuratorius, coupled w. invocation of divine power.

comple totum psalmum..cum ~iis [ME: *halsinde*] oracionibus in loquela propria *AncrR* 109.

adjutor [CL], helper.

auctor ante omnes atque ~or opusculi hujus BEDE *HE pref.*; inveniebant stiremannum et unum alium ~orem *DB* I 1; propinquus erat ~or et propitius GIR. *GE* II 7; **1383** pro juribus..Sancti recuperandis..~or et operator assiduus *Ac. Durh.* 440.

adjutorium [CL], help, aid, support. **b** aid (financial), customary payment.

~io usus..regis, convocavit episcopos BEDE *HE* II 2; ita tamen ut..faciens servitium regis haberet ~ium.. fratris sui *DB* I 354; ymago..nulla ex parte ~iis constringentibus vel extendentibus fulciebatur W. DAN. *Ailred* 47; spem suam..in ~io Dei..ponentes AVESB. 122. **b** facit ~ium cum aliis burgensibus invenire caballum in exercitu *DB* II 48; **1111** dono..consuetudines omnino et ~ia et si que alia sunt que pater meus..vel ego ipse habuimus in ea [civitate] (*Ch. Hen. I*) *MonA* II 267 (*Regesta* 988); precipio prepositis meis..ut..nemo cogatur eis ad firmae ~ium [AS: *to feormfultume*] aliquid dare (*Quad.*) *GAS* 357; **c1140** a gablis sive ~iis atque omnibus exactionibus reliquis omnino quietos *Reg. Ant. Linc.* II no. 324; **c1160** quiete..omni seculari servitio excepto danegeld et murdra et ~io regis, si communiter positum fuerit super comitatum *Eng. Feudalism* 278; **1204** quieta et soluta de omnibus geldis et †socchis [l. scotthis] et ~iis et ab auxiliis vicecomitum et prepositorum nostrorum *RChart* 118 (cf. *Feod. Durh.* 96); **1241** cives Londonienses..non sub nomine aut titulo liberi ~ii sed tallagii..regi..numerare sunt coacti M. PAR. *Maj.* IV 95; **1357** solvet dim. m. in ~io pontium ville *Rec. Leic.* II 107.

2 humerus bone.

fractura ~ii, i. partis brachii supra cubitum versus spatulam, [requirit] 40 dies GAD. 124 v. 1; ~ium est os brachii a cubito usque ad spatulas *SB* 9.

adjutrix [CL], helper, helpful (f.).

ipsa..~ix disciplinae regularis eidem matri existere.. curabat BEDE *HE* IV 9; **s878** cum sola provincia Sumersaetun; nec aliae..ei ~ices ÆTHELW. IV 3; ~ix est virtutum tribulatio NECKAM *NR* II 42; **s1237** ad..opus promovendum..manum porrexerunt ~icem M. PAR. *Maj.* III 391.

adjuvamen, help, aid.

~ine Christi visus datus est ÆTHELW. III 2; compositio hujus electuarii per ~en divinum est.. GILB. VII 329. 1; **1289** in portagio aque et aliis ~inibus in coquina, ij d. *Ac. Swinfield* 35; **s1453** petiit ab ipsa succursum sibi dari et ~en *Reg. Whet.* I 110.

adjuvamentum, help aid.

hec ~a facit aqua frigida GILB. II 105. 1.

adjuvare [CL], to help, aid: **a** (trans.); **b** (absol.); **c** (w. dat.).

eum ut in regnum perveniret adjuvit BEDE *HE* II 12; sub eis sunt c bordarii qui ~ant eos ad persolutionem *DB* I 203; quomodo id quod nullum habebat esse adjuvit aliquid ut perveniret ad esse? ANSELM (*Mon.* 8) I 22; **s1091** rex ~aret eum ad omnia..conquirenda H. HUNT *HA* VII 2 (= BROMPTON 986: †adjuraverat eum et omnia); **1269** ita ~et me Deus et S. Maria *CBaron* 77; **1452** lego Waltero ..ad ~andum eum transire ad scholas Oxonie..xx s. *MunAcOx* 647. **b** Domino ~ante BEDE *HE* II 9; ~abat in exercitu regis *DB* I 368; **1226** ad munitionem civitatis.. de bosco nostro promisimus ~are *Lit. Cant.* III 380; **1376** fuit ~ans et consenciens ad feloniam faciendam *SelCCoron* 93. **c** **a755** si..vel tibi vel alicui tuorum possim ~are (CENE) *Ep. Bonif.* 97.

adjuvatio, help, support.

in ~onem et sustentacionem..pauperum *Entries* 68b.

adjuvativus, helpful (against). **b** (sb. n.) assistant.

fel..taurinum..morbi est ~um GILB. IV 178 v. 2; item humiditas est ~a BART. ANGL. IV 4. **b** inter membra.. spiritualia cor est principium; ..cujus ~a sunt pulmo, panniculi, lacerti et arterie *Ib.* V 1.

adl- v. et. all-.

†adluricum [? *for* ad ludicrum], plaything.

pleyynge thynge, ..~um *PP*.

admallaratus v. admirallatus.

admallare [cf. mallum], to bring before a moot.

iste [tainus] poterat deinceps jurare pro domino suo..et accusationem ejus recte ~are [AS: *his onspæce geræcan mid rihte*] (*Quad.*) *GAS* 457.

admallum v. esmallum.

admannire [AS *amanian*], to claim, exact.

episcopus †admoneat [AS: *amonige*] overhyrnessam illam a preposito in cujus hoc mannitione sit (*Quad.*) *GAS* 165; ~iat scyre presul [AS: *amanige pære scyre biscop*] emendam illam ad manum regis *Ib.* 201.

admarallatus v. admirallatus.

admassare, to knead in or together.

tunc pulverisata †a massa [? l. amassa] cum modica †porcine [l. porcina] asungia donec sit sicut terra, ..et amassetur cum ea media pars salis petre M. SCOT *Lumen* 264.

admeliorare, to improve, ameliorate.

1342 salva..sacerdoti.., tuo..arbitrio de permutanda et ~anda.., pro suis victualibus..de..ecclesie..proventibus congrua porcione *Lit. Cant.* II 254.

admelioratio, improvement, amelioration.

1253 hec concordia [de tholoneo] facta fuit ad ameliorationem..civitatis *Mem. York* I 117.

admensare, to lay on the table.

non admensetur frustum piscis sine pelle D. BEC. 2603.

admensuramentum, admeasurement, apportionment.

1203 querat breve de amensuramento dotis *CurR* II 198

admensurare, a to measure. **b** to moderate, restrict. **c** to admeasure, apportion.

a **1216** ammensurari faciatis per perticam nostram xl acras terre in foresta *Cl* 279a; **1218** ad construendam domum religiosam per..easdem metas per quas nuper fuit amensurata *Ib.* 368b; cum..pastura fuerit..~ata *Fleta* 263; **1300** in uno busselo frumenti empto pro mensuris amensurandis coram marescallo *Rec. Leic.* I 256; **c1300** modus amensurandi terram, pratum, boscum..et hujusmodi *StRealm* I 206; **1378** ad eundem boscum..amensurandum, viz. quantum idem boscus seu haia in se continet per numerum acrarum *IMisc* 215/4 r. 1 (cf. ib. r. 2: ~avimus boscum predictum). **b** omnis judex justus..dicat emendationem secundum culpam, et eam tamen ~et propter indulgentiam (*Quad.*) *GAS* 474; **c1182** precipio quod omnia molendina..ita attemperari et ~ari faciatis ut molendina Cantuariensis ecclesie..plenarie molere possint (*Ch. Hen. II*) ELMH. *Cant.* 462; **1227** (v. admensuratio 1b); **1232** stagnum illud amensuratum fuit per consideracionem hundredi et per querelas liberorum hominum *BNB* II 538; **1262** gurgites..amensurari et artari faciant *Cl* 32; **1290** [senescallus] amensurare debet superoneracionem instauri bestiarum *Fleta* 160. **c** si mulier aliqua plus habeat in dotem quam habere debeat.., precipiatur vicecomiti quod id amensurari debeat GLANV. VI 17; **1201** de dote ipsius.. amensuranda *CurR* I 416; **1224** [dos] sicut justum fuerit ammensuretur *Pat* 430; **1285** ad dotem ~andam *Reg. Malm.* I 78.

2 to assess: **a** a liability; **b** a person or estate held liable.

a **c1103** ipse ~et servitia vavassorum suorum ad proficuum ecclesie *Chr. Rams.* 220; **1220** custodia castrorum amensurabitur..secundum statum locorum et temporum tam in expensis quam in aliis *Pat* 264; **1226** dabimus vobis mille m. ..pro bono adventu vestro, nisi per consilium comitum..possit ad minorem summam amensurari *Pat* 100; **1228** quod tallagium super eum assisum ita rationabiliter faciant amensurari quod se sentiat alleviatum *Cl* 139; **1271** mandamus quatinus terminos suos..taliter ~etis quod..possunt nobis..satisfacere *Cl* 338; **1336** quodlibet amerciamentorum predictorum amensuretur ad xx li. (*ExtractR*) *Foed.* IV 683. **b** **a1100** precipio vobis ut ita bene ~etis abbatiam de Thorneia..de omnibus consuetudinibus sicut melius ~atus est aliquis honor in tota Anglia qui tantundem terre habet *Regesta* p. 136; **c1103** sicut vavassores aliorum abbatum regni..~ati sunt *Chr. Rams.* 220; **a1123** Serlo ~atus fuit de misericordia regis ad x s. (*Cart. Merton*) *EHR* XIV 426; **1186** si vero xij nummos..dare non poterit, ..ita ~etur quod persolvere valeat *BBC* (*Coventry*) 154.

admensuratio, a measurement. **b** moderation, restriction. **c** admeasurement, apportionment.

a **c1230** facta est ~o pasture.., ita quod assignate fuerunt unicuique bovate terre xv capita..boum *Meaux* I 414; **1238** F. ..attornavit T. ..contra A. ..de amensuratione pasture *Cl* 126; **1285** non sunt ibi nisi una acra et dim. terre per amensuracionem *SelPlForest* lxxxi n. 3; ~o nihil aliud est quam reduccio ad mensuram; illis autem qui communiam tantum habent in fundo alicujus aliud remedium non competit nisi ~o *Fleta* 262; personam ecclesie.., qui †per pasturam superhonerabat, ad ~onem pasture coegit DOMERH. *Glast.* 507; 1378 per ~onem illam boscus predictus..continet in se.. *IMisc* 215/4 r. 3. **b** 1227 constituimus vos justiciarios nostros..ad..amensurandum..gurgites qui ad impedimentum navium..levati sunt..; et [vicecomites] scire faciant omnibus qui gurgites habent..ut..sint coram vobis ad audiendum inquisitionem et amensurationem *Pat* 162. **c** 1196 loquela..de amensuratione dotis *Pipe* 186; 1202 de placito audiendi recordum et judicium de ~one dotis sue *CurR* II 118; si [dos] ulterius quam rationabiliter constituatur, id quod excedit per ~onem revocabitur BRACTON 93; ubi plures habuerit terras in diversis comitatibus, oportet quod procedat ~o [dotis] in curia domini regis et quod omnes terre extendantur et apprecientur *Ib.* 314; quando vir dotat uxorem suam..de majori [quam tercia parte] et remanebit ei quousque admensuretur et reddatur ei per breve de ~one HENGHAM *Parva* 2.

2 **a** assessment (of liability). **b** assessed liability (of persons).

a 1230 (v. admensurator). **b** 1358 quod..teneant de ipso P...omnia vasta ad predictam villam pertinencia sine ~one ipsius P...reddenda *IMisc* 176/27 r. 3.

admensurator, assessor.

1230 cum..M...et R..., qui dati fuerunt amensuratores cujusdam amerciamenti.., amensurationem illius amerciamenti ad Scaccarium miserint, eam faciant inrotulari *Cl* 288.

†admercandizare, to spend in trade.

1354 recepit..xx li. de denariis..episcopi †~andas [? l. ad mercandizandum] et proficuum..episcopi inde faciendum *Reg. Heref.* 205.

admerciabilis, liable to amercement.

distringantur ulterius plegii..et nichilominus amerciabiles sint eo quod non habuerunt [quos plegiaverunt] *Fleta* 133; 1334 quod si non fecerit, amerciabilis est ut supra *Surv. Denb.* 151 (cf. ib.: puniendi sunt per misericordiam xv s.).

admerciamentum [OF *amerciement*], amercement.

1168 (v. admerciare b); 1180 ~a de gildis adulterinis *Pipe* 153; 1198 amerciamenta de Hertford': de hundredo de Hodesdon' j m. pro murdro *CurR RC* I 168; 1228 concessit dominus rex eis licentiam concordandi absque amerciamento *Cl* 34; s1242 per illa amerciamenta et per alia auxilia..omnes de regno..gravantur M. PAR. *Maj.* IV 187; 1254 taxantur nomine ammerciamenti vj s. viij d. *Rec. Leic.* I 68; 1275 cepit emerciamenta servisie *Hund.* I 280; 1285 predicte ville sunt guyldabiles cum hundredo ad regem, sc. ad turnum vicecomitis et ad amerciamenta justiciariorum *Aids* II 23; nec apprecientur quantitates amerciamentorum nisi per sacramentum parium suorum *Fleta* 63; 1313 de..ballivis qui bis vel pluries ceperunt denarios ab alico pro unico amerciamento *Eyre Kent* 63; *a mercyment*, amerciamentum, misericordia *CathA*; 1583 releviis, heriettis, finibus, amerciamentis *Pat* 1235 m. 19.

admerciare [OF *amercier*], to amerce, assess for fine at the mercy of the court (*cf. misericordia*). **b** (p. ppl. as sb. m.) person amerced.

1188 Bonefei Judeus Wirecestre debet j m. auri pro respectu usque coram rege de se ~iando de misericordia pro nova assisa *Pipe* 182; 1198 de Reginaldo..amerciando ad scaccarium *CurR RC* I 170; 1215 liber homo non amercietur pro parvo delicto nisi secundum modum delicti *Magna Carta* 20; 1225 amercatus fuit ad x m. pro vino vendito *LTRMem* 7 r. 13; 1244 de novis placitis corone:..de illis qui sunt in misericordia domini regis et non sunt amerciati *MGL* I 79; 1258 si iidem clerici..amerciati fuerint a judice seculari, prelati ad hujusmodi amerciamenta solvenda predictos clericos non compellant *Conc. Syn.* 578; 1278 si aliquis tenencium..suorum..sit ~iatus coram rege, ..abbas et monachi omnes mercias et amerciamenta..habeant *PQW* 276; 1278 sciat quod graviter amerciatus est, eo quod preceptum domini regis non est executus, et gravius amerciabitur nisi.. *Reg. Heref.* 72; 1295 curia..amerciata fuit pro falso judicio *Reg. Carl.* I 65; 1336 amerciatus fuit in c m., eo quod non venit ad parliamentum nostrum tentum apud Dubliniam (*ExtractR*) *Foed.* IV 683; 1448 ubi..homines..fines facere vel fecisse, amerciari vel amerciatos fuisse..contigerit (*Ch. Hen. VI*) *Reg. Whet.* I 35; *to mercy*, amerciare *CathA*; a1540 ubi non deberent amersiari..nisi in tempore guerre (*De Pidele Trenthyde*) *Winchester Coll. MSS.* **b** 1166 hic annotantur ammerciati pro navibus oneratis *Pipe* 30; 1168 de ix li...de ~iatis [v.l. admerciamentis] pro forisfacto foreste *Pipe* 44; 1230 ita quod predictam misericordiam cum aliis ammerciatis debeat participare *LTRMem* 11 I. 6d.; 1236 faciat inquisicionem qui fuerunt ballivi..per quorum visum dicti justiciarii amerciaverunt amerciandos qui amerciati non inveniuntur in comitatu *KRMem* 15 r. 16 (2).

admerciatio, amercement.

furtum ypocriticum ut palliata injuriacio temporalium per leges humanas, que est injusta exaccio, amerciacio, multacio vel quomodocunque aliter nominetur WYCL. *Mand. Div.* 368; 1539 presentacionem et amerciacionem et levaciones amerciamentorum *Entries* 426.

admerciator, amercer, assessor of fine.

ad hoc fideliter affidabunt amerciatores BRACTON 116b.

admetiri [CL], to measure, survey.

Julius Cesar..consulatus est omnem orbem per prudentes viros ~iri *Eul. Hist.* II I (= HIGD. I 5: dimetiri).

admictio v. adjunctio 2.

adminiculari [CL], to give support.

da verborum regulas, quae palimbachii legibus pariter amminiculentur ALDH. *PR* 124 p. 172; 786 divino ~ante favore ALCUIN *Ep.* 3 p. 28; 990 Altithrono amminiculante Anglorum..basileus *CD* 684; s1064 si mihi te in hoc ipso ~aturum spoponderis EADMER *HN* 8; discipline subalterne dicuntur quarum una ~atur alii, ut arismetica et musica NECKAM *NR* II 173; s1311 item ~atur XL^{mus} testis, qui dicit quod ipse..audivit.. *Ann. Lond.* 183; amminiculor, A. *to helpe* WW.

adminicularius, supporter, ally.

metuebant ne cum ~iis invincibiles inimici Ascalonem intrarent ORD. VIT. IX 17.

adminiculatio, provision, resources.

quicquid tibi..de propria ~one defuerit, ego..supplebo *V. Dunst.* B. 14.

adminiculum [CL], **a** prop, buttress. **b** support. **c** supporting document, adminicle.

a ecclesiam cathedralem..perfecte de plumbo cooperiet cum omnibus suis ~is *Proc. v. A. Kyteler* 37; s1415 quantum canelle nostre ex fortalicio seu muris..exarmassent de die, ipsi de nocte..fasciculis congestis..et ~is aliis rearmarunt ELMH. *Hen. V* 24. **b** abminiculum, adjutorium *GlC* A 1; mortalium diffidens amminiculo et angelorum fretus suffragio ALDH. *VirgP* 26 p. 262; regio fultus ~o BEDE HE I 33; 800 absque ullo scribendi ~o verbum Dei praedicabat ALCUIN *Ep.* 213; ut..peregrinis..in suis necessitatibus pio profuisset aminiculo *V. Dunst.* B. 37; epistole..ita sunt manifeste..quod minus videantur egere historiali ~o A. TEWK. 26; ut subjecti caloris amminiculo sanguis efficacius accedat digestioni ALF. ANGL. *Cor* 3; c1273 †aminuculo vestre diligencie *AncC* VII 109; 1306 sine quarum [ecclesiarum] amminiculo procuracionem..persolvere minime potuisset *Reg. Carl.* I 271; Deus..creat effectum sine ~o se juvantis WYCL. *Dom. Div.* I 10; institutionis..execucio que contingit per aditionem hereditatis et per subsequens ~um, sc. per apprehensionem et possessionem corporalem UPTON 47. **c** 1250 mandavit dominus rex justiciariis.. quod recordum predicte loquele sibi submitterent cum omnibus ~is loquelam illam tangentibus *CurR* 139 r. 7d.; 1251 cum recordo predicto et aliis amminiculis attinctam illam tangentibus *Cl* 545; 1263 cum brevi nostro originali et aliis ~is *Cl* 302; 1312 cum atachiamentis et omnibus aliis ~is appellum istud tangentibus *SelCCoron* 66; 1330 consideratis deposicionibus testium productorum ac aliis ~is que pro domino episcopo faciunt in hac parte *Reg. Roff. Ep.* f. 130b.

administrare [CL], to supply, make available. **b** to administer (sacraments etc.).

fortuna amisso gladio ei bipennem aministraverat G. MON. I 12; 1206 debet..celerarius ea..fratribus per manus subcelerarii ~are (*Const. Evesham*) *MonA* II 24b; s1238 in militia non minima, quantam et qualem omnes ejus amici..potuerunt ~are M. PAR. *Maj.* III 518; 1243 Martino converso faciant ~ari in aliqua villa ubi possit..de fide catholica..erudiri *RGasc* I 177; cum [luna] est crescens lumine in secunda quarta, jam ex propriis radiis suam amministrat virtutem BACON VI 61. **b** 1258 quod archidiaconi..nichil omnino exigant..pro ~ando aliquo sacramento *Conc. Syn.* 613; 1361 ipsius inhabitatoribus sacramenta ecclesiastica et sacramentaria ~ari *Mem. Ripon* I 204; 1451 ad ~andum sacramenta et sacralia *Reg. Heref.* 13.

2 to administer, operate: **a** (an office); **b** (laws or affairs); **c** (absol.).

a cum..episcopatum ~aret BEDE *HE* III 23. **b** leges..divinae per angelos ~atae sunt ERIUG. *Per.* 544C; s1509 Henricus..sibi consiliarios delegit..ad quos rerum ~andarum curam detulit P. VERG. *Camd.* 149n.; satagunt reges..pacem tueri..quo locus sit ~andi justitiae FERR. *Kinloss* 5. **c** 1210 noverit..dignitas vestra in officio sacerdotali eum ~asse *FormOx* 274.

3 to administer an estate: **a** (trans.); **b** (w. *de* or absol.).

a peto ut reddat rationem tutele mee de bonis ~atis quia tutor meus fuit..legitimus W. DROGHEDA *SA* 178 (cf. ib. 210: cujus negotia eo absente..~avi); a1265 prius quam de bonis ipsis aliquid ~ent *Conc. Syn.* 716; 14.. ad recognoscendum..si predictus I. ~avit diversa bona et catalla que fuere predicti W. tempore mortis sue ut executor testamenti ipsius W. *Reg. Brev. Jud.* 30b; 1452 ut nullus executorum suorum habeat bona eis legata..si non..actualiter ~averint execucionem testamenti *MunAcOx* 656; ~abis omnia et singula bona ejusdem defuncti *Praxis* 10. **b** c1258 si quis..de rebus cujuscumque defuncti disponere, ordinare seu ~are presumpserit *Conc. Syn.* 619; 1261 ne..executori permittatur ~are de bonis testatoris nisi.. *Ib.* 681; 1287 donec ista fient.., executores minime ~ent *Ib.* 1047.

administratio [CL], supply, provision. **b** administration of sacraments etc.

eis..cum ~one victus temporalis licentiam quoque praedicandi non abstulit BEDE *HE* I 25; aquae ~o non aspernatur *ReguIC* 64; ADEL *QN* 55 (v. administrativus); commissa est ei cura amministrationis aque, ignis et luminarium ecclesie parochialis *Found. Waltham* 1. **b** s1200 legatus Romane ecclesie..multos ab ~one altaris amovendos judicavit *Plusc.* VI 38; 1549 contra eos qui adversus ipsa sacramenta..in sacramentorum ~one obganniunt *Conc. Scot.* II 120.

2 **a** administration, management. **b** (public) office. **c** arrangement, settlement. **d** province (Franciscan).

a de proprietatibus divinae ~onis ERIUG. *Per.* 566D; ne unquam aliquid usque ad knipulum in ~one cancellarie sue pro mercede acciperet GIR. *GE* II 26; 1228 vidit eum habere liberam ~onem ejusdem ecclesie tanquam custodem *Feod. Durh.* 296; 1261 priores seu administratores [celle]..qui curam, ~onem seu regimen ab..episcopo..recipient *Reg. Malm.* II 79; 1543 antiquissimi regni hujus ~onem ad nos detulit..Scotorum..consensus *Mon. Hib. & Scot.* 614b. **b** Dominus, adhuc adolescens non habens potestatem publice ~onis, vendentes et ementes ejecit de templo GIR. *GE* II 26; 1214 sacerdotes..qui fuerunt..executores sevorum [preceptorum] aliquando in publicis ~onibus *Conc. Syn.* 25 (cf. ib. 1022 [1287]: ne clerici..seculares ~ones recipiant); jusjurandum quod prestatur ab his qui ~ones suscipiunt W. DROGHEDA *SA* 136 p. 162; s1514–15 Volsaei ~o talem ab initio justitiae umbram in vulgus habuit P. VERG. *Camd.* 230. **c** a1180 si lis..evenerit, liberam..habeat potestatem ut ~ones concordes fiant *BBC* (*Wells*) 112. **d** provisum fuit ut tantum xxxij ~ones essent in ordine, xvj scilicet ultra montes et xvj citra ECCLESTON *Adv. Min.* 54.

3 administration of estate: **a** of ward; **b** of deceased person.

a si tutores vel curatores vel alie quedam sint persone que ~onem alienarum rerum auctoritate legitima gerunt RIC. ANGL. *Summa* 28. **b** 1232 non impediat..executores testamenti..quin liberam habeant amministrationem de omnibus catallis que fuerunt ipsius comitisse *Cl* 76; 1261 non permittatur aliquibus executio seu ~o in bonis defunctorum nisi talibus qui debitam ~onis sue possint..reddere..rationem *Conc. Syn.* 682; de bonis ipsius A. per executores nulla fiat penitus ~o *FormMan* 10; si reus..non allegavit plenam ~onem bonorum defuncti, viz. bona sufficientia ad solvendum legatum petitum non remanere penes se *Praxis* 98.

administrativus, apt to maintain.

si..semper [aquae] praecedentis [aqua] sequens est ~a, tota erit haec administratio infinita ADEL. *QN* 55; ejus [sc. voluntatis] proprium est..causati a se conservativam et ~am esse *Ps.*-GROS. 382.

administrator [CL], administrator, manager. **b** (w. *generalis*).

1261 super..modo instituendi et destituendi priores seu ~ores in cella memorata *Reg. Malm.* II 78; 1414 custodes et ~ores spiritualitatis in eisdem civitatibus et diocesi *Reg. Cant.* III 291; 1543 ut novos [monasteriorum commendatorum]..~ores deligere..valeamus *Mon. Hib. & Scot.* 614b; 1549 abbates, priores, commendatorios, ~ores locorum exemptorum *Conc. Scot.* II 92. **b** 1337 quilibet custos et prepositus seu generalis ~or cujuslibet aule *StatOx* 139; 1535 J. archiepiscopus ~or generalis monasterii de Dunfermling *Reg. Dunferm.* p. 385.

2 administrator of estate: **a** of minor; **b** of deceased person.

a 1289 Petrum..~orem Bernardi et Petri, filiorum suorum *RGasc.* II 431. **b** c1258 ne quis ipsos [religiosos] executores, consiliarios vel ~ores in suo constituat testamento *Conc. Syn.* 619; 1345 habeat archidiaconus..testamentorum..approbacionem, ..~orum liberacionem seu quietacionem *MunAcOx* 150; 1451 jocalia..ad manus..regis devenerunt, ut ~oris..ducis, quod..dux obiit intestatus *Reg. Whet.* I 65; proximi consanguinei..poterunt vocare ~orem defuncti decedentis ab intestato ad exhibendum inventarium *Praxis* 71.

administratorie, as an administrator.

heredes regni Deus constituit..ministratores bonorum fortune: et additur '~ie', quia omnis creatus dominus est solum ministrator..muneris ut capitalis Dominus limitat WYCL. *Civ. Dom.* I 35.

administratorius, a ministering (of angels). **b** appointing an administrator. **c** (sb. m.) minister, servant.

a opus ministerii sortientes..~ios spiritus AD. SCOT *Serm.* 30. 280D; fortassis aliquis angelus ~ie virtutis exstitit R. COLD. *Cuthb.* 90; c1236 angelicos spiritus ad Conditoris nutum ~ios GROS. *Ep.* 36 p. 126. **b** 1587 litere ~ie *Entries* 680. **c** s1135 infinitam eris copiam..regis ~ii repererunt *G. Steph.* I 4.

administratrix, administratrix (of estate).

1356 Agnetem relictam Ade H...~icem in bonis ejusdem Ade nuper ab intestato deodatis deputavimus *Test. Karl.* 9; 1573 ~ix bonorum et catallorum *Pat* 1105 m. 31.

adminus v. ad 4b, 6e.

1 admirabilis [CL], **a** wonderful, deserving or causing wonder. **b** admirable.

a memor gloriosae tuae resurrectionis et ~is ascensionis ANSELM (*Or.* 2) III 7; s1143 lapides murorum ecclesie..guttas sanguinis emiserunt, unde per totam Angliam rumor abiit ~is *Chr. Rams.* 330; GIR. *TH* I 15 (v. admirari 3b); s1403 utriusque sexus ~is multitudo *Dieul.* 146. 2. **b** c625 quantumve sit ~e quod..praemium consequi meruisti (*Lit. Papae*) BEDE *HE* II 11; mira quidem et supra modum ~i sobrietate H. Bos. *Thom.* IV 14.

2 admirabilis v. admirallus. admirabilitas v. admirallitas.

admirabundus, overawed.

~um a novitate et congressu seniorum FERR. *Kinloss* 63

admirajusus v. admiravisus.

admiralla, flagship.

s1335 maxima navis, que classis predicte ~a [v.l. admiralia] dicebatur, super scopulos..confracta est *Plusc.* IX 31

admirallatus, admiralty, office or jurisdiction of admiral. **b** prize dues.

1438 custodes et admiralli in locis custodie et ~us suorum *RScot* 310b; 1460 compotantes omiserunt se onerare de xl s. receptis de officio admarallatus *ExchScot* 594. **b** 1459 de xl li. x s. receptis a R. M., Brittone, de †admallaratu duarum navium captarum per eundem ab Anglicis *Ib.* 495.

admirallitas, admiralty, office or jurisdiction of admiral.

1339 dum tamen dicte naves pro flota nostra navium ~atis versus partes boriales in comitiva admiralli profecturarum ordinate non fuerunt *RScot* 568b; **1383** quod.. propositus et homines ejusdem ville de Aldestowe aliquam curiam seu jurisdiccionem ~atis ibidem habent (*CoramR*) *SelPlAdm* I xlix; **1392** processus loquele..in curia ~atis *Ib.* 2; **1437** quod eo casu nullus mercator vel nauta de hansa judicium ~atis subire teneatur (*Pat*) *Foed.* X 668; **1444** in curia admiralitatis nostre tenenda apud Cromere juxta fluxum maris loco debito *BBAdm* I 261; **1482** de hiis que ad curiam principalem ~atis nostre pertinent (*Pat*) *SelPlAdm* I lv; **1587** mandato judicis curie admirabilitatis nostre Anglie *Pat* 1300 m. 15.

admirallus, ~ius, ~is [OF *amiral* < Ar. *amir*, *infl. by* admirari], emir, Arab commander or governor; w. *Murmelin* or sim. (< Ar. *Mu'minīn*) = caliph. **b** Italian governor, *podestà*.

s807 Chumeid amiras, missus ab Aaron rege Persarum Diceto *Chr.* 130; Abdallas amiras, rex Saracenorum Ord. Vit. V 9; Jerosolymorum admiratus *Ib.* IX 10 p. 543; procuratori suo, quem admiralium vocant *Ib.* p. 557; **s1097** Aoxianus civitatis [Antiochie] admiratus W. Malm. *GR* IV 360; **s1098** venerant interea multi de gente amiralii Babilonis in Antiochiam H. Hunt. *HA* 224; **s1164** conductus ab amiralio Babilonico Torigni *Chr.* 223; **1188** Conradus.. magnum Alexandrie admiraldum cum octo aliis admiraldis cepit (*Lit. Preceptoris Templi*) *G. Ric. I* II 41; **s1192** Saffatino cum plurimis admiralibus..ad regem veniente Devizes 43; cum vicina sibi paganorum civitate.., cui quidam admirabilis..presidebat Map *NC* III 4 p. 130; Salius, natione rituque gentilis, filius admirandi majoris, quem admirabantur pater ejus..et tota nacio *Ib.* IV 14; **s622** Machometus..in regno Saracenorum quatuor pretores statuit, quos admiralios vocavit M. Par. *Maj.* I 272; **s1103** procurator civitatis qui..*emyr* dicitur *Ib.* II 126; **s1195** rex de Marroch.., quem mirabilem mundi vulgus, vel qui melius admiralium Murmelin, id est bellicosum et victoriosum, nominant *Ib.* II 410 (cf. ib. V 232: admirabilem mundi); **s1238** venerunt Saracenorum legati solemnes, estimati ab orientalium primatibus, soldanis et admirabilibus *Id. Min.* II 409; **1250** ivimus cum quodam admirato, qui nos conduxit *Ann. Burton* 288; tres admīrālii linquunt in litore vitam Garl. *Tri. Eccl.* 133; quas admīrāti treugas statuere tenendas *Ib.* 138; **s1271** quidam admiralius nacionis Sarracenice, que dignitas apud nos consulatus vocatur Rish. 69; **1290** dominus regum et soldanorum, participator ammiralium fidelium (*Lit. Soldanorum*) B. Cotton 216; admiraldi filiam advenisse, quam cuncti sequentes admirabantur, nunciavit *NLA* (*Thos. Becket*) II 375; **s1391** hii iiij fuerunt martyrizati a Kadi..una cum confessoribus amiraldi et soldani *Mon. Francisc.* I 527. **b s1244** hiis galeis prefuit potestas Janue, quem admiratum vocant M. Par. *Min.* II 485.

2 admiral, naval commander: **a** (Sicily); **b** (Fr. and Gasc.); **c** (Eng. and Scot.; *cf. SelPlAdm* I xi–xiii).

a s1157 rex Sicilie Willelmus navali expeditione cepit per admiralios suos civitatem Sibillam Trevet 42; **s1177** Walterus de Moac..regii fortunati stolii admiratus *G. Hen. II* I 171. **b 1274** dilectus miles noster Florencius de Warenne, nostri navigii amirallus (*Lit. Reg. Franc.*) *Leg. Ant. Lond.* 134; **1295** constituimus ipsum Berardum [de Sescars] ~um maritime Baionensis et capitaneum nautarum et marinariorum nostrorum ejusdem ville *RGasc* III no. 3883 (cf. ib. 3892 = *Foed.* II 691: senescallis, marescallis, admirantis, castellanis..); **1297** placuit regie majestati ipsum esse in officio admirati navigii Baione *Ib.* p. clxxxix; **s1385** rex Francie..misit [in Scociam]..~um Francie cum notabili armatorum comitiva *Plusc.* X 7. **c 1300** Gervasio Alard, amerallo flote Quinque Portuum *Ac. Wardr.* p. 72; **1303** amirallus flote nostre navium *CalPat* 131; **1306** de ~is flotarum navium constitutis *Pat* 127 m. 21; **1310** cum constituerimus..S. de Monte Acuto amirallum flote navium nostrarum quas pro expedicione guerre nostre Scocie.. sumus transmissuri *RScot* 93a (cf. ib. 115b); **1313** quo ad libertatem essendi ~us [ville Dovorr'].., dicit quod dominus rex nunc..fecit..Willelmum de Leyburne ~um *PQW* 321b; **1315** venit navigium vestrarum gencium de Anglia, cujus amiratus existebat dominus B. (*Lit. Baionensium*) *Foed.* III 509b; **s1340** [comes] Huntingdon' qui fuit dux et ~us [v.l. admirabilis] navium de Quinque Portubus et dominus R. de Morley qui fuit ~us [v.l. admirabilis] et dux navium borealium Ad. Mur. 106; **1360** constituimus ipsum [Johannem de Bello Campo] ~um nostrum omnium flotarum navium australium, borialium et occidentalium.., dantes ei plenam..potestatem audiendi querelas..de hiis que officium ~i tangunt et cognoscendi in causis maritimis (*TreatyR*) *Foed.* (*ed.* 1825) III 505; **1390** tenor recordi.. cujusdam placiti in curia Admirallitatis Johannis comitis Huntyngdonie ~i domini regis [nostri in] partibus occidentalibus moti (*Chanc. Misc.* 6/7) *SelPlAdm* I 2; **s1294** rex.. navigium ad custodiendum mare in tres classes distinxit, tres preponens sibi admiralios Wals. *HA* I 47; **s1387** comes Arundelie..constitutus est admirallus instantis termini *Ib.* II 153; **s1379** dominus H. de Calverley et dominus T. Persy ..facti admiralii maris oceani *V. Ric. II* 11; **s1408** comes Cancie..~us maris Anglicani *Eul. Hist. Cont.* III 413; **s1411** donec ammirallius, qui pro tunc fuit regni cancellarius, naves armasset *Chr. S. Alb.* 59; **1416** T. Beauford, ~us Anglie, Acquietanie, Hibernie (*Chr.*) *EHR* XXIX 511; si †qua supra altum mare extra corpus cujuslibet comitatus regni illius fiant que postmodum in †placitato [l. placito] coram ~o Anglie deducantur Fortescue *LLA* 32; **1450** Geo. de Creichtoun, ~us Scocie *RMSScot.* 334; **a1460** de hiis qui ordinati fuerint ad serviendum domino regi super mare..et se illicite ab eodem servicio absentaverint.., si dominus rex sive ~us suus graciam eis..non fecerint *BBAdm* I 235 (cf. ib. 234: finis facienda per capitalem ~um et non per locumtenentes suos); **s1459** dicto..amarallo [sc. comiti Warwyci] pro tam pingui spolio..Kalisius apportato sint laus, honor et potestas *Reg. Whet.* I 331; Admiralii Curia res maritimas tractat: in hac numerantur Admiralius Angliae, locumtenens et judex, scribae duo, serviens curie, viceadmiralii Angliae Camd. *Br.* 143.

admirande, marvellously, admirably.

de quibus tamen..Ptolemeus et ceteri sapientes operati sunt non nimis ~e Bacon *Maj.* I 392; **s1304** vere Dominus erat secum, admirantissime (*sic*) coram omni populo servans eum *Flor. Hist.* III 317.

admirandus v. admirallus 1a, admirari 3.

admiranter, w. wonder.

ex modo quodam docendi quem in his ~antius comperient in priorum libris exercitati Balsh. *AD* 8.

†admirantia, wonder.

s1347 rex..in talem ~iam [v.l. admirationem] et querimoniam prolapsus est, dicens..*Eul. Hist.* III 213 (cf. admirativus).

admirantus v. admirallus 2b.

admirari [CL], to wonder, marvel. **b** (w. acc. and inf.). **c** (act. form).

ammirans nimium sic fatur semet ad ipsum: / "rem miram video" Wulf. *Swith.* II 153; ~ans vehementer ~or super tue tyrannidis protervia ('*Lit. Lucii*') G. Mon. IX 15; ~antibus cunctis de Herwardo *G. Herw.* 334b; **s1170** ~atus archiepiscopus nuncio hujuscemodi ad propriam ecclesiam est reversus *Meaux* I 194. **b 1166** ~or curiam Romanam ita manifeste operari contra me (*Lit. Regis*) *Becket Mat.* V 362. **c 1237** vos quam plurimam ~asse..de eo quod.. noluit castrum reddere (*AncC* V 65) *RL* I 321; **1330** premissa..fratribus nostris..communicavimus, ..de quibus non mediocriter †~ant *Lit. Cant.* I 305.

2 (trans.) to marvel at. **b** to admire.

~or rerum subtilitatem Eriug. *Per.* 527D; Salius.., quem ~abantur pater et mater..pre sciencia in puero matura Map *NC* IV 14. **b** cum..virginalem urbanitatis disertitudinem magnopere ~arer Aldh. *VirgP* 2.

3 (gdv.) **a** deserving wonder. **b** provoking wonder (i.e. w. sense of pr. ppl. pass.).

a ~andi hujus suavitas odoris Bede *HE* V 12; illa ~ande animositatis abbatissa [Ebba] M. Par. *Maj.* I 392. **b** istam [generationem] non minus admirabilem, minus tamen ~andam, quia sepe imitatrix natura ministrat Gir. *TH* I 15.

admiratio [CL], **a** wonder. **b** admiration. **c** source of wonder, marvel.

a hinc dolor, hinc gemitus, hinc ammiratio crescit Wulf. *Swith.* I 583; ~one quam maxima ductus, ..palatium subit Eadmer *Wilf.* 27; **1166** quod..audivimus, canonicos cum monialibus in una ecclesia commorari, ..in vehementem nos ducit ~onem *Canon. G. Sempr.* 91; solis ortum, ..quo nihil..stupore dignius, ..sine omni ~one preterimus Gir. *TH* I 15. **b s1299** erat ei [Margarete] tanta pulchritudo ut aspicientes in ~onem duceret *Ann. Ang. & Scot.* 395; **s1378** solus J. Philipot ore omnium laudabatur et ~oni habebatur Wals. *HA* I 370. **c** in quo illud quoque ~oni nonnullis fuit, quod idem aurifrigium..nec majus nec minus inventum est Eadmer *Mir. Dunst.* 23.

admirativus, wondering, puzzled.

s1347 rex..in talem ~am queremoniam prolapsus est.. Higd. VII 44 p. 344.

admirator [CL], admirer, devotee.

studiorum non fucatus ~or Ferr. *Kinloss* 80.

1 admiratus v. admirallus.

2 admiratus, admiralty, (area of) jurisdiction of admiral.

1344 mandamus quod..naves..de ~u vestro predicto.. liberari faciatis *RScot* 654b; **1351** in singulis portubus et locis infra ~um vestrum (*TreatyR*) *Foed.* V 720; **1357** castrum de Brest..ac eciam villam de S. Matheo cum brevibus et custumis ejusdem ville ac ~u, piscariis..et omnibus aliis..proficuis ad predicta villam et dominium spectantibus *Ib.* VI 70; **1379** pro custodia maris et costerarum ~us de la North (*Pat*) *RParl* III 391a.

†admiravisus, ~ius [? l. admirajusus; cf. Ar. *amir aj-juyūsh*], military commander.

s1099 Babylonicus ~us Ascalone est et ibi contra nos ingens bellum preparat Ord. Vit. IX 16; **s1099** dux Normannorum.., ~ii standardum a longe considerans, ..ipsum deprehendit ibidem esse M. Par. *Min.* I 154.

admirificus, marvellous.

mervelous, admirabilis, ammirificus in factis *CathA*.

admiscēre [CL], to mingle, mix (with). **b** to have sexual intercourse.

angelorum coetibus ~itur (*sic*) Aldh. *VirgP* 25 p. 260; nulla [proles] sic dignitur ut nulla admixta dissimilitudine omnimodam similitudinem parentis exhibeat Anselm (*Mon.* 40) I 57; res non nutribilis nutribili admixta Neckam *NR* II 98 p. 182; cujus [solis luna] virtutem ~et suo lumine Bacon VI 61; cataplasma dicitur cum herbe pultibus ~entur *SB* 36. **b 597** viris suis non debent ~eri (*Lit. Papae*) Bede *HE* I 27 p. 55; cum nec etiam generis multiplicandi causa..liceat uxoribus ~eri J. Sal. *Pol.* 520D.

admissarius [CL = *stallion*], charger, courser; *v. et. amilarius*.

14.. hic ~ius, equus qui portat arma WW; *a courssor*, ~ius, cursarius *CathA*.

admissibilis, admissible, acceptable.

non est..~is ignorancia scripturarum Paul. Angl. *ASP* 1554; **1486** invenimus..causas fuisse veras..et in hac parte ~es (*Decr. Ep. Linc.*) *Croyl. Cont. D* 592; **1549** si quas [raciones] non ~es produxerit *Conc. Scot.* II 122.

admissio [CL], admission (of person): **a** to a benefice or sim. (eccl.); **b** to court (leg.); **c** to the peace (leg.); **d** to a degree or sim. (acad.).

a 1229 admissus fuit et persona institutus..et profert.. cartam..archidiaconi de ~one *BNB* II 303; **c1350** capellanus..admissus statim post ejus ~onem et institucionem.. prestet..juramentum *FormA* 266; **c1520** curatorum ~ones *Conc. Scot.* I cclxxiii. **b** petens ~onem in forma pauperis *Praxis* 189. **c 1337** potestatem..litteras de pardonacione ..inimicicie necnon de..~one ad pacem nostram eisdem hominibus..faciendi *RScot* I 509b (cf. *Reg. Brev.* 295). **d a1350** quiscunque ascensurus gradum qualemcumque in universitate in ejus ~one sacramentum prestet..item idem observetur in ~one advocatorum et serviencium communium *StatOx* 70; **1514** in eorum [studencium] ~onibus, incepcionibus vel composicionibus *Ib.* 329.

2 acceptance: **a** of request; **b** of office or remuneration; **c** of something imposed.

a 1293 ~o..resignacionis *DCCant* Q f. 5a; **14..** peticionis ~o *Reg. Brev.* 16. **b** nec me [Deus] propter rerum temporalium et redditum ~onem sive novorum adjectionem.. abduci permittat Gir. *Symb.* 20; **c1400** cancellarius in sui officii ~one..sit juratus *StatOx* 19. **c s1278** annus.. Wallensibus odibilis propter ~onem dominationis insuete Wals. *HA* I 18.

3 commission, perpetration.

nec te inpresentiarum alicujus criminis ~one notamus Eadmer *Wilf.* 27.

admissivus, admissible.

1485 nisi..~am excusacionem pretendere habeant *Reg. Brechin.* 211.

admissorius, granting admission.

s1454 abbas..concessit..ei licenciam gradiendi ad cellam de Bynham..et de hac sua licencia scripsit priori loci illius litteras ~ias *Reg. Whet.* I 144 (cf. ib. II 67).

admissus, approach, access.

[Editha] eloquio cum quovis non facilis, ~u eque difficilis Ciren. II 221.

1 admittere [CL], to admit (a person): **a** to a building; **b** to a status or office; **c** to a benefice (eccl.); **d** to court (leg.); **e** to an inheritance; **f** to the peace; **g** as surety; **h** to a degree or sim. (acad.).

a ammisso micuit sintagma berillo [v.l. benigno] Frith. 1159; femineus hic sexus non ~itur Gir. *TH* II 4; **1217** mandamus..quod Adam.~atis in castris nostris cum ad vos venerit..ad salvacionem castrorum nostrorum *Pat* 33. **b 1277** Michaeli..balistario admisso ad vadia regis *KRAc* 13/17 m. 1; **1313** ipsum in clericum nostrum et de consilio nostro duximus ~endum *RGasc* IV 1123; **1334** mandavimus eisdem..quod vos..in socium ~ant *RScot* 298a (cf. ib. 937b: admisimus ipsum..in burgensem); **1407** quod nullus imposterum †amittatur [? l. admittatur] nec †recipiatur eum pro cive *BBWinchester* f. 36. **c** ne quis alius extra consensum suum in eandem ecclesiam ~eretur per episcopum instituendus *Chr. Battle* 125; **1218** habeat breve ad archidiaconum quod ~at clericum *Eyre Yorks* 426; **1220** presentatus fuit episcopo et admissus ad ecclesiam eam *SelPl Crown* 136; **1459** donec ad temporalitatem episcopi ~antur *Conc. Scot.* II 79. **d 1285** (v. amicus 2b); [non debet] de cetero ~i ad aliquam responsionem dilatoriam *State Tri. Ed. I* 76; **1309** si uxor..venerit parata petenti respondere.., ~atur uxor *Year Bk. 2 Ed. II* 77; testes super articulis objectis..recipi, ~i, jurari..debent *Praxis* 316. **e 1296** peciit ~i ad tenementum integraliter *SelPlMan* 174. **f 1337** qui cum eis [Scotis] contra nos de inimicicia fuerunt.. et quos ad pacem et fidem [nostram] fore viderunt..~endos *RScot* 509b. **g** optulit..sufficientes manucaptores..quos ..~ere recusavit *State Tri. Ed. I* 14 (cf. *SelPlMan* 170). **h 1268** forma..sub qua bachilarii arcium determinaturi ad determinandum..forent ~endi *StatOx* 25; **c1450** ad effectum quod possit ~i ad opponendum in..theologia *MunAcOx* 732.

2 to admit (of), allow. **b** to acknowledge (as true). **c** (w. inf. or acc. and inf.) to consent.

hujuscemodi versum..modernus usus in exametro.. non libenter ~it Aldh. *Met.* 10 p. 93; philosophia..nec opulentia gaudens nec inopiam ~ens Gir. *TH intr.* p. 4; **1284** ~atur illa responsio (*Stat. II Westm.* 20) *StRealm* 82; **1314** prohibitum est..abbati ne interim ~at purgacionem ipsius *Eyre Kent* 113; **1321** major..petebat libertatem suam ~i de..servientibus [habendis] *MGL* II 297; lonchitis.. folia vulneribus imposita tumorem non ~unt *Alph.* 105; rejiciendo testes vel materiam defensionis de jure ~endae *Praxis* 231. **b** non itaque hoc ~endum, sed quod unaquaeque res tempus et ordinem spectet credendum Osb. *Mir. Dunst.* 1; **1308** quesitus..si verificacionem patrie quam A. et M. pretendunt velit ~ere, dicit revera quod non *PIRCP* 170 v. 54. **c** quod tandem..se facturum admisit Gir. *Galf.* II 7; **1450** pro eo quod..comes..dictos..denarios ..percipere ~it *Cl* 300 m. 8 (*but* cf. *Cal.* p. 149).

3 to accept: **a** a thing; **b** an office; **c** an appointed day.

a s1306 ut..adessent..admissuri singuli omnem ornatum militarem..de regia garderoba *Flor. Hist.* III 131. **b 1279** per preces gildanorum ~it senescalliam *Gild. Merch.* II 290; **1298** devenit ballivus manerii.., curam et administracionem omnium bonorum ~ens *MGL* II 95; **13..** ne quis..clericus beneficiatus administracionem alicujus laici..gerere presumat..vel ~ere *Conc. Scot.* II 67; **1419** aldermanni..officium majoritatis ~ere metuentes *Ib.* I 30; curas admittunt pingues Gower *VC* III 1345. **c 1327** ad audiendum judicium suum quare diem quem alias admisit..non servavit *LTRMem* 99 r. 104; **1333** vicecomes..in propria persona admisit diem essendi hic *Ib.* 105 r. 32.

4 to commit (an offence). **b** (p. ppl. as sb. n.) offence.

criminis admissi testis et ipsa mei Nig. *SS* 3020. **b** admissum, peccatum vel receptum *GlC* A 272. **c 765** (12c) quamvis parva..sint que pro amissis offerimus *CS* 194; ejusmodi et similibus ammissis, id est peccatis, procedit animadversio spiritalis *Cust. Cant.* 253.

2 admittere v. amittere.

admittibilis, admissible, acceptable.

omne possibile est ~e, posicione presignante illud concedendum Wycl. *Act.* 93; predicta defensio..non est sufficiens exitus nec ~is *Entries* 151b.

admixtio [CL], admixture. **b** sexual intercourse.

cum omnis substantia ~onis differentiarum..sit susceptibilis Anselm (*Mon.* 26) I 44; eo simplicior est [intellectus] quo simpliciora sine aliorum ~one perspicit singulatim J. Sal. *Met.* 877D; ~o syrupi Gilb. II 95 v. 1; ex amixtione Bart. Angl. IV 11 (cf. ib. 9). **b 597** licita amixtio conjugis sine voluntate carnis fieri non potest (*Lit. Papae*) Bede *HE* I 27 p. 57.

admixtus v. admiscere.

admodicus, small.

portiones comparatione fructuum ex eis habunde provenientium ~as suscipiens *Chr. Battle* 130.

admodum [CL; al. div., cf. ad 9g], to some extent, very, quite.

mellitae dulcedinis gustum ammodum inconparabiliter praecellit Aldh. *VirgP* 7; fratres..~um anxiati G. Mon. III 9; quidam tamen homines terre illius..redduntur ~um [*tolerably*] religiosi W. Dan. *Ailred* 38; vocans eum monachum, non quia castus tunc ~um [*completely*] fuit, set quia valde humilis *Id. Ep.* 62*d.*; **s1196** milites..ad modum xl occidit *Ann. Cambr.* 60.

1 admonere v. admannire.

2 admonēre [CL], to warn, urge.

c705 ut..de his..implendis..possis ammoneri Aldh. *Ep.* 8; visione..in qua ~itus est..insistere Bede *HE* III 19; ammonens quia nulla ratione conveniat *Ib.* II 12; eum amonuit desistere sub interminatione Map *NC* IV 6 p. 163; **a1205** ammonita in somnis ut emplastrum..apponeret *Canon. G. Sempr.* 163v.; de contumacibus precipit regula quod semel et secundo amoneantur secrete *Cust. Cant.* 392; cui ut pontificale decus susciperet vehementi petitione ~uit Ciren. II 92 (= Osb. *V. Dunst.* 29: innuit).

admonitio [CL], admonition, warning. **b** summons (leg.).

plebem..~onibus saluberrimis ad caelestia vocabat Bede *HE* IV 28; habet sacerdos gregi commisso excessus suos annuntiare et primo per secretas ~ones corripere, deinde per publicas, si opus fuerit, increpationes arguere Gir. *Symb.* 21 p. 257; **1215** post ternam ammonitionem..archiepiscopi, precedente eciam mandato apostolico *RChart* 208; **12..** post trinam ammonicionem excommunicetur *Conc. Scot.* II 23; **c1230** sine ammonicione, citacione aut aliquo strepitu judiciali *Reg. Dunferm.* no. 203; correccio..que ..tendit ad emendacionem..delinquentis per simplicem ammonicionem Ockham *Dial.* 543. **b** ter in anno teneri placita episcopi sine ammonitione *DB* I 87b.

2 erron. for AS *mænigeo* (= multitude, number) conf. w. *manung*.

secundum societatis †~onem [AS: *be pæs geferscipes mænio*] (*Quad*) *GAS* 177.

admonitiuncula, mild rebuke.

ne qualemcumque ~am scriberem Gildas *EB* 1.

admonitor [CL], warner. **b** watch-dog, 'wappe'.

correptores suos et ammonitores Ockham *Err. Pap.* 964. **b** [canes degeneres] inutiles.., nisi quod..advenas latratu excipiant..et eorum adventu domesticos commonefaciant, unde canes ~ores appellamus Caius *Can.* 9b.

admonitorius, admonitory.

c798 ammonitoria aeternae salutis verba Alcuin *Ep.* 136; **s1247** verba transmisit consolatoria et ~ia *Flor. Hist.* II 331.

admonitus [CL], admonition, prompting.

concilium magnum coegit Anglie ejusdem Bonefatii ~u W. Malm. *GP* I 4.

†admorari, to reside.

1289 clericis..in nostro servitio ~antibus *Conc.* II 171b (= *Conc. Syn.* 1087: commorantibus).

admortificare, to alienate in mortmain.

1283 regamus vos quatinus permittatis [fratribus illis].. in dicta villa remanere..et locum ex parte vestra amortificare (*Lit. Regis Franciae*) *AncC* XLVII 116; **1422** ad amortificand' terras ad fabricam ecclesie *Ac. Durh.* 407.

admortizamentum [cf. OF *amortissement*], alienation in mortmain.

1386 lego d m. argenti ad empcionem et amortizamentum advocacionis j ecclesie *FormA* 429; **1426** sine aliqua licencia regia inde unquam obtenta seu aliquo amortisamento inde facto *Cl* 276 m. 5; **14..** apposuit grandes expensas pro amortizamento terrarum *Chr. Evesham* 306.

admortizare [cf. OF *amortir*], to amortize, alienate in mortmain.

c1350 quas [acras]..religiosi facient eidem vicarie amortizari suis sumptibus *Reg. S. Aug.* 186; **1386** volo quod ..advocacio unius ecclesie..ematur et approprietur domui hospitalis de Welle et amorticietur sumptibus meis *FormA* 428; **1418** terre, tenementa, ..rura..prioratui..pro perpetuo possidenda data et concessa et amortisata..jacent inoccupata *Reg. Heref.* 49; **1430** qui redditus nunc est amortizatus ad priorem *Feod. Durh.* 67; **1435** volo quod omnia..tenementa mea..amortizentur pro una cantaria de eis facienda *Test. Ebor.* II 57; **1467** erga monasterium nostrum de N. dedisse, concessisse, ~asse et..confirmasse.. omnes..terras.. *Reg. Newbattle* no. 293; **1488** donacionem ..ratificamus, ~amus et..ad manum mortuam..confirmamus *Reg. Aberd.* I 321.

admortizatio, amortization, alienation in mortmain.

c1412 pro amortizacione manerii de Snelshale pro iiij[xx] li. *G. S. Alb. Cont.* III 390; **1440** amortizaciones, maxime temporalium, omnibus nunc odiose sunt et non dubito post hec vix futurum iri ut alique concedantur Bekynton I 116; **1505** presenti carte nostre confirmacionis et ~onis *Reg. Brechin* 222.

admortuare, to alienate in mortmain.

1348 prior de Brommore tenet de eodem dim. feodum, quod amortuatur *IPM* 85/6 r. 12.

admortuatio, alienation in mortmain.

pro amortuatione predicti manerii *Entries* 691b.

1 admovēre [CL], to move towards. **b** to post, station. **c** (fig.) to attach, apply.

ut..admotum ab hostibus urbi regiae ignem orando amoverit Bede *HE* III 16; leves..cohortes / admovet Frith. 545; pedibus anterioribus simul solo amotis et admotis W. Fitzst. *Thom. prol.* 11; eminus inspectam statuam condemnat Apelles; / admotam †proprius [l. propius] nobile censet opus Neckam *DS* III 952. **b** janitorem archiepiscopi amoverant, suum ~erant W. Fitzst. *Thom.* 136. **c** genitor.. / lubrica mundanis admovit gaudia pompis Aldh. *VirgV* 1145; Dunstanus..cenobii restaurationi.. egregiam curam ~it W. Malm. *GP* V 255; utrique animum ~it Ferr. *Kinloss* 14.

2 admovere v. amovere.

admullonare [cf. mullo], to stack.

1375 debent illud [fenum] levare et ~are *IMisc* 206/11.

admur' v. adunire b.

admustrisona [cf. OF *amostrer, mostraison*], muster.

1223 clamant quod burgenses..non cogantur..~am facere coram seneschallo *Lib. Prim. Kilken.* 79.

admutuatio, borrowing.

1329 in ammutacione argenti apud Berwicum pro molacione bladorum, xviij s. *ExchScot* 216.

adn- v. et. ann-. adnasc- v. agnasc-.

adnepos [CL], great-great-great-grandson.

~os, *fifte sune* Ælf. *Sup.*; atnepos Bracton 64b (v. abnepos).

adneptis, great-great-great-granddaughter. **b** great-great-niece.

~is, *fifte dohter* Ælf. *Sup.* **b** Henricus..~em Edwardi Matildem duxit uxorem Ciren. II 290 (= W. Malm. *GR* V 393: Edwardi..abneptis).

adolari, ~atio, ~ator, v. adul-. adoleo v. ardalio b.

1 adolēre [CL], to kindle or burn. **b** (fig.), of passion. **c** to offer as a sacrifice.

timiama diis ut ~eret Aldh. *VirgP* 47; extinctas adolere faces Neckam *DS* III 235; thuribulum in quo thus ~etur Ferr. *Kinloss* 73. **b** ut qui priores ~evistis in eam ignes crebris non fraudemini cupitis Map *NC* IV 5 p. 196. **c** canorem spiritualem mihi dederat, in †quos [? l. quo] ei [sc. Christo] laudes et preces ~erem Rolle *IA* 233.

2 adolēre [cf. adolescere], to grow.

1376 mirari cogimur quod..lollium inter purum triticum **..**permittatis pullulare et..eciam ~ere (*Bull*) *Ziz.* 242.

adolescens v. adolescere 2.

adolescentia [CL], youth.

ab ~ia incipit homo posse generare Bede *TR* 16; ab ineunte adulescentia monachicum..nomen adsumsit *Id. HE* IV 27; **8..** in ~ia, *in giohðhade* WW; jamque vernans aetas ~iae decus induerat Osb. *V. Dunst.* 8; non solum ~iam sed et omnem decet etatem Gir. *PI* I 3; adholocenciam dicit [medicus quidam] illam primam partem vite in qua calidum et humidum magis dominantur, et hoc dicunt terminari in 25 anno aut in 30 ad plus; et dicitur adolocencia ab *adolos* Grece, quod est 'crementum' Bacon VI 6.

adolescentula [CL], girl. **b** (fig.).

respiciens sociam operis ~am Ailr. *Ed. Conf.* 783C; quod juvenes aut ~e in eadem villa consistunt R. Cold. *Cuthb.* 108; huic aliquamdiu herebat ~a Dei ancilla Ositha *NLA* (*Osyth*) II 232; hec ~a, puella xiiij [annorum] WW. **b 1200** ecclesias alias tanquam ~as suas..adornat (*Lit. Papae*) *Reg. Dunferm.* no. 279.

adolescentulatio, childish prank.

eos ponens sub tutela virtuosorum..sacerdotum, ..ne scilicet indomite ~ones succrescerent Blakman *Hen. VI* 9.

adolescentulus [CL], boy. **b** serving lad, henchman.

erant hi duo ~i ambo Gir. *EH* 1. 4; **s799** Leoni adhuc ~o de lascivia penitenti M. Par. *Maj.* I 366. **b 1571** cum.. rex..dederit..officium docendi..adulescentulos suos vocatos *henchmen Pat* 1076 m. 21.

adolescere [CL], to grow. **b** (of plants). **c** (fig.). **d** (?) to become wanton.

a690 ubi..adulto tenus pubertatis aevo adoleveras Aldh. *Ep.* 5 p. 490. **b** segetes..jam in spicas et aristas ~entes Gosc. *Aug. Maj.* 58. **c** quamvis tanto jam tempore in terra ista fundata fides adoleverit Gir. *TH* III 26. **d 10..** ~eret, *wlancode* WW.

2 (pr. ppl.) youthful. **b** (as sb.), youth, lad.

c705 licet ~ens aetate existas Aldh. *Ep.* 8 (10). **b** in cor ~entis Eddi *Wilf.* 3; ut ipse adulescens in Hibernia.. monachicam..vitam..agebat Bede *HE* IV 3; ~ens vel investis..*geong man* Ælf. *Sup.*; quales infantes, tales pueri, quales pueri, tales ~entes H. Los. *Ep.* 39; quindecim ~entes imberbes animosos Gir. *TH* III 40.

3 (pr. ppl. compar.) more full of youthful vigour. **b** younger.

stabilior jam ex eo tempore animoque ~entior existere coepit Bede *Cuthb.* 1. **b** ~entiores fratres..instituebantur Gerv. Cant. I 8.

adoliare [? cf. dolium, *or more prob.* OF *aoillier* < *adoculare, cf. oillare], to pour into a barrel.

1180 pro vij tonellis vini Franci portandis..et pro vino.. ~iando *RScacNorm* I 1.

adolocentia v. adolescentia.

Adonai [Heb.], Lord.

Adonaique pio clamore citavit Frith. 513; confortator.. tuorum fidelium, ~ay indeficiens (*Duellum*) *GAS* 431; qua pater suus ~ai coronavit ipsum ante secula H. Bos. *LM* 1344.

Adonicus [*Ἀδώνειος*], Adonian (metre).

s1077 epitaphium ~o metro, quod dactylo spondeoque constat, editum sic exaratum est: 'hic jacet Hugo Lexoviensis clarus honore..' Ord. Vit. V 3.

adopatum v. adipare.

adoperire [CL], to cover (? w. double acc.).

hanc vestem quam famula tua..pro conservandae castitatis signo se ~iendam exposcit Egb. *Pont.* 113; [diabolus] fallax fallacem hominis ~tus imaginem Osb. *V. Dunst.* 14.

adoptare [CL], to adopt, take to oneself: **a** as heir; **b** as godchild; **c** (?) as wife; **d** (fig.).

a s1153 Henrico duce Normannorum, quem rex Stephanus ~avit sibi in filium et constituit heredem et successorem regni R. Howd. I 212; [Sichelinus Loth] sibi in regnum succedere ~averat M. Par. *Maj.* I 239; femine secundum leges..non possunt ~are nec postulare nec fidejubere Ockham *Pol.* I 163. **b 735** alterius filium de sacri baptismatis fonte elevans ~avit sibi in filium Bonif. *Ep.* 33 p. 57; **s994** quem [Anlafum Æthelwardus] rex honorifice suscepit, confirmari ab episcopo fecit, sibi in filium ~avit, regiaque munera donavit Fl. Worc. I 152. **c s1193** rex [Francie].. eam..matrimonio solempniter contracto thoro †adaptavit Brompton 1244. **d** homo..in baptismo..in filium ~atur Dei Alcuin *Ep.* 166 p. 272; bonus Filius audiat Matrem pro fratribus, unigenitus pro iis quos ~avit Anselm (*Or.* 7) III 24.

2 to win (favour).

s1366 graciam domini regis sibi ~avit; rediit dilectus ad propria J. Reading 187.

3 to choose, desire. **b** (w. inf.). **c** to wish on to (by imprecation).

s792 inimicum vestrum, cujus regnum tam diuturno ~astis desiderio (*V. Off. II*) M. Par *Maj.* I 355; **s1192** filia Boyac..dilexit eum [Sanctium] in tantum quod vehementer ~avit eum sibi in maritum R. Howd. III 90; **s1312** hec ~ata nativitas tempore accepto nobis advenit *V. Ed. II* 188; **1340** quam..promissionem expecto..in effectum ~atum fore producendam *FormOx* 307; femineum si miles adoptet amorem Gower *VC* V 261. **b †948** (14c) ut..se ovili Dominico..mancipare..~at *CS* 872; quem injusta nece dampnare ~at G. Mon. IV 8; **s1451** potius.. minister dici quam magister appellari ~avit *Reg. Whet.* I 6. **c** crepitum dedit, quem statim viri naribus, cujus causa vexabatur, verbis et votis ~avit Gir. *IK* I 11.

adoptativus [cf. adoptivus], adoptive (? of a foster father).

956 (14c) meo ~o parenti, vocabulo Aebrico, xx mansas.. concedo *CS* 941.

†**adoptimus** [? *for* adoptivus], optional.

willfulle, ~us, benevolus, . . voluntarius *CathA*.

1 adoptio v. adeptio.

2 adoptio [CL], adoption: **a** (as heir); **b** (as godson); **c** (fig.); **d** (theol.).

a s**1153** Stephani regis Anglie et Henrici ducis Normannie concors ad invicem facta est ~o GIR. *EH* II 31; legitimantur quandoque per ~onem de consensu et voluntate parentum BRACTON 63b (= *Fleta* 13: per ~onem [v.l. †adeptionem]). **b** egressus de fonte, loco filii susceptus est; in cujus signum ~onis duas illi provincias donavit BEDE *HE* IV 13; s**878** quem [Guthrum] rex in filium ~onis sibi suscipiens de fonte sacri baptismatis †elimavit [? l. elevavit] FL. WORC. I 96. **c 1284** thesaurum. . quem spiritualis Dei ~o. . in vestro collegio reposuit PECKHAM *Ep.* 610 p. 846. **d** c**798** de ~one. ., quam quidam injuriose Christo Deo ingerere contendunt ALCUIN *Ep.* 137 p. 211; dicit [Felix] propter adsumptionem Christum esse adoptivum, minus considerans non omnem adsumptionem ~onem esse, licet omnis ~o quedam sit adsumptio *Ib.* 166 p. 269; dicimur filii per ~onem: ~o enim est per voluntatem que communis est Patris et filii, que voluntas est Spiritus Sanctus HALES *Qu.* 44 p. 754.

2 choice, desire.

in ~one petentis erit. . deducere placitum suum vel non HENGHAM *Magna* 3; positus igitur in ~one eligeret minus malum WYCL. *Ver.* II 22; *a desyre*, ~o *CathA*.

†**adoptior** [? *for* adoptatior], more desirable.

nos sumus ~oris condicionis quam judaizantes WYCL. *Ver.* III 254.

adoptive, by adoption (fig.).

plantatio Wallie nec naturaliter nec ~e sed violenter inserta GIR. *GE* II 34 (cf. *Id. Invect.* I 4: falsos fraterculos nostros ecclesie nostre nec ~e nec naturaliter insertos).

adoptivus, adoptive: **a** (of heir); **b** (of godchild); **c** (fig.); **d** (w. ref. to Adoptionist heresy).

a [Dalfinus] sibi illum in ~um filium eligere voluit EDDI *Wilf.* 4; s**1153** ipsum [Henricum] rex in filium suscepit ~um et heredem regni constituit H. HUNT. *HA* VIII 37 (cf. ib. VI 13: simus fratres ~i regnumque partiamur). **b** paternum memini me nomen adeptum teque ~ae dignitatis vocabula cum caelestis gratiae praerogativa sortitum ALDH. *Met.* 1; puer regius. . pontifici nostro filius ~us factus est EDDI *Wilf.* 59; **735** viduam. . cujus filium in baptismo ~um suscipiebat BONIF. *Ep.* 32. **c** ~as regenerantis gratiae filias ex fecundo ecclesiasticae conceptionis utero. . progenitas ALDH. *VirgP* 2. **d 800** nec Christus ullatenus credendus proprius et ~us Dei patris filius ALCUIN *Ep.* 204 p. 334 (v. et. adoptio 1d).

2 (sb.) adoptive son. **b** (fig.).

offerebat ut. . eum loco ~i semper haberet BEDE *HE* V 19. **b 1268** dignitas ~orum sponse et gloria filiorum. . matris ecclesie *Conc. Syn.* 747.

ador [CL], spelt or emmer wheat.

ador, genus †faras *GlC* A 243 (= *EE* 346. 45: genus farris vel frumenti); genus quoddam frumenti quod far vel ador dicitur BELETH *RDO* 42. 51; hoc ador, indeclinabile, A. *flowyr* WW.

†**adoramentum**, (?) object of reverence (or *f.l.* for *adornamentum*).

tunc enim cetus apostolorum protulit rudimenta fidei sicut ficus, et discipuli Christiani florentes virtutibus ut palmites vitis vere dederunt ~a sancte matri ecclesie WYCL. *Eccl.* 198.

adorare [CL], to pray. **b** (trans.) to pray to, beseech.

~at ad crucem *Hist. Abb. Jarrow* 27; s**1016** fuit occisus in guerra. . apud Essdoune, cum ibi esset ad ~andum pro exercitu Anglicano *Chr. Rams.* 339; "sit pax vobiscum" presul adorat GARL. *Myst. Eccl.* 506. **b** Dominum Silvester adorat / ut plebs. . haud fallatur ALDH. *VirgV* 583.

2 to worship: **a** pagan idols; **b** Christian God or Christ; **c** the Host; **d** Christian images or sim.; **e** the Cross (esp. on Good Friday).

a coeperunt fana. . restaurare et ~are simulacra BEDE *HE* III 300; interdicimus. . lignum viride. . ~are (*Inst. Cnut.*) *GAS* 313; s**1311** quidam. . fratres ~abant idolum (*Dep. Templar.*) *Ann. Lond.* 193. **b** Deum verum et vivum. . ~o semper et colo BEDE *HE* I 7; hymniferi Christumque chori veneranter adorant WULF. *Swith.* I 425; item probatur quod dignior est [Christus] angelis, nam ~atur ab eis LANFR. *Comment. Paul.* (*Heb.* 1 6) 377; nobilis hunc cetus colit et †reveratur [l. reveretur *or* veneratur] adorans NECKAM *DS* I 71; Christus. . debet latria soli Deo debita ~ari WYCL. *Incarn.* 183. **c 1240** quando elevatur corpus Christi, ~et stando (*Stat. Ep. Lichf.*) *MonA* VI 1259; postea, ubi dicit "~amus sanctum corpus tuum", utrumque ~ando obnixe contempletur *Cust. Cant.* 285. **d** Romam venire ad ~anda beatorum apostolorum ac martyrum Christi limina BEDE *HE* V 5; s**791** quod pene omnium Orientalium. . unanimi assertione est diffinitum, imagines ~are debere, quod omnino ecclesia catholica execratur M. PAR. *Maj.* I 354; que colit ac memorat sacra presbiter omnis adorat SERLO WILT. 63. 2. **e** ~o, veneror et glorifico in te crucem illam ANSELM (*Or.* 4) III 11; s**1223** frequenter ~atur et colitur crux prefata [de Bromholm] non solum a gente Anglicana WEND. II 276; crucis ~ate dies advenerat DEVIZES 40; a**1256** in die Parasseves omnes parochiani veniant ad crucem ~andam (*Cust. Sal.*) *Conc. Syn.* 512; **1309** filius suus primogenitus fuit natus die Crucis ~ate *IPM* 18/6; post hec crux honorifice collocetur et ab omnibus ~etur et primo ab episcopo *Pont. Exon.* 227; **1413** in oblacionibus domini regis factis ~ando crucem in die Parasceves (*KRAc* 406/21 f. 19) *Rois Thaumaturges* 446.

3 to prostrate oneself before (an earthly ruler or sim.).

s**1272** [Saraceni] stantes a longe ~averunt Edwardum proni in terram; et ait Edwardus in Anglico: "vos quidem ~atis me, sed non diligitis" W. GUISB. 210; revertitur ad baculum quem in locum regis constituerat, et inclinans se ~avit eum super terram *Latin Stories* 4.

adorasta v. adarasca.

adoratio, worship.

930 docemus. . ut quilibet sacerdos. . prohibeat fontium ~onem et necromantiam et auguria et incantationes *Conc.* I 226; s**1311** alius clericus deponit de ~one vituli (*Dep. Templar.*) *Ann. Lond.* 193; 1313 inhibeas. . ne quis. . pro ~one dicte imaginis [B. Virginis] ad prefatam ecclesiam. . accedat *Conc.* II 423; s**1413** circa ~onem S. Crucis dixit [J. Oldkastelle]. . quod solum corpus Christi, quod pendebat in cruce, debuit adorari WALS. *YN* 444; c**1430** B. Gregorius . . in. . epistola Sereno episcopo Massiliensi, qui imagines propter populi nimiam ~onem fregerat et de ecclesia dejecerat. . AMUND. I *app.* C 418.

adorator, worshipper.

sancte crucis aliorumque Christiane religionis sacramentorum vel sacrorum cultor et sedulus ~or BLAKMAN *Hen. VI* 6; veri ~ores in spiritu et veritate GARDINER *VO* 719.

adoratrix, 'oratress', petitioner, offerer of prayers (f.); *cf. oratrix.*

1435 ~tricis vestre perpetue Universitatis nostre in proficuum et decorem *EpAcOx* 115.

adordinare, to set in order, dispose.

est inter illas [animam activam et animam passivam] tanta connexio, nedum quod eadem persona sit eadem essencia materia prima et anima, sed quod ille essencie propter se reciproce ~entur WYCL. *Compos. Hom.* 7.

adordiri [? *conf. w.* adoriri], to begin. **b** to address, speak (to).

†adoritur, nascitur *GlC* A 247; orator adorsus: / "ter centum memini. . " FRITH. 272; ita ~sus est fari OSB. *Mir. Dunst.* 15; preliari contra Normannos ~si sunt ORD. VIT. XII 18 p. 359. **b** suos sic demum ~sus est GIR. *EH* I 7; *to speke*, ~iri, ex-, loqui *CathA*.

adoreus [CL], made of emmer wheat, (sb.) obley, wafer, offering (cf. Virgil *Aen.* VII 109).

~ea, libamina *GlC* A 238; *ubly, bredd to seyne with messe*, nebula, . . ~ia *PP*.

adoria [CL], glory.

his [Dunstanus] gloriosus triumphis, victoriosus ~eis, . . translatus est ad superos W. MALM. *GP* I 19 p. 31.

adoriri [CL], to attack. **b** to undertake.

~itur, adgreditur *GlC* A 247 (cf. ib. 211); s**1066** Normanni. . dispersos ~iuntur et in fugam cogunt W. MALM. *GR* III 242. **b** si pugnam ~iretur, opimas manubias referebat *Id. GP* I 51.

adornare [CL], to adorn, equip. **b** to prepare.

monasterium. . quod. . augustioribus aedificiis ac donariis ~arunt BEDE *HE* III 19; virgines Deo dicatae. . texendis. . indumentis operam dant, quibus. . se ipsas. . ~ent *Ib.* IV 23; s**1050** ab eodem duce decenter est armis ~atus ORD. VIT. III 1 p. 40; o vere tunc beata Anglorum ecclesia, quam innumerabilium monachorum et virginum ~abat integritas! AILR. *Gen. Regum* 362; capella. . hedere nexibus ~ata GIR. *IK* 1 3; **1438** damus vobis. . unum pretiosum apparatum pro altari, quod. . habebis ipsum satis honorifice ~are (*Ch.*) AMUND. II 193. **b** suo populum sermone salubri / instruit, exercet, renovat, meliorat, adornat WULF. *Swith.* I 855; ~atis omnibus in hunc usum necessariis FERR. *Kinloss* 64.

adornatio, adornment. **b** an ornament.

1488 ad melioracionem et ~onem ipsius [hostrie] expendit in. . coopertoriis pro lectis. . ultra summam v m. *Reg. Whet.* I *app.* D 456. **b 1438** damus vobis has que sequuntur ecclesie ~ones (*Ch.*) AMUND. II 193.

adornativus, ornamental.

12.. qui studioso labore suo opera ecclesie nostre ~a post se reliquerunt *G. S. Alb.* I 233.

adornatus, adornment.

non indigent aurum vel gemme exteriori ~u, quibus propria sufficit pulchritudo H. LOS. *Ep.* 39.

adorinsicus v. odorinsecus. adorti v. aorta. adp- v. app-. adq- v. et. acq-. adque v. atque. adr- v. et. arr-. adreciare, adressare, v. addretiare.

†**adria**, stone.

a stane, ~ia Grece; adriacus, petrosus *CathA*.

adrianum (adrion') v. hadrianum.

adriare [cf. arraiare], (?) to set in order, trim.

1297 idem computat in haiis parci erigendis, ~iandis, supponendis et per diversa loca emendendis cum claustura *Ac. Cornw.* I 5 (cf. ib. 45).

adriatica v. hadriatica.

†**adripes** [? *for* aëripes], fleet-footed.

wight, †alicer, acer, . . ~es, alipes *CathA*.

adrop [Ar. *usrubb* < Pers. *usrup*], lead (alch.).

scito igitur quod immundum corpus est plumbum, quod alio nomine ~p interpretatur ROB. ANGL. *Alch.* 518b; ~p est plumbum *LC*.

ads- v. et ass-. adsc- v. asc-. adsida v. 2 assisa.

†**adsimilia**, (?) *f.l.*

†~iam [? l. ad similia] sperantes MILEMETE *Nob.* 97.

adsp- v. asp-. adst- v. et. ast-.

adstatim [al. div.], immediately. **b** (w. *ut*) as soon as.

1418 ~im post adventum tuum *Cl* 268 m. 20; **1421** volo quod executores ~im audito de morte mea faciant mille missas infra mensem pro anima mea *Reg. Cant.* II 252; s**1388** regem. . ad statim sub nova gubernacione ordinarunt AD. USK 6; **1494** quendam R. Charnok. . ilico et ad statim in priorem. . prefecit *DCCant* S f. 396b. **b 1476** ~im ut habuerimus noticiam de. . die *FormA* 336.

adt- v. et. att-. adtheleta v. athleta c.

adtunc [al. div.], at that time.

s**1386** M. de la Pole. . atunc cancellarius Anglie FAVENT 1; **1401** si. . Thomas ~c superstes fuerit *FormA* 406; **1406** alias ad tunc solvent dictam summam *ExchScot* 4; **1440** Willelmum . . ~c nostre congregacionis priorem *Meaux* III 239; quorum consolacionibus ad tunc, sicut eciam alias, potitus fuit BLAKMAN *Hen. VI* 21; **1484** ipsum Stephanum ad tunc et ibidem. . percussit *Mem. Ripon* I 310; c**1545** in vacacionibus diversorum tenementorum, eo quod nemo ea ~c conducere velit *Cart. Osney* III 288.

aduber, plentiful.

s**1170** grates tibi refero ~eres de labore tuo, licet inutili M. PAR. *Min.* I 360.

adul [? Ar. *ad-dulb*], (?) plane-tree or sycomore.

insitio †artemisie in adul silvestre ALF. ANGL. *Plant.* I 16.

adulanter, flatteringly.

quisquis pravis operibus alicujus ~er applaudit J. SAL. *Pol.* 485B.

adulari [CL], **a** to fawn, wag. **b** to flatter. **c** (fig.).

a s**870** leporarius. . regi ~ante cauda applaudere satagebat M. PAR. *Maj.* I 394. **b 717** per blandimenta adolantium verborum BONIF. *Ep.* 9; quid alium arguit adulationis qui sibimet ~atur? J. SAL. *Pol.* 485A; dici Serlo miser merui, non Serlo magister; / sic scit adulari scola discola mosque sinister SERLO. WILT. 77. 2; non habet causas mentiendi, id est ~andi, mendicandi, familiaritatem potentum adquirendi GIR. *GE* II 22. **c** vultuque sereno / tempus adulatur pelago VINSAUF *PN* 811.

adulatio [CL], flattery, deference, coaxing.

~o fallax inimici ALDH. *VirgP* 58; c**745** si. . adolationis gratia falso securitatem populis pronuntient (*Lit. Ep. Wint.*) *Ep. Bonif.* 64 p. 133; ~o, *liffetung* ÆLF. *Sup.*; ratione sola, auctoritatis ~one seclusa, audire desidero ADEL. *QN* 76; qui linguam ~onibus polluit J. SAL. *Pol.* 484D; cum canes. . nec vocatione nec ~one. . ad se introducere posset GIR. *IK* I 11.

adulativus, flattering.

blandis et ~is sermonibus *Entries* 636b.

adulator, [CL], flatterer. **b** (w. *warennae*) (?) poacher.

793 quid est adolator nisi blandus inimicus? ALCUIN *Ep.* 17; ~or vel favisor, *liffetere* ÆLF. *Sup.*; ~or. . eo magis cavendus est quo sub amantis specie nocere non desinit J. SAL. *Pol.* 481C; pravus adulator tibi non sit consiliator D. BEC. 594. **b 1396** ~or garenne (*MinAc Wethersfield*) *MFG*.

adulatorie, flatteringly, so as to curry favour.

plenitudinem potestatis quam sedem apostolicam occupantes sibi. . usurparunt et quam plures ~ie et erronee sibi tribuere moliuntur OCKHAM *Pol.* I 285; s**1329** proditor ad regem Anglie. . hec denuncians ~ie *Plusc.* IX 25.

adulatorius [CL], flattering. **b** (sb. f.) art of flattery.

ad despectum. . laudis ~ie H. HUNT. *HA* II 18; verbum ~ium O. CHERITON *Fab.* 37; parvulus. . non sapit nisi placentia et ~ia *V. Ric. II* 211. **b** in eo ~ie vis magna consistit, si omissis propriis aliena commoda curare videaris J. SAL. *Pol.* 497D.

adulatrix, flattering, coaxing (f.).

~ix lingua A. TEWK. *Ep.* 10; blanda quadam et ~ice verborum utens forma NECKAM *NR* I 19; **1207** qui sub ejus cubito manu ~ice pulvillos consuunt (*Lit. Papae*) *Conc.* I 523.

adulatus, flattery.

12.. per ~um falluntur *Latin Stories* 145.

adulesc- v. adolesc-.

adulosus, flattering.

1349 per sermones ~os *Cal. Pl. & Mem. R. Lond.* 231.

adulter [CL], adulterous. **b** (sb. m. or f.) adulterer, adulteress. **c** illicit, unauthorized.

quaecunque mulier adulterium perpetravit, in potestate viri est si velit reconciliare mulieri ~erae THEOD. *Pen.* II xii 11; rex habet hominem ~erum, archiepiscopus feminam

DB I 26; nec quod delectet honestos / conjugis attractus oculus delibet adulter HANV. IX 388. **b 747** ipsi pagani.. fornicatores et ~eros puniunt BONIF. *Ep.* 73 p. 150; **747** perpauce sunt civitates..in Gallia in qua non sit ~era vel meretrix generis Anglorum *Ib.* 78 p. 169; **10..** ~er, *forligr*, **14..** hic ~er, *a spowsbreker*, **14..** †eria [l. ~era], *a spowsbrekere* WW; in meretricios ~ere sinus accubuit *G. Steph.* II 77; suus occurrit secumque coivit adulter *V. Merl.* 291. **c 1189** prohibemus ne forum C. aliquo foro ~ero impediatur *BBC* (*Colchester*) 201; **s1154** munitiones ~ere, que erant improborum receptacula et spelunce latronum W. NEWB. I 32.

adulterare [CL], to commit adultery. **b** (dep.). **c** (p. ppl.) adulterous.

1307 adivit..ad ~andum cum uxore ipsius *Gaol Del.* 39/1 r. 9; **1397** recusat cohabitare cum uxore sua legitima..et ~at cum Matilda (*Vis. Heref.*) *EHR* XLIV 281; Agnes..et Ricardus..~ant adinvicem *Ib.* 453. **b** numquid fornicari vel ~ari..licet cum pluribus cum nec etiam..liceat uxoribus admisceri? J. SAL. *Pol.* 520D; **1207** plures ~abantur cum ea *SelPlCrown* 55; **s1226** qui..cum regina Blanchia ~abatur *Flor. Hist.* II 186; **1300** dicunt quod pro sua voluntate ~etur cum Juliana *CourtR Hales* 404; **1448** Johannes.. ~atur cum Matilde *Eng. Clergy* 216. **c 742** episcopales sedes traditae sunt ~atis clericis, scortatoribus et publicanis BONIF. *Ep.* 50 p. 82.

2 to adulterate, contaminate. **b** (fig.).

balsami guttam ~ant admixto oleo cyprino NECKAM *NR* II 72. **b** arte invida et invisa ipsam turpiter ~ante naturam GIR. *TH* III 35.

adulterator, adulterer. **b** forger. **c** contaminator, perverter.

1207 fuit domi quando ~ores fuerunt in domo *SelPlCrown* 55. **b** falsarius faber egregius et sigillorum ~or expeditus GIR. *Symb.* 28 p. 300. **c** sacri eloquii interpretes falsidici et divini verbi ~ores nequissimi CHAUNCY *Passio* 52.

adulteria v. adulter b, adulterium.

adulterinus [CL], adulterous. **b** bastard (fig.), spurious, mock.

quos ~ae titillationis calcar incesti crimine cruentabat ALDH. *VirgP* 44; puella nobilis, quam ipse ~is amplexibus adamabat GIR. *GE* I 48; **a1350** in amplexionibus fornicariis seu ~is *StatOx* 151. **b** in utroque avium genere..quedam inveniuntur aves..quasi ~e..et non vere GIR. *TH* I 17; vetulas quasdam..se in leporinam transformare formam ut ~a sub specie lac..surripiant *Ib.* II 19; repudiatis ~is amplexibus mundane scientie P. BLOIS *Ep.* 76. 234B; quidam nominis Christiani bajulus ~us R. COLD. *Cuthb.* 129; **s1233** apparuerunt in celo quatuor soles ~i preter verum solem M. PAR. *Maj.* III 242.

2 counterfeit, forged: **a** (of key); **b** (of seal or document).

a ecclesiam cum clave ~a aperuit R. COLD. *Cuthb.* 129; **c1530** quod sere ostiorum..adeo reformentur ut antiqui (*sic*) claves seu ~i, quibus canonici retroactis temporibus usi sunt, ullo modo aperire non possint (*Vis. Leic.*) *EHR* IV 307. **b 1242** impetrata..quadam carta ~a de feoffamento ejusdem manerii *Cl* 58; **1258** pro quodam brevi sigillo ~o signato *Liberate* 34 B m. 2; **1274** de cartis ~is captis in manu majoris *Leg. Ant. Lond.* 166.

3 unauthorized, illicit: **a** (of school); **b** (of guild); **c** (of castle).

a a1123 conquesti sunt nobis canonici de Huntingdon, quod quidam..presumunt ~as scolas regere absque eorum licencia (*Reg. Hunt.*) *EHR* XVIII 713; **1328** scholas ~as infra..jurisdiccionem nostram *Reg. Whet.* II 307. **b 1180** ad·nerciamenta de gildis ~is in civitate *Pipe* 153. **c s1140** rex..plurima ~a castella..subvertit *G. Steph.* I 49; **s1173** apud Alvertonam firmavit opidum, impetrato a rege ut inter ~a, que tunc sparsim per Angliam destrui jubebantur, hoc solum privilegium integritatis optineret G. COLD. *Hist. Durh.* 7; **1217** statuimus..quod omnia castra ~a, viz. ea que a principio guerre..constructa fuerint vel reedificata, statim diruantur (*Ch. Libert.* c. 47) *StRealm* I 19; **1220** quod [castrum meum] non sit ~um, cum constructum fuerit per assensum..regis (*AncC* I 204) *RL* I 141; **s1272** arbitrati sunt illos malificos esse manifeste contra pacem domini regis, qui fecerunt castrum ~um in civitate sua *Leg. Ant. Lond.* 146.

adulterior v. ulterior.

adulterium [CL], **~ia**, adultery. **b** (fig.). **c** fine for adultery. **d** miscegenation (of animals).

quaecunque mulier ~ium perpetravit THEOD *Pen.* II xii 11; **742** qui a pueritia sua semper in stupris semper in ~iis.. vitam ducentes..venerunt ad diaconatum BONIF. *Ep.* 50 p. 82; ~ium vel raptum faciens viii sol. et iiii den. emendat homo et femina tantundem *DB* I 26; nec incestus ullos nec ~ia vitans GIR. *EH* II 11; **1203** Robertus genuit ex ea in ~ia *CurR* III 36; **1280** convictus fuit super ~ium ad capitulum cum quadam muliere *SelPlMan* 97; **1397** Thomas B. committit ~ium cum Margareta H. (*Vis. Heref.*) *EHR* XLIV 444. **b** WYCL. *Mand. Div.* 347 (v. affidare 6b). **c** de ~io vero per totum Chenth habet rex hominem et archiepiscopus mulierem *DB* I 1. **d** leopardus est bestia.. ex leena et pardo per ~ium generata BAD. AUR. 111.

adulterius, adulterer.

si pater filiam maritatam in adulterio deprehendit, ..licet ei †~ium [? l. ~um] occidere (*Leis Will.*) *GAS* 514; **1313** A. cum suo ~io venit Londiniam..; ~ius et A. atachiati *Eyre Kent* 81.

adultio, growing up, reaching maturity.

secundum istud voluntas in primo instanti sue creacionis non posset libere velle quicquam. nec voluntas antiqua in primo instanti ~onis seu evigilacionis a somno BRADW. *CD* 670C.

adultus [CL], grown up, mature, adult. **b** inveterate. **c** (fig.) ripe, fully fledged, arrived at culmination of career.

706 usque ~ae pubertatis florem ALDH. *Ep.* 9; ~i jam filii pie satis..a patrum domiciliis expelluntur GIR. *TH* I 12; fere omnes ~i detraccionis vicio..sunt impliciti OCKHAM *Dial.* 670. **b** ~a ulcera et illisa vulnera ANSELM (*Or.* 9) III 31. **c a690** in flore philosophicae artis ~o ALDH. *Ep.* 5 p. 493; est apprenticius, sergantus post et adultus; / judicis officium fine notabit eum GOWER *VC* VI 249.

adumbrare [CL], to screen, shelter. **b** to represent by a likeness, counterfeit. **c** to offend, give umbrage to.

[serpens] per estum interceptus ~ari a fervore non potuit MAP *NC* III 2 p. 122. **b** ~ata quedam imago glorie, cui nulla virtutis..subest soliditas W. FITZST. *Thom.* 29. **c s1333** magnates ~abantur plurimum de hujusmodi presumptuosis suggestionibus et procuracionibus domino pape factis *G. S. Alb.* II 288.

adumbratio, shade, shelter. **b** outline, sketch (fig.).

earum [virtutum] foliis veluti amoenae arboris ~one velati BEDE *TR* 64. **b** Dei gratia sunt illustrata eorum corda, in quibus eadem figurata legis ~o finem accipit *Id. Tab* I 9.

adumen v. abdomen.

adunare [LL; cf. adunire], to unite, unify, combine. **b** to annex.

ignes..in inmensam ~ati sunt flammam BEDE *HE* III 19; **797** ut ecclesie unitas..pacifice ~etur ALCUIN *Ep.* 128; effectus causis ~antur, quoniam in uno genere, in creatura dico, unum sunt ERIUG. *Per.* 528A; liquet..papam..minus congrue ~asse cuculle capucium A. TEWK. *Addit. Thom.* 345; non..~antur in rivum gutte MAP *NC* IV 11 p. 182; homo quem..studium celeste..celestibus animis in Dei filio et consociat et ~at AD. MARSH *Ep.* 28; donec [luna] soli ~etur in uno gradu BACON VI 59; quod si omne mundi gaudium in uno loco fuerit ~atum ROLLE *IA* 220. **b 1188** Deus ~avit nobis regiones affluentius, sicut et coadunavit eas longe lateque sub potestate nostra (*Lit. Saladini*) GIR. *PI* III 18 (= WEND. I 148: adjuvavit; M. PAR. *Min.* I 451: adunabit); **s1201** rex Francie..eandem patriam [sc. Normanniam] sibi ~avit *Plusc.* VI 39; **1354** si..possessiones predictas vicarie dicte ecclesie..~ari..contigerit *Lit. Cant.* II 324.

2 to amass, collect, get together: **a** (money); **b** (materials); **c** (hay); **d** (corn).

a s1194 regi..quem sub obtentu liberationis sue immanes copias didiscerat ~asse G. COLD. *Durh.* 9; **1242** de..pecunia regi perquirenda et ~anda *RGasc* I 16. **b 1226** maeremium ..quod ~ari fecerunt..ad reparationem domorum *Pat* 29; **1293** in placiis..fima collecta sunt et ~ata in villa (*CoramR*) *MunCOx* 293; **1409** uxori Johannis G. petras minere ferri †adimanti [l. ~anti] (*Rec. Aud. Durh.*) *EHR* XIV 522. **c 1251** falcabit uno die, ~abit fenum alio die (*Cust.*) *Cart. Rams.* I 311; **1253** una medietas ~atur et ponitur super quemdam tassum *SelPlForest* 110; **1265** pro prato..~ando et preparando (*RHosp*) *Manners* 71; **1275** inveniemus boves nostros ad trahendum dictum pratum cum fueret ~atum *Reg. Heref.* 27; **1279** quando fenum ~atum est in curia *Hund.* II 750; **1302** faciunt..colligere et †adimare [l. ~are] fenum iiij acrarum prati falcabilis *Suff. Hund.* 70. **d 1345** messuerunt, ligaverunt et ~averunt..cxij acras *Comp. Swith.* 150.

3 to bring together, assemble (persons). **b** to reconcile.

spatium quo totum suum congregaret atque ~aret exercitum BEDE *HE* II 12; **s1138** rebellem multitudinem..in exercitum inopinabilem ~ans *G. Steph.* I 26; voce preconia citati cives..~antur MAP *NC* I 21; ut..in funeris sui obsequium duos reges ~atos haberet AD. EYNS. *Hug.* V 1; **s1253** ~ato magno parlamento M. PAR. *Abbr.* 326; **1326** nec est verisimile quod magnus exercitus subito valeat ~ari *Lit. Cant.* I 173. **b** amici..invicem ~antur in individuum beate vite consortium AD. MARSH *Ep.* 166; B. Augustinus.. ad vivendum communiter fratres ~avit *Obs. Barnwell* 34; **1382** discordes tantomodo fratres adunavit (*Contra Religiosos* 188) *Mon. Francisc.* I 598.

adunate, collectively, as a group.

separatius..distingui hec..inutile; sunt enim quibus minus est ad doctrinam multiplicem quam nullam fieri distinctionem, quare ~ius quelibet eis distinguendum quam in his que sunt ex arte potentioribus abundare BALSH. *AD* 81.

adunatim, collectively.

1293 cum statuta nostra ~im contigerit recitari *StatOx* 104.

adunatio, union, unification, concentration. **b** annexation. **c** (means of) connection, link.

de universali universalis naturae divisione et ~one ERIUG. *Per.* 528B; virtus visibilis, que fit propter coarctationem, id est, congregationem et ~onem BACON *Maj.* II 84; plenum non est causa distantie sed potius convenientie et ~onis *Id.* VIII 197; dicitur..annus lunaris spatium temporis in quo luna xij menses, qui sunt †per [? l. post] ~onem cum sole usque ad aliam ~onem, ..perficit BACON VI 51. **b 1354** stantibus..~onibus prejudicialibus..hujusmodi [cantarie possessionum beneficio] *Lit. Cant.* II 324. **c 794** scio me per sacri baptismatis ~onem de illius esse ovili pastoris ALCUIN *Ep.* 27; homo..medietas atque ~o omnium creaturarum ERIUG. *Per.* 536B.

2 getting together: **a** (of hay); **b** (of corn).

a 1252 tempore falcationis..continuus erit in ~one feni cum cottariis (*Cust.*) *Cart. Rams.* I 304; **c1315** in falcacione, levacione et aduniacione xx acrarum prati *Cart. Boarstall* no. 629; **1322** in falcacione, levacione et ~one magni prati *Estates Crowland* 263. **b 1449** pro messione, ligacione et †adimacione [l. ~one] cujuslibet acre *Crawley* 488.

3 united force, assemblage (of persons).

1097 post placitum quod totius regni ~one contra te.. habitum est (*Lit. regis*) EADMER *HN.* 95; **s1179** predictis.. sollempniis rex..interesse decernens, illam nobilium ~onem singulari sue presentie prerogativa..illustravit DICETO *YH* I 439; **1188** ~o..legis Christianorum bis venit super nos (*Lit. Saladini*) GIR. *PI* III 18; **13..** tanta hominum ~o *Latin Stories* 100.

adunativus, unitive, comprehensive.

nisi omnia..sophismatum genera infinitorum ~a discretione distinxerimus BALSH. *AD* (*rec.* 2) 40; quod non est contrarium per se ipsum est ~um DASTIN *Ros.* 2.

adunator v. adamator.

aduncare, to hook, catch.

s1168 rex..multos milites cepit, inter quos etiam senescallus..comitis ~atus est TORIGNI *Chr.* 238; quibuscumque modis ipsam ille temptaverat, ..ipsum ~are conatur MAP *NC* IV 11 p. 180; hamo voracem extrahis aduncatum J. HOWD. *Cant.* 15 174 (cf. ib. 41 558); ~o, A. *to drawe wyth an hooke* WW.

aduncinare, to hook.

s885 demones advolantes cum uncis igneis..voluerunt me ~are (*Visio Caroli III*) W. MALM. *GR* II 111 (= *NLA* II 186: aduncare).

aduncus [CL], hooked.

~is, *gebegdum GlC* A 199; vir longae staturae..naso ~o pertenui BEDE *HE* II 16; nasus aduncus ei, frons torva, pedes caprearum NIG. *Paul* 47v. (*Speculum* VII 420); huic natura pedem digitis armavit aduncis NECKAM *DS* II 687.

adundare, to abound in.

cum quatuor elementis componantur, eo magis ~ant quod ad vitam..magis aptum est ADEL. *QN* 74.

aduniatio v. adunatio 2a.

adunire [cf. adunare], **a** to annex. **b** to collect. **c** to get together (corn or hay).

a 1488 croftum unum..annexuit sive ~ivit manerio eidem *Reg. Whet.* I 464. **b 1276** collegit et †admur' [l. aduniri] fecit ad domum suam in burgo circiter iiij saccos lane *Hund.* II 134. **c 1284** in blado metendo, ligando et ~iende *MinAc* 1237/3 r. 1; **1314** omnes custumarii debent ~ire et tassare fenum domini *IPM* 43/32.

adurere [CL], **a** to burn, scorch. **b** to brand. **c** to cauterize. **d** to singe (fig.). **e** to inflame (fig.).

a poenis Acherontis adusti FRITH. 289; palmam turgore vident carbonis adustam WULF. *Swith* II 393. **b** [Paterini] adusti et virgis cesi disparuerunt MAP *NC* I 30. **c** artaria timporis, que quandoque flebotomatur, quandoque inciditur, quandoque extrahitur, quandoque ~itur *Ps.*-RIC. *Anat.* 44. **d** tanquam alis presumptuosi ingenii..adustis GIR. *TH* I 13. **e** maligni, / igne venenosus quos livor adurit edaci WULF. *Swith.* I 1107.

2 to overheat (bodily humours), make 'adust' (med.).

naturalem interius ex adusto humore calorem..trahunt GIR. *DK* I 15; cito ~itur in eis [sc. avibus rapacibus masculis] cholera et transit in melancholiam NECKAM *NR* I 79 (cf. *Id. DS* II 271: cholere..humor aduste); sperma non ~itur in prima mansione nec ultimate infrigidatur, est tamen in ~i quo ad aliquas partes GAD. 37 v. 1; quando pro speciebus calidis ~itur sanguis *Id.* 42 v. 1.

3 (p. ppl. *adustus*) **a** (w. *creta*) burnt lime. **b** (w. *vinum*) brandy.

a 1502 pro quatuor quarteriis crete ~e *Cant. Coll. Ox.* II 234. **b 1674** navem..vinis ~is..onustam (*Comm. HCA*) *W. Sussex Archives Ad. MS.* 5380.

adusque [CL], all the way to. **b** (w. *mittere*) to send (a messenger) to.

taedis late lucentibus / ..ad usque caeli cardinem (ÆTHELWALD) *Carm. Aldh.* 4. 30; tandem pacatos devenit adusque Sicambros FRITH. 1231; si regius ortus, adusque / innumeros decurrat avos HANV. VI 332; **1432** exierunt obviam..regi ~e quendam locum vocatum Blakehethe (J. CARPENTER) *MGL* III 456. **b** misit ad usque ducem, postulat et precibus G. AMIENS *Hast.* 578.

adustare, to reclaim (land) by beat-burning (*cf. bateiceum*).

1475 totam terram fossatam, ~atam ac zabulatam vocatam *bete* (*MinAc Cornw*) *Arch. J.* V 121.

adustibilis, combustible.

minora mineralia a metallis extranee sunt nature; ..debilioris sunt virtutis et ~ia *Correct. Alch.* 10; ex tale sulphure ~i *Spec. Alch.* 379.

adustinus v. adustivus.

adustio, burning, burn. **b** firing (of lime-kiln). **c** branding. **d** cauterization. **e** conflagration (fig.).

illos omnino non tetigit ignis, nec etiam in vestibus ~o vel modica inventa est MAP *NC* I 30. **b 1420** pro ~one unius ustrine calcis *Ac. Durh.* 270. **c 1458** pro ~one et *le stokyn* equorum indomitorum *ExchScot* 438. **d** in caput a medicis affertur adustio caeci WULF. *Swith.* II 697. **e** si tali ~oni ignee superadderem faculas verborum comminancium *NLA* (*J. Bridl.*) II 69.

2 overheating (of humours), making 'adust' (med.).

si in hepate putrefactio esset, ..urina rubea et tenuis minaretur ~onem et ad nigredinem pertineret P. BLOIS *Ep.* 43. 127A; per ~onem ex colera fit melancolia BART. ANGL. IV 6; in omni febre est aliqualis ~o humorum pravorum GAD. 4 v. 1; vestra complexio..colerica existit, ..que..per ulteriorem ~onem..in melancoliam convertetur KYMER 3.

adustionalis, caused by 'adust' humours.

si sit terciana nota de materia adusta, tunc potest sciri per morbos precedentes ~es non plene purgatos GAD. 15 v. 2.

adustivus, a incendiary. **b** making humours 'adust' (med.).

a s1415 ollas plenas pulveribus †adustinis sulphuris et calcis vive ad immittendas oculis nostrorum..ac vasa furencium pulverum oleorumque et pinguium †adustinorum pro combustione et consumpcione ordinacionum nostrarum ..hostilis calliditas..paraverat ELMH. *Hen. V* 24. **b** ita quod virtus et non substancia [colloquintide] transeat ad potum, quia substancia est ulcerativa ~a GAD. 66. 2.

adustor, burner (of bricks).

c1400 operarii quidam de Beverlaco, qui tegularii dicebantur, fabricatores et ~ores laterum *Meaux* III 179.

adustus v. adurere. advalare v. avalare a. advant- v. avant-.

advectare [CL], to bring.

animarum manipulos..quos angelici messores..caelestis regni horreo catervatim ~abunt ALDH. *VirgP* 28; c770 marinis aestibus [libros] terram ~antibus (*Lit. Arch. Ebor.*) *Ep. Bonif.* 124 p. 261; misit legatos ad inquirendum utrum pacem vel guerram ~asset G. MON. I 12; [auce majores] in grege magno, flante aquilone, ~antur GIR. *TH* I 23.

advectio, immigration.

illa ~o ex tribus provinciis, quae tum eminentiores habebantur Germaniae, venisse leguntur (*sic*) ÆTHELW. I 3; ipsa [Danorum] ~o erat prima *Ib.* III 1.

advectivus, bringing, conductive.

1550 [aqueductu] ad dictum messuagium ab antiquo adcurrente et ~o *CalPat* III 357.

advectrix, bringer (f.).

jam exsulum ~ix stabat in littore prora W. CANT. *V. Thom.* II 8.

advectus, arrival.

exercitus paganorum, cujus ~um supra memoravimus ÆTHELW. IV 2.

advehere [CL], to bring. **b** (pass.) to arrive.

bucellam..quam penniger praepes..advexerat rostro ALDH. *VirgP* 28; advexit illo plurimam congeriem trabium BEDE *HE* III 16; advectos inde pulveres GIR. *TH* I 6. **b** a690 Hibernia quo..classibus advecti confluunt ALDH. *Ep.* 5 p. 492; advecta est subito Danorum..classis ÆTHELW. III 1.

advelatio v. avolatio b.

1 advena [CL], outsider, foreigner, immigrant. **b** (adj.) extraneous.

grandescere populus coepit ~arum BEDE *HE* I 17; pro quo eis, quasi pro suae gentis ~is, orabat ad Dominum *Ib.* IV 14; de..ejusdem [gentis] per ~as expugnationibus GIR. *TH intr.* p. 8; educatum aiunt Galonem inter advenas sed 'ad venas' et cor penetrat MAP *NC* III 2 p. 109; a1205 ~e et domestici adverterunt, quotquot advenerant, ..ipsius passionem *Canon. G. Sempr.* 167v. **b** sol ex se lucet, lune lux advena GIR. *Vers.* I (I p. 344).

2 advena v. avena. advenagium v. alnagium.

advenantum [OF *avenant*], (instalment of) rent.

1166 lx solidatas terre cum avenanto suo de v s. de redditu molendini de Frankelawe et cum avenanto suo de ij s. de costoma unoquoque anno *Reg. Ant. Linc.* III no. 895; 11.. reddendo..xx d. pro omnibus serviciis..excepto servicio domini regis, quod deffendet per avenantum iiij acrarum *AncD* A 11092; 1181 constituo ut unoquoque Sabbato reddat prepositus avenantum de illis c li. *Act. Hen. II* II 216.

advenienter, (?) in due time.

a1130 ut sit ad placita..abbatis..quotienscumque fuerit ~er submonitus *Cart. Burton* 32 (cf. *EHR* XX 281).

advenire [CL], to come to, arrive. **b** (w. inf.). **c** (trans.) to approach.

tunc procus advenit ALDH. *VirgV* 1957; jussit Augustinum ..ad suum..~ire colloquium BEDE *HE* I 25; si contra pacem regis..navis ~iret *DB* I 262b; Ranulfo ad veniente, de fuit Radulfus *Ib.* II 424; 1228 ~iente postea episcopo versus illam villam *Feod. Durh.* 250; s1254 nescierunt intelligibiliter intimare qui, cur, unde vel qualiter ~issent M. PAR. *Abbr.* 332; 1283 cuilibet magistro cedente vel decedente, dabit pro herietto et relevio novus ~iens x s. *Cust. Battle* 94; s1190 rogans eum Romam domino pape ~turum *Meaux* I 253. **b** s1398 ad monasterium ~it personaliter visitare..abbas de Fontibus *Ib.* III 267. **c** 1473 ~it me.. Johannes *Cant. Coll. Ox.* III 113.

2 to come about, arise, occur. **b** to accrue, be added.

in annum..quo redemptio gentium..~isse traditur ALDH. *Met.* 2 p. 69; ~iente diluculo BEDE *HE* IV 8; si forte alicunde quid auxilii, quo salvarer, ~iret *Ib.* V 12 p. 306; aeris nebulositas..ex aquarum terrarumque propinquitate ~it ERIUG. *Per.* 550A; s1312 (v. adoptare 3a). **b** illa persona que minus discreta est ~it illis que majorem discretionem habent ad augendum discretionem earum BACON XV 47; potencie radicantur in una essencia, et superponitur eis habitus, et tercio ~iunt actus PECKHAM *Quaest.* III 38A. 3 p. 213.

3 (w. *ad*) to come by, acquire.

1318 requisiti qualiter ~erunt ad predictum statutum suspectum (*CoramR*) *Law Merch.* III 45; 1328 allocutus qualiter ~it ad predictum falsum sigillum *SelCKB* V 33; 1382 nec sciunt qualiter ~it ad certa punchons *IMisc* 228/12.

adventagium v. avantagium 2a. advental- v. aventailum.

adventare [CL], to come. **b** (p. ppl.) having arrived.

torrido ~ante autumni fervore ALDH. *VirgP* 9; clangit vox clara tubarum / adventante Deo *Id. VirgV* 281; inter ceteros qui ~averant ADEL. *QN intr.* p. 1; rex percitus illuc ~ans *G. Steph.* I 31; ~antibus mulierum turbis de vicinia.. ad festum GIR. *IK* I 2; s1192 nunciatum est regem..~asse COGGESH. 57; cotidie ~ancium caterve *V. Har.* 3 f. 7. **b** illis in Angliam ~atis *G. Steph.* I 34; s875 vij naves nuper ~atas deprehendens M. PAR. *Maj.* I 408.

adventatio, (frequent) arrival.

s1296 sine ~one Anglorum in Flandriam..negociari profectualiter non valemus *Flor. Hist.* III 290; c1412 pro expensis excessivis racione ~onis dominorum et hospitum insolite confluencium *G. S. Alb. cont.* III 390.

adventicius [CL], extraneous. **b** (leg.) not derived from parents. **c** (?) extra.

stellae quae non proprio..sed adventitio et a sole mutuato lumine fulgent BEDE *TR* 6; usque ad nostra..tempora, quibus..~ia dignitas evanuit GIR. *IK* II 1. **b** ~ia dos dici poterit maritagium quod ab aliis datur quam a patre vel matre BRACTON 92; 1446 bona..adipiscenda quacumque via ac titulo, viz. hereditario, ~io, provecticio *MunAcOx* 554. **c** c1350 quandam aulam longam et latam, de barris, tabulis †avenaciis [? l. aventiciis] et cameris adjacentibus ornatam *MunCOx* 119.

2 of foreign origin, (sb.) newcomer.

c1218 si aliquis ~ius qui fidelis sit in terras eorum venerit et ei placuerit ibidem morari (*Ch. Com. Cestr.*) *EHR* XXIX 43; c1250 ~ius malefactor nunquam recipiatur *Stat. Cantab.* 211; 1255 de terris propriis..dabunt ~iis volentibus se casare ibidem concatum pro vj d. *RGasc.* I sup. 15; 1281 nec ipsi nec antecessores fuerunt ~ii in predicto manerio [*Steventon, Berks*], immo sunt de sanguine sokemannorum procreati *CoramR* 60 r. 33*d.*; 1290 eo pretextu quod vir suus ~ius dictam hereditatem suam ipsa invita vendidit (*Reg. S. Edm.*) *EHR* I 735; 1307 sunt ibidem [*Tenbury, Worcs*] sex burgenses ~ii *IPM* 4/1 r. 3; 1326 extranei ~ii, qui mansiones suas conducant (*sic*) de variis, ..communicant in marisco [de Ely]..et illi vocantur *undersetles CBaron* 146; 1366 consuetudines diversorum..~iorum tenencium terras nativas [*Norf*] *Cl* 204 m. 2*d.*; 1366 antecessores sui fuerunt ~ii de Hibernia et gratis posuerunt se in advocaria domini *Rec. Caern.* 216 (cf. ib. p. xi); neque per habitare neque per justorum participare est quis civis; hiis participant ~ii et qui contractibus participant BURLEY *Comment. Pol.* 277; s1455 vir quidam ~ius..inhabitans infra villam de Watteforde *Reg. Whet.* I 199.

1 adventio v. adinventio 2.

2 adventio, coming, approach. **b** appearance (of suitor in court).

que..~o ad predictum J. D. ..*Entries* 612. **b** 1379 per ..sectam curie ad duas ~ones *IMisc* 221/3.

adventitare, to come repeatedly.

undique ~abant et cum gaudio accelerabant *V. Osw.* 436.

adventivus, not derived from parents (*cf. adventicius* 1b).

~a dos est quam ipsa mulier dat pro se, vel aliquis alius a patre vel avo *Fleta* 341.

2 of foreign origin (*cf. adventicius* 2).

c1400 ~os et forinsecos homines qui..in advocariam domini devenire voluerint *Rec. Caern.* p. xi.

adventura, casual profit. **b** (w. *maris*) flotsam and jetsam (C.I.).

1267 placita et perquisita cum omnibus aventuris et eschaetis valent per annum xxx li. *IPM* 34/8; 1332 concessionem..de omnibus homagiis liberorum hominum et villanorum suorum, cum omnibus sequelis suis et catallis suis et cum omnibus aliis ~is (*Pat*) *MonA* VI 890. **b** 1254 abbatia Montis S. Michaelis consuevit..percipere..werequum et ~as maris *CartINorm* 28; 1309 ea que reperta sunt in alto mari.., si per laborem marinellorum leventur a mari et ponantur in navi..et sic..ducantur ad terram, non possunt dici wreckum, set sunt tantummodo de ~is maris, de quibus nullus potest aliquid clamare nisi salvatores et dominus rex vel ille cui dominus rex concesserit libertatem percipiendi hujusmodi ~as *S. Jers* XVIII 221 (cf. *PQW* 829: aventuras maris).

2 risk (in trading).

1253 que..vina dicti cives debent nobis..reddere conducta ad suam aventuram apud Burdegalam *RGasc* I 329; 1458 se obligat omnia onera, expensas, rixicum et aventuram supportare *Cl* 309 m. 40*d.*; 1489 ut liberi sint.. de solucione..custume..bonorum..que ad..partes extramarinas..destinaverint..eorum propriis aventuris pro empcione victualium *Reg. Glasg.* 468.

3 adventure of arms, joust.

1233 quod nec sub nomine torn' neque sub nomine aventurar'..arma ferant *Pat* 43 m. 4; 1242 nulli conveniant ad turneandum vel ad burdiandum vel ad alias quascunque aventuras *Cl* 483 (cf. M. PAR. *Maj.* VI 209); 1262 cum.. quidam de regno nostro ad arma ire proponant, viz. ad torneandum aut aventuras querendum *Cl* 133; 1353 ne quis..turneare, burdeare, justas facere, aventuras querere seu alia facta armorum exercere presumat (*Cl*) *Foed.* (*ed.* 1825) III i 258.

4 accidental death.

1353 habeurunt coronatores infra burgum [S. Edmundi] ad..visus aventurarum ibidem supervidendos *ChartR* 138 m. 1; 1359 per aventuram corpora mortua infra predictam placeam..inventa humata fuerunt in cimiterio B. Marie de Grimesby *IMisc* 179/7; 1377 rotulus..unius coronatorum de ~is mortis hominum per ipsum visus (*sic*) *SelCCoron* 105.

adventurare, to venture (as a trader). **b** (refl.) to venture.

1471 mercatores..[regi Castelle] subjecti in regnum nostrum cum navibus, rebus et mercandisis suis accedere et ~are formidant (*TreatyR*) *Foed.* XI 720. **b** s1337 quadam nocte obscura apud fortalicium de Bas se aventurans, refugium victualium..ab eodem loco reduxit *Plusc.* IX 36.

adventurarius, engaged in trading ventures.

1597 vestrae majestatis subditos negotiatores, quos mercatores ~ios vocant, illorumque collegium sive societatem (*Lit. Consulum Emdae*) *Foed.* XVI 323; civitatem nostram mercatoribus ~iae societatis Anglicanae, si..e Stadensi oppido forte emigrandum foret, non defuturam (*Lit. Consulum Groning.*) *Ib.* 326.

adventus [CL], coming, approach, arrival. **b** (w. *bonus*) welcome. **c** (of justices in eyre).

ad primum hostium ~um..terga vertens BEDE *HE* II 2; canebat..de Spiritus Sancti ~u *Ib.* IV 24; in ipso primo ~u ejus in Angliam *DB* I 1; de..singulis..diversarum nationum tam ~ibus quam defectibus GIR. *TH intr.* p. 8; a1330 de mittendis pro ~u vestro eveccionibus et familia J. MASON *Ep.* 32. **b** 1226 (v. admensurare 2a); 1258 recepit a burgensibus Colecestr'..illas xx m. quas..regi dudum promiserunt pro bono ~u suo ad partes illas *Liberate* 34B m. 2. **c** 1198 summoneatur quod sit in ~u justiciariorum inde responsurus *CurR* I 35; 1202 non fuit captus..nisi pridie contra ~um justiciariorum *SelPlCrown* 153; 1225 [vicecomes] ponat coram vobis in proximo ~u vestro in partes illas loquelam.. *Pat* 589.

2 appearance in court: **a** of sheriffs etc. at Exchequer; **b** of suitors.

a 1208 ~us vicecomitum per totam Angliam in crastino Clausi Pasche *LTRMem. PR* p. 31; 1306 ~us vicecomitum ad Scaccarium in crastino S. Michaelis *LTRMem* 99 r. 1 (cf. ib. r. 1*d.*: ~us escaetorum). **b** 1285 rex recuperet seisinam suam de predicta secta [ad hundredum] et aliis ~ibus et prestacionibus *PQW* 250b; 1306 debent tres ~us ad tres curias generales per annum *Ext. Hadleigh* 231; 1311 debet..~um de laghedeyes *Cust. Battle* 147; 1323 per servicium faciendi iij ~us ad curiam de Bamburgh' per annum *IPM* 81/2; 1329 ab..omnimodis curiis, sectis, ~ibus ad visum franci plegii (*Pat*) *MonA* VI 1564; 14.. quod ~us franci plegii racione residencie tantummodo debeatur *Reg. Brev.* 175b.

3 a coming of the Saviour. **b** his second (or third) coming. **c** Advent (period covering the four Sundays preceding Christmas). **d** (pl.).

a prophetarum oracula..Salvatoris ~um vaticinantia ALDH. *VirgP* 4; praedicat adventum Christi paranymphus in orbe *Id. VirgV* 407; ~um suum ideo Christus usque ad sextam distulit etatem ut nove legis plenitudinem prolixitas temporis non auferret M. PAR. *Maj.* I 81. **b** s874 in ecclesia S. Marie honorifice sepultus ~um Domini primamque cum justis resurrectionem expectat FL. WORC. I 92; dubitatur utrum in tercio ~u Domini celum stabit WYCL. *Serm.* I 14 (cf. ib. IV 124). **c** ~us Domini..tempore hymni ejusdem cultus legitime decantentur *RegulC* 28; canantur ymni Dominicis diebus usque ad ~um Domini LANFR. *Const.* 87; 1074 prima Dominica die ~us Domini in festivitate S. Andree *Regesta* 20; ab ~u Domini usque ad octavas Epiphanie pacem Dei et sancte ecclesie per omne regnum (*Leg. Ed. Conf.*) *GAS* 628; in Domini ~u, qui mundo fuit tam..acceptus, vester non pariter in terram adventus tranquillitatis deberet esse H. BOS. *V. Thom.* V 5; s1195 erat hiems, et Dominici Natalis sollemnis exspectatio, que ~us Domini dicitur, erat in januis W. NEWB. V 17; 1201 facient serviri predictam capellam iij diebus qualibet ebdomada..et in ~u..diebus iiij *CurR* I 459; s1220 imminente tempore ~us Dominici *Flor. Hist.* II 171; ~us Domini semper habet tres (*sic*) Dominicas ante diem Natalem, et accidit semper quod Dominica prima ~us Domini est Dominica proximior festo B. Andree, qui est pridie Kalendas Decembris; ..et illud retinetur per hos versus: 'Andree festo vicinior ordine quovis / Adventum Domini prima colit feria' GROS. *Comp.* 266; ~us Domini quatuor semper continet Dominicas..propter quadruplicem Domini ~um in scripturis promissum BACON VI 112; 1455 xij Kal Jan. Dominica iiija ~us Domini *Invent. Ch. Ch. Cant.* 162. **d** sub fine ~uum cani debere septem antiphonas secundi toni BELETH *RDO* 63. 70 (cf. ib.: juxta dies ~uum).

4 occurrence. **b** accrual.

perfecta dicitur esse illa pausatio que non transmutat modum propter sui ~um GARL. *Mus.* A 103; quemcunque privari omni jure suo sic ut, antequam sententia execucioni mandetur, nullus posset eum (*sic*) revocare propter quemcunque ~um, neque est licitum neque justum OCKHAM *Dial.*

901. **b** non hoc tollit deperdicionem potencie Dei sine ~u nove equivalentis WYCL. *Act.* 63.

adverbialis, adverbial.

nec interrogativa dictio nominalis nec similiter alie ~es exigunt sua responsiva BACON XV 153; oportet quod hoc ~e 'antequam' preponatur in constructione *Id. CSPhil.* 481; hanc sentenciam quam inferunt iste ~es determinaciones [sc. substancialiter, corporaliter, presencialiter] (TYSS.) *Ziz.* 172.

adverbialiter, adverbially.

[verbum] per nominativum determinatur quando nominativus ille ponitur ~er, ut hic: 'incedit supinus', id est 'supine'. VINSAUF *AV* II B 82; nomen cum preposicione equipollet adverbiali determinacioni et ~er tenetur BACON XV 154; importat illas easdem res, quamvis non nominaliter sed ~er tantum OCKHAM *Summa* I 59 f. 20B.

adverbiare, to use adverbially.

'infra' vero et 'supra', cum ~iantur, pro adverbiis comparativi gradus, 'inferius' et 'superius' LINACRE *Emend. Lat.* 103.

adverbium [CL], adverb. **b** (in a pun on *Verbum Dei*).

exempla [spondeorum] ab ~io qualitatis et quantitatis, ut 'sancte, . . longe' ALDH. *PR* 114 p. 157; 'tunc' temporis ~ium est, 'tum' ordinis BEDE *Orth.* 2802; ~ium 'solummodo' nequaquam posuit LANFR. *Corp. & Sang.* 419B; inter ~ia loci motum et statum designantia male distinguens GIR. *GE* II 36; **1286** omnia . . verba et ~ia superius memorata, que designacionem presentis temporis representant *TreatyR* I 79. **b c1220** conjugio Christo nexos 'adverbia' dico H. AVR. *Poems* 103 p. 59.

adversabilis, subject to opposition.

omnis scriptura foret a quotlibet hominibus . . ~is WYCL. *Ver.* I 111.

adversantia, opposition. **b** (?) occurrence.

numquid credimus papas aliquos adversantes Christo in sua voluntate in illa ~ia interire? WYCL. *Chr. & Antichr.* 679. **b** cujus modestam pacienciam . . consequens experiencie ~ia certissime declarabit *NLA* (*J. Bridl.*) II 69.

adversari [CL], (w. dat.) to conflict (with).

his adversantur vitiorum castra maligna ALDH. *VirgV* 2456; omne quod est misero ~atur ANSELM (*Or.* 10) III 35; **1205** quorum rotuli aliis ~antur de recordo illo *CurR* III 301; repugnanciam assercionum, quarum una alteri ~abatur OCKHAM *Dial.* 528.

2 (pr. ppl.) opposing, hostile. **b** (as sb.) opponent.

cujus regni principia . . tantis redundavere rerum ~antium motibus BEDE *HE* V 23; maliciose impugnaciones mihi ~ancium inimicorum ROLLE *IA* 249; **a1350** jurabis quod ~antem quemcumque statutis . . non fovebis consilio *StatOx* 19. **b** ~ancium frustrato conatu *CollectOx* I 10.

adversarius [CL], hostile. **b** (sb.) adversary, opponent. **c** the Devil.

nunciatum est regi . . ~iam potenciam esse in multis millibus ex altera parte fluminis ELMH. *Hen. V* 46. **b** Finanum . . acerbiorem castigando et apertum veritatis ~ium reddidit BEDE *HE* III 25; donec ~ius ad curiam veniens aliud breve perquirat GLANV. II 10; **c1250** ne in plures ~ios distringatur qui cum uno contraxit *Stat. Cantab.* 215 (cf. ib. 327); **1440** monachus ~ius prioris *Pri. Cold.* 110. **c c1006** confitentes quicquid tota ebdomada impugnante ~io commiserint *Comp. Swith.* 176; ~ius noster Diabolus intravit in corda quorundam ELMH. *Hen. V* 10.

adversatio, opposition.

1197 quoniam nobis imminet fortune adversitas [et] ejus comitantium aversio, immo ~o *Ep. Cant.* no. 415.

adversative, in opposition.

s1138 ad . . castellum quod Willelmus . . ~e tenuerat obsidendum FL. WORC. *Cont.* A II 110.

adversativus, expressing opposition (gram.). **b** (sb.) opponent.

per hanc conjunccionem 'sed' aut aliam similem, que secundum grammaticos . . et secundum communem modum loquendi dicitur ~a, eo quod adversando priori sentencie ponit ejus oppositum BRADW. *CD* 678D. **b** et [presules] virtutis penitus sunt adversativi; / vendunt non dant redditus hospiti vel civi *Ps.*-MAP 151. 19.

adversator, opponent.

protervus ecclesie Menevensis sueque dignitatis impugnator et ~or GIR. *Spec.* III 3 p. 149; **s1304** constabularius castri Roffensis, monachorum ~or ibidem in quantum potuit *Flor. Hist.* III 121.

adversio, a transgression, breach. **b** (?) misfortune. **c** (?) opposition or disobedience. **d** (? for *animadversio*) rebuke or punishment.

a 1102 Gualensis episcopi causam sacris . . canonibus obviare non nescis; ceterum, quia inter barbaros barbarice . . promotus est, in tue fraternitatis arbitrio ponimus, sic tamen ut de cetero . . hujusmodi non presumatur ~o (*Lit. Paschalis II Papae*) EADMER *HN* 160. **b** huic pape [Paschali II] multe ~ones [v.l. adversitates] ingruerunt, sed Deo volente illos [v.l. illas] prostravit *Eul. Hist.* I 267. **c 1255** de facto suo et ejus ~one vel mora ac ceteris ejus negociis et agendis *Cl* 196. **d 10..** ~one, *ðrean* WW.

adversitas, hostility, enmity. **b** (mode of) attack or injury.

8.. misericordiae tua muro ab hostium ~ate . . munitus (*Pontific.*) *Rec. Coronation* 4; **1298** ne . . inquietudinis dispendia ex parcium hujusmodi ~ate valeant . . contingere *Reg. Cant.* I 290; **s1454** quicquid contra ipsos sive diabolice sive humane moliuntur ~ates *Reg. Whet.* I 137. **b** vermium hujusmodi, quot genera sunt, tot venena, . . quot varietates, tot ~ates GIR. *TH* I 36.

2 adversity, misfortune. **b** a (specific) misfortune, affliction.

706 ingruente calamitatis ~ate ALDH. *Ep.* 9; **9..** in ~ate, *on wiþerwerdnesse* WW; vel de rerum prosperitate . . vel de ~ate earum OSB. *V. Dunst.* 46; si ~as earum rerum quas servus Dei contemnere debet vos contristat ANSELM (*Ep.* 78) III 201; **s1154** multo labore et ~ate confractus *Chr. Rams.* 336; fortune didicit impetus et ~atis insultus equanimiter sustinere GIR. *RG* III 17; **s1254** viderant . . regis [Francie] in ~ate patientiam M. PAR. *Abbr.* 331; **s1308** nihil nocebit ~as ubi nulla iniquitas dominatur AD. MUR. 13. **b 1216** in hujus ~atis tempore *Pat* 200a; quamlibet ~atem reputabat in gloriam G. COLD. *Durh.* 13; **s1251** sic ~ates diverse regem affixerunt M. PAR. *Min.* III 105; **1318** inter tot et tantas universitatis . . ~ates *FormOx* 40; **1323** variis ~atibus corporis . . prepeditus *Lit. Cant.* I 93; tribulaciones et ~ates, quas sustinere posset communitas fidelium OCKHAM *Dial.* 951.

adversum [CL], against.

allophilorum exercitus . . ~um Israhelitas . . hortantur ALDH. *VirgP* 13; ~um illos qui aliter facere volebant zelo . . accensus BEDE *HE* IV 24; commota est terra, exasperata ~um vos H. BOS. *V. Thom.* V 5; **c1184** duas culturas . . quas clamaverunt ~um me *Cart. Osney* IV 34.

1 adversus [CL], against. **b** at the expense of.

hoc opus adversus querulos defendite scurras ALDH. *VirgV* 2833; rebellarunt ~us regem BEDE *HE* III 24; qui cum illo prius erant, amodo ~us illum H. CANTOR 7v; ~us . . tot inimicos GIR. *PI* II *pref.*; **s1347** (v. advocare 1a). **b** hunc hominem detinuit ~us Godricum *DB* II 278.

2 adversus v. advertere 3.

†advertare, (?) *f.l.* for *adventare.*

s1300 cum Scoti eos †~asse contemplabantur, mox irruerunt in illos *Ann. Ed. I* 445.

advertentia, attention.

c1283 officium ecclesiasticum dicitur sine reverencia, diligencia et ~ia J. WALEYS *V. Relig.* I 6 f. 231; scio . . quanta ~ia exortacionis mee tu ponderas qualitatem FORTESCUE *LLA* 3; [vocativus] absolute semper consistit, quasi cum ~iam effecerit officio defunctus LINACRE *Emend. Lat.* 16.

advertere [CL], to turn (fig.), pervert.

1219 si aliquis medicorum suadet aliquid quod ~atur alicui in periculum anime sue, non admittat illud *Conc. Syn.* 57.

2 (sc. *animum*) to notice, grasp, realize; *cf. animadvertere.*

rumorem adverte parentum ALDH. *VirgV* 2058; quod a malitia inhabitantium . . contigisse . . omnes . . facillime potuerunt ~ere BEDE *HE* IV 23; ~it . . abbas difficultatem eventus SERLO GRAM. *Mon. Font.* 113; **1201** avertit quod . . curatus est *Canon. G. Sempr.* 146; animis discretis ~endum quanta . . veneratione . . curabant GIR. *Spec.* IV 23; **1296** ~ens . . quod mater sua . . amisisset jus *SelPlMan* 173; incipio magis ~ere sentenciam memoratam OCKHAM *Dial.* 431 *bis*; animo ~endum est quod . . appellans potest prosequi appellationem *Praxis* 269.

3 (p. ppl. *adversus*) **a** opposite. **b** adverse, unfavourable. **c** (sb. n.) opposite direction, contrary (side).

a ~i dentes, *þa eahta forworden teþ betwux tuxum* ÆLF. *Gl.*; ex ~a parte ERIUG. *Per.* 459C; **c1205** manus in ~am brachii partem reflexa *Canon. G. Sempr.* 163; **1239** Mediolanenses . . abigere studuit . ., quos tamen ~a parte ad unitatem trahere potius debuit (*Lit. Papae*) M. PAR. *Maj.* III 596. **b** replicavit . . quae sibi ~a quaeve in ~is solacia provenissent BEDE *HE* IV 22; in omnibus que undatim ingruebant ~is . . infractus *G. Steph.* I 61; parati . . pro ipsa veritate ~a equanimiter tolerare AD. EYNS. *Hug.* V 13; **s1197** diversas non ~as proferebant rationes GERV. CANT. I 549; in quibus quam plurima . . racioni naturali . . contraria pariter et ~a patenter inveni OCKHAM *Pol.* III 2; **a1350** ~a valitudine detenti *Stat. Cantab.* 322. **c** quasi ab ~o pectentes, veniunt contra mentem auctoris J. SAL. *Met.* 877A; **a1400** in cathedra . . preparata exadverso *Miss. Westm.* II 684; **1426** contra fratrem W. . . in ipsa cedula principalem ex ~o nominatum *Reg. Cant.* III 139.

advesperare, (impers.) to grow late.

ubi jam ~ante noctis adessent empora *Enc. Emmae* II 10; *to wax even*, vesperare, ~are *CathA.*

advesperascere [CL], to grow late, approach evening. **b** (fig.).

8.. †advesperescente die, *geæfenedan deige* WW; **s1296** in quodam conflictu . . ~ente die conserto *Flor. Hist.* III 100; **s1381** eo die ~ente *V. Ric. II* 31. **b** mihi jam ~it et accelero ad vite transeuntis occasum P. BLOIS *Ep.* 236 568C; **a1440** viro illi cum jam ~it dies vite *Reg. Whet.* II 405.

adviatio, method of approach.

ars quelibet suas habet metodos, quas nos figuraliter ~ones vel aditus possumus interpretari J. SAL. *Met.* 870D.

advidēre, to observe, catch sight of (fig.).

cum exercende malicie locum ~erint, utinam vel non invidierint vel potius nihil viderint GIR. *TH* III 21.

Advincula (Petri), feast of St. Peter's Chains (*S. Petri ad Vincula*), 1 August; *cf. vinculum.*

c1250 inter Pentecosten et ~am S. Petri *DCCant* H f. 160; **c1300** ad avincculam S. Petri *Reg. S. Aug.* 60; **s1322** in avincula S. Petri *Eul. Hist.* III 197; **s1364** circa ~am S. Petri *Ib.* 235; **1425** die Martis proximo post festum ~e S. Petri *Cl* 275 m. 2.

advisagium v. avesagium.

advisamentum [cf. OF *avisement*], advice. **b** consultation, deliberation.

1295 sitis coram nobis . . parati et instructi nobis et consilio nostro super premissis . . consilium vestrum una cum avisamento vestro impensuri *RParl* I 140b; **1302** juxta ipsorum . . avisamentum et informacionem *RGasc* III 406; **1312** dicunt . . quod stat . . interpretacio per avisiamentum barnagii (*Ordin. Reproband.*) *Ann. Lond.* 213; **1313** paratus est per avizamentum aliquorum de paribus suis . . reddere ea (*Tract. Ed. II*) *Camd. Misc.* XV 7; **1327** de consilio et avisiamento prelatorum, comitum et baronum WALS. *HA* I 187 (= *Foed.* IV 243: de . . avisamento); **1344** consilium, auxilium, avisamentum vestrum . . habere volumus *Reg. Heref.* 6; ita quod ipsi [pares] . . considerent inter se qualiter melius et justius procedi poterit in casu illo . . et suas responsiones et avisamenta reportent in scriptis *Mod. Ten. Parl.* 18; **1379** per ~um et assensum militum qui ad parliamentum . . venerunt *Rec. Leic.* II 189; **1420** secundum aviseamentum executorum meorum *Reg. Cant.* II 184; **1424** de avizamento domini regis et omnium dominorum tam spiritualium quam temporalium AMUND. I 192; **1437** spretis . . sanis et celebribus . . precipuorum catholice fidei et ecclesie pugilum ac defensorum avisamentis BEKYNTON II 43; rex de ~o concilii sui eligere solet unum de servientibus ad legem FORTESCUE *LLA* 51; **1466** quod se maritabunt per avisamentum et agreamentum . . uxoris mee *Test. Ebor* II 277. **b 1321** quod justiciarii inde habeant avisiamentum *PQW* 452; **1394** datus est dies illis . . accusatis positis in avisamento justiciariorum super materiis unde accusati fuerunt *ArchOx* II 116; qui confestim brevi †avisitamento [v.l. avisiamento] in sua peticione predicto regi obtemperavit *Plusc.* VIII 12; sine ulteriore dilacione vel avisiamento [v.l. avisamento] responderunt *Ib.* IX 46.

advisare, ~iare [OF *aviser*], **a** to advise or inform. **b** (refl.) to seek advice or information. **c** to recommend.

a statutum est quod clericus [camerarii] . . semper aviset regem in omnibus *Iter Cam.* 52; **1441** alterum, contra quem facta fuerit suggestio hujusmodi, plane et plene ~abit et singula sic suggesta ei denunciabit BEKYNTON I 142; **1443** ut regem . . per literas . . ~avi *Ib.* 176; **1456** avisaveram . . et instruxeram nostrum exercitum ut . . omnes Jhesum . . acclamarent *Ib.* II 156; **1470** si . . servicio Jacobi pro tempore non egebunt, tunc ipsum . . Jacobum . . de super avisabunt *Pri. Cold.* no. 222. **b 1305** nos studeatis ad plenum certificare, ut per hoc nos avizare possimus *RGasc* III 470; **1329** consueverunt habere . . respectum xl dierum . . ut consultius et providius avisare se possint cujusmodi recordum . . fuerit faciendum *MGL* I 440; **1440** adicitis quod ego . . ~arem me bene quid emanet sub sigillo meo BEKYNTON I 111; **1466** concessiones . . prefato J. L. ad se avisandum et informandum efficacius . . exhibuit *Reg. Paisley* 150. **c 1457** eedem communitates . . ~arunt, ordinaverunt et appunctuaverunt, limitaverunt et assignaverunt certum numerum . . sagittariorum cuilibet comitatui (*Pat*) *Lit. Cant.* III 226 (cf. ib. 225: oportunitatem ad avisandum et providendum qualiter . . iidem . . sagittarii haberentur).

2 (pass.) **a** to be advised, receive advice or information. **b** (?) to be minded or resolved. **c** (of actions) to be advised, recommended.

a 1366 respectuatur . . eo quod curia nondum inde ~iatur *G. S. Alb.* III 25; **1366** quousque in proximo parliamento possit super hoc maturius avisari (*Stat. Dav.* II) *APScot* 139b; **a1380** tunc maturius avisati responsa . . fieri fecimus *Pri. Cold.* no. 53; **c1390** quia curia nondum avisiatur *Mem. York* 133b; **1391** quam summam . . rex ~atus cum suo consilio . . remisit *ExchScot* 255; **1392** eo quod justiciarii inde medio tempore avisiarentur *ArchOx* II 97; **1407** plenius avisati . . cum cujusmodi . . auxilio . . nobis . . voluerint . . deservire (*Cl*) *Foed.* VIII 466; **s1425** cum visis meis privilegiis melius avizatus fuerit, penitebit ipsum AMUND. I 197; **14..** volumus super contentis in peticione . . plenius avisari *Reg. Brev.* 281. **b 1306** non est avisatus mutare locum prisonarum suarum *RParl.* I 193a; **1381** partem Scocie quam . . credebat super hoc avisatam quod exprimeret sibi articulos *RScot* 38a; **1560** curia . . ad presens non ~atur ad judicium reddendum *Entries* 192. **c 1474** quicquid per . . nostros . . commissarios . . communicatum, ~atum, appunctuatum . . seu conclusum fuerit *RScot* 443b (cf. ib. 456b).

advisatio, advice. **b** information. **c** recommendation.

1401 certa nostra sciencia et assensu ac avisacione nostri sanioris et digesti consilii (*TreatyR*) *Foed.* VIII 215; **1492** matura avisacione prehabita *Reg. Aberd.* I 330. **b 1441** veritate . . per ~onem et denunciacionem hujusmodi . . cognita seu comperta BEKYNTON I 142. **c 1457** de omnimodis avisacione et provisione, solucione et onere, in, de, pro vel ad exhibicionem dictorum . . sagittariorum (*Pat*) *Lit. Cant.* III 226 (cf. advisare 1c).

advisator, adviser.

1422 cum deliberacione, ut asseruit, avisatorum dixit . . *Conc.* III 409.

advisatus, (?) aiming (cf. OF *aviser*).

1313 cementario . . operanti . . in turrello . . ad elarganda batillamenta pro springaldis in eodem turrello situandis et pro avisatibus et squach' eorundem springaldorum melius habendis *KRAc* 469/1 f. 3 (= *Building in Eng.* 90: †amsatibus).

advisio, advice.

1354 apporci[o]nacio..facta..per sacramentum..collectorum..et per avisionem..justiciariorum..ad inquirendum de servientibus (*Exch. Lay Subsidy*) *Enf. Stat. Lab.* 358.

advisus, advice.

1324 de consensu et ~u tocius capituli ecclesie nostre cathedralis *Reg. Carl.* II 226.

advivere [CL], to survive. **b** (?) to live by, owe livelihood to.

nosti quantum mihi infestus abbas..dum ~eret exstiterit Osb. *Mir. Dunst.* 24; s**1135** adjecit et regem Henricum, cum ~eret, ..constrinxisse..*G. Steph.* I 4; juret mihi quod..Cartusiensibus, dum ~am, minime sociabitur Ad. Eyns. *Hug.* I 8; **1453** dicebant..locum..sic bene esse..locupletatum..quod successori, dum ~eret.., nullum opus esset *Reg. Whet.* I 103. **b** avicule..nunquam ab ejus divelli karitate potuerunt quo advixerunt (*V. Aldhelmi*) W. Malm. *GP* V 247.

advoare, ~atio, v. advoc-. advocacia v. advocatia.

advocamentum [cf. OF *avoement*], avowal, acknowledgement (of suzerainty) (Gasc.).

1293 homines..parrochie se avoarunt esse nostros, ..carta avoamenti..penes nos..remanente *RGasc* III 72; **1313** supplicavit..quod cum..quoddam avouamentum de terra sua..gentibus nostris..per ignoranciam..fecisset, quod quidem avouamentum domino de M. de jure fecisse..debuisset, avouamentum predictum..remittere..velimus, ut intrare possit racione terre predicte in homagium et fidelitatem dicti domini *Ib.* IV 998.

†**advocantia,** advowson (*cf. advocatia, advocatio*).

1437 quod dictum manerium de Thorp Moryeux et ~ia ejusdem ville..de nobis..tenentur *Cl* 288 m. 16 (cf. ib.: manerium de T. M. una cum advocacione ecclesie).

1 advocare [CL, cf. OF *avoer*], to call (to oneself), summon. **b** to attract.

ut ipsis quoque qui eos ~averant indigenis essent terrori Bede *HE* I 17; gentem..ad agnitionem veritatis ~ans *Ib.* II 9; advocat et fratrem socios accersit et omnes Wulf. *Swith.* II 355; advocat ipse duces, comites terraeque potentes G. Amiens *Hast.* 169; currunt..cursores unus alterum prius ut ~arent ad praesentiam regis *Latin Stories* 4; s**1347** cum sacerdotes parcium borealium ~arentur adversus Scotos in prelium Knighton II 44. **b** institute sunt nundine, ut quos non invitabat confessoris sanctitas vel mercium ~aret aviditas W. Malm. (*V. Aldh.*) *GP* V 269.

2 to vouch to warranty (AS *tyman*), meet a charge of possessing stolen property by appeal to a person from whom one claims to have bought it.

si captale intercietur furtivum, et ille super quem intercietur ~et [AS: *sio hond tiemð*] inde, si ~atus nolit hoc recipere et dicat quod nunquam hoc ei vendidit sed aliud, tunc licebit ~anti ipsam manum in verum mittere quod [advocatus] nullum aliud vendidit ei (*Quad.*) *GAS* 123; si mortuum hominem ~et [AS: *to deadan tyme*], ..manifestet hoc cum testibus, si possit, quod recte ~et *Ib.* 226 (cf. ib. 111–12, 224, 397).

3 to vouch: **a** as overlord or feoffor (cf. 8 below); **b** as patron of benefice (*cf.* 17f below).

a de ista terra ~at Walterus regem ad protectorem et Henricum de F. ad liberatorem *DB* I 276b; hoc manerium tenet Walscinus de regina, et inde regem ~at *Ib.* 111b; **1164** si uterque ~averit de feudo illo eundem episcopum vel baronem, erit placitum in curia ipsius *Const. Clar.* 9. **b** **1194** Benedictus de B. venit et ~avit Nicholaum de S. de ecclesia S. Marie..cujus advocacionem Theobaldus W. clamat; Nicholaus summoneatur..inde responsurus *CurR RC* I 1.

4 to vouch for, acknowledge (a person). **b** to support, back up.

1227 Johannes per cartam suam illam concessit ad maritandum ut filiam suam..et ita ~avit eam pro filia sua *CurR* XIII 24; **1237** Jordanus..nunquam ~avit eum pro suo [filio] *BNB* III 244; **1255** homines bene ~avit et factum eorum warantizavit *SelPlForest* 78; est enim wayvium quod nullus ~at, nec princeps eam [feminam] ~abit nec tuebitur cum fuerit rite wayviata Bracton 125b; **1281** Willelmus..proposuit quod, cum..esset juratus..communie, respondere minime teneatur; ac..major..insule..Willelmum, ..tanquam juratum suum advoans, ..ad examen suum remitti peciit *RGasc* II 149. **b** s**1257** intellexerunt per murmuracionem populi quod ipsi nollent ~are aldermannos in responso per illos facto *Leg. Ant. Lond.* 35.

5 to avow, accept responsibility for (an act). **b** (w. *quod*).

1220 non ~amus factum Leulini..unde..nos vocavit auctorem *Pat* 254; **1224** licet non ~aret factum, nihilominus obtulit quod faceret Willelmum..de facto satisfacere (*Lit. Leulini, AncC* IV 19) *RL* I 229; **1255** quod factum forestarii domino comiti..intimaverunt, qui factum illud bene ~avit *SelPlForest* 13; **1257** R. ..cepit..tres cervos, ..quorum capcionem acceptat et ~at *Cl* 33; ipsi [procuratores] erunt principales quousque domini eorum factum eorum ~averint ..vel deadvocaverint Bracton 204b; **1278** theþingmannus ..in misericordia, quia theþinga sua non ~avit presentacionem suam *Hund. Highworth* 93; **1289** dantes [procuratoribus]..potestatem..avoandi..nostro nomine actum quod dicitur esse per homines nostros..perpetratum *RGasc* II 408; **1292** ipse in curia sua terminavit apella, sicut ipse ~at *PQW* 121a; **1293** de Martino..pro falsa presentacione, eo quod presentavit quod..Lecia occidit Olivam.., que presentacio non fuit ~ata de decennariis *Leet Norw.* 44; **1307** omnes excessus predictos in plena curia illa contemptibiliter ~averat *Pat* 128 m. 34*d*.; **1313** si alique prisiones sunt facte contra formam tractatus, rex non avoat eas nec ratas habet (*Tract. Ed. II*) *Camd. Misc.* XV 10; c**1320** cepit ad opus suum proprium centenam hujusmodi piscis pro j d. ..et capcionem hujusmodi ~at..ut de antiquo feodo constabularie *Lond. Ed. I & II* II 182; **1324** dicit quod..imposicionem predicte custume..~are non possint auctoritate brevium domini regis *MGL* II 331; **1351** abbas pro se et aliis..bene ~at capcionem illam [v equorum etc.] et juste etc. *Reg. S. Aug.* 331. **b** **1236** querit si predictus R. velit ~are quod narrator suus narrat pro eo; et R. dicit quod bene ~at *CurR* XV 1767; c**1300** ~at quod habet tronam *MGL* II 116.

6 a to avow, acknowledge (documents) as authentic. **b** to vouch for (goods) as genuine. **c** (w. acc. and inf.) to avow, aver.

a s**1274** ~avit..omnes cartas quas fecerat tempore majoratus sui *Leg. Ant. Lond.* 164; **1286** quesiti si ~ant predictum recordum, dicunt quod sic (*PlRCP*) *Law Merch.* II 43. **b** **1311** capellarios..capellas falsas..pro bonis et legalibus ~antes et vendentes *MGL* II 102. **c** **1289** ~at bladum suum esse de feodo prioris *Leet Norw.* 24; **1319** ij oves matrices..~avit ei esse sanas, que quidem oves expirarunt pro putredine *CBaron* 128; **1321** bene ~ant illam piscariam..esse communam *Ib.* 133.

7 to avow, claim, as one's own. **b** (w. acc. and inf.). **c** (w. inf.) to claim (the right) to.

1202 nolumus quod ipse ~et alterius catalla quam sua *Pat* 10a (cf. ib. 12b); **1288** assuetus est ducere mercandizas extraneorum extra civitatem et ~at eas pro suis bonis *Leet Norw.* 15; porcellos..posuit in lardario suo et eos ~avit tamquam weyf *State Tri. Ed. I* 70; **1311** rentarius S. Antonii ..non ~abit aliquos porcos euntes infra civitatem (*LBLond* D) *MGL* I 591; **1348** ita quod lanas..pro suis non ~ent *RScot* 716b; **1375** blada ~averunt tanquam sua *Leet Norw.* 62. **b** **1289** ~at bona Ranulphi..esse sua dominica *Ib.* 28; **1291** mercatores de Alemannia..quosdam mercatores extraneos..cum mercimoniis suis.. venientes receptant et mercimonia illa esse sua propria sepius ~ant *MGL* II 196; **1321** ita quod aliquem qui de gilda ipsorum..non extiterit nec ejus..mercimonia de gilda sua esse ~ent ullo modo *PQW* 455b. **c** **1272** juramentum fidelitatis..quod ipsi [Lemovicenses] fatentur et avohant debere nobis (*Pat*) *Foed.* I 875; **1331** ipsi ~ant capere de intrinsecis unum tolnetum et de extrinsecis..duplum, quod est contra commune jus *PQW* 160b.

8 to claim to hold (land or sim.) as feudal tenant. **b** (w. acc. and inf.) to avow oneself a tenant.

aecclesiam..S. Cutberti ~at idem W. de Hugone comite et vii minutas mansiones *DB* I 298; **1164** si recognitum fuerit [tenementum]..pertinere..ad laicum feudum, nisi ambo de eodem episcopo vel barone ~averint, erit placitum in curia regia *Const. Clar.* 9 (cf. 3a above); **1166** regnum meum quod a nemine nisi a solo Deo ~o (*Lit. regis, Ep.* 185) *Becket Mat.* V 362; **1230** Rogerus et Sarra ~ant terram illam ut suam..et..Willelmus ut suam *CurR* XIII 2350; **1279** [cum] Bernardus..nitatur a..Willelmo possessionem dicte domus avocare *RGasc* II 94; **1283** cum..vicecomes..castrum suum de F. de comite P. ~averit, quod de feodo nostro existere asserimus *Ib.* 182; **1285** Amanevo..asserente se..legitime advoasse a nobis omnia supradicta *Ib.* 255. **b** **1281** super hiis que..Amaneus advohat a nobis se tenere *Ib.* 148; **1283** cum..quicquid habent avohent se tenere a nobis *Ib.* 214; **1285** (v. advocatio 3c).

9 (refl.) **a** (w. *de*) to avow or claim (a liberty). **b** (w. *per* or dat.) to vouch or claim as overlord (*cf.* 3a and 8 above). **c** (w. *per*) to claim as patron of benefice (*cf.* 3b above). **d** to claim or appeal to as protector.

a **1298** alii quicunque, ~antes se de libertate eorundem et de libertate eorundem gaudere volentes, contribuant *BBC* (*Cinque Ports*) 139. **b** **1227** homines de Baiona non ~ant se per vos nec per vestrum dominium nec per vestros (*AncC* V 63) *RL* I 319; **1261** [Lemovicenses] in vestra fidelitate existunt et nulli alii se ~ant nisi vobis nec alium nisi vos habent dominum (*AncC* IV 13) *Ib.* II 181; **1280** restituit nobis..seisinam hominum questalium..vicecomitis qui se nobis avocaverant *RGasc* II 107. **c** poterit esse contentio..si persona vel is qui se personam gerit in ecclesia ipsa ~et se per unum advocatum et alius credens se esse rectiorem advocatum ejusdem ecclesie clamet eandem advocationem Glanv. IV 7. **d** **1253** Salomon..[est] malefactor in eisdem boscis..et se ~at per..senescallum foreste *SelPlForest* 109; **1265** quidam malefactores se per nos..~antes *Cl* 128; **1275** Johannes..et Willelmus.., avocantes se per..vicecomites London', †telarios [? l. celarios] proborum hominum cervisiam vendencium sigillaverunt *Hund* I 406; **1282** quidam regratarii..se per quosdam ministros nostros ~antes (*Pat*) *Mon. Francisc.* I 623.

10 (intr.) to plead as advocate.

prohibentur..clerici coram seculari judice..~are W. Drogheda *SA* 35; **1423** viriliter, quesumus, ..apud ipsos..ministros ~are velitis; et nos pro vobis apud ipsum habebitis ~antes qui est propiciacio pro peccatis nostris *Reg. Whet.* II 409; **1461** suspensi sunt ab omni officio procurandi et ~andi *MunAcOx* 683; nec licet..alicui advocato ~are pro eodem [contemptore] nisi.. *Praxis* 63.

11 to appeal against, challenge.

si quis judices suspectos habeat, ~et aut contradicat (*Leg. Hen.*) *GAS* 564; injusto..judicio contradici poterit.., presertim si in reddicione fuerit ~um *Ib.*

12 to advoke (an action) from an inferior court.

1542 emanavit decretum ad ~andum causam pendentem coram..deputato..viceadmiralli *HCA Warrant Bk.* I f. 35.

13 (inf. as sb.) avowal (*cf.* 5 above).

1351 abbas per ~are suum supponit fidelitatem ipsius W. eidem abbati aretro fore *Reg. S. Aug.* 334; a**1400** abbas..in ~are suo predicto advocavit capcionem suam predictam pro relevio predictorum W. et I *Couch. Furness* I 406; ad ~are suum predictum respondere non potuit *Entries* 225.

14 (p. ppl. as sb. n.) (?) land claimed (*cf.* 8 above).

c**1138** quod..resaisias omnes illas terras que fuerunt de aocatis domni tui de blado et feno *AncD* L 2 (= *Anc. Ch. ed.* Round, p. 58: †accatis).

15 (p. ppl. as sb. f.) patroness. **b** patron saint.

quedam matrona Alfwara..[dedit] Ramesie ecclesiam de Elesworth, cujus erat ~ata *Chr. Rams.* 84; **1189** donationes Matillidis comitisse de Warrewico ~ate sue [sc. monachorum de Sallaye] *CalCh* II 164; ducis animum erga bonos viros illos exasperatum mitigare solebat, tanquam specialis existens precipuaque eorum ~ata Gir. *Spec.* II 1; s**1272** obiit ~ata nostra de Hibernia, domina Basilia de Wigornia, et sepulta est in ecclesia S. Marie Oseneie *Ann. Osney* 249. **b** s**1201** Innocentius papa..a B. Maria ejusdem [sc. Cisterciensis] ordinis ~ata..correptus *Flor. Hist.* II 123; **1434** ob honorem S. Frideswide alme universitatis Oxon' specialis ~ate *Reg. Cant.* III 256.

16 (p. ppl. as sb. m.) advocate, pleader (not in courts of Eng. common law). **b** 'next friend' at law (AS *mundbora*). **c** advocate (fig.), spokesman. **d** intercessor (of Christ; cf. 1 *John* ii 1).

~atus, *pingere GlC* A 283; causidicus, ~atus, *forespeca* Ælf. *Gl.*; quondam venerabile nomen..~ati notabili venalitate vilescit P. Blois *Ep.* 26 92A; ~atus linguam habet venalem Neckam *NR* II 188; **1243** magister W. de Becco non venit..; et vicecomes mandavit quod idem magister est ~atus itinerans *CurR* XVII 2011; ~atus..dici potest ille qui quoquo studio causis agendis operatur W. Drogheda *SA* 33; c**1259** in Romana curia ~ato (*AncC* III 22) *RL* II 144; **1301** magister J. dicit quod ipse est communis ~atus et pro suo dando stetit cum..magistro W. [coram archidiacono Linc'] *Abbr. Plac.* 295b; **1338** ~atus in consistorio archiepiscopi Cantuariensis *Hosp. in Eng.* 208; a**1350** ex malicia ~atorum..introductum est quod indirecte fiant ~ati per hoc quod admittuntur tanquam procuratores *Stat. Cantab.* 323; **1420** ~ato consistorali (*Lit. Reginae Siciliae*) *Foed.* IX 865; judicibus tuis et ~atis qui in regno Anglie servientes ad legem appellantur Fortescue *LLA* 8; **1452** curie Cantuariensis de Arcubus ~atus *MunAcOx* 640; **1461** ~ato domine regine *ExchScot* 59; si..~ati utriusque partis informationes dederint judici tam in facto quam in juris questionibus, ita quod non habent quod ulterius dicant in causa *Praxis* 293. **b** ~atus, patronus vel interpellator, *forspeca* vel *mundbora* Ælf. *Sup.*; si ordinatus vel alienigena seducatur in aliquo de pecunia vel vita, tunc debet ei esse rex..et episcopus ipsius gentis pro cognatione et ~ato [AS: *for mæg and for mundboran*], nisi penitus alium habeat (*Quad.*) *GAS* 135 (cf. ib. 592); qui sibi facit ~atum contra dominum suum per superbiam perdat quod de eo tenet (*Leg. Hen.*) *Ib.* 569. **c** **1239** pro se veritas non invenit ~atum (*Lit. Papae*) M. Par. *Maj.* III 592. **d** cum ~ato et redemptore nostro Aldh. *VirgP* 30; si mediatorem Dei et hominum haberet ~atum Osb. *V. Dunst.* 42; mi ~ate tutissime Anselm (*Or.* II 81) III 9.

17 (p. ppl. as sb. m.) patron, protector: **a** (w. ref. to saint); **b** (w. ref. to Mohammed); **c** (w. ref. to the Emperor); **d** (of religious house; *cf.* S. M. Wood: *English Monasteries and their Patrons.. pp.* 17–18); **e** of town (? as deputy of count); **f** (of church, *cf.* 3b above).

a s**1138** ob declaranda merita sanctorum Andree apostoli et Wilfridi episcopi et confessoris, ~atorum ejus, et ceterorum patronorum..et aliorum sanctorum in eadem ecclesia quiescentium Ric. Hex. *Stand.* 41; in vigilia S. Petri ad Vincula..pulsentur insimul due majores campane..quia ~atus noster est *Cust. Westm.* 310. **b** s**1348** dummodo contra ~atum suum Machometum et leges ac ritus eorum depravando non †obsequerentur [? l. obloquerentur] J. Reading 106. **c** s**800** papa..dignitatem patriciatus contulit ei [sc. Carolo Magno].., ut imperator semper esset pater urbis et ~atus R. Niger 67; **1239** [papa] nos tanquam defensorem et ~atum ecclesie requisivit quod contra Romanos..procedere deberemus (*Lit. Imp.*) M. Par. *Maj.* III 581; licet..imperator sit specialis ~atus, id est defensor, ecclesie Romane, sicut et patroni ecclesiarum sunt ~ati earum Ockham *Pol.* I 93. **d** **1149** S Marie ecclesia, cujus fundator pater meus extitit et cujus ego patronus et ~atus sum *Cart. Osney* IV 28; a**1160** tamquam ejusdem ecclesie protector et ~atus *Cart. Eye* f. 23; **11..** ipse autem sanctimoniales [de Sewardelege] michi firmiter promiserunt quod in recipiendis sanctimonialibus meo tanquam ~ati consilio utentur *AncD* B 3229; incliti quondam ducis Ailwini, ~ati nostri *Chr. Rams.* 11; a**1160** P. de Golsa, fundator ejusdem abbacie [*Newhouse*]..; R. de Baius, ~atus predicte abbacie *Danelaw* 239; s**1177** comes Flandrie misit ~atum Bitunie Robertum [i.e. *Robert de Béthune, patron of the abbey of St. Vaast in Arras*]..ad..regem Anglie R. Howd II 119; **1200** Willelmus ~atus de Beton' *CurR* I 174; [Grandimontani] neminem ad sepulturam domus preter solum ~atum suum..admittere solent Gir. *Spec.* III 21; **1279** cum dominus rex sit ~atus predicte domus [Dei] Dovor' *PQW* 344b; s**1290** abbas..prioratum de Wymundham visitare disposuit; sed dominus R. de Tateshale, dicti loci ~atus, ..dictum prioratum intravit et januas contra abbatem claudi jussit *G. S. Alb.* II 23. **e** homo quidam erat diversarum villarum ~atus.., faciens graves exactiones in sibi subditos *Latin Stories* 70.

f **1160** Reginaldus se..ecclesiam de Porestok' presentatione Roberti de Arundel, ejusdem ecclesie quondam ~ati, ..adeptum ipsam diutius possedisse..asseverabat *Ch. Sal.* 31; summonebitur..assisa ad recognitionem faciendam, sc. quis ~atus tempore pacis ultimam personam mortuam ad ecclesiam illam presentaverit Glanv. IV 1; **1225** ad recognoscendum quis ~atus [etc.] *Pat* 592; **c1218** (v. advocatia); **12..** statuimus ne ~ati ecclesiarum seu quilibet laici impediant..personas..quominus de decimis suis.. libere valeant disponere *Conc. Scot.* II 23.

18 (p. ppl. as sb. m.) **a** warrantor vouched as vendor (*cf.* 2 above). **b** warrantor vouched as feudal overlord (*cf.* 3a above).

a omnis homo sciat ~atum suum [AS: *his getyman*] de hominibus et de equis et de bobus (*Quad.*) *GAS* 129. **b** ipse reclamat ~atum episcopum Baiocensem *DB* I 30; in eadem villa tenebat H. ii acras de terra abbatis de quibus non habet ~atum nec liberatorem *Ib.* 191; istam mansionem tenet Walscinus de regina, et inde vocat regem ~atum *DB Exon.* 346; **1103** si vero externus ibi inventus fuerit, qui tamen ~atum sibi monachum [de Staningis] dicat, adducetur ad eum; quem, si pro suo cognoverit, accipiet de eo rectum *MonA* VI 1083; **c1150** ego et heredes mei predictam terram adquietabimus apud omnes ~atos perpetuo *Reg. St. Bees* 317; **11..** hanc donationem..concessit..in curia Roberti G., qui ~atus est ipsius feudi *Danelaw* 459.

2 advocare v. annotare 1a.

advocaria [cf. OF *avoerie*], avowry, patronage, protection. **b** protection extended in return for payment (or the payment itself). **c** protection extended to certain tenants in boroughs (W. Marches). **d** protection (W. *arddel*) extended to new settlers or payment therefor (W. & Chesh; cf. *EHR* XXIX 41–55).

1255 Hospitalarii..habent unum tenementum in Brug' [*Bridgnorth, Salop*] et Templarii habent duo tenementa; et habent tenentes qui tenent illa tenementa ad vitam suam et non permittunt se talliari nec volunt scottare cum hominibus de Brug' de merchandia quam faciunt in dictis domibus propter ~iam Hospitalariorum et Templariorum *Hund* II 60 (cf. 1b infra); **1293** forestarii [Rogeri de Munbray] per preceptum et ~iam predicti Rogeri..ceperunt chiminagium de transeuntibus per medium..chacearum *PQW* 218b; **1295** idem Hugo habuit ~iam omnium menestrallorum et meretricium in Cestrisir' de tenura..comitis *IPM* 70/1 r. 2 (cf. *CalCl* 416). **b** **1181** ecclesia de Baldecamp est in donatione canonicorum, de qua Robertus clericus est persona ex donatione decani et capituli; et dicit se reddere annuam marcam Ruffo firmario non nomine ecclesie sed propter avoeriam *Dom. S. Paul.* 148; **1255** Radulfus le Butiller cepit advocar' et emendas de warenna, set nescimus quo waranto; ..Ricardus..dat iiij d. pro ~ia Radulfo Pincerne per annum *Hund.* (*Salop*) II 58b (cf. 1c infra); **1279** predictus magister [Templariorum] capit in ~ia sua homines qui non sunt sui tenentes nec aliquid de eis tenent nec sunt de feodo suo; et [Templarii] capiunt ab eis per annum denarios pro ~ia illa *PQW* (*Suss*) 761b; **1321** de hiis qui capiunt mercedem de aliquibus pro ~ia habenda cum non sint eorum tenentes nec residentes in tenuris suis (*Artic. Itineris*) *MGL* II 362. **c** **1262** concesserunt dicti cives quod omnes homines dictorum episcopi, decani et capituli qui manent in eorum terris et feodis in civitate predicta [*Hereford*] libere emant et vendent et marchandisas suas faciant et quieti sint de tolneto..excepta gente de ~ia (*Compositio*) *CalPat* 1391–6 423 (= *Reg. Heref.* 1275–82 92); **12..** sunt ibidem [*Dymock, Glos*] lxvj burgenses qui dant per annum de redditu lxv s.; item de minuto opere filiorum et filiarum bondorum per annum et aliorum pro awoaria j m. *IMisc* 19/28. **d** **1294** de quodam annuo redditu ~ie concelato et recuperato coram..justiciario (*Rent. & Surv.* 768, *Anglesey*) *Tribal System app.* 23; **1299** habeant..omnia maneria..cum homagiis, ..villanis et eorum sequelis, ~iis, wardis, releviis (*Ch. Vale Royal*) *MonA* V 710b; **1303** [baillivus de Weverham debet] districciones facere et ~ia levare (*Leger Bk. Vale Royal*) *Hist. Chester* II 165; **c1359** [comes] clamat racione dominii sui et constabularie sue.. habere ~ias suas per totum comitatum Cestrie de omnibus qui se in ~iis suis se (*sic*) ponere voluerint et habere omnia proficua et libertates que ad illas ~ias pertinent (*DL Coucher*) *Ib.* I 704; **1334** nullus erit nativus nec aliquis alius adventicius residens inter eos, nisi terram teneat, quin det domino pro ~ia sua habenda secundum quod poterit cum senescallo seu ragloto ~ie convenire *Surv. Denb.* 318; **c1370** de hominibus †anowarie [l. avowarie] ipsius domini principis in Northwallia *Rec. Caern.* 171; **1384** clamant esse libere condicionis, eo quod antecessores sui fuerunt adventicii de Hibernia et gratis posuerunt se in ~ia domini; set si poterit eos..disracionare pro villanis suis, ammoveantur de ~ia *Ib.* 216; **c1400** raglottus ~ie.., cujus officium est adventivos et forinsecos homines qui..in ~iam domini devenire voluerint..recipere *Ib.* xi; **1387** suscepimus in proteccionem et defensionem nostram A. T...qui nuper gratis se posuit in ~iis nostris (*Pat. Chest.*) *EHR* xxix 50; **1505** ~ia nostra aliter vocata *arthell* et denarii ~ie aliter vocati *arian arthell Pat* 597 m. 19.

2 (?) right possessed in manor by patron of appurtenant advowson.

1238 Ricardus venit et dicit quod petit manerium illud, sc. id quod tenet in dominico in dominico et in servicio in servicio et quod in ~ia in ~ia, et unde dicit quod illa hida terre fuit in ~ia predicti Jordani *BNB* III 244; item dicere poterit tenens et respondere quod nihil inde tenet omnino nec in dominico nec in servicio nec in elemosina nec in ~ia, et hoc probato cadit breve Bracton 432b (cf. ib. 433b: si quis manerium petierit cum omnibus pertinenciis ad quod pertineat advocatio).

3 avowry, claim that a distraint is justified (cf. *Stat. 21 Hen. VIII*, c. 19).

a1564 tenementum predictum in ~a predicta specificatum *Entries* 561.

advocarius, a (adj.) paying for lord's avowry. **b** tenant in avowry. **c** bailiff (W. *rhaglaw*) of avowry (*cf. advocaria* 1d).

a **1510** de redditu tenencium advocar[iorum] nihil, quia nulli tenentes advocar[ii] sunt ibidem *MinAc* (*Brecon*) 4704. **b** **1218** si aliquis adventicius..in terras eorum venerit.., liceat baroni ipsum..retinere, salvis michi ~iis qui sponte ad me venerunt (*Ch. Com. Cestr.*) *EHR* XXIX 43; **1352** omnes alii nativi et ~ii domini principis istius commoti solvent staurum domini principis annuatim *Rec. Caern.* 9; **1366** ad communem peticionem factam hominum de advocaria principis..responsum est quod justiciarius informet se de statu et condicione ~iorum *Ib.* 214. **c** **1335** officium ~ii cum redditibus hominum qui sunt in advocaria valet..xxv s. *Surv. Denb.* 209.

advocatia, patronage (eccl.).

1172 ut infra territoria de Glasgu [etc.]..nullus dominium, ~iam vel conductum aut quodlibet jus sibi vindicare audeat nisi vos et episcopus vester (*Lit. Papae*) *Reg. Glasg.* I 26; **c1218** diffinitum est quatinus, si patroni vel advocati aut feodotarii seu vicedomini alicujus ecclesie rectorem vel alium clericum ipsius ecclesie..occidere..presumpserint, patroni jus patronatus, advocati ~iam, ..amittant *Conc. Syn.* 95; **s1244** papa..inhibebat ne qui occasione juris patronatus, ~ie seu custodie quam in..domibus ordinis nostri [sc. Cisterciensis] se habere proponunt, ..bladum.. et res alias pro..usibus eorundem a nobis exigerent *Meaux* II 66; **1259** porrecta nobis ex parte tua peticio continebat quod J. rex Anglorum ~iam decanatus ecclesie S. Marie de Peneris [*Penkridge*]..concessit..archiepiscopatui Dubliniensi *Mon. Hib. & Scot.* 81b; **1422** quod nullus patronus ecclesiasticus..~iam seu jus patronatus aut jus aliquod quod habet in aliquo beneficiorum hujusmodi fraudulenter ..alienabit *Reg. Durh.* III no. 558.

advocatio, summons, invitation.

ipsa enim capparum distributio eorum est ad regendum chorum ~o Lanfr. *Const.* 148 (cf. *Cust. Westm.* 29); **s1254** venit..rex Francie.., vocantibus eum urgentissime magnatibus sui regni..; veniens igitur..tractavit qualiter..dissensionem, ~onis sue causam, ..pacificaret M. Par. *Abbr.* 337.

2 (vouching to) warranty (AS *team*; *cf. advocare* 2).

si [mortuus] amicos habeat, qui audeant hoc facere [sc. eum mundificare], tunc deficit ~o [AS: *þonne berst se team*], sicut si ille viveret ac negaret (*Quad.*) *GAS* 226; non sit quisquam alicujus ~onis dignus [AS: *ne beo ænig man æniges teames wyrðe*], nisi credibile testimonium habeat unde venerit ei quod cum eo deprehenditur (*Const. Cnut.*) *Ib.* 327.

3 **a** avowal, acknowledgement (*cf. advocare* 5). **b** claim (*cf. advocare* 7). **c** claim to hold (*cf. advocare* 8).

a cum [dominus ante mortem] non advocavit, sic transit ~o disseisine usque ad heredes, ut sic advocent factum [procuratoris] vel non advocent Bracton 204b. **b** **1279** rex..aut senescalli sui..nunquam recipient avocaciones aliquas de bonis..que sunt infra civitatem *RGasc* II 59; **1289** nove avoaciones decimarum que sunt de feodo [episcopi]..per gentes nostras recipiebantur ac eciam impediebant eundem super percepcione novalium *Ib.* 477; **14..** pro eo quod predictus B. averia sua propria esse advocat, ..nolentes quod idem A. per hujusmodi falsam ~onem de averiis suis..defraudetur, ..tibi precipimus quod.. *Reg. Brev.* 83. **c** **1282** causa..mota..super indebita ~one castri de Fronciaco *RGasc* II 169; **1285** cum questio verteretur..super eo quod..A. advoaverat se tenere..a nobis..omnia supradicta.., in recompensacionem omnium que..J. racione feodi, advoacionis, homagii, deadvoacionis et tocius questionis ac controversie..petere poterat a dicto A., idem A...det..dicto J...lx li. *Ib.* 255; **1289** avoavit se tenere..a..rege..vicecomitatum.., quibus recognicione et avocacione factis [etc.] *Ib.* 313; **1286** eorum tenentes habeant communam in..communibus pasturis..sine aliqua ~one seu recognicione mihi..facienda *BBC* (*Bakewell*) 8.

4 **a** encouragement. **b** authorization.

a fragilis [anima]..indiget mansuetudine, ..hilari ~one ..et pluribus hujusmodi Eadmer *V. Anselm.* I 22. **b** **1297** si aliquis per ~onem domini regis..seu..magnatum quorumcunque decetero hujusmodi prisas facere presumpserit, ..capiatur *MGL* II 72; **1318** P..., qui non est communarius, falcavit in communa vj^{e} lesch' sine ~one alicujus communarii *CBaron* (*Ely*) 125.

5 (payment for) avowry, patronage, protection (*cf. advocaria*). **b** (W. & Marches). **c** (Ir.; cf. G. J. Hand: *English Law in Ireland* 197–8).

1215 liberavimus R. C...captum pro eo quod inventus fuerat sine ~one in com. de Suhamton' cum N. de W. *Pat* 133a; **c1230** si aliquis sue ~onis infra autumpnum egressus fuerit domum suam ad serviendum.., denarium dabit (*Cust. Wretham*) *Doc. Bec* 117; **1247** dabit iij gallinas annuatim..pro habenda ~one domini et recipitur in thedinga *SelPlMan* (*Weedon Beck, Northants*) 11; **1275** communitas Lenn' [*Norf*] aliter utuntur libertate sua quam facere debent, eo quod recipiunt in avocacione sua extraneos occasione gilde †sua [l. sue], ita quod extranei sunt quieti alibi de toloneis *Hund.* I 461b; **1296** sunt v nativi de tenencia prioratus S. Andree Northamt'; et debent de consuetudine dare ad Natale Domini pro ~one habenda x capones *IPM* 80/6 (*Cal.* p. 283); **1317** onerat se..de iij s. de censura hominum que vocatur ~o (*MinAc*) *Peramb. Dartmoor* 297; **1349** capitagia..de J. atte Dole et filio ejus pro ~one habenda ad terminum vite (*Ext. Brightestone*) *Arch. J.* VI 165; **p1375** [tenentes ad vitam] quibus non licebit ponere se in ~one alterius domini in prejudicium domini abbatis (*CourtR Cranfield, Reg. Ramsey*) *Ib.* **b** **1199** liberos meos spadarios et homines de ~one mea (*Ch. Lewelini*) *Rec. Caern.* 147; **1218** nativos suos qui ad ~onem meam venerint..quietos concedo (*Ch. com. Cestr.*) *EHR* XXIX 44; **1251** plures sunt in dicto manerio [*Stretton, Salop*] qui ceperunt domus vel mesuagia et nichil reddunt domino regi nisi ij d. vel iij vel iiij pro ~one *IMisc.* 5/28; **1283** de hiis qui sunt in ~one domini, per annum x s. *IPM* (*Carm*) 35/4 r. 14; **1331** Ewias: ..est ibidem alia consuetudo que vocatur ~o hominum *IPM* 29/7 r. 14. **c** **1306** de Huet O Laythgan pro esse in ~one domini per annum iiij d.; ..de quadam Flory Hybernica de Joeliston de testagio pro esse in ~one domini per annum iiij d. *RBOrmond* 40–1.

6 **a** patronage of religious house. **b** patronage of benefice (w. right of presentation), advowson. **c** (w. *decimarum*) (?) right to assign tithes.

a **1259** rex..concedit quod idem episcopus [Bathon'] et successores sui ~onem abbacie [Glaston']..possideant, et quotiens abbaciam vacare contigerit inde, prout ad patronum pertinet, ordinent et disponant *Cl* 411. **b** **†1141** dedisse..jus ~onis et dominationis ecclesie ejusdem Terdebig [*Worcs*] *Regesta* III 115; **1154** concessisse..totum manerium de Cressynge cum ~one ecclesie ejusdem manerii in liberam elemosinam *Rec. Templars* 147 (cf. ib. 261: [**1177**] de †adductatione ecclesie de Roueston); jus ~onis aut patronatus ecclesie quid prohibet distrahi? J. Sal. *Pol.* 677c; si super ultima presentatione tantum fiat contentio, ..tunc per assisam de ~onibus ecclesiarum proditam loquela illa tractabitur Glanv. IV 1; **1199** petit versus Adam..quod permittat ei presentare idoneam personam ad ecclesiam de S., que vacans est, cujus ~o ad eum habet pertinere, sicut illam que fundata est super feudum suum et ad quem omnes antecessores sui presentaverunt personam post conquestum Anglie *CurR* I 111; **1200** petit..~onem ecclesie sue de H., ut illam que sita est in feudo suo de H. et quam antecessores sui a conquestu Anglie dederunt et quam..pater suus dedit cuidam R. persone *Ib.* 211; cum jus ~onis et jus presentandi semper remaneat cum patrono Bracton 53; unica ~o dividi non poterit, quamvis ecclesia..in plures partes dividatur.. ratione diversarum baroniarum *Ib.* 76b; **1281** extunc ipsius ecclesie patronatus seu ~o ad nos..tanquam ad verum ipsius patronum revertatur *Reg. Heref.* 294b; **1419** rogo.. quod..alia tenementa..aut certe ~ones ecclesiarum ad valenciam xl li. per annum perquirantur et approprientur *Wills NCountry* 26. **c** **13..** ne placitum tenerent inde in curia Christianitatis donec discussum esset in curia domini regis ad quem parcium pertineret ~o decimarum retentarum *Meaux* II 291.

advocator, a summoner. **b** patron of church (*cf. advocare* 17e). **c** agent.

a accitor, ~or *GlC* A 126. **b** **1288** ~or ecclesie de Wodham *IPM* 50/27 r. 3. **c** pro cujus operis perfeccione reliquit..~orem suum.., propterea quod ipsemet fuit a consiliis regi Henrico VIII, adeo ut res suas episcopatus Dunelmensis illic agere non potuit *Hist. Durh.* 151.

advocatorie, as an advocate, by advocacy.

c1430 vigil in causis..nichil sinit sompnolenter quiescere quod..suis valuerit viribus ~ie promovere *Reg. Whet.* II 456.

advocatrix, a advocate or intercessor (f.). **b** patron saint (f.). **c** patroness (of religious house).

a **s1459** sedente pro tribunali..rege..assurexit ~ix justicia proposuitque contra dominos dictos replicatorie sub ista forma *Reg. Whet.* I 345. **b** **c1160** dedi Deo et S. Marie et B. Bege ~ici mee totam terram que vocatur S. *Reg. St. Bees* 384; **1458** ~icis nostre Marie..laudem (*Ch. Episc. S. Andr.*) *Mon. Hib. & Scot.* 407b. **c** **12..** ista est Alicia ~ix de Fontibus de Crostwait et de Wattendelangre *MonA* v 394b; **14..** que nunc se clamat ~icem domus de Sibeton..et de Bliburg' *Ib.* III 636.

1 advocatus v. advocare 16–18.

2 advocatus, protection.

s1008 Galfridus comes [Britannie] Romam proficiscitur, totam Britanniam duobus filiis..sub ducis [Normannie] ~u reliquit Diceto *Abbr. Norm.* 256.

advohare v. advocare.

advolare [CL], to fly up, soar. **b** (fig.). **c** to resort to.

~antibus apibus flores diversorum colorum mella distribuunt G. Mon. I 2; olor novus et nunquam ibi antea visus ~avit Gir. *Rem.* 29 p. 73. **b** ingeniorum..tria sunt genera, sicut Carnotensis senex Bernardus..tradere consuevit: aliud enim ~ans, aliud infirmum, aliud mediocre est. ~ans quidem eadem facilitate qua percipit recedit a perceptis nec in aliqua sede invenit requiem J. Sal. *Met.* 838D; sunt gregarie virtutes; simul ~ant et evolant, ut columbe Gir. *PI* I 11. **c** nec visitat egrum / copia Parnasum, sublimior advolat aulas Hanv. III 277.

advolitare, to resort.

saepiusque advolitat.. / turba nefanda Æthelwulf *Abb.* 6. 49.

advolvere [CL], to roll up. **b** (pass.) to prostrate oneself before.

s1348 dominarum cohors..cum capuciis brevibus et liripi[pi]is ad modum chordarum circa caput advolutis Knighton II 58. **b** pedibus ejus ~itur Bede *HE* I 7; pedibus ejus advolutus veniam..exorat Map *NC* III 3 p. 127.

advovēre, to dedicate.

Malcolmus [IV]..uxorem ducere renuit, suam..Deo ~ens virginitatem *Plusc.* VI 20.

advunculus v. avunculus.

adytum [CL < ἄδυτον], inner sanctuary.

~a, interiora templi *GlC* A 270; postquam in isto me deposuit adito Lantfr. *Mir. Swith.* 2. 335c; et quis in hoc adito mulierem clauserat istam? WULF. *Swith.* II 156; sint etiam limen, cardines et †hec ~um templi NECKAM *Ut.* 119.

adzur- v. azur-. aeccles- v. eccles-. aecremannus v. ehtemannus.

aedes [CL], **a** house, building. **b** church, chapel, or religious house. **c** hall (acad.). **d** (fig.).

clientelae resonant singultibus aedes ALDH. *VirgV* 2254; multi de fratribus ejusdem monasterii qui aliis erant in ~ibus BEDE *HE* III 8; **8..** in ~ibus, *on hofum* WW; Diogenes fixus animo sed mobilis ede HANV. VI 331; mus murem suscipit, edem / commodat WALT. ANGL. *Fab.* 12; **c1410** cleri qui sunt in hac ede / pauca volunt facere sine donis (*Vers. Exch.*) *EHR* XXXVI 60. **b** basilicam Domino restaurans aede renata ALDH. *VirgV* 854; **972** ego Aðelwold Wintoniensis presul edis *CS* 1282; **s1119** nonnulli senes..religiosi in ede sancta prestolabantur ORD. VIT. XII 25; majori cedes intranti templa vel edes D. BEC. 182; relliquie, quas ede sacrata / sacras ille colit GARL. *Tri. Eccl.* 22; edificari mandavit..edem binam super Thamisiam flumen, unam Cartusiensibus viris religiosis, ..alteram sacris mulieribus Beate Brigide LIV. *Hen. V* V 2b; **1504** coram crucifixo in ede B. Virginis *StatOx* 320; **1528** in ede dive Virginis *Ib.* 335; **1559** apud ~em Dominicanorum Fratrum *Conc. Scot.* II 176. **c 1556** (v. 1 aula 6a). **d** Petrus apostolicae qui culmen praesidet aedis ALDH. *VirgV* 530.

aedicare v. aedificare 1b.

aedicula [CL], **~um,** small house. **b** tomb. **c** chapel. **d** small religious house.

~a, *lytel hof* ÆLF. *Sup.* **b** venit..ad almi patris Augustini ~am..oraturus *V. Dunst. B.* 36. **c 1502** lego edificacioni ~i S. Johannis in parte boriali [ecclesie] (*Test. R. Chapman, Bledlow*) *Rec. Eton.* **d** ~am que in honore B. Laurentii constructa est introiens W. CANT. *Mir. Thom.* II 78; fraterculorum mendicantium ~am adjunxit CAMD. *Br.* 285.

aedificabilis, edifying. **b** (sb. n.) ability to build.

1549 quodque utilius et pro tempore ~ius *Conc. Scot.* II 105. **b** ~e potest existere in edificante in potencia DUNS *Metaph.* V ii 46c.

aedificamen, building (w. ref. to brigbote and burhbote).

†**c960** (12c) cuncta illius monasterii possessio nullis sit gravata oneribus.., nec pontis et arcis ~ine (*Ch. Westm.*) *CS* 1228.

aedificare [CL], to build (or cause to be built). **b** (fig.). **c** (absol.). **d** to build on (a site). **e** to signalize by building. **f** to build up, fashion.

praeparatis fundamentis..coepit ~are basilicam BEDE *HE* II 14; capellam ~avit propriis sumptibus ECCLESTON *Adv. Min.* 26; abbas [Willelmus, ob. 1367]..~avit dim. partem majoris grangie, tam in columnis et muris lapideis quam in meremio *Chr. Evesham* 296; **1372** dedi..xij carectatas turbarum ad quodlibet astrum super dicta burgagia ~andum (*Ch. Roby*) *EHR* XVII 296; **1460** turrim.. cum petris et calce..~are et facere *ChartR* 190 m. 1. **b** ut regnum caeli.. / aedificet plantetque ALDH. *VirgV* 317; dona gratiae quibus..~atur..ecclesia ERIUG. *Per.* 565B; Christi ecclesiam eorum melius ~at mors quam vita GIR. *TH* I 21; magnum est..fundamentum quod firmiter †edicari [l. ~ari] queat fideliter extruere *Id. RG prol.* **c c1185** ex illa die qua in villa ~are ceperint per biennium de omnibus quieti sint (*Ch. Coventry*) *EHR* XVI 99; **1289** ~abit super dicta roda *SelPlMan* 33; **1463** pro..laboribus et expensis ~ancium per ix ebdomadas *ExchScot* 179. **d 1165** terris que in foresto meo ~ate sunt vel ~abuntur *Reg. Paisley* 6; **1252** tenet unam acram ~atam *Cart. Boarstall* no. 608; unum predium ~atum *Lib. Eli.* II 16 p. 92; **1282** quod placeas predictas ~are et arentare possint (*Pat*) *MGL* II 274; **1281** placias ibidem assideatis et eas..baronibus ~andas committatis *BBC* (*Winchelsea*) 2; **1285** tenet j croftam ~atam continentem dim. rodam terre *Cust. Suss.* II 112; **1326** sunt ibi v tofta non ~ata *IPM* 96/5 r. 2; **1343** venella vocata Eldebowelane..~ata est..et sic impeditur in latitudine v pedum *MGL* II 450; **1430** ij messuagia ..unum vastum et aliud ~atum *Feod. Durh.* 24. **e** R. NIGER 18 (v. aetas 5d). **f** Dominus tulit unam de costis ejus..et..illam ~avit in mulierem *Eul. Hist.* I 19.

2 (inf. as sb.) building material (Norm.).

a1150 habeat suum hardere et suum ~are in foresta mea de Tisone *Regesta* III 381.

3 (p. ppl.) settled, domiciled.

1313 Henricus..et Johannes frater ejus manentes et ~ati in Norwyco..sunt villani domini regis de manerio predicto et se subtraxerunt per triennium *IMisc.* 73/3.

4 to edify (*cf.* 1 *Cor.* x 23). **b** (w. *ad*) to pave the way to (fig.).

601 subditorum mores..boni operis exempla monstrando ~a (*Lit. Papae*) BEDE *HE* I 32; de sacra..lectione materia loquendi sumpta convescentes ~abat EADMER *V. Anselm.* II 10; theologice discipline fructum elicere possum vel me ipsum ~ando vel qualiter alios ~em addiscendo GIR. *GE* II 37; ut ipsi..habeant unde in propria vocatione..~entur ECCLESTON *Adv. Min.* 1; clericus..artis scribendi..ignarus ..presentes tantum ~at R. BURY *Phil.* 6. 98; non ~at audientes quoad fidem vel eciam quoad mores dicere..quod nunc licitum est circumcidi (KYN.) *Ziz.* 64. **b** contra conscientiam..scienter agens nonne palam ~avit ad Gehennam? GIR. *Inv.* I 7 p. 110; **c1260** quicquid impunitum in filiis nostris ~at ad Gehennam (*Sententia excom.*) *Ann. Durh.* 91; foris omnia ~ant ad Gehennam OCKHAM *Dial.* 900; aliquod verum..~ans ad salutem *Ib.* 838.

†**aedificarius** [? *for* aedificatorius], edifying.

paucissimis eloquiis, ut verbis ~iis vel ceteris utilibus, omnino usus fuerat BLAKMAN *Hen. VI* 15.

aedificatio [CL], building. **b** (w. ref. to brigbote and burhbote). **c** establishment.

de ~one templi BEDE *HE* V 24; **c1160** concessisse.. ecclesie B. Marie Linc' e[and]em libertatem quam rex W... concessit ~oni predicte ecclesie (*Ch. Hen. II*) *EHR* XXIV 310; **1514** in expensis factis circa novam ~onem lapideam trium tenementorum *Ac. Durh.* 663. **b 877** (12c) excepta expeditione et pontis ~one *CS* 544; **927** (12c) exceptis expeditione pontis arcis[ve] ~one *CS* 660; **c1125** nulla.. persona..aliquid ab hominibus et terris et possessione Radingensis monasterii exigat, non equitationem sive expeditionem, non pontium vel castrorum ~onem *MonA* IV 40; **1254** liberi de domuum regalium ~one et omnimoda operacione (*Ch. Hen. III*) *PQW* 376a. **c** ipse est omnium stationis et ~onis causalis qui est super omnem ~onem et stationem ERIUG. *Per.* 523A.

2 edification: **a** (of church, religion etc.); **b** (of persons); **c** (absol.).

a ad ~onem catholice religionis AD. MARSH *Ep.* 75 p. 184; **1317** ad honorem Dei et ~onem corporis Christi *FormOx* 33; libros eis..ad tocius ~onem ecclesie contulerunt R. BURY *Phil.* 6. 90; **c1400** nec papa..potest licite aliquid agere contra ~onem ecclesie (*Concl. Lollard.* 16) *EHR* XXVI 744. **b** ad memoriam ~onemque sequentium BEDE *HE* IV 7; quid eum ab humani cordis ~one flectere niteris? EADMER *Wilf.* 38; studio fuit..ad posteritatis ~onem vite perfectioris exemplum oblivioni subducere AILR. *Nin. prol.*; quamvis..unusquisque..famam suam..ad ~onem proximi ..servare teneatur OCKHAM *Dial.* 738; **1377** ad ~onem populi (WYCL.) *Ziz.* 263; **1451** quod ejus recepcio clero et populo non modicam ~onem afferat *Mon. Francisc.* II 83. **c** frater E...fuit majoris ~onis quam alii quantum ad ingressum ordinis, ..quia fuit nobilis et dives ECCLESTON *Adv. Min.* 64; **1253** apostolice sedis sanctitas non potest nisi que in ~onem sunt et non in destructionem GROS. *Ep.* 128; **1423** miramur..cur..presumit, ..que sibi ad ~onem tantummodo data est, taliter in destitucionem abuti potestate sua *Reg. Whet.* II 409.

aedificativus, edifying.

apud eos quorum interiores oculi..excecantur..verba vite ~a vesanie ascribuntur P. BLOIS *Ep.* 10. 32; [S. Edmundus, arch. Cant.] in fallaciarum animadversione fuit circumspectus, ..in legendo ~us HIGD. VII 35 p. 222.

aedificator [CL], builder, originator of buildings. **b** edifier.

Lud.., gloriosus ~or urbium existens, renovavit muros urbis Trinovantum; ..precepit etiam civibus ut domos et edificia sua in eadem construerent G. MON. III 20; si cupis agricola fieri novus edificator, / edificare velis vicinos inter honestos D. BEC. 2161; **c1374** arduus allator et optimus edificator (ROB. SYRESTON *de J. Fossore*) *Hist. Durh.* 134. **b** verborum Dei seminator et eorundem strenuus ~or RICH *Edm.* 619.

aedificatorius, concerned with building. **b** edifying.

ars ~ia est mechanica geometrie et non est pars philosophie BACON *CSPhil.* 420. **b 1235** novimus quod zelus domus Dei vos comedit [cf. *Psalm* lxviii 10] et desiderium illius edificande vehementer accendit; suppetit quoque vobis..eminenter ars ~ia GROS. *Ep.* 16 p. 62; ad quam [desidiam] excutiendam debet vacare verbo ~io vel utili studio J. WALEYS *V. Relig.* 12 f. 238; si quando lector cessaret, aut de hiis que legerat aut de ~iis aliquibus cum assistentibus tractabat *NLA* (*Richard*) II 332; in divinis libris et anime ~iis *Cust. Cant.* 157; veritas caritative ~ia ad salutem WYCL. *Ver.* I 343.

aedificatrix, edifying (f.).

c1100 metuendum est ne..vox spiritualium ~ix raucescat (*Lit. Mathildis reginae*) *Ep. Anselm.* (242) IV 150.

aedificium [CL], building. **b** (w. ref. to brigbote). **c** (fig.). **d** (*s. dub.*).

cum monasterio propinquarent et ~ia illius sublimiter erecta aspicerent BEDE *HE* IV 25; ~ium, *getimbrung* ÆLF. *Gl.*; ibi fuit dominicum ~ium *DB* I 222; in edifitiorum spetie sullimium W. MALM. *GP* II 74 p. 152; **1142** cum.. libertate..materierum ad ~ia construenda *Regesta* III 116; **1255** plateam..cum edeficiis *RGasc* I *sup.* 33; **1256** utilis sustentacio ~iorum ibidem exigit per annum c s. *Reg. Roff.* 63; interius villa [*Harfleur*] ornatur perpulcris ~iis prope sitis ELMH. *Hen. V* 18; **1430** in papiro scripto pro expensis ~ii collegii *Reg. Cant.* II 445. **b 940** (12c) preter..tria, exercitus aditum, pontis edifitium, munitionis castellique auxilium *CS* 761. **c** alimenta corporalia quae [trinitas nostrae naturae] extrinsecus in ~ium corporis accipit ERIUG. *Per.* 581C. **d** cui [sc. Godrum] rex cum suis omnibus multa et optima †~ia [*ed.*: beneficia] largiter dedit ASSER *Alf.* 56 (cf. ib. 91: de..~iis aureis et argenteis incomparabiliter..fabricatis).

aedilis [CL], overseer of buildings. **b** sacristan.

~is, *hofweard* vel *byriweard* vel *botlweard* ÆLF. *Gl.* **b** aedilisque [v.l. aedituusque] graves oppandit agillimus aedes FRITH. 1141; *a sacristane*, sacrista, †elidis [v.l. edilis] *CathA*.

aedilitas [CL], (?) supervision of buildings.

edilitatem, †*hainscire* [? l. *hamscire*] *GlC* E 35.

aeditua, sacrist of nunnery.

sanctimonialis ecclesiae ~a.., cum perditas claves sacrorum..anxie quesisset GOSC. *Wulfh.* 16.

aedituus [CL], **a** keeper of (Jewish) temple. **b** sacristan. **c** churchwarden. **d** champion of church.

a ~us, †custus templi *GlC* E 27 (cf. ib. A 325); Pompeius ..~is precepit ut locum sacrum a sordibus mundarent GIR. *PI* I 17 p. 61. **b** ~us basilice S. Remigii (*Mir. S. Vedasti*) ELMH. *Cant.* 210; [Carolus Magnus] ecclesiam mane et vespere ingrediebatur, valde monens ne quid in ea indecens linquerent ~i R. NIGER 149; FRITH. 1141 (v. aedilis b); infantibus ecclesiam intrantibus ~us primum sonet signum *RegulC* 20; ut ~us templi ipsius cloccam personaret Altissimo *V. Osw.* 426; si ~i [AS: *hiwan*] magis opus habeant ecclesiam suam [v.l. ecclesie sue], custodiant eum in alia domo (*Quad.*) *GAS* 53; **c1200** in cena Domini annatim ~us S. Augustini l sol. denariorum secretario S. Salvatoris Dorobernie reddebat *MonA* I 128b. **c 1583** ecclesiae Houghtoniensis ~is (*Reg. Paroch. Houghton le Spring*) *EHR* XX 677. **d** decentis ~i, almi sc. Dunstani, merita monumenta protelare *V. Dunst. B.* 1.

2 keeper or officer of household, steward.

accessit ad thecam ~us in qua es regium servabatur AILR. *Ed. Conf.* 746B; quedam [liberationes] sunt servientium,.. quales sunt ~i [*gl.*: hoc est custodes domus] regii, tibicines..et hujusmodi *Dial. Scac.* II 6; **s1245** David [f. Lewelini] ..jussit prerupta montium artissima..per ~os suos custodiri *Flor. Hist.* II 286; *hows kepare*, ~us, m., ~a, f. *PP*.

aedonea [ἀηδών], nightingale.

10.. aidoneae, *hearpen* WW.

aefum v. aevum. aegeator v. ageator.

aeger [CL], sick, ill. **b** spiritually ill. **c** anxious, distressful. **d** weak (fig.). **e** (of food) poor, coarse.

egra, *slaece GlC* E 101; cum scabies morbi pulpas irrepserit aegras ALDH. *Aen.* 94. 5; in loco in quo eger jacebat BEDE *HE* IV 14; ~er vel aegrotus, *adlig* ÆLF. *Gl.*; egrotavit in itinere et accubuit eger nimis apud manerium suum DEVIZES 38; **1485** sanum mente licet egrum corpore *Reg. Aberbr.* II 240. **b** ni desperatus medicantem [sc. Christum] spreverit aeger ALDH. *VirgV* 2660. **c** inter egra tremens suspiria BEDE *HE* III 13; amicorum..egrior solet esse et acerbior persecutio *G. Steph.* I 32; cum majori tumultu et egriori sollicitudine J. SAL. *Pol.* 392B; stomacho succedit inani / egra fames HANV. VI 337. **d** qui accusantur.., si diem sic condictum subterfugiant respectuatum, partem suam, etsi non mortuam, faciunt tamen egriorem (*Leg. Hen.*) *GAS* 562. **e s1298** [R. de Broys] per..silvarum et rupium abdita latibula cum egro victu et aspero vestitu se obumbrans *Plusc.* VIII 28.

†**aegesta, aegella** [? cf. eglentia], gorse.

7.. aegesta, **9..** aegella, *gorst* WW.

aegilips [αἰγίλιψ], precipitous crag.

~lippon, Grece saxum eminens quo nec capellae valent ascendere *GlC* A 306.

aegilops, ~opa [αἰγίλωψ], **a** ulcer at corner of eye, sty. **b** (?) darnel (bot.).

a ~opa habet fieri in angulo opposito, qui caprinus dicitur; *egle* enim 'capra' dicitur GILB. III 135. 1; ~opa est quedam infirmitas cum †minus [? l. unus] angulus rotundatur intus crescente carne *SB* 18 (cf. *Alph.* 52); *styany*, ~opa *PP*. **b** ~ops herba est folia habens triticeis foliis similia sed mollia *Alph.* 52.

aegis [αἰγίς], aegis, shield of Athene. **b** shield. **c** (?) goat-skin.

assumat..Pallas egidem MAP *NC* III 2 p. 116 (cf. ib. IV 6 p. 164). **b** hii se defendunt et in hostes egida tendunt GARL. *Mor. Scol.* 80; *a schelde*, clipeus, ..eges, scutum *CathA*. **c** capra aegida, *gatbuccan* †*hyrde* [? l. *hyde*] ÆLF. *Gl.*

aegit v. agere 2a.

aegoceros [αἰγόκερως], Capricorn (astr.). **b** (kind of) rhinoceros.

urebat binis sol Egoceronta diebus G. WINT. *Epigr. Hist.* 4; augeturque dies Cancri contraque minorem / deprimit Egoceron HANV. VIII 373 (cf. ib.: caput Egocerontis); egoceros madidis se concessisse diebus / admirans NECKAM *DS* I 461. **b** de rinocero..hujus fere multe sunt species, sc. rinoceron, monoceron, egloceron BART. ANGL. XVIII 89; *an unycorne*, egloceros, capricornus, rinoceron', unicornis *CathA*.

aegre [CL], **a** w. difficulty, scarcely, grudgingly. **b** w. grief or indignation (*cf. aegriferre*).

~e, *earfedlice GlC* A 94; quod dum ~e impetraret ab ea BEDE *HE* IV 11; concessis regi, licet ~e et invite, ..pecuniarum copiis *G. Steph.* I 36. **b** suspirabat tam ~e ut..ad racionem poneretur cur hoc MAP *NC* II 16; **c1460** ~e atque ~e fero..vitam castissime urbis a te..impugnari CHAUNDLER *Laud.* 114; dux..egreferens datam fuisse Henrico causam P. VERG. *Vat. app.* III p. 205.

aegrescere [CL], to become ill. **b** (of the mind). **c** to be exhausted.

morbo correptus ĕgrescit ALDH. *CE* 3. 29; homo cujus otium erat ~ere W. MALM. *GR* IV 385. **b** anime morbo ~entes *G. Steph.* I 1; ~it profecto ingenium nisi jugi lectione reparetur GIR. *EH pref.* **c** non egresco datis, dare non fastidio rerum / continuans partus HANV. IX 384.

aegretarius v. aegrotare.

†**aegriferre** [cf. aegre], to be displeased.

s1399 tenentes illius ville, fideles regi et regno et de eis ~entes *V. Ric. II* 166.

aegritudo [CL], illness. **b** (w. *regis*) king's evil.

decussa molestia ~inis convaluit BEDE *HE* III 27; instrumentum volendi..numquam ita est affectum ut aliquando velit ~inem ANSELM (*Praesc.* 11) II 279; solent eas [arterias] cirurgici ad plurimas incidere..~ines RIC. MED. *Micr. Anat.* 222; **1220** fecit ei cartam illam in ~ine unde obiit *CurR* VIII 288; **c1228** usque ad lectum ultime ~inis sue *Feod. Durh.* 230; signa qualitatum et ~inum et sanitatum corporum humanorum BACON VI 1; spasmus est ~o nervosa *SB* 40; **1435** in lecto sue ~inis personaliter institutus, sanus mente, ..corpore tamen eger *Reg. Cant.* II 530. **b 1278** pro xxx egrotis egritud[ine] regis, xxx d. (*Chanc. Misc.* 4/1 f. 9 (13) v) *Rois Thaumaturges* 98.

aegriuscule, w. a little reluctance.

paulum remorata virum propter conjugalem in Christo fidem ~e reliquit ANDRE *Hen. VII* 75.

aegrotare [CL], to be ill. **b** (dep.).

~antibus sospitatem contulerunt ALDH. *VirgP* 34; tetenderunt ei ~anti tentorium BEDE *HE* III 17; coepit vehementius ~are in anhelitu CUTHB. *Ob. Baedae* clxii (= M. PAR. *Maj.* I 335: ~ari); ~ans forte poma desiderabat GIR. *TH* II 28; **a1268** †egretarius [? l. egrotantis] passio (*Lit. Ottobon.*) *EHR* XV 116; **1314** effigies..quibus cibus et potus sicut ~antibus sunt allati (*Rec. Eng. Dominicans*) *Ib.* V 109; **s1415** ~avit..ex fluxu sanguinis ELMH. *Hen. V* 27. **b 1305** magistri et scolares..frequenter ~antur et infirmantur *BBC* (*Oxford*) 376.

aegrotativitas, sickliness.

illa naturalis impotencia, mediante qua non potest aliquis nichil pati, ..est ut egro[ta]tivitas, si liceat nomen fingere BACON XV 228.

aegrotativus, sickly, (sb.) invalid.

quedam que sanis conferunt et obstant ~is J. SAL. *Pol.* 659C; hominem ~um morborum incursu assiduo *Ib.* 738D; molestari cepit, cooperante cibo et somno complexioni ejus, †qui [? l. quia] et tener et ~us erat W. CANT. *Mir. Thom.* V 9; **s1235** episcopus, qui jam senuerat valitudinarius et ~us M. PAR. *Min.* II 383; [cause mutationis] aliter sunt.., in corpore sano ~o [v.l. in corpore egrotanti], aliter in corpore sano hora presenti BACON IX 78.

aegrotus [CL], sick, ill, (sb.) invalid. **b** spiritually ill.

claudum restaurat ĕgrotum ALDH. *CE* 4. 2. 18; referre est solitus..hujus gustum..multis sanitatem ~is et hominibus et pecoribus conferre BEDE *HE* V 18; **12..** deferat corpus Dominicum ad ~um *Conc. Scot.* II 34; **1426** quod invenirent in eodem manerio v lectulos ~orum et in quolibet lecto ij ~os *Cl* 276 m. 5. **b** hunc morbum aegroti medicantur gaudia cordis ALDH. *VirgV* 2651.

Aegyptiacus [CL], Egyptian. **b** inauspicious (of two days in each month).

faba ~a, i. lupinus *SB* 20 (v. et. acanthus). **b s1189** Ricardus primus Londoniis est consecratus..tertio nonas Septembris, qui dies ex prisca gentili superstitione malus vel ~us dicitur; dies enim ille Judeis exitialis fuisse dignoscitur et ~us magis quam Anglicus, cum Anglia..repente illis in Egiptum..verteretur W. NEWB. IV 1; de diebus ~is dicunt quod in illis non debet fieri flebotomia quia luna in ascensu suo et descensu acquirit immutationem ab aliquo maligno planeta secundum quem alterat corpora GILB. I 74. 1.

Aegyptianus, gypsy.

1577 contra formam statuti pro punicione vagabundorum vocancium seipsos ~os *Baga Secr.* 44/8.

Aegyptius [CL], Egyptian (adj. or sb.).

c710 excussum ~iae servitutis jugum (*Lit. Ceolfridi*) BEDE *HE* V 21 p. 341; apud ~ios antiquos..menses secundum cursum lune determinabantur BACON VI 88; a Mesreum ~ii dicti sunt Mesrei HIGD. II 7 p. 254.

aeira v. aerea. aeisamentum v. aisiamentum. aelicus v. caelicus.

†aellio, kind of falcon.

aliud genus [falconum] est illud quod herodius vel vulgariter girfalcus dicitur; istud enim genus communius est genere ~onis et carius habetur propter moderanciam cibi et vite UPTON 188.

Aëllo [Ἀελλώ], a Harpy.

reparat Aëllo, / que vivit bello, vi, raptu, strage, flagello GARL. *Mor. Scol.* 221.

aemilianus, (?) type of gladiator (*cf.* Horace: *Ars Poetica* 32).

hinc mimi, ..balatrones, emiliani, gladiatores, palestrite J. SAL. *Pol.* 406A.

aemulabilis, inspiring emulation.

in opere Dei..tam ~i, tam acceptabili AD. MARSH *Ep.* 50.

aemulari [CL], to emulate, vie with. **b** to contend. **c** to envy, grudge.

quem [Vergilium] Lucanus ~ans ..imitabatur ALDH. *Met.* 10 p. 89; exemplum..pietatis illius coepit ~ari BEDE *HE* I 7; **9..** ~ari, i. imitari vel *ellenwodian* WW; ~ate sunt alie civitates..fidem Londoniensium DEVIZES 25v. **b 10..** ~abantur, *wæran sacende* WW. **c s1190** eorum vel ~ando felicitatem vel inhiando fortunis W. NEWB. IV 7.

aemulatio [CL], emulation, zeal. **b** contention, strife.

apostolicum illum..sermonem, quod '~onem Dei habebant, sed non secundum scientiam' BEDE *HE* V 22 (cf. *Rom.* x 2); laudabili ~onis invidia GIR. *TH pref.* p. 21; inflammatus celicis ~onibus AD. MARSH *Ep.* 246 c. 8; talis mendicitas.. non potest prudenter et sancte assumi, quamvis secundum ~onem Dei possit assumi RIC. ARMAGH *Def. Cur.* 1409. **b 9..** ~o, i. dissensio, *anhering* WW.

aemulator [CL], emulator, aspirant, zealot, champion. **b** contender. **c** envier, enemy.

beatae vitae ~ores ALDH. *VirgP* 14; caelibes integritatis ~ores et spurcitiae contemptores *Ib.* 45; omnes hi ~ores sunt legis BEDE *HE* III 25; audite me, fratres, Dominice legis ~ores T. MON. *Will.* I 6; vehementi ~ori non satis fuit..erubescere J. FORD *Wulf.* 23; regis optimi Lodowici laudabilis ~or effectus GIR. *PI* I 20; **s1252** papale mandatum, omnibus regni ~oribus exosum et detestabile M. PAR. *Maj.* V 324; Christiane religionis sincerus..et fervidus ~or OCKHAM *Pol.* I 121; **c1430** zizannie satores et ~ores discordie *Reg. Whet.* II 392. **b 10..** ~ores, *onhyrgend* WW. **c** ab his qui probitatis illius improbissimi ~ores exstiterant OSB. *V. Dunst.* 11; **s1460** introducti..in castrum..per dies non paucos secure ab ~oribus permanserunt *Reg. Whet.* I 368.

aemulatorie, maliciously.

c1430 erga susurrancium sibilos, qui ~ie faces [amoris] nituntur retrahere et causare fumum *Reg. Whet.* II 413.

aemulatrix, imitative (f.). **b** zealot (f.).

penne ~ices nature aquile corrodunt alias pennas NECKAM *NR* 1 23. **b c1300** domina M...devota carismatum ~ix *Lit. Cant.* I 11.

aemulus [CL], emulous, vying, similar. **b** envious, (sb.) enemy. **c** devil.

Scotia et Wallia..Hiberniam in modulis ~a imitari nituntur disciplina GIR. *TH* III 11 (cf. ib. 24: ~a malorum doctrina); citrinitas faciei et color viridis aut emul[us] GILB. VI 235. 1. **b** aemula scaevorum vitat figmenta virorum ALDH. *VirgV* 1025; ~us, *gesaca* vel *gewinna* ÆLF. *Sup.*; muscipulas nostis quas obicit aemulus hostis FRITH. 1344 (cf. ib. 1184: aemula.. / actio pravorum); cum illum.. ~i ejus et inimici Dei pagani cepissent EADMER *V. Anselm.* I 30 p. 51; cum quidam ~i ipsius, objectis falso querelis, conati sunt terram..preripere R. COLD. *Cuthb.* 46; **s1238** dictum etiam fuit ab ~is suis ipsum F. imperatorem plus consensisse in legem Machometi quam Jesu Christi M. PAR. *Maj.* III 921; **1295** ecclesia que pacis ~os reprimit *Reg. Carl.* I 46; **s1340** regis rancorem suorumque invidiam ~orum timens AVESB. *Ed. III* 93b; **s1459** jussit..exercitum..progredi..in itinere, in ~orum captivacionem *Reg. Whet.* I 342. **c** praestigias quas lividorum..~orum factio.. ingerebat ALDH. *VirgP* 26.

aënarius, brazier, brass-worker.

1561 ahenarius (*SPDom. Eliz.* 17/33) *Huguenot Soc.* X 274.

aëneator [CL], trumpeter.

~ores, tubicines, ..cornicines *GlC* A 302, 350.

aëneola, ~um, brazen cauldron.

braspote, †emola *PP*; *a calderon*, caldria, ..eniola, ..enium, †enulum [v.l. eniolum] *CathA*.

aenesc- v. aesnec-.

aëneus [CL], brazen. **b** (sb. n.) cauldron.

cuncti pariter velut aenea signa rigebant ALDH. *VirgV* 1527; enea ceu pelvis cutis est mea NIG. *SS* 1609; septem cerei candelabro eneo imponuntur *Offic. Sal.* 5; vesica enea GILB. V 227 v. 1; **1331** pro una olla..et una patella ennea *PQW* 18a; **1383** vasa †cunea [l. ennea] *Rec. Norw.* II 25; **1449** unius olle enie *Cl* 300 m. 27*d.*; **1467** vasa ennea et stannea *Cl* 319 m. 19*d.*; **1478** cum duobus cereis supportatis per duos angelos †cenneos [l. aenneos] tanquam candelabra (*Ch. Dundee*) *Scot. Grey Friars* II 125; duos cacabos aheneos ad cerevisiam conficiendam FERR. *Kinloss* 76. **b** (v. aëneola).

aenigma [CL < αἴνιγμα], allegory, riddle. **b** obscurity, disguise.

ordo rerum exigit ut promissa ~atum problemata luculentae urbanitatis versibus patefacias ALDH. *Met.* 10 p. 96; ~a est obscura sententia per occultam similitudinem rerum BEDE *ST* 616; ut..certiora essent experimenta rerum quam ~ata figurarum EGB. *Pont.* 2; multa dicimus que proprie sicut sunt non exprimimus, sed per aliud significamus.., ut cum per ~ata loquimur ANSELM (*Mon.* 65) I 76. **b** quia nunc per speculum et ~a videmus in aenigmate gloriam LANFR. *Comment. Paul.* (2 *Cor.* iii 18; cf. 1 *Cor.* xiii 12) 226; ista pervigil oculo corporeo et sub nullo ~ate vidit R. COLD. *Cuthb.* 38; perceptis hic erroribus sub lucis ~ate GARL. *Mor. Scol. prol.*

aenigmatice, allegorically, in a riddle. **b** obscurely.

~e proloqui GIR. *DK* I 17; quid ei super hoc ~e pariter et irrisorie scriptum fuerit audiatis *Id. Inv.* I 8; solummodo ~e et sub similitudinibus et figuracionibus rerum in scripturis divinis revelata sunt a Deo OCKHAM *Dial.* 833; **s1464** fratrem S. Swynshed, ..qui capam..dedit..in suo pectorali nomen ejus ~e preferentem *Croyl. Cont. B* 536. **b** quem ~e et sub aliena specie cernimus *AncrR* 10; quasi diceret manifeste: "vos qui nunc ~e creditis..tandem cognoscetis certissime veritatem" BRADW. *CD* 777B.

aenigmaticus, riddling, allegorical, figurative.

ut pote qui eas [calamitates futuras] non ~o fuco sed aperto eloquio..pronuntiaverit W. MALM. *GP* V 255; quid quod scientia quevis ~a quedam est ignorantia? NECKAM *NR* II 155; aliqui per characteres et carmina occultaverunt multa, aiii vero per verba ~a et figurativa BACON *NM* 8 p. 544; dominium [bonorum] Romane ecclesie reservatum est simplex, id est palliatum nudum et ~um OCKHAM *Pol.* III 7 (*citing bull* 'Ad conditorem'); non credent absque sciencia que non erit ~a sed per speciem BRADW. *CD* 764B; noticia specularis vel ~a WYCL. *Ver.* I 215.

aenigmatista, speaker in riddles.

he þat spekis rydels, ~a *CathA*.

aenigmatizare, to speak in riddles.

dicebant nonnulli illum [Merlinum]..more demonum obscure et amphibologice ~asse exemplo Balan *Flor. Hist.* I 237; exponit [Aristoteles] fabulam ~ancium Oceanum circulariter fluere circa terram BRADW. *CD* 102C; *to rede rydels*, ..*to speke mystely*, ~are *CathA*.

aënum [CL], (brazen) vessel. **b** (fig.).

enum, *cetil GlC* E 193; in coquina sint..cacabus, ~um [*gl.*: *paele*], patella [*gl.*: idem].. NECKAM *Ut.* 97; ahenum est vas metallicum ex cupro aut ferro duorum pedum altitudinis..cusum *LC*. **b** sit amoris coctus aëno SERLO WILT. 31. 4.

aeolicus [Αἰολικός], windy.

~is..flatibus et pluvialibus inundationibus..hec [terra] exuberat GIR. *TH* I 6.

†aeolus [(?) *conf. w.* eous], the east.

1578 [pecia horti] extendens orientaliter ad pomarium episcopi..ad eolum *Reg. Brech.* II 320.

aeon [αἰών], age, eternity. **b** aeon (personified).

995 (12c) regnante in eona eonum coeli terraeque dispositore *CD* 692. **b s141** heresis Valentiniana et Marcionis..cujus pestis inventores eonas, id est secula quedam, in originem creatoris inducunt M. PAR. *Maj.* I 139.

aequ- v. et. equ-.

aequabilis [CL], comparable.

par quoque jam veteri signumque aequabile signo ALCUIN *Carm.* I 1362; percunctativa..videbuntur..executive interrogandis ~ia esse; sed hoc falso BALSH. *AD* 141.

aequaevus [CL], of like age, coeval.

~us vel coetaneus, *efneald* ÆLF. *Gl.*; aequevos habitu studuit superare venusto FRITH. 52.

†aequalentia [? *for* aequivalentia], equality.

an evyn-hede, equalitas, equanimitas, equipollencia, equalencia *CathA*.

aequalis [CL], equal. **b** on a level. **c** contemporary.

invidiae pestis.. / quae solet aequales tumido contemnere fastu ALDH. *VirgV* 2715; **c710** dies septimanae non ~i cum luna tramite procurrit (*Lit. Ceolfridi*) BEDE *HE* V 25 p. 337; ~i sibi [sc. homini] ad angelos..gnostica scientia ERIUG. *Per.* 535A; nullum bonum quod per aliud est ~e aut majus est eo bono quod per se est bonum ANSELM (*Mon.* 1) I 15; in quinque portiones fere ~es GIR. *TH* I 7; [circuli] porcio *CB*..sit ~is porcioni *DE* WALLINGF. *Quad.* 102; **a1350** si duo in scrutinio habeant ~es voces, preferatur senior *StatOx* 66; de cruce ~i: ille qui hec arma possidet portat de argento cum una cruce plana ~is longitudinis ex omni parte UPTON 211 (cf. BAD. AUR. 192). **b** lapis terrae ~is obtectus cespite tenui BEDE *HE* V 6. **c** cum..de parente meo suis et ~ibus..meminissem LIV. *Hen. V* 1a.

2 a fair, impartial (*v. et. manus aequalis*). **b** constant, uniform. **c** equable, unruffled.

a c786 ut mensuras aequas et pondera ~ia statuant omnibus ALCUIN *Ep.* 3 p. 26. **b** sonitu quodam quasi tonitrui, longiore tamen et ~iore GIR. *PI* III 28; cum omnibus stellis et planetis qui sunt in eo motu ~i et uniformi per diem et noctem GROS. 13. **c** Thomas.. nec tristior effectus est nec sollicitior sed ~is permansit H. BOS. *Thom.* IV 26.

aequalitas [CL], equality. **b** levelness, evenness.

per ipsam ad angelos scientiae ~atem ERIUG. *Per.* 535A; cum dexteram nec sinistram Deus habet, ~atem ejus et Filii dexterae sedem appellamus LANFR. *Comment. Paul.* (*Heb.* i 13) 376; tanta Pater et Filius et utriusque Spiritus ~ate sese complectuntur..ut eorum nullus alium excedere ..probetur ANSELM (*Mon.* 59) I 70; fac..lineam *TD* ad ~atem *ST* WALLINGF. *Quad.* 109. **b** habebit funiculus.. l cubitos longitudinis: x videlicet ascensionis.., x ~atis secundum longitudinem domus, x rursus descensionis AD. SCOT *TT* 649D; superficies muri trulle ~atem..representet NECKAM *Ut.* 104.

aequaliter [CL], equally. **b** evenly, (?) straight.

satrapas..qui ingruente belli articulo mittunt ~er sortes BEDE *HE* V 10; diviserunt dominicam terram patris sui ~er et pariliter *DB* I 375; quaecunque dicuntur aliquid, ita ut ad invicem magis vel minus aut ~er dicantur, per aliquid dicuntur quod..idem intelligitur in diversis, sive in illis ~er sive inaequaliter consideretur ANSELM (*Mon.* 1) I 14; equaliter orbem / sectio distinguit HANV. IX 378; **1370** ita quod proporcionenter ~er *Hal. Durh.* 97; **1384** solvit velj li. ~er in auro et argento *ExchScot* 118. **b 1320** et de dicta cruce ~er transeundo ultra legam de L. usque G. *Cart. Cockersand* 298.

aequamentum [LL], levelling.

hostimentum, id est ~um vel exagium trutinae ALDH. *PR* 140 p. 199.

aequanimis, even-tempered, calm; *cf. animaequus.*

s1106 cui [Henrico I] pater: "~is esto, fili, et confortare in Domino" M. PAR. *Min.* I 206.

aequanimitas [CL], equanimity, even temper.

est philosophantis animi fructus nobilis generosa ~as mentis J. SAL. *Pol.* 587A.

aequanimiter, calmly, w. equanimity. **b** like-mindedly. **c** equally.

insectationes..inflexi cordis constantia ~er perferebat ALDH. *VirgP* 32 p. 274; cetera quae agitis..~er cuncta tolerabimus BEDE *HE* II 2; **s1106** [rex juravit] se omnia damna ~ius toleraturum quam Anselmi decessum EADMER *HN* 216; fructus philosophie eximius est ut..quis..leto animo ~er omnia portet J. SAL. *Pol.* 587B; **s1183** filie.. regis..alienationem a nativo solo forsitan eo sustinent ~ius quod..nupserint..viris illustribus DICETO *YH* II 17; a quo, cum leto leditur, / nec verbum ire jacitur, / set migrat equanimiter J. HOWD. *Cyth.* 127; sequaces pape heretici, quando salva pace nequeunt coherceri, sunt ~er tolerandi OCKHAM *Dial.* 691; **c1390** ad..onera..~ius supportanda *FormOx* 228. **b c1430** vobiscum in hiis vestris doloribus ~er tristaremur *Reg. Whet.* II 425. **c 1261** de redditu.. villanorum et liberorum..qui ~er solvunt ad iiij terminos anni *DLCourtR* 128/1919; **c1310** xxv li...de exitibus manerii..recipiendas, viz. ad festum S. Mich. medietatem et ad Pascham medietatem ~er *Chr. Rams.* 392.

aequare [CL], **a** to level. **b** to fit. **c** to equalize, make equal. **d** to equate, regard as equal. **e** to equal.

a ~atis, *efnum GlC* A 295; **s1066** tot ibi inimicorum conculcavere ut cumulo cadaverum planitiem campi ~arent W. MALM. *GR* III 242; **1350** ad equand' muros..antequam cooperti essent de stramine marisci *KRAc* 459/16. **b** faber..non capiet argentum pro novo vomere ~ando ad cheppum *Cust. Suss.* II 4. **c** quatinus ~atus gratia suo intercessori..una..sede..perpetuae beatitudinis meruisset recipi BEDE (*V. Cuthb.*) *HE* IV 27; semel ~atis hujus con-positi qualitatibus ADEL. *QN* 44; ubi flectit habenas / sol noctique diem punctis finalibus equat HANV. VIII 375; non sis solus ěques; tibi me per equum, precor, ěques SERLO WILT. 2. 36; hic ěquus insons [sc. feretrum] / omnibus ěquus ěquis omnes ěquans ěquitantes D. BEC. 333; non etiam si te ruperis Octaviano in thesauris ~aberis GIR. *GE* II 21. **d** undarum fluctibus aequat / ..sontes ALDH. *CE* 4. 12. 20; ordinavit Ithamar, ..eruditione antecessoribus ~andum BEDE *HE* III 14. **e** ut dominum propriis aequaret viribus audax ALDH. *VirgV* 2740; dignaque solis ěquis, quos ěquet passibus ěquis SERLO WILT. 12. 3.

2 (pr. ppl. m., sc. *circulus*) equant (astr.).

~ans lune est circulus concentricus cum terra et in superficie ecliptice; ..deferens et ~ans cujuslibet planete sunt equales SACROB. *Sph.* 114; dyameter epicicli..non transit per centrum ~antis nisi cum centrum epicicli est in auge aut in oppositione augis eccentrici BACON IV 451; inveniantur centra deferentis et ~antis Saturni WALLINGF. *Albion* 352.

aequatio [CL], **a** correspondence. **b** equation (math.). **c** balance (in account).

a aliquorum potest esse unus actus dupliciter, uno modo per unionem et conformitatem.., alio modo per ~onem solum BACON VII 27. **b** earum cum suis radicibus generatur ~o ROB. ANGL. *Alg.* 70. **c 1409** summa totalis iiij^{xx} iij li. j d.; et debet iiij li...que onerantur in compoto sequenti; et ~o est (*Rec. Aud. Durh.*) *EHR* XIV 528.

aequator, celestial equator.

figit utrumque polum paribusque utrumque diei / respicit equator spatiis HANV. VIII 372; est equinoctialis circulus quidam dividens speram in duo equalia..equedistans ab utroque polo, ..unde appellatur ~or diei et noctis, quia adequat diem artificialem nocti; et dicitur cingulus primi motus SACROB. *Sph.* 86; circuli qui equidistant ~ori et sunt eisdem concentrici BACON IX 194; nodos..orbis novi existentes in ecliptica apud ~orem et tropicos WALLINGF. *Rect.* 337; sub ~oris linea..ab utroque latere, quantum fere spatii solis orbita complectitur MORE *Ut.* 30 (cf. ib. 239).

aeque [CL], equally. **b** at an equal distance. **c** on equal terms. **d** in balance (in account).

Latinam Graecamque linguam ~e ut propriam..norunt BEDE *HE* IV 2; ut..te..eque laudet ut Actius Ulixem laudat J. SAL. *Pol.* 633C; Deus..majores atque minores / posset, si vellet, eque fecisse beatos D. BEC. 253; **c1228** in foresta in qua est ~e bonum meremium *Feod. Durh.* 236; si fratres post professionem sunt ~e solliciti circa temporalia sicut in noviciatu fuerunt OCKHAM *Pol.* III 6 (cf. id. *Dial.* 932: ~e bene..sicut..). **b** ~e inter aquas maris et Humbrie *Meaux* II 30. **c** non eque ludo si non consentio ludo SERLO WILT. 58. 3. **d 1274** major reddidit compotum de aula gilde de vj li. ix s. iij d...; tantum aula custavit in omnibus, unde ~e est versus communitatem *Rec. Leic.* I 115; **1356** summa que supra; et ~e *Crawley* 274; **1476** et sic ~e de pecunia *ExchScot* 329.

aeque- v. aequi-. aequiale v. equiale.

aequiangulus, equiangular.

figuris quinque..que regulares vocantur et sunt ~e et equilatere BACON *Maj.* I 159; oportet quod triangulus totalis *KCE* sit equilaterus; aliter enim [isti] non essent ~i WALLINGF. *Quad.* 107; in Deo est potentia..ad inscribendum..infinitorum angulorum rectilineorum figuram equilateram et ~am circulo assignato BRADW. *CD* 842D.

aequibonus, equal in goodness.

1497 sunt personarum [Trinitatis] operationes communes, quae sunt equisapientes, ~ae COLET *In 1 Cor.* 202.

aequicolus [cf. ἰσόκωλος], composed of equal members.

~am quoque, id est equimembrem, definito oportet fieri definitionem J. SAL. *Met.* 907B.

aequidialis [CL gl.], equinoctial.

~es, aequinoctiales, id est isymerinos Grece *GlC* A 296; [cena] ab hora diei nona usque ad xij noctis, et hoc tempore ~i, protracta J. SAL. *Pol.* 735D.

aequidies, equinox.

equator solem statione reflectit / equidiemque facit HANV. VIII 373 (cf. ib. IX 379: dies hec plenior, illa / equidie brevior).

aequidistanter, a at a constant distance apart, parallel. **b** at an equal distance.

a a fine illius dimensionis ducatur linea..~er linee terminanti primum clima GROS. 25; si..ducantur due linee a centris eorum [corporum] ~er usque ad tertium corpus BACON *Tert.* 156. **b** in linea *DB* signentur alia duo centra ~er ipsi *O* WALLINGF. *Albion* 362; cujus media linea mediatrix..dicitur, habens 2 latera..equedistanter mediatrici lineata *Turquet* 371.

aequidistantia, a constant distance. **b** equal distance.

a cum ipse linee sint equedistantes..res visa secundum equedistantiam a termino diametri non videbitur major quam sit ipse diameter J. BLUND *An.* 91; ducantur linee per ~iam BACON IV 315. **b** inter album et rubium non potest esse aliquid equedistans simpliciter, quare ~ia simpliciter habet respectum ad extremos UPTON 105.

aequidistare, to remain at a constant distance.

cum circulus articus secundum quamlibet sui partem ~et [v.l. eque distet] a polo mundi SACROB. *Sph.* 93; corpus motum..habet prius et posterius in suis partibus, et ~ant semper BACON *Tert.* 151; turno..sic disposito quod ~et orizonti *Turquet* 372.

2 (pr. ppl.) **a** remaining at a constant distance, parallel. **b** equidistant.

a nulle linee ~antes videntur ~antes NECKAM *NR* II 153; quidam circulus ~ans equinoctiali, qui vocatur parallelus, eo quod est ~ans GROS. 14; cum grave movetur deorsum movetur secundum lineas equedistantes, quia partes sunt equedistantes in toto BACON XIII 396; tunc protrahatur linea *FGK* ~ans *AB* WALLINGF. *Quad.* 108. **b** color rubeus est color medius ab extremis albedinis et nigredinis ~ans BAD. AUR. 98; color equedistans inter extremos UPTON 105.

aequidium, equinox.

dulce bis equidium, bis solsticiale juvamen GARL. *Tri. Eccl.* 12; *equinoccion'*, equinoccium, ~ium *CathA*.

aequifaciliter, with equal ease.

cum hoc operari possumus cum omnibus stellis erraticis.. ~er sicut cum stellis fixis WALLINGF. *Albion* 365.

aequiformiter, correspondingly.

vinum habet melius esse in homine..; ~er homo habet altius esse et verius in Deo quam in genere proprio NETTER *DAF* I 22C.

aequigena, twin.

~ae, gemini *GlC* A 318.

aequilaterus, equilateral.

elmuhahin est..~um, sed rectangulum non est ADEL. *Euclid* 10; triangulum ~um BACON VIII 14; *Id. Maj.* I 159 (v. aequiangulus).

aequilibra, balance, pair of scales. **b** (fig.).

si unum F suspendatur ex una parte ~e et aliud F omnino equale ex altera BRADW. *CD* 129D; **1427** ij ~as pro ponderibus majoribus et minoribus *MunAcOx* 284. **b** sub ~a, sub librato judicio *GlC* S 678; deprimat pia manus brachium ~e qua nostra..merita pensabuntur R. BURY *Phil.* 20. 251.

aequilibrare, to weigh out, apportion (fig.). **b** to judge, esteem.

nec de meis excessibus tua judicia ~es P. BLOIS *Ep.* 139 414B; cum sit Deus justus retributor, scit ~are premia et penas meritis atque delictis GROS. 155. **b 1452** sententia hec, equelibrans me non minus inter ceteros omnes tui amantissimum quam fateor te..mihi beneficentissimum BEKYNTON I 273.

aequilibris, evenly balanced.

si ~is fuerit positio equalis, equis ponderibus appensis ab equalitate non discedet BACON *Maj.* I 169.

aequilibritas, even balance (fig.).

ratione et ~ate debet nostra subsistere natura W. MALM. *GR* IV 334; **s1205** ut..legatarii sui juxta ~atem conscientie sue potestatem haberent [testamentum] corrigendi COGGESH. **106b.**

aequilibriter, in even balance.

donec ~er se habeat examen cum pondere *Dial. Scac.* I 6 H.

aequilibrium, level.

14.. equilibrum, *a lewel* WW.

aequilocus, (?) evenly matched.

s882 contra paganicas naves in mari congressus est; ex quibus ipse ~us duas potenti virtute exsuperavit S. DURH. *HR* II 86.

aequimanus [LL], ambidextrous.

~us, species gladiaturae quae utraque manu depugnat *GlC* A 349; *that wirkis with bothe the handis*, ~us *CathA*.

aequimembris, composed of equal members.

J. SAL. *Met.* 907B (v. aequicolus).

aequimodus, formally correct (log.).

J et V consonantes non magis proficiunt ad sillabam quam adjectiva secunde impositionis primis substantivis apposita ad rectam et ~am locutionem J. SAL. *Met.* 843A.

aequinoctialis [CL], equinoctial. **b** (sb. m., *sc. circulus*) equator.

~is dies omni mundo aequalis et una est BEDE *TR* 31; sole in aequinoxiali degente linea ADEL. *QN* 71; super circulum ~em e directo meridiani tabule ~is recte ad meridiem eleva ~em [sc. tabulam] donec..*Turquet* 372; punctus equinoxialis [i.e. *point of intersection of equator and ecliptic*] WYCL. *Log.* III 39. **b** latitudo est ab ~i et longitudo ab oriente BACON *Maj.* I 187; medietas inferior mundi est ab ~i usque ad polum arcticum WYCL. *Log.* III 9.

aequinoctium [CL], equinox. **b** (w. *S. Michaelis*) autumnal equinox.

dicentes viii kal. Apriles in ~io verno Dominum conceptum et passum..; item beatum praecursorem et Baptistam Domini viii kal. Octobres in ~io autumnali conceptum BEDE *TR* 30; **1233** hujusmodi circulus in spera recta vocatur equator diei, super quo quandocumque venerit sol perambulans sub zodiaco dicitur esse ~ium, eo quod tunc dies equantur noctibus BACON VI 19; equinoxium autumpnale W. MERLE 4. **b 1233** debent..in ~o S. Michaelis iiij s. et ij d. *CurR* XV 137.

aequiparabilis, equal, comparable.

tot virgo radiis..fit..aut minor aut ~is GOSC. *Edith* 68; **1509** in numerositate comparandum sit et ~e *Reg. Merton* 380.

aequiparantia, equivalence, correlation.

sequitur de 3° predicamento, in quo est relacio genus generalissimum..sub quo sunt due species subalterne, primo ~ia, [secundo] nonequiparancia sive inequiparancia, ut nomen fingatur BACON XV 221; relatum ~ie est equivocum DUNS *Metaph.* V 6 p. 32 A; **c1301** veritas est adequacio rei ad intellectum et est relacio ~ie *Quaest. Ox.* 338; affirmacio de positivo fundatur in paritate vel ~ia WYCL. *Log.* I 221; relaciones ~ie mutuo se inferunt *Id. Ente Praed.* 207.

aequiparare [CL], **a** to equalize, make equal. **b** to equate, regard as equal. **c** to equal. **d** (pass.) to be logically equivalent (of negatives; *cf. aequivalere* 1c).

a si omnes horas aequiperare, hoc est aequinoctiales habere, volumus BEDE *TR* 3; in cujus [harundinis] fastigio aequiperatas scedulas aequali lance pendentes..cerneres FELIX *Guthl.* 37; **1234** pro summa tallagii Lond' ~ando (*sic*) tallagio Eboraci, quod prius excessit *CurR* XV 1118. **b 787** illorum meritis aequiperari dignus efficiaris in coelis ALCUIN *Ep.* 4; [vinum] subtilitati Parvipontane veritatis ~etur NECKAM *Ut.* 103; asserens duas epistolas ubique uni posse evangelio ~ari GIR. *GE* I 48. **c** dum cupidus gestit normam aequiperare magistri ALDH. *VirgV* 801; nullus eum ~are potuit BEDE *HE* IV 24; aequiperans tantum fidei fervore magistrum FRITH. 667; **955** (12c) largiflui signum trophaei equiperans consignavi *CS* 905; Scotia non tantum magistram ~avit Hiberniam verum etiam in musica peritia longe prevalet GIR. *TH* III 11. **d a1250** nullus, non aliquis, omnis non, equiparantur (W. SHIRWOOD) *GLA* III 13; ipsis [negacionibus] positis, perit omnis ordo cognoscendi, cum omnes veritates equeparantur WYCL. *Act.* 97.

aequiparativus, expressing correlation.

si [proposicio] est secundum modum respectivum positivum non commensurandi seu equiparandi, hoc est dupliciter, vel secundum modum respectivum, eciam qui de se nec ~am nec disquiparativam importat, vel secundum modum respectivum, qui disquiparativam importat WYCL. *Quaest. Log.* I 242.

aequipensum, ~ium, equipoise.

~um, *ebnwege GlC* A 352; **9..** ~ium, *efenwæge* WW.

aequiper- v. aequipar-.

aequipollenter, with equal force. **b** with like significance.

c1110 ut [ecclesia] orbata..Anselmi..emigratione Herberti..corroborata suffragio ~er vigeat H. LOS. *Ep.* 59. **b** hoc est dicere ~er: ergo volo vos esse sine uxore; nam volo vos esse sine sollicitudine seculi LANFR. *Comment. Paul.* (1 *Cor.* vii 27) 178; si adjectiva ~er in alia resolvantur, ..appositionem equipollentis termini nequaquam horrebit animus J. SAL. *Met.* 843B; taliter vel ~er OCKHAM *Dial.* 430.

aequipollentia, equivalence, like amount or extent. **b** logical equivalence, like significance, equipollence.

cum de pelliciis nigros [monachos] derideant, [albi] plurimis et suavissimis habundant ad ~iam tunicis MAP *NC* I 25 p. 41; **c1230** debent..ad communia dona et auxilia scotare et lotare, sc. iij d. ob. quad., et ~iam ad scotum hundredi *Doc. Bec* 110; *an even-hede*, equalitas, equanimitas, ~ia, equalencia *CathA*. **b** in quantum possum per ~ias propositionum tego artem [sc. dialecticam], ne videar magis arte quam veritate..confidere LANFR. *Corp. & Sang.* 417A; ~ias philosophi dicunt semper tenere nisi aliquid speciale.. repugnet BRADW. *CD* 723B; ~ia est equivalencia duarum proposicionum adinvicem, causata per negacionem WYCL. *Log.* I 22.

aequipollēre [LL], to have equal force or value, be equivalent. **b** to be logically equivalent, equipollent.

si quid humane rationis possit allegari quod ~entibus argumentis valeat enervari W. MALM. *GR* IV 334; **c1178** iiij marcatas terre vel redditus ~entes *FormA* 3; tanquam multis minoribus delictis ~ente statim uno GIR. *PI* I 10; **1215** quousque ei in ~enti vel uberiori beneficio providerimus *Cl* 221b; **1235** toftum cum crofto ~et bovate *Reg. Linc.* III 79; **s1247** ut tres ex his [denariis] in statera publica positi duobus sanis et integris vix aut nullatenus ~ere possent *Ann. Wav.* 339; **s1250** ut eorum [sanctorum] testimonium canonizationi ~eret M. PAR. *Min.* III 318; breve de ingressu ~et brevi assise mortis antecessoris BRACTON 350b; **1350** habebit iiij panes..vel aliquid quod ~eat *Reg. S. Aug.* 79; **s1404** probans quod ipsi, ..cum sint armigeri et bachalarii, baronibus in diviciis ~ent *Eul. Hist. cont.* III 400; adquirere [feudum] per investituram traditivam vel ~entem; et voco ~entem fictam tradicionem in casibus feudorum approbatis UPTON 38. **b** percurrunt..que [propositiones] determinate vere sint aut false, que quibus ~eant, que consentiant sibi, que dissentiant J. SAL. *Met.* 900A; lata..sententia per hec verba..'de pecunia sua' idem est ac si 'de tota pecunia' dixissent; laicorum enim indefinite [propositiones] non..particularibus sed semper universalibus ~ent *Dial. Scac.* II 16; vox hec..videtur ~ere voci huic 'alleluia' BELETH *RDO* 79. 85; **a1250** quodlibet signum ~et suo contradictorio cum negatione preposita (W. SHIRWOOD) *GLA* III 13.

aequisapiens, equal in wisdom.

1497 (v. aequibonus).

aequisonus, harmonious or (?) antiphonal.

indidit aequisonas divinis auribus odas FRITH. 1146.

aequitas [CL], **a** even balance. **b** equity. **c** (dist. from common law). **d** just due. **e** just decision.

a alioquin..exametri regulae legitima ~atis lance carentes..vacillarent ALDH. *Met.* 6. **b** qui..judicaturus esset orbem in ~ate [cf. *Psalm* ix 9] BEDE *HE* III 22; [Æthelstanus] ~atis legibus serviens regnum strenue gubernabat EADMER *V. Osw.* 2; ex ~ate maxima prodita est legalis ista constitutio [sc. magna assisa] GLANV. II 7; reservatur juri positivo quod suum est, ita ut ~as stricto juri preferatur NECKAM *NR* II 189; **1278** insuper concesserunt de ~ate..quod narrassent..in principale (*sic*) placito *SelCKB* I 41; in tanta ~ate justiciam exsequebatur RICH *Edm.* 620; leges..recusant reduci ad ipsam synteresim, ~atis originem R. BURY *Phil.* 11. 172. **c** fora ~atis sunt Cancellaria, Curia Requestarum, Concilia in limitibus Walliae et parte Boreali CAMD. *Br.* 143. **d** **1155** ecclesiis singulis suam conservetis in omnibus ~atem *Lit. Cant.* III 366; **s1325** ut res Francie..redderet sibi statim..terras in Aquitania de quibus fuerat placitatum et de aliis †~atis [? l. ~atibus]..faceret sibi justicie complementum AD. MUR. 43. **e** **11..** litis contentionem..hujus ~atis prudentia diffiniendo in perpetuum terminavimus *Feod. Durh.* lx.

aequitibiale, last for leggings, expl. (? erron.) as shoe.

allutarii..conservant sibi †forumpedias, ~ia et spatulas [*gl.*: ~ia dicuntur *estivax*, ab equus, ~a, ~um, quia adequantur tibie] GARL. *Dict.* 125; *a laste of a sowter*, formula, ..formipedia, ..~e pro ocreis *CathA*.

aequitrinus, equal in trinity.

[Plato] unam summam ~am indivisam divinitatem..ita esse convicit BACON *Maj.* II 229.

aequivalenter, to an equal extent or value. **b** to a like effect.

terrarum cultura per temporum incongruitatem singulis annis minime ~er respondet *Fleta* 157; **s1292** abbas..in manerio..est seysitus ~er OXNEAD *Chr.* 286; negantes Deum habere realiter, ~er vel supereminenter omnem virtutem BRADW. *CD* 3E (cf. ib. 20B); ~er et eciam prevalenter); iste terminus..nec papam nec episcopos excludit.., imo eosdem ~er vere includit CONWAY *Def. Mend.* 1413; **1436** c sol. sive in pecunia sive alias quovismodo ~er seu ultra *Reg. Heref.* 208. **b** nusquam dicit quod creature antequam fierent erant, nisi addat quod non erant, vel ~er NETTER *DAF* I 21B.

aequivalentia, equivalence, equal amount or value. **b** logical equivalence.

obtulit ei Herefordensem episcopatum ampliare fundis ad ~iam archiepiscopatus predicti MAP *NC* V 6 p. 234; divisa est..Wallia totalis in tres partes tanquam equales, plus ~ie tamen quam juste quantitatis..habita consideratione GIR. *DK* I 2; **c1189** ville Bathoniensis excambium, pro Glastonia factum, ~iam, quam nobis asseruerat idem episcopus, non effecit (*Lit. Regis*) DOMERH. *Glast.* 375; **1226** deponemus c milia unciarum auri vel ~iam in argento (*Lit. Papae*) *Reg. S. Osm.* I 194; **1382** ut predaretur regnum..sine ~ia pecunie recompense (WYCL.) WALS. *HA* II 51; **1432** de ipsorum [obsidum]..sufficiencia vel ~ia in hac parte..plenius informati *RScot* II 277a. **b** ecclesia..per omnes argumentorum sedes, conversionum modos, ~iarum articulos sine offendiculo paralogismi liberrimo pede transcurrit NETTER *DAF* I 25A.

aequivalēre, to be equivalent to (w. dat.). **b** (w. acc.). **c** to be logically equivalent, equipollent (*cf. aequiparare*).

1285 ut..archiepiscopum Ebor'..cum cruce erecta in suis ecclesiis non admittant nec ipsius benedictionem recipiant, quam maledictioni ~ere credimus PECKAM *Ep.* 649; **1458** summa hujus expense ijᶜxxix li., que ~ent oneri remissionum deliberatarum compotanti *ExchScot* 486. **b** **1205** litteras domini regis patentes de protectione que ~ent j cartam *RChart* 108; **1254** duas carettas longas ~entes carettas predictas *RGasc* I 531; quatinus..terras..nobis assignaret que dictam extentam ville..~erent *Meaux* II 188. **c** **a1250** ~ent 'omnis', 'nullus non', 'non aliquis non' (W. SHIRWOOD) *GLA* III 13; ~ent apud me 'Deus non est nunc' et 'Deus non est pro mensura presenti' (KYN.) *Ziz.* 23.

2 (pr. ppl.) equivalent, of equal value. **b** corresponding. **c** logically equivalent, of like significance. **d** (as sb. n. w. *in*) in effect.

pro duabus ecclesiis ~entibus GIR. *Symb.* 22 p. 263; **1213** ut in ~enti beneficio vel uberius vobis provideamus *Pat.* 105b; **1259** in ~enti statu vel in meliori *Reg. S. Thom. Dublin* no. 211; integram et ~entem..piscis..porcionem *Cust. Westm.* 73; **1291** ~ens escambium *RParl.* I 68a; **a1350** caligas aut anulos vel quid aliud ~ens *StatOx* 28; tenementa alia eis ~encia *Meaux* II 186; **1423** personas obsidum..aut alias ~entes in possessionibus et redditibus *RScot* II 241b. **b** nec ipse armarius debet libros accommodare nisi accipiat ~ens memoriale *Obs. Barnwell* 62. **c** cum verbum tribuendi et ~encia quoad significacionem ibidem sepius inserantur OCKHAM *Pol.* I 53; non hoc tollit deperdicionem potencie Dei sine adventu nove ~entis WYCL. *Act.* 63. **d** iste error fuit in ~enti damnatus per Alexandrum IV CONWAY *Def. Mend.* 1419.

aequiveloci̇ter, at the same speed.

c1340 sive ponatur quod in *c* instanti velocius remittetur *a* quam *b*, sive tardius, sive equevelociter, sequitur quod *a* tunc erit intensior *b* (R. SWINESHEAD *Lib. Calc.*) *Sci. Mech.* 299.

aequivocabilis, ambiguous.

c1301 aut est agens ~is; tunc non causat aliquid in se, sicud patet de sole et fantasmate *Quaest. Ox.* 355.

aequivocalis, ambiguous.

est ergo dare motum velocissimum possibilem ut motum ~em WYCL. *Log.* II 143.

aequivocare, to use in an ambiguous sense. **b** to equivocate, speak ambiguously, play with words.

cum ~ari possint duo modis sex, tria decem..et deinceps similiter BALSH. *AD* (*rec.* 2) 42 p. 28; ideo cognitio..erit in brutis; propter quod ~atur hic, vel magis est vitium translationis, que non habet vocabulum proprium ad hunc modum cognoscendi BACON *Maj.* II 128; duplex est equivocum, sc. equivocum ~ans et equivocum ~atum: ~ans dicitur quod sub se ~antur multa supposita..; equivocum ~atum est cui competit ~ans secundum diversam racionem dici cum aliis, ut quelibet res mundi ~atur sub transcendente cum aliqua alia WYCL. *Ente Praed.* 15–16; **s1447** quia sepe Latinarum vocabula diccionum ~antur ad sensus.., presul decreti sui arbitrium in Anglicano idiomate tradendum censuit *Croyl. Cont. B* 522. **b** iste est sensus istius protestantis et ~antis OCKHAM *Dial.* 744; Eliphaz..~avit cum Job, putans quod oportet quemlibet punitum peccare in persona propria proporcionaliter ad penam, quod non est verum WYCL. *Ente* 298; Aristoteles.., arguens contra ideas Platonis, ~avit in logica, stulte concipiens quod idea sit essencia absoluta distincta ab essencia divina *Id. Dial.* I 8 f. 12v; quibus nominibus..utitur ecclesia, utantur ipsi, ut unanimes non ~ando..Deum honorificemus (TYSS.) *Ziz.* 135.

aequivocatio, ambiguity, application of the same name to different objects. **b** equivocation, deceitful use of ambiguous language.

1132 ~o est eadem diversorum non eadem ratione appellatio; ~onum autem genera sunt sex..BALSH. *AD* 42; habita ratione ~onis, qua ens vel esse distinguitur pro diversitate subjectorum J. SAL. *Met.* 885D; ~one deceptus, inter Judam et Judam male distinxit GIR. *GE* II 35; decepti sunt in ~one nominis, non distinguentes inter mathematicam veram et falsam BACON *Tert.* 27; **s1204** predictum fuerat illam urbem [Constantinopolim] capi non posse nisi per angelum; sed, hostibus per murum ubi erat angelus depictus intrantibus, indigene per ~onem angeli se deceptos cognoverunt HIGD. VII 32; tanquam si cujusdam ~onis multiplicitate fallatur simplex monachica plebs moderna, dum Liber pater preponitur libro patrum R. BURY *Phil.* 5. 79; expedit ~onem termini prenotare; et multipliciter capitur 'titulus' in jure PAUL. ANGL. *ASP* 1528. **b** **1098** id remota omni ~one ac sophismate faciat EADMER *HN* 109; sic arguendo esset fallacia ~onis (KYN.) *Ziz.* 13; **c1430** postquam seriose et absque fallacia ~onis audiveritis *Reg. Whet.* II 380.

2 identity of name.

dilectissimo magistro suo Petro Blesensi Petrus Blesensis ..salutem. ~oni vestre toto corde congratulor; nec reor hoc accidisse sine dispensatione divina, ut nobis esset uniformitas nominum P. BLOIS *Ep.* 77. 238.

aequivoce, ambiguously, in more than one sense. **b** metaphorically, improperly.

~e 'quaestum' accipit LANFR. *Comment. Paul.* (1 *Tim.* vi 5–6) 359; 'argumentum' ~e dicitur, tum ratio qua aliquid probatur, tum narratio ficta et verisimilis BALSH. *AD* 59; aut ~e aut univoce aut denominative..singula predicantur J. SAL. *Met.* 895A; non est ~e dictum sed univoce GROS. 80; hujusmodi nomina, 'dominium', 'dominus' etc...in diversis facultatibus ~e et variis modis accipiuntur OCKHAM *Pol.* I 307; substancia et quantitates sunt univoce universalia sed ~e encia WYCL. *Ente Praed.* 16; videtur quod 'spirituale' non univoce sed ~e vel amphibologice dicatur de sacramentis PAUL. ANGL. *ASP* 1550. **b** **1382** talis frater fictus / est frater equivoce, sicut frater pictus (*Contra Religiosos* 246) *Mon. Francisc.* I 599.

aequivocus [LL], ambiguous, used (or understandable) in more than one sense. **b** (sb. n.) ambiguous word, ambiguity.

'modius' est nomen ~um ad mensuram et ad illud instrumentum super quod erigitur navis malus NECKAM *Ut.* 114; quosdam †nutos [? l. nutus] ~os faciebat *Latin Stories* 78; verba legis, propter aliqua verba ~a vel multiplicia in ipsa contenta, possunt habere diversos sensus OCKHAM *Dial.* 628; 'gith' est nomen ~um, sc. ad ciminum Ethiopicum et ad nigellam *SB* 22. **b** ut hec tria, sc. ~a, univoca et denominativa, asserat Isidorus categoriarum instrumenta J. SAL. *Met.* 893A; equivocum celat sub eadem plurima voce GARL. *Syn.* 1577B; principium processus ponam in distinccione multiplici, ne in ~o procedatur CONWAY *Def. Mend.* II 1411; WYCL. *Ente Praed.* 15 (v. aequivocare a); ne magister meus et ego tota die simus in ~is (KYN.) *Ziz.* 39; procedit ex ~o, probans quod omne preteritum vel futurum existit in tempore suo *Ib.* 84.

2 bearing the same name, (sb. m. or f.) namesake.

licet..ibi..competenter locata veneraretur ejus ~a sancta Ædgith *V. Ed. Conf.* 49v; Humbram congressum regibus equivocis *Ib.* 53; diaconus Leofricus et alter presbyter ejus ~us HERM. ARCH. 1 p. 30; hoc quidem frater idem retulit michi ~o sibi *Ib.* 38; **s738** [Egbertus] habuit fratrem ~um W. MALM. *GR* I 65; duo fratres ~i, sc. duo Alfelmi *Lib. Eli.* 83.

3 figurative, metaphorical. **b** misnamed.

debet intelligi mistice ad sensum ~um WYCL. *Ver.* III 147. **b** felices merito fuissetis..si prolem non degenerem nec ~am reliquisse..licuisset R. BURY *Phil.* 5. 77.

4 ambivalent, having more than one possible cause or effect.

rigor..de signis est ~is GILB. I 14. 1; alia [actio] est ~a, ut lux generat calorem et vitam et in contrarium putrefactionem et mortem BACON *Tert.* 115.

aequor [CL], **a** plain. **b** sea. **c** (fig.).

a seges lini vernans ex aequore campi ALDH. *Aen.* 74. 1; jocunda planitie delectati juvenes..precantur..ut liceat eis equos suos in eodem probare inoffenso campi ~ore FOLC. *J. Bev.* 8. **b** scrutor maris aequora ALDH. *Aen.* 16. 2; tumida ~ora placavit BEDE *HE* V 1; insanos fluctus turbidi ~oris periculoso navigio tranare *V. Dunst. B.* 23; ecce precor, transcurras ocius equor SERLO WILT. 39. 9. **c** retibus angelicis raptos ex aequore mundi ALDH. *VirgV* 537; non arescente loquendi / equore HANV. VIII 369.

aequoreus [CL], marine, of the sea. **b** (fig.). **c** watery.

Gregorius.. / arida mellifluis perfundens arva fluentis, / de quibus aequorei potus hausere Britanni ALCUIN *Carm.* I 88; Britannici Oceani orbis ~eus GOSC. *Aug. Min.* 743; ~eas vias ponti..transiliens *V. Dunst. B.* 23; illum prodigium Nicolaum Pipe, hominem ~eum, qui sine spiraculo diu..intima ponti cum piscibus frequentabat indempnis MAP *NC* IV 13; equoreus piscis humores nutrit amaros D. BEC. 2745; sumne cetus aut vis equorea? J. HOWD. *Phil.* 664. **b** jam tempus cogit currentes cludere versus / ..terminus aequoreo dum venit margine metri ALDH. *VirgV* 2803. **c** Baptista Tonantem / diluit aequoreis mergens in gurgite limphis *Ib.* 410.

1 aequus [CL], equal, even. **b** calm, unruffled.

a680 pro meritorum diversitate dispar retributio ~issimis judicii lancibus trutinabitur ALDH. *Ep.* 4 p. 486 (cf. *Reg. Aberbr.* I 168 [**1249**]: ~a lance procedere cupientes); quibus [annis] ~a partitione divisis BEDE *HE* IV 23; cum..nec in equo permeet equos / tempore sol arcus orbis HANV. IX 379; surgant alii quantumlibet hostes! / non mihi sunt equi VINSAUF *PN* 525; **c1430** dixistis..nequaquam pugnam litis esse ~am 'ubi tu pulsas, ego tantum vapulo' [Juvenal III 289] *Reg. Whet.* II 380. **b** alienas auribus equis / ..accipe laudes HANV. VIII 366; felix quod sors fert animo qui pertulit equo GIR. *Vers.* 36 p. 379.

2 fair, just, equitable (*v. et. manus aequa*).

si quid..controversie nascebatur, ~issimo..statu componebat G. CRISPIN *Herl.* 96; **c1198** nulla lex equior, / nec gratior, / quam quas tu statueris / leges (*De W. Ep. Eliensi*) *EHR* V 318; judices quos bonos et ~os credidit LIV. *Hen. V* 2b; **1439** ad eam que utrimque ~a et justa sit conclusionem BEKYNTON I 76.

3 (sb. n.) equality. **b** equity. **c** (dist. from common law).

non ex ~o tum affirmationis tum negationis ad hec fit responsio BALSH. *AD* 178; **s1459** (v. Areopagita b). **b** non est dignus ĕquo, cui carior est ēquus ĕquo SERLO WILT. 2.35; amplius equo / amplificans sumptus HANV. VI 336; tres tria conservant, rex, miles, rusticus: equum / rex, miles pacem, rusticus arva bonus GARL. *Hon. Vit.* 107. **c** fora temporalia sunt duplicia, juris sc. et ~i CAMD. *Br.* 141.

2 aequus v. equus.

1 aër [CL < ἀήρ], air, atmosphere, weather. **b** (n. pl.). **c** blast of air. **d** (w. *in*) (?) draught.

irrigat et terram tenebrosis imbribus āër ALDH. *VirgV* 2045; Hibernia..salubritate ac serenitate ~um multum Brittaniae praestat BEDE *HE* I 1 p. 12; inferior pars [mundi]..a terra usque ad lunam aer dicitur ERIUG. *Per.* 549C; non dubito omnem hanc mundi molem..constare ex terra et aqua et ~e et igne ANSELM (*Mon.* 7) I 21; cum..celum terre..~um temperie debitum prestaret officium AILR. *Gen. Regum* 362; spondet opes, medicos, ..salubris / aëris accessum NIG. *SS* 1032; Britannia Hiberniam ~is tam serenitate quam subtilitate longe precellit GIR. *TH* 1 3; **s1240** ventus..validus et violentus totum aera perturbavit M. PAR. *Maj.* IV 10; **1380** ex fetore..aier..inficitur *FormOx* 255; **c1395** malum aierem de fimo..venientem (*Anc. Indict.*) *Pub. Works* II 62; generatur albedo ex aiere vaporose declinante ad humiditatem aqueam BAD. AUR. 154; **c1400** pro serenitate eris *Miss. Rosslyn* 89; **1415** pro serenitate aieris *Reg. Heref.* 86; hic aier, *the wethyr* WW.

b limpida letiferis corrumpens āera venenis ALDH. *VirgV* 2388 (cf. ib. 14). **c** [musica] etiam in chordis sive ~ibus et malleis..vim suam..habet ADEL. *ED* 25. **d** c**1150** jejunans debet sedere in ~e ante mensam et commedere bisum panem suum super scamnum sine panno (*Reg. Reading*) *MonA* IV 44.

2 aer [cf. OF *aire* < area; v. et aether 2], **a** (?) threshing floor. **b** (?) floor.

a 1282 in iij hominibus..facientibus ~em grangie dominicalis *MinAc* 1070/5 r. 1. **b 1283** in xx carett[atis] arsilli ad torchiand' ~em in domo..gaole ultra portam *KRAc* 467/11; c**1300** in j trappa facienda in summo aer' ejusdem turell'; ..in eodem aer' de novo plastrando cum alba terra *MinAc* 863/8; **1314** in plastracione cumuli alte camere nove turris subtus plumbum, cum plastracione, ~is medie camere ejusdem turris *DLMinAc* 1/3 r. 12.

1 aëra, air.

que mare, terra parit, meliora vel aera format / sunt mihi prompta foro GOWER *VC* III 831; hec aera, *the wethyr* WW.

2 aera [LL], a Spanish era (from 38 B.C.). **b** era, basis of reckoning time.

a 1176 facta carta..era anno MCCXIIII, VIII Kal. Sept. (*Conventio regum Castelle & Navarre*) *G. Hen. II* I 143 (cf. ib. 150); invenimus annos Romanorum quos eram vocant, eo quod incipiunt ab eo tempore quo Cesar Augustus primo tributa eris imposuit provinciis subditis Romano imperio BACON VI 85. **b** ante principium ere Arabum, que incipit Anno Domini 622 *Ib.* 167; astronomi..habentes eram, radices et tabulas a tempore diluvii institutas BRADW. *CD* 141B.

2 tax (Sp.).

1290 per loca terre nostre ad defensionem ejusdem adjutorium sive era colligitur et prestatur (*Lit. regis Aragon*) *Foed.* II 461.

aeramen, copper.

fricus [i.e. Phrygius] lapis..iij habet species: una est †metallitica [l. metallica] que in Cipro nascitur, altera est fex †craminis [l. eraminis] *Alph.* 67.

aeramentarium, copper vessel (for brine).

1633 ~ia, A. *salt pannes Pat* 2622 m. 27.

aeramentum [CL], copper or bronze work. **b** (fig.). **c** bell.

aurum vero, quantum sono succumbit, tantum splendore praestat ~o BEDE *Tab.* III 11; **10..** ~um, *argeweorc* WW. **b** virginitas aurum, castitas argentum, jugalitas ~um ALDH. *VirgP* 19. **c** post ipsum classicum nullum pulsetur ~um ante sanctum Sabbatum *Cust. Westm.* 316.

aerare v. aeriare.

aerarium [CL], treasury. **b** (fig.).

10.. ~ium, *maþmhus* WW; [Henricus I] leges justas.. populo dedit, carta confirmavit..et in ~io suo apud Wintoniam conservari precepit RIC. HEX. *Stand.* 37b; vacantium proventus ecclesiarum in fiscale ~ium mittens GIR. *EH* I 46; nudis ecclesie tribuens eraria GARL. *Tri. Eccl.* 9; omnis ejus substancia pauperum ~ium semper fuit *NLA* (*Kentigern*) II 118; s**1291** ut..eligerentur iiij custodes qui.. res et redditus regales in errario regis Scocie reconderent W. GUISB. 233; **1346** Scoti vim faciunt, vastant erraria, jura, / occidunt, rapiunt, faciunt incendia plura *Pol. Poems* I 43; **1401** percipiant singulis annis ad Scaccarium nostrum de errario nostro *Cl* 248 m. 8; **1411** unum ob. de..communi errario..applicandum *Reg. Heref.* 80. **b** pandebat ei ~ia et cellaria Christi GOSC. *Aug. Maj.* 88.

1 aerarius [CL], coppersmith, brass-founder. **b** moneyer.

habeo fabros ferrarium, ..~ium [AS: *arsmiþ*], lignarium ÆLF. *Coll.* 99; **10..** ~ius, *mæslingsmiþ* WW; s**1091** duas skelettas quas Fergus ~ius de S. Botulfo nobis nuper contulerat *Croyl.* 101; **14..** ~ius, A. *a brasyer* WW. **b** *monyowre*, nummilarius, monetarius, errarius *PP*.

2 aerarius [cf. aerea, aeriare], nesting, breeding.

1245 de cignis eyreriis de instauro..cariari faciat usque Windesor' sex paria cignorum *Liberate* 21 m. 13; a**1260** habebunt eciam..canonici cignos suos errarios, quantos voluerint, natantes et nidificantes cum pullis et cineolis eorum, depascentes et errantes in omnibus aquis meis *Cart. Newnham* 2 (= *MonA* VI 375); **1277** et remanent iij auce errarie *MinAc* 997/3; **1308** duos cygnos ~ios et tres pullos *CalPat* 169; **1340** respondent de xxxvj cignis herrariis..repertis in ripariis regis de Thamisia, Colney et Waya et aliis ripariis.. inter pontem London' et villam de Habendon'..et de x cignis herrariis adjunctis de staggis *MinAc* 1120/10 r. 4*d.*; **1351** de remanentibus xij anates, unde v errarii; ..et remanent vj anates, unde iij eir' (*MinAc*) *Econ. Condit.* 69 (cf. ib. 84 [**1368**]: de remanentibus v, quarum iiij †cirrar'); **1380** cigni: presentatum est..quod v aierarii mortui sunt in morina apud Croulandmore *CourtR* 88/1200 r. 22*d*; **1394** unum cignum ayrarium cum tribus pullis asportavit *ProcJP* 137.

aeratus [CL], fitted w. bronze.

quamlibet aerata praecellat forte lucerna ALDH. *VirgV* 212.

aerea, ~ia, ~ius [OF *aire*], aerie, eyrie (nest or brood).

ibi..silva sexcentorum porcorum et una area accipitris *DB* I 152; ibi iiij aeirae accipitrum *Ib.* 172; ibi est airea accipitris *Ib.* 180; silva..in qua sunt ij haiae et aira accipitris *Ib.* 252b; **1199** canonici elongabunt animalia sua ab eiriis spervariorum nostrorum *RChart* 29 (cf. ib. 206b: ab aeriis); c**1200** preter eria sperveriorum *MonA* V 503; c**1200** salvo cervo et cerva, ..et aera accipitris *Couch. Furness* II 523; **1212** custodiunt aeria ancipitum domini regis in foresta Karleoli *Fees* 197 (cf. ib. 267); **1217** unusquisque liber homo habeat in boscis suis aereas ancipitum, spervariorum et falconum, aquilarum et de heyruns (*Ch. Forest.*) *StRealm* I 21; **1229** vidende sunt aerie osturorum et espervariorum et falconum, in quibus boscis fuerint et quis ea habuerit (*Artic. Forest.*) *Pat* 287; **1232** ingressus est boscum..et duas arias sperveriorum contra pacem nostram asportavit *KRMem* 11 r. 7; **1235** liberari faciat..falcones de aerio regis de Brug'..deferendos ad regem *Cl* 80; **1243** eyriam falconum gentilium *Cl* 95; **1272** nichil crevit de heyr' de falconibus.., sed unus erius spervariorum fuit in parco *IMisc* 17/18; **12..** debet habere falcones, espervarios, muskettos et omnes ayerias preter ancipitres, que remanent domino regi *Ib.* 20/14; s**1289** salvaginam cum ayreis avium in parco GRAYSTANES 22; **1325** unum tercelettum de erea nostra *Cl* 143 m. 31; **1370** ad custodiendum ayerium anticipetrum *IPM* 213/5.

aëreitas v. aëritas.

1 aereus, nesting.

1301 quilibet custumarius..habens aucas ereas dabit.. j aucam vocatam *lesegos AncExt* 8 m. 7.

2 aereus [CL], made of bronze or brass. **b** (?) (sb. f.) brass vessel.

aerea portarum quassavit claustra ALDH. *VirgV* 457; ut..ob refrigerium viantium..~eos caucos suspendi juberet BEDE *HE* II 16; tube vocem ignoras eream J. HOWD. *Ph.* 604; heres..habebit..ollam eream, patellam, cratem ferream *Leg. IV Burg.* 116; **1311** j springald' cum..j nuce erea *Pipe* 156 r. 49*d.*; **1331** onerat se de ij magnis ollis erreis *ExchScot* 379; c**1520** pro x li. lamine eree *Arch. Hist. Camb.* III 432. **b** a**1183** terram..in vico ubi faciunt heras *Eng. Feudalism* 266.

3 aereus v. aërius. aeria v. aerea.

Aërianus, follower of the heretic Aërius.

s**454** orti sunt Heriani pro mortuis non sacrificantes R. NIGER II 131.

aeriare, ~are [cf. aerarius, aerea], to nest.

1235 preterea aerium accipitrum et sperveriorum, ita quod monachi maliciose non impediant quin eo loco quo ~iant possint ~iare quamdiu habuerint consuetudinem ibidem ~iandi *Melrose* 198; **1277** percipiant..†aucipitres [l. ancipitres] et nisus et omnia alia genera avium aeriancium in..separalibus boscis suis *Cart. Sallay* 244; **1322** heyrones aerantes ibidem evacuabantur per forgeas in dicto parco euntes (*MinAc* 1145/21) *VCH Yorks* II 349; **1351** [*two pairs*] cignorum aeriorum [*of which one*] aeriat [*on the north side of the water*] (*Cart. Lewes*) *Norf. Rec. Soc.* XII 7.

aerifilum, brass wire.

14.. erifilum, A. *braswyre* WW.

aërimantia [ἀερομαντεία], divination by air, aeromancy.

Varro..quattuor species divinationis ab elementis mutuatus est, piromantiam sc., ~iam, ydromantiam et geomantiam J. SAL. *Pol.* 407C; similiter alie magice artes, ut ydromancia que fit in aqua..et ~ia in aere, ..sunt erronee BACON V 7 (cf. M. SCOT *Phys.* 97: †acrumantia).

aëritas, airiness, nature or quality of air.

color indicus..est color blavius, ..plus habens aquitatis et aereitatis admixtum cum partibus terrestribus BART. ANGL. XIX 21; igneitati debetur caliditas et siccitas, ~ati calor et humor GILB. VI 245 v. 1; animal est omne genus quod movetur et sentit.., et ~as in ipso magis dominatur BACON V 129; he quidem forme disparate esse possunt, sicut igneitas et ~as, opposite vero sibi esse non possunt *Ps.*-GROS. 347; color terreus..non tantum participat de albedine sicut de nigredine, plus habens terrestreitatis quam aieritatis UPTON 120.

aerium v. aerea.

aërius [CL < ἀέριος], **~eus**, airy, belonging to (or rising into) the air. **b** (w. *ignis*) wild fire.

tempestates potestatum ~iarum BEDE *HE* II 7; supposuit lunari corpore fulgens / aerium celum, quod per loca celsa redundat / spirituum cuneis *V. Merl.* 772; avibus aquaticis natione, ~eis habitatione GIR. *TH* I 11; in summis ..~eorum arduorumque collium verticibus *Ib.* 4. **b** s**1047** ignis ~ius, vulgo dictus silvaticus, ..villas et segetes multas ustulavit FL. WORC. I 201.

2 airy, of the nature of air. **b** (sb. n.) perceptible air (mixture of elements w. air predominant).

ignis nisi ~io spiritu insuffletur..cito extinguitur ERIUG. *Per.* 498A; spiritus in corporibus ~eis, que assumunt ex divina permissione, ludibria..faciunt GERV. TILB. III 61; hanc extensionem et contractionem ingredientem profunditatem materie et precipuo id quod est ~eum subtile in corpore sonativum esse intelligo GROS. 3; terrestres partes dissolvit et aquosas et ~eas BART. ANGL. IV 1; substanciam ~eam..et..substanciam terream BACON V 115; ignis qui vocatur a philosophis aliquando sulphur faciale, aliquando oleum, aliquando humor ~eus *Id. NM* 9 p. 546. **b** nec terra, nec aqua, nec aer, nec ignis, ..sed terreum, aquaticum, ~eum, igneum dicenda sunt; ex eo tamen quod in singulis magis abundat appellationem hanc sortita sunt ADEL. *QN* 1.

3 sky-blue (cf. *Esther* i 6).

aeri[i], jacintini *GlC* A 356; dedit [G. abbas, ob. 1146].. dossale magnum, in quo intexitur Inventio S. Albani, cujus campus est ~eus *G. S. Alb.* I 94; volucres duos, alterum albi, alterum coloris ~ii W. CANT. *Mir. Thom.* V 22; **1396** vestimentum..~ii coloris pro virginibus (*Invent.*) *Meaux* III lxxxi; a**1414** sapphirum coloris ~ei intensi (*Invent.*) AMUND. II 331.

aeruginamentum, burnishing (fig.).

illa arma induti sunt omnes milites Christi, ejus imitacione tamquam ducis exercitus pugnantes et recipientes eadem ~a WYCL. *Dom. Civ.* 112.

aeruginare [bibl.], to tarnish, rust (fig.). **b** to burnish. **c** (*? f.l.*).

s**1185** in brevi aurum ~avit, argentum versum est in scoriam GERV. CANT. I 34; **1198** ut qui eum [sc. gladium Petri] pre nimia miseria ~asse et hebetasse reputant.. acutum sentiant *Ep. Cant.* 481. **b** cultellos..~are et lavare *Cust. Westm.* 100; *to frubische*, elimare, ~are, erubiginare *CathA*. **c 1554** occasione invasionis sui confratris ..cum diga seu pugione †~ata [? l. evaginata] *Midlothian* 221.

aeruginator, burnisher.

†euruginatores [*gl.*: *furbyars*] gladiorum cumulant denarios vendendo gladios †euruginatos GARL. *Dict.* 124; hic ~or, A. *forbushere* WW.

aeruginosus, a (?) tinged w. verdigris. **b** stocked (or tainted) w. money.

a apostema de colera ~a adusta GAD. 121 v. 1. **b** cardinalium, quos ad auram ~i marsupii trahi posse videbat in cujusque turpidinis cenum J. SAL. *Hist. Pont.* 49.

aerugo [CL], copper rust, verdigris.

erugo, *rust GlC* E 297; **9..** ~ine, i. rubigine, *of ruste* vel *ome* WW; ~o.., quando simpliciter [ponitur], de ~ine eris vel cuperi vel auricalci intelligitur *SB* 20; ~o vel viride eris *LC*.

2 (conf. w. *eruca*) canker, blight, or caterpillar.

catrypel, a worme amonge frute ,erugo, ..*myldew*, arugo *PP*; **1476** thesaurus..qui..nec effoditur per fures nec per tineas sive ~ines..demolitur [*cf. Matth.* vi 20] *FormA* 336; *the meldewe*, aurugo, ~o, rubigo *CathA*.

aerumna [CL], anguish, distress.

herumna, labor *GlC* H 48 (cf. ib. A 313, E 275); ab erumna perpetuae damnationis BEDE *HE* IV 13; excepi mestas tenero olim somate ĕrumnas [v.l. rimas] FRITH. 701; [Dunstanus] Eielredo regi futuram ~am..predixit W. MALM *GP* I 19 p. 30; **12..** nisi in paupertatem deciderint vel erumpnam *Deeds Newcastle* 43; vidit mulierem..que, extincto paulo ante filio, fratrem ejus jam morti proximum tenebat..et preteritam pariter et presentem testabatur erumpnam *NLA* (*Cuthb.*) I 229; **1434** post hujus exilii erumpnas *Pri. Cold.* 108.

aerumnare, to harass.

1559 insectatores..statum..sanctae Scoticanae ecclesiae ..in totum ~are, tollere et subvertere nitentes *Conc. Scot.* II 141.

aerumnose, wretchedly.

ignominiose nimis et ~e, tanquam talione suscepta, stirpitus [expelli] meruerunt GIR. *PI* III 30.

aerumnosus [CL], wretched, distressing.

961 in hoc erumpnoso dejectus seculo *CS* 1066; vae ~us dolor de ~o errore filiorum Adae! ANSELM (*Ep.* 117) III 253; istius †erumni [? l. erumnosi] seculi laudem querunt (*Text. Roff.* 70) *MonA* I 165; ~am..vite istius viam..contemnere docent GIR. *TH* I 12; hec..anima..rapietur ab illuvione terrena et erumpnosa cohabitacione nostra *NLA* (*Edith*) I 312.

aes [CL], copper, bronze, or brass. **b** (w. *ductile*) copper wire. **c** (w. *ustum*) calcined copper. **d** (w. *viride*) verdigris.

aes tinnit ALDH. *PR* 131 p. 180; [Brittania] venis metallorum, aeris, ferri et plumbi et argenti fecunda BEDE *HE* I 1; est [tintinnabulum] de antiquo veterum opere, ubi minus stagni adicitur, plus de ere R. COLD. *Cuthb.* 81; originalia.. in quibus aqueitas et terrestritas magis dominatur, sicut aurum, argentum, es, ferrum BACON V 129; **1316** in renovacione eris cujuslibet molendini simul cum iiij li. eris emptis ad idem *Cart. Glam.* 832; hoc es, ~ris, A. *brasse* WW. **b** *wyre*, ereductile [? *for* ere ductili] *CathA*. **c** calcucecumenon, i. es ustum; calciton idem *SB* 14; esustum, A. *brende bras, calcemonie* WW. **d** argelzarus, viride es idem *Alph.* 16.

2 money. **b** (esp. w. *alienum*) debt.

ad thecam..in qua es regium servabatur AILR. *Ed. Conf.* 746B; ut exiguo dominum mutaverit ere HANV. IV 306; ēris servus ēris, si te species trahit ēris SERLO WILT. 2. 37. **b** ~e alieno, *geabuli GlC* A 321; liberales sunt qui..es alienum amicorum suscipiunt W. MALM. *GR* IV 313; **1260** ere alieno oneratus *Cl* 217; s**1302** quod..eum eiceret ab omni ere alieno W. GUISB. 352; **1360** monasterium..ere alieno depressum *Cart. Ciren.* I no. 140; **1527** cogor effari ex hac humanitate tua me tam in aere tuo esse ut.. (*Lit. L. Cox*) *Ep. Erasm.* VII 1803.

aesca v. esca.

aesculum, fruit, (?) medlar.

s**1257** coctana, escula, cerasa et pruna et omnes fructus qui in testa continentur..perierunt annullata M. PAR. *Maj.* IV 660.

aesculus [CL], (?) kind of oak. **b** beech. **c** (?) medlar.

quem..decumbere sub umbra vident ~i tortuose W. MAP *NC* IV 11 p. 180; quercus et horrenti crudescit conjuga rusco / esculus Hanv. IV 293; antiquis gratas quondam dedit esculus escas Neckam *DS* VIII 57. **b** ~us, *boece GlC* A 304 (cf. ib. 342: aesolus, genus arboris); ~us, *boc* Ælf. *Gl.* **c** hec mespulus, *a meltre*; hoc mespulum, fructus ejus; hec esculus, fructus ejus WW.

aesia v. aisia, hesa. aesiamentum v. aisiamentum.

aesnecia [OF *ainzneece*], 'esnecy', privilege of eldest coheir.

si fuerit liber sokemannus [qui moriatur], tunc quidem dividetur hereditas inter omnes filios..per partes equales .., salvo tamen capitali mesuagio primogenito filio pro dignitate aesnescie sue Glanv. VII 3; **1195** Hawisa..petit.. medietatem tocius terre..et hainesciam ut soror primogenita *CurR PR* XIV 30; **1198** aisnecia..sicut ei qui habet primogenitam *CurR RC* I 147; **1199** pro habenda parte sua de terra..ex parte Margarete uxoris sue cum esnecia *Pipe* 253; **1200** salva asnecia ipsius Matillidis *CurR* I 350; **1201** illam terram que habet ei descendere a C. filia R...cum einescia *Ib.* 447; **1200** idem comes assignavit filie sue priori natu capud honoris sui..cum esneseya *RChart* 52b; **1204** concessimus Ricardo et Ade uxori sue aysneciam ipsius Ade *Ib.* 132a; **1204** pro habenda rationabili parte que contingit Agnetem..et pro habenda etnesceia terre illius *Pipe* 77; **1220** dicit quod ipse est de sorore primogenita et petit aesneciam *CurR* VIII 215; **1233** salva..esnechia de hereditate *Cl* 540; **1240** cum primogenita nihil petere possit plus quam minor nisi capitale mesuagium nomine eylnesce (*Breve Regis*) M. Par. *Maj.* IV 13; **1241** tam in terris et tenementis quam in libertatibus et liberis consuetudinibus ad esneciam pertinentibus (*ChartR* 15) *EHR* XXXV 54; per sortem assignetur utrique parti sua medietas, salva tamen ipsi A. sua aesnescia Bracton 73; **1260** ille qui habet einesciam hereditatis illius unicam faciat sectam..et participes sui pro portione sua contribuant ad sectam illam faciendam *Cl* 146; **1267** juxta eineciam suam *Cl* 367; **1280** tenent de inechia heredum *JustIt* 762 r. 60 (cf. ib. 759 r. 7: ennech[ia]); preferenda erit soror antenata nepoti vel nepti ex filia primogenita [ante parentes mortua] quantum ad aesneciam *Fleta* 314; **1292** ut ei qui habuit statum eynecye *PQW* 113a; ille qui eneyam, id est capitalem partem, hereditatis illius habet unicam sectam faciat (*Fragm. Collecta* 20) *APScot* I 368.

aesnecius, eldest. **b** (sb. f.) eldest coheiress.

1198 defendit totum sicut homo qui etatem excessit vel per filium suum esnecum *CurR* I 39; **c1330** si dominus.. eyniceam filiam suam maritaverit et petat auxilium *MonA* III 41b; **1268** Aliciam..eynesciam heredem..Walteri *Cl* 546; **s1316** Johannam enecyam, unam earum [sororum], desponsavit filius domini W. (*Chr. Croxden*) *MonA* V 661; **1324** exivit de Isabella, eynecia sorore..Adomari *IPM* 83 r. 33; **1327** eynecia filia et una heredum Ricardi *KRMem* 103 r. 189; **1358** filia enesia *IPM* 139/21 r. 4; **1364** Isabella, que fuit soror eignecia, vel heredes sui haberent primam presentacionem *Reg. Heref.* 19; **1497** Philippe unius et ennicie filiarum..Johanne *FineR* 308 m. 9. **b 1233** Ricardus exivit de masculo et de aennescia *CurR* XV 797; **1281** Willelmus est de aenecia *PQW* 768a; **1315** petiit propartem..Alienore uxoris sue sibi et eidem Alienore tanquam einecie deliberari *RParl* I 353b.

2 pertaining to the eldest.

1348 eyneciam partem *CalIPM* IX p. 93; **14..** ille qui habet eniciam partem hereditatis illius sectam illam faciet *Reg. Brev.* 176b.

aesnus [AS *æsne*], poor man or serf.

uni ~o [AS: *anan esne*] (id est inopi) contingunt ad victum xii pondia bone annone (*Rect. 8, Quad.*) *GAS* 449.

aestas [CL], summer. **b** (w. *magna*) great summer (astrol.).

prole virens aestate, tabescens tempore brumae Aldh. *Aen.* 1. 4; ~as, illo [sole] superfervente calida [est] et sicca Bede *TR* 35; nolo pascere eos [equos] in ~ate [AS: *on sumera*], eo quod nimium comedunt Ælf. *Coll.* 96; dabant iii denarios in hieme et ii in ~ate *DB* I 1; ver, autumpnus, hyems, estas dominantur in anno D.Bec. 2793; estas tunc incipit quando sol ingreditur primum gradum Cancri et continet 92 dies et 23 horas et terciam partem hore unius, hoc est a 23 die Junii usque 24 diem Septembris Bacon V 77; Lyndw. 194b (v. aestuare 1d). **b** ab istis [corporibus celestibus] orbis terrarum plage..certis temporum vicibus suas magnas hyemes et ~ates (ut Aristotelico utar verbo) recipiunt: magna autem ~as dicitur cum aliqua provincia ex nimia siccitate et fervore ita sterilescit ut diutius inhabitatores fovere nequeat Robyns: *Com.* 51.

aestifer [CL], torrid.

estifere radiis ardere Sienes Hanv. VII 345.

aestimabilis, reckonable. **b** apprehensible by judgement. **c** 'estimative' (*cf. aestimativus*).

in quibus multa circa idem varie estimata aut ~ia, ut 'an dies sit tempus a mane usque ad mane' Balsh. *AD.* 176. **b** ultra istam maneriem noscibilium sunt aliqua ~ia ut appendicie rerum materialium, quas nec sensus nec ymaginacio sufficit apprehendere, sed estimativa potencia Wycl. *Dom. Div.* II 3 p. 185. **c** secundum comparationem virtutis active ad virtutem ymaginabilem et ~em J. Blund *An.* 335.

aestimantia, judgement, discernment.

nullum brutum cognoscit omne ens sensibile sensu exteriori vel interiori, ut sunt omnia sensibilia, et habitudines quas animal natum est elicere secundum ~iam, ut sunt amicicie et inimicicie cum similibus multis Wycl. *Ente* I i 1 p. 9.

aestimare [CL], to value, esteem, appraise. **b** to estimate (the amount of).

non es, o crux admirabilis, ~anda secundum intentionem crudelis insipientiae Anselm (*Or.* 4) III 11; abbas [Robertus, ob. 1166]..munera, que fere ad cc marcas ~abantur, ..distribuit *G. S. Alb.* I 127; **c1283** ~atur dictum cariagium ad xv dolea *Cust. Battle* 15; isti parum reputant de persona pape, licet forte de officio pape multum ~ent Ockham *Dial.* 735; **1373** equitatis tramite benigniter extimato (*TreatyR*) *Foed.* VII 18; **1463** pro custuma lxx pellium.. venditarum absque custuma sed ~atarum.. in numero dictarum pellium *ExchScot* 220; **1510** consueverunt..carnes in eorum macellis lacerare et extimare publice *RBOssory* 264. **b 1254** sive bladum vendatur mensuratum sive extimatum *RGasc* I 546.

2 to judge, adjudge, suppose. **b** (w. compl., acc. and inf., or *quod*) to consider. **c** (w. inf.) to intend.

extimat, suspicatur *GlC* E 521; Romam adire curavit, quod..magnae virtutis ~abatur Bede *HE* IV 23; quod ~ato frequentius accidit Balsh. *AD* 105; ~aretur ut mortuus *Mir. Montfort* 78; actu eciam ~abit de convenienti Duns *Metaph.* I 2 p. 13a. **b** ~abat eum insanire Bede *HE* II 13; ne ~arentur primordiales causas..creatoris earum..cognitionem..superare Eriug. *Per.* 552C; alii Eadmundum..~ant preferendum Ailr. *Edw. Conf.* 741D; extimant quidam putrefactionem..accidere non posse nisi.. Gilb. I 9. 1; **1288** cum extimari posset et dici hec propter injusticiam illatam..civi nostro..evenisse (*Lit. Consulum etc. Bononiae*) *AncC* LV 10; congregacionem que a multitudine fidelium generale concilium ~atur Ockham *Dial.* 826; **s1352** ~antes Anglici quod fiebat nusquam verum esse J. Reading 163. **c** extimavi secreta nature intelligentibus revelare (M. Scot *Alch.* 1) *Med. Sci.* 151; **c1350** estimat elatus Anglorum corda vorare *Pol. Poems* I 42.

aestimatio [CL], valuation, reckoning.

est mensura ejusdem insulae juxta ~onem Anglorum MCC familiarum Bede *HE* IV 16; **774** hujus terrae ~o v aratrorum esse videtur *CS* 213; ~o, *æhtunge* Ælf. *Sup.* 190; **1251** obviaverunt quibusdam malefactoribus..per ~onem duodecim *SelPlForest* 99; **p1254** ~o ecclesiarum decanatus Landavie facta per Eneam *Val. Norw.* 314; **1255** si.. dampnificaretur in redditibus.., volumus quod bona ~one servetur indempnis *RGasc* I 11; **1333** due partes purpresturarum destructe..fuerunt ad ~onem valoris ij parcium earundem *LTRMem* 105 r. 33; **1358** summa infra ~onem (*Ac. Ox.*) *EHR* XXIV 743; **1454** xxx librarum..secundum communem ~onem *Reg. Brechin.* 400; **1504** pro..detentione ..proficuorum extendentium ad xx li...ad bonam ~onem *Reg. Paisley* 62; **1546** gardinum continens per ~onem plus minus rodam terre *Cart. Osney* III 3.

2 judgement, discernment, apprehension (*cf. ALMA* XXII 171–83).

accipe..rationem quae non solum praescientia sed et ~one aut qualibet suspicione suum eum [apostatam angelum] praesensisse casum excludit Anselm (*Casus Diab.* 21) I 267; [ira et acedia] veram de proximis exstinguunt ~onem Ad. Scot *TT* 701D; intentio est res accepta ab ~one non cadens in sensum, ut mediante sensu apprehendatur ab anima J. Blund *An.* 257; ultra omnem ~onem..uxorem sanam..reperit *Hist. Meriadoci* 354; omne animal, sicut habet sensum ita et aliquam extimacionem Duns *Metaph.* I 3 p. 13a.

aestimative, by estimation. **b** in imagination or hope.

1372 in empcione iiij doliorum vini..~e varii precii, xliiij li. *ExchScot* 369; **1395** unde valor ~e xx li. *Invent. Ch. Ch. Cant.* 100; **s1415** acies illa..~e erat tricesies plures quam omnes nostri Elmh. *Hen. V* 49. **b** cor eodem modo ardere non ~e sed realiter [ME: *not hopingly bot verraly*] sentitur Rolle *IA* 185.

aestimativus, 'estimative', concerned w. judgement or discernment (*cf. aestimatio* 2). **b** (sb. f.) estimative faculty.

cum per vim ~am possit perpendi quid sit verum et quid sit falsum J. Blund *An.* 259; virtus anime sensitive longe nobilior et potentior, et hec vocatur estimatio seu virtus ~a, ut dicit Avicenna.., quam dicit sentire formas insensatas circa sensibilem materiam Bacon *Maj.* II 8 (cf. ib. 75); virtus imaginativa vel ~a apprehendit rationem amicitie vel inimicitie Peckham *Quaest.* I 7 p. 78; Wycl. *Dom. Div.* 185 (v. aestimabilis b). **b** ovis, cum videt lupum, quem nunquam viderat, fugit..propter impressionem factam in ~a Hales *Qu. app.* 1571; a cogitatione et estimatione quibus ovis sentit speciem complexionis lupi inficientem et ledentem organum ~e Bacon *Maj.* II 421; sic species in intellectu..aut in imaginativa vel ~a 'forma' dicitur *Ps.*-Gros. 323; hic non distinguit [Aristoteles].. inter sensum et extimativam Duns *Metaph.* I 3 p. 13a; **a1384** dirigendo ~am ad particularia (Wycl. *Determ.*) *Ziz.* 474.

aestimator, appraiser, reckoner.

aquae Creator atque ~or universitatis Bede *Gen.* (i 18) 21; ~or, *æhtere* Ælf. *Sup.*; sicut modestus ~or asseruit Gir. *PI* III 21.

aestimatus, appraisal.

dictu et ~u indicibilis copia *G. Steph.* I 62.

aestivale v. stivale.

aestivalis, of (occurring in) summer. **b** (of migrant birds). **c** (? w. ref. to May-day king). **d** for use in summer (*v. et. stivale*).

s959 in festo S. Martini ~is Diceto *Chr.* 148; **s1097** die solstitii ~is..imperatori se dedidere W. Malm. *GR* IV 357; **s1241** imminente tempore ~i *Flor. Hist.* II 246; **s1257** continuitas pluviarum ~ium et autumnalium Oxnead *Chr.* 215; ne..contingeret intemperies hiemalis in signis ~ibus Bracton 359b (cf. *BNB* III 301); **1315** navium..in instanti seisona ~i profecturarum *RScot* 138a; summa operum yemalium cccxx; summa operum ~ium c *FormMan* 27; **1330** xl salmones de capcione ~i *ExchScot* 365 (cf. ib. 306: de capcione †estuali); **1345** de pastura ~i super montanam vendita *Comp. Swith.* 146. **b** meruli minuti et ~es hobeli Gir. *TH* I 12. **c** cui [Roberto Bruz] illa: "estimo quod rex ~is sis; forsitan hyemalis non eris" *Flor. Hist.* III 130. **d** ad habitacula vernalia et †aestualia [? l. ~ia] *V. Cuthb.* I 6; **†a1087** homines de Walda debent unam domum ~em quod Anglice dicitur *sumerhus*, invenire *Cart. Bilsington* 15*n.*; abbas [Willelmus, ob. 1367]..fecit aulam ~em *Chr. Evesham* 296; ista sunt inordinata claustralibus..viz.: culcita, ..coperlectile, tunica ~is *Cust. Cant.* 362; **1356** in una supertunica ~i *Ac. Durh.* 22; **c1390** simul cum veste sua ~i et yemali *Mem. York* I 43; **1396** omeliarium unum ~e et aliud omeliarium yemale (*Invent.*) *Meaux* III lxxxiv; **c1457** custodes cistarum ~ium *MunAcOx* 746.

aestivatio, summer pasturing (of cattle).

iiij s...pro ~one ij vaccarum (*MinAc. Stebbing*) *MFG.*

aestivus [CL], of (occurring in) summer. **b** for use in summer. **c** (n. pl.) shady place.

siccior aestivo torrentis caumate solis Aldh. *Aen.* 100. 73; ~os..dies longioribus, brumales vero brevioribus horis includi Bede *TR* 3; ~us dies, *sumorlic dæg* Ælf. *Sup.*; calor..~us maturat Balsh. *AD* 158; tempore ~o reviviscunt Gir. *TH* I 20. **b 798** velut vermes fenestris involant ~is Alcuin *Ep.* 143; ibi molinum hiemale non ~um *DB* I 254b. **c** *schadowyng place*, umbraculum, ~a, ~orum, ..*swale*, umbra, umbraculum, estiva *PP.*

2 hot.

tibi quoque ~i Acherontis voragines..hiscunt Felix *Guthl.* 31.

aestualis, concerned w. heat or (?) *f.l.* for *aestivalis* (*v. et. aestivalis*).

ista signa dicuntur ascendentia, item calida et sicca, juvenilis, estualis, colerica Bacon IX 199 (in figura).

aestuanter, hotly (fig.), fiercely.

s1455 dux de Eboraco..~er iracundie faculam in camino sui pectoris incendebat *Reg. Whet.* I 160.

aestuare [CL], to blaze. **b** to burn w. fever. **c** (trans.) to glow with. **d** to usher in summer.

~antibus solis ignibus Gir. *TH* I 13; **1457** tempore quo ignis ~abat in regali collegio *Arch. Hist. Camb.* III 12*n.* **b** quartanarii magis ~ant..ad partes exteriores Gad. 15 v. 2. **c** rex [Oswaldus]..indutus chlamydem vel auro rigentem vel Tyricos murices ~antem W. Malm. *GR* I 49 p. 52. **d** aestas incipit ibi [in festo S. Urbani, viii Cal. Jun.] et terminatur ix Cal. Sept. in festo S. Bartholomei..: unde versus: 'dat Clemens hyemem; dat Petrus ver Cathedratus; / estuat Urbanus; autumnat Bartholomeus' Lyndw. 194b.

2 to burn with desire. **b** (w. inf.). **c** (w. *ad*).

doce me..qua satietate ~abas Anselm (*Or.* 13) III 53; fatetur sodalibus in amore..virginis sese nimium ~are *G. Herw.* 325; servus..desiderio esus..avium ~abat R. Cold. *Cuthb.* 27. **b** discordia orta est inter fratres propter regnum, quia uterque totam insulam possidere ~abat G. Mon. II 6 (cf. ib. I 9: adire ~abat). **c** praeter haec libidinis ardens sine intermissione ~abat ad coitum Osb. *V. Dunst.* 25; **1290** abbas ..ad parentum suorum divicias accumulandas ~ans *Mon. Hib. & Scot.* 155a.

aestuarium [CL; cf. OF *estier*], tidal inlet or channel, estuary.

~ia, *fleotas GlC* A 319; **1288** per quod esterium derivatur aqua ad Gyrundam vel mare *RGasc* II 289; **1291** ab esterio in quo est fons novus *Ib.* III 25.

aestuarius, tidal, surging, boiling (fig.).

1515 plus quam ~iis irarum fluctibus *Conc.* III 659.

aestuatio, heating. **b** fever heat.

cavendum est ei ne..importunis ~onibus vexet illud [argentum] atque consumat *Dial. Scac.* I 6 G. **b** iste finis habet tria tempora, sc. tempus ~onis et commotionis, tempus principii evacuationis materie et tempus consumptionis materie Bacon IX 187; [in febre quartana] diutius durat ~o Gad. 15 v. 2.

2 tidal ebb and flow. **b** upheaval.

in mari fiunt per certas lunationes ~ones fluxus et refluxus inundationes, ut in mari Britannico apertius apparet Gerv. Tilb. I 5. **b** sub gravissimi temporis ~one *Cart. Glam.* 90.

aestus [CL], heat. **b** (fig.; *cf. Matt.* xx 12).

597 contra ~um auras, contra frigus vestem..quaerere (*Lit. Papae*) Bede *HE* I 27 p. 56; ~us vel cauma, *swolop* Ælf. *Sup.*; non auram..~u periculosam..formidamus Gir. *TH* I 37. **b 1234** ut portantibus pondus diei et estus abbas..vel..prior..faciant procurari (*Vis. Bury*) *EHR* XXVII 733.

2 tide. **b** (fig.) fluctuation, perturbation.

~us oceani nunc vespertinus post xv dies fit matutinus Bede *TR* 29; ~us, recessus et accessus maris, *yst* Ælf. *Sup.*; navim mitius ventus et ~us inquietabant W. Cant. *Mir. Thom.* III 47. **b** quod..tam interioris hominis ~us quam exterioris gestus..sanaretur Aldh. *VirgP* 25 p. 258; multis cepit cogitationum ~ibus affici Bede *HE* II 12; frons, oculi, gestus exponunt pectoris estus Serlo Wilt. 2. 21.

aesus v. esus. aesya v. aisia. aet v. et.

aetas [CL], age (human). **b** tender age, childhood. **c** old age. **d** age group.

aetatis decimus necnon et tertius annus ALDH. *VirgV* 1928; multitudinem..condicionis diversae et ~atis BEDE *HE* I 7 p. 20; si cum materia calida complectio calida, tempus anni, regio, etas conveniant RIC. MED. *Signa* 34; etas..dicitur..tercio modo pro parte determinata vite humane: ..dicunt quidam esse 4 etates vite humane, alii 6, alii 7 BACON VI 5. **b** ~ate tenellus ALDH. *VirgP* 53; innocuae..parvulorum ~ati BEDE *HE* II 20; profundius disputas quam ~as nostra [AS: *yld ure*] capere possit ÆLF. *Coll.* 101; a prima etate annisque pueritie GIR. *TH* III 48; si..judicetur minoris etatis, minoris gaudebit privilegio GLANV. XIII 17; **1345** ita tenere etatis sunt quod nesciunt adhuc seipsos gubernare *Hal. Durh.* 18. **c** Theodorus.. vir..~ate venerandus, id est annos habens ~atis lx et vi BEDE *HE* IV 1; non etas Nestora sed mens / fecit eum SERLO WILT. 15. 27; **1225** postea cecidit in etatem et fuit impotens sui, et tunc posuit se in custodiam..nepotis sui *CurR* XII 1075; **1408** in magna etate existens, sanitate votiva non perfruens *Lit. Cant.* III 108. **d** facto ab omni ~ate, ab omni sexu..concursu W. CANT. *Mir. Thom.* VI 26; **s1190** venit contra regem omnis ~as, populus sine numero DEVIZES 29.

2 legally defined age: **a** majority (over 21, 15 etc.); **b** age of judicial combat (under 60).

a cum heres, nunc minor, legittime etatis adeptus beneficia sibi suisque disponere noverit *Dial. Scac.* II 10c; tene[n]tur heredes ipsi esse sub custodia dominorum suorum donec plenam habuerint etatem, ..quod sit post xxj annum completum si fuerit heres et filius militis vel per feodum militare tenentis; si vero heres et filius sokemanni fuerit, etatem habere intellegitur cum xv compleverit annos; si vero fuerit filius burgensis, ..cum discrete sciverit denarios numerare et pannos ulnare et alia negotia paterna similiter exercere GLANV. VII 9 (cf. ib. 12: donec plenariam habeant etatem); **1199** pro habenda custodia terre et heredum.. donec heredes etatis fuerint *Pipe* 16; **1200** ad recognoscendum si ipse fuit etatis vel non, scilicet de xxj annis *CurR* I 362; **1216** cum [talis heres] ad etatem pervenerit, sc. xxj anni, habeat hereditatem suam *Magna Carta Hen. III* 3; **1219** assisa..ponitur in respectum usque ad etatem domini regis *CurR* VIII 5; dicit quod non debet ei respondere, quia videtur ei quod est infra etatem; et, si curia consideraverit quod habeat etatem, libenter ei respondebit *Ib.* 11; **1220** dicit quod est infra etatem et petit etatem suam; et ipsi.. dicunt quod non debet esse majoris etatis, quia terra illa est socagium *Ib.* 226; **1228** si..ante rationabilem etatem suam in fata decesserit *Pat* 183; etas..dicitur..alio modo pro statu vite hominis in quo secundum tempus potest ad opera legitima recipi BACON VI 5; femina plene poterit esse etatis in socagio..cum possit et sciat domui sue disponere et ea facere que pertineant ad dispositionem..domus, ut sciat que pertineant ad *cove and keye*, quod quidem esse non poterit ante xiiij vel xv annum, quia hujusmodi etas requirit discretionem et sensum BRACTON 86b; **1269** omnes masculi laici habentes etatem xij annorum..debent esse in franciplegiagio vel thewinga *CBaron* 68; **1295** fuit plene etatis secundum usum [manerii] quando terram..reddidit sursum; ..et est etas mulieris xiij anni et dim. et etas virilis xiiij anni et dim. *SelPlMan* 121; **1364** non est ad plenam etatem *Hal. Durh.* 34; **1417** volo quod..T. H. habeat wardam cum maritagio W. L. ad terminum etatis sue *Reg. Cant.* II 127; **1468** usque completam ~atem regis xxj anni *ExchScot* 575; tributum in capita..hominum, qui id etatis essent quam jurisconsulti legitimam vocant, impositum est P. VERG. XX 402. **b** declinare potest accusatus in hujusmodi placitis per etatem, per mahemii judicium; etas autem talis esse debet quod sit lx annorum vel supra GLANV. XIV 1; **1198** (v. aesnecius 1a); **1201** offert probare per quendam liberum hominem..qui filiam suam habet in uxorem, pro eo desicut ipse transivit etatem lx annorum *SelPlCrown* 18 (cf. ib. 27: ut homo qui preteriit etatem); **1218** defendit.. feloniam..sicut homo qui etatem transiit et mahematur *EyreYorks* 268; per hoc quod transiit etatem, declinare poterit duellum BRACTON 138b (cf. 142b).

3 age (of animals).

c1280 dabit..ad pannagium pro bestia de etate vj d. et de dim. etate iij d. pro bovetto (*Cust.*) *Crawley* 233; **c1283** debent..pannagiare porcos..sc. pro porco plene etatis ij d. *Cust. Battle* 75 (cf. ib. 89: porcos plenarie etatis).

4 phase or cycle (of moon). **b** annual cycle (of sun).

non aliud quam lunae ~as significatur BEDE *TR* 11 p. 203; luna, ubi suam perfecerit ~atem *Ib.* 18 p. 218; **798** quomodo computare velint ~ates lunares a xv Kal. Maias, ubi quarta decima lune novissimi anni fuit.. ALCUIN *Ep.* 145; *Miss. R. Jum.* 35 (v. altivagus); in prima et tertia etate lunae GILB. II 110. 1. **b** bis novem scribens aetatum lustra ALDH. *VirgV* 332.

5 period of time: **a** lifetime, generation (or people belonging to it); **b** duration of (specified) life; **c** indeterminate period, lapse of time; **d** age (epoch) of world history; **e** eternity (or total duration of time).

a illis decedentibus, cum successisset ~as tempestatis illius nescia GILDAS *EB* 26; per succiduas saeculorum aetates ALDH. *Met.* 5; nec diffidendum est nostra etiam ~ate fieri potuisse quod aevo praecedente aliquoties factum fideles historiae narrant BEDE *HE* IV 17 p. 243; quae res quem sit habitura finem posterior ~as videbit *Ib.* V 23; etas..dicitur..uno modo pro spacio vite cujuslibet hominis BACON VI 5; inter omnes ~atis nostre reges Henricum.. fama anteire LIV. *Hen. V* 1a. **b** iii hidas vendiderat.. cuidam taino..ad ~atem trium hominum; ..et postea debebat redire ad dominium *DB* I 66b; hoc manerium emit ..ad ~atem trium hominum *Ib.* 177a. **c** quod crastina diruat etas / instruit instanter labor irritus HANV. IV 299; illis..que nulla valeat etas destruere GIR. *TH pref.* p. 21. **d** sex ~atibus mundi tempora distinguuntur BEDE *Temp.* 16; primam ~atem mundi Adam inchoavit, secundam Noe innovavit, tertiam Abraham aurora fidei illustravit, quartam Moyses data lege ordinavit, quintam Salomon edificavit, sextam Christus hereditavit R. NIGER 18; primam etatem mundi..dicunt sancti terminatam in diluvio..; secundam..dicunt terminari in confusione linguarum..; terciam incipiunt ab Abraham et terminant in Saul..; quartam incipiunt a David et terminant in transmigracione Babilonis..; quinta incipit a complecione 70 annorum captivitatis et terminatur in Johannem Baptistam..; in Christo sexta etas incepit et durat usque in finem BACON VI 8. **e** aevum vel ~as perpetua, *widerfeorlic* vel *ece* ÆLF. *Gl.*; ejus [summae naturae] ~as, quae nihil aliud est quam ejus aeternitas, non est tota simul sed est partibus extensa per temporum partes ANSELM (*Mon.* 21) I 37; aliter dicitur etas..de toto tempore et statu temporis in mundo isto sensibili BACON VI 7.

aetatula [CL], early age.

tenerrima ~a infantis ALDH. *VirgP* 32 p. 273; ejus ~e pusio W. MALM *GP* I 19 p. 29; in ~a infancie W. DAN. *Ep.* 61d; non sexui parcentes vel parvulorum ~e FORDUN II 25.

aeternabiliter, for eternity.

1472 ~er stabiliri *Mon. Hib. & Scot.* 465b.

aeternalis [LL], eternal, everlasting.

memoria quorum fuerit ~is HERM. ARCH. *prol.*; nobili.. largitate ~is..memorie fructum..comparans *Chr. Rams.* 63; unum est principium ~e BACON VII 57; racio res cum conderet eternalis / et lege sub recta locaret enorme J. HOWD. *Cant* 596; **1435** ut [sit]..anime vestre ~e meritum *FormOx* 445.

aeternalitas, timelessness.

ante mundum sola eternitas non 'ante' temporalitatis vel eviternitatis sed 'ante' solius ~atis fuit *Ps.*-GROS 410.

aeternaliter, eternally, timelessly. **b** for ever, in perpetuity.

[Deus] est..finis omnium quae eum appetunt, ut in eo ~er immutabiliterque quiescant ERIUG. *Per.* 526c; melior est gloria quam ~er possidet inter angelos ALCUIN *Will. P.* 32; **841** sub iram Dei aeterni judicis..~er incumbunt *CS* 432; ad Deum vadetis ~er cum illo victuri OSB. *V. Dunst.* 38; solus Deus ~er est GROS. 140; **1236** Dominus Jesus.. personaliter natus ante tempora ~er de Deo patre *Id. Ep.* 23 p. 84; Deus ~er intuetur omne creatum (KYN.) *Ziz.* 40; ad finem quem Deus ~er ordinavit WYCL. *Ver.* II 69. **b** **c1070** rex..in dotem perpetuam ~er eandem hereditavit ecclesiam *Regesta* I 120; **s1090** Northambrensis comes.. dedit..abbati [S. Albani] ecclesiam de Thinemue pro salute sua et antecessorum suorum ~er possidendam M. PAR. *Min.* I 42; **s1225** ut [Falcasius] Angliam ~er abjuraret omnes..addixerunt *Id. Maj.* III 94; **1453** pro certis continuandis precibus pro anima ipsius ~er sine fine *Reg. Whet.* I 94.

aeternare, to perpetuate, immortalize.

gaudebit..vitale Johannes / eternare jubar HANV. VI 331; hec et consimilia facta, scriptis et laudibus ~anda, fecit abbas Samson BRAKELOND 133 v.; **13..** actus nostros ..quantum possumus ~are debemus (*Hist. S. Crucis*) *Bannatyne Misc.* II 13.

aeternativus, immortalizing.

veris eternativa juventam / floribus ipsa loci deitas nativa perennat HANV. VI 326.

aeternitas [CL], eternity, timelessness. **b** eternal life. **c** everlasting remembrance.

c625 summae divinitatis potentia..quae..invisibili atque investigabili ~ate consistit (*Lit. Papae*) BEDE *HE* II 10; ~as sui similis est ac tota per totum in se ipsa una simplex individuaque subsistit ERIUG. *Per.* 459A; vera ~as principii finisque meta carere intelligitur ANSELM (*Mon.* 24) I 42; illa transeunt, ista cum ~ate contendunt GIR. *EH intr.* p. 214. **b** hereditariam legitimae ~atis sobolem ALDH. *VirgP* 5; ut..ad ~atis gratiam venire concupiscat BEDE *HE* II 1; **1488** sic..quod..cum sanctis..mereatur sortem habere..in perpetuas ~ates *Reg. Whet.* I 453. **c** regis naturam..~ati depingere non indignum reputavi GIR. *EH* I 46.

aeternus [CL], eternal, timeless, everlasting. **b** (sb. n., s. or pl.) eternity. **c** (sb. n. as adv.) eternally.

aeterno regi regum ALDH. *VirgV* 1973; ~a caelestis regni gaudia BEDE *HE* II 5; non est illud praesens temporale, sicut nostrum, sed ~um, in quo tempora cuncta continentur ANSELM (*Praesc.* I 5) II 254; eternos gratia nodos / vix recipit nisi quos eterna pecunia nectit HANV. V 317; ad veram illam invariabilem ~amque felicitatem GIR. *TH* I 12; **1228** ita quod preter mercedem ~am a nobis grates reportare debeant *Pat* 174; **1292** ~am [sc. salutem] in Domino *RScot* 11a. **b** vivens in ~um ALDH. *Met.* 2 p. 63; ruinam de ~is ad temporalia ERIUG. *Per.* 540A; **a799** quid sit inter ~um et sempiternum et perpetuum..et aevum et tempus ALCUIN *Ep.* 163; proficuum ad ~a OCKHAM *Err. Papae* 960; mundus non fuit ab ~o *Id. Dial.* 909; **s1216** nunquam ab ~o fuit visum Anglorum regem..a rege [Scocie] auxilium postulare *Plusc.* VII 7. **c** hostia.. / de qua qui comedent eternum non morientur P. BLOIS *Euch.* 3. 1139C.

aether [CL < αἰθήρ], ether, fiery region above the air. **b** (n. pl.).

cum nimbi fugiunt et fervet torridus aether ALDH. *VirgV* 217; superior [pars mundi] a luna usque ad siderea extremae sperae ~er [dicitur] ERIUG. *Per.* 549C; ~er, *hroder* ÆLF. *Sup.*; licet angelicos stabiliret in aethre ministros WULF. *Swith. prol.* 409; in igne etiam, id est superiori ~ere, ignea animalia..vivunt ADEL. *QN* 5; [Ptolemeus] celum vocat ~era in quo dicit sidera collocari, et corpus contiguatum ~eri dicit aerem BACON *Maj.* II 473. **b** aethera celsa tonant ALDH. *VirgV* 429 (cf. ib. 1989).

2 (?) ceiling (cf. 2 *aer*).

1306 ad bord' sarrand' de uno quercu ad etherem istius solar' *MinAc* (*Norf*) 935/19.

aethera, ~alis, v. aethra, ~alis.

aethereare, to search the ether.

1432 scienciarum liberalium, ..quarum quelibet secum habebat famosissimum preceptorem artis sue, puta..geometrica Euclidem metientem, astronomia Albumazar ~eantem (J. CARPENTER) *MGL* III 460.

aetherius, ~eus [CL < αἰθέριος], ethereal, of ether. **b** of (or rising into) air. **c** celestial. **d** (?) sky-blue.

~ium spatium ERIUG. *Per.* 477A; **10..** ethereus, *se roderlice* WW; ~ei caloris igne GIR. *TH* I 6; circa elementarem regionem ~ea [sc. regio] lucida, a variatione omni sua immutabili essentia immunis existens, motu continuo circulariter incedit SACROB. *Sph.* 79. **b** aethereo non possum vivere flatu ALDH. *Aen.* 16 (*Loligo*) 4; in valle.. montibus ~eis orbiculariter undique conclusa GIR. *IK* I 3. **c** unus ut aethereos per caeli culmina campos / alter sic herebum lustrat ALDH. *VirgV* 764; regis ut aetherei matrem jam credo sequaris BEDE (*Hymn*) *HE* IV 18; idem ipse nunc velut animalis corporis.., nunc velut ~ei, ..supra sidera scandens H. BOS. *LM* 1383. **d** violarum livor ethereus J. HOWD. *Ph.* 1073.

Aethiopicus, Ethiopian.

inter mare Rubrum et mare ~ um BACON *Maj.* I 325; ciminum ~ um *SB* 22; olivam ~ am *Alph.* 3.

Aethiopissa, Ethiopian woman (*cf. Num.* xii 1).

c1120 nigra dicitur hec Ethyopissa quam Moyses noster duxit uxorem OSB. CLAR. *Ep.* 1 (cf. HIGD. II 13 p. 322).

Aethiops [Αἰθίοψ], Ethiopian. **b** dusky, blackened.

1237 nobiscum, qui Greci sumus, conveniunt.. illi qui in prima parte orientis habitant ~es (*Lit. archiep. Constantinop.*) M. PAR. *Maj.* III 460; multi sunt alii ~es his tribus populis..copulati BACON *Maj.* I 313; a Chus usque nunc ~es dicti sunt Chusei HIGD. II 7. **b** Phebe ferrugine vultus / ethiopes odit HANV. V 323.

aethra [CL < αἴθρα], sky, heaven. **b** weather.

adduci merear Christo regnante per aethram! ALDH. *VirgV* 2904; angelicum superam numen recucurrit ad ethram FRITH. 1257; **s1119** hec [merita]..defunctum..super ethra tulerunt W. MALM. *GP* II 74 p. 152; **1345** †etheram [v.l. citharam] exultacionis in luctum tristicie..convertentes (*Lit. Papae*) AD. MUR. 185. **b** hec ethera, *the wethyr* WW.

aethralis, coming from the sky. **b** heavenly.

Helias..iniquorum terrae imbres adimens aetherales GILDAS *EB* 71. **b** quem Deus aethrali ditavit gratia gratis ALDH. *VirgV* 526; arbiter aethralis jussit me hoc semper habere BONIF. *Aen.* 1 124; altus auctor ~ium atque aeterne rex angelorum EGB. *Pont.* 127; **964** (11c) Christus pace qui perhenni regnat ~i in arce (*Lit. Ep. Worc.*) *CS* 1136; aethralem vitam testatur jure sequendam FRITH. 1330.

aetiatus [αἰτιατός], caused.

[Johannes] Damascenus [*Fid. Orthod.* I 8]..'differenciam ..' inquit '..personarum in solis tribus proprietatibus, anetio, sc. incausabili et paternali, et †etiaci, id est causabili et filiali, et causabili et processibili..' DUNS *Sent.* I 26. 4.

aetiam v. etiam.

aëtites [ἀετίτης], 'eagle-stone'.

in mensa fraudes hostis manifestat ëtites, / quem gratum nosti, prepes adunce, tibi NECKAM *DS* VI 247; aquila ponit in nido lapidem nomine †achathem [ME: *achate*], quia nichil venenosum potest lapidem contingere *AncrR* 42; aetitis sex sunt species *LC* 220.

aëtus [ἀετός], eagle (? Aristotle's μελανάετος).

preter quandam speciem aquile quam Aristo[teles] vocat †athat, que cogitat de pullis suis magno tempore BART. ANGL. XII 2.

aevatio, measure of duration of heavenly beings.

alia [vita] est celestium, que dicitur evum; unde dicitur quod ~o mensura vite nobilis que a celestibus participatur BACON VII 32.

aevitaneus, everlasting.

14.. evitaneus, A. *withoute end* WW.

aevitas [CL *var. of* aetas], age.

~as, aetas, aeternitas *GlC* A 336.

aeviternitas, continuance throughout time (*cf. aevum* 2b).

Ps.-GROS. 410 (v. aeternalitas).

aeviternus, enduring throughout time (but not timeless). **b** (sb. n.) infinite duration.

[opiniones vulgate] ponunt quod.., sicut forma variatur in rebus, sic evum multiplicatur in ~is BACON *Maj.* I. 165; quecumque temporalia ~aque, localia, preterita presentiaque futuraque intelligere *Ps.*-GROS. 443; dicunt alii quod sunt plura eva, quia sunt plura ~a que non reducuntur ad unum DUNS *Metaph.* V 10 61C; angelus dicitur ~us, quia non coexistit toti tempori possibili fuisse in preterito sed quia coexistit toti tempori futuro et possibili fore; Deus autem dicitur eternus, quia non potest non coexistere cuicumque tempori existenti vel possibili fuisse vel possibili fore *Ps.*-Ockham *Princ. Theol.* 104. **b** cum duratio ~i, ut cujuslibet mensurati evo, sit infinita Bacon *Tert.* 192; si in ~o idem est fuisse et fore, impossibile est cogitare ipsum non fore Duns *Sent.* II ii. 6.

aevum [CL], period of time, esp. human life-time or generation. **b** age, stage in growth or maturity.

aevus, tempus *GlC* A 303 (cf. ib. 341, E 357); integris totum servantem legibus aevum Aldh. *VirgV* 303; Bede *HE* IV 17 (v. aetas 5a); aevoque sequenti / addidit Arctois borealia sceptra triumphis Frith. 555. **b** cum forte foret felix praecursor adultus / atque prophetali jam maturesceret aevo Aldh. *VirgV* 406; quamvis in tenero pulcher pubesceret aevo *Ib.* 1263; rugosa genam producto dactylus evo Hanv. IV 294.

2 time without end. **b** (dist. from timeless eternity).

arbiter aeternum mihi jam miserescat in aevum Aldh. *VirgV* 2876; os gehennae, in quo quicumque semel inciderit numquam inde liberabitur in ~um Bede *HE* V 12; quid sit inter..saeculum et aevum et tempus.. Alcuin *Ep.* 163; **822** liberata permaneat in aefum *CS* 870; quid Julio.. gloriam in evum accumulavit? Gir. *EH* II 31. **b** intellectus noster..habet posse ad 'semper', non temporis sed evi Hales *Qu.* 563; evum vel solum habet dimensionem linearum, si ponamus evum esse divisibile; ..tunc sic est de evo sicut de tempore, propter quod erit unum et non plura; aut evum erit indivisibile, et tunc erit ad eviterna sicut locus indivisibilis ad puncta Bacon *Maj.* I 166; alii dicunt quod evum est unum omnium Duns *Metaph.* V 10. 61B; evum angeli est omnino simplex, coexistens toti tempori *Id. Sent.* I xxxix 1. 10.

afeit- v. affait-.

Afer [CL], African (adj. or sb.). **b** (w. *avis*; *cf.* Horace: *Epod.* 2. 53).

Hadrianus, vir natione Afir Bede *HE* IV 1; Rogerius in gladio suo inscribi fecit id triumphale..: 'Appulus et Calaber, Siculus mihi servit et Afer' Gerv. Tilb. III 19 p. 943; Africa dicitur ab uno posteriorum Abrahe, ut dicit Hieronymus, ..qui vocatur Afer; qui dicitur..ejus posteros Afros..nuncupasse Bacon *Maj.* I 315; radius solaris per continuam permanenciam super Afros exhauriendo eorum humores efficit corpore breviores, cute nigriores, crine crispiores Higd. I 7. **b** Afram avem..non querant appositis que ibi inveniuntur deliciis W. Fitzst. *Thom. prol.* 10.

afet, afeys-, afeyt-, v. affait-.

affaber [LL], skilful.

crafty, artificiosus, faber, ~er; ..*wyse*, ..effaber, faber *CathA*.

affabilis [CL], affable, courteous.

671 vestrae caritatis ~i praesentia frui Aldh. *Ep.* 1; ~is omnibus qui ad se consolationis gratia veniebant Bede *HE* IV 26; ~is, *wordwynsum* Ælf. *Gl.*; Godwynus..jocunda et promta affabilitate omnibus ~is *V. Ed. Conf.* 38 v; lenis et ~is, mitis et amabilis, injuriarum..indultor Gir. *TH* III 49; hilaris et amabilis valde, omni [v.l. omnibus] †effabilis, benignus et modestus *Plusc.* IX 31.

affabilitas [CL], affability, courtesy.

hujus sancte ~ati se commendare gloriatur Gosc. *Edith* 63; cum primum mortales per agros passim et ferali more sine mutua ~ate..vagarentur Adel. *ED* 18; quicquid ~atis, facetie, largitatis a quovis..nobili potest expeti Map *NC* V 3.

affabiliter, affably, courteously.

celsitudinem vestram ~er alloquens Aldh. *Met.* 5; **995** (12c) pro fidissimo quo mihi ~er obsecundatus est obsequio *CD* 692; **10..** ~er, *luflice* WW; **1413** cui nos ~er et suaviter recitavimus quomodo excommunicatus..est (*Proc. v. J. Oldcastel*) *Ziz.* 443.

affabre [CL], skilfully

~e, *cræftlice* vel *smicere* Ælf. *Sup.*

affadillus v. asphodelus.

affaitare, ~iare [OF *afaitier*; cf. affectare 6], to 'enter', train: **a** hounds; **b** hawks.

a a**1190** pro uno bracheto..afietando ad porcum et cervum inveniendum ut limer *E. Ch. Chesh* no. 7; **1222** per servicium ~andi j limarium *LTRMem* 4 r. 3 (5); **1235** ad currendum ad cervos..cum canibus cerverettis ad illos afeyteiandos *Cl* 84; **1250** affetandi et custodiendi j limerium *Fees* 1200; **1275** per servicium afeysandi quemdam berselettum *Hund* II 6. **b** **1204** ad follos falcones suos ~andos *Pipe* 63; **1221** ad afeitiandum quendam stultum girefalconem nostrum *Cl* 449b; **1239** ad aves affeitiendas *Cal. Liberate* I 420 (cf. ib. 64 [**1228**]: affetiandos); **1243** ad ~andos falcones nostros..donec predicti falcones ~entur *Liberate* 19 m. 2.

affaitatio, training (of hawks).

1243 pro expensis suis..in afeitacione cujusdam girofalconis nostri et pro duobus equis quos amisit in ~one ejusdem girofalconis *Liberate* 19 m. 6.

†affaitus [OF *afait*], wrought.

1281 in ferris †aseitis [? l. afeitis] ad equum domini W. (*Ac. Pri. Wint.*) *EHR* LXI 103.

affalcare, (?) to trespass against in mowing.

1280 vadit legem Philippo..de quadam transgressione eidem facta, quod ~averit illum die S. Johannis Baptiste *CourtR Hales* 148.

affaleisire [cf. falesia, infalisiare], to punish by throwing over a cliff (Cinque Ports).

1234 recordum [hundredi de Fasebergh', Suss'] tale est.. quod ~itus fuit sine vicecomite et sine coronatoribus *CurR* XV 1106.

affamen [LL], address, salutation.

angelus Domini.., gratiosus incessu, dulcis ~ine Gosc. *Aug. Maj.* 87; dulci eam precari et ortari cepit ~ine ut surgeret *Arthur & Gorlagon* 154.

affari [CL], to address, speak to. **b** to be interrogated. **c** (p. ppl. as sb. n.) matter discussed.

levavit eum et quasi familiari voce ~atus..inquit.. Bede *HE* II 12 p. 110; visum est illi [Bruto] deam ante ipsum astare et sese in hunc modum ~ari G. Mon. I 11 (= *Eul. Hist.* II 211: sibi..~ari); secrecius ~atur rex Parium Map *NC* III 3 p. 127. **b** **1259** cum a..senescallo.. fueritis requisiti seu ~ati *RGasc* I *sup.* lxxxviii; s**1257** responderunt..de predictis articulis et multis aliis unde ~ati fuerunt *Leg. Ant. Lond.* 32; ~atus simpliciter a quodam cenobita cur non uteretur regalibus vestimentis, respondit.. J. Lond. *Commend. Ed. I* 5. **c** s**1353** inter alia ~ata dicti parliamenti fiebant statuta popularium, viz... J. Reading 164.

affarium [OF *afaire*], estate, tenement (Gasc.).

1255 ~ium suum..de Rion et alias possessiones suas *RGasc* I *sup.* 46; **1289** que ad nos pertinent..racione ~ii seu tenementi de N. *Ib.* II 369 (cf. ib. 356: pro auffario de B.); **1312** de redditibus et exitibus castri et ~ii de Sono *Ib.* IV 977.

affata, v. affari c, cassare 1 c.

affatim [CL], plentifully. **b** (? by conf. w. *affari*) eloquently. **c** (? by conf. w. *statim*) at once.

e quibus affatim saturantur pectora plebis Aldh. *VirgV* 2034; quod fuit affatim factum, donante Tonante Alcuin *SSEbor.* 75; **10..** ~im, *genihtsum*, ..*genihtsumlice* WW; familia..spoliis ~im jam refecta Gir. *EH* II 17; castellum.. quod armis et victualibus ~im communivit *V. Ric. II* 60; *fulsomly*, fatim *CathA*. **b** adfatim, optime loquens *GlC* A 219; aphatim pro 'abunde' corripitur, sed pro 'facunde' producitur Bacon *Tert.* 260. **c** adfatim, habundanter, mox vel statim *GlC* A 213; hinc quasi apertis celis..~im rapitur ad sanctorum sollemnia Gosc. *Edith* 52.

1 affatus [CL], conversation. **b** written communication.

rex..~u jucundus et moribus civilis Bede *HE* III 14; puellarum ~ibus et cithararum modulis usque ad vesperam delectantur Gir. *DK* I 10. **b** **1297** licet epistolares ~us.. tanto patri..dirigendos..non scripserimus *Reg. Cant.* II 531.

2 affatus v. cassare 1 c. affeagium v. affidagium.

affectabilis, desirable.

valeat vestre sanctitatis ~is incolumitas in Christo Ad. Marsh *Ep.* 82.

affectanter, keenly, eagerly.

1220 cupientes ~er vos videre (*AncC* IV 33) *RL* I 99.

affectare [CL], to desire, strive (after). **b** (w. dat.). **c** (w. inf.). **d** (w. acc. and inf.). **e** (w. *quod*). **f** to intend.

veram patriam..totis nisibus ~are Gir. *TH* I 12; cor non affectat quod non oculi nota spectat Serlo Wilt. 1. 1; anime sunt nomina plura: / ..cor est / quando quid affectat Garl. *Syn.* 1578A; **1262** vestram prosperitatem..tanquam propriam ~antes (*AncC* III 41) *Foed.* I 741; cum..regis comodum pocius ~are debuisset quam..abbatis *State Tri. Ed. I* 50; **1302** absolucionem et inhibicionem..ad vestram ~atam, sicut credimus, noticiam censuimus deducenda[s] *Reg. Cant.* II 764; nihil sibi impossibile videtur de omnibus que ~at Rolle *IA* 194. **b** **1254** tenemur..fratris nostri utilitatis augmento animosius ~are *RGasc* I 474. **c** Anglorum affectantes opibus substitui Serlo Gram. *Bell. Stand.* 59; affectant..nostras invadere terras Garl. *Tri. Eccl.* 136; **1293** multum ~at terram..Walteri habere *RParlIned.* 42; **1338** ~antes gratitudinem vestram..premiare (*RGasc.*) *Foed.* V 17; comes Flandrie..talem bullam..abbati transmittere ~abat Elmh. *Cant.* 123; **1509** te magnificare ~amus *Reg. Merton* 380. **d** **1452** ~avit..nos eligere viam procedendi secundum statuta *MunAcOx* 631. **e** quod constitucionis conditor respondeat, ardenter ~o Ockham *Pol.* I 293. **f** **1294** omni mora ~ata postposita (*Tractatus*) B. Cotton 242.

2 to affect, assume ostentatiously.

in habitu mediocritatem est secutus, ita ut..nec essent exquisite sordes nec ~ate delicie H. Bos. *Thom.* III 6.

3 to register emotion.

nullius histrionis sales..adeo placent mihi ut istius infantuli: cum ~at, letitia afficior [*gl.*; ~are est affectus animi vultus mutatione declarare] Neckam *NR* II 157.

4 to inspect, approve.

1268 legamus..xx li. ..pro anniversario nostro annis singulis faciendo, quod anniversarium ~etur per visum domini P. [et al.] antequam satisfiat eis de pecunia supradicta (*Testamentum*) *Camd. Misc.* XIV 4.

5 to offer, make available.

tumor Thamesinus..intrare volentibus non nisi navigio aliquam ~abat viam Flete *Westm.* 40.

6 to train (hawks); *cf. affaitare.*

1243 ad quendam girefalconem ~andum *RGasc.* I 254.

affectatio [CL], effort.

nolebat summus artifex..plus illud [lignum] distorqueri aut infructuosis ~onibus exhumectari G. Crispin *Herl.* 88.

affectativus, arousing desire.

quando offertur artifici forma operis, complacet sibi primo simpliciter in ea; secundo afficitur ex complacentia ad produccionem ejus, et ex tali affeccione dicitur amor ~us qui oritur ex primo Duns *Sent.* II i. 1. 2.

affectator, desirer. **b** pretender; *v. et. assectator.*

adfectatoris, adpetitoris vel amatoris *GlC* A 231. **b** cum illi taliter contrahendo clandestina conjugia non expertes sciencie vel saltem ~ores ignorancie videantur *Fleta* 12.

affecte, eagerly.

prodest boves..stergere cum vispilione, eo quod ~ius se lambebunt *Fleta* 166; **1279** rogantes ~ius Peckham *Ep.* 6; **1410** ~ius quo valeo supplicans *FormOx* 191.

affectio [CL], feeling, emotion. **b** affection, liking. **c** volition, inclination. **d** tendency.

fortes species que immutant animam sensitivam fortiter, ut moveatur ~onibus timoris et horroris et fuge vel contrariis Bacon *Maj.* II 8. **b** adolescens..quem speciali quadam ~one archiepiscopus diligebat Osb. *Mir. Dunst.* 19 p. 146; vulnerate..dilectioni renovata cicatricem obducit ~o Gir. *EH* I 12; **1311** unde necessarius victus, fama et ~o subtrahitur ab eis (*Digby Rolls* I) *CollectOx* II 220; **1442** propter specialem benevolenciam et ~onem quas ad magistros..gessit *StatOx* 266. **c** in adfectione, in voluntate *GlC* I 324 (cf. ib. A 237); quas aptitudines in voluntate possumus nominare ~ones..~o hujus [sc. volendi] instrumenti est qua sic afficitur..ad volendum aliquid, etiam quando illud quod vult non cogitat, ut, si venit in memoriam, aut statim aut suo tempore illud velit Anselm (*Praesc.* 11) II 279; ipsos spiritus corporeos nullo alio corpore medio movet, sed sola ~one Gros. 116. **d** terram ..ponderosam esse a primarum ~one qualitatum novimus Adel. *QN* 48.

2 disease.

humida proprietas a tali eam ~one defendit Adel. *QN* 41.

affectionalis, volitional.

angeli ad corpus assumptum que [est] colligatio, ut ejus ~em motionem sequatur in assumpto corpore comproportionalis motio corporalis? Gros. 117 (= *Ep.* I p. 13).

affectionatus, inclined, (well) disposed.

c**1350** cui monasterio adeo ~us erat ita quod..donaria ad ejus necessaria..transmisisse dinoscitur (*Chr. Wigmore*) *MonA* VI 353b; **1407** si mirabuntur..aliqui ex aliter ~is unde nobis ista licent Bekynton II 128; excipit contra testes..quod..sunt..~i, partiales, minus indifferentes..et de roba et stipendio partis producentis *Praxis* 149.

affectiose v. affectuose.

affective, earnestly.

s**1396** archiepiscopus ~e rogatus..celebravit magnam missam Thorne 2198.

affectivus, 'affective', volitional. **b** (sb. f.) volition. **c** earnest, heart-felt.

quedam [res] ad speculativam partem anime magis relate, quedam vero ad ~am vel motivam *Ps.*-Gros. 300; a**1290** an sit principalius in vi cogitativa animi an ~a *Quaest. Ox.* 127; praxis dicitur communiter ad scienciam factivam et ad ~am, que est operacio Duns *Metaph.* I 8 20D; quarta via dicit theologiam esse ~am; quod bene intelligi potest si ~a ponatur esse quedam practica; si autem ~a ponatur tercium membrum distinctum [sciencie] contra practicum et speculativum, sic est contra dicta in primo articulo *Id. Sent. prol.* 4. 26. **b** ociositas est anime quo ad suam ~am maculativa J. Waleys *V. Relig.* I 2 f. 22D. 1. **c** **1328** dominacioni vestre preces agimus ~as quatenus.. *Conc.* II 551.

†affector, killer.

adfector, interfector *GlC* A 182.

affectualis, 'affectual', concerned w. or appealing to the emotions, heart-stirring.

ex sedula carissime necessitudinis instantia, sicut fieri assolet in ~ibus causarum optabilium fragranciis Ad. Marsh *Ep.* 4; habitus ~is propinquior est potencie intellective quam actus ejus; quod patet quia potencie radicantur in una essencia, et superponitur eis habitus, et tercio adveniunt actus Peckham *QA* III 38 (A) 3 p. 213; **1293** expedit quod vos habeatis tractatum ~em et effectualem.. cum..episcopo *Reg. Cant.* II 1287.

affectualiter, earnestly, w. sincere feeling.

eas [laudes et horas] dicat ~er cum mentis devocione J. Waleys *V. Relig.* III 7 f. 249. 2; s**1413** tam rex quam pontifex non ejus [J. Oldkastelle] interitum sed vitam cupiebant ~er Wals. *YN* 446.

affectuose, earnestly, w. sincere feeling.

601 ita illum dilectio vestra..~e dulciterque accipiat (*Lit. Papae*) Bede *HE* I 28; ~e quaerit quis et cujus nominis sit Herm. Arch. 41; s**1151** Pictavienses..campestria nec fastidiunt nec nimis appetunt ~e DICETO *YH* I 294; **1171** ~issime supplicans ut saltem familia sua servaretur illesa (*Lit. archiep. Senon.*) *Becket Mat.* VII 431; tanto se sperat obsequium prestare Deo placencius et ~ius acceptari MAP *NC* V 5 p. 231; certo certius est ipsos [equos] dominos suos ~e diligere NECKAM *NR* II 158; **1254** rogat †affectiose..quatinus.. *RGasc* I 347; inseruntur verba ~e significancia, que moveant in desiderium et execucionem boni BACON *Mor. Phil.* 258; si..~e cantare proponat, a priore claustri licenciam postulabit *Cust. Westm.* 159; secrecius et ~e loquantur de conversacione ejus in seculo *Cust. Cant.* 254; **1401** vos corditer et ~e requirimus quatinus (*Lit. Oeni de Glendordee*) AD. USK 73; **1420** nostrorum negociorum vestro in transitu ad Normanniam ~issime admissorum *Lit. Cant.* III 139.

affectuositas, sincere feeling, sensibility.

singula quorum, si quis sine invidia relegat, grata ~ate plena inveniet ADEL. *ED* 21.

affectuosus [LL], charged w. emotion, earnest, heart-felt. **b** friendly disposed.

in rhetorice ~a elocutione ADEL. *ED* 4; cogitatio..~a.. ad voluptuosas pristinarum iniquitatum recordationes AD. SCOT *TT* 764A; super tali..desiderio suo literas direxit ~as viris venerabilibus AD. EYNS. *Hug.* V 14; **1219** rogamus..precibus ~is quatinus.. *Pat* 209; que ad agendum proponuntur indigent sermonibus ~is, qui magnifice inmutant affectum in opus BACON *Mor. Phil.* 253; **1295** movet animam..sincera et ~a dileccio *Reg. Carl.* I 47; **1304** ~a instancia supplicamus quatinus.. *FormOx* 6; **s1469** rex, ~is allectus nimium regine suggestionibus, singulos ejusdem..propinquos..immensis ditabat muneribus *Croyl. Cont. B* 542. **b c1219** terram vestram vastant.. et sic erga vestros se habent quod apparet..quod de servitio vestro non sunt ~i (*AncC* IV 103) *RL* I 37; **c1370** papa Clemens semper fuit Gallicis ~us et non Anglicis [J. BRIDL. *gl.*] *Pol. Poems* I 151.

affectus [CL], emotion, feeling. **b** disposition, frame of mind. **c** impulse, desire, intention.

sermonem habuit..prolatum cum ~u cordis et corporis multa fatigatione W. DAN. *Ailred* 49; nihil amplius [musica] humanos vel jocundat vel delectat ~us GIR. *TH* III 12; philosophorum ~us ligati erant plus cum transitoriis quam cum eternis GROS. 1253. **b** ne quis me ~u cunctos spernentis..edicturum putet GILDAS *EB. pref.*; pro contribulibus dolitura compatientis ~u ALDH. *VirgP* 57; simplex actu, purus ~u AILR. *Ed. Conf.* 742. **c** ut ad thalami taedas..ferreos juvenculi ~us..inclinarent ALDH. *VirgP* 36 p. 281; ob magnum castigandi corporis ~um BEDE *HE* V 12; quid..illum ~um..in contrariam convertit actionem? ADEL. *QN* 13; [Albion] ameno situ locorum.. ~um habitandi Bruto..inferebat G. MON. I 16; potat ad affectum, qui presto videt sibi lectum SERLO WILT. 17. 2; laudem mereri poterit, etsi non opus, vel operantis ~us GIR. *TH intr.* p. 8; **1217** ~um in partes suas se transferendi *Pat* 113; **1414** tribuens ~u unicuique quod suum est *Reg. Cant.* III 321.

2 affection, devotion.

~us, *megsibbe* vel dilectione *GlC* A 371; Johannes..quem Salvator..peculiariter pio dilexit ~u ALDH. *VirgP* 23; qui familiari quodam ~u dominum Dunstanum semper dilexerat OSB. *Mir. Dunst.* 19; quid justius quam ut ille cui datur pretium majus omni debito, si debito datur ~u, dimittat omne debitum? ANSELM (*Cur Deus* 20) II 132; hucusque verba venerabilis Bede presbyteri de eo [Wilfrido], quem miro venerationis et dilectionis ~u excolebat et amplectebatur RIC. HEX. *Pri. Hex.* 14; perseverat inter eos sine actu conjugali conjugalis ~us AILR. *Ed. Conf.* 748; non novercali sed materno diligens ~u GIR. *EH* I 42; dum amo, ~us cujusdam intime dulcescentis mihi conscius sum *Id. Symb.* 9 p. 232; ei ecclesiasticum beneficium..~u vicario contulit BRAKELOND 132 v; **1218** salutem et sincere dilectionis ~um *Pat* 185; **1559** majori pietatis ~u *Conc. Scot.* II 165.

affeffamentum [cf. feoffamentum], enfeoffment.

c1250 prout per particulas distinguntur in quadam carta quam idem Henricus habuit de me et per ~um meum *Reg. Ant. Linc.* no. 542.

affeit- v. affait-. affenatus v. affeuatus. afferamentum v. afferantum, afforamentum.

afferantum [OF *aferant*], 'afferant', quota, due share.

1250 [totum] afferentum [suum in Brakanhouker] *Cart. Fount.* II 537; **1251** si..adjudicata fuerit possessio fundi dicte pasture alicui exigenti, monachi de Sallai habebunt inde ~um suum. ..de Litton ita provisum est quod.. habebunt..~um suum terre sue.., sc. justam estimacionem et visum bonorum et legalium virorum *Cart. Sallay* 411; **1254** faciant habere Baldewino..afferentum suum de termino S. Mich. *Cl* 278; **1275** prius solvit plenum ~um suum secundum quod agistabatur ad dictum auxilium regis *Hund* I 448 (cf. ib. 449: postquam solvit †afferamentum suum).

afferare, ~ator, ~entia v. affora-. afferentum v. afferantum. afferesis v. aphaeresis.

afferre [CL], to bring: **a** (persons); **b** (things).

a [virguncula] ante theatrales spectaculi clatros..allata ALDH. *VirgP* 46; nonne allatus eo poteris rogitare Tonantem? WULF. *Swith.* II 1032. **b** astulae..ad infirmos adlatae citam illis solent adferre medellam BEDE *HE* IV 6; **10..** adfero, *ic tobere* WW; veniente comitissa in manerium, ~ebantur ei xviii orae den. *DB* I 253b; ANSELM III 29 (v. auferre 1a); attuleram plenam, vacuam queror esse crumenam SERLO WILT. 21. 1; **s1307** allatum est corpus regium a Burgo..usque ad Waltham. *Ann Paul.* 257.

2 a to bring forward (a plea). **b** to bring about (an effect), inspire. **c** to herald, usher in.

a a1350 reus per se suam ~at defensionem *Stat. Cantab.* 323. **b** cui tantum attulit securitatis..quantum Romanis intulerat formidinis MAP *NC* II 17. **c** purumque aurora sciendi / allatura diem HANV. VII 352.

affertor [*for* allator], importer.

1492 per se aut factorem suum hernesiarum et aliarum mercandisarum predictarum in hoc regnum nostrum ~orem (*TreatyR*) *Foed.* XII 471.

afferua [OF *aferue*], share.

a1250 concessi..quintam partem tocius ~e mee in marisco extra forinsecum Fendic..contingentis manerium meum de Gedene [*Lincs*] *DL Cart. Misc* 2/227.

afferus v. averus. affet- v. affait-.

affeuatus [cf. feudare], enfeoffed tenant (Gasc. & Sp.).

1289 terras..plurium ~orum *RGasc* II 532; **1366** quatinus dictum principem [Aquitanie et Wallie]..ponatis.. in..sayzinam..rerum per nos eidem concessarum..cum omnibus suis redditibus, ..hominibus questialibus et ~is (*Ch. regis Castelle, DipDoc*) *Foed.* VI 526; **1433** a quibuscumque nostris ligeis feudatoriis, †affenatis, emphiteotis, censuariis et tenenciariis (*RGasc*) *Ib.* X 544.

affibulare, to fix, fasten. **b** (fig.) to implant.

regnantem affibulat clavus irrisum J. HOWD. *Cant* 390. **b** alea vel scacci si ludo dampna ministrent, / pectore non sevos affibulet ira furores D.BEC. 1420.

afficere [CL], to affect, produce an effect on. **b** (w. dat.). **c** to burden, assail (w. something).

consul..acri angore ~itur ALDH. *VirgP* 42; Brettones fames sua magis magisque adficiens BEDE *HE* I 14; multis coepit cogitationum aestibus ~i *Ib.* II 12; musa mihi gravis est et eam color afficit ire SERLO WILT. 3. 3; letitia ~ior NECKAM *NR* II 157; origo interjeccionis est ut audito aut viso aliquo delectabili vel tristabili extrinsecus intus ~iatur BACON XV 99; melle tuo mel verum afficis J. HOWD. *Ph.* 50. **b** tria ab eis subtraxit per que et in quibus plus nobis ~ere potuerunt ELMH. *Hen. V* 74. **c** affectus quovis verbere NIG. *SS* 64; **s1216** conviciis affectus est M. PAR. *Min.* II 190; genera penarum quibus ~iuntur malefactores sunt hec BRACTON 104b; **1274** affecit uxorem suam verbis contumeliosis *CourtRWakefield* I 5.

2 (*cf. affectare* 1) to affect, strive after. **b** (w. inf.).

mundanos quos †afficiatis [v.l. affectatis] honores NECKAM *VM* 180. **b** civitates..igne succendere ~iunt G. MON. VIII 21.

3 (pass.) to be disposed in some way (towards). **b** to be well disposed, devoted. **c** (w. inf.) to be minded (to).

c1205 numquid, sicut ad motiones corporis ad quod prave ~itur patitur et torquetur spiritus malus, sic ad motiones corporis ad quod bene ~itur potest pati delectabiliter spiritus bonus? GROS. *Ep.* 1 p. 15. **b 1300** consului magistrum J. ..quem novi secretum et affectum ad vos *Lit. Cant.* I 28; qui habet terrena nec tamen ~itur ad [ME: *luvieð*] ea *AncrR* 136; **1360** consilium peritorum..communitati..specialiter affectorum *MunAcOx* 223; **1388** volentes dictis burgensibus nostris quibus ~imur graciam facere specialem *ExchScot* 200; **1453** cui ~iebatur ex visceribus *Reg. Whet.* I 94. **c 1415** ~ior illius [littere] tenorem..adimplere *FormOx* 433.

afficha [OF *afiche*], buckle, clasp.

c1160 lego..Johanni filio meo unam ~am auri *Cart. Worc.* 70. 2; **1432** una capa preciosa de campo rubii cerici cum (?) pe[ndicul]is de †ofichis aureis *Reg. Glasg.* 333.

affidagium [cf. OF *afiage*], payment exacted (?) as pledge (Gasc.).

1236 quod haberet terram [in insula Oleronis]..cum affeagiis navium ibidem *Cl* 301; **1253** ~ia et mala tolta quas ..percipiunt..in insula..Oleronis *RGasc* I 380.

affidare, to 'affy', pledge faith (to): **a** (w. *quod*); **b** (w. acc. and inf.); **c** (w. acc. and gdv.); **d** (w. *ad* and gdv.); **e** (w. inf.); **f** (w. sb. or pron. as obj.); **g** (absol. w. *de* or *pro*).

a s1141 juravit et ~avit imperatrix episcopo quod omnia majora negotia..ejus nutum spectarent; ..nec dubitavit episcopus..ei..~are quod..ipse quoque fidem ei custodiret W. MALM. *HN* 491; **c1165** afidavimus Tome quod..terram warantizabimus *FormA* 296; **p1212** ex parte domini J. .. ~atum est quod eos fideliter..tractabit *BBC* (*Corbridge*) 240; **1214** posuerunt eum per fidem et per redempcionem s. et insuper fecerunt ~are quod non appellaret H...pro hoc facto *SelPlCrown* 69; **1228** redeuntem fecerunt forestarii ~are quod nichil [ducentes meremium] ceperant nisi.. *Feod. Durh.* 279; fuit inhibitum ne breve de transgressione cuiquam concederetur..nisi ~at quod bona asportata valeant xl s. ad minus *Fleta* 65. **b a1130** quod omnes res.. quas homines eorum ~are †poterint se emere ad dominicum opus monachorum..sint quiete de theloneo *Cart. Bath* p. 49; **a1155** in omnibus rebus quas homines eorum poterunt ~are esse ad opus ecclesie sue (*Ch. com. Heref.*) *Camd. Misc.* IV 36; **a1190** omnes res monachorum de Kirkebi quas homines eorum poterunt ~are esse suas proprias *FormA* 294. **c 1182** pax..~ata fuit utrobique tenenda (*Lit. Hen. II*) GIR. *PI* II 16; **s1190** hoc reges in propriis personis ~averunt firmiter et fideliter servandum R. HOWD. III 59; **1202** hanc ..treugam firmiter et fideliter tenendam ~abunt *Pat* 21a; **c1250** hoc fideliter observandum pro me..~avi *Reg. Aberbr.* I 91. **d a1231** ad hoc fideliter observandum..pro me et heredibus meis ~avi *Reg. Heref. 1344–61* 185. **e 1203** A... in misericordia, quia ipse noluit sequi cum uxor ejus ~aret sequi *SelPlCrown* 28; **1219** non invenit plegios de prosequendo, immo ~avit sequi *CurR* VIII 12; **12..** predictos iij s. nobis solvere ~avit *Meaux* I 359. **f a1170** hoc ~avit Willelmus..et plegius fuit quod condicio predicta teneretur *Rec. Templars* 239; **a1216** super pacem quam ipsi ~averunt et vadiaverunt in comitatu *SelPlCrown* 77; **1206** ~avit legem gilde et quietus per totum *Rec. Leic.* I 19; **1239** omnes homines de M. qui sunt in gilda mercanda de M. et hoc ~are voluerint *BBC* (*Marlborough*) 257. **g 1218** Henricus.. versus Mariam..de placito dotis.. ~avit *Eyre Yorks* 3; **1237** [vicecomites]..non capiant fidem senescallorum qui ~averunt pro debitis dominorum suorum et non venerunt.. sicut ~averunt *KRMem* 15 r. 23 (1); **1333** unus executor.. ~avit..pro diversis debitis exactis *LTRMem* 105 r. 54d.

2 to pledge faith by symbolic act: **a** by joining hands; **b** by corporal oath.

a 1141 hanc conventionem..tenendam ~avi manu mea propria in manu ipsius comitis *Regesta* III 275; **c1150** hanc ..donationem firmiter..tenendam ~avit..propria manu sua *FormA* 1; **a1181** hec fideliter..tenenda..manu mea ~avi primo in manu Rogeri..et postea in manu Radulfi.. in curia comitis de Richemund *E. Ch. Yorks* IV 93; **1182** hanc donationem..acquietare et defendere ~avi in manu J. de J. *Ch. Gilb.* 103 (cf. ib. xxix); **c1223** pro hac conventione..tenenda..~avi in manum Simonis *Deeds Newcastle* 46; **1223** ~at hic in manu marescalli quod faciet pacem de debito suo *LTRMem* 6 r. 1(2)*d.*; **s1256** ~averunt in manus vicecom' esse fideles *Leg. Ant. Lond.* 24; tu, essoniator Ricardi, ~a habendi warantum tuum hic..; et tu, Willelme, serva eundem diem, ~ato in manibus vel super virgam clamatoris HENGHAM *Magna* 6; **1467** super hoc ~avit et fidem fecit cum manu sua dextera in manum dexteram majoris *BBWinchester* f. 36. **b 1238** hanc compositionem..fideliter tenendam..corporaliter ~averunt *Ch. Sal.* 247.

3 (refl.) to pledge oneself.

abbati nostro [Ade, ob. 1339]..persolvit et se et heredes suos ad illius annui redditus solucionem ~avit et..obligavit *Meaux* II 301.

4 to bind by oath of fealty. **b** (p. ppl. as sb.) one so bound.

1202 de predictis terris..debent predicti R. et heredes sui esse ~ati et jurati mihi et heredibus meis *Pipe* 143. **b c1160** pro hac donatione dedit mihi R. de Luci iij m. argenti de recognitione..quando devenit meus ~atus *FormA* 42; **1208** nunc devenit ~atus ejus *Fines Warw* no. 164; **1211** devenit inde ~atus ipsius..in eadem curia [domini regis] *Fines P. Lincs* 319; **c1230** de prefato prato est predictus W.~atus meus *AncD* A 3466; **12..** [inde est] adfidatus [Willelmi] *Cart. Fount.* II 718.

5 to assure by pledge of faith.

c1100 rex..bene ~avit eum per litteras suas quod.. nullum illi dampnum eveniret (*Vexatio Will. Ep.*) S. DURH. *Durh.* I 174.

6 to affiance, pledge oneself to marry. **b** (fig.).

1224 ~avit quandam feminam et eam duxit ad domum suam *CurR* XI 1945; **1236** locuti fuerunt cum eo de maritagio filie sue et ita quod in tantum processum fuit quod debuit ~ari *Cl* 509; Helewisa, cui quidam Eudo donationem fecerat postquam eam ~averat et cum qua publice postea contraxit BRACTON 29; **1276** Symon..captus fuit per amicos..Matilde..fornicando cum ipsa, ..per quod compellebatur unum de tribus facere, vel uxorem ipsam ~are, vel vitam suam amittere, vel ipsam Matildam retro osculari; ita quod..dedit..Matilde fidem suam quod ipsam desponsare debuit *CoramR* 25 r. 7*d.*; **1330** si ad matrimonium contractum vel contrahendum se obligaverint vel ~averint aliquam mulierem *Lit. Cant.* I 321; **s1376** compertum est eam ~atam fuisse..Willelmo de Windeshore; unde..regi notificare curarunt qualiter compererunt eam esse alterius viri sponsam *Chr. Angl.* 97; si quis clandestinum contrahat matrimonium et postea coram testibus mulierem aliam ipse ~averit FORTESCUE *LLA* 32; **s1425** ad contrahendum matrimonium per verba de futuro cum predicta Margarita, †affitando [v.l. ~ando] eam..Delphino *Plusc.* XI 3; filiam comitis Marchiae ~avit seu subarravit MAJOR 281. **b** cum omnis pure homo debet ~ari sponso ecclesie, que affidacio per quodcumque mortale disrumpitur, patet quod omne crimen est spirituale adulterium vel mechia WYCL. *Mand. Div.* 346.

7 (w. *foris*) v. forisaffidare.

affidatio, pledging of faith, affidavit. **b** lease. *V. et. forisaffidatio.*

cum maritus suus inde nullum homagium..facere debeat, sed cum ~one fidelitatem tantum GLANV. VII 12 (cf. BRACTON 88); **1262** credatur eis super hoc per solam ~onem suam sine aliqua alia difficultate *Reg. Heref.* 92; **1333** de ~one recedat quietus *LTRMem* 105 r. 57; **1428** ~one sua firmando dicit (*Exeter*) *Law Merch.* I 120. **b** piscator mercenarius salmonum piscationem a domino terrae illius Cathenensis certa pecunie summa in ~one possidebat (*V. Gilb. Moray*) *Brev. Aberd.* 84.

2 affiance, betrothal. **b** betrothal (fig.). **c** (*s. dub.*).

propter mutuam ~onem que fieri solet quando aliquis promittit se ducturum aliquam mulierem GLANV. VII 18; **c1518** decernimus pretensam ~onem inter dictos Jacobum et Alisonam contractam per verba de futuro esse nullam.. causante impedimento affinitatis *Offic. S. Andr.* 16. **b** (v. affidare 6b). **c** honorem temporalem et specialiter ex ~one [v.l. dotacione] copiosa temporalium debet homo nolle WYCL. *Sim.* 2 p. 22.

affidere, to confide.

s1214 rex, cognito quod is jam subtractus fuisset super quem ejus animus non parum ~ebat *Meaux* I 394.

affiduciare, to pledge faith (Norm.).

1151 predictas concessiones ~iavit G. dux Normannorum ..se tenere et pepigit quod faceret ~iare uxorem suam *Regesta* III 729.

affidus, loyal.

†**944** (13c) flaminum invectione ~orum *CS* 1151.

2 (?) *f.l.* for *affidatus* (*cf. affidare* 1c).

c1160 hec conventio..est tenenda †~a [? l. ~ata] et jurata super altare (*Cart. Brecon*) *Arch. Cambr.* (4) XIII 308.

affigere [CL], to affix, fasten. **b** to fix (fig.). **c** to post up (a notice). **d** to fit, deck. *Cf. affixere.*

flamma..foramina ingrediens quibus [destina] aedificio erat adfixa BEDE *HE* III 17; crucem quam antea spreverant in carne sibi invicem jam ultronei affixerunt GIR. *IK* II 7; **s1381** sumentes caput archiepiscopi ac caput Johannis..diu super pontem Londoniarum affixum deponentes, loco ipsius pro ludibrio affixerunt *V. Ric. II* 27; **1418** psalterium affixum analogio ad feretrum *Ac. Durh.* 461. **b** eandem [lunae] mutationem primo anno circuli..adfigunt BEDE *TR* 42; **s718** in nomine Domini spem sibi totam ~ens *Chr. Evesham* 16; cum diu lecto affixus..desperaretur W. CANT. *Thom.* III 4; veritas vocis soli patet auditui.., affixaque subtilissimo motui incipit et desinit quasi simul R. BURY *Phil.* 1. 24. **c** libellos..~i in portis ecclesiarum OCKHAM *Pol.* I 294; **1552** insordescentes..velut abominabiles in cancellis.. ~antur et ibidem fixa [remaneant eorum nomina] *Conc. Scot.* II 133. **d** **s1415** gradatum..ascensum..regni et ejus principum armis undique affixum AD. USK. 128.

affilacium [cf. filacium], file (of documents).

1376 imponendo et affilando quandam cedulam cirograffatam ad modum cujusdam finis in ~iis finium (*CoramR*) *EHR* XXXV 415 (cf. ib. 416: cepit ~ia..et ea secum asportavit).

1 affilare [cf. filare], to file, thread on a cord or thong.

1327 in albo corio pro..foliis talliarum ~andis *IssueR* 225; **1345** brevia..remaneant ~ata inter recorda de anno xix *Mem. Ripon* 229; **1356** presentaciones predicte ~antur in baga Middlesex' (*KBControlmt. R*) *EHR* XXIII 512; **1369** invenerunt in quadam ligula de finibus quandam cedulam ~atam suspectam (*CoramR*) *Ib.* XXXV 413 (cf. ib. 415: cedulam in ligula..posuit et ~avit); **1461** panellum huic rotulo residet ~atum (*CoramR*) *Law Merch.* II 118.

2 affilare [OF *afiler*], to 'affile', sharpen. **b** (p. ppl.), pointed.

to filoure.., to strake, ~are *CathA.* **b** ~atam sibi barbam fecerat..et †glutinnie secretissime contextam capite est plexus *Dieul.* 143v.

affilatorium, whetstone.

a filoure, ~ium *CathA.*

affiliare, to adopt as son.

adoptat, adfiliat *GlC* A 215.

affina, refinery.

14.. hec ~a, *a werkhowse* WW.

affinantia [cf. finantia], ransom.

1358 in partem solucionis m m m vij^c florenorum in quibus idem dominus rex michi tenebatur..racione ~ie..comitis de Juny nuper prisonarii mei *AncD* WS 705.

affinare, to refine: **a** salt (alch.); **b** metal.

a cum aqua ita facta poteris ~are sales tuos qui in luna operantur (M. SCOT *Alch.*) *Med. Cult.* 155. **b** de eis qui emerint platas tonsure non ~atas; ..de fundatoribus qui retonsuram vel platas ejusdem ~averint (*Cap. Coronae*) *Fleta* 30; **1294** de..turbis tannitis emptis ad inde faciendos cineres pro dicto plumbo ~ando *KRAc* 260/3; **c1295** in decasu..argenti in ~ando *Ib.* 5; **1300** [pollardi] mittebantur usque Turrim Lond' ad ~andum *Ac. Wardr.* p. 57; **1304** pecie ~ate de pollardis vel alia moneta contrafacta *KRAc* 288/30 r. 7; **1323** quod quidem plumbum fertile idem T. liberavit affinatoribus ad ~andum et album argentum inde extrahendum *Pipe* 170 r. 53.

affinatio, refinement: **a** of salt (alch.); **b** of metal.

a hec est ~o salium qui in arte alchimie operantur (M. SCOT *Alch.*) *Med. Cult.* 155. **b** cum aurum per calcinationes vel assationes aut ~ones virtutem acquirit ignis *Id. Sol* 716; **1293** in ~one plumbi extracti..*KRAc* 260/3; **1323** de plumbo sterili proveniente de dicto plumbo fertili post ~onem et extraccionem argenti albi *Pipe* 170 r. 53

2 refinery.

1304 Johanni Lond' scindenti blockes et minutam buscam pro ~onibus *KRAc* 260/7 r. 1d. (cf. ib.: conflantibus folles.. ad iiij astra ~onum); **1323** de vij follibus pro ~onibus *Pipe* 170 r. 53.

affinator, refiner (of metal).

c1295 magistro Elye et sociis suis ~oribus *KRAc* 260/5; **1297** minatores et ~or, quos dominus rex misit in Hiberniam, ..negligentes fuerunt in operando minas ibidem *Ib.* 230/27 r. 18; **1323** (v. affinare b); **1325** Willelmo Coppynhod ~ori..; tribus coadjutoribus ~orum.. *LTRMem* 95 r. 128; **1566** adducturum xx homines metallicos, nempe fossores, fabros ferrarios, latores, excoctores, ~ores atque alios..rei metallicae recte tractandae expertos *SPDom. Eliz.* 40 no. 73.

†**affinicola,** (?) foreigner.

afiniculum, a finibus procul, *ellende GlC* A 357.

†**affinicus,** refined (? *f.l.* for *affinatus*).

1237 pro auro ~o ad predictas operationes argenteas deaurandas *Pipe* 81 r. 15.

affinis [CL], neighbouring, (sb.) neighbour. **b** (n. pl. as sb.) neighbourhood.

10.. adfinis, *nehgebur* WW; ~es omnes igne et depredatione..vexabat *G. Steph.* I 14; pinguia concedens que sunt affinia carni NIG. *SS* 91; naute..de Bebburch notissimi et ~es R. COLD. *Cuthb.* 31. **b** plebeia communitas in diversis Anglie partibus, puta in Cancia et ejus ~ibus FAVENT 21.

2 (one) allied or related, esp. by blood or marriage.

quod genitor ~ium et contubernalium relatione comperit ALDH. *VirgP* 35 p. 277; **10..** adfinium, *neahmaga* WW; regis barones, quotquot sibi erant ~iores *G. Steph.* II 85; quod universi fideles per Hiberniam constituti, repudiato cognatarum et ~ium contubernio, legitima contrahant matrimonia GIR. *EH* I 35; **1200** quosdam milites..qui non sunt afines consanguinitate predicti R. *CurR* I 246; **1201** xij de legalioribus militibus de comitatu, qui neutri parti sint ~es *Ib.* 377; **c1248** Henrico..~e predicte Margerie allegante contra cives *Leg. Ant. Lond.* 15.

affinitas, neighbourhood, adjacency.

tam Deo dignae ~atis delectatus vicinitate O. CANT. *Pref. Frith.* 36; **974** (12c) ab ~ate..circumjacentium agellulorum haec..terra giratur teritorio *CD* 1301; habitationem sibi in ~ate sacri templi constituens OSB. *V. Dunst.* 15; habebant in emendationem forisfacture, ubi supradicti comitatus [legis Danorum] habebant x et viii hundreda, isti x et dimidium, et hoc ~ate Saxonum (*Leg. Ed. Conf.*) *GAS* 660.

2 kinship, relationship (esp. by marriage), alliance. **b** similarity. **c** kindred matter.

non..parvi pendenda est haec dextris firmata ~as ALDH. *Met.* 4; **10..** adfinitate, *gesibnesse* WW; felices se reges alienigene..putabant si vel ~ate vel muneribus ejus [Ethelstani] amicitias mercarentur W. MALM. *GR* II 135; canones quidam prohibentes aliquos in secundo vel in tertio genere affinitatis conjungi GIR. *GE* II 33; **c1230** quod non ibi sit compaternitas, consanguinitas vel ~as vel aliquod aliud impedimentum *Conc. Syn.* 221; **1203** vicecomes apponat sex legales homines..quorum nullus predictos ~ate contingat *CurR* II 222; si qui occasione cujuscumque ~atis vel alia racione quacumque fugaverint in parcis.. aliorum.. (*Cap. Coronae*) *Fleta* 27; de..ballivis..qui prece, precio vel quacumque ~ate concelaverint..felonias factas *Ib.* 29; **1292** post confederacionis ~atem inter nos et eosdem regem Scocie et regnicolas habitam (*Pat. Regis Francie*) *Plusc.* VIII 20; convenerunt ut, habita honoris ratione, alia quaereretur ~as P. VERG. *Vat. app.* III 206; si quis contraxerit..matrimonium in gradu consanguinitatis vel ~atis..de legibus hujus regni non permisso, ..competit utrique..causa nullitatis matrimonii *Praxis* 107. **b** tam armorum quam morum ~as GIR. *TH* III 7. **c** **1357** quoddam instrumentum super deliberacione corporis Caroli de Bloys et aliis ~atibus (*LTRMem*) *Cal. Exch.* I 181.

affiniter, closely.

ecclesiarum possessiones.., ubicumque suis ~ius coherebant municipiis, ..tributis atrocissime premere *G. Steph.* II 78.

affirare v. afforare.

affirmare [CL], to make firm, build up. **b** to establish, reinforce.

c1190 licenciam..vivaria sua ~are.., ita quod numquam ibi fiat molendinum *Ch. Derb.* 1274; **1237** (v. 2 baia). **b** **1332** ivit ad mercatum de T. et ibidem emebat et vendebat et illud mercatum ~abat in prejudicium ville..de Andevere *Gild Merch.* II 328; **s1333** contra dictam villam..sedem.. ~avit *Plusc.* IX 28; **s1335** obsidionem ibidem intendens ~are *Ib.* 34.

2 to fasten. **b** to tether. **c** to attach (fig.).

s1251 optulit duo monilia..et jussit ea feretro..clavis fortiter ~ari M. PAR. *Maj.* V 258; **1297** in bordis serrandis ad ponenda desuper plumbacia cum clavis emptis ad dictos bordos ~andos *Ac. Cornw.* I 65; **1354** pro c dim. grossorum clavorum emptis pro pedibus cuplarum magne aule ~andis *KRAc* 471/6 r. 18; **1445** in viij spiknaylis emptis pro tignis ~andis *Comp. Swith.* 447. **b** **1279** in..virgis ad boves ~andos *Ac. Stratton* 102; **1345** de..iij seruris cum cathenis ferreis pro equis ~andis *MinAc* 1120/12 r. 4 (1). **c** **s1335** totam patriam ad fidem regis David ~avit *Plusc.* IX 34.

3 to confirm. **b** to affirm, assert. **c** (w. *in manum*; *cf. affidare* 2a).

†**691** (13c) signum manus Edilredi regis Merciorum dum ille adfirmaverat [v.l. infirmaverat] terram nostram *CS* 42 (cf. ELMH. *Cant.* 234); dedit vadimonium ad ~andum quod antecessor Alani..habuit vj bovatas *DB* I 377b; **14..** si contingat primum judicium ~ari *Reg. Brev.* 129b. **b** taliter affirmans perfecto famine ALDH. *VirgV* 746; dicito *gae*, quod est lingua Anglorum verbum adfirmandi et consentiendi, id est 'etiam' BEDE *HE* V 2; alii totius sensibilis creaturae.. creationem his verbis indicari ~ant ERIUG. *Per.* 545D; ~ant homines de T. quod archiepiscopus debet habere hanc socam *DB* 375b; sunt interrogabilium alia ad que hinc ~ando inde negando respondetur BALSH. *AD* 176; hominis generationem..tertiam solam, ex mare scilicet et femina, ..approbas et ~as GIR. *TH* I 15; non intelligens qui loquitur neque de quibus ~at OCKHAM *Pol.* I 294; **1373** ~antes se non teneri ad contribucionem *ExchScot* II 422. **c** **a1160** in verbo sacerdotis in ejusdem manum ~avit se amplius non moturum aliquam calumpniam *Danelaw* 287.

4 to farm out, grant at farm. **b** to take at farm.

istud manerium..fuit ~atum..pro xx li. per annum et traditum Alicie *RDomin.* 8; **1194** ad wardas et excaetas.. instaurandas et appretiandas et ~andas (*Cap. Coronae*) R. HOWD. III 265; **1205** scias quod velimus quod W... habeat ad firmam manerium de B...; et S...ei sic ~abit manerium illud *Cl* 24a; **1242** de redditibus..positis ad firmam cum dominicis ~atis *Pipe* 8; **c1305** de piscaria de Tamisia ~ata (*Rent. Linc.*) *Ambrosden* I 506; **1531** resolucio pro terris ad firmam ~atis *Househ. Bk. Durh.* 23. **b** **1348** molendinum quod nichil valet hoc anno eo quod..stat vacuum nec aliquis illud ~are vult *IPM* 104/23.

affirmatio [CL], a fastening. **b** confirmation. **c** affirmation, positive statement.

a **1400** cum imposicione et ~one tocius novi meremii eorumdem novorum operum *Doc. Leeds* 122. **b** **1301** in ~one hujus donacionis et concessionis *SelPlMan* 126. **c** [Dionysius] bipertitam theologiam asserit esse, id est καταφατικὴν et ἀποφατικήν, quas Cicero in 'intentionem' et 'repulsionem' transfert, nos autem..in '~onem' et 'negationem' maluimus transferre.. ERIUG. *Per.* 461B; 'essentia est', ~o; 'essentia non est', abdicatio; 'superessentialis est', ~o simul et abdicatio *Ib.* 462C (cf. *GLA* II 21); quod.. dialectica verba, ~onem, praedicatum, subjectum ceteraque ..tractatui tantae rei laboras inserere LANFR. *Corp. & Sang.* 418D; ad quid facta est ~o? ad significandum esse quod est ANSELM (*Ver.* 2) I 178; quia semper est negatio fortior quam ~o [AS: *onsagu*] (*Quad.*) *GAS* 226; comparant illos duos status secundum racionem ~onis et negacionis LUTTERELL *Vis. Beatif.* 94.

affirmative, affirmatively, positively.

statue caput..quod non nisi interrogatum loqueretur sed verum ~e vel negative pronuntiaret W. MALM. *GR* II 172; ad ~e respondendum, non ad negandum BALSH. *AD* 167; **s1243** ~e divulgatum est quod [imperator] numquam divina audire curabat M. PAR. *Min.* II 474; ostendimus veritatem complexam..rem esse intellectus ~e seu negative aliquid formantis *Ps.*-GROS. 296; **1323** omnis libertas..habet probari per usum ~e et non per abusum *MGL* I 442; si papa haberet..hujusmodi plenitudinem potestatis, nec ~e nec negative auctoritates scripture sacre dicentes legem evangelicam esse legem libertatis valerent intelligi OCKHAM *Pol.* I 234; **s1452** ad quam..questionem quia quidam responderint ~e *Reg. Whet.* I 19.

affirmativus, affirmative, positive. **b** (sb. f.) affirmative proposition.

καταφατική [pars theologiae] omnia quae sunt de ea [sc. divina essentia] praedicat et ideo ~a dicitur ERIUG. *Per.* 458B; **a1250** dividitur enuntiatio secundum qualitatem in ~am et negativam (W. SHIRWOOD) *GLA* III 13; condicionum ..alia duplex et fit partim verbis negativis et partim ~is BRACTON 19; non est negatio, licet adverbia valentia negationes imponantur, sc. 'antequam' et 'priusquam', sub specie ~a BACON *CSPhil* 481; vix esset respondendum ad aliquod argumentum..in proposicionibus ~is..nisi cum distinccione (KYN.) *Ziz.* 13; multe alie nature generales tam ~e quam negative sunt in feudis UPTON 39; **1573** quiquidem burgenses in hujusmodi parliamento habebunt voces suas tam ~as quam negativas *Pat* 1104 m. 30. **b** ista negativa ex ~a precedenti non sequitur OCKHAM *Pol.* II 498; quantum ad ~am supradictam CONWAY *Def. Mend.* 1423.

affirmator, affirmer, asserter.

1286 eorum [articulorum] ~ores ..excommunicatos esse ..denunciamus PECKHAM *Ep.* 661 (= *Conc.* II 124).

†**affirmatorius,** confirmatory.

s1420 simili modo..faciet super eisdem suas litteras patentes approbatorias, et ~ias..fratrum suorum [cf. ib. supra: confirmatorias] WALS. *HA* II 333.

affirmatura, lease.

1304 damus..Arnaldo [notario]..potestatem..litteras sigillandi sigillo..ducis..in contractibus et casibus quibuscumque, ~as recipiendi et condempnaciones..inde faciendi *RGasc* III 456.

affitare v. affidare 6a.

†**affixere** [*for* affigere], to fix in place.

candelas ~endas..undique in muris..inveniet *Cust. Cant.* 103.

affixio, affixing. **b** posting up (of notices).

1485 pro..deauracione unius coclearis et ~one ejusdem feretro *Fabr. York* 89. **b** **1582** si [publicatio] fieret per bedellum sive per affixtionem ad ostium ecclesiae *StatOx* 423; **1592** per ~onem quaestionum..valvis ecclesiae *Ib.* 445.

†**affixmalium** [cf. firmaculum], (?) brooch.

a1200 unum †~ium [? l. affirmalium] auri..dedit *Danelaw* 338.

afflagitare, to pray for.

cum de te cogito, / frater, et merito / mortem afflagito HIL. RONCE. XI 45.

afflamen, breath or inspiration.

mox..juvenis ille vite spiraculum attrahere videbatur et redivivo hanelitus ~ine parturire novella spiritum gratia probabatur; et merito..S. Cuthbertus homini spiritus afflatum reddidit, cujus signo virtutis et gratie S. Spiritus ~ina consolationis..a Domino impetrasse presignavit R. COLD *Cuthb.* 92.

afflare [CL], to blow, breathe or shower upon. **b** to inspire; *v. et. efflare.*

atflarat, *onsueop GlC* A 868 (cf. ib. 359); spicula / quibus .. / afflant necantes imbribus / telorum emicantibus (ÆTHELWALD) *Carm. Aldh.* III 33; igneus [paralyticae]..calor venas afflavit apertas Alcuin *WillV*. 30. 10; ~averat..rumor aures ejus W. Malm. *GP* II 83 p. 183; bestie terribiles, ..solum odore florum et Francorum ~ate, statim in fugam sunt converse Gir. *PI* III 30; s**1386** aspiravit aura que classem ~avit in Britanniam Wals. *HA* II 143. **b** profetico ~atus spiritu Aldh. *Met.* 2 p. 69; caelesti ~atus spiraculo *Id. VirgP* 3; ~atus rore Spiritus Sancti *V. Osw.* 428.

afflator, inspirer.

inflatus per ~orem malitiae (*Jud. Dei*) *GAS* 407.

afflatus [CL], breath. **b** inspiration.

vel fotu solis vel aeris ~u Bede *Cuthb.* 46; R. Cold. *Cuthb.* 92 (v. afflamen); fulmen ab ore volat, urbis afflatibus ardet Gower *VC* I 325. **b** ea quae apostoli ac prophetae ~u S. Spiritus scripserunt Bede *Egb.*17; cum ipse esset speciale S. Spiritus organum et ejus ~u resonans *Offic. R. Rolle* xxvi.

afflectere, to bend, crook.

cum dicis tria, tertium [digitum] similiter adflectes Bede *TR* I p. 179.

afflictare [CL], to afflict.

ex quo paradisi terrestris primicola..debita moleste caepit ~ari sollertia O. Cant. *Pref. Frith.* 12; quamvis cotidiano regiorum prelio..~aretur W. Malm. *HN* 500.

afflictio, affliction, distress.

saevissimis plagarum ~onibus Aldh. *VirgP* 4; temporales adflictiones aeterna mercede mutavit Bede *HE* IV 9; quot crucibus corporee ~onis carnis sue incentiva [S. Oswoldus] edomaverit *Chr. Rams.* 23; s**1175** in vigiliis, in ~onibus, in oratione pernoctans Diceto *YH* I 399; mavult beneficio meritorum amari quam carceris ~one timeri Map *NC* III 4; s**1321** dum in ejus animo..cogitaciones non pacis sed afflixionis assidue sic volverentur *Flor. Hist.* III 199; **1339** ut..tristis mater..de filio gaudeat consolata, nec ~onem ~oni accumulet (*Lit. Regis*) Ad. Mur. 93; s**1416** ~oni sociorum in Harfleu per famis inediam Elmh. *Hen. V* 86.

afflictivus, distressing.

licet..in statu innocencie non fuisset fames, sitis et hujusmodi nonnulli defectus ~i Ockham *Pol.* II 731.

afflictus, conflict.

s**1319** W. de Ermine..in eodem ~u [*Myton*] captus est *Ann. Paul.* 287.

affligare v. affugare.

affligere [CL], to strike. **b** to afflict, distress. **c** to inflict.

afflictus flagris et stipitis ictu Aldh. *VirgV* 1320; hostes aut machinis ~ere aut fame afficere putabat *G. Steph.* I 39. **b** adfligit, *gehnaeh GlC* A 232; ne forte vos..temporalibus damnis..~at Bede *HE* IV 25; correpti..morbo..et gravissime adflicti *Ib.* III 27; o cor..de quo, cum ~eretur, tam copiosa misericordia supereffluebat Anselm (*Or.* 13) III 52; magis afflictos exhilarare magis Nig. *SS* 2984; duritiis.. ~i carnem eligunt Gir. *TH* I 12; per mutuas cedes, flagella et tormenta seria se invicem ~entes *Plusc.* IX 1; **1407** afflictiones afflictis apponi *Lit. Cant.* III 103. **c** simili pena in eos ~enda [qui].. *Conc. Scot.* II 66.

afflixio v. afflictio. affluenta v. affluentia.

affluenter [CL], copiously, abundantly.

opulentias ~er cumulantem Aldh.*VirgP* 24; annonas sibi ~ius ministrare cogunt Bede *HE* I 15; cogor ~er glutire acerbos haustus meae infelicitatis Anselm (*Or.* 13) III 54; **1187** Deus..qui nobis de calice predecessorum nostrorum propinat ~er *Ep. Cant.* 82; hos..deliciis ~er exhibent Map *NC* I 25 p. 40; balsamum stillando..~er emittunt S. Sim. *Itin.* 58; s**1345** copia..victualium abundabat satis ~er Ad. Mur. *app.* 249.

affluentia [CL], overflowing. **b** abundance. **c** fullness (of heart), generosity.

ad lacrimarum ~iam moti fuerunt Gir. *IK* I 11; **1306** in *le flodgates* ejusdem molendini fractis per ~iam aque emendandis *MinAc* 830/13. **b** diliciarum ~ias Aldh. *VirgP* 38 p. 289; provinciae..in maxima omnium rerum ~ia praefuit Bede *HE* III 14; ~ia, *oferflowendnys* Ælf. *Gl.*; cecidit pluvia sanguinea et muscarum †affluenta [v.l. ~ia] homines moriebantur G. Mon. II 16; cum inopinabili extere gentis ~ia illic..coadunata *G. Steph.* I 65; licet petita suscipiat rapiatque negata, nulla potest ~ia sedari Map *NC* IV 6 p. 168; immoderantiam in epularum ~iis Ad. Marsh *Ep.* 37; **1296** gens Anglorum..rerum copiosis ~iis redundabat *Reg. Cant.* I 144. **c** cognovi piam vestri pectoris ~iam Ad. Marsh *Ep.* 78.

affluere [CL], to flow in, rise (of tide). **b** to abound. **c** to accrue.

mare per id temporis vicies novies adfluit semel et remeat Bede *TR* 29. **b** abundantiarum copiis insula..~ebat Gildas *EB* 21; affluat et pretio cultuque arrideat ori / copia Hanv. VI 333. **c** **1458** quecunque bona et catalla mihi.. infuturum accidencia seu ~encia *Cl* 309 m. 35*d*.

2 (pr. ppl.) amply supplied **b** lavish, generous.

inter ~entissimas dominorum mensas G. Crispin *Herl.* 93; terram fertilem omnibusque copiis ~entem reddidere *G. Steph.* I 8. **b** s**1305** inopum plus quam divitum ~ens recreator *Flor. Hist.* III 129.

affluus, abundant.

puteorum uberes venas ~isque aquarum rivulis semper destillantes *G. Steph.* I 18.

affodillus v. asphodelus. affolia v. offalia. affonitrum v. aphronitrum.

afforamentum, 'affeerment', allowance, assessment.

1252 solebant communicare *horn under horne*, quilibet secundum afferamentum suum et quantitatem boscorum *CurR* 146 r. 9*d*.; c**1270** omnes homines de manerio..debent sequi ad curiam de W. ad quodlibet ~um curie (*Cust. Droxford*) *Reg. Wint.* *1282–1304* II 658; **1321** vicecomites.. recognoverunt quod amerciaverunt homines in curiis suis ad voluntatem suam sine affuramento parium suorum *MGL* II 410; **1352** amerciavit J. B. in hundredo de S. pro quodam parvo debito in x s. sine affuramento parium *Proc. J.P.* 74.

afforantia, 'affeerance', assessment, valuation.

1443 secundum afferenciam propartis sue *Pat* 456 m. 28; **1452** unde ipse haberet solucionem..de quarterio in quarterium..secundum afferenciam *RScot* 355a; **1458** solvant..summam xlv li. vel ratam earundem secundum afferenciam temporis quo..monasterio remanebunt amortizate (*Pat*) *Reg. Whet.* I 302; **1485** secundum pondus et puritatem argenti, printam sive sculpturam, formam, afferenciam et ratam *Pat* 564 m. 18 (7).

afforare [< ad+forum; cf. OF *aforer*], to fix the price of, appraise. **b** (absol.). **c** to conclude (a purchase).

s**1269** averia †qui [l. que] ~antur per libras..solebant ponderari per..stateras *Leg. Ant. Lond.* 118; **1287** affuraverat navem..ad cariandum j doleum vini (*St. Ives*) *Law Merch.* I 23 (cf. ib. 25: affuraverunt et emerunt..equum.. pro v m.); **1319** quod..victualia que venalia invenire poteritis..ad opus nostrum ~etis et saisiatis *RScot* 194b; c**1300** nullus pistor..aliquam navem ascendat ad bladum ~andum ante primam pulsacionem (*Halimotum Pistorum*) *MGL* I 356. **b** **1258** nullus eat..contra naves ferentes mercandisas ad..villam ad ~andum aut alloquendum mercatores *BBC* (*Grimsby*) 295. **c** **1291** per argentum Dei ..empcionem equi..affuravit (*St. Ives*) *Law Merch.* I 45.

2 to 'affeer', assess: **a** (an amercement or sim.); **b** (a person amerced).

a **1316** quod amerciamenta..tenencium ~entur et taxentur per sacramentum parium suorum (*Compositio*) Thorne 2034; **1319** pro amerciamentis ad opus regis affurendis (*LTR Mem.* 89 r. 100) *Hist. Exch.* 590; **1369** custos foreste afferat presentaciones presentatas per forestarios in swanemotis..per semetipsum absque..aliis afferatoribus ad hoc juratis *SelPlForest* xlix; **1408** amerciamenta..per eos affirentur *Doc. Bev.* 9; **1451** amerciamenta super ipsos assessa sive affurata *Cl* 301 m. 3*d*.; **1469** amerciamenta.. super quascumque personas..adjudicata, assessa sive afferata (*Pat*) *Foed.* XI 644b. **b** **1176** de x m. pro forefactura foreste de quibus ~atus fuit *Pipe* 129; **1178** reddidit de hac misericordia xx s. antequam esset afferatus ad x m. *Pipe* 63; **1189** de illa misericordia [burgensis] sit afferatus juramento..burgensium *BBC* (*Colchester*) 151; **1327** ~atur per justiciarios ad dim. m. (*CoramR*) *Law Merch.* III 108; **1387** ipse in misericordia et ~iatur per justiciarios ad xl den. (*Ib.*) *Pub. Works* I 18.

afforatio, 'affeerment', assessment.

1364 si aliquis..reprobet affratores de *brewestergild* pro affracione ejusdem *Doc. Bev.* 41.

afforator, 'affeerer', assessor: **a** (of amercements); **b** (of measures).

a **1290** afferatores, Ricardus B., Willelmus K. *Leet Norw.* 34 (cf. ib. xxxii); **1352** amerciatos illos amerciare fecit pro voluntate sua sine affuratoribus *Proc. J.P.* 75; **1353** eundem priorem ad xxx li...auctoritate sua propria amerciasse et absque aliquibus afferatoribus afferasse *Pat* 239 m. 20; **1364** affratores (v. afforatio); **1433** affuratores jurati *Banstead* II 99; ob quam defaltam idem amerciatus extitit.. per W. S. et T. H. tunc afferatores ejusdem visus ad hoc electos et juratos ad v s. *Entries* 553. **b** **13..** assiator et afforiator mensurarum *Little RBBristol* I 38.

afforc- v. effort-.

1 afforestare, to 'afforest', put under forest laws.

†a**1153** facite recognosci quos boscos episcopi Heref' Henricus rex ~avit in vita sua (*Breve Stephani*) *Reg. Heref.* *1282–1317* 50; **1217** omnes foreste quas H. rex avus noster ~avit videantur per bonos et legales homines; et, si boscum aliquem alium quam suum dominicum ~averit ad dampnum illius cujus boscus fuit, deafforestentur (*Ch. Forest*) *StRealm* 20; **1219** illi de comitatu tuo [Hunt'] deambulacionem fecerunt..de tota foresta nostra in bailliva tua, nichil nobis relinquentes ~atum nisi haias nostras de W. et de S. *Cl* 386a; s**1225** qui..novas a veteribus discernerent forestas, ut omnes ille que invente fuerint ~ate post primam coronationem Henrici II..statim deafforestarentur M. Par. *Min.* II 269; **1293** exceptis circiter cc acris bosci et more..que solent ~ari et postea per dominum regem nunc fuerunt deafforestate *PQW* 587a; Willelmus..Rufus, eo quod accipitrum et canum ludicris se totum dederat, totum fere regnum Anglie..primus ~avit Wykes 14; **1329** comes Glouc'..ipsos..ejecit.., eo quod affectavit dictas terras et tenementa ~are (*Inq.*) *Cart. Glam.* 1156; aforestare est forestam facere *CathA*; incredibile est quantum terrarum reges Angliae passim incultum jacere permiserint et feris inclusis dicaverint vel, ut nostri loquuntur, ~averint Camd. *Br.* 254.

2 †afforestare, (?) *f.l.* for *arrestare*.

1206 mittatis separatim in quemlibet portum bonos nuncios..ad ~andas naves *Pat* 63a.

afforestatio, 'afforestation', subjection of land to forest laws.

s**1299** petierunt ut..~ones, quibus plebs angariebatur, ..fierent discrete *Flor. Hist.* III 108.

afforiare, ~iator v. afforare, ~ator. afforis v. aforis. afforismus v. aphorismus.

afformare, to fit.

quasi ocreas pedibus et tibiis ejus ~ans, manu artissima pertractabat *Chr. Wallingf.* 63.

affors-, affort- v. effort-. affra v. 2 astrum, avera. affractus v. anfractus. affragium v. averagium. affrai- v. effrai-. affratio, ~ator, v. affora-.

affrangere [CL], to break (by contact).

demon..os quo exire compellebatur latius suffocando aperuit et..partem aliquam..in diripiendo..affregit R. Cold. *Cuthb.* 17.

affrect-, affreight- v. affrett-.

†affrenatus, bridled beast or (?) *f.l.* (*cf. averus*).

1283 reddere iiij d. pro unoquoque ~o et bove quem habebat in festo S. Martini vel arrare cum unoquoque ~o et bove dim. acrum terre ibidem ad opus domini (*Ch. Wexford*) *EHR* XXIII 217.

affrenitum v. aphronitrum.

affrettamentum (affrect-), freight, cargo. **b** affreightment, boat-hire.

1434 dedimus..navem cum..batello et toto apparatu ac ~o eisdem navi..et batello..spectantibus *Cl* 284 m. 5*d*. **b** **1447** citra naulum sive †affreightamentum (*Lit. Regis*) *Foed.* XI 157; **1460** pro rata nauli sive ~i hujusmodi mercium (*TreatyR*) *Ib.* 442b; **1470** in quadam causa maritima de et super ~o v doliorum vini *Pat* 525 m. 9*d*.

affrettare (affrect-) [OF *afreter*; cf. frettare], to freight, load (for). **b** to load, consign (goods).

1264 cum..major..ville de Depe..navem illam affretasset ad quendam militem ad partes Hibernie in eadem ducendum *Cl* 81; **1390** ~avit unam crayeram *SelPlAdm* I 15; **1440** navis..existentis in portu London' et ibidem ~ate ad velificandum deinde..usque portum Bayonie *Cl* 290 m. 5*d*. **b** **1549** cum dictis 4500 *kintals* in eadem navi ~atis *Entries* 409b.

2 (?) to sail.

1276 dum..in terram Wallie crederet per mare nostrum †affretare [MS. (?) offretare; (?) cf. transfretare] *TreatyR* I 55.

affrettatio (affrect-), freighting, loading.

1277 contra consuetudines in ~onibus navium hactenus observatas (*Pat* 96) *Law & Cust. Sea* I 51; **1290** scribaniam super affretacione navium Burdegale *RGasc* II 557; **1394** occasione ~onis, conduccionis sive locacionis cujusdam navis versus le Bay *Pat* 339 m. 25.

affricare [CL], to rub off on, rub against (fig.).

quod pociori non potuit, pejori fucum sue maledictionis ~uit Map *NC* III 3 p. 123; discretio talis / affricuit [v.l. applicuit] limam dempta rubigine verbis Vinsauf *PN* 871.

affricus v. Africus. affrinus v. averinus. affrodicia v. aphrodisia. affrodillus v. asphodelus. affronicum v. aphronitrum.

affrontare [cf. OF *afronter*], to delimit.

1289 in justiciatu..tocius territorii superius ~ati *RGasc* II 440.

affrotrum v. aphrotum.

affugare [cf. aufugare], to put to flight, banish. **b** to drive off.

s**1136** ipsum ab Anglia ~ans exilio condempnavit M. Par. *Min.* I 255; s**1250** devicto et ~ato..W. de Holande *Ib.* III 71 (= *Flor. Hist.* II 365: †affligato]; **1341** in liberacione j hominis ~antis frues..de bladis seminatis *MinAc* 1120/11 r. 11*d*.; s**1399** 'infidos cervos'..penitus regno ~avit Ad. Usk 25. **b** **1274** ~avit duas vaccas ad opus domini regis *Hund.* I 136; **1349** averia..pacifice abfugantur sine imparcacione *Cart. Sallay* 168; districcionem captam.. abfugare *Entries* 184.

1 affugere [cf. aufugere], to flee, run away.

hostes ipsum putaverunt deum Romanorum et ~erunt Bacon VI 102; ut..post professionem..~iat dampnatus *Cust. Westm.* 224; **1309** si..inde ~isset ita quod non potuisset deprehendi *TreatyR* I 193; s**1340** exceptis paucis [navibus] que ~erant *Eul. Hist.* III 205.

2 affugere [? < ad+fugere], to flee to.

s**537** [Vigilius] ad ecclesiam S. Sophie ~it, de qua extrahitur *Eul. Hist.* I 207.

affulare [cf. OF *afoler*], to strike on the head.

strykyn hedys, ~o *PP*.

affundere [CL], to pour upon. **b** to prostrate, subdue.

ut oleo flamme affuso Gosc. *Edith* 58. **b** absolvit Phrygiis affusa Britannia Grecos Hanv. I 244.

affundrare [OF *afondrer*], to founder, sink down.

1281 quendam pullum, qui de pedibus anterioribus ~avit, ita quod..Johannes cecidit ultra caput dicti pulli in fossatum *IMisc* 40/30.

affur- v. affor-. afietare v. affaitare. afiniculum v. affinicola. afingea v. axungia. Afir v. Afer. afoho v. aphlopho. aforc- v. effort-.

aforis [al. div.], outside.

dum pernoctant ~is presbyteri domo Herm. Arch. 11 p. 41; fecit..valde a foris illam [insulam] undique munire *G. Herw.* 333b; unguatur a foris cum sandalo Gilb. IV 200. 2; **1283** quamvis [pecunia] in sacculis..ejusdem molis apparencia, ut sublata fuerat, afforis videatur Peckham *Ep.* 496; **s1299** erat [Margareta] omnium morum tam intus quam afforis, intuencium oculis, nectare imbuta Rish. 395; vestimentis afforis mediocribus utebatur *NLA* (*Maglorius*) II 157; **s1357** Anglicis..portas afforis servantibus J. Reading *Chr.* 163; *wyth-oute*, foras, foris, af- *CathA*.

aforismus v. aphorismus. afr- v. et. affr-, aver-. aframentum v. aisiamentum 1b.

†africana, (?) *f.l.* (*cf. avera*).

1277 remane[n]t..iiij boves, vj mutilones et vj †~e femine, ij pullani †femini, viij boves, xj vacce *Ambrosden* I 405.

Africanus [CL], African (adj. or sb.).

s1195 Boyac Almiramimoli, imperator ~orum, ..intravit fines Christianorum R. Howd. III 302; sal ~um Gilb. II 108 v. 1; Phenices..Numidas ac Getulos et ceteros ~os coarctaverunt Bacon *Maj.* I 317.

Africus [CL], south-west wind or quarter.

ab Affrico, *suðanwestan GlC* A 89; **796** (12c) sic ab ipso confinio ab affrico vel a fauno habet..sepe transversum *CS* 282; ~us, *suðan westan wind* Ælf. *Gl.*; Affricus in dextra zephyri regione locatur Neckam *DS* II 83; hic affricus, *the sowth est* (sic) *wynd* WW.

afro- v. aphro-. afrus v. averus. agabo v. agapo.

agagula [LL], wanton woman.

gygelot, wynch, ~a *PP*.

agaitus v. awaita.

†agalantia [? cf. acalanthis], plover (bird).

14.. agalancia, A. *a plover*, ..hec agalauda, A. *plowere* WW.

agalaster v. agelaster.

agalma [ἄγαλμα], image.

en rutilum liquido summae virtutis agalma Frith. 1204; ~a vel iconisma vel idea, *anlicnes* Ælf. *Gl.*; **†969** (13c) ego Dunstanus hanc libertatem crucis ~ate consignavi *CS* 1228 (cf. ib. 1264); martyris ecce zoma servat Michaelis agalma (*Inscr.*) Brakelond 154.

2 high place.

an heghte, sublimitas, ..fastigium, ~a est sedes alta, jugum, summitas *CathA*; ~ata, i. alta sedes WW.

agamus [ἄγαμος], unmarried.

presbiter est agămus, pariter nos sic et agāmus Serlo Wilt. *app.* II a, a6; *sengyl, nowt marryd ne weddyd*, ~us *PP*.

agape [ἀγάπη], love, charity. **b** alms. **c** love-feast, banquet.

tum agape pro numinis / ..Petri petunt suffragia (Æthelwald) *Carm. Aldh.* 2. 65. **b** dum universi facultatum reditus..ad ~em pauperculis mendicantibus venirent Aldh. *VirgP* 52 p. 308 (cf. ib. 27 p. 260: ~em egentibus erogantem); ~e, *ælmesse* Ælf. *Gl.*; mane iterum veniens agapem dispersit egenis / fratribus Wulf. *Swith.* I 772; turbatis rebus que ad victum et vestitum et ~en servorum Dei date erant Ord. Vit. III 3 p. 52; **s1298** mortuo quodam predivite Lundoniarum cive..urbis plateis per pauperes ut ~em acciperent constipatis (*Chr. S. Edm.*) *EHR* LVIII 70. **c** ~em, *swoesendo GlC* A 405; ~is, *dægmete* WW; **s1097** Goisfredus quippe de presulatu jam securus erat jamque copiosas ~es pro sublimatione sui preparaverat Ord. Vit. X 7; usque intro in atrium magnum, ubi ad ~em multi ex comprovincialibus congregati sunt *G. Herw.* 337; *feest or fedyng of mete or drynke in holy chyrche*, ~es *PP*.

agapeta, (?) fellow guest, toasted in 'loving-cup' (*cf.* J. Sal. *Met.* ed. Webb p. 238).

in ipsa..~arum consuetudine planum est invenire superstitionem qua nominis sollicitatur gratia et quasi religiosis precibus invitatur J. Sal. *Pol.* 729a.

agapis v. achates.

†agapo [(?) *for* agaso], harbinger.

~o, qui negotia aliena anteambulat *GlC* A 383; †agabo, qui negotia praecedit *EE* 34. 46.

agard- v. esward-. agarectare v. esgarrettare.

Agarenus, descendant of Hagar (cf. *Gen.* xxi; *Ps.* lxxxii 7), Saracen, Moslem.

c790 maledicti Saraceni, qui et ~i (Alcuin *Ep.* 14) W. Malm. *GR* I 91; detestabiles ~i..Christianorum limites jamdudum transierunt Ord. Vit. IX 1; pagani qui Saracenos se mentiuntur cum sunt ~i (*gl.*: possunt tamen se dicere Saracenos, cum sint filii Agar, eo quod, ut dicit Augustinus, uterus Agar accommodatus est sed Sare accessit auctoritas) Neckam *NR* II 158; constanter cecitatem infidelium ~orum objurgaverat Ad. Eyns. *Hug.* IV 13 p. 65; qui verius dicuntur ~i quam Saraceni, quia de Agar ancilla matre Ismaelis sunt progeniti Higd. I 15; quod et putant Saraceni seu ~i Bradw. *CD* 96a.

agareunare v. awarennare.

agaricus [ἀγαρικόν], agaric, tree-fungus.

addito polip' agar' Gilb. I 21. 2; ~us purgat omnes humores specialiter, tamen flegma principaliter Gad. 15. 2; ~us, fungus abietis, cor album abietis *Alph.* 3; fungus ~us crescit in arboribus, G. *moscherones*, A. *paddocstol Ib.* 70.

agasaeus, 'gaze-hound' (cf. *King's Serjeants* 278).

quod visu lacessit, nare nihil agit sed oculo, ..~um nostri ..vocant Caius *Can.* 3; a verbo nostrati *gase..gasehunde* appellatur nostris quem ante ~um nominari diximus *Ib.* 11.

agaso [CL], groom.

agasson, minister officialis *GlC* A 378; ~o, *horspen* Ælf. *Gl.*; proverbialiter dici solet quia misera terra est quam ~o vel mulio depopulatur J. Sal. *Pol.* 612b; quisque summariorum suum habebat ~onem W. Fitzst. *Thom.* 18 p. 30; se a longe ostenderunt..~ones; quorum aspectu.. territi Scoti..abiere Boece 201.

agastrum v. ogastrum. agates v. achates.

agathus [ἀγαθός], good.

si quis..accipiat ad intellectum, et non ad quem balbutit ..Empedocles, inveniet Amorem quidem causam esse agatorum [*gl.* bonorum], Litem vero malorum Bradw. *CD* 13b.

†agausea, (?) magpie (OF *agace*) or plover (*agalantia*).

erant tales pitantie unicuique canonico: ..xij merule, aut ij ~ee aut ij perdices *Found. Waltham* 15.

agayt- v. awaita.

†ageator, instigator.

~or, hortator *GlC* A 384; †aegeator, hortator *Ib.* 308.

agelaster [ἀγέλαστος], unlaughing.

sad or sober withoutyn laughynge, agillaster vel agalaster *PP*.

agella v. agellus, agnella.

agellarius, hayward. **b** husbandman.

1397 quoddam pratum viride quod vocatur Heywardsmere, eo quod pertineat ad officium agillarii domini Lestraunge (*Terrier*) *Ambrosden* II 191; **1425** in solutis diversis hominibus..conductis ad sarculanda diversa blada, ut patet per tallium contra agillarium (*Ac. Bicester*) *Ib.* 255; *heyward*, ~ius, ..abigeus *PP*; agelarius, A. *a hayward* WW; **1519** agillarius vocatus *le heyward CourtR* 183/116 r. 5. **b** *a tylle man*, ~ius, agricola *CathA*.

agellicus, arable.

c960 (11c) concessimus..aliquas ~as portiones pro remedio animae nostrae *CS* 1007.

agellulus, tiny plot of land.

796 (12c) hujus ~i hec sunt certa termina *CS* 282; **†821** (13c) omnia loca..cum omnibus ~is ad prefata loca pertinentibus *CS* 366; **†938** (14c) dignatus sum largiri sex mansas †aseluli..cum pratis paschuisque *CS* 728; **974** (12c) ab affinitate..circum jacentium ~orum *CS* 1301; **s1173** persona fortune injuria miserabilis, si vel ~um possideret vel asinum, urgebatur conferre Diceto *YH* I 372.

agellus [CL], **~a,** small plot of land.

mundani cultor agelli Aldh. *VirgV* 2750; nil propriae possessionis excepta ecclesia sua et adjacentibus ~is habens Bede *HE* III 17; **811** pro mutua commoda (*sic*) vicissitudinis ~orum nostrorum quorundam *CS* 332; **842** (14c) termini vero harum †asellarum ista sunt *CS* 438.

agen v. agmen c. agener- v. aggener-.

agenfriga [AS], owner (of animals).

si [porci] non fuerunt ibi [in pasnagio] sepius quam semel, det ~a [AS: *agenfrigea*] (id est liber cujus habentur) j. sol. et inveritet (*Quad.*) *GAS* 111 (cf. ib. 109: recipiat ~a corium ejus).

agentaculum v. jentaculum.

agentia, agency, action (in active aspect).

secundum id quod agit, magis proprie videtur dici ~ia et percutientia, et secundum id quod patitur actio et percussio Anselm (*Ver.* 8) I 187; providentia ex sua significatione non tantum permissionem sed aliquem actum sive ~iam quandam importat Bradw. *CD* 283a; tercio modo accipitur accio pro ~ia, que est forma accidentalis qua agens formaliter et actualiter denominatur agens, et ex tali ~ia procedit motus Wycl. *Act.* 38; in ~iis injustis, cujusmodi sunt ~ie contra consilia Domini *Id. Civ. Dom.* 40.

ager [CL], field, arable plot. **b** (fig.). **c** field for (Christian) action (cf. *Matth.* xiii 38).

fructus agrorum viridi de cespite ruris / carpo Aldh. *Aen.* 24 (*Locusta*) 2; quod [hordeum] dum..eodem in agro sereret Bede *HE* IV 28; novalis ager, *brocen land*, ..squalidus ager, *forlætan æcer* Ælf. *Gl.*; compascuus ager, *gemæne læs* Ælf. *Sup.*; ibi aecclesia cui pertinet una hida..et medietas agrorum *DB* I 38b; **11..** ille molendinos, hic nostros surripit ăgros (*Quer. Cleri*) *Sat. Poets* II 217; spondet opes et ăgros, Nig *SS* 3657; cum a silvis ad agros, ab agris ad villas ..humani generis ordo processerit Gir. *TH* III 10. **b** in hac sententia spinas dubitationum ab agro mentis mee eradicasti Adel *QN* 69. **c** pius agri spiritalis cultor Bede *HE* II 15; qui [prelati] in agro sunt dum terram mentis nostre aratro doctrine sue proscindunt Pull. *Sent.* 931a; **1327** salutem et in agro dominico jugiter prosperari *Lit. Cant.* I 259; **1559** ad dominici agri culturam *Conc. Scot.* II 141.

2 specific area of land, acre. **b** (?) Cornish acre. *Cf. acra.*

850 (13c) dimidium agrum quod nostra linga dicimus *Healve aker CS* 460; **963** (12c) unam mansam cum xij agrorum quantitate *CS* 1121; omni die debeo arare integrum agrum [AS: *fulne æcer*] aut plus Ælf. *Coll.* 90; habet abbas..vj agros nemoris et vj agros prati *Dom. Exon.* 182 (= *DB* I (*Devon*) 103b: vj acras prati); Heringod habet inde i sullinc decem agros (*sic*) minus *Dom. Cant.* 2v; **a1112** hec est conventio quam P. de S. ..fecit de feudo suo, id est terra unius hide et terra xxviij agrorum *Cart. Rams.* I 129 (= *Chr. Rams.* 236; cf. ib. 266). **b** geldabat pro j agro terre; terra est iii car' *DB* I (*Cornw.*) 122; geldabat pro dimidio ferling; ibi est unus ager; terra j car' *Ib.* 122b; geldabat pro uno agro; ibi tamen est una virga terre *Ib.* 124.

3 county.

in Angliam transire per agrum Salopiensem P. Verg. *Vat. app.* III 207.

agerarius v. aggregarius.

agere [CL], to drive. **b** (w. *iter*) to direct. **c** to urge, induce. **d** to pass, spend (a period of time). **e** to emit, yield up, bring forth.

errantes fluctibus actos / ..ad litora duco Aldh. *Aen.* 92 (*Pharus*) 7; inimicis qui..praedas in terra agebant Bede *HE* I 14; nubes..ventorum viribus acte *V. Merl.* 758; opilio pastas oves agebat †ac [? l. a] pascuis W. Cant. *Mir. Thom.* IV 43; navis motu suo acta preterit W. Fitzst. *Thom. prol.* 15; per juga, per sepes Jovis egit ad oscula se pes Serlo Wilt. 18. 48; **s1297** molendino cuidam quod vento agebatur Trevet 359. **b** iter agentes Bede *HE* V 6; quando rex iter agit *Domus Reg.* 133. **c** catervas / quantas exemplis egerunt credere Christo Aldh. *VirgV* 1185; Hadrianus ad suscipiendum episcopatum actus est Bede *HE* IV 1; laicos ..ut ad discendum psalmos intenderent agebat G. Crispin *Herl.* 104; audacia agebat Brittones in hostem; fortitudo vero hostis agebat imprudentiam eorum in confusionem H. Hunt. *HA* II 12; aguntur petulancia R. Bury *Phil.* 17. 218; **s1463** pudore actus, non voto, ad ecclesiam festinavit *Croyl. Cont. B* 537. **d** quadragesimae tempus agere Bede *HE* IV 30; in magna perfectione vitam egerat *Ib.* V 9; **1504** dum diem in humanis egerit *Conc.* III 649. **e** prostratum ac jam animam agentem Beleth *RDO* 4. 17; **1309** agendo penitencie dignos fructus *Lit. Cant.* I 34 (cf. *Luke* iii 8).

2 (trans.) **a** to do, perform (in general sense). **b** to perform, practise (a specific act), to conduct, apply (procedure). **c** to execute (an official act or document). **d** to play the part of.

a aegit, *wraec GlC* A 316; **680** totum hoc contra evangelii praecepta..agere noscuntur Aldh. *Ep.* 4 p. 484; cuncta quae agenda didicerat sollicitus agere curabat Bede *HE* III 19; digna viro vir ago, si te colo, summa virago Serlo Wilt. 18. 85; **1312** de predicto appello nichil ulterius actum fuit *SelCCoron* 66. **b** **610** ad sola missarum sollemnia agenda (*Lit. Papae*) Bede *HE* II 29; missae solemnibus actis Aldh. *VirgV* 979; joci varietatem..agere ceperunt *V. Cuthb.* I 3; jejunium agere Bede *HE* IV 14; pontificatum agente Sergio *Ib.* V 7; Deo gratias agens *Ib.* 21; missa matutinalis pro eo festive agatur Lanfr. *Const.* 186; amplis.. edificiis modicas expensas agunt W. Malm. *GR* III 245; **1166** pridie quam ad hanc causam agendam venimus *Canon. G. Sempr.* 90v.; excubias agere Beleth *RDO* 21. 33; cum nocturnas..agunt vigilias Gerv. Tilb. III 61; medico cuidam..qui ejus tunc curam agebat Gir. *PI* III 14; **1245** qualiter concilium agi debeat (*Invent. S. Paul.*) *Arch.* L 498; vices agens subdiaconi M. Par. *Maj.* III 339; ad agendam penitentiam *Ib.* 512; **1325** qualiter..agatur nocturna laus; ..qualiter matutini agantur *Ac. Durh.* III 717; **1328** dominacioni vestre preces agimus *Conc.* II 551; in crastino in capitulo agat inde clamorem *Cust. Cant.* 78; **c1400** si volueritis michi agere communem legem (R. Wyche) *EHR* V 539. **c** **673** actum in mense et indictione supra scripta (*Syn. Hertf.*) Bede *HE* IV 5; **681** (12c) actum in mense Octobri indictione nona *CS* 57; **858** hactum est *CS* 496; **938** (14c) acta est hec prefata donatio..indictione xi *CS* 728; **1307** actum fuit istud testamentum die Jovis *Deeds Balliol* 56. **d** fratrem..admonuit ut comitem, non monachum, ageret W. Malm. *GR* V 398; egit officialem Ferr. *Kinloss* 39.

3 (absol.) to act, conduct proceedings. **b** (w. adv. or sim.). **c** (w. *ut*) to effect, contrive, design. **d** (w. inf.) to strive, venture. **e** to take legal action. **f** to celebrate mass.

genera..et species..cum se in diversas species..multiplicent agere videntur Eriug. *Per.* 472b (cf. ib. 463a: haec a Graecis vocantur..πράττειν..quae Latialiter dicuntur agere); Anselm I 187 (v. agentia); Adel. *QN* 44 (v. 7b infra). **b** ut prave agere metuat Bede *HE* II 1; quasi unus e convivis agebat *Ib.* V 5; **†1082** (12c) senes..qualiter.. apud Sanctum ageretur Cuthbertum..exquisiti *Feod. Durh.* xxxviii; dicis agisque bene Serlo Wilt. 23. 6; quos in vita neglegentius egisse novimus Pull. *Sent.* 917a; civitas semper civiliter agens Devizes 25v.; errassem..si aliter egissem Rolle *IA* 239; **1450** cum tua voluntas omnis in bene agendo bonis studentibus diversetur *Let. Ch. Ch.* 16. **c** actum est ut aliqua videre possemus Osb. *Mir. Dunst.* 1; agit unusquisque pro gradu suo..ut regem..non taedeat Ailr. *Ed. Conf.* 751b. **d** **s1065** quatinus lector agnoscat quanta cura rex egerit a periculo..absolvi Ciren. IV 16; si bene sibi cavet, a tanta sententia ipse viderit et aliis improperare turpia parcius agat Gir. *Symb.* I 31 p. 324. **e** Ric. Angl. *Summa* 4 (v. actio 4a); **1268** ita..quod..attornatos facere possint tam agendo quam defendendo *MGL* II 253; **1285** consules..debent..facere, ducere et agere in judicio contra ..impedientes *RGasc* II 261; **1357** de..agendo, defendendo, excipiendo, replicando *MunAcOx* 193; si jus accreverit homini agendi in judicio Fortescue *LLA* 23. **f** agitur illa hebdomada de S. Trinitate *RegulC* 59.

4 (absol. w. prep.) **a** (w. *ad*) to promote. **b** (w. *contra*) to contravene. **c** (w. *cum*) to deal with. **d** (w. *de*) to deal with, treat of. **e** (w. *in*) to be in (a condition or place).

a **c1318** ad ipsorum exheredacionem ex certo proposito agebamus J. Mason *Ep.* 16. **b** ecclesiam nostram vestre subjicere contra decreta..agit H. Cantor 5v. **c 1220** misericorditer agitur cum eo *SelPlCrown* 127. **d** in contrarium agatur de illo qui permanet in sua malicia *Cust. Cant.* 251; phisica est sciencia agens de natura rerum *SB* 36. **e** eo in extremis agente, ..conveniant omnes ad tuendum exitum ejus *RegulC* 65; **1325** episcopo in rebus humanis agente *Lit. Cant.* I 156; **1406** dum ageret in humanis *Ib.* III 98; Gurmundo in Britannie regno..jam in sceptris agente Gir. *TH* III 38; **c1228** tunc aberat et agebat in transmarinis *Feod. Durh.* 295; **1374** tenens locum..decani..in remotis agentis *Cart. Boarstall* no. 844.

5 (gdv. as sb. f. s., *sc. missa*) celebration of mass.

altare..in quo..a presbytero loci illius agendae eorum sollemniter celebrantur Bede *HE* II 3; dum agendam mortuorum sedulus orator passim deambulando cantaret Gerv. Tilb. III 17.

6 (gdv. as sb. n. pl.) **a** celebration of mass. **b** conditions, terms. **c** legal proceedings. **d** affairs, business.

a intra missarum agenda prorupit in lacrimas W. Malm. *GR.* II 218; in agendis parvulorum mortuorum 'requiem' oramus Pull. *Sent.* 917A; pontificalem benedictionem agendis interserens, missam more solenni..peregit Ad. Eyns. *Hug.* V 12. **b** hec sunt pacis agenda [AS: *ðis is ðæt frið*] (*Quad.*) *GAS* 127. **c** tertius [liber] est de statu et agendis causarum (*Quad. Argumentum*) *GAS* 535; si quis in curia sua vel in quibuslibet agendorum locis placitum tractandum habeat (*Leg. Hen.*) *Ib.* 564. **d** de statu et agendis regni (*Quad. Argumentum*) *GAS* 532; **1191** precipimus ut secundum dispositionem vestram de omnibus agendis regni nostri..faciatis (*Lit. regis*) Diceto *YH* II 91; **1214** pro agendis dilecti et fidelis nostri G. de M. *Pat* 107b; **1218** ad agenda nostra parcium illarum feliciter disponenda *Pat* 152; **1219** propter quod removeremur a consilio et agendis filii nostri (*AncC* II 5) *RL* I 34; risum proscribit luctus, ludum dolor, ira / mensuram, somnum clamor, agenda stupor Garl. *Tri. Eccl.* 16; **s1262** ipse major omnia agenda sua per illos [cives] agebat *Leg. Ant. Lond.* 55; **1342** agenda nostra vestre propiciacionis manibus..recommendamus (*RomanR*) *Foed.* V 313b; **s1321** [rex] retinuit..Hugonem le Spenser sibi secretarium et per eum ductus..fuit multociens in agendis Avesb. *Ed. III* 77; **1381** quod major pars..populi..nostro..consilio in agendis potissime regulantur (*Lit. IV Ordinum*) *Ziz.* 294.

7 (pr. ppl.) **a** active, actual (phil.). **b** (as sb. n.) agent (phil.). **c** (as sb. m.) agent, deputy.

a intellectus agens dicitur qui influit in animas nostras illuminans ad scientiam et virtutem, ..licet intellectus possibilis possit dici agens ab actu intelligendi Bacon *Maj.* III 45; variatur per potenciam quamdam agentem et aliam possibilem, quia respectu ejusdem objecti aliud principium oportet esse potenciam activam, ut faciat objectum in actu cujus est agens.. Knapwell *Not.* 187. **b** 'occido', quod est patientis et agentis ut 'ruo' Aldh *PR* 140 p. 196; agentia et percutientia ab agente et percutiente dicitur, quae sc. agens et percutiens..activa sunt Anselm (*Ver.* 8) I 187; quidquid..in aliud agit, ..a patiente tamen in agens agitur Adel. *QN* 44; agens naturale multiplicat virtutem suam a se usque in patiens Gros. 60; agentia nobilia non possunt [complere suas species], ut angeli et celestia et homines et cetera animata Bacon *Tert.* 109; **c1301** agens est prestancius paciente *Quaest. Ox* 346. **c 1542** per me J. H. presbiterum..agentem *Wills Richmond* 36.

8 (p. ppl. *actus* as sb. n.) **a** act, deed. **b** (record of) proceedings. **c** act of Parliament.

celsis ubi floruit actis Bede (*Hymn*) *HE* IV 18; actio et percussio ab ~o et percusso, quae passiva sunt, derivantur Anselm (*Ver.* 8) I 187; **a1350** omnia ~a judicialia, sine quibus ad sententiam perveniri non poterit, sine scriptura procedant *Stat. Cantab.* 325; **1435** ~um corporale..incontinencie *MunAcOx* 509. **b 1231** nullam sectam producit nec ~a ostendit *CurR* XIV 1394; **1237** nisi [procurator] apud ~a fuerit constitutus *Conc. Syn.* 256; **c1530** ex ~is..visitacionis nostre nobis constat (*Vis. Leicester*) *EHR* IV 308; **1546** requisivit..officialem ad delendum..~a et contractus una cum ~o assignacionis, cessionis et translacionis *Offic. S. Andr.* 157. **c 1549** sub penis ~orum Parlamenti *Conc. Scot.* II 120.

agest- v. agist-. ageus v. hagius. agga v. erga.

aggaudēre, to delight in.

ad I. ..quasi ad unicum filium adgaudebant Bede *Gen.* (xxi 10) 189; adgaudens nominum auspiciis Gosc. *Aug. Maj.* 53; O decus..virginitatis, cui sic adgaudet natura..angelice dignitatis Osb. *V. Dunst.* 40; Willelmus rex..~ebat et ei [Lanfranco] et aliis quos in bono fervere audisset W. Malm. *GP* I 42; **s1114** affabilitas que ad cunctos in eo vigebat..honori ejus ~ere bonum quemque faciebat Eadmer *HN* 267.

aggenerare, to generate, produce (in sequence).

in speculo..secundum motum ymaginantis successive non nova ydea adgeneratur Gilb. III 128. 1; calor ageneratur ex motu solis Bacon VIII 118; stupe ardentes que in ventosa calorem ~ant *Ib.* 208.

aggeneratrix, generative (f.).

in istis inferioribus resistentia medii non est caloris ageneratrix in moto Gros. 82.

agger [CL], heap, stack. **b** earthwork, embankment, motte. **c** highway. **d** mill-dam. **e** ridge of 'rig and fur' field (cf. D. Murray: *Early Burgh Organization in Scotland* (1924) I 103).

Alpes / aggeribus niveis et montis vertice saeptas Aldh. *CE* 3. 25; jurans quod potius praesentis littora portus / illi committet aggere sub lapidum G. Amiens *Hast.* 584; **s1216** [Savaricus] omnia blada..sicut erant..aggerata combussit, ipsomet docente quod in imis ~erum incendiarii ignem supponerent M. Par. *Min.* II 190. **b** cum..mansionem angustam circumvallante ~ere construxisset Bede *HE* IV 26 p. 271; aggeribus crassis nisa est gens Picta rebellis / Anglorum solitas jam tunc non ferre catenas Frith. 539; castellum..editissimo ~ere sublatum *G. Steph.* I 16; in turrim cumulato terrarum ~ere sitam Gir. *IK* I 4; **s1297** cingitur villa [Wincheleseia] non muro lapideo sed ~ere de terra facto Trevet 359. **c** ~er, *eorðbyre* vel *geworht stræt*, strata vel delapidata Ælf. *Gl.*; [rex Elfredus] pacem infudit provincie, ut etiam per publicos ~eres..armillas aureas juberet suspendi que viantium aviditatem riderent W. Malm. *GR* II 122; cum..~erem calcaret publicum (*Mir. S. Edm.*) Ciren. I 354. **d s1318** fecit unum novum molendinum..stans prope aquam, cujus ~er perficitur ex petra veluta ad modum parietis Whittlesey 165. **e 1487** de sex ~eribus jacentibus contigue super le Comon Lonyng *Reg. Glasg.* 453.

aggerare [CL], to heap up. **b** to accumulate.

s1216 blada..sicut erant circa festum S. Mich. ~ata M. Par. *Min.* II 190. **b** agerat, adicit *GlC* A 259; in ~andis thesauris mirus W. Malm. *GR* III 277.

aggeratio, heap. **b** accumulation.

fecit..illo advehi multam struem..atque ex omni materia ~onem *G. Herw.* 334b (cf. aggregatio 2a). **b 1367** matrimonia clandestina..solemnizancium..temeritatem..penarum ~one reprimere *Conc.* III 71.

aggerere [CL], to bring.

aggerem aggestis de fossato sablonibus..dici etimologia declarat Aldh. *PR* 140 p. 195; donec adgesto a militibus pulvere [crux] terrae figeretur Bede *HE* III 2.

aggeries, heap.

turres aequabit harenis; / elatam turrem destruet aggerie G. Amiens *Hast.* 678.

agestare v. agistare.

aggestio, accumulation.

sola est de qua nonnihil culpetur pecunie ~o, quam undecunque..congregabat W. Malm. *GR* III 280.

aggist- v. agist-.

agglomerare, to attach.

milites..orthodoxorum falangibus ~antur Aldh. *VirgP* 36 p. 283; **10..** adglomerantur, *togeðeoddan* WW.

agglutinare [CL], to attach. **b** (fig.).

quibus [cintris] amotis testudo nimis tenaciter ~ata devolvi cepit W. Cant. *Mir. Thom.* VI 49. **b** militibus..secum in castello ~atis *G. Steph.* I 14.

aggraciliare, to thin, shrink.

alia agraciliantur et arescunt quia nutrimenti habent inopiam Ric. Med. *Micr. Anat.* 227.

aggratulari, to give thanks (to or for). **b** to give a welcome.

quisquis..hujusmodi voluntate preditum se sentit, dono Dei ~etur Pull. *Sent.* 894A; **1188** prudentie tue et probitati agratulantes, tibi..securum transitum..concedimus (*Lit. Imp.*) Diceto *YH* II 53; pro..beneficiorum exhibitionibus putavi vestre liberalitati potius agratulari silentio quam eloquio regratiari Ad. Marsh *Ep.* 78. **b** risu gratissimo fratri Willelmo ~ans J. Ford *Wulf.* 72.

aggratulatio, thanksgiving. **b** welcome. **c** congratulation.

ecclesiam..puto, jucundatam sub locutione debita preci ~one quadam, non ingratam auctori Pull. *Sent.* 917B. **b** qui cum introduxisset eam, in multa hilaritate..suscepta est, adeo ut ipsa, ..tam insperata tanti viri ~one admirans .. J. Ford *Wulf.* 65. **c 1232** recepta epistula tua..pie ~onis..non modicum refocillatus est spiritus meus Gros. *Ep.* 9.

aggravamen, oppression. **b** grievance.

1275 ne quis illorum suas firmas levare possit sine ~ine populi *Hund.* I 251. **b s1431** exposuit suo superiori per ordinem totum ~en suum Amund. I 305.

aggravare [CL], to make heavier. **b** (fig.) to make more oppressive (*cf. Job* xxiii 2 *etc.*). **c** to aggravate, make more culpable.

spirituum evaporatio, ex quorum presencia corpus levigabitur, quibus evaporatis per ipsorum absenciam ~atur Bart. Angl. IV 1. **b 1149** quamvis..contra eos..manus nostras ex rigore canonum.. ~are possemus (*Lit. Papae*) Elmh. *Cant.* 399; **s1194** Anglos militaribus armis instructos ..in verberibus ~andis Diceto *YH* II 120; **s1265** ~ato super eum pondere prelii Trevet 266; **s1273** cujus super se manum senciens ~ari dedidit se eidem *Ib.* 285; ~antibus ejus [prioris] jugum guerris Graystanes 30. **c** injuriam..per tot circumstantias..plectibiliter ~atam Gir. *GE* I 34.

2 to aggravate (a sentence of excommunication). **b** to subject to aggravated excommunication.

c1270 quod..possit..excommunicare..et dictam sententiam ~are prout crudelius voluerit *Cart. Bilsington* no. 38. **b 1288** suspensus, excommunicatus et ~atus, incorrigibilem penitus se reddebat *MunAcOx* 44; **1506** si..excommunicacionis sententiam pertinaciter sustinuerint..omnes ipsos..in hiis scriptis ~amus (*Lit. Papae*) *Cart. Beauly* 180; **c1520** excommunicandi, ~andi, reaggravandi *Conc. Scot.* I ccxlii.

3 to oppress, aggrieve. **b** to become more oppressive.

prioribus adgravata doloribus et rapta confestim de mundo Bede *HE* IV 19; me sopor adgravat ingens Wulf. *Swith.* I 381; haec est..alleviatio quam omni populo meo previderi volo in quibus nimis omnino fuerant ~ati [AS: *gedrehte*] (*Quad.*) *GAS* 357 (= *Inst. Cnut.* ib.: gravati); **1249** cum..se conqueratur contra justitiam ~atum super terra quadam (*AncC* III 61) *RL* II 326; **1276** per magistros ..hospitalis nimium ~atur et deterioratur dictus burgus *Hund.* I 61; **s1381** ~atus tandem lethali morbo *Hist. Durh.* 3; **1465** sub pena x li., ..solvendo unam partem..officio cancellariatus, secundam partem universitati et terciam parti ~ate *MunAcOx* 714. **b a1175** post tempus ~ante michi stomacho quisivi adjuvamen *Lib. Landav.* 4.

aggravatio, increase of weight. **b** (fig.) weighing down. **c** adding weight (to proposals). **d** (fig.) burden.

[caliditas] agendo in substantia rei..leviores partes consumit et †removentibus [? l. remanentibus] partibus grossioribus fit compactio et per consequens ~o Bart. Angl. IV 1. **b** corpus primi hominis non aggravabat revera animam; ~o enim dicit depressionem in statum naturalem que facta est per culpam Peckham *Quaest.* I 12 p. 104. **c s1459** quibus..in ~onem sue materie..per eum..expositis *Reg. Whet.* I 335. **d 958** (13c) donum liberum ab omni ~one secularis servicii *CS* 1041.

2 aggravation: **a** of guilt; **b** of penalty or sentence.

a c1236 ad ~onem peccati..accedit quod..excommunicati sunt Gros. *Ep.* 72* p. 230; in exprobracionem et ~onem ac detestacionem peccati Jeroboam Ockham *Dial.* 582. **b** cum pene ~one corporalis Bracton 118b; **1342** per censuras ecclesiasticas et ~ones earum *Conc.* II 693; **1423** ratificacio condemnacionis..et ~o contra..participantes (*Ord. Conc. Sien.*) Amund. I 167n.; **1545** excommunicationis et ~onis sententias *Conc. Scot.* I cclxiv.

aggravativus, increasing weight. **b** oppressive (med.).

accidentaliter est caliditas ~a Bart. Angl. IV 1 (cf. aggravare 1a). **b** dolor ~us medii pectoris Gilb. IV 190. 2; humor..agravativus melancolicum significat Bacon V 85; si causa est..frigida, [est dolor] ~us, nisi materia sit ventosa Gad. 25 v. 1.

aggravatorius, designed to aggravate (a previous sentence).

1423 procedere intendimus per denunciaciones solempnes et ~ias sentencias *Reg. Heref.* 36; **1523** quasdam litteras nostras ~ias et citatorias *Form. S. Andr.* I 94.

aggrea- v. agrea-.

aggredi [CL], **a** (intr.) to draw near (menacingly). **b** (trans.) to approach. **c** to attack, assail.

adgrediuntur, *geeodun GlC* A 217; numquam aggreditur rugis sulcata senectus Aldh. *VirgV* 2289; in ira commoti armis in fine aggressi sunt *G. Herw.* f. 337b. **b** heremi vastitatem aggressus Aldh. *VirgP* 37; cum..amator..lupanar..~eretur *Ib.* 45. **c** juvenem atrocioribus tormentis ac terroribus ~iuntur Gosc. *Mir. Aug.* 534; dux..cum paucis multos audacissime aggressus est H. Hunt. *HA* VII 25; **1263** Lewelinus..et complices sui..terras nostras..hostiliter sunt agressi *Cl* 303; cum flos confringitur / et mors vite venam aggreditur J. Howd. *Ph.* 949.

2 to undertake, embark on. **b** (w. inf.).

ut hoc opus adgredi auderem Bede *HE pref.* p. 7; iter adgressuri *Ib.* III 15; **10..** adgreditur, *onginneð* WW; **s938** astu exploratoris munus aggressus W. Malm. *GR* II 131; id unanimiter ~iamur Gir. *EH* I 9; surge..festinus; ~ere [v.l. egredere] callem prematurus (*V. S. Edm.*) Ciren. I 354. **b** aggressi sunt impugnare insulam *G. Herw.* 335; mirum qua temeritate bis in die..conficere quidam ~i presumant Gir. *GE* I 49.

3 (pass.) to be attacked or accused. **b** to be urged. **c** to be undertaken.

s1097 urbs aggressa est H. Hunt *HA* VII 6; **s1305** [Willelmus le Waleis] per..justiciarium domini regis..pro traditore ejusdem regis aggressus *Ann. Lond.* 139; **s1318** coram rege multipliciter aggressus *Ann. Paul.* 283; in pugna illa non est deliberatio ex parte aggressi generaliter, set ex parte ~ientis tantum vel neutrius Upton 72. **b 1298** agressus fuit ut faceret legem, et dixit quod noluit facere *Rec. Leic.* I 224. **c** sicut providus in ~iendis sic pertinax erat in aggressis Gir. *EH* I 43.

aggregare [CL], to call together, assemble. **b** to recruit.

in pugna Australium Saxonum, quos contra eum Edric..adgregarat Bede *HE* IV 26; ~ati tandem ascendunt puppes *Enc. Emmae* 106; aggregat et strictim compellit abire quirites G. Amiens *Hast.* 309; ut..viros..ibidem ~are placuerit Osb. *V. Dunst.* 18; **1381** ~ata sibi magna potestate de communitate..ville *RParl* III 106b; **1573** cum aliis..proditoribus..~atis, assemblatis et armatis *Pat* 1105 m. 7. **b** [Eugenia] sanctorum coetibus ~atur Aldh. *VirgP* 44; **1415** te..nostrorum..capellanorum consorcio favorabiliter ~amus (*Lit. Papae*) *Reg. Cant.* III 451.

2 to heap together, accumulate. **b** to add (together), combine. **c** to add to, increase.

cum alites..adgregatis quisquiliis nidum fundarent Felix *Guthl.* 39; quibus [vaporibus elevatis], ~atis et condensatis in nubes Bart. Angl. IV 1; **1265** in asportatione pecunie de regno nostro undique ~ate (*AncC* II 46) *RL* II 292; ysopus humida est sordicies ~ata super lanam yliorum ovium *SB* 25. **b** nomina quae..accumulantes ~avimus

Aldh. *PR* 136; **10..** adgregatur, *wæs togerimed* WW; si tricennale unius vel anniversarium tricennale alterius annumeretur vel ~etur, injuriabitur alteri Gir. *GE* I 49 p. 133; quadragenarius ex partibus suis aliquotis ~atis surgit in quinquagenarium Bacon VI 117; extendo hoc nomen 'aliquid' ad omne ens, vel per se vel ~atum Wycl. *Trial.* 39. **c** in contrarium agatur de illo qui permanet in sua malicia.., quod semper sua penitencia ~etur *Cust. Cant.* 251; s**1336** concesserunt regi..de qualibet sacca lane..ij m.; et..summa cujuslibet sacce usque ad xl s. excrevit, que nunc ad l s. est continue ~ata *Meaux* II 378; utinam non sit capitaneus cleri dotati temporalibus dicti dominii agregati! Wycl. *Ver.* III 268.

3 (p. ppl.) corporate (leg.). **b** (as sb. n.) aggregate, assemblage (of words).

licet persona ~ata posset presentari parti sue plus habili ad beneficium cujus est patronus, ymo persona simplex posset in casu presentare se ipsam Wycl. *Sim.* 90. **b** hoc ~atum quod sequitur disjunctive captum Paul. Angl. *ASP* 1528.

aggregarius, sheep-dog, cur.

agerarius, A. *a curdogge*, ..hic ~ius, *a scheperd dog* WW; *a cur dog*, ..*a scheperde doge*, ~ius *CathA*.

aggregatio, congregation, assembly. **b** addition to flock (fig.), recruitment.

c**1210** multa ~one servorum Dei (*Leg. Hen. add.*) *GAS* 554*n*. **b** **1247** exultant cives celibes de celebris ~one concivis (*Lit. Papae*) M. Par. *Maj.* VI 121; **1415** nulli..hominum ..liceat hanc paginam nostre recepcionis, ~onis..et dispensacionis infringere (*Lit. Papae*) *Reg. Cant.* III 452.

2 heaping together, accumulation, concentration. **b** aggregation, adding together.

adductis..structuris lignorum et lapidum et ex omni genere struis ~onem in palude..straverant *G. Herw.* 331 (cf. aggeratio a); quod stella non differt ab orbe nisi per majorem ~onem et minorem lucis..falsum est Bacon *Tert.* 118. **b** si ~onibus hujusmodi et generalitate quasi pro specialibus uti liceret Gir. *GE* I 49 p. 133; accidentia..per ~onem differentiarum cum genere in quolibet predicamento accidentium Bacon VII 21; **1381** quod dictum sacramentum [sc. altaris] sit accidens, qualitas, quantitas aut earum ~o (Wycl. *Concl.*) *Ziz.* 106.

3 (?) covenant, agreement (? *cf. agreare*).

1459 volo..quod quedam convencio de maritagio.. perimpleatur secundum veram intencionem ~onis inde inter me et Radulfum..facte *Test. Ebor.* II 243.

aggregative, collectively.

sexto accipitur substancia ~e pro multis collectis Wycl. *Ente Praed.* V 38; quandoque dicunt ~e multos actus *Id. Ver.* II 88.

aggregativus, consolidative, concentrative.

~us [dolor] est de melancolia Gilb. II 89 v. 1; color niger nihil aliud est quam privatio albedinis, et ideo nigredo est species visibilis ~a et ejusdem repercussiva Bad. Aur. 101.

aggressio [CL], attack. **b** undertaking, tackling.

1239 ~onis hostilis furore deposito (*Lit. Imp.*) M. Par. *Maj.* III 565; s**1302** hostilium ~onum magnificus triumphator *Flor. Hist.* III 112; impugnaciones hostiles et ~ones iniquas *Plusc.* VIII 20. **b** non sine..maximarum difficultatum ~onibus Ad. Marsh *Ep.* 30 p. 125; ne vos absterreat tanti laboris ~o Garl. *Tri. Eccl.* 96; **1321** causam instantis ~onis sui itineris versus marchiam..novit *Lit. Cant.* I 56; **1336** morum generositate et magnorum operum ~one nobilitatus *Ib.* II 116.

aggressor, robber.

agressor, *strudere* vel *reafere* Ælf. *Gl.*

aggressus, attack. **b** undertaking, tackling.

si..pontifices ~u precipiti confligere temptaverint contra ..vite temporalis inquietationes Ad. Marsh *Ep.* 147 c. 43; **1299** ad hostiles ~us et incursus procedens regnum nostrum invasit (*Lit. Arch. Cant.*) *Ann. Lond.* 119; **1338** pericula †aggressium alienigenarum hostium *RScot* 552a (cf. ib. 453a: ~ibus..resistendum); **1341** coacti sumus..ab inchoatis magnanimiter hostium ~ibus..desistere (*Lit. Regis*) Avesb. *Ed. III* 95; s**1401** Oenus..per intraneos ~us..in fugam pulsus est Ad. Usk. 71. **b** utinam..principes nostri in hujus expeditionis ~um proficisci meruissent Gir. *EH* II 29; **1282** ante ~um principalis negocii *Conc. Syn.* 923.

agguis v. anguis. agiamentum v. aisiamentum 1a.

agibilis, practicable, (sb. n.) object of action (πρακτόν). **b** (pl.) practical affairs, business.

sicut prudencia est habitus cognoscitivus circa ~ia, ita ars circa factibilia Duns *Metaph.* I 5 17 B; judicium est de particulari ~i *Id. Sent.* I xli. 1. 15; omnem de ~ibus questionem consilium probat esse R. Bury *Phil. prol.* 2; prudencia est ~ium, cujusmodi sunt consiliari, ordinare, precavere et ceteri actus hujusmodi immanentes Wycl. *Ente Praed.* XV 134. **b** s**1294** senescallus Francie, ..vir quidem in ~ibus admodum circumspectus Rish. 146; **1328** priori in ~ium administracione assistatis *Reg. Exon.* II f. 59; **1377** viri..in †agilibus providi *FormOx* 380; **1444** consilio expertorum virorum qui in armorum ~ibus conversantur *Cl* 294 m. 6*d*.; **1456** pro expensis..existencium apud Perth in ~ibus domini regis versus Forfare *ExchScot* 245.

agilis [CL], mobile, agile, nimble; *v. et. agibilis* b.

volubilis et ~is polorum vertigo Aldh. *Met.* 2 p. 63; c**750** accipitres..qui..ad..artem [arripiendi grues] animo ~es ac bellicosi educantur (*Lit. Regis Cantiae*) *Ep. Bonif.* 105; aedituusque graves oppandit agillimus aedes Frith. 1141; gens hec gens levis et ~is Gir. *DK* I 8; tertia [navis].. ~ior illis, retorta in altum, diffugit periculum Devizes 33v.; Hardiknotus corpore erat agillimo Major 92.

agilitas, mobility, agility. **b** (of mind).

gimnicorum..qui ~ate corporis theatrales..pompas.. adipiscuntur Aldh. *VirgP* 3; omnes coetaneos in ~ate et petulantia superans *V. Cuthb.* I 3; que quidem forma vel causa in igne, cum sursum fertur, vocatur levitas; ..in aere igitur vocetur ~as Adel. *QN* 60; equi..~ate pervicaci feruntur W. Fitzst. *Thom. prol.* 11; bucee, ..vasa magne capacitatis et ~atis Devizes 28v; ~as est conformitas corporis ad animam Hales *Qu.* 1326. **b** s**1139** episcopus Eliensis, ..ut erat animi versutioris ~atisque expeditioris *G. Steph.* I 35; animus..~atis innate beneficio quatuor mundi cardines uno momento complectitur Gir. *EH pref.*

agiliter, swiftly, nimbly.

properans ~er ad novam vitam *V. Osw.* 415; s**1138** cum.. viderimus..ignitos..globos..variis in locis ~er sese et densanter movere *G. Steph.* I 24; cum currerent agillime Brinton *Serm.* 11 p. 41; **1408** cum..solum restet execucio juramenti, quam ~er potest expedire *Conc.* III 302.

agillarius v. agellarius. agillaster v. agelaster. agimonia v. agrimonia. agiographus v. hagiographus.

aginare [LL], (?) to hawk goods.

†agonantes, explicantes *GlC* A 386.

agista [cf. gista], joist.

1271 in grosso meremio et cheveronibus et ~is emptis *Pipe Wint.* 159299 r. 5*d*.

agistamentum [OF *agistement*], agistment, (right of or payment for) pasturage.

1184 incipit ~um domini regis xv dies ante festum S. Michaelis et durat xv dies post festum S. Michaelis (*Assisa Foreste* 7) R. Howd. II 246; **1188** debent dim. m. pro transgressione ~i *Pipe* 125; **1200** custodiam..boscorum ..et agistiamentum porcorum in ipsis boscis *RChart* I 76b; habeant adgistamenta sua et pasnagium suum libere *Ib.* 82b; **1221** summone..agistatores quod ibi sint cum ~is suis *Cl* 475b; a**1230** sciatis me dedisse..burgensibus meis.. pasturam in bosco meo sine ~o vel panagio *BBC* (*Barnard Castle*) 71; **1281** de xxiiij s. receptis de proficuo et agistiamentis animalium in boscis *Cart. Glam.* 825; a**1310** concessimus..Thome..quod liceret sibi..l oves..contra defensas agistare, ita tamen quod nullum faceret agistiamentum.. nisi in separalibus suis vel pastura sua *Meaux* II 220; **1310** salva..communia pasture ad decem jumenta..pascencia in eadem foresta toto tempore anni sine ~o vel impedimento *FormA* 384; **1350** nichil de aggistamentis plus in parco, quia ad bestias de venacione *Surv. Durh. Hatf.* 237; **1373** pro firma et agestiamento averiorum suorum *Hal. Durh.* 121; **1504** de porcis agistatis..nihil..quia nulla pessona; set respondent de xvj s. de ~o vaccarum *Crawley* 492; **1604** accipiebat in adjestiamentum oves.. *CourtR Tempsford* (*Beds RO*) r. 1.

2 raising of water level. **b** (?) (erection of) lists or stands.

a**1250** dedit..molendinum..cum..agistiamento aque et attachiamento molendini *Cart. Chester* 320; **1268** cum refluxu et agistiamento aque *Ib.* 330; **1271** cum..aqueductu et agistiamento vivarii *Ib.* 422; **1316** pro licencia..agistiamenti aque stagni predicti W. super terram et pratum predicti Lewelini ad altitudinem stagni..molendini *AncD* (*Wales*) C6310. **b** **1397** pro diversis operibus factis pro ~is et ludis regis et regine..contra festa Natalis Domini *LTR AcWardr.* 5 r. 7*d*. (cf. ib.: circa cariagium dictorum ~orum et operum de London' usque Coventre).

agistare, ~iare [OF *agister*], to agist (animals), put to pasture or assess for pasture duty. **b** to agist (woodland etc.), assess or use for pasturage. **c** to assess (pasture duty).

1185 reddit compotum de xl s. pro porcis suis ~atis contra assisam *Pipe* 108; c**1200** pro qualibet vacca ~ata.. iij d. per annum *Rec. Leic.* I 5; **1217** quod unusquisque liber homo possit ducere porcos suos per dominicum boscum nostrum..ad ~andum eos in boscis suis (*Ch. Forest*) *StRealm* I 21; **1233** ipsa eos [porcos] misit ad pessonam et.. nomine suo recepti fuerunt a forestariis et.. per forestarios fuerunt adgestati *CurR* XV 905; inquiratur qui receperint finem pro extraneis animalibus ~andis in foresta (*Cap. Forestae*) *Fleta* 90; **1326** quod presentant..quot averia quilibet habet ut possunt (*sic*) ~ari ad proficuum domini *CBaron* 147; **1335** adgistavit bidentes extraneos in campum *CourtR* 188/33 r. 1; **1337** *utlaier* de Laysyngby..de averiis villate.. noctanter ~atis in foresta *KRAc* 131/27 m. 6; **1350** de iij bobus..aggistatis in parco in estate *Surv. Durh. Hatf.* 237; **1384** neque..possunt agestare animalia extraneorum in vastis communibus *Surv. Denb.* 107. **b** **1184** iiij milites ponantur ad ~andum boscos suos et ad recipiendum pannagium..; et defendit rex quod nullus ~et boscos suos infra metas foreste antequam bosci regis ~entur (*Assisa Foreste* 7) R. Howd. II 246; **1217** unusquisque liber homo ~et boscum suum in foresta..et habeat pannagium suum (*Ch. Foreste*) *StRealm* I 20; pasturam..cum averiis suis.. †agitasset et occupasset *Entries* 151. **c** **1301** negavit recipere et colligere agistiamentum ~iatum per villam *CourtR Hales* 418.

2 (? infl. by *aggestio*) to build up (? w. joists). **b** to raise the level of (water). **c** to overflow.

1237 muros ejusdem [cancelli] exaltari et bene ~ari et planchiari..facias *Cal. Liberate* VI 2431; **1249** faciat habere..carpentario regis xxv fusta ad turrim Judeorum in castro regis Wintonie aggistandam *Cl* 146; **1324** plures perticate predictorum fossatorum..sunt..irreparate, pro eo quod terre pro quibus ille perticate ~ate fuerunt..sunt distracte *Terr. Fleet* lviii; **1359** fossate maris..sunt nimis debiles; ..ideo necesse est quod de novo adjestentur (*CoramR*) *Pub. Works* I 252; **1375** fossata..debent de novo ~ari et reparari (*Anc. Indict.*) *Ib.* 271. **b** c**1270** dedit.. porcionem suam aqueductus..ad stagnum levandum..et aquam super terram suam ~iandum quantum voluerit *Cart. Chester* 447. **c** **1316** propartem suam prati super quam aqua stagni..~at *AncD* (*Wales*) C6310.

3 to assign or annex land.

1234 tenet j croftam que quondam abstracta fuit de dominico et ~ata eidem tenemento *Cust. Glast.* 67.

4 to assess (person or tenement) for payment or service.

s**1296** milites ad custodiam maris deputati ~arunt episcopos..secundum valorem terrarum suarum ad equos et arma, viz. ad xx libratas terre unum equum coopertum B. Cotton 312; **1297** assignatus fuit..ad custodiam maris faciendam, racione cujus custodie faciende..tenementa hominum ejusdem comitatus [Kancie] ~ata fuerunt ad certam pecunie summam..solvendam *PlR CP*121 r. 72 (74); **1306** cum contigerit aliquem..grossas mercandisas exercentem inter cives [Norwyci] secundum quantitatem mercandise sue ~ari et de porcione ipsum contingente ad auxilia..satisfacere noluerit.., moneatur prior..ut ipsum sic racionabiliter ~atum ad porcionem..contribuendam.. distringat *ChartR* 93 m. 21; **1311** ad solvendum xl s. pro communi contribucione facienda per communem consensum omnium nostrum ~ati estis *Doc. Eng. Black Monks* 170; **1355** de hominibus ~atis ad arma in leta de Berstret *Rec. Norw.* I 393; c**1360** Johannes..~atus et arrayatus est ad unum hominem peditem armatum cum purpont.. (*Leet Roll Norw.*) *Norf. Arch.* XIV 314.

agistatio, pasturing of animals or duty paid therefor.

1220 de ~one bosci de Brembelwud' *Cl* 433b; **1239** ab omni depastione et ~one..simus exclusi *BBC* (*Leicester*) 72; **1257** quod..averia ville..possint uti pastura..sine ~one *FormA* 309; c**1300** quod porci..liberam haberent ~onem in..bosco tam tempore †pestionis quam in alio tempore (*Reg. Wetheral*) *MonA* 590b.

2 assessment (for service).

c**1360** arrayacio et ~o hominum armatorum et sagittariorum in leta de Wymer (*Leet Roll Norw.*) *Norf. Arch.* XIV 314.

agistator, 'agister', official charged w. allotting pasturage in forests and collecting duty paid therefor.

a**1190** capiat pannagium de hominibus suis quando ~ores nostri ceperint pannagium nostrum *CalPat 1461–7* 58; **1190** W. S. cum ~oribus debet vij s. ..pro pasnagio *Pipe* 137; **1212** venire facias omnes..~ores ballive tue ad agistandos predictos boscos *Cl* 125a; **1217** in principio xv dierum ante festum S. Mich., quando ~ores conveniunt ad ~andum dominicos boscos nostros, et circa festum S. Martini, quando ~ores nostri debent recipere pannagium nostrum (*Ch. Foreste*) *StRealm* I 20; **1224** agistores foreste de Wochewode *LTRMem* 6 r. 8 (cf. ib. r. 20: †agitoribus); **1329** absque omni occasione..forestariorum, viridariorum, ~orum, regardatorum et quorumcumque ministrorum nostrorum foreste *Pat* 172 m. 12; *a gister*, ~or *CathA*.

1 agitare v. agistare 1b.

2 agitare [CL], to drive or chase. **b** to set in motion. **c** to hasten (intr.).

in summis cignos agitabo fugaces Aldh. *Aen.* 57 (*Aquila*) 4; **1326** averia ~are *BB St. David's* 262; **1406** pro garcione ~ante aratrum *Ac. Durh.* 222; **1428** ~anti currum prioris *Ib.* 621; **1527** ad ~andum..eosdem [boves] *Reg. Aberbr.* II 474. **b** cernua quae graditur tremulis agitata lacertis Aldh. *VirgV* 599; dum se sic agitat, dum sic evadere sperat Serlo Wilt. *app.* IIIb 29. 31. **c** ~ate, *onettad GlC* A 401.

2 to urge, vex, disturb. **b** (p. ppl.) keyed up, alert. **c** to concern, engage.

matrona stimulis agitata maligni Aldh. *VirgV* 1918; supremo eum ~ante mortis articulo *G. Steph.* I 4; ita sensu excesserat ut..miserabiliter cerebri turbatione ~aretur W. Cant. *Mir. Thom.* VI 3; s**1463** horrore valido cepit †~are [? l. ~ari] *Croyl. Cont. B* 537. **b** s**1194** ut [milites].. vegetatiores, ~atiores, exercitatiores reddantur ad prelium Diceto *YH* II 120. **c** hii quos ~at mundi labor dicunt solis et lune defectus facere aliquid non significare Devizes 33 r. p. 35; hi quos ~at talis labor Neckam *NR* II 166.

3 to pursue (legal action).

pro dape pugnetur, pro conjuge lis agitetur Serlo Wilt. *app.* III B 11. 1; quod..causam coram aliquibus monachis constitutis judicibus..~arent Ockham *Dial.* 917.

agitatio, driving. **b** movement, disturbance.

1438 pro ~one martorum regis..a partibus borealibus usque Perth *ExchScot* 58. **b** ~o, *unstilnis GlC* A 399; post multam animi ~onem vigilando conceptam Ferr. *Kinloss* 16.

2 prosecution (of a legal action).

1356 habeat in dicto hundredo..cognicionem, ~onem et decisionem omnium causarum *MunAcOx* 176.

agitator, mover.

Speh [*River Spey*] loca mutantis preceps agitator arene Neckam *DS* III 909.

agitor v. agistator. agius v. hagius.

agmen [CL], line of march, procession, queue. **b** company. **c** swarm (of bees). **d** (w. *Trojanum*) joust.

per turmas pariter procedent agmine denso ALDH. *VirgV* 2881; cujus corpus honorifico ~ine. .suam defertur ad urbem BEDE *HE* I 21; ~en, *gangend feða* ÆLF. *Gl.*; facto ~ine regem pariter adeuntes *G. Steph.* I 19; cum militum ~ine pulcherrimo GIR. *EH* II 15; qui tandem in ~inibus, aciebus et turmis. .stationem fecerunt ELMH. *Hen. V* 46. **b** ~en, *weorod GlC* A 407; electorum est sociatus ~inibus BEDE *HE* IV 14; Stephane, fortis miles Dei, primus in beato ~ine martyrum Dei ANSELM (*Or.* 13) III 50; nil probo virosum, tamen agmen laudo virosum SERLO WILT. *app.* IIa, 5. 1. **c** [apes] aethereos repetentes agmine nimbos ALDH. *VirgV* 663; †agen, *beogang* WW. **d** cum prosilient ad Trojanum ~en vel ad troinapium vel ad tornamentum NECKAM *Ut.* 104.

agna [CL], ewe lamb. **b** (fig.) nun. **c** *agnel d'or* (coin).

non lupus esuriens una satiabitur agna SERLO WILT. 20. 13; hec ~a, *a new lame* WW. **b** sic ~as evertit in lupas MAP *NC* V 3 p. 210. **c** 1341 xiij coronas auri et ij ~as auri in eodem sacco (*DipDocE* 63) *Foed.* V 259.

agnascentia, natural attachment, contiguity (phil.).

continuacio talium cum corporibus disparis speciei adnascencia vel contiguacio nominatur WYCL. *Log.* III 83.

agnasci [CL], (p. ppl. agnatus) agnate, (person) related in male line. **b** naturally attached, contiguous (phil.).

~i, *fædern magas* ÆLF. *Sup.*; convocat agnatos, sic verba precantia fundens: / "o cari fratres" WULF. *Swith.* I 1212; proximis de eorum sanguine, . .~i fuerint seu cognati FORTESCUE *LLA* 44. **b** continuacio vel adnascencia talium [elementorum] in mixtis est de perfeccione universi, eo quod inordinacio esset si omnia mixta essent cathenata, eciam minima naturalia non adnata WYCL. *Log.* II 165.

1 agnatio [CL], kindred (coll.); *v. et. agnitio b.*

concessit sibi et ceteris de ~one sua leonem rubeum. .in campo aureo BAD. AUR. 42.

2 agnatio, lambing.

1364 de quibus [ovibus] in morina ante tonsuram et ~onem xvij *Banstead* 347.

agnatus v. agnasci.

agnella, ewe lamb.

10. . †agella, *lam* WW.

agnellare [cf. OF *agneler*], to lamb.

12. . dominus inveniet alium bercatorem ad custodiendum oves matrices et agnos †que agnilaverunt *Cust. Bleadon* 207; 1297 ix oves vendebantur ante agnelacionem et xiij de adjunctis non agnelaverunt hoc anno *Ac. Cornw.* I 11.

agnellatio, lambing.

c1230 toto tempore agnelacionis bercarius auxiliari debet (*Cust. Chisenbury*) *Doc. Bec* 56; 1234 pastor. .habebit dim. quarterium ordei ad agnelacionem et agnum et vellus *Cust. Glast.* 167; 1276 oves. .de quibus in morina ante tons[ionem] et agnilacionem vj et post angnilacionem et ante tons[ionem] xij *Ac. Stratton* 78; 1307 in liberacione alterius hurdeke. .in principio agnilacionis custodientis agnos pro avibus et aliis malis *Doc. Bec* 154; 1341 in j lib. et dim. candelarum empt' ad supervidendas oves matrices noctanter tempore ~onis *MinAc* 1120/11 r. 1; 1417 morina tempore ~onis *Ac. Durh.* 317.

agnellinus [cf. OF *agnelin*], of a lamb.

1206 robas. .cum penulis agnelinis *Cl* 73a; 1332 pro. . furris ~is (*KRAc* 386/7) *Arch.* LXXVII 127; 1335 in . .furruris agnelinis emptis *Comp. Swith.* 236; 1415 pro . .carnibus †agnellis ix d. (*Expense*) *Analog. Cant. Pilg.* 3.

agnellulus, lambkin.

s1455 fugerunt. .non aliter. .quam ~i, cum lupum viderint venientem *Reg. Whet.* I 169.

agnellus [CL], lamb. **b** (fig.). **c** lambskin; *v. et. agnellinus.*

androgia. .que ~os morbidos. .in sua teneritate lacte foveat alieno NECKAM *Ut.* 101; 1355 de j multone. ., j ove et angnell' *Sacr. Ely* II 171; 1375 cepit unum ~um de straio vagantem *Leet Norw.* 67. **b** ne ~i sui perditos suorum curialium actus vel mores saperent BLAKMAN *Hen. VI* 12. **c** 1388 j pilch' nigri ~i. .de russet furrat' cum albo ~o *IMisc.* 239/10 r. 2; 1416 unam togam de nigro russet furratam cum nigris ~is *Reg. Cant.* II 93.

agnicellus, ~cellulus, little lambkin.

diminutiva diminutivorum inveniuntur, ut. .agnus, agniculus, ~us, ~ulus ALDH. *PR* 132; c1250 summa agnorum, iiij^{xx} et xj; valebit dim' agnicillus, qui vocatur *gadlamb Reg. S. Aug.* 26.

1 agnicium [OF *agniz*; cf. *Year Bk. 12 Ed. II* pp. 83, 85], parchment tag to which seal is attached.

1268 prior dixit quod aliquo tempore predictum sigillum fuit impressio sigilli sui, set tamen predicta cera ~io predicti scripti maliciose apposita fuit *Exch. Jews* 40; 1290 †aguicium quo pendet sigillum capituli ex uno latere in transverso ruptum existit *Reg. Heref.* 232.

2 agnicium v. alniceus.

agniculus, little lamb, lambkin. **b** (fig.). **c** lambskin.

ALDH. *PR* 132 (v. agnicellus); [Joabel] primus. .greges ordinavit. ., separans greges. ., ut ~os a maturioribus GERV. TILB. I 20; quid est quod ut agniculus obmutescis? J. HOWD. *Cant.* 70. **b** 798 quid inter leones ~us? ALCUIN *Ep.* 145; Judas mitem vendens agniculum J. HOWD. *Ph.* 102. **c** 1224 cum furruris de ~is *Cl* 609.

agnilare, ~atio, v. agnell-.

agninus [CL], of a lamb. **b** lamb-like.

carnes agnine, porcelline, vituline D. BEC. 2565; 1188 pro x penulis ~is ad opus regis *Pipe* 23; 1283 penulas. .amiciarum caprinas esse volumus vel ~as (*Pat*) *MonA* VI 1332; 1329 de. .supertunicis ~is *ExchScot* 143; capicium servientis pellibus ~is semper albis duplicatur FORTESCUE *LLA* 51. **b** agninus facie non sis vir, mente lupinus D. BEC. 1500; 1435 a morsu fere pessime preservetur ~a simplicitas sue prolis *EpAcOx* 126.

agnitio [CL], recognition, awareness. **b** acknowledgement. **c** acquaintance or (?) kinship (*cf. agnatio*).

gentem Anglorum ad ~onem veritatis perducebant BEDE *HE* II 1; ~o quidem certitudinem habet et vel in scientia vel in fide consistit J. SAL. *Pol.* 479B; tanquam crimen et virtus. .parem ~onis discrecionem admittant W. DAN. *Ep.* 61C; ~o [= 1 *Cor.* iv 6: scientia] est cooperante cogitativa; doctrina [est] cooperante interpretativa HALES *Qu.* 304; c1239 ad pastorem spiritualium ovium spectat earum differentias. .agnoscere, quarum ~o. .haberi non poterit nisi inquisitione GROS. *Ep.* 127 p. 375. **b** 1217 fidei catholice ~o et professio *Conc. Syn.* 61. **c** 1251 non malecredunt ei. .de latrocinio predicto, eo quod ignotus fuit cum nemine prefate civitatis habens ~onem *IMisc.* 5/25.

agnitivus, concerned w. recognition.

solus Avicenna phantasiam esse potenciam ~am. .estimavit *Ps.*-GROS. 479.

agnitor, one who knows, acquaintance.

martyris consecretalis cubicularius a suis vocabatur ~oribus HERM. ARCH. 4 p. 35.

agnizare, to be lamb-like.

tolerat patientia, simplicitasque / agnizat GARL. *Epith.* VII 142.

agnomen, byname, nickname. **b** surname.

rusticus in socios non sis agnominis auctor D.BEC. 888; quod in vita non habuit, post mortem eventus ~en dedit GIR. *TH* II 28; duce Johanne, agnomine *þe Wode*, quod Latine sonat Insano vel Vehementi *Id. EH* I 21; a Barri scilicet primo ~en, postea cognomen de Barri suscipientes *Id. IK* I 6; agnomen florens contulit illa mihi GARL. *Hon. Vit.* 97. **b** Willelmus nomine sed *Serjant*, quod servientem sonat, ~ine R. COLD. *Cuthb.* 194; 1221 juratores testantur quod quidam H., cujus ~en ignorant, fuit tunc in molendino *PlCrGlouc* 329.

agnomentum, surname.

nostrum [saeculum aureum], cui Aureus Mons [i.e. *Richmount*] ~o est, Saturno felicior. .regnandi sua tempora in aevum prorogabit ANDRE *Hen. VII* 64.

agnominare, to distinguish by a nickname or surname. **b** to nominate. **c** to assign.

s814 Karolus. .moritur, . .qui pro magnitudine operum ~atus est Magnus DICETO *Chr.* 133; Joannes ille Marescallus ~atus *G. Steph.* I 64; [Henricus II filium] quartum, natu minimum, Johannem scilicet 'Sine Terra' ~ans W. NEWB. II 18; Philippus. .per totam terram nostram ~atus est 'Falsus', sicut et alius eorum testis, sc. Golloenus, per totam Walliam ~atus est 'Follus' GIR. *Inv.* I 13; proprios annominat hostes / Gallica lingua GARL. *Tri. Eccl.* 42. **b** quarto conventu annominentur [AS: *sceawie man*] qui eum. .sub fidejussore ponant (*Cons. Cnut.*) *GAS* 329; secundum supernam infusionem ab ~ato choraula moventur semper stelle BRADW. *CD* 191C. **c** coloni. .fundorum illorum qui corone annominantur *Dial. Scac.* I 4A; [comitatus] qui antiquo jure corone regie annominantur *Ib.* 7D.

agnominatio, alliteration.

pre cunctis rhetoricis exornationibus, annominatione magis utuntur, eaque precipue specie que primas dictionum literas vel syllabas convenientia jungit GIR. *DK* I 12; est annominatio quando diverse dictiones sibi assimilantur in litteris vel in syllabis. .ut in predicto exemplo, 'parva domus sed prava fuit; res apta, sed arta' VINSAUF *AV* II 64 (cf. *Id. CR* 323).

agnoscere [CL], to recognize (person or thing). **b** to recognize or know (fact).

maculatus egreditur et. .a propriis parasitis non ~itur ALDH. *VirgP* 50; an hoc signum ~eret requisivit BEDE *HE* II 12; 1239 vidit. .tres alios cum eo quos non agnovit *SelPl Forest* 73; a duobus viris. .agnitus *V. Har.* 5; s1381 periculosum erat ~i pro clerico WALS. *HA* II 9. **b** agnoscens propriam tanta virtute salutem ALDH. *VirgV* 2440; ut quid de te fieri deberet ~erem BEDE *HE* V 12 p. 309; 986 in penis aeternis se talionem passurum agnoverit *CD* 654; ~o hanc esse sententiam justitiae ANSELM (*Or.* 9) III 32; cum nihil oculata fide. .agnoverint GIR. *TH* I 6.

2 to acknowledge: **a** (something as right or true); **b** (a fault or obligation).

a agnita observatione catholici Paschae BEDE *HE* III 26; 1259 agnita plenius veritate premissorum *Cl* 479. **b** 597 bonarum. .mentium est et ibi aliquo modo culpas suas ~ere ubi culpa non est (*Lit. Papae*) BEDE *HE* I 27 p. 56; archiepiscopus [Thomas, ob. 1304] diffinivit ut, in oneribus. .~endis, vicarius. .quartam partem taxacionis subiret. .et nos tres partes taxacionis. .~eremus *Meaux* II 230; 1373 summa. . arrerag' xl mill. librarum per nos de. .provincia [Cantuar'] agnitarum *Conc.* III 94.

agnoscibiliter, recognizably.

vidi praefulgidum hierarcham, ~er Yvonem, sublimi solio principaliter praecellentem GOSC. *Mir. Iv.* lxiv.

1 agnus [CL], lamb. **b** (fig.). **c** lambskin. **d** runt lamb given to St. Anthony, 'tantony'. *V. et. lingua agni.*

debet per consuetudinem unam ovem cum ~o *DB* I 92; 12. . [prepositus] habebit secundum meliorem ~um femellum post dominum, qui dicitur †*stilom*, quando separent ~os domini *Cust. Bleadon.* 209; 1281 unacum decima lane angnorum *Reg. Ebor.* 77. **b** rex leo, rex agnus, rex armis paceque magnus SERLO WILT. 16. 23; non. .congressio sed ~orum fuga pre lupis MAP *NC* II 17; dixit senex: "edi quidem sunt qualis ego; ~os vero Dei quis scit?" *NLA* (*Egbinus*) I 370. **c** 1200 supertunicam viridem furratam cum angno *CurR* I 230; 1259 unam furruram de ~is *Cl* 380; 1415 togam. .furratam de ~is nigris *Reg. Cant.* II 84. **d** c1400 de m^{l} vij^{c} j ~is exitus. .: dat' S. Antonio pro eorum meliori sanitate habenda ante tonsionem, vj (*MinAc Foulness*) *ERO* D/DHt M 45 m. 1d. (cf. *Ac. Durh.* 319 [1447]: cum. .j *Antonlam*).

2 Paschal lamb. **b** Christ as Lamb of God. **c** Agnus Dei (part of liturgy). **d** figure of Agnus Dei. **e** Agnus Dei on coin (*agnel d'Or*).

c710 XIIII die in cujus vespera ~us est immolatus (*Lit. Ceolfridi*) BEDE *HE* V 21 p. 335; jam non per Moysen agnus populo datur assus; / agnus Christus adest pro nobis in cruce passus P. BLOIS *Euch.* 4. 1140A; 1381 sic ~us paschalis fuit sacramentum et figura Christi preteriti passi (WYCL. *Concl.*) *Ziz.* 108. **b** conclamant carmina Christo / Agnum sectantes ALDH. *VirgV* 2897; nullus ab altithroni comitatu segregat Agni / . . BEDE (*Hymn*) *HE* IV 18; 8. . adjuro te. .per cxliiii milia qui secuntur ~um (*Jud. Dei*) *GAS* 411; dum gloriosi ~i paschales epulas celebraret *V. Osw.* 406; celestis ~i carnibus saginatus AILR. *Ed. Conf.* 767C; federa rupisti quibus Agno juncta fuisti NIG. *Mir. BVM* 23b; tunc pius est Agnus morti se tradere promptus GARL. *Myst. Eccl.* 301. **c** Sergius [I] papa constituit ut. .'~us Dei' a clero et populo decantetur ALCUIN *Div. Off.* 497; a1150 donec dicatur '~us Dei' usque 'miserere nobis' (*Jud. Dei*) *GAS* 417; 'Agnus' ter fertur GARL. *Myst. Eccl.* 611; 14. . ab evangelio usque post '~us Dei' *StatOx* 2. **d** 1295 casula. . cui inserantur. .iiij alemandini et in medio ~us paschalis *Vis. S. Paul.* 322; 1368 item pixis eukaristie argentea. .j ~us pa[s]chalis (*Invent. Norw.*) *Norf. Rec. Soc.* XIX 26 (cf. ib. p. xcix); 1383 una bursa de rubeo velveto brodata cum ~o Dei *Ac. Durh.* 427; 1390 de uno magno disco. .aymellato in fundo cum uno ~o, scripto circa ~um '*al is for þe beste*' *Ac. Foreign* 25G; 1430 j par precum de corall' cum. .j ~us Dei aureo et j corde aureo *Test. Ebor.* II 8; 1499 in placito detencionis. .unius ~us Dei de argento et deaurati *Rec. Nott.* III 52. **e** c1300 xxx florenos ad ~um *AncC* LV 14 (cf. ib.: exceptis xxx florenis ~i. .supradictis).

2 agnus [ἄγνος], agnus castus (*Vitex*). **b** (variously identified).

agno / casto vim similem castoreoque dabis NECKAM *DS* VII 75; est arbor quam ~um castum nominant, cujus ramus, si capiti dormientis supponatur, visiones capitis phantasticas non sentiet dormiens GERV. TILB. III 109; ~us castus dicitur quedam herba calida et sicca BART. ANGL. XVII 15; si viator portet baculum de agnocasto non offendet ad lapides. .pedes suos GAD. 20 v. 1; nonne castratio, . .~us castus. .et similia extinguunt veneris appetitum? BRADW. *CD* 119B. **b** ~us castus, frutex est, i. *bischopeswort*; . .~us sperma, i. semen salicis marine *SB* 9; ~us, fructus juniperi idem *Alph.* 11 (cf. arceuthis); 14. . ~us castus, A. *toutsayne* [? *Hypericum*] WW.

3 agnus v. hagnus. ago v. agere, agon.

agolum [CL], **~us**, crook.

schepperdys croke, pedum. ., ~us *PP*; agulus, A. *a shephoke* WW.

agon [CL < ἀγών], **ago**, (gymnastic) contest. **b** disputation (acad.). **c** dispute, action (leg.). **d** battle. **e** (w. ref. to crusades).

qui. .Olimpiaci agonis triumphum. .nanciscuntur ALDH. *VirgP* 2; infinitum est sicut dies et ago, ut dicit [Aristoteles, *Phy.* III 6. 206A] BACON XIII 147. **b** c1320 sola inter nos superest scolastici certaminis in agone pia contencio de profectu *FormOx* 58. **c** jura volunt quod homo facinus qui mittit et alter / qui consentit ei sint in agone pares GOWER *VC* I 1124. **d** 963 (14c) preter arcem construendam atque pontem componendum agonisque miliciam *CS* 1112; s1066 Heraldus. ., ut Normannos in Angliam ingressos esse audivit, iterum se ad agonem preparavit ORD. VIT. III 14; s1346 ante belli. .exordium vel quasi agonis principio (J. TYNEMOUTH *Hist. Aurea*) *EHR* XLIII 212. **e** de multitudine gentium sed. .non concordi hoc in agone superbire GIR. *EH* II 29; [Baldewinus] inter tot agones. . singulari ictu paganum armatum. .in duo frusta diviserat GERV. TILB. II 20.

2 (earthly life regarded as) spiritual struggle, tribulation, martyrdom. **b** throe.

Christianorum agonem. .gimnicorum ALDH. *VirgP* 3; post multiplices militiae caelestis agones ad praemia remunerationis supernae suspirans BEDE *HE* V 11; agonem martyrii conferre EGB. *Pont.* 98; fatigatos pro Christo in multis agonibus pugiles ORD. VIT. X 11 p. 78; regis Stephani . .multo graviores invenies tribulationes et agones *G. Steph.* I 32; Christi athletam [sc. B. Thomam] et ipsius agonem. . depinxit A. TEWK. *Prol. Thom.* 300; s1074 [Editha] diu. .in agone mortis semivivens migravit ad Dominum M. PAR. *Min.* I 20; te constantem Deus hoc in agone notavit GARL. *Mor. Scol.* 306; ad tam desiderabilem tante salutis agonem AD. MARSH *Ep.* 49; post diuturnum. .hujus vite agonem *NLA* (*Kyneburga*) II 130; c1430 post contencionem in agone premium victorie suscipere *Reg. Whet.* II 449. **b** agones morientium vel extasim patientium imitari Ailr. *Spec. Char.* 571.

agonare v. aginare.

agonia [ἀγωνία], (gymnastic) contest. **b** agony of Christ's passion. **c** death agony. **d** agony, tribulation. **e** sacrifice. **f** (?) anger.

[tetrasyllabica] quedam longantur, ut agonīa Bacon *Tert.* 257; qui pro gymnasticis et corporalibus ~iis premia statuerunt R. Bury 2. 31. **b** c**1430** duo angeli..Dei Patris Filium in ~ia sue passionis consolaturi Amund. I *app.* C 420. **c** egro..in agonia posito et..jam jam morituro famulus..signum crucis..faciat Lanfr. *Const.* 182; factus in ~ia egrotus Osb. *Mir. Dunst.* 4; [Eadmundus] ~ia peracta in domo Domini multiplicatur Herm. Arch. 1; quasi per ~iam raptus ad superos W. Dan. *Ailred* 64b; tanto..diutius talis ~ie martyrium duxit Gir. *GE* II 10; s**1376** princeps..in ~ia mortis positus *Chr. Angl.* 89. **d** indicavit eis ~iam animi sui Eccleston *Adv. Min.* 17; s**1311** Petrus in Angliam rediens..toto (*sic*) regno ~iam reportavit *Ann. Lond.* 202; s**1463** consimili passionis ~ia semetipsum conturbavit *Croyl. Cont. B* 537. **e** ~ia, hostia *GlC* A 387. **f** ~ia, A. *anger* WW.

agonista [ἀγωνιστής], champion.

egregius ~a et divini sermonis dogmatista [S. Paulus] Aldh. *VirgP* 2; **939** aegregius ~a sermocinatus est *CS* 734; ~a providus concupivit..fieri athleta castus *V. Osw.* 415; ~a Dei *V. Dunst.* B. 16; **1171** ad tumulum ~e [B. Thome] (*Lit. regis Franc.*) Fl. Worc. *Cont.* B 147; **1378** ~as catholice fidei *FormOx* 233.

agonistica [ἀγωνιστική], art of winning.

juniores..campestria prelia ludunt et ~am exercent militarem W. Fitzst. *Thom. prol.* 14.

agonitheta v. agonotheta.

agonizare [ἀγωνίζεσθαι], to struggle. **b** (dep.).

1281 ~ante olim Dei militia et se laudabiliter periculis exponente Peckham *Ep.* 97; rex..ut fortis athleta indefesse ~avit J. Lond. *Commend. Ed. I* 19; per paucitatem nostram ~antem pro justicia Elmh. *Hen. V* 57. **b** s**1278** libertates ecclesie tuetur ac pro eisdem ~atur tota virtute *Flor. Hist.* III 51.

2 to suffer death pangs (esp. in martyrdom). **b** (dep.).

cum palma virginitatis triumpho martirii ~arunt Aldh. *VirgP* 34; invenit egrotum..ultimo anhelitu in exitum ~antem Gosc. *Mir. Iv.* lxi; S. Spiritum..~anti femine..vidit adesse W. Malm. *GP* I 19; s**1101** eo quod..sodales suos in martyrio Christi ~antes deseruerit Ord. Vit. X 19 p. 118; mitti faciat ad ~antem sex fratres *Cust. Cant.* 343. **b** decubuit, ~atus est, defungitur Osb. *V. Dunst.* 17.

agonizatio, struggle.

angeli..intuentur..totam nostram ~onem Wycl. *Ver.* III 103.

agonotheta [ἀγωνοθέτης], overseer of contest (esp. of Christ). **b** champion, martyr.

agonitheta, princeps illius artis *GlC* A 374; praesidente agonitheta theatrales pancratiariorum pompae..peraguntur Aldh. *PR* 121; a vero agonitheta cursum certaminis contemplante *Id. VirgP* 18; eduxit eos agonithetes Deus in celeste refrigerium M. Par. *Maj.* III 453; Christi..nostri ~ae Bekinsau 733. **b** anthletis et agonithetis Christi Aldh. *VirgP* 36 p. 283; **10..** agonteta, *ellenlæce* WW; repedat [Edmundus] agonitheta sua mansionaria Herm. Arch. 15 p. 45; probo agonithete, quanto acrior erit pugna, tanto gloriosior erit victoria Ord. Vit. V 14 p. 417; perstans mente et corpore ~a Dei fixit ex adverso gradum W. Cant. *V. Thom.* II 41.

agra- v. et. aggra-.

agrammatus [ἀγράμματος], unlettered (person).

spretum a gravibus detur agrammatis *Ps.*-Map *Poems* 127 l. 706; *layman or woman, no clerk, ..lewd, not lettyrd,* illiteratus, ~us *PP*; *lewde,* agramatus *CathA* (cf. ib.: *unlettyrde,* agramaticus).

agrarius [CL], living in the country. **b** holding land or belonging to land. **c** (sb. f.) land-tax or rent.

~ius ut †lines [l. limes] *GlC* A 391. **b** s**925** rex Henricus trans-Renanus, ~ios milites recensens, edixit ut octo eorum in agris et nonus in urbe moraretur Diceto *Chr.* 144; s**1159** rex..nolens vexare ~ios milites.., sumptis lx sol...de feudo uniuscujusque lorice, ..capitales barones suos cum paucis secum duxit, solidarios vero milites innumeros Torigni *Chr.* 202. **c** **1289** cum juribus, deveriis, serviciis, feodis et agreriis ipsorum tenementorum *RGasc* II 493 (cf. ib. 380: aggrerias, ..census, redditus); agrum locat ut ~iam accipiat Ockham *Pol.* I 319.

agreabilis [OF *agreable*], agreeable, welcome.

1458 vocantes ad nos de magnis †prelatibus regni nostri.., quod nobis valde ~e fuit, ad intelligendum ipsorum bonas disposiciones versus..pacem *Reg. Whet.* I 300.

agreamentum [OF *agreement*], agreement, assent. **b** (terms of) agreement, covenant. **c** settlement.

1428 nec aliquam partem..includere facient..absque assensu, voluntate et aggreamento..Thome (*Indent.*) Amund. I 259; **1458** sine aggreamento partis propter cujus securitatem..recognicio fuit facta (*Pat*) *Reg. Whet.* I 307; **1466** ita quod se maritabunt per avisamentum et ~um..uxoris mee *Test. Ebor.* II 277; **1472** absque voluntate, assensu, licencia et agremento supradictis *Enr. Chester* 144 m. 7. **b** **1434** indenturam..testificantem..diversas convenciones, concessiones, condiciones et ~a inter partes predictas *FormA* 353; **1514** si..observaverint..convenciones et aggreamenta ex parte sua performanda *Cart. Glam.* 1784. **c** **1425** cum..assignaverimus vobis..summam ij milium m. in partem satisfaccionis et aggreamenti..de..debito *RScot* 253a.

agreare [OF *agreer*], to agree (to or upon): **a** (w. dat. or absol.); **b** (w. *pro*); **c** (w. *quod*); **d** (trans.); **e** (refl. w. *ad*).

a **1411** eisdem decreto et judicio plenarie concenserunt et aggreaverunt *RParl* III 652b; **1446** cum..adhibuerimus assensum ac integre et plenarie aggreaverimus eisdem [dimissioni et liberacioni] *MunCOx* 209; **1417** cum..subsidia..solvissent et ~eassent *Cl* 267 m. 4; **1466** sciatis nos..omnibus predictis concessisse et aggreasse per presentes *Mem. Ripon* 177. **b** **1587** si..non agriabunt pro precio..premissorum *Pat* 1301 m. 7. **c** **1573** ~eatum fuit inter partes predictas..quod.. *Pat* 1104 m. 9. **d** **1456** ipsos pro quibus..exceptiones..super actu predicto facte, ~eate et..certificate existunt (*Breve regis*) *Reg. Whet.* I 263. **e** **1384** finem illum approbavit, acceptavit et ad illum se aggreavit et assentivit *IMisc* 229/17; s**1467** ~eavit se ad concludendum matrimonium W. Worc. *Ann.* 788; **1472** ad que dampna..se aggreaverunt (*PlRExch*) *Law Merch.* II 125.

2 to settle, pay.

1417 cum..custumas et subsidia pro lanis predictis debita..solvissent et ~eassent *Cl* 267 m. 4.

agrecula, agredula v. acredula. agredi, agreg-, agress- v. aggr-. agremonia v. agrimonia.

agresta [cf. OF *aigrest*], sour juice (esp. of grapes), verjuice or vertsauce. **b** (?) sour fruit.

pampinus et palmes et turio, botrus, agresta Neckam *DS* VIII 29; non redit nisi ad eandem acetositatem que fuit in ~a ante maturacionem Gad. 135. 1; **1315** si..furatus fuerit racemos, ~am de vineis, poma..et talia comestibilia *RGasc* IV 1626 (xxxiii); [sanguis Domini] de ~a non conficitur, i. succo uvarum immaturarum J. Burgh *PO* 3. 17v;. *veriowse, sauce,* ~a *PP*; *vert sawse,* viridis salsa, †agretas *CathA*. **b** teneat malum granatum aut ~am in manu, quam masticet in motu rejectionis Gilb. I 17 v. 2.

agresticus, rustic.

urbanus [mus murem] ~um cepit hilarare *Latin Stories* 143.

1 agrestis [CL], wild. **b** (of fruit) sour. **c** earthy. **d** rustic. **e** (fig.). uncultivated, barbarous. **f** pagan.

ut pecus agrestes ex prato vellicat herbas Aldh. *VirgV* 2775; ~is, *wildae GlC* A 396; **10..** ~es, *wudulice oððe wilde* WW; aquatica et ~ia volatilia R. Cold. *Cuthb.* 27; allium domesticum..A. *garleke*; allium ~e, ..A. *crowelek Alph.* 5. **b** acetosa et ~ia [caliditas] convertit in dulcia, ut est videre in fructibus Bart. Angl. IV 1. **c** tumulus ~ibus glaebis coacervatus Felix *Guthl.* 28. **d** cultor agrestis Aldh. *Aen.* 78. 9. **e** rudi..et ~i stilo Gir. *TH intr.* p. 8. **f** **724** curavi..qua potissimum ratione obstinationem ~ium convincere promptus queas (*Lit. Ep. Wint.*) *Ep. Bonif.* 23.

2 agrestis v. agrostis. agretas v. agresta.

agriaca [? < ἀγρία γαλῆ], (colour of) a kind of jaundice.

ex colore prassino vel viridi..fit viridis que vocatur ~a Gilb. VI 257. 1.

agriare v. agreare.

agricola [CL], husbandman, peasant (serf or free).

quamvis agricolis non sim laudabilis hospes Aldh. *Aen.* 34 (*Locusta*) 1; **1012** (12c) his terminis praefata tellus circumdata ~is testibus dinoscitur *CD* 1307; **10..** ~a, *æcerman* WW; c**1100** dedit quendam ~am et terram iiij boum *Cart. Chester* 20; dum et optimis agris desunt ~e Gir. *TH* III 10; a duobus..mediocribus viris quos francalanos sive ~as vocant *V. Har.* 5 f. 9; **14..** hic et hec ~a, *a londtyllere* WW.

agricolari, to cultivate, till (the earth).

quinta hebdomada septimi anni, quo toto populus ab ~andi opere legis imperio vacabat Bede *TR* 8 p. 198; agricolare, Dei tumidus contemptor, ubique; / nullos vis fructus reddere justitie Neckam *VM* II p. 191; s**1073** quidam suas porciones ~antes, quidam ad fenum conservantes *Croyl.* 94.

agricolatio, agriculture.

si omnes ibi novi ~onisque rudes essent, aliquid in annona..peccaretur More *Ut.* 121.

agricolator, husbandman.

a tylle man, ..agricola, ~or, agricolonus, agricultor [v.l. agricultator], colonus *CathA*.

agricolatus, tillage.

1095 ibi Christicole.., pauperculo ~u transigentes inediam, nefandis illis vectigal pensitant (*Sermo Papae*) W. Malm. *GR* IV 347 p. 395.

agricolonus v. agricolator.

agricolosus, arable.

1604 in agro agriculoso Anglice *le tylthe feild CourtR Tempsford* (*Beds RO*) r. 1.

agricolus, (figure of) husbandman.

1468 uno agriculo, Anglice *a plowghman,* de auro garni siato cum dyamoundys *Pat* 522 m. 8.

agricultor, husbandman.

~ores, pastores, aratores et plures ceteri R. Cold. *Cuthb.* 139; sicut naute et ~ores..per vias astronomie considerant tempora electa in quibus operentur Bacon *Tert. Sup.* 12; s**1454** quidam ~or firmarius vendidit x quarteria frumenti pro xx s. (*Chr.*) *Camd. Soc. NS* XXVIII 151; *CathA* (v. agricolator).

agricultura [CL], agriculture. **b** ploughland. **c** (fig.; *cf.* 1 *Cor.* iii 9).

†quales [? l. qualis] tibi videtur inter artes seculares retinere primatum? ~a [AS: *eorptilp*], quia arator nos omnes pascit Ælf. *Coll.* 99; nemora studio ~e succisa Gir. *TH* III 2; artes mechanice sunt laneficium, ..venatio, ~a, medicina Bacon XV 193. **b** a**1160** in pratis et pascuis, in ~is et aquis (*Ch.*) *EHR* XXXII 248; ut..tota..~a ad urbem [Ascalonem] pertinens fidelibus remaneret Devizes 43; **1216** infra divisas ~e sue in foresta *Cart. Chester* 104. **c** homines quibus talis cultura impenditur ~am Dei vocat apostolus; est autem semen hujus ~ae verbum Dei Anselm (*Praesc.* 6) II 270 (cf. id. III 33).

agrielaea [ἀγριελαία], oleaster.

agrielea quam multi cathium [κότινον] dicunt, alii olivam Ethiopicam, Latini oleastrum *Alph.* 3.

agrifolium v. acrifolium. agrilopa v. anchilops.

agrimonia [ἀργεμώνη], (?) agrimony (bot.). **b** (variously identified).

10.. ~ia, *garclife*; **12..** ~ia, i. *agremoine,* i. *garclive*; **14..** hec agremonia, A. *ogremoyne,* hec egromonia, *egromonym* WW; balsamite, agrimo[nie].. Gilb. I 56. 2 (cf. id. II 97 v. 2: sambuci..et acrimonie); ~ia in cibo sumpta splenem consumit Gad. 17. 2; ~ia i. *egremoyn SB* 9. **b** ~ia, *sticwyrt* Ælf. *Gl.*; lappa incisa, i. ~ia *SB* 26; agimonia vel ~ia..secundum quosdam genus est apii *Alph.* 3.

†agrimulatum, tare, (?) corncockle.

acrimulatum vel ~um, melancium, gyth i., ..et est equivocum ad cyminum Ethiopicum et ad nigellam; viridem habet stipitem, aliquantulum grossum, foliis circumdatum et in extremitate divisum, et flores albos *Alph.* 2; melancium, i. gith, ..agrimatum vel ~um idem; crescit in segetibus, semine utimur *Ib.* 111.

agripenna v. aripennis.

agrippa [*personal name*], sort of ointment.

unguentis calidis sicut ~a, arogon.. Gilb. III 170. v. 2; ~a est quoddam unguentum Alph. 3; **1414** unguentum ~a, ij lib., xij d. *EschF* 1066/1.

agrister, agricultural.

1414 do et lego cuilibet famulorum meorum agristrorum.. *Reg. Cant.* II 6.

agriunculus, small plot of land.

857 (11c) ad censum..regi reddatur in anno de ~o illo xii denarios (*sic*) *CS* 492.

agrius v. staphis. agroaticus v. acroaticus. agromellum v. acromellum.

agrostis [ἄγρωστις], couch grass.

poligonus masculus herba est virgas habens..super terram †spansas sicut †agrestis [l. ~is] *Alph.* 147.

aguaria v. 2 acuare. aguicium v. agnicium. agulare v. aculare.

agularius [cf. OF *aguillier*], (?) needler.

c**1200** his testibus: ..Hugone filio Radulfi ~ii; Henrico ~io *E. Ch. S. Paul.* 199.

agulettus [OF *aguillete*], aglet, metal point, tag.

1342 pro ij laqueis serici ynde cum uno ~o argenti *KRAc* 389/14 m. 7; **1349** xxxij aguyllett' cum punctis de cupro (*KRAc* 391/15) *Arch.* XXXI 39; ciiij^{xx}xij ~i de serico cum punctis argenti *Ib.* 55.

agulus v. agolum.

aguzorium [cf. OF *aguisier*], (?) sharpener for quills.

1235 pro..~iis, pumicis et aliis minutis expensis *Liberate* (*Exch.*), 1203 m. 2.

agya v. atia. ah v. 2 a. ahen- v. aën-.

†ahoho [? for *adohoc* < Ar. *ad-dūgh* < Pers.], buttermilk.

~o, i. lac acetosum de quo extractum est butirum *SB* 9.

aicla v. situla. aidonea v. aëdonea. aier, aier-, v. aer, aer-. aimal-, aimel-, v. esmal-.

ain, Hebrew letter.

generatur..aleph in ore, ain in gutture Bacon *Maj.* I 74.

aio [CL], I say.

tunc ait audacter depromens fata futura /.. Aldh. *VirgV* 1559; at ego aperiens oculos aio: "etiam" Bede *HE* V 6; aiens eum petiisse Romam Herm. Arch. 25; bellum, ut aiebat, adversus eum promoturus abscessit *G. Steph.* I 9; quidam aiunt utrumque verbum..necessarium Gir. *GE* I 8; inter se deliberantes Persone aierunt: "faciamus hominem" *Eul. Hist.* I 11.

aira, airea v. aerea. airale, airiale, v. areale.

aisantia, easment (Norm.).

c1152 concessi..pasturas suas et pasnagia omnesque ~ias suas in omnibus sibi necessariis *Act. Hen. II* I 43.

aisia [OF *aise*], profit, advantage. **b** easement.

a1120 qui divisionem habet juxta terram regis..dilectione aut pretio adquirat, si voluerit aliquam in terra illa ~iam habere (*Inst. Cnut.*) *GAS* 614; **c1140** ita quod loca per eos superedificata reparent et ad ~ias suas reficiant *Regesta* 637; **a1185** sic quod nullus aesyam inde habeat preter me et.. burgenses *BBC* (*Swansea*) 58; **c1190** ponent..in defensione unam partem nemoris ad ~iam suam *Kelso* I no. 249; **c1228** quod daret monachis meremium ubi posset ad majorem esiam eorum et minus dampnum foreste *Feod. Durh.* 245. **b 1208** cum omnibus ~eis eidem terre pertinentibus *CurR* V 317.

aisiamentum, easement, right enjoyed in land other than one's own. **b** convenience or provision enjoyed in a house or household.

1144 dedisse..in forestis meis..omnia ~a sua, pasturam sc. ad averia sua et ligna et materiem et pasnagium ad suos proprios usus *E. Ch. Scot.* 141; **c1155** esiamenta ad faciendum omnimoda cariagia sua et ad caciandum et recaciandum..animalia sua *Danelaw* 120; **c1155** eisiamenta aque *Ib.* 195; **c1187** in semitis, in communiis et in omnibus aliis asiamentis *Ib.* 123; permittat habere H. ~a sua in bosco et in pastura GLANV. XII 14; **1199** que essiamenta et que pertinentia..solebant pertinere ad predictam firmam *CurR RC* II 149; **c1200** ut habeant in Hereth..aeisamenta.. in aquis, in piscationibus (*Ch.*) *Chr. Holyrood* 12; **c1200** cum omnibus justis pertinenciis suis et hesiamentis que ad terram illam spectant *Reg. Aberbr.* I 44; **s1210** rex..bona eorum [Cisterciensium]..ac terras et ligna de forestis suis..et omnia alia ~a que pater ejus dedit..illis abstulit W. NEWB. *Cont.* 4 p. 511; **1231** quod permittat..homines suos..habere estoverium suum ad husbote et heybote et pasturam ad averia sua et alia ~a in foresta regis *Cl* 564; **a1240** cum omnibus communibus ~is ville *Reg. St. Bees* 280; **c1240** omnia †asaysamenta..de jure spectantia ad tenementa *Ch. Sal.* 271; **1241** aesiamentum de bosco ad domos et edificia sua *BBC* (*Newport, Pem.*) 64; **c1270** reddendo.. unum hominem..ad metendum ad cibum domini pro essciamento habendo infra terram domini *Cart. Glam.* 730; **1272** cum omnibus libertatibus et ayciamentis *Ib.* 768; **1277** cum eisiamentis undique eundi et redeundi *MGL* III 450; **1277** in..asyementis et approviamentis *Cart. Chester* 428; **1293** forbarrat ripam..ita quod caballi non possunt habere aysiamenta sua *Leet Norw.* 44; **1296** communia et eysiamenta *BBC* (*Kirkham*) 84; **1301** terram..cum.. †agiamentis [? l. asiamentis] *DocScot* 437; **1343** ..~a sua de aqua haurienda et aliis rebus ducendis *MGL* II 444; **1556** terras et solum et easiamenta (*Pat*) *Arch. Cant.* XLIX 214. **b 1296** ita quod omnia castra..nostra in eodem regno [Scocie]..ingredi et in eis morari et asiamenta sua habere possit *RScot* 27b; **13..** Alicia habeat pro franco banco suo..principalem cameram..et eciam commune asiamentum in coquina, in stabula, communi cloaca et curtilagio *MGL* I 393; **1384** panes..pro liberacionibus, esiamentis sociorum..et aliis oneribus consuetis *Ac. Obed. Abingd.* 43; coquinam..cum cameris pro conservacione.. stauri et asiamentis officiariorum [abbas J., ob. 1401] construxit *G. S. Alb.* III 442; **1458** in suis expensis ordinariis, viz. esculentis et poculentis ac cameris et ipsius collegii †aframentis [v. l. asiamentis] (*Ch. Ep. S. Andr.*) *Mon. Hib. & Scot.* 408b; **1466** absque aliquo easimento lecti aut ignis sive esculenti sive poculenti *Entries* 268b.

2 profit, advantage, convenience. **b** (?) fitment. **c** (w. *domus*) privy. **d** (w. *prisonum*) relaxation of prison conditions (*cf. suavitas, sueta*).

a1190 ut habeant unam viam..super terram meam, ubicunque ad opus suum et ~um melius esse providerint.. ad deducendum victum suum *Danelaw* 120; **s1190** mariscos edificare, excolere et omnia aisamenta sua inde facere *Croyl. Cont* B 456; **1223** ad commune ~um burgi *BBC* (*Inverkeithing*) 342; **1277** utrum fons..sit communis ad aesiamenta singulorum aut separalis fratrum [Minorum Colecestrie] (*Inq. AQD*) *Mon. Francisc.* II 285; **1288** [escambia] sunt ad commodum et aysiamentum utriusque partis (*Inq. AQD*) THORNE 1950; pro aysiamento juratorum *State Tri. Ed. I* 82; **1302** placea..jaceat vasta..ad commune asiamentum omnium hominum de O. *CourtR Hales* 457; **1321** allecia..emere volentibus pro utilitate et ~o tocius populi *MGL* II 400; **1338** illud mane sic temperetur ut nulli sit onerosum, sed ad assiamentum [v.l. †assisiamentum] omnium infirmorum (*Artic. domus S. Juliani*) *G. S. Alb.* II 505. **b 1377** in vadiis..carpentariorum operancium.. super factura unius nove camere cum omnibus aysiamentis in eadem factis *Banstead* 354. **c 1497** domum ~i tenementi in coopertura..ruinos' *CourtR Lygh* II f. 7v. **d 1353** nichil capiant..de eisdem servientibus pro feodis suis vel ~is prisonum (*LTRMem*) *EHR* XXV 307.

aisiare, to accommodate, provide facilities for.

1277 una cum eisiamento kaii dicte domus ad eorum res proprias..eisiandas, carcandas et discarcandas *MGL* III 452; **1300** pro expensis suis et unius exploratoris..morando extra curiam per v dies..pro dicto exploratore eisiando *Ac. Wardr.* p. 281; **1358** in qua alta strata omnes hostilarii ejusdem ville..ad recipiendum, hospitandum et aysiandum dictam communitatem..sunt commorantes *SelCKB* VI 122.

aisio, profit, convenience.

12.. [ij carrucate] de terra mea propropinquiori ad eisionem canonicorum predicte ecclesie perficiantur *Reg. S. Thom. Dublin* 38.

aisn- v. aesnecia, aesnecius. aissella v. axilla. aius v. hagius.

aizoon [ἀείζωον], houseleek (bot.).

12.. aizon, i. *sinfulle* WW; zion, semperviva idem *SB* 44; ayzon, semperviva idem, et dicitur ab *ay*, quod est 'semper', et *zeo*, quod est 'vita' *Alph.* 18; †scicados [l. sticados], ayzon, semperviva.., A. *erwrt* vel *housleke* vel *sinegrene Ib.* 175.

aj- v. adj-. akatum v. accatum. akermannus, akirmannus v. acremannus. aket-, akedonus, v. alcoto. akortare v. accurtare.

1 ala [CL], wing. **b** (artificial). **c** (fig.). **d** fin.

mergula nec penitus nigris contemnitur alis ALDH. *VirgV* 222; ad quid pignus ălis, o Dedale, quod caret ālis? SERLO WILT. II 14; gravior est brucus quam locusta.., quia ei desunt ale J. SAL. *Pol.* 590C; cignus.. / ludenti similis paulisper sublevat alas NECKAM *DS* II 371; in his cherubin alas suas extendunt ut intellectus studentis ascendat R. BURY *Phil.* 1. 17. **b** ingenium per quod ale artificialiter composite aerem verberent BACON *NM* 533. **c** Zephiri velocior alis ALDH. *Aen.* 100. 35; sufficiunt alae fidei in palatio regis ALCUIN *Ep.* 28 p. 70; tamquam alis presumptuosi ingenii..adustis GIR. *TH* I 13; sub umbra alarum parentum latuit scholaris NECKAM *NR* II 40; GARL. *Tri. Eccl.* 108 (v. aquila 1c); **s1355** ut..sub alis domini pape manerent in tuto AVESB. *Ed. III* 127b. **d** fulcior haud volitans veloci praepetis ala ALDH. *Aen.* 71 (*Piscis*) 3; **a1100** dexteram alam de crasso pisce (*St. Vigor, Cérisy*) *MonA* VI 1074b; **c1266** habebit..sub brancia [salmonis] quantum latitudinis tres digiti vel ala piscis amplectitur extendendo (*Cust. Westm.* iv 8) FLETE *Westm.* 66.

2 wing, (military force stationed on) flank, cavalry. **b** horse.

legio, *fepu*; alae, *fedes* ÆLF. *Gl.*; plurimas equestrium alas ad predandum quaquaversum direxit *G. Steph.* II 69; ponens aciem suam anteriorem..pro ala..a dextris ELMH. *Hen. V* 50. **b** ala, aequus *GlC* A 488.

3 a sail of windmill. **b** 'wing' (shoulder-band) of gown.

a 1287 in xxx ulnis caneveci emptis ad alas molendini *Pipe Wint.* (159308) r. 12*d*. **b 1576** pro factura alarum duplic' pro una toga *AcLChamb.* 67 f. 8v.

4 aisle: **a** of church; **b** of other building.

a sub medio longitudinis aule..due turres erant, prominentes ultra ecclesie alas (EADMER *S. Audoen.*) GERV. CANT. I 8; murus..qui, chorum cingens et presbiterium, corpus ecclesie a suis lateribus, que ale vocantur, dividebat *Ib.* 13; **1234** quod persona..ecclesie et parochiani sui faciant quandam alam ad construendum ibi quoddam altare *Cl* 365; **1264** quercus aptas ad maeremium ad alam ecclesie sue inde faciendam *Cl* 7; **1293** in pleno comitatu sub alis capelle in castro Huntingdon' habito *Reg. Ant. Linc.* III 836; **1343** (v. aluratio); **c1350** ascendat..super plumbum alarum..ad supervidendum *Mon. Exon.* 271; **1358** in loco emineneciori et devociori dicti porticus sive ale, in quo quidem loco idem miles intendit sepeliri (*Reg. Ebor.*) *Fabr. York* 335 (cf. ib.: porticus sive aule); **1430** ad clausuram capelle sive ale S. Gabrielis *Reg. Cant.* II 479; **1431** fabrice cujusdam ele ex parte boriali ecclesie *Ib.* 465; latitudo brachiorum duarum elarum super duplices columpnas W. WORC. *Itin.* 280. **b 1141** latitudo hujus grangie xv pedes, preter alam que habebat iiij pedes *Dom. S. Paul.* 136; ale hujus orrei sunt latitudinis vj pedum et dim.; altitudo alarum vj pedum et dim. *Ib.* 123; **c1155** una domus xxiiij pedum in longitudine cum una ala (*Ext. Leighton Buzzard*) *Beds. Hist. Rec. Soc.* VIII 22; **1233** ad scindulas emendas.. ad alas aule regis ibidem [*Woodstock*] cooperiendas *Liberate* 10 m. 10; **1254** ale dicte grangie minantur ruinam *CalI Misc.* I 205; **1313** de xxv ringis de una ala siliginis..magne grangie *Rec. Elton* 220; **1322** salva..libertate habendi corbell' in muro predicto, si ad eum aliquam alam facere voluerit *Cart. Osney* II 286.

5 measure of length (? upper arm, ell; *cf. alna, ulna*).

1382 unam peciam panni..continentem v alas, aliam peciam de mixto continentem vij alas (*Cl*) *Foed.* VII 356a.

2 ala, ale.

[hippelaphus] bibit..alam seu beram avidissime.., idque sine ebrietate CAIUS *Anim.* 11.

3 ala v. alga a.

alabandina [LL], kind of garnet.

1222 textus unus aureus..continens..alemandinas xviij et gennettas viij *Reg. S. Osm.* II 127; **1245** [crux] ornatur lapidibus..et alamandina in medio (*Invent. S. Paul.*) *Arch.* L 471; mitra..breudata stellis.., in stellis utrinque sunt topatii et almandine *Ib.* 473.

alabastarius v. arbalistarius. alabastratum v. alabastrum 1.

alabastrinus, made of alabaster.

s1372 fecit novum opus marmoreum et ~um sub feretro S. Cuthberti *Hist. Durh.* 2.

alabastrites, (?) onyx.

lapis ~es virtutis est laxativi *Alph.* 92.

alabastrum, ~us [ἀλάβαστρος], (stone) box (for ointment).

~um, *stænen elefæt* ÆLF. *Gl.*; alabastrum cum recens frangitur J. HOWD. *Ph.* 289; **1315** in filacterio argenteo.. cum gemmis, cum alabaustro Magdalen' *Invent. Ch. Ch.* 82; *boyst or box*, pixis, alabaustrum *PP*; ~um, A. *a box* WW; *a buyste*, ~um, ~atum, pixis *CathA*.

2 alabaster.

~us, ut dicit Ysidorus.., est lapis candidus intertinctus variis coloribus ex quo evangelici illius ungenti vasculum factum fuit BART. ANGL. XVI 3 (cf. ib. 67: sunt et alia.. genera [marmoris] ut ~um); in ~o, quod est genus marmoris candidissime micantis *Ps.*-GROS. 630; **1333** unam cuppam de alabaustro *DCCant* DE 3 f. 45b; **s1344** episcopus ..feretra..de marmore et ~o fecit renovare (W. DENE *Hist. Roff.*) *Anglia Sacra* I 375; **1369** pro..asportacione lapidum de alabasto a navi pro monumentis *ExchScot* 348; **1420** una ymago B. Marie sedentis cum filio suo de alabaustro *Fabr. York* 296; **1442** una tumba de alebastro sive marmore *Reg. Cant.* II 628.

alabrisare, to reel.

relyn with a rele, ~o *PP*.

alabrum [LL], reel (for spinning).

alibrum, *hreol* ÆLF. *Sup.*: videbamus..globellos et mataxas, alibra [v.l. alabra; *gl. traules, reles*] BALSH. *Ut.* 52; *a rele*, ~um et alibrum, abductorium *CathA*.

alacer [CL], **~ris,** brisk, alert.

~er, *swift GlC* A 446, ~ris, *snel Ib.* 445, *blidi Ib.* 341; **673** ~ri animo libentissime servare (*Conc. Hertf.*) BEDE *HE* IV 5; se in expeditionem promoturum letus et ~er promittebat *G. Steph.* II 101; **s1214** comes David, ..quamvis nec ~ris animo nec corpore vegetatus *Plusc.* VII 5; **s1386** [H. Percy] gentem inquietam..sua ~ri inquietudine multotiens fatigavit WALS. *HA* II 144.

alacrimonia, joy. **b** briskness.

~ia, laetitia *GlC* A 469; **993** nos..ad supernorum ~iam patrimoniorum advocans *CD* 684; *joy*, adoria, amenitas, ..~ia, alacritas *CathA*. **b** *wightnesse*, alacritas, ~ia, celeritas *Ib.*

alacrita v. alarica.

alacritas [CL], briskness, liveliness.

delectabatur antistes prudentia verborum juvenis, ..~ate actionis BEDE *HE* V 19; summa cum ~ate recessit T. MON. *Will.* V 13; ab exteriore vicissim vexatione spiritus ~ate respirare GIR. *TH intr.* p. 8.

alacriter [CL], briskly, eagerly.

~er terrena quaeque transiliens BEDE *HE* II 7; alacerrime quidam praecurrens nuntiat illum redire G. CRISPIN *Herl.* 98; ceteris ad opus injunctum ~er redeuntibus AILR. *Ed. Conf.* 764A; [Willelmus I] solito more alacerrime Archas obsedit dissuadentibus amicis W. MALM. *GR* III 232; **s1377** Londinienses ~er in donis variis..respexerunt *Chr. Angl.* 151; **1439** quas ~er et gratulabunde intuiti sumus BEKYNTON I 206.

alahacab [Ar. *al-a'qāb*], sinew.

quedam [ligamenta] sunt quibus appropriatur nomen quod est ~ab; ..quod continuatur inter duo extrema ossium aut inter alia membra anectendo unum alii firmiter et ligamentum et ~ab appellatur *Ps.*-RIC. *Anat.* 5.

†alaharih [?Ar. *al-aqrīṭī* = *Cretan seseli*], (?) hartwort (*Tordylium*).

~ ih, i. †cordeon *SB* 10.

†alahehi [? l. adahebi < Ar. (*as-sarkhas*) *adh-dhahabi* = golden fern; cf. Sp. *doradilla*], ceterach (fern).

~i, i. ceterac *SB* 10.

alamandina v. alabandina.

Alamannicus, German.

s1098 homines ~i regis EADMER *HN* 106; **s1120** propter Alemagnicum regem, qui Romanam ecclesiam persequebatur H. CANTOR 20v; **s1219** de S. Elizabetha Alemannica M. PAR. *Maj.* III 51; **1456** pro cervisia Almanica *ExchScot* 114.

Alamannus, German.

742 homines idiotae, ~i vel Baioarii vel Franci, si juxta Romanam urbem aliquid facere viderint ex his peccatis.. BONIF. *Ep.* 50 p. 84; Carolus ~orum rex ASSER *Alf.* 70; Lotharingi et ~i et ceteri Transrhenani populi qui imperatori Teutonicorum subjecti sunt, magis proprie se Francos appellari jubent W. MALM. *GR* I 68; **s1134** Henricus Teutonicus rex multitudinem Saxonum, Alemannorum, Lotharingensium aliarumque gentium coacervavit ORD. VIT. VII 4; **s1189** dum Alemanni ad predas hiantius convolant *Itin. Ric.* I 29; in cujus tempore [**1217–28**] erat persecutio super regnum Anglie ab Alemannis et aliis *Ch. Sal.* 266; **1265** pro eo quod quendam Alemannum cum gladiis et armaturis in..navi invenit, mercandisas.. arrestavit *Cl* 107; **1336** homines ad arma..Almanni *CalScot* III p. 360.

alambicum v. alembicum. alaneraris v. lanarius.

Alanius, (?) henchman of Alan de Neville, forester.

ut declinarem..importunam..~iorum exactionem *Dial. Scac.* I 11 F.

†alanus, (?) *f.l.* (*cf. alauda*).

1392 fugaverunt perdices, †~os [? l. alaudas] et fesianos *CourtR Carshalton* 34.

alapa [CL], blow, buffet. **b** (given by wind or wave). **c** (fig.).

~as, flagra..et coronam spineam BELETH *RDO* 50. 56; **1191** populus totus eum..verbis et ~is et sputis..turpiter tractavit (*Lit. Ep. Coventr.*) R. HOWD. III 147; **1321** in dictum Willelmum..insultum fecit et ipsi quandam ~am dedit *JustIt* 546 r. 44*d*.; **1584** cum pugna sua dedit..Antonio ..tres allapas super faciem et auriculas de quibus..titubavit *Pat* 1249 m. 2. **b** alternant ălăpas Tethis et ventus GARL. *Tri. Eccl.* 131. **c** ipsi bursa grandi paca bonam ~am, et vacillabit quocunque volueris MAP *NC* I 22.

alapatio, buffeting.

nonne semper versabatur inter persequuciones et ~ones? NETTER *DAF* II f. 147A.

†alapha [? cf. ἔλαφος], (*s. dub.*).

1292 liberat' hominibus qui presentaverunt ~am ad dominum G., vj asper' *KRAc* 308/14 r. 4.

alapiciosus v. alopeciosus.

alapsa [Ar. *al-'afs*; cf. Syr. *'afṣā*], oak-gall or leather tanned with gall.

~a quandoque est galla, quandoque est alluta *Alph.* 4.

alare, to wing, furnish w. wings. **b** (p. ppl.) winged. **c** (fig.) fleeting.

hanc [Venerem] de more filius suus comitatur, / nudus, cecus puer est, facies alatur *Ps.*-MAP *Poems* 26. **b** cicade quedam alate GIR. *TH* I 21; [vermiculi] post pauca tempora ad instar papilionum alati..avolare parant GERV. TILB. III 56; ut alati..more seraphico super cherubin scanderetis R. BURY *Phil.* 4. 47. **c** avis dicta mundi vanitatem transitoriam et alatam designat NECKAM *NR* I 76.

alaria v. avalaria.

†alarica, socket (of spear etc.) or spearhead; (?) *cf. falarica.*

sokette or candel styk or odyr lyk, allerica vel ~a *PP*; ~a, A. *a coronel* WW; *a sokett*, ~a .., *a spere*, hasta.., †alacrita [v.l. ~a] *CathA*.

alario [? cf. valeria], 'alerion', kind of eagle.

aquila, sicut rex avium est, si non ~onem excipias, que forte aquilarum species potentissima est J. SAL. *Pol.* 410C.

alaris [CL], auxiliary force. **b** horseman.

gencium errores audierat, nocturnasque phalanges demonum, ..Dictinnam et cetus Driadum et ~es MAP *NC* II 12; ~is, A. *a company of hors* WW. **b** ~is, cabbalarius *GlC* A 472.

alaso v. alleucho.

†alaste [Ar. *al-ḥāshā*], garden thyme (*Thymus*).

~e, i. ysopus ortolanus *SB*.

†alastogia [? Ar. *ad.* συστοιχία], parallel series.

Pythagoras duas ~ias, systichias, coelementaciones seu coordinaciones..dicitur posuisse, ..sicut breviter tangitur in 12 Metaph. 37, ubi in †nona [l. nova] translacione habetur 'coelementacio', in translacione vero quam Averroes exponit '~ia' BRADW. *CD* 13B.

alathia v. alethia.

alator [LL], beater (of game).

~or, A. *a wanelasour* WW.

alatorium (cf. OF *aleor*], 'alure', rampart walk.

1091 nulli licuit in Normannia fossatum facere in planam terram, nisi tale quod de fundo potuisset terram jactare superius sine scabello, et ibi non licuit facere palicium nisi in una regula et illud sine propugnaculis et ~iis (*Consuet. Norm.*) *EHR* XXIII 507.

alatura [cf. alura, OF *aleure*], 'alure', rampart walk, gallery.

1320 circa diversos defectus existentes in vicio et ~is nove capelle S. Stephani *KRAc* 469/1.

alatus v. alare.

alauda [CL < Gall.], lark. **b** (w. *fera*) pipit.

allauda, *lauricae GlC* A 497; ~a, *lauerce* ÆLF. *Gl.*; laudat alauda diem, prenuncia leta diei NECKAM *DS* II 765; alauda / exiguo promit gutture grande melos H. AVR. *Poems* 20. 155; **1285** ingenium quod vocatur *tonel* ad ~as et perdricia capienda *PQW*249b; **1289** in ~is, j d. quad. *Ac. Swinfield* 5; aves parve, sicut ~e et tales, sunt pure digestionis GAD. 10 v. 1; **1384** (v. avis 1c); nuncius aurore modulans volutabat alauda / desuper et summi cantat in aure Dei GOWER *VC* I 95. **b** alterum genus [galeritae]..a nostris fera ~a, a Germanis *heid Lerch* nominatur TURNER *Av.* 40.

alaudarius, hobby (hawk).

hobehawk, ~ius, alietus *PP*; *an hoby*, ~ius *CathA*.

alausa [LL; cf. OF *alose*], shad (or other fish).

alosis prepinguibus..Sinnenus abundat GIR. *TH* I 9; [lumpe] jocundus sapor est, pinguedine vincit alosam NECKAM *DS* III 625; **1233** homines Glouc' reddiderunt regi ..xij alosas per quas cum xij lampredis finem fecerunt *Cl* 219; **1258** omnes lampredas et allosas que inveniri poterunt in gurgitibus regis *Cl* 192; **a1285** gordario..pro prima alosa, j [panis] *Reg. Pri. Worc.* 125b; olosa, A. *a breme or an alose*, ..hec ~a, *a loch* WW; *a loche*, ~a, fundulus, piscis est *CathA*.

alayum v. allaium.

alaz [Ar. *al-ās* (*al-barrī*)], (?) butcher's broom (*Ruscus*).

quedam [plante habent] spinas, ut alaz ALF. ANGL. *Plant.* I 13.

alba v. albus 8.

†albacalay [Ar. *al-Balkhī*], kind of vitriol (from Balkh).

dicit [Avicenna] in 4 canone in fen decorationis vii [946D] quod si ʒ j draganti rubei ~ay potetur potentissime depilat canos et loco eorum facit nigros renasci BACON IX 4 (cf. ib. 137: dragagantum albilaki [v.l. albalaki]).

albalastrum, albalist- v. arbalist-.

albanellus, a bird of prey (? hobby).

si avis que vulgo dicitur ~us pretervolans viam a sinistris feratur ad dextram, de hospitii hilaritate ne dubites J. SAL. *Pol.* 411C.

albanaria, *aubaine* (*v. albania*).

1384 J. Letani..dabit domino pro ~ia sua quolibet anno pro voluntate domini..ij s.; et fecit fidelitatem prout nativus *Hal. Durh.* 185 (cf. ib. xvii).

albanarius, *aubain*, outsider (*v. albanus*).

1307 de ij s. de Rogero Markebroun albanar'; et de vj d de annuali recognicione alban' in quarterio de Stocton (*ReceiptR Durh.*) Boldon Bk. p. xxix.

albania [OF *aubaine*], payment by alien serf for right to reside on manor.

1307 (v. albanarius); **1376** fecit fidelitatem domino prout ad nativum pertinet et concedit solvere domino ij s. annuatim (*in margin*: ~ia, ij s.) *Hal. Durh.* 137.

Albanice, in Gaelic.

ken 'caput'.., *tyern* ~e 'dominus' Latine interpretatur J. FURNESS *Kentegern* 33.

Albanicus, Scot.

c1210 qui leges apostabit, si fuerit Anglicus vel Dacus vel Waliscus vel ~us aut Insulicola, were sue reus sit erga regem (*Leg. Edw. Conf. Lond.*) *GAS* 657.

albanus [OF *aubain*], stranger, outsider.

a1150 si parentes non haberet, dominus ejus eas [marcas] haberet, aut felagus, si haberet..; si autem neutrum istorum haberet, rex regni, sub cujus dominio et pace degunt omnes ~i, haberet vj marcas cum suis xl (*Leg. Edw. Conf.*) *GAS* 642.

Albanus, Scot.

s1138 exclamavit simul exercitus Scotorum insigne patrium et ascendit clamor usque in celum: "~i, ~i" H. HUNT. *HA* VIII 9.

albaras [Ar. *al-baraṣ*], leprosy.

morphea..differt ab ~as quia morphea solum est in cute ..sed ~as est in carne et cute usque ad os. ..~as nigra et ~as alba non proporcionantur sicut morphea alba et nigra GAD. 85 v. 1; ~as est morfea alba ut lac *SB* 10.

albardeola [cf. ardea], spoonbill (bird).

~am, quae Graece λευκερῳδιός dicitur, semel tantum in Italia vidi. ..hanc si non vidissem, Anglorum shovelardam ~am esse judicassem TURNER *Av.* 15.

albare, to whiten. **b** to deck or dress in white (esp. for baptism). **c** to 'blanch' (*cf. albus* 6).

nichil differt '†hominum [l. hominem] esse album et hominem ~ari', vel 'album esse aut fieri hominem' WYCL. *Ente* 47. **b** baptizati sunt..alii.., quorum primi ~ati adhuc rapti sunt de hac vita BEDE *HE* II 14; albanturque suis lustrata altaria peplis FRITH. 452. **c 1227** preceptum est vicecomiti quod ingrediatur in manerium de Hedindon'..ad ~andum firmam *LTRMem* 9 r. 8*d.*; **1275** reddendo domino regi pro dicta civitate [London'] cum comitatu predicto cccc li. plene, ubi solebant reddere nisi ccc li. et xv li. pro eis ~are *Hund.* I 403.

albareda v. arboretum.

albatio, whitening. **b** tawing. **c** whitewashing.

species albedinis est color, quia ~o est coloratio WYCL. *Ente* (*Spec.*) 343. **b** in ~one corei equini iiij d. *FormMan* 33; **1323** de vj coreis.., de quibus in ~one ij *Ac. Wellingb.* 135. **c 1392** [pro] ~one chori ecclesie *Invent. Ch. Ch.* 113; **1470** in lathamis conductis pro ~one capituli *Ib.* 114.

†albatorium [? cf. habrotonum], southernwood (bot.).

hoc ~ium, *sothernwode* WW.

albeareum v. alveare.

albederagi [Ar. *al-bādharuj* (?) < Pers.], basil (*Ocimum*).

succus alvederagi, basiliconis et columbine GAD. 9. 1; ~i, i. basiliconis vel columbine secundum Gaddesden *Alph.* 6.

albedo [LL], whiteness. **b** white of eye (*cf. albus* 9a). **c** dairy produce (*cf. albus* 9c).

idem medius aër ~ini simul et nigredini subjectus erit ADEL. *QN* 23; frigiditas mater est ~inis et palloris BART. ANGL. IV 2; **1248** [leporarius] techellatus ~ine et nigredine *SelPlForest* 77; **1282** estimant quod multum sit de argento in illo plumbo propter ~inem ejus et sonoritatem *AncC* XLVIII 177; ~o..habet multos gradus infra suam speciem, quorum nobilissimus et completissimus candor, secundo ~o communiter dicta, tertio flavum sive lividum BACON XIV 75; **s1284** [errores] in naturali philosophia: ..~o intensa et remissa differunt secundum speciem *Ann. Osney* 299; ultra ~inem non intensissimam est intensior OCKHAM *Dial.* 744; et sic [post transsubstanciacionem] simul manet ~o et non manet ad sensum LUTTERELL *Occam* 133v; **s1377** [socii Johannis Wyclef] tenuerunt..quod omnes alie sanctorum regule non plus perfeccionis addunt evangelio quam addit ~o parieti WALS. *HA* I 324; **s1382** quod sacramentum altaris..est verus panis et verum corpus Christi, et illa rotunditas que videtur et ~o..sunt panis (*Concl. Wycl.*) *Ib.* II 54; ad hoc quod caro Christi et sanguis sint eucharistia requiritur panis, sicut ad hoc quod album sit requiritur ~o (TYSS.) *Ziz.* 161; homo albus, equus albus..conveniunt in ~ine PAUL. ANGL. *ASP* 1550. **b** hec ~o, *the whyte of the ee* WW. **c 1325** respondet de iiij s. de ~ine unius vacce vendita (*Ac. Merstham*) *DCCant.*

albefacere, to whiten.

accipe auripigmenti partem et pone in aceto donec ~fiat BACON V 173; natura..seipsam ~facit et rubore decorat DASTYN *Ros.* 12.

albefactio, whitewashing.

1520 pro opere ij dierum circa ~onem magne camere *Arch. Hist. Camb.* II 26*n.*

albeolus, youth, (?) prince, atheling.

Cunutus..filios Eadmundi, elegantes ~os, in Daciam relegavit ORD. VIT. I 24 p. 178; **s1120** tener ~us..relapsus in pontum obiit *Ib.* XII 26 p. 414 (cf. XI 37).

albēre [CL], to be white.

~et, splendet *GlC* A 484; corvos / vertit in albentes glauco sine felle columbas ALDH. *VirgV* 492; ille qui specialiter integritate carnis virginalis ~et byssus retorta est BEDE *Tab.* II 13; querere an sol splendeat, ~eat nix J. SAL. *Pol.* 649A.

alberg- v. hauberc-, hauberg-, herberg-.

1 albescere [CL], to be white, gleam.

7.. flavescit, *glitinat*, ~it *GlC* F 252; agros cultissima segete ~entes *G. Steph.* II 78; ~ente aurora AILR. *SSHex.* 179; nocte tota supra horizontem polus ~it GIR. *TH* II 25.

2 albescere v. allubescere. albest- v. arbalist-, asbest-. albeum v. alium.

albezardi [Ar. *al-bārzad* < Pers.], galbanum (bot.).

~i [v.l. albesardi], i. galbanum *Alph.* 5; albetud est galbanum *LC*.

albicolor, silver (play on *bicolor*).

W. FITZST. *Thom.* 39 (v. bicolor).

albidare, to whiten.

to mak whyte, albare, ..~are, candidare *CathA*.

albidus [CL], pale.

invenitur purpureus cereus ~us viridis GOSC. *Aug. Maj.* 52; yposelinum, quod alii apium agreste vocant, ..melius ortino et ~ius *Alph.* 197.

Albiensis v. Albigensis.

albificare, to whiten. **b** to taw (leather). **c** to make silvery (alch.).

hec omnia ~ant et clarificant et mundificant..faciem BACON IX 122; cerusa qua mulieres ~ant se *Id.* XIV 75; frigus ~at humidam materiam et denigrat siccam BAD. AUR. 154 (= UPTON 102). **b 1284** de whittawyariis..qui corea bovina et equina furata scienter ~ant, ut sic non agnoscantur (*Stat. Rhuddlan*) *Rec. Caern.* 120; **1313** †albisitat corea..furata et ea sic †albisitat ut non agnoscantur *Leet Norw.* 55. **c** mundant cum eo corpora et ~ant ea sufficienti albedine et reddit ea clara et lucida M. SCOT *Lumen* 248; rubificare est facere aurum et ~are est facere argentum BACON *Tert. Sup.* 84.

albificatio, whitewashing.

1465 pro iij cersinis calsis albe emptis pro ~one camerarum infra hospicium *Ac. Durh.* 154.

Albigensis, Albigeois, (heretic) of Albi (*dép.* Tarn).

s1178 heretici quos ~es vocant..conveniunt circa Tholosam, male sentientes de sacramento altaris, de matrimonio et aliis sacramentis TREVET 89; **s1209** Abigei, homines nepharii, ..deleti sunt in partibus Tolosanis *Ann. S. Edm.* 18; **s1210** hoc anno concrematus est quidam Ambigensis apud Londonias *Leg. Ant. Lond.* 3; **s1213** hereticorum pravitas qui ~es appellantur in Wasconia, Arvernia et Albegesio..invaluit; ..dicuntur autem ~es ab Alba civitate WEND. II 87 (cf. ib. I 118: de..Albegensibus); adhereant faucibus suis ~ium lingue, qui dicunt duos esse Dominos, bonum a quo bona, malum a quo punitiones malorum GERV. TILB. I 2 (cf. ib. III 103: internecio Albiensium); **s1238** ipsos nomine vulgari Bugaros appellavit, sive essent Paterini, sive Joviniani vel ~es vel aliis heresibus maculati M. PAR. *Maj.* III 520; hinc Albigensis, hinc Tartarus arma resumit GARL. *Tri. Eccl.* 67; hic Abigēa manus canonis ense petit [? l. perit] *Id. Hon. Vit.* 183.

albigineus v. albugineus. albilaki v. albacalay.

1 albinus [cf. albanus], stranger, outsider (Northumb.).

1333 nec levasse potuit..v s. de redditariis qui vocantur ~i per annum *LTRMem* 105 r. 184*d.*

2 Albinus, silver personified as a saint, bribery (*v.* P. Lehmann: *Die Parodie im Mittelalter* 44); *cf. Rufinus.*

se tutos interventu fecerunt ~i coram omnium judice MAP *NC* I 25 p. 50.

1 Albion, Britain.

Brittania..cui quondam ~on nomen fuit BEDE *HE* I 1; **982** (12C) ego Æðelredus..totius ~onis basileus *CD* 632; **s974** regnante Edgaro regum ~onum candidissimo *Lib. Eli.* II 53; **s1101** totius ~onis regnum tranquillitate pacis tripudians siluit ORD. VIT. X 18 p. 115.

2 albion, sort of astronomical instrument.

1326 albyon ad instar planisperii tocius spere celistis concentricos, eccentricos et eciam epiciclos pro variis stellarum motibus machinatos..mira continet brevitate WALLINGF. *Albion* 349; [Ric. de Walingforde] precipuum instrumentum astronomie, antea invisum, 'albion', quasi totum per unum [*all by one*], etymologice vocitavit *G. S. Alb.* II 207.

albipedius, white-footed.

~ius, *huitfoot GlC* A 436.

albisitare v. albificare.

Albiston, a place in Rome (church of St. Balbina in Albiston).

in †Albisterio quod dicitur mutatorium Cesaris, ubi fiebant albe stole imperatorum, fuit candelabrum factum de lapide albeste, qui semel accensus..nulla arte potuit extingui HIGD. I 24 p. 222.

albium v. alveus 1a.

Albius, of Albi (*cf. Albigensis*).

enucleatus erit error prius Albius GARL. *Tri. Eccl.* 67.

alblast- v. arbalist-. albocyn v. albotim.

albor, whiteness.

lingua quoque splendoris, †lava [l. lana] rubricata suspensa in Templo convertebatur in ~orem BRADW. *CD* 53A.

albotim [Ar. *al-buṭm*; cf. botam], terebinth (bot.).

oleum de ireos cum glutine ~im, i. terbentina GAD. 65 v. 2; †albocyn, id est terebentina *Alph.* 5; ~im vel ~ai, albotra helcalibat [Ar. *'ilk al-anbāṭ*.], est terebinthina *LC*.

albrastarius v. arbalistarius. albubit v. alkibrit. albucies v. albuties.

albucum [CL], **~ium, ~ia,** asphodel (bot.).

folium albutii tere et herbam cum toto succo suppone GILB. V 232 v. 1; affodillus, centum capita, ~ium idem *Alph.* 3; *affadyl, herbe,* affadullus.., ~ia *PP*.

albuga v. albugo.

albugineus, belonging to the white of the eye.

illa animalia que die quam nocte minus vident ~eum humorem abundanter habent, minus vero nigrum ADEL. *QN* 12; humor cristallinus est in medio, ..cui anterius ministrat ~eus, ..posterius vitreus RIC. MED. *Micr. Anat.* 215; †albigineus humor GILB. III 125. 2; †-enum humorem BART. ANGL. V 4; humor ~eus BACON *Maj.* II 17.

albugo [CL], white spot or film on eye, cataract. **b** white of eye.

†albulo, *flio GlC* A 417; cujus oculi..fulvis ~inis nubibus tegebantur FELIX *Guthl.* 53; **10..** †albuga, *flig* WW; ~o, *eagflea* ÆLF. *Gl.*; ~ine que virginis oculos tanquam ovi membrana obduxerat dissoluta T. MON. *Will.* V 17; altero oculorum..nihil videbat; ~o quippe lumen obduxerat W. CANT. *Mir. Thom.* VI 45; ~o est macula minuta nascens in cornea GILB. III 135. 1; ~inem habens in oculis †ambobis *Mir. Montfort* 69; ex obtalmia male curata surgit ~o, et est illa macula GAD. 108 v. 1. **b** sub patentibus oculorum hiatibus sole ~ines prominebant R. COLD. *Cuthb.* 63; sebel, vene rubie que sunt in ~ine oculorum *SB* 38; hec ~o, A. *wyte of the hea* WW.

2 white of egg.

~o ovi BART. ANGL. XIX 7; apparent muscillagines in modum vitri liquefacti ut ~inis ovi GILB. I 38 v. 2; misce cum equali mensura ~inis ovi BACON IX 72.

albula, a kind of fish (? whiting or bleak). **b** white spot on eye (*cf. albugo* 1a). **c** small alb (*cf. albus* 8a). **d** (w. *regia*; *cf. hastula regia*) woodruff (*Asperula*).

a escas diminuis †nocuos febrisque calorem, / a candore nitens albula nomen habens NECKAM *DS* III 646. **b** ~a, i. macula in oculo *SB* 10. **c** **1524** casula de albo serico.. cum..~is ejusdem; item ~a de crimson *Cant. Coll. Ox.* I 66. **d** malve, †~e regie quam Angli †woerovam vocant, plantaginis, millefolii, equales mensuras in butiro coque ADEL *CA* 14.

albulo v. albugo a. album v. albus 9.

albumen, white of egg.

albumen durum, pressum palmis, spoliatum / a conchis D. BEC. 2627; humor similis ~ini ovi BACON *Maj.* II 17; ~en ovi coctum est album, quia non tangitur ab igne propter testam UPTON 105.

†alburgon [? ἀλουργόν], red or purple colour.

per ~on, quod ponit in lictera et per †karapon, quem nominat commentator secundo De Anima et medici similiter, possunt alii duo intelligi, ut per ~on 'rubeum', quoniam per karopon videtur intelligi glaucus magis BACON XIV 71.

alburneus, made of 'auburn' (*v. alburnus* b).

non arcu utuntur corneo, non ~eo, non taxeo GIR. *IK* I 4; **1297** de xij d. de j arcu auburneo, iij sagittis barbatis provenientibus de tenemento quondam Almarici de S. Amando in Grendon' vend' de redditu assiso per annum *Ac. Cornw.* I 142 (*cf. IPM* [**1300**] 96 r. 3); **1327** per servicium reddendi ..unum arcum eburneum sine corda cum tribus sagittis barbatis *IPM* 3/2 r. 9 (cf. ib.: aburneum).

alburnus, white, gleaming. **b** (sb. n.; CL = sapwood) 'auburn', kind of wood used for bows (? *Viburnum*). **c** (sb. m.) kind of fish (? bleak).

705 notus propter ~um dictricis Romaniae decorem *Ep. Aldh.* III (9) p. 498. **b** **1209** [per servitium] unius arcus de ~o per annum reddendi ad Phasca *Fines Warw.* 172; **1239** solvit..j arcum de auburno *KRMem* 18, r. 12 (cf. *Fees* 586; *CalCh* I 277). **c** variata piscis..magnitudine et forma est ~i CAIUS *Anim.* 25b.

albus [CL], white. **b** (as by-name) fair, blond. **c** (in plant names). **d** (w. ref. to food or drink; *cf. infra* 9b).

me dudum genuit candens onocrotalus albam ALDH. *Aen.* 59 (*Penna*) 1; sermone Scottico Inisboufinde, id est 'insula vitulae ~ae' BEDE *HE* IV 4; locellum de marmore ~o.. factum *Ib.* 19; ~us, *hwit* ÆLF. *Gl.*; esto..ut..duo corpora ~a unius sint magnitudinis, ..una tamen ~ior alia ADEL. *QN* 34; allumen zucharinum est ~issime nature M. SCOT *Lumen* 255; **1359** cccc arcus depictos et cc arcus ~os *Cl* 197 m. 9; Gallicia..a candore populi illius regionis sic nominata; pre ceteris hominibus illi dicuntur esse ~iores *Eul. Hist.* II 101; **1368** item j vestimentum integrum ~um de serico *Invent. Norw.* II 7 (cf. infra 8a); **1503** pro factura xiiij petrarum candelarum ~arum et nigrarum *Ac. Durh.* 102. **b** ut pro diversa capillorum specie unus Niger Heuuald, alter ~us Heuuald diceretur BEDE *HE* V 10; Robertus ~us *DB* I 219; **11..** Stephano ~o clerico *Feod. Durh.* 141; **1188** Godefridus ~us *Pipe* 176. **c** (v. helleborus, spina, vitis). **d** **c1150** exceptis infirmis qui, si voluerint, ~um [sc. panem] comedere poterunt in Adventu (*Inst. Sempr.* 26) *MonA* VI 946* xxxiii (cf. GAD. 38. 2: recipe micam panis ~issimi); **1187** pro ij doliis ~i vini et ij rubei vini *Pipe* 203; **1220** albior his vitis liquor est acceptior et qui / vix patet argento H. AVR. *Poems* 2. 233; **1281** in ij lib. et dim. zinziberis ad ~um pulverem faciendum (*Ac. Pri. Wint.*) *EHR* LXI 104; **1299** in decima soluta..pro ~o pisce *MinAc* 978/19 (cf. albula a); **1327** pro xiij bollis grossi salis, una celdra ~i salis *ExScot* 66; **1340** in xx li. ..succuris alb' *Ac. Durh.* 36; **1358** in alleciis rubeis et ~is (*Ac. Univ. Ox.*) *EHR* XXIV 739 (v. et. piper, pisum).

2 (of leather or parchment) **a** tawed. **b** (w. ref. to inner surface of skin used for recto of membrane) front (*cf.* 9e *infra*). **c** blank (*cf.* 9f *infra*).

a **1257** in harnasio emend[and]o cum ~o corio *Crawley* 216; **c1300** quod nullus..coria ~a vel tannata..vendere debeat *Reg. Malm.* II 393; **1305** unum par ~arum cirothecarum *Cart. Glam.* 982. **b** presentem affero descriptionem in ~iori parte pellis BACON *Maj.* I 300; **1372** ex parte ~a.., ex parte nigra *LTRAcEsch.* 13. **c** **1257** cum xx cedulis ~is et vacuis sigillo regis sigillatis (*Pat*) *Foed* I 633; **1267** rex ~o cardinali salutem *Cl* 362; **1296** invente fuerunt plures littere ~e sine scriptura bullate *Reg. Carl.* I 31; **1368** transgressiones quas fecit faciendo sex ~as cartas sive litteras patentes et eas sigillo nostro..signando *Pat* 277 m. 8; **s1399** ad ~as chartas..eosdem..apponere sigilla sua compulit WALS. *HA* II 231 (cf. *EHR* LXVI 384).

3 (of glass) colourless.

cum ~um vitrum ac detersissimum intuemur ADEL. *QN* 29; **1351** de vitro glauco, ~o et rubeo *Ac. Durh.* 381.

4 dressed in white. **b** (of Cistercians). **c** (of Austin canons and canonesses). **d** (of Servites). **e** (w. ref. to the wearing of albs on the Sunday after Easter; *v. infra* 8d).

apparuit ei quedam formosa domina cum duobus armigeris ~is *Mir. Montfort* 108. **b** si fuero monachus albus, generalia dura / hi pulmenta duo, sed bene cocta, dabunt NIG. *SS* 2111; **1234** ut viri religiosi tam albi quam nigri solito honestius recipiantur (*Vis. Westm.*) *EHR* XXVII 738; nec canonici nec monachi albi sedebunt nobiscum *Cust. Westm.* 259; **1251** ~i monachi de Karlyon *IMisc* 5/29; **1257** priorisse ~arum monialium de Wygornia [*Whistones in Worcester*] *Cl* 95; **s1208** [Johannes rex] destruxit omnes domos ~orum monachorum *Leg. Ant. Lond. app.* 201; **s1220** R. comes Cestrie..edificavit..abbaciam de Deulecres ~i ordinis HIGD. VII 34. **c** duas domos canonicas fecit, unam..de canonicis nigris, ..altera[m] vero..de canonicis ~is GIR. *Spec.* III 19; **1537** monasterium ~arum monialium de Brewood *Val. Eccl.* III 193. **d** **s1404** in villa de Paris prope ecclesiam ~e religionis que..vocatur Gallice *les Blans Manteaux Plusc.* X 22. **e** usque ad Dominicam que ~um Pascha dicitur *Chr. Battle* 60.

5 (of metals) **a** (w. *ferrum*) white (tin-coated) iron (*cf.* Fr. *fer blanc*). **b** (w. *stannum*) (?). **c** (w. ref. to lead) carbonate (wheatstone or ceruse). **d** (w. ref. to mercury or supposed transmutation into silver). **e** (w. ref. to silver) plain, ungilt. **f** of silver (*cf.* 10 *infra*).

a **1464** j sconse de ~o ferro *Ac. Durh.* 639. **b** **1305** stannum tam ~um quam nigrum (*Pat*) *Rec. Stan.* 16; **1411** xxx pecias stanni ~i *Cl* 260 m. 1. **c** **1300** de cccij li. ..receptis tam de mina ~a quam nigra *Pipe* 145 (*Devon*); **1301** vj disci de minera plumbi azur'..et vj disci de ~a ? sc. minera] plumbi (*Comp. Camer. Cestr.*) *Pipe Chesh. app.* 203; cerusa, plumbum ~um *SB* 15; **1472** pro necessariis ad picturam magni campanilis viz. ..vij lib. et dim. plumbi ~i *Fabr. York* 77. **d** fumus rubeus et fumus citrinus et fumus ~us ROB. ANGL. *Alch.* 517b; opus rubeum fermento indiget rubeo, sicut opus ~um ~o DASTYN *Ros.* 5. **e** **1208** j cuppam deauratam et planam, ..j cuppam ~am (*Invent. Exch.*) *LTRMemPR* 124; **1244** tres calices, unum deauratum et alios ~os *Liberate* 20 m. 4; **1245** phiale..quarum una est tota deaurata, altera ~a (*Invent. S. Paul.*) *Arch.* L 466; **c1250** calix argenteus ~us *Vis. S. Paul.* 6; **c1322** v botons de argento albo *IMisc* 87/25; **1409** duos..~os ciphos de argento *Pat* 382 m. 16. **f** offerens ~um nummum justoque labore quesitum W. CANT. *Mir. Thom.* II 82.

6 (of silver) 'blanched' (tested by assay, or w. allowance to offset impurity). **b** payable in 'blanched' money. *Cf. blancus.*

valet xxii li. de ~is denariis ad pensum hujus comitis *DB* I 137; reddebat x li. ad numerum; modo reddit xvi li. de ~o argento *Ib.* 143; reddit lx sol. albas (*sic*) *Ib.* 39b; **1212** in ~a moneta *Fees* 80; **1225** debet xl li. alb' et xx li. numero de firma *LTRMem* 7 r. 7d.; **1297** de xl li. ~is de reddito burgenciali Walyngford'..et xl s. pro dealbacione dictarum xl li. *Ac. Cornw.* I 111 **b** tantum reddit de firma ~a *DB* I 39b; **1199** vij li. et v s. de ~a firma *CurR RC* II 149; **1219** occasione cujusdam ~e firme quam terra illa debuit *CurR* VIII 79; **1440** vij li. ..de ~a firma *Cl* 290 m. 13; **1455** onerat se..de iiij s. albefirme unius tenandie *ExchScot* 56; **c1283** ~us redditus domini regis *Cust. Battle* 124; **13..** de auxiliis ~is dim. m. (*Cust. S. Edm.*) *Cust. Rents* 109.

7 a (w. *candidus*) pure white. **b** (w. other colour) light, pale.

a ~us candidus, A. *mylke whyte* WW. **b** **1310** unam tunicam de ~o blueto..unam tunicam de nigro blueto *Arch. Bridgw.* 47; **1316** pro restauro..unius equi ~i ferandi, ..unius equi ~i liardi *RGasc* IV 1679; **1396** ij pec' de ~o blod[io] *KRAc* 338/3 r. 6.

8 (sb. f. or n., sc. *vestis*, *vestimentum*) white robe, alb. **b** (?) altar hanging (or alb worn by ministrant at altar). **c** (pl.) (wearing of) baptismal robes. **d** (pl.) week following Easter (when white robes were worn) incl. Low Sunday (*cf. supra* 4e).

hanc planetam, ..~am ac stolam..benedicere..digneris EGB. *Pont.* 17; diaconus..exuat casulam et duplicans eam circumponat sibi in sinistra scapula, annectens alteram summitatem ejus cingulo ~ae *RegulC* 34; **s1105** presbyteri induti ~is et sacerdotalibus stolis regi..nudis pedibus occurrerunt EADMER *HN* 203; dedit unum ~um optimum cum stola et manipulo *Chr. Rams.* 199; utuntur [Cartusienses] ~a et amictu, stola, fanone atque planeta planis et candidis AD. EYNS. *Hug.* IV 10; sacerdos..pro lorica totum corpus cooperuit ~a BELETH *RDO* 32. 43; **1232** mandatum est W. scissori quod capam de choro et ~am et dalmaticam..liberari faciat..capellano *Cl* 25; ymaginem cere indutam ~a et casula ad modum sacerdotis *Mir. Montfort* 106; **1317** ~a cum aurifrigiis *Reg. Heref.* 42; abbas ..erit in vesperis [festorum principalium] solempniter revestitus, sc. in ~a, capa, mitra, cirothecis et anulo *Cust. Cant.* 45; **1368** unum ~um cum paruris de rubeo velveto pulverizatum cum *boterfleyes* de auro *Invent. Norw.* 1; ~a, A. *an awbe*, ..*a haube*, ..*a nawbe* WW; **1467** de..j parolla unius aube blodii coloris *Ac. Obed. Abingd.* 134; **1503** una ~a viridis coloris *Invent. Ch. Ch. Cant.* 130 (cf. ib. 159: una auba de velvete). **b** **c1240** custodi ~arum monasterii Rameseie ..xx s. ..ad emendum et sustinendum paruras ~arum ad sex altaria ex utraque parte chori sita *Cart. Rams.* II 225; **1518** non habent..pallia et ~as pro altaribus consecratis *Vis. Linc.* I 11. **c** **c690** [Caeduualla] post albas igitur morbo correptus egrescit ALDH. *CE* 3. 29; **s689** [Caedualla] in ~is adhuc positus, langore correptus..solutus a carne..est BEDE *HE* V 7. **d** **s1153** celebrata sollemnitate paschali, post ~as ad civitatem propriam properavit W. NEWB. I 26 (cf. ib.: post ~as paschales); **1175** invenimus..x prefationes in sacro cathalogo recipiendas, unam in ~is paschalibus.. (*Conc. Westm.* 14) GERV. CANT. I 254; **s1194** rex Ricardus.. in ~is gloriose coronatus est *Ann. Cestr.* 44; **s1194** usque ad xv Kal. Maii, sc. Dominica in ~is FORDUN *GA* 21; **c1250** hec sunt festa duplicia in ecclesia Salisbur', viz. ..dies Pasche cum tribus sequentibus diebus, Dominica in ~is.. *Conc. Syn.* 323; **s1172** Dominica in ~is, octavo die Pasche HIGD. VII 22 (= GIR. *EH* I 40: Dominica que vulgo Clausum Pascha vocatur); **c1430** erga Dominicam in ~is jam post Pascha proximam *Reg. Whet.* II 448; **1463** die Lune proxima post Dominicam in ~is (*CourtR*) *Rec. Eton* XXVIII no. 61.

9 (sb. n.) **a** white of eye. **b** white stone, marble. **c** dairy produce. **d** white skin of vair (fur). **e** front of membrane (*cf.* 2b *supra*). **f** album, entry-book of names. **g** (? by conf. w. 9f) pen. **h** blanch-farm (*cf.* 6b *supra*).

a ~a oculorum citrina fiunt GILB. VI 235. 1. **b** **1255** ~orum scissor (*KRAc* 467/4) *Antiq. J.* XXVIII 147. **c** **1243** exitu ~i, sc. de xxvj vaccis xl s. *MinAc* 825/16 r. 7; **1270** consistit..vicaria..in decima..ovorum, pomorum, ~i, vitulorum *Reg. Linc.* 151; **1296** de xxx s. de ~o x vaccarum positarum ad firmam, deducta decima *DLMinAc* 1/1 r. 2; **s1315** carnes..incipiebant deficere, ova et cetera ~a evanescere TROKELOWE 92; **1322** de ~o xxxiiij ovium matricium non respondet, quia steriles erant hoc anno *LTRAc* 16 r. 29. **d** **1189** pro penula de ~o varii *Pipe* 17; **1432** nullus studens..utatur pellura de minutis variis seu de puro ~o *StatOx* 239. **e** **1267** adhuc staurum de Bouecumbe in ~o alterius rotuli *MinAc* 984/1 r. 1d. **f** aethralis litteraturae ~o descriptos ALDH. *VirgP* 34 (cf. *Phil.* iv 3); mansionario praecepisti ut in ~o vestrae sanctae congregationis meum nunc quoque nomen apponeret BEDE *Cuthb. prol.*; in ~o [i.e. libro confraternitatis] beatitudinis vestre ALCUIN *Ep.* 67; **10..** ~o, *nombred*, in quo consulis nomen scripserant WW; meus a modo eris et meo ~o insertus laudabilis militie premia reportabis W. MALM. *GR* IV 309. **g** ~o, penna *GlC* A 495. **h** quantum de ~o firme pro singulis libris solvere teneantur *Dial. Scac.* I 4A; **1198** debet ..lxj s. de ~o ville de Benton' de anno preterito *Pipe* 191; **1224** cives Ebor' habent diem..ad audiendum judicium de ~o quod exigitur de firma ville sue *LTRMem* 6 r. 4 (3) *d.*

10 (sb. m.) small silver coin (Fr. *blanc*).

1409 rex..concessit..domino..alferitz de Navarra..quod levare posset..v ~os pro quacumque tarqua coriorum (*DipDocE* 374) *Foed.* VIII 576.

albuties, whiteness. **b** white of eye.

albucies, *white of þe face* WW; *whittnesse*, albedo, albucies, candor *CathA*. **b** hec albucies, ..hec †abbcies, A. *the qwyt of the ye* WW.

albutium v. albucum.

alcaldus, ~is [Sp. *alcalde* < Ar. *al-qāḍī*], civic magistrate (*cf. cadius*).

c**1149** Alcaiz OSB. BAWDSEY clxxviii; **1309** †escabinos [MS: escaldos], consules et communitates villarum (*Cl*) *Foed.* III 153 (cf. *Cl* 127 m. 21*d*.: escaldis et consulibus de Bermeio); **1317** prepositis, ~is et inhabitantibus in..villa de Bermey *Cl* 135 m. 17*d*.; **1311** ~us..domini nostri regis Castelle *RGasc* IV 562 (cf. ib.: per ~os et juratos dictarum villarum); **1322** littera alcadi regis Arragon' *TRBk* 187 p. 114; **1386** mittet..decem galeas..bene armatas, viz. de uno patrono, tribus ~ibus, sex arraizis (*DipDocE* 309) *Foed.* VII 521; c**1394** magne prudencie viris alcadis et algasullis civitatis Ispalensis *DipCorr. Ric. II* no. 209.

alcanamia v. alchiminum.

alcanna [Ar. *al-ḥinnā, al-ḥanna*(*t*)], henna (*Lawsonia*). **b** alkanet (*Anchusa, Alkanna*).

~a hujusmodi virtutis est.. Gilb. II 77. 1; super..egritudines nervorum frigidas..oleum de euforbio est optimum ..et oleum de ~a Gad. 65 v. 2; ~a herba est que ultra mare et precipue in Sicilia invenitur *Alph.* 7 (cf. ib. 182: tapsia nos inflat sed nos alcanna colorat); ligustrum Grece dicitur *cyprus*; officinae vocant ligustrum ~am aut *henne* Turner *Herb.* B ii v. **b** *alkenet, herbe*, alcanea *PP*; ~a, A. *alkenet* WW.

alcannetta, (?) henna or alkanet.

1380 unam balam de arquinetta (*Cl*) *Foed.* VII 233.

1 alcanus v. 1 altanus. alcarinus v. altarmus.

†alcasse [? Ar. *al-kūr*, misr. as *al-kūz*], bdellium (bot.).

~e, i. bdellium *SB* 10.

alcassinum [Ar. *al-khazzī*], coarse silk.

a**1100** xl albas: harum iiij sunt de osturino et tres de ~o et tres deorsum parate de pallio ad pedes *Process. Sal.* 184.

alcato v. alcoto.

alcedo [CL], 'halcyon: **a** gull'; **b** (?) coal-tit.

a alcido, *meau GlC* A 478; ~o vel alcion, *mæw* Ælf. *Gl.*; *semew, byrd*, aspergo, ~o *PP*. **b** *colmose, byrd*, ~o *PP*; ~o, A. *a colmose* WW; *a collemase*, ~o *CathA*.

alces [ἄλκη], elk.

hoc animal Norvegia *elend* et *elke* nominat..; equidem hippelaphum..dicerem; ~em esse non putem, cum ~i.. nec cornua his similia nec..juba sit apud veteres Caius *Anim.* 11b.

alchalim v. alkali.

†alchemer [? l. *alcheier* < Ar. *al-khiyār* (*shanbar*) = cassia fistula], senna.

~er, i. *sene SB* 10.

alcheozoidos v. arceuthis.

alchimia [Ar. *al-kīmiyā'* < χυμεία], alchemy. **b** (?) philosophers' stone. **c** alloy resembling gold (cf. alchiminum).

scientia de alckimia, que est scientia de transformatione metallorum in alias species D. Morley 34; hec ars.. / argento copiat et aurilegio / plus quam alkimie vana traditio (*Palpo* 24) *Ps.*-Map *Poems* 107; in hac arte que alkimia nuncupatur M. Scot. *Lumen* 240; supponunt doctores ~ie quod in unoquoque corpore naturali et complexionato inest quinta essentia Gros. 36; hec scientia est alkimia speculativa, que speculatur de omnibus inanimatis et tota generatione rerum ab elementis; est autem alkimia operativa et practica, que docet facere metalla nobilia et colores et alia multa melius et copiosius per artificium quam per naturam fiant Bacon *Tert.* 40; s**1320** contigit eum [priorem de Bynham] familiaritatem contrahere cum quodam fratre de ordine Mendicantium, qui promisit se sibi pecunias inestimabiliter multiplicaturum per artem que alkomia vocatur *G. S. Alb.* II 132; **1329** per artem alkemonie sciunt metallum argenti conficere (*Pat*) *Foed.* IV 384a; **1351** recepit..d scuta auri xx libras argenti ad comodum regis inde faciendum per artem alkemie *SelCKB* VI 73; **1373** fecit pecias predictas cum arte alconomie de auro et argento et aliis medicinis *Ib.* 165. **b** quoniam quid sit alchymia..nondum vestra cognovit Latinitas, in presenti sermone elucidabo. posui istud verbum, licet ignotum et admirabile, ut sub diffinitione claresceret; Hermes vero philosophus, et alii qui post ipsum fuere, hoc vocabulum diffiniunt..: alchymia est substantia corporea ex uno et per unum composita preciosiora ad invicem per cognationem et effectum conjungens et eadem naturali commixtione ingeniis melioribus naturaliter convertens Rob. Angl. *Alch. pref.* p. 509. **c 1287** conscensiens fuit controfaccioni monete..et misit alkemiam et falsum metallum..usque A. *Gaol Del.* 36/1 r. 24*d*.

alchimicus, alchemistic. **b** (sb. m.) alchemist.

argentum vivum sitit aurum sicut sitiens aquam, ut habetur in libris allzimicis Gilb. VII 351 v. 2; de scientiis experimentalibus et alkymicis et mathematicis Bacon *Min.* 327; fuit [Hermes]..in astrologia clarissimus..et in alkimicis magicisque famosus *Ps.*-Gros. 277; liber..de arte †alkumita *Cant. Coll. Ox.* I 26. **b** occultis et enigmaticis verbis tam Hermes quam ceteri alkimici sequentes philosophiam suam velaverunt *Ps.*-Gros. 637; sicut plumbum non sit aurum secundum alkymicos nisi.. Wycl. *Ver.* I 60.

†alchiminum [cf. ME *alkamine*], alloy resembling gold.

alcanamye, metalle, alcanamia *PP*; alchinum vel alchimum, A. *alkemoyn* WW; **1604** xxx pecias cunei de falso mixto metallo viz. de argento cupro et alcumine *Pat* 1655 m. 9 (cf. *CalPat 1452–61* p. 182).

alchimista, alchemist.

apud omnes filosoficas permutationes ratum arbitror quicquid in hac arte conditum subsistendi vicem alkemiarum vel alkemistarum (M. Scot *Alch.* 2) *Med. Cult.* 152; alchemiste in minoribus mineralibus laborantes.., volentes ex his tincturas perficere *Correct. Alch.* 10; per solem potest intelligi aurum et per lunam argentum, et hic est mos alkimistarum Bacon V 116; Callistenes alkimista famosus *Ps.*-Gros. 279; lac virginis artificiale quod faciunt archimiste Gad. 131. 1; erit res optima quam recipere possunt alchymiste ut ex ea faciant aurum Dastyn *Ros.* 18; sicut etiam alchymiste multa grossa et gravia subtiliant sic per ignem Bradw. *CD* 115e.

alchimistice, alchemistically.

†Hermogenes [l. Hermes] dixit: '..omnes res generantur ab una sola substancia, ..quarum pater est sol, quarum mater est luna'..istud potest exponi ~e et figurative de auro et argento Bacon V 116.

alchimisticus, alchemistic.

est alkimisticus intellectus sub figurativis locucionibus Bacon V 116; scit naturalia per experientiam et medicinalia et alkimistica *Id. Tert.* 46; nonne aurum naturaliter vel artificialiter generatum a philosophis naturalibus.., sc. alchymisticis, imputribile..affirmatur? Bradw. *CD* 116e; **1550** (v. alchimistria).

alchimistria, falsification (of metal).

1550 perdonavimus..†alkimisticam [MS: alkimistriam] multiplicacionem et pejoracionem sive imbasionem cunie nostre (*Pat*) *Foed.* XV 206a (cf. *CalPat* III 186).

alchior v. alcion. alchites, alchiticus, v. ascit-.

alchitram [Ar. *al-qiṭrān*; cf. *kitran*], resin of cedar or sim.

~am i. pix *SB* 9; alquitran, pix liquida idem *Ib.* 10; ~am est oleum juniperi, pix liquida *LC*.

Alchoram, ~an, v. alcoran. alchorismus v. algorismus.

alchubugi [Ar. *al-qabaj* < Pers. *kabh*], red-legged partridge.

recipe fellis galli aut perdicis aut fasiani qui vocatur ~i a Mess[ue] Gad. 111 v. 2.

alcinoe v. alcyon.

†alcinus, (?) of alder (*cf. alniceus*).

ingentes palos quercinos et ~os..humo defigi fecit *Croyl.* 4.

1 †alcion, (?) iron or a kind of bird (*cf. alcyon*).

~on, *isern*, *GlC* A 422 (= *EE* 339. 10: alchior).

2 alcion v. alcyon. alciorare v. altiorare. alcius v. alte.

alcohol [Ar. *al-kuḥl*], powder used as eye-salve, kohl (galena or antimony). **b** spirit, alcohol.

distemperentur cum alcofol quod fit cum stipitibus feni melle repleti Gilb. III 139, v. 1; alcol est collirium vel pulvis indifferenter Gad. 109. 1; ~ol i. pulvis ad oculos; alcofol idem *SB* 10; ~ol est antimonium sive stibium *LC*. **b** alcol vini est aqua ardens rectificata *LC*.

alcollum [Ar. *al-qulā'*], ulcer in mouth.

~a, i. pustule parve que fiunt in ore *SB* 10.

alcon [etym. dub.], maidenhair (*Adiantum*). **b** cuckoo-pint (*Arum*).

alloon [v.l. aloon), capillus Veneris idem *Alph.* 4. **b** ~on. †rarus [v.l. iarus], pes vituli idem, ..A. *cokkowespitte Ib.* 5.

alconnium v. alcyonium. alconomia v. alchimia.

Alcoran, ~anus [Ar. *al-Qur'ān*], Koran.

incipit lex Saracenorum quam Alchoran vocant, id est collectionem preceptorum Rob. Angl. *Koran* 3; ordinavit ut mense [Romodan] completo totus Alchoran perlegeretur *Id. Chr. Mend.* 219; s**618** [Mahimetus] edidit Alchoram, id est collectaneum preceptorum, sicut instructus erat a quodam Judeo et a Sergio monacho apostata Nestoriane heresis R. Niger II 142; ipse quidem Machometus in Alchoran, qui est liber legis sue, dicit Christum natum de Virgine Maria sine commixtione hominis Bacon *Mor. Phil.* 218; de ~ano, id est lege Machometi *Ps.*-Gros. 283; **1443** liber Alkeron *EpAcOx* 233.

†alcotar [Ar. *al-qulquṭār*], iron peroxide; *cf. colcotar*.

deice super ipsum parum ydragor resolutum in aqua et coagula, vel parum lapidis ~ar preparati M. Scot. *Lumen* 250.

alcoto, ~onus, ~ona [Sp. Ar. *al-quṭūn*], 'acton', padded jacket.

1209 pro vij ulnis linee tele ad faciendum j ~onem..et pro cotone ad illum ~onem *Misae* 124; **1213** in cotone ad auketonum domini regis, sc. j li. et dim., xij d.; in eodem auketuno suendo, xij d. *Misae* 269; **1215** fieri facias duos.. †acotimos [l. acotunos] *Cl* 240b; **1223** ad unum †acoconem [l. acotonem] cooperiendum *Ib.* 550b; **1226** chalonem.. impignoravit pro quodam alketono *CurR* XII 2138; **1235** ad ij alkethon' cend[allo] cooperiendas *Chanc. Misc.* 3/3; s**1190** suscepit rex Ricardus..a Saladino..unum alcatonem satis levem, nulli spiculo penetrabile[m] M. Par. *Min.* II 18; **1271** de uno aketuno *SelCCoron* 29; lego..arma mea cum akedono *FormMan* 17; **1297** in precio duorum haketonum *DocScot* II 138 (cf. ib.: unius haketone); **1305** aketoni: et pro iij hacketonis emptis pro municione eadem *MinAcW Wales* I 404; **1315** erunt illi homines pedites armati aketonis et bacinettis *RParl* I 351a; **1318** quod durante guerra quilibet homo de terra laicus..habeat pro corpore suo unam sufficientem aketonam [v.l. actonem].., et qui non habuerit aketonam..habeat unum bonum hobirgellum vel unum bonum ferrum pro corpore suo (*Stat. Rob. I* c. 27) *APScot* 113; **1322** de vij aquiton' debilibus *MinAc* 1145/21 r. 40; c**1322** ij actones *IMisc* 87/25; c**1325** quod tu uteris ij aketonibus, uno pro diebus ferialibus et alio pro festivis (*Vis. S. Petr.*) *EHR* LVII 270; **1327** per duas actonas liberatas serjandis regis *ExchScot* 64; **1336** ad eligendum.. hobelarios, quorum quilibet habeat..unum aketonem vel platas *RScot* 408a; c**1350** legavit..j aketonem cum platis *Reg. S. Aug.* 302.

alcubd v. alzubd.

alcufar [Ar. *al-kabar* < κάππαρις], caper (bot.).

~ar, i. capparis *SB* 10.

alcumen v. alchiminum.

alcyon [ἀλκυών], **~one,** 'halcyon', sea-bird, gull.

alcion avis est que stagna marina frequentat / edificatque suos hiemali tempore nidos *V. Merl.* 1357; mergus, alcion, cignus archana nature frequenter aperiunt J. Sal. *Pol.* 417a; alcinoe nautis gratissima Neckam *DS* II 229; alcion, A. *a semewe* WW.

†alcyonitus, 'halcyon', calm.

cum circa medium hyemis alciones nidificare..con spexeris, de xv dierum..serenitate ne dubites; ..dicunturque dies ~e, quibus vix vel tenuis aura sentitur J. Sal. *Pol.* 417b.

alcyonium [ἀλκυόνιον], 'halcyon's nest', identified w. sponge, coral, salty efflorescence (*adarce*), etc.

alconnium, †adaras, †coro [l. caro] marina idem secundum nos; secundum alios alconnium est plumbum ustum, vel quedam avis marina, vel quedam superfluitas arboris in mari crescentis *Alph.* 7 (cf. ib. 179: est et tercium genus [spongie]..; comburuntur sicut †calcionium); halcyonium est nihil aliud quam maris spuma concreta [etc.] *LC*.

aldea [Sp. *aldea* < Ar. *al-ḍay'a*], village, hamlet.

1282 eidem..domicelle..pro arris damus..Jactam..et Pertusiam, cum omnibus villis, ~eis, pechis, †moneticis, Judeis et Saracenis ibidem habitantibus (*Lit. regis Aragon.*) *Foed.* II 210.

aldermannatus, ward governed by alderman.

s**1248** major cepit ~um illum in manum suam, ipso [aldermanno] omnino amoto *Leg. Ant. Lond.* 15; s**1273** †precepitur [l. preceptum] est viris in illo ~u manentibus ut ipsi eligerent virum idoneum *Ib.* 169.

aldermanneria, aldermanry, office of (or ward governed by) civic alderman: **a** (London); **b** (elsewhere).

a 1241 ponunt se super xlij homines de tribus ~iis propinquioribus loco ubi..inventus fuit occisus *MGL* I 102; s**1258** regis consilium decrevit..aldermannos..de ballivis et ~iis esse derogandos *Ann. Lond.* 50; s**1273** degradatus fuit de ~ia sua *Leg. Ant. Lond.* 169; **1376** renunciacio Johannis Wrothe de aldermanria sua (*LBLond.* H) *MGL* I 576. **b** a**1198** sciatis nos concessisse..Baldewyno de V. quicquid ad nos pertinet de aldermanria de Westgate infra muros civitatis Cantuarie *BBC* 130; **1198** Baldewynus.. debet xx m. pro habendo eo quod ad donationem regis pertinet in ~ia de Westgate *Pipe* 210; **1281** tenuit apud Cantuariam c s. annui redditus de quadam aldremanneria vocata Westgate, quam aldremanneriam..vendidit magistro H. .., reddendo sibi dictos c s. *IPM* 27/7; **1283** alremariam [in civitate Cant'] *CalIPM* no. 469; **1265** mandamus ..quatinus gentes ville vestre [*Bridgnorth*] per aldemanerias et constabularias ordinetis *Cl* 122; **1382** per sacramentum.. aldr[emanni] de Novo Vico [*Salisbury*] et iiij hominum vicinorum ejusdem aldr[emanrie] *SelCCoron* 107; **1236** fuit in ~ia majoris de Magno Vico [Winton'] *JustIt* 775 r. 20; **1423** consuetudo civitatis Wyntonie semper fuit..[quod] quedam aldermanria infra civitatem inveniret iiij homines sufficientes ad vigilandum.. *BBWinchester* f. 24.

2 office of alderman of guild.

1305 S. pistor intrat in aldremanriam Johannis le Knygt (*Andover*) *Gild Merch.* II 341.

aldermannia, office of (or ward governed by) civic alderman: **a** (London); **b** (elsewhere).

a s**1302** restitutus est..in honore ~ie Londoniarum et factus est aldermannus de Basseishawe *Ann. Lond.* 104; **1321** prior [S. Trinitatis]..est aldermannus medietatis illius warde [de Portesokene], racione cujus ~ie idem prior et predecessores sui semper hactenus ad husteng' civitatis.. venerunt *PQW* 472a. **b 1217** habere facias Johanni de H. talem saisinam de ~a Lincolnie cum pertinentiis qualem habuit A. advunculus ejus *Cl* 340b; s**1278** abbas..dimisit cuidam magistro N. ..~iam de Westgate [*Canterbury*] Thorne 1927.

2 office of alderman of guild.

c**1380** qui quidem aldermannus sic electus officium ~ie sue et custodie magne gilde predicte habere et exercere debet ad totam vitam suam (*King's Lynn*) *Gild Merch.* II 168.

aldermannus [AS], 'ealdorman', royal official or nobleman.

†**974** (13c) quidam vir dilectissimus mihi, Ailwinus alderman nomine *CS* 798; dona ipsius ~i [vv.ll. ealdormanni, aldremanni] *Ib.* (cf. *Chr. Rams.* 182, 186); †**998** hic requiescit Ailwinus..totius Angliae ~us (*Epitaph.*) *MonA* II 546; si homo siþcundus agat cum rege vel cum regis ~o [AS: *wið kyninges ealdormannan*] pro familia sua (*Quad.*) *GAS* 111; burhbrece episcopi et ~i, quem Latine comitem vel seniorem dicunt *Ib.* 73; si aldremannus suus [AS: *his ealdorman*] ei concedat (*Quad.*; *Rect.* 17) *Ib.* 451; **12..** temporibus Romanorum in regno isto Britannie vocabantur senatores qui postea temporibus Saxonum..vocabantur ~i, non propter etatem sed propter sapientiam et dignitatem (*Leg. Ed. Conf. Lond.*) *Ib.* 655; **1419** antiquis legibus..regum Saxonum '~us', qui nunc dicitur judex et justiciarius, vocabatur *MGL* I 32.

2 alderman, civic official: **a** (London); **b** (elsewhere in England); **c** (Wales); **d** (Ireland); **e** (Calais); **f** (Scotland; = provost).

a **1111** Turstenus ~us de la warde (*Ch. S. Paul.*) *HMC Rep* IX 68a; **a1123** coram..Ebrardo sellario alderman' illius warde (*Cart. B. Scriptoris*) *EHR* XIV 429; **1196** in reparacione Turris..per visum..Walteri ~i *Pipe* 290; **s1196** voluerunt..excellentiores civium, quos majores et ~os dicimus, seipsos servare indemnes..et pauperiores intolerabiliter apporriare M. Par. *Maj.* II 418; **1227** quod singuli ~i..omnia debita que nobis debentur in singulis wardis colligant *Pat* 132; **s1229** omnes ~i et magnates civitatis *Leg. Ant. Lond.* 6; sine ~is per quos judicia in Londonia redduntur *State Tri. Ed. I* 79; **1319** quod ~i civitatis..de anno in annum et precipue die S. Gregorii Pape sint amobiles, et..alii eligantur per easdem gardas de quibus sic amoti prius ~i fuerunt (*Pat*) *MGL* II 269 (cf. *CalPat 1374–7* p. 387); **s1386** major et aldremannei civitatis Londonie Favent 6; **c1393** custos precedit comitantur eumque quater sex / quos aldirmannos urbs habet et proceres (Ric. Maidstone) *Pol. Poems* I 284; **1419** ~i per etymologiam nomine seniores dicti sunt; *alde* enim Saxonice 'senex' et *alder* 'senior' est; et sic..quod apud Romanos 'consul' vel 'senator' dicebatur apud nos dicitur '~us' *MGL* I 32; major urbis cum senatoribus suis quos ~os vocant Liv. *Hen. V* 9b; regiones quas 'custodias' nuncupant, quibus singulis singuli praesunt '~i', id est, senatores P. Verg. XIV 244. **b** **1200** aldremannus et prepositi Linc' *CurR* I 259; **c1200** ego R. ~us Radyngate in Cantuaria *Reg. S. Aug.* 164; **1255** quattuor ~i fiant in Oxonia *BBC* 367; **1382** per sacramentum..aldr[emanni] de Novo Vico [*Salisbury*] *SelC Coron* 107; **c1393** major et xij ~i *Mem. York* 56b. **c** **1421** quod..eligantur xij burgenses..qui..prestent sacramentum ad burgum nostrum [de Kaerdif] bene et fideliter gubernandum; et quod iidem..nominantur ~i *Cart. Glam.* 1487. **d** **1412** major..sacramentum suum..prestet coram illis qui in villas predicta [de Drogheda] hactenus vocabantur jurati, quos..~os decetero volumus nominari *ChartR* 179 m. 2. **e** **1376** concessimus..quod loco baillivi, scabinorum et †cornemannorum..habeatis in eadem villa unum majorem et xij ~os (*TreatyR*) *Foed.* VII 116a. **f** **1326** camerarius Scocie ~o et..ballivis de Rokesburgh *Dryburgh* 255; **1329** Huctrido dicto Pistore, tunc aldirmanno dicte ville *Kelso* II no. 483; **1373** Adam Forest aldirmannus de Edynburgh *Reg. Paisley* 43; **1405** per solucionem factam aldirmanno et communitati burgi de Perth..ad sustentacionem pontis de Tay *ExchScot* 640.

3 bailiff or beadle of hundred.

presit..hundreto unus de melioribus et vocetur aldremannus, qui Dei leges et hominum jura vigilanti studeat observancia promovere (*Leg. Hen. I*) *GAS* 554; **c1253** debent invenire ~um ad hundredum de Burn' pro tota villa de Burne [*Eastbourne*] *IMisc.* 8/23; **1275** [subballivi] unacum Benjamino ~o hujus hundredi [*Hawksborough, Suss.*] venerunt in borgham *Hund.* II 217 (cf. ib. 214: hundredum de Rutherebrugg': ..est ibi quidam bedellus qui vocatur *aldreman*).

4 warden: **a** of guild; **b** of hospital.

a **1130** Thomas de Everwic..debet j fugatorem ut sit ~us in gilda mercatorum de Everwic *Pipe* 34; **1156** ne prepositus meus..de gilda eorum se intromittat nisi proprie ~us et minister eorum *BBC* (*Wallingford*) 204; **1180** de gilda piperariorum [Lond'] unde Ædwardus est ~us *Pipe* 153; **1288** tannatores habent quandam gildam inter se, quod si aliquis confratrum forisfecerit alicui conqueretur aldermano *Leet Norw.* 13; **a1295** condempnetur et puniatur secundum arbitrium aldirmanni, feryngmannorum, decani et aliorum confratrum gilde *Stat. Gild. Berw.* 6; **1320** concessiones quas W. le Chen ~us de gilda mercatorum Oxen'..fecit *MonA* VI 254; **1424** ~us et confratres..gilde [SS. Simonis et Jude] [*Boston*] *Reg. Cant.* II 284; **1451** ~us cujusdam gilde sive fraternitatis..in honore Nativitatis B. Marie Virginis (*Lit. Testimon.*) *Croyl. Cont. B.* 528. **b** **1447** quoddam hospitale unius ~i et xiiij fratrum et sororum infra Flixton' [*Yorks*] *MonA* VI 614.

aldio [Lomb.], semi-servile vassal.

si ~o..accusatus fuerit super aliquo crimine, patronus ejus ipsum defendere debet Upton 79.

Aldsaxo, Old Saxon (*cf. Saxo*).

omne genus Ambronum, id est ~onum Nen. *HB* 207.

1 alea [CL], dice or board-game. **b** (fig.) chance, risk. **c** gamester (? for *aleo*).

alea, *tebl GlC* A 414; alea, *tæfel*; aleae, *tæfelstanas* Ælf. *Gl.*; alii cum aleis ceterorumque jocorum diversitate contendentes G. Mon. IX 14; alea..mendacii, perjurii, furti, sacrilegii mater est P. Blois *Ep.* 74. 228c; **1188** nullus ludat ad aleas vel ad decios (*Capit. Crucesig.* 5) Gerv. Cant. I 409; ălea vel scacci si ludo dampna ministrent D. Bec. 1419; de bragmanno..in aleis ludente Gir. *GE* I 32; cum ad aleas omnia..amisisset *Ib.* II 32; **14..** pertica, scaccarium, ălea [*gl.*: *tabelere*], decius quoque, talus WW. **b** verebatur aleam incisionis W. Cant. *Mir. Thom.* VI 54; ancipiti semper bellorum alea Gir. *EH* I 13; **s1455** (v. alearis). **c** alea, prodigus *GlC* A 465.

2 alea v. aleia. 3 alea v. alium.

alealis, of dice (fig.).

s991 dum ~is tabule tessera nutat, dum vicinum jam mortis terminum vivi adhuc..operimur *Chr. Rams.* 91.

alearis, chancy, risky.

s1455 stabimus..sub jactu alee, ~isque pocius quam aularis..erit nobis vita nostra et omnino absque securitate *Reg. Whet.* I 166.

aleator [CL], gamester, gambler.

~or, *teblere GlC* A 416; ~or lusor cupiditatis *Ib.* 466; ~or calculis et tesseris ludens per aleam Aldh. *PR* 120 p. 164; ~or, *tæflere* Ælf. *Gl.*; nonne tibi videtur ~or ineptus qui..omnem jactum sortis sue presulem facit? J. Sal. *Pol.* 399a; emulus ejus, quondam vero socius ~or R. Cold. *Cuthb.* 67; hic aliator, A. *hassardore* WW.

aleatorium, gaming-house.

1553 suspiciosas domos, tabernas, diversoria, ~ia *Pat* 863 m. 13.

aleatrix, gambler (f.).

s975 o quam callida ~ix mors, quam arguti et incerti jactus tesserarum! *Chr. Rams.* 72.

alebastrum v. alabastrum.

alebris [CL Gl.], nutritious.

†alerius, nutritor *GlC* A 452; †alibre, nutrimentum *Ib.* 454.

alebrodium, alebrot, v. alembrottum. alec v. allec.

alectoria, ~ius, ~io [ἀλεκτόρειος], stone found in gizzard of cock.

allectorio, qui invenitur in ventribus gallorum, invictum facit portantem se Neckam *NR* II 89; [gallus] lapidem nomine †allectricium calcedonio similem gignit Bart. Angl. XII 17 (cf. ib. XVI 15: allectoria sive allectrius); allectorius..gestatus in ore ardorem sitis extinguit J. Godard *AP* 260; lapis preciosus..qui allectorius dicitur assumptus artificiose de ventriculo antiqui caponis Upton 121.

alef v. aleph.

†**alefeniati** [Ar. *al-afāwiyat* < *al-afāwīh*], aromatics.

Avicenna..vocat ibi aromatica '~i', sicut cassialignea, costum, zafranum, amomum Gad. 50. 2.

aleia [OF. *alee*], covered walk. **b** rampart walk (*cf. alura*). **c** alley, passage-way, or lane.

1237 fieri faciat..unam aleam inter cameram regis et cameram regine *Liberate* 12 m. 13; **1239** in quadam alea ab hostio camere regine in eodem castro [Winton'] usque ad hostium capelle regine *KRMem* 17 r. 9; **1241** habere facias..carpentario nostro maeremium ad faciendum quandam ~am de coquina nostra de Windesor' usque ad aulam nostram *Cl* 266. **b** **1238** quod gradus aleyarum et kernellos in castro de Wyndesor'..reparari faciat *Liberate* 12 m. 10. **c** **1368** que quidem tenementa..situantur in latitudine inter quandam aleyam..et vacuam placeam terre *FormA* 200; **1400** robuse pro viis ~arum gardini elevandis *Ac. Bursar. Coll. Wint.*; **1404** in quodam aleio ibidem sunt vij cotagia *Bridge House Rental* (*London City R.O.*) I f. 55; **1426** lego fabrice cujusdem alee in parochia S. Botulfi extra Aldrichgate [Lond'] *Reg. Cant.* II 365; **1440** in aleya..vocata Norton Aley *Cl* 291 m. 31d.; **1574** in quadam allea sive venella vocata Shippe Alley *Pat* 1121 m. 29.

Alemagnicus v. Alamannicus.

alemanda [OF *alemande*; cf. amanda, amygdala], almond.

1205 quod mittas nobis..cc libras de ~is *Cl* 22a; **1220** faciatis habere..j fraell' alemand', j fraell' ficuum et racemorum *Ib.* 412a; **1424** j ob. pro alimanda (*Mun. Barnstaple*) *HMC Rep* IX 205b.

alemandina v. alabandina. Alemann- v. Alamann-.

alembicum [Ar. *al-anbiq* < ἄμβιξ], alembic, (upper part of) vessel used for distilling.

pone in cucurbita cum ~o, et quod distillaverit serva M. Scot *Lumen* 266; extractio per ~um Gilb. III 139. 1; sublimetur per alembicum *Id.* VII 319. 1; aqua vite simplex fit de vino forti per viam distillationis in ~o Gad. 66 v. 2; ponantur in ~o vel distillatorio, quod idem est *Id.* 112. 1; ~um, i. vas distillatorium in quo fit aqua rosacea et hujusmodi *Alph.* 6.

†**alembrottum** [? misr. of †Ar. *al-zi'baq*], chloride of mercury and ammonium.

de sale alebrot: sal allebrot album sali acro assimilatur in colore M. Scot *Lumen* 250; iste [sal agrum] a quibusdam philosophis alibrot appellatur *Ib.* 248; allumen rubeum..a quibusdam philosophis albebrot rubeum vocatur *Ib.* 254; de ~is (*Id. Alch.*) *Med. Cult.* 156; *albri or albery*, alebrodium *PP*; alembroth est sal mercurii vel sal philosophorum *LC*.

alenaceraris v. lanarius.

alenatius [OF *alenaz* < Frk.], 'anlace', small dagger.

s1226 eum occidit cum quodam anelacio *MGL* I 85; **1234** percusserunt Willelmum quodam alennatio *CurR* XV 1100; **1247** vulneravit..Johannem quodam alnacio in brachio *JustIt* 56 r. 44d.; **1253** vulneravit..Rogerum quodam alenatico in collo (*JustIt*) *SelCWW* 77; **s1234** percussit eum in posteriora..cum quodam genere cultelli quod vulgariter anelacius nuncupatur M. Par. *Maj.* III 279 (= *Id. Min.* II 368: hanelacius); gestans anelacium ad lumbare, quod clericum non decebat *Ib.* 295; **s1253** extrahens sicam quam bajulavit sc. hanelacium *Ib.* V 386; anelacias Anglicorum [*gl.*: *alenaz*, ab Alano inventore qui fuit pirreta regis Ricardi] Garl. *Dict.* 130; **1268** de una anlacia mancie yvorie *Rec. Norw.* I 205; **1269** cum alnacio suo extracto voluit occidere..Henricum *Cl* 22; **1275** cepit..unum †avelacium [l. anelacium] de ebore precii iij s. *Hund.* I 204; **1288** asportaverunt..annelacum suum *Leet Norw.* 9.

aleola, dice.

a dice, taxillus, alea, ~a, decius *CathA*.

aleph, Hebrew letter. **b** (fig.) teaching.

in hoc principio *be resiz* sex littere sunt tantum apud Hebreos, ..viz. *bez, rehs, alef, sin, joz, thave* Neckam *NR* I 1; sunt autem sex vocales, viz. aleph, ain, he, heth, iot, vau Bacon *Maj.* I 74. **b** *techynge*, doctrina, aleph, aqua, informacio *CathA*.

aleptes v. aliptes.

alere [CL], to feed, nourish, foster. **b** (fig.) *V. et. altus.*

heremita..membrorum vitalia..quinque caricibus..sustentasse et aluisse describitur Aldh. *PR* 114; insula..alendis apta pecoribus Bede *HE* I 1; **1185** pro frumento empto ad alendas columbas *Pipe* 215; principes filios suos generosis de terra sua viris diversis diversos alendos tradunt Gir. *DK* II 4; celi panis jejunos aluit J. Howd. *Ph.* 935; [muliercula] liquore tantum cervisie..septem diebus puerum suum cogebatur alere *NLA* (*Osmund*) II 247. **b** dolum intus alentes [AS: *facn wiðinnan tyddriende*] Ælf. *Coll.* 101; legendi studio quasi quotidiano cibo alitur et pinguescit oratio Gir. *EH pref.* p. 223.

aleria v. aliera. alerius v. alebris.

ales [CL], bird.

spiritu in simulacro alitis descendente Aldh. *VirgP* 23 p. 254; ad hoc ova ab alitibus..foventur Eriug. *Per.* 554b; alitum istorum [sc. falconum] exemplo..filios instruunt Gir. *TH* I 12; [aves] alites quasi alates id est alis se levantes, a plurimis nominantur Bart. Angl. XII 1; Hebrea plebs velut alites / Rubri Maris exsiccat gurgites J. Howd. *Ph.* 933.

alesta v. arista 3.

†**aletafur** [cf. Ar. *al-kāfūr*], (?) camphor tree.

quod guttatim manat remanet in forma sua et erit ut arbor que dicitur ~ur Alf. Angl. *Plant.* II 15.

alethia [ἀλήθεια], truth (personified).

s1308 fistulam falsitatis personuit Pseustis.., cujus..clamoribus lyra veritatis interdum Alathie conticuit *Flor. Hist.* III 143.

aletta [OF *alete*], *ailette*, shoulder-plate.

1303 ad unam tunicam de armis..sibi faciendam pro hastiludiis, ..ut in..serico, sindone et carda, corio pro ~iis et aliis rebus *KRAc* 363/18 f. 23; **1348** unum cotarium barrez cum ~is *IMisc* 161/9.

aletudo [CL Gl], nourishment.

alitudo, *fothur GlC* A 491.

aleuzco v. alleucho.

alevoso [Sp. *alevoso*], traitor.

1167 si aliquis regum vel baronum istas treugas fregerit..sit perjurus et ~o (*Conventio regum Castellae et Navarrae*) *G. Hen. II* I 150.

1 alexander, 'borde-alexander', silken material.

1521 j vestimentum de ~ro *Fabr. York* 278.

2 alexander, ~ria, ~rum, alexanders (*Smyrnium olusatrum*).

~er vel olixatrum, i. petroselinum Macedonicum, G. *alisandre*, A. *stanmersh Alph.* 5; ~ria, i. *stanmarche SB* 10; hoc ~rum, *alysandyre* WW.

Alexandrinus a (w. *daphne*) a species of butcher's broom (*Ruscus*). **b** (w. *lignum*) brazil wood. **c** (w. *nux*) walnut.

a camedafnes, quam multi ~am vocant, folia habet lauro similia sed tenuiora et viridiora *Alph.* 28; dampne, quam alii ~am vocant vel ypoglosson, folia habet eximursine similia sed majora et albidiora *Ib.* 48. **b** *brasyl*, gaudo vel lignum ~um *PP*. **c** carena basilica, i. nux ~a, quam multi Persicam dicunt *Alph.* 31.

alexandrum v. 2 alexander. alexantes, ~i, v. alosanthi.

†**alexinus** [? *for* Alexandrinus], (w. *panis*) biscuit.

panis ~us, panis bene coctus idem *Alph.* 135.

alexir v. elixir. aleya v. aleia.

†**alfa** [? cf. acalephe], (?) stitchwort.

~a, *æðelfyrdingwyrt* Ælf. *Gl.*

alfabetum v. alphabetum.

alfachinus [Ar. *al-faqīh*], 'alfaqui', one versed in Islamic law.

alphachini et cassini, ministri scilicet nefandi erroris, episcopi et presbyteri secundum opinionem Saracenorum *Expug. Terrae Sanctae* 16b (cf. ib. 15b).

†alfagi [Ar. *al-faqd*], agnus castus (bot.).

~i, i. agnus castus *SB* 10.

alfarsungi [cf. Sp. Ar. *al-isfāranj* < ἀσπάραγος], asparagus.

~i, i. speragus SB 10.

alfeborda, sort of board.

1267 in xxiij fitherbord' et xxvj alfebord' sarrandis *Pipe Wint.* (159308) r. 7.

alfefe [Ar. *al-fa'fa'* = stammer], defect of tongue (or speech).

~e, i. egritudo lingue *SB* 10.

alfefur v. alphesora.

alferezia [Sp.], office of *alférez* (standard-bearer).

1254 ~ia domini regis vacat (*Ch. Regis Castelle*) *Dip. DocE* 1210 *in sigillo* (cf. *Foed.* I 531, *facsimile*).

alferiz [Sp. *alférez* < Ar. *al-fāris*], (mounted) standard-bearer.

1405 Karolus de Beaumont, ~iz de Navarre *Cl* 254 m. 14*d*; **1409** (v. albus 10).

alfetum [AS], ordeal kettle.

si aquae judicium sit, calefiat donec excitetur ad bullitum; et sit ~um [AS: *þæt ālfæt*] ferreum vel ereum vel plumbeum vel *lemen* (*Quad.*) *GAS* 386.

alficus v. alfinus.

alfinus [Ar. *al-fīl*], 'alfin', bishop (at chess). **b** (fig.).

senex Nestoris personam gerens explorator est, qui vulgo alphicus [v.l. alficus] dicitur: regine geminat cursum, gressum obliquans tanquam insidiator Neckam *NR* II 184; ~i sunt cornuti exemplo episcopi, ..isti ~i oblique currunt et capiunt, tria puncta pertranseundo (J. Waleys *Commun.* I x 7) *Speculum* VI 464; **14..** alphicus in triviis parat insidias inimicis; / saltans incedit; per obliquum sic quoque ledit (*Modus Ludi Scacc.*) H. Murray: *Hist. Chess* 519; alphinus, A. *an awfyn* WW. **b s1215** ecce rex sine regno..; ecce alficus nauci et angularis, rota quinta in plaustro M. Par. *Maj.* II 611.

alfita, alfus v. alph-.

1 alga [CL], sea-weed. **b** (as type of worthlessness). **c** "moss" (ed.), but (?) ice (<*algere*). **d** (by conf.) sandhill.

~a, *waar GlC* A 434; velut scopulis refluis ~arum illisionibus et undarum..vorticibus fatigatus Aldh. *PR* 142 p. 203; ~a, *sæwaur* Ælf. *Gl.*; [bernace] tanquam ab ~a ligno coherente..per rostra dependent Gir. *TH* I 15; inde / algidus et algor, pariter maris †ala vocatur Garl. *Syn.* 191; ut capiant ~am maris ad impinguendam..terram *Cart. Newm.* 55; **14..** algea, *fletwort* WW. **b** spretis vilior algis Aldh. *Aen.* 100. 26; lepus ad Martem fit vilior alga D. Bec. 1703; aurum et ~am equiparando Gir. *PI* I 20. **c** nemus ingressus fuerat rituque ferino / vivebat, paciens concrete frigoris †alge *V. Merl.* 417. **d** ~a, *scaldhyflas* vel *sondhyllas GlC* A 440.

2 alga v. algea.

algarab [Ar. *al-gharab*], lachrymal abscess and fistula.

valet ad ulcera oculorum et ad ~ab, i. ad fistulam ibidem Gad. 114. 1.

algardum v. halgardum.

algare [cf. Sp. *algar* < Ar. *al-ghār*], hollow, cavern (Gasc.).

1289 cum..landis, nemoribus, ~ibus, aquis et pascuis *RGasc* II 445.

algarismus v. algorismus. algarum v. laganum.

algasullus [Sp. < Ar. *al-wazīr*], *alguacil*, magistrate.

1394 [scribitur] alcadis et ~is civitatis Ispalensis *Dip Corr. Ric. II* no. 209.

1 algea v. alga.

2 algea, ~eus [cf. OF *auge* < alveus], trough, vat. **b** trough of water-mill, penstock. **c** cistern.

c1160 vij cuve et ij alge et unum plumbum super fornacem *Dom. S. Paul.* 132; **12..** habebunt meliorem caseum qui jacet in augeo ad saliendum *Cust. Bleadon* 204; **a1280** item ~eas duas magnas *AncD* A 796; **1295** in iij ~eis emptis ad deferendum intus mortarium ad cementarios *KRAc* 462/14 m. 1; **c1300** Constantinus tannator habuit..cuvas et ~eas et alia utensilia pro officio suo in eadem [tannaria] *RParl* I 246a; **1340** de..j ~eo pro pasto *MinAc* 1120/10 r. 5; de..j ~eo pro porcis *Ib.* r. 6*d.*; de..ij ~eis de petra pro lardario *Ib.* 15; **1365** vasa lignea, sc...unam ~eam, unum keler *IMisc* 189/26; **c1400** in brasina..~eam vulgariter *le trowch Reg. Moray* 367. **b 1209** in ~eo faciendo iiij s. ij d.; in rungis factis ad molendinum, vj d. *Pipe Wint.* 60; **1237** in ferro emendo et clavis faciendis ad magnam augiam affirmandam *KRAc* 501/18 r. 2 (cf. ib. r. 1: pro loco deliberando ubi augea debet jacere); **12..** A. cecidit de una auga in aquam de C.; auga apreciata pro iiij d. (*Consuet. Divers. Curiarum*) *SelCWW* ccii; **1312** in operacione cujusdam ~ee longitudinis xxiiij pedum pro aqua incurrenda *KRAc* 486/25; **1321** in 1 clavis de bordnayl emptis ad emendacionem ~ee sub rota aquatica..molendini *MinAc* 992/11; **1322** in..~ea subtus rotam molendini per inundacionem asportata..de novo facienda cum sarracione meremii ad eandem *Ib.* 1146/11 r. 7. **c 1433** quandam augeam sive cisternam..de petra et calce..erigere et fabricare *Pat* 434 m. 3; **1443** augee, ventose, suspirales, fistule, pipe et alie machine per quas tota aqua veniens et discedens a capitibus et fontibus..recipitur et currit (*Pat*) *Foed.* XI 29.

algebra [Ar. *al-jabr*], restoration (med.), restorative. **b** algebra (math.).

~a, restauracio carnis *SB* 10; *a restoratyve*, ~a *CathA.* **b** liber ~e et almucabola de questionibus arithmeticis et geometricis Rob. Angl. *Alg.* 66.

algema [ἄλγημα; *conf. w.* algor], pain.

†974 (14c) fessus extitit †algena piscarioque labore biliosus *CS* 1311 (= *Chr. Rams.* 183: †algeva); **14..** †algenia, A. *the coold ache* WW; *calde*, frigus, ..algor, †algeria *CathA.*

algēre [CL], to be cold. **b** (fig.).

597 aestuare, ~ere, lassescere ex infirmitate naturae est (*Lit. Papae*) Bede *HE* I 27 p. 55; **9..** ~eo, *ic cealdige* WW; ferventes medullarum ardores aquis ~entibus extinguere Gir. *GE* II 10; **1201** cepit tremere et fremere sed tamen non alsit *Canon. G. Sempr.* 150 v. **b** pietas tepet, alget honestas Hanv. VI 326.

algeria v. algema.

algescere, to grow cold. **b** (fig.).

magis algescunt quo plus incendia crescunt Nig. *Laur.* f. 43. 2. **b** quamvis.. / jamdudum sterili matrix algesceret alvo Aldh. *VirgV* 418; charitate erga Deum ~ente Beleth *RDO* 20. 32.

algeus v. algea. algeva v. algema.

algidus [CL], cold.

algida ventosis crepitabant carbasa flabris Aldh. *CE* 3. 22; numquam ipsa vestimenta uda atque ~a deponere curabat Bede *HE* V 12; non ardor Phebi, non algida tempora brumae Frith. 567.

algor [CL], cold. **b** (fig.).

9.. ~ore, *cyle* WW; ne ~or senilis corporis frigidi elementi infusione auctus incurabilem morbum contraheret W. Malm. *GP* III 100; pluviam perpessus et ~orem W. Cant. *Mir. Thom.* II 31; aque..~oris aerei nexibus astricte Gir. *TH* I 6. **b** minimus, ~or torporis et ignavie a virtutis ..suffocat..vigore J. Godard *Ep.* 220.

algorismus [Ar. *al-Khwārizmī*], 'augrim'], Arabic notation (math.).

alchorismus Adel. *Alch.* (*title*); studiosa compotatio ~i in suis speciebus (M. Scot. *Part.*) *Med. Sci.* 291; **c1225** ~us vulgaris Sacrob. *Alg.* (*title*); Hyades est dispositio stellarum ad modum septime figure ~i Bacon IV 396; questiones que tangunt in parte augorismum *Leg. Ant. Lond. app.* 179; sicut in ~o cifra per se posita nihil significat, sed addita alteri figure facit eam significare Ockham *Summa* I 4 (*cf. GLA* III 363 n. 825); **1409** ad determinandum pro se nullus bachillarius admittatur nisi prius algarismum integrorum.. audierit *StatOx* 200; **c1410** hec presens ars dicitur ~us ab Algore rege ejus inventore; vel dicitur ab *algos* quod est 'ars' et *rodos* quod est 'numerus', que est ars numerorum vel numerandi, ad quam artem bene sciendum inveniebantur apud Indos bis quinque..figure (Thos. Newmarket *Comment.*) *EETS* (*ES*) 118 p. 72; **a1444** secundum ordinem specierum ~i Killingworth *Alg.* 713; *augrin*, algarismus *PP*; ~us, A. *augrym* WW.

algoristicus, concerned w. Arabic notation.

tempus dictum continet 29 dies et 12 horas et 44 minuta unius hore, sicut opus ~um expediet Bacon *Maj.* I 196.

algosus [CL], seaweedy. **b** mossy.

algosis verrebat caerula remis Aldh. *CE* 4.5.5; se algosis mergat in undis Æthelwulf *Abb.* 16. 7; **10..** ~ is, *þæm warihtum* WW. **b** †briocteris [l. dryopteris] nascitur in locis ~is *Alph.* 27.

†alhel [Ar. *abhul*], juniper berry.

~el, i. fructus juniperi *SB* 10.

alhidada [Ar. *al-'idāda*], 'alidade', sighting-rod.

1326 hallidada est virgula longa..mota super paxillum motu elevacionis et depressionis ut per foramina in ejus tabellis altitudo syderum discernatur Wallingf. *Rect.* 343 (cf. ib. 346: allidada); **a1350** tercia pars instrumenti est allidada quadrangula fortis et eque spissa; et dicitur allidada zodiaci sive turnus proprie *Turquet* 371.

Alhigera [Ar. *al-hijra*], Hijra, Hegira, Arabic era (A.D. 622).

ubi feria secunda mensis Rabe primi xii die in quarto sc. Ietrib primum ingressus est, vitam [Machumet] expiravit; illius igitur ~am integre decenne spacium mensum est Rob. Angl. *Chr. Mend.* 217; **1184** annus Alligere quingentesimus septuagesimus secundus; qui est etiam annus millesimus centesimus octogesimus sextus ab incarnatione Domini vestri Christi (*Lit. Pharamel. Cordub.*) R. Howd. II 297; **s1184** Saladinus et Safadinus, reges Saracenorum, scripserunt domino Pape de relevatione captivorum anno Alligere DLXXVIII Fl. Worc. *Cont.* II 155.

aliaria, garlic mustard.

alliaria est herba..allium odore mire referens; hec est (ni conjectura fallor) *sauce alone*, aut ut alii *jak of the hedge* Turner *Herb.* A ii.

aliarius [< alium], garlic-seller.

a garleke seller, allearius *CathA.*

alias [CL], (of time) **a** a second time, afterwards. **b** previously. **c** form of writ, w. ref. to neglect of previous one.

a 1273 facient monicionem..semel et ~as *Rec. Leic.* I 114; **1290** propter quod predicti piscatores ~as piscem ad villam ducere noluerunt *Ib.* 213. **b 1203** ut loquela..summoneatur coram rege..in statu quo ~as remansit *Pipe* 21; **1220** captus pro malo retto cognovit quod ~as captus fuit *SelPlCrown* 134; **1344** B. Folyn ~as indictatus *Lib. Kilken.* 6; **1476** de firmis..~as concessis *ExchScot* 339. **c s1433** jussit eum..tria brevia regia..a Cancellaria accipere..; et de hiis tribus est ipsius quod vocatur '~as' tenor talis: '..vobis mandamus, sicut ~as mandavimus'..Amund. I 311.

2 (of place) **a** elsewhere. **b** to another place. **c** to another (feudal) lord.

a arcam oblitus claudere, quidpiam operis ~as facturus egreditur Ailr. *Ed. Conf.* 746B. **b** languore corripitur.., per quem se intellexit ~as de ista vita vocari Eadmer *V. Osw.* 33; tres episcopatus ex antiquis sedibus transiere ~as W. Malm. *GR* IV 338. **c** nec poterat ~as ire sine abbatis licentia *DB* I 32b.

3 (of manner etc.) **a** otherwise, in other respects. **b** (w. *sin*, = *minus*). **c** otherwise (if something is not done). **d** *alias*, otherwise named.

a artes..liberales..magis palpando sensit quam bibendo gustavit; ..~as autem omne tulit magisterium secum W. Dan. *Ailred* 18; **1300** scholaris vel serviens ejus aut ~as jurisdiccionis dicti cancellarii subjectus *MunAcOx* 79; si.. princeps est alienatus a sensu vel ~as infirmus Ockham *Dial.* 701. **b** si mihi divina gratia..donaverit, ..ibi morabor; sin ~as, ad vos revertar Bede *HE* IV 26. **c 1347** vestimenta..in cista universitatis reponantur.., quia ~as .., consumptis vestimentis que jam habet, universitas possit destrui *StatOx* 149; minatur se ~as prisonarium occisurum (*Stat. Hen.* V) Upton 141; [rex] commune bonum super omnia diligat..; ~as nuncquam diligetur a subditis suis *Plusc.* VII 18; divina humanaque..retinentur, ~as in nihilum abitura Ferr. *Kinloss* 7. **d c1306** una acra prati juxta Roberteswode, ~as Rokeswode *Cust. Battle* 18; petitum est a plebeis ut signa, ~as stigmata dominorum.. deponerentur *V. Ric. II* 121; Estrilda ~as Elfrida *Eul. Hist. annot.* V 90.

aliator v. aleator.

aliatus, flavoured w. garlic. **b** (sb. f.) garlic sauce.

s1254 macta eos [sc. filios meos]..et unum eorum coctum elixum devora piperatum et alium assatum et alleatum M. Par. *Maj.* V 440; quando pro speciebus calidis aduritur sanguis, sicut cum piperatis et alliatis Gad. 42 v. 1. **b** assa carnis suille..condimentum dedignatur aliud quam purum salem vel simplicem ~am [*gl. alye*] Neckam *Ut.* 102; bibat fortissimam alliatam cum forti vino Gilb. II 123 v. 2.

alibi [CL], elsewhere.

non ~i quam in medio eorum..sepulta Bede *HE* IV 19; ut idem magister ~i ait Eriug. *Per.* 530C; ibi sunt xii carrucae villanorum et ~i iiii carrucae in dominio *DB* I 90; piscium genera que nusquam ~i reperiuntur Gir. *TH* I 10; **1255** viridarii quieti quia ~i [sc. amerciantur] *SelPlForest* 28; tam de Galwidia quam †alubi *Plusc.* IX 28 (cf. ib. X 15)

alibre v. alebris. alibrot v. alembrottum. alibrum v. alabrum. alica v. aliqui. alices v. allec, alyces. alicitor v. haliaëtus. alicium v. cilicium. alico v. aliqui, aliquis. alicotus v. aliquotus. alictarius v. alutarius. alictum v. 1 alnetum b.

alicubi, somewhere. **b** anywhere (excl.). **c** anywhere (incl.). **d** to any place (excl.). **e** to any (feudal) lord (excl.).

summa essentia aut ubique et semper est, aut tantum ~i et aliquando, aut nusquam et numquam Anselm (*Mon.* 20) I 35; queritur de aliquo..an sit ~i et aliquando Balsh. *AD* 137; **c1205** angelus..quandoque ~i dicitur esse Gros. *Ep.* 1 p. 15. **b** cum nil ~i praesidii nisi in fuga esse videretur Bede *HE* II 20; nequivit ~i conquiescere nisi in Kynlos Ferr. *Kinloss* 37. **c** omnes qui ~i..hac aegritudine laborant Bede *HE* IV 14. **d 674** ut nullus clericorum..passim quolibet discurrat neque ~i veniens.. suscipiatur (*Conc. Hertf.* 5) Ib 5. **e** nec ~i potuit recedere *DB* I 38.

alicujusmodi, of some kind.

queritur de aliquo..an ipsum sit alicujus qualitatis aut, si quis forte uno nomine uti volet, an sit ~i Balsh. *AD* 137.

alicunde, from any source.

si forte ~e quid auxilii..adveniret Bede *HE* V 12.

alicxir v. elixir. aliegena, aliegina v. alienigena. aliementare v. alimentare.

alienare [CL], to alienate (possessions).

terras quas Hugo..~averat..revocavit Gir. *EH* II 25; **1269** quod ~atum fuit de jure domini mei..per ballivos antecessores meos revocabo *CBaron* 77; **1280** abbas ~avit terras, maneria, decimas *Reg. Ebor.* 23; **1309** extraneus cui tenementa ~ata fuerunt ipsum non permisit intrare *Year*

Bk. 2 Ed. II 49; **1333** de fine pro licencia ~andi laicum feodum..ad manum mortuam *LTRMem* 105 r. 139; quia ipsa jura eas [decimas] volunt ~are Wycl. *Compl.* 91.

2 (w. pers. obj.) to detach, estrange. **b** (refl.). **c** to drive out of one's mind.

s1141 [imperatrix] erecta in superbiam intolerabilem.. omnium fere corda a se ~avit H. Hunt. *HA* VIII 19; **a1188** ero..a consorcio eorum..in perpetuum ~atus *Feod. Durh.* 128. **b** cupiens se ab omnibus saeculi hujus.. negotiis ~are Bede *HE* III 19; **s1386** ab illo tempore ~avit se rex a cetu procerum *V. Ric. II* 77. **c** nec mirum si illi qui spiritum Domini..subito suscipiunt a terrene mentis interim statu ~ari videantur Gir. *DK* I 16; succus consolide..epilenticis et ~atis valet Gad. 132 v. 1; si princeps est ~atus a sensu Ockham *Dial.* 701; **s1384** frater..finxit se ~atum a mente *V. Ric. II* 51.

3 to alter, transform.

licet..frequenter ad motum ~emur, ad quietem statim naturali desiderio revocamur Adel. *QN* 72; **1220** pluries ~avit loquelam suam *CurR* VIII 278; **1310** ingressus ordinem Templariorum, fuit ~atus et ita sublatus infra duos annos quod nec comes..nec alii amici potuerint scire quid de eo fiebat *Conc.* II 362.

2 alienare v. alleviare 3b.

alienatio, alienation, conveyance (of possessions).

1235 quod de predicta terra nullam faciat venditionem vel ~onem *Cl* 99; **1318** quod regnum suum depauperetur per ~ones bonorum †deportatas extra regnum (*Stat. I Rob. I* c. 24) *APScot* 113 (= *RegiamM* 33 v: alienatores..disportatorum); **1332** iiij acras terre..que occasione ~onis quam..fecerunt prefato R. sine licencia..regis..nunc in manu regis existunt *LTRMem* 105 r. 8*d.*; **1537** hariettabunt ad quamlibet ~onem vel decessum cujuslibet tenentis *MinAc* 3352 r. 9*d.*

2 removal, separation. **b** driving out of one's mind, madness.

s1183 filie..regis..~onem a nativo solo..eo sustinent equanimius quod.. Diceto *YH* II 17. **b** que major mentis esse potest ~o? Gir. *GE* II 3; **1201** incidit in mentis ~onem *Canon. G. Sempr.* 152; accidentia mala..sc. sitis, vigilia, dolor capitis, frenesis vel ~o vel sincopis Gad. 5. 1; si primo esset alienatus a sensu, sibi non deberet hujusmodi jus conferri..sic ut possit stante ~one actum potestatis exercere Ockham *Dial.* 931; paracopa, i. ~o mentis *Alph.* 135.

3 alteration.

moveri ipsum [Deum] pie arbitrandum non secundum delationem aut ~onem aut alternationem aut conversionem Eriug. *Per.* 523ab.

alienativus, eliminative, tending to banish..

alienativa quietis / agmina concurrunt Hanv. VI 339.

alienator, alienator (of possessions).

debent..~oribus bonorum patrimonii Crucifixi resistere Neckam *NR* I 18; advocaciones..ecclesiarum sine corporibus alienari non possunt, ..nec cum corpore possunt alienari nisi ~ores in seisina presentandi extiterint *Fleta* 204; **1318** (v. alienatio 1).

aliene, detachedly, without connection.

sunt etiam, ut non minus ~e dicatur, ..similes indistinctiones que ad disputationem constituendam non idonee videntur Balsh. *AD* (*rec.* 2) 62.

alienigena, ~us [CL], alien (adj. or sb.). **b** belonging to aliens.

ut hoc vitio..etiam ~e huc advecti..involvantur Gir. *TH* III 24; **1241** quod clerici..neque †aliegine neque indigene aliquid contribuerent ad subsidium domino pape prestandum *Cl* 345; **1265** †aliegene nobis..adversantes *Cl* 34; †ablienigene repelli debent in Anglia ab agendo *Fleta* 439; **1322** mercatores lanarum alienigini seu indigini (*Chanc. Misc.*) *EHR* XXXI 600; populorum concursu ~orum S. Sim. *Itin.* 52; **1373** quod ipsi ut indigene et non ~e teneri..et de..demandis que ab eis..ut de ~is exigi possent quietari..valerent (*Pat*) *MonA* V 15. **b 1448** prioratum de Penbroke ~am *Reg. Whet.* I 46.

alienigenare, to estrange, banish.

1004 (11c) sciat se a celesti ~ari gloria *CD* 710.

alieniloquium, allegory.

dicitur allegoria ~ium, vel potius inversio, cum aliud verbis aliud sensu ostendimus Beleth *RDO* 113. 118.

alienitas, otherness.

si A instans erit prius quam reliquum instans erit, aliquod instans erit reliquum ab A; et sic per idem alteritas vel ~as unius instantis ad alterum est signanda Wycl. *Ente Praed.* 204.

alienus [CL], alien (adj.), detached, belonging to or concerned w. others. **b** alien (sb.), outsider or foreigner.

probos propriis prosternere telis / nititur et strages alienis factitat armis Aldh. *VirgV* 2709; cuncta hujus mundi velut ~a spernendo Bede *HE* I 26; summam..substantiam.. necesse est ~am esse a natura et jure omnium quae ipsa de nihilo fecit Anselm (*Mon.* 22) I 39; a predicta distinctione ~a videntur 'a quo' et 'secundum quid'..et alia hujusmodi plura Balsh. *AD* 153; jam bene me freno, jam sum meus ex alieno Serlo Wilt. 31. 12; multa..aliis regionibus ~a Gir. *TH pref.*; quis..vel amicis ~ior vel ~is amicior? *Ib.* III 51; **1201** nisi ~o auxilio de lecto moveri non potuit *Canon. G. Sempr.* 142v.; **a1250** relinquent..terram edificatam plenarie ad valenciam estimacionis predicte nisi igne ~o [*started in another's property*] combusta fuerit *AncD* A1932; **1307** clamant tenementum liberum in..~o solo *Year Bk. 1 Ed. II* 5; quod sordidis muneribus essent †alienii Upton 16. **b** hic tamen indigenis sol parcit, non alienis Serlo Wilt. 24. 57; comes Lincoln' habet hujusmodi protecciones de ~is *Hund.* I 381 (cf. *Arch. J.* VI 169); **1375** ceperunt de J. S. ~o xl d. per extorsionem *Leet. Norw.* 64.

2 rambling, mad.

loquens ~a tentus est donec..suis redderetur, qui eum ligaverunt W. Cant. *Mir. Thom.* III 47.

aliera [cf. OF *alier* = *service-tree*], a tree w. hard wood, (?) hawthorn.

1225 maeremium de alier' ad telarios faciendos ad balistas nostras *Cl* 50; **1257** sex fusta de alier vel de huls'..ad..balistas inde reparandas *Liberate* 33 m. 10; **1260** in eodem parco [de Havering'] faciat habere..attiliatori balistarum regis apud Turrim Lond' duas alyeras ad reparacionem balistarum *Cl* 25; **1263** de aleriis ad telarias balistarum: ..faciat habere..factori balistarum regis de cornu xij ~as ad teleras balistarum regis inde faciendas *Cl* 238.

alietas, otherness.

quod si aliquis cavillando dicat non esse ~atem nisi inter simul existentia Gros. 195; hec divisio materie non est secundum ~atem veram sed apparentem et secundum nomen Bacon *Tert.* 123; ad quam biformem proprietatem necessario sequitur ~as vera relationis unius ad reliquum *Ps.*-Gros. 383; tunc omne idem esset diversum, primo quia per se racio referendi idem sibi est ~as, ex hoc quod intellectus attribuit aliquid racionis utrique termino Ockham *Metaph.* V 12. 67d.; si unum instans est aliud quam reliquum, tunc est dare ~atem qua est aliud Wycl. *Ente Praed.* 205.

alietum v. 1 alnetum b. alietus v. haliaëtus. aligancia v. alligantia.

aliger [CL], winged, feathered. **b** (fig.).

aliger hunc praepes.. / paverat Aldh. *VirgV* 788; aligeros inter socios summosque ministros / Michael princeps Alcuin *Carm.* 88. 25; **10..** ~ger, *fiðerberende* WW; dum pacata equora ~gero sulcabant remigio R. Cold. *Cuthb.* 23. **b** ~ger amator..Vuiltoniam revolavit Gosc. *Wulfh.* 3.

aligerare, to feather, fledge.

sagittas..recisis / aligerat pennis Hanv. II 261.

aliginnasium v. gymnasium. alimanda v. alemanda. alimen v. alitus.

alimentare, to nourish, sustain.

1513 ad prefatam Agnetem..juxta juris exigenciam †aliementandam *Offic. S. Andr.* 4; maritus allegat..quod uxor..habeat aliunde de quibus sufficienter ~ari possit *Praxis* 36.

alimentatio, sustenance, victualling.

1457 ipsi hospitacionem et ~onem habeant *Mon. Exon.* 407b; **c1525** habere ~onem unius mulieris et unius pueri *MonA* IV 89b; **1623** pro ejus [navis] provisione, reparacione et ~one *HCA. Libel* 81/9.

alimentum [CL], nourishment.

volucrum turbae.. / dulcia de ramis carpunt alimenta ciborum Aldh. *VirgV* 342; ut tota septimana absque ~o corporis perdures Bede *HE* IV 25; ~a corporalia..per.. venarum nervorumque meatus..distribuendo Eriug. *Per.* 581c; fragile corpus hominis tunc demum..convalescit quando nature sufficienti sustentatur ~o *G. Steph.* I 19; ex succo ligneo..~a simul incrementaque suscipiunt Gir. *TH* I 15.

aliminare v. illuminare.

alimonia, ~ium [CL], nourishment, sustenance. **b** (fig.). **c** mensal land. **d** wife's alimony.

cujus ~ia, immo parsimonia, tam frugalis fuisse ferebatur ut..herbarum fasciculis..vesceretur Aldh. *VirgP* 38 p. 287; elimosynas in ~iam inopum dare Bede *HE* V 4; unde ..fratribus..sufficientem usque ad autumnum ~iam divina miseratio ministraret Gir. *IK* I 7; **1221** quod ipsi canonici.. ad hospitum suscepcionem et pauperum ~iam [v.l. †alumpniam] fructus omnes..convertant *CurR* X 40; annonam dicit ~iam ciborum et victum omnem monachorum *Cust. Cant.* 132. **b** refectionis domum letabundus ingrediens omnes ad se confluentes et cibo corporis et spiritualis vite ~ia saginavit Osb. *V. Dunst.* 43; hora illa qua spiritalis ~ia assistentibus tradebatur Ailr. *Ed. Conf.* 748d; in ~ium spiritus manna celestis refectionis colligebat H. Bos. *V. Thom.* III 11; tu es intellectus celestis ~ia R. Bury *Phil.* 1. 15. **c 1126** terram que ad ~iam illius ecclesie pertinet *Regesta* II p. 354. **d** in dicta taxatione ~iae, judex solet allocare uxori terciam..partem annui valoris bonorum immobilium *Praxis* 36.

alimotum v. halimotum.

alio [CL], to another place, in another direction. **b** to another (feudal) lord.

ut ~o, quo necessitas vocaret, admoveret suos *G. Steph.* II 89; nonne melius est ~o, ut cum amore et pace sim, migrare? Ad. Scot. *OP* 501d; est bona fontis aqua que tendit solis ad ortum / ac ad meridiem; tendens alio nocet omnis D. Bec. 2785; illo / devenisse dolet; alio festinat Hanv. II 274. **b** has hidas tenuerunt vii alodiarii de episcopo nec poterant recedere ~o *DB* I 52b.

†aliolus, weary.

wery ~us ,defessus itinere *CathA.*

alioquin [CL], otherwise (if something is not done).

ne..virginitatis nobilitas..vilescat, ..multimoda mandatorum varietate decoretur..! ~in..cum fatuis virginibus.. multabitur Aldh. *VirgP* 15; respondendum ita; ~in in Pascha non acciperet populus Corpus Christi Gir. *GE* I 8; **1327** ~in onerabitur in fine compoti *Mem. R. 1 Ed. III* no. 2255; ~in jam non sumus ipsius membra Rolle *IA* 199; **1351** statuimus ut..'aliōquin' penultima longa [pronuncietur] *G. S. Alb.* II 429; **1395** dictum est..ballivis..quod celerem justiciam exhibeant; †alioquim redeant etc. *Mem. York* I 147.

aliorsum [CL], to somewhere else, in another direction. **b** (fig.) to something different.

nec usquam aut ~um ulterius progredi valentes Aldh. *VirgP* 38 p. 288; numquid credibile est lunae statum.. posse ~um quam fuerat converti? Bede *TR* 25; non enim credendum est aliunde venisse [Jesum] localiter ut suis discipulis appareret et ~um recessisse quando non appareret Eriug. *Per.* 538c; praesciverat hunc aliorsum / vomere salvifico sulcare novalia Christo Frith. 182; **10..** ~um, *elles hwider* WW; fuit..~um destinatus *G. Steph.* I 11; nec flamma ~um poterat divertere quam in solum sepulcrum R. Cold. *Cuthb.* 45. **b 955** (12c) singrafam..immutare ~um quam constituimus *CS* 906; id quod opponis ~um respicit Adel. *QN* 34.

alipes [CL], (swift-footed) steed.

~pedes, veloces, ut equi *GlC* A 489; sessores ~pedum pueri, ..docti equis imperitare W. Fitzst. *Thom. prol.* 11; cratibus et craticulis opus est, †ut [? l. ne] pulsatio crebra ~pedum [*gl.: astif*] compaginem navis dissociat (*sic*) vel dissolvat Neckam *Ut.* 114.

alipiados v. alypias.

alipta [τὰ ἀλειπτά], ointment, salve.

~a muscata..aut galla muscata..informentur Gilb. III 158 v. 2 (cf. ib. VII 301 v. 2: calamite, ~e..); magdaleon ex ~is muscatis formatis secundum longum Gad. 51 v. 2; ~a confita, i. mixtura, confectio est; et quia †muscus recepit dicitur ~a muscata *Alph.* 4.

aliptes [ἀλείπτης = *anointer or masseur*], physician etc.

aleptes, *leche*, ..*a surgyon or a chamerleyne* WW.

aliqualis, of some sort. **b** of any sort (excl.). **c** of any sort (incl.).

†a1230 (15c) post ~e intervallum *Ch. Sal.* 213; in ~es cogniciones spiritualium Bacon III 235; **s1289** uxorem.. ad graciam suscepit ~em *Ann. Worc.* 499; **s1333** post ~em numerum occisorum..universi Scoti sunt in fugam conversi Ad. Mur. 68; patrum..non imago sed vestigium remanet ~e R. Bury *Phil.* 5. 80; illa..que necessario sunt ~ia, sunt certius talia quam illa que contingenter..tantum sunt talia Bradw. *CD* 755c; **s1379** arridere cepit ~is aura serenior.. pape Wals. *HA* I 395. **b 1281** nec vos..procedere potestis nec debetis ad execucionem ~em *Chr. Peterb.* 49; **1304** omnes vicarii.., priusquam statu vicarie gaudeant ~i, prestent sacramentum *Mem. Ripon* 120; **1348** ita quod.. versus..Edmundum..~em accionem..habere nequeunt (*sic*) *FormA* 62; hec rapiunt, nec eis lex aliqualis obest Gower *VC* I 486; **1459** absque cohercione ~i eis inde fienda *Test. Ebor.* II 245. **c 1451** ut..~is displicencia vel..indignacio..deponatur *Pri. Cold.* 172.

aliqualiscumque, of whatever sort.

historia..que fuerunt oblivioni tradita..renovat..et ~icunque quasi morte separata vivificat Knighton *pref.* p. 2.

aliqualiter, in some way, to some extent. **b** in any way (excl.). **c** in any way (incl.).

ut [oculus] obliquetur ~er a loco suo Bacon *Maj.* II 33; **s1300** intelligens..cor..episcopi..ab eo ~er elongatum *G. Durh.* 4; duabus racionibus positis, ..pertracto eas ~er Duns *PW* 5; Leo IX, cum conscienciam haberet cauteriatam quod ~er fuisset intrusus Higd. VI 22 p. 170; **s1345** erat.. dapsilis valde, sed ad habendum ~er cupidus *Hist. Durh.* 3; sedes..episcoporum ~er explanabo, ut potero *Eul. Hist.* II 173; **1417** cum..cooperculo coronato ~er deaurato *Reg. Cant.* IV 180. **b** putaverunt res non posse dinosci ~er per odores Bart. Angl. XIX 37; **1280** inhibentes..ne..capellanum..~er..inquietare seu molestare presumat Peckham *Ep.* 111; **c1290** nolens..mandatis superiorum meorum.. ~er refragari *Cart. Glam.* 900; Christus non est ~er in sacramento altaris qualiter non est ibi sacramentaliter (Wycl. *Conf.*) *Speculum* VIII 505. **c a1180** (1292) pro omnibus serviciis que de eodem tenemento ~er possent provenire *CalCh* II 431; **s1399** quod quilibet..~er suo jure privatus..esset restituendus Ad. Usk 36.

aliquamdiu [CL], for some time. **b** (w. *post*).

apud eos aliquandiu demorabatur Bede *HE* III 25; ~u in oratione perstitit T. Mon. *Will.* VI 7; his visis ~u reverencius exhibitus est, et tandem inventus est falsus Map *NC* V 6 p. 240. **b** post ~u Gislebertus presbiter tenet *DB* I 32.

aliquando [CL], sometimes, at some time. **b** at last. **c** (?) thereupon.

ascendente aqua..usque ad lumbos, ~o usque ad collum Bede *HE* V 12; capio..capreos et ~o [AS: *hwilon*] lepores Ælf. *Coll.* 92; xl porc' cum oneratur et ~o lxvi porc' *DB* I 154b; nec mutabiliter est [idem spiritus] aliquid quod ~o aut non fuit aut non erit Anselm (*Mon.* 28) I 46; **1220** multociens venit ad domum suam et ibi moram fecit per octo dies ~o, ~o plus, ~o minus *SelPlCrown* 121; **c1228** ~o prior Willelmus ~o cellerarius petierunt ab eo meremium *Feod. Durh.* 244; sacerdotes celebrantes post confeccionem hujus sacramenti †alitando [? l. alicando] dicimus Wycl. *Ver.* I 133. **b** ubi vix ∼o inpetravit, intravit monasterium Bede *HE* IV 19; Peckham *Quaest.* II 3 A5 (v. aliquotiens a). **c** **s1348** corpora junctim sepeliebant et, uno gradu ita disposito, terram injecerunt, ∼o gradum eodem modo reincipientes J. Reading 159.

aliquantillulus, a very little. **b** (sb. n.).

s1455 per morulam temporis ∼am..fuerat eventus dubius *Reg. Whet.* I 168. **b** **1453** per ∼um temporis quo nos rexerimus *Ib.* 109; **s1455** rexit se per ∼um temporis satis pacifice *Ib.* 199.

aliquantillus, a very little.

∼o elapso tempore *G. Steph.* I 23.

aliquantisper [CL], for some time. **b** to some extent.

ubi fatigatus infirmitate ∼er moratus est Bede *HE* IV 1; **s1087** [Willelmus], contractis inimicitiis cum rege Francorum, ∼er se continuit W. Malm. *GR* III 281; cum deinceps ∼er soli stetissent Elmh. *Hen. V* 101. **b** **a690** sciolos, quorum..tua sagacitas dogmatum favo ∼er abusa est Aldh. *Ep.* 5 p. 493; gratiam episcopatus admonet eum resuscitare; ..∼er enim timidus et negligens erat Lanfr. *Comment. Paul.* (2 *Tim.* i 6) 361; motus ille ∼er..inquit Osb. *V. Dunst.* 23 p. 96; uno suorum, ∼er..exercitato in his, accito H. Bos. *Thom.* III 11; psittacus..cujus forma ∼er falconem representat Neckam *Sac.* 862.

aliquantulus, some small. **b** (pl.) some few.

quorum exempla ∼a explanatione digessimus Aldh. *PR* 125; ut..ecclesia..∼am..pacem habuerit Bede *HE* I 8 *rub.*; **808** tibi dabo ∼am partem terrae juris mei *CS* 322. **b** ∼a metrorum munuscula..subjunxi Aldh. *Met.* 5.

2 (sb. n.) a little. **b** (acc. as adv.) for a short time. **c** (acc. as adv.) a little way, to a slight extent.

cum..∼um itineris confecissent Bede *HE* I 23; cum ∼um horae..maneret *Ib.* IV 3; xx acrae prati, silvae ∼um *DB* I 166b. **b** coeperunt illi mox idolatriae, quam ∼um intermisisse videbantur, palam servire Bede *HE* I 5; dimicando ∼um restitit *G. Steph.* II 74; nec bene potest moveri donec ∼um stetit *SB* 41. **c** ∼um quassatis cymbae compagibus Aldh. *VirgP* 10; ∼um..paucis diebus timere.. coeperunt Bede *HE* IV 23; Hibernia..in medio ∼um substricta Gir. *TH* I 3; ∼um remota erat a mensa *Latin Stories* 13; folia habet rotunda ∼um *SB* 44.

aliquantus [CL], some amount of. **b** (pl.) some, a certain number.

post ∼um utriusque partis conflictum Bede *HE* V 19; ∼i..temporis interjecto spatio T. Mon. *Will.* II 5; **a1225** fuit cum eo per ∼um tempus *SelPlCrown* 126; post ∼am stationem premisit..familiares suos Elmh. *Hen. V* 101. **b** ex quibus ∼i jam dormierunt in Domino Bede *HE* V 11; aliquae harum terrarum erant quietae ab omni consuetudine praeter geldum et ∼ae a geldo sunt quietae *DB* I 270; Galterus omnes fere..fructus..messuit, Bucardus qui suberat ∼os Map *NC* V 5 p. 223.

2 (sb. n.) a certain amount. **b** (acc. as adv.) to some extent. **c** (abl. as adv.) in some degree.

ibi ∼um prati *DB* I 84. **b** ad eorum..rationem intuendam..∼um conor assurgere Anselm (*CurDeus, commend.*) II 40; **s1126** spes sua eum ∼um decepit H. Cantor 30v. **c** videbatur illa per biduum ∼o levius habere Bede *HE* IV 17; **s1126** qualis meaverat set ∼o..hillarior remeavit H. Cantor 30v; in nonnullis..∼o majorem terrorem incussit *G. Steph.* II 80.

aliquatenus [CL], to some extent. **b** to any extent (excl.), at all.

597 in his qui per ignorantiam fecerunt, culpa ∼us toleranda est (*Lit. Papae*) Bede *HE* I 27 p. 51; [anima mea] vidit te ∼us, sed non vidit te sicut es Anselm (*Prosl.* 14) I 111; que..secundum elementorum federa prenotata sunt.. ∼us novimus Map *NC* IV 6 p. 168. **b** nulli est ∼us a[m]bigendum ununquemque fidelium corporis..Dominici ..esse participem Lanfr. *Sermo* 640B; **1176** si quis..ei [mandato] ∼us contraire presumpserit (*Lit. Papae*) Elmh. *Cant.* 416; **1218** nec ∼us omittatis quin.. *Pat* 179; nec se debet..circa talia aliquatinus interponere *Cust. Westm.* 152; quod nullus..a justicie tramite ∼us declinare presumat *Fleta prol.*; ne ∼us requies presumpcionis materiam ministraret hostibus Elmh. *Hen. V Cont.* 133.

aliqui [CL], some. **b** any (excl.). **c** any (incl.). *V. et.* 2 *aliquis*.

per ∼quod tempus Bede *HE* II 13; omnibus annis.. ∼qua sanitatum miracula..solent..ostendi *Ib.* 16; egregium ∼quod..memoriale Gir. *TH intr.*; uno ∼quo die, nondum decennio elapso Gerv. Tilb. III 90; ∼quem turpem ribaldum diligit plusquam maritum O. Cheriton *Fab.* 14A; hic erit ∼ca improprietas Bacon XV 56; cum.. ∼co modo tribulantur J. Sheppey *Fab.* 23; de edificatoriis ∼quibus..tractabat *NLA* (*Richard*) II 332; patiens sedet in decoccione ∼quarum herbarum *SB* 20. **b** sine ∼quo puritatis offendiculo Aldh. *VirgP* 14; ut ne minimam quidem lucis ∼cujus posset particulam videre Bede *HE* IV 10; **1220** respondit quod non habuit ∼quam sitim set tamen..libenter cum eo biberet *CurR* VIII 382; **1223** hoc non dimittent pro ∼qua re *Pat* 403; si ∼ca animalia generarentur per putrefactionem Bacon VII 10; nec ∼quod judicium inde voluerunt reddere *State Tri. Ed. I* 19. **c** ita ..ut..ubicumque clericus ∼qui [v.l. ∼quis]..adveniret, gaudenter..exciperetur Bede *HE* III 27; **1189** cum omnibus libertatibus quas habet ∼quod burgum in terra nostra de tota Anglia *BBC* (*Bath*) 380.

2 (sb. n.; *aliquod* = *aliquid*) something. **b** anything (excl.).

precept..∼quod..pauperi Christiano erogare *Croyl.* 26. **b** ita quod nec ego nec aliquis..pro me ∼quod juris vel clamei..poterimus..vendicare *FormMan* 8.

aliquiculi (pl.), some few.

per Anglicos et quandoque ∼quosculos alios Knighton *pref.* p. 2.

aliquilibet, any (excl.).

1239 nec ista dissimulasse ∼quolibet modo hactenus.. credatis (*Lit. Imp.*) M. Par. *Maj.* III 563.

aliquimodus, of any sort (excl.).

1485 non capient..in futurum ∼a theoloneum seu alia onera quovismoda *Rec. Nott.* II 350.

aliquis [CL], someone, (n.) something. **b** anyone, anything (excl.). **c** (w. *in*) in any way. **d** (w. *quam*) anyone else (excl.). **e** (n. acc. as adv.) to some extent.

c705 te..aliquotiens de ∼quibus ammonere curavi Aldh. *Ep.* 8; nec dubium remansit..quin ∼quis de illa congregatione citius esset moriturus Bede *HE* IV 9; sive nihil sit ∼quid, sive nihil non sit ∼quid, consequi videtur ut quidquid factum est factum sit de ∼quo Anselm (*Mon.* 8) I 22; nunc oblique intuetur ∼quem arrogans, nunc.. alium despicit Neckam *NR* II 190; est aliquid puro vincere fonte sitim *Id. DS* III 292; contingit quod ∼qua habet pulchrum maritum O. Cheriton *Fab.* 14A; **c1230** si ∼quis manerii vendat equum..infra manerium *Doc. Bec* 42. **b** consilium..utilius quam ∼quis de tuis..cognatis umquam audivit Bede *HE* II 12; nec ipse..proficere ∼quid valebat *Ib.* III 11; quod..non ∼cui nisi ei de quo tenebat vendere.. liceret *DB* I 45b; haec terra nunquam reddidit ∼quid consuetudinis *Ib.* 2; ab Hibernia potestne ∼quid boni esse? Gir. *TH intr.* (cf. *John* i 46); **1233** nec ballivus vicecomitis nec ∼cujus alterius *BNB* II 564; nec indigens..∼co alio Bacon VII 5; non permittat quod ∼quis vel ∼qua in androchiarium..ingrediatur ∼quid ablaturus *Fleta* 172. **c** **1160** si quis..ei in ∼quo obviare conatus fuerit *Lit. Cant.* III 356; **1216** licet..in ∼quo erga vos deliquerit *Pat* 4; ne aliqua negligencia eveniat de servicio Dei in ∼quo *Obs. Barnwell* 58; **1434** hujusmodi statuto..in ∼quo non obstante *StatOx* 257; **s1454** nec velle illius in ∼quo misereri *Reg. Whet.* I 140. **d** qui coronatur ab ∼quo quam ab illo qui antiquitus coronare consuevit Ockham *Pol.* I 171. **e** ut ∼quid sciatis quo Franco devenerit W. Map *NC* II 23 p. 96.

2 (adj. = *aliqui*) some. **b** any (excl.).

nisi quia ibidem sanctior..vir ∼quis fuisset interfectus Bede *HE* III 10; si ∼quis heres petat..aliquam terram Bracton 324. **b** neque ∼quis regno eorum annus [deberet] adnotare Bede *HE* III 9; **1227** ita quod vicecomes.. vel ∼quis alius ballivus scotallum non faciat *BBC* (*London*) 108; **1322** nec faciet ∼quid wastum *Lit. Cant.* I 82.

aliquitas, 'somethingness' (that whereby something is something).

illud quod aliquid est dicitur ratitudo ejus; quo autem ipsum est quod est vel aliquid dicitur ∼as ejus Duns *Sent.* I iii. 5. 7; asserunt quod foret in ista transsubstanciacione anichilacio, nisi panis ∼as remaneret in carne Christi Wycl. *Euch.* 60; nulla ∼as panis Netter *DAF* II 137.

aliquomodo [al. div.], in any way (excl.).

nulla lex loci..naturam ullam ∼o cogit quam nullus locus..claudit Anselm (*Mon.* 22) I 39.

aliquorsum, in some direction. **b** somewhere.

ne aliquis lignum nudatum cum ossibus ∼um proiceret W. Malm. *GP* (*V. Aldh.*) V 255. **b** quotiens eum aliquamdiu ∼um perhendinare contigisset *Hist. Meriadoci* 357.

aliquot [CL], (pl.) some, a certain number of. **b** (?) (sg.) some, a certain amount of.

cum ∼ot annos Deo serviret Bede *HE* V 19; ita ut ∼ot laesi, omnes territi, ..cessarent *Ib.* III 16; ubi diebus ∼ot.. perendinavimus Gir. *IK* II 12. **b** Aldhelmus..ad pedes Adriani..per tempus ∼ot [? l. aliquod] studuit *Eul. Hist.* I 225.

aliquotiens, ∼ies [CL], several times, sometimes. **b** at any time (excl.), ever.

'circum' praepositio *m* ∼ies amittit, ut 'circuitus' Aldh. *PR* 140 p. 198; ∼ies equo sedens, sed saepius pedes incedens Bede *HE* IV 27; quod Alredus virginitatem suam ∼iens defloraverit W. Dan. *Ep.* 62c; omne finitum per..diminutionem proportionabiliter ∼ies multiplicatum aliquando finitur et consumitur Peckham *Quaest.* II 3 A5. **b** **1363** nisi pro negociis..hospitalis..ipsum oporteat ∼iens absentari *Lit. Cant.* II 438; nec..diviciis..∼iens illicito amore captus fuerat Blakman *Hen. VI* 9; nullam personam quantumcunque sibi noxiam voluit ∼ies mulctari *Ib.* 18.

aliquotus, aliquot, forming an integral factor. **b** (sb. f., *sc. pars*) aliquot part.

cujuslibet ∼e pars est non ∼a Neckam *NR* II 173; **1254** quingentas libratas terre vel ∼am partem earumdem *RGasc* I 474; quadragenarius ex partibus suis ∼is aggregatis surgit in quinquagenarium Bacon VI 117; **a1350** si detur quod nulla est pars alicota AQ cujus medius gradus precise tantum distat.. (J. Dumbleton *Summa Log. Nat.*) *Sci. Mech.* 321; ut senarius non habet partem ∼am nisi trinarium, binarium et unitatem Wycl. *Temp.* 108D; partes ∼e sunt que multociens sumpte precise reddunt suum totum Hothby 328. **b** numerus finitus numeri infiniti ∼a vel aliquot ∼e esse non potest Gros. 53; **s1455** quatenus.. posset..exiguam ecclesie dotem in quota augmentare, ∼a et augere *Reg. Whet.* I 187.

alitando v. aliquando.

aliter [CL], otherwise, differently. **b** otherwise (if something is not done). **c** (repeated) in one way, in another.

ut penitus ∼er..vivere nequiret quam..dignitas..permitteret Aldh. *VirgP* 30; non ∼er quam vivebat cum suis ipse docebat Bede *HE* III 5; an tibi ∼er videtur? Eriug. *Per.* 441A; **10..** ∼er, *on ænige oðre wisan* WW; dum alius sic et alius ∼er de salute communi deliberant T. Mon. *Will.* I 8. **b** ∼er autem qui domum incenderit et inde accusatus fuerit per xl homines se defendit *DB* I 179. **c** ∼er sedet in carruca praefecturae dignitas, ∼er mulionis vilitas, ∼er qui pedibus continet mulas Aldh. *VirgP* 19; ∼er placitatur ..coram justiciariis de Banco, ∼er coram justiciariis itinerantibus, ∼er in aliis curiis *CBaron* 68.

alitilis v. altilis. alitudo v. aletudo.

1 alitus, nourishment.

a nuryschynge, ∼us, alimen, fomes *CathA*.

2 alitus v. halitus.

aliubi [CL = *elsewhere*], to another (feudal) lord.

non potuit ire ∼i *DB* I 40.

alium [CL], garlic.

alium, *gaarleec GlC* A 419; allia deposcunt porci vacceque recentes D.Bec. 2629; allia si piperi sociata fideliter assint Neckam *DS* III 453; herbis nimis calidis, ut porris, cepis, alleis..et hujusmodi Bart. Angl. IV 10; **12..** alleum, i. *ail*, i. *garlec* WW; **1284** de quolibet summagio ceparum et allearum *Pat* 103 m. 7; **1290** pro xix racemis alleorum *Doc Scot.* I 139; **1298** de duobus miliaribus †albei aut ceparum venalibus, j ob. *Reg. Carl.* I 116; **1324** in cepis emptis ad plantandum..; in alleo empto ad idem *MinAc* 992/13; **1350** in j bunche de alea empt' *Sacr. Ely* II 144; scordion, i. allium agreste..; similis est allio ortolano, florem habet indum, A. *crowelek SB* 38.

aliunde [CL], from elsewhere, from another source. **b** to another place, to others. **c** for another reason. **d** otherwise, in or about other things.

811 cum fructibus interius exteriusque vel ∼e usquam ad eas rite vel umquam pertinentia (*sic*) *CS* 335; Eriug. *Per.* 538C (v. aliorsum); [summa substantia] nihil omnino ∼e assumpsit unde..eorum quae factura erat formam.. compingeret Anselm (*Mon.* 11) I 26; **1236** habet respectum.. de debito quod regi debet tam de prestito Hibernie quam ∼e *KRMem* 14 r. 8*d*; *Praxis* 36 (v. alimentare). **b** precipiens quod ∼e secederet et fidem..predicaret Brinton *Serm.* 28 p. 108; **s1237** legavit corpus suum sepeliendum in monasterio nostro.., dispositis ∼e rebus suis *Meaux* II 59. **c** neque ∼e dives ille evangelicus dampnatus est nisi quod.. epulabatur cotidie splendide Serlo Gram. *Mon. Font.* 16. **d** bene se memorem tam de tempore quam ∼e fore..dicebat Gir. *JS* III 551; **1237** faciat..desium..aule tam coloribus quam ∼e emendari *Liberate* 12 m. 14; **1266** expensas..quas posuit in custodia..castri..Dovor'..et ∼e *Cl* 198; **1426** dominus ∼e occupatus..Roffensi episcopo..commisit vices suas *Reg. Cant.* I 101.

2 (w. *ab*) (from) elsewhere.

quoniam ab ∼e venisse comperiri non potuit Gir. *GE* II 18.

alius [CL], other, another. **b** the other (of two). **c** the next. **d** (w. *ab*) other than, different from.

tempore mox alio Aldh. *VirgV* 1494; aut sibimet ipsi au alio cuicunque dare voluisset Eddi *Wilf.* 15; ut..nil aliud ageret quam..plebem..instruere Bede *HE* II 15; utrum de se an de alio aliquo diceret *Ib.* IV 3; tradidit ast alio caras super omnia gazas / librorum nato Alcuin *SSEbor.* l. 1525; Piria et alia Piria *DB* I 1; inveniebant stiremannum et unum alium adjutorem *Ib.*; non solum..isti sed et alii nonnulli *G. Steph.* I 42; **1202** alia vice..retraxit se *SelPl Crown* 40; **1335** in reparacione..alii navis *KRAc* 19/14 r. 7; **1586** unius tenementi.., alii tenementi jacentis.., necnon unius acre *Reg. Brechin.* II p. 355. **b** e quibus alter.. amisit camellum, alius..asello..perfruitur Aldh. *VirgP* 37; duas domus..unam foris, aliam intra civitatem *DB* I 2; quarum una adminiculatur alii Neckam *NR* II 173; **s1259** alter pocione et alius injurie convincebatur frequentacione *Flor. Hist.* II 422; **1284** eligant unum ballivum de uno burgo et alium de alio burgo *BBC* (*Nottingham*) 355; **1464** cum duabus campanis, una majore et alia minore *Ac. Durh.* 639. **c** **1290** summoneantur uno die quod compareant ad alium diem, et non aliter *MunAcOx* 54. **d** hae duae personae propriis vocibus aliae ab invicem aperte designantur Anselm (*Incarn. A*) I 285; **1230** si alius ab eo eum implacitaret *CurR* XIV 811; **1286** exceptis religiosis aliis a domo nostra *BBC* (*Burton on Trent*) 50; dominium..est aliquid aliud a potestate utendi Ockham *Pol.* I 338.

2 (repeated) one..another, some..others. **b** one..the other (= CL *alter*). **c** different.. different. **d** (w. ∼*que*) one after another.

ut alius..luctamina..exercere studeat, alius..spicula.. dirigit (*sic*) .., alius..vectus cornipede..spatia..metitur Aldh. *VirgP* 2; neque enim possunt carmina..ex alia in aliam linguam..transferri Bede *HE* IV 22; castella..alia.. subvertit, alia..suis permisit *G. Steph.* I 44; constat quod alia herba est Jovis barba, alia est barba Jovis Neckam *NR* II 166. **b** **1323** in..duabus robis, alia cum pellura et alia cum linura *IPM* 82/7 r. 8. **c** estne credendum esse unum aliquid, per quod unum sint bona quaecumque bona sunt, an sunt bona alia per aliud? Anselm (*Mon.* 1) I 14. **d** sed et aliis aliisque..temptamentis me [demones]..deterrere.. conabantur BEDE *Cuthb.* 22.

aliusmodi, of another kind.

alterius vir animi et ideo ~i deditus fini H. HUNT. *HA* IV 16.

aliva v. alura. aliwerus v. alloverius. alkakengi v. alkekengi.

alkali [Ar. *al-qalī*], soda, alkali.

sal ~i..facit coagulare alios sales; iste autem sal fit de herba salsifera que juxta mare..invenitur M. SCOT *Lumen* 242; salis alzali GILB. VII 318 v. 1; amoniaci ʒ ix, alchaloim quantum sufficit, hec omnia tere *Ib.* 314 v. 2; calcem.. aquis ~i et aliis aquis acutis purifica BACON *NM* 9 p. 545; ~i, cinis clavellatus *SB* 10; ~i est lapillus salis modo ex calcibus reverberatis per humorem extractus dissipatoque humore coagulatus *LC.*

alkekengi [Ar. *al-kākanj* < Pers.], winter cherry (*Physalis*).

~i, ii species solatri *SB* 10; halicacabus a Latinis solanum vesicarium, ab officinis alkakengi et vulgo dicitur *alcakenge* TURNER *Herb.* B i v.

alkem- v. alchim-. alketonus v. alcoto.

alkibrit [Ar. *al-kibrīt*], sulphur (*cf. Gabricus*).

Maria quoque dicit: quando..laton cum allzebric, id est sulphure, comburatur ROB. ANGL. *Alch.* 514b; quod fit de †albubit, i. sulphure vivo GILB. VII 341 v. 2; alkibrie, alcabrick, algibich est sulphur vivum *LC.*

alkien [Ar. *al-kiyān* < Syriac], essence (alch.).

~en terra, id est quedam generacio secreta in terra; et est sicut ~en in homine; illud virtute sua preparativa clarificat et dividit sicut scit et nutrit DASTYN *Ros.* 7.

†alkiffil [Ar. *al-iklīl* (*al-jabalī*)], rosemary (*Rosmarinus*).

~il, i. ros marinus *SB* 10.

alkim-, alkom- v. alchim-. alla v. olla.

allabi [CL], to glide towards. **b** to glide by.

Germani..tribus longis navibus..Britanniam ~untur W. MALM. *GR* I 5; ad litus idem..defensor ~itur MAP *NC* II 17 p. 83; ~entibus fluctuum alluvionibus R. COLD. *Cuthb.* 23. **b** fluvius..qui illac ~itur W. FITZST. *Thom. prol.* 5.

allaborare [CL], to perform (for). **b** to contrive.

omnia te..coronant quae Domino ~asti GOSC. *Aug. Maj.* 51. **b** **1106** ~avi..ut caput..totius episcopatus de Summerseta sit in urbe Bathonia *Cart. Bath.* 53.

allacium [etym. dub.], ivy.

~ium [v.l. aliacum] est edera *Alph.* 4.

allacrimari, to weep over.

ille desiderata vota complectens ~atur ei MAP *NC* III 3 p. 131.

allactare v. allectare.

allactanter, receptively (as though taking suck).

allactancius GOSC. *Wulsin* prol. (v. appotare b).

allactatio, suckling (fig.).

~onis nutrimenta quam pia aviditate..hauserit GOSC. *Aug. Maj.* 74.

allagallica v. aloe d. allaia v. allaium.

allaiare [OF *aleier*], to alloy (metals).

p**1280** †pono [? l. pone] quod debeam ~are monetam ad ix d. de allaio (*Tract. Nov. Mon.*) *RBExch* III 997; **1295** summa ccxj li. xj s. vij d. per pondus, quod potest allayari ad standardum mon[ete] per xij li. xv s. vij d. per pondus *KRAc* 260/7 r. 4.

allaiatio, alloying.

p**1280** ad magistrum monete pertinet bilhonis et argenti congnicio et ejusdem empcio et ~o et omnimoda monete disposicio (*Tract. Nov. Mon.*) *RBExch* III 1002.

allaiator, alloyer.

p**1280** cum he regule assaiamenti et probacionis allaii sunt infallibiles, discretus ~or ex sola materia falli poterit (*Tract. Nov. Mon.*) *RBExch* III 998.

allaium [OF *alei, aloi*], **~a,** alloy.

1245 scrutari faciat omnes domos de Sandwiz donec falsa aluvia, que prohibita fuit ne duceretur in Angliam, ..inveniatur *Cl* 376; **1280** apponitur in ipsa moneta magis de eslaio quam in sterlingis *RBExch.* III 986; p**1280** quodlibet argentum aut moneta ad certum numerum ~i esse dicitur secundum quod continet de argento computando a xij denariis usque ad nichil pro grana (*Tract. Nov. Mon.*) *Ib.* 996; **1295** summa..argenti cum allayo quod potest apponi ccxxiiij li. vij s. j d. *KRAc* 260/7 r. 4; **1304** pro monetagio.. denariorum monetatorum..de predicto argento, tam de billone argento cismarino quam de argento transmarino cum ~o apposito *Ib.* 288/30 r. 1; **1326** adduntur cuilibet libre vij d. ob. pro alayo secundum standardum sterling' predictum *IssueR* 218 m. 13; **1353** monete ille bone sunt et legales in ~a et pondere *Pat* 239 m. 12; **1355** quedam moneta..que in pondere minor et ~a debilior existit in.. regno Scocie de novo est cussa (*Cl*) *Foed.* V 813; **1414** aurum predictum est debiti ~i juxta assaium inde factum per petram *Pat* 412 m. 29; **1449** j par *touches* vocat' *nedels* continens dcxlvij pecias auri diversorum ~orum *KRAc* 294/6.

allambere [CL], to lick (fig.), wash.

in civitatem que propter fluvium Exam, qui muros lapsu suo ~it, vocatur Execestra W. MALM. *GP* II 94; e quibus maris una est Ramesmere..ipsius [insule] oram..pulchre ~ens *Chr. Rams.* 8.

allapa v. alapa. allapare v. alopare b. allaqueare v. illaqueare.

allateralis, companion.

s**1176** Johannem..gloriosi Thome martyris quondam ~em DICETO *YH* I 410.

allaterare, to bear at one's side. **b** to walk beside, accompany. **c** to adjoin. **d** (w. dat.) to be beside. **e** (dep. w. dat.) to approach.

s**1162** dummodo cancellarius curie sinistro lateri sigillum ~et nunc regis nunc imperatoris DICETO *YH* I 308. **b** sequebatur preeuntes, adlaterantibus eum viris duobus AILR. *Ed. Conf.* 770A; videbam..quendam abbatem, quem duo..episcopi ~antes comitabantur *Croyl.* 75. **c** **1306** que quidem placea jacet adlaterando tenementum ipsius J. *CourtR Hales* 543. **d** s**1324** rex..in reginam sibi adlaterantem virus sue malicie refundere conabatur *Flor. Hist.* III 229. **e** s**1119** quo egrediente e monasterio..clerici nostri..~ati sunt illi H. CANTOR 17; **1189** mihi ~atus.. Willelmus..proditorem me vocavit *Ep. Cant.* 307.

allatio, translation, bringing. **b** motion (φορά).

in ~one reliquiarum ejus [Cadwalladri], status Britonum pristinus..reparabitur R. NIGER 135; s**1223** de cujus crucis ~one et domui illi collatione siquis historiam scire desiderat.. M. PAR. *Min.* II 258. **b** dicitur secundo De Generatione quod ~o adducit generans sc. solem BACON XIII 412; duplex..~o solis sub obliquo circulo *Id. Maj.* I 181.

allativus, bringing.

s**1423** dicens hunc sibi fuisse de Anglia missum, bonorum ..nunciorum ~um AMUND. I 176.

allator, bringer, contributor.

allator luminis / noctem necat nostre caliginis J. HOWD. *Ph.* 12; p**1381** pius auxiliator, / arduus allator et optimus edificator (ROB. SYRESTON *de T. Hatfeld*) *Hist. Durh. Script.* 2 p. 134.

allatus v. afferre. allay- v. allai-. allea v. aleia, alium. allearius v. aliarius, alveare. alleaster v. oleaster. alleatus v. aliatus. allebrot v. alembrottum.

allec, ~ecia, ~ecium [CL *usu.* hallec], herring.

quid capis in mari? ~eces [AS: *hæringcgas*] et isicios.. ÆLF. *Coll.* 94; ~ec vel iairus vel taricius vel sardina, *hæring Id. Sup.*; reddebat..xl milia de ~ecibus ad victum monachorum *DB* I 10b; valuit..c ~ectia *Ib.* II 406 (cf. ib. 407: modo..c et lx ~ectii); et halecia et ostrea mire in ea redundant H. HUNT. *HA* I 1; c**1160** cum vetere decima ~eciorum *Lit. Cant.* III 371; a**1163** vj retia ad ~ecia capienda *Reg. Paisley* 2; a**1164** cum deductis sumptibus xv millia alecium exspectant J. SAL. *Ep.* 31; c**1165** unum millenarium de ~ectiis *AncD* A 3354; exierant in altum.. naute, quos amor lucri et ~ecis capiendi cupido..in fata trahebant W. CANT. *Mir. Thom.* III 46; a**1200** de servicio de ward'fee et ~ece *CurR* I 11; [pisces] diversi sunt utpote mugiles, ..alecia [*gl. arangue*], gamarus NECKAM *Ut.* 98; allec, cui cibus est aqua vitaque, mater et aula *Id. DS* III 467; **1202** capiendo..de careta hallecium v ~ecia *SelPl Crown* 21; **1298** de x mille ~icum *DocScot.* II 327; c**1320** assunt festa paschalia; / gaudet mater ecclesia; / foras procul allecia (? RIC. LEDEREDE) *RBOssory, HMCRep.* X *app.* V 245; ad instar balene que cum alicibus et aliis pisciculis mare absorbuit FORTESCUE *LLA* 22; **1453** decimalia ~eca de Innernes *Reg. Aberbr.* II 84.

2 herring dist. as: **a** fresh; **b** dried; **c** smoked; **d** salted or pickled; **e** w. or without roe.

a **1257** de sex millibus ~ecis frisci *Cl* 153; c**1280** de ~ece frisco a festo Assumpcionis B.M.V. usque festum S. Mich. xij pro den. *MGL* II 119; **1288** duo miliaria ~ecis viridis *Rec. Norw.* II 9; nichil ei [A. Bek, ob. 1310] carum erat quod ejus gloriam magnificare posset: pro xl ~ecibus recentibus xl s. Londonie semel solvit GRAYSTANES 18. **b** a**1100** tria concessi..millearia siccorum ~ectium *FormA* 239 (= *MonA* III 433: †sticarum ~ecium); **1334** in mccc allec' siccis emptis xj s. j d. *Ac. Durh.* 18. **c** **1231** preter..~ec ruffum quod venit de Scocia *CurR* XIV 1518; **1250** ballivis Suhampton'..de ij lastis ~ecis ruffi *Cl* 385; ~ecia fumata fetent; sufficit..pisciculus..recens J. GODARD *Ep.* 222; c**1280** milliarium melioris ~ecis †sorni et poudrati pro iiij s. *MGL* II 119; **1297** j lastam ~ecis sori *DocScot.* II 127; **1284** ~ecia rubea *IPM* 39/9 r. 2; **1302** de iiij meysis rubeorum allec' receptis de stauro *MinAcW. Wales* I 468; c**1320** de singulis decem lastis ~ecis rubei venientibus de Jernemuth' (*Eyre*) *Lond. Ed. I & II* II 182; **1375** iiij cades et ij c allec' rub', viz. de *codheryng IMisc* 207/16; **1391** pro ij kempes de rubiis ~ecibus *Ac. H. Derby* 77; **1405** pro xj millibus ~ecum rubeorum..et costagiis, sale et siccacione eorundem *Exch Scot.* 638; **1531** ij millia ~ecum sororum xviij s. *Househ. Bk. Durh.* 9. **d** **1244** si forinsecus..~eciam salsatam in navi sua adduxerit *MGL* I 240; c**1280** ~ecis..poudrati *Ib.* II 119; **1309** adduxit ~ecium album *EEC* 365; **1344** iiij[c] allec' pulv[erizati] *KRAc* 390/11 r. 15; **1364** cum quadam navi dim. lasto ~ecium alborum carcata *IMisc* 188/15; **1360** duos barellos ~ecis albi vocati *skoneheryng' Pat* 259 m. 17; **1375** unum barellum de ~eciis albis de Skone [*Skania*]..furtive cepit *SessP. Lincs* 67; **1390** pro dc ~ecibus poudr' *Ac. H. Derby* 29. **e** **1394** ~ec rubeum plenum (*Ac. Cust.*) *Bronnen* 736(77); **1472** ~ecia vacua *Ib.* 1662 I (2); **1550** pro uno lasto ~ecis albi pleni val. iiij li.; ..pro uno lasto ~ecis vacui val. xl s. *EEC* 626.

3 (w. *os*) herring-bone (pattern).

1571 cum laqueo..juxta formam oss' halec' *Ac LChamb* 62 f. 6v.

allecho v. alleucho. allecia, ~ium, v. allec.

alleciarius, used for curing herring.

1430 R. M. burgensis de Hertilpole tenet ibidem ad firmam ij mesuagia et j magnam domum ~iam *Feod. Durh.* 24 (cf. *Ac. Durh.* 500 [**1299**]: in reparacione domus allec' de Jaru).

allectare [CL], to cajole.

s**1289** magnates..Scocie..dulci eloquio †allactabat exhortando ut concordarent *Plusc.* VIII 10.

allecticius v. allectivus a.

1 allectio [< allicere], allurement, enticement.

10.. ~o, *tyhtend* WW; sinistra [virgo] ita vulgari ~oni subjacebat ut et eam solam assequerentur ADEL. *ED* 5; **1304** ad attraccionem seu ~onem hominum ad superspicionis vanitatem *FormOx* 8; in principio non est nisi ~o ad amorem *AncrR* 78.

2 allectio [< allegere], appointment.

1300 cum..intellexerimus vos velle Johannem..consiliarium vestrum facere, ..inhibemus ne id quod..circa ejus ~onem facere concepistis ad effectum..perducatis *Reg. Cant.* I 378 (= *Lit. Cant.* I 28).

allectium v. allec.

allectivus, alluring, attractive. **b** (sb. n.) temptation.

quae [litterae] remissae consilio quorundam..fuerunt ~ae HERM. ARCH. 26; s**1291** precibus et premiis ~is B. COTTON 208; **1356** mentes fidelium ad pietatis et caritatis opera per ~a indulgenciarum munera excitamus *FormA* 321 (cf. *Reg. Heref.* [**1348**] 148: per †allecticia indulgenciarum munera); **1373** baculus pastoralis in summitate est ~us ut desides alliciat BRINTON *Serm.* 23 p. 95; **1466** missarum celebracio ..sit..divine misericordie ~a *Mem. Ripon* 168. **b** quod mens humana videtur necessitari ad peccandum ex infeccione corporis et aliis extrinsecis ~is WYCL. *Ente* 142; **1413** coram te despice dici / allectiva malis (ELMH. *Hen. IV*) *Pol. Poems* II 120; hec sunt ~a regum et principum CAPGR. *Hen.* 16.

Allecto [CL], one of the Furies. **b** valkyrie.

polluit Allecto mentes, linguasque venenat / Thesiphone GARL. *Tri. Eccl.* 13. **b** **10..** ~o, *wælcyrige* WW.

allectorium, inducement.

initium et ~ium ad hec decimandum..datum fuerat per Giraldum GIR. *RG* I 4; putantes eam [missam] efficax esse ~ium ad oblationes *Id. GE* I 49.

allectorius, ~tricius, v. alectoria.

allecula, (?) pilchard.

1565 pro v lastes halicularum *PortBk.* (*Dartmouth*) 925/5 f. 5 (cf. LEVINS: *Manipulus Vocab.* [**1570**]: halecula = *pilcharde, smelt, sprot*).

†allefias [Ar. *al-asfiyūs*], fleawort.

~ias, i. psillium *SB* 9.

allegabilis, adducible.

s**1281** descendetur postmodum ad excepciones.., super quibus debite et provide prospiciantur ~es raciones *Chr. Peterb.* 52; non foret nobis remanens aliqua scriptura sacra ~is WYCL. *Ver.* I 285.

allegantia v. alligantia.

1 allegare [CL], to recommend (fig.). **b** (?) to depute.

offerens filium, cujus necessitatem ipsa debilitas etiam sine precibus adlegabat (*V. Germani*) BEDE *HE* I 22. **b** **1312** erit prepositus et bedellus et alleg[abit] fil[ium] et filiam *Cust. Tolleshunt Tresgoz* (*Essex R.O.*) *MFG.*

2 to cite in evidence, appeal to: **a** a person; **b** an authority.

illi ~antur in disputationibus et lectionibus sicut auctores BACON *Min.* 327; secundum..Johannem monachum, quem ~at super hoc CONWAY *Def. Mend.* 1426; c**1400** episcopus ~avit michi Berengarium et preceptum eius michi revocacionem ejus (R. WYCHE) *EHR* V 535; ut Beda testatur, quem pro hac parte ~at W. Malmesberiensis ELMH. *Cant.* 235. **b** ut docet capitulum ~atum PECKHAM *Ep.* 55; c**1370** istam historiam ~at auctor pro rege Anglie (J. BRIDL. *gl.*) *Pol. Poems* I 146.

3 to submit in evidence, advance as an argument. **b** to plead, put forward as a justification. **c** (w. *forum*) to claim, assert (jurisdiction).

contra eos..possent plurima ~ari J. SAL. *Met.* 931D; cum utramque harum urbium S. Thomas illustraverit, ..habet altera versus alteram quod amplius ~et W. FITZST. *Thom. prol.* 4 (= *MGL* II 3: †~iet); petitionem Lincolniensis ecclesie, regias preces, monitionem archipresulis, scriptis verbisque ~ant AD. EYNS. *Hug.* III 4; pro quibus B. Thomas glorioso certamine, multis ante ~atis, demum caput ~avit, sacerdotum jura tuendo GIR. *Symb.* 22 p. 260; **1321** nisi..aliquid alligetur unde curia..non poterit.. placitum illud terminare *PQW* 449b; **1382** contra quos cum venerant nihil allegabant (*Contra Religiosos* 290) *Mon. Francisc.* I 601; **1519** sententiam tulisse secundum ~ata et probata *Form. S. Andr.* I 20. **b** **12..** ne quis possit ignorantiam ~are, ..hoc statutum publicetur *Conc. Scot.*

II 60; **1286** longa seisina sua, quam waranto alligat, non debet ei valere *PQW* 294a; **13..** regem provocantibus et temporis congruenciam et venandi complacenciam ~antibus *Found. Holyrood* 15. **c** non erat aliqui qui in principio litis ex parte conventus forum ~aret BRAKELOND 151v.

4 (absol.) to plead, argue. **b** (w. *pro*). **c** (w. *in*). **d** (pr. ppl. as sb.) pleader.

cum inter archiepiscopos de..honore virgis, baculis et pugnis ~atum fuisset GIR. *Rem.* 28; **s975** imago Dominica.. expresse locuta ita ~abat quod clericos..confusos reddidit .., cum magno conflictu hinc inde ~antium res ageretur M. PAR. *Maj.* I 469; **1255** venit coram justiciariis et ~avit, dicens quod.. *SelPlForest* 25; **1518** jurisdictiones et privilegia ~andi et defendendi *Form. S. Andr.* I 22. **b** uno ~ante pro pace populi, altero vero pro libertate cleri H. Bos. *Thom.* III p. 179 *n.*; cepit ~are pro socio DEVIZES 40; **s1216** sperandum est quod quedam bona, que [rex] fecit in hac vita, ~abunt pro eo ante tribunal Jesu Christi M. PAR. *Maj.* II 668; **s1296** prohibitis..placitatoribus in lege sua peritis..pro personis ecclesiasticis ~are *Flor. Hist.* III 291; veritas magis splendescit in lucem cum pro utraque parte..~atur OCKHAM *Pol.* I 293. **c** meticulosa res in illum ~are qui potest relegare GIR. *TH* III 51. **d 1231** vitiosa allegatio quam potest adversarius in ~antem retorquere GROS. *Ep.* 4; errant ~antes predicti cum dicunt.. OCKHAM *Pol.* I 51.

5 to allege, assert as fact. **b** (w. acc. and inf.). **c** (w. *quod*). **d** to confirm.

pars contra quam lata est..sententia..potest ~are nullitatem ejus *Praxis* 302 (cf. ib. 278: de forma ~andi desertionem appellationis). **b** se diutius non posse morari ..~avit LANFR. *Ep.* 33; **s1072** quod ~as, voluisse Gregorium ut Augustinus resideret Lundonie, fluctuat plane W. MALM. *GP* I 41; **1341** mortis sibi periculum..imminere.. minus veraciter ~avit (*Lit. Regis*) AVESB. 96; **1489** ~ant se in superplus tantum oneratos quod non possunt..solvere *Ac. Durh.* 479. **c s1196** cepit..quod eorum fraude fisco plurimum deperiret potenti eloquio ~are W. NEWB. V 20 p. 468; **1284** quamvis ~emus..quod vestra sentencia.. non se extendit.. *AncC* 47/96; illi ~anti quod ecclesia.. deberet sublevari, rex [Henricus I]..ecclesie..plurima contulit HIGD. VII 9 p. 386; **14..** ~ans quod habet omnes redditus *Reg. Merton* 93. **d** *to conferme*, confirmare,.. ~are, ut 'ille ~at literas meas' *CathA*.

6 to bequeath (CL *legare*).

s1086 Willelmo secundo filio suo Anglie monarchiam ~avit ELMH. *Cant.* 345.

2 allegare v. alligare 1b.

1 allegatio, deputation.

c750 ut..beatitudinem tuam..fidelium legatorum ~one alloquar (*Lit. Regis Cantiae*) *Ep. Bonif.* 105; **s1163** rex contra eum misit in ~onem archipresulem..et alios, qui nihil omnino ad votum..regis peregerunt R. NIGER 170.

2 plea, argument, assertion.

s1098 supervenit nuncius a rege directus qui ~ones Anselmi enervaret W. MALM. *GP* I 54; **s1107** privilegia.. per que abbatem suum non nisi in sede sua ordinari debere manifesta ~one se probaturos asseruerunt EADMER *HN* 224; **s1142** archidiaconus..scriptas gerens ~ones abbatum in eum J. HEX. *HRCont.* 14; **1177** petitiones et ~ones utriusque partis..audivimus (*Lit. Regis*) DICETO *YH* I 419; sic una brevisque viri justi obtinuit ~o quod vix unquam crederetur obtinere..causidicorum multitudo AD. EYNS. *Hug.* V 13; **1257** grates..referentes..pro ~onibus et responsis que nunciis regis Castelle..fecistis *Cl* 118; **s1313** ~ones facte per cives coram rege, quod non debent talliari (*LBLond.* D 164) *MGL* I 593; **ut**, utriusque partis ~onibus intellectis, ipsa veritas..elucescat OCKHAM *Pol.* I 293; procurator partis adversae est melius instructus quid et qualiter responderet ad hujusmodi ~onem quam ejus dominus *Praxis* 77.

2 allegatio v. allegiatio.

allegative, (?) as a deputy, by (divine) commission.

Constantinus..illam inordinatam potestatem, qua forte antea ~e utebatur, humiliter ecclesie resignavit OCKHAM *Dial.* 885.

allegator, arguer.

secundo respondetur ad allegacionem predictam quod [etc.]. ..cum vero accipiunt ~ores predicti quod [etc.] OCKHAM *Pol.* I 50.

allegatrix, defending, advocating (adj. f.).

s1051 cum epistolis innocentie et restitutionis sue ~icibus W. MALM. *GP* I 22.

allegiantia [cf. OF *ligeance*], allegiance.

1384 nullus..conventiculam faciat..vel confederaciones ..per que (*sic*) cancellarius..universitatis..poterit perturbari, sub allegientia sua et sub forisfactura omnium bonorum suorum *MunAcOx* 235.

1 allegiare v. allegare 3a.

2 allegiare [OF *alegier*, (?) < *exlitigare], to clear by oath or ordeal. **b** to admit as accuser.

si se velit adlegiare [AS: *hine sylfne treowsian*], secundum regis weregildum hoc faciat (*Quad.*) *GAS* 51; eat ad ferrum calidum et ~iet manum [AS: *ladige þa hond*] que inculpatur *Ib.* 159; ejusdem censure digni sunt, ..nisi..se possint adlegiare eodem cyrað vel ordalio predicto *Ib.* 236; si Anglicus bellum nolit, Francigena compellatus adlegiet se [AS: *ladige hine*] jurejurando contra eum secundum legem Normannie *Ib.* 483; diaconus in simplici compellatione cum duobus..diaconibus se ~iet (*Leg. Hen. I*) *Ib.* 585. **b** nemo sine testibus sive..cogentibus circumstanciis in ceteris accusationibus ~iandus est *Ib.* 583.

allegiatio, oath of clearance.

juramenta legitima fidelitatis, repetitionis, ~onis (*Quad.*) *GAS* 397 *rub.*; episcopo pertinet..in compellationum adlegatione [AS: *æt tihtlan ladunge*] edocere, ne quis alii faciat injuriam..in jusjurando vel in ordalio *Ib.* 477.

allegientia v. allegiantia.

allegoria [CL < ἀλληγορία], allegory.

evangelicae relationis dicta..secundum historiam, ~iam, tropologiam, anagogen digesta ALDH. *VirgP* 4; ~ia [v.l. alligoria] est tropus, quo aliud significatur quam dicitur BEDE *ST* 615; **10..** ~iam, *gebecnendlicum* WW; ab eadem re sepe ~ia fidem, tropologia mores variis modis †edificet [? l. edificat] J. SAL. *Pol.* 666B; historialis / est unus; sequitur post allēgŏria GARL *Myst. Eccl.* 225; **s1179** Petrus Comestor obiit, qui utriusque Testamenti historias in uno volumine et ~ias in alio compilavit TREVET 91.

allegorice, allegorically.

quamvis..latentem..in litteris sensum perscrutantes ~e ad sinagogae tipum retulerint ALDH. *Met.* 4; hec omnia ~e intelligenda AD. SCOT. *TT* 633; ~e, tropologice ex hujusmodi enigmatice revelatis eliciunt [sensus] OCKHAM *Dial.* 835.

allegoricus [ἀλληγορικός], allegorical.

Arcturus..rigidam priscae legis austeritatem ~is enigmatibus praefigurat ALDH. *Met.* 3 p. 72; de aedificatione Templi ~ae [v.l. alligoricae] expositionis libros BEDE *HE* V 24; 'sermones' vocat ~as prolationes LANFR. *Comment. Paul.* (1 *Cor.* xii 10) 195; quatuor sunt sensus scripture sacre, viz. hystoricus, ~us, tropologicus et anagogicus OCKHAM *Err. Papae* 957.

allegorizare, to express allegorically. **b** to interpret allegorically.

sapientes qui ante nos fuerunt multas nominaverunt confectiones et multa pondera et multos colores; et sic super vulgus dicta sua ~averunt ROB. ANGL. *Alch.* 514b. **b** ~at historiam Moysi tangentis petram virga NETTER *DAF* f. 154.

allehbut [? Ar. *lubb al-ḥūt*], choice part (of a fish), roe.

primum ingressis vescendum proponitur jecur piscis ~**ut**, cibus ultra quam mirari possis delectabilis S. SIM. *Itin.* **30**.

alleluia [Heb.], hallelujah, song of praise (sung in mass, except between Septuagesima Sunday and Easter).

lingua Brittaniae..Hebreum coepit ~ia resonare BEDE *HE* II 1; ad eandem missam super ~ia cantitantes vocale organum..insonuit W. MALM. (*V. Aldh.*) *GP* V 269; Dominica prima Septuagesimae ~ia ex toto dimittatur; loco ~ia per singulas horas 'Laus tibi..' usque ad pascalis vigiliae vesperas dicatur LANFR. *Const.* 97; **1199** petiit terram suam..per plevinam die Sabbati quo clausum est ~ia *CurR* I 108 (cf. ib.: die Lune proxima post clausum ~ia); '~ia', 'gloria in excelsis' hymni sunt in missa cantandi GIR. *GE* I 7; secunda [pars officii] est epistola, gradale, ~ia, evangelium *Ib.* II 20; gradale, ~ia vel responsorium non cantabit *Cust. Westm.* 199; Greci inchoant suum jejunium octo septimanis ante Pasca a Dominica que vocatur Sexagesima et simul cum esu carnium tunc ~ia dimittunt KILWARDBY *Jejun.* 165 (cf. ib. 168: tunc..claudant ~ia); **c1290** quia ~ia clausum erat, non processit ipse ad assisam (*Anc. Pet.* 2070d.) *SelCKB* I cxlv.

2 wood sorrel (*Oxalis*).

~ia, i. *wodesour SB* 10; panis cuculi, ~ia, trifolium silvestre idem, A. *wodesour Alph.* 134; oxys sive oxytriphillon, a Latinis dicitur trifolium acetosum, ab officinis ~ya; vulgus etiam vocat *alleluya, wodsore* & *cuckowes meat* TURNER *Herb.* B iv.

alleluiaticus, of hallelujah.

illos [Saxones S. Germanus] ~o cantu fudit W. MALM. *GR* I 22; **1345** unus liber ~us et gradaliticus *Sacr. Lichf.* 114.

†allematus, *s. dub.* (? *cf. alemanda*).

13.. de xiiij balis amigdalarum et grani ~i (*Ac. Cust. Sandwich*) *EEC* 183.

allemotum v. hallemotum. allenetum v. alnetum. allenus v. alnus. alleo- v. alloeo-. allepecia v. alopecia. allerectum v. holeretum.

alleria [cf. alatorium, aleia, alura], rampart walk, gallery.

1241 veterem portam prosterni et de novo muro reparari cum ~iis faciatis *Liberate* 15 m. 17.

allerica v. alarica.

†alletum [? cf. aulaeum], curtain, hanging.

1501 unus pannus sive ~um cum arboribus et bestiis ad caput aule *Cant. Coll. Ox.* I 33.

alleucella, cog (of mill-wheel).

1263 volens ungere ~as cujusdam molendini aquatici *JustIt* 874 r. 27d.

alleucho [OF *alleuchon*], cog (of mill-wheel).

1241 B. molendinarius.., sicut voluit ungere aleuzcones ipsius molendini *JustIt* 55 r. 21; **1268** volens ungere alasones rote cujusdam molendini *Ib.* 1051 r. 10; **1331** de meremio dicti molendini..dominus rex debet invenire tortas et allechones pro roeto (*KRAc* 89/15) *S. Jers.* I 9.

alleum v. alium.

alleurare [OF *aleurer*], to allure (falc.).

1333 falconem predictum sic eirantem..per leuras suas ~arunt *CoramR* 294 r. 62.

alleuratio, allurement (falc.).

1333 falcones..ad hujusmodi deductum..jactatos..per ~ones, recia, ingenia seu aliquibus aliis modis ad se attrahere, capere et asportare sunt consueti *CoramR* 294 r. 62.

allevabilis, leviable.

1478 liberantur..computanti xij d. de amerciamentis ~ibus prioris de Bernewell, eo quod feodum ad presens ignoratur *MinAc Whittlesford* (*Cambs RO*).

allevamen v. alleviamen.

allevare [CL], to lift up. **b** to lift (hay). **c** to set up (a commune).

illum [etherem] calor ~at ADEL. *QN* 62; Ycarus..dejectus est dum ~aretur J. SAL. *Pol.* 812D; [Theodorus Ceaddam] propriis manibus ~avit in equum ELMH. *Cant.* VII 23. **b 1279** falcabit totum pratum domini sui in magno prato, aleviabit, tassabit et cariabit *Hund.* II 461. **c 1234** exitus preposituге..de Olerun, qui.. diminuti sunt occasione commune que ~ata fuit tempore domini J. regis *Pat* 44 m. 9.

2 to levy: **a** a sum of money; **b** an impost; **c** a fine.

a s1193 episcopus dimidium precii de calicibus sumpsit et dimidium de proprio suo ~avit OXNEAD *Chr.* 93. **b 1230** permittatis homines nostros de..Gereseya..res suas venales ducere extra insulam et..reducere sine aliqua consuetudine facienda aliter quam fieri consuevit..usque ad tempus quo H...consuetudinem ~avit *Cl* 409; **1276** ~avit prisam vini primo in com. Cornub' *Hund.* I 57. **c 1425** jus suum.. vendidit per finem ~atum coram justiciario domini regis *Reg. Cant.* I 229.

1 allevatio, lifting, unloading (of cargo).

1511 pro naulo xiij barrell'..salmonum a Barvico..usque Novum Castrum..una cum ij s. solutis ministris pro ~one a puppe usque Gateshede *Ac. Durh.* 661.

2 allevatio v. alleviatio 2c.

alleviamen, relief.

hoc est allevamen [AS: *lihtinge*] quod universe genti mee parcere volo (*Cons. Cnut.*) *GAS* 357 (cf. alleviatio 3b); ut.. reatus sui et languoris consequeretur allevamen KETEL *Mir. J. Bev.* 283; satis est ecclesiastico quod fidelis occupet bona ecclesie, cum scit tunc illum cujus sunt bona ipsa ad sui ~en debite occupare WYCL. *Civ. Dom.* I 337; **s1404** ad ~en Quadragesime jam mediate, papa in missa unum.. rosarium..manu sua gerit AD. USK 96.

alleviamentum, (?) (due for) lightening, unloading (of ships). **b** relief.

1205 quod navem..quietam esse faciatis de ~o *Cl* 46b. **b** Baldwinus..Jerosolimam contendit..pro peccatorum ~o W. MALM. *GR* III 257; cellararius..clamitabat..sperasse se nuper aliquod ~um pro tot elationibus funerum *Ib.* 293.

1 alleviare v. allevare.

2 alleviare [LL], to lighten, make lighter. **b** (fig.).

fumus ~iatur et depuratur BART. ANGL. IV 1; **s1196** jussit pondus armorum episcopi et archidiaconi..in tantum ~iari ut lorice eorum deponerentur M. PAR. *Min.* II 60. **b** archiepiscopatus sui pondus ~ians W. MALM. (*V. Aldh.*) *GP* V 223 p. 376; si [alea]..curarum pondus ~iet J. SAL. *Pol.* 400A; dispensando tamen sacer ordo, salubribus usus / consiliis super his, alleviavit onus NIG. *SS* 2302; **1224** donec Deus onus debitorum ~iet (*AncC* VI 51) *RL* I 284; scire ista non est pondus aggravans sed ~ians, sicut plume avium sunt BACON *CSPhil* 433; **1343** †allienare [? l. alleviare].. onerum..gravitatem (*Lit. Regis*) AD. MUR. 145; **1438** sarcine vicarii Jesu Christi ~iatur moles BEKYNTON I 62.

2 to alleviate, allay, relieve: **a** toil or task; **b** loss or lack; **c** pain, grief or sickness; **d** a sentence; **e** sin.

a omnes species olei corpora confortant et motum ~iant BACON IX 68; **1435** in his que vestrum opus ~iant *FormOx* 450; labores diffusos ~iando AD. USK 83. **b 1184** citius ~iatur [damnum] cum horum.. providentia in melius reformatur (*Lit. episcoporum*) DICETO *YH* II 23; **s1191** navem..per cujus adventum ~iata est..cibariorum penuria *Itin. Ric.* I 79. **c** rogo vos..ut mea saltem temptetis ~iare tormenta W. MALM. *GR* II 204; **s1452** poterit..languoris.. imbecillitas curari vel in toto vel saltem in parte ~iari *Reg. Whet.* I 22; **1466** ut omnis erumna legitime ~ietur *Mem. Ripon* 173. **d p1380** eorundem convictiones deberent ~iari infra octo dies post eorum convictionem *StatOx* 187*n.* **e s1463** peccatum ejus..~iare volens, ..exegit..ut..hoc ipsum denuo peccatum apertissima proderet confessione *Croyl. Cont.* B 539.

3 to lighten, relieve (a thing) of a load. **b** to relieve (a person) of a charge, care or sim.

sic incole aliquorum expulsione matrem [sc. terram] adlevant [v.l. ~iant] W. MALM. *GR* I 5; **s1087** jocatus in ejus ventrem quem potione ~iarat *Ib.* III 281; alleviat ventres labor inflatos moderatus D. BEC. 2532; **1289** de.. batellis intendentibus ad ~iandum naves cum..mercandisis venientes *RGasc* III 582; **s1380** trabes confractas, que semet ipsas ferre non poterant ~iate a campane sarcina *Chr. Angl.* 265. **b** quo martyr adest..~ians eum ponderis mestitia HERM. ARCH. 6; **1100** sicut tam magno gravamine ~iati sunt (*Ch. Hen. I*) *GAS* 522; constat, qui hanc unctionem fideliter..percipit, et in corpore et in anima ~iari, si tamen expedit ut in utroque ~ietur GIR. *GE* I 4; **1216** quod Hugonem..~iet de prisona sua, salva tamen bona custodia ipsius *Cl* 288a; **s1217** rex fecit eis cartam de foresta, per quam multi fuerunt ~iati de gravamine et molestia *Leg. Ant. Lond. app.* 204; **1285** nec excusabitur aut ~iabitur ille qui injuste rapuit hujusmodi heredem de pena..per mortem heredis (*Stat. I Westm.* c. 35) *St Realm* I 88 (= *Reg. Malm.* I 100: †alienabitur); **1300** quod..de dicto debito nos ~iando..securitatem nobis faceret *Chr. Rams. app.* 393; **1400** si..papa interdiceret nostrum regnum, ..per hoc ~iati essemus ab ejus legibus observandis (PURVEY) *Ziz.* 403.

4 "to levy" (ed.) or (?) to relieve (by reducing quota demanded).

1346 (*supersedeas for levying*) alleviand' (*the said men*) *Rec. Leic.* II 65 (cf. ib. 66).

5 to make light of, pass lightly over.

de veritate non ~iabitur hic quippiam GIR. *PI* III 2 p. 232; aut..sancte ita precepit, et habent ostendere cur, ~iando tante sanctitatis pondus, non respexerint.. RIC. ARMAGH *Def. Cur.* 1402.

alleviatio, lightening, making lighter. **b** (fig.).

frigiditas..accidentaliter levigat, quia facta eductione humiditatis que gravabat totius substantie fit ~o BART. ANGL. IV 2. **b 1239** in ~onem sui oneris dati sunt ei coadjutores GROS. *Ep.* 127.

2 alleviation: **a** of expense; **b** of pain or sickness; **c** of punishment; **d** of prison conditions (*cf. suavitas*).

a s1248 rex..ad ~onem sumptuum ipsorum..exegit.. m m li. *Flor. Hist.* II 356. **b 1201** exivit una sola gutta sanguinis de ore ejus et sensit ~onem *Canon. G. Sempr.* 144v; quartane perpessus accessionem..post ~onem qualemcunque..expectat..remedium AD. MARSH *Ep.* 186; sola Jesu rememoratio / fit dolorum alleviatio J. HOWD. *Ph.* 394. **c s1199** hec..pietatis opera..maximam penarum suarum [sc. regis] †allevationem, ut speramus, prestabunt COGGESH. 97 (= OXNEAD *Chr* 107: alleviationem); **s1300** afflicta doloribus, B. Thomam..pro ~one tante pene suppliciter invocavit WALS. *HA* I 81. **d 1296** de xix s. de finibus quorundam pro ~one prisone *DLMinAc* 1/1 r. 17; **1358** maximas pecuniarum summas pro manucapcione sua et ~ione prisone habenda..extorsit *Pat* 255 m. 8*d*.

3 clearance (of things). **b** relief, easing (of persons).

1508 solut' operantibus fodiendo in ~one aque ductus *Ac. Durh.* 660. **b** hec est ~o [AS: *lihtingc*] quam omni populo meo previderi volo (*Quad.*) *GAS* 357 (cf. alleviamen); utrumque cooperatur ad conferendam ~onem corporis et anime GIR. *GE* I 3; **1226** quatinus cum ~one nostra ipsi T. satisfaciendo..de terminis..transeatis *Cl* 164b; **1234** de ~one prisonum: ..prisonam Mathei..et Serlonis..faciant ~iari de oneratione ferramenti, dum tamen salvo custodiantur *Cl* 423; **1290** cc li...fratribus..liberari faciatis..ad ~onem eorundem super amissione *RGasc* II 557; **1304** justiciarii..eant..ad juratas et inquisiciones capiendas..in ~onem populi regni *RParl* 161a; **1447** erigantur nove cruces de lapidibus in locis ubi solebant corpora defunctorum portandorum ad sepulturam deponi pro..~one portancium *MunAcOx* 559.

alleviativus, tending to lighten. **b** tending to allay.

[caliditas] naturaliter est gravium ~a BART. ANGL. IV 1. **b** cura est triplex, sc. tentativa, ~a vel mitigativa, et eradicativa GAD. 33 v. 1.

alleviatorium, relief.

1375 in manibus vestre potencie captivitatis mee conspicio ~ium intercludi (*Lit. abbatis*) THORNE 2150.

alleya v. aleia. allia v. alium. alliaria v. aliaria. alliata, ~us v. aliatus. alliaticus v. alloeoticus. allibentia v. allubentia.

allicere [CL], to attract, induce.

ut conjunctius sibi ~eret..eos libere progredi..permisit *G. Steph.* I 20 p. 28; multi de plebe ad crucis obsequium sunt allecti GIR. *IK* II 7; **s1197** adiit regem..ut consensum ejus ad pacem ~eret W. GUISB. 140; **1373** (v. allectivus a); miraculum estimo cum quis per graciam Dei..hec ~iencia perfecte †contempnitur [? l. contempnit] ROLLE *IA* 166; **s1383** cupiditate pocius..ducti quam salute animarum suarum sunt allecti *V. Ric. II* 46.

allices v. alyces. allictarius v. alutarius. allicum v. allec. allidada v. alhidada.

allidere [CL], to knock against. **b** (fig.). **c** to crush.

adlido, †*tonwinto GlC* A 218; **10..** conlidit, i. ~it, *ætspearn*, offendit WW; selle testes ejus allisi sunt et contritus est alter W. CANT. *Mir. Thom.* V 5; cum [campana] feritur interius, ~itur aer NECKAM *NR* I 22; spiritus animalis..ibi passus ab aere alliso in voce vel sono recurrit ad fantasticam [cellulam] RIC. MED. *Micr. Anat.* 217; **s1296** ~ente tota mole capiti suo, penitus est quassatus *Flor. Hist.* III 289. **b** contrariis cogitationum fluctibus ~or ERIUG. *Per.* 601D. **c** ut..in ima vitiorum lapsos ~at et confringat GIR. *TH* I 22.

2 (p. ppl. *allisus, cf.* OF *alis*) unleavened.

1312 vj panes ~os, precio cujuslibet panis xij d. Burd[egalenses] *RGasc* IV *app.* II p. 548.

allienare v. alleviare 1b.

alligamentum, tying on (as amulet).

non hec [fiunt remedia]..herbis aut herbarum ~is, sed hec omnia operante..Deo GERV. TILB. III 28.

alliganter, by alliance.

1405 ad rebelles nostros Wallicos adinvicem ~er et assuranter fortificandos *Cl* 254 m. 6.

alligantia, bond, obligation. **b** marriage tie. **c** alliance. **d** conspiracy. **e** faction, group of allies or dependants.

1356 relaxamus et quietum clamamus..prefato domino.. omnimodas ~ias, promissiones, convenciones et contractus inter ipsum et nos..initos sive factos *RScot* 789b. **b 1325** nobis exposuit vestram magnificenciam affectare inter vestram et nostram soboles aliquos iniri contractus conjugales; verum, quia de tantis ~iis tractare non decet absque majori presencia nunciorum.. (*Cl*) *Foed.* IV 157. **c 1337** ad tractandum..super aliganciis et federibus *RScot* 515a; **s1414** missis..ambassiatis ad..alios principes Christianos amicicias et ~ias mutuas contraxit cum eis ELMH. *Hen. V* 8; **1416** si in uberioris hujusmodi ~iarum roboris fulcimentum nos in Parliamento nostro ~ias ipsas..ratificaverimus, ..tunc presentes ~ie in suo perpetuo robore permaneant in effectu *RParl* 98b. **d 1345** multiplicantur contra nos.. conspiraciones et ~ie (*Lit. Regis*) AD. MUR. 167; **1357** in alleganciis injustis, falsitatibus, forstallariis, dampnis (*Pat*) *EHR* XXVII 233; **1377** remisimus..sectam pacis nostre pro omnimodis..cambiperciis, ambidextriis, ~iis, falsarum querelarum manutenenciis.. (*Pat*) *Foed.* VII 166; **1588** de quibuscunque prodicionibus, ..falsis alleganciis, transgressionibus, riotis, routis *Pat* 1321 m. 4. **e 1215** nec debemus..monachos..nec eorum †allingantiam de..terra ..dehospitari *Reg. S. Aug.* 381; **s1329** arettati fuerunt super eo quod cum aliis de ~ia et confederacione eorum venerunt ad domum Ricardi.. *Ann. Lond.* 244; **1400** Francigenis aut aliis quibuscumque de eorum ~ia existentibus (*Cl*) *Foed.* VIII 147.

1 alligare v. allegare.

2 alligare [CL], to bind, fasten (to). **b** (fig.). **c** to impose.

sua vulnera..ipse ~avit BEDE *HE* IV 22; sub talaribus suis ~antes ossa W. FITZST. *Thom. prol.* 17; non fasciis ~antur GIR. *TH* III 10. **b** o tu cupiditas, ..quam innumerabilibus cathenis voluptatis tue istum regem generosum †allegasti! *V. Ric. II* 147. **c 1231** nos non tantum judicare sed etiam condempnare intendunt, ~antes onera importabilia (*Lit.*) M. PAR. *Maj* III 209.

2 to moor. **b** (absol.) to moor (fig.).

navem..funibus precepit ~are R. COLD. *Cuthb.* 23; naves navibus ~antur LIV. *Hen. V* 11a. **b 1337** sanum est.. inconstancie fluctibus importune depulsis ad portum salutis ~are *FormOx* 92.

3 (refl.) to ally onself. **b** (p. ppl.) associated. **c** (p. ppl. as sb. m.) ally, confederate.

1296 provocavimus dominum nostrum..regem Anglie.. in eo quod..~avimus nos regi Francie [Fr.: *de fere aliaunce au roy de Fraunce*] (*Transl. lit. regis Scocie*) *Foed.* II 718 (cf. *Anglo-Scottish Relations* p. 73); **s1325** Rogerus de Mortuo Mari..se cum..domina Isabella..~avit AVESB. 77; **s1342** se fecit..regi Anglie..~ari *Ib.* 98b. **b s1197** hec est omnium preter unius episcopi sententia, eo quod [ille] vicinior esset et ~atior Cantuariensi GERV. CANT. I 549; **s1397** rex peciit ab eo..per quos eis ~atus vel associatus extiterat *V. Ric. II* 140. **c 1294** est maximus conspirator et habet ~atos ad se *JustIt* 1095 r. 1; **1313** pro dictis comitibus et baronibus, suis adherentibus et suis manageriis suisque ~atis (*Tract. Ed. II*) *Camd. Misc.* XV 18; **s1340** ad tractandum cum ~atis suis AVESB. 89; **1389** quod possitis nos utpote ~atum vestrum pro posse defendere et juvare *Dip. Corr. Ric. II* 73; **1415** invicem boni, firmi et stabiles erimus..amici, ~ati et confederati *RParl* 97b.

alligatio [CL], braid, plait (of hair).

793 non tortas crinium ~ones, sed rectas morum conligationes ALCUIN *Ep.* 15.

2 bond, obligation. **b** marrage tie. **c** alliance. **d** conspiracy.

cum te ipsum Deo totum vovisti..per monachicam professionem, solvisti omnia minora vota..quae prius sine jurejurando et fidei ~one promisisti ANSELM (*Ep.* 188) IV 74 (cf. V 241); noverit..se mea auctoritate ab hac ~one solutum AILR. *Ed. Conf.* 152D. **b 1331** ad tractandum.. super ~onibus inter ipsum [regem Francie] et nos per fedus conjugale..ineundis (*RomR.*) *Foed.* IV 502b. **c s1321** ad tractandum qualiter comes possit confederaciones et ~ones jam inceptas cum extraneis annullare *G. Ed. II Bridl.* 64; **s1325** inter..regis primogenitum comitemque Anonie talis ~o facta fuit quod.. AVESB. 77. **d 1321** ~ones et confederaciones per sacramentum vel aliis modis ad invicem.. fecerunt in status nostri subversionem (*Lit. regis*) *Lit. Cant.* III 404; **1321** litera regis ne cives aliquam covinam vel ~onem facerent cum comite Lancastrie (*LBLond* E) *MGL* I 648; **1326** vlneraverunt..J. de O. ..per preceptum et abectum, per confederacionem et ~onem illicitam Johannis le Shirreve *JustIt* 309 r. 3.

alligatura, amulet.

quasi missam a Deo conditore plagam per incantationes vel ~as vel alia quaelibet daemonicae artis archana cohibere valerent BEDE *Cuthb.* 9 (cf. W. CANT. *Mir. Thom.* V 11).

alligera v. alhigera. alligoria v. allegoria. allingantia v. alligantia e. allipiados v. alypias.

allileti [? Sp. Ar. *al-hīlat* for *al-hāla(t)* < ἅλως], halo.

halo sive ~i, qui est circulus coloratus circa solem et lunam et stellas BACON V 10.

allisio, striking, blow. **b** (fig.).

miles..ad ~onem lapidis hostii sub manu seminudum lesit brachium HERM. ARCH. 48; sitiens levi ~one baculi ad silicem elicuit laticem W. MALM. *GP* (*V. Aldh.*) V 247; sic campanam preceps allisio reddit / fissam NECKAM *DS* VI 85; ut melior fieret ~o proportionata ~oni extrinsecе; propter siccitatem enim et duriciem cordarum melius resonant vielle et citare GILB. III 144 v. 2; lapis pirites lapis est a quo per alisionem calibis..evolat ignis *Alph.* 90. **b 1106** communis casus ~onem indifferenter subibo (*Lit. Mathildis regine*) *Ep. Anselm.* (400) V 344.

†allistrigium [? cf. allec], mease (measure of 1,000 herring).

a mayse of herynge, millenarius, ~ium *CathA*.

allisus v. allidere.

allitare [< ad+litus], to come ashore.

s1101 [Robertus] ~ans apud Portesmuthe, copias suas.. effudit W. MALM. *GR* V 395.

allium v. alium. allivio v. alluvio.

allocabilis, a allowable in account, to be credited (*cf. allocare* 3a). **b** allowable in law, admissible (*cf. allocare* 4a).

a 1296 omnes dies festivales et ~es debent allocari in numero predictorum operum *IPM* 80/6; **1391** summas pecunie ad usum regine.., prout patet in suis compotis.., ~es habuerunt *ExchScot.* III 253; **1420** computantes presentaverunt unam literam domini camerarii..de lxiiij li., que pro tunc non videbatur eis ~is *Ib.* IV 316; **1442** omnibus computatis computandis, allocatis et allocandis.., compertum est quod racionabiles parcelle ~es..magistro J. excedunt racionabiles parcellas ~es..abbati AMUND. II *app.* B 282. **b** si [exceptio] non sit ~is, sequitur quod juratores..[sunt] puniendi *Fleta* 30; **1318** per calumpnias non ~es multi..defendentes fuerunt..amerciati (*Stat. Rob. I* 14) *APScot* 110; ordinatum est..quod talis essonia non sit ~is nec recipiatur (*Ib.* 26) *Ib.* 113.

allocabilitas, allowability in account (fig.).

homo ergo non est reus ignis eterni propter peccatum de quo penitet fructuose, quia de isto reddet racionem ~atis in die judicii WYCL. *Mand. Div.* 340.

allocabiliter, allowably, so as to be credited. (fig.).

episcopi possunt..absentare se a suis diocesibus..excusabiliter et meritorie et ~er penes Deum PECOCK *Abbr.* 617.

allocamentum, allowance in account.

1225 summa ~i pro stauro..; summa totius ~i *DCCant Ass. Scacc.*; **1252** summa ~orum pro hostilagiis xxiij li. *Ib. Reg.* H f. 173a; **1285** summa tocius expense..sine ~is faciendis in maneriis *Cant. Cath. Pri.* 221.

allocantia, allowance in account.

1290 petit quod rex faciat ei ~iam de iiij marcis annuis.. que ei decidunt de firma sua *RParl* 56b; si quis de talsa ~ia convincatur, de tanto regi respondeat quanto fuerit summa allocationis *Fleta* 85; **1300** debitam ~iam sibi in firma sua faciatis *Reg. Carl.* I 139; **1576** cum omnibus feodis, vadiis, commoditatibus et ~iis (*Pat*) *Foed.* XV 760.

allocare [< ad+locare; cf. OF *aloer*], to place, stow, store.

1222 ~abit blad' in grangia *MinAc. Essex* (*Tillingham*); **1234** quod libere..~are possint cleias suas de..gurgite in chimino..cum necesse fuerit, ubi carecte..ire possunt, ..et non alibi *E. Ch. S. Paul* 262; **1243** galias..in domo.. de la Rye ad custodiam ipsorum (*sic*) facta..~ari faciatis *Cl* 45; **1243** domus..in qua bacones nostri..~ati fuerunt *Liberate* 19 m. 6; **12..** concessimus abbati..de Bruer' ~are et elongare gabulum boverie sue..versus stratam et murum utrobique juxta portam *FormA* 313.

2 to let, hire out. **b** to take on hire. **c** to hire (a labourer or mercenary).

1253 venerunt ad terram Willelmi..quam..Henricus.. ei ~averat (*JustIt*) *SelCWW* 75; **1292** si contingat..domum vel cameram vel aliquid domus alicui ~ari *MunAcOx* 59; **1363** septem shope..si ~arentur valerent quiete per annum lxx s. *Pat* 268 m. 23. **b 1274** morina bidencium in patria communis fuit et nemo pasturam ~are voluit *Ac. Stratton* 58; **1343** computat in j navi ~ata de Novo Castro usque Berwycum *Pri. Cold. app.* p. xvi; **s1364** miles..navim.. adiit quam sibi perprius ~averat *Eul. Hist.* III 238 (cf. ib. I 165: [S. Paulus] horreum publicum ~avit); **1424** in ~anda carta et pro allocatione equi xxix s. *MunCOx* 283. **c 1303** in vadiis iiij sahetorum ~atorum ad..maeremium saheandum *KRAc* 579/6; **s1364** multitudo gentis..quos..sibi ~averant *Eul. Hist.* III 233; **1427** volo quod executores mei ..gubernent et sustentent servientes meos ~atos et apprenticios *Reg. Cant.* II 402.

3 to allow (in account), credit (an expense or sim.). **b** (fig.). **c** (w. *pro*) to count (as). **d** to credit (a person w. an expense).

1233 mandatum est baronibus quod ~ent eidem H...x s. ..quos solvisse debuit ad Scaccarium (*KRMem*) *Cal. Liberate* I xi; **1259** Petrus..liberavit per preceptum regis magistro H. ..unum dolium vini; ..et mandatum est baronibus de Scaccario quod eidem Petro illud dolium vini ~ent *Cl* 360; **1275** ita quod A. ei ~aret de eadem pecunia valorem unius libre lane que de pondere viij librarum.. deficiebat *SelPlMan* 140; **1278** elemosinam nostram.. persolvant de firma.., quam eis..in eadem firma volumus ~ari *BBC* (*Dunwich*) 320; **1298** vobis faciemus expensas racionabiles ~ari *Mem. Ripon* 296; **1332** quod predicte xx li. ~entur prefato J. in debitis que..regi debet *LTRMem* 105 r. 14; **1425** in ~atis eidem [collectori redditus nostri] pro amerciamentis illevabilibus hoc anno vj d. (*Ac. Prior.*) *Ambrosden* II 251; **1449** petit sibi allogari pro..cameris vacantibus..iiij li. *Cant. Coll. Ox.* II 173; **1469** ~ate computanti per solucionem [? l. persolucionem] factam fratribus S. Trinitatis *ExchScot* 649. **b** ipsa affectio intrinseca benevolencie..apud gratum dominum plus debet accipi et ~ari quam quodlibet aliud donum MILEMETE *Nob.* 56; tota mea pena in cruce nichil me gravat in hujusmodi comparacione, quod sic ~o [ME: *ic þus biteo*] quicquid feci *AncrR* 160. **c** **12..** dedi..tres damas in parco meo..; et si damum vel brokettum tempore firmationis ceperint, ~abitur ei pro dama *FormA* 304; **1469** in c li. grossorum monete Flandrie, ~ando pro qualibet libra lv sol. *ExchScot* 662. **d** **1275** isti fuerunt ~ati de denariis quos mutuaverant communitati *Rec. Leic.* I 148; **1338** nullus taxator nec collector..quieti sint nec ~ati de eorum tallagiis *Ib.* II 44; **1451** [collectores] xxvj s. viij d. ..nomine feodi sui retinere ac inde in compoto suo..~ari..usi fuerunt *Reg. Whet.* I 62; **1523** auditores eidem Simoni debita ~averunt et idem Simon inde ~atus fuit (*PlRExch.*) *Law Merch.* II 130; **1546** habebunt potestatem..~andi et acquietandi.. computantem pro singulis per eum..solutis *StatOx* 341.

4 to allow, admit, accept as valid. **b** (w. *quod*).

1258 essonia sua non fuit ~ata *SelPlMan* 67; **1305** ~atis comitatibus in quibus..R. exactus fuit *SelCCoron* 72; **s1313** coram quibus [justiciariis] ~ata est subscripta libertas THORNE 2015; **1325** petunt libertatem suam predictam eis ~ari (*Plac. Aulae*) *MGL* I 305; **s1425** exponens [regi].. quam difficiles reddebant se sui barones [de Scaccario] ad ~andum chartam illam *Reg. Whet.* I 26; **1583** quamquidem sursumreddicionem acceptamus et ~amus *Pat* 1235 m. 19. **b** **1196** [S.] petit quod hoc ei ~etur quod [R.] modo dicit quod tenet feodum illud de abbate *CurR* I 23; **1219** petit sibi ~ari quod ipse posuit se in magnam assisam *Ib.* VIII 90; **s1272** nichil ~atum fuit civibus quod prior et complices sui fuerunt..causa tocius illius infortunii *Leg. Ant. Lond.* 147; **1291** petit sibi ~ari quod J. nullam fecit mencionem in appello suo de die.. *Eyre Kent* 111.

5 (imp. *allocate*) form of writ addressed to the Exchequer (cf. *Cal. Liberate* I xi). **b** form of Exchequer bill.

1257 cum eas [marcas] liberaveris, breve nostrum de ~ate tibi inde habere faciemus *Cl* 29; **1266** nisi..sibi eas [marcas] ~ari fecerimus per brevia nostra de computabitur vel ~ate *Cl* 199. **b** **1333** (v. 2 billa 2b).

6 (p. ppl. as sb. m.) deputy or (?) hireling (C.I.).

1274 homines ejusdem insule male tractantur..per ~atos ..ballivi (*Chanc. Misc.* 10/5/3) *S. Jers.* II 40.

allocatio, hire.

1294 burgenses nihil dabunt pro ~one prisone mee vel ferrorum meorum *BBC* (*Chesterfield*) 210; **1330** in ~one unius lardarii pro..allecibus reponendis *ExchScot* 305; **1358** in ~one unius equi (*Ac. Ox.*) *EHR* XXIV 737.

2 allowance in account. **b** allowance of food.

1221 litteras nostras de ~one ad Scaccarium nostrum *Cl* 464b; **1259** multas fecit impensas..de quibus nullam habuit ~onem vel restitutionem *Cl* 389; **1292** sacrista petit ~onem de xiij s. iiij d. perditis de bidentibus emptis de domino episcopo pro *candelsilver Sacr. Ely* II 8; **1313** visores operacionum..magis computaverunt..quam posuerunt racionabiliter et super hoc falsas ~ones fieri procuraverunt *Eyre Kent* 38; **1327** de quibus sibi solvuntur per ~onem sibi factam in compoto custumariorum..l s. *ExchScot* 67; **1448** nec pluris quam de eis per ipsos juste expenditur ~onem petendo *StatOx* 270; **1449** summa..expensarum et allogacionum *Cant. Coll. Ox* II 173. **b** **1489** quod dies dedicacionis ecclesie et Corporis Christi fiant dies †appeitancie [l. appietancie] que prius erant dies ~onis tantum *Reg. Merton* 126.

3 allowance (leg.), acceptance as valid.

[defendens] petat sibi fieri ~ones et proponat excepciones BRACTON 146b; **s1292** si nullus respectus fieri debeat postgenitis propter equalitatem juris quod descendit omnibus tanquam in recompensacionem seu ~onem juris eorum *Ann. Regn. Scot.* 354; **s1293** omnes illi qui habent cartas de libertatibus post tempus ~onum predictarum THORNE 1962; **s1340** Londonienses noluerunt..respondere quousque libertates eorum allocarentur nec super hujusmodi ~one facienda potuerunt brevia regia..habere AD. MUR. 118; quod unum breve sufficiat in Scaccario et in qualibet placea domini regis ad ~ones cartarum suarum (*Ch. Ed. III*) *MGL* I 146.

allocatorius, granting allowance (in account).

1435 ut patet per literas domini ~ias sub signeto suo *ExchScot* 661.

allocpare v. alopare.

allocutio [CL], address, conversation, discussion.

~o excusativa ad regem ALDH. *Met.* 142 *rub*; cum ~one ejus refecti..domum rediremus BEDE *HE* V 1; nihil..vel intellectu difficilius vel mutua ~one inexplicabilius est ADEL. *QN* 20; exactiva responsionis ~o, ut si quis querat an ars sit scientia BALSH. *AD rec.* 2, 12.

allocutive, in conversation.

palam est hujusmodi non solum ~e sed et considerabiliter ut ad alterum per se inquiri BALSH. *AD* 130.

allocutus v. alloqui. allod- v. alod-, aulodium.

alloeosis [ἀλλοίωσις], symbolism.

alleosin figuram quidam admiserunt; ..at alleosin symbolorum et rerum hic nobis regulator primus invexit GARDINER *CC* 565.

alloeoticus [ἀλλοιωτικός], alterative (med.). **b** (?) (sb. f.) symbolism.

alliatica virtus dicitur digestiva et interpretatur †minutans [l. immutans] *Alph.* 55. **b** iste modus loquendi figurative est et apud grammaticos vocatur †alleotheta [MS: †assotheca] (KYN.) *Ziz.* 9.

allogallica v. aloe d. allogare, ~atio, v. alloc-.

allogiamentum, lodging.

1511 omnibus stipendiariis nostris liberum transitum et ~um cum victualibus honesto precio..dabunt (*Lit. regis Francie*) *Foed.* XIII 303b.

allogiatus [cf. OF *alogie*], encamped.

s1300 Scoti ~i delituerant in quodam passu fortissimo *Ann. Ed. I* 441.

†allogium [? cf. alloquium *or* elogium], (?) word, utterance.

delectatus..rex peregrinus hujusmodi responsi ~iis *NLA* (*Edmund*) II 576.

allomnare v. illuminare. alloon v. alcon. allopare v. alopare. allopedes v. alopedes.

allophylus [ἀλλόφυλος], foreigner, esp. Philistine (*cf. Psalm* lv 1).

inormem allophilorum gigantem ALDH. *VirgP* 53; ipse cum tota gente periit ~orum BEDE *TR* 10; David in funda et lapide..allophilum stravit J. SAL. *Pol.* 618c; ~us ille.. corporis sui mole parvitatem meam despiciens H. BOS. *Ep.* 3. 1425.

allopiamentum, ~iare, v. alop-. allopicia v. alopecia. allopides v. alopedes.

alloppare, to lop off.

1539 ~are ramos suos de arboribus dependentibus regiam viam *CourtR* 173/46 r. 13 (cf. ib.: ut loppant ramos suos).

alloqui [CL], to address, speak to: **a** (trans.); **b** (w. dat.); **c** (w. *ad*).

a ambas alloquitur tali cum voce puellas ALDH. *VirgV* 2371; proprio eam nomine quasi presentem ~ens, 'Eadgyd' BEDE *HE* IV 8. **b** ei suppliciter in genibus astat et reverenter ~itur MAP *NC* IV 9; diabolus..transeuntibus est allocutus B. COTTON 56 (= W. MALM. *GR* IV 331: transeuntes); **s1217** magnates quidam..Londoniensibus ~ebantur *Meaux* I 399; **1432** inter exercitus angelorum..regi transeunti taliter ~encium (J. CARPENTER) *MGL* III 462. **c** Lucius imperator..his verbis ad suos allocutus est *Eul. Hist.* II p. 350 (= G. MON. X 8: eos allocutus est).

2 (p. ppl. pass. *allocutus*) addressed, questioned, or required. **b** arraigned.

1309 separatim ~i qualiter se velint..acquietare *SelC Coron* 121; **1325** quandocumque de hoc per senescallum fuerit ~us *CBaron* 141; **1380** in ipsum A., prius per ipsos scolares verbis contumeliosis ~um, graves fuerunt insultus *FormOx* 252. **b** **1292** nullus de cetero debet facere legem cum hominibus ~is nec suspectis *Rec. Leic.* I 218; **1321** coram justiciariis inde ~us..bene cognovit quod.. (*Eyre*) *MGL* II 372; **s1329** coram justiciariis..super hoc ~us sive accusatus quod erat particeps prede *Ann. Paul.* 346; **1369** attachiatus fuit et ~us de hoc quod.. *MunCOx* 144.

alloquium [CL], address, discourse, conversation. **b** urging, appeal. **c** summons.

ut..mentem..cotidie per studiosae lectionis roboraret ~ium BEDE *HE* II 1; precor ut..[libellum] alterum non ~ium sed *Proslogion* tituletis ANSELM (*Ep.* 109) III 242; ad partem sollicitudinis ejus oris ipsius invitatus ~io W. FITZST. *Thom. prol.* 1; vultum avertit, ..declinat ~ia MAP *NC* III 3 p. 127; actibus, alloquiis vir verax, mitis, honestus D. BEC. 42. **b** tunc patris alloquio rex censuit, omnis et ordo, / servent ut pariter Wilfridi dogma FRITH. 1290; hujus ob alloquium nobis miserere precamur WULF. *Poem* 142. 5. **c** hoc morientis..certum est signi indicium et..inevitabile mortis ~ium R. COLD. *Cuthb.* 32.

allosa v. alausa.

†allotay [? l. alhocav < Ar. *al-'uqāb*], sal ammoniac.

~ay, i. sale armo[niaco] GILB. VII 341 v. 2.

allottare [OF *aloter*], to allot.

auxilia de coperticipibus, qui reddent pro rata si tenementum coperticipum allotatum evincatur FORTESCUE *LLA* 53; maneria..~ata et assignata *Entries* 363.

allouare [OF *aloer* < allaudare], (?) to please.

1214 nolumus quod ab eodem abbate aliquid capiatur ad opus illorum [equorum], quia in nullo super hoc ~ati essemus *Cl* 174b.

alloverius, ~a [OF *aloiere*], pouch.

si das †almerium [v.l. †almiolum] cuiquam, joculare sit intus, / aureus anulus aut firmacula D. BEC. 909; in suis sotularibus, cirotecis, ~iis, bursis seu pautoneriis vel sacculis *Fleta* 170; **1300** unum alverum magnum perlis broudatum.. de armis Anglie, Flandrie et Barr' *Ac. Wardr.* p. 343; **1302** unus alverus de perlis datus regi per comitissam Flandrie *KRAc* 357/13 m. 2; **1307** xx s. in uno alvero *Doc. W. Abb. Westm.* 208; **1313** armurario regis Navarre portanti ad regem j cingtorium et j aliwerum de serico *KRAc* 375/8 f. 32; **1332** unam †alneriam de serico consutam (*KRAc* 386/7) *Arch.* LXXVII 139.

allowantia [OF *alouance*; cf. allocantia], allowance in account.

1400 item ~ia pro redditibus aretro portantibus *Ac. Churchw. Bath* 17.

allox v. allus.

allubentia [LL], consent.

a consenting, allibencia *CathA*.

allubescere [CL], to be favourable. **b** to win favour.

956 (14c) divina alubescente gratia *CS* 941 (cf. 987); **963** (11c) †albescente et consentiente Eadgaro basileo *Ib.* 1111; **s1190** ~ens favonius rates attulit armatis onustas *Itin. Ric.* I 41. **b** talibus et aliis paucis verbis ~it, orataque mulier ad sua facile desideria trahitur MAP *NC* III 4 p. 133.

allucēre [CL], to shine.

solaris splendoris columna coram omnibus alluxit GOSC. *Aug. Maj.* 87.

alluces, ~ia, ~ium v. ablutium. allucum v. alutum.

alludenter, allusively.

Abbennus..monasterium..fundavit, cui nomen Abbendoniam vel a nomine suo vel a loci vocabulo ~er imposuit *Chr. Abingd.* I 2.

alludere [CL], to play or jest with. **b** (tr.) to mate with.

sibi familiaribus assistentibus ~ens, in hoc prorupit eludium DEVIZES f. 27v. **b** vitulus matris est cujuscumque taurus alluserit (*Leg. Hen. I*) *GAS* 594.

2 to recite.

ver prior adlusit ternos modulamine versus ALCUIN *Carm.* 58. 9; haec piis amicis ~endo et pie commendando oramus.. GOSC. *Aug. Maj. prol.* 45.

3 to allude (to). **b** (w. *ad*) to pun (on).

quasi his ~ens que in manibus habemus AD. SCOT. *Serm.* 159; ~ens illi ..Merlini proverbio GIR. *EH* I 38; ut poeticis ~amus figmentis NECKAM *NR* I 51 p. 102; hiis concilium Carthaginiense ~ere videtur OCKHAM *Pol.* I 22; ut verbis ~amus Boecii R. BURY *Phil. prol.* 6. **b** ille adludens ad nomen [Aelli] ait: "alleluia..illis in partibus oportet cantari" BEDE *HE* II 1 p. 80; **s1235** qui, ut verbo ~amus, vere Caursini quasi capientes et ursini nuncupantur M. PAR. *Maj.* III 331.

4 to refer to, consult.

1424 regi..non statim ~ens, ..tante cure sarcinam satis acute ponderabit HEETE *Wykeham* 298.

alluere [CL], to wash (of sea, etc.). **b** (fig.) to pollute.

aestus..terras adluit et resilit BEDE *TR* 29 (cf. ib. 5: aquarum diffusio omnem ~entium terram); continens munitionem hinc marino gurgite ~ente inaccessam *G. Steph.* I 37; de Castro Novo quod fluvius Thynus ~it W. CANT. *Mir. Thom.* VI 75; palus..que menia urbis aquilonalia ~it W. FITZST. *Thom. prol.* 17. **b** criminum quibus humanum genus adluitur causa FELIX *Guthl.* 45.

†allugo, ~inatus [? *for* uligo], mould, mouldy.

~o, *fyne*; ~inatus, *fynig* ÆLF. *Sup.*

allumen v. alumen. alluminatio v. illuminatio. allura v. alura.

allus [CL Gl.], **allux, allox,** big toe.

~ox, *tahae GlC* A 494; ~ux, †pollux in pede *Ib.* 427; dum..pedum ~oces truciter adnecterent ALDH. *VirgP* 36 p. 284; ~ox, *micele tan ÆLF. Gl.*; U ante C producitur, ut.. ~ux, ~ucis BACON *Tert.* 264; hic ~ux, A. *a grete too*: ..'est manuum polles, sed dicatur pedis allux' WW.

allusio [LL], play.

10.. ~o, *plegan* WW.

allusus, play, sport (fig.).

[Willelmus II] in omnibus usus est placido ~u fortune W. MALM. *GP* I 50.

allut- v. alut-.

alluvies [CL], swamp.

~ies, locus cenosus *GlC* A 424.

alluvio [CL], flood, surge. **b** (fig.).

aquarum ~o, *wætera gewæsc* ÆLF. *Sup.*; **s1170** ossa cujusdam gigantis in Anglia per ~onem detecta sunt TORIGNI 244 (= *Eul. Hist.* III 72: †allivione); allabentibus fluctuum ~onibus R. COLD. *Cuthb.* 23; **s1314** tante fuerunt ~ones pluviarum et inundaciones aquarum *Flor. Hist.* III 160; **s1379** armiger..~one maris dum flueret violenter avellitur ab ipsa petra WALS. *HA* I 425; Willelmus abbas [cessit **1396**]..terras plurimas..per ~ones aquarum perdidit *Meaux* III 228. **b** **1093** credas me in maxima lacrimarum ~one ista scripsisse (OSBERN) *Ep. Anselm.* (152) IV 14.

2 silting. **b** increase.

ut pars aliqua ripe olim avulsa..paulatim postea per ~onem incrementa susceperit GIR. *IK* II 9; **1277** cum per multas et diversas maris ~ones paulatim factas cursus aquarum de ripa de Wirmegeye impediatur *Pat* 96 m. 12d.; **c1290** per ~onem maris nata fuit quedam parva insula *IMisc* 49/22. **b** [Henricus II] scutagiis, recognitionibus et variis angariarum ~onibus fere omnes depressit R. NIGER

168; **1222** Dominus..benedicens viaticum peregrinationis vestre, quanto magis illud..in usus pauperum distribuitis, tanto magis celesti ~one multiplicat (*Lit. Papae*) *Reg. Newbattle* 239.

alluvium, flood.

~ium, *wætergewæsc* ÆLF. Sup.; *warpynge of the see or of oder water*, ~ium *PP*.

allux v. allus. allzali v. alkali. allzebric v. alkibrit. allzimicus v. alchimicus. alma v. almus, 1 alva.

almacenus [Ar. *al-ma'qān* (dual)], corner of eye, canthus.

quorum [musculorum] unus movet oculum sursum, alius deorsum, alii duo ad duos ~os, unus ad angulum domesticum sive lacrimalem, alius ad angulum silvestrem *Ps.*-RIC. *Anat.* 26.

†almachor, (?) sea-eagle (ἁλιάετος; cf. Aristotle *H.A.* IX ix 3, xxii 3; Ambrose *Hexaemeron* 18).

dicit Aris[toteles]..quod amachel [v.l. almaches] manet juxta maram et juxta magnos lacus..dicit etiam Ambro[sius]..quod quedam species aquile quam vocat ~or [v.l. almothec] est acuti visus valde.. BART. ANGL. XII 2.

Almagesti [Ar. *al-mijisṭī* < μεγίστη], Ptolemy's *Almagest.*

unde commodior ad Almajesti, quo precipuum nostrum aspirat studium, pateret accessus (ROB. ANGL. *Judicia Alkindi*) *EHR* XXX 63; decem reges..Egypto imperaverunt et omnes uno Ptholomei nomine fuerunt vocati, ex quibus unus..librum quendam, in quo totum corpus astronomie continetur, sc. ~i, Yonica lingua scripsit D. MORLEY 28; positiones Ptolomei in Almagesto GROS. 100; teste Ptolomeo in prologo ~i R. BURY *Phil.* 1. 21; **1565** explicabunt..astronomiam vel Johannis de Sacro Bosco..vel Ptolomei Almogestam *StatOx* 378.

almagra [Ar. *al-maghra*], red ochre or (?) bronze.

~a quoque est laton, licet superius eam esse terram rubeam diceremus ROB. ANGL. *Alch.* 518b; ~a est bolum, cuprum, laton et lapis ipse, vel terra rubea, lotum vel lotio *LC*.

almagrip [Ar. *al-maghrib* = *west*], a point of the astrolabe.

c1110 quia de astrolabio scientibus loquor, primam partem Tauri eidem altitudini superposui in parte ~ip, ..notato loco quem designabat almeri (WALCHER MALVERN. *Tab. Lun.*) *EHR* XXX 57.

†almahar [? Ar. *al-martak* or *al-mardār* (both < Pers.)], litharge, lead oxide.

~ar, i. litargirium *SB* 10.

Almajesti v. Almagesti.

almalia [OF *almaille* < animalia], (pl.) cattle.

c1200 dedi eis communem pasturam..ad cc oves et xl ~ia *AncD* AS 225.

almanac [Sp. Ar. *al-manākh*; etym. dub.], almanac.

antiqui astronomi ponunt principium anni circiter principium Octobris, sicut patet in expositione tabularum que ~ac vocantur BACON *Maj.* I 192; he tabule vocantur ~ach vel tallignum, in quibus semel sunt omnes motus celorum certificati a principio mundi usque in finem.., ut homo possit inspicere omnia que in celo sunt omni die, sicut nos in calendario inspicimus omnia festa sanctorum *Id. Tert.* 36; Johannes de Norhamptona edidit anulum philosophicum elegantem..qui perpetui ~ac (ut vocant) vicem suppleat BALE *Index* 234.

almandina v. alabandina. Almanicus, Almannus, v. Alamann-. almaria, v. armarium, elemosynaria. almariolum, ~ialum v. armariolum. almarium v. armarium. almatica, ~ula v. dalmatic-. almererium v. elemosynaria. almeri v. almuri.

†almericum, *s. dub.*

s1265 erat castrum [de Kenilwrthe]..machinis et tormentis jaculator[i]is, ~is et sindonis necessariis admodum munitum (RISH.) WALS. *HN app.* 549.

almerium v. alloverius, armarium c. almicanterath v. almucantarath. almicium v. almucia.

almificus, bountiful, beneficent.

multis ~i Yvonis signis GOSC. *V. Iv.* 16; ad transferendum corpus ~um [S. Alchmundi] S. DURH. *HR* 52; tuam ~am paternitatem suppliciter efflagito *NLA* (*Fiacrius*) I 442; **1403** caritatis magnifice et ~e *FormOx* 199; **1418** ~o spiramine ducta *Reg. Heref.* 34.

almifluus, flowing w. bounty.

tumba ~a GOSC. *V. Iv.* 16; post longas visionis ~e delicias AD. EYNS. *Hug.* V 10; vitam hujus ~i patris *NLA* (*Deusdedit*) I 266; stat patris almiflui domus hec, puer ut veneretur ELMH. *Cant.* 93; **a1424** ~a clemencia..Plasmatoris *Reg. Whet.* II 392.

almiger, bountiful.

796 (12c) sub..dominice defensionis ~a dextera *CS* 282.

almipara, maternally bountiful.

Virginis almipare cameraria semper in armis GARL. *Epith.* IX 347; almipare matris inter miracula lecta *Id. Tri. Eccl.* 123.

almipater, paternally bountiful (of S. Benedict).

tu monachos deduxeris ante tribunal / celsithroni regis, almipater, proprios ALCUIN *Carm.* 51 6.

almiphonus, gracious-sounding, dulcet.

neupmatis almiphŏni GARL. *Hon. Vit.* 9; dum canentis cor igne celico funditus exuritur et in ejus similitudinem figuratur in quo ~um est ROLLE *IA* 174 (cf. ib. 200: ~um amoris arcanum); almiphŏnis jubilate tonis per rura colonis ELMH. *Cant.* 93.

almipotens, bountiful in might.

a713 apud ~entem Dominum (ÆLFLED) *Ep. Bonif.* 8; angelus almipotens celi ALCUIN *Ep.* 243.

almisonus, gracious-sounding, dulcet.

almisonaeque preces claris cum laudibus una / clam pereunt BONIF. *Aen.* 344.

almitas, benignity, grace. **b** benign presence. **c** benignity (as title).

793 per caritatis ~atem obtestor ALCUIN *Ep.* 19. **b** pontificis ~ati..adhaerebat *V. Dunst. B.* 8. **c a705** cognoscat vestra ~as ALDH. *Ep.* 6; **705** domino reverentissimo ..tuae ~atis suplex servulus salutem *CS* 115; **794** pro his.. qui vestrae ~ati se..commendant ALCUIN *Ep.* 27.

almivolus, benevolent.

797 a vestrae autoritatis ~a pietate ALCUIN *Ep.* 125.

almizadar v. alnuzadir. almogesta v. almagesti. almonera, ~ia, almosneria v. elemosynaria. almor- v. armar-.

almucabola [Ar. *al-muqābala*], 'almachabel', algebra (or equation).

liber algebre et ~a de questionibus arithmeticis et geometricis ROB. ANGL. *Alg.* 66.

almucantarath [Ar. *al-muqanṭarāt* (pl.)], almucantar, celestial latitude.

solis progressionis, que ~ath dicuntur, ..lineas J. GODARD *Ep.* 222; **1326** fiant perfecte azimuth et almuchantarath, ita tamen quod non confundant nimis gradus zodiaci in longitudine et latitudine nec appareat quicquam in circulo equinoxiali aut de tropicis nisi sub almucanterath inter lineas horarum WALLINGF. *Albion* 364 (cf. ib. 365; almicanterath).

almucia, ~ium [etym. dub.; (?) *infl. by* amictus], almuce, hood.

nullus clericorum de superiori gradu ~ia utatur nisi nigra *Offic. Sal.* 19; **a1272** capucium.. / alioquin dequadratur, / de quadrato rotundatur, / transit in almucium *Pol. Songs* 53; **1277** almiciis..linitis sindone non utantur *Doc. Eng. Black Monks* 65; **1283** penulas..amiciarum caprinas esse volumus vel agninas *MonA* VI 1332; accipiens..pallium et ~iam super caput suum *Obs. Barnwell* 122; **c1300** in yeme tamen, urgente frigore de nocte, liceat illis gestare ~ia simplicia de panno nigro ultra colli medium protensa *Reg. S. Paul.* 67; habeat in capite pileum foderatum; ..et sit quasi ~ium descendens usque ad spatulas GAD. 133 v. 2; **s1330** quesivit episcopus..in quali habitu esset [apostata]; et responsum est quod in tunica de burneto et ~ia sine cuculla THORNE 2057; ~ie due, una sc. furrata..et alia non furrata *Cust. Cant.* 401; **1331** superpelliciis et aumuciis induti matutinas ..dicant *MonA* VI 705; **c1335** almicias nigras nigris fururis furratas *Eng. Clergy* 269; **1336** pro factura..v amuciarum *Ac. Durh.* 533; **1366** non capucia sed ~ia vel birreta tenentes in capite *Reg. Aberd.* II 4; **1397** presbiteri per totam villam incedentes amisiis utuntur, quin verius abutuntur, nulla auctoritate abbatis *Reg. Heref.* 141; **1400** pro j superpellicio, ij amusiis *Test. Ebor.* III 13; **1406** in habitu decente, saltem in superpelliciis et nigra almusia furrata de pellibus agninis *Midlothian* 315; *amuce*, almicium *PP*; **1451** puniant illos qui viciosi fuerint..portare..~ia alba sive rubea, sive de panno vel de tela (*Abbr. Stat.*) *Mon. Francisc.* II 89; **1453** tibi..nunc abbati..licenciam damus uti hujusmodi ~ia instar decani ecclesie collegiate *Cart. Osney* III 95.

Almuharran [Ar. *al-Muḥarram*], first month of Islamic year.

s1138 prima dies ~an primi mensis Arabici J. WORC. 53.

almuri [Ar. *al-mur'ī*], almury, pointer of astrolabe or sim.

c1110 notato loco quem designabat almeri (v. almagrip); ~i quidam denticulus egrediatur a medio meridiani lateris basilice a directo linee meridiane super gradus tabule equinoctialis, cujus officium omnino est hic ut in astrolabio *Turquet* 371.

almus [CL], fostering, gracious. **b** (w. ref. to university; cf. P. N. Denifle: *Universitäten des Mittelalters* 33–5).

cum caeli coetibus almis ALDH. *VirgV* 2442; sed blanda, sed alma, sed aurea, nectit / blanda dolos, alit alma malum, petit aurea donum J. EXON. *BT* II 303–4; rogat ut veniam protector ei daret almam J. HERD *Hist. IV Regum* 98. **b 1411** in causis coram domino cancellario hujus ~e universitatis matris nostre *MunAcOx* 260; **1440** ad decus decoremque ~e matris vestre [sc. Universitatis Oxon'] (*Lit. regis*) BEKYNTON I 101; **1491** rectore ~e universitatis Glasguensis *Reg. Paisley* 155; **1520** in hac ~a universitate sua S. Andree *Conc. Scot.* I cclxxi.

2 holy, blessed. **b** (w. ref. to ecclesiastical courts).

sic rexit regnum plures feliciter annos, / donec conversus cellam migravit in almam ALDH. *CE* 3. 13; alma Deus Trinitas BEDE (*Hymn*) *HE* IV 18; inclinate suppliciter ad ~as aras [AS: *to halgum wefodum*] ÆLF. *Coll.* 103; piam petitionem pro ~a virgine de Karru AD. MARSH *Ep.* 108; exinde post ~e Trinitatis solemnia ELMH. *Hen. V* 82. **b** officialis ~ae curiae Cantuariensis de Arcubus *Praxis* 3.

almusia v. almucia.

almustakim [Ar. *al-mustaqīm*], equinoctial circle.

aplanos his circulis distinctus est, quorum primus Arabice ~im, Latine equinoccialis nuncupatur..dicitur ~im ab Arabibus, id est rectus, eo quod motus ejus a motu aplanetici corporis nulla ratione distat D. MORLEY 35.

almuthemen [Ar. *al-muthamman*], total amount to be expended, orig in commercial transactions (math., *cf. althemen*).

tertius [numerus] ~en, id est ignotus ROB. ANGL. *Alg.* 120. 24*n*.

†almuzarar [l. almuzahar < Ar. *al-musa''ar*], unit of measure (math.).

horum numerorum primus juxta Arabes ~ar..nominatur ROB. ANGL. *Alg.* 120. 22*n*.

alna [OF *aune* < Frk. *alina*; cf. ulna], ell. **b** ell-measure.

c1180 pro..vj ~is de blancheto *FormA* p. xv; **1277** de quadam placea..xxxix ~as ad ~am seu mensuram ville Baione usitatam in latitudine et lx ~as..continente in latitudine *RGasc* II 29; **1410** de ij towells unius pecie, long' viij aln' *Test. Ebor.* III 45. **b 1283** quicumque tenuerit.. falsam mensuram vel falsam ~am.., in lx s. puniatur (*Stat. bastide, Lib. B*) *Foed.* II 262.

alnacius v. alenatius.

alnagium [OF *aunage*; cf. ulnagium], alnage, duty on cloth (*cf. VCH Hants* V 24).

1369 indentura..de aunagio pannorum forisfactorum in com. Warr', Leyc' [etc.] (*Lib. Mem. Cam.*) *Cal. Exch.* I 224; **1398** [de] xxvj li. receptis de J. F. de †avenagio [? l. aulnagio] pannorum *Ac. Chamb. Winchester*; **1513** †advenagium concessum civitati per dominum regem distribuitur sequentibus, viz. ballivi habeant annuatim xx m. et major habebit x m. et x m. camerariis *BBWinchester* 125 (cf. *Pat* 449 m. 4: concessimus..majori et communitati xl m. ..de exitibus.. de ulnagio et subsidio nostro pannorum venalium infra.. civitatem..Wynton').

alnatus, (?) measured in ells or planted with alders.

12.. donacionem illius partis petere..ab ~a fronte quantum ipsa petera se extendit versus australem partem et per illam viam quam..monachi fecerunt ab ~a fronte, que se extendit per costeram montis versus occidentem *Reg. Newbattle* no. 102 (cf. ib. nos. 101, 104–5).

alnea v. 1 alneus. alneria, v. alloverius. alneta, v. 1 alnetum, alnetus.

1 alnetum, ~a, alder-holt. **b** alder-timber.

~a, *alerholt* GlC A 433; unum pratum et unum ~um *DB* I 2b; alnetum in ea [*Athelney*] permaximum cervos et..id generis bestias continet W. MALM. *GP* II 92; insula de Heorty cum specioso simul et spacioso auneto [v.l. aulneto] *Id. Glast.* 108 (= J. GLAST. 15: †anneto); sonat Penguern caput ~i GIR. *IK* I 10; **1250** usque cornerium de augneto marisci *TR Bk.* 57 f. 9; **1278** clausturam de alleneto *CallMisc* I 1128; **1279** duas ~as..que continent iiij acras *Hund.* II 661; **1298** una grava de ~o continens xvj acras de curraúth' (*Ir.*) *KRAc* 233/6; **s1302** adquisivit unum ~um, Anglice j *holt* WHITTLESEY 155. **b 1185** de xl s. de ~o de Scrobi vendito *Pipe* 79; **1223** quod de spinis et ~o facias habere..J. Russel..xl carectatas ad focum suum *Cl* 538b; **1317** meremium de ~o et salice (*St. Ives*) *Law Merch.* I 104; **1324** tenementa tenentur de episcopo Elyensi per servicium xx discorum de †alieto ad Natale *IPM* 82/9 r. 8 (= *Cal.* p. 311: †alicto; cf. *IPM Hen. VII* 7/58: xxiiij discos ligneos).

2 alnetum, (?) wine of Aunay.

1205 ad cariandum vinum nostrum.., sc. usque F. iij dolia vini albi et iij dolia de ~o, usque L. ij dolia albi et iiij dolia de ~o *Cl* 41b.

alnetus, ~a, alder-tree.

1307 cepit de bosco domini ~as et alia genera arborum *CourtRHales* 593; **c1312** in stipendiis x carpentariorum.. prosternend' ~os in bosco *LTRAc.* 19 r. 29.

1 alneus, of alder, (sb. f.) alder-tree. **b** (sb. n.) (?) buckthorn (*Rhamnus*).

1287 amputantes..querulos vel spinetas vel telam vel ~eam vel hussum *SelPlForest* 63. **b** ~eum, *fulaetreo* GlC A 430.

2 alneus v. alveus 2b.

alnicetum, alder-holt.

an ellyrtre, alnus; ~um est locus ubi crescunt *CathA*.

alniceus, of alder. **b** (sb. n.) alder-holt.

1393 prostracio..non..fiat nisi..virgarum anicearum, quas primo die mensis Octobris prosterni permittimus *Lit. Cant.* III 20. **b a1222** dim. acram terre mee cum agnicio desuper astante *Cart. S. Greg. Cant.* no. 130 (*endorsed*: de dim. acra terre de alneto).

alnus [CL], alder. **b** danewort.

~us, *aler GlC* A 428; ~us, *alr* ÆLF. *Gl.*; silva ~orum *DB* I 351b; riguisque libentior alnus / ascendisse vadis HANV. IV 293. **b** allenus, *veal vyrt* vel *ellen vyrt Gl. Durh.*

alnuzadir [Ar. *al-nūshādir*], sal ammoniac.

cum sale anatron..et †almizadar, cujus complexio est frigida et sicca, fiximus albedinem ROB. ANGL. *Alch.* 514b; almizadar, almisadar, amizadir..est sal armoniacus praeparatus *LC*.

alo v. alere, halo, halos. aloa v. aloë. aloarius v. alodiarius.

alodialis, held in freehold (Anjou).

c1175 vinee arpenta tria allodialia *Act. Hen. II* II 65.

alodialiter, in freehold (Gasc.).

1156 monachi illud semper allodialiter possideant *Act. Hen. II* I 120.

alodiarius, free-holder: **a** (Fr.); **b** (Eng.).

a quibus [monachis] dux Willelmus [ob. 943] Gemmeticum dedit, abbatique locum tradidit cum tota villa, quam ab allodariis auro redemit DICETO *Abbr. Norm.* p. 248; **c1160** illud quod tenuerunt..~ii *G. Hen. II* II 65. **b** has forisfacturas habet rex super omnes ~ios totius comitatus de Chent et super homines ipsorum; et quando moritur ~ius rex habet relevationem terrae..*DB* I 1; tres aloarii tenuerunt de rege E. et potuerunt ire quolibet *Ib.* (*Suss.*) 26b; septem alodarii tenuerunt de Goduino *Ib.* 28b; x hidas tenebant ~ii villae, qui cum suis terris quo volebant recedere poterant *Ib.* (*Surr.*) 31b; tres ~ii tenuerunt in paragio de rege E. et iij aulae fuerunt *Ib.* (*Hants*) 46a; has hidas tenuerunt vii ~ii de episcopo [Winton'] nec poterant recedere alio *Ib.* 52b; **c1105** sciatis me dedisse Deo et S. Augustino [Cantuar'] et fratribus ut habeant..consuetudinem que dicitur *teames* et supra omnes allodiarios quos eis habeo datos (*Ch. Hen. I*) *CalPat 1461–7* 404 (= *Regesta* II 817); **1189** super omnes allodarios (*Ch. Ric. I*) *CalCh* V 434.

alodium [Frk. *al-ôd*], allod, freehold (tenement): **a** (Fr. & C.I.); **b** (Eng.).

a c1080 terram quam de me tenet G. M. in territorio Cadomi tam in ~io quam in feodo *Regesta* I p. 124; **c1160** terram quam apud Brolium [*Breuil, Norm.*] de ~io suo habebat *CalCh* III 308 (cf. ib. 310: terram quam..tenebant ..sicut ~ium suum); **p1200** de ~iis, x bossellos frumenti *CartINorm* 262; **1242** castrum..quod..tenuerunt in allodio *RGasc* I 161; **1298** certum est quod..terra Vasconie non erat..de feodo regis Francie set de allodio regis Anglie (*Ch. Misc.* 29/4/9) *EHR* XLII 578; **c1300** terra Vasconie aliquando fuit libera et dumtaxat tenebatur in allodium et dominus ipsius habuit in ea merum et mixtum imperium et omnimodam jurisdiccionem (*Ib.* 29/4/20) *Bull. IHR* XXI 206; **1305** de omnibus que in francum allodium tenere noscuntur *RGasc* III 455. **b †a1075** habeant [monachi Westm']..tam bene..sicuti Turstanus de eodem rege in allodium libere tenuit *Regesta* I p. 121; iiij^xx acras terrae..quas tenebant burgenses [Cantuariae] in ~ia de rege *DB* I 2; in hoc manerio mansit Godricus et tenet xx acras de ~io suo *Ib.* 11; Godessa tenuit in ~ium et dedit inde S. Augustino xxv d. in elemosina *Ib.* 12b; Aluuinus tenuit sicut ~ium *Ib.* 21b; duo liberi homines tenuerunt de rege E. in alod' *Ib.* (*Berks*) 60; si liberalis homo, quem Angli *þegen* vocant, habet in ~io (id est *bocland*) suo aecclesiam (*Inst. Cnut.*) *GAS* 295; istae sunt consuetudines regum inter Anglos: ..carta ~ii ad aeternam haereditatem; forisfactura ~ii; et pretium eorum qui habent ~ium, quando ita profunde forisfaciunt se ipsos *Ib.* 613; **s1093** precepit rex ut..civitas Cantuaria quam Lanfrancus in beneficio a rege tenebat, et abbatia S. Albani..in ~ium ecclesie Christi Cantuariensis..perpetuo jure transirent EADMER *HN* 43; *an heretage*, allodium, hereditas, ..*a maner*, allodium, manarium, mansorium, predium *CathA*.

aloë, ~es [ἀλόη], aloe. **b** dist. as *caballinus, Cicotrinus* (of Socotra), †*citrinus* (? var. of *Cicotrinus*) and *hepaticus*. **c** (w. *lignum*), lignaloes (*Aquilaria*). **d** (w. *Gallica*) gentian. **e** (?) wormwood (cf. *aloigna*). **f** (fig.) bitterness.

aloëque saporis amari NECKAM *DS* IV 838; ysopus humilis, .. / aloës alta J. HOWD. *Cant.* 643; si os fractum habuerit avis tua.., aloe calidum superliga UPTON 190. **b** aloe dicitur cujusdam herbe succus, que herba aloem appellatur; ..tria sunt genera, sc. citrinus, epaticus et caballinus..et discernuntur ex colore BART. ANGL. XVII 6; recipe..aloes epatici vel cicotrini GILB. II 99 v. 2; Latini medici..non habent..aloen epaticum nec citrinum..nec lignum aloes purum BACON IX 153; aloe caballinum valet pro oculis equorum et bovum; set aloe succatrinum valet pro oculis hominum GAD. 109. 2 (cf. ib. 108 v. 1: de aloe succotrino); **1307** istud unguentum fuit iterum factum pro domino rege cum balsamo et aloen cicotrino (*KRAc* 368/30) *Arch. J.* XIV 279 (= *EHR* LXVII 174: †cicotervo); aloen, azabare idem; ex succo cujusdam herbe fit, que similiter appellatur, et tria sunt genera, videlicet cycotrinum [v.l. cytrinum], epaticum et caballinum *Alph.* 6; aloe quando simpliciter epaticum intelligitur, licet apotecarii pro citrino intelligant *SB* 9; **1414** aloes citrini j unc' precii ij d. *EschF.* 1066/1. **c** aloa arbor est aromatica que in India generatur, ..cujus particula vice thimiamatis altaribus adoletur BART. ANGL. XVII 5; aloes lignum, cujus sunt tria genera, viz. cume, cameatis et same, reperitur in magno flumine Babilonie *Alph.* 7; *xilo* interpretatur 'lignum', inde xilo aloes, i. ligni aloes *SB* 43; **1414** lignum aloes j li. precii xxd. *EschF.* 1066/1. **d** allagallica i. genciana *SB* 9; allogallica, genciana idem, G. et A. *genciane Alph.* 4. **e** aloen, i. *wermode SB* 10. **f** plus aloes intus quam mellis habens GIR. *TH* III 52.

alogia [ἀλογία], disregard.

990 anathematis ~ia ambro [sc. Adam] pomum momordit vetitum *CD* 684.

2 banquet [LL].

~ia, convivium *GlC* A 420.

alogus [ἄλογος], **a** without speech, infant. **b** irrational (math.).

a infans vel ~os G., *unsprecende cild* ÆLF. *Sup.* **b** de..principiis corporum, de progressu multitudinis et magnitudinis sectione an terminos omnino non habeant an eos dumtaxat ~os tandem inveniant J. SAL. *Pol.* 640B; sicut in ingenuis artibus multa reperiuntur analoga, ita et multa ~a seu paraloga [*gl.*: irregularia] NECKAM *NR* II 173 p. 297.

aloigna [OF *aluisne* < ἀλόη ὀξίνης; cf. aloxis], wormwood.

centena cere..amigdolarum et ~e continet xiij petras et dim. *Fleta* 73.

†alonaxdi, alonazontes [f.l.], monks.

super Rogerium Cluniacenses †alonaxdi [? l. MONAXOI] tale scripserunt epitaphium ORD. VIT. XI 32; Guillelmus Ebroicensium comes..decrevit in proprio fundo domum edificare in qua electi †alonazontes [? l. MONAZONTES] cum vera religione Regi Regum congrue possent militare *Ib.* 33.

alopamentum, elopement, abduction.

1277 capti..pro suspicione allopiamenti M. le F., que infra etatem fuit *Gaol Del* 71 r. 16.

alopare, ~iare [? ME], to elope with, abduct. **b** to seduce (cf. *EHR* XVIII 781). **c** to entice away (a servant). **d** to run away.

1218 ~averat amicam Ricardi..et adhuc eam detenet *Eyre Yorks* 351; **1351** Henricus Bonet..~iavit Johannam uxorem Thome Row..nocte diei Lune *Proc. J. P.* 65; **a1384** amabat quandam mulierem..quam †allocpavit post in Cestresir' et eam tenuit tanquam suam et de ea genuit extra exponsalia..quandam Annoram nomine (*Inq.*) *Pat* 318 m. 41. **b 1309** Margareta filia Johannis..allopatur; ideo in misericordia *CourtR* (*Lincs*) 85/1159 r. 1; **1380** Margareta filia Galfridi..allapata est cum Thoma Priour; dat domino pro leyr[wit'] *Ib.* 88/1200 r. 1. **c 1299** nec alicui liceat allopare seu tenere servientem vel ancillam vicini sui seu alterius sine voluntate illius cum quo prius steterit *StatIr* I 216 (cf. *EHR* XVIII 509); **1301** allopiavit [eam] *CourtRRuthin* 47; **1356** alloppiavit Edwardum Tyrel servientem Ricardi Sort a servicio suo *CourtR* (*Stannary*) 161/81 r. 8. **d** ipsam Katerinam ad elopandum de viro suo et ipsum relinquendum tentavit et procuravit *Rec. Nott.* III 214.

alopecia [ἀλωπεκία], baldness, mange. **b** blondness.

~ia, *feaxfeallung* ÆLF. *Gl.*; curat omnem lepram, non modo tyriam, leoninam sed elephantiam et allopitiam W. CANT. *Mir. Thom.* IV 20; Tyriaque condeletur; / condeleri prohibetur / putris allopicia GARL. *Mir. BVM* 85v; pulvis magnetis..valet contra..allopiciam BART. ANGL. XVI 61; lepra que est de sanguine..allopicia nuncupatur GILB. VII 339 v. 2; [caro viperina] cum administratur in allopicia magnum confert juvamentum BACON V 107; lepre ..secunda species dicitur allopitia ab *alopice* que est vulpes propter depilacionem suam similem depilacioni vulpis GAD. 45. 2; allopicia est fluor capillorum *SB* 9; **1468** unamquamque ejus morbi [sc. lepre] speciem, que quatuor sunt, alopicia videlicet, Tiria, leonina et elefancia *Cl* 320 m. 17*d*. **b** *yalownes of hare*, allepecia *CathA*.

alopeciosus, bald.

alapiciosa, calwa *GlC* A 459.

†alopedes, mange.

restat adhuc lepra quam designant nomine certo / allopedes NECKAM *DS* IV 863 (864); hic morbus qui allopides dicitur GILB. II 79 v. 2.

alopia- v. alopa-. alopicia v. alopecia.

†alopitis, (?) brawn.

14.. ~is. A. *the braun* WW.

alos v. halos. alosa v. alausa.

alosanthi [ἅλος ἄνθη], finely ground salt.

alexanti, i. flos salis; molitur sal cum mola et illius flos alexanti dicitur *SB* 9; alexantes, flos salis idem, *alos* i. 'sal', *anthes* i. 'flos' *Alph.* 5; alexanthi..est flos aeris; ..alosanthi est flos salis *LC*.

alotare v. alutare.

aloxis [ἀλόη ὀξίνης; cf. aloe e, aloigna], wormwood.

si multo mellis modicum miscetur aloxis, / mellis amarescit dulcor H. CANTOR *Vers.* 222.

alpha [ἄλφα], first letter of Greek alphabet. **b** beginning.

unde ~a describitur per designacionem linearum, quia hec littera unitatem signat apud Grecos BART. ANGL. XIX 123; **1250** j magnus saphirus cum ~a et O *Pipe* 94 r. 7; potest ipsilo consequi ~a, sic *av* BACON *Maj.* I 76. **b** alfa i. initium, *angin* ÆLF. *Gl.*

alphabetum [ἀλφάβητος], alphabet, alphabetic order, ABC.

Hieremiae ruinam civitatis suae quadruplici plangentis ~o GILDAS *EB* 1 (cf. *Lament.* i); primam ~i literam BEDE *TR* 1; juxta alfabetum Hebraicae linguae ALCUIN *Ep.* 243; et regit alphăbĕtum rector uterque suum WULF. *Swith. prol.* 156; posito ~o super altare S. Baptiste, ..prima elementa perdocuit literarum AD. EYNS. *Hug.* V 14; **1211** capitulorum tenorem..sub alfabeto distinctum (*Lit. Papae*) GERV. CANT. II *app.* cxiv; **1242** pro auro..ad firmaculum nostrum cum ~o faciendum *Liberate* 16 m. 6; hoc alphābēti geminus discriminat ordo GARL. *Syn.* 1578A; **s1201** factus est..adeo laicus ut nec ~um legere sciret M. PAR. *Min.* II 90; ~um Hebreum, ..~um Grecum BACON *Maj.* I 74, 75; **1396** tractatus diversarum auctoritatum, distinctus per ~um *Meaux* III *app.* lxxxvi; hoc ~um, *a nabse* WW.

alphachinus v. alfachinus. alphe v. acalephe.

†alphesora [Ar. *al-fāshirā* < Syr.], white bryony (*Bryonia*, app. conf. w. turnip).

~a, amphelion, prassion, vitis alba, brionia idem, G. *navet*, A. *wildnep Alph.* 5; †alfefur, i. radix vitis albe *SB* 9.

alpheus v. alveus 1a. alphicus, alphinus, v. alfinus.

alphiscabiosus, (?) afflicted w. white mange.

Yeraruffini usualis..curat impetiginosos et ~os GILB. VII 346 v. 1.

alphita [ἄλφιτον], barley-meal.

gumi, enule, alfite, ysopi.. GILB. IV 187 v. 2; ~a, farina ordei idem *Alph.* 7; *barlymele*, ~a *PP*.

alphus [ἀλφός], skin disease, morphew.

~os..purgat GILB. VII 346 v. 1; alfus i. morfea *SB* 9; ~us, morphea idem, inde alphuemelas i. morphea nigra et alpholeucas id est morphea alba *Alph.* 4.

alpinus [CL], mountainous, (*sb. f. s. or n. pl.*) wold.

the walde, ~a *CathA*.

alrafed v. araseth. alremannus v. aldermannus. alremaria v. aldermanneria.

alsiosus [CL], sensitive to cold.

~us, frigoriosus *GlC* A 458.

†alszarar [? l. alszahar < Ar. *al-si'r*], price per unit.

alter [numerus] ~ar, id est secundus per primum dinotus, appellatur ROB. ANGL. *Alg.* 120. 23*n*. (cf. almuzarar).

alta nutrix v. assassinus. altalagium v. altaragium.

1 altanus [CL = *wind from the land*], whirlwind, squall.

†alcanus, *þoden*, *GlC* A 482; ~us, *þoden* ÆLF. *Gl.*; *storme, weddyr*, nimbus, procella, ~us *PP*.

2 altanus [cf. OF *hautain*], high-flying (falc.).

1211 debet duos bonos falcones haltanos pro quietantia c m. de misericordia sua *Pipe* 63; j falconem hauteinum bonum *Ib.* 243; **1212** duos falcones hautenos bonos *Pipe* 15; **1225** falcones haltanos *LTRMem* 7 r. 8*d*.

altar v. 2 altare.

altaragium [cf. OF *autelage*], altarage, revenue derived from endowment of altar or offerings thereat.

c1190 alia annua..ad vicariam ejusdem ecclesie assignavimus cum terris, ..redditibus et ~iis (*Ch. Ep. Linc.*) *Cart. Rams.* II 176; **p1200** de altelagio xv s. et dimidium cymiterium *Cart. INorm.* 262; **c1209** vicaria..consistit in altelagio et terra ecclesie *Reg. Linc.* I 2; **a1218** domus de Theokesbiria retinuit in manu sua curam de spiritualibus, ~ium et jus presentandi vicarium *Cart. Glam.* 227; **1220** vicarius habeat nomine vicarie x m. aut totum alteragium cum terris et omnibus aliis ad alteragium pertinentibus *Reg. Glasg.* I 98; **1220** carta de quadam portione autelagii (*Invent.*) *Reg. S. Osm.* I 293; **1228** assignabitur sexta pars illius estimationis in obventionibus alteriagiorum perpetuis vicariis *G. S. Alb.* I 279; **1237** in capellis..presentabunt domino archiepiscopo ydoneos capellanos perpetuos ad alteragia, ita tamen quod singula alteragia valeant x m. *CalCh* I 240; **1245** portiones ejus [sc. vicarii], viz. omnes minutas decimas et oblationes et ~ia *Reg. S. Thom. Dublin* p. 341; **s1248** vicarius de Landithwith habebit totum altalagium cum decimis majoribus et minoribus *Ann. Tewk.* 136; **c1250** alteragia dari ad firmam quibuscunque personis ..inhibemus *Conc. Syn.* 491; **1270** altellagium, id est provenciones ad altare, valet per annum x li. *Cart. Glast.* I 61; **1281** percipiet omnes decimas et oblaciones ad alteragium ecclesie quoquo modo pertinentes *Reg. Ebor.* 34; **1285** altilagium ecclesie *Reg. Exon.* 339; **1294** nichil adhuc percepit de ecclesia sua..nisi tantummodo alteragium, quod vix sufficit ad sustentacionem deserviencium in ecclesia *Reg. Carl.* I 9; **1328** oblaciones et obvenciones utriusque alteragii, tam ecclesie quam capelle *Lit. Cant.* I 266; **c1520** capellani capellanias seu ~ia habentes *Conc. Scot.* I cclxxxviii.

altaraxacon [Ar. *al-ṭarakhshaqūn* < Pers. *talkh-chakūk*; cf. taraxacon], chicory, sowthistle, or other plant.

endivia hortulana et silvestris, que crescit in locis non altis sicut ~on, i. rostrum porcinum vel cicorea GAD. 73 v. 1; alterasecon, i. rostrum porcinum vel endivia silvestris quod idem est *Ib.* 71. 1; ~on i. rostrum porcinum; endivia silvestris idem *SB* 10; rostrum porcinum..A. *sowethistel*..vocatur ataraxacon secundum Gaddesden *Alph.* 155.

1 altare [LL], to lift, exalt.

~ato..sceptri in vertice celydro ALDH. *Ep.* 3 (cf. W. MALM. *GP* V 214); **1331** nescit..qui humilia respicit..propter se taliter inclinatos talariter non ~are *Reg. Exon.* II f. 76b.

2 altare [CL], altar: **a** (pagan); **b** (Jewish).

a illud ~e quod gentes construxerant atque sanctificaverant non emundaverunt sed..destruxerunt G. CRISPIN *Simon.* 115. **b** torridus altaris ni sumtus forcipe carbo / ..

emundet spurca labella Aldh. *VirgV* 76 (cf. *Is.* vi 6); Noe.. edificato ~i obtulit holocaustum Domino R. Niger 3 (cf. *Gen.* viii 20).

2 altar (Christian). **b** (w. *magnum*, etc.) high altar (for use on festivals). **c** (w. *portatile, etc.*) portable altar, altar-slab. **d** revenue of altar (*cf. altaragium*). **e** (used for) church.

pallia.. / quae sunt altaris sacri velamina pulchra Aldh. *CE* 3. 71; evasit ignem ~e quia lapideum erat Bede *HE* II 14; c**750** utrum talis ministerium sacri ~is impleat Bonif. *Ep.* 91; altar vel ara, *weofod* Ælf. *Gl.*; sacerdotibus cum ministris ~is benedicta aqua sacra ~ia lavantibus *ReguIC* 40; hoc manerium..donavit aecclesiae per unum textum positum super ~e quia *DB* I 177b; s**1120** si [papa] duo ~ia in ecclesia una consecraturus erat, alterum illi..consecrare precipiebat H. Cantor 20 v.; ut ea ipsa die, qua quisque militari cingulo decoratur, ecclesiam solenniter adeat gladioque super ~e posito et oblato..seipsum obsequio ~is devoveat J. Sal. *Pol.* 602A (cf. P. Blois *Ep.* 94. 294B); **1222** provideant..archidiaconi ut lintheamina et alia ornamenta ~is sint..honesta *Conc. Syn.* 111; abbas.. accedat ad ~e thurificet illud et postea faciat inclinacionem devotam coram ~i et erigens se osculetur ~e *Cust. Cant.* 47; ~e super quod celebrandum est non debet esse terreum vel ligneum sed lapideum..; quod intellige de superiore tabula que dicitur mensa ~is, que omnino debet esse lapidea, quia ~ia que non lapidea chrismatis unccione non consecrantur J. Burgh *PO* VII f. 23v; **1392** capellano celebranti ad ~e S. Laurencii in ecclesia parochiali *ExchScot* 296; **1409** ornamenta pertinencia ad ~e annuale [*? for anniversaries*] sunt debilia *Fabr. York* 245; hoc ~e, *a nawtyr*, ..*a hawtere* WW. **b** c**1128** omnes oblationes que ad majus ~e ejus [ecclesie de Dunfermlin] offerentur *E. Ch. Scot* 74; jacuit..in lectica ..sancti viri corpus ante ~e ecclesie majus H. Bos. *Thom.* VI 15; a**1200** juxta cornu magni ~is *Chr. Rams.* 339; magnum ~e, quod prius concavum erat, ..et spacium illud quod erat inter feretrum et ~e solidari fecit lapide et cemento Brakelond 155v; **1229** nomen dedicantis et nomen sancti in cujus honore dedicata est ecclesia..scribantur circa majus ~e..; idem fiat circa minora ~ia *Conc. Syn.* 172; **1266** principale ~e *Reg. Aberd.* I 28; Godefridus [ob. 1321] dedit..unum frontale magnum cum mappa adjunctum..que magno ~i principalibus festis apponuntur Whittlesey 167; **1342** licet locus in quo majus ~e consistit cancellus dici debeat (*Vis. Totnes*) *EHR* XXVI 111; **1425** lego autentico ~i unam togam de panno aureo *Reg. Cant.* II 326; s**1387** cum tabulis deauratis summi ~is et ~is matutinalis [*morrow-mass altar for use on week-days*] *Ann. Bermondsey* 481; c**1520** cereis super summum ~e accensis *Conc. Scot.* I cclxxxiii. **c** a**1170** duo ~ia marmorea ad deferendum cum argento parata (*Invent.*) *Chr. Steph.* II 759; ~e portabile, cui lapis firmiter infixus tante quantitatis ut pedem calicis et pateram ample contineat Gir. *GE* I 10; **1315** ad..~ia portatilia consecranda *Reg. Heref.* 499; **1423** ut..supra ~e portatile missas celebrare..valeant (*Supplicatio*) Amund. I 155. **d** ecclesia de Withekirke est in dominio, preter ~e quod Paulinus sacerdos tenet pro iij m. *Rec. Templars* 127; **1337** tenementum..appropriatum.. ~i B. Marie *RScot* 492a; **1426** timetur quod plures retrahentur a solucione hujusmodi decimarum in maximam.. vicariorum, qui tantum ex ~i vivunt, ..depauperacionem *Reg. Cant.* III 143. **e** **12..** episcopus..condempnavit parochianos ~is S. Oswaldi ad claudendum..cimiterium *Cart. Chester* 117.

altaria v. altarium.

altariolum, small altar or altar-slab.

s**1235** [Fratres Minores] fabricato ex ligno altari superpositoque ~o lapideo benedicto secum allato missas clandestinas..celebrarunt M. Par. *Maj.* III 333; **1440** lego ..collegio..omnia vestimenta et ~a de capella mea ibidem *FormA* 433.

altarista, altar attendant.

c**1230** de pueris..chori et ~is quilibet habebit obolum *Ch. Sal.* 204; **1256** in die obitus mei..recipiet quilibet canonicus Sar' qui servicio interfuerit iij d.; ..et quilibet ~a j ob. *Reg. S. Osm.* I 393; **1310** computant..ij ~is juvantibus predictos presbiteros missas celebrare vj d. *Ac. Exec. Ep. Exon.* 23; **1319** consueverunt..~e..chorum cum vicariis frequentare *Stat. Sal.* 254 (cf. ib. 379n.); **1435** ..vicariis perpetuis, ~is, ceterisque presbiteris, clericis.. (*Lit. auditoris papalis*) Amund. I 381; **1448** ~e interiores *Fasti Sal.* 237n.; c**1520** vicarios perpetuos, porcionarios, pensionarios ac ~as capellanias..habentes *Conc. Scot.* I cclxxxv.

altarium, ~ia, altar. **b** revenue of altar. **c** (?) altar-slab. **d** (?) altar ornament.

s**1095** pontifex summus ad celebranda missarum solennia ..~io presentatur Eadmer *HN* 83; super Martinum.. adsistentem ~io Ben. Pet. *Mir. Thome* III 1; ecclesiastica beneficia..quorum possessores non palatio..sed..~io convenit deservire Ad. Eyns. *Hug.* III 9; **1587** duas rodas terre ..appunctuatas ad manutencionem ~ie *Pat* 1299 m. 22. **b** sicut qui ~io deserviunt ~io jure participantur Ad. Eyns. *Hug.* III 11; **1289** sub pena privacionis ~iorum suorum *Reg. S. Paul.* I 20; altari deservientes, cum ~io participantes R. Bury *Phil.* c. 4. 48. **c** instauramenta ecclesie sunt hec: ..vestibulum sive vestiarium, altare, ~ium Neckam *Ut.* 119; ~ium, A. *a superaltarye* WW. **d** tenor scripture ornamentorum et jocalium que Osmundus [ob. 1099] dedit ecclesie de Sar': ..quatuor ~ia argentea deaurata *Stat. Sal.* 34.

altarmus [Sp. Ar. *al-tarmus* < Ar. *al-turmus* < θέρμος], lupin (bot.).

†alcarinus, i. lupinus *SB* 10.

alte [CL], at or to a height. **b** (fig.). **c** deep (fig.). **d** (cut) close. **e** loudly. **f** at a high rate. **g** (w. *basse*) completely.

ut lapis..~ius ipso in loco reponeretur Bede *HE* III 8; adduxerat..equos dextrarios..ingredientes ~ius W. Fitzst. *Thom.* 119; ~ius elevati Gir. *TH* I 6; altea..laciora habet folia quam alia malva et alcius crescit *Alph.* 22. **b** perversitatis procella ~ius intumescat A. Tewk. *Ep.* 10; s**1162** quod ~ius in cor regis ascendit Diceto *YH* I 307; inter nobiles urbes..civitas Londonie..una est que..caput ~ius extollit W. Fitzst. *Thom. prol.* 2. **c** ut ~ius repetens ab origine pandam Aldh. *VirgP* 54; deliciosa minus alteque in scrinia mentis / digna venire parum Hanv. III 279. **d** clerici non nutriant longos capillos sed ~e tonsos Beleth *RDO* 39. 49. **e** tuba raucisonis reboat clangoribus alte Aldh. *VirgV* 372; pueri..primitus ~e legant et postea.. cantent Lanfr. *Const.* 87 (cf. ib. 106: canentes ~e); canere ~issime et serenissime W. Fitzst. *Thom.* 120. **f** **1381** petierunt..quod nulla acra terre que in bondagio vel servicio tenetur ~ius quam ad iiij d. haberetur (*Pat*) *Foed.* VII 317. **g** c**1170** illam villam..teneat..in perpetuum.. ~e et basse subtus terram et supra terram *E. Ch. Yorks* IV 52; **1256** stare ordinationi nostre ~e et basse *AncD* A 14261; **1304** submittendo se..diffinicioni nostre ~e et basse *Reg. Aberbr.* I 181.

altea v. althaea. altelagium, altellagium v. altaragium.

altellus, foreign.

aliene, straunger of a-noder lond, a[l]tellus, altella *PP*.

alter [CL], second. **b** doubled in length (mus.). **c** (fig.) a second (distinct but comparable). **d** (w. neg.) (no) second or other. **e** (w. *se*) accompanied by one other. **f** every other, alternate. **g** (w. *die*) the other day, a few days ago. **h** (w. *melior*) second best.

prior felix Rufina vocatur, / altera posterior florens aetate Secunda Aldh. *VirgV* 2281; tertio vel ~ero anno Bede *TR* 9; ~era [occasio] nec merito minus quam numero secunda Gir. *TH intr.* p. 4; fuerunt occisi tunc dominus J. S. miles.. cum dcc hominibus ~erius gradus *V. Ric. II* 181. **b** ultima brevis valet duo tempora et vocatur ~era brevis Haudlo 385b; longarum duplicium quedam sunt duplices longe que recte vocantur et quedam sunt duplices longe que ~ere nominantur Hauboys 410b; pars aliquota bis sumpta dicitur aliquota media vel ~era Hothby 329. **c** ecce Thomas noster, Joseph ~er, ..~er in spiritu et virtute Helyas H. Bos. *Thom.* III 6; Hibernia..quasi ~er orbis Gir. *TH* I 2. **d** **673** quod si quisquam propriam expulerit conjugem.., nulli ~eri copuletur (*Syn. Hertf.* 10) Bede *HE* IV 5; proco..quo non praestantior alter Aldh. *VirgV* 2066; gravidam me..reliquit nec est ~er qui juvenem istum genuerat M. Par. *Maj.* I 197. **e** ad hoc Robertus venerat ut..pene se ~ero vagaretur W. Malm. *GR* IV 389; **1215** mittimus ad vos Henricum de R. se ~um *Cl* 197b; **1257** Johanni de A. se solo..; Radulfo M. se ~ero..; Willelmo de F. se tercio *Cl* 140. **f** a**1300** debent habere unum tassatorem per ~erum annum in horeo domini abbatis in autumpno *Reg. S. Aug.* 119; **1434** quolibet ~ero anno dabunt..iiij virgas panni *Cl* 284 m. 1d. **g** **1170** venit ~era die usque Cadomum (*Ep.*) *Becket Mat.* VII 673. **h** **1279** habebunt a domino maneriі ~erum meliorem multonem *Hund.* II 722; **1285** habebit..j multon' alteram (*sic*) meliorem in falda domini *Cust. Suss.* II 19.

2 the other (of two). **b** (w. *unus*). **c** (repeated).

se..vitae ~erius ingressui paravit Bede *HE* IV 22; de his omnibus habet Willelmus medietatem et rex ~eram *DB* I 26; nec potuit..gesticulatio..exprimere quantum eorum uterque gauderet ex ~ero Devizes 29r; **1496** Jacobo †altri compotancium *ExchScot* 613 (cf. ib. 614: ~eri compotancium). **b** unus ut aethereos..campos, / alter sic herebum lustrat Aldh. *VirgV* 765; [cometarum] una diei, ~era noctis praecurrebat exortum Bede *HE* VII 23; harum unam habet episcopus, ..presbiter vero habet ~eram *DB* I 76; duas..insulas, unam majorem et ~eram minorem Gir. *TH* II 4. **c** quorum alter Cosmas, Damianus dicitur alter Aldh. *VirgV* 1079; postea emit ~er ab ~ero partem suam *DB* I 233; sunt duo..genera largorum: ~i prodigi, ~i liberales dicuntur W. Malm. *GR* IV 313; ~ero humero seipsum precedere videtur, ~ero sequi Neckam *NR* II 190; s**1312** ~er ~erius maritali federe conjungi affectavit Trokelowe 71.

3 either. **b** each (of two).

1240 si ~era dictarum Mabilie vel Angnetis in misericordiam..inciderit *KRMem* 18 r. 15; **1310** vel eorum ~eri qui diucius vixerit *Deeds Balliol* 145. **b** sic duo non duo sunt, sic alter vivit utrumque (? Serlo Wilt.) *Eur. Love Lyric* II 511; **1437** in denariis solutis J. W...et J. S.., ~eri eorum xij d., ij s. *Ac. Durh.* 624.

4 a (esp. gen.) other (not of two). **b** another person of the same name. **c** other (than), different.

a **673** ut nullus episcoporum se praeferat ~eri (*Syn. Hertf.*) Bede *HE* IV 5; prosit unusquisque ~eri arte sua Ælf. *Coll.* 100; navigium vertis litus ad alterius G. Amiens *Hast.* 47; stellarum coreas applicationesque unius ad ~eram J. Sal. *Pol.* 408d.; **1233** hominum ~erius religionis *BNB* II 568; **12..** melius forum dabit domino quam ~eri homini *Cust. Bleadon* 208; **1300** pro stranglino et polan et [milliario] cujuslibet ~erius nigri operis *MGL* II 94; **13..** nullus ~erius diocesis..admittatur ad celebrandum divina *Conc. Scot.* II 65; sic fuit hoc hydrae scissum caput; attamen altrum / illi succrevit J. Herd *Hist. IV Regum* 167. **b** c**1170** testibus hiis, Alano constabulario, Eudone ~erius [sc. Eudonis] filio *E. Ch. Yorks* IV 52. **c** alter et est hodie quam fuit orbis heri Nig. *SS* 2946; dicitur mixtio miscibilium ~erorum unio Peckham *Quaest.* II 15 p. 131; licet dominium Dei sit ~erius racionis a dominio humano Ockham *Pol.* II 641; aureus axis erat, nec temo fit alter ab auro Gower *VC* I 21.

alterabilis, alterable, changeable.

gratus est aulicis palpo vertibilis, / ad quorum volitum est alterabilis (*Palpo* 264) *Ps.*-Map 114; quattuor [sphere] existentes..~es, augmentabiles, generabiles et corruptibiles, utpote incomplete Gros. 56; non omne ~e est generabile Bacon *Maj.* II 446; cum dico '~e alteratur', exprimitur subjectum appropriatum *Ps.*- Ockham *Princ. Theol.* 63; erunt ibi corpora hominum ~ia ad infirmitates et ita forsitan alterata Bradw. *CD* 57A; et intelligencie sunt ~es alteracione communiter dicta, acquirendo..qualitates spirituales Wycl. *Log.* III 119.

alterabiliter, so as to be changeable.

si [Deus] illa [sc. mutabilia] cognosceret sicut homo ~er passibiliterque ab eis Bradw. *CD* 7D.

alteragium v. altaragium.

alterare [LL], to alter, change (trans.). **b** to make other, distinguish. **c** to double in length (mus.). **d** (?) to reverse. **e** (w. *habitus*) to become a monk.

res Anglorum ~ari cepit Herm. Arch. 23; Elfricus..in episcopum Cridiensem ~atus W. Malm *GP* V 254; s**1191** sumpsit habitum muliebrem, sed..incessum ~are non potuit quin vir..appareret Diceto *YH* II 101; [caliditas] vapores varios..~at in varias species Bart. Angl. IV 1; s**1224** cum a quamplurimis viris.., licet in multis ~atus fuisset, cognosceretur M. Par. *Maj.* III 90; si tantum de aqua ponatur quod ~etur vinum a suis naturalibus saporibus *Cust. Westm.* 216; quod..~et aquam cum melle Bacon IX 47; locus ligetur..cum fasciis latis..ne ab aere ~etur Gad. 125. 1; differencia est inter..~ari et ~atum esse Ockham *Pol.* II 602; pars illius mixti..recipit quotlibet qualitates secundas, et illud mixtum ~atur secundum partem Wycl. *Log.* III 127; alterat error eos Gower *VC* I 534; s**1428** ex hiis [ecclesiis] ~atis et transmutatis fortalicia..facta sunt *Plusc.* X 29. **b** **11..** alteritas sexus quos alterat, unio mentis / omniter unificans vix sinit esse duos (? Serlo Wilt.) *Eur. Love Lyric* II 511. **c** ultima..brevis valet duo tempora et vocatur altera brevis; que magis proprie potest dici brevis ~ata Haudlo 385; quelibet nota minor alia ~ari potest Hauboys 410b. **d** s**1235** corpus pontificalibus similiter adornatum, baculo ~ato..tumulavit *G. S. Alb.* I 305. **e** placet..ut benedictione percepta tonsorationis ~etur habitu religionis Herm. Arch. 37; [Elphegus] adolescens ~avit habitum W. Malm. *GP* II 76.

2 (pr. ppl. as sb. n.) cause of change. **b** alterative (med.).

si inter primum ~ans et ultimum ~atum fuerit medium Gros. 82; sic in alteracione cessante ~ante non statim cessat alteracio Duns *Metaph.* V ii 46A. **b** operandum est per contraria ~antia et infrigidantia Gilb. I 35 v. 2.

alterasecon v. altaraxacon.

alteratio, alteration, change. **b** doubling of length (mus.).

scientia Dei..~onis vices ignorat J. Sal. *Pol.* 445C; s**1191** cum se variata..assertione respondissent esse Genuenses..et supra ea ~one responsi cunctis ambigentibus *Itin. Ric.* II 42 p. 206; in qualitate ~o Bacon VII 7; sperma..mediantibus multis ~onibus materia est..hominis *Ps.*-Gros. 304; Duns *Metaph.* (v. alterare 2a); **1511** pro ~one mitri et baculi de nova cappa ij s. *Midlothian* p. 164; piscium..augmentationes, diminutiones et ~ones Robyns *Com.* 52. **b** alio modo assignatur ~o in semibrevibus ligatis Hauboys 431b.

alterative, by way of alteration.

non movetur a suis effectibus objective, et multo minus localiter, augmentative vel ~e Wycl. *Incarn.* 106.

alterativus, productive of change. **b** alterative (med.); *cf. alternativus a.*

est..fetor..nervorum infectivus et naturalis consistencie in innaturalem ~us Bart. Angl. XIX 38; virtus.. ~a omnes reliquas species motus circuit et sequitur *Ps.*-Gros. 595. **b** de medicina egritudinis ~a Gilb. I 35 v. 2; potest dari potus ~us et laxativus Gad. 6. 1.

altercari [CL], to dispute, fight. **b** (impers. pass.).

quatenus cum rege..alternis vicibus disputans ~aretur Aldh. *VirgP* 33; ~antibus de crucis susceptione fratribus Gir. *IK* II 4. **b** s**1226** cum hinc inde fuisset plurimum ~atum M. Par. *Maj.* III 106; s**1314** gladiis circa capita tinnientibus ~atum est Trokelowe 85.

altercatio [CL], dispute.

680 hujuscemodi ~onis opprobrium apostolica compescit buccina Aldh. *Ep.* 4 p. 482; s**1123** inter episcopos et monachos Cantuarie de eligendo archiepiscopo ~o grandis existit H. Cantor 26v; **1220** post multas et longas ~ones utraque pars..subjecit se..disposicioni..v virorum prudencium *Reg. Glasg.* I 97; **1358** habita super hoc aliqua altercassione inter vicecomitem et predictum D. *Cart. Glam.* 1296.

alteriagium v. altaragium.

alteritas, otherness, difference. **b** change, variation. **c** alternation.

Eur. Love Lyric II 511 (v. alterare b); Pitagoras et Aristoteles duo omnium principia dicebant, unitatem, id est Deum, et ~atem, id est naturam D. Morley 14; dixit [Alanus] quod in supercelesti..est unitas, in celesti, sc. in orbibus, ~as, id est diversitas, accidentalis Bacon VII 66. **b** videt sanitatem quam presensit; certioratur de ~ate de qua dubitavit W. Cant. *Mir. Thom.* III 20; recipit fomenta ciborum / alteritate fames, diversaque fercula gustus / invitant Hanv. II 264; aqueus liquor.., / obtusus, liquidus, †inundans [l. mundans], gravis alteritati, / parens diaphanus Neckam *DS* IV 234; omnes existencium essenciales substancie, ..immutabilitates, ~ates, similitudines, dissimilitudines Bradw. *CD* 173D. **c** [jejunium] aliud reperitur..~atis, ut sic dicam: ..alternationis esse dicitur jejunium cum quis alternatim jejunat, nimirum si cum hoc die abstinuerit sequenti comedat Beleth *RDO* 11. 25.

alteriusmodi [cf. alter 4a], of another sort.

1221 xiiij quarteria bladi tam frumenti quam ~i *PlCr Glouc* 26; anni ~i BACON VI 79; **1266** non teneatur ad ~i sectam in comitatu Sumerset' quam in aliis comitatibus *Cart. Glast.* I 101.

alternalis, successive, of one from another.

infinitum..malitiae dedecus et a summa defectus essentia nec sub ~i generatione producitur nec cert[o] multitudinis fine concluditur (*Quad. Dedic.*) *GAS* 529.

alternare [CL], to alternate (trans.), set or move or use alternately. **b** to occur in alternation. **c** to vary, alter (trans.). **d** (dep.) to interchange.

~antium, *staefnendra GlC* A 451; sus.. / alternare nequit crasso sub gutture rumen ALDH. *VirgV* 2778; quamvis.. quidam..incensiones earum [sc. lunarum] medio diei et medio noctis..~ent BEDE *Temp.* 12; nemora quorum in saltibus et ~andis animalium pastibus gramina conveniunt G. MON. I 2; alternatque latus HANV. VI 340; **1201** actionis et contemplationis vices ~abat *Canon. G. Sempr.* 131v; **c1430** habentes..hanc..medelam duplicem; ..~are applicareque curetis ad morbos *Reg. Whet.* II 431. **b** spondeus isdem locis ~are cognoscitur ALDH. *Met.* 10 p. 88. **c** [damna] ~antur omnia, loco.., tempore.., persona (*Leg. Hen.*) *GAS* 586; **s1177** jurantibus..quod de corpore illo nihil retinerent sed idem corpus non ~atum redderent *G. Hen. II* I 179; **c1365** temporis nostri dispendium considerantes, in majoris profectus compendium ~antes *FormOx* 367. **d** *to entyrchaunge*, ~or *CathA*.

alternatim, alternately, in turn. **b** successively. **c** mutually. **d** (of seals) interchangeably (OF *entrechangeablement*; *cf. AncD* A 2133).

arsis et thesis quibus discriminibus ~im temporum particulas sequestrant? ALDH. *PR* 139; **s1100** lectis ~im lectionibus Grece et Latine W. MALM. *GR* IV 379; fidicinem previum habens, et precentorem cantilene notulis ~im in fidicula respondentem GIR. *IK* I 4; **1219** R. debuit semel ecclesiam illam dare et N. alias, et ita ~im *CurR* VIII 100; **s1228** ita..ut deinceps episcopos ~im eligant, monachi primum et canonici..alterum M. PAR. *Min.* II 300; **1265** de quibus novem tres ~im seu vicissim..sint presentes *MGL* II 663; processiones ordinare..et eos qui non ordinate incedunt corrigere et ~im disponere *Obs. Barnwell* 60; **1451** assignetur hebdomadarius, qui missam ~im pro vivis et mortuis celebret *Mon. Francisc.* II 116. **b** hoc modo decupla scematum species ~im inserta supputatur ALDH. *Met.* 10 p. 85; in parte Israelita Ochozias, Joram, Jehu ~im subito discesserunt *Eul. Hist.* I 48. **c** cum ~im confabularentur ALDH. *VirgP* 42; ~im concitant iras; arma movent ÆTHELW. IV 2; eis ~im verum de se testantibus (*Leg. Hen.*) *GAS* 571; discurrentibus nunciis ~im pax stabilitur DICETO *Abbr. Norm.* 246; [gaudium et molestia] sese ~im magnificantes GROS. *Ep.* 76 p. 246; hanc consideracionem inter se ~im habere debent *Cust. Westm.* 118; priusquam ad mutua eorum cordium voluntaria declaranda ~im confabularentur FAVENT 12. **d** **1226** ut hec concordia rata permaneat in perpetuum, dicte partes ~im huic scripto sigilla sua apposuerunt *Reg. Dunferm.* p. 136; **1265** utraque pars..scripto sigillum ~im apposuit *Cl* 98; **1273** partes ~im huic scripto cyrographato sigilla sua apposuerunt *Rec. Leic.* I 60; **1317** sigilla parcium ~im sunt appensa *DLCart. Misc.* II 251; **1449** per cedulam inter eos indentatam et eorum sigillis ~im sigillatam *Test. Ebor.* II 150; *entirchawngeably*, ..*sunderly*, ~im *CathA*.

alternatio [CL], alternation, interchange. **b** (?) vicissitude.

per revolventem dierum ~onem ALDH. *Met.* 2 p. 68; reciproca duarum sillabarum ~one variantur *Id. PR* 141; **s1158** qui cum admirabili omnibus dilectione et dilectionis ~one simul comedissent TORIGNI *Cont. Bec.* 319; sanctorum monitus vocat alternatio psalmi GARL. *Myst. Eccl.* 204; loca ..quedam in estate nostra projiciunt umbram in austrum, ..in hyeme nostra..ad aquilonem..; et hec ~o umbre fit per senos menses BACON *Maj.* I 306; **s1428** vendico ut conveniam cum predecessore meo habere [animalium fugaciones] annis singulis absque alio consorcio ~onis AMUND. I 256. **b** moveri ipsum [Deum] pie arbitrandum non secundum delationem aut alienationem aut ~onem aut conversionem ERIUG. *Per.* 523A; **c1430** mansuetudo, ..austeritas et discrecio sint vobis apothecarii materiamque ministrent in omni ~one vestra *Reg. Whet.* II 431.

2 (w. *sub*) alternatively, interchangeably. **b** (of seals) interchangeably.

1252 constituentes eosdem sub ~one conservatores treugarum (*Pat*) *RL* II 391; **1258** ponit loco suo E. et W. sub ~one in loquela *Cl* 287; **1285** ut assignetur unus vel duo sub ~one justiciarii *Conc. Syn.* 956; **1423** attornavit..loco suo J. ..et R. ..sub ~one (*Pat*) AMUND. I 124. **b** **1291** presentibus sigilla sua sub ~one apposuerunt *Deeds Newcastle* 73.

alternativus, (?) used alternately. **b** (sb. f.) agreement involving alternative choices.

in capite..†~a [? l. alterativa] ponantur..ut aqua decoctionis ro[sarum] viol[arum] et cortices papaveris GILB. III 152.2. **b** **1527** quod dicta ~a super matrimonio..Marie.. in personam..ducis..determinetur, hoc est ut inter eundem ..ducem..et..Mariam..matrimonium suo tempore sorciatur effectum (*DipDocE* 1112) *Foed.* XIV 204b.

alternus [CL], alternate. **b** alternating, interspersed. **c** mutual, reciprocal. **d** (pl.) both. **e** (abl. pl.) alternately.

dactilo et spondeo..~a interpositione variatis ALDH. *Met.* 10 p. 82; singulis diebus vel ~is W. CANT. *Mir. Thom.* II 52; dimittens a se fratrem, qui versibus ~is suppleverat hymnodiam *Ib.* VI 22; [priora et posteriora] sine lite licenter / alternas sedes capiunt VINSAUF *PN* 96; **s1428** vendicatis vos singulis ~is annis habere..omnium animalium fugaciones AMUND. I 256. **b** alternoque gelu sitientem submovet aestum HANV. IX 381; sapientis est proprium.. fastidiosa quelibet ~a delectatione distinguere GIR. *TH intr.* **c** **634** quoties..unianimam dilectionem quadam contemplatione ~is aspectibus repraesentat (*Lit. Papae*) BEDE *HE* II 18; ut disertissimi oratores..virginis ingenium ~o experire conflictu vererentur ALDH. *VirgP* 35 p. 278; virum..~e pacis federe sibi astrictum *G. Steph.* II 97 p. 126; litibus alternis quando bellantur amantes VINSAUF *PN* 880; eorum utrique qui ~as prosperitates ut fratres uterini.. ambierunt ELMH. *Hen. V* 90. **d** naribus alternis tenuis vix flabat anhelus ALCUIN *SSEbor.* 1142. **e** ~is, subauditur 'vicibus', ut modo †qui [? l. hoc], modo illud *GlC* A 477.

†altersandarei [Ar. < *al-barsiyāndārū*], (?) knotgrass (*Polygonum aviculare*) conf. w. teasel (*Dipsacus*); *cf. 2 asar.*

~ei, i. virga pastoris *SB* 10.

alteruter [CL], one or the other, either (incl.). **b** (excl.). **c** (n. w. *in*) in either direction.

11.. mortuus alteruter cogit utrumque mori (? SERLO WILT.) *Eur. Love Lyric* II 511; duorum..~trum eligamus GIR. *EH* I 15; super hoc..non multum trahimus ex ~tra parte funem *Chr. Wallingf.* 40. **b** **1201** ita ut caput in ~tram partem torquere non posset *Canon. G. Sempr.* 146v. **c** **c1170** respuit hec veri verus amoris honor; / nescit in †alterutrem [l. ~um] flecti (R. PARTES) *Speculum* XII 233.

2 each other, one another. **b** (adj.) each other's, each the other's.

701 hortamur vos..in omnibus Dei mandatis ~tros excitare (*Lit. Papae*) W. MALM. *GP* V 221; [audientes] coeperunt ~trum requirere quis esset ille BEDE *HE* V 19; ne sibi obessent ~tra ADEL. *QN* 70; **s1312** valedicentes se mutuo unus ~tri nunquam visurus digressi sunt ab ~tro *Flor. Hist.* III 151; reclinabantur in ~trum, in sanctum sanctus ELMH. *Cant.* IV 3. **b** **s1198** quod homines utriusque regis et mercatores per terras ~tras et nundinas..ire et redire..potuissent M. PAR. *Maj.* II 450; **c1235** hoc scriptum in modum cyrographi confectum sigillis mutuis hinc inde munitum penes partes ~tras est divisum *AncD* A 2156.

3 (acc. n. as adv.) mutually.

a786 mutuis ~trum solaciis (CYNEWULF) *Ep. Bonif.* 139; multis ~trum diu habitis internuntiis *Enc. Emmae* II 17; illis ~trum dissentione mutua concertantibus *G. Steph.* II 93; cohabitantibus Anglicis et Normannis et ~trum uxores ducentibus vel nubentibus *Dial. Scac.* I 10B.

alterutrare, to try alternately. **b** to alter.

c1212 alterutrare vices A. MEAUX *Susanna* 204. **b** **c1170** sint licet exuvie, facies, status alterutrata, / te tamen assidue mens, manus, os recolunt (R. PARTES) *Speculum* XII 227 (cf. ib. 228: talos alterutrat sortis iniqua manus).

alterutrim, mutually.

insidias et necem ~im moliri *G. Steph.* I 1; tabernaculum carnalis concupiscentie et virginalis castimonie..sibimet ~im contradicunt R. COLD. *Cuthb.* 8.

†alteterera [? misr. of Ar. *al-shinār*], (?) horehound (*Marrubium*).

~a, i. armoniacum *SB* 10.

althaea [ἀλθαία], marsh-mallow or hollyhock.

altea vel eviscus, *seomint* ÆLF. *Gl.*; **10..** arthea, *merscmealewe*, ..athee, *sæminte*, **12..** althea, i. *ymalve*, i. *holihoc* WW; emplastrum super pectinem ex radice altee cocta GILB. I 27 v. 1; mucillaginis altee et mucillaginis fenugreci partes convenientes GAD. 40 v. 1; bismalva, alta malva, altea idem, laciora habet folia quam alia malva et alcius crescit; A. *wymalue* vel *marshmalue Alph.* 22; altheam aliqui ebiscum sive ibiscum nominant, officinae malvam, bis malvam, nostrates *holy oke* TURNER *Herb.* A. iia.

althemen [Ar. *al-thaman*], total amount to be expended, orig. in commercial transactions (math.); *cf. almuthemen*.

quartus [numerus] ~en, id est per primum et secundum dinotus ROB. ANGL. *Alg.* 120. 24*n*.

althemisis v. anthemis.

altiboare, to proclaim aloud.

963 (12c) alme auctoritatis agiographa nos ~bohando corroborat dicens.. *CS* 1114.

alticordis v. altus 6c.

altiduplex, double, solemn (of church festivals).

in omni ~plici festo *Cust. Cant.* 74.

altilagium v. altaragium. altilia regia v. hastula.

1 altilis, ~e [CL], (fattened) fowl, capon (*v. et. vettonica*).

~is, avis dicitur †a volando [l. ab alendo] *GlC* A 418; ~e, *fedels* ÆLF. *Gl.*; **1189** eidem Ricardo pro custodia ~ium regis vj s. *Pipe* 204; altilis in thalamo nutrit natura lapillum NECKAM *DS* VI 181; ~es sive ~ia [*gl.*: *chapunz*] *Id. Ut.* 106; **1232** cepit..l ~ia pretii viij s. iiij d. *CurR* XIV 2187; **12..** consueverunt reddere.. ad Natale duo ~ia *Cart. Rams.* III 249; **1279** tenet j placiam et reddit per annum vj d. et ij ~es *Hund.* II 494; gentes ad arma comedunt altilia sua, ita ut vix ova eorum ipsis relinquantur FORTESCUE *LLA* 35; *polayle, bryddys or fowlys*, ~e *PP*; hoc †astile, *a capon*, ..~e, *a capun* WW.

altilis v. stylus.

altiloquus, eloquent. **b** boastful.

magnus et ~us poeta Lucanus M. PAR. *Min.* II 384; **s1179** [abbas Joachim] miraculose factus est subito de simplici et fere laico ~us theologus *Flor. Hist.* II 91. **b** **s1397** jactacio per militem Anglicum..hec fuit: ..quidam Anglicus miles ~us..dixit: .. *Extr. Chr. Scot.* 205.

altiorare [< altus], to raise, heighten.

1184 in muris circa motam..~andis *RScacNorm* I 110; **1299** in terra extra parietes ~anda pro pluvia jactanda a muris *MinAc* 1079/16 r. 2.

altipotentia, exalted power.

s1298 quis eum [W. Wallas] ordinavit..talia presumere contra magnificenciam et ~iam regis Anglie? *Plusc.* VIII 28.

altisonare, to sound loudly.

sic chorus altisonet quod musica consonet illi D. BEC. 171.

altisonus [CL], loud-sounding.

[tube] clangor ~us congrediendi signum cunctis indicat GIR. *TH* III 12; ab omnibus Deus..voce ~a collaudatur AD. EYNS. *Hug.* III 1; verbis altisonis GARL. *Tri. Eccl.* 91; vocibus altissonis *Plusc.* VI 36.

altithronus, throned on high. **b** (sb.) God.

altithronus quadrati conditor orbis ALDH. *VirgV* 1289; nullus ab altithroni comitatu segregat agni BEDE (*Hymn*) *HE* IV 18; **903** (10c) regnante..~i patris sobole *CS* 603. **b** filius Altithroni ALDH. *CE* 2. 25; **856** (12c) ~i favente clementia *CS* 491; **1445** unum de Altitroni astantibus septem principibus *Reg. Heref.* 267; **1452** summi ~i nomine *MunAcOx* 639.

altitonare [CL], to thunder aloud, bellow. **b** (pr. ppl. as sb.) God.

altitonare cave "*wesheil*" nisi precipiatur D. BEC. 944; Pragensium urget querela pastores, quam ~ant sub his verbis.. NETTER *DAF* II f. 146 v. 2. **b** **956** (12c) ~antis providentia..rector *CS* 963; formido sit Altitonantis D. BEC. 136; **1426** ad os Moysy fari dignabatur ~ans *Reg. Cant.* III 135.

altitudinalis, of height.

quarum posicionum radix est triplex †dynameter [l. dyameter] mundi sc. longitudinalis, latitudinalis et ~is WYCL. *Log.* III 44.

altitudo [CL], height. **b** altitude (astr.). **c** exalted rank or status. **d** high degree, extremity. **e** spiritual height.

priusquam ~o parietis esset consummata BEDE *HE* II 14; ~o ante et retro protenditur ERIUG. *Per.* 464B; edificia minaci ~ine murorum erecta W. MALM. *GP* III 117; **s1297** villa de Wincheleseia..super montem sita est prerupte ~inis TREVET 359; ab ~ine..castri usque deorsum ELMH. *Hen. V* 66; **1459** pro factura murorum..ad iiij ulnas..in ~ine *Ac. Durh.* 638. **b** **c1110** (v. almagrip); astrologia.. speculativa certificat numerum.. stellarum et magnitudines earum et ~ines a terra BACON *Tert.* 30; **1387** ~o meridiana cum gradu ascendentis in meridie (ELVEDEN *Cal.*) *SB* 5. **c** **1093** ~o illorum [regis et reginae].., divitiae illorum nec illos servaverunt nec cum illis abierunt ANSELM (*Ep.* 169) IV 47; destructionem..omnis ~inis et extollentie AD. SCOT. *TT* 618C. **d** ex paupertatis ~ine, quam vovent Fratres Minores, ipsis non licet pro temporalibus..litigare OCKHAM *Pol.* II 820. **e** qui in ~ine rectae actionis Domino assistere curavimus BEDE *Tab.* I 1; primitiva principia tanta ~ine.. omnem intellectum superantia ERIUG. *Per.* 555A; nec nomen essentiae mihi valet exprimere illud quod per singularem ~inem longe est supra omnia ANSELM (*Mon.* 65) I 76; **1285** novitates..citra xx annos in ~ines theologicas introducte PECKHAM *Ep.* 645 p. 901.

altivagus, wandering on high.

qua luna aetate kalendas / ..altivago rutulans transcurrit culmine caeli *Miss. R. Jum.* 35.

altor [CL], fosterfather, nourisher. **b** (fig.) teacher.

pater omnipotens, devotae virginis altor ALDH. *VirgV* 1761; ~or, *fostorfæder GlC* A 493; altor egentium WULF. *Swith. prol.* 267; animarum pastor et altor *Ib.* I 789. **b** cujus [Athanasii] ~or et dogmatista beatus Alexander.. extitisse memoratur ALDH. *VirgP* 32 p. 272; nec tamen Wigornensi sedi renuntiare permissus est, ne monachorum recens habitatio ~oris sui destitueretur fomento W. MALM. *GP* III 115 p. 249.

altrimodus [cf. alteriusmodi], of another sort.

cibarie [leges] gulam jugulant, sumptuarie ~am, ut ait Portunianus, luxuriam cohibent J. SAL. *Pol.* 731C.

1 altrinsecus [CL = *on the other side*], on both sides, at both ends. **b** mutually. **c** (of seals) interchangeably

~us, *on ba halfe GlC* A 435; ~us corrumpuntur, id est tam praepositio quam ceterae orationis partes ALDH. *Met.* 140 p. 194; **982** (13c) jugera ~us copulata adjacent *CD* 1278; **10..** ~us, *on twa healfa* WW; notare licet in pavimento.. lapides ~us..positos W. MALM. *GR* I 20; secus utrumque femur..caro..ita computruit ut duo ~us foramina apparerent AD. EYNS. *Hug.* IV 2; disponuntur acies ~us NECKAM *NR* II 184; **1377** utinam Christiani..non forent ista heresi.. ~us irretiti (WYCL. *Responsio*) *Ziz.* 270. **b** cum metrica leporis elegantia et rhetoricae disertitudinis eloquentia tantum ~us discrepent quantum.. ALDH. *VirgP* 60 p. 321. **c** **1249** partes resenti scripto cyrographato inter eas diviso sigilla sua ~us apposuerunt *Cart. Osney* II 113.

2 altrinsecus, (adj.) situated on both sides.

lamina media..cum suis limbis ~is WALLINGF. *Albion* 350.

altriplex, double-faced.

false, ..versipellis, ..~ex *CathA.*

altrix [CL], fostermother, nourisher (f.). **b** (fig.).

10.. ~ix, *festermodor* WW; ~ix reparatoris carnis meae, lactatrix Salvatoris ANSELM (*Or.* 7) II 19; ~ix militaris matrona prolis OSB. CLAR. *Ep.* 33 p. 118; altricis mentita fidem J. EXON. *BT* II 544. **b** altrix cunctorum quos mundus gestat ALDH. *Aen.* 1 (*Terra*) 1; Ermenburgis.. totius criminis altrix FRITH. 949.

altus [CL < alere], high, tall, extending upwards. **b** high, situated far up. **c** (sb. n.) height. **d** (w. *bassum*) entirety, completeness.

altos / belliger impugnans elefantes ALDH. *Aen.* 60. 5; murum..viii pedes latum et xii ~um BEDE *HE* I 12; lucem ..ad caelum usque ~am *Ib.* III 11; hic pinus graciles succingitur alta capillos HANV. IV 293; visum est..quod.. arbor staret ~issima usque ad sidera *Chr. Wallingf.* 13; sic opus in basso tenementum construit altum GOWER *VC* IV 857; **1442** abuttantes..super ~am ripam *Cl* 292 m. 4*d*.; **1495** pro custodia animalium in ~a silva tempore tempestatis *Ac. Durh.* 653; **1565** nullus..prefectus..in camisiis suis ~ioribus plicaturis..utetur *StatOx* 386. **b** [Judas] laqueo suspensus ab alto ALDH. *CE* 5. 8; altior, en, caelo rimor secreta Tonantis *Id. Aen.* 100 (*Creatura*) 21; dum caelum respicit altum FRITH. 1381; **a1250** totam terram..tam in sablone quam in ~a terra *Ch. Gilb.* 45; **1385** vina ~e patrie ducatus nostri (*RGasc*) *Foed.* VII 471a; **1464** iiij scabella pro ~a mensa *Feod. Durh.* 191. **c** his convexa poli merito lustrantibus alta ALDH. *VirgV* 1227; ad caeli se ~a subduxit BEDE *HE* IV 7; crispatus in altum / contrahitur nasus HANV. III 279 (cf. ib. nunc tollit in altius alas); candelam ita exstinctam..ut fumum copiosum in ~um porrigeret BEN. PET. *Mir. Thom.* III 1; ne in ~um tendens cadas ab ~o GIR. *TH* I 13; pōpulus alta petit NECKAM *DS* VIII 51; est mediatoris ortus signatus ab alto GARL. *Myst. Eccl.* 503; **1241** faciatis..cameram nostram in ~o depingi *Liberate* 15 m. 17; sit balneum edificatum in ~o et in loco ventoso BACON V 96; **1289** construere solaria et domos in ~o *RGasc* II 332; **1322** usque ad ~um de Yowberg' *Cl* 139 m. 2*d*. **d 1264** cum..nos de ~o et basso submiserimus (*AncC* XLVII 5) *RL* II 276; **s1265** de dicto ejus ad ~um et bassum firmando *Flor. Hist.* III 257; **1315** talliando ipsos ~o et basso pro voluntate sua *Year Bk. 8 Ed II* 160; **1427** promiserunt..quod in ~o et in basso starent..laudo *FormOx* 459.

2 deep. **b** (of the sea; *cf.* also 'high sea'). **c** (fig.) deep, profound, in the depths. **d** (sb. n.) depth, deep, high sea.

nec putei laticem spernendum ducimus altum ALDH. *VirgV* 218; ut..ablata exinde terra fossam ad mensuram staturae virilis ~am reddiderit BEDE *HE* III 9; puteus ~us xx pedum ab aqua sursum W. CANT. *Mir. Thom.* VI 136; fossata..~a nimis GIR. *TH* III 37; **1399** in medio ~i fili grossarum ripariarum *Pat* 351 m. 16. **b** alta pererrant / marmora FRITH. 357; **s1270** anchoraverunt in ~o mari plusquam uno milliario a terra W. GUISB. 206; **1325** felonice depredati fuerunt navem..in ~o mari (*CoramR*) *Law Merch.* II 99. **c** ceteris..~o sopore pressis BEDE *HE* II 12; ingenii..~ioris et magis exercitati BALSH. *AD* 36; dissimulatas diu injurias ~aque mente repostas vindicem ad animum revocantes GIR. *EH* I 1; **1239** angit nos ~iori mente turbatio (*Lit. Imp.*) M. PAR. *Maj.* III 549. **d** suspenso velo..in ~um maris descendere H. BOS. *Thom.* III 5; ventus..eos ad maris ~a propellebat R. COLD. *Cuthb.* 30; [tempestas] naves in ~um progredi compellebat *Ib.* 33; hoc ~um, A. *see* WW.

3 high (of price). **b** (sb. n.) high rate.

propter firmam quae nimis est ~a *DB* I 66b. **b 1294** non amercietur ad plus vel ~ius..nisi ad iij d. *BBC* (*Chesterfield*) 200.

4 extreme (of poverty).

habere aliqua in communi quoad proprietatem non derogat ~issime paupertati OCKHAM *Frat. Min.* 6; in ~issima paupertate ~issimas divicias sapiencie thesaurizatas invenimus R. BURY *Phil.* 8. 135; **14..** vivere in voluntaria et ~issima paupertate (*Concl. Lollard.*) *EHR* XXVI 747.

5 full, far advanced (of time).

ibi usque ad ~am primam expectes KNIGHTON I 22; **1412** cancellarius..valeat librariam, dummodo ~a die, cum sibi placuerit, visitare *StatOx* 219; **1486** quia ~a dies erat, continuavit..convocacionem usque ad..crastinum *Conc.* III 619.

6 a (w. *manus*) high, forceful, (compar.) upper. **b** haughty. **c** (w. *cor*) stout. **d** (w. *vox*) loud. **e** (sb. n.) loudness.

a c1400 antequam nos ~iorem manum in hac parte haberemus (*Lit. Oeni*) AD. USK 73; **c1430** quomodo..vult nos aliter..dimittere nisi in fortitudine manus ~e *Reg. Whet.* II 468. **b** Henricus..abstulit altos / Francigenis animos H. HUNT. (*Vers.*) *HA* VII 31; [humilitas] mitigat iratos, altos inclinat GARL. *Epith.* IX 221. **c** more majorum †alticordis [? l. ~i cordis], sed in re militari ineptus MAJOR VI 7. **d 1377** incipiebat archiepiscopus ~a voce ympnum 'Veni Creator Spiritus' (*Cl*) *Foed.* VII 159; **1503** psalmum 'de profundis' ~a et audibili voce dicet *FormA* 339. **e** elata in ~um voce BEDE *HE* III 9; hec omnia in silentio dicuntur; ..letaniam in ~o dicant LANFR. *Const.* 114.

7 high, important: **a** (of roads) main; **b** (of mass) solemn; **c** (of jurisdiction etc.) authoritative; **d** (of charge or offence) serious.

a a1216 versus ~um chyminum *Couch. Furness* II 451; **1271** fuerunt in pace..in ~o itinere domini regis *SelCCoron* 18; **1276** obstruxit unam ~am viam descendentem de regia via *Hund.* I 61; **1304** insultavit ipsum..in ~a strata ville *CourtRHales* 482; **1376** quandam vacuam placeam jacentem in ~o vico in parochia S. Martini Oxon' *Cart. Osney* III 3. **b 1377** usque summum altare ad ~am missam celebrandam accesserunt (*Cl*) *Foed.* VII 159; **c1530** nec ~am missam in diebus solemnibus quibus tenebaris per x annos celebrasti (*Vis. Leic.*) *EHR* IV 305. **c 1283** habeant bassam justiciam et eciam magnam sive ~am (*RGasc* II 206; **1313** cum.. jurisdiccionibus ~is et bassis (*RGasc*) *Foed.* III 372b; **1307** brevi de recto.., quod breve supremum est et ~ioris nature quam..aliud breve *Year Bk. 1 Ed. II* 3; **1281** non tenetur respondere [in hundredo], eo quod de eadem fuga inplacitavit eundem R. coram justiciariis, que est ~ior curia *Hund. Highworth* 190; **c1440** ~a Curia [Prioris] *Cant. Cath. Pri.* 90. **d** quodlibet appellum de felonia et seduccione sit de tam ~a natura quod.. *State Tri. Ed. I* 44; **1400** racione ~e prodicionis contra regiam majestatem nostram..perpetrate (*Pat*) *Foed.* VIII 163.

8 high in public esteem: **a** (of rank or person); **b** (of tenure); **c** (of reputation).

a s1141 consul Cestrensis, ..~iora se machinans H. HUNT. *HA* VIII 17; quanto ab ~iori gradu, tanto proniore casu in ima vitiorum lapsos GIR. *TH* I 22; **1232** ab ~ioris dignitatis gradu descensio GROS. *Ep.* 9; **s1460** alicui alteri, ~o vel basso, parvo vel magno *Reg. Whet.* I 358. **b c1186** habet per illam terram libertates de ~o socagio *Kal. Samson* 22. **c** alias..assecutus est famam ~ioris glorie W. MALM. *GP* II 88.

9 spiritually exalted, heavenly: **a** of virtue; **b** of thought; **c** of reward; **d** of God; **e** (superl. as sb. m.) God (bibl.).

a si aliquis diceret castitatem quam moniales..voverint non esse ~iorem castitate conjugii.. OCKHAM *Dial.* 433. **b** plus persuadebis ~iores in hac re rationes latere si aliquam [rationem] te videre monstraveris quam si..nullam ANSELM (*Cur Deus* II 16) II 117. **c** ~ioris praemii gloriam promereri BEDE *Cuthb.* 4; ut..duplicis honoris dignitatem vobis cumulet ~issima retributio AD. MARSH *Ep.* 86. **d** regi famularier alto ALDH. *VirgV* 2072; en Deus altus adit BEDE (*Hymn*) *HE* IV 18. **e** quum apud ~issimum fuerit refugium tuum A. TEWK. *Ep.* 10; **1196** obsequium..~issimo prestitum (*Lit. Archiep.*) DICETO *YH* II 147; **1242** cum nos constituerit ~issimus ecclesie defensorem *Cl* 435; **1410** cum spiritus vitales resignaverit ~issimo *StatOx* 210.

alubi v. alibi.

alucinari [CL], to be dazzled. **b** to be deluded.

ne oculis sideris fulgore percussis et ob id lippientibus et hallucinantibus certamen inirent BOECE 112. **b** foede hallucinantur qui putant brancam ursinam esse *bearefote* TURNER *Herb.* A ii.

alucinatio, daze, darkness.

a mirknes, †ablucinacio, lucis alienacio *CathA.*

alucium v. ablutium. aluctus, ~or, v. haliaëtus. alucurus v. calamaucus 2.

aludel, ~ellum [Ar. *al-uthāl*], aludel, vessel used for sublimation (alch.).

pone totum in vase ~el seu alembico ad sublimandum primo cum lento igne donec humiditas per foramen capitis vasis recedat CUTCL. *CL* 190; ut..in ~ello nullum sit foramen *Ib.*; ~el et alutel est vitrum sublimatorium *LC.*

aluma [OF *alum* < alumen], alum.

1226 querelam..de falsa ~a *Pat* 36; **1263** warenciavit et bullivit in ~a *Rec. Leic.* I 102; **1276** cum..emissent in Vasconia..lij balas ~e (*CoramR*) *Law Merch.* II 14.

alumen [CL], alum (incl. plume, roche and saccharine alum).

~en vel stipteria, *efne* ÆLF. *Gl.*; eris splendorem prebet alumen ei NECKAM *DS* VI 122; allumen Jammeni triplex vocatur: Jammenum, de pluma, Scagloli. aportatur..de Spania, est autem frigide nature et sicce, hoc bonitatis in se continens ut, si jungatur cum re rubea, facit ruborem acquirere in ea. ..allumen rubeum apportatur de Buzea [[? *Bougie, Algeria*]; depillatur autem ut allumen de pluma; istud autem a quibusdam philosophis allebrot rubeum appellatur. ..allumen de Maroc est pulvis subrufus acetositatem parvam in se continens. ..allumen zucharinum est albissime nature, acetositatem mordacem in se continens. .. allumen de rocco est in massa redactus (*sic*), acetositatem subtilem in se continens M. SCOT *Lumen* 254–6; sal alkali.. fit de herba salsifera..sive de allumine †gattivo [l. gattino] quod extrahitur de supradicta herba *Ib.* 242; accipe.. allumen naturale vel allumen Romanum, idem allumen zuccherinum, allumen de Castiglio, ..allumen de Tunixe, quod est rubeum et album et salsum (*Id. Alch.*) *Med. Sci.* 153; ~inis †scisci [l. scissi] GILB. VII 308 v. 2; **1261** quidam de rebellibus regis venire faciunt in Angliam armaturas in doliis cum ~ine et aliis mercandisis *Cl.* 489; **1267** de ij quintallis †alumpini [? alumpnii] et iij quar', v d. ob. *MinAc* 1031/20 r. 3; ~en..est..frequentius in colore album, et cum assatur distillat ab eo sicut salgemma; quoddam vero est longum scissibile argento simile, quoddam siccum et rotundum in corpore parum a priore †difficile, quoddam siccum petrosum declinans ad citrinitatem; suntque omnia facile †pulverinabilia et calida sicca, multum exsiccancia et constrictiva, preter tercium. est eciam quedam ejus species unctuosa, sicut Britannie, quod est multum cremabile, cujus quandam speciem dicunt esse naptam *Ps.*-GROS. 643; **1303** allumen nichil debet *EEC* 166 (= *Doc.Scot.* 459: †~inum); **1317** cum..emisset j balam ~inis de plume..compertum fuit in eadem bala argillum et terra mixta cum allumine (*St. Ives*) *LawMerch.* I 106; constipentur..cum modico ~inis de pluma GAD. 4 v. 2; recipe ~inis plume partes 5, ..~inis roche partem 1 *Ib.* 131. 2; de ~ine glaciali vel zuccarino fiat pulvis *Ib.* 126. 2; ~en Janem, ~en scissum, ~en de pluma idem; ~en rotundum, ~en zuccarinum idem *SB* 9; allumen Lapparis, i. allumen liquidum, de Lappario [*Lipari*] insula ablatum *Alph.* 94; ~en..est Jamenum, roccum, scissum, rotundum, zacharinum, de Belgamo, Genuensium nitrum, fossile, fusile, plumosum, liquidum, capillare, commune, placodes, ustum, Liparinum.. *LC.*

aluminator v. illuminator.

aluminosus, containing alum. **b** (?) clayey.

[liquores] quidam ex venis terre hauriuntur, ut aqua salmantina, †vitrosa [l. nitrosa], ~a BART. ANGL. XIX 49; ista que claudunt poros racione stipticitatis, ..sicut est balneum aque ~e GAD. 20. 1. **b** est..aratrum difficilis regiminis cum..in terra gipsea vel alumpniosa [*gl.*: lutosa] sit impressum NECKAM *Ut.* 112.

alumna [CL], foster-daughter, pupil, ward (f.). **b** (fig.).

~ae, *fostorbearn GlC* A 450; sorores monasticae, ~ae scholasticae ALDH. *VirgP* 60 p. 323; quoddam makementum maritagii inter quandam †alumpniam ipsius..H. et quendam G. *State Tri. Ed. I* 17. **b** ~am Spiritus Sancti GOSC. *Edith* 51; delicati aeris semper ~a et amica Venus GIR. *TH* I 37.

2 foster-mother, nurse, patroness. **b** (fig.).

s1118 Matildis regina..pauperum ~a..obiit *Croyl. Cont. A* 129. **b s1229** a nutrice philosophie et alumpna sapientie civitate Parisiaca recedentes clerici M. PAR. *Maj.* III 168; **s1455** quis..in tota etate sua [sc. regis] tenera suus verus.. fuerat alumpnus ac eciam alumpna nisi dux Gloucestrie? *Reg. Whet.* I 180.

alumnare, to nurse, nourish. **b** (fig.).

Zephyris ubi succuba tellus / veris alumnat opes HANV. IV 293; *to nuryche*, nutrire, ..alumpnare *CathA.* **b c1430** nec hanc recognoscimus esse matrem que lacte regularis discipline suos naturaliter non ~at *Reg. Whet.* II 401.

alumnaria, nurse or nursery.

a nurische or a nurische house, alumpnaria, nutricia *CathA.*

alumnatio, rearing, upbringing.

s1461 viri..militares de alumpnacione patrie borealis *Reg. Whet.* I 397.

alumnulus, nurseling (fig.), disciple.

convenit suis ~is gaudere *V. Osw.* 399; Socraticosque bibit Xenocratis alumnulus imbres HANV. VIII 368.

alumnus [CL], foster-son, *protégé*, ward. **b** (fig.). **c** disciple, pupil, student.

10.. alumpnus, *fostercild* WW; solum vero ~is et collactaneis, si quid habent amoris vel fidei, illud habent GIR. *TH* III 23; **1285** Poncetum filium nostrum..et vestrum armigerum et alumpnum (*AncC* XIX 121) *RGasc* III 445*n*.; **1295** lego L. camerario et alumpno meo (*Test.*) *EHR* XV 526; **s1359** dominus R. de S., quondam alumpnus domini regis primogeniti J. READING 171b; **c1430** cum..tenear.. pupillis succurrere, ..rogo ut id quod noster attornatus in vestrum alumpnum exercuerit..non displiceat *Reg. Whet.* II 424. **b** infula terrenos nisi caeli comat alumnos ALDH. *VirgV* 2692; laudis alumpnus / Alcides J. EXON. *BT* I 64; **s1380** milites, Martis ~i *V. Ric. II* 19; **14..** ecclesia Scoticana..propriis eciam quos parturivit alumpnis spernitur *Cop. Pri. S. Andr.* 204; **1480** W. Wyntoniensis episcopus ..Christiane religionis alumpnos..intendens ampliare *Lit. Cant.* III 306. **c** egregius Christi regnantis alumnus ALDH. *CE* 4. 5. 10; Nicholaus spetialis ejus [Wlstani] ~us W. MALM. *GP* IV 147; **1324** de statu Edmundi..alumpni vestri *Lit. Cant.* I 126; **1337** nostre communitatis alumpnos *FormOx* 89; **1551** quemcumque voluerit academiae ~um *StatOx* 361.

2 foster-brother.

10.. ~us, *fosterbroþor* WW.

3 foster-father, nourisher, patron, sponsor.

~us, *fosterfæder* ÆLF. *Sup.*; a domini..accessu..suum ~um [olor] non mitius ceteris..propellebat AD. EYNS. *Hug.* III 7; **1428** studencium..quorum semper extitistis singularis alumpnus *EpAcOx* I 41; illo ~o qui puerum in Christo educandum suscepit COLET *Eccl. Hier.* 269.

alump- v. alimonia, alumin-, alumn-, illumin-.

†alunbes [? cf. palumbes], kind of bird.

aves cortis sunt hec: ..grues, fulice, ~es, mergites NECKAM *Ut.* 106.

alura [OF *aleure*; cf. alatura, aleia], 'alure': **a** rampart-walk; **b** covered passageway; **c** (?) aisle or gallery.

a 1188 pro ~is castelli de Norwico emendandis *Pipe* 54; **1215** ad turres civitatis [Winton']..gistandas et ~as faciendas *Cl* I 240a; **1240** fieri faciatis super eandem turrim [London'] in parte australi superius versus austrum unas ~as de bono et forti meremio et per totum bene plumbari, per quas gentes videre possint usque ad pedem ejusdem turris et ascendere et melius defendere *Liberate* 15 m. 20; **1243** fieri faciat gradus ligneos quibus eatur ad ~as muri mote *Cl* 24; **1266** barreras, kernellos, ~as [*Cal.* p. 663: †*alivas*] et defectus muri et fossati reparantes *Pat* 84 m. 20*d*.; **c1300** super muros..quasdam ~as fecit construi *Reg. Malm.* II 365 (cf. ib.: fecit..~as in circuitu capituli). **b s1438** fecit illam cameram solemnem que se protendit a capella dicta usque ad illam ~am que ducit a coquina AMUND. II 199 (cf. *Reg. Whet.* I 456). **c 1292** pro xvj fenestris factis de novo in superioribus alluris ecclesie *Sacr. Ely* II 9; **1329** de..xxij pedibus petre de Cadamo operat' pro *scutchtables* pro nova ~a; ..pro duobus hostiis in nova ~a pendendis (*Ac. capelle S. Steph.*) *KRAc* 467/6/1; **1331** pro novis ~is magne aule S. Thome faciendis *DC Cant. Ac. Thes.* II.

aluratio, fitting w. an 'alure'.

1343 in opere cementariorum..circa ~onem australis ale ecclesie *Ac. Durh.* 379.

aluta [CL], **~um,** (piece of) tawed leather.

1225 tria paria hosarum de †alluco [l. alluto] (*AncC* IV 169) *RL* I 263; **1252** alluta xvij duodene et viij pelles *DCCant* H f. 172; **1272** nec basanarius de opere alluti se intromittat *MGL* III 441 (cf. ib. 444: ~um..male courea-tum); unum par botarum de ~o feltr' *Obs. Barnwell* 196; **1343** xxiij pelles ~e non parate et ij pelles ~e parate *Ac. Durh.* 171; **1365** de albo ~o, ..nigro ~o *Pl. Mem. R. Lond.* II 46; alumen ibi [in Mari Mortuo] reperitur; est enim terra †que [l. qua] tingitur alluta, id est cordewan *Eul. Hist.* I 33; *cordwayne*, ~a *PP*.

1 alutare, to taw.

erant [ocree] pulcherrime omnium quas unquam videret et alotate W. CANT. *Mir. Thom.* II 39.

2 alutare [? < ad+lutum], (?) to defile, dirty.

14.. ~are, *to fyle* WW.

alutarius, tawyer, cordwainer, shoemaker.

in limine domus cujusdam ~ii W. CANT. *Mir. Thom.* III 37; **a1210** Osmundo allutario *AncD* A 2665; allutarii sunt qui faciunt calciamenta de alluta GARL. *Dict.* 125; allutarius ..quando..botas parat yemales *Cust. Westm.* 74; **s1267** parmentariis et ~iis *Leg. Ant. Lond.* 100; **1272** quod nullus allutarius de opere basani..se intromittat *MGL* III 441; **1294** Willelmi †allictarii *Ib.* 622 (= *Cal. Pat.* 106: allutarii); **1294** de J. R. pro officio †ablutarii exercendo *CourtRRams.* 207 (cf. ib. 200: J. R. est conreator corii); **s1278** a Johanne L. †alictario *Mon. Francisc.* I 500; **1352** nonnulli nostre civitatis Exonie inprudentes filii ludum noxium..in.. opprobrium allutariorum..in theatro..civitatis..publice peragere proponunt *Reg. Exon.* II 1120; **1442** ~io operanti duas pelles equinas pro campanis *Ac. Durh.* 410; *sowtare or cordynare*, sutor, allutarius *PP*.

alutoria, shoemakers' quarter.

1354 in schopa..in allutoria Oxon' *Cart. Osney* I 239.

alutum v. aluta.

alutus, tawed.

1304 quatuor balas corii ~i rubei *Cl* 196 m. 6.

aluvia v. allaium.

1 alva [OF *alve*], side-flap of saddle.

sagitta per partem illam selle que ~a vocatur usque in ipsum equum letaliter transpenetravit GIR. *IK* I 4; **1213** pro duabus bargis et una ~a et duabus contracingulis *Cl* 153b; **1220** ad carectam coquine nostre duo paria tractuum, ..unam bargiam, duas †almas [? l. alvias] *Ib.* 440b.

2 alva, ~us, part of water-mill (apparently smaller than the penstock; *cf.* 2 *algea* b, *alveus* 1e).

1209 in bordis emptis ad ~os faciendos et rotas molendini ..reparandas *Pipe Wint.* 54; **1211** in ~is ad rotam molendini *Pipe Wint.* 155 (cf. ib. 14: ad ~as faciendas); **1312** custus molendini..clavis ad ~as attachiandas *DCCant Ac. Bocking*; **1320** in maeremio empto pro exteriori rota de novo facienda, vj s. ij d.; in xx novis ~is emptis ad idem, vij d.; in clavis ligneis emptis pro eisdem ~is, ij d. *KRAc* 482/1 m. 4d.

alvea v. alveus.

alveare, ~ium [CL], beehive. **b** (fig.).

~ia, *hyfi GlC* A 460; examen..angusta ~ii vestibula.. egressum ALDH. *VirgP* 4; uti apes..in uno ~io *RegulC* 5; canistrum vel ~ium, *hyf* ÆLF. *Gl.*; **10..** allearii, *hyfe* WW; quasi frequentissima ex apium ~iis examina prodierunt *G. Steph.* I 62; ut fieret in monasterio quod fucus in ~io W. CANT. *Mir. Thom.* VI 9; **1304** de duabus lagenis mellis provenientibus de uno alvear' apum domini *MinAc W. Wales* I 312; capiatur sordicies ~is apium GAD. 29. 1. **b a690** oracula..in ~iis sofiae..servanda ALDH. *Ep.* 5 p. 491; quatenus..ceu prudentissima apis..in sui pectoris albeareo..virtutum favos construeret ALCUIN *WillP* 4.

alvederagi v. albederagi.

alveolus [CL], trough, basin. **b** river-bed, channel. **c** beehive (*cf. alveare*). **d** paunch.

alviolum, *aldaht GlC* A 439; **10..** ~um, *treg* WW; solum scopis, parapsidibus, ~is et aliis rusticanis utensilibus incumbentes rejiciebant W. CANT. *Mir. Thom.* III 1; [puer] rotatur in ~o ut nausea provocetur BEN. PET. *Mir. Thom.* IV 62; discoopertus est loculus stans super ligneum ~um BRAKELOND 154; **1351** Johanni Plumber..pro olla erea de bracina et alviolis plumbo furandis *Ac. Durh.* 552. **b** consimiliter dux noster progreditur versus eum, usque obviassent..in medio ~o dulcis aque ELMH. *Hen. V* 101; [Secana fluvius] intrat divisim sub muris per medium ville in una janua fluviali et duobus collateralibus ~is testudinatis *Ib.* 16. **c c1110** concessit..decimam (*sic*) ~um apum i. ruscam (*Lib. Alb. Windsor*) *EHR* XL 77. **d** *CathA* (v. 3 alvus a).

alveris v. alveus 1a. alverus v. alloverius.

alveus [CL], **~ea, ~eum,** trough, tub, basin (for cooking, brewing, etc.). **b** drinking trough. **c** fuller's trough. **d** cooling trough (in smithy). **e** mill trough, penstock (*cf.* 2 *algea* b, 2 *alva*).

aluuium, *meeli GlC* A 437; **10..** albium, *mele* WW; labra que etiam ~ea dicuntur BALSH. *Ut.* 51; **1233** recepit..tres ~eos prec' vj d. *Cl.* 191; **1270** unum plumbum prec' ij s., ij alwee prec' iiij d., duo cuvi prec' iiij d. *RCoron.* 1 r. 6; **1285** debet quelibet hida..facere j. cupham prec' xviij d. et j ~eum prec' viij d. *Cust. Suss.* II 36; lego..unum doleum cum uno cado et iiij ~eos *FormMan* 17; **1324** de..vij cumelinis, ij alpheis, j cista *MinAc* 1126/5 r. 1; **1338** concessit..bracinam.., j †alverim [? l. ~eum] de plumbo, xj kemelinos (*MSS St. Paul's*) *HMC Rep.* IX *app.* I p. 20b; **1345** in sarracione meremii pro quodam ~eo in coquina *Ac. Durh.* 41; *dow-trough*, ~eus *PP*; alvus, A. *a trowe*, ..hoc ~eum, A. *trogh* WW. **b 1292** fecit tres ~eos de quercu in.. parco *IMisc* 51/19; **1297** [carpentario] emendanti presepia longi stabuli et facienti stallos et ~eas pro pullanis ibidem *Ac. Cornw.* I 133. **c 1337** nullus eorum [fullonum] laboret in ~eo *Guild Cert.* 41/153 (cf. *EETS* XL 180). **d** ferrugo secundum quosdam est arena †relicto [? l. relicta] in fundo ~ei aque fabrorum *SB* 21. **e 1320** in j plaunck' empt' pro fundo ~ei aquatici *KRAc* 482/1 m. 5d.

2 river-bed, channel of watercourse. **b** eddy. **c** sea-bed. **d** channel (fig.). **e** (?) depth (fig.) or *f.l.* for *album* (*cf. albus 9f*).

~eus, *streamraad GlC* A 447; alveus ut Tiberis mersisset gurgite glauco ALDH. *VirgV* 2333; prope fluvium..qui tunc ..late ~eum suum, immo omnes ripas suas, transierat BEDE *HE* III 24; in ~eo lapideo aqueductus ad usus officinarum per mediam villam decurrebat RIC. HEX. *Pri. Hex.* 3; rivulus..non tam aquarum profunditate quam ~ei concavitate..non nisi certa per loca..transmeabilis GIR. *IK* I 6; **c1230** usque ad ~eum fossati super quem abbatia fundata est *Cart. Beaulieu* (*BMLoan*) f. 1; si quis..aliquid fecerit..per quod ~eum fluminis mutetur *Fleta* 271; **1384** per quod brek' cursus ejusdem aque totaliter defluebat, †alvo ipsius aque ducente ad molendina omnino sicco *Doc. Leeds* 115; dux Burgundie cepit passim prosilire ultra crepidinem arentis ~ei ELMH. *Hen. V* 101. **b** ~eum, *eduaelle GlC* A 490. **c** ut..aestus oceani..tot aeque vicibus suum relabatur in ~eum BEDE *TR* 29; arbores ille sunt in †compidine [l. crepidine] †alnei [l. alvei] marini BACON *Min.* 387. **d** per doctrine..~eos hoc..dirivasse OCKHAM *Err. Papae* 963. **e 804** quatenus illius nomen in †~eo fraternae dilectionis transcribere jubeatis ALCUIN *Ep.* 269.

3 boat.

1233 omnes batellos et ~eos..de aqua Sabrine quos.. venire fecit usque Glouc'..libere descendere permittat et ascendere cum victualibus *Cl* 546; **1299** de viij s. de piscaria cum ~eis hoc anno *MinAc* 978/19; **1325** in bordis sarrandis pro j ~eo ad piscandum faciendo *MinAc Wint.* (*Michelmersh*).

alviolum, ~us, v. alveolus.

1 alvus v. 2 alva. 2 alvus v. alveus 2a.

3 alvus [CL], belly, bowels. **b** womb.

~us, *rif* ve *lseo inre wamb* ÆLF. *Gl.*; per ~i, quo ciborum digestiones continentur, medium R. COLD. *Cuthb.* 128; radix ejus [lappe]..sistit ~um, sed folia adjecto sale solvunt BART. ANGL. XVII 93; *a wambe*, ..venter viri est, uterus feminae pregnantis, ~us de utroque dicitur, et ~us virginis est, alviolus ventricosus *CathA*. **b** ALDH. *VirgV* 418 (v. algescere b); en Deus altus adit venerandae virginis alvum BEDE (*Hymn*) *HE* IV 18; dum matris in ~o gestaretur GIR. *IK* II 7; nec effusum pregnanti porrigit alvo / curvatura sinum HANV. I 356.

alwea v. alveus 1a.

alyces [ἀλύκη], tossing about, convulsive movement.

†abicies, turba *GlC* A 62; oscitationes et alices superveniunt GILB. I 55 v. 1; de quo loquitur [Hippocrates] in expositione illius afforismi [vii 56] 'alices et oscitationes' BACON IX 60; **s1244** oscitans, tibias et brachia ad se attrahens, alices faciens et suspirans *Flor. Hist.* II 284; ossitacio et allices propter fumos exeuntes et aerem inficientes GAD. 42. 1.

alyera v. aliera.

alypias [ἀλυπιάς], daphne.

foliorum ozi[mi], alipiad[os].. GILB. VII 316. 1; allipiados, ang[e]lica, herba catholica, laureola idem, ..G. et A. *lauriole Alph.* 4.

alzubd [Ar. *al-zubd*], butter.

acub, i. butirum *SB* 9; acubd, alumbair, est butyrum crudum *LC*.

amabilis [CL], lovable, beloved. **b** (as forename) Amabel, Mabel. **c** (w. *dies*) love-day (*cf. amor* 5b).

occisus est Aelfuini..utrique provinciae ~is BEDE *HE* IV 19; **9..** deliciosa, i. ~ior, leta, *epgeorn* vel *estful* WW; ~is et laudabilis est omnis qui studet bonus esse ANSELM (*Ep.* 189) IV 75; **s1244** vir bonus, ab omnibus ~is *Flor. Hist.* II 281; **1390** ~ium Deo patrum..cardinalium *FormOx* 191. **b 1221** Amabilem uxorem Gileberti de Aivill' *CurR* X 43. **c 1410** ad equitandum cum eo..pro querelis suis manutenendis sub colore tractandi et dies ~es tenendi in eisdem querelis *CoramR* 596 r. 76.

amabiliter, affectionately.

placuit..ipsum [librum] Philobiblon ~er nuncupare R. BURY *Phil. prol.* 13.

amachel, v. almachor. amadrias v. hamadryas.

amaisiamentum [OF *amasement*], perpetual rent.

c1160 alodium Rogeri de B. in quo sita est domus sua cum toto amaisiamento suo *Act. Hen. II* I 271.

amal- v. et. esmal-.

amalgama [Ar. *al-mulgham*; cf. μάλαγμα], amalgam (alch.).

aliqui hic graviter errant operando, qui solvunt ~a nostrum in aqua forti CUTCL. *CL* 195; ~a est impastatio.. metalli cum argento vivo *LC*.

amamen, love. **b** love-gift.

palpo mobilior quam verna flamina / ..hac arte principum emit amamina *Ps.-*MAP (*Palpo* 526) 122; *a lufe*, ..amacio, ~en, amor *CathA*. **b** *yyfte yove to a dere frend*, ~en *PP*.

amanda [OF *amende*; cf. alemanda, amygdala], almond.

1157 pro pipere et cumino et canella et ~is ad opus regine *Pipe* 175.

amandare [CL = *to send away*], to commend.

~at, commendat *GlC* A 541.

amanēre, to stay outside.

~et, extra manet *GlC* A 552.

1 amans [OF *aimant*; cf. adamas, diamas], **a** (?) lodestone. **b** diamond.

a sicut intenditur..virtus ferri appropinquantis ad amantem [? l. adamantem] BACON XIII 179. **b 1272** firmaculum cum duobus amantibus de eodem thesauro (*Pat*) *Foed.* I 879a.

2 amans v. amare.

amanter, lovingly.

quam consolari ceperat..~er excolit MAP *NC* III 2 p. 118; **c1239** castigationem..~er et obedienter suscipere et tanto ~ius et obedientius a patribus spiritualibus quam a carnalibus quanto.. GROS. *Ep.* 127 p. 405; **s858** ipsa.. quendam magistrum ~issime diligebat *Eul. Hist.* I 243.

amantilla [cf. It. *amantilla*], valerian (bot.).

~a, †portentilla, marturella, fu, valariana idem, G. (et A.) *valeriane Alph.* 8.

amantivitas [cf. amativus], ability to love.

cum..anima Christi videatur creatura entitatis finite, quare et capacitatis, intellectivitatis, ~atis et cujuslibet virtutis finite respectu cujuslibet habitus et actus creati sive creabilis BRADW. *CD* 463c.

amaracinus [ἀμαράκινος], of marjoram.

oleum †amarissimum [l. ~icinum], i. de succo majorane *Alph.* 128.

amaracus, ~a, ~ium [ἀμάρακος], **a** marjoram. **b** mayweed (feverfew) or stinking camomile.

a 10.. ~ium, †*sealscyn* [l. *sealfcyn*] WW; virginibus gratam dat mollis amārācus umbram NECKAM *DS* VII 367; ~us, majorana, ..colimbrum idem; ..inter omnes herbas †major est odorifera (G. et A. *majorane*) *Alph.* 7. **b 1283** in amerok' extra frumentum extrahend' *MinAc* 840/3; **1312** in amaroco et walrith' extrahendis de frumento *Ib.* 843/3 (cf. 843/5: amaroca); **1296** in amaruc' extirpand' per manus *DL MinAc* 1/1 r. 5 (cf. r. 6: amarusc'); amarusca, ameroke idem; i. *maythe SB* 10; moreclium, amarusca idem, A. *maythe Alph.* 119; fetida, id est amarusca *Ib.* 64; *crowysfote*, amarusca vel amarusca emeroydarum, ..*maydewode*, amarusca *PP*; amarusa, A. *a mathge*, ..*doufinkylle* WW.

amarallus v. admirallus.

amarantus [ἀμάραντος], amaranth (bot.).

crisogon vel crisantum vel ~um, virga ejus est alba recta, folia habens angusta in circuitu sicut abrothanum *Alph.* 42.

amarauda v. esmeraldus.

1 amare [CL], to love (persons). **b** (sexually). **c** (spiritually). **d** (refl.).

qui noverant eam religiosi..sedulo eam visitare, obnixe amare, diligenter erudire solebant BEDE *HE* IV 21 p. 253; cum..ita se modeste..gereret ut merito a majoribus quas unus ex ipsis amaretur, veneraretur, amplecteretur *Ib.* V 19 p. 322; amare motus quidam agentis est, amari vero patientis ERIUG. *Per.* 467BC; si vos multum non amarem, multum vos increparem ANSELM (*Ep.* 237) IV 145; hic fratrem, ille filium carnaliter amantes H. CANTOR 7v. **b** unus homo Wihenoc amavit quandam feminam..et duxit eam *DB* II 232; amasti amantem te..Alanum? ANSELM (*Ep.* 169) IV 47; binas amō, ducere conor / unam, vel neutram; nec mihi constat utram SERLO WILT. 8. 1; **1201** ipsa dixit quod ipse tam per minas quam per..pulcrum loqui tantum fecit quod ipsa eum amavit et ipse illam *CurR* I 389. **c** cum..ipse [Deus] omnem naturam se vere amantem amet ANSELM (*Mon.* 69) I 79; sic sic amans ut nequeat enarrari, / divino cor nostrum amore succendas J. HOWD. *Cant.* 713; totam intencionem nostram constituamus Deo obedire, Deo servire, Deum amare ROLLE *IA* 227; **1397** est nichil hic certum preter amare Deum GOWER *VP* 287. **d** inter tot..se amantes et voluptatum suarum amatores H. BOS. *Thom.* III 7.

2 to love (animals).

[Willelmus I] amavit feras tanquam pater esset earum H. HUNT. *HA* VI 39.

3 a to love, desire (possessions or experiences). **b** to love, esteem (places, institutions, qualities or sim). **c** (w. inf.).

a ut nequeam prorsus quicquam carnalis amare ALDH. *VirgV* 1725; nil hujus mundi quaerere, nil amare curabat BEDE *HE* III 5; ad caelestia, quae semper amabam ac desiderabam, praemia *Ib.* IV 3; qui haec [divitias, potestates, voluptates] amat saepe facit aliquid contra Deum et contra proximum ANSELM (*Ep.* 112) III 246; **s1135** rex..semper eas [murenas] amabat H. HUNT. *HA* VII 43; ut super omnes potiones medonem amaret *Chr. Wallingf.* 41; si nummorum summas..amassemus R. BURY *Phil.* 8. 123. **b** Eoas partes amo ALDH. *Aen.* 81 (*Lucifer*) 4; †**597** non pro locis res sed pro bonis rebus loca amanda sunt (*Lit. Papae*) BEDE *HE* I 27 p. 49; qui catholicas ecclesiae regulas sequi semper et amare didicerat *Ib.* V 19 p. 325; haec in [Aidan] multum complector et amo *Ib.* III 5. **c** interemptorum spolia diripere amant W. POIT. I 44; mesta senectus / atra veste tegi nuncia mortis amat NECKAM *DS* II 333.

4 (pr. ppl.): **a** (adj.) enamoured, devoted; **b** (superl. in passive sense) beloved (*cf.* 6a *infra*); **c** (as sb.) lover.

a Deus omnipotens famulam protexit amantem ALDH. *VirgV* 2107; nullus ea tempestate justior erat aut amantior equi G. MON. III 16 (= *Eul. Hist.* II 245: justior aut omnibus amantior). **b** amantissime fili mi ALDH. *Met.* 5; juvenis amantissimae..venustatis BEDE *HE* V 19; domino amantissimo W. MALM. *HN prol.*; **s1260** vir..universis et singulis amantissimus *Flor. Hist.* II 442; amantissimas divine legis sentencias exestuans *NLA* (*J. Bridl.*) II 70. **c** si queris quis amet, sum tibi verus amans GIR. *Symb. Metr.* 8. 28; est secretus amor furor intestinus amantum D. BEC. 2441; decentissime ipse amatur qui omnia in se continet que querenda sunt ab amante ROLLE *IA* 269.

5 (p. ppl.) beloved. **b** (as sb. m. or f.).

tu es antistes meus amatus BEDE *HE* V 6; mi amatissime magister AD. MARSH *Ep.* 105. **b** amans ad limen amate / ocius igne volat HANV. III 284; amantem et amatum simul esse manifestum est GROS. *Ep.* 2 p. 18; electus ad amorem omnino solum Christum optans seque in amatum transformans ROLLE *IA* 235.

6 (gdv.) beloved. **b** (as forename).

sospes soboles vobis comitatur amanda ALDH. *VirgV* 1488; **c1430** vestre..amandissime..paternitati *Reg. Whet.* II 381. **b** **a1200** Amandus Pincerna *CurR* I 5.

amarē, bitterly (fig.), sorrowfully.

~issime flere OSB. *Mir. Dunst.* 19 p. 148; flens ~e MAP *NC* III 2 p. 114; **1347** animarum ~ius plangenda pericula que..guerre..producunt (*Lit. Papae*) AVESB. 111.

amarefactus, embittered (fig.).

s1198 monachi ~i..famam archiepiscopi..denigrarunt M. PAR. *Min.* II 69.

amarellus [cf. Germ. *Ammer*], bird, (?) yellowhammer.

14.. volatilia sana: perdix, frigellus, parex, tremulus, amarellus [gl.: *cobart*] (*Diet.*) *EETS* XXXII ii 56.

amarescere, to become bitter. **b** (fig.).

mellis amarescit dulcor H. CANTOR *Vers.* 222; ~unt gustui mel et manna R. BURY *Phil.* 1. 14; aque statim ~unt et fetent *Eul. Hist.* II 129. **b** omnia mundi dulcia.. ~unt J. SAL. *Pol.* 386A; in vestro amore ~itis AD. SCOT *TT* 815C.

†amariis, (?) *l. amarus* (*cf. Psalm* ciii 7; *Eccles.* vii 27).

exultet Anglia Christo, cum suis sicatricibus et squalorosis reliquiis nostris †~iis laqueus contritus est FAVENT 24.

amaricare [bibl.], to make bitter. **b** (fig.) to embitter (w. anger or grief). **c** to be embittered.

continua salsedine fluvius influens ~atur GIR. *TH* II 2; ~atur os GILB. VII 311 v. 1; vitis amara nimis quam primus amaricat hostis GARL. *Tri. Eccl.* 79. **b** invidia..excitati contra suum abbatem, in tantum ~ati sunt ut..dominum suum..proderent ASSER *Alf.* 96; **s1087** cum raperet suis sua .., in intimis cordium ~abantur et tabescebant H. HUNT. *HA* VI 39; **1120** non audeo..cor vestrum in nos ~are (*Lit. archiep.*) EADMER *HN* 332; **s1191** licet..fuerimus ..exacerbati, cum oblationes sepulture redierint.., ~atum animum nostrum dulcorabunt GERV. CANT. I 83; **1222** nolentes hujusmodi vexationibus eorum Sabbati ~ari quietem (*Lit. Papae*) *Reg. Newbattle* 243; **1297** nostra ex hoc †amaritantur intrinseca *Reg. Cant.* I 177; **1424** contra consilium Achitophel volentis dulcedinem ~asse in odium BEKYNTON I 280; **c1430** ~atam doloris materiam quam intus geritis in visceribus *Reg. Whet.* II 425. **c** **1198** magis ac magis dolorum ~ante et accrescente cumulo *Ep. Cant.* 492.

amaricatio, bitterness. **b** (fig.) anger or grief.

oris ~o GILB. II 90. 2; pomi mortis amaricatio J. HOWD. *Ph.* 273. **b** quoties sub voluptate aut ~one incitati.. pravitati acquiescimus PULL. *Sent.* 856A; **1188** puer delicate nutritus..laborum †amaritationes, dolorum symptomata penitus ignorat *Ep. Cant.* 207; **s1171** o infelix..coronatio, quam sequebatur..regni..perturbatio, prelatorum excommunicatio, summi pontificis ~o! M. PAR. *Min.* I 366; **1321** non sine cordis ~one *FormOx* 69.

amariorare, to embitter.

quis sermones meos maledice objurgationis ~aret absinthio? P. BLOIS *Ep.* 238. 541A.

amarissimus v. amaracinus. amarit- v. et. amaric-.

amaritudo [CL], bitterness. **b** (fig.) grief.

cum ~o..sit dulcis privatio, sic facit speciem saporis BACON XIV 83. **b** **982** (13c) aeternae dampnationis ~inibus involvatur *CD* 1278; volutare in gurgite ~inis, qui delectatus es in volutabro turpitudinis ANSELM (*Med.* 2) III 81; non sine magna mentium ~ine GIR. *EH* I 28; hec [mors] est sagitta ~inis toxicata que viscera mea transfixit S. SIM. *Itin.* 74; in multorum ~ine et lacrimis ELMH. *Hen. V* 27.

amaroca, ~us v. amaracus.

amarulentia, bitterness.

1517 Stygem arbitror non longe illinc abesse, ea est aquarum nigritudo et ~ia (C. TUNSTALL) *Ep. Erasmi* III 663.

amarus [CL], bitter. **b** (fig.). **c** (sb. n.) bitterness.

cortice vescor amara ALDH. *Aen.* 56 (*Castor*) 9; venenosas et ~as..taxos GIR. *TH* I 6; fructus mirabalanorum in principio sunt dulces, in medio sunt pontici et in fine ~i BACON XIV 80. **b** desperatio mentis / opprimit incautam obtentu rancoris amari ALDH. *VirgV* 2647; **a1190** ex hac vita mihi longo tempore ~a et tediosa *Canon. G. Sempr.* 100v; **1267** vere dicitur [B.V.M.] Stella Maris, ut nos dirigat ad portum salutis, et ~um mare, qui in omni..amaritudine temporali vixit in hoc mundo BACON *Maj.* I 93; **s1420** ~i doloris aculeis sauciatus ELMH. *Hen. V Cont.* 143. **c** quis ejus amarum ut mella propinat? J. HOWD. *Cant.* 297.

amarusca, ~usa v. amaracus. amasarca v. anasarca.

amascere, to fall in love.

inchoativa: ..~o, lavasco, gelasco ALDH. *PR* 124.

amasia, sweetheart, mistress.

miles..in gremio ~ie obdormivit GERV. TILB. II 12; **s1284** pro eodem facto..Alicia ~ia..Radulfi clerici fuit combusta *Ann. Lond.* 93; **1291** appellat H. de L. et E. ~iam suam de eadem roberia *SelCCoron* 130; cum juvenis quidam ..surrexisset ut crucem sumeret, ejus ~ia ipsum tenuit *NLA* (*Edmund. Ep.*) I 320; **s858** magister ille..~iam suam in veste virili semper tegebat *Eul. Hist.* I 243; *lemman, concubina*, ~ia *PP*.

amasius [CL], **~io, ~iunculus**, lover, minion.

quedam mulieres cereas sive luteas formant imagines, ut sic hostes vel ~ios torqueant et incendant P. BLOIS *Ep.* 65. 192A; **c1370** ex quo..impetu provenit amanti opprobrium, ~io [P. de Gavastone] obloquium..et regno detrimentum (J. BRIDL. *Gl.*) *Pol. Poems* I 133; *specyal concubyne, lemman*, ~ius *PP*; *a lechour*, ~io, ~ius, amaciunculus, ambro *CathA*.

amassare v. admassare. amatides v. amiantus.

amatio, love.

quod esset dicere spiritum in spiritu, ~onem in ~one ejusdem de eodem NETTER *DAF* II 98; *a lufe*, ..~o, amamen, amor *CathA*.

amatista v. amethystus.

amativus [cf. amantivitas], capable of love.

potencia ~a non potest excitari ad amorem nisi per cognicionem BACON III 299; erit..triplex perfectivum voluntatis create: ..id est principium cognitivum respectu veri; principium ~um respectu boni absoluti, jucundi scilicet ac voluptuosi; principium potestativum respectu boni ardui *Ps.*-GROS. 449; **1412** quicunque est..ecclesie servitivior et in amore Christi quoad suam ecclesiam ~ior, ille est in ecclesia militante major *Conc.* III 345.

amator [CL], lover (of persons), adherent, friend. **b** (sexual). **c** (spiritual).

Londoniarum civis.., regis et regni specialis ~or *V. Ric. II* 6; **1494** quod..pannarii et cissores..amodo..boni ~ores fuerint et invicem amicabiles *Doc. Bev.* 102. **b** quo devenit ille amatus ~or tuus? ANSELM (*Ep.* 169) IV 47; nil, quia nil habuit, pauper amator agit (? SERLO WILT.) *Eur. Love Lyric* 510; vincĭtur et semper graviter vincītur amator GIR. *Symb. Metr.* 3. **c** audiat quid..dicat..animarum ~or piissimus AD. MARSH *Ep.* 247 c. 9; amor in te prevaluit, o amator J. HOWD. *Cant.* 710; quod odit omnis sanctus Dei ~or ROLLE *IA* 251.

2 lover (of things, places or sim.).

lector libri solers et gnarus amator ALDH. *VirgV* 2773; rex ille caelestis regni ~or factus est BEDE *HE* III 18; **961** (13c) universa visibilia..ornamenta hujus cosmi cotidie ab ipsis ~oribus transeunt *CS* 1075; pacis ~or et auctor GIR. *TH* III 48; non sis auditor tantum legis sed amator D. *BEC.* 26; Bacchus..collis amator NECKAM *DS* VIII 23.

amatorie, in amorous style.

aliquando procedat herotice, quod est ~ie GARL. *Dict.* 133.

amatorius [CL], provocative of love, amorous. **b** (sb. n.) love-song.

virum suum interfecit..Lucilia poculo ~io P. BLOIS *Ep.* 79. 244C; **c1229** nec [moniales] auctores vel quoscumque versus ~os post susceptum religionis habitum publice legant vel privatim *Conc. Syn.* 153. **b** si videas graviores ~ia, que ab ipsis dicuntur elegantius stulticinia, personare J. SAL. *Pol.* 402C.

amatrix [CL], lover (f.): **a** (sexual); **b** (of something).

a mihi queque secundat amatrix, / que volo, que cupio, conjux que fallere nescit D. BEC. 1957. **b** effigies.. Veneris, stuprorum ~icis ALDH. *VirgP* 47; novitatis levitatis amatrix NIG. *Mir. BVM* 56. 1; novitatis ~ix mulier MAP *NC* III 4 p. 133; mulier..gule ~ix et petulantie M. PAR. *Maj.* I 381; divina pietas, que fraterne dileccionis est auctrix et ~ix *Cust. Cant.* 294.

amaubragium v. amobragium.

Amazo, Amazon (fig.), of the women of Toulouse.

ad flammas peltis armantur Amazones GARL. *Tri. Eccl.* 86.

Amazonicus, like that of an Amazon.

s752 fortissimi gladiis et securibus ~is rem agentes H. HUNT. *HA* IV 19.

†amazus, (?) *f.l.* for *amarus*.

o mira, miseranda et ~a vesania ELMH. *Hen. V* 4.

†amba [?], part of mill.

1232 in fusillo et in ~a molendini fract' per bis reparand', xx d. *Pipe Wint.* (159283) r. 11.

ambac- v. ambasc-.

†ambades, (?) *f.l.* for *anates* or *barnaces*.

utrum liceat vesci ~es in Quadragesima KNAPWELL *Quodl.* 28.

ambages [CL], out-of-the-way place, recess. **b** twist, winding. **c** tangle (fig.), complication.

ad remociores regni ~es..regem duxerunt FAVENT 4. **b** ~es, *ymbsuaepe GlC* A 522; cadaver prolixis fasciarum ~ibus conexum ALDH. *VirgP* 36 p. 283. **c** haec..tantis verborum ~ibus deprompsimus *Id. Met.* 4; mutatis ex tempore..intercalationum ~ibus cunctis BEDE *TR* 14; multiplicem ~em in certitudinem redigit ADEL. *ED* 21; ignotis sermonum ~ibus et intricatis quibusdam verborum involucris GIR. *EH intr.*; in amphiboliis et ~ibus ELMH. *Hen. V* 104.

ambagiosus, circuitous.

~us, circulosus *GlC* A 523.

ambanum [cf. OF *embanie*], (?) stall in front of house (Gasc.).

1276 ~a, perjecta et stillicidia domorum, fenestre et antefenestre, que sunt ante mercatum, sint libere burgensibus quibus fuerint..domus *RGasc* II 15; **1284** credit inbannum domus ponterii Baionensis diruere, que domus, c anni vel amplius sunt elapsi, sicut nunc est cum dicto inbanno hedificata extitit *AncC* XLVII 96; **1289** domorum, prejectorum, enbannorum, sedilium, stillicidiorum *RGasc* II 415; **1315** placee sive soli in quibus fient domus habeant ~a et perjecta et stillicidia contigua mercato; ..et tenebuntur dicta ~a et perjecta sub eisdem censu et sporla de quibus supradicitur *Ib.* IV 1626 (ii).

ambarata [? < barra], (?) suburbs (Gasc.).

1254 milites et burgenses dicti loci [*Genciac*] debent habere vendagium ple[i]durarum et domorum qui (*sic*) tenentur ab eis in burgo vel in ~is *RGasc* I 546 (= *CalPat* 357).

ambariam v. ambifariam.

ambascia [cf. OF *ambasse*], embassy.

s1420 convenit quod ex parte sua notabilis ~ia virorum nobilium versus..Carolum et ducem Burgundie mitteretur ELMH. *Hen. V Cont.* 134.

ambasciare, to send as ambassador.

pontifices clerus ambassiat Anglicus illuc [sc. Constanciam] ELMH. *Metr. Hen. V* 205 (cf. ib. 827).

ambasciata [cf. OF *ambassee*], embassy. **b** (fig.) mission.

1340 Romanam curiam..in ambassata nostra adveniens (*RRom.*) *Foed.* V 188b; **1388** inter cetera capitula sub eorum ambassiata contenta *Dip. Corr. Ric. II* no. 59; **1400** eidem Ade pro una alia ambaxiata per ipsum factam in regno Anglie *ExchScot* 487; **s1404** ad Bonefacium papam.. solempnis pro unione ecclesie venit ambassiata AD. USK 87; **1406** militi de terra Dacie venienti in ambaciatam pro maritagio.. (*KRAc* 406/10) *Arch.* LXVII 176; **s1425** missi sunt a rege Francorum in ambassada regi Scocie *Plusc.* XI 3; **s1433** una taxacio pro †ambassanda [v.l. ambassada] hujus contractus [matrimonii] *Ib.* XI 2; **s1459** ad communicandum..cum..prelatis et proceribus super ambassiata mittenda in Ytaliam *Reg. Whet.* I 323. **b** **1395** hec est nostra ambascata quam Christus precepit nobis prosequi (*Concl. Lollard.*) *Ziz.* 368.

ambasciatio, embassy.

1241 tres dicti legati..cum ambaxiationibus civitatum rebellium Lumbardie, qui ad prefixum ire concilium properabant (*Lit. Imp.*) M. PAR. *Maj.* IV 128.

ambasciator [cf. OF *ambasseor*], ambassador, envoy.

1297 ambassatores celebriores..non duximus destinandos *Reg. Cant.* I 531; **1318** accedentibus..ambassatoribus seu nunciis ex parte Edwardi regis (*Lit. regis Franc., Cl*) *Foed.* III 703a; **s1326** bassatores domini pape et nuncii..regis Francie *Ann. Paul.* 312; **1334** deferenti litteras ambassatoris regis Anglie existentis in partibus Francie eidem domino regi *KRAc* 387/9; **s1345** quod concilium regis congregaretur ..ad audiendum ea que ambassiatores pape dicere voluerunt AD. MUR. 161; **1370** ambaxiator et nuncius ad presenciam.. regis Anglie (*DipDocE* 261) *Foed.* VI 673b; **1406** ambaciatoribus regis Dacie venientibus in Angliam (*KRAc* 406/10) *Arch.* LXVII 179; hos per rumores adeunt ambassiatores / regem querentes GOWER *CT* III 107; **1408** pro expensis

~orum laborancium versus curiam Romanam pro unione habenda *Rect. Adderbury* 2; **s1426** evenit Londonias unus nebulo fingens se embassiatorem ab imperatore domino regi..missum *Chr. S. Alb.* 7; **1487** oratores, ambassiatores, procuratores et nuncii speciales (*DipDocE* 591) *Foed.* XII 320.

ambasciatorius, ambassadorial.

1327 litteris vestris ambassatoriis lectis *Ann. Paul.* 336; (**s1066**) **c1480** cum ipse esset in transmarinis partibus circa negocia regia imbassatoria (*Chr. Tewk.*) *MonA* II 60a.

ambasciatria, embassy.

1399 cum..fecerit certa viagia guerre et ambassatrias *Pat* 352 m. 20; elegit..dominos et magnates quos solenni ambassiatria ad adversarios suos Francie destinavit *Ps.-*Elmh. *Hen. V* c. 14.

ambasciatrix, ambassadorial (f.).

s1427 ut dignaretur votis eorum annuere quatenus scriberet litteras †inbastiatices summo pontifici missuras *Chr. S. Alb.* 17.

ambasciatum, embassy.

1491 pro suis financiis faciendis pro ambasiato *ExchScot* 304.

ambasciatus, embassy.

legacionibus crebris functi..ad mundi diversa dominia.. tediosis ambassiatibus..mittebamur R. Bury *Phil.* 8. 124; **1477** episcopo Aberdonensi existenti in ambassiatu domini regis *ExchScot* 463.

ambass-, ambax- v. ambasc-. ambelerius v. ambularius. ambicus v. anubicus.

ambidexter, ambidextrous. **b** (fig.); *v. et. ambisinister.*

Aoth, qui cum esset ~er..Israel liberavit M. Par. *Maj.* I 14 (cf. *Jud.* iii 15). **b** **1161** (v. ambilaevus); **1191** utpote qui regni potestatem et sedis apostolice auctoritatem quasi ~er habebat (*Lit. Ep. Coventr.*) R. Howd. III 142; athleta fortis nostrique temporis ~er probatissimus, utraque pro dextera uti doctus Ad. Eyns. *Hug.* IV 6; **1396** videtur quod hermaphroditus vel ~er essent bona nomina pro talibus hominibus duplicis status [sc. temporalis et spiritualis] (*Concl. Lollard.*) *Ziz.* 363.

2 receiving profit from two sources. **b** (one) taking fees from both sides (leg.).

ut ecclesiam una cum terra tanquam ~er lucrari possit Gir. *Symb.* 22 p. 262. **b** de..ballivis ~is qui capiunt ex utraque parte Bracton 117; **c1320** Robertus..est ~er et cepit de Henrico..ad ipsum Henricum fovendum et manutenendum contra Petrum..; et postea revertebatur ad predictum Petrum et cepit de eo x li. pro parte ipsius Petri contra predictum Henricum manutenenda (*Eyre*) *Lond. Ed. I & II* II 171; **1355** sunt communes ~res (*sic*) in omnibus querelis in comitatu..motis *SelCKB* VI 104; **1367** ex utraque parte ut ~er falso munera sumpsit *Pat* 275 m. 2*d*.

ambidextraliter, equivocally.

ubi palam dicit [Augustinus] totum hominem non nisi ex anima et carne constare, nisi per synecdochen ~er Netter *DAF* I 107.

ambidextria, taking of fees from both sides (leg.).

1353 placita corone de..decepcionibus, minis, ~iis, cambiperciis, concelamentis *ChartR* 138 m. 1; **1448** habeant omnes fines pro..manutenenciis, ~iis, falsitatibus (*Ch.*) *Reg. Whet.* I 33.

ambifariam [LL], on both sides.

†ambariam, pro ambobus partibus *GlC* A 588; **s1433** cum magno peritorum consilio ~iam congregato *Croyl. Cont. B* 517.

ambigena, hybrid.

~e non generant, teste Hippocrate; quod igitur genitalia in mulo faciunt, hoc sandalia in abbate P. Blois *Ep.* 90. 283.

Ambigensis v. Albigensis.

ambigere [CL], to dispute. **b** to doubt. **c** (w. inf.) to hesitate.

obviare..principiis..sive de his ~ere..est..vecordis J. Sal. *Pol.* 650b; de qua..ab antiquis non mediocriter ~ebatur Gir. *TH* II 15. **b** non ~o..sed confido quod.. Aldh. *Met.* 1; haec Deo placuisse non ~o Bede *HE* III 17; nulli est..†abigendum [v.l. ~endum] unumquemque fidelium corporis..Dominici tunc esse participem Lanfr. *Sermo* 640b; neque..quod ~ebam dissolvis Adel. *QN* 15; quin hec figmenta nostre famulentur instructioni non ~o J. Sal. *Pol.* 387d; **1330** ea occasione in aliquas †censuaras [l. censuras] ecclesiasticas non ~imus incidisse *Lit. Cant.* I 335; **1414** ubi eisdem ligeis nostris celeris justicie complementum fieri non ~imus *Cl* 264 m. 22*d*. **c** **1254** cum..cives jocalia ..penes se..~ant detinere *RGasc* I 347.

2 to speak ambiguously, equivocate.

in abstracto ~ere potest aliquis Duns *Metaph.* VIII 2. 117b; quod propheta non †ambiguit cum dixit Paul. Angl. *ASP* 1554.

†ambigua [? *for* ambigena *or* ambegna], ewe w. two lambs.

14.. hec ~a est ovis portans duos agnos WW.

ambigue, ambiguously.

principium sophisticum est quo tum de uno tum de alio enuntiare ~e incipiendum Balsh. *AD* 46 (cf. ib. 27: ad ~e argumentandum).

ambiguitas [CL], doubt, uncertainty. **b** doubtful point, difficulty (leg.).

sine ancipiti ~atis scrupulo veraciter credendum est quod.. Aldh. *VirgP* 11; nebulas ~atis ex acie intentionis tuae penitus depelle Eriug. *Per.* 546c; **8..** tu ei sis..in ~ate consilium (*Pontifical*) *Rec. Coronation* 6; ut hanc ~atis contentionem certitudo dirimeret Gir. *TH* II 12; [Judei] profitentes..se sue [Christi] cedis auctores cordibus suis non minimam ~atem inde ingerunt S. Sim. *Itin.* 29. **b** **1295** ad judicia ob difficultates seu ~ates in eadem curia respectuata circumspeccius reddenda *CalIPM* III p. 145; recordum et processum cujusdam nove disseisine..justiciariis nostris..racione ~atis [*gl.*: *pur difficultie*] per vos.. missa *Entries* 78.

1 ambiguus v. 1 abigeus.

2 ambiguus [CL], doubtful, uncertain. **b** (sb. n.) doubt, doubtful point.

inter ~as Fariseorum traditiones Aldh. *VirgP* 54; nihil.. obscurum videtur esse seu ~um praeter hominis divisionem in masculum et feminam Eriug. *Per.* 542c; ~i et adversi humanarum rerum..eventus H. Bos. *Thom.* II 10. **b** sine ~o Aldh. *PR* 128; inprimis istud ~um dissolve Adel. *QN* 14; **1579** cujus [questionis] ~a et dubitationes dum.. enucleaverint *StatOx* 345.

†ambila [? *for* alium], leek.

~a, *laec GlC* A 545; **10..** de herbis: ..~a, *leac* WW.

ambilaevus, doubly left-handed (fig.).

1161 sicut quidam in virtutis exercitio ambidextri sunt, sic isti ~i convincuntur ab avaritia et rapina J. Sal. *Ep.* 79 (118).

†ambilatio, wearing of a sort of ornament, (?) a kerchief (*anabola*).

sub A [pertinens ad partes corporis] sunt ~io, torquatio, inaurities et hujusmodi Bacon XV 232.

ambiloquus, equivocal.

dubylle-tonged, ~us, bifarius, bilinguis *CathA*.

ambire [CL], **a** to go round. **b** to surround, girdle. **c** to wrap round. **d** to envelop, contain. **e** to embrace (fig.). **f** to skirt round (fig.).

a Beleth *RDO* 81. 86 (v. amburbale). **b** partem indumentorum quae corpus sanctum ~ierant Bede (*Cuthb.*) *HE* IV 28; **10..** ~it, *ymbgyrdeð* WW. **c** galliculae rubricatis pellibus ~iuntur Aldh. *VirgP* 58; utrumque humerum orario ~iens H. Bos. *Thom.* III 6. **d** tenebris obscurior atris / atque latebrosis, ambit quas Tartarus, umbris Aldh. *Aen.* 100. 56. **e** **959** (13c) priscorum atque modernorum lepidissimam ~iens facundiam, ..angelus..stupenda cecinisse videtur carmina *CS* 1046. **f** sed rem circuiens longis ambagibus ambi / quod breviter dicturus eras Vinsauf *PN* 232.

2 to delimit. **b** (fig.).

956 istis terminis ~itur praedicta tellus *CS* 926; **c1205** non quod [angelus] ~iente locali superficie claudatur Gros. *Ep.* 1 p. 15. **b** [artes] suis locis, id est propriis diffinitionibus, ~iuntur Eriug. *Per.* 475a.

3 to desire. **b** to desire for someone else, concede freely. **c** to resort to.

nil de mortalium opibus praeter salvandas animas ~iebant Gosc. *Aug. Min.* 750; hic..summum sacerdotium ~ierat, sed..Christus ambitionem illius impediebat Osb. *V. Dunst.* 32; istis et illis discordiam ~ientibus *G. Steph.* II 95; O sincera animi puritas, non honorem ~ientis, nec respuentis tamen H. Bos. *Thom.* III 1; inter spem et metum anxii, dum et timent et ~iunt Gir. *GE* II 38; alternas prosperitates ut fratres..~ierunt Elmh. *Hen. V* 90. **b** quid ~it homo domino suo si secus ei non ~iat et competentiam? (*Quad.*) *GAS* 395. **c** [neque] illicitum coitum ambeat [AS: *forligru begange*] (*Cons. Cnut.*) *Ib.* 291.

ambisinister, doubly left-handed (fig.).

perversi non sunt ambidextri cum Aoth [cf. *Jud.* iii 15] set ~ri sunt, dextera carentes Neckam *Eccles.* 8. 85c (cf. Gir. *GE* II 28 p. 308); qui cum †Abioth ambidexter esse debuerat, cum diabolo factus ~er de dextera sinistram fecit P. Blois *Serm.* 760ab; simul utroque gladio niti solet ut, tanquam ambidexter vel potius ~er, quod una potestate non prevalet altera nimirum exequatur Gir. *Invect.* I 4; **c1430** iste ~er, dextralem mee cause particulam in posicionem contrariam pellere..sollicitus *Reg. Whet.* II 379.

†ambitatio, soliciting.

ad tales [magnates] accedere ob..honoris ~onem.. periculosum est J. Waleys *V. Relig.* III 10 f. 251b.

ambitio [CL], retinue.

episcopus..cum multa equestrium ~one regem adivit *G. Steph.* I 41.

2 delimitation.

1188 consecratum est [opus] illa prima sacratione que fit per crucis..†fictionem [? l. fixionem] locique ~onem *Ep. Cant.* 555; **c1205** cum legimus spiritum incorporeum circumscriptum, non est hec circumscriptio localis superficiei ~o Gros. *Ep.* 1 p. 14.

3 **a** pomp, splendour. **b** ambition, self-aggrandizement. **c** desire.

a ut qui Haugustaldensem fabricam vident ~onem Romanam se imaginari jurent W. Malm. *GP* III 117. **b** **673** ut nullus episcoporum se praeferat alteri per ~onem (*Conc. Hertf.*) Bede *HE* IV 5. **c** **943** donatio libera ab omni regali servitio et ab aliena ~one mundialium curarum *CS* 780; iniquitas est superba mundane vanitatis ~o Anselm (*Ep.* 117) III 253.

ambitiose, ingratiatingly.

ab his que ei displicerent ~e ob ejus..favorem abstinerent Gir. *GE* II 20.

ambitiositas, ambition.

1472 avaricie vel ~atis sectatores *Melrose* II 577.

ambitiosus, **a** showy, ostentatious. **b** ambitious, seeking advancement. **c** desirous. **d** corrupt.

a elegit abjecta esse in domo Dei sui magis quam habitare in tabernaculis ~ae concupiscentiae Gosc. *Edith* 69; codices et pixides ~i Gir. *EH intr.* p. 212; [tempora] tam sumptuosa sunt et ~a *Ib. pref.* p. 222. **b** quod [Vulferus] primus regum Anglorum sacrum episcopatum Londonie cuidam Wyne ~o daret W. Malm. *GR* I 76; **s1388** Willelmus Duglas, qui et ipse fuit juvenis ~us Wals. *HA* II 176. **c** **1432** principales aularum..lucri ~i *StatOx* 243. **d** **a1350** illi qui ..clanculas conspiraciones..faciunt seu pacta ~a iniunt (*sic*) *Stat. Cantab.* 329.

†ambitire, to surround.

10.. ~iuntur, *ymbhwyrfte, ymbhammene* WW.

ambitus [CL], circuit. **b** (?) passage-way (cf. Isidore *Etym.* XV 16). **c** encirclement, envelopment. **d** (fig.) circumlocution.

sol annuum caeli ~um..non in ccclxv diebus sed superadditis sex horis adimplere cognoscitur Bede *TR* 38 p. 251; genera et formae ex uno fonte *ΟΥΣΙΑΕ* manant inque eam naturali ~u redeunt Eriug. *Per.* 494b. **b** ~us, *twicen* Ælf. *Gl.* **c** utriusque humeri [orario] ~us H. Bos. *Thom.* III 6. **d** **671** prolixo ~u verborum ratiocinari Aldh. *Ep.* 1.

2 compass, circumference, extent. **b** cloister. **c** region, neighbourhood. **d** (fig.) limit, sphere of action.

in triquadro terrarum ~u Aldh. *VirgP* 22; extremus mundi ~us Eriug. *Per.* 549b; inter ~um Britannicae insulae *RegulC* 1; modo vero majori ~u continetur de terra quam tunc arabatur *DB* II 372b; **1155** terra..que est infra ~um illius vie *Feod. Durh.* 121; castrum..Soldani..habet in ~u unum miliare S. Sim. *Itin.* 53; **1432** cuilibet ecclesie parochiali infra ~um decanatus Bathoniensis *Reg. Cant.* II 463. **b** bonum cellarum numerum constructum habuimus et claustrum sive ~um Chauncy *Passio* 152 (cf. *Lit. Cant.* I 115 [**1323**]: nec ~um monasterii introibit). **c** castra metati sunt ob ~u London urbis Æthelw. IV 3. **d** omnis regula et universitas omnis alicui generi accommodata est, cujus ~um si lasciviendo excesserit illico vitiatur J. Sal. *Met.* 898b; perfectum potest considerari..in se et secundum omnem sui ~um Bacon XV 16; **1549** singuli regentes et non regentes qui in academia commorantur maxime et infra ~um academiae sunt *StatOx* 355.

3 (w. ref. to time) cycle. **b** period, neighbourhood.

denique quadriduanum post ~um Eðered rex adest cum exercitu Æthelw. IV. 2. **b** in eodem anno post Pascha in ~u letanias cometa apparuit *Ib.* IV 3.

4 ambition. **b** desire.

s1052 [Stigandus] adversus ~um nichil dignitati sue consulens W. Malm. *GP* I 23; modestia..ad ~um animi sedandum specialius applicatur Gir. *PI* I 13. **b** **s1075** affluebant sibi tanta que quantumlibet ~um possent et explere et vincere W. Malm. *GP* I 43; **s1109** ~u pecunie allate..occisus est ab hospite suo Higd. VII 25 p. 90.

ambizare, to buzz.

apes ~ant vel bombizant Aldh. *PR* 131.

amblyopia [ἀμβλυωπία], dim-sightedness.

†ampliopio, i. obscuritas visus *Alph.* 9.

1 ambo [CL], both. **b** (sg.) each of two.

par labor ambarum, dispar fortuna duarum Aldh. *Aen.* 66. 3; reges ~o, pater scilicet et filius Bede *HE* III 25; precium ~arum terrarum xl sol. *DB* I 50b; una tantum manu et non ~abus in securi percutiunt Gir. *TH* III 10; **1287** via..que tangit ~as theþingas de Straton' et Straton' *Hund. Highworth* 320; **1382** de quibus ~abus summis executores..respondebunt *ExchScot* 86; **s1388** ~o milites, ~o juvenes, set ~o proditores Wals. *HA* II 174. **b** introeant totidem ex ~a parte [AS: *of ægðre healfe*] et consistant ex utraque [v.l. amba] parte [AS: *on twa healfe*] judicii (*Quad.*) *GAS* 386; dato..in ~a parte federe *Eul. Hist.* II 322 (= G. Mon. IX 11: utraque [v.l. amba]).

2 ambo [ἄμβων], lectern, pulpit, desk.

imposito super ~onem evangelio *RegulC* 42; abbas ~onem ascendens populo narravit Ord. Vit. III 13; graduarius..eo quod in gradus ascendi debeat atque isthic cantari in ~one (dicitur autem ~onis ab 'ambio', eo quod locus ille ambitur gradibus, vel ab 'ambo, ambe, ambo', quod nimirum due sunt vie isthic), hoc est in pulpito, quod situm est ante eum locum ubi recitatur evangelium Beleth *RDO* 59. 65; **s1222** Joannes [de S. Egidio], sermonem faciens ad clerum, ..descendens de ~one habitum fratrum recepit Trevet 211; **1434** in mercede j fabri reparantis ~onem ferri in choro *Fabr. York* 55; **1443** cum j tuella de panno lineo pro ~one *Cant. Coll. Ox.* I 1; **1466** obligavit se ad faciendum ~ones cum formulis pro novis scholis sacre theologie Oxonie, viz. xxxvij ~ones cum scabellis correspondentibus *MunAcOx* 716–17; **1475** sub ~one in cancello ecclesie *Test. Ebor.* III 216; *a lettron'*, ~o, discus, lectrinum; ..*a pulpyte*, ~o, amon, amonicus.., pulpitum *CathA*; **c1550** ~onem evangelicum *Reg. Aberd.* II 104.

ambolare v. ambulare.

1 ambra [AS *amber*; ? cf. amphora], measure of volume (4 bushels, *infra* 1280 but (app.) not 1274): **a** (of salt); **b** (of other products).

a **832** (13c) reddere debet cxx mensuras quas Angli dicunt *ambres* de sale *CS* 402; ibi v salinae de cx ~is salis *DB* (*Suss*) I 28 (cf. ib. 28b: x ~ae salis); Willelmus..de Braiosa [temp. Will. I]..ecclesie de Bello..dedit..annuatim centum ~as salis *Chr. Battle* 35; **1211** in venatione salanda iiij sextaria ij ~e *Pipe Wint.* p. 119; **1234** de centum ~is salis quos (*sic*) singulis annis percipere consuevit abbas de Gresteng' de salinis marisci de Pevensell' *Cl* 496; **1274** de iiij^xx^xix wichewerk' et ij ambr', que faciunt ccxxij quart' vij bus' ij ambr' *MinAc* (*Old Lymington, Hants*) 984/3 r. 1; **1275** do..†unoquoquo [l. unoquoque] anno xx ~as salis (*Ch. Leeds, Kent*) *MonA* VI 217b; **1280** redditus ibidem [*Crowhurst, Suss*] xxiiij ~e salis que faciunt xij quarteria secundum mensuram London' *Reg. Richm. app.* 44; **1283** debet cariare v ~as salis et j bussellum de..Hastinges usque Bellum *Cust. Battle* 4 (cf. ib. 14: j ~am, j bussellum et pek). **b** de x hidis ad corredium debent reddi..xij ~e [AS: *ambra*] cervisie Wylisce, ..plena ~a butiri (*Quad.*) *GAS* 119; de duabus nihtfirmis detur ei singulis mensibus una ~a farine *Ib.* 148; **12..** quando triturat frumentum, triturabit unam mensuram plenam que dicitur amer' *Cust. Bleadon* 202.

2 ambra, ~um [Ar. *'anbar*], ambergris. **b** (?) ambergris or storax (*Liquidambar* = Ar. *'anbar sā'il*). **c** amber. **d** (w. *pomum*) pomander (OF *pome ambre*).

cetus..effundit semen in undis; / ambre censeri nomine fama refert Neckam *DS* III 414; addendum est quod a mari projicitur et est ~a, que est sperma cete, res mire virtutis Bacon *Maj.* II 210. **b** ~e grana sex Gilb. II 119. 2; **1307** pro uno emplastro pro collo regis cum ladano et ~a orientali (*KRAc* 368/30) *EHR* LXVII 173. **c** ambram nonnulli †grumiam [? l. gummam] nucis esse fatentur Neckam *DS* III 415; **1313** paternoster de ~a (*DC St. Paul's*) *HMC Rep.* IX *app.* I 29b; ~a dicitur sperma bellue marine, i. cete; sed proculdubio gumma arboris est in mari crescentis *Alph.* 8; **1411** unus anulus cum uno lapide coloris de aumbro *Lit. Cant.* III 113; **1415** paternoster de curallo cum gaudiis de ~o (*Test.*) *Foed.* IX 276; **1504** pro dim. lib. de ~o val. xx s. *EEC* (*imports from Dantzig*) 677. **d** **s1219** perceperunt..magnam partem divitiarum Egypti in auro et argento, perlis, pomis ~e, filis aureis M. Par. *Maj.* III 55; pomum ~e fiat et..portetur in manibus vel sinu Gilb. III 159. 2.

ambrachion [? Ar. *abarīqūn* < ὑπέρεικον], shrub.

plantarum quedam sunt arbores, quedam inter arbores et herbas, nominanturque ille ~ion Alf. Angl. *Plant.* I 12; olus et ambrathion, que sunt media inter arborem et herbas; set olus majus vicinatur herbe et ambrathion arbori Bacon XV 218.

ambratus, (?) flavoured w. ambergris or storax.

masticentur gariof', muscati, ~i.. Gilb. VII 362. 2.

ambria v. elemosynaria.

ambro [CL *tribal name*; *cf. History* XX 259], glutton, lecher (or as adj.). **b** (applied to English by Britons).

~ones, *gredge GlC* A 519; ~onis Orci faucibus Aldh. *VirgP* 12; [Adam] buccis ~onibus et labris lurconibus *Ib.* 11; dum vetitum ligni malum decerperet ambro *Id. VirgV* 2498; **717** (v. aurilegus); ~o, *gifere* vel *frec* Ælf. *Sup.*; **990** anathematis alogia ~o pomum momordit vetitum *CD* 684; lascivire cum eis voluerunt; quod cum abnegassent puelle, irruerunt in eas ~ones G. Mon. V 16; *tastowre*, gustator, ~o *PP*; *a gluton*, ~o, catilio..; *a lechour*, amasio, ..~o *CathA*. **b** illi priores inimici ac si ~ones, lupi.. rabidi Gildas *EB* 16; numquam addiderunt Saxones ~onum ut a Pictis vectigal exigerent Nenn. *HB* 203 (cf. ib. 206: omne genus ~onum [*gl.*: id est Aldsaxonum]); redite Scoti et Picti, redite ~ones Saxones G. Mon. XII 15 (cf. ib. VIII 6, 23).

ambrogium v. amobragium.

ambroninus, gluttonous, lecherous.

lykerows, ~us, delicatus *PP*; *gluterus*, ~us, castrimargiosus, ..*lecherous*, ..~us, dissolutus, fornicarius *CathA*.

ambrosia [ἀμβροσία], divine food, delicacy. **b** (applied to various herbs).

~ea, *suoetnis GlC* A 529; [Ambrosius] qui nomen gerit ambrosiae de nectare ductum Aldh. *VirgV* 654. **b** **10..** nomina herbarum: ..~ia, *hyndhælepe* [? *Eupatorium*] WW; suavior ambrosie flore recentis erat A. Meaux *Susanna* 156; fiat locio..de vino decoccionis plantaginis, ..et balaust' et ~ie et celidonie Gad. 118. 1; ~ia minor, i. millefolium *SB* 10; ~ia, lilifagus, eupatorium, salvia agrestis idem; G. *ambreise*, A. *wildesauge Alph.* 8.

Ambrosianus, of St. Ambrose. **b** (sb. n.) hymn-book.

1415 ymnum ~um 'te Deum laudamus' devote cantantes *Reg. Cant.* III 366. **b** que cordetenus a monachis sunt scienda, viz. ..cantica tam ecclesiastica quam monastica, ~um, id est ymnarium *Cust. Cant.* 420.

ambrosius, ambrosial, divinely sweet.

~io dictionalitatis collemate O. Cant. *Pref. Frith.* 45.

ambrum v. 2 ambra.

ambubaja [CL], **~us,** harlot. **b** (?) (m.) glutton.

mascularii, ~e, farmacapole, ..balatrones—'hoc genus omne'—totas [Londonie] replevere domos Devizes 39v. p. 65. **b** vinum gariofilatum lambris et ambubagis [*gl.*: *glutuns*], quorum sitis est incompleta, appetibile Neckam *Ut.* 98.

ambulabilis, able to walk. **b** (sb. n.).

continua fuit necesaria cordi aeris atractio, ut in animalibus ~ibus *Ps.*-Ric. *Anat.* 41. **b** superficies levium predominantur [v.l. ~atur] in avibus respectu natatilium et ~ium et reptilium Neckam *NR* I 39.

ambulacrum [CL], walk, passage.

~um, spatium ambulandi *GlC* A 542; **1530** in quodam superiori ~o sive in quadam superiori galeria (*DipDocE* 1001) *Foed.* XIV 390; **1535** in reparacionibus factis circa tecta, muros, fenestras Edis Sacre, aule, ..campanilis, ~i et ceterorum edificiorum infra collegium [*Magdalen, Ox.*] *Val. Eccl.* II 288.

ambulare [CL], to walk. **b** (bibl.) to follow a course of life. **c** (of disease) to creep, spread. **d** (fig.) to occur.

opus evangelii magis ~ando quam equitando perficere Bede *HE* IV 3; ceu rura soli premeret, sic ambulat undis Alcuin *SS Ebor.* 1369; nudis pedibus ~ant Gir. *DK* I 8; **s1297** ne [via]..descendentes..repere pocius manibus quam ~are cogat Trevet 359; **1308** via est tam stricta..quod homines propter latronum insidias vix audent ~are (*JustIt* 262) *EHR* XL 417. **b** causa cur 'non secundum carnem ~ant' Lanfr. *Comment. Paul.* (*Rom.* viii 1) 129; **s1193** non '~avit in magnis' [*Ps.* cxxx 2].., clamores equa lance dijudicans Diceto *YH* II 112; **1327** electis Dei 'in veritate ~antibus' [*3 Joh.* 4] *Lit. Cant.* I 230; Petrus..aliquando 'ad veritatem' minime '~avit' [*Gal.* ii 14] Ockham *Dial.* 843; si..anime purgate post claustrum corporum..vident Deum, sequitur quod non '~ant' tunc 'per fidem' [*2 Cor.* v 7] *Ib.* 764; ~ans in viis patrum suorum [*1 Kings* xv 26 etc.], omni virtute repletus *Plusc.* VI 16. **c** aliquando sunt pustule multe que ~ant et ulcerant Gad. 29 v. 1. **d** **s1231** libertates civitatis et vita et membra civium pari passu ~ant *MGL* I 90.

2 (pr. ppl.) ambling (of horses).

juvat videre gradarios succussatura nitente suaviter ~antes, pedibus lateraliter simul erectis quasi a subalternis et demissis W. Fitzst. *Thom. prol.* 11; equo insideat.. neque succussanti neque cespitanti..sed bene ~anti [*gl.*: *amblaunt*] Neckam *Ut.* 99; **1264** unum pullum bene ~antem *Reg. Whet. app.* II 320; **1335** de uno palfredo suaviter ~ante *Lit. Cant.* II 95; **1378** in precio unius equi ambolantis (*DC St. Paul's*) *HMCRep.* IX *app.* I 42a; **1428** xxvj equos ~antes..ad opus..regis Portugalie (*Cl*) *Foed.* X 392; **14..** v eque, quarum iiij ~antes et una trottans *Feod. Durh.* 188.

3 (p. ppl. as sb. n. pl.) beaten bounds.

1320 una cum v acris terre arabilis prout jacent in roddevallo per suas certas metas et bundas et sua ~ata *AncD* D7990.

ambularius, ~aris, ambling; *v. et. amilarius.*

1401 cum manuopere..viz. ..uno equo ambelerio ac una sella cum freno (*CoramR*) *G. S. Alb. cont.* III 510; **1423** pro uno equo bay ambeler' *Test. Ebor.* III 80; **1425** lego..unum equum ~arem *Reg. Cant.* II 312.

ambulatio, a walking the bounds, perambulation. **b** following a course of life (*cf. ambulare* 1b). **c** (of disease) creeping, spread.

a **1195** [dicunt] quod divisa per ~onem sint..*CurR PR* XIV 37; **1258** bosci..qui per ~onem proborum hominum deafforestati fuerunt (*Pet. Baronum*) *Ann. Burton* 440; distinguendi sunt fines agrorum inter vicinos..per rationabiles divisas vel per ~onem Bracton 102b; **1300** quicquid per istam ~onem ponitur extra forestam *Cart. Rams.* II 307. **b** ut..in sollicita divini comitatus ~one..ordinentur universi Ad. Marsh *Ep.* 140. **c** prohibet ~onem putridorum morborum Gad. 28. 1.

ambulativus, creeping, spreading (of disease).

formica est omne apostema in cute ~um quod latitudinem non habet Gad. 29. 1.

ambulator, walker, (w. *nocturnus*) prowler. **b** ambler, saddle-horse. **c** horse-trainer.

1389 si aliquis masculus vel femella dicte fraternitatis pro malafactore, ..pugnatore, nocturno ~ore..teneantur *Guild Cert.* (*Hull*) 46/451. **b** *aumlar, hors*, gradarius, ~or *PP*. **c** **1290** cuidam ~ori informanti duos pullanos domini *Ac. Swinfield* 179.

ambulatorius, movable, variable. **b** (sb. n.) walk, passage.

1269 decime garbarum sunt de anno in annum ~ie *Reg. Exon.* 42b. **b** **1241** minorem turrim circa magnam turrim [Hereford'] emendari, ..~ia eciam ibidem decencius ordinari facias *Liberate* 15 m. 14; [abbas J., ob. 1316] fecit longam cameram pro minutis cum volta, super quam edificatur ~ium *Chr. Evesham* 287; [abbas R., ob. 1418] constituit..ut reparare debent..~ium a camera prioris usque ad sartariam *Ib.* 309; **s1423** circa vitracionem..iij [fenestrarum] in medio ~ii juxta cellam magistri studii *Mon. Francisc.* I 520; **1535** terre..adjacentes collegio [*Magdalen, Ox.*]..et ~ium muratum ubi solent pueri ludere *Val. Eccl.* II 273.

ambulatura, passage.

1531 sic inter cellulas erit ~a octo pedum latitudinis *Reg. Aberd.* I 401.

ambulum, compass, extent (*cf. ambitus* 2a).

1209 habeant..piscarias suas..et volatilia sua infra ~um ville [*Lewisham, Kent*] *RChart.* 184a.

amburbale [LL], lustral ceremony in Rome.

erat antiquitus Rome consuetudo ut..in principio Februarii urbem lustrarent, eam ambiendo cum suis processionibus gestantes singuli candelas ardentes, et vocabatur illud ~e Beleth *RDO* 81. 86; Agapitus [ob. 536] statuit ibi [in Bizantio] Ypapanton celebrari pro mortalitate hominum, quum ante Rome celebraretur propter ~[i]a tollenda R. Niger 135.

amburere [CL], to scorch. **b** (fig.) to enflame (passion). **c** to enflame (eyes).

ruit in praeceps ambusta cacumina linquens / congeries lapidum Aldh. *VirgV* 1773; nuntians abbati domus ambustas et matrem ejus inibi esse combustam G. Crispin *Herl.* 94; trabes..ambuste deciderunt ad solum W. Malm. *GP* IV 149. **b** expleri rabies ambusta negatur Aldh. *VirgV* 2619. **c** vultumque cruentat / ignibus, ambustis oculis Hanv. III 279.

ambuttare v. abuttare. amdodus v. avidotus. amelior- v. admelior-. amell- v. esmall-. amelum v. amylum.

amen [Heb.], so be it: **a** (as conclusion); **b** (as separate utterance); **c** (defined).

a valete, ..sorores monasticae..et caelestis patriae participes! amen! Aldh. *VirgP* 60; Deo laus et gratiarum actio per infinita secula seculorum amen Osb. *Mir. Dunst.* 26; cui est honor et gloria in secula seculorum amen Ailr. *Ed. Conf.* 776B; explicit Philobiblon..ad laudem Dei feliciter et amen R. Bury *Phil.* 20. 253. **b** oscula dando tamen dixit asellus 'ămen' Nig. *SS* 1440. **c** assertio dicitur āmen Garl. *Myst. Eccl.* 589; ista dictio 'amen'.. aliquando est adverbium affirmandi.., id est 'vere'..; aliquando est nomen..secundum quod significat idem quod 'sine defectu', unde dicitur sic ab *a* quod est 'sine' et *menos* quod est 'defectus'..; aliquando est verbum et significat idem quod hoc verbum 'fiat' Bacon XV 176.

amenare v. amoenare. amend- v. emend-. amenerium v. elemosynaria. amenitas v. amoenitas. amenium v. aminaeus.

amens [CL], demented. **b** scared out of wits. **c** madly excited.

~s, *emod GlC* A 532; bacchatur [puer]..vagabundis passibus amens Aldh. *VirgV* 1482; **9..** demoniacus, ~s, insanus, *gewitleasa* WW; Map *NC* IV 16 (v. arrepticius b); tanquam ~tes et extra se facti representare solebant Gir. *GE* I 54; semper amans amens, semper amarus amor *Id. Symb. metr.* 3; aut est [mania] cum furia et alienacione et vocantur dementes vel ~tes Gad. 132. 1. **b** amens, si tibi mus parvus oberret, eris *Babio* 28. **c** **s1386** [Londonienses] currunt..~tes ad muros, contiguas domos dilacerant *V. Ric. II* 73.

amensur- v. admensur-. amentalis, ~atus v. ammentatus.

amentare, to dement.

nisi virtute divina protegeretur, ..ipso tumultu ~aretur *NLA* (*Purg. S. Patr.*) II 294.

amenter, madly.

insilit ~er inprovidus Map *NC* II 19.

amentia [CL], madness. **b** mad excitement.

9.. furia, insania, ~ia, *wodscip, repnes* WW; ~iae quicquid agebat reputabatur G. Crispin *Herl.* 89; nisi quem.. percussit Dominus ~ia et furore Ad. Marsh *Ep.* 92 p. 213; *wodenes*, ~ia, demencia *CathA*. **b** cives urbis inique, furore debacchantes ~ie Gir. *EH* II 3.

amentialis, causing madness (of deadly nightshade).

vinum et cerevisiam solatro ~i..miscent Boece *Hist.* 257.

1 amentum [etym. dub.], tartar, wine lees.

~ idulcis.. Gilb. III 167. 1.

2 amentum v. ammentum. amenus v. amoenus. ameos v. ami. amera v. 1 ambra b, Amerinus. ameraldus, ameraudus v. esmeraldus. amerallus v. admirallus. amerc- v. admerc-.

Americus, American.

1564 ad Indos vel ~os non illi esse philosophandi gratia peregrinandum fatebitur Dee *Monas pref.* 186.

Amerinus [CL], kind of willow.

†amera, genus salicis *GlC* A 515; **10..** †amera, *sealh* WW.

amerokus v. amaracus. amersiare v. admerciare.

ames [CL], beam, pole. **b** fishing-rod. **c** of cart pole.

amites, *laergae GlC* A 502, *fugultreo* vel *reftras Ib.* 535; †anate, *clader-sticca Ib.* 625; trudes vel amites, *spreotas* Ælf. *Gl.* **b** pisces..gurgustio..vel †amitte levi vel nassa in vivario †depressi [v.l. deprensi] Neckam *Ut.* (ed. Scheler) p. 60. **c** **1353** unam carettam.., unum amitem precii dim. m., duas cellas precii xx s. *Pat* 239 m. 20.

amessare, ~iare, v. amissare. ameta v. amictus, amita.

amethystus, ~a [ἀμέθυστος], amethyst.

topaziorum flamma vel ametistorum viola W. Malm. *GR* IV 337; **1245** in pede calicis apponuntur amatiste (*Invent. S. Paul.*) *Arch.* L 464; **1267** una amatista in capsa aurea *CalPat* 138.

ameum v. ami. amf- v. et. amph-. amfract- v. anfract-.

†amfrida [? cf. Virg. *Aen.* VI 398: Amphrysia], verses.

~is, versiculis *GlC* A 505.

ami, ameos [ἄμι], ammi (bot.).

apii, amei, levistici.. GILB. II 100. 1 (cf. ib. 112 v. 2: ameos); idromel in quo coquuntur isopus, calamentum, ameos et similia GAD. 12 v. 1; ameos agreste, similis fraxinarie, A. *wodewhisgle Alph.* 8; carui agreste, cumnella, ameos, cordumeon..idem *Ib.* 30.

amiantus [ἀμίαντος], asbestos.

cum ~on, quod ligni genus est vel ligni habens similitudinem, quanto plus arserit, tanto mundius inveniatur BEDE *Tab.* II 11 (= AD. SCOT. *TT* 668A: †amyton); amatides est lapis vel gemma a qua si vestis fuerit contacta contra ignem resistit, et si igni imponatur non ardebit BART. ANGL. XVI 17; amianthus est lapis alumini scissili.. similis; igne non uritur, quapropter et salamander appellatur *LC*.

amica v. amicus 3, amita.

amicabilis [LL], friendly (of compacts or sim.). **b** (of persons). **c** (as forename; *cf. amabilis* b). **d** congenial (of things).

825 pro amore Dei et ~i amicitia illius regis (*Conc. Clovesho*) *CS* 384; **1163** sopita est discordia et ~i fine terminata (*Concordia*) DICETO *YH* I 306*n.*; **1191** sub hac forma pacis de sepedicta querela ~is compositio facta est *Ch. Sal* 51; per ~em compositionem BRACTON 310b; **s1265** de nova pace ~i consensu partium ordinata *Flor. Hist.* III 262; **s1301** ad coronacionem hujus regis vocatus..ut ei presenciam ~em..amicus exhiberet WALS. *HA* I 85; **1347** per ~em tractatum *RScot* 704b; **1489** ~i locucione *Entries* 51b. **b** **s1098** qui videbant Christiani ipsos [bellatores], ~es et favorabiles in spiritu cognoscebant M. PAR. *Min.* I 125; **1279** arbitratores seu ~es compositores *RGasc* II 58; **c1370** aliqua mulier..que erit uxor galli vel forte sibi ~is (J. BRIDL. *Gl.*) *Pol. Poems* I 213; **1382** regentes in artibus non fuerunt ~es vel benevoli doctoribus determinantibus contra Nicolaum Herforde *Ziz.* 308; **s1453** vir probus et..abbati multum ~is *Reg. Whet.* I 92. **c** **1210** Milo de B. C. et ~is uxor ejus *CurR* VI 47. **d** sanguis.. inter quatuor humores laudabilior et nature ~ior est BART. ANGL. IV 7.

amicabilitas, friendship. **b** (of things) affinity, congeniality.

s1296 comes Flandrie, passus injuriam a rege Francie domino suo, recessit ab ~ate ejus KNIGHTON I 331; **s1295** nobis efficaciter assistere gratuita ~ate disponens (*Tract. Franc. & Scot.*) *Plusc.* VIII 20; *a frenschip*, amicicia, ~as *CathA*. **b** res non nutribilis nutribili admixta accidentalem contrahit ~atem, qua potest nutrire subjectum NECKAM *NR* II 98; aliorum humorum malicia sanguini admixta propter ~atem ejus ad naturam non se ita subito manifestat BART. ANGL. IV 8.

amicabiliter, in a friendly fashion. **b** (of things) favourably.

discesserunt ~er sine juditio *DB* II 402; **s1109** valedicentes ~er digrediuntur H. CANTOR *Hist.* 8; rex Francorum..urgebat ~er regem Anglie dicere primum MAP *NC* V 6 p. 240; **1214** ut ~er et legitime componerent inter partes *Reg. Dunferm.* 67; **1217** sub hac forma coram nobis ~er conquievit *Reg. S. Thom. Dubl.* 326; ecce quam ~er [ME: *sweteliche*] alloquitur sponsus sponsam *AncrR* 30; **1343** ad tractandum..non in forma..judicii sed extrajudicialiter et ~er (*Pat*) AD. MUR. 137; **1360** briga ~er et ex consensu..discussa et..terminata *MunAcOx* 222; **1441** fraternaliter et ~er inter nos..dirigi faciemus BEKYNTON I 142. **b** dum..ventus ~er sufflasset in frontem velorum ELMH. *Hen. V* 86.

amicalis [LL], friendly.

nunc persolvo debitum..fidele..et ~e Christi tironibus, grave vero..apostatis GILDAS *EB pref.*; ~i et quasi fraterno consilio BEDE *HE* III 22.

amicare, to make a friend of, conciliate. **b** (of things) to make congenial, adapt. **c** (intr.) to be a friend. **d** to be well disposed.

talis amicetur tibi qualis amicus habetur D. BEC. 676; [humilitas] mitigat iratos, altos inclinat, amicat / hostes GARL. *Epith.* IX 221; amicat / oppositum opposito conciliatque suo *Latin Stories* 198; **c1470** qui plus solent adversari quam ~ari *Reg. Whet.* I 429; *to make frende*, ~are, amicum facere *CathA*. **b** radicibus arborum..aqua.. attrahitur, quia arbori ~atur NECKAM *NR* II 98. **c** *to be frende*, ~are *CathA*; cum regibus ~are SKELTON I 349. **d** non adversandum littere arbitror sed ~andum J. SAL. *Met.* 888A.

amice [CL], in a friendly fashion.

carius..et ~ius..regis Henrici filiis compatiebatur *G. Steph.* I 34.

amicia v. almucia, amictus.

†amicialiter, in a friendly fashion.

Saxones, ~er [v.l. amicabiliter] locuti, in mente..vulpicino more agebant NENN. *HB* 190.

amicire [CL], to clothe. **b** to don the garb of. **c** (fig.) to cover.

†amictit, vestit, texit *GlC* A 537; qui vellent habitare cultius, ~iri elegantius W. MALM. *GR* V 400; amictu meliore necesse habuit ~iri J. GODARD *Ep.* 231. **b** ille, qui nondum ~isset monachum, constantius reniti [in primatem sullimari] W. MALM. *GP* I 14. **c** Alpes nive sempter amictas NECKAM *DS* V 329.

amicitia [CL], friendship, amity. **b** (as title). **c** (w. *mundi*) worldliness (*cf. James* iv 4). **d** friendly settlement (leg.).

frater, amicitia numquam fraudabere nostra ALDH. *VirgV* 725; presbyter..viro Dei spiritualis ~iae foedere copulatus BEDE *HE* IV 27; conjunctus est ~iis regis *Ib.* V 19; amor est connexio et vinculum quo omnium rerum universitas ineffabili ~a..copulatur ERIUG. *Per.* 579B; foedus amiciciae nostrae dissolvit inique G. AMIENS *Hast.* 233; has iiii libras dant burgenses gratis et †amiticia *DB* II 118b; potest esse vera ~ia..etiamsi numquam instet flagitandi necessitas ANSELM (*Ep.* 20) III 127; divinitus conceditur..omnibus veri nominis amicis in supersimplicem originem fontalis ~ie superseculariter pergere AD. MARSH *Ep.* 166; **1377** amicisciam et..concordiam *FormOx* 381. **b** **1242** rex B. regine Castelle, salutem...~iam vestram rogamus.. *RGasc* I 27; **1303** vestre ~ie [i.e. priori Predicatorum] affectuose consulimus *Reg. Cant.* I 450; **1317** vestram reverendam ~iam ..exoramus *FormOx* 15; **1322** dilectam ~iam vestram.. rogamus *Lit. Cant.* I 69. **c** pericia..que disponit peculiariter ad ~iam hujus mundi R. BURY *Phil.* 11. 168. **d** ubi tainus habet duas optiones, ~ie vel lage [AS: *lufe oððe lage*], et ~iam elegerit, stet hoc ita firmum sicut ipsum judicium (*Quad.*) *GAS* 232; ubi aliquis eorum opcionem habet per justitiam ~ie vel lage et ~iam eligit (*Leg. Hen.*) *Ib.* 574.

amicitialis, bound by friendship.

obsistit..absentia corporalis ~ibus animis AD. MARSH *Ep.* 166.

†amicitior, more friendly. **b** (sb. m.) closer friend; *v. et. amicus* 1.

1459 qui..nobis magis amicabiles fuerant ~oris largicionisque dragmas in tipicam nostram Jerusalem intulere *Reg. Whet.* I 326. **b** vereor quod fucorum fictiones in me etiam ~ores mei suspicentur AD. MARSH *Ep.* 245.

amiclas v. Amyclas. amicta v. amictus.

amictorium [CL], **~ia,** garment, wrap.

~ium, vestimentum *GlC* A 538; **14..** ~ia, A. *a coverture* WW.

amictus [CL; cf. OF *amit*; (?) *infl. by* almucia], **~um, ~a,** garment, robe. **b** (fig.).

lacernae gracilis ~u ac mastrucae tegmine incompto utatur ALDH. *Ep.* 3; involutum novo ~u corpus BEDE (*Cuthb.*) *HE* IV 28; vidit quendam albo indutum ~u versus chorum tendere FOLC. *J. Bev.* B 324; habent..economum ..qui eis..annuatim ~ui commoda suggerat W. MALM. *GP* II 91. **b** ut rude thema nove forme sibi sumat amictum VINSAUF *PN* 1684.

2 (eccl.) amice (kerchief or shoulder-wrap): **a** (decl. 4); **b** (decl. 2, m. or n.); **c** (f. forms).

a sacerdos..~u pro galea caput contegit BELETH *RDO* 32. 43; utuntur [Cartusienses] alba et ~u, stola, fanone atque planeta, planis et candidis AD. EYNS. *Hug.* IV 10; octavum responsorium a v pueris in superpelliceis et ~ibus capita velatis..cantatur *Off. Eccl.* 55; **1240** in qualibet ecclesia in ornatu altaris sint tres albe cum amitibus et stolis et manipulis *Conc. Syn.* 296; **1245** trans humeros designat amictus utrumque GARL. *Myst. Eccl.* 428; **1520** ~us duos *Invent. Ch. Ch. Cant.* 44. **b** **c1160** sexdecim ~os auro venuste paratos *Cart. Rams.* II 273; **1186** pro..j dalmatica et j tunica et ij ~is *Pipe* 198; **1245** ~i plures, sc. duo de filo puri auri tracto.., alius breudatus aquilis..super nigrum sendatum, ..alius consutus de serico cum griffone.. (*Invent. S. Paul.*) *Arch.* L 490; **1250** una stola cum fanone..; unum ~um *CallMisc* I p. 31; **1251** electo de Persora faciat habere unam capam..cum amito decenti ad tantum virum *Cl* 431; **12..** induantur episcopi albis et ~is *Conc. Scot.* II 4; **1315** ~i de aurifrigio gemmis ornati *Invent. Ch. Ch. Cant.* 60; **1368** j amitum glauci coloris poudratum cum capitibus capri *Invent. Norw.* 12; ~um, ..hic amittus, A. *amytte* WW. **c** **c1216** nos..suscepisse..de testamento domini M. ..unam albam, unam ~am et sandalia *Couch. Furness* II 712; **1251** emi faciat quandam albam et unam amitam..ad capellam..deserviendam *Cl* 464; **1290** ij dalmatice, j amicia per se, j stola *Reg. Wint.* II 705; **1310** vij s. de ij †amicis [? l. amitis], quarum j de serico et alia broudata *Ac. Exec. Ep. Exon.* 4; **1313** unam albam amitam cum diversis scutis in paruris *Pri. Cold.* 9; **1339** j albam cum †aurica *Bec* 20*n.* (cf. *Rec. Eton* 30 no. 1); **1407** tres amittas cum paruris (*DC Sal.*) *HMC Var. Coll.* I 350; **1436** cum albo et ameta *Reg. Aberd.* II 139; **1455** pro iij ulnis de panno lineo emptis pro amisiis *Cant. Coll. Ox.* II 175; **1457** lego vestimentum meum ..viz. albam, ~am, stolam, manipulum, casulam *Test. Ebor.* II 206.

3 (*s. dub.*).

juxta altare sit finaculum, examitam (*sic*) vel †amicum NECKAM *Ut.* 119.

amiculum [CL], garment, robe.

~o, *hraegli GlC* A 546; peplorum ~a..nequaquam a sanctis artubus spoliari valuerunt ALDH. *VirgP* 50 p. 306; regillum vel peplum vel palla vel ~um, *riccræ wife hrægl* vel *deorwurðe wæfels* ÆLF. *Gl.*; anaboladia deerant et ~um et teristrum BALSH. *Ut.* 53.

amiculus [CL], humble friend.

ad magnum munus prefulsit amiculus unus / conderet ut funus GARL. *Mor. Scol.* 609.

amicus [CL], friendly. **b** (of things) congenial.

filia mox matrem fatu correxit amico ALDH. *VirgV* 1805; gaudet amica cohors de virgine matre tonantis BEDE (*Hymn*) *HE* IV 18; gentem innoxiam et nationi Anglorum semper ~issimam *Ib.* IV 26; me ~um vestrum ~iorem vobis reddetis ANSELM (*Ep.* 275) IV 190; illam ~is sedavit verbis G. MON. X 3; **s1247** exempti..omnibus fratribus grati existentes †amicitiores[MS amiciores] extiterant M. PAR. *Min.* III 19. **b** est inimica mihi quae cunctis constat amica/..lampas..Phoebi ALDH. *Aen.* 97 (*Nox*) 7; diligit.. quod sibi ~um est; quod vero natura simile est, id ~um esse necesse est ADEL. *QN* 43; **1178** ludus et sollicitudinum depositio ~issima sunt nature P. BLOIS *Ep.* 15. 56A; natura corporis adhuc viventis sanguinem ut sibi ~um attraheret NECKAM *NR* II 98.

2 (sb. m.) friend. **b** kinsman. **c** (w. *spiritualis*) agent (of friar), proctor.

quia nulla ratione conveniat tanto regi ~um suum optimum..auro vendere BEDE *HE* II 12; vocato filio suo.. et pluribus ~is suis, dixit: "audite vos, ~i mei" *DB* I 177; ~us velut medicus in necessitate probantur (*sic*) ANSELM (*Ep.* 275) IV 190; invento..tertio ~o, quem parum dilexerat.., quasi dimidium ~um eum reputabat *Latin Stories* 97; ~i speciales ipsius Willelmi *State Tri. Ed. I* 10. **b** **c1150** ~i extrahant mortuum, deponentes in feretrum (*Leg. Ed. retr.*) *GAS* 667 (cf. *Leg. Ed. ib.* 666: parentes interfecti ex utraque parte generis sui); **1285** in omni casu quo minores ..implacitari possunt, ..si..minus personaliter sequi possint, propinquiores ~i admittantur ad sequendum pro eis (*St. 2 Westm.* 15) *StRealm* I 82 (= *Ib.* 38: *prochein ami*); **1507** racionabilem dotem suam..in presencia propinquorum ~orum..heredis..infra etatem existentis..assignari faciatis *Cl* 373 m. 5. **c** **14..** postea [alii fratres] conduxerunt sibi per ~os spirituales domum quandam in Cornhyll (*Reg. Fr. Min. Lond.*) ECCLESTON *Adv. Min. app.* 156.

3 (sb. f.) friend. **b** sweetheart, mistress. **c** (fig.) advocate, patroness.

~a mea in Deo et in vera amicitia ANSELM (*Ep.* 169) IV 50. **b** dulcis amica, vale! (? SERLO WILT.) *Eur. Love Lyric* 511; interdumque thoro sit amica tibi generosa D. BEC. 2819; qua ratione vocatis ~as que potius inimicissime proculdubio vobis existunt? GIR. *GE* II 3; **1303** sacrista optulit filie Willelmi..unum firmaculum..per sic quod deveniret ~a sua (*KRAc* 332/8) *Cal. Exch.* 254. **c** philosophia.. mediocritatis ~a GIR. *TH intr.*

amid-, amigd- v. amygd-, amyl- amil- v. et. amyl-.

†amilarius [? cf. admissarius *or* ambularius], horse.

~ius, *mearh GlC* A 536.

amilasatus v. esmallare.

aminaeus [CL = *a kind of vine*], white. **b** (sb. n.) white wine.

amineae, sine rubore [i.e. minio] *GlC* A 501; aminea vitis, *hwit wingeard* ÆLF. *Gl.*; nomina colorum: amineus vel albus, *hwit Ib.* **b** **14..** hoc amuennum, A. *wyte wyne* WW; *whyte wyne*, amenium *CathA*.

aminic- v. adminic-.

†aminitare [? cf. OF *amenuisier* < *adminutiare], to diminish.

1199 concelavit propresturam..unde firma domini regis posset ~ari de xxx m. *CurR RC* I 387.

amir- v. admir-, esmeraldus. amisfractis v. arceuthis.
amisia v. almucia, amictus 2c.

amissare, to let slip.

1288 Walterus Scot amessavit leporarios quos..tenuit ad quendam cervum *TR Forest Proc.* 45 r. 7*d.*; **1293** amessiaverunt leporarios suos ad unam herdam damorum *Ib.* 82 m. 3 (cf. *SelPlForest* 133).

amissibilis, able to be lost.

non videtur..quod omne jus spirituale ~e per hereticam pravitatem amittatur absque constitucione ecclesie OCKHAM *Dial.* 939.

amissio [CL], loss. **b** discontinuance.

amisionem, *forlor GlC* A 504; videns..se suosque..suorum ~one..desperanter afflictos GIR. *EH* I 19; **1250** licet damna non modica..fuere perpessus..propter temporis amisionem *FormOx* 487; **1328** sub pena ~onis..arreragiorum *Reg. Paisley* 28. **b** origo est iniquitatis ~o bonitatis ALCUIN *Ep.* 137 p. 211.

amissis v. amussis.

amissor, loser.

si de escambio fieri debet extentio, estimari debet res amissa in eodem statu in quo fuit quando primo data fuit, quia melioracio ~oris †sui [? l. si] post feoffamentum ampla construxerunt edificia *Fleta* 422.

1 amita v. amictus.

2 amita [CL], (paternal) aunt.

monasterium Aebbae abbatissae, quae erat ~a regis BEDE *HE* IV 17; ~a mea, *min faþu*; ~a mea magna, *minre faþa moder* ÆLF. *Sup.*; **1125** presbiteris..feminarum contubernia..inhibemus, preter matrem, sororem, ~am, sive illas mulieres que omni careant suspicione (*Conc. Lond.* 13) J. WORC. 21; caveant..cum mulieribus cohabitare, nisi forte cum matre, sorore vel †amica [l. amita] GIR. *GE* II 15; cuidam Aline, ..que fuit ~a predicti Ricardi *CurR* XIV 1875 (= *BNB* II 468: †amica); soror patris dicitur ~a BRACTON 68b; hec ameta, *a nawntt* WW; **1495** pro expensis domine Margarete, †emite domini nostri regis *Exch. Scot.* 483.

amiticia v. amicitia.

amitinus, ~a [CL], cousin.

si ex amita procedat filius vel filia, dici poterunt quantum ad nepotem †proprior [? l. propior] †amitivus [l. ~us] et †proprior †amitiva BRACTON 68b.

1 amittere v. admittere.

2 amittere [CL], to let go. **b** (passive) to escape. **c** to hand over. **d** to do away with, destroy.

qui furem plegiatum amiserit (*Leg. Hen.*) *GAS* 558. **b** si ~atur [AS: *gif he losige*], sit forsbannitus et excommunicatus (*Quad.*) *GAS* 49. **c 1203** porcos..imparcavit et eos optulit ~ere per vadium et plegium *SelPlCrown* 48; quod quidem breve [Salamon] amisit Ricardo, ..qui quidem Ricardus.. breve..dilatavit *State Tri. Ed. I* 11. **d** qui magorum molimina funditus everteret et medullitus ~eret Aldh. *VirgP* 43.

2 to lose, be deprived of. **b** (p. ppl. as sb. n.) thing lost, loss.

'circum' praepositio M aliquoties ~it, ut 'circuitus' Aldh. *PR* 140 p. 198; ut visum caeco, quem amiserat, restitueret Bede *HE* II 2; metuens amittere naves G. Amiens *Hast.*141; Willelmus manerium amisit *DB* I 129b; confunditur qui ludum [scaccorum] amisit Neckam *NR* II 184; **1201** si quid admiserint (*sic*) occasione illius defalte, id eis restitui faciant *CurR* I 464; **1219** si H. ~at [sc. terram] per assisam, recuperet *Ib.* VIII 82; si [obligatio] ab una persona transfusa fuerit in aliam que obligari non possit, ammittitur Bracton 101; **1385** pro delicto suo vitam vel membrum admittere debeant *Cl* 225 m. 19. **b c1226** de amissis hominum domini regis que amiserunt in terra nostra inquiri faciatis (*AncC* XI 45) *RL* I 305.

amitus v. amictus. amixtio v. admixtio. amma- v. et. adma-. ammaylatus v. esmallare. amme- v. et. adme-.

ammentatus [CL], hurled w. a throwing-strap.

s1138 amentatis missilibus et lanceis super aciem..loricatam percutiunt H. Hunt. *HA* VIII 9 (= W. Coventr. I 161: amentalibus; M. Par. *Min* I 259: aumentatis [*ed.* †augmentatis]); ludentes..amentatis missilibus ultra metam expediendis W. Fitzst. *Thom. prol.* 16.

ammentum [CL], throwing-strap (of spear). **b** nock (bow-tip).

~um, *scept[l]og GlC* A 517, amentis, *sceptloum Ib.* 548; regis dirum patefecit āmentum, / toxica loetiferae volitant quo tela pharetrae Frith. 1081 (cf. *ALMA* XXV 77); amentum, *wegures gewiðsperes* Ælf. *Gl.*; **1188** Frisonia in amento prevolans (*Lit. Imp.*) R. Howd. II 358 (= Gir. *PI* III 17: volans). **b 14..** amentum, *nok* WW.

ammi- v. et. admi-. ammicdala v. amygdala. ammittere, v. admittere, amittere. ammo- v. et. admo-. ammob- v. amob-. ammodo v. amodo.

ammoniacus [ἀμμωνιακός], (w. *sal*) sal ammoniac. **b** (sb. n.) gum obtained from a desert plant (*Ferula* or *Dorema*). **c** (sb. f. or n.) (applied to various herbs; *cf. armoracia*).

sal armoniacum est magne virtutis, quoniam ex †fumositate eq'a [? l. fimositate equina] fit; est autem multiplex naturale et ficticium M. Scot *Lumen* 244; sophisticantur metalla..mediantibus spiritibus, quorum species sunt 4, sc. argentum vivum, sulphur, auripigmentum et sal ~um (*Id. Part.*) *Med. Sci.* 295; sal armoniacum [fit] ex cinere allzali Gilb. I 52. 2; corpus calcinatur quando humor in eo corrumpatur per salem et sale ~o et aceto Bacon *NM* 548; sales, maxime sal armoniacum *Ps.*-Gros. 626. **b** gutta ad modum galbani est cujusdam herbe vel arboris lacrima que alio nomine armoniacum appellatur Bart. Angl. XVII 78 (cf. ib. 77: galbanus habet plures guttas sicut †armonialem); cum squilla cocta et amoniaco Gilb. VI 264. 1; contra duriciem splenis armoniacum in aceto liquefactum..utilissimum est Gad. 17. 1; ferula: hujus multe sunt species.. gumme sagapinum, amoniacum, galbanum *SB* 21; amoniaci due sunt species, s. albus et purpureus similis rose *Alph.* 8. **c** alteterera i. armoniacum *SB* 10; armoniaca, i. *selfhele*, .. armoniacum, i. marubium *Ib.* 11.

ammonit- v. admonit-. ammoriolum v. armariolum. ammot-, ammov- v. amot-, amov-. ammutatio v. admutuatio.

amnestia [ἀμνηστία], forgetting. **b** amnesty.

~iam, †obolitionem [l. ab-] *GlC* A 514; *a forgettynge*, annescia, oblivio *CathA*. **b 1484** offensarum acerbitas reducta ~ia, verbo Greco, id est injuriarum oblivione, jocunda inter principes relacione celebranda est (A. Quhytelaw) *Bannatyne Misc.* II 47.

amnicus [CL], fluvial.

omnis pene ~orum piscium generis..est copia W. Malm. *GP* IV 183.

amnifluus, torrential.

tu..qui paulo ante finem ~i cursus rusticus expectabas Adel. *QN* 55 (cf. Horace *Ep.* I ii 42).

1 amnis [CL], river. **b** water.

ceu viridis lentescit papirus amne Aldh. *VirgV* 1219; mansio..ab ecclesia..interfluente Tino ~e separata Bede *HE* V 2; transire per amnem G. Amiens *Hast.* 353; militem ..~is impetuosi violentia raptum ad ima Gir. *EH* II 7; **1516** operantibus super ampnem molendini *Ac. Durh.* 664. **b** antempne sunt corde quasi ante ~em [*gl.*: *eve*, i. aquam] posite Neckam *Ut.* 115; sperso signatur presulis amne / mersio baptismi triplex Garl. *Myst. Eccl.* 107 (cf. ib. 319).

2 †amnis, (?) *f.l.*

antequam [apes] a meo alveo †vel ~e [? l. velamine] includantur *Fleta* 175.

amnuere v. abnuere.

amobilis [cf. amotibilis, amovibilis], removable, subject to dismissal.

1319 quod aldermanni civitatis..de anno in annum..sint ~es (*Pat*) *MGL* II 269; **s1330** priorissa semper fuit..dativa et ad domini abbatis voluntatem ~is et ponenda *G. S. Alb.* II 212; **1416** prior dativus et ad nutum abbatis..ammobilis *Reg. Cant.* III 396.

amobragium [W. *amobyr*], payment for bondwoman's marriage or incontinence.

1284 de filiabus expedorum suorum habebunt..prior et fratres [Hospitalis] medietatem ~ii, cum acciderit; de propriis hominibus, totum *IMisc* 43/15; **1301** de filia Gogan ..pro amaubragio..xij d. *Pipe Chesh. app.* 204; **1316** quod illa consuetudo que vocatur ~ium decetero non exigatur nisi infra annum a tempore cognicionis delicti pro quo dicta consuetudo solvi debeat (*Pat*) *Foed.* III 548; **c1370** per illam clausulam 'et habere ammobragium etc.' clamat quod, si aliqua nativa sua maneriorum suorum..de fornicacione fuerit accusata et inde se coram seneschallo suo legitime purgare non poterit, habere [debeat] de qualibet..dim. m. *Rec. Caern.* 167; **1378** †ambrogium *CalPat* 156.

amobrarius, collector of *amobyr*.

1334 amobr' istius commoti cum feodis ~ii valet cx s. *Surv. Denb.* 209.

amobrium, *amobyr* (Wales).

1334 quicumque eorum [nativorum] filiam maritaverit vel quecumque mulier nativa se maritaverit dabit domino pro mercheto v s.; vel quecumque earum [in]nupta convicta fuerit super fornicacione dabit domino pro letherwito v s.; et eciam quecumque fuerit uxor alicujus nativi et fuerit super adulterio convicta, vir ejus dabit pro ea domino pro letherwyto v s.; et vocantur iste consuetudines ~ia *Surv. Denb.* 60.

amodo [al. div.], from now, henceforward.

a modo torpentes decet evigilare Camenas G. Amiens *Hast.* 28; **c1070** clamo eos quietos ~o ab omnibus querelis *Regesta* p. 120; **s747** decreverunt ut episcopi sollicitius ~o viverent W. Malm. *GP* I 5; qui cum illo prius erant, ~o adversus illum H. Cantor 7v.; amodo quid credam, quid dicam nescio certe Nig. *Laur.* 39. 1; **s1236** mandat vobis.. rex quod, hactenus quicquid fecerit, ex hoc nunc et ~o vestrum omnium..consiliis se subdet indubitanter M. Par. *Maj.* III 380; **c1300** ut omnium..operum pietatis que.. fiunt et ~o fient in futuro sit particeps *Lit. Cant.* I 11; **1455** mandatur compotantibus quod ammodo non solvant dictam summam usque ad novum mandatum *ExchScot* 27.

amoenare, to sweeten, make lovely.

cicada viatoris promovet gressum et initiatorum ~at exitum J. Sal. *Pol.* 412D; dat opes dolus amplas / causidicis, mellit successus, ditat, amenat D. Bec. 1508; nimphula cujus facies talamum serenet et ~et Neckam *Ut.* 101; si Camenam amenat, / si mens philomenat Garl. *SM* 1153; regionem..quam..Zephyrus..leniter aspirans ~et Bradw. *CD* 101E.

amoene, agreeably.

multi odoris thi[mi]amata satis ~e redolentia R. Cold. *Cuthb.* 38.

amoenerium v. elemosynaria.

amoenitas [CL], loveliness, amenity.

in cujus ~atem loci cum nos intraturos sperarem Bede *HE* V 12 p. 308; veris ~ate temperieque Gir. *TH* I 33; **1279** virginalis ~as re vel fama faciliter leditur Peckham *Ep.* 70; **s1419** de cujus [ville] ~ate, diviciis et utilitate rex scripsit.. *Chr. S. Alb.* 123.

amoenus [CL], lovely.

de ~issimo scripturarum paradiso Aldh. *Met.* 1; monasterium silvarum et maris vicinitate ~um Bede *HE* III 19; amenus locus, *luffendlice stede* Ælf. *Gl.*; sancta dat crumena, sancta fit amena (*De Nummo* 60) *Ps.*-Map *Poems* 228; ~issima ville suburbia edificiis honestissime decorata Elmh. *Hen. V Cont.* 112.

amogd- v. amygd-.

amoliri [CL], **~ire,** to remove. **b** (pass.).

amulire, abducere *GlC* A 528. **b** necdum sic ab humeris ipsis ~itum est onus adversitatis W. Cant. *Mir. Thom.* II 15.

amolum v. amylum.

amomatum, a spicy electuary.

serapinum, ~um [*gl.*: i. electuarium factum ex pluribus confectionibus] Neckam *Ut.* 109.

amomum [ἄμωμον], a kind of spice.

hunc lacrime thuris recreant et succus amomi Neckam *DS* II 205; ~um..est vocatum eo quod habet odorem veluti cinamomum; ..medicinis solet ~um sepe adhiberi Bart. Angl. XVII 8; ~um genus est herbe †adoratissime [l. od-] cujus fructus similis est butruo et est triplex, sc. ~um, frutex, Armenicum ceteris melius, aurosi coloris *Alph.* 8; hoc ~um, *canylle* WW.

amon [cf. 2 ambo], **amonicus,** pulpit.

a pulpyte, ambo, amon, amonicus *CathA*.

amon- v. et. admon-. amont- v. amunt-.

amor [CL], love. **b** (sexual). **c** (spiritual).

cuidam virginum..quae illam immenso amore diligebat Bede *HE* IV 23; amor est conexio et vinculum quo omnium rerum universitas..copulatur Eriug. *Per.* 519B; omnes vobis in amore fraternitatis conglutinate Anselm (*Ep.* 165) IV 39; est igitur sedes anime dignissima cordis / hospitium; nam vis regnat amoris ibi Neckham *DS* IX 350; est amor continua cogitacio cum ingenti desiderio pulchri bonique amabilis Rolle *IA* 268. **b** luxuriae stimulis caeco et correptus amore Aldh. *VirgV* 2226; accepit Mathildem.., cujus amori jampridem animum impulerat W. Malm. *GR* V 393; castam non amo rem, quia nil amo preter amorem Serlo Wilt. 18. 6; liberor a morte! mea, jam meus urit amor te *Ib.* 101; Gir. *TH* II 24 (v. amplecti a); de genere melancolie est amor hereos in istis mulieribus et viris qui inordinate diligunt Gad. 132. 1; **c1370** ille proprie dicitur infatuatus qui propter amorem alicujus viri vel mulieris cui adheret non curat quid faciat (J. Bridl. *Gl.*) *Pol. Poems* I 133. **c** Christum miro veneratur amore Aldh. *VirgV* 1890; jam credentes amplius in fide atque amore Christi confirmavit Bede *HE* III 19; rogo..propter timorem et amorem Redemptoris nostri *Ib.* IV 5; refrigescit in eo amor caelestis Anselm (*Ep.* 418) V 364; hunc [Dei] amorem non poteris habere perfectum nisi evacuaveris cor tuum ab omni alio amore *Id.* (*Ep.* 112) III 245; remanens dividant pro amore Dei [AS: *Godes pances*] (*Quad.*) *GAS* 178; **1199** pro amore Dei..et pro salute anime nostre *RChart.* 3b; sint ibi fixa tibi spes, amor atque fides Gir. *Symb. metr.* 5.

2 (personified) a Cupid. **b** God.

a cur Amor huic parsit? michi fac ut vulnere par sit! Serlo Wilt. 18 12. **b** Deus per metaforam Amor dicitur Eriug. *Per.* 512D; Amor potens omne quod voluit J. Howd. *CA* 8.

3 desire of or for something.

virginitatis amor flagrans in corde puellae Aldh. *VirgV* 1979; homines ab amore scelerum abstrahere Bede *HE* IV 21; amor persuadendi (*V. Cuthb.*) *Ib.* 25; reviviscit amor mundi Anselm (*Ep.* 418) V 364; amor studii non illaudabilis Gir. *TH intr.*; quisque quidem proprii lucri preponit amorem D. Bec. 2269; amputacionem amoris inordinati ad temporalia Ockham *Err. Papae* 958.

4 favour.

cum abbas eam [hidam] dederat ob amorem regis *DB* I 208; oportebat omnibus obsequi regis nutui si amore ejus ..vellent perfrui H. Hunt. *HA* VI 39; **1220** qui nec odio nec amore veritatem celare velint *SelPlCrown* 140.

5 amicable settlement of dispute. **b** (w. *dies*) love-day, time for amicable settlement.

si quis cum socio vel compari causam habuit et inter eos super hiis ex amore et testimonio convenerit (*Leg. Hen.*) *GAS* 574 (cf. ib. 572: pactum legem vincit et amor judicium); **1236** convenit quod per sacramentum sex vel octo legalium hominum vicinorum de consensu partium electorum in amore inquiratur utrum.. *AncD* A3431. **b 1230** dies amoris captus est inter eos (*AncC* VI 112) *RL* I 361; **1239** habent diem amoris..de quadam contencione.., ita quod convocatis amicis suis dicto die..de pace tractent inter eos *KRMem* 18 r. 14d.; si post defaltam factam ante judicium capiatur dies amoris.., videtur per hoc quod petens tacite renunciat defalte Bracton 369; **1372** est communis manutentor de champertrie et cum bonis..abbacie sustentat dies amoris inter quamplures partes, unde magna odia..sepius generantur *IMisc* 202/1.

amoracea v. armoracia. amoratum v. moratum.

†amorfolia [? cf. antofilus *or* aurisfolia], (?) burdock (bot.).

nomina herbarum: ..~ia, *clate* Ælf. *Gl.*

amorifer, charged w. love.

gentis amorifere Venerem Cyprus insula dudum / excoluit Garl. *Tri. Eccl.* 131; o pectus amoriferum, / quod cum intrat rex syderum, / factus nobis vicinior J. Howd. *Cyth.* 120 (cf. ib. *pref.*: verbis ~is).

amorosus, amorous.

s1327 quot ~a †teleumata [? l. celeumata] voce submissa ..concinuit Baker 106b; in hominibus ~is, qui [= Upton 108: in quibus] pre amoris magnitudine estuantes dilati cordis spiritus incipiunt evaporare Bad. Aur. 102.

amort- v. admort-.

amotibilis [cf. amobilis, amovibilis], removable, subject to dismissal.

sunt..quidam priores et procuratores qui ~es sunt Bracton 12; **1287** prior..~is ad voluntatem abbatis *PQW* 9a; **1337** omnes ballivi istarum curiarum sunt ~es ad voluntatem domini ducis *Capt. Seis. Corn.* m. 28.

amotio [CL], removal, withdrawal. **b** dismissal.

summum remedium..esset ~o oblationum Gir. *GE* I 49; **c1230** post ammocionem bladorum quando averia domini stipulas pascunt (*Cust. Ogbourne St. A.*) *Doc. Bec* 38; **1316** si aliquis burgensis..in solucione annui census cessaverit.., quod per capcionem pignorum vel amocione[m] porte domus satisfacere compellatur *RGasc* IV 1626; causa ammocionis sue ab uno lecto ad alium *Cust. Cant.* 194; **1369** pro ~one et asportacione lapidum..a navi *ExchScot* 348. **b** nullus per talem ~onem [juratorum]..dampnum habere potuit *State Tri. Ed. I* 36; **1332** post ammocionem..nuper vicecomitis *LTRMem* 105 r. 12d.; **1399** per subitas et frequentes ammociones et expulsiones priorum (*Pat*) *Foed.* VIII 101a; **1416** ammocio prioris Dovorr' et subrogacio alterius loco sui *Reg. Cant.* I 151; **1561** sub pena ~onis ab universitate *StatOx* 376.

amotivus [cf. amotibilis], removable, subject to dismissal. **b** (sb. m.) removable curate.

1395 prior de Neuport Paynell' dativus et ammotivus ad voluntatem abbatis de Mermoustier' *RParl* III 332b; ~i.. ad voluntatem..comitis *Entries* 388b. **b 1519** deservitur cure per ammotivum *Vis. Linc.* I 50.

amotor, remover.

c1275 abbas inveniet eis ovile et ~orem illius *Ac Beaulieu* 21v.

amovēre [CL], to take away, remove. **b** (fig.) to clear away, dispel. **c** to raise (a siege). **d** (leg.) to transfer (an action). **e** (w. *manus*) to withdraw restraint from, release from possession.

placuit..ut lapis..~eretur et altius.. reponeretur BEDE *HE* III 8; W. FITZST. *Thom. prol.* 11 (v. admovere a); **1207** omnia catalla amota fuerunt de domo *SelPlCrown* 55; **1242** ammota est..draperia a loco illo in quo esse consuevit *Cl* 449; **1275** nec voluit se de eodem loco ~ere *SelPlMan* 142; s1385 versus partes Scocie castra sua ammovit *V. Ric. II* 61. **b** qui..caliginis incommodum ab oculis ~erent BEDE *HE* IV 17; res procul amote tristes, si dicis "amo te" SERLO WILT. 18 55; ad dubitacionem ~endam BACON XV 161. **c** **1342** ad proficiscendum..pro obsessione..~enda *RScot* 626a; s1352 iter arripuit..ut obsidionem ammoveret J. READING 162b. **d** **1312** breve nostrum tibi venit ad predictum appellum coram nobis..~endum *SelCCoron* 72; a1460 placitum retrahendo et ~endo a lege terre coram admirallo pertractabunt *BBAdm.* I 227. **e** **1347** tibi precipimus quod manum nostram de baronia predicta.. ~eas *RScot* 700a; **1366** ~eat manum suam de arrestu predicto *Hal. Durh.* 57.

2 to remove from office, depose, dismiss.

amotis subregulis, ..suscepit imperium BEDE *HE* IV 12; s1147 Willelmum..ab archiepiscopatus Eboracensis officio et beneficio ammovendum censuit J. HEX. *Pri. Hex.* 154; **1219** ~et M. ..et O. ..quos prius posuerat loco suo versus J. ..de placito terre *CurR* VIII 35; **1248** illum admovebimus et alium..loco suo subrogabimus *BBC* (*Poole*) 353; **1416** fratrem W. ..ab administracione..prioratus duximus ammovendum *Reg. Cant.* I 151.

amovibilis [cf. amobilis, amotibilis], removable, subject to dismissal.

1419 olim non erant ~es aldermanni ab officiis suis *MGL* I 36; **1465** priorem prioratus de Coldingham..et suos monachos ibidem ad nutum prioris..ecclesie Dunelmensis ex solito ammovibiles *Pri. Cold.* 207; **1534** per curatum.. ~em ad nominacionem nostram..deputandum *Reg. St. Bees* 370.

amovitio [cf. amotio], removal.

c1375 de temeraria capcione et ~one duorum monachorum *Pri. Cold.* 53.

ampar- v. empar-. ampeleos, ~ion v. ampelos.

ampeloprason [ἀμπελόπρασον; CL = kind of leek], white vine (or bryony) conf. w. wild turnip.

ampelon prassion, vitis alba idem *SB* 10; alphesora, amphelion prassion idem, vitis alba, brionia idem, G. *navet*, A. *wildnep Alph.* 5.

ampelos [ἄμπελος], vine (or bryony).

brionia vel ~os leuce, *hwit wilde wingeard*, ..brabasca vel amplos male, *blac wingeard* ÆLF. *Gl.*; ampelion vel anapelion vel crampeleon, vitis agrestis.., ampeleon melanis vel melas, i. vitis nigra, et ampeleos ynipheros, i. vitis †vermifera [v.l. vinifera] *Alph.* 6.

amperium v. hanaparium. ampha v. nympha. amphelion v. ampeloprason.

amphemera, quotidian ague.

cum fortitudo que solet in amphimera evenire non apparet GILB. I 57 v. 2.

amphemerinus [ἀμφημερινός], quotidian (med.).

urina tenuis et alba..in febribus amphimerinam deficientem significat GILB. I 37 v. 2; flegma putrefactum..in toto corpore..facit amphimerinam, effi[merinam] et quotidianam continuam, quod idem est GAD. 11 v. 2; flegmatica aut amphimerina ab *amphi*, quod est 'dubium', vel *amphi* et *meron*, 'terminacio', quia dubie terminacionis, i. periculose, febris, quia est morbus periculosus *Ib.*

amphi [ἀμφί], on both sides.

~i, utrimque *GlC* A 510.

amphibalus, ~um [cf. ἀμφίμαλλος], rough cloak.

sub sancti abbatis ~o GILDAS *EB* 28; ~us, †hircus bellosus [? l. birrus villosus] *GlC* A 551; ~um, *ruhhrægel* ÆLF. *Gl.*; *duddyd cloth..*, *roowe clop, as faldyng or odyr lyke*, ~us *PP*; amphibulus, A. *a sclavayn or faldyng* WW; *a slavyn'*, ~us, birrus, †caracalca *CathA.*

amphibena, ~bim v. amphisbaena.

amphibius [ἀμφίβιος], amphibious, (sb. f. or n.) seal or porpoise.

[pisces] diversi sunt, utpote mugiles, †amphinia [*gl. soles*, (?) l. *seles*; *but* v.l. amphimera, cf. ephemera] NECKAM *Ut.* 97; **14..** amphivia, A. *seles*, ..hec †amphinia, *a porpas* WW; *a seyle*, amphivia, piscis est *CathA.*

amphibolia [ἀμφιβολία], ambiguity, equivocation.

quos non rumor ambiguus per ~ie diverticula distrahebat W. CANT. *Mir. Thom.* III 11; est quoque in talibus secundus modus equivocacionis vel ~ie, eo quod diccio vel oracio accipitur transsumptive BRADW. *CD* 188D; opinio populi dat eum tenuisse regem nostrum..in ~iis et ambagibus ELMH. *Hen. V* 103.

amphibolicus, ambiguous.

assumptum ejus est ~um WYCL. *Ver.* III 214.

amphibologia, ambiguity, equivocation (*v. et. amphibolia, amphilogia*).

rex dimissionem de suis episcopis..quesivit, sed non nisi in ~ia assecutus H. CANTOR f. 24; est ~ia plurium sententiarum per unam orationem designatio; et dicitur ab *amphi*, quod est dubium, et *bole*, 'sermo'; ..fallacia ~ie est deceptio proveniens ex idemptitate orationis secundum materiam et formam BACON XV 333; fallacia equivocacionis vel ~ie DUNS *Sent.* I ix 1. 4; differencia..inter diversos sensus proposicionum talium secundum ~iam OCKHAM *Dial.* 802; cum duce colloquia secreta nimis tenuit rex; / amphibologia danda veretur ibi ELMH. *Metr. Hen. V* 1007.

amphibologice, ambiguously, equivocally.

dicebant nonnulli illum [Merlinum]..more demonum obscure et ~e enigmatizasse *Flor. Hist.* I 237; videtur quod spirituale non univoce sed equivoce vel ~e dicatur de sacramentis PAUL. ANGL. *ASP* 1550.

amphibologicus, ambiguous, equivocal.

s1219 papa interpretabatur hanc locutionem ~am ['reginam interficere nolite timere bonum est'] in melius M. PAR. *Min.* II 233; a1250 sub duplicitate ~a (J. GODARD *Ep.*) *Anal. Cisterc.* X 228; licet parabole evangelice et ~e Jesu Christi possint accipi ad multiplicem et dubium intellectum BRADW. *CD* 791E; illa tamen universalis 'omnis homo futurus est animal' est ~a, eo quod hoc totum 'futurus est' potest supplere vicem hujus verbi de futuro 'erit' et tunc est vera WYCL. *Log.* I 90.

amphibolus [ἀμφίβολος], ambiguous.

tunc esset dubitatio an conversio egrederetur a 'captivitate' in 'Dominum' vel e contrario, et tunc esset sermo ~us BACON XV 161.

amphibrachys [ἀμφίβραχυς], amphibrach.

vocitatus est ~us quod ex utraque parte brevibus ambiatur sillabis..: ergo *amphi* 'utrimque', *brachus* 'brevis' interpretatum dicitur ALDH. *PR* 121; ~us ex brevi et longa et brevi temporum quattuor, ut 'hărēnă' BEDE *AM* 2364.

amphibulus v. amphibalus. amphicapa v. amphitape.

amphicyrtos [ἀμφίκυρτος], (of the moon) showing a double curve, i.e. almost full. **b** (fig.).

luna..in neomenia..dicitur neonides, in majori incremento diaconios, in circuli perfectione amphikyrtos, in plenilunio pansilenos GERV. TILB. I 6. **b** sicut in astrologia Martiani luna..cum accedit ad circulum dicitur ~os, ..sic Dei ecclesia..in adventu Christi ~os..poterat nuncupari P. BLOIS *Ep.* 8. 22B.

amphilogia [ἀμφιλογία], doubt, dilemma.

1237 si tribulationem..inveniremus, ..[Dominus] nobis ..adesset, sicut in medio discipulorum jampridem pacificans discordes et cogitationum corrigens ~iam [v.l. amphibologiam] (*Lit. Archiep. Constantinop.*) M. PAR. *Maj.* III 450.

amphimacrus [ἀμφίμακρος], amphimacer, cretic.

~us..vocabulum sumpsit quod ab utraque parte longis sillabis [brevis] cingitur; nam *macra* 'longa'..dicitur ALDH. *PR* 122; ~us ex longa et brevi et longa temporum quinque, ut 'impōtēns' BEDE *AM* 2364.

amphimer- v. amphemer-. amphinium v. amphibius.

amphisbaena [ἀμφίσβαινα], (mythical) two-headed snake. **b** Satan (*cf. Arch. J.* LXVIII 285–316).

dat natura tibi geminum caput, amphisebena NECKAM *DS* IX 293; alii [serpentes] habent duo capita, ut amphibena BART. ANGL. XVIII 8; hec emfimenia, serpens cum duobus capitibus, ..hoc amphibim est serpens cum tribus (*sic*) capitibus..hec apaphsibena, *a nedyr with ij hedes* WW. **b** ludit et illudit mortalibus †amphisilena, / decipiendo quibus Paradisi tollit amena ORD. VIT. XI *pref. vers.*

amphiscius [ἀμφίσκιος], throwing a shadow either way (north or south).

dicit Ambrosius: 'sunt..et ~ii, id est circum umbrati' BACON *Maj.* I 308.

amphistrum v. aplustre.

amphitape [ἀμφιτάπης], cloth w. pile on both sides.

~e genus vestimenti utrimque villosum et hirsutum dicitur ALDH. *PR* 121; lectisternia..simplis et ~is coornata erant BALSH. *Ut.* 47; *bankar*, scannarium, amfitaba *PP*; amphicapa est tapeta ex utraque parte villosa WW; *a chalon'*, amphitapetum *CathA.*

amphitheatrum [ἀμφιθέατρον], amphitheatre.

amphitetron, circumspectac[ul]um *GlC* A 516; dicitur.. ~um, ubi altrinsecus scenicorum ludibria histrionumque ridiculosa commenta exercentur ALDH. *PR* 166; in amfitheatrum sanctos..carnifex imperat duci *Id. VirgP* 36 p. 284; ~um, *syneweald wafungstede* ÆLF. *Gl.*; **10..** ~i, *plegstowe* WW.

Amphitrite [Ἀμφιτρίτη, *sea goddess*], sea. **b** ocean girdling earth from pole to pole.

~e, mare *GlC* A 529 (cf. ib. 509, 609). **b** cingunt duo maria totam terram; et illud quod cingit terram sub polis ~es vocatur, reliquum vero Oceanus. hec duo maria dividunt terram in quattuor partes GROS. 24.

amphivia v. amphibius.

amphora [CL < ἀμφορεύς], liquid measure [*cf.* 1 *ambra*]. **b** vessel (esp. hooped vessel of wood or leather).

anfora quattuor modios tenet *GlC* A 585; **c805** (12c) dent ..x anforas de melle *CS* 324; amfora, *sester* ÆLF. *Gl.*; abbas ..debet mittere ad Ecclesiam Christi xxx panes tales..et iii amphoras plenas ii de meda et tertiam de cervisa *Dom. Cant.* 1 (cf. THORNE 1804); s1194 similiter et de batis vel ~is seu metretis vulgo galones [rex] legitime jussit fieri mensure *Itin. Ric.* VI 38 p. 448; ~a ab ansis est vocata, quibus hinc inde levatur; et recipit frumenti vel vini modios ytalicos tres. cadus est ~a continens tres urnas BART. ANGL. XIX 125. **b** anfora, *crocca* ÆLF. *Gl.*; **1286** debuisset haurire aquam cum quadam †ansera [? l. anfora] *Rec. Norw.* I 216; **1448** J. Couper pro factura unius nove ~e et R. Smyth pro ligatura ferrea ejusdem *Ac. Durh.* 275; **1454** iij ~e de corrio et iiij de ligno *Ib.* 148; ~a, *tankard* WW.

amphorismus v. aphorismus.

amplare, to enhance, invigorate.

c1450 mentem spes animat, jubet, instat, fervet et amplat *Vers. Ed. Conf.* 5.

amplastr- v. emplastr-.

ample [CL], fully, thoroughly.

quod..Gallia ~issime contestatur G. CRISPIN *Herl.* 103; lapis..tante quantitatis ut..pateram ~e contineat GIR. *GE* I 10 p. 35.

2 (compar.) more fully, further, in addition. **b** moreover. **c** (of time) longer. **d** any more, henceforward.

crepitant incendia flammis / amplius ALDH *VirgV* 2621; suis ~ius ex virtutum exemplis prodesse curabat BEDE *HE* V 9; puer trium circiter non ~ius annorum *Ib.* IV 8; quid ~ius [AS: *hwæt mare*] facis in die? ÆLF. *Coll.* 91; valet vii sol.; nil ~ius *DB* I 31b; ut..dulcedinem amoris senciam ~ius ROLLE *IA* 185; butirum ovinum melius est, quod..est ..~ius pingue *Alph.* 25. **b** potestas spiritualis et laicalis.. in eodem esse non possunt; ~ius, potestates ille.. OCKHAM *Pol.* I 14. **c** s1338 per annum et ~ius moram traxit AVESB. 83b; s1382 stella cometa apparuit in occidente ~ius quam per quindenam WALS. *HA* II 68. **d** hanc penam iis [excommunicatio] infligit: gratia Dei..illis ~ius subtrahitur GIR. *GE* I 53; **1350** juravit quod ~ius hujusmodi empciones non committeret *Leet Norw.* 81; **1398** ita quod..~ius inde justam queremoniam non audiamus *Reg. Paisley* 96.

†amplectari, to embrace. **b** (gdv.) to be cherished.

tempus..quo collum caritatis vestrae ~er ALCUIN *Ep.* 10 p. 36. **b** c745 domino..merito ab omnibus orthodoxis ~ando (*Lit. Ep. Wint.*) *Ep. Bonif.* 64 p. 132; venerando patri nobis cum summo honore ~ando [v.l. ~endo] ALCUIN *Ep.* 196 p. 323.

amplecti [CL], **~ere,** to embrace. **b** to comprise. **c** (fig.) to welcome, cherish, adhere to.

dum eam nefandus ille ~eretur G. MON. X 3 (= *Eul. Hist.* II 339: amplectaretur); hic [leo] fatuam quandam.. bestiali amore ~i solebat GIR. *TH* II 24. **b** 'crepuerunt, tonuerunt'..non epitritum primum sed ionicum minorem ~untur ALDH. *PR* 137. **c** martiris amplexus felix oracula puber ALDH. *VirgV* 1397; studium tuae sinceritatis ~or BEDE *HE pref.*; ut merito a majoribus..amaretur, veneraretur, ~eretur *Ib.* V 19; si [hoc opus] cum supercilio ~unt ÆTHELW. IV 2; s1172 [Hibernienses] episcopi..circa matrimonium..que Anglia..observat se firmiter amplexuros..promittunt DICETO *YH* I 351; fide certissima est ~endum GIR. *TH* II 19; s1315 cum [rex]..solatium in remigando infra diversos lacus amplexisset *Flor. Hist.* III 173.

†amplestia, ~ria, plenty. **b** gluttony.

plenty, abundancia, ~ia, ..plenitas *CathA.* **b** *a glutony*, ~ria, castrimargia, ..gula *Ib.*

†amplex, (?) wide (or *f.l.* for *duplic*[*atus*]).

1315 par unum..de sindone de purpureo †amplici *Invent. Ch. Ch.* 57.

amplexabilis, estimable, to be prized.

quod est..obstupescibile et predignatione incomprehensibili ~e, sic est Verbum in carne H. BOS. *LM* 1378; civitatem famosissimam Alexandrie et mercatoribus cunctis ~em S. SIM. *Itin.* 24.

amplexari [CL], **~are,** to embrace, entwine. **b** to comprise. **c** to embrace (fig.), welcome.

in capella..hedere nexibus ~ata GIR. *IK* I 6. **b** ~antibus singulis [temporibus] medio moderamine quae circa se sunt BEDE *TR* 35 p. 246; omnia quae intra decem categoriarum terminos ~antur ERIUG. *Per.* 593B. **c** abbatissa, ~ata gratiam Dei in viro BEDE *HE* IV 22; devotam viri subtilitatem cum admiratione ~atus est GIR. *IK* I 8; huc accedunt..†~enda [? l. ~anda] sanctorum exempla AD. MARSH *Ep.* 102; fontem lucis amplexans inclitum J. HOWD. *Ph.* 881; studium sacre pagine..bracchiis fidei ~atus est RICH *Edm.* 618.

amplexatio, embrace (fig.).

c1236 me vestrum specialiter vestra suscipiat benigne caritatis ~o GROS. *Ep.* 36.

amplexio, embrace (fig.), acceptance.

honor scripture consistit..non in verbali ~one WYCL. *Ver.* I 341.

1 amplexus v. amplecti.

2 amplexus [CL], embrace. **b** (fig.) union, alliance.

jocosos ludorum ~us ALDH. *VirgP* 35 p. 278; cum dicis triginta, ungues indicis et pollicis blando conjunges ~u BEDE *TR* 1; considera..quantum distent viriles ~us ab ~ibus Christi ANSELM (*Ep.* 168) III 44; amicam suam ~ibus regis herentem videt MAP *NC* II 19; si tibi sit carus, amplexus, oscula prestes D. BEC. 2345. **b** ..negotii salutaris urgentiam..in misericordie et veritatis occursu et ~u justitie et pacis ad..consummationem..producere AD. MARSH *Ep.* 85.

ampliamentum [cf. implementum, OF *emplement*], stock.

1286 pontifices..~a successoribus suis dimiserunt infrascripta, viz. apud S. xliij boves, apud R. xvj boves.. *Ch. Sal.* 364.

ampliare [CL], to enlarge, increase. **b** to enhance, enrich (w. something). **c** to spread, disseminate. **d** (log.) to extend (*cf. amplicare, ampliativus*).

a710 (11c) ~iet Deus partem ejus in regione viventium *CS* 122; ut non areas ~iari sed ex toto domos amoveri oporteret ECCLESTON *Adv. Min.* 55; **1276** ita quod..ad debitorum solucionem et ad hospi[ta]litatem ~iandam totaliter convertantur (*Cart. Glast.*) *MonA* I 32a (cf. ib.: ad..hospitalitatis graciam †appliandam); **1481** veraces fidei cultores intendens ~iare *Lit. Cant.* III 306. **b** aedificium.. mirificis ~iavit operibus BEDE *HE* V 20; comprovinciales ecclesiam..in rebus et redditibus ~iabant BRAKELOND 140; [Alfredus] peregrinos..pecuniis simul et possessionibus ~iabat M. PAR. *Maj.* I 406; **s1297** rex..eos in magnis muneribus ~iavit et honoravit *Eul. Hist.* III 165. **c** sicut patet ~iantibus verbum WYCL. *Ver.* III 219. **d** si sit verbum ~iandi, potest subjectum supponere pro non ente, ut 'homo laudatur'; hoc est verum pro Cesare et est verbum ~ians cujus res potest inesse non existenti (W. SHIRWOOD) *GLA* III 19; magister meus..~iat significacionem hujus verbi 'est' (KYN.) *Ziz.* 64.

2 (w. dat.) to grant in addition. **b** to leave room (fig.), give scope.

[Augustus] imposuit coronam capiti ejus [sc. Herodis], ~ians illi..Samariam..et maritimas civitates M. PAR. *Maj.* I 76. **b** si celaverit [mortem furis] et fiat deinceps quandoque notum, tunc ~iavit mortuo ad juramentum [AS: *rymeð he ðam deadan to ðam aðe*], quod licet parentibus suis purgare eum (*Quad.*) *GAS* 99.

ampliatio, widening. **b** enlargement (in size). **c** increase (of number). **d** prolongation (of time). **e** enhancement, furtherance. **f** (log.) extension (*cf. ampliativus*).

silvestrium semitarum..~one GIR. *EH* II 36; **1262** ad ~onem transituum *Cl* 120. **b** **s1228** emit..terram..pro ~one aree fratrum *Mon. Francisc.* I 496; **1279** inquiratur de ~one..warenne *PQW* 190; **s1279** fuit statutum factum ne religiosi in ~onibus terrarum crescerent *Ann. Lond.* 89; **c1470** in..~onem et elargacionem dominii terrarum *Reg. Whet.* I 428. **c** **1301** ad..~onem numeri eorum [scolarium] *Reg. Cant.* II 737; **1425** propter ~onem numeri sociorum *Reg. Cant.* I 344. **d** quare scriptura tam frequenter utitur..figurativo modo loquendi, et precipue in extensione vel ~one temporis (KYN.) *Ziz.* 31. **e** unctio interior que..virtutum ~onem perficit GIR. *GE* I 4; **1197** ut..desideraret que ad pacem essent et ~onem Rothomagensis ecclesie (*Lit. Archiep. Rotom.*) DICETO *YH* II 157; **1212** si..in ~onem divini cultus illud invenerint posse fieri *Reg. Moray* 40; **1216** quo exemplo..~onis libertatum vestrarum ceteri ad obsequium nostrum forcius..aspirabunt *Pat* 196a; **1440** quantum..universitatis nostre omniumque vestrum ~onem, honorem profectumque..zelemus (*Lit. regis*) BEKYNTON I 101. **f** abutuntur eis [scripturis] nimia verborum affirmativorum ~one, sub eis falso assumendo, sicut qui preceptum de honorandis parentibus extendit ad prohibendum religionis ingressum PECKHAM *Exp. Thren.* II 30 p. 633; ex modo loquendi quem oportet habere de tempore et aliis successivis patet ~o verbi de presenti WYCL. *Ente Praed.* 189; solum signum quantum ad significacionem recipit hujusmodi ~onem (KYN.) *Ziz.* 64.

ampliativus, ampliative, extending a conception (log.). **b** supplementary, explanatory.

proposicionum de inesse quedam sunt in quibus ponitur aliquis terminus ~us subjecti vel predicati ad supponendum ..pro suppositis possibilibus preteriti vel futuri aut cujuslibet temporis indifferenter (DUNS *An. Pri.* I 12. 3) *GLA* III 227 n. 189; 'posset'..est secundum logicos verbum ~um, quare sub voce presentis temporis potest extendi ulterius ad futurum BRADW. *CD* 839E; **1363** nec impeditur similitudo propter hoc verbum ~um (KYN.) *Ziz.* 34. **b** **1522** in secundo brevi apostolico ~o *Form. S. Andr.* I 236.

ampliator, enricher, benefactor.

1439 domine clementissime necnon ~or nostri gloriosissime *EpAcOx* 185.

amplicare, to extend or (?) be extended (log.); *cf. ampliare* 1d.

'esse' est commune ad omnia talia [sc. presens, preteritum vel futurum]; igitur et 'posse' ad quecunque talia tempora signanda, ut pro illis ~et WYCL. *Act.* 62.

amplicative, by way of extension (log.).

1363 quero..quomodo accipitur ibi hoc verbum 'vident', numquid pro presenti solum vel ~e (KYN.) *Ziz.* 12.

amplicativus, ampliative (*cf. ampliativus*).

omne verbum, quantumcunque presens non ~um fuerit, connotat omne tempus in hoc quod connotat tempus presens in communi; igitur multo magis hoc verbum ~um 'potest' WYCL. *Act.* 62.

amplificare [CL], to enlarge, increase. **b** to enhance, enrich (w. something).

superfluis..argumentis addere et ~are ALDH. *VirgP* 56; **704** (9c) si quis..hanc donationis nostre munificentiam augere et ~are maluerit *CS* 111; quicquid ejus famam ~are potuerat, illud adimplere..satagebat GIR. *EH* I 4; [cor] ~at se continue secundum circulos crescentes *Ps.*-RIC *Anat.* 21; [materiam] hominis manus interioris / ducit ut amplificet vel curtet VINSAUF *PN* 218. **b** tuus incipiat fieri meus iste libellus, / ut careat vitiis et laudibus amplificetur G. AMIENS *Hast.* 14.

amplificatio, enrichment, profit.

1350 ut..in divini cultus augmentum ac ministrorum dicte ecclesie ~onem quedam cantaria perpetua ordinetur (*Reg. Ebor.*) *Fabr. York* 168n.

amplitudo, width. **b** extent.

locus..habet ingressum ~inis quasi jactus fundae BEDE *HE* IV 13; est Hibernia..circa capita..in ~inem dilatata GIR. *TH* I 3. **b** cujus ~ini aut diuturnitati nulla meta.. opponitur ANSELM (*Mon.* 22) I 39; **s1194** papa..fretus sua potestate, de cujus ~ine disputare fas non est R. HOWD. III 230; ordinem per orbis ~inem longe lateque diffusum GIR. *GE* II 13; tempus extra non ampliat, eo quod ~o ejus non subjacet potestati illius (KYN.) *Ziz.* 64.

amplus [CL], broad. **b** extensive. **c** (compar. pl.) more (in number).

in viam planam et ~am BEDE *HE* V 6; [Hibernienses] utuntur..securibus..~is..quas a Norwagiensibus..sunt mutuati GIR. *TH* III 10; **1456** per vendicionem v ~arum sagittarum *ExchScot* 142. **b** princeps imperium qui Romae rexerat amplum ALDH. *VirgV* 1039; ~iora beneficia BEDE *HE* II 13; ~issimam ac nobilissimam bibliothecam *Ib.* V 20; in ~iorem tam pretiosi finis laudem H. BOS. *Thom.* VI 7; fers ampla trophea SERLO WILT. 37. 5; **1276** affeccione qua possumus ~iori *TreatyR* I 57. **c** **1235** dicit quod plures venerunt in domum, circiter duodecim vel ~iores *CurR* XV 1438.

2 (sb. n.) extent. **b** (compar.) anything more.

c1393 non fuerant vise tabule prius orbis in amplo (R. MAIDSTONE) *Pol. Poems* I 295. **b** obsecro ne ~ius quam haec solummodo proxima nox intersit BEDE *HE* IV 9; **1285** (v. amuntare b).

amplustr- v. aplustre. ampnis v. amnis. ampollarius v. ampullarius. amponenth v. emponenth. ampsoca v. hamsoca.

ampulla [CL], ampulla, cruet, small flask, esp. for holy oil. **b** liquid measure.

adsumta ~a misit de oleo in pontum BEDE *HE* III 15; archidiaconus ascendens cum chrismate ampulam auream cum pallio albo habens in manu sua EGB. *Pont.* 120; **796** misi..~am et patenam ad offerendam..oblationem ALCUIN *Ep.* 102; ejus [secretarii] sollicitudinis est ~as vinarias et aquarias bis in ebdomada..lavare LANFR. *Const.* 150; **a1170** una ~a argentea ad serviendum altari de j m. et iij unciis et ij d. (*Invent.*) *Chr. Steph.* II 759; aliquid staminis.. de quo facta fuerat ~a W. CANT. *Mir. Thom.* VI 155 (cf. ib. 9); **1222** ~e iij argentee ad oleum; item ~e ij..bene operate et ornate lapidibus pretiosis (*Invent.*) *Reg. S. Osm.* II 128; cola et distilla per filtrum et serva in ~a vitrea GAD. 131. 2; **1315** tres ~e..unde j deaurata *Invent. Ch. Ch.* 73. **b** ~a est modica liquoris mensura, quasi ampla bulla. similis..est in rotunditate bullis que ex spumis aquarum fiunt BART. ANGL. XIX 125.

2 bubble, swelling.

vapor ampullis testibus alta petit NECKAM *DS* IV 545; urina colorata magis et quedam ~e minute in superficie GILB. I 33. 1; [aer] ascendit..in ampulla ex ipsa aqua GROS. 88; ~as tumentes et ingurgitantes aquas maris BACON *Maj.* I 140.

ampullare, to bubble. **b** (p. ppl.) puffed up, bombastic.

repone donec ~averit et appareant ampulle GILB. VII 324. 2. **b** [Lanfrancus] mundi fumos et ~ata gentilium eloquia parvipendens W. MALM. *GP* I 24.

ampullarius, (?) dealer in flasks.

13.. de domo que fuit Henrici Ampollarii *Reg. S. Aug.* 336.

ampullatio, swelling, formation of blisters.

~o et vesicatio cuti vicina GILB. VI 250. 1.

ampullose, bombastically.

s1217 ad hoc verbum ~e prolatum appositam chartam.. dilaceravit *G. S. Alb.* I 257; **s1453** respondebat ~e satis comminabaturque verbis grandibus *Reg. Whet.* I 96.

ampullosus, pot-bellied.

venter honustus..et corpus ~a carnositate compactum J. GODARD *Ep.* 226.

2 bubbly, frothy. **b** bombastic, grandiloquent.

quod sit spuma ~ior M. SCOT *Sol & Luna* 721; urina tenuis et glauca vel livida et ~a GILB. VI 265 v. 1. **b** si ~is dictionibus paginam illinissem G. MON. I 1; **s1190** verba jaculans ~a et contentiosa *Itin. Ric.* II 18; **s1106** neque.. minas ampulosas..pertimesco M. PAR. *Min.* I 203; turgidus et inflatus est ille qui nimis duris et ~is utitur translationibus VINSAUF *AV* II 3 147; **1378** dimittendo ~am apparenciam sophisticam WYCL. *Ver.* I 89; **a1400** quod nullus se jactat verbis ~is *Gild Merch.* (*Grimsby*) I 27; **1440** stupore.. concutior quod tam supercilioso stilo, ut..~us didascolus, ..'correctorem in deviis' te appelles BEKYNTON I 116.

ampullula, little flask.

protulit..~am in cujus fundo parvissimum quid [balsami] resederat W. MALM. *GP* I 66.

amputabilis, able to be cut off. **b** (of woodland) fit for clearing.

s1100 est collum cameli..talis scematis et substantie ut vix sit ~e M. PAR. *Min.* I 184. **b** **1347** sunt..c acre bosci ..unde subboscus potest amputari quolibet decimo anno, et sic decimum quarterium est ~e quolibet anno *IPM* 85/5 r. 4.

amputare [CL], to cut off (part of body). **b** to amputate (med.). **c** to steal by cutting loose.

letali vulnere brachium ~avit GIR. *EH* I 41; **1265** ~avit partem capitis cum cerebro *SelCCoron* 2; **1345** manum suam dexteram amittat, et ~etur *SelCKB* VI 42. **b** membrum ~are oportet GAD. 125. 2. **c** **1291** inventus fuit.. ~ando unam bursam (*St. Ives*) *Law Merch.* I 42.

2 to lop or fell. **b** to clear (woodland). **c** to reap (corn).

1269 fraxini..~ate erant in curia sua propria *SelPlForest* 52; **1293** ~avit summitates ij quercuum *TRForest Proc.* 82 m. 3. **b** **1305** est ibidem quidam boscus; ..pannagium inde non extenditur, quia tarde ~abatur *Ext. Hadleigh* 229; **1324** sunt ibidem tres parve gravette..et possunt ~ari quolibet sexto anno *IPM* 83 r. 17; **1367** suboscus nullus, eo quod raro ~abatur *IPM* 196/10 r. 4. **c** **1269** ~avit unam quantitatem bladi in dicta divisa et adduxit ad curiam suam *CBaron* 86.

3 to dock (an item). **b** to rescind (a statute). **c** to remove, eliminate.

1329 allocantur eidem ij celdre per superfluam oneracionem in compoto vicecomitis..et que a dicto vicecomite debent ~ari *ExchScot* 186. **b** **1565** illa statuta que pertinent ad missas..prorsus abscindimus et ~amus *StatOx* 385. **c** **11..** omnem perturbationis materiem ~are conamur *Feod. Durh.* xlvii.

amputatio [CL], amputation, dismemberment. **b** theft by cutting loose.

1345 execucio judicii de ~one manus..respectuetur *SelCKB* VI 42. **b** pro ~one cujusdam cultelli cujusdam hominis extranei..abcisi *Ib.* 49.

2 lopping or felling. **b** reaping.

1308 boscus non est amputatus, ..per quod via est tam stricta pro defectu ~onis quod.. (*JustIt* 262) *EHR* XL 417; **1336** pro ~one..virgarum pro wattelyngs *Cal. Scot* III 349; **1422** pro ~one xij arborum..pro scaffaldyng *Fabr. York* 45. **b** **1269** bene cognovit ~onem illius bladi *CBaron* 86.

3 elimination.

disponitur ad caritatem per ~onem solicitudinis quam ipsa temporalia..exigunt OCKHAM *Err. Papae* 958.

amsages v. amseges. amsatus v. advisatus.

amseges [CL gl. = owner of land adjoining highway], butt or headland.

14.. hec amsages, *a but of lond* WW; *an hede lande*, †aviseges, †artifinium, bifinium *CathA*.

amtes v. antes.

†amua [? cf. hamula], wine jar.

1383 vasa nec ~e vini de Rino non continent mensuram de certo (*Cl* 222) *RParl.* III 395a (= *Foed.* VII 378a).

amucia, ~ium v. almucia. amuennum v. aminaeus. amula v. hamula. amulatus v. esmallare.

†amulinga, (?) fence, boundary (*cf. ambulatio* a).

1146 de his divisis: ..inter boscum de Saltre et boscum de Waltone usque ad †~am [? l. aumlingam] de Waltone Hacche *Cart. Rams.* I 162 (= *MonA* V 524).

amulire v. amoliri.

amuntantia, extent.

1279 abbas Ramesie tenet banleucam suam..usque ad petram extra domum Johannis de R. ad amuntanc' ij leucarum *Hund.* II 605.

amuntare [OF *amonter, amunter*], to amount to. **b** (w. *ad*).

1205 cum frumento sumpto pro avena, quod ~at xvij li. *DCCant* D 4 f. 15b; **1252** †aumuntant lvij li. *Ib. Reg.* H f. 174a; **1285** summa istarum..ebdomadarum ~at mcc li. *Cant. Cath. Pri.* 132; **1333** xxxi florenos..qui amontant in denariis v li. iij s. iiij d. *DCCant* DE 3 f. 48b. **b** **1205** preter sparnum quod ~at ad xl li. *Ib.* D 4 f. 15b; **1285** allocamentis ..que ~abunt forte usque ad c li. vel amplius *Cant. Cath. Pri.* 221.

amuntia, amount.

s1262 habuimus defectum de cervisia, et mutuo accepimus brasium de H. Chadde ad ∼iam xx librarum *Ann. Dunstable* 219.

amurca [CL < ἀμόργη], oil lees.

∼a, *elesdrosna* ÆLF. *Gl.*; vite hujus prosperitas, que quasi ∼a fluit per plateas oleo in torculari presso H. Bos. *Thom.* IV 13; fex olei olivarum que vocatur ∼a GAD. 65 v. 2; ∼a fex est olei nigra et aquosa cum premitur *Alph.* 9; [porcis] nil sedimen vel amurca placet GOWER *VC* I 359.

amurcalis, mixed w. lees (fig.), impure; *v. et. auriculum.*

705 vestrae Latinitatis panagericus rumor, ..sine sanna aut ∼i impostura notus (CELLANUS) *Ep. Aldh.* 3 (9).

amus v. hamus. amusium v. almucia.

amussis [CL], builder's square. **b** (fig.) canon.

c975 (12c) istis limitibus prefatum resentum ex ∼im (*sic*) circum giratur *CS* 1319; surgit..altitudo muri..secundum legem ∼is et perpendiculi NECKAM *NR* II 172; amissis, *a squyre* WW; *a swyre,* ∼is, perpendiculum *CathA.* **b 1549** ut..ad veterum doctorum ∼im et catholice fidei veritatem ..[theologie legende] incumbant *Conc. Scot.* II 105.

Amyclas, type of pauper (cf. Lucan: *Phars.* V 539).

p1183 floruit Henricus quasi Carolus; alter Ulysses / sensu; Cresus erat opibus; post pauper Amiclas (W. NEWBURGH) R. L. Poole: *Studies in Chronology & History* 245 *n.* 3.

amygdala, ∼um, ∼us [CL < ἀμυγδάλη; cf. alemanda, amanda], almond. **b** almond tree. **c** (fig.; *cf. Eccl.* xii 5).

1171 in conductu amigdalarum et cere regis *Pipe* 40; dabit tibi et nobilis hortus..aurea mala, ∼a, dactylos NECKAM *NR* II 166; **c1250** in ammicdalis j d. et ob. *FormOx* 491; **1252** unum bullionem amigdolarum *Cl* 127; **1265** amogdala per viij dies, xij li. (*RHosp.*) *Manners* 12; amigdalarum dulcium excoriatarum BACON IX 73; infortunium adeo..regem contristavit ut cibum per tres dies preter lac amigdalorum non sumpserit *NLA* (*T. Becket*) II 397; **1350** in dim. c amigdenarum empt' vj s. vj d. *Sacr. Ely* II 142; **1358** in ij li. amidol' v d. (*Ac. Ox.*) *EHR* XXIV 74; amigdale amare competunt medicine *Alph.* 8; **1390** in amiddel' et rys v d. *HMCRep.* IX 204b; afferente..servitore..nuces vel ∼a *Croyl.* 50. **b** amigdala vel †nutida, *magdala treow* ÆLF. *Gl.*; et nux / nobilior gustu quam gessit amygdalus HANV. II 273; amigdalus est arbor mature florens; et dicitur 'hec amigdalus' pro arbore et 'hic amigdalus' pro fructu BART. ANGL. XVII 3. **c** respergor canis, jam floret amigdalus, aures / surdescunt NECKAM *DS* II 445.

2 tonsil (*cf.* Ar. *lawzatān* (dual)).

due amigdale sunt quasi due auricule ante os meri, ..claudentes cibum in media via inter se *Ps.*-RIC. *Anat.* 31; apostema gutturis et uve et duarum amigdalarum in radice lingue GAD. 18 v. 2; amigdale..caro dicitur superflua quae nascitur ad linguae radicem *LC.*

amygdalatus, (sb. f. or n.) an almond drink.

a1250 pugillum polente de avena excorticata vel modicum amigdalate J. GODARD *Ep.* 222; detur sorbile aliquod ut amigdalatum, id est amigdale coquinate cum lacte amigdalarum et zuccara GILB. I 27 v. 2; hoc amigdalatum, *almund mylk* WW.

amygdaleon [? ἀμυγδάλιον], almond or (?) almond oil (ἔλαιον).

amigdaleon amarum GILB. III 147 v. 2.

amygdalinus [ἀμυγδάλινος], of almond.

calculus..∼e quantitatis et forme W. CANT. *Mir. Thom.* II 64; scrabo semel volavit per amigdalinas arbores florentes O. CHERITON *Fab.* 28A; oleum amigdalinum..ex amigdalis amaris *Alph.* 128.

amygdalum, ∼us v. amygdala.

amylum [CL < ἄμυλον], fine flour, starch.

7.. †amilarius, *mearh* WW; species aromaticas et amolum [*gl.*: *flur de furment*] NECKAM *Ut.* 97; si..distemperentur amidum et farina fabe cum aceto GILB. III 168 v. 1 (cf. ib. IV 201. 2: amili); comestionem que fit de amido et farina BACON IX 92; flores frumenti, si assentur, vel farina riçi vel amidi valent GAD. 6. 2; amilum vel amidum, id est medulla frumenti sine mola facti *Alph.* 8; *teere of flowre,* amelum *PP*; *floure,* ador..simila, amolum *CathA.*

amyton v. amiantus.

an [CL], (in dir. qu.) interr. particle (= *num*). **b** (w. *non,* = *nonne*). **c** (repeated, expr. alternatives). **d** or.

an mei oblitus es exempli? BEDE *HE* II 6. **b** an non sufficiunt tibi haec? ANSELM (*Med.* 1) III 78; annon et ipsam sententiam..autor ipse fidei..autorisat? BRADW. *CD* 708E. **c** utrum victoriosius oro, an post gravem luctam ..tandem hostem superare an statim..triumphare? GIR. *GE* II 8 p. 206. **d** presumptuosus itaque dicar an providus? GIR. *TH intr.* p. 5.

2 (in indir. qu.) whether. **b** (repeated) whether..or. **c** or.

consulentes an..suas deserere traditiones deberent BEDE *HE* II 2; dubito ne sit et an sit ita NIG. *SS* 2916; cum.. expeteret..an..cartas haberent GIR. *TH* III 26; queritur ..an sit dictio vel oratio BACON XV 95; ignoro an sit homo vel animal brutum OCKHAM *Dial.* 434; **1446** petivit..an omnia illa intendebat et vellet observare *Reg. Brechin.* 106. **b c790** testis est..an illius pietas prius alterum nominaret an ego precarer ALCUIN *Ep.* 58 p. 101; nesciunt de quo, an de aecclesia an de comite, ..hanc terram tenuit *DB* I 238. **c** nec interest utrum corripiatur an producatur ALDH. *Met.* 10 p. 82; quod utrum de se an de alio aliquo diceret, nobis manet incertum BEDE *HE* IV 3; unusquisque scit si flagellatus erat an non [AS: *oppe na*] ÆLF. *Coll.* 102; inquirere utrum usui eorum sit oportunus anne non *Cust. Westm.* 98.

1 ana [ἀνά], at the rate of. **b** in an equal quantity (with). **c** (sb.) equal quantity.

1235 triginta millia marcarum argenti..ana tresdecim solidos et iiij d. per marcam *TreatyR* I 1; recipe radicem rafani, piretri ana ʒ [i.e. unciam] GILB. I 21 v. 2; recipe sal petre, vitrioli Romani ana lib., id est libram unam de quolibet CUTCL. *LL* 3 (cf. Id. *CL* p. 189: recipe salis petre et vitrioli Romani ana libras duas). **b** granum celeste fert ana dona fide GARL. *Tri. Eccl.* 88. 32. **c** quisquis ipsum [salem communem]..cum ana sui ydragor sublimati in aquam redire fecerit M. SCOT *Lumen* 242; carnis tyri ana et parum musci BACON IX 100; ana, i. sursum vel equale, si rectum interpretatur *Alph.* 10.

2 ana v. anas.

Anabaptista, Anabaptist.

1538 cum nonnulli..∼arum errore[s]..in..Anglie regnum clam irrepserunt *Conc.* III 836; ∼arum damnavit heresim BEKINSAU 753; **1561** utrum se Lutheranos profiteantur an Zwinglianos an etiam ∼as (N. SANDERS) *Cath. Rec. Soc.* I 7.

anabasis [ἀνάβασις], horse-tail (*Equisetum*).

hipporis aut †anabis nascitur in locis humidis et mont[u]osis, hastas habet rufas et asperas et nodosas *Alph.* 82.

anabathrum [ἀνάβαθρον], platform, step. **b** curtain, hanging, dorser.

cum sit ana sursum †ba[n]chique gradus anabastrum GARL. *Syn.* 1584A; **14..** anabatrum, A. *a style* WW; *a pulpyte,* ambo, ..anabatum, ab *ana* quod est 'sursum' et *vatum,* 'gradus' *CathA.* **b** vela vel aulea, cortine sunt anabastra GARL. *Syn.* 1584A; **1425** in bolt' rubei say..propter anabatam faciendam *Ambrosden* II 254; *doorcere,* anabatrum *PP*; hoc anabatum, A. *a docer* ad dorsum WW; *a curtyn,* anabatum, ansa, curtina..*a sylour,* anabatrum *CathA*; **1516** ij anabatra parvi valoris *Ac. Durh.* 253.

anabibazon [ἀναβιβάζων], retracing steps (fig.).

utendum puto ∼on verbo, quod significat 'sursum scandens'; hoc est quod superius dimisimus repetere placet *V. Osw.* 427.

anabis v. anabasis.

anabola [ἀναβολή], wimple, kerchief.

∼a, *winpel* ÆLF. *Gl.*

anaboladium [ἀναβολάδιον], cloak or kerchief.

∼ium vel sindo, *linen heafodes wrigels* ÆLF. *Gl.*; ∼ia [*gl.*: pallium superauratum, *cuverche a dames*] deerant et amiculum et teristrum BALSH. *Ut.* 53; **14..** anabolandium, A. *a rochet* WW; *a colar,* ..*a nekkyrchefe,* ∼ium *CathA.*

anabulla [etym. dub.], spurge (*Euphorbia*) or (?) spurge laurel (*Daphne*).

dicitur: 'lac anabūla parit, catapucia semine gaudet' BART. ANGL. XVII 56; adde..radicem laureole et ∼e GILB. VI 254 v. 1; cum succo anabule et celidonie GAD. 126. 2; titimallus: hujus tres sunt species quibus utimur, sc. ∼a, esula et catapucia; de ∼a quidem utimur lacte *SB* 42; ∼a major, spurga, mezereon, ..leo terre, species est titimalli, oblonga habet folia versus terras, flores multos in summitate parum croceos, cujus semen vocatur catapucia; G. et A. *spurge*; ∼a minor, titimallus, verrucaria, labulla idem; G. *veroine,* A. *wartwort Alph.* 9; *sporge, herbe,* catapusia, esula, ∼a *PP.*

anacardinus, made of marking nuts.

purgetur cum Theodorico cuper' vel ∼o GILB. I 52 v. 2; mel ∼um rumpit [apostema]; quod fit de anacardis positis inter duo ferra ignita GAD. 28. 2; inungatur cum oleo ∼o *Ib.* 66 v. 1.

anacardus [cf. ἀνακάρδιον], marking nut (*Semecarpus anacardium*).

cum melle †ancardi GILB. VII 324. 2 (cf. ib. I 48. 2: pulveris ∼i); cum ∼i ponuntur in tyriaca corrumpunt carnem tyri BACON IX 113; ∼i et mel eorum aufert verucas GAD. 29. 2; ∼us pediculus elefantis vel fructus est arboris cujusdam *SB* 10; †ancicardi fructus cujusdam arboris in India, quos imperiti †modici [? l. medici] testiculos vocant *Alph.* 9.

anacephalaeosis [ἀνακεφαλαίωσις], recapitulation.

anacephaleosin, repetitionem vel recapitulatio *GlC* A 628; Deuteronomius, hoc est lex altera, cujus velut quamdam tradit anacephaleosin vel recapitulationem BELETH *RDO* 61. 67.

anachites v. anancites.

anachoresis [ἀναχώρησις], withdrawal from the world, life of recluse.

anchoresis, remotio vel recessio *GlC* A 596; theoricam ∼eos exercuit vitam ALDH. *VirgP* 37; in secessu ∼eos positus BEDE *Cuthb.* 8; **10..** ∼eseos, *on anacorselle* WW; monachatus sui [Cuthberti] anno tricesimo quinto, ∼eos nono RIC. HEX. *Pri. Hex.* x; viri venerabilis, quem in ejusdem ∼eos inhabitatione habuit successorem, verbis.. exprimetur *V. Har.* 15 f. 20b.

anachoreta [ἀναχωρητής], anchorite, recluse. **b** (f.) anchoress.

Heribercto anchoritae BEDE *HE* IV 29; claruit his etiam venerabilis Echa diebus, / ānachŏreta sacer, eremi secreta secutus ALCUIN *SSEbor.* 1388; ∼a, *ancra* ÆLF. *Gl.*; Benignus confessor, qui non longe hinc anachorita fuerit W. MALM. *GP* II 91; **1192** anacorite ecclesie S. Jacobi de Colecestr' *Pipe* 175; cum audiret..aliquem prelatum cedere oneri pastorali et fieri anachoritam, in hoc eum non laudavit BRAKELOND 131v; **c1225** prohibentes..ne religiosi, monachi, ..anachorite vel heremete subditum alicujus audeant ad penitentiam admittere *Conc. Syn.* 146; **1259** faciat habere anachorite de Dovor' manenti in rupe xl s. *Cl* 223; **1300** pro..putura fratrum, monialium et †annocorinatum [? l. annocoritarum] *Ac. Wardr.* p. 358 (cf. ib. 361); **1360** lego..anachorettis de Donecastro vj s. viij d. *Test. Karl.* 30; **1428** lego pro missa celebranda pro anima mea x s. ..per ankerethum de Mellenyth..servientem aliis presbyteris celebrantibus *Reg. Heref.* 107; *an hermett,* anachorita, heremita, ..reclusus *CathA.* **b** aliqua mulier anachorita laica que litteras non didicerat W. FITZST. *Thom.* 154; **c1250** decanis nostris.. injungimus ut omnes capellanos ecclesiis ubi degunt anachorite deservientes sacramento astringant quod infra septa domorum earundem cum ipsis non loquantur *Conc. Syn.* 359; **s1253** facte sunt inquisitiones..an aliqua ∼a facta fuit.. sine assensu episcopi *Ann. Burton* 310; **1321** Alicie..que ∼e vitam ducendo cupit Altissimo famulari apud ecclesiam S. Egidii *Reg. Heref.* 205; **1438** Juliane..anachorite *Reg. Cant.* II 600; **s1479** quedam generosa nomine Elizabet Katerina Holsted, vidua, admissa fuit et professa in anachoritam S. Petri infra villam de S. Albano *Reg. Whet.* II 202.

anachoretanus, of a recluse.

s603 venerunt ad quendam virum sanctum qui apud eos anachoritanam ducebat vitam M. PAR. *Maj.* I 258 (= BEDE *HE* II 2: anachoreticam).

anachoretice, as a recluse.

xij fratres anachoritice viventes ibidem repperiens congregavit W. MALM. *Glast.* 19; venerunt ad quendam virum sanctum, qui apud eos anachoritice vixit *NLA* (*Augustine*) I 94; Alwinus quidam apud saltum Malvernie anachoritice vivens HIGD. VII 8.

anachoreticus [ἀναχωρητικός], of a recluse.

∼am ducere vitam BEDE *HE* II 2; ipse ab omnibus mundi rebus liber in anchoretica conversatione vitam finire disposuit *Ib.* III 19; ad anchoriticae contemplationis silentia *Ib.* IV 26; quatinus resignata dignitate..anachoriticam solitudinem aut heremiticam..vobis finaliter eligeretis GIR. *S. Langton* p. 401; **1315** Isabelle..que anachoriticam vitam duoendo cupit Altissimo famulari *Reg. Heref.* 501; **s1415** quidam reverendus heros [sc. B. Guthlacus] anachoritico schemate indutus sibi propius assistens *Croyl. Cont. B* 502; **1418** contemplativam vitam seu anocariticam ducere *Reg. Heref.* 34.

anachorissa, ∼ista, anchoress.

c1272 cum ipsa ordinem anacoriste voverit et in eo proficisci voluerit apud ecclesiam S. Leonardi de Bruges *AncC* VII 45; **1321** commissio pro reclusagio ∼iste *Reg. Heref.* 205; **1483** domum sive mansionem..annexam ecclesie S. Michaelis..in qua domina Margareta Smythe ∼issa jam residet *Reg. Whet.* II 257.

anachorit- v. anachoret-.

†anacoccus [? misr. of Ar. *ath-thāriqa* = laurel; infl. by κόκκος], laurel berry (*cf. daphnococcus*).

anacochi, i. bacce lauri *Alph.* 10.

anacor- v. anachor-.

anacreonticus [cf. Ἀνακρεόντειος], anacreontic (metre).

metrum iambicum tetrametrum colobon, quod ∼um dicitur BEDE *Met.* 2379.

anacrotulus v. onocrotalus.

anadiplosis [ἀναδίπλωσις], reduplication.

∼is est congeminatio dictionis in ultima parte praecedentis versus et prima sequentis BEDE *ST* 609.

†anadonia, gentian (? *cf. anemone*).

∼ia, *feldwyrd* ÆLF. *Gl.*; **10..** avadonia, *feltwyrt,* .. **14..** annodoma, *feltwort* WW.

anadosis [ἀνάδοσις], distribution of digested food in bloodstream.

secunda degestio dicitur †madosis, tercia ∼is *Alph.* 144.

anadrogia v. androchia.

anaetius [ἀναίτιος], causeless.

DUNS *Sent.* I 26. 4 (v. aetiatus).

anafora v. anaphora.

anagallicum, comfrey (bot.).

∼um seu anagallis, i. consolida major *SB* 10; consolida major, ∼um, anangalla vel anagallum, †symphicum [l. symphytum] idem, longa habet folia et flores subalbos; G. et A. *comfilie Alph.* 45.

anagallis [ἀναγαλλίς], pimpernel. **b** nettle (? *recte* myrtle). **c** comfrey.

14.. anagallus, A. *pympernelle* WW. **b** anagalidos, †netyllesede WW. **c** (v. anagallicum).

anager v. onager. anaglaf-, anaglif- v. anaglyph-. anaglogium v. analogium.

anaglypha [ἀναγλυφή], (carved) image. **b** crest.

anagliffa, sculpta species *GlC* A 622; **10..** anagrippa, *anlicnes* WW. **b** *creest of a wark*, anaglipha *PP*.

anaglypharius, concerned w. embroidery or (?) sculpture. **b** (sb. m. or f.) broiderer.

acus..parvas et subtiles ad opus anaglafarium [*gl.*: *tripharye*] NECKAM *Ut.* 101; peritus esse debet..tam in opere fusili quam in opere anaglafario *Ib.* 118. **b** *a brothester*, anaglafarius, anaglafaria *CathA*.

anaglyphatus, embroidered.

1433 legavit..unum lectum de viridi cerico cum aquilis anaglafatum *Reg. Cant.* II 496.

anaglyphus [ἀνάγλυφος], carved.

10.. anagliva, *agrafene oðōe aholede*, ..anaglifa, *heahgræfte* WW; crisentida et ~a [v.l. anaglaffa; *gl.*: vasa sculta] BALSH. *Ut.* 51; cum ea scrinii antiqui argento viderimus impressa, eo genere artifitii quod anaglifum vocant W. MALM. (*V. Aldh.*) *GP* V 212; prima hujus dictionis γλυφή longa est secundum Grecos: ergo cum in hac dictione ~a penultima est longa, ..acuetur illa penultima BACON *Tert.* 236.

anagnostes [ἀναγνώστης], reader.

in templo erant cantores: apud nos sunt lectores sive ~es BELETH *RDO* 13. 27.

anagodan [? cf. Pers. *angudān* = leaves of asafoetida], sumach (bot.).

petrosilini, antigodam i. sumac, malabatri GILB. V 225 v. 1; anogodan, i. sumach *Alph.* 10.

anagoge [ἀναγωγή], **a** bringing up, vomiting. **b** anagoge, spiritual uplift by mystical or eschatological explanation.

a ~e, i. rejeccio sursum per os †sanitatis [? l. sanguinis] *Alph.* 9. **b** ~en, superior sensus *GlC* A 634; quadrifaria evangelicae relationis dicta..secundum historiam, allegoriam, tropologiam, ~en digesta ALDH. *VirgP* 4; ~ae, id est, ad superiora ducens, locutio est quae de praemiis futuris ..disputat BEDE *Tab.* I 6; quae rerum figura futurarum juxta ~en..mundi terminum..portendere manifestatur *Id. Met.* 2 p. 70; **10..** ~en, *gastlecum andgite*, ..*ðæm godcundan heahstan* WW; ~e quoque multipliciter sursum ducit, ut litteram non modo verbis sed rebus ipsis instituat J. SAL. *Pol.* 666B; in hoc nomine Jerosolyme..[invenitur] ~e denique, ut Jerosolyma celestis BELETH *RDO* 113. 118; in opusculis..tropologie deservientibus presudare decrevi antequam arduarum subtilitatum ~es apicibus operosam exhibeam diligentiam NECKAM *NR pref.*; sequenter / est tropologia; dicetur post anagoge GARL. *Myst. Eccl.* 226.

anagogia, anagoge (? infl. by *analogia*).

injectae deperationis †angilogias intrito universalitatis epithemate et ambrosio dictionalitatis collemate indulcabo O. CANT. *Pref. Frith.* 43; ~ia sive velatis sive apertis dictis de eternis superne patrie gaudiis tractat et..legentem.. excitat..ad desiderium superne felicitatis AD. SCOT *TT* 697A; magnus dies festus figurat..festum suum perpetuum per ~iam WYCL. *Ver.* I 27.

anagogice, anagogically, eschatologically.

intellige..Christi transitum ~e non allegorice in predictis BELETH *RDO* 113. 118; possumus magnificos sensus exprimere moraliter et allegorice et~e BACON *Maj.* I 185.

anagogicus [ἀναγωγικός], anagogic, eschatological.

verba coelestis oraculi vel historico intellectu vel allegorico vel tropologico..vel certe ~o solent accipi BEDE *Tab.* I 6; †**959** (13c) Arrianas Sabellianasque proterendo nenias ~o infrustrans famine *CS* 1046; ut..in sensu illo quadripartito, historiali videlicet, allegorico, tropologico,~o..dulcedinem ..percipias..cujusdam quadruplicis panis AD. SCOT. *Serm.* 198A; sensus..~us BACON *Min.* 389; scriptura habet quatuor sensus, sc. ~um, tropologicum, allegoricum et literalem DUNS *Sent. prol.* 3. 1 (cf. OCKHAM *Err. Papae* 957).

anagogium v. analogium. anagrippa v. anaglypha. analaria v. avalaria. analectica v. analytica.

analepsia [cf. ἀνάληψις, ἐπιληψία], analepsy, gastric epilepsy.

epilensia..tria..stillicidia..diffundit: ..tertium manat a stomacho, quod vocant analempsiam W. CANT. *Mir. Thom.* II 6; aut fit vicio stomachi et dicitur analempsia GILB. II 109 v. 1; si [materia] venit a stomaco, tunc vocatur analensia, ab *ana* quod est 'conversio' et *lesis*, 'lesio', quasi lesio conversiva de stomaco ad caput et e converso GAD. 60. 2; †analeucia [l. analencia] species est †epileucie. ..analempsia est gutta caduca a stomaco *SB* 11; ~ia species est epilencie de vicio stomachi *Alph.* 10.

analepticus, analeptic.

valet..cathalepticis et analenticis cum vino GILB. II 119 v. 1.

analet- v. analyt-.

†analis, kermes oak.

arbor vermiculum generans vulgo ~is nuncupatur GERV. TILB. III 55.

analogia [ἀναλογία], analogy, ratio, (reasoning from) parallelism.

excipiuntur anomala 'sinistimus' et 'dextimus'..; nam secundum ~iam 'sinisterrimus' et 'dexterrimus' diceretur ALDH. *PR* 134; in numeros innumerabiles infinitosque, immutabilibus tamen naturae suae ~iis finitos ERIUG. *Per.* 577D; in regulis artis grammatice, in ~iis, ..in tropis et schematibus P. BLOIS *Ep.* 101. 313B; ignis..in multiplici ~ia est: ..gerit similitudinem cum sapientia; ..quandam habet similitudinem cum igne Spiritus Sancti NECKAM *NR* I 17; per anologiam vel proportionem BACON VII 2; materia non sit a nobis cognoscibilis nisi per anologiam ad formam WYCL. *Form.* 163.

analogicare, to describe analogically (*cf. analogizare*).

laboraverunt priores doctores ad habendum in suis descripcionibus nomina significancia simul, licet equivoce, tam exemplaria eterna quam eciam exemplata, ut veritas, justicia, liberum arbitrium; et persona ~atur secundum Anselmum et Boecium sub istis nominibus WYCL. *Incarn.* 131.

analogice, analogically, by way of analogy.

c1238 [monachicus ordo] sacrorum principatuum perfectivis virtutibus comprehensus..et in..sacre scientie eorundem consummatam perfectionem ~e deductus GROS. *Ep.* 57; quando [vox] univoce significat et tamen potest significare infinita, licet..nec equivoce nec ~e secundum modos communes analogie BACON *Tert.* 101; quod causa dicitur equivoce vel annologice de 4 causis *Id.* VIII 71; ut ens contingit analoyce substancie et accidenti, cum substancia sit per se ens WYCL. *Ente Praed.* II 18; **c1430** vos ~e nimis..ampliastis terminos vestros, dum infra limites [nostre] libertatis..erexistis vobis furcas *Reg. Whet.* II 415.

analogicus [ἀναλογικός], analogous.

natura est similiter annologica ad materiam et formam BACON VIII 71.

analogium [ἀναλογεῖον], reading-desk, lectern.

prosternant se cuncti in terram, lector etiam ante ~ium LANFR. *Const.* 93; secretarii..parent duo ~a, unum quod in capitulo est et alterum in monasterio, quod ante collationem in refectorium deportetur *Ib.* 110; lector..veniens ante ~ium aperiat librum (*Inst. Sempr.*) *MonA* VI 946* xxix; pulpitum sive anologium NECKAM *Ut.* 119; **1277** ad libros supportandos †anaglogia convenienter aptentur super formas *Doc. Engl. Black Monks* I 67; **s1369** lecciones legerunt duo seniores..super anologium in chori medio *G. S. Alb.* III 276; **1418** j psalterium affixum ~io ad feretrum *Ac. Durh.* 461; **a1447** ex altera parte ~ii ibidem versus orientem jacent corpora sex abbatum AMUND. I *app.* 435; *a pulpyte*, ambo, ..anologium *CathA*; **1517** ~ium..sive aquilam eneam ..procurari fecit *Invent. Ch. Ch. Cant.* 123; donavit.. †anagogium aeneum MYLN *Dunkeld* 45.

analogizare, to describe analogically (cf. *analogicare*).

ymaginari..quod ~atur ad actum intelligendi Dei WYCL. *Ver.* II 125.

analogus [ἀνάλογος], analogous, conformable to (or based only on) analogy.

sicut in ingenuis artibus multa reperiuntur ~a [*gl.*: regularia], ita et multa aloga seu paraloga NECKAM *NR* II 173; quedam est ~a causalitas BACON VIII 11; ~um in omnibus ..amicitiis..fieri oportet, puta meliorem magis amari quam amare, et utiliorem, et aliorum unumquodque similiter BRADW. *CD* 627C; in secundo gradu equivocatorum sunt ~a, sive secundum esse sive secundum operacionem vel aliam proprietatem accidentalem WYCL. *Ente Praed.* II 18; tota difficultas consistit de communitate descripcionis, quod est nimis anologa *Id. Sim.* I 3.

analoyce v. analogice.

analysis [ἀνάλυσις], analysis (log., w. ref. to Aristotle's *Analytics*).

anālysis illa / posterior NECKAM *DS* X 65.

analytica [ἀναλυτικά], Aristotle's *Analytics*.

analeticorum perutilis est sciencia et sine qua quisquis logicam profitetur ridiculus est. ut vero ratio nominis exponatur, quam Greci *analeticen* dicunt nos possumus 'resolutoriam' appellare, familiarius tamen assignabimus si dixerimus 'equam locutionem'; nam illi *ana* 'equale', *lexim* 'locutionem' dicunt J. SAL. *Met.* 916D; dicit Aristoteles in Posterioribus Analecticis NECKAM *NR* I 6; audiat..Priores Analetichos (*Id. Sac.*) *Med. Sci.* 373; similiter logica: syllogismus, ..topica, ~a BACON *CSPhil.* 444; **1549** Aristotelis ~a *StatOx* 358.

analytizare, to explain by analysis.

interpres meus, cum verbum audiret ignotum, et maxime in compositis, dicebat "analetiza hoc", quod volebat equivalenter exponi J. SAL. *Met.* 917A.

anamel-, anamil- v. enamel-. anancia v. avantia.

anancites [CL < Gk.], diamond.

reperiuntur in Laudonia..gemmae, cyanenus, rubinus, anachites, qui et adamas LESLEY *RGScot* 15.

anapaesticus [ἀναπαιστικός], anapaestic.

exempla ~is regulis..subjecta.., utpote 'dĕītās, pĭētās' ..ALDH. *PR* 119.

anapaestus [ἀνάπαιστος], anapaest.

anapesto aequa divisio competit, quia totidem tempora arsis sibi usurpat quot in thesi continentur ALDH. *PR* 119; ~us ex duabus brevibus et longa, temporum quattuor, ut 'pĭĕtās' BEDE *Met.* 2364.

anapelion v. ampelos.

anapepticus [cf. πεπτικός], fully digestive.

pepsis interpretatur degestio..; inde peptica degestio et anapetica, i. recta degestio *Alph.* 144.

anaphora [ἀναφορά], anaphora, repetition.

anafora..est relatio, cum eadem dictio bis saepiusve per principia versuum repetitur BEDE *ST* 609.

anaphus v. hanapus.

anapleroticus [ἀναπληρωτικός], anaplerotic (med.).

anapoletica [v.l. anapopletica] sunt que replent vulnus carne *Alph.* 10.

anarchia [ἀναρχία], anarchy.

~ias, sine principatu vel ubi nullius potestas *GlC* A 591; **1523** omnes [contendunt] ex aequo reges; nam eo tendit libertas illa Christiana, quam nullis hominum legibus asserunt obnoxiam. quo quid aliud quam ~iam parant? (C. TUNSTALL) *Ep. Erasmi* V 1367.

anarchus [ἄναρχος], without beginning.

Deus..~us, hoc est sine principio ERIUG. *Per.* 516A.

anaria v. avenarius c. anaroxia v. anorexia. anarum v. avarus 2a.

anas [CL], duck (or drake).

anates teritisant ALDH. *PR* 131; anas, *ened* ÆLF. *Gl.*; **10..** anax, *æned* WW; accidit ut..motam de flumine †anam [? l. anatem *or* avem] accipiter insequeretur GRIM *Thom.* 9; anates minores que vulgari vocabulo cercelle vocantur GIR. *TH* II 29; ardei et anetes *Lib. Eli.* II 105; **s1295** precepit rex..quod nullus caperet ova annatum B. COTTON 299; **1351** xij anates, unde v errarii (*MinAc*) *Econ. Cond. app.* 69; **14..** anas, *mallard* WW.

anasarca [ἀνὰ σάρκα], subcutaneous dropsy.

qualiter ~as aut vitium matricis significet..ostendetur GILB. I 33 v. 2; sarcos, i. caro, inde ~a [v.l. †amasarca], i. yposarca *Alph.* 163.

anastasis [ἀνάστασις], resurrection. **b** (? by conf. w. *anachoresis*) seclusion, withdrawal.

~in, resurrectionem *GlC* A 652; in vigiliis paschalibus, quando..~is dominica solitae sollemnitatis tripudio celebratur ALDH. *VirgP* 32 p. 271. **b** ~is, *dygelnyssum* ÆLF. *Gl.*

anastomosis [ἀναστόμωσις], anastomosis, interconnection of veins etc.

venas findit..per anastomasim, id est apertionem ex multitudine GILB. III 152 v. 1; resudat extra ad modum roris; ..et signum ipsius est rubedo et claritas in colore, et vocatur anastamosis *Ib.* IV 194 v. 1.; per eadem [tympora] secundum †anathomiarum spiritus vitalis per quasdam arterias a corde ad cerebrum demandatur BART. ANGL. V 11.

anastropha, ~e [ἀναστροφή], inversion. **b** gastric spasm.

~e est verborum tantum ordo praeposterus BEDE *ST* 614. **b** ~a, que est velox expulsio cibi per superius GAD. 58 v. 1; anostropha i. conversio stomachi sursum per vomitum *Alph.* 11.

anata, ~ia [*for* anas], duck.

aneta, *enid GlC* A 569; **10..** aneta, *æned*.., **14..** ~a, *a doke*.., hec anacia, anas WW.

anatarius, duck-hound.

eo [cane] aves in aquis aucupamur et praecipue anates, unde etiam ~ius dicitur CAIUS *Can.* 5.

anate v. ames. anatene v. anatome. anathanasia v. athanasia.

anathema [ἀνάθημα, ἀνάθεμα], **a** something offered to God (*cf. Joshua* vii). **b** accursed object (*cf.* 1 *Cor.* xvi 22). **c** curse, esp. excommunication.

a legebam..palliolum aurique parum de ~ate praesumptum multos stravisse GILDAS *EB* 1; Achar..de ~ate.. pallium sibi usurpans ALDH. *VirgP* 55; consultus Dominus respondit populum ~ate esse pollutum W. NEWB. I 20; qui de ~ate regulam aureamet clamidem coccineam tulerat M. PAR. *Maj.* I 13; E ante M longatur..; sed ~a secundum Grecum corripitur, licet usus habeat contrarium BACON *Tert.* 260; adversus numen imperatoriae majestatis auro velut ~ate propitiandum MORE *Ut.* 83. **b** **779** (12c) si quis..hanc donationem meam infringere temptaverit, sit ~a maranatha *CS* 228; **1032** (12c) sit ~a maranatha, hoc est alienatio a consortio Christianorum *CD* 746; **c1090** quicumque blasphemiam, quam supra posui me audisse a Roscelino dici, pro veritate asseruerit, sive homo sive angelus, ~a est ANSELM (*Ep.* 136) III 280; pro fratribus a Christo ~a esse optavit H. BOS. *Thom.* II 9; dicit apostolus, '~a sit' hoc est tanquam ~a sit habendus OCKHAM *Dial.* 574 *bis*; **a1400** a S. Trinitate anatema sit *Mon. Francisc.* I 591. **c** ut templa .., quae sine fructu utilitatis sacravimus, ocius ~ati et igni contradamus BEDE *HE* II 13; judicio Domini cunctos anathēmate plecti FRITH. 776; **1070** si quis huic nostre donationi contraire praesumpserit, ~ati subjacebit *Regesta* I 120; excommunico eos qui..cervum meum interfecerunt eo ~ate quo Deus iratus percutit animas impiorum. .. habeant ~a maranatha, nisi cito resipuerint! H. LOS. *Ep.* 35 p. 71; **1182** papa hanc divisam..sigillo suo confirmavit sub interminatione ~atis *FormA* 423; percellitur ~ate, nec timet MAP *NC* IV 6 p. 167; **s1238** archiepiscopus..totum conventum..non tantum suspensionis sed etiam ~atis vinculis innodavit M. PAR. *Maj.* III 493; percussus totiens comes est anathēmate GARL. *Tri. Eccl.* 84; **1279** contra proclamacionem et bannum interminacionis ∼atis ne quis in ordinibus clam se ingereret *Reg. Ebor.* 20; ∼atis vulnere.. feriatur R. Bury *Phil.* 4. 51.

anathemare, to anathematize.

∼atum, abhominatum *Erf.* 2. 265. 60; **812** noverit se ∼atum esse et ante tribunal..Christi rationem redditurum *CS* 341; *to curse,* ∼are, anathematizare, devotare.. *CathA*.

anathematizare [ἀναθεματίζειν], to anathematize (curse, condemn, or excommunicate).

∼ato omni idolatriae cultu Bede *HE* II 6; sacramenta regni caelestis..∼ando prodidit *Ib.* III 1; **10..** ∼are, *frendian* WW; aut ∼et venenum quod proferendo evomit aut ∼etur ab omnibus Christianis Anselm (*Ep.* 136) III 280; **s1131** in hujuscemodi scismate anathema formidandum est, quod difficulter a quibusdam precaveri potest, dum unus alium..cum fautoribus suis feraliter ∼et Ord. Vit. XIII 11; si ideo ∼at ut ∼ato male cedat, prius nocet sibi quam illi Pull. *Sent.* 899C; ∼avit omnes qui..facultatem exequendi quod jusserat..executoribus denegare tentassent Ad. Eyns. *Hug.* V 16; excommunicamus, ∼amus et a †luminibus [l. liminibus]..ecclesie sequestramus omnes illos qui amodo ..ecclesias..spoliaverint jure suo (*Sententia Arch. Cant.*) *MGL* II 43 (= *Fleta* 93); propter detencionem temporalium per se non debet quis anathematisari Wycl. *Civ. Dom.* I 336; **s1381** J. Wyclef hereticus reassumpsit ∼atas opiniones Berengarii Wals. *YN* 333.

anathematizatio, (pronouncement of) curse, esp. excommunication.

de ∼one sine nomine et de illo anathemate quod fit nominatim Pull. *Sent.* 663C; sacerdotum..suspensio, ∼o, occisio H. Bos. *Thom.* IV 30 p. 460; **1310** ∼o facta in Ecclesia Christi Cantuar' per dominum R. archiepiscopum pontificalibus indutum *DCCant* Q 53v.; **a1400** sub pena ∼onis *Doc. S. Paul.* 94.

anatho- v. et. anato-. anathomiarum v. anastomosis.

anathymiasis [ἀναθυμίασις], rising of vapours.

passiones provenientes ex caliditate sitis fumosas eructuationes, anatimiases, lippothomias Gilb. V 206 v. 2; anathimiasis est stomachi passio molesta.. *Ib.* 213 v. 1; anathimiasis [v.l. †anathumatis] delacio fumi stomachi sursum capud *Alph.* 10.

anatileon v. anethelaeon. anatinulis v. anatulus.

anatinus [CL], of a duck. **b** of the nature of a duck.

anetina ova ovis gallinaciis sunt majora Bart. Angl. XIX 80. **b** aves omnes cum pedibus integris, sicut anserine, ∼e Gad. 35. 2.

anatole [ἀνατολή], east.

sensit salutaria..fluenta..novi Jordanis qui de capite novi martyris emergens derivatur in disim, allabitur arton, anathole[n] mesembriamque non preterit W. Cant. *Mir. Thom.* II 56.

anatome [ἀνατομή], cutting up, opening.

anathomen, apertionem *GlC* A 573; **14..** anatene, A. *upcuttynge* WW.

anatomia, anatomy, dissection.

∼ia est interiorum maxime et exteriorum recta et equalis divisio; dicta est ab *ana*, quod est 'equalis', et *thomos*, quod est 'divisio' Ric. Med. *Micr. Anat.* 212; **s1216** facta de corpore suo [sc. regis] phisicali anathomia per..abbatem.. seposita sunt viscera M. Par. *Min.* II 193; reumatismus fit inferius, ut in anathomia apparet Gilb. II 101. 2; sic apparet anotomia oculi Gad. 107 v. 1; tomos i. divisio; inde anathoma, i. recta divisio *Alph.* 187; **1549** medicine chirurgiaeque studiosus..duas ∼ias faciet *StatOx* 346.

anatomice [ἀνατομική], anatomy.

haec sunt quae..introductionem hanc in ∼en justa prolixitate finiant D. Edw. *Anat.* 2.

anatomicus [ἀνατομικός], anatomical, (sb. m.) anatomist.

tercia ∼orum circa nutritiva est consideratio post animata et spiritualia membra Ric. Med. *Micr. Anat.* 222.

anatomizare, to dissect.

oves que patiuntur epilepsiam cum a cerebris suis anothomizantur Gilb. II 109 v. 1; de simia sua et gallo suo, quos anothomizavit et invenit humores grossos..inter cor et cassulam suam Gad. 67 v. 2.

anatron v. nitrum.

anatropa [ἀνατροπή; cf. anastropha], gastric spasm.

anatropha est subversio stomachi superius cum vomitu Gilb. V 213 v. 2.

anatulus, duckling.

1341 respondet..de vj anatibus de exitu, de quibus in vend' super compotum vj annatuli *MinAc* 1120/11 r. 5*d.*; †anatinulis, id est pullus anatis *CathA*.

anatus, ∼ius, drake or teal.

14.. anacius, A. *a tele*, ∼us, A. *a mallard* WW.

1 anax v. anas.

2 anax [ἄναξ], king.

fungitur interea regno post ānăx in arce Æthelw. IV 9.

anb- v. amb-.

1 anca [? cf. ancyla *or* ME *ancle*; *but* cf. hanca], ankle or knee-bone.

14.. ∼a, ..hec †anta A. *knebon*, ..∼a, *ancle* WW.

2 anca [? cf. OF *anche*], bezel, setting.

aurifabrorum industria..includit gemmas preciosas infra ∼as anulorum Garl. *Dict.* 128 (? cf. WW: ancha, A. *a tache*).

3 †anca, sort of vessel.

14.. nomina pertinencia ad coquinam: ..hec olla, A. *potte*; hec anca, A. *potere* WW.

4 anca v. ansa 1a. 5 anca v. auca. ancaragium v. ancoragium. ancardus v. anacardus.

1 ancella, ∼um [OF *ancelle, lancelle* < lancella], 'auncel', balance.

1281 se facit emptorem lane et vadit per diversa loca cum quodam ansero *Gaol Del.* 35 B v. 41*d.*; **1303** [*trons..examined by*] Thomam factorem aunserorum *Cal. LBLond.* C 113; **1349** j auncer' cum j par de balaunez pro rebus ponderandis (*KRAc* 391/15) *Arch.* XXXI 81; **1357** J. Pount utitur auncella contra formam statuti *Enf. Stat. Lab.* 223*; **1371** emunt lanam per anceram et vendunt per stateram *Proc. J.P.* 207; **1391** j ancel' (*Ac. Cottesford*) *Rec. Eton* XXVI 44.

2 ancella v. ancilla 1c.

1 anceps [CL], two-edged. **b** (sb. m.) two-handed sword.

ancipites inspicant acrius enses Frith. 843. **b** ancipitis, gladiolum quae in medio habet manubrium *GlC* A 598; **14..** hic anceps, A. *a towhand swerd* WW.

2 doubtful.

anceps, *tuigendi GlC* A 656; sine ancipiti ambiguitatis scrupulo..credendum est Aldh. *VirgP* 11; ille ex longo languore anceps propriae vitae *V. Dunst.* B. 20; ancipiti discrimine permotus W. Malm. *GR* IV 357; ancipiti semper bellorum alea Gir. *EH* I 13.

2 anceps [*for* accipiter], hawk.

1212 aeria ancipitum *Fees* 197; **1388** onerat se de vj s. viij d. vel de uno rubro †aucipite [? l. ancipite] redditus assise *ExchScot* 165.

3 anceps v. auceps. ancer, ancer- v. anser, anser-. ancera v. ancella.

ancesseria [OF *ancesserie*], ancestry, ancestral tenure.

1200 libere tenentes de prebenda ipsius thesaurarii ab ∼ia *CurR* I 264 (cf. ib.: sunt..liberi tenentes.., ipsi et antecessores sui a conquestu Anglie); **1204** terram..tenet ipse de anceseria *JustIt* 1039 r. 4*d.*; **1219** tenet in capite..dim. carucatam terre..de anceseria *Eyre Lincs & Worcs* no. 559.

ancessor v. antecessor. ancha v. 2 anca, hanca. ancharare v. ancorare. anchile v. ancile.

anchilops, ∼opa [ἀγχίλωψ], sty (at inner corner of eye); *cf. aegilops.*

angilopa est inveterata egilopa *SB* 11 (= *Alph.* 52: †agrilopa).

anchofilus v. antofilus. anchor- v. et. anachor-, ancor-.

†anchorum, ∼ium [? cf. antora], madder (bot.).

10.. nomina herbarum: ..∼um, *mædere* WW; ∼ium, *medere Gl. Durh.*

anchusa [ἄγχουσα], alkanet (bot.).

balneum dissintericum ex..encusa, tapso.. Gilb. V 225. 1.

ancianus v. antianus. ancicardus v. anacardus.

ancile [CL], shield. **b** (fig.).

∼ia, scuta, arma caelestia *GlC* A 581; remissis / acclines rogitant ancilibus ut benedicat Frith. 797; **10..** achile, *scyld*, ..anchile, *scelde* WW; missilibus eorum leva objectans ∼ia J. Sal. *Pol.* 598D; assint et lancee, catapulte, †antillia [*gl.: talevaz*] Neckam *Ut.* 104; **14..** hec antile, A. *halnase* WW. **b** gestantes..ancile duelli / et machĕram Verbi Aldh. *VirgV* 2463.

ancilla [CL], female slave or serf. **b** maidservant. **c** (w. *Dei* or sim.) nun. **d** maiden.

si quis liber ∼am in matrimonio acciperit, non habet licentiam dimittere eam Theod. *Pen.* II xiii 5; **716** ut ∼am quandam, quam in potestate communiter possederunt, pro anima ejus manu mitteret Bonif. *Ep.* 10 p. 13; omnes.. unda baptismatis abluit, inter quos servos et ∼as ducentos Bede *HE* IV 13; ibi quidam miles habens viii inter servos et ∼as *DB* I 6; cum a libero ducitur ∼a putante se ducere liberam Neckam *NR* II 179. **b 12..** (14c) garcionem prioris et ∼am infirmorum *Cart. Chester* 299; **1269** quia ∼a sua saltavit parcum domini *CBaron* 79; **1275** in liberacione j †anelle [MS: ∼e] lactantis oves *Ac. Stratton* 65; **1307** ad sectam Sabine ansille *Gaol Del.* 39/2 r. 1*d.*; **1333** ∼a aule *Hal. Durh.* 13; **1355** xxiiij fratribus et sororibus in firmar', cum stipendio ∼e *Ac. Durh.* 208. **c c720** (v. abbatissa); eam monasterii partem qua ancellarum Dei caterva a virorum erat secreta contubernio Bede *HE* IV 7; verae Christi ∼ae..Mahtildi Æthelw. *prol.*; **1240** ex fidelium devotione aliqua ∼e Christi beneficia percipiunt *FormA* 60. **d** misit..Maximianum..ut ipse ∼am illam Britannicam cum regno possideret *Eul. Hist.* II 269.

2 (fig.) minister, subordinate.

ut sit virginitas regina castitas domina, jugalitas ∼a Aldh. *VirgP* 19; te mihi cuncta debere nemo negabit, cujus animam in corde tuo tenes ∼am tue Map *NC* III 2 p. 117; Deus artifex et ∼a natura R. Bury *Phil. prol.* 5; **1346** hec lex ancilla [sc. Salica] merito privatur amicis *Pol. Poems* I 33.

ancillare, to enslave (fig.).

1166 illam [sc. ecclesiam rex] non est veritus ∼are J. Sal. *Ep.* 151; abbas..advenit..ut..ecclesiam de Bello sibi subjugando ∼aret *Chr. Battle* 50; **c1236** potestates et judices seculares..liberam [ecclesiam] ∼ant et captivant Gros. *Ep.* 72* p. 218; sponsam Christi ∼are nituntur Ad. Marsh *Ep.* 247 c. 35; **1340** non deceret matrem per filias ∼ari *Lit. Cant.* II 225; **s1378** Christiani..domum Dei..non tantum ∼are sed insuper polluere..non verentur Wals. *HA* I 375.

ancillari [CL], to serve (as handmaid). **b** (fig.) to serve, help. **c** (?) to possess.

∼antur, *hyrsumiað* Ælf. *Sup.*; [ille] cui quantum licebat ∼abar Map *NC* III 2 p. 107; male acquiescens dominatrici [sc. uxori], cui ordine prepostero diu consueverat ∼ari Ad. Eyns. *Hug.* IV 5. **b** orthodoxae fidei famulitio ∼atis O. Cant. *Pref. Frith.* 1; animam que tot labyrinthis intricata est necesse est frequentius ∼ari P. Blois *Ep.* 16. 59; que est hec pax, si quiescit ancilla et domina sub jugo gravi.. ∼atur? *Ib.* 138. 412; ∼atur ratio dum blanditiis sensualitatis illicitis consentit Neckam *NR* II 109; **s1293** ∼ante, immo principante, summa centum m..librarum, ..prosperabatur opus *Flor. Hist.* III 88; ecclesia..nulli parti oracionis parcit quam sermonibus suis ∼ari non cogit Netter *DAF* I 25a. **c** ardebat..Gerbertus librum quoquo modo ∼i W. Malm. *GR* II 167.

ancillatio, enslavement, servitude.

s1216 doleo de regni ejus ∼one, cum princeps provinciarum fiat sub tributo M. Par. *Min.* II 176; native libertatis ∼o Ad. Marsh *Ep.* 52; **s1381** tractare ceperunt de ∼one monasterii Wals. *HA* I 467; **s1425** pocius..quam ecclesiam hactenus liberam premi permitteret servilis obsequiis ∼onis Amund. I 198.

ancillatus, menial service.

conjugem suam feminis humillimae ∼um famulae.. exhibere praecipiens *Hist. Abb. Jarrow* 34.

ancillula [CL], maidservant.

arripuitque citum fugiens ancillula cursum Wulf. *Swith.* I 1187; accessit..ad consedentes ∼as, observatrices dominae suae *V. Dunst.* B. 11.

†ancillum, (?) cell.

a1135 dicis quia monasteria, eo quod a monachis inhabitantur, locus et carcer sunt damnatorum, et ideo jure vocantur ∼a (Theob. Etampes) *Educ. Charters* 104.

ancilus v. ancyla. ancionarius v. actionarius. ancipiter, ∼trus v. accipiter (cf. 2 anceps).

anciput, forehead.

∼put, *forheafod* Ælf. *Gl.*

ancistrum [ἄγκιστρον], hook.

est admodum lubricum draconem in ∼o tenere ne effugere valeat H. Bos. *Ep.* 1462.

ancla v. antlia.

anclare [CL < ἀντλᾶν], **∼ari,** to draw water. **b** to steal. **c** (?) to exhaust (or *f.l.* for *anhelare*).

to drawe water, ∼ari, ex-, haurire, ex- *CathA*. **b** *to steyle*, †acari, furari, ..∼ari *Ib.* **c** abduxit eam [equam]..portitor multis vigiliis et laboribus †antlatam Map *NC* VII 9.

anclatio v. anhelatio.

anclator, thief.

a thefe, †auclator, ..grassator, fur *CathA*.

anclea v. antlia.

†anclidia [? cf. antlia], ordeal kettle.

si quis ad *ceace* pertrahatur, id est contamen vel fauces vel ∼iam (*Quad.*) *GAS* 25.

ancon [CL < ἀγκών], hook.

†∼onos, urcenos [? l. ∼ones, uncinos] *GlC* A 575.

anconicum v. aconitum. ancopa v. accopa.

1 ancora [CL < ἄγκυρα], anchor. **b** (fig.).

tentabant nautae anchoris in mare missis navem retinere Bede *HE* III 15; **1198** de duabus ∼is et uno cabulo..que fuerunt de navi regis *Pipe* 182; opus est anchora, sic dicta eo quod contra chorum [i.e. caurum] Neckam *Ut.* 115; **1216** tam de ∼abus quam de aliis..que inventa fuerunt in ..navibus *Cl* 260b; **1283** quod dictum ancrum nunquam furatus fuit *Gaol Del.* 35 B r. 17; **1294** pro empcione ij ancrarum, iiij m. *KRAc* 5/2 m. 3; **1295** pro xxxij duodenis petrarum ferri fabricandis ad ∼as *Ib.* 5/8 m. 8; **c1390** navis infra portum..invenerunt cum ankuris *Mem. York* 132b; quidam..requieverunt in anchoris Elmh. *Hen. V* 105; **1438** navem..per ∼am jacentem (*KRMem*) *Bronnen* 1117; **1452** de ij ∼is, viz. una ∼a grossa..continente in longitudine xvij pedes et ij pollices et in latitudine xj pedes dim.; et virga ejusdem ∼e continet in circuitu ex parte anteriori ij pedes et ij pollices et in fine posteriori j pedem ac dim.; ac palme ∼e continent, viz. utraque earum, in latitudine ij pedes et j pollicem *Ac. Foreign* 86 r. G. **b** anchora fluctivagam nunc sistat metrica barcam Aldh. *VirgV* 2809; hunc portum teneas, hic fixa sit anchora mentis Vinsauf *PN* 1062; **1341** clementissimi Patris benignitas, in cujus soliditate fixa est immobiliter anchora spei nostre (*Lit. Regis*) Avesb. 96.

2 ancora v. antora.

ancoragium, (payment for) anchorage.

1286 de iiij s. vj d. ob. de ∼io et batellagio hoc anno *MinAc* (*Topsham*) 827/39 r. 3; **1288** pro ∼io seu ripagio [Burdegale] *CalCh* VI 302; **1304** de ankoragio iiij d. *EEC* 168; **1331** ∼ia navium in..portu applicancium *Pat* 177 m. 14*d.*; **1394** ∼ium vocatum..*yeveltol IMisc* 254/13; **1417** de ankerag' diversarum navium applicancium in portu *DL MinAc* 3910; **1439** de ancaragio ij navium apud Shelez *Ac. Durh.* 68; **1448** hankeragium, kayagium et groundagium *ChartR* 190 m. 46.

ancorare, to anchor: **a** (intr.); **b** (tr.); **c** (fig.).

a 1234 quelibet navis veniens ad portum cum marchandisa ∼abit ex utraque parte portus prout sibi necesse fuerit (*DL Misc. Bk.* 5) *Eng. Justice* 132; **s1270** anchoraverunt in alto mari W. Guisb. 206 (= Knighton I 259; anchoriaverunt); **1316** in aliis portubus ∼antes *RScot* 154a; **s1407** cxx naves anchorantes..ceperunt Wals. *HA* II 275; in abruptis rupium anchorare Elmh. *Hen. V* 105. **b 1276** burgenses de Scardeburg' ceperunt teolonium de navibus ∼atis extra portum *Hund.* I 132; **s1290** anchoravit eam magister navis in mediis fluctibus W. Guisb. 226; **1321** ad quandam navem ..per distanciam dim. leuci a terra ankoratam *IMisc* 87/41; **s1321** xv naves.., cum ancharate fuerunt ad terram,.. combusserunt *Ann. Paul.* 298; **1333** diverse naves..ante portum ville..∼antur *RScot* 252a; **1337** naves..tam velantes supra mare quam ∼atas (*RGasc*) *Foed.* IV 742; *to fest*, alligare, ∼are, annectere *CathA.* **c 1427** adest magni consilii angelus, per quem..tante deliberacionis anchoratur maturitas ut.. *EpAcOx* 33.

ancorarius, (?) anchor-master.

1565 capitaneus, magister, correctores, anchorarii, naute et marinarii dictarum navium *SelPlAdm* II 131.

ancra, ∼um v. ancora.

anculus [CL *Gl.* = servant], (?) cup-bearer.

†antulus, *caecbora GlC* A 659; **10..** †antulum, *ceac*, †anthevilus, *ceacbora* WW.

ancyla [ἀγκύλη], knee-joint (*cf.* 1 *anca*).

†ancilus [? l. ancilas], poplites *GlC* A 600.

ancyromachus [LL < Gk.], sort of ship. **b** stern.

archiromacus, *swiftscip* Ælf. *Sup.* **b** *a sterne of a schype*, anquiromagus, clavus *CathA.*

andabata, blindfold gladiator.

1527 ne antabatarum more cum ejusmodi larvis [sc. M. Lutheri libris] lucteris, ignorans ipse quod oppugnes *Conc.* III 712.

andanicus [cf. 1 andena], (w. *ferrum*) ondanique; *cf.* 1 *andena*.

ex vilibus et muracido ferro fit ferrum ∼um M. Scot (*Part.*) *Med. Sci.* 295.

andapila v. sandapila. andarium v. andera.

†andatus [? cf. It. *andata*], (?) alley.

qui nullam penitus offert pecuniam, / andatus circuit, forum, ecclesiam *Ps.*-Map (*Cruce Den.* 71) 225.

andeda v. andera.

Andegavensis, Angevin, of Anjou; *cf. Angevinus.*

monaci S. Nicholai ∼is *DB* I 214b; Ligeris.. / Andegavense solum placidis interfluit undis Neckam *DS* III 767; **1181** omnis homo habens in catallo xl vel xxx..li. ∼is monete ad minus (*Assisa Arm.*) R. Howd. II 253; alii denarii ∼es erant, alii sterlingi Gir. *GE* II 35; **1214** debet l li. pro cc li. ∼ibus *Pipe* 40; **1215** si forte vinum ∼e non habueritis, j tonellum boni vini Wasc' ei habere faciatis (*Cl*) *LTR Mem. PR* p. 133.

Andegavus, Angevin.

∼i, Turoni, Pictones, Burdegala, multae regiones, civitates plurimae W. Poit. I 15; Pictavus, Andegavus, Normannus et Anglicus instant Garl. *Tri. Eccl.* 51.

andegravius v. landegravius. andela v. 2 andena.

Andelucianus, Andalusian, Spanish Moslem.

s1114 Amoravii et ∼i de Africa missi a rege Alis Ord. Vit. XIII 4.

1 andena [Ar. *hunduwānī* = *Indian blade, sword, etc.*], high-grade steel, ondanique; *cf. andanicus.*

tertium [genus ferri] est quod vocatur ∼a, cujus rarior est usus apud Latinos Bacon *Min.* 383; ∼a est calybs ex regionibus orientalibus advecta, quae liquescit igne *LC.*

2 andena [OF *andaine*], measure of meadowland, swathe; *cf. ando, dayna, handayna.*

a1200 septem ∼as prati et dim. ∼am in Westmore *Danelaw* 25; **c1200** iiij ∼as prati *Cart. Dunstable* no. 496; **1244** dimisit..tres ∼as prati..et quandam perticatam de prato *Reg. Ant. Linc.* IV 73; **a1245** unam andelam apud novum pratum *Ib.* VII 43; **1500** [cum] xvij †audoenis [prati] *CalPat* 196.

3 andena, andeona v. andera.

andera, ∼ium [OF *andiere, andier*], andiron, firedog or gridiron.

andeda, *brandrod*, *GlC* A 562; andena vel tripes, *brandisen* Ælf. *Gl.*; **10..** ardeda, *brandrida* WW; **1283** de caldeis, de ∼iis, de patellis *RGasc* II 211; **1286** de..ander' ferreis *IMisc* 45/25; **1303** de duobus aunder' et una craticula venditis *Ac. Exec. Ep. Lond.* 70; **1307** pro duobus novis andariis magnis emptis..xviij s. *KRAc* 501/22 r. 3 (1); **1388** de..vij paribus de andernis *LTR Ac. Esch.* 10 r. 5; **1390** unam par forpicum, unam andenam *PIRCP* 519 r. 499; **1396** in lectisternio abbatis..∼e iij paria (*Invent.*) *Meaux* III lxxix; **1406** in ij magnis andenis ferreis ponderis lx lib. *Comp. Swith.* 288; **1409** screne ferri cum ij †andeonis *Test. Ebor.* III 48; *aundyryn*, andena, ipopurgium *PP.*

andivia v. endivia.

ando [cf. 2 andena], swathe.

a1290 dedit..sex ∼ones prati falcabilis in ploulond Odonis *CarteNativ.* 464; tres ∼ones prati..que extendunt se versus forarium Simonis..et j ∼onem et dim...in Warinplougeland *Ib.* 468.

†andra [? cf. Sp. Ar. *al-qārra*], (?) betony (*Stachys betonica*).

∼a, *bishopeswort SB* 10.

andrachne [ἀνδράχνη], purslain (bot.).

andrago, portulaca *SB* 10; portulaca.., andrago vel andragnis, pes pulli idem, G. et A. *porsulaigne Alph.* 149.

andrafraxa v. atriplex.

†andreporesis [? cf. ἀνδρόπορνος], androgyne, hermaphrodite.

∼is, i. homo utriusque generis, *bæddel* Ælf. *Gl.*

†andreseya [? cf. androchia], (?) dairy or a place-name.

1255 summa decimationis decime feni de parochia de Burthonia iiij s.; de cantaria, viij d. ob.; de ∼a, ij d.; de sacrista, j m. *Ann. Burton* 365.

andricon [cf. ἀνδρικός], sort of electuary.

debilibusque viris et tristibus est bona pliris [*gl.*: alio modo dicitur ∼on, id est *princes*, quia precipuum est illud electuarium et nobilissimum] Garl. *Mor. Scol.* 594.

androchia [etym. dub.], dairy-maid.

androgia, que gallinis ova supponat pullificancia, ..que agnellos morbidos..lacte foveat alieno.. Neckam *Ut.* 101; ∼ia..esse debet..in officio daerie sapiens et experta..; ejus officium est..lac per talliam recipere.., caseum facereque butyrum.., curamque de poletria optinere *Fleta* 172; abbas Michael [ob. 1349]..manerium de Bradewey reparavit, faciens ibidem de novo..coquinam domumque ∼ie et pistrinum *G. S. Alb.* II 362; *deye*, ∼ia; hec genetharia idem est *PP*; anadrogia, A. *a deye* WW.

androchiarium, ∼ianum, ∼iatorium, dairy.

androchia..non permittat quod aliquis vel aliqua in ∼iarium sibi ingrediatur aliquid ablaturus *Fleta* 172; *deyry*, ∼ianum, ∼iarium, armendarium *PP*; hoc ∼iatorium, *a deyry* WW; *a derye*, ∼iarium, bestiarium, genetheum *CathA.*

androchius, dairy-man.

deye, ..hic ∼ius *PP*; *a deye*, ∼ius, ∼ea, genatarius, genetharia *CathA.*

androgia v. androchia.

androsaemon [ἀνδρόσαιμον], *Hypericum androsaemum.*

arbor que vocatur androsmon, que nascitur in terra Sin, ..complexa habens folia sicca et parva nimis et semina nimis parva, rotunda, intrinsecus alba Bacon V 122.

†anduca [? cf. sambuca], sort of musical instrument.

14.. nomina ludorum: ..hec idraulis, A. *waterpype*; hec ∼a, A. *belepype* WW.

andullia [OF *andoille*], sausage.

1245 in exitibus..porcorum et boum lavandis, faciendo salsag', pund', andull' et aliis *Pipe Wint.* (159287) r. 12*d.*

anealare v. esmallare. aneel- v. 1 anelare, anelatio. anelacius, ∼ia v. alenatius.

1 anelare [ME *anelen*], **a** to kindle. **b** to anneal.

a 1370 non respondet de pluribus furnis..propter magnam habundanciam pluvie in autumpno, quia non permisit eos plures furnos ∼are *MinAc* 900/14. **b 1422** in anelacione xxxvj lib. veteris auri ∼ati per predictum campsorem *KRAc* 302/1; auri veteris non aneelati *Ib.* 301/19.

2 anelare, ∼ere v. anhelare. 3 anelare v. esmallare.

anelatio, annealing.

1422 in aneelacione mdxlij lib...auri veteris non aneelati *KRAc* 301/19 (cf. ib. 302/1: in ∼one); **1458** pro factura et anulacione de clx mille tegularum (*Ac. Tattershall*) *HMC Rep.* LXXVII 198.

anelitus v. anhelitus. anella v. ancilla.

anellus [LL], **∼um,** little ring. **b** ring for confining prisoners.

anelus, *lytel hring* Ælf. *Gl.* **b 1221** in viij paribus ∼orum ad opus prisonum *Cl* 450b; **1236** quoddam ∼um percussum fuit de quodam probatore *CurR* 116A r. 7; **1250** in stipendiis fabri qui ponit et deponit ∼os prisonum *Pipe* 94 r. 18.

anemellare v. enamellare.

anemone [ἀνεμώνη], poppy.

anomon, papaver idem *Alph.* 10.

aneria v. avenaria. aneron v. meron.

anesis [ἄνεσις], relaxation.

dilatatus ergo [thalamus] aërem inmittit, digestum emittit, neque admittit ∼im Alf. Angl. *Cor* 6; ∼im, id est requiem, prestat Gilb. VI 273. 2; anesis, i. resis, i. requies *Alph.* 10.

anesum [ἄνησον; cf. anethum], anise.

anisum et sinapis..nonnullam hortulano conferunt utilitatem Neckam *NR* II 166; **1265** pro anisio empto..iiij d. (*RHosp.*) *Manners* 64; cuminum dulce, anisum idem; G. et A. *anyse Alph.* 40; anethum vulgus appellat *dyll*, anisum vero *anys* aut *anyssede*; quare toto errant coelo, quia anethum interpretantur *anys* Turner *Herb.* A ii v.

aneta v. anata, anethum. anetes v. anas.

anethelaeon [ἀνηθέλαιον], oil of dill.

oleum laurinum, .., anatileon [*gl.*: factum de succo] et epithimata Neckam *Ut.* 110; pectus unguatur cum anatileon Gilb. IV 198 v. 2; ungantur cum..anetil[eon] *Ib.* II 108. 1; ungantur renes cum †aveleon alias †avetileon Gad. 101 v. 1.

anethinus [ἀνήθινος], of dill.

cum oleo ro[saceo] vel anetino Gilb. II 81. 2; ungatur cum oleo anetino, camomellino, rosaceo Gad. 34 v. 1; oleum anetinum, i. oleum aneti *Alph.* 129.

anethum [ἄνηθον], dill. **b** anise.

anetum, *dili GlC* A 571; anetum, *dile* Ælf. *Gl.*; ubera nutricis sumptum fecundat anetum Neckam *DS* VII 97; **1303** saccus anete ij d. *EEC* 161; cum oleis..aperientibus, sicut oleum de aneto Gad. 20 v. 1; decimantibus mentam et ciminum et annetum Wycl. *Ver.* I 221 (cf. *Matth.* xxiii 23); meu, i. anetum agreste *SB* 30. **b** Turner *Herb.* (v. anesum).

aneticus [ἀνετικός], relaxing.

anesis, ..inde ∼a, i. mitigatoria *Alph.* 10.

anetileon v. anethelaeon. anetinus v. anatinus, anethinus. anetius v. anaetius. anetum v. anethum. anfora v. amphora.

anfractuose, tortuously.

[intestinum] quod magis amfractuose reflectitur et ideo ileon appellatur quasi propter revolutiones confusum et confundens Ric. Med. *Micr. Anat.* 224.

anfractuosus, twisting, tortuous (also fig.). **b** (fig.) involved.

in distorte et amfractuose vie et vite hujus nocte H. Bos. *Thom.* III 3; enfractuosus est ejus meatus, ut per tam breve spacium prolongetur *Ps.*-Ric. *Anat.* 27; quis ejus..amfractuosi serpentis perniciabile virus non exhorreat? Ad. Marsh *Ep.* 92 p. 213; dicitur vulpes quasi 'volupes', quia volubilibus pedibus et amfractuosis cursibus incedit Upton 171. **b** que antiqui ∼is adinvencionibus effoderunt R. Bury *Phil.* 9. 145.

anfractus [CL], twist or turn, winding path (also fig.). **b** (fig.) manœuvre, trick, wile.

neglecto tramite Christi / errorum anfractus salebroso calle sequuntur Aldh. *VirgV* 2291; lucida nigratis fuscans anfractibus arva *Id. Aen.* 59 (*Penna*) 5; **10..** ∼ibus, *ymbgongum, bogetungum, hilcum* WW; Normannia..turbatores suos..in Franciam liberis ∼ibus emittens W. Malm. *GR* V 397; amfractus vito, semita recta placet Neckam *DS* VII 10; veri via despicit orbis / †affractus, planum diligit Garl. *Epith.* VII 138; vallis in †amfractis [? l. ∼us] tendit *Id. Tri. Eccl.* 21; super serpentem..tortuosum propter multiformes callide varietatis amfractus Ad. Marsh *Ep.* 92 p. 215. **b s1141** dimicabant..non congressibus acierum sed militarium ∼uum circuitionibus H. Hunt. *HA* VIII 19; **s1219** pleni ∼ibus Saraceni M. Par. *Maj.* III 46; **1300** litigiorum amfractibus..subductis *Reg. Carl.* I 124; **1316** per varios litis amfractus durante lite diucius *Reg. Newbattle* p. 129; post..scrupulosos causarum ∼us R. Bury *Phil.* 8. 125.

angaria, ∼ium [ἀγγαρεία], compulsory service, *corvée.* **b** toll. **c** fasting (w. ref. to ember days). **d** constraint, duress.

1077 ab omni..∼ia regalium et episcopalium ministrorum ..sint perpetim expediti (*Ch. Will. I*) *Chr. Rams.* 202; **1139** nec [monasterium] ecclesiasticis conditionibus seu ∼iis..subjaceat (*Lit. Papae*) Elmh. *Cant.* 370; [milites] in ∼iis plurimum detinendi sunt, ..ut corporibus eorum robur accedat et animis J. Sal. *Pol.* 594A; fere tota ejus [Henrici I] progenies Anglos ∼ia foreste vehementer oppressit R. Niger 165; [Henricus II] tributum..monasteriis nunquam indixit, quibus etiam ab ∼iis et exactionibus publicis..immunitatem servavit W. Newb. III 26; concussiones, rapinas, ∼ias..exercere Ad. Marsh *Ep.* 21; **1258** servi ecclesie non debent ∼iis aut novis oneribus fatigari (*Privil. Cler.*) *Ann. Burton* 427; **1321** abbas de Gant..clamat. esse quietus.. ab omni..opere seu †augaria regalium ministrorum *PQW* 462b; **1418** absque solucione alicujus..pedagii..∼ii vel perangarii *Mon. Hib. & Scot.* 370a; **1453** immunes..ab omnibus tributis, ..∼iis et perangariis *Reg. Glasg.* 399. **b a1100** ut homines mei..absque omni ∼ia clausurarum et theloneariorum..securi Romam eant (*Notif. Cnut.*) *GAS* 276; **1498** (v. angariagia). **c** quartum [celebratur jejunium] in Decembri in quarta feria post festum Lucie..; si vigilia Nativitatis fuerit in Sabbato, tunc celebratur jejunium in septimana precedente.., et hec possunt sciri per hos versus: 'dat Crux, Lucia, Cineres, Karismata Dia / quod sit in angarīa quarta sequens feria' Bacon VI 115 (cf. *Conc. Scot.* II 75); *embyrday*, ∼ium vel dies iiij temporum *PP.* **d** me ..quasi per ∼iam in sue cupiunt suspicionis impellere voraginem W. Dan. *Ep.* 61a; rex..commodius ratus est juvenum animos..premiis allicere quam ~iis preceptorum urgere *Itin. Ric.* III 13; crux..quibusdam perditis amara et onerosa est; eam enim in ~iam portant P. Blois *Serm.* 674c (cf. *Matth.* xxvii 32); portabat vero, sed in ~ia, crucem hujusmodi actionum Ad. Eyns. *Hug.* V 5; experti conjuges horrent conjugia, / qui crucem bajulant, sed in angarīa *Ps.*-Map (*Conjunx* 56) *Poems* 79; ne †augmentat scandalum major angarīa, / se consulte transtulit fuge, fultus via *Poem S. Thom.* 74.

2 grief, distress.

s1121 ipse..in ~ia ista pro ecclesia nostra fideliter stetit H. Cantor *Hist.* 26; **s1186** quod..factum est necessitate cogente ad utilitatem, jam in ~iis revocatur ad memoriam Gerv. Cant. I 46; **s1215** [rex] in ~ia mentis aliquandiu constitutus excogitavit quo contra barones ultionis genere uteretur Wend. II 135; **1222** fecit invitus et in ~ia positus pactum de reddenda Damieta (*Lit. Ph. de Aubeney*) M. Par. *Maj.* III 70; in tanta tam mesti cordis ~ia cum lacrimarum profluvio..rogavi Ad. Marsh *Ep.* 49 p. 156; cum in angarīa / leti libasti calicem J. Howd. *Cyth.* 85; **s1392** comes Oxonie.. diem clausit extremum in mentis anguria [v.l. ~ia] rerumque penuria miseranda Wals. *HA* II 212; *angwysh*, angustia, agonia, angurria *PP*.

†angariagia, toll.

1498 vectigalia, pedagia, †augariagias ac custumas qualia mercatores Hanze Teutonice solvere tenentur (*TreatyR*) *Foed.* XII 702b (cf. ib.: †augarias et custumas solvent).

angarialis, distressing.

s1253 annus iste..pape et papalibus arctus et ~is M. Par. *Maj.* V 420 (= Oxnead 197: †angularis).

angariare, to constrain. **b** to burden, oppress.

s1139 ad resignandas munitiones quas exstruxerat ~iatus est W. Newb. I 6; **s1097** rex..incolas ad constructionem aule..injuriose nimis ~iavit M. Par. *Min.* I 97; cum ~iante mille passus ire et alia duo Ockham *Pol.* II 803 (cf. *Matth.* v 41); beneficia..resignare ~iant et compellunt Brinton *Serm.* 4 p. 3; alios..[terram] eis vendere ~iaverunt *Plusc.* VII 17. **b** **a1070** conquestus sum..quod mei archiepiscopi in tantum ~iabantur immensitate pecuniarum quae ab eis expetebatur (*Notif. Cnut.*) *GAS* 276; a..rege..plurimis exactionibus ~iati *G. Herw.* 331; ~ians eum jejunii tormento H. Hunt. *HA* VIII 10; **s1187** multi, et maxime pauperiores, ~iantur et affliguntur *Ann. Waverley* 245; quis est quem sic angarias / et crucis curvas sarcina? J. Howd. *Cyth.* 133; **s1299** afforestaciones quibus plebs †angariebatur *Flor. Hist.* III 108; **1485** ecclesiam..anguriare pecuniariis imposicionibus injustis *Reg. Aberbr.* II 242.

2 to grieve, distress.

s1000 sinistris ~iate nunciis, puppes relique Londoniam redierunt H. Hunt. *HA* VI 5; estuant ~iati, quibus non dabatur requies *Itin. Ric.* IV 18; **1452** nos ~iant et circumvallant adversitatum..occasiones *Conc.* III 561.

angarius, bailiff or sim.

arester or atacher or a cacherel or a cachpolle, ..*baly or servaunt man arestynge*, ~ius, apparitor *PP*.

angarizare, to constrain.

si te subterfugientem..episcopum ~arem et ad apostolicam sedem tendentem retinerem Eddi *Wilf.* 28.

†angaronia [? angaria, *infl. by* agonia], hardship.

c1300 rigide et cum magna ~ia deducebatur ad prisonam *Year Bk. 30–31 Ed. I app.* II 543.

angela, angel (f.).

illa tam innocenter..respondit ut credas ~am locutam que possit angelum quemvis ad vota fallere Map *NC* IV 9 p. 174.

angelatus, ~ettus, v. angelotus. Angelice v. Anglice.

angelicus [ἀγγελικός], of an angel or angels. **b** having the nature of an angel. **c** like or worthy of an angel, angelic.

sicut in quodam volumine ~a relatione refertur Aldh. *VirgP* 19; ~a meruit visione perfrui Bede *HE* III 19; cum hymnus ~us, sc. 'gloria in excelsis', inciperetur *Mir. J. Bev.* A 299; choris immistum ~is Ailr. *V. Ed. Conf.* 777b; in nullo aliter sentire quam res se habeat [est] ~a vel divina perfectio J. Sal. *Pol.* 428a; hymnus ~us, 'sanctus, sanctus' Gir. *GE* II 20; post hunc angelicus est ultimus ordo H. Avr. *Poems* 43. 5; **s1240** festo ~o [*29 Sept.*] sollempnizato M. Par. *Min.* II 438; ~a natura nullam habet dependenciam a materia Bart. Angl. II 2; ~a presidia Ad. Marsh *Ep.* 49; per ~um ministerium Bacon *Tert.* 186; **1393** dicent..psalmum 'de profundis' cum oracione dominica ac salutacione ~a *Lit. Cant.* III 18. **b** angelicus princeps et protus Lucifer Aldh. *VirgV* 2734; ut..~is spiritibus mererentur associari Osb. *V. Dunst.* 3; per aliam personam sive ~am sive humanam Anselm (*Cur Deus* 1) II 48; sub numero certo claudit sapientia cives / angelicos Neckam *DS* IV 301. **c** se ~ae castitatis comitem fore gratulatur Aldh. *VirgP* 17; bene [vocantur Angli]; nam et ~am habent faciem Bede *HE* II 1 p. 80; egerat angelicam sub carnis tegmine vitam Nig. *Paul* f. 47a; ad alios autem ~i affectus suavitatem semper habuit Eccleston *Adv. Min.* 110; **1336** erat in ecclesia ~us, in aula splendidus, in mensa dapsilis *Lit. Cant.* II 117; [abbas Michael, ob. 1349] toto conamine laborabat ut ~o nomini vitam ~am copularet *G. S. Alb.* II 300.

2 (sb. f.) angelica (bot.). **b** daphne.

senecion, ~a, que et regina, coriandrus..herbe note sunt Neckam *NR* II 166; ~a [etc.] coquantur in vino Gilb. II 86. 1. **b** allipiados, †anglica [v.l. ~a], herba catholica, laureola idem..G. et A. *lauriole Alph.* 4.

angelotus [OF *angelot*; cf. angelus 2a], half angel (coin).

1532 tres coronas de sole, unum angelettum, ..et duos angelos aureos vocatos *angelles KRMem* 311 *rec. Mich.* r. 13; **1535** Cromwellus..tibi dedit viginti angelatos (T. Bedill) *Ep. Erasm.* XI 3058.

Angelsaxo v. Anglosaxo.

angelus [ἄγγελος], angel. **b** (w. *malus* or sim.) fallen angel, devil.

~us limpidissimo lucis radio resplendens Aldh. *VirgP* 38 p. 288; apparuit ei ~us Domini in forma stabilis viri.., sicut..Abrahae..~i in forma virorum apparuerunt Bede *Cuthb.* II 2; vidit animam..comitantibus ac ducentibus ~is ad caelum ferri *Id. HE* IV 21; ~us est essentialis motus circa Deum et rerum causas Eriug. *Per.* 444b; ~us vel nuntius, *engcel* Ælf. *Gl.*; licet ~i nomen ab officio sumptum sit, quia ~us nuntius dicitur, tamen, sicut anima pro specie substantiae accipitur, ita et ~us Anselm (*Incarn.* 2) II 13; **1095** ad magni consilii ~um curram (*Ep. Anselmi*) Eadmer *HN* 65; novem sunt officia ~orum, quorum nomina sunt hec: ~i, archangeli, virtutes, potestates, principatus, dominationes, throni, cherubin atque seraphin Pull. *Sent.* 885b; angelus ex vultu, corpore cum sit homo Nig. *Mir. BVM* 7 v. 1; spiritus..quando a Deo mittitur tunc primo ~us proprie nuncupatur; cui..~o licentia pictoris alas tribuit in quarum subito motu celer est Bart. Angl. II 1; venerunt duo demones et sederunt ad sinistram, et unus bonus ~us stetit ad dextram Eccleston *Adv. Min.* 71; **1338** quem..auctor..pacis..ad..Anglicane ecclesie et regni pacem tanquam pacis ~um destinavit *FormOx* 102; Wycl. *Civ. Dom.* I 422 (v. assumptibilis); **c1430** ille satelles Sathane, qui se in ~um lucis transformaverat *Reg. Whet.* II 381 (cf. 2 *Cor.* xi 14). **b** ~i damnati non possunt servari nisi per ~um deum Anselm (*Cur Deus* 21) II 132; **11..** cum diabolo et ~is ejus *Feod. Durh.* xliii; potestatem forsitan dedit Dominus ~o illius perditi malo ut in corpore illo mortuo se exagitet Map *NC* II 27; **1208** a variis suggestionibus penitus avertentes auditum, que profecto sunt immissiones per ~os malos (*Lit. Papae*) Gerv. Cant. II xci; **c1370** 'corruit in terram' cum illo ~o damnato (J. Bridl. *gl.*) *Pol. Poems* I 174.

2 angel (gold coin). **b** sort of cup (? w. image of angel).

1345 summa totalis auri empti: ccclxxv li. ..de auro Franc' et angel' scut' et in alio diverso billon' *KRAc* (*Mint*) 290/28; **1509** in ~is auri in gross' lxv li. *Fabr. York* 234; **1527** summa lx li. in ~is secundum antiquam computacionem (*DCCant.*) *HMC Var. Coll.* I 225; **1533** misit.. unum ~um aureum *Cant. Coll. Ox.* III 267. **b** **1328** cuppe xij cum uno cooperculo, que vocantur ~i (*Invent.*) *Hist. Cath. Cant. app.* VII p. xviii.

angere [CL], to crush. **b** to harass, distress. **c** (pass.) to take pains (over).

fictilis olla / rupta fit in testas, dum lapis angit eas Gower *VC* VII 138. **b** anthletam Domini.. / udis et crudis nervorum nexibus angens Aldh. *VirgV* 1191; spiritus..circumdederunt me atque..de ore..ignem putidum efflantes ~ebant Bede *HE* V 12; juste ~itur reus Dei inter malum et pejus Anselm (*Or.* 8) III 28; dum te mortis timor continuus ~eret Gir. *GE* II 20. **c** id ego semper ~ebar, quare huic studio forem attentior Adel. *QN intr.* p. 4.

2 (pr. ppl.) grievous. **b** (as sb.) briar, bramble.

angens sceptri ludibrium J. Howd *Cyth.* 30. **b** anguens, *breer GlC* A 576; **10..** anguens, *bremel* WW.

Angevinus, Angevin, of Anjou; *cf. Andegavensis.*

Osmundus ~us *DB* II 2b; numisma vulgo dictum ~um *Itin. Ric.* I 75; **12..** duos solidos de ~is *FormA* 249.

anggrena v. gangraena.

angildum [AS], simple weregeld.

si tuus geneat..furetur et amittetur tibi, si habeas plegium, admone eum de ~o [AS: *mana þone þæs angyldes*]; si non habeas, redde tu ~um (*Quad.*) *GAS* 99.

angilogia v. anagogia. angilopa v. anchilops.

angina [CL], quinsy.

~a apostema est sub gula, dictum ab ango, -is *Alph.* 11; brancho atque ~a morbis correptus est Boece 173 v.

anginasticus v. acmasticus.

angiportus [CL], narrow street. **b** harbour. **c** (fig.) tight corner.

~us, angustus locus *GlC* A 615; Turci experrecti..fugam per ~us invadunt W. Malm. *GR* IV 363. **b** angeportus, refrigerium navium *GlC* A 621; ~us, i. refrigerium navium, *hyð* Ælf. *Gl.* **c** in ~u magno nos inclusistis..hac prohibitione vestra W. Fitzst. *Thom.* 56.

Anglecheria v. Anglescheria.

Anglensis, English.

dum se ~es ita turbulenter..continerent *G. Steph.* I 2.

Anglescheria, Englishry: **a** English status of slain man (exempting community from payment of murder-fine); **b** English tenantry or (area of) tenure (Wales and Marches).

a **1185** vicecomes reddit compotum de v m. pro murdro per defectum probationis Englescherie *Pipe* 123; **1186** pro defectu probationis ~ie *Pipe* 164; **1188** quia non presentavit Englescheriam ad horam *Pipe* 145 (cf. ib. 162: pro falsa presentatione Englisherie); **1202** presentator Englescherie.. obiit *SelPlCrown* 25; **1221** in hoc comitatu debet Englescheria presentari per duos ex parte patris et per unum ex parte matris *PlCrGlouc* 1; **1229** nulli Englengeria presentatur in civitate London' *CurR* XIII 2272; **1255** nec aliquam Englescheriam presentaverunt racione assise foreste *SelPlForest* 19; **1258** cum..villate de ita mortuis nihil sciunt nec dicunt nisi quod casu..moriuntur, et quia nihil de huthesia [? nec] Englescheria assignatur, amerciatur patria ..tanquam de murdro (*Pet. Baronum*) *Ann. Burton* 442; murdrum est occulta extraneorum hominum occisio..; extraneorum dico quia, sive interfector cognitus fuerit vel incognitus, dicitur Francigena nisi Englescheria, id est quod Anglicus sit, probetur per parentes et coram justiciariis presentetur Bracton 134b; **1285** nulla Englashiria presentatur in hoc burgo (*Eyre*) *DocCOx* 194; Anglischeria in inquisicione et visu coronatoris corpore non sepulto debet presentari *Fleta* 46; **1313** Englescheria presentatur in comitatu isto de feloniis tantum et hoc de masculis *Eyre Kent* 13. **b** **1205** terre et tenementa infra..burgum..tractentur per legem Bretoll'.. et legem Anglischerie secundum quod..solent tractari per predictas leges *BBC* (*Shrewsbury*) 137; **1268** quia Griffinus ..est de Anglecheria nostra, vobis significamus ut, si de deliberacione illius..in curia nostra loqui volueritis, parati sumus vobis inde justiciam exhibere *Cl* 497; **1278** hoc parati sunt verificare per homines de Englescheria ejusdem manerii [*Bangor Iscoed, Flint*] *Welsh R.* 254; verificacio.. per homines juratos de marchia in medio existentes inter Englesheriam et Walesheriam *Ib*; **1282** recognoscit dictum tenementum esse Englescheria (*sic*) et sic secundum legem communem inde esse procedendum *Ib.* 335; **1292** dominus rex intendit predictas villatas [in com. Salop']..†textitere in Englecheriam, quas predictus P. subtraxit in Walechriam *PQW* 681b.

Anglia, England. **b** silver or pale gold.

~ia vetus sita est inter Saxones et Giotos, habens oppidum capitale quod..Slesuuic nuncupatur..; ideoque Brittannia nunc ~ia appellatur Æthelw. I 4; **†c1030** (13c) omnibus fidelibus totius Anglie *CD* 1326; **1067** W. rex Anglorum omnibus vicecomitibus suis ~ie, salutem *Regesta* I p. 118; insularum nobilissima cui quondam nomen Albion fuit, postea vero Brittannia, nunc autem ~ia H. Hunt. *HA* I 2; argenti venas coquit Anglia Garl. *Tri. Eccl.* 2. **b** vocatur argentum ~ia, quia ibi habundat argentum; similiter et aurum minus rufum vocatur ~ia quia ibi oritur Bacon *Tert. Sup.* 84.

Angliacus, English.

lux, decus Angliaci, spes †et [? *omit*] augustissima regni (*Collect*) *NLA* (*Lethardus*) II 148n.

Anglicanus, English. **b** (w. *ecclesia*).

s1191 sibi nihil esse cum rege ~o *Itin. Ric.* II 32; **1219** in episcopatibus ~is (*Lit. Arch. Rotomag.*) *Ch. Sal.* 87; **s1305** [W. Waleys] nemini qui lingua ~a utebatur pepercit *Ann. Lond.* 141 (cf. ib.: legibus ~is); **c1324** charta Willelmi Bastard..per verba ~a *MGL* II 25; **1332** testificatum fuit quod ~us fuit *SelCCoron* 82; ~a perspicacitas R. Bury *Phil.* 8. 134; **1413** monete nostre ~e *RScot* 209a; **1431** unum librum ~um de Pers Plughman *Test. Ebor.* II 34. **b** auctoritate regia ab omnibus curie nexibus absolutus liber ~e ecclesie redditur H. Bos. *Thom.* III 2; **1213** negocium quod inter ecclesiam ~am et ipsum regem versatum est *Lit. Cant.* I 21; **1215** quod ~a ecclesia libera sit *Magna Carta* 1; **1316** pro defensione regni nostri et ecclesie ~e *RScot* 166a; **1437** secundum..computacionem ecclesie ~e *Mem. Ripon* 131; **1539** anno regni regis Henrici VIII..in terra supremi capitis ~e ecclesie XXX *Sanct. Bev.* 465; **1600** contra canones et constitutiones ecclesiae ~ae *StatOx* 456.

Anglicare, to Anglicize. **b** to English, translate into English.

1297 similiter mandatur Scotis ~atis *RScot* 50; **s1296** congregati sunt apud Sconam omnes magnates Scocie cum aliis ~atis *Plusc.* VIII 25. **b** **1413** libri et tractatus novelli ab ortu schismatis ~ati *Conc.* III 365.

Anglicatio, Englishing, translation into English.

1413 de ~one librorum *Conc.* III 365; **c1450** ~o cartarum ..omniumque aliorum de lingua Latina debet fieri sicut littera jacet et sapit in communi usu loquendi ad auditorium *TRBk* 330 f. 23a.

Anglice, in English. **b** by English reckoning.

Deura Bernech ~e Deira et Bernicia Nenn. *HB* 205; **947** (12c) bis denas mansas, quod Angelice dicitur *twentig hida CS* 834; **c1070** ab omni mea consuetudine et censu pecunie que *geld* et *Danegeld* ~e vocatur *Regesta* 120; [quidam fantasticus spiritus] loquebatur ~e secundum idioma regionis illius Coggesh. 89b; non est sub lege, id est *inlaghe* ~e Bracton 125b; **1323** dictas litteras..Latine, Gallice et ~e faciatis nunciari *Reg. Carl.* II 219; **c1370** ventis aurum, ~e *Wyndesor*' (J. Bridl. *gl.*) *Pol. Poems* I 135; **1440** ij vehiculatoriorum, ~e *hweylbarwys Cant. Coll. Ox.* II 156. **b** hic numerus ~e computatur i centum pro cxx *DB* I 336.

Anglicus, English. **b** (sb. m.) Englishman. **c** (sb. f.) Englishwoman.

s892 volant rostra ad ~as partes Æthelw. IV 3; ~i burgenses ibi manentes *DB* I 179; in patrium id est in ~um sermonem Osb. *V. Dunst.* 1; si ~us homo [AS: *Ænglisc man*] Dacum occidat (*Quad.*) *GAS* 222; membrana..elementis ~is..conscripta W. Malm. *GP* IV 156; reges pugnant, hinc Gallicus, inde / Anglicus Garl. *Tri. Eccl.* 16. **b** tenet..unus ~us iii hidas *DB* I 65b; si ~us [AS: *Englisc man*] Dacum servum occidat (*Quad.*) *GAS* 222; immisit ultio divina Brittannie..tertiam [plagam] per ~os, qui eam debellaverunt et obtinent H. Hunt. *HA* I 4; **s1087** ita etiam ut ~um vocari esset opprobrio *Ib.* VI 38; sic permixte sunt nationes, ut vix decerni possit hodie, de liberis loquor, quis ~us quis Normannus sit genere *Dial. Scac.* I 10b; **1215** quando ~i venerunt in Hiberniam *Cl.* 186a; pro ~o, vero et de quo constare possit quod ~us sit, non dabitur murdrum Bracton 135b; **s1345** vertitur in proverbium quod ~i sunt boni asini, omnia onera eis imposita..supportantes Ad. Mur. 175; **1346** Anglicus angelicus Edwardus, juris amicus (*In Franciam*) *Pol. Poems* I 39; ~i dicuntur quasi 'Inglici' vel 'igne electi' Bad. Aur. 108; et ~i..in ludis hujusmodi et compotis linguam loquuntur †Gallicanum Fortescue *LLA* 48. **c** Suttunam tenet Alvid quedam ~a *DB* II 45.

2 (sb. n) English language: **a** (sg.); **b** (pl.).

a ut nos loquimur ~um, Gallicum et Latinum Bacon *CSPhil.* 433; **1298** ut hoc..in ~o exponatur *Reg. Cant.* I 271; nec bene possent [per Angliam transire] nisi ~um scirent *Latin Stories* 128; **1431** lego..unum librum de ~o vocatum 'Gower' *Test. Ebor.* II 14; terminos quosdam, quos plus proprie placitantes in Gallico quam in ~o exprimunt Fortescue *LLA* 48; **1484** [scolares] non locuntur Latinum in scola sed ~um *Vis. Southwell* 49. **b** **1415** libros scriptos in ~is *Conc.* III 372; **1416** legendam sanctorum in ~is *Reg. Cant.* II 124; **1529** recitavit hec verba in ~is *Deeds Balliol* 127.

Angligena, English-born, English. **b** (sb. m.) Englishman.

dilectis..~is fratribus Abbo *QG pref.*; **1068** Angligenis turmis concedat dona salutis (*Coron. Matilde*) *Mon. Rit.* II 88; ut omnes futuri temporis ~ae populi agnoscant.. Osb. *Mir. Dunst.* 1; Aldredus..ultimus ~a archiepiscopus H. Cantor 8v; **c1216** invocat Angligenas Anglorum lacrima vires (*Guerra Joh.*) *Pol. Songs* 22; **1382** a viris Angligenis non est Christus notus (*Conc. Lond.*) *Pol. Poems* I 254. **b** **943** (12c) ego Eadmundus ~arum rex ceterarumque gentium in circuitu persistentium *CS* 789 (cf. ib. 833); pons est inde suis pervius Angligenis (Abbo *QG prol.*) *Chr. Rams.* xxvii; sunt hospitati in Hantone lxv Francigenae et xxxi ~ae *DB* I 52a; hinc sunt illae leges..quo ~arum corda suspirant (*Quad. Arg.*) *GAS* 533; **s1309** rex omnes ~as sibi notos pro tanta tolerancia..increpavit Trokelowe 68; **p1377** sed Deus Angligenas bene salvans sit benedictus (*Epitaph. Ed. III*) *Pol. Poems* I 221.

Angligenensis, English.

c1370 partes burgenses non cedent Angligenenses (J. Bridl.) *Pol. Poems* I 149; Princeps Wallensis, regni decus Anglig[en]ensis Elmh. *Metr. Hen. V* 52.

†Angligenus, English.

c1302 cujusdam magnatis ~i (*Chr. S. Edm.*) *EHR* LVIII 69 (cf. ib. 76: magnates Angligene); **s1400** stragem maximam populo ~o..contulit Elmh. *Cant.* 257; Angligeni majestas inclita regni J. Herd *Hist. IV Regum* 75.

Anglischeria v. Anglescheria.

Anglosaxo, Anglosaxon.

Aelfred Angul-Saxonum [v.l. Anglorum Saxonum] rex Asser *Alf.* 1; **a940** (10c) cum consensu..Æðelstani Angelsaxonum Denorumque gloriosissimi regis *CS* 648 (cf. ib. 659); **956** (12c) ego Eaduuig imperiali Anglo-Saxonum diademate infulatus *Ib.* 932; **956** ego Eadwig egregius Angul-Saxonum basileus *Ib.* 961; ex diversis ~onum finibus Lantfr. *Mir. Swith.* 2. 335D; Isca..in ~onum potestatem ante annum cccclxv ab eorum in Britanniam ingressu non devenit Camden *Br.* 168.

Anglus, Angle. **b** Englishman. **c** (?) (adj.) English.

de ~is, hoc est de illa patria quae Angulus dicitur, .. Orientales ~i, Mediterranei ~i, Merci, tota Nordanhymbrorum progenies ceterique ~orum populi sunt orti Bede *HE* I 15; frater Æthelwoldi principis Orientalium ~orum *V. Osw.* 429; anno..ccccxlix venere ~i et Saxones Britanniam W. Malm. *GR* I 1. **b** **601** Aedilbercto regi ~orum (*Lit. Papae*) Bede *HE* I 32; quinque gentium linguis, .. ~orum videlicet, Brettonum, Scottorum, Pictorum et Latinorum *Ib.* I 1; **735** rogo ut mihi studeatis indicare in quoto anno..praedicatores primi missi a S. Gregorio ad gentem ~orum venissent Bonif. *Ep.* 33; **774** ego Offa rex totius ~orum patriae *CS* 214; **c1067** (v. Anglia); homines de hundredo, Franci et ~i *DB* I 32; nullus hodie ~us vel dux, vel pontifex, vel abbas W. Malm. *GR* II 227; per Normannos, qui eam [Brittanniam] devicerunt et ~is impresentiarum dominantur H. Hunt. *HA* I 4; **s1271** ait unus, natione ~us W. Guisb. 209; ad tres Cesareos apud Anglos sceptrigerantes (*Epitaph. Ed. III*) *Pol. Poems* I 219. **c** **1101** dabit..l libras †~orum denariorum in feodo *DipDoc I* p. 4.

2 (w. *Saxo*) Anglosaxon (*cf. Anglosaxo*).

957 (15c) rex ~orum Saxonum *CS* 995; ut mos est Anglis Saxonibus Wulf. *Swith.* II 786; ~i Saxones..Britonibus.. imperium..abstulerunt Ord. Vit. IV 7 p. 230.

angmasticus v. acmasticus. angn- v. agn-.

angor [CL], pain, grief. **b** spite.

acri ~ore afficitur Aldh. *VirgP* 42; cum diu tacitis mentis ~oribus..carperetur Bede *HE* II 12; magno ~ore correptus *V. Dunst.* B. 7; anguor et ex anguore quidam stupor animos cunctorum obsedit G. Crispin *Herl.* 108; ~oribus conflictatus W. Malm. *GP* I 44. **b** **s1141** [imperatrix] irritata muliebri ~ore regem..in compedibus poni jussit H. Hunt. *HA* VIII 19.

angoreus, painful.

docens per ~eas hujus vitae semitas..esse transiendum *V. Dunst.* B. 15.

anguens v. angere 2b.

anguicomus [CL], snaky-haired.

Gorgonis anguicome modo monstra vigent nisi come Garl. *Mor. Scol.* 113.

anguilla [CL], eel. **b** (w. *rubea*) smoked eel.

anguilla, *el GlC* A 651; Elge..a copia ~arum, quae in eisdem paludibus capiuntur, nomen accepit Bede *HE* IV 17; [capimus] ~as [AS: *ælas*] et lucios..et qualescunque [pisces] in amne natant Ælf. *Coll.* 94; habet rex..ij sticas ~arum *DB* I 1; fecunde..piscibus, et precipue..~is lutosis Gir. *TH* I 9; **1247** per serjantiam..solvendi..tres angwillas in ieme *Fees* 1405; **1265** xij sticke angulle *CalIMisc* I 674; **1344** iij ~e grosse, iij s. vj d.; l shaft', vij s. vj d. *KRAc* 390/11 r. 15; **1350** Johanni..deferenti ~os (*sic*) priori *Ac. Durh.* 550. **b** **1421** pro ij dim. barellis ~arum salsarum rubearum *EEC* 508; **1425** navis..onerata..cum ~is rubeis et piscibus salsis (*KRMem*) *Bronnen* 999.

anguillaris, of or for eels.

collectis..retibus ~ibus Bede *HE* II 13; cum..pastillum ~em pro parte dracus nutrici dedisset Gerv. Tilb. III 85; **1576** pro argento ~i Anglice vocato *elesilver Pat.* 1142 m. 16.

anguillarium, eel-bed.

an ele bed, ~ium *CathA*.

anguillosus, abounding in eels.

c970 anguillosa palus nescit habere modum (Abbo *QG prol.*) *Chr. Rams.* xxviii; ambitur isdem locus paludibus ~is *Ib.* 8.

anguillula, little eel.

inquisita..vermis natura, invenerunt..anguem modicum, ~e nigre formam preferentem Gir. *TH* I 36.

anguillus v. anguilla.

anguina [? cf. It. *anchini*], rope, stay.

nomina navium et instrumenta earum: ..~a, *cops* Ælf. *Sup.*; ventus contrarius percussit proram..et erupte sunt ~e W. Cant. *Mir. Thom.* II 30; **s1217** [presciderunt rudentes et] antennas, et maxime ~as, malum et velum sustinentes M. Par. *Abbr.* 241 (cf. *Id. Min.* II 219).

anguis [CL], snake. **b** (astr.) Draco. **c** (fig.).

~is, serpens aquarum *GlC* A 590; **10..** ~is, *wæternædre..*, **14..** hic agguis, A. *a wateradder* WW; Gir. *TH* I 36 (v. anguillula); angue diu socio nemo pericla cavet *Babio* 466; angues carminis arte novant Garl. *Tri. Eccl.* 102. **b** videns Plaustrum quo labitur axem, / haec cum detinuit conversis vultibus Anguem Æthelwulf *Abb.* 22.56; ore minax Anguis geminas intersecat Ursas Neckam *DS* I 359. **c** **s1295** semper latuit ~is tortuosus, portans in cassidili toxicum mellitum *Flor. Hist.* III 282.

angula v. angulus 1d, cingulum.

angulare, to cause to converge. **b** to corner, drive into a corner. **c** to play hide and seek.

omnes linee per quas formatur visus uniuntur et quasi ~antur in pupille cono Bart. Angl. V 7. **b** **1320** ~averunt dictum R. inter cimiterium..et fossatum..ecclesie *SelCKB* II 93. **c** *pleyyn bukhyde*, ~o *PP*.

2 (p. ppl.) **a** bent. **b** indented. **c** gyronny (her.).

a dimittat cubitum ~atum secundum quantitatem quam tolerat Gad. v. 2. **b** **a1413** cape..habent orfreys de nigro velvetto cum circulis ~atis de auro (*Invent.*) Amund. II 343. **c** sunt eciam arma inangulata, quasi contrario modo ~ata, ut conus contra conum in medio Bad. Aur. 129.

angularicus, angular, having angles.

angulus naturalis est principium mensurans posicionem et quantitatem figure ~e Wycl. *Log.* III 49.

1 angularis v. angarialis.

2 angularis, situated at a corner. **b** outlying. **c** angular (geom.).

1236 turrem ~em in..ballio [castri] *Cal. Liberate* VI 2422; **1246** domum ~em *CalCh* I 301; **1267** de una selda ~i *Cart. Osney* I 84; **1352** de uno cotagio ~i..in introitu de Ingramestwychen *Pat* 238 m. 8; **1420** pro ij stodys ~ibus oratorii *Arch. Hist. Camb.* II 443. **b** quiescente in pacis quiete universali Britannia cum adjacentium regnorum monarchiarumque ~ibus insulis *V. Ed. Conf.* f. 40; Angliam.. ~ibus Saxoniae populis denominaverunt Andre *Hen. VII* 10. **c** quilibet triangulus minimus habet tres angulos, in quolibet trium punctorum conalium, quorum quilibet dicitur ~is respectu basis sibi immediate Wycl. *Log.* III 49.

2 (w. *lapis*) corner-stone. **b** (fig.) Christ (*cf. Eph.* ii 20).

s1114 primum..lapidem ~em orientalem contra boream posuit ipse..abbas *Croyl. Cont. A* 118; in quem [Henricum II] velut lapidem ~em Anglici generis et Normannici gaudemus duos parietes convenisse Ailr. *Ed. Conf.* 738c. **b** †**c707** in ~i duorum testamentorum lapide Aldh. *Ep.* 10; Dominus Jesus Christus..vocatur..lignum, petra, lapis ~is, multaque in hunc modum Lanfr. *Corp. & Sang.* 438D.

3 (sb. ? n.) corner-plate.

1245 feretrum totum cristallinum bene preparatum cresta argentea et ~ibus argenteis bene deauratis (*Invent. S. Paul.*) *Arch.* L 465.

angulariter, at an angle.

intellige parietes ad centrum terre tendere, et reperies ipsos parietes ~er sibi sociari Neckam *NR* II 172; pupilla omnia sub angulo comprehendit, quia, sive radii a pupilla exeant ad rem visam sive a re visa ad pupillam redeant, semper in pupille..centro tanquam in cono ~er uniuntur Bart. Angl. V 7.

angulatim, from corner to corner.

serpens ille tabidus, quem..diximus latenter per aulam et ~im serpsisse, manifeste exserit caput H. Bos. *Thom.* III 31.

angulator [ME *angler*], angler.

1508 J. N. est communis ~or piscium in aqua dominorum *CourtR* 206/34 f. 82.

angulla v. anguilla.

angulosus [CL], angular, having corners. **b** (fig.) devious, crooked.

[apes] multiformem favorum machinam ~is et opertis cellulis construunt Aldh. *VirgP* 3 p. 232. **b** isti..~i veritatis exsufflatores H. Bos. *Ep.* 1462.

Angulsaxo v. Anglosaxo.

angulus [CL], corner. **b** extremity, outlying part. **c** angle (geom.). **d** plot of land lying at a corner.

aquam..in ~o sacrarii fuderunt Bede *HE* III 11; acu torta immissa per caprinum ~um [oculi] Gilb. III 137. 1 (cf. *Alph.* 52: simile est in oculo capre, cujus ~us exterior est major interiore); muri terrei..armati ~is et propugnaculis pro defensione Elmh. *Hen. V* 15; **1430** j cotagium super Westrawe in quodam ~o *Feod. Durh.* 29. **b** cum suis paucissimis et in extremo mundi ~o positis Bede *HE* V 15; **736** qui tenebrosos ~os Germanicarum gentium lustrare debet Bonif. *Ep.* 30; ~us unus terrarum, sc. Hibernicus orbis Gir. *TH intr.* p. 6. **c** lineae ex uno centro progredientes ~orum..causae dinoscuntur Eriug. *Per.* 602B; de puncto et linea, de ~o acuto vel obtuso Gir. *GE* II 37; nomen habens a contactu miracula prebet / angulus Neckam *DS* X 150; quanto ~us contingentie remotior est, tanto videtur major *Id. NR* II 153; aliter dicitur ~us contingentie pars ~i recti Gros. 54; omnis ~us corporalis est ex tribus superficiebus ad minus Bacon *Tert.* 137. **d** calumniatur ipse H. iii masuras et ~um prati *DB* I 45; **a1184** dedi eciam ..duos~os terre *Ch. Gilb.* 81; **12..** confirmavi..illam ~am terre mee que..est juxta magnam viam *FormA* 197; **1311** tenet..j peciam terre apud la Lak et j ~um apud brueram *Cust. Battle* 158.

2 crookedness (fig.). **b** trick, contrivance.

1168 veritas quia directa est, non habet ~os J. Sal. *Ep.* 266. 308c; plica duplicitatis et ~i in vita hominis Wycl. *Ver.* III 85. **b** **1325** querit~os usquequaque: pridie vero petebat quod possit in claustro..residere; nunc autem petit quod possit in infirmitorio facere penitenciam *Lit. Cant.* I 160.

anguor v. angor.

1 anguria [etym. dub.], water melon.

in ipsa [Candia]..papiniones, ~ie, cucurbite minimo precio comparantur S. Sim. *Itin.* 22.

2 anguria, ~iare v. angari-.

angustare [CL], to whittle down, diminish. **b** to oppress; *cf. angustiare.*

974 (12c) ut nemo successorum meorum ~are temere presumat quod ego amplificans..dilatavi *CS* 1302. **b** animum..inopia non ~ante *Chr. Battle* 32; **1244** populus.. periculis plurimis ~abatur (*Lit. Patriarchae Jerusal.*) *Chr. Melrose* 158.

angustatio, confinement, narrow limit.

1268 major est anime cedes quam corporis, cum illa perpetua sit, hec autem brevis temporis ~one depereat *Conc. Syn.* 750.

angustia [CL], narrowness, cramped space. **b** slightness, weakness.

671 de his prolixo ambitu verborum ratiocinari stricta epistularis ~ia minime sinit Aldh. *Ep.* 1; propter ~iam loci in quo monasterium constructum est Bede *HE* IV 10; in ~ias inaccessorum montium *Ib.* 24; per foraminis ~iam Gir. *TH* I 27. **b** illa nihil contra; nam jam ~ia valitudinis vocem precluserat W. Malm. *GP* III 101; pro sensus nostri ~ia H. Bos. *LM* 1371.

2 pressure. **b** affliction, anguish.

quod, nisi..remota fuerit obsidionis ~ia, castellum.. redderetur Elmh. *Hen. V Cont.* 114. **b** improperia et ~ias passuri Lanfr. *Comment. Paul.* (*Heb.* xiii 13) 406; o nimis gravis ~ia! si me inspicio, non tolero me ipsum; si non inspicio, nescio me ipsum Anselm (*Or.* 8) III 28; ~iam cordis et furorem mentis clamor et suspiria prodiderunt Ailr. *Ed. Conf.* 746D; Map *NC* III 3 (v. augustiae); quantum mihi merorem quantasque doloris ~ias..casus incusserit Gir. *Symb.* 23; erumpnosi exilii †anguscie ardorem..interpolant Rolle *IA* 146.

angustiare [bibl.], to constrict, squeeze. **b** to put in a difficult position, embarrass. **c** to oppress, afflict; *cf. angustare.*

ex superfluitate cibi ~iatur stomacus et pectus similiter Bacon V 72; **s1424** Anglici, inter bella Longobardorum et Francorum ~iati *Plusc.* X 29. **b** ~iatus Judeus ex his vix obtinuit ut..pecunie..sibi medietas laxaretur Eadmer *HN* 115; ~iatus..miles, quoniam solvendi debiti non suppetebat facultas, ..solutionis renovabat indutias T. Mon. *Will.* II 13; **s1190** sic ~iatis Turcis, advenerunt tres naves onerarie *Itin. Ric.* I 37; **c1242** tunc oportebit me.. adversus vos stare, si me ~iaveritis et labores meos abstuleritis Gros. *Ep.* 96; **s1254** [regina] lesa utrobique et ~iata, quid ageret excogitat M. Par. *Abbr.* 335; **s1319** donec ~iati pro modico forsan offerant quod pro magno prius vendidisse poterant *V. Edw. II* 247. **c** noli ~iari de morte carorum Alcuin *Ep.* 198; **1001** (14c) dirissimis hostium..~iatus flagellis *CD* 706; quasi passus extasim, positus in mentis excessu ~iatur vicissim Herm. Arch. 40; Deus electos suos ~iari permittit Ad. Scot. *Serm.* 379; **s1216** pater..compassus est filio dolenti et ~iato M. Par. *Min.* II 178; **s1383** ~iabant nempe eos tot mortes, non plebeianorum sed exercitatorum militum Wals. *HA* II 102; **s1454** hiis dictis attonitus non modice ac eciam..in se ~iatus *Reg. Whet.* I 133.

angustiose, painfully.

ex multitudine materie suffocantis calorem ~e se nitentem exonerare Gilb. II 124. 2; gemunt ~e *Ib.* VII 301. 2.

angustiosus, painful. **b** anxious, painstaking. **c** embarrassing.

tussis et ~a febris Gilb. I 27. 2; suspiria..ordinata et non ~a *Id.* II 114. 2; colica passio appellatur ~a cibi detencio corrupti *SB* 17. **b 1263** S. Passelewe cujus ~a diligentia et assidua illum non permisit quiescere (*Lit. Ep. Exon.*) *Foed.* I 758b. **c 1422** cum ~um sit..aut legem statuere..aut indifferenter concedere.. *Conc.* III 416.

angustus [CL], narrow, cramped. **b** (w. ref. to *Matth.* vii 14). **c** (fig.) pressing.

cum..mansionem ~am, ..id est oratorium et habitaculum commune, ..construxisset Bede *HE* IV 26; ~ior compes tibias grossiores circumplecti non poterat W. Malm. *GP* III 101; duplo fere ~iore spatio mare coarctatur Gir. *TH* I 1; virga..folia habens ~a *Alph.* 42. **b** ad superas arces angusto tramite tendens Aldh. *VirgV* 1315. **c** ecce miserum in ~o periculo, in periculosa angustia! Anselm (*Or.* 13) III 51.

angwilla v. anguilla.

anhelanter, w. breathless haste.

ad archiepiscopum..nec equis parcens nec calcaribus ~er accessit Gir. *Inv.* I 7.

anhelare [CL], to breathe (heavily), pant. **b** to emit heat.

nullus anhelanti procedit viscere flatus Aldh. *Aen.* 72 (*Colossus*) 5; continuis febribus ~abat Bede *HE* II 1; ~abit in oculos ejus G. Mon. VII 4 p. 392*n.*; sacerdos in aquis suaviter ~at Beleth *RDO* 110. 113; asma est difficultas hanelandi *SB* 12; anelo, A. *to panty & blowe* WW. **b 716** vidi..flammam immensae magnitudinis ~antem et terribiliter..ascendentem Bonif. *Ep.* 10 p. 9.

2 to pant for (fig.), desire ardently: **a** (w. *ad*); **b** (w. *in*); **c** (w. dat.); **d** (w. acc.); **e** (w. inf.).

a ad summum virginitatis fastigium ~at Aldh. *VirgP.* 37; cum videam..infideles ad hoc totis viribus hanelare ut.. J. Sal. *Pol.* 548c; vitandam..societatem..ad schismata ~antium Ad. Eyns. *Hug.* III 11; cucullatum cave, quoniam suspirat, hanelat, cupit et ambit..totis ad hoc nisibus Gir. *Inv.* I 9; **1309** alios ad enervacionem..eorundem jurium.. conspicimus anelare *Reg. Carl.* II 12; **1332** ad destruccionem status nostri..prodicionaliter anelebat (*Pat*) *Foed.* IV 506; quorum..mentes..ad dilectum anhelebant Rolle *IA* 152; ad easdem preservandas..omni studio ~abant Elmh. *Hen. V Cont.* 113. **b 802** opes..in quas mentis nostrae intentionem spiritus sanctus..†~ari [v.l. ~are] prohibuit Alcuin *Ep.* 251 p. 406; totis in Hiberniam tendens nisibus, totis in illam ~ans suspiriis Gir. *EH* I 12; [Conanus] omni nisu in regnum ~abat M. Par. *Maj.* I 169. **c s1016** dux perfidissimus, qui patrie sue semper ~abat insidiis Diceto *Abbr. Norm.* I 169; impossibilibus ~ans H. Hunt. *HA* VIII 17; pii pectoris clementiam salvandis animabus ~are conspicio Ad. Marsh *Ep.* 71; propriis comodis nimis anelantes Milemete *Nob.* 91. **d** [insulam Wehtam] ritus sacrilegos adhuc ~antem W. Malm. *GR* I 76; [Henricus II] totus in auro, aurum esuriebat, sitiebat, ~abat R. Niger 169; **s1402** dux Baverie..Romam pro coronacione anelans Ad. Usk 75. **e** servus tuus..~at videre te Anselm (*Prosl.* 1) I 98; **1412** nisi aliquis sit extraneus..qui librariam hanelaverit visitare *StatOx* 219.

anhelatio, ardent desire.

nullus ambigit quin †anclacio [v.l. hanelacio] ad ista est precipue propter commodum temporale annexum Ric. Armagh *Unusq.* 68.

anhelitus [CL], breath, gasp. **b** ardent desire. **c** (?) endurance.

[draco] pestifero spiritus ~u aethera corrumpens Aldh. *VirgP* 25 p. 258; quod..magno staret Edmundus hanelitu crebroque reductu spiritus Map *NC* V 4 p. 213; anelitum continendo Ric. Med. *Micr. Anat.* 230; jacuit sine anelitu *Mir. Montf.* 85; orthomia est rectus anelitus *Alph.* 131; **s1333** in ascensu..monticuli Scoti anelitu deficientes *Plusc.* IX 28; ad extremum ~um nobiliter dimicavit Elmh. *Hen. V Cont.* 150. **b** nimirum hoc avide amplecteretur atque ardentissimo exoptaret ~u Rolle *IA* 146. **c** si dominus extraxerit sanguinem supra ~um servi sui *RegiamM* II xii 8.

anhelosus, short of breath.

gargarizata prodest ~is Gilb. VII 357 v. 1 (cf. ib. IV 174. 2: hanelosis).

anhelus, panting, breathless. **b** ardently desirous.

quem febris torsit anhela Aldh. *CE* IV 2. 20; nunciis hanelis et literis vocatus anxiis Map *NC* I 17 p. 82; quo.. spiritus ~us..et fessus in robur respiret Ad. Eyns. *Hug.* V 1. **b** anima..~a in transitum eternitatis flagrabat Gosc. *Edith* 93; anime luctamen anhelum / pressa labella juvant Hanv. III 279; **s1239** nec mirum si..admirarentur.. quod adhuc tam ~o spiritu ad episcopatum..aspiravit M. Par. *Maj.* III 539.

aniceus v. alniceus. anichil- v. annihil-.

anicula [CL], old woman.

apparuit ei in visione..quaedam ~a satis decrepita Aldh. *VirgP* 25 p. 258; **10..** ~a, *eald cwene* WW; ~am partium istarum, que per triennium ante ceca fuerat Gir. *IK* I 11; salutantes se pannosas etiam ~as mitissime resalutabat Ad. Eyns. *Hug.* V 11 p. 141.

anigerulus v. avigerulus.

anilis [CL], of an old woman. **b** (? infl. by *annus*) ancient.

recta locutio..et utilis, non ~is [AS: *idel*] aut turpis Ælf. *Coll.* 89; ~is fabula, *ealdra cwena spell Id. Sup.*; ~ium somniorum figmenta W. Malm. *GP* I 66; cum..anum prestigiosam..adissemus, ibique ~ibus imbuti sententiis.. moraremur Adel. *QN* 58; ~es fabulas et nenias pueriles P. Blois *Ep.* 76. 237b; nondumque infundit aniles / brumula prima nives Hanv. IX 395; cuticulam..in rugas ~es evo longiore contractam Gir. *GE* II 4. **b** haec..accipiens ab annili vetustate Æthelw. IV 2; annilem dividunt inter se thesaurum *Ib.* 3.

anima [CL], (in man) **a** breath. **b** 'soul' (phil.), source of life, sentience and reason. **c** seat of emotion, 'heart'. **d** life.

a gementes / exhalant animas ossa cutisque vagas H. Hunt *HA* VIII 12; prostratum ac jam ~am agentem Beleth *RDO* 4. 17. **b** [homo] partem..sui..cum sensibilibus possidet in quantum corpus est, partem cum intelligibilibus in quantum ~a Eriug. *Per.* 530c; si non esset ~a tota in singulis membris sui corporis, non sentiret tota in singulis Anselm (*Prosl.* 13) I 111; non est ratio vel voluntas tota ~a, sed est unaquaeque aliquid in ~a *Id.* (*Praesc.* 11) II 279; quod [infans] mox ab ipsa conceptione rationalem ~am habeat, nullus humanus suscipit sensus *Id.* (*Orig. Pecc.* 7) II 148; caro vivit ab ~a, cum aliunde corpori vita esse non posset J. Sal. *Pol.* 477c; illud quod movetur voluntarie..movetur per aliquid quod est aliud a natura corporis: quicquid illud sit, illud est ~a J. Blund *An.* 2; est igitur sedes anime dignissima cordis / hospitium Neckam *DS* IX 349; spiritus animalis, qui est unicum instrumentum ~e Ric. Med. *Micr. Anat.* 215; corpus humanum..proprium ~e rationalis organum Bart. Angl. IV 1; [caput] ipsius ~e, que consistit corpori, quodammodo personam gerit *Ib.* V 2; ~a rationalis..est ubique in corpore et in singulis partibus, sed tamen non localiter sed ut forma et perfectio corporis Bacon *Tert.* 185; **a1290** utrum in homine ~a racionalis, sensibilis et vegetabilis sint una substancia simplex *Quaest. Ox.* 132; subversio ~e est continuus appetitus nauseandi *SB* 41; ubi..dicit totum hominem non nisi ex ~a et carne constare Netter *DAF* I 107. **c** quid ~a in occulto passa sit, caro palam praemonstrabat Bede *HE* III 19; duplici contritione anxiata est in ~a H. Hunt. *HA* VII 3; suam in patientia ~am possidens W. Fitzst. *Thom.* 139 (cf. *Luke* xxi 19); **s1298** data sunt Wallensibus duo dolia vini ad refocillandas eorum ~as W. Guisb. 325; nova audita cor multum letificant et ~am recreant *Eul. Hist.* I 297. **d** me sine.. / vix artus animaeque carerent tramite mortis Aldh. *Aen.* 70 (*Tortella*) 6; ut..nullius ~a hominis pro interfecto regis fratre..daretur Bede *HE* IV 19; **s1196** quod frater suus in ~am ejus conjurasset W. Newb. V 20; ut confessione..certioraretur, si in ~am suam aliquid machinarentur filii M. Par. *Maj.* I 86.

2 (in animal) 'soul', vital spark.

eorum [sc. brutorum] ~e, simul ut a corpore separantur, pereunt Adel. *QN* 14; sicut generatur ~a in putrefactis per solam illam virtutem [celestem] Bacon XIV 112.

3 (in universe or heavenly body) 'soul', vital principle.

~a est generalis vita quae omnia quae in motu atque in statu sunt vegetat atque movet Eriug. *Per.* 476c; sicut illa extime sphere ~a omnibus conditorum ~abus..prestantior est Adel. *QN* 25; super hos duos polos..circumvolvitur celum cum omnibus stellis et planetis, qui sunt in eo motu equali et uniformi.., cujus motus causa efficiens est ~a mundi Gros. 13.

4 'soul', individual, person (bibl.).

supersunt fideles ~ae quae ipsum..testantur se..conspexisse Gosc. *Mir. Iv.* lxxv; Joseph..patrem suum cum lxxij ~abus venientibus recepit R. Niger 5 (cf. *Gen.* xlvi 26); in navi cclxxvj ~e fuerunt Ord. Vit. II 3 p. 246 (cf. *Acts* xxvii 37); **s1270** collise naves..perierunt et submerse sunt plusquam cxx cum equis et armis et ~abus multis W. Guisb. 207.

5 soul (in Christian sense): **a** (during life); **b** (after bodily death); **c** (prayers or alms for); **d** (oaths by); **e** (w. *ventris*); **f** (pl. w. *dies* or sim.) Feast of All Souls (2 Nov.); **g** (w. *collegium*).

a hoc carneum ~ae ergastulum Aldh. *VirgP* 60 p. 321; **601** idcirco haec signa de fine saeculi praemittuntur, ut de ~abus nostris debeamus esse solliciti (*Lit. Papae*) Bede *HE* I 32; nec timore mortis hi qui supererant a morte ~ae, qua peccando sternebantur, revocari poterant *Ib.* I 14; reliquit.. ~arum curam fratri suo Fullano *Ib.* III 19 p. 167; oporteret te ~abus eorum pastorali discretione consulere Lanfr. *Ep.* 29; diabolus, qui semper circa hoc satagit, qualiter in ~abus hominum maxime latrocinari possit (*Cons. Cnuti*) *GAS* 307; corpus..non perire dicis, ~am vero, ducem ac dominam incorpoream agentemque naturam, totalem non particularem perire deliras Adel. *QN* 14; **s1191** episcopus..electo curam ~arum commisit Diceto *YH* II 100; ne prolixior ecclesie..viduatio damnum irreparabile pariat ~abus Ad. Marsh *Ep.* 5; necessarium ad salutem ~e Ockham *Pol.* I 296; in ~a tua vide alia duo, peccatum et ignoranciam, quia sepe quod putas bonum est malum et mors ~e [ME: *soule murðre*] *AncrR* 103. **b** ad superas anima remeante catervas Aldh. *VirgV* 2161; locus..in quo recipiuntur ~ae eorum qui in bonis..operibus de corpore exeunt Bede *HE* V 12 p. 308; ignea inferni animabus Tartara complet Bonif. *Aen.* 9. 189; est necesse omnem humanam ~am aut semper miseram esse aut aliquando vere beatam Anselm (*Mon.* 73) I 82. **c** cuidam virginum, ..quae..eas ad orandum pro ~a ejus, etiam priusquam cetera congregatio ejus obitum cognovisset, excitaverit Bede *HE* IV 21 p. 258; **c1000** munera..defunctorum ~abus congruentia [AS: *saulsceat*] puteo inpendantur aperto (*Syn. Decr.*) *GAS* 253; **a1085** concedo ecclesie S. Martini..terram.. sicut dominium monasterii pro ~abus patris et matris mee *Regesta* 126; hanc terram..concessit S. Petro pro sua ~a *DB* I 32; **1100** si ipse ..pecuniam suam non dederit, ..parentes et legitimi homines ejus eam pro ~a ejus dividant (*Ch. Hen. I*) *GAS* 522; **a1163** pro ~a regis David..constituam quandam domum religionis *Reg. Paisley* 1; **1227** ad sustentandum quemdam militem in Terra Sancta, quem illuc mittet pro ~a sua *Pat* 169; **1344** pro..oracionibus, elemosinis et hospitalitatibus in locis ubi ecclesie fundate fuerunt pro ipsorum fundatorum..et omnium fidelium defunctorum ~abus faciendis (*Lit. Regis*) Ad. Mur. 234; **1406** ut nostre provisionis remedio..transeuncium ~arum quieti succurramus..et saluti *Lit. Cant.* III 98; **1420** cujus ~a concivis et coheres supernorum civium fieri letetur Elmh. *Hen. V Cont.* 162; **1432** celebrabit..unam missam pro ~abus omnium predictorum *StatOx* 253; matutinas canonicas dicere..cum ~arum commemoracione *Plusc.* X 31; **1549** in..concionum fine oretur pro ~abus defunctorum in recepta ecclesie consuetudine *Conc. Scot.* II 121. **d 1176** cum unum et idem putemus sacramentum quod vel manu propria fit vel in ~a jubentis et presentis juratur (*Lit. Regis Siciliae*) Diceto *YH* I 414; **1220** compositionis..a..patre nostro..facte et in ~am suam jurate *Pat* 243; non fiet ita in ~a mea *Latin Stories* 114; ab abbate nostro [ob. 1269] in sua et conventus ~abus..de dicenda veritate juramento recepto *Meaux* II 80; **1323** comes Pembrochie precepto nostro in ~a nostra ad sacra Dei Evangelia corporale prestitit sacramentum (*Treuga*) Blaneford 138; **1343** in..regum predictorum ~as ..prestiterunt..juramenta (*Treuga*) Ad. Mur. 137; **1347** in ~as ipsorum regum in nostris manibus corporaliter juraverunt (*Treugae*) Avesb. 117. **e** per ~am ventris mei magis sum letus..quam *BR Will. I* 2. **f** latuit..usque ad diem ~arum H. Bos. *Thom.* IV 3; **1194** in crastinum festivitatis ~arum *CurR RC* I 25; **1201** usque in crastinum ~arum *CurR* II 22; **s1280** justiciarii sederunt..a crastino ~arum usque ad Natale Domini *Chr. Peterb.* 40; in die ~arum fit processio circa cimiterium cum psalmis commendacionis *Obs. Barnwell* 150; **s1329** quod in die Parasceve et in commemoracione omnium ~arum ab omni servili opere cessaretur Ad. Mur. 59; **1348** post festum commemoracionis ~arum *Conc.* II 743. **g 1442** capella collegii ~arum omnium fidelium defunctorum de Oxon' *Cart. Osney* I 194.

6 prayer for the dead.

1358 ad ~as M. et M. filiarum suarum..in loco eminenciori ..ale, in quo quidem loco idem miles intendit sepeliri, .. transferendum (*Reg. Ebor.*) *Fabr. York* 335; **c1400** et ipse poneret ~am suam in parte pro me et specialiter oraret pro me in missa per unum annum (R. Wyche) *EHR* V 533; **1472** suffragiis, laudibus et ~abus, si que fuerint, ..omissis (*Vis.*) *Fabr. York* 251; **1503** omnes easdem ~as..publice recitans et Deo devote recommendans *FormA* 339.

7 confidential enclosure in letter.

1259 ista clausula scripta fuit in quadam ~a et inclusa in littera prefati episcopi *Cl* 5; **1353** ~a missa..domino archiepiscopo interclusa in littera secunda *Lit. Cant.* II 318.

animadversio [CL], punishment.

bestiam [sc. draconem]..perpetuae ultionis ~one.. multavit Aldh. *VirgP* 25 p. 258; magna ~one atque anathemate..prohibentes *RegulC* 10; **s1135** [Henricus I] in publicis ~onibus cervicidas ab homicidis parum discernebat W. Newb. I 3; **s1191** Saraceni capitis ~one multati sunt Diceto *YH* II 94.

animadvertere [CL], to note. **b** to proceed against.

~e, quaeso, perplexam metricae artis subtilitatem! Aldh. *PR* 136; dum..~eret quantum..praestaret *Id. VirgP* 35 p. 277; ~endum est quod..bona aliqua fecit Bede *HE* V 13; **s1095** intellexerunt quod prius non ~erunt nec ipsum advertere posse putaverunt, videlicet archiepiscopum..a solo papa judicari posse Eadmer *HN* 70; hoc ~et lectoris discrecio Elmh. *Hen. V Cont.* 142. **b** non esse tutum.., in reos tantum ~endo, animositatem irritare ceterorum *Chr. Rams.* 141; graviter ~itur in transgressores Gir. *TH* III 33.

animaequus (bibl.), calm, easy in mind; *cf.* *aequanimis.*

ne timeas, ..~ior esto Bede *Cuthb.* 14; ~ior exhinc facta mulier, ad rogandum regem..se totam convertit Ailr. *Ed. Conf.* 788a; **s1095** gavisi exinde sumus et ~iores effecti Eadmer *HN* 70; quatinus, communicato cum viris sanctis consilio, ..~ior..rediret Ad. Eyns. *Hug.* II 1; **s1306** exinde ~iores effecti..recesserunt *Flor. Hist.* III 132.

animal [CL], living creature (incl. man). **b** animal (excl. man). **c** farm animal. **d** head of cattle.

formam hominis..erectam, caeterorum vero ~alium.. pronam Eriug. *Per.* 494d; [hominis] universalem essentiam, quae est '~al rationale mortale' Anselm (*Mon.* 10) I 25; nihil aliud est ~al quam substantia animata sensibilis *Id.* (*Gram.* 3) I 147; ~alis esse nihil aliud est quam anime et corporis conjunctio Adel. *QN* 46. **b 601** nec diabolo jam ~alia immolent (*Lit. Papae*) Bede *HE* I 30; cuncta..quasi mundum ~al ruminando in carmen convertebat *Ib.* IV 24; quando bruta ~alia illis [appetitibus] consentiunt, non dicuntur injusta Anselm (*Orig. Pecc.* 4) II 144; **s1087** Deus ..inmisit..tonitrua, quibus multos hominum occidit nec ~alibus nec pecori pepercit H. Hunt. *HA* VI 38; arbores et herbas multum ~alia bruta precedunt Gir. *TH* I 13; placitum istud [detentionis namii] dilationem non capit propter ~alia muta Bracton 155v. **c 1283** habebunt v bidentes..et cetera ~alia sua *Cust. Battle* 51; **1332** ceperunt ..~alia de stauro, sc. boves, vaccas et oves *LTRMem* 105 *rec.* r. 18; **1344** viij carrat' feni pro majoribus ~alibus; item viij carrat' pro minoribus *Ac. Durh.* 206; **1430** communem pasturam pro xvj ~alibus bovinis et equinis et pro c ~alibus ovinis *FormA* 286. **d** ~al, *ælc cuce þinc* vel *nyten* Ælf. *Gl.*; in dominio ii runcini, v ~alia, xviii porci, xxxvi oves *DB* II 22; villani [habent] ..vi ~alia in carr[uca] *DBExon* 320; viginti vi ~ia ociosa *Inq. Ely* 12b; adquirat ex illis sex [hominibus] unum pro ~ali uno [AS: *æt anum hryðere*] (*Quad.*) *GAS* 139; **1130** de cornagio ~alium episcopatus *Pipe* 131; **a1200** communem pasturam quatuor ~alibus et uno equo et lx ovibus *Danelaw* 32; **1573** communiam pasture pro sex equis, xij ~alibus et octoginta ovibus *Pat* 1107 m. 40.

animalculum, wretched animal.

quum venator ab miseri ~i caede..nihil nisi voluptatem petat MORE *Ut.* 201.

animalis [CL], animate. **b** concerned (or infused) w. the 'soul' or vital principle. **c** (?) dear to the soul (or heart).

psalmista 'omnia ligna silvarum exultasse' [*Psalm* xcv 12] ..ab ~i ad inanimale metaforice retulit ALDH. *Met.* 7. **b** opinionem..que in brutis est non ~e sed corporale subjectum exigere certum est ADEL. *QN* 14; ~es virtutes, sc. sensus, qui dicuntur corporis et sunt anime J. SAL. *Pol.* 428D; quatuor humores, tot virtutes animales NECKAM *DS* IV 326; absque alimentorum juvamine quibus ~e corpus sustentari solet GIR. *TH* I 20; in illo [cerebri] rethi digeritur spiritus ~is et per ipsum spiritum fit penetratio virtutum cerebri ad alia membra BART. ANGL. V 3; pulsus..alius in vigilante, qui est conjunctus cum operationibus ~ibus *Ps.*-RIC. *Anat.* 20; stupor est disposicio mentis quando instrumenta sensuum ad sensum parata ~em sensu privantur *SB* 41; **1497** corpore reformato anima factoque, ut ita dicam, ~i COLET *Rom. Enarr.* 177. **c 796** dilectissimo filio atque ~i meo.. salutem ALCUIN *Ep.* 88.

2 (bibl.) natural, concerned w. man's 'animal' (not spiritual) nature.

ruinam..a spirituali homine in ~em ERIUG. *Per.* 540A; qui secundum carnem vivit, carnalis sive ~is est ANSELM (*Incarn.* 1) II 8; gratia preveniens hominem, non mens animalis, / dat bona velle viros NIG. *Laur.* 32. 2; nos ~es et carneos H. BOS. *Ep.* 1418; **c1236** nonne clerus et populus.. sunt sicut duo homines, quorum alter est spiritalis et reliquus carnalis sive ~is? GROS. *Ep.* 72* p. 217; mundanos incursus superabimus si subigamus impetus ~es AD. MARSH *Ep.* 56; **1374** superbi et ~es BRINTON *Serm.* 34 p. 143; **a1384** contra ~em sapienciam mundanorum (WYCL.) *Ziz.* 453.

3 bestial.

nautas animales / inveni, tales Theseus catulos Stigiales GARL. *Mor. Scol.* 603.

animalitas, vitality, animal nature.

ut [resultat] ex corpore et anima ~as *Ps.*-GROS. 335; si Christus non sit multa animalia racione multarum ~atum ypostatice conjunctarum WYCL. *Incarn.* 210.

animalus v. animula b.

1 animare [CL], to infuse w. life or 'soul' (*anima*). **b** (fig.). **c** (p. ppl.) animate, possessed of 'soul'. **d** (pr. ppl. intr. as sb. n.), living creature, animal.

cum mundus habeat animam, totus mundus et quelibet ejus pars ~abitur et regetur ab eadem anima J. BLUND *An.* 358; carnem et sanguinem ejusdem [Domini]..sibi..ad animarum vegetationem sacramentaliter associant, non autem sibi incorporant sed potius, ut ita dicatur, †antanimant [? l. aut animant] aut inflammant GIR. *Spec.* IV 23. **b** consonantes..velut exanime corpus jacent quousque illas singulae vocalium..~ando movent ABBO *QG* 11. **c** utrum stellas ~atas an inanimatas esse intelligas ADEL. *QN* 74; vivo carens anima..; / miror quod vivo non animatus homo *Babio* 186; ~ata et spiritualia membra RIC. MED. *Micr. Anat.* 222; est mirandum quod..colorem vermiculatum recipit..sola vestis que ex vivo animanteque vel quovis ~ato decerpitur GERV. TILB. III 55; quelibet pars animalis ~ata in corpore suo..manet ~ata anima totius BACON XIV 112; homines et cetera ~ata *Id. Tert.* 109; imperator lex ~ata vocatur OCKHAM *Dial.* 871; **s1381** [J. Wyclef] multo prestanciorem esse fatebatur rem ~atam quam que carebat anima WALS. *YN* 334. **d** in irrationabilibus ~antibus ERIUG. *Per.* 581A; **c1152** de ovibus et porcis et omnibus aliis ~antibus *Cart. Boarstall* no. 295; corpora ~antium sunt leviora post prandium quam ante propter caloris confortationem BART. ANGL. IV 1; ~antium tam domestica quam silvestria BRADW. *CD* 191C.

2 to inspire w. courage or resolve (*animus*), incite. **b** (?) to recommend. **c** (p. ppl.) minded, resolved.

flagellis simul et exhortationibus ~atus BEDE *HE* II 6; ad eum depredandum inflatiore spiritu ~atus erat W. MALM. *GP* I 51; **1187** ~emini..ad certamen monitu..martyris *Ep. Cant.* 130; **1226** eos..ad Terre Sancte succursum..sollicite †annuare [l. animare] (*Lit. Papae*) *Reg. S. Osm.* I 195; ~abuntur periti..opera facere exquisita OCKHAM *Dial.* 871; **s1381** [J. Ball] populum ad..insurrecciones ~averat et induxerat *V. Ric. II* 33; **a1460** inquiratur si quis cum armatura..fortificavit seu ~avit inimicos..regis *BBAdm.* I 222. **b 1421** de..articulis..qui (*sic*)..proponi et ~ari et tractari et concludi contigerit *Conc.* III 403. **c 1244** quam sitis ~ati dedecus nostrum..vindicare *Cl. Suppl.* 1.

2 animare v. annuere 1b.

animatio, infusion w. 'soul', vitality.

sicut sensus non nisi circa animatum corpus est, ita et sine anima (quoniam et sine anima ~o non est) esse non potest ADEL. *QN* 13 p. 17; cum calor naturalis et humidum subtile extincti fuerint, cessat ~o WYCL. *Log.* III 66.

2 encouragement, incitement.

s1066 ad eorum confusionem et ad suorum ~onem SILGRAVE 77; ~o ad exeundum M. PAR. *Min.* I 118; **1423** si pro fortificacione exigui corporis ~oneve spiritus pusillanimis..preces effuderitis (*Lit. Abbatis*) AMUND. I 128.

animose [CL], courageously.

eos cum clamore..viriliter et ~e insequentes *G. Steph.* I 9; **s1377** armiger..tam viriliter, tam ~e pugnavit WALS. *HA* I 342.

animositas, (act of) courage. **b** magnificence. **c** ill will, grudge, dislike, animosity.

dum in talibus adhuc juvenculus..~atum progressibus.. proficeret *G. Herw.* 320v; **s1187** ut suis..timorem incuteret et hostes..~ate incitaret *Itin. Ric.* I 5; ~atem archidiaconi et virilitatem multis laudibus efferebant GIR. *RG* I 6 p. 38; illa admirande ~atis abbatissa M. PAR. *Maj.* I 392; **s1320** in ..armentis..taurus corpore et ~ate prestancior ceterorum erit..ductor *V. Edw. II* 252; **s1398** nimia bellicosa ~ate exercitum..precedens AD. USK 19; militem non minus armorum exercicio quam ~ate preclarum ELMH. *Hen. V* 20. **b s1020** [Cnuto] supra corpus B. Edmundi..basilicam ~ate regia construxit W. MALM. *GR* II 181. **c** ~atum tumore, jurgiorum contentione..carpebantur GILDAS *EB* 21; **s1016** convenire prudentie ut depositis ~atibus Angliam partiantur W. MALM. *GR* II 180 p. 217; pro sedandis quorundam ~atibus quas ad dejectionem monachorum conceperant EADMER *HN* 23; **1188** erunt secte, dissensiones, ~ates, que omnia plurimum valebunt ad perditionem animarum *Ep. Cant.* 242; vis irascibilis est respuitiva ejus quod putatur esse nocivum; ..et ab Aristotele in *Topicis* quandoque hec vis appellatur ~as J. BLUND *An.* 55 (cf. ib. p. ix); **1325** [alienigene] causam non habent nec eciam ~ates aggrediendi talia *Lit. Cant.* I 162; **1343** qui heresi pertinaci ~ate adheret OCKHAM *Dial.* 407; **c1430** tabes..~atis Abirine *Reg. Whet.* II 462 (cf. *Num.* xvi 12).

animosus [CL], courageous. **b** resolute or (?) minded. **c** (?) harsh.

quarum [rerum] lectio..laudabili emulationis invidia tam ~is conferet quam ignavis GIR. *TH pref.* ii p. 21; ~i ducis nimium accensa ferocitas ELMH. *Hen. V Cont.* 150. **b 1441** ut..reddatis..nos ad grata quevis..impendenda obsequia ~um BEKYNTON I 212. **c** gis melia est..dura gustu ~a atque siccans linguam *Alph.* 77.

animotenus v. animus 1a.

animula, (poor little) soul. **b** butterfly (ψυχάριον).

1002 (11c) pro redemptione ~ae meae *CD* 1297; muliebribus modis..stupentes ~as emollire nituntur J. SAL. *Pol.* 402C; sequere, o ~a mea, sequere hunc solem NECKAM *NR* I 13. **b** †animalus, *fifaldae Gl. Leid.* 43. 47.

animus [CL], mind or heart (source of thought, feeling and will). **b** character. **c** courage. **d** pride. **e** purpose. **f** animosity.

ebrietas animos solet enervare virorum ALDH. *VirgV* 2501; toto ~o intendens BEDE *HE* II 9; dum sincere..humanus ~us ad Deum perveniet ERIUG. *Per.* 534D; rerum omnium quae..~o percipi possunt vel intentionem ejus superant *Ib.* 441A; ~us, *mod* vel *geðanc* ÆLF. *Gl.*; amplexus ~otenus scripta..legi ÆTHELW. *prol.*; ut esset ipsa..laeto ~o *DB* I 179b; accepit Mathildem..cujus amori jampridem ~um impulerat W. MALM. *GR* V 393; dum corpore langueret, sic ~o vigeret H. HUNT. *HA* VII 34; felix quod sors fert animo qui pertulit equo GIR. *Symb. Metr.* 36 p. 379; que clausum reserent animum sunt verba reperta / ut quedam claves animi VINSAUF *PN* 1065–6; pulchritudo sapientie.. habet naturaliter ut plena admiratione ~os nostros alliciat et suspendat BACON *CSPhil* 394; sedet ~o..tollere quotidie crucem suam *V. Har.* 6 f. 10; **c1430** ab avaricie glutino, quod multorum inviscat ~os *Reg. Whet.* II 461. **b** ~o ac moribus barbarus BEDE *HE* II 20; puer simplicis ac mansueti ~i *Ib.* IV 14; alterius vir ~i H. HUNT. *HA* IV 16; Dacus, ..vir factiosus, ..Anglorum ~os ex suo ponderans *Chr. Rams.* 140. **c** ~o recuperato unanimiter invadunt hostes H. HUNT. *HA* VII 10. **d** majores inde ~os contraxit quam opportunum esset suis *Ib.* VIII 26 (cf. altus 6c). **e** si mallent animo nutum complere nefandum ALDH. *VirgV* 2228; erat barbaro ~us ut Christianos..obsideret W. MALM. *GR* IV 371; omnes unum habentes ~um *G. Steph.* I 62; mihi inest ~us..ea..commendare *Mir. J. Bev. A* 293; sic perquisitis incumbens ~um possidendi deseruisse non creditur *Dial. Scac.* II 10G; ut..ab ~o predandi predonem revocaret W. CANT. *Mir. Thom.* VI 168; **1361** non habuit ~um tunc interficiendi uxorem ejus *RCoron* 18 r. 57. **f** quis tibi [Mars] tunc animus, quanta cupido mali! G. AMIENS *Hast.* 348.

2 (w. *celestis*) angelic being, intelligence.

homo quem..studium celeste non tam electis animabus quam celestibus ~is in Dei Filio..consocat AD. MARSH *Ep.* 28.

anisum, ~ium v. anesum.

anitas [< an], 'whetherness', existence.

Avicenna..concludit: nostra igitur dispositio erga illa est sicut dispositio surdi qui nunquam audivit..delectationem armonicam, cum ipse sit certus de ~ate ejus, id est an sit seu quod sit BACON *Mor. Phil.* 25; simplex alia est [scientia] ~atis rei, alia quiditatis uno modo *Ps.*-GROS. 299; quod Hero..per clepsedras et siphones..~atem vacui nititur declarare, non est..reprobandum *Ib.* 417.

ankeragium v. ancoragium. ankerethus v. anachoreta. ankor-, ankur- v. ancor-. anlacius, ~ia v. alenatius.

anlepimannus [ME *onlepi man = bachelor*], (?) bondsman without tenement in manor (Norf.); *cf. Cust. Rents* 173 and F. G. Davenport *A Norfolk Manor* xxxi.

1270 de viij s. de chevag' ~orum per annum *MinAc* (*Framingham*) 935/20; **1272** de chevag' annelepemennorum *Ib.* 23; **1272** de viij s. vj d. de chevagiis de v^{xx}ij ~orum reddencium chevagium *Ib.* (*Forncett*) 935/3 m. 1; **1293** de capitag' den. de *anlepymen* manencium extra manerium *Ib.* 13; **c1348** medietas omnium villanorum vocatorum *onlepymen IPM* (*Ingham*) 93/2.

annalis [CL], annual, yearly. **b** (sb. m., *sc. rotulus*) Pipe Roll.

annuales ad festum ejus institute sunt nundine W. MALM. (*V. Aldh.*) *GP* V 269; campus in quo ~e forum quoquo anno congregari solet DICETO *Chr.* 14; **1194** per annualem pensionem *CurR RC* I 18; **1284** remanencia firmarum..comitatuum..scribantur in rotulis ~ibus, et onerentur inde vicecomites (*St. Rhuddlan*) *St. Realm* I 69; **1340** cum plenitudine sue rate annualis *FormOx* 302; **s1356** clerus decimam ~em.. concessit AVESB. 135; **1448** pro suo ~i stipendio per annum ..iiij m. habeat *StatOx* 270; **1491** quandam annuitatem sive annualem redditum x librarum *RScot* 494a. **b** cum scribatur in ~i 'in operatione illa c libras' *Dial. Scac.* II 8A.

2 concerned w. a year (astr.). **b** (sb. m.) calendar.

computus eorum [sc. Graecorum] ~is BEDE *TR* 14; innitatur alphabetis quae in ~i videt libello juxta cursum distincta *Ib.* 23. **b** juxta quod eorum [sc. Aegyptiorum] ~em describentes signavimus *Ib.* 14.

3 concerned w. the events of a year. **b** (sb. n.) calendar of obits. **c** (sb. m. or n. pl.) annals.

lege historias et libros ~es GIR. *GE* II 8. **b** requisivit in ~e suo et invenit eadem ipsa die Osualdum regem fuisse peremptum BEDE *HE* IV 14 p. 235. **c** cronica in qua per annos dominicales regum Anglorum repperiri possunt ~es HERM. ARCH. 8; **1437** quo nullus unquam seculis nostris princeps beatior.., si universa revolvamus ~ia, poterit inveniri BEKYNTON I 246; in annualibus capelle de Walsingham continetur quod.. CAPGRAVE *Hen.* 164; **s1459** cepit revolvere res gestas varias ~iaque multa *Reg. Whet.* I 338; ut ~ia probant ecclesiastica BEKINSAU 747.

4 lasting for a year. **b** effective for a year. **c** to be taken for a year (med.).

finis annualis laboris est collectio fructuum BACON *Tert.* 210; **s1339** post moram plus quam ~em AVESB. 86v; decollatus est Johannes [Baptista] post annualem incarcerationem *Eul. Hist.* I 77. **b** non competit restitutio per assisam ei qui tenet ad voluntatem alicujus de anno in annum, quia..voluntas concedentis est annualis BRACTON 170. **c** oleum regum, que (*sic*) dicitur medicina annualis, que anno integro sumi debet BACON IX 129.

5 (of mass or sim.) repeated daily for a year. **b** (sb. n.) 'annal', sequence of daily masses (esp. for the dead) continued for a year. **c** (sb. n.) payment for such masses. **d** (adj.) appointed to say such masses. **e** (sb. n.) daily alms for a year on behalf of a specified person.

1309 in hujusmodi missis certis annualibus sic celebrandis *Conc. Syn.* 1257; **1451** recipientur in annuali servicio et tricennali *Cart. Osney* I xviii. **b 1214** ne pro annualibus vel..septennalibus missarum faciendis laici vel clerici dare aliquid vel legare in testamento cogantur *Conc. Syn.* 30; **1216** obventionibus..de..trentalibus et annualibus *Reg. Linc.* I 138; **1240** legavit..ad perficiendum unum annuale l s. *FormA* 425; **12..** clericus ad religionem transiens habeat annuale suum sicut et alii qui in Domino moriuntur *Reg. Aberd.* II 9; **1256** aliquis vicarius..percipiet annuatim xl s. ad celebrandum annuale pro anima mea *Ch. Sal.* 326; **1281** nec presumat aliquis ~ia celebranda suscipere nisi pro defuncto celebret cotidie vel procuret specialiter celebrari *Conc. Syn.* 895 (cf. LYNDW. 228 *s, t*: ~ia, i.e. missas celebrandas per anni spacium. ..loquitur in casu quo sacerdos sit conductus per annum ut specialiter celebret pro anima alicujus defuncti; et idem intelligas si convenerit per annum celebrare pro vivente); **s1291** obiit..janitor noster.., pro quo fecimus celebrari per canonicos duo annualia *Ann. Dunstable* 370; **1320** dedisse..ecclesiam..a die obitus.. Willelmi rectoris ejusdem ecclesie..et fine ~is ejusdem usque in sempiternum *Reg. Glasg.* 226; **1393** extunc.. capellanus unum annuale per unum annum, vel duos ad magis, celebrare poterit *Lit. Cant.* III 16; **1415** volo quod capellanus idoneus celebret unum annuale missarum pro vivis ac mortuis omnium parrochianorum meorum ac eciam pro anima mea..statim post obitum meum *Reg. Cant.* III 403. **c c1238** inhibemus..ne aliquis rector ecclesie faciat hujusmodi pactum cum suo sacerdote, viz. quod ipse sacerdos preter cetera stipendia poterit recipere annualia vel tricennalia GROS. *Ep.* 52* p. 158; **1245** sacerdotes..nullum ~e vel †tercennale [= THORNE 1894: tricennale] de parochianis de Faversham..recipient *Reg. S. Aug.* 510; **1259** articuli inquirendi in domibus religiosorum: ..an recipiant annualia vel tricennalia *Ann. Burton* 486; **1415** capellanos cantarias perpetuas seu annualia..obtinentes *Reg. Cant.* III 441; **1438** non intendo quin posset habere unum ~e per idem tempus, dicendo pro anima mea in qualibet missa mea, "Deus, cujus misericordie non est numerus.." *Ib.* II 563; **1420** ego R., rector ecclesie de P., lego..executoribus meis annuale ecclesie..seu fructus ejusdem *Wills N. Country* 30; **1559** ubi defuncti pars ad x li. ..tantum se extenderit, vicario illius ecclesie in composicionem pro ~i seu mortuario persolvi solito..solvantur xl s. tantum *Conc. Scot.* II 168. **d 1214** ne capellanos suos ~es..studeant amovere *Conc. Syn.* 30. **e 1206** si obitus monachi vel abbatis alterius domus, si fuerint de capitulo Eveshamensi, evenerint, ad ~e pro abbate et †tritennale [l. tricennale] pro monacho de cellario panis et cerevisia, sicut et monacho, alicui pauperi erogentur (*Consuetudines*) *Chr. Evesham* 220.

6 anniversary (adj.). **b** (sb. n.) an anniversary.

s1459 ad observandum..post nostrum decessum diem ~em obitarium nostrum *Reg. Whet.* I 325. **b** Olimphas est quintum annuale BACON *CSPhil.* 443.

7 one year old, in second year (of animals). **b** (sb. m. or n.) yearling.

1195 pro lx porcis annualibus..et pro porcis junioribus *Pipe* 51; pro xij bobus ~ibus *Ib.* 251; annuales agni GILB.

I 36. 1; **1338** cumj pullano ij annorum et alio pullo ~i *Ac. Durh.* 199. **b** **1232** de boviculo iij annorum iiij d. et de ~i ij annorum ij d. *Crawley* 201; **1283** de iiij ~ibus de remanenti, quorum ij masculi (*MinAc*) *Surrey Rec. Soc.* XV 52; **1290** vij vacce, ..octo ~ia *Reg. Wint.* II 704; **1297** remanent vj-~es, quorum iij femelle *Ac. Cornw.* I 39; **1316** ij ~es et iiij vitulos *Cart. Glam.* 1036; **1328** j taurus, ..unum ~e *Reg. Exon.* 571; **1388** habuit..j taurum, vj bovettos, xj ~es et xxiij vaccas *IMisc* 240/21.

annaliter, annually. **b** for a year.

divitiarum quae annualiter ad eum..pervenire consueverant Asser *Alf.* 99. **b** multiplicis ~er et eo plus infirmitatis attritus molestia Herm. Arch. 36.

annamel- v. enamel-.

annare [CL (*adnare*)], to arrive by swimming or floating.

GlC A 273 (v. annatare); plures illo mures ~asse, corticibus malorum granatorum..inclusos W. Malm. *GR* III 291.

annata [cf. OF *annee*], annate, first year's revenue of see or benefice, payable to Pope.

1441 de firmis aque borealis de Done pertinentibus ad ~am ecclesie Aberdonensis, sede vacante *ExchScot* 95; juramenta in camera fiunt pro ~is Paul. Angl. *ASP* 1552; **1453** qui..fructus primi anni..ordinariis solvere renuunt..fore reformandos et [ad] hujusmodi ~am..persolvendam compellendos *Conc.* III 571; **c1450** circa ~as seu annalia *Reg. Aberd.* II 89; **1497** ~is aut mediis fructibus *Ib.* 314; tribuit [regnum Angliae] ~as non debitas Gardiner *Si Sedes* 194a p. 38.

annatare, to swim to.

adnavimus, †adnotavimus [l. adnatavimus] *GlC* A 273.

annatim v. annuatim. annatulus v. anatulus. annatus v. 2 annuare 2a.

annavigare, to sail to (? or on). **b** to swim beside.

Wilfridus..proram in Eurum obvertit..ut Fresiam ~aret W. Malm. *GP* III 100; nautis..a Saxonia..mercem advectantibus et jam mare Britannicum ~antibus W. Cant. *Mir. Thom.* VI 77. **b** animalia juxta carinam ~antia priora ad terram perveniunt W. Malm. *GR* III 290.

anne v. an 2c.

annectere [CL], to attach, append. **b** (fig.). **c** to annex.

malus navis..cui..rudentes adnectuntur Aldh. *PR* 113 p. 152; **10..** adnecterent, *gewrǣstan, gecnyttan* WW; **c1330** in cedula..litteris certificatoriis †~anda [? l. ~enda] *Lit. Cant.* I 8; **1459** per indenturam..huic compoto annexam *Ac. Durh.* 638; **1476** licebit quemdam aqueductulum parvum ..aqueductui ipsorum..~ere *FormA* 128. **b** verba quae ..subter adnectere..formula compellet Aldh. *PR* 112; cum ea de quibus dicitur transposite et internexe sibi ~i licet Balsh. *AD* 102; **s1151** [Aquitania] sic lingue satisfaciens ut in salibus condiendis licet mordacibus plurimum habeat civilitatis annexum Diceto *YH* I 294; abbas, nullas moras ~ens, confirmationem regis Stephani..obtinuit *G. S. Alb.* I 117; plurima oracula..ex dictis prophetarum..legi Machometh callide..annexit M. Par. *Maj.* III 352; in quo [sc. Aristotelis ingenio] nature complacuit experiri quantum mortalitati racionis posset ~ere R. Bury *Phil.* 10. 159; **s1397** quod potestas regis esset sibi unita, annexa et solida *V. Ric. II* 131. **c** **1254** ut aliam prebendam eidem dignitati episcopali..posses †~are *Reg. S. Osm.* I 197; **1274** ecclesiam de M. ..archidiaconatui..~endam duximus, ipsamque eidem anneximus *Reg. Malm.* I 424; **1293** clamat ..emendas assise panis fracte..tamquam †anexes [l. annexas] et pertinentes mercato *PQW* 220a; **1365** unum mesuagium cum..gardino eidem mesuagio annexo *Deeds Balliol* 243; ecclesiam in usus nostros proprios ~ere conabamur *Meaux* II 229; **1449** vicariam..ecclesie de Wye..collegio vestro..univimus, annexuimus, incorporavimus *Lit. Cant.* III 200; **1502** quod..consolidare, ~ere et unire..possint terras et alias possessiones *StatOx* 301.

2 (p. ppl. *annexus*) **a** adjoining. **b** bound, allied. **c** (?) predetermined.

a Wallo..in quodam vado civitati ~o precipitatur, ..quod usque hodie vocatur Wallebroke *Eul. Hist.* II 226. **b** **s1346** justiciarii..in tantum fuerunt ~i magnatibus terre per pensiones..et alia donaria quod justicia penes mediocres ..non potuit habere processum Ad. Mur. 245. **c** **s1281** curiam illam illudere intendebant, cum eorum causa erat ~a Graystanes 17.

annectio v. annexio. annelacus v. alenatius. annelepemennus v. anlepimannus. annellare v. esmallare. annetum v. alnetum, anethum.

annexare, to attach, append. **b** to annex.

1373 cum duabus cameris eidem aule ~atis *Banstead* 352; **1538** cedula indentata, ~ata et filata cuidam carte *FormA* 415. **b** **1279** inclusit..c acras bosci.., et ~antur ad leucatam de Tonebrigge *PQW* 339a; **1549** in ecclesiis ipsis monasteriis ~atis *Conc. Scot.* II 101; **1588** cotagium..cum curtilagio eidem ~ato *Pat* 1319 m. 3.

annexatio, attachment. **b** annexation.

fiat ligatura cum ~one forti Gad. 128 v. 1. **b** **1240** ~o prebende de B. ad dignitatem cancellarii Sar' *Ch. Sal.* 259; **1449** de ~one et appropriacione vicarie ecclesie..de Wye..ad dotacionem collegii *Lit. Cant.* III 198.

annexio, connection. **b** annexation.

causa est ~o scientiarum, quia quelibet ab alia quodammodo dependet Bacon *Maj.* III 79. **b** **s1288** contra adnexionem ecclesiarum ad prebendas de Westbure bulla venit *Ann. Worc.* 498; **1448** super assignacione et ~one schire nostre de Gaytmylk *Reg. Dunferm.* p. 308; **1465** affectantes..ecclesiam..de Bogonore..ecclesie de Berstede ..uniri et annecti, ..unioni et annectioni faciende nostrum prebemus consensum *Lit. Cant.* III 241.

annexitas, (?) constipation.

[Herodes] vehementi plexus ~atis incommodo Gir. *PI* I 17.

1 annexus v. annectere.

2 annexus [CL], link (fig.).

concordie dissoluto ~u *G. Steph.* I 42.

annichil- v. annihil-.

annictare [CL], to wink (at).

~o vel annuto, *ic wincie* Ælf. *Gl.*; **14..** annicito, A. *to twynkele* WW.

anniculus [CL], one year old: **a** (of men); **b** (of animals); **c** (sb. f. or m.) (yearling) heifer or steer.

a infantulus ~us..a matre illuc allatus *Canon. G. Sempr.* 165. **b** ~us, unius anni *GlC* A 577; agnellos, non dico ~os Neckam *Ut.* 101; **1232** de bovetto ~o *Crawley* 201; **1412** cum vitulis suis ~is *Couch. Furness* II p. 22. **c** ~a vel vaccula, *heahfore*; ~us vel trio, *steoroxa* Ælf. *Gl.*

annihilabilis, annihilable.

si est ~e in quantum finitum, multo magis est corruptibile Peckham *Quaest.* I ii a p. 15; tota substancia integralis est sue partes quantitative, cum aliter materia prima esset anichilabilis per divisionem Wycl. *Ente Praed.* 46; si [creatura] sit de se adnihilabilis et tendens ad non esse Netter *DAF* II 116.

annihilantia, act of annihilation.

adnichilacio, cum sit forma, requirit subjectum quod formaliter denominat, cum sit accidens correspondens adnichilancie Wycl. *Ente* 289.

annihilare [LL], to annihilate (phil.), reduce to nothing.

cum plus sit ~ari quam mori vel corrumpi Peckham *Quaest.* I ii a p. 15; Wycl. *Act.* 7 (v. annullare 1); quod Deus non potest ~are creaturam (Wycl.) *Ziz.* 2.

2 to destroy, demolish, bring to nothing: **a** (material objects); **b** (persons); **c** (abstractions).

a **s1135** disce contempnere..quicquid sic adnichilatur [sc. corpus humanum] H. Hunt. *HA* VIII 2; **1220** quatinus id quod firmatum est in dicto castello..dirui et ~ari..jubeatis (*AncC* III 54) *RL* I 108; **1241** quando mare superundavit et wallia illa cepit anichillari *JustIt* (*Kent*) 359 r. 13d.; ita consumi possent divise et adnihilari Bracton 167; **s1260** fruges..ita adnihilabantur quod vix sufficiebant messores suos remunerare M. Par. *Abbr.* 453. **b** [Henricus II] illustres..patrimoniis privavit vel..decrustando sensim adnihilavit R. Niger 167; mors pietate carens communis habetur / omnibus; adnichilat omnes D. Bec. 316; **s1383** omnem suam familiam..quisbusdam captis, quibusdam occisis, ..adnichilavit *Plusc.* X 5. **c** †**1031** Deo..qui..inimicorum nostrorum potentiam adnihilet (*Lit. Cnutonis*) W. Malm. *GR* II 183 p. 223; alia lex..habens alias observationes per quas observationes tuae ~entur Lanfr. *Comment. Paul.* (*Rom.* iii 27) 117; **1105** ordo sancte religionis in eis [ecclesiis] neglectus ~atur (*Lit.*) Eadmer *HN* 196; quem simulatio fingit / vel timor extorquet, adnichilatur amor Nig. *Mir. BVM* f. 22; **p1188** licet status noster jam pene nullus est, immo penitus adnihilatus *Ep. Cant.* 173; [ignorantia] ~at totius humani generis dignitatem Bacon *CSPhil* 394; hec verba..heretica omnipotenciam Dei limitancia, imo ~ancia..sunt Ockham *Err. Papae* 972; ne aliquod peccatum in ipso duret quod non statim igne amoris adnihiletur Rolle *IA* 208; **1400** ita quod ob defectum operis sui artificium pannarii ammodo non adnichiletur seu deterioretur *Mem. York* 143.

3 to annul, quash (leg.). **b** to cancel.

~atis omnibus quae..iniquis fuerant legibus decreta Osb. *V. Dunst.* 29; **c1150** nullatenus sit in potestate canonici ..hanc institutionem immutare sive adnichilare *Reg. S. Osm.* I 344; **1202** ad adnichilandum apellum suum *CurR* II 115; **1218** ad adnichilandum placitum *Eyre Yorks* 19; **1231** finis teneatur donec secundum legem terre adnichiletur *CurR* XIV 1473; quod per ultimam assisam posset adnihilari quod rite actum esset per primam Bracton 167b; **1285** judicia in curia regis reddita per istud statutum non adnichilentur (*St. Westm.* 5) *StRealm* I 76; **1514** ad examinandum, reformandum et adnichillandum..statuta *StatOx* 328. **b** **1302** prepositus monetariorum..dictum breve scidit et adnihilavit ne retornaretur *MGL* II 186; **1331** obligaciones inde confecte restitute erant et dilacerate et adnichillate *ExchScot* 403.

4 to make light of.

to sett at noghte, ..vilipendere, adnullare, adnichilare *CathA*.

annihilatio, annihilation (phil.). **b** destruction, undoing.

clare sciemus quid [J. Witcleff] de ~one desipuit Netter *DAF* I 53. **b** **s1300** ignis..qui..toti manerio exicium et ~onem minabatur *Ann. Ed. I* 476; **1305** in decepcionem partis petentis et debiti sui retardacionem et adnihilacionem *MGL* I 121; **s1405** ut ordinetur remedium contra subjecciones vel subacciones et adnihilaciones in quo verisimile est regni dominos periclitari Wals. *HA* II 422; **1439** in ipsorum mercatorum adnichilacionem manifestam *RScot* 314b; **s1458** quos..discordia..pene usque ad ultimum deduxit terminum adnichilacionis *Reg. Whet.* I 297.

annihilativus, annihilative.

Deus..non habet potestatem super peccata, quia sunt adnichilative privaciones facte sine ipso Wycl. *Ente* 169; argumentum Witcleff contra potenciam Dei adnihilativam tale est Netter *DAF* I 54.

annihilatrix, destroyer (f.).

[superbia] universe, que est in anima vel esse potest sanctitatis ~ix est Ad. Scot. *Serm.* 382a.

1 annilis v. anilis.

2 annilis [cf. annalis], yearly.

priusquam sol bis senis voluminibus ~em circumvolverit orbem Felix *Guthl.* 52.

annisus, effort.

601 adnisum illius..adjuvate, ut regni sui vos ipse faciat esse participes (*Lit. Papae*) Bede *HE* I 32; ipse gravi reclamationis adnisu ne id fiat obsistere nititur Eadmer *Wilf.* 720d; [Birinus] cum divino nutu tum suo ~u..Kinegilso..lavacrum salutare impertiit W. Malm. *GP* II 75 p. 158; non suo sed maligni spiritus ~u rupit vincula T. Mon. *Will.* V 13; miles ille, quem..semivivum pagani reliquerant, ~u quo potuit, montem manibus reptando conscendit (Will. S. Alb. *V. S. Alb.*) M. Par. *Maj.* I 152; pro beneficio..veneficia illi omni mentis ~u rependere satagitis *Chr. Battle* 98; quidam lapides ~u brachiorum certatim longius prohicere decertabant R. Cold. *Cuthb.* 87; **1238** equorum..sessores eosdem equos toto ~u sponte currentes nihilominus calcaribus urgent Gros. *Ep.* 61.

anniti [CL], to be supported, rely. **b** to strive. **c** to support, help.

textor..duarum streparum adnitens apodiamento Neckam *Ut.* 106; nos orationibus tuis †adniti [? l. adnisi *or* adnixi] de exterioribus curam geremus Serlo Gram. *Mon. Font.* 76; per Deum celi, cujus annixus sum gracie Elmh. *Hen. V* 47. **b** adnitentibus, *tilgendum* *GlC* A 584; pro pace in regno revocanda plurimum adniti *G. Steph.* I 7; ille annitendo surgere voluit R. Cold. *Cuthb.* 20. **c** **s1135** ~entibus nonnullis regni primoribus..ab archipontifice Cantuarie..coronatur *Chr. Battle* 64.

annivelarius v. annualarius.

anniversalis, annual. **b** (sb. n.) anniversary mass or sequence of such masses.

annua, ~is *Erf.* 2. 266. 34. **b** **a1190** [*the canons perform in common*] ~e missarum [viz. *every canon 10 masses*] *Wells MSS* (*HMC Rep.* 12) I 31; **1339** manuceperunt uno die in anno..celebrare ~e cum solempnitate, qua decet..magistri M. de G. *Reg. Dunferm.* p. 260.

anniversarius [CL], annual, concerned w. the passage of the years. **b** extending over last year. **c** anniversary (adj.), celebrated annually, esp. in commemoration of a death or retirement.

~ia temporum vicissitudo Aldh. *Met.* 3; **c750** super lectionarium ~ium Bonif. *Ep.* 91. **b** ~io tempore plurimas..direxi litterulas Alcuin *Ep.* 253 p. 408. **c** **c1220** quod die ~io depositionis nostre..vicarii..habebunt pitancias *Ch. Sal.* 102; abbas hanc..specialitatem habet, quod dies ~ius mortis ejus singulis annis..cum duabus capis ad missam festive celebrabitur *Cust. Westm.* 5; tunc pronuncientur annue ~ie festivitates sanctorum (*Cust. Cant. Abbr.*) *Ib. app.* 264; **1357** si..unam missam ~iam..annuatim faciat celebrari *MunAcOx* 202; **1473** exequias ~ias *Lit. Cant.* III 264; **1504** cujus ~ium deposicionis diem commemoramus *StatOx* 313.

2 (sb. ? m. or n.) anniversary, day on which obit or sim. is commemorated. **b** (sb. n.) record of anniversary. **c** (sb. n. or f.) year's mind, mass or alms in celebration of anniversary. **d** (sb. n.) payment for such celebration.

c1183 singuli decani x s. in ~io ejusdem decani..ad pitantiam..persolvent (*Lit. Ep. Lond.*) Diceto II lxxiii; in ~iis episcoporum..tenetur exequi officium *Offic. Sal.* 2; **s1341** pro pitancia..in die ~ii sui facienda *Hist. Durh.* 2 p. 131; **14..** officium mortuorum in ~iis *Reg. Brev.* 250; *a yere*, annus; ..~ium est quando repetentibus annis idem dies recolitur *CathA*. **b** nomen ejus notetur in ~iis *RegulC* 68; **c1150** pro fratribus defunctis hoc utrimque servabitur: ~ium in martyrologio scribetur *MonA* II 26; **1343** j quaternus continens ~ia *Ac. Durh.* 205. **c** **1168** monachis..pro ~io Johannis episcopi faciendo *Pipe* 168; **c1182** vj m. ..unde ~ium..episcopi in perpetuum faciemus *Ch. Sal.* 44; quidam etiam vivi ~ia pro se faciunt celebrari, quibus obviant suffragia..pro defunctis instituta et non pro vivorum animabus Gir. *GE* I 49 p. 137; **1206** capellariam datam a..rege J. ..ad iiij prebendas..ad facienda ~ia patris sui et fratrum *Cl.* 70a; **s1276** episcopus..duos instituit de novo obedienciarios, infirmarium videlicet et custodem ~iorum *Ann. Wint.* 123 (cf. 3 infra); **1306** onerati ad perficiendam quandam ~iam pro anima Alianore quondam regine Anglie *RParl* I 196a; **c1316** ut ~ium nostrum singulis annis ..libencius celebretur et memoria anime nostre in una collecta omni die ad magnum altare..habeatur, damus..*Kelso* I 309; **1395** in pane eroga to pauperibus..pro qualibet ~ia *Comp. Swith.* 203; **1414** capellani annuatim tenebunt unum ~ium in ecclesia parochiali *Reg. Cant.* II 21; **1438** concessimus pro animabus omnium supradictorum unum ~ium novem leccionum, viz. placebo et dirige, semel in anno imperpetuum celebrandum (*Cart. Boarstall*) *Ambrosden* II 328; **1521** faciat celebrari omni anno..~ium, viz. *saulmes* et dirige *Reg. Aberbr.* II 434. **d** **12..** tricennale dividatur inter personam et capellanum, et sic ~ium *Conc. Scot.* II 44; **1567** super domibus, ..proficuis, emolumentis, ..obitibus et ~iis..que pertinuerunt..ad capellanias..aut prebendas, ubicunque prefate domus, ..~ia, ..proficua et emolumenta jacent *Scot. Grey Friars* II 255.

3 obedientiary in charge of anniversary celebrations.

1239 committant..Philippo, qui fuit refectorarius, officium ~ii et refectorarii [Winton'] *Cl* 158; **c1270** episcopus ..consuevit..instituere..magistrum operum, ~ium, infirmarium et hostillarium *Reg. Wint.* II 655; **c1300** redditus pertinentes ad ~ium *Cant. Cath. Pri.* 24n.; **1395** compotus fratris J. ..~ii et custodis manerii de B. *Comp. Swith.* 202.

annocatio v. annotatio. annocorinatum v. anachoreta. annodoma v. anadonia. annolog- v. analog-. annomin- v. agnomin-. annon v. an.

annona [CL], grain (esp. as rent; *cf.* A. Ballard *The Domesday Inquest* 194–5). **b** harvest (fig.).

de ~a ad caballos modia quattuor Alcuin *Ep.* 298 p. 457; molinus reddens x modia frumenti et x modia grossae ~ae *DB* I 23; ~ae, id. *bled*, clxii acras *Ib.* 69; unusquisque sochemannus qui habet i hidam aut plus reddit unam summam ~ae huic ecclesiae *Ib.* 143b; de circet xi s.; de ~a unius anni xxx lib. *Ib.* 154b; **1106** volo ut..abbas..reddat.. totam pecuniam suam sc. in ~a sicca et in peculibus, quam apportavit ad terram suam de terris aliis; de domibus vero et ~is viridis..fiat rectitudo (*Breve regis*) *Chr. Abingd.* II 93; **1157** decimam ~e *Reg. Aberd.* I 6; cum ~am equis apponendam..manu..purgaret Gir. *TH* I 36. **b** ne, ..dum in ~a depressa peritura olera extirpare nituntur, justa potius plantaria cum malis..eradicando precidant *V. Dunst.* B. 1; quatinus, dum sui ad fruges temporales..vacarent, ille..carpende..invigilaret ~e spiritus Ad. Eyns. *Hug.* IV 14.

2 supply of food. **b** allowance (mon.). **c** lunch (infl. by *nona*). **d** earnest, payment to clinch bargain.

[Saxones] ~as sibi eos [Britannos] affluentius ministrare cogunt Bede *HE* I 15; solet tunc [in Maio] ~a deficere Beleth *RDO* 127. 133; [cignus] consueverat..ministrante ..edituo ~am percipere Ad. Eyns. *Hug.* III 7; de exigua tritici ~a..multiplicati fuerant panes Blakman *Hen. VI* 20. **b** in refectorio [subprior]..dupplicem ~am habebit *Obs. Barnwell* 54; **s1324** [rex] jussit..bona..religiosorum.. exterarum..nationum..seisiri, constituens prelatis ex his ~am..nimis brevem, tres videlicet per septimanam solidos ..ac religiosis singulis xviij d. *Flor. Hist.* III 226; fratribus constitutam ~am..offerat: ..~am dicit alimoniam ciborum et victum omnem monachorum; hora enim nona veteres commedere solebant, et ideo a tempore ipso hore none..omnis victus hominis..nomen accepit '~a' *Cust. Cant.* 131. **c 9..** ~a, *nonmete* WW. **d p1285** (v. annonare); **s1404** hic [in curiam Romanam] non intrat aliquis nisi facta annona (*Vers.*) Ad. Usk 89.

annonare, to pay earnest (*cf. annona 2d*).

p1285 quod nullus carnifex [etc.]..nullo modo emant nec per denarium nec per argentum Dei ~ent nomine annone, id est *arnest*, attachient..aliquod..venale *Rec. Norw.* I 186.

annositas, old age. **b** antiquity.

c1093 ~atem provectus ad sexagenariam H. Los. *Ep.* 1. **b** [Sergius I] invenit crucem argenteam in loco obscuro multe ~atis *Eul. Hist.* I 224.

annosus [CL], full of years, aged. **b** long-lived. **c** long-established. **d** lasting many years.

notus voce cānis, annosaque tempora cānis Serlo Wilt. 2. 21. **b** cornix est avis ~a Bart. Angl. XII 10. **c** nec violenter jure debuit antiquo serpenti..possessionis ~a spolia..tollere R. Cold. *Cuthb.* 17. **d s1224** Baldewinus.. post ~am et morosam incarcerationem..rediit in Flandriam M. Par. *Maj.* III 90.

2 (sb. f.) (?) giant fennel (*Ferula*).

annuosa, *æscprotu* Ælf. *Gl.*

1 annotare v. annatare.

2 annotare [CL], to note down, record. **b** to append as a note. **c** to take notes (? in shorthand).

martyrologium..in quo [martyres] omnes..qua die.. mundum vicerint..adnotare studui Bede *HE* V 24; miraculum..quod..~ari non immerito videtur nobis Herm. Arch. 32; ~atis omnibus debitis illic seriatim *Dial. Scac.* II 1b; cum quis se ita subtraxerit propter crimen.., sententia festinari non solet, sed †advocari [v.l. adnotari], non utique ad penam sed ut potestas sit ei purgandi se Bracton 125; debet nomen recipientis et libri traditi..in rotulo suo ~are *Obs. Barnwell* 62; **s1212** ab hoc anno.. institucio ordinis Fratrum Minorum..incipit ~ari Trevet 185; **1553** per unum quaternum..ubi nomina..cum eorum summis plenius ~antur et declarantur *Ac. Durh.* 730. **b 1239** decrevit literas transmittendas, pro parte inferius ~atas (*Lit. Papae*) M. Par. *Maj.* III 572; placet cartam dicti regis [Edgari]..huic operi ~are Ciren. II 96. **c** si mihi manus conferantur, non dico scribe velociter scribentis, sed et notarii velocissime ~antis Ben. Pet. *Mir. Thom.* IV 1.

2 a to distinguish by a mark. **b** to annotate. **c** to write up, rewrite.

a [litteris] similiter nudis, id est nullo puncto adnotatis Bede *TR* 23. **b** habetur in eodem librario psalterium..in cujus primo folio incipiunt Meditaciones quedam devote.. taliter ~ate.. (*Invent.*) Elmh. *Cant.* 97. **c c803** quo.. libellum stilo simpliciori digestum..cultius adnotarem Alcuin *Ep.* 306.

3 to assign: **a** (persons); **b** (time).

a ipsius [cantoris] est omnes fratres in tabula ad omnia officia ~are Lanfr. *Const.* 147. **b** ut nomen apostatarum ..aboleri deberet neque aliquis regno eorum annus adnotari Bede *HE* III 9.

4 a to notice. **b** to bring to notice.

a in ceteris personarum declinationibus amphimacrus crebro insertus ~atur, ut 'cōnglōbās, cōnglōbānt' Aldh. *PR* 122. **b c1093** ut..etatis ineptias senescentis non debeam ~are meorum successorum judiciis H. Los. *Ep.* 1; primus error presentibus ~andus in constitucione 'ad conditorem' contentus est Ockham *Frat. Min.* 2.

annotatio, noting down, indication. **b** record, history. **c** note. **d** comment, criticism.

numquam in adnotatione festi Paschalis errabit (*Ep. Ceolfridi*) Bede *HE* V 21 p. 334; **1309** presentis scripti †annocacione et sigilli mei apposicione *PQW* 839a; horum numeri ~onem, ut aliquantulum ceteris certiorem, sequar *Chr. Wallingf.* 11. **b** incipit quedam brevis ~o..Ricardi prioris Hagustaldensis ecclesie de..statu ejusdem ecclesie Ric. Hex. *Pri. Hex. intr.* **c** ~ones aliquot in aeras Ferr. *Kinloss* 45. **d** cum [virtutes] per eas [sc. Scripturas] facillime et actuum exemplo et vocum ~one valeant agnosci J. Bury *Glad. Sal.* 4 p. 583.

annotinus [CL], of the previous year. **b** yearly.

†arnotinus, hornotinus, quorum primitiva sunt..†arnus, horno Aldh. *PR* 132. **b** quarta decima luna..primo circuli decemnovenalis anno..xii diebus ~um cursum praecurrere solet Bede *TR* 60; *a yere*, annus..; annualis, annuarius, ~us *CathA*.

2 (w. *Pascha*) **a** (celebrated at) paschal full-moon (*cf. annus c*). **b** anniversary of Baptism.

a ~um Pascha dicimus ubicunque quarta luna concurrit [cum die Dominica]; unde in quibusdam ecclesiis, quamvis non concurrat cum die Dominica, cantatur 'resurrexi' cum toto paschali officio Gerv. Tilb. I 6. **b** vocatur Pascha ~um quando aliquis diem quo baptisma suscepit annuatim celebrat Beleth *RDO* 84. 88.

annualarius [cf. OF *annueler*], responsible for anniversary masses. **b** (sb. m.) priest so responsible.

1416 domino M. B., presbitero annuellario in ecclesia cathedrali Wellensi *Reg. Bath* 263. **b 1310** computant.. xxx annuvellariis et aliis presbiteris..cuilibet vj d. *Ac. Exec. Ep. Exon.* 23; **1337** si annivelarii ecclesie..in omnibus commendacionibus, placebo et dirige in choro dicendis personaliter intersint *Reg. Exon.* II 859; **1411** licet capellani, stipendiarii et ~ii ad deserviendum ecclesiis parochialibus.. possint..per ordinarios compelli *Conc.* III 335; **1430** lego.. cuilibet..annivelario presenti in exequiis meis iiij d. *Reg. Cant.* V 503 (cf. ib. II 477: cuilibet annuellario); **1444** ~ii [ecclesie de Taunton] *Reg. Bath.* I 16.

annualis, ~iter v. annal-. 1 annuare v. animare 2a.

2 annuare, to renew yearly.

to newe yerly, ~are *CathA*.

2 (p. ppl.) **a** one year old. **b** annual.

a pro hogastris annatis et juvenibus *Fleta* 167. **b s1399** fuerunt in monasterio in firmis perpetuis et resolucionibus aliis ~atis xxxiiij li. *Meaux* III 275; **1440** ~ata pensio.. genitori nostro..promissa tot terminis constitutis soluta non extitit Bekynton I 180; **1517** ~atum munus *Cant. Coll. Ox.* III 137.

annuarius, yearly. **b** responsible for anniversary masses.

munuscula ~ia vice tributi..exigere *G. Steph.* I 13; **1262** feodum x librarum ~iarum *Cl* 36; *CathA* (v. annotinus). **b 1405** clerus..concessit regi unam decimam et vj s. viij d. a quolibet ~io sacerdote *Conc.* III 282 (cf. *Eul. Hist. cont.* 409).

annuatim, annually.

coepit ~im..regis..natalicius dies..venerari Bede *HE* IV 14; habent..economum..qui eis diatim necessaria victui, ~im amictui commoda suggerat W. Malm. *GP* II 91; terra..valet ~im xv li. *RDomin.* 1; potationes quas ~im.. facere consuevistis Gir. *GE* II 19 p. 258; **c1200** in cena Domini annatim edituus..reddebat.. *MonA* I 128b; **1254** solvent..†annuatum [l. ~im] ij m. *Reg. Aberbr.* I 323; **1340** scolarium..apud Godstowe in festo Nativitatis B. J. Baptiste ~im confluencium *FormOx* 173; **1502** continuabit lecturam..~im quolibet anno *StatOx* 303.

annuatio v. antenatio.

annuere [CL], to summon by a nod. **b** to enjoin by a sign.

sacerdotem ~ens et asciscens Gir. *IK* I 4 p. 52. **b** Fansy †animat [l. annuat] silentium cum manu Skelton I 236.

2 to assent (to), agree, allow: **a** (w. dat. or absol.); **b** (w. acc.); **c** (w. inf.).

a faventibus cunctis et adnuentibus fidei Bede *HE* III 22; **a1085** ~ente..Gaufrido *Regesta* p. 125; annue poscenti (Nig. *S. Laur.*) *Spec.* VII 420; **s1297** [rex] votis eorum ~it in premissis et omnia concessit W. Guisb. 313. **b** hoc non ~unt monachi *DB* I 10; burgensibus ~erunt leges..quae sunt in Hereford *Ib.* 269; [Arthurus] eis veniam concessit et ~it postulata *Flor. Hist.* I 262; nulli layce persone ~etur ingressus *Cust. Cant.* 113; **s1297** [rex] ~it peticionem ipsorum *Eul. Hist.* III 168. **c a1035** (12c) filiabus meis ~o Stevecheworde dum vivant tenere *CD* 932; **s1164** ~it de consilio regie voluntati parere W. Cant. *V. Thom.* I 15.

annuitas, annuity, annual payment. **b** anniversary service.

c 1400 quamdiu..Willelmus..non haberit aliquam cantariam, ~atem aut aliud beneficium ecclesiasticum *Mem. York* I 246; **1404** G. H. ..ea habuit..dum vivebat concessione cujusdam ~atis xl li. *RScot* 167b; **1420** solvendo ~ates predictas *MonA* VI 617b; **1533** reddendo inde annuatim.. fratri dicti J. quamdam ~atem vj s. viij d. per annum durante vita ejusdem T. *Banstead* II 104; **1547** habebit.. dictam ~atem sive annualem redditum *Cart. Glam.* 1978. **b s1435** concessit..dominus relaxacionem facere..pro certa sibi concessa suffragiorum ~ate Amund. II 107.

1 annularis, (?) yearling.

1269 respondet de ij de exitu, quia tercia vacca erat anularis *MinAc* 1006/29; **1350** respondet de xxij vitulis de exitu xxij vaccarum vitulancium hoc anno; et non plus quia omnes vacce ~es *Rec. Elton* 380.

2 annularis v. anularis.

annullabilis, liable to be annulled.

omnis volicio Dei ad intra est immobilis, et per consequens non est trahibilis, curvabilis, anullabilis, obeditiva Wycl. *Dom. Div.* 149.

annullare, to annihilate (phil.), reduce to nothing.

quandocunque aliqua res absoluta..corrumpitur, tunc adnullatur vel adnihilatur Wycl. *Act.* 7.

2 to destroy, demolish, bring to nothing: **a** (material objects, incl. animals); **b** (persons); **c** (abstractions).

a quomodo tanta ferarum milia..tam repente fuerint adnullata *G. Steph.* I 1 (cf. ib. I 30: consumi omnia et adnullari); **s1267** omnes municiones circa illam [sc. insulam de Ely]..fecit dominus rex prosternere et adnullare *Leg. Ant. Lond.* 95. **b** dispartitur, minuitur et adnullatur piratica..gens Danica a sua [sc. Anglie] infestatione Herm. Arch. 1; ipse omnium [curialium] aspiratione ~atus est H. Hunt. *CM* 6; iste totum [populum] funditus adnullavit Map *NC* I 15 p. 22; **c1239** emulorum..nostram parvitatem ..adnullare molientium ora livida Gros. *Ep.* 66; **s1259** obiit ..pre dolore mentis..adnullatus *Flor. Hist.* II 420. **c** ad quod frangitur ~atus episcopi sermo Herm. Arch. 25; legis..institutis..ex toto neglectis, immo et adnullatis *G. Steph.* I 1; **s1240** cum vidisset sic justiciam manifeste vacillare et tot labores ~ari *Flor. Hist.* II 237; **1265** nitens ..constituciones..anullare *Cl* 125; **s1304** nihil inventum est quod de jure videretur statum illorum [sc. Templariorum] ~are T. Stubbs *Chr. Ebor.* 413; **s1320** pro feria abbatis.. minuenda et adnullanda *Chr. Rams.* 350; nituntur potestatem summi pontificis ~are Ockham *Dial.* 485; **1395** private religiones..essent..digne ~ari (*Concl. Loll.*) *Ziz.* 361; ut emulorum..opinionem frivolam..valeam ~are Elmh. *Cant.* 202.

3 to annul, quash (leg.). **b** to invalidate (persons).

s1252 detulit breve regis, ..quod narrando adnullavimus *Ann. Dunstable* 185; **1268** quatinus..appella..cassetis penitus et anulletis *Cl* 441; **1280** peticio de adnullandis.. procuracionibus..ecclesiarum *Reg. Heref.* 257; assisa..adnullata fuit *Fleta* 302; fuit idem irrotulamentum postea rasum et adnullatum *State Tri. Ed. I* 36; abrogare et ~are easdem [leges] Ockham *Pol.* I 58; **1358** pro..privilegiis anullandis super hominibus ville Oxonie (*Ac. Univ. Ox.*) *EHR* XXIV 738; **1383** statuta..penitus revocamus, cassamus et ~amus *Lit. Cant.* II xxxi; **1451** predicte littere patentes..virtute predicti statuti adnullate et evacuate existunt *Reg. Whet.* I 63. **b** si [executores mei]..relaxaverint aliquod debitum meum.., volo quod..~entur *Reg. Cant.* II 297.

4 to make light of, despise.

a1300 hec scripsimus..propter eos qui rei geste simplicem ~are solent stilum, nisi variis verborum fucis veritas depingatur *Chr. Evesham* 16; adulator..in presencia peccatoris diminuere peccatum vel anullare nititur *AncrR* 23; *CathA* (v. annihilare 4).

annullatio, destruction, undoing, ruin.

s1102 Gausfrido manerii de Wi ~onem..exponente *Chr. Battle* 49; Judei de sui..adnullatione consilii condolentes T. Mon. *Will.* I 3; **1305** in machinacionem mortis..domini regis et in corone et regie majestatis sue ~onem et enervacionem manifestam (*Plac. de W. Waleys*) *Ann. Lond.* 141; **1338** post adnullacionem Templariorum *Hosp. in Eng.* 133.

2 annulment.

s1270 ex dilacione..puplicacionis statuti.., Judeis forsitan et eorum fautoribus ad ejus adnullacionem insistentibus *Leg. Ant. Lond.* 235; **1306** contra..revocacionis, ~onis, cassacionis, irritacionis et decreti nostri tenorem (*Lit. Papae*) *Reg. Carl.* I 266; **1343** super adnullacione finis *Reg. Brev.* 13b; **1396** recordum..adnullacionis cujusdam judicii nuper erronice redditi *Mem. York* I 224; **s1424** reducentes ad memoriam cassacionem et ~onem omnium libertatum illis temporibus..extortarum Amund. I 192.

annullativus, tending to invalidate.

1399 quidquid viciosum, ~um et destructivum contra predicta juramenta probata fide videremus insurgere *Misc. Scrope* 292.

annullatorie, by way of annulment.

ne procedatur ~ie Conway *Def. Mend.* 1428.

†annullitas, annulment.

1377 alias procedet contra vos ad ~atem pretensi juris vestri Thorne 2188.

annulosus, annulus, v. anul-.

annumerare [CL], to reckon (in a total), include. **b** to count out, pay.

nos decem et septem genitae sine voce sorores / sex alias nothas non dicimus annumerandas Aldh. *Aen.* 30 (*Ele-

mentum) 2; viij annos, adnumerato etiam illo Bede *HE* III 9; hujus terrae pecunia superius est ~ata *DB* I 235; rubeum colorem inter extremos ~abis Neckam *NR* II 22; si tricennale unius vel anniversarium tricennale alterius ~etur et aggregetur Gir. *GE* I 49 p. 133; ut in cathalogo sanctorum eum anumerare..dignemini *Canon. G. Sempr.* 126v. **b** pro redemptione peccati auxiliaribus ~ata pecunia honori restitutus est W. Malm. *GP* II 91 (cf. ib. I 45: rex..omnes sibi redditus ~abat).

annumeratio, reckoning, inclusion.

s1423 cum undecim electis duodecimus annumeratus est ipse abbas, superque sua ~one has..recepit epistolas cerciorantes Amund. I 99.

annuntiabilis, proclaimable.

bonum est annuntiare Christum cum peccato; ergo bonum est peccare annuntiando: ista enim sunt ~ia S. Langton *Quaest.* 248v.

annuntiare [CL], to announce, proclaim, ascribe: **a** (w. obj.); **b** (w. acc. and inf.).

a verbum Dei omnibus adnuntians Bede *HE* III 19; [sensus exterior] dicitur quod..ea quae extrinsecus introducit..interiori sensui ~iet Eriug. *Per.* 570A; sicut sacerdos nuntiat, sic etiam ~iat; habet enim sacerdos gregi commisso suos excessus ~iare Gir. *Symb.* 21 p. 257; **s1430** laudem et gloriam Domino ~iantes pro..beneficiis suis *Plusc.* XI 5; anuncio, A. *to shewe* WW. **b** ~io..amicis meis tristandum de mea morte non esse Osb. *V. Dunst.* 16; interroga patres tuos, et ~iabunt tibi ..se nusquam sanctum legisse venatorem J. Sal. *Pol.* 395B.

2 to add by proclamation.

c1204 ut [S. Caradocus] canonizaretur et consortio sanctorum †~iaretur [? l. annumeraretur] operam adhibens Gir. (*De se ipso*) I p. 399.

annuntiatio, announcement, proclamation. **b** Annunciation (25 March).

c625 frigiditatem cordis ipsius Sancti Spiritus adnuntiatione accende (*Lit. Papae*) Bede *HE* II 11; **795** nos vestrae prosperitatis ~one laetificabat Alcuin *Ep.* 41; **1102** non tyrannorum violentia..a veritatis ~one desistis (*Lit. Papae*) Eadmer *HN* 154; **1225** apostolus gaudet in Dei ~one Gros. *Ep.* 2 p. 19. **b** sunt aliae festivitates quae magnifice celebrantur..; sunt autem hae: Epiphania, Purificatio S. Mariae, festivitas S. Gregorii, ~o Christi Lanfr. *Const.* 130 (cf. ib. 131: Dominicae ~onis); contulit ut.. in festivitate S. Marie que ~o Dominica dicitur majorem missam in conventu celebraret W. Malm. (*V. Lanzonis*) *GR* V 443; Sergius [II instituit]..litanias in ~one R. Niger 73; **1189** eo anno quo ~o Domini in die Pasche continget (*Lit. nuntiorum*) Diceto *YH* II 59; **s1191** die Sabbati post ~onem B. Marie *Itin. Ric.* II 26; **1201** dederunt ei diem a sexto die post ~onem S. Marie in j annum *CurR* I 455; in festo ~onis Virginis gloriose Bacon *Maj.* I 271; incipimus annum ab ~one Dominica Kilwardby *Jejun.* 168; **c1283** a tempore ~onis usque post tempus falcacionis *Cust. Battle* 51; **14..** [qui dies debeant a clero et a populo observari ab opere servili] in Marcio dies ~onis B. Marie tantum *Conc. Scot.* II 74.

annuntiator, announcer, proclaimer.

1250 cum nos..simus ex officii debito verbi Dei ~ores Gros. *Ep.* 130; quid est facere opus evangeliste nisi ut ~or salutis, quod veritas docet, hoc confirmet..? Ad. Marsh *Ep.* 111.

annuosa v. annosus 2.

annus [CL], year. **b** (dist. acc. method of computation). **c** (w. *magnus* or sim.) 'great year' (astr.).

ea quae totius ~i circulus in celebratione dierum festorum poscebat Bede *HE* IV 16 p. 241; una vice in ~o *DB* I 1; ~us est spatium quo sol ad idem zodiaci punctum revertitur Adel. *Alch.* I 18; **c1150** si civis Lundon' terram aliquam per ~um et diem unum sine calumpnia tenuerit.. (*Lib. Lond.*) *GAS* 674 (cf. *CurR* VIII 215 [**1220**]: Ricardus fuit seisitus ~is et diebus); sicut ~os remissionis vel jubileos a remissione vel a jubilo scimus esse dictos, ~os sc. remissionis et gracie Map *NC* I 15; ver, autumpnus, hyems, estas dominantur in anno D. Bec. 2793; **1265** solvent..de ~o in ~um xxxvij m. ..ad totam vitam..Margerie *Cl* 131; **1298** cujus proficuum valet communibus ~is xv li. *IPM* 81/17; ~um juxta morem Romani calendarii a principio Januarii exordimur Trevet 3; **1313** puniantur per prisonam unius ~i *Eyre Kent* 42; **1432** unum ~i donum [*New Year's gift*], par sc. cultellorum *Cant. Coll. Ox.* III 90; **1456** sic quod nullus eorum ultra ~um et mensem in custodia..ciste..se continuet *StatOx* 280; **1468** de ~o computi *ExchScot* 540. **b** est ~us lunaris, est et solaris, est et errantium discretus stellarum Bede *TR* 36 p. 249; ex ~is quotlibet Romanis (Adel. *Tab.*) *EHR* XXVI 494; sunt uniuscujusque populi ~i proprii, unde Arabes ~os lune secuntur *Id. Alch.* I 18; **s1138** ~us Arabicorum ex quo inceptus est, Arabicorum dico collectorum dxxxvij, †plavorum [? l. planorum] vero xxij J. Worc. *Chr.* 53; Judei tres ~os distinguunt; usualem, qui a Januario incipit..; legitimum, quo utuntur in legitimis que agunt et distinguunt per lunationes, cujus est Aprilis lunatio prima; et ~um emergentem, quem..computant ab exitu de Egypto Gerv. Tilb. I 6; ~orum alius solaris, alius lunaris, alius artificialis, alius naturalis, alius usualis Bracton 359; ~us solaris dicitur quem sol suo motu efficit in circuitu spere proprie. ..per accidens dicitur ~us alius Egyptiorum, alius Grecorum, alius Latinorum, alius Arabum, ..alius Indorum Bacon VI 8–9; ut in ~o bisextili computetur unus dies plus in ~o quam in aliis ~is communibus *Id. Tert.* 274–5; quis nesciat quod duplex est ~us, solaris et lunaris, et solaris, hic quidem Egypcius, sine quadrante, quo utitur Ptolomeus in Almagesti? Bradw. *CD* 107D. **c** ibi ~um magnum, hoc est planetarum cursum, exordium finemque sortiri Bede *TR* 6 p. 193; magnus ~us, de quo philosophi disserunt Neckam *NR* I 6; nunc ~us magnus, qui planetis omnibus ad sua loca creationis reversis completur, quod fit demum post dxxx annos; nunc ~us mundanus, qui completur omnibus stellis ad sua loca primitiva reversis, quod fit, ut ait Josephus, post v millia ~orum Gerv. Tilb. I 6; annus..alius secundum stellam fixam, qui dicitur major ~us sive mundialis Bacon VI 8.

2 (in reckoning dates) **a** year of Christian era. **b** year of office (incl. regnal year).

a ~o ab urbe condita dcxciii, ante vero incarnationis dominicae tempus ~o lx^mo Bede *HE* I 2; quarto imperii sui [Claudii] ~o.., qui est ~us ab incarnatione Domini xlvi *Id.* 3; **735** in quoto ~o ab incarnatione Christi praedicatores primi missi a S. Gregorio ad gentem Anglorum venissent Bonif. *Ep.* 33 p. 58; ~o millesimo quadragesimo tertio dominicae carnis Herm. Arch. 17; ~o millesimo octogesimo sexto ab incarnatione Domini *DB* II 450; ~o incarnati Verbi quadringentesimo vicesimo quinto W. Malm. *GR* I 68; praesens habeatur Anglorum cronica, in qua per ~os dominicales regum Anglorum repperiri possunt annales Herm. Arch. 8; ultra posse nostrum est..in his..ad annum usque millesimum centesimum quadragesimum septimum quantum ad ~os dominicales solvere dissonantiam Diceto *Chr. prol.* 19; ~o Gratie millesimo centesimo xiij R. Niger 178; quidam [scriptores] ~os Domini incipiunt computare ab Annuntiatione, alii a Nativitate, quidam a Circumcisione, quidam vero a Passione Gerv. Cant. *Chr.* I 88; **1268** ~o Domini mcclxvij *StatOx* 27; **1285** ~o incarnacionis Domini mcclxxxv *RGasc.* II 245; ~i presentis viz. ~i Christi 1444 Killingworth *Alg.* 715; **1476** data..~o a dominico Natalicio mccccclxxvi *FormA* 336; **1517** ~o incarnate Deitatis secundum..computacionem Anglicane et Hibernicane ecclesiarum mcccccxvii *Mon. Hib. & Scot.* 519a; ut illi nobis indicent..quo ~o salutis facta sint omnia Ferr. *Kinloss* 10; ~o reparationis humanae 1533 Chauncy *Passio* 56; ~o restauratae salutis nostrae 1534 *Ib.* 64. **b** cujus [Theodosii II] ~o imperii viii Palladius ad Scottos..mittitur; ~o autem regni ejus xxiii Aetius..gessit consulatum Bede *HE* I 13; ~o regni Ecgfridi nono *Ib.* IV 19; **s752** ~o regni sui xij° Cuthredus Westsaxonum..rex..Fl. Worc. 53; **1072** ~o ab incarnatione Domini millesimo septuagesimo secundo, pontificatus autem domni Alexandri papae undecimo, regni vero Willelmi gloriosi regis Anglorum.. sexto (*Const. Regis*) *Eng. Royal Writs* pl. xxix (= *Regesta* no. 64); **1208** rotulus compoti ~i quarti pontificatus domini Petri Wintoniensis episcopi *Pipe Wint. titul*; ~o regis nunc xix° *State Tri. Ed. I* 15; **1299** consecracionis nostre ~o sexto *Lit. Cant.* I 27; cum in serie regum Romanorum duo numeri signentur, superior ~os designat imperii, inferior vero regni Trevet 3.

3 (pl.) age, period of life.

virgineis cum jam pubesceret annis Aldh. *VirgV* 2065; **1173** non contrahatur matrimonium inter aliquos infra ~os *Conc.* I 475; si quilibet..decedens minorem ~is heredem reliquerit *Dial. Scac.* II 10D; a tenerioribus ~is incipiens P. Blois *Ep.* 27. 94C; ut proximus consanguineus habeat wardam pueri..usque ad ~os discretionis Brakelond 151v; **c1228** sicut audivit in ~is suis juvenilibus *Feod. Durh.* 225; **1346** dum sic eramus in ~is minoribus (*Cl*) *Foed.* V 496; **1431** quod..filii mei dum in ~is puerilibus steterint sint in custodia..usque ipsi pervenerint ad ~os discrecionis *Reg. Cant.* II 444.

4 a year's rent or profit. **b** year's profit accruing to crown or royal grantee from lands of felon. **c** year's study.

a 1203 debet xl m. pro habendo cambio Anglie ad firmam ..pro tanto quantum R. ..inde consuevit reddere, salvo eidem R. ~o suo *Pipe* 11; **1513** volo quod T. et W. ..habeant insimul omnes ~os et terminos meos in firma mea de S. ..et quod executores mei non..alienent predictos ~os meos (*Test.*) *Crawley* 545. **b †1190** quod habeant..felones †freinthe..cum ~o et vasto predictorum *CalCh* II 306; **1241** abbas de S. Eadmundo clamat..murdrum, catalla fugitivorum, ~um, diem et vastum infra octo hundreda et dim. *KRMem* 20 r. 7; **1241** finem fecit cum rege pro habendo ~um regis et diem de terris que fuerunt R. ..et W. .. suspensorum pro latrocinio *ExcRFin.* I 340; **1267** concessimus..terras..que sunt escaeta nostra per feloniam.., una cum ~o et die ad nos pertinentibus de eisdem *Cl* 316; **1318** vendidit..~um et vastum unius mesuagii..quod fuit Johannis..pro felonia suspensi *Couch. Furness* II 478; **1400** ipse dux haberet quascumque forisfacturas, ~um, diem et estreppamentum *Rec. Leic.* II 212. **c 1450** supplicat.. quatenus tres ~i in philosophia..possint sibi stare pro completa forma *MunAcOx* 732.

annutare [CL], to nod (to).

annicto vel ~o, *ic wincie* Ælf. *Gl.*

annutivus, expressive of assent.

'et' [est]..modo adnutiva et compromissiva, [ut] 'dic quibus in terris *et* eris mihi magnus Apollo' Bonif. *AG* 541.

annutus, (nod of) assent.

1521 afflictos ut..potencie tue adnutu consolarere *Conc.* III 698.

annuus [CL], annual, yearly. **b** anniversary (adj.). **c** (w. *Pascha*) celebrated on Sunday, whether or not coincident w. Paschal full moon (*cf. annotinus 2a*).

~a, *gerlice GlC* A 618; cum tempus festis paschalibus aptum / annua Christicolis renovaret vota Aldh. *VirgV* 904; quatenus..cursum canendi ~um..edoceret Bede *HE* IV 18; de..~a per septenne spatium celebratione Gir. *TH* II 43; salva nobis ~a pensione x m. Brakelond 134v; **1313** iiij d. ~i redditus *Leet Norw* 55; **s1345** quod divicie que ad sedem apostolicam..de Anglia transferuntur erarium regis Anglie ~um..excedunt Ad. Mur. 175; **1516** de ~a dividenda in pauperes *StatOx* 333. **b** ~us..Wilgilsi sanctae migrationis dies Alcuin *WillP* 137; **1504** regis..cujus hodie ~a dies agitur *StatOx* 315. **c** ab anno dicitur ~um Pascha et annotinum: ~um Pascha quod celebratur singulis annis die Dominica; non tamen semper concurrit lunatio paschalis cum die Dominica Gerv. Tilb. I 6.

annuvellarius v. annualarius. anocar-, anocor- v. anachor-.

anodynare, to make less painful.

saccellationes eorum..anodinat et paragorizat Gilb. VII 314 v. 2.

anodynus [ἀνώδυνος], allaying pain, anodyne.

efficax valde et anodinum et maturativum Gilb. V 216. 2; anodina sunt illa que..mitigant dolorem *SB* 10; anodinum, i. mitigativum *Alph.* 11.

anogodan v. anagodan. anolog- v. analog-.

anomale, irregularly.

s1422 alius..ad ecclesiam Christi Cantuarie non minus ~e quam apostatice commigravit Amund. I 89.

anomalus [ἀνώμαλος, *infl. by* norma], anomalous, abnormal, irregular: **a** (gram.); **b** (in other contexts); **c** (pun on a and b).

a 'faxo', quod ~um [v.l. anamalum] est Aldh. *Met.* 116; ~a, quae..subtiliter analogiam tricant Bonif. *AG* 488. **b** partuque timendo / lineat ānŏmălos larvosa puerpera vultus Hanv. I 248; ne solus inter vos ~us videar Gir. *RG* II 2; ~os falsosque fraterculos nostros *Id. Inv.* I 4; est etiam inter alia essonia essonium anormalum, eo quod non sequitur regulam aliorum essoniorum Bracton 363b; **1371** a processu vestro..anormalo, ut suspicor, et inepto..provoco *Reg. Moray* 173; nisi ut [Witcleff] ecclesie Christi reddatur totus anormalus et Pauli consorcio alienus Netter *DAF* I 481; **s1422** quanta exhibita fuerat vagandi occasio per tuum recessum..et anormalam exorbitacionem! Amund. I 88; **c1430** anormala scandalosaque fercula extraordinarie sibi sumunt *Reg. Whet.* II 388; *withowten rewle*, abnormis, anormulus *CathA*. **c** pars Incarnato discordat, ănōmăla verba, / quilibet hereticus H. Avr. *Poems* 103 p. 59; **s1291** que ..in monasterio..monacharum..superficialem aut sophisticum habitum gessit; ut congruenter dici posset verbum, sed anormalum, presertim cum non sequeretur regulam aliarum conjugacionum *Ann. Osney* 329; **c1430** non.. proponit..esse verbum anormalum, immo pocius..mavult sequi regulam aliarum conjugacionum *Reg. Whet.* II 393.

2 (? by conf. w. *νόμος*) unlawful.

~um, inlegale *GlC* A 565.

anomoeomereus [ἀνομοιομερής], consisting of unlike parts.

nonne individua in universo ponerentur quasi partes omeomeree, et species quasi anomeomeree? Duns *Metaph.* VII 20.

anomon v. anemone.

anonis, ~ia, ~ium [ἀνωνίς, ὀνωνίς], rest-harrow (bot.). **b** deadnettle.

†onomia, quam multi †anomiadam dicunt, ..urinam provocat *Alph.* 130. **b** anonium dicitur lamium, ..urtica. mortua Turner *Herb.* A ii v.

anorexia [ἀνορεξία], loss of appetite.

ardorem et †anaroxiam, flegmonem et similia Gilb. V 206 v. 2; fastidium sive †avarexia, abominatio sive nausea et vomitus simbolum habent adinvicem et differentiam *Ib.* 210 v. 2; ~ia, i. fastidium *SB* 10; *orexis* interpretatur 'appetitus'; inde †onorexia ab *a* quod est 'sine' et *orexis*, i. stomachi appetitu, vel cum fastidio *Alph.* 131.

anormalus, ~ulus v. anomalus. anostropha v. anastropha. anothom-, anotom- v. anatom-. anowaria v. advocaria 1d. anph- v. amph-.

anquina [CL < ἀγκοίνη, = *halyard*], bow-string.

~a, *bogenstreng* Ælf. *Gl.*

anquirere [CL], to seek out.

~it, valde quirit *GlC* A 597; **†973** (13c) piscator..sedulo ~ens lina sua..proiciendo..aliquid capere nitebatur *CS* 1311.

anquiromagus v. ancyromachus.

1 ansa [CL], handle (of vessel). **b** stilt (of plough). **c** chair-arm. **d** curtain-ring (*cf. Exod.* xxvi and xxxvi).

nomina vasorum: ..~a, *sal* Ælf. *Gl.*; **1349** j patella argent' cum j †hausa [? l. hansa] (*KRAc* 391/15) *Arch.* XXXI 58; **1501** j calefactorium cum duabus ancis *Cant. Coll. Ox.* I 33. **b** quoddam aratrum unica aure vel ~a contentum est Neckam *Ut.* 112; **c1280** (*Cart. Coton*) *Antiquity* XXVII 167. **c** scripturus in cathedra sedeat, ~is [*gl.*: *braces*] utrinque elevatis pluteum sive asserem sustinentibus Neckam *Ut.* 116. **d** apte quinquagenas ~as habebant cortinae, quibus invicem necterentur Bede *Tab.* II 2; *a rynge of a curtan*, ~a *CathA* (cf. ib.: *a curtyn*, anabatum, ~a).

2 tag or tape of bandage. **b** "truss". **c** loop, twist, knot (fig.).

extrema debent ligari cum institis..et cum ~is, quod de facili aperiantur, vel cum nodis Gad. 10. 1. **b 14..** ansea, A. *a trusse* WW. **c** ad ~am calumpniae solvendam Abbo *QG* 21; quamvis abbreviata..eloquia..interdum simplicibus occasionem errandi ministrent et, dum ~am occulte solvunt, nodum manifeste ligare putentur Ockham *Pol.* I 230.

2 ansa v. hansa.

ansatus [CL], fitted w. a thong, (sb. f.) dart. **b** (fig.).

~ae, *aetgaere GlC* A 603. **b** oratio quasi..propugnaculum contra venenatas aemulorum ~as fore creditur Aldh. *VirgP* 60 p. 322.

ansea v. ansa 2b.

anser [CL], goose, gander. **b** (w. *Bassanus*) gannet.

~er, *goos GlC* A 627; ~er, auca, id est *gos Erf.* 2. 266. 20; ~er silvatica, *gregos Ib.* 54; ~eres crinciunt vel trinsiunt ALDH. *PR* 131 p. 179; ~er, *ganra* ÆLF. *Gl.*; vir apud quem ab ovo ~er eductus est W. CANT. *Mir. Thom.* IV 48; aves cortis sunt..altilia, anceres [*gl.*: *gars*], anates NECKAM *Ut.* 106; ~es albi illic [in septentrionem] volant a medietate Martii *Comm. Sph.* 16 p. 336; **1296** iiij aucas et ij anceres.. et x aucilas *Anc. Ext.* 81/1 m.2; **1403** unus ancer et due auce veteres *Test. Ebor.* III 24; ancer, A. *a gandyr* WW. **b** chenerotes..aut berniclae aut Bassani ~es sunt, aut mihi prorsus ignoti TURNER *Av.* 10; Scotorum Bassanus ~er, qui in Basso Scottorum insula nidum ponit CAIUS *Anim.* 18.

1 ansera v. amphora.

2 †ansera, goose.

1552 aucam sive †auceram [? l. anceram *or* ancerem] *CalPat* IV 290.

anserculus [CL], gosling.

tertium genus..nuper ab ovo exclusum aufert ~um TURNER *Av.* 97.

anserinus, of a gander (or goose). **b** of the nature of a goose. **c** (w. *pastus*) shepherd's purse (*Capsella*).

caro ~a GAD. 10 v. 1. **b** aves..~e *Ib.* 35. 2. **c** sanguinaria, pastus ~us idem *Alph.* 162.

anserulus, gosling.

c1250 decima..~orum *Mon. Exon.* 255b; **1283** de lj aucis de remanenti, quarum iiij †marioli [l. mariole] et ij †aucerole [? l. anceroli] (*MinAc*) *Surrey Rec. Soc.* XV 52; **1454** iij auce, ciij anceruli *Ac. Durh.* 150; *a geslynge*, ancerulus *CathA*; **1530** custodit unam suem irracionabilem ad devorandum ancerilos vicinorum suorum *CourtR* 183/20 r. 1*d*.

anserum v. ancella. ansifer v. anxifer. ansilla v. ancilla 1b.

ansorium, cobbler's shaping knife.

alutarii secant cum rasorio vel ~io [*gl.*: cultrum ipsius sutoris] corium GARL. *Dict.* 125; *shapyng knyfe of sowtare*, ~ium *PP*; ~ium, *a shavyngknyf or a trenket* WW.

ansportare v. asportare.

ansula, little handle. **b** hook (cf. *Exod.* xxvi 4–5).

[tintinnabulum] inter brachiola ~arum in regione superiori foramen gerit non modicum, ab ~e prima origine incipiens R. COLD. *Cuthb.* 81. **b** curtinae..tabernaculi.. diversis ~arum nexibus assutae ALDH. *Met.* 2 p. 64; ~is ergo hyacinthinis cortinae invicem copulantur BEDE *Tab.* 428.; **1308** aperturis tunice et camisie sibi invicem connexis ~is argenteis *Lib. Regal.* 12.

ansum v. hansa. anta v. acanthus, 1 anca. antabata v. andabata.

antagonista [ἀνταγωνιστής], opponent.

~a, recertator *GlC* A 601.

†antale [? misr. of Ar. *al-ṭalq*], (?) talc.

~e, lapis quidam *SB* 11 (cf. *Alph.* 11).

antanimare v. animare 1a.

antapoche [ἀνταποχή], countertally, foil of tally (*cf. anticopa*).

†apote et †antapote, G. *taile et contretaile* (NECKAM *Sac.*) *Med. Sci.* 363.

antapodotice [cf. ἀνταποδοτικός], antiphonally.

canat antipodotice, id est responsorie GARL. *Dict.* 133.

antarcticus [ἀνταρκτικός], antarctic.

sub opacis ~i poli finibus GIR. *TH* II 17; polus oppositus dicitur antarticus, quasi contra articum positus SACROB. *Sph.* 2 p. 87; versus polum †entarticum BACON XIII 175; ibi polum ~um, quem nec oculus vidit nec auris audivit, inspicimus R. BURY *Phil.* 15. 199.

ante [CL], (adv. of place) in front, fore (naut.). **b** forwards (esp. w. ref. to ceremonial bowing). *V. et. inante.*

ante catervatim per limphas duco cohortes ALDH. *Aen.* 62 (*Famfaluca*) 6; **s1114** [casulam] ~e et retro cum lista bruslatam *Flor. Hist.* II 44; **1235** membrum ejus visum est pelle coopertum ~e in capite (*CurR*) *SelPlJews* xlvi; **1234** debet ferare ij avveros in pedibus ~e de ferro domini *Cust. Glast.* 54; **1295** pro ferura vj equorum ~e et retro et ij jumentis ~e ferandis *MinAc* 765/17*d.*; **1290** cum dominus rex capiat..prisas suas..viz. de qualibet navi vini duo dolia ~e et retro *RParl.* I 27a (cf. infra 3a); **1325** cum castello navis et hurdicio ~e et retro *Cal. Pl. & Mem. R. Lond.* 8; **s1349** supra caput singuli habentes singulos capellos cruce rubea ~e et retro signatos AVESB. 119b; **1376** claudant gardina ~e et retro *Hal. Durh.* 138; **1430** a via regia ~e usque ad *le heddyke* episcopi retro *Feod. Durh.* 6. **b** missam matutinalem †celebrantur [l. celebraturi] ~e et retro faciant LANFR. *Const.* 87; habent..corpora..moveri ..dextrorsum et sinistrorsum et ~e et retro ex aere et aqua ADEL. *QN* 13; hominem..se ~e et retro continua passione moventem GIR. *IK* II 7.

2 (adv. of time) before, previously. **b** (as conj. followed by sub. cl.). *V. et. antequam.*

hunc Gabrihel..praedixerat ante ALDH. *VirgV* 2292; quales numquam ~e videram BEDE *HE* IV 14; ut qui subjectus fuerat paulo ante caducis / rebus WULF. *Swith.* I 184; **1226** donationem..quam longe ~e fecerat *CurR* XII 2641 (= *BNB* III 587: antefecerat longe). **b 1218** ante ipse G. captus fuit, ..invenerunt.. *Eyre Yorks* 299; **1253** Petrus Welp venit de cervisia eadem hora ante Willelmus cepit..Gaufridum *SelPlForest* 107.

3 (prep. of place) in front of. **b** in (or into) the presence of. **c** (w. *manum*) beforehand.

astrorum..situs..~e frontem aethralis Tauri locatus ALDH. *Met.* 3 p. 73; sepultus est..in ecclesia ~e secretarium BEDE *HE* II 1; illud genus vexilli..~e eum ferre solebat *Ib.* 16; feminam quam ~e domum suam filare vidit MAP *NC* IV 15 p. 192; **1294** ~e bordam navis *Stat. Gild. Berw.* 49; **1260** antiqua prisa nostra vini, unius viz. tonelli ~e malum et alterius retro malum (*Ch. regis*) *Leg. Ant. Lond.* 103; **1327** unum dolium vini ~e mastum et aliud retro mastum (*Cl*) *Foed.* IV 273; vertigo est obvolutio visibilis speciei ~e oculos *SB* 43; **1366** habeant primum bellum sive *delanterre* ~e omnes mundi Christianos (*Lit. regis Castellae*) *Foed.* VI 532. **b** gregatim gradituri ~e angelicum caelestis theatri consessum ALDH. *VirgP* 22; **c1072** quod..omnes milites quos mihi debent paratos habeant ~e me (*Breve regis*) *EHR* VII 17; **a1087** si aliqui sunt qui vobis obedire noluerint, mittite ~e me et ego rectum faciam eis *Regesta* 68; ~e archiepiscopum..recognovit se injuste accepisse *DB* I 2; ecce ~e vos onustus peccatis mundi ANSELM (*Or.* 8) III 29. **c** hii tamen ante manum, quicquid de fine sequetur, / sepius immerito premia ferre petunt GOWER *VC* VI 185 (cf. ib. 438, 680, 870).

4 (prep. of time) before : **a** (a time or event) ; **b** (another person) ; **c** (w. adv.).

a ante diem qui vitae lumina claudit ALDH. *VirgV* 2820; anno ~e hunc proximo BEDE *HE* I 13; electus fuit in abbatem..biennio ~e Conquestum *G. S. Alb.* I 44; **1366** ~e solis occasum *SelCCoron.* 53; **1379** in nocte ~e gallicantum *Ib.* 92. **b** Alricus qui ~e eum fuit prepositus *DB* II 371; Britones olim ~e ceteros..insederunt G. MON. I 2. **c** ~e modo non vidi regem humilem *NLA* (*Oswin*) II 270 (= BEDE *HE* III 14: ~e haec); ~e sero penitus pigeat ociari R. BURY *Phil.* 6. 100; **1507** ~e diu vos visam *Reg. Merton* 341.

5 (prep. of degree) above, more than.

erat..~e omnia divinae caritatis igne fervidus BEDE *HE* IV 26.

6 (? quasi-sb. or abbrev. for *antecessore*) predecessor.

i liber homo sub †~e Rogeri Bigot *DB* II 204.

antea [CL], (adv.) before; *v. et. inantea, perantea.*

tantum profectus.., quantum numquam ~ea potuere, ceperunt BEDE *HE* V 8; sunt in eisdem masuris lx domus plusquam ~ea fuerant *DB* I 23; que per triennium ~ea ceca fuerat GIR. *IK* I 11; **s1328** David filius Roberti le Bruys, per annum ~ea mortui AVESB. 78.

anteactus [CL], past.

aliquo..~e vite merito id exigente GIR. *IK* I 4; **s1359** retencionem..qualem..non audivimus factam nostris ~is temporibus KNIGHTON II 105; **s1384** in hac expedicione non minus quam..~is expedicionibus WALS. *HA* II 112.

antealtare [al. div.], altar frontal.

14.. ante altaria de serico ad majus altare iiij (*Cart. Reading*) *EHR* III 116.

antebiblium v. antibiblium. anteca v. antela.

Antecanis, Procyon (astr.).

sub Cane aut sub Anticane NECKAM *Ut.* 113; in celo sunt plures stelle que dicuntur Canes, sc. Anticanis, quasi contra Canem Syrium.. *Comm. Sph.* 12 p. 323.

antecastellum, siege-work.

s1138 ad alia..castella..obsidenda divertit, ibidemque ~is extructis et manu militari munitis discessit J. WORC. 50.

antecedenter, in advance, in anticipation. **b** antecedently (theol.).

1415 abusionibus suis reprobatus animos decipiens ~er *Reg. Heref.* 86; **1422** de tuis commissis incipias conteri.., quod nos ~er appetimus tibique credimus..necessarium ut conclusionaliter exequaris (*Lit. abbatis*) AMUND. I 97. **b** ipse non dedit graciam ~er DUNS *Sent.* II xxxvii 2. 24; ~er voluntati divine de se non fit futurum BRADW. *CD* 213B; certum est quod ~er fecerunt graciam in predestinatis WYCL. *Ver.* III 153.

antecedentia, foreordainment (*cf. antecedere 2a*).

~ia, de qua hic fit sermo, est eventus futuri secundum cursum nature necessarii preordinacio BRADW. *CD* 600C.

antecedere [CL], to go in front of. **b** to advance (in time). **c** to precede (in time). **d** to anticipate. **e** to surpass.

ut..equitantem..~ere signifier consuesset BEDE *HE* II 16; Levitae..quos ~ebant iiij pueri *V. Osw.* 447. **b** equinoctium..ascendit plus et plus, ita quod..erit V Idus Martii et sic ulterius ~endo versus principium Martii BACON *Tert.* 280. **c** ~it in ordine nature..preparatio cordis preparationem cerebri *Ps.*-RIC. *Anat.* 20; patet per datam brevium, que est per iiij dies ~ens diem qua.. *State Tri. Ed. I* 35; in omni accione communi voluntatum increate et create, increata creatam naturaliter ~it BRADW. *CD* 578A. **d** mortis..sententiam..meruit, quia in gustu mellis constitutum edendi tempus antecessit AD. SCOT. *OP* 529. **e** qui, cum honestatis forma eminentes quosque ~ere deberet W. POIT. I 53.

2 (pr. ppl.) **a** antecedent (theol.). **b** (as sb. n.) antecedent (gram.). **c** (as sb. n.) antecedent (log.). **d** (as sb. m. or f.) ancestor, ancestress.

a [Deus] est causa ~ens, sc. preordinans secundum cursum nature [ut] eveniat aliqua res de necessitate, ut quod futura est eclipsis..; et est causa conjuncta, sc. ut cum sunt faciat ea esse (GROS. *Quaest. Theol.* I ii) *Powicke Studies* p. 196; **c1350** voluntas divina non est respectu cujuslibet effectus futuri necessitas ~ens (J. BUCKINGHAM) *Wycl. & Ox.* 51*n*. **b** relativum construitur cum simpliciter diverso a suo ~ente in proposito BACON XV 37. **c** sunt loci dialectici a genere, a specie, a nomine, ab ~entibus, a consequentibus ERIUG. *Per.* 474D; si ab ~enti [causam] non reperis, a consequenti consideres ADEL. *QN* 71; ~ens potest habere sensum verum et consequens nullum sensum habet verum OCKHAM *Pol.* I 328. **d** de legittimacione Isabelle ~entis sue *Plusc.* VIII 8.

antecellere [CL], to surpass: **b** (w. acc.); **c** (w. dat.).

~it, praecedit *GlC* A 645. **b** [sacramentum] quod cetera cuncta incomparabiliter ~it GIR. *GE* II 39. **c** si Petrus hac authoritate reliquis apostolis ~uerit BEKINSAU 743.

antecenium [CL], meal preceding dinner, lunch.

infamem fecit cenam, et ~ium vel..paracenium tanta instruxit luxuria ut.. J. SAL. *Pol.* 735B; *nunmete*, merenda, anticenium *PP*; hoc †auncinium, hec †imranda, hoc merarium, *a myddyner, undermete* WW; *a nune mete*, ~a, ~um, merenda *CathA*.

antecessatrix, ancestress.

1225 Sabina ~ix sua *BNB* III 116; **1230** quedam Beatricia †antecessix sua *Ib.* II 331; **1231** per quandam Brictivam antecessistrem ipsarum *Ib.* 389 (= *CurR* XIV 1101).

antecessio, precession (astr.).

necesse est quod Pascha fieret circa principium Martii vel in Februario, et sic antecedendo secundum ~onem equinoctii BACON *Tert.* 280.

antecessivus, progressive.

stellarum..motus ~us ab occidente in orientem fieri supponitur *Ps.*-GROS. 583.

antecessix v. antecessatrix.

antecessor [CL], **a** front-line soldier (fig.). **b** (?) beadle. **c** predecessor. **d** ancestor.

a ut..qui in sancto proposito successor extiterat..efficiatur ~or ALDH. *VirgP* 10. **b 1320** ita quod omnes et singuli..sine impedimento..decani et capituli et ~orum seu ministrorum ecclesie [S. Pauli] ejusdem ecclesie liberum ingressum habeant (*Pat*) *MGL* II 342. **c** ordinavit Ithamar..eruditione ~oribus suis aequandum BEDE *HE* III 14; **751** ~or..precessoris vestri..Gregorius [II] BONIF. *Ep.* 86 p. 192; **c1080** concedo Lanfranco archiepiscopo omnes consuetudines in ecclesia de N. quas solebant habere ~ores ejus *Regesta* p. 124; **1520** cancellum..ecclesie..~or ejus imperfectum reliquerat *Invent. Ch. Ch. Cant.* 44. **d** R. E. tempore et omnium ~orum suorum *DB* I 137b; clamat Erfastus..dim. sepem quae jacebat ad manerium ~oris Erfasti *Ib.* 211b; R. Pictaviensis j d[omum] quam tenuit Alflet sua ante cessor *Ib.* II 106b; est quedam recognitio que vocatur de morte ~oris: ..cum quis moritur saisiatus de aliquo libero tenemento, ..heres..saisinam ~oris sui.. petere potest GLANV. XIII 2; **1200** petit..advocationem ecclesie..ut illam..quam ancessores ejus a conquestu Anglie dederant *CurR* I 152; **c1200** pro salute anime mee et ~orum meorum *Cart. Glam.* 448; **1243** de dono anticessorum domini regis *Fees* 737; nec..ipse nec ullus de ~oribus suis nativus suus fuit *State Tri. Ed. I* 90; **1502** ob..animarum parentum, progenitorum et ~orum nostrorum..salutem *StatOx* 300.

antecessus [CL], (payment in) advance. **b** excess.

dat ei miser aleator tesseras in ~um NECKAM *NR* II 183. **b** habemus de maneriis nostris liij firmas..; tot ergo habemus firmas quot sunt septimane in anno, et unum in ~um *G. S. Alb.* I 74.

antechristus v. antichristus.

antecrescere, to be added as a prefix.

[in 'cĕcīdi'] tantum penultima diphthongus mutatur in productam I, manente priore syllaba correpta quae ~crevit, sicut in omnibus ejusmodi praeteritis ABBO *QG* 13 (cf. ib.: ~crescentem syllabam).

antecubitus, forearm (of image).

jactu lapidis ~um per medium fregit GIR. *GE* I 32.

antedenuntiatus, previously denounced.

1169 precipimus..quatenus ~os excommunicatos evitetis (*Lit. T. Archiep.*) *Becket Mat.* VI 578.

antedictus, aforesaid.

presbiter ~us AILR. *SSHex.* 12; **1199** abbas..~e ecclesie *RChart* 5b; **1222** in presencia ~orum nunciorum *Pat* 366; **s1343** super contentis in literis ~is AD. MUR. *app.* 230.

antedo- v. antidotum. antefacere v. ante 2a.

1 antefactus, done before, (sb. n.) past deed.

quando Christus dominus judicabit omnem hominem ex ~is suis [AS: *be ærran gewyrhtan*] (*Quad.*) *GAS* 369.

2 antefactus v. antefatus.

antefatus, aforesaid. **b** (sb. n. pl.) words aforespoken.

930 (14c) ad nanciscendam jam ~ae gloriae coronam *CS* 669; in ~o congressionis loco *Chr. Battle* 7; **a1285** super vicariis in †antefactis ecclesiis constituendis *Reg. S. Thom. Dublin* p. 275; **1453** ~us..rex Scotorum *RScot* 364a. **b** ~a, *forewyrde GlC* A 579.

antefenestra, space or ledge in front of window (Gasc.).

1276, 1315 (v. ambanum).

anteferre [CL], to carry in front. **b** to rank above. **c** (inf. pass.) precedence. **d** (p. ppl.) (?) aforementioned.

crucem coram illo ~ri..contulerat R. COLD. *Cuthb.* 52. **b** cuncticreator Deus..creaturis omnibus incomparabiliter ~tur GIR. *TH* I 13. **c 1362** cum reservacione, inhibicione et decreto, acceptacione et ~ri ac aliis clausulis consuetis (*Rot. Magist. Ox.*) *EHR* XV 529 (v. et. antelatio). **d 1407** plurimorum †antelate [? l. antefate] civitatis [Ebor'] mercatorum *Lit. Cant.* III 100.

†antefissus, (?) for *-fixus*, fastened in front.

conversi laici corrigiatos et ~os habeant sotulares *Cust. Cant.* 401.

antefluere, to flow onward, approach (of time).

cometa..stella, quam nonnulli existimant rusticanorum esse temporum ~ium omen ÆTHELW. IV 3.

antefossatum, moat lying in front (Gasc.).

1281 pro domibus..faciendis in ~is et aliis locis vacuis *RGasc.* II 138.

antegarda v. antewarda.

†antegenitor, ancestor.

1290 ~ores [? l. antecessores] et progenitores nostri reges Anglie (*Lit. regis*) *Ann. Lond.* 112.

antegenitus, (one) previously begotten.

1236 plus videtur posse bonum matrimonii subsequentis in ~um quam bonum matrimonii presentis in eum quem vir non genuit nec generaturus fuit GROS. *Ep.* 23 p. 83.

anteguarda v. antewarda.

antehabitus, previous.

ne infirmiores animos conturbationis ~e memoria aliquatenus moveret J. FORD *Wulf.* 101.

antehac [CL], previously.

numquam ~c locutus sum LANTFR. *Mir. Swith.* I 331D (cf. ib. 335B: ante hac); **1583** mesuagia..pro missis ibidem celebrandis ~c concessa *Pat* 1235 m. 9.

anteire [CL], to precede. **b** to excel.

s991 si michi non datur ~ire remorantem, detur utinam sine dilatione subsequi precedentem *Chr. Rams.* 100. **b** inter omnes etatis nostre reges Henricum..fama..~ire LIV. *Hen. V* 1a.

anteis v. inanteis.

antejuramentum, 'foreoath', preliminary oath of accuser.

nullum umquam ~um [AS: *foraþ*] condonetur (*Quad.*) *GAS* 327; continget ~um non dari, non frangi, per alterum fieri (*Leg. Hen.*) *Ib.* 584.

antela [cf. LL antilena], breast girth or forepeak of saddle (saddle-bow).

antena, *boga GlC* A 610; ~a, *forðgyrd* ÆLF. *Gl.*; sellarum antellas et postellas deauratas videbamus BALSH. *Ut.* 50; arculi duo, sc. antella [*gl.*: *arsun devant*] et postella, suas habea[n]t antellas [*gl.*: *peytereus*] et postellas NECKAM *Ut.* 100; **s1191** ut [equites], ..cedentes tusionibus, brachia ceteraque membra..super sellarum inclinarent antellas stupidi *Itin. Ric.* IV 19; **1229** L. de Bedeford' misit ad scaccarium..duo paria †antecarum ad sellas *LTRMem* 11 r. 1(1)*d.*; **1395** in uno freno cum ~a *Ac. Durh.* 599; ~a, *paytrelle* WW.

antelatio, precedence, priority; *cf. anteferre c.*

exorbitantes gracie, que nunc fiunt et appellantur..nunc 'perpetuum silencium', nunc 'clausula anteferri' vel '~onis', nunc 'de proprio motu Pape' PAUL. ANGL. *ASP* 1533; **1473** quacumque ~onis prerogativa muniti *Mon. Hib. & Scot.* 470a; **1529** reservatis..omnibus..dignitatibus, ..~onibus et preeminentiis..quibus..utebatur *Form. S. Andr.* I 323.

antelatus v. anteferre.

antelectus, read out before.

fateberis..non esse ~um id alii sanctorum tociens contigisse *NLA* (*Osmund*) II 250.

†anteleuce, small thistle.

10.. ~e, *smæl þistel* WW.

antella v. antela.

anteloquium, office of spokesman. **b** (?) prerogative.

consurgentes prefati v proceres eorum †~um [MS: ~ium] Roberto Plesyngton, militi prudenti, meminerunt FAVENT 14. **b 935** (12c) ego Æðelstanus..antiloquium [*altered to* antilogium] predecessorum meorum et regalium infularum non obliviscens *CS* 707.

antelucanare, to rise before dawn.

to ryse before day, ~are *CathA.*

antelucanus, preceding dawn. **b** (sb. n.) time just before dawn. **c** (sb. n. pl.) matins. **d** (sb. f.) lark.

erat hora quinta ~a W. CANT. *Mir. Thom.* VI 111. **b** maluerunt horam mutare medie noctis in ~um, ut sinaxis una cum nocte finem habeat MAP *NC* I 24 p. 37; accidit abbatem in ~o vigilantem, in lecto suo sedere *G. S. Alb.* I 103; *dawnyng of þe day*, ~um *PP.* **c** explicitis ~is ad hospicium reversa *NLA* (*Edmund*) II *app.* 628. **d** ~a, *a larke* WW.

antelupus v. antilops.

antema [ME < *anteme* < OF *antefne* < antiphonum], anthem.

1458 interessentibus missis et ~ate de nomine Jhesu coram ymagine crucifixi..cantandis *Fabr. York* 240; **1483** incipitur anthemia de Trinitate a succentore *Ib.* 211.

antememoratus, aforementioned.

†871 (13c) est..~a terra libera.. *CS* 568; Eduyno [i.e. Owen] prefati regis avo paterno ~o ANDRE *Hen. VII* 11.

antemeridianus [CL], before noon, (sb. n.) forenoon.

totum illud ~um datur ludo puerorum vacantium W. FITZST. *Thom. prol.* 13.

antemittere, to add as preface.

1424 filiali recommendacione humiliter ~missa *Conc.* III 432.

antemna [CL], sailyard. **b** halyard or cable. **c** hoisting tackle.

~a, *seglgaerd GlC* A 588; ~e, *waede Ib.* 587; antemnas.. solvens de parte rudentum ALDH. *VirgV* 2808; antenna, *segelgyrd* ÆLF. *Gl.*; laxis fastigia spumea verrunt / otius antemnis pelagi FRITH. 338; antemne gravidus stipes roburque volatus / sustinet *V. Ed. Conf.* 40v; carbasus a malo profluxerat et fluctibus jam exsaturata antennas deducebat W. CANT. *Mir. Thom.* IV 14; quendam virorum ad ~am sullevandam..per mali fastigia sursum dirigunt R. COLD. *Cuthb.* 32; **s1218** quatuor malos et totidem antempnas erexerunt in illis [cogonibus] M. PAR. *Maj.* III 37. **b** antempne sunt corde quasi 'ante amnem' posite, quarum superiores extremitates cornua dicuntur NECKAM *Ut.* 115; hee ~e, *gret cabyls*, ..hec ~is, *a hedrope* WW. **c 1449** pro antempna ad trahendos lapides in campanile *DocCOx.* 326 (cf. *Building in Eng.* 326).

antemuralis, lying in front of a wall. **b** (sb. n.) outer wall, outwork, barbican. **c** (fig.).

cum..vix ~es civitatis domos fugiendo liquissent *G. Steph.* I 62. **b** palatium regium..cum ~i et propugnaculis W. FITZS. *Thom. prol.* 5; vidi..nucem grandem in horto juxta..~ia GERV. TILB. III 11; **s1099** ut..~ibus confractis cogerent defensores retroire M. PAR. *Min.* I 139; in civitate Tholose..vidi ~ia [*gl.*: *barbycons*], ..turres, propugnacula GARL. *Dict.* 130; **s1295** fracto ~i civitatis [Burdegale] suburbium intraverunt *Flor. Hist.* III 285; **1380** pro opere..~is quod dicitur *barvicane* castri de Strivelyn *Exch. Scot.* 654; hoc ~e, *a †harchcame* [l. *barbicane*] WW. **c s1219** est Damiata..~e tocius Egypti TREVET 205; **s1455** illa municio [sc. dux Gloucestrie]..que..fuit ei [sc. regi] alter murus et eciam ~e *Reg. Whet.* I 179.

antena v. antela.

antenatio, 'esnecy', privilege of eldest coheir.

1198 salva ipsi Beatrici ~one sua *AncCh.* 109 (= *RChart.* 90a: †annuatione).

antenatus, elder, eldest. **b** older (of document).

1198 feodum..tenendum de..Olivero ut de ~o *FormA* 77; **1218** fratres sui cognoscunt se esse villanos, quorum ambo sunt ~i *Eyre Lincs & Worcs* no. 78; cum jus proprietatis descendat ad ~um propinquiorem BRACTON 3; **1287** habuit tres filias et heredes, viz. Matill[idem] ~am.. *PQW* 2a. **b 1237** habent libertates illas per cartam..que ~a est *BNB* III 203.

antenna v. antemna.

antenovissimus, penultimate.

cum crescens E productam ~am syllabam habuerit, ut merces, ..mercēdis BEDE *AM* 2359.

antepaenultimus, antepenultimate, last but two. **b** (sb. f.) antepenultimate syllable (or word accented thereon).

qui [accentus] tribus locorum limitibus clauduntur, id est ultimo, paenultimo, ~o ALDH. *PR* 112 p. 152; tertium et ~um Pascha utrumque tantum octies revertitur in eodem dicto tempore BACON VI 264; **1408** ~o die mensis Decembris *Eng. Clergy* 201; **1529** mensis..Septembris die ~o *Deeds Balliol* 127. **b** ~a accentu notatur ALDH. *PR* 117 p. 162; ~a est nomen ante duas sillabas habens a fine accentum *Ib.* 141 p. 200; dictio trisyllabica acuitur in ~a cum habet penultimam correptam BACON *Tert.* 236.

antepedale, vamp (of shoe).

hoc ~e, A. *wampe* WW.

antepedare, to buck.

equitaturus..equo insideat..neque repedanti neque ~anti [*gl.*: *trop avaunt alaunt*] sed bene ambulanti NECKAM *Ut.* 99.

antepedes, toe-cap of greaves (OF *trumelieres*).

1246 †estruvielers [l. estrumelers] cum antipeditibus *Cal. Liberate* III 30.

antepedia, vamp (of shoe).

nec debent [soleis] ~ie nove apponi..nisi nove semelle apponantur *Cust. Cant.* I 197.

antependium, curtain, altar frontal.

15.. ~ium magni altaris ex tela aurea coloris viridis *Reg. Aberd.* II 192 (cf. ib.: cum mensa ad deferendum..sacramentum cum mappula et ~io).

antepestilentialis, dating from before the plague.

1412 libri et cetere ~es cauciones, que antiquitate temporis..corrumpuntur *StatOx* 212 (cf. ib. 228: cum caucionibus ante primam pestilenciam incistatis).

antepetitus [al. div.], sought before.

s1217 cum..libertatibus ~is *Flor. Hist.* II 166 (= M. PAR. *Maj.* III 31: ante petitis).

antephalerica v. antifalarica.

anteponere [CL], to put in front (of). **b** to prefer.

nox omnis ex quo Dominus..resurrexit sequentis diei temporibus ~itur, non autem praecedentis apponitur BEDE *Wict.* 3; lux apertionis..perstrictis hujus libri summitatibus lectori diligenter ~enda est H. HUNT. *HA* V 31; nichil..invenire prevaluit quod hospitibus ~ere potuit R. COLD. *Cuthb.* 22; **s1415** nolebant permittere eorum.. balistarios accidere ad vangardiam..sed se ipsos ad honorem anteposuerunt *Plusc.* X 23. **b** gazis gloriam ~ens GIR. *EH intr.*

antepos v. antipodes.

antepositio, priority in setting.

a1280 remisi..totam libertatem quam habui..in aqua de Ribbil, sc. ~onem omnium recium *Cart. Cockersand* p. 445.

antepraedicamenta, matters preliminary to predicaments (Aristotle: *Categ.* 1–3).

confirmatur per illud Philosophi in ~is.. DUNS *Sent.* I xix 2. 1.

antepraemissa, chapter before the previous one.

per ~am, sc. quintam hujus WALLINGF. *Rect.* 7 (cf. ib.: per premissam et ~am).

anteprisa, fine for taking prise before the king.

12.. *forfeng*, id est quietus esse de ~a, in quo Londonienses cadunt qui capiunt prisam ante regem *Leg. Angl. Lond.* 1.

antequam [CL; al. div.], before (conj.): **a** (w. ind.); **b** (w. subj.).

a ~am Wido fuit saisitus de terra *DB* I 367; ~am attigit flumen illud, pertransiit unum mariscum ELMH *Hen. V* 43. **b** ante praesentis quam nosset lumina vitae ALDH. *VirgV* 308; hortabatur ut vel tunc, ~am moreretur, paenitentiam ageret BEDE *HE* V 13; ut..ante ad vitam raperetur aeternam quam..cogeretur.. *Ib.* 15; ~am rex E. dedisset illum S. Kin' reddebat regi xv li... *DB* I 3; Willelmus filius Willelmi natus est..pluribus annis ~am pater Angliam adiret W. MALM. *GR* IV 305; **1170** faciatis habere ei et suis.. omnes res suas sicut habuerunt tribus mensibus ~am exiret ab Anglia (*Lit. regis*) DICETO *YH* I 339; credo quod hoc non fiet ~am audiverimus in tuba novissima vocem archangeli (WYCL. *Ente*) *Wycl. & Ox.* 189; ~am..fluvium transnatassent, ostenderunt se Gallicani equites ELMH. *Hen. V* 44.

antera v. anthera.

anterior [LL], front (adj.), fore. **b** (w. *flator*) 'foreblower' (in tin mine). **c** (w. *glacialis*) lens of eye.

[mulier] ab ~ori parte capillos ab invicem separat LANFR. *Comment. Paul.* (1 *Cor.* xi 5) 191; a coquina properans in ~orem domum W. CANT. *Mir. Thom.* II 47; spectant emptores [equorum]..motum citatiorem, qui est.. pedibus ~oribus simul amotis et admotis W. FITZST. *Thom. prol.* 11; cum..jugum ascendunt equi, aptetur honus carri.. ~ori parti conjunctum NECKAM *Ut.* 108; anteriore tamen panis si parte locatur GARL. *Myst. Eccl.* 575; **s1286** caballus regis..tibiis ~oribus in sabulo infossatis titubavit *Plusc.* VII 32; **1316** lego..unam aulam cum selda ~ori *RR K.'s Lynn* I 75; **1349** ad sagittandam unam sagittam ad ~orem exercitum Wall' *CalIPM* IX p. 359; **1559** nostri ~oris horti *Scot. Grey Friars* II 115. **b 1332** solut' ~oribus flatoribus pro opere suo (*MinAc* 890/24) *Arch.* LXIV 156 (cf. ib. 158: *forblouweris*). **c** altera pars ~or [sc. corporis glacialis] est similis glaciei..et vocatur ~or glacialis, non habens aliud nomen proprium apud auctorem perspective BACON *Maj.* II 17 (cf. ib. 23: foramen uvee est parvum et ~us glaciale minus, quia interius est).

2 (sb. n. pl.) the fore parts. **b** the front, the van. **c** what lies ahead.

vas cavatum..acquirit, cui nates..injiciens..~ora manibus sustentabat, posteriora quasi per terram navigando trahebat AILR. *Ed. Conf.* 775D; licet ipse nobis..ad instar apis mel in ~oribus effundat, in posterioribus vero aculeum proferat AD. SCOT. *Serm.* 147. **b** nullus retro respiciendo penset..quam multos praecedat, sed indeclinabiliter in ~ora intentus sollicite consideret si.. ANSELM (*Ep.* 2) III 100; **s1144** dux impiger ad ~ora se extendens.. aggressus est expugnare castellum TORIGNI *Chr.* 148. **c** ut pia legentis devotio ad percurrenda singula promtior ad ~ora nunquam desistat anelare T. MON. *Will. prol.* p. 6; nec retro respiciens sed semper se in ~ora protendens GIR. *RG* II 1.

3 former, earlier: **a** (of dates or events); **b** (of persons).

a inaudita ~oribus saeculis strage ALDH. *Met.* 2 p. 68; **1293** fiat limitacio in narracionibus..de tempore regis Ricardi et de tempore subsequenti et non de tempore ~ori *PQW* 352b; **1321** in predicto brevi ~oris date *MGL* II 332; **c1370** anterioris facta doloris nam reboabunt (J. BRIDL.) *Pol. Poems* I 141; **s1386** in ~oribus parliamentis dictum est *Eul. Hist. Cont.* III 360; **1452** de ~oribus beneficiis tuis BEKYNTON I 268. **b s1005** sicut ~or ejusdem nominis abbas Godricus..prefuerat quondam monasterio *Croyl.* 55.

4 more advanced (in merit or esteem).

ut..qui existimabatur posterior, deinceps..caritatis flamma succensus existat ~or ALDH. *VirgP* 10; Christi.. alumnus / omnibus anterior *Id. CE* IV 5. 11.

anteriorare, a to advance (trans.). **b** to put earlier. **c** to anticipate.

a ponatur quod, facta prima distribucione per alternas animas modo predicto, anime residue preter primam ~entur per unum gradum versus primam BRADW. *CD* 122D. **b** mundus non potest ~ari nec posteriorari tempore quoad sue creacionis inicium WYCL. *Temp.* 105b. **c** propter limitacionem temporis quo voluit [diabolus] ~are suum commodum WYCL. *Ente Praed.* 176.

anterioratio, a advancement, bringing forward. **b** anticipation, hastening.

a fiat alterna distribucio animarum..secundum ordinem ..corporum..prelibatum, et fiat ~o remanencium animarum BRADW. *CD* 123A. **b** sic Christus docet per ~onem sanacionis [leprosi] quod ista ostensio sacerdotibus cessare debuit pro tempore nove legis NETTER *DAF* II 230 v.

anterioritas, priority, previous existence.

substancia hujus mundi in ejus superioritate, posterioritate et inferioritate, sive altitudine, ~ate et profunditate una est BACON V 157; nec potencia [fuit] ante actum, saltem ~ate temporali WYCL. *Log.* III 226.

†anteritus [? *for* antesitus], (?) past.

10.. ~us, *æreldo*, ..antisitus, *æryeldo* WW.

anterius, in front. **b** in the past.

in palla qua altare coopertum est et cujus pars ~ius pendet LANFR. *Const.* 173; **1245** capa..breudata gladeolis duplicibus foliis †anteriis [? l. ~ius] (*Invent. S. Paul.*) *Arch.* L 477; cappa..cum..lapidibus ~ius in parte superiori ornata ELMH. *Cant.* 99; **s1428** capam..que circumtexit suum palefridum usque ad aures ~ius *Chr. S. Alb.* 26; **1440** extendit se a predicto vico ~ius usque ad tenementum ..posterius *Cl* 290 m. 11*d*. **b** nonne.., si mundus est eternus ~ius, et species ac generacio humana similiter? BRADW. *CD* 120A.

1 antes [CL], (pl.) vine-rows. **b** vine-shoots.

antes, *oemsetinne wiingeardes GlC* A 534; antes, extremi ordines vinearum *Ib.* 626; vinitor et spoliat frondentes falcibus antes ALDH. *VirgV* 179; letum celeuma decantant vinitores cum ad extremos ~es perveniunt NECKAM *NR* II 167. **b 10..** ~es, *leaf*, ..~es, *owæstmas* WW.

2 †antes, (?) *f.l.* for *ante et.*

apparuit [S. Thomas] male habenti, ..in habitu monachili et, cum ~es retro circumduxisset, ait 'quid clamas ad me?' W. CANT. *Mir. Thom.* VI 13.

antescriptus, written before.

c1283 memorandum de allocacionibus faciendis de ~is *Cust. Battle* 48; allegacio ~a non procedit OCKHAM *Dial.* 865; **1489** lecta fuit..per ~um Stephanum *Lit. Cant.* III 314.

antesellum, front peak of saddle.

14.. ~um, A. *for asyon of the sadell* WW.

antesidēre [cf. obsidere], to besiege.

s1418 abbatiam validissimam..sitibus armiferis ~sedit ELMH. *Hen. V Cont.* 124.

antesignanus [CL], front-line soldier or standard-bearer.

s1054 reliquos fuga eripuit cum ~is W. POIT. I 31; **s1097** visis ~is optimatum venientium, nostri..prodeunt W. MALM. *GR* IV 357.

antesignatus, †~atius, standard-bearer.

prohibitus..a domino papa..ne in provincia Cantuariensi crucem ~ius ejus ferret W. FITZST. *Thom.* 48; **1245** dominus de Monteforti, qui regni vexillifer erat et ~us (*Lit. Imp.*) M. PAR. *Maj.* IV 301.

antesituatus, situated in front.

1405 in toto illo tenemento bracineo vocato *le Garlaunde on the Hoop* cum tribus shopis ~is *Cl* 254 m. 24*d*.; **1446** seisita de uno tenemento et de una shopa ~a *Cl* 296 m. 32.

antespastus v. antispastus.

antespecificatus, specified before.

1526 visitacione..per ~um vicarium generalem celebrata *Vis. Wells* 221.

antestare [CL = *surpass*], to stand in front. **b** to hold authority (as bishop).

clericus corone in medio parliamenti..predictos articulos festinanter lectitando antestetit FAVENT 15. **b** orthodoxae fidei famulitio ancillatis eisdemque ecclesiastico antistantibus proposito, ..tam instantibus quam futuris O. CANT. *Pref. Frith.* 2.

antestes v. antistes. antetresturnum v. trestornum.

antevertere [CL], to outdo.

ut non solum majores suos ~ere sed etiam..posteritatem evincere concupierit FERR. *Kinloss* 15.

antevigilia, eve of the eve.

s1338 in ~ia Annunciacionis B. Marie W. GUISB. *Cont.* 315.

antewarda [cf. avantwarda], vanguard.

c1212 ibunt..in exercitu Scocie, sc. in eundo in ~a et in redeundo in retrowarda *Fees* 351 (cf. ib. 199: in eundo in anteguarda); **1239** per serjanciam sc. eundi..in exercitu versus Scociam in antegarda *BNB* III 279; **1274** ad conducendam antegardam exercitus domini regis quosciens.. ierit in Westwalliam *IPM* 4/11 r. 3.

anthema v. antema.

anthemis [ἀνθεμίς], camomile.

camamilla, althemesis idem ut in Alexandrino athemis [v.l. ~is]..G. et A. *camamille Alph.* 28.

antheodoricon v. theodoricon.

anthera [ἀνθηρά], confection of flowers. **b** anther (of roses).

viola et antera GILB. III 131 v. 1; antera est medicina tracta de hyacinthis..et similibus *LC*. **b** ~a, sc. semen rose, valet summe GAD. 6. 2; antera dicitur flos rose; est autem quiddam quod reperitur in rosa interius *SB* 10.

anthevilus v. anculus.

anthismos [ἀνθισμός], flowery language.

antismos [*gl.*: urbanitas] abest; sit, peto, protectio praesens *V. Osw.* 401.

anthleta v. athleta. anthlia v. antlia. anthonom- v. antonom-. anthora v. antora.

anthos [ἄνθος], flower. **b** (?) flower (fig.). **c** rosemary.

~os pro quolibet flore secundum Grecos *Alph.* 9. **b 1346** patria collecta.. / hymnis insistens.. / in sulcis cantos [? l. cantus] fecit divinitus †antos (*Neville's Cross*) *Pol. Poems* I 43. **c** florum borrag' anthos salvie sicce GILB. II 121 v. 1; antos flos roris marini BACON IX 174; pliris et similia que recipiunt majoranam et ~os et conserva florum..herbe paralesis GAD. 65 v. 2; ros marinus frutex est cujus flos ~os dicitur *Alph.* 155.

anthrax, ~aca [ἄνθραξ], carbuncle (med.).

furunculus vel antrax, *angseta* ÆLF. *Gl.*; mulier..cujus majorem pedis articulum antrace consumpserant W. CANT. *Mir. Thom.* III 32; savine virtus anthrăcis vim fugat atram NECKAM *DS* VII 107; **c1300** [scabiosa] amplastrata foris necat antrăcem tribus horis *Reg. Malm.* II lvii; antrax est apostema parvum venenosum in quo colera nigra dominatur adusta aliqualiter et ideo ulcerat; et propter hoc vocatur antrax, i. faciens antrum, i. foveam; et vocatur Anglice *felon* GAD. 29 v. 1; **1319** accidit sibi..infirmitas que vocatur †autrax, Gallice *felun*, ..ad modum parvarum vesicarum rubearum (*Mir. Rob. arch. Cant.*) *Conc.* II 490; antrax, *the felon* WW.

anthropocaedus, man-slayer.

sicarii, multatores, enectores, antropocedi [*gl.*: homicide] NECKAM *Ut.* 105.

anthropologice, in human terms.

isto modo dicitur Deus ~e quiescere in se eternaliter, quia est finis ultimus non potens in aliquem extra se ad ejus indigenciam tendere WYCL. *Log.* III 218.

Anthropomorphita [Ἀνθρωπομορφίτης], heretic attributing human form to God.

cor Dei humani corporis membrum juxta ~as BEDE *1 Sam.* 579; ~ae dicti pro eo quod..Deum habere humana membra ..arbitrantur; *anthropos* enim Graece Latine 'homo' interpretatur LANFR. *Annot. Cassian.* 443B; eo tempore [c 350].. prodierunt ~e, qui lineamenta corporea ponebant in Deo R. NIGER 39; **s352** heresis ~arum M. PAR. *Maj.* I 164 (cf. ib. 458).

anthropomorphus [ἀνθρωπόμορφος], having a human form (of mandrake). **b** Anthropomorphite heretic.

hanc [mandragoram] poete vocant †antropomoros, eo quod habeat radicem forme hominis quodammodo similantem BART. ANGL. XVII 103. **b** ~i..sunt heretici qui.. contendebant Deum ab eterno habuisse talia membra materialia qualia nos habemus (TYSS.) *Ziz.* 136.

anthropospathos [cf. ἀνθρωποπαθής], attribution (to God) of human emotions.

usu quodam loquendi iracundie opera dicuntur quecunque solent..ex justitie rigore..provenire; unde et..divino quoque numini interdum ira..attribui solet, quam figuram antropospaton, hoc est 'humanam propassionem' vocant GIR. *PI* I 6; diebus istis cum sitis..circa questus intenti, presumpcione probabili credi potest, si per anthropospatos sermo fiat, Deum circa vos minorem sollicitudinem gerere R. BURY *Phil.* 6. 91; figura que antropospatos dicitur, quando scilicet humana passio Deo attribuitur, ab *antropos* 'homo' et *patos* 'passio' WYCL. *Incarn.* 115.

anthropus [ἄνθρωπος], man.

9.. antropus, *mann* WW; **940** nobis jacentibus in infimis ad antrapon [? i.e. ἀνθρώπων] salutem concessit duo inesse.. *CS* 748 (cf. ib. 714); **†974** (14c) sicut..melius..prekaraxati nobilissimi possederunt antropi *CS* 1311; **c1198** (v. archiepiscopa).

anthypophora [ἀνθυποφορά], refutation of anticipated objection.

'etsi sunt qui dicantur dii'..sola ~a infidelibus LANFR. *Comment. Paul.* (1 *Cor.* viii 5) 181; antipofora est: diceret enim quis..; huic tacite objectioni respondet NECKAM *Eccles.* 8 f. 85c.

antia, forelock.

~iae, *loccas GlC* A 572; ~iae frontis et temporum concinni calamistro crispantur ALDH. *VirgP* 58 p. 318.

antianus [It. *anziano*], senator, civic dignitary.

1288 ~i et consules populi..civitatis Bononie *AncC* LV 10; **1346** ancianos, mercatores et communitatem tam dicte civitatis [Pise] quam ville de Luk' *Cl* 178 m. 17*d*; **1441** mandamus universis et singulis..capitaneis, ~is, potestatibus.. ceterisque nostris et Imperii sacri subditis (*Lit. regis Romanorum*) BEKYNTON II 102; **1484** ~is, gubernatoribus, presidibus..ceterisque nostris fidelibus (*Lit. Imp.*) *Foed.* XII 210.

antibacchius [ἀντιβάκχειος], antibacchic foot.

antibachius vel palimbachius..contrarius bachio..[ut] nātūră, fōrtūnă ALDH. *PR* 124; ~ius ex duabus longis et brevi, temporum quinque, ut 'nātūră' BEDE *AM* 2364.

antibiblium [ἀντιβιβλίον], pledge for book.

antebiblium, pignus codicis *GlC* A 630.

antica [cf. postica], front gate (porch or hatch).

videbamus..basilicam, in qua analogium..ab ~a et postica eque distabat BALSH. *Ut.* 50; **1373** pendere quandam ~am vocatam Hepwodeshache de meremio domini (*MinAc*) *MFG*; *heke or hech of a dour*, ~a *PP*; haec ~a, A. *a porche* WW; *a yate*, janua, ..valva, ~a, postica *CathA*.

Anticanis v. Antecanis.

anticardinalis, cardinal adherent to antipope.

s1385 papa cum cardinalibus non privatis..excommunicavit..antipapam et ~es WALS. *HA* II 123; **1406** dummodo ~es..velint cum eisdem dominis de sacro collegio sic.. concordare quod ex hoc collegio sacro..sequatur juste canonica eleccio unici summi pontificis *Conc.* III 286.

anticenium v. antecenium. anticepeter v. accipiter. anticessor v. antecessor.

antichristine, in the manner of antichrist.

quanto magis †antichristive [l. ~ine] peccat qui..impedit alios..ne currat libere sermo Dei WYCL. *Chr. & Antichr.* 670.

antichristinus, ~ianus, antichristian.

quotlibet tales conclusiones subdolas, hereticas et †antichristivas [l. ~inas] innuunt in effectu WYCL. *Ver.* III 21; **1412** statuuntur quedam leges ~iane ad pecunias extorquendas *Conc.* III 343; ~inum quod non sit sacramentum quod sensus confunderet NETTER *DAF* II f. 78; ad..illum ~ianum supremum et extremum totius Christianae veritatis inimicum Crumwellum CHAUNCY *Passio* 98.

antichristus [ἀντίχριστος], the Antichrist. **b** opponent of Christ.

contra Antichristum gestant vexilla Tonantis ALDH. *VirgV* 277; Enoc..translatus esse dicitur in paradisum, unde venturus esse preconatur novissimis diebus..ad confligendum cum ~o R. NIGER 2; **1178** injungimus quatenus ..ipsos [Tolosanos] tanquam hereticos et ~i preambulos.. expellatis (*Lit. cardinalis*) *G. Hen. II* I 206; hoc factum est contra dies ~i BACON *Tert.* 67; tempore ~i electi miracula minime sunt facturi OCKHAM *Dial.* 463; hic antechristus, *ancryst* WW. **b s1292** Predicatores et Minores mali interpretatores caveant ne in hoc facto jure dici debeant ~i *Ann. Worc.* 510; Cyprianus Novacianum extra ecclesiam et inter adversarios et ~os reputavit computandum OCKHAM *Dial.* 956; videtur multis peritis probabile quod iste papa sit precipuus ~us WYCL. *Chr. & Antichr.* 671; **s1413** [J. Oldkastelle] dixit quod dominus noster papa est verus ~us WALS. *YN* 444.

antichthones [ἀντίχθονες], inhabitants of southern hemisphere.

†antictores, contra positi *GlC* A 647.

anticidum v. antidotum.

anticipabilis, pre-eminent.

tot virgo radiis et titulis anticipabilis / fit rerum minimis aut minor aut equiparabilis GOSC. *Edith* 68.

anticipare [CL], to anticipate, act before (a time). **b** to outstrip. **c** to attain or occupy prematurely. **d** to forestall, prevent. **e** (w. inf.) to make the first move, hasten.

~ant illi tempus in lege praescriptum BEDE *HE* V 21; nunc Hermes gaudet anticipare diem NECKAM *DS* I 486; **s1202** summo mane, ~antes horam canonicam, celebravimus capitulum nostrum *Chr. Evesham* 116. **b** jam dudum id facere satagerem, nisi scrupulosae interrogationes tuae ~antes festinationem meam vi quadam praeoccuparent ALDH. *Met.* 10 p. 96; ut dudum superiorem..victorem ~et *Id. VirgP* 10. **c** futura angelicae vitae celsitudo ab illaesae virginitatis sectatoribus..jam quodammodo violenter ~atur ALDH. *VirgP* 18; quarta decima luna paschalis locum prioris quartae decimae XI diebus ~at ALCUIN *Ep.* 126 p. 186; finis..intret / primus et anticipet sedem VINSAUF

PN 114. **d** ut..doloris sensum mors ~et Gir. *TH* I 13. **e 1119** rex..~avit pacem facere cum comite J. Worc. 14; in laudem..Henrici.., quem licet minime peritus laudare ~avi, aliqua tractare necessarium duxi Blakman *Hen. VI* 3.

2 to seize or encounter prematurely.

s1138 [Scoti] mulieres gravidas findebant et fetus ~atos abstrahebant H. Hunt. *HA* VIII 6; **s1335** Brandani..a vicecomite..~ati, ..videntes se..circumvallatos.., vicecomitem..cum lapidibus..occiderunt *Plusc.* IX 31; ~avit eos infelix Tresilian, qui..inter tegulas latitans reperiebatur Favent 17.

3 to arrest (AS *forfon*, conf. w. *forefon*).

si ei nolit preesse qui captale suum pro eo dedit antea, et hoc ~averit [*and he hine þonne forfehð*], perdat captale suum (*Quad.*) *GAS* 117.

anticipatio, anticipation. **b** prolepsis. **c** overtaking. **d** priority. **e** advance payment.

per ~onem, *ðorh obst GlC* P 578; his per ~onem praelibatis Bede *TR* 9; similem..prophetiam Edwardus moriens exhibuit, quam hic per ~onem dicam W. Malm. *GR* II 226; sicut antequam describatur modus formacionis Eve per ~onem dicitur Deum creasse feminam, ita per ~onem dicitur Deum masculo et femine benedixisse Ockham *Pol.* II 489. **b** quod S. Albanus protomartyr Anglorum vocatur, ..hoc omnino dici oportet interpretative et per ~onem, quia necdum Angli in Britanniam venerant Elmh. *Cant.* 182. **c** velocitatis et, ut ita dicam, ~onis..mensura nequaquam latet Bede *TR* 42. **d** ut..esset inter..episcopos mutua gratie vicissitudo et foret amplitudo prior honoris ~o ordinationis W. Malm. *GP* I 40. **e 1416** facta est ~o solucionis decime domino regi alias concesse *Reg. Cant.* III 16; nunc fiunt ~ones datarum, nunc date cardinalium conceduntur, nunc date pape Paul. Angl. *ASP* 1533.

2 (reward for) rescue (AS *forfang*, confused w. *forefang*).

de ~one [AS: *forfang*] sapientes consiliati sunt ut per totam regionem simile judicium teneatur, id est, pro homine xv nummi, pro equo tantumdem, sive ultra unum comitatum sive ultra plures... sin autem in repostaculo reperta [fuerit pecunia furata], tunc poterit census ~onis [AS: *pæt forfangfeoh*] moderatior esse (*Cons. Cnut.*) *GAS* 391.

anticipativus, anticipatory.

s1191 eodem tempore Clemens papa..diem clausit extremum, cui successit Celestinus. ..sed hec parumper ~a digressio est M. Par. *Min.* II 20.

anticipter, ~iter v. accipiter.

anticopa [cf. antapoche], countertally, foil of tally.

in fine summa generalis omnium [recepcionum] debet poni per quamdam talliam, sc. accopam et antocopam *FormMan.* 12; tallia..divisa in accopam et antocopam *Ib.* 14 (v. accopa); *countyrtaly*, ~a *PP*; *a tayle*, acopa, ~a, apoca *CathA*.

anticristivus v. antichristinus.

anticrocus, safflower (*Carthamus*).

~us est cardo habens flores similes croco *Alph.* 10.

anticrux, rival cross.

s1164 archiepiscopus Eboraci, qui..et suam e regione ~crucem sibi preferri faciebat, quasi 'pila minantia pilis' W. Fitzst. *Thom.* 48.

antictores v. antichthones. anticularius v. auricularius.

1 †anticus [? *for* antiquitus], of old.

1316 ubi fuit ~us via a domo Wydonis *Terr. Fleet* 23.

2 anticus v. antiquus. antidodum v. antidotum.

antidonum, guerdon, recompense.

~um, G. *werdun* (Neckam *Sac.*) *Med. Sci.* 363.

antidorum [cf. ἀντιδωρεά], recompense.

ad ~a teneri et vel mentaliter ac naturaliter obligari plurimum cavens Gir. *Rem.* 26; **c1219** cum naturale sit quemlibet teneri ad ~a obligatum (*AncC* II 150) *RL* I 67; **1303** memores beneficiorum..receptorum.., que ad ~a nos obligant vinculo naturali (*Lit. Ep. Lond.*) *Chr. Rams.* 380.

antidotarius, ~ium, book of antidotes.

quod in ~io majori reperitur Gilb. VI 239 v. 1; **a1350** incepturi in medicina.., quantum ad practicam, ..~um Nicholai legisse tenentur *StatOx* 41; incipit primum capitulum ~ii quem [v.l. antitodarii quod] fecit R. Bacon Bacon IX 103; **1451** volo quod..habeat unum ~ium secundum magistrum Bartholomeum de Mantiniana (*Test.*) *MunAcOx* 614.

antidotum [ἀντίδοτον], antidote, remedy for poison or disease. **b** (fig.).

†antedo, *wyrtdrenc GlC* A 602; tiriaca vel ~a quae letiferum virus auferre solent Aldh. *VirgP* 13 p. 243; **10..** ~a, *wyrtdrencas* WW; eodem quo prius occurrisset ~o perfecte reddita sanitati Ailr. *Ed. Conf.* 788b; prebet et antidotum serpens infecta veneno Neckam *DS* IX 267; dosis, i. dacio..; inde ~um quasi contra vicium alicujus egritudinis datum *Alph.* 51; *treacle*, tiriaca, antitodum *PP*. **b** huic [juveni] ~um fratres exhibuerunt monasticum *V. Osw.* 422; nunquam sera venit morbi medicina cruenti, / quolibet antidoto dummodo curet eum Nig. *SS* 1474; non desunt consolationis ~a, si rationem vis doloris admitteret P. Blois *Ep.* 167. 462a; oculus et auris divine perceperunt recreationis ~um T. Mon. *Will.* III 13; si conficis istud / antidotum verbi, facies juvenescere vultum Vinsauf *PN* 764; est ancilla Dei simplex elemosina, mortis / antitodum Gower *VC* VI 828.

2 recompense (*cf. antidorum*).

innuit antidotum fieri decursus amoris Walt. Angl. *Fab.* 41 *add.* 1; **a1350** ex mutua vicissitudine obligamur ad ~a *StatOx* 53; **1350** eidem pro..beneficiis que..nobis impendidit merito †anticida [? l. antitoda] astringimur rependere *Lit. Cant.* II 307; **1437** siqua per nos impendi queant beneficiorum antidoda Bekynton I 12.

antifalarica, portcullis.

poorte colyce, antephalerica, cecerniclum *PP*.

antifolium v. antofilus. antifon-, antifras- v. antiph-.

1 antigenus, earlier born.

†actigeni [*EE* 345. 52: ~i], †prior geni [? l. prius geniti] *GlC* A 649.

2 antigenus, of a contrary kind.

subdita primorum generum sibi symmetra non sunt, / nec simili antigena sub ratione cadunt J. Sal. *Enth. Phil.* 960.

antigodam v. anagodam.

antigrapharius, controller.

familiae illius censor erat meritissimus sive ~ius vel, ut vulgari vocabulo utor, controlator vigilantissimus Chauncy *Passio* 136.

antigraphus [ἀντιγραφεύς], scribe, secretary. **b** controller.

antigrafus, *writere* Ælf. *Sup.*; **s1139** summus illius [sc. regis] ~us [sc. Rogerus cancellarius] *G. Steph.* I 35. **b 1549** familiae nostrae ~um seu contrarotulatorem *StatOx* 342.

antile, antillia v. ancile. antilogium v. anteloquium.

antilops, ~us [ἀνθόλοψ], antelope (esp. her.). **b** Chester herald (bearing insignia of antelope).

quoddam animal vocatur ~s; ludit cum virgultis cum cornibus suis O. Cheriton *Fab.* 17; **s1415** in altero [propugnaculo pontis stat] antelupus cum armis regis circumcollatus Ad. Usk 128; **s1415** summitas columne in dextro latere effigiem antilupi erectam habuit Elmh. *Hen. V* 62; antilopis formam retinebat dextra columna *Id. Metr. Hen. V* 615; **1417** de..j signo de worstede cum j ~e ascendenti super uno bekyn *Ac. Foreign* 54 G1; **1472** cum ij antyloppis et scriptura *Test. Ebor.* III 202; **1509** due albe..quarum una cum antlappis *Cant. Coll. Ox.* I 89. **b s1415** quod..a Gallorum rege sepius rogasset, id ipsum petitum Antylopum in Galliam misit Redman *Hen. V* 38.

antilupus v. antilops.

antimonium, ~ia [*etym. dub.*], antimony (sulphide). **b** (?) clay.

~ium in minima [quantitate] Gilb. II 111. 2; ~ium est vena terre similis plumbo *SB* 12; ~ium vena est terre et assimulatur metallo precipue †scampno [v.l. stagno] *Alph.* 10. **b** est aratrum difficilis regiminis cum †~ia [*gl.*: i. dura terra] vel in terra gipsea..sit impressum Neckam *Ut.* 112.

antinomastice v. antonomastice.

antinotator, controller.

~or regiae domus Andre *Hen. VII* 106 (cf. ib. 115: Caleti ~or).

antipapa, antipope, rival pope.

s1168 obiit Guido Cremensis ~a R. Niger 171; **s1177** Johannes..qui et vocatus fuerat papa Calixtus, qui etiam tertius et ultimus hujus schismatis ~a exstiterat, degradatus est *G. Hen. II* I 185; **s1177** vicennali schismate jam cessante et tribus ~is divinitus extinctis Gir. *EH* II 20; imperatore Frederico et..~a Octaviano, schismaticis tam insignibus H. Bos. *Thom.* IV 11; **s1121** Mauricium..quem Henricus imperator ~am constituerat M. Par. *Maj.* II 149; **s1237** ~a creatus est in Grecia *Ann. Tewk.* 106; **1382** contra..Urbanum..summum pontificem Roberto ~e dampnabiliter adherere *RScot* 45b; **s1406** quod..renunciaret papatui si et quando ~a qui est et pro tempore fuerit consimiliter renunciaret Wals. *YN* 419.

antipapalis, adherent of antipope.

s1379 occisi sunt ex ~ibus v millia sive plures Wals. *HA* I 393.

antipapista, adherent of antipope.

1406 tunica Domini inconsutilis..~arum scissuram diuturnam et lamentabilem patitur *Conc.* III 303.

antiparies, breastwork.

s1304 immensa tormenta ictu unius lapidis duos ~etes de arce in vertice rupis fundatos..perforarunt *Flor. Hist.* III 319.

antiparistasis v. antiperistasis. antipasis v. antispasis. antipedes v. antepedes.

antipera [cf. antipirgium (DuC.)], screen. **b** churn.

~a, A. *a screne* WW; *a screne*, ~a *CathA*. **b** hec ~a, A. *kyrne* WW.

antiperistasis [ἀντιπερίστασις], interchange, reciprocal replacement.

Deus..non vult peccatum nisi..in quantum..valet ad exercicium bonorum, ad punicionem malorum, ad pulchritudinem universi per ~in contemplandam Bradw. *CD* 301b; [Septentrionales] calidiores sunt propter antiparistasim frigoris circumstantis Major V 20.

antipharmacon [ἀντιφάρμακον], antidote. **b** (?) *Vincetoxicum* (bot.).

hedera..~on ebrietatis est Neckam *NR* II 84. **b** recipe ..ossis de corde cervi, mummie, antifarmaci ana ʒ j Gilb. VII 357. 1.

antiphenarium v. antiphonarium.

antiphona [ἀντίφωνος; cf. antema], antiphon, anthem.

dulcibus antifŏnae pulsent concentibus aures Aldh. *CE* 3. 46; quomodo juxta ritum primitivae ecclesiae assono vocis modulamine, binis adstantibus choris, persultare responsoriis antifonisque reciprocis instruerem Eddi *Wilf.* 47 p. 98; dum nequaquam omnes..antifonas sive responsoria dicere nossent *Hist. Abb. Jarrow* 11; ambulans in circuitu..canendo antifonam: 'asparges me, Domine, ysopo' Egb. *Pont.* 36; cantent ~am de cruce, inde ~am de S. Maria *RegulC* 19; composita quattuor ~arum cantilena Herm. Arch. 32; ~e sunt quasi cantilene ad animorum recreationem divinis laudibus inserte Beleth *RDO* 25. 37; officium misse quinquepartitum est: pars prima est ~a ad introitum misse 'kyrie eleison' Gir. *GE* II 20 p. 267; secundum morem ipsius patrie [Majoris Britannie] ipsi layci ipsam ~am †qui [l. que] incipit 'ave, rex gentis angelorum' circa ignem loco benedic[i]te frequentant O. Cheriton *Par.* 145; antiphŏne signant flammas ardentis amoris Garl. *Myst. Eccl.* 205; ~a dicta quod sit 'vox reciproca' et per eam psalmus intonatus de choro ad chorum revertetur Odington 217; **1426** (v. antiphonista); cum una zona nigra texta litteris aureis continentibus †~a Flete *Westm.* 72; †antiphora, A. *evensonge* WW.

antiphonale, antiphoner, book of anthems.

1368 j ~e antiqui usus sine rubricis.., j ordinale per se et j ~e in scribendis *Invent. Norw.* 40; **1420** lego ecclesie parochiali de Hyde v m. ad empcionem unius ~is *Reg. Cant.* II 210.

1 antiphonare, to sing antiphonally.

rursus statuit ut antifonatae psalmodiae cursus restauraretur *Hist. Abb. Jarrow* 14; **s425** Celestinus..constituit ut psalmi †~ancium [? l. antiphonatim] decantarentur a choro in chorum *Eul. Hist. Chr. Brev.* 271.

2 antiphonare, antiphoner, book of anthems.

1329 recepi..unum ~e modicum cum notis, item xxxvij pecias de uno ~i sine notis (*Mun. DC Sal.*) *HMC Var. Coll.* I 357; **1506** in..ligacione..missalium et ~ium *Cant. Coll. Ox.* II 246.

antiphonarius, containing anthems. **b** (sb. m. or n.) antiphoner, book of anthems.

B. Gregorius in suo ~io et missali libro Egb. *Dial.* 16; **c1250** item liber ~ius bonus et notatus *Vis. S. Paul.* 6; libros necessarios ac ~ios *Cust. Westm.* 36. **b** quod.. nostra testantur ~ia Egb. *Dial.* 16; canentes antiphonas quae in ~io continentur *RegulC* 34; Rainaldus..septem antiphonas edidit, que in Uticensibus ~iis scripte repeiuntur Ord. Vit. III 7; ~ius certum habet initium Beleth *RDO* 59. 65; [Thomas, ob. 1236] invenit omnia necessaria ad iiij ~ia cum ipsis notariis, excepto quod fratres monasterii scripserunt ea *Chr. Evesham* 268; **1269** infra annum ~ium sciant et psalterium corde tenus *Reg. Heref.* 119; **c1316** unum †antifonium [l. antifonerium] per se *CalIMisc* II 73; **1388** ij antiphenaria *IMisc* 332/55; **1427** ad emendum duos ~ios *Mem. Ripon* 329; memoriale meum in..tropario, sequencia, ~io, ..cum novis addicionibus et notis compositis, ..relinquo Ad. Usk 56; hic antiphonerius, *a antyphonere*, ..hoc antifonarium, *a amphanere* WW.

antiphonatim, antiphonally.

[Wilfridus] respondit..se primum fuisse qui verum Pascha in Northanimbria..docuerit, qui cantus ecclesiasticos ~atim instituerit W. Malm. *GP* III 104; Celestinus [I]..constituit..ut psalmi..ante sacrificium ~im canerentur Fordun III 8.

antiphonista, leader in singing antiphon.

1426 in incepcione antiphonarum non prius presumat precentor tonare psalmum..quam ~a plenum pneuma, vel tonum saltem perfectum, cantaverit (*Const. Tynemouth*) Amund. I 213.

antiphonum, antiphora, v. antiphona.

antiphrasis [ἀντίφρασις], use of words in a contradictory sense.

~is est unius verbi ironia Bede *ST* 615; increvit.. Malvernense monasterium, quod mihi per antifrasin videtur sortitum esse vocabulum; non enim ibi *male* sed bene.. religio *vernat* W. Malm. *GP* IV 158; per antiphrasim quia somnia sepe resolvi / consuevere Nig. *SS* 1641; officium illud ..ab officiendo non per ~in sed proprie dictum Gir. *TH* II 54; tu es avis pulcherrima per antifrasin, quoniam turpissima O. Cheriton *Fab.* 55; immo per antifrasim, tanquam derisio, quando / corpore deformem Paridem.. cognomino Vinsauf *PN* 931; **1382** quid dicam de monachis sancti Benedicti, / dicti per antiphrasim, sed sunt maledicti? (*Contra Religiosos* 140) *Mon. Francisc.* I 596.

antiphrasius, having a name contrary to the reality.

illum ~ium Beatum Alcuin *Ep.* 182.

antiphrastice, by way of contradiction.

sororum triplicium [Parcarum]..que sumptis a parcendi vocabulo suis nominibus ~e ponuntur P. Blois *Ep.* 172. 467; mundus antifrastice 'mundus' nuncupatur; / nam fetet horrifice Peckham *Def. Mend.* 85.

antipodes, ~ae [ἀντίποδες], antipodes (pl.). **b** (sg.) (?) fabulous being.

neque..~arum ullatenus est fabulis accommodandus assensus BEDE *TR* 34; respondent patres suos solem apud ~as non vidisse J. SAL. *Pol.* 570C; dum strato Phebus ab axe / antipodum surgat HANV. III 282; nonne et ~es sub pedibus nostris esse dicuntur? NECKAM *NR* II 49. **b** hic antepos, hec lamea, A. *fayery* WW.

antipodotice v. antapodotice.

antipontifex, antipope, rival pope.

quis..fuisse simul alias duos, alias tres, quatuor etiam aliquando ~fices nesciat? BEKINSAU 751.

antipophora v. anthypophora.

antiptosis [ἀντίπτωσις], substitution of case (gram.); *cf. antithesis.*

inter omnes figuras antithosi frequentius atque licentius uti solet, casum pro casu ponens et precipue accusativum pro nominativo GIR. *Inv.* I 5 p. 100; illi / devia barbaries antitŏsisque placent GARL. *Hon. Vit.* 49; simul cum concepcione est antithesis, quia ponitur ibi ablativus pro nominativo BACON XV 68.

antiquare [CL], to repeal. **b** to make obsolete. **c** (pass.) to age, grow old. **d** (p. ppl.) aged, outworn, of long standing.

1549 ut..~atis semibarbaris..statutis..regiis deinceps legibus pareatis *StatOx* 342. **b** usus verborum rarescendo ~atus BALSH. *AD* 7; antiquas quasdam et tineis adesas leges, longa desuetudine ~atas MORE *Ut.* 89. **c s1178** R. de Lucy, mente revolvens..quia quod ~atur et senescit prope interitum est, ..novam edificavit ecclesiam GERV. CANT. I 277. **d** culmina ~ata tecti EDDI *Wilf.* 16; fragmenta veteris ferri de biga..vel ~ate (*sic*) suppellectilis avulsi secum deferebat MAP *NC* IV 13; quendam capellanum.. citra omnem juris ordinem..antiquo sed et ~ato more suspendit GIR. *Symb.* 8; Roma..nil habens honorabilis vetustatis preter..~atam lapidum congeriem GERV. TILB. II 17 p. 932; in bibliis ~atis BACON *Maj.* III 97; **1319** non in figmentis poeticis seu cronicis ~atis *FormOx* I 49; ~ate tonsure..parvum prefert signaculum R. BURY *Phil.* 4. 54; **c1430** ~ate societatis unico ac sincere affeccionis consocio *Reg. Whet.* II 456.

antiquarius, skilled in writing. **b** (sb. m.) scribe.

Theodosius..alimoniam..~ii scriptoris mercimonia indeptus est ALDH. *PR* 142 p. 203. **b** non..dictandi tenorem notariis excipientibus et ~iis describentibus usurpare praesumpsimus ALDH. *VirgP* 59; librarius vel bibliopola vel ~ius vel scriba, *writere* ÆLF. *Gl.*; per supradictos et per alios, quos ad hoc opus flectere poterat, ~ios..omnes libros Veteris et Novi Testamenti..Uticensium bibliothece procuravit ORD. VIT. III 3; [Radulfus, ob. 1151] primitus~iorum domum.. prudenter rexit, librorumque copiam huic ecclesie contulit *G. S. Alb.* I 106.

antique, formerly, of old.

1373 prout ~e solebant *Hal. Durh.* 122.

antiquitas [CL], antiquity, age. **b** antiquity of tenure. **c** the ancient (Classical) world. **d** ancient history.

obumbratae ~ate legis ALDH. *Met.* 2 p. 68; alia..flumina predictis..non minora et, nisi sola temporis ~ate, non secunda GIR. *TH* I 7; rex iste [Henricus I]..de modernis est, nec ei fecit auctoritatem ~as MAP *NC* V 5 p. 220; **1412** libri ..~ate temporis adeo corrumpuntur quod processu temporis ad nichilum redigentur *StatOx* 212. **b 1311** eandem ecclesiam tenuit de dicto domino J. in capite per ~atem *IPM* 26/10. **c** sacra quae..Bachanalia..nuncupari Veterum ~as verae religionis expers decreverat ALDH. *PR* 123. **d** dum per successionum seriem ~atem ecclesie temptabo suspicionibus eruere W. MALM. *Glast. pref.* 4.

1 antiquitus [CL], of old.

quod sacra Geneseos auctoritate ~us praefigurabatur ALDH. *Met.* 2. p. 68; gens Occidentalium Saxonum, qui ~us Geuissae vocabantur BEDE *HE* III 7; **c1070** sicut tempore meo juratum est eos ~us illud habuisse *Regesta* p. 120; haec [terra] ~us pro iii hidis fuit libera *DB* I 175b; **1300** sicut ipsa aqua ~us currere solebat *SelPl Forest* 119.

2 †antiquitus, ancient. **b** aged.

1300 ut ~us numerus monachorum..impleretur (*Vis. Ely*) *Camd. Misc.* XVII 14 (cf. ib. 1: ad numerum antiqum). **b** *agyd*, ~us, senectus, veteranus *PP* 7 (= ib. 802: antiquatus).

antiquus [CL], ancient, of long ago. **b** (sb. n. w. *ab* or *ex*) from of old.

cum..in ~um chaos omnia redire cogerentur ALDH. *VirgP* 29 p. 267; antiquae cum narret littera legis *Id. VirgV* 244; ~os diversarum gentium populos BEDE *TR* 37; Augustinus..recuperavit..ecclesiam quam inibi ~o Romanorum fidelium opere factam fuisse didicerat *Id. HE* I 33; miraculum memorabile et ~orum simile *Ib.* V 12; ~a tempora majori innocentia..laudabilia GIR. *TH* II 24; memor dierum ~orum WALS. *YN prol.* 4. **b s1174** castellum ab ~o constructum sed tunc temporis dirutum reedificavit DICETO *YH* I 379; **1240** inquirat..si..ab ~o ita feoffati fuerint *KRMem* 18 r. 15*d.*; **1407** cum..teneantur ab ~o..in annua pensione *Lit. Cant.* III 99; **1434** cum omnibus..commoditatibus eidem debitis et **ex** ~o consuetis *Cl* 284 m. 7*d.*; **1508** cum villanis eisdem terris..ab ~o spectantibus *Cl* 374 m. 3*d.*

2 (sb. m. pl.) the Ancients (esp. w. reference to Classical times). **b** logicians writing before the discovery of Aristotle's *Analytics* and *Topics* (*cf. GLA* II 116).

~issimi non 'vetus' sed 'veter' protulere, ut Ennius ALDH. *PR* 134; prout vel ex litteris ~orum vel ex traditione majorum..scire potui BEDE *HE* V 24; laudabili ~orum industria GIR. *TH* III *intr.* p. 138. **b** nec dedignatus sum modernorum proferre sententias, quos ~is in plerisque preferre non dubito J. SAL. *Met.* 825A (cf. GIR. *GE* II 37: de logicis disputationibus ~is et modernis earumque comparatione).

3 old established or previous: **a** (of assessments or sim.); **b** (of custom or tenure; *v. et. dominicum*); **c** (w. *ecclesia*) mother church.

a 1269 secundum ~am taxacionem (*Pat* 87 m. 23*d.*) *Val. Norw.* 80*n.*; **1296** reddendo per annum ~am firmam *Hal. Durh.* 4; **1404** proficua ~e custume lanarum *RParl.* III 528b; **1433** in contribucione ~a assignata ad fabricam magni campanilis *Ac. Durh.* 232; **a1400** faciendo servicia ~a pro predicto..cotagio (*CourtR Wilburton*) *EHR* IX 438. **b** ~a lex Anglorum fuit [AS: *hit wæs hwilum on Engla lagum*] (*Inst. Cnut.*) *GAS* 457; **1166** debeo..servicium dim. militis..de ~o tenemento a conquestu Anglie *RBExch.* 400 (cf. *EHR* VII 13); **1215** exceptis piscationibus..quas alii habent ex ~a tenura *Cl* 219a; **1275** dicunt..quod Rex Adelstanus aliquando tenuit manerium de Axemue in manu sua de ~o dominico regis *Hund.* I 63; **1276** de terris tenencium de ~o dominico corone *Ib.* 12. **c** omnes decime reddantur ~is ecclesiis [AS: *þam ealdan mynstre*] ad quas juste parrochiani pertinent (*Inst. Cnut.*) *GAS* 197 (= *Quad. ib.*: ad matrem ecclesiam).

4 inveterate (med.). **b** (w. *hostis* or sim.) the Devil.

in..pocionibus contra tussim ~am *Alph.* 138. **b** ~us humani generis grassator ALDH. *VirgP* 32 p. 271; nostram gentem..de dentibus ~i hostis eripiens BEDE *HE* II 1 p. 78; Deus qui..unicum filium tuum..de hoste ~o triumphare fecisti (*Duellum*) *GAS* 430; **1220** versucias hostis ~i *Lit. Cant.* III 26.

5 aged. **b** (compar.) senior. **c** (compar. as sb. m.) elder.

de melioribus et ~is hominibus totius comitatus *DB* I 44b; **1166** extra comitatum nisi v milites, sicut ~i testantur *RBExch.* 274; armiger antiquus, leporarius, istrio, rethor, / Thais, venator, viles numerantur ubique D. BEC. 1299; mimus..cecus et ~us effectus *Latin Stories* 127; **1412** ~i, qui..ex causa excusande libidinis..copulantur adinvicem, non vere matrimonialiter copulantur *Conc.* III 345; **1431** lego..antico servienti meo v m. *Reg. Cant.* II 439. **b c1095** in curia regis Willelmi ~ioris *Regesta* p. 137; **12..** petet dyaconus benedictionem a conservatore, si presens fuerit, vel ab ~iore episcopo, si sit absens *Conc. Scot.* II 4; **1429** domine Murielle ducisse Albanie ~iori *ExchScot* 466. **c 1228** audivit ab ~ioribus quod omnia spectant ad episcopum *Feod. Durh.* 226; **1428** ad declaracionem faciendam per ~iores de clero *Conc. Scot.* II 77.

antiscipeter v. accipiter.

†antisiastice, (?) for *antusiastice* (*cf.* οὐσία) or *antistasiastice* (*cf.* ἀντιστασιαστής).

procedat..aliquando ~e, id est contra substantiam, id est contra se ipsum GARL. *Dict.* 133.

antisigma [ἀντίσιγμα], inverted sigma (ɔ), used as a critical mark.

sciat notarius..ubi scribere debeat antisima [*gl.*: i. x] NECKAM *Ut.* 117.

antisitus v. anteritus.

antispasis [ἀντίσπασις], draining off of humours (med.).

si sanguineus est, precedat omnem rem minutio per antipasim GILB. II 118 v. 1.

antispasticus [ἀντισπαστικός], antispastic (metre).

metra principalia..choriambicum, ~um BONIF. *Met.* 585.

antispastus [ἀντίσπαστος], antispast.

antespasti..proferantur exempla: hărēnōsŭs, lăcērtōsŭs.. ALDH. *PR* 129.

antistare v. antestare.

antistes [CL], high priest. **b** bishop or archbishop.

Lupercorum bacchantum ~ites ALDH. *Ep.* 3. **b** antestis, pontifex *GlC* A 588; antistes sacrato more dicatus *Id. VirgV* 985; **724** antestiti Bonifatio Daniel *Ep. Bonif.* 23; pulsus est idem ~es a sede sui episcopatus BEDE *HE* IV 12; sic pius antistis primum Paulinus habebat ALCUIN *SSEbor.* 210; ceterum consecrationis ministerium non quasi super ~item Wicciorum sed sicut super archiepiscopum Cantuariorum..absolvit OSB. *V. Dunst.* 29; Lanfrancus, indignus ~es LANFR. *Ep.* 9; **s1095** reputans..nihil in..susceptione Romani ~itis se profecisse EADMER *HN* 79; ille Thomas qui quondam Cantuariorum ~es sed nunc jam non urbis sed orbis primas est H. Bos. *Thom.* I 1; si sis primalis antistitis officialis D. BEC. 1838; hic [episcopus] etiam ~es quasi 'ante stans' dicitur, qui populo preminere videtur; hoc etiam ab *anti*.., quod est 'contra', inde ~es quasi 'contra stans' dicitur, quasi hereticis..contrastare..cernitur GIR. *PI* I 19; ~item iterantem sacramentum baptismi OCKHAM *Pol.* I 55; **1414** cum..papa..venerabilem fratrem nostrum dominum J. K. ~item consecraverit ipsumque eidem ecclesie Menevensi..prefecerit in episcopum et pastorem *Reg. Cant.* I 15; **1440** dum..ecclesia orbata fuisset †antiste [? l. antistite] suo BEKYNTON I 28; ~es, *prelatte or byschop* WW.

Antisthenicus, disciple of Antisthenes, Cynic.

Aristoteles approbando ~os improbat Platonis ideas DUNS *Metaph.* VIII 1. 115A.

antistitium, bishopric.

ibi [Antiochie] B. Petrus primi ~ii cathedram sedit W. MALM. *GR* IV 359; **1280** quia testimonium habere ab hiis qui foris sunt antisti[ti]o est studendum PECKAM *Ep.* 119; quod hoc ~ium sit illi precibus impetrandum MORE *Ut.* 8.

antitesis, antitetis v. antiptosis, antithesis.

antithesis [ἀντίθεσις], objection (*cf. antitheton*). **b** (gram.; *cf. antiptosis*). **c** opposition, contradiction.

cum porrigerent pape literas cum multis sigillis, dixerunt: 'hee sunt †antitetes prelatorum totius Angliae contra Giraldum' GIR. *Inv.* VI 16. **b** synthesis, antithesis, conceptio, zeuma, prolemsis / gaudent grammatice subdere colla jugo NECKAM *DS* X 45; ~is, zeugma, syntaxis BACON *CSPhil.* 444. **c** consonat †architesis in amore; sciencia nescit; / ira jocatur; honor sordet; habundat egens GOWER *VC* V 45.

antithetarius, defendant bringing countercharge.

de ~io (*Quad.*) *GAS* 537 (cf. ib. 331: qui in placito se vel hominem suum distortis compellationibus [AS: *mid wiðertihtlan*] defendere presumpserit).

antithetum [ἀντίθετον], opposite.

antibachius 'contrarius bachio', sicut ~a 'contraposita' ALDH. *PR* 124.

antitodum v. antidotum. antitosis v. antiptosis.

antitypum [ἀντίτυπον], antitype.

ea..signa, symbola, typos, ~a..appellamus JEWEL *Apol.* 24.

antlappus v. antilops. antlare v. anclare.

†antlerans, (?) antlered beast.

1501 j alba..intexta aquilis aureis et ~antibus *Cant. Coll. Ox.* I 35.

antlia [ἀντλία], water-wheel (for pumping). **b** cup.

anthlia, rota auritoria *GlC* A 567; gelida cisternae limpha quam anthlia, hoc est rota hauritoria exanthlamus ALDH. *VirgP* 9; laticem.. / anthlia quem sursum solet exanthlare cisternis *Id. VirgV* 219; **10..** anthlia, *hlædhweogl* WW; *a drawynge whele*, ancla, ..*a wheylle of a drawe wele*, anclea *CathA*. **b** nomina vasorum: ..anthlia, *hnæp* ÆLF. *Gl.*

antocopa v. anticopa.

antofilus [? cf. ἄνθος, φύλλον], clove.

dyacameron facit..imbecillitati stomachi: recipe antifolii zinziberis ana ℥ v.. GILB. IV 200 v. 2 (cf. ib. 201. 1: antofol'); anchofili vel anstofili, gariofili magni idem *Alph.* 10.

antonomasia [ἀντονομασία], antonomasia: **a** use of description instead of personal name; **b** (use of general term in) special sense.

a ~ia est significatio vice nominis posita; ex accidentibus videlicet propriam significat personam BEDE *ST* 613. **b** [Pascha] per ~iam atque excellentiam vocetur solemnitas solemnitatum BELETH *RDO* 113. 119; hec..vocatur scientia experimentalis quia per ~iam utitur experientia BACON *Tert. sup.* 43.

antonomastice, by antonomasia: **a** by use of epithet as proper name; **b** by specialized use, *par excellence*; **c** (?) metaphorically; **d** as a surname.

a ita viguit [Aristoteles] ut commune nomen omnium philosophorum anthonomasice, id est excellenter, sibi proprium esse meruerit J. SAL. *Pol.* 647D; ut non archiepiscopus, non primas, sed sanctus homo ~e, id est excellenter, velut proprio nomine vocaretur *Id. V. Anselm.* 10. 1028B; 'Conanum', id est imperatorem Fredericum, qui Conanus, id est rex, dicitur..†autonomasice quia summus (*Proph. Merlin*) M. PAR. *Maj.* I 208; de te dixit propheta [*Psalm* xliv 15], 'adducentur regi virgines post eam'; signanter et antinomastice dixit eam [sc. BVM]..omnes alias precellentem J. GODARD *Ap.* 264; Christus non solum unctus est unccione materiali sed spirituali. ..ideo, si hoc nomen sit commune, tamen Christo competere potest antonomice, sc. per quandam excellenciam, et ideo appropriatur sibi tanquam proprium H. HARTLEPOOL 196 (cf. OCKHAM *Pol.* II 675; WYCL. *Incarn.* 12); 'veritas' quandoque sumitur ~e pro Deo WYCL. *Ente* 17; bonus cardinalis †automatice et per excellentiam..dici meruit CHAUNCY *Passio* 152. **b** que domus..S. Maria Rotunda vocatur, †antonomasite quidem a prima et potiori parte, cum sit omnium sanctorum ecclesia GREG. *Mir. Romae* 21; **s1238** dies Paraceves, sc. dies Veneris, que antonomasice dicitur 'Sancta' M. PAR. *Min.* II 416; **1258** quoniam ecce 'reges terre congregati sunt' [*Psalm* xlvii 5], convenerunt in unum Romanorum, Francorum et Anglorum reges, dici possunt †autonomaice 'reges terre' (*Lit. nuntii*) *Ann. Burton* 461; moralis philosophia sola dicitur †autonomatice et proprie practica BACON *Tert.* 48; isti [recti corde] dicuntur boni anthonomatice *AncrR* 5; sepe moris est scripture aliquod negare ab aliquo cui primo et principalissime seu anthonomatice non convenit OCKHAM *Dial.* 853; vos [clerici] ~e ipsa ecclesia Dei dicimini R. BURY *Phil.* 4. 48; dicitur predicamentum quod †autonomice per se et principalissime predicatur WYCL. *Ente Praed.* 12; isto modo habet Christus †autonomatice potestatem dimittendi peccata *Id. Ente* 173; maximus numerus, quem hic vocat antonomatice 'numerum' NETTER *DAF* I 45. **c** terra illa

~e est 'ignis' M. Scot. *Sol* 716. **d** s**1377** iste rex Edwardus ..dictus †autonomatice 'Gloriosus' [? l. Graciosus], quia virtute gracie..suos..predecessores..prefulgebat Ad. Mur. *Cont. A* 225; s**1377** rex iste..dictus †autonomasice 'Graciosus' propter graciam singularem qua precelluit Wals. *HA* I 327; a**1447** dominus Adam Cellerarius, dictus athonomatice 'Lyons' Amund. I *app.* 435.

antonomasticus, antonomastic.

[appellatio] ~a, quando terminus stat pro aliquo individuo cui maxime convenit nomen, ..ut, cum dicimus 'philosophus', hoc dictum intelligitur de Aristotele Bacon XV 287.

antora [? < ἀντιφθορά; (?) *infl. by* αὔθωρος, '*quick-working*'; cf. ancorum, andra], species of aconite (*Aconitum antora*). **b** 'sanicle' (? auricula).

anthora est herba quasi contra toram, i. herbam venenosam *Alph.* 10. **b** ancora i. sanicla Gilb. II 85 v. 2; anchora, i. sanicula gilba *Alph.* 11.

antos v. anthos. antra v. antrum. antrapon v. anthropus. antrax v. anthrax. antrop- v. anthrop-, Atropos.

antrorsum [cf. retrorsum], forwards.

dum intrat in eas [cavernas ventus] non revertitur retrorsum, ymo flat ~um (M. Scot. *Part.*) *Med. Sci.* 296.

antrum [CL], cave. **b** (fig.). **c** cell, chamber. **d** recess, cavity. **e** 'den' (Scot.), dingle, hollow.

per cava telluris clam serpo celerrimus antra Aldh. *Aen.* 84 (*Fons*) 1; spelunca vel specus vel ~um, *scræf* Ælf. *Sup.* **b** mortis in antra ruit Garl. *Tri. Eccl.* 102. **c** ut exitus omnes et ~a [theatri] ex uno solidoque lapide sculpta sint Greg. *Mir. Romae* 11. **d** quem Deus a nostri detrudat pectoris antro Aldh. *VirgV* 2865; spiritus internis animans dulcoribus antra / cordis amara mei Frith. 6 (cf. ib. 384: in antra cerebri); expellere de cordis ~o venenum dissensionis *V. Osw.* 449; repleto ~o [in carne], si fieri potest, ad subtilem cicatrizationem ungatur Gilb. III 174. 1; Tholosa / mittit munitos urbis ad antra viros Garl. *Tri. Eccl.* 85; dum timor exsiccat pectoris antra viri Gower *VC* I 1238. **e** **1541** rivulum descendentem per ~um sive *by den* vulgariter nuncupatum *Reg. Brechin* 229.

2 pit, ditch. **b** pitfall.

1311 terram..sicut canonici precinxerunt ~o propriis manibus *ChartR* 97 m. 4; hec ~a, *a dyke* WW. **b** c**1112** ut faciat ~a circumquaque [per] parcum ad capiendos lupos (*Ch. Hen. I*) *Regesta* 1025.

antulus v. anculus. anu- v. et. annu-.

†anubicus, chatterer, tell-tale (? *cf.* Virgil *Aen.* viii 698).

blabbe..or bewryere of cownselle, futilis, ~us, ..*discurar of cowyncel*, †ambicus *PP.*

anula [cf. anicula], old woman.

10.. ~a vel vetula, *eald wif* WW.

anulare, to invest w. a ring. **b** to fit (a dog) w. a collar. **c** to ring (a pig; *cf. anulus* 4b). **d** to hoop w. metal. **e** to emblazon w. annulets (*cf. anulus* 7).

~atum, chirothecatum et mitratum incedere Gir. *Spec.* II 16; **1388** eos [reges Anglie] attente rogantes ut placeat eis in coronacionibus suis cum predicto anulo..insignari sive ~ari (*Invent. Westm.*) *Arch.* LII 282. **b** c**1400** tercia vice [spiritus] apparuit eidem scissori..in figura canis ~ati (*Ghost Stories*) *EHR* XXXVII 415. **c** **1287** in xvj porcis ~andis, j d. ob. *Pipe Wint.* (159308) r. 7; **1355** nulli porci pergerent infra..altas stratas ~ati nec inanulati *Rec. Leic.* II 103; **1433** quod iidem tenentes ~ent et yochiant porcos suos *CourtR* 177/54 r. 18*d.*; **1511** quod nulli tenentes..permittant porcos suos ire in communi pastura nisi sint annulati et jugati *Ib.* 208/28 f. 12. **d** **1320** (v. anulus 4a); **1326** pro jugis ferro ~andis *MinAc* 1148/23; **1388** de..iij capistris ~atis *LTRAcEsch.* 10 r. 5. **e** de armis ~atis Upton 241 (*rub.*).

anularis, ring-shaped, annular.

si fiat reflexio..a superficie ovalis figure vel annularis Bacon *Tert.* 112.

2 (w. *digitus* or as sb. m.) ring finger.

medicus vel annularis, *goldfinger* Ælf. *Gl.*; **10..** ~is, *hringfinger* WW; tertius digitus..nominatur impudicus.., quartus ~is *Text. Roff.* 26 p. 40; medius digitus..super eum qui medicinalis vel annularis dicitur cecidit W. Cant. *Mir. Thom.* II 36.

1 anulatio v. anelatio.

2 anulatio, ringing (of a pig).

1445 ad porcos..racione non ~onis sive non peggacionis fodientes..imparcandum *FineR* 252 m. 12.

anulosus, ring-shaped or formed of a succession of rings. **b** (w. ref. to animals).

trachea arteria..est..~a, ut quasi cum quadam mora in anulis aer temperiem accipiat Ric. Med. *Micr. Anat.* 221; corpora que habent superficies concavas vel convexas..sunt spherica vel pyramidalia vel columnaria vel ovalia vel annulosa vel lenticularia Bacon *Maj.* II 466. **b** de animalibus ~is: ..corporum ~orum novem sunt genera; ..horum generum sunt vermes et vespe et apes et formice Gilb. VII 356 v. 1; licet partes ~i corporis inveniantur animate post decisionem Bacon XIV 112; non formidabit agiles ad predandum, / ..non colubrum annulosum J. Howd. *Cant.* 109; apis est animal multipes et breve, inter omnia animantia ~i corporis in multis obtinens principatum Upton 152.

anulus [CL], (finger) ring: **a** as ornament or object of value; **b** as badge of rank (esp. royal or episcopal); **c** as token of espousal (incl. nun's espousal to Christ); **d** used as signet; **e** sent to authenticate message.

a ista..gemmiferis digitorum ~is comi concupiscit Aldh. *VirgP* 17; c**794** melius est..bonorum operum in manibus portare lucernas quam digitos ~is ostentationis radiare Alcuin *Ep.* 34; **1130** reddit compotum de..j ~o auri et j ~o argenti *Pipe* 38; c**1186** pro hac donatione..dedit mihi..unum..~um aureum *Cart. Worc.* no. 100; **1200** cepit..pannos uxoris sue et ~os..et proprios ~os extraxit de digitis *CurR* I 255; **1224** computate..xviij ~os aureos cum smaragdinibus optimis; ..xxiij ~os cum saphiris et xv ~os cum diamandis; ..unum ~um cum grosso et bono rubeto; ..ix ~os cum gernettis..et unum ~um gemellum cum duobus lapidibus *Cl* 602ab; **1242** emi faciat..dc mercatas ~orum et firmaculorum qui consistant in opere ponderis cum pulcris lapidibus *Cl* 407; **1267** duo baculi continentes xxij ~os *CalPat* 136; **1401** pendent ibidem diversi ~i oblati per peregrinos *Ac. Durh.* 451. **b** accipe ~um pontificalis honoris ut sis fidei integritate munitus Egb. *Pont.* 3; post unctionem dedit ei [regi] archiepiscopus ~um *V. Osw.* 438; **10..** accipe ~um, signaculum videlicet sanctae fidei, soliditatem regni, augmentum potestatis *Rec. Coronation* 18; **11..** accipe regie dignitatis ~um *Ib.* 35; idem papa Anglorum regi annulum aureum in investiture signum presentavit Gir. *EH* II 5; c**1260** clerici..fibulas non ferent..nec ~os, nisi quibus competit ex officio dignitatis *Conc. Syn.* 565; **1408** in emendacione unius annuli magni pontificalis *Ac. Durh.* 401. **c** Christi.., / qui se rite subarravit cum dote fidei, / anulus et cujus sacravit membra puellae Aldh. *VirgV* 1945; rex convivii..~um sponsalitium digito extento statue eree..composuit W. Malm. *GR* II 205; c**1218** nec quisquam annulum de junco vel quacumque vili materia vel pretiosa jocando manibus innectat muliercularum ut liberius cum eis fornicetur, ne dum jocari se putat honeribus matrimonialibus se astringat *Conc. Syn.* 87; **1222** sola monialis consecrata deferat annulum et uno solo sit contenta *Ib.* 119; **1225** Alicia dicit quod revera fuit desponsata eidem Jacobo in domo sua in egritudine sua, ita quod ipse inposuit ei ~um digito *CurR* XII 705; s**1238** ~um quo se Christo subarravit vel potius desponsavit assumpsit M. Par. *Maj.* III 487; **1542** decernimus dictum D. H. ad..deliberandum dictis Agneti et Johanni ejus sponso pro suo interesse unum annulum aureum sponsalitium *Offic. S. Andr.* 143. **d** apposito naribus patientis ~o habente sigillum a Salomone monstratum W. Malm. *GR* II 169; **1399** [rex R.] annulum auri de signeto suo patenti de digito suo..extraxit et digito dicti ducis apposuit *RParl.* III 417a; **1403** dominus rex destinavit cancellario Anglie quendam ~um pro intersigno quod ipse quasdam litteras patentes..fieri faceret et consignari (*PS Warrant* 1385/5) *Great Seal* 87; **1465** lego fratri meo..annulum meum argenteum sigillatorium *MunAc Ox* II 711; **1472** custos jurisdiccionis vendicat..unum ~um signetum, cum testator nullum habeat *Fabr. York* 255. **e** **1425** per liberacionem factam Johanni..servitori domini regis per annulum regis auditoribus directum *ExchScot* 391.

2 ring, worn as a cure for cramp etc. (esp. after royal blessing). **b** worn round neck. **c** used to make the sign of the cross over invalid.

1219 petit..tres ~os aureos.., unde ostendit quod..Alicia fuit infirma..et petiit..pro Deo ut dimitteret ei ~os pro infirmitate *CurR* VIII 35; **1369** in denariis solutis pro eisdem oblacionibus reassumptis pro ~is medicinalibus inde faciendis (*KRAc* 396/11) *Rois Thaumaturges* 176; c**1462** aurum et argentum, sacris unctis manibus regum Anglie in die Parasceve divinorum tempore..tactum devote et oblatum, spasmaticos et caducos curant, quemadmodum per annulos ex dicto auro seu argento factos et digitis hujusmodi morbidorum impositos..crebro usu expertum est; que gracia reginis non confertur, cum ipse in manibus non ungantur (Fortescue *Def. Lanc.* 3) *Ib.* 178; **1554** Deus..hos ~os propitius benedicere et sanctificare digneris ..ut omnes qui eos gestabunt sint immunes.. *Conc.* IV 103. **b** demptis ~is et brevibus que causa salutis collo morientis appenderant W. Cant. *Mir. Thom.* II 39; **1221** peciit..ut saltem ~um ei dimitteret, qui erat circa collum..Alani pro eo quod oculus suus infirmus fuerat *CurR* X 214. **c** **1397** sex ~i pro infirmis signandis, cum cristallis appensis *Ac. Durh.* 445.

3 ring worn round wrist or ankle: **a** as ornament; **b** as shackle.

a portant [mulieres Saracene]..in tybiis inferius circa pedes et in brachiis circa manus ~os grossos et concavos ad instar compedum, qui sunt communiter de auro vel argento S. Sim. *Itin.* 36. **b** Benedictus homini compedibus vincto †approprians [? l. appropians] digitum in ~o ferreo inter duas compedes medio misit *Lib. Eli.* 268; **1162** pro ~is obsidum xij d. *Pipe* 37; ~is ferreis per ambas tibias constrictum *Mir. J. Bev.* A 303; **1200** inprisonaverunt eos et in ~is posuerunt *CurR* I 264.

4 metal ring: **a** for hooping a stake; **b** put in a pig's nose; **c** for hanging an altar veil; **d** for hanging a club; **e** for crozier; **f** for tilting at; **g** as handle or knocker of door (esp. w. ref. to conveyance of seisin).

a **1320** pro eisdem stakis ferrendis ad ambo extrema et eisdem anulandis circa medium cum grossis ~is ferreis *KRAc* 99/38. **b** **1366** injunctum est..quod custodiant porcos suos et ordinent quod habeant ~os in nasis suis *Hal. Durh.* 50. **c** **1449** pro velo quadragesimali capelle..una cum..factura, filo, suicione et ~is *Ac. Durh.* 276. **d** in quarum [sellarum] qualibet parte anteriori est unus ~us in quo clava ad..equitis tutamentum..ponitur S. Sim. *Itin.* 53. **e** **1404** j ~us pro baculo pastorali *Ac. Durh.* 394. **f** s**1508** hastiludia exercuit preclara ad annulum Andre *Hen. VII* 124. **g** quidam ex fratribus..annulum ostii excutiens ad sanctum Domini intromissus est (*Passio S. Thom.*) *Becket Mat.* II 287; fieri debet traditio [domus] per ostium et per haspam vel per ~um, et sic erit in possessione de toto Bracton 40; **1396** cepit ~um porte..in manu sua et tradidit dicto domino Galfrido in manu sua nomine seisine *RecogR. Chester* 69 r. 11; **1418** pro iij serruris cum clavibus et annulis emptis pro iij hostiis cancelle *Rect. Adderbury* 20.

5 link (of mail shirt).

filo in ~os lorice inducto J. Ford *Wulf.* 9 (cf. ib. 10: ~os ex ~is..explicabat).

6 part of stone cross.

1292 W. imaginatori..pro factura imaginum ad crucem de Norhamtona, virge, capitis et ~i (*KRAc* 353/1) *Manners* 120.

7 segment of tube (trachea).

canna pulmonis superior componitur ex ~is quibusdam, inferius autem ex ~is perfectis *Ps.*-Ric. *Anat.* 41.

8 annulet (her.).

sunt certa signa rotunda que non sunt solida, ut annuli; ..et qui ista signa portat..portat [e.g.] sex annulos aureos in campo rubeo, et G. sic: *il port de goules sex annulets d'ore* Bad. Aur. 132.

9 (?) measure of lampreys.

1298 in lampred[ar]um †annulo nobis ex vestra liberalitate missarum vestris precordiis presentes existimus *Reg. Carl.* I 116.

10 dancing ring.

s**1305** adduxi vos ad annulum. saltate et karolate ad melius sicut scitis Rish. 226.

1 ānus [CL], ring. **b** anus, fundament.

anus, anellus *GlC* A 608; anos, *hringas* Ælf. *Gl.* **b** ruptis extalibus ani Aldh. *VirgP* 977; non tacitos flatus sub femore proferat anus D. Bec. 1100; maledicta religio que develat anum! Map *NC* I 25 p. 49; sextum [intestinum] est et ultimum longaon vel anus, qui etiam rectum intestinum nuncupatur Ric. Med. *Micr. Anat.* 224; cibus per anum injectus..potest ad stomachum ascendere Gad. 6 v. 2.

2 ănus [CL], old woman. **b** (fig.).

anus, *ald uuif* *GlC* A 646; anum prestigiosam Adel. *QN* 58; construxit sanctimonialium cenobium.., quibus preposuit Etheldredam virginem anum W. Malm. *GP* II 78; anus..et institores gemmarum..si intromiseris, periculum pudicitie est J. Sal. *Pol.* 750D; forma senilis ănus, pars quedam corporis ānus Serlo Wilt. 2. 11; exulat.. / †anus [l. anu] cum edentula puer recens natus *Poem S. Thom.* 75. **b** anus decrepita haec est civitas..nomine Bizantium Aldh. *VirgP* 25 p. 259; plena dierum vetula, mors seculi scilicet, anus improba, litigiosa, querula P. Blois *Ep.* 27. 93B.

anxagia v. axungia.

anxiamen, expression of grief.

absentia corporalis..non sine planctuum ~mine ferenda Ad. Marsh *Ep.* 166.

anxiare [LL], **a** to constrict. **b** to straighten (fig.), impoverish. **c** to distress, harass. **d** (pr. ppl.) worried.

a coangusta et ~iata vincula circumamplectere membra non poterant Eddi *Wilf.* 38. **b** si quis..adeo ~iatus sit [AS: *swa geswenced weorðe*] amicorum penuria quod fidejussorem habere nequeat (*Cons. Cnut.*) *GAS* I 337. **c** regina duplici contritione ~iata est in anima H. Hunt. *HA* VII 3; tanto plus illa ~iabatur ut sciret *G. Ric. I* 196; occurrebant tam Judei quam Christiani, exigentes debita, turbantes et ~iantes eum Brakelond 129; **1264** dampna de quibus ~iari fuistis *Cl* 79; de..hujusmodi injuriis..supra modum †~iebamur *Meaux* II 190; cepit eum dolor intolerabilis ~iare *NLA* (*Guthlac*) II *app.* 712; **1390** pro quo dolet clerus, gemunt principes, populus ~iatur *FormOx* 192; **1412** cum..stacionarius..multiplici laborum cura et occupacionibus indies ~ietur *StatOx* 211; dumque fui memor dierum antiquorum.., ~iatus est in me spiritus meus Wals. *YN prol.* 4 (cf. *Psalm* cxlii 4). **d** ~ianti super hoc et multum conturbato abbati..consolator accessit G. Crispin *Herl.* 99; si quando ~ianti eveniret ministrantibus indignari Ad. Eyns. *Hug.* V 16.

anxiatrix v. auctionator.

anxie [CL], anxiously. **b** implacably.

divitie, / tam anxie / quas acquiris cum tormento P. Blois *Poems* 1134C; talia..mihi..diu..in animo ~ie volventi Gir. *TH intr.* p. 6; s**1273** dum mortem patris ~ius quam filii plangeret Trevet 284. **b** injurias..vindicem ad animum ~ie revocans *Id. EH* I 11; non solum hoc..~ ie ab eodem repetunt Ad. Eyns. *Hug.* IV 7.

anxietas [CL], anxiety, worry, tribulation. **b** obligation.

sopitis ac relictis curarum ~atibus Bede *HE* II 12; vidit visionem consolatoriam, quae omnem ei ~atem memoratae sollicitudinis auferret *Ib.* IV 11; tam suorum quam sui non mediocriter ~ate turbati Gir. *EH* I 22; [Christi] pietas, lex, anxietates, / pax, sindo, festum..juratio non sit D. Bec. 1434; quarumvis ~atum..superuberent inundationes Ad. Marsh *Ep.* 61; **1326** ~ates et angustias..perpessus *Lit. Cant.* III 402. **b** **809** (13c) liberas ab omnibus saecularibus ~atibus exceptis communi expeditione, pontis et arcis constructione *CS* 329.

anxietudo, severity (of disease).

1202 si..didicisset quanta esset febrium ~o *Canon. G. Sempr.* 75.

anxifer [CL], distressing.

ansiferis [*EE* 345. 42: ~is], mestificis *GlC* A 636.

anxima v. axioma.

anximonia, distress.

nulla maestitia sine consolatione, nulla ~ia sine consilio ab illo reversa est Felix *Guthl.* 45.

anxius [CL], anxious, oppressed. **b** hazardous, oppressive. **c** (? compar.).

~ius, *sorgendi GlC* A 617; germana..deplorans anxia curis Aldh. *VirgV* 2048; una tenebris / anxia nocturnis privataque lumine solis / nil videt Wulf. *Swith.* II 206; cum hoc ..pervigil et ~ius expectaret Gir. *GE* II 11; cum [moriens] propriis edibus ~ia quadam parentum et filiorum festinatione propellitur Ad. Eyns. *Hug.* V 1; mens..anxia pugnat; / pugnat enim secum Vinsauf *PN* 1750; **s1304** de morte ipsius Roberti de Broys ~ius †pertractarunt [v.l. pertractavit] *Plusc.* IX 5; ~ii de flagellis lapidum et pene desperantes de succursu habendo Elmh. *Hen. V* 30. **b s676** siquidem ille Mercios, iste Britannos ~ia clade perculerint W. Malm. *GR* I 33; Gilebertus febrium molestia..~ia pulsabatur *Canon. G. Sempr.* 75; vulneribus duris in me, dolor anxie, sevis Vinsauf *PN* 1628; **s1461** in tam ~ia necessitate periclitantem ecclesie naviculam *Croyl. Cont. B* 534. **c** nonne illa vox est ad pastores inter alias decem millia †~iores? Ad. Marsh *Ep.* 88.

anxungia v. axungia. aocatum v. advocare 14. aolagium v. oillagium.

aorasia [ἀορασία; *conf. w.* ἀκρισία], failure of vision, temporary blindness.

duo discipuli euntes in Emmaus, acrisia sublata, .. Dominum cognoverunt P. Blois *Ep.* 29. 99; inter medios hostes..quasi acroisia percussos, ad instar Elizei transierunt (*V. Gilb. Sempr.*) *MonA* VI 946 xvii; caligine videndi et non discernendi que Greco eloquio aorosia dicitur R. Cold. *Cuthb.* 13; **s1219** velut aurisia percussi, oculis apertis nihil videbant Wend. II 246; alii narrant..regem [Ealfredum] acrisia percussum *Chr. Wallingf.* 28; generatur in oculis.. visus disgregatio, quam appellat aoriziam sacra scriptura J. Godard *Ep.* 238; [didascalus] suorum percussus acrisia Netter *DAF* II 67 v.

aoristus [ἀόριστος], aorist (gram.).

loquatur..de perfectis per †loriston Garl. *Dict.* 134.

aorta [ἀορτή; *form infl. by OF variants* (*aorer, adorer,* etc.)], aorta.

[auriculam] sinistram, a qua procedit adorti, que est mater et origo omnium arteriarum Ric. Med. *Micr. Anat.* 219; alia vena egrediens a corde est illa que dicitur adorti *Ps.*-Ric. *Anat.* 41; a magna ~a arteria cavam venam subeunte D. Edw. *Anat.* B 3.

apageum v. hypogeum. apal- v. hapal-. apaphsibena v. amphisbena. apar- v. et. appar-.

aparctias [ἀπαρκτίας], north wind.

aparcias, septemtrionum ventus *GlC* A 713; †aparciate seu borea flante ad Angliam applicuit Ord. Vit. III 14.

aparine [ἀπαρίνη], cleavers, goosegrass (*Galium Aparine*).

10.. nomina herbarum: ..apasina, *clife* WW; galion.. folia habet et hastam similia apparine sed erecta *Alph.* 71; apparine Turner *Herb.* A ii v (v. aspergula).

aparitus v. apparatus. aparkare v. apparcare. apasina v. aparine. apastinata v. pastinaca. apatissamentum v. appaticiamentum.

apechiamentum [ME *apechement*; cf. impechiamentum], hindrance, interference.

1294 volens eorundem jura et libertates..sine ~o aliquo imperpetuum augmentare *Reg. Paisley* 93.

apecula v. apicula.

†apeletum [*? for* abellanetum], (?) buckthorn (*Rhamnus frangula*).

10.. de lignis: ..~um, *spracen* WW.

apell- v. et. appell-.

Apella, (type of a) Jew (*cf.* Horace: *Sat.* I v 100).

dum circumcisa pro pelle merentur Apelle / nomen Garl. *Tri. Eccl.* 112 (*cf. Id. Stella Maris* p. 115: vir Apella); **a1272** juncturarum rupto filo, / pellis circumciditur; / sic mantellus fit Apella (*De Sartoribus*) *Pol. Songs* 54.

Apellaios [Ἀπελλαῖος], Macedonian month.

vocatur apud eos [Graecos] ipse December apileos Bede *TR* 14.

apen- v. appen-.

aper [CL], boar. **b** (w. *liber*) privilege of owning boar (man.).

aper, *eobor GlC* A 670; canes..stipant latratibus aprum Aldh. *VirgV* 1649; capio cervos et apros [AS: *baras*] Ælf. *Coll.* 92; aprorum capita primo tot tanta feruntur, / ut si quodque nemus assit regionis habundans H. Avr. *Poems* 2.212; tunc temporis non celebrabantur magna convivia sine apro, et adhuc apud modernos eadem optinet consuetudo Bacon XV 53; **1257** ad capiendum in foresta regis de Dene xx apros silvestres et lx laias..contra festum Natalis Domini *Cl* 163; dicitur aper quasi 'afer', id est 'a feritate' Bad. Aur. 114; **1517** pro apre (*sic*) vj s. viij d. *Cant. Coll. Ox.* II 272. **b c1280** tenet..liberum aprum et taurum *Suff. Hund.* 6 (cf. ib. 28: libertatem tauri et apri).

apercularius v. apertularius.

aperculus, little boar.

porculus en porcum furiens et aperculus aprum / consequitur Gower *VC* I 305.

aperiamentum v. operimentum.

†aperiatio (*s. dub.*).

1295 de aperyacione x porcorum..xij s. *Comp. Worc.* I 27.

aperire [CL], to open. **b** (fig.). **c** to clear, unblock (ditches). **d** (alch.) to unlock, release from qualitative restrictions.

illa ~iens januam monasterii exivit Bede *HE* III 11; os et oculos ~uit *Ib.* IV 9; has aperit clausas iterumque has claudit apertas Wulf. *Swith. prol.* 153; **1201** in tantum ut.. oculos elevatis palpebris †~iri [? l. ~ire] non posset *Canon. G. Sempr.* 50; **1212** ceperunt clavem..et ~uerunt serruram domus regis *SelPlCrown* 65; [vena] basilica..que solet ~iri pro passione inferiorum Ric. Med. *Micr. Anat.* 227; **1438** os informacionis sinistre..adperire ausus est *EpAcOx* 167. **b a690** orthodoxiae ~ito gurgitem et sitientia rigato arva mentium Aldh. *Ep.* 5 p. 491; ut..implorarent ~iri viam inveniendi..veritatem (*V. Gilb. Sempr.*) *MonA* VI 946 xvii; utinam imperator..~ire nobis dignetur..hoc vas [peregrinationis] H. Bos. *LM* 1327; **1202** quod..via nobis hostibus resistendi potentior apperiatur *Pat* 18a; suis et ipse diebus edificare..contendat suisque posteris materialem arcam apperiat Gir. *RG. prol.* **c s1443** fossata sua perficere et inficere, claudere et ~ire prout melius sibi viderit *Croyl. Cont. B* 520. **d** per solam solutionem [corporum in mercurium] seratum ~itur propter ingressum unius nature in aliam *Correct. Alch.* 15.

2 (p. ppl.) open. **b** (of wounds) gaping. **c** (of letters) patent. **d** (of costume). **e** (of birds' feet) unwebbed. **f** (of land) unenclosed. **g** (w. *tempus*) season when land is thrown open for pasturage. **h** (sb. f.) receipt.

materia duplici palmis plasmabar apertis Aldh. *Aen.* 52 (*Candela*) 1. **b** pro ~to et hiante vulnere Bede *HE* IV 17; si inveniantur plage ~te vel brussure per ictus orbos Bracton 122. **c 1285** cum nostris litteris ~tis *RGasc* II 251; **1436** ut patet per literas domini regis ~tas *ExchScot* 677. **d 1342** nolumus prohibere quin clerici ~tis et patentibus supertunicis..uti valeant *Conc.* II 703. **e** alterum pedem unguibus armatum, ~tum et rapacem, alterum vero clausum et pacificum Gir. *TH* I 16. **f 1567** una pastura vocata lez Heath que olim jacebat ~ta et modo in separale posita est, viz. in iij clausis *Surv. Pembr.* (*Dorset*) 503. **g 1276** includit boscum suum de Inwode, ubi homines domini regis de Berton' communare solebant cum averiis suis tempore ~to *Hund.* I 175. **h** *a quytance*, acquitancia, accopa, apocha, apperta *CathA.*

3 to open (med.), loosen, dissolve. **b** (pr. ppl. as sb. n.) an aperient.

kromios..calidam et extenuatoriam habet substanciam, unde emoroydas apperit imposita *Alph.* 88; uti expedit.. rebus impedientibus reuma, ..epar et splenem ~ientibus Kymer 3. **b** emplastrationes et ~ientia Gilb. I 23 v. 1.

4 to lay bare, reveal. **b** disclose, make clear, explain. **c** (p. ppl.) open, undisguised, manifest. **d** (w. *placitum*) (?) made in open court. **e** (w. *campus*) pitched battle. **f** (p. ppl. as sb. n.) the open.

vidit ~ta Tartara Bede *HE* V 14; ~to vertice..sacram vulneribus coronam obtendit Gir. *EH* I 20; **1267** [Dominus] vultum sue pietatis ~uit (*Lit. Cardinalis Ottob.*) *EHR* XV 118. **b** his verbis..magister ~it.. Eriug. *Per.* 532B; quam [causam] cum ille incunctatus ~uisset W. Malm. *Glast.* 25 (= J. Glast. 87: †apparuisset); sic cooperta venit sententia; non aperitur / res plene Vinsauf *PN* 1536. **c** acerbiorem castigando et ~tum veritatis adversarium reddidit Bede *HE* III 25; sancti spiritus in sensu ~tissima lucescit similitudo Eriug. *Per.* 579B; *open pyfp* (id est ~tum furtum) et *æbere morð* (id est ~tum murdrum).. inemendabile est (*Quad.*) *GAS* 353; mulier quae..adulterata fuerit, et ~tum factum sit [AS: *and hit open weorðe*] (*Inst. Cnut.*) *Ib.* 349; *rán*, quod Angli dicunt ~tam rapinam quae negari non potest (*Leg. Will.*) *Ib.* 487; res ~tissima negari non potuit H. Hunt. *HA* VII 36; ~tior et lectori gratior existam *Ib.* II 40; ubi verba..statuti..sunt satis clara et ~ta Lyndw. 246*u*. **d c1248** cum..aliqua placita ~ta contra eos..fuerint emersa *BBC* (*Poole*) 201; salvis.. querelis et placitis ~tis ad libertatem suam pertinentibus *Reg. Malm.* II 179. **e s1099** in ~to liberi campo concurremus Ord. Vit. IX 15; **s1485** ut in regno suo ~to campo interficeretur *Croyl. Cont. C* 575. **f** ecce sonat in aperto vox clamantis in deserto Becket *Sim.* 177; [lepores Hibernici] semper in denso..et in operto non in ~to diffugiunt Gir. *TH* I 24; **1419** legere debet clericus in ~to warantum *MGL* I 37.

5 to initiate, inaugurate.

adeo ut relictis sive destructis fanis..~irent ecclesias Bede *HE* II 30; **1338** ordinavimus quod..sigillum..de coket in portu predicto..~iatur et extunc ~tum teneatur *RScot* 533a; **1383** quia jam treuge sunt finite et guerra est ~ta *ExchScot* 666.

aperitio v. apertio.

aperitivus, concerned w. opening up, anatomical. **b** loosening, solvent, aperient (med.). **c** (sb. n.) an aperient.

mortuorum divisio ~a Adel. *QN* 16. **b** nunc invenitur [caliditas]..liquefactiva et ~a et econverso nunc condensativa Bart. Angl. IV 1; cum medicinis diureticis ~is Bacon IX 111; per evaporacionem, sicut per medicinas ~as Gad. 27. 2; diaforesis dicitur pororum apercio, et inde diaforeticum, i. pororum apertivum, et sudor *SB* 18. **c** curatur cum ~is Gilb. II 94. 2; oleum..compositum cum quibusdam calidis ~is sicut nardinum, costinum, camomelinum Gad. 13 v. 2.

apertura v. apertura.

aperte [CL], openly, clearly.

planius et ~ius..patefacere Aldh. *Met.* 9 p. 81; ~e et lucide monstravit Bede *Pleg.* 310; sicut in libro Numerorum ~issime scribitur *Id. HE* V 21; qui murdrum ~e perpetrabit [AS: *gif open morð weorðe*] (*Quad.*) *GAS* 349; promontoria.. satis ~e sereno tempore prospici possunt Gir. *TH* I 1; longe plenius et ~ius quam alter prophetasse perhibetur *Id. IK* II 8; res ita se demonstrat aperte / ut quasi sit presens oculis Vinsauf *PN* 1272; **s1342** anime sanctorum..videbunt..visione intuitiva.., divina essencia immediate, nude et ~e eis ostendente *Meaux* III 39.

aperticius, opening.

~ius, †asperens [l. aperiens] *GlC* A 705.

apertilis, openable.

bifores..facili tractu manus ~es..quemvis intromittunt More *Ut.* 130.

apertio, (act of) opening. **b** (fig.). **c** (place of) opening, aperture, mouth.

in prima ~one sepulchri *V. Cuthb.* IV 14; vulnus, si in artariis et venis †contingerit [l. contigerit], vocatur ~o Gad. 122. 1; **s1332** precepit ut..litteras..clausas..sine ~one priori ostenderet Graystanes 46 p. 114; sicut apericio oculi *AncrR* 27; usque ad ~onem hostii celestis Rolle *IA* 189; **†1401** (recte **1404**) quod..ambassiatorem.. regis Portugalie sine apericione manticarum, valesiorum, cofrorum et fardellorum suorum transire permittatis (*Cl*) *Foed.* VIII 178 (cf. Amund. I 125); **1461** absque aliqua apparicione seu scrutinio eorundem [bonorum etc.] *RScot* 403a; **1451** de cellarum dormitorii ~onibus et clausuris *Mon. Francisc.* II 88. **b** in hujus vasis [peregrinationis] ~one H. Bos. *LM* 1327; **c1310** quia promittitur ~o, ..adhuc ad vestre pietatis januam pulsare presumo *Chr. Rams. app.* 408. **c** si in vase superius penitus integro inferius fiat ~o Adel. *QN* 58; [monachus] lapsis pedibus..subito totus in ~onem illam resupinus intravit Gir. *Spec.* II 7; **1189** debet ~o..fovee distare spatio ij pedum et dim. a terra vicini sui (*Assisa clausturarum*) *Leg. Ant. Lond. app.* 208; **s1264** ita quod ~o galonis extransverso contineat iiij pollices *Ib.* 70; **s1037** ~o vulneris..quatuor pedum et semis habens longitudinis M. Par. *Maj.* I 511 (= W. Malm. *GR* II 206: hiatus); verus odor invenitur hic in ~one narium Bacon *Maj.* II 57.

2 opening (med.), loosening. **b** clearing (of ditch). **c** throwing open (of pasture).

ex opilatione splenis accidit fastidium.., sicut ex nimia ~one accidit verolismus *Ps.*-Ric. *Anat.* 37; per..pororum ~onem Bart. Angl. IV 1. **b 1226** ex ipsius fossati vacuacione et ~one *Cl* 120b; **1301** via..deterioratur per defectum ~onis fossati *CourtR Hales* 428. **c c1230** salvo eo quod post ~onem campi intrabit cum aliis de manerio.. quando communiter intrant in dictam pasturam *Cart. Worc.* 12.

3 disclosure, revelation.

lux ~onis ex ordinata abbreviatione genita H. Hunt. *HA* V 31; in spiritualium gaudiorum ~one vox humana raucescit H. Bos. *Hom.* 1404; de vero intellectu cujuscunque contenti in lege divina..et de ~one talis intellectus per scripturas vel revelationem congregatis in concilio generali Ockham *Dial.* 827; **1438** veritatis ~o Bekynton I 23.

apertivus v. aperitivus.

apertularius [cf. DuC.], house-breaker.

an howse breker, apercularius *CathA.*

apertura [CL], (act of) opening. **b** (place of) opening, aperture. **c** (fig.).

1426 in prima appertura portarum circa quartam horam de mane *Reg. Cant.* III 176. **b** turribulum..habet in superiori parte foramina et ~as Gir. *GE* II 25; **1300** exitus et introitus..custodiantur.., ne quid mali..per hujusmodi ~as..valeat perpetrari *Vis. Ely* 18; **1308** ~is tunice et camisie sibi invicem connexis ansulis argenteis *Lib. Regal.* 11; caro tua quem fructum profert in omnibus suis aperituris [ME: *openunges*]? *AncrR* 103. **c 1358** inter omnes artes et sciencias hec est singulariter commendanda, sicut janua et ~a ad omnes alias *MunAcOx* 211.

apes v. apex, apis.

apex [CL], peak, top. **b** (doctoral) cap. **c** (fig.) summit, crowning dignity. **d** (applied to a person). **e** climax.

rotundum sperae apicem Aldh. *VirgP* 36 p. 283; apex, summitas galeae, *helmes top* Ælf. *Gl.*; crux templi quae.. sui gemina hinc et inde sustentatione mediae turris celsum apicem fulciret *V. Ed. Conf.* 49; coma primula comit / arboreos apices Vinsauf *PN* 550. **b 1352** illi qui in arte medicinali..magistralem apicem sunt adepti *StatOx* 41; **1448** doctoralem vel magistralem apicem in universitate adepti *Ib.* 272; apes, *cappe* Stanbr. *Vulg.* 8. **c** quatenus.. ad summum pontificatus apicem..perveniret Aldh. *VirgP* 43; **706** cum praesule proprio, pontificatus apice privato *Id. Ep.* 9; qui post illum regni apicem tenebat Bede *HE* III 11; summum conscendit apicem philosophiae Folcard *J. Bev.* 1; tuus usque nunc honor ad regie celsitudinis apicem..accrevit Gir. *EH* II 27; **s857** Ethelbaldus..Occidentalium Saxonum apicem crudeliter gubernavit M. Par. *Maj.* I 387; versum fuit illi [Lucifero] mane repente / in sero, bonitas in pejus, apex in abyssum Vinsauf *PN* 1452; illis qui..episcopalis apicis ministerium suscepere Ad. Marsh *Ep.* 209; **s1329** quem si papa vidisset, nunquam eum ..ad tantum apicem promovisset Ad. Mur. 61; **1421** et tanti patris apicem pastoralem conservet summus pastor *Reg. Cant.* III 71. **d** Johannes, / pontificalis apex Alcuin *SS Ebor.* 1086; **c1400** Eduardum..qui postea princeps /

Wallorum fuerat, inclitus orbis apex *Pol. Poems* I 455. **e** ut in oratione apex affectualis nullatenus subsistat quousque super linguam et spiritum in mentem conscendat Ad. Marsh *Ep.* 247 c. 14; **1319** intencionis sue devote dirigens apicem ad suprema varia miraculorum insignia *Lit. Cant.* III 399.

2 tittle (*cf. Matth.* v 18). **b** fine point (of the law), nicety.

ita regule incubantes ut nec iota unum nec apicem preter-eundum putent W. Malm. *GR* IV 336; usque ad iodim et apicum impletionem Dee *Monas pref.* p. 182. **b** Boloniam..revertar, / legales apices conciliare mihi Nig. *SS* **1202**; apices juris intelligere volens audiat codicem Justiniani.. (Neckam *Sac.*) *Med. Sci.* 375; **1297** ut..apicibus ipsius [juris] postpositis, libere procedere valeant (*Lit. Papae*) *Couch. Furness* I 553.

3 letter (of alphabet). **b** (usu. pl.) letter (epistle), writing. **c** (pl., w. *sacri* or sim.) holy scripture. **d** (?) word.

flexis litterarum apicibus in quadrata parietis pagina caraxatis Aldh. *VirgP* 21 p. 251; magnam prolixe cartule rotellam..densim apicibus conscriptam *V. Dunst. B.* 33; **1166** [littere] eo spiritu videntur esse concepte ut singula verba et fere singuli apices signis fidelibus protestentur J. Sal. *Ep.* 168. 158d; si apices capitales singulorum versuum ex ordine conjunguntur *Id. Pol.* 430a; **s1274** litteram aperiens..invenit ibi aureis apicibus..hoc inscriptum.. Wals. *HA* I 13; *a lettyr*, apex, caracter, ..littera *CathA*. **b 680** epistulares litterarum apices Aldh. *Ep.* 4 p. 481; **717** humillimis mediocritatis meae apicibus..precor Bonif. *Ep.* 9; **948** (15c) litteratoriis apicibus roboravi quod..tradidi .. *CS* 868; **1005** (12c) memorie..futurorum..veracibus litterarum apicibus insinuare curavi quod.. *CD* 714; **s1093** nunciis apicibusque directis Eadmer *HN* 49; **s1100** abbas commonitorios apices [*gl.*: scedulas] edidit et..regi direxit Ord. Vit. X 14 p. 84; quia aliorum literis..innotescit, nostris apicibus non indiget illustrari *Chr. Rams.* 16; **s1173** apices summi pontificis..recitati sunt Diceto *YH* I 369; [columba] portat adhuc apices in partes ista remotas Neckam *DS* II 703; vos stilus hic parvus reprehendit, cartula juste / castigat, gracilis crimina prodit apex Garl. *Tri. Eccl.* 58; **1327** prout in vestrarum apicibus litterarum.. vidimus contineri *Lit. Cant.* I 258; **1433** cum sacratissimos apostolice celsitudinis apices..receperimus *FormOx* 447. **c** cum ad sacratissimos evangeliorum apices venisset Aldh. *VirgP* 35 p. 277; in sacris litterarum apicibus insertum legitur *Id. Met.* 7; inter sacrorum apicum volumina Bede *HE* IV 2; ea quae sacrorum apicum attestatione..directa sunt Egb. *Dial. pref.*; cum..sacris apicibus studiosum animum applicuisset Gir. *RG* II 1; **1518** in sacris apicibus illuminatissimus erat (*Necrol. Aberd.*) *Mon. Francisc.* II 123. **d** Simfosius..enigmatum propositiones..ludibundis apicibus legitur cecinisse Aldh. *Met.* 6.

aphaeresis [ἀφαίρεσις; cf. ἄφεσις], docking of initial syllable. **b** (facet.) decapitation, killing.

que ex nemoribus..debentur, quorum non est tam firmus ..questus set est in eis ascensus et descensus, ..census dicuntur, et sic per afferesim redditus hos censeri dicunt *Dial. Scac.* I 5u. **b** mors, que per ~im cunctis aufert mortalibus caput P. Blois *Ep.* 174. 469c.

aphaltum v. asphaltum. aphatim v. affatim.

aphlopho [ἀφλοφό (Dioscorides)], mercury (bot.). **b** mercury (metal).

mercurialis, ..†calfu idem, G. *mercurie*, A. *scandany Alph.* 116 (cf. ib. 181: †thalphi, ..mercurialis idem). **b** afoho i. argentum vivum *SB* 9.

aphonia [cf. ἀσυμφωνία], discord.

habet nescio quid latentis ~ie, id est inconsonantie J. Sal. *Met.* 844a.

aphorisma [ἀφόρισμα], aphorism. **b** rule.

innumeras numeris reddunt aphorismata leges Neckam *DS* X 123; habet..arismetica aporismata, ..medicina aphorismos (*Id. Corrog.*) *Med. Sci.* 363. **b** spernunt baptisma, fidei calcant aporisma [*gl.*: doctrinam, id est regulam fidei sancte, id est decalogum; ab 'aperio' Garl. *Mor. Scol.* 547.

aphorismus [ἀφορισμός], aphorism, pithy definition or rule. **b** (w. ref. to medical writers, esp. Hippocrates).

†**974** (14c) ut meis hiis credat aforismis [v.l. mandatis] *CS* **1311**; in hac tabula plura legi, set pauca intellexi; sunt enim afforism[i], ubi fere omnia verba subaudiuntur Greg. *Mir. Romae* 33; amphorismus est sermo brevis integre rei perfectum sensum demonstrans *SB* 10. **b a1079** glosas Aforismi si omnes potes scribere, gaudeo; sin autem, eas quae sunt Graecorum aut inusitatorum nominum ne deseras admoneo Anselm (*Ep.* 60) III 174; ut precepta Christi non teneamus ad vitam eternam nec Aforismos Ypocratis ad temporalem Map *NC* I 15 p. 24; dicit Galienus in commento super hunc Amforismum Ric. Med. *Micr. Anat.* 33; hic, Ypocras, hic, Galiene tace.. / est afforismus Christi Garl. *Tri. Eccl.* 93; Johannes Damascenus in suis Amphorismis Bacon IX 18; **13..** Liber Afforismorum Viatici [Isaac Judei] (*Invent.*) *Chr. Rams. app.* 357; **c1430** nec.. tradiderat tantam medelam Ypocras..in Afforismis *Reg. Whet.* II 421.

aphrodillus v. asphodelus.

aphrodisia [cf. τὰ ἀφροδίσια], sexual maturity. **b** kind of orchis.

pueri et eunuchi facile non podagrisant, pueri autem non ante afrodisiam Gilb. VII 311 v. 1; pueri non podagrizant ante afrodisiam, i. ante tempus quo possunt spermatizare Gad. 35 v. 1; inde affrodicia, i. etas veneria *Alph.* 3. **b** orchis, quam alii..affrodisiam..dicunt, tirsim habet †bipalmen [l. bipalmem], folia similia olive *Alph.* 131.

aphronitrum [ἀφρόνιτρον], saltpetre or soda. **b** yeast.

loco ipsius [sc. alebrot] potest poni sal acrum; item et afronitrum M. Scot *Lumen* 252; sternutaciones fiant cum affonitro Gilb. II 115 v. 1; nitrum..cujus spuma affrenitum nuncupatur Bart. Angl. XVI 68; affronitruum, spuma †vitri [l. nitri] idem *SB* 9. **b** *yeste*, affronicum, fusma, spuma *CathA*.

†**aphrotum** [*cf.* Isid. *Etym.* xx 2. 29], curds.

posset, balducta, effrotum *PP*; *a possett*, affrotrum, balducta *CathA*.

apiago, balm-mint (*Melissa*). **b** (?) honeysuckle.

~o, *beowyrt* Ælf. *Gl.* **b** *honysokyl*, ~o *PP*.

apiarius [CL], bee-keeper.

10.. ~ius, *beocere* WW; **a1182** j summam mellis cum vasis qui dicuntur *costarez*..ab ~iis dicte foreste [*Marigné, Maine*] ..solvendam *Act. Hen. II* II 160.

apiaster, apiastrum [CL], balm-mint (*Melissa*). **b** an umbelliferous plant (*cf. apium*).

~rum, *biowyrt GlC* A 672; mellissa, apiasia..melago idem; herba est pigmentaria, A..*bouruurt* vel *beuurt Alph.* 115. **b** ~er, *wudumerce* Ælf. *Gl.*; **10..** ~er, *swines mearce* WW.

apica [CL < ἄποκος, sheep with no wool on belly], scabbed sheep.

scabbyd schyppe, ~a *PP*.

apicelli, (pl.) little letter.

acceptes, obsecro, ..horum ~orum tenuem congeriem.. tuae specialiter sublimitati collatam *V. Dunst. B. prol.*

apicula [CL], little bee,

thesaurum..reconditum..non solum ~arum officio sed etiam angelorum ministerio; ..pie nimirum credi potest quod..angeli per ~a[s] operati sunt Gir. *GE* I 11; hirundo ..muscarum et apecularum infestatrix Neckam *NR* I 52.

apicularius, bee-taker.

1180 de ~iis foreste Silve Drue *RScacNorm* I 27.

apidiscus v. aspidiscus.

†**apies** [? cf. abies], aspen.

10.. apies, *æps* WW.

†**apiferum,** sail-yard.

yerdrope or sayle yerde, ~um *PP*.

Apileos v. Apellaios. apina v. arma.

1 apis [CL], **apes,** bee.

apes si occidunt hominem ipsae quoque occidi debent festinanter Theod. *Pen.* II xi 6; apes ambizant vel bombizant Aldh. *PR* 131; apis vel †melle, *beo* Ælf. *Gl.*; custos apium *DB* I 180b; vasa apum *Ib.* II 136; melle suo delinit apes quod postmodo pungit *V. Merl.* 712; Ailr. *Nin.* 2 (v. argumentosus a); apes..sine pedibus nascuntur, unde et nomen suum sortiuntur Neckam *NR* II 162; ingeniosus apum labor ingenuusque laborem / humanum vincit *Id. DS* IX 223; velut apes domestica vel secundaria rimando cavernulas favi intestinas R. Cold. *Cuthb.* 107; ut apes prudentissima Ad. Eyns. *Hug.* I 13; apis est animal multipes et breve Upton 152.

2 *venter apis*, millfoil (*Achillea*).

venter apis, millefolium..A. *nosebledles Alph.* 190.

2 apis v. apium 1a.

apisci [CL], to acquire.

~itur, utilitate consequitur *GlC* A 701.

apistus [ἄπιστος], infidel.

qui super altare Christi masculum puerum ~um fecit celebrare Netter *DAF* II. 7v.

apium [CL], celery or parsley (or other umbelliferous plant). **b** alexanders (*Smyrnium olusatrum*) or Macedonian parsley (*Athamanta macedonica*). **c** water dropwort (*Oenanthe*). **d** lovage (*Ligusticum*).

apio, *merice GlC* A 673; apium, *merce* Ælf. *Gl.*; **10..** apis silvatica, *wudu merce* WW; cum vivant apio tantum et feniculo P. Blois *Ep.* 46. 134b; his apium, maratrum ponatur, petroselinum D. Bec. 2658; virtutes apii dignas reor esse relatu Neckam *DS* VII 79; apium domesticum sive ortolanum, cujus semen selinum sperma dicitur, †similis est petrosillini sed minus est; foliis, semine utitur; G. *mennache*, A. *smalache Alph.* 11; apium, A. *ache* (vel *merche*), ..hoc apium, *smalege* WW; †*chernel* [l. *chervel*], cerifolium, apium risus *PP*. **b** apium silvestrum vel montanum, petrosilinum Macedonicum idem, G. *alixaundre*, A. *stanmerche Alph.* 11; yposelinum quod alii apium agreste vocant, sive ut Latini olixatrum *Ib.* 197. **c** apium †ravinum [l. raninum] ligatum super pulsus preservat a febre Gilb. I 18 v. 1; apium ranarum sive apium rampnum crescit in pratis et habet folium rotundum aliquantulum oblongum *Alph.* 11. **d** apium levisticum, i. *loveache SB* 11.

2 a pilewort (*Ranunculus ficaria*). **b** celery-leaved crowfoot (*R. sceleratus*).

a apium emeroidarum secundum quosdam †similis est rampne, nisi quod habet guttas nigras in foliis *SB* 11; apium emeroidarum, pes corvi idem..crescit in aquis (A. appellatur *crowefet*) *Alph.* 11. **b** apium risus et pes columbinus multum valet Gilb. III 173 v. 1; apium risus, herba scelerata vel murtillana sive brutacea..; extra corpus utuntur foliis et radice, non intra, quod mortifera est *Alph.* 11; ranunculi..secundum genus ab herbariis vocatur apium risus, ab historicis herba sardonia, unde risus sardonius originem traxit; quidam putant vocari nostrati lingua *ache* Turner *Herb.* C 1.

3 (?) foxglove.

fox glove, apium, branca vulpina *CathA*.

aplanes, ~os [ἀπλανής], firmament, sphere of fixed stars.

firmamentum, quod ~os dicitur, a quibusdam etiam ultima spera vocatur Adel. *QN* 25 (cf. ib. 76: de ipso ~o); quicquid mobilis celestisque quantitatis infra ~em continetur *Id. ED* 32; fixarum circuli et ~os suprema sphera *Id. Alch.* 17n.; ~em nullius erroris participem faciunt J. Sal. *Pol.* 440b; octava [spera] stellarum fixarum, quam Greci ~on, quasi sine errore, vocant D. Morley 35; empyreo celo celum supponitur illud / quod Grecissantes aplanon esse ferunt Neckam *DS* I 230; mergit in occasum motu nunquam variato / aplanos et secum sidera mota rapit *Ib.* 624; ex motu applanes generatur motus circulorum Gilb. III 157 v. 1; applanos occurrit testante Platone planetis Garl. *Tri. Eccl.* 34.

aplaneticus, of the firmament.

nescit vulgus ~e continentie circumferentiam Adel. *QN* 49; vis..in rerum natura nulla molestior est quam ~i corporis conversio *Ib.* 74; [pars mundi] que a circulo lune usque ad ~am protenditur regionem D. Morley 15; qui [planete] dum naturali motu contra volubilitatem ~i corporis nituntur *Ib.* 21.

aplanos v. aplanes. aplauda v. apluda.

†**aplesta** [cf. aplanes], (? fixed) star.

10.. ~a, *steorra* WW.

aplestia [cf. ἀπληστία], superfluity.

~ia, crapula *GlC* A 680; **10..** ~ia, *oferfyl* WW.

apluda [CL], groats. **b** sauce, caudle.

~es vel cantalna, *hwæte gryttan* Ælf. *Gl.* **b** *gancely, sauce for gosys flesch*, applauda *PP*; hec aplauda, *a mese*, ..*a cawdelle* WW.

aplustre, ~um [CL < ἄφλαστον= *stern-post*], rudder.

~a, *geroeðro GlC* A 667; ~e, *gereðru* vel *scipgetawu* Ælf. *Gl.*; derelictum navis applustre arripiens, proram ad continentem convertit T. Mon. *Will.* VII 17; obstupescente navis rectore, qui ad ~e residebat W. Cant. *Mir. Thom.* IV 50; cimbam crucis vexillo pro velo et justi sui precibus pro amplustribus instructam *V. Har. prol.* 2; amphistrum, A. *a sterne or an helme*, ..amplustrum, *a rodyr* WW.

apocalypsari, to reveal.

to schewe, ..annunciare, apocalipsari, aporiare, enucliare *CathA*.

apocalypsis [ἀποκάλυψις], the Apocalypse of St. John. **b** (fig.).

~eos, revelationem *GlC* A 688; ut Apocalipseos animalia altrinsecus oculata Aldh. *PR* 135; imagines visionum apocalipsis B. Johannis Bede *HA* 6; **c1006** in Dominica post octavas Pasce legimus apocalipsin *Comp. Swith.* 194; Johannem..damnavit exilio in Pathmos insulam, ubi scripsit †Apochryphen R. Niger 24; **c1160** de hac veste in Apochalipse scriptum est Osb. Clar. *Ep.* 42 p. 168; proferens ex testimonio ~is solutum fuisse Sathanam post annos Domini mille (Tyss.) *Ziz.* 134; hic Apocălypsis circumcinctus patet hostis Elmh. *Metr. Hen.* V 96. **b c1350** intrat in eclipse fines ejus David ipse, / virus dans dipse frustrabitur āpocalipse (*Neville's Cross*) *Pol. Poems* I 46.

apocap- v. apocop-. apocare v. appotare.

apocatastasis [ἀποκατάστασις], return to previous position (astr.).

nec..intencio fragilitatis humane..potuit..originem mundi racione facili concipere.., presertim cum trecentum annorum major ~is per hypyrosim vel cataclysim fiat Bradw. *CD* 135e.

apocatastaticus [ἀποκαταστατικός], returning to place (astr.).

apocatasticus, adstans *GlC* A 661 (cf. ib. 169: †acatasticus).

apocha, ~e [ἀποχή], quittance, receipt (*cf. accopa*).

†apote et †antapote, G. *taile et contretaile* (Neckam *Sac.*) *Med. Sci.* 363; **1305** recepta ab eo sufficienti ~a de soluto *RGasc.* III 453; **1340** ~as de soluto..stacionario super.. librorum recepcione *FormOx* 123; **1381** potestatem..summas..recipiendi ac quietancias seu †apoccias de solucione pro summis..receptis dandi *RScot* 36b; *quytaunce*, acquitancia, apoca *PP*; **1457** ~am eis concedendi que plene liberacionis, absolucionis et quietacionis vigorem obtineat *Mon. Hib. & Scot.* 404a.

apochris v. apodixis.

apochyma [ἀπόχυμα, *conf. w.* ὑποκιστίς], coating washed off a ship, or linseed oil.

apoquinatos sive apoquistidos succus est seminis lini; secundum quosdam sordes sunt †manuum [l. navium] *Alph.* 12.

apociasticus v. apocrusticus. apocopa v. apocope.

apocopare, to dock (a word) by apocope. **b** to cut short, retrench.

c1213 papa, si rem tangimus, nomen habet a re: / quicquid habent alii, solus vult papare; /vel, si verbum Gallicum vis apocopare, / *paez, paez, dit le mot,* si vis impetrare *Ps.*-Map 38. 51 (= *Pol. Songs* 17); mos est barbarice locucionis et maxime Saxonum verba et nomina..transformare.. ~ando, ac sepius syncopando, ut pro Thoma *Tomme* sive *Tomlin,* pro Johanne *Jankin* sive *Jacke* Elmh. *Cant.* 338. **b** [amorem] sincopet hunc nec leta dies nec apōcopet atra (R. Partes) *Spec.* XII 228; ante tamen quam sic āpocopata foret [cauda] Nig. *SS* 86 (cf. ib. 1709); nervi succisus apōcopat usum Hanv. IX 387; non sua terra dolis āpocopanda foret Garl. *Tri. Eccl.* 53; plures sua jura recidunt, / āpocapata novo que quasi jure silent Gower *VC* IV 354; ~antes immensitatem magnitudinis infinite Netter *DAF* I 52; ut declinantem vitam tuam jam iracundie ac invidie veneno apocupare..nitaris Chaundler *Laud.* 104.

apocopatio, cutting short, retrenchment.

c1430 cum per nostri apocapacionem juris ad flagella virgam juris erigerent *Reg. Whet.* II 469.

apocope, ~a [ἀποκοπή], apocope, docking of final syllable. **b** cutting short.

cum dictum est quod vocalis non aspiratur a parte post, non est instantia in hujusmodi interjectionibus indignandi, 'vah', 'ah'..; nam ~a facta extreme vocali †cui [? *omit*] additur aspiratio, unde perfecta est vox '*vah*[*a*]', '*aha*' Bacon *CSPhil* 510; in omnibus talibus ~e et syncope quasi apponuntur epenthesis et paragoge Elmh. *Cant.* 338; **s1423** absque syllabe syncopa vel diccionis ~a, tota stabit integra vestre clausula libertatis Amund. I 145. **b** decaudat fraus minuendo / fena per āpocapen Gower *VC* V 820.

2 receipt (? *cf. apoche*).

1516 scripsit..te misisse litteris episcopi inclusam ~en quae tibi solutam [pecuniam] declararet (More) *Ep. Erasmi* II 424.

apocrif- v. apocryph-.

apocrisiarius [ἀποκρισιάριος], nuncio, (papal) envoy. **b** chancellor. **c** (?) sacristan.

Constantinopolim ~ius ab apostolica sede directus Bede *HE* II 1 p. 75; **991** accersivi quendam apocrisarium nostrum Leonem..et misi eum illuc cum litteris nostris exhortatoriis (*Lit. Papae*) *Mem. Dunstan* 397 (= W. Malm. *GR* II 166: apocrisiarium); **s644** Constantinopolitanus episcopus.. †apocrypharios Rome, qui ad ejus correpcionem missi fuerant, ..verberibus affecit *Eul. Hist.* I 219; **1438** Romeorum imperator una cum Constantinopolitano patriarcha et aliarum patriarchalium sedium ~iis Bekynton II 32. **b** obtinuit..novi regis constitui cancellarius; et tantum quidem principem talis ~ius optime decuit *V. Thom. B* 5; huic [episcopo]..annulus quasi †ypocrifario, id est secretorum sigillatori, traditur Gir. *PI* I 19; *a chawnceler,* cancellarius, secretarius, †apocripharius *CathA.* **c** apocrisarius Brunstanus nomine..ad sancti mausoleum accedit *NLA* (*Edmund*) II *app.* 609.

1 †apocrisis [? cf. ἐπίχρυσος], gilding.

a giltynge, ~is, deauracio *CathA.*

2 †apocrisis [? ἀπόκρουσις *conf. w.* ἀπόκρυψις], repulsion or concealment.

~is, depulsio, absconsio *GlC* A 690.

apocrofus v. apocryphus 1c.

apocrusticum [ἀποκρουστικόν], repellent (med.).

capite raso apponuntur ~a ad repercutiendum fumum ascendentem Gilb. II 102. 2; †apociasticum, i. repercuss[iv]um *Alph.* 13*n.*

apocryphare, to pronounce uncanonical.

si licet pape dispensare contra Apostolum, tunc licet dispensare quod omnes epistole sue non sunt autentice, quia auctoritate pape canonisantur et apocrifantur libri de Biblia Wycl. *Civ. Dom.* III 330.

apocryphe v. apocalypsis.

apocryphus [ἀπόκρυφος], apocryphal, uncanonical (of professed scriptures). **b** unauthentic, spurious. **c** (of a person). **d** (?) cryptic, w. a hidden meaning.

cum in decretis Romanorum pontificum sacrisque canonibus ~ae scripturae nominatim damnatae sunt Lanfr. *Corp. & Sang.* 435D; si dicatur quod hi libri [Esdras et Liber XII Patriarcharum] sunt ~i, id est de quorum auctoribus non est certum, hoc non tollit veritatem Bacon *Maj.* II 391; liber ille [Enoch] reputatus est ~us, nec ecclesia eum recipit in canonem scripturarum (Kyn.) *Ziz.* 5; nil obest quedam ~a esse eque vera sicut scriptura nostra canonica (Wycl. *v. Kyn.*) *Ib.* 455. **b 1068** kartula que apocrifas quaslibet vel anteriores..irritas faciat esse *Land.-Ch.* 433 (= *Regesta* 23); hos Anne trinube assertores, velut aliquorum ~orum deliramenta sectantes, omittamus H. Bos. *Ep.* 1. 1418B; cum passiones vel conversationes miraculave sanctorum leguntur, fictitia vel apocrifa ab imperitis et incredulis esse dicuntur Gerv. Cant. I 17; quoniam non sub certi auctoris nomine liber editus est, merito dicitur esse apocriphus Gir. *Catal. Brevior* I p. 422; quia hii libri sunt apocrifi, ergo non potest aliquid probari per eos Bacon III 282; solent de isto Offa multa narrari que ..relinquimus pro incertis et apocriphis *Chr. Wallingf.* 11. **c 1382** omnia solvebat / que Petrus sic apocrofus in scholis tangebat (*Contra Religiosos* 274) *Mon. Francisc.* I 600. **d** apocrifa, occulta *GlC* A 689; Dominus narrat eam [historiam] tamquam parabolicam sive apocrifam Wycl. *Ver.* I 83.

2 (sb. n. pl. or f. s.) Apocrypha (of scripture).

apocriforum naenias..nequaquam catholica receptat ecclesia Aldh. *VirgP* 54; **10..** apocrifa, *dyrngewrita* WW; quicquid neutericis confinxit apocrifa biblis Frith. *Wilf.* 1210; **1396** †Apocrisa Esdre *Meaux app.* III xcv.

apocupare v. apocopare. apocus v. abacus. apodentium v. apodyterium. apodiare v. appodiare.

apodictice, demonstratively.

a philosophis jam pridem multipliciter et etiam ~e esse comprobatum H. Bos. *LM* 1357.

apodicticus [ἀποδεικτικός], demonstrative. **b** (sb. f.) logical demonstration.

pereuntque mali sophismata civis; / ..additur atque bonis virtus apodictica victrix Frith. 1296; numquid Aristotelem de circuli quadratura syllogismus ~con (*sic*) latuisset si..? R. Bury *Phil.* 7. 111. **b** dialecticam et ~am, quam nos demonstrativam dicimus, precedentia docent J. Sal. *Met.* 928C; [Aristoteles] ~am et dialecticam restricto vocabulo..scripsit Neckam *NR* II 173.

apodixa [cf. ἀπόδειξις and (?) ἀποδοχή], (certificate of) receipt.

1237 de predictis xv m marcarum presentem ~am fieri fecimus sigillo majestatis nostre munitam (*Instr. Imp.*) *KRMem* 15 r. 24*d.*; **1454** apodissis super singulis summis in singulis capsis repertis, manibus eorundem..subscriptis aut subsignatis *Mem. Ripon* 302.

apodixis [ἀπόδειξις], demonstration (log. or geom., esp. w. ref. to Aristotle's *Posterior Analytics*). **b** demonstration, proof. **c** power.

hic error sublatus est de medio per beneficium ~eos; docet enim ~is Aristotelica quatuor esse genera questionum Neckam *NR* II 173; est autem logice pars tentativa, .. / pars †apochris [? l. apodixis;] eam consummat Analysis illa / Posterior *Id. DS* X 65; audiat..Cathegorias Aristotilis ..et Priores Analetichos et Apodoxim ejusdem (*Id. Sac.*) *Med. Sci.* 373; commentariorum in iiij libros ~ium Euclidis Ferr. *Kinloss* 46. **b** ~en, fantasia vel ostentatio *GlC* A 660; ~es exemplum, probatio *Ib.* 668; quidam hirsutus de Barbarie..~en medicinalis peritie super desperatum juvenem exercere cepit Ord. Vit. XI 9 p. 197; *a provynge,* ~is, experimentum, ..*a schewynge,* ~is, ostensio *CathA.* **c** *a powere,* ~is [v.l. apodoxis], brachium, dicio, facultas, ..*a vertew,* virtus, ..apodoxis, mores *Ib.*

apodyterium [ἀποδυτήριον], disrobing room, drying room.

†apolitarium, ubi ponuntur res †labentium [l. lavantium] *GlC* A 669; ~ium, *baðiendra manna hus,* i. domus quo vestimenta balneantium ponuntur, ..apoditerium, *breawern* Ælf. *Gl.*; †apodentio [v.l. apodeuterio] haustra per vallem mediam aquam administrabant [*gl.*: locus ubi vestes pendent ad desiccandum, *lavenderie*] Balsh. *Ut.* 50.

apof- v. apoph-.

apollinaris [CL = hyoscamus], mandrake. **b** foxglove.

apolinaris, mandragora idem *SB* 11. **b 10..** ~is *glofwyrt* WW.

apollogium v. apologia.

apologeticus [ἀπολογητικός], defensive, justificatory. **b** (sb. m. or n.) defence, apologia.

apologitica verborum veritate Aldh. *VirgP* 32 p. 274; ferrato apologiticae defensionis clipeo *Ib.* 44; **796** accepi litteras..apollogiticam tenentes rationem Alcuin *Ep.* 82; **10..** apologitico, *aladiendre* WW; nec de fuga hac opus est sermonem ~um texere H. Bos. *Thom.* IV 1. **b** cogente illo evangelistae testimonio, meo videlicet ~o O. Cant. *Pref. Frith.* 34; ~us, *beladung* Ælf. *Sup.*; **1166** spero non esse opus nunc..allegare metus argumenta et fuge mee ~um scribere (H. Bos. *Ep.*) *Becket Mat.* V 289; **s172** Mellitus.. imperatori pro Christianis ~um tradidit M. Par. *Maj.* I 127; **1390** Bernardus..ad milites Templi;..~us ejusdem (*Invent.*) *Meaux* III *app.* xci; **14..** tractatus Bernardi..et ~um ejusdem (*Cart. Reading*) *EHR* III 122.

apologia, ~ium [ἀπολογία], defence, apologia.

680 se..tali excusationis ~ia defendentes Aldh. *Ep.* 4 p. 482; **c695** (12c) absque ulla excusationis apollogio *CS* 89; non pro fuga hac ~ia necessaria H. Bos. *Thom.* IV 1; B. Ambrosius in ~ia David Capgr. *Hen.* 54.

apologicum, fable.

dum de leone loquor, occurrit mihi illud ~um Neckam *NR* II 148.

apologiticus v. apologeticus.

apologos [CL < ἀπόλογος], story, fable.

nec ~os refugit aut narrationes aut quecunque spectacula, dum virtutis..habeant instrumentum J. Sal. *Pol.* 406C; refert in ~o quodam Apuleius Neckam *NR* II 126.

apomel [ἀπόμελι], honey water.

~mel, i. aqua frigida in qua favus mellis abluitur *Alph.* 12.

aponeurosis [ἀπονεύρωσις], tendon.

subtenditur his [musculis] ~is sive potius membrana quaedam spissa et tenax quam aliqui falso peritonaeum appellant D. Edw. *Anat.* A 3v.

apopempeus v. apopompaeus.

apophaticus [ἀποφατικός], negative, (sb. f.) negation.

ut omnia quae de eo [sc. Deo] praedicantur per catafaticam eum esse negemus per apofaticam, id est negationem Eriug. *Per.* 522B.

apophlegmaticus, purgative of phlegm.

[dicitur] apofleumaticus ab *a* quod est 'sine' et *fleuma,* quasi deponens fleuma *Alph.* 13.

apophlegmatisma, ~us [ἀποφλεγματισμός], purgation of phlegm.

fiat..apofl[egm]atisma, quod sic fit.. Gilb. II 100. 1; apoflemnatismus dicitur esse omne quod per os vel per nares flema [v.l. fleuma] deponit a capite, sive fit [v.l. sit] gargarizacio sive masticacio sive fricacio interioris oris sive capud purgamentum [v.l. caputpurgium] per nares immissum *Alph.* 13 (cf. ib. 171: sinape..apoflegmatismis utile est).

apophoresis [ἀποφόρησις], draining off (of blood).

flebotomatur longa incisione per apoforesim Gilb. I 45 v. 1.

apophoreticus, expressive of conquest.

Rogerius in gladio suo inscribi fecit id triumphale et apoforeticum: 'Appulus et Calaber, Siculus mihi servit et Afer' Gerv. Tilb. III 19 p. 943.

apophoretum [ἀποφόρητον], fruit-dish, punnet.

mala..in ~is allata Balsh. *Ut.* 48.

apophthegma [ἀπόφθεγμα], pithy saying, apophthegm.

illud cujusdam sapientis ~a, 'nihil est ex omni parte beatum' Chauncy *Passio* 138.

apoplexia [ἀποπληξία], apoplexy, stroke.

10.. ~ia, *færdeap* WW; per totum corpus ~ia gravi tactus Ketel *Mir. J. Bev.* 279; que sanitas tuta esse poterit a furtivo ingressu ~ie? Neckam *NR* II 155; quando strangulatio hunc intercipit spiritum vel ~ia, est suffocatio Alf. Angl. *Cor* 3; in ~ia, in qua superflua humiditas sic occupat omnes ventriculos cerebri quod non permittit.. spiritum animalem..suas peragere actiones Bart. Angl. IV 4; epilempsia..a quibusdam ~ia parva vocatur Gilb. II 109. 1 (cf. ib. III 151 v. 1: in appoplesia et paralisi); ~ia vera est que fit ex opilacione non integra ventriculorum non principalium cerebri; non vera est que fit ex eorum constriccione Gad. 60 v. 2; ~ia, i. subita effusio sanguinis que suffocat *SB* 12.

apopompaeus [ἀποπομπαῖος], averter of evil (as divine title).

mox Apopempeo grates persolvere summo / accelerant Frith. 1388.

apoquinatos, ~quistidos v. apochyma. aporatio v. aporiatio.

aporema [ἀπόρημα], contradictory argument.

est..aporisma syllogismus dialecticus contradictionis J. Sal. *Met.* 913B.

1 aporia [ἀπορία], **a** doubt. **b** annoyance, difficulty.

a 10.. apporia, *inca* WW. **b** acerbae cervicositatis ~ias ..ambrosio dictionalitatis collemate indulcabo O. Cant. *Pref. Frith.* 43; pedestri accessu despectos risu et apporia afficiebat Gosc. *Aug. Min.* 745; *an hevynes,* ~ia, ..molestia, ..*a noye,* angor, angustia, ..~ia, ..*a travelle,* labor, ..vexamen, †operia [v.l. ~ia] *CathA.*

2 aporia v. aporrhoea.

1 aporiare, to impoverish, ruin. **b** to despoil (of). **c** (?) to disfigure or wound (? *cf. aporrhoea*).

~iamur, *biað preade GlC* A 671; ~iamur, *we synd bereafod* Ælf. *Sup.*; ~ior nunc..sed tunc angelos judicabo *Trop. Wint.* 28; '~iamur sed non destituimur': *poros* Graece, 'dives' Latine; *aporos,* id est 'pauper', inde '~iamur' Lanfr. *Comment. Paul.* (2 *Cor.* iv 8) 228; **1197** ~iati sed non destituti (*Lit. Archiep. Rotomag.*) Diceto *YH* II 157; nimiam egestatem in itinere pertulerunt et pene usque ad mortem ~iati sunt Ord. Vit. X 11 p. 69; [paupertas] prima beatitudinum, ..quatenus hic ~iata ditetur in Patria W. Cant. *Mir. Thom.* II 78; fratres proprios fraudulenter apporians Gir. *Inv.* VI 23 p. 224; **s1070** rex..omnia Anglorum monasteria.., auro spolians et argento, insatiabiliter apporriavit M. Par. *Min.* I 13; **c1257** monachos.. sumptuosis expensis ~iatos *Mon. Francisc.* II *app.* 271; **s1379** ferunt quidam eundem J. ..pauperes multipliciter offendisse, apporiasse, vexasse *V. Ric. II* 16; **s1380** eo quod totiens non tam apporiassent quam despoliassent patriam diversis taxis Wals. *HA* I 445; *to make †pure* [v.l. *pore*], ~iare, depauperare *CathA.* **b 1166** cum ad traiciendum in Tolosam exercitum tot ipsam [ecclesiam] marcarum millibus ~iastis (G. Foliot) *Becket Mat.* V 525; **s1210** [rex Francorum] adeo eos [Judeos] omnibus apporiavit ut nec sibiipsis possent subvenire *Chr. Melrose* 109. **c** intuens.. puerum..capite rasum et puncturis innumeris ~iatum T. Mon. *Will.* I 10.

2 (? by conf. w. *abhorrere*) to abhor, shun.

~iens, *anscungendi GlC* A 666; Johannes..polluta..contubernia ~ians asperrimae invectionis severitate coercuit Aldh. *VirgP* 23 p. 254; aporriatis vitreorum fontium limpidis laticibus, lutulentas limphas..potare *Id. Ep.* 3; **10..** ~ians, *onscuniende* WW; **966** in refectorio..secularium delicias ut melancoliam ~iantes..licitis..utuntur cibariis *CS* 1190 (= *Conc.* I 435: †apportantes); vitia carnalis petulantie velut quisquiliarum peripsema ∼ians *V. Osw.* 416; *dyffyyn or utterly dyspysyn*, ..sperno, apporio, .. *revylyn*, apporio *PP*.

2 †aporiare [? *conf. w.* aperire], to reveal.

opyn, apertus, ∼iatus, evidens, ..*to schewe*, ..∼iare, enucliare, ..aperire *CathA*.

aporiatio, impoverishment.

1268 ne domus nostra..in aliquo casuram patiatur vel ad aliquam..apporiationem..deveniat (*Lit. abbatis*) *EHR* XXXIII 224; **s1255** consencientibus in apporiacione Anglicane ecclesie *G. S. Alb.* I 379 (*rub.*); in †aporacionem maximam monasterii *Ib.* III 399; **c1380** relictis..proceribus qui continue eorum apporiacioni studebant WALS. *HA* I 445.

aporiator, impoverisher, despoiler.

s1100 Ranulphum..quem..rex Willelmus episcopum fecerat Dunelmensem et regni Anglie apporriatorem M. PAR. *Min.* I 182.

aporisma v. aphorisma, aporema.

aporrhesis [ἀπόρρησις], denial.

apparasin, negatio *GlC* A 665.

aporrhoea [ἀπόρροια], flowing or pouring out. **b** wound, sore.

apporia, defluens *GlC* A 682; *strynkyllynge*, aporia, aspergo, ..perfusio *CathA*. **b** †apporeor *GlC* A 711 (v. apostema); *a wounde*, apporia, apparigo, ..vulnus, .. lesio *Ib.*

aporriare v. aporiare. aport- v. apport-, asport-. aposchematio v. apostematio. apostare v. apostatare.

apostasia [ἀποστασία], apostasy, renunciation of Christian faith. **b** renunciation of Jewish faith. **c** dereliction of duty (by cleric), rejection of eccl. authority. **d** rejection of rule of religious order. **e** renunciation of a vocation.

†apotasia, *fraetgengian GlC* A 676; Julianus qui tyrannidem et ∼iam pariter arripuit ALDH. *VirgP* 38 p. 288; relictis Christiane fidei sacramentis ad ∼iam conversus est BEDE *HE* III 30; **10..** †apotassia, *fretgenga*, ..∼ie, *fleamlastes* WW; Petrus..factus..ex ∼ia fidelior H. BOS. *Thom.* III 30; nisi [clericus]..convictus fuerit de ∼ia, quia tunc primo degradetur et postea per manum laicalem comburatur BRACTON 123b; **1308** fratres..milicie Templi..contra ipsum Dominum in scelus ∼ie nefandum et hereses varias erant lapsi (*Lit. Papae*) *Conc.* II 305b (= *G. Ed. II Bridl.* 28: apostacie); ex quo..idolis immolavit [B. Marcellinus] fuit de ∼ia perfidie..suspectus OCKHAM *Dial.* 516. **b** alterum [regem Salomonem] in ∼ie crimen amor induxit GIR. *TH* I 22. **c s1095** episcopi confusione vultus sui operti sunt, intelligentes..∼iam suam..a cunctis detestari EADMER *HN* 74; unus erat [episcoporum] quem suspicio istius ∼ie [sc. simonie] insimulabat W. MALM. *GR* III 265; **1236** vinum, i.e. omne quod inebriat, ..principium est ∼ie aliaque mala procreat innumera GROS. *Ep.* 22 p. 73; **1382** civitatem Anagnum et alias terras pape occupare..presumpserunt, crimen heresis, scismatis, lese majestatis et ∼ie incurrendo (*Lit. Papae*) WALS. *HA* II 74. **d** Godfridus clericus qui ∼iae calumniam habet LANFR. *Ep.* 24. 528C; **11..** si quis in ∼ia ordinatus fuerit, ordinibus male susceptis perpetuo carebit (*Cap. Arroacense*) *EHR* LII 273; a sceleratioris ∼ie piaculis perditissimis..revocatum AD. MARSH *Ep.* 189; de ∼ia et de reditu cujuscumque fratris ad seculum *Cust. Cant.* I 41; **1282** [prior Malvernie] depositus fugam init et scandalo addidit ∼iam *Ann. Worc.* 484; **1382** quod nullus religiosus de privata religione debet sumere gradum in universitate sub pena ∼ie (HERFORD) *Ziz.* 305; **s1454** nomina..fratrum qui recesserunt ab ecclesia..diverteruntque se ad ..laxiorem modum conversandi: ..frater W. S. per viam ∼ie, in qua decessit *Reg. Whet.* I 147. **e** liberalibus artibus habiles..quasi quadam ∼ie specie ad artes mechanicas..revertuntur R. BURY *Phil. prol.* 7.

apostasis [ἀπόστασις], rejection of monastic rule (= *apostasia* c).

12.. ut †∼i [? l. ∼ia] sua relicta ad monasteria redeant *Conc. Scot.* II 60.

2 ulcer (= *apostema*).

in laboriosis febribus ∼es fiunt GILB. I 69. 2.

apostata, ∼us [ἀποστάτης], apostate, renouncer of Christian faith (m. or f.). **b** renegade from Islam to Christianity. **c** rebel against eccl. authority. **d** runaway monk or friar.

persolvo debitum..amicale..Christi tironibus, grave.. ∼is GILDAS *EB* 1; earundem..∼arum cicatrices..ita.. curavit ut..ad martirii palmam praecederent ALDH. *VirgP* 47 p. 302; ut nomen et memoria ∼arum de catalogo regum Christianorum prorsus aboleri deberet BEDE *HE* III 9; de ejus [diaboli] corpore, quod maxime in impiis et ∼is et in hereticis denoscitur constitutum ERIUG. *Per.* 559C; **8..** homo ∼a, *afliged mon*, i. retrogradiens WW; **964** (12c) sit pars ejus cum..Juliano ∼a aecclesiarum Dei oppressore *CS* 1135; pessima fex hominum Julianus apostata, regum / pessimus NIG. *Mir. BVM* 8. 2; **s1189** [Benedictus] Judeis est redditus ∼a Christianus W. NEWB. IV 1; Christiani ∼e.. detractari debent et conburi *Fleta* 54; ∼a..a fide inter hereticos computatur OCKHAM *Dial.* 459; hic, hec apostita, qui bene incipit et statim recedit WW. **b** metu mortis ∼e Turcorum, contempta superstitiosa vanitate, ad Christiane relligionis fidem conversi, regi Ricardo se subdiderunt *Itin. Ric.* IV 30. **c** quod [Anselmus]..Urbanum apostolicum, alterum ∼am pronuntiaret W. MALM. *GR* IV 333; deposito ∼a archiepiscopo Stigando M. PAR. *Min.* I 13; a tempore quo divisa est ecclesia per †∼os [? l. ∼as] introductos (WYCL. *Conf.*) *Speculum* VIII 506; **s1382** [J. Wicliff] emisit viros ∼as, de fide catholica pessime sencientes, ad dogmatizandum WALS. *HA* II 53; **s1413** regis pietas miserentis milicie dicti ∼e [J. de Veteri Castro] distulit mortis..sententiam ELMH. *Hen. V* 3. **d c1218** quoniam quidam ∼e..de ordine suo egredi sine licentia prelatorum suorum et in seculo seculariter conversari, abjecto religionis habitu, non verentur *Conc. Syn.* 93; **1295** attendentes pericula..∼as ad certos ordines recipiendi (*Lit. Papae*) *Reg. Carl.* I 50 (cf. B. COTTON 268); **s1310** frater Augustiniensis erat et ∼us est GRAYSTANES 34; **1314** ∼arum qui in.. ordinis Fratrum Minorum scandalum relicto habitu religionis sue..infra regnum..vagantur (*Pat*) *Mon. Francisc.* I 615; **1327** nuper..commonachus ecclesie nostre, nunc autem ∼a et fugitivus *Lit. Cant.* I 230; **1340** predictus W., secundum formam regule sue detentus, se justiciari et castigari non permittens set..muros..prioratus Dunolmie noctanter ut ∼a transcendens *RScot* 581a; **1358** ipsum ∼am ordinis [de Monte Carmeli]..nequiter affirmantes *Pat* 254 m. 28; **s1454** tenemini..∼as vestros cum lacrymis revertentes..iterum recipere *Reg. Whet.* I 140.

apostatare, to renounce the Christian faith. **b** (refl.). **c** to renounce the Jewish faith. **d** to break faith, renounce allegiance. **e** to reject the rule of a religious order.

feminis..quae a Christi consortio ∼averant ALDH. *VirgP* 47 p. 301; **10..** ∼are, *æswician* WW; refugientes ad Turcos ∼are non dubitaverunt *Itin. Ric.* I 74; **s1098** alii..ad hostes Crucis se ∼antes..contulerunt M. PAR. *Min.* I 113; **s1275** quidam de ordine Predicatorum..∼avit et ad Judaismum convolavit FL. WORC. *Cont.* C 214; **s1287** rex Hungarie †apostavit RISH. 115 (*rub.*); qui ∼ant ore et mente a fide OCKHAM *Dial.* 437; **a1384** hereticum ∼antem a religione Christi (WYCL.) *Ziz.* 489. **b** de quodam diacono qui se ∼avit pro quadam Judea BRACTON 124. **c** immolavit Israel, ∼ans a salutari suo, filios et filias suas demoniis J. SAL. *Pol.* 725D. **d** illos [angelos] qui ex illo ∼averunt nomine PULL. *Sent.* 887D; **s1260** comes Glovernie quasi ∼avit, recedens a consilio..magnatum quibus juramentum fecerat *Ann. Dunstable* 217; **c1265** que [misericordia].. humane nature preciosum est ornamentum, cujus expers homo ∼at et degenerat *Ann. Durh.* 199; **s1404** [diaconus] qui miliciam sortemque Christi deserens in sortem Martis ∼ando transierat WALS. *HA* II 266. **e 11..** quicumque ∼averit, si intra xl dies non redierit, excommunicabitur (*Cap. Arroacense*) *EHR* LII 272; **s1217** [Eustachius] relicto habitu et ordine suo ∼averat et existens pirata..multis.. fuit..cruentus M. PAR. *Maj.* III 29; effeminatus..honoribus et a se ipso alienatus ab ordine miserabiliter ∼avit ECCLESTON *Adv. Min.* p. 14; **1290** cum frater W. ..ab ordine fratrum Minorum..∼ando recesserit (*Lit. Arch. Cant.*) *Mon. Francisc.* II 31; **1332** ab eodem Minorum ∼antes ordine *Bull. Francisc.* V 528 (= *Scot. Grey Friars* II 2: †apostantes); **c1380** cum fratres professi ordinis Predicatorum ..a statu sue professionis appostataverint *Conc. Scot.* I ccxxxvii.

2 to break, violate (a law).

qui leges istas ∼abit [v.l. apostabit; AS: *wyrde*] quas rex modo nobis omnibus indulsit (*Quad.*) *GAS* 367; qui legem ∼abit (*Leg. Hen.*) *Ib.* 558.

apostatatio, rejection of monastic rule.

13.. idem Willelmus.., post secundam ∼onem respectus divinitus rediit supplex ad portam monasterii *G. S. Alb.* II 303.

apostatatus, apostasy (from Christian faith).

s925 [Sihtricus] Christianitatem abiciens idolorum culturam restauravit et post modicum temporis ∼us vitam miserabiliter terminavit M. PAR. *Maj.* I 446.

apostatice, as an apostate (runaway friar or monk).

qui..cum meretricibus devoravit substantiam suam, ∼e vivens in regione dissimilitudinis AD. MARSH *Ep.* 211; **s1422** alius [monachus S. Albani]..modulacionis incrassatus pinguedine, ..ad Ecclesiam Christi Cantuarie non minus anomale quam ∼e commigravit AMUND. I 89.

apostaticus [ἀποστατικός], of an apostate, pagan, rebellious, blasphemous. **b** (w. ref. to pope or antipope). **c** (w. ref. to runaway friar).

Dianae..∼o ritu turificare ALDH. *VirgP* 52 p. 309; **804** erumpunt..∼a [MS: †apostolica] seducti calliditate pseudodoctores ALCUIN *Ep.* 280; in agmine Petrus / plebis apostaticae constans WULF. *Swith. prol.* 472; cadentibus angelis ∼is AD. SCOT *Serm.* 154D; verbum ∼um..inpudenter emisit GIR. *PI* III 24 p. 283. **b 1159** Octavianum ∼um et schismaticum..execrare..presumpserunt (*Lit. Papae*) *Conc.* I 433; qui noscitur sedem apostolicam occupare, quantumcunque esset verius ∼us reputandus OCKHAM *Pol.* I 282; papa inhabilis quoad Deum..non est apostolicus sed ∼us WYCL. *Ver.* III 76; **s1378** [nuncii] repulsi sunt ∼i et admissi papales WALS. *HA* I 381. **c** quatenus..quondam ..fratrem nostrum A. de B., licet reum ∼e prevaricationis, ..recipere..non ducatis indignum AD. MARSH *Ep.* 201.

apostatizare, to apostatize.

omnis peccator ∼at, primo omnium ex superbia, dum peccans renuit numeros suos numeris Dei subicere WYCL. *Mand. Div.* 488.

apostatrix, apostate (f.), heretical. **b** (fig.) rival, upstart.

s1306 quidam hereticus apostata..surrexit in Venecia.., coadunans secte sue unius[cujus]que ordinis gentes ∼ices *Flor. Hist.* III 135. **b s1198** timuerunt quod dignitas Cantuariensis ecclesie minueretur et ad capellam illam ∼icem [apud Lamhee] transferri videretur R. HOWD. IV 48.

apostatus v. apostata.

apostema [ἀπόστημα], impostume, abscess.

†∼am [? l. ∼a] commune, †apporeor [? cf. aporrhea], *onsteuum*, quibus ejus viscera †coinquinentur [*EE* 346. 7 coquerentur] et inde loquendo exalavit odorem, foetorem *GlC* A 711; ∼a, *swyle* ÆLF. *Gl.*; sub acella ∼a nimii tumoris excreverat W. CANT. *Mir. Thom.* IV 39; ăpostemata rumpit/ ..nigella NECKAM *DS* VII 281; ex ∼ate vel ex †pusculis in lingua accidentibus BART. ANGL. V 21; frenesis est ∼a ignitum in anteriori parte cerebri GILB. II 100. 2; dicitur ∼a a 'post' et 'tumor', i. tumor superveniens post disposicionem naturalem; vel dicitur partis tumor vel preter naturam tumor GAD. 24 v. 1; species ∼atum sunt multe, sc. sex in generali secundum materias sex ex quibus fiunt, sc. quatuor humores, aquositas et ventositas *Ib.* 24 v. 2; ∼a interpretatur 'collecció' *Alph.* 13; *postym, seknesse*, postema *PP*; medicus..asseruit dictam A. infectuosam esse de tribus postumis in corpore *Entries* 463b.

apostemari, to suppurate, be affected w. abscesses.

quandoque ∼atur diafragma et impeditur a suo motu *Ps.*-RIC. *Anat.* 41; fit gravedo lingue et stomachi et ∼atur cor GILB. VII 351 v. 1; [hec medicina] non permittit aliquem locum ∼ari nec collectionem humorum facere BACON V 104; quia tumor extra naturam potest esse in omni membro, ideo quodlibet membrum potest ∼ari GAD. 24 v. 1.

apostematio, suppuration, formation of an abscess. **b** (fig.).

in discrasia febrili cum calore magno epatis sine ∼one GAD. 5 v. 1. **b** non fit vera sanacio set verius †aposchemacio, sanato vulnere exterius, ferro interius remanente RIC. ARMAGH *Serm.* 9. p. 40.

apostemosus, affected w. (or in the form of) abscesses.

materia colica in membro ∼o GILB. IV 191. 1; ulceracionem ∼am in vesica GAD. 26. 2.

apostilla, ∼are v. postill-. apostilli v. apostolus 2a. apostita v. apostata.

apostola, apostle (f., w. ref. to Mary Magdalene).

que fuerat..peccatrix, ..non solum liberari meruit a peccatis sed fieri ∼a et evangelista, imo..apostolorum ∼a festinans ad annuntiandum apostolis resurrectionem Domini P. BLOIS *Ep.* 234. 567A; ista est apostolorum ∼a Maria Magdalena *NLA* (*Godric*) I 484.

apostolatus, apostleship. **b** (postbiblical).

1157 ecclesia..apostolorum principis ∼u insignita *Conc.* I 431; ad ∼um vocatus est Paulus J. SAL. *Pol.* 395C; nec enim eorum quisque quos Imperator [sc. Christus] ipse ad ∼um elegit permansit H. BOS. *Thom.* VII 1(23); [habuerunt a Deo] duodecim apostoli ∼um OCKHAM *Pol.* I 74. **b** signaculum ∼us ejus [sc. Gregorii] nos sumus in Domino BEDE *HE* II 1 p. 73.

2 papacy. **b** (papal title).

s1098 Wibertus archiepiscopus Ravennas..de ∼u quem contra jus invaserat pulsus EADMER *HN* 106; **s1119** si contra hoc ipse [Calixtus] ∼us sui jure niti vellet W. MALM. *GP* III 124; **1191** licet nobis aliquando, ∼us exigente officio, cum personis religiosis..misericorditer dispensare (*Lit. Papae*) *Reg. Malm.* I 375; **1301** ante provisionem nostram ad summum ∼us officium (*Lit. Papae*) *MGL* II 159; in ∼u possunt esse plures apostolici OCKHAM *Dial.* 814; **s1463** successor ejus in sede Romana Paulus mox in ∼us inicio.. *Croyl. cont. B* 534. **b 883** relatum est ∼ui nostro quod.. (*Lit. Papae*) W. MALM. *GP* V 240; **1250** ∼ui nostro innotuit *FormA* 24; **1308** eorum confessiones..nostro ∼ui deferre (*Lit. Papae*) *Reg. Carl.* II 5; **1326** quedam miracula que..vestri dignissimi ∼us culmini..duximus presentare *Lit. Cant.* III 402.

3 archbishopric.

Dunstanus candida ∼us sui stola a Romano pontifice.. infulatus OSB. *V. Dunst.* 34.

apostolicatus, papacy.

s1181 cui in ∼u successit Imbaldus..et vocatus est Lucius papa III *G. Hen. II* I 282; **1421** ∼us officium..quo ecclesiarum omnium regimini presedemus..utiliter exequi.. cupientes (*Lit. Papae*) *Reg. Heref.* 1.

apostolice, w. apostolic authority or force.

1227 rogavit dominum papam quod..appostolice assensum impendat *Pat* 166; presbiter..canat ∼e, id est suasorie GARL. *Dict.* 133; quod ille [Augustinus] ∼e plantavit, iste regifice confirmabat *NLA* (*Ethelbert*) I 409.

apostolicus [ἀποστολικός], apostolic, of an apostle or the apostles. **b** faithful to the apostles. **c** (sb. m.) apostle.

ut..∼ae [sc. Pauli] jubilationis tripudio carmen triumphale..decantet ALDH. *VirgP* 18; coeperunt ∼am primitivae ecclesiae vitam imitari BEDE *HE* I 26; haec evangelica et ∼a traditio *Ib.* III 25; inito opere ∼o *Ib.* V 9; tempore quo ∼ae tonsurae indicium suscepit FELIX *Guthl.* 20; **†796** (12c) ut ∼um testatur oraculum *CS* 279; praeferebat scientiam pietatis quae in evangeliis et ∼is continetur litteris OSB. *V. Dunst.* 8; **1121** amici mei..qui propter ∼um diem [sc. festivitatem Petri et Pauli] huic adestis curie *Cart. Bath* 49; **c1220** cetus apostolicus../ pura mente Deum coluit H. AVR. 43. 63; **s1239** cogitans de illo ∼o, scilicet 'qui bene administrat..' [1 *Tim.* iii 13] M. PAR. *Maj.* III 542; huic et apostolica gesta ligata tuli GARL. *Tri. Eccl.* 101; doctrine que absque scripturis ∼is ad nos pervenit OCKHAM *Dial.* 422; **1552** vera, catholica et ∼a fides *Conc. Scot.* II 136. **b** eligebantur ∼i sacerdotes (*V. Germani*) BEDE *HE* I 17; Cuthbertus.. / doctor apostolicus fuit hinc et presbyter almus ALCUIN *SSEbor.* 650; voluit Dominus..ut apostoli et ∼i viri se et sua darent pro Christo..et pro fide ejus

BACON *Maj.* III 51. **c** Simon zelotes.. / inter apostolicos Petri cognomine functus ALDH. *CE* 4. 11. 2; **1353** in crastino S. Matthie †~i [? l. apostoli] *Reg. Rough* 251.

2 deriving authority from the apostle Peter, papal. **b** (sb. m.) pope. **c** (?) episcopal.

contra ~a statuta et legalia scita ALDH. *VirgP* 55 p. 314; ad pontificem Romanae et ~ae sedis BEDE *HE* II 1 p. 80; cum ~o papa Bonifatio *Ib.* II 4; auctoritatem B. Gregorii papae sedis ~ae *RegulC* 50; [Willelmus I] non pati volebat quemquam..constitutum Romane urbis pontificem pro ~o nisi se jubente recipere EADMER *HN* 12; voluit..ut fratres.. publicis meritis se potius tuerentur quam ~is privilegiis ECCLESTON *Adv. Min.* 92; **1300** constitucionibus ~is contrariis non obstantibus (*Lit. Papae*) *MunAcOx* 80; **1347** regi Anglie salutem et ~am benedictionem (*Lit. Papae*) AVESB. 111; **1477** Roberto B. publico auctoritate ~a notario *Sanct. Durh.* 3. **b** facilius..~um ejus rationes susceptorum si suam illum sententiam cognoverit reveritum ANSELM (*Ep.* 65) III 182; **s1119** ne ab ~o consecrationem acciperet H. CANTOR 18; inde Romam cum ~o reversus est J. SAL. *Anselm* 10. 1027D; duos ~os non habebo GIR. *Galf.* I 7; hic [sc. papa] quoque ~us nominatur, quia principis apostolorum vice fungitur GIR. *PI* I 19; cum a potestate ~a derivetur in episcopos episcopalis potestas, quemadmodum in ipsum ~um a Christo potestatis plenitudo GROS. *Ep.* 127 p. 367; ~us ..potest eos ..condemnare OCKHAM *Dial.* 461. **c** quot..vidimus..tantum proborum virorum pietate suffultos ~as cathedras meruisse R. BURY *Phil. prol.* 10.

3 (sb. n.) apostles' ointment, apostolicon.

~um cyrurgicum..; recipe picis navalis,..picis Grece.., galbani.. GILB. II 87 v. 1; apponatur ~on, vel aliquod simile emplastrum supponatur *Ib.* III 183. 1; rupto apostemate, si materia sit viscosa, apponatur ~on GAD. 28. 2; **1322** ~on *CalScot* III 766.

apostolus [ἀπόστολος], (biblical) apostle. **b** the apostle (i.e. St. Paul). **c** (w. ref. to festivals). **d** (w. *limina*) papal curia. **e** (postbiblical) apostle, missionary.

680 sicut praedicaverunt..sancti ~i et prophetae et doctores (*Conc. Hatfield*) BEDE *HE* IV 15; exemplum sequebatur primi pastoris ecclesie, hoc est beatissimi ~orum principis Petri *Ib.* II 4; per ~orum successores ERIUG. *Per.* 530A; ~us, *ærendraca* ÆLF. *Gl.*; quamvis post ~os sancti patres et doctores nostri..tanta de fidei nostrae ratione dicant ANSELM (*Cur Deus, commend.*) II 39; in his..verbis de ordinacione ~orum nulla fit mencio; sed magis, cum dicit in principio 'convocatis duodecim discipulis suis', eos quasi antonomatice 'discipulos' appellando, supponit eos fuisse prius ~os ordinatos OCKHAM *Pol.* II 752; **1495** coccclearia argenti cum ~is super eorum fines *Test. Ebor.* IV 106. **b** juxta promissum ~i dicentis . BEDE *HE* III 4; ut ait ~us ERIUG. *Per.* 532A; legitur ~us, 'si consurrexistis' [*Col.* iii 1] *RegulC* 49; **1440** instantia vestra quotidiana est, cum ~o, 'omnium ecclesiarum solicitudo' [*2 Cor.* xi 28] BEKYNTON I 16; juxta illud ~i, 'conversacio nostra in celis est' [*Phil.* iii 20] BLAKMAN *Hen. VI* 16. **c** usque ad festum ~orum Simonis et Jude [*28 Oct.*] *RDomin* 61; **1199** in die S. Thome ~i [*21 Dec.*] *CurR* I 79; **1259** post festum ~orum Philippi et Jacobi [*1 May*] *Cl* 358; in omnibus festis ~orum et aliorum festorum festis duplicibus BIRCHINGTON *Arch. Cant.* 13; **1399** in festo S. Barnabe ~i [*11 June*] *Reg. Malm.* II lxxxvii; in festo ~orum Petri et Pauli [*29 June*], '~orum passio' ELMH. *Cant.* 97. **d** equum . in quo..in urbe Roma ~orum et martirum limina circuisti ALDH. *VirgP* 25 p. 259; **c1302** maturato diffinitores ~orum petunt limina (*Chr. Edmundsbury*) *EHR* LVIII 69; **1422** ~orum limina, Romana curia existente citra singulis bienniis, ultra vero montes singulis trienniis, visitabo per me aut per nuncium meum *Reg. Cant.* I 80. **e** [Gregorius] quem recte nostrum appellare possumus et debemus ~um BEDE *HE* II 1 p. 73; **1070** ecclesie S. Augustini Anglorum, ~i *Regesta* 119; **1444** S...Wilfridi..merita extolli cupientes, ..precipue eis in partibus quibus quasi ~us vita et miraculis claruit *Lit. Cant.* III 188.

2 (pl.) letters authorizing appeal (eccl. law). **b** (w. *refutatorii*) letters disallowing appeal.

1245 si quis .super interlocutoria vel gravamine ad nos duxerit appellandum, causam appellationis in scriptis assignare deproperet, petat ~os [v.l. †apostillos], quos ei precepimus exhiberi (*Conc. Lugdun.*) M. PAR. *Maj.* IV 470; **1282** quamquam nulla appellacio fuisset..recitata nec ~i juxta juris exigenciam requisiti *Reg. Heref.* 267; **1292** in hiis scriptis provoco et appello et ~os peto *DCCant* Q f. 1b; **1395** peciit a..domino episcopo ~os super appellacione.. *Reg. Glasg.* 294; **1426** ordinavit suum..procuratorem..ad.. appellandum, ~os petendum et recipiendum.. *Reg. Cant.* I 238; **s1434** scripsit litteras deprecatorias domino officiali.. ut ille..procuratorem benivolo vultu admitteret concederetque.. ~os AMUND. I 374; **1549** ne dentur citationes et inhibitiones super appellatoriis nisi visis ~is *Conc. Scot.* II 126; pars contra quam lata est sententia potest..in hunc modum appellare: 'ego dissentio sententiae hujusmodi prolationi..~osque peto' *Praxis* 234. **b** si judex..cum appellatur..assignaverit ~os refutatorios.., si..non appellaveris a denegatione vel assignatione ~orum refutatoriorum, succumbes in causa *Ib.* 240 (cf. *EHR* XXIX 739).

apostropha, ~e, ~us [ἀποστροφή, ἀπόστροφος], apostrophization, ref. to person (or personified object) in second person.

sit apostropha quarta morarum / qua rem detineas VINSAUF *PN* 264.

2 semicircular mark indicating omission of final vowel.

apostrofus est signum extritae vocalis ALDH. *PR* 141 p. 200; sciat [notarius]..ubi apostrofus subscribi debeat vel dici NECKAM *Ut.* 117; prima istarum passionum [prosodie] vocatur *apostrofos* secundum Grecum, et Latinus dicit '~us' vel '~e'; et notat dictioni precedenti..deesse.. ultimam ejus vocalem; et est quasi pars circuli dextra BACON *CSPhil* 514; ~a est species accentus que tollit ultimam vocalem diccionis cum sequens diccio inchoat a vocali ODINGTON 214.

3 reversion.

~a vel ~es, regressus, reversus..; reciprocus, *strophos* Grece *CathA*.

apostrophare, to apostrophize, address as if present.

versus..in Giraldi laudem tanquam ad ipsum apostrofando GIR. *Inv.* IV 15 (*rub.*); ad dictum abbatem..verbis authenticis ~emus: 've qui predaris, nonne et predaberis?' [*Is.* xxxiii 1] *Id. Spec.* III 1 p. 133; collige plene / quam rem, qua forma, quis casus apostrophet apte VINSAUF *PN* 275; est apostrophatio quando ~amus nos vel aliquam aliam personam *Id. AV* II 2. 24.

2 (dep.) to turn away (from virtue).

to turne agayn the gudnes, ~ari, advertere, recidivare.

apostrophatio, apostrophization.

est ~o ..quando convertimus sermonem ad nos vel ad aliquam aliam rem animatam vel inanimatam; in ~one quatuor incidunt exornationes, sc. exclamatio, conduplicatio, subjectio, dubitatio VINSAUF *AV* II 2. 24; more poetarum qui solebant facere ~ones in carminibus suis GARL. *Mor. Scol.* 253 (*gl.*).

apostrophe, ~us v. apostropha. apotasia, ~tassia v. apostasia. apote v. apocha.

apotheca [ἀποθήκη], storehouse. **b** (fig.). **c** reliquary. **d** container for wine. **e** drug store.

~a vel horreum, repositio *GlC* A 662; dum alii materiali fructu frumenti, vini et olei suas exteriores satagerent replere ~as AD. EYNS. *Hug.* V 13 p. 153. **b** merulenta defecati nectaris defruta ~is caelestibus recondenda ALDH. *VirgP* 30; ~am cordis tribus implevit speciebus W. DAN. *Ailr.* 13; si oleum esse desideras, torcularis pressuram sustineas necesse est donec ex torculari in ~am defluas H. BOS. *Thom.* IV 13; quo liberius carpende et in intimis anime sue ~is recondende invigilaret annone spiritus AD. EYNS. *Hug.* IV 14. **c** crepans ~a nocturna silentia..inquietabat indignansque sanctuarium custodie †sua tenebras increpabat W. CANT. *Mir. Thom.* II 89. **d** ~a, domus vini *GlC* A 687; appotheca, *winfæt Ib.* 710; ~a, *winhus* ÆLF. *Sup.*; **10..** ~a, *winfæt, winhorn* WW. **e** apotecarii in apoteca habent.. zinziberum GARL. *Dict.* 129; posito quod habeant res medicinales in apotecis communibus BACON IX 163; **1323** de quolibet balo zucre sive alterius rei in ~a iiij d. *EEC* 209; magis voluptuose consedimus quam fecisset medicus delicatus inter aromatum ~as R. BURY *Phil.* 8. 121; **1398** de furto..cujusdam capse cum pipere et aliis rebus de ~a J. W. apothecarii de Leominstria *Reg. Heref.* 158; *a spycere schoppe*, ~a vel ipotheca *CathA*.

1 apothecaria, ~ium, storeroom. **b** apothecaries' quarter.

Josephus et Augustinus dicunt iiij fuisse cameras in arca [Noe], Rabanus vero v: una[m] hominum, ..iiij[tam] ~iorum *Eul. Hist.* I 26; **1318** in longis stabulis, pincernariis, ypotecariis et in aliis diversis locis infra palacium [Westm'] *KRAc* 468/20 f. 19. **b** duo famuli..apud Cantuariam ad ~iam pro quibuscumque medicinalibus incedere debent *Cust. Cant.* I 328; **1388** shopa in parochia Omnium Sanctorum Oxon' juxta magnam portam in appotecaria *IMisc* 240 22 r. 2.

2 apothecaria, apothecary, spicer (f.).

14.. hec apoticaria, A. *a spyser wyfe* WW.

apothecarius, a treasurer. **b** apothecary, druggist, spicer. **c** (fig.).

a **s1198** Ricardus Nigelli quondam Eliensis episcopi filius et regis Henrici apotecarius *Ann. Wint.* 70. **b** GARL. *Dict.* (v. apotheca e); qualis debet esse ~ius sive herbarius BACON V 30 (cf. ib. 59: debes habere fidelem virum cognoscentem genera specierum et qualitates); rusticis ~iis *Id.* IX 150; **1260** domus Thome apotecarii *Cart. Osney* III 104; **1290** R. L. ipotecario Norhampton' pro inplastris et aliis medicinalibus *Ac. Wardr.* (*Chanc. Misc.* 4/5) f. 11d.; libra electuariorum et hujusmodi apotecariorum confecte *Fleta* 73; **1303** soluta cuidam ypothecario pro croco, gingiberi, sucro et aliis speciebus *Ac. Exec. Ep. Lond.* 100; **1367** de bonis cujusdam apoticarii apud Edynburgh *ExchScot* 214; **s1382** ne de cetero ullus eorum . qui de numero sunt ~iorum eligantur in majores civitatis [London'] WALS. *HA* II 71; **1393** hic apotēcārius, pistor, pictor, lathomusque (R. MAIDSTONE) *Pol. Poems* I 284; **1392** pro diversis speciebus emptis de Anton' potecario *Ac. H. Derby* 219; **1439** cuidam potecario London' pro diversis medicinis ab eo emptis *KRAc* 503/7 m. 2; **1462** cum..concesserimus..J. C. apoticario civitatis nostre London' quod sit appoticarius noster *Cl* 314 m. 29; **1524** de J. S. poticario *DocCOx.* 70; **1573** dictum J. ~ium nostrum ordinarium facimus *Pat* 1106 m. 23. **c** **s1452** rogamus vos, fratres, esse nobis pro baculo in hoc nostro senio, pro ~io vero in morbo nostro gravissimo *Reg. Whet.* I 22.

apozema [ἀπόζεμα], (unsweetened) decoction.

pillulis et appozimatibus..usus W. CANT. *Mir. Thom.* II 32; utendum est apozimatibus GILB. II 76 v. 2; fiat hoc apozima vel decoccio GAD. 101. 1; apozima dicitur quando decoquuntur alique herbe vel medicine in aqua, ita quod virtus herbe aque mandetur..; et dicitur apozima ab *apos* quod est 'decoccio' et *zeo* quod est 'ferveo'...sed non omnis decoccio dicitur apozima, sed illa sola ubi non ponitur mel neque zuccarum *SB* 11.

†appalia (pl.), (?) *f.l.* for *mappalia.*

786 trado terram..cum ~ibus quae pater ejus habebat *CS* 248.

appaltator [It.], agent, contractor.

1506 A. C. mercatori Senensi, ..†appalcatori aluminum sive minarum aluminum Camere Apostolice (*Pat*) *Foed.* XIII 159.

appalus v. hapalus.

apparamentum, fitting, equipment. **b** (item of) apparel, costume.

1295 navem cum ~is et mercimoniis existentibus in eadem *RGasc.* III 316; **1312** extimavit lofirnam et alia ~a dicte navis cc li. Morlanorum *Ib.* IV 562 p. 162; **1458** pro reparacione aule castri de Edinburgh, in ferro, panno lineo pro fenistris et aliis ~is ibidem factis erga parliamentum *ExchScot* 385. **b** **1310** vestimentum..cum omnibus ~is suis, viz. capa chori [etc.] *Reg. Cant.* II 1340; **1349** ad facienda ~a sua de panno serici tartaryn (*KRAc* 391/15) *Arch.* XXXI 85; **1410** domine Egidie..pro aparamento suo *ExchScot* 106; **1421** in ~is corporis sui et aliis necessariis *Reg. Cant.* II 253; rex ipse inter hec laudum preconia et ~a civium indutus veste purpurea..incedebat ELMH. *Hen. V* 68; **1466** unum ~um sacerdotale, quod Anglice appellatur *a sute Wills N. Country* 46.

apparantia v. apparentia.

apparare [CL], to prepare, see to. **b** to equip, fit (with). **c** to annotate (= *apparitare*).

bellum utrimque ~atur G. CRISPIN *Herl.* 88; **a1128** debent falcare..et adparare fenum et adjuvare ad ducendum *Chr. Peterb. app.* 163; Israel laborabat in ~ando reditum BELETH *RDO* 77. 83; **1220** pro robis nostris ~endis (*sic*) *Cl* 414b; **1296** in vineis cindendis et ~endis (*sic*) *MinAc* 997/11. **b** **1336** galeas et usceria hominibus et armis ~ata (*Pat*) *Foed.* IV 710; **1411** una zona de serico nigro ~ata cum stipis argenteis et deauratis *Lit. Cant.* III 113. **c** **1331** Decretales nove ~ate tercie ..; item Decretales nove quarte non ~ate (*Invent. Ch. Ch.*) *Arch. J.* LIII 262.

2 (p. ppl. as sb. n.) fitting, furnishing.

1250 deest totum ~atum, et totus murus in parte interiori castri decasus est *CalIMisc* I p. 30.

apparasin v. aporrhesis.

apparatio [CL], preparation, provision. **b** fitting, equipment.

apparitione, *getiunge*, *GlC* A 684; aparitio.., *gethingio*, *Ib.* 708; **10..** ~o, *gepingio* WW; **1333** super providencia et ~one c balistarum *LTRMem* 105 r. 199d. **b** de ~one ecclesiarum (*Quad. rub.*) *GAS* 185n.; ornamenta..que..ad ~onem ecclesie aut capituli pertinent *Cust. Westm.* 42 (= *Cust. Cant.* 101: apparicionem); **1512** pro †apporicione iij par le orfas iij albarum *Ac. Churchw. Bath* 102.

1 apparator, (?) fitter (arch.; *cf. apparellator*). **b** (? *f.l.*) arrayer (of troops). **c** (? *f.l.*).

1292 Michael ~or (*Fabr. Westm.*) *Med. Mason* 96; **1376** ~ori operanti et ordinanti opus carpentarie *KRAc* 464/30. **b** **1327** rex †~oribus hominum tam equitum quam peditum ..in Estrithingo..et eorum †subapparatoribus *RScot* 206a (cf. ib.: eodem modo mandatum est arraiatoribus et subarraiatoribus in comitatibus subscriptis). **c** **1334** assignavimus..clericum..ad supervidendum naves predictas et earum apparatus..nec non ad certificandum nos de numero dictarum navium et earum †~oribus [? l. apparatibus] *Ib.* 305b.

2 apparator v. apparitor.

apparatorium [CL], place of preparation.

~ium, ubi res quaecumque parentur *GlC* A 704.

apparatura, furniture, (?) bedding. **b** apparel, costume.

1432 habeant literas licenciales..eskippandi sargeas, lectos, ~as..et alia domus utensilia *Foed.* X 516. **b** **1423** ecclesia..habeat sectam de panno aureo nigro, viz. apparituram pro sacerdote, diacono et subdiacono *Reg. Cant.* II 238; **1517** duas casulas..ad eadem funera solempniter curanda cum antiqua apparitura..reparavit *Invent. Ch. Ch.* 124.

apparatus [CL], preparation, provision. **b** preparation of the mass (eccl.).

~um, *geprec GlC* A 709; aparatu, *aexfaru Ib.* 696; ~us *gearcung* ÆLF. *Sup.*; [filii Israel] in ~u redditus [i.e. reditus] suas colligendo sarcinulas multum laboraverunt BELETH *RDO* 77. 82. **b** sedebunt..ordinate donec tangatur parvulum signum ad ~um misse capitalis; nec debet aliquis, priusquam fiat idem sonitus, ad ~um ingredi *Cust. Westm.* 144; in Dominicis et festis diebus fiet semper ~us ad missam matutinalem immediate post capitulum *Cust. Cant.* 110 (cf. ib. 111: solempnior ~us magni altaris); **1432** in vestimentis ordinatis ad ~um divinum *Reg. Cant.* II 467.

2 **a** trapping, decking (of altar). **b** furniture (of room, incl. hangings and bedding). **c** adjunct (of garden). **d** stage-property.

a **1234** honestas circa altaria in omnibus ~ibus servetur ad altaria pertinentibus (*Vis. Bury*) *EHR* XXVII 736; **c1284** ij toweles pro ij altariis cum ~u (*Invent.*) *Arch. Soc. Salop* I 358; **1424** do..~um altaris de rubeo velvetto *Reg. Cant.* II 281; frontale, i.e. ~um pendentem in fronte altaris, qui ~us alias dicitur palla LYNDW. 252i; **1501** ~us pro iiij altaribus..cujus octo sunt partes *Cant. Coll. Ox.* I 34. **b** **1329** pro ~u camere regine *ExchScot* 213; **1419** lectus de worsted' cum ~u *Ac. Durh.* 615; **1432** [lego] lectum cum toto ~u, viz. matras, blankettys, linthiaminibus, mappis et manutergiis *Reg. Cant.* II 469; **1434** lego..unum aulare seu ~um de rubeo worstede *Ib.* 541. **c** **1305** ex turbis viridibus et aliis aparitibus ad hujusmodi herbaria et virgulta spectantibus *Cl* 122 m. 15. **d** **1389** excepto solum ~u pro dicto ludo disposito, qui quidem ~us ad aliquem alium usum..modicum vel nichil potest proficere *Guild Cert.* 46/454.

3 a apparel (eccl.), ornamentation of vestment. **b** apparel (lay), (article of) costume. **c** accoutrement (of fighting man).

a executor officii solempni ~u se induat *Offic. Sal.* 72; fecit etiam [prior Thomas, ob. 1229] duas albas cum ~ibus auro textis *Chr. Evesham* 269; **1260** capam de choro cum decenti ~u de latis aurifrigiis *Cl* 234; **1295** casula de fustia[n], cujus totus ~us est de fustian; ..item unum vestimentum cum toto ~u de pal *Vis. S. Paul.* 332; **1365** cum toto ~u empto..pro uno vestimento integro faciendo *Ac. Durh.* 567; **14..** vestimentum novum cum casula cum †operatu rubii coloris de panno de auro *Invent. Norw.* 42. **b 1330** pro diversis ~ibus pro capite..sororis domini regis *ExchScot* 339; **1380** henxstman domini regis pro vestura et apparat' suis *KRAc* 400/4 r. 23; qui in ~ibus cultioribus domini sui faciem..viderent Elmh. *Hen. V* 62; **1489** lego..totum ~um meum pertinentem corpori meo *Cart. Boarstall* 290. **c 1168** in ~u cujusdam probatoris *Pipe* 126; **1261** secum ducat balistarios equites quotquot habere poterit de bono ~u *Cl.* 496; **1305** pro ~u militum de novo factorum (*KRMem.* 79) *EHR* XLVIII 88.

4 preparation, equipment (mil.). **b** store (mil.), ordnance.

cum infinito duelli ~u Aldh. *VirgP* 48; preparato tanti conaminis ~u Gir. *EH* I 16; ad committendum bellum cum eo..cujus dispar ~us..imparatum nonnunquam exterminat *V. Har.* 6 f. 10. **b** ingentem machinam, quam berfredum vocitant, ..erexit et copiose bellicis ~ibus instruxit Ord. Vit. VIII 16; **1550** machine bellice cum omni suo ~u, sc. pulverum, boulletorum, mortariorum (*DipDoc* E 1054) *Foed.* XV 213.

5 harness, equipment (of horse, cart or sim.).

equus cum ~u suo [AS: *hors and his geræda*] (*Quad.*) *GAS* 359; pro duabus carectis ferratis cum earum ~u *Cl* 38a; **1331** pro expensis cujusdam equi..cum garcione suo..unacum ferura et aliis aparatibus *ExchScot* 382; **1374** in..factura unius litere..cum custagiis sellarum, frenorum et aliorum ~uum necessariorum pro eadem *Ac. Durh.* 579; **1392** capitale aratrum cum toto ~u suo *Cl* 234 m. 28*d.*; **1411** in j corpore carecte..cum toto ~u *Crawley* 307; de iij carrucis cum iij paribus ferramentorum et toto ~u ferri pro xvj bobus *Ib.* 312; **1454** cum toto ~u pro iij equis trahendis *Ac. Durh.* 150.

6 outfit (naut.), tackle. **b** 'parrel', cordage securing yard to mast (*cf. Sea Terms* II 9–11). **c** fishing tackle.

1204 in..~u vj navium, sc. de funanis et ancoris et aliis necessariis *Pipe* 125; navi opulentissimo instructa ~u *V. Har.* 1 f. 3b; **1384** valorem..balengere predicte cum toto ~u *Cl* 225 m. 35; **1388** de navibus predictis, attillariis et ~ibus earundem *Cl* 228 m. 8*d.*; **a1460** si quis interfectus..fuerit..super mare per aliquem ~um vel attilionem ancorarum *BBAdm.* I 242. **b 1401** de sailyerd cum ~u *KRAc* 42/39 m. 4*d.*; **1422** j apparat' integr' pro mal' j toppecastell' *Ib.* 49/29 m. 9. **c 1309** ad capiendum muletum cum propriis batillis et proprio ~u *IPM* 16/9 r. 6.

7 (?) design, workmanship.

1431 lego..vj ciphos argenteos flat de uno aparatu, *les brynkes* deauratos *Reg. Cant.* II 439.

8 commentary.

respondeo in verbis ~us Peckham *Puer. Obl.* 427; **s1274** contulit..totum Corpus Juris †opperatu ordinario glosatum Thorne 1922; **1303** librum codicis sine ~u *DCDurh. Misc. Ch.* 4799; quicunque..super ipsam [diffinicionem]..glossas, ~us, literam vel scripta quecunque componeret Ockham *Dial.* 674; **1434** lego..minus missale ac unum ~um misse pro sacerdote et librum qui dicitur 'Pupilla Oculi' *Reg. Cant.* II 540.

apparcare, to impound. **b** to impark, enclose; *cf. imparcare.*

1276 presentat quod auce aparkate in parco Jacobi..evaserunt *Hund. Highworth* 41. **b 1428** peciam prati..imperpetuum poterit ~are *Rec. Leic.* II 240.

appare, exemplar in like terms.

c1100 Herbertus Ingulfo, Willelmo et Stano ~aribus H. Los. *Ep.* 14; **1191** Ricardus rex Anglorum Willelmo cancellario suo, Gaufrido filio Petri..et Willelmo Briwerre ~aribus (*Lit. Regis*) Diceto *YH* II 90.

apparella v. apparellum.

apparellare [OF *appareillier*], to fit.

1510 communis cista †apellata [? l. aperellata] cum duobus ceris *Cant. Coll. Ox.* I 53.

apparellator, (?) fitter (arch.); *cf. apparator.*

1325 Willelmo de U. carpentario appariliat[ori] et tenenti locum magistri carpentarii *KRAc* 469/8 m. 16; **1333** cementario et apparilatori *Ib.* 12 m. 18; **1351** apparilator operum cementariorum *Ib.* 492/27.

apparellum, ~a [OF *appareil*], a 'apparel', furniture (of bed). **b** 'parrel', tackle (naut.).

a 1414 lectum..cum toto ~o *Reg. Cant.* II 13. **b 1444** bargea predicta cum tota ~a sua..valebat l li. *Pat* 458 m. 17*d.*

apparenter, evidently. **b** in appearance (only).

nisi sumatur translatio ab talibus, quesunt expressime et ~issime similia, ut ipsa expressio et apparentia similitudinis faciat evidentiam translationis Vinsauf *AV* II 3. 17. **b** in eis..que..vere vel ~er sunt nociva J. Blund *An.* 411; cum omnia ista ~er sint metalla et non existenter *Correct. Alch.* 10; recitabis quomodo vere et realiter aut ~er seu sophistice valeat reprobari Ockham *Dial.* 849.

apparentia, appearance (of person) in court (leg.). **b** name of a court (Penwortham, Lancs). **c** personal appearance, aspect, looks. **d** showing oneself, apparition (of demon).

c1272 faciant curie nostre tres apparancias annuatim *BBC* (*Congleton*) 198; **1286** sint quieti a secta curie mee.., salva una ~ia ad magnam curiam meam post festum S. Michaelis *Ib.* (*Bakewell*) 180; adjudicaverunt quandam defaltam versus..abbatem mortuum post ~iam *State Tri. Ed. I* 2; **1288** post apparanciam, si fecerint defaltam, quod capiatur terra in manum domini *SelPlMan* 107; nec tenenti nec petenti post ~iam nullum essonium allocetur *Fleta* 226; facit duas †apprehencias, precium cujuslibet vj d. *FormMan* 27 (cf. ib.: sequitur curiam bis per annum, precium utriusque vj d.); **s1392** diem ~ie sue..conscribi fecerunt *Croyl. Cont. B* 488; **1423** cum duabus ~iis ad duas magnas curias ibidem de anno in annum *Cl* 274 m. 16*d.*; **1483** nec unquam pater ejus habuit ~iam *Reg. Aberbr.* II 204. **b 1521** curia ~ie de Penwurtham tenta ibidem..coram..capitali senescallo *DLCourtR* 78/1011 r. 4. **c** vidit et alium cum eo militem..quantum ad ~iam gradu dignitatis inferiorem Brakelond 140v.; homo est stature decentis et personalis ~ie *Ib.* 160; **s1213** invenerunt milites..secundum ~iam robustiores et ferociores et plures prioribus M. Par. *Maj.* II 560; **1340** (v. apparere 4a). **d** ille ~ie quas aliquibus interdum demones per se faciunt..aut innocenter transeunt aut nocenter Map *NC* II 13.

2 appearance, becoming visible (astr.). **b** visibility, perceptibility. **c** visible image, phenomenon.

s1316 propter quam caristiam et comet[ar]um ~iam multa extunc mortalitas hominum *Flor. Hist.* III 340. **b** si hoc esset, nulla esset generatio [formarum], set solum alteratio quedam, unde solum exirent de latentia ad ~iam Bacon VIII 21. **c** ~ia accidentis solum est in speculo et oculo, non forma Gilb. III 128. 1; moderniores mathematici ad salvandum ~iam epicyclos posuerunt *Ps.*-Gros. 565; omnis demonstracio naturalis est ab ~ia sensitiva effectus †convincientis ejus causam Wycl. *Act.* 119.

3 show of truth, evidentness.

ad tercium [argumentum] dico quod, si aliquam ~iam haberet, magis concluderet contra opinionem illam Duns *PW* V 118; doctrina istius..ab omni veritate est vacua, plena erroribus, nullam habens ~iam vel colorem Ockham *Pol.* I 370; **1516** due versantur opinaciones, quarum prior est Gregorii de Arikino; ..judicio meo modica est ~ia in suo modo dicendi (J. Major *In P. Hisp.*) *GLA* IV 248*n.* 423.

4 mere appearance (as dist. from reality). **b** display, ostentation. **c** likeness, counterfeit.

bonus et comis in ~ia, que..habebat probra tegebat Map *NC* V 3 p. 209; **s1190** restitutis cunctis et quantum ad exteriorem ~iam firmiter pacificatis *Itin. Ric.* II 21; manifestam hypocrisis notam et simulatricis ~ie, ubi non subest existentie veritas Gir. *Spec.* III 13 p. 213; ex argento et ramo dealbato cum medicina fit plus argentum in ~ia (M. Scot *Part.*) *Med. Sci.* 295; **1230** nos cum magno gaudio et honore in ~ia suscepisset (*AncC* VI 155) *RL* I 366; **c1239** incidit anima decepta in hec loca 'in die nubis et caliginis' [*Ezek.* xxxiv 12], id est in quadam imaginaria ~ia qua concupita apparent esse vera bona Gros. *Ep.* 127 p. 375; cum merdam seminaveritis, merdam metere visi estis et ~ias sophisticationum *Correct. Alch.* 14; sic esset tantum equidistancia..secundum ~iam et non simpliciter secundum veritatem Upton 105. **b** ad quasdam que magis quadrivium redolent questiones ~ie causa se transferentes Gir. *GE* II 37 p. 355 (cf. ib. 348: ad ~iam sibi scientias comparaverunt); nunc de vanitatis ~ia, nunc de voluptatis intemperancia circa litteras notabamur R. Bury *Phil.* 18. 230. **c s1415** gradatum ascensum grosso lineo variis..petrarum coloribus ad murorum..~iam velatum Ad. Usk 128.

1 apparere v. aperire 4b. 2 apparere v. apparare 1a.

3 apparēre [CL], (of persons) to appear, show oneself. **b** to appear in court. **c** (w. adv. or gen.) to present an appearance. **d** to appear in a vision. **e** to attend, minister.

postquam..in hac eum provincia ~uisse et apud regem..habitare cognovit Bede *HE* II 12; **s1192** ~uerunt nuntii *Itin. Ric.* VI 31; **s1284** in Alemannia ~uit Fredericus quondam imperator, secundum opiniones diversas sophisticus sive verus *Flor. Hist.* III 61; **s1364** ~uit subito rex Philippus cum exercitu copioso *Meaux* III 58; si ad prefixum terminum non ~erent qui viris inclusis auxiliativos prestarent succursus Elmh. *Hen. V Cont.* 131. **b** utroque litigantium iterum ~ente in curia Glanv. III 3; **12..** ut coram nobis..~eant *FormOx* 277; **1268** coram eis [justiciariis] non ~et *Cl* 449; **1288** quod habeant tres summoniciones, tres districciones et tria essonia antequam ~eant *SelPlMan* 107. **c** ut..ceteris..clericis se conforment, ut unius cum aliis ~eant honestatis Peckham *Ep.* 561 p. 738; **s1308** [coronacioni interfuit] Petrus de Gavestone, qui nobiliter ~uit omnes transcendens Ad. Mur. 12. **d** ~uit ei..quaedam anicula Aldh. *VirgP* 25 p. 258; unus ex eis in visione nocturna ~uit cuidam de sociis suis Bede *HE* V 10; W. Malm. *GR* III 285 (*v.* apparitio 3d); [demones] sibi multotiens ex aëre corpore sumpto / nobis apparent *V. Merl.* 782; sunt qui dicunt hujusmodi phantasias ex animi timiditate et melancholia hominibus ~ere videri Gerv. Tilb. III 93. **e** ~et qui videtur, adparet qui obsequitur, non regulae ratione sed discernendi gratia intellectus Bede *Orth.* 2778.

2 (of objects or events) to appear, be seen. **b** (astr.). **c** (med., of symptoms). **d** (in a vision).

quicquid ~et per formam ~et Eriug. *Per.* 479B; ~uit non procul facies terre cujusdam Gir. *TH* III 26; non solum ~entia coram oculis cognoverunt sed absentia Bacon *Maj.* II 393; **1442** ita quod..offendiculum aliquod..infra..listas..non emineat nec appareat quovismodo (*Ac. Foreign*) *Analog. Cant. Pilg.* 24. **b** eclipsis solis facta..et ~uerunt stellae pene hora dimidia ab hora tertia diei Bede *HE* V 24; tercio modo accipitur mensis lunaris ex prima apparitione lune post conjunctionem suam cum sole donec iterum secundo ~eat Bacon VI 59. **c** oculum ita sanum..invenit ac si nil umquam in eo..tumoris ~uisset Bede *HE* IV 30; rubor et pustule que ~ent in facie juxta nasum *SB* 11. **d** ~uit..quasi fulgor stellae micantis inter tenebras Bede *HE* V 12 p. 306; quod..cuidam..obitus illius in visione ~uerit *Ib.* IV 21; **s1236** ~uerunt in aere portenta militum armatorum..velut hostiliter congruentium M. Par. *Min.* II 391.

3 to be evident. **b** (impers.).

ex hoc ~et improbacio illius quod dicitur in precedenti opinione Duns *PW* 28. **b 1283** prout per bundas et metas..plenius ~et *Chr. Peterb.* 65; **1313** prout in litteris..evidenter ~et *Reg. Heref.* 487; **1421** mitigacio..statutorum nimium, ut ~uit, astrictorum *Reg. Cant.* III 69.

4 (w. compl.) to appear, be seen to be, seem: **a** (of persons); **b** (of objects); **c** (of abstractions); **d** (? w. acc.).

a [Guillelmus II] perdomitis hostibus..~uit..qualis apud se latuisset W. Newb. I 2; **1340** de quibusdam, qui secundum sui habitus apparenciam scolares ~ere videntur, qui contra pacem..nequiter incedunt *FormOx* 159. **b** linteamina..integra ~uerunt et ita nova ut ipso die viderentur..ejus membris esse circumdata Bede *HE* IV 17 p. 246; corpus Dominicum inter manus ejus cruentum..~uit Eadmer *V. Oswald* 3; possunt sic figurari corpora ut maxima ~eant minima et e converso Bacon *NM* 534. **c** ita haec vita hominum ad modicum ~et Bede *HE* II 14; prime..allegaciones contra istum modum inefficaces ~ent Ockham *Dial.* 952; **1549** nisi cause in appellatorio contente relevantes ~uerint *Conc. Scot.* II 216. **d** quia preclarum virum in cunctis ~es *G. Herw.* 327b.

5 (pr. ppl.) evident, clear, manifest. **b** (?) outstanding. **c** (w. *heres*) apparent, evident, recognized. **d** (w. *lex*) revealing the truth (by ordeal; later by duel or grand assize.).

ista responsio videtur mihi ~ens Ockham *Dial.* 421; puto quod ~enciores raciones pro ipsa [assercione] non est facile invenire *Ib.* 578. **b 1238** venire faciat..xij homines de comitatu suo..tam milites quam libere tenentes de magis ~entibus, parati (*sic*) recognoscere.. *LTRMem* 12 r. 11 (1). **c 1202** quo justiorem vel ~entiorem heredem non novimus de comitatu *Pat* 8; **s1238** cum sim heres solus ~ens M. Par. *Maj.* III 477; **1406** declaramus prefatum principem Henricum, filium nostrum primogenitum, heredem nostrum ~entem, nobis in corona, regnis et dominiis..successurum *RParl* III 581b. **d** per legem ~entem purgandus est vel omnino ab imposito crimine absolvendus Glanv. XIV 1; non habet appellum femina, nisi de morte viri sui inter brachia sua interfecti vel de corpore suo proprio, per quod alicui judici debeat lex ~ens Bracton 125.

6 (pr. ppl.) apparent, seeming (as dist. from being).

videtur similitudo quedam, ~ens quidem specie, non existens autem in re W. Fitzst. *Thom.* 29; utinam [clerici]..fuerint..tam puri quam duri, tam existentes quam ~entes Gir. *TH* III 27; amicus / apparens, hostis tectus Vinsauf *PN* 1298; sunt qui motu veloci membrorum ~entia fingentes..multa mortalibus proponunt miranda Bacon *NM* 1 p. 523; **1475** instrumenta ferrea..cum quibus ipse M. nobilia et alias pecias aureas ~entes, cum sic non fuerunt, ..fabricavit *Ac. Chamb. Cant.* 143.

apparescere, to appear, come into sight.

subito ~unt carbasa non multa in medio mari *Enc. Emmae* II 3.

apparibilis, conspicuous.

ex venis sunt signa [dispositionis] oculi: si sint ~es et plene humoris, multitudo humoris egritudinis causa est Bacon V 85.

†apparigo, wound.

a wounde, apporia, ~o *CathA*.

apparilator, ~iator v. apparellator. apparine v. aparine.

apparitare [cf. apparare 1 c, apparatus 8], to annotate, provide w. a commentary.

c1290 quedam Decretales bene ~ate..ac omnes addiciones plenissime continentes *Ann. Durh.* 130; **1328** Decreta ~ata cum casibus et historiis in margine *Reg. Exon.* 563; juvenes impudentes qui..incipiunt fieri glossatores incongrui et, ubi largiorem marginem circa textum perspexerint, monstruosis ~ant alphabetis R. Bury *Phil.* 17. 222; **a1350** libros..ordinarios ~atos juris civilis *StatOx* 43.

1 apparitio v. apertio 1a. 2 apparitio v. apparatio.

3 apparitio, (of persons) appearance, showing oneself. **b** appearance in court (leg.).

s1284 de ~one Frederici *Flor. Hist.* III 61 *rub.* (cf. apparere 1a). **b c1240** sic erit dies ~onis [in j annum et j diem] et incipit ab hora nona die solari [trecentesimo] sexagesimo sexto *BNB* III 300; si unus ex pluribus warrantis defaltam fecerit ante ~onem Bracton 385; quibus dilacionibus potest tenens litem differre ante communem ~onem in curia Hengham *Magna intr.*; **s1392** utrique parti..diem ~onis constituere *Croyl. Cont. B* 490.

2 appearance, visibility. **b** (astr.).

Pictagorici vocaverunt colorem *epiphaniam*, sc. 'supra ~onem', eo quod sit extremitas corporis perspicui terminati

Bart. Angl. XIX 7. **b** quedam stelle sunt sempiterne ~onis, sc. que accedunt ad polum articum Sacrob. *Sph.* 82; **s1113** cometa ingens apparuit; quod in triste auspicium evenit, ut testatur..Claudianus, qui de comete dicit ~one.. M. Par. *Min.* I 218; propter multiplicationem ~onum stellarum Bacon *NM* 534.

3 (supernatural) apparition, manifestation: **a** (magical); **b** (angelic); **c** (divine). **d** Epiphany (6 Jan.).

a a fantasia, quod est ~o transiens, dicitur fantasma Map *NC* II 13; corpus Domini..sumere videbatur ~o revera, et non veritas fuit Gir. *GE* II 13; **s1236** de quibusdam ~onibus fantasticis M. Par. *Min.* II 391 *rub.*; **s1402** sic dicta fantastica vel fatalis ~o sepius delusit plurimas accedere cupientes Wals. *HA* II 254. **b** dixit..quod ~o Seraphyn facta fuit S. Francisco in quodam raptu contemplationis Eccleston *Adv. Min.* 93; non est tam crebra talis ~o angelorum Wycl. *Civ. Dom.* I 422; **1521** dorsorium..cum ~onibus angelorum *Cant. Coll. Ox.* I 64. **c** [Jesus] peracto momentaneae ~onis spatio mox in intellectualem invisibilemque..redibat Eriug. *Per.* 539A; de hac ~one et subsequenti nihil ab evangelistis dicitur Lanfr. *Comment. Paul.* (1 *Cor.* xv 6) 209; divine iste ~ones que theophanie dicuntur H. Bos. *LM* 1369. **d** aderat sacratissima dominicae ~onis dies Bede *Cuthb.* 11; ipse die Epiphaniorum moriens, .."hodie", inquit, "in die ~onis sue apparebit mihi Dominus meus Jesus Christus" W. Malm. *GR* III 285; erat autem vigilia dominice ~onis Ailr. *Ed. Conf.* 786D; dies ~onum sive epiphaniarum, que plures leguntur fuisse eodem die annis tamen diversis; quarum..una effecta est per stellam decimo tertio die a nativitate Christi, atque hec proprie dicitur 'epiphania'..; altera vero facta est per vocem Patris eodem die anno tricesimo et appellatur 'theophania'..; tertia denique nominata est 'bethania'.., apparuit enim in domo per transformationem aque in vinum Beleth *RDO* 73. 79 (cf. *Eul. Hist.* I 74: Christus..baptizatus est VI idus Januarii die Dominica, ..que vocatur Epiphania Domini tribus de causis: prima causa est ~o desursum per stellam).

apparitor [CL], **a** royal official, attendant, bailiff. **b** eccl. official, serjeant, summoner. **c** (acad.) bedel.

a apparator, ministrator, auxiliator *GlC* A 699; ~orum, adjutorum *Ib.* 664; **835** dabo aliquantulam partem terrae Badonoðe ~ori meo *CS* 449; hec sunt dominica placita regis; nec pertinent vicecomitibus vel ~oribus vel ministris ejus.. in firma sua (*Leg. Hen.*) *GAS* 556; suggestum est ab ~ore ut furtum rebus aliis, quasi furtivis, augeret W. Cant. *Mir. Thom.* II 3; [Henricus II] ex cubiculariis et aule nugatoribus episcopos [? et] abbates factos auctoritate propria ad officium ~orum revocavit R. Niger 167; **s1094** ilico cum transfretasset [Anselmus], ~ores omnia ecclesie ejus bona fiscalibus commodis addixerunt M. Par. *Min.* I 52; **s1295** missis ~oribus, confestim captus..non negavit facinus *Flor. Hist.* III 282. **b** **1219** statuimus..ut nullus decanus habeat ~orem nisi fuerit ille clericus ad minus ordinatus in acolitum *Conc. Syn.* 54 (cf. ib. 333*n.*); **1239** ballivi domini regis citati ad capitulum.. fingunt causas ut ~ores, decanos vel capellanos per quos citati sunt capiant *Ib.* 283; **1240** volumus quod ~ores communiter per officialem nostrum et archidiaconum eligantur *Ib.* 308; **c1258** precipimus quod decetero tam decani quam apparitores nobis..prestent fidelitatis juramentum *Ib.* 609; **1278** testibus..Stephano ~ore Oxonie *Cart. Osney* II 415; **1281** amoveatur ~or, preparatus ad predam, et compleatur ejus officium per decanum *Reg. Ebor.* 215; **1317** ad officium ~oris in archidiaconatu *Reg. Heref.* 33; **1335** cuidam apparatori de Arcubus *Comp. Swith.* 239; **1342** ~oris officium in..Cantuariensi curia *Lit. Cant.* II 251; **1401** apparatoribus consistorii..pro labore circa processionem *Ac. Durh.* 448; ~ores, sic dictos quia faciunt reos apparere in conspectu judicum Lyndw. 91*f*; **1446** scientes Thomam.. fore ~orem generalem..Lincolniensis episcopi *Eng. Clergy* 208; *a sominder*, citator, ~or, summonitor *CathA*; per praeconem curiae, viz. ~orem vel bedellum curiae *Praxis* 262. **c** **c1250** duo tantum bedelli seu ~ores juramento astricti habeantur.., universa semper parati mandata cancellarii adimplere *Stat. Cantab.* 207; **a1350** in bedellorum seu ~orum eleccione *Ib.* 320.

apparitura, ~us v. apparat-.

appaticiamentum [OF *apaticement*], tribute levied by victor in war.

1433 de et super appatissamentis capiendis et levandis in terris, patriis et dominiis inimicorum et rebellium..domini regis ultra flumen Ligeris (*DipDocE* 441) *Foed.* X 558a; **1446** absque hoc quod..molestentur..per captivitates, apatissamenta Gallice dicta *appatis*, cursus, fouragia.. (*Ib.* 504) *Ib.* XI 135a; **1444** in parte et modo solvendi ~a ab eisdem exigi consueta..qui in armorum agibilibus conversantur et ~a predicta disponere consuerunt *Cl.* 294 m. 6*d.* **1457** appatizamentum (v. appaticiare).

appaticiare [OF *apaticier*; cf. pacticius], to levy tribute from enemies.

1457 damus potestatem..ad quecumque loca et patrias inimicorum nostrorum, ubi..melius fieri poterit, appatizandi et in eisdem appatizamentum facere absque impeticione (*Pat*) *Foed.* XI 406a.

appaticiatio, imposition of tribute by victor.

dedimus..bonum et salvum conductum ac..securitatem appatisationis vel aliorum Upton 88.

†appediamentum [? *for* appodiamentum], 'foot' (support) of dam.

1259 concesserunt..fossatum..simul cum pede †apposita [? l. apposito] stagno..juxta vivarium.., salva..libera potestate frangendi stagnum suum cum ~o..quotiens.. placuerit *Cart. Colch.* 559 (cf. *MFG*).

appella v. appellum.

appellamen, appellation, name.

979 (11c) militi meo Eadwine ~ine *CD* 623.

appellamentum, 'appeal', accusation; *cf. appellum.*

1292 qui maliciose illud ~um fieri procuravit *Doc. Scot.* 358.

1 appellare v. apparellare.

2 appellare [CL], **a** to greet or summon. **b** to call, name. **c** (refl.). **d** to predicate (log.).

a eum salutans ac suo ~ans nomine Bede *HE* IV 22; **s1403** ~avit capitaneum et..alter alterum aggreditur Fordun *Cont.* XV 15. **b** in loco qui sermone Pictorum 'Peanfahel', lingua autem Anglorum 'Penneltun', ~atur Bede *HE* I 12; mirum quare stultum ~are velitis laborem nostrum *Ib.* III 25 p. 184; principia rerum causae quae primordialium causarum nominibus ~antur Eriug. *Per.* 552A; in ipso manerio Roelend est factum noviter castellum similiter Roelent ~atum *DB* I 269; appellativum nomen cujuslibet rei nunc dico quo res ipsa usu loquendi ~atur Anselm (*Gram.* 12) I 157; **1320** Willelmum S. Andree..et David Moraviensem episcopos, quos venerabiles fratres nostros ~are non possumus *Mon. Hib. & Scot.* 206b. **c** **1219** Willelmum le Champeneys, qui alio cognomine ~at se Willelmum de Arches *CurR* VIII 10. **d** **a1250** terminus ex parte subjecti supponit et ex parte predicati ~at (Shirwood) *GLA* III 19.

2 to vouch (vendor of property) to warranty (AS *tyman*); *cf. advocare 2.*

qui aliquid emit, emat cum testibus; et, si ~andum sit inde [AS: *hit eft tymon scyle*], recipiat hoc a quo emit (*Quad.*) *GAS* 165; si [venditor] recipiat, tunc adquietat eum cum quo fuerat deprehensum; ~et deinceps [AS: *cenne he syððan*] unde venerit ei *Ib.* 224.

3 to appeal against judgement (esp. eccl. law): **a** (trans.; obj. = person appealed to); **b** (absol.); **c** (w. *ad*); **d** (trans.; obj. = person appealed against); **e** (pr. ppl. as sb.) appellant; **f** (p. ppl. as sb.) adversary of appellant.

a de hac..quaestione..fiducialiter sedem ~o apostolicam Eddi *Wilf.* 47 (cf. ib. 63; Bede *HE* V 19); **s1146** orta simultate inter..archiepiscopum Cantie et..episcopum Wintonie, ipsi adversum alterutrum apostolicum ~averunt J. Hex. *HR Cont.* 319. **b** **s1203** ante sententiam ~avi *Chr. Evesham* 128; **s1265** abbas clausis januis episcopum exclusit.., ~ans auctoritate nove indulgentie nostre; sed episcopus non deferens appellationi eum excommunicavit *Ib.* 149; **1218** appellationem..gratam habemus; ..nichilominus ad majorem cautelam, ne quid inde fiat in prejudicium juris nostri, ~amus per has litteras nostras patentes *Pat* 148; **1228** sic procurator predicti P. recessit ~ans *Feod. Durh.* 280; **1235** ita..quod nulla fiat appellatio extra regnum, si de necessitate contingat ~ari *BNB* III 136; **a1322** si contingat aliquem..a sententia cancellarii in pacis perturbacione ~are *StatOx* 87; pro causa..heresis licet a papa eciam catholico ~are Ockham *Pol.* I 295; **a1350** dabis fidem quod contra statuta universitatis non ~abis *Stat. Cantab.* 313; si ~atur extrajudicialiter coram notario in scriptis *Praxis* 307. **c** **1194** ipsa ~avit ad curiam Romanam *CurR RC* I 57; a minori ad majorem ~ari solet Gir. *PI* I 17 p. 58; **1221** ne aliquid statuatis in prejudicium nostrum.., ad dominum papam..~amus *Pat* 311; **1233** ipsi ~averunt ad officialem episcopi Lond' *BNB* II 585; **s1312** episcopus ad sedem apostolicam ~avit Ad. Mur. 18; **1442** a denegacione justicie..~at ad..Lincolniensem episcopum *FormOx* II 469; **1456** sensato gravamine, immediate ~et ad universitatem regencium et non regencium *StatOx* 279. **d** **s1151** in Anglia appellationes in usu non erant donec eas H. Wintoniensis episcopus, dum legatus esset, malo suo crudeliter intrusit; in eodem namque concilio ad Romani pontificis audientiam ter ~atus est H. Hunt. *HA* VIII 31; **1446** libellus appellatorius..a parte ~ata admissus *Pat* 463 m. 23; citatio partis pro qua lata est sententia, ..quae dicitur pars ~ata *Praxis* 259. **e** **s1203** quum vestrum sit tueri ~antes *Chr. Evesham* 128; aliter accipit 'usum' ibi Augustinus et aliter ~ans Ockham *Pol.* II 547; **1593** cautionem..teneantur procuratores.., casu quo ~ans obtineat, eidem restituere *StatOx* 449; non sufficit ~anti dicere, aut in appellatione allegare, ~antem talem dedisse materiam et judicem eam rejecisse *Praxis* 248. **f** si ~atus credit ~antem juste ~asse, expedit ut idem ~atus..fateatur gravamina *Ib.* 252.

4 to 'appeal' (common law), accuse (*cf. appellum*). **b** (pr. ppl. as sb.) appellor. **c** (p. ppl. as sb.) appellee. **d** (pr. ppl. pl.) Lords Appellants.

si Anglicus ~et [AS: *beclypað*] Francigenam de utlagaria et hoc super eum inveritare velit (*Quad.*; *Inst. Will.*) *GAS* 484; si quis ~atur [OF *si home apeled auter*] de furto (*Leis Will.*) *Ib.* 503; **1130** habeat pacem de morte Willelmi..; et, si quis eum ~averit, defendet se legali lege *Pipe* 102; si ~etur minor de felonia aliqua, ..dum fuerit infra etatem non tenebitur respondere, sed demum factus major Glanv. VII 9; **1198** Erneburga ~avit Gill'..quod rapuit eam in pace domini regis *CurR* I 33; **1243** si forte contigerit quod appelentur de vita vel membris *BBC* (*London*) 168; cum taliter captus ..productus fuerit et de crimine ei imposito accusatus. ..si ..crimen defenderit precise et sit aliquis qui eum ~et per verba legitima appellum facientia, ..habebit electionem utrum se ponere velit super patriam..vel defendendi se per corpus suum Bracton 137; **1313** Matilda que fuit uxor T. ~avit Michaelem et sequebatur appellum usque ad iiij comitatum *Eyre Kent* 67; **1377** archipredones..penis / taliter absolvit ut presidis ante tribunal / discipulos appellarent agerentque duello (*Epitaph. Ed. III*) *Pol. Poems* I 223; **s1380** (v. appellator a); **1583** impetiri, ~ari, rectari *Pat* 1235 m. 23. **b** si ~ans diem suum non fuerit prosecutus, tunc plegii quoque in misericordiam regis incident Glanv. XIII 38; **1208** W. B. ~ans et H. B. ~atus de verberatione ponunt se in misericordiam pro habenda licencia concordandi *SelPlCrown* 24; **1228** placita..de pace fracta inter G. ..~antem et W. ..defendentem *Feod. Durh.* 218; **1236** per sic quod R. .., qui ~atus est de..roberia, tradatur in ballio, ..vel quod rex det ei licenciam concordandi cum ~antibus si ~antes voluerint *ExcRFin* I 293; si ~ans victus fuerit [in duello], gaole committatur tanquam calumniator puniendus Bracton 137. **c** semper victus, sive fuerit ~ans sive ~atus, in misericordia domini regis remanet Glanv. XIII 38; **1208** convenit inter J. .. ~antem et H. ..~atum de morte D. *SelPlCrown* 102; si omnia bene concurrant que jungant duellum, tunc det ~atus vadium defendendi..; et, si ~atus victus fuerit, capitalem subibit sententiam Bracton 137; **1265** probatores una cum ~atis eorum..in prisona custodias *Cl* 44; dicti ~ati fuerunt quieti de illa morte *State Tri. Ed. I* 82; **1309** postea *le appelour* et ~atus fuerunt manucapti *Year Bk. 2 Ed. II* 43. **d** **1388** cum..T. ..dux Glouc', H. comes Derb', R. comes Arundel' et T. comes War'..~averint A. archiepiscopum Ebor' [et al.] ipsique ~antes appellum suum predictum se optulerint ..prosecuturos (*Cl*) *Foed.* VII 567; tunc appellantes fuerant octo dominantes, / qui tres appellant Gower *CT* II 77.

3 appellare v. appellere.

appellatio [CL], **a** hailing, greeting. **b** utterance, expression. **c** name (esp. designative of class). **d** invitation, summons by bell (mon.). **e** feast after blood-letting (mon.).

a **752** haec fuit occasio tarditatis litterarum et ~onis paternitatis vestrae Bonif. *Ep.* 108. **b** hec ~o 'peccavi in Domino' dupliciter accipitur S. Langton *Quaest.* f. 171. **c** ut..aliter..vivere nequiret [Benedictus] quam propriae ~onis dignitas..permitteret Aldh. *VirgP* 30; alii terrae ~one mundi hujus inchoationem suadere conantur Eriug. *Per.* 545C; **a1250** ~o est presens convenientia termini, i.e. proprietas, secundum quam significatum termini potest dici de aliquo mediante hoc verbo 'est' (Shirwood) *GLA* III 17. **d** cum parvo signo..debet fieri pulsacio que vocatur ~o *Obs. Barnwell* 74. **e** **1457** minucio tercii prioris; ..in die Dominica nisi iij capones pro magna ~one *Ac. Almon. Peterb.* 96.

2 voucher (of vendor) to warranty; *cf. appellare 2.*

admoneat eum ille qui suum prosequitur ut ad singulas ~ones [AS: *to ælcan teame*] habeat credibile testimonium (*Quad.*) *GAS* 226.

3 appeal (esp. eccl. law). **b** appeal, supplication.

s1145 in ~one adversus..archiepiscopum Eboraci J. Hex. *HR Cont.* 318; **s1151** (v. appellare 3d); cum legibus illis ~ones ad Romanam ecclesiam inhibite forent H. Bos. *Thom.* IV 18; ~o est ad majorem judicem facta proclamatio; vel ~o est inique vel suspecte sententie date vel dande protestatio Ric. Angl. *Summa* 81; cum in quendam sibi familiarissimum..capitalem..sententiam ferret, in vocem ~onis ille prorumpit Gir. *PI* I 17; **s1203** ut sine ~one judicium ejus subiret *Chr. Evesham* 128; **1228** si castra.. restituta non fuerint infra xv dies, ego in pristinam sententiam recidam, ~one remota *Pat* 211; **1235** ita quod in inquisicione illa cesset omnis ~o, sicut in omni alia inquisicione de bastardia de qua inquisicio fuerit transmissa ad curiam Christianitatis *BNB* III 136; ille ~ones nichil erroneum continebant Ockham *Pol.* I 299; **s1434** ne pendente sua tuitoria ~one presumeret aliquid prejudiciale attentare Amund. I 371; **1516** si contingat aliquem..a sententia cancellarii in pacis perturbatione appellare, materia ~onis non valet *StatOx* 333; ~o vel est a gravaminibus..vel a sententia diffinitiva seu decreto interlocutorio *Praxis* 241. **b** **s1183** sepelierunt eum [Henricum] in eodem loco contra voluntatem et ~onem eorum qui corpus ejus deducebant Torigni *Chr.* 306.

4 'appeal', accusation; *cf. appellum.*

si contigerit presbyterum..calumniari de latrocinio.., missam celebret et per corpus Domini solus de una ~one, quam Angli vocant *anfealde spæce*, se purget (*Inst. Cnuti*) *GAS* 285; **1151** nullus eorum respondeat pro ~one alicujus latronis recognoscentis vel aliquo crimine convicti *Regesta* (*Norm.*) III 729; **1167** reddit compotum de c s., quia defecit de ~one de morte sororis sue in murdro *Pipe* 83; **1253** se defendant ab omnibus ~onibus per juramenta xxxvj hominum *BBC* (*Scarborough*) 187; **s1312** heres..Roberti defuncti prosequebatur ~onem versus E. W. *Ann. Lond.* 219; **1321** de ~one sive indictacione de morte hominis ponenda sive dimittenda *MGL* II 373.

appellativus, designative, indicative. **b** (sb. n., *sc. nomen*) common noun.

quod genus dictandi ab undecima ~orum nominum specie translatum reor Aldh. *Met.* 9 p. 81; **†931** (13c) in loco celebri ubi ruricolae ~a relatione nuncupant Maeldumesburg *CS* 671 (cf. ib. 708); **939** in illo loco cui ruricolae ~o usu..nomen indiderunt Æt Meapham *CS* 741; per acciones et locuciones et motus inde [sc. ex mente] provenientes convincimur cujus meriti sit homo.., et ita ~a interioris hominis est facies ad denoscendum ipsum in merito Kilwardby *Jejun.* 170. **b** haec..tam propria quam ~a in singulari numero pentaptota sunt Aldh. *Met.* 140; 'Turbo', si sit proprium, 'Turbonis' facit; si ~um, 'turbinis' Bede *Orthog.* 2803; ~um nomen cujuslibet rei nunc dico quo res ipsa usu loquendi appellatur Anselm (*Gram.* 12) I 157; aliud esse quod ~a significant et aliud esse quod nominant J. Sal. *Met.* 881A; aliud genus denominationis quando ponitur ~um pro proprio Garl. *Ex. Hon. Vit.* 166; habebunt ergo plurale tam ~a quam propria, set differenter Bacon XV 173.

2 designated, nominated.

1283 ne per ~os custodes bona ecclesie consumantur Peckham *Ep.* 427.

appellator, appellor, accuser (*cf. appellare* 4). **b** (w. *regis*) 'approver', criminal used as king's evidence. **c** thief.

~or [OF: *li apelur*] per vij legales homines ex nomine jurabit quod nec ex odio nec alia aliqua causa hoc ei imponit nisi tantum ut jus suum adipiscatur (*Leis Will.*) *GAS* 503; si ~or fuerit victus [in duello], in misericordia domini regis remanet Glanv. XIV 1; **1198** vadimonia duelli data fuerunt per G. . .defensorem et W. . .~orem *FormA* 185; **1201** si opus scelerosum et apertum inter eos [sc. Judeos] emerserit, . .licet nullus eorum inde ~or fuerit, nos ipsam querelam faciemus per legales Judeos nostros Anglie inquiri *RChart* 93b; det. .~or vadium disrationandi Bracton 137; **1269** defensor a sinistris primo jurabit tenens ~orem qui erit a dextris sic *CBaron* 77; **1285** procurant falsa appella fieri. .per ~ores nichil habentes (2 *Westm.* 12) *StRealm* I 81; s**1380** vocatus est armiger. .tali forma: "Thoma Katringtone, defensor, compareas defensurus causam tuam, pro qua dominus Johannes de Annesee, miles et ~or, te publice et in scriptis appellavit" Wals. *HA* I 432. **b 1259** in qua. .prisona confessus est et devenit appelator regis *Cl* 406. **c 1315** in qua quidem prisona [de Newegate] idem J. inter ~ores et latrones per biennium moram traxit *RParl* I 322a; **1316** placet domino regi ut latrones [? et] ~ores. .possint sacerdotibus sua facinora confiteri (*Artic. Cleri* 10) *StRealm* I 173; s**1382** descissa cesarie ad modum furum quos ~ores dicimus Wals. *HA* I 65; *pelowre, thefe*, ~or *PP*.

appellatorius, concerned w. appeals (eccl. law). **b** (sb. m. or n.) appeal. **c** (sb. f. pl.) letters of appeal.

libellum ~ium. .archipresuli transmiserunt H. Bos. *Thom.* IV 18; **1264** huic libello ~io sigilla plura apponi procuravi (*Apell. episcoporum*) Gerv. Cant. *Cont.* 242; **1446** ita quod dicta appellacio. .fuerit. .admissa. .libellusque ~ius legitimus. .porrectus et propositus et a parte appellata admissus *Pat* 463 m. 23. **b 1549** nisi cause in ~io contente relevantes apparuerint *Conc. Scot.* II 126. **c 1167** recepit ~ias vestras et alias nomine episcoporum J. Sal. *Ep.* 216.

appellatrix, appellor, accuser (f.).

s**1284** Christiana ~ix nunquam fuit uxor dicti Simonis desponsata; per quod appellum suum in hac parte non potest nec debet valere *Ann. Dunstable* 308; **1301** quia. . ~ix nullum attachiatorum predictorum de facto principali ~et *RParl* I 145b; **1315** Margareta ~ix. .appellat. .Johannem et alios. .de morte. .Roberti quondam viri sui, occisi inter brachia sua per hec verba. . *CoramR* 220 r. 105.

appellatus, 'appeal', accusation.

1201 si Judeus ab aliquo appellatus fuerit sine teste, de illo ~u erit quietus solo sacramento suo super librum suum; et de ~u illarum rerum que ad coronam nostram pertinent similiter quietus erit solo sacramento suo super rotulum suum *RChart* 93a.

1 appellere [CL], to drive (beasts) to. **b** to drive (a ship) towards. **c** to come ashore.

si quis prohibeatur. .pecus ad aquam ~ere Bracton 233. **b** navem. .quae. .tribus in provinciis in terram appulsa est *Hist. Abb. Jarrow* 31; ad portum quo. .sedecim naves appulit ventus G. Crispin *Herl.* 101; s **1386** surgente vento secundo appulsi sunt in Hispanniam Wals. *HA* II 143. **c** ~ens, †adplicens *GlC* A 702; †appulissit, applicavit *Ib.* 703; s**495** duces duo. .quinque navibus in Britanniam sunt advecti et in loco qui Cerdicesora nominatur ~antes (*sic*) . .dimicaverunt Fl. Worc. 4; nesciebant qui essent qui appulerant vel cur appulissent H. Hunt. *HA* IV 25; cursu prospero navis Anglie littoribus appulit T. Mon. *Will.* IV 10; **1590** in portu de Pullchelly. .cum navi. .invitos ~asse (*sic*) *SelPlAdm* II 170.

2 appellere v. aspellere.

appellitare, to name.

ut omnis fere medecinae ac artium quas mechanicas ~itant cura intermitteretur Boece 20 v.

appellum [OF *appel*], 'appeal', accusation brought by injured party (common law). **b** appeal against sentence (civil law).

nec in propria persona licebit petitori prosequi ~um suum, quia id fieri non potest nisi per testem idoneum audientem et videntem Glanv. II 3; **1196** de placito ~i *CurR* VII *app.* 333; **1200** de placito finis facti in curia domini regis de ~o de pace domini regis et violentia *Ib.* I 148; **1202** apellum de pace domini regis infracta, unde R. . .apellat L. *Ib.* II 100; **1215** nullus capiatur aut imprisonetur propter ~um femine de morte alterius quam viri sui *Magna Carta* 54; **1217** si episcopus admisit ipsum J., hoc fecit injuste et contra ~um. .Alani. .qui aramiavit assisam ultime presentationis de eadem capella *BNB* III 314; in omnibus ~is majoribus vel minoribus non potest appellans variare vel ~um suum in aliquo mutare Bracton 140b; coronatores querelam illam sive ~am (*sic*) irrotulare debent et omnia verba ~i per ordinem *Ib.* 154b; **1316** quidam seculares judices clericos. .reatus. .enormes. .coram eis confitentes admittunt ad accusacionem aliorum, quod ipsi communiter vocant ~um (*Artic. Cleri* 16) *StRealm* I 174; **1388** (v. appellare 4d). **b 1315** occasione cujusdam ~i quod procurator suus. .de curia nostra in ducatu predicto ad curiam regis Francie nomine ipsius B. fecit, in quo ~o cecidit *RGasc.* IV 1391 (cf. ib.: in eadem appellacione).

appencium v. appendicius 2a.

appendentia, appurtenance.

hec sunt que ad justitiam vel indulgentiam regis et fiscum proprie censentur cum apendenciis [v.l. appendiciis] suis (*Leg. Hen.*) *GAS* 559; ea de causa et ejusdam cause circumstanciis et ~iis *Entries* 468b.

1 appendēre (~ĕre), (intr.) to hang on, be attached to. **b** (of seals).

phialam. .parieti ~entem W. Cant. *Mir. Thom.* II 47; phalera, attillamenta et hernesia minuta carectis ~encia *Fleta* 172; **1303** duo lapides situati. .in auro invicem ~entes per laqueum de serico (*KRAc* 363/6) *DocExch* 280. **b 1217** scriptum. .cui sigillum domini regis. .~et *Cl* 342a.

2 (of land or sim.). **a** to belong to (a person). **b** to pertain, be appurtenant (absol. or w. dat.). **c** (w. *ad*). **d** (pr. ppl. as sb. n. pl.) appurtenances.

a s**1213** fugiente domino cui plurima castra ~ebant Wend. II 88. **b** †**1051** (16c) cum omnibus juribus et aliis rebus ~entibus *CD* 795 (cf. *Croyl.* 87); **1070** ex omnibus redditibus que michi redduntur ex hiis mansionibus et omnibus ibidem ~entibus *Regesta* p. 119; plurima desunt huic manerio quae T. R. E. ~ebant ibi *DB* I 219b; haec appreciata est in manerio cui ~et *Ib.* 320; huic manerio ~unt (*sic*) v soche in aliis hundret *Ib.*291; Hedenham. .cum omnibus xl hidis terre que ~ent *Text. Roff.* 225; a**1180** si quis burgensium meorum. .domum vel terram que eidem ville ~at (*sic*). .tenuerit *BBC* (*Pembroke*) 72; **1199** Jarreiam [in Pictavia] cum terris sibi ~entibus *RChart* 9a; **1425** cum. .commoditatibus et proficuis. .manerio. .pertinentibus, ~entibus sive spectantibus *FormA* 270. **c** hae iii mansiones append[en]t ad Wachetone *DB* I 100; **1212** duas hydas terre. .~entes ad baroniam de Heselbere *Fees* 80; **1275** unum feodum militis. .solebat ~ere ad villam de Polsted' *Hund.* II 142 (cf. ib. 144: est ~ens ad manerium de P.); de manerio. .ad quod advocacio ecclesie predicte est ~ens *Entries* 503b. **d** totum manerium cum ~entibus *DB* I 319.

3 (of persons) to belong to (hold land in).

omnes consules et meliores barones qui ~ebant ad Bedefordiam H. Hunt. *HA* V 16.

2 appendĕre [CL], (trans.) to hang up, hang on. **b** to append, affix (seals). **c** to attach (schedules). **d** to hang (malefactors). **e** to fit, adorn.

adpendens linteolum. .in una posta parietis Bede *HE* III 10; nobilis appensum pretiatur purpura velum *V. Ed. Conf.* 40 v.; cithara ejus paxillo appensa W. Malm. *GP* I 19; s**1190** appensorum in singulis proris scintillantibus radiis scutorum *Itin. Ric.* II 13; quintanam erigi fecerat, clypeum videlicet. .posti firmiter appensum Gir. *RG* II 4; s**1255** membra [malefactoris]. .ad iiij portas. .civitatis sunt appensa Oxnead *Chr.* 202; nulli licitum est. .pannum. . lineum suo lecto habere appensum *Cust. Cant.* I 194; arma sponsi. .in camera sua. .~ebat *Latin Stories* 133; **1397** sex anuli. .cum cristallis appensis *Ac. Durh.* 445; pro retibus suis ad pisces in stallis illis capiendos ~endis *Entries* 667. **b** s**1206** quod dispositio nostra. .esset duratura, quamvis sigilla nostra tunc non ~erentur *Chr. Evesham* 204; **1225** secundum formam scripti. .cui eorum sigilla fuerint appensa *Pat* 558; **1231** tunc habuit aliud sigillum et in alia forma quam sigillum fuit quod prolatum fuit in judicio et cartis appensum *CurR* XIV 1681; s**1238** appensa sunt tam legati quam aliorum magnatum sigilla M. Par. *Maj.* III 478; **1347** huic scripto indentato sigilla dictorum abbatis et. .Willelmi . .alternatim sunt appensa *G. S. Alb.* II 329; **13..** quod. . nullum testamentum ad probacionem admittatur nisi sigillum testatoris sit appensum vel appositum *MGL* I 403. **c 1302** inquisitionem. .vobis in schedula transmittimus hiis appensa *Ib.* II 232. **d** s**1095** ille appensus est admirando fortitudinis spectaculo W. Malm. *GR* IV 319; illum furcis ~ere voluit R. Cold. *Cuthb.* 129. **e** sella et phalera ejus bestiolis et aviculis auro paratis. .~ebantur Ailr. *Ed. Conf.* 377.

2 a to weigh out, pay. **b** to weigh, put on the scales. **c** (fig.). **d** to weigh, have a weight (of). **e** to ponder.

a s**1173** marcis ccc a civibus numeratis et appensis Diceto *YH* I 376. **b** in lance utraque. .~antur pondera equalia Bacon *Maj.* I 170. **c** sed non aequatis appendit lancibus aequi / testamenta Dei Frith. 262. **d** precipimus ne quis pecuniam puram et recte ~entem sonet (*Quad.*) *GAS* 234 (cf. ib.: impurum et minus ~ens); ut. .majoretur judiciale ferrum ut ~at lx sol. [AS: *þæt hit gewege þry pund*] *Ib.* 389; oblata imagine argentea xiij solidos ~ente W. Cant. *Mir. Thom.* VI 51; s**975** [moneta] vetus. .adeo erat corrupta ut vix nummus obolum ~eret in statera M. Par. *Maj.* I 467; s**1040** quilibet. .duas habebat armillas aureas xvj. .uncias ~entes *Ib.* 514 (= Fl. Worc. 195: pendentes); emina ~it libram unam Bart. Angl. XIX 125. **e** impii. .vilipendunt antequam ~ant Map *NC* II 3 p. 130.

appendicius, attached, adjoining. **b** appurtenant.

11.. hec fuerunt ibi edificia que [tenens] cum manerio reddet: sc. una aula et una camera ~ia et una coquina. . *Dom. S. Paul.* 136; in proprio Lateranensi palatio ecclesiam . .fabricavit et basilicam ~iam Gir. *Spec.* IV 4. **b 955** (12c) terras ~ias que per loca diversa ad eandem villam pertinent *CS* 906; multa sedis sue ~ia predia. .ad jus legitimum trahere W. Malm. *GP* I 17; s**1263** castra. .in deditionem accepit; que cum provincia appenditicia Rogero. . tradidit ad custodiendum *Flor. Hist.* II 486.

2 (sb. n. or f.) attached building, lean-to, penthouse (*cf.* OF *apentiz*). **b** (w. *curia*) Pentice Court, Chester. **c** ornament of robe. **d** ornament of curtain, hanging. **e** appendage, fitment. **f** (?) book-cover (*cf. appendix a*).

1141 recepit bonam hallam et cameram et j ~ium ad hallam versus sud' *Dom. S. Paul.* 136; [Wilfridus] ipsum corpus ecclesie appentitiis et porticibus undique circumcinxit Ric. Hex. *Pri. Hex.* 3; **1175** in operatione unius coquine et j appenticii ubi regina junior audit missam *Pipe* 188; **1212** fieri facias apendicias ad eundem murum. ., in quibus omnia ateiuriamenta navium. .possint custodiri *Cl* 117a; **1231** habere faciant J. carpentario regis maeremium. . ad quoddam appenticium faciendum ultra furnum *Cl* 14; **1237** pro appencio wallando et cooperiendo *KRAc* 501/18 r.2; **1240** appenticium supra illas fenestras plumbo cooperiri facias; aperturas etiam duorum apenticiorum inter aulam nostram et cameram regine nostre. .bordiri. .facias *Liberate* 15 m. 23; **1276** levavit unum ~ium nimis bassum (*Eyre*) *Lond. Ed. I & II* 141; **1288** J. . .Taverner habet apenticiam ad parvam tabernam suam ad nocumentum ibidem equitancium *Leet Norw.* 7; s**1310** omnia appenticia nociva que invenerant concito cum ligonibus fecit prosterni *Ann. Lond.* 175; **13..** quod appenticia sint ita sublimia quod homines potuerint faciliter sub illis ire et equitare *MGL* I 259; si hujusmodi tenens aliqua appenticia seu alia asiamenta. .in domibus fecerit et ad meremium. .domus per clavos ferreos vel ligneos attachiata fuerint, . .semper remanebunt domino soli ut parcella ejusdem *Ib.* 432; *pentyse off a hows eende*, . .*schud, to-fal*, . .~ium *PP*; *a pentis*, appendix, ~ium, appendiculum, appenticium *CathA*. **b 1403** curia Portmoti seu Appenticii Cestr' *Plantagenet & Tudor Chester* 199 (cf. *Gild Merch.* II 44). **c** a**1100** tres clamides ad opus acolitorum, quarum videlicet una cum duobus ~iis auro brusdatis *Process. Sal.* 184; **1416** unum vestimentum integrum quadragesimale de serico albo cum ~iis de panno lineo *Reg. Cant.* III 417; ~ium, A. *a lady trayne* et A. *a pendaunt of a gyrdyll* WW. **d 1459** j novum ~ium pro capite aule stragulatum ex rubio et viridi *Cant. Coll. Ox.* I 16; **1493** cortinas de duplici tartara. .cum ~iis suis et ceteris necessariis (*Invent.*) *Bannatyne Misc.* II 26. **e 1258** navem cum atillio et ~iis suis *Cl.* 318; sciantur. .geometricalia super omnia hec, ut arca Noe, tabernaculum cum omnibus ~iis suis. . Bacon *Min.* 358. **f 1417** lego. .unum librum vocatum Ferrum cum ~iis suis *Reg. Cant.* II 119.

3 (sb. n.) dependency, appurtenance (of land, tenement or sim.). **b** adjunct, associated matter.

856 (12c) xx cassatos. .cum omnibus ad se rite pertinentibus ~iciis *CS* 491; s**1043** stabilit locum cum suis ~iis libertate regia data Herm. Arch. 17; c**1070** habeant manerium suum. .cum omnibus rebus et ~iis suis *Regesta* p. 120; de ~iis hujus manerii tenuit xx hidas *DB* I 58; hoc manerium cum suis ~iis et consuetudinibus reddit firmam unius noctis *Ib.* 75; hec iii maneria reddebant firmam hunius noctis cum suis ~iis *Ib.* 87; c**1087** manerium cum omnibus ~iis suis *Foed.* (*ed.* 1816) I 5 (cf. *Regesta* no. 290 = *FormA* 176: appenticiis); **1091** cum tota decima ejusdem ville et cum ceteris ~iis, exceptis monachorum decima et sepultura *Reg. S. Osm.* I 198; Ethelwulfus. ., avito. .regno contentus, cetera que pater subjugaverat ~ia filio Ethelstano contradidit W. Malm. *GR* II 108; Dunstanus, . .omnia quondam ~ia et iis multo plura nactus, abbatiam composuit [Glastonie] *Id. GP* II 91; a**1150** terram. .cum molendino et apentisiis suis *Reg. S. Aug.* 385; a**1150** dedisse . .A. burgensem meum. .et duas carucatas terre. .cum omnibus consuetudinibus et appenticiis *Deeds Newcastle* 49; de jure et de ~iis corone regni Britannie (*Leg. Ed. Lond., rub.*) *GAS* 635; dicitur insula nunc esse in com. Cantebrigie ij centuriatuum, sed unum est cum ~iis que deforis sunt *Lib. Eli. prol.* p. 3; **1282** cum Snaudon' sit de ~iis principatus Wallie Peckham *Ep.* 358; **1300** curiam burgensium. . cum omnimodis libertatibus pertinenciis et apendiciis suis *BBC* (*Warrington*) 182. **b** [Cistercienses] horas canonicas indefesse continuant, nulla ~ia extrinsecus adjicientes preter vigiliam pro defunctis W. Malm. *GR* IV 336; qualiter circa hanc [eucharistie venalitatem] delinquitur primum videamus, et postea de ~iis aliqua dicamus Gir. *GE* II 24; intellectus. .apprehendit formam abstrahendo eam materia et ab apendiciis materie J. Blund *An.* 233; formas absolute, prout a motu et materia omnibusque ~iis per intellectum nostrum agentem abstrahuntur *Ps.*-Gros. 359; s**1344** ad quod quidem [sc. Mensam Rotundam] observandum, sustinendum et promovendum in omnibus suis ~iis comites. .consimile fecerunt juramentum Ad. Mur. *app.* 232; idem est concedere scripturam esse impossibilem secundum partem hujusmodi et concedere illam esse impossibilem cum aliis ~iis inconvenientibus recitatis Wycl. *Ver.* II 113; **1387** istud kalendarium. .habet. .duas tabulas; . .et adjungitur sibi tabula festorum mobilium cum suis ~iis durans in eternum (Elveden *Cal.*) *SB* 5.

appendiculum, a (?) plumb-line (*cf. perpendiculum*). **b** penthouse.

a libra equaliter teneatur per ~um, ut stet ~um ad angulos rectos super regulam libre in centro revolutionis Bacon *Maj.* I 170. **b** *a pentis*, appendix, appendicium, ~um *CathA*.

appenditicius v. appendicius 1b.

appendium, reel.

14.. ~ium, A. *a yernwynder or a reel* WW.

appendix [CL], **a** (?) book-cover. **b** penthouse (*cf. appendicius 2a*). **c** dependency.

scriptor. .cedula sive apendice tam superiori parte quam inferiori folia habeat conjuncta Neckam *Ut.* 116. **b** *schud, to-fal*, ~ix, appendicium *PP*; *a pentis*, ~ix, appendicium *CathA*. **c** nunc urbes Majoris Britannie cum suis ~icibur explicemus Gerv. Tilb. II 10.

2 adjoining (? *f.l.*).

s**1380** cum. .innumerabiles de †~icibus [? l. ~entibus *or* ~iciis] comitatibus. .confluxissent Wals. *HA* I 438.

appendulus, dependent, appurtenant.

1181 capella non alicui vicinarum ecclesiarum ~a *Dom. S. Paul.* 152 (cf. *Vis. S. Paul.* [c**1250**] 4).

appensio, hanging (of bells). **b** appending, affixing (of seals).

1414 in expensis factis circa ~onem sex campanarum antiquarum *Ac. Durh.* 404. **b 1226** tenorem litterarum. . imperatoris. .~one bulle ipsius auree munitarum (*Lit. Papae*) *Reg. S. Osm.* I 193; **1231** ut hec omnia rata et inconcussa permaneant, sigillorum nostrorum ~onibus ea communimus *Reg. Malm.* I 390; **1281** in cujus rei testimonium presentem paginam sigilli nostri fecimus ∼one muniri Peckham *Ep.* 488; **1346** hoc scriptum signorum nostrorum ∼one roboravimus *Reg. Paisley* 10; **1441** presencium sub nostri regalis sigilli ∼onis testimonio litterarum (*Lit. Regis Romanorum*) Bekynton II 103; **1452** datum .. quoad sigilli nostri ∼onem, octavo die mensis Maii *Reg. Whet.* I 18; **1526** restringimus ut in ∼one sigilli communis.. sufficiat consensus prioris et majoris atque sanioris partis capituli (Wolsey: *Vis. Worc.*) *EHR* XL 91; **1616** pardonavimus..controfacturam magni sigilli nostri Anglie et ejusdem proditoriam ∼onem..litteris patentibus *Pat* 1686 m. 15.

2 weight.

panis ordeaceus esse debet siccus et caseus caprinus aridus, †que [? l. quorum, *as Text. Roff* 33] ∼o sit unius uncie (*Jud. Dei*) *GAS* 425*n.*; *a weynge*, libramen, ..∼o *CathA*.

3 pension (eccl.).

1189 ecclesiam de Tatecastre cum annua ∼one ecclesie de Neutona *Cart. Sallay* 623.

appensor, weigher.

a weyer, ∼or, librator, ..ponderator *CathA*.

appent- v. appendicius. apper- v. et. aper-. apperivare v. approuare 2b.

appersonare, to institute as parson (*cf. impersonare*).

rex et comes..Alexandro episcopo Lincolniensi [ob. 1147] Gilebertum..presentaverunt, postulantes ut predictam ecclesiam ei concederet et eum ∼aret *G. S. Alb.* 114.

appertinere, to appertain (of land). **b** (?) to annex (or *l. ad pertinendum*). **c** to belong.

adpertinebant adhuc huic manerio vii acrae *DB* II 4. **b** **1270** jus et clamium quod habui..in manerio de Purle, ..quod clamavi habere adpertinendum manerio de Hamstede *Cl* 249. **c** **1403** confirmavit quod medietas navis.. necnon xvij laste allecium..sibi ∼eant (*Lit. consulum Lubic.*) *Foed.* VIII 287.

appetere [CL], to desire. **b** (w. inf.). **c** (w. *post*). **d** to claim, demand. **e** (fig.) to seek out, be drawn to.

[animus] cum se..ad exteriora sparserit, etiam cum interiora ∼it, ad haec..minor redit Bede *HE* II 1 p. 74; ipsum [Deum] omnia ∼unt Eriug. *Per.* 451D; omnis ∼endi conatus perit ex desperatione consequendi Gir. *TH intr.* p. 5; Bacon II 112 (v. appetitivus a). **b** [mundi processionem] formari ∼entem Eriug. *Per.* 549B; quis sic amet justitiam, veritatem, beatitudinem..ut iis frui non ∼at? Anselm (*Mon.* 70) I 80. **c** c**1430** nec ulterius Judaice ∼ant post ollas carnium *Reg. Whet.* II 388 (cf. *Exod.* xvi 3). **d** [Arturus] imperatoribus..mandavit se..Romam aditurum..ut ex illis ∼eret quod ab illo judicio suo ∼ere decreverunt G. Mon. IX 20. **e** multoties dignitatis sublimitas sui solet appetitores contemnere, ∼ere contemptores Ad. Scot. *Ord. Prem.* 599B; gloria.., appetitores sui deserens, ∼it contemptores Gir. *EH* I 4.

2 to attack.

si quis aliquem clericorum in accusatione fornicacionis ∼it (*Leg. Hen.*) *GAS* 550.

appetibilis [CL], desirable. **b** desirous.

in habitu, quem oculis intuentium preferebat, et decens et ∼is compositio inerat Eadmer *V. Oswald* 6; quanto.. solicitudine ∼ior est tranquillitas Gir. *TH* I 40; reprobis, ut debita sibi diutius differant, ∼is est longevitas *Id. GE* II 8 p. 207; posite sunt virtutes naturales in membris generativis cum delectatione nimia et sapore ∼i ut vigeat appetitus Gilb. VII 282 v. 1; divitiarum..possessio.., cum sit ∼is secundum naturam corruptam viventibus Ockham *Pol.* II 615; quid..plus ∼e quam habere vitam eternam? Wycl. *Ver.* II 170; quis..dubitabit terminum vie, ad quam attenditur, esse ∼iorem quam ipsam viam? Paul. Angl. *ASP* 1547. **b** vindicta, cujus precipue sancti illi ∼es esse videntur Gir. *TH* III 33 (= *IK* I 2).

appetibilitas, desirability. **b** (?) urge to approach.

quecunque condiciones tradantur de fine magis nate sunt ostendere ∼atem finis Duns *Sent. prol.* 4. 29. **b** actio est.. estimationis in his intentionibus [operari] per modum †inconvenientie [? l. convenientie] et ∼atis, disconvenientie et fuge *Ps.*-Gros. 478.

appetitio, (gratification of) desire; *v. et. appetitudo*.

mysticum thymiama tanta inhibetur districtione ne fiat in usus humanos perversum ad ∼ones temporalium Ad. Marsh *Ep.* 247 c. 12.

appetitivus, a attrahent, attractive. **b** provocative of appetite (for food). **c** provocative of desire. **d** desirous. **e** meant to attract.

a humor..ab arborum radicibus ∼a quadam virtute attrahitur J. Sal. *Pol.* 427D; [virtutem] motivam de loco ad locum dividunt medici in tres, sc. ∼am, que trahit rem necessariam ad locum, et expulsivam ..et retentivam *Ps.*-Ric. *Anat.* 14; materia..habet in se aliquod principium.. ∼um, unde appetit terminum generationis completivum, sicut mulier virum et turpe bonum, et sic est principium motus intra per appetitum naturalem fortem quo desiderat compleri Bacon II 112. **b** cepit cogitare de cibo, et statim pulso fastidio vis ∼a ad cibi desiderium excitatur Ailr. *Ed. Conf.* 786B; defectum virtutis ∼e Gilb. V 208 v. 1; crocus dejicit virtutem ∼am Gad. 10 v. 1. **c** vis ∼a non illud apprehendit quod anima secundum eam appetit J. Blund *An.* 74; queritur si in singulis viribus est propria voluntas sive proprius appetitus, aut si est una potentia voluntaria sive ∼a diffusa per totum Gros. 265; c**1260** potentia mentis rationalis create cognitiva et †appetiva non tantum est activa sed et receptiva; ideo..potest recipere adjutorium cognoscendi et appetendi sive diligendi infinitum (T. Docking) *Doc. Francisc.* 110; appetitus est motus ab anima; et ideo est in ∼a [sc. virtute] secundum racionem propriam appetibilium; que, quia differunt secundum genus appetibilis, necesse est differre vires ∼as eciam secundum racionem [generis] Peckham *Quaest.* I 7 p. 79; virtus hominis ∼a interior per peccatum originale ita viciata est ut sibi viciorum suavia et virtutum aspera opera sapiant Fortescue *LLA* 4. **d** dicitur vis esse concupiscibilis secundum quod anima dicitur esse ∼a rei delectabilis J. Blund *An.* 71. **e** per opuscula vana..plausus popularis aucupativa..et ∼a Gir. *LS* 419.

appetitor, desirer (*v. et. appetere 1e*). **b** claimant. **c** visitor.

∼or honesti, turpitudinis executor Osb. *V. Dunst.* 8; ut ∼ores mali pravas actiones nequaquam exercere praesumant Lanfr. *Ep.* 37. 535C; Aidanus, ∼or silentii et sancte paupertatis W. Malm. *GP* III 126; s**1147** vir mollis et thalamorum magis quam militie ∼or *G. Steph.* II 110; vir docilis..et litteralis eruditionis ∼or Gir. *RG* II 2. **b** s**1147** Henricus .., justus regni Anglorum heres et ∼or, ..Angliam advenit *G. Steph.* II 107. **c** inter quamplures curie [Henrici I] ∼ores..Majoris Monasterii abbas..advenit *Chr. Battle* 50.

appetitrix, desirous (f.).

s**1327** communitas regni, veterum fastidiatrix, novorum ∼ix Baker 106b.

†appetitudo, (?) desire.

Deus..operatur exteriores operaciones..secundum imperium suum et a se partitas distribuciones potestatum et †∼ines [v.l. appeticiones; ? l. aptitudines] commoditatum Bradw. *CD* 171C.

appetitus [CL], attraction. **b** desire. **c** appetite (for food). **d** (w. *caninus*) unnatural appetite, 'bulimy'.

duorum..ad se invicem ∼us Eriug. *Per.* 470A (cf. ib. 603B). **b** ∼us, *gidsung GlC* A 683; appetitus turpis lucri Aldh. *VirgV* 2578; pro ∼u aeternorum bonorum liberius laborare Bede *HE* IV 23; nec ipsi ∼us..justi vel injusti sunt per se considerati Anselm (*Orig. Pecc.* 4) II 144; cum sis..curialis gratie appetitor, ∼us hic.. celestis ..gratie fluenta siccavit P. Blois *Ep.* 107. 331A; duplex est ∼us: unus qui est in conjunctione convenientis et hic dicitur delectatio; alter qui est in separatione convenientis..et hic dicitur tristitia Hales *Qu.* 262; s**1386** ceteris nobilibus.. indigne ferentibus tante promocionis ∼um in viro tam mediocri Wals. *HA* II 148; sine ∼u et desiderio ad coitum *SB* 35; sine gravi pena, que multociens..de cordibus audiencium ∼um audiendi extinguit *Plusc. prol.* **c** *orexis* interpretatur ∼us; unde †onorexia ab *a*, quod est 'sine', et *orexis*, i. 'stomachi ∼u' *Alph.* 131. **d** caninus ∼us dicitur quia, sicut nunquam canis saciatur set continue comedit usque ad vomitum, ..sic faciunt isti Gad. 89 v. 2; †cinorodoxa, i. gula canina, i. caninus ∼us *Alph.* 41.

appetivus v. appetitivus c.

appietantia [cf. pietantia], pittance (mon.).

1362 [lego] conventui Karl' ad unam ∼iam j bovem *Test. Karl.* 64; **1417** lego meliorem peciam meam deauratam.. collegio [de Merton'] ad serviendum custodi in diebus ∼ie *Reg. Cant.* II 215 (cf. ib. 175: ad ∼iam sociorum); **1489** quod vigilie Nativitatis Domini et Pentecostes sint dies allocacionis, que priscis temporibus erant ∼ie minores *Reg. Merton* 126.

appingere [CL], to paint on, add colour. **b** (fig.).

femina..sandaliis suis non aurum tantum appinxerat sed et varium et grisium insuerat W. Cant. *Mir. Thom.* VI 69. **b** forme tam picte si vis appingere cultum Vinsauf *PN* 600.

applacitare, to claim.

Arnisius..feretrum S. Ecgwini cuidam..custodiendum commendabat; quod ut abbas Ageluuius [ob. 1077] cognovit, ..recto jure illud debere esse proprium hujus sancte ecclesie adplacitavit *Chr. Evesham* 94.

applanare, to level, smooth.

si timpora..∼entur, ..moriendo loquentur, sed loquendo moriuntur Gilb. IV 196 v. 2; locum aurore roseatum ostendit, / et iter in momento lucis applanat J. Howd. *Cant.* 374.

applanes v. aplanes.

applar [CL *s. dub.*], ear-pick.

∼are, *eorscripel GlC* A 706.

applauda v. aplu da.

applaudenter, w. applause.

1286 clerus..tricesimam suorum proventuum..vestre concessit magnificencie ∼er *Conc. Syn.* 981; cuncta regi nostro ∼er subministrant elementa *Chr. S. Edm.* 62; quicunque..recipit a vobis aplaudenter benediccionem Wycl. *Sim.* 19.

applaudere [CL], to applaud (w. dat. or absol.); **b** (w. clapping wings, fig.). **c** to arrogate.

adplaudat, *on hlior rouuit GlC* A 267; venienti Stigandus processu et favore applausit W. Malm. *GP* I 23; dum tibi ∼unt ceci et videntes minantur Map *NC* IV 3 p. 148; **1296** eleccioni et electo ineffabiliter ∼abant (*sic*) *Reg. Cant.* II 1275; s**1399** populo pre nimio gaudio fortiter ∼ente *V. Ric. II* 290. **b** cum ei jam pene victoria letis ∼eret alis H. Hunt. *HA* IV 18. **c** qui [aruspices]..sibi frustra latentium rerum peritiam ∼unt Aldh. *VirgP* 44.

applausor, applauder.

Kenwlphi regis munificencie ∼or Elmh. *Cant.* 338.

applausorius, applausive.

exultationis clamor ∼ius Neckam *NR* II 155.

applausus, applause, congratulation, approval. **b** (?) song of triumph.

processit..non sine ∼u benedicentium ei J. Ford *Wulf.* 53; s**1190** reficiuntur exercitus mutuis ∼ibus et colloquiis Devizes 29; **1271** cum consensu et ∼u omnium qui aderant *Ch. Sal.* 351; **1318** ista, quesumus, dilectis filiis nostri capituli ad eorum ∼uum solamina, que eis inducere cupimus, nuncietis (*DCCant*) *HMC Var. Coll.* I 269; **1345** dum speraretur pacis tranquillitas provenire, ecce, tranquillitatis ∼us in subitam transiit tempestatem (*Lit. Regis*) Ad. Mur. 169; si..dominarum ∼ui vacassemus R. Bury *Phil.* 18. 235; s**1461** cum maximo ∼u et complausu tocius plebis.. consummavit sollemnia coronacionis *Reg. Whet.* I 401. **b** s**1323** [rex] episcopos..expoliavit, super quibus clam inter sceleratos crebro furiosos composuit ∼us et ridiculosos *Flor. Hist.* III 219.

†applectatus, folding.

1553 de..una parva mensa ∼a, A. *on litle folding table*, ..una parva cathedra ∼a, A. *one lytell foldinge chayer Pat* 852 m. 28.

applegiamentum, surety.

1282 racione aplegiamenti quod W. de C. de vi et injuria contra..Willelmum T...fecerat super manerio de M. *RGasc.* II 148.

applegiare, to become pledge or surety for.

quod..acquietet R. de centum m. versus R., unde eum ∼iavit Glanv. X 4; **1309** latronibus..indictatis et pro magna parte coram ballivo ∼iatis ad assisas (*JustIt*) *S. Jers.* 18 p. 32.

appilare v. ampliare 1a.

applicabilis, applicable, readily applied.

mentem..liberalibus studiis aptabilem valde et ∼em Gir. *JS* 7 p. 335; intellectus..qui ad infinita est ∼is omnino est illimitatus Duns *Prim. Princ.* IV 76 p. 681 (ed. Wadding p. 773); intencio secunda vocatur aliquid in anima rebus ∼e predicabile de nominibus rerum (Ockham *Sent.* I 23. 1D) *GLA* III 342.

applicare [CL], to bring into contact, lay on, join. **b** (fig.) to bring nearer. **c** (refl. w. *ad*) to strike. **d** (intr.) to come into 'application' (astr.; *cf. applicatio 1b*).

adplicuit, *gepuidde GlC* A 288; lampadarum flammas ∼avit Aldh. *VirgP* 47; orbis terrarum et paradisus in unam terram ∼abantur Eriug. *Per.* 534AB; cum ∼uisset emplastrum W. Cant. *Mir. Thom.* VI 6; cum [rex]..buccellam ori ∼uisset M. Par. *Min.* I 166; cathaplasma..inter durum et liquidum super membrum tepidum ∼atur *SB* 15; injurias..antedictas pro perpetuo remittant..ac manus ad invicem ∼ent, de cetero super his litem..minime moturi *MunAcOx* 722. **b** omnis paulatim loeto nos applicat hora Alcuin *Carm.* 62. 80. **c** fulmina..ad ea que in terris sublimiora reperiunt..se frequentius ∼ant Gir. *IK* I 12 p. 95. **d** luna Veneri applicans in mansionibus humidis ymbres futuros nunciat Rob. Angl. (II) *Sph.* 165.

2 to bring ashore. **b** (intr.) to come ashore, land. **c** to land at, reach by sea.

1320 cum [naves] ad kaias ∼ate fuerint *MGL* II 393; s**1345** cum grandi comitatu armatorum transfretaverunt versus Vasconiam; quibus ibidem..∼atis, attraxerunt sibi ..dominos illius terre Ad. Mur. *Cont. A* 161; S. Augustino sic ∼ato Thorne *prol.* 1759; **1388** diversa..bona..que ∼uit in aqua de Trent *IMisc.* 239/7 r. 1; rex cum majori parte exercitus sui in naviculis, batellis et cymbis terre se ∼uit Elmh. *Hen. V* 14; **1448** de custuma brasii et vini ∼atorum ad portum de Lethe per Anglicos *ExchScot* 316. **b** in hac [insula] applicuit..Augustinus Bede *HE* I 25; de exitu aquae ubi naves ∼abant rex habebat ii partes *DB* I 32; **1201** alie naves que egresse erant de portu cum illa non ∼uerunt eodem die *Canon. G. Sempr.* 19. 151v.; applicat armipotens ibi rex Garl. *Tri. Eccl.* 131; **1261** ballena que nuper ∼uit apud Somercote *Cl* 459; **1276** de bonis cujusdam felonis ignoti, qui ∼uit in thethinga de Coverton' et, cum perpendebat se ∼uisse, abivit antequam potuit attachiari *Hund.* I 56; **1368** impignorari faciat..omnes qui ∼ant cum velis super solum domini *Hal. Durh.* 75. **c** a**690** vestram.. ambrosiam..territorii marginem Britannici ∼uisse..comperimus Aldh. *Ep.* 5; **1289** cum ipsos..cum navibus et.. mercimoniis suis..portum ∼are contigerit *RGasc.* II 340; s**1399** dux Henricus..in loco ∼ari insolito..∼uit Ad. Usk 25.

3 a to appoint (to a task). **b** to subject (to a penalty). **c** to subject (to authority).

a **1236** fas non est publicarum rerum nexibus implicatos divinis serviturosm ∼are ministeriis Gros. *Ep.* 28 p. 110; **1298** monachi..ad repetendum divinum servicium ∼entur *Cant. Cath. Pri.* 46*n*. **b** s**1323** certos milites..diris tormentorum suppliciis precepit ∼ari *Flor. Hist.* III 215 (cf. ib. 205: nobiles..suppliciis et neci..∼andi). **c** **1262** auxilium apponant..quod presumptuosa dominatio predicti David [fratris Lewelini] deprimatur et jurisdictioni regie ∼etur *Cl* 143.

4 to apply or devote to a purpose: **a** (of things, esp. money); **b** (of principles or knowledge); **c** (of the mind or the writer's pen); **d** (refl.).

a c1230 dedisse..ecclesie..de D. ..terram..usibus suis ~andam *Dryburgh* 115; libros..ad alium usum nisi ad..studium nullatenus ~abunt R. Bury *Phil.* 19. 242; 1349 sub pena dupli illius quod sic solutum..fuerit.., illi qui ex hoc se senserit gravatum..~andum (*sic*) (*Stat. Lab.*) *StRealm* 307; 1370 si testamentum non fecerint, ..bona collegio ~entur *Lit. Cant.* II 503; 1412 ordinavit quod c s... in dicti capellani sustentacionem..~entur *StatOx* 217; 1424 mille m. ~andas et exponendas super reparacionibus..profundarum viarum *Reg. Cant.* II 299; c1520 sub pena..confiscacionis quarte partis fructuum..fabrice hujus ecclesie ~andorum *Conc. Scot.* I cclxxii. **b** quicquid oportet sciri secundum vias alkimie et naturalis philosophie et medicine, que radices ~ari debent ad omnium rerum generationem Bacon *Tert.* 42. **c** cuicunque studio animum ~ueris ingenium auget Gir. *TH* III 12; c1470 calamus..ad opus propositum ~atur *Reg. Whet.* I 423. **d** sicut operi se studiosus ~averat W. Cant. *Mir. Thom.* III 1; leve quid jocus est cui se jocundior etas / applicat ex facili Vinsauf *PN* 1914.

5 to apply (a test). **b** to relate, compare.

unum retulisti quod..forte utile erit et ad multa genera hereticorum ~ari poterit Ockham *Dial.* 449. **b** meliusque saporat in aure / quando quod effectus sibi vendicat applico cause Vinsauf *PN* 977; 1327 nullus..sane mentis factum et casum dicti H. in hac parte facto et casui fratris T. .. poterit ~are nec aliqualiter coequare *Lit. Cant.* I 240.

6 to involve in (payment of).

1389 in j libra cere sciat se ~atum nisi sit excusandus *GildCamb.* 87.

applicatio, bringing into contact. **b** 'application' (astr.).

13.. cum aplicacione candele accense ad cauntum inferius *RBOssory* 254. **b** stellarum coreas ~onesque unius ad alteram J. Sal. *Pol.* 408d; 1184 computent proportionaliter habitudines stellarum, respectus, ~ones, separationes (*Lit. Pharamel. Cordub.*) R. Howd. II 298; si in mansione sicca fuerit conjunccio et non fuerit ~o cum superioribus, ymbrium cessat significacio Rob. Angl. (II) *Sph.* 165.

2 landing, coming ashore. **b** landing due.

†1067 (1335) de uno hwearfo quod est ad ~onem navium ad capud pontis illius civitatis [London'] *CalCh* IV 333; navium que de Hibernia eo in portu crebris ~onibus suscipi consueverant Gir. *EH* I 2; 1239 per inundationem aquarum et ~onem navium et opere manuum..ampliata est trenchia *BNB* II 539; 1267 civitas nostra..per ~onem predictam plurimum deteriorata est *BBC* (*Waterford*) 244; 1325 de ~one vestra apud Whytsand *Lit. Cant.* I 137. **b** 1108 portum cum ~one navium et lofcop' *Regesta II* p. 322; 1121 cum..navium ~one et omnibus consuetudinibus *FormA* 291; 1321 in redditibus et portu suo et ~one maris *PQW* 472b.

3 application to a purpose: **a** (of things); **b** (of principles or knowledge).

a 1309 per legatorum [*bequests*] in subsidium Terre Sancte ~onem et appropriacionem (*Lit. Baronum*) *Ann. Lond.* 163. **b** in ~one mathematice ad ecclesiam Bacon *Maj.* II 389; que ibi tango de istis radicibus cum ~one ad metalla *Id. Tert.* 42.

4 application (of an instance to a generalization).

respondetur primo quod [exemplum] incongrue sumptum est, secundo quod ejus ~o frivola et vana judicatur J. Bury *Glad. Sal.* 578.

applicatus, arrival. **b** landing.

s871 nec non discriminatio longa ~us eorum [paganorum] in Readingon locum Æthelw. II 3. **b** 1320 piscenarii ibidem residentes, eorum [victualium in navibus] ~um pre ceteris percipientes *MGL* II 393.

applicium, lodging, encampment.

milites regis, qui jam fuerant in ejus societate, sed unusquisque in suo ~io ut semper solebant, fecerunt impetum Æthelw. II 18; ~ium sumunt hyemale in loco Cippenhamme *Id.* IV 3.

applorare [CL], to bewail.

s1140 plures ..efflabant animas, ..Deo miserias suas ~antes W. Malm. *HN* 483.

applumbatura, soldering.

est et alia [accessio] que fit..per adjunctionem unius speciei ad aliam, ejusdem generis vel diversi, per ~am vel ferruminationem, secundum quod in Institutis legitur.. Bracton 9b (= *Fleta* 176: per aplumbat').

applustre v. aplustre.

†applutus, *s. dub.*

hec habet, hec et habens plus ardet habere Cuminus / nobis applutus, remque furore probat L. Durh. *Dial.* II 246.

†appodencium, sweep (for raising water).

a tumrelle of a wele, ~ium, ..ciconia, tollinum *CathA*.

appodiamentum, buttress, prop. **b** support (physical). **c** support (moral). *V. et. appediamentum.*

1275 levavit iiij ~a lapid[ea] super terram domini regis *Hund.* I 203; s1287 cum..castrum..cepissent suffodere, ita quod magna pars muri ruere putaretur et pars suffossa ~is suppositis nimis tamen debilibus fulciretur Wykes 310. **b** textor..duarum streparum adnitens apodiamento Neckam *Ut.* 106; in sue erectionis initio vicine pyramidis usus est ~o *Mir. J. Bev. C* 332. **c** peccator confidens de isto ~o [sc. oleo adulacionis] deflexus ad malum se ipsum illaqueat Wycl. *Mand. Div.* 425.

appodiare [< ad+podium; cf. OF *apoiier*], to prop, buttress, support. **b** (fig.).

baculo quem bajulabat ~iatus, immobilis stetit Ord. Vit. VIII 17 p. 368; muri supereminentes columpnis exterius apodientur Neckam *Ut.* 104; qui quidem [nervus] ut apodietur vestitur carne *Ps.*-Ric. *Anat.* 41; Gad. 73. 2 (v. appodiatio); cum hujusmodi edificia fuerint ~iata J. Acton *Comment.* 1130. **b** 1291 culpabiles uniti et congregati insimul erant, ~iati super fortitudinem generacionis ipsorum (*Lit. Soldani*) B. Cotton 218.

2 (refl.) **a** to support oneself, lean. **b** (fig.) to be based.

a conatur..se arroganter super eam [securim] ~iare Herm. Arch. 21; in sinistro genu se apodiat Gilb. VII 306. 1; 1254 A. [triturator] ~iando se super flagellum suum dormitavit *JustIt* 872 r. 36; sicut patet frequenter studentibus et diu sedentibus uni lateri se apodiantibus Gad. 26. 2. **b** omnes..secte ~iant se ad sectam Judeorum, quia hec..est radix aliarum Bacon *Maj.* I 256.

3 (intr.) to lean.

s1271 assacinus quidam..ipsum [dominum Edwardum] ad fenestram quandam ~iantem ex improviso cultello vulnerat venenato Trevet 277 (cf. Rish. 69); *to lene*, accumbere, ..~iare, ..inniti *CathA*.

appodiatio, support. **b** leaning.

adjungitur cartilago quedam..ut sit quasi ~o carnis pendentis circa foramina narium *Ps.*-Ric. *Anat.* 28. **b** propter..casum super latere dextro vel ~onem ad illud, sicut in studentibus contingit qui continue jacent super uno latere et ad aliud appodiantur Gad. 73. 2.

appodium [cf. OF *apui*], prop.

s1097 fossores..eam [turrim]..suffodientes et ligneis ~iis ad horam sustentantes M. Par. *Min.* I 82 (= *Id. Maj.* II 62: materiis).

appoisonare [? OF; cf. *empoisoner*], to poison.

s1258 ~atus..ad jentaculum Edwardi.., obiit Willelmus de Clare *Ann. Tewkesb.* 165; 1324 Robertus P. leprosus rectatus de sedicione facta ad homines ~andos *JustIt* 1164 r. 2d. (cf. *J. Arch. Soc.* XXII 326).

appolus v. hapolus.

1 apponere [CL], to apply, put beside, against, or before. **b** to set before (fig.), bring to notice. **c** (w. *manum* or *manus*) to take action, intervene.

680 neque pedibus ad lavacrum pelvis ~itur Aldh. *Ep.* 4 p. 484; laevam medio pectoris supinam ~es Bede *TR* 1; suppositi eidem feretro vel adpositi curantur egroti *Id. HE* IV 6; valde edax es, cum omnia manducas que tibi ~untur Ælf. *Coll.* 102; s986 apposuit juxta ossa..fialam W. Malm. (*V. Aldh.*) *GP* V 255; unguentum sibi non apposuit W. Cant. *Mir. Thom.* II 65; 1221 apposuit ignem in domo B. ..pro odio quod habuit versus eandem B. *PlCrGlouc* 58; 1228 vidit ignem appositum ad hostia *Feod. Durh.* 267; de tempore.. ventose ~ende Bacon V 32; comites, ..cum viderint regem sine freno, frenum sibi ~ere tenentur *Fleta* 17; a1350 ~at manum super librum *Stat. Cantab.* 312. **b** quem [Alfredum Neotus]..de suis pravis actibus increpavit, penas ignis eterni apposuit M. Par. *Maj.* I 412; 1334 archa nostra.. pecunia non habundat, et hoc pre oculis vestris ~atis *Lit. Cant.* II 71. **c** 1218 ne pro defectu vestri manus ad hoc nos oporteat ~ere *Pat* 150; in nullo te intromittas de honore illo nec ad illum in aliquo manum ~as *Ib.* 158; 1219 servientes episcopi non permittunt vicecomitem ~ere manum in libertate episcopi *CurR* VIII 11; 1230 nec permittas quod ..abbas de cetero manum ~at ad hujusmodi boves *LTRMem* 11 r. 10d.; s1272 (v. bracchium 2a); 1285 si tercio deliquerint, alii non ~ant manum quam dominus rex *Reg. Malm.* I 106; 1323 rex..ad custodiam..prioratus manus apposuit *Lit. Cant.* I 115; 1340 si Summus Moderator Omnium manum non apposuerit adjutricem *FormOx* 303.

2 to affix (a seal); *cf.* 2 *appendere* 1b.

s1192 nec earum [litterarum vidimus] transcriptum sigillis appositis et authenticis consignatum *G. Ric. I* II 242; 1241 huic scripto..alternatim sigilla sua apposuerunt *DL Cart. Misc.* 83; in testimonium et approbationem rei geste ~it donator signum Bracton 38; presenti scripto sigillum meum appossui *FormMan* 17; 13.. nisi sigillum testatoris sit appensum vel appositum *MGL* I 403; 1449 quia sigillum meum quampluribus est incognitum, ideo sigillum majoratus ville Oxon' presentibus ~i procuravi *Ambrosden* II 384.

3 to add. **b** to adduce. **c** (of tenements or tenants) to annex, tack on. **d** (w. *patribus*) to gather to, bury w. (*cf. Dan.* xiii 65). **e** (w. *clamium*) to put in, assert. **f** to add to a charge (leg.). **g** to attach (a penalty). **h** to attach (a predicate).

1214 hae littere dupplicate fuerunt, apposito quod [ecclesia] spectat ad sacristariam S. Edmundi *Pat.* 125a; 1221 ad porcionem Theobaldi..appositi sunt xx s. *BNB* II 124; ~ere unitatem unitati ut crescat numerus Bacon XIII 161; alios juratores poni fecit in panello, ..que quidem nomina in aliis panellis prius per vicecomitem non fuerunt apposita *State Tri. Ed. I* 21. **b** 799 si minus quid exemplorum habeant.., Beselel..de paternis versibus adponere poterit Alcuin *Ep.* 172; ea que duo viri..super eodem [libro]..dixerunt..hic ~emus Gir. *JS* 7 p. 335; 1422 ~imus tercio librum Legis (*Lit. abbatis*) Amund. I 96. **c** Robertus apposuit eam [dim. virgam] huic manerio *DB* I 46b; manerium fuit; modo est appositum in alio manerio *Ib.*; ibi apposuit rex W. vj sochemannos pertinentes ad Rapendune *Ib.* 273. **d** adpositus est ad patres suos *Hist. Abb. Jarrow* 32; s1326 Rogerus [de Mortuo Mari]..diem clausit extremum apud Bristolliam delatus et patribus appositus est ibidem Blaneford 147. **e** 1201 Constancia ..venit et ~it clamium suum *CurR* I 416; 1218 apposuit clamium suum in dicto tenemento *Eyre Yorks* 28; si dominus infra annum clameum suum qualitercumque apposuerit, si fugitivus post annum redierit, licite retinere poterit, ..cum res per clamium appositum litigiosa efficiatur Bracton 7; 1328 nec liceat alicui..aliquid juris seu clamei in †predicto [? l. -a] domo ~ere seu vendicare *Reg. Whet.* II *app.* 306. **f** 1201 ipse non apposuit in appello suo visum et auditum nec eciam feloniam *SelPlCrown* 67; 1223 dicit quod apposuerunt feloniam et roberiam et quod W. debuit venire cum equis et armis *CurR* XI 574. **g** 1281 illam [ordinacionem]..observare, sub commissione pene in compromisso apposite, partibus precepimus supradictis *RGasc.* II 121. **h** ut conveniens principio ~atur assignatio Balsh. *AD* 85.

4 **a** to pledge, mortgage. **b** to let at farm, lease. **c** to lay out, expend.

a s1096 [Robertus], accepta a fratre Guillelmo summa non modica, Normanniam illi apposuit W. Newb. I 2; s1160 comes Pictavensis..illi..civitatem Tolosam apposuerat atque in fata concedens absolvendi appositi operam ad filium transmiserat *Id.* II 10. **b** 1198 terra Thome..sc. iij carucate..valet annuatim xxiiij s. et non amplius, unde nequit aponere bovatam ad firmam nisi per xij d. per annum; item..terra Roberti..valet..xxx s., ..unde nequid ~ere bovatam nisi per xij d. *Fees* 5. **c** 1204 custum quod ad hoc faciendum aposueris computabitur tibi *Cl* 1b; 1237 non fuit certum precium super eos [boves] appositum *KRMem* 15 r. 6d.; 1263 salvis..estoveriis suis que eos circa predicta blada..colligenda..~ere oportebit *Cl* 244; 1267 multas apposuit expensas in edificiis *Cl* 309; domus..si non sepius reparatur..veterascit, quare..oportet locantem expensas ~ere Ockham *Pol.* I 323; 1447 in custibus appositis super quamdam domum *Fabr. York* 63; 1477 cum omnimodis custibus et expensis circa construccionem..turris factis et appositis *Ac. Durh.* 646.

5 to expend, devote (thought or effort).

tanto studiosius..attentionem ~ere necesse Balsh. *AD* 29; 1219 rogamus..quatinus de mutuo illo..perquirendo curam diligentem ~atis *Pat* 199; rogavit ut partes suas sollicite ~ant ut assignatio illa..teneatur illesa *Ib.* 203; 1239 dicunt quod ad presens nichil sciunt set ma[gnam] diligenciam ~ent istud inquirendi *SelPlForest* 69; 1242 agendis nostris..consilium efficax ~ere *RGasc.* I 3; diligenciam..~ant ad obviandum navi *Ib.* 7; opera huic apposita Hengham *Magna intr.*; 1317 vires ~ere et precibus instare ut..*FormOx* 30; 1351 quatenus..partes vestras ad hoc effectualiter ~atis *Conc.* III 17a; 1410 ut..ad pacem conservandam suos labores ~ant *StatOx* 207; c1430 quod parens fraudis in partu pereat proprie prolis, omnem vestrarum virium sollicitudinem..~atis *Reg. Whet.* II *app.* 412.

6 (absol.) to resolve, set out, proceed: **a** (w. *ut*); **b** (w. inf.).

a itane..in perpetuum irascetur Deus et 'non ~et ut complacitior sit adhuc?' Ailr. *Ed. Conf* 743A (cf. *Ps.* lxxvi 8); s1191 apposuit ut comprehenderet illos *G. Ric. I* II 232. **b** apposuit..martyr..vidue apparere W. Cant. *Mir. Thom.* IV 26; ~entes peccare adhuc H. Bos. *Thom.* IV 15; apposuerunt denuo ligare hominem J. Ford *Wulf.* 61; s1198 his auditis obstupuit rex..nec apposuit super hoc eos denuo sollicitare Gerv. Cant. I 566; s1206 facti sumus amici adinvicem nec apposuimus amplius invicem nos in aliquo gravare *Chr. Evesham* 199; ecclesiam..parochialem ..a persona suscipere consequenter apposuerunt Gir. *Spec.* III 1 p. 135.

7 to predicate (gram.). **b** (p. ppl. as sb. n.) predicate.

cum hic [in oratione 'video hominem'] sit appositum sufficiens quod ~itur secundum vocem Bacon XV 18; ~ens et cui ~itur erunt sub ydemptitate generis *Ib.* 52. **b** cum sic se habent suppositum et appositum apud gramaticum sicut subjectum et predicatum apud logicum *Ib.* 124.

8 (refl.) to set oneself against, oppose.

quis asserenti se non ~eret..pastorem avium futurum ovium tam bonum..pastorem? H. Bos. *Thom.* III 2; s1455 si insurgeret contra eum [regem] hostis..extrinsecus, quis contra eum se ~eret nisi heres ipsius proximus? *Reg. Whet.* I 179.

2 apponere [cf. ME *apposen* = *opposen*], to 'appose', interrogate, put on trial.

utrum..debeat ~i modo per regem vel interim moratur *Year Bk. 2 Edw. II* 43.

apponibilis, able to be added (to).

queritur an numerus sit divisibilis in infinitum aliquo modo sicut ~is Bacon XIII 166.

†apponsagium [? cf. OF *apondre, aponse*; v. et. sponsagium], (?) landing due (Cinque Ports).

1381 [quieti a]..rivagio, aponsagio *CalCl* 427; 1447 quieti sint ab omni lastagio, tallagio, passagio, caiagio, rimagio, ~io et omni wrecco *Pat* 469 m. 9.

appoplesia v. apoplexia. apporciacio v. apportionatio. apporia, ~are, ~atio v. apori-, aporrhoea. apportio v. apparatio.

apporrectus [CL], outspread.

[arbor] frondibus in gyrum ~is valde decora (*V. S. Ethelberti*) Ciren. I 281.

1 apportare v. aporiare 2.

2 apportare [CL], to bring (to). **b** to contribute. **c** to derive profit.

1106 volo ut..abbas..reddat..totam pecuniam suam..quam ~avit ad terram suam de terris aliis (*Breve Regis*) *Chr. Abingd.* II 91; cum..tres summe ~ate per decem pelves in die pauperibus darentur GIR. *PI* II 13; allumen Jammeni..aportatur de Spania M. SCOT. *Lumen* 254; ad pitanciam moros asportavit *Latin Stories* 169; **s1459** pro tam pingui spolio..Kalisius ~ato *Reg. Whet.* I 331. **b 1196** salvis nobis serviciis que rex Anglie nobis debet de feodis quos de nobis tenet, sicut feodi ~ant *DipDoc* I 18 (= *Foed.* I 92); **1298** inquiras qui..monachi..apportum seu pecuniam aliquam in subsidium abbatum..~arunt *Cl* 115 m. 6*d*. **c c1350** tota decimacio acrescit rectoribus..et vicarius inde nichil ~at *Reg. Rough* 296.

3 apportare v. asportare.

apportatio, bringing, transport.

1361 allocantur..pro diversis cariagiis et ~onibus diversarum literarum *ExchScot* II 59; **1417** pro ~one rotulorum ad scaccarium *Ib.* IV 288; **1399** pro asportacione bullarum *Fabr. York* 16; **1476** cum..asportacione lapidum extra mare..ad molendinum *Ac. Durh.* 646 (cf. ib. 241).

apportatus, a revenue. **b** contribution (for Templars).

a c1100 concessisse..ad servitia magni altaris..totum ~um magne crucis totius anni.. (*Ch. Westm.*) *MonA* I 307b; **c1195** cum divisis morientium et asportatu altaris *Couch. Furness* II 734. **b 1266** concessisse..preceptori de Couele manerium nostrum de Samford', ..tenendum..tota vita sua sine aliquo ~u inde faciendo nisi id quod facere voluerit *Pat* 84 m. 18; **1296** ipsum fratrem Brianum..transfretare et ~um suum secum ducere permittatis *Cl* 113 m. 9*d*.

apportionare, to apportion, allot, assess.

1315 ad peticionem..quod terre et tenementa quorundam tenencium com. Cornub'..cum terris dictorum tenencium com. Devon'..in auxilium debiti regis ~ari possint *RParl.* I 330a; **1331** murdra non aporcionantur in isto itinere, per quod contribucio de murdro fieri debeat *PQW* 135b; **1416** cum..homagium habuerunt (*sic*) diem ~andi iij acras terre.., modo ad hanc curiam ~averunt quamlibet acram ad ix d. *CourtR Banstead*; **14..** vij li. ad quas dicte iiij hide terrae pro reparacione pontis ~ate sunt *Reg. Brev.* 154b.

apportionatio, apportionment, assessment.

1297 ~o facta de tenentibus terrarum..que fuerunt Philippi..defuncti pro quodam debito *SelPlExchPl* 155; **1315** †apporciacio..de eisdem terris com. Cornub' cum illis de com. Devon' facta *RParl* I 330a; **1341** denarios de illis ..saccis..nobis..concessis..juxta ~onem de lanis illis..factam *RScot* 612a; **1354** apporci[o]nacio de lviij li...facta ..per sacramentum..collectorum (*Exch. Lay Subsidy*) *Enf. Stat. Lab.* 357 (cf. ib. 325: †apporciacio).

apportum, ~us [cf. OF *aport*], revenue (eccl.). **b** payment by daughter house (mon.).

c1235 vicaria [de Grimesby] consistit in ~u panis et cervisie, decimis.. *Reg. Linc.* III 58; **1298** vicarii..oblaciones..cum ~o panis et denariorum sponsalium..percipient *Reg. Heref.* 347; **s1452** quod..actus resumpcionis..non extenderet..alicui persone..in vel de aliquibus..pensionibus, porcionibus annuis, ~ibus annuitatibus, ..que ..habuit..racione alicujus doni..per..regem facti pro aliqua causa que intelligi..posset concernere..collegium regale..de Eton *Reg. Whet.* I 74; **1502** quod lector..et successores sui..possidere..possint..porciones, ~us et annuitates *StatOx* 301. **b 1298** (v. apportare b); **1305** ne quis abbas..seu quivis alius religiosus..censum aliquem per superiores suos..impositum..extra regnum..sub nomine redditus, tallagii, ~i seu imposicionis cujuscumque..transmittat *StRealm* I 151; **1337** si forte aliqui ad dictum portum..declinaverint, ..scrutinium super ipsos..tam de litteris quam de ~is que secum detulerint secreciori modo quo poteritis faciatis (*Cl*) *Foed.* IV 729b; **1348** ita quod proficua manerii et ecclesie..nomine ~i quolibet anno..abbati et conventui [de Cesaris Burgo in Normannia] in subvencionem sustentacionis sue..solverentur (*IMisc* 160/18) *MonA* VI 1029; **1353** ne aliquod hujusmodi ~um ad..partes transmarinas..mittant (*Breve Regis*) *Couch. Kirkstall* p. 312; **1378** nunquam a principio guerre nulla dictarum domorum fecit aportum..prout alienigene fecerunt *IMisc* 214/9 r. 2; **1404** firme, ~us, exitus et proficua quecumque prioratuum alienigenarum in regno nostro Anglie *RParl* III 528b.

apposite [CL], appositely, aptly.

sin vero minus ~e dixi OSB. *Mir. Dunst.* 26; rhetorica docet loqui ornate et ~e ad persuadendum NECKAM *NR* II 173; monachum ad literas ~e natum FERR. *Kinloss* 80.

appositio, laying on, application. **b** posting (of a guard). **c** application (of a remedy, fig.).

tumorem..horum [capillorum] adpositione..mollire curabat BEDE *HE* IV 30; de tempore..ventosarum ~onis BACON V 30; **14..** appossisio, A. *puttyng to* WW; per ~onem illam parietes..concavi devenerunt *Entries* 442. **b 1228** de ~one custodie concordat cum eodem, eo addito.. *Feod. Durh.* 267. **c 1333** celeris ~one remedii sic attemptata per nostros curabimus *RScot* 233b.

2 affixing (of seal).

c1160 id ipsum presentis scripti testimonio et sigilli nostri ~one communire..curavimus *Ch. Sal.* 32; **1190** sicut capitularis forma continet, quod vobis misimus sigilli nostri ~one signatum (*Lit. Regis*) *G. Ric. I* 135; **1200** presentis scripti attestatione et sigilli nostri †apposione *RChart* 78b; **1238** presens scriptum signorum nostrorum ~one roboravimus *Reg. Paisley* 26; **1312** ego J. notarius presenti procuracioni, constitucioni sigillorumque ~oni..presens interfui (*Digby R.* I) *CollectOx* II 248; **1428** presens publicum instrumentum..ejus [notarii] signi ~one sigillique nostri officii appensione..fecimus..communiri (*Script. W. Lyndewode*) AMUND. I 252; **1437** domino W...pro ~one sigilli sui ad instrumentum ij s. *Ac. Durh.* 233.

3 addition. **b** (her.). **c** insertion, inclusion. **d** attachment (of penalty).

augmentum fiet per additionem vel ~onem BACON VIII 206; queritur an sit ~o ad magnitudinem in infinitum *Id.* XIII 161 (cf. VII 30); posset augeri per ~onem unitatis et multitudinis finite BRADW. *CD* 126A. **b** tractavi de ~one armorum regis Francie facta armis..regis Anglie per..principem Edwardum..post capturam dicti regis Francorum ..in bello de Poyters, que quidem ~o licita fuit UPTON 257. **c** per successionem regum et cartarum ~onem agam propositum W. MALM. *GP* V 232. **d 1296** confederacionem et amiciciam..per pene ~onem assecurandas et roborandas *TreatyR* I 124; **1487** ut ordinacio..confirmetur, cum ~one penarum in quoscumque volentes..ordinacionem..violare *Reg. Whet.* II 288.

4 juxtaposition, esp. as epithet or predicate.

dicitur in hujusmodi compositis esse apostrophe, sicut in ~one dictionum BACON *CSPhil* 516; est ~o duplex: [quedam] inmediata ut 'animal homo', quedam mediata ut 'homo currit, verbi gracia Socrates' *Id.* XV 43; ~o consistit in adjunctione unius ad aliud propter speciem et constructionem faciendam *Ib.* 50; omne habens se per modum ~onis respectu alterius inferius est eo WYCL. *Log.* I 13 p. 46.

appositivus, predicative. **b** tending to attach itself.

hec est nugatio et nullo modo ~a constructio BACON XV 44. **b** intellectus componit ~um et collativum, qui quietari non potest nisi per lucem eternam PECKHAM *QR* 14.

1 appositor, applier, one who lays on.

1212 dealbatores et luti ~ores et torchiatores *MGL* II 86.

2 appositor [cf. 2 apponere, oppositor], apposer (Exchequer official).

1327 de Nicholao de Teukesbury admisso in officium appos[itoris] in Scaccario *LTRMem* 99 r. 56.

apposta, post, prop.

ut ~a ecclesiae..flammis absumi nequierit BEDE *HE* III 17 *rub.* (= ib.: destina).

appotare, to drink. **b** (fig.).

ut adpotantium aqua mundet corpora EGB. *Pont.* 129. **b** Wlsini..merita didiceram..a presentibus fratribus qui a suis prioribus..allactancius †apocarunt [? l. apotarunt] GOSC. *Wulsin prol.*

appotec-, appotic-, v. apothec-.

appraebendare, to make a prebend of, grant as a prebend.

1220 episcopus Cicestr' presentavit predictum W. et aprebendavit ecclesiam illam, et W. obiit canonicus *CurR* VIII 358; **1269** appropriamus et ~amus abbati et monachis Lirensibus porciones ecclesiarum quas habent in diocesi nostra *Ch. & Rec. Heref.* 121; **1332** ecclesias..appropriatas et ~atas *Reg. Heref.* 20.

appraebendatio, grant as a prebend.

1268 si domini..predictam donationem sive adprebendationem..laudare voluerint et grantare *Test. Ep. Heref.* 3; **1269** abbatem Lyrensem, quantum ad dictarum ecclesiarum appropriacionem et ~onem, ..canonicum ecclesie constituimus, assignantes eidem stallum in choro et locum in capitulo *Ch. & Rec. Heref.* 122.

appraestare [cf. OF *aprester*], to advance or lend (money). **b** (p. ppl. as sb. n.) advance payment, imprest.

13.. (v. appraestatio); **1415** dicit quod ipse..aprestavit predictas x m. Simoni *March. S. Wales* 56. **b 1354** que vestimenta habuerunt de aprestito *SelCKB* VI 95.

appraestatio, advance payment or loan.

1345 quod ipsi †aprestacione [? l. a prestacione] theolonii sint de cetero quieti *PQW* 821b; **13..** de apprenticiis seu mercatoribus qui bona et mercandisas apprestant magnatibus longinquis..ordinatum est..quod..respondeant..dominis..de dampnis..que per hujusmodi ~ones sustinueri[n]t *Little RB Bristol* I 78 (cf. ib. 67).

†appraestum, advance payment.

1377 per quod ipsum avum nostrum opportebat communitatem regni et cleri per viam subsidii et apprestorum [? l. apprestitorum] onerare (*Pat*) *Foed.* VII 164.

apprasare v. appretiare 1f. apprehend- v. appraebend-. apprec- v. appret-. apprehencia v. apparentia 1a.

apprehendere [CL], to seize, occupy. **b** to take possession of. **c** (dep.). **d** to arrest. **e** to reach, arrive at. **f** to take on, assume (a form).

[equus] partem feni tectorum avide adprehendens traxit ad se *V. Cuthb.* I 6; adprehendens eum de mento BEDE *HE* V 2; stupor adprehendit audientes *Ib.* 19; **c710** etsi [Pascha] saltim unum ex eis [diebus], hoc est ipsum septimum, adprehenderit (*Ep. Ceolfridi*) *Ib.* 21 p. 337. **b 1255** damus licenciam..priori et fratribus..~endi, implendi seu adequandi..fossata *RGasc.* I *sup.* 50; **s1310** ~erunt prior et capitulum jurisdiccionem GRAYSTANES 33. **c** antequam dominus apprehensus fuerit possessionem BRACTON 25. **d** si abierit domum non apprehensus vel divadiatus *DB* I 1. **e** tempore regis Willelmi I, abbas Baldewinus, ..cum civitatem Italie quo Lucas dicitur ~isset *NLA* (*Edmund*) II *app.* 618; **s1401** exactor.. ,per vulgus invasus, vix mare per naviculam captatam ~it AD. USK 62. **f** ~ere est suscipere speciem alicujus in quantum illius est species; ideoque nec aër speciem..coloris ~it, quia non suscipit eam in quantum est species ejus *Ps.*-GROS. 490.

2 to grasp, understand (without full 'comprehension'). **b** to apprise, inform.

671 haec [metra]..brevi temporis intercapedine ~i nequaquam valebunt ALDH. *Ep.* 1 p. 477; per estimationem ~untur universalia; possunt ergo bruta animalia ~ere universalia J. BLUND *An.* 258; desideratum et intellectum apprehensibilia sunt vel apprehensa BACON VII 42. **b s1248** apprehensus rex, quasi motus in iram, fecit eos venire coram se *Leg. Ant. Lond.* 15.

apprehensibilis, apprehensible, able to be grasped or understood.

inter apprehensivam virtutem et ~e est mutua actio et passio BACON VII 42.

apprehensibilitas, ability to be assumed (v. *apprehendere 1f*).

per modum intencionis, id est ~atis speciei in quantum hujus vel illius est species *Ps.*-GROS. 490.

apprehensibiliter, apprehensibly, in a form that can be grasped.

in his [sc. libris] incomprehensibilis ipse Deus altissimus ~er continetur R. BURY *Phil.* 1. 18.

apprehensio, seizure, capture. **b** taking possession. **c** (obligation or right of) arrest. **d** (w. *colli*) share of weregeld due to next of kin (AS *halsfang*).

continet occupatio piscationem, venationem et ~onem BRACTON 8b. **b 1285** supplicantes..regi..ut..dominam ..ad ~onem possessionis..omnium..predictorum dignetur juvare *RGasc.* II 246; **s1310** credebant se Deo et ecclesie sue obsequium prestitisse in jurisdiccionis ~one GRAYSTANES 33; **1438** cessabit..omnes capciones, ~ones sive prisas personarum, bonorum, ..castrorum et aliorum locorum *RScot.* 307b; omnium corporalium [possessionum]..~o corporalis PAUL. ANGL. *ASP* 1531. **c †1005** (13c) illius monasterii possessio nullis sit obnoxia fiscis, sc...nec juris regalis fragmine nec furis ~one *CD* 672; **†1060** (13c) ut nullis graventur oneribus..nec furis ~one et emissione *CD* 809 (cf. *PQW* 65a); **a1188** dictas concessiones..teneant..in mercato, in theolonio, in feria, in furis ~one et evasione, in sanguinis effusione *CalCh* II 333 (cf. ib. I 425, III 484). **d** *halsfang* ejus sunt v mance..est autem verbum Anglicum quod Latine sonat '~o colli': si quis ad iiij li. persolvendus occidatur et ad id res veniat ut precio natalis ejus componendus sit, primo debent reddi xij s. et vj d. et in wera numerari; reddantur vero patri..vel qui propinquior est de patre (*Leg. Hen.*) *GAS* 593.

2 apprehension, grasping, understanding (less complete than 'comprehension').

agitur..vita intellectus in ~one formarum intelligibilium AD. MARSH *Ep.* 247 c. 14; dicit quod equalis est †volumptas [l. voluptas] Dei in sui ipsius comprehentione vel contemplatione et delectatio anime in sui ipsius apprehentione BACON VII 53; secundum Philosophum..ea que sunt maxime cognitionis secundum se sunt minime ~onis quoad nos *Id. Maj.* III 2; terminus respectivus connotans ~onem alicujus potencie intellective (KYN.) *Ziz.* 11; nos hoc opus..incepisse..propter auditorum facillimam ~onem HAUBOYS 403. 2.

apprehensivus, apprehensive, able to grasp or understand. **b** (sb. f., *sc. virtus*) faculty of apprehension.

est tactus ~us qualitatum que sunt ab elementis primis J. BLUND *An.* 212; virtutes ordinate sunt adinvicem, sicut ~a de intus ad ~am de foris GILB. III 129. 2; quod ex eadem virtute ~a vel desiderativa veniant diverse operaciones in corpore BACON IV 399; divina essencia non videtur visione comprehensiva ab intellectu creato; ..ergo nec videtur visione ~a PECKHAM *QA* II 22(A) 3 p. 167; non ipse [species] sed earum idola virtutem ~am moverent, veriusque idola quam species ipse comprehenderentur *Ps.*-GROS. 298; inter actus intellectus sunt duo actus quorum unus est ~us et est respectu cujusque quod potest terminare actum potencie intellective sive sit complexum sive incomplexum (OCKHAM *Sent. Prol.*) *GLA* III 333 n. 753; vocetur prima sua sciencia sive noticia incomplexa seu simpliciter ~a aut intuitiva, vel simplex apprehensio aut intuicio BRADW. *CD* 221A; dare potenciam ~am in anima WYCL. *Dom. Div.* 191. **b** philosophorum..~a, in phantasmatibus mutabilium detenta, simplicitatem eternitatis attingere non potuit GROS. 105; hanc appetitivam [virtutem] movet ~a convenientis vel nocivi WYCL. *Log.* III 213.

apprehensor, seizer, arrester.

s1191 dederunt anathematis sententiam in omnes ~ores archiepiscopi GERV. CANT. I 507.

2 one who grasps or understands (without full 'comprehension').

creature dicuntur ~ores ad alium sensum, quoniam secundum ultimum sue potencie cognicione quicquam cognoscunt WYCL. *Ente* 69; num tunc leges..toto conamine addiscende sunt, dum felicitatem..earum ~or obtinebit? FORTESCUE *LLA* 4.

apprehensus, apprehension, recognition.

multa sunt facilia que sunt de humana salute, ut ~us virtutum et vitiorum BACON *CSPhil* 427.

apprenticia, apprentice (f.).

1384 Amiciam Craan ~iam ipsius Roberti..abduxit *Proc. J. P.* 393; **1456** se habebit..tanquam bona et fidelis

~ia se habere debet secundum usum et consuetudinem civitatis Lond' *AncD* D 1176.

apprenticiagium, apprenticeship.

1412 nullus commorans infra civitatem..qui est extra gildam mercatoriam non faciat apprenticium sibi obligatum sub pena amisionis servicium (*sic*) ~ii predicti *BB Winchester* 31.

apprenticialitas, apprenticeship.

1364 nullus recipietur in libertatem civitatis nisi per ~atem (*LB Lond* G 140) *MGL* I 665.

apprenticiatus, apprenticeship.

1378 annos ~us sui fideliter complevit *RR K.'s Lynn* II 135; **1387** nullus forinsecus..recipiatur in libertatem..civitatis per viam ~us nisi prius juret quod est liber homo *MGL* I 452; **1408** durante termino ~us †sue *FormA* 98; **1417** apprenticius qui non complevit terminum et annos ~us sui *Mem. York* I 156.

apprenticietas, apprenticeship.

1449 lego W. apprenticio meo..meliorem diploidem meam et alia instrumenta cum pecuniis sicut fit mencio in indentura sue ~atis *MunAcOx* 596.

apprenticius [OF *aprentiz*], apprentice, indentured servant learning a craft (*cf. Trans. R. Hist. Soc.* 3rd Ser. V 193–208).

1272 dabit ~ius allutario pro sua doctrina xls. *MGL* II 442; s**1275** ut ~iorum nomina abbreviarentur in papirio *Ann. Lond.* 85; **1286** cum ipse pepigisset pro predicto Ada per xl s. quod staret cum eo et foret ejus ~ius per triennium in officio ferronis *JustIt* 579 r. 68*d.*; **1293** de sutoribus, quia habent gildam contra defensionem domini regis, eo quod capiunt de ~iis suis ij s. *Leet Norw.* 42; **1299** predictum J. emere mercandisas diversas a diversis extraneis sub quopertura libertatis sui ~ii *Cal. Mayor's CourtR. Lond.* 47; **1300** omnes ~ii qui..infra primum annum a dominis suis non intrentur in papyro *MGL* II 93; **1331** cum..servientes ac ~ios de mestero illo [textoris] secum adduxerit (*Pat*) *Foed.* IV 496; **1333** Johanni le Bakere cementario ~io *KRAc* 469/12 r. 2; **1345** Alicia tradidit Agnetem filiam suam prefato R. more ~ii commoraturam..usque ad finem trium annorum *AncD* A 8267; **1353** prout ~io competit magistro suo deservire *Reg. Rough* 289; **1371** eidem ligatus ad commorandum cum eo tamquam ejus ~ius (*PlRCP*) *Enf. Stat. Lab.* 424*; s**1381** plures ~ii civitatis decollatis magistris suis abierunt cum illis Knighton II 136; s**1383** de Londoniis multi ~ii..sumptis albis capuciis et rubeis crucibus in parte dextera..invitis magistris et dominis sunt profecti Wals. *HA* II 95; **1392** allutarios..ipsorumque †apprintitios *Conc.* III 218; **1392** J. Tannere..fuit ~ius per vij annos in arte de tannere *ArchOx* II 115; c**1400** si aliquis magister artificii predicti [barbitonsorum] receperit vel allexerit aliquem servientem vel ~ium alterius magistri..priusquam servierit magistro suo priori ad tempus et terminum inter ipsos limitatum *Mem. York* I 208; sic apprenticius plebem clamore reducit / ad secreta doli, quando magister adest Gower *VC* V 751; **1412** quod omnes cives, quando faciant novum ~ium, ducent illum ad Curiam cum indenturis suis *BB Winchester* 31; **1417** cognicionem..placitorum..de servientibus et ~iis a serviciis magistrorum suorum recessis vel elongatis (*Chanc. Misc.*) *Law Merch.* II xcix; c**1420** pocius eligunt filios suos ~ios facere vel constituere in aliqua arte temporali vel seculari quam ad aliquam universitatem pro clericis fiendis mittere *Misc. Scrope* 302; **1421** erga magistrum et suos humiliter, reverenter et benigne se habebit prout ~io condecet *AncD* C 5018; *preyntyse*, ~ius *PP*; **1493** in shoppis suis tenere †~ia et servientes *Doc. Bev.* 100.

2 apprentice at law, (junior) barrister (*cf. Hist. Eng. Bar*).

a**1290** hoc apprenticiis ad barros †ebore munus / gratum juridicis utile mittit opus Horn *Mir. Just.* (*pref. vers.*) (cf. ib. liv); c**1290** de attornatis et ~iis *RParl.* I 84b; in curia..regis sunt servientes, narratores, attornati et ~ii *Fleta* 87; s**1326** orta est magna dissensio apud Westmonasterium inter ~ios de Banco Domini Regis, viz. inter Norenses et Suthrenses *Ann. Paul.* 313; **1336** item aliis narratoribus et ~iis placitantibus pro eodem *Ac. Durh.* 527; **1345** dimisit..mesuagium..~iis de Banco *IPM* 75/1 r. 23; s**1380** episcopus..justiciarios et ~ios regni legisque doctores..in partem suam trahere..laboravit *Chr. Angl.* 259; s**1381** redierunt ad Novum Templum et ibi..cistas..in cameris ~iorum inventas fregerunt Knighton II 135 (cf. ib. 136: juratos civitatis et juris regni..~ios..interfecerunt); locum qui vocatur Temple Barre, in quo ~ii juris morabantur nobiliores, diruerunt Wals. *HA* I 457; **1389** clerici Cancellarie..non [morentur] inter ~ios legis, attornatos seu alios extraneos *Chanc. Orders* 4; [abbas T., ob. 1396] scholarem monachum..apud Oxoniam et juris terre ~ium apud Londonias..exhibuit *G. S. Alb.* III 391; est apprenticius, sergantus post et adultus; / judicis officium fine notabit eum Gower *VC* VI 249; **1419** recordator civitatis Londoniarum erit et solebat esse unus de peritissimis et virtuosissimis ~iis legis tocius regni (*Lib. Alb.*) *MGL* I 42; s**1429** per virum argutum J. Lynsfelde, de jure canonico prenticium *Chr. S. Alb.* 36; relinquantur illa..advocatis..et aliis juris peritis quos ~ios vulgus denominat Fortescue *LLA* 8; s**1449** ~ius in lege W. Worc. *Ann.* 770; **1456** unus maximorum notabilium et famosorum ~iorum legis domini regis *Entries* 50.

appresc-, appress- v. appret-. apprest- v. appraest-.

appretiabilis, assessable.

cum..judicio divino sit standum quoad valorem ~is sequitur quod habere virtutem, quod est Deo carius, sit melius quam habere quecunque naturalia Wycl. *Civ. Dom.* I 91.

appretiamentum, valuation.

1567 ab existente tempore ~i turbarum et petarum *Rutl. MSS* (*MinAc 4–9 Eliz. 35*).

appretiare [LL], **~iari,** to value, appraise (in terms of money). **b** (dep.). **c** (w. acc. of value). **d** (dep. w. *pretium* and gen.). **e** (?) (w. abl. of value). **f** (w. *ad*). **g** (dep. w. *ad*). **h** (w. *pro*). **i** (w. *per*).

Walchelinus..habet xxvii hagas de xxv sol. et sunt ~iatae in Bricsteuuelle *DB* I 56; thainus..adlegiet se cum xi parium suorum et cum uno regis thaino..in omni causa que major sit quam iiii mance; et, si non audeat, solvat eam tripliciter, sicut adpretiabitur [AS: *swa hit man gewyrðe*] (*Quad.*) *GAS* 127; **1184** nos ~iabimus captivos nostros..et Christiani ~ient suos, et que pars minus habuerit restituetur ei ab altera (*Lit. Saladini*) Diceto *YH* II 25; **1219** queritur quod [terra] male ~iata est *CurR* VIII 137; **1287** manuopus statim ~ietur per..viridarios et [attachiatus] reddat precium viridariis *SelPlForest* 63; **1302** quod †aprasiari [MS: apresiari] faciant totum bladum *CourtR Hales* 467; **1311** mittimus..clericum nostrum..ad ~iandum equos vestros *RScot* 106a. **b** a**1380** teneantur stacionarii..cauciones..fideliter ~iari *StatOx* 186. **c** modo [villa] ~iatur xl libras *DB* I 1; modo tantumdem ~iatur *Ib.* 14; dicit comitatus quia, si deliberatum esset hoc manerium, ~iari posset sexies xx libras *Ib.* 180; a**1128** grangia et placita ~iantur xvj libras *Chr. Peterb. app.* 161; **1169** v ladas frumenti ~iatas iiij s. ij d. *Pipe* 143; **1218** catalla ~iata sunt xxiiij solidos *Eyre Yorks* 187. **d** s**1311** imperatorem..letifero sibi veneno propinato nequissimi prostraverunt, mortis precium ~iati quingentorum milium florenorum *Flor. Hist.* III 150. **e** **1443** unum pamplette..~iatum tribus denariis; ..item una clamis..~iata duobus solidis *MunAcOx* 532. **f** **1221** catalla ejus ~iata fuerunt ad xxij s. *PlCrGlouc* 95; s**1270** catalla ~iata fuerunt plusquam ad xl mille m. *Leg. Ant. Lond.* 127; pro catallis..~iandis..ad minus quam ad verum valorem *Fleta* 21; **1294** averia †apprasantur [MS: apressantur] ad x s. *CourtR Hales* 292; **1321** si ~iassent bona homicidarum..ad minus precium quam fuerit..irrotulatum *MGL* II 370; istud manerium..fuit appressiatum ad xix li., ut patet in Domesday Thorne 1864; s**1422** capam..fieri fecit ad valorem c marcarum sepius ~iatam *Croyl. Cont. B* 515. **g** **1461** ~iati sunt equum..ad xiij s. iiij d. *MunAcOx* 687. **h** **1199** catalla non fuerunt ~iata nisi pro xj li. *CurR* I 110; **1287** vasa et utensilia ~iata..pro v s. (*St. Ives*) *Law Merch.* I 31; pro quanto quelibet acra †vasture communiter possit apressiari *FormMan* 26 (cf. ib.: pro quanta pastura quelibet acra possit apreciari). **i** **1242** quod..catalla..per racionabile precium appreciari..faciat *Cl* 424.

2 to value, prize, esteem. **b** (dep.). **c** (dep. w. acc. of value).

non ideo minus is [sc. Dunstanus]..debet ~iari Osb. *Mir. Dunst.* 26; s**1296** viri ecclesiastici..infelix commercium, commutantes proteccionem regis terreni pro celestis, appressiaverunt *Flor. Hist.* III 292; **1441** rex..proposicionem tuam..tanquam unum aliquod maxime laudatum habet; ..alteram..parum ~iat Bekynton I 231. **b** regulas verborum..adstipulor, ~ior, intueor Aldh. *PR* 185; quam [legem] cum ipse rex Willelmus audivit..maxime ~iatus est eam (*Leg. Ed.*) *GAS* 661; nemo sue carnis spolium plus apprecietur / morte triumphali Nig. *Laur.* 28b; dicens se propter hoc factum non minus archidiaconum ~iari Gir. *RG* I 6 p. 38; s**1251** nec appretiebantur (*sic*) aulici et regales donativa nisi pretiosa M. Par. *Min.* III 99*n.*; omnes..~iabuntur tuam clementiam Bacon V 55; nec ~iati sunt eam [felicitatem corporum] comparacione hujus felicitatis Bradw. *CD* 56e; c**1400** nec aliquis Christianus plus ~iari debet eorum censuras quam sibilum serpentinum (Purvey) *Ziz.* 403; **1422** si..nostris scriptis non adheseris nec ~iaris sermonem (*Lit. abbatis*) Amund. I 96. **c** **1167** quorum juramenta contra voluntatem domini sui Franci nostri non ~iantur obolum J. Sal. *Ep.* 244; **1169** rex..dixit..“ego neque vos neque excommunicationes vestras ~ior vel dubito unum ovum” (*Lit. ignoti*) *Becket Mat.* VII 73.

3 (p. ppl.) equivalent.

s**1099** quedam pretiosissima..extulit; sed postmodum..vel eadem vel ~iata loco restituit W. Malm. *GR* IV 370.

appretiatio, valuation, appraisal.

1199 nomina eorum qui interfuerunt ~oni et per quos appreciata fuerunt catalla *CurR* I 110; **1222** ~o est xj li. x s., set..videtur justiciariis quod ~o minus sufficienter facta est *BNB* II 124; **1226** quod..per ~onem proborum et legalium hominum..emi faciant..l ulnas.. *Cl* 116b; **1257** facta appresciacione omnium catallorum suorum *Cl* 180; **1260** W...et A...assignavimus ad estimationem seu ~onem terre Agenensis *Cl* 221 (= *RL* II 160); vendunt [vina] sine ~one prius facta *Iter Cam.* 18; **1336** ad valorem c s. per racionabilem ~onem *RScot* 399b; s**1456** valor..utensilium..juxta ~onem expertorum xx li. *Reg. Whet.* I 246.

appretiator, valuer, appraiser.

1240 ~ores bonorum..comitis..longe minoris valoris ea faciunt et estimant quam valeant et vendi possunt *Cl* 223; **1254** in singulis portibus..sint duo ~ores jurati *RGasc.* I 344; **1305** quod ~ores habeant bona appreciata pro precio imposito *MGL* I 121; ~ores carnium..in burgo *Iter Cam.* 1; **1452** per communes taxatores et ~ores *MunAcOx* 628; **1459** valor..prede..capte, juxta supputacionem doctiorum ~orum *Reg. Whet.* I 331; **1493** apprisatores unius blodii kirtell..valoris xvj d. *DLCourtR* 128/1937 r. 1.

appridare [cf. pridare (W. *prydau*)], to take (land or acknowledgement of loan) by way of mortgage.

1416 omnes terras..~avit in manu de dicto David pro vij li. pre manibus solutis..usque ad iiij annos, et sic de iiij annis in iiij quousque dictus David..vel sui assignati..satisfacerent..de dictis vij li. (*Rental*) *Arch. J.* VI 394; **14..** dictus Gruffut..solvit seu ~avit de David Vychan xiij s. iiij d. super tenementum quod vocatur Erw Eignion *Ib.*

apprime [CL], extremely, especially.

erat..piis studiis ~e imbutus Eadmer *V. Osw.* 14; adprime luxuriosus..videri potest cui..hec tanta in epulis..ponantur J. Sal. *Pol.* 731c; cum morum venustas cuilibet ad se regendum ~e in vita sit utilis Gir. *PI* I 1; **1446** quod ~e desideramus Bekynton I 184; materiam..historiae texendae †~o necessariam Ferr. *Kinloss* 11 (cf. ib.: amicus adprime candidus).

apprimus, excellent.

[vir] ~e lectionis et eloquentissimus W. Fitzst. *Thom.* 98.

apprintitius v. apprenticius.

apprisa, ~ia [OF *aprise*], report.

1280 assignavimus vos ad certificacionem et aprisam faciendam..per quas leges..antecessores mei..consueverant.. *WelshR* 2 m. 6; **1280** quia..volumus quod aprisa hujusmodi per vos fiat, ..mandamus quod..aprisam diligentissime faciatis *RGasc* II 116–17; **1281** inquisiciones seu aprisie *Ib.* 125; **1301** pro redditu suo per estimacionem et aprisam captam *Pipe Chesh.* 200; **1306** per examinacionem, confessionem, informacionem seu apriziam *RGasc* IV 235; **1313** inquestam seu ~iam factam de terminis territorii..per ballivum nostrum *Ib.* 1032.

apprisator v. appretiator.

apprisonare [OF *aprisoner*], to imprison.

1315 nullus burgensis..pro aliquo debito..capiatur ve aprisonetur nisi.. *RGasc* IV 1626 (xiii).

appriva-, approa- v. approua-.

approbabilis, worthy of approval, commendable.

c**600** cum rectum sit quod agitur, non est tamen adprobabile quod in eo animus perturbatur (*Lit. Papae*) Bede *HE* I 27 p. 58; quid..hic stabile et sincerum? ac per hoc quid ~e et appetendum? Ad. Scot. *Serm.* 305; nec ~e est hoc nec imitabile Gir. *GE* I 8; **1407** nisi ex causa racionabili et per magistrum suum alias ~i fuerit..impeditus *StatOx* 194.

1 approbare [CL], to approve, regard as good, think fit: **a** (of persons); **b** (of acts, usages, or institutions); **c** (absol.); **d** (w. *quod*); **e** (w. acc. and inf.); **f** (w. inf.).

a Aristoteles ~ando Antisthenicos improbat Platonis ideas Duns *Metaph.* VIII 1 p. 115a; s**1306** excommunicando jusjurandum illud observare volentes, dirumpentes vero illud ~at et absolvit *Flor. Hist.* III 130; **1597** si quis presentatus testimonio novem deponentium de certa scientia ~atus fuerit, tunc admitteretur ad determinandum *StatOx* 455. **b** da exemplum auctoritate ~atum Aldh. *Met.* 10 p. 94; [voluntas] ~ans est quae ~at aliquid quod dicitur velle Anselm (*Praesc.* III 11) II 281*n.*; si Deus ~at istud dominium, per idem ~at usum illius dominii Wycl. *Civ. Dom.* I 8. **c** ut Prisciani auctoritas ~at Aldh. *PR* 125. **d** quod..Pascha non suo tempore observabat..non adprobo nec laudo; in quo tamen hoc adprobo quia..non aliud praedicabat quam quod nos Bede *HE* III 17. **e** **1412** Deus non ~at quemquam dominari civiliter *Conc.* III 347. **f** s**1162** curie curis interesse non ~ans, ut eximeretur a curia..nuntium..regi direxit Diceto *YH* I 307.

2 to believe, regard as true. **b** (w. *quod*). **c** (w. acc. and inf.).

tertiam solam [hominis generationem]..~as et affirmas Gir. *TH* I 15. **b** Wycl. *Ver.* II 2 (v. approbative). **c** [Deum] esse aliquid eorum quae sunt et quae non sunt denegans et omnia quae de ipso praedicantur non proprie sed translative de eo ~ans Eriug. *Per.* 574b.

3 (w. compl.) to regard, repute (as). **b** (refl.) to show oneself (as).

Constans nullius valoris ~atur; totum Vortigerno reputatur *Eul. Hist.* II 275 (cf. G. Mon. VI 7). **b** omnium in commune se ~at inimicum Gir. *EH* I 7.

4 (w. *testamentum*) to approve, confirm.

1351 testamentum..fabricatum coram..commissario episcopi Londoniensis in capitulo fratrum de Chelmersford ~are fecerunt *SessPEssex* 134; **1449** probatum fuit presens testamentum coram nobis..hujus..universitatis cancellarii commissario generali..ac per nos ~atum, †insumatum [l. insinuatum] legitimeque pronunciatum *MunAcOx* 595.

5 (p. ppl.) approved, highly regarded. **b** accepted, established.

1299 ~atissime circumspeccionis viro *Reg. Cant.* II 559; aliquem de senioribus et ~acioribus fratribus *Ib.* 830; s**1455** tanquam dominum magis ~atum et idoneum *Reg. Whet.* I 160. **b** **1228** requisitus qua auctoritate hoc faciunt, dicit quod hoc faciunt ex antiqua et ~ata consuetudine *Feod. Durh.* 281; **1255** ex consuetudine ~ata et obtenta *Cl* 167; [rex] habet in potestate sua ut leges et consuetudines et assisas in regno suo provisas et ~atas et juratas faciat..firmiter observari *Fleta* 16.

2 approbare v. approuare.

approbate, w. approval or authority.

ut vetus error ~atius fulciretur Ord. Vit. IV 6.

approbatio [CL], approval, authority, confirmation. **b** (w. *testamenti*).

si S. Gregorii..auctoritas veraque rationis ~o talia credere non prohiberet Eriug. *Per.* 456d; c**1150** commenta falsitatis veritatis ~one destruere est pacis solide fundamenta construere *Feod. Durh.* lxii; c**1254** universitatis vestre communionem..apostolice ~onis munimine prosequentes *MunAcOx* 26; Ockham *Dial.* 419 (v. approbative). **b** **1341** pro probacione vel ~one seu insinuacione testamentorum..nihil per episcopos..recipiatur *Conc.* II 675; **1345** habeat archidiaconus..testamentorum..insinuacionem et ~onem *MunAcOx* 150; **1446** habet diem..ad exhibendum testamentum ejusque ~onem *Eng. Clergy* 220; ad judicem Curiae Praerogativae spectant probationes, ~ones et insinuationes testamentorum *Praxis* 4.

approbative, by way of approval or authorization.

si aliqua veritas ideo est catholica quia est a Deo revelata, et revelacio divina nullatenus dependet a summo pontifice ~e nec ex approbacione tocius ecclesie OCKHAM *Dial.* 419; contra Doctorem Profundum concedentem quod Deus vult ~e et causative peccata; nam per idem approbaret quod dicta sua sunt mendacia et quod fallat peccatores WYCL. *Ver.* II 2.

approbativus, capable of approving.

constat quod sapiencia, sciencia et discrecio ~a vel reprobativa preclarissime sunt virtutes BRADW. *CD* 6c.

approbator, one who approves.

sequitur quod Deus sit auctor et ~ator peccati, ..quod est blasphemum dicere WYCL. *Civ. Dom.* I 1 p. 8.

2 'approver' (leg.), accuser of accomplice (*cf. probator*).

1280 W. S. ~or appellat T. P. ..de diversis latrociniis *Gaol Del.* 35B r. 40.

approbatorius, expressing approval.

1420 quod [rex Francie]..super premissis..regi Henrico dabit et faciet..suas litteras patentes..necnon litteras patentes ~ias et confirmatorias..ducis Burgundie et aliorum procerum (*Tract.*) WALS. *HA* II 333; **1423** quod [rex Scotorum] literas suas ~ias et confirmatorias de et super omnibus et singulis hujusmodi concordatis..regi Anglie.. tradi faciet *RScot* 242a (cf. ib. 482b).

approbi-, approc-, approe-, approi- v. approu-.

appromptare [cf. OF *aprompter*], to borrow.

s1192 Wintoniensis episcopus restituit ecclesie sue magnam partem tesauri quem appruntaverat DEVIZES 38v; unicum erat refugium..abbati denarios appruntare, ut saltem sic honorem domus sue posset sustentare BRAKELOND 121 (cf. ib. 162: ut pecuniam sufficienter appruntaret).

appropatio v. appropiatio.

approperare [CL], to hasten (to).

nec minus approperant opicizi emblemata proni / arcus incultos hialino claudere velo FRITH. 448; **s1462** [Edwardus] Bristollie ~ans a civibus ejus honoratissime receptus est *Compilatio* 175.

appropiabilis v. approximabilis. appropiamentum v. approuamentum.

1 appropiare [LL < ad prope; cf. OF *aprochier*; *infl. by* appropriare], to draw near, approach. **b** (w. *ad*). **c** (w. dat.). **d** (w. inf.). **e** (fig.).

nocturnis adpropiantibus umbris FELIX *Guthl.* 52; huc celer appropia WULF. *Swith.* I 517; †appropriens digitum in anulo ferreo..misit *Lib. Eli.* 268; ~ians vulnera..contrectavit W. CANT. *Mir. Thom.* IV 26; quandocunque †appropriaret Gallorum exercitus ELMH. *Hen. V* 42. **b** mox ut adpropiabat ad fanum BEDE *HE* II 13; antequam ad propria unde venerit adpropiet habitacula HERM. ARCH. 6; **s1317** Anglorum comperta desidia ad dictum locum †appropriare minus curancium (J. TYNEMOUTH *Hist. Aur.*) *EHR* XLIII 208. **c** quia mysteriis coelestibus ministraturi ~iemus BEDE *Tab.* III 14; cum dies sibi mortis..vel vitae magis..adpropiaret introitus *Id. HE* IV 27; ~ia, Domine, tu nobis G. HOYLAND *Ascet.* 258; **s1190** incautius muro ~ians W. NEWB. IV 10; **s1273** cui [Edwardo] tandem abjecto gladio ~ians collum..brachio circumduxit TREVET 285. **d 1423** licet ipse ~iet, et cum eo turba multa.., me comprehendere (*Lit. abbatis*) AMUND. I 80. **e** non ad materiam tantam sine prefatiuncula ausus sum accedere, ne irreverenter †~iens projiciar a tanta dignitate CAPGR. *Hen.* (*dedic.*) 3.

2 to bring near (w. dat.).

1220 defendit..quod propter eum non misit..nec per ipsum fuit morti ~iatus nec a vita elongatus *CurR* IX 168.

2 appropiare v. approuare.

appropiatio, approach.

s1319 distensis lacius..rumoribus de..Scotorum †appropriacione versus civitatem, ad arma prosiliunt cuncti *Flor. Hist.* III 189.

appropinquare [CL], to draw near (in space or time), approach (absol. or w. dat.). **b** (w. acc.). **c** (fig.) to approximate, resemble.

~ante jam stili termino ALDH. *PR* 142 p. 201; **c601** adpropinquante..mundi termino (*Lit. Papae*) BEDE *HE* I 32; ubi adpropinquare sibi citharam cernebat, surgebat a media caena *Ib.* IV 24; plus omnibus aliis approximans et ~ans GIR. *Spec.* II 7; **a1350** [frater] pani et cervisie non †~at [? l. ~et] tangendo vel aliquo modo tractando (*Artic. Hosp. S. Juliani*) *G. S. Alb.* II *app.* 506. **b** per ipsam [justitiam homo] domesticat terribile et ~at remotum BACON V 123; **1263** ita quod cursus..aque nullam putredinem ~et *Cart. Harrold* p. 121; ~avit eundem Rogerum et petiit ab eo.. *State Tri. Ed. I* 52; **s1317** ~ante..rege castrum *Flor. Hist.* III 181. **c 1432** quia artes scribendi..loquendique Gallicanum idioma..magis grammatice et rhetorice quam aliis scienciis..~ant *StatOx* 240.

appropinquatio, approach.

quanto major est ~o ad unum terminum tanto est major elongatio ab alio termino J. BLUND *An.* 107; tunc illa stella ..non potest videri propter ~onem solis ROB. ANGL. (II) *Sph.* 175.

appropriabilis, specifically attributable.

ipse [Creator] est verissime primus motor..istius immediati motoris, immediatius tamen..movens, non tamen isti mobili sicut motor ejus creatus omnino ~is *Ps.*-GROS. 560; appropriatum persone [Trinitatis]..est ibi quasi pars ejusdem..; nec tantum hoc, sed eciam ~e, licet non acceptum ut appropriatum, adhuc est ibi quasi pars ejusdem DUNS *Sent.* I iii 5. 6.

appropriamentum v. approuamentum. 1 appropriare v. 1 appropiare.

2 appropriare [LL], to grant or assign (as property). **b** (w. *ut*) (?) to grant. **c** (eccl.) to appropriate (a benefice to a religious house or college). **d** (w. *missam*) to appropriate (to a saint).

potior insule Britannice pars regibusque antiquitus ~iata GIR. *TH* I 2; quod mihi jus ~iat, juste tuli MAP *NC* V 6 p. 244; terras / appropriant homini lex ratioque fori GARL. *Tri. Eccl.* 15; **1277** mansionem..decanatui ~iatam *Ch. Sal.* 356; **1284** predicte mole sue sunt communes et nulle eorum alicui apropriate *Chr. Peterb.* 65; **1285** illud tenementum est de tribus feodis que ~iantur in unum per empcionem Johannis *Deeds Balliol* 13; **1337** de quodam tenemento.. quod ~iatum est altari B. Marie *RScot* 92b; **1367** terras.. abbati [et] conventui fore applicandas et perpetuis eorum usibus apropriandas *Reg. Paisley* 29; **1455** de annua pensione v librarum..~iatarum dicte domui *ExchScot* 33. **b 1236** rex..assensum prebuit, ~iavit et concessit ut mercatores..nullas merces exponant venales..in cemeterio Omnium Sanctorum GROS. *Ep.* 21. **c** monasteria Walensica..parochias ecclesiarum matricum et baptismalium occupare solebant et..mutilare vel etiam ex toto..~iare GIR. *Spec.* III 10; **1225** quod permittat priorem [et conventum]..pacifice possidere ecclesias que eis ~iate fuerunt *Cl* 28b; **1262** Magna Reynes..~iatur monachis de Stratford' per perpetuum *Val. Norw.* 355; **s1274** [episcopus] ecclesiam de M. monachis de Fynkall in augmentum sex monachorum ~iavit GRAYSTANES 16; **1381** quod ipsi dictam advocacionem a prefato episcopo..dicto custodi et scholaribus..in liberam..elemosinam imperpetuum..tenendam recipere et ecclesiam illam ~iare et eam sic ~iatam in proprios usus tenere possint *Rect. Adderbury* 88; **1386** advocacio unius ecclesie valoris xl li. per annum ematur et ~ietur domui hospitalis de Welle *FormA* 428; quod Christiani domini.. debent subtrahere..decimas a pinguibus ecclesiis ~iatis divitibus monachis et aliis fictis religiosis per..media illicita (PURVEY) *Ziz.* 394; **1443** quatinus..prefatam ecclesiam.. collegio nostro unire, ~iare ac..concedere dignetur apostolica celsitudo BEKYNTON I 222; **1583** rectoria ~iata de Llanarth *Pat* 1236 m. 35. **d 1451** pro hospitibus qui in itinere fratres recipiunt infra octavam B. Francisci in honorem ipsius sancti ~ietur missa conventualis unius diei et una privata a quolibet sacerdote, et a quolibet clerico l psalmi et a quolibet laico c 'pater noster' (*Abbr. Stat.*) *Mon. Francisc.* II 117 (cf. ib. 116: celebret unam missam vel ~iatam collectam mortuorum).

2 to appropriate (to oneself), make one's own. **b** (w. *sibi*). **c** (w. *ad se*).

1179 prohibemus ne [prelati]..partem redditunm ~iare presumant (*Decr. Papae*) *G. Hen. II* I 225; **s1098** si hoc posses..optinere quod civitatem..tibi..traditam ~iare et in tuos usus convertere valuisses et voluisses M. PAR. *Min.* I 105; **1423** inter officiarios..quidam sunt..qui bona eis in ministracione concessa..taliter ~iant ut claustralibus exituris nec equum..nec aliquid aliud..necessarium accommodare velint (*Ordinatio abbatis*) AMUND. I 111. **b** quare potius..Occidentalis oceanus quam..Mediterraneus.. fluxus et refluxus..sibi ~iaverit GIR. *TH* II 3; **1220** res.. omnes contentas in..navibus sibi ~iare presumit *Pat* 242; si sibi ~iare voluerit aliquam partem que communis est BRACTON 216b; si..forma ~iat sibi suam materiam BACON *Tert.* 121; **1278** R. B. ..~iavit sibi injuste iij sulcos ad unam rodam suam de omnibus sell[ionibus] abuttantibus super illam rodam *SelPlMan* 93; **1287** ~iavit sibi..visum franci plegii *PQW* 13a; **1321** ~iaverunt sibi et ecclesie sue quandam placeam terre de solo domini regis *MGL* II 338; **1334** indigne sibi nomen ~iant hominum ad arma cum pocius pugnatores nominari debeant †funorales *RScot* 285a; jus et equorum / injuste cupiunt appropriare sibi GOWER *VC* I 198. **c 1272** W. de S. ..solum ejusdem commune ad se et ad homines suos de Staworth' ~iare nititur (*AncC* V 37) *RL* II 341.

3 to attribute or apply specifically. **b** (p. ppl.) specifically applied, proper, appropriate.

motor ad mobile coartatur et ei ~iatur; set substantia eterna non coartatur nec ~iatur alicui BACON VII 25; in demonstratione communia [principia] non possunt ~iari *Id.* XI 114; [definicio] ~iatur sic.. OCKHAM *Dial.* 456; nescio unde ~iatum est hoc vocabulum [collirium] ad designandum id tantum quod in oculis ponimus *SB* 16. **b** nulla magis proprie sibi vendicat appropriata / quam que cognovit vili de pulvere nata NIG. *Laur.* 34. 1; **1202** ex diuturna et apropriata regni nostri consuetudine *Pat* 9a; quod commune fuit proprium sit nomen amanti! / res utinam votis appropriata foret! GIR. (*Ad Laetitiam*) *Symb. metr.* 8; quanquam..Cluniacensibus lascivia videatur ~iata *Id. Spec.* II 15; in re communi communis, in appropriatis / sit sermo proprius VINSAUF *PN* 1091; crux, cambuca, liber sunt instrumenta fidelis / presulis, officiis appropriata suis GARL. *Ex. Hon. Vit.* 164; quelibet actio habet suas exceptiones ~iatas secundum formam actionum BRACTON 399b; alio modo potest nominari aliquid non nomine omnino ~iato BACON VII 63; *Ps.*-OCKHAM *Princ. Theol.* 63 (v. alterabilis); quam [scienciam] licet geologiam ~iato vocabulo nominare R. BURY *Phil.* 11. 174; **s1422** qui propter siliquas porcellis appropriatas / valde salutiferas monachatus spreverat escas (*Versus de apostata*) AMUND. I 98; quod vix eorum [justiciariorum] aliquis sine exitu discedat quod instar magne et quasi ~iate benedic[c]ionis Dei est FORTESCUE *LLA* 51.

3 appropriare v. approuare.

appropriate, properly, appropriately. **b** by specific attribution.

est actio voluntas [Creantis] et in sua voluntate agit ~issime loquendo BACON VII 51; ~ius quantitas cum omnibus speciebus suis a substancia materie erit qualitas nec a forma substantiali *Ps.*-GROS. 343; spiritus racionales celestes non movencie seu motores a movendo sed intelligencie ab intelligendo ~ius nuncupantur BRADW. *CD* 87D; preter istos tres modos essendi corporis Christi est dare tres alios modos realiores et veriores quos corpus Christi ~e habet in celo (WYCL.) *Ziz.* 117; accipiendo dictos terminos ~e pro professoribus talium sectarum privatarum WYCL. *Compl.* 89. **b** Spiritus Sanctus ex vi productionis sue non quidem proprie sed ~e est amor omnis amati necessario DUNS *Sent.* I xxxii 2. 11; licet forma Dei accipiatur communiter pro deitate vel essencia cuilibet harum trium personarum, tamen forma Dei aliquando accipitur personaliter ~e pro Verbo WYCL. *Form.* 173.

1 appropriatio v. appropiatio.

2 appropriatio, assignment. **b** (eccl.) appropriation (*cf. appropriare 1b*).

1309 (v. applicatio 3a). **b 1237** quod..abbas et conventus †nil [? l. non] amplius in..ecclesiis quas nunc in proprios usus non habent aliquam ~onem de jure vendicent in futuro nisi de novo eis concedantur *CalCh* I 240; **1268** episcopis..inhibemus ne quis eorum ecclesiam sibi subjectam alteri episcopo vel monasterio seu prioratui ~onis jure conferat vel assignet nisi..legittima causa subsit quod talis ~o non tam juri contraria quam pietati consona..censeatur *Conc. Syn.* 770; quod, quando..ecclesie fuerunt auctorizate per ~onem diversis locis, fides, spes, caritas inceperunt fugere de ecclesia nostra (*Concl. Lollard.*) *Ziz.* 360; **s1399** statutum fuit editum in parliamento..quod omnes ~ones ecclesiarum in quibus vicarii perpetui instituerentur nisi [etc.]..casse[n]tur, et pro nullo habeatur hujusmodi ~o *Ann. Bermondsey* 483–4; **1439** in agendis suis, quantum ea ~onem parochialis ecclesie de Wottona..concernent BEKYNTON I 68; **1504** bulla †qua [? l. que] restituit canonicatum..de Kincardyn..et..†appropacionem revocavit *Reg. Aberd.* I 350.

2 appropriation (to oneself), making one's own. **b** area appropriated (*cf. approuatio*).

1279 post annum completum a tempore quo hujusmodi empciones, donaciones aut alias ~ones fieri contigerit, terras et tenementa..capiemus in manum nostram (*Mortmain*) *StRealm* I 51; **1295** mercha, retencio, ~o [bonorum] *RGasc* III 294; quia nulla fuisset inter eos [Apostolos] quantum ad dominium ~o rerum OCKHAM *Pol.* II 483. **b 1278** quo warranto apropriavit sibi chaciam a via regali.. usque ad Shafton', infra precinctum cujus apropriacionis continentur villate de M. [etc.] *PQW* 185a.

3 specific attribution or application. **b** making appropriate, adaptation.

hec tria [sc. exigens et promissio et solvens] per ~onem reperiuntur in tribus personis Patris et Filii et Spiritus Sancti GROS. *Quaest. Theol.* III 28 p. 205; **1236** licet opera Trinitatis sit indivisa, puto tamen quod per quandam ~onem 'dedit Pater omne judicium Filio' [*John* v 22] *Id. Ep.* 72* p. 217; inter movens et mobile oportet esse aliquam proportionem et ~onem ratione quorum hoc movet, illud movetur, sicut inter agens et patiens BACON VII 25; cum forma commune nomen sit forme substanciali..et forme accidentali..et forme que habitūs per ~onem dicitur *Ps.*-GROS. 351; in..~one istarum [legum humanarum] jacet periculum WYCL. *Sim.* 4 p. 51. **b** sufficiente preparatione et ~one existente ut anima ei [sc. corpori] infundatur J. BLUND *An.* 361.

appropriator v. approuator.

appropriatorius, of appropriation (eccl.).

1313 cum..parochiam..appropriaverimus in usus proprios..possidendam.., prout in litteris ~iis evidenter apparet *Reg. Heref.* 487.

approprietarius, holder of appropriated benefice.

illi parochiani pro quibus ~ii orant non recipiunt subsidium temporale ab eis GASCOIGNE *Loci* 109; **1537** universis et singulis ~iis, rectoribus et vicariis per decanatus de N. etc. *Conc.* III 829a.

approuamentum [OF *aproement*; *infl. by* appropriare], (source of) profit, revenue.

c1132 dedit..burgum..cum..foris, nundinis, libertatibus et ~is quibuscumque *MonA* VI 240; **12..** hameletum.. cum..redditibus et servitiis, consuetudinibus, catallis et omnimodis aliis approwamentis et pertinentiis suis *Ib.* 883; **12..** totum jus meum..in tota piscaria sua cum omnibus appropriamentis inde provenientibus *Cart. Osney* IV 145; **1259** quod, si terra in socagio teneatur, ..ad opus heredis salvo custodiatur, ita quod..custos de exitibus et de aproiamentis [OF: *des pruz*] ejusdem rei fideliter sibi respondeat..et quod non possit dare vel vendere maritagium nisi sit ad heredis aproiamentum [OF: *al pru*] (*Provis. Baronum*) *Ann. Burton* 482; **s1291** Scoti..tradiderunt regi Edwardo regnum Scocie..posueruntque custodes, qui medio tempore exitus et approuiamenta terre ad opus illorum quorum interesset custodirent RISH. 128 (= *Meaux* II 256: †appropuiamenta); **1294** debet vicecomes onerari in compoto suo de xj s. iiij d. de residuo dicte extente una cum approwamento *Tribal System app.* (*Anglesey*) 23 (cf. E. A. Lewis: *Medieval Boroughs of Snowdonia* 95); **1300** appropriando vobis perquisita curie vestre, gersumas et approuyamenta viridis cere recepistis *Reg. Carl.* I 120; **s1443** abbas ac..firmarii de maneriis..suis pro aisiamento, commodo et appruamento abbatis..diversa loca in..fossatis repararverunt *Croyl. Cont. B* 520.

2 'improvement', exploitation (of land), enclosure (for cultivation).

1252 convenit..quod quilibet posset facere appruiamenta in willis suis de pratis et pasturis *CurR* 146 r. 7; **1252** que aproamenta possunt fieri de assartatione foreste *Cart. Boarstall* no. 608; **1261** salvis..appruamentis ante composicionem istam..in villa peractis *Cart. Cockersand* 148; **1262** una cum approiamento quod per ipsum fieri contigerit in terris et feodis *ChartR* 52 m. 3 (= *Cal.* p. 42: †appropiamento); **1269** dicit quod..idem R. extra ~um predictum habet sufficientem pasturam ad..tenementum suum *JustIt* 643 r. 2; **1276** ad gaynagium terrarum et exitus grangiarum et alia ~a maneriorum habeatis cor directum *Reg. Heref.* 110; **1278** salvis..omnimodis approuiamentis suis in eisdem brueris.., ita tamen quod per nimia approuiamenta ipsorum predicti..non impediantur quin habeant racionabilem pasturam..animalibus suis *Cart. Chester* p. 208; **1283** quod de..pastura..fiat appruamentum *Chr. Peterb.* 65; **1292** si me..aliquod ~um..facere contigerit in loco ubi..viam habere deberent, volo..quod..viam suam.. habeant..cum introitu, transitu et exitu illius appruamenti *Couch. Furness* II 541; **c1295** appruiamenta facere *Cart. Sallay* 406; **c1300** communam pasture in marisco nostro.. exceptis clausis et approyamentis nostris *DLCartMisc* II 257; **1306** prostravit approyamentum domini apud Offemor *CourtR Hales* 542; **1317** abbas..includere fecit..xl acras in solo suo more predicte et eas appropriavit [et]..per hujusmodi appropriamentum et separale inde factum ille xl acre more ad manum mortuam..devenerunt *Cart. Glast.* I 228; **1364** quod..teneant..omnia approwiamenta sua in eadem [villa] nova et vetera et quod de residuo vastorum suorum se approwiare possint pro voluntate sua *Cart. Cockersand* 387.

approuare, ~iare [OF *aproer* < ad+prod-; *infl. by* approbare, appropriare], to profit, enrich, endow.

1279 abbas..respondet..quod invenit ecclesiam suam seisitam et aproiatam de predicta terra *JustIt* 1245 r. 21; nulli ballivo sit vile si de rebus domini dominum possit appruare, ut de suis ordeis braseum..fieri..faciat *Fleta* 164; **1327** (v. approuator 1b).

2 to enrich oneself, make a profit (esp. by bringing land into cultivation): **a** (refl. w. *in* or *super*); **b** (refl. w. *de*); **c** (absol. w. *sibi*).

a 1256 quod..burgenses se possint appruare in terra et in aqua infra libertates suas *BBC* (*Shrewsbury*) 62; **a1290** possent libere apprueare se in magnis vastis suis *Terr. Fleet* 158; **1292** predecessores..prioris se appruaverunt in predicto vasto et fecerunt ibi mansiones *PQW* 125b; **1309** dominus J. rex..concessit eis quod se †aprocare [? l. aproiare] possent super mare et alibi infra civitatem *Chain Bk. Dublin* f. 33 (cf. *RChart* 79a [**1200**]: quod quilibet eorum [civium Dublin'] possit se emendare quantum poterit in edificiis faciendis..super ripam); **1310** quod bene liceat..Marie..se ~are in..foresta *FormA* 384. **b c1200** licebit approbare nos de omnibus terris nostris *BBC* (*Walsall*) 60; **1247** volens approiare se de vasto suo, fecit assartare quandam partem.. bosci et illam redegit in culturam *JustIt* 454 r. 9*d*.; **12..** quod ipsi libere se possint approwiare de vastis, boscis, pratis, pascuis et pasturis ac aliis terris..includendo, assartando, excolendo, arentando et commodum suum faciendo *ChartR* 135 m. 3; **1257** quod permittat M. ..~iare se in manerio de S. ..de vasto ad idem manerium pertinente *Cl* 77 (= *Cal. Scot.* I 2081: †apperivare); **1272** ~iabunt se de quadam placea terre..ad arandum et faciendum omnimodam commoditatem suam *Cart. Chester* 386; **1285** cum in statuto edito apud Merton concessum fuerit quod domini boscorum, vastorum, pasturarum appruare se possent de boscis [etc.]..dummodo tenentes..haberent sufficientem pasturam.., statutum..locum habeat decetero inter dominos..et vicinos (II *Westm.* 46) *StRealm* I 94 (= *Merton* 4 ib. p. 2: commodum suum facere); **1287** †apropwyavit [l. approwyavit] se de vasto suo..prout ei bene licuit per statutum *SelCKB* I 115; **1300** vacuas placeas..edificare et alias se inde †apprivare [l. appruiare] ac commodum suum facere *BBC* (*Chester*) 337; **1306** licenciam quod possit appruare se de proprio territorio suo usque ad cc acras *RParl* I 198b; **1399** se approware..de parcella more *FormA* 405; **14..** de terra propinquiore..se appruantes, diversas parcellas ad usum suum proprium incluserunt *Feod. Durh.* 193*n.*; *to approwe*, approare, sicut domini se faciunt de vastis *CathA*. **c 1248** quod bene liceat predicto W. appruare sibi et suis infra dictas divisas *MonA* V 357; **1269** dicit quod ipse ~avit sibi de vasto, sicut bene ei licuit.., et..quod R. extra approuamentum..habet sufficientem pasturam pertinentem ad..tenementum suum *JustIt* 643 r. 2.

3 to 'approw', 'improve', exploit (land), enclose (for cultivation). **b** to make by 'improvement' of waste.

c1245 licebit michi..vastum meum colere et appruare *Reg. St. Bees* 321; **1254** quod possint approbiare vastum suum *MonA* III 559; **1253** quod..burgenses licite possint omnes vastas placeas..edificare et approbare *BBC* (*Scarborough*) 337; **1256** manerium infra divisas suas edificare, includere et ~are *Ib.* (*ib.*) 61; **1256** villam edificare et appropriare *Ib.* (*Orford*) 61; **1265** terras..excolere, seminare et appruiare *Cl* 143; **c1273** terras que..~iari et reddituari †poterint *BBC* (*Congleton*) 49; **1279** potestatem..aproandi seu meliorandi..paludes *RGasc* II 86; **1280** liceat..terram illam assartare, curare, pratum inde facere, assidere, arentare seu alio quocumque modo..approwiare *DLCart Misc.* I 223; [ballivi] faciant..terras dominicas marlari, conpostari, ..faldari, appruari et emendari *Fleta* 162; **1304** potestatem..vasta..†appropiandi, emendandi, in feodum ..concedendi *RGasc.* III 439; **1305** quamdiu..bruera remanserit inculta et non ~iata *Cart. Chester* 98; **1312** quod ipse terras..et alias res suas..approuviare, meliorare ac de novo adquirere et commodum suum inde facere possit *RGasc.* IV 680; **1317** (v. approuamentum 2); **1338** quamdiu ..pastura non inclusa vel non ~ata extiterit *Couch. Furness* II 348 (cf. ib.: non appruuatum); **1501** constituimus vos commissarios nostros ad appruandum et ad firmam dimittendum..terras [etc.] infra villam nostram Berwici *RScot* 545a. **b 1302** abbas..approwyavit in..marisco unam culturam *Cart. Glast.* I 230; **c1419** pro firma unius clausure ..de novo appruate *Ac. Durh.* 616; **1430** infra ij shoppas appruatas super vastum regis *Feod. Durh.* 2.

4 (?) to acquire at a profit.

1523 ferrum, ceram et alia bona..emendo et appruando et versus regnum Anglie conducendo *Law Merch.* II 129.

approuatio, 'improvement', exploitation (of land).

1334 amercietur pro appruacione sine licencia *Surv. Denb.* 121; **1392** si quod amplius habent, hoc utique habent de ~one et assartacione vastorum (*Reg. Stoneleigh*) *Villainage in Eng.* 430.

approuator [*infl. by* appropriare], 'apprower', 'improver', exploiter, manager of estate. **b** (royal official).

ballivus cujuscumque manerii esse debet..pro discreto appruatore cognitus *Fleta* 161; prepositus tanquam appruator et cultor optimus per villatam electus *Ib.* 164; **1303** constituimus..W. ..attornatum et appropriatorem nostrum de omnibus terris et tenementis que..habeamus de dono domini nostri [Edwardi I], ..ita quod idem..de exitibus et appruiamento terrarum et tenementorum..de anno in annum..respondeat *Reg. Carl.* I 207; **1314** de..apruatore prepositure Leicestr' (*MinAc*) *EHR* XLII 197. **b 1261** racionabilia stipendia..de toto tempore quo fuit approuiator regis..comitatus [Suthamt'] et..civitatis Wintonie *Cl* 492; **1262** appruator [de Windesor'] *CalPat* 226; **1266** cum ..habuerit custodiam comitatus..Wiltes' tanquam appropriator noster ejusdem *Cl* 187; **1267** de tempore quo idem Fulco fuit vicecomes et approeator..comitatus [Kancie] (*LTRMem.*) *Hist. Exch.* 674*n.*; **1272** allocate..vicecomiti et †approetari comitatus nostri Linc'..tantum..quantum hujusmodi vicecomitibus et †approetatoribus allocari consuevit *Liberate* 48 m. 5; **1279** approuiator [terrarum regis] (*Chanc. Misc.* 10/13/21) *Cal. Doc. Ir.* II p. 323; **1284** [justiciarius Cestr'] respondet tanquam approiator [v.l. appruyator] *Pipe Chesh.* 147; **1301** constituit dominum W. T. justiciarium suum et approwyatorem com. Cestrie et Flynt *Ib.* 193; **s1293** fecit..rex E. R. et H. le B. appropriatores regis in civitate..et precepit illos colligere..consuetudines et tolnetum et stalagium *Ann. Lond.* 102; **1327** cum commiserimus..Johanni custodiam terrarum..ita quod de terris..illis nos approuiaret prout ad commodum nostrum fore videret faciendum..idemque J. tanquam approuiator noster..cc oves matrices pro manerio de H. instaurando.. emisset *LTRMem* 99 r. 50; **c1465** pascendo..cum averiis suis..absque licencia approatoris..regis *Terr. Fleet* 185; **1515** appruat[ori] comitatus *Cart. Glam.* 1794.

2 manager, overseer: **a** of ironworks; **b** of ulnage; **c** of a swannery.

a 1409 compotus..custodis et appruatoris cujusdam forgee ferri (*Ac. Aud. Durh.*) *EHR* XIV 516; **1542** summa compoti..ballivi sive appruatoris eorundem molendinorum [ferrariorum] *Rutl. MSS* (*Ac. Bail. Yorks etc. 33–4 Hen. VIII r.* 12). **b 1465** appruatorem subsidii et ulnagii pannorum venalium in civitate London' *FineR* 274 m. 14. **c 1472** custodi, supervisori et appruatori omnium cignorum mere nostre vocate Wytlesmer' *Pat* 529 m. 18*d*.

approximabilis, liable to approach.

sunt duo lacus hodie, / quorum unus erraticam / in se concludit insulam, / ventis hinc inde mobilem, / rupis approximabilem (*De Wallia*) HIGD. I 38 (= *Eul. Hist.* II 138: appropiabilem).

approximantia v. apraximeron.

approximare [bibl.], to approach (absol. or w. dat. or *ad*). **b** (fig.). **c** (w. acc.).

cum [ad] hoc spectaculum †accederat [l. accederet] plus omnibus aliis ~ans et appropinquans GIR. *Spec.* II 7; **s1135** [fetor] homines letaliter infecisset ~antes M. PAR. *Min.* I 250; ~are possunt regno cum fuerint implacitati, elongare autem non BRACTON 338b; **1263** eo quod sic vobis ~at gressus †nostros [? l. noster] (*AncC* IV 175) *RL* II 248; ~averunt per stadium unum usque ad spatium unius quadrige BACON *Maj.* I 304; ad locucionem conventus nullus secularis debet ~are *Obs. Barnwell* 170; cum pisces incaucius illi quasi nichil premeditanti..~averunt UPTON 184. **b** his [ministris] invitantibus ~at ad nos Jesus AD. SCOT. *Serm.* 423C; **s1303** ingressus rex Anglie Scociam, ut 'in camo et freno maxillas' comprimeret eorum qui 'non ~antes ad' pacem suam eam infregerant *Flor. Hist.* III 311 (cf. *Psalm* xxxi 9); sic erat dura corde quod ipsius amori nullatenus ~are potuit [ME: *ne muhte he never beon ðe neorre*] *AncrR* 153. **c** quos [terminos ventus].., ne datas sibi metas excedat, non ~at GERV. TILB. III 34; **c1400** [canalis] aquilonarem partem vie tenet, aliquando et minus domos ~ans *Mon. Francisc.* I 510.

2 to bring near. **b** (p. ppl.) (?) intermediate.

orbis ecentricus habet partem aliquam ejus maxime elongatam a terra, et ei oppositam maxime ~atam BACON IV 434; sit A unum corpus calidum..cui et ~etur B contrarium combustibile BRADW. *CD* 130B; quantumlibet forte agens ~atum pro primo instanti generacionis forme substancialis in materia exspectabit amplius quam per instans WYCL. *Log.* III 219. **b** omne quod ~atum fuerit inter albedinem et ebenum ALF. ANGL. *Plant.* II 14.

approximatio, approach, drawing near. **b** (fig.).

s1217 cum per fideles exploratores de ~one eorum plenius edoceretur M. PAR. *Min.* II 217; **c1260** montes..plures suscipiunt radios meridionales propter majorem eorum ~onem ad corpus solare (DOCKING *Deut.*) *Doc. Francisc.* 116; per ~onem ad locum excitatur virtus ipsius gravis per virtutem loci BACON XIII 409; **s1380** in adventu et ~one Britannie WALS. *HA* I 442; **s1455** propter assistenciam, circumstanciam et ~onem virorum forcium regi adherencium *Reg. Whet.* I 166. **b c1236** secundum gradus majoris ~onis..consummatius in ejusdem Patris assurgit incessabiles gratiarum laudes GROS. *Ep.* 36.

approy-, apprua-, apprui-, v. approu-. appruntare v. appromptare.

appulsio, driving towards. **b** landing.

c1240 propter appulcionem pecorum ad diversarum parochiarum pasturam *Conc. Syn.* 382 (cf. ib. 1054). **b s839** piratas Danorum..inopinatis ~onibus littora omnia infestantes W. MALM. *GR* II 108.

appuncta- v. appunctua-.

appunctuamentum, settlement, agreement.

1402 ultimum ~um in[ter] ambassiatores Anglie et Francie (*Lib. Mem. Cam.*) *Cal. Exch.* II 65 (cf. ib. 67 [**1403**]: appunctamentum indentatum inter ambassiatores); **1414** certa..inter ipsos proposita apunctamenta fideliter observari..jurare consenserunt *Reg. Moray* 217; **1426** contra formam ~i finalis pacis inter duo regna nostra..concluse (*Cl*) *Foed.* X 360; **1444** rex confirmavit..evidenciam certi ~i..facti et initi inter A. ..et R. ..milites *RMS Scot.* 728; **s1390** rex..tale fecit ~um quod duo principales..capitanei ..in campo clauso..pugnarent *Plusc.* X 11; **s1459** reddiderunt..Turrim obsidentibus, sub ~o quod obsessi starent legi W. WORC. *Ann.* 773; **1464** ad conservandum predictum ~um et contractum *Reg. Newbattle* no. 291.

appunctuare [cf. OF *apointer*], to settle, agree, decide. **b** (w. *ut, quod,* or acc. and inf.). **c** (trans.). **d** (p. ppl. as sb. n.) decision.

1439 asseruit se ad sic ~andum nulla fore potestate fulcitum BEKYNTON I 76; **1454** volo quod tumba mea sit facta de petra marmorea.., sicut inde in vita mea appunctavi *Test. Ebor.* II 200; **1466** commissio prioris..ad ~andum et concordandum inter ipsos et abbatem..super..oblacionibus *Reg. Dunferm.* no. 471. **b 1420** ~atum et ordinatum existit..ut..scolares..jurent *StatOx* 226; **s1420** ea que.. appunctata fuerint et concordata WALS. *HA* II 332; **1429** domini de Consilio ~arunt et concordarunt quod W. Paston ..sit unus justiciariorum *Act. PC* IV 4; **1441** consilium ..nostrum..~avit et ordinavit litteras nostras..fore dirigendas *Cart. Glam.* 1575; **1465** ~atum extitit..quod.. magister R. ..manebit cum dicta decima *Reg. Aberbr.* II 144. **c 1380** ad melius providendum pro quiete..populi utriusque regni et eis que deducta erant in questionem congruencius ~andis *RScot* 30a; **s1416** litere..que..dederunt plenum consensum ad articulos ~atos per Concilium Anglie ELMH. *Hen. V* 83 (cf. ib. 20: ex ~ato consilio); hiis sic ~atis *Plusc.* IX 45. **d 1437** literas..responsiones..ad deliberata et ~ata ultimate inter nos..et ambassiatores..continentes BEKYNTON I 220.

2 to appoint, fix: **a** (a thing); **b** (a person).

a 1383 quedam summa denariorum ~ata pro reparacione castri *RScot* 55b; **s1458** limitato..die et apunctuato pro incepcione concilii *Reg. Whet.* I 296; **1583** mesuagia..pro missis ibidem..celebrandis antehac concessa seu ~ata existencia *Pat* 1235 m. 9. **b 1423** in..cleri convocacione.. ~ate fuerunt certe persone ad proximum generale consilium transmittende (*Lit. Archiep.*) AMUND. I 99; **1546** magister sive pedagogus per..gubernatores..nominandus et ~andus (*Pat*) *Mon. Exon.* 420a; **1551** per commissionarios..assignatos et ~atos (*Pat*) *MonA* II 542.

appunctuatio, settlement, agreement, decision.

1399 cum copia cujusdam ~onis in percamino (*Lib. Mem. Cam.*) *Cal. Exch.* II 54; **s1420** omnes articuli et appunctaciones premisse concordie WALS. *HA* II 334; **1423** recipiens certificatorias super cleri eleccione ~oneque regis (*Lit. Abbatis*) AMUND. I 100; **1426** quedam ~o inter eos extitit ordinata *RParl* IV 296b; **s1455** ut totam ~onem, quam prius fecerat cum duce.., revocaret in irritum *Reg. Whet.* I 160; **1482** paccionibus..et apunctuacionibus *Mem. Ripon* 251.

appuramentum [cf. puramentum], liquidation (of debt).

1276 scrutatis rotulis ~i, ..si eas [v marcas] inveneritis non esse de debitis predicti Isaac.. *Cl* 93 m. 11.

appurare [cf. purare], to liquidate (a debt).

1274 que quidem duo debita apurantur ad xx li. *SelPl Jews* 79; **1284** unum debitum..quod ~atur ad xxx li. *Ib.* 132.

apra [cf. aper], wild sow.

1235 habebunt tantum cervum et cervam, aprum et ~am, capreolum et capreolam *Melrose* 198.

aprasiare v. appretiare 1a.

apraximeron [? ἀπραξία μερῶν], sexual impotence.

deficit omnis operatio membri et virtutis generative et vocabitur aproximeron GILB. VII 285 v. 2; †approximancia, que est defectus coitus GAD. 74 v. 1.

aprebendare v. appraebendare. apreci-, apresi-, apress- v. appreti-. aprest- v. appraest-.

apricitas [CL], sunniness, brightness (? by conf. of *calor* w. *color*).

~as, color, *hio GlC* A 707; **10..** ~as, *hleowð, ..hiw* WW.

apricus [CL], sunny. **b** sheltering. **c** benign, genial.

~a, aestiva, calens *GlC* A 674; ~am, calor sine vento *Ib.* 675; ~um, locus temperatus *Ib.* 678; **10..** ~us locus, *hleowstede* WW; hiis dantur vici, campi colles et aprici GARL. *Mor. Scol.* 108. **b** fruitur foliis pro aprico tegmine pepli ALDH. *VirgV* 784; **10..** pro ~o, for *ðære wearman* WW. **c 1346** sis rex..pius atque pudicus, / justus munificus, clemens, moderatus, apricus (*In Franciam*) *Pol. Poems* I 39; **s1346** [eum] littera magnificum reddebat, sensus apricum, / munera munificum (R. SYRESTONE *de T. Hatfeld*) *Hist. Durh.* 2 p. 133.

Aprilis [CL], April.

[apud Anglos] ~is *Eosturmonath*.., qui nunc paschalis mensis interpretatur, quondam a dea illorum quae Eostre vocabatur et cui in illo festa celebrabant nomen habuit BEDE *TR* 15; dum sol illustrat Aprilem GARL. *Tri. Eccl.* 137; **s1248** videres..in Februario..aviculas velut in ~i canendo lascivire M. PAR. *Min.* III 43; mense ~i, tempore videlicet quo omnia aperiuntur, warectandi erit tempus *Fleta* 162.

aprimium v. aprunum.

aprinus [CL], of a boar, of brawn. **b** like that of a boar.

dentur galline, leporine post et aprine / carnes D. BEC. 2566; **c1327** vobis mittimus..quatuor scuta ~a J. MASON *Ep.* 29 p. 210. **b** hippotamus..~is dentibus NECKAM *NR* II 30.

†apriola, wild sow or (?) *f.l.* for *capreola*.

fere ibi [in Boemia] abundant, sc. ursi, pardi, cervi, ~e, bubali *Eul. Hist.* II 72

apriolus, young boar.

1388 nec respondet de..uno apro et ij ~is *LTRAc. Esch.* 10 r. 5; **1389** de ij apris..et de ij ~is..et de j recepto de adjunct' porcellorum *MinAc* 1126/6 r. 3*d*; **1441** de xij d. de precio unius ~i *DLMinAc* 645/10461 r. 1; **1478** extrahure: ..unus ~us coloris albi precii vj d. *CourtR Lygh* I f. 12v.

aprisa, ~ia v. apprisa. apro- v. et. appro-. apropimum v. aprunum. aprotanum v. habrotonum. aproximeron v. apraximeron.

aprunum [etym. dub.], sweet apple.

†apropima vel †aprimia, i. melimela, solvunt †ventris [v.l. ventrem], ardorem commovent *Alph.* 12.

apsida v. apsis.

apsinthiose, bitterly.

s1465 plurima evenerunt incommoda et sumptuosa, quod multum et absinthiose dolendum HERRISON *Abbr. Chr.* 9.

apsinthium [CL < ἀψίνθιον], wormwood (*Artemisia*). **b** (fig.) bitterness, grief.

absinthium, *wermod GlC* A 9; dirior..quam glauca absinthia campi ALDH. *Aen.* 100. 32; scientes quod absinthium et thimum argumentosa degustet apis MAP *NC* III 2 p. 122; **c1225** mons Salisberie.. / nil equidem preter absinthia gignit amara H. AVR. *Poems* 20. 7; artemesia..trita cum †azimbia dolorem pedum..mitigat BART. ANGL. XVII 16 (cf. id. 12; abscinthium); absinthum, quod est cujusdam floris species BACON V 82; cum istis ponatur de sale, centaurea, absinthio, abrotano GAD. 6 v. 2; absinthium, G. *aloine*, A. *wermode Alph.* 1 (cf. ib. 38: secundum quosdam abscincium ponticum est centonica). **b 796** qui dura invectione indigeat, bibat ex absinthio ALCUIN *Ep.* 114; **1283** ex hujusmodi torcularibus amaritudinis hausimus absinthium PECKHAM *Ep.* 453.

apsis, apsida [CL < ἀψίς], arc. **b** apse or vault. **c** edge of well.

lunam.. cum infimas sui circuli ~idas plena petierit BEDE *TR* 7; auge refulget / sol fervens, radiat abside dulce micans NECKAM *DS* I 490. **b** absida, sacrarium *GlC* A 4; absedas, aedificii latiores †conaculas [? l. conchulas] *Ib.* 61; Romani reconciliant hominem intra absidem; Greci autem nolunt THEOD. *Pen.* I xiii 1; hanc Petrus absīdam sanctorum sorte coronat ALDH. *CE* 4. 1. 1 (cf. ib. 3. 41); absida, *sinewealt cleofa* vel *portic* ÆLF. *Sup.*; limphis perfunditur absis FRITH. 451; in turri muris contigua ad superiores fenestrarum absides cum duabus puellis stabat *Hist. Meriadoci* 384. **c** *beerd or brynke of a welle or oder lyk*, margo, absidia *PP*.

aptabilis, applicable. **b** apt.

est harum appellationum prima disciplinalibus ex equo etiam nunc ~is BALSH. *AD* 127. **b** mentem..literalibus studiis ~em valde et applicabilem GIR. *JS* 7 p. 335.

aptamen, cover (of book).

c1080 xij textus et ~ina duorum textuum *Lib. Eli.* II 114 (= *MonA* I 447b).

aptanter, fittingly.

s1264 loco..~er considerato, murum leviter prosternentes, urbem ingrediuntur WALS. *YN app.* 516.

aptare [CL], to fit (in place). **b** (w. *in*) to fashion (into). **c** (w. dat.) to adapt. **d** (absol. w. *ut*) to arrange.

abtemus, †adjungemus *GlC* A 58 (cf. ib. 64, 663); frenum ..quod faucibus suis ~averat W. CANT. *Mir. Thom.* VI 141; pedibus suis ~antes..ossa W. FITZST. *Thom. prol.* 17; ~atis et sitis machinis suis..sub muris ELMH. *Hen. V* 21; **1431** fenestras..dolabit et ad posicionem earum complete ~abit *Arch. Hist. Camb.* I 73. **b 1427** quem quidem apparatum [ad lectum pertinentem] ~ari volumus in capas *Reg. Cant.* II 391. **c** introitus et exitus occultos..insultibus ~ans GIR. *EH* I 5; [virtus] assimilativa, cujus est quod confuse unitum est distinguere et nutriende particule ~are *Ps.*-GROS. 525; **1434** lego..vestes meas usui meo ~atas *Test. Ebor.* II 25. **d** unde ~avit ut unus tractaret specialiter de Christi sacerdocio et alius.. WYCL. *Ver.* I 247.

2 (w. *sibi*) to prepare. **b** to win.

apto mihi baculum quo baculabo canem GARL. *Epith.* VI 572. **b** abtavit, conparavit, adquisivit *GlC* A 75; **s1366** comes..clam se transtulit versus partes illas [Lettowe], ut consimile nomen sibi ~aret J. READING 188.

3 to train (hawks or hounds). **b** (refl.) to accommodate oneself.

illud cave ne antequam †privatus [? l. firmatus] sit ad manum clames vel ~es vel volare facias ADEL. *CA* 2; **1198** Wido venator tenet..ij carucatas per servicium ~andi unum limerium *Fees* 4; **1313** pro eisdem [falconibus gentilibus] ibidem custodiendis, trahendis et ad volandum ~andis *KRAc* 375/8 f. 45. **b** dicebat minando quod ipsum.. suspendi faceret nisi se ~aret comiti *State Tri. Ed. I* 10.

4 to assign. **b** to apply, refer.

frustra virginitas laudem rumoribus aptat ALDH. *VirgV* 2758; singulis his [articulis] singulos ~antes annos BEDE *TR* 55. **b** quo sensu [liber Job] unicuique fidelium sit ~andus *Id. HE* II 1 p. 75; huic regi non inconvenienter ~atur quod scriptum est.. AILR. *Ed. Conf.* 754A; cuilibet aptes / talem juncture seriem VINSAUF *PN* 1612.

aptatio, fitting (in place). **b** build (of body). **c** fitting together, union. **d** adaptation. **e** conformable action. **f** contrivance, design.

1424 pro ~one xij parium de *les over leders Mem. York* I 193; **1431** pro formacione et ~one cujuslibet fenestre *Arch. Hist. Camb.* I 73. **b 1361** quidam extraneus cujus nomen..ignorant, set, ut intelligunt.., secundum ~onem corporis sui fuit predictus J. *IMisc* 184/6. **c** unde tam honeste ~onis inutilis separatio? ADEL. *QN* 44. **d** ~o corporis ad species rerum salubrium recipiendas BACON *Maj.* I 143. **e** magister suus [sc. novicii] talis sit qui in signis, in moribus et in ceteris ~onibus..possit eum..salubriter monere *Cust. Cant.* 258. **f** ille qui frustrat ~onem et voluntatem Dei WYCL. *Sim.* 47.

aptatorium, shaping board.

a schapynge burde, sculpatorium, ..~ium *CathA*.

aptatrix, constructive (f.).

alia [virtus motiva] est effectiva vel ~ix composicionis absolute nominate, alia vero composicionis vite tantum sensitive *Ps.*-GROS. 594.

aptatura, workmanship (*cf. aptura*).

s1266 machina..contra quam quedam petraria ~a satis artificiosa viriliter reverberavit WALS. *YN app.* 554.

apte [CL], fitly, fittingly.

locum in quo cum suis ~e degere potuisset BEDE *HE* IV 1; locellum..operculo..similis lapidis ~issime tectum *Ib.* 19; nonne [nostra natura] ~issime Sancto Spiritui copulatur? ERIUG. *Per.* 568C; apte / praefecit sedi longum pastore vacanti FRITH. 433; quam rem qua forma quis casus apostrophet apte VINSAUF *PN* 275.

apterium v. asceterium.

aptificare, to adapt.

fuit..necesse ut [melancolia] cum sanguine misceretur, ut ~aret sanguinem ad membra multiplica nutrienda BART. ANGL. IV 11; ~atur materia arefactioni GILB. VI 267 v. 2.

aptificatio, adaptation.

cum..4 sunt virtutes naturales..et procedunt ab epate, quamvis fit sensus ex parte anime et ~o ex parte instrumenti ipsius cum opere non fit nisi incipiat natura GILB. IV 186 v. 1.

aptitudinalis, having an aptitude or tendency, potential.

hoc forte consuevit dici de inherencia actuali et ~i: prima non semper inest accidenti, secunda semper inest DUNS *Metaph.* VII 1. 82C; illa extensio consistit in duplici relacione ~i, sc. conformitatis et prioritatis naturalis; ..dixi '~i' quia neutra relacio requiritur actualis *Id. Sent. prol.* 4. 6; cum morbo hereditario ~i stat sanitas, non hereditario actuali GAD. 36 v. 2; nulla est ibi rebellio actualis nec ~is NETTER *DAF* I 442.

aptitudinaliter, w. ref. to aptitude or tendency, potentially.

tunc diffinitur [accidens] ~er per substanciam DUNS *Metaph.* VII 4. 85D; infirmus generat infirmum ~er, licet actu sit sanus GAD. 37 v. 1.

aptitudo, aptitude, tendency, proclivity. **b** fitness (for). **c** capability, talent. **d** aptness, appropriateness. **e** (?) potential significance. **f** fitting occasion, opportunity.

si non sit in eo [corpore] organum cum ~ine vitam recipiendi, [Deus] non infundit ei animam J. BLUND *An.* 364; naturalem potentiam vel ~inem ad habitum hujusmodi BACON VIII 2; hec ~o [sc. sursum elevari] non potest esse in terra *Id. Tert.* 141; morbus accidentalis non est hereditarius: quia, si filius regat bene se, non incurret has passiones; sed, si erret in regimine, tunc ~o ista duceretur in actum GAD. 36 v. 2. **b 1542** in sociis eligendis solum considerent virtutem et ~inem discipline *Deeds Balliol* 321. **c** cum..natura..in singulis tibi membris ~inem suam eleganter impresserit MAP *NC* III 3 p. 126; verus homo, nichil inhumanum in membris..habens, trans hominem acceperat ~inem piscium *Ib.* IV 13; ibi..scriba indoctus ~inem penne probat R. BURY *Phil.* 17. 222; **1312** nec videtur racionabile quod..debeat..~o studencium in ea [sc. theologia] per hujusmodi [inferiores sciencias] judicari *Collect. Ox.* II 257; **1442** non puto facile inveniri posse qui in ~ine, habilitate et merito ad tantum regimen commode subeundum meritis sibi possit equari BEKYNTON I 147. **d a1520** delectantur congerie dictorum ab aliis, in quibus magis student numero quam ~ini COLET *Ep.* 209. **e s1430** consideratis..paucitate populi, prenosticorum quoque ~ine, omnia ad felicem ordinem reducuntur CAPGR. *Hen.* 128. **f** voluptati querentibus ~inem occurrit..effugere presentiam obtrectantium MAP *NC* IV 6 p. 164.

aptotus [ἄπτωτος], indeclinable (gram.).

~um, inflexibile vel incas[u]ale *Gl. Leid.* 43. 56; neutra haec tantum quae in singulari numero ~a sunt et in plurali declinantur BONIF. *AG* 487.

aptura, fitting (*cf. aptatura*).

1431 pro dolacione et ~a majoris ostii *Arch. Hist. Camb.* I 73; **1438** carpentario pro ~a tegularum pro tectura capelle *ExchScot* V 59; **1462** cum diversis pannis.., harnesiis, ~a vestimentorum.. *Ib.* VII 150.

aptus [CL], apt, fit, suited: **a** (absol.); **b** (w. dat.); **c** (w. *ad*); **d** (w. *pro*); **e** (w. inf.).

a plecto mihi retia et pono ea in loco ~o (*on stowe gehæppre*) ÆLF. *Coll.* 92; qui oculos ~os habent et non vident *SB* 22. **b** tempus festis paschalibus aptum ALDH. *VirgV* 903; insula..alendis ~a pecoribus BEDE *HE* I 1; carmina.. pietati ~a *Ib.* IV 21; silva est ibi non pastilis ~a venationi *DB* I 273; frons est apta minis NIG. *Poems* 420; **s1385** vir plus ~us mercimoniis quam milicie WALS. *HA* II 141. **c 1287** ut [clerici] ~iores et magis ydonei fierent ad majora *Conc. Syn.* 1026. **d** de terra..pro captura piscium ~a ALDH. *Ep.* 10; **1359** maeremium et boscum pro sagittis inde faciendis ~a *Pat* 258 m. 9*d*. **e** hoc non fieret nisi terra ~a nata esset sursum a centro elevari BACON *Tert.* 141.

2 trained.

c1225 cum sex canibus ~is ad vulpes capiend' (*AncC* VI 83) *RL* I 278.

apud (aput) [CL], at, near. **b** at the house of. **c** among, in the country of, acc. the usage of. **d** (w. *acta*) w. or to the authority of (records). **e** at (the time of).

~d Romam ALDH. *VirgP* 25 p. 257; ~d Cantuariam *DB* I 1; **s1147** consecrans H. archiepiscopum..apud civitatem Treveris H. CANTOR *Cont.* 225; **s1186** ad palatium suum quod ~d Wudestoke habetur..redibat AD. EYNS *Hug.* III 1; **1211** de v quarteriis siliginis ~d ultra montem venditis *Pipe Wint.* 74; **s1228** rex..festum Dominice Nativitatis ~d Eboracum celebravit WEND. II 333; **1324** in ij summis albi piscis emptis ~d mare *Ac. Durh.* 14. **b** illi..exulanti ~d Redualdum BEDE *HE* II 12; hospitari ~d te [AS: *mid þe*] ÆLF. *Coll.* 99; **1277** in multis locis Anglie ~t diversos homines erat pecunia de dicta decima (*Instr. Notar.*) *EHR* XXXII 73; **1420** pro sclattynge de uno flore ~d W. Osborne *Ac. Churchw. Bath* 27; **1438** ~d Fratres Predicatores *CalPat* 166. **c 680** erat genus quoddam hereticorum ~t Orientales ALDH. *Ep.* 4 p. 483; ~d homines sum iterum vivere permissus BEDE *HE* V 12; quod usque hodie ~d Pictos constat esse servatum *Ib.* I 1; dominus solvat legis transgressionem ~t Danos [AS: *mid Denum*], plenam forisfacturam ~d Anglos (*Cons. Cnut.*) *GAS* 345 (= *Quad.*: cum Danis, ..cum Anglis). **d s1237** mandatum..per scripturam probetur autenticam, nisi ~d acta fuerit constitutus M. PAR. *Maj.* III 437; **1549** ~d acta fiat publicatio *Conc. Scot.* II 125; pars contra quam lata est sententia potest..~d acta coram judice..appellare *Praxis* 234. **e** fovea..dilatatur ~d dilatationem cordis et constringitur ~d sui constrictionem *Ps.*-RIC. *Anat.* 23.

2 to (a place). **b** (lying) towards (a compass point).

c1225 ut [ferrum] ducatur ~d Gloverniam (*AncC* VI 88) *RL* I 279; **s1240** quidem cives perrexerunt ~d Wodestok' *Leg. Ant. Lond.* 8; **c1283** debent..averare ~d Wynton' *Cust. Battle* 54; **1290** emit..pisces..venientes ~d forum *Leet Norw.* 34; **s1327** venerunt..cardinales sic ~d Dunelmum GRAYSTANES 38; **s1350** tenentes..non solvunt bladum..nec ducunt ~d Cantuariam *Reg. S. Aug.* 62. **b 1228** adversus duas cruces que sunt ~d aquilonem *Feod. Durh.* 259; **c1230** jacent propinquiores juxta terram B...~d aquilonem *AncD* A 1907; **s1165** apparuerunt due comete, una ~d austrum, alia in aquilone *Plusc.* VI 21 (= FORDUN *GA* 5: ad austrum).

3 in relation to: **a** (a person); **b** (an abstraction); **c** (oneself).

a cum..verbo exhortationis ~d homines..ageret BEDE *HE* II 12; nunquam se quietavit ~d regem *DB* I 6; accusatus ~d..districtum judicem Deum ANSELM (*Or.* 10) III 33 (cf. ib.: ~d Deum esse magnae potestatis); priusquam innocens sit ~d omnem manum [AS: *wið ælce hand*] (*Quad.*) *GAS* 145; cxx sol. reus sit ~d regem [AS: *wið þone cing*] *Ib.* 174; **1184** cognovimus magnum amorem quem ~d nos habetis (*Lit. Saladini ad Papam*) DICETO *YH* II 25; **1236** adquietaverunt me..~d Judeos de xx m. *Starrs* I 44. **b** ut ~d misericordiam..Conditoris impetraret se..absolvi BEDE *HE* IV 9; presbiteri simplices..~d judicium ecclesie moderne debent contentari simplici victu (*Concl. Lollard.*) *EHR* XXVI 747; **s1453** obeunte..terrarum..possessore.. nec relinquente post se heredem ullum ~d noticiam villanorum *Reg. Whet.* I 95. **c** in diversas meditationes inductus deliberavit ~t se qualiter locum faceret memorabilem G. MON. VIII 9.

4 in the opinion of.

equivalent ~d me 'Deus non est nunc' et 'Deus non est pro mensura presenti' (KYN.) *Ziz.* 23.

Apulia [CL], S.E. Italy. **b** fine gold (alch.).

[R. Guiscardus] profecit ut se ducem ~ie et Calabrie.. faceret W. MALM. *GR* III 262. **b** aurum bonum dicitur Hispania vel ~ia vel Polonia vel alia regio ubi bonum aurum abundat BACON *Tert. sup.* 84.

Apulus [CL], Apulian.

Rogerius in gladio suo inscribi fecit id triumphale..: 'Appulus et Calaber, Siculus mihi servit et Afer' GERV. TILB. III 19 p. 943.

apunct-, apur- v. app-. aput v. apud.

†apylois, 'mortrel', milk pudding.

morterews, dyschmete, peponum, ~is, mortaricium *PP*.

aqua [CL], (sg. or pl.) water. **b** (as element). **c** river, stream, (stretch of) running water. **d** sea or tidal water. **e** watering-place.

in cumulum salsarum fluxus aquarum / concrevit ALDH. *VirgV* 823; ultimam vitae aetatem pane cibario et frigida ~a sustentat BEDE *HE* V 12; estate. .~a marina salsior est quam hieme ADEL. *QN* 51; ~e salse diligenti depuratione dulces redduntur NECKAM *NR* II 1; cisterna non habet ~am perpetuam nec ~am vivam BRACTON 233; **1290** emit smeltes. .et alios pisces ~e rescentis *Leet Norw.* 34 (cf. ib. 80: pisces ~e †dulce); **1453** per ~as salsas vel recentes *RScot* 360a; **1403** propter destruccionem molendini. .per tempestatem aquarum *Ac. Durh.* 216; ~am ipsi [Angli] non bibunt, nisi qui ob devocionis et penitencie zelum aliquando ab aliis abstinent FORTESCUE *LLA* 36. **b** homo quatuor elementis constat, id est igne, aere, ~a et terra EGB. *Dial.* 16; omne corpus visibile quattuor partibus constare. .ex igne videlicet, aere, terra et ~a ERIUG. *Per.* 487C; non dubito omnem hanc mundi molem. .constare ex terra et ~a et aere et igne ANSELM (*Mon.* 7) I 21. **c** Elge undique est ~is ac paludibus circumdata BEDE *HE* IV 19; **779** (12c) mariscem pertinentem ad aridam et ad ~ae ripam *CS* 228; **c1070** manerium suum de A. . .cum omnibus suis pertinentibus, in bosco et plano, ~is et ~arum decursibus *Regesta* 120; fecit quandam domum super ~am regis *DB* I 1; totam terram quae jacebat trans ~am quae De vocatur *Ib.* 283b; **c1143** totam decimam. .de his piscatoriis ~is de H. *E. Ch. Scot.* 154; adolescens. .ad molendinum. .~e tractu perlatus GRIM *Thom.* 9; **c1250** ibidem sunt tria molendina ad ~am *Cart. Rams.* I 486; **s1262** ~a Thamisie tota pertinet de rivo ad rivum ad civitatem usque ad Newe Were *Leg. Ant. Lond.* 52; **1276** per mediam †atr [MS: aquam] de Wheye *Hund.* II 228; **c1290** alio capite abuttante super ~am currentem *Carte Nativ.* 369; jus ~e ducende *Fleta* 266; **1315** cum ~is refluentibus in eisdem molendinariis *RGasc* IV 1454; **1346** juxta ripam cujusdam ~e periculose. .et profunde (*Lit. confessoris regis*) AD. MUR. 213 (= AVESB. 105b: *sur une river qe feust mal a passer*); **1363** pro decima de. .temporalibus infra ~as [*Tyne & Tees*] *Ac. Durh.* 178; **1402** ~am Thamisie modo guerrino de cetero intrare magis timeant (*Pat*) *Foed.* VIII 271. **d** **s1326** rex. .venit. .ad Strogoyl. .et posuit se in ~am cum. .valde paucis AD. MUR. 47; **1400** ballivus ~e maritime de Bristoll' *Cl* 245 m. 16; turres inter quas ~a influit et refluit ELMH. *Hen. V* 18; **1445** tenemento. .in Gravesende. .situato inter. .regiam stratam. .et bassam ~am Thamisie *Cl* 295 m. 18*d*. **e** **c1300** pertinet ad istum mariscum et terram una ~a pro averiis. .adaquandis *DC Cant* J 79.

2 (eccl.) **a** water of baptism. **b** holy water. **c** water used in ordeal.

a didicit se ~a baptismatis non esse regeneratum BEDE *HE* III 23; licet illud baptisma vetus. .in ~a fuerit ANSELM (*Azym.* 4) II 228; Domine Deus. ., qui baptismum in ~a fieri jussisti (*Jud. Dei*) *GAS* 423; num. .liceat in cocta ~a. . aliquem baptizare BELETH *RDO* 110. 115; terra sancte ecclesie fundata est super ~as baptismales NECKAM *NR* II 49; ~a lustrationis non tantum fuit significativa delationis culpe, sed spiritus etiam HALES *Qu.* 877; baptizatur aqua; set aquam baptizat GARL. *Epith.* IX 497; Christus. .~am et sanguinem. .affluere. .permisit, ~am in lavacrum, sanguinem in redempcionem BRINTON *Serm.* 8 p. 25. **b** **601** ~a benedicta fiat, in eisdem fanis aspergatur (*Lit. Papae*) BEDE *HE* I 30; ~a benedicta domus suas aspergent quotiens voluerint qui habitent in eis THEOD. *Pen.* II i 11; aecclesiae . .~a exorcizata aspergantur *Ib.* ix 2; monachi. .benedicte ~e aspergine prestigias inimici effugarunt W. MALM. *GR* IV 323; ~a lustrali, quam benedictam vocant, aspergat BELETH *RDO* 2. 16; ~a benedicta est visibilis forma significativa invisibilis gratie, quia significat interiorem ablutionem HALES *Qu. app.* 1479; sunt et alii. .qui. .nec ~a nec exorcismis arcentur GERV. TILB. I 18; **1243** in qualibet ecclesia [sit]. .unum vas ad ~am benedictam *Conc. Syn.* 296; **c1230** volumus ut scolares ferant ~am benedictam per villas rurales si sint qui postulent et indigeant *Ib.* 211; **a1256** dabunt beneficium ~e benedicte clerico pauperi scolari *Ib.* 514; **1397** Henricus. ., quum venit ad ecclesiam, perturbat divinum officium, . .recusat ~am benedictam (*Vis. Heref.*) *EHR* XXIV 452; **1421** lavacrum pro ~a benedicta *EEC* 478; **1514** sanctum crisma et oleum, ~am Gregorianam *Eng. Clergy* 199. **c** si quis judicium ferri vel ~e vadiaverit [AS: *gif hwa ordales weddige*], accedat. .ad presbiterum qui debet sanctificare eum (*Quad.*) *GAS* 163; si ~a sit [*gif hit þonne wæter sy*], calefiat donec excitetur ad bullitum *Ib.* 386; **1134** concedimus. .monachis. .omnes regias libertates, murdrum, . .~am et ignem (*Ch. Bec*) *EHR* XXIV 211; **1166** si aliquis fuerit captus, qui fuerit saisitus de. .latrocinio, . .eat ad ~am (*Ass. Clarendon*) R. HOWD. II 250; **1166** debet x m. soca de A. pro homine quem posuerunt ad ~am sine serviente regis *Pipe* 49; **1168** de catallis fugitivorum et eorum qui perierunt ad ~am *Pipe* 90; **1176** si . .retatus fuerit, quamvis ad ~am mundus fuerit, . .a regno exeat (*Ass. Northampt.*) R. HOWD. II 89; judicio ~e adjudicatus est, ne quoquo modo evadere posset W. CANT. *Mir. Thom.* II 3; adverte. .hic usualiter nuncupari. .judicia. . leges candentis ferri vel ~e *Dial. Scac.* II 7A; tenetur se purgare accusatus [de mahemio] per Dei judicium, sc. per calidum ferrum vel per ~am, . .per ~am si fuerit rusticus GLANV. XIV 1; **1198** purgent se ~a et igne *CurR RC* I 204; **1201** purgent se masculi per ~am *SelPlCrown* 3; **1219** abbas dominus eorum. .fecit eos ire ad ~am in curia sua *CurR* VIII 42.

3 (? bibl. allegory) sorrow, learning, people.

14.. hec ~a, A. *sorow*, . .*lernyng*, . .*folke*: 'est aqua qua fruimur doctrina, dolor, populusque' WW; *a sorow*, . . mesticia, ~a, . .*techynge*, doctrina, ~a, . .*pepille*, ~a, gens, . .populus *CathA*.

4 water flavoured w. juice or sim., decoction. **b** (w. *ardens*) distilled fluid, spirit. **c** (w. *vite*) alcohol, brandy or whisky, (?) also mercury vapour (alch.).

1188 Saladinus. .fecit templum Domini ~a rosata. . lavari (*Lit. Praeceptoris Templi*) *G. Hen. II* II 41; utrum [sacramentum]. .in clareto. .vel ~a vinata confici valeat, questio est GIR. *GE* I 8; ~a †vitis GILB. III 132. 2 (cf. infra 4c); intingatur in ~a sanguinis draconis GAD. 52 v. 2; ~a ordei, i. ptisana *SB* 11; embrocatio dicitur cum membrum ponitur in ~a calida sive simplici sive decoccionis herbarum *Ib.* 19; stemento, i. pura ~a fabarum *Alph.* 168; **1380** unam †vergentam zinzibiris facti cum ~a limonis (*Cl*) *Foed.* VII 233; **1436** unum puff argenti pro ~a rosarum spargenda *Test. Ebor.* II 15. **b** ~e vite, i. de distillacione vini vel ~e ardentis GAD. 39. 2; alembicum, i. vas distillatorium in quo fit ~a rosacea et ~a ardens et hujusmodi *Alph.* 6; **1390** magistro W. Cook pro ~a ardente *Ac. H. Derby* 60. **c** terantur simul cum ~a vite, cujus proprium est dissolvere omnes res alias BACON *NM* 550; alii accipiunt 4 elementa, que vocantur ~a vite et humor aereus et virtus ignea et calx *Id. Tert. sup.* 88; ~a vite gubernat et dealbat omne corpus, vertens totum in suum colorem; ille namque fumus albus est DASTYN *Ros.* 14; ~a vite simplex fit de vino forti per viam distillacionis in alembico cum lignis salicis vel serpentaria GAD. 66. v. 2; **1439** in precio. .trium lagenarum ~e vite, precii lagene iiij s. *KRAc* 503/7 m. 1 (cf. *Bodleian Quarterly Rev.* VI 197–200); **1469** in reparacione. .stillatorii pro ~a vite stillanda *Ac. Durh.* 280; ~a vite simplex hoc modo debet fieri: accipe vinum electum. .et pone in olla et claude os olle. . (*RBOssory* 62b) *HMC Rep.* X *app.* V 254; utuntur pro panchresto medicamine ignito quodam vino. . quod communiter ~a vitae dicitur STANIHURST *Hib.* 38.

5 (alch.) mercury, acid, alkaline, or other fluid (often *s. dub.*).

riga cum ~a fetida ROB. ANGL. *Alch.* 518a (cf. *LC*: ~a foetida est ~a mercurii); metallorum ~a, ut ferri, arsenici, vitrioli, calcis et virideramini, corodit et frangit calibem (M. SCOT. *Part.*) *Med. Sci.* 295; solvitur in spiritum, id est in ~am mineralem *Correct. Alch.* 11; ~a philosophorum, ex qua viva fiunt elementa *Ib.* (cf. *LC*: ~a philosophica nominatur quibusdam acetum sublimatum, aliis vinum circulatum, aliis ~a perennis); virtus mercurii cum ~a viscosa fumum sulphureum commiscens vivum efficit argentum GROS.6; quidam [liquores] ex venis terre hauriuntur ut ~a salmantina, †vitrosa [l. nitrosa], aluminosa BART. ANGL. XIX 49 (cf. *LC*: ~a salmatina est de sale facta); ex potatione ~e solis [*'potable gold'*] purissimi BACON IX 133; calcem ~is alkali et aliis ~is acutis purifica *Id. NM* 545; jubeo ~am vivam coagulare, corpore suo miscere et coquere quousque exsiccetur DASTYN *Ros.* 14; quando crudum est, vocatur argentum †virum [l. vivum], ~a permanens, plumbum, sputum lune, stannum. . *Ib.* 4 (cf. *LC*: ~a permanens. .dicitur etiam ~a coelestina et mercurius philosophorum); ~a nigra fit de calce viva et auripigmento rubeo simul in ~a temperatis GAD.134 v. 2; funde desuper ~e fortis vel ~e maris. .lib. viij *Ib.* 40 1; recipe libram unam salis petre et tantundem vitrioli Romani et extrahe ~am fortem. .et dissolve eum [mercurium] in illa ~a forti super cineres calidos in amphora vitri clausa CUTCL. *CL op.* 2 (cf. *LC*: ~a fortis est quae ex acribus et corrosivis. .violentis ignibus distillatur. .).

aquab-, aquad- v. aquae-.

aquaebaillivus, water bailiff (*cf. baillivus* 3b).

1475 [officium] aqueballivi [*Malahide, Ir.*] *CalCh* VI 244; **1507** aqueballivus ibidem. .presentavit quod R. C. insultum fecit super W. F. . .super aquam *CourtR* (*Devon*) 166/21.

aquaebajularius, holy water clerk.

1395 aquebagillarius [ecclesie] *Cal. Recog. R. Chester* 98.

aquaebajulatrix, water-carrier (f.).

1355 Johanna Fetyz ~ix *JustIt* 312 r. 1 (= *Enf. Stat. Lab.* 174*: †aquebanilatrix).

aquaebajulatus, office of holy water clerk.

1427 Ricardum aquebajulum et suos. .antecessores officium ~us in eadem aula. .exercuisse *FormOx* 463; decernit quod officium ~us conferatur ut beneficium ecclesiasticum LYNDW. 142 p; **c1530** officium ~us ecclesie parochialis *Augm. Bk.* 91 f. 1v.

aquaebajulus [cf. bajulus 3c], holy water clerk.

1291 decrevimus ~um. .in ecclesia de Haxay. .non per parochianos. .set per loci vicarium. .deputari *Reg. Linc.* III 104; **1334** officium ~i conferat vicarius *Reg. Heref.* 67; **1393** nullus istorum scolarium erit ~us. .ecclesie de B. *Lit. Cant.* III 20; **1397** clericus aquebagilus *Cat. AncD* VI C 5383; vult parochianos compelli ad prestandum ipsis ~is elemosinas consuetas LYNDW. 142 p; hic aquebachelus *a halywater clerke* WW; *a parysche clerke*, clericus parochialis aquabajulus *CathA*; **1518** vicarius ibidem non habet aquebagilum *Vis. Linc.* I 14.

aquaeductile, conduit, gutter. **b** spout.

1348 licenciam prebuit ultra terras suas fodere et quoddam aquaductile disponere per quod cursum aque licite sub eisdem terris possint habere *AncD* A 8113; aquaductile, A. *a condyt*, . .hoc ~e, *a guttur* WW; *a cundyth*, aquaductile, . .*a gutter*, . .aqualicium, aquaductile, aqueductus *CathA*. **b** **1509** unum pelvem cum uno ~i *Reg. Merton* 384.

aquaeductor, water-carrier.

hic ~or, *a waterleder* WW.

aquaeductulus, small (branch) water-pipe.

1476 licebit quemdam ~um parvum plumbeum, cum foramine magnitudinis unius straminis frumenti, aqueductui ipsorum. .apponere et annectere *FormA* 128.

aquaeductus, ~um [CL; *al. div.*], aqueduct. **b** mill lade. **c** drainage tunnel (of mine; *cf. avidotus*). **d** water-pipe, conduit, or gutter.

perpes ~uum decursus. .celsis arcuum fornicibus in edito sublimatus ALDH. *VirgP* 9; murus. .ex latere occidi. .qui immensis fornicibus aque ductum sustentat GREG. *Mir. Rom.* 18. **b** **10..** ~um, *wætergelada* WW; **c1174** ab aquiloni parte ~us veteris molendini *CalCh* IV 131; **c1240** ad stagnum et ~um. .molendini reparandum *Cart. Tutbury* no. 141; **1252** alnetum inter duo inferiora molendina sua et inter bolhagium et aque ductum *MonA* VI 430; **1294** quod liberum ductum aque de E. habeant ad molendina sua. .et quod libere possint facere et reficere dictum ~um *Reg. Paisley* 95; **1368** in factura cujusdam ~us lignei in stagno molendini *Ac. Durh.* 128; **1469** percipienti. .j m. annui redditus pro ~u ad molendinum *ExchScot* 653. **c** **1357** manuceperunt ad faciendum quemdam aque ductum in minera nostra de Vaynol *Recog. R. Chester* 39 r. 1; **1376** in expensis factis circa ~u[m] carbonum de Raynton *Ac. Durh.* 583; **c1415** circa lucracionem ~us minere [de Raynton] *Ib.* 708. **d** canalis vel colimbus vel ~us, *wæterpeote* ÆLF. *Sup.*; transfossus est [collis], ut aque ductum patulo sinu receptum traduceret per directum W. CANT. *Mir. Thom.* III 1; eluviones et ~us in vicis W. FITZST. *Thom. prol.* 12; **1259** plumbum quod rex. .dedit Fratribus Predicatoribus London' ad ~um suum faciendum *Cl* 10; **1301** fistulas. . plumbeas ~us. .fecit excidi *Reg. Cant.* II 597; **1365** quendam ~um subterraneum a fonte predicto usque ad mansum suum in Salopia facere fistulasque ~us illius subtus terram . .ponere *Pat* 272 m. 29; **c1375** in plumbo empto pro uno ~o *Ac. Durh.* 47; **c1400** ~um de piscina communis lavatorii . .adduxit *Mon. Francisc.* I 508; ad turrim ~us in Cornehille ELMH. *Hen. V* 64; hoc ~um, *a guttur* WW; **1471** pro reparacione †~i que (*sic*) descendit a coquina. .ad portam *Cant. Coll. Ox.* II. 194; **1511** pro uno plancke posito super ~am (*sic*) prope coquinam *Ib.* 253.

aquaefluus, flowing w. water.

868 (12c) prata longe et lato alta et ~a *CS* 518.

aquaelicium [CL = *rain-making*], gutter, drain.

a1285 quod possint de aqueletio seu lavatorio nostro aquam ibidem superabundantem extrahere *Cart. Glouc.* I 172; *a gutter*, . .aquagium, aqualicium, aquaductile *CathA*; **1514** faciet aquagia et aqualitia mundari *Reg. Merton* 448.

aquaemanile [? *for* aquae manale], wash-basin.

†aquemale, *lebel GlC* A 716; **10..** ~e, *lævel* WW; subdiaconus cum ordinatur. .de manu. .archidiaconi accipiat urceolum cum aquamanili ac manutergium EGB. *Pont.* 14; urceolus. .est vas superius unde lavandis manibus aqua infunditur. aquamanile sive ~e Italici unam partem dicunt, vocaturque lingua eorum vas inferius in quod manibus infusa aqua delabitur LANFR. *Ep.* 13. 520D.

†aquaenomio, spout.

aquenomio, A. *a spute* WW.

†aquagagia, (?) payment for upkeep of dikes (*cf. aquagium* 1a, *watergangia*).

1359 [ballivus] omnes collectores et expenditores tam generales scottas quam speciales ~ias, assessas ut predictum est, onerabit. .levare, expendere et computare *Laws Romney Marsh* 69.

aquagium [CL], watercourse, mill-lade. **b** conduit or gutter. **c** (?) holy water stoup.

1209 reddit compotum de xx s. de ~io molendini de hospitali S. Crucis *Pipe Wint.* 77; **1298** lestus marisci de Romenal tentus apud Borewaremersh: abbas. .optulit se. . versus. .homines. .~ii de Heth' *Reg. S. Aug.* 610; **1359** non liceat alicui facere. .impedimenta in aliquibus landeis, †watergageis, fossatis sive ~iis communibus in marisco *Laws Romney Marsh* 71; **1453** pro duobus *scottes* assessatis ad reparacionem ~ii de Burwardmerssh *MinAc* (*Kent*) 1129/3 r. 4; *water lesu*, ~ium *PP*. **b** ~ium, *wæterpeote* ÆLF. *Gl.*; plumbarius sive conductarius, quociens ~ium reparatur infra muros ecclesie, . .bina fercula recipiet *Cust. Westm.* 74; *chanel of a strete*, canalis, ~ium *PP*; ~ium, A. *a gutur or a condyt* WW. **c** **a1200** †obsecretarius. .†~ium [? l. aquarium] feret ubicunque in capitulum, in dormitorium *Chr. Abingd.* II 383.

2 toll for passage by water (Norm.).

1172 dono. .quietantiam vendendi, emendi et transportandi per terram et per aquam. .absque passagio, pontagio, ~io, theloneo et consuetudine aliqua *Act. Hen. II* I 463.

aqualiculus [CL], pot-belly.

adolescens. .fortitudinis probate, quanquam exilis corporis et pinguis ~i W. MALM. *GR* IV 389; Johanni cuidam. . immoderato tumore ~um distento aquam. .propinavit W. CANT. *Mir. Thom.* III 51.

aqualitium v. aquaelicium.

aqualium, top of head.

an hede, ~ium est summa pars capitis *CathA*.

aquamanile v. aquaemanile.

1 aquare [cf. CL aquari], to water (animals). **b** to dilute w. water. **c** to wet (wool). **d** to water (cloth).

1254 jacebit. .inculta. .ut animalia. .chaciam suam habeant. .ad ~andum et pascendum *Cart. S. Fridesw.* II 273; **1257** habeant. .ingressum. .ad ~andum averia eorum *Reg. Malm.* II 203; **c1270** pro iij frenis emptis ad ~andum palefridos regis *Chanc. Misc.* 3/7/24; **1327** quo minus. . averia sua. .chaciare valeat †ad ~anda [? l. ad ~andum *or* adaquanda] *MonA* I 53b. **b** ~atam potionem recte dicimus quae aquam aliunde recipiat, aquosum autem locum qui ex se aquam fundat BEDE *Orth.* 2778; vinum non ~atum bibas GIR. *TH* I 35. **c** **1299** acculpatus quod ~avit lanam et imposuit sabilonem apud S. Botulfum *Rec. Leic.* I 226. **d** **1437** bonum pannum et habilem, ita tamen quod omnino teneat in latitudine infra listas ad minus ij virgatas, plenum, ~atum et scissum *Doc. Bev.* 33.

2 aquare, watering-place (*cf. aquarius* 2b).

1476 lego ad faciendum unum ~e. .juxta viam. .vj s. viij d. *Test. Ebor.* III 220.

1 aquaria, ewery, office of ewerer.

1361 J. Wafrer et Ade de ~ia, garcionibus officiorum hospicii regis *KRAc* 393/11 f. 71; 1399 [servienti regis] ~ie [sue] *CalPat* 307; c1472 de officio ~ie *BBHouseh.* 78; 1574 A. Mathewe, generosum ~ie nostre *Pat* 1117 m. 18.

2 aquaria v. aquarius 2a.

aquariolum, sink.

~um, *synke* Stanbr. *Vulg.* 10.

aquarius [CL], (adj.) for holding water. **b** driven by water. **c** dealing w. water. **d** (w. *canis*) water-dog.

ampullas vinarias et ~ias Lanfr. *Const.* 150; 1229 duo vasa, unum vinarium et aliud ~ium *Conc. Syn.* 171; c1250 vas ~ium stagneum *Vis. S. Paul.* 6; 1402 bacinus ~ius *Invent. S. Paul.* 514. **b** 1265 molendinis tam ~iis quam ventoriis *Melrose* I 322. **c** dum minister ~ius superiora foramina..obturabat, nil aque..emanabat Adel. *QN* 58. **d** [canes] grandes et graviores etiam rotae amplioris circumactu aquam ex altis puteis ad usus rusticos hauriunt, quos ~ios appellamus ex officio Caius *Can.* 8.

2 (sb. n., m. or f.) ewer. **b** watering-place or (?) water-meadow. **c** trough. **d** gutter.

c1250 deest ~ium *Vis. S. Paul.* 21; 1317 in j ~io argenteo empto pro priori, xx s. *Ac. Durh.* 573; 1328 unus ~ius ejusdem secte *Reg. Exon.* 569; 1330 una olla argentea que dicitur ~ia *ExchScot* 323; s1330 cum discis et salsariis et ~eo argenteo Thorne 2057; abbas [Johannes, ob. 1379]..acquisivit..unum ~ium pro aqua benedicta cum aspersorio de argento *Chr. Evesham* 301; 1400 pro j alto cipho cum j ~io amellato et deaurato *Test. Ebor.* III 10; 1431 unam ~iam deauratam *Wills N. Country* 40. **b** c1182 concessisse ..~ias suas de S. [*Norm.*] *Act. Hen. II* II 247; 1308 assignata fuit eidem..tercia pars unius gardini..et eciam unum ~ium *IPM* 124/3; 1326 in liberacionibus..j formanni seminantis semen, facientis ~ia et custodientis campum *MinAc* 1148/22 (cf. ib.: facient' aqueria); 1445 cum..moris, mariscis, ~iis, faldagiis et omnibus aliis commoditatibus *Cl* 295 m. 9*d*. **c** Harduinus..ingens saxum..in domum suam devexit, ibique ~ium sibi suisque jumentis facere voluit; sed post inceptam cavationem in languorem cecidit Ord. Vit. VI 10 p. 112. **d** ~ium, A. *a gutur* WW.

3 (sb. m.) ewerer, official of household (esp. royal) concerned w. provision of water. **b** water-carrier. **c** (astr.) Aquarius. **d** holy-water clerk (*cf. aquaebajulus*).

~ius [capit] duplicem cibum; et quando rex iter agit, j d. ad pannos exsiccandos; et quando rex balneat, iiij d. *Domus Reg.* 133; 1212 Brianus ~ius *Fees* 122 (cf. ib. 591: Brianus le Ewer); 1234 concessimus Simoni ~io nostro liberationem j d. *Cl* 40; 1259 Colino ~io regis *Cl* 449; 1391 lotrici lavanti mappas ~ii *Ac. H. Derby* 81. **b** 1221 Ketelburtus ~ius de Ravenestorp *Rec. Leic.* I 25; c1270 Radulfo ~io [v.l. le Ewer] *Ib.* 135; 1293 Hychecoke le Waterledere..manucapitur per Hugonem ~ium et Rogerum ~ium *PlRChester* 6 r. 10. **c** [inchoat oriri] undecimum ~ii sidus a parte solari mediantis Januarii Bede *TR* 16; casualiter Saturno cedit ~ius J. Sal. *Pol.* 442A; Neckam *NR* I 23 (v. astrologia b). **d** 1348 lego..capellano parochiali..vj d.; item lego ~io iij d. *AncD* B 9629; hic ~ius, *a halywater clerke* WW; *an halywater clerke*, ~ius, aquebajulus *CathA*.

aquaticare, to drain or irrigate. **b** to steep, ret (flax).

1321 debet ~are super terram domini per j diem et dim. *Cust. Suss.* III 65 (cf. ib. 49). **b** 1340 de villanis de Ayshtone [*Wilts*] pro lino ~ando ad festum S. J. Baptiste, vj d. *Rent. & Surv.* 699 m. 5*d*.

aquaticus [CL], aquatic, growing in water. **b** living or born in water. **c** (sb. m., sc. *canis*) water spaniel. **d** (sb. m.) Moses.

menta ~a, A. *horsment SB* 30; ipsmia..herba ~a est *Alph.* 86. **b** avibus ~is natione, aereis habitatione Gir. *TH* I 11. **c** post hunc subsequitur ~us, hoc est *a water-spainel* Caius *Can.* 12. **d** velud Josue sub eximio ~o *V. Osw.* 411 (cf. ib. 399).

2 a water-filled. **b** for carrying water. **c** for holding water. **d** (sb. n.) ewer.

a 1367 fossatum ~um *CalIPM* XII no. 170. **b** s1331 conduxerunt omnes carectas ~as civitatis ad irrigandum campum *Ann. Paul.* 354. **c** 1307 in j buketto ~o *Crawley* 253; 1336 in..j urceolo ~o deaurato *Ac. Durh.* 527. **d** 1431 [lego] unum ~um argenteum trussyng' [i.e. *designed for packing*] cum v gobelettes; item..unum ~um argenteum cum vj gobelettes infra dictum ~um contentis *Reg. Cant.* II 439.

3 adjoining water: **a** (of mill wall); **b** (of gate); **c** (of town).

a 1320 in emendacione parietis ~e *KRAc* 482/1 m. 4*d*.; 1372 in uno arbore empto pro tabulis ad parietem ~am *CourtR Meltham.* **b** 1359 dederunt..Thome moram suam in..domo juxta portam †~um ad illam portam custodiendam *Lit. Cant.* II 384; 1411 trahentes..eundem [canonicum] per portam ~am et per viam inviam *FormOx* 188. **c** 1306 de tallagio bondorum de villis ~is *Cust. Rents (Beverley)* 96; 1397 cum villis ~is subsequentibus, viz. Thorn', ..et Snorholme *IMisc (Yorks)* 268/10.

4 driven by water (of mill); **b** (of mill-wheel); **c** (w. *arca*) *s. dub.*

1196 de uno molendino ~o in campo de Wotton' [*Warw*] *Fines P. Ric. I* 91; 1199 unum molendinum ~um cum tofto sibi adjacente *CalCh* IV 163; 1255 W. L. ..fuit prope stagnum molendini ~i..et cecidit in..aqua et oppressus fuit rote (*sic*) illius molendini *JustIt* 872 r. 27*d*.; 1284 de quodam molendino †aquato *PQW* 94a; 1311 duo molendina ~a cum cursu aque valent.. *Cust. Battle* 137; 1378 tria molendina aquatiqua *IMisc* 213/4 r. 4; 1412 quoddam molendinum ~um..fregerunt et *le forpount* et *lez flodeȝates* ejusdem prostraverunt *Proc. J.P.* 316. **b** 1297 in stipendiis ij carpentariorum..emendancium..rotas ~as reficiendas *Ac. Cornw.* II 193; 1321 ad emendacionem algee sub rota ~a..molendini *MinAc* 992/11; 1325 in bordis sarrandis pro sroudura rote ~e j molendini ~i *Ib.* 1147/23 r. 7; 1409 in stipendio..operantis et de novo facientis unam rotam ~am pro dicta forgea (*Ac. Aud. Durh.*) *EHR* XIV 517. **c** 1320 (v. arca 2a).

5 a used in water. **b** used for flushing water-fowl. **c** used for watering animals. **d** used for draining. **e** (w. *vir*) waterman.

a s1295 xxx de galeis et aliis vasis ~is combusserunt *Flor. Hist.* III 284; 1388 j rethe ~um precii dim. m. *IMisc.* 239/6 r. 2. **b** 1287 pro viij taburellis ~is emptis pro ostoriis regis ad ripariam *KRAc* 351/24 m. 1. **c** 1368 in uno freno ~o empto pro palefrido prioris *Ac. Durh.* 569; 1384 locus ~us..in quo..averia..solebant adaquari *PlRCP* 497 r. 233. **d** 1352 in via ~a minere de Raynton de novo facienda *Ac. Durh.* 553 (cf. ib. 176); 1587 hereditamenta.. prope ..rivulum Humbrie..adjacencia, racione cujus muri marittimi littora, ripe et opera ~a eorundem..sine magnis ..sumptibus reparari..non queant *Pat* 1303 m. 15. **e** 1411 aldermanni et seneschalli arcium.., viz. ..allutariorum, virorum ~orum, tinctorum *Doc. Bev.* 34.

6 a watery, originating from water. **b** rainy (astr.). **c** (w. *sapphirus*) water sapphire. **d** (fig.). **e** (sb. n.) perceptible water (mixture of elements w. water predominant).

a ex terrenis ~isque vaporibus Eriug. *Per.* 550A. **b** Jove existente in signo ~o *Ps.*-Gros. 587. **c** unum [anulum]..habentem saphiri ~i gemmam viliorem..nobis contradidit Ad. Eyns. *Hug.* V 16 p. 192; 1349 anulus auri cum zaphiro ~o (*Mem. Thes.*) *CalExch* I 165. **d** cor quod fuit sapore ~um [ME: *wateri*]..convertetur in vinum *AncrR* 147. **e** Adel. *QN* 1 (v. aerius 2b).

aquatilis [CL], aquatic, living in water. **b** (sb.) aquatic animal.

c798 non terrestrium seu ~ium animalium carnem comedit Alcuin *Ep.* 134. **b** s1392 [delphines] contra naturam ~ium soli linguas suas movent Wals. *HA* II 204.

aquatio, watering (of animals).

1365 pro ~one averiorum *Hal. Durh.* 38.

aquatorium, watering-place.

1256 salvo..libero introitu et exitu ad quoddam ~ium quod..vocatur Therspettes et libera chacia sua ad aquandum ibidem omnimoda averia sua *Fines* (*Northumb*) 180/5/145.

aquatus v. 1 aquare, aquaticus 4a. aqueb-, aqued-, v. aquae-.

aqueitas, wateriness, moisture.

si inveniatur continuatio in materia ~atis, dicitur ~as una; si pluralitas, dicitur ~ates plures, cum ~as in se simplex sit et indivisibilis Gilb. VI 245. 1; color indicus ..est color blavius..plus habens †aquitatis et aereitatis admixtum cum partibus terrestribus Bart. Angl. XIX 21; non congelatur sola aqua nisi siccitate, que alteravit ~atem et terrestreitatem *Correct. Alch.* 5; ex humiditatibus congelatis in concavitatibus cavernarum, in quibus ~as et terrestritas magis dominatur Bacon V 129; cetera simplicia, ut celum, ignis et aqua et similia, formam, que est natura quedam et pars compositi, in sui compositionem recipiunt eodem nomine cum forma substantiali mancipatam, ut celeitas, igneitas, ~as *Ps.*-Gros. 336; sudor est ~as sanguinis cui pus colericum est admixtum Gad. 44. 2.

aquem-, aquen-, v. aquae-. aquesta v. acquestus.

aqueus, aqueous, consisting of water. **b** wet, rainy.

sub hoc [celo aereo] est celum ~eum quod terram contingit et humectat Gerv. Tilb. I 1; causa finalis iridis est dissipatio humiditatis ~ee Bacon *Maj.* III 52; de vitro vel quocunque omogenio, quantumlibet fortiter commixto, contingit partem subtilem ~eum (*sic*) vel aereum extrahi Wycl. *Log.* III 77; in qua [materia florum], si predominantes partes fuerint ~ee et aerie, color erit albus; et, si fuerint partes prevalentes ~ee cum terrestribus, erit color griseus Upton 113. **b** s1450 ille mensis ~eus in quo, ut in herbis.., ita eciam in..hominibus solent humores increscere *Reg. Whet.* I 156.

aquie- v. acquie-.

aquifolia [CL], holly.

baccis ~iae arboris..et similium arborum vescitur Turner *Av.* 27.

1 aquila [CL], eagle. **b** lectern (in form of eagle). **c** (imperial) standard. **d** 'eagle', base coin. **e** Aquila (astr.).

~ae clangunt Aldh. *PR* 131; vidit ~am volantem in aere *V. Cuthb.* II 5; ~a, *earn* Ælf. *Gl.*; velut si..noctuae..de meridianis solis radiis disceptent contra ~as ipsum solem.. intuentes Anselm (*Incarn.* 1) II 8; c1138 a nido ~e usque ad fontem Egardi *Cart. Newm.* 1; ~arum..non minorem hic copiam quam alibi mivorum videas Gir. *TH* I 13; corpore par aquile phenix Neckam *DS* II 185; ~a..velut regina inter volucres optinet principatum; ..est..~a ab acumine oculorum dicta; ..est..avis naturaliter calida et sicca, prede avida et supra aliarum avium vires fortis et animosa Bart. Angl. XII 2. **b** post epistolam unus ceroferariorum..~am in pulpito ad legendum evangelium ornando preparet *Offic. Sal.* 92 p. 150; in hac feria [sc. secunda in Adventu] evangelium non in pulpito in ~a [legitur] sed in presbiterio super pulpito [ad] hoc parato *Ib.* 94 p. 160. **c** ~ae, *segnas GlC* A 717; o sancti.. / victrices aquilas caeli qui fertis in arcem Alcuin *SSEbor.* I 10; Christi victrices aquile, que sunt crucis ale Garl. *Tri. Eccl.* 1; s1214 imperator cum vexillo ~e deaurato..in quadriga erecto *Plusc.* VII 2. **d** s1299 mercatores alienigeni introduxerant in Angliam monetas plurimas et pessimi metalli pollardorum, ..~arum, ..et aliorum diversorum nominum W. Guisb. 333. **e** Neckam *NR* I 23 (v. astrologia b).

2 (alch.) sal ammoniac or mercury vapour.

~a volans per aerem et bufo gradiens per terram est magisterium Dastyn *Ros.* 9; ~a..usurpatur nomine pro sale armoniaco propter levitatem in sublimationibus... ~a mercurii spiritus *LC*.

2 aquila v. aquola. aquilaria v. aquileia.

aquilaris, of an eagle (fig.).

sicuti inter quatuor aurigas currus evangelici Johannes ~i volatu pre ceteris subtiliora Trinitatis misteria pennis contemplacionis..propalavit *NLA* (*J. Bridl.*) II 71.

aquileia [etym. dub.], columbine or celery-leaved crowfoot.

herbam que †avigilia [v.l. angulia] dicitur ei da eumque ab inflatione et vento curabit Adel. *CA* 11; feniculum, levisticum, ~eiam Gilb. II 112 v. 2; ~eia, columbina idem secundum Laurencium; ..aquilaria vel ~eia unum stipitem habet et folia fissa..et florem album; secundum antiquos apium risus appellatur *Alph.* 13.

aquiletta [cf. aquila 1d], 'eagle', base coin.

1258 de auquilatis faciendis et currendis in civitate vestra [*Bayonne, Gasc.*] *Cl* 323; 1297 pauca moneta..est in Hibernia et fere tota..que currit ibidem est de extraneis partibus, Flandr' et aliunde, quam vocant quidam ballards, pollards, rosar[ios] vel aquilett' *KRAc* 230/27 r. 17.

aquilex [CL; cf. aquaelicium], **~licus,** water-diviner.

~lici, scrutatores aquarum *GlC* A 718.

Aquilianus [CL], Aquilian (leg.).

1347 per acceptilacionem et ~am stipulacionem verbis solemnibus introductam liberacionem fecerunt (*Pat*) *Foed.* V 570.

aquilinus, aquiline, of an eagle. **b** (w. *Aula*) Eagle Hall (Oxford). **c** (*s. dub.*).

renovatus more ~o *V. Osw.* 417; forma leonina Rome, virtus aquilina Garl. *Mor. Scol.* 145. **b** 1498 tenementum Thome Ape, viz. Aula ~a *Cart. Osney* III 280. **c** scirra †~us, sciurus, *acwern* Ælf. *Gl.*

aquilium v. aculeus 2a. aquilus v. 1 aquilus. aquillus v. arquillus c.

aquilo [CL], north wind. **b** (fig.). **c** north. **d** (adj.) northern.

801 surgat ~o vel auster Alcuin *Ep.* 215; ~o vel boreas, *norðan westan wind* Ælf. *Gl.*; aquas aquilo congelat atque ligat Neckam *DS* II 94. **b** circa tempora Antichristi erit una gens de stirpe Gog et Magog contra ubera ~onis, circa pontum Euxinum Bacon *Mor. Phil.* 16; 1281 appellacionem..fundatam in veritatis injuria aut ~onis vacuo fundamento Peckham *Ep.* 192 (cf. *Job.* xxvi 7). **c** ex aquilone Aldh. *VirgV* 2735; cometae duae..portabant.. facem ignis contra ~onem Bede *HE* V 23; c1220 terram meam in parrochia S. Petri versus orientem in magna platea versus ~onem *Cart. Osney* I 290; 1300 quantum comitatus Surreie durat versus ~onem *SelPlForest* 118. **d** c1174 ab ~oni parte aqueductus veteris molendini *CalCh* IV 131; 1206 usque ad reditum domini regis ab ~onibus partibus *Prests* 275; s1261 cum per crucem ex ~one parte chori..transire conaretur Graystanes 7.

aquilon v. diaquilon.

aquilonalis, northern. **b** (of persons).

boreo ~is poli cardine Aldh. *Met.* 3; natio Anglorum quae ad ~em Humbre fluminis plagam habitabat Bede *HE* II 9; ad ~es partes Britanniae Nenn. *HB* 37; palus illa magna que menia urbis ~ia alluit W. Fitzst. *Thom. prol.* 17; s1173 rubor quidam videbatur in aere inter orientem et occidentem in parte ~i Gerv. Cant. I 241; c1300 ascendendo per illum rivulum ex parte ~i *Reg. Paisley* 102; ad cornu altaris ~e *Cust. Cant.* 424. **b** presbiter..qui ab omnibus ~ibus Anglis patris loco colebatur Ailr. *SS. Hex.* 190.

aquilonaris, northern. **b** (of persons). **c** (sb. m. or f.) north.

insultus venti ~is Neckam *Ut.* 117; 1222 quod cheminus ille decetero sit extra domum suam ejusdam ville a parte ~i *Cl* 518a; sedere solet..prior primus in ~i parte [claustri] juxta ostium locutorii *Cust. Cant.* 202. **b** regnum Australium Merciorum, qui sunt..discreti fluvio Treanta ab ~ibus Merciis Bede *HE* III 24; s1260 (v. australis 2a). **c** selda.. exterius proxima versus ~em *Cart. Osney* III 103.

aquilonicus, northern.

hac sub fortuna presens aquilonica luna / non fuit ad sortem [*gl.*: comes Northumbrie, cujus signum fuit luna crescens] Gower *CT* I 55.

aquilonius, northern.

aestivo..decurrens in circulo, [sol]..brevem sub ~ia terrae loca noctu facit digressum Bede *TR* 34.

1 aquilus [CL], dark.

~ium [*Erf.* 2. 267. 9: ~um], fuscum vel subnigrum *GlC* A 714.

2 aquilus, aquiline, hooked.

aliud est hoc accidens ~us [*gl.*: qui habet nasum recurvum], aliud est hoc accidens ricum NECKAM *NR* II 173.

aquiscium v. arquitium. aquisi- v. acquisi-. aquit- v. et. acquiet-. aquitas v. aqueitas. aquito v. alcoto.

Aquitanus, ~icus, ~iensis, Aquitanian, Guiennois.

s1066 instigerant eis Cenomanici, Francigenae, Britanni, ~i W. POIT. II 192; **s1151** Henricus dux Normannorum.. sic factus est dux ~orum DICETO *YH* I 293; **s1204** inter Pictavenses et ~icos magnus conflictus..exstiterat COGGESH. 101; **s1346** multitudinem arcubalistariorum ~iensium *Meaux* III 59; **s1411** cum Wasconibus et ~nicis WALS. *YN* 432.

aquola [CL], a little water.

a water, aqua, aquila diminutivum, rivus *CathA*.

aquositas, wateriness, moisture.

que est..tante ~atis copia que jam pridem non foret excursa? ADEL. *QN* 55; pluvialis ~as GIR. *TH* I 6; pisces.. crudos inter manus fortiter comprimebat, donec omnis ~as consumeretur, et sic eos edebat COGGESH. 88; transit ad renes ~as et ibi separatur et formatur urina RIC. MED. *Micr. Anat.* 226; illa unctuosa que habent majorem ~atem minus pertinent ad naturam aeris BART. ANGL. XIX 41; semina.. resolvunt flegma in ~ates GILB. I 35. 1; cum [sanguis] ad ~atem tendit BACON IX 48; hernia..aquosa curatur cum medicinis evacuativis ~atis GAD. 130. 1.

aquosus [CL], watery, moist. **b** dilute. **c** (fig.). **d** rainy (astr.). **e** (w. *sapphirus*) water sapphire.

ni fallax caupo strofas infundat aquosas ALDH. *VirgV* 2796; BEDE *Orth.* 2778 (v. 1 aquare b); post oscula frontis aquose FRITH. 1223; terra..mollis et ~a GIR. *TH* I 4; gustus recipit saporem quia gustus est ~e nature J. BLUND *An.* 218; relinquitur ~a superfluitas in ramosa RIC. MED. *Micr. Anat.* 226; simili censenda tenore / sicca dies et aquosa tamen pro parte VINSAUF *PN* 1036; ydrogogum, i. purgans ~os humores *SB* 24; **1353** pratum acosum et sepius enundatum *IPM* 124/4; **1371** quoddam puteum ~um in eodem campo *SelCCoron* 45. **b** vina alba ~a aliqualiter aromaticata GAD. 22 v. 1; materia ~a *Ib.* 30. 2. **c 717** ut..divini intellectus..ignem ~o luto..terrene cupiditatis..non extinguas BONIF. *Ep.* 9. **d** planetas humidos..considerabis, ..maxime si in primo aspectu aspexerint se..in signis ~is GROS. 51. **e 1315** anulus cum saphiro quadrato ~o *Invent. Ch. Ch.* 71.

1 ara [CL], altar: **a** pagan; **b** Jewish; **c** Christian; **d** (fig.).

a aras et fana idolorum BEDE *HE* II 13; **10..** ara, *wiggebed* WW. **b** Judei, ubicunque dicimus aram, dicunt aream: quod nos ereum..altare propter laminas asseribus affixas dicimus, illi parietes aree appellant AD. SCOT. *TT* 666B; corpus dominicum in ara consecrando non vitule rufe cineres spargunt GIR. *Spec.* IV 23. **c** qua fulgent arae bis seno nomine sacrae ALDH. *CE* 3. 40; inclinate suppliciter ad almas aras [AS: *to halgum wefodum*] ÆLF. *Coll.* 103; ante aram..se prostraverant W. MALM. *GR* III 264; **c1137** ubi sacerdos ad aram debebas procedere OSB. CLAR. *Ep.* 12; ut videam clare quis sacre sit cibus are P. BLOIS *Euch. prol.* 1137C; are majori missam cantare rogatus H. AVR. *Poems* 2. 129. **d c1150** in ara mentis OSB. CLAR. *Ep.* 33; [avarus] omnia que sua sunt commendat demonis aris D. BEC. 2465.

2 ara [cf. AS *ār*], (?) oar.

1342 de ara batelli de wrecco *MinAc* 1091/6.

3 ara v. hara.

Arabicus, Arabian, Arabic (*v. et. gummi*). **b** (sb. n.) Arabic language.

cum diebus annorum et mensium et dierum ~orum (ADEL. *Tab.*) *EHR* XXVI 494; **s1192** Saphadinus duos equos nobilissimos ~os regi..destinavit *Itin. Ric.* VI 22; nonnulli librorum..~am magis loquacitatem quam..Grecam eloquentiam..pretendunt *Ps.*-GROS. 283; hic ensis [Constantini imperatoris] fuit de nobilissimo auro ~o KNIGHTON I 20 (cf. W. MALM. *GR* II 135). **b** liber Aristotilis.. translatus est de Greco in ~um et de eo in Latinum BACON *Mor. Phil.* 265; scientia linguarum sapientialium a quibus tota Latinorum sapientia translata est, cujusmodi sunt Grecum, Hebreum, ~um et Chaldeum *Id. CSPhil* 433; idem de ~o in plerisque tractatibus astronomicis..est censendum R. BURY *Phil.* 10. 166.

arabiem v. 2 arabilis.

1 arabilis [CL], arable, cultivable or cultivated. **b** (sb. f., sc. *terra*) ploughland. **c** (w. *bos*) plough ox. **d** (w. *dies*) ploughing day.

villani plus habent car[ucarum] quam ~em terram *DB* I 181b; ccxxxi acras terrae ~is inland et c acras prati *Ib.* 336; **c1150** unam carucatam terre ~is *Reg. Dunferm.* no. 12; **a1190** quantum ibi habent brullii possint excolere et convertere ad terram ~em *MonA* VI 1066b; **1201** xxv acras terre arrabilis in dominicis culturis *RChart* 86a; **1217** unusquisque liber homo..faciat..in terra sua quam habeat in foresta terram ~em extra †cooperatum in terra ~i (*Ch. Forest*) *St.Realm* I 21; **s1233** in campis ~ibus et fructiferis.. et aliis insolitis locis proruperunt fontes WEND. III 49; **1263** habeant in quolibet burgagio tres acras terre, sc. duas acras ~es et unam in burgo ad inedificandum *BBC* (*Agardsley*) 47; **1346** dedi..unam dim. acram capitalem terre ~is *AncD* C 4222; **1587** sex selliones sive landas terre arrabilis *Pat* 1300 m. 43. **b 1269** tota arrabilis pertinens ad.. ecclesiam, ix acre *Cart. Glast.* I 60. **c c1185** de unoquoque bove ~i *Rec. Templars* 23; **1232** multi boves erunt ~es *Crawley* 201. **d 1285** debet quilibet istorum bovariorum invenire j hominem ad carucam domini qualibet die ~i *Cust. Suss.* II 25.

2 arabilis, ~us [OF *airable* < acerabulus], maple.

hic deficiunt castanus et fagus ferhles, aralus et buxus, fructum non ferentes, scyphos tamen et manubria largientes GIR. *TH* III 10; **1215** quod habeant..unum summarium in forista nostra de Chipeham..deferentem duo summagia in die de bulo et alno et fraxino et arabil' *Cl* 220a; **1223** clausturam et palos de spinis et arabulis et subbosco *Ib.* 564a; **1229** tres carectatas busce de spinis, alno et ~i ad focum suum *Cl* 212; **1232** per †arabiem qui est super montem (*Ch. Dore*) *MonA* V 556a; **1232** habere faciat ..arables in foresta de Wichewude ad justas faciendas *Cl* 97; **1236** in quibus locis..forgie levari possint ad ~em et spinam, corulum et mortuum boscum *Pat* 47 m. 11 (cf. *Cl* 416); **1285** quercus, fagos et ~es *IMisc.* 44/25; **1306** de xxvij ~ibus et vij fraxinis venditis *MinAc* 1079/17 r. 3; **1308** pro arrab' amputat' *CourtR Wakefield* II 154; **1315** succidendo et vendendo..ducentas ~es precium cujuslibet ij s. *Year Bk. 8 Ed. II* 120.

arabo v. arrabo.

Arabs [CL], Arab.

s1095 Turci et Perse, ~es et Agareni, ..ipsam Jerusalem ..invaserant ORD. VIT. IX 2 p. 466; dilucidas ~um sententias D. MORLEY 7; **1232** primus Aristotilis satagens perquirere libros, / quando recenter eos Arabes misere Latinis H. AVR. *Poems* 127. 79; a tempore..quo gens ~um per Machometum ~em pseudoquepropheta seducta.. Egyptum Africamque subegit, in gente illa preclarissimi philosophi extiterunt *Ps.*-GROS. 279.

arabulus v. 2 arabilis.

arachne [ἀράχνη; cf. aranea], spider.

massam / ..quasi telam rupit aragnae WULF. *Swith.* II 581.

aracionatus v. arrationare. aracium v. haracium. aracuincula v. aratiuncula. aradicare v. abradicare.

†araenum, *s. dub.* (? cf. *Atrebatensis*).

1396 in lectisternio abbatis: ..coopertoria duo de rubio, quorum [j] est de opere ~i (*Invent.*) *Meaux* III lxxix.

aragiatus [OF *aragie*], mad.

1205 Juliana..debet c s. pro liberando viro suo..qui est ~us [v.l. arragiatus] in carcere *Pipe* 267.

aragium v. arreragium, averagium. aragna v. arachne. aragon v. aregon. Aragonensis v. Arrago. arai- v. arrai-, arram-. araldus v. heraldus. aralus v. 2 arabilis. aram- v. armare 3, arram-, arren-.

aranea [CL < ἀράχνη; cf. arachne], spider. **b** (fig.).

10.. ~ea, *gongelwafre* WW; bibit sanguinem [Christi] cum ~ea nec lesus est; immo postea integra per brachium exivit GIR. *GE* I 45; ~ea filum extrahit, telam orditur, totam se eviscerat, ut unicam muscam capiat O. CHERITON *Fab.* 15A; hec arena, hec ~ea, *a nerane* WW; **s1138** omnis virtus eorum [Scottorum] quasi arenarum contexio contrita est BROMTON 1027; de primo modo sunt basiliscus, †armaria, aspis GILB. VII 349. 1. **b 717** (v. aurilegus); absit quod fallacia antichristi seducat mundi principes et claudat tela ~ee manus suas WYCL. *Sim.* 6.

2 a (usu. w. *tela*) front of retina. **b** (?) herpes, shingles (med.).

a humor cristallinus est in medio.., cui anterius ministrat albugineus, media est ~ea [v.l. mediante tela ~ea], posterius vitreus nullo medio RIC. MED. *Micr. Anat.* 215; ab eodem loco nascitur alia tunica, que ~ea appellatur, perficiens speram in retina circumdantem cristallinum humorem; et dicitur ~ea ad modum tele ~ee *Ps.*-RIC. *Anat.* 26; quarum [tunicarum oculi] prima dicitur tela ~ea BART. ANGL. V 4; aliqui septem tunicas posuerunt; sed falsum est, quia telam ~ee pro tunica computaverunt BACON *Maj.* II 16; [retine] correspondet a parte anteriori ipsius oculi tunica ~ea, que est sicut tela ~ee GAD. 107. 2. **b** nisi febris conjungatur cum ~ea rubea *Ib.* 42 v. 1.

aranealis, (w. *tela*, resembling that) of a spider (? w. ref. to retina or to herpes).

indiget medicinis quarum proprietas est †eurare [l. curare] scabiem oculorum et maculam et telam ~em GAD. 108 v. 2.

aranga, ~us [Pers. *nārang*], orange (fruit or tree).

non recedit color nisi cum succo pomorum agrestium vel arenge GILB. II 77. 1; **1290** ad emenda..xv poma cedrina, vij poma de orenge *ChancMisc.* 4/5 f. 1; semina citrangulorum, i. pome de orenge GAD. 113 v. 2; viridariis.., palmis altissimis, milonibus, ~is..bene dotata S. SIM. *Itin.* 40; ~e, citromilum idem *Alph.* 15.

arapag- v. harpag-. araragium v. arreragium.

arare [CL], to plough (land). **b** (absol.). **c** to plough up (unlawfully; *v. et.* sursumarare). **d** (p. ppl. as sb. f. or n.) day's ploughing (*cf. aratura*).

omni die debeo arare integrum agrum [AS: *erian fulne æcer*] aut plus ÆLF. *Coll.* 90; pastura unde araverunt extranei homines vi acras terrae *DB* I 9; haec terra appreciatur in T., quia illuc arata est cum dominicis carrucis *Ib.* 13; terram nullus ărет in qua spes seminis ăret SERL. WILT. II 13; **1199** tenetur arare domino regi xvj acras terre, viij de hibernagio et viij de tramesio *CurR* I 77; **1269** quia male †aruit terram *CBaron* 76; **1270** debet arrare duas acras in yeme *Reg. Wint.* II 658; **1283** arare j acram ad frumentum *Cust. Battle* 28; **1417** in expensis..carucarum arrancium terram domini *Ac. Durh.* 317. **b** in dominio v boves arantes *DB* I 14; arat cum dim. carruca *Ib.* 206; ibi est j villanus cum ij bobus arans *Ib.* 242; terra ad arandum *Ib.* 280; v villani non arantes *Ib.* 346b; **1088** cum consuetudinibus sicuti homines ejusdem ville faciebant, sc. arare, kariare, ..bladum secare *MonA* IV 623; **s1187** erant in domo Waverleie..caruce arantes circiter xxx *Ann. Waverley* 244; **c1280** si tenuerit carucam per totum annum et tempestas evenerit, ita quod errare non poterit, operabit dim. opus (*Cust.*) *Crawley* 235; **1302** si non arrant, nihil dabunt pro arrura *Suff. Hund.* 68; **1431** de qualibet caruca †arente *Cl* 282 m. 17*d*. **c 1167** de iiij m. pro via regis arata *Pipe* 91 (cf. ib. 160: quia aravit terram regis); **1278** aravit viam; ideo..pro transgressione in misericordia *SelPlMan* 90; **1313** quidam terram habens juxta viam regalem arando et sibi appropriando de eadem..viam artavit *Eyre Kent* 84. **d 1196** dabunt ij s. annuatim..pro tribus aratis et una bidripa *Fines* (*Beds* 1/1/5) *RC* I 3.

2 (fig.): **a** to plough through water; **b** to furrow, scratch; **c** to write (*cf. exarare*); **d** to labour; **e** to transact.

a vaga per freta navis arat GOWER *VC* I 1730. **b** dumus aret vultus, boree furor ora flagellet HANV. I 252. **c †801** (13c.) ego Beorhtricus rex..signum crucis aravi *CS* 282; Deus quasi calamo scribe velociter scribentis legem naturalem in ejus [Ade] mente araverat GERV. TILB. I 21; **c1370** federa declarat que patrum cura patrarat, / postea firmarat, ipse patenter arat (*Bell. Hisp.*) *Pol. Poems* I 105; **1439** dum ararentur hi apices BEKYNTON I 206; **c1470** tacuisset si sibi scriba, / nec complanasset tabulas graphio nec arasset *Reg. Whet.* I 423. **d 1443** amici mei..una tecum arabunt BEKYNTON I 174. **e** qui lites agitare sitit, sibi litigiosum / querat consimilem, cum quo lis possit arari D. BEC. 516.

araseth [Ar. *ar-rashād*=cress], water-cress.

~eth, i. nasturtium *SB* 11; alrafed, id est narstucium *Alph.* 5.

aratio [CL], ploughing. **b** ploughing up (unlawfully).

~o, *eriung* ÆLF. *Gl.*; **1305** si..possit dicta bruera in culturam redigi et per ~onem, inclusionem vel alio modo approuiari *Cart. Chester* 98; **1499** pro ~one cum aratro apud Q. ..per vj dies *Ac. Durh.* 655. **b 1392** omnes mete et balkes..integre conserventur..absque minoracione seu ~one *Feod. Durh.* 166.

arationare v. arrationare.

aratiuncula, furrow, channel (cf. 1 *Kings* xviii 32).

10.. ~a, *sulincela* WW; quasi †aracuinculam [l. ~am] modicam circumducens peccora circumcinxit AILR. *Nin.* 8; quod nos dicimus arulam Judei dicunt ~am vel sulcum quemdam in medio parietum altaris fuisse AD. SCOT. *TT* 666C (cf. ib. 681D: †areunculam); *grype or a gripyll qwher water rennyth away in lond*, ~a *PP*.

arator [CL], ploughman. **b** stirrer up.

quando ~or [AS: *se yrþlingc*] disjungit boves ÆLF. *Coll.* 91; **14..** hic ~or, *a tyller* WW. **b** juxta carbones residens cinerosus arator / non sis in cinere D. BEC. 1217.

aratorius, used for ploughing. **b** (fig.; *cf. Jud.* iii 31).

1220 bestias ~ias occupando dissipat (*AncC* I 163) *RL* I 96. **b** hoc est vomer ~ius Samgar P. BLOIS *Ep.* 76. 237A.

aratralis, concerned w. ploughs. **b** used for ploughing.

10.. decimationes frugum..necnon et ~es elemosinae [AS: *sulhælmessan*]..Domino..temporibus rependantur congruis, elemosinae viz. ~es xv diebus post Pascha peractis (*Paraphr. Syn. Decr.*) *GAS* 253. **b 12..** boves ~es (*MinAc. Waltham Abbey*) *MFG*.

aratrum [CL], plough (less freq. than *carruca*, but app. not clearly dist. from it). **b** (w. *terra*) ploughland. **c** (?) unit of land, ploughland.

sulcos obliquat adinstar aratri ALDH. *Aen.* 32 (*Pugillares*) 5; ~i gressum stiba regendo BEDE *HA* 8; jungo eos [boves] ad ~um [AS: *iugie hig to syl*] ÆLF. *Coll.* 90; **s1085** rex..inquirere fecit..quot..jugera uni ~o sufficientia per annum essent in unaquaque villa et quot animalia H. HUNT. VI 36; **c1150** carriabit fimum secundum hoc quod habet in ~o (*Ext. Binham*) *Med. E. Anglia* 271; stant ibi apte ~is, trahis et bigis eque W. FITZST. *Thom. prol.* 11; pascua..in que nullus ~um ausus est mittere GIR. *TH* II 36; desiderat ~um ad sui constitutionem burim, stivam, temonem, aures binas, cultrum, vomerem NECKAM *NR* II 169; **c1350** debent querere rotas †aratorum [? l. ~orum] apud Cantuariam *Reg. S. Aug.* 79; **1392** capitale ~um cum toto apparatu precii vij s. *Cl* 234 m. 28*d*.; **1406** pro garcione agitante ~um *Ac. Durh.* 222; **1474** per *le upcast* ~i usque ad..ranam *Reg. St. Bees* 485. **b 697** terram iiij ~orum quae dicitur Wieghelmestun *CS* 97; **774** aliquam partem terrae trium ~orum quod Cantianice dicitur *threora sulunga CS* 214; **811** terram duorum aratrum (*sic*). Coenuulf rex..donare..dejudicavit *CS* 335; concessit in eadem villa [*Parnes, Norm.*] terram unius ~i et decimam carruce sue ORD. VIT. III 12 p. 132. **c †674** (13c) monasterio B. Petri contuli possidendum unum ~um, in quo mina ferri haberi cognoscitur *CS* 73; **732** terrula quaedam, id est quarta pars ~i unius *CS* 148; **s1198** collectum est caruagium in Anglia, sc. iij s. pro quolibet ~o *Ann. Dunstable* 27 (cf. *EHR* IV 109).

2 plough (fig.), (instrument of) labour (*cf. Luke* ix 62).

caelestis ~i stibarius et evangelici seminis sator ALDH. *VirgP* 28; ~a eorum non recte incedunt; oportet autem.. ad rectum haec tramitem revocare BEDE *HE* V 9; ad ~um celestis paradisi manum mittentes GIR. *TH* I 13; hodie ad sulcum ultimum meum pervenit ~um M. PAR. *Maj.* I 381; **c1470** ut manum retractam ab ~o rursus ad eum (*sic*) remitteret *Reg. Whet.* I 423.

aratura [cf. OF *areure*], ploughing. **b** ploughing service. **c** (w. *gabuli*) 'gavelearth'. **d** payment in connection w. ploughing service. **e** (?) right to plough (w. lord's plough). **f** ploughland.

c1194 sicut decime solent pervenire ecclesie sine omni deductione expensarum ~e et seminis *Ch. Sal.* 53; **1276** fecit purpresturam super regalem viam..per arruram super dictam viam *Hund.* I 51; una acra pro frumento trinam erigit aruram *Fleta* 170 (= *Husbandry* 18: *treys arrures*); **1366** J. invenit ij acras bine arrure et j acram trine arrure *Hal. Durh.* 51; cum tercia arrura vocata *striking' Entries* 184. **b** aliquotiens debet [geburus] esse paratus ad multas operationes voluntatis domini sui et ad *benyrðe*, id est ~am precum (*Quad., Rect.*) *GAS* 448 (cf. benhirda); **1193** clamavi burgenses quietos..de arura et aliis servilibus consuetudinibus *BBC* (*Lancaster*) 95; **1199** intravit in consuetudines, ..sc. in unam ~am ante Natale et in aliam ante Pascha ad cibum suum *CurR RC* I 358; ut..celerarius haberet ~as et alia servitia, sc. ~am unius rode pro qualibet acra sine cibo Brakelond 150; **1201** quolibet anno debet habere terciam partem..~e carucatarum *CurR* II 46; **1203** consuetudines et servitia de feodo..sc. aruras et messiones *Ib.* III 190; **1228** debuit villanas consuetudines..sicut arruras et messuras *Ib.* XIII no. 508; **1231** fecerunt omnes..abbati unam ~am secundum quod boves habuerunt, plures vel pauciores *Ib.* XIV 1281; **1234** debet aruram que dicitur *gareshurthe Cust. Glast.* 135 (cf. grashurtha); virgatarii solebant operari et arare aruras consuetudinarias..; W. abbas.. permisit eos esse ad gabulum *Ib.* 149; idem debet in quadragesima arare unam aruram que dicitur *type Cust. Bleadon* 202; **1279** tenet dim. virgatam..faciendo arruram cum caruca sua qualibet die Veneris *Hund.* II 656b; **c1283** quequidem arrura (*sic*)..non possunt hic extendi, quia non fecerunt opus per longum tempus *Cust. Battle* 15 (cf. ib. 6: valet arura unius acre xij d.); donec aruras suas legitime compleverint *Fleta* 161; de xxiij arruris vocatis *ben* provenientibus de dictis custumariis, de quibus computat in relaxacione terre sue proprie j arrurum (*sic*) *FormMan* 49; **1390** de arura xxv acrarum proveniente de..virgatariis et ..semivirgatariis.., quorum quilibet carucam habens integram arabit j acram sicut jacet ad semen yemale vel quadragesimale, percipiendo..pro arura cujuslibet acre j d. *Crawley* 289. **c** de ~a gabli sui [AS: *his gavolyrðe*] arabit iij acras (*Rect.*) *GAS* 447; **1363** in allocacione valoris.. serviciorum suorum de xv acrewar' terre cust[umarie] preter aruram gabuli *MinAc* 840/25 r. 2 (cf. ib. 840/26; pro arura xxxj acrarum terre domini vocat' *gavelerthe*). **d 1242** in..acquietandis aruris que debentur carrucariis qualibet die Sabbati de consuetudine quando non sunt ad liberationem, viz. iij ob. pro qualibet carruca *Pipe* 137; **c1300** de eisdem sullingis ad Purificacionem B. Marie aranda est una acra de quolibet sullingo et hec arrura solvi debet sulmannis per assensum tocius curie cum firma Pasce *Reg. S. Aug.* 59. **e c1280** si tenuerit carucam per totum annum, et tempestas evenerit post festum S. Mich., ita quod non errare (*sic*) poterit, operabit dim. opus; et habebit arruram ad viij acras de caruca domini ad iiij terminos..; si autem custodierit multones.., habebit arruram v acrarum de caruca domini..; et recipiet arruram suam sicut caruce tenentur (*Cust.*) *Crawley* 235. **f** xlj acre de ~a *DB* II 2b; **1401** parcellam terre continentem vij dietas arure *FormA* 328.

araula v. arula c. arax v. arx. arba, ~agium, v. arvum, herb-.

arbalista [OF *arbaleste*, *albaleste* < arcuballista], arblast, crossbow.

1160 pro m quarellis et apparatu arbelast' *Pipe* 2; **1190** pro quarrellis de arbelest' et *pilez*..et pro mmmdc fleccis de arbalest' *Pipe* 3; **1194** pro ducendis ad regem hominibus arbalesteriorum regis cum arbalastis et harnasio eorum *Pipe* 176; **1212** Radulfus arbelastarius consuevit servire domino regi in castello de arbelasta sua *Fees* 120; **1266** in arblast' et bauder' emend' cum cor' filo empt' *MinAc* 1087/6 r. 1; **1275** asportaverunt..arcus et arblastas et hujusmodi arma †munita [? l. minuta] *Hund.* I 492; **1297** in ..j magno arbalistro ad viz' *Ac. Cornw.* II 163; **1298** xxxvj baston' de *hiffe* pro albast' *KRAc* 7/1 m. 3; **1335** pro ccc quarellis pro arblastis..de novo pennandis *Ib.* 19/16 m. 2; **1336** iij albalistas de vice *Cl* 157 m. 11 (= *Cal.* 622; †arbalistas); **s1340** domus [apud Bononiam] plena remis, velis et armis et ~is..pro..galeis armandis Ad. Mur. 104; **1352** ij alblastos (*CoramR*) *Collect. Staffs.* XIV 79; **1380** asportavit arma, viz. ..arblastus, arcus, sagittas et secures *IMisc* 221/13 r. 2; **1418** xxv ~as de torno, xxv ~as de tibia *RNorm* 237; **1516** valectum †arkastell' nostrarum (*Pat*) *L. & P. Hen. VIII* II 1715; **c1540** W. ..cum telo albalastri ..vulneratur *Extr. Chr. Scot.* 175.

arbalistaria, crossbow service. **b** arrowslit.

1190 sciatis nos concessisse..Turpino arbalastario nostro totam terram de Hakuneby, ..tenendam..per servitium arbalisterie *CalPat 1345–8* 373; **1198** de serjantia ~ie *Fees* 5; **1199** tenent xl s. redditus per arbalasteriam *Ib. app.* 1325; **1212** per servitium arbalisterie *Ib.* 128; tenet per alblastariam *Ib.* 190; **c1227** debet xl dies alblasterie ad castrum de Norwico pro terra sua *Ib.* 388. **b 1203** pro arbalastareia facienda in monasterio *RScacNorm* II 548; **c1219** facit illud [castellum de Fulkilgham] torchiare [cum] albesteriis et lancearis et breteschiis de ligno per loca (*AncC* XI 98) *RL* I 64; **1251** duas turellas ad duos angulos ballii predicti apertas versus castrum cum arblasteriis *Liberate* 28 m. 17.

arbalistarius [cf. OF *arbalestier*], arblaster, crossbowman.

Bernerus ~ius *DB* II 267b; Walterus Arbalastarius *Ib.* 324; Nicholaus Arbalestarius *DBExon.* 473; **c1103** Walterus arbolasterius meus de Everwic *Regesta* 642; **s1123** super murum presidii eminebat machina, unde sagittarii et alabastarii preliabantur S. Durh. *HR* 209; **1177** R. de Burc ~ius debet j accipitrem *Pipe* 126; quas clamat tenere..per liberum servitium inveniendi tibi unum arbelastarium in exercitum domini regis per xl dies pro omni servitio Glanv. XII 3; **s1192** nunciatum est regem..advenisse, nec amplius quam lxxx milites, exceptis ~is suis cccc, in comitatu habere Coggesh. 57; **s1198** comprehendit de militibus regis Francie ad minus octoginta tres, preter servientes alabastarios R. Howd. IV 59; **1212** de feodo Helpe Albrastarii *Fees* 178 (v. et arbalista); **1266** in robis predictorum..in castro existentium arblastariorum *MinAc* 1087/6 r. 1; **1276** Algreto Albalestario *Hund.* II 25; **1291** W. dictum arblastarium *Melrose* no. 353; **1331** xx homines ad arma, x albalistarii *Cl* 151 m. 13; *alblaster*, alabastarius [v.l. alblastarius] *PP*.

arbalistata, (distance of) crossbow-shot.

1204 ipse non habet terram prope illam piscariam de iij arbelastatis *CurR* III 158.

arbatae v. artaba. arberosus v. arborosus. arbina v. arvina.

arbiter [CL], eyewitness, spectator. **b** observer. **c** arbiter, judge (*cf. arbitrator*). **d** (as divine title).

pedes egenis omni die semotis ~tris lavabat W. Malm. *GP* II 75; ~tro omni remoto Neckam *NR* II 188. **b** pauciores illos credo peragrasse philosophos qui nature ~tro mathematicum..coequant J. Sal. *Met.* 897a (cf. ib. 896c: nature scrutator). **c** judex vel censor vel ~ter, *dema* Ælf. *Gl.*; non compromittitur in ~tros sed in arbitratores et amicabiles compositores *RegiamM.* II 6; **1317** tanquam in ~tros, arbitratores et amicabiles compositores..extitit concorditer compromissum *FormOx* 20; **1434** per nos.. officialem Curie..de Arcubus, ~trum, arbitratorem sive amicabilem compositorem a partibus..communiter electum (*Compositio*) Amund. II 91. **d** arbiter aeternus dum sontum crimina punit Aldh. *VirgV* 969; in conspectu interni ~tri Bede *Tab.* III 3 (cf. ib. I 7: summi ~tri).

arbitra [CL], arbiter (f.).

femine secundum leges..non possunt esse judices..nec fidejubere nec procuratrices nec ~e esse Ockham *Pol.* I 163.

arbitrabilis, decidable, subject to decision.

utrimque id quod queritur responderi a talia disquirentibus varie ~e Balsh. *AD* 128.

arbitralis, of an arbiter.

1291 controversiis..nostra ~i sentencia terminatis *Mon. Francisc.* II 47; **1448** ordinacionem seu sentenciam ~em *Reg. Dunferm.* 424.

arbitramentalis, of arbitrament.

1461 quod concordia ipsa post quandam ~em sentenciam ..inter partes latam..extitit inviolabiliter observata *Reg. Aberbr.* II 118.

arbitramentum, arbitrament, decision of an arbiter.

1430 ut patet per ~um indentatum quatuor fide dignorum *Feod. Durh.* 21; **1475** tulit arbitrium, ~um sive amicabilem composicionem *Reg. Heref.* 18.

arbitrari, ~are [CL], to judge, decide. **b** to think.

1221 reservata judicibus potestate confirmandi quod fuit [? l. fuerit] ~atum *Ch. Sal.* 112; **1317** inter cetera in.. arbitrio continetur quod..arbitri ~ati fuere ut.. *FormOx* 20; **1449** arbitri..laudaverunt, ~averunt, sentenciarunt quod.. *MunAcOx* 598. **b** sed magis arbitror quod sic errata reorum / Nitria purgavit Aldh. *VirgV* 1465; curavit conferre quid de his agendum ~arentur Bede *HE* II 9; non enim, ut ~or, te potest latere Eriug. *Per.* 546c; accedentes tam prope ut applicare se jam ~ati fuerint Gir. *TH* II 12; ut sibi servire regnare feliciter ~entur Elmh. *Hen. V Cont.* 116.

arbitrarie, at discretion.

1282 cervices indomitas..corrigas, in minoribus ~ie, in gravioribus autem de consilio seniorum tibi assidencium Peckham *Ep.* 308 p. 399; **1284** nihilominus, si post monicionem se correxerit, pro preteritis ~ie puniendus *Ib.* 561 p. 739 (= *Conc.* II 105).

arbitrarius [CL], exercised by an arbiter. **b** discretionary, imposed at discretion.

s1265 fuit..in regem Francorum compromissum; ..cumque..rex..provisiones..~ia potestate cassasset, ..comes Leycestrie et ejus complices..presumpserunt eas..sustinere *Flor. Hist.* III 258; **1320** perpetuum silencium ~ia auctoritate nostra imponentes *AncD* A 2857. **b** ~ie sunt penitentie et pro motu prelati imponende Gir. *GE* I 46; **c1230** quia penitentie ~ie sunt, non diffinimus vobis aliquas certas penitentias quas debetis injungere *Conc. Syn.* 224; in hoc erit dilatio ~ia Bracton 334; prefixio dierum..fuit ~ia ad voluntatem justiciariorum *State Tri. Ed. I* 23; **1327** rigor observanciarum et consuetudinum religiosarum, que sunt ~ie, bene poterit moderari *Lit. Cant.* I 233; an.. apud imperatorem in exercendo justiciam omnes pene..sint ~ie, ut liceat ei pecuniariam penam vel aliam pro quocunque crimine infligere Ockham *Dial.* 885; **1559** sub pena ~ia.. arbitrio ordinarii injungenda *Conc. Scot.* II 155.

arbitratio, arbiter's decision.

1298 vestre ordinacioni, arbitracioni, dicto seu laudo..nos ..submittimus (*Lit. Regis ad Papam*) *Foed.* II 809; **1428** quibus quidem decreto, ordinacioni, ~oni, pronunciacioni et declaracioni rector..adquievit (*Replicatio*) Amund. I 246.

arbitrator, umpire (allowed more discretion than *arbiter*).

1279 compromiserunt..in nos..tanquam in ~ores seu amicabiles compositores *RGasc* II 58; **1291** ~or et amicabilis compositor communiter et concorditer electus (*Instr. Notar.*) *Mon. Francisc.* II 43; *RegiamM.* II 6 (v. arbiter c); **1314** in..J. ..et T. ..tanquam in arbitros et ~ores, laudatores, diffinitores seu amicabiles compositores..compromittimus (*Pat*) *CollectOx* II 266; **1427** nominaverunt..T. .. in arbitrum, ~orem, laudatorem sive imparem *FormOx* 459.

arbitratus [CL], arbiter's decision. **b** judgement, discernment.

1291 renunciando..appellacioni, proclamacioni ac boni viri ~ui et omni juri per quod contra predicta..posset.. obviari (*Compositio*) *Mon. Francisc.* II 36; **1427** promiserunt ..partes..quod..starent..decreto, laudo, arbitrio, ~ui, pronunciacioni sive sentencie dictorum..R. et T. *FormOx* 459. **b** ibi edifitia..erecta.., ~u quidem multa [Wilfridi] proprio, sed et cementariorum..magisterio W. Malm. *GP* III 117.

arbitrium [CL], decision, judgement. **b** discretionary power. **c** choice, will.

1201 rex testatur quod..posuerunt se super ~ium suum de terra de A. *CurR* I 374; **1221** pars que ab ~io resilierit xl m. nomine pene parti adverse persolvet *Ch. Sal.* 112; ~ium est actus legitimus personarum super civili questione et querela †in quasi [v.l. quasi in] judicio contendencium *RegiamM.* II 2; **1428** vigore cujusdam compromissi ~iive seu decreti in ea parte lati (*Replicatio*) Amund. I 246. **b** membra et vita ejus in ~io regis erunt si captus fuerit *DB* I 154b; **1167** volo..ut tota terra inculta..in..monachorum sit potestate et ~io *Feod. Durh.* 141; sola natura.. artus..pro sui ~io..disponit Gir. *TH* III 10; **c1250** absque ulla dilatione vel ~io creditorum *Stat. Cantab.* 213. **c** ut potioris sit meriti munus quod libero spontaneae voluntatis ~io offertur quam quod..imperio complendum jubetur Aldh. *VirgP* 18; liberae voluntatis ~ium Eriug. *Per.* 540b; hoc ~ium, quod et judicium dici potest, liberum est Anselm (*Praesc.* 6) II 257; charitas..et alie virtutes infuse viatori sunt opera Dei et tamen per liberum ~ium dissolvi possunt Ockham *Dial.* 492.

arbitrix, arbiter (f.).

c1263 curiam Romanam, que omnibus pro †justiciam exhibendo [? l. justicia exhibenda] se promittit ~icem principibus et mundi nobilibus (*AncC* III 175) *RL* II 105.

arbitum, ~us, v. arbut-, arx. arblast-, arbolast- v. arbalist-.

arbor [CL], tree. **b** branched ornament, tree of Jesse. **c** (w. *Mariae*) mugwort (*Artemisia*) or tansy. **d** (w. *solis* or *sicca*) *arbre sol*, *arbre sec*, a fabulous oriental tree. **e** (fig.; *cf. Matth.* iii 10).

~orum silvestrium natura Aldh. *VirgP* 19; opima frugibus atque ~oribus insula Bede *HE* I 1; ~or, *treow* Ælf. *Gl.*; siquis ~orem stantem extra viam intra prostraverit *DB* I 1; gloria vitis / herbis precellit arboribusque simul Neckam *DS* VIII 26; **a1232** concedo..Willelmo..suum *restingtre* et residuum pomorum meorum post excucionem ~orum gardini mei (*Ch. R. comitis*) *RecogR. Chester* 70 r. 3*d.*; **1309** grossas ~ores et subboscum *Year Bk. 2 Ed. II* 102; **1431** prostraciones ~orum portancium fructus (*Cl*) *Foed.* X 488; **1450** cum..~oribus mortuis ac ~oribus vento cadentibus sive ad terram prostratis *Cl* 300 m. 20*d.*; cedrus harbor unde fit pix cedrina *Alph.* 36; *a tre*, ~or dicitur esse [omne] lignum, ~os tantum fructifera *CathA.* **b 1303** jocalia: ..de una ~ore ramata cum v linguis serpentinis *Ac. Exec. Ep. Lond.* 55; **1432** ex altera parte..~oris quedam alia de generacione Salvatoris a radice Jesse..apparebat (J. Carp.) *MGL* III 462. **c** febrifuga, i. ~or S. Marie, arborarie idem *SB* 21; radix ~oris Marie, i. atanasia *Ib.* 36. **d** de ~ore solis.., quia qui fructu ejus vescitur sicut rex Alexander Aristoteli scribit, vitam extendit in inmensum Gir. *TH* II 4; **1188** quod..una pars Turcorum gladio peribit, altera fugiet ultra ~orem siccam (*Lit. Nuntiorum*) *G. Hen. II* II 53. **e** minatur securim ad radicem ~oris ponendam W. Fitzst. *Thom.* 100.

2 a mill-shaft. **b** wooden saddle-base.

a 1211 in j ligamine ferreo ad ~orem rote molendini *Pipe Wint.* 14; **1232** in rota molendini infra domum et in ~ora (*sic*) liganda ferro *Ib.* (159283) r. 11; **1331** meremium pro faciendo rotam et ~orem..molendini (*KRAc* 89/15) *S. Jers.* I 34. **b 1368** in j ~ore pro sella carectaria empta, iiij d. *MinAc Wint. Silkstead*; **1377** in j ~ore [*corr.* to ligno] pro sella carectarie *Ib. Whitchurch*; **1396** in una ~ore selle carectarie *Ib. Chilbolton.*

arboracia *v.* armoracia

arborarius, (?) timber merchant.

c1120 hida illa de Fleta quam Henricus ~ius tenet *E. Ch. S. Paul* 27; **1155** Henrico ~io x li. ad reparandam gaiolam *Pipe* 4.

arboraticus, growing among trees.

12.. †felix [l. filix] ~a, i. *pollipode*, i. *eververn* WW.

arboratus, embroidered w. figures of trees.

1245 capa vetus de albo baldekino et ~a purpura gracili cum ymaginibus malefactis *Invent. S. Paul.* 480.

arboretum [CL; cf. It. *albereto*, Sp. *arboleda*], plantation of trees.

1289 ad vineas et albaredas plantandas seu edificandas *RGasc* II 312; **1315** de omnibus vineis, ..viminariis et albaredis..in civitate Burdeg' *Cl* 132 m. 6*d.*; *a wodde*, arbustum, ~um, boscus *CathA.*

arboreus, growing on trees. **b** of a tree.

utitur arboreo fructu morisque rubeti *V. Merl.* 79; arborei fructus D. Bec. 2220; edera ~ea, G. *yere*, A. *yvy Alph.* 52. **b** coma primula comit / arboreos apices Vinsauf *PN* 550.

arboriferus, borne on trees.

de Westfalia: ..nuces et poma et omnis fructus ~us ibi abundat *Eul. Hist.* II 74.

arborosus, (?) branched.

agrestis flosmos virgas habet longas in se et ~as [v.l. arberosas] *Alph.* 69.

arbos v. arbor 1a. arbula v. herbula.

arbuscula [CL], small tree, shrub.

in littore maris ~e nascuntur ad quantitatem salicum GERV. TILB. III 133.

arbustum [CL], **~a,** copse, covert, plantation. **b** (? conf. w. *arbuscula*) sapling.

~a, ..*treowstede* ÆLF. *Gl.*; ~um dicitur locus ubi arbores concrescunt BART. ANGL. XVII 1; ut..hispidum exterius silvescat ~um GIR. *IK* II 3; **1335** in stipendio..custodis ~i *Sacr. Ely* II 68; **1398** ita semper quod sufficiens ~um ibidem pro ferina foreste..remaneat *Pat* 351 m. 36. **b** ~um, *iung treow* ÆLF. *Gl.*; [herba] in arborem novellam et teneram convalescit et est dicta ~a quasi arboris hasta BART. ANGL. XVII 1.

arbutum [CL = *fruit of strawberry-tree*], crab-apple.

14.. arbitum, A. *a crabbe* WW; **1481** solut' pro arbitis, xviij d. *Ac. Durh.* 96; *a crab,* arbitum vel arbota *CathA.*

arbutus [CL = *strawberry-tree*], crab-apple tree. **b** poplar.

14.. arbutus, A. *a crabtre* WW; **1467** excecabunt omnes arbores infra..pasturam crescentes, tantum exceptis quercis (*sic*), fraxinis et arbitis *AncD* A 8414; *a crabtre,* arbitus, macianus *CathA.* **b** ~us, *æspe GlC* A 735.

1 arca [CL; cf. OF *arche*], casket, coffer, strong-box. **b** coffer containing Jewish bonds (starrs). **c** (fig.) repository.

~arum clustella reserantur ALDH. *VirgP* 42; ~a libraria *Id. Aen.* 89 (*title*); sit thesaurus tuus ecclesia et ornamenta illius non archa singularis ALCUIN *Ep.* 282; ~a vel scrinium, *scrin* ÆLF. *Gl.*; **1161** ad conducendum ~am de Winton' ad Lond' *Pipe* 56; **1180** in custamento ducendi archam monetariorum *Pipe* 136; thecam obfirmatam archa reposuit et..arche clavem secum asportavit T. MON. *Will.* V 10; **1201** fregerunt archam ipsius A...et in roberia ceperunt scrinium suum *SelPlCrown* 60; **1240** peccunia..apud prioratum S. Frideswyde..in archa communi..reponatur *StatOx* 75; **1249** nec archam habeant nec clavem *Doc. Eng. Black Monks* 38; ~a jam facta, si resolvatur et iterum conjungantur partes, eadem ~a erit BACON *Maj.* II 549; **1446** j magna archa cum ferro ligata *Feod. Durh.* 191*n*. **b 1194** altera pars [cirograffi] remaneat in ~a communi, in qua sunt tres serrure (*Capitula Judeorum*) R. HOWD. III 266; **1230** versus predictos Judeos ipsum H. inde quietum esse faciatis; cartas etiam et pedes cyrographorum..ab archa extrahi et ei deliberari faciatis *Cl* 439; **1237** de..debitis..in quibus ..alicui Judeo tenebatur per archam domini regis apud Eboracum *Couch. Furness* II 448; **1239** quod custodes †archiarum Londoniarum..amoveantur et..eligantur duo alii de legalibus et discretioribus Christianis et duo alii de legalibus Judeis Londoniarum quibus archa committatur custodienda (*Lit. Regis*) *Leg. Ant. Lond.* 237; **1244** archa cyrographorum Londonie *SelPlJews* 8; **1272** archa Judeorum *Ib.* 66. **c 804** melius est te Deum habere in archa cordis quam aurum in archa cubilis ALCUIN *Ep.* 282; **c1170** hoc igitur memori figatur pectoris arca (R. PARTES *Henr.*) *Speculum* XII 244; **s1389** perfidie promptuarium, sentina avaricie, ..~a malicie, ..Michael atte Pole WALS. *HA* II 187.

2 a receptacle for flour etc. (esp. in mill). **b** 'trunk' for catching fish. **c** (?) chest used in making breakwater.

a 1320 j archa ad bultandum *Rec. Leic.* I 376; **1320** in clavis ferreis pro reparacione arche farinalis *KRAc* 482/1 m. 5*d*. (cf. ib.: in j serrura pendente empta pro archa multure; ..pro reparacione arche aquatice); **1373** de A. Multure pro ~a pro multura reservata asportata de molendino *Hal. Durh.* 122; **1384** unum spowte per quod farrina descendit a molar' in ~am multure *DLMinAc* 507/8228 m. 16. **b 1297** de j d...pro quadam ~a ponenda in aqua domini *Ac. Cornw.* I 48; **1336** de ~is anguillarum *CalScot* III 331; **1454** licenciam..piscandi per ~as, recia aut alia instrumenta *Inchaffray* 145. **c 1394** archas omnes pro portu ordinatas..implebunt et locabunt ac lapidibus onerabunt *Reg. Aberbr.* II 41.

3 sarcophagus or reliquary.

cujus corpus..adposuerunt desuper ~am in qua incorrupta ejusdem patris membra locaverant BEDE (*V. Cuthb.*) *HE* IV 28; incenset..~am in qua continentur reliquie *Offic. Sal.* 25.

4 (bibl.) **a** Noah's ark. **b** ark of the Covenant.

a de mundis [animalibus] septena septena..bicameratam et tricameratam leguntur ~am gregatim ingressa ALDH. *Met.* 2 p. 63 (cf. GERV. TILB. I 24); cum cuncta animantium semina in arca conclusa fuerint GIR. *TH* II 16; omnium mortalium finis..preter eos qui salvandi erant in archa *Canon. G. Sempr.* 79; anno vite Noe c, inundante diluvio, cum septem animabus archam intravit M. PAR. *Maj.* I 4; o libri! ..vos [estis] ~a Noe et scala Jacob R. BURY *Phil.* 1. 29; **1395** per hunc cubitum [geometralem] archa Noe fabricata est *Mem. York* I 142. **b** veluti Oza ~am testamenti..contingere non metuens ALDH. *VirgP* 45; arca Dei.. / ducta per Azotos *Id. VirgV* 1358; [Levite] portabant ~am federis AD. SCOT. *TT* 657; arca Philisteis cessit GARL. *Tri. Eccl.* 25; 'tollite librum istum et ponite illum in latere ~e federis Domini' [*Deut.* xxxi 26]. O locus idoneus et bibliothece conveniens! R. BURY *Phil.* 17. 227.

2 arca v. arcus 4. arcacis v. arthrisis.

1 arcagium, (?) contribution to, or payment for use of, coffer (mon.).

c1075 trado..ecclesiam de Montleiscent, ..necnon monasterii ~ium, quantum G. tenuit, decimamque molendini mei (*Ch. S. Ebrulf, Norm.*) ORD. VIT. V 15 p. 425.

2 arcagium, payment to builders on completion of arch (cf. arcus 4).

1326 dat' cementariis super murum in camera predicta cum archag' et potacione ex curialitate *Sacr. Ely* II 55; **1333** liberat' cementariis pro arcag' eorum die qua magna gabla perclusus (*sic*) fuit, quod habere debent de antiqua consuetudine *KRAc* 469/12 (*Westminster*).

arcane, profoundly.

1441 satis ~e et non parum exquisite exploratum id habeo BEKYNTON I 225.

arcangel- v. archangel-.

arcanus [CL], secret, mysterious. **b** (sb. n.) secret, mystery. **c** (sb. n. pl.) personal possessions or (?) documents.

spectaculum..spiritali et ~o praecordiorum intuitu..cernere promeruit ALDH. *Met.* 2 p. 66; archanus [? *play on* archangelus] Michael nitido lampabilis ore FRITH. 1245; **c1105** archano humane redemptionis consilio H. LOS. *Ep.* 11. **b** misteriorum ~a ALDH. *Met.* 2 p. 64; dignus..cui Dominus specialiter sua revelaret ~a BEDE *HE* IV 3; ut..tamen crederes quae in tanto ~o humani ingenii vires excedunt LANFR. *Corp. & Sang.* 439D; **c1093** marcet animus nec.. archana phylosophiae penetrat H. LOS. *Ep.* 1; non cunctabor cordis mei ~um vobis reserare ORD. VIT. X 23 p. 145; cum multa..†areana [l. ~a] scrutantium..revolverem H. BOS. *Ep.* 1470; in almiphono amenitatis archano in animum suum hauriunt felicem ardorem ROLLE *IA* 152. **c s1194** regis fugientis plaustra et clitellas cum quibusdam ~is et gaza multiplici..comprehendit W. NEWB. V 2.

arcare v. 1 artare.

†arcarium [? *for* arcanum *or* archivum], treasury.

s1296 insignia regalia regni Scocie..apud Westmonasterium in archariis regis sunt recondita et signata *Flor. Hist.* III 288.

1 arcarius [CL], treasurer, guardian of treasury.

~ius, dispensator *GlC* A 814; **796** regalis palatii ~o Megenfrido..salutem ALCUIN *Ep.* 111; †**833** (14c) archarius meus omnes expensas..pro fisco integre acceptabit *CS* 409; heram suam cum archariis prestolantem ante turrim invenerunt. mox illa custodibus ait.. ORD. VIT. X 23 p. 147.

2 arcarius v. arcuarius.

Arcas [Ἀρκάς], Arcadian (fig.), champion (*cf.* Virgil *Ecl.* VII 4).

Archades hinc ambo voto statuere sub uno FRITH. 87.

arcbuttans [Fr. *arc-boutant*], flying buttress (*cf. arcubutericius*).

1385 pro xl doliatis petre de Stapulton' emptis pro archbuttant' ex parte orientali magne aule inde faciend' *KRAc* 473/2 m. 4.

arce v. 1 artus 2b, arx. arcecosus v. acetosus.

arcella, casket.

14.. ~a, A. *a forser* WW.

arcellus v. arquillus. arcenarium v. arcionarius b. arcenator v. arcionator. arcenio v. artemon. arcenocum v. arsenicum. arceotide v. arceuthis.

arcēre [CL], to fend off, keep away. **b** to constrain.

limpida sed tenebras arcebant lumina furvas ALDH. *VirgV* 1404; ob ~endos barbarorum impetus BEDE *HE* III 2; procul a nostris arcemus finibus hostem P. BLOIS *Euch.* 4. 1140B; **12..** usque ad dignam satisfactionem ab ecclesia ~eatur *Conc. Scot.* II 55; **a1350** ut eos..ab hujusmodi appellacionibus..~eamus *Stat. Cantab.* 325; **s1377** abbas..[Gallicos] viriliter ~uit ab ingressu ville *V. Ric. II* 2; policaria..~et pulices *SB* 34. **b c1250** cimiteria claudantur a parochianis..et ad hoc ~eantur *Conc. Syn.* 461; **1298** quod episcopi..negligentes..ad denunciaciones faciendas per..archiepiscopos ~erentur *Ib.* 1193; si communitas..fuerit..negligens.., arciantur per capitulum et corrigantur *Reg. Glasg.* 240; **1451** ~eatur ad veritatem dicendam; si vero testis fide dignus..appareat contra eum, ..~eatur gravius in domo discipline (*Abbr. Stat.*) *Mon. Francisc.* II 102.

arcerunt *for* arserunt v. ardere 4b.

arcessere, ~ire [CL], to fetch, summon. **b** to elicit.

~itus, *feotod GlC* A 807; **634** dum quis eorum de hoc saeculo ad auctorem suum fuerit ~itus (*Lit. Papae*) BEDE *HE* II 17; Diocletianus..Christi pedisequas..arcersiri praecepit ALDH. *VirgP* 50; jubet..vatem.. / protinus arcessi porro de finibus istuc *Id. VirgV* 1004; principibus..in locum synodalem accersitis EDDI *Wilf.* 34; accersit qui evocat, ~it qui accusat BEDE *Orth.* 2777; cum ~itis [v.l. accersitis] Christi ancellis..eas..ammoneret *Id. HE* IV 23; cantatorem ad se suosque instituendos accersiit *Ib.* V 20; Angli a Brettonibus accersiti [v.l. arcesiti] *Ib.* 24; **10..** arcersivit, *laðode* WW; nuncios..qui..Dunstanum accersiant OSB. *V. Dunst.* 24; per incantationes diabolo accersito W. MALM. *GR* II 167; **s1180** papa..legato..precepit..ut accersiret [v.l. assericet]..archiepiscopum *G. Hen. II* I 263; accerciatur..ocius..hospes tuus *NLA* (*Milburga*) II 189; **1341** quem..in..vinculum federis accersivit (*Lit. Regis*) AVESB. 96b. **b s1255** accersita..a rege veritate super statu suo.., eam civiliter..consolabantur M. PAR. *Abbr.* 347.

arcetum v. artemon.

arceuthis [ἀρκευθίς], juniper berry.

10.. arciotidas, *fyrses berian* WW; alcheozoidos, i. bacce juniperi minoris *Alph.* 4; †amisfractis [? l. ami fructus], archocides, i. fructus juniperi *Ib.* 8; arceotide, juniperus idem *Ib.* 14.

archa v. arca, archangelicus 2, arcus 4. archacon v. acaron. archagium v. arcagium. archall' v. argilla.

archaeogonia [ἀρχαιογονία], antiquity of origin (cf. Jerome *Vir. Illust.* 38).

†arxhotanian, antiquitatem vel principatum *GlC* A 811.

archangelicus [ἀρχαγγελικός], archangelic, of an archangel.

~a Michaelis visitatione EADMER *Wilf.* 35; est archangelicus octavus in ordine cetus, / agminis angelici princeps H. AVR. *Poems* 43. 47; hinc archangelicis simul angelicis puerorum / agminibus cuneus assimilatur ibi ELMH. *Metr. Hen. V* 655 (cf. ib. 669).

2 (sb. f.) deadnettle (? *Lamium album*).

~a, *blinde netle* ÆLF. *Gl.*; **12..** arcangelica, i. *mort ortie,* i. *blinde netle* WW; in aqua decoquatur..urtica mortua vel ~a, que est specialis contra quartanam GAD. 17. 1; in dolore de lapide vesice..ponatur morsus galline et celidonia domestica et urtica minor vel †area anglica *Ib.* 97. 2; archa angelica, i. *blinde netle,* habet flores albos *SB* 11; ~a vel barba anglia, G. *archangle,* A. *dedenetle Alph.* 14.

archangelus [ἀρχάγγελος], archangel.

Daniel..ob indaganda secretorum arcana ab ~o..vocitatus ALDH. *VirgP* 21; quidam candido praeclarus habitu, dicens se Michahelem esse ~um BEDE *HE* V 19; ~us, *heahencgel* ÆLF. *Gl.*; 'supra..omne nomen quod nominatur', id est super angelorum et ~orum nomina LANFR. *Comment. Paul.* (*Eph.* i 20) 290; †**1081** tuba ~i perstrepente (*Ch. Malm.*) *Regesta* 136; ~i forte dicti non solum quod annuntiant principalia verum etiam quod principantur nuntiantibus minora PULL. *Sent.* 885D; **s1158** venerunt uterque rex ad Montem B. ~i [*Mont St. Michel*] TORIGNI 198; mentitus est ille [Mahumet] quod accideret habito colloquio cum ~o Raphaele R. NIGER 58; considera quam feliciter sancti angeli in notitia divinorum judiciorum, ~i in cognitione internorum consiliorum excellant AD. SCOT. *Serm.* 292B; ad primam ~i vocem emergent GIR. *TH* I 19; in tertia [hierarchia] primo principatus, secundo ~i, tertio angeli AD. MARSH *Ep.* 246 c. 1 p. 417; WYCL. *Ente* (v. antequam b); **1332** die S. Michaelis Arcangeli [*29 Sept.*] *Lit. Cant.* I 499; **1411** capa..brodata cum ~is aureis *Ib.* III 112; in summo positus archangelus aureus astat ELMH. *Metr. Hen. V* 665.

2 dead-nettle (*cf. archangelicus* 2).

deefe nettyl, ~us *PP.*

archanus v. arcanus. archarium v. arcarium. archarius v. arcarius, arcuarius. Archas v. Arcas. archbuttans v. arcbuttans. archea v. arcus 4. archearius v. arcuarius. archeatus v. arcuare 2b. archecyregraphariuS v. 2. chirographarius a. archemacherus, ~mecherus, ~merus, v. archimagirus. archemisia v. artemisia. archepresul v. archipraesul. archer- v. arcuar-. archeratus, v. acanthus. archericus, ~eticus v. arthriticus.

archetypus [ἀρχέτυπος], archetypal.

[Plato] quid essent [res] antequam in corpora prodirent expressit, ~as rerum formas..definiens ADEL. *ED* 11; in mundo invisibili et principali Academicorum, viz. ~o H. BOS. *LM* 1299 (cf. D. MORLEY 9); cum..terre faciem linearriter aperuisset, fabricam [ecclesie] ~am sensili quodam modo circumponens GIR. *EH* II 36; pater architipo complectens omnia cosmo A. MEAUX *Susanna* 273; status ejus / est prius archetypus quam sensilis VINSAUF *PN* 48; mundus sensibilis factus est ad similitudinem mundi architipi SACROB. *Sph.* 1 p. 80; **s1268** sphericus architypum globus hic monstrat macrocosmum (*Versus in pavimento*) FLETE *Westm.* 113; ut mundum ~um demonstraret auctori, quo de superno exemplo mundus sensibilis duceretur R. BURY *Phil.* 7. 104.

1 archia v. arca 1b.

2 archia [-αρχία], government, principality. **b** beginning.

~ia, principatus *GlC* A 762; *a prynshede,* ~ia, principatus *CathA.* **b** ~ia, initium *GlC* A 724.

3 archia v. arcus 4.

archiabbas, 'arch-abbot'.

s1178 Willelmus abbas Ramesiensis ,Cluniacensium curam suscipere detrectans multis diebus, ad ultimum adquievit, ditiorem non ambiens abbatiam, nisi quod hec cujus erat collocandus in sede, dum abbatias plures sue subici noverit dispositioni, quandam ex hoc sibi vendicet prerogativam, ut prelatus Cluniacensis non abbas solummodo nominandus sit sed ~as DICETO *YH* I 424; Willelmus abbas Ramesie fit ~as Cluniacensis TAXTER 154.

archiadversarius, arch-enemy.

archidiaconi..fere cuncti dignitati S. David..adversantes necnon et ~ius ipse..ab hac terra sunt absumpti GIR. *Spec.* III 3 p. 150.

archiantistes, archbishop.

964 (13c) ego Dunstan Dorovernensis ecclesie ~es *CS* 1143.

archiarius v. arcuarius.

archiater [ἀρχιατρός], master physician, (spiritual) healer.

~tros, *healecas GlC* A 773; celeberrimos..caelestis medicinae ~tros Cosmam et Damianum Aldh. *VirgP* 34; **s1087** G. Luxoviensis episcopus et G. Gemeticensis abbas cum quibusdam aliis ~tris sedulo excubabant et de spirituali ac corporali salute regis sollicite tractabant Ord. Vit. VII 14.

archibal- v. arcubal-. archibuteracius v. arcubutericius.

archicancellarius, arch-chancellor. **b** lord chancellor.

s1162 audierat quod Maguntinus archiepiscopus in Theutonica sub rege, quod Coloniensis archiepiscopus in Italia sub imperatore, nomen sibi vendicent ~ii Diceto *YH* I 308; **1294** Colonensis ecclesie archiepiscopo, sacri imperii per Italiam ~io *TreatyR* I p. 103; **1439** Coloniensi archiepiscopo..ac sacri Romani imperii per Italiam ~io Bekynton I 73. **b** post..contumelias..cum ab ipso Crumwello cum ab ~io..eis irrogatas Chauncy *Passio* 76.

archicantor, ~ator, principal chanter.

s676 [Benedictus et Ceolfridus] Johannem ~orem Romanae aecclesiae abbatemque monasterii B. Martyni secum Brittanniam ducunt, qui nos abundanter ordinem cantandi per ordinem et viva voce simul et litteris edocuit *Hist. Abb. Jarrow* 10; [Benedictus] ordinem cantandi, psallendi atque in aecclesia ministrandi juxta morem Romanae institutionis suo monasterio contradidit, ..accepto ab Agathone papa ~ore aecclesiae beati apostoli Petri..Johanne Bede *HA* I 6; **s680** intererat huic synodo.. Johannes ~ator ecclesiae sancti apostoli Petri *Id. HE* IV 16; accepit et Johannem, ~orem B. Petri Apostoli, Britanniam perducendum, ut in monasterio suo cursum canendi edoceret Fl. Worc. 34 (cf. ib. 36).

archiceraunus [ἀρχικέραυνος], lord of the thunderbolt.

propter quod non male dicitur in Orphicis Jupiter '†arigikeminus', secundum aliam translationem 'princeps fulminum' Bradw. *CD* 169e.

archicoquus, chief cook, chef.

1461 archicoco pro ore nostro *CalPat* 80; *a cuke*, archimacherus, archicocus, cocus *CathA*; **1589** pro Johanne Smythson archiquoquo..regine *Ac. LChamb* 80 f. 35.

archidapifer, chief steward (seneschal).

1440 Henricus..rex Anglie..Ludowico comiti Palatino Reni, sacri..Romani imperii ~fero, Bekynton I 182.

archidecanus v. archidiaconus.

archidiabolus, arch-fiend.

1169 una cum ~o illo Galfrido Ridel [archidiacono Cantuarie] (H. Bos. *Lit. in persona T. Archiep.*) *Becket Mat.* VII 20; Gaufridus ~us noster (T. Becket *Lit.*) *Ib.* 59; ut archidiaconi nomen tanquam ~i cum horrore quodam auribus insonet audientium Gir. *GE* II 33; ille ~us—'archidiaconus' deberem dicere, ..sed lingua in udo est et de facili labitur Vinsauf *AV* II 3. 167.

archidiaco, archdeacon.

s1097 clerus Hildebertum ~onem in cathedra pontificali residere compulit Ord. Vit. X 7 p. 41; **1102** de..~onibus.. qui uxores suas derelictas..in maneriis suis ponunt (*Lit. Archiep. Cant.*) *Conc.* I 384; **1125** cum ~onibus..tue diocesis *Ib.* 408; **s1153** per..Wazonem ~onem J. Hex. *HR Cont.* 26.

archidiaconalis, archidiaconal. **b** (sb. n. pl.) archdeacon's rights or dues.

1222 is qui pro tempore fuerit rector..ecclesie omnia onera consueta et consuetudines episcopales et ~es sustinebit *Ch. Sal.* 120; **1228** episcopus H. et episcopus P. fuerunt in possessione juris ~is et posuerunt decanos suos *Feod. Durh.* 251; **1249** ne..presumant..impedire quominus.. archidiaconus visitationis officium et jura ~ia exerceat in ecclesiis supradictis (*Proc. in Curia Romana*) *G. S. Alb.* I 360; **1259** cum..expressa..mentio fieret de vicariorum qui pro tempore in concessis servirent ecclesiis, portionibus, ex quibus..possent..episcopalia, ~ia et cetera ecclesiarum.. onera supportare (*Lit. Papae*) *Ann. Burton* 489; **s1323** ita quod prior habebit totam jurisdiccionem ~em in ecclesiis de Jarow et Weremouth Graystanes 40; **1470** sustinebunt ..omnia onera ordinaria et extraordinaria episcopalia et ~ia *Lit. Cant.* III 250. **b 1249** ne impediant..archidiaconum visitare et exercere ~ia in ecclesiis supradictis (*Proc. in Curia Romana*) *G. S. Alb.* I 356; **1268** salvis nobis..omnibus episcopalibus, ~ibus, synodalibus et omnibus que..percipere solebamus in eadem [ecclesia] *Dryburgh* 6; **1300** vicarius et successores sui..sustinebunt omnia onera et ~ia *Reg. Carl.* I 189.

archidiaconatus, archdeaconry, office or jurisdiction of archdeacon. **b** area of such jurisdiction.

[Fulconis] ~um, quem in feudo..ab episcopo Rotomagensi tenebat, monachis dedit Ord. Vit. III 12 p. 132; **s1102** statutum est..ut ~us non dentur ad firmam W. Malm. *GP* I 64; **s1108** qui vero archidiaconus vel decanus hec jurare nollet, ~um vel decaniam..perderet Eadmer *HN* 232; subdecani officium est..curam ~us in urbe et suburbio gerere *Offic. Sal.* 7; **1372** quorum [beneficiorum] quatuor sunt dignitates, viz. decanatus, cantoria, cancellaria et thezauraria; quintum vero, viz. ~us, officium est *Reg. Brechin* I 19. **b 1080** archidiaconi per ~us suos semel in anno presbyterorum suffraganeorum suorum vestimenta, et calices et libros videant (*Conc. Illebon.* 5) Ord. Vit. V 5; **c1130** W. thesaurarius in cujus ~u est ipsa ecclesia *E. Ch. Yorks* II 445; [Turstinus, ob. 1140] dedit illi ecclesie..c s. per annum de ~u de Westrithinc Ric. Hex. *Pri. Hex.* II 11; **c1192** universo clero per ~um Oxenefordie constituto *Cart. Eynsham* I 67; **1229** in archideaconatu Norwic' *LTRMem* 11 r. 2d.; **1287** singulis archidiaconis precipimus ut..~uum suorum singulis annis singulas ecclesias studeant visitare *Conc. Syn.* 1034; **1486** in presencia..archidiaconi nostri Leicestrie, infra cujus ~us procinctum et ambitum dicta ecclesia parochialis..fore dignoscitur situata (*Decr. Ep. Linc.*) *Croyl. Cont. D* 592; archidiaconi, qui oculi dicuntur episcopi, tenentur et solent annuatim personaliter vel per eorum officiales visitare eorum ~us *Praxis* 309.

archidiaconus [ἀρχιδιάκονος], archdeacon (*cf. archidiaco*). *v.* A. H. Thompson *Diocesan Organization* (*Proc. Brit. Acad.* 1943).

ad amicitiam viri..sanctissimi Bonifatii videlicet ~i Bede *HE* V 19; in Edwardum urbis Lundonie ~um Osb. *Mir. Dunst.* 23; **c1072** mando..ut nullus episcopus vel ~us de legibus episcopalibus amplius in hundret placita teneant [v.l. teneat] (*Leg. Will. Episc.*) *GAS* 485; presbyter ab episcopo vel ~o suo accusatus (*Leg. Hen.*) *Ib.* 585; **1125** nullus in ~um nisi diaconus promoveatur (*Conc. Lond.* 7) J. Worc. 21; scelus archidiaconus audet, / presbyteros Domini dum radere rodere gaudet H. Hunt. *HA* XI 164; qui decani sunt vel ~i nisi illi..in quorum manibus iniquitates sunt? J. Sal. *Pol.* 580a (cf. *id. Ep.* 156); ~i officiales sunt domini episcopi quorum officium in exterioribus administrationibus consistit *Offic. Sal.* 6; ~us dicitur summus diaconus. ..~orum autem officium olim in ecclesia grande fuerat. ..super clericos autem omnes exteriores et rurales archipresbyteros et decanos ~us modernis quoque temporibus administrationem habet Gir. *PI* I 19 pp. 112–13; *Id. GE* II 33 (v. archidiabolus); **a1265** occasione consuetudinis per quam..~i a singulis ecclesiis sui archidiaconatus xij d. annuos extorserunt, quam..alii donum, alii lardarium, alii vero porcum ~i ficto nomine jam appellant *Conc. Syn.* 721; **1287** singulis ~is precipimus ut ab ecclesiis quando personaliter non visitant procuraciones exigere..non presumant. ..et, quamquam nostre sollicitudinis cura per ipsos tamquam oculos nostros in quampluribus habeat relevari, nolumus [etc.] *Ib.* 1034–6; **1289** pro..Bertrando majore ~o Agennensi *RGasc* II 467; **1291** abbatibus, prioribus, decanis et †archidecanis [? l. ~is] (*Lit. Papae*) B. Cotton 223; **c1300** ~orum quatuor potestas et officium in exteriori jurisdiccione consistit, ut subditorum curas gerant, eorum causas justo libramine dirigentes, mores reformantes et excessus corrigentes *Reg. S. Paul.* I 50 p. 20; episcopi ponunt capellanos super parochias, ~os et officiales super capellanos; capellani devorant parochianos, ~i et officiales parochianos et capellanos J. Sheppey *Fab.* 72; **1382** introducti sunt ~i magis patenter superflui Wycl. *Serm.* I 402; hic ~us, *a narsdekyn*, ..*a arsdekyn* WW; **s1450** quod Petro Paulus fuerat quando non recte..ambulabat, hoc illi [abbati] erat ipse ~us *Reg. Whet.* I 148; *Praxis* 309 (v. archidiaconatus b).

archididascalus, head teacher.

1541 omnis scholasticorum numerus in v aut vj ordines seu classes distribuatur; horum inferiores tres instituat hipodidascolus, superiores autem archididascolus instituat *Educ. Ch.* 464; **1560** sint duo preceptores, quorum alter ~us vocetur *Ib.* 496.

archidominus, abbot.

1299 ~us monasterii vestri [S. Edmundi] *Reg. Wint.* II 545.

archiducalis, archducal (w. ref. to Austria).

1496 regalem vel ~em licenciam (*DipDoc* E 624) *Foed.* XII 584.

archiducissa, archduchess.

1513 illustrissima domina Margareta ~a Austriae *Mon. Hib. & Scot.* 512a.

archiductor, chief leader.

964 (12c) cum suo ~ore, viz. episcopo, qui eos defendere.. debet ab omni perturbatione *CS* 1135 (cf. ib. 1136); **a1000** (11c) illius ~oris dominatui et voluntati qui episcopatui praesidet *CD* 1287.

archidux, archduke.

1487 Maximiliani..et Philippi Dei gracia ~ducum Austrie (*DipDocE* 591) *Foed.* XII 320; **1508** Karoli..~ducis Austrie *Spons. Mariae* 2.

archiepiscopa, female archbishop (fig.).

c1198 hec [sc. avaritia] ut archiepiscopa regnat super episcopos, / in exemplum pontificum †hinc servitionis [? l. huic servientes] antropos (*Avar. Praesulum*) *EHR* V 321.

archiepiscopalis, archiepiscopal. **b** (sb. m.) adherent of an archbishop. **c** (sb. n. pl.) archbishop's functions.

in sedem meam ~em superstitem et heredem vivens te constituam Eddi *Wilf.* 43; cathedram est ~em indeptus Eadmer *V. Osw.* 22; est ibi in ecclesia B. Pauli episcopalis sedes; quod fuit metropolitana et adhuc futura creditur, ..nisi forte B. Thome titulus ~is..dignitatem illam Cantuarie..conservet W. Fitzst. *Thom. prol.* 4; **1243** prior et conventus Ecclesie Christi Cantuarie, vacante nunc ultimo sede Cantuariensi, jurisdictionem et potestatem ~em..in episcopos et alios Cantuariensis provincie sibi vindicantes Gros. *Ep.* 110; **s1273** archiepiscopus Cantuarie..intronizatus est et positus in cathedra ~i *Leg. Ant. Lond.* 160; **1317** ~es et episcopales ecclesie *Reg. Carl.* II 159; **1413** opiniones suas defendit, ..potestatem ~em et episcopalem multipliciter contemnendo (*Proc. v. J. Oldcastel*) *Ziz.* 436. **b s1191** in Neustria..nemo ex ~ibus communicabat cancellario Devizes 38. **c** exstitit consuetudo inter duos metropolitanos Anglie ut altero defuncto alter in provincia defuncti ~ia faceret, utpote episcopos consecrare.. H. Cantor 2v.

archiepiscopaliter, as befits an archbishop.

supra que habuit ~er tunicam, dalmaticam, casulam, pallium cum spinulis, calicem, chirothecas, annulum, sandalia, pastoralem baculum W. Fitzst. *Thom.* 151.

archiepiscopari, to be made archbishop.

1166 in cancellarium.., qui nunc aut ~atur, ut credo, aut ~ari contendit, ut emuli mentiuntur (J. Sal. *Ep.* 145) *Becket Mat.* V 379; episcopus Londoniensis, ..~andi, quod plurimi suspicantur, ambitione tractus (*Ib.* 183) *Ib.* VI 15.

archiepiscopatus, archbishopric: **a** office; **b** see (w. appurtenances); **c** province.

a hunc antistitem ordinandum Romam miserunt, quatinus accepto ipse gradu ~us catholicos per omnem Brittaniam ecclesiis Anglorum ordinare posset antistites Bede *HE* III 29; siquando in metropoli Eboraco, ~us sc. sui sede, eum contigisset morari Folcard *J. Bev.* 11; iterum preces de ~u Dunstano funduntur Osb. *V. Dunst.* 32; **s1070** honorem..exhibuimus non quem ~u tuo sed quem magistro..debuimus Eadmer *HN* 13; Stigandus.. primus in habitu clericali ~u functus est Diceto *Abbr. Chr.* 17. **b** hoc manerium tenuit Stigandus archiepiscopus, sed non erat de ~u *DB* 9b; ubi fuerit ~us tempore Britonum cognitio labat W. Malm. *GP prol.*; regnum Anglie..habet ~us duos (*Leg. Hen.*) *GAS* 552; principales ecclesie, sicut ~us et episcopatus (*Inst. Cnuti*). *Ib.* 283; **1164** cum vacaverit ~us..de dominio regis, debet esse in manu ipsius (*Const. Clarendon* 12) *Becket Mat.* V 77; Bilingeia est de ~u Eboracensi *RDomin.* 3; rex..obtulit ei Herefordensem episcopatum ampliare fundis ad equivalenciam ~us [Eboracensis] Map *NC* V 6 p. 234; **1224** recipiat omnes exitus ejusdem ~us *Pat* 434; **1439** non est intencionis nostre quod ipse per assumpcionem..cardinalatus destituatur ecclesia et ~u Eboracensi Bekynton I 44. **c c1051** in ceteris ecclesiis ~us sui que sunt trans Humbram *Chr. Pont. Ebor*, A 344; **s1108** cum ~us sui monasteria frequenter visitaret Ric. Hex. *Hist. Hex.* II 7; **s1206** archiepiscopus Eboracensis..omnes.. qui in ~u suo hanc rapinam facerent..anathematis sententia innodavit M. Par. *Maj.* II 511; sicut archiepiscopus in ~u..est caput primum Ockham *I. & P.* 26.

archiepiscopium, archbishopric (office). **b** archbishop's palace.

pater regis illud dedit archiepiscopo [Lanfranco] in vita sua tantum, ut sullimatus fuit in ~io *Text. Roff.* 88; protestans se non illius ~io sed magisterio litterarum tantum deferre *NLA* II (*Lanfranc*) 141. **b** Cuthbertus..jussit suis ut apud ~ium infoderetur W. Malm. *GP* I 7.

archiepiscopus [ἀρχιεπίσκοπος], archbishop.

Augustinus Brittaniarum ~us ordinavit duos episcopos Bede *HE* II 3; Cantuārios archī quī rexit episcopus olim Wulf. *Swith.* I 1460; [Willelmus I] primatem regni sui, ~um dico Cantuariensem seu Dorobernensem, ..non sinebat quicquam statuere..nisi que sue voluntati accommoda ..essent Eadmer *HN* 12; **c1102** [crucem ante se portari facere] non pertinet nisi ad ~um a Romano pontifice pallio confirmatum Anselm (*Ep.* 278) IV 192; ibi [Cantuarie] prima sedes ~i habetur qui est totius Anglie primas et patriarcha W. Malm. *GP prol.*; **s1154** Rogerus Cantuariensis archidiaconus..in Eboracensem ~um consecratus est a Theobaldo Cantuariensi ~o apud Westmonasterium, sed professionem non fecit Diceto *YH* I 298; mysterium grande est illud insigne [sc. pallium], illud ~i singulare W. Fitzst. *Thom.* 25; ~us dicitur summus episcopus vel princeps episcoporum; *archos* quippe summus vel princeps dicitur. ..horum officium est episcopos consecrare, concilium congregare, jura dilapsa reparare Gir. *PI* I 19 p. 108; non enim primas proprie vel patriarcha dici potest..nisi qui ~um unum vel plures subjectos habuerit *Id. JS prol.* p. 113; **1225** erchiepiscopus *KRMem* 8 r. 11(1)*d.*; **1237** quid ad venerabiles patres ~os et episcopos incumbat ex officio faciendum, nomen dignitatis eorum, quod est *episcopus*, id est superintendens, exprimit evidenter *Conc. Syn.* 255; **1281** cum beneficiorum declaratur vacatio per dominum ~um, ipsa beneficia quantumcunque vacaverint, patronorum, episcoporum vel capitulorum suorum negligentia non probata, per ~um conferuntur, per quod jus enormiter leditur predictorum *Ib.* 925; hic ~us, *A. a arsbyschop* WW; **1438** J. divina providencia ~us Armachanus et Hibernie primas Bekynton I 3; **1536** J. miseratione divina ~us Sanctiandree totius regni Scotie primas *Conc. Scot.* I ccxlvii.

archierarchus, pope.

annuit et scriptis legalibus archiierarchus / Theodoro regique jubet sancita notari Frith. 773.

archifactor, ~fector, ~fer, ~ferarius v. arci-. archifenium v. arcifinius.

archiflamen, high priest (pagan). **b** archbishop.

fuerunt tunc in Brittannia xxviij flamines, set et iij ~ines, quorum potestati ceteri judices morum atque phanatici submittebantur. hos etiam ex precepto apostolici †ydolatriam [v.l. ydolatrie] eripuerunt, et ubi erant flamines episcopos, ubi ~ines archiepiscopos posuerunt G. Mon. IV 19; **1169** Londoniensis episcopus..protestatus est..quod cathedram metropoliticam illuc transferri faciet ubi eam esse debere fingit.., sc. ad ecclesiam Londoniensem, ubi ~inem gloriatur sedisse dum Jovialis religio colebatur (J. Sal. *Ep.* 189) *Becket Mat.* VII 10; Helenus Priami filius, qui ~en eorum erat Gir. *DK* I 16; civitates illas [in Palestina etc.] olim flaminum et ~inum, istas fecit [Dominus] esse cathedrales episcoporum Gerv. Tilb. II 3 (Vol. II p. 760). **b** Thomam Beket Londoniarum praesulem Cantuariae ~inem et Angliae Cancellarium creat Major III 15.

archiforestarius, head forester.

s1399 foreste de Knarisborow ~ius..advenit cum ducentis forestariis Ad. Usk 25.

archigrammateus [ἀρχιγραμματεύς], lord chancellor.

~aeus, seu communiori vocabulo supremus regni cancellarius Chauncy *Passio* 74.

archihaereticus, arch-heretic.

prepositi qui declinando a Cristi consiliis..sunt ~i Wycl. *Ver.* III 287.

archiierarchus v. archierarchus.

archijustitiarius, chief justiciar.

s1179 rex..Wintoniensem, Helyensem, Norwicensem episcopos ~ios regni..constituit DICETO *YH* I 435.

archilatro, arch-robber.

plebis predones et in insidiis latitantes / archilatrones, murdrantes, mansa cremantes, / damnat, suspendit ELMH. *Metr. Hen. V* 122.

archilevita, archdeacon.

pastor ovem propriam, natum pater, archilevitam / presul ama NIG. *Laur.* 29. 2; pontifex Theobaldus Thomam, quem prius..ad alios inferiores ordines, postea in levitam, simul etiam et ecclesie sue ~am..ordinavit H. BOS. *Thom.* II 6; **1188** levita, imo ~a, ego sum P. BLOIS *Ep.* 20 p. 73; dum..peteretur ab archidiacono Oxenofordensi..quatinus juvenem..ydoneum, familie ipsius ~e prepositum, ad gradum promoveret subdiaconatus AD. EYNS. *Hug.* V 10; nec melior pontifex quam archilevita *Ps.*-MAP (*Contra ambitiosos* 69) 155; R. Foliot Herefordensis ~a GIR. *Symb.* 23; **a1220** archilevita Thōmas et cancellarius Anglis / regia divino jura tenore dabat H. AVR. *Poems* 27; **s1423** pontifici vellus, decano cedit ocellus; / ren, quia pingue sapit, archilevita capit (*Versus*) AMUND. I 75.

archileviticus, archidiaconal.

ad vehementiorem omnium admirationem.., ~am contulit eidem dignitatem GIR. *JS* 7 p. 346.

archilio [? cf. ἀρχέλαος], (?) leader.

naviter increpitans pigrum decus archilionum FRITH. 1324.

Archilollardus, Arch-Lollard.

illius satellitis infernalis heresiarche sive ~i, Johannis de Veteri Castro ELMH. *Metr. Hen. V prol.* p. 82.

†archimaga, (?) mistress of witchcraft.

Gorgones †artimagas et visus stringere sagas R. CANT. *Malch.* IV 441.

archimagirus [ἀρχιμάγειρος], chief cook, chef.

habeat archimacherus capanam in coquina..ubi species aromaticas..reponat NECKAM *Ut.* 97; **1443** David Lloit unus archemacherorum coquine nostre *Pat* 456 m. 29; **1445** archemecherorum *CalPat* 343; archimacherus, A. *a mayster cooke*, ..hic archemerus, *a master cuke* WW.

archimandrita [ἀρχιμανδρίτης], keeper of sheepfold. **b** archimandrite, abbot. **c** (*s. dub.*; (?) *f.l.* for *archipresbyter*). **d** (fig.) pope.

custodes ovium nos dicimus opiliones, / archimandritos quos constat esse vocates GARL. *Syn.* 605; *schepheerde*, opilio, pastor, ..~a *PP*; hic archimendritas, *a schepard* WW. **b** [Apollonius] quingentorum circiter monachorum ~a et rector extiterat ALDH. *VirgP* 38; **a705** Aldhelmo ~ae (CELLANUS) *Ep. Aldh.* 3 (9) (cf. *CS* 114); **988** (12c) ego Ælfwold Cridiensis aecclesiae ~a *CD* 665; **10..** ~a, *heahleareow* WW; defunctis presulibus et ~is, satellites regis ecclesiasticas possessiones et omnes gazas invadebant ORD. VIT. X 2 p. 9; Fulcheredus..Scrobesburiensis ~a *Ib.* 14 p. 85; **s1403** in finibus cujusdam dominii quod ad ~am loci illius [S. Albani]..pertinuit REDMAN *Hen. V* 17; archimandrita [*gl.*: princeps omnium, pastor ecclesie] sit celebs eusebiusque (*Verse*) WW. **c s1173** Nicholaus Romane ecclesie subdiaconus, a domino papa transmissus, ab archiepiscopis, episcopis, abbatibus, .. prioribus, †~is, plurimam collegit pecuniam DICETO *YH* I 379. **d 796** probatissime ~a ALCUIN *Ep.* 94 (*ad Papam*).

archimarescallus, chief marshal.

1440 Frederico duci Saxonie, sacri Romani imperii ~o BEKYNTON I 105.

archiminister, chief minister (of king).

exceptis quibusdam regis Henrici..amicis, quos..in tantum..sibi..astrinxit ut eos..omnium palatinorum ~tros efficeret *G. Steph.* I 12.

archimista v. alchimista. archiolus v. arciolus.

†archioritas, polemic (misinterp. of Jerome *Vir. Illust.* 13: '*scripsit libros duos ἀρχαιότητος adversus Appionem*').

~as, conflictus *GlC* A 725 (cf. ib. 779: archioretis, libros duo).

archipastor, chief shepherd. **b** archbishop.

1438 pro feodo ~oris pro gubernacione gregum regis a scabie, xxxv s. *ExchScot* 58. **b †974** (12c) ego Dunstan ~or †salutifere stigmate gabuli..subscripsi *CS* 1301.

archipater, archbishop.

pius archipater Metensis gloria plebis ALCUIN *Carm.* 103. 3. 3; archipater gaudet heredem nactus opimum, / cui queat eudoxas moriens committere caulas FRITH. 180.

archiphilosophus, prince of philosophers (Aristotle).

~o attestante R. BURY *Phil.* 2. 30.

archipirata [ἀρχιπειρατής], arch-pirate, viking. **b** arch-robber. **c** admiral.

ut barbarus praedo vel crudelis ~a spretus est ALDH. *VirgP* 42; **955** (12c) tempore quo ~ae totam hanc insulam devastantes pervagati sunt *CS* 906; archipiratra, *yldest wicing* ÆLF. *Gl.*; **10..** archipiratta, *heah sæpeof* WW. **b** quatuor ~is ecclesie Menevensis..primos..redditus sibi vacantes..conferre curavit GIR. *JS* 7 p. 346. **c †971** (12c) ego Mascusius ~a confortavi [donum] *CS* 1277.

archipolites, archbishop.

cursores sed jam praemiserat archipolites / Theodorus FRITH. 733.

archipolus, (?) heavenly ruler. **b** (applied to archbishop).

c850 (10c) in nomine arcipoli conditoris *CS* 429. **b** hic sponsus gloriae urbem sibi novam Jerusalem per ~um Augustinum..molitur GOSC. *Aug. Min.* 750.

archipontifex, archbishop.

811 praesulatus Uulfredi ~ficis anno vj *CS* 335; **10..** ~fices una cum ceterorum consensu pontificum (*Syn. Decr. paraphr.*) *GAS* 249; Laurentius..primus ab ipso [Augustino] adhuc vivente ordinatus ~fex GOSC. *Transl. Aug.* I 16; **s960** Dunstanus jamdudum ~fex divino presignatus oraculo W. MALM. *GP* I 18; **s1123** Turstino Eboracensi ~fice J. WORC. 17; **s1135** Stephanus..ab ~fice Cantuarie..regio diademate coronatur *Chr. Battle* 64; prefatus ~fex [Cantuarie] AD. MARSH *Ep.* 191; **s1381** cum staret ~fex inter eos..circumdatus nebulonum millibus WALS. *HA* I 460.

archipontificalis, archiepiscopal.

1442 Cantuariensis archiepiscopus..pro impetranda apud sanctitatem vestram sue dignitati et cure ~i in sacras manus vestras cedendi licencia BEKYNTON I 148.

archipontificatus, archbishopric.

747 fratri ~us infula sublimato coepiscopo Cudberhto Bonifatius BONIF. *Ep.* 78 (*title*).

archipraedo, arch-robber.

1377 archipredones captos post crimina penis / taliter absolvit ut presidis ante tribunal / discipulos appellarent (*Epitaph. Ed. III*) *Pol. Poems* I 223.

archipraefectus, chief civic dignitary (Riga).

1498 cum..~o, proconsulibus, consulibus et senioribus..civitatis Rigensis (*TreatyR*) *Foed.* XII 701.

archipraesul, archbishop. **b** pope.

965 (11c) ego Oswoldus ~sul *CS* 1166 (cf. 1167); ~sul et martyr Domini Ælfegus HERM. ARCH. 20; **1089** Lanfranco ~sule machinante *Regesta* 314; ~sules Theonus Lundoniensis et Tadioceus Eboracensis G. MON. XI 10; **s1163** rex..misit .. ~sulem Eboracensem Rogerum R. NIGER 170; venerabili Dublinensium ~suli GIR. *RG* II 12; **1272** contra electionem monachorum S. Trinitatis Cantuarie et ejus formam de futuro ~sule preficiendo *Pat* 90 m. 18 (cf. *Cal.* p. 639); **1373** [Thomas] mortuo archiepiscopo in archepresulem canonice est electus BRINTON *Serm.* 30 p. 120; ~sul, *archebyschope* WW; **1449** commissario..~sulis Cantuariensis *Reg. Whet.* I 154; **1507** ecclesie metropolitice ~sul *Lit. Cant.* III 337. **b** supremum pastorem et sacrosanctae sedis apostolicae ~sulem..dominum papam CHAUNCY *Passio* 66.

archipraesularis, archiepiscopal.

1253 in singulis ecclesiis cathedralibus Hibernie.., viz. in ecclesiis ubi sedes est ~is..et in ceteris ecclesiis cathedralibus *Cl* 402.

archipraesulatus, archbishopric.

984 (11c) ~us adeptus culmen in Eboraca *CD* 644; **s1013** Livingus ~um Dorobernie suscepit FL. WORC. I 166; Altissimo supplicans postulaverat ut ~us sui tempore.. nemini preterquam digno consecrationis..imponeret manum H. BOS. *Thom.* III 21; **s1177** Cristianus..successit.. Coenredo in ~um Maguntinum et pallium suscepit a Widone de Crema *G. Hen. II* I 186; ecclesiam..Mediolanensem ubi Ambrosius ~um obtinuit BELETH *RDO* 84. 88; **c1240** de Eadmundo..qui a gremio ecclesie nostre ad ~us dignitatem est translatus *Ch. Sal.* 272; **s1508** de ~u Eboracensi jam diu vacuo ANDRE *Hen. VII* 125.

archipresbyter, 'archpriest' (of collegiate church), bishop's vicar, rural dean. **b** (as nickname). **c** 'archpriest' of Roman Catholic community in England after Reformation.

640 Hilarius ~er et servans locum sanctae sedis apostolicae (*Lit.*) BEDE *HE* II 19; **s1180** ~er Brivatensis domini papae litteras..inseruit manui defuncti DICETO *YH* II 4; notemus..quod ~er ordinandos prius debeat offerre archidiacono, unde hic etiam dicitur vicarius, quoniam in hoc vicem supplet sacerdotum BELETH *RDO* 134. 139; **1203** episcopo Agenensi, abbatibus, archidiaconis, ~eris et capellanis et universis clericis per episcopatum Agenensem *Pat* 23b; ~er dicitur quasi summus presbiter vel principalis, quem quidam eundem putant quem et decanum, presbiteris aliis et clericis causa administrationis jure prepositum; alii dicunt ~um principalem in plebanis ecclesiis, ubi plures tam presbiteri quam clerici ministrant inferiores, quales in Italia multe sunt ecclesie que plebane vocantur GIR. *PI* I 19 p. 110; ecclesia S. Petri [Rome]..habet ~erum cardinalem clericis singulariter ibidem deservientibus prepositum et prestitutum *Id. Spec.* IV 2; **1216** ut..in [chorepiscoporum] locum eligerentur..~i *Conc.* I 547; **1236** Vitalis ~er de Inter Duo Maria, preceptor totius militie Templi in Wasconia *Cl* 351; **1249** decanis, prepositis, ~eris, officialibus et aliis ecclesiarum prelatis (*Lit. Papae*) *Reg. Newbattle* no. 227; **1261** assumpto nomine Urbanus..ab ~ero Ostiensi munus benedictionis recepit (*AncC* III 176) *RL* II 189; **1275** ~er ordinet precentorem *Comp. Swith.* 203*n.*; **1293** dominus Benjamyn ~er ecclesie de Olecumbe *DCCant Q* f. 5a; **1320** ita quod unus capellanorum.. quem ~erum, eo quod aliis presbiteris preerit servientibus ibidem volumus nominari.., per dominos manerii de F. ..presentetur *Reg. Exon.* 140; **1439** concessimus..Waltero T. ~ero oratorii S. Trinitatis in Insula Vecta..quod ipse..v mesuagia.., que in jure archipresbyteratus sui oratorii S. Trinitatis..tenet, ..dare possit *Pat* 444 m. 25. **b s1358** quidam natione Vasco surrexit, vulgariter nuncupatus ~er, ducens secum unam comitivam per diversas partes Francie ipsas..devastando AD. MUR. *Cont.* A 191 (cf. WALS. *YN* 302). **c 1621** novam illam et antea inauditam ~eri potestatem pro episcopis et ordinaria jurisdictione clero Anglicano obtrusit (J. BENNETT) *Cath. Rec. Soc. Misc.* XII 135.

archipresbyteralis, of an 'archpriest'.

1440 deputati per..sanctum synodum cardinalatus †archiprisbitrali, episcopali, abbaciali dignitatibus..insigniti (*Lit. Antipapae*) *Cop. Pri. S. Andr.* 194.

archipresbyteratus, office of 'archpriest'. **b** (in England after Reformation).

1243 universis clericis, baronibus et militibus Inter Duo Maria..et..per ~um Sernensem constitutis *Cl* 60 (cf. *RGasc.* I 212); **1320** si cedente..archipresbitero..~us vacaverit *Reg. Exon.* 140; **1417** resignacionem domini W. F. archipresbiteri ecclesie collegiate de Ulcombe..de ~u suo *Reg. Cant.* I 156; **1439** (v. archipresbyter); **1547** *CalPat* 159. **b 1621** ultimum archipresbyterum..saepe et diu deliberasse de ~u deponendo (J. BENNETT) *Cath. Rec. Soc. Misc.* XII 138.

archiprinceps, prince elector.

s1486 Maximilianus..quem..~cipes sacri imperii electores in regem Romanorum..elegerunt *Eul. Hist.* I *Cont.* 295.

archiprior, chief prior.

tangere Landonem quia mens pavet archipriorem, / tangimus Hugonem R. CANT. (*H. suppriori S. Pancratii* 15) 260.

archiquoquus v. archicoquus. archiromacus v. ancyromachus. archis v. ascites.

archisacerdos, archbishop.

pontificalis apex meritis archique sacerdos ALCUIN *Carm.* 2. 1; **798** (13c) michi Athelhardo Dei gratia ~dot (*Conc. Clovesho*) *CS* 291; **813** ego Uulfredus misericordia Dei ~dos *CS* 342; **927** (12c) pro honore ~dotis Wlfhelmi *CS* 660.

archischismaticus, leader of schism.

s1165 justitiarius regis illum archiscismaticum [Reginaldum Coloniensem] in osculum non recepit DICETO *YH* I 318.

archischola, official (chancellor) in charge of school (*cf. Educ. Ch.* 74).

1091 ~a debet lectiones auscultare et terminare, sigillum ecclesie portare, literas et cartas componere et in tabula lectores notare *Reg. S. Osm.* I 214; **p1408** ordinavit in ecclesia Wellensi..thesaurarium et cancellarium quem vocant archiscolam *Hist. Wells* 62.

archisigillarius, keeper of Great Seal.

Regis Henrici secundi ~io GIR. *Galf.* II 10.

archisophus, prince of philosophers.

Phebum philosophorum, ~um Aristotelem R. BURY *Phil.* 7. 103.

archispeculator, archbishop.

986 (17c) ego Dunstan Dorobernensis ecclesiae ~or *E. Ch. S. Paul.* 1.

archisterium v. asceterium.

archistrategos [ἀρχιστράτηγος], commander, ruler.

archistrāteios solio prospectat ab alto FRITH. 808.

archisynagogus [ἀρχισυνάγωγος], ruler of synagogue (*cf. Mark* v 22). **b** (fig.).

Christum..suscitasse filiam ~i ALCUIN *Ep.* 138 p. 219; de duodenni ~i filia AD. SCOT. *Serm.* 139D; ~ae (*sic*) filiam BEKINSAU 754. **b 1188** desideramus ut ecclesia debita gaudeat libertate, ut idolum ~i conteratur *Ep. Cant.* 269.

architecta, architect (fig., f.).

illa proverbialis aula [cf. *Prov.* ix 1] cujus ~a [v.l. ~us] et opifex..sapientia legitur extitisse ALDH. *Met.* 2 p. 64.

architectare [CL], to construct.

in aula mea ~ari feci trapetas, solivas, lacunaria GARL. *Dict.* 137.

architectonicus [ἀρχιτεκτονικός], architect, master builder (fig.).

c1240 lapides fundamentales edificii cujus estis ~i..libri sunt prophetarum GROS. *Ep.* 123; [nos libri] ~i reputari debemus in scienciis R. BURY *Phil.* 4. 67.

architector, architect, master builder. **b** the Creator. **c** (infl. by *tector*) thatcher.

s992 in domo quam..sapienter sibi edificaverat, venerande sapientis ~oris [Ælphegi] exuvie..venerabiliter deposite *Chr. Rams.* 107; imaginare..in mente ~oris formam et similitudinem domus fabricande GROS. 109; **c1250** patri suo ac domino R., architectori prudentissimo *FormOx* 346*n.*; *a wryghte*, ~or, ~us, carpentarius *CathA*. **b 956** (12c) providentia summi ~oris *CS* 973. **c 1380** uni ~ori operanti super coopertura et reparacione unius grangie in parco cooperte cum stramine pro feno ferarum tempore yemali *KRAc* 499/1; **1461** pro..stipendiis latamorum, carpentariorum, ~orum et eorum servienscium *ExchScot* 78; hic ~or, A. *thekare* WW; *a theker*, ~or, tector *CathA*.

architectorius, architectural. **b** creative.

s1224 artifices regis castellum fecerunt ligneum, altum et ~ia [*corr. from* geometrica] arte fabricatum M. Par. *Maj.* III 86. **b 940** (14c) regnante Deo imperpetuum ~io qui omnia disponit *CS* 754 (cf. *CD* 690).

architectura [CL], architecture. **b** construction.

quid ~a, quid mercatura, . .nisi vite subsidia sub quadam providentia curant? Gir. *PI* I 12. **b** cista. .puelle [Rosamunde] vix bipedalis mensure sed mirabilis ~e ibidem cernitur Higd. VII 22.

architectus [CL], architect, master builder. **b** (fig., iron.).

almae oraminum aedes ~i ingenio fabre conduntur Aldh. *Ep.* 5 p. 489; ~os sibi mitti petiit qui juxta morem Romanorum ecclesiam de lapide. .facerent Bede *HE* V 21 (cf. *Hist. Abb. Jarrow* 7); ~us, *yldestwyrhta* Ælf. *Gl.*; ~us cum instrumentis materiam prequirit, in qua se et illa exerceat J. Sal. *Met.* 910a; prudens ~us in omni structura artis forissece R. Cold. *Cuthb.* 47. **b** noster regularum ~us Gardiner *CC* 563.

architenens v. 1 and 2 arcitenens. archites v. ascites. architesis v. antithesis, arcithesis.

archithalassus [ἀρχιθάλασσος], lord high admiral.

Edmundus qui Angliae ~us. .anno salutis 1408 occubuit Camd. *Br.* 309.

archithrenius [cf. θρῆνος], chief mourner.

architrenius Hanv. 130 (*title*).

archithronatus, enthroned in supremacy (w. ref. to archbishop).

c1381 mactatur temere sine judicio patriarcha, / ecclesie princeps, patronus et archithronatus (*Mors Simonis*) *Pol. Poems* I 227.

architicus v. asciticus. architipus v. archetypus.

architriclinium, parlour.

1551 in architricluneo vocato *a parlour Pat* 840 m. 14.

architriclinus [ἀρχιτρίκλινος], governor of the feast (*cf. John* ii 8–9). **b** marshal. **c** (adj.) appropriate to a governor of the feast.

~ium, domus major *GlC* A 797; **c800** ex quo ~o Turonicae civitatis. .miscendum quis ignorat? Alcuin *Ep.* 192; proponetur querela de inofficioso. ., nisi ~us usque ad nauseam . .cum hospitibus suis bibendi bella continuet P. Blois *Ep.* 102. 319a; hausto [vino] atque ad ~um deportato Ad. Scot. *Serm.* 414a. **b** ex ea progenie [sc. Keth] in qua nunc est, regii ~i, vulgo mariscalli, magistratus haud paucos insignes patriae assertores prosiluisse Boece 251v. **c 1432** magni fontes vivacissimi scaturiebant aquas ~as in vinum conversas (J. Carpenter) *MGL* III 461.

archityrannus, chieftain. **b** archtyrant.

s1185 principales. .architiranni Galuwidiensium *Plusc.* VI 32. **b** jubente ~o illo Crumwello Chauncy *Passio* 108.

†**archius** [?], weary.

~ius, gravatus *GlC* A 749; arcius, lassus vel grabatus *Ib.* 820.

archivum [CL < ἀχρεῖον], **a** treasury. **b** archive, repository of records etc. **c** (fig.). **d** register, record.

a s1182 post mortem archiepiscopi [Ebor'] quecunque reperta sunt suis in ~is. .confiscata sunt, quorum summa fuit xj milia li. argenti Diceto *YH* II 12; **s1484** qui. .per fas et nefas maximas pecuniarum summas de omnium pene statuum regni ~is abraderent *Croyl. Cont. B* 572. **b** bibliotheca vel armarium vel ~um, *boochord* Ælf. *Sup.*; has [litteras] quas vobis transmitto, in ~is. .servatum iri praecipio Lanfr. *Ep.* 12. 519d; **s1106** secundum quod in antiquarum monimentis litterarum, que. .in ~is ecclesie. . servabantur, scriptum repperit Eadmer *HN* 213; legi ego scriptum quod in ~o. .ecclesie continetur index facti W. Malm. *GR* II 179; **s1164** scriptum dictas consuetudines [de Clarendon] continens recipit. .; alteram vero scripti partem suscepit Eboracensis archiepiscopus, rex vero ipse tertiam in regum ~is reponendam H. Bos. *Thom.* III 29; **1310** in singulis locis insignibus ~um publicum constituatis, et in eo preficiatis aliquem virum idoneum prothonotarium, in cujus libris instrumenta que per notarios circumvicinos recepta fuerint. .transcribantur, alias viribus perpetuo caritura *RGasc.* IV 395; **s1317** rex Anglie in Scotorum ~iis quesivit. .formam. .pacis sub pallio treugarum *Flor. Hist.* III 181; **s1320** immanis sceleris exordia. .ex. .~iis Judeorum. .et Agarenorum in exterminium Christianitatis mundo palam producta. .horrorem. .populis. .incusserunt *Ib.* 195; **1335** rotulorum uno. .retento alter remaneat communibus in ~is (*Stat. Sibthorpe*) *Eng. Clergy* 270; instrumentis productis ex ~is publicis Ockham *Dial.* 840; **1354** scrutatis. .registris et munimentis aliis in ~is. .ecclesie *Reg. Heref.* 221; **s1430** precepit. .ut tollerent librum voluminis hujus ponerentque in ~is sue domus Amund. I 286; *cloos lybrary*, ~um *PP*; **1441** recorda nostra, rotulas (*sic*), custumaria et evidencias nostras in ~is nostris existencia. .scrutari fecimus *Cl* 292 m. 24*d.* **c** quasi in ~is memorie depositam J. Sal. *Pol.* 449d; quin. .intimo pectoris ~o arcana sibi perplurima . .reservaret Gir. *TH* I 13. **d** id cenobium [*Bardney*] fuit . .affinitate. .nostro, id est Malmesberiensi, conjunctum, sicut in ~is utriusque reperitur ecclesie W. Malm. *GP* IV 155; **1300** scrutatis. .omnibus cronicis, ~is et secretis domus vestre *Cl* 117 m. 3*d.* (cf. *Ann. Ed. I* 454); unum. .directivum intrinsecum, quod in ~is presentis monasterii reperi Elmh. *Cant.* 309; **1448** in registris et ~is nostris scribetur *StatOx* 276.

†**archivus,** *s. dub.* (? cf. *arcarius* or *arcuarius*).

s1431 ~us domini regis apud Lovers interfectus est *Chr. S. Alb.* 63.

archocides v. arceuthis.

archon [ἄρχων], ruler (w. ref. to king, archbishop or noble).

~ontes, principes *GlC* A 745; arcontus, princeps *Ib.* 746; **840** (11c) coram suis ~ontis *CS* 430; **947** ego Wulfstanus ~ons divinae servitutis officio mancipatus Eboracae civitatis archiepiscopus *CS* 820; **956** Eadwig numine caelesti gentis Geuuisorum ~ons *CS* 926; **956** (12c) cum consensu meorum sapientium ~ontumque *CS* 964; **964** (12c) cum consensu principum et ~untorum meorum *CS* 1135; gemmata vehitur archontum more curuli Frith. 351 (cf. ib. 1213); perprudenti domino ~onti Albrico [archiep. Ebor.] *V. Dunst. B.* 1.

archoniare v. archonizare.

archoniatio, stacking.

1466 pro. .lucracione et arconiacione feni decimalis *Exch Scot* 383; **1467** pro. .~one feni *Ib.* 482.

archonista, ~us, stacker (? conf. w. *arcuarius*).

~us, A. *a mowyer*, . .hic ~a, *a †bower* WW.

archonius, ~ium, 'mow', stack (of corn or hay).

1380 de exitu grangie per talliam de uno arconio anni precedentis *Reg. Rough* 217; *golf off corne*, ~ium, acervus, . .*reeke or golfe*, ~ius, acervus *PP*; **1434** pro clausura circa †arcomos feni regis *ExchScot* IV 592; **1456** cum. .arconio granorum *Ib.* VI 144; **1463** pro duobus ~iis feni emptis. . pro equis domine regine *Ib.* VII 189; **1471** in agardo de Tawelaght vij arconios sive cumulos granorum *Wills Dublin* 25; hic †arcomus, *a haystak*, . .*a stathele* WW; *a cok of hay or of corne*, arconius, . .*a mughe*, ~ius, . .*a stowke*, arconius, congelima *CathA*.

archonizare, archoniare, to stack.

c1240 in antiquo statuto iconomi grana decimalia acsi propria arconizabant et ad sua fenilia ducebant (*Syn. Sodor.*) *Conc.* I 665a (= *MonA* V 253); *stakkyn*, arconiso *PP*; ~izo, *to moweye*, . .arconio, A. *to stake* WW; *to mughe hay*, archoniare, ~izare *CathA*.

archonizator, stacker.

a mugher of hay, ~or *CathA*.

†**archonomolum,** stack.

c1240 modernis diebus rectores grana decimalia in arconomolis accipiunt ob majorem iconomorum commoditatem (*Syn. Sodor.*) *Conc.* I 665a (= *MonA* V 253).

archonticon [ἀρχοντικόν], sort of electuary.

electuaria dentur ut pliris, artoricon. . Gilb. II 111. 2; arcoticon, dyaciminum. . *Ib.* 124. 1; pliris [*gl.*: interpretatur arconticon, id est principale, et valet ad frigidum tollendum] Garl. *Mor. Scol.* 594.

archticus v. arthriticus. archus, ~ualis, v. arcu-.

arcicula [cf. arx], turret.

a towre, ~a, arx, turris, turricula *CathA*.

arcifactor, ~fector, bowyer.

1369 fletcharios, fabros pro capitibus sagittarum faciendis, archifactores, armurarios et *fourbours*. .pro operacionibus nostris in Turri nostra *Pat* 279 m. 14; **1466** officium supervisoris archifectorum nostrorum infra Turrim Londonie ac custodis arcuum nostrorum *Cl* 318 m. 17; **1568** officium archifectoris nostri ac supervisoris archifectorum *Pat* 1044 m. 36.

arcifer, ~ferarius, bow-bearer (*cf. arcubajulus*).

1446 [officium] archiferi *CalPat* 438; **1453** officium rangeatoris et archiferi haiarum de Allerwas Hay. .et Gauley Hay *Cl* 304 m. 18; **1470** officium archiferarii foreste nostre de Danby *Pat* 526 m. 12.

† **arciferrum,** (?) iron for bows.

1302 in xvij petris ferri emptis. .; item in iiij garbis arcifer' emptis. ., precium cujuslibet garbe xj d. *KRAc* 482/20 r. 20 (cf. ib.: in v garbis ascer' emptis, . .precium cujuslibet garbe viij d.).

arcifinius, ~ium [CL = adjoining boundary], land at edge of field, headland (in open field), croft.

adjacebant agris sationalibus ~ii [*gl.*: *foreres*] squalidi et uliginosi juxta novalia Balsh. *Ut.* 46; **13..** concessimus. . tria ortiphinia terre nostre in villa de Hatton' jacencia, quorum unum ortiphinium vocatur Bissepesecrofte et aliud ortiphinium Orchardestede *AncD* A 8893; hoc archifenium, *a crofe* WW; *an hede lande*, †aviseges, †artifinium, bifinium *CathA*.

arcillum v. argilla.

1 arcio [OF *arçon*], saddle-bow. **b** (?) bracket for altar curtain.

1217 Laurencius filius Thome sellatoris venit et tulit duo paria arconum de fine terre sue *KRMem* 1 r. 3*d.*; **1232** L. Sellator de Bedeford misit ad scaccarium duo paria ~onorum *Ib.* 12 r. 16; **1233** duo paria arcunorum *Ib.* 13 r. 12*d.*; **1237** in arzonibus. .et alio apparatu unius selle ad opus regine *Liberate* 11 m. 3; **c1285** prior de Neuenham tenet dim. hidam terre. .reddendo regi unum par arsonum alborum ad unam sellam *Aids* I 4; **1292** decem arbores de charme ad arsones sellarum regis inde faciendos *Cl* 109 m. 2. **b c1080** ij tapetas ad altaria, ij capitalia et iiij arcones et vj limbos cortinarum *Lib. Eli.* II 114 (= *MonA* I 477b).

2 arcio v. arsio.

†**arciolus** [cf. arculus], little arch.

aula. .columpnis et archiolis undique erat constructa, quasi monachorum claustrum *NLA* (*Patrick*) II 294.

arcionarius [cf. OF *arçonier*], for a saddle-bow. **b** (sb. ? n.) (?) cover of saddle-bow. **c** (sb. m.) (?) maker of saddle-bows.

1213 pro iiij ulnis et j quarterio de *blou* ad unam huciam ~iam ad unum equum domini regis *Misae* 239. **b 1208** vj d. pro canevac' et vj d. pro †artuuero [? l. arcunero] et xxv d. pro burra *Cl* 109a; **1349** unum hernes' de bokeram'. .viz. cropar', pectorale, testar' et arcenar', extencellat' cum argento (*KRAc* 391/15) *Arch.* XXXI 43; et j aliam sellam pro eadem domina operatam cum arsoneriis cum cornu cervino et coopertam cum velvetto *Ib.* 82. **c c1230** Savore Arzonario *Cart. Osney* II 356; **12..** terram Turberni Arconerii *AncD* A 7354.

arcionator [cf. OF *arçoneor*], (?) maker of saddle-bows.

c1230 Wydone Arcenatore *Cart. Osney* II 271.

arciotidas v. arceuthis. arcipitrarius v. accipitrarius. arcire v. arcere b.

arcirma [CL = *sort of vehicle*], wheelbarrow.

1573 unam †acirmam vocatam *a whelebarowe Pat* 1103 m. 2.

arcis v. ars 2a, arcus 3a, arx.

†**arciselus,** (*s. dub.*).

949 (14c) dedi cuidam meo homini. .~us ob studium quam mihi. .deservit. . *CS* 879.

arcista v. artista.

arcister, ~es [cf. arquites], archer.

~er, *strelbora GlC* A 810; ~is, sagittarius *Ib.* 758; arcister contorquens spicula ferri Aldh. *Aen.* 603; **c690** utpote belliger in meditullio campi ~er legionum falangibus saeptus aemulorum spissis *Id. Ep.* 5 p. 493.

arcisterium v. asceterium.

†**arcistria,** lectern.

a lettron, ambo, discus, lectrinum, ~ia *CathA*.

1 arcitenens [CL], archer. **b** bowyer. **c** captain or prince (? conf. w. *archi-* or w. 2 *arcitenens*).

s1124 in prima fronte xl architenentes caballos occiderunt Ord. Vit. XII 39 p. 458; **s1136** virilis pectoris ~entes usque ad quingentos conducens *G. Steph.* I 10; **1255** percepit unum architenentem cum arcu et sagittis *SelPlForest* 115; **1285** per sergentiam inveniendi domino regi in guerra architenentem. .per xl dies *PQW* 252b; **1325** ultra domum architenensium infra. .castrum *MinAc* 1147/23 r. 3; **1327** solebat invenire unum hominem armatum qui deberet esse dux xxx architenencium *Kelso* II no. 471; **s1337** misit. . multos armatos et architenentes et Wallenses Ad. Mur. 80; **s1386** factum est parliamentum Londoniis, ad quod venerunt armati et architenentes de tota Anglia *V. Ric. II* 74; architenens, A. *a narcher* WW; **s1461** per paucos. .architenentes. .compulsi erant retrorsum recedere *Reg. Whet.* I 390; **1469** pro gagiis. .trium architenencium stabuli *Exch Scot* 655. **b** ad portam S. Lazari manent architenentes qui faciunt balistas, arcus de acere, viburno, taxo, sagittas et hastas Garl. *Dict.* 124. **c** *a captan*, . .*a cheftane*, architenens, capitaneus, . .*a prince*, ~ens, dictator, presul, princeps *CathA*.

2 arcitenens [? < arcem tenens], Lord of Heaven.

dum pater arcitenens concessit Aldh. *Aen.* 100. 19; sic sator arcitenens dissolvit competa clausa *Id. VirgV* 1538; architenens altor, qui sidera clara gubernas Bonif. *Aen.* 2. 34; **972** (12c) perhennem gratulationem. .quam architenens hylariter a sui devotis accipiet *CS* 1285; **10..** ~ens, *heofenhæbbenda* WW.

†**arcithesis,** bowcase or quiver (*cf. arquitium*).

a whywer for bowes, architesis *CathA*.

†**arcitula,** bowstring.

hec ~a, *a bowstryng* WW.

arcium v. ars, arx. arcius v. archius, arte, artius. arco, ~onerius v. arcio, ~ionarius. arcom-, arconi- v. archoni-. arcontus v. archon. arcoticon v. archoniticon. arcta-, arcte v. art-.

arcticus [ἀρκτικός], arctic, northern.

ventorum ~orum constrictio Adel. *QN* 64; in extremis borealis oceani secessibus longe sub ~o polo Gir. *TH* II 17; polus mundi qui nobis semper apparet dicitur polus septentrionalis, articus vel borealis; . .articus quidem dicitur ab Arthos, quod est Major Ursa Sacrob. *Sph.* 87; non. .solum circa polum entarticum set etiam circa polum articum Bacon XIII 175; articus polus non †novebat [? l. noverat] Arturum J. Howd. *Cant.* 556.

arctitas, ~tudo, v. arti-.

†**arctoes** [? cf. plaustrum arctoum], cart-shaft.

archtoes, *waegnepixl GlC* A 743; temo vel ~es, *pisl* Ælf. *Gl.*

arctophylax [ἀρκτοφύλαξ], bearward. **b** Arcturus (astr.).

CAIUS *Can.* 7 (v. arctylus). **b** de ~ace, inicio septentrionalis circuli et solsticii estivalis NETTER *DAF* II 93.

arctos v. 1 arctus.

arctous [CL < ἀρκτῷος], arctic, northern.

mare ~um, *norðsæ* ÆLF. *Gl.*; latitudo ~as minoratur ad partes GIR. *TH* I 2; arthous boreas austro plus obstat GARL. *Tri. Eccl.* 131.

Arcturus [CL < Ἀρκτοῦρος], Arcturus, Boötes, or Charles' Wain (*Ursa Major*).

~us. .qui boreo aquilonalis poli cardine volvitur. .septiformi temonis et plaustri sidere signatur ALDH. *Met.* 6 p. 72; ~us, Orion et Canis. .caeteraque militia caeli BEDE *TR* 34; zodiacus ubi plus declinat ad austri / arcturique polos HANV. VIII 373; arcturum solus novit septentrio plaustrum NECKAM *DS* I 351; hic Pleiades conjungere, / girum Arthuri terere / suis valebit viribus J. HOWD. *Cyth.* 132 (cf. *Job* xxxviii 31); *Charelwain*, arthurus, plaustrum *CathA.*

1 arctus [CL < ἄρκτος], pole star. **b** north.

s1171 in regione Anglorum, †qui respicit ad Arthon *Becket Mat.* IV 167; quanto est erectior arctos [v.l. arthos] HANV. VIII 373; tranquillum pelagus promittit puppibus arthos GARL. *Tri. Eccl.* 30. **b** evacuatque suos populorum viribus arctus *V. Merl.* 1506; sensit salutaria. .fluenta. . novi Jordanis, qui de capite novi martyris emergens. . allabitur arton H. CANT. *Mir. Thom.* II 56; s1461 Austro tunc cesserat Arctos (*Versus*) *Reg. Whet.* I 413.

2 arctus v. 1 artus.

arctylus [ἀρκτύλος], bear-cub.

[canes villaticos] nostri. .ursos, tauros, ~os aliaque fera animalia, praefectis certaminum arctophylacibus, . .exagitare. .docent CAIUS *Can.* 7.

arcualis, bow-shaped, curved, arched. **b** of a bow.

si sic esset, non esset iris omnino ~is figure GROS. 76; aliquando basis pyramidis lucis solaris occupantis corpus lune apparet linea ~is. ., sed in septimo [die] apparet linea recta BACON *Maj.* II 109; ostendam quod in lineis ~ibus est proporcio secundum proporcionem suarum cordarum WALLINGF. *Quad.* 99; s1250 prope tumbam. .Malcolmi, in boreali parte navis ulterioris ecclesie sub testudine †arthuali [v.l. archuali] jacentis *Plusc.* VII 15. **b** 1420 (v. baculus 2f).

arcualiter, in a curve.

Humbra. .ab australi parte Eboracensium ~er decurrens HIGD. I 46.

1 arcuare [CL], to curve, arch. **b** to encircle.

cernuus ~atis poplitibus flexisque suffraginibus ALDH. *Ep.* 3 p. 479; cum postremo nasus ~ato acumine summitatis superficiem stimulabat R. COLD. *Cuthb.* 63 p. 124; molles aut arcuat artus / in talos refuga cervice VINSAUF *PN* 652. **b** 1376 est mensura garbe quantum homo potest ~are cum uno brachio tenendo zonam suam cum manu sua *IMisc.* 208/4.

2 (p. ppl.) curved, arched, twisted. **b** arched, vaulted. **c** (as sb. m.) jaundice.

usus calceorum cum ~atis aculeis W. MALM. *GR* IV 314; pedem rigidum et ~atum supportare W. CANT. *Mir. Thom.* II 11; s1199 sic ~ato vulnere telum dilapsum est deorsum COGGESH. 78; c1250 ne [velum] ~ata tangat supercilia J. GODARD *Ep.* 233. **b** 1292 in vadiis carpentariorum. . operancium quandam portam archeatam *KRAc* 486/7 (cf. ib.: cum. .iiij fenestris, quarum due sunt archeate); ibi [in Wokyhole] pendent pinnacula in *le voult* archuata mirabiliter de petris W. WORC. *Itin.* 288. **c** elephanticus vel hicteris vel †artuatus, *sydmycleadl* ÆLF. *Gl.*; dicitur morbus auriginosus et ~atus ab yride, id est ab arcu celesti GILB. VI 257 v. 2.

2 arcuare v. artuare.

arcuaria [cf. OF *archerie, archiere* < arcaria], archery. **b** arrow-slit, loophole. **c** (?) wickerwork.

1198 tenet in serjantia archerie *Fees* 5 (cf. ib. 1157); 1234 J. le Archier, qui de domino rege tenuit in capite per serjanteriam archerie *Exc. R. Fin.* I 262; 12. . foresta. . destructa est de bestiis per forestarios, per canes et archeream *CallMisc* I p. 144 (v. et. arcuarius b). **b** 1253 duo armariola, viz. unum ex una parte camini et aliud ex altera, cum duabus archeris *Liberate* 29 m. 12; 1260 in infimo stagio nove turelle. .tria ostia et tres archerias, per que lumen intrare possit, fieri facias *Ib.* 36 m. 6 (cf. ib. m. 5: tres archeras); 1304 domum fortem cum cranellis et arqueriis *RGasc.* III 428. **c** videbamus. .capsum contextum archera viscata BALSH. *Ut.* 50.

arcuariare, to practise archery.

1290 duobus archeriis regis euntibus ibidem. . ad archeriandum *Ac. Wardr.* (*Chanc. Misc.* 4/4) f. 48.

arcuarius [CL], bowyer. **b** bowman, archer.

1436 armurarii, ~ii, petiliarii et alii diversarum misterarum. .armaturam. .et alia habilitamenta guerre ad vendendum habentes *Cl* 286 m. 5; hic archarius, *a bowere* WW; 1473 J. M. factori armorum. .et N. P. ~io *ExchScot* 189; 1575 officium flechiarii sive archiarii *Pat* 1137 m. 5. **b** Willelmus ~ius *DB* I 48b; Rainaldus arcarius *Ib.* 160b; 1130 Sueinus archarius *Pipe* 75; de archeariis qui portabant arcum regis, unusquisque [debet habere] v. d. in die; et alii archearii tantundem *Domus Reg.* 135; Baldricus. . comitis archearius ORD. VIT. III 2. p. 35; 1156 in liberationibus archiariorum regis in exercitu *Pipe* 89; 1173 in liberatione x ~iorum *Pipe* 107; ut semper arcarii [v.l. sagittarii] militaribus turmis mixtim adjiciantur GIR. *EH* II 37 (cf. ib. I 11); 1198 duobus archeriis equitibus *Pipe* 172; 1214 sex archeriis qui venerunt ad servitium domini regis *Cl* 212a; 1228 faciendo inde domino regi. .servicium duorum archeriorum *Pat* 202; 12. . vallis. .multum deterioratur. .per archeriam Rogeri forestarii maxime et aliorum archeriorum de Lonisdaille *CalIMisc* I p. 144; 1290 pro vadiis. .archeriorum peditum *DocScot* p. 206; s1345 cum grandi comitatu armatorum et archeriorum AD. MUR. *app.* 243; s1455 pro. .militibus scutiferis, archariis, sagittariis ac omnibus aliis qui secum ad villam S. Albani venerant *Reg. Whet.* I 183.

2 arch-maker.

1518 [ab omnibus] lathomis, . .vitrariis, ~iis, tectoribus et domorum vallatoribus *Form. S. Andr.* I 6.

arcuatio, arch, vault. **b** arch (of eyebrows).

ubi fonticuli per occultas fistulas aquas. .ex abstrusis terre visceribus sursum in receptaculum per cameratas ~ones gloriose dispositum emanant *G. Steph.* I 28. **b** superciliorum ~o GILB. VII 340. 1.

arcuator, archer.

1465 propter gravem multitudinem ~orum cum rege contra nautas (*Act Bk. Rochester*) *Arch. Cant.* LIII 59.

arcubajulus, bow-bearer (*cf. arcifer*).

s1100 W. Tyrel, ~us regis et miles M. PAR. *Abbr* 178; 1471 officium ~i septem haiarum circa le Cankewode in com. nostro Stafford' *Pat* 527 m. 11.

1 arcubalista [< arcus+ballista; cf. arbalista], arblast, crossbow.

c1185 [habeat] minutorum quilibet unam lanceam, unam ~am et xv s. argenti *Ps.-Cnut*) *GAS* 621; sunt in eis [oppidis]. . / arcus, lorice, galee gladiique, sagitte, / archībāliste, saxorum pondera dura D. BEC. 1865; s1199 tetendit ~am atque quoddam quarellum violenter direxit ad regem COGGESH. 77b; 1212 G. Balistarius [tenet] vj carucatas de dono regis J. per duas archibalistas *Fees* 227; s1346 cariagia et currus ~is, telis. .et aliis armis onerata *Meaux* III 59; *stonebow*, ~a *PP*.

2 arcubalista, arblaster, crossbowman.

s1099 funditores lapidibus, sagittarii jaculis, ~e telis, quisque suum exercentes officium, instare W. MALM. *GR* IV 368; s1199 quidam ~a. .traxit sagittam de castello R. HOWD. IV 82.

arcubalistarius, arblaster, crossbowman.

Nicholaus Archibalistarius *DB Exon* 67b (= *DB*: N. Arbalestarius); s1138 architenentes et ~ii gentis Anglorum equitibus permixti, imbre sagittarum. .Scotos quos inermes repererunt penetrabant M. PAR. *Min.* I 260 (= *Id. Maj.* II 169: sagittarii); s1339 magistrum ~iorum regis Francie *G. Ed. III Bridl.* 148; s1341 cum mmmm armatis et mcccc Januensibus arcubalisteriis *Meaux* III 50; s1346 multitudinem ~iorum Aquitaniensium jussit. .decollari *Ib.* 59.

†arcubilus, archer.

~us, A. *an archer* WW.

arcubius [CL], **arcubus,** sentinel.

~ius, . .hic †arculius, *a wayte* WW; *a sawdyour*, ~us, qui cubat in arce *CathA.*

arcubutericius [cf. arcbuttans, butericius], flying buttress (*cf. Building in England* 97, 135).

1320 cementario operanti circa archibuteracium camere Marculfi, qui buteracius fuit debilis et in puncto corruendi *KRAc* 469/1.

arcudium v. armicudium.

arcula [CL], **~us,** coffer, coffer-lid.

mozitia vel ~a, *tæg* ÆLF. *Gl.*; *a corfyrlyd* [v.l. *cofer leyd*], ~us *CathA.*

arculius v. arcubius. 1 arculus v. arcula.

2 arculus, saddle-bow (*cf. arcio*). **b** oxbow. **c** fiddle-bow.

~i duo, sc. antella et postella; suas habeat antellas et postellas, ut vestes bene disponantur in mantica NECKAM *Ut.* 100; ~us, A. *the arsyon of a sadelle* WW; *a sadylle bow*, ~us *CathA.* **b** 1350 in viij ~is emptis pro bobus, ij d. (*MinAc*) *Surv. Durh. Hatf.* 257. **c** *a fidylle stik*, ~us *CathA.*

arcunus v. arcio.

arcuositas, curvature.

creatura superbiens, . .si reputaverit se humiliter in medio mundi sensibilis secundum corpus maxime distans a circumferencia infinita, tunc erit secundum ~atem maximam plenissima gracia WYCL. *Mand. Div.* 145.

arcuosus, curved.

et huic figure [quadrato iiij punctorum] convenit circulus sive spera, et illa spericitas est maxime ~a, multiplicata per totum, cum sit primus gradus et simplicissimus WYCL. *Log.* III 60; geometris qui norunt aquam in vase non superficiem planam sed ~am expetere *Id. Mand. Div.* 145.

arcura [OF *archure*], wooden shield of mill-wheel (C.I.).

1328 in meremio empto pro ij novis alveolis et pro ij ~is cum bordis et clavibus ad ij molendina. .reparanda *KRAc* 89/11 m. 3.

arcus [CL], bow. **b** (dist. acc. make). **c** stone-bow. **d** crossbow. **e** (w. *pravus*) 'deceitful bow' (cf. *Psalm* lxxvii [lxxviii] 57).

sagittarum spicula de. .feretrae latibulis depromens, . .pando strepente ~u et nervo stridente ad destinatum. . dirigit locum ALDH. *VirgP* 2 p. 230; ~us, *boga* ÆLF. *Gl.*; 1209 inventus fuit in chimino magno in foresta cum ~u sine corda *SelPlForest* 6; 1236 per serjantiam unius arci, v sagittarum et j buzenn' *Fees* 601 (cf. ib. 586: per servicium j ~us de auburno); a1250 ad. .aditum [del Odd] de Ald Ravenserre via patebat arenosa. .latitudinem quantum ~us jacere potest vix habens *Meaux* II 30; 1264 in cordellis emptis ad archos *KRAc* 3/3 r. 2; 1298 pro. .quarellis pennandis et ~is emendandis (*KRAc* 7/1 r. 6) *DocScot* 322; hircina. .herba aspera est, qua solent polliri pectines et archus *Alph.* 82; distat ab insula Man per tres sagittaciones ~us W. WORC. *Itin.* 152. **b** non autem ~u utuntur corneo, non alburneo, non taxeo; solum ex ulmellis silvestribus ~us formant GIR. *IK* I 4; unde et ~us taxei dicuntur NECKAM *NR* II 70; s1191 tot ~us Turkenses *Itin. Ric.* IV 19; 1235 ij ~us Turkes' cum ij cordis de corio *Chanc. Misc.* 3/4; 1315 tenens unum ~um qui vocatur Turkeys de taxu de Ispania facto (*sic*) de j corda tento in manum suam sinistram de longitudine j ulne regis et dim. et de grossitudine in girum v pollicum hominis *CoramR* 220 r. 105*d.*; Turci quorum ~us sunt de cornu curvi S. SIM. *Itin.* 53; 1306 xxix ~us manuales de omello *KRAc* 486/20; 1315 pro factura d quarellorum ad ~um de pilo *Cl* 132 m. 19; 1359 cccc ~us depictos et cc ~us albos (*Cl*) *Foed. ed.* 1825 III 454; 1390 pro vj ~ubus latis *Ac. H. Derby* 34; 1391 lx ~us pro bosco, . .iiij duodenas sagittarum pro bosco (*Cl*) *Foed.* VII 699. **c** 13. . nullus infra civitatem. .portet ~um de petra [OF: *arc a perre*], viz. *stonebowe MGL* I 251 (cf. ib. 278). **d** 1224 recepisse. .ij ~us ad balistam de cornu ad j pedem et j alium ~um ad j pedem crudum *Pat* 453; 1328 c ~us balistos ad pedem et xx ~us balistos ad troll' (*Cl* 147) *Foed.* IV 367; 1416 j ~um vocatum *arblast Reg. Cant.* II 103; 1513 cum. .~ubus planis et cruciferis *Reg. Butley* 29; 1532 sagittacionem in quodam ~u cruciato *KRMem* 311 *Rec. P.* r. 8. **e** 1167 mentiuntur Romanam ecclesiam nobis conversam esse in ~um pravum (J. SAL. *Ep.* 204) *Becket Mat.* VI 198; s1187 tantam unitatis constantiam converterent in ~um pravum GERV. CANT. I 354; s1189 Constantinopolitanus imperator versus in ~um pravum non est adhuc ad cor reversus *Flor. Hist.* II 103; in ~um. . pravum conversus, duo. .agere attemptavit OCKHAM *Err. Papae* 958.

2 rainbow.

10. . yris vel ~us, *renboga* WW; arcus celestis imitatur gemma colores NECKAM *DS* VI 303; quod Aristotiles dicit ~um varium apud ortum et occasum solis parve esse mensure GROS. 77; GILB. VI 257 v. 2 (v. 1 arcuare 2c); usus armorum erat post diluvium, cum tunc primo apparuit ~us celestis, id est iris, diversi coloris BAD. AUR. 144.

3 (*cf. arculus*): **a** saddle-bow; **b** ox-bow; **c** handle of bucket.

a 1226 homines de Bedeford' tulerunt ad scaccarium duo paria ~uum ad sellam de redditu Lamberti Sellarii *LTRMem* 9 r. 1 (1) *d.*; colliget unam summam virgarum. .; et habebit †arcem que est ultra cellam unde summa ligatur, pariter et alterum baculum qui est ex altera parte equi portantis summam in occulo dicte ~is *Cust. Bleadon* 203; 13. . de ~ubus sellarum [OF: *arzons de seles*] equestrium *MGL* II 50 (cf. ib. 80). **b** 9. . boia, ~us vel *geoc* WW; debet ire in wodelonde. .propter juga boum et ~us *Cust. Bleadon* 203; 1261 inveniet funes et ~us ad carucas domini *MinAc Wint.* (*Chilbolton*); 1267 in meremio ad ij carucas scapellando cum ~ubus et hart' ad easdem *MinAc* 824/6 r. 1*d.*; 1270 in. . xiij jugis, xviij ~ubus et meremio ad duas novas carucas *Ac. Stratton* 32; 1293 in ~ubus boum *DCCant* (*Ac. Cliffe*) (cf. ib.: *in oxseboghes*); 1295 de ~ubus ad juga boum *Pipe* 141 r. 28*d.*; 1341 in ij ~ubus bovinis emptis, j d. *MinAc* 1120/11 r. 8; 1454 xxx ~us boum *Ac. Durh.* 150. **c** c1400 in iiij ~ubus emptis pro iiij warepaill', ij d. *MinAc Essex* (*Foulness*) r. 1.

4 arch or vault (in building). **b** (of bridge or tunnel). **c** (w. ref. to burial). **d** (triumphal) arch. **e** arched recess. **f** (w. ref. to church of St. Mary le Bow). **g** (w. ref. to Court of Arches, originally held at St. Mary le Bow).

~us, *forbigels* ÆLF. *Gl.*; 9. . camera, ~us, fornax, *bigels*, *boga*, *incleofa* WW; ambitus ipsius edis dupplici lapidum ~u ex utroque latere hinc et inde fortiter solidata operis compage clauditur *V. Ed. Conf.* 49; infra ~us supra introitum cancelli positos *Mir. J. Bev.* A 298; 1192 de duabus domibus sub archa *CurR RC* I cvi; 1237 archiam in aula nostra ibidem reparari facias *Cal. Liberate* VI 2436; 1238 quod archeam subtus privatam cameram regis. .barris ferreis barrari faciat *Cl* 99; 1249 levabunt novum gablum. . cum una archa vel duabus. .in eodem loco *Cart. Osney* I 363; 1275 prostrabit totum murum inter ecclesiam. .et cancellum usque ad ~um lapideum *SelPlMan* 150; 1387 super reparacione. .turrium, archiarum, murorum et contramurorum infra castellum *KRAc* 183/12 f. 30*d.*; hec archus, *a vowt* WW; in aliis duobus panellis. .sunt due arche W. WORC. *Itin.* 401. **b** c1170 Roberto de Ponte Archarum *FormA* 48; s1209 hoc anno fuit fundatio arche pontis Londonie *Ann. Berm.* 451; 1221 pons ille jam peractus est preter unam ~am *SelPlCrown* 114; 1233 fieri faciat archias in introitu et exitu bovarum castri Dovr' *Liberate* 10 m. 9; 1307 pro emendacione j arche pontis borealis *Rec. Leic.* I 262; 1340 in reparacione archie stagni *Ac. Durh.* 538; c1430 preter communem semitam. .inter ~as domibus contiguas adjacentes et terras dicte fosse adjacent AMUND. I *app.* 429; 1448 pro reparacione. .arche lacus de Linlithgow *ExchScot* 304. **c** s1113 postea. .in secretario. .ecclesie, Acca quidem ad dextrum cornu altaris et Alchmundus ad sinistrum, decentius in duobus ~ubus positi sunt RIC. HEX. *Pri. Hex.* 4; **1415** lego..corpus meum ad sepeliendum in archa nove capelle ecclesie *Reg. Cant.* II 70; **1420** lego..corpus meum sacre sepulture..in primo archu dicti claustri *Ib.* 230. **d** ~us triumphales tunc proficiunt illustribus viris..cum..quorum sint impressa docet inscriptio J. SAL. *Pol.* 385B; **s1415** apparuit..quasi castrum..circa eam [crucem de Cheepe].. habens ex utraque parte ~us testudinatos..sub quibus.. populus velut per duas janua equitabat ELMH. *Hen. V* 65. **e** **1189** licet vicinus habeat in..muro..~us sive almeria, ..nihil amplius potest in predicto muro exigere (*Assisa Domorum*) *MGL* I 326 (cf. ib. 322: si ~us habere voluerint, facient ex utraque parte). **f** tectum ecclesie S. Marie que 'ad ~us' dicitur W. MALM. *GR* IV 324; **c1140** scolas S. Marie de Archa *E. Ch. S. Paul* 217; **s1271** campanile lapideum B. Marie de ~ubus in foro Londoniarum cecidit *Ann. Lond.* 81; **1377** custodibus operis ecclesie B. Marie de ~ubus *IMisc* 213/6 r. 4. **g** **1267** decanus de ~ubus *Cl* 309; **1289** quod..procuretis dictam causam alicui discreto committi extra ~us (*DCCant*) *HMC Var.* I 253; **1323** auditoribus causarum curie vestre et consistorii vestri de ~ubus Londoniensis *Lit. Cant.* I 98; **1335** cuidam apparatori de ~ubus *Comp. Swith.* 239; **1338** bedellus de ~ubus capit per annum..vj s. viij d. *Hosp. in Eng.* 209; **s1452** transferri facit..solucionem questionis ad doctiores jurisperitos totius curie de ~ubus *Reg. Whet.* I 19; officialis almae curiae Cantuariensis de ~ubus est judex competens ad cognoscendum de causis ecclesiasticis quibuscunque..necnon in causis appellationum..a quibuscunque episcopis.. *Praxis* 3.

5 something bow-shaped or arched, curve. **b** arc (geom.).

geminos intersecet arcus [*eyebrows*] / lactea forma vie VINSAUF *PN* 564; nunc brachia curvat in arcum / infurcata manus lateri *Ib.* 657. **b** nec minor et medie qui nocti ascribitur arcus / dimidiumque diem metiri dicitur arcu HANV. VIII 372; GROS. 20 (v. ascensio 2a); isti circuli [quos describit sol] dierum naturalium appellantur: ~us autem qui sunt supra orizontem sunt ~us dierum artificialium; ~us vero qui sunt sub orizonte sunt ~us noctium SACROB. *Sph.* 102; communiter sumpta altitudo rei super horizontem dicitur ~us circuli altitudinis interceptus inter rem elevatam et inter horizontem BACON *Maj.* II 176; **1326** linea *GI* est corda recta ~us anguli *AEF* WALLINGF. *Rect.* II *pref.*

†arcutere [? *infl; by* percutere], to shoot w. a bow.

s1284 insidiavit cum uno arcu de *yf* tendito, unde corda fuit *caume*, in manu sinistra, nequiter et in felonia arcussit ad eum cum una sagitta *barble Ann. Dunstable* 309.

arcutus v. arrentare a.

†arcuus, of a bow.

1385 judicium collistrigii pro falsis cordis ~is [? l. arcus; *but* cf. *Cal. LBLond. H* 272] *MGL* I 608.

ardalio [CL < ἄρδαλος], trouble-maker, trickster. **b** glutton.

s1417 tanta fuit ~onis [sc. J. Oldcastill'] demencia ut putaret se post triduum a mortuis resurrecturum *Chr. S. Alb.* 117; *lowmysman or woman, ..slyman and doggyd,* ardulio *PP.* **b** †adoleo, glutto *GlC* A 242.

ardaliosus, crafty, deceitful.

lowmysh, arduliosus *PP.*

ardalitas, craftiness, deceit.

lowmyshnesse, ardulitas *PP.*

†ardamare, to taste.

~o i. gusto, *ic gesmecge* ÆLF. *Gl.*

ardator [cf. 2 ardor, arsor], burner (of lime).

1351 vij ~oribus calcis..vigilantibus super combustione creti pro calce inde faciendo *KRAc* 492/27 r. 5.

ardea [CL; *infl. by* arduus], heron.

~ea, *hragra* et dieperdulum *GlC* A 729; ~ea, *hragra* ÆLF. *Gl.*; ~ea rerum arduarum auspicium est J. SAL. *Pol.* 411B; ardea visa fuit fluviali proxima ripe NIG. *SS* 2793; ~ea quasi ardua dicitur NECKAM *NR* I 63; ardea.. / ardet adire Jovem, petit ardua, nubibus ardet *Id. DS* II 651; accipitrem suum optimum ad ~eam..leva projecit GIR. *GE* I 54; **1399** pro duobus falconibus pro ardua *IssueR* 561 r. 14; **1451** piscariis, aucupacionibus, proficuis..arduorum *Cl* 301 m. 21*d.*; hec ardua, A. *heyrune*, ..hec ardia, *a haron* WW.

ardearius, used in the pursuit of herons (*cf. tardearius*).

1242 tres leporarios nostros ~ios custodiri [facias] *Liberate* 16 m. 10; **1242** quod omnes aves regis, tam gyrofalcones quam ancipitres et falcones ~ios..volare faciat *Cl* 514; **1253** tenuit..per serjantiam..a domino rege, ita quod debet custodire falcones lanarios ~ios *IPM* 14/1; **1257** falcones ~ios et leporarios *Cl* 170; **1290** falco arduarius *CalIPM* p. 473.

ardeda v. andera.

Ardena, liberty of the forest of Arden (cf. *Eyre Lincs & Worcs* 447).

1275 fecit de novo quoddam cunicular' in bosco de Mandeveleye, quod fuit libera ~a *Hund.* (*Worcs*) II 284 (cf. ib. 285).

ardenter [CL], ardently.

veritas..quae quanto studiosius..inquiritur, tanto ~ius deligitur ERIUG. *Per.* 572C; puella..in ipsum..petulantes oculos ~er injecit GIR. II 17.

ardentia, ardent passion.

migret amor amens, ardentie / totum habens, nihil ucentie J. HOWD. *Phil.* 466.

ardeola, (young) heron.

an heron', ardea, ~a, *an heron' sewe,* ardiola *CathA.*

ardēre [CL], to burn (intr.), be on fire. **b** (pr. ppl.) burning, hot (*v. et. aqua* 4b). **c** (w. *lapis*) coal. **d** (inf. as sb.) fuel (Norm.).

~ebat, *scaan GlC* A 801; nec crepitante foco nec scintillante favilla / ardeo ALDH. *Aen.* 15 (*Salamandra*) 4; calor ~entibus ~endi est causa ERIUG. *Per.* 602C; partem candele peruste alteri arsure compegit *Canon. G. Sempr.* 76v; **1236** nichil amplius cepit ad *husbote* et *haybote* et ad ~endum *BNB* III 179; **1271** estoverium..ad ~endum, claudendum et domos..reparandas *Cl* 366; **s1258** arsit monasterium FERR. *Kinloss* 25. **b** in ~entes thermarum vapores ALDH. *VirgP* 51; ardens carbo fuit Laurentius, ignis in igne P. BLOIS *Euch.* 23. **1151** C; ardenti spolio vestitur sidere celum HANV. VIII 371; **1397** tenentur invenire unam lampadem ~entem coram †ymaginem B. Virginis (*Vis. Heref.*) *EHR* XLIV 450. **c** **1313** unum plaustrum lapidum ~entium (*Yorks Deeds*) *VCH Yorks* II 339. **d** **a1150** habeat suum hardere et suum edificare in foresta mea de Tisone *Regesta* 381.

2 (fig.) to burn, glow: **a** (w. desire); **b** (w. anger or grief); **c** (pr. ppl.) ardent, fierce; **d** (pr. ppl.) *s. dub.*; **e** (pr. ppl. pl.) etym. of seraphim.

sicut quis ~et in corpore per inlicitam voluptatem, ita solutus corpore ~ebit per debitam poenam BEDE *HE* III 19; quod explices ~ens exspecto ERIUG. *Per.* 599D; non mea lux ardet, accendere si tua tardet P. BLOIS *Euch. prol.* 1137D. **b** **801** episcopus multum ~et super nos ALCUIN *Ep.* 248; collamentantur et ardent / funditus internis cruciatibus usque dolendo *V. Merl.* 196. **c** ~ens mentis desiderium ALDH. *VirgP* 14; ~entis fidei defensaculo fretus *Ib.* 28; ~ens devotio mentis BEDE *HE* I 7; dolor.., omnis et de brachio, ubi ~entior inerat, ..ablatus est *Ib.* V 3. **d** **1213** j furrura de grisio ~enti ad supertunicam domini regis de russetto *Misae* 258. **e** vult Deus ut.. simus ~endo seraphim; seraphim enim interpretatur '~entia' P. BLOIS *Serm.* 39. 680A.

3 (trans.) to burn, destroy (a building). **b** (fig.) to harm.

c1249 deprecamur quatenus..detis nobis..vestras patentes litteras..sicut fecerat dominus rex Ricardus, que arserunt cum capella..que erat in castro quod arsit vicecomes (*AncC* III 73) *RL* II 59. **b** **1329** considerantes quod hoc forsitan fumo flammam ignis producet qui invitos ~ebit *Lit. Cant.* I 297.

4 (trans.) to burn: **a** (candle or torch); **b** (fuel); **c** (charcoal); **d** (land, by beat-burning; *cf. batare*); **e** (lime); **f** to anneal (clay); **g** to smelt (ore).

a candelam ~ebis totam (*Mir. Brit.*) DICETO *Chr.* 13; **c1300** iiij cereos..ad missam..~endos *Reg. Malm.* II 374; **1451** duorum torticorum quos ordinavi ~endos *MunAcOx* 618. **b** **1236** de vivo boscho in dictis terris non ~ebunt nec dabunt nec vendent *BBC* (*Ayr*) 336; **1242** arcerunt turbas..in mora *Assize R. Durh.* 27. **c** **1195** hunc autem carbonem ~ebit predictus faber quamdiu ipse voluerit (*Ch.*) *Hist. Brit. Iron & Steel Ind.* 341; **1308** quod possit.. ~ere carbones de omni genere bosci (*Indent.*) *Pat* 321 m. 26; **1337** de H. Coliere pro licencia ardend' carbon' de mortuo bosco *KRAc* 131/27 m. 6. **d** **1236** potuit eam [terram] howare, ~ere et excolere *BNB* III 165. **e** **1277** quod calcetum mensuretur per sportam que tenet dim. quarterium, bene arsa et fideliter mensurata (*LBLond. A* 130) *MGL* I 729; **1396** ita quod..calcem ~eant in predicto *lympette* omni tempore apto ad calcem ~endum *AncD* C 5304. **f** **1277** quod tegule sint bene arse et bene plumbate (*LBLond. A* 130) *MGL* I 729. **g** **1196** in custamento ~endi minam *Pipe* 261; **a1314** ad ~endum mineram *ChartR* 101 m. 12.

5 to fall short in assay by 'blanching' (*cf. blancus* 2). **b** (p. ppl.) 'blanched'.

tunc inscribitur idem examen, desuper ducta creta, hiis verbis: 'Everwicscira: libra arsit tot vel tot denariis'; et tunc illud essaium dicitur *Dial. Scac.* I 6H; **1238** libra novorum denariorum cambii Lond' lacat in examine viij d. ..; argentum non fuit pure examinatum, quia si pure esset examinatum ~eret usque ad x d. *KRMem* 17 r. 1. **b** hoc suburbium reddit xx libras arsas et pensatas et iii molina reddunt x libras ad numerum *DB* I 132; **1212** reddendo inde ad scaccarium annuatim xlij li. argenti arsas et ponderatas *Fees* 71; **1275** solebat reddere..iiij^{xx} libras arsas et ponderatas per annum *Hund.* II 297.

ardescens, burning. **b** (fig.) glowing, ardent.

pendeo.. / ignibus ardescens necnon et gurgite fervens ALDH. *Aen.* 49 (lebes) 3; rogus ardescens *Id. VirgV* 1758. **b** mens virgineis ardescens torrida flammis *Ib.* 1986; ardescente fide WULF. *Swith.* I 1052.

ardia, ~iola, v. ardea, ~eola. ardicomata v. ortygometra.

arditus [cf. Sp. *ardite*], *hardi*, coin of Guienne.

1409 levare posset de omnibus personis transeuntibus septem †ardicos [l. ~os] pro quocumque †conello [l. tonello] de *gaide*, duos †ardicos cum dim. pro quacumque pipa vini (*DipDocE* 374) *Foed.* VIII 576; **1410** v †ardicos Guiaynes (*Ib.* 375) *Ib.* 580.

1 ardor [CL], fire, heat. **b** passion. **c** intensity, ferocity.

laxis ardor fornacis regnat habenis ALDH. *Aen.* 80. 3; nullo solis ~ore BEDE *HE* I 1; percussa febribus acri coepit ~ore fatigari *Ib.* IV 21 p. 256. **b** **634** Christianitatis vestrae integritas..fidei est ~ore succensa (*Lit. Papae*) BEDE *HE* II 17; torrido castitatis ~ore flagrans ALDH. *VirgP* 23 p. 254; semper bibis cum delectabili ~ore ipsum desiderium ANSELM (*Or.* 13) III 54; nisi naturalis cupidinis ~or et amor animum alliceret GIR. *GE* II 2; puella ab adolescentis ~ore liberata WEND. II 294. **c** **s1272** accidit..aeris tempestas, ..in cujus tempestatis ~ore flamma fulgoris diversa loca incendit *Plusc.* VII 28.

2 ardor [OF *ardeor* < ardator; cf. arsor], smelter.

1213 mittatis ad..H. Dublin' archiepiscopum in Hibernia quatuor bonos ~ores de mineria nostra ad morandum ibidem in mineria nostra *Cl* 146b; **1290** impedit et defendit predictos mineritores solvere minerium suam illis emptoribus qui vocantur ~ores *KR Ext. & Inq.* (*Derb*) 3/2/16.

ardua v. ardea.

arduare, to lift.

educit cubitum, flexam procul arduat ulnam HANV. V 311.

arduarius v. ardearius.

ardue, w. an effort.

s1226 ut..ostenderent comitem tam ~e penitentem ad lucis filios pertinere WEND. II 298.

arduitas [CL], steepness. **b** difficulty.

saxa montis ejusdemque cacuminis ~as Britonibus defensio erat G. MON. IV 9; desperantemque relabi / arduitas cogat HANV. III 281. **b** in tantam ~atem excrescent negotia GIR. *Inv.* I 4 p. 95; **1260** istius negotii ~atem ponderantes *Cl* 273; **1334** considerata tanti ~ate negocii *RScot* 298b; **1424** negocia..quorum quedam propter eorum ~atem ..remanserunt inexpedita *Reg. Heref.* 59.

2 power to ascend, uplift. **b** (as title of justiciar) eminence (Gasc.).

1488 eidem patri in tribus nature donis aptissime poterit aquila convenire: ..in animi regimine est rectoris nobilitas, in visus acumine sensus subtilitas et in alarum libramine precellens ~as *Reg. Whet.* I 454. **b** **1220** nobilitatis et strenuitatis vestre ~atem preclaram specialius exorare audemus (*AncC* I 164) *RL* I 139.

ardul- v. ardal-. 1 arduus v. ardea.

2 arduus [CL], steep. **b** erect, tall, long. **c** (n. pl. as sb.) heights (esp. fig.).

montem..in uo nihil repente ~um, nihil praeceps, nihil abruptum BEDE *HE* I 7 p. 20; pauperem vitam in montibus, silvis vel rupibus ~is..agebant *Ib.* I 14; in summis..aereorum ~orumque collium verticibus GIR. *TH* I 4. **b** †artuus, erectus *GlC* A 789; †artoa, excelsa atque alta *Ib.* 754. lancea dextram suam [Arturi] decorat, que nomine Ron vocabatur; hec ~a erat lataque lancea cladibus apta G. MON. IX 4; dextrarios..cervicibus ~is W. FITZST. *Thom. prol.* 11. **c** volitans super ardua pennis ALDH. *Aen.* 36. 2; monuit.. / ardua sectari necnon devexa caveri *Id. VirgV* 762; longos per gyros semper ad ~a tendentes GIR. *TH* I 12; NECKAM *DS* II 653 (v. ardea).

2 arduous, difficult. **b** hard-won.

ad exemplum rigidae conversationis et ~i formam propositi animos militantium Christo instigantes ALDH. *VirgP* 8. **b** ardua lucra labor pariens non est honerosus D. BEC. 1251.

3 large. **b** weighty, important.

advecta est subito Danorum ~a non nimia classis, dromones numero tres ÆTHELW. iii 1; ~o (*sic*) cum manu *Ib.* iv 3 (cf. ib. p. xlviii). **b** **1257** non decere illam divinissimam sedem decreta..suorum predecessorum absque ~a et rationabili causa..in irritum revocare *Mon. Francisc.* II *app.* 272; **1292** sine ~a causa *MunAcOx* 59; **1376** munimenta ~a, que transeunt sub illo sigillo, registrentur *Conc.* III 111 (cf. *Cant. Cath. Pri.* 67n.); **1432** ob ~am causam *March S. Wales* 82.

1 area v. aerea. 2 area (Anglica) v. archangelicus 2 3 area v. 1 ara b.

4 area [CL], open space, plot. **b** building site. **c** churchyard. **d** castle bailey. **e** garden bed (also fig.). **f** battlefield or lists. **g** (w. *molarum*) millstone quarry (Norm.) **h** (w. *tentoriorum*) tenter-yard. **i** area (math.).

tota campi area..beneficium..stercorationis ecorum.. sentiat NECKAM *Ut.* 112; **a1236** notum sit..me..dedisse.. unam aream prati..que continet xx pedes in..latudine *Reg. Ant. Linc.* IV 89 no. 1206; **1283** tradiderunt..unam aream terre et unum stabulum, que continent in longitudine x ulnas regias *Cart. Osney* I 94. **b** aree facies equatur chelindro NECKAM *NR* II 172; **s1225** Cantuarie contulit eis [fratribus] aream quandam et edificavit capellam..magister hospitalis sacerdotum ECCLESTON *Adv. Min.* 25; **1244** faciat habere fratribus Minoribus Ebor' xl m. ad fabricam nove aree sue *Liberate* 20 m. 14; **1255** de xl m. quas..gardiano et conventui [fratrum Minorum Burdeg'] concessimus ad quandam aream inde emendam ad situm domus sue ampliandum *Ib.* 32 m. 12; **1254** †areram vastam..que extendit in longum juxta viam *RGasc* I 418; **1280** aream competentem..in qua vicarius possit domos facere *Reg. Heref.* 238; **c1280** recipiet a domino aream ad componendum messuagium (*Cust.*) *Crawley* 238; **1443** unam aream sive fundum *Deeds Balliol* 125. **c** postquam corpus ejus tanquam mortuum in area collocatum [est] *Mir. Montfort* 77. **d** arcem palatinam.., cujus et area et muri a fundamento profundissimo exsurgunt W. FITZST. *Thom. prol.* 5. **e** area salvie corona rute cingi..debet NECKAM *NR* II 121; GIR. *Rem.* 20 (v. areola b); area sermonis ut floreat his speciebus / florum VINSAUF *PN* 1585. **f** **s1066** dux victoria consummata ad aream belli regressus est ORD. VIT. III 14 p. 151; nonne est stolidus miles qui quietem querit in pugna et ediam in area [ME: *eise iþe place*] ? *AncrR* 139. **g** aream molarum in silva Bole dedit S. Marie, ita ut ex singulis molis ij d. dentur ad luminaria ecclesie Ord. Vit. V 19 p. 449. **h 1384** unam aream tentoriorum..que est modo predictum gardinum *Cl* 225 m. 49. **i** amplior excludit egresse cuspidis orbem / area zodiaci Hanv. VIII 373.

2 threshing-floor. **b** (fig.).

area, ..*flor on to perscenne* Ælf. *Gl.*; fleverunt eum..in area Athan [cf. *Gen.* l 10] Beleth *RDO* 159. 159; in area triturare aut ab area..gelimas..collectas horreis commendare Neckam *Ut.* 113; ubi segetes triturabantur in area *Latin Stories* 6; **1312** decime stantes in area durante autumpno *Reg. Aberbr.* I 284. **b** sanctae messis manipulos..metens in area tortoris triturandos Aldh. *VirgP* 36 p. 282; predicatoris..in area ecclesie separationem palearum a granis triturantis Gir. *GE* II 33.

3 salt-floor, salt-pan.

in Spallinge habebat..aream salinarum reddentem iiii den. *DB* I 368; **a1195** unam salinam..cum tribus areis salinariis que a vulgo *flores* dicuntur *CalCh* III 85; **a1200** dedi unam middam salis de feodo meo.., sc. de area quam W. tenuit de me *Ch. Gilb.* 87; **1316** tenent quarterium..et continet xv acras et unam acram aree et hoge *Terr. Fleet* 4; tenent..unam hogam cum area pro qua dant ij modios salis *Ib.* 7 (cf. ib. lxii); **1321** est ibidem una salina cum una hoga et area *IPM* 67/4 r. 5; **1338** una acra aree et hoge est pertinens huic dim. bovate *Cl.* 161 m. 12; **1399** *CalCl* 374.

4 floor. **b** flooring (of planks), storey. **c** deck (naut.).

[monialis vitiosa] in area refectorii sine mappula et mensa comedat ut confundatur et peniteat (*Inst. Sempr.*) *MonA* VI 947* xlix; **1184** pro exaltanda area dominice aule regis apud Westmonasterium *Pipe* 137; jusserat quaque die novo stramine vel feno in hieme, novis scirpis vel frondibus virentibus in estate, sterni hospitium suum, ut militum multitudinem quam scamna capere non poterant, area munda et leta reciperet W. Fitzst. *Thom.* 11; in ecclesia de Houedene persone..concubina tumbe..lignee in sedilis modum super aream eminenti, ..insedit Gir. *IK* I 2; pueri ..stent ante alios in area ex utraque parte pulpiti *Offic. Sal.* 30; cecidit [candela] in aream [coquine], ubi multum straminis..colligebatur *Canon. G. Sempr.* 76v.; **1365** pro vij mil' tegul' de Flandr' emptis pro pavimento arearum..; pro vj mouncellis plastri Parys' emptis pro areis..turris.. plasterandis *KRAc* 472/14 r. 1; **1397** rector tenetur invenire stramina..pro area ecclesie (*Vis. Heref.*) *EHR* XLV 97; **1461** pro *le pavyng* aree coquine *Ac. Durh.* 90; **1472** aria capelle est quodammodo defectiva *Fabr. York* 252. **b** area, *breda piling* Ælf. *Gl.*; unam nobilem domum..construxit abbas [Johannes, ob. 1260]..; quia duplicem habet aream, in superiori sui parte ministris abbatis liberioribus, et pars inferior lardario, ..deputatur *G. S. Alb.* I 314; **1384** in maremio tectorum et arearum solariorum putrefacto pro defectu coopperture *IMisc* 230/6 m. 4; **1396** pro areis in turre, tabulis, ostiis, fenestris faciendis *DocCOx* 311; **1444** j pecia meremii..empta ad supponendum aream supra cameram puerorum *Cant. Coll. Ox* 166. **c s1191** aqua ebulliente repletur dromunde non tantum carina et sentina set et limbus ejus propugnaculatus et area M. Par. *Min.* II 23.

areale, building site, urban plot (Gasc.).

1279 quorundam airalium seu placearum pro domibus vel pro ceteris *RGasc* II 90; **1289** ayrialium *Ib.* 314; **1291** infeudare..sub annua pensione plateas seu ayralia vacancia *Ib.* III 23.

areana v. arcanus b.

areata, measure of straw from threshing-floor (C.I.).

1247 habebit quolibet die unam areiatam straminis de xxv garbis (*Inq. Guerns.*) *Cl* 546 (cf. *CalIMisc* I p. 16 = *Ext. Guerns.* 25: †arietatam).

arect- v. arrett-, arrigere. areddatio v. arrentatio a.

arefacere [CL], to dry. **b** to wither, paralyse.

congregatis aquis..arefecit terram Bede *Gen.* (viii 1) 99; quedam carnes glandulose que parant †hanitatem [? l. humiditatem] organis oris, ne ex nimio motu arefiant *Ps.*-Ric. *Anat.* 29; **1459** pro tribus petris cere..deliberatis..ad cerandum canubium ad arificiendum pulveres bumbardorum *ExchScot* 495. **b** manus ~te restituuntur Aelnoth *Cnut* V 70; percurrente per artus molestia, ~ti nervi contrahuntur T. Mon. *Will.* VI 12.

arefactio, drying. **b** withering, palsy. **c** parching (of grain).

sitis ad extremum..intolerabili ~one extenuati *G. Steph.* I 19; cum ~one cutis Gad. 22. 1; carnis putredine, oculorum ~one cruciatus Ad. Usk 119. **b** patitur manus materialiter, sc. contractionem, ~onem, pustulationem Bart. Angl. V 28. **c 1511** pro ~one avenarum pro lentibus fiendis *Ac. Durh.* 661 (cf. *Househ. Bk. Durh.* 17).

aregon [ἀρηγών], a sort of ointment.

cum mixtura unguentorum calidorum, sicut arogon, marciaton..Gilb. I 36 v. 1 (cf. ib. III 171. 1); spina dorsi debet inungi contra horripilacionem..cum aragon et marciaton acuitis cum piretro Gad. 17. 1.

areiata v. areata. aren- v. aran-, arren-, haran-, haren-.

areola [CL], **~us,** garden bed. **b** (fig.). **c** enclosure.

~i aromatum, horti *GlC* A 723; **14..** ~a, A. *a lykbedde* [*leek-bed*] WW. **b 802** inriga florentes bonae voluntatis in eis ~as Alcuin *Ep.* 262; in horto celesti veraque deliciarum area, per ~as congrue distincta Gir. *Rem.* 20. **c** auriola, *stigu GlC* A 893.

2 (?) sheaf.

~i, *sceabas GlC* A 726.

Areopagita [Ἀρειοπαγίτης], Areopagite. **b** head of synagogue. **c** (fig.) jurist.

Johannes [Scotus]..Hierarchiam Dionisii ~e de Greco in Latinum transtulit M. Par. *Maj.* I 416. **b** aripagita, archisynagogus *GlC* A 750. **c s1459** ubi ab equo contendunt justicia simul et misericordia, ibi tam juxta rethores quam juxta Ariopagitas pars majoris pietatis preferenda est *Reg. Whet.* I 353.

areos v. arum. arera v. 4 area 1b. areragium v. arreragium.

arēre [CL], to dry up, wither. **b** (pr. ppl.) dry. **c** (pr. ppl.) withered, paralysed; *cf. arescere.*

cessante anima a vivificatione..arent ossa Ailr. *Anima* 86; nunc stat et abstat homo, flat et efflat, floret et aret *Babio* 417 (= Gower *VC* II 9). **b** de arente terra Bede *HE* IV 26 *rub.*; qui ante fontes, nunc rivuli vel potius alvei arentes et exhausti Gir. *PI* III 19. **c** senserat..quendam ..reflectendo manum arentem ab omni lesura contractionis absolvere R. Cold. *Cuthb.* 108.

ares v. 1 areticus.

arescere [CL], to become dry. **b** to wither (fig.). **c** to pine, esp. to be paralysed.

aruerant lacrime J. Exon. *BT* VI 402; aquarum inopia tellus ~it Gir. *TH* II 7. **b** principium floret, arescit finis amarus D. Bec. 1510; in primis diebus vite dicti regis [Alexandri III]..vicium aruit, virtus crevit *Plusc.* VII 33. **c** spumant labia, strident dentibus et ~it Ailr. *Ed. Conf.* 784A; alii agraciliantur et ~unt quia nutrimenti habent inopiam Ric. Med. *Micr. Anat.* 227; sensit dextrum pedem suum..emarcuisse et aruisse *Canon. G. Sempr.* f. 141.

arest- v. arista, arrest-.

arete [ἀρετή], virtue.

~e, quod est virtus Bacon *Tert.* 261.

1 areticus, virtuous, efficacious.

ares, i. virtus, inde ~a [v.l. arotica], i. virtuosa *Alph.* 14.

2 areticus v. arthriticus.

aretro [al. div.; cf. OF *arere* < ad retro], on the back. **b** behind, in the rear. **c** (?) back (again). **d** (w. *ad*) again.

fiat tunc collatio de carta brevis capiendi terram et de die captionis indorsato a retro brevis illius retornati Hengham *Magna* 8 p. 21. **b 1346** naute a retro manentes..villam.. combusserunt (*Lit. Confessoris Regis*) Ad. Mur. 212; ut ipsa ..ecclesia.., notabili distancia a retro existens, ..quatertur *Ps.*-Elmh. *Hen. V* 42; **c1430** qui aspirat ut in grege sit precessor, subsequetur a retro *Reg. Whet.* II 377; dixerat.. cuidam in secretis, aliis tamen a retro hoc audientibus Blakman *Hen. VI* 20. **c 1480** *takyng done* de *le tymbir entreclose* cum veteris pertinenciis et *settynge uppe* de eisdem a retro, xij d. *Ac. Churchw. Bath* 82. **d 1420** ibidem expectaverunt et ad aretro ad custodiendum mare velando omnino recusaverunt *KRAc* 49/33.

2 heretofore, in the past. **b** (?) retrospectively. **c** behindhand (in payment), in arrear, overdue (*cf arreragium*).

1231 prohibitum est Margerie quod, quicquid a retro actum sit [v.l. fuerit], quod (*sic*) de cetero vastum non faciat *CurR* XIV 1555; **s1307** tanta in diebus ejus caristia tritici..extitit quanta a retro seculis visa vix fuerit Higd. VII 41 p. 300. **b 1300** ut..se..personaliter representet, nostris..pariturus mandatis ac facturus a retro..quod ordo exegerit racionis *Reg. Cant.* I 380. **c 1199** petit..que ei a retro sunt de rationabili dote sua *CurR* I 85; **1200** unde idem Milo fuit pejoratus et ~o fuit ad quendam compotum quem debuit *Ib.* 247; **1212** pro defectu servicii domini sui, quod ~o fuit *SelPlCrown* 61; **1219** ei ~o sunt vij li. *CurR* VIII 120; **1236** si v quercus ei ~o sint, ..tunc illas ei habere facias *Cl* 273; **s1270** qui redditus a retro fuit per plures annos *Leg. Ant. Lond.* 126; quater viginti et xiij li. que ei arretro fuerunt de quodam annuo redditu xxj marcarum *State Tri. Ed. I* 92; **1292** de arreragiis firme ville..assignavimus.. persone..xiij li. et x s. qui ei a retro sunt de vadiis suis *RScot* 14b; **1302** ~o fuit tempore ballive sue de iiij li. *Rec. Leic.* I 239; **1336** quocienscunque contigerit predictos iiij s. a retro esse in parte vel in toto post aliquem terminum per xl dies *Feod. Durh.* 26 *n.*; **1534** cumulationem solvant bedello..cum debitis a retro detentis *StatOx* 336.

arett- v. arrett-. areuncula v. aratiuncula.

1 arga [Lomb.], cuckold.

est ordinatum per leges Lumbardorum..quod pro veritate duellandum est..si unus vocaverit alium ~am, ninerum vel cuculum Upton 78.

2 arga v. erga.

argalia [ἐργαλεῖον], catheter.

si..urina non exierit..stranguria permanente ~iam fieri necesse erit, ut cum ipse lapis de collo vesice moveatur et urine aditus et descensus aperiatur et urina egrediatur Gilb. VI 270 v. 2.

argast- v. ergast-. argella v. argilla.

argelzarus [Ar. *al-jinzār*], verdigris.

~us, viride es idem *Alph.* 16.

argemon [ἄργεμον], white spot on eye.

orminon..facit ad..oculorum argema vel leucomata *Alph.* 132 (cf. ib. 105: vulnera oculorum et argemecta [v.l. argemeta]).

argencia v. argyranchia.

†argens, of silver.

1423 j cista, in qua habetur j equus ~ens super quo sedet j miles ~ens *Ac. Obed. Abingd.* 99.

argentare v. argentatus, arrentare c.

argentarius [CL], concerned w. silver. **b** (w. *miles*) pesour (Exchequer official). **c** (w. *terra*) Lemnian earth (*cf. argenteus* 1d). **d** (sb. m.) silversmith. **e** (sb. m.) moneyer. **f** (sb. f.) silver-mine.

habeo fabros, ferrarium, aurificem, ~ium [AS: *seoloforsmip*] Ælf. *Coll.* 99; missus est cyphus magistri..ad quendam..artis ~ie peritum *Canon. G. Sempr.* 76v. **b** miles ~ius ab inferiore scaccario ad superius defert loculum examinandi argenti *Dial. Scac.* I 6F. **c** terra sigillata, terra ~ia, t. Saracenica, chimolea idem *SB* 41. **d** utimur cinere qui invenitur supra fornaces ~iorum *SB* 40. **e** furum rapacitas, ~iorum falsitas, capitali dampno cohercita W. Malm. *GP* I 18. **f s1152** querelam fecit apud Karleol'..super forestam suam, quam vastaverunt homines regis qui operabantur in ~ia J. Hex. *HR Cont.* 328.

argentatus [CL], silver-plated.

1338 ij cruces ~e *Ac. Durh.* 376; **1379** unam securim ~am *Test. Karl.* 123.

argenteus [CL], silvern, of silver. **b** woven w. silver. **c** silvery, white. **d** argent (her.). **e** (w. *terra*) Lemnian earth (*cf. argentarius* c).

aureis atque ~eis vasis Bede *HE* IV 1; **c750** caucum ~eum intus deauratum (*Lit. Regis Cantie*) *Ep. Bonif.* 105; dum puteos argenteos / larga diffundit Anglia P. Blois *Contra Clericos* 1133A; filum ~eum quo ciphi fracti apte consui vel contrahi possint Neckam *Ut.* 118; **a1275** de vasis ~eis absque deauratione *RB Exch.* III 979; **1360** in folio aureo et ~eo *Ac. Durh.* 384; **1361** abstulerunt..c pecias ~eas (*Chr. Abingd.*) *EHR* XXVI 734; **1414** ij osculatoria ~ea et deaurata *Reg. Cant.* II 40; **1479** pro relaxacione vasorum suorum ~iorum deauratorum *ExchScot* 627; calicem unum ~eum auroque incrustatum Ferr. *Kinloss* 32 (cf. ib.: cum gutturnio †~eio). **b 1451** pro pannis sericis ~eis et aureis *ExchScot* 436. **c** ~eus, albus *GlC* A 771. **d 1384** cum armis de Lucy, que de goules cum tribus luciis ~eis consistunt *Pat* 317 m. 16; portat tres fusulos rubeos in campo ~eo; et G. sic: *il port dargent trois fusilles de goules* Bad. Aur. 135. **e** terra sigillata..et..dicitur terra Sarracenica sive ~ea Bart. Angl. XVI 96.

2 silver (of coins). **b** (sb. m.) silver coin, esp. penny). **c** (w. ref. to *Matth.* xxvi 15).

reddat..pro presbitero octingentos siclos, pro diacono sexingentos, pro monacho vero quadringentos ~eos Egb. *Dial.* 12 (cf. ib. 8: †duplicato [v.l. duplicata] xxx siclorum pecunia, hoc est lx ~eos); **13..** provisum fuit quod.. denarius ~eus, sc. sterlingus, quociens necesse exposceret, divideretur in obolum et quadrantem *MGL* II 105; denarium ~eum, quod vulgo *sterlyng*..vocitatur P. Verg. XVI 309. **b s793** dedit ad sustentationem gentis regni sui illuc [Romam] venientis singulos ~eos de familiis singulis (*V. II Off.*) M. Par. *Maj.* I 360; **8..** pro mercede pecuniae suae, id est quatuor milia ~eis *E. Ch. S. Paul.* 8; *Dial. Scac.* I 5K (v. aureus 2b); rex exigit..pecuniam quam, ut asserebat, cancellarius..a se acceperat mutuam, ~eorum videlicet libras quingentas H. Bos. *Thom.* III 34; in memoriam recepte sanitatis unum ~eum singulis annis ad tumbam ipsius..deportat *Canon. G. Sempr.* 154v; sive debeatur aurum sive argentum in pecunia numerata, ut si dicatur reddendo inde per annum x aureos vel x ~eos sive x solidos Bracton 35. **c** cum triginta ~ei pretium sanguinis essent Gir. *GE* II 24; vendere..Deum pro triginta ~eis Paul. Angl. *ASP* 1551.

3 (sb. f.) lily.

12.. ~ea, i. *argentine*, i. *lilie* WW.

argentifilum, silver wire.

14.. ~um, *sylver wyre* WW.

argentifrigium [cf. aurifrigium], silver embroidery.

c1080 ij stolas cum argentifriso et vj manipulos cum argentifriso *Lib. Eli.* II 114.

argentilla, a herb, (?) clary (*Salvia sclarea*).

~a sumpta in potu purgat maculam Gilb. III 136. 2; ~a orvalis; hec potata ossa fracta consolidat. (Gilb.) *Alph.* 16.

argentius v. argenteus.

argentosus, silver-bearing.

1325 commisimus..custodiam minere regis plumbi ~e in manerio de Coumartyn in com. Devon' *FineR* 124 m. 7.

argentum [CL], silver. **b** (fig.).

non ergo argenti squalescit spreta libella / ..quamvis auratis praecellat fibula bullis Aldh. *VirgV* 205; Bede *HE* I 1 (v. aes 1a); planete sunt metalla: ..nam plumbum dicitur Saturnus, ..~um Luna Bacon *Tert. Sup.* 83; *Ib.* 84 (v. Anglia b); a **1275** genera ~i, viz. de Monte Pessulano, quod est adeo bonum quod decidit libra examinata nisi in uno denario, vel in duobus ad plus; ..~um de Alemannia fere totum purum; ~um de Brucela et de Flandria, de quo libra decidit iiij d. (etc.)..; et hec omnia de ~o in platis *RBExch.* III 979 (cf. ib. 994–5); cum ymaginibus..de ~o deaurato Whittlesey 168. **b** Aldh. *VirgP* 19 (v. aeramentum b).

2 silver (as currency or medium of exchange). **b** money, cash, payment. **c** (w. *fractum*) broken silver vessels or coinage.

argenti spondendo plura talenta Aldh. *VirgV* 1935; **a940** (13c) pro duobus denariorum milibus ~i *CS* 640; de una marka ~i *DB* I 10b; reddit xii lib. et xii sol. et unum den. de albo ~o *Ib.* 86b; **1330** in duobus milibus librarum bonorum sterlingorum ~i *ExchScot* I *pref.* 183. **b** argenti sonus est placidus vincitque Sirenes NECKAM *DS* VI 73; **1301** nullam sibi [candelam mittere] voluit sine ~o *SelC Coron* 69; **1393** in ~o servientibus deliberato *Ac. Durh.* 50. **c 1406** crateres et coopertoria argentea..cum alio ~o fracto *Ib.* 400; **1446** in alia bursa continetur de ~o fracto ponderis vij unciarum (*Invent. S. Paul.*) *Arch.* L 519 (and *n.*).

3 silver or penny (in names of customary rents). **b** (w. *Dei*) God's penny, earnest money.

1286 ~um de decenna [*tithing penny*] *IPM* 46/1 r. 7; **1307** de ij s. iij d. de ~o vinee [*vineyard silver*] (*MinAc*) *Econ. Condit. app.* 20 (cf. ib. 74, 90); **1358** reddendo primo anno xviij s. ad scaccarium prioris et ~um terrarii *Hal. Durh.* 25; **1576** pro ~o anguillari Anglice vocato *elesilver Pat* 1142 m. 16. **b 1275** super quas pelles dederat eis ~um Dei in arris pre manibus *SelPlMan* 151; **1291** equum.. arravit per ~um Dei de prefato A. (*St. Ives*) *Law Merch.* I 44; super quam empcionem solvit ei j quad. in ~o Dei et unum potellum cervisie ad beveragium *Ib.* 52; **1307** in ~o Dei j d. (*MinAc*) *Econ. Condit. app.* 28; **1360** conduxit unam domum ad terminum annorum..; et super hoc recepit ~um Dei prout consuetudo requirit *CourtR Carshalton* 24.

4 argent (her.).

1395 de certis armis de *goules* cum tribus *cheverons* de ~o *Pat* 341 m. 8; hic portat de ~o cum sex lodisingis de rubeo; G. *il port dargent six losinges de goul* BAD. AUR. 135.

5 (w. *vivum*) quicksilver, mercury.

10.. ~um vivum, *cwicseolfor* WW; argenti vivi vires, miracula, motus, / effectus multis scribere cura fuit; /..auro vestiri facies nequit ulla metalli / ni vis argenti mobilis addat opem NECKAM *DS* VI 89; ~i vivi extincti GILB. III 156. 2; spiritus dicuntur qui evolant ab igne, ut ~um vivum, sulphur, sal ammoniacum et auripigmentum BACON *Tert. Sup.* 83 (cf. ib. ~um vivum [dicitur] Mercurius); **1277** lx bagas vivi ~i *Law Merch.* III 139; operari cum ~o vivo vel sublimare ipsum..et similia que ledunt pectus GAD. 52. 2; **1307** in uncto, vivo ~o et coperose emptis *Crawley* 253; ~um vivum generatur in terra et tale quale apparet a terra quasi aqua fluens producitur *Alph.* 14; ~um (*sic*), *quyksylver* WW; *quyksylver*, ~um vivum, marcurius *CathA*.

6 name of a comet.

~um habet radium pulcherrimum album ad modum ~i purissimi..; signat autem annos fertiles, maxime si apparuerit Jove existente in signo aquatico *Ps.*-GROS. 586 (cf. GROS. 37*n.*, 38*n.*).

argilla [CL < ἄργιλλος], **~um,** clay, loam. **b** potter's clay. **c** fuller's earth.

argella, *laam GlC* A 730; ~a, *thoae Ib.* 748; sumpto foeno vel ~a..stipaverat rimulas BEDE *Cuthb.* 46; ~a, *laam* ÆLF. *Gl.*; invenies..insitam fractam, a qua eluta defluxit ~a W. CANT. *Mir. Thom.* II 4; **1239** invenire facias arzyllum ad operacionem illam [magni fontis] *Liberate* 14 m. 25; **1279** in arcillo empto ad torchiandum *KRAc* 467/7/4 (cf. ib. 7/7: pro arisillo ad fabricas); **1284** pro stipendiis iiij carr[etariorum] cariancium ~am de campo Rothelan usque in castrum ejusdem loci ad quoddam stagnum faciendum *Ib.* 351/9 m. 5; **1292** j carecta ad car[iandum] arcillum *Ib.* 468/6 r. 28; **1282** in arsillo fodiendo ad parietes [aule] *MinAc* 843/22; **c1300** in quodam homine..locato ad archall' erigend' et apponend' in predicta cagia *Ib.* 863/8; **1306** de arsilio et petris fodiendis *Ib.* 856/15 m. 2*d.*; recipe ~am vocatam Anglice *clei*, et est terra rubea, viscosa et tenax GAD. 80 v. 2; **1352** ~um, viz. *gravel Rec. Leic.* II 78; **1363** in vadiis.. laboratorum..rameancium argill' subtus..flodgates *MinAc* 1015/12; hoc ~um, *clay* WW. **b** ~a et cera atque hujusmodi que susceptioni forme et impressioni se offerunt P. BLOIS *Ep.* 101. 312A; **c1182** Osbertus potarius reddit pro ~a sua per annum viij d. *RBWorc.* 37; **c1288** de firma arsilli pro tegulis et ollis faciendis *Ib.* 28; **1349** Hanleye [*Worcs*]: ..pottarii qui solebant reddere pro arzillo habendo xiij s. ..mortui sunt; ideo nunc nichil reddunt *IPM* 105 r. 14; **1501** de firma fodicionis ~i figulatorum *DLMinAc* (*Cowick, Yorks*) 8692 r. 10. **c c1182** fullones de Wygornia †reddent [? l. reddunt] xxxij d. per annum pro ~a sua *RB Worc.* 38; fullones..fullant pannos..in alveo concavo in quo est ~a et aqua calida GARL. *Dict.* 131; **1260** non fullabunt pannos coloratos in arzilio *Rec. Leic.* I 89.

argillarium, clay-pit.

a clapitte, ~ium *CathA*.

argillarius, dauber.

dawber or cleyman, ~ius *PP*.

argillosus [CL], clayey.

10.. ~a, *ðoihte* WW; **1258** muro terrestri, qui fiat de litera et bona terra arzilosa *Liberate* 35 m. 7.

argisterium v. ergasterium.

arguella [OF *argoil*], 'argol', tartar of wine.

c1250 dolium de ~a, iiij d. (*Cust. Sandwich*) *DCCant H* f. 162a; **1281** duos barillos arguille precii xx m. *Law Merch.* II 31; **1296** quia vendit †vitrum [? l. nitrum] mixtum cum *vertegrez* et arguel' mixtum cum fecibus vini *Leet Norw.* 47; **1340** pro quolibet doleo..coperose, cardonum, asseris, arguel' *IMisc* 140/5; **14..** de qualibet centena sulphuris, argoil', attramenti *EEC* 213.

1 arguere [CL], to charge, accuse, blame.

o quantus quosdam..pallor ob detectum sceleris reatum ~it! ALDH. *VirgP* 32 p. 273; quae [epistolae] meorum foenus votorum infectum ~ebant *Ib.* 59; episcopum cum ~eret non fuisse rite consecratum BEDE *HE* IV 2; nullus ~ere nos poterit quod non recte..suscepimus.. (*Lit. Ceolfridi*) *Ib.* V 21 p. 337; **742** ut..per responsum apostolicum convincantur et ~antur peccatores BONIF. *Ep.* 50 p. 83; **1166** quesivimus cur eas [litteras] falsitatis ~isset *Canon. G. Sempr.* 96; dum novitatis ~itur, desinit esse novum GIR. *TH* II *pref.* p. 76; **s1272** (v. argutio a); **13..** hic, contrarius juvenili consilio dominorum, regem ~it, ..asserens regiam majestatem.. campis vagari..non debere *Found. Holyrood* 15.

2 to argue, reason. **b** to maintain (to be).

de necessitate puer ~it sic apud se: 'quod est pulchrius est melius, et quod est melius est magis eligendum; ergo pomum pulchrius est magis eligendum'..et tamen nescit quid vocetur argumentum; ex quo concludit auctor quod homo ~it a natura sine difficultate et labore BACON *Tert.* 103; contra primum motivum de creacione ~itur sic DUNS *Sent.* II xviii 1. 4; licet dominium Dei sit alterius racionis a dominio humano, tamen contingit sepe ~ere ab uno ad aliud OCKHAM *Pol.* II 641; **1379** quod doctores ~ant in eisdem [vesperiis] *StatOx* 177; **1409** se..disputando, ~endo et respondendo doctrinaliter exercentes *Ib.* 200; pro hac conclusione sic ~itur J. BURY *Glad. Sal.* 2 p. 576. **b** de fortalicio, quod Gallorum superbia semper invictissimum ~erat ELMH. *Hen. V* 28.

3 to creak.

charkyn, as cart or barow or oder lyk, ~o..; alii dicunt stridere *PP*.

4 (p. ppl.) loud. **b** shrewd, subtle.

arguta simul cantans luscinia ALDH. *Aen.* 68. 7; sceptrorum flagra beatus / ictibus argutis..non sensit *Id. Virg V* 1217; **9..** ~is, *pæm swogendum, hleoþregendum* WW. **b** argutus fertur dixisse poeta ALDH. *VirgV* 29; **10..** ~us, *se gleawa..*, ~o, *scearpe* WW; est, hujusmodi equivocatio ceteris ad fallendum ~utior BALSH. *AD* 59; cum alias avium sint omnium [cornices] ~utissime, in sola nidi positione.. istas ingenio natura destituit GIR. *TH* I 22; fur ~utissimus MAP *NC* II 23 p. 93.

2 arguere [? conf. w. augēre], to enlarge.

~ere, ampliare *GlC* A 786.

arguilla v. arguella. arguit- v. argut-.

argumentabilis, arguable.

ex quibus locis sint problemata primus aperit [liber Topicorum]; sequentes unde et quomodo probentur exponunt, et que propositio magis aut minus ~is sit et quare J. SAL. *Met.* 904C.

argumentalis, logical.

divisio cum illatione ~i: '..ne piger esse velis, es piger; ergo male' GARL. *Hon. Vit.* 211.

argumentari [CL], **~are,** to argue, resolve by argument.

Aristoteles..perplexa..enigmata..~atur ALDH. *Met.* 6; ~antur solem terra esse majorem BEDE *TR* 7 p. 194; hoc etiam ex scriptura Geneseos possumus ~ari ERIUG. *Per.* 563C; non facto manifesto quid est quod positum est, non est facile ~ari J. SAL. *Met.* 912A; GIR. *IK* I 5 (v. argute); pro primo istorum ~atum est multipliciter supra OCKHAM *Dial.* 585; **1382** sed, cum hic nescierat plus argumentare, / Nichol solvens omnia jussit Bayard stare (*Contra Religiosos* 207) *Mon. Francisc.* I 598.

argumentatio [CL], argument, reasoning.

671 sagaci ~one colligantur ALDH. *Ep.* 1 p. 477; [Aristoteles] acutissimas Periermeniarum scriptitans ~ones ALCUIN *Ep.* 155 p. 250; monstravi me..satis necessaria ~one probasse..ANSELM (*Resp. Ed.* 10) I 138; loci argumentandi et dividendi diffiniendique plerumque communes sunt; sed vis artis in ~onibus amplius viget J. SAL. *Met.* 911B; artis dialectice instrumentum ~o GIR. *GE* II 37; **s1193** [rex] veritatem..veridicis assertionibus et probabili ~one ..in lucem propalavit COGGESH. 63b.

argumentative, by way of proof.

notatur de hac materia ~e UPTON 109 (cf. BAD. AUR. 103).

argumentator, arguer, one who adduces evidence.

'scribae' sunt moralium et naturalium librorum auctores et actuum saecularium scriptores, id est, de ipsis artibus praecepta dantes; 'conquisitores' sunt ~ores ex praeceptis ipsarum artium aliquid approbantes LANFR. *Comment. Paul.* (1 *Cor.* i 20) 158.

argumentose, assiduously. **b** ingeniously. **c** convincingly.

eundem [abbatem Robertum, ob. 1168]..~e fraudibus impedivit *G. S. Alb.* I 112; **s1244** Griffinus.., qui in Turri Londoniensi captivus tenebatur, ..cogitavit ~e qualiter inclusionem poterat evadere carceralem M. PAR. *Maj.* IV 295; satis ~e tam..regine quam comitisse..sollicitudo.. satagunt (*sic*)..operam impendere AD. MARSH *Ep.* 226. **b s1075** interemerunt..homines..edoctos pecuniam ~e a simplicibus extorquere M. PAR. *Min.* I 22. **c s1193** rex.. ita luculenter et ~e peroravit ut omnibus admirationi.. haberetur COGGESH. 63b.

argumentosus, assiduous, busy (epithet of bee). **b** persuasive, plausible, convincing. **c** ingeniously contrived.

instar apis ~e ex diversis doctorum sententiis, quasi ex multi generis floribus, sapientie sibi favos composuit AILR. *Nin.* 2; quasi apis ~a per campos volitabat virtutum W. DAN. *Ailr.* 13; volo sis ~e api similis, que mel elicit ex urtica MAP *NC* IV 3 p. 155; apes ~e fabricantes jugiter cellas mellis R. BURY *Phil.* 8. 136. **b** dum..fides in necessitatibus ~a clamaret J. FORD *Wulf.* 64; infelicitas nostri temporis, ..ubi adulterium ~um probitatis indicium effertur GERV. TILB. III 97; nisi..~a pietas de cetero vigilandum censeat AD. MARSH *Ep.* 36; **s1244** non erat hoc factum pre timore imperatoris, immo ut occurreret pecuniam afferentibus, asserunt ~i *Flor. Hist.* II 276. **c s1098** contempnentes Sarracenorum ~a tela aut strepitus artificiosos M. PAR. *Min.* I 123; **s1230** cunctis imprecantibus ut eventu careat tam ~a extorsio OXNEAD *Chr.* 159.

argumentum [CL], rebuke, denunciation.

1320 tanta prudencia commissum sibi gregem regebat ut..ad consolacionem humilium pietas non deesset nec rigor in rebellium ~um *FormOx* 59.

2 argument, proof, piece of evidence. **b** syllogism. **c** disputation (ac.).

farisaicae temptationis calumniam verae responsionis ~o confutans explodit ALDH. *VirgP* 18; ad ~um hortandae suasionis apostolicis utuntur oraculis *Ib.* 36; mandatis memoriae veteribus illis Aegyptiorum ~is (*Lit. Ceolfridi*) BEDE *HE* V 21 p. 341; considerans illud [opusculum] esse multorum concatenatione contextum ~orum, coepi mecum quaerere si forte posset inveniri unum ~um quod nullo alio ad se probandum quam se solo indigeret ANSELM (*Prosl.*) *proem.* I 93; **11..** veritatis ~o innitentes *Feod. Durh.* lxii; hujus..eventus ~um est non improbabile quod piscatores aque illius turres..sub undis..conspiciunt GIR. *TH* II 9. **a1350** recitans ~a principalia *Stat. Cantab.* 313. **b** cum.. filosoforum sillogismos..atque Aristotelis ~a didicisset ALDH. *VirgP* 44; sophisma est syllogismus litigatorius, philosofima vero demonstrativus, ~um autem syllogismus dialecticus J. SAL. *Met.* 913B; scientia de ~is est nota homini per naturam: ..a natura scimus arguere et..dissolvere ~a per interemptionem propositionum falsarum et per divisionem et distinctionem malarum consequentiarum BACON *Tert.* 104; non igitur refragabor ~o quod vocant 'a conjugatis' GARDINER *VO* 729. **c 1407** nec disputet magister aliquis disputaturus problema ultra ~um unicum cum sophista *StatOx* 194; **1462** supplicat..quatinus viij ~a, viij responsiones, ..sermo examinatorius [etc.] sufficiant sibi ad effectum quod possit admitti ad incipiendum in sacra theologia (*Reg. Ac. Ox.*) *Grey Friars Ox.* 336.

3 device, engine of war. **b** (fig.).

s1097 non prosunt inclusis..tela ignita, ..non missilia formidabilia, non alia excogitata ~a defensionis M. PAR. *Min.* I 83. **b** catholicae fidei propugnaculum saecularis ~i ballista quassatum ALDH. *VirgP* 36 p. 282.

4 matter, theme.

oblato hujus supputationis ~o ALDH. *Met.* 4 (cf. ib. 7: novo..et inusitato dicendi ~o); **8..** hoc ~um forsorii Oeðelwalch episcopus decerpsit *Lib. Cerne* 174.

argus [? ἀργός, *conf. w.* argutus], slothful. **b** inconstant.

slawe, accidiosus, desidiosus, ..lentus, ~us [v.l. ~utus] *CathA*. **b** *un sstabylle*, ~us, vagus, instabilis, inconstans *Ib.* (s.v. *stabylle*).

argute [CL], shrewdly.

~e, acute *GlC* A 737; a signis quibusdam conjecturalibus argumentando de predictis, ~e futura conjectat GIR. *IK* I 5.

argutia [CL], shrewdness, sophistry: **a** (pl.); **b** (sg.).

~iae, *prauuo GlC* A 731; ~iae, *gleaunisse Ib.* 736; ad reticulatas logicorum ~ias GIR. *GE* II 37 p. 350. **b** Antheos fortes et quos argutia ducit / Anglia producit GARL. *Tri. Eccl.* 60; ista blasfema ~ia cecat multos WYCL. *Sim.* 91; talis est turpis ~ia ab una proposicione de possibili ad suam de inesse *Id. Ver.* I 213 (cf. ib. 351).

arguties, subtlety.

nec valet ~ies adversarii J. BURY *Glad. Sal.* 6 p. 586.

argutio, rebuke. **b** reasoning, disputation. **c** trick, contrivance.

c1239 quam efficaciter [apostolus] persuadet filios patrum disciplinam non negligere neque fatigari ab eorum ~one GROS. *Ep.* 127 p. 405; **s 1272** [rex] unum de comitibus suis.. negligencius se habentem..arguit et ~oni minus..obedienti minas adjecit TREVET 282; sic de Baptista quoad arguicionem Herodis WYCL. *Ver.* I 318; ~ones discolice quibus seminatur scandalum in ecclesia *Ib.* 344. **b 1362** si..aliquis sit in domo, habeat primam disputacionem..et post arguicionem suam †redeat [l. reddat] propria argumenta, sicut in vico scolarum fieri consuevit *Cant. Coll. Ox.* III 170 (= *Conc.* III 57); non valet ~o tua, o Witclef NETTER *DAF* I 484; qualiter tibi videri potest cum sola arguicione aut tentativa inquisicione procedere *Ib.* II 4. **c** unde..abbatem Johannem [ob. 1214] oderat et prenotatam ultionis ~onem facilius machinabatur *G. S. Alb.* I 223.

argutiuncula, quibble.

an non forte et aliter..dici potest quod ista ~a sciencie divine non obviat..? BRADW. *CD* 185E.

argutive, by reasoning, inferentially.

similitudo expressa partis non est similitudo tocius, quia neque secundum racionem tocius in se nec eciam qua totum immediate cognoscitur, sed arguitive tantum ex hoc quod cognoscitur illud representatum esse aliquid illius DUNS *Sent.* I iii 5 3; non enim Deus arguitive tantum et non intuitive scit futura BRADW. *CD* 226B; inquisitive aut ~e multa dicit que asserere non proponit NETTER *DAF* II 4; **c1430** cujus causacionis motivum eo magis arguitive dubitativa patris opinio formaverat in alumpnum quo.. *Reg. Whet.* II 453.

argutor, (false) reasoner.

istis ~oribus et eorum argumento per viam instancie redargutis BRADW. *CD* 728B.

argutus v. arguere 4.

†argyrancia [ἀργυράγχη], choking caused by silver (facet.).

non squinanciam sed †argenciam pateris, quoniam argentum vocem tuam obturavit O. Cheriton *Par.* 105.

aria v. aerea, area. ariagium v. averagium.

Arianus, Arian (heretic).

993 Arrianas Sabellianasque proterendo nenias *CD* 684; Clodovicus..Alaricum †arrione sexto [? l. Arriane secte] occidit R. Niger 133; **s321** heresis Arriana exoritur, dicta ab Arrio Alexandrino presbitero qui..diversas in Trinitate substantias astruxit M. Par. *Maj.* I 159; Gothos ~os Higd. I 27; ~a malicia fere totam eclipsarat ecclesiam R. Bury *Phil.* 10. 164; convertantur aridi Arriani, ..qui.. personarum divinarum substanciam separant ipsasque inequales et non coeternas coaffirmant Bradw. *CD* 19B; heretici solent initi dominis secularibus, ut patet de Arrianis Wycl. *Ver.* I 351.

†ariax, (?) stag-beetle.

14.. nomina vermium et muscarum: ..~ax, *a hert horne* WW.

aribeticus v. arthriticus.

aridatus, withered.

germina de qualibet..fraxinorum excrescencia mortificata et ~a devenerunt *Entries* 699.

aride, (?) fruitlessly.

c1415 Oxonie affuisti ad tuorum amicorum non modicas expensas, proprio quasi proficuo arride pululante *FormOx* 434.

ariditas [CL], dryness. **b** withered part of body.

ignem..caliditas ~ati, ..terram frigiditas ~ati copulata conficiunt Eriug. *Per.* 596A; siccitas vel ~as, *drugaþe* Ælf. *Sup.*; terre sitientis ~as Ketell *J. Bev.* 271; nullus panem intinctum accipiat excepto infirmo qui propter ~atem aliter nequeat deglutire Gir. *GE* I 9; arilli sunt arida uvarum grana et dicuntur ab ~ate *Alph.* 14. **b** ~as sucum, nervi officia receperunt (*V. Germani*) Bede *HE* I 21.

aridulus, dry, barren (fig.).

optat ut arctois infusum manna Britannis / cedat et irriguum Normannis influat, urbis / aridule deserta rigans sitientia Hanv. I 246.

aridus [CL], dry. **b** (fig.). **c** dry-eyed. **d** dried (of fish or hides). **e** (?) remote from navigable waterways. **f** withered, paralysed.

aridus ut nullis roraret nubibus aether Aldh. *VirgV* 260; fontis hujus arene petrose sitibundis et ~is ori imposite sitim extinguunt Gir. *TH* II 7 p. 88. **b** arida divinis irrorans corda scatebris Aldh. *CE* 4. 10. 14; [verba] tam inter eloquentes ~a quam inter scientes usitata Gir. *TH intr.* p. 6; Bradw. *CD* 19B (v. Arianus). **c** respuit in primis lacrimosas arida, blandas / aspera, clamosas surda puella preces Vinsauf *AV* II 3. 86. **d** **1429** pro piscibus ~is *Exch Scot* IV 505 (cf. ib. VII 240); **1496** de custuma certorum corriorum ~orum *Ib.* X 612. **e** **1392** ad singulos portus.. regni [Anglie], ..omissis civitatibus et villis in locis ~is constitutis *Cl* 233 m. 10. **f** arida marcescens dum torpet dextra lacerti Aldh. *VirgV* 2423; contracto poplite..~um et enervem..sanitati restituit Gir. *GE* I 23; **1446** virorum pauperum debilium et impotencium, sc. cecorum, claudorum, ~orum *Pat* 463 m. 9.

2 (sb. f.) dry land.

~a, terra *GlC* A 766; **779** (12c) adiciam mariscem pertinentem ad ~am et ad aquae ripam *CS* 228; **c1180** unum ferlingum terre..in plano et prato, in ~a et aquis (*Cart. Tavistock*) *EHR* LXII 364; **s1191** nisus..lupum..natantem ..sub undis..intercepit et super ~am..se cum nova preda recepit Diceto *YH* II 102; **s1242** a naufragio vix ereptus, ..ad ~am jactatus *Flor. Hist.* II 259; circueuntes mare et ~am R. Bury *Phil.* 8. 133; *a dry erth*, ~a *CathA*.

arierefeodum [cf. retrofeodum], *arrière-fief*, tenure under mesne lord (Fr.).

1281 castrum de You [*Burgundy*] cum suis appenditiis, prout..avunculus noster tenet a nobis ~um (*Lib. B*) *Foed.* II 162.

aries [CL], ram. **b** (w. *ovis*). **c** Aries (astr.). *V. et. lingua arietis.*

~etes crissitant vel blaterant Aldh. *Met.* 131; reddit hoc manerium vj vaccas et xc porcos et xx ~etes *DB* II 249; in armis ~etum dextris..futura prospiciunt Gir. *IK* I 11; **1205** habeat in pastura..cc oves matrices cum ovibus earum [abbatisse et conventus] et x ~etes cum ~etibus earum *RChart* 162a. **b** **1548** unus ovis ~es vocatus *a rambe tegge* (*Court Bk. Apledram*) *Mun. Petworth* MCR 60 f. 71; **1513** volo ut habeat pro labore suo xx ariet' oves (*Test.*) *Crawley* 545. **c** primum..~etis signum in illa celi parte quam in medio Martii mensis sol tenet oriri incipit Bede *TR* 16; casualiter..cedit..~es Marti J. Sal. *Pol.* 442A; renovantur in eis [signis] quatuor complexiones principales omnium rerum, sc. calida et humida in ~ete Bacon *Maj.* I 377; Bradw. *CD* 450E (v. ascendere 4b).

2 battering ram. **b** builder's ram. **c** sort of quintain. **d** blow w. a ram (also fig.).

~es, genus tormenti expugnati *GlC* A 22; cum [Rollo] in ejus [Luthecie] expugnatione cum balistis et ~etibus intenderet Diceto *Abbr. Norm.* 246; castri gnarus obsessor vel unum eruere lapidem ~etis ictu crebro studet Neckam *NR* I 60; vinea, trux aries indomitusque catus Garl. *Tri. Eccl.* 86. **b** **1286** pro uno ~ete empto ad opus cyment[arie] .., xiij s. iiij d. *KRAc* 485/28 r. 3. **c** **1139** pravam turpemque consuetudinem ~etum, sc. panum et potus extorsionem, ..penitus removemus (*Lit. Papae*) Elmh. *Cant.* 370; **c1239** ne quisquam levet ~etes super rotas vel alios ludos statuat in quibus decertatur pro bravio *Conc. Syn.* 274 (cf. Gros. *Ep.* 22 p. 74; 52 p. 162); **1240** prohibemus clericis ne.. sustineant ludos fieri de rege et regina nec ~etes levari *Ib.* 313; **a1250** interdicimus levationes ~etum super rotas *Ib.* 432; **s1253** an aliqui laici elevaverint ~etes vel fieri faciant schothales vel decertaverint de preeundo cum vexillis in visitatione matricis ecclesie (*Artic. Cler.*) *Ann. Burton* 307. **d** catholicae fidei propugnaculum..atrocis machinae ~etibus subrutum Aldh. *VirgP* 36 p. 282; constantia quae tot diaboli ~etibus impulsa labare non poterat G. Crispin *Herl.* 94; inequalitas superficiei ~ete crebro vincitur Neckam *NR* II 172.

arieta, ewe.

1575 reddent..unam pinguem ~am *Pat* 1129 m. 23.

arietare [CL], to charge.

s1098 Turchi..foras exiliunt, in nostros aliquantisper ~antes W. Malm. *GR* IV 366.

arietata v. areata.

arietinus [CL], of a ram.

sepum ~um W. Cant. *Mir. Thom.* V 21; carne ~a [*gl.*: *mutun*] Neckam *Ut.* 104; non arietine mensis ego gaudeo carnis Garl. *Epith.* III 449; in quo decoquantur carnes ~e Gad. 6. 2.

arietulus, young ram.

a schepe, aries, ~us diminutivum *CathA*.

arificere v. arefacere. arigikeminus v. archiceraunus.

arillus [cf. Sp. *arillo*], grape seed.

ex tribus componitur uva, sc. ex folliculis, glarea et ~is: ..~i..dicuntur alio nomine acini Bart. Angl. XVII 180; emplastrum factum de pulvere ~orum immaturatorum Gilb. V 222. 2 (cf. ib. VII 296. 1; ~arum immaturarum); pullos gallinaceos nutritos ex ~is racemorum Bacon IX 37; nuclei vel ~i uvarum passarum desiccentur Gad. 6. 2; *Alph.* 14 (v. ariditas).

arim- v. arithm-. ariol- v. hariol-. aripagita v. Areopagita.

aripennis [OF *arpent* < Gall.], measure of land, esp. of vineyard.

†943 (14c) ad villam quae dicitur Bodenewel [*Cornw*] tres arpennas; ..in Pendre unam arpennam *CS* 785; **c1080** habet unum clausum vinee et continet quatuor arpent' (*Mem. Pri. Eastry*) *MonA* I 103; ibi ii arpendi vineae et viii acrae prati *DB* I 7b; ibi una arpenna vineae *Ib.* 67b; ibi i arpenna prati *Ib.* 73; ibi iiii arpenni vineae noviter plantatae *Ib.* 128; ibi ii aripend' vineae *Ib.* 142b; j arpentum vineae *Ib.* II 418; **c1100** censum trium semis agripennarum in vinea Mainerie (*Chirog., Norm.*) Ord. Vit. V 19 p. 441; unum ~em vinee *Ib.* p. 454; duo arpenta terre *Ib.* p. 463; stant simul, in angusto sc. terre ~o, ecclesia, molendinum..et pomerium Gir. *IK* II 3; unum arpennum habentem xvj pedes in longitudine, xvj in latitudine Neckam *NR* II 173; **1200** x arpennos vinee de vineis nostris *RChart* (*Anjou*) 71b; **1246** lx arpennos [terre] *CalCh* (*Norm.*) I 308; **c1280** xx acras terre de dominico †arpenti de Wedgarstun (*Cust.*) *Crawley* 238; **1289** xij arpentorum terre *RGasc* II 425.

aripere v. abripere. ariragium v. arreragium.

†arisbot [misr. of Ar. *ad-dashbadh* < misr. of Pers. *dushbil*, *dushpil*], osseous growth at junction of bone fracture.

in tali tempore incipit ~ot, i. porus, generari et indurari secundum Avicennam Gad. 124. v. 1.

arisillum v. argilla a. arism- v. arithm-.

arista [CL], awn or 'beard' of corn. **b** ear of corn. **c** (fig.).

~a, *egla* Ælf. *Gl.*; sata jam in spicas et ~as maturescentia Gosc. *Aug. Min.* 747; spica latet grano cum nodis, culmus, arista Neckam *DS* IV 432 (433); faciat..affros et equos.. prebendari, ita quod prebenda..stramine avene misceatur vel frumenti; ~e enim straminis ordeacei rugitus eorum inpedirent *Fleta* 165; ~a, A. *an eyle*, ..hec ~a, *a nawn* WW. **b** *an ere of corne*, spica, ~a, aristella *CathA*. **c** unde horrenda seges diris succrevit aristis Aldh. *Aen.* 88. 3 (cf. *Id. VirgV* 2500).

2 ridge, rib or outer corner in building (cf. *Building in Eng.* 378). **b** (?) ridge or rib in cloth.

flamma que, vario prius agitata discursu, domus super quam stabat lambebat ~as Ben. Pet. *Mir. Thom.* IV 6; abbas [Willelmus, ob. 1235]..turrim..retegi fecit, ..collateralibus additis ornamentis, viz. octo linearibus elevationibus a tholo usque ad murale extensis, ut octogona turris manifestius appareret, ..et linee ipse predicte, que vulgariter ~e nuncupantur, turrim et mirabiliter roborabant et roborantam decorabant et imbres certius cohibebant *G. S. Alb.* I 281; **1260** arestas de cumulo in summa turrella plumbo cooperiri *Liberate* 36 m. 8*d*. **b** **c1370** tunc taxet listas, pannus quia tendit aristas (J. Bridl.) *Pol. Poems* I 192.

3 (w. *pannus* or sim.) a rich fabric (? ribbed).

1215 pannos sericos de aresta..ad robam..perficiendam *Cl* 214a; **1223** pro uno baldekino de aresta ad quisserias et spalderas nostras *Ib.* 550b; **1238** pannus sericus de aresta *CalLiberate* 316; **1244** regi mittat in Angliam..c pannos de alesta sine auro, xl ad aurum de levi precio, xx de majori, de predictis pannis *Cl* 175; **1245** capa..de panno de ~a rubeo cum aviculis albis *Invent. S. Paul.* 480; pannus de aresta cepeatus, tabulatus rubeo et indico *Ib.* 493; **c1250** vestimentum..cum casula de ~a et paraturis de eodem *Vis. S. Paul.* 2; **1257** unam culcitram punctam de aresta *Cl* 33; **1260** unum pannum ad aurum et iiij pannos de aresta ad coyntisas..faciendas *Cl* 116; **1300** tres cape chori veteres broudate, linate de panno de ~o *Ac. Wardr.* p. 352; **1310** de j casula de panno de lareste *Ac. Exec. Ep. Exon.* 4.

1 aristare, to glean.

to glene, ~are, conspicare *CathA*.

2 aristare, ~amentum, ~atio, v. arrest-.

aristator, gleaner.

a glener, ~or, conspicator *CathA*.

aristella, ear of corn.

an ere of corn, spica, arista, ~a, ..*a glene*, arista, ~a conspica *CathA*.

aristocratia [ἀριστοκρατία], aristocracy.

hoc magis fit si princeps fuerit una persona quam si plures exstiterint, quemadmodum accidit in ~ia Ockham *Pol.* I 110; ~ia foret prestancior, cum cura multorum virtuose regencium magis proficeret Wycl. *Civ. Dom.* I 205.

aristocratice, aristocratically.

tunc nullus est ad summum pontificem eligendus, sed assumendi sunt plures excellentiores aliis, qui ~e vel politice omnes alios regant Ockham *Dial.* 799.

aristocraticus [ἀριστοκρατικός], aristocratic.

principatus regalis, quo una persona prefulget, tam principatum ~um quam politicum, in quorum utroque president plures, ..precellit Ockham *Pol.* I 109; utrum †expedicius [? l. expediencius] sit communitatem regi tantum secundum legem Domini a judicibus quam secundum legem civilem [? a] regibus vel contra; prima enim policia vocatur ~a vel naturalis et secunda vocatur monarchica vel regalis Wycl. *Civ. Dom.* I 185.

aristolochia [ἀριστολόχεια, -λοχία], birthwort.

tres †astrologie species herbe note sunt Neckam *NR* II 166; aristologie speciem medicina rotundam / dicit; nam radix esse rotunda datur *Id. DS* VII 221; aristologia rotunda cocta in aqua et sumpta tussientibus prodest Gilb. IV 196. 1 (cf. ib. III 174. 1: aristologia longa); pulvis radicum aristo[logie] ro[tunde] et longe in potu datus valet ..contra morsus reptilium Gad. 68 v. 1; aristologia, i. paciens, alia longa, alia rotunda; quando simpliciter, rotunda *SB* 11 (cf. *Alph.* 14).

aristophorum [ἀριστοφόρον = breakfast bowl], portable bottle.

coostreed or costreel, gret botel, onophorum, ~um *PP*.

Aristotelicus, Aristotelian (adj. or sb.).

fortassis ~us dicit: "corpus fuit, ergo coloratum fuit" D. Morley 11; stilum ~um *Ps.*-Gros. 283; putabam antea per ~a dogmata..veritatis tue me penetrasse abyssos Ric. Armagh *AP* 20.

aristum v. arista 3.

arithmeticus [ἀριθμητικός], arithmetical. **b** (sb. m.) arithmetician. **c** (sb. f.) arithmetic.

798 per campos ~ae artis Alcuin *Ep.* 144; per arimeticam [sc. medietatem] Ocreatus *Helceph.* 134; hujus autem hec est ratio secundum consuetum cursum scaccarii non legibus arismeticis *Dial. Scac.* I 5L; demonstrare conclusiones geometricas et arsmetricas Wycl. *Sum. Ente* I 107. **b** medietates tres quas considerat ~us reperiuntur in divinis scripturis Bacon *Tert.* 228; binarius secundum arismetricos est infamis Wycl. *Dom. Div.* 22. **c** arthimetrica, divinitio [*FE* 337. 15: difinitio] vel numeralis *GlC* A 719; philosophorum disciplinas, hoc est ~am, geometricam, ..astronomiam Aldh. *VirgP* 59; ~ae ecclesiasticae disciplinam Bede *HE* IV 2; **798** quam dulcis est in rationibus ~a! Alcuin *Ep.* 148; ~a est numerorum contemplationibus animi succumbentium rata intemerataque disciplina Eriug. *Per.* 475A; **10..** ~a, *rimcræft* WW; primus gradus est ab ~a [v.l. arismetrica] numerorum virtutem mutuare J. Sal. *Pol.* 439C; arsmeticam Boecii et Euclidis legat (Neckam *Sac*) *Med. Sci.* 374; facta ratione per geometriam et arismetricam ei diximus summam miliariorum (M. Scot. *Intr.*) *ib.* 290; arsmetrica nominis interpretacione est sciencia de numero Odington 183; Ricardus abbas [ob. 1335].. doctrinalibus mathematicis..operam magnam dedit, viz. circa speculacionem conclusionum arsmetrice et geometrie, astronomie et musice *G. S. Alb.* II 182; **1432** in..consistorio septem scienciarum liberalium, quarum quelibet secum habebat famosissimum preceptorem artis sue, puta.. arsmetrica †Pigtagoram numerantem (J. Carpenter) *MGL* III 460.

ariv- v. arriv-. arkastella v. arbalista. arkillus v. arquillus. arkmannus v. avermannus. arlechatus v. harnesiare.

1 arma, (f. s.) weapon or piece of armour. **b** tool (*cf.* 2 *arma* 4).

isti portant ~as in naves *Tap. Bayeux* XL; **1295** meliorem ~am *CalIPM* III p. 190; **1514** puncto cujusdam ~e vocate *a poleaxe Entries* 49. **b** permittat..eosdem homines.. colligere sekkiliones sine secure et ~a moluta *Cl* 514.

2 arma [CL], (n. pl.) arms (weapons) or armour. **b** (w. *ferre* or sim.). **c** (dist. as offensive and defensive). **d** war, fighting. **e** (fig.).

Aldh. *PR* 140 (v. armatura 1a); cum moriebatur, habebat rex equum et ~a ejus *DB* I 179; si quis alteri prestet ~a sua [AS: *his wæpnes*] in occisione alicujus (*Quad.*) *GAS* 61; nihil damnabilius est in milite quam otium, per quod usus ~orum dediscitur P. Blois *Ep.* 94. 294D; clamant, "~a, ~a, viri!" W. Fitzst. *Thom.* 136; **s1181** rex Angl i fecit hanc assisam de ~is habendis in Anglia *G. Hen. II* I 278; **1198** venit cum vi sua et ~is et cum hominibus suis armatis ad domum domini sui *CurR* I 63; **s1226** ut omnes qui possent ~a movere se cruce signarent Wend. II 305;

1275 cum maciis et aliis †apinis [l. armis] *Hund.* I 292; **s1295** monstratis ~is et numeratis capitibus que apta essent ad bella procedere *Lanercost* 169; **1324** jurati sunt in ~is et arreati per constabularios pacis *IMisc.* 99/10 r. 2; **1327** ad abbaciam [de S. Edmundo] vi et ~is, sc. lanceis, gisarmis, hachiis, gladiis, arcubus et sagittis, accesserunt (*JustIt*) *MonA* III 109b; **s1332** Scoti..clamaverunt statim "ad ~a, ad ~a!" et preliari ferociter ceperunt Knighton I 463; **s1385** l paria ~orum integralia, cum totidem lanciis et targiis *Plusc.* X 7; **1410** pro extraccione ~orum violenta *StatOx* 205; **1471** pro..tribus paribus ~orum dictorum *forharnes ExchScot* 120; **1533** pro cingulis et preparacione aliorum ~orum equorum *Ac. Durh.* 197. **b** non..licuerat pontificem sacrorum..~a ferre Bede *HE* II 13; sacerdotes ..~a portantes ut laici erant G. Crispin *Herl.* 89; tractandum est..de modo portationis vel positionis ~orum (*Leg. Hen.*) *GAS* 602; tunc Hugo ~a pro senio non ferebat Ord. Vit. VIII 16 p. 363; **1268** quicunque in clericali ordine constitutus ~a detulerit..vinculum excommunicationis incurrat *Conc. Syn.* 752; **a1322** noctivagus, percuciens aliquem, portitor ~orum et consimiles *StatOx* 87; **1340** occasione delacionis ~orum, que contra pacem detulerat *FormOx* 138; **1457** convictus de lacione ~orum *MunAcOx* 668 (cf. ib. 717: de portacione ~orum); **1476** quod nulla persona..gerat ~a, viz. duploida, defensum, gladium, arcus, sagittas, lanceas, secures guerre *March S. Wales* 86. **c** ~is offensivis et defensivis Alb. Lond. *ID* 303; **1322** quod omnia convictorum ~a, sive defensiva sive offensiva fuerint, ..procuratoribus..liberentur *StatOx* 125 (cf. ib. 293 [**1482**]: quod nullus uteretur ~is invasivis aut defensivis.. infra precinctum universitatis); **s1350** cum multis navibus ..cum telis et ~is aliis defensivis munitis Avesb. 121. **d** armis diffisus Aldh. *VirgV* 2080; insulani..~a ~is repellebant Bede *HE* IV 24; illum in ~is omnique rei militaris usu..attollebant G. Crispin *Herl.* 87; **1100** quodsi ipse preventus vel ~is vel infirmitate pecuniam suam non dederit (*Ch. Hen. I*) *GAS* 522; **s1086** rex Willelmus, quem ~a confregerant et cure ardue sollicitaverant M. Par. *Min.* I 30; **1262** cum..quidam..ad ~a ire proponant, viz. ad torneandum aut aventuras querendum *Cl* 133; **1341** ne quis.. turneare, burdeare, justas facere seu alia facta ~orum exercere presumat (*Cl*) *Foed.* V 223; **1347** secundum jus ~orum *TreatyR* 25 m. 8. **e** ~orum instrumenta bellica, ..hoc est divini macheram verbi et loricam fidei Aldh. *VirgP* 11; ut diris certaret demonis armis *Id. VirgV* 1858; accinctus ~is militiae spiritalis Bede *HE* I 7; instrue spiritualibus ~is virtutibus inermem Anselm (*Or.* 15) III 64; oratores..quibus acuenda precipue sunt ~a facundie Gir. *TH intr.* p. 6; quinque ~a spiritualia que recitat Augustinus Wycl. *Ver.* I 167.

2 arms as mark of rank or class: **a** (of freeman or serf); **b** (of adult); **c** (of knight); **d** (of serjeant or man-at-arms).

a qui servum suum liberat..lanceam et gladium vel que liberorum ~a sunt in manibus ei ponat...si quis in servum transeat, ..in signum transitionis hujus billum vel stumblum vel deinceps ad hunc modum servitutis ~a suscipiat (*Leg. Hen.*) *GAS* 594; **c1210** tradat illi libera ~a, sc. lanceam et gladium; deinde liber homo efficitur (*Leg. Will. retr.*) *Ib.* 491. **b** **s1149** Henrico nepoti suo David rex Scotorum virilia tradidit ~a...Eustachius vero filius regis Stephani..eodem anno virilia sumpserat ~a H. Hunt. *HA* VIII 29. **c** de harieta lagemannorum habuit..unius militis ~a *DB* I 189; regis armiger factus ei servivit donec ab eo ~a militaria accepit Ord. Vit. III 9 p. 109 (cf. ib. VI 10 p. 105: ~a militiae ab eo accepit); hunc [filium Henrici I] Lanfrancus.., dum juvenile robur attingere vidit, ad ~a pro defensione regni sustulit eumque lorica induit et galeam capiti ejus imposuit eique ut regis filio..militie cingulum..cinxit *Ib.* VIII 1 p. 267; **1260** quod omnes illos..qui tenent de nobis in capite et milites esse debent et non sunt distringas ad recipiendum a nobis ~a militaria *Cl* 171; **1277** a die quo dictus comes [Lincolnie] ~a militaria a domino Henrico rege patre nostro cepit et cinctus fuit gladio comitatus illius (*Breve Regis*) *Ambrosden* I 408; **s1327** Edwardus [rex] juvenis suscepit ~a militaria per..comitem Lancastrie Wals. *HA* I 188. **d** **1225** in liberationibus servientum ad ~a *KRAc* 364/1 m. 4; **1264** rogamus quatinus..aliam gentem ad ~a regnum illud..invadere..nullatenus permittatis *Cl* 396; **1266** stipendiis militum et servientum ad ~a *Cl* 234; **1297** generalem servientem hominum nostrorum ad ~a *RGasc* III 372; **s1343** comites et barones et alii homines ~orum Avesb. 101b; **s1351** dc viri ~orum congregati in Vasconia *Ib.* 121; **s1346** captivatis..centum militibus ac hominibus ad ~a sexcentis J. Reading 155; **s1346** putans regnum Anglie gentibus ~orum omnino evacuatum *Plusc.* IX 40; **s1405** fugit papa cum sua ~orum gente ad Viterbium Ad. Usk. 99; omnes ville et burgi [Francie] solvunt regi annuatim ingentes summas..pro stipendiis hominum ad ~a Fortescue *LLA* 35 (cf. ib.: si gentes ad ~a comedunt alitilia sua); **1496** nostrum servitorem ad ~a *Pat* 578 m. 11.

3 arms (her.), blazon. **b** (w. *Domini*) representation of the instruments of the Passion.

1237 pro j platello..ad opus regine..et pro auro ad deauranda scuta in ipso platello de ~is regis *Pipe* 81 r. 15; **1243** emi faciant unum pulcrum lapidem ponendum super corpus Geroldi..justiciarii Hibernie, in quo fieri faciant scutum ipsius G., cum ~is suis *Liberate* 20 m. 19; **c1250** vexilla nova parata aureis pellis de ~is regiis *Vis. S. Paul.* 15; **1261** scutum de ~is suis propriis *KRMem.* 34 r. 8 *d.*; **1303** cyphus cum aymallo de ~is regis Anglie (*KRAc* 363/6) *DocExch.* 277; **1315** casula..consuta ~is diversorum *Invent. Ch. Ch.* 52; **1320** pro armis domini regis faciendis ad quatuor portas *Rec. Leic.* I 333; **s1339** ~a gerit quadrata de ~is Francie et Anglie compaginatis Baker 117; **1357** cuidam heraldo ~orum *Ac. Durh.* 557; **s1326** vestierunt eum [H. Dispensatorem] uno vestimento cum ~is suis reversatis missa corona de urticis in capite ejus Knighton I 436; **s1377** inter cetera probra que duci [Lancastrie] intulerat ~a ejus in foro sunt publico reversata Wals. *HA* I 325; **1386** cum uno homine armato de ~is meis, cooperto de russeto cum *scochons* de ~is meis *FormA* 429; **1391** pro j scuto ~orum domini *Ac. H. Derby* 107; **1395** in quadam causa ~orum..de certis ~is de *goules* cum tribus *cheverons* de argento *Pat* 341 m. 8; imagineris te esse retro illa ~a et quod essent super pectus tuum ante te, et sic potes cognoscere dexterum latus a sinistro Bad. Aur. 143; potest.. portare ~a illa duplicata que fuerunt patris sui una cum ~is matris sue *Ib.* 136; ~a et insignia ad cognoscendum homines sunt inventa Upton 59; [T. abbas, ob. 1396] penticium cum ~is diversorum dominorum..lucidissime depinxit *G. S. Alb.* III 389; **1404** item x panni de blueto de ~is *Ac. Durh.* 395; [W. episcopus, ob. 1406] de omnibus edificiis suis arma sua, viz. vj virgas vicissim flexatas in forma cribri, imposuit *Hist. Durh.* 5; **1415** ego Ricardus Brigge alias dictus Lancastr' rex ~orum *Reg. Cant.* II 186; **1417** homines qui in viagiis nostris..~a ac tunicas ~orum vocatas *cotearmures* in se sumpserunt (*Cl*) *Foed.* IX 457a; **1447** volo quod executor meus..ponet supra sepulcrum meum..lapidem marmoreum ..cum ~is meis suprasculptis supra eundem *MunAcOx* 557. **b** **1448** j tecam cum ~is Domini gemmis textam..cum duobus corporalibus in eadem (*Invent. All Souls*) *Arch. J.* LI 120.

4 tools, instruments, organs.

Brigidam..domum reversam, relictis ibidem quibusdam insigniis suis, viz. pera, monili, nola et textrilibus ~is W. Malm. *Glast.* 24; si aliquam vi oppressisset, genitalibus privabatur ~is H. Hunt. *HA* VI 39; **1251** siccum quod jacuit per terram, quod colligere possent manibus suis sine ~is emolitis *IMisc.* 5/24.

armacudium v. armicudium. armagium v. arrivagium.

armamentarium [CL], storehouse or armoury.

Aldh. *PR* 140 (v. armamentum); ~ium, *wæpnahus* Ælf. *Gl.*; spatiando videbamus primo ~ium, secundo bibliothecam sive armarium, quod idem est Balsh *Ut.* 49; hoc †armentorium, locus ubi fiunt arm[a] WW.

armamentum [CL], equipment, tackle: **a** (of ship); **b** (of plough).

a locus receptaculi, quo ~a reconduntur, armamentarium nuncupatur, quod ad naucleros proretasque pertinet Aldh. *PR* 140; **s1040** trierem..~is optimis instructam Fl. Worc. I 195; pro ferreo ~o [sc. anchora] ejusdem forme W. Cant. *Mir. Thom.* III 44; estus maris..de navis ~is videbatur abtrahendo consumpsisse R. Cold. *Cuthb.* 33; **1243** galias nostras cum omnibus ~is suis *Liberate* 20 m. 19; ~um, A. *takelyng*, ..a *hal takylle* WW. **b** **c1230** de maeremio domini parare debet aratrum cum omni ~o *Doc. Bec* 55.

ararmarius v. armurarius.

armare [CL], to arm, equip w. arms or armour. **b** (fig.).

in ipso proaulo seorsum se ~at W. Fitzst. *Thom.* 136; **s1297** [princeps] jussit ~ari suos et ipse confestim ~atus processit in publicum W. Guisb. 322; **1381** ducere possit.. certas armaturas..ad ~andum inde ad omnes pecias pro listis R. M. armigerum *RScot* 35b. **b** qui solet assiduis castos armare triumphis Aldh. *VirgV* 2020; qui B. Hilarium hac ~asti virtute ut tibi militaret in fide Egb. *Pont.* 91; episcopus quasi in specula locatur, ut populum contra hostes demones et hereses ~are nitatur Gir. *PI* I 19 p. 108.

2 (p. ppl.) armed or armour-clad. **b** (as sb. m.) armed man, man-at-arms. **c** (of animals). **d** (of fortified towns).

~atas peltarum testudine catervas Aldh. *VirgP* 38 p. 289; legio ~ata Bede *HE* I 12; **742** episcopi qui pugnant ~ati Bonif. *Ep.* 50 p. 83; **9..** quasi vir ~atus, *swa gewepned wer* WW; **1199** milites et gentes ~atos *Pipe* 154; **1214** ~atus lorica et purpuinto et capello ferreo *SelPlCrown* 71; si sint ista infirmantia in homine ~ato, oportet dilacerare arma Gad. 122 v. 1; ~atus usque ad dentes multiplici armatura tam linea quam ferrea *Proc. A. Kyteler* 25; **1355** unus constabularius ~atus cum dublet plat' bacinett' cum *pisan* et *aventail* et *bratz* et cerotecis *Rec. Norw.* I 391 (cf. ib.: plene ~ati, ..dimidie ~ati); **1375** communes noctivagi..incedentes..~ati ad modum guerre *Leet Norw.* 68; **1386** (v. arma 3a). **b** ita '~atus' significat substantiam, quia significat habentem substantiam, id est arma Anselm (*Gram.* 19) I 164; **1229** amotis custodiis balistariorum et aliorum ~atorum (*Lit. Patriarch.*) M. Par. *Maj.* III 183; **s1383** numerus tam ~atorum quam peditum..cotidie accrescebat *V. Ric. II* 44; cogebantur in fugam per nostros, cesis quibusdam ex eis et captis duobus ~atis Elmh. *Hen. V* 41. **c** armatos dentibus apros Aldh. *Aen.* 39. 1; aves ~atas, venaticos canes J. Sal. *Pol.* 674A; accipitres..quibus..pedes unguibus ~atos natura dedit Gir. *TH* I 12; illic [in Oceano Britannico] miles [? *swordfish*] ~atus equitat Gerv. Tilb. III 63. **d** villa..~ata et circumcincta muris externis angularibus Elmh. *Hen. V* 16.

3 (w. *duellum*) to arm (combatants) for (ordeal by battle).

1200 unde placitum fuit inter eos..et duellum invadiatum et ~atum (*Fine*) *Reg. Malm.* I 449; **1218** duellum fuit inde invadiatum, ~atum et percussum *Eyre Yorks* 40 (cf. *PlCrGlouc* 22 [**1221**]: venerunt ~ati..et duellum percussum fuit inter eos); **1228** vidit in curia prioris duellum vadiatum et ~atum et concordatum *Feod. Durh.* 275; **1292** duellum vadiatum, †aramiatum [MS ~atum] et percussum fuit (*JustIt* 137 r. 13*d.*) *Doc. Scot.* 363.

4 to fit out or man (a ship). **b** to fit (nets w. ropes). **c** to fit (a mill-wheel) w. (?) cogs.

s1383 hostes ~averunt v vasa bellica que balingarie appellantur Wals. *YN* 338; **1386** inveniet..x galeas..bene ~atas, viz. de uno patrono, ..xviij marinariis, xxx balastariis, ciiij^xx remigibus (*DipDoc* E 309) *Foed.* VII 521; **1400** aliquam navem, bargeam sive balingeram de guerra ~atam (*Cl*) *Ib.* VIII 147. **b** **1238** fieri faciatis..duo retia ad piscandum et funibus ~ari *Liberate* 13 m. 25. **c** **c1334** in stipendio j carpentarii reparantis et ~antis dictam rotam [aquaticam] *MinAc* 992/22 (cf. ib. 13 [**1324**]: armant' de novo rotam aquaticam).

5 to incite. **b** (p. ppl.) earnest.

Guillelmus Clito, Roberti ducis Normannorum filius, ~atus est ut patrem suum..liberaret Ord. Vit. XII 18 p. 358; conatus est..ut..~asset manum laicam in spoliacionem ecclesie Elmh. *Hen. V* 6. **b** J. de Kirkeby [ob. 1290]..precibus rogavit ~atis ut..obligarent *G. S. Alb.* I 468 (cf. ib. II 91: peticioni ~ate).

6 (gdv.) suitable for use as armour, defensive (*cf.* 2 *armarius*).

1224 recepit de lineis armaturis..coler' et coifam et tunicam ~andam *CurR* XI 1913 (cf. *Cl* 109a [**1208**]: tunicas nostras ad ~andum paratas).

7 (p. ppl. as sb. f.) armed force: **a** armada (naut.); **b** army (OF *armee*).

a **1349** congregata quadam ~ata nostra navium apud Sandewicum pro passagio nostro versus partes transmarinas *Pat* 227 m. 15; **1360** potestatem arraiandi..et gubernandi omnes naves tocius ~ate (*TreatyR*) *Foed.* VI 170; **1472** cum quandam ~atam potenciam ad proficiscendum super mare.. ordinaverimus, ..eis..potestatem..committimus ad ~atam predictam conducendam *Pat* 529 m. 9; **s1473** rex omnem ~atam suam..Calesiam usque transvexit *Croyl. Cont. C* 558. **b** magis vir beatus didicit in eo confidere per quem reges regnant quam in ~ata exercitus sui (*V. Ethelberti*) Ciren. 274; omnes ville et burgi [Francie] solvunt regi.. ingentes summas..pro stipendiis hominum ad arma, sic quod ~ata regis..pascatur..de stipendiis suis per pauperes villarum..regni Fortescue *LLA* 35.

1 armaria v. aranea.

2 armaria, armoury (*cf. armarium* e).

1436 per deliberacionem..in duobus pipis..plenis harnesiis armorum..constabulario castri.., locatis in ~ia..castri per eundem *ExchScot* 680.

3 armaria v. armarium.

†armariculum [? *for* armariolum], small cupboard.

1409 de iij s. de j ~o appreciato *Test. Ebor.* III 48.

armariolum [CL], **~a, ~us,** small cupboard or chest for storing valuables, ambry (esp. eccl.). **b** book-case. **c** study. **d** (fig.).

s1217 (v. armarium a); **c1270** custodem ~e de celario *Reg. Wint.* II 655; **s1272** (v. armarium a); **1342** fabro..facienti ceruras..pro ~o *Sacr. Ely* II 109; **1354** pro seruris..vj hostiorum cujusdam almariole pro vestimentis in revestiario in eodem (*sic*) custodiendis *KRAc* 471/6 r. 15; **1368** unum almariolum bene ferratum pro vestimentis *Invent. Norw.* 124; **1414** in pictura ~e S. Andree *Ac. Durh.* 224; **1433** ad fabricam ~i noviciorum *Ib.* 468; **1434** super facturam almoriolorum infra capellam *Ib.* 711; **1436** unum tabernaculum pro eodem altari..cum ~o de tabulis orientalibus pro vestimentis conservandis *Reg. Aberd.* II 137; **a1440** in factura illorum almarialorum que ponuntur sub capella pro custodia minutorum Amund. II *app.* 272; **1458** pro expensis factis in castro de Edinburgh super garderoba et ammoriolis ejusdem *ExchScot* 387; ~um, ..hoc almariolum, A. *almary*, ..hoc armoriolum, *a nalmry*, ..almoriolum, A. *almery* WW. **b** versus ~o librorum Giraldi quo composuit suprascripti Gir. *Symb. metr.* 24 *rub.*; [P. abbas, ob. 1093] dedit..xxviij volumina notabilia.., sine..aliis libris, qui in ~is habentur *G. S. Alb.* I 58; debent reponere in almariolum in claustro libros suos *Cust. Cant.* 10; **c1350** ~i fortes fiant in stallis.. ad reponendum..libros *Mon. Exon.* 270; **1361** carolas in claustro et librorum ~as fregerunt (*Chr. Abingd.*) *EHR* XXVI 733; [J. abbas, ob. 1401] sub volta capelle..almariola pro munimentis conventus reponendis facere proposuit *G. S. Alb.* III 442; **1435** subtus..altare unum almarriolum [fiat] pro libris et vestimentis..conservandis *Test. Ebor.* II 53; **c1470** in ~o in choro pro custodia psalteriorum limitato *Reg. Whet.* I 430. **c** **1601** in quodam ~o suo vocato *his studdy KR Spec. Comm.* 1350. **d** patrum canones..in sacro pectoris sui ~o devote recondens Ailr. *SS Hex.* 6; non nisi in solo pectoris secreto ~o spiritus vite halantis substiterat R. Cold. *Cuthb.* 92 p. 203.

armarium [CL; cf. OF *aumaire*], **~a,** cupboard or chest, ambry (esp. eccl.). **b** bookcase. **c** recess in wall. **d** shelf. **e** contents of chest or (?) armoury.

†aumatium vel ~ium, *ælces cynnes cæpehus* Ælf. *Sup.*; **s1217** ecclesias..spoliantes, arcas omnes cum ~iis..confregerunt Wend. II 218 (= M. Par. *Maj.* III 23: cum almariolis); **s1272** omnia preciosa, tam in thesaurario, vestiario, refectorio, quam eciam in ceteris ecclesie illius officinis, et almaria, ea minutim confringentes.., asportarunt Fl. Worc. *Cont. C* 208 (= Oxnead *Chr.* 241: almariola); **s1289** inventum est quoddam ~ium de serico in bonis suis [Ade de Stratton], in quo fuerant parure unguium hominum..et alia diabolica B. Cotton 172; servitores ecclesie stabunt continuo inter professionem ante almare, portantes turribulum et cereos *Cust. Cant.* 386; **1359** in una nova cerra pro almaria capelle *Ac. Durh.* 266; **1359** almorias, *quivers* et cistas in Turri..pro reposicione et salva custodia eorundum arcuum, sagittarium et cordarum *Pat* 258 m. 9*d.*; **c1400** vestibulum..elongavit et..adornavit ~iis *Mon. Francisc.* I 508; **1423** j almarie (*sic*) pro vestimentis inponendis *Ac. Obed. Abingd.* 98; **1423** j almoria *Test. Ebor.* III 89; **1432** [lego] unum almarium et unum *copbord Ib.* II 36; **1480** ubi..~ia sunt ad res altaris reponendas *Lit. Cant.* III 301; **1588** officium custodis garderobe nostre lectorum nostrorum et ~ie nostre infra castrum nostrum de Wyndsor *Pat* 1320 m. 10. **b** **804** si forte [illi libri] in ~io imperiali inveniantur, quaerite, legite Alcuin *Ep.* 309; bibliotheca vel ~ium vel archivum, *boochord* Ælf. *Sup.*; **a1160** x s... quos..Walterus donavit ~io ad reparationem librorum ecclesie *Chr. Rams.* 272; libentius voluisset fieri magister almarii et custos librorum quam abbas Brakelond 130v; qui eosdem libros videre desiderat, in almario picto quod est in ecclesia..repositos poterit reperire *G. S. Alb.* I 184; ~ium, in quo libri reponuntur, intrinsecus ligno vestitum esse debet, ne humor parietum libros humectet vel inficiet *Obs. Barnwell* 64; **1360** pro..factura novarum almoriarum

pro rotulis..inibi custodiendis (*Cl*) *Foed.* VI 173; **c1450** ad officium precentoris pertinet committere juvenibus custodiam ~iorum et eadem reparare; et..libros reponat si forte..obliti fuerint (*Reg. Evesham*) *MonA* II 39b. **c 1189** licet vicinus habeat in predicto muro corbellos vel trabes ad sustentandum solarium suum, vel etiam arcus et almeria, ..nihil amplius potest in predicto muro exigere.. (*Assisa Domorum*) *MGL* I 326 (= *Leg. Ant. Lond.* 209: almaria). **d** *schelf*, epiaster, epilocarium, ~ium, repositorium *PP*. **e a1120** quecunque acquisivi in ornamentis ecclesiasticis.. et plenarium ~ium meum, pannos etiam meos *Cart. Bath* I 53; **1415** lego J. fratri meo totum ~ium meum exceptis ij loricis *Reg. Cant.* II 89.

1 armarius, librarian.

in decano bonitatem invenit, ..in ~io cognitionem futurarum rerum *V. Osw.* 423; cantor qui et alio nomine ~ius appellatur, eo quod de libris curam habere solet qui in armariis continentur *Cust. Westm.* 28; precentor, qui eciam ~ius dicitur, binomium habet, unum quia habet custodiam librorum et aliud quia ad ipsum pertinet regere chorum *Obs. Barnwell* 58.

2 armarius, used as armour, defensive (*cf. armare* 6, *armatrix* b).

1208 ciij s. ..pro cendal' ad tunicas ~ias et banerias.. et j m. ad tunicas ~ias domini regis liniandas per xxxij ulnas de linea tela *Cl* 109a; **s1297** dicunt..Angli quod rex non fuit ibidem in persona propria, sed alius..indutus consimiliter in sua tunica †armorica *Plusc.* VIII 27.

3 armarius v. armurarius. armata v. armare 7.

armatio, arming, donning or wearing armour. **b** provision of armour. **c** (w. ref. to animals).

1258 noveritis me..me obligasse ad duellum vadiandum ..pro eis [abbate et ecclesia Glaston']..pro xxx m. .., de quibus..abbas..mihi solveret in vadiatione..duelli x m., in tonsione mea v m.; et residuum..die ~onis mee tradatur alicui bono viro in equalem manum (*Script. Glast.*) UPTON *app.* (*notes*) 36; sub †inductione [? l. induitione] sunt hujusmodi species, ~o, vestigatio..; sub ~one sunt hujusmodi, loricatio, calcatio BACON XV 232. **b 1327** quod illi qui insufficientes fuerint ad pugnandum contribucionem faciant..expensis et ~oni aliorum *RScot* 222a. **c** creavit Deus dentes..quibusdam animalibus propter ~onem, sicut in apris *Ps.*-RIC. *Anat.* 30.

armator, armourer.

1292 pro retibus emptis..per Gilkinum ~orem suum *Doc. Scot.* 374; **1333** ~ori regis..pro diversis..expensis circa facturam diversorum harnesiorum *LTRMem* 105 r. 111; quod aurifabri et ~ores et omnimodo artes non necessarie homini..destruerentur (*Concl. Lollard.*) *Ziz.* 368; **1549** linee armature ~ores *CalPat* III 87.

armatrix, protective (f.). **b** (w. *tunica*) coat of arms (*cf.* 2 *armarius*).

saphirus est gemma ~ix castitatis UPTON 108. **b 1268** Petrus fuit contra dominum regem..et tulit tunicam ~icem Willelmi le Marsal et eidem Willelmo adhesit *JustIt* 618 r. 4.

armatura [CL; cf. armura], **~um,** armament (arms and armour). **b** armour, suit of armour. **c** (dist. as iron or linen). **d** (fig.). **e** (her.).

arma unius militis, ~a autem totius expeditionis ALDH. *PR* 140; **743** servis Dei..~am portare prohibuimus BONIF. *Ep.* 56 p. 99; **1229** balistas et ~as..pro defensione terre reservatas..fecit clam in navi deponi (*Lit. Patriarchae*) M. PAR. *Maj.* III 183; **1233** balistas et omnes alias ~as que fuerunt in castro *Cl* 212; **1307** pro municione castrorum et villarum..balistis et aliis ~is..indigemus (*Pat*) *Foed.* III 16; **1314** castrum..una cum ~is, victualibus et omnibus aliis rebus *RScot* 134a; **1326** lego filiis meis..omnia ~a mea inter eos dividenda *RR K's Lynn* I 118; **1342** pro ~is..pro municione gallee *Ib.* 201; **1344** ne qui..~as quascunque.. Hibernicis..ministrent *Stat. Ir.* I 364; **1554** ~is tam defensivis quam invasivis *Entries* 413. **b 1166** pro scutis probatorum et ~is, vij s. *Pipe* 72; **1230** in ~a ij latronum *Pipe* 98; **1283** invenerunt..de ~is vj loricas, vj capellos ferreos, unum par coopertoriorum et supertunicam..de ferro *Reg. Heref.* 86; **1295** lego..totum atirum de meliori ~a mea ad corpus suum et equum cooperiendum (*Test. N. Longespee*) *EHR* XV 526; **1336** ~as pro xl hominibus que esse volumus dubletta cum platis, bacinettis et cirotecis ferreis vel eciam aketones et hauberjones cum bacinettis et cirotecis predictis *Cl* 99 m. 11; **1390, 1436** (v. armurarius). **c** sicut, ubi militares acies de plano conveniunt, gravis illa et multiplex ~a tam linea quam ferrea milites egregie munit et ornat, sic, ubi solum in arcto configitur.., longe levis ~a prestantior GIR. *EH* II 38; **1209** ad emendas ~as lineas *Misae* 123; **1224** hee sunt ~e quas..recepit..: unam loricam, ..j *gardecors* de ferro, j cohoperturas ferreas, j caligas ferreas, j galeam, j cap[ellum ferreum], j paelett'; et de lineis ~is j purpunctum et j espaulleram de nigro cendalo, ..quiseram et coleram et coifam et tunicam armandam et duo paria cohopertoriorum.. *CurR* XI 1913; **1243** ~as ferreas *RGasc.* I 171 (= *Cl* 5); *Proc. A. Kyteler* 25 (v. armare 2a); **1549** (v. armator). **d** spiritalis ~ae spiculis ..certandum ALDH. *VirgP* 11; sic est quintuplex ~a secundum quam defendi potest [scriptura] a callidis sophistis WYCL. *Ver.* I 167. **e** [reges Francorum] clypeos et vexilla cum ceteris ~is simplicibus tantum gladioli flosculis signant et ornant GIR. *PI* III 30 p. 321; **1328** omnes ~as tam *cotearmurs* quam alias (*Cl*) *Foed.* IV 371.

2 manufacture of arms. **b** (?) arms factory. **c** armoury. **d** (?) armed force, army.

artes mechanice sunt laneficium, ~a, navigatio BACON XV 193. **b 1392** dati ~e [apud Venis] pro j pare de vambraces et emendacione aliorum..harnisiorum *Ac. H. Derby* 280 . **c 1437** officium ~e nostre linee infra Turrim nostram de London' *Pat* 441 m. 1; **1440** officium servientis ~e nostre infra Turrim nostram *Cl* 290 m. 3 (= *PS*: *armery*). **d 1583** vadia..que..alii..equites de ~a nostra in regno Hibernie perceperunt *Pat* 1235 m. 29.

3 defensive (or aggressive) equipment (of animals).

falcones..[predas] prepositis talorum ~is..confodiunt GIR. *TH* I 12; aliquibus et dantur [dentes] ad ~am, sicut apris, sicut cornua dantur aliis ad ~am *Ps.*-RIC. *Anat.* 30.

4 equipment, gear (naut.). **b** (fig.).

nauta ~am regiminis, qua navis disponi debuerat, amisit R. COLD. *Cuthb.* 23; nunquam potest barcha bene ascendere nisi cum vento et velo vel bona remorum ~a S. SIM. *Itin.* 41. **b** scripturarum flectenda sunt gubernacula totiusque navigii ~a atque instrumenta paranda (*V. Aldh.*) W. MALM. *GP* V 199.

†armaturus, armoured.

c1288 preter equis ~is [? l. et ~is] *KRAc* 231/26 r. 3.

armebolta, 'arm-bolt', handcuff.

1486 incarceratos..in gaola..custodiet..in compedibus, collariis ferreis, ~is..et aliis vinculorum generibus *Reg. Heref.* 102.

armelausa, armelus v. armilausa. armell- v. armill-.

Armenicus, Armenian. **b** (w. *bolus*) earth containing iron oxide. **c** (w. *lapis*) carbonate of copper. **d** (? *sc. sichen*) southernwood (*Artemisia*).

amomum †armonicum [v.l. ~um] cet[e]ris melius *Alph.* 9. **b** bolus †Armenitus BART. ANGL. XVI 83 (v. 1 bolus 2b). **c** lapis ~us dicitur a regione illa *SB* 27. **d** *sothrenwod*, abrotonum, ~us, herba est *CathA*.

Armenius [CL], **Armenus,** Armenian (adj. or sb.).

s1097 in Syros et ~os, civitatis [Antiochie] indigenas W. MALM. *GR* IV 361; **s1102** in illis regionibus Syri et ~ii barbaris mixti habitabant; in casalibus passim degentes, Turcis serviebant..et Christianam nichilominus legem.. devote servabant ORD. VIT. X 19 p. 129; **s1252** quidam ~ii ..ad S. Albanum venerunt; ..est autem, ut dicunt, terra eorundem ~iorum distans a Jerusalem xxx diebus et ultimi fines eorum attingunt usque ad primas partes Indie M. PAR. *Maj.* V 340–1; audiveram..indoctorum ~orum..tumultum (RIC. ARMAGH *Quaest. Armen.*) *Wycl. & Ox.* 91.

armentalis, concerned w. cattle.

coniza lata vel ~is *Alph.* 43.

armentarium, ~ariolum, herd of cattle.

a drawe of nowte, armentum, ~ium, ~iolum *CathA*.

armentarius [CL], herdsman.

[est] armentum quod ~ius seu bubulcus procurat ALDH. *PR* 140 p. 139; subtrahuntur..compascua ~iis J. SAL. *Pol.* 396B; **1461** ~io domine regine, ad armenta ejusdem, vij marte *ExchScot* 92.

armentorium v. armamentarium.

armentum [CL], herd of cattle.

mitem armento fecit succedere taurum ALDH. *VirgV* 598; **805** hec duo aratra..a quibusdam 'Campus ~orum', id est *Hriðra Leah*, appellantur *CS* 322; **10..** ~a, *hryðera heorde* WW; gregum et ~orum depredationi *G. Steph.* II 83; **1460** ultra proprias terras domini regis deputatas ad ~a sua *ExchScot* 646.

Armenus v. Armenius. armiclausa v. armilausa.

armicudium [? < arma+cudere], dagger.

1448 sepius fregit pacem, cum †armiscudio et armis proximos suos invadens *MunAcOx* 581; **1448** †aruncudium (*Rye MSS*) *HMC Rep* V 490a; **1463** extraxit sanguinem super..Willelmum injuste cum armic' precii viij d. (*CourtR Everdon*) *Rec. Eton* XXXVIII no. 61; **1461** quod, ..~ium cum quo..Ricardum noscitur usque ad sanguinis effusionem percussise sursum in manu sua gestans, ..processionem.. antecederet, ~ium ad feretrum S. Thome..offerendo *Reg. Heref.* 98; ~ium, *a dagger*, ..; armiturium, A. *a dagar* WW; **1549** †arcudio sive dagario *CalPat* 241; **1573** vi et armis, viz. gladiis, scutis, armacudiis, falcastris et aliis armis invasivis *Pat* 1105 m. 8.

armiductor, ~doctor, military commander.

s1297 sic ipse [W. Wallace] ~doctor et gencium ductor effectus est *Plusc.* VIII 26; **s1402** ex eo quod valenciores ~doctores [v.l. ~ductores]..superasset *Ib.* X 19; **s1409** de parte Insulanorum cecidit ~doctor Maclane nomine FORDUN *Cont.* XV 21; **s1306** Symon Fraser, ille nobilis ~ductor *Extr. Chr. Scot.* 133.

armifaber, armourer.

1393 hic cultellārius, tonsor et armifaber (R. MAIDSTONE) *Pol. Poems* I 284.

armifodrita, ~fraudita, v. hermaphrodita. armigaisa v. armilausa.

armiger [CL], bearing arms.

rex noster cum sua fideli gente ~gera ELMH. *Hen. V* 5; **1549** precones ~geri *StatOx* 352.

2 (sb. m.) armour-bearer, squire (in service of knight or sim.). **b** (w. *Jovis*) eagle. **c** (w. *pro corpore*) esquire for the body. **d** household servant (esp. mon.).

~ger, *wæpenbora* ÆLF. *Gl.*; **a1123** David et Radulfus ~geri Bernardi (*Reg. Pri. Merton*) *EHR* XIV 420; barones ..milites suos et proprios servientes sub friborgo habebant; et ipsi suos ~geros vel alios servientes suos sub suo friborgo (*Leg. Ed.*) *GAS* 647; ORD. VIT. III 9 (v. 2 arma 2c); equos qui ~geris magis conveniunt, durius incedentes sed expedite tamen W. FITZST. *Thom. prol.* 11; **a1185** ubicunque ~geri mei herbam ad equos meos ceperint *BBC* (*Swansea*) 58; arma subitus ab ~gero rapit MAP *NC* IV 7; **1234** quoddam buhurdicium captum est inter ~geros (*Pat*) *Foed.* I 332; **1248** venit dominus W. ..et iiij ~geri et tres garciones veniebant post ipsum ducentes tres leporarios *SelPlForest* 87; **s1321** magnates..diversa indumenta super arma ad cognoscendum turmas sibi providentes, viz. pro militibus cotucas, A. *quartleys*, pro ~geris vero *bendes* TROKELOWE 109; **s1370** inter scutiferos legis vires dominantur, / jura per armigeros subjectis dum reserantur (J. BRIDL.) *Pol. Poems* I 138; **1419** solvet iiij d. aldermanno, nisi sit miles, ~ger, femina, legis apprenticius vel clericus, aut aliquis alius qui 'non habet hic manentem civitatem' [cf. *Heb.* xiii 14] (*Lib. Albus*) *MGL* I 38; *a squyere.* ~ger, domicellus, dominellus, scutifer *CathA*. **b** armiger infausti Jovis et raptor Ganymedis ALDH. *Aen.* 57. 1. **c 1484** Willelmi C. ..pro corpore domini regis ~geri *Reg. Whet.* II 268 (cf. *Cl* 361 [**1501**] m. 10*d*.). **d s1124** G. L., a quodam rustico captus, arma sua illi pro redemptione sua dedit et ab eo tonsus instar ~geri, manu palum gestans, ..confugit ORD. VIT. XII 39 p. 459; **s1283** juris civilis professor, in veste stragulata quasi ~ger fuisset, laicum se fingens GRAYSTANES 19; **1312** dabit..unam robam honestam, sicut ~geri..abbatis capiunt *Reg. Aberbr.* I 286; **1322** camberlanus, marescallus et alii ~geri prioris *DCCant* J 518 (cf. *Cant. Cath. Pri.* 31); **1425** in blodeo panno empto pro ~geris et valectis prioris Burcestr') *Ambrosden* II 256.

3 esquire (as title), person entitled to bear arms (her.).

1420 Johannes Goldsmyth de Hertylpole, ~ger *Feod. Durh.* 24; **1440** Johannem de Enczberd, ~gerum BEKYNTON I 182; *squyer, gentylman*, ..*sweyn*, ~ger *PP*; **1472** Johanni Bromston, ~gero *Lit. Cant.* III 258; his [militibus] proximi fuere ~geri, qui et scutiferi hominesque ad arma, ..qui vel a clypeis gentilitiis, quae in nobilitatis insignia gestant, vel quia principibus et majoribus illis ab armis erant nomen traxerunt. ..~geri primarii hodie censentur equitum auratorum filii natu maximi et eorum itidem filii maximi successive; secundo in loco habentur filii natu maximi minorum filiorum baronum et aliorum superioris ordinis..; tertio ordine sunt quibus rex ipse cum titulo insignia donat aut ~geros creat, collum torque SS vel sigmatico argenteo et candidis et argentatis calcaribus exornans, unde hodie .. vocantur *whitespurres*..; quarto loco ~geri habentur quicunque aliquo publico..munere funguntur vel principi honestiori conditione famulantur CAMD. *Br.* 140.

armilausa, ~ia [LL < Germ.], sleeveless tunic or cloak. **b** clasp.

~ia, *serce GlC* A 755; **†605** (12c) †armilcaisia oloserica *CS* 6 (= THORNE 1762: †armigaisia); colobia, levitonaria, †armillansas [*gl.*: quasi armiclausas, G. *curtepiez*] BALSH. *Ut.* 53; **1376** judicium et pena aldermanni, eo quod ~a sive cloca sua fuit simplex et non furrata (*LBLond* H) *MGL* I 609; **1375** insultum fecit Johanni B. et ibidem ~am suam delaceravit *SessPLincs* 225; **1386** unam ~am duplicatam et alia vestimenta ad corpus dicte Matillidis spectancia *Pat* 321 m. 9; **c1390** quod oportet provideri dicto T. de..ocreis et calcaribus et curta ~a gradui sui competentibus *FormOx* 236; **1418** lego meam hoplandam et ~am meam viridis coloris *Reg. Heref.* 44; **1419** capucio..et armilousa, A. dicta *a cloak*, qua..induebatur..ab eo depositis *Conc.* III 405; **1430** lego ..armilousam, sed remota ipsius armilouse furrura *Reg. Cant.* II 478; *cloke*, ..*hayeste garment or huke*, armelus, armelausa, lacerna *PP*; **1461** idem famulus recepit ab eo gladium, frenum et ~am de russeto in suam custodiam *MunAcOx* 685; **1473** pro j †armilansa simplici de scarlet *Test. Ebor.* III 73; armelausa, A. *a cloke*, ~a, *a sclavayn*, ..hec armiclausa, *a clok* WW; *a scaplory*, †armilansa, †armilans, scapularium *CathA*; abstulit..unam †armilansam duplicatam..et eam induit *Entries* 266. **b 14..** hoc armiclausum, *a claspe* WW.

armilla [CL], **~um,** bracelet. **b** stole bracelet (worn in coronation). **c** (fig.; *cf. Job* xl 21). **d** (?) book-clasp. **e** armillary sphere (astr.). **f** ring for hanging up.

armellae, brachialia *GlC* A 722; prostitutae..quae obrizo rutilante periscelidis ~aque lacertorum tereti..comuntur ALDH. *Ep.* 3; **796** duas direxit ~as auri obrizi pensantes xxiiij d. ALCUIN *Ep.* 96; **s876** [Dani] ei statuunt jusjuramentum in eorum ~a sacra ÆTHELW. IV 3; [rex] aliquando dat mihi equum aut ~am [AS: *beah*] ÆLF. *Coll.* 93; **9..** dextrocerium i. brachiale, ~um vel torium, *earmbeag* WW; ~as bajulans in brachiis ambobus superbe HERM. ARCH. 21; **s1040** Godwinus regi..dedit trierem..electis lxxx militibus decoratam, quorum unusquisque habebat duas in suis brachiis aureas ~as xvj uncias pendentes FL. WORC. I 195; **c1260** tactis sacrosanctis et super ~am S. Bege corporali me prestiti juramento *Reg. St. Bees* 314; hoc ~um est ornamentum WW. **b 11..** accinctus ense similiter, ~as accipiat, dicente metropolitano: "accipe ~as sinceritatis et sapientie divineque circumdationis indicium" (*Consecr. Regis*) *Lib. Regal.* 15; iste ~e in modum stole circa collum et ab utraque scapula usque ad compages brachiorum erunt dependentes *Ib.* 15. **c** Cuthbertus ~a sue clementie maxillam tue nequitie perforat R. COLD. *Cuthb.* 63. **d s780** Offa rex dedit ecclesie Wygorniensi..magnam bibliam cum duabus ~is ex auro *Ann. Worc.* 366. **e** instrumenta quibus experimur ea que sunt in celestibus cujusmodi vocantur ~e vel alia BACON *Maj.* I 131; rectangulum in remedium tediosi et difficilis operis ~arum..concepimus ad rectificandum cursus et loca stellarum WALLINGF. *Rect.* 337. **f** aptemus ~am unam suspensoriam sive portatilem *Id. Albion* 369.

2 (?) arm-pit.

ex parte sinistra a planta pedis usque ad ~as turgida fuit quasi ydropyca *Mir. Montf.* 108.

armillatus, adorned w. rings.

s1388 in apparatu festivali in robis talaribus, stolis ~is, ad cenam sedentes *Plusc.* X 9.

armillum [CL], wine-jar.

armellum, vas vinarium *GlC* A 782.

armilustrium [CL], purification of arms. **b** armed assembly. **c** tournament.

∼ium, quod armis locus lustretur *Erf.* 2. 267. 54. **b** miles..in ∼io a manerio suo non multum distante cum suis complicibus causa mali perpetrandi existens O. CHERITON *Fab. add.* A 12. **c** hic ∼lustras, *a turnament* WW.

†arminilis, *s. dub.*

expulsus est [Britus] ab Italia et ∼is [vv.ll. armillis etc.] fuit NENN. *HB* 152.

armiportator, armour-bearer.

armiger, ∼or *GlC* A 798.

armipotens, strong in arms.

689 Caedual armipotens (*Epitaph.*) BEDE *HE* V 7; rex ∼ens Eadgar *V. Osw.* 425; nobilitas innata tibi probitatis honorem, / armipotens Alfrede, dedit H. HUNT. *HA* V 13.

armiscudium v. armicudium.

armistitium, armistice.

1335 concordatur quod ∼ium fiat ex utraque parte in archiis regnorum *RScot* 335b.

armistri v. armus b. armiturium v. armicudium. armon- v. ammon-, armen-, harmon-.

armoracia [CL], kale or charlock (*cf. ammoniacus c*).

arboracia vel lapsana, *cal* ÆLF *Gl.*; amoracea, rapistrum *Alph.* 8; rapistrum, armoceren, A. *kenekel* vel *carlokes Ib.* 153.

armor- v. et. armar-, armur-.

†armoria, (?) alms (*cf. elemosynaria*).

[Adelstanus] in perpetuam elemosynam dedit S. Johanni ..quatuor travas de unaquaque caruca per totum Austriding .., si quidem ex priorum regum statutis persolvebatur communiter..regiis equis et emissariis suis predicta ∼ia *Sanct. Bev.* no. 3.

1 armoricus v. 2 armarius

2 Armoricus, Breton.

hi sunt Brittones ∼i NENN. *HB* 167; in ∼a Britannia G. MON. VIII 3; Scotos, Cambros et Cornubienses / Armoricosque viros sociabunt *V. Merl.* 970; Cornubia et ∼a Britannia lingua utuntur fere persimili, Kambris tamen.. fere cunctis intelligibili GIR. *DK* I 6.

armura [OF *armëure* < armatura], armour.

1306 cum esset captus..amisit equos, ∼am, hernasium et quicquid habuit *RParl* I 193a; **1381** asportaverunt certas ∼as pro tubiis (*sic*) (*Anc. Indict.*) *Peasants' Rising* 8; **1418** lego..loricam meam et omnes alias harnesias meas sive ∼as pro corpore meo *Reg. Cant.* II 168.

armurarius [OF *armëurier*], armourer. **b** (w. *lineus*) linen-armourer.

1333 cum..∼ii nostri per nos onerati existant ad diversas armaturas..ad nos..ducendas *RScot* 227a; **1355** armararii et alii qui armaturas..habent vendendas (*Cl*) *Foed.* V 817; **1377** billa missa ∼iis quod vendant ad racionabile precium (*LBLond. H*) *MGL* I 653; **1390** cuidam armourerio pro emendacione diversarum armaturarum domini *Ac. H. Derby* 45; **1436** ∼ii armaturas suas cariori precio vendere proponunt (*Cl*) *Foed.* X 648; **1477** J. Tait †armario domini regis *ExchScot* VIII 465 (cf. ib. X 142 [**1489**]: J. Tayt, armerario); **1606** officium brigandarii sive armorarii sui..infra turrim suam London' *Pat* 1714 m. 21. **b 1327** scissores et ∼ii linearum armaturarum..London' *Pat* 166 m. 22; **1380** ∼ius lineus *CalPat* 544; **1452** officium brouderarii et linei ∼ii nostri *Cl* 302 m. 21; **1461** [officium] lenei ∼ii *CalPat* 15.

armus [CL], shoulder or shoulder-blade (of animal). **b** shoulder or upper arm (of man). **c** (?) bough.

in ∼is arietum dextris, carne nudatis et non assis sed elixis, ..futura prospiciunt GIR. *IK* I 11; non spumantis in belli stadio / armos equi fodis calcario J. HOWD. *Ph.* 605. **b** ∼us, *boog GlC* A 765; **a1100** maledictus sit..in humeris, in harmis, in brachiis, in manibus (*Excomm.*) *GAS* 440; nunc ∼os a corpore, nunc brachia separabat GIR. *EH* II 17; utrosque clamis tegat armos D. BEC. 153; debent..collo in corio vituli suspendi..et post harmo epileptici suspendi GILB. II 111 v. 1; humeri et †armistri necessarii sunt etiam ad spiritualium membrorum defensionem BART. ANGL. V 26. **c** nidum in †∼is [? l. ramis] arborum..dependent UPTON 198.

arna v. mna. arnaglosa v. arnoglossa.

Arnaldensis, ∼inus, a local currency (Gasc.).

1282 promiserunt..receptori redituum..in Agenensi mille libras ∼enses in pecunia numerata *AncC* LV 17A; **1281** duos..denarios ∼enses vel unum Morlanensem *RGasc* II 120; **1283** ad precium novies viginti et x li. ∼inorum *Ib.* 215; **1285** v sol. Arnaudensium *Ib.* 262; **1289** xxx li. Arnoldensis monete *Ib.* 319; **1289** pro xxxv li. Ernaldensium *Ib.* 528.

†arnaldia, a disease, (?) Syrian sickness.

s1191 uterque regum Anglie et Francie in infirmitatem que dicitur ∼ia inciderunt, in qua fere usque ad mortem laborantes capillos suos deposuerunt *G. Ric. I* 170; [rex Ricardus] gravissimam incurrit egritudinem, que vulgo arnoldia vocatur, ex ignote regionis constitutione cum ejus naturali complexione minus concordante *Itin. Ric.* III 4.

arnementum [? OF *arrement* < atramentum], 'arnement', vitriol.

1284 pro arnamento empto et melle pro lingua dextrarii nigri ungenda *KRAc* 97/3 r. 11; **1335** in ∼o empto pro equis *Sacr. Ely* II 69.

arnes- v. harnes-.

arnoglossa, ∼us [ἀρνόγλωσσον], waybread, plantain (*Plantago major*).

arnaglosa, *wegbrade GlC* A 763; **12..** arnoglosa, i. *plauntein* WW; ∼a decocta GILB. I 26 v. 1; caputpurgium fit cum succo arnoglose et virge pastoris GAD. 9. 1; ∼a, lingua agni, lingua arietis, plantago major idem, G. *planteyne*, A. *weybrode Alph.* 14; *weybrede*, ∼us, ∼a, plantago, herba est *CathA.*

arnold- v. arnald-. arnotinus, arnus, v. annotinus. arogon v. aregon. arollius v. arrolius.

aroma [ἄρωμα], perfume, fragrant spice. **b** (fig.).

altare hoc..∼atibus divinae sanctificationis infunde EGB. *Pont.* 42; clero cereis et ∼atibus omnique genere gaudiorum occurrente OSB. *Mir. Dunst.* 17; tanta odoris fragrantia..ut..in sepulcro ∼ata scaturire putarentur AILR. *Ed. Conf.* 782B; phenix / ..ingentes ab aromate jungit acervos *V. Merl.* 1348; non odore spiritualia temperando, sicut faciunt ∼ata M. SCOT. *Sol* 722; ∼a dicitur de 'aer'..et 'oma'.., quod est odor in ∼atibus, quasi 'aeris oma', id est bonus odor aeris GARL. *Mor. Scol. prol. gl.*; R. BURY *Phil.* 8 (v. apotheca e). **b** cur nunc virtutum tuarum ∼ata non spirant? OSB. *Mir. Dunst.* 19; diligis..Circen, que tibi suspirate suavitatis ∼ate gaudia plena perfundit MAP *NC* IV 3 p. 143; austro spirante..fluxerunt ∼ata justitie AD. MARSH *Ep.* 189; ∼ata affeccionum et thimiamata precum offerant *Commend. Ed. I* 18.

aromatarius, spicer, apothecary.

1516 cum A. medico..fabulatus sum in officina ∼ii (J. WATSON) *Epp. Erasm.* II 450; **1542** F. Aikman, ∼ius (*Test. Regis Scotiae*) *EHR* XXI 113.

aromaticatus, spiced.

vina alba aquosa aliqualiter ∼a GAD. 22 v. 1.

aromaticitas, fragrance.

potest rosa tam ∼ate quam ruboris gratia destitui si diu superponatur fumositati sulphuris accensi NECKAM *NR* II 66; humores in juncturis et articulis existentes consumuntur ejus [mirri] ∼ate BART. ANGL. XVII 102 (cf. ib. 2: arbor aromatica aliquando habet †aromaticem [? l. ∼atem] in cortice); ∼as non est ex primis qualitatibus sed ex effectibus secundariis GILB. III 50. 2; de simplicibus medicinis valet ysopus, rutha, thimus, spica nardi racione terrestreitatis et ∼atis GAD. 71. 1.

aromaticus [ἀρωματικός], spicy, fragrant. **b** (sb. n.) spice. **c** (sb. m.) a kind of tree. *V. et. calamus.*

rursus aromaticum vis ignea prebet odorem NECKAM *DS* VII 305; cum..transisset apud Montem Pessulanum per vicum ubi diverse species ∼e terebantur O. CHERITON *Par.* 47; non discernunt inter medios odores, sed inter extremos tantum, sc. inter fetidum et ∼um *Ps.*-RIC. *Anat.* 28; **1220** ferina.. / panis aromaticis nunc fertur cocta sepulchris H. AVR. *Poems* 2. 223; **1423** victualia species ∼as..sive res alias..adducentes (*Ord. Senensis*) AMUND. I 166. **b** vapor calidus sicut de ∼is et fumosis GAD. 69 v. 2; muscus nomen est equivocum ad idem ∼um et ad illam lanuginem que vestit arbores *SB* 30; dulci mero et saccaro conditis ∼is *Spons. Marie* 28. **c** BART. ANGL. XVII 101 (v. acanthus).

aromatizare [ἀρωματίζειν], to spice, perfume, anoint. **b** (fig.).

coletur.., ∼etur cum musci 3 1 GAD. 66. 1; *to uynte*, ∼are, ..ungere *CathA.* **b** quando divinitas Christi fuit illapsa apostolis, tunc ejus humanitas ∼avit ecclesiam WYCL. *Ver.* I 294 (cf. *Cantic.* i 11).

2 to exhale fragrance (of). **b** (fig.).

sophiste accipiunt de sanguine illo et miscent cum partibus granorum maturatorum, et sic decipiunt; sed nigrior fit color nec sic ∼at BACON IX 173; *to savyr wele*, ∼are, redolere *CathA.* **b** aeternamque dilectionem ∼abat GOSC. *Aug. Min.* 760; [Augustinus] tam verbis quam factis ∼ans ELMH. *Cant.* 107.

aromatopola [ἀρωματοπώλης], spicer.

∼a, *grosser* WHITTINGTON *Vulg.* 66.

arondo v. harundo. aroticus v. 1 areticus. arp- v. et. harp-. arpen- v. aripennis. arquelus v. arquillus. arqueria v. arcuaria b.

arquillus, ∼a, bow of a cross-bow. **b** saddle-bow (*cf. arcio*). **c** ox-bow.

1205 remanent ij baliste ad duos pedes et vij arkill' et vj telar' (*Lit.*) *Pipe 8 John* p. xxvii; **1213** baculos ad arkillos balistarum faciendos *Misae* 231; **1213** arkillos de cornu crudos ad turnum *Cl* 145b; **1225** pro xxiiij telariis et totidem arkillis ad xxiiij balistas..faciendas *Cl* 50a. **b 1225** homines de Bedeford tulerunt duo paria arcellorum, que debuerunt domino regi de hoc termino *KRMem* 8 r. 11(2); *sel, hors-harneys*, ∼us *PP.* **c** plaustra, quorum partes.. limones et temones, juga cum ∼is [*gl.* (? *erron.*): id est circulis qui circumdant colla boum vel pecorum ne intrent sepes] GARL. *Dict.* 129; in x ∼is emptis ad boves, ij d. ob. *FormMan* 32; **1338** xvj ∼e nove, precia iiij d. *Ac. Durh.* 200; aquillus, A. *an oxebowe*, ..arquelus, *a noxbowe* WW; *an oxe bowe*, ∼us, columbar *CathA.*

arquinetta v. alcannetta.

arquites [CL], (pl.) archers.

arquītes, equites ad propugnacula fortes D. BEC. 1882.

†arquitium, (?) bow-case (*cf. arcithesis*).

hoc †aquiscium, *a quyver* WW.

arra [CL], earnest money, pledge. **b** bride-price. **c** (fig.).

∼a, *gylden wedd* vel *feoh* ÆLF. *Gl.*; **†1032** (16c) in ∼as hujus meae satisfactionis..offero..unum calicem *CD* 748; **1184** Bonenfant Judeus reddit compotum de x m. pro habendis erris suis quas dederat pro predicta domo *Pipe* 107; **1205** quod..faciatis inarrari..omnes naves..et quantum posueritis in ∼is illarum nobis scire faciatis *Cl* 29a; **1237** emit..totam lanam..de hac prima tonsione, ..unde reddidit..pre manibus ∼arum nomine xxx m. *CurR* XVI 11; **c1250** si quis emerit..mercimonia et dederit denarium Dei vel aliquod argentum in ∼is, pacabit mercatori..secundum forum prius factum *Stat. Gild. Berw.* 28; **1271** quod..bona Flandrensium..simul cum ∼is et debitis ipsorum (*Breve Regis*) *Leg. Ant. Lond.* 138; **1275** (v. argentum 3b); **s1275** recepimus in ∼is xxx m. *Ann. Dunstable* 265; **1342** cum.. ..magistris navium earundem certas pecuniarum summas nomine errarum de veniendo ad certum diem..solvi fecerimus *Cl* 171 m. 27*d.*; ∼a simonie prius data gravatur WYCL. *Sim.* VI 71. **b** desponsata probo pactis sponsalibus arrae ALDH. *VirgV* 2068; **1282** damus potestatem..recipiendi..concessionem ∼arum faciendam per..regem Arragonum..racione matrimonii inter [filiam nostram]..et.. domicellum Alfonsum *RGasc.* II 161. **c** scandens in ligno Christus dedit arram vitae ALDH. *Met.* 10 p. 85; 'dedit pignus spiritus..', id est arrham sui vel aeternae hereditatis LANFR. *Comment. Paul.* (2 *Cor.* i 22) 220; hec te generatio querit, Domine Deus, quia et eam ad te querendum excitas, consecrans eam arrha tua et dedicans pignore tuo AD. SCOT. *TGC* 825B; —a eterne remunerationis..dotatur R. COLD, *Cuth.* 2; **s1068** rex Willelmus..cepit..mortis ∼am cum infirmitatibus presentire M. PAR. *Min.* I 30; **c1350** tremor, error et arra doloris (*In Franciam*) *Pol. Poems* I 36; **1441** literas..tuas, uti primas amoris in me tui ∼as, letabundus excepi BEKYNTON I 170.

arrabilis v. 1 and 2 arabilis.

arrabo [CL < ἀρραβών], earnest money, pledge.

arrabona vel ∼o, *wedd* vel *wedlac* ÆLF. *Gl.*; *a hanselle*, arabo, strena, ..*a wedde*, pignus, ..arabo *CathA.*

arraciare [OF *arachier* < abradicare], to pull up.

1234 castellani..∼iari fecerunt plumbos in Crawmerse et deferri apud Wallingford' *BNB* II 637.

Arracium v. Atrebatensis. arragium v. arreragium 2a.

Arrago, ∼onius, ∼onicus, ∼onensis, Aragonese (*cf. Tarraconensis*).

Hildefonsus ∼onum rex ORD. VIT. XIII 2; ∼onii.. Francos iterum accersierunt *Ib.* 4; ∼onensis rex *Ib.* 6; ∼ones..regionem..spoliatam invenerunt *Ib.*; **1165** pro instructibus Arragonorum *Pipe* 31; **1179** de..∼onensibus, Navariis et Basclis..qui tantam in Christianos immanitatem exercent (*Decr. Papae*) R. HOWD. II 179; Tholose princeps Aragŏnica regna movebat GARL. *Tri. Eccl.* 80 (cf. ib.: rex / Arragŏnum); **s1245** regni Francorum introitus.. et ∼onum denegabatur M. PAR. *Maj.* IV 410; **s1288** quod.. Carolus a domino Papa pacem Aragonensibus impetraret TREVET 314; **s1324** de stipendiis militibus Hispanis, ∼onicis et Gasconensibus WALS. *YN* 261.

arraiamentum [OF *areement*], fitting out (naut.).

1335 in paracione de guerra et ∼a (*sic*)..navis vocata (*sic*) *la Trinite* ut in *ofcastel, topcastel* et *forcastel KRAc* 19/14 r. 7; **1386** compotus..clerici araiamenti navium et bargearum regis (*Ac. Foreign*) *Med. Admin. Hist.* IV 459.

2 drawing up (of a list), enrolment. **b** drawing up, drafting (of account or sim.).

1385 calumpniant arraimentum panelli.., quia dicunt quod panellum..arraitum fuit per B. M. *PlRCP* 495 r. 486; **1387** calumpniat ∼um panelli jurate infraconte, quia dicit quod panellum illud arraiatum fuit..ad denominacionem J. D. .. (*CoramR*) *Pub. Works* I 49; hic abbas [ob. 1401] obtinuit breve regium de ∼o cleri jurisdiccionis S. Albani episcopo Lincoln' solito committi *G. S. Alb.* III 437; **1419** bedellus monstrabit aldermanno unum panellum per constabularios warde arraiatum de probis hominibus..per quos inquisicio debet fieri; quod ∼um, si aldermanno videbitur expedire, ipse poterit emendare *MGL* I 37. **b 1312** nichil penes se habent ut in..memorandis..per que..poterunt..certificari super ∼o et redditione compotorum predictorum *Doc. Ir.* 314; **1335** circa ∼um rotuli ad liberandum dicto W. T. *Rec. Leic.* II 28; **1337** ∼um [compoti] *CalScot* III 1240.

arraiare [OF *areer* < Frk.], to array, muster, marshal (troops). **b** to equip, accoutre, fit. **c** to fit out (naut.).

1322 mandamus quod..omnes..homines dictorum comitatuum..congregari et araiari facias ad resistendum.. inimicis nostris (*Pat*) *Foed.* III 961 (= *Parl. Writs* I 599); **1324** jurati sunt in armis et arreati per constabularios pacis domini regis *IMisc* 99/10 r. 2; **1327** ita quod quilibet dictorum hominum bene et sufficienter armetur et ∼etur *RScot* 206a (cf. ib. 436a); **1356** quod..xx homines Walenses ..eligi et ∼ari et arcubus, sagittis et lanceis..muniri faciatis (*Breve Regis*) *Reg. Heref.* 241; **s1318**..tam pulchram multitudinem hominum in equis sic bene araiatorum KNIGHTON I 412; **1415** recepit breve regium pro monstro faciendo cleri.., tam regularibus quam secularibus.. sufficienter araiari faciendis, ita quod prompti sint et araiati ad resistendum..infestacioni inimicorum..ecclesie regisque *Reg. Heref.* 87; **1437** tenentes..abbatis..in non modico numero aggregati et modo guerrino ∼ati vi et armis..venerunt (*Artic. Querelae*) AMUND. II 132; **1457** quod omnes hujusmodi homines sagittarii..sint parati sufficienter et defensive arriati prout pertinet sagittariis

Lit. Cant. III 228; **1511** assignavimus vos..ad..homines ad arma ac homines armatos..et alios homines..defensibiles..~andum et triandum..et ad monstrum eorumdem..faciendum..ita quod.., sic ~ati et muniti, prompti sint ad deserviendum nobis.. (*Pat*) *Foed.* XIII 300b. **b 1375** corpus predictum ibidem vestibus honestis et calcaribus..de novo ~averunt *SessPLincs* 142; **1385** zonas de serico ~atas cum argento et deauratas *CoramR* 497 r. *6d.*; **1386** quod unus equus sit ~atus pro guerra cum uno homine armato de armis meis (*Test.*) *FormA* 429. **c 1347** littera ad ~andam unam navem (*LBLond.* F) *MGL* I 651; **1375** preceperat..~are quandam navem vocatam *la Barge* de Lincoln' versus mare in defencionem regni *SessPLincs* 66; **1378** predicta bargea fuit dimissa..male araita et defuit tam velum quam gabell' *Mem. York* I 30; **1413** navem..cum sufficienti estuffamento..araiari faciant (*Ac. Foreign*) *Bronnen* 917.

2 to draw up: **a** (a list); **b** (an account or sim.); **c** (an assize or a writ of assize; *cf. arramare*).

a 1385, 1419 (v. arraiamentum 2a). **b 1327** ita fuit occupatus..quod compotum suum..facere seu ~are nondum potuit *KRMem* 103 r. 184; **1333** dicit eas [extractas] nondum esse ~atas neque paratas *LTRMem* 105 r. 89; **1376** ad ~andum et reddendum [compotum] *CalCl* 323; **1412** ordinatum est quod paupirum de cartis..esset de novo ~atum et ligatum *BBWinchester* 32. **c 1327** intelleximus quod R. B. ..†arraiv' [? l. arramiavit] coram vobis per breve nostrum quandam assisam nove disseisine *RScot* 217a; s**1385** breve originale assise predicte..in omnibus secundum vim, formam et effectum ejusdem †~atum [? l. ~ate] et †executum *G. S. Alb.* III 250; s**1455** b. originale assise predicte, in omnibus secundum vim, formam et naturam ejusdem brevis †~atum [? l. ~ate] et †executum *Reg. Whet.* I 207; brevia assisarum..secundum formam et naturam eorundem modo debito ~atarum *Reg. Brev.* 30.

arraiatio, array, muster (of troops). **b** fitting, setting in order. **c** fitting out (naut.).

1327 mandamus quod..homines..tam equites quam pedites juxta ~ones alias per vos..factas venire faciatis ad nos *RScot* 206a (cf. ib. 222a); **1332** occupati..in eleccione et ~one hominum ad arma *LTRMem* 105 r. 12; **1404** assignavimus vos..ad dictos homines ad arma ac homines armatos et sagittarios sic arraiatos et munitos continue in ~one, ut in millenis, centenis et vintenis et alias prout conveniens fuerit et necesse, teneri et poni faciendos *RParl* III 527a; **1415** ad nos de ~one et municione ac numero personarum cleri predicti sic arraiandi..certificandum *Reg. Cant.* III 326; **1442** pro monstracione et ~one hominum armatorum *DCCant Ac. Chamb.* 139. **b 1434** pro araiacione et *le scowrynge* diversorum armorum cum unccione *Ac. Durh.* 147; c**1460** pro perforacione de *le burelston* et pro †araiecione de iij aubis et reparacione j bere *Ac. Churchw. Bath* 131. **c 1330** assignavimus..Walterum..ad supervidendum naves pro passagio..Johannis..provisas ac ~onem passagii illius (*Pat*) *Foed.* IV 442; **1335** in reparacione et ~one de guerra alii (*sic*) navis *KRAc* 19/14 r. 7; **1394** ad anchoras..ac omnia pro ~one emendacione et reparacione necessaria..emenda *Pat* 339 m. 6; **1395** circa ~onem, emendacionem et reparacionem navis regis vocate *la George IssueR* 554 m. 9; **1452** de precio unius olle enee..ordinate pro calcacione et ~one navium regis *Ac. Foreign* 86G.

2 drawing up (of an account or sim.).

1337 circa ~onem compoti sui *Cl* 158 m. 25; **1376** circa ~onem rotulorum et memorandorum (*IssueR*) *EHR* XXXV 418; **1434** pro pergameno, scriptura et ~one hujus compoti *Ac. Durh.* 711.

arraiator, commissioner of array, marshal: **a** (of troops); **b** (of horses); **c** (of game); **d** (naut.).

1322 assignavimus ipsum comitem capitalem custodem comitatuum..et superiorem ~orem et ducem tam hominum ad arma quam peditum (*Pat*) *Foed.* III 973; **1326** arrayatoribus pacis *IssueR* 218 m. 11; **1327** ~oribus et subarraiatoribus in comitatibus subscriptis *RScot* 206b; **1342** dominus rex mandavit ~oribus hobelariorum istius comitatus..quod nullus hujusmodi hobelariorum ad partes predictas proficisceretur *SelCKB* VI 17; **1536** araiator seu triator hominum ad arma, hobiliariorum seu sagittariorum *Pat* 668 m. 24. **b 1326** supervisori et capitali arrayatori omnium equorum et haraciorum domini regis *IssueR* 218 m. 10. **c 1443** officium capitalis custodis ferarum..necnon ~oris et gubernatoris venacionum et deductus nostrorum [sc. archiepiscopi] *Reg. Cant.* I 124. **d 1335** unus custodum portuum maris Suthwallie et ~orum navium et marinariorum *KRAc* 19/14 r. 7.

arraiatus, array, gathering, procession.

1425 volo quod vigilie mortuorum communi modo immediate post mortem meam fiant, cessantibus pomposis exequiis et ~ibus *Reg. Cant.* II 312.

arrain- v. arram-, arren-.

arraizus [Sp. *arraez* < Ar. *ar-rā'is*), naval officer.

1386 inveniet..x galeas..regis Portugalie sumptibus..bene armatas, viz. de uno patrono, tribus alcaldibus, sex ~is (*DipDoc E* 309) *Foed.* VII 521.

arralis, involving an earnest or pledge (fig.).

in Christo, qui est gigas gemine substancie, quarum una..decrevit..assumere hominem..et naturam communem in illo supposito reconciliavit per modum ~is comercii Trinitati Wycl. *Dom. Div.* III 235.

arraliter, by way of earnest or pledge (fig.).

divina dispensacio, qua voluit Verbum suum ad tempus esse corpus, non plene sed quasi ~er tunc beatum Wycl. *Incarn.* 70.

arramare, ~iare, ~ire [OF *aramir* < ad+ Frk. *hramjan*; *forms w.* arrain- *or* arrani- f.l., *or infl. by* arrenare (cf. ME *arrayn*)], to 'arraign', summon: **a** (an assize); **b** (a jury or sim.); *v. et. armare* 3.

1199 de assisa nove disseisine quam ipse aramiavit versus eum *CurR* I 71; justiciariorum..coram quibus assisa illa ~iata fuit *Ib.* 72; **1203** W. ..debet..iiij m. pro amovendis a jurata magne assise quam idem W. aramivit sex militibus *Pipe* 58; **1204** juratores [assise] de nova dissaisina quam..W. aramiaverat super R. *Pipe* 185; **1205** †arainiaverat assisam *Cl* 32b; **1205** dat v m. pro convincendis xij juratoribus per xxiiij, qui fuerunt recognitores in assisa nove dissaisine †arrainiata..de libero tenemento *RFin.* p. 323; **1218** ad assisam nove disseisine capiendam quam L. ..aramavit versus V. *Pat* 165; si..ille ~averit super eum assisam nove disseisine Bracton 18; **1277** †arrainabit assisam ultime presentacionis *Reg. Heref.* 144; **1281** ita quod impossibile esset quod predicta assisa debito modo esset †arrainita *Cart. Rams.* III 44; **1305** †arraniavit *Reg. Cant.* I 487; **1319** †arraindavit assisam nove disseisine (*Chain Bk. Dublin*) *Doc. Ir.* 432 (cf. ib. 429: †arraindaverunt diversa brevia assisarum); **1448** coram..justiciariis nostris ..ad assisas.., captas seu capiendas, assignat' seu assignand', ~iatas seu ~iandas *Reg. Whet.* I 39. **b 1201** dies datus est jurate que aramiata est de libertatibus domini regis *CurR* I 452; **1203** debet xv m. ut recognitio de morte antecessoris quam aramiavit versus magistrum R. ..procedat *Pipe* 6; **1277** quia tale sit jus suum, sectam aramiavit *CourtR Hales* 88; **1329** super quo brevi idem G., modo †arranians istam attinctam, fuit convictus de transgressione facta *MGL* I 444; **1380** iste custodie cum constabulariis †arainiate et ordinate fuerunt *Mem. York* I 151.

†arramatio, summoning (of assize).

1342 coram..justiciariis domini regis ad omnes assisas in com. predicto †arraniationem capiendam [? l. arramatas capiendas]..assignatis *Cart. Rams.* I 180; titulus..medius inter dictam †arrain' predicte assise..et recuperare supradictum *Entries* 59b (cf. ib. 429b: post quam quidem †arrain' assise illius).

arramentum v. erramentum. arrantare v. arrentare b. 1 arrare v. arare.

2 arrare, to pay earnest money for. **b** to plight, betroth.

1269 liberate..ccc li. ad minuta hernesia nostra in instantibus nundinis S. Ivonis inde emenda et alia necessaria nostra ibidem ~anda *Liberate* 45 m. 8; **1291** equum..~avit per argentum Dei de prefato A. *Law Merch.* (*St. Ives*) I 44; **1356** pro mercandisis forstallandis, emendis aut alio modo ~andis *Cl* 194 m. *6d.*; *to yife erls*, ~are, in-, sub- *CathA*. **b** quam sibi Salvator sponsam copularat adultam / sanguinis arratam conquirens dote puellam Aldh. *VirgV* 1813; **10..** ~atam, *beweddad* WW; tu pontificis manum audes contingere, qui virginem deitatis munere ~atam non timuisti preripere? Osb. *V. Dunst.* 35.

Arras v. Atrebatensis,

†arrastrium [cf. astrium], (?) hearth.

1351 in factura ~ii dicte fabrice, xvj d. (*KRAc* 485/11) *Arch.* LXIV 158.

arratellus v. martellus. arraticus v. erraticus.

arrationare [cf. arrenare], to arraign, accuse.

1274 idem P. super hoc ~atus concessit quod limites..ad statum debitum reducantur (*Chanc. Misc.* 10/5/1) *S. Jers.* II 20; **1293** aracionati quod sanarent suas defaltas *CourtR Hales* 241; **1295** aracionatus de injusta inhibicione.., recessit a curia sine responsione *Ib.* 325; **1300** de predicta transgressione aracionatus *JustIt* (C.I.) 1158 r. 9.

array- v. arrai-. arreagium v. averagium c. arreare v. arraiare. arrect- v. arrett-, arrigere. arredare v. arrentare.

arregniare [OF *aresner, aregnier*], to tether.

corpus solito defunctorum more componat, et lanceam suam figat et arma circummittat et equum adregniet (*Leg. Hen.*) *GAS* 600.

†arremittere [? *for* abremittere], to omit (payment).

1373 si contingat predictum redditum..a retro existere, ..liceat..districciones..capere..et retinere quousque..de predicto redditu et ~missis et expensis, si que fuerint, plenarie fuerit satisfactum *Cant. Coll. Ox.* III 29.

arrenamentum [OF *araisnement*], arraignment, accusation.

1327 absque arenamento et responsione..contra legem terre..morti extitit adjudicatus *RParl* II 5a; **1385** non obstante aliquo arainamento, processu vel judicio contra ipsum comitem..reddito sive facto (*Pat*) *Foed.* VII 463.

arrenare [OF *araisnier* < arrationare], to arraign, accuse.

1292 coram ipso domino rege..de diversis transgressionibus..~atus, in inquisicionem patrie se inde posuit *RParl* I 81b; **1301** nec per aliquem ballivum ~atus fuit quod se attachiaret alicui..responsurus *Law Merch.* II 67; **1325** ~atus de eo quod portavit arma in nundinis domini regis *Ib.* I 108; **1320** †aramatus [? l. arainatus] ad sectam dicti J. de..latrocinio *Rec. Leic.* I 376; s**1323** episcopus Herefordensis, coram rege et cunctis regni proceribus constitutus, †arrannatus [? l. arrainiatus] extitit et examinatus de prodicione Blaneford 140; s**1326** Hugo Spenser areniatus est coram eo [justiciario] ad barrum Knighton I 437; s**1329** arenandus fuit de aliis dominum regem tangentibus *Ann. Lond.* 245; **1330** tenentes ejusdem manerii arennare solebant talem captum pro hujusmodi felonia ad sectam sequentis *PQW* 612b, **1337** ballivus [de la Escluse] ~avit malefactores predictos super facto predicto *Cl* 158 m. 21; s**1344** rex reconcessit per chartam suam..quod nullus clericus sit arenatus coram justiciariis suis, sive ad sectam suam sive partis, si clericus sue clerimonie se submittat Wals. *HA* I 264 (= *Id. YN* 283: arreynatus]).

arrend- v. et. arrent-.

arrenda, lease.

1423 Bonifacius..abbati..monasterii..necnon rectoribus ecclesiarum..ab ipso monasterio dependencium..ut..fructus et cetera ad monasterium..pertinencia quibuscunque personis, eciam laicis, cum quibus..condicionem meliorem efficere possent, arrendare, locare, seu ad firmam vel annuam pensionem concedere, ipsisque laicis ut fructus et cetera hujusmodi in ~am recipere et retinere val[er]ent..duxit indulgendum (*Supplicatio*) Amund. I 156; **1521** duas tercias partes terrarum..quas..habent in ~a *Reg. Aberbr.* II 433; **1546** exceptis decimis garbalibus..quas..in ~am seu locacionem habuerant ad..monasterium..pertinentes *Dryburgh* 287.

arrendatorius v. arrentatarius.

arrentamentum, (letting out at) rent.

1262 quod predicte xxxiiij li. ..eidem Hagino et Leoni..allocentur in parte ipsos contingente de arentamento Judaismi *Cl* 35; **1265** de xx s. annuis qui..exiguntur..de arentamento cujusdam serjantie..et de xv s. annuis..pro arentamento assartorum *Ib.* 56; **1289** arrendamentum per..vicecomitem..factum..fratribus..ad novem annos de redditibus.. *RGasc* II 535; **1308** summa arrendamenti omnium beneficiorum tocius provincie Cantuariensis (*Lit. Collectoris Papalis*) *EHR* XLI 353; **1440** sic quod communitas pro quolibet anno prescripti arrendamenti seu firmarie abbati..l m. persolvat ad terminos in eadem arrendacione expressatos *Reg. Dunferm.* p. 292.

arrentare [OF *arenter*], to rent out. **b** to tax or assess (a source of revenue or a liability). **c** to commute (a service). **d** to commute the service of (a serjeant).

s**1262** venellas..obstupatas et quibusdam arentatas nitebantur aperire *Leg. Ant. Lond.* 56; **1282** concessimus..quod placeas predictas edificare et arentare possint (*Pat*) *MGL* II 274; **1297** cartarum..de domibus et placeis ~andis *RScot* 40a; **1307** caput boreale xx acrarum †arcutarum [l. arentatarum] eisdem (*Pat*) *MonA* II 310b; **1308** summa debitorum cujuslibet dyocesis provincie [Cantuariensis] de beneficiis arrendatis (*Lit. Collectoris Papalis*) *EHR* XLI 353; **1328** ad locandum et †arredandum..maneria *Conc.* II 554; **1388** vie arentate ibidem valent per annum vj d. ob. *IMisc.* 240/16; [T. abbas, ob. 1396] obtinuit..privilegium arendandi seu libere dimittendi quibuscunque personis decimas et bona ecclesiastica..monasterii *G. S. Alb.* III 378; **1457** ut fructus, redditus..et obvenciones..ecclesiarum..appropriatarum..personis idoneis..ad firmam †avendere [MS: arendere], locare sive dimittere..valeatis *FormA* 334; **1524** declaramus..cameras superiores..allocandas et arrendandas fore *Reg. Brechin.* II 177; **1559** ne quis..ecclesiasticus ..terras ad suum beneficium pertinentes..locet, concedat vel arrendet in emphiteosim vel assedacionem *Conc. Scot.* II 168. **b 1251** abbas quietus est de murdro et de essartis suis arentandis *Cl* 396; **1258** de assartis factis infra metas foreste de terris suis propriis et tenementorum suorum de novo arentatis (*Petitio Baronum*) *Ann. Burton* 440; **1260** de l m. assessis super communitatem Judeorum regis de talliagio suo arentato de termino S. Mich. *Cl* 96; **1267** per istam constitutionem non tolluntur fines seu prestationes arentate a tempore [etc.] (*Marlb.* 11) *St. Realm* I 23 (cf. *Fleta* IV 5 p. 224); **1280** sex millia librarum quibus..pedagium fuerat arendatum *RGasc* II 106; **1285** petunt quod ~are possint predictas trabes ad xij d. per annum (*JustIt*) *DocCOx* 220; **1287** ita quod homines de hundretis predictis ad solucionem dictorum c s. non teneantur nec terre vel tenementa eorundem ea occasione arententur Thorne 1944; **1314** quod ballive, redditus et alia quecumque..ad nostrum commodum arendentur et ascensentur *RGasc.* IV 1230; **1314** reddendo nobis lvj s. ad quos predicte cxx acre..per J. et socios suos ad vasta et assarta sua [sc. regis] in diversis forestis arentanda assignatos arentabantur *MonA* VI 417b; **1332** de quibus debent resolvi domino regi.., quod dicitur donum arentatum, vj s. iij d. *IPM* 31/24; **1334** de veteribus assartis ab antiquo arrantatis *Ib.* 40/8 r. 10. **c 1252** serjantia, sc. conducendi thesaurum domini regis, ..fuit arentata..ad j m. per annum *IMisc* 6/15; **1259** inquiratur de alienatione servientum, si qua fuerit alienatio adhuc non arentata et quantum possit arentari de cetero (*Form. Inq.*) *Ann. Burton* 480; **1260** assignati ad ~andum serjancias regis alienatas *Cl* 304; **1285** tenet j coteriam, cujus servicia sunt arentata *Cust. Suss.* II 18; **1333** de consuetudinibus vocatis *scatpeny, maltpeny*..et scatavena operibus..~atis (*MinAc Durh.*) *Cust. Rents* 37; c**1420** †argentare [? l. ~are] (*MinAc*) *MFG*; **1504** opera customaria non arentata pertinent firmario cum firma sua *Crawley* 497. **d 1275** solebant portare in adventu domini regis in foresta de Dertemore j arcum cum iij sagittis; et nunc arentati sunt in v s. solvendis in festo S. Mich. vicecomiti Devon' *Hund.* I 85.

arrentaria, hire.

1297 de iiij s. iij d. de ~ia proprie caruce hoc anno locat' *Ac. Cornw.* I 49.

arrentatarius, rent-paying tenant, farmer.

1479 arrendatorios..et feudatorios..mense episcopalis Artfertensis *Mon. Hib. & Scot.* 485a; **1518** omnes..dicti monasterii..feudatarios, arrendatarios, censuarios et tenentes..terrarum ejusdem *Form. S. Andr.* I 2.

arrentatio, (letting out at) rent. **b** assessment (for taxation). **c** commutation (of service).

c**1250** reddunt..pro †aventatione croftarum xxj d. per annum *Cart. Rams.* I 489; **1281** ad assidendas placias..et eas per certam ~onem..probis hominibus..committendas (*Breve Regis*) *BBC* 1; **1285** tunc primo cepit predictam ~onem quam..monachi..percipere consueverunt *PQW* 252a; **1344** venella arentatur domino regi, ..que quidem arentacio nocet communitati *MGL* II 452; **1356** supplicarunt nobis burgenses [Berewici]..quod..velimus..burgagia, domos et placeas vacuas..de novo arrentari ipsisque burgensibus et aliis..qui eadem burgagia ad firmam habere voluerint per hujusmodi ~onem in feodo et ad terminum vite vel annorum committi jubere *RScot* 790b; **1394** habuerunt..scrutacionem, areddacionem et emendacionem aque de Derwent..de mari usque ad capud *IMisc* 254/13; **1440** arrendacionem fructuum..ecclesie *Reg. Dunferm.* p. 292; **1546** locacio et arrendacio..decimarum *Dryburgh* 288. **b** **14..** per certum servicium ad scaccarium nostrum annuatim reddendum de ~one..R. et sociorum suorum ad vasta nostra..arrentandum..assignatorum *Reg. Brev.* 12. **c** **1266** arentacionem octo li...factam pro alienacione quam P...fecit de serjantia de B. *Cl* 177 (cf. *CalCh* II 131); **1322** fecit finem cum domino pro omnibus operibus suis et arruris.., ita tamen quod ipse reddet omnem redditum suum assisum..; et pro ista arentacione dat domino per annum xxx s. *CBaron* 135.

arrentator, rent-paying tenant, farmer. **b** assessor (of service, for commutation).

1308 sub eodem censu quo per arendatores locorum predictorum nunc tenentur *RGasc* IV 146; **1435** arrendator dicte ecclesie *Reg. Brechin.* I 74; **1521** parochiani arrendatores, decimatores, reddituarii, ..censuarii, receptores, debitores, possessores et detentores fructuum *Form. S. Andr.* I 103. **b** **1271** arentatoribus serjanciarum nostrarum per Angliam *Cl* 438.

arrepticius [LL; cf. arripere 2a], possessed by a spirit: **a** inspired; **b** demented.

a [divinatores], super aliquo consulti ambiguo, statim frementes spiritu quasi extra se rapiuntur et tanquam ~ii fiunt Gir. *DK* I 16. **b** abrepticius, furiosus *GlC* A 19; arepticium, demoniosum *Ib.* 795; vidimus..~ium..divina miseratione curatum T. Mon. *Will.* V 13; tu nos deliros dicis, et nos te amentem; voca vicinos tuos et, cum tibi dixerint quod nos, crede quod ~ius es Map *NC* IV 16 p. 201; s**850** spiritus malignus..per os cujusdam ~ii..protestatus est M. Par. *Maj.* I 380; s**1265** cives Londonienses, ..qui fere per biennium demoniaca delusione facti fuerant ~ii, per mortem comitis [Leicestrie] et suorum quasi miraculose subito a dementia seu furia curabantur Wykes 176; *fonde*, arepticius, astrosus, ..*wode*, arepticius, abrepticius, ..demens, demoniacus *CathA*.

arreptio, seizure. **b** bout (of fever). **c** (w. *itineris*) undertaking, setting out.

est avis..aliis avibus capiendis avida, a quarum ~one [? l. acceptione] accipiter, id est raptor, est vocata Bart. Angl. XII 3. **b** quidam testificantur se vidisse ~ones febris de anno in annum Gilb. I 54. 2. **c** **1163** quamvis.. in hujus itineris ~one Pictavensium meorum contempserim loquacitatem (*Ep. J. Pictav.*) *Becket Mat.* V 37; **1229** ante ~onem itineris illius [versus Terram Sanctam] *CurR* XIII 2107; c**1250** licet damna non modica ab [? l. ob] incepti itineris areppcionem (*sic*) fuero perpessus *FormOx* 487; **1424** inutilis esset..ad tam remotas partes itineris ~o Bekynton I 286.

arreragium [OF *arerage*; cf. aretro, reragium], (pl.) rear (of building), back premises.

1270 non optulit canobum ad vendendum in ~iis (*St. Ives*) *Law Merch.* I 2; **1287** habuit unum fossatum in ~iis ad nocumentum transeuncium *Ib.* 18; locavit duas domos suas in ~iis ex opposito aque *Ib.* 34.

2 (usu. pl.) arrears. **b** (w. *in*) in arrears.

1197 castellano..et aliis..ad perficiendum areragium feodi comitis Flandrie *Pipe* 62; **1200** de placito ~iorum firme *CurR* I 294; **1212** ceperunt averia illa..pro ~io servicii *SelPlCrown* 61; **1224** vicecomes habet diem ad †arragia et ad debita sua reddenda *LTRMem* 6 r. 11d.; **1236** compotum [vicecomitis] de †aragiis comitatus *Fees* 597; **1246** dedit..viij li. sterlingorum pro araragiis suis *Couch. Kirkstall* 224; **1253** de arreragiis compoti *RGasc.* I 307; s**1270** reddendo ei quantum solebat reddere imperatori..et ~ia que a retro fuerunt *Leg. Ant. Lond.* 132; **1279** solvet arriragia de gilda *Gild Merch.* II 290; de †arrerariis illis *State Tri. Ed. I* (cf. ib.: de predictis ~iis); c**1300** ~ium vocatur illa quantitas que de liberacionibus faciendis tunc non dum soluta est nec solvitur in instanti (*Regula Comp. Belli Loci*) *Seignorial Admin.* 170; **1314** aliquarum ~iarum *Deeds Balliol* 145; **1316** si contingat..cantariam per communem guerram impediri, ..quam cicius..fieri poterit solvant..~ia missarum que aretro fuerint *FormA* 263; **1323** liberatus fuit..prisone..pro arriragiis compoti sui *SelCCoron* 79; **1355** tam de ~iis, si que fuerint, quam principali debito *RMS Scot* 56; **1538** de ~iis et resta pedis ultimi sui compoti *Rent. S. Andr.* 3. **b** **1230** debet inde per annum x s.; et..est in ~iis xv s. *LTRMem* 11 r. 15d.; unde remansit in ~iis de xxxvj li. *State Tri. Ed. I* 52; si sit in errerag' *FormMan.* 36; **1299** ipsi qui fuerunt vicecomites et super compota sua reman[s]erunt in ~iis erga dominum regem *MGL* II 92.

arrerarium v. arreragium 2a. arrescere v. accrescere 2. arresta v. arrestum.

arrestabilis, subject to arrest.

1292 licitum est ballivis..ipsum..arestare, si non sit prisonabilis sed arestabilis *Year Bk. 20–1 Ed. I* 127.

arrestamentum [cf. OF *arestement*], arrest.

si..se non permiserint arestari, tunc vigilatores..ipsos insequantur, ita quod ipsi vigilatores pro hujusmodi arestamento non..graventur *Fleta* 35; **1449** libere exeundo absque impedimento vel ~o *RScot* 336a; **1495** nolebat obedire aristamento ipsius..subballivi *Sanct. Durh.* 59.

arrestare (arest-) [cf. OF *arester*], to stop, halt. **b** to hold fast, tether. **c** to lay hold of. **d** (w. *bellum*) to withstand, face. **e** to hold back, deter.

1274 arestitit carettas abbatisse ad unam wardam quousque solvisset xij d. *Hund.* I 138; si conventus debeat extra scepta ire cum processione, ..liberi servientes debent equos et carettas e contra venientes, ne per medium conventus transeant, seorsum divertere vel quousque conventus transierit ~are *Obs. Barnwell* 170; s**1300** cum prior veniret pro cariagio ~ato locuturus, eum attachiarunt Graystanes 23. **b** **1315** in j pari compedum empto pro stottis ~andis in pastura eorum *MinAc* 918/13; **1340** de..iiij cordis pro equis ~andis in eorum pastura *MinAc* 1120/10 r. 17d. **c** **1302** Thomas..~avit Margeriam..dum Ricardus ..verberavit..illam *CourtR Hales* 465. **d** s**1370** 'ad sua confugient' sc. castella.., non audentes ~are bellum contra eum (J. Bridl. *gl.*) *Pol. Poems* I 147. **e** c**1396** quia domini et domine sunt ~ati propter timorem suorum confessorum (*Concl. Lollard.*) *EHR* XXII 302.

2 (leg.) to arrest, detain (persons). **b** to impress (for forced labour). **c** to seize, impound (things). **d** to lay under embargo (naut.). **e** to stay (proceedings).

1194 si invenerint aliquem torneantem qui non satisfecerit, corpus suum ~abunt et bailivo domini regis liberabunt capitali justitie transmittendum (*Breve regis*) Diceto II lxxxi; **1200** ~atus est per preceptum domini regis *CurR RC* II 166; **1202** ~avit eum donec inveniret plegios standi recto..de vulneratione *SelPlCrown* 18; **1244** non fuit captus nec inprisonatus set tantummodo ~atus simpliciter *JustIt* 201 r. 2; **1279** assignavimus eosdem..ad dictos aurifabros ..ac eorum bona et catalla..~andos, capiendos et salvo custodiendos (*Pat*) *Chr. Peterb.* 27 (cf. Fl. Worc. *Cont.* C 221); **1292** ita quod propter hoc non aristentur set dent simplex vadium quousque dampnum videatur *Couch. Furness* II 540; **1304** culpabiles..~ari et in prisona nostra salvo et secure custodiri faciant *Parl. Writs* I 407b (cf. W. Guisb. 360); **1313** ~averunt ij extraneos transeuntes in borgha de W. cum bonis et catallis et eos detinuerunt per unum diem et unam noctem et postea permiserunt eos abire, retinendo bona et catalla *Eyre Kent* I 76; c**1350** Copland arestat David, cito se manifestat (*Halidon Hill*) *Pol. Poems* I 46; **1437** H. Vorrat..~atus extitit et sic sub arresto usque modo detentus et impeditus existit Bekynton I 216. **b** pro latomis ~atis ad opus domini regis *DocCOx* 313. **c** precipiatur vicecomiti quod catalla et fructus per preceptum domini regis vel ejus justitiarum interim ~atos faciat habere illi qui desaisinam probavit Glanv. XIII 38; **1197** debet v m. ut catalla hominum comitis de Hoilland' ~entur donec satisfactum fuerit ei de l m. *Pipe* 73; **1201** ipsum P. cepit et alios Judeos..et eorum catalla que potuit invenire..per visum legalium civium Eboraci ~avit *CurR* I 389; **1225** catalla Reginaldi B. posita fuerunt in manus executorum ante quam vicecomes fecit ea aristari *KRMem* 7 r. 15; **1228** si talis inventus fuerit, equos, arma et hernasium ipsius ~ari facias *Cl* 106; **1283** rectorem ecclesie.., cujus bigam et equos [clericus ballivi Cycestrensis] nuper cepit et ~avit contra libertatem..personis ecclesiasticis concessam Peckham *Ep.* 436; **1296** qui..apud edes sacras deposita ecclesiarum vel ecclesiasticarum personarum ~averint, saisiverint seu occupare presumpserint (*Lit. Papae*) *Foed.* II 707a; **1298** appropriavit apes super terram suam ~atas *Cust. Taunton intr.* lx; **1313** ballivus de lasto.. ~avit ij quarteria frumenti de blado Hamonis..ad opus domini regis *Eyre Kent* I 76; **1414** ad ~andos et capiendos omnes libros Anglicanos *Anc. Indict.* 204/11 r. 104; **1442** quod lane mercatorum vestrorum in galeis vestris carcande ..auctoritate nostra ~ate et intromisse fuerint Bekynton I 127. **d** **1228** navem quam ~ari fecerunt..deliberari faciant *Cl* 20; **1317** posuit servientes suos ad portus qui ~abant †baichas [l. barchas] sive naves sale oneratas (*RGasc.*) *Foed.* III 685; **1440** navis..~ata est et hucusque sub arresto detenta Bekynton I 194. **e** si super aliquem istorum articulorum ~etur loquela, poterit ex incidenti.. ad duellum recte perveniri Glanv. II 6.

arrestatio (arest-), arrest (of person). **b** seizure (of goods). **c** embargo (naut.). **d** (?) right to seize or stop or to levy a toll.

1242 ita quod nullus occasione hujusmodi ~onis vel captionis extraneorum per vicecomitem..occasionetur *Cl* 482; **1285** habito respectu ad prisonam seu ~onem quam occasione hujusmodi appellorum sustinuerunt appellati (2 *Westm.* 12) *StRealm* I 81 (= *Reg. Malm.* I 85; adrestationem); †**1201** (14c) inhabitantes..gravare per aliquam citacionem, monicionem aut ~onem *Cart. St. Fridesw.* I 45; **1327** potestatem..contrarios..per ~onem corporum et bonorum suorum puniendi *RScot* 212b; **1389** ab omni obligacione..et ~one in persona tua vel fidejussorum tuorum habitis te..liberamus *Reg. Heref.* 9; **1396** nec paciemur fieri dampnum, ..molestiam, ~onem nec disturbacionem..per tempus nostre convencionis (*Juramentum Regis Francie*) Wals. *HA* II 220; **1495** in aristacione ipsius J. ad pacem *Sanct. Durh.* 59. **b** **1253** significet regi causam illius ~onis [vinorum] *Cl.* 201 (= *RGasc.* I 377); **1265** quod vos quasdam ~ones lanarum et aliorum bonorum mercatorum vestrorum..factas..tenetis molestas *Cl* 46; c**1370** 'sponsus celestis taxatur et insula restis', i. communitas terre taxabatur per ~ones vel per restas, i. per funes et cordas (J. Bridl. *gl.*) *Pol. Poems* I 143; **1375** fregit sigillum eorum [taxatorum] quod posuerunt nomine ~onis *Leet Norw.* 67; **1405** qua ~one facta, mercatores Anglici.. quorum bona arrestata fuerunt inierunt nobiscum pactum *Lit. Cant.* III 92. **c** **1228** non obstante..~one quam.. fecit de navi, ..habere faciant civibus..vina sua que habent in navi *Cl* 131; **1337** non obstantibus ~onibus et inhibicionibus nostris.., quamplures naves..sunt profecte *RScot* 476b; **1389** ab hujusmodi..~onibus navium et batellorum..desistentes (*Breve Regis*) *MGL* I 416. **d** **1437** officium de waterbaillye ville nostre Cales'..cum pontibus pro equis et ~onibus eidem officio pertinentibus *Pat* 441 m. 13 (= *PS*: *arrestes*).

2 (?) remainder.

1282 summa receptorum de restis seu ~onibus que erant penes collectores (*Lib. Collectorum Papalium*) *EHR* XXXII 53 (cf. ib.: de predictis areragiis et restis).

arrestatus, arrest.

1315 si..~um fregerit, ..pro arresto fracto xx s...solvere teneatur *RGasc.* IV 1626 (xxxii).

arrestum, ~a (arest-) [OF *arest*, *areste*], arrest (of persons). **b** seizure (of goods). **c** embargo (naut.). **d** (*s. dub.*).

1369 in expensis..comitis de Marr tempore quo fuit sub ~a regis apud le Bass *ExchScot* 357; **1434** cum arrestatus est..fugit, unde..iterum..captus est, ..et sic in Bocardo positus est, quia fregit ~am commissarii *MunAcOx* 506; **1422** vicecomes respondebat..quod ipsam [Agnetem] teneret sub ~o quousque.. *Mem. York* I 204; **1438** absque ~o seu aliqua..justa execucione..pede liberi quo vellent ire ..sinebantur Bekynton I 252; **1475** non inferentes eis.. malum, molestiam, injuriam, violenciam, ~am, dampnum aliquod seu gravamen (*Doc. Scot.*) *Foed.* XI 843. **b** **1294** quod..nobis scire faceres..~um quod de rebus predictis [lanis etc.] fecisses et quantum de rebus singulis arrestasses (*Breve Regis*) B. Cotton 245; **1309** vinis illis remanentibus in ~o domini regis *PQW* (*C.I.*) 830a; **1315** predicta.. mercimonia sub ~o morari debent *Law Merch.* II 87; **1318** de omnibus firmis terrarum..et possessionum suarum..cum arreragiis..de temporibus quibus erant sub ~a nostra *Reg. Aberd.* I 45 (cf. *Reg. Brechin.* I 146 [**1500**]: ~a de terris); **1404** quorum bona..sub ~a detinentur *Lit. Cant.* III 83; **1412** que bona Willelmus..frangendo ~am abduxit *ExchScot* 144; **1505** hec fuit causa ~ie sive attachiamenti dictorum ..pecunie summarum *Law Merch.* II 133. **c** **1335** quod.. naves..arestari faceretis et sub ~o hujusmodi..detineri *RScot* 321b; **1359** naves et batellos..arestari facitis, eos sub ~o hujusmodi..detinendo (*Breve Regis*) *MGL* I 415; **1440** (v. arrestare d). **d** **1217** mittimus conbarones vestros [sc. baronum de V Portubus] ad videndum quod omnes vestri, qui inimicos nostros nuper in mari spoliaverunt, habeant inde quod habere debeant, et ad †arestam de lucro illo id quod ad nos de jure spectat habendum *Pat* 88.

2 decree, *arrêt* (Fr.).

1312 pro perquirendis..quibusdam ~is..domini regis Francie..que sunt sub sigillo..senescalli *RGasc.* IV *app.* p. 561; **1322** contra ordinaciones et ~a progenitorum vestrorum *TreatyR* I 241; **1336** demandis, controversiis, ~is seu debatis..in curia..regis [Francie] pendentibus *Conc.* II 582; **1343** ad tractandum..super universis..controversiis, ~is, demandis et †delatis [l. debatis]..que mutuo competunt (*TreatyR*) Ad. Mur. 137.

Arretina, pot of Arretine ware.

†asierina, *readde læmene fatu* Ælf. *Gl.*

arretragium v. arreragium 2a. arretro v. aretro.

arrettamentum, bringing to justice.

1295 probavit ea esse suum fidele catallum..et pro arettamento dat domino vj d. *CourtR Hales* 327; licuit judici illi usque post annum illum arrectamentum sive disraci[on]acionem mulieris illius [de morte mariti sui attincte] respectuasse Fortescue *LLA* 53.

arrettare [OF *areter* < ad+reputare; cf. rettare], to bring to justice, arraign. **b** to adjudge, repute.

1267 si clericus aliquis pro crimine aliquo vel recto [v.l. retto] quod ad coronam pertineat †arestatus [v.l. ~atus] fuerit et postmodum..in baillium traditus..extstiterit (*Marlb.* 27) *StRealm* I 25; **1268** ad eos disrationandos qui de rebus ad coronam spectantibus appellati fuerint vel arrectati (*Ch. Regis*) *Leg. Ant. Lond.* 103; **1268** detenti in prisona regis pro morte Ricardi..unde ~ati sunt *Cl* 482; s**1329** arettatus super eo quod per minas habuit..c s. *Ann. Lond.* 245; **1330** abbas..capi et arretari fecit quosdam..de burgaria domus *PQW* 519a; nec..sunt..~ati de crimine aliquo qualitercumque..enormi nisi secundum leges terre illius et coram judicibus Fortescue *LLA* 36; **14..** si aliquis..pro aliqua felonia ~atus fuerit *Reg. S. Aug.* 149. **b** **1392** quia..Thomas arectatus fuerit in culpa, quod non potuit se excusare de hac culpa, ideo commissus est gaole *Mem. York* I 173; **1400** ordinamus quod nullus homo incipiat ad operandum in officio magistrali nisi pro justo viro..inter vicinos suos cognoscatur et ~etur *Ib.* 242.

arreynare v. arrenare. arrha v. arra. **1** Arrianus v. Arianus.

2 arrianus [Ar. *ar-rīḥānī*], sort of aromatic wine of great purity.

[Haly] dicit quod potest sumi..cum 30 ʒ vini ~i; et Avicenna dicit 'cum vino rubeo'. sed vinum ~um est rubeum; alii dixerunt quod vinum ~um est vinum forte Bacon VIII 65.

arriare v. arraiare. arride v. aride.

arridentia, tranquillity.

s**1455** in illa ~ia temporis qua cum matre ecclesia sub pacis silencio starent bene omnia et nox in suo cursu tranquillum perageret iter *Reg. Whet.* I 202.

arridēre [CL], to smile at, say w. a smile. **b** (fig.) to be gracious or propitious.

rex..~ebat ei [Ygerne] multociens et jocosa verba interserebat G. Mon. VIII 19; archiepiscopus vocato..Constantino ei in hec verba arrisit: "Christus vincit" *Ib.* VI 4. **b** adridente, *tyctende GlC* A 198; ubi oportunitas adridebat temporis Bede *HE* V 2; **764** cum tempus adrideat (*Lit. Abb. Jarrow*) *Ep. Bonif.* 116; in his [accidentibus]..eorum [sensibilium corporum] pulchritudo maxime ~et Eriug. *Per.* 544B; mundum sibi jocundissime ad votum ~entem.. recusavit G. Crispin *Herl.* 87; **1197** ut amici fortuiti fortune ~enti ~eant *Ep. Cant.* 415; s**978** ipsi [Edwardo]..ignobiliter sepulto arriserunt divina miracula Higd. VI 12 p. 36; pessimum signum est quando talibus peccatoribus publicis ~et perseveranter mundi prosperitas Wycl. *Mand. Div.* 396.

arrigere [CL], to raise. **b** to prick up. **c** (p. ppl.) alert.

indutos artus agresti de spatulo surgens arrexit Felix *Guthl.* 19. **b** **10..** arrectas, *upp arehte* WW; lete aures

~ebant..qui sibi assentiebantur *G. Steph.* II 107; phocas.. ad auditum aures ~ere Gir. *TH* III 12. **c** arectas, *hlysnendi GlC* A 805.

arriol- v. hariol-.

arripere [CL], to seize, lay hold of. **b** (fig.) to take upon oneself. **c** to grasp (fig.), realize.

fertur quia, facta.. cruce, ..ipse..hanc ~uerit Bede *HE* III 2; c**750** falcones quorum ars..sit grues velle.. captando ~ere et ~iendo consternere solo (Ethelbert) *Ep. Bonif.* 105; **8..** ~e, *gegrip* WW; frigus adest, juvenes, frondes nunc †arripite silve Alcuin *Carm.* 55. 8; de manibus ejus illud [cornu] ~uit Gir. *TH* III 34; si arrip[u]eris hunc lapidem et posueris eum in alio lapide Bacon V 118; arreptis securibus..hostes prostraverunt Elmh. *Hen. V* 53. **b** Julianus qui tyrannidem et apostasiam pariter ~uit Aldh. *VirgP* 38 p. 288; tantis lucubrationibus elaborandum mihi onus ~ui Gir. *TH intr.* p. 5. **c** statim ~iens mente de rege esse dictum *V. Cuthb.* III 6.

2 a to seize (of demoniac possession; *cf. arrepticius*). **b** to attack (of disease). **c** to assail (verbally).

a subito a diabolo arreptus, clamare, dentibus frendere, spumare..coepit Bede *HE* III 11. **b** infirmitate corporis arreptus *Ib.* 19; cum..Albinus..febribus ~eretur *Canon. G. Sempr.* 75v; tanta infirmitas ~uit eam *Ib.* 144. **c** scripta defendencium veritatem..conatur pervertere et ~ere eos in verbis, ut sic eos cogat a veritate consona cessare Ockham *Dial.* 657 (757).

3 to start, set out on (a journey). **b** (fig.). **c** (w. *fugam*) to take flight. **d** (w. *gressus*) to direct one's steps. **e** to cover (a distance).

iter arreptum..tetendit *G. Herw.* 325; **1203** die qua iter peregrinationis sue ~uit versus Jerosolim *CurR* III 34; **1217** iter ~iet eundi versus S. Jacobum *Pat* 108; s**1213** [rex] summo diluculo iter furibundus ~iens versus Notingham properavit Wend. II 83; **1258** infra tres dies ~iat iter versus illum qui ceperit namia illa *BBC* (*Grimsby*) 233; **1334** infra duos dies..iter ~iant veniendi *RScot* 293b; **1407** viam ~uit in portum *Lit. Cant.* III 100; **1411** ~ere..viagium..versus Franciam *Conc.* III 334. **b** ille viam sideream ~ere, incedere et permeare nititur qui..Deum in Sion contemplatur J. Sal. *SS* 949c; nondum tante perfectionis iter ~ui ut possim tantis injuriis non moveri Gir. *Symb.* 28 p. 298; viam perfeccionis ~ere Ockham *Pol.* II 607; desuper in celis arripe fortis iter Gower *VC* VII 694. **c** arripiendo fugam citius properavit ad almum / pontificem Wulf. *Swith.* II 1130; s**1173** Anglie magnates..regem Scotie subito fugam ~ere coegerunt Diceto *YH* I 376; s**1381** fugam latenter ~uit, legum censuram timens *G. S. Alb.* III 313; **1426** carceres..fregit et fugam furtive ~uit *Reg. Cant.* III 143. **d** versus Dunelm' ~iet gressus suos *FormOx* 236. **e** adeo ut mulier tria milliaria Cantuariam ingressura pedes ~eret W. Cant. *Mir. Thom.* II 5.

4 to put ashore (*cf. arrivare*).

s**1415** rex Henricus..cum armatorum magna multitudine in partibus Normannie ~uit *Plusc.* X 23.

arriragium v. arreragium 2a.

arrisus, smile. **b** (fig.).

vultusque modestia raro / gratior arrisu Hanv. IV 295. **b** despicantes..patrii soli dulcem ~um W. Poit. I 55.

arrius v. varius.

arrivagium [OF *arivage*], landing due.

1279 clamat..habere villam et portum de Schorham et ~ium cum theolon' et aliis rectis consuetudinibus ad illud (*sic*) portum et ~ium pertinentibus ab antiquo *PQW* 760b; **1328** de ~io navium et batellorum in portu de Donewico applicancium seisiti fuerunt *Pat* 170 m. 24*d.*; **1361** ad.. protegendum..jura et libertates nostras..apud Wythsand et alibi in regno Francie, quocienscunque contigerit nos.. pro passagio vel †armagio [? l. arivagio] seu aliis consuetudinibus..molestari *Lit. Cant.* II 408; c**1370** quietos esse de ~io in omnibus portubus domini principis in Northwallia *Rec. Caern.* 133.

arrivare [OF *ariver* < ad+ripa], to come ashore. **b** to bring ashore, strand.

transnavigantes in Normanniam ad portum Dive ~averunt *BR Will. I* 18; **1308** [clamat habere] theolonium de quibuscumque merchandisis arivantibus super terram dominicam..manerii [de Whitstaple] *PQW* 321a; s**1459** reversus est..de Hibernia et ~avit apud Redbanke prope Cestriam W. Worc. *Ann.* 774. **b** **1279** cum balena ~ata fuerit in terra sua de Useflet *PQW* 192b.

Arroacensis, Aroasian.

c**1170** secundum institutiones ecclesie S. Nicholai de Arrowasia *Regesta Scot.* II 56; **1251** abbates ordinis ~is *Chanc. Misc.* 19/2 r. 10 (cf. *Cal. Doc. Ir.* I 3150); **1519** canonici regulares vocati Arusianses (*sic*) et Victorini, quos audivimus a ceteris segregatos *Conc.* III 684.

arroganter [CL], arrogantly, presumptuously.

adrogantissime, *wlonclice GlC* A 235; isti..fiducia virginitatis inflati ~er intumescunt Aldh. *VirgP* 10; **10..** ~er, *gilplice* WW; urbem..solito ~ius cum armato milite ingredi *G. Steph.* I 15; quos pueros secum in expeditionem ~er adduxerat Gir. *IK* I 9.

arrogantia [CL], arrogance, presumption.

si tumentis ~iae spiculo sauciatur Aldh. *VirgP* 16; nec harum apices litterarum ~iae supercilium esse suspiceris Bede *Egb.* 1; **9..** fastus, ..elatio, vel *gepungennes* vel *gelp* vel ~ia, .. **10..** ~iae, *gilpes* WW; pro nobis..contra ~iam et intemperantiam modus et modestia dimicabunt Gir. *EH* I 8; quid..apud viros ecclesiasticos..uspiam aspicimus nisi aut ~ias dignitatum aut avaritias facultatum aut immoderantias voluptatum Ad. Marsh *Ep.* 75 p. 183.

arrogare [CL], to claim. **b** (w. inf.). **c** to adopt.

fragmenta..a subelemosinario colligi debent, priusquam a refectorio coclearia ~entur *Cust. Westm.* 124. **b** **1107** cum ecclesie ostium reges esse ~ant (*Lit. Papae*) *Conc.* I 385. **c** s**1152** ducem Normannorum rex in filium ~avit Diceto *YH* I 296.

2 (pr. ppl.) proud, arrogant.

8.. omnis ~ans, *elc upahafenes* WW; clericus non debet esse superbus, non ~ans Ælf. *Ep.* 1. 175; arrogantia superbie species est; est autem ~ans qui neminem pre se hominem ducit Neckam *NR* II 190; *prowde*, ampullosus, ~ans, attollens *CathA*.

†arroinanare, (?) to arraign (*cf. arrationare, arrenare*).

12.. redduntur dicte experquerie domino regi inutiles, dictique piscatores ex parte ballivorum domini regis ~ati super hoc composuerunt apud partes arrognon' cum domino rege in recompensacionem dictarum experqueriarum *AncC* (*Pet. Guernsey*) LV 4.

arrolius [cf. Sp. *arrollar*], roll of cloth (Sp.).

1470 carricaverunt xxxvj arollios sive pecias de marfaca, de quo fiunt sacci valoris j li. cum dim. pro quolibet ~io sive pecia (*TreatyR*) *Foed.* XI 675b.

arrumare [LL], to bring news.

adrumavit, rumorem obtulit *GlC* A 248 (cf. *Erf.* 2. 261. 24: adromavit, rumorem adtulit).

arruptus v. abrumpere 2c. arrura v. aratura.

ars [CL], art, skill or technique or accomplishment in making things, esp. things of beauty. **b** human handiwork (contrasted w. nature). **c** product of art or craft. **d** artifice, trick. **e** (w. *pars*) 'art', (responsibility for) contrivance. **f** skill exercised by animals.

de terrae gremiis formabar primitus arte Aldh. *Aen.* 61 (*Pugio*) 1; artes esse aeternas et semper animae adhaerere Eriug. *Per.* 486c; opus quod fit secundum aliquam artem.. semper est in ipsa arte non aliud quam quod est ars ipsa Anselm (*Mon.* 34) I 53; est de eo omnis ars cujus in ea docetur scientia Balsh. *AD* 9; in diversicoloribus picturis, ubi lenocinante splendore fucorum ars spectabilis rapiebat animos W. Malm. *GP* I 43; est ars ratio que compendio sui naturaliter possibilium expedit facultatem J. Sal. *Met.* 838a; 'artes' dicte sunt eo quod 'artant' regulis et preceptis; vel a virtute, que Grece *ares* dicitur et animos roborat ad percipiendas vias sapientie; aut a ratione, cui alimenta et incrementa prestant, que a Grecis *arso* nominatur *Ib.* 839d; sin autem..longe penitius ad artis arcana transpenetraveris, tam delicatas et subtiles..notare poteris intricaturas ut.. Gir. *TH* II 38; cum doceas artes, sit sermo domesticus arti; / quelibet ars gaudet propriis Vinsauf *PN* 1087–8; ars non facit nisi formam artificialem Bacon *Maj.* II 549; essencia divina est ars seu racio vel species vel ydea cujuslibet rei create vel creande (Ric. Armagh *Sent.*) *Wycl & Ox.* 85*n.*; ex istis elicitur quod innocens nec arti liberali nec mechanice intendisset. constat quidem quod ars, in quantum hujusmodi, dicit quamdam erudicionem anxiam preter noticiam theoricam Wycl. *Mand. Div.* 495. **b** arte invida et invisa ipsam turpiter adulterante naturam Gir. *TH.* III 35; natura se ab arte superari conqueritur Neckam *NR* II 172; natura potentior arte Vinsauf *PN* 579; ars utens natura pro instrumento potentior est virtute naturali; ..quicquid autem est preter operationem nature vel artis aut non est humanum aut est fictum et fraudibus occupatum Bacon *NM* 523; natura cum paucis artibus sufficit ad necessitatem hominis (*Concl. Lollard.* 12) *Ziz.* 368. **c** dentibus ex ferro longisque ferocibus omnes / corrodunt artes, quod nichil obstat eis Gower *VC* I 474. **d** heu fortuna ferox quae me sic arte fefellit! Aldh. *Aen.* 60 (*Monocerus*) 6; terras quas vi vel arte multis abstulerat H. Hunt. *CM* 8; exquisitissimo dolo et arte maligna W. Fitzst. *Thom.* 35; venenis vincere solet quam viribus et arte magis quam marte vigere Gir. *TH* I 37; [mulier] cleros dum decipit arte pudicos D. Bec. 1975; [hyena] vocem simulans humanam, nomine noto, / servum quem fallax evocat, arte necat Neckam *DS* IX 98. **e** **1221** deadvocavit stagnum [adiratum] quod in eo non habuit partem nec artem *CurR* X 105; **1295** optulit se ad probandum..quod dictus H. artem nec partem non habuit in predicto equo (*St. Ives*) *Law Merch.* I 68. **f** arte mea crocea flavescunt fercula regum Aldh. *Aen.* 20 (*Apis*) 3; desidero..duos falcones, quorum ars et artis audatia sit grues velle libenter captando arripere (Ethelbert) *Ep. Bonif.* 105; [castores] ex salicum ramis in castrorum constructione ligna connectunt..ut..hispidum exterius silvescat arbustum, tota interius arte latente Gir. *IK* II 3.

2 mechanical or practical art, craft. **b** handiwork, design. **c** community or guild of craftsmen.

nisi..arte plumaria omne textrinum opus diversis imaginum thoracibus perornent Aldh. *VirgP* 15; [frater] fabrili arte singularis Bede *HE* V 14; o salinator, quid nobis proficit ars tua [AS: *cræft þin*]? Ælf. *Coll.* 97; puella nobilis..scientia liberalitatis multum dedita in mechanicaque arte etiam peritissima *G. Herw.* f. 325; bellatorie artis industria P. Blois *Ep.* 231. 527b; practicus obtusus medicalis nescius artis D. Bec 1797; quid aliud agricultura, quid architectura, quid mercatura, quid artes mechanice tam varie, ..nisi vite subsidia sub quadam providentia..curant? Gir. *PI* I 12; queritur utrum secundum artem possit fieri verum aurum M. Scot. *Sol* 713; s**1224** castellum..ligneum.. architectoria [*corr. from* geometrica] arte fabricatum M. Par. *Maj.* III 85; artes mechanice sunt laneficium, armatura, navigatio, venatio, agricultura, medicina Bacon XV 193; hec [geometrica practica] se habet ad alias [scientias] sicut navigatoria ad carpentariam et sicut ars militaris ad fabrilem *Id. Maj.* III 221; **1363** ut quilibet..artem sagittandi discat et exerceat (*Cl*) *Foed.* VI 417; **1389** dispositorem operacionum artem cementar' tangencium *CalPat* 122; *Ziz.* 368 (v. armator); **1402** de xij d. receptis de J. L. pro decima †arcis [? l. artis] sue (*Ac. Harrold*) *Beds. Rec. Soc.* XLIX 46. **1449** ad artem fabricalem exercendam *Crawley* 476; **1471** sive mechanico officio..insudent sive aliis artibus vivendi et negociacionibus intendant (*Pat*) *Foed.* XI 729. **b** **1392** J. P. habet *wyldewar* de qualibet arte supradicta *IMisc* 251/5. **c** **1380** ars peletrie, ..ars bocherie *Doc. Bev.* xxxii; s**1388** comparuerunt plures artes civitatis Londonii conquerendi causa se de pluribus injuriis Favent 17; **1427** lego communi pixidi artis mercerie London' in sustentacionem pauperum ejusdem artis xx m. *Reg. Cant.* II 406; **1440** quilibet molendinarius solvat..vj s. viij d., viz. dim. muro et dim. art i molendinariorum *Leet Coventry* 193; **1463** procuratores artis coquorum universitatis *MunAcOx* 701; **1451** quandam fraternitatem sive gildam artis mercatorum civitatis Dublin'..de novo..facere *Gild Merch.* II 60; **1554** qui non sunt alicujus artis manualis *Ib.* 361.

3 liberal art, comprised in trivium (grammar, rhetoric, logic) and quadrivium (arithmetic, geometry, astronomy, music). **b** (pl.) faculty of arts (acad.). **c** compendium of logic or other art. **d** (w. *verbum*) technical term.

non solum artes grammaticas atque geometricas bisternasque omissas fisicae artis machinas Aldh. *Ep.* 5; quem cum parentes..tam dialecticae artis compotem quam rethoricae artis participem fecissent *Id. VirgP* 36; disertos arte sophistas *Id. VirgV* 619; ut puer indolis librorum disceret artes *Ib.* 1127; canendi artem didicit Bede *HE* IV 22; de metrica arte *Ib.* V 24; de licitis artibus, arithmetica, musica et astronomia et geometria, nihil attinet dicere W. Malm. *GR* II 167 (cf. ib.: stellarum..arte); publicas scholas professus, artem magisterii attigit *Ib.* 168; [filie regine Scotie] litteratoriam artem edidicerunt Ord. Vit. VIII 22 p. 399; cum artium multa sint genera, ingenio philosophantis animi prime omnium liberales occurrunt. he quidem omnes aut trivii aut quadrivii ratione clauduntur J. Sal. *Met.* 839c; oratores..curantes artis precepta servare W. Fitzst. *Thom. prol.* 9; artes ingenue sunt septem lumina mundi Neckam *DS* X 37; inter liberales artes invigilare desiderans audiat..cathegorias Aristotilis (*Id. Sac. Med. Sci.* 373); in humanis operibus..ad perfectionem deductiones sunt artes septene Gros. 1; c**1250** nec licet alicui suprascriptorum, invito domino et nesciente, filios suos arte clericali informare *Cart. Rams.* I 466; dicuntur artes liberales vel quia liberant homines a curis temporalibus vel quia tantummodo liberi et nobiles solent eas adiscere Bacon XV 194; **1432** pertransibat usque..tabernaculum domine Sapiencie.., ubi..videbat ipsam dominam..sedentem in.. consistorio septem scienciarum liberalium, quarum quelibet secum habebat famosissimum preceptorem artis sue. ..in hoc tabernaculo Musica cum Boecio practicam artis sue per diversorum instrumentorum modulamina propalabant (*sic*) (J. Carpenter) *MGL* III 460–1; **14..** [volumina] ordinaria audienda sunt hec: primo sc. in veteri arte Liber Universalium Porphyrii (*Stat. Glasg.*) *EHR* XIV 251. **b** laudabiliter rexerat in artibus et decretis et fuit cancellarius Oxonie Eccleston *Adv. Min.* 64 (*insertion*) (cf. ib.: magister artium); **1253** universitas Oxonie corroborat quod nullus..incipiat in theologia nisi prius rexerit in artibus in aliqua universitate *StatOx* 49; commissarii ordinaverunt quod..hac vice frater T. inciperet [in theologia] non obstante impedimento objecto eidem, sc. quod in artibus non rexerit Ad. Marsh *Ep.* 192 p. 346; **1325** quod facultas arcium plene deliberet de tractandis in congregatione generali *MunAcOx* 117; **1340** nullus licencietur..ad incipiendum in artibus nisi prius juret se legisse duos libros logicales ad minus *Ib.* 142; **1358** dans intellegere quasi ij essent sophiste qui student in artibus *Ib.* 211; a**1350** ordinatum est quod nullus magistrorum quemquam ad lecturam alicujus libri facultatis arcium presentare presumat nisi presentandus se artes ad minus per quadriennium audisse in scolis ubi viget ejusdem facultatis studium generale proprio firmaverit juramento *StatOx* 24; **1431** septem artes liberales et tres philosophie..a magistris arcium..pro forma scolarium legantur *Ib.* 235; **1549** ne ulli ad scholas dialectices sive artium recipiantur nisi qui Latine et grammatice loquuntur *Conc. Scot.* II 105. **c** **10..** Ars Sedulii (*Invent.*) *EHR* XXXII 389; nec in transitu vel semel dialecticorum attigi scripta que vel in artibus vel in commentariis aut glosematibus scientiam pariunt aut retinent aut reformant J. Sal. *Met.* 889a. **d** est ex usu et artis verbis equivocatio cum alterius in usu loquendi, alterius ad artem docendi fit eadem appellatio, ut 'exemplum'.. Balsh. *AD* 42.

4 art of government or guidance.

ars artium est: si placere vis, frequenter dato J. Sal. *Pol.* 487d; in nave gubernanda necessaria videtur ars moderandi; quanto magis in regno regendo Gir. *PI* I 19 p. 105; **1237** cum 'ars artium', teste B. Gregorio [*Reg. Past.* I i], sit regimen animarum, non cessat antiquus sophista sua girare volumina fraudis.., quo valeat concludere hujus artis discipulos *Conc. Syn.* 250.

5 forbidden or black art.

doctus in horrenda sceleratorum arte magorum Aldh. *Virg V* 1855; per incantationes vel fylacteria vel alia quaelibet demonicae artis arcana Bede (*V. Cuthb.*) *HE* IV 25; ad artis demoniace deliramenta declinasti W. Cant. *Mir. Thom.* V 11; magicas Medee curret ad artes D. Bec. 1964; multi libri cavendi sunt propter carmina..et hujusmodi, quia pure magici sunt, ut Liber De Officiis Spirituum..et liber De Arte Notoria, qui nec artis nec nature continent potestatem sed figmenta magicorum Bacon *NM* 532; **1331** invenerunt ..quosdam..operando circa invocaciones malorum spirituum et de aliis artibus nigromancie *SelCKB* V 54; non videmus aliquid mutacionis in aliqua creatura que est sic exorcizata nisi per falsam fidem, quod est principale artis diabolice (*Concl. Lollard.* 5) *Ziz.* 362.

arsacida v. assassinus.

arsare, to make a rattling noise (erron. expl. as 'to go').

arsantesque grues proturbo sub aetheris axe ALDH. *Aen.* 57. 5; **10..** ∼antes, *þa gegcndan* WW.

arsenicum [ἀρσενικόν], (compound of) arsenic, dist. as white (trioxide, sublimate), yellow (trisulphide, orpiment), and red (monosulphide, realgar).

∼i tres sunt species, sc. croceum, rubeum et album: croceum cum teritur lucens apparet, ut aurum foliatum quasi ut talcum; rubeum non ita folliatur, immo est in massam reductum..; album est aliquantulum crocei subalbique coloris. ..istud de Turcie partibus apportatur, reliqua vero duo de Armenia M. SCOT. *Lumen* 264; ∼um auripigmentum dicitur ob colorem auri BART. ANGL. XIX 29; fumus argenti vivi et arcenici BACON IX 47; [elixir] per spiritum occultatum in partibus animalium..sulphure et ∼o permiscetur cum liquescit *Id. Min.* 314; ∼i plures sunt species, id est album, citrinum quod et auripigmentum vocatur; rubeum est autem terre nature coagulationem habens cum sulphure *Ps.*-GROS. 642; medicine cauterizantes, sicut calx non abluta, ∼um citrinum et rubeum et sal armoniacum GAD. 34 v. 1; ∼um, lompnias i. auripigmentum citrinum *Alph.* 13; **1415** item pro arcenoco empto pro ratonibus interficiendis *Ac. Durh.* 610.

arsietura v. herciatura. arsilium, arsillum v. argilla.

arsina [cf. OF *arsin*], arson.

1283 si ∼e vel alia maleficia clam fiant *RGasc* II 209.

arsio [cf. arso], burning (of building), arson. **b** smelting. **c** 'blanching' (of silver; *cf. ardere* 5).

s1194 regi Francorum..∼ones et spolia multa perpetranti *Meaux* I 276; silve..deteriorantur..per vaccarias et per arciones vaccariarum *CallMisc* I p. 144; **1366** de arcione seu incendio grangie *Reg. Rough* 173. **b 1278** circa lavacionem cinerum plumbi et ∼onem *Ac. Durh.* 485. **c** viii libras cum pondere et ∼one *DB* I 337b.

arsis [ἄρσις], arsis (metr.), accentuation. **b** dilation (of heart), diastole.

∼is interpretatur elevatio, thesis positio; sed ∼is in prima parte nominis seu verbi ponenda est, thesis in secunda ALDH. *PR* 112; ∼is est vocis elevatio, ..thesis est positio BART. ANGL. XIX 128. **b** hoc [cor] habet duos motus contrarios, sc. dilatationis et constrictionis, que dicuntur diastole et sistole apud Grecos vel ∼is et thesis, id est elevatio et depressio RIC. MED. *Micr. Anat.* 226.

arsivus, burning, (sb. f.) burning fever.

in istis acutis ∼is non est expectanda digestio antequam detur aqua GAD. 5.2.

arsmet- v. arithmet-. 1 arso v. arcio.

2 arso, ∼ona [OF *arson* < arsionem], arson.

1228 placita ad coronam spectantia, viz. de ∼ona *Feod. Durh.* 218 (cf. ib. 270: ivit ad polam..pro ∼ona); **1274** minantur..Ricardum de vita et membris et ∼one *Hund.* II 92.

arsonerium v. arcionarius b.

arsor, burner (*cf. ardator*).

1320 ∼or calcis *KRAc* 487/3.

arsura, burn (on body) or cauterization. **b** burning (of building), arson.

incandens arsura replevit et ingens / illius volam WULF. *Swith.* II 348; **10..** ∼a vel ustulatio, *bærnet* WW. **b** burgenses..omnino vastati..propter ∼am *DB* II 117b; **1192** ut sit quietus de eo quod imponebatur hominibus suis de ∼a domus monialium *Pipe* 173; **1383** cum quamplurima homicidia, depredaciones, ∼e variaque alia injurie dampna ..in partibus marchiarum..perpetrata existant *RScot* 59a; **1389** de..∼a domorum..vel aliqua alia felonia *Guild Cert.* 46/451.

2 a burning (of lime). **b** smelting, calcining. **c** 'blanching' (*cf. ardere* 5). **d** residue of precious metal from sweepings of workshop.

a 1333 ∼a calcis: in stipendio j hominis ardentis calcem *KRAc* 542/4. **b 1409** colier iiij duodenas carbonis †vocatur [? l. vocati] *charcole* [com]burenti pro ∼a ferri minere (*Rec. Aud. Durh.*) *EHR* XIV 519. **c** reddit l libras ad ∼am et pensum, quae valent lxv libras *DB* I 16. **d** has reliquias corradebant..et pretiosam massam extorquebant, in tali negotio..emptas ex more copiosas ∼as, quas dicunt scopaturas, ad..flumen ferebant diluendas GOSC. *Mir. Aug.* 549.

arsurus, arsus v. ardere.

artaba [ἀρτάβη], measure of flour. **b** sifted (? misinterp. of *Dan.* xiv 2: *similae* ∼*ae*).

∼a, mod[i]i tres *GlC* A 813. **b** †arbatae, *sibaed Ib.* 769.

artabilis, subject to constraint.

strenabylle, ∼is, coercibilis *CathA.*

artago [? cf. Lomb. *arzadega*], teal.

artogo, artogis, i. avis Tolosana habens optimas carnes ad comedendum *Alph.* 14.

†artanita, (?) *f.l.* for *artemisia.*

succus cepe vel ∼a vel panis porcinus..supponatur et aperit GAD. 60. 1.

artanter, urgently.

cum..instet ∼er ex cura quam gerunt per istius sacramenti remedium infirmo succurrere J. BURGH *PO* VII 2 f. 91.

artanulus v. artavulus.

†artaratus, (?) decorated.

1419 unum parvum baslardum de brasele ∼um cum argento *Reg. Cant.* II 223.

1 artare (arct-) [CL], to narrow, constrict. **b** to confine, restrict. **c** to besiege, blockade. **d** (?) to force, drive.

1239 [per] levationem illam [fossati] †arcata [l. artata] est communis via et chacia in longitudine unius perticate *BNB* III 267; **1366** injunctum est..tenentibus..quod ∼ari faciant cursum aque..quod teneat †antiquam cursum *Hal. Durh.* 57; **1364, c1387** (v. artatio 1a). **b** genitor..filium.. latibulis carceralibus ∼andum..includit ALDH. *VirgP* 35; **s1307** episcopum..squalore carceris coartavit, ∼atum omnibus bonis..spoliavit TROKELOWE 63; **1314** (v. artator). **c s1238** adeo urbem..Valentiam..aggravavit ut undique ∼ata ad supremas conditiones est compulsa M. PAR. *Maj.* III 517. **d s1386** v..naves..ceperunt..; †∼atas [v.l. attractas] autem ad terram ceperunt eas exonerare victores *V. Ric. II* 73.

2 to constrain, compel. **b** (w. *ad*). **c** (w. *ut* or *quod*). **d** (w. inf.). **e** to restrain, prevent.

numquid, queso, nulla lege ∼atur quem lex ista constringit? J. SAL. *Pol.* 519B; ∼atus evidenti ratione, hac tandem seipsum responsione deludit AD. EYNS. *Hug.* IV 5 p. 21; **s1298** de exercitu pedestri non curavit rex.., eo quod non ∼abantur aliqui nisi qui gratis venire voluerunt W. GUISB. 324; **s1322** informatus fuit per malos consiliarios quod ipsum prefata citacio seu monicio non ∼abat AD. MUR. 40; reges pagani..de consuetudinibus Christianorum non ∼antur OCKHAM *Pol.* I 160; taliter..faciunt non veritatis causa sed solum urgentibus torturis ∼ati FORTESCUE *LLA* 22. **b** invenies armatam militiam non minus quam spiritualem ex necessitate officii ad religionem et Dei cultum ∼ari J. SAL. *Pol.* 600A; **1162** ipsum G. a juramento quo ad illas pactiones tenendas ∼abatur absolvimus *E. Ch. St. Paul's* 151; **1237** ∼are possumus per ballivos nostros.. executores ad solvenda nobis debita *KRMem* 15 r. 21; **1276** nisi dominus rex ∼aret se ad faciendum ea que facere non tenetur (*Cl*) *Foed.* II 69; si alios ad suum..defendendum errorem..quovis modo ∼are molitur OCKHAM *Dial.* 461; **1387** qualem penam merentur illi qui compulerunt sive ∼arunt regem ad consenciendum confeccioni..statuti? *RParl.* III 233a; **1405** cives..ad difficiliores..probaciones gravaminum suorum..non ∼abunt seu compellent *Lit. Cant.* III 96; **1514** ad..statuta..scribenda..se noscat fore ∼atum *StatOx* 329. **c 1293** quod..magistri..missam.. dicere teneantur bona fide promittimus et tenore presencium nos ∼amus *Ib.* 103; **1350** noscant..magistri..se ∼ari..auctoritate statuti ne..ipsis incepturis..suas revelent consciencias *Ib.* 31; presbyteri..∼ant..piscatores ut Petri sancti decimacionem [esiciorum] sibi conferant CIREN. I 94. **d 1166** cum ∼aretur Cantuariensis..Romanam audientiam appellare (BECKET *Ep.*) *Becket Mat.* V 494; qui..pacem ecclesie infringeret, lxxij li. persolvere ∼aretur *NLA* (*J. Bev.*) II 63; **s1331** quis ∼aret eum convivare domi? GRAYSTANES 44; nec eis aliter populi credere ∼abantur OCKHAM *Dial.* 432 *bis*; nonne..cum eadem consummare matrimonium ∼abitur? FORTESCUE *LLA* 32. **e** Ambrosius imperatorem excommunicavit et ab ingressu ecclesie.. ipsum ∼avit GIR. *PI* I 18 p. 92; si gutta †arcentur [? l. artentur; *but* cf. arcere b] ita quod gradus dormitorii ascendere nequeant, seu alio..incommodo sint detenti *Cust. Westm.* 234.

3 to oppress, afflict.

parentes..flebilibus orbitatis questibus acriter ∼abantur ALDH. *VirgP* 52; **9..** non demum artemur malis / pro qualitate criminis *Anal. Hymn.* LI i 48; **s1236** ecclesia Romana sollicitudine et angustiis nimis ∼abatur M. PAR. *Maj.* III 362.

2 †artare [cf. arthrisis], to suffer from cramp.

14.. pes patitur ∼are, A. *my fothe ys a slepe* WW.

artari v. arteri-.

artate, strictly.

1288 ad ipsius processus observacionem..nos ∼e et inevitabiliter cogunt..juramenta *AncC* (*Bologna*) LV 10.

artatio, narrowing, constriction. **b** narrowness, cramped quarters. **c** confinement. **d** siege, blockade.

1232 ad assisam capiendam..de ∼one vie *Pat* 522; **1364** artavit quasdam aquas.., per quam ∼onem J. S. ..et tres alii..submersi fuerunt *Pat* 270 m. 7; **c1387** via..in tantum artata est quod homines cum carectis et equis..transire non possunt ob defectum mundacionis fossati necnon †∼onis [? l. ∼onem] vie *Pub. Works* II 83; **1391** manutenet plurima ligna..fixa in regia ripa de messuagio suo..in obstupacionem et ∼onem dicte ripe *Leet Norw.* 73; **14..** ad predictas aquam et seweras et earum ∼ones et obstrucciones supervidendum *Reg. Brev.* 128. **b 1280** conspicientes.. ∼onem vestri dormitorii *Reg. Ebor.* 96. **c** hec duo pertinent ad anachoritam, ∼o [ME: *neruhðe*] et amaritudo *AncR* 148. **d s1238** de ∼one Valentie civitatis M. PAR. *Maj.* III 517 (*rub.*).

2 restraint, restriction. **b** constraint, compulsion (esp. canon law).

potentia divina non habet ∼onem et limitationem BACON *Maj.* I 145; **1281** grandis est superbie in subdito nolle..ad eandem reduci ∼onis regulam ad quam abbas se humiliter inclinat PECKHAM *Ep.* 189; **s1303** videbatur..quod statutum..editum fuit in ∼onem duorum ordinum..et in favorem nimium prelatorum *Lanercost* 202; **1325** credo quod vos non intenditis ad..solite disposicionis mee..sublevacionem, ∼onem vel restriccionem..procedere *Lit. Cant.* I 152; **1412** ne inclemens ∼o residendi custodes [librarie].. faciat lassescere *StatOx* 219. **b 1301** an [hec verba] debeant vim habere denunciacionis, monicionis, citacionis seu ∼onis *Anglo-Scot. Rel.* 89; **1310** quod Templarii abinvicem separarentur..et iterum examinarentur..et, si per hujusmodi ∼ones et separaciones nihil aliud quam prius vellent confiteri.. *Conc. Syn.* 1290; cogentes sibi subjectos ad tenendum opinionem hujusmodi et tali ∼oni seu coaccioni consencientes OCKHAM *Dial.* 844; **1344** quod juramentum.. civiliter et absque capcione et ∼one scripulosa (*sic*) jurantis intelligi volumus (*Stat. Cotterstock*) *Eng. Clergy* 282.

artator, gaoler.

1314 prioribus [Predicatorum] et ∼oribus ac incarceratorum custodibus imponitur..quod..singulos custodiant sicut volunt pro corporibus respondere, ..propter quod in fratres artatos seu incarceratos exercentur tirannides..graviores (*KR Eccl. Doc.* 1/12) *EHR* V 111.

artavulus, little knife.

mulier..zonam pueri reperit et a zona dependentem cum †artanulo vaginam et acus et thecam T. MON. *Will.* II 9.

artavus [*etym. dub.*], knife.

ut..∼um suum sub pede..poneret NENN. *HB* 189 (cf. *Ib. intr.*: cultros); **10..** ∼us, *cnif* WW; **s946** nebulonis ∼o intra inguina infixo rex [Edmundus] evisceratus est *Ann. Wint.* 11; dominus..∼um longitudinis palmi gutturi [agni] infixit W. CANT. *Mir. Thom.* IV 30; condiscipuli..impegerunt me et incubui ∼o *Ib.* V 30; artavum porto fidelem *Babio* 335; ∼i quibus pisces possunt exenterari NECKAM *Ut.* 97; **14..** hic ∼us, *a penknyfe* WW.

arte (arcte) [CL], firmly, closely. **b** (fig.). **c** strictly.

10.. ∼ius, *fæstlicor* WW; quem..vinculis ferreis ∼issime perstringi impetraverat R. COLD. *Cuthb.* 46; **s1379** monachi ..diversis abbathiis..custodiendi ∼ius diriguntur *V. Ric. II* 14. **b** memoriam misericordiarum Dei cordibus eorum ∼ius impressurus OSB. *V. Dunst.* 42; timens..ne..pompa splendidior animum..sibi..inclinaret, ∼ius solito se collegit ad se AILR. *Ed. Conf.* 767D. **c** quos regendos acceperat, ∼issime sed more patrum priorum regebat G. CRISPIN *Herl.* 93; **1218** inhibet ∼ius ne..procedant *Eyre Yorks* 399; excommunicationis sententia estis innodati, per quod ab omnibus ∼ius vitari debetis *Cl* 51; **1446** quod per censuram..∼ius compellantur *Reg. Aberbr.* II 154.

artel- v. artill-.

artemisia [ἀρτεμισία], wormwood or mugwort.

∼ia vel matrum herba, i. *mugwyrt* ÆLF. *Gl.*; distinguunt.. inter ∼iam et ∼iam nostram que febrifugium dicitur NECKAM *NR* II 166; matricis vitium levat artēmīsia *Id. DS* VII 11; artemesia est mater herbarum dicta BART. ANGL. XVII 16; arthemesia GILB. II 98. 1; ad preservandum a labore itineris portetur arthemisia a laborante et non senciet laborem ab intus GAD. 20 v. 1; †archemesia, matricaria, ..mater herbarum idem; tota herba utimur; G. *armoise*, A. *mugwort* vel *mugwed Alph.* 13; artemisia, A. *moderwort*, ..hec ∼ia, *mugwortt*, ..hec artimatia, *wodrofe* WW.

Artemisios [Ἀρτεμίσιος], Greek (or Macedonian) month.

vocatur apud eos [Graecos]..Maius Artemiseos BEDE *TR* 14.

artemon [ἀρτέμων], sail or mast. **b** (fig.) ship.

∼on, *obersegl* vel malus navis *GlC* A 753; malus vel ∼o, *mæst* ÆLF. *Gl.*; casus agitans artĕmo minaces FRITH. 360; suspenso velo, ∼one erecto, ..in altum maris descendere H. BOS. *Thom.* III 5; *bonet of a sayle*, †arcenio [v.l. ∼o] *PP*; *a sayle*, arthenio, artenum, arcetum, ..velum *CathA.* **b** ∼one petunt Gallias partes ÆTHELW. IV 3 p. 43.

artemta (artepta) v. artopta.

†artena, bow.

∼a, *boga* ÆLF. *Gl.*

arteria [CL < ἀρτηρία], wind-pipe. **b** artery. **c** (fig.).

∼ie, *windæddran* ÆLF. *Gl.*; cicade..∼ias sub gutture apertas habentes quibus voces..emittunt GIR. *TH* I 21; ut raucitas arctaret ∼ias W. CANT. *Mir. Thom.* II 35; pars ore canoro / nativas ostentat opes contentaque nervis / artĕrie non artis opem.. / ad vocis mendicat opus J. EXON. *BT* II 96; pulmoni continuatur trachea ∼ia, que usque ad gulam extenditur et guttur appellatur; et est membrum durum, cartilaginosum et semper patulum, ut aer libere ingrediatur RIC. MED. *Micr. Anat.* 220; viam aeris que [dicitur] trachea ∼ia BART. ANGL. V 24; vocis raucitatem ex humiditate nimia ∼iam gutturis infundente *Ib.*; propter ulcus trachee ∼ie seu cannalium pulmonis GAD. 52 v. 2; ∼ie, *smal pypys*, ..hec ∼ia, A. *the hole of the throt* WW. **b** venis omnibus et ∼iis cum via spiritus et halitus organo pariter precisis GIR. *IK* I 4; dolor cerebri..oculorum et pupillarum ∼ias..infusa caligine scintillanti languore obscurabat R. COLD. *Cuthb.* 99; vite consulens Deus vene ∼iam supposuit ALF. ANGL. *Cor* 3; omnes ∼ie dicuntur oriri a corde et cordi deservire, ministrando scilicet vitalem calorem omnibus membris RIC. MED. *Micr. Anat.* 222; spiritum suscipiunt ∼ie a corde et deferunt ad pulsum faciendum BART. ANGL. V 1; sunt vene omnes ex una tunica facte, non ex duabus sicut ∼ie *Ib.* 61; si..in magna vena aut ∼ia sagitta fixa fuerit GILB. V 233. 2; si artarie rumpuntur in cerebro vel alibi tunc [fluxus] est cum saltu et continue GAD. 8. 2; a qua venalis ~ia progrediens pulmones subit D. EDW. *Anat.* B 4v. **c** radices obsoletas, studiosis tamen accommodas et que possent, digesta barbarie rancida, pectorales ~ias eloquencie munere medicari R. BURY *Phil.* 8. 141.

2 †arteria, *s. dub.*

1437 pro carpentariis et aliis operariis conductis circa facturam nove librarie et nove ~ie hoc anno (*Ac. Pri. Cath. Cant.*) *Arch. Cant.* LVIII 33.

arteriacus [ἀρτηριακός], bronchial, or afflicted w. bronchitis. **b** (sb. f.) bronchitis. **c** (sb. f.) remedy for bronchitis.

ab †arteriata passione..convaluerat W. CANT. *Mir. Thom.* III 30 (*rub.*: de abbatissa †arteriata); diairis valens asthmaticis, ~is, tussientibus vocem perditam restaurat GILB. IV 189 v. 2; ~i sunt quibus fauces reumatizant. . . ~a passio dicitur quando aliquis loquitur cum magna difficultate propter siccitatem trachee arterie *SB* 11. **b** grossum flegma..quo fiunt..artherice diuturne GILB. I 37. 1. **c** ~a, *gebrecdrenc* WW.

2 (conf. w. *arthriticus*), (?) arthritic.

artericus vel artriticus, *liðadl* ÆLF. *Gl.*

arterialis, arterial.

in ventriculo dextro nascitur vena que penetrat ad pulmonem, et..eam venam venam ~em vocant *Ps.*-RIC. *Anat.* 23; ex artariis et venis in quibus deffertur sanguis ad nutrimentum fetus, venalis sanguis epati, ~is cordi *Ib.* 40; in sanguine ~i extracto GILB. VI 248. 1; de epilepsia nervali et artariali cerebrali GAD. 60 v. 1; a quo et vena ~is in pulmones copiosum sanguinem eructat D. EDW. *Anat.* B 4v.

arteriasis, bronchitis.

~is, *sweorcopu* ÆLF. *Gl.*

arteriatus, artericus, v. arteriacus.

arteriosus, rich in arteries. **b** affecting the arteries.

si cancer fuerit in nervosis locis et ~is GILB. VII 331. 2. **b** in febre artariosa in articulis et circa maxillas fiunt apostemata GAD. 25 v. 2.

artesis, ~eticus v. arthri-. arth- v. et. art-, arct-, arith-.

†arthrisis, cramp.

14.. †arcacis, A. *a slepe of the fothe* (cf. 2 artare); *a malady*, arthesis, . .*slepynge in the lymmes*, artesis *CathA.*

arthriticus [ἀρθριτικός], arthritic, caused by or afflicted w. gout or sim. **b** (sb. f.) gout or sim. ailment. **c** (fig.).

sanctus vir..artetica passione novos pristinis adjectos persensit..cruciatus W. DAN. *Ailred* 31; ciragra dicitur eadem passio in manibus que et podagra in pedibus nuncupatur; . .talis infirmitas est longa †archerica que..vix curatur BART. ANGL. V 28; dragantum..†acchiricos juvat *Id.* XVII 51; pedes podagricorum et †archticorum *Ib.* 136; benedicta..proficit †aribeticis et podagricis GILB. VII 316. 2; **s1285** Honorius IV..cui pedum ac manuum fere ossa abstulerat artetica egritudo RISH. 109; artetica passio est dolor juncturarum: et dicitur artetica ab 'artus' et 'teneo', quasi artus vel juncturas tenens; . .et a laicis dicitur gutta GAD. 35. 1; arthetici dicuntur qui paciuntur in juncturis *SB* 11. **b** ptisis et artetica [v.l. †aretica], serpigo, fistula cancer D. BEC. 2022; succus ebulli valet contra †archeticam et contractionem nervorum manuum atque pedum BART. ANGL. XVII 60; ab artubus..arthetica appellatur GILB. VII 309 v. 2; ista artetica habet sub se species: sc. sciaticam, podagram et ciragram GAD. 35. 1; valet in podagra et sciatica et arthretica *RB Ossory* 255. **c** artheticam paciuntur nonnulli de nobis [sc. libris], sicut extremitates retorte insinuant evidenter R. BURY *Phil.* 4. 63; **s1461** perrexit princeps..usque ad Eboracum..ac ipsam [urbem] morbum arteticum, tam in manibus quam in pedibus, opere hoc est ac eciam cogitacione, pacientem comperiens, mox ipsam..consanare studuit *Reg. Whet.* I 411.

2 (sb. f.) primrose.

~a officinis est primula veris que ab Anglis dicitur *a prymerose* TURNER *Herb.* A ii v.

arthualis v. arcualis. Arthurus v. Arcturus. artice v. artite.

articula, art.

a crafte, ars liberalis, sciencia, ~a *CathA.*

articulare [CL], to articulate, fit w. joints.

ut pedes tam flexibiles tamque delicaciter ~atos haberet quod articulorum proceritate pariter et flexibilitate..acu suere consueverit GIR. *IK* II 11.

2 to write down in articles or clauses. **b** (usu. dep.) to draw up (a charge or sim.) in articles.

1505 concedunt..quod nomina eorum..in martirologio inscribi, ~ari, recitari et commemorari debeant (*Indent.*) *MonA* III 60; **1558** de aliqua dispensacione habita..inter eos super gradibus libellatis et ~atis inter eosdem *Offic. S. Andr.* 168. **b 1317** potestatem..quodlibet genus sacramenti in animam nostram prestandi, ponendi et ~andi, posicionibus et articulis respondendi (*Lit. Procur.*) *Reg. Heref.* 6; **1320** comparet rector, ~avit eidem, et habet diem..ad respondendum articulo *Reg. Roff. Ep.* 207; **1397** super quo dominus primas prefato M. . .vocato et comparenti judicialiter ~avit *Vis. Derry* 40; **1425** tibi ~amur, obicimus et opponimus..omnia et singula infrascripta..prout in articulis subscriptis seriosius exprimuntur *Reg. Cant.* III 105; **1425** dominus..~abatur eidem de dilapidacione *Reg. Heref.* 73; **1526** ~amur tibi..quod.. expulisti quosdam tenentes tuos (*Vis. Thame*) *EHR* III 705; **1549** statuantur articuli ad ~andum et probandum *Conc. Scot.* II 124; si allegata vel materia cui respondere tenetur sit ~ata, tenetur articulatim eisdem respondere *Praxis* 164.

3 (p. ppl.) articulate (of speech).

duas..vocis species..hoc est ~atam et confusam ALDH. *PR* 131; ymnistae crebro vox articulata resultet *Id. CE* III 48; **10..** ~ata, *rihtliðlicu* WW; sermonem aliquem vel vocem ~atam proferre non potuit W. CANT. *Mir. Thom.* VI 23; cum sint ~ate voces earum que sunt in anima passionum note GIR. *EH intr.* p. 208.

articularis, arthritic, affecting the joints. **b** reckoned by means of finger-joints.

ejus vi morbus articularis obit NECKAM *DS* VII 52. **b** de..computu ~i utrarumque epactarum BEDE *TR* 55 *rub.*

2 articulate.

lingua..dicta est..quia per eam ~is sonus verba ligat BART. ANGL. V 21.

articulariter, in articles or clauses. **b** in detail.

s1360 concordiam.., ceteris convencionibus ac concessionibus ~iter collectis.., circumspectissime compositam J. READING *Chr.* 173. **b s1471** ut rex aliquem..mittat qui, mentem ducis ~ius intelligens, omnia regi referat *Croyl. Cont.* C 557.

articulate, articulately.

1552 alta et intelligibili voce, distincte, clare et ~e.. legere ac de libro..recitare *Conc. Scot.* II 137.

articulatim, by means of finger joints. **b** (?) one by one. **c** article by article.

est et alterius modi computus ~im decurrens BEDE *TR* 1. **b** ut quid ~im annos futuros te judice supputas? NECKAM *NR* I 13. **c s1213** carta [fuit] ~im distincta et utrobique concessa M. PAR. *Min.* II 135; **1333** quod in pleno comitatu faciatis ~im proclamari ea que inferius inseruntur *LTRMem* 105 r. 138; *Praxis* 164 (v. articulare 2b).

articulus [CL], **~um,** joint, knuckle, bit between joints, finger, or toe. **b** finger-joint used in reckoning.

dum liciis..digitorum ~os et palmarum pollices obvolverent ALDH. *VirgP* 36; **949** (11c) hanc..kartulam..propriis digitorum ~is perscripsi *CS* 880; **10..** ~us, *lipincel, lytel lip* WW; dextri pedis majorem ~um defigebat in terram W. CANT. *Mir. Thom.* II 11; calceus..pedis instar factus, ut ipsos / exprimat articulos HANV. II 261; GIR. *IK* II 11 (v. articulare 1); possunt [manus mortui]..reflecti et ~i singuli more viventis in carne movendo plicari R. COLD. *Cuthb.* 42; **s1216** Scotos per pedes et manus et quosdam per manuum et pedum ~os cruciando *Plusc.* VII 4; ~i, *tooyn*, . .hic artuculus, A. *tho*, . .hic ~us, *a lytyle too* WW. **b** quidam..utriusque ordinem circuli, et solaris videlicet et lunaris, transferunt in ~os. nam, quia manus humana ~os habet adjunctis unguibus x et viiij, . .lunarem cursum in laeva manu..consummant. item, quia manus binae ~os exceptis unguibus habent xxviij, his singulos annos singulis aptant BEDE *TR* 55.

2 decad (ten or multiple of ten).

veniente plagarum ~o BEDE *Tab.* I 8 (cf. *Exod.* vii–xi); progressionem numerorum ~is quasi quibusdam unitatibus ad infinita crescere..videmus ALCUIN *Ep.* 133; in digitis et ~is abaci numerabilibus ADEL. *ED* 11; omnes numeri qui sunt in ceteris limitibus preter primum ~i solent appellari OCREATUS *Helceph* 132; digitus continet numeros ab uno usque ad x; ~us continet x et reliquos denarios; compositus amplectitur digitum et ~um, ut xj, xij, xiij et sic de aliis usque ad xx qui est secundus ~us BART. ANGL. XIX 121; omnis numerus perfectus, . .digitus, ~us compositus, sive cujuscunque alterius disposicionis laudabilis, est finitus BRADW. *CD* 120C; scribe..figuram ~i sub duabus proximis figuris KILLINGWORTH *Alg.* 714.

3 article, section, or clause: **a** (in agreement, grant, or regulation); **b** (in claim, complaint, or accusation); **c** (in inquisition); **d** (in creed).

a 1220 ita quod secundum tenorem compositionis..m li. ..deberet recipere annuatim, prout hoc cum quibusdam aliis ~is in carta..continetur *Pat* 243; **1236** apud Mertonam, ubi tractatum fuit de communi utilitate regni super pluribus ~is dominum regem et regnum tangentibus *BNB* III 134; **s1249** clamabant omnes..quod in nullo ~o a libertatibus suis usitatis discedere voluerunt *Leg. Ant. Lond.* 16; **1255** libertates..quas burgenses..habent tam de tallagiis.. quam aliis ~is *BBC* (*Portsmouth*) 13; **s1264** regem.. rogantes quod saltem unicum..remittat ~um, viz. quod alienigenis ab Anglia remotis per indigenas gubernetur *Ann. Lond.* 61; **1325** in gracis concedendis et aliis negociis expediendis..nullus ~us nec graciosus nec alius.. pertractetur nisi.. *StatOx* 128; **1358** cartas in omnibus punctis, condicionibus, ~is et circumstanciis suis..ratificamus *Inchaffray* 126; **c1370** nota quod hic habetur ~um quod iste non erit Gallus (J. BRIDL. *gl.*) *Pol. Poems* I 193; **s1420** ~i magne concordie pacis de verbo in verbum ELMH. *Hen. V Cont.* 137. **b** si super aliquem istorum ~orum arrestetur loquela GLANV. II 6; **1227** instructus super variis ~is pro quibus..citaveritis eundem (*Lit. Papae*) *Reg. S. Osm.* I 386; **1278** in nullo ~o est culpabilis *SelCMan* 95; petit judicium ..si debeat..ad illum ~um respondere *State Tri. Ed. I* 21; **s1280** proponit contra abbatem..quod vult uti littera sua provisoria seu executoria loco narracionis libelli seu ~i cum hac adjeccione peticionis *Chr. Peterb.* 86; **1300** quod possint eos..ad..premissorum observacionem absque ~i seu libelli peticione..compellere *Ambrosden* I 490; **1301** ~i liberati domino E. regi ex parte..cleri Anglie in parliamento suo *Conc. Syn.* 1206; **s1311** factum fuit concilium provinciale Londoniis contra Templarios super heresi et aliis ~is..nefandis AD. MUR. 14; **s1322** conduxerunt.. advocatos ad componendum ~os contra eum GRAYSTANES 39; cum hec suggestio coram..archiepiscopo [Ebor', ob. 1352] proponeretur, ipse eam admittere differebat quoad usque..cognosceret si predicta ~a rei veritatem continerent *Meaux* III 8; **1461** volumus quod quilibet prosequi valeat ~um eciam per alium inchoatum (*Lit. Papae*) *Reg. Aberbr.* II 124. **c 1228** circa hunc ~um requisitus nichil scit *Feod. Durh.* 221; **s1252** facta est inquisitio per..Lichfeldie diocesim super ~is subscriptis *Ann. Burton* 296; **1283** ubi non est aliquod placitum sed tantum presentaciones fient de ~is corone *SelCKB* I 128; **1409** omnes episcopi Dunelmenses..venire solebant per ballivos suos obviam..justiciariis itinerantibus hic in primo ingressu suo in..comitatum..et ibi petere ~os corone *PQW* 604b; **1549** ~i super quibus..inquisitores suas inquisiciones formare potissimum deberent *Conc. Scot.* II 119. **d** sic Creator..magis improbabiles probate fidei ~os..firmat exemplis GIR. *TH* I 21; **c1218** precipimus quod..fidem rectam teneatis, parochianos vestros in ~is fidei..instruentes *Conc. Syn.* 61; **s1239** imperator respondit se esse virum catholicum Christianum sane de omnibus orthodoxe fidei ~is sentientem M. PAR. *Maj.* III 626; non tenentur fideles credere quod omnis determinacio ecclesie Romane est undequaque..ab ecclesia tanquam ~us fidei capienda (*Concl. Lollard.*) *EHR* XXVI 746.

4 a (gram.) connecting link. **b** clause not linked to others by conjunction, asyndeton. **c** (mus.) phrase.

a infinitivus..supponere potest loco nominativi; set ~us constructionis, sc. casus, advenit infinitivo in significatione gerundii BACON XV 86. **b** ore brevi dispendia lata coartet / articulus punctum cesus VINSAUF *PN* 695; ~us est quando singula verba singulis intervallis distinguntur cesa oratione, ut hic: 'armis, classe, cibo dives mala castra petisti; solus, inermis, inops, inglorius ecce redisti' *Id. CR* 322. **c** lascivientis vocis luxu..muliebribus modis notularum ~orumque cesuris stupentes animulas emollire nituntur J. SAL. *Pol.* 402C (cf. ib. 402D: replicatio ~orum).

5 (critical) moment, crisis, emergency; **b** (w. *necessitatis*); **c** (w. *mortis* or sim.).

ingruente belli ~o BEDE *HE* V 10; in ~o temporis estu marino..abreptus est W. CANT. *Mir. Thom.* VI 146; qui in ipso doloris ~o gaudium simulat GIR. *TH* III 12; **s1217** doluerunt valde illum in tali ~o fuisse constitutum WEND. II 221; **s1314** ordo [Predicatorum]..fuit in ~o subversionis et damnacionis ab ecclesia militante *Meaux* II 320; si aliquis fuerit in tali ~o constitutus quod, nisi veste sibi presente se cooperuerit, morietur OCKHAM *Pol.* I 325; *a thryngyn downe*, ~us, pressura *CathA.* **b** si necessitatis non incumbit ~us J. SAL. *Pol.* 592B; **1265** in necessitatis ~o solebant amici specialiores requiri (*Petitio*) *EHR* XXXIII 224; **1327** considerantes quod in tante necessitatis ~o nullus se excusare poterit *RScot* 214a; excepta suscepcione baptismatis in necessitatis ~o OCKHAM *Dial.* 729. **c** in ipso tandem mortis ~o ad paenitentiam confugiunt BEDE *HE* V 12; mihi mortis amarae / articulus properat ALCUIN *SS Ebor.* 469; **c1150** in ~o mortis, intelligens se..inconsiderate peccasse *Cart. Rams.* I 257; imminente letali ~o GIR. *TH* I 19; regum sublimitas non..evitare poterit brevis sepulture ~um S. SIM. *Itin.* 75.

articus v. arcticus.

artifex [CL], artificer, craftsman. **b** artist (in music or literature), performer. **c** master of artifice. **d** the Creator.

nobilium ~fices imaginum ALDH. *VirgP* 60; murum.. non tam lapidibus quam cespitibus construentes, utpote nullum tanti operis ~ficem habentes BEDE *HE* I 12; ~fex, *cræftica* ÆLF. *Gl.*; **982** (11c) meo fideli ~fici Wulfhelm *CD* 634; terra Rabelli ~ficis *DB* II 269b; [vasis] miratur in illis / artificis natura manum HANV. IV 302; GROS. 95 (v. artificialis a); **c1260** quod decime solvantur de ~ficibus.. et omnibus aliis stipendiariis operariis *Conc. Syn.* 796; **1349** batellarii, carectarii et quicumque alii ~fices et operarii *MunAcOx* 789; urbs stat communis de gentibus ecce duabus: / sunt mercatores, sunt simul artifices GOWER *VC* V 664; **a1460** inquiratur de carpentariis et aliis manuum ~ficibus *BBAdm.* I 228. **b 764** delectat me quoque citharistam habere, . .quia citharum habeo et ~ficem non habeo (*Lit. Abb. Jarrow*) *Ep. Bonif.* 116; turpis rei narratio, quanquam preferat artem, devenustare tamen videtur ~ficem GIR. *TH* III 25. **c** consilio..capellani sui, quem optimum sciebat in subtilibus ~ficem, . .sigillum..aperuit MAP *NC* V 4 p. 217 (cf. ib.: mortis ~fex). **d** filium artem omnipotentis ~ficis vocitamus ERIUG. *Per.* 479B.

artificatorius v. ratificatorius.

artificiabiliter, by art.

1419 lapis de birillo ~er in coreo nigro suspensus *Reg. Cant.* III 55.

artificialis, artificial, produced by human skill. **b** skilled, artistic, involving craftsmanship. **c** (med.) prescribed by art, scientific. **d** (sb. m.) craftsman.

animus secreta sua molimina..in..aliorum animorum notitiam naturalibus ~ibusque progressionibus proferre non retardat ERIUG. *Per.* 552A; lanam..que nivei candoris efficitur..antequam tinctura ~is superinduatur NECKAM *NR* II 164; forme ~es habent esse in actu in materia et esse in potentia in anima artificis GROS. 95; omnia ~ia representant artem in mente artificis BACON *CSTheol.* 39; naturalis [materia] est que solum subjectibilis per se et primo est forme naturali; ~is vero que subjecta est forme in arte in quantum tali *Ps.*-GROS. 303. **b** ~i verborum compositione KETEL *J. Bev.* 279; textoris prudentia ~i R. COLD. *Cuthb.* 42; nullus..serviencium debet..altari appropinquare..nisi pro..opere ~i exercenda (*sic*) quod per fratres fieri non possit *Cust. Westm.* 57. **c** in duobus modis operandi, sc. ~i et emperico GAD. 126. 1; non est tamen valde ~e uti laxativis cum cibis *Ib.* 7. 1. **d** ~is, A. *a craftiman* WW.

2 (w. *dies*) **a** working day (from sunrise to sunset). **b** day of 24 hours (associated w. *annus* ~*is, s. dub.*).

a dies naturalis 24 horis concluditur; dies autem usualis vel ~is 12 horis terminatur GERV. TILB. I 5; [sub polo arctico] una medietas anni est una dies ~is et alia medietas est una nox SACROB. *Sph.* 102 (cf. arcus 5b); vulgus theologorum estimat quod dies ~is precessit noctem et lux tenebras in principio mundi BACON *Tert.* 211; clerus [Hibernie]..abstinencie per diem ~em indulget HIGD. I 36 (= GIR. *TH* III 27: ut..usque ad crepusculum jejunent); [Alexander III Scotiae] constitucionem..fecit ut unusquisque longitudinem et latitudinem sui corporis omni die ~i foderet, id est vij pedum *Plusc.* VII 33. **b** c1250 est annus naturalis et ~is, et est dies solaris et dies lunaris et ex hiis duobus diebus fit unus dies ~is. ..computande sunt igitur xxiiij hore ex conjunctione diei solaris et lunaris ab aurora usque ad aliam auroram..et inde fit dies ~is *BNB* III 300; annorum alius solaris, alius lunaris, alius ~is, alius usualis BRACTON 359b; computatur nox sequens cum die precedente pro uno die ~i *Ib.* (cf. ib. 264: efficitur unus dies qui dicitur ~is ex die precedente et nocte subsequente, qui constat ex xxiiij horis).

artificialiter, artificially, by human skill. **b** skilfully, artistically. **c** acc. rules of art, intelligently.

num possit aliqua virtus seminaria ~iter procreari M. SCOT *Sol* 713; possunt fieri instrumenta volandi, ut homo sedeat in medio instrumenti revolvens aliquod ingenium per quod ale ~iter composite aerem verberent BACON *NM* 533. **b** 1402 turribulum magnum ~iter operatum argenteum deauratum *Invent. S. Paul.* 513. **c** a1345 nulla sciencia potest haberi ~iter absque logica, quia quicunque scit ~iter aliquam conclusionem scit se scire illam (BURLEY *Exp. Art. Vet.* 2A) *GLA* III 298 *n.* 580; oportet nos clericos uti ~ius cautelis Cristi quam laicos WYCL. *Ver.* III 165.

artificiare, to construct by art, manufacture. **b** (pr. ppl. as sb. m.) artificer. **c** (p. ppl. as sb. n.) artefact.

habent mel in triplici differencia, unum commune, videlicet apium, et ~iatum duplex S. SIM. *Itin.* 84. **b** verius est animam esse in semine sicut ~iatum in ~iante *Ps.*-GROS. 363. **c** unde ~iatum est, oportet quod constituatur in esse specifico per ipsam compositionem quam ars introducit BACON *Maj.* II 549; si est peccatum in forma artificis, erit peccatum in forma ~iati GAD. 36 v. 2; cum ista individua habent determinatum esse, necesse est ut nulla eorum sit intellecta apud abstractam formam cujus proporcio ad illam est sicut proporcio †artificii [? l. ~ficis] ad ~iatum BRADW. *CD* 153A; homines inordinate vagari in talibus edificiis et curiositatibus instrumentorum, indumentorum vel quorumcunque aliorum ~iatorum WYCL. *Log.* II 175.

artificiarius, artificer, craftsman.

1351 coram..justiciariis domini regis super laborarios et ~ios (*JustIt* 267) *EHR* XXI 528; 1393 justiciarii laboratorum, serviencium et ~iorum in tribus trithingis infra comitatum Ebor' *Mem. York* I 144; 1407 pro solucione vadiorum soldariorum, ~iorum et aliorum officiariorum ville et castri nostrorum Calesii (*Cl*) *Foed.* VIII 489; 1424 discordia..inter magistros et ~ios de *wevers crafte* civitatis Coventrie ex parte una et *le jornemen* dicte artis ex parte altera *Leet Coventry* 91.

artificiolum, craft.

ex concilio Cartaginensi:..clerici omnes qui ad operandum invalidi sunt et ~a et litteras discant BART. EXON. *Pen.* 168 v. 2. (cf. WYCL. *Ver.* III 81).

artificiose [CL], skilfully, artistically. **b** (of animals). **c** acc. rules of art.

9.. fabre, i. perfecte, arteficiose, ingeniose, *cræftig* WW; [torques] ex quatuor frustis..~e conserta GIR. *IK* I 2; tempore abbatis J. [ob. 1214]..facta est magna tabula cujus pars est de metallo, pars de ligno ~issime perfecta *G. S. Alb.* I 232; gentiles..conversi..quo certius [gentium errores] noverunt, eo ~ius hoc expugnare..didicerunt BACON *Maj.* III 44; quoddam molendinum equinum..~e inceptum sed non consummatum WHITTLESEY 166; 1432 in quodam..vase aureo ad modum sportule ~e composito (J. CARPENTER) *MGL* III 463. **b** quedam [hirundines] in fenestris vitreis nidos limo oblitos ~e suspendunt NECKAM *NR* I 52. **c** his..modis principia ad disserendum ~e variare oportebit BALSH. *AD* 121; disputans acute et ~e cum literatis et disertis GIR. *IK* I 12 p. 94.

artificiosus [CL], exercising or involving art, skilful, ingenious, elaborate: **a** (of persons or faculties); **b** (of works or actions).

a non aliud dicimus consilium praeter ~ae mentis conceptum ERIUG. *Per.* 577B; tam ~os quam virtuosos.. animosi pectoris impetus GIR. *TH* III 50; vir ~us opere et prudens architectus R. COLD. *Cuthb.* 47; [amor] eciam in terra subtilis et ~us est, qui homines olim amabiles fuscos facit et pallidos ROLLE *IA* 270. **b** dulces..aquas in sal verti caloris decoctione ~a sepe visum est ADEL. *QN* 51; quanto in ipsis principiis latentius sophisma, tanto ~ius BALSH. *AD* 39; ut fugitivam aviculam..nec ~a nec longa fuga tueatur GIR. *TH* I 12; cujus operis industria satis ~a fuisse videtur R. COLD. *Cuthb.* 42; considera gladii ~am compositionem NECKAM *NR* II 47; ut clarius apostoli sermo intelligatur, qui in hoc loco ~issimus est COLET *In 1 Cor.* 166.

2 crafty, tricky.

ille ~us serpens [sc. diabolus] *Latin Stories* 85.

artificium [CL], artistry, craftsmanship. **b** product of art or craft. **c** craft, handicraft. **d** community or guild of craftsmen.

hec ymago..tam miro et inexplicabili perfecta est ~io ut magis viva creatura videatur quam statua GREG. *Mir. Rom.* 12; [castores] tanto ~io ligna connectunt ut nec aque stilla..subintret GIR. *IK* II 3; hesitatur an ex senio diuturno seu alio ~io vel donante sic natura color illius nigredinis contrahatur R. COLD. *Cuthb.* 43; ubi..ymago extremi examinis..eleganter satis pro modulo humani exprimitur ~ii opere sculptoris AD. EYNS. *Hug.* V 11 p. 140; velabatur turris..canopeo intextis nubibus et multum artificiose congestis; ..et quatuor postes, super quibus canopeum vehebatur, quatuor angeli non minoris ~ii supportabant ELMH. *Hen. V* 67. **b** c1205 dicitur forma exemplar ad quod respicit artifex ut ad ejus imitationem et similitudinem formet suum ~ium GROS. *Ep.* 1 p. 4; 1481 quod quilibet forincicus artifex..non monstrabit in..opella ~ium suum in primo introitu suo *Gild Merch.* (*Andover*) II 345. **c** 1229 ut de negotiatione vel ~io ecclesie illius parochie in qua quis domicilium habet decimas det, licet in alia parochia negotietur vel ~io utatur *Conc. Syn.* 176; 1376 misit eum versus Eboracum pro ~io sellarii *Hal. Durh.* 138. **d** [rex] adhesit cantoribus, tragedis, aurigis, navigiis et aliis hujuscemodi ~iis mechanicis *G. Ed. II Bridl.* 91 (= HIGD. VII 41: ceteris artis mechanice officiis); s1346 ad Turrim procedens, subsequente populo et quolibet ~io pro se in propria secta vestitus distincto adducitur KNIGHTON II 46; s1356 quodlibet ~ium per totam civitatem vexillum sibi proprium ordinavit AVESB. 134b; qui omnes juxta eorum ~ia certas habuerunt divisas cultiores, que unumquodque ~ium notabiliter ab alio distinguebant ELMH. *Hen. V* 61; 1445 ordinatum est..de unanimi consensu.. omnium ~iorum *Mem. York* I 136; s1461 urbem [London']..ingrediens, ..ab omni ~io tocius urbis letantissime suscipitur *Reg. Whet.* I 404; 1491 ceteri ipsius fraternitatis sive ~ii [scissorum] *StatOx* 298.

2 artifice, trick.

philosophi multa posuerunt ~ia ad artis sue veneracionem seu occultacionem DASTYN *Ros.* 6 (cf. assare e).

artifinium v. arcifinium.

artiga, ~ale [cf. Prov. *artigau*], newly reclaimed land, assart.

1288 ab ~a seu terra sua *RGasc* II 289; 1291 eundo inter ..vineam et ~ale sive novale *Ib.* III 11.

artillaria, ~ium [OF *artillerie*], artillery, engines of war or the chase. **b** gear, equipment.

1377 licencias..de..vasis aureis vel argenteis, armaturis, artellariis..extra regnum..educendis (*Pat*) *Foed.* VII 166; 1381 cuidam artifici facienti arcus, balistas et alia instrumenta artelerie infra castrum *ExchScot* 82; 1384 concessimus ei..licenciam..fugandi et interficiendi cum..canibus ac cum ~iis..de cervis..leporibus ac omni alia fera cum canibus et arcubus fugabili (*Pat*) *SelPlForest* cxxx *n.*; 1384 camerarium..Berewici..ac custodem victualium et ~iorum ibidem *RScot* 64a (cf. ib. 68b: de..asportacione..~ie); 1416 exceptis..armaturis, ~iis et omnibus aliis hernesiis et habilimentis guerre (*TreatyR*) *Foed* IX 400; 1417 proviso.. quod..castrum predictum in fortitudine et ~ia nullo modo pejoretur *RNorm* 158; 1430 artillerias et alia invasiva et defensiva instrumenta *ActPC* IV 33; s1435 perditis omnibus nobilibus magnis machinis, tam cannalibus quam fundalibus artilliariis *Plusc.* XI 7; 1459 magistro artilarie *ExchScot* VI 496; 1462 cum..bumbardis ac arteleria missis ad castrum..pro municione ejusdem *Ib.* VII 152; 1474 pro artilyearia regis *Ib.* VIII 216; 1486 pro..expensis factis circa artilyeriam *Ib.* IX 435; 1466 ordinacionem pro defensione patrie in artilleria, viz. colubrinas, librillas.. (*Declaratio bonorum J. Fastolf*) *Paston Let. app.* 979; 1548 de thesauro nostro municionum, ~iorum, tentorum, pavilionum (*Pat*) *Foed.* XV 175. **b** 1435 unum parvum tintinnabulum pro missa et duas fiolas argenti et omnes alias ~ias..competentes (*TreatyR*) *Ib.* X 600.

artillarius [OF *artiller*], maker or supervisor of artillery.

1382 artilario castri de Edinburgh *ExchScot* 660; 1400 W. B. ~ius suus *War. Issue* 15/279; 1420 addicio ad constituciones ~iorum..: ordinatum est per magistros artifices de *bowercrafte*.. *Mem. York* I 199; 1454 unum janitorem, unum artilarium et unum vigilem infra..castrum *Pat* 479 m. 10.

artillatio, fitting out (naut.).

1481 pro reparacione, artelacione et sustentacione predictarum navium sive balyngerarum *KRCustAc* 19/16 (cf. *Mariner's Mirror* XVI 198).

artillator, maker of artillery (*cf. attilliator*).

1360 in xij springaldis factis et reparatis per magistrum J. B., artilatorem domini nostri regis (*KRAc* 392/14) *EHR* XXVI 691.

artimaga v. archimaga. artimatia v. artemisia.

artista, artificer. **b** student of the (liberal) arts (acad.).

forma substantialis solis non est a colore solis vel ignis quo utuntur †talis ~e M. SCOT. *Sol* 713. **b** c1250 quibusdam ~is, in omnibus..honorifice..magister R. exhibuit necessaria *FormOx* 481; quod huic statuto subscriberent.. omnes magistri regentes in sacra scriptura..et duo rectores pro ~is AD. MARSH *Ep.* 192; quales..sunt ~e istius temporis tales sunt theologi BACON IX 158; hoc argumentum non est notum vulgo ~arum apud Latinos, quoniam libri Aristotilis..nondum sunt in usu studencium *Id. Mor. Phil.* 251; alios homines reputant asinos et insanos, qui vacant cavillationibus juris et sophismatibus ~arum *Id. Tert.* 41; 1292 veniant magistri non promoti..ad cancellarium et procuratores vel seniorem theologum et seniores ~as, qui.. aliquos de melioribus illorum admittant ad..collegium *MunAcOx* 61; 1347 ad reparacionem vestium tam arcistarum quam gramaticorum (*Mun. Merton*) *Educ. Ch.* 298; a1350 incepciones non nisi die disputabili vel saltim apud arcistas festine legibili celebrentur *StatOx* 36; a1350 bedellus arcistarum *Stat. Cantab.* 321; 1409 jurent se..in scolis ubi viget studium generale facultatem arcium audivisse; jurabunt eciam quod ante responsionem suam..ad minus per annum arciste fuerant generales *Ib.* 200; *arceter or þat lernyth or techyth art,* archista *PP*; arcista, *an arcetere, ..a arcister* WW; 1451 in S. Andree civitate, ..loco.. ydoneo..in quo..quoddam notabile theologicorum et ~arum collegium existeret *Mun. Hib. & Scot.* 384a.

artiste v. artite.

artitas, constriction.

1374 se excusans..ab oracionibus propter pectoris ~atem BRINTON *Serm.* 34 p. 141; 1520 dicta M. est ita arcta quod non possit a prefato D. ..cognosci propter ~atem in membro secreto *Offic. S. Andr.* 11.

artite, w. art, skilfully.

facibus quos ad machinas eorum ustulandas..regis artifices prudenter et †artice [v.l. artiste] immittebant *G. Steph.* I 19; vasa..ex auro †artice [v.l. artiste] et gloriose celata *Ib.* 46.

artitudo, narrowness, confined space. **b** strictness, harshness, austerity.

propter vie ~inem equum..circumflectere minime poterat *Hist. Meriadoci* 388; 1314 loca eis sub cloacis preparantur .., quorum locorum vix ultra spacium lecti..continet ~o (*Instr. de Praedicatoribus*) *Flor. Hist.* III 163 (cf. *EHR* V 109); s1066 qui propter loci ~inem..ab Haraldo se subtraxerunt HIGD. VI 29 p. 246; s1400 plures [puerorum].. pedibus calcati locorumque ~ine oppressi moriebantur AD. USK 45; s1411 dum meticulose fugiunt, per ~inem tabularum cadentes in flumine demerguntur WALS. *HA* II 286 [= *Id. YN* 434: in flumen]. **b** s1244 in insulam Farne secessit, ..ubi in religionis ~ine..residuum vite egit GRAYSTANES 5; religiosos nonnullos ad majorem ~inem quam regula eorum contineat obligando OCKHAM *I. & P.* 44; a1389 exaltabit te contra ~inem miserie BRINTON *Serm.* 9 p. 29; *starknesse,* rigiditas, ~o *PP*.

artitus, skilfully wrought, artistic. **b** artful.

tam delicatas et subtiles, tam arctas et ~as, ..notare poteris intricaturas GIR. *TH* II 38. **b** *wyse,* altus, argutus, ~us, astutus *CathA*.

artius [ἄρτιος], even (of numbers).

arcii id est pares sunt 4, 6, 10, 20 BACON IX 203.

artocapus v. artocopus.

artocaseus, cheesecake.

jungitur arthocrea, simul arthocaseus illis GARL. *Syn.* 561; *chesekake,* ~eus, artocuria, artocria, ..*flawne, mete,* flamicia, flato, ~ius *PP*; hic ~ius, cibus factus ex pane et casio, ..hic artocacius, *a flawne* WW.

artocopa v. artocreas b.

artocopus, ~a [ἀρτοκόπος], **a** baker or pantler. **b** fine loaf, simnel cake.

a promus et arthocopus [*gl.*: *bakere* vel †*panttere*] WW. **b** artocopus primo scindatur, dente teratur D. BEC. 935; panes, artocopus, pastilla, liba, placenta GARL. *Syn.* 560; 1293 panis ~i, i. simenel, ponderabit minus wastello per ij s. (*Assisa Panis*) *MGL* III 411 (cf. ib. II 106); c1300 j patellam eneam pro ~is coquendis *RParl* I 247b; ~us, A. *a symynel*, ..hic artocapus, *a symnylle* WW.

artocreas [ἀρτόκρεας], meat-pie. **b** *torteau,* roundel argent (her.).

regula que statuit, velim mihi dicas, / placentas, artocreas et cornutas micas (*Maurus et Zoilus* 146) *Ps.*-MAP *Poems* 247; GARL. *Syn.* 561 (v. artocaseus); pronunciant de nocte gafras et nebulas et ~creas [*gl.*: *roissoles*] vendendas in calatis *Id. Dict.* 126; accipe testiculos arietum et..minutim incidentur, ac si deberent fieri ~cree ex eis GAD. 77 v. 1; *pye, pasty,* ~crea, pastillus *PP* (v. et. artocaseus); hec ~cria, *a tartelat*, hic ~crius, *a pye*, ..~crea, A. *a tart* WW. **b** quedam sunt pile rotunde. ..sunt et alia..que dicuntur ~criata, et sunt rotunde ad modum pile, sed sunt de argento ut hic: et portat tres †artocopas in campo rubeo, G. sic: *il port de goul trois torteus dargent* BAD. AUR. 132.

artogo v. artago.

artopta [CL < ἀρτόπτης], bread-pan.

†artemta [*EE* 338. 37: artepta], genus vasis *GlC* A 752.

artoricon v. archonticon.

artos [ἄρτος], bread.

in Greco, ubicumque legitur in Evangelio de hoc sacramento [sc. altaris], invenitur secundum eos 'arton'. ..nihil aliud est [arton] de principali intentione sui quam panis HALES *Qu.* 909, 911.

artous v. arduus.

†**artuare,** to carve (fowl).

spoylyn or dysmembryn, as men done caponys or oder foulys, †arcuo [v.l. ~o] *PP*.

artuatus v. 1 arcuare 2c. arcuculus v. articulus 1a.

artuosus, (?) clean-limbed.

a lymme, artus, ~us, membrum, membratus *CathA*.

1 artus (arctus) [CL], narrow. **b** (w. ref. to *Matth.* vii 14). **c** (w. *campus*) *champ clos,* lists (for trial by combat).

examen ~a fenestrarum foramina..egressum ALDH. *VirgP* 4; cymbulam..~am et oblongam GIR. *TH* III 26 (cf. ib. I 3: Britannia..oblongior et ~ior esse dignoscitur); 1374 de clj ulnis tele late.., de ccliij ulnis tele ~e *ExchScot* 466; pertransiens ~o satis passagio rivulum ELMH. *Hen. V Cont.* 150. **b** sit via prudens, via fortis, arcta, / justa seu solers, bene temperata ALCUIN *Carm.* 121. 14. **c** connectantur insimul manus reprehensi sub flexis poplitibus ad modum hominis in campum ~um intrantis (*Jud. Dei*) *GAS* 418.

2 tight, firm. **b** stringent, rigorous, austere. **c** difficult. **d** close, intimate.

arta catenarum constringunt vincla lacertos ALDH. *VirgV* 1210; ~issima digitorum impressione cepit oculos perfricare OSB. *Mir. Dunst.* 11; **s1232** vinculis ~ioribus constrinxerunt illum vicecomites WEND. III 38. **b** ~a castitatis continentia ALDH. *VirgP* 9; illum..flagellis ~ioribus afficiens BEDE *HE* II 6; districtio vitae ~ioris *Ib.* IV 23; **s1144** Arnaldus de Brixia, ~issimam vitam ducens TREVET 18; **s1232** sub ~a custodia deputatur WEND. III 38; **c1370** fundis falsorum premet arcta [*gl.*: magna] fames famulorum (J. BRIDL.) *Pol. Poems* I 190; **s1398** post primas cartas alias statuit magis artas GOWER *CT* III 67; **s1420** alii ..†arce [l. arte] carcerali mancipantur custodie ELMH. *Hen. V Cont.* 145; *starke*, ~us *PP*. **c 671** jurisconsultorum secreta..et, quod his multo ~ius et perplexius est, centena sc. metrorum genera ALDH. *Ep.* 1. **d** ut..credentes ~iori dilectione..amplecteretur BEDE *HE* I 26; exclamat cetus assidentium, auspitia future sanctitatis exosculatus in puella; pater ipse ~ioribus basiis dignatus sobolem..inquit .. W. MALM. *GP* II 78; ~iori eum sibi amicitia federeque conjunxit AILR. *Ed. Conf.* 745B.

3 (sb. n.) confined space, hollow (of hand). **b** close confinement. **c** (fig.) 'tight corner', difficulty (*cf.* 1 *Sam.* xiii 6).

cum..dicis unum, minimum in laeva digitum inflectens in medium palmae ~um infiges BEDE *TR* 1 (*but* cf. 2 artus a); digiti illius ad ~um palme inferioris..se procurve inflexerant R. COLD. *Cuthb.* 108 (cf. ib.: ~um palme illius..compressit); **s1242** incepit conflictus..in ~is viarum M. PAR. *Maj.* IV 213. **b s1232** Ranulphum..deponens tenensque in ~o ad gravissimam compulit redempcionem *Flor. Hist.* II 203 (= *Ann. Lond.* 31: in artho). **c** in ~o res sita est H. CANTOR 10V; **s1181** in ~o positus..patrem suum..consuluit *G. Hen. II* I 271; **1188** supplicamus quatenus..nobis in †arctu positis..subvenire..studeatis *Ep. Cant.* 175; **c1367** senciens se in ~o positum *Couch. Furness* I 528.

2 artus [CL], joint (of body). **b** limb.

cum dicis decem, unguem indicis in medio figis ~u pollicis BEDE *TR* 1 (v. et. 1 artus 3a). **b** Sunamitis sobolem..~us ~ubus membraque membris copulans suscitaverat ALDH. *Met.* 2 p. 64 (cf. *2 Kings* iv 34); diris ut rodant muliebres morsibus artus *Id. VirgV* 2000; imbecilles ~us baculo sustentans BEDE *HE* IV 29; ~us, *þa maran liða* ÆLF. *Gl.*; resupinus humi consumptos deicis artus *V. Merl.* 112; videre erat quomodo ~us spiritui famulabantur W. FITZST. *Thom.* 142; sola natura quos edidit ~us..componit et disponit GIR. *TH* III 10.

artuuerum v. arcionarius b. artuus v. arduus 2b. aruginosus v. auruginosus. arugo v. aerugo. aruit v. arare, arescere.

arula [CL], little altar. **b** brazier or grate. **c** (?) tinder-box or tinder.

ut..in eodem fano et altare haberet ad sacrificium Christi et ~am ad victimas daemoniorum BEDE *HE* II 15; fuere qui dicerent inter parietes altaris craticulam positam.. et sub ipsa craticula ~am parvam formatam et in eadem ignem exstrui AD. SCOT. *TT* 666A. **b** ~a, *fyrþonne GlC* A 751; ~a, vas †apium at [l. aptum ad] focum *Ib.* 768; ~a vel batilla, *fyrþanne* ÆLF. *Gl*; **10..** †asula, *iren hiorð* WW. **c** *tundyr*, †incentinum, †araula, napta, receptaculum ignis *CathA*.

arum [ἄρον], arum (*cf. barba 2a*).

aaron GILB. II 119 v. 1; recipe radicum feniculi, ..ireos, areos, aristo[logie] GAD. 73 v. 2; aaron, iarus, pes vituli *SB* 9.

aruma v. arvina. aruncudium v. armicudium.

aruncus [CL < ἤρυγγος], beard (of animal).

cum..mari [hippelapho] ~us sit CAIUS *Anim.* 11b.

arund- v. harund-. aruptus v. abrumpere 2. 1 arura v. aratura.

2 arura [ἄρουρα], ploughlands.

~a Graece dicitur Latine arvum BEDE *Orth.* 2775.

Arusiensis v. Arroacensis. arusp- v. harusp-.

arvalis, rural. **b** of ploughland, arable.

~is, rusticus, agrestis *GlC* A 788. **b** inundantibus.. populis, ..conculcatae, attritae et comminutae sunt illius ~is aequoris annonae GOSC. *Aug. Min.* 747.

arvambulus, "land-leaper" (? arval priest). **b** (sb. n. pl.) ambarvalia.

~us, A. *a londlepar* WW. **b** gentilis populus faciens arvambula Rome / excoluit festum Cereris GARL. *Myst. Eccl.* 340.

arvina [CL], fat, grease. **b** (fig.) grossness.

arbina, adeps, axungia *GlC* A 770; ~a *risel Ib.* 796; ut.. papirus in centro positus velut fomes ~a vel sevo madefactus solito clarius lucesceret ALDH. *VirgP* 22; in vitro resplendens arvina scrofae *Id. VirgV* 978; ~a vel adeps, .. *hrysel* vel *gelend*, vel *swind*, vel *swines smere* ÆLF. *Gl.*; **10..** arbina, *swind* WW; in ethica primo consumitur adeps recens..; deinde antiquior consumitur mixta cum carne, et ista vocatur ~a GAD. 21. 1; ~a est pinguedo cuti adherens *SB* 11; **1475** [de qualibet centena] cepi et †arume [l. ~e] *CalCh* VI 248. **b** Raimundus primus omnium laicorum crucem accepit, adjiciens voto ut..duraturo..labore ~am [v.l. ruinam] preteritarum iniquitatum extenuaret W. MALM. *GR* IV 388.

†arvingis [? cf. AS *yrf* vel *eriung*], unit of land (*cf. Econ. Hist. Rev.* 2nd S. X 201).

c1150 R. cum Barba habet xxx acras et dim., sc. tres ~es pro iij s. ..fuerunt tres predicte aervi[n]ges divise per tres homines in diebus Henrici regis *Cart. Rams.* III 285.

arvinosus, fat.

fatte, pinguis, ~us, bussus, crassus *CathA*.

arvinula [bibl.], fatness.

a fatness, arvina, ~a, crassitas *CathA*.

†arvisium, look-out post.

a tute hylle, ~ium montarium [v.l. montorium], specula *CathA*.

arvum [CL], ploughland. **b** field (of pasture). **c** field (mil.). **d** (pl.) earth.

arba, terra que aratur *GlC* A 728; arvorum gelido qui cultus fonte rigabis ALDH. *VirgV* 8; rediet viridantibus ~is annus laetus et frugifer BEDE *HE* IV 13; frugibus ~a abundant GIR. *TH* I 5. **b** herbas arvorum buccis decerpo virentes ALDH. *Aen.* 86. 2; includuntur..in terra illa [Anglia] pasturarum ~a fossatis et sepibus FORTESCUE *LLA* 29. **c s1420** rex suos exercitus revocavit in ~a ELMH. *Hen. V Cont.* 142. **d** veni, ut simul gaudere valeamus in astris sicut pariter gaudebamus in ~is *V. Osw.* 442.

arx [CL], citadel, stronghold, castle. **b** Tower of London. **c** Heaven. **d** (fig.) top, eminence, capital, supremacy. **e** (fig.) authority.

arx, *faestin GlC* A 740; †arbitus [l. arcibus], *faestinnum Ib.* 808; statuitur ad haec in edito arcis acies, segnis ad pugnam GILDAS *EB* 19; eversa ruunt urbis fastigia fractae, / quae dudum steterant, septenis arcibus amplae ALDH. *VirgV* 2616; arx, *se hihsta wighus* ÆLF. *Gl.*; porte sublimes sunt in arce, per quas in aulam poteritis per lapideos gradus descendere ORD. VIT. X 23; hec arax, *a towre* WW. **b** habet ab oriente arcem palatinam maximam et fortissimam W. FITZST. *Thom. prol.* 5; **s1267** rex..arci †cartate cominus appropinquans WYKES 202. **c** civibus angelicis junctus in arce poli (*Epitaph. Theodori*) BEDE *HE* V 8; quem Deus infidum caeli clamavit ab arce ALDH. *CE* 2. 5; aethereas lustravit spiritus arces *Ib.* 12. 27; **14..** ejus cultores ditet Deus arce polorum *Couch. Furness* I 22. **d** exametri.., quod ceterorum omnium arcem et infulas possidet ALDH. *Met.* 10; Hii, ubi plurimorum caput et arcem Scotti habuere coenobiorum BEDE *HE* III 21 (cf. ib. III 3: Hii..cujus monasterium in cunctis pene septentrionalium Scottorum ..monasteriis..arcem tenebat); **961** nos [pastores]..in sullimiore arce ceteris dijudicamur (*Lit. Papae*) W. MALM. *GP* I 39; si vehemens calor arcem capitis..invaserit P. BLOIS *Ep.* 43. 127B; tandem in arce victorie plene constitutus GIR. *EH* II 18. **e** stat vini quarta quam dat sors arce sub arta [*gl.*: sub certis regulis] GARL. *Mor. Scol.* 261.

2 fortification (AS *burh*). **b** (w. ref. to *burhbote*; cf. *Bull. IHR* XXXI 117–29).

8.. ad arcem et ad moenia, *to burge and to wealle* WW; **s893** [barbari] arcem fundant in Cantiae fines ÆTHELW. IV 3 p. 49; **s913** ad locum qui Sceargete dicitur venit ibidemque arcem munitam construxit FL. WORC. 122. **b †680** (c1000) absque trimoda [v.l. †trinoda] necessitate totius Christiani populi, id est arcis munitione, pontis emendatione, exercitu (*sic*) congestione liberam *CS* 50; **s748** concessit rex Ethelbaldus ut omnia monasteria et ecclesie regni sui a publicis vectigalibus in operibus et oneribus absolvantur, nisi struccionibus arcium vel poncium, que relaxari non solent, contingat ELMH. *Cant.* 314 (= *Croyl.* 5: archium); **749** (12c) nisi sola quae..edicto regis facienda jubentur, id est instructionibus pontium vel necessariis defencionibus arcium contra hostes non sunt renuenda (*Conc. Gumley*) *CS* 178; **770** praeter instructionibus pontium vel necessariis defensionibus arcium contra hostes *CS* 203; **814** preter arcem et expeditionem pontisque constructionem *CS* 346; **844** (13c) sine..arcis munitione *CS* 447; **878** (11c) absque..arcis et pontium structura *CS* 545; **c900** (13c) constructione regalis arcis *CS* 581; **904** (12c) arcis et pontis constructione et †conductione [? l. conditione] *CS* 611; **927** (12c) pontis arcis[ve] edificatione *CS* 660; **931** (12c) pontis arcisve renovatione *CS* 670; **940** pontis arcisve coaedificatione *CS* 753; **947** (10c) pontis arcisve instructione *CS* 820; **955** ruris particulam..ab omni servitio preter arcem, pontem, expeditionem liberam..concessi *CS* 903; **956** (12c) pontis arcisve restauratione *CS* 919; **956** (13c) arcis munimen *CS* 925; **956** (10c) nisi pontis et arcis..juvamine *CS* 926; **957** (14c) poncium arcisve cooperacione *CS* 997; **†969** (12c) cuncta illius monasterii possessio nullis sit unquam gravata oneribus, ..nec pontis et arcis edificamine *CS* 1228; **s1244** nec adeo [reges] libertati dederunt hujusmodi possessiones quin tria sibi reservarent, ..viz. expeditionem, pontis et arcis reparationes vel refectiones M. PAR. *Maj.* IV 312.

arxhotania v. archaeogonia. arzil- v. argil-. arzo v. arcio. arzonarius v. arcionarius c.

as [CL], unit (of weight), coin. **b** (w. *ex*) entirely.

asses scorteas, *liprine trymsas GlC* A 836; libra vel as sive assis: xii unciae BEDE *TR* 4; aut solidum assem usurpant sibi aut..trientem dumtaxat archidiaconis..cedunt J. SAL. *Pol.* 580C. **b** quis enim elementorum naturam ex asse metitus est? FRIDUG. 129; periclitatur oratio, dum quod ex asse verum diffiniam non habeo W. MALM. *GR* II 108.

asa [*supposedly* Pers. *azā, but* etym. dub.], gum mastic, asafoetida.

galbano, serapino, asa fe[tida] GILB. VII 293 v. 1 (cf. ib. II 119. 2: galbani, ase, serapini); assefetida gummi est gravis odoris *SB* 11; asar lazarum, quinancium, sulphitum sanancium, ferula, silfiium, [?] inde opus silphii, i. asafetida *Alph.* 15.

asaldus [OF *a saut*], 'assaut', rutting (of stallions).

1330 (v. assultare 1).

asamac [Ar. *aṣ-ṣimākh*], auditory meatus, opening of ear.

est †asaniat auris, id est foramen, ad ipsam aurem in conparatione pupille ad oculum *Ps.*-RIC. *Anat.* 27.

asaphatum [Ar. *as-saʿfa(t)*], skin disease, psoriasis.

[tinea] dicitur eciam ab Avicenna in 4º et a Mesue asafati GAD. 130 v. 2; ~i, i. rubor et pustule que apparent in facie juxta nasum *SB* 11; ~um est serpigo vel impetigo aut intercutanea scabies in poris generata *LC*.

1 asar v. asa.

2 asar [Sp. Ar. *ʿaṣāh* or Ar. *ʿaṣā (ar-rāʿī) = knotgrass (lit. "shepherd's staff")*], (?) knotgrass (*Polygonum aviculare*) conf. w. teasel (*Dipsacus*); *cf. altersandarei*.

asar, i. virga pastoris *Alph.* 15.

asara, ~us, ~um [ἄσαρον; cf. baccara], hazelwort (*Asarum*).

~am bacharam, que vulgago dicitur NECKAM *NR* II 166; cum decoctione..~ebaccare GILB. I 17 v. 2 (cf. ib. II 96. 2: asari); experimentum optimum contra quottidianam et quartanam, vinum decoccionis assare bacchare detur ante accessionem GAD. 13. 1; ~um, †rafanus *SB* 11; gariofilus agrestis, i. ~um *Ib.* 22; ~abaccara, vulgago, gariofilata agrestis, ~us idem *Alph.* 15; ~us, †quam multi nardum agrestem vocant, folia habet edere similia tenera et rotunda, flores inter folia juxta radicem purpurei coloris *Ib.* 16; **1414** azarum ij unc' prec' ij d. *EschF* 1066/1; ~um, perpensa, vulgago, sanguis martis, rustica nardus et vulgo azarabaccara dicitur. eram eo loco ubi vocaretur *folfot* TURNER *Herb.* A iii.

asaysamentum v. aisiamentum 1 a.

asbestos, ~on [ἄσβεστος], asbestos. **b** quicklime.

asbestos lapis est qui Vesta judice nescit / extingui NECKAM *DS* VI 271; qui munitam vult habere navem, albestum [*gl.*: *une pere*] habeat, ne desit ei beneficium ignis *Id. Ut.* 114; est in Arcadia ~on lapis, qui semel accensus exstingui non potest GERV. TILB. III 3; continuat flammam flammarum fomite vivo, / albeston lucet igne serena domus GARL. *Epith.* VI 599; albeston Archadie est lapis ferrei coloris ab igne nomen sortitus, eo quod semel accensus numquam extinguitur BART. ANGL. XVI 10; HIGD. I 24 (v. Albiston); hic abbestus, A. *a fyirstone* WW. **b** albesten vel albestum, ..i. †calix [v.l. calx] viva *Alph.* 7.

ascaeta v. escaeta. ascaldare v. escaldare.

Ascalonia [CL, sc. caepa], scallion.

~ium, *ynnelaec GlC* A 841; scolonia, *cipe Ib.* S 112; **10..** ascolonia, *cipe* WW; scalonia, *cype leac Gl. Durh.*; **1211** in alliis et scalonibus emptis ad plantandum, xvj d. *Pipe Wint.* 154; cepe..et ~ia bis faciunt folia BART. ANGL. XVII 42; **1323** in cepe et allea, ij d.; ..in scalionibus, ob. *Ac. Wellingb.* 125; **1324** in semine petrocill' empto ad idem [gardinum], ob.; ..in scalon' empt' ad idem, j d. *MinAc* (*Suff*) 992/13; vitare debetis..commestionem rerum vaporosarum, sicut porrorum, ceparum, allii, †stalangarum KYMER 3; hec ascolonia, *a holleke* WW.

ascapura v. escapura. ascarabia v. scarabaeus.

ascaris, ~ida [ἀσκαρίς, *conf. w.* ἄκαρι], threadworm. **b** louse or tick.

xxx circiter ~ides et lumbrici varie quantitatis expulsi sunt W. CANT. *Mir. Thom.* II 15 (cf. ib. III 51: ab eo xl lumbricos cum sanie et ~es ejecit); si [vermes]..in inferioribus et grossioribus [intestinis] sunt nutriti, ~es dicuntur et cucurbini BART. ANGL. VII 49; generantur..ex flegmate lumbrici et ~ides in intestinis GILB. V 228 v. 1. **b 9..** ~ida, *hnitu* WW; *schepyslows*, pego, ~ida, ..*tyke, wyrme*, ascarabia, ~ida *PP*; ~ida, *teke*, †astayda, A. *a tyke*, ..hec ~ida, *a scheplows* WW.

ascedula v. †acidula. ascella v. astella, axilla. ascellaris v. axillaris. ascemor v. aschemon.

ascendere [CL], (intr., of persons) to ascend, climb up. **b** (fig.). **c** to ascend into Heaven. **d** to ascend in musical scale.

cum audiret unum de fratribus ad locum..~ere disposuisse BEDE *HE* III 2; H. BOS. *Thom.* V 1 (v. ascensorium a); **1211** fecit eum ~ere retro super equum *SelPl Crown* 58; **1313** ~it super rotam [carecte] *Eyre Kent* 96; quousque fratres..in dormitorium assenderint *Cust. Cant.* 105; **1391** cum scala quadam ~it ad fenestram domus sue *Leet Norw.* 70; **1465** in secunda linea ~endo *Pri. Cold.* 206. **b** AD. SCOT. *Serm.* 314C (v. ascensor a). **c** ad caelestia regna.. ~it BEDE *HE* II 20; pro salute nostra Christus carnem assumpsit, pependit, resurrexit, ~it LANFR. *Ep.* 33. 533B; cum ista evangelii lectio pronunciaretur et post hec quemadmodum..Christus in celum ~erit subjiceretur OSB. *V. Dunst.* 42. **d** cantare..tam ~endo quam descendendo HOTHBY 333.

2 (intr., of things) to rise. **b** to slope up. **c** (of inheritance) to pass to an older generation. **d** to amount.

~ente aqua fluminis usque ad lumbos BEDE *HE* V 12; **716** flammam..ad superiora ~entem BONIF. *Ep.* 10 p. 9; **s1242** ~it clamor usque Xantonas ad regem M. PAR. *Maj.* IV 213; **1266** ignis assendit in ..domo *SelCCoron* 2. **b** acutus tonus est nota per obliquum ~ens in dexteram partem ALDH. *PR* 141; **1458** croftam..que se extendit ab angulo.. cemiterii..superius per..torrentem assendendo *Reg. Glasg.* 408. **c** terra ista..naturaliter quidem ad heredes hereditabiliter descendit, numquam autem regulariter ~it GLANV. VII 1; **1205** Agneti, de qua terra illa ~it Alicie, ..quia ipsa nullum habuit heredem de corpore suo *CurR* IV 2.

d c**1170** tenendum..per servicium quinte partis unius militis et hoc perficiend'..michi in denariis sicut servicio ~erit *AncD* A 2097; **1239** receptis libris illius monete solummodo que ad l marcarum numerum non ~unt (*Lit. Imp.*) M. Par. *Maj.* III 58; s**1270** bona per eos inventa..~ebant ad vij m li. *Leg. Ant. Lond.* 142; s**1086** fecit..inquirere de urbibus et viculis ad quid in solidum ~erent *Flor. Hist.* II 11; s**1232** ~it summa collecta in duplam fere quantitatem *Ib.* 207; s**1264** cum militia que ad cccc loricatos adscendit Trevet 260; c**1300** misericordia in curia nostra non ~et ultra xij d. (*Cust. Preston*) *EHR* XV 497; **1432** si ad tantum ~ant expense *Reg. Cant.* II 488.

3 (trans.) to climb, go up (a ladder or hill). **b** (of climbing plants). **c** to mount (a horse or sim.). **d** to embark on (a ship). **e** to take one's place at (table).

scalam Jacob ~ens Aldh. *VirgP* 25 p. 260; montem ~it Bede *HE* I 7. **b** ligustrum est quasi agreste lilium, i. flos minoris volubilis ~ens sepes *SB* 28. **c** ~e illum equum tuum Aldh. *VirgP* 25 p. 259; ~ens equum Bede *HE* V 6; levam streparum levis ascendas Garl. *Mor. Scol.* 565; **1255** ~it equum et transivit pontem *SelPlForest* 115. **d** ascensa..navi venit ad insulam Bede *Cuthb.* 24; ego ~o navem [AS: *ic astige min scyp*] cum mercibus meis Ælf. *Coll.* 96. **e** post gracias ~ent mensas *Cust. Cant.* 7.

4 to ascend, be in the ascendant (astr.). **b** (pr. ppl. as sb.) ascendant.

sol..sic procedendo venit in Cancro, quo non altius ~ere potest *V. Osw.* 443; Gros. 20 (v. ascensio 2a); illi conjunccioni prefuit Mercurius dominus Virginis, quod signum tunc temporis ~ebat Bradw. *CD* 73c. **b** prima domus vocatur ~ens, quia oritur et ~it super terram et terrena Bacon V 22; videatur quis sit dominus ~entis Rob. Angl. (II) *Sph.* 196; quendam cujus nativitatis ~ens fuit prima facies Arietis Bradw. *CD* 450e; **1387** prima linea kalendarii ..docet ~ens medie noctis (Elveden *Cal.*) *SB* 5; proximo sequuntur ~entes *Ib.*

5 to go upstream. **b** to come ashore, disembark. **c** (w. *terram*).

nunquam potest barcha bene ~ere nisi cum vento et velo S. Sim. *Itin.* 41 (cf. ib.: per fluvium ~itur et descenditur absque labore). **b** xl navium..Danorum exercitus ~erat *Enc. Emmae* II 6 (cf. ib. II 3). **c** fixit anchoras..circiter tria milliaria ab Harfleu, ubi proposuit terram ~ere Elmh. *Hen. V* 14.

6 to graduate (acad.). **b** (w. *gradum*).

1461 nullus sophista, si solus ~at, expendat in sua ascensione ultra xvj d.; si duo simul ~ant in eodem loco, ij s. non excedant *MunAcOx* 684. **b** a**1350** quiscumque assensurus gradum bachillarii dimidiam communam suam universitati solvat *StatOx* 58.

7 (bibl.) **a** (w. *ex adverso* or sim.) to oppose, attack (cf. *Ezek.* xiii 5; *Josh.* xxii 33). **b** (w. *caput*) to be used on (cf. *Jud.* xvi 17). **c** (w. *in cor* or absol.) to occur (cf. 1 *Cor.* ii 9 *etc.*).

a s**1164** unum..qui pro ecclesia Dei..ausus fuit ex adverso ~ere A. Tewk. *Thom.* 25; **1321** quietem studencium.. fovere et exadverso ~entibus obviare *FormOx* 70; s**1409** dux ..et cardinalis..cum grandi exercitu contra regem Neopolitanum ~erunt *Eul. Hist. Cont.* III 416. **b** ferrum caput ejus [S. Jacobi Minoris] non ~it *Eul. Hist.* I 82. **c** viam..temptare in cor adolescentis..~it Eddi *Wilf.* 3; **1259** cum nunquam..res hujusmodi ~eret in cor nostrum *Cl* 479; c**1400** nunquam cogitavi nec fuit intencio mea nec unquam ~it jurare illud juramentum (R. Wyche) *EHR* V 540.

8 (dep.) to go upstream. **b** (p. ppl.) having ascended. **c** (p. ppl.) having mounted.

1289 sal..~i faciatis de Burdegala per aquam apud Agennum *RGasc* II 497. **b** Christo crucifixo et in celum ascenso *Eul. Hist.* I 162. **c** ascensus equo *G. Herw.* 329b; cursatiles ascensi equos *G. Steph.* I 62; s**1295** ascensis sex lictoribus equos *Flor. Hist.* III 282.

ascensa- v. accensa-.

ascensio, ascent, rising. **b** (fig.). **c** Ascension (theol.). **d** Ascension Thursday (40 days after Easter).

prora ad ~onem maris descensura sub undis W. Cant. *Mir. Thom.* III 46. **b** theophaniae..fiunt ex descensione divinae sapientiae et ~one humanae angelicaeque intelligentiae Eriug. *Per.* 449d. **c** canebat de incarnatione dominica, passione, resurrectione et ~one in caelum Bede *HE* IV 22; qua passio Christi / sculpta beata nitet simul et resurrectio necnon / ejus ad astriferos veneranda ascensio caelos Wulf. *Swith.* II 14; nisi..Dominum crucifixissent, crux Christi et resurrectio et ~o ejus praedicata et credita in mundo non esset Lanfr. *Comment. Paul.* (*Rom.* xi 12) 141; per xlij annos post Christi ~onem (Wycl. *Resp.*) *Ziz.* 271. **d** s**988** dies ~onis Christi festivus diem clarificationis B. Dunstani precessit tertius Osb. *V. Dunst.* 41 (cf. ib.: dum sacros dominicae ~oni honores..impenderet); c**1006** canimus hymnum..usque ~onem Domini *Comp. Swith.* 190; in die..~onis *DB* I 262b; in ipsa sacrosancte ~onis Domini.. vigilia W. Malm. (*V. Aldh.*) *GP* V 261; s**1213** acta sunt hec.. in vigilia dominice ~onis, ..instabat autem dies ~onis Domini in crastino Wend. II 76; s**1219** dies ~onis, viz. xvij kalendas Junii M. Par. *Maj.* III 43; nec Rogationes nec ~o..celebrantur hoc anno suis temporibus Bacon *Tert.* 289; die Martis proxima ante Assencionem Domini *State Tri. Ed. I* 4; **1354** in octabis Assensionis (*Pat*) *EHR* XXI 533; circa dominice ~onis mysteria Elmh. *Hen. V* 79.

2 ascension (astr.). **b** latitude.

arcus de equinoctiali circulo qui ascendit cum aliqua parte zodiaci dicitur ~o ejusdem partis Gros. 20; sex signa que sunt a principio Cancri..usque in finem Sagittarii habent ~ones suas simul junctas ~onibus reliquorum sex signorum Sacrob. *Sph.* 103. **b** clima, i. plaga, ~io, *epl* WW; per tabulam ~onum ville vel climatis ubi magis intendimus commorari Wallingf. *Albion* 362.

3 graduation.

1461 (v. ascendere 6a).

4 elation, ambition; *cf. Psalm* lxxxiii 6 (lxxxiv 5).

quid tecum cogitas et ~ones turbant animum tuum? Gir. *GE* II 11 p. 220; sic [Saladinus] ~ones in corde suo disposuit et jam cepit regno majora sperare *Itin. Ric.* I 3; c**1430** ne..concupiscencia disponat in cordis visceribus ~ones *Reg. Whet.* II 469.

ascensive, at an increasing rate.

1397 pro domo..cujus pensio..se extendit..ad xx s. .., obolum; si ad xl s., ..denarium; et sic ~e pro rata pensionis ..offerre teneantur *Conc.* III 231.

ascensor, climber (fig.). **b** rider.

si tante turri humilitatis vim inferre contendis et eousque in eam pius invasor et infatigabilis ~or..ascendere decernis Ad. Scot. *Serm.* 314c. **b** equis et ~oribus in mare projectis H. Bos. *Serm.* 1413a; in ipso ascensu..tam equum quam ~orem ejus lancea perforavit Gir. *EH* I 41.

ascensorium, mounting-block. **b** stair, step. **c** (fig.).

jungens se ad latus equitantis illius, amplexatus est pedem simul cum ~io cui videbatur inniti Osb. *Mir. Dunst.* 20; non expectato ~io sonipedem insiliens W. Malm. *GR* II 309; rex [archipresuli] ascendenti ~ium aptavit et tenuit H. Bos. *Thom.* V 1. **b** ~ium, *stæger* Ælf. *Gl.*; s**1174** in ipsis cocleis et super ipsas ~ia ex lapide et deambulatoria machinari fecit Ric. Hex. *Hist. Hex.* 3; **1413** pro iij hostiis, viz. cancelle, vestibuli et assensorii *Rect. Adderbury* 7; **1499** in ij paribus †assensorum [MS.: assensoiorum (*sic*)] pro aliis sedelibus (*MinAc* 691) *MonA* IV 564. **c** hanc [crucem] nobis proposuit misericordie propitiatorium, virtutum ~ium et scalam..ad jocunditatem celestium gaudiorum P. Blois *Serm.* 575a.

ascensorius, kind of falcon, hobby.

falco ~ius [*gl.*: *auteyn*] Neckam *Ut.* 100; hic acensorius, A. *a hoby* WW.

1 ascensus, ascent, climbing. **b** upward direction (at table). **c** rising (of tide). **d** rising (astr.).

pede timido ~um [sc. graduum] attemptavit T. Mon. *Will.* VII 18; Gir. *EH* I 41 (v. ascensor b); c**1220** gravis est ascensus ad astra H. Avr. 103 *epil.* 5. **b** nullus in ascensum det pocula sic sibi missa, / sive dapes in descensum gustent comedentes D. Bec. 1062. **c** s**1109** concesse sunt ei inducie xl dierum et unius ~us maris et refluxus M. Par. *Min.* I 212. **d** luna in ~u suo et descensu acquirit immutationem ab aliquo maligno planeta Gilb. I 74. 1.

2 Ascension Day (*cf. Ascensio 1c*).

benedictio in ~u Domini Egb. *Pont.* 69; **1268** quo tempore? festo / Ascensus Domini *MunAcOx* 37.

3 stair.

cum in eo nullam januam vel fenestram vel ~um alicubi conspiceret Bede *HE* V 12; circuitus, ~us, *gewind* Ælf. *Gl.*; cum vias castri cunctas turriumque gradus et ~us cordis oculo jam tenuisset Gir. *IK* I 11.

2 ascensus v. assensus. ascer- v. acer-, asser-.

ascesis [ἄσκησις = *training*], understanding (cf. Jerome *Vir. Illus.* 41).

†arcesi, intellectui *GlC* A 775; ~i, ingeni[o] *Ib.* 851.

asceterium [ἀσκητήριον], monastery.

955 (12c) eandem villam prefato arcisterio [*Abingdon*] ad usus predicti abbatis fratrumque inibi Deo servientium.. restituo *CS* 906; †**974** (13c) Ailwinus..in insula que.. Ramesia promulgatur..arcisterium construxit *CS* 1310; †**981** (13c) arcisterium cui notabile *at Tavistoc* fulget vocabulum *CD* 629; sacra archisteria [v.l. consistoria] scandit Frith. 1149; postquam adiit claustra arcisterii *V. Osw.* 418; ovem..quam gestans in humeris..deferre gliscebat secus arcisterium S. Durh. *HR* 6; s**1171** accepistis..qualiter ibi ecclesie..vacent, ..lugeat religio, arcisteria desolentur (*Lansd.* 3) *Becket Mat.* IV 167; aditum templi, quod idem sunt, basilica, oratorium, cancellum, ecclesia, monasterium, †apterium [v.l. assisterium], capella Neckam *Ut.* 119.

asceticon [ἀσκητικόν], understanding (cf. Jerome *Vir. Illust.* 116).

†ascetron, intellectum *GlC* A 848.

ascheit- v. escaet-.

aschemon [ἀσχήμων], ugly.

†ascemor, inhonestum *GlC* A 834.

aschit- v. ascit-.

ascia [CL], axe, adze (*cf.* 1 *axa, aza, hachia*). **b** (?) lancet.

securim atque ~iam in manu ferens Bede *HE* IV 3; ~ia, *adesa* Ælf. *Gl.*; Ord. Vit. IX 6 (v. biduvium); **1201** per hascia[m]..amputaverunt ei capud *CurR* I 395; ascia, falx, fede quos roderat atra rubigo, / gestantur Gower *VC* I 855; hec acia, *a thyxylle* WW. **b** si est arthetica, ~ia superius aperiatur epatica a parte opposita in principio Gilb. VII 314. 2.

asciare [CL], to shovel or sharpen.

ascio, A. *to thwyte or schyrpe* WW.

asciatio, chopping.

1450 pro assiacione..meremii in grosso..; et pro assiacione..vij lignorum *DocCOx* 336.

asciculus v. acisculus, asciola. ascid- v. accid-. ascilla v. axilla. ascinaria v. asinarius c. ascingtus v. accinctus.

asciola, little axe.

1359 cum quadam ~a Willelmum..percussit *RCoron* 102 r. 15; *an hachet*, ascia, ~a, ascis, asciculus *CathA*.

ascire [CL], to engage as assistant. **b** (fig.).

filius adscitur Alhtridi Frith. 1285; clericus constabularie magnus et officiosus in regis curia ad Scaccarium etiam ad majora queque cum magnis ~itur *Dial. Scac.* I 6d. **b** impossibile est tale [sc. ens infinite bonitatis et sufficiencie essencialis] esse et nullum tale esse, quia tunc posset produci et non a finite minori, quia illud non posset sibi tantum esse dare, quia non haberet ut adsciret ipso Wycl. *Quaest. Log.* 283.

ascis v. acisculus, asciola.

asciscere [CL], to summon, engage as assistant, appoint to office. **b** (w. inf.). **c** (dep.). **d** to enlist (fig.).

[Andream] Deus.. / caelitus adscivit Aldh. *CE* 4. 3. 5; pater.. / undique deserti turmas assciscere jussit *Id. VirgV* 1578; ambo de monachorum collegio in episcopatus gradum asciti Bede *HE* IV 12; **9**.. adsciti, *gegaderade* WW; hujus.. urbis primus institutor ~itur Augustinus Gosc. *Aug. Min.* 750; clero in unum conventum..ascito [? l. accito] *G. Steph.* II 80; ascitis nobiscum viris religiosis *Canon. G. Sempr.* 89; ascito [? l. accito] ad hoc spectaculum presbytero Gir. *GE* I 11 p. 42; sacerdotem annuens et ~ens *Id. IK* I 4. **b** asciverat..regem ceterosque Grecos parti sue favere G. Mon. I 3. **c** rex..ascitus..archiepiscopum ad Rollonem dirigit Diceto *Abbr. Norm.* 246. **d** a**1205** sancti virtutem in sui ascissit adjutorium *Canon. G. Sempr.* 158.

2 to acquire (in addition.) **b** to endue. **c** to use.

ipse sibi in hoc mortem adscivit..quod.. Bede *Gen.* (iv 23) 77; post resurrectionem ejus [Domini] scientia vel sanctitas non est aucta sed felicitas ascita Pull. *Sent.* 650d; ascitis sibi..caracis..et aliis..navibus Elmh. *Hen. V* 79. **b** integritatis clamide, qua angelicae puritatis liniamento velut domestica soliditate adsciscebatur Aldh. *VirgP* 29 p. 268. **c** quamvis [antibachius] in ceteris..declinationibus ~atur *Id. PR* 124.

ascisinus v. assassinus.

ascites [ἀσκίτης], ascites, abdominal dropsy.

[ydropisis] que est ex sanguine vocatur archis vel archites; *archis* [ἀσκός] enim uter est, sonat enim venter ad modum utris semipleni Gilb. VI 248 v. 1; denominatur aschites quasi uter; *aschites* enim uter dicitur *Ib.* 250. 2; architen, timpaniten, ydropicos curat *Ib.* VII 360. 1; secunda species [idropisis] vocatur †asclites; et est illa in qua est materia aquosa effusa in spatium ventris inferioris Gad. 30. 2; aschites species quedam ydropisis est *SB* 12; alchites sive alkites..dicta ab *alkis* quod est uter *Alph.* 6.

asciticius, adventitious.

Romani pontificis authoritatem ~iam et..praerogativas fictas Bekinsau 748.

asciticus, (one) afflicted w. ascites.

in aschiticis et timpaniticis Gilb. VI 251 v. 2; alchitici et tympanithici confirmati non curantur in introitu gravissime *Ib.* 255 v. 1; quedam vetula multos liberavit cum succo plantaginis..qui erant fere architici *Ib.* 260 v. 1; venter aschitici percussus resonat ad modum utri semipleni *SB* 12.

ascius [ἄσκιος], shadowless (of equatorial region).

~ios, exumbres *GlC* A 838; quedam loca sunt in nostro habitabili que ~ia dicuntur, id est sine umbra Bacon *Maj.* I 305.

asclepias [ἀσκληπιάς], snakeweed (*Dracunculus*).

draguncea, ~ias, viperina, G. et A. *dragaunce Alph.* 48.

asclites v. ascites. ascolonia v. ascalonia.

†ascopa [ἀσκοπήρα], wine-flask.

~a, *kylle GlC* A 852; asscopa, *flaxe oþþe cylle* Ælf. *Gl.*

ascribere [CL], to write (beside). **b** to record (for). **c** to invite in writing.

[versus] in Priapeio metro..adscriptus Aldh. *Met.* 10 p. 93; quibuscumque diebus E literam videris adscriptam Bede *TR* 19; c**740** quia..nomen tuum adscriptum habuissem..simul cum nominibus episcoporum nostrorum (Sigebald) *Ep. Bonif.* 36. **b** quis nostri temporis..inclite gesta perpetuis literarum vinculis eternitati ~it? Gir. *IK* I *pref.*; [Herodes] combussit omnes libros in quibus nobilitas gentis illius in templo servabatur ascripta M. Par. *Maj.* I 78. **c** non credo latere vestram fraternitatem quam ob rem ad hunc..conventum eam ascriberim (*sic*) Eddi *Wilf.* 29.

2 to devote (resources). **b** to consign. **c** to consecrate, enlist (persons). **d** (p. ppl. w. *glaebae*) bound to a tenement, (as sb.) serf, villein (*cf. ascripticius*).

illud lucrum precipuum arbitrantes emendis vel edendis codicibus adscripserunt R. Bury *Phil.* 6. 90. **b** cum illum regalis impietas exsilio ascripsisset Osb. *V. Dunst.* 29; cur ascripta malis est tantis mansio talis? Garl. *Mor. Scol.* 498. **c** se suosque liberos..satagunt magis..monasterialibus adscribere votis quam bellicis exercere studiis Bede *HE*

V 23; qui ascripti fuimus clericali milicie ELMH. *Hen. V* 53. **d** denarium annuum B. Petri, qui nunc a solis ascriptis glebe..datur in Anglia W. FITZST. *Thom.* 65; qui glebe ibidem ab antiquo ascripti fuerant GIR. *PI* III 30.

3 to assign. **b** to accredit. **c** to ascribe (as cause).

singulis [signis] tricenae partes, ob tricenos dies quibus a sole lustrantur, adscribuntur BEDE *TR* 16; *Ib.* 48 (v. attitulare a); homines illius provincie [Gallicie] Grecam sibi ~unt originem *Eul. Hist.* II 101. **b** eum viriliter egisse testabantur †ei et [? l. et ei] magnifice in laudem ~ebant H. CANTOR 11. **c** multi asscripserunt ei cordis imbecillitati quod non asperius..egerat pro archiepiscopo *Ib.* 19v; nolo que miraculo peregrinantes ~unt..inter miracula non computare W. CANT. *Mir. Thom.* VI 136; **a1350** eorum absenciam contemptui vel arrogancie ~ere *StatOx* 57; que, ..si dignabitur benignius excusare, distraccioni mentis.. aut inadvertencie..~at OCKHAM *Pol.* I 221.

ascripticius [LL; cf. ascribere 2d], bound to a tenement: **a** (sb. m.) serf, villain; **b** (sb. f.).

a c1168 qui anti conversionem suam ~ii glebe fuerunt *Canon. G. Sempr.* 100; exceptis ~iis qui villani dicuntur, quibus non est liberum, obstantibus dominis suis, a sui status conditione discedere *Dial. Scac.* I 10B; **1258** eodem modo procedatur contra eos qui ~iorum et aliorum servilis conditionis testamenta impediunt *Conc. Syn.* 585 (= *Conc.* I 740: †ascriptorum); opponi poterit de ~io, ut dicitur, quia vere liber est licet quodam servitio sit astrictus BRACTON 4b; fuerunt in conquestu liberi homines qui.., cum per potentiores ejecti essent, postmodum reversi receperunt eadem tenementa sua tenenda in villenagio, faciendo inde opera servilia sed certa et nominata; qui quidem dicuntur glebe ~ii et nihilominus liberi, quia..opera..non faciunt.. ratione personarum sed ratione tenementorum; ..et ideo dicuntur glebe ~ii quia tali gaudent privilegio quod a gleba amoveri non poterunt quamdiu solvere possunt debitas pensiones *Ib.* 7; hujusmodi villani sokemanni proprie dicuntur glebe ~ii *Ib.* 209; tales nativi ~ii lege imperatoria nuncupantur *RegiamM* II 12. 3. **b** si mater sit ~ia licet pater sit liber LYNDW. 172 q.

ascult- v. auscult-. ascunditus v. abscondere 2a. aseitus v. affaitus. 1 asella v. agellus.

2 asella [CL], (young) she ass.

vocibus humanis fantem testantur asellam ALDH. *VirgV* 56; sic iter Axa sue regit et moderatur aselle NIG. *Paul.* 46v (cf. *Josh.* xv 18).

3 asella v. axilla.

asellus [CL], (young) ass, foal.

ruditus proprie ~orum est ALDH. *PR* 131; **10..** ~us, *weorf* WW; pelle leonina dic quid asellus agat J. SAL. *Enth. Pol.* 383A; **1211** reddunt compotum de vij asinis remanentibus anno preterito; de ij asselis anni preteriti; ..de ij pullis asinariis proventis hoc anno *Pipe Wint.* 67.

aselulus v. agellulus.

asep [Ar. *ash-shabb*], alum.

mos erat sapientium quod suum †assos de eo et cum eo semper faciebant: †assos Arabice alumen interpretatur Latine ROB. ANGL. *Alch.* 514b; asep, i. alumen *SB* 4; aseb, asep est alumen *LC*.

aser v. asser. aserra v. acerra. asiamentum v. aisiamentum. asierina v. Arretina. asilum v. asylum.

asilus [CL], gadfly. **b** drone.

~o, *briosa GlC* A 832. **b 14..** hic ~us, *a drane* WW; *a drone*, ~us, fucus *CathA*.

asimus v. azymus.

asina [CL], she ass.

10.. asinus vel ~a, *assa* WW; cum asino non suppetit facultas accedendi ad ~am NECKAM *NR* II 159; Axa regens asinam NIG. *Paul* 46v. (cf. *Josh.* xv 18); lac]~e coctum da GILB. IV 177 v. 2; ut asinos et ~as monasterii venderet *Latin Stories* 41; **14..** hic asinus, A. *a nas*; hec ~a, uxor ejus WW.

asinalis v. asinarius a.

asinare, to ride on an ass. **b** to make an ass of (fig.).

mittebatur..ad curias sedens asinum, ..quia metuebat seculo irretiri nec equitare jam volebat, ~ando serviens domino sine cujus permissu discedere nolebat G. CRISPIN *Herl.* 89; ipse ~avit et filium tenerum eum sequi permisit *Latin Stories* 129; **1451** tollatur abusus ~andi preterquam in casu necessitatis (*Abbr. Stat.*) *Mon. Francisc.* II 95. **b** invenies asinum si tu cupias asinari; / optatus veniet non cito sponte leo WALT. ANGL. *Fab.* 17 *add.* 5.

asinarius, of or for an ass. **b** (w. ref. to *Matth.* xviii 6). **c** (sb. f.) mill driven by ass. **d** (sb. m.) ass-driver.

1211 (v. asellus); *an asse*, asinus, ..asellus; asininus, ~ius, asinalis, participia *CathA*. **b** mola ~ia ad collum suspensa FERR. *Kinloss* 8. **c** ascinaria, *esulcweorn* WW. **d 1198** in costamento asinorum et ~iorum *RScacNorm* II 310.

asininare, to behave like an ass.

secundo ~ant cum querunt quomodo materia hinc inde distinguatur BACON *Tert.* 126; hic ~ant et sunt infirmi et imbecilles *Id. CSPhil* 401; *to be dulle*, ~are, ebere *CathA*.

asininus [CL], asinine, of a donkey. **b** (in plant names). **c** (w. *lapis*) a kind of gem.

~us *CathA* (v. asinarius a). **b** (v carduus 2a, cucumis, daucus). **c 1290** cum..unum lapidem preciosum, qui dicitur ~us, ..legaverit *Reg. North.* 90.

asinitas, asinine nature.

ista nomina, humanitas, animalitas, ~as, Socratitas, Platonitas, ..non sunt concreta set abstracta BACON XV 207; corrupta forma speciei remanet forma generis, sicut corrupta ~ate remanet forma corporeitatis *Ps.*-GROS. 332.

asinus [CL], ass, donkey. **b** (type of dullness or patient stupidity).

~i oncant vel rudunt ALDH. *Met.* 131; ~us, *assa* ÆLF. *Gl.*; in dominio supradicti manerii est i runcinus et i ~us et xxx porci *DB* II 1b; ~us..respectu multitudinis laborum quos sustinet parum gratie consequitur NECKAM *NR* II 160; [Egyptus]..in ~is vivacissimis et velocissimis est habundanter dotata S. SIM. *Itin.* 44; onager, ~us silvestris idem *Alph.* 129. **b** O. CHERITON *Fab.* 43 (v. asperitas 1b); **s1345** vertitur in proverbium quod Anglici sunt boni ~i, omnia onera eis imposita..supportantes AD. MUR. 175.

2 cod (fish).

color universo corpori [ceruchi] qui ~o nostro, quem coddum nostri vocant, ut et caro similis CAIUS *Anim.* 28.

asitabulum v. acetabulum. asma, ~aticus, v. asthm-. asmal- v. esmal-.

†asmonia [? *for* armonia], harmony.

hec [virgo] luxuriam secuit ense ~ie *Miss. Westm.* ii 1102.

asnasare [AS], to pierce, wound.

si quis habeat lanceam super humerum suum et aliquis ~etur vel impungatur [AS: *and hine mon asnaseð*], solvat weram ejus sine wita. si ante oculos ~et, reddat weram ejus (*Quad.*) *GAS* 69.

asotus [ἄσωτος], dissipated.

~us, luxoriosus *GlC* A 883.

asnecia v. aesnecia. asonus v. assonus. asorium v. azurum.

aspalathos [ἀσπάλαθος], tragacanth (*Astragalus*).

est alia arbor [cipro] similis que dicitur aspalatos..et in parte redolet ut castoreum; a multis vocatur sceptrum Helisei BART. ANGL. XVII 26.

aspaltum v. asphaltum.

asparagus [ἀσπάραγος], asparagus. **b** some other herb. **c** toadstool.

apii, brusci, sparagi GAD. 32 v. 2; alfarsungi, i. speragus *SB* 10; de oleribus ad fecunditatem valent menta, sparagus, pastinaca, erica, rapa KYMER 9; ~um officine sparagum vocant, vulgus autem *sperage* TURNER *Herb.* A iii. **b** sparagi agrestis, *uude cearfille*, sparago, *nefle Gl. Durh.*; **10..** speragus, *wudu cærfille*, .. **14..** speragus, *colverfot* WW; allion, speragus idem *Alph.* 5. **c** unum significat boletus, tubera, fungi, / ..additur asparagus; his sensus convenit unus GARL. *Syn.* 1583A; *a paddokstole*, boletus, ~us *CathA*.

aspargere v. aspergere. aspatilis v. aspratilis. aspatum v. asphaltum.

aspectare [CL], to look upon. **b** to gaze.

aspectant immensos corporis artus ALDH. *Aen.* 99. 7; aspectans certantis bella puellae / arbiter *Id. VirgV* 1948. **b** ~ans in caelum BEDE *HE* IV 9.

aspectio, aspect (astr.).

aspectus lune in his etatibus diversus est a priore aspectu; aliam igitur habet ~onem in elementis GILB. II 110. 2.

aspector, beholder (*cf. arbiter d*).

recte vivere gratiamque interni ~oris promereri satagunt BEDE *Tab.* III 7.

aspectus [CL], look, gaze, glance, view. **b** (fig., w. *mentis*). **c** view (leg.). **d** look out, wait.

634 unianimam dilectionem..alternis ~ibus repraesentat (*Lit. Papae*) BEDE *HE* II 18; **716** ut cunctas terrarum partes et populos..sub uno ~u contueretur BONIF. *Ep.* 10 p. 8; ad satisfactionem unius tam parvi peccati sicuti est unus ~us contra voluntatem Dei ANSELM (*CurDeus* I 21) II 88; [Anselmus] pueritiam egressus numquam vel lasciviori ~u castimoniam turbavit W. MALM. *GP* I 45; humano terras non subtrahens ~ui..interfluens mare GIR. *EH* I 2; **12..** ne intuentium..offendant ~um *Conc. Scot.* II 13; **s1297** inter cujus [aggeris] propugnacula patet ad naves ~us TREVET 359; **1334** ad has..litteras..vestre dominacionis ~ibus presentandas *Let. Ch. Ch.* 1. **b** purae mentis ~ibus ERIUG. *Per.* 464A; opera nostre potestatis aut in mentis ~u aut in ejusdem affectu..consistunt GROS. 1. **c 1211** de xij d. de Estmundo pro ~u hundredi habendo *Pipe Wint.* 22. **d 1271** insultavit W. ..et ~u et insultu premeditato *SelCCoron* 18; **1397** jacuerunt in ~u ad interficiendum Willelmum *Proc. J. P.* 409.

2 appearance.

vir..venerabilis simul et terribilis ~u BEDE *HE* II 16; angelicorum agminum et ~us intueri et laudes..audire *Ib.* III 19; ~u pulsus subtilis et velox et spissus BART. ANGL. IV 10.

3 aspect (astr.).

~us oppositus est cum fuerit planeta in aliquo signo et alius in signo directe opposito. ..trinus autem ~us est cum duo planete sunt in signis consimilibus et continent inter se tertiam partem firmamenti. ..quartus autem ~us est cum fuerint inter duos planetas tria signa integra. ..sextilis autem ~us est cum fuerint inter duos planetas duo signa integra GROS. 44–5; bonitas et malitia planetarum..augmentantur vel remittuntur vel temperantur per eorum ~um vel ~us adinvicem BACON V 18; 8 sunt ~us sive figurationes, 4 accedendo et 4 recedendo *Id.* IX 189; quadruplex est ~us signorum et etiam planetarum in signis, sc. oppositio, ~us sextilis, quartilis et trinus ROB. ANGL. (II) *Sph.* 9 p. 175; nonne motus..~us, proprietates et virtutes celestes sunt note fidelibus sicut infidelibus astrologis? BRADW. *CD* 42B.

aspellere [CL], to drive away.

hic ad duo matris sue sponse ubera diutissime dependens tandem ablactatus est a lacte, appulsus ab uberibus H. BOS. *Thom.* VII 1 p. 523.

1 asper [CL], rough, rugged. **b** (fig.). **c** (of style). **d** (of sounds).

~era, *unsmopi GlC* A 859; plano superficiem constans asperrima rerum ALDH. *Aen.* 21 (*Luna*) 4; in arduis ~erisque montibus (*V. Cuthb.*) BEDE *HE* IV 25; locis saxosis et ~eris *Alph.* 102. **b** quasi vias vestras dirigens, ~era queque complanans GIR. *TH* III 48; qui vias currens asperas / vie torrentem liberas J. HOWD. *Cyth.* 72. **c** sermonis †aspersi [? l. ~eri] magis et blandi minus..veniam peto GIR. *Symb.* 28 p. 292. **d** ABBO *QG* 9 (v. aspiratio 1b).

2 harsh, disagreeable, troublesome. **b** stern.

non est tam ~era hiemps [AS: *swa stearc winter*] ut audeam latere domi ÆLF. *Coll.* 90; pane ~eriori vescebatur G. CRISPIN *Herl.* 89; veritas ~era est et plerumque molestiam parit J. SAL. *Pol.* 486B; clamore horrendo, ..precipiti cursu, crebris quoque jaculorum ictibus gens ~errima GIR. *DK* II 3; rascacio est ~era spasio educcio vel expulsio *SB* 36; **s1397** desideravit de hiis..~eram correccionem sumere *V. Ric. II* 131; qui ~errimam vitam duxerant ROLLE *IA* 230; FORTESCUE *LLA* 4 (v. appetitivus c). **b** ~errimae invectionis severitate ALDH. *VirgP* 23; ~era illos invectione corrigebat BEDE *HE* III 5.

2 asper [ἄσπρος], Greek silver coin.

1292 cclxviij aspres *KRAc* 308/13 r. 3; cij besaunt', qui valent dx asper *Ib.* 15 r. 2.

3 asper v. 2. asser a.

asperare [CL], to roughen.

cilicio testantur consciae matres ~atam GOSC. *Edith* 70.

asperativus, causing roughness.

~us [dolor] est ex humore sicco GILB. II 89 v. 1; [siccitas] naturaliter est ~a; ..accidentaliter tamen quandoque lenificat BART. ANGL. IV 3; virtutes relique, id est ~a et lenitiva, ultimam superficiem rei nutrite, ut in debita forma et figura inveniantur, respiciunt *Ps.*-GROS. 525.

aspere [CL], harshly, painfully.

pro quo mortis deberes ruere / in puncturas et penas aspere J. HOWD. *Ph.* 1014; ~erius et amarius verba recitans *Latin Stories* 109.

aspergere [CL], to sprinkle (a fluid). **b** (absol.). **c** (fig.).

601 aqua benedicta..in eisdem fanis ~atur (*Lit. Papae*) BEDE *HE* I 30; **s1095** aspersa aqua benedicta, episcopus discessit W. MALM. *GR* IV 319. **b 13..** j instrumentum ad ~endum *Invent. Norw.* 15. **c** Arriana heresis..perfidiae suae virus..insularum ecclesiis aspersit BEDE *HE* I 8.

2 to besprinkle (w. fluid or powder).

aqua benedicta domus suas aspargent THEOD. *Pen.* II i 11; saginantur..sale aspersis holerum fasciculis ALDH. *VirgP* 38; cum..eis [aquis] languentes homines..asperserint BEDE *HE* III 2; **1006** ~entes se aqua sanctificata et lectulos eorum *Comp. Swith.* 175; si..viridaria..pulvere ipsius ~antur GIR. *TH* I 30; herba trutannorum de qua trutanni solent facies suas ~ere ut leprosis assimulentur *SB* 41.

asperginosus, applied by sprinkling.

haec [membrana] tuetur cor..ne ~o fomento careat quo fervori suo moderetur D. EDW. *Anat.* B 4v.

aspergo [CL], sprinkling.

706 pulverulenta sablonis ~ine ALDH. *Ep.* 9; opera nautarum, qui olei ~ine perspicuum sibi profundum maris efficiunt BEDE *TR* 5; monachi..benedicte aque ~ine prestigias inimici effugarunt W. MALM. *GR* IV 323.

2 (trailing) female garment.

non autem limata. sed ~ines, sparta et sirmata NECKAM *Ut.* 101.

3 sea-bird.

semew, byrd, ~o, ..alcio *PP*; ~o, *a cormeraunt* WW.

aspergula [cf. spergula], goosegrass (*Galium aparine*).

apparine..ab officinis ~a vel mella vocatur, ab Anglis *goosgyrs* aut *gooshareth* TURNER *Herb.* A ii v.

asperialus v. sciurellus.

asperies, stiffness.

asseris senescentis ~iem..movendo intorquere R. COLD. *Cuthb.* 2; [artus] rigoris ~ie indurescunt *Ib.*

asperiolus v. sciurellus.

asperitas [CL], roughness, ruggedness. **b** (fig.).

itineris ~atem et nimiam prolixitatem pretendebat KETEL *J. Bev.* 279; lingue ~as RIC. MED. *Signa* 33; dracoma [τράχωμα] dicitur ~as palpebrarum *SB* 18; *Alph.* 15 (v. aspratilis a). **b** plerumque contigit quod in magno conventu..non sunt nisi bestie, ..asini per segniciem, heric[i]i per ~atem O. CHERITON *Fab.* 43.

2 harshness, hardship. **b** sternness.

tantam frigoris ~atem..tolerare BEDE *HE* V 12; si homo per suavitatem peccat, an non convenit ut per ~atem satisfaciat? ANSELM (*Cur D.* II 11) II 111; **1254** in ovibus sustinendis tempore fetus propter temporis ~atem (*Pipe Wint.*) *Econ. H. R. ser.* 2 XII 371; **1384** exponantur..~ates et onera dicte gilde *Rec. Gild. Camb.* 75. **b** cum.. / nec tamen asperitas patris compesceret ulla / ..natos ALDH. *VirgV* 1355.

aspernanter, disdainfully.

[Anselmus] non ~er a Lanfranco susceptus W. MALM. *GP* I 45.

aspernari [CL], to despise, disdain.

680 ut..traditionem ecclesiae Romanae..nequaquam.. arroganter ~emini ALDH. *Ep.* 4 p. 485; quorum communionem sedes ~aretur apostolica W. MALM. *GP* III 100; hoc perversi ingenii est et suum ~antis profectum J. SAL. *Met.* 849D; nescit martyris misericordia contritos ~ari W. CANT. *Mir. Thom.* I 13.

aspernator, despiser.

s870 cujus [Hinguari] potentiae si ~or extiteris, et vita indignus et regno judicaberis M. PAR. *Maj.* I 396; **s1195** dum idem dux [Austrie] mandati apostolici ~or existeret *Ib.* II 409 (= WEND. I 38: spernator); **s1219** sic superborum ~or ab eisdem recedet WEND. II 247.

aspernere, to despise.

~it, contemnit *GlC* A 833 (cf. ib. 41: abspernit).

aspersio [CL], sprinkling: **a** (w. miraculous water). **b** (w. holy water). **c** (w. baptismal water). **d** (w. dust).

a hujus [aquae] gustum sive ~onem multis sanitatem egrotis..conferre BEDE *HE* V 18. **b** donec..aque benedicte..~one..fontem reconciliaverit GIR. *TH* II 7; laicos hinc inde stantes aspergat; peracta ~one redeat sacerdos *Offic. Sal.* 68; ~o aque benedicte videtur solummodo humanitus instituta OCKHAM *Pol.* I 167. **c** mersio baptismi triplex, aspersio trina / nomine facta patris nati quoque pneumatis almi GARL. *Myst. Eccl.* 108; **1559** ~onem, oleum et alia inter baptizandum observari solita *Conc. Scot.* II 175. **d** nostros oculos..Belgici pulveris..ventuosa ~o caliginare facit ALCUIN *Ep.* 170 p. 281.

2 splash.

si palla altaris inde [sc. sanguine consecrato] tincta fuerit, recidenda est illa particula.., quantum videlicet ~o sanguinis comprehenderit *Cust. Cant.* 287 (= *Cust. Westm.* 219: aspercio).

3 (?) scattering, dispersal.

1486 pro aspercione *les molhylles* in pratis *Ac. Durh.* 98.

aspersorium, sprinkler (for holy water).

det ei abbas ~ium cum aqua in manum LANFR. *Const.* 139; sublato thorali cum ~io jacentem rigavit W. CANT. *Mir. Thom.* VI 13; cum..aquam in ecclesia benediceret et ~ium deesset J. FORD *Wulf.* 35; **c1250** vas stagneum ad aquam benedictam cum ~io *Vis. S. Paul.* 10; cum hyssopus pro ~io fingatur BACON *Tert.* 263; **1328** j aquarium argenteum cum ~io deargentato *Reg. Heref.* 378; **1358** solut' R. Aurifabro pro j ~io argenti faciendo *Sacr. Ely* II 177; **1368** vas aque benedicte cum ~io de laton' *Invent. Norw.* 4; hoc ~ium, A. *strynkylle*, ..*a sprenkylle* WW.

aspersura, sprinkling.

presenti subvenitur sancti presencia, absenti vero pulveris de ligno in quo sanctus jacuerat ~a *NLA* (*Erkenwald*) I 397.

aspersus v. asper 1c, aspergere. aspertare v. asportare. aspervarius v. sparvarius.

asphaltum [ἄσφαλτος; (?) *conf. w.* ἀσπάλαθος], bitumen.

aspaltum [*EE* 340. 23: aspaltum], *spaldur GlC* A 839; glutinum aphalti quod nec ferro dissolvitur nec aquis..dispergitur BART. ANGL. IV 8; potest..suffumigari de aspato GILB. III 151 v. 2 (cf. ib. II 76 v. 2: cum aspalto vel anacardis); aspaltum dicitur quoddam genus gummi nigri quod a quibusdam dicitur bitumen Judaicum *SB* 12.

asphodelus [ἀσφόδελος], asphodel (*Asphodeline*), ramson (*Allium*) or daffodil (*Narcissus*).

affodillus, *uude h[r]ofe*, ..apodiliis, *uude rove* vel *bara popig Gl. Durh.*; accipe succi affodillorum vel ermodatilorum et eleboris albi extracti cum aceto M. SCOT *Lumen* 252; affrodillorum GILB. I 38 v. 2 (cf ib. III 151 v. 2: affodillorum contritorum); affodillus resolvit ea [apostemata] aperiendo cum abstersione GAD. 30. 1; centum capita, affodillus idem, A. *clansing gresse SB* 15; affodillus, centum capita, albucium idem; saporem habet flos, plures flores albos; ..folia ejus similia foliis porrorum; A. *ramesen Alph.* 3; *rammys, herbe*, affadillus *PP*; ~us a Latinis hasta regia et albucum dicitur, a barbaris et Latine lingue corruptoribus aphrodillus et affodillus, ab Anglis *affadyll* et *daffadilly* TURNER *Herb.* A iii.

aspiatilis v. aspratilis.

aspicere [CL], to see, look at. **b** (fig.) to perceive (mentally). **c** to look for, expect. **d** (astr.; *cf. aspectus* 3).

puellas, / quas ille adspiciens torvis obtutibus horret ALDH. *VirgV* 717; aspicit infantum..turmas / mistica dona Dei ludo simulare *Ib.* 981; insulam..quam..de longe ~ere solemus BEDE *HE* I 1; Dominus..jejunia propitius aspexit *Ib.* IV 14; aspexit..lucem omnia replevisse *Ib.* 21; invisibilis..quia homo qui eam [terram] ~ere posset nondum.. eruperat ERIUG. *Per.* 548C. **b** [mentis] aspectus primo ~it; secundo aspecta sive cognita verificat GROS. 1. **c** diem mortis..laetus aspexit BEDE *HE* IV 3. **d** si in primo aspectu aspexerint se planete humidi in signis aquosis GROS. 51; si stelle superiores lunam aspexerint ROB. ANGL. (II) *Sph.* 165.

2 to look, gaze. **b** (w. *in*) to look at.

si..aliquis tibi diceret '~e illuc' et Deus e contra 'nullatenus volo ut ~ias' ANSELM (*Cur Deus* I 21) II 88; **1203** ipsa venit ad hostium suum et intus aspexit *SelPl Crown* 34. **b** **716** tam magnae claritatis..angelos..ut nullatenus..in eos ~ere potuisset BONIF. *Ep.* 10 p. 8; astronomi ~ientes in astris BACON VIII 124; **1313** ut ~ientes in eum [serpentem]..sanarentur *Conc.* II 423 (cf. *Num.* xxi 9).

aspidalis, of an asp.

s1251 improbos Romanos literas provisionis afferentes quasi venenum respuit ~e M. PAR. *Min.* III 113.

aspidiscus [ἀσπιδίσκος], hook of weaver's beam.

apidiscus, *webhoc* ÆLF. *Gl.*

aspidochelone [ἀσπιδοχελώνη], (?) giant turtle.

est belua in mari que Grece aspido †delone dicitur, Latine vero aspido testudo, cete eciam dicta ob immanitatem corporis: est enim sicut ille qui excepit Jonam *Best.* 55a.

aspinet' v. diasperatus.

aspirare [CL], to breathe, blow. **b** to aspirate.

rursus ~ante vento G. CRISPIN *Herl.* 101; ventus..sua contrarietate significans quia non sine numine periclitantibus ~aret W. CANT. *Mir. Thom.* VI 77; **s1386** ~avit aura que classem afflavit in Britanniam WALS. *HA* II 143; *to ande*, afflare, asspirare, spirare *CathA*. **b** ad prosam pertinet debitus modus accentuandi et ~andi syllabas BACON *Tert.* 324.

2 to inspire, give a blessing. **b** to favour, approve. **c** (trans.) to bestow.

~ante superna gratia BEDE *HA* 1; facundae munia linguae / aspirante Deo gestis explebat apertis FRITH. 54; quoniam illic divina ~at gratia *Enc. Emmae* II 17. **b** †**793** (16c) ego Ceolburga abbatissa de Berden ~avi *CS* 268; si Deus conamini suo tam fortunate ~aret *G. Steph.* I 49; **s1291** rogavit prior magistrum..ut per pomerium suum.. transire liceret; hoc magistro concito ~ante, subdit: "et ultra stratum meum, si necesse foret" *Flor. Hist.* III 73. **c** nostris aspira ceptis charismata mira P. BLOIS *Euch. prol.* 1137D.

3 to aspire, long (for): **a** (w. *ad*); **b** (w. *in*); **c** (w. *ut*).

a ad laudes hominum vanas sibi conciliandas / qui nimis aspirat insipienter agit NIG. *SS* 1777; illo quod perpetuum in nobis esse dignoscitur ad perennitatis gloriam ~emus GIR. *EH pref.* p. 223; **s1436** comes Atholie.., qui a longo tempore callide ad coronam ~abat *Plusc.* XI 9. **b** **s1217** milites sexcenti.., qui omnes ~abant in aliena WEND. II 209. **c** **c1430** qui ~at ut in grege sit precessor *Reg. Whet.* II 377.

aspiratio, breath (of slander). **b** (pronunciation of) aspirate.

sicut sal anguillarum destruitur humore, sic ipse omnium ~one annullatus est H. HUNT. *CM* 6. **b** humanus spiritus earum [mutarum] sine ~one leves cum ~one asperas facit, id est C, P, T ABBO *QG* 9; ~ones bene vos Angli pervidere potestis, qui pro Θ frequentius †B [l. Þ] scribitis *Ib.* 12 (cf. *Proc. Brit. Acad.* X 174); hec Britannice Haveren..vocata est; unde et Latine mutatione ~onis in S..dicta est Sabrina GIR. *DK* I 5; **1321** [nomen] Huberti archiepiscopi..in.. literis ejusdem..per solam ~onis notam designatur *Conc.* II 510.

2 inspiration.

[Egwinus] illustratione veri luminis et S. Spiritus ~one irradiatus *Chr. Evesham* 3.

3 aspiration, longing, ambition.

spiritus dicuntur, id est ~ones que precedunt virtutes J. SAL. *SS* 954B; **c1300** ~o ad illum statum sue conspiracionis fuit causa *G. Durh.* 29; ad peticionem et ~onem eorum [fratrum], non ad vocacionem ecclesie, istud curatorum officium acceperunt RIC. ARMAGH *Unusq.* 61; **c1430** [laqueator] ante eorum vestigia jacit ambitionis involucra, superaddit ~onis reticula *Reg. Whet.* II 460.

aspis [CL < ἀσπίς], venomous snake, asp.

aspidis ut morsum spernebat basia ALDH. *VirgV* 2136; **747** furor draconum vinum eorum et furor ~idum insanabile BONIF. *Ep.* 75 (cf. *Deut.* xxxii 33); [Henricus II] heredes omnium quos avus suus extulerat..[tam]quam ~ides exosos habuit R. NIGER 168; infestant ~ides et vipere GIR. *TH* I 36.

aspium v. asplenos.

asplenos, ~ion [ἄσπληνος], a fern (? *Ceterach*). **b** (?) other plant.

scolopendria, i. lingua cervina, spleneon idem *SB* 38; ~is herba est splendilidion similis et in exterioribus et in virtute scolopendrie *Alph.* 15. **b** †splemon, *brunuyrt* [? *Scrophularia*] *Gl. Durh.*; hoc †aspium, *a gresse* WW.

1 asportare v. apportare.

2 asportare [CL], to take away, remove. **b** to steal. **c** to withdraw (land). **d** to withdraw, refuse payment of (toll).

†ansportat, abducit, avehit *GlC* A 599; quemadmodum.. mellifluum examen..flava bajolans gestamina ~at ALDH. *Ep.* 5 p. 490; in opus Dei absportare conabatur quicquid pretiosum poterat G. CRISPIN *Herl.* 89; **s1137** illa..que ad edificationem nove ecclesie coadunata fuerant absportavit GERV. CANT. I 101; **1221** villata..cognovit quod corpus ~atum fuit in villam suam et quod sepultum fuit sine visu.. coronatorum *SelPlCrown* 100; res suas..clam ab ipsa domo absportaverat et subtraxerat *FormMan* 23; totam predam leonis improbitas asportavit J. SHEPPEY *Fab.* 4; **1415** qui rotuli ~ati fuerunt extra castrum *March SWales* 69. **b** **1194** blada sua que injuste aportaverunt *CurR RC* I 4; **1200** cepit et ~avit bladum suum *CurR* I 144; **1201** in roberia ~averunt scrinium uxoris sue *SelPlCrown* 2; **1221** catalla..fuerunt ~ata a malefactoribus *PlCrGlouc* 62; **1308** de carnibus..furtive ~atis *Ac. Durh.* 2; **1313** fecit hampsok super J. .., apportando unum pannum extra domum suam *Leet Norw.* 59; **1375** unam markam in pecunia numerata.. cepit et ~avit *Ib.* 66. **c** de una mansione [Uctredi].. dicunt burgenses Willelmum..~asse sibi in castellum; ipse vero W. terram ejusdem U. negat se habuisse, sed per H. comitem domum ipsius dicit se in castellum tulisse *DB* I 298. **d** si vero in aliam sciram ipsum theloneum ~abat *DB* I 268; **1194** qui theloneum domini ~avit in forisfacto remanebit *BBC* (*Pontefract*) 179; **c1300** misericordia..non ascendet ultra xij d. nisi de tolneo ~ato (*Cust. Preston*) *EHR* XV 497.

1 asportatio v. apportatio.

2 asportatio [CL], removal, carrying off, theft.

12.. illos qui res alienas in locis sacris depositas violenter asportaverint..seu ab aliis factam suo nomine ~onem ratam habuerint vel acceptam *Reg. Dunferm.* p. 143; **1384** de destruccione, elongacione et ~one cujuscumque artillarie infra villam et castra predicta *RScot* 68b.

asportator, remover, stealer, abductor. **b** exporter (of goods from town).

si quis convictus fuerit de bonis viri robbatis vel asportatis ad sectam..viri cujus uxor cum hujusmodi ~ore recesserit *Fleta* 58; **1377** fructuum, redditum et aliorum bonorum.. ~ores *Mon. Hib. & Scot.* 359a; **1525** sunt ~ores focalium, viz. ..spinarum..crescencium in *le heth CourtR* 197/55. **b** **1416** W. ..abstulit v dacras coriorum sine solucione custume; et est communis ~or lane ut supra *ExchScot* 251.

asportatus v. apportatus.

aspratilis [LL], spiny (fish). **b** stickleback.

pisces aspatiles GILB. IV 195 v. 2; aspatiles dicuntur pisces squamosi ab asperitate squamarum vel spinarum vel locorum in quibus degunt *Alph.* 15. **b** aspiatiles, A. *stikelinges SB* 12.

1 †assa, ~ia [cf. assula], plank, board.

framyd tre, ~a, cadia *PP*; hec ~ia, A. *a burde* WW.

2 assa v. assus.

assabilis, fit for roasting. **b** (alch.) able to be calcined.

1451 in j anguilla ~i, ij d. *Ac. Almon. Peterb.* 20. **b** nitrum..est ~e in igne *Ps.*-GROS. 643.

assacinus v. assassinus. assacula v. assatura. assag-, assaia-, v. essai-. assahilare, assail-, v. assilire.

assaisiona [cf. saisiona], season.

1290 pro mutacione eorum [austurcorum] de asseysona anni presentis *KRAc* 352/20 r. 3.

assaisionare, to plan the cultivation of (land). **b** (?) to ripen (hay).

1282 fregit pactum..de una acra terre..arrando et seminando illam et aliter assaysienando [? l. assaysionando] quam fecisse debuerat *CourtR Hales* 212. **b** **1230** licitum erit eis fenum prati infra clausum..ad desiccandum.. immittere et illud ibidem..~are donec desiccatum et eductum fuerit *E. Ch. S. Paul's* 163.

†assaisire [cf. saisire], to seize.

1168 de terra..de H. postquam fuit ~ita [v.l. saisita] in manu regis *Pipe* 125.

assaium v. essaium. assalire, ~iare, v. assilire. assalt- v. assult-. assara v. asara.

assare [LL], to roast. **b** (fig.). **c** (of human victims). **d** to torture. **e** (alch.) to heat, calcine.

salamandras quas naturaliter torrentes prunarum globi ~are vel cremare nequeunt ALDH. *VirgP* 34; nos ipsi possumus coquere quae coquenda sunt et ~are quae ~anda sunt [AS: *brædan þa þinge þe to brædene synd*] ÆLF. *Coll.* 98; si sit opus, volucres tales assentur in aula D. BEC. 2675; **1220** nunc elixa venit, nunc est assata ferina H. AVR. *Poems* 2. 221; **s1274** magna coquina in qua volatilia debent ~ari igne est tota discoperta in sumitate sua, ut ..fumus possit exire *Leg. Ant. Lond.* 173; monachis nigris, qui ~ata et frixa comedunt nunquam saciati W. GUISB. 143; si [pitancia] sit frixa vel elixa vel ~ata *Cust. Cant.* 136; **c1410** pones / costas †assastas, pisces pinguesque capones (*Vers. Exch.*) *EHR* XXXVI 61; **1521** verutas..pro avibus ~andis *Cant. Coll. Ox.* I 64. **b** **796** pisces..igne sancti spiritus..ad epulas aeterni regis ~are ALCUIN *Ep.* 113. **c** quamquam tortores assarent igne tenellam ALDH. *VirgV* 1822; jam satis assatum rex verte notaque crematum NIG. *Laur.* 43b; **s1097** Turcos aliquot..mandat jugulari et, copioso igne supposito, quasi ad opus cene ~ari M. PAR. *Min.* I 95; **s1217** a ministris Sathane, qui etiam vivos captivos inter cetera ~averunt facinora *Ib.* II 203. **d** quare Dei filius sic est humanatus, / ut in crucis cornibus fieret assatus (*Praedic. Goliae* 4) *Ps.*-

Map 31. **e** philosophi multa posuerunt artificia ad artis sue veneracionem sive occultacionem.., ut sunt commiscere, coquere, sublimare, ~are..; hic sunt nomina plura quorum tamen regimen est coquere tantum Dastyn *Ros.* 6.

assarium, ~ius [LL], as (coin).

constabant singuli de duabus decimis Ephi, quas Josephus duos ~ios vocat Ad. Scot. *TT* 677c.

assart- v. essart-.

assassinus [Ar. *ḥashīshī*], Assassin, follower of the 'Old Man' (Sheikh) of the Mountain, Neo-Ismaili (conf. w. *Arsacides*). **b** assassin, murderer.

vir auctoritatis maxime, qui Senex vocatur, Axasessis, quasi..'sub axe consessis', inperat, qui fuit fons religionis et fidei gentilium Map *NC* I 22; per manum Bonefacii marchionis de Monteferrato, quem..duo Hassasisi occiderunt *Ib.* V 6 p. 241; **s1192** duo juvenes Hausassisi..duobus cultellis..exsertis..lethaliter ipsum [Conradum de Monte Ferrato] vulnerantes..pretervolabant *Itin. Ric.* V 26; duo de servientibus regis Accinorum, id est de Assasis, ..interfecerunt Conradum R. Howd. III 181; a duobus Sarracenis, quos Hautasis appellant Coggesh. 54b; **s1195** accesserunt.. quidam Accini numero xv *Ib.* 283; Marchisius [de Monte Ferrario]..ab Assisinis Arsacidis interfectus est Wend. I 201; **s1195** ut idem marchio ab Assacinis interemptus esset R. Niger 100; **s1150** hos tam Saraceni quam Christiani Assisinos appellant M. Par. *Maj.* II 185; **s1238** confessus est se missum illuc ut regem more Assessinorum occideret *Ib.* III 498; **s1257** Tartari detestabiles Assessinos detestabiliores, quos cultelliferos appellamus, destruxerunt *Ib.* V 655; **c1272** hic Assessinus Veteris de Monte ferebat / nuncia conficta..; / ingreditur thalamos, precludens hostia, cultro / vulnera vulneribus impressit (T. de Wyta *Edw. I* 75) *Pol. Songs* 132; **s1272** rex Judeorum, qui vulgo Vetus de Monte dicitur, ..unum de sicariis suis, quos vulgo Assessinos vocant, misit in Syriam ut..Edwardum..jugularet Wykes 249; **1283** letiferas inimici hominis asisini..insidias evasisti (*Lit. Papae ad Regem*) *Foed.* II 236; **1291** vulnerum..sibi ascisini cujusdam insidiis inflictorum memoria (*Lit. Papae*) *Ib.* 514; Hassacinus quidam..ipsum [Edwardum]..cultello vulnerat venenato Wals. *YN* 165; **s1192** creditur quod fuerunt de genere †Alte Nutricis, qui mortem non metuunt ut jussa majorum adimpleant Brompton 1243; Saraceni Arsacidas vocant sicarios P. Verg. XVI p. 319. **b** *a manslaer*, assisini, grassator, homicida *CathA*.

assatio, roasting. **b** roast meat. **c** (alch.) calcination.

[amara] adhibita ad ignem efficiuntur dulcia per digestionem, que est epsesis vel ophthesis vel ~o *Ps.*-Gros. 514; **1456** pro loco ~onis et [c]occionis alimentorum de novo facto *Cant. Coll. Ox.* II 178. **b 1449** in uno capone, ij d. ob.; in una ~one, A. *a rooste*, j d. ob. *Ac. Almon. Peterb.* 14. **c** cum aurum per calcinationes vel ~ones aut affinationes virtutem acquirit ignis M. Scot *Sol* 716; calcem..pluribus ~onibus concrema Bacon *NM* 545.

assativus, (?) fully cooked.

ovis duris et ~is Gilb. IV 195. 2.

assator, roaster.

1443 stipendia famulorum: catour, cocus, ~ores, carnifex *Ac. Durh.* 82.

assatorium, toasting-fork.

a toste yren, ~ium *CathA*.

assatura [LL], roast, roast meat.

cocturam vel ~am alimentorum in focularibus praeparatam Aldh. *VirgP* 38 p. 288; assura vel ~a, *bræde* Ælf. *Gl.*; cibi eorum sint ~e, et non detur cum brodio Gilb. V 221 v. 2; debes tunc [in hyeme] redire ad cibos calidos et materias calidas, ut sunt pulli columbarum, arietina caro et ~e Bacon V 80; **s1400** cena parata, cum ~is non paucis ad ignem decoquendis *Plusc.* X 15 (cf. *Extr. Chr. Scot.* 207: †assuraturas); †assacula, A. *an hastelet* WW; **1480** pro ~a caponis, auce et cuniculorum *Ac. Chamb. Cant.* 136.

2 (w. *renum*, by conf. of AS *bræd* = breadth w. *bræde* = roast) lumbar region.

si ~a renum, quam Angli vocant *lendenbræde*, omnino incisa fuerit, lx sol. emend[etur] (*Inst. Cnut.*) *GAS* 85.

assaturis, gridiron.

1283 de patellis, de ~ibus, de cauderiis *RGasc* II 211.

assatus, roasting.

1467 soluti in iiij costis bovinis et in ~u predictarum costarum *Ac. Chamb. Winchester.*

assaysienare v. assaisionare. assecla v. assecula. assecretis v. ab 8 b.

assectator [CL = *disciple*; *but* cf. affectator], emulator.

adsectator, imitator *GlC* A 241.

assectatio [CL], pursuit.

vestre discretionis honestatem nec caduci honoris ambitio ..nec fluide voluptatis ~o damnabiliter illexit Ad. Marsh *Ep.* 77.

assecula [CL], follower, attendant, servant (m. or f.). **b** tradesman.

adsaeculum, *pegn*, minister turpitudinis *GlC* A 209; assecla, *folgere* Ælf. *Sup.*; assecla Domini Gosc. *Aug. Maj.* 76; sequitur canis assecla fidus Neckam *DS* I 412; assecla mense / vilis et illepidus Vinsauf *PN* 1773; *wench*, assecla, ancilla *PP*. **b** *grocer, merchawynt*, grossarius, assecla *PP*.

assecurantia, assurance, pledge (esp. of peace).

1383 contra specialem ~iam factam et concordatam inter ipsos (*Doc. Scot.* 102/36) *Foed.* VII 403; **s1399** [Henricus] Angliam intravit sub securitate et ~ia..dominorum [de Percy] modico tempore demorando *Plusc.* X 12; **s1400** volentibus ~iam pro eorum domibus, bonis, personis vel fortaliciis *Ib.* 16; **s1402** capitaneus castri de ~ia accessit ad Percy et obtulit se duello Fordun *Cont.* XV 15; **1451** in cujus..dominio hujusmodi fugitivus..receptatur seu assecuratur, requisitus..tenebitur..omnem ~iam et salvum conductum hujusmodi fugitivo concessum annullare *RScot* 352a.

assecurare [< ad+securus; cf. assurare], (w. pers. obj.) to assure (by pledge), make sure. **b** (refl.) to pledge or commit oneself.

1174 rex Scottorum..et barones..eos inde ~averunt (*Conventio*) *Anglo-Scot. Rel.* 2; si..pactiones..minus quam oporteret ~atus..tamen, ut videtur, rerum necessitate coactus inierit Ad. Marsh *Ep.* 161; **1295** ipsam bene ~abit de dotalicio..percipiendo ab eo post matrimonium contractum (*Concord.*) W. Guisb. 266; **s1297** non videtur..quod sit ad bonum regis quod transeat in Flandriam nisi plus esset ~atus de Flandrensibus pro se et pro gente sua Trevet 362; in ista comutacione stulta vendicio non sufficit ~are ementem Wycl. *Sim.* 87; **s1397** rex, hoc negans, ~avit eum, jurando sibi super corpus Christi *Eul. Hist. Cont.* III 371 (cf. ib. 376: te ~o quod..revocaberis); **1518** [Delphinus Mariam] de eodem doario..certam et securam reddet et ~abit (*DipDocE* 817) *Foed.* XIII 635a. **b s1138** principales..viri sese adinvicem sacramentorum obligatione ~ant et confirmant quod nullus eorum..alium desereret Ric. Hex. *Stand.* f. 43; **1293** quod occasione..presentis mandati non ~ent se de intrando alicubi in portu..in quo..possit eis periculum imminere *Cl* 110 m. 8.

2 to confirm (by pledge), guarantee. **b** (w. *quod*). **c** (w. inf.). **d** (w. acc. and inf.).

1189 voluntatem..vestram et propositum super hoc nuntiis nostris..~ari faciatis nosque..certificetis; idem vero nuntii nostri super hoc vobis securitatem prestabunt (*Lit. Regis Franciae*) Diceto *YH* II 71; **1202** de hiis que in scripto illo continentur ~andis *Pat* 8a; **1228** mandamus quatinus..treugas..observari et a vobis et imprisiis nostris in ballia vestra ~ari faciatis *Pat* 215; **s1264** ad hec firmanda et ~anda tradiderunt castra..fere omnia *Flor. Hist.* II 504; **1346** mandamus quod de..condicionibus ejusdem tractatus, priusquam per vos..firmetur vel ~etur, nos.. certificetis *RScot* 676b. **b 1164** si exierint, ..~abunt quod nec in eundo..nec in redeundo perquirent malum..regno (*Const. Clar.* 4) Gerv. Cant. I 178; **c1177** quieti..de omni theloneo de omnibus rebus quas..possunt ~are quod emant vel vendant ad proprios usus..ipsorum *Danelaw* 179; **1174** rex filius..~avit in manu domini regis patris sui quod..nec malum nec damnum..faciet (*Concord.*) *G. Hen. II* I 77; **1189** providit rex Francie quod per sacramentum hominum terre ~atum esset quod..soror sua tradita sit comiti Ricardo *Ib.* II 70; est apud illos commune commercium quod velint ~are propter stipendium quod ponent animas suas..pro animabus [etc.] (Wycl. *Versut.*) *EHR* XLVII 102. **c** ita quod ~abit inde warantum suum habere ad talem diem Glanv. I 23; **s1291** rex ~at reddere regnum Wals. *HA* I 37 *rub.* **d s1119** mandavit ei rex quatinus veritatis assercione ~aret se post Pascha iturum H. Cantor 16; **c1150** ipsam..convencionem sacramento fidei sue ~avit Rogerus se tenere (*Pactio*) *Eng. Feudalism* 261; **c1160** hec omnia..nos per omnia servaturos..~avimus *Ch. Sal.* 33; **a1190** omnibus rebus quas ipsi potuerunt ~are suas esse dominicas *BBC* (*Newcastle upon Tyne*) 185; **1251** theloneum ..cujuscunque rei unde (*sic*) homines..abbatis..~are poterunt ad abbatem..pertinere *MonA* II 309b.

3 to secure, safeguard. **b** (w. dat.) to ensure, guarantee (possession of). **c** to insure (naut.).

1231 rex misit J...ad salvam custodiam apponendam.. castris..et ad partes illas ~andas *Pat* 427; **1303** pro statu eorundem [mercatorum] plenius ~ando *MGL* II 205 (= *EEC* 260); **1297** quousque status terre illius ~atus esset *RScot* 49b; **1308** concessimus vobis firma[m] ville [de Perth] ..habend[am] ad eandem villam et pontem illum inde afforciandum et ~andum, ita quod firma illa in assecuracione et afforciacione ville et pontis..convertatur *Ib.* 56a. **b 1101** volo ut ~etis michi sacramento terram meam Anglie, ad tenendum et defendendum contra omnes homines et nominatim contra Rotbertum..fratrem meum (*Breve Regis*) *EHR* XXI 506; **s1100** principes et proceres.., factis regi hominiis et fidelitatibus juratis, regnum ei ~averunt H. Cantor 3; **1141** comes Andegavie..~abit ei manu sua propria illud eidem tenendum *Regesta* III 634. **c 1565** navem..ejusque apparatus..necnon periculum viagii..fiendi ~asse *SelPlAdm* II 132.

assecuratio, safeguarding, protection. **b** guarantee, pledge. **c** (document embodying mutual) assurance. **d** (document guaranteeing) safe-conduct.

1297 ad morandum..in dictis partibus pro salvacione et ~one parcium earundem *RScot* 49b; **1300** pro ~one [= *Eul. Hist.* III 181: †assecuritate] regni nostri accessimus ad confinium regni utriusque, mandantes Johanni tunc regi Scocie ut..ad nos accederet super premissis et aliis ~onis statum tranquillitatem et pacem regni utriusque contingentibus tractaturus (*Lit. Regis*) W. Guisb. 343; **1308** (v. assecurare 3a). **b s1277** pro ~one istorum [concessorum] tradidit princeps [Wallie] decem obsides Trevet 297; **s1339** rex.. uxorem cum liberis..apud Andewarp..dimisit, quasi in ~onem [v.l. asseuracionem] reditus sui Higd. VII 44 p. 334. **c 1152** facta est hec carta et compositio et ~o inter.. episcopum et comitem *Ch. Sal.* 24. **d 1417** ad concedendum et nomine nostro faciendum literas salvi conductus et ~ones quibuscunque personis de Scocia..melius videbitur expedire *RScot* 221b; **1440** nobiles viri, ..salvi securique passagii sui ~one in scriptis redacta spreta prorsus, capti.. sunt Bekynton I 93.

assecuritas v. assecuratio a.

assecutio, acquisition, attainment.

1235 ad ~onem sui propositi..vestra dignetur paternitas eis..consilio subvenire (*Const. S. Alb.*) *Conc.* I 632a; talis artis est difficilis et laboriosa ~o Bacon *Maj.* I 244; **1298** littera..super justa ~one ecclesie de H. *Reg. Cant.* I 294; **1339** quod pro nostrorum tuicione et ~one jurium..fecimus (*Lit. Regis*) Ad. Mur. 96; **1424** per ~onem vicarie perpetue ..per fratrem T. W. ..canonice factam *Reg. Cant.* I 320; **1440** cum..paternitatem vestram ad nostre intencionis ~onem multum conferre posse sciamus Bekynton I 15; **14..** in ~onis dotis sue retardacionem *Reg. Brev.* 7.

assecutivus, subsequent.

disciplinalium hec inceptiva, illa ~a nominentur: inceptiva ideo quoniam ceteris disciplinalium secundum genera sua usu priora sunt; ~a ideo quoniam et reliqua tria interrogabilium genera secuntur et interrogantis propositum et ad cetera respondentis diffugium assecuntur Balsh. *AD* 163.

assedare, to rent, lease (Scot.).

13.. tenuit ij carucatas et dim. que nunc ~antur pro c s. *Pri. Cold. app.* xc; **1348** terras..capelle..quanto..utilius poterit ad utilitatem..capellanorum..~et *Reg. Brechin.* I 11; **1365** sciatis nos..~asse et ad firmam dimisisse..Thome L. totam terram nostram de R. ..tenendam et habendam sibi et uni heredi masculo..de nobis..ut ad firmam..reddendo inde annuatim nobis..octo s. *Reg. Aberbr.* I 229; **1370** de terra molendini solita ~ari cum molendino *Conc. Scot.* I cxci *n.*; **1413** non ~abunt, non impignorabunt, non alienabunt dictam terram *Reg. Newbattle* no. 280; **1469** de firmis de le Halch de Brechin, que consuevit ~ari pro ij celdris *ExchScot* 631; **1539** in augmentacionem firme terre ecclesiastice..~ate domino de M. *Rent. S. Andr.* 39.

assedatarius, lessee (Scot.).

1566 omnibus et singulis feudatariis, ~iis, tenentibus et parrochianis quarumcumque terrarum, ecclesiarum, locorum et prediorum dicto episcopatui pertinencium *Reg. Brechin. app.* II 329.

assedatio, renting, leasing (Scot.).

1329 onerat se de vj li. per firmam dicti burgi de predicto termino..ex ~one camerarii *ExchScot* 164; si aliquis ballivus in ~one profectuum domini regis fuerit particeps capcionis (*Art. Cam.*) *APScot.* 317; **1342** per..~onem terrarum *Cart. Lindores* cxxxiv; **1378** non obstantibus impignoracione ad feodifirmam, ~one, donacione aliqua, infeodacione *Reg. Aberd.* I 123; **1405** infra terminum ~onis predicte *Reg. S. Andr.* 423; **1485** de vj li. pro grassuma et introitu Willelmi ..ad ~onem loci de C. *ExchScot* 318; **1525** cujusquidem ~onis septem anni currendi sunt *Reg. Aberbr.* II 447; **1549** emphiteutarie locaciones vel ad longum tempus ~ones *Conc. Scot.* II 94.

assedella v. assidella. assedere v. 1 assidere.

asseditor [cf. 1 assidere 4], stone-layer.

1253 in stipendiis..vij marmor[ariorum], v ~orum, ix carpent[ariorum] (*KRAc* 467/1) *Ac. Build. Hen. III* 282.

assedula v. 1 acidula. assefetida v. asa.

assegiare [OF *assegier*], to besiege.

1279 si castrum honoris Waling[ford] fuerit ~iatum, invenient j hominem..per xl dies ad dictum castrum *Hund.* II 777.

asseisina v. assisa 6c, essaium. asselare v. 1 acerare. asseler' v. asshelarium. assella v. axilla.

assellare [LL], to go to stool, evacuate the bowels.

si [patiens] nullo istorum modorum ~averit Gilb. I 32. 1; si constipatus est et non potest ~are Bacon IX 95; nec urinet nec ~et quousque cum viro coiverit Gad. 79. 1.

assellatio, evacuation of the bowels.

supposuit..minister in ~onis foramine domino suo veru ferreum acutum et grande Map *NC* V 4 p. 215; cum ductum fuerit ad tres ~ones Gilb. II 98. 1; quod ventres eorum liniantur cum rebus purgantibus fleuma..cum duabus vel tribus ~onibus Bacon IX 93; laxabuntur fere usque xxx ~ones Gad. 7. 1.

assellator, one who evacuates the bowels.

sitque decorus / assellatorum thalamus D. Bec. 2205.

assemare, ~atio, v. essaim-.

assemblare, ~iare [OF *assembler* < assimulare], to assemble: **a** (trans.) to bring together; **b** (intr.) to come together.

a 1389 fratres et sorores dicte confraternitatis sunt convocandi, convocati, ~ia[n]di seu ~ati secundum quasdam ordinaciones (*Gild Cert.* 310) *Eng. Gilds* 29; **1573** major et gubernatores ville..in curia sive convocacione predicta pariter congregati et ~ati *Pat* 1104 m. 27. **b 1569** insimul insurrexerunt, convenerunt, ~averunt et univerunt, ad bellum..contra..reginam..paraverunt *Entries* 413; **1573** proditorie insimul congregaverunt et ~averunt *Pat* 1105 m. 12.

assemblatio, assembly.

1573 ~ones *Pat* 1105 m. 7; **1593** et in omnibus aliis locis ubi solemnis ~o gentium foret *Entries* 406.

assemblea, ~eia, ~ia [OF *assemblee* < assimulata], assembly, gathering.

1338 ~eia tenenda ad finem Carniprivii *Hosp. in Eng.* 211; **1397** perdonavimus..sectam pacis nostre et quicquid ad nos occasione congregacionis, adunacionis et ~ee gencium, servientum et familiarium predictorum ac monstri predicti pertinet *Pat* 347 m. 20; **1501** prior S. Johannis

Jerusalem in Anglia..et ejusdem confratres..in ~ia sua *Cl* 361 m. 11*d*.

ssendere v. ascendere. assensa, ~are, ~aria, v. accens-. 1 assensio v. ascensio.

2 assensio [CL], assent.

1320 in contestacionis nostre supplementum, quam vestre assencionis comparacione minorem reputamus infirmam *FormOx* 64; **s1389** juvit multum ad animos sedandos rebellium et ~o procerum Scotorum *V. Ric. II* 111 (= WALS. *HA* II 183: assercio).

assensivus, expressive of assent.

apprehendo rem sub modo cognoscendi ~o et assertivo WYCL. *Log.* II 234.

assensor v. assessor 1b. assensorium v. ascensorium b.

assensus [CL], assent, agreement. **b** complicity, abetment. **c** body of accomplices, faction.

praebuit palam adsensum evangelizanti..Paulino rex BEDE *HE* II 13; ~um fecerunt cuncti ut cum illo irent G. MON. III 7 (= *Eul. Hist.* II 240: ~um prebuerunt omnes cum illo ire); **a1200** ascensu et concensu heredis mei *Danelaw* 90; **1227** licentiam eligendi et in electos ~um prebendi *Pat* 125; **1253** rogavit ipsum quod collacioni regis ~um suum adhiberet *Cl* 179 (= *RGasc.* I 361: †assentum); **1285** hoc fecit per ~um communitatis *CBaron* 120; **1373** ordinatum est ex communi ~u *Hal. Durh.* 118; **1566** partes litigantes..ex suis unanimis et voluntariis consensubus et ~ubus submiserunt se *Act PC Ir.* 160. **b 1277** indictatus ..de societate et ~u latronum *Gaol Del.* 85 r. 10. **c 1295** quod..capitaneus flote Baionensis et omnes illi de eadem flota unius sint ~us cum..aliis capitaneis flote regis Anglie *RGasc.* III 322; **s1379** E. de Brounfeld..xiij monachos..ad suum ~um attraxit *V. Ric. II* 14.

assentaneus, assenting, in agreement. **b** (sb.) adherent. **c** similar, consonant.

assignetur ei..de..fratribus cautus et providus, qui conscius sit et ~eus in hiis que vendiderit vel emerit (*Inst. Sempr.* xi) *MonA* VI 946 xxxixb; Willelmus..cum militibus sibi ~eis..restitit *G. Steph.* II 74. **b** rex.., ascitis sue partis ~eis *Ib.* 70. **c** est..Dacorum genere multum permixta illa provincia [Eboracensis] et multum ~ea in loquela *Chr. Wallingf.* 61.

assentari [CL], **~are,** to flatter. **b** to assent.

adsentatur, adolatur, blanditur *Erf.* 2. 261; 38 (*but* cf. assentator); cum multiplex sit vitium adulandi, aliis vultu, aliis verbo, aliis vel opere vel munere ~antibus J. SAL. *Pol.* 487D; *to fage*, adulari, ~ari, assenciare, assentiri *CathA*. **b** his infortunis rebus perplurimi ~abant et non cohibebant *V. Osw.* 445; **1571** concesserunt et ~averunt quod dicte convictiones..forent approbate *Entries* 645.

assentatio [CL], flattery, deference. **b** mark of respect.

hec in ~onem Egfridi fiebant W. MALM. *GP* III 102; non est utique perniciosior ~o quam ea que affectionis inductione procedit J. SAL. *Pol.* 503C; ~ones curialibus appropriatas longe post terga relinquens GIR. *PI pref.* 1 p. lix. **b** corpus B. Alphegi..dignis ~onibus veneratus est CIREN. II 176.

assentator [CL], flatterer, 'yes-man'. **b** assenter.

adsentator, adolator, blanditor *GlC* A 258 (*but* cf. assentari); quod ~oris proprium est, qui ad alterius vivit nutum J. SAL. *Pol.* 482B. **b c1150** hujus donationis et confirmationis mee testes et ~ores sunt hii *E. Ch. Scot.* 189.

assentatorie, obsequiously.

quidam ~e regi faventes..instabant ut regie voluntati obsequeretur H. CANTOR 1 v.

assentatorius, obsequious.

de illis..qui mendaciis ~iis..Dominum..extollunt H. BOS. *Thom.* III 13; magnis et ~iis acclamationibus BOECE 59.

assentatrix, obsequious (f.). **b** assenting (f.).

~ix, unde Prosper, cum de crimine adulationis loqueretur, subjunxit.. ALDH. *PR* 176. **b 10..** ~ix, *sio gepafigende* WW.

assentiare v. assentari. assentio v. ascensio 1d.

assentire [CL *usu. dep.*], to agree (to or with): **a** (w. dat. or absol.); **b** (w. *ad*); **c** (w. *in*); **d** (w. acc. and inf.); **e** (w. inf.); **f** (w. *quod*).

si non vis adsentire nobis in tam facili causa BEDE *HE* II 5; illa, licet hoc perfici posse desperet, ~it MAP *NC* IV 16 p. 199; voluntas libere ~it cuilibet bono DUNS *Sent.* I i 4. 16; quibus omnibus multitudo Fratrum Minorum.. favet et ~it et adheret OCKHAM *I. & P.* 3; **s1327** rex..~ivit *Meaux* II 354; **s1402** rex..non ~iit *Eul. Hist. Cont.* III 395. **b 1384** ad illum se aggreavit et ~ivit *IMisc* 229/17. **c 1268** comitatus Ebor'..et Lanc' ~iunt in Johannem..et Adam.. ut ipsi ordinent.. *Cl* 557; **s1451** [volo] vos..in virum probum.., ut ipse illam [majoritatem] reaccipiat, ..cordialiter ~ire; ut igitur in ipsum ~iatis..do vobis..consilium *Reg. Whet.* I 7. **d** que omnia nemo potest ~ire competere negacioni WYCL. *Act.* 90. **e s1312** ~ivit occidere Robertum *Ann. Lond.* 219. **f 1318** ordinatum est et assensum [*DuC.*: assisatum] statuente domino rege quod..justicia fiat.. *Stat. Rob.* I c. 3) *APScot* 107.

2 (trans.) to abet.

s1305 latrones, ..~iente eos quodam Juda de fratribus, ..rapuerunt cccc [li.] argenti *Flor. Hist.* III 128.

assentus v. assensus.

assequi [CL], to overtake, catch up. **b** to catch. **c** to acquire, attain, achieve. **d** (w. *ut*). **e** (*s. pass.*).

hi precedentibus instant nec ~untur W. FITZST. *Thom. prol.* 14. **b** quas [predas] dum ~untur [falcones]..ictu concutiunt violento GIR. *TH* I 12. **c** ut..~ar hujus satietatis desideratum bonum ANSELM (*Or.* 12) III 46; propositum assecutus est W. FITZST. *Thom.* 20; **s1264** habito ..magno tractatu super pace regni ~enda *Flor. Hist.* II 505; **1279** ut is qui plura beneficia..fuerit assecutus ultimum beneficium sic optentum retineat *Conc. Syn.* 839. **d** si ~atur [AS: *peah he gepeo*] ut habeat loricam..et deauratum gladium (*Quad.*) *GAS* 461. **e 1345** assecuta pacis dulcedine (*Lit. Papae*) AD. MUR. 188.

2 to follow, fulfil, carry out. **b** (*s. pass.*). **c** (pr. ppl.) subsequent (*cf. assecutivus*).

1417 mandatum vestrum..sum reverenter assecutus *Reg. Cant.* II 34. **b 1225** conventio illa nunquam assecuta fuit *CurR* XII 1527. **c** ~entiora..sunt, sicut initialibus inceptiva, inceptivis executiva, sic assecutivorum simplicibus multiplicia et coartate conquisita, quale est illud 'quid, qualiter, ad quid doceatur', que tria in disciplinarum principiis demonstrare solemus BALSH. *AD* 164.

1 asser v. 3 acer.

2 asser [CL], **~era,** board, plank, lath. **b** board for book-binding. **c** book-rest. **d** pax-board.

~eres, *latta* vel *reafteres* ÆLF. *Sup.*; fenestris lucem dabant vel panni linei tenuitas vel multiforatilis ~er W. MALM. *GP* III 100 p. 217; ~erem illum..quem Pilatus summitati crucis Dominice titulo sue passionis inscriptum affixerat MAP *NC* IV 11 p. 181; ei [dolio] operculum.. ex ~eribus adaptavit GIR. *GE* II 10; **1208** pro..pluribus ~eribus furratis *Pipe* 127 (cf. forare); unicuique [fratri].. ~erem tractabilem latitudinis quarterii et dim. unius ulne per lecti sui introitum habere permittitur *Cust. Cant.* 194; **1296** in †asperibus [emptis ad domum] *Rec. Norw.* II 33 (cf. ib. 35: ~eribus); **1364** pro ~eribus et ferro ad reparacionem batelle *ExchScot* 167; **1374** in stipendio j hominis findentis dc ~eras [*corr. to* lattes] pro parietibus *DL MinAc* 507/8227 m. 27; **1418** unam ~erem sive tabulam principalem pro aula *Reg. Cant.* II 157; **1452** sinistrum altare cum ~eribus pertinentibus *MunAcOx* 629; **1455** pro cc ~eribus de Prusia emptis ad fabricam castri de Edynburgh *ExchScot* 4; ~er, *a latt*, ..hec ascera, *a lytil chyp*, ..hic aser, *a borde* WW. **b 1220** unus troparius per se in ~eribus *Reg. S. Osm.* I 276; **c1250** bona legenda in duobus voluminibus paribus et ligatis in ~eribus *Vis. S. Paul.* 22; bene..faciatis componi libros.., ablatis ~eribus, in panno cerato AD. MARSH *Ep.* 213; **1267** de uno libro cum ~eribus j d. *MinAc* 1031/20 m. 3; **1322** Decreta mea in †vitulinio scripta in ~eribus nigro corio coopertis (*Test.*) THORNE 2037; **1432** liber..non cathenatus carens ~ere *Reg. Glasg.* 338; **1495** lxx volumina in ~eribus bene ligata (*Necrol.*) *Mon. Francisc.* II 139. **c** librarius.. cathedram habeat cum ansis porrectis ad sustinendum ~erem cui quaternus superponendus est; ~er autem centone operiatur cui pellis cervina maritetur (NECKAM *Sac.*) *Med. Sci.* 361; in evangelio, quod non in altari sed in ~ere vel..lectorio..legi oportet BELETH *RDO* 37. 45. **d 1287** sit..~er ad pacem *Conc. Syn.* 1006; **1342** ~er ad pacem non est depictus (*Vis. Totnes*) *EHR* XXVI 111 (cf. ib. 113; ~er ad pacem male depictus).

assera v. acervum. asserare v. 1 acerare. assercire v. arcessere.

asserere [CL], to assert, maintain (a right). **b** (w. compl.) to maintain, keep.

plerique validius ~unt quam impugnant J. SAL. *Met.* 906C; si quis se juri meo presumpserit adversarium opponere, presto sum illud ~ere MAP *NC* V 6 p. 244. **b s1192** nihil ulterius tentandum, quia tot millia hostium littoris aditum ~ebant impossibilem TREVET 141.

2 to assert, affirm, allege. **b** (w. acc. and inf.). **c** (w. *quod* or *quia*). **d** (inf. as sb.) assertion.

quod nequaquam..adseri potest ALDH. *Met.* 10 p. 89; **s925** ipse..verba legatorum ~uit W. MALM. *GP* II 134; ANSELM *Ep.* 136 (v. anathema b); **1204** sicut Hugo ~it *CurR* II 316; ad quod poterit mulier ~ere contrarium.., ut fiat inquisitio BRACTON 309; **1559** contrarium pertinaciter ~ere hereticum est *Conc. Scot.* II 163. **b 680** diversas ob causas Petrum..hunc ritum sumpsisse ~imus ALDH. *Ep.* 4 p. 483; unum quod..a fidelissimis..fratribus sibi relatum ~ere solebat BEDE *HE* IV 14; in quo ~itur salvari hominem per solam fidem LANFR. *Comment. Paul.* (*Rom.* iii 28) 117; nec fidem somniis adhibendam ~uit AILR. *Ed. Conf.* 762C; id se factorum..~uit AD. EYNS. *Hug.* V 11 p. 141; protestans et ~ens loquelam illam in curia sua debere tractari BRAKELOND 140; ~endo..hereticum quod..constitucio.. catholicum ~it et catholicum quod constitucio..hereticum declaravit OCKHAM *Pol.* I 294; non sine causa eulogium illud ~o *Eul. Hist.* I 4. **c** ~uit quia..hoc ipsum facere non pretermitteret GIR. *RG* II 7; quidam ~uerunt constanter quod..nollent se Galli subtrahere ELMH. *Hen. V* 38; nonnulli..~unt quod tota ejus exultacio..erat in Dei laudibus ..persolvendis BLAKMAN *Hen. VI* 15. **d 1382** sed ejus asserere vel suum [v.l. sui] negare / non est factum aliquod liquide probare (*Contra Religiosos* 219) *Mon. Francisc.* I 599.

3 (p. ppl.) alleged. **b** (as sb. n.) assertion, allegation.

1494 quidam dominus T. P. prior dicti prioratus ~tus *DCCant S* 396b; **1520** postquam dictum ~tum matrimonium fuit..contractum *Offic. S. Andr.* 11; **1527** a quodam domino ~to religioso *Form. S. Andr.* I 205. **b 1425** aliquamdiu conatus ipsa ~ta sua..defensare, tandem..se submisit *Conc.* III 438.

assergeanticus [cf. serjans], serjeant (at arms).

1444 venit hic in camera Guihalde Johannes Combe ~us civitatis..ad arma *Pl. Mem. Lond.* A 70 m. 7.

assertare v. essartare.

assertibilis, capable of assertion.

sic iste terminus 'deus' de sua intencione primaria hominem et omne ~e significat WYCL. *Incarn.* 216.

assertio [CL], assertion, vindication. **b** corroboration. **c** (?) demonstration.

retulit nobis quidam miles testimonio legalium virorum in veritatis ~onem HERM. ARCH. 48 p. 89; etiam Judeis vita hodie indulgetur, ..dum ad ~onem nostre fidei prophetas circumferunt P. BLOIS (*Perf. Jud.* 1) 825C; **s1170** ait [archiepiscopus]: "ego mori paratus sum, vite preferens ~onem justitie" DICETO *YH* I 343; **1521** ~o septem sacramentorum HEN. VIII (*title*). **b c1130** ego H. rex Anglorum concedo et sigilli mei ~one confirmo *Norm. Inst.* 96 (= *Regesta* II 1702). **c** comicus ideo Gnatonem introduxit servum militis gloriosi, ut..innueret quoniam et in vita hominum et in ~one morum subest Gnatonica Trasoniane J. SAL. *Pol.* 711B.

2 assertion, affirmation.

non nostris ~onibus sed scripturae astipulationibus ornatus feminarum rapina virorum vocatur ALDH. *VirgP* 57; fideli innumerorum testium adsertione cognovi BEDE *HE pref.* p. 7; precor ut..quid super hoc tenendum sit ecclesiasticis ~onibus edoceatis G. CRISPIN *Simon* 111; argutis verborum ~onibus se tales non esse..affirmabant EADMER *V. Anselm* II 14; violentissimas [Aldhelmi] ~ones exornat color rethoricus W. MALM. (*V. Aldhelmi*) *GP* V 196; quod fuerit hec ejus opinio, certum est; quod vere non fuerit ejus ~o hec, ipse testatur J. CORNW. *Eul.* 3. 1052; quorundam ~o est eum..vocari prepositum AD. SCOT. *OP* 566C; preter publice fame ~onem J. FORD *Wulf.* 84; si concorditer affirmaverint eos descendisse de eodem stipite.., super hoc stabitur ~oni GLANV. II 6; **s1191** cum demum eorum ~ones perpendisset esse verba *Itin. Ric.* IV 31; **1262** asserunt se velle observare treugas.., licet contrarium faciunt sue ~oni *Cl* 272; **1265** per ~onem..episcopi intelleximus *Cl* 51; **1339** ex ~one intelleximus nonnullorum *RScot* 567a; plus me monebit una racio evidens..quam ~o tocius universitatis mortalium OCKHAM *I. & P.* 3; **s1389** (v. assensio); **1396** cum antiquum sit proverbium et est assersio Sapientis quod.. *FormOx* 414; **s1413** [Johannem de Veteri Castro] propria confessione, immo violenta et obstinata ~one, convictum ELMH. *Hen. V* 3; **1437** ~onibus hujusmodi tam variis tamque contrariis..Christi fidelium animos nutantes redditis et perplexos BEKYNTON II 40.

assertive, as an assertion of fact, positively.

quidam non ~e verum opinanter aiunt beneficia..ad hec..prodesse PULL. *Sent.* 916C; ipsum..non diu postea fore superstitem ~e proponebat GIR. *Inv.* VI 23 p. 225; **s1252** Lincolniensis episcopus ~e protestabatur quod papa ita ecclesiam..nequaquam subderet servituti M. PAR. *Min.* III 125; **a1279** voluntatem vestram..finaliter ~e et precise singnificetis *Ann. Durh.* 89; **1279** non debet jurare de credulitate set ~e *CourtR Hales* 111; non omnia dicta a philosophis ~e erant eis probata per racionem necessariam naturalem DUNS *PW* 148; vel potuit Christus hoc ~e dixisse vel non BRADW. *CD* 786D; supposicio simplex est illa qua terminus solum ~e supponit pro re universali ad extra WYCL. *Log.* I 40; scriptura sacra nihil ~e ponit nisi verum (KYN.) *Ziz.* 7.

assertivus, involving an assertion, positive, declaratory.

si tamen ad multorum ~am relationem pro certo sic H. BOS. *LM* 1298; **s1242** comes regem..per nuncios.. pluries vocavit et per cartas ~as et obligatorias persuadens ..ut in Pictaviam transfretare non omittat M. PAR. *Min.* II 460; **1293** ex ~a relacione..fidelium nostrorum *RGasc.* III 72; nullum intelligibile simplex intelligitur intelleccione ~a DUNS *Metaph.* IV 3 p. 41*d.*; **1341** qui nos..inauditos et indefensos..oppressores..falso et maliciose verbis ~is descripsit (*Lit. Regis*) BIRCHINGTON *Arch. Cant.* 37; WYCL. *Log.* II 234 (v. assensivus); intendo..capere pro ~o argumenti mei illud quod est verum (WYCL. *v. Kyn.*) *Ziz.* 474; credunt Christi fideles..quod ille oraciones "hoc est corpus meum" et "hic est sanguis meus" sunt ~e et conversive, et assercio sequitur modum conversionis (TYSS.) *Ib.* 148.

assertor, maintainer, champion. **b** affirmer.

contra hereticos pro te adstitit ~or EGB. *Pont.* 91; **c1128** hujus et †privilegia [l. privilegii] testes et ~ores sunt *E. Ch. Scot.* 74 (cf. ib. 209); regie sanctitatis ~or AILR. *Ed. Conf.* 764A; validior hic expugnator extitit quam ~or J. SAL. *Met.* 906C; hos assertores fidei stabilesque columnas NECKAM *DS* V 107; **1322** omnes ejusdem convencionis ~ores, fautores et valitores (*Indent.*) *G. Ed. II Bridl.* 83; est errorum suorum defensor pertinax et ~or OCKHAM *Pol.* I 327. **b** assertor verax ALDH. *VirgV* 940; omnis igitur ~or veritatis, te auctore, inimicus est veritatis LANFR. *Corp. & Sang.* 412C; que tantum demissa per aures.., horum non ~or sed recitator existo GIR. *TH* II *pref.* p. 75; **s1387** quia erat veritatis ~or, dicit plurima semet adversa passurum WALS. *HA* II 158.

assertorius [LL], involving an assertion, declaratory.

juramentum..~ium ut de preterito vel presenti *Fleta* 334; juramentum quoddam est ~ium et quoddam promissorium: ~ium quo juratur de veritate nobis determinata ..de presenti et de preterito, ut quando juratur quod sic est vel fuit WYCL. *Mand. Div.* 196; **s605** Augustinus..regem ad hoc inducens ut prius concessa cartis confirmaret ~iis ELMH. *Cant.* 109 (cf. ib. 144: carta ~ia).

assertum v. asserere 3b, essartum. asserum v. acerum.

asservare [CL], to preserve, watch over.

nec erat qui presideret introrsus et religionem ~aret M. Crispin *Lanfr.* 5. 31c.

assessa, ~um [*p. ppl. of* 1 assidere *as sb.*; cf. assisa], assessment, assessed payment. **b** regulation (*cf. assisa* 4).

c**1202** ~um tinctorii, textorii, fullonii debet fieri per visum xij burgensium (*Ch. Egremont*) *BBC* 160; **1359** firmas, redditus et antiquas ~as *Doc. Bev.* 1. **b** c**1202** ~um [MS.: (?) assesum] panis et cervisie debet fieri per xij burgenses *BBC* (*Egremont*) 159.

assessare, to assess: **a** (cost); **b** (person).

a 1446 reparacio aule, capelle, unius grangie et deire ibidem ~antur (*sic*) ad xxvj li. *Feod. Durh.* 184*n*. **b 1480** pro diversis personis qui ~ati fuerunt, viz. quidam eorum ad v s. et quidam ad x s., et non solverunt *Ac. Chamb. Cant.* 133; **1540** tenentur solvere pro sustentacione hominum dictorum *gallowglasses*, quando ~antur, per annum vj s. *SP Ir.* 3(3) f. 79; **1573** operarios pro vectura et portacione victualium. .~are et onerare poterit *Pat* 1104 m. 32.

assessatio, assessment.

1467 si. .dubitet de vera ~one. .expensarum *Doc. Bev.* 54.

assessibilis, liable to assessment.

assideret. .hundreda ad hoc ~ia ad certam summam solvendam *Entries* 664b.

assessinus v. assassinus.

assessio [CL], sitting near. **b** sitting, session (of court).

sedile tuum in excelso celorum fastigio eorum exornat ~o Osb. Clar. *Anne* 6. **b** s**1443** per. .attornatum suum ad singulos ~onis assignatos dies. .comparebat *Croyl. Cont.* B 520.

2 assessment.

1229 ipsos assessores et collectores habeas cum rotulis suis de ~one et recepta sua coram baronibus de Scaccario nostro *LTRMem* 11 r. 3*d*.; s**1265** quicquid per illud breve levatum fuerat assessum fuit per visnetum more debito; et. . †toto [l. tota] illa ~o. .non ascendebat ad m li. *Leg. Ant. Lond. app.* 240; **1277** vos. .ad consenciendum cuidam auxilio seu †collecto [? l. collecte] super. .clerum. .assidendo. .intendit. cum igitur hujus auxilii et collecte ~o sive consencio, si super bonis †vestrorum [l. vestrarum] domorum. . fierent (*sic*). . (*Breve Regis*) *MGL* I 123; **1309** super ~one victualium *RScot* 65b; **1457** ad contribucionem. .juxta ~onem. .commissionariorum *Lit. Cant.* III 228; **1574** (v. assessionabilis).

assessionabilis, liable to assessment.

1574 visus rotuli assessionum maneriorum. .~ium existencium coram commissionariis domine regine *AssessR. Cornw.* 3/2 (*heading*).

assessium, (?) assembly or 'assize' (*cf. assisa* 2b or 6f.) (Scot.).

s**1255** regni ~ium seu concilium exspectare formidabant Major IV 12.

assessor [CL], companion (at table). **b** assessor (leg.), colleague. **c** (*s. dub.*).

Christus. .cum apostolis et ceteris ~oribus et familiaribus suis Gir. *PI* III 30 p. 325; s**883** assederat [J. Scotus] ad mensam ante regem. . .nec vero rex verbis ejus commotus est, sed potius ipsum cum ~oribus suis commovit ad cachinnum M. Par. *Maj.* I 416. **b** †adsensore [*EE* 341. 25: adsessore], *fultemendum GlC* A 201; **10**. . adsessore, *fultemendum* WW; **1371** quod nullus electus ad consilium. . alium non electum. .sibi consiliarium vel ~orem. .adducat (*Stat. Rob. II*) *APScot* 183. **c 1218** remanentibus in officio monetarie nostre custodibus cuneorum, ~oribus, monetariis et ceteris baillivis *Pat* 138.

2 rider.

equi aurei cum ~oribus aureis W. Malm. *GR* II 170; strepe sive scansilia ~ori tergum equi prementi juvamen prebent et cingula sellam regit, maxime cum ~or rudis est in equitandi peritia Neckam *NR* II 158; s**1217** balistariis. . qui. .equos cum ~oribus suis prostraverunt in terram M. Par. *Maj.* III 21 (= Wend. II 215: sessoribus); s**1291** contigit equo cespitante ~orem. .in terram allidi W. Guisb. 233; s**1315** terra. .liquefacta. .equos Francorum. . cum suis ~oribus vivos absorbebat *Flor. Hist.* III 171.

3 one who puts in place, (w. *ferculorum*) server.

senescallus convenire debet singulis noctibus. .servientes, ~orem ferculorum, pincernam, panetarium *Fleta* 78; officium hostiarii est fercula conpotare que aulam ingrediantur et inde testimonium ~ori perhibere in compoto cotidiano *Ib.* 79.

4 assessor (of tax or sim.).

1232 provisum est. .quod. .quadragesima hoc modo assideatur et colligatur: viz. quod de qualibet villa. .eligantur iiij de. .legalioribus hominibus una cum prepositis. . per quorum sacramentum quadragesima pars omnium mobilium. .assideatur. .in prescencia militum ~orum ad hoc assignatorum. . .et deponatur pecunia per eosdem ~ores in aliquo loco tutiori ejusdem ville *Cl* 155; **1313** levacio tallagii. .assessi super eosdem homines per ~ores nostros *Reg. Carl.* II 80; **1321** per ~ores et consensum poletariorum emendata fuit assisa *MGL* II 306; **1335** rex ~oribus et receptoribus illius pecunie summe quam homines de com. Kanc' nobis concesserunt *RScot* 369a; s**1342** ~ores et collectores. .none. .in com. Ebor' per regem commissi. .nos. .injuste distrinxerunt *Meaux* III 25.

assessum v. assessa. assessus v. 1 assidere.

assestrix [CL; *infl. by* assistere], one who sits beside (f.). **b** (w. ref. to *Wisdom* ix 4). **c** helper (f.).

letatur mater †assistria [? l. assistrix] quod famula sua desuper visitatur W. Cant. *Mir. Thom.* V 13. **b** s**1309** sedium Domini assistricem exhibuerunt sibi sapienciam *Flor. Hist.* III 146; s**1399** illud. .Salamonis votum, in quo. . preoptavit. .assistricem Dei sapienciam Capgr. *Hen.* 108; **1432** pertransibat usque. .tabernaculum Domine Sapiencie, . .ubi. .videbat ipsam dominam celestem sedentem assistricem (J. Carpenter) *MGL* III 460. **c 1248** ut habeas. . Romanam ecclesiam prompto patrocinio assistricem *Mon. Hib. & Scot.* 49b; assistrices et coadjutrices in rebus tam arduis assignavit *Ps.*-Elmh. *Hen. V* 75.

assetum v. acetum. asseuratio v. assecuratio b.

asseverare [CL], to asseverate, affirm.

nobis. .laborem modi hujus gratum nobis. .fore ~antibus Bede *Cuthb.* 37 p. 278; tam facinorosam actionem ipsius consilio. .patratam fuisse ~amus T. Mon. *Will.* II 14 p. 100; **1177** episcopi in verbo veritatis ~abunt et laici jurabunt quod. .hoc inter nos dicent (*Tractatus*) Gir. *PI* II 5; adstruit, affirmat, asseverat, tria sunt hec, / asserit est quartum, que signant quatuor unum Garl. *Syn.* 99. 1579c.

asseviare, assew- v. essew- asseym- v. essaim-. asseysona v. assaisiona.

asshelarium [OF *aisselier* < axillaris], ashlar, squared stone.

1253 pro mm . .pedibus de asseler' *Ac. Build. Hen. III* 226; **1318** quarrerario pro petra de Reygate ab eo empta, . .viz. pro crestis, scutis, corbellis, angularibus, ~iis et aliis diversis necessariis. .ad batellamenta parve aule *KRAc* 468/20 f. 13*d*.; **1420** pro ccc achellariis ex convencione cum eo [latamo] †facto [? l. facta] xlv s. *Ac. Durh.* 270; **1450** pro xxxvj ulnis de perpent' achillar'. .; pro factura lv ulnarum de parapent' achillari *Hist. Durh. app.* cccxxvi.

assia v. 1 assa. assiamentum v. aisiamentum. assiatio v. asciatio. assiator v. essaiator.

assibilare [CL], to whisper. **b** to blow softly. **c** (fig.) to flatter.

s**1091** fuit vir ille [H. Losinga] magnus. .simonie fomes, . .principum favori non leves promissiones ~ans W. Malm. *GR* IV 338. **b** assibilat Eurus Hanv. III 276. **c** non sum . .cujus facunda smaragdus / disputet in digitis, vulgique adsibilet aures / attonitas gemmis *Ib.* I 243.

assiccare [CL], to shrivel.

membris ~atis vigor succrevit W. Cant. *Mir. Thom.* II 43.

1 †assida, ~ia, ostrich.

est animal quod dicitur ~a, quod Greci stratcamelon vocant, Latini vero struction; habet quidem pennas, set non volat, pedes autem cameli similes *Best.* 35a (cf. ib.: ~ia).

2 assida v. 2 assisa.

assidatus, settled, occupied.

12. . unam placeam terre nostre adhuc non ~am *AncD* C 3881.

assidella [CL gl. mensa assidela], sideboard, table or (?) trestle.

syde borde or tabyle, ~a PP; **1446** unam longam tabulam mensalem cum duabus ~is *Cl* 96 m. 26*d*. (= *MonA* VI 1427b: †assidillis); assedella, A. *a table dormant* WW; *a burde dormande*, . .*a syde burde*, . .*a tabyldormande*, ~a *CathA*.

assidentia, putting (material) in place.

1266 in constructione vij^{c} perticatarum novi parci de Kincairdin, cum cariagio et ~ia *ExchScot* 21.

1 assidēre [CL; *some forms might be referred to* 2 assidĕre; v. et. assessa], to sit beside. **b** to sit (beside) in court (leg.). **c** to occupy a see (eccl.).

faverunt adsidentes quique sive adstantes Bede *HE* III 25 p. 189; dum adsiderem illi *Ib.* V 3; corpori flentes adsederant *Ib.* V 12; **793** magistris adsidete [v.l. adsedete] Alcuin *Ep.* 19 p. 55; ad pedes archiepiscopi ~ebat W. Fitzst. *Thom.* 48; a**1250** duo seniores qui dextra levaque ei [abbati] habent assedere (*Cust. Cant. Compend.*) *Cust. Westm. app.* 263. **b** vobis qui adsidetis presentibus protestor quia hoc observare tempus. .volo Bede *HE* V 21 p. 345; †**1084** (12c) ~entibus et assentientibus. .archiepiscopis *Feod. Durh.* xlvii; inter duos principaliter. .pugna committitur, thesaurarium scilicet et vicecomitem qui ~et ad compotum residentibus aliis tanquam judicibus *Dial. Scac.* I 1b; principaliter resident, immo et presidet, . .capitalis justitia; huic autem ~ent. .quidam qui majores. . videntur in regno. . .~ent, inquam, ad discernenda jura *Ib.* I 4 bc; **1205** quod assedebo ad Scaccarium suum per xv dies. .quando michi preceperit *Pat* 55b; **1238** nullus baronum nostrorum ibidem [in Scaccario]. .residentium vel eorum qui. .ibidem deservire et ~ere tenentur *LTRMem* 12 r. 9*d*.; **1309** tunc debent justiciarii una cum militibus et magnatibus assedentibus in Banco ad placita facere recordum hujus (*JustIt*) *S. Jers.* XVIII 31 (= *PQW* 826a: †assindentibus); **1334** in contemptu regis et justiciariorum suorum hic ~encium *SelCKB* V 80; a**1350** quod in correccionibus faciendis rectores debent ~ere cancellario *Stat. Cantab.* 322. **c** s**1093** [Anselmus] VII kal. Octobris Cantuarie assedit W. Malm. *GP* I 49.

2 to sit on, bestride (a horse). **b** to sit before, besiege.

1387 ~ens bonum equum. .aufugit *Dieul.* 143v. **b** assint et lancee, . .sudes ferri, clave nodose, . .quibus assultus ~entium elidantur Neckam *Ut.* 104; **1221** de castro de S. ~endo et diruendo *Cl* 474b; **1271** quando. . percepit quod domus insultata fuit et assessa *SelCCoron* 29.

3 to seat, cause to sit (leg.). **b** to settle (a resident). **c** to post (a guard).

1219 quia vicecomes assedit comitatum infra tres septimanas, in misericordia *BNB* II 39; **1265** ipsos in loco quo placita Judeorum. .consueverunt teneri tanquam justiciarios ad placita illa tenenda assignatos vice nostra ~eri faciatis *Cl* 52; **1321** postquam major et cives assessi fuerant *MGL* II 295. **b 1204** assedit ipsam Agnetem in domo sua, donec amota fuit per Hugonem *CurR* III 126; **1207** pro licentia faciendi domos et homines ~endi super terram suam. .ad defensionem bosci sui *Pipe* 124. **c** [marescallus] in crepusculo insidias assedebit et in aurora eas levabit *Fleta* 69.

4 to set in place. **b** (?) to fit together. **c** (p. ppl.) settled, compact.

1189 ille qui velit arcum habere inveniet liberam petram. . et arcus de communi custo ~eatur (*Assisa domorum*) *MGL* I 322 (= *Leg. Ant. Lond. app.* 207: assedeatur; cf. et. *EHR* XVII 507); c**1200** tria retia libere ~enda in aqua de Rible *Cart. Cockersand* 410; **1243** iiij imagines fieri faciat in. . capella deauratas et eas ~eri locis quibus prius hujusmodi imagines rex poni disposuerat *Cl* 39; **1259** ~eri faciat lapides preciosos et camautos in feretro B. Edwardi *Cl* 223; **1292** pro virga, capite et imaginibus. .crucis. .~endis (*KRAc* 353/19) *Manners* 132; s**1305** caput sic abscissum †assedatur [? l. assedeatur] super pontem Londoniensem *Ann. Lond.* 142; **1327** cuidam cementario pro reparacione murorum pro dicto maeremio ~endo *LTRMem* 99 r. 122*d*.; si tamen assessa sint pre manibus tua dona, / tunc potes assisis sumere lucra tuis Gower *VC* VI 425. **b 1273** in carucis carpentandis et ~endis xiiij d. *MinAc* 931/22. **c** [tempus erit] ad seminandum cum terra fuerit assessa et non concava *Fleta* 162.

5 to settle or stock (land). **b** to settle (land or rent) upon someone, to let or lease (*cf. assedare*). **c** (absol.) to make a settlement. **d** to assess (land) for taxation.

in ipsa terra. .moris est ut ad terram ~endam [AS: *to landsetene*] dentur ei duo boves et una vacca et vj oves et vij acre seminate in sua virgata terre (*Quad., Rect.*) *GAS* 447. **b 1154** manerium rex Stephanus dedit et assedit eis pro c m. *Regesta* III 206; **1203** mandamus vobis quod in escaetis nostris ~eatis Hasculillo. .xl li. redditus quas ei dedimus pro servicio suo *Pat* 23a; **1214** assedebimus. .Roberto. .cc libratas terre *Ib.* 138a; **1218** ~eatis rationabiliter Margarete . .tres carrucatas terre *Pat* 162; **1254** exceptis d li. terre quas ~ere tenemur. .Galfrido. .in terra vasta Hibernie *RGasc.* I 309 (cf. *CalPat* 270); **1227** salvis firmis suis assisis in toftis. .et salvis illis toftis quos dictus W. B. et heredes sui postea assedebunt *BBC* (*Chesterfield*) 54; **1281** mandavimus quod. .placias ibidem ~eatis et. .baronibus edificandas et inhabitandas committatis *Ib.* (*Winchelsea*) 2; **1294** ad terras extend[endas] et †assend'. . .ad terras †sedend', . .ad terras predictas †assend' *KRAc* 331/2 (cf. *Doc. Scot.* p. 430); **1359** allocantur computanti, pro expensis locum tenentis camerarii assedentis terras regis *ExchScot* 581. **c 1292** rex Scocie. .md li. . .annui redditus in dotalium. .assignare tenebitur, de quibus. .in locis infrascriptis. .~ebit (*Confoederatio*) *Plusc.* VIII 19. **d** s**1284** fuit scutagium levatum . .et fuit quodlibet feudum militare integrum assessum tunc ad xl s. Thorne 1939.

6 to fix, appoint (a day). **b** to fix (a standard; *cf. assisa* 4).

c**1205** assedi in eo [burgo] quolibet die Sabbati diem fori *BBC* (*Ayr*) 172; **1217** assedit eis diem in curia sua *BNB* III 306. **b 1228** assisam de pane et cervisia, quam episcopus ~et in burgo suo, prior et ballivi sui. .~eri et servari faciunt in terra sua *Feod. Durh.* 283.

7 to assess, impose (a tax, fine or sim.). **b** to assess (a price). **c** to assess, put a price on (commodities). **d** to assess (damages).

1175 de c s. de T. D., quia assedit tensariam in dominio regis *Pipe* 69; **1217** talliagium ~entes super dominica nostra *Pat* 170; **1222** debet hec collecta ~eri in qualibet villa. .per capellanum et duos probos. .homines. .et colligi in festo S. Mich. *Cl* 516b; **1227** occasione tallagii quod nuper ~eri fecistis. .in episcopatu Dunelmensi, super feoda ipsius [Ricardi]. ., cum hujusmodi feoda talliari non debeant, tallagium assedistis *Cl* 9; **1229** quod predicta pecunia ~eatur per totam universitatem civitatis Dublin' secundum facultates singulorum *Cl* 186; **1232** provisum est. .quod predicta quadragesima hoc modo ~eatur et colligatur: . .quadragesima pars omnium mobilium. .taxetur et ~eatur super singulas [villas] in presentia militum assessorum ad hoc assignatorum *Cl* 155 (cf. M. Par. *Maj.* III 231); **1258** ~et tota curia. .ad expensas dictorum iiij militum. .ad quamlibet hydam ij sol[idos] *SelPlMan* 62; **1260** racione xij denariorum assessorum per annum ad opus regis super eadem terra *Cl* 71; **1309** x quarteria frumenti. .assedenda. . super terras *S. Jers.* XVIII 205; **1313** (v. assessor 4); s**1318** malefactores. .collectas et tallagia diversa inter se assederunt ad summam xxvj li. Thorne 2035; omnes. .burgi [Francie] solvunt regi annuatim ingentes summas super eos assessas pro stipendiis hominum ad arma Fortescue *LLA* 35 (cf. ib.: tallagia. .assessa ad opus regis); **1469** amerciamenta, fines, forisfacturas et deperdita. .super quascumque personas. .adjudicata, assessa sive afferata (*Pat*) *Foed.* XI 644b; **1559** amerciamentorum. .super hujusmodi delinquentes. .~endorum et imponendorum (*Pat*) *Gild Merch.* II 88. **b 1356** precium vinorum assessum (*LBLond.* G) *MGL* I 710; non patitur rex [Francie] quenquam regni sui sal edere quod non emat ab ipso rege precio ejus solum arbitrio assesso Fortescue *LLA* 35. **c 1309** vos. .victualia nostra eis super vadiis suis liberata in eisdem vadiis suis in nimis gravi precio assedetis *RScot* 65b. **d 1356** ~ent damnum ipsius abbatis. .ad dim. m. (*PlRCP*) *G. S. Alb.* III 46; **1436** ~ent damna ipsius. .ad xx s. (*Assisa*) Amund. II 125; **1472** ~ent dampna. .per tres sol. (*Piepowder*) *Law Merch.* I 129; asseserunt (*sic*) damna ipsius A. ad iiij m. *Entries* 59.

8 to assess (persons): **a** (for payment); **b** (for arms).

a s**1272** illis civibus qui ultra †contra [l. quod] facultates sue sufficerent fuissent assessi in prestitis antea factis *Leg. Ant. Lond.* 149; **1315** vos..homines et tenentes..episcopi.. ad quintamdecimam..nobis prestandam..~eri facitis et taxari *Reg. Heref.* 516 (cf. ib.: proviso quod prefati homines ..ad vicesimam ad opus nostrum prestandam ~eantur et taxentur); **1350** in auxilium solucionis summarum ad †quos eedem ville seu homines earumdem ad decimam et quintamdecimam jam currentes sunt assessi (*Pat*) *Foed.* V 695. **b** **1333** pro remissione..de uno hobelario et sex sagittariis ad quos per arraiatores hominum..assessi fueritis *RScot* 228a; **1333** ad ipsos..armis competentibus muniri et ad arma ~eri faciendos *Ib.* 250a; **1338** xij sagittarii..ad quos homines de dictis partibus..assedistis *Ib.* 552a; **1511** ad monstrum..faciendum, ..assignavimus quoscumque duos aut tres vestrum ad omnes alios et singulos vestrum similiter mutuo et se invicem triandum, ~endum et arraiandum .., ita quod..triati, assessi, arraiati, armati et preparati prompti sint..ad nobis..serviendum (*Pat*) *Foed.* XIII 300b.

2 assīdĕre [CL], to sit (leg.).

1336 pro stipendio domus sue ubi justiciarii ad billas ~erunt *SelCKB* V 88.

2 to seat. **b** to cause to sit (leg.).

1292 assisus fuit inter duos fratres ad faciendum legem *Rec. Leic.* I 224; **1336** ipsam ~erunt super quendam palefridum suum sellatum *SelCKB* V 91. **b** **1233** sequi debent curiam predicti G. rationabiliter assisam et summonitam *CurR* XV 137; s**1234** officium cancellarii..et omnia officia regia ordinata sunt et assisa in Scaccario M. Par. *Maj.* III 296n.; **1275** [rex] recipit..de turno vicecomitis assiso ad eundem terminum vij s. j d. *Hund.* I 97.

3 to set in place, site. **b** to set (gems).

1235 ~erunt domos suas versus villam *CurR* XV 1768. **b** **1216** zonam de corio..cum petris preciosis intaillatis assisis in cassa *Pat* 173a.

4 to settle (land or rent), to rent or lease.

1181 fuerunt due hyde apud Luffehale, quarum una fuit in dominio, altera assisa *Dom. S. Paul.* 141; **1185** apud Couele..habentur iiij hide, quarum due sunt in dominio et due assise ab hominibus. ..apud Meritune..sunt vij hide, quarum due sunt in dominio et v assise de hominibus *Rec. Templars* 41, 44 (cf. *Ambrosden* I 197); **1200** libratas terre.. quas Hugo dedit..tenendas..pro quibusdam calcaribus deauratis annuatim reddendis eidem Hugoni vel heredibus suis assisis *RChart* 50b; **1215** donec in alio loco tantam terram ei ~erimus *Cl* 215b; **1222** essarta assisa tempore W. thesaurarii firmarii *Dom. S. Paul.* 12; **1260** cum xxx acris terre assisis in eadem villa de villenagio nostro per O. quondam firmarium de H. *BBC* (*Helston*) 336.

5 to fix, establish, ordain: **a** (a fair); **b** (a day); **c** (w. *quod*).

a c**1220** in nundinis assisis in nativitate S. Johannis Baptiste *BBC* (*Chester*) 214. **b** precipietur vicecomiti quod ~at diem certum quod sit coram justiciariis *Fleta* 379. **c** **1204** assisum est per consilium fidelium nostrorum quod omnes mercatores..possint salvo venire..; item assisum est quod nullus forinsecus mercator aliquem falsum denarium..apportet..in Angliam *Pat* 42b; **1205** assisum est de moneta quod vetus moneta currat unde.. *Ib.* 54b.

6 to assess, impose, levy (a tax or fine); **b** (p. ppl. *assisus*) fixed (of rent or payment).

1184 cives Londonienses debent..de auxilio civitatis quod prius assisum fuit per wardas civitatis *Pipe* 139; in terra sua de R. sunt v m. assise in terris et molendinis *RDomin.* 20; **1201** de talliagio quod assisum fuit super communam Lincolnie *CurR* I 418; **1220** duo milites per quos [caruagium] illud in balliva mea est assisum (*AncC* I 82) *RL* I 163; **1225** reddent vobis milites illi, statim ex quo quintadecima fuerit assisa, scripta et rotulos suos inde †factas *Pat* 561; s**1229** juramento..prestito quod rationabiliter ~erent tallagium.., ~erunt tantum lxiij s. *Ann. Dunstable* 121; s**1235** assisum fuit scutagium per totum regnum, sc. de quolibet feodo ij m. M. Par. *Min.* II 380; **1269** justiciarii..super..Eliam c s. ~erunt *Cl* 170; c**1270** abbas..debet c s. de tallagio super eum assiso *Reg. S. Aug.* 6; provisum est quod communes misericordie vel fines comitatuum..per sacramenta..proborum hominum de comitatu eodem ~antur super eos qui contribuere debent *Fleta* 64; non ferentes gravamina regis Anglie Johannis et ejus abusivas consuetudines nequiter assisas *Plusc.* VII 4; justiciarii ~erunt finem *Entries* 348b. **b** **1176** baillivi domini regis respondeant ad Scaccarium..de ~o redditu (*Ass. Clarendon*) *G. Hen. II* I 110; recepit inde xij li. de ~o redditu *RDomin.* 2; reddidit..xv li. de firma ~a *Ib.* 19; **1201** de tanta pecunia quanta perveniet per tres annos de liberationibus asisis quas idem R. habet per annum de predicta custodia [domorum de Westm' et gaole de Flete] *Pat* 4b; **1203** r. c. ..de xl s. de auxilio ~o *RScacNorm* II 507; **1234** elemosinarius..elemosinam..integre in clericos et scolares, reclusas et liberationes ~as et in pauperes mendicantes exspendat (*Vis. Bury*) *EHR* XXVII 736; **12..** reddendo inde nobis..iij s. ..et iiij d. de gabulo ~o *Reg. Malm.* II 69; **1242** salvo nobis..quicquid augere poterimus in redditibus ~is in burgagiis in terris nostris forinsecis *BBC* (*Plympton*) 312; **1322** ita tamen quod ipse reddet omnem redditum suum ~um, set non..erit in servicio domini *CBaron* 135.

7 to assess (persons) for payment.

s**1229** ditiores [sc. burgenses] burgi non erant assisi nisi ad iij s. *Ann. Dunstable* 121.

assidiare [cf. insidiari], to waylay.

1195 in felonia ~iavit eum et voluit eum percutere et occidere *CurR PR* XIV 97 (cf. ib.: ~iaverunt et eum robaverunt).

assidilla v. assidella.

assidualiter, assiduously.

1415 qui circa me ~er tempore infirmitatis mee existebant *Reg. Cant.* II 75.

assiduare, to practise assiduously. **b** (w. inf.) to continue, persist.

jejunia, vigilias, orationes, elemosinas..~abant Gosc. *Aug. Maj.* 65A; ~abat piissime devotionis orationem R. Cold. *Cuthb.* 51; seviens ac furens hunc ritum ~averat *Ib.* 114; quod ~et vomitum cum repletur Bacon IX 47. **b** non ~et intueri rem unam a qua non avertat [oculos] *Id.* V 85.

assiduatio, prolonged practice or use.

~o comestionis ejus Bacon IX 71; ~o odoris rute est experta in hoc Gad. 117. 2.

assidue [CL], assiduously, persistently, constantly.

quos magus assidue strofosus misit ad almam Aldh. *VirgV* 1859; mulier ista..curiam ~e sequebatur Gir. *TH* II 20; **1251** W. de D. cum nullo est ~e, set aliquando huc aliquando illuc *SelPlForest* 102.

assiduitas [CL], perseverance, constant practice.

illius quoque opinio crebra lectionis ~ate divulgetur Aldh. *VirgP* 49.

assiduus [CL], assiduous, persistent. **b** (of person) constant, permanent. **c** (w. dat. or gen.) persistently devoted. **d** (sb. m.) regular retainer.

cantibus assiduis et psalmi carmine crebro Aldh. *VirgV* 1304; orationibus..~is, vigiliis et jejuniis serviendo Bede *HE* I 26; caetera quae [trinitas nostrae naturae] de sollicitudine ~a animae circa corpus suum..accipit Eriug. *Per.* 581C; horrea..~a non adjectione referta Gir. *EH pref.* p. 223. **b** quicunque manens in villa ~us *DB* I 1. **c** **1383** scolares disciplinE sue imposterum sint ~i *Lit. Cant.* II xxxii. **d** s**1141** ~orum paucos adducens, convenarum dispersam multitudinem congregans H. Hunt. *HA* VIII 17.

assieta [OF *assiete*], condition (C.I.).

1368 si tria alia quarteria frumenti censualis fuerint vendicioni exposita in bona assisia et ~a *Cart I. Norm.* 214.

2 assignment of dowry (Fr.).

1475 Ludovicus..Elizabetham..ad lx millia li. redditus annui in ~a..annuatim dotabit (*Chanc. Misc.* 30/10) *Foed.* XII 20.

assignabilis, assignable, attributable.

infinitum est quod omne finitum datum secundum nullam mensuram terminatam precise excedit sed ultra omnem habitudinem ~em adhuc excedit Duns *Prim. Princ.* IV p. 778.

assignamentum, assignment, grant.

1391 in una tallia de Recepta Scaccarii regis facta domino de majori summa de quodam ~o sibi facto per ipsum regem *Ac. H. Derby* 142; **1425** cum nos..assignaverimus vobis.. summam mm m. .., de quo quidem ~o vos solucionem summe predicte nondum habere potuistis *RScot* 253a; a**1509** collacionum, ~orum et concessionum aliquorum debitorum aut summarum monete per litteras patentes *Entries* 102.

assignanter, specifically.

1483 pro suis serviciis..et ~er..pro certa summa pecunie nobis..persolutis *Reg. Aberbr.* II 192.

assignare [CL], to assign, allot, grant. **b** to assign a debt (*cf.* A. Steel *Receipt of the Exchequer*, Cambridge 1954, pp. xxix *seqq.*). **c** (w. *ad*) to assign for a purpose. **d** to assign, appoint (a time). **e** (fig., w. *locum*) to assign a place.

insule..pars..quam..a..Locrino, cui ~ata fuerat, Loegriam dixere Gir. *TH* I 2; **1214** reddendo annuatim dicto R. et heredibus suis vel cui assignare voluerit ij s. vj d. *FormA* 116 (cf. ib. 158); **1221** ~avit ipsis hominibus aliam viam *PlCrGlouc* 81; **1258** assingnavimus in subsidium.. sustentacionis scolarium..c li. *Deeds Balliol* 331; **1301** ante obitum suum ~avit et in testamento suo legavit totam terram suam perquisitam..filiis predicti R. *SelPlMan* 127; **1329** percipienti annuatim [xx li.]..pro toto tempore vite sue sibi ~atas per camerarium *ExchScot* 168; **1330** manerium ~atum fuit..Marie..nomine dotis; et reversio..manerii.. ~ata fuit..comiti Athol' *PQW* 640a; **1539** de ecclesia.. nichil, quia ~atur fratribus nostris studentibus in Oxonia *Feod. Durh.* 328; ~amus appellanti totum et integrum processum *Praxis* 238. **b** **1217** habere faciatis..Falkesio.. debitum quod..patri nostro debuistis, quod ipse pater noster eidem F. de vobis ~avit capiendum *Pat* 29; **1292** de illis clxviij li. in quibus nobis tenemini, ..~avimus magistro J. ..xx li. percipiendas per manus vestras *RScot* 13a; **1327** de debito predicto ~antur executoribus testamenti J. nuper episcopi Norwyci cxlix li. *LTRMem* 99 r. 150. **c** **1252** custodi domorum que ~ate sunt ad..hospicium bajulatoris sigilli regis *Cl* 44; **1283** de redditu ad bracinum ~ato *Dom. S. Paul.* 166; **1431** in una pietancia solita dari conventui.., modo ~ata ad sustentacionem vestimentorum altaris S. Nicholai *Ac. Durh.* 288. **d** parti petenti brevis dies fuit ~atus *State Tri. Ed. I* 23; a**1350** magistri..certum diem eis [procuratoribus] ~ent *Stat. Cantab.* 319; **1516** ~etur ei unus solus terminus ad producendum..testes *StatOx* 332. **e** sinaphe Phitagoras inter ea..laudat et primum locum ~at *Alph.* 172.

2 to assign, refer (by inclusion). **b** to assign, attribute (a cause or reason). **c** (w. acc. and inf.). **d** to specify. **e** to predicate, attach as predicate or epithet.

placuit..ut..idem annus sequentis regis..regno adsignaretur Bede *HE* III 1; utpote..illam in Pascha diem adsignent primam (*Lit. Ceolfridi*) *Ib.* V 21. **b** medici.. fracto interius apostemati causam saniei ~abant et causam non curam inveniebant W. Cant. *Mir. Thom.* VI 37; cause quare sancti sic affirmant..possunt ~ari Bacon *Maj.* III 44; cum hujus [Pape] raciones quare hoc voluit ~antur Ockham *Pol.* I 22. **c** quidam..siccitatem et humiditatem causas istorum motuum esse ~ant Gilb. II 124. 1; hanc [racionem] ~at fuisse studium in originalibus sanctorum Ockham *Dial.* 752. **d** super allegoriis circa avium naturas ~atis in prima Topographie distinctione Gir. *RG* II 20; **1245** causam appellationis in scriptis ~are deproperet (*Conc. Lugdun.*) M. Par. *Maj.* IV 470; dicendo quod omnes fuerunt procurati absque ~ando certam calumpniam contra quamlibet personam *State Tri. Ed. I* 35; volentes diffinicionem dominii ~are, de dominio secundum quod accipitur in jure distinguunt Ockham *Pol.* I 308. **e** considerandum ..si huic ut in alio genere assignationum, illi ut in alio, velut si uni ut ad quid sit ~andum, alii ut ad quale vel quantum vel aliquod reliquorum secundum que genera assignationum variari docebimus Balsh. *AD* 52.

3 to appoint (a person to office or task). **b** (w. inf.). **c** (w. *coram*) to summon to appear. **d** to assign (a creditor) as recipient of a sum. **e** (w. *ad*) to appoint as keeper of (land). **f** to appoint (a friar) as lector to convent (*cf. Doc. Francisc.* pp. 62–3).

1173 ad arbitrium abbatis de C. et..archidiaconi Sar' vel aliorum legitimorum per regem ~atorum (*Chirog.*) *G. Hen. II* I 41; **1242** G. ..~atus est ad recipiendum aurum regine *RGasc.* I 13; **1279** coram justiciariis assingnatis ad assisas capiendas *PQW* 759b; **1292** Rogero..et Osberto..ad querelas..conquerencium infra..regnum Scocie ~atis *RScot* 8a; **1359** justiciarii ~ati de operariis et mensuris (*DL Chanc. R.*) *EHR* XXI 525; **1374** J. M. et J. S. ~antur prepositi *Hal. Durh.* 123; **1511** (v. arraiare 1a). **b** **1219** rex ~avit Michaelem..esse servientem suum ad custodiendum forestas *Pat* 196. **c** **1262** volumus quod..milites..ponantur in defaltam seu coram vobis [justiciariis] ~entur *Cl* 23. **d** **1269** fiant littere patentes de subscriptis mercatoribus ~andis ad denarios primo levandos de proximo itinere justiciariorum.. *Cal. Liberate* VI 914 (cf. ib.: de quibus m et xxx li. [mercatores] petunt ~ari ad predicta itinera). **e** **1217** concedimus ut..F. et filium ejus ad totam terram quam de vobis tenemus ~etis, quousque de predicto debito ..eis fuerit satisfactum *Pat* 115. **f** mihi bonum videtur quod [frater Thomas] ~etur fratribus Oxonie pro lectore Ad. Marsh *Ep.* 198.

4 to commit, entrust: **a** (a person); **b** (oxen).

a filiam suam Christo consecrandam Paulino episcopo adsignavit Bede *HE* II 9. **b** primo mane adsigno eos [boves] aratori [AS: *ic betæce hig þam yrþlincge*] Ælf. *Coll.* 91.

5 (p. ppl. as sb. f.) authority, licence. **b** (p. ppl. as sb. m.) assignee, assign, grantee.

convencio talis erit quod mihi cartam unam de sanguine tuo facias quod, si diem inter nos non tenueris, ~atam libere habeam sine condicione omnes carnes tui corporis evellere *Latin Stories* 116. **b** c**1200** ipsi et heredes sui vel sui ~ati *BBC* (*Walsall*) 49; **1208** volo..quod..Christiana et heredes sui vel ~ati sui habeant et teneant..in perpetuum omnia predicta tenementa *RChart* 182b; **1221** cccc libras.. reddet eidem episcopo..vel ejus ~ato *Pat* 319; c**1250** non solum terram illam dedit..Gaufrido set ~atis suis, et recognitum est..quod Gaufridus fecit ~atum de..Willelmo *BNB* III 298 (cf. ib.: Gaufridus eandem terram ~avit.. Willelmo..et..per assignationem illam fuit..Willelmus in seisina); **1256** solvemus illi quamdiu vixerit et ~atis suis post mortem suam *Ch. Sal.* 325; **1266** mihi..sive meis assingnatis *Cl* 252; **1327** terram..Ade et asingnatis suis.. warantizabimus *FormA* 120; s**1387** per sufficientem securitatem inde dicto duci et ~atis suis factam *Eul. Hist. Cont.* III 359; **1560** cessionarium, donatarium et ~atum *Scot. Grey Friars* II 247.

6 to sign or seal. **b** to mark (? w. a stamp or print).

1042 (12c) hanc territoriam scedulam signo sanctae crucis diligenter adsignare curavi *CD* 763; **1089** haec carta manu sua firmata est ac sigillo suo ~ata *Regesta* I 310. **b** **1517** duo dorsaria ~ata cum canibus *Ac. Durh.* 293.

assignatio [CL], assignment, allotment, transfer, grant. **b** (of debt). **c** appointment, allocation (of place). **d** appointment (of time), assignation, tryst.

1269 dominus S. ..fecit homagium..abbati..de quarta parte feodi j militis per resignacionem et assingnacionem domini R. ..et..intravit dictus dominus S. ad faciendum dicto..abbati..per predictam resignacionem et assingnacionem dicti R. servicium j paris calcarium deauratorum *Reg. S. Aug.* 604; **1270** liberate..viij^xx li. ..juxta ~onem quam eisdem militibus fecimus pro feodo suo quod de nobis percipere consueverunt *Liberate* 46 m. 6; **1291** cum G. .. assignasset..Aysivo..c li. ..percipiendas annuatim, unde ..Aysivo a retro sunt ccccl li. de ~one eidem facta per.. G. *RGasc.* III 9; **1297** mandamus vobis quod..assignari faciatis..Marie..x marcatas terre per..extentam faciendam, ..proviso..quod feoda militum..que nobis volumus reservari infra extentam de ~one predicta faciendam nullatenus sint contenta *RScot* 38a; **1323** ultra donacionem et assingnacionem predictas *Couch. Kirkstall* p. 301; **1330** libertates..quas..Maria tenet in dotem..ex ~one..patris sui *PQW* 640a; **1513** in pensionibus et stipendiis ex imposicione et ~one..prioris in..sustentacionem famulorum *Ac. Durh.* 662. **b** **1269** fiat ~o mercatoribus de Ypra de dcxl li. ..pro pannis ab eisdem captis ad opus domini regis *Cal. Liberate* VI 914 (cf. assignare 3d); **1292** mandamus quod predictas xx li. prefato J. habere faciatis juxta ~onem nostram predictam *RScot* 13 (cf. assignare 1b); **1313** salvis.. civibus..~onibus eis per nos..factis pro debitis de quibus (pro nobis) satisfacere manuceperunt (*Pat*) *MGL* III 434; **1327** de arreragiis illis habere faciant prefato A. ciiij^{xx} li., que ei a retro sunt de ~one predicta *LTRMem* 99 r. 135; **1336** vobis inde festinam solucionem sive ~onem..faciemus *RScot* 446a; **1447** pro omnimodis debitis et compotis nobis debitis..que vigore litterarum nostrarum..aut per estallamenta sive ~ones respectuata existunt *MonA* III 357; **1583** vigore..litterarum ~onis in ea parte concessarum *Pat* 1235 m. 25. **c** **1426** contra ~onem loci hujusmodi.. obiciendo *Reg. Cant.* I 100; **1429** proviso quod seniores socii dicte domus in ~one camerarum..preferantur (*Otryngham Book*) *Arch. Hist. Camb.* II 677; **1432** nemo post sessionem magistrorum sedere presumat..nisi per ~onem servientum communium *StatOx* 245. **d** **c1337** quod nullus veniat ad civitatem ad attrahendos homines in ~ones (*LBLond.* F 161) *MGL* I 641.

2 assignment (of cause).

in causarum ~one nec sufficienti nec competenti, ne verum ex toto publicaret GIR. *GE* I 18; argumentum facit fidem in re dubia per ~onem cause et rationis BACON *Tert.* 103.

3 appointment (of a person): **a** (to office); **b** (to a task); **c** to a lectorship (*cf. assignare* 3e).

a **1335** cum assignaverimus Robertum..ad eligendum.. hobelarios, ..in eleccione..hominum predictorum male se gessit..diversos..excessus colore ~onis predicte faciendo *RScot* 377a; **s1399** vendicavit sibi regnum..ex ~one..regis Ricardi, qui eum ore proprio assignaverat CAPGR. *Hen.* 108. **b** **s974** ejus [precentoris] ~onibus in choro tam abbas et prior quam tota cetera congregatio humiliter obediat *Croyl.* 50; proclamari fecit quod omnes..juxta ~onem capitaneorum suorum se pararent..ad assultum ELMH. *Hen. V* 29. **c** rogavit me frater Hugo..ut non displiceat sanctitati vestre fratribus injungere, quibus est assignatus pro lectore, ut..ipsum ab obligatione dicte ~onis..†absoluto [? l. absolvi] non querantur AD. MARSH *Ep.* 198.

4 commitment.

cum..habuisset nutrituram corporis Johannis filii Petri per ~onem ejusdem Petri *State Tri. Ed. I* 53.

assignator, director.

W. de Chamai, ..regalis militie dux et ~or *G. Steph.* II 93.

2 (? for *assignatus*; *cf. assignare* 5b) assignee, assign.

1285 quietumclamavi pro me et heredibus meis et †~oribus meis *Reg. Heref.* 54.

assilire [CL], **~iare** [cf. OF *assaillier*], to leap upon, mount (of stallions).

1341 pro expensis suis existent' ibidem cum stalonibus pro jumentis assaliandis *KRAc* 459/24.

2 to assault, assail: **a** (a person); **b** (a building or sim.).

a si quis alicujus curiam vel domum violenter effregerit vel intraverit ut hominem occidat vel vulneret vel assaliat, c s. regi emendat *DB* I 154b; **1091** nulli licuit in Normannia in forestis ipsius domini hominem assailire vel insidias ponere (*Consuet. Norm.*) *EHR* XXIII 507; custodiat eum [inimicum suum] septem noctibus intus nec assalliat eum [AS: *hine on ne feohte*], si ille velit immorari (*Quad.*) *GAS* 75; hamsocna est si quis alium in sua vel alterius domo cum haraido assailliaverit (*Leg. Hen.*) *Ib.* 597; rapidis furit in hostes irruptionibus, frequenter ~it et in instantia perdurat MAP *NC* IV 7; **s1306** Robertum gladio ~ivit *Meaux* II 276; ~o, *to stroke* WW. **b** Daci terram..insilientes et ~ientes H. HUNT. *HA* V *prol.* (cf. ib. VIII 18: sicut castellum solet ~iri); **s1159** ob reverenciam presencie ipsius dictus est rex Anglie..civitatem Tolosam non ~uisse DICETO *YH* II 303; **1332** navem..~ierunt *Meaux* II 365; si quis aliquem calumniari velit de haimesuckin, oportet quod propria domus ubi calumnians est manens die et nocte assaliata sit *RegiamM* IV 9. 1; **s1336** castrum de Cupro..~ire noluit *Plusc.* IX 35; **s1400** castrum de Edinburgh obsedendo ~iavit *Ib.* X 16; **1413** non erunt aliqua castra..nec aliqua fortalicia obsessa, assahilata, debellata, escalata clandestine nec furtive capta *Cl* 262 m. 13 (cf. *Foed.* VIII 618); **s1471** portam terribiliter assalientes *Croyl. Cont.* C 556.

assimilabilis, assimilable, able to be made like.

dico sicut Philosophus dicit quod 'intellectus est quodammodo omnia', id est ~is omnibus et..communicat cum corpore in passionibus, ..ipso naturali colligacione se corpore assimilante PECKHAM *QR* III 3 p. 47; causa perfeccior magis assimilat effectum ei cui est ~is quam imperfeccior DUNS *Sent.* I iii 8. 4.

assimilare [CL], to assimilate, make like. **b** to assimilate, digest (food). **c** to liken, compare. **d** (pass.) to resemble.

per omnia se Francigenis..~are AELNOTH *Cnut* 127A; ut sis celestis, non assimilare scelestis SERLO WILT. II 19; qui et in pugna sua et in palma milites suos sibimet ipsi ~at sic H. BOS. *LM* 1339; ~abitur persona verbi persone nominativi BACON XV 3; PECKHAM *QR* (v. assimilabilis); hec [necessitas sequens] ~atur consequenti logicali in consequencia logicali BRADW. *CD* 724A; omne quod vivit ~ari cupit cause prime FORTESCUE *LLA* 39. **b** inferior venter domus est organorum in quibus ~atur nutrimentum *Ps.*-RIC. *Anat.* 24; dum calor naturalis..non plene ~at sed in parte digerit adnatam pingwedinem WYCL. *Log.* III 100. **c** cui [Abimelech]..ramnorum surculus..ab Joatham adsimilabitur ALDH. *VirgP* 2 p. 68; avibus aliis ~ari possunt qui..duritiis affligi carnem eligunt GIR. *TH* I 12. **d** si potentia materie ~atur potentie divine infinite, multo magis potentia forme, quia nobilius nobiliori magis ~atur BACON *Tert.* 128; sulphur et vivum argentum, quorum primum..†~iatur semini paterno et secundum menstruo mulieris *Ps.*-GROS. 625; origanum et pulegium ~antur *SB* 32; spuma maris..assimulatur pulpe coloquintide *Ib.*40.

2 to go or come together (*cf. assemblare*).

[via regia] tanta debet esse ut inibi..bubulci de longo stumbli sui possint assimulare (*Leg. Hen.*) *GAS* 596; cum se invicem assimulassent ex utraque parte *V. Ric. II* 180.

assimilatio, assimilation, making like. **b** assimilation, digestion (of food). **c** resemblance.

oportet quod persona nominativi sit prima vel secunda cui fiat ~o BACON XV 3; intelleccio est quedam ~o ad intelligibile; sed intelligibile sufficienter de se causat sine alio agente suam ~onem in intellectu, ex quo illa ~o non est ad intellectum sed tantum ad intelligibile T. SUTTON *Quodl.* 357. **b** propter malam complexionem cutis est defectus ~onis in ipsa GILB. III 170. 2; maximus homo possibilis non posset augeri per ~onem alimenti WYCL. *Log.* II 167. **c** fleuma..vitreum sic dictum propter †caloris [? l. coloris] vitri ~onem BART. ANGL. IV 9.

assimilativus, able to assimilate, make like. **b** assimilative (of food).

esse ~um dicit racionem activi respectu assimilabilis DUNS *Metaph.* VI 3 79C. **b** virtutem ~am ut in consumptivis et ethicis confortat GILB. I 36 v. 1; virtuti digestive due obsequuntur, id est immutativa cibi..et informativa; informative autem actiones sunt quinque, et juxta eas quinquepartita virtus, sc. ~a, concavativa, perforativa, asperativa, †levitiva [l. lenitiva] *Ps.*-GROS. 469; quamdiu manet vis ~a nutriti, ut membrum secundum terre dyametrum fiat majus, tamdiu manet augmentacionis potencia WYCL. *Log.* III 113.

assimilis [CL], similar.

s1384 responderunt quod tempore treugarum nostri in mari naves depredassent..; quare..eis licuit ~e, hoc est unum pro alio, nobis inferre *V. Ric. II* 56.

assimulare v. assimilare. assindere v. 1 assidere 1b.

†assirare [(?)], to wrap.

1337 in wyvelyng' panno de canabo ad assirand' ij oneribus straminis ad bord' vertend' *Pipe* 182 r. 39*d*.

assis v. as.

1 assisa, ~ia, ~um [*p. ppl. of* 2 assidere *as sb.*], assessed tax, aid or sim. **b** assessment. **c** (w. *redditus*) fixed rent (*cf.* 2 *assidere 6b*). **d** fixed penalty.

a1120 quod ipsi canonici..liberi sint..de omnibus geldis et scotis et witis et ~is *CalCh* V 265; **1155** vic. r. c. de xv li. ..de assisa comitatus. ..idem vic. r. c. de v m. argenti de ~a de Gipeswiz *Pipe* 9 (cf. ib. 11: de vij li. ..de ~a episcopi Cicestrensis); **1157** reddent communiter cum civibus meis Lincolnie gelda mea et ~as civitatis *BBC* 108; **c1160** nec ..aliquibus operibus aut exactionibus, angariis aut ~is aliquibus homines..canonicorum gravare *Ch. Sal.* 33; **1165** vic. r. c. de ccc..li. ..de auxilio exercitus Wallie..; monetarii Lund' r. c. de xl m. de ~a ejusdem exercitus *Pipe* 33; **1168** r. c. de c li. de ~a facta super dominia episcopatus ad maritandam..filiam regis *Pipe* 168 (cf. auxilium 4a); **a1171** clamo omnes terras et homines H. episcopi Wint' quietos de tota ~a †quam per justitias meas facta est per Angliam (*Ch. Wint.*) *EHR* XXXV 399; fiunt interdum per comitatus communes ~e a justitiis errantibus, ..que ideo dicuntur communes quia, cognita summa que de comitatu requiritur, communiter ab hiis qui in comitatu fundos habent per hidas distribuitur *Dial. Scac.* I 8D (cf. *PQW* 640b [**1330**]: abbas de Rupe..clamat tenere..tenementa sua..quieta..de omni misericordia et communi ~a); **a1200** tales consuetudines capiet de hominibus regni mei quales capiuntur apud Rokesburg excepta ~a baronie sue *E. Ch. Scot.* p. 308; ut nulla exigentia omnino in dono, vel in ~a vel alia consuetudine ab episcopo vel a quolibet alio fiat in prebendis eorum [canonicorum] *Offic. Sal.* 9; **1227** nisi sit in lotto et scotto et in ~is et tallagiis cum eisdem burgensibus *BBC* (*Shrewsbury*) 286; **1255** salvis nobis talliagiis, redditibus, escaetis, wardis, maritagiis, prisis et aliis ~is nostris in villa *Ib.* (*Bamburgh*) 315. **b** **1291** tunc estimabitur quantum valere debeat annui redditus pars vendita, secundum ~iam que consuevit fieri de nemoribus in partibus illis (*Lit. Papae*) B. COTTON 192 (= *Conc.* II 180: assissam); **1310** potestatem ..assizias terrarum que nobis debent assideri..faciendi *RGasc.* IV 393. **c** de certo redditu ~e per annum *Form Man.* 12; **1412** de redditu ~e *MinAc* 856/25 m. 1. **d** **c1198** si quis eorum cessiderit (*sic*) in misericordia nostra pro assisa panis vel cervisie fracta ter, non dabit pro qualibet misericordia nisi vj d.; et si quarta vice cesiderit, faciet ~am regis *BBC* (*Walsall*) 158; **1253** faciet ~am ville pertinentem ad tale delictum (*Ch. Bolton*) *EHR* XVII 292.

2 'assize', regulation (or procedure prescribed thereby). **b** (Scot.). **c** 'assize' of the forest (*cf. StRealm* I 243). **d** (w. *aquae*) regulation of flow of water. **e** (w. *antiqua*) (?) a set of rules for chess.

s1091 (14c) Aldwinus..fecit ~as Rames' *Chr. Rams.* 340 (cf. ib. 347: iste fecit ~am domus Ramesie); [Henricus II], abolitis antiquis legibus, singulis annis novas leges, quas ~as vocavit, edidit R. NIGER 168; **1164** hec est ~a quam dominus rex Henricus consilio archiepiscoporum et episcoporum et abbatum ceterorumque baronum suorum statuit pro pace servanda et justitia tenenda (*Ass. Clarendon*) R. HOWD. II 248; **1166** homines de Tichesoura debent v m. quia noluerunt jurare ~am regis *Pipe* 65; **s1176** venit.. rex usque Northamtoniam..et per consilium comitum et baronum et militum et hominum suorum hanc subscriptam ~am fecit et eam teneri precepit *G. Hen. II* I 107; **s1181** rex ..fecit hanc ~am de armis habendis in Anglia *Ib.* 278; quanta [misericordia] esse debeat per nullam ~am generalem determinatum est GLANV. IX 10; **s1189** dicta provisio et ordinatio [super clausturis faciendis etc.] vocata est ~a; ad quam ~am persequendam et ad effectum perducendam electi sunt xij viri, aldermanni de civitate *MGL* I 320; **1194** jurandum est ab omnibus quod non torniabunt antequam domino regi de pecunia sua secundum ~am domini regis inde factam..satisfecerint (*Forma Pacis*) DICETO II lxxxi; **1201** purget se per aquam per ~am [sc. de Clarendon'] *Sel PlCrown* 1; **1219** de catallis..que amovit de..terra contra ~am regni *CurR* VIII 175; **1232** coronatores..mittat..ad videndum quod quidam latro..faciat ~am et abjurationem regni secundum consuetudinem terre *Cl* 99; **1232** ij m. quas ..promiserunt regi pro facienda ~a de..latrone qui se receptaverat in ecclesia *MemR. Hen. III* 1413; **1236** corpus ipsius secundum ~as Scaccarii debebat arestari *KRMem* 15 r. 16(1)*d.*; **1239** †prohibimus ne aliquis Judeus aliter pecuniam suam mutuo det quam per ~am communiter Judeis a nobis ..concessum est (*Lit. Regis*) *Leg. Ant. Lond. app.* 237; **1272** secundum ~am et consuetudinem Judaismi *SelPlJews* 65; de illis qui ceperunt denarios ab illis qui extraneos hospitati sunt contra ~am inde factam BRACTON 116b; **1282** W. ..et R. ..districti pro extraneis herbigatis extra ~am *CourtR* 170/57 r. 2*d.* **b** **c1180** dominus terre illius..auxilium habere faciat ad vestigia latrocinii sui prosequenda secundum ~am meam [sc. regis] de Galweia *Melrose* I no. 18; ~a facta per dominum regem in Laudonia (*Assise Willelmi* 1) *APScot* I 49; **c1200** terram..que secundum assysam regni.. perambulata mihi..fuit *Reg. Aberbr.* I 60. **c** **1184** rex precepit quod omnes forestarii sui jurent quod..tenebunt ~am ejus qualem eam fecit de forestis suis (*Ass. Woodstock* 6) R. HOWD. II 246; **1266** solebant habere in bosco domini regis *housbote* et *heybote* cum omnibus feodis forestario pertinentibus secundum ~am foreste (*Inq.*) *Ambrosden* I 375; **1393** proviso quod..clausuram..copiciorum juxta ~am foreste sustinere faciant *Pat* 338 m. 21 (cf. *Cl* 143 [**1325**] m. 31: si ipse secundum ~am chacee predicte replegiabilis sit). **d** **1440** volunt quod ~a aque fiat per majorem et consilium suum..et quod quilibet molendinarius solvat pro quodlibet (*sic*) transgressione vj s. viij d. *Leet Coventry* 193. **e** responsum est [inter disputationes antiquas et modernas] hoc interesse quod inter bene ludentes cum omnibus scaccis, sc. ~is antiquis, et ludentes solum in ludis partitis GIR. *GE* II 37 p. 356.

3 (regulation governing) allowance of drink (esp. mon.). **b** regulation of food-prices etc. (mon.).

hec est ~a quando pro cervisia vinum debent habere, unusquisque sc. habere debet duas caritates in die W. MALM. *Glast.* 120; coquinarius scire debet quid et quantum per singulos dies conventui dare oportet secundum ~as antiquas *Obs. Barnwell* 186; **1381** constabularius percipiet ~am cervisie, sc. xij lagenas cervisie pro iij d. ..per totam warennam *IMisc.* 223/17. **b** **1252** ~a scaccarii: frumentum iiij s.; ..pensa casei x s.; stoppa mellis xviij d. *DCCant* H f. 172a (cf. *Cant. Cath. Pri.* 19).

4 assize of bread etc., (enforcement of) regulations governing quality and price of food-stuffs: **a** (bread); **b** (ale); **c** (wine).

a **c1185** hec est ~a de pane faciendo et vendendo que probata est per pistores domini Henrici secundi *Growth Eng. Indust.* I 568; **a1190** habeant..omnes terras..cum..~a panis et cervisie, cum furcis, pilloriis.. *MonA* II 351a; hec est ~a facta..per regem Ricardum *RBExch* II 750; **c1198** (v. 1d supra); **s1202** rex fecit generaliter acclamari ut legalis ~a panis..sub pena collistrigiali observaretur M. PAR. *Maj.* II 480; **s1256** justitiarii..per loca ~am panis, vini et cervisie sub forma tradiderunt subsequenti *Ann. Burton* 375 (cf. *StRealm* I 199 [? recte **a1250**]); **s1280** quo warento clamat habere emendas de ~e panis et cervisie fracte *Chr. Peterb.* 44; **1300** pistores vendunt unum panem pro sterlingg' et alium pro poll[ardis] et sic faciunt duas ~as *Leet Norw.* 50; **1316** ceperunt de quodam pistore..ij s. pro delicto ~e panis invento *Reg. Heref.* 510; **1321** oboli de..custuma..allocantur.. in examinacione panis et ~a inde tenenda et..occasione dicte custume ~a panis in pondere decrescit et minoratur *MGL* II 327; **1379** non mutatur ~a sive pondus panis (*Pat*) *EHR* XIV 504. **b** **c1160** habeant libere curias suas cum.. ~a panis et cervisie *Act. Hen. II* II 441; **1221** juratores cognoverunt quod non tenuerunt ~am panis et cervisie ad nundinas suas *PlCrGlouc* 50; **1359** nihil hic de vj s. viij d. per defaltam ~e bracine de I., quia est in assedacione cum terris regis thanagii de C. *ExchScot* 548; **1366** conservatores..secundum valorem dicte cervisie inde ponant ~am *Cl* 204 m. 6*d.*; **1371** brasiatores..frangunt ~am vendentes care *CourtR Winchester*; **1396** J. P. vendit celiam in domo sua propria sine signo exposito et eciam vendit cum discis et ciphis non signatis contra ~am *Rec. Nott.* I 316. **c** **s1199** si vinatorem qui vinum vendat ad brocam contra hanc ~am invenerint R. HOWD. IV 99; **1202** P. Vinitor [et alii] vendiderunt vinum contra ~am *SelPlCrown* 24; **1221** custodes ad placita corone custodienda similiter custodiant ~am vini *Ib.* 151; **s1226** inventum fuit quoddam dolium vini in cellario..ubi multa dolia vinorum vendebantur contra ~am *MGL* I 83; de vinis venditis..ubi vina vendita sunt contra ~am BRACTON 116b; **1400** quod..dux..faceret et haberet assaiam et ~am panis, vini et cervisie *Rec. Leic.* II 215.

5 'assize' (regulation) of measures. **b** (of cloth). **c** measure of woad. **d** regulation governing mesh of fishing-nets. **e** standard linear foot. **f** (standard) size.

1255 justitiarios..ad placita mercati nostri tenenda, ad ~as mensurarum constituendas, ad videndum transgressiones mensurarum et ~arum *Pat* 69 m. 1; **1255** in transitu suo per partes illas rectas ~as et mensuras in eadem civitate [Lincoln'] constituant *Cl* 142; **1287** probat mensuras et capit emendas de ~a fracta *PQW* 5. **b** **a1214** nullus faciat extra burgum meum pannum tinctum..contra ~am regis David *BBC* (*Inverness*) 170; **1221** ~a de latitudine pannorum non est servata *PlCrGlouc* 24; si ~a de latitudine pannorum servata sit sicut fuit provisum et si quis denarios ceperit pro pannis contra ~am venditis BRACTON 116b; **1296** de quolibet panno integro de ~a venali, j ob. *Pat* 115 m. 8; **c1320** quando [ulnator]..invenerit illos [pannos] non esse recte ~e, ..pro donis permittit eos [mercatores] vendere pannos illos (*AssizeR*) *Lond. Ed. I & II* II 157; **1408** de quolibet panno dimidium pannum de ~a per tres ulnas et amplius excedente qui pannus de ~a integer non fuerit *FineR* 213 m. 15 (cf. *Stat. 2 Ed. III* c. 14, *25 Ed. III* c. 3); **1587** pannus de ~a *Pat* 1299 m. 1. **c 1275** de qualibet ~a wayde *Pat* 94 m. 17; **1367** de qualibet ~a waide vendita j d. *Pat* 275 m. 13. **d 1290** capiunt pisces in aqua rescenti cum retibus que non sunt de assissa *Leet Norw.* 34; **1293** habent recia contra assissam cum quibus capiunt *fry* et destruunt ripam *Ib.* 42. **e 1379** viam..latitudinis sex pedum de ~a *Poulesfete* nuncupatorum *FormA* 33; **1393** per spacium c pedum ~e plus et ultra spacium quod..pons ad presens continet *Mem. York* 56b; **1400** parcella continet in longitudine lxxiiij pedes ~e.., in latitudine xv pedes ~e *Reg. Heref.* 163. **f 1285** pro unoquoque opere Augusti solebat habere j garbam per corrigiam de ~a *Cust. Suss.* II 20; **1304** omnes mensure tam bladi quam brasei..sint unius ~e et ejusdem quantitatis..secundum standardum busselli et lagene regis *Cant. Cath. Pri.* 210; **1330** remansit in arreragiis de uno salsario argenteo de majori ~a et de uno alio salsario, ut creditur, de eadem ~a *ExchScot* 323; **1414** unum lectum de parva ~a *Reg. Cant.* II 39; **1428** ij lectos cum curtinis de maxima ~a.., iiij lectos de media ~a (*Cl*) *Foed.* X 392.

6 assize, (regulation establishing) procedure for settling dispute by jury, action by this procedure (esp. before justices itinerant). **b** assize of right, grand assize (*cf. Royal Writs* 87). **c** possessory assize (mort dancestor, novel disseisin, darrein presentment). **d** assize of nuisance. **e** assize *utrum*. **f** criminal assize. **g** limit of action allowed by assize. **h** assize jury.

1166 (v. 2a supra); **1168** debet v m. pro habenda ~a de terra quam R. M. tenuit *Pipe* 137; **1170** debent j m. quia petierunt ~am sicut liberi et fuerunt rustici *Pipe* 149; judex ecclesiasticus..placita de debitis laicorum vel de tenementis in curia Christianitatis per ~am regni ratione fidei interposite tractare non potest GLANV. X 12; girovagando conciliis omnibus, ~is et conventiculis..non invitatus interesse curavit GIR. *Symb.* I 1 p. 210; **1229** coram justiciariis nostris quando venient in villa..ad ~as capiendas *BBC* (*Drogheda*) 357; **1313** justiciarii..ad ~ias capiendas in dictis insulis assignati *Cart. INorm* 98 (cf. 7a infra); **c1290** generalis atornatus in omni placito, asysa et hundredo *Ann. Durh.* 129; **1321** die Martis..omnes ~e et bille quassate sunt et adnullate *MGL* II 425; **1452** apud Ebor' tempore ~e *Test. Ebor.* III 148; ~ae, quas dicimus, in quolibet comitatu bis anno habentur, in quibus duo ~arum justitiarii ad hoc deputati..et de civilibus et de criminalibus cognoscunt CAMD. *Br.* 143. **b 1182** posuerunt se in ~am de Windlesor' utrum illi an predictus T. majus jus in terram illam haberet *E. Ch. Yorks* II 1220; **1184** r. c. de iij m. pro habenda magna ~a versus W. M. *Pipe* 106; in electione..tenentis erit se versus petentem defendere per duellum vel ponere se in magnam ~am domini regis inde et petere recognitionem quis eorum majus jus habeat in terra illa GLANV. II 3; **1196** summoniti fuerunt ad eligendum xij milites ad magnam ~am faciendam inter S...petentem et A...tenentem de viij parte feodi j militis *CurR* I 16; **1200** de placito magne ~e *Ib.* 134; **1203** (v. arramare 1a); **s1240** xij milites..fuerunt electi in asisa..; et consenserunt partes in x, quia duo non venerunt M. PAR. *Maj.* IV 53; placitum de recto ultimum sibi locum vendicat in ordine placitorum, quia quicunque in hoc placito semel amiserit per judicium vel per ~am vel per duellum nunquam ad aliam actionem habebit regressum BRACTON 328; **1284** placita de terris in partibus istis non habent terminari per duellum neque per magnam ~am (*Stat. Walliae* 8) *StRealm* I 65; **1456** per magnam ~am xxv nobilium..reperte fuerunt dicte terre fore eschaetam (*sic*) domino regi *ExchScot* 264. **c 1166** T...debet xx s. pro disseisina super ~am regis *Pipe* 65; que [saisine]..ex beneficio constitutionis regni que ~a nominatur in majori parte transigi solent per recognitionem GLANV. XIII 1 (cf. ib. 2: est quedam recognitio que vocatur de morte antecessoris); debitor habere poterit ~am de nova desaisina *Ib.* X 11; per ~am de advocationibus ecclesiarum proditam loquela illa tractabitur *Ib.* IV 1; **1196** dies datus est..de ~a mortis antecessoris *CurR* I 18; illam terram recuperavit per ~am nove diseisine et non habet inde plenam seisinam *Ib.* 21; de placito ~e ultime presentacionis *Ib.* 30; **1198** ~a de nova presentatione ad ecclesiam *Ib.* 42; **1199** (v. arramare 1a); **1227** mandatum est M...et sociis suis quod ~as mortis antecessoris, nove disseisine, ultime presentationis et magnas ~as et alia placita..ponant in respectum *Cl* 6; **1236** quicumque hujusmodi feoffati a quibuscumque..~am nove disseisine deferant (*Merton* 4) *St. Realm* I 2 (= M. PAR. *Maj.* III 342: †asseisinam nove disseisine; cf. B. COTTON 119); **1254** post ~am nove disseisine captam *Cl* 302 (= *RGasc.* I 448: post †assuagium); ~a nove disseisine cum sit triplex, personalis sc. propter factum et penalis propter injuriam et delictum et persecutoria, sc. quod res restituatur disseisita.. BRACTON 218b; mandetur justiciariis ad ~as [v.l. †asseisinas] *Fleta* 151; est ~a in jure possessorio quedam recognicio xij hominum juratorum per quam justiciarii cerciorentur de articulis membri contentis *Ib.* 213; **1320** cum ..partes hujusmodi ad ~am placitaverint et ~a capi debeat, veniunt frequenter juratores ~e et dicunt simpliciter..quod hujusmodi querentes sunt disseisiti *MGL* I 448; **1333** ~a frisce forcie capta coram..ballivis libertatis civitatis Cantuarie *Reg. S. Aug.* 184. **d** si exaltetur stagnum alicujus molendini infra ~am domini regis ad nocumentum liberi tenementi alicujus GLANV. XIII 34; **1198** ~a..de quadam domo levata..ad nocumentum ipsius *CurR* I 33; ~a de nocumento extendit se ad fundum alienum..in eo quod nociva est et injuriosa BRACTON 234b; **1397** coram.. justiciariis nostris ad ~as..capiendas assignatis in quadam ~a nocumenti non comparuit *Pat* 347 m. 19. **e 1194** assisa venit recognitura si terra..sit liberum tenementum prioris.. an libera elemosina pertinens ad ecclesiam *CurR PR* XIV 1; **1199** ~a ad recognoscendum utrum j virgata terre..sit laicum feodum Willelmi..an libera elemosina Simonis.. ponitur in respectum..pro defectu recongnitorum *CurR* I 82; **1230** S. persona de W. optulit se versus..A. de W. de placito quod esset auditurus ~am..utrum unum mesagium et v acre terre..sint libera elemosina pertinentes ad ecclesiam suam..an laicum feodum *Ib.* XIV 800; est.. quedam ~a que multum habet possessionis et juris...per istam ~am recognoscitur utrum tenementum de quo agitur laicum sit feodum tenentis vel libera elemosina BRACTON 285b (cf. GLANV. XIII 23: de recognitione..utrum..). **f 1166** vic. non r. c. de catallis fugitivorum, quia de illis non fuit facta ~a in com. illo *Pipe* 60; **1169** de catallis fugitivorum et suspensorum per ~am de Clarendon' *Pipe* 118; **1176** hec ~a atenebit a tempore quo ~a facta fuit apud Clarendonam..usque ad hoc tempus et amodo quamdiu regi placuerit in murdro et proditione et iniqua combustione (*Ass. Northampton*) *G. Hen. II* I 108; si..vir..metu arctioris ~e quam rex propter sceleratos constituit a sede sua fugerit, ..et postmodum comprehensus per legem ~e constitutam reus sceleris convictus fuerit, ..mobilium.. pretia..ad scaccarium deferuntur et in annali sic annotantur: 'ille vic. r.c. de catallis fugitivorum vel mutilatorum per ~am' *Dial. Scac.* II 10F; de occultatione inventi thesauri fraudulosa..ob infamiam non solet aliquis..per legem apparentem se purgare, licet aliter per ~am fieri posset GLANV. XIV 2; hoc modo assissium vocant: quando de alicujus morte ambigitur rei, vicinos xij aut in numero majore evocant, qui rei casum ancipitem interpretantes eum aut liberandum aut protinus occidendum declarant MAJOR VI 12; **1549** excessus tam publicos quam privatos sibi per ~as et inquisiciones utrobique †delatas [? l. delatos] *Conc. Scot.* II 94. **g** cum quis infra ~am domini regis, id est infra tempus a domino rege de consilio procerum ad hoc constitutum.., alium injuste..desaisiaverit GLANV. XIII 32; **1201** dicunt quod jurata inde non debet fieri, quia est contra ~am rengni *CurR* I 439; burgenses.. responderunt se esse in ~a regis, nec de tenementis †qui [? l. que]..tenuerunt..in pace uno anno et uno die..se velle respondere contra libertatem ville BRAKELOND 143; **1219** si R. ..injuste..disseisivit H. ..de tenemento suo..infra ~am *CurR* VIII 8; cum legales homines sint et infra ~am domini regis *Ib.* 41. **h s1189** debent duo viri de ~a.. ibidem accedere *MGL* I 326; **1196** ~a venit recognitura quis advocatus..presentavit personam ultimam *CurR* I 24; **1200** ~a tota atachietur quod tunc sit ibi *Ib.* 131; **1224** fuerunt recognitores illius ~e *Cl* 633; **1242** socii sui recognitores cujusdam ~e *Pipe* 20; **1265** cum..sit tediosum clericis laicum feodum habentibus poni in ~is, juratis seu recognitionibus *BBC* (*Oxford*) 188; senes lxx annorum et ultra..in minoribus ~is non ponantur *Fleta* 223; **s1357** per ~am electam condempnatus, pena capitali punitus est *Plusc.* IX 44; **1455** personis ad ~am electis *ExchScot* 94.

7 (act or session of) court of assize: **a** (Norm.); **b** (Gasc.).

a c1145 recognosci faciatis secundum ~iam meam de feodo Guillelmi B. quis inde saisitus erat *Regesta* III 55; **a1150** comprobatum fuit per meum preceptum in ~ia mea apud Valonias quod..tenuerant.. *Ib.* 245; **a1182** pasturam suam de L. que ipsi adjudicata est in ~ia apud Rothomagum in curia mea *Act. Hen. II* II 170. **b 1283** si..senescallus Vasconie..~ias suas teneat in civitate..Vasatensi de hominibus commorantibus extra civitatem, omnis jurisdiccio et justicia extraneorum qui ad ~am et pro ~a venient ..sint propria senescalli ~a durante *RGasc.* II 205; **1312** ad ~ias Vasatenses et Burd' tenendas *Ib.* IV *app.* p. 556 (cf. ib.: pro ~is tenendis); quem..citari fecerant ad ipsam assiziam *Ib.* p. 560; **1313** cause nos tangentes..nunc ad particulares assizias trahuntur et ventilantur extra civitatem *Ib.* no. 1110.

8 (?) session of justices (*cf. EHR* LXXIII 673). **b** session of guild. **c** entrance-fee of guild.

1220 ad primam ~am coram justiciariis *Cl* 473b; **1225** mandatum fuit eis quod assisa illa ponatur coram justiciariis ad primam ~am cum in partes illas venerint *Pat* 79; **1321** omnia placita que posita sunt ad primam ~am coram justiciariis *MGL* II 286. **b 1210** isti intraverunt [gildam] ad ultimam ~am *Gild. Merch.* (*Shrewsbury*) II 211; **1252** rotulus de ghylda mercatoria in burgo Salop' ad novam ~am: primus dies sessionis fuit dies Mercurii *Ib.* 212. **c 1210** de illis quorum patres fuerunt in gulda, una ~a de xxij d. apponitur *Ib.* 211.

9 membership of tithing.

1278 thethingm[annus] presentat quod L. heres habeat H. famulum suum extra ~am *CourtR* (*Sevenhampton*) 209/51 m. 3; **1284** H. molendinarius attachiatus est quod est extra ~am *Ib.* 54 m. 5; **1287** R. pistor in misericordia quia tenuit R. filium suum extra ~am, qui fuit etatis *Ib.* (*Highworth*) 208/81 m. 22; **1288** R. nepos prioris non est in decenna; de eodem R. quia non est in assissam *Leet Norw.* 15 (cf. ib. 19: H. de C., qui mansit in civitate per longum tempus, non est in assissa).

10 land leased or farmed (*cf.* 2 *assidere* 4).

1158 duas carucatas terre.., unam de dominio et alteram de ~a rusticorum *Danelaw* 251.

11 shaped block of stone, (?) segment of column (*cf. azeisa*).

1253 pro..l ~is, pretii ~e v d. *KRAc* 467/1; **1293** [vij pedes de buscelles..faciunt v] ~as (*Merton Roll* 4059) *Building in Eng.* 114.

2 assisa [cf. accessus 1c, adsisa (*Hisperica Famina* D 7)], flood-tide or wave.

†accire, maris fluctus *GlC* A 153; interpretatio nominum Ebraicorum et Grecorum: ..†adsida, *flood Ib. app.* no. 34 p. 189.

assisagium, (area of) jurisdiction of court of assize (Gasc.).

1316 scribaniam..de ~iis curie senescalcie..de Villa Franca et de Bello Monte et de omnibus aliis locis, villis et bastidis ad dicta ~ia pertinentibus *RGasc.* IV 1622.

1 assisare v. assentire 1f.

2 assisare, to assess.

1270 isti sunt electi ad eligendum xx legales homines ad taylagium ~andum *Rec. Leic.* I 146; **1281** quod..~ant dictam pecunie summam super quamlibet societatem predictam (*CoramR*) *Law Merch.* II 37.

assisarius, assessor (leg.).

1509 suscepimus in salvum conductum..commissarios.. regis Scotorum..preter et ultra querentes et defendentes ac assisar[ios] *RScot* 572a.

assisator, assize juror. **b** (?) assessor (of tax or sim.).

1294 R. ..est vetus et communis ~or, capiens lucrum ex omni parte, ita quod qui plus ei dederit pro ejus parte dicet *JustIt* 1095 r. 1 (cf. ib. r. 1d.: falsus ~or capiens ex omni parte). **b 1350** de viij s. iiij d. receptis de diversis ~oribus hundredi de Eddebur' *MinAc* (*Chesh*) 783/15 r. 4.

assisatus, ~um, (area of) jurisdiction of assize court (Gasc.).

1308 scribaniam assisiatus senescalli nostri Agenensis *RGasc.* IV 35; **1316** scribaniam senescalcie Agennensis in assisiatu Candom' *Ib.* 1620a; de scribania registri..senescalcie de ~is Caturcinii *Ib.* 1625.

assisia, ~iatus v. assisa, ~atus. assisinus v. assassinus.

assisor, assize juror. **b** assessor (of tax or fine). **c** assessor of the assize of ale (*cf. assisa* 4b).

1348 conspiratores, perjuros, falsos ~ores, qui prece vel precio..aut promissionibus corrupti contra justiciam in alterius prejudicium..falsum dixerint *Conc.* II 747b. **b 1225** omnes ~ores et receptores denariorum de fine quem milites..fecerunt pro habenda custodia foreste *LTRMem* 8 r. 1(2)*d.*; **1445** ~ores nominati per cancellarium Oxonie ..qui juraverunt quod fideliter..quemlibet servientem scholaris..taxarent..pro dimidio quintedecime vel taxe domino regi concesse *MunAcOx* 549. **c c1445** cancellarius ..solvit vj s. viij d. impositoribus vel ~oribus assise cerevisie *Ib.*

assissa, ~ium v. assisa. assistare v. assistere.

assistator, assistant.

1538 quelibet talis persona vel persone sic agentes, .. eorum auxiliatores, ~ores, confortatores, abbettatores (*Pat*) *Foed.* XIV 596.

assistentia, presence, participation. **b** assistance, guidance.

cum civilis possessio corporalem ~iam non mendicet P. BLOIS *Ep.* 26. 91A; ut..mei quoque non negetur ~ia personalis ad id ipsum AD. MARSH *Ep.* 182; **1318** si.. nostram in hac parte ~iam duxeritis eligendam *FormOx* 42; quamvis Deus specialiter assistat ad generale concilium congregatum in nomine Christi, tamen per talem ~iam divinam in fide nullatenus confirmantur quin possint labi in errorem OCKHAM *Dial.* 495; **1377** si dominus noster papa non foret ex ~ia curialium..instigatus (WYCL. *Resp.*) *Ziz.* 268; **a1400** ut caveant posteri cum ignotis personis secedere in loca privata sine ~ia famulorum *G. S. Alb.* II 177. **b** [Adam] ab extrinsecis nocumentis custodiebatur providencia divina et ~ia angelica PECKHAM *QA* II 20 p. 164; **1281** viros..providos..de quorum consorcio et ~ia possitis merito confidere *Id. Ep.* 208; **c1280** semper regebatur curia regum Anglie principaliter..per clericos beneficiis et honoribus ecclesiasticis spaciose ditatos, per quorum ~iam non solum regno Anglie set et ecclesie salubri circumspeccione consulitur (*DipDocE*) *Doc. Exch.* 369; **s1328** non potuit..ab eis petere subsidium seu ~iam GRAYSTANES 42; **1341** propter habendum nostrum et aliorum principum contra.. inimicos fidei ~iam et succursum (*Lit. Regis*) AD. MUR. *app.* 270; per..magni Dei..cooperacionem seu ~iam specialem BRADW. *CD* 788A; **1425** mandamus quatenus vobis.. impendant ~iam *Conc. Scot.* I lxxxix *n.*; **1446** nec ea committentibus dabit ~iam *Eng. Clergy* 211; **1453** quod.. inimicis regis ~iam, servicium..aut juvamen nullo modo prestent *RScot* 362b; **1573** potestatem..marcialem legem.. cum ~ia duorum..illi assistencium exequendi *Pat* 1104 m. 31.

assistere [CL; *some forms might be referred to* astare], to stand beside. **b** to be with, attend, be present (at) or privy (to). **c** (of things). **d** (w. inf.) to be ready.

ut..quasi regina a dextris divinae majestatis..jugiter ~ere..mereatur ALDH. *VirgP* 15; aris adsistere ac daemonibus hostias offerre BEDE *HE* I 7; collocatis in lectis suis ~ant magistri dum sint cooperti LANFR. *Const.* 178; cuidam..B. Thomas per visum astitit W. CANT. *Mir. Thom.* IV 51; astitit ei angelus in somnis GIR. *TH* II 39. **b 597** quando de Galliis episcopi veniunt, qui in ordinatione episcopi adsistant? (*Lit. Papae*) BEDE *HE* I 27 p. 52; **s1136** rex..quosdam de ~entibus sibi..ad eos..reducendos transmisit *G. Steph.* I 12; **1166** ~entibus in presentia nostra.. canonicis *Canon. G. Sempr.* 89v; rex..divinis laudibus devotus ~ebat AILR. *Ed. Conf.* 748D; majores de regno, qui familiarius regis secretis ~unt *Dial. Scac.* I 4B; **1318** si nostre sollicitudinis presenciam corporalem..in eodem tractatu pocius eligeritis (*sic*) astituram *FormOx* 42; **1329** expedit vos habere in consilio ~antes (*sic*) viros..prudentes *Lit. Cant.* I 302; **s1388** usque ad parliamentum futurum, quo suis astituri erant responsis WALS. *HA* II 173; nonnulli quondam eidem ~entes asserunt quod.. BLAKMAN *Hen. VI* 15. **c 1514** ~ente ibidem vexillo S. Cuthberti *Ac. Durh.* 663. **d c1314** intelleximus vos..~ere..universitatis onera.. supportare *FormOx* 11.

2 to stand by (fig.), assist (w. dat.). **b** (w. acc.). **c** (pr. ppl. as sb.) assistant.

rogans ut illi, in quocunque negotio vestri opus habuerit, ~atis EADMER *Wilf.* 731A; qui ei [Henrico I] in subigenda Anglia constanter adsistebant R. NIGER 168; **1226** mandamus vobis..quatinus..~atis..hominibus nostris.. existentibus in predicta navi, ..consilium et auxilium eis prebentes *Pat* 14; **1255** [aldermanni] sint ~entes et consulentes majori et ballivis nostris *BBC* (*Oxford*) 367; **1301** vos rogamus quatinus consilium vestrum..mittatis..consilio nostro corditer †assisturum *Reg. Cant.* II 1323; **1545** proditorum ipsis inimicis..~encium *Conc. Scot.* I cclvii. **b** **1288** episcopum..defensionis subsidio ~atis *RGasc.* II 115. **c 1545** heresium..fautores, auctores, ~entes *Conc. Scot.* I cclxi.

3 (trans.) to stand, place (a thing). **b** to bring (persons) before (a court or sim.). **c** (?) to bring (a case) into court. **d** (w. *adversus*) to set against (cf. *Psalm* ii 2).

quando aliquis fratrum sentencialiter ad..scabellum ponitur, quod a latere inter duos choros ~i consuevit *Cust. Westm.* 200. **b s1317** misit rex nuncios suos ad curiam Romanam, presencie summi pontificis ~endos *Flor. Hist.* III 182; **s1321** dominus T. Lancastrie inter suos commilitones regi ~itur, quos continuo rex in compedibus..precepit alligari *Ib.* 205; **s1322** comes..coram judicibus ~itur tribunali *G. Ed. II Bridl.* 83. **c s1169** ita declamabat [episcopus Lond'], sed causa †~ata est nullo adversario W. FITZST. *Thom.* 83. **d s1340** quidam..astiterunt adversus eum [sc. archiepiscopum] Christum Domini ac contra eum prefatum dominum regem excitarunt AVESB. 93b.

assistrix v. assestrix. assisum v. assisa. assisus v. abscidere 1d, 2 assidere. assitabulum v. acetabulum. assizia v. assisa 7b.

associare [CL], (of persons) to associate, unite, add to others (as colleague or sim.). **b** (w. *sibi*). **c** (refl.).

susceptum in monasterium..fratrum cohorti adsociavit BEDE *HE* IV 22; ut..angelicis spiritibus mererentur ~iari OSB. *V. Dunst.* 3; **s1159** Mathildem..illi [Remelio] ~iaverunt, ex qua genuit unam filiam TORIGNI 200; **1218** unus ex militibus..ad hoc ~iatus eidem Philippo *Pat* 174; **1251** non fuit cum eis.., quia non est ~iatus eis *SelPlForest* 100; duobus hominibus, qui dicuntur ~iati fuisse in uno itinere BACON V 144; Robertus justiciarius in itinere ultimo.. Salomoni..~iatus *State Tri. Ed. I* 68; **1300** ita quod per majorem duo aldermanni †eligentur [? l. eligantur] et ~ientur camerario *MGL* II 93; **a1350** cum contingat in incepcionibus magis potentum plures bachilarios ~iari *StatOx* 68. **b** ~iaverunt illum [Corineum] sibi et populum cui presidebat G. MON. I 12; **s1181** pontifex ~iavit sibi plus quam xx millia Braibacenorum *G. Hen. II* I 276; **1215** ne aliqui religiosi..~ient sibi principes *Pat* 140a; **s1233** ~iatis sibi quibusdam magnatibus, ad regem audacter accessit WEND. III 49; constituimus vos justiciarium nostrum una cum aliis quos vobis duxeritis ~iandos vel assumendos (*Breve*) BRACTON 111; **1454** quos sibi voluerint ~iare *Melrose* II no. 568. **c 1269** ~iavit se cuidam servienti.., ad cujus domum sepius conversabatur *SelPlForest* 45; **1287** cum dicto latrone se ~iavit *PQW* 258b.

2 (of animals) to unite (to a flock). **b** (fig.).

[anser] gregi suo ~iatus est W. CANT. *Mir. Thom.* IV 48. **b** animal irrationale..rationalium gregi quis ~iabit? GIR. *TH* II 21.

3 (of things) to join, unite, set beside. **b** to combine, incorporate. **c** to group (among).

juxta lectum cathedra locetur, ..cui scabellum subjungatur, cui lectica ~ietur NECKAM *Ut.* 100 (cf. ib. 114: asseribus opus est proportionaliter ~iatis); per eum [nervum] spiritus animalis anime ~iatus decurrit ad concava aurium RIC. MED. *Anat.* 217; **1264** si posse predictorum potentie mee et amicorum meorum in partibus predictis fuerit ~iatum (*AncC* IV 105) *RL* II 255; quia Jude Scariothis vitam scripserim, vitam Pilati illi ~iabo *Eul. Hist.* I 84. **b** [Jesus] omnem vitam nutritivam et auctivam in se ipso ~iavit ERIUG. *Per.* 542A; quandocumque..timemus ne digestio.. frangat virtutem ejus [medicine], ~iamus ei medicinam que eam conservet BACON IX 111. **c** decet eas [notas] inter longas simplices et duplices et inter se ~iari HAUBOYS 462b.

4 to join, associate oneself with: **a** (w. acc.); **b** (w. dat.).

a nec letitiam convivii ~iabo, nec gaudiis nuptiarum participabo *G. Herw.* 323; **1291** qua hora capta fuit civitas Achon, Tyrus eam ~iavit (*Lit. Soldani ad Regem Armeniae*) B. COTTON 218; de occisoribus B. Thome.., et de illis qui ~iaverunt eos OCKHAM *Dial.* 705. **b c1300** qui non habet integram carrucam associabit alii socco ad arrandum *Cust. Battle* 76; **1457** juravit..quod..non..scissoris uxori suspiciose..~iabit *MunAcOx* 670.

associatio, association (of persons), enlistment, fellowship, company.

c1115 per sacramentum xij burgensium sine ~one alicujus extranei omnia placita terminabant *BBC* (*Dunstable*) 124; in quo casu..fit tali justiciario ~o alterius justiciarii..ut captio assise differatur; ..si talis..non [venerit], nihilominus procedat assisa, quia plus habet auctoritatis breve patens de capiendo assisam quam breve clausum de ~one BRACTON 111; **1260** cum nuper vobis associaverimus R. de T. ad assisam nove disseisine capiendam, ..nolentes quod occasione dicte ~onis dicta asssisa indebite prorogetur capienda.. *Cl* 171; furum associacio, / fel, sputum et illusio J. HOWD. *Cyth.* 29; **1450** illicitis ~onibus, congregacionibus et coadunacionibus *Lit. Cant.* III 206; **1466** se invicem in mutuam fraternitatem et †associetacionem perpetuam susceperunt *Reg. Dunferm.* no. 472.

associative, by way of association (gram.).

hec proposicio 'cum' aliquando tenetur ~e, et sic non facit conceptionem; aliquando copulative, et sic potest suplere officium copulationis, quia copulatio potest similiter teneri ~e vel copulative BACON XV 70.

assolēre [CL], to be accustomed. **b** (impers.). **c** (p. ppl.) accustomed.

quadam die, ut adsolebat, ..usque insulam..pervenit FELIX *Guthl.* 40; his duobus simul, ut ~ent, recubantibus GIR. *EH* I 4. **b** non ex harum coitu, ut ~et, ova gignuntur *Id. TH* I 15; sicut fieri ~et AD. MARSH *Ep.* 4. **c** presbyter parochianus sacra mysteria populo celebrare ~itus Gosc. *Aug. Min.* 761; rex Martiis altercationibus ~itus H. HUNT. *HA* VIII 5.

assolut-, assolv-, v. absol-. assoni- (assoin-) v. essoni-.

assonus [cf. CL assonare], harmonious.

asono vocis modulamine, binis adstantibus choris, persultare responsoriis EDDI *Wilf.* 47.

assor v. effortiamentum. assos v. asep. assuagium v. assisa 6c. assuare v. esseware.

assub [Ar. *ash-shuhub* (pl.)], falling star. **b** (fig.). **c** 'star-slime', nostoc.

impressiones, inflammate in aere ex vaporibus ignitis in similitudinem stellarum, que vocantur Arabice ~ub ascendens et descendens, sunt corpora parve quantitatis BACON *Maj.* II 102; sicut unius oculi aspectu videmus quartam celi fere et omnes stellas in ea collocatas, ita quod intendentes in stellam quamcumque videamus, i.e. visu advertamus, ~ub volare PECKHAM *QA* III 209; dicit Albumasar quod adventus ignium et ~ub et stelle comate est ex dominio Martis ROB. ANGL. (II) *Sph.* 5 p. 166. **b** heu quod..planeta progrediens regiratur retrograde ac naturam..vere stelle pretendens subito decidit et fit ~ub! R. BURY *Phil. prol.* 8. **c** *sterre slyme,* ~ub *PP*; *a sterne slyme,* ~ub *CathA*.

assueare v. esseware.

assuefacere, to accustom, habituate. **b** (p. ppl.) customary.

1166 hic est qui..multorum animas..Christi jugo ~fecit *Canon. G. Sempr.* f. 94; **1454** ~faciat igitur se frater..in jam dictis, et absque difficultate aliqua feret illa omnia que sunt ponderis gravioris (*Lit. Abbatis*) *Reg. Whet.* I 145. **b** in Suine est novum theloneum ~factum *DB* I 375b.

assuefactio, habituation.

usque dum ipsa ~one minus terreantur anates NECKAM *NR* II 125; valent etiam [bona opera] ad augmentum caritatis et ad dimissionem pene et ad ~onem in bono S. LANGTON *Quaest.* f. 221; oportet supponere quod consuetudo vel ~o est naturam esse consuetam ad aliquid WYCL. *Mand. Div.* 442; **1423** eisdem viciis..assuetos, ..que quidem ~o ex ipsa iteracione decernatur *Reg. Cant.* III 518; **1430** volentes tanti sceleris ~oni, ne nimium invalescat, pio occurrere remedio *Reg. Durh.* no. 847; nec habetur [magnitudo] per ~onem, quemadmodum virtutes morales..acquiruntur PAUL. ANGL. *ASP* 1544.

1 assuēre v. assuescere 1a.

2 assuĕre [CL], to sew on. **b** (fig.).

adsutae, *gesiuwide GlC* A 177; curtinae tabernaculi.. diversis ansularum nexibus ~utae ALDH. *Metr.* 2 p. 64; capitio ~uto tunicae induatur LANFR. *Const.* 169; fimbria que vesti isti ~itur BELETH *RDO* 110. 114; non capucio ~uto tunice..nec tunica cuculle indecenter ~uta *Cust. Cant.* 257. **b** cavete ne..inextricabile malum ~atis capitibus vestris BOECE 34v.

assuescere [CL], to grow accustomed. **b** (refl.) to accustom oneself. **c** (trans.) to grow accustomed to.

nichil utilius est quam ei quod fieri ex arte oportet ~ere J. SAL. *Met.* 856A; parentes filios.., ut bonis ~ant, ad divini luminis intuitum..oculos dirigere docent interiores GIR. *TH* I 13; *to be wonte,* assuere, ~ere, ..solere *CathA*. **b 1454** dissueti sepius tediose magis claustrale jugum deferunt, et propterea faciatis ipsum se illi ~ere (*Lit. Abbatis*) *Reg. Whet.* I 145. **c** solam barbariem, in qua et nati sunt et nutriti, sapiunt et ~unt et..amplectuntur GIR. *TH* III 10; precepit militem..levem armaturam ~ere *Croyl.* 68.

2 (p. ppl. *assuetus*) accustomed. **b** customary.

[apes] domesticis ~ae deliciis ALDH. *VirgP* 6; **10..** adsuetae, *gewunede* WW; hominem ~um obsequiis W. MALM. *GP* II 83; [pulli] nondum freno bene ~i W. FITZST. *Thom. prol.* 11; **1288** R. C. est fur et ~us est furari aucas *Leet Norw.* 5; **1423** (v. assuefactio). **b** adsueto more FELIX *Guthl.* 31; die Veneris, que est dies ~a ad faciendam †dayuam [l. daynam] *Cust. Bleadon* 203.

assuetudo, habituation, practice.

si ex industria et ~ine possit aliquod animal uti voce alterius BACON XV 233.

assugia v. axungia.

†assula [CL; cf. assa, astula], chip (of wood).

schydd or astelle, ~a vel astula *PP*; **1456** de vj d. pro ~is venditis *Ac. Chamb. Winchester.*

assultare [CL], to leap upon, mount (of stallion).

1330 afri asaldi..grossa jumenta nostra..assaltarunt et pullanos minus decentes..procrearunt *Chanc. Misc.* 11/8/4.

2 to assault, attack: **a** (person); **b** (building or town).

a 1199 cum ipsi post missam auditam equitarent versus forestam.., venerunt..R. et H. ..et ~averunt eos et vulneraverunt et maimaverunt *CurR* I 91; **1221** venit cum vi sua et..vi et nequiter et in felonia eum ~avit *PlCrGlouc* 16 (cf. ib. 100: eum assaltaverunt et tres plagas ei fecerunt in capite); **1235** assaltavit eundem servientem *SelCWW* 64; **1266** misit duas filias suas ad domum suam pro quodam beke ad eum assaltandum *IMisc.* 13/22. **b 1198** venerunt ..ad domum suam et eam ~averunt et combusserunt *CurR* I 49; **1221** ~averunt domum suam et illam fregerunt *PlCrGlouc* 26; **1265** castellum ville [Glovernie] audaciter bellando assaltant (*AncC* XI 72) *RL* II 288; **1269** nocturno tempore domum suam ~avit et suffodit in pace Die et domini regis *CBaron* 73; quod adversa navalis potencia.. conclusisset januam portus de Portesmothe.., que et ~are tentasset hanc interiorem partem ELMH. *Hen. V* 83.

assultatio, assault (on town).

s1264 dum una pars exercitus..circa portas [Norhamtune] more ~onis occuparetur (RISH.) WALS. *YN app.* 516.

assultus [CL], assault, attack (mil.): **a** (on person); **b** (on building or town).

a 1289 homines..regis se defendebant et, magnis ~ibus inter ipsos habitis, ipsum et homines suos..fugiendo ceperunt (*Chanc. Misc.* 22/1/10) *DocScot* I 75. **b 1130** vic. r. c. ..de quater xx..li. ..pro assaltu navium et domorum Lond' *Pipe* 146; **1138** balistis et aliis machinis et variis ~ibus oppidum expugnare aggressus est RIC. HEX. *Stand.* 40 b; **s1191** muris civitatis [Achon] appropiant et ferocissimos ingerunt ~us *Itin. Ric.* III 5 (cf. *Plusc.* VI 34: nec illic rex Anglie gentes suas ad assaltum urbis [Achon] ire..permittere volebat); **s1206** acerrimo ~u illud [castellum] inquietans *Flor. Hist.* II 132 (= *Ann. Lond.* 13: assaltu).

2 assault (criminal). **b** jurisdiction (w. perquisites) in case of assault.

si in via regia fit ~us super aliquem, *forestal* est (*Leg. Hen.*) *GAS* 596; pax chiminorum et aquarum..sub majori judicio..continetur..de assaltu (*Leg. Ed.*) *Ib.* 639; **a1185** qui effuderit sanguinem [det]..xij d. de forisfacto, excepto assaltu meditato et forestallo *BBC* (*Swansea*) 153; **1185** r. c. de x m. pro ~o (*sic*) facto cum armis versus canonicos de S. Oswaldo *Pipe* 71; **1190** de exitu terrarum..eorum qui aufugerunt pro ~u Judeorum *Pipe* 75; **1201** excessus qui inter eos [Judeos] emerserint, exceptis hiis que ad coronam nostram pertinent, ut..de assaltu premeditato *RChart* 93b; **12..** roberia et pax fracta..et assaltus †propensatus [? l. prepensatus], omnia..talia defendenda sunt ante consilium captum et post consilium *MGL* I 114; **1444** in Agnetem.. insultum fecerunt..et quampluribus vicibus assaut' super dictam Agnetem fecerunt *Pat* 458 m. 18. **b †1020** (13c) ut habeant..pacis fracturam et pugnam in domo factam, vie assaltus et latrones in terra sua captos *CD* 756; **1121** ut.. teneat cum..domus invasione et ~u in suo jure *FormA* 291 (= *Regesta* 1249); **c1158** habeat..omnes ~us in suo jure, in via et extra *Ib.* 45 (= *MonA* III 434); **c1160** habeant.. sanguinis effusionem et omnes ~us et *forestal CalCh* II 369; **1203** habeant..pugnam in domo factam et vie assaltus *RChart* 105b (cf. ib. 125a: omnem justiciam de assaltu).

3 (sexual) advance, approach. **b** (w. *Inimici*) temptation by Devil.

a regina nimium amabatur et vehementissimis impetebatur ~ibus in verbis et signis MAP *NC* III 2 p. 105. **b c1300** quia graves fuerunt ei indies ~us Inimici ad tolerandum *MonA* VI 893b.

assum v. adesse.

†assumare [? *for* assignare], (?) to appoint.

c1400 ~avit me ut crastino comparerem (R. WYCHE) *EHR* V 540.

†assumatio [? *for* assignatio], appointment.

c1400 dies ~onis ad comparendum coram episcopo (R. WYCHE) *EHR* V 537.

assumentum [bibl.; cf. 2 assuere], patch. **b** (fig.; *cf. Mark* ii 21).

1440 unum parvum saccum cum ~is *Pat* 446 m. 13; *a clowte,* ~um, repecium, ..*a pece of leder or of clathe,* ~um *CathA*. **b 800** volentes rudis panni ~um veteri inmittere vestimento ALCUIN *Ep.* 212.

assumere [CL], to take (in addition), acquire (a thing). **b** (w. *habitum*) to adopt the religious life. **c** (w. *crucem*) to become a crusader. **d** to take as arms (her.). **e** to take (extract) a root (math.). **f** to 'take up', turn up (cloth). **g** (w. *cameram*) to be brought to child-bed. **h** (w. *carnem*) to become incarnate. **i** to derive.

eadem 're' praepositio..D litteram crebro ~it ALDH. *PR* 140 p. 197; manum suam inmittere ac partem pulveris inde adsumere BEDE *HE* IV 3; iterum adsumentes, flagellis ..eum verberare coeperunt FELIX *Guthl.* 31; de vii hidis quas comes Moriton' ~psit *DB* I 142; ipse [mundus] ~i debet a te ad usum AD. SCOT. *OP* 453D (cf. ib.: si sibi [mundum] in affectu ~erent); Julius..qui..primus in unitate persone ~psit imperium R. BURY *Phil.* 1. 20; **1372** si predicta summa argenti..capellano..assignata non possit ~i *IPM* 227/10; **s1399** ego Henricus..tronum regium, ..coronam et regnum ..clamo, ~o et eundem ascendi [v.l. ascendo] *V. Ric. II* 160. **b** monachicum..adsumsit..habitum BEDE *HE* IV 25; si vero habitum religionis ~pserit, tunc breve..variabitur GLANV. XIII 5; **s1238** licet habitum cum velo non ~pserit mulier, anulum tamen, quo se Christo..desponsavit, ~psit M. PAR. *Maj.* III 487. **c 1217** ita..crucem ~ant ad partes suas contra inimicos Dei et ecclesie defendendas *Pat* 34. **d** ~psit v merulos aureos, portans eos sine pedibus UPTON 129. **e** hujus collectionis radice ~pta ROB. ANGL. *Alg.* 72. **f 1587** par manicarum de satten scissarum et ~ptarum cum taffata *Ac. LChamb.* 78 f. 5v. **g c1470** regina Elizabeth gravida suam ~psit cameram..et..peperit filiam HERRISON *Abbr. Chr.* 9. **h** pro salute nostra Christus carnem ~psit LANFR. *Ep.* 33. 533B; Jesus Christus..misericorditer carnem ~ens M. PAR. *Maj.* I 80. **i** duo scemata..a Vergilio adsumpta ALDH. *Met.* 10 p. 90; ea quae conscripsi partim ex eis quae de illo prius..scripta repperi adsumsi BEDE *HE pref.* p. 7; ratiocinationis exordium ex divinis eloquiis ~endum ERIUG. *Per.* 545B; [summa substantia] nihil omnino aliunde ~psit unde..eorum quae factura erat formam..pingeret ANSELM (*Mon.* 11) I 26.

2 to take (a person) as companion or helper. **b** to admit to an order or office. **c** to take up (w. ref. to *Matth.* iv 8). **d** (w. impers. subj.) to seize, attack.

adsumtis his qui se sequi voluerunt BEDE *HE* III 26; [Lanfrancus] ab ipso Normanniae duce W. consiliarius ~itur G. CRISPIN *Herl.* 97; **1214** ~psit secum legales homines *Sel PlCrown* 74; ~ptis que per loca varia disperse fuerant viribus bellicosis ELMH. *Hen. V Cont.* 122. **b** patefecit quales ad ecclesiae regimen adsumi..debeant BEDE *HE* II 1 p. 76; **1187** quatenus paupertas ordinis unde ~ptus estis debeat..commendari *Ep. Cant.* 87; **1268** in senatorem urbis unanimi consensu Romani populi sumus ~pti *Cl* 560; **1276** Hospitalarii ~unt diversos homines per chevagium *Hund.* I 96; **s1325** archiepiscopus Ebor' ad officium thesaurarie ~ptus fuit in parlamento Westmonasterii *Hist. Roff.* 365; nos..faciemus quod ad officia..~entur persone habiles ELMH. *Hen. V Cont.* 141; **1427** Thomas..ad..arbitrandum ..electus et concorditer ~ptus *FormOx* 460. **c** temptator ..Christum ~psit..semel tantum in montem excelsum OCKHAM *Pol.* I 344. **d** catarrus, qui regnum pervagatus est et multos ~psit W. CANT. *Mir. Thom.* VI 2.

3 to take up into Heaven: **a** (Christ; *cf. Mark* xvi 19 *etc.*); **b** (the Virgin); **c** (a Christian soul).

a 'praedestinatus est'..Christus ut Filius Dei esset in virtute divinitatis Dei qua ~ptus est LANFR. *Comment. Paul.* (*Rom.* i 4) 167; Christus..est ~ptus in celum OCKHAM *Dial.* 422. **b** credo quod ~ta fueris in celum cum anima et carne tua, resurrexione plena celebrata J. GODARD *Ap.* 247; **s49** Beata Maria mater Domini obiit anno vite sue lxiij..; vixit..post [sc. assumpto Domino]..secundum alios xij annis, ut sic sexagenaria sit ~pta HIGD. IV 8 p. 388. **c** vidit animam Ceddi..descendere de caelo et adsumta secum anima ejus ad caelestia regna redire BEDE *HE* IV 3 p. 211; ad sempiterna animarum gaudia adsumtus in caelum *Ib.* 13 p. 234; videbatur..illi se patrem ipsum..de presenti vita ~ptum..advertere EADMER *Mir. Anselm.* 385; Britannorum rex Lucius, in bonis actibus ~ptus, ..ab hac vita migravit ad Christum M. PAR. *Maj.* I 149; **1292** postquam ~pti fuerimus ab hac luce (*DCCant*) *HMC Var.* I 261.

4 **a** to assume, take on (an attribute, identity, name, or role). **b** (w. *in vanum*) to take in vain (cf. *Exod.* xx 7). **c** (w. *cordi*) to take to heart. **d** to assume (log.), take for granted. **e** (p. ppl. as sb. n.), minor premiss.

a monachicum..nomen adsumsit BEDE *HE* IV 25; Christus..re ipsa omnia quae ~psit adunavit ERIUG. *Per.* 545A; Deus ~psit hominem et homo ~ptus est a Deo J. CORNW. *Eul.* 1047; divinam naturam pro mundi salute humanam naturam ~psisse GIR. *TH* II 19; **c1200** (v. abacus 2b); non solum opponentis..sed eciam respondentis personam ~ere OCKHAM *Dial.* 850. **b** **1300** cum non ~ere nomen Dei in vanum dominicum sit preceptum *Vis. Ely* 14. **c** **1332** nos iter [ad Terram Sanctam] ~entes multum cordi *Lit. Cant.* I 439. **d** ~pto ex eis que predicta sunt cujuslibet generis initialia tot esse quot ea sunt de quibus interrogabilia sunt BALSH. *AD* 143; dicendum per interempcionem ad utramque ~ptarum [sc. proposicionum] PECKHAM *Puer. Obl.* 436; prima proposicio quam ~unt et quam ipse dicit esse falsam OCKHAM *Pol.* II 833; non video quod aliunde.. ~ere poterit populum Judaicum specialiter..fuisse Petro commissum *Id. Dial.* 849. **e** probatur ~ptum RIC. ARMAGH *Unusq.* 60; argumentum et ~ptum patet ex secunda supposicione secundi capituli CONWAY *Def. Mend.* 1422; **c1430** quasi de totidem dialecticorum premissis conclusive infertur non dubium sed debitum ex ~pto *Reg. Whet.* II 439.

5 to undertake. **b** (w. inf.). **c** (w. *iter*). **d** (w. *in se* or *super se*) to take upon oneself. **e** (w. *ad* in writs initiating procedure by *assumpsit*).

1338 cum..~psisset..custodiam castri de Edenburgh *RScot* 553b. **b** **1342** cum T. W. ~pserit coram nobis et consilio nostro invenire xx homines ad arma *Ib.* 627a (cf. ib.: cum..~pserit..morari). **c** **s1270** rex Francie..pro recuperacione Terre Sancte iter ~psit *Meaux* II 165; **s1321** rex..iter suum ~psit versus Wygorniam *Flor. Hist.* III 345. **d** **1258** cum in vos curam regni Scocie..~pseritis *Cl* 461; **1262** alium..qui negocium illud in se ~at *Cl* 154; **1344** ipsi per se non sunt ausi ad talia super se ~enda nisi xij.. meliores ville ea secum velint presumere *SelCKB* VI 38; **1567** parcellam terre..super quam ~psit super se edificare unam domum *Surv. Pembr.* 398. **e** **14..** ostensurus quare, cum idem B. ..ad sanandum predictum A. de morbo.. ~psisset.., idem B. ..ipsum..non curavit *Reg. Brev.* 105b (cf. ib.: 108, 109b, 110, 110b).

assummare, to add up, total. **b** (fig.) to settle the account of, kill.

s1166 inventa est ecclesia tot debitis gravata quod ad dc m. summa inveniretur, sicut regiis famulis fuit ~ata *G. S. Alb.* I 183; **1259** quod omnes empciones..assumari faciat per tallias *Cl* 431; **1263** ~atis omnibus particulis solucionis *Cl* 295; cotidie quid et quantum expenderit fideliter scribere et totam septimanam ~are *Obs. Barnwell* 186. **b** **1266** arripuit quoddam magnum palum..et voluit ~are ipsum sic jacentem *IMisc.* 13/21.

assummatio v. essaimatio.

assumptibilis, to be taken.

caput ecclesie, sicut ordinavit massam sanctam ~em ad medelam veneni serpentis, sic ordinavit angelos bonos in forma corporea sponse sue assistere; sed post assumpcionem illius nature in unione ypostatica..non est tam crebra talis apparicio angelorum WYCL. *Civ. Dom.* I 422.

assumptio, taking (into the body). **b** attraction.

quidam [morbi] extra adveniunt aut per eorum ~onem aut obviationem, ut venena GILB. I 1. 2. **b** magnetes lapides..circumquaque habebantur et [ferreum simulacrum] hinc et inde in ~one proportionalit rahebatur GREG. *Mir. Rom.* 9.

2 admission to office. **b** taking up (w. ref. to *Matth.* iv 8).

in predictis casibus esset ~o cujuscumque ad mundi imperium differenda OCKHAM *Dial.* 877; **1417** de..~one et eleccione..pape..celebrata *Reg. Cant.* III 33. **b** Lucas.. istas duas [Christi] ~ones recitat ordine contrario OCKHAM *Pol.* I 344.

3 taking up into Heaven: **a** (of Christ); **b** (of the Virgin, celebrated on 15 Aug.).

a **799** si necesse est propter adsumptionem adoptivum esse Christum ALCUIN *Ep.* 166; [Christus] per ~onem in caelum..caelum unificavit et terram ERIUG. *Per.* 540C; **1315** cum..corporali cum crucifixo et ~one brudato *Invent. Ch. Ch.* 77; Petrus et Jacobus et Johannes post ~onem Salvatoris prelati fuerunt a Domino pene omnibus OCKHAM *Dial.* 848. **b** **1006** de ~one et Nativitate S. Marie *Comp. Swith.* 191; quinque sunt praecipuae festivitates, id est Natale Domini, Resurrectio ejus, Pentecostes, ~o S. Dei genetricis Marie.. LANFR. *Const.* 126; in ~one vel Nativitate S. Mariae *DB* I 262b; paucis ante ~onem B. Dei genetricis diebus W. MALM. *HN* 500; **1196** apud Wigorniam de termino ~onis B. Marie *CurR* I 30; scripsi in vigilia ~onis litteram AD. MARSH *Ep.* 50; nulle festivitates ipsius nisi ejus ~o et Nativitas rite debent celebrari *Cust. Westm.* 91; ~onis tue tam in corpore quam in anima J. GODARD *Ap.* 249; S. Edwardus rex et confessor contulit..zonam quam ipsa [Virgo] propriis manibus operata est et utebatur atque S. Thome apostolo in ~one sua dimisit FLETE *Westm.* 70; **1455** consecravit altare..in honore ~onis B. Marie *Invent. Ch. Ch.* 162; in festis..Ascensionis, ~onis Nostre Domine.. *Plusc.* VII 19; de ~one B. Marie in corpore et anima BLAKMAN *Hen. VI* 20.

4 **a** taking on (of attributes or sim.). **b** assumption (log.), minor premiss.

a quid repugnant quorundam quae accidentia dicuntur susceptibilitas et naturalis incommutabilitas si ex eorum ~one nulla substantiam consequatur variabilitas? ANSELM (*Mon.* 25) I 43; ita distinxit Boetius quod Deus est natura et non ex ~one, homo vero ita est natura quod ~one J. CORNW. *Eul.* 1068; **s452** Eutices..qui Christum post humanam ~onem negavit existere de duabus naturis sed solam divinam in eo asseruit esse naturam M. PAR. *Maj.* I 119; gaudium..quod habebunt [sancti] de..~one corporum gloriosorum OCKHAM *Dial.* 743. **b** particularis sit negatio tua, 'non omnis affirmatio constare poterit parte subruta'; rursus ~o tua, 'panis et vinum altaris solummodo sunt sacramentum..': his duabus particularibus praecedentibus poterisne regulariter concludere parte subruta ea non posse constare? LANFR. *Corp. & Sang.* 417D; 'si autem quod non videmus speramus, per patientiam expectamus': ~o, 'sed speramus quod non videmus' *Id. Comment. Paul.* (*Rom.* viii 25) 132.

5 undertaking, acceptance (of office). **b** undertaking, promise. **c** undertaking, setting out (w. play on 4b).

1264 faciant omnes ballivos suos in ~one ballive jurare quod..justitiam exhibebunt (*Pat*) *Foed.* I 795. **b** **1382** remisimus..quascumque condiciones, manucapciones et ~ones quas ipsi..racione earundem recognicionum debebant vel tenebantur *RParl* III 135b; ~oni dicti R. †fideliter [? l. fidem] adhibens *Entries* 4. **c** nichil aut minimum prodest sana ~o, si consequens vita dissentit J. SAL. *Pol.* 793D.

assumptive, by way of assumption.

accipitur ~e vel suppositive GAD. 21 v. 1.

assumptor, taker up, supporter (of complaints).

1333 falsi juratores et falsarum querelarum ~ores *Conc.* II 562; **1355** communes ~ores et manutentores falsarum querelarum *SelCKB* VI 103; **1362** non contenciosi, non querelarum aut litium ~ores *Lit. Cant.* II 425.

assumptus [cf. CL sumptus], cost.

1334 consideratum est..quod ~us et expense existunt versus priorem in placito *Gild Merch.* (*Andover*) II 330.

assuniare v. essoniare. assungia v. axungia. assura v. assatura.

assuranter, by assurance.

1405 (v. alliganter).

assurantia, conveyance (of land).

asseruit..quod idem R. daret eidem T. ..mmm li. ..ad confeccionem ~ie predicti manerii *Entries* 594 (cf. ib. 691b: in perpetuam eleemosynam et ~iam); **1587** colore cujuscumque prescripcionis sive ~ie de aliquo statu..perceperunt annuales redditus..sive proficua *Pat* 1298 m. 7.

assurare [OF *asseurer* < assecurare], to convey (land). **b** (?) *f.l.*

dari in perpetuam eleemosynam et ~ari *Entries* 691b. **b** **a1389** (v. assurgere 1a).

assuratura v. assatura.

assurgere [CL], to stand up for (as mark of deference). **b** (w. *ad gratias* or sim.) to express thanks. **c** to strive for, devote oneself to.

si vobis adpropinquantibus adsurrexerit, ..obtemperanter illum audite BEDE *HE* II 2; mox assurgebat complaudebatque sorori *VMerl.* 577; hospitibus tua sit conjunx assurgere docta / assurgatque tibi D. BEC. 2250–1; **a1389** non tenentur filii parentes honorari in †assurando [? l. ~endo] vel aliter reverenciam exhibendo sed in omni necessitate supportando BRINTON *Serm.* 7 p. 21. **b** **1226** ut ..vestre debeamus ~ere diligentie cum..speciali gratiarum actione *Pat* 104; **1259** ad gratias vobis ~imus quas possumus ampliores *Cl* 476; **1261** super immensis beneficiis..quibus ..invenimus nos..honoratos, vobis..ad quas valemus gratiarum ~imus actiones *Cl* 96. **c** **1293** taliter..honorem nostrum..conservantes quod ad..ecclesie vestre jurium conservacionem affectuosius ~amus *RGasc.* III 73.

2 (of things) to rise, increase.

aestus oceani..vespertinus adsurget BEDE *TR* 29; si.. repente flatus venti major adsurgeret *Id. HE* IV 3.

3 (w. *ad*) to attain to.

si [Waliscus] non ~at [AS: *gif he ne geþeo*] nisi ad dim. hidam, sit wera ejus lxxx s. (*Quad.*) *GAS* 461.

assurrectio, standing up (as mark of deference). **b** deference.

nec vero in sessione vel ~one..cognoscitur homo Dei Gosc. *Aug. Maj.* 78 (= ELMH. *Cant.* 105: assurrexione). **b** testis est hec epistola, quam pro nominibus potentissimorum et omnium ~one dignissimorum nemo..vel vix aliquis potest perlegere H. HUNT. *CM* 16.

assurus v. azureus.

assus [CL], roasted. **b** (as sb. f.) a roast.

hunc in carne Deum sumptus piscis probat assus (NIG. *Laur.*) *Speculum* VII 419; quatenus ova ~a secarent in quadrantes W. CANT. *Mir. Thom.* VI 2; ferinam tam ~am quam coctam GIR. *GE* II 32 p. 320. **b** ~a carnis suille, diligenti tractu assata, ..condimentum dedignatur aliud quam purum salem NECKAM *Ut.* 102; ~a, *a rost mete* WW.

Assyrius, Saracen.

ordo duplex, alba cruce pugnax et cruce rubra, / Assyrios mittit ad stygiale chaos GARL. *Tri. Eccl.* 135.

ast [CL; cf. at], but (expr. contrast). **b** (w. no definite contrast). **c** (after concessive clause).

quorum [sc. Abel et Melchisedech] prior..passionem.. praefiguravit; ast vero Melchisedech..nonne..libamina litaturus redemptoris..personam praefigurans obtulit..? ALDH. *VirgP* 54; unus / .. / alter.. / tertius ast testis.. *Id. VirgV* 935; **a1000** (11c) ast si quid praefatorum..defuerit jurum.. *CD* 1287; ast alii plures? aliis sunt hi meliores! G. AMIENS *Hast.* 541; pes graditur recte..; / claudicat ast animus NIG. *SS* 1297. **b** contigit..plures ad eum..confluxisse; ast ille tres sportulas..exhibuit ALDH. *VirgP* 38 p. 290; **c717** karitatis tuae copulam, fateor, ast dum per interiorem hominem gustavi..hic sapor insidet (EGBURG) *Ep. Bonif.* 13; convocat ast hominem Flodoaldus luce sequenti WULF. *Swith.* II 352. **c** licet..gratissimus extiterat, ast tamen..minora..praeconia crebrescunt ALDH. *VirgP* 53 p. 312; quamvis caecatus sentiret damna pupille, / ast tamen..vidit *Id. VirgV* 499.

asta v. hasta.

astaco [ἀστακός = *crayfish*], grasshopper.

de nominibus insectorum: ..locusta, ~o, *gærstapa* ÆLF. *Gl.*

astalagium v. stallagium. astall- v. astell-. astantivus v. stantivus.

astare [CL; v. et. assistere], to stand by or near: **a** (of persons); **b** (of things).

a EDDI *Wilf.* 47 (v. antiphona); vidi adstantem mihi subito quendam BEDE *HE* IV 23; ~antes et ministrantes Deo caelestes virtutes legimus ERIUG. *Per.* 574D; ecce enim ~at reus ante tremendum judicem! ANSELM (*Or.* 13) III 50; a quodam marescallo, qui cum virga sua ~abat W. FITZST. *Thom.* 48; ut sentiam tibi ~are adulterum *Latin Stories* 78; **1321** semper duodene fuerunt ~antes ad barram coram justiciariis *MGL* II 370; R. regnum vastat, vindex et in omnibus astat GOWER *CT* III 472. **b** littera quindecima praestat quod pars domus adsto ALDH. *Aen.* 86 ([*p*]*aries*) 8; ~abat prope quandam mons G. MON. IV 9; [res] fluctuat intus / et foris, hic et ibi, procul et prope, distat et astat VINSAUF *PN* 255.

2 to be helpful or amenable.

eciam in hoc presenti seculo deliciis fruitur qui Salvatoris sui desideriis ~are delectatur ROLLE *IA* 216; non curant quomodo causa / stat, set ut illa lucris fertilis astet eis GOWER *VC* VI 26.

astata v. hastata. astayda v. ascaris.

asteismos [ἀστεϊσμός], urbanity, elegance (of speech).

astismos, quidquid simplicitate rusticana caret *GlC* A 847; ~os est tropus multiplex..: namque ~os putatur dictum omne quod simplicitate rustica caret et faceta satis urbanitate expolitum est BEDE *ST* 616.

astella, ~um [cf. astula, hastile], stick (esp. for firewood). **b** cart-pole, shaft. **c** splint (med.).

1221 de caretta honerata de bosco, unde solebant capere unam astelam, capiunt majus lignum *Eyre Lincs & Worcs* no. 1167 (cf. *SelPlCrown* p. 90); **1233** petit terciam partem unius ~e de qualibet carettata busce *CurR* XV 738 (cf. *Reg. Malm.* II 318); **1235** Agatha uxor Gilberti..percussit eundem Gilbertum quodam ~o *JustIt* 864 r. 17*d.*; **1275** Robertum percussit subtus auriculam cum..astilla *IMisc.* 33/39; **1286** in c astell' ad vivificandum ignem sub carbone, v d.; in cariagio illorum astell' per mare usque Ore, j d. *KRAc* 460/27 A(3); **1289** in piris per ventum prostratis findendis pro ~o faciendo *MinAc* 840/6; **1293** in viij[m] hastal' amputandis et faciendis in Herboldeswode *Ib.* 7; non fuit necesse ut [igni] supponerent multa ligna sed tantum duas †ascellas BRADW. *CD* 53B; **1361** maeremium, astell', faget'..furatus fuit *Pat* 128 m. 19. **b** c**1160** dedit ..~am summarii et gloam quadrige *Act. Hen. II* I 260; **1213** in j caretta..et j pari ~orum *Cl* 128b; **1214** iiij paria ~arum..ad carettam *Ib.* 160b; **1242** pro xij ~is limonariis *Liberate* 16 m. 6; **1285** in v collariis novis ad eandem [carettam] cum astill' novis *KRAc* 351/18 m. 1; **1290** pro..v paribus ~orum, iij paribus tractuum..pro equis de curru regine *Ac. Wardr.* (*Chanc. Misc.* 4/5) f. 3v; **1316** pro..ij pervant' et cor' ad hastell' de secundo curru domicellarum *KRAc* 99/21 m. 1. **c** si ossa..vel vene sint lese, ligentur ~e vel tabule tenues et rigide ex utraque parte GAD. 122 v. 2.

astellaria, ~ium [cf. OF *astelier*; v. et. hastellaria], workshop.

1222 pro una mola ad habendum in astelerio *KRAc* 491/13; **1252** fieri facias..unam astelariam ad opus cementariorum *Liberate* 28 m. 14; **1279** in cccc de durebord' emptis ad..hostia hastilariorum..in vj mill' cc et dim. calami ad hastilaria, muros et quarellos contra yemem cooperiend' *KRAc* 467/7/4; **1293** arondinis..ad coopperturam hastilarii magistri M. et..cementariorum *Ib.* 468/6; **1315** sunt in manu regis pro astallaria cementariorum et carpentariorum facienclum operaciones regis ibidem *Pipe* 118 r. 55; **1319** illud penticium quod est pro loggis cementariorum in ~ia *KRAc* 469/1; **1320** circa..emundacionem placee a superfluis pro ~ia [*gl.*: i. domus cementar'] ibidem edificanda *Ib.* 482/1 r. 5; **1325** portitoribus tractantibus petras cum baiard' de ponte usque astelr' *Ib.* 469/8 r. 4; **1371** in operacione iij *buketts* in astillar' et in vestiario *Fabr. York* 12.

astenta v. extenta. aster v. auster.

asteriscus [ἀστερίσκος], asterisk.

~is, stellis *GlC* A 849 (cf. Jerome: *Job pref.*); ~os et obelos in libris suis..depingebant D. MORLEY 6; transvolutis ab hoc obelo usque ad †astericum foliis..ad ulteriora..depreperent GIR. *GE* I 24 p. 64; Origenes..translationem LXX obelo et ~o correxit R. NIGER 120; Origenes non fecit aliquam translationem, licet Magister Historiarum dicat Origenem transtulisse cum ~o et obelo. ..sed non potest translatio dici cum ~is et obelis; nam, cum ~us ponatur, ut illuminet sicut stella et ostendat ubi aliqua omissa.., constat quod nullus in opere suo, cum alieno, hoc facit BACON *Min.* 337; *tokyn or signe where a booke lakkyth*, ~us *PP*; ut sic liber.. ~o vel obelo consignatus, securius ad alios descendat, tanta auctoritate vallatus CAPGR. (*Dedic.*) *Hen. app.* 222.

asthma [ἆσθμα], asthma.

s**1173** tussis asthmatica omnes fere..occupavit..; contra quam [pestem] quidam hujusmodi prece..liberantur: Christe, tuum plasma, me torquet tussis et asthma; / asthmatis et tussis, Christe medicus mihi tu sis FORDUN *Cont.* VIII 21 (cf. *Plusc.* VI 25); uva..tangit epiglotum et summitatem trachee, unde sepe raucedinem et asma..et plures pectoris facit passiones, quociens elongatur et accurtatur RIC. MED. *Micr. Anat.* 221; sirupus optimus ad.. asma GILB. IV 187 v. 1; asma..est sicut anhelitus in homine fatigato cum magno cursu et est difficultas in expellendo aerem GAD. 54 v. 2; †disma [l. disnia] est species asmatis, sed †disma fit ex siccitate, asma ex humiditate *SB* 18.

asthmaticus [ἀσθματικός], asthmatic.

hic locus astmaticos sanat NIG. *SS* 3193; asmaticosque juvat nepta NECKAM *DS* VII 114; dyadragagantum..valet ..asmaticis GILB. IV 174. 1; comitissa Glovernie habuit palefridum asmaticum G. *porsif Mir. Montf.* 68; pacientes cadunt in constriccionem anhelitus..et sunt asmatici GAD. 52 v. 1; asmaticus dicitur qui non habet vocem claram *SB* 12; s**1421** obiit frater J. W. ex asmatica passione STONE *Chr.* 11b.

astiatus v. astratus. astile v. altile. astill- v. astell-, hastell-. astiludium v. hastiludium.

astipulari [CL], **~are,** to confirm, corroborate, demonstrate. **b** to affirm, assert. **c** to pretend. **d** (w. dat.) to support, assist.

septiformis sacramentorum numerus sacrosanctis.. oraculis..adstipulatur ALDH. *Met.* 1; apis..virginitatis tipum ..scripturarum auctoritate asstipulatur *Id. VirgP* 5; †**974** (12c) vivifici signaculo triumphi idem adstipulavi *CS* 1301; c**1022** ego Ælfsige episcopus adstipulavi *CD* 736; **10..** adstipulamur, *we trymmað* WW. **b** Athanasius.. quantas..machinas expertus sit, decimus liber..adstipulatur ALDH. *VirgP* 32 p. 273; **10..** ~atur, *is seðende and cweðende* WW; quidam cecus sompno suasum sibi ~abatur quia.. *V. Ed. Conf.* 54v; **1443** quod communis amicus noster..dilectionem tuam mihi ~averit..magnipendo BEKYNTON I 173. **c** ni fallax caupo strofas infundat aquosas / ..taliter adstipulans natos de vite racemos ALDH. *VirgV* 2799. **d** **10..** adstipulans, *fylstende and geecende and gewemende* WW; s**1146** ~abantur ei..suffragia Romani senatus J. HEX. *HR Cont.* 19; accedens miles..ad pontificem, ~antibus sibi viris discretis, ..omnem rei..pandit rationem AD. EYNS. *Hug.* IV 5 p. 21; c**1430** cui eciam concordat et ~atur illud Salomonis dictum *Reg. Glasg.* 355.

astipulatio [CL], confirmation, corroboration, support. **b** affirmation, assertion.

ut evidentioribus adhuc ~onibus..comprobetur GILDAS *EB* 93; [nomina] quae poetica exemplorum adstipulatione.. indigent ALDH. *PR* 116; c**738** duorum pontificum..adstipulationem et consensum..accepi BONIF. *Ep.* 46; **800** veritatis adstipulatione ALCUIN *Ep.* 201; †**866** (11c) scripta est et corroborata hec cartula sub ~one testium idoneorum *CS* 514; omnium ~one nobilium ASSER *Alf.* 12; **10..** adstipulationibus, *trymnessum* WW; [miracula] eodem modo quo scripta sunt, fixa ~one, velut ex lectione, exponebat Gosc. *Aug. Maj.* 58; a**1105** quaecunque illis..habenda concessit, sigilli mei ~one corroboro *Regesta* II p. 310; ecclesiastica electio prius debet ab ipsis subjectis..fieri et postmodum ~one patrum..confirmari ORD. VIT. IV 7 p. 227. **b** prophetarum oracula certis adstipulationibus..Salvatoris adventum vaticinantia ALDH. *VirgP* 4; *Ib.* 57 (v. assertio 2); Anglorum ~oni divinitas assentiri videtur W. MALM. *GP* IV 182.

astipulator, confirmer, corroborator. **b** supporter, adherent.

adstipulator, idoneus testis *GlC* A 223; **980** (11c) his testamentorum ~oribus quorum nomina..aperte videntur *CD* 625; **981** (11c) istis ~oribus corroborata est haec donatio *Ib.* 631. **b** misit ei Radulfus nuntios sue partis ~ores W. MALM. *GP* I 70; omnes Balduini ~ores..ei [regi] se supplices contulerunt *G. Steph.* I 17.

astismos v. asteismos. astmaticus v. asthmaticus. astop- v. astup-. astovarium v. estoverium. astque v. atque a. astra v. 2 astrum.

astraba [cf. ἀστράβη], foot-board, foot-rest.

~a, *fotbret* ÆLF. *Gl.*

astracare [ME *straken*], to 'strake', blow the hunting-horn.

1271 si contingat quod canes..in warenna..intrant, venatores seu bernatores..ad..divisam..demorabunt et ibidem pro canibus cum cornu ~abunt seu haulohabunt *AncD* A 306.

astracta v. extrahere. astraeus, astralis v. astrosus.

astrarius [cf. 2 astrum 2], (son or brother) resident at paternal hearth, acknowledged heir. **b** (?) householder or household servant.

1239 iste Matheus, ut ~ius et qui expectavit hereditatem patris sui et fuit cum ipso quando obiit, consecutus est hereditatem ut suus rectus [heres] *CurR* XV 959; **1244** Petrus antenatus obiit ante patrem ipsorum; et..Thomas postnatus remansit in eadem terra sicut ~ius *Ib.* XVIII 1087; **1250** Henricus..successit..Jordano ut frater ejus ~ius *Ib.* 139 r. 7d.; **1257** predicte terre..restituentur.. comitisse.., si ita fuerit quod predictus M., filius dicti M. postnatus, ..predictas terras..non clamaverit ut jus suum per..feoffamentum..patris sui vel alio modo, sc. ut ~ius ipsius patris sui *Cl* 288; videndum si nepos et avunculus sub eadem potestate antecessoris simul fuerint ~ii tempore mortis, eo quod ambo reperiuntur in atrio sive in astro BRACTON 267b; **1279** quod prefati Willelmus et Johanna haberent astrum et ea que ad ~ium pertinent *Cl* 96 m. 4. **b** *frithborghe* est laudabilis homo ~ius testimonii *Fleta* 62; s**1291** obiit Thomas Pictor.., de quo domina de la Yorne habuit melius averium nomine herietti, quia ~ius ejus fuit *Ann. Dunstable* 371.

1 †astratus, (?) starry.

†gipsa terreos [? l. gesasterios], i. terra ~a [v.l. †astiata], ..rubeus bolus armenicus *Alph.* 76.

2 astratus [cf. 2 astrum], occupied by a hearth-site, inhabited (Somerset).

1567 tenent per copiam..unum tenementum..continens xvij acras de antiquo austratas *Surv. Pembr.* 476; unum toftum de antiquo austratum *Ib.* 480.

astraura v. straura. astreciare v. estreciare. astrepare v. estrepare.

astrepere [CL], to join in a cry.

cum..alii anseres..ingressi domum interstreperent, cepit [anser] qui evectus fuerat ~ere W. CANT. *Mir. Thom.* IV 48.

astricola, dwelling among the stars.

licet astricolas inter numerere catervas FRITH. 1249.

astricte, under obligation, devotedly.

1230 me ad omnia..que vestrum..tetigerint.. honorem semper habebitis..~issime famulantem (*AncC* VI 130) *RL* I 380.

astrictio, obligation.

visum est omnibus.., ex ~one ligii homanagii quod domino regi archiepiscopus fecerat, ..quod parum esset.. excusatus W. FITZST. *Thom.* 40; **1327** molendino..cum ~one multure ejusdem *Reg. Dunferm.* 370; **1493** potestatem ..committimus..omnes..securitates, ..penas ~ones et literas sigillatas..promittendi (*TreatyR*) *Foed.* XII 524b.

astrictus, obligation.

1399 legios homines meos..a juramentis fidelitatis.. omnique vinculo legiancie..vel quolibet ~u absolvo (*Lit. Ric. II*) *Reg. North.* 427.

astridulus, whistling, hissing.

10.. adstridulae, *ðære hristendan toswege* WW.

astrifer [CL], starry, starlit.

sacer astrifera gauderet spiritus arce ALDH. *VirgV* 1770; astriferas ego nocte fovebo latebras *Id. Aen.* 35 (*Nycticorax*) 4.

astrifugus, putting the stars to flight.

sol jubar astrifugum mundum circum[m]eat HANV. IX 379.

astriger [CL], starry. **b** heavenly.

invocat astrigero qui regnat in axe tonantem WULF. *Swith.* II 557; nec enim Jove major ad axes / imperat astrigeros HANV. V 314. **b** nec semel astrigeris sonuerunt agmina dictis ÆTHELWULF *Abb.* 685.

astringere [CL], to bind. **b** to congeal. **c** to confine, contain. **d** (w. *sibi*) to annex, appropriate.

in nodosi cippi claustrum..tibias et suras adstringunt ALDH. *VirgP* 35 p. 279; inerguminum..catenarum nexibus asstrictum *Ib.* 52 p. 309; cranii vacuitate cooperta cum lineo mundo, pileolo desuper ~ente W. FITZST. *Thom.* 149. **b** aque..algoris aerei nexibus astricte GIR. *TH* I 6. **c** irrupit..populus..quantum ecclesie spatiositas potuit ~ere G. CRISPIN *Herl.* 107. **d** miles quidam..tria maneria de dominio sibi astrinxerat DOMERH. *Glast.* 306.

2 to bind (fig.), constrain, oblige. **b** (w. inf.). **c** (w. *ad*). **d** (w. *quod*).

artioribus se necesse habent..continentiae frenis ~ere (*Lit. Ceolfridi*) BEDE *HE* V 21 p. 343; sacramento jurisjurandi eum astri[n]xit ne unquam aliquid..pro mercede acciperet GIR. *GE* II 26 p. 292; c**1218** nec quisquam annulum de junco..jocando manibus innectat muliercularum, ..ne, dum jocari se putat, oneribus matrimonialibus se ~at *Conc. Syn.* 87 (= *Ch. Sal.* 154: †abstringat); papa..a legibus imperialibus minime est astrictus OCKHAM *Dial.* 513; s**1387** in fide et ligeancia quibus eidem [regi] ~ebantur *V. Ric. II* 86. **b** **1201** preceptis divinis ~imur annuntiare..gloriam ejus *Canon. G. Sempr.* 118 v.; **1268** preter quartum librum Topicorum, ..quem audivisse non ~antur *StatOx* 26; nec Romanum pontificem ~erentur consulere OCKHAM *Pol.* I 266; s**1399** in dictos..abbates..compromiserunt, promittentes et fide media ~entes parere..arbitrio eorundem *Meaux* III 264; **1467** astrinxit..custodem..obviare vicario *Reg. Whet.* II 74. **c** **1257** ad hanc conventionem fideliter observandam meam fidem astrinxi *Reg. St. Bees* 356; **1280** ad quorum..articulorum..observacionem..dicunt omnes magistri..se esse adstrictos *MunAcOx* 43; est attachiamentum quoddam vinculum legitimum per quod pars defendens invita ~itur ad standum juri *Quon. Attach.* 1 2; **1399** ad que..perimplenda dictus..major..et..Adam predictus..per fidem suam [se] †astruncerunt *Mem. York* I 206. **d** a**1350** ~antur..procuratores..quod..nullam fraudem committant *StatOx* 30.

3 (p. ppl. *astrictus*) morally bound, constrained. **b** attached (by ties), devoted. **c** strict.

se excusans..quia episcopatu propriae civitatis..teneretur adstrictus BEDE *HE* III 7. **b** sed forte falsarius ille aliquibus vestrum carnaliter ~us erat GIR. *Symb.* I 31 p. 318; **1280** ipsum exercicium armorum cum liberalitate magnifica fecit militibus carissimum sibi in magna ~orum multitudine PECKHAM *Ep.* 118. **c** **1421** mitigacio certorum statutorum..nimium, ut apparuit, ~orum *Reg. Cant.* III 69.

astrium v. 2 astrum.

astrivagus, moving among the stars.

torserat astrivagum..Phebum / annua mobilitas J. EXON. *BT* VI 115.

astrolabicus, concerned w. the astrolabe.

sunt et alie metiendi corpora demonstrationes; sed, quoniam ille..magis..geometrice quam ~e dici possunt, eas preterimus (ADEL. *Astr.*) *Med. Sci.* 21.

astrolabium [ἀστρολάβος], astrolabe.

quia de ~io scientibus loquor (WALCHER *Exp.*) *Med. Sci.* 114*n.*; hec quam vides..dextra radium, leva vero ~ium gestantem ADEL. *ED* 32; Gerbertus..vicit scientia Ptholomeum in ~io W. MALM. *GR* II 167; Hermannus Contractus inventor ~ii BELETH *RDO* 38. 46; sumpto ~io vel quadrante .., notetur graduum in qua steterit mediclinium multitudo SACROB. *Sph.* 85; si fieret taliter ~ium quod esset aliquod rete in ~io in quo divideretur circulus equinoctialis integer ROB. ANGL. (II) *Sph.* [illegible]; ad rectificandum cursus et loca stellarum..una cum c[illegible]teris que investigari poterunt per armillas, ~ium aut turketum WALLINGF. *Rect.* 337.

astrolapsus, astrolabe.

apprehenso ~u, hora qua totam nigredo caliginosa lunam absorbuerat..inspexi (WALCHER *Exp.*) *Med. Sci.* 115; libellus..Alardi Bathoniensis de opere ~us (ADEL. *Astr.*) *Ib.* 28.

astrologia [CL < ἀστρολογία], astronomy. **b** applied astronomy, astrology.

philosophorum disciplinas, hoc est arithmeticam, geometricam, musicam, astronomiam, ~iam et mechanicam ALDH. *VirgP* 59; **798** Abraham..ex ~iae ratione creatorem Deum intellexisse ALCUIN *Ep.* 148; ~ia est caelestium corporum spatia motusque reditusque certis temporibus investigans disciplina ERIUG. *Per.* 475A; in stellis stellas astrologia notat NECKAM *DS* I 288; sic in matematicis, sc. in abstralogia BACON VII 6; ~ia componitur ex hoc nomine *astron*, quod est 'stella', et hoc nomine *logos*, quod est.. 'sermo', quia est sermo de stellis *Id.* (*Math.*) *Maj.* I 242*n.*; ~ia..speculativa certificat numerum et figuram celorum et stellarum et magnitudines earum et altitudines a terra et spissitudines et ortus et occasus signorum et stellarum et motus et eclipses et quantitatem et figuram terre habitabilis et partes ejus magnas que sunt climata mundi *Id. Tert.* 106. **b** utrosque alterutra ~ia eruditionis sue recipit professores J. SAL. *Pol.* 439D; quamquam secundum ~ie fabulosam traditiunculam Aquila signum sit sidereum Aquario oppositum, ..secundum veritatem..astronomie Leo signum est oppositum Aquario NECKAM *NR* I 23; ~ia practica docet et preparat instrumenta et canones et tabulas, quibus certificantur ad omnem horam ea que in celestibus renovantur et in aëre, cujusmodi sunt comete et irides.., et preparat vias ad judicia facienda de omnibus inferioribus et ad opera mira et utilia in hoc mundo que fieri habent in certis electionibus constellationum in actibus hujus vite BACON *Tert.* 106.

astrologice, astronomically.

descripsi hec loca in universali et in particulari et ~e et naturaliter BACON *Min.* 358; c**1410** ~e satis patet quod Jovis mansueta benignitas per zodiaci circulum locum Martis vendicat revolutum *FormOx* 425.

astrologicus [ἀστρολογικός], astronomical (or astrological).

671 cum ~ae artis peritia et perplexa oroscopi computatio doctoris indagatione egeat ALDH. *Ep.* 1; **13..** instrumenta ~a magistri J. E. (*Invent. York*) *N. & Q. ser.* 1 I 84.

astrologus [CL < ἀστρολόγος], astronomer. **b** astrologer.

inferiores orbes septem planetarum moventur contra firmamentum secundum omnes ~os *Comm. Sph.* 282. **b** ~us vel magus vel mathematicus, *tungelwitega, geberdwiglære* ÆLF. *Gl.*; hoc ipsum astronomie sue beneficio sibi ~us repromittit J. SAL. *Pol.* 440C; ~us, phisicus et medicus de tempore, licet varie, considerant: ille, ut effectum superiorum motuum, et ut causam naturalium inferiorum BACON VI 1; veri mathematici et astronomi seu ~i, qui philosophi sunt, non ponunt necessitatem et infallibile judicium in rebus contingentibus de futuro *Id. Maj.* I 246.

astronomia [ἀστρονομία], astronomy. **b** astrology.

ALDH. *VirgP* 59 (v. astrologia); ~iae et arithmeticae ecclesiasticae disciplinam BEDE *HE* IV 2; **10..** ~ia, *tungelcræft wisan* WW; est ~ie nobilis et gloriosa scientia, si clientelam suam intra moderationis metas cohibeat J. SAL. *Pol.* 440A; **1432** (v. aethereare); **1439** tam de quibuscunque..discordiis et litibus inter ipsos..habitis..quam de certis opinionibus certorum articulorum sciencie astronomie inter partes predictas *Cl* 290 m. 27*d.*; **1453** scola ~ie alta secunda *Cart. Osney* III 252. **b** **1188** hec prophetia et ~ia Turcorum est quod infra hoc triennium una pars Turcorum gladio peribit (*Lit. Nuntiorum*) *G. Hen. II* II 52; illi qui sydereis motibus vim et efficatiam negant adeo sunt impudentis amentie ut, antequam scientie disciplinam habeant, ejus doctrine incipiant derogare; unde quidam ex solo nomine ~iam odio habent D. MORLEY 34; ~ia dicitur lex stellarum et *nomos* est lex; unde, quia lex..sonat in practicam, ..~ia est practica astrologie BACON (*Math.*) *Maj.* I 242*n.*; certior est via judicandi de futuris quam per ~iam, et hoc est per experientiam *Id. Tert.* 44.

astronomice, astronomically.

expono loca in tractatu et figura, et hoc dupliciter, sc. ~e et naturaliter BACON *Min.* 318.

astronomicus [ἀστρονομικός], astronomical, astrological. **b** (sb. m.) astronomer, astrologer. **c** (sb. f.) astronomy.

junxit se Gerebertus cuidam illius artis [astrologie] perito, qui libros ei ~os prebuit ad scribendum M. PAR. *Maj.* I 476; per ~am considerationem BACON XI 183; possumus cognoscere primationem lune secundum veritatem ~am *Id. Tert.* 288. **b** vocavit obvium sibi ~um qui Cesarem moriturum in kalendis predixerat GREG. *Mir. Rom.* 29; s**1229** ~i Tholetani omnibus Christi fidelibus..literas direxerunt WEND. II 356; Ptholomeus ~us tunc floruit *Eul. Hist.* I 324. **c** **1498** scola ~e alta secunda *Cart. Osney* III 278.

astronomus [ἀστρονόμος], astronomer. **b** astrologer.

secundum ordinem temporum naturalem principium anni est in lunatione Octobris; et hoc ~i orientales Egyptii et Greci et Perse et omnes considerant, qui a patriarchis et prophetis habuerunt astronomiam BACON *Tert.* 209. **b** ~us, cum futuros rerum eventus prescierit, poterit eorum noxia repellere D. MORLEY 34; hic [Fredericus], licet astronomus esset, non vidit in astris / se deponendum GARL. *Tri. Eccl.* 124; sic homo, utens..intellectu ad causas futurorum inspiciendo..multa futura precognoscit sicut ~i aspicientes in astris que mundum ordinant BACON VIII 124; *Id. Maj.* I 246 (v. astrologus b); sum peritissimus ~us; ..scio futura predicere *Latin Stories* 98; secundum ~os lunam habent [Angli] planetam proprium, que in motu et lumine est magis instabilis (WYCL. *Resp.*) *Ziz.* 270; s**1394** inter ceteras cometas..~i pessimam eam esse dixerunt *Eul. Hist. Cont.* I 287; s**1476** quidam magister J. Stacy dictus ~us, cum etiam magnus nercromanticus extiterat *Croyl. Cont. C* 561.

†**astrosia** [? cf. atrophia], waist.

the waste of a mannis body, ~ia *PP*.

astrosus [CL], **~aeus, ~alis,** maddened by stellar influence.

fonde, arepticius, ~osus; ..*a steron*, ..astrum..sydereus, ~eus, ~alis, ~osus, i. lunaticus; ..*wode*, arepticius, ..~alis, ~osus *CathA*.

astructio, demonstration.

Lanfrancus..edidit..libellum..vere intelligentie ~one de eucharistia copiosum ORD. VIT. IV 6 p. 211.

astruere [CL = *to add* (*in building*)], to edify.

quis..nostri temporis mores adstruit? GIR. *IK pref.* p. 4.

2 to affirm, assert. **b** (w. acc. and inf.). **c** (w. *quod.*).

adstruere [est] adfirmare BEDE *Orth.* 2784; c**1148** era[n]t ibi predictus R. et A. ubi, ut iste juvenis ~it, habuerunt ..colloquium..cum inimicis regis (*Reg. S. Edm.*) *EHR* XXXIX 569; nihil..ambiguitatis de his que piscator ~xerat..potuit residere AILR. *Ed. Conf.* 757; torporis.. fomitem subministrant, ut ~itur, ..quidam pestilentes AD. MARSH *Ep.* 239; GARL. *Syn.* 99 (v. asseverare); **1285** non cessavimus..imperterrite irreprehensam ~ere veritatem PECKHAM *Ep.* 645; de..hereticis asserentibus sese doctrinam veram ~ere OCKHAM *Dial.* 573; **1381** ergo qui istud astruunt / ecclesiam destituunt (*In Lollardos* 29) *Pol. Poems* I 240. **b** beati doctores..eisdem..sententiis..concorditer ~xerunt hereticum esse.. LANFR. *Corp. & Sang.* 416B; s**1139** ~ens fide data eum omni cibo cariturum donec.. H. HUNT. *HA* VIII 11; s**1146** templa se abolere..fixe ~ebant *G. Steph.* II 99; si Deus est et homo, duo sunt, prout astruis esse NIG. *Laur.* 38 v. 2; quod..se ~ebat nunquam in alia curia vidisse *Hist. Meriadoci* 372; **1339** cimiterium..per..episcopum..dedicatum esse ~entes *Reg. Exon.* II 899. **c** coepit..regi adstruere quod ipse..obtinuerit ut.. BEDE *HE* II 9; **1166** constanter ~ebat quod neminem..coegit *Canon. G. Sempr.* 90; fratres ~xerunt ..quod huic ministerio..non est annexa facultas exigendi vite necessaria.. RIC. ARMAGH *Def. Cur.* 1400.

3 to demonstrate, prove. **b** (w. *quod*). **c** (w. indir. qu.).

cujus..prophetiae veritatem sequens rerum astruxit eventus BEDE (*Cuthb.*) *HE* IV 27; nolo te..iis quae diximus inhaerere, si quis validioribus argumentis haec destruere et diversa valuerit..~ere ANSELM (*Gram.* 21) I 168; Walenses orationum frequentatione et multiplici sermone id procul-dubio ~unt et corroborant W. MALM. *Glast.* 26; si tam patenter ~eret propria quam potenter destruxit aliena J. SAL. *Met.* 906C; quod cum plurimis ~i queat rationibus NECKAM *NR* II 173; obtulerunt..quod vel corporali duello ..vel quibuscunque modis aliis quos curia decerneret.. ~erent..suarum propositionum articulos AD. MARSH *Ep.* 30 p. 125; eandem assercionem auctoritate Urbani pape.. nituntur ~ere OCKHAM *Dial.* 468. **b** sunt plures qui suis velint argumentis ~ere quod..nullus liber sit.. *Dial. Scac.* I 11C; quod abbatis electio non fuerit prima..veris assertionibus sic adstruimus GIR. *Inv.* IV 3 p. 167. **c** quanti meriti fuerit apud Deum, certis miraculorum ~it argumentis AILR. *Ed. Conf.* 786C.

4 to persuade. **b** to inform.

1259 multis persuasionibus..~ere et inducere..nitebatur nos..ut eundem A. ..restitui pateremur *Cl* 491. **b** **1321** dixerunt..quod de hujusmodi rebus non fuerunt astructi *MGL* II 370; **1438** ad presens satis luculenter et evidenter sumus astructi qualiter.. *Cl* 289 m. 33.

5 (?) to endeavour.

c**1380** quomodo..pervenerunt..tam luculenter quam veraciter ~imus presentibus †nunicare [l. nunciare] *Pri. Cold.* 53.

1 astrum [CL < ἄστρον], star. **b** sky.

ut globus astrorum plasmor teres atque rotundus ALDH. *Aen.* 100 (*Creatura*) 57; percipit inde decus reginae et sceptra sub astris; / plus super astra manens percipit inde decus BEDE (*Hymn*) *HE* IV 18; chorus ~orum suam immutatam observat sedem ERIUG. *Per.* 477C; que per ~orum ortum, occasum et motum significata [sunt] MAP *NC* IV 6 p. 168; GARL. *Tri. Eccl.* 124 (v. astronomus b). **b** ~um, caelum *GlC* A 840.

2 astrum, ~ium, ~a [cf. OF *astre*], hearth. **b** (for burning charcoal). **c** (for smelting iron). **d** measure of pitch (? boiling).

1221 de petris quas ipsi deferri fecerunt ad ~ium quoddam faciendum *SelPlCrown* 90; **1284** in factura unius hastri in magna turri [Lond'] ad opus mercatorum ibidem emprison[atorum] *KRAc* 467/9; **1297** in una ~a reficienda in camera exteriori cum petris ad idem cariandis *Ac. Cornw.* I 73; c**1300** quod libere possit turbam..†quantum sufficit ad aliud solum ~um..capere fodiendo *Cart. Chester* 418; **1345** circa construccionem..cujusdam nove domus pro quatuor cameris inde habendis constructe cum ij caminis de duobus ~is de petra et morterio in eadem *MinAc* 1120/12 r. 2(1). **b** **1269** ad plura ~a sustinenda ad carbonem †faciendam *SelPlForest* 44; **1336** habuit quatuor ~a ad carbones in dicto cooperto ad destruccionem foreste *Cl* 157 m. 23*d.* **c** **1270** concesserunt lapidem mine..ad unum ~um *Couch. Furness* I 263; **1308** unam..forgiam..cum duobus ~is de loco in locum transferend' pro ferro suo faciendo (*Indent.*) *Pat* 321 m. 26; **1353** in j ~io de novo faciendo pro dicta fabrica (*KRAc* 485/11) *Arch.* LXIV 161. **d** **1338** pro iij barell' et iiij ~is picche pro eadem nave *KRAc* 20/27 r. 1.

2 hearth as unit of habitation, household (*cf. astrarius, atrium* 1d). **b** (w. *vetus* or *antiquum*) 'old auster', (tenement annexed to) old-established habitation (w. specific rights and obligations).

s**1221** facta est promissio..in subsidium Terre Sancte, ita quod..quodlibet ~um j d. *Ann. Dunstable* 67; **1251** rex perderet..tallagium cum collectum esset in civitate eadem [Cantuaria] per ~a *IMisc* 5/13 (= *Cal* p. 35: †ostria); cum sit heres apparens unus vel plures unum jus habentes, ..sive inveniantur in ~o sive non, ..habeant seisinam hereditatis BRACTON 71b; villanis in ~o commorantibus non competit..remedium [per breve nove disseisine] versus veros dominos HENGHAM *Parva* 8; **1279** si quis sit viduarius et fuerit filius natus in ~o, dum est viduarius habeat totum tenementum; et, si velit uxorare, ..filius de ~o habeat partem terre ad vivendum *CourtR* 209/57; qui..extra ~um suum villanum ad loca remotiora se transtulerunt *Fleta* 217 (cf. ib.: villanis in veteribus ~is suis commorantibus); **1297** de omnibus ~is seu tenementis *Cart. Osney* II 459; (?) a**1300** ipse R. inventus fuit in †affra [? l. astra] et plena etate (*Inq.*) *CalPat* 1381–5 434; **1355** viij ~a et dim. et viij virgate *Cart. Boarstall* 161; **1372** (18c) dedi..xij carectatas turbarum ad quodlibet ~um super dicta burgagia edificandum (*Ch. Roby*) *EHR* XVII 296. **b** **1347** ad..faciendum pro quolibet tenemento integro, quod ab antiquo erat vetus ~um et herietabile, ..unum heriettum (*Indent., Middx*) *G. S. Alb.* II 328; **1343** Petrus.. de dominis de fine..pro uno messuagio et una ferdella terre antiqui astri..habend' et tenend' in villenagio *CourtR N. Curry* (*Somerset RO* DD/CC 131903/2); **1438** tenementum.. quod idem W. prius tenuit de nobis..in Hampton' [*Som*].. secundum consuetudinem manerii de antiquo ~o *Pat* 443 m. 23; **1463** unum tenementum continens dim. virgatam terre de antiquo ~o *Reg. Bath* I 401; **1548** [cotagium] de antiquo ~o [*Som*] *CalPat* 45; **1607** tenet per copiam curie.. unum messuagium continens v acras terre de antiquo ~o cum suis pertinenciis *LR Misc. Bk.* CCII (*Som*) f. 212 (cf. ib.: de antiquo austro).

3 astrum v. auster b. astrunc- v. astringere.

†**astuit** (?) *f.l.* for *astitit* (*cf. assistere* 1a) or *affuit* (*cf. adesse* 1c); *cf.* †*austat.*

1201 dormienti..~it senex venerandus *Canon. G. Sempr.* 167.

1 †**astula** [CL; cf. assula *or* hasta], chip (of wood).

multi de ipso ligno sacrosanctae crucis ~as excidere solent BEDE *HE* III 2; s**811** pons..ita..conflagravit ut ne una quidem hastula super aquam remaneret DICETO *Chr.* 133; absentibus infirmis per hastulas inde [sc. a feretro] abscisas..salus sepius advenit *NLA* (*Erkenwald*) I 394; **1389** de x s. de ~is *Ac. Obed. Abingd.* 52; *schyyd or astelle*, assula vel ~a *PP*; hec ~a, *a chype* WW.

2 astula v. hastula.

astuppare, ~iare [cf. stuppare, obstuppare], to stop up, block.

dicitur purprestura..quando aliquid super dominum regem injuste occupatur, ut in dominicis regiis vel in viis publicis astopatis GLANV. IX 11; **1255** dicunt quod..alta via et generalis inter Brehull' et Pidinton'..omnino esset astopata (*Inq.*) *Ambrosden* I 353; **1266** veniat responsurus quare astupavit quoddam fossatum *Rec. Lewes* 36; **1275** vicus S. Martini Orgor' ~iabatur per..clericum vic. Lond' et adhuc ~iatur *Hund.* I 421; astoppavit viam reg' per fossatum levatum *Ib.* II 311.

astur [cf. asturcus], bird of prey, (?) goshawk.

~ur, *haesualwe GlC* A 864.

asturcaria, service of supplying or keeping goshawks.

1198 tenet..per servitium serjantie hostricerie *Fees* 8; **1201** per servicium austurcarie *RChart* 93a; **1207** quod saisies..terram..pro defectu servicii ostriciarie *Cl* 96a; **1208** terram que capta fuit..pro defalta austurciarie *Ib.* 100a; **1211** Albreda..debet ij palefridos ut R. nepos ejus et J. filius B. possint supplere vices ejus hoc anno de serjanteria austurcarie quam regi debet *Pipe* 240; **1212** tenuit eam [terram] de dono Henrici regis antiqui per austriceriam *Fees* 130; **1234** servitium austurcarie, quod debetur de terra quam W. de L. tenet.., factum fuit domino J. regi *Cl* 16; **1240** dies datus est Galfrido de Insula versus regem de officio hosteracarie *CurR* XVI 1338.

asturcarius [cf. OF *ostricer*], keeper of goshawks, 'ostringer'.

c**1150** Hugone osturcario *Danelaw* 363; **1159** Hugoni ~io *Pipe* 32; **1160** in passagio..austurcariorum et falconariorum regis *Pipe* 23; **1178** in pluribus passagiis austurcariorum.. ut pro hugiis ad aves eorum *Pipe* 112; **1212** tenet..in servicio ostricerii *Fees* 219; **1213** in expensis Roberti B. ostricar' *Misae* 249; **1239** Henrici..austurciarii nostri *Cal. Liberate* 410; **1284** rotulus..vadiorum..falconariorum, austurcariorum.. *KRAc* 351/11; **1300** domino J. de Bikenore, militi, ~io regis, pro vadiis suis per xliij dies per quos fuit extra curiam cum asturcis regis ad ripandum per vices..percipiendo per diem ij s. *Ac. Wardr.* p. 304.

asturcia, service of supplying goshawks. **b** hawking w. goshawks.

12.. Warinus Ostricer per serjantiam ostrucie *Fees* 346 (cf. ib. 347: per serjantiam austurcie). **b** **1243** Waltero Wobode..eunti..ad summonendos omnes qui nobis debent servicium austurcorum contra instantem seisonam austurcie *Liberate* 19 m. 2.

†**asturcinus,** goshawk.

1320 redditus..unius †austurkini [? l. *austurkun*; cf. 2 asturco] sori per annum *Cl.* 138 m. 12.

1 asturco [CL], ambling horse.

ex Francia..sturconem..egregium cum suo †sessori.. advexit ANDRE *Hen. VII* 101; cum muneribus, equis ~onibus, canibus sagacibus.. BOECE 96v.

2 asturco, goshawk.

reddit..i ~onem et xx li. blancas comiti *DB* II 117b; accipiter a capiendo nomen accipit, sicut nomen austurconis ab australi plaga contraxit que Austria dicitur NECKAM *NR* I 25; **1279** unum austurconem vel fauconem *RGasc.* II 59.

asturcus [cf. OF *ostor*], goshawk. **b** (dist. as 'sore' or mewed). **c** image of goshawk.

1159 debet v austurc[os] et v girf[alcones] *Pipe* 64; **1194** unum hostarcum *CurR RC* I 35; c**1200** dominus de Coupland feoffavit O. ..de quarta parte de Crostwhait pro custodia ~orum suorum *MonA* III 584b; **1205** quod in quolibet adventu suo in Angliam dabit nobis j austurcum *Pat* 53a; **1210** cum..osturco et espervario et cum omni venatione *Couch. Furness* II 569; **1213** nunciis..qui venerunt cum austurcis de Hibernia *Misae* 235; **1213** cum osturci et girefalcones nobis fuerint presentati de Nortwaya *Cl* 156b; **1217** pro..uno hasturo et uno girefalcone *Ib.* 346b; **1219** reddendo unum hosturium *Fees* 273; **1223** duos bonos auxturos et duos bonos spervarios bene volantes *KRMem* 6 r. 2; **1224** per servicium portandi auxurum *Ib.* 7 r. 14; **1229** videnda sunt aerie osturorum et espervariorum et falconum, in quibus boscis fuerint et quis ea habuerit *Pat* 287 (cf. *Fleta* 89); c**1231** ut mittatis mihi quendam bonum outorium Norreis (*AncC* IV 139) *RL* I 390; **1236** finem fecit ..per xl m. et per bonum asturgum suum *CurR* XV 1928; **1244** per custodiam aerie hosturcii domini regis in foresta Cumbr' *Fees* 1149; **1259** custodi austercorum regis *Cl* 398; **1272** pro capcione unius anatis in primo volatu austurci noster *Liberate* 48 m. 9; **1274** columbelle: ..hostoriis comitisse viij *MinAc* 984/4 r. 5; **1290** pro lumine eorundem ostoriorum..eundo versus mutas *Ac. Wardr.* (*Chanc. Misc.* 4/4) f. 51*d.*; **1297** falconario comitis, ..qui morabatur cum rege cum quodam ~o, †quod [? l. quem]..comes dederat regi, ..durante seysona ~orum (*Ac. Wardr.*) *Doc. Scot.* 137; **1333** per servicium mutandi unum ostorium *LTRMem* 105 r. 80; **1346** qui falcones, austurcos, vertivellas et gescias ..ceperunt (*Cl*) *Foed.* (*ed.* 1825) III i 67; **1402** per servicium custodie j osterii regis sumptibus suis propriis *Aids* I 57. **b** **1180** duos absturcos mutarios *RScacNorm* I 28; **1200** per liberum servicium unius osturi sori *RChart.* 69a; **1204**

reddendo..unum austore' sorum *Ib.* 135a; **1205** de placito servitii ij austeriorum sororum *CurR* III 263; **1212** tenet.. per j austurium sorum *Fees* 82; **1218** reddendo annuatim.. nobis..unum austurcum mutatum pro omni servicio *Pat* 142; **1224** consideratum est per justiciarium quod precium osturci sor sit xx s., precium osturci mutati xl s.; et, si austrurcus (*sic*) sor non reddatur primo anno, in anno sequenti dicatur et reddatur mutatus *LTRMem* 7 r. 1B *d.*; per servitium unius ~ii sori Bracton 328b; **1281** tenuit.. per serjanciam portandi unum austurum sorum *PQW* 443a; **1287** habuit manerium..per austurcum sorum vel xx s. per annum *Ib.* 264a; **1292** cum manerium..pro uno haustoro soro in xx s. ..annuatim teneatur (*Reg. Bury*) *DL Misc. Bk. V* f. 83; **14..** †asturti sori *Reg. Brev.* 2b. **c 1237** in j austurco argenteo faciendo et deaurando ponendo ultra altare S. Edwardi Westm' *Pipe* 81 r. 15.

astus [CL], craft, guile. **b** skill.

~u, *facni* vel *fraefeli GlC* A 844 (cf. ib. 855: ~us, calliditas); cum pueris, astus quos arte fefellit Aldh. *VirgV* 1897; **985** (12c) turgidos..atque gazifero hujus saeculi ~u arridentes *CD* 648; **10..** ~us, *gebrægdnes, wærlotes* WW; ille ~u quo callebat..in suas partes eosdem traduxit W. Malm. *GR* III 232. **b** documenta librorum / ..discipulus scripsit scholasticus astu Aldh. *VirgV* 1264.

2 (in Lombard law; 2nd decl.) malice. **b** (adj.) malicious.

quod quidem juramentum in Lumbarda vocatur juramentum de ~o, quod idem est quod juramentum de calumpnia in judicio contencioso fori civilis Upton 73; si quis suam propriam uxorem incriminatus fuerit ~o absque certa causa quod adulterata sit *Ib.* 81. **b** si quis alienam puellam ..fornicariam aut strigam clamaverit et probatum est quod non ~o animo neque per furorem hoc dixit *Ib.*

astute [CL], craftily.

9.. fraudulenter, i. ~e, *facenlice* WW.

astutia [CL], craft, trick, wariness.

9.. cautela i. ~ia, *wærscipe* WW; venatoris ~iam vitare molitur Gir. *IK* II 3; edoctus preliorum ~ias, varietates et casus Map *NC* III 5; **1201** ipse tam per minas quam per †estucciam et per pulcrum loqui tantum fecit quod ipsa eum amavit *CurR* I 389; **1279** vicarius, ob hastuciam quorundam de parochia, liberam librorum vel calicis administracionem ..habere nequit *Reg. Ebor.* 12; **1294** ne..lupi rapacis austucia eorum oves rapiat *DCCant* Q f. 23; **1314** calliditatibus et hastuciis variis ad..renunciandum suis..appellacionibus inducuntur (*Rec. Eng. Dominicans*) *EHR* VI 752; **1335** per suppressionis veritatis haustuciam *Reg. Exon.* II 801; **c1360** hostis hastucia ruit vi fraudium (*Planct. Univ.* 127) *CollectOx* III 175.

astutus [CL], crafty, cunning.

cum simulatam legationem ore ~o volveret Bede *HE* II 9; vultis esse..in loquelis ~i, versuti [AS: *on spræcum on glæwlice hindergepe*], bene loquentes et male cogitantes? Ælf. *Coll.* 101 (cf. *Id. Gl.*: sagax vel gnarus vel ~us vel callidus, *petig* vel *abered*); Willelmus [I]..erat sapiens, sed ~us H. Hunt. *HA* VI 39; vir eloquens et ~us Gir. *TH* III 52.

asula v. arula.

†asur [Ar. *'uṣfūr*; (?) Sp. Ar. *'aṣfūr*, cf. Sp. *alazor*], safflower (*Carthamus*).

asur, i. crocus orientalis *SB* 11.

asur- asuur- v. azur-.

asylum [CL < ἄσυλον], **~ium,** asylum, sanctuary.

asilum, templum refugii *GlC* A 846; ~um, *friðhus* vel *generstede* Ælf. *Sup.*; ad Norwicensis ecclesie confugit ~um T. Mon. *Will.* V 10; qui propter homicidium nuper ad crucem ductus in asilum evasit Map *NC* IV 16 p. 201; fundatorum monasterium quod..universis propitiabile fiat asilum *Chr. Battle* 4; **a1220** rex tamen Henricus Ludowicum pulsat, asilum / ne velit ulterius exulis esse sui H. Avr. *Poems* 27. 75; **1229** ad ipsius patris preclaram prudentiam tanquam ad asilium et presidium nostrum singulare..convolare *Reg. S. Osm.* II 157; **s1294** municipium de Ryuns, in qua pars exercitus Anglicani asilium sibi construxerat *Flor. Hist.* III 92; **1334** sperantes in tante securitatis asilo tuti subsistere *CollectOx* I 28; **c1430** ad vestrum fugiendo consultacionis asilum *Reg. Whet.* II 398; *holy halwyd place,* asilum *PP*; **1521** azili immunitatem ibidem ob hujusmodi homicidium obtinens *Reg. Heref.* 126.

asymmeter [ἀσύμμετρος], asymmetric.

temporis atque loci non est proportio nota, / mensurae ratio ponderis esse nequit. / praedictis numerus asymmeter est, et in istis / quinque suum munus philosophia gerit J. Sal. *Enth Phil.* 963; est assimetra coste /in duo quadratum partita diametros aut est / par impar numeris Hanv. III 280; in dictis disciplinabilibus, ut 'diametrum esse coste asymmetrum' Gros. 194.

asyndeton [ἀσύνδετον], asyndeton (gram.).

dialyton vel ~on est figura..carens conjunctionibus Bede *ST* 611.

aszeisua v. azeisa.

at [*less freq. than in* CL; cf. ast; v. et. attamen], but (expr. contrast). **b** (w. no definite contrast). **c** (w. *enim.*, expr. hypothetical objection). **d** (after concessive clause or sim.) yet.

[palimbachii] famulatum minime repudiant, ut..'mergendus', 'sumendus', 'mittendus'; at vero 'legendus', 'agendus', 'videndus' amphibrachio mancipantur Aldh. *PR* 124; Penda..Christiani erat nominis ignarus; at vero Caedualla, quamvis nomen..haberet Christiani, ..erat.. moribus barbarus Bede *HE* II 20; a pulmone et calidi et frigidi..procedunt aeres; at non confuse Adel. *QN* 33; [tunc anima] similiter se habebit et in maxima culpa et sine omni culpa. ..at hoc satis patet quam sit inconveniens Anselm (*Mon.* 71) I 81; contingit ad utrumque integra locutione responderi hac 'sol est lucidissimus'; at sufficit ad alterum principio, ad alterum reliquo responderi Balsh. *AD* 94; alii Basilium, alii Benedictum, hi Augustinum, at isti singularem magistrum habent Dominum Jesum Christum J. Sal. *Pol.* 699c. **b** quem videns..non parum expavit; at ille accedens salutavit eum Bede *HE* II 12; at comes Eustachius.. / ad ducis auxilium festinat G. Amiens *Hast.* 519; pastores..Dunstanum..adeunt. at ille..inquit Osb. *V. Dunst.* 36; fluvium transire festinant. at in transeundo.. periclitantur G. Mon. I 5; de saturitate libido, de libidine immunditia..generatur. at ex his nichil nisi dolor..sequitur J. Sal. *Pol.* 748D. **c** formosus est? expecta paulatim et non erit. at enim bonis artibus doctus et adprime est eruditus et..boni consultus *Ib.* 633B. **d** ex quibus [digitis] ecce quater denis de carne revulsis / quinquies at tantum video remanere quaternos Aldh. *Aen.* 90. 4.

ata v. hachia. atach-, ataci- v. attach-. atacus v. attacus.

atamita, paternal great-great-great-great-aunt.

Bracton 68b (v. atavus a).

ataraxacon v. altaraxacon.

atavia [CL], **atava,** great-great-great-grandmother. **b** great-great-grandmother. **c** great-grandmother. **d** grandmother.

Bracton 68b (v. atavus a). **b 1224** unde cartam Hawisie de Ripariis ~ie sue..habet *BNB* III 28. **c 1432** consanguineo et heredi Alicie Wake attave mee *Cl* 282 m. 6*d.*; hec attava, *the thyrd modyre* WW. **d** [Eadgarus] Dunstanum in..honorem restituit, similiter et atavam suam et nonnullos alios *V. Dunst.* B. 24.

atavunculus, maternal great-great-great-great-uncle.

sic gradatim vocandi sunt abavunculus magnus et abmatertera magna et ~us magnus et atmatertera magna Bracton 68b.

atavus [CL], great-great-great-grandfather. **b** great-grandfather. **c** ancestor (unspecified).

10.. us, *fifta fæder* WW; percunctationum alia..est.. triplex, ut 'quis quando cujus fuerit attavus' Balsh. *AD* 100; istis [abavo et abavia] deficientibus ex parte patris, [vocandi sunt] frater [et soror] ~i et atavie, qui dicuntur atpatruus magnus et atamita magna et eorum heredes in infinitum Bracton 68b. **b** adavus, patris avus *GlC* A 277; **1158** carte regis Henrici ~i mei et Stefani comitis avi mei *E. Ch. Yorks* IV 47; ~us meus [sc. Henrici II] rex Willelmus W. Fitzst. *Thom.* 107; **1219** petit..advocationem..ut jus suum unde W. ..~us suus fuit seisitus..; et de illo W. descendit jus..J. filio suo et avo istius *CurR* VIII 159; hic attavus, *the thyrde fadyre* WW. **c** paternae generationis prosapia per ~os et tritavos Aldh. *VirgP* 12; Felix..ejus [Gregorii] fuit ~us Bede *HE* II 1 p. 73; tirannos..avis et ~is suis indomabiles Devizes 41v.; non solum avos, ~os et tritavos sed usque ad sextam vel septimam et ultra procul generationem Gir. *DK* I 17.

ategia v. attegia. ateinta v. attingere 9a. ateiuriamentum v. attiramentum. aten- v. atten-, attin-.

1 ater v. 1 acer 2b.

2 ater [CL], black, dark. **b** (fig.) gloomy. **c** (sb. n.) the dark.

vilescit graculus ater Aldh. *VirgV* 234; candidum codicem protulerunt angeli, deinde atrum daemones Bede *HE* V 13; atra caligine Alcuin *Carm.* 9. 106; ater, teter, *sweart* Ælf. *Gl.*; mesta senectus / atra veste tegi nuncia mortis amat Neckam *DS* II 333. **b** qui liquor..atrum fantasma fugabit Aldh. *VirgV* 1201; tales ex atro dum rupit pectore voces *Ib.* 2683; est in meditullaneis Brittanniae partibus immensae magnitudinis aterrrima palus Felix *Guthl.* 24 (cf. 1 acer 1b; v. et. ib. 31: in atrae paludis coenosis laticibus). **c** condita non atro sunt hec set scripta theatro Garl. *Mor. Scol.* 461.

atermin-, atest- v. att-. ateyuriamentum v. attiramentum.

†atha [AS *áþ*], oath.

†944 (12c) consuetudines et..forisfacturas omnium terrarum suarum, id est burhgerita [v.l. burgebrice] et hundredsetena, athas, ordelas *CS* 794; **†971** (12c) aðas et ordeles *CS* 1277; si dominus ejus dicat quod neutrum ei fregit vel *ap* vel *ordel* (*Quad.*) *GAS* 217.

athach-, athag- v. attach-.

athanasia [ἀθανασία], medicament to prolong life. **b** tansy (*cf. tanacetum*) or other herb.

reumaticis ygia, fluidis valet āthanasīa [*gl.*: interpretatum immortale, id est electuarium †eum [? l. cum] succo plantaginis] Garl. *Mor. Scol.* 596; hec sunt vera nisi plures radices diversas respiciunt egritudines, ut in atonasia majori, quia tunc quelibet radix suam recipit operationem diversam ab alia Bacon IX 107. **b** †anathanasia cum flore cameleonte Gilb. V 214. 1 (cf. ib. IV 195. 2: ~ie partes); herba S. Marie, i. febrifuga vel secundum quosdam idem est quod ~ia *SB* 24; atanasia vel athasia, tanacetum idem.., G. *tanesie*, A. *bemerfan Alph.* 16 (= *Ib.* 181: *banifan*); ~ia que Grece tagetes, Latine tanacetum, A. dicitur *tansey* Turner *Herb.* A iii.

athanatos [ἀθάνατος], immortal.

ecclesiastica vocabula [Greca] sunt..*agios*, sanctus, ..~*os*, immortalis Bacon *CSPhil.* 444; ut, quamdiu liber supererit, auctor manens ~os nequeat interire R. Bury *Phil.* 1. 21.

atharafa [Ar. *aṭ-ṭarfā'*], tamarisk.

plantarum..quedam in humido loco et quedam in arido et quedam vivunt in utroque ut salix et ~a Alf. Angl. *Plant.* I 13.

athat v. aëtus. athelabs, athelebus v. attelebus. athemis v. anthemis. athenum v. attrenum. athia v. atia.

Athir, Egyptian month.

Aegyptii..quorum..tertius [mensis] ~ir v Kal. Nov. .. die sumit exordium Bede *TR* 11.

Athlas v. Atlas.

athleta, ~us [ἀθλητής], athlete, wrestler. **b** champion. **c** martyr.

ut alius strenua anthletarum luctamina cum aemulo sinuosis laterum flexibus desudans Aldh. *VirgP* 2; **10..** anthletae, *oretmæcgan* WW. **b** convaluere nimis diorismata fortis / athletae Frith. 1294; agonista providus concupivit ..fieri ~a castus *V. Osw.* 415; **10..** anthletarum, *cempena* WW; Dei ~ae, immemores constantiae suae, surripiuntur vaniloqua hominum fama Gosc. *Aug. Maj.* 54B; **s1123** Rannulfum..constituit in Eboraurum turri..aliosque probos ~as in aliis locis ad tutandam regionem Ord. Vit. XII 38; ad ejus [diaboli] tirannidem debellandam strenuus ~a accingitur Ailr. *Nin.* 6; athlete fidei reges concurrite cuncti Garl. *Tri. Eccl.* 7 (cf. ib. 130: crucis athletas); **a1270** commissum est duellum..a mane usque ad vesperum, atleta nostro paulatim succumbente *Meaux* II 101; **s1346** quos Christus, ~a fortissimus, ..contra Scotos prevalere concessit Avesb. 111; **s1360** ubi est Rotolandus, Oliverus et ceteri proceres et ~i nobiles de temporibus transactis? *Plusc.* IX 45; **1309** inter omnes alios vivacissimus atleta *Reg. Merton* 380. **c** crudus āthleta Dei Cyprianus Aldh. *VirgV* 1880; rigidos saevi tormenta tyranni / anthletas Christi cogebant ferre cruenta *Ib.* 2195; sui Deus adthelete miseratus agones Nig. *Paul* 50 v. 2; signa operum..que.. ad imitandum data sunt..vobis presertim a Deo vocatis.. tanti ~e inire pugnam, subire curam, implere cathedram H. Bos. *Thom. Ep. dedic.* p. 156; **1445** gloriosus Dei ~a [Thomas] *Lit. Cant.* III 191.

athom- v. atom-. athonia v. atonia.

†athronizare [cf. inthronizare], to enthrone (a bishop).

s1362 episcopum consecraverunt ipsum ~antes et more Romane curie coronantes, ..Urbanum V illum nominantes Fordun *GA* 182 p. 380*n.*

atia [OF *aatie*], hate, spite (*cf.* N. D. Hurnard *The King's Pardon*, Oxford 1969, pp. 339 *seqq.*).

1191 r.c. de x m. pro habenda inquisitione..si appellatus fuit per attiam necne *Pipe* 110; **1194** consideratum est quod est acia *CurR RC* I 36; **1196** utrum..appellent eum de roberia..per invidiam vel atiam an non *Pipe* (*Chanc.*) 186; **1198** offert..xx s. pro habendo vero dicto patrie, utrum sc. athia sit necne; et duo milites qui debuerunt videre plagam dixerunt quod nullam plagam viderunt *CurR* I 39; **1201** R. facit hoc appellum versus eum per attiam et per vetus odium, unde tres causas ostendit *SelPlCrown* 41; **1205** utrum appellat eos per aatiam an eo quod sunt culpabiles *Pipe* 57; **1227** si..rectati sint odio et athia et non eo quod.. culpabiles sint, tunc tradat eos in ballium *Cl* 7; **1255** willate de..S. et A. odio et hatya illud crimen falso dicto Hugoni et aliis inposuerunt *SelPlForest* 37; fieri solet inquisitio utrum hujusmodi imprisonati pro morte hominis culpabiles essent de morte illa vel non, et utrum appellati essent odio vel atya; et breve de hujusmodi inquisitione nulli debet denegari. ..si autem dicat inquisitio quod per odium et per atyam et contineatur causa..quo odio vel qua atya, diligenter erit causa examinanda Bracton 123; **1275** ut ipsum dimitteret per plevinam a tempore quo breve de †agya fecit pro eo *Hund.* I 513 (cf. ib.: breve de acya); **1285** habeant breve de odio et atya (II *Westm.* 29) *StRealm* I 85 (cf. *Fleta* 39); **c1324** de discordiis et atyiis ortis in civitatibus *MGL* II 19 *rub.* (cf. ib.: *guerre et hayne est si multipliee..en cytez*).

atil- v. attill-. atincar v. tincar. atir- v. attir-, azurum.

Atlantides, (pl.) Pleiades.

quid referam ~as, ..quas Graecorum traditio..pliadas, Latina..vergilias..nuncupaverat? Aldh. *Met.* 3.

Atlas [Ἄτλας, *Titan supporting heavens*], (fig.) a pillar.

pondus et informes Athlantes ferre priores / jussit Frith. 450.

atleta v. athleta.

atmatertera, maternal great-great-great-great-aunt.

Bracton 68b (v. atavunculus).

atnepos v. adnepos.

atomalis, atomic.

omnes nature sunt corpora, sc. corpuscula illa atomorum, et inane, id est vacuitas intersepta, per cujus partes ingredi possunt ~ia corpora Netter *DAF* II 124v.

atomosus, in the form of a speck.

pulveree resolutiones..~e aliquantulum grosse in urina mulieris apparentes Gilb. VII 306. 1.

atomus [CL < ἄτομος], indivisible.

unde album non est comparabile nigro, quia non conveniunt in specie athoma set solum in genere, ut in colore Bacon XIII 361.

2 (sb. f., m. or n.) atom, indivisible minimal particle of matter. **b** minute particle, speck, mote. **c** midge. **d** (fig.). **e** (in pun on *Thomas*) minimal amount (of difference).

specialissimis speciebus quae ~a, id est individua, dicuntur Eriug. *Per.* 472c; uno moto corporis ~o in infinitum procedet motio Adel. *QN* 61; ~os esse cum Democrito dicentes Balsh. *AD* 87; videtur quod athomus, si sit res naturalis et indivisibile, non poterit moveri per punctum nec mutatur Bacon XIII 332; licet [angelus] non commetiatur se illi [loco] indivisibili per situm, sicut indivisibile corporale, quod est punctus vel ~us *Id. Tert.* 170. **b** minor exiguo..verme / aut modico, Phoebi radiis qui vibrat, atŏmo Aldh. *Aen.* 100. 67; longa dies oculos atra caligine claudit / solivagos athomos quae numerare solet Alcuin *Carm.* 9. 106; **796** nec unius parvissimi et variis motibus vibrantis in sole spurcitiam athomi offendimus *Id. Ep.* 60; **10..** ~o, *mote* WW; spirituales creaturas ita..ebullire in aere tamquam minimas ~os in splendore solis Beleth *RDO* 154. 154; quot ludunt atomi radiis, quot in orbe lapilli / novit Neckam *DS* IV 310; exiles atomi particuleque leves *Ib.* V 62; urina tenuis..cum resolutionibus albis et rotundis velut athomis Gilb. VII 311 v. 2; *mote in sunne*, atthamus *PP*. **c** s**1389** convenerunt in curia..multe turme attomorum et..fecerunt maximam stragem invicem, adeo ut scopis et pertis mundarent locum de interfectis Knighton II 311. **d** **799** meum est de terrae gremio..auri effodere ~os Alcuin *Ep.* 171. **e** c**1220** honor sit sanctificans ut / te non *a Thoma* separet ulla *athomos* H. Avr. *Poems* 44. 2.

3 minimal period of time. **b** instant, moment. **c** determinate fraction of a minute (*ostentum*).

minimum omnium et quod nulla ratione dividi queat tempus ~um Graeci, hoc est indivisibile sive insectibile, nominant Bede *TR* 3 p. 183 (cf. ib.: p. 184); in ipsis [temporis partibus] dum inter se invicem conferuntur, ..horae ad punctos, puncti ad momentum, momenti (*sic*) ad ~a Eriug. *Per.* 467b; probavit..quod nulla quidem res facta vel athomo subsisteret temporis nisi per provisionem ..Dei W. Dan. *Ailred* 10. **b** cum figura mundi in ictu et ~o evanuerit Aldh. *VirgP* 28; **864** (11c) qui..cum suo nutu ..gyrando omnia gubernat in icto ~o *CS* 509; **10..** in ~o, *in breahtme* WW. **c** hora..dividitur..quinto in ostenta, quorum lx faciunt horam..; et sexto dividitur in athomos, in quibus stat divisio ipsorum [compotistarum], unde *athomos* Graece 'indivisibile' dicitur Latine.., et est ~os trecentesima septuagesima sexta pars ostenti Bacon VI 48 (cf. 291).

atonasia v. athanasia.

atonia [ἀτονία], slackness, enervation (med.).

†tonotiron [l. tonoticon], i. corroborativum; inde athonia, i. debilitas *Alph.* 187.

atorn- v. attorn-.

atpatruus, paternal great-great-great-great-uncle.

Bracton 68b (v. atavus a).

atque, ac [*less freq. than in* CL; ac *not only before consonant*], and. **b** (w. *etiam*). **c** also.

~e, *end suelse GlC* A 204; ut..patefacias ac deinceps.. inculces Aldh. *Met.* 10 p. 96; nupti qui jam conubia spernunt / ac indulta sibi scindunt retinacula luxus *Id. VirgV* 93; miracula gessit / atque arcana..prompsit *Ib.* 252; ut nullis roraret nubibus aether / atque negarentur latices *Ib.* 261; qui caput et princeps ac pugnae signifer atrox / extiterat *Ib.* 1556; libentissime ab omnibus suscipiebatur ~e audiebatur Bede *HE* IV 2; docendo ac dictando *Ib.* V 15; c**1040** quam brevis..est delectatio spurcae carnis †astque quam ignominiosum..esse dignoscitur ut.. *CD* 769; nostra corda timore labant; / atque manus populi.. / urbis ad auxilium segniter arma movet G. Amiens *Hast.* 703; senescente me ac taciturnitati operam dante Osb. *V. Dunst.* 36; vir.. magnus satis et dives, notus atque famosus W. Cant. *Mir. Thom.* VI 6; expellit, removet, diligit adque fovet Serlo Wilt. 16. 18; vult iter ac actus reserare D. Bec. 2062; sonitu repentino ac impetuoso *Cust. Westm.* 139; **1314** cablis, anchoris, malis et cordis ac alio attilio *RScot* 126a; propter leccionum longitudinem ac oracionum lassitudinem *Eul. Hist.* I 2; **1542** diebus Dominicis et festivis ac aliis temporibus *Deeds Balliol* 321. **b** **1291** adinvicem stipulantes ac eciam promittentes (*Compositio*) *Mon. Francisc.* II 36; **1334** fecimus et constituimus ac eciam ordinavimus *Lit. Cant.* II 69; **1542** mandamus quod unusquisque.. scolaris..sit obediens magistro..; ac quod..caste vivant..; aceciam quod non accedant..ad..domos suspectas *Deeds Balliol* 322. **c** obligantur pro nostris defunctis orare sicut ~e nos pro suis *Obs. Barnwell* 218.

2 as: **a** (after words expr. likeness); **b** (w. *si*).

a omnibus, id est nobilibus simul atque ignobilibus Bede *HE* III 14; aeque orando ac benedicendo *Ib.* V 6 *rub.*; simul ac iter arripuit W. Cant. *Mir. Thom.* III 21; pro communi commodo simul ac proprio Gir. *S. Langton* 402; haec assignatio..habet eandem vim..atque monitio ad interessendum *Praxis* 233. **b** quantum securitatis ..ac si non esset quod timeretur increverat Gildas *EB* 1; Franci, bellare periti, / ac si devicti, fraude fugam simulant G. Amiens *Hast.* 424; s**1164** adversarius..objicit quoniam..esset apostolice sedis..diminutio, ac si nesciat quod..dissimulandum erat pro tempore Diceto *YH* I 315; imago se perforabilem reddidit, ac si esset caro Gir. *GE* I 30; **1218** inventus fuit..vulneratus..v plagis.., ac si esset de cultello *Eyre Yorks* 184; **1267** qui vice nostra plenam habebunt potestatem tractandi vobiscum..pro parte nostra ac si presentes essemus *Cl* 375; **1310** virtute recognicionis, ac si rite facta fuisset cum non esset *Law Merch.* III 27; procedas ac si papa esset hereticus Ockham *Dial.* 646; acsi gemitibus ..veniam petens *Arthur & Gorlagon* 156; s**1377** Ricardus.. inter omnes mortales, ac si secundus Apsalon, pulcherimus Ad. Usk 1; **1453** cum videremus fratrem illum..transire indifferenter, acsi dicta materia nullo modo videretur ad eum pertinere *Reg. Whet.* I 106.

atr' v. aqua. Atrabatus v. Atrebatensis.

atrabilis, black bile, melancholy.

lien eundem [sc. sanguinem] repurgat ab ~e D. Edw. *Anat.* B 1.

atract-, atrah- v. attr-.

atramentarium, ink-pot, ink-horn. **b** (fig.). **c** ink, black dye.

1188 inveni ~ium a renibus dependens humore sicco repletum *Ep. Cant.* 197; pergamenum, attramentum cum ~io et pennario, colores..liberentur precentori *Cust. Cant.* 362; ~ium scriptoris gestabat in renibus R. Bury *Phil.* 6. 98 (cf. *Ezek.* ix); s**1381** periculosum erat agnosci pro clerico, sed multo periculosius si ad latus alicujus ~ium inventum fuisset Wals. *HA* II 9; attramentarium, *blacchepot* WW; *an inke horne*, ~ium, calamarium, incausterium *CathA*; **1534** item atramentorium unum (*Invent.*) *Cant. Coll. Ox.* I 83. **b** **1192** in amaritudine est anima mea, que totum hujus epistole cursum mihi de doloris ~io subministrat P. Blois *Ep.* 143. 429b (cf. ib. 386a. 504d). **c** alutarii secant..corium ~io [*gl.*: *arnement*] denigratum Garl. *Dict.* 125.

atramentosus, inky.

ferrum ex argento vivo terrestri..et sulphure immundo terrestri ~o componitur *Ps.*-Gros. 641; ~i sarctoris, *a bletchy sowter* Whittington *Vulg.* 86.

atramentum [CL], black pigment, ink. **b** (fig.). **c** darkness.

797 apices..~o formati Alcuin *Ep.* 126; incaustum vel ~um, *blaec Ælf. Gl.*; **988** (12c) ~o caraxamus quae stare firmiter optamus *CD* 662; **1314** usi pro calamo stramine et pro attramento sanguine proprio cum urina permixto (*Pet. Frat. Praedic.*) *EHR* V 110; *Cust. Cant.* 362 (v. atramentarium); contra diaboli surrepciones illicitas calamo et ~o pugnare R. Bury *Phil.* 16. 207; signum est quedam figura vilissima..cum arundine et ~o depicta, quam ipse Soldanus ..depingit S. Sim. *Itin.* 78; *bleke or blech*, attramentum, ..*inke*, encaustum, ..attramentum *PP*; attromenta, *blacche* WW. **b** saecularis scoriae ~o foedatos Aldh. *VirgP* 10; caccabatum furvae fuliginis ~um exhorruit *Ib.* 44; **1042** (12c) libellulum falsae cupiditatis ~o praetitulatum *CD* 762; sicut testamenti sic et scripti auctoritas mortis ~o confirmatur Gir. *IK pref.* p. 5; crasso tenebrarum fuscatus ~o Map *NC* IV 3 p. 146. **c** quid tali hujus ~o aetatis facturus est? Gildas *EB* 1.

2 vitriol or sim. (*cf. arnementum*). **b** (w. *citrinum*) iron peroxide. **c** salve for animals.

~orum sunt multe species, colcotar, calcadis, vitriolum nigrum, capernum viridis cuperose M. Scot *Lumen* 260; ~a composita sunt ex sale et sulphure et lapidibus. creditur in eis esse vis mineralis aliquorum liquabilium, que ex eis fiunt, vel chalcanthum et colcotar, que generantur ex majoribus granis ~i *Correct. Alch.* 8; ~orum species sunt multe: aliud namque est album, aliud rubeum, aliud citrinum, aliud viride, aliud fuscum, quo utuntur scriptores, ..et secundum omnes species medium est lapidum et metallorum *Ps.*-Gros. 642; attramentum, calcantum idem, quedam terra in Gallia cujus due sunt species, viz. vilior species est attramentum, nobilior species est vitriolum *Alph.* 17. **b** si vis aliquid corrodere, adde modium de colcotar, i. de ~o citrino Gad. 118. 1; calcater, i. ~um citrinum *SB* 13. **c** **1248** in j ~o ad boves sanandos *MinAc. Wint.* (*Wroughton*); **1301** in vertegrez, melle, ~o emptis ad reparacionem equorum *Ac. Durh.* 502; **1344** in..gummis et attramento pro quodam equo..infirmo *Ib.* 502.

Atrebatensis, of Arras (w. ref. to tapestry).

s**1345** dedit..unum magnum dorsare pro aula operis de Arrace *Hist. Durh.* 3 p. 139; s**1396** preciosi..panni de Aras ..pro apparatu aule regine *V. Ric. II* 129; **1432** magnus pannus Arrace de vita S. Kentigerni *Reg. Glasg.* 334; **1435** (v. aurum 1d); **1436** tapisario fabricanti pannos de Attrabato apud Bruges *ExchScot* 678; **1461** pannus de Arracio (*Chanc. Proc.*) *Prejudice & Promise* 185; **1470** pannos istos sollemnes et artificiosos qui pro nunc in sua dependent camera majori in estivo tempore pannique de Araas vulgariter sunt vocati *Reg. Whet.* I 426; **1475** Johanni Dolas, textori Atripotenti *ExchScot* 315; **1478** magistro J. Dolace textori Attrabatensi *Ib.* 568; **1479** textori Attripotenti *Ib.* 630; **1527** tentoria viridaria et Atrabata opera, *arrais uerkis* vulgariter nuncupata *Form. S. Andr.* I 202.

atrenum v. attrenum. atrichiare v. attachiare 2.

atricus [etym. dub.], haemorrhoid, pile.

secundum aliquos †atriti nihil aliud sunt quam emoroyde inflate Gilb. V 223 v. 1; emoroyde, ficus, condilomata, ~i, apostema, ragadie passiones sunt ani *Ib.* 231. 1; ~i sunt nigre collectiones ani *Ib.* 233. 2.

atriensis [CL], door-keeper.

~is, janitor *GlC* A 871.

atriplex [CL < ἀτράφαξυς], orach. **b** weld (*Reseda*).

9.. crysolachan i. aureum olus vel ~plex, i. *tunmelde* WW; quo rigidum pallescit olus, quo fercula festo / atriplicis libanda die Hanv. III 277; creantur..ex ~plicibus rane Neckam *NR* II 163; atriplici parent ignis sacer atque podagra *Id. DS* VII 173; blitus, attriplex et spinachia Bacon IX 94; **12..** ~plex, i. *arasches* WW; attriplices trite vel fronti vel capiti emplastrate dolorem tollunt Gad. 5 v. 2; beta major vel bleta.., ~plex agrestis vel domestica idem; G. *arache blanc Alph.* 22; sanction..folia sunt †andrafraxe similia *Ib.* 161; *arage, herbe*, attriplex *PP*. **b** *weld or wold, herbe*, sandix, attriplex *PP*.

Atripotens v. Atrebatensis. atritus v. atricus.

atrium [CL], outer room, hall. **b** courtyard or plot. **c** (fig.). **d** household, hearth (*cf.* 2 *astrum* 2).

aule Graece ~ium dicitur Bede *Orth.* 2775; cum illa.. intraret ~ium domus in cujus interioribus daemoniosus torquebatur *Id. HE* III 11; atria gazarum rumpunt regalia Alcuin *Carm.* 1. 53; ~ium, *mycel and rum heall Ælf. Sup.*; **10..** ~ium, ..*inburh* WW; offendens ad limen domus quam subitura erat, prona cecidit..; ~ium namque subsidebat inferius limine W. Cant. *Mir. Thom.* II 49; [aula] ~ium habeat, quod ab atro dicitur Neckam *Ut.* 109. **b** **801** pro ~io intra muros civitatis unde fratribus S. Petri habitatio honesta construi potuisset Alcuin *Ep.* 211; ~ium, ..*cafertun Ælf. Sup.*; **11..** in capella..quam feci in ~io meo *Cart. Darley* 439; c**1200** ortum ante portam ~ii *MonA* VI 336; **1236** concessimus..quod aliquibus placeis, ~iis, litiis.. et aliis civitatis Burdegalie paduentiis uti possint..ad pannos faciendos (*Pat*) *RL* II 11; **1322** J. fugit, et eum secuti sunt usque ad ~ium W. filii A. *SelCCoron.* 75; **1671** ad partem pomarii et ~ii sive curtelagii *Crawley* 540. **c** superni ~ia paradisi et caelestis regni vestibula patefecit Aldh. *VirgP* 39 (cf. ib. *V.* 1306: pulsantes atria caeli); veritas..per..imaginacionis ~ia transiens thalamum intellectus ingreditur R. Bury *Phil.* 1. 25; pontifex..populum..super paludes heresium ad ~ia vite ducit Gir. *PI* I 19 p. 109. **d** **1224** talis est consuetudo manerii domini regis de Bray quod postnata filia que remanet in ~io retinebit totam hereditatem patris sui *BNB* III 7; naute, qui sunt in villa eradicati et ~ium habentes in villa habebunt rectum secundum usum et consuetudinem hominum ville vel provincie (*DL Misc. Bk.* 5) *Eng. Justice* 136; Bracton 267b (v. astrarius a).

2 (eccl.) churchyard, precinct, or forecourt. **b** (?) porch, galilee.

istius antiqui reparavit et atria templi Wulf. *Swith. prol.* 41 [*but cf. Arch. J.* CXIV 44–6]; **1080** in cimiteriis: ..si.. aliqui..ibi faciant mansionem dum guerra duraverit et ipsi propter guerram in ~io manserint (*Conc. Illebon.* 8) Ord. Vit. V 5; nec in sanctificato ~io aliquo [AS: *binnon nanum gehalgodum lictune*] aliquis jaceat si moriatur (*Quad.*) *GAS* 165; expectante eum [sacerdotem] plebe cum fure..in ~io ecclesiae (*Jud. Dei*) *Ib.* 420; quicunque reus..ad ecclesiam pro presidio confugerit, ex quo ~ium ingressus fuerit, securus sit (*Leg. Ed.*) *Ib.* 630; **1136** infra ~ium ecclesie *Regesta* 975; ~ium templi..muro circumvallavit Ric. Hex. *Pri. Hex.* 3; per medium aule fugientes a facie armatorum aperta eis janua ~ium introeuntium W. Fitzst. *Thom.* 137; **1191** ecclesiam B. Pauli in ~io monasterii..sitam *Reg. Malm.* I 375; **1198** debet xl m. super terram suam in ~io S. Petri *Pipe* 57; circuendo extrinsecus totam ecclesiam et ~ium *Offic. Sal.* 74; **1201** nullatenus ecclesiam..et ~ium ecclesiae negotiaturi intrare..presumant *BBC* (*Wells*) 173; **1202** abbas de Persora dicit quod ~ium ecclesie sue est et non liberum tenementum abbatis de Westmonasterio *CurR* II 93; **1240** cimiteria..inhoneste credimus..sordibus deturpari; propter quod..rectoribus..inhibemus ne ipsi in dictis ecclesiarum ~iis animalia sua pascant *Conc. Syn.* 297; **1245** in xv millibus pauperum pascendis in ~io S. Pauli die Conversionis ejusdem *Liberate* 21 m. 7; in..capellis earumque ~iis populi.. obtruncati jacuerunt *Mir. Montfort* 67; **1295** attendentes ~ium ecclesie Linc' tam angustum esse quod propter.. multitudinem moriencium illatorum commode non sufficit ad sepulcra *Reg. Antiq. Linc.* II 466; s**1312** quidam.. cardinalis interfectus fuit prope ecclesiam S. Pauli in ~io *Ann. Paul.* 272; hoc ~ium, *a kyrkyerd*, ..hoc simutorium, hoc ~ium, *a schererd* WW; *a kyrkegarth*, cimitorium, poliandrum, ~ium *CathA*. **b** **1468** ~ii ejusdem capelle parietes..construxit *Invent. Ch. Ch.* 163; **1522** pro inferiori cubiculo ex parte boriali ~ii *Cant. Coll. Ox.* II 258 (cf. ib.: pro *le slatyng* in duobus angulis in ~io).

atrocitas [CL], atrocity, savagery. **b** atrocious act.

Dei famulas satis crudescente poenarum ~ate vexandas Aldh. *VirgP* 50; quin universos ~ate ferina morti per tormenta contraderet Bede *HE* II 20; tunc demum gladius est judicis exserendus quando..~ate delicti..provocatur Gir. *PI* I 10 p. 34; c**1250** nisi facti ~as..magistrorum requirat conniventiam *Stat. Cantab.* 197. **b** ut..pervasionum ~ates exerceat Ad. Marsh *Ep.* 92 p. 213.

atrociter [CL], atrociously, savagely.

..grassatoribus obvia quaeque ~er vastantibus Aldh. *VirgP* 31; ecclesiarum possessiones..tributis ~issime premere *G. Steph.* II 78; prole propria..in parentes ~er armata Gir. *PI* III 30 p. 321.

atrophia [ἀτροφία, *conf. w.* ἀτροπία], atrophy, malnutrition.

~ia, *meteafliung Ælf. Gl.*; squaliditas Grece †atrosia [l. atrofia] dicitur, i.e. 'sine succo' vel 'sine conversione' Gilb. IV 196 v. 1; species cathexie, que sunt sinthesis, smaragmos, †atrosia, squaliditas.. *Ib.* VI 261. 1; nutrimentum..deficit in ~ia vel in sinthesi que est extenuata macies Gad. 45. 1; attropia, i. extenuacio, et interpretatur 'sine conversione' vel 'sine succo' *Alph.* 17.

Atropos [Ἄτροπος], one of the Fates. **b** death.

ingreditur campum dominans elegia, pallens / Atropos Garl. *Tri. Eccl.* 60. **b** *dede*, antropos [v.l. attrapos], decessus, ..fatum *CathA*.

†atrorbus, type of syzygy.

alternantes sinzigiae replicationes, ..quarum vocabula haec esse noscuntur: prolixius, ..phymarus, ~us, rivatus.. Aldh. *PR* 141.

atrox [CL], atrocious, savage. **b** (?) sour.

lupus horrendis non frendet rictibus atrox Aldh. *VirgV* 1670; inter ~ocissimarum gehennarum tormenta Felix *Guthl.* 31; **1002** (13c) in poenis ~ocibus se esse passurum *CD* 1296; **10..** ~ox, *seo grimme* WW; [monachus vel clericus] ~ocissima verberum contusione defatigatus *G. Steph.* II 78; vulnus ~ox acceperat in corpore..et vulnus ~ocius pertulerat in mente W. CANT. *Mir. Thom.* VI 30 (cf. ib. 13: ~ociorem conceperat indignationem); corpus suum defendendo vel ~ocem injuriam corporis sui prosequendo GLANV. II 3; canis..ob catulorum ~ox defensionem GIR. *GE* II 11 p. 226: **c1225** fures ~ociores *Conc. Syn.* 151 (= Conc. I 597: †attrectatores); **a1350** crimina non attrocia tanquam attrocia criminaliter proponentes *Stat. Cantab.* 315. **b** **1284** de iiij s. de lacte ~oci vendito *MinAc* 1027/17 r. 2.

atta [CL Gl.], walker on tip-toe.

~a, qui primis plantis ambulat *Erf.* 2. 269. 14.

attabernalis, keeper of next-door shop. **b** frequenter of taverns.

attubernalis, vicinus †proximae [l. proxime] taberna[m] habens *GlC* A 872. **b** *CathA* (v. attabernio).

attabernare, to expose for sale in a tavern (C.I.).

1324 quod atabernatores debent poni ad afforandum seu ~andum vina et cervis' pro respectu juratorum *JustIt* 1165 r. 7*d*.

attabernator, tavern-keeper (C.I.).

1324 (v. attabernare).

attabernio, frequenter of taverns.

a tawern ganger, ~io, attabernalis *CathA*.

attacare, attachare v. attachiare 3 a. attaccatio v. attachiatio.

attachia [OF *atache*; cf. tachia], fastening, cord.

c1170 reddendo mihi annuatim..quasdam ~ias de serico pro omni servicio *Danelaw* 244 (cf. ib. 245: predictas athachias); **1213** pro duobus duodenis ~iarum et laqueorum de serico..ij s. vj d. *Misae* 240; **1220** pro laciis et ~iis que..W. emit ab eo *Cl* 412b; **1309** salvis semper domino regi principalibus rebus antiquitus exceptis, ut aurum non operatum, serica non operata.., mantellum sine ~ia, ..et hujusmodi *SJers.* XVIII 23.

attachiabilis, liable to attachment (leg.).

c1290 pro pacis regni..conservacione..~es in eisdem terris..inventos omni tempore licite possunt attachiare, arestandos arestare, capiendos capere *ChartR* 77 m. 14; omnes..~es licet vicecomiti in prisona custodire donec.. fuerint replegiati *Fleta* 38; **1314** si quos malefactores..juxta formam statuti [de Wyntonia, 13 Ed. I] ~es inveneritis, ipsos attachiari..faciatis (*Breve*) *MGL* III 439; **14..** corpus ..defendentis ~e est *Cust. Fordwich* 25.

attachiamentum [OF *atachement*; cf. tachiamentum], abutment or embankment: **a** (of mill-dam or weir). **b** (of bridge or causey).

a **c1240** reddendo..dim. m...pro athachiamento stangni ..molendini *Cart. Sallay* 441; **a1250** in..molendinis et molendinorum sedibus, ~is et aque transversionibus *Reg. S. Thom. Dublin* 188; **c1250** molendinum..cum..agistiamento aque et ~o molendini *Cart. Chester* 320; **1268** dedit.. j acram dominice terre..una cum ~o stagni et molendini eorum ad terram predicti W...ascendendo per aquam cum refluxu et agistiamento aque *Ib.* 330; **c1270** dederunt.. medietatem suam aqueductus de L. et ~um stagni ad terram suam, cujuscunque voluerint altitudinis et latitudinis *Ib.* 446; **1330** est quoddam ~um apud Tengemouth [*Devon*] et reddit per annum v s. *IPM* 23/22; **1331** dedi.. ~um gurgitis molendini sui fulleretici *AncD* A 8514; **1358** licenciam faciendi attachamentum suum ipsius gurgitis in terra mea et mora de Tregilyou [*Cornw*] *Ib.* 9989; **1389** adquisivit..~um stagni cujusdam piscarie in aqua de Loone super terram..prioris..et..dictum ~um..continebat in longitudine unam perticatam terre *Couch. Furness* II 207; **1497** [que terra est] ~um fossati defensorii sive capitis stagni vocati *a were AncD* C 3968; **1507** cum..atachamento unius molendini aquatici *Cl* 373 m. 19*d*; **1552** pro ~o sive legac[ione] ex una parte gurgitis ibidem *Pat.* 849 m. 13. **b** **1272** faciant pontem vel calceam..ultra sichetum..et.. habebunt atachiamentum super terram..abbatis et conventus *Cart. Chester* 386; **c1275** dedit..~um cujusdam pontis latitudine quam voluerint in solo suo..ultra le Pul.., ita quod, si dictus pons in loco ubi constructus fuerit subsistere..comode non poterit, liceat eis in alio loco..ipsum attachiare, construere et sustentare *Ib.* 376.

2 attachment (leg.), binding (of party) by pledge, distraint or arrest to appear in court. **b** (w. *placitorum coronae*) attachment in crown plea. **c** (? w. *assisae*). **d** (?) writ of attachment.

1195 j m. pro injustis atachiamentis *Pipe* 172; **1200** quod ipse [vic.] attachiet quosdam appellatos de pace regis per breve primum, quod ei allatum fuit et per quod nullum ~um factum fuit, quod sint..in octabis S. Johannis *CurR* I 195; **1224** quod per homines tuos et per ballivum..episcopi facias athachiamenta communiter in feria proximo ventura apud Divisas, ..donec plenius inquisierimus ad quem pertinea[n]t atachiamenta predicta *Cl* 633a; **1236** nulla attagiamenta infra burgum attachiata sint *BBC* (*Berkeley*) 156; si..personalis causa fuerit criminalis.., nulla erit ibi solennitas ~orum, sed statim capiatur corpus BRACTON 439; **1267** eadem lex de ~is faciendis in omnibus brevibus ubi ~a jacent de cetero quoad districtiones faciendas firmiter observetur, ita tamen quod secundum ~um sit per meliores plegios *Leg. Ant. Lond. app.* 231; **1269** duplex est ~um, per corpus videlicet et per manucaptores sive per plegios *CBaron* 79; **1278** pro summonitoribus inveniendis ad faciendum districciones, summoniciones et ~a infra libertatem *Reg. St. Bees* 375; **1321** dubitavit de ~o corporis sui *DocCOx* 171; est ~um quoddam vinculum legitimum per quod pars defendens invita astringitur ad standum juri et respondendum parti de se querenti *Quon. Attach.* I 2; **1375** athagatus fuit per..constabularium et post athagamentum..insultum fecit..Ricardo *SessPLincs* 225. **b** **1228** querelam quam habent versus abbatem..de atachiamento placitorum corone de hundredo *Cl* 14; **1256** coronatores..ad ~a placitorum corone nostre..facienda *BBC* (*Bristol*) 358; **c1320** cum rex transmiserit litteras suas ad ~a corone sue summonenda *MGL* I 52. **c** **1456** preceptum fuit vic. .. quod venire faceret coram justiciariis..die Martis..breve originale assise predicte, proviso..quod ~um inde fieret per xv dies ante predictum diem Martis *Reg. Whet.* I 207. **d** **1308** cum..probator noster..appellat C. ..et G. ..de morte duorum hominum..detentos in prisona nostra Wyntonie, ..tibi precipimus quod predictos C. et G. et eorum ~a..duci faciatis usque Neugate (*Breve*) *MGL* II 110; **1349** habeas ibi..summonitores cum ~is parcium querelatarum *Reg. Rough* 60; **1448** quod ballivus..libertatis.. omnia juratas, panella, inquisiciones, attachementa et intendencias..justiciariis..faciat, retornet et intendat *Reg. Whet.* I 42.

3 pledge for observance of contract (C.I.).

1270 debent accipere ab unaquaque parte..atachementum sufficiens ad partes ligare bene et fideliter quod.. firmum tenebunt..dictum..eorum *Cart. I. Norm.* 179.

4 seizure of goods. **b** (w. *forinsecum*) foreign attachment, seizure of goods or money claimed to be due to defendant in plea of debt. **c** (right of) seizure of stray beasts.

s1262 constabularius Turris voluit occupare contra illos libertates suas arestando in Tamisia naves ante Turrim et capiendo prisas. ad hoc cives dixerunt quod ~a in Thamisia pertinent solummodo ad vicecomites Londoniarum *Leg. Ant. Lond.* 52. **b** **1419** de forinsecis ~is: ..*tieux arrestes de biens et defenses des deniers sount appellez foreyns attachiementz MGL* I 207; quartam fecerunt defaltam et se justificari non permiserunt per forinsecum ~um *Entries* 157. **c** **1273** de hominibus de Merston' pro licencia arandi quoddam pratum quod suum est, in quo prato comitissa habet ~a a Purificacione usque festum S. Mich. *Ac. Stratton* 40; **1285** R. ..versus ballivum de ~o bidencium in stipula ter in Emed *CourtR A. Stratton* no. 79 (cf. ib. no. 20); **1296** de ~is averiorum ibidem [*Colne, Lancs*] in Trochden' *DLMinAc* 1/1 r. 17*d*.

5 (in forest law) attachment of offenders for vert and venison. **b** perquisite of attachment for minor offences of vert. **c** court of attachment (*cf. SelPlForest* xxx–xxxvii).

1217 singulis xl diebus..conveniant viridarii et forestarii ad videndum ~a de foresta, tam de viridi quam de venacione, per presentationem ipsorum forestariorum, et coram ipsis attachiatis (*Ch. Forest* 8) *StRealm* I 20; **1255** omnes forestarii qui faciunt ~a in foresta [*Bernwood, Bucks*].., cum venerint coram senescallo ad swanimotum et ibi presentent ~a, senescallus interrogat eis..utrum spine fuerint pertinentes ad dominum regem vel ad forestarium *Hund.* I 26; **1289** ~a apud Hoby [*Galtres, Yorks*] (*TR Forest Proc.* 237) *SelPlForest* xxx n. 2; **1295** perquisita de ~is foreste de Engilwode (*Ib.* 6) *Ib.* **b** **1230** tenet j hidam..per serjantiam custodiendi forestam de Bernewode..et..debet habere feodum in bosco domini regis, viz. ~um de spinis de bosco suo et de bosco qui vento prosternatur; et recipit pannagium et clamationes et indictationes, si que fuerint, viz. de viridi et venatione (*Inq.*) *Cart. Boarstall* 169 (cf. *Ambrosden* I 295); **1266** habet..racione..ballive [foreste de Bernwode] omnia ~a et exitus ~orum factorum de minuta spina *SelPlForest* 122 (cf. *CalIMisc* I p. 305); **1254** herbagium et pannagium cum ~is valent communibus annis x m. *IPM* 10/18; **1266** placita et perquisita curie cum attach' boscy valent per annum j m. in omnibus, quia sine attach' boscy non valerent ij s. *IMisc* 13/6; **1277** respondebunt de omnibus ~is exeuntibus de..custodia [bosci de Westwode] *Reg. Heref.* 146; **1388** boscus..cujus ~a et profectus nichil valent.. ultra feodum custodis *IMisc* (*Southwell*) 240/13; **1388** fines et perquisita curie cum ~is bosci valent per annum..vij li. *Ib.* (*Sherburn in Elmet*) 240/17; **1445** cum *wyndfallyn wode dere fallyn wode* cabliciis, ..~is forestariorum (*IPM*) *Sel PlForest* xxxv n. 2. **c** **1285** si..animalia ibidem venerint per eschapiam, dabitur pro eisdem [etc.], etsi hec inveniantur bis infra duo placita ~orum foreste; quod si tercio inveniantur infra duo ~a, tunc debent appreciari ad opus regis *TRForest Proc.* 1/5 r. 15*d*.; **1316** ~um tentum apud Calverton [*Sherwood*] (*KRAc* 134/16) *SelPlForest* xxxii; **1323** de duobus ultimis ~is tentis in..foresta [*Inglewood*], viz. in wardis de Penreth' et Gaytescales..nichil respondet *KRAc* 131/22 r. 7.

6 object seized (? as exhibit in crown plea).

1220 servientes [quos misi]..†sumerant arcum suum cum sagitta sanguinolenta et perchias cervi sanguinolentas. ..servientes duxerunt ad me malefactorem cum attaciamento; ..ego vero incontinenti feci convenire omnes probos homines cujusdam ville vestre de eadem foresta [in Hybernia] et feci ducere malefactorem illum cum ataciamento coram eis et ataciamentum coram eis inbreviari (*AncC* III 106) *RL* I 83; **1253** venire facias..H. le Serjant captum..pro combustione grangiarum, unde suspectus fuit, cum omnibus ~is suis *Liberate* 29 m. 10; **1331** ipsos ibidem attachiaverunt et.. ducti fuerunt..coram consilio domini regis..cum ~is cum predicto..R. inventis, viz. cum quibusdam platis de cupro sculpatis in forma hominum et quibusdam figuris de cera virginea conpressatis *SelCKB* V 54.

7 (?) tenement (apparently misconstruction of *le seon* w. *attachement*).

infangthef est infra suum ~um capere reum, P. *dedeyntz le seon* [? sc. *tenement*] *attachement de laron* BROMPTON 957.

attachiare [OF *atachier*; cf. tachiare], to attach, fasten. **b** to tie, moor, tether. **c** to attach (a document). **d** (refl.) to entangle oneself. **e** to set, stud (w. gems).

1234 trahere †retta [l. retia] sua..sine impedimento.. burrochiarum vel stachiarum quibus ~iabuntur..burrochie *E. Ch. S. Paul.* 261; **1235** in clavis ad attagiend' tegulas circa pomella *Pipe Wint.* 159284 r. 10; **1244** cuppas deauratas..ultra altare..~iari faciat *Liberate* 20 m. 4; **1250** desunt ..due fenestre cum gumphis et vertivellis et alio ferramento unde borde ~iari debent *CalIMisc* I p. 30; **s1265** postes quibus..catene ~iate fuerunt *Leg. Ant. Lond.* 78; **1311** uni carpentario ad ~iandum seruram super..portam *MunCOx* 256; **1337** pro pomellis attagiandis *Sacr. Ely* 84; **1355** pro lx clavis emptis pro vitro ~iando *Ib.* 170. **b** **1228** [cathena ad] ~iandum [batellum] *Cal. Liberate* 83; **1275** ammoverunt unum batellum de loco ubi dictus R. ~iavit illum batellum *Hund.* I 308; **1253** brokettum dami trahentem unum pelum una corda ~iata ad pedes *SelPlForest* 112; **1295** in corda de *weft* ad ~iandum equos in herba *DCCant* (*Ac. Cliffe*); **1325** in j corda empta ad ~iendum ad bukett' de predicto fonte hauriend' *MinAc* 1147/23 m. 3; **1364** due corde de crine pro equis ~iatis in pastura *Banstead* 351. **c** **1231** cujus cirographi transcriptum ~iatum est in fine istius rotuli *CurR* XIV 1155; transcriptum huic rotulo est ~iatum *State Tri. Ed. I* 9; **1306** breve patens..~atur in rotulo *Reg. Malm.* II 404; **1352** patet in panello huic precepto ~iato *Mem. Ripon* 340. **d** **1253** [brokettus] fugit versus boscum et in bosco athachavit se inter duo ligna *SelPlForest* 112. **e** **1245** capa ..atachiata est de minutis perlis *Invent. S. Paul.* 478.

2 to build up an abutment, embank.

c1250 construxit molendinum..et stagnum attagiavit *Chr. Dale* (= *MonA* VI 894b: †atrichiavit); **c1275** (v. attachiamentum 1b); **c1300** libertatem ~iandi calcetum, murum vel stagnum in solo suo *Cart. Chester* 378; **1304** ~iarunt [stagnum molendini] *Cart. Fountains* II 586; **1342** pro maeremio stagni molendini sui ~iando *MinAc* 1091/6 m. 1.

3 to attach (leg.), bind (a party) by pledge, distraint or arrest to appear in court. **b** (w. gen. of gd.). **c** (w. *placitum* or sim.) to attach parties in. **d** (w. *corpus*) to arrest.

1170 inquiratur si forestarii vel bailivi eorum aliquem acceperint vel attacaverint per vadium et per plegium..et postea sine justitia per se relaxaverint (*Inq. Vic.* 7) GERV. CANT. I 218 (= *SelCh* 177: ~iaverint); **1188** debet dim. m. quia non ~iavit quos debuit *Pipe* 162; **1194** plegii ejus ~ientur *CurR RC* I 8; **1195** attagiendi sunt quod sint apud Westm' *CurR PR* XIV 128 (cf. ib. 129: attagiandi); **1196** preceptum est vic. quod atachiat Galefridum *CurR* I 23; catallum reddet pro quo fuit ~iatus [OF: *dunt il est retez*] (*Leis Will.*) *GAS* 495; **1201** A. ~iata fuit per W...et J...et non venit; et ideo plegii in misericordia et ipsa capiatur *SelPlCrown* 134; **1202** loquela fuit..in comitatu; et ideo non fuerunt ~iati ad esse coram justiciariis *Ib.* 8; **1215** mercatores..de terra contra nos guerrina..~ientur sine dampno corporum et rerum donec sciatur.. *Magna Carta* 9; **1220** servientes scrutaverunt domum si possent invenire in domo sua †perinde esset melius ataciandus (*AncC* III 106) *RL* I 83 (cf. attachiamentum 2e); **1228** apellum..de quo idem N. ~iatus est ad respondendum coram vobis *Cl* 41; **1243** mandatum est..preposito de Vasato quod ~iari faciat G. ..et alios malefactores..et de eis bonam capiat securitatem quod sint coram senescallo Wasconie ad respondendum regi.. *Cl* 66; **1248** non possunt ~iari quia manent extra forestam *SelPlForest* 90; **s1251** appellatus est de..proditione..unde et retentus, quod vulgariter dicitur athachiatus M. PAR. *Maj.* V 213 (cf. ib. 234: atachiabatur, ut verba convenientia curie habeamus); **1265** attachientur depredatores..per corpora sua *Cl* 132; **1275** subvicecomes..dictum felonem W. capere et attagiare recusavit *Hund.* I 313; cum aliquis..verberaverit aliquem, tunc per corpus debet ~iari et non per bona transgressoris *Quon. Attach.* I. 6; **1391** ~iavit ..debitorem suum et eum deliberavit sine licencia ballivorum *Leet Norw.* 72; **1455** ~iatus fuit per corpus pro pigacione unius burse *FormA* 18; *to tache*, ~iare *CathA*. **b** ~iatus fuit veniendi coram justiciariis *SelPlCrown* 144; **1268** ~iantur respondendi super delicto suo *JustIt* 618 r. 8*d* (cf. ib. 14*d*.: ~iati veniendi hic); **1332** ~iati fuerunt essendi hic ..ad liberandum hic extractas finium *LTRMem* (*Comm.*) r. 12; **1340** preceptum est vic. quod ~iet eos essendi coram ..justiciariis *SessPCambs* 11. **c** **1195** in liberatione ij servientum ad attagianda et summonenda placita *Pipe* 159; **1195** loquela ista athagchiata ad Scaccarium *CurR PR* XIV 103; **1215** quod ipse et heredes sui atachient..omnia placita corone nostre in..[Waterford'] tanquam constabularius civitatis nostre *RChart* 210b; **1215** salvis.. placitis corone que ~iari debent per eosdem cives nostros usque in adventu justiciariorum nostrorum *BBC* (*Hereford*) 121; **1217** forestarius..~iet placita de foresta (*Ch. Forest* 16) *StRealm* I 21; **1221** ~iata fuit loquela usque in adventum justiciariorum *SelPlCrown* 172; **1228** placita ad coronam pertinencia..semper vidimus per servientes prioris..~ari et in curia eorundem..presentari et deduci *Feod. Durh.* 219; **1229** placita corone ~iabunt et custodient donec illa placitari faciamus *BBC* (*Montgomery*) 357; **1265** in loquela que ~iata est coram rege *Cl* 104. **d** **1212** operarii extranei, qui..predictam considerationem sequi noluerint, corpora eorum ~iantur (*sic*) *MGL* II 87; **1325** corpus dicti J. ~ietur per senescallum *CBaron* 141.

4 to seize in distraint. **b** to seize (beast) as stray in meadow or sim. **c** to seize (bread) for breach of assize.

1221 ballivi comitis non permiserunt eos ~iare navem nec illos qui in navi fuerunt *SelPlCrown* 132; primo debent res et bona partis defendentis ~iari et teneri quousque fecerit securitatem per plegios ad respondendum et standum juri parti conquerenti *Quon. Attach.* I. 5. **b** **1274** pro licencia.. cujusdam prati frussandi in quo comitissa solebat attachiare a Purificacione usque festum S. Mich. *Ac. Stratton* 51 (cf. attachiamentum 4c); **1276** A. ..in misericordia pro ij bobus ~iatis in prato *CourtR A. Stratton* no. 97; **1288** ad respondendum de ovibus in blado domini ~iatis *Ib.* 97; **1283** predicti prioratus capi et ~iari fecisti averia PECKHAM *Ep.* 452. **c** distringatur respondere ballivo pro pane suo ~iato *CourtR A. Stratton* no. 149.

attachiatio, attachment (leg.).

1185 debet xij d. pro injusta attaccatione *Pipe* 153; **1258** si dominus rex..ad ~ones vel districtiones processerit eorundem [prelatorum], tunc..ballivi ipsos attachiantes et distringentes per eosdem attachiatos et districtos..

excommunicentur; ..clerici autem, qui hujusmodi brevia ~onum seu districtionum dictaverint..excommunicentur *Conc. Syn.* 574; **1324** ut..prelatos ecclesie per ~ones vel manucaptiones ad suas trahant curias seculares *Proc. v. A. Kyteler* 7; **1376** si..judex in causa procedat ulterius, datur ~o contra judicem, advocatum et partem *RParl* II 357b; athachiacio, A. *athachyment or arestynge* WW.

attachiator, officer making attachment (leg.).

1258 si attachiationes et districtiones intervenerint, ad remedia contra ~ores et distringentes superius premissa habeatur recursus *Conc. Syn.* 582*n.*; attachiamentum habet fieri per ballivos vel eorum ministros presentatos in curia et juratos. tales itaque erunt ~ores eorum cum necesse fuerit ad capiendum rebelles et fugitivos *Quon. Attach.* 1. 3.

1 attactus [CL], touch. **b** touching, taking (of food).

~us tuus peccatores justificat ANSELM (*Or.* 10) III 41; ejusdem [Erkenwoldi] lectice ~u imbecilles multos curatos auctor est Beda W. MALM. *GP* II 73; lactis ad attactus morbus fugit NIG. *Mir. BVM* f. 10; quod pre nimietate doloris †actatum [? l. ~um] manus sue proprie abhorreret *Canon. G. Sempr.* 146v. **b** ante quorumlibet ciborum ~um..Deo persolvebat devociones BLAKMAN *Hen. VI* 13.

2 attactus v. attingere 1.

attacus [bibl. < ἄττακος], drone or solitary bee. **b** caterpillar.

atticus, ~us, *dora GlC* A 873; **10..** adticus, *feldbeo* WW. **b** *a cale worme,* atacus *CathA.*

attaediare [< ad+taedium], to weary, disgust, bore.

1335 ne ~ietur, si placet, dominacio vestra, si frequenter ..vobis scribam *Reg. Exon.* I 293; **s1399** unus dixit melius esse ibi expectare quousque communitas ~iaretur de eorum pervagatione per regnum *Eul. Hist. Cont.* III 381.

attaediatio, weariness, disgust.

non est ita insatiabilis appetitus justitie sicut amor pecunie; nam in istis est appetitus sine satietate, in illa est satietas sine ~one P. BLOIS *Serm.* 603C; **1452** intelligentes quanta incomoda et expense, ~ones vexacionesque et impedimenta utrique parti..hujusmodi jurisdiccionis occasione..devenerunt *Reg. Glasg.* 394.

attaedium, (source of) weariness, burden.

1437 creditur quod..eciam ad extremas quasque mundi partes, spretis laborum ~iis, esset..cum gaudio proficiscendum BEKYNTON II 45.

attag- v. et. attach-, attaleare.

attagen [CL < ἀτταγήν], kind of game-bird (cf. Horace *Epod.* 2. 54).

Afram avem vel ~enem non querant W. FITZST. *Thom. prol.* 10.

attaintus v. attingere 7–9.

attaleare, to tallage, tax.

1352 si contingit..Johannem..pro predictis xx s. attagliari vel gravari *Reg. Rough* 252.

attamen [CL; al. div.], but, however. **b** (after concessive clause) yet.

nunc mea divinis complentur viscera verbis / ..at tamen ex isdem nequeo cognoscere quicquam ALDH. *Aen.* 89. 3; accendite ergo lucernam illam..; ~en scitote quia non est mea BEDE *HE* IV 8; Dunstanus..jam..post tergum omnia posuerat; ~en..hoc..responsionis jaculum vibrat OSB. *V. Dunst.* 36; ineptum eum ad hoc intelligit; ~en, quia non potest alias, ipsi confitetur MAP *NC* IV 7; es maximus; attamen esto / flexilis VINSAUF *PN* 2097; **c1380** Oxonie.. persevero; propter ~en subsidii..defectum sum..perturbatus *FormOx* 322. **b** cui licet in terris stirpis generamina surgant, / attamen in caelis virtutum culmina scandit ALDH. *VirgV* 144; quamlibet non esset expertus vulnera ferri, / ..attamen illustrem meruit confessio palmam *Ib.* 705.

attaminare [LL], **attamiare** [cf. OF *atamer*], to contaminate, defile, dirty. **b** (fig.) to debase. **c** to dung.

~at, inquinat *GlC* A 867; tentantium vitiorum sorde ~ari BEDE *Tab.* 430; **s552** corruptior..celi tractus egrescentibus elementis civitatem ~inans DICETO *Chr.* 97; non audebat..indumentorum pontificalium sancta immundis contactibus ~inare R. COLD. *Cuthb.* 26; *to defoulle,* ~inare, †attarere, ..coinquinare *CathA.* **b** ni..hujus opusculi diffinitionem degeneri vitiorum stilo..~inando foedarem *V. Dunst. B.* 1. **c 1376** ~inabunt mariscum cum vaccis, bovettis et boviculis *IMisc* 208/4.

2 to broach (casks or liquor). **b** to open up (a cargo). **c** (?) to cut into (w. ref. to felons' chattels; *cf.* 3 *infra*). **d** to broach (fig.), begin discussion of.

adtaminat, usurpat *GlC* A 188; precones vini clamant gula yante vinum ataminatum [*gl.*: *atamyd, affore*; (?) *pun on* 1a supra] in tabernis GARL. *Dict.* 126; **1290** item ij sextaria vini de uno doleo primo atamiato *Ac. Swinfield* 107; **1291** volens ~iasse dictum doleum et vendidisse (*St. Ives*) *Law Merch.* I 52; **1292** precipimus quod conventus noster habeat ..singulis annis unum doleum vini clari et purissimi et quod illud doleum primo ~ietur die anniversarii nostri *Reg. Malm.* II 380; **1305** j kempe allec' ~eat' de stauro *Middleton MSS* (*HMC*) 326 (cf. ib. 324: athameat'); *ataymyd, as a vessel with drink,* ~inatus *PP.* **b 1290** discarcata nave vel ~inata..de venalibus percipiet dominus rex custumam suam *RParl* I 28. **c 1368** clamat habere omnes pannos talliatos seu ~iatos [*Collect. Staffs* XVI 20: †attanuatos] et omnes carnes ~iatas et totum braseum infra quarterium et omnia blada inventulata infra j quarterium *PlRChester* 71 r. 32*d.* **d 1313** ad omnia placita hac vice..~inata terminandum *Eyre Kent* I 1 (cf. ib. p. 15: *le plee attame*; v. et. atterminare 1b); **1360** ita quod nulla querela in eodem hundredo de villis predictis ~iari potuit *Pat* 259 m. 4; **1367** neque resortum aliquod coram eo propositum seu ~iatum fuit (*LTRMem* 139) *Camd. Misc.* XIX (*Sovereignty of Aquitaine*) 53.

3 to bolt, sift (flour).

1326 bedellus habebit de farina in quocumque vase ~inata *BB St. Davids* 238; bedelli consueverunt habere de bonis felonum farinam ~inatam *Ib.* 256; *bultyn flowre,* ~ino *PP.*

attaminatio, broaching.

attaymyng of a vessel with drink, ~o *PP.*

attarere v. attaminare 1a. attashere v. attrahere 1d.

attastator [cf. tastator], taster.

1442 ~or cervisie (*MinAc*) *MFG.*

attav- v. atav-. atted- v. attaed-.

attegia [CL (?) < Gall.], hut or tent.

s877 ategias figunt in oppido dicto Gleaucestre vario ictu ÆTHELW. IV 3.

atteinctus v. attingere.

attela [OF *atele*], swingletree.

1350 in virgis emptis pro reparacione ~e carucarum..ij d. (*MinAc.*) *Surv. Durh. Hatf.* 238.

attelebus [ἀττέλεβος], immature locust (also fig.).

ex locusta nascitur brucus..; exinde succrescentibus alis, cum ceperit volitare, vocatur athelebus. ..in officialibus eundem brucum, athelebum invenies et locustam J. SAL. *Pol.* 590C; primo est athelabs et postquam crescentibus alis fit locusta.. BART. ANGL. XII 25; brucus, acelaber, res una locusta vocatur; / hinc tres etates tria nomina dant animali: / tunc brevis est brucus; cum de tellure levatur, / dicitur acalaber; postquam fit adulta, locusta GARL. *Syn.* 1582D.

attemperamentum, tempering, moderation.

quia non decet imperatorem in omnibus ferocem esse, sed in quibusdam mitem, assumpsit sibi pro ~o colorem aureum BAD. AUR. 107.

attemperare [CL], to adjust, moderate.

c1182 precipio quod omnia molendina..ita ~ari et admensurari faciatis ut molendina Cantuariensis ecclesie.. plenarie molere possint (*Breve Regis*) ELMH. *Cant.* 462.

attemptamentum, attack.

1402 pro aliis diversis ~is contra dictas libertates ecclesiasticas..in regno vestro ad presens plus solito pululantibus *RParl* III 494a (= *Conc.* III 271b).

attemptare [CL], to attempt undertake, venture upon. **b** (w. inf.). **c** (w. *ad* and gdv.).

1096 sine regimine nec exercitus bellum nec navis marinum audet attentare periculum *Ep. Anselm* (201) IV 92 (= EADMER *HN* 87); ut..simile opus..nullatenus ~aret EADMER *V. Osw.* 5 p. 9; **s1176** constat quod quicquid circa presens negotium est ~atum sub universitate concluditur *Chr. Battle* 178; nec tamen modernis tantum temporibus scelera hujusmodi sunt attentata GIR. *TH* II 24; cum milites..fugam ~assent *Id. IK* I 12; tam..prepostere.. negocium ~are WYCL. *Civ. Dom.* II 1; **1442** si..fraude.. clam aliquid..~atum aut usurpatum sit BEKYNTON I 128; **1503** quod nunquam aliquam sui causam coram majore..~et *StatOx* 309. **b 681** (12c) ut nulla regalis auditia..decretum nostrum confringere ~et *CS* 58; **s1176** attentavit impetrare ..licentiam eundi in peregrinatione *G. Hen. II* I 114; libellos suos..ad diversas mundi partes..destinare ac ipsos affigi (*sic*) in portis ecclesiarum..~avit OCKHAM *Pol.* I 294; noluit quod C..se intromittere ~aret *Id. Dial.* 632; **1376** auri nitorem tantis nebulis opponere ~avit *Chr. Angl.* 94; **s1384** juravit quod..ecclesiam..ingredi ~aret *V. Ric. II* 54. **c 1409** in stipendio J. G. *smythman*.., incipientis et ~antis ad fabricandum ferrum (*Rec. Aud. Durh.*) *EHR* XIV 519.

2 (w. *contra* or sim.) to take action against, attack. **b** (absol.). **c** (p. ppl. as sb. n.) hostile undertaking, attack, offence.

1213 quod nec per se nec per alios contra personam.. nostram aliquid attemtabunt *RChart* 193b; **c1254** decernimus irritum..si quid super hoc contra protectionis..nostre tenorem ab aliquo fuerit temere attentatum *MunAcOx* 28; **1341** multa alia..~are presumpsit in status nostri detrimentum (*Lit. Regis*) AVESB. 97. **b 1417** sedem apostolicam, contra quam nullatenus ~are intendimus *Conc.* III 382b; judex a quo processit in dicta causa a[t]emptando contra dictam inhibitionem *Praxis* 265. **c 1237** ita quod regi respondere possint..super ~atis contra pacem regis per hujusmodi malefactores *Cl* 532; **1265** occasione aliquorum per nos..contra ipsum [regem] et suos attentatorum (*Lit. Pat. Princ. Wallie, Chanc. Misc.* 17/1/17) *RL* I 284; **1339** contra nos illum non provocat aliquod factum nostrum vel ~atum per nos aliquod contra eum (*Lit. Regis*) AD. MUR. 92; **s1345** nuncii pape..hortabantur..quod..rex.. ~ata in contrarium revocaret *Ib.* 161; **1342** †attentatorum [? l. attentatum] post et contra appellacionem.., si de illo articuletur specialiter et probetur, per modum attentati poterit revocari *Conc.* II 686–7; **1417** occasione guerrarum, hostilitatis, reprisaliarum vel ~atorum contra treugas *RNorm.* 211; ideo peto hujusmodi ~ata..revocari *Praxis* 265.

3 to challenge, dispute, impugn.

1242 si forte prefatus heres vel heredes sui, cum ad etatem pervenerint, presentem conventionem non ~averint, omnia predicta..tenementa..simili modo revertentur *CurR* XVI 2196; **1404** si qui presumpserint ~are vel posteriare ordinacionem factam de textoribus..affirmando quod predicta ordinacio est in punctu cotidie esse fracta *BB Winchester* 4.

4 (?) to approve, confirm.

1266 nos, assignacionem..Alicie factam de maneriis.. ~antes, ..precipimus quod..Alicie de maneriis..seisinam ..rehabere faciatis *Cl* 185; **1278** qui forme pacis..assenserunt et eandem per instrumentum aut sigillum autenticum ~arunt et admiserunt *RGasc* II 48.

attemptatio, undertaking, enterprise. **b** offence.

1233 non erit locus..vos excusandi quin manifestam relinquatis suspitionem quod predicta ~o a conscientia et voluntate vestra emanaverit *Cl* 325; **1236** litteras..super ~one Lumbardorum..recepimus (*TreatyR*) *Foed.* I 364; **s1397** ne separata negocii ~o..discrimina provocaret *Meaux* III 249. **b 1463** quodsi..contingat aliquem..dictas inducias violare..aut contra easdem quicquam attemptare, de tali ~one seu violacione sufficienter informati parti.. lese †redderi [l. reddi] faciemus justicie complementum *RScot* 409b.

attemptator, offender.

1284 si..aliqua fuerint attemptata indebite..in prejudicium molendini, ..taliter attemptata in statum pristinum.. revocetis, ..in ipsos ~ores procedentes *RGasc* II 231; **1438** ad puniendum quoscumque ~ores et malefactores in contrarium *RScot* 303b.

attendentia, attention, consideration. **b** attendance (upon), service. **c** attendance (at), presence.

illud perficiamus et a vetito abstineamus absque ~ia ad leges ordinatas noviter, et est satis NETTER *DAF* II 235 v.; **1448** ad hoc..officiarii..maximam dederunt ~iam (*Court Bk. Ep. Linc.*) *Eng. Clergy* 224. **b s1399** sibi legiancie, fidelitatis, subjeccionis, ~ie et cujuscumque obediencie juramentum et fidelitatem totaliter reddiderunt, ipsum diffidendo nec pro rege..habituri AD. USK 32; **1431** pro ~ia sua circa personam regis *ActPC* IV 79; **1475** pro ~iis suis super personam regis in servicio suo guerre ultra mare profecturo (*IssueR*) *Foed.* XI 847. **c 1447** pro..~ia et resorto populi nostri et officiariorum ibidem causa officii *Pat* 464 m. 11; **1459** pro custubus et expensis..in..~ia apud civitatem.. Dunolmi *RScot* 391a; ad diurnam comparenciam vel ~iam ad respondendum legi *Entries* 600b.

attendere [CL], to exert, direct. **b** to apprise. **c** (pl. ppl.) directed, intent (*v. et. attinere* 6).

s1326 plures, ..~entes malam voluntatem versus.. abbatem, dictum abbatem false..accusabant *Chr. Rams.* 351. **b 1250** monstravit illum [austurcum] cuidam armigero, et ille armiger dominum suum atendidit (*sic*) *IMisc* 4/19. **c** ut studiose inventione attentos, sic facili cognitioni non promptos disputatores BALSH. *AD* 40; [cognitio] habebitur ex attenta consideratione eorum que similia videntur, non sunt autem *Ib.* 115.

2 to pay attention, be attentive, take pains. **b** (w. *quod*). **c** (w. dat.). **d** (w. *ad*). **e** (w. *super*).

si humiliter per caritatem volueris ~ere, ..perspicies *Ep. Aldh.* 1(6); ut..diligenter adtenderet ne quid ille contrarium veritati..introduceret BEDE *HE* IV 1; quod..ignoranti incredibile, ~enti dubium, intelligenti certum BALSH. *AD* 10; non ~entibus sed quasi videndo non videntibus GIR. *TH* III 11. **b a1350** debent ~ere quod scolares sui regulam observent *StatOx* 21. **c 1147** quietas ab omni servitio..excepto exercitu regis unde monachi erunt ~entes ipsi regi *E. Ch. Scot.* 178; **1379** qui quidem clericus eciam ~et camerariis *Rec. Leic.* II 193; **1487** solvet..clerico..pro officio suo ~endo (*Indent.*) *Crawley* 468; **1552** predicacionibus diligenter ~ant *Conc. Scot.* II 132. **d** usum disserendi et sic ad disserendo explicata ~endi BALSH. *AD* 6; **1299** quod ad providendum sibi de viro idoneo..eligendo..~ant *Reg. Cant.* I 300. **e 1471** quod ipse sit ~ens super prelocutorem *Pat* 527 m. 19; **1497** in expensis..~encium super vexillum S. Cuthberti *Ac. Durh.* 654; **1583** conduccionem.. equitum ad ~endum super municiones *Pat* 1316 m. 28.

3 to consider, note: **a** (w. indir. qu.); **b** (w. acc. and inf.); **c** (w. *quod*); **d** (impers. pass. in abl. absol.).

a studioque adtende sagaci / an sint vera WULF. *Swith.* I 349; ~atur..et de quo quid queratur BALSH. *AD* 152; abbas, ~ens qualiter celerarius turpiter ibat per villam ad colligendum *repselver* BRAKELOND 149. **b s1173** ..regis filii cesserunt in partem, non quia causam ejus justiorem ~erent DICETO *YH* I 371; ut ex his ~i valeat et deprehendi nihil in terris..[esse] beatum quod plena queat felicitate gaudere GIR. *TH* I 27; **c1240** ~ens in hoc meam utilitatem fuisse factam *Reg. Moray* 143; **1263** ~entes..honori regis plurimum fuisse detractum (*Arbitrium Regis Franciae*) *Leg. Ant. Lond.* 59; **s1328** rex ~ens justum esse..quod.. *Croyl. Cont. B* 482; **1452** ~entes..Thomam nullo modo probare potuisse intentionem suam *MunAcOx* 636. **c** ~e..quod flegma..nominatur naturalis humor GILB. I 33 v. 1; **1287** est ~endum quod in fine..compoti est quoddam memoriale (*Comp. Collect. Apostol.*) *EHR* XXXII 57; **1311** ~entes.. quod..archiepiscopus jam parari fecerit viam (*Pat*) *MGL* I 127. **d 1390** attento quod de pura gracia..ei subvenitur *FormOx* 236; **1399** attento quod..regnum non prestiterit suum consensum (*Quaestiones*) AD. USK 49; **1407** attento.. vestram dominacionem..affectare bonum pacis *Lit. Cant.* III 103; **1468** attento quod fecit expensas.. *ExchScot* 544.

4 (trans.) to observe, abide by. **b** to mark, pay attention to, consider, recognize.

c (p. ppl. in abl. absol.). **d** to reckon (acc. a standard).

illud cautissime ~endum est, ut ea..inviolata serventur LANFR. *Const.* 85; si terminum a preposito datum non ~ebat *DB* I 269b; **1101** de istis conventionibus atendendis dedit comes R. regi Henrico istos obsides *DipDoc* I p. 3. **b** nostras adtende loquelas WULF. *Swith.* I 516; si sapientie Dei immensitas..~atur J. SAL. *Pol.* 446B; martyr voventes ~it et promissa respicit W. CANT. *Mir. Thom.* IV 15; si in nobis [episcopis] ordinationem ~itis, et in ipso [archiepiscopo] similiter ~ere debetis W. FITZST. *Thom.* 40; **1217** nos vero, ~entes fidele servicium suum.., benigne..exaudivimus *Pat* 117; **1227** episcopus..mandavit quod..fecit inquisitionem per quam dicti W. legitimationem non ~ens, ipsum W. non habuit pro legitimo *CurR* XIII 77; **1380** ex causa considerata et diligenter attenta *ExchScot* 655. **c** **1356** attenta debilitate nostri corporis (*Pat. Ed. Balliol*) AVESB. 132; **1404** premissis debito intuitu attentis et ponderatis *Cl* 254 m. 30*d*.; **1416** attenta evidente utilitate.. collegii *Deeds Balliol* 124. **d** primus modus febris composite; secundus modus ~itur secundum modum affligendi GILB. I 7 v. 2; notandum est penes quid ~itur velocitas in motu quo ad causam (R. SWINESHEAD) *Sci. Mech.* 208*n*. (cf. ib. 221).

5 to wait. **b** (trans.) to await, expect. **c** (w. inf.) to expect, plan. **d** (pr. ppl.) stationary, persistent.

dum pater ~eret ut manuum indicio solito more suo filius patri innueret KETEL *J. Bev.* 286; ~e et dormi O. CHERITON *Fab. add.* B 11; s**1399** [dux] ibidem ~ebat quousque rex exisset de interiori parte castri *V. Ric. II* 155. **b** id solum intendentes, id ~entes, spem singularem..habebant GIR. *RG* I 9; [Edwardus II] inimicos suos in campo ~ere vix audebat *Meaux* II 355. **c** **1305** quia ~imus applicare apud Burdegalam die Sabbati proximo post Assencionem Domini, mittimus ibidem A. ..et N. ..ad preparanda hospicia nostra *RGasc.* III lviii *n.* **d** **1428** ubi aqua stans est, ~ens [*PS*: *attendante*] ac immutabilis *CalPat* 478.

attenerare, to make tender.

caro..~ata et mollificata ex facili excoriaretur et lederetur GILB. II 78 v. 1.

attenta- v. attempta-.

attente [CL], attentively, earnestly. **b** seriously, gravely.

quod dum ~ius consideraret BEDE *HE* IV 21; non minus ~e considerandum BALSH. *AD* 13; a**1190** ~ius divinam clementiam precibus..implorando *Canon. G. Sempr* 101; prudenter et ~e struit insidias MAP *NC* III 2 p. 121; **1264** ~e rogamus quatinus.. *Cl* 397; **1409** libros logice..in scolis ..audire paciatce et ~e *StatOx* 200. **b** **1330** gravamina que ..viri ecclesiastici ~ius sunt perpessi (*Lit. Papae*) *Lit. Cant.* I 326.

attenticus v. authenticus 2a.

attentio [CL], attention, mental application. **b** (w. indir. q.) observation, awareness. **c** care, looking after.

tanto studiosius..~onem apponere necesse; acuat igitur attendendi necessitas industriam, superet ~onis industria difficultatem BALSH. *AD* 29; curandum ne, aliquo sophismatum genere alicubi comperto, comperiendi cesset ~o *Ib.* 104; cum docilis sis et in te nondum tepuerit ~onis industria *Dial. Scac.* II *prol.* **b** quem..qualiter haec sint primo edita latere non potuit ~o BEDE *Wict.* 10. **c** **1564** pro ~one et custodia..librí matriculationis per discretionem custodum ciste *StatOx* 395.

1 attentus v. attendere.

2 attentus, extension, augmentation.

c**1170** notum sit..me concessisse..Reginaldo B. meo †milite in atentu sue garison' villam totam de Est Witton (*AncC* I 27) *E. Ch. Yorks* IV 52.

3 attentus v. attinere.

attenuare [CL], to thin, emaciate. **b** to diminish. **c** to extenuate (a fault). **d** to make light of. **e** (fig.) to fine down.

adtenuatus, subtilis *GlC* A 205; macer..effectus, puta quem..tenuis dieta et noctes insomnes non mediocriter ~averant GIR. *GE* II 13; *to make thinne*, ~are, ..subtiliare *CathA*. **b** s**796** privilegia omnium ecclesiarum que seculo suo genitor [Offa] ~averat..revocavit W. MALM. *GR* I 94; s**1320** †regios [? l. regis] vires adeo ~arunt ut ejus assensu saltem umbratice adhibito..Dispensatores exlegarent HIGD. VII 42. **c** ignorancia juris in hoc casu non excusat, licet forte ~et OCKHAM *Dial.* 683. **d** ceteris laudantibus, rex, factum jocular iter ~ans, diabolice fortitudini non humane virtuti attribuit W. MALM. *GP* II 95. **e** **1321** eterne sapiencie..altitudo..vicarium reliquit in terris..ut ..recreacionis gracia ad principium velud ad cor ~atum, spiritus quociens indigencia hoc exigit, redeant universi *FormOx* 75.

attenuatio, slimming, emaciation. **b** (fig.). **c** diminution, weakening.

carnis jejunium dici potest si quando quispiam..jejunat ne corpore supra modum pinguescat; verum illud nulle virtutis est, †adeoque [? l. ideoque] dicendum est potius esse ~onis BELETH *RDO* 10. 22; alcanna..valet ad mundificacionem et ~onem *Alph.* 7; s**1423** cum..consuleret ut.. racione sue ~onis in egritudine de aere se subtraheret AMUND. I 181. **b** s**1454** patimini..febrem..consumpcionis in corpore vestro mystico adeo gravem quod, ubi dudum..habebat ipsa ecclesia membra..lx.., vix pro nunc attingit quinquagenarium. ..nunquid..hec consumpcio gravis, ..hec ~o grandis, ..hec inanicio tam..formidabilis quod..fiet..mors istius ecclesie? *Reg. Whet.* I 142. **c** mahemium esse dicitur ossis cujuslibet fractio vel teste capitis per incisionem vel abrasionem ~o GLANV. XIV 1; **1283** status archidiaconalis ~o vel dejeccio PECKHAM *Ep.* 425; ex quo [radiorum] concursu fit ~o vaporis, ut pluviam inde consumat *Id. Persp.* III 21.

attenuativus, causing thinness, attenuant.

siccitas est naturaliter ~a BART. ANGL. IV 3; addantur ~a subtiliativa cum sirupo GILB. I 32. 2 (cf. ib. VII 352. 1: ~a dieta); Avicenna..dicit quod subtiliativa et ~a idem est GAD. 12 v. 1.

atterere [CL], to wear away, bruise. **b** to fritter away (time). **c** to crush, oppress. **d** to dishearten, demoralize.

misella / stringitur adtritis ingenti compede plantis WULF. *Swith.* II 97; accipitrem evexit fracto crusculo, quod ungula equi..attriverat W. CANT. *Mir. Thom.* V 19; abrasa et attrita dorsorum depilatione GIR. *TH* I 26. **b** jumentum suum inaniter vexans et tempus ~ens W. CANT. *Mir. Thom.* V 11. **c** nascentem..heresim..attrivit BEDE *HE* II 1 p. 75; provinciam illam saeva caede..attrivit *Ib.* IV 14; **1266** (v. attonitus b). **d** nec ipsi machinis ~ebantur nec obsidione..flectebantur *G. Steph.* I 45.

2 (p. ppl. *attritus*) shameless, brazen. **b** crushed in spirit, 'attrite' (less strong than *contritus*).

quantus quosdam ~ae frontis pallor ob detectum sceleris reatum tremibundos arguit! ALDH. *VirgP* 32 p. 273. **b** spiritus attrite mentis plusquam caro sana NIG. *Laur.* 28 v. 1; resipiscat..dimittendo opus extrinsecum, ~us de peccato, quousque plenarie conteratur, et post compleat opus suum meritorie in gracia WYCL. *Civ. Dom.* I 344; c**1430** admiramur quibus mente, corde et spiritu ducti estis ut..taliter..in ~um hominem exacerbastis *Reg. Whet.* II 433.

atterminare, to fix a day (leg.). **b** (trans.) to fix a day for (a plea or sim.). **c** to adjourn. **d** to provide (party or petitioner) w. a day for hearing plea or sim.

diximus cujus dignus esset qui rectum alicui disfortiet vel in bocland vel in folcland; et ut ei adterminetur [AS: *ðæt he him geanddǵode*] in folcland quando rectum velit ei facere coram proposito suo (*Quad.*) *GAS* 141; volumus ut rectum judicetur in omni causa et adterminetur [AS: *andagie*] quando hoc impleatur *Ib.* 194. **b** **1220** facias.. clamari..quod omnes assise et omnia placita que sunt ~ata et non finita coram justiciariis nostris apud Westm' tunc sint coram prefatis justiciariis apud Hertford' in eo statu in quo remanserunt apud Westm' *Cl* 473b (cf. BRACTON 109, 426; *Fleta* 437: †actannata); **1237** quod tunc esset ibi ad audiendum assisam illam in eodem statu quo aterminata fuit coram justiciariis apud Westm' ad predictum terminum *BNB* III 207; **1246** mandamus quod omnes loquelas unde W. Mar'..vocatur ad warantum coram nobis et alia placita ipsum tangencia aterminetis coram nobis in octabis S. Hyllarii *Cl* 471; primo de placito [v.l. die placiti] ~ato ad Bancum foris comitatum per pone potest tenens essoniari de malo veniendi HENGHAM *Magna* 5; **1286** quod omnia placita..que in eodem itinere ~ata coram vobis non fuerint [? sc. finita] una cum processu eorundem..justiciariis nostris de Banco mittatis (*Breve Regis*) *PQW* 84b; loquela.. ~ata fuit coram rege per breve ipsius regis *State Tri. Ed. I* 9. **c** **1292** adhuc ibi [in Scaccario] pendet loquela..et est ibi ~ata usque ad quindenam S. Mich. *PQW* 387b; **1313** mandamus vobis quod omnia negocia dictos B. ..et M. ..in itinere predicto tangencia usque in proximo parliamento nostro ~etis (*Breve Regis*) *Ib.* 322b. **d** **1243** quod sint coram.. senescallo Wasconie die et loco quibus alii loquelas habentes coram eodem ~ati sunt ad respondendum regi et aliis de.. injuriis per eos perpetratis *Cl* 66; **1285** in consimili casu.. indigente remedio concordent clerici de Cancellaria in brevi faciendo vel ~ent querentes in proximo parleamento (*Westm.* 24) *StRealm* I 83.

2 to attermine (fix terms for payment for): **a** (a debt); **b** (a debtor).

a **1253** quod debitum lvij m. ..~etur ad c s. per annum reddendos predictis Judeis *Cl* 198; **1258** de x m. quas regi reddere tenetur ad Scaccarium suum Pasche proximo futurum de xx m. ad quas rex ~avit debita que regi debet *Cl* 207; **1266** quod quidem relevium inter alia debita que eadem I. nobis debet ad Scaccarium nostrum ~avimus liberandum custodi operacionum nostrarum Westm' *Cl* 213; **1290** petit quod dominus rex velit ~are xxxvj li. quas ei debet, sicut ei ~are promisit *RParl* I 54b; **1292** de illis cccc li. in quibus nobis tenemini..et que vobis per..custodem Garderobe nostre ~ate sunt ad certos terminos nobis solvende *RScot* 13a; **1339** volentes quod debita nostra sic ~ata vel respectuata..leventur (*Pat*) *Foed.* V 109b. **b** **1238** P. filius Gilberti Medici ~atus de debito suo ad xxx s. per annum solvit anno xxj xxxv s.; anno sequenti reddat xxv s., et habeat terminos suos *LTRMem* 12 r. 7*d*.; **1239** preceptum est vic. quod distringat homines de W. et omnes alios ~atos in com. suo ad respondendum per manum suam, quousque breve regis vel talliam ostenderint de terminis suis servatis *KRMem* 17 r. 9; **1327** major ville predicte ~atur de debito predicto in rotulo finium *LTRMem* 99 r. 113*d*.

atterminatio, fixing a day (for plea).

1331 episcopus dicit..quod quedam libertates..apud Derb' presentate atterminate fuerunt coram prefato J. .. apud Lincoln' in octabis S. Trinitatis; ..et W. ..qui sequitur..dicit quod..episcopus..ostendit..nullam restitucionem inde sibi..fuisse factam, ostendendo nisi tantum ~onem predictam *PQW* 150b; **14..** [assisa] summonita fuit coram prefatis justiciariis..et postmodum capta..per ~onem justiciariorum..predictorum *Reg. Brev.* 30.

2 attermination (fixing terms for payment).

1297 atterminarunt predictum debitum xx li. et super ~one illa solverunt domino regi c s. *PlRExch* 21 r. 12*d*.; **1302** mitigetur aterminacio..et interim cesset execucio judicii *RParl* I 158b; **1310** cum plures de regno nostro nobis in diversis debitis teneantur, ad que nobis solvenda.. absque status eorum depressione non sufficiunt hiis diebus, ac videatur nobis quod per ~onem inde in Scaccario.. faciendam commodius quam per viam aliam poterimus dicta debita recuperare *Cl* 127 m. 2; **1333** predictus G. solvit.. de fine juxta ~onem eidem G. prius concessam *LTRMem* 105 r. 57; **1339** ~ones seu astallamenta et respectus debitorum nostrorum..revocamus (*Pat*) *Foed.* V 109b; **1352** quod prefatis N. et M. de predictis c li. hujusmodi ~onem.. habere et terminos illos..irrotulari..faciant *RScot* 747b.

atternare v. attornare 7a.

attestari [CL], **~are,** to attest, bear witness. **b** (w. dat.) to support by testimony.

quamvis alii duas esse vocis species ~entur ALDH. *PR* 131; id ipsum apostolo ~ante *Id. VirgP* 54; sicut ipse postea flendo solebat adtestari BEDE *HE* II 1 p. 74; praedictis eisdem atestantibus testimoniis ERIUG. *Per.* 536A; **796** ~ante veritate ALCUIN *Ep.* 99; hunc adolescentem non esse quod fuit ~aris OSB. *Mir. Dunst.* 19; ipso auctore sceleris ~ante W. CANT. *Mir. Thom.* VI 14. **b** hoc manerium reclamat abbas..et hund[ret] ~antur (*sic*) ei *DB* I 10; sed homines de scira non ~antur eis *Ib.* 133b; cum..interminabiles inimicitie mihi ex vestra parte.. intenderentur et his vester habitus circa me et dissaisitio qua me..spoliastis ~arentur, necessario dimisi quod..retinere non potui EADMER (*Lit.*) *HN* 351; **1280** illum nominet.. pro hoc officio cui majus et fidelius testimonium ac major fratrum numerus ~antur *Cant. Cath. Pri.* 34*n*.

2 to call to witness, invoke. **b** to swear (by a saint).

1239 cardinales per sanguinem Jesu Christi et sub attestatione divini judicii per literas nostras..~amur ut generale concilium..debeant evocare (*Lit. Imp.*) M. PAR. *Maj.* III 587. **b** s**1291** ~avit rex per S. Edwardum quod jus regni sui et corone S. Edwardi..habere deberet W. GUISB. 235.

attestatio, attestation, sworn testimony of witness (civil or canon law). **b** testimony, evidence. **c** (w. ref. to document). **d** (w. ref. to seal).

nisi de reliquo se caste victurum canonica ~one promittat LANFR. *Ep.* 21. 526C; **1177** cum..publicatis ~onibus utrobique esset renunciatum *Ch. Sal.* 41; si deducens testes.. nondum perlegerit ~ones RIC. ANGL. *Summa* 47; auditis.. ~onibus et allegationibus partium, ..electionem cassavimus utriusque GIR. *Inv.* IV 4; acceptis juramentis a sexdecim legalibus hominibus et auditis eorum ~onibus, dixit abbas.. BRAKELOND 147* p. 93; **1223** in foro ecclesiastico..testes produxit et publicatis ~onibus..*Cl* 629b; s**1308** concilium.. super iniquitatibus..Templariorum.., in quo..recitari fecit ~ones enormitatum *Flor. Hist.* III 144; **1317** testibus ..diligenter examinatis ipsorumque ~onibus publicatis *FormA* 11; **1390** eorum ~ones nobis et curie nostre sub sigillis eorum clausas..debito modo transmittendas *SelPl Adm.* I 12; c**1430** queruntur de longinquo testes, quorum ~onibus habeat iniqua ferri sentencia *Reg. Whet.* II 371. **b** in ~one veritatis quam praedicant in nullo ab invicem discrepant BEDE *Tab.* 405; certissima fidelium virorum adtestatione *Id. HE pref.* p. 8; ex fratribus Ramesiensis cenobii, quod B. Yvo corporali presentia signorum ~one collustrat GOSC. *Mir. Iv.* lxiii; fides..tua secundum Jacobi ~onem [*James* ii 17]..mortua est AELNOTH *Cnut* 132F; ~one miraculi fidem verbis fecit AILR. *Ed. Conf.* 779A; qui literam papalem habuit in ~one tanti miraculi BACON *Maj.* II 213; est ergo Deus qui facit illa gloriosa miracula Christiana in ~onem fidei Christiane BRADW. *CD* 47A; s**1385** sibi fidelitatem promittentibus sub jurisjurandi ~one WALS. *HA* II 120; in ~onem sue eximie devocionis ad Deum BLAKMAN *Hen. VI* 16. **c** **1155** presentis scripti ~one notum facimus quod controversia..terminata est *Lit. Cant. app.* III 367; **1200** eam [concessionem] presentis scripti ~one et sigilli nostri appositione communivimus *RChart* 41b. **d** **1148** ipsam [concessionem] episcopali auctoritate et sigilli nostri ~one confirmavimus *Reg. S. Osm.* I 216; c**1160** sigilli ~one firmamus *Melrose* I no. 5; **1193** que omnia predicta..sigillorum nostrorum ~one roboravimus (*Forma Pacis*) R. HOWD. III 220.

2 voucher to warranty for stolen property (*cf. advocare* 2). **b** calling to witness, invocation.

absque vero utro, nulla ei ~o [AS: *team*] indulgeatur [*gl.*: id est, liceat ei trahere aliquem ad tutelam quod ab eo habeat] (*Cons. Cnut.*) *GAS* 193. **b** s**1178** qui in periculo anime et sub ~one tremendi judicii asserebat se ipsum martirem..vidisse M. PAR. *Maj.* I 404; **1239** (v. attestari 2a); juramentum est affirmacio vel negacio de aliquo ~one sacre rei firmata *Fleta* 334.

atteuiriamentum v. attiramentum. atteyntare v. attinctare. atticus v. attacus. attile v. attillum d.

attillamentum [OF *atillement*], fitting, equipment: **a** (of ship or boat); **b** (of cart).

a **1212** in custod' x battellorum cum omnibus attiliamentis suis *Pipe* 75; **1258** quia alibi invenire non possumus attilyamentum ad galyas nostras quam in partibus vestris, vobis mandamus quod galyas illas attiliari faciatis *Cl* 197; batellus cum onere et omni ~o *Fleta* 37. **b** ejus [carectarii] est scire phalera, attilamenta et hernesia minuta carectis appendencia preparare et emendare *Ib.* 172.

attillare, ~iare [OF *atillier*], to fit (out), equip: **a** (ships); **b** (crossbows or quarrels).

a **1215** parari faciatis duas bonas galias bene atillatas et eskippatas bona gente *Cl* 214a; **1233** [ad galias regis] atillandas *CalLiberate* 204; **1258** (v. attillamentum a). **b** **1242** v milia quarellorum..bene impennari et attiliari faciatis *Liberate* 17 m. 3; **1252** ad balistas nostras apud Turrim Lond' conservandas et atilliandas *Ib.* 28 m. 9; **1254** provideat quod illas xx balistas ad duos pedes habeat rex bene atyllatas *Cl* 231; **1255** [ad balistas] ~iandas *CalLiberate* 257.

attillia v. attillium.

attilliator, maker of artillery (*cf. artillator, attiriator*).

1246 injungat atilliatori balistarum regis in eadem Turri quod et sit in auxilium donec predicte baliste reparentur *Cl* 446; **1247** mandatum est constabulario de Windlesor' quod attylliatori balistarum regis moranti in castro. .inveniat baculas ad balistas et alia que necessaria sunt ad officium suum *Cl* 6; **1266** attiliatori flechiarum regis in Turri Lond' *Cl* 280; **1272** Henrico attilliari (*sic*) balistarum regis *Cl* 492; **1277** j attillatori et j suo garcioni pro vadiis eorundem *KRAc* 3/11; **1284** xxx homines defensabiles, de quibus sint x balistarii, . .unus ~or, unus faber (*WelshR* 5) *EHR* XXXIII 349; **1293** carpentariorum, fabrorum, attiliatorum et aliorum. .artificum missorum per regem. .in Vasconiam *RGasc* III cxl *n.*; **1300** pro stipendio unius attillatoris facientis unam lengam. .pro eodem ingenio *Ac.Wardr.* p. 267; **1332** in domibus nostris pro officio attiliatoris deputatis in diversis castris nostris in ducatu nostro Aquitanie plures defectus existunt. ., ita quod ingenia nostra. .deteriorantur (*RGasc*) *Foed.* IV 510; **1337** in stipendio j fabri ~oris cum suo garcione existentis in eodem castro ad diversa ferramenta et instrumenta *KRAc* 40/19 m. 10 (cf. *CalScot* III 366).

attillio, fitting, gear (naut.).

1446 quod nullomodo omittatis. .quin capiatis. .quamdam navem. .alias *a catche*, ipsamque navem cum toto apparatu et ~one eidem pertinentibus sub salvo et securo custodiatis arresto *BBAdm.* I 262; **a1460** si quis interfectus . .fuerit aut mortuus super mare per aliquem apparatum vel ~onem ancorarum, cabulum, cordulam aut aliquam quamcumque navi deservientem *Ib.* 242.

attillum, ~ium, ~ia, fitting, equipment, gear: **a** (naut.); **b** (of cart, plough, or sim.); **c** (of crossbow or other armament); **d** (various).

a 1213 quod. .liberari faciatis. .navem cum toto attillio quam R. . .de Bristoll' duxit usque Porecestr' cum ingeniis nostris *Cl* 148a; navem de xx remis. .cum atillo *Ib.* 152a; **1257** de una galia ad lvj remos et una bargia ad xxviij remos cum toto attilio earum *Cl* 155; **1269** navem. .cum ~o ejusdem *Cl* 52; **1291** in diversis navibus emptis ad quendam pontem Anglesie inde †factam cum attilio ad easdem (*Ac. Wardr.*) OXNEAD *Chr. app.* 334; **1295** precipimus quod naves et batellos. .religiosorum [alienigenarum]. .ad terram trahi et totum attilium eorundem. .facias. .amoveri (*Breve Regis*) *Reg. Wint.* 520; **1296** in stipendiis vj marinariorum laborancium circa attilium galee ordinandum *Ac. Galley Newcastle* 183; **1298** quieti sint. .de corporibus propriarum navium suarum et earum attilio prestandis *BBC* (*Yarmouth*) 119; **1311** quia pro expedicione guerre nostre. . †namium [l. navium] attillie (*sic*) et apparatu sufficienti et . .marinariis. .indigemus (*Ch.*) *Hist. Chester* 23; **1314** tres naves. .quas. .providit. .ad opus nostrum minus sufficienter cablis, anchoris, malis et cordis ac alio attilio. .preparantur *RScot* 126a; **1337** bargiam illam. .et attilia. .que pro gubernacione ejusdem necessaria fuerint *Ib.* 479b; **1343** navem illam cum attileo ejusdem (*Cl*) *Foed.* V 384; **1391** de valore navis. .cum attilio et apparatu suo *Mem. York* I 233. **b 1251** fieri faciat duas longas carettas cum toto atilio et harnesio que pertinent ad hujusmodi carettas *Cl* 520; **1265** pro. .j sella carette, . .j dosserio, j crupario, cum atilo pertinente *Manners* 55; **1275** capere fecit. .viij boves junctos cum caruca et toto attilio *Hund.* I 67a (= ib. 71a: cum baculo, stimulo et ferramento); **1277** cum alio atillo ad carucas *Banstead* 312; **1290** ij carecte. .unde j ferrea cum †aciliis *Reg. Wint.* II 704; **1310** ad capienda necessaria mea de meremio ad carucas, carras, carectas, hercias, attilia et alia minuta *FormA* 384; **c1350** per servicium inveniendi. . in omni guerra. .unam carectam ferratam cum uno equo carectario liminari et †acilio seu apparatu ad v equos carectarios *MonA* V 380a (= *MonExon* 344: atilio); **1419** de carucis cum totis ~iis *Wills N. Country* 23. **c 1256** faciat habere. .xx s. ad attilium necessarium ad reparationem balistarum regis *Cl* 26; **1264** unam balistam de cornu de truil' cum attilio et cc quarellis *Cl* 337; **1265** rex dedit E. filio suo ad tuitionem castri de Odyham v balistas de cornu cum eorum attillio *Cl* 149; **1287** duas balistas cum toto ~o *IMisc* 46/3; **1318** quod. .habeat. .unam. .aketonam, unum bacinetum et chirothecas de guerra cum lancea et gladio. ., ita quod quilibet sit paratus cum actiliis predictis. .; et quicunque. .non habuerit. .omnia armorum actilia predicta . . (*Stat. Rob. I*) *APScot* 113; **1336** x balistas cum attilio ad eas pertinente *RScot* 438b. **d 1244** xj pampiliones regis. . cum cordis et toto atylo cariari faciat London' *Liberate* 36 m. 9; **1298** j zona de serico cum attilia argenti *Rec. Leic.* I 363; **1387** in uno attile de *laton* pro cereo suspendendo coram altari *Ac. Durh.* 266.

attillura, (?) item of harness.

1242 Ricardo Rotario. .pro ij duodenis attillurarum, viz. pro qualibet ij d. *Liberate* 16 m. 6.

attincta v. attingere 9.

attinctare, to attaint.

s1461 [rex] parleamentum suum inchoavit, ubi indictati et atteyntati sunt Henricus vocatus nuper rex Anglie. ., duces eciam Somerset et Exetre *Compilatio* 175; **1569** manifeste apparebat quod predictus dux et alie persone predicte legitime et juste de prodicionibus predictis convicti et ~ati fuissent *Entries* 413b.

attinctio, attaint, attainder.

1400 perdonavimus. .conviccionés, ~ones, judicia et execuciones judiciorum (*Pat*) *Foed.* VIII 166; **s1461** ~o quarundam personarum illustrium aliorumque nobilium plurium causaque ~onis eorundem *Reg. Whet. rub.* I 419; **1465** dedit. .omnia proficua. .archidiaconatus a tempore ~onis ejusdem [J. Moreton] (*Pat*) *MonA* IV 6*n.*

attinctura, attainder.

1540 emolumenta officii predicti [magni camerarii] a tempore ~ure et condempnacionis nuper comitis Essexie (*Pat*) *Foed.* XIV 703; **1587** *Pat* 1301 m. 39.

1 attinctus, attaint (of jury; *cf. attingere* 8b).

1260 optulit se versus H. . .per breve de ~u, . .unde queritur quod juratores prime assise. .falsum fecerunt sacramentum. . .milites de ~u. .dicunt quod juratores prime assise predicte falsum non fecere sacramentum *PlR Chester* 1 r. 3.

2 attinctus v. attingere.

attinentia, affinity, relationship, tie.

1325 ob connexitatem ~ie que (*sic*) inter vestram et nostram domus regias. .recolimus viguisse (*Cl*) *Foed.* IV 157b.

2 retinue. **b** appurtenance. **c** (?) tenancy.

s1381 ut nullus miles aut armiger se auderet dicere de ~ia domini ducis Lancastrie aut ejus signum puplice portare *Chr. Kirkstall* 125. **b 1475** terram cum suis ~iis *Scot. Grey Friars* II 212. **c 1543** ad. .possessionem liberam et expeditam et illarum [domorum] ~iam eidem dimittendum *Form. S. Andr.* II 298.

attinēre [CL], (?) to hold. **b** (intr.) to hold good.

a1135 precipio quod ecclesia. .et abbas. .†atenent sokam et sakam. . .ita bene. .sicut melius tenuerunt tempore patris. .mei *Regesta* 1642 (= *Doc. Bury* no. 48: teneant). **b 1176** hec assisa atenebit a tempore quo assisa facta fuit apud Clarendonam continue usque ad hoc tempus et amodo quamdiu domino regi placuerit (*Ass. Northampton*) *G. Hen. II* I 108 (= R. HOWD. II 89: attenebit).

2 (*cf. attingere* 2b and c) to be akin or allied to (w. acc.). **b** (w. dat.). **c** to be dependent (on).

proles procreata ex matrimonio infidelium in secundo gradu consanguinitatis se ~encium J. BURGH *PO* VIII 17 f. 144. **b 1252** de vobis habentes fiduciam specialem, attendentes etiam quod Arnaldo. .~etis (*Pat*) *RL* II 86; **s1263** S. de Monteforti predari cepit bona regi adherencium et precipue eorum qui regine ~ebant, qui per eam fuerant in Angliam introducti *Eul. Hist.* III 121; **c1520** Robertus. . carnaliter cognovit quandam Margaretam †sibi [? l. ipsi] Elizabethe †~enti [? l. ~entem *or* attingentem] in secundo et tercio gradibus affinitatis et sic dicti R. et E. sibi invicem in eisdem gradibus attingunt *Offic. S. Andr.* 19. **c** non minorem diligenciam adhibere solebat. .circa alios sibi ~entes ut vicia declinarent BLAKMAN *Hen. VI* 9.

3 to pertain, belong: **a** (w. dat.); **b** (w. *ad*).

a tenet. .iiii hidas quietas. .ab omni consuetudine que regi ~et *DB* I 176; huic manerio ~ebat j soc[amannus] *Ib.* II 33; R. COLD. *Cuthb.* 91 (v. attractivus a); officium eis ~ens WYCL. *Sim.* 62. **b** xx acre que ~ebant ad ecclesiam *DB* II 60; **†1084** (12c) ab omnibus consuetudinibus. .quecumque ad coronam regis in perpetuum ~uerint *Feod. Durh.* xlix; **1254** de potagio conventus quantum ad quatuor homines ~et *Cart. Osney* III 82; **1492** ducatus. .ad nos de jure hereditario ~entes (*Pat*) *Foed.* XII 487.

4 (w. *ad*) to concern. **b** (impers.).

in eis que ad disciplinas ~ent inquisitionibus BALSH. *AD* 130; licet hec ad suscepta negotia. .non ~eant *Dial. Scac.* I 10B; quantum penetraret. .non multum ad rem reor ~ere W. CANT. *Mir. Thom.* VI 136. **b** quantum ad praesentis quaestionis ~et negotium ERIUG. *Per.* 542B; **1299** de nominibus. .citatorum. ., quatenus ad vos ~et, nos certificare curetis *Conc. Syn.* 1201.

5 (w. dat.) to befall.

ex hoc sepe consulenti immensum ~et dampnum MILEMETE *Nob.* 75.

6 (pass. w. *de*) to become possessed (perhaps referable to *attendere*).

1340 parum et parum furatur semen, unde attentus fuit de j bussello frumenti *CBaron* 10.

attingere [CL < ad+tangere; *some forms and senses infl. by* attingere < ad+tingere = *stain*], to touch, lay hold of. **b** to encounter. **c** (*s. dub.*). **d** to touch (fig.), affect (w. abstr. subj.).

credens suum oculum capillis viri Dei, quibus adtactus erat, ocius esse sanandum BEDE *HE* IV 30 p. 280; attigit locum infirmitatis W. CANT. *Mir. Thom.* VI 134; omne agens ~it aliquam partem patientis quam potest alterare BACON *Maj.* II 438; **1272** in marchaucia j stotti attincti in arsura ij ped' ante *MinAc* 994/28; **1298** insultum fecerunt in omnes laicos quos ~ere potuerunt *SelCCoron* 90. **b 1326** attinxerunt plures ignotos venientes. .versus abbatiam *Rec. Leic.* I 380. **c c1250** debet quilibet [croftarius] qui equum habuerit herciare avenas domini quousque caruce †attincte [? l. adjuncte] fuerint (*Cust. Povington*) *Doc. Bec* 65*n.* **d** virgo. .eadem adtacta infirmitate BEDE *HE* IV 8; respectu divino attactus, . .coepit. .Deum timere *RegulC* 1; pestis eam. .non attigit W. CANT. *Mir. Thom.* V 26; **1335** si . .sanior deliberacio. .nos ~at *Lit. Cant.* II 77.

2 to touch, adjoin. **b** to be akin or allied to. **c** (absol. or w. dat.).

aliqui dicunt Paradisum ~ere lunarem circulum HIGD. I 10 p. 76; quedam fragilis treuga sepius rupta. ., per quam ~entes ad invicem regnorum fines misere premebantur *Plusc.* VI 22. **b 1203** xij legales milites. .qui neutram partem ~ant *CurR* II 278; **1212** legales milites. .qui non. . eum nec ipsos A. et R. affinitate ~ant *SelPlCrown* 61; qui nec Willelmum. .nec Henricum. .aliqua affinitate ~ant *State Tri. Ed. I* 30. **c** cum. .numquam ipsius. .familiaris socius fuisset aut specialis ei aliqualiter ~ens *Ib.* 41; **1397** sunt illegitime conjugati, eo quod ~unt in quarto gradu (*Vis. Heref.*) *EHR* XLV 460; **c1520** (v. attinere 2b).

3 to reach, attain, achieve, catch up with. **b** (absol., w. *usque*). **c** (w. ref. to time). **d** (w. abstr. subj.). **e** (phil.) to attain knowledge of, apprehend.

attigit obtatum lassus de gurgite litus ALDH. *VirgV* 2806; Gerbertus, . .cum Pytagoricum bivium attigisset W. MALM. *GR* II 167; cum scapha littus attigisset W. CANT. *Mir. Thom.* V 7; statim ut terram ~unt GIR. *TH* II 4; **s1190** prius rediit quam ceteri regem attigissent HIGD. VII 26; sicut homo balbutiens quedam verba ~it. ., quedam non *Ps.*-GROS. 640; quod quicunque ad finem stadii. .cucurrerit bravium quantumcumque de facili attingibile quomodocunque ~eret WYCL. *Dom. Div.* III 228; dictam attigerunt caracam ELMH. *Hen. V* 97. **b** si contingat aliquos tarde in refectorium venire, ita quod usque ante justas suas ~ere nequeant priusquam incipiatur Gloria Patri *Cust. Westm.* 109. **c 1420** scolarium famuli discrecionis annos ~entes *StatOx* 226. **d** fama viri. .Hiberniae partes attigit BEDE *HE* III 13; ut infamia. .sceleris aures ipsius attigit G. MON. XI 1. **e** nulli conditae substantiae naturaliter inest virtus per quam possit. .Deum immediate per se ipsam ~ere ERIUG. *Per.* 576B; quod ergo non ~at Deum sub omni racione sub qua est inteiligibilis, provenit ex aliqua trium racionum predictarum. . .exemplum est in puncto, quem quicumque intelligit totum intelligit, non tamen totaliter, in quantum est attingibilis PECKHAM *QA* II 175.

4 (w. *ad*) to reach, attain (to), achieve. **b** (w. ref. to time). **c** (w. abstr. subj.). **d** to amount to. **e** (refl.). **f** (w. *usque ad*) to extend (*cf. Wisd.* viii 1).

1318 circa unitatis fedus. .solidandum, prout ad id pre ceteris ~ere cupimus *FormOx* 46; non poterant ad intelligendum tam subtiles difficultates theologie. .~ere OCKHAM *Dial.* 432; **1345** super modis. .quibus melius. .posset ~i ad pacis reformacionem (*Lit. Papae*) AD. MUR. 183; ad cujus veritatis noticiam. .adipiscendam. .non poterit ~ere lumine naturali intellectus humanus *Plusc. pref.* p. 3. **b** ad quam etatem nondum ~ebat (*Fragm. Coll.* 6) *APScot* 373. **c s1319** cum [minacio] ad aures magnorum attigerat *Flor. Hist.* III 188. **d 1221** si forte hee terre. .ad summam. . m libratarum ~ere non possint *Pat* 309; **1271** ad quantum dampnum. .illud per annum posset ~ere *Cl* 350; **1285** de porcionibus decimarum que ad terciam. .partem bonorum ecclesie non ~unt *Conc. Syn.* 965; **a1350** si numerus regencium. .ad xij non attigerit *Stat. Cantab.* 316; **s1452** decima. .regi. .debita. .~it ad summam lxiij li. *Reg. Whet.* I 72. **e 1451** omnes. .summe. .debite. .ad xxxiij li. . .et non ultra in toto se ~unt *Ib.* I 58; **1461** que quidem dampna in toto se ~unt ad xl li. *Law Merch.* II 119; **1530** [arreragia] se ~unt ad xl li. *Cant. Coll. Ox.* III 217. **f 1337** rex pacificus in sublimi extulit clemencie vestre tronum, cui diligencia provida contra jacula inimici ~it undique a fine usque ad finem fortiter *FormOx* 97 (cf. ib. 29).

5 to undergo, submit to (ordeal or oath). **b** (refl.) to undertake (? *f.l.* for *accingere*).

simplex purgatio ~atur [AS: *ofgá man anfealde lada*] simplici prejuramento (*Cons. Cnut.*) *GAS* 325 (= *Quad. ib.*: inducatur simplex lada); calumpniatus triplex Dei judicium adeat; quod calumpniator sic ~at [AS: *ofgá*] *Ib.* 333; **1205** debet xx s. pro ~endo falso sacramento de assisa nove dissaisine *Pipe* 155. **b 1383** qui. .ad prelatorum scismaticorum exterminium se †~erent *Reg. Heref.* 29.

6 to treat of, deal with.

haec. .breviter attigimus BEDE *HE* III 19; **1283** hundredum vocant congregacionem masculorum. .ad pacem domini regis ~endam *SelCKB* I 128.

7 to establish, decide. **b** (w. indir. qu.). **c** (w. acc. and inf.). **d** (w. *quod*).

1211 ut hoc atingatur obtulit. .Aliz iij m. *CurR* VI 118; **1226** mandamus. .quod. .in ipsa curia nostra de forisfacto ipsius patris sui [sc. regis Connacie]. .rei veritatem ~atis *Pat* 48; **1227** nec aliquid inde per juratores attinctum fuit *BNB* II 197; **1236** nos fecit securos de ~endis predictis omnibus. .contra predictum R. *KRMem* 14 r. 12*d.*; **1318** si aliter sit attaintum, sint amerciati tam indictatus quam plegii ejus (*Stat. Rob.* I 6) *APScot* 108. **b 1196** offert domino regi j m. ut ~atur si ita sit necne *CurR* I 28; **1212** quod ~atur per sacramentum legalium xxiiij hominum si Alanus. .tenuit. .Aviciam pro uxore sua *Ib.* VI 237; **1234** cum. .attinctum non sit an idem W. culpabilis sit. . quod illum occiderit. .an quod per infortunium submersus sit *Cl* 492; **1235** donec per sacramentum xxiiij. .legalium hominum [Insularum de Gernes' etc.] ~atur utrum culpabiles sint necne de retto. .eis inposito *Cl* 177; **1267** ~atur utrum hujusmodi feoffamentum bona fide factum sit vel in fraude (*Marlb.* 6) *StRealm* I 21. **c 1231** duxerunt eam [plagam] talem quod per eam bene potuit ~i pacem regis esse infractam *CurR* XV 1737 (cf. *BNB* II 456). **d 1211** si illa ullum illorum potest ~ere quod homo suus fuit vel parens *CurR* VI 118; **1225** si attinctum fuerit per inquisitionem. .quod ipsam [terram] de nobis tenuit in capite *ExcRFin* I 133; **1230** atinctum fuit coram ipso et viridariis quod ipsi. .abstulerunt dictos denarios *LTRMem* 11 r. 8*d.*; **12. .** attingtum fuit quod dicta terra debuit serviles consuetudines *Cart. Rams.* III 315; **1275** dimisit illum abire, ubi attinctum fuit per inquisicionem quod ipse fuit culpabilis *Hund.* I 320.

8 to establish a charge against, convict. **b** to attaint, convict (jurors) of false verdict (*cf. convincere*). **c** to attaint (convict) of felony or treason. **d** (w. *sanguis*) to taint.

1198 qui. .canes duxerit sine copula per forestam regis et inde attaintus fuerit, erit in misericordia regis (*Ass. Forest.* 14) R. HOWD. IV 65 (= W. COVENTR. II 132: atteinctus); **1204** si quis attinctus fuerit quod ballivos nostros. .in aliquo deceperit *Pat* 42b; **1276** attinctus fuit quod ponderavit lanas cum falsa petra *Rec. Leic.* I 169; **1419** si defendens. .in aliqua querela transgressionis, verberacionis. .aut alterius accionis personalis. .fecerit defaltam, tunc defendens ut attinctus judicetur *MGL* I 174. **b 1205** de v m. quas domino regi promisit pro quadam assisa de ~endo xij homines per xxiiij *Cl* 24a; **1218** dat domino regi xx s. pro habendo brevi de ~endis coram justiciariis apud Westm'.. juratoribus nove dissaisine capte apud Norewic' *ExcRFin* I 17; **1221** abbas..nondum habuit juratam xxiiij de ~endis xij *LTRMem* 4 r. 5; **1225** assisam..ad ~endos xij juratores assise..qui falsum..fecerunt sacramentum *Pat* 590; **1230** pro habendo brevi de ~endis xij juratoribus *Pipe* 235. **c 1208** quod nulli..malum faciant vel dicant viris religiosis vel clericis contra pacem nostram et, si quem inde ~ere possimus, ad proximam quercum eum suspendi faciemus *Cl* 111a; **1225** boves Hugonis.., qui nuper attinctus fuit de felonia in curia domini regis per probos et legales homines, appreciari faciat *ExcRFin* I 129; **s1279** Judei accusaverunt quam plurimos Christianos, et quot diffamati et attincti dati sunt ad suspendendum (*Chr. Barlings*) *Chr. Ed. I & II* II cxviii; si sui attincti punientur fune revincti (*Versus*) *State Tri. Ed. I* 99; **1337** duo homines..fuerunt indictati et per assisam †activati [? l. attincti]..de tribus equis furatis *ExchScot* 436; si tu exeas de carcere, tu obligas te et vitam tuam fore attayntum et tanquam convictum sine aliquo.. judicio (*Fragm. Coll.* 19) *APScot* 375; vidi..mulierem de morte mariti sui..attinctam..et combustam FORTESCUE *LLA* 53; **s1449** Communibus in Parliamento per billam desiderantibus de rege ut tanquam proditor attinctus puniretur W. WORC. *Ann.* 766; **1465** de altis prodicionibus attinctus emolumenta..forisfecit (*Pat*) *MonA* IV 6n.; **1540** catalla felonum..attinctorum (*Pat*) *MonExon* 105; **1583** condemnari, convinci, ~i *Pat* 1235 m. 23. **d s1483** quod sanguis fratris sui G. ducis Clarencie fuisset attinctus, ita quod hodie nullus certus et incorruptus sanguis linealis ex parte R. ducis Eboraci poterat inveniri nisi in persona dicti R. ducis Glocestrie *Croyl. Cont. C* 567.

9 (p. ppl. as sb. f. or n.) attaint, attainder: **a** (of jury); **b** (of felon or traitor).

a 1210 quod..daret domino regi de suo pro habenda inde ateinta *CurR* VI 73; **1251** quia rex non potest..aliquem.. dimittere qui cum R...judicio reddendo in ~a quam T... prosequitur versus H. ..valeat interesse, mandatum est eidem R. quod..judicium illud proroget.., eundem diem prefigens partibus et juratoribus assise nove disseisine.. quod sint coram rege..recordum illius ~e audituri *Cl* 545; nota ~am esse capiendam per defaltam ubi ille qui recuperavit est infra etatem *BNB* (*marg.*) III 125; de convictione sive ~a juratorum qui male juraverint BRACTON (*marg.*) 288b; **1259** omnes assisas..et ~as et placita de dote *Cl* 142; **1267** si adeo necessarium sit eorum juramentum quod sine eo justicia exhiberi non possit, veluti in magna assisa..aut in ~is.., jurare cogantur (*Marlb.* 14) *StRealm* I 23 (cf. *Reg. Malm.* I 46: atteinctis); **1269** de placito terre unde ~a xxiiij ad convincendum xij per etc. *CBaron* 82; **s1274** contra adversarios pro nobis lite terminata, ..ad curiam domini regis †festinanter [? l. festinantes] breve super ~a studiose impetrarunt [MS.: †perpetrarunt] *G. S. Alb.* I 412; dato quod assisa transierit contra minorem, minor cum ad etatem pervenerit non posset facere ~am HENGHAM *Parva* 8; **s1281** cum falsa assisa adjudicasset Johanni..advocacionem capelle.., prior..impetravit atinctam in curia domini regis *Ann. Worc.* 481; justiciarios..ad assisas, ..certificaciones et ~as..deputatos *Fleta* 66; **1328** ante statutum [1 Ed. III c. 6] de ~is in brevibus de transgressione concedendis nullum jacuit breve de ~a secundum legem..de transgressione *MGL* I 441; si pars altera, contra quam veredictum hujusmodi prolatum est, conqueratur se per illud esse injuste gravatum, prosequi tunc potest pars illa versus juratores illos, et versus partem que obtinuit, breve de ~a FORTESCUE *LLA* 26. **b s1485** facte sunt proscripciones, quas vulgares ~a vocant, de xxx personis *Croyl. Cont. D* 581.

attingibilis, a attainable. **b** (phil.) apprehensible.

a WYCL. *Dom. Div.* III 228 (v. attingere 3a). **b** PECKHAM *QA* II 175 (v. attingere 3e); licet ens, ut est quoddam intelligibile uno actu, ..sit naturaliter ~e, ..non tamen ens, ut primum objectum, ..potest poni naturaliter ~e DUNS *Sent. prol.* 1. 32.

attiramentum [OF *atteirement, atirement*], fitting, equipment: **a** (of ship); **b** (of cart or plough).

a 1208 cum omnibus necessariis †atteuiriamentis que ad navem pertinent *Pat* 85a (cf. *Cl* 103a: in omnibus ateyuriamentis); **1212** fieri facias apendicias ad eundem murum [excluse de Portesmue].., in quibus omnia ateiuriamenta navium nostrarum salvo possint custodiri *Cl* 117a. **b 1325** in iiij fasciculis virgarum emptis pro ~o carucarum *Rec. Elton* 273; in uno feramento cum toto ~o empto pro uno pare rotarum *Ib.* 274.

attirare [OF *atirier*], to fit, equip (a cart). **b** to attire, adorn, dress.

1303 in corpore carecte autumpn[alis] atirando contra autumpnum *MinAc* 991/26. **b 1301** in roba domini comitis ~anda..cum cindone empto ad eandem *Ib.* 991/25; **1310** in solucione facta..adsurgico pro labore suo circa corpus domini, mundandum et ~andum post decessum ejusdem *Ac. Exec. Ep. Exon.* 22.

attiriator [cf. attilliator], fitter, maker (of crossbows).

1257 liberate..~ori balistarum nostrarum apud Turrim nostram London' xl s. ad attillium..emendum *Liberate* 33 m. 1.

attirum, ~ium, attire, outfit.

1295 lego..totum atirum de meliori armatura mea ad corpus suum et equum cooperiendum (*Test. N. Longespee*) *EHR* XV 526; ibi tractatur de vestibus et atyrio monachorum J. ACTON *Comment.* 144a.

attitulare [< ad+titulare], to ascribe. **b** to assign, consign. **c** to dedicate, devote. **d** to appoint (eccl.).

ut eundem annum unus historicus ejusdem regis adscriberet temporibus, ..alter vero historicus eundem successori illius potius ~andum putaret BEDE *TR* 48. **b** attitulat vento quod prestat inops opulento D. BEC. 2342; **s1192** reliquos..redditus in prebendas partitus est, quarum quasdam Romane perpetuo adtitulatas ecclesie dedit appropriatas quibusdam cardinalibus DEVIZES 40; se transtulit abbas J. [ob. 1214]..ad alia opera, relictis..auxiliis operi priori.. ~atis *G. S. Alb.* I 220; **1276** servicia eorum ~antur ad firmam ballivi hundredi *Hund.* II 179; cum antiphonis psalmis et collectis eidem ministerio ~atis *Cust. Cant.* 257. **c** ubi videt..rex..urgueri se ad exitum, fune[b]ribus exequiis ~at se commendatione et precibus summorum Dei fidelium *V. Ed. Conf.* f. 55. **d** episcopus..illum..sacerdotali gratia promovit, ~ans ecclesiae B. Mariae Virginis OSB. *V. Dunst.* 12; illam cui tu noviter ~atus es ecclesiam (OSB.) *Ep. Anselm.* (149) IV 9; Swithunus..a S. Helmstano.. sacris est ordinibus ~atus FL. WORC. I 68.

attollere [CL], to lift up, raise. **b** to promote, advance. **c** to elevate, dignify. **d** to extol. **e** to enrage.

mare..aestum solet ~ere BEDE *TR* 29; **1201** potuit illud [caput] attolere in sullime *Canon. G. Sempr.* 163v. **b** multis eos qui fidem suscipere vellent beneficiis adtollens BEDE *HE* V 10; illum..in armis omnique rei militaris usu.. ~ebant G. CRISPIN *Herl.* 87. **c** ut exilitatem materie gravior stilus ~at GIR. *TH intr.* p. 6. **d** virginitatis gloria ..debitis ~enda est praeconiis ALDH. *VirgP* 7; cum..vituperemus que ignoramus..ut ea modica que scimus ~amus BACON *Maj.* I 20. **e** ut mare ventis, ita maledictis ~itur et intumescit MAP *NC* IV 6 p. 167.

attom- v. atom-.

attondēre [CL], to trim, cut the hair of. **b** (eccl.) to tonsure. **c** (p. ppl. as sb. m.) tonsured clerk.

Frisones..in coma circulariter sunt attonsi, quia quanto nobiliores tanto rotundiores arbitrantur †~i [? l. ~eri] *Eul. Hist.* II 75. **b** adtondebantur omnes in coronam ministri altaris ac monachi BEDE *HE* V 21; attonsus in clericum AILR. *Nin.* 12 p. 156; **s794** [Offa] Romam..attonsus celica regna devotus conscendit *Flor. Hist.* I 357 (= M. PAR. *Maj.* I 320: monachus effectus); Dunstanus..in gradum clericalem est attonsus J. GLAST. 115; **c1400** in canonicum regularem..attonsus *G. S. Alb.* II 373. **c** sive adtonsi seu laici BEDE *HE* III 5.

attonitus [CL], thunderstruck (fig.). **b** amazed, dumbfounded.

in occiduis oceani finibus Jove tonante..occidentales reguli, tonitruis ejus ~i, pacis adepte beneficio fulminis ictum prevenerunt GIR. *TH* III 9. **b** ~us, *hlysnende, afyrhte GlC* A 876; omnem..tragoediam..~is spectatoribus resurgens..patefecit ALDH. *VirgP* 36 p. 283; cum aliquantulum horae quasi adtonitus maneret BEDE *HE* IV 3; monachi..pro tali..tumultu tam pavidi quam ~i W. FITZST. *Thom.* 138; **1266** ingressus †accritam [? l. attritam] et †actomuam [? l. attonitam] regionem (*Lit. Cardinalis*) *EHR* XV 97; per longa secula in sepulcris soporata volumina expergiscunt ~a R. BURY *Phil.* 8. 120.

attornamentum [cf. OF *atornement*], attornment, tenant's acknowledgement of new lord. **b** transfer as token of seisin.

1333 ~um ipsius tenentis: ..J. ..super hoc attornavit.. abbati..in plena curia civitatis..ut tenens ipsius abbatis redditus predicti *Reg. S. Aug.* 185; **14..** dedimus vobis potestatem recipiendi cognicionem [quid juris ipsa I. clamat habere in terra predicta] et testificandi atturnamentum †que [? l. quod] prefata I. coram vobis facere voluerit..; et cum eam receperitis et ipsa coram vobis..se atturnaverit, ..socios vestros..certificetis, predictum atturnamentum testificantes *Reg. Brev.* 168 (cf. ib. 251); **1459** de quo.. redditu..priorem et conventum in realem possessionem posui..per ~um..Johannis..tenentis in feodo mesuagii *FormA* 334. **b 1443** nomine seisine eorundem bonorum et catallorum posui predictos..in possessionem per ~um unius eque et unius vacce eis deliberatarum *Cl* 293 m. 24d.

2 (w. *generale*) appointment as attorney (for all pleas).

1288 habet litteras regis de generali ~o *RGasc* II 289; **1389** generale vero ~um recipiant clerici de prima forma *Chanc. Orders* 4.

attornare, ~iare [< ad+tornare; cf. OF *atorner*], to turn, direct (a watercourse). **b** to direct (a writ).

c1176 debebant molendinum illud novum facere..et aquam ad molendinum ~are *Kelso* 383. **b 1268** breve illud retornavi ad diem in illo brevi contentum..una cum aliis brevibus ad dictum diem ibidem atornatis per nuncium *Cl* 9.

2 to turn (sour or bad).

si vis ut vinum redeat postquam †actornatur, hoc potest fieri in principio quando incipit acescere GAD. 135. 1; aliquando urinam antiquam ~atam ego misceo cum istis; et tunc est penetrativum et consumptivum *Ib.* 39 v. 2.

3 (w. *ad*) to alter (to). **b** (w. *in*) to account, reckon (as).

1223 tunc se essoniavit de Hibernia, et attorn[atum] fuit essonium ad essonium de malo veniendi *BNB* III 478. **b 1207** mandamus vobis quod..absentiam suam die illo ~etis eis in defaltam *Pat* 77a.

4 to get ready, equip, fit: **a** (ships); **b** (weapons, tools or sim.); **c** (corn); **d** (a larder); **e** to dress (food); **f** (vines); **g** (wool or cloth); **h** to array, adorn.

a 1205 naves nostras quas atornastis de Gippewico ad eundum in servicium nostrum..muniri faciatis *Cl* 33b; **1242** sine dilacione atornari et bene muniri faciant in omnibus quandam navem *Cl* 392; **1243** ix li. xviij s. quos posuerunt..in navibus..~andis canevacio, clavis et latis *Liberate* 19 m. 6. **b 1213** mittimus..xxiiij arkillos ad duos pedes quos..parari et bene atornari faciatis *Cl* 145b; **1257** in vomeribus emptis xiiij d.; in eisdem ~iandis ij d. *Crawley* 216; **1258** in ij vomeribus..atornandis *Ib.* 224; **1270** in dictis ferramentis acuendis et aturnandis *MinAc* 768/5 r. 2; **1271** in carris emendandis et ~andis contra autumpnum *Pipe Wint.* 159299 r. 3d.; **1283** ~are meremium ad carucas *Ac. Man. Wint.* (*Houghton*). **c 1285** metet iij dim. acras bladi, aturnabit et ligabit *Cust. Suss.* II 19. **d 1283** in xxiiij baconis necandis et lardario inde ~ando *Ac. Man. Wint.* (*Michelmersh*). **e 1233** salmones escawardos.. in panem poni faciant et bene ~atos ad regem transmitti *Cl* 349; **1255** capi faciant..xl damos et eos saliri, atornari et cariari faciant usque Eboracum *Cl* 123. **f 1233** in.. stipendiis..vineatorum et in vineis apud Tenham..excolendis et ~andis *Liberate* 10 m. 9; **1270** in expensis Nicholai le Wynur..ad wyneam plantandam et aturnandam *MinAc* 768/5 r. 3; **1283** in vineis cedendis et ~andis *Ac. Man. Wint.* (*Michelmersh*). **g 1261** bene liceat pannos in hospicio suo habere et plicare et ~are *Rec. Leic.* I 95; **1318** in lana saccanda et ~anda *Ac. Man. Wint.* (*Houghton*); **1345** in stipendio j hominis saccantis et ~antis lanam domini *Comp. Swith.* 149. **h s1255** rex [venit] in propria persona sua, civitate Londoniarum nobilissime aturnata et acurtinata *Leg. Ant. Lond.* 22; **s1259** civitate optime ~ata et curtinata *Ib.* 41; **s1272** corpus suum nobiliter ~atum, sicut decet reges, datum est sepulture *Ib.* 153; **s1274** de nobilitate ~ata contra coronacionem domini Edwardi *Ib.* 172.

5 to train (falc.).

1237 circa aves nostras custodiendas et ~andas *Liberate* 12 m. 16; **1243** liberate Henrico de H. v m. ad se sustentandum dum ~averit quendam girofalconem nostrum ad volandum *Ib.* 19 m. 9; **1252** *Cal. Liberate* IV 30.

6 (w. *male* or sim.) to maltreat.

1202 vicini venerunt ad clamorem et viderunt eum taliter ~atum *SelPlCrown* 15; **1218** talem (*sic*) ~avit avunculum suum quod ipse obiit *Eyre Yorks* 224; **1221** captus fuit et male ~atus *PlCrGlouc* 43; **1224** ita ~ata fuit quod dimissa fuit pro mortua *CurR* XI 2715; **1234** viderunt..puerum circumcisum..et ita aturnatum sicut predictum est *Ib.* XV 1320; **1276** male aturnavit eum et abstulit pannos ejus *Hund.* II 175.

7 to assign, pledge, devote: **a** (money); **b** (rent, service, or homage); **c** (land or sim.); **d** (an altar); **e** (p. ppl. as sb. f.) pledging (of money) or sum pledged.

a 1266 expense..de quibus ~antur xl m. magistro P. cementario..ad reparandum domos *ExchScot* 31; **s1415** fertur..quod despoliatus sit de lxxv milibus li. argenti et auri quas sibi atternaverat pro tutela *Chr. S. Alb.* 85. **b 1201** venit..ad regem..et impetravit ab eo quod ipse ~avit servitium illud ad manerium de Merleberge *CurR* I 424; decrevit ut xx s. darentur singulis annis celerario ad *portmanemot*..a burgensibus, qui ~averunt redditum ad hoc solvendum BRAKELOND 149v; **1215** concessimus quod servitium vestrum quod nobis debetis de terris quas de nobis tenetis in capite atornatum sit de cetero..W. comiti de F. *Cl* 194b; **1224** nunquam ingressum habuit per Aliciam, sed revera servitium suum ~atum fuit eidem Alicie in dotem *CurR* XI 2662; **1231** ipse ~avit servitium illud predicte domui *CurR* XIV 1875; **1235** allocentur episcopo Baton'..xx s. pro uno osturco soro de servitio Willelmi.., quod quidem servitium dominus rex ~avit episcopo *KRMem* 14 r. 3d.; servitium ~ari poterit in omni casu et contra voluntatem tenentis, licet homagium non possit nisi in casibus supra dictis BRACTON 82; **12..** predictos xij d. [annuatim reddendos] prefato W. ..atturniavi, tenendos sibi et heredibus suis *FormA* 158; **1275** quos quidem iiij s. et ij s. de tenementis predictorum A. et T. ~avi ad unam pietanciam faciend' in conventu Oseneye..in die anniversarii mei *Cart. Osney* VI no. 942; **1277** ~avi..abbati Cestrie homagium et servicium que michi facere solebatis *Cart. Chester* 423; ut fidelitas et servicium tali donatori ~entur *Fleta* 183. **c 1200** de placito quo jure et waranto ~avit feodum ipsius abbatisse in elemosinam Hospitalariorum *CurR* I 161 (cf. ib. 203); de terris..que..~ate fuerunt in feodum dim. militis BRAKELOND 163; **1219** per defectum ipsorum..amiserunt seisinam et vellent recuperare ad terram suam, que bene ~ata est *CurR* VIII 78; **1222** debuit eam [ecclesiam] ~asse ad sustentationem ejusdem conventus *BNB* II 140; **1232** ~avit..feodum de P. ad manerium de D. *Ib.* 534. **d a1190** de terra quam T. tenuit ad opus illius altaris quod in eadem ecclesia est atturnatum ad cantandum pro defunctis *Danelaw* 124. **e 1163** vic. r. c. de c m. de ~ata quam debuit Rob[ertus] Baioc' *Pipe* 23; aturnata Wilelmo Cade dc et vj li. et viij s. et ij d. *Ib.* 46 (cf. *EHR* XXVIII 220); **1203** Robertus r. c. de xx li. de debitis Aaron; ..set Thomas..debet amodo respondere pro eo per ~atam quam..Robertus fecit coram baronibus *Pipe* 8.

8 to pledge (a person, to make a payment). **b** to attorn (a tenant), make liable for obligations due to lord. **c** to acknowledge oneself liable as tenant (refl.). **d** (absol.).

1168 M. ..debet cc li. de veteri firma de Essexa; ..sed est ~atus inde ad faciendam abbatiam unam *Pipe* 36; G. M. xv li. ..unde ~atus est in camera curie *Ib.* 174; episcopus Judeus recognovit..quod Willelmus..pers[ol]verat Isaac Judeo dccc m. ..unde fuerit ei atturnatus de debito quod debebat regi *Ib.* 222; **1197** r. c. de lxviij s. et viij d. de terra unde atornatus fuit reddere ad firmam in camera regis *Pipe* 95. **b 1215** nobis significetis utrum voluerit super hoc comiti predicto atornari *Cl* 194b (cf. 7b supra); **1231** to atturnet eosdem..de servicio illo et feodo eidem Thome et heredibus suis inperpetuum *BNB* II 478; **1232** nec ipse nec antecessores sui umquam ~ati fuerunt ad faciendum predicto R. aliquod forinsecum servitium *CurR* XV 17; **1233** dimisit se in plena curia et ~avit ipsos ad faciendum servitium suum predicto J. *BNB* II 597; **1234** ~avit quendam R. .., qui tenementum illud tenuit ad firmam, quod redderet eidem J. firmam suam *Ib.* 664; **a1258** nota quod ille qui medius est potest se demittere propter paupertatem de feodo suo et ita quod tenens suus sit de cetero ∼atus superiori domino capitali *Ib.* 520 (*marg.*); prospiciat tenens, cum fuerit ∼andus, quod de eo cui fuerit ∼atus cartam habeat sufficientem BRACTON 82b; **1285** cum.. ∼atus sit tenens respondere capitali domino, medio omisso, necesse habebit tenens respondere..de serviciis..que medius ei prius facere debuit (2 *Westm.* 9) *StRealm* I 79; **1294** nec ipse unquam ∼atus fuit ad solvendum dictum redditum dicte Avicie *SelPlMan* 83. **c** poterit tenens, si voluerit, oblato homagio..et precise recusato, ∼are se superiori domino capitali et, si ipse homagium recusaverit, alteri superiori, et ita de domino in dominum quousque perveneril ad ipsum regem BRACTON 82b; **1293** cognovit quod ipse tenuit predictum manerium ad terminum vite..; et se ∼avit domino regi *PQW* 706a; **1315** servicium predicti R... assignatum fuit eidem Alicie in dotem, per quam assignacionem predictus R. se ∼avit eidem A. *Year Bk.* XVII 70; **1323** de cetero se ∼et et sit intendens..Henrico..racione dicti manerii *Lit. Cant.* I 95; **1332** virtute cujus concessionis ..Henrico se ∼avit et fidelitatem sibi fecit *Cl* 151 m. 1; *Reg. Brev.* 168 (v. attornamentum 1a). **d** **1333** (v. attornamentum 1a); **1345** W., qui statum habuit in tenemento ad terminum vite noluit eidem M. ∼are nec statum suum sursum reddere *Rec. Leic.* II 63; ipse paratus est prefato E. C. de fidelitate sua ∼are *Entries* 460.

9 to appoint, depute. **b** (w. inf.) to direct, require. **c** to appoint as attorney or proxy. **d** (p. ppl.) (?) concerned w. appointment of attorney.

ad quam [recognitionem] capiendam..∼astis alios loco vestro GLANV. XII 19; **1200** abbas de Sagio atturnat Willelmum..ad esse senescallum suum, ut faciat que ad senescallum facere pertinent *CurR* I 323; **1207** quos ∼avimus justiciarios nostros ad addresciandum..ea que addresciari non possunt per justiciarios nostros quos prius ∼avimus *Pat* 72a; **1212** persona ecclesie..fide corporaliter prestita ∼avit nobis ad solutionem faciendam terminis statutis A. capellanum suum *FormA* 82; **1221** primo apposuit eos [servientes] pro terra sua custodienda et postea ∼avit ad comitatum custodiendum *SelPlCrown* 110; **s1261** certificaverunt illos qui ad hoc per dominum regem ∼ati fuerunt.. que bona comitissa ceperat *Leg. Ant. Lond.* 142. **b** **s1267** comes habuit introitum civitatis per consilium et assensum legati, cujus consilio cives per preceptum domini regis.. fuerunt ∼ati obedire *Ib.* 90. **c** hec est finalis concordia facta..inter priorem..et W. ..per A. filium suum, quem ipse ∼avit in curia domini regis ad lucrandum et [v.l. vel] perdendum GLANV. VIII 2; **1199** missi ad videndum et audiendum quem Matillis ∼avit loco suo ad lucrandum vel perdendum versus Rogerum.., dicunt quod posuit loco suo Hugonem .. *CurR* I 77; **1231** bene possunt ∼are sokerevum in hustengo, et ibi in hustengo debent placitare *MGL* I 64; **1258** mandatum est baronibus de Scaccario quod ∼atum quem loco suo ∼are voluerit coram eis ad perreddendum compotum suum..loco ipsius..recipiant *Cl* 235; **1282** fuerunt atornati per..regem ut..Rogerum..sequerentur *Reg. Heref.* 76; **1366** ∼atos custodis..aule de Merton..quos coram nobis loco suo ∼are voluerit *MunAcOx* 791; **1501** sciatis me..∼asse et in loco meo posuisse..R. G. et T. C. meos veros et legitimos ∼atos..ad intrandum in omnibus predictis..terris *Cl* 362 m. 1 *d*. **d** **1543** warranta †∼ata recepta *KB Warrants of Attorney* 34/4 *rub.* (= *Ib.* 6/1 etc.: warranta attorn' [? *for* ∼atoria *or* ∼acionis]).

10 (p. ppl. as sb. m. or f.) attorney, proxy, legal representative (*v. et.* 9c *supra*). **b** (dist. as 'general', i.e. for all pleas, or 'special'). **c** professional attorney. **d** (w. *regis*). **e** attorney general (royal official).

1200 J. non venit vel se essoniavit nec ejus ∼atus *CurR* I 304; **1220** Petrus..dicit quod traxit virum suum [sc. Mabilie] in placitum in curia Christianitatis..et..sententiatum fuit..contra eam, eo quod ipsa fuit ∼ata viri sui *Ib.* IX 9; **1228** mandatum est vic. ..quod illum quem abbas Glouc' de hiis que ad dominum regem pertinent in eodem com. ∼are voluerit..loco ipsius abbatis tanquam ∼atum suum ad hoc recipiat *Cl* 33; **1236** heredibus seu actornatis suis *Melrose* I 297; **c1250** dicto S. vel ejus atorniatis *Ib.* 295; **1255** cc li. ..Elie vel ejus aturneato..nos promittimus soluturos *RGasc.* I *Suppl.* 42; **1256** venerunt..atornati episcopi Lync' ad recipiendos clericos a prisona *SelPlForest* lxxxix; **1270** perambulacio facta..in presencia..∼ati.. justiciarii forestarum *Ib.* 118; **1268** eidem vel ejus certo atturnato *Cl* 520; **1274** nil aliud scit nisi quod dominus suus misit ipsum pro eo et precepit ei quod..offerret eum ∼atum ipsius domine; ..et ignorat utrum ∼atus verus sit vel falsus (*Husting Roll*) *London Ed. I & II* II 248; **1279** debet unicam sectam pro maneriis de la M. et de T. ad com. Oxon' et ad hundredum de C., quas facit per J. ..atornatum suum ad hoc antiquitus feoffatum *Hund.* II 733 (cf. *EHR* III 418); **1279** S. ..et R. ..nostros constituimus ∼atos ut ipsi vel eorum alter..ipsum supleat officium vice nostra *Reg. Ebor.* 12; **1288** abbas per †attornum [? l. ∼atum] suum dicit.. *Reg. Malm.* I 263; **1294** quilibet liber homo qui sectam debet ad curiam domini sui libere possit facere ∼atum suum ad sectam illam faciendam pro eo *SelPlMan* 79; **1300** de Emma P. .., ∼ata uxoris Johannis R. *Leet Norw.* 51; **a1341** dominum N. ..procuratorem nostrum ∼atum et nuncium specialem facimus..ad vendendum..garbas *Pri. Cold.* 29; **s1399** cogendo regem R. resignare coronam in Parliamento ..per ∼atum *Misc. Scrope* 305; **1459** dicto A. L., tutori et ∼ato domini de G. *ExchScot* 510; **1530** cum..∼avimus..G. et R. nostros..∼atos ad..*Deeds Balliol* 129. **b** Willelmus ..generalis ∼atus abbatis de S. Ebrulpho *State Tri. Ed. I* 91; **1291** queritur de J. de T. de com. Ebor', generali ∼ato coram rege, de eo quod predictus J. concessit predicto R. patrocinium consilii sui ad appellandum priorem de Tinemewe *SelCKB* II 40 (cf. ib. IV lxxi); **1298** ∼atus meus legitimus et specialis *Ib.* I xcvi; **1330** J. de Helpeston' generalis ∼atus Oliveri de Hengham *PQW* 501a; **1333** H. de W., generalis ∼atus prefate regine *LTRMem* 105 r. 25; **1337** concessimus..eidem abbati quod ipse.., quamdiu dicta infirmitate detentus fuerit, facere possit in curia nostra ∼atum vel ∼atos generalem vel generales ad libertates suas in quibuscunque curiis Anglie calumniandas (*Pat* 191 m. 26) *Reg. Brev.* 27 (cf. ib. 9); **1389** (v. **c** infra). **c** **1312** in salariis narratorum et ∼iatorum in curia regis et in civitate Londinii (*Lit. Collect. Apostol.*) *EHR* XLI 357; **1336** J. de Lutterworth' de com. Leic', ∼atus in Communi Banco, fecit breve predictum absque aliquo waranto *SelKCB* V 83; **1389** nullus cursista..fiat ∼atus inter partem et partem in aliquibus placitis..in aliqua curia extra..Cancellariam nec sese aliquibus attornamentis intromittat, nisi per litteras domini regis patentes fuerit generalis ∼atus *Chanc. Orders* 6; ib. 4 (v. apprenticius 2); **1419** major et aldermanni pro civitate posuerunt unum de Scaccario ∼atum..civitatis ad calumniandas et clamandas suas libertates; ..et consimiliter in Communi Banco posuerunt unum de illa placea ∼atum civitatis. in Banco vero Regis ponere solebant duos ∼atos conjunctim et divisim *MGL* I 25. **d** **1430** servientibus et ∼atis regis ad legem *ActPC* IV 71; **1507** J. Ernley ∼ato.. regis *Cl* 373 m. 9*d*. **e** **1497** generalis ∼atus domini regis qui pro domino rege sequitur in hac parte *Entries* 48; **1535** Cristoferum Hale, generalem ∼atum domini regis *FormA* 236; in qua [Curia Wardorum] Magister Generalis judicat, subsunt autem supervisor Liberationum, ∼atus Generalis, Receptor Generalis.. CAMD. *Br.* 142.

attornatio, refitting (of ships).

1214 in ∼one navium ad opus equorum *Pipe* 129.

2 assignment, pledging (of money). **b** (of rent or service). **c** attornment, acknowledgement of new lord by tenant. **d** transfer as token of seisin.

c1166 de atornatione de Lundonia xx libras (*KR Misc.* 1/1b) *EHR* XXVIII 227; **1168** Abraham Judeus clamavit quietum Ricardum..de plegiis debiti patris sui episcopi Eliensis coram baronibus..quando recepit cartum episcopi ..et atturnationem ministrorum ejusdem de debito eodem reddendo *Pipe* 222; **1191** D. filius Aaron debet compotum de ∼one quam Aaron eis fecit *Pipe* 24. **b** **1202** dedimus Gregorio..primum redditum ecclesiasticum vacantem..de donatione nostra, non obstante aliquo mandato nostro vel atturnatione super aliquo redditu ecclesiastico alicui clerico conferendo *Pat* 16a; **1205** concordia talis est, sc. quod.. archidiaconus reddidit ei saisinam suam inde et recepit homagium, ..ita quod de cetero per ∼onem ipsius N. ballivi archidiaconi reciperent redditum et omnia pertinentia salvo unicuique tenentium tenemento quod tenere debet *Cur R* III 250; **1223** jurata venit recognitura..si..Leticia..fecit .. Warino servitium per ∼onem..Willelmi de eodem tenemento vel non...juratores dicunt quod non possunt inquirere quod..Willelmus unquam attornasset..Leticiam.. Warino *Ib.* XI 1206; **a1228** me..dedisse..redditum xv s. .. quos..frater meus et heredes sui per atturnationem meam annuatim dictis canonicis..persolvent *Reg. S. Thom. Dublin* 396; **c1250** nos..dedisse et attornasse..decimas.. de B. ..ad ista providenda; ..et ut hec nostra..donatio, ∼o ac carte nostre confirmatio..robur obtineat.. *MonA* III 35b; si..homagium..recuperavit verus dominus racione alicujus finis vel ∼onis *Fleta* 206; **s1294** dedimus ei..annis singulis per ∼onem dicte communitatis..vj d. *Ann. Dunstable* 392. **c** **1383** quiquidem W., licet aliquem statum per ipsum J. alicui factum (*sic*), nullam fecit ∼onem durante vita predicti J. *IMisc* 229/12. **d** **1449** per deliberacionem et ∼onem unius olle enie *Cl* 300 m. 27*d*.

3 appointment as attorney or proxy.

1203 Amabilia..ponit loco suo David virum suum...non est recepta ista ∼o; set David dicit quod ipsa attornaverat eum loco suo *CurR* II 270; **1455** littera ∼onis..ad recipiendum vice et nomine..abbatis seisinam et possessionem manerii *Reg. Whet.* I 189 *rub.* (cf. ib.: noverint universi nos ..in loco nostro posuisse..J. W. nostrum verum et legitimum attornatum).

attornator, attorney or proxy (*cf. attornare* 10a).

in feodo N. de F. ∼oris domini ad certam curiam pro eodem faciendo xx s. per talliam *FormMan* 35; **s1300** prior Westm' fecit R. H. confratrem suum ∼orem ad recipiendum seisinam W. WORC. *Anecd.* 528.

attornatorius, of attorney (*cf. attornare* 10a).

1330 pro impetracione litere ∼ie, xv d. *Pri. Cold. app.* viii; **s1386** littere †∼ia Johannis W. *G. S. Alb.* III 248 *rub.*; **1428** litteram ∼iam generalem sub nomine suo eidem Johanni factam ad..debita sua..recipienda..liberavit (*Exeter Staple*) *Law Merch.* I 119; trado pro facto meo parti agenti..literas atturnatorias nomine meo sibi factas et concessas ad agendum et recuperandum *Praxis* 170.

1 attornatus v. attornare 10.

2 attornatus, appointment of attorney or proxy.

1325 habet litteras regis de ∼u (*Pat*) *Foed.* IV 162b; **1432** habet litteras de generali ∼u (*TreatyR*) *Ib.* X 500; **1450** cuidam clerico scribenti dictas cartas cum literis ∼i (*sic*) *Fabr. York* 65; **1497** literam actornatus *Melrose* II no. 584.

attorniare v. attornare. attornus v. attornare 10a. Attrabatum v. Atrebatensis. attractare, ∼abilis (∼ibilis), v. attrect-. attractatus v. tractatus.

attractio [LL], attraction, drawing towards. **b** enticement. **c** appropriation, usurpation.

ex quatuor oppositis..oceani partibus violenta quedam maris ∼o GIR. *TH* II 3; ex natura multipliciter fit ∼o, aut vi caloris, aut virtute, aut naturali qualitatum similitudine, aut lege vacuitatis NECKAM *NR* II 98; ptisanaria massa.. per compressionem et adtractionem venit ad epar RIC. MED. *Micr. Anat.* 226; ∼o [fit] per calidum et siccum BACON III 298; in ratione qua virtus attrahentis unit sibi virtutem ejus quod attrahitur ∼o tam activa quam passiva omnino est naturalis *Ps.*-GROS. 614; WYCL. *Log.* II 161 (v. adamas a). **b** **1304** ad ∼onem seu alleccionem hominum ad superstitionis vanitatem *FormOx* 8. **c** **1358** vobis [sc. custodi V Portuum] mandamus quod..majores et ballivos Portuum..†convisciones [? l. connisciones *for* cognicionem] querelarum de hiis †qui [? l. que] in eisdem portubus emerserint absque impedimento vel ∼one vobis inde facienda habere..permittatis *Reg. Rough* 129; ib. 125 (v. attrahere 2a).

attractivus, attractive, drawing towards itself. **b** (sb. f.) attractive force.

eo quod de impulsiva [aeris] formatione fit, ..similitudo affectus etiam in ∼a formatione intelligenda est ADEL. *QN* 21; quod sibi dulce putat vis attractiva, libenter / attrahit atque sibi fida recondit humus NECKAM *DS* IV 454; ejus cure attinebat..oblationis elemosine collectio attrectiva R. COLD. *Cuthb.* 91; [caliditas est] inferiorum ad superiora reductiva et ∼a BART. ANGL. IV 1; in eo viget virtus ∼a GILB. II 101. 2; potentia ∼a BACON VIII 175; cum clisteri ∼o GAD. 53 v. 1; R. BURY *Phil.* 8. 144 (v. adamas b); [anima vegetativa] quam illustravit..Deus septem viribus, que sunt vis ∼a, retentiva, digestiva, expulsiva, nutritiva, generativa, informativa BRADW. *CD* 138D; est color viridis ..visum delectans et ad sui viriditatem aspectum (*sic*) oculorum atractivus et reparativus UPTON 113. **b** lutum tantam habens ∼am quod, si..quamcunque solidam materiam..infixeris, nulla vi..potest extrahi GERV. TILB. III 19; defectus ∼e epatis, ut in cachechia GILB. V 219 v. 1; nutritive deserviunt ∼a, retentiva, digestiva, expulsiva *Ps.*-GROS. 469.

attractorium, trace (of harness).

14.. ∼ium, A. *a trayne*, sed melius *a trays* WW.

attractrix, attractive (f.).

vis ∼ix in eis [sc. renibus] pollet plurimum D. EDW. *Anat.* B 3 v.

attractus [cf. OF *atrait*], haulage or accumulation (of building materials). **b** (?) store, stock.

1171 pro ∼u calcis et lapidum ad operationes de Hasting' *Pipe* 128; **1190** ad faciendum ∼um de petra et calce et sabulo ad opus castelli de Cantebr' in ipso castello *Pipe* 7; **1195** in liberatione quadrigarum que fecerunt adtractum in castrum *RScacNorm* I 137; **1201** pro firmandis castellis.. fossatis, palis..et aliis reparationibus et ∼ibus *Pipe* 253; ∼um fecit magnum de lapidibus et sabulo ad magnam turrim ecclesie faciendam BRAKELOND 123; **1204** quod omnem ∼um quem facere poteritis de lapide et calce facias ad firmandum castellum nostrum de Eboraco et ∼um illum venire facias super aquam usque Usskel' *Cl* 4b; **1215** mandamus quatinus..totum ∼um quem habetis apud Knapp'.. attrahatis usque Bremble et domum illam muniatis *Pat* 137b; **1222** rotulus de ∼u ad aulam infra ballium *KRAc* 491/13 r. 2; **1241** l m. ..faciat habere custodibus operationum de Windlesor' ad atractum faciendum de petra et calce ad castrum..claudendum *Cl* 268; **1259** in ∼u calcis et petre contra estatem *Liberate* 35 m. 6. **b** **c1190** quod ipse in eodem tofto manebit et ibi ∼um rerum suarum faciet *E. Ch. Yorks* I 369; **1213** tu omnem ∼um victualium et omnia mercata ballivarum tuarum venire facias, ut sequantur exercitum nostrum (*Breve Regis*) WEND. II 67; **1256** permittat Johannem..hospitari cum uxore et familia sua in duobus vel tribus maneriis predicti archiepiscopatus [Dublin']..et ∼um suum in eis facere ad perhendinandum ibidem sumptibus propriis *Cl* 417.

2 bringing in, admission (of persons). **b** enticement, allurement.

s1091 prohibuimus..servientibus nostris..ne faciant.. aliquem ∼um secularium virorum, puerorum vel mulierum in infirmitorium *Croyl. Cont. A* 131; **s1308** ∼us..alienigenarum et retencio..a domino suo rege corda magnatum distrahebant *G. Ed. II Bridl.* 32. **b** nec quod delectet honestos / conjugis attractus oculus delibet adulter HANV. IX 388; procacitas cum nutu vel tactu vel ∼u [ME: *tollunge*], cum stolido risu, cum oculo meretricio *AncrR* 72.

attrahere [CL], to attract, draw towards oneself. **b** (w. *spiritum*) to draw breath. **c** to shorten, contract (in pronunciation). **d** to haul (building material etc.), lead in (harvest).

tertia [forma naturae] secundae similitudinem ∼it, eo quod creatur ERIUG. *Per.* 525C; duo ex nautis..stantes in prora ∼ebant funem W. CANT. *Mir. Thom.* III 44; aque in nubibus attracte et conglobate GIR. *TH* I 6; [navis] rapitur et ∼itur fluctuum violentia *Ib.* II 14; NECKAM *DS* IV 455 (v. attractivus a); caliditas accidentalis per fricationem in lapide pretioso ∼it paleam *Ps.*-GROS 614; ne..∼ant ad locum materiam apostematis GAD. 127 v. 2. **b** ad spiritum ∼endum BART. ANGL. V 13. **c** tonus aut pertrahitur aut ∼itur ALDH. *PR* 141. **d** **a1128** [sunt] ij caratores qui ∼ant petras ad opus aecclesiae *Chr. Peterb. app.* 167; **c1180** focalia sua suis bigis †attashere [? l. ∼ere] poterunt *Melrose* I 108; **c1182** cum ∼unt bladum de marisco, ter in die ibunt *RBWorc.* 409.

2 to take to oneself, appropriate (to a use), usurp. **b** (w. *sibi*).

812 Aet Sueordhlincum et Ecgheanglond Uulfredo..concedens donabo, sibi ipsi habendum ac perpetue fruendum ac sic ad trahendum [? l. adtrahendum] ut semet ipso utillimum esse videretur *CS* 341; **1164** si calumnia emerserit inter clericum et laicum de ullo tenemento quod clericus ad elemosinam ∼ere velit, laicus vero ad laicum feudum *Const. Clar.* 9; ut vicinorum..victum atque pecuniam ∼erent et coacervarent *Mir. J. Bev.* 302; **1276** attraxit ad tenementum suum..sectam que solebat fieri ad wapp[entacum] *Hund.* I 105b (cf. ib. 104b); attraxit de via regia ad berc[ar]iam suam, set nesciunt quantum); **1358** custos V Portuum..atrahebat coram se ad ecclesiam S. Jacobi de Dovorre diversa placita extra loca Portuum..in eorumdem prejudicium *Reg. Rough* 125; **1415** dicta loca dicte civitati usurpando super dominum regem attraxerunt *Rec. Norw.* I 323. **b** **c1087** interdico ut nullus..eandem soknam sibi ∼at nisi S. Edmundo et abbati *Regesta* p. 138; **1100** regales ministri tempore vacantis abbatie nullam potestatem sibi ∼ant in maneriis..conventus (*Ch. Bury*) *EHR* XXIV 425; **1262** inhibentes ne..de tenuris predicti aliquid..vobis ∼ere, usurpare vel appropriare presumatis *Cl* 120; **1309** rex habet iij acras de communa ..; et R. ..et C. ..atraxerunt inde sibi per carucam suam *S. Jers.* XVIII 257; **1317** abbas..communarios a communa sua impedivit et..per hujusmodi impedimentum attraxit sibi seperale in locis predictis tanquam ad manum mortuam *Cart. Glast.* I 228.

3 to bring in (outsiders). **b** to entice, seduce.

a1190 concessi..quod nullum hominem attraam in territorio et pastura de C. ad detrimentum animalium.. *Ch. Gilb.* 109. **b s1274** perrexit per vicos..predicando et †~iando populum..ut adhererent ei contra majorem *Leg. Ant. Lond.* 165.

4 to handle, treat (*cf. attrectare*).

princeps quasi pauper egenus / turpiter attractus jacet et sine jure subactus GOWER *CT* II 40.

5 (refl.) to withdraw (*cf. retrahere*).

1293 attraxerunt se de appello *GaolDel.* 36 r. 2*d*.

attrament- v. atrament-. attrana v. attrenum.

attrectabilis, touchable, palpable.

s1044 claras sacri susceperat maculas cruoris, quas usque hodie et oculis conspicabiles et osculis ~es ostendit *Chr. Rams.* 158.

2 attractive.

934 (10c) fortuna..saeculi..quae, quamvis arridendo sit infelicibus adtractibilis, ..ad ima Cociti..est decurribilis *CS* 702 (cf. ib. 54, 704, 716, 718).

attrectare [CL], to touch, handle. **b** to treat.

~are, †malae [l. male] tangere *GlC* A 869; demone possessus.., se ipsum et quibus ~ando contingere potuit morsibus dilaniare contendit R. COLD. *Cuthb.* 17; *to grape*, attractare, ~are, ..palpare *CathA*. **b s1272** honorifice.. attractavit [v.l. ~avit] eos et post biduum dimisit in pace W. GUISB. 210.

2 to draw in. **b** to usurp.

1198 qui nisi in castrum..a custodibus attractatus fuisset, ..comprehensus fuisset TREVET 158. **b 1353** sic attractando sibi ipsi regalem potestatem *Pat* 239 m. 20.

attrectatio, treatment, dealing.

si invidie ~ones metuant ADEL. *ED* 3.

attrectator v. atrox. attrectivus v. attractivus.

attremere [CL], to tremble before.

s1070 ut nichil minus quam B. Petro successoribus ejus et minantibus ~ant et..benignitatem indulgentibus..applaudant W. MALM. *GP* I 41.

†attrenum [? misr. of Ar. *al-qaṭṭāra*], vessel used in distilling.

ponitur in †atuum vel †egem, que sunt vasa distillationis in operibus alkimie BACON IX 157; ~um vel atrena [v.l. athenum vel attrana] vas alembico valde simile *Alph.* 17.

†attria [? misr. of Ar. *al-ḥadīd* = iron], a kind of pyrites

marcasita, cujus tot sunt species quot metalla, et ab illis denominantur: ~ia, electrum, tuchia.. *Ps.*-GROS 626.

attribuere [CL], to grant; **b** (in response to prayer).

634 ea quae..pro vestris sacerdotibus ordinanda sperastis, haec..gratuito animo adtribuere..praevidemus (*Lit. Papae*) BEDE *HE* II 17; si quid de ipsis cuicunque homini ..~tum vel prestitum fuisset *DB* I 172b. **b 1268** si.. unanimes.., quod Deus ~at, effici valeatis *Cl* 497.

2 to assign, allot (a task). **b** to attribute, ascribe (a power, quality or sim.). **c** (p. ppl. as sb. n.) attribute.

quanto singularius hoc negotii suscepti difficillimum.. ~etur, tanto studiosius singularem attentionem apponere necesse BALSH. *AD* 29. **b** quid veluti specialiter Patri, quid Verbo, quid S. Spiritui ~endum videtur ERIUG. *Per.* 562C; illi cui specialis fit injuria convenientius ~itur culpae vindicta aut indulgentia ANSELM (*Cur D.* 9) II 105; ea vicissitudo, que rerum est ad sermones sermonumque ad res, que sibi invicem quasi collatione mutua suas proprietates ~unt J. SAL. *Met.* 846D; nec ei [visui] ~itur judicium de aliis [sensibilibus], sed aliis virtutibus anime BACON *Maj.* II 426; dicit Averroes quod hec omnia [salubria] ~untur eidem [sc. sanitati] tanquam eidem fini.., distinguens tres modos quibus aliqua ~untur eidem BRADW. *CD* 565A. **c** desistant pictores Dei ipsum variis qualitatibus, ~tis, habitibus vel actibus..depingentes *Ib.* 20D.

3 to impute (w. inf.).

illa..sentencia..nec ordini [Minorum]..~it usurpasse potestatem quam non habuit nec.. OCKHAM *Dial.* 427.

attributalis, expressive of (or of the nature of) an attribute.

s1301 queritur utrum distinccio racionum communium in divinis presupponat distinccionem racionum ~ium *Theol.Ox* 297; cognicio illius essencie est perfeccior cognicio quam cognicio proprietatis ~is DUNS *Sent. prol.* 3. 10; aut significant [nomina] illam [rem] diverso modo et racione diversa, et tunc..possunt vocari nomina dispositiva..aut nomina ~ia, sicut theologis magis placet, cujusmodi sunt potencia, clemencia, sapiencia et similia dicta de Deo BRADW. *CD* 564C; contingens..per se et primo accipitur uno modo tantum, et ad illum primum omnes alii velut ~es accessorii reducuntur *Ib.* 652B.

attributio [CL], attribution, ascription.

omnia ex ~one se habent uni primo, quod est materia; ergo materia erit principium omnium tam substantiarum quam accidentium BACON VII 24; potest conceptus aliquis alius a conceptu lapidis creati formari, ad quem conceptum lapidis, ut est idea in Deo, habet lapis iste ~onem DUNS *Sent.* I iii 2. 10; hujusmodi ~o sive transumpcio est quidam color rhetoricus quem..[Tullius] denominacionem appellat BRADW. *CD* 565B.

attriplex v. atriplex. Attripotens v. Atrebatensis.

attritio [LL], attrition, wearing away, bruising. **b** pounding (alch.). **c** chafing (fig.). **d** friction (fig.).

s1194 equo cecidit et pedis ~one subita sauciatus ad necem..pede truncatus est DICETO *YH* II 124. **b** prius est pulverisatio cum congelatione, deinde resolutio..; et postea est sublimatio cum ~one et mortificatione BACON *Min.* 314. **c** sic est [imago tua] abolita ~one vitiorum, sic est offuscata fumo peccatorum ANSELM (*Prosl.* 1) I 100. **d** in hujus discussione plurima ~o est, quoniam contrariarum concursus rationum dubitandi materia est J. SAL. *Met.* 908B.

2 tribulation, hardship. **b** attrition (as step towards contrition).

ut in rerum augmento crescat humilitas et in ~one patientia roboretur MAP *NC* V 5 p. 231; **1384** sinceritatem.. mittentis.., variis tribulacionibus et ~onibus tam afflicti, ..attendentes *Conc.* III 189. **b** ~o non dicit nisi tritionem, que debet ad contritionem terminari.., quia sine amore est ..qui attritus est HALES *Qu.* 1032; **1301** quia tam manifesta..delicta..manifestis ~onibus, penitenciis et correccionibus expiare..convenit *Reg. Cant.* II 888; idem actus ~onis factus in gracia posset esse contricio, et sic actus meritorius et virtuosus WYCL. *Civ. Dom.* I 344; **c1430** virum ..~onis contricionisque lacrimis plenum *Reg. Whet.* II 434.

attritor, corroder.

inter vos quidam..subintraverunt..religionis ~ores et absumptores H. LOS. *Ep.* 52.

1 attritus v. atterere.

2 attritus [CL], scrubbing, polishing.

surarum pagina leves / pumicis attritus refugit HANV. II 260.

attromentum v. atramentum. attropia v. atrophia. attrox v. atrox. attuala v. cetewalla. attubernalis v. attabernalis. atturn-, aturn-, v. attorn-, tornus. atunc v. adtunc. atuum v. attrenum. atyl- v. attill-. auba v. albus 8. aubergellus v. halbergellus. aubulcus v. bubulcus. auburn- v. alburn-.

auca [LL], goose. **b** (dist. as tame or wild etc.). **c** (paid as rent). **d** (w. *Mariola*) (?) unmated goose. **e** (w. *rosaria* or sim.) kind of water-fowl, (?) sheldrake (cf. W. Bibblesworth: *Gl.* 781: *un ouwe roser*, wilde ges).

~am illam..coquite et comedite BEDE *Cuthb.* 36; volitantum more strepentes / aucarum WULF. *Swith.* I 553; ~a, *gos* ÆLF. *Gl.*; milvus societur olori, / accipitres merulis, bubonibus auca sinistris *Simon Her.* 34; sete [hystricis].. similes pennis ~arum ubi desinunt plume W. MALM. *GR* V 409; [Anglici] Parisius ovis incubantes aucas et anseres sibilis ac gestibus simulare solent GIR. *Inv.* I 4 p. 94; ~a pinguis et ponderosa rogavit corvum quod juvaret eam ut in altum posset volare O. CHERITON *Fab.* 36; **12..** pulli ~arum decimantur *Conc. Scot.* II 44 (cf. *Conc. Syn.* 511); **1277** et remanent iij ~e errarie *MinAc* 997/3; **1280** de quolibet manerio ubi ~e nutriuntur habeant infirmi duas ~as *Reg. Ebor.* 137; **1296** item iiij aucas et ij anceres, precium cujuslibet iiij d., et x aucilas, precium cujuslibet ij d. *Anc. Ext.* 81(1) m. 2; **s1314** quod..~a crassa [vendatur] pro ij d. ob. *Ann. Lond.* 233; **1321** in liberacione j ancille.. custodientis ~as et gallinas *MinAc* 992/11; accidit ut oga transeunti obvia occurreret *NLA* (*Winwaloeus*) II 461; ancer et ipse suam, cum qua se miscuit, aucam / linquit GOWER *VC* I 549; **1417** de quacumque ~a preter ~as †*brodoges* [l. *brodeges*] vulgariter nuncupatas sex pennas alarum suarum pro sagittis..faciendis..capi..facias (*Cl*) *Foed.* IX 436; **s1417** rex fecit capi et colligi de qualibet ~a non feta sex pennas pro sagittis (*Chr.*) *EHR* XXIX 512; **1440** heu lupus agnellis, heu vulpes predicat †ancis (*Versus Abbatis*) AMUND. II 221. **b** bernace..~is palustribus similes, sed minores GIR. *TH* I 15 (cf. STANIHURST 231: 'ancis'; quid hoc verbo significetur prorsus ignoro, nisi forte legendum sit 'anatibus'); ~e minores albe, †qui et gantes dicuntur *Ib.* 23; auce silvestres cenate cum piperatis D. BEC. 2640; notum est girofalconem cum cohorte multarum ~arum silvestrium de transmarinis adventare partibus NECKAM *NR* I 28; ~a domestica..aliatam fortem desiderat *Id. Ut.* 102; **1274** sic emat quod possit dare..a Pascha usque festum Pentecostes †ancam domesticam pastam meliorem pro v d. .. *MGL* II 82; **1344** ij ~e de ripa, x d. *KRAc* 390/11 r. 16; cum ~e indomite in eodem loco..agros occupantes depascerent et passim depopularent *NLA* (*Milburga*) II 191; **c1375** in vij ~is indomitis ij s. ix d. *Ac. Durh.* 46. **c a1128** reddunt per annum xj ~as et lxv gallinas *Chr. Peterb. app.* 160; **1237** dabit ad Natale octo gallinas et preterea iiij augas ad festum S. Mich. *CurR* XVI 122; **1277** exigebant ab eisdem iij ~as ubi ei non recognoverunt nisi unam *Reg. S. Aug.* 253; **1295** racione octodecim auccarum quas dominus rex percipere solet nomine sergancie de quodam tenemento *Ann. Dunstable* 401; **1297** in *rypgos* iiij ~e per talliam (*MinAc*) *Econ. Condit. app.* 15; **1299** (17c) goselandi: T. W. tenet j forland per servicium vj ~arum ad Nativitatem B. Marie *RBWorc* 78; **1301** quilibet custumarius villate de Staford' [*Som*] habens ~as ereas dabit de consuetudine ad gulam Augusti j ~am vocatam *lesegos* *Anc. Ext.* 8 m. 7; **1306** tenet j parvam peciam terre..et debet j ~am precii ij d. *Cust. Battle* 19; **1307** in ~is ad obolum [(?) *compulsorily sold by tenant at* ½d.] liberatis cursori, v s. *Ac. Durh.* 5; **1417** in xix ~is obulatis et v ~is rent', ix d. ob. *Ib.* 55; **1408** in xx ~is †st'bulatis [? l. obulatis] x d. *Ib.* 53. **d 1244** de vj ~is mariol' et ij anseribus *MinAc* 766/19; **1247** de v ~is mariol' et ansere exierunt hoc anno xij aucule et de emptis xxxj; de eis remanent vij ~e mariol' et ij anseres *Ib.* 740/7; **1340** j ancer, v ~e unde iij mariole, xxviij aucule *Ib.* 1120/10 r. 10; **1388** de..x ~is †morol' *Ac. Esch.* 10 r. 5; **1391** j ~am marol' (*Ac. Cottesford*) *Rec. Eton* XXVI no. 44. **e c1190** reddendo..de eadem virgata pro omni..consuetudine v s. et x ~as rosarios (*sic*) *Carte Nativ.* 511; **1247** eodem modo scribitur vicecomiti Wiltes' de ..ccc gallinis, ..c perdicibus in pane, et de ~is roseris et avibus de ripera quotquot poterit *Cl* 47 (cf. ib.: de ~is †reres'); **1274** quod possit dare..~am roseram meliorem pro iiij d. *MGL* II 82; **1326** in iij ~is rosettis *Ac. Durh.* 15; **1339** in iiij ~is rosatis emptis, xxij d. *Ib.* 536.

aucare v. hircare.

aucarium, goose-house.

1268 exitus ~ii: idem computat de xv anatibus..et..de xviij aucis remanentibus *Ac. Wellingb.* 9.

aucarius, goshawk. **b** goose-herd.

~ius, *goshafoc* ÆLF. *Gl.* **b 14..** ~ius, *gosherd* WW; *a guse herde*, ~ius *CathA*.

aucella [cf. aucula], gosling.

1321 decimas..porcellorum et ~arum *Reg. Heref.* 181; **1380** de xv aucis et j ~a *Reg. Rough* 225.

auceparia v. aucuparia. 1 auceps v. 2 anceps.

2 auceps [CL], bird-catcher, fowler. **b** (adj.) preying on birds. **c** (fig.). **d** (?) fowling-place.

†aupex, qui aucupia exercet *GlC* A 888 (cf. ib. 958); sicut avem nectit nodosis retibus auceps ALDH. *VirgV* 1937; **c800** nec unus passer cadat in laqueum aucupis ALCUIN *Ep.* 198; quid dicis tu, ~s [AS: *fugelere*]? quomodo decipis aves? ÆLF. *Coll.* 95; **a1128** ibi est j ~s qui tenet vij acras et dim., unde reddit x anseres salvages *Chr. Peterb. app.* 162; **c1153** testibus..Hugone †Aucipite *Cart. Chester* 232; nisus ..dimissus ad predam aucupis evasit aspectum W. CANT. *Mir. Thom.* V 20; auceps si fueris, sis fraudibus usus opertis: / viscum viscet aves, latitantia retia flectant D. BEC. 1763; eos [phasianos] sic seducunt aucupes NECKAM *NR* I 42; **1279** pro vadiis ij †aucip' prec' per diem vj d. *Chanc. Misc.* 4/1; **1287** Jacke †ancipiti regine et Ade veauterario regine *KRAc* 351/24 m. 5; **1330** cuidam aucupi..vj s. viij d. *ExchScot* 327. **b 1529** accipitres aut aves aucupes *Conc.* III 721. **c** aucupes novitatum rumusculos congerunt J. SAL. *Pol.* 483D; aucepsque favoris / eloquium HANV. IV 295. **d 814** cum campis, ..paludibus, aucupibus, aquis, mariscis *CS* 348.

Aucerensis, Aucerr' v. Autisiodorensis. aucerola v. anserulus. aucila v. aucula.

aucinus, of a goose.

carnes aucine, pulli pinguesque capones D. BEC. 2564; **1325** garcionibus pennantibus quarell' cum pennis ~is *KRAc* 165/1 m. 2; **1450** pro alis †aucium [? l. aucin'], brosches et scopis emptis pro purgacione..murorum ecclesie *Fabr. York* 65; caro ~a, *goseflesche* WW.

aucion- v. auction-. aucipiter v. accipiter. aucipium v. aucupium. auclator v. anclator. aucment- v. augment-.

auco [cf. pavo], gander.

1312 ~ones ij, auce v (*Ac. Bocking*) *DCCant.*

aucoxum v. auxilium 3b.

auctarium [CL], supplement.

reward at mete qwane fode faylyth at þe servyse, auctorium *PP*; *bute*, auctorium, augmentum, *as in cosynge CathA*.

aucte, increasingly.

~ius, amplius *GlC* A 918.

auctent- v. authent-.

auctio [CL], auction sale. **b** enlargement, supplement.

~o, puplica venditio *GlC* A 913; auctio dum decuplat asses, decrescere sentit / pregnantem loculum Parisiana cohors GARL. *Epith.* II 209. **b** autio, crementum *GlC* A 926; **1549** statutis illis nostris..haec paucula, seu interpretationes, seu emendationes, seu ~ones denique, adjicienda praecipimus *StatOx* 358.

auctionari [CL = *to sell by auction*], to retail.

~abatur [*EE* 345. 56: †actionabatur], puplice vendebat *GlC* A 946; **14..** auccionor, A. *to hukke* WW.

1 auctionarius v. actionarius a.

2 auctionarius, ~ia, retailer, huckster. **b** purchaser.

auxionarii [*gl.*: G. *regrateres*] mittunt servos et servas per vicos ad decipiendum clericos, quibus vendunt nimis care cerasa, pruna..et poma immatura GARL *Dict.* 126; placente ..jacent ad fenestras augxionariorum *Ib.*; **1268** de tota terra mea juxta aquam de Tyne inter bothas auxionariorum *Deeds Newcastle* 117; **1290** auxionarii et auxionatrices panis et cervisie et aliarum rerum *RParl* I 28; **s1315** gravi pena in puletarios et alios auxionarios provisionem non observantes inflicta TROKELOWE 90; **1419** certificari solebat aldermannus de nominibus hostellariorum, ..vitellariorum et auxionariorum in eadem warda manencium *MGL* I 38; *an hukster*, ~ius, ~ia *CathA*. **b** ~ius, qui emit *Erf.* 2. 44.

auctionator (m.), **~atrix** (f.), retailer, huckster. **b** (fig.) exaggerator.

†actionator, qui de pretio contendit *GlC* A 96; **1290** (v. auctionarius); **1371** est communis hospitator, oxionator et..

vigilator *Sess. PLincs* 158; **1395** omnes †anxiatrices Notingham vendunt allium..casios et hujusmodi nimis caros *Rec. Nott.* I 270; *hukstare*, auxionator m., auxionatrix f. *PP*; ~or et ~ix, *an hukker & an hukkester*, ..hec auxiatrix, *a hukster*, ..hec auxionatrix, *a hoxter* WW. **b** c**1200** dum confiteris, non sis fraudulentus diminutor nec iniquus ~or W. Rams. *Cantic.* 341. 218.

auctivus, productive of increase.

extremam..animae partem, nutritivam dico et ~am vitam.., quae pars..corpus nutrit et auget Eriug. *Per.* 444A.

auctor [CL; *infl. by* authenticus (cf. *ALMA* III 81–6)], author, originator. **b** (authoritative) writer. **c** (in divine epithet; *cf. Heb.* ii 10, xii 2). **d** (in epithet of Devil).

680 quis primus ~or..tonsurae extiterit Aldh. *Ep.* 4 p. 482; **706** quomodo examina apum.., earum ~ore linquente brumalia..receptacula, ..cohortes..glomerant *Ib.* 9 p. 501; didicerat a doctoribus ~oribusque suae salutis Bede *HE* I 26; ~or ipse belli..interemtus est *Ib.* III 24 p. 178; si is a quo tollitur occupatum ~or est facti *Dial. Scac.* II 10B; s**1381** omnes..qui viderent ipsum regem esse velut ~orem nostre commocionis Wals. *HA* II 10. **b** argumenta ex libris ~orum prolata Aldh. *Met.* 10 p. 87; Basilius quondam doctorum maximus auctor *Id. VirgV* 730; scripsit..librum..cujus ~or erat docendo ac dictando Arcuulfus Bede *HE* V 15; de Virgilio et aliis ~oribus.., exceptis his in quibus aliqua turpitudo sonat Anselm (*Ep.* 64) III 181; logicam diviserunt ~ores in scientiam inveniendi et scientiam judicandi J. Sal. *Met.* 860D; hec summis ~oribus prima fuit..scribendi occasio Gir. *TH intr.* p. 4; iste [Albertus] per modum authenticum scripsit libros suos, et ideo totum vulgus insanum allegat eum Parisius sicut Aristotelem aut Avicennam aut Averroem et alios ~ores Bacon *Tert.* 31 (cf. *Id. Min.* 327–8); videtur per ~orem sex principiorum [sc. *Gilbert de la Porrée*] Duns *Sent.* II ii 9. 27; ~ores indifferenter quandoque utuntur his nominibus *SB* 35; **1549** lecture probatorum authorum.. vacent *Conc. Scot.* II 105. **c** auctorem lucis tenebroso corde negantes Aldh. *CE* IV 8. 6; omnipotens auctor, nutu qui cuncta creavit *Id. Aen.* 91. 1; Dominus beatitudinis ~or atque largitor Bede *Cuthb.* 42; mundi mitissimus auctor Alcuin *Carm.* 28. 8; tanquam..habitatoribus indignam ~or nature judicasset Gir. *TH* II 9; **1219** salutem in ~ore salutis *Pat* 197; **1354** tandem, authore ecclesie superante, ..se ad unitatem ecclesie converterunt *DocCOx* 259; **1559** ~or aeternus *Conc. Scot.* II 140. **d** auctorem sceleris populo praesente revincens Aldh. *VirgV* 1917; pro dolor.. quod tam lucidi vultus homines tenebrarum ~or possidet! Bede *HE* II 1 p. 80; s**1453** recedit a Deo acceditque ad eum qui fautor est ficcionis autorque mendaciorum *Reg. Whet.* I 121.

auctorabilis, authoritative.

p**1250** divino ~i inviolabili dictamine (*Const. Frat. Paenit.*) *EHR* IX 123; **1345** consensu nostro ~i *Mem. Ripon* 154.

auctoramentum [CL], bargain.

~um, quod est indicium *GlC* A 941 (cf. *Erf.* 2. 269. 52: †autornamentum, fiduciam).

auctoratio, sale.

aucturatio, venditio *GlC* A 959.

auctoratus, hallowed.

erga / auctorata volans altaria Frith. 150; auctorata ferens Petri vexilla beati *Ib.* 803.

auctoris- v. auctoriz-.

auctoritas [CL], authority, power or right to command obedience. **b** (as title). **c** (w. gen.) right (of action). **d** tradition, accepted usage. **e** authoritative pronouncement or text.

indubitata scripturarum ~ate Aldh. *VirgP* 5; ecclesiarum ordinatio in vestrae apostolicae ~atis pendet arbitrio Eddi *Wilf.* 29; lectorem admonemus trimoda ratione computum temporis esse discretum..et ipsa quidem ~ate bifarie divisa: humana videlicet ut Olympiadas quattuor annorum..celebrari; ..divina autem, ut septima die Sabbatum agi Bede *TR* 2; litteras..magna ~ate atque eruditione plenas *Id. HE* II 19; memoravi..~atis tuae, qua inter homines es Christus Dei Folcard *J. Bev. prol.*; dubitandum non est, quamvis hoc ~as divina aperte non pronunciet Anselm (*Cur D.* 16) II 119; rerum inclite gestarum memorabilis ~as Gir. *TH intr.* p. 4; Johanni de S. ..Osenie ~ate vestra commoranti Ad. Marsh *Ep.* 19; **1280** ~ate ordinaria..canonice assignamus *Reg. Ebor.* 71; **1293** ~ate sua propria feofavit..filium suum de..tenemento *SelPlMan* 166; ita ut que fidei sunt intellectum nostrum..non convincant..; sed propter ~atem ecclesie creduntur Lutterell *Vis. Beatif.* 92v; **1344** formam..authoritate apostolica roboratam *Pri. Cold.* 31; s**1394** crucem..per authoritatem domini regis et Parliamenti..erectam *Croyl. Cont. B.* 492; s**1454** peciit autoritate Parliamenti illud manerium sibi.. restitui *Reg. Whet.* I 137; **1549** articuli..contra negantes authoritatem concilii generalis in decernendis dogmatibus *Conc. Scot.* II 120; **1580** repudio quascunque peregrinas jurisdictiones, potestates, celsitudines, praeeminentias et authoritates *StatOx* 416. **b** a**786** litterae ~atis tuae, quas ..ad nos direxisti (Botwin) *Ep. Bonif.* 131. **c** data sibi ordinandi episcopos ~ate a pontifice Bede *HE* II 8. **d** hoc ~ate magis quam ratione valet Aldh. *PR* 122; Graeci et Romani, quorum in hujusmodi disciplinis potius quam Hispanorum ~as sequi consuevit Bede *TR* 35; nil.. aliud videtur mihi esse vera ~as nisi rationis virtute reperta veritas et a sanctis patribus ob posteritatis utilitatem litteris commendata Eriug. *Per.* 513B; c**798** hic si..queritur ..ratio, non est ambigua; si ~as, non est incerta Alcuin *Ep.* 132; ratione sola, ~atis adulatione seclusa, audire desidero Adel. *QN* 76. **e** unde dicimus hanc ~atem potius intelligendam sic.. J. Cornw. *Eul.* 1070; facile est respondere ~atibus que viderentur dicere contraria S. Langton *Quaest.* f. 171; videtur ex ~atibus Augustini diligenter inspectis Gros. 133; sicut patet in illa longa ~ate tercio hujus scripta Bradw. *CD* 172B.

auctoritative, w. (ultimate) authority.

aliquo modo aliter operatur Pater quo modo non operatur Filius, quia ~e Duns *Sent.* I xv 1. 4; hoc..~e et judicialiter judicare..spectat ad summum pontificem in consilio sapiencium Ockham *Pol.* I 59; absolvitur muliebris sexus ne ~e possit docere Netter *DAF* I 374.

auctoritativus, authoritative.

unde 1 Tim. vi 17 'divitibus' inquit 'hujus seculi precipe': ecce ~a potestas Wycl. *Civ. Dom.* I 139 (cf. *id. Ver.* I 406: contendimus de ~a potestate); istud est preceptum pocius executivum illius quod primo statutum est quam ~um Lyndw. 11c.

auctorium v. auctarium.

auctorizabilis, (able to be) made authoritative, authorized.

esset omnis scriptura sacra..~is a scriba Wycl. *Ver.* I 111; talis dotacio..utrimque est a tota trinitate ~is et fundabilis in scriptura *Id. Eccl.* 300; *worthy*, augustus, autenticus, autorozabilis (*sic*), commendabilis *CathA*.

auctorizabiliter, in a way that can be sanctioned by authority.

aut quis in loco tali ~er facit sibi celebrari divina, et talis eciam irregularitatem non evadet? ..tantum enim vel plus peccat autorizans sicut et faciens J. Acton *Comment.* 7t.

auctorizare, to make authoritative, ratify, approve. **b** (w. acc. and inf.). **c** to canonize. **d** to authorize (a person), invest w. authority.

s**965** papa J. hanc ipsam paginam Rome in generali synodo ~avit W. Malm. *GR* II 150; quamquidem historiam ..ipse..pro amore martiris..~avit, ~atamque in ecclesia Dei legi cantarique instituit Eadmer *Anselm* I 30 p. 54; **1285** obligaciones..ratificare, confirmare et ~are *RGasc* II 246; s**1306** responsum est cardinali, ..presente domino rege et responsum authorizante W. Guisb. 371; annon et ipsam sentenciam..autor ipse..fidei fideliter autorisat? Bradw. *CD* 708E; tunc capitulum Bonifacianum 'super cathedram' non fuit sacro instante et approbante concilio roboratum et ~atum Conway *Def. Mend.* 1340 (8 pp. *after* 1428); **1369** ad..permutaciones hujusmodi quascunque auctorisandum *Reg. Heref.* 55; c**1363** quod nescimus..utrum [liber Enos] fuit a Spiritu Sancto ~atus (Wycl. *v. Kyl.*) *Ziz.* 455; **1382** ~are incarceracionem hominis propter hoc quod facit ut debet foret opus demonii meridiani (*Propos. J. Wicliff*) Wals. *HA* II 52; **1395** quod quando..ecclesie fuerunt ~ate per appropriacionem diversis locis, fides, spes et caritas ceperunt fugere (*Concl. Lollard.*) *Ziz.* 360; **1408** ad.. eleccionum negocia..inventa rite facta..approbandum et ~andum *Eng. Clergy* 190; in largicione elemosine Christiane autorizare scrutinium Netter *DAF* I 520; s**1435** una cum prefatis transumptis..collacionatis, ascultatis ac decreti nostri interposicione ~atis Amund. II 56; **1549** ne tales infeudaciones..per ordinarios vel capitula admittantur vel authorisentur *Conc. Scot.* II 94. **b** **1442** studium Cadomense..ad Dei laudem..erectum..fuisse vestra beatitudo auctorisare et approbare dignata est Bekynton I 123. **c** s**1174** B. Bernardus..a domino papa..sollempniter auctorisatur et in cathologo memoriam ejus scribi auctoritate apostolica constituitur *Chr. Melrose* 87. **d** cambiatores..monete non ad hoc ~ati..omnia sua catalla..regi forisfaciunt *Fleta* 33; tirones scholastici soliditatem doctrine..non attingunt, quantumcunque..~entur habitibus R. Bury *Phil.* 9. 154; s**1397** suplico quod me..~are dignemini Ad. Usk 12; **1486** viros..quos..rex Scotorum per literas commissionis sue ~are voluerit ad veniendum..in hoc regnum *RScot* 471b; **1494** per procuratorem suum plene et sufficienter in hac parte auctorisatum *DCCant* R 400b.

auctorizatio, recognition as authoritative. **b** authorization (of a person or an act), ultimate responsibility (for).

de ~one libri Job patet prima Cor. iii..; et B. Jacobus v cap. transmittit nos ad scripturam Job tamquam autenticam Wycl. *Ver.* I 222. **b** ad objecta que arguunt de autorizacione peccatoris a Deo et quomodo Deus non sit prima causa peccati, quia non est prima causa imputabilis ad culpam.. Bradw. *CD* 304A; cum ergo ad omnem speciem naturalis accionis ordinatur a Deo potencia et appetitus ad intendendum naturaliter pro illa complenda, patet quod si aliqua talis esset per se mala, talis malicie auctorisacio redundaret in auctorem nature, quod est impossibile Wycl. *Ente Praed.* 158; **1384** quod..predecessores vestri.. premissa, permutacionum [sc. beneficiorum] ~onibus et fructuum beneficiorum percepcionibus duntaxat exceptis, in diversis diocesibus..exercuerunt *Conc.* III 190; **1441** composicionem..auctoritate nostra ordinaria admittimus, auctorizamus et confirmamus..; quibus..factis.., partes predicte ~onem, confirmacionem et decreta nostra predicta..admiserunt *Reg. Cant.* I 314.

auctrix [LL], authoress, originator (f.), source.

regina gravis hujusce scismatis auctrix Frith. 820; [seditio] ~ix et genetrix..malorum *V. Osw.* 448; cum interna gratia, que puritatis ejusdem ~ix et donatrix est in cenobio Ad. Scot. *Serm.* 403A; mee salutis ~ix [sc. amica]..in januis est Map *NC* III 2 p. 114; a**1230** divina pietas que fraterne dilectionis est ~ix et amatrix *Ch. Sal.* 214 (cf. *Cust. Cant.* 294); **1239** cum Roma sit caput nostri et ~ix imperii (*Lit. Imp.*) M. Par. *Maj.* III 546; luna..est autrix humidorum Wycl. *Ver.* III 151.

auctuario, bird (identified w. corn-bunting).

secundus passer magnus ~o dicitur et in summis arborum ramis plerumque solet sedere: hunc..Anglorum..buntingam..esse suspicor Turner *Av.* 71.

auctumn- v. autumn-. aucturatio v. auctoratio. auctus v. augere.

aucubaculare, to 'batfowl', catch birds after dark.

batfowlyn, ~o *PP* (*ed.* 1865) (cf. ib.: *batfowlere*, ~ator ..*batefowlyng*, ~atus).

aucula [cf. aucella], gosling.

gallinis pabula, anatibus, aucis et ~is [*gl.*: *oysuns*] Neckam *Ut.* 110; **1266** per ix^{xx} ~as emptas, cum liberacione custodum *ExchScot* 17; **1296** item iiij aucas, ij anceres..et x aucilas *Anc. Ext.* 81/1 m. 2; **1308** de xv ~is receptis de exitu *Doc. Bec* 168; **1388** de precio..iij aucarum precii xij d., xviij ~arum precii xviij d. *LTRAcEsch.* 10 r. 1*d.* (= *IMisc* 332/25: xviij auce juniores, precii capitis j d.); hec ~a, A. *geslyng* WW.

aucupamentum v. acculpamentum. 1 aucupare v. acculpare.

2 aucupare, ~ari [CL], to catch birds, go fowling. **b** (fig.). **c** to seek, search for.

juvenis miles..studio captus ~andi W. Cant. *Mir. Thom.* V 20; Upton 188 (v. aucupativus a). **b** excussi dumos; aucupat alter aves *Babio* 184. **c** aurum assidue intra muros ~antes Gir. *EH* II 36.

aucuparia, fowling place.

1388 ibidem [sunt piscaria] et †auceparia *IMisc* 239/36.

aucuparius, fowler.

1279 Stephanus ~ius *Hund.* II 344; **14..** (v. aucupator a).

aucupatio, (right of or place for) fowling or hawking. **b** (fig.) trap.

815 cum omnibus, ..piscationibus, ~onibus, aquis, mariscis *CS* 353; [insule Camarge] Rhodano..clauduntur, ..piscationibus, ..venationibus..et ~onibus..incomparabiles Gerv. Tilb. II 3; **12..** quod decime de..venacione, ~one et aliis hujusmodi integre persolvantur *Conc. Scot.* II 21; **1251** assignant liberam ~onem et venacionem in communis villarum *Cart. Harrold* p. 21; **1314** tenendam.. cum omnibus..aisiamentis..in ~onibus, venacionibus, nemoribus et piscariis *Inchaffray* 115; s**1344** rex se dedit solaciis et ~onibus versus partes Suthfolchie Ad. Mur. 160; s**1371** [Robertus II] in venacionibus et ~onibus multum delectabatur *Plusc.* X 1; ~o, A. *fowlynge* WW; **1582** piscaciones, ~ones..ac omnia alia..privilegia..manerio pertinencia *Pat* 1234 m. 39. **b** ~one, *setunge GlC* A 898; verborum tendicula proponuntur et ~ones sillabarum J. Sal. *Pol.* 579A.

aucupativus, used in hawking. **b** (fig.) 'fishing', intended as bait (for).

tercioli sunt minime volucres ~e pro sexu et natura sua, set ad aucupandum promptissimi Upton 188. **b** plus per opera bona quam per opuscula vana..plausus popularis ~a..et appetitiva Gir. *LS* 419.

aucupator, fowler. **b** seeker, wooer.

1378 J. C. canonicus dicte capelle..est venator et ~or (*Vis. Windsor*) *Conc.* III 133; ~or et aucupatrix et aucuparius idem sunt, A. *fowlers* WW; *a fewler*, auceps, ~or, avicularius, aucupiscus *CathA*. **b** s**1043** Æthelstanus Rameseie abbas, ..vir aliene affectionis industrius ~or *Chr. Rams.* 155; s**1173** vidit rex senior..quam stulte egerit, ..minus attendens quod novarum rerum ~ores regem proclivius sequerentur juniorem W. Newb. II 27; utinam.. adeo divinitatis amator sicut et vanitatis ~or Gir. *Retract.* 427.

aucupatrix v. aucupator a.

aucupatus, fowling, hawking.

in venatu ut decebat et in ~u edoctus G. Mon. III 6; *a fewlinge*, aucupacio, ~us *CathA*.

aucupictor v. acupictor. aucupiscus v. aucupator a.

aucupitium, fowling, hawking.

s**1194** asserebant eum, omne episcopale officium vilipendentem, ~io, venationi et aliis curis militaribus esse deditum R. Howd. III 230; c**1300** quod..parochiani.. decimas..persolvant..de proventibus..bestiarum, warenarum, ~ii, ortorum *Conc. Syn.* 1390; hodie multi milites lasciviis vacant, ociis et ~iis sunt effeminati Upton 12.

aucupium, (right of or place for) fowling.

auceps qui ~ium exercet Aldh. *PR* 114; **791** (14c) cum.. campis, silvis, pascuariis, ~iis *CS* 262; **10..** ~ium, *fuglung*, ..*yltwist* WW; commisit rex..cuidam Radulfo volucres ~ii sui W. Cant. *Mir. Thom.* VI 147; onustus..xenniis equorum, canum, accipitrum et omnium que venatui vel ~io prestantiora videntur Map *NC* I 11; s**1272** cum [rex] juxta quandam ripariam falconum ~io se exerceret Trevet 282; hoc aucipium, *a hawkynge* WW.

audacia [CL], daring, courage. **b** audacity, presumption. **c** (w. gen.). **d** (w. inf.).

invocate Christum ut audatiam adhibeat G. Mon. VI 2; [apri] exigui.., nec minus ~ia et animositate quam corporis compositione degeneres Gir. *TH* I 24; Dominus..ab eis [Gallis] subtraxit..~iam ex incussione timoris de terribilibus..plagis in stragibus hominum Elmh. *Hen. V* 74. **b** strofosam muliebris ~iae muscipulam parvi pendens Aldh. *VirgP* 53; ut superbiam eorum dissipet et conturbet ~iam Bede *HE* IV 3 p. 211; impudenti ~ia contempsi vos Anselm (*Med.* 2) III 81. **c** s**1311** cernentes quod eorum paciencia..Petro [de Gavestone] ~iam malignandi prestabat Trokelowe 68; **1545** ne facilitas pene audatiam tribuat delinquendi *Conc. Scot.* I cclxiv. **d** **1390** concepta ..fiducia michi parit ~iam vobis scribere *FormOx* 238.

audacitas, daring, courage. **b** audacity, presumption. **c** encouragement (*cf. audatio*).

gentes..tante audacie et ~atis ut nudi cum armatis congredi non vereantur Gir. *DK* I 8; satis tibi [sc. Bruto] inest de fortitudine, de decore, de vigore, de ~ate *Eul. Hist.* II 206. **b 681** (12c) ut nulla..regalis ~as..contra decretum nostrum confringere temptaverit *CS* 58. **c 1356** in ipsorum operariorum..perniciosum exemplum et ad confortacionem et ~atem eis exibendas *SelCKB* VI 110.

audacter [CL], **~iter,** bravely. **b** presumptuously, w. effrontery.

coenubialis militiae pugiles frontem vexillo crucis armatam ~iter aemulorum agminibus offerentes Aldh. *VirgP* 11; ~ter coram eis processit, vultu intrepido palam affirmans omnia..fore vera *V. Ric. II* 51; quasi spiritum malignum ~ter alloquendo locutus est Elmh. *Hen. V* 16. **b** audet atrox sanctam, spurco flammatus amore, / audacter cellam stolidis irrumpere plantis Aldh. *VirgV* 2235; hostis antiqui..malitia..ad summa dignitatis culmina..provectos ~ius aggreditur Gir. *TH* I 22.

†**audatio,** encouragement (*cf. audacitas* c).

1344 post feloniam predictam factam in ~onem, consolacionem et confortacionem..malefactorum *SelCKB* VI 37.

audax [CL], brave, venturesome. **b** bold, presumptuous. **c** used w. courage, warlike.

setigero rursus constans audacior apro Aldh. *Aen.* 100. 10; cum larbam et mascam miles non horreat audax *Id. VirgV* 2859; valde ~ax [AS: *þryste*] fuisti tunc Ælf. *Coll.* 93; quo fortior sive audatior nullus..aderat G. Mon. I 15; vir bellicosus et ~ax in gente sua Gir. *EH* I 6. **b 1221** clamari fecerunt in villa quod non esset ita ~ax aliquis qui ipsi abbati..aliquam mercandisam venderet, super forisfacturam x s. *SelPlCrown* 115. **c** oliva / concilians, cornus venatrix, fraxinus audax J. Exon. *BT* I 509.

1 audentia [CL], daring, courage.

videntes alii Apostolum in vinculis non timentem verbum Dei loqui, abundantiorem ~iam sumebant sine timore loqui verbum Dei Lanfr. *Comment. Paul.* (*Phil.* i 14) 308; venaticum quendam..~ia..supra communem canum facultatem ..insignem Boece 97.

2 audentia v audientia 2b.

audēre [CL], (w. inf. or acc.) to dare, venture. **b** to presume, make so bold. **c** (w. inanimate subj.).

ausus, *gedyrstig GlC* A 900; neque..in proelium venire ~ebat Bede *HE* I 34; non est tam aspera hiemps ut ~eam [AS: *þæt ic durre*] latere domi Ælf. *Coll.* 90; quomodo fuisti ausus [*hu wære þu dyrstig*] jugulare aprum? *Ib.* 93; **1271** que non audivit (*sic*) nec potuit contradicere eum *SelCCoron* 30 (cf. ib. 10: non ausus fuit intrare); foras suas fores exire non auderunt (*sic*) Strecche *Hen. V* 166. **b 597** omnes qui ad fidem veniunt admonendi sunt ne tale aliquid ~eant perpetrare (*Lit. Papae*) Bede *HE* I 27 p. 51; Aldh. *VirgV* 2234 (v. audacter b); Osb. *V. Elph.* 131 (v. audientia 1a); **c1090** defendo ne aliquis sit ausus ei..inde super hoc aliquam injuriam facere *Regesta* p. 135; unum tale directivum..habeo, quale non plures, ~eo dicere, nostre gentis chronicatores previi habuerunt Elmh. *Cant.* 309. **c** famulas..sacratas.. / quas prius exusti non audent urere torres Aldh. *VirgV* 2334; sedentem ad tumbam sancti infirmitas..in tantum..aufugit ut nec secunda die..neque umquam exinde ~eret contingere Bede *HE* III 12; **s1091** majus quoque scelus furor ventorum ausus, tectum ecclesie ..levavit W. Malm. *GR* IV 324 (= *Eul. Hist.* III 50: †ausius).

2 to venture: **a** (w. *ut*); **b** (w. gen. of gd.); **c** (w. *ad* and gdv.).

a neque Romani ausi sunt ut venirent Brittaniam Nen. *HB* 167. **b 1234** non fuit ausus veniendi ad dominum regem *CurR* XV 1126; **1235** non fuit ausa exeundi *Ib.* 1438. **c 1344** ipsi non fuerunt ausi ad predictos felones attachiandos *SelCKB* VI 38 (cf. ib.: si ipsi ballivi sint ausi ad eos arestandos).

3 (p. ppl. as sb. n.) venture, enterprise.

ulciscebatur digne pro talibus ausis Aldh. *VirgV* 1841.

audibilis [LL], audible. **b** auditory.

musica alia vertitur circa ~e, alia circa visibile; ..que vero est circa ~ia habet partes duas Bacon *Maj.* I 237; *hereabylle*, ~is *CathA*; **1503** alta et ~i voce *FormA* 339. **b** a fantastica [cellula] oritur nervus obtalgicus, id est ~is, qui bifurcatus tendit ad utramque aurem Ric. Med. *Micr. Anat.* 217.

audientia, hearing, earshot. **b** audience, assembly of listeners. **c** hearing (granted to petitioner), audience, interview. **d** (acad.) cursory lecture.

ut nemo in ~ia illius obscenum verbum proferre.. auderet Osb. *V. Elph.* 131; **c1148** testibus subscriptis, in quorum ~ia hec carta facta fuit, lecta et concessa *Cart. Sallay* 2; **s1244** hec cum ad ~iam domini regis et suorum magnatum pervenissent M. Par. *Maj.* IV 399; **1294** ad ~iam apostolatus nostri pervenit quod (*Lit. Papae*) *Reg. Cant.* I 7; ~ia, A. *an hurynge* WW. **b c1090** quae..in totius conventus ~ia legantur Anselm (*Ep.* 136) III 281; naute] accersitis..fratribus ecclesie quid inter navigandum acciderat..seriatim in communi proferunt ~ia Ketel *Mir. J. Bev.* 290; narrationem audivi de..conviciis ad eum dictis, que, si mihi nihil habenti in tanta ~ia dicta fuissent, semimortuum me ducerem H. Hunt. *CM* 1; **s1162** sub ~ia cardinalium in consistorio postulatione facta Diceto *YH* I 307; **s1175** coram legato..in publica ~ia sunt protestati Gir. *RG* I 8; **s1385** in eodem..Parliamento in communi ~ia omnium Dominorum et Communitatis rex..fecit proclamari *Eul. Hist. Cont.* III 361; concionantur ergo symbola, secundum illos, sed ~iae surdae Gardiner *CC* 140. **c 1218** audito..literarum tenore et data eis ~ia petierunt.. *Pat* 183; apud Edinburgh versus regem [Willelmum]..venientes, ..~iam pecierunt *Plusc.* VI 40. **d a1350** lecciones cursorias, quas vocant ~iam abusive *StatOx* 23.

2 (leg.) hearing, audience. **b** (court of) audience (papal). **c** (eccl.). **d** (w. ref. to royal Council or Chancery). **e** (Gasc.). **f** (Fr.).

a1350 cause de atrocibus delictis, que requirunt penam carceris et bannicionem alicujus magistri.., ~iam cancellarii requirunt simul et magistrorum *Stat. Cantab.* 321. **b s1206** quum [indulgentie] in publica ~ia legerentur, ..omnibus contradixi. ..et, quum in crastino ad ~iam contradictarum convenissemus, ..dixi.. *Chr. Evesham* 199; eadem die qua lecta fuit litera in ~ia, qua decreverat dominus Innocentius IV octo sentencias Eccleston *Adv. Min.* 118; **s1451** referendarius domini pape, auditor aud[i]encie contradictarum Stone *Chr.* 52; **1456** ad..domini pape ~iam..appellare et non ad alterius judicis infra regnum ~iam *StatOx* 278. **c c1202** presentiens eum velle apellare ad ~iam domini nostri decani Linc' (*DC Norw.*) *Becket to Langton* 197; **1344** que causa vertitur..in ~ia domini [archiepiscopi] *Lit. Cant.* II 277; **1384** pro eo quod ..archidiaconus [Richemond'] de justicia eidem W. .. facienda defecit, ..idem W. ..appellavit inde ~ie ipsius archiepiscopi [Ebor.] *PlRCP* 495 r. 312; **1415** magistro W. Lyndewod..nostre ~ie causarum et negociorum auditore *Reg. Cant.* II 35; **1416** in querele negocio ad nos et nostram ~iam..devoluto *Ib.* I 147; auditor curiae ~iae Cantuariensis habet..consimilem cum..officiali de Arcubus jurisdictionem, fuitque ab antiquo..vicarius in spiritualibus generalis..archiepiscopi; eoque intuitu ad eum ulterius spectat omnis..jurisdictio..cujuscunque dioecesis vacantis ..que ad ipsos episcopos sedibus plenis pertinuit *Praxis* 3. **d 1426** cum..ab eadem sentencia..ad nos et ~iam nostram legitime appellaverit *Pat* 418 m. 14 (cf. *Plusc.* VIII 18: ad ~iam regis Anglie, quasi ad superlativam ~iam, ..appellabat). **e 1304** scrivaniam de ~ia in castro.. Burdegale *RGasc* III 424. **f 1188** rex Francorum..in communi ~ia recognovit quod..custodia abbatie..ad me pertinet *Act. Hen. II* I 193; **1277** cum..ad vestram ~iam se assereret appellasse *RGasc* II 38; ut..omnes isti senatores [Parisienses] cessacionem ~ie in Parleamento publice proclamarent *Plusc.* VII 17.

3 audit (of account).

1327 quousque fuerint intendentes ~ie compotorum terrarum forisfactarum *LTRMem* 99 r. 121*d*.

audire [CL], to hear (sound, speech, or speaker). **b** (absol. w. adv.). **c** (absol.) to listen, give ear. **d** (w. inf.) to hear tell or sim. **e** to hear (a document), esp. as witness. **f** (pr. ppl.) witness by ear. **g** (p. ppl.) current (of words). **h** (?) (p. ppl. as sb. f.) sense of hearing.

qui cupit instanter sitiens audire docentes Aldh. *Aen.* 30. 6; ~ita..dogmatistae doctrina *Id. VirgP* 46; ~iendi verbi Dei causa veniebant Bede *HE* III 26; discipulos qui eum..docentem ~ierunt Eriug. *Per.* 530A; aliquando ~io signum [AS: *ic gehyre cnyll*] et surgo Ælf. *Coll.* 103; **1166** ~ivi preceptum vestrum in Herefordia *RBExch* 280 (cf. *EHR* VI 427); ~imus ex omni parte sonos sine fractione et sine reflexione ut proferens ~it vocem propriam Bacon *Maj.* II 56; ~iens voces Anglicanas *V. Ric.* II 12. **b s1214** non video pure; mihi nil sapit; audio dure (*Versus*) *G. S. Alb.* I 247. **c** dixit: "~ite vos amici mei" *DB* I 177. **d** quia..crebro eum ~ierit de mirandis..narrare Bede *HE* III 13; regnum caelorum de quo praedicari..~ivi *Ib.* V 12; **1201** ~ivit dici quod idem R. disracionavit quandam terram *SelPlCrown* 43; **1223** dicit quod ~ivit dici quod mortuus est *CurR* XI 452; **1309** nunquam ~ivit loqui de talibus *Conc.* II 339. **e** testante wapent[ac] qui brevem regis inde vidit et ~ivit *DB* I 373b; **c 1147** notum sit omnibus legentibus vel ~ientibus litteras has *Cart. Sallay* 1; **1189** debet dim. m. .. pro ~iendo cyrographo *Pipe* 140; **1228** dicit quod nescit, quia cartam ejus nunquam ~ivit *Feod. Durh.* 242. **f 1220** quod hoc verum sit probat per quendam ~ientem et alium videntem *SelPlCrown* 125; **1269** prefatus N. habet hoc ~ientes et videntes A. B. C. *CBaron* 75. **g** hoc..observandum..si [verbis utamur] parum ~itis, ut notabiliora sint quam ut quid eis designetur facile sit ignorare Balsh. *AD* 113. **h** resumpta †~ita, caput erexit *Hist. Meriadoci* 376.

2 to hear (of), learn by hearing (w. acc. and inf., indir. qu., *quod* or *quia*). **b** (absol. w. adv.). **c** (w. *de*). **d** (w. obj.).

a680 ~itum..et..compertum nobis est quod sacerdotes ..minime concordent Aldh. *Ep.* 4 p. 482; **706** cur..percurram, ~ite *Ib.* 9 (12) p. 502; ~ivit ab eo..qualia essent quae..videret Bede *HE* V 12; hanc..tonsuram, quam plenam esse rationis ~imus *Ib.* 21; **747** ~ivimus quia.. personam hominis non timeas Bonif. *Ep.* 74; memorat se a B. Theodoro..audisse..periculosam esse quartam lunam in minuendo sanguine Folcard *J. Bev.* 5. **b 799** addatur ..ut fratres..sub manu vestra..secundum sanctitatem.. vivant; nec ego aliter ~ivi Alcuin *Ep.* 184 p. 310. **c s1160** ~ito de morte Theobaldi *Flor. Hist.* II 76; **s1272** ~iens..de morte patris *Meaux* II 161. **d** virtutes sanctorum quos.. clariores nosse vel ~ire poterat Bede *HE* II 1 p. 76; ad nuper ~ita caelestis regni gaudia *Ib.* IV 2; postquam.. Æthelbald..obitum..Guthlaci ~ivit Felix *Guthl.* 52; **742** majorem laetitiam..nobis non ~ivimus Bonif. *Ep.* 50 p. 81; ~ita..seriatim..exilii..causa Gir. *EH* I 1; ~ivimus demones incubos et succubos et concubitus eorum periculosos Map *NC* II 12.

3 (leg.) to hear: **a** (pleas or sim., esp. w. ref. to oyer and terminer); **b** (parties); **c** (judgement or sim.).

a 1202 ~ita querela sua in comitatu..misit vic. legales homines ad domum suam *SelPlCrown* 26; **1237** (v. atterminare 1b); **c1250** cancellarius..per se tantum, si voluerit, causas scolarium ~iat universas *Stat. Cantab.* 197; **1252** omnes contenciones inter eos motas in suspenso teneat usque adventum Roberti W., cui rex precepit quod eas ~iat et terminet secundum legem et consuetudinem partium illarum *Cl* 230; **1253** ad placita..tam ad terras et tenementa quam ad coronam regis pertinencia ~ienda et terminanda *Pat* 64 m. 16*d*.; **1278** ballivi domini regis venire solebant ad curiam baronum et ibidem sedere et ~ire placita *CoramR* 37 r. 14*d*.; **1281** quod..plenam habeant potestatem ordinandi, disponendi, ~iendi, arbitrandi et finaliter terminandi *State Tri. Ed. I* 12; **1306** coram justiciariis nostris ad felonias [et] transgressiones in diversis comitatibus regni nostri contra pacem nostram factas ~iendas et terminandas assignatis (*Breve Regis*) *MGL* II 152; **14..** ~ita querela *Reg. Brev.* 114 (cf. ib. 149); **s1468** in guihalda civitatis Londonie ad magnam sessionem de ~iendo et terminando W. Worc. *Ann.* 790. **b c1250** litigatores non ~iantur exceptis in universitate rerum inmobilium possessoribus *Stat. Cantab.* 209; **1313** *il dit qe il fut clerek* et non potuit ~iri *Eyre Kent* 154. **c 1196** dies datus est..fratribus..et comiti..ad ~iendum judicium suum *CurR* I 24; ipse J. sit ibi ad illam electionem ~iendam *Ib.* 23; **1198** dies datus est..ad ~iendum recordum et judicium *Ib.* 41; **1224** dies datus est eis de ~iendo judicio *CurR* XI 1671; **1290** datus est dies ad proximam curiam ad ~iendum judicium et recordum suum *SelPlMan* 35; haec assignatio ad ~iendum sententiam facta in praesentia partis habet eandem vim..atque monitio ad interessendum *Praxis* 233.

4 (acad.) to study (a subject), attend (a course of lectures).

apices juris intelligere volens ~iat Codicem Justiniani.. celestem paginam ~ire volens..~iat tam Vetus Instrumentum quam Novum (Neckam *Sac.*) *Med. Sci.* 375; **a1231** ita quod saltem unicam lectionem ordinarie ~ierit singulis diebus in scolis suis *StatOx* 82; **a1275** inhibemus.. ne aliqui cursorie legant neque ~iant de hiis que ad jus civile vel canonicum pertinent illis horis *Ib.* 109; **a1350** ita quod..scolares possint ~ire cursus suos *Ib.* 28; **1409** jurabunt..libros logicales..se leccionatim integre ~ivisse *Ib.* 200; **1408** an aliqui monachi ejusdem monasterii ~eant (*sic*) leges vel phisicam *Eng. Clergy* 298; **1421** scolares in jure canonico debent ~ire Decretales complete *Reg. Cant.* III 72.

5 (eccl.) to hear: **a** (mass); **b** (confession).

a 1199 cum ipsi post missam ~itam equitarent versus forestam *CurR* I 91; venit rumor..quod cancellarius vellet transire per S. Ædmundum apud nos missam in crastino ~iturus Brakelond 135; **s1214** cum..in missis ~iendis fuissent occupati W. Newb. *Cont.* 516; **s1271** in ecclesia Fratrum Minorum..missarum solempnia ~ientes *Leg. Ant. Lond.* 134; [Henricus VII] attente ~iebat quotidie binas ternasve missas quas vocamus P. Verg. XXVI 617. **b 1214** confessiones mulierum ~iantur in propatulo quantum ad visum hominum, non quantum ad auditum *Conc. Syn.* 32; **1221** quod in nullo jura dicte ecclesie, vel ~iendo confessionem parochianorum..vel divina eis celebrando.. diminuet *Ch. Sal.* 116; **1228** sacerdos de A. ~it confessiones iiij villarum *Feod. Durh.* 228; **s1300** archiepiscopus..octo Predicatoribus et octo Minoribus tantum dedit licenciam predicandi et confessiones ~iendi cum per rectores vel sacerdotes ecclesiarum ad hoc officium sint vocati *Ann. Worc.* 546; **c1520** potestates et facultates ~iendi et faciendi confessiones *Conc. Scot.* I cclxxiii.

6 to check (a text) by ear.

1411 Decretales glosate et bene ~ite *Lit. Cant.* III 121.

7 to audit (accounts).

1216 mandamus vobis quod..~iatis compotum civium.. de Dublin' de areragiis finium..que nobis debuerunt *Pat* 12; **c1226** nunc circa festum S. Mich. instat tempus compoti ~iendi (*AncC* VI 133) *RL* I 294; **1238** rex mandavit baronibus quod..compotum ipsius G. plene ~iant et terminent *LTRMem* 12 r. 6*d*.; **1336** quod..dentur auditores compoti quinque..qui raciocinia dictorum custodum..~iant *StatOx* 135; **a1350** duobus procuratoribus hujusmodi scrutinium ~ituris *Stat. Cantab.* 317 (cf. ib. 319: ad..finalem compotum ~iendum); **1357** quod compotum..~iatis et quod natura compoti requirit..faciatis *RScot* 801a; **1451** receptori..pro expensis suis usque Dunelm' pro compoto suo ~iendo et terminando *Ac. Durh.* 189.

auditio [CL], hearing. **b** (acad.) study. **c** audit (of account).

exeunt..juvenes..in ~onem vel ascultationem, ut Theudus.., qui furtim accedens ad domum Meilerii audivit intro unum ex sedentibus..dicentem.. Map *NC* II 23 p. 92; **1259** ad ~onem nostram jam pervenit quod.. *Cl* 427; visio, ~o, olfaccio, gustacio et taccio vocantur actus sensuum particularium Wycl. *Act.* 1. **b 1311** quilibet socius infra septennium sue ~onis in scolis opponat *Mun AcOx* 89; **a1350** statuto super ~one theologie..edito *StatOx* 49; **1407** cursoria ~o..alicujus libri Metaphisice *Ib.* 193; **1409** ita tamen quod in primo biennio..hujusmodi ~onem leccionariam..aggredi non presumant *Ib.* 200. **c 1334** pro ~one compotorum servientum *Ac. Durh.* 523; **1345** habeat archidiaconus..computi ~onem *MunAcOx* 150; **1397** in expensis garcionum..auditorum compotorum.., qui continuaverant ~onem usque ad finem Scaccarii *ExchScot* 432; **1412** ut patet per parcellas Johannis B. in presencia.. custodis inde examinati super ~onem compoti istius probatas *Rect. Adderbury* 5; **1549** racio omnium reddatur prout ad id admonendi sunt tam in confirmacionibus quam in ~one computorum *Conc. Scot.* II 111.

†**audititidestos,** (*s. dub.*; *cf. ALMA* XXV 87).

dulsos coenosi lichinos audititidestos Frith. 1118.

auditivus, auditory.

in tali mixto aere complantato, et non in aere alieno contento in spongiosioribus, subjectatur vis anime ~a Wycl. *Log.* III 84.

auditor [CL], hearer. **b** disciple.

[contionatores] attonitis ~oribus ignarisque auscultatoribus arcana mentis ipsorum recludentes Aldh. *VirgP* 27; ~oribus sive lectoribus hujus historiae Bede *HE pref.* p. 5; non sis auditor tantum legis sed amator D. Bec. 26; omnis ~or quod ab alio celandum accipit amico alii secure committit Map *NC* I 12. **b** doctores suos vicissim ~ores sui faciebat Bede *HE* IV 22.

2 (leg.) hearer (of pleas or sim.): **a** (papal); **b** (eccl.); **c** (common law); **d** (Parliamentary).

a 1255 monachi Winton' vos..coram domino papa vel ~oribus suis in curia Romana trahunt in causam *Pat* 69 m. 5*d.*; **1256** contradictorum ~or *Pat* 70 m. 16*d.*; **1279** procurator..sequenti die, cum in prima ~oris copiam habere non posset, dictum..revocavit *Mon. Hib. & Scot.* 118b; **s1316** electus fuit J. ..in papam, qui fuit..episcopus.. Avinoniensis et ~or palacii Ad. Mur. 24; **s1319** Lucas cardinalis sex ~ores majores de palacio consuluit qualiter esset procedendum *Hist. Roff.* 359; **1349** patefacta justicia questionum mearum..apud palacii apostolici ~ores Ric. Armagh *AP* 20; **s1361** cui [sedi Lond'] papa providit de magistro S. de Southburia, tunc ~ore in curia Romana J. Reading 178; **s1378** [papam] elegerunt episcopum Barensem, ~orem causarum *Eul. Hist. Cont.* III 341; **1438** causarum sacri palacii apostolici ~or Bekynton I 57; **s1451** (v. audientia 2b). **b 1399** pro..uno jantaculo facto ~oribus consistorii *Ac. Durh.* 446; **1415** (v. audientia 2c); *Praxis* 3 (v. ib.); coram J. S. ~ore causarum et negociorum ipsius archiepiscopi *Entries* 139. **c** [rex] habet..curiam suam coram ~oribus specialiter a latere regis destinatis.., quibus non conceditur potestas audita terminare sed regi deferre *Fleta* 66; **1291** placita coram ~oribus querelarum apud Westmonasterium *State Tri. Ed. I* 5. **d 1322** coram ~ore peticionum in ultimo Parliamento *Lit. Cant.* I 68.

3 auditor (of accounts).

1277 computavit..prepositus..de manerio de C. de omnibus receptis et expensis per ipsum factis..coram dominis..suppriore [et al.] ~oribus deputatis *Ambrosden* I 405; **1285** si ad curiam venerint, dentur ~ores compoti (2 *Westm.* 11) *StRealm* I 80; **1328** per expensas ~orum compotorum per totum tempus compoti *ExchScot* 118; **1333** admissus est..ad officium ~oris forincecorum compotorum hic in Scaccario *LTRMem* 105 r. 23; **1485** ~oribus hunc compotum audientibus *Comp. Swith.* 298.

auditoriatus, office of (papal) auditor.

1417 coram nobis J. de C. ..officium ~us curie causarum camere apostolice regente *Reg. Cant.* II 128; **1543** per.. dominum J. ..curie causarum camere apostolice generalem ..auditorem..ac suos in ~us hujusmodi officio successores *Form. S. Andr.* II 261.

auditorium [CL], place in which speech can be heard, esp. lecture-hall. **b** parlour (mon.).

~ium, *spræchus* Ælf. *Sup.* 184; in curia..constitutus, in publico ~io verbum hoc indignanter emisit Gir. *EH* I 21; magistrum Mainerium in ~io schole sue Parisius dicentem ..audivi *Id. GE* II 37; qui theologicis vacabat ~iis..in.. Parisiaca civitate Ad. Eyns. *Hug.* V 13 p. 156. **b** silentium teneatur in claustro.., excepto ~ii loco, qui et ab hoc maxime eo censetur nomine quod ibi audiendum sit quid a praeceptore jubeatur *RegulC* 56; **1006** consuetudo docet ~ium habendum in monasterio ut in eo liceat loqui pro necessitate aliqua, quando fratres vacant lectionibus seu post vesperam *Comp. Swith.* 192; cum hostis antiquus dampna sibi in capitulo illata in ~io sibi proponat restitui, rarum ingressum sed necessarium in ~io nostro concedimus (*Inst. Sempr.* 32) *MonA* VI 947 l*; qui levem se exhibet in choro, ..rixantem in capitulo, detrahentem in ~io Ad. Eyns. *Hug.* I 14 p. 43; quando sol est in angulo ultra hostium ~ii communis *Cust. Westm.* 257.

2 audience-hall, court-room: **a** (papal); **b** (eccl.); **c** (Gasc.); **d** council chamber (royal); **e** (fig.).

a 1181 si de his fuerint in ~io nostro convicti, duriorem sententiam reportabunt (*Lit. Papae*) Elmh. *Cant.* 446; **1195** super causa tam difficili vertitur ut..debeat ~io Romane ecclesie reservari (*Lit. Papae*) Diceto *YH* II 130; ea que vel in pape consistorio vel cardinalium ~io.. publice propositi Gir. *Invect.* I *proem.*; **s1331** procurator.. literas revocatorias in ~io publicavit Graystanes 46. **b** pontifex..mox ~ium intrat et sedet ut judicet..; et..ad ~ium hoc fratres suos universos et presertim comprovinciales suos episcopos vocat ut sibi assideant H. Bos. *Thom.* III 14; **1297** causa..in nostro ~io..mota *Reg. Cant.* I 164; **1427** per appellacionem ad dictum..episcopum seu ejus ~ium *Reg. Glasg.* 320. **c 1290** xv li. de exitibus ~ii [regis Burdegale]..eidem..faciatis persolvi *RGasc* II 560. **d 1207** a regalis celsitudinis ~io non est ita lectio divinorum librorum..aliena quin.. (*Lit. Papae*) Gerv. Cant. *app.* II lx; **13..** vos..qui in regis ~io gradum digne precipuum obtinetis (†*Lit. Abbatis*) *Croyl. Cont. A* 108. **e** quasi secretior Dei thalamus et familiare ~ium Spiritus Sancti P. Blois *Serm.* 561D.

3 audience (of students).

1333 aliter..magistri pauperes.., quos colligere oportebit, erunt debito ~io, quod alias habituri essent, frustrati *StatOx* 132.

auditrix, hearer, disciple (f.).

scito te [anima] eorum [sc. seniorum tuorum] ~icem, non judicem Ad. Scot. *Sol.* 851C; Mammea..~ix fuit Origenis *Eul. Hist.* I 329.

auditura, (acad.) attendance at lecture.

1453 habitis lecturis et ~is librorum ad formam determinatorum pertinencium, poterit pro se determinare *MunAcOx* 739.

1 auditus [CL], (sense of) hearing. **b** listening, attention. **c** hearsay. **d** earshot. **e** ear.

auditu surdos et claudos gressibus ornat Aldh. *VirgV* 860; particula capitis quae proprie auris dicitur ex ~u denominatur, quoniam instrumentum ~us est Eriug. *Per.* 481A; ~us, *hlyst* Ælf. *Gl.*; **10..** ~us, *gehirnes* WW; in omni sensuali motu qualitas corporis commutatur, aut accedendo ad aliud, ut in visu et tactu, aut alterius ad ipsum accessu, ut odoratu, gustu, ~u Adel. *QN* 13; quantum aut visus aut etiam ~us extenditur Gir. *TH* I 12; spiritus animalis.. decurrit ad concava aurium et ibi passus ab aere alliso in voce vel sono recurrit ad fantasticam [cellulam], ubi anima de vocibus et sonis judicat, et sic ~us completur Ric. Med. *Micr. Anat.* 217. **b** verbis..horum..diligenter ~um praebebant Bede *HE* III 26; fidei adhibendus est ~us et ~ui praedicatio Lanfr. *Comment. Paul.* (*Rom.* x 17) 140; qui.. ad audienda..miracula patulum converterint ~um *Mir. J. Bev.* C 327; ~us uniuscujusque sit jugiter ad lectorem *Cust. Cant.* 174. **c 1228** de pensione xv s. nichil scit nisi de ~u *Feod. Durh.* 222. **d** proviso..quod nullus ausus sit..stramen lecti sui..movere, sed neque aliquem pannum in ~u excutere *Cust. Westm.* 141. **e 1271** jecit dictum W. ..cum manu sua dextra sub ~um a parte sinistra cum una petra *SelCCoron* 19; **1284** ipsum percussit sub ~u *CourtR Rams.* 156; **1285** percussit dictum J. in capite sub ~u *IMisc.* 44/34.

2 oyer (right to hear). **b** audience (right to be heard).

1224 H. ..vocavit ad warantum W. .., qui presens est et petit ~um carte quam warentizare debeat *BNB* III 11; **1387** petunt ~um brevis predicti et eis legitur *PlRCP* 504 r. 117. **b 1419** ambassiatoribus ipsius regis pro maturando negocio pacis..desideratus..non concedebatur ~us (*Artic. Juris Reg.*) *Foed.* IX 790.

3 audit (of account).

1448 in vino dato confratribus in dono communi in ~u compoti *Ac. Durh.* 87; **1533** tempore ~us compotorum *Comp. Swith.* 223.

2 auditus v. avidotus. audoena v. andena.

Audynaios [Αὐδυναῖος], Greek (or Macedonian) month.

vocatur apud eos [Graecos] ipse..Januarius †Eudymios Bede *TR* 14.

auferre [CL], to take away, remove. **b** to steal. **c** (p. ppl. *ablatus* as sb. n. pl.) seized or confiscated possessions.

ablata, *binumine GlC* A 15 ut nullus posset membris auferre ciclades Aldh. *VirgV* 2263; dolor..de brachio..ablatus est Bede *HE* V 3; lepra..corporis non ~t aciem mentis Eriug. *Per.* 531C; Rannulfus..~t eis unum pratum *DB* I 2; de isto manerio ablatum est unum pratum *Ib.* 2b; tunc ii car[ucatae] terrae, modo i; mare abstulit alia *Ib.* II 311b; qui abstulisti peccata quae attuli nascendo, tolle peccata quae contraxi vivendo Anselm (*Or.* 8) III 29; **1219** maliciose et ut assisam suam ~rent fecerunt eum indictari *CurR* VIII 10; **1254** abstulerunt ab eis..lxiij li. .., eo quod credebant eos..non esse de fidelitate regis *Cl*(*Gasc.*) 290; **1284** rex non concedit nisi quod suum est nec †austat [MS: aufert] ab aliquo curiam suam *SelCKB* 132; tutia..~t ruborem *SB* 42. **b** qui aliquid rerum..ecclesiae..furto ~ret Bede *HE* II 5; **c1070** defendo ne aliquis de prefato jure ecclesie..aliquid ~at vel minuat *Regesta* p. 120; **11..** qui hanc elemosinam meam ~re voluerit, ~at ei Deus regnum vite *Feod. Durh.* 132*n.*; mulier..non afferre quicquam sed ~re parata Gir. *IK* I 2; **1201** cum gladio quodam quem ipse eis abstulit et retinuit *SelPlCrown* 79; **1221** voluit se perjurare ut ~ret ei catalla sua *PlCrGlouc* 6. **c 1213** de ~is autem plenam restitutionem et de damnis recompensationem sufficientem omnibus impendemus tam clericis quam laicis ad hoc negotium pertingentibus (*Pat*) Wend. II 72; **1213** si super dampnis vel ~is..questio fuerit de facto suborta.., ante relaxationem sententie interdicti publice terminabitur *RChart* 193b (cf. *Cl* 154b); **1214** in multis vobis tenemur et maxime de hiis que nobis dedistis tempore interdicti, que nunc ~a vocantur *Pat* 124a; **1217** si..justiciario..satisfeceritis de dampnis et ~is et interceptionibus per vos.. terre nostre illatis, bene placet nobis *Pat* 26; **s1341** pro adjutorio ad tuendum ducatum [Aquitanie] et recuperandum ~a Ad. Mur. 122.

2 (or persons) to carry off, abduct. **b** to withdraw, oust (a tenant). **c** (as euphemism for death).

1220 vi et armis abstulerunt eis..domicellam *SelPlCrown* 135; **s1397** filius..ducis Gloucestrie..per quendam mercatorem..furtim ablatus est et ultra mare provectus *V. Ric. II* 142. **b** unde abstulit rusticum qui ibi manebat *DB* I 30; **1201** abstulerunt ei quendam nativum suum *SelPlCrown* 2. **c** plangere ceu solet ablatum matrona maritum Aldh. *VirgV* 2130; Aidan..de saeculo ablatus Bede *HE* III 14.

auffarium v. affarium.

aufugare [cf. affugare], to drive out, banish.

s1069 rex..Dacos ~avit H. Hunt. *HA* VI 32; **s793** Ethelboldo..successit Bronred.., sed brevi; Offa enim eodem anno ~avit eum Diceto *Chr.* 127*n.*; **s1092** Duncanus.. patruum suum ~avit M. Par. *Min.* I 43; **s1066** militia pulsus et quasi abhominabilis ~atus *Flor. Hist.* I 596.

aufugere [CL; cf. 1 affugere], to run away, flee, escape. **b** (trans.) to escape, avoid.

[virgo] vicit, contempsit et cum palma virginitatis ~it Aldh. *VirgP* 53; noctu eum, ne ~eret, vinciri praecepit Bede *HE* IV 22; terram..non habuisse Herewardum die qua ~it *DB* I 376b; **1195** set ~it et W. B. habet terram per regem *Pipe* 167. **b** [apes] per aethera evolantes..mortalium visus ~iunt Aldh. *VirgP* 26; quo ~is aciem mentis meae? Anselm (*Or.* 7) III 21; **1239** nepos regis Thunyci, non ut baptizaretur sed ut ~eret mortem, ..de Barbaria fugit in Siciliam (*Lit. Nuntiorum*) M. Par. *Maj.* III 558.

auga v. algea b, auca c. augaria, ~iagia v. angari-. augea v. algea.

augēre [CL], to increase, enlarge, enhance.

plurima dum flammis augerent pabula pagi Aldh. *VirgV* 1826; **a690** Pacificus [Salomon]..almo auctus spiramine *Id. Ep.* 5 p. 491; auxit procellam hujusce perturbationis..mors Sabercti Bede *HE* II 5; **805** si quis hanc largitionem illi ~eat, ~eatur illi a Deo vita *CS* 322; non quia idem motus substantialis ~eri vel minui in se ipso possit Eriug. *Per.* 570B; aula decora nimis..Guest vocitata..; / post Petri nomen auxit ab ecclesia G. Amiens *Hast.* 668; **11..** monachi ..ex occasione hujus donationis nostre ~ebunt conventum ..de duobus monachis *Feod. Durh.* 157*n.*; reprobis leo, mitibus agnus, / hostes antiquos qui terret et †augit [? l. ~et] amicos Gower *CT* III 341; ut, sicut aucta fuerint ei graciarum dona.., sic ~eret ipse laudum rependia Elmh. *Hen. V* 91.

augescere [CL], to increase, grow larger.

ubi lux corpore exilior, ibi umbra sine termino ~it Bede *TR* 7; ~ente dolore nimio *Id. HE* III 9; de talibus disserendi usu ~ente, augetur et eorum notio Balsh. *AD* 107.

augeus, augia v. algea. augis v. aux.

†augistrum, cupping-glass.

1200 si quis ~o, quod ab augendo dicitur et alio nomine 'ventosa' a suspirio vocatur, minui voluerit, infirmario indicabit *Chr. Abingd.* II *app.* 408.

augmasticus, ~aticus v. acmasticus.

augmentabilis, susceptible of increase. **b** (sb. n.) susceptibility of increase.

sphere..quattuor..alterabiles, ~es, generabiles et corruptibiles, utpote incomplete Gros. 56; hic oportet notare minimum subjectum ~e; et per ipsum oportet intelligere gradum augmentacionis mole indivisibilem multiplicari Wycl. *Log.* III 117. **b** videtur necesse ponere ipsum [vacuum] propter corpora locanda, sive in loco sive in nutribili et ~i Bacon III 206.

augmentare, to increase, enlarge: **a** (in number or amount); **b** (in bulk or extent); **c** (in power or intensity).

a omnis Europa..religionis Cluniacensis numerum per eum ~atum non nescit W. Malm. *GR* III 265; **1139** ad illam communam ~andam et sustentandam dono eis..x libratas terre *Ch. Sal.* 10; **1191** ad libitum vestrum pensiones earundem [ecclesiarum] ~are..vobis indulgemus (*Lit. Papae*) *Reg. Malm.* I 375; propter elemosinam ampliandam et ~andam tanta..admissa est ferculorum numerositas Gir. *RG* II 5 p. 53; **1215** de garnisione castri..aumentanda *Pat* 156b; **1232** quomodo potestatis mee sunt que, cum voluero..apprehendere, evanescunt, ~are, diminutionem capiunt? Gros. *Ep.* 9; **1283** non faciunt servicium qui aumentaverunt redditum suum *Cust. Battle* 71; ceterorum collata..de suo proprio largissime ~avit Oxnead *S. Ben. Holme* 292; **1297** super augmen[tan]do numero monachorum *Lit. Cant.* I 24; **1306** procuravit..vicariam usque ad..x librarum valenciam..aumentari *Reg. Cant.* II 1079; **1496** pre multitudine..parochianorum..~ata *Eng. Clergy* 127. **b** cervisia vires / prestat, augmentat carnem generatque cruorem D. Bec. 2723; **1250** pro..horeo aumentando *DC Cant* H 178b; sic ~antur caro et os et ingrossantur Bacon *Tert.* 158; **1269** licebit..alia clausa in..foresta facere vel eadem clausa aumentare *Cart. Sallay* 37. **c** fundamenta ecclesiae, quae nobiliter jacta vidit, ~are..et.. provehere curavit Bede *HE* II 4; si vera virtus..in melius ~atur Lanfr. *Ep.* 37. 535B; caritas ab aliis aumentari dicitur per hoc quod intenditur Knapwell *Not.* 187; injuria quam..W. fecit..est ~ata et non correcta *State Tri. Ed. I* 3; **1300** divinus cultus tanto magis ~atur quanto plures ministri..sunt constituti *Vis. Ely* 14; **s1328** nequissimas nobis.. ~ans injurias *Croyl. Cont. B.* 483; posset tota illa multitudo adhuc peccando ulterius adaugeri, possetque in malicia ~ari Bradw. *CD* 21E; **c1370** ejus honor et virtus.. semper ~abuntur et crescent (J. Bridl. *gl.*) *Pol. Poems* I 139; illi amores mutuo se ~ant et minuunt ex adverso Wycl. *Civ. Dom.* I 60; mites augmentet regni justos animando Elmh. *Metr. Hen. V* 1308.

2 to add.

etiam bissexti diem postquam transierit ~are memento Bede *TR* 22.

3 to enrich, endow.

s1040 dux [Willelmus] dum multis probitatum commodis quotidie ~aretur W. Jum. VII 17; Lucius..aumentavit eas [ecclesias] amplioribus et agris et mansis G. Mon. V 1; **1272** labores..per quos ipsum monasterium in spiritualibus et temporalibus..~asti (*Lit. Episc.*) *Ann. Durh.* 29.

augmentatio, increase, enlargement: **a** (in number or amount); **b** (in bulk or extent); **c** (in power or intensity). **d** (w. *Curia*) Court of Augmentations.

a c765 (13c) hanc donationem ad monasterii edificationem et Deo..ibi servientium ~onem..subscripsi *CS* 197; gaudebunt naves ~one tanta G. Mon. VII 4; dum etatis fit augmentatio J. Howd. *Phil.* 54; **1283** de aumentacione redditus sui *Cust. Battle* 69; **1305** in ~onem firme sue *BBC* (*Norwich*) 341; **c1400** adquisivit..terram..ad aucmentacionem tunicarum..et habituum conventus *Chr. Rams. app.* 348*n.*; **1564** pro ~one rentalis mei *Scot. Grey Friars* II 5. **b 1212** rex..dedit Baldrico..manerium..in aumentacione baronatus *Fees* 135; **1240** quod vicus..includeretur in ~onem cimiterii *Cl* 185; **12..** terras quas..ad ~onem gardini mei comparavi *Reg. S. Thom. Dublin* 373; hec ~o non est in rebus animatis sed in lapidibus Bacon *Tert.* 158; de..~one curie et curtilagii *Fleta* 215. **c 1216** exemplo ~onis libertatum vestrarum ceteri ad obsequium nostrum.. libentius aspirabunt *Pat* 196a; **c1236** hujusmodi dispensatione abutitur quisquis ad alium finem quam ad fidei et caritatis ~onem [v.l. augmentum] eadem utitur Gros. *Ep.* 25; **s1248** reprehensus est de..rerum dilapidatione sine sui emendatione vel regni aucmentatione M. PAR. *Min.* III 33; caloris naturalis ∼one BACON IX 1; s**1382** non ad emendacionem malorum sed ∼onem WALS. *HA* II 60; **1440** ad.. boni regiminis tam in spiritualibus quam in temporalibus ∼onem BEKYNTON I 121. **d 1542** recorda et irrotulamenta Curie ∼onum revencionum Corone nostre *Deeds Balliol* 164; **1546** solicitator Curie ∼onum revencionum corone domini regis *FormA* 344.

2 addition, supplement.

1320 pro ∼one duorum monachorum ultra consuetum numerum recipiendorum *Reg. Dunferm.* p. 245; scienciarum ingencia corpora ad immensas..quantitates successivis ∼onibus succreverunt R. BURY *Phil.* 10.158.

3 enrichment, endowment.

c**1250** aumentacio thesaurarii facta per..abbatem *Reg. S. Aug.* 2.

augmentativus, augmentative, causing increase. **b** (fig.).

omne augmentum est a vi ∼a, et istud augmentum est a vi nutritiva; ergo vis nutritiva est vis ∼a J. BLUND *An.* 48; [potentiam] hanc vocat J[ohannicius] nutritivam; ab aliis vocatur ∼a GILB. VI 242. 1; tunc in rebus inanimatis oporteret ponere virtutem ∼am, sicut in animatis, ut per aliquod corporale veniens convertendum in rem inanimatam virtus illa ∼a duceret illam rem ad debitam quantitatem BACON *Maj.* II 438; potentie vegetative partes principales sunt tres, sc. nutritiva, ∼a, suique similis in specie generativa *Ps.*-GROS. 469; c**1301** an in Christo potencia nutritiva et augment[at]iva sint una potencia *Quaest. Ox.* 331; vis ∼a per infusionem cibalis hujusmodi paulative remittitur WYCL. *Log.* III 113. **b** s**1245** transiit annus..regno Francorum prosper et aucmenta[ti]vus M. PAR. *Min.* II 511.

augmentator, enlarger, amplifier.

Octavianus Augustus, Romani ∼or pre omnibus imperii GERV. TILB. II 16; de Constantino Magno, Christiane religionis ∼ore *Plusc.* VII 14.

augmentatus v. ammentatus, augmentare.

augmentum [CL], increase, enlargement, addition: **a** (in number or amount); **b** (in bulk or extent); **c** (in power or intensity). **d** (*sc. firmae*) payment by sheriff for right to farm the county.

a collati sunt in aucmentum predictorum [victualium] unicuique canonico redditus xl s. *Found. Waltham* 16; c**1160** ad aumentum hujus elemosine *Cart. Sallay* 222; **1240** redacto in scripturam ∼o ejusdem pecunie *StatOx* 76; **1281** mandamus quatinus..matrimonium..compleatis. arras autem non ∼um [sc. dotis] eligimus et per vos eligi precipimus *RGasc* II 164 (= *Foed.* II 173). **b** in ionico majori.. duplum temporis ∼um arsis usurpat et simplum thesis gubernat ALDH. *PR* 132; quanto fuerint augmenta rogorum, / tanto plus sitiunt *Id. VirgV* 2621; **8..** aumenta, *eacan* WW; **798** omnibus lunae et siderum ∼is vel detrimentis explosis ALCUIN *Ep.* 145 p. 232; s**761** dedit..episcopo Roffensi terram..unius et semis jugeri..ad ∼um monasterii B. Andree *Flor. Hist.* I 384; s**1136** deditque ei rex Stephanus burgum quod vocatur Huntedonia in ∼um H. HUNT. *HA* VIII 4; **1201** dederunt..in aumento medietatem predicti tofti *Cart. Malton* f. 206v.; anima que facit motum aumenti terminat ipsum propter quietem in quantitate debita BACON II 117; **1298** concessimus..tenementa..includenda dicte ville..in ∼um, emendacionem et securitatem..ville *BBC* (*Newcastle*) 41; c**1300** dimisisse..abbati..quandam placeam terre..in aumentum placee sue *Cart. Sallay* 569. **c** cum..vitae caelestis institutio cotidianum sumeret ∼um BEDE *HE* III 22; virtutum ∼a nutriebat OSB. *V. Dunst.* 8; sunt cujuslibet egritudinis tempora iiij: principium, ∼um, status et declivium RIC. MED. *Signa* 32; adjicientur..in ∼um pulcritudinis..preciosiores philacterie *Cust. Cant.* 111; **1271** salutem cum sincere dileccionis in Christo semper ∼o (*Lit. Archiep.*) *Leg. Ant. Lond. app.* 234; **1340** salutem in ∼o Salvatoris *FormOx* 128; si Anglicana perspicacitas..quicquam ad ∼um sciencie..promulgabat R. BURY *Phil.* 8. 134; **1475** ad ∼um divini cultus *Scot. Grey Friars* II 212. **d** comitatus Oxeneford reddit firmam trium noctium, hoc est c libras; de ∼o xxv libras ad pondus *DB* I 154b.

2 piece added (? patch).

1222 cognoscunt tunicam illam per pannum et per quoddam ∼um factum super humeros *BNB* II 116.

3 lineage.

reges usque duos, de quibus nos ∼um sumpsimus ÆTHELW. IV 2; **9..** crementum, i. ∼um, *wæstm, cip* WW.

augnetum v. alnetum. augorismus v. algorismus.

augur [CL], augur, diviner. **b** (fig.).

∼ur, qui aves colit *GlC* A 906; ∼ur, *haelsere Ib.* 953; nec cantus volucrum servet vanissimus augur ALCUIN *SSEbor* 161; stans volucres augur solitus servare sinistras FRITH. 374; ∼ur vel auspex, *fugelweohlere* ÆLF. *Gl.*; ∼ur vel ariolus, *wicca Id. Sup.*; est augur surdus, aruspex / cecus et ariolus amens VINSAUF *PN* 350. **b** ∼ure conscientia, jam sibi de fama metuit MAP *NC* I 12.

augurari [CL], to divine. **b** to suppose, opine. **c** (w. inf.) to expect.

∼ans, ominans *GlC* A 885. **b** qui se multorum fidei committere curat, / auguror hunc leviter posse carere fide NIG. *SS* 1020. **c** esca sed et rapidis auguror esse lupis *Ib.* 1622.

augurialis, ominous.

detestor auguriale nefas GARL. *Tri. Eccl.* 33.

augurium [CL], augury, omen.

qui ∼ia, auspicia sive somnia vel divinationes quaslibet secundum mores gentilium observant, ..quinquennio peniteant THEOD. *Pen.* I xv 4; caverat ne in aliquam domum ad se introirent, vetere usus ∼io BEDE *HE* I 25; c**738** lucorum vel fontium ∼ia..omnino respuentes BONIF. *Ep.* 43; ∼ia quoque et avium cantus..vetanda sunt ALCUIN *Ep.* 267; **10..** ∼ia, *hælsunga* WW; ∼ium, quod est in avium observatione, Phriges invenisse traduntur J. SAL. *Pol.* 409B; ∼ia sunt in canonibus ecclesie vetita; tamen dicimus quod quedam accipiuntur per obviationem hominis vel alterius animalis vel per auditum vocis M. SCOT. *Phys.* 57; augurii fallax elegia GARL. *Tri. Eccl.* 33.

augustalis [CL], imperial. **b** royal. **c** (sb. m.) imperial gold coin.

sustulit imperator [Alexius] maleficio quem virtute nequibat, uxori ipsius conubium ∼e mentitus W. MALM. *GR* III 262; si times conscientiam tuam, quasi injustitiam propter sacramentum ∼e patiatur GERV. TILB. II 19 p. 944. **b** Thoma nostro in aula summa ∼i..ceteris longe prefulgente H. BOS. *Thom.* III 1. **c 1254** aurum..in bisanciis, ∼ibus et aliis..monetis *RGasc* I 484 (cf. *CalPat* 314).

augustaliter, imperially.

regnum est imperiale, Romanis Caesaribus ∼er regnatum GOSC. *Aug. Maj.* 51.

auguste, augustly, solemnly.

pater auguste regnorum sceptra gubernans ALDH. *VirgV* 2059; illud Augusto datum ∼e consilium non ignorans GIR. *TH* III 48.

augusteus, imperial.

hec tercia carta ∼ea regia majoris forme dici poterit, que ..prima est et precipua inter cartas ELMH. *Cant.* 113.

augustiae, honours (play on *angustiae*).

quot toleravit ex Lausi prosperis adversa, ..ex ∼iis angustias MAP *NC* III 3 p. 129.

Augustinianus, ∼inensis, ∼iniensis, of St. Augustine (w. ref. to Austin Friars); *v. et. canonicus 6b, ordo.*

1249 fratres Heremitarum ordinis S. August[in]i venientes in Angliam *Pat* 60 m. 3; **1255** suscepimus in protectionem et defensionem nostram priores et fratres Heremitarum ordinis S. Augustini in Anglia commorantes *Pat* 69 m. 13; **1284** de..responsione..∼inianorum..nobis..rescribatis PECKHAM *Ep.* 607 (cf. ib.: plurimos fratres de ordine S. Augustini, qui et alio nomine Heremitanos se faciunt aliquociens appellari); Gregorius [X]..aliquos status de ordinibus mendicantium approbavit..; aliquos toleravit, utpote Carmelitas et ∼ienses; aliquos reprobavit.. HIGD. VII 37 p. 258; anno Domini mccxxiiij obtinuerunt primo fratres Predicatores loca habitandi in Anglia; et tercio anno sequente Minores venerunt primum in Angliam ..; et post hec Carmelite quasi xxx annis; et ultimo ∼ienses *Meaux* I 435; **1349** fratribus ∼ianis *Cart. Osney* II 62; **1353** fratribus Minoribus ville Novi Castri super Tynam do et lego xx s.; item fratribus Predicatoribus ∼iensibus et Carmelitis dicte ville per equales porciones do et lego xx s. *Feod. Durh.* 6n.; a fratre T. Wyntirton, ordinis ∼iensium *Ziz.* 181; s**1428** sermoni interfuerunt..cujus thema, fratris ∼iniensis predicantis, fuit.. AMUND. I 31; **1429** fratribus †∼inentibus [l. ∼inencibus] (*Test. Ad. Usk*) *EHR* XVIII 316.

1 augustus [CL], august, venerable. **b** imperial. **c** (imperial title). **d** (royal title).

augusti quassata mole sacelli ALDH. *VirgV* 1390; majorem et ∼iorem de lapide fabricare basilicam BEDE *HE* II 14; augustis augusta viris angustia, felix / copia paupertas HANV. VII 348. **b** Dioclitianus imperator ∼ae potestatis monarchiam gubernans ALDH. *VirgP* 41; ducitur augustam quapropter praesul ad aulam *Ib. V.* 1048. **c 1256** Ricardus Dei gratia Romanorum rex, semper ∼us (*Lit.*) *Leg. Ant. Lond.* 26; **1341** Lodowicus Dei gracia Romanorum imperator semper ∼us (*Lit. Imp.*) AVESB. 97b. **d** nihil deliciis et divitiis illis ∼i [sc. Henrici II] et sarcine huic pastorali H. BOS. *Thom.* III 30 (cf. ib. III 2: officiales ∼i).

2 (month of) August.

[apud Anglos] ∼us *Uueodmonath*..mensis zizaniorum, quod ea tunc maxime abundent BEDE *TR* 15; iii diebus in ∼o secabat *DB* I 179; in quibusdam terris operatur opus septimanae duos dies..et in ∼o [AS: *on hærfest*] iij dies (*Quad., Rect.*) *GAS* 446 (cf. ib. 450: manipulus ∼i [AS: *hærfesthandful*]); **1142** recepit..ij acras terre per..operationem viij dierum in †∼a [MS.: ∼o] *MonA* V 455a; **1279** faciet arruram..qualibet die Veneris..a festo S. Mich. usque ad gulam ∼i *Hund.* II 656b; c**1370** Augusti portis [*gl.*: in fine mensis ∼i] veniet pars optima sortis (J. BRIDL.) *Pol. Poems* I 168, 170.

2 augustus, augury.

augustus, ∼ti, ∼to, Cesar vel mensis habeto; / augustus, ∼tus, ∼ui, vult divinatio dici GARL. *Aequ.* 1589D.

auketonus, ∼unus v. alcoto.

1 aula [CL < αὐλή: *infl. by* AS *heall and* OF *halle* < Frk.; cf. halla], hall, (large) room, esp. dining-room. **b** (fig.).

infans..antiquorum disciplinis ∼is [v.l. ∼eis] in paternis inbuebatur FELIX *Guthl.* 11; fratribus hac requiem dulcem concedat in aula ALCUIN *Carm.* 96. 1. 3; ∼a, *heall* ÆLF. *Sup.*; **1167** in operationem..domorum regis de Westm', sc. nove ∼e et camere regine *Pipe* 1; **1223** de maeremio..cariando.. ∼e et camere regis..ad operationem ∼e..castri [de Sireburn'] *Pat* 370; c**1224** ∼a ad elemosinam (*Chanc. Misc.* 10/13/2) *Cal. Ir.* I 1227; **1254** ∼a elemosinaria et magna ∼a domini regis et parva ∼a et camere [castri Hereford'] indigent coopertorio in pluribus locis *CalIMisc* I 205; s**1259** dominus rex existens in magna ∼a Westmonasterii..fecit legi aperte..compositionem factam per barones *Leg. Ant. Lond.* 42; in ∼a ij mense mobiles et ij immobiles (*Invent.*) *FormMan* 21; **1304** exceptis.. expensis ∼e circa ciphos..reparandos *Ac. Durh.* 112; **1308** de quo manerio capitalis ∼a cum cameris et coquina et aliis edificiis valet per annum ij s *IPM* 4/2 r. 2; abbas [Willelmus, ob. 1367]..fecit..∼am estivalem cum parva capella et camera sibi annexa *Chr. Evesham* 296 (cf. *Ac. Durh.* 159 [**1506**]: pro factura unius *le synke* subtus ∼a estivali in hospicio); **1377** in alba ∼a regii palacii Westmonasterii (*Cl* 217) *Rec. Coronation* 132; **1463** cum..ij mensis et formulis pro minori ∼a [*Dunbar*] *ExchScot* 179. **b** Pluton..qui../ ..inferni furva regnavit in aula ALDH. *VirgV* 1379; supernorum reboat concentibus aula *Ib.* 1888; transit ad aetheream laetus feliciter aulam ALCUIN *SSEbor* 1567; caelestis aulae nobiles (WULFSTAN 141. 1) *Anal. Hymn. LI* 164; ∼a universalis propitiationis, ..vas et templum vitae et salutis universorum ANSELM (*Or.* 7 *ad S. Mariam*) III 20; ubi Filius Dei ∼am uteri virginalis intravit OSB. CLAR. *Anne* 6. 38.

2 church building. **b** nave (*cf. ala* 4a).

hic Petrus et Paulus.. / carminibus crebris alma venerantur in aula ALDH. *CE* 1. 4; s**709** hanc Domino qui aulam ductus pietatis amore / fecit et eximio sacravit nomine Petri (*Epitaph.*) BEDE *HE* V 19; c**1056** Odda dux jussi[t] han[c] regiam ∼am construi atque dedicari (*Inscr.*) *Arch.* L 70; abbas..habuit..secundum jussum regis [Willelmi I] pretaxatum numerum infra ∼am ecclesie victum cotidie de manu celerarii capientem atque stipendia *Lib. Eli.* II 134; **1261** faciat habere..sex quercus aptas ad maeremium ad sex postes inde faciendos ad quandam ∼am inde construendam apud ecclesiam..de Eton' *Cl* 330. **b** s**1122** est..in medio ∼e majoris ecclesie decenter sepultus EADMER *HN* 354; inde ad occidentem chorus psallentium in ∼am ecclesie porrigebatur GERV. CANT. I 8; ab hac versus occidentem navis vel ∼a est ecclesie subnixa utrinque pilariis octo; hanc navem vel ∼am finiunt due turres sublimes *Ib.* 9.

3 royal (or papal) residence, palace, court. **b** (fig.) favour, usage. **c** court of royal Marshalsea or Verge.

∼a Latine domus regia est, *aule* Graece atrium dicitur BEDE *Orth.* 2775; Sanctus apostolicam tenuit tunc Sergius aulam ALCUIN *WillV* 4. 2; reddebat: alias minutas consuetudines in ∼a et in camera regis *DB* I 161; qui..in ∼a regis [AS: *on cyninges sele*] domino suo serviret (*Quad.*) *GAS* 457; **1116** sicut rex W. ..ei dedit in excambium pro terra illa in qua aedificavit ∼am suam in urbe Winton' *MonA* II 444 (= *Regesta* 1126); unum genuit filium..qui, litteris imbutus, inter regales capellanos usque hodie demoratus est in ∼a Willelmi et Henrici Anglie regum ORD. VIT. V 13 p. 412; H. BOS. *Thom.* II 8 (v. aulicus a); in ∼a quadam regia visus est sibi videre quasi principem in throno sedentem GIR. *PI* III 30 p. 324; **1251** capellano de ∼a domini regis *Cart. Osney* II 115; s**1392** perduxerunt regem et reginam in ∼am Westmonasteriensem KNIGHTON II 320. **b** fuerunt quidam qui dixerunt quod in omni emitriteo putrescit flegma intus et extra; quorum opinio ab ∼a recessit, eo quod non consonat nomini GILB. I 57. 2; solet hoc aliquando cum protestatione fieri quod, si hoc non sufficeret, tenens diceret aliud; quod quidem modo recessit ab ∼a, quia vocatio illa aliquando frivola inventa fuit et quasi nulla BRACTON 389b. **c** de placitis ∼e regis *Fleta* 67 (cf. ib. 75: clerico placitorum ∼e pro rege (cf. ib. 79: de officio marescalli ∼e); **1315** placita ∼e domini regis apud S. Dunstanum infra Barram Novi Templi Lond'.: A. B. opposuit se versus W. le F. ..de placito transgressionis infra virgam *MGL* I 300; **1326** placita ∼e domini regis apud Turrim Lond' coram..senescallo et marescallo hospicii domini regis *Ib.* 303; **1400** placita corone ∼e hospicii domini regis tenta in castro Oxon'..in presencia ipsius regis coram senescallo et marescallo hospicii sui *PlR Marshalsea* 28 (*title*).

4 hall used as lawcourt, hall of justice. **b** guild-hall (*cf. gildhalla*). **c** guild-hall of Hanse merchants, Steelyard.

1272 (v. b infra); **1291** ipsum..traxerunt per capillos in ∼am ubi tenent comitatum in eadem villa [Stafford'] (*JustIt* 541A) *EECounty Court* 151; c**1320** quod die tercia ante placita corone ingrediantur Turrim ad visitandos bancos magne ∼e, quod sint integri *MGL* I 59; **1320** in ∼a placitorum Lincolnie *SelCKB* IV 94; **1344** venerunt ad ∼am placitorum in..villa [Gippewici] et ibidem sedendo super gradus ejusdem ∼e proclamare fecerunt.. *Ib.* VI 37 (cf. ib. 47); **1348** senescalli et ballivi nostri..in ∼a placitorum ville de Hedon' tenere possint wapentachium de Holdernesse *ChartR* 135 m. 14; s**1397** fecerat..rex ante..parliamentum in medio palacii apud Westmonasterium unam ∼am inter turrim et hostium magne ∼e situatam, ad judicia sua ibidem exercenda..; quam quidem ∼am finito parliamento prosterni fecit et penitus inde asportari *V. Ric. II* 131. **b** convocata civium multitudine in ∼a publica, que a potorum conventu nomen accepit GIR. *Galf.* II 8; a**1260** ut ..teneant unam placeam in eodem burgo ad quandam ∼am gillatoriam erigendam *BBC* (*Dunheved*) 343; **1272** omnia placita civitatis..teneantur in ∼a placitorum civitatis.. que Gyldehalle vocitatur *Ib.* (*Lincoln*) 154; **1305** ita quod eos haberet..apud gildam ∼am *GaolDel.* 39 r. 1; **1373** de.. receptis ∼e, et omnibus aliis receptis ad..villam [*Guildford*] pertinentibus *Gild Merch.* II 102; **1378** pro..shopis subtus gildam ∼am Oxon' *DocCOx* 303; **1386** pro xiiij libris cere de ∼a gilde..in Ebor' *Ac. Durh.* 390. **c 1300** quod mensuratores non cedant pro blado mensurando ultra ∼am Teutonicorum *MGL* I 243; **1321** aldrem[annus] de societate predicta [mercatorum Alemannie]..inde faciet justiciam in ∼a Alemannorum (cf. ib.: ∼a †Aldermannorum) *PQW* 455b.

5 hall, manor-house, manor. **b** demesne (*cf. Med. E. Anglia* 283).

duo sochemanni tenuerunt T. R. E. sine ∼is et dominiis *DB* I (*Kent*) 11; A. ..tenet Acres, quod tenuerunt duo fratres et quisque habuit haulam; modo est pro uno manerio *Ib.* 11b; tres aloarii tenuerunt de rege E. ..; unus ex his habuit ∼am *Ib.* (*Suss*) 86; ibi est una virga ubi comes habet ∼am suam *Ib.* 48; in dominio ∼e sunt x bovate de hac terra *Ib.* (*Notts*) 283; terra j carucae cum saca et soca sine ∼a *Ib.* 286b; **1127** sit una cultura et una firma in dominio ∼e de Hovetone nec inde unquam separetur *Reg. S. Ben. Holme* p. 72; si quis pugnam inierit in ∼a comitis, xx sol. emendet; et, si hoc fit in domo hominis quem Angli vocant *ceorlman*, ..vj sol. (*Inst. Cnut.*) *GAS* 73; reddunt..

lx celdras de *avermalt* ad mensuram ∼e de Heighyngtona *Boldon Bk.* 22; **c1195** concedo..monachis ut habeant..ad dominicam ∼am suam de Minori Heseldene quodlibet *fuail* in mora mea *Feod. Durh.* 132*n.*; **c1283** in Brunesfordwendo sunt x juga, sc. ∼a de Brunesford' cum veteri tenemento j jugum.. *Cust. Battle* 123; **1284** tenet ∼am suam, croftum et boscum..de rege in capite, reddendo per annum xvj d. *Aids* IV 218; **1292** reddendo inde annuatim j d. argenti ad ∼am de le Glen *RScot* I 11a; **1430** prior habet magnam ∼am et vij acras terre quondam Johannis K. per forisfacturam *Feod. Durh.* 61; **1463** de firmis ∼e de T. *ExchScot* 197. **b** ad hujus manerii ∼am pertinent Catenai et Usun *DB* I (*Lincs*) 338b; in ∼a dominica tunc viij equi, modo v *Ib.* II (*Norf*) 257b; in P. tenet idem xxiiii acras terre; sed fuerunt in ∼a S. Edmundi *Ib.* 263b; **a1107** super duas acras que pertinent ad ∼am de Thurgertona *Reg. S. Ben. Holme* p. 169 (cf. *EHR* XXXVII 226); **c1130** concessise..decimam de ∼a mea de Ormesby (*Norf*) *CalCh* I 152.

6 hall of residence or college (acad.). **b** (of vicars choral).

1260 ∼a Leonum major proxima in venella..; ∼a minor ibidem proxima *Cart. Osney* III 106; **1272** ex opposito illius ∼e que vocatur ∼a S. Helene *Ib.* II 414; **1313** quod quilibet principalis inhabitator..tam ∼arum quam camerarum.. sacramentum prestent corporale quod, si noverint aliquem de societate sua conventiculas tales facientem.., cancellario ..denuncient *StatOx* 111; **1337** statuimus..mansum illud ∼am Scolarium Regis Cantebrigie nuncupari (*Pat*) *Foed.* IV 821; libros..donamus..communitati scholarium in ∼a N. Oxoniensi degencium...quinque de scholaribus in ∼a prefata commorantibus assignentur per ejusdem ∼e magistrum quibus omnium librorum custodia deputetur R. Bury *Phil.* 19. 237–8; **s1355** universitate Oxonie..dissoluta, .. singuli scholares ad propria declinarunt, scholaribus ∼e de Mertone et aliarum ∼arum consimilium..exceptis Avesb. 124; **1367** tenementum magistri et sociorum ∼e de Balliolo *Deeds Balliol* 121; **1379** custos et scholares collegii, domus sive ∼e predicte [*New College*] *Pat* 305 m. 33; **s1382** mandatum [archiepiscopi] datum cancellario Oxonie..inquirendi per omnes ∼as de fautoribus earundem [conclusionum damnatarum] *Ziz.* 309 *rub.*; **1410** quod singuli scolares universitatis in ∼a vel collegio universitatis ubi commune ponuntur sive in ∼is eisdem annexis..commorentur *StatOx* 208; **1432** quod quilibet principalis alicujus ∼e vel introitus saltem non collegii..de cetero sit graduatus, moribus et sciencia suos coaulares idoneus ad regendum *Ib.* 243; **1438** hec sunt nomina principalium ∼arum pro quibus exposite sunt cauciones..: principalis ∼e Brasenose magister R. Grey .. *MunAcOx* 519; **1556** curet commissarius..ne artium et juris studia in ∼is confundantur, hoc est, ne in aedibus juristarum scholares dare operam liberalibus artibus, nec econtra in artistarum ∼is juri civili vacare permittantur *StatOx* 372. **b** **1442** ordinaciones facte per procuratores et communitatem vicariorum ecclesie B. Marie Sar'..pro bona gubernacione mercanciarum necessariorum et victualium in eorum ∼a communi infra clausum Sar' *Stat. Sal.* 324; **1475** quidam vicarii temporibus quibus in eorum ∼a communi in mensa et in aliis degunt multociens rixantur *Process. Sal.* 157.

7 halling, hanging, curtain (*cf. aulaeum*).

1315 legavit summo altari..∼am suam de pennis de *ostrech* et tapestria nigra *Invent. Ch. Ch.* 97; **1349** unam ∼am de worstede operatam cum *papagailles* (*KRAc* 391/15) *Arch.* XXXI 78; **1380** in expensis factis circa ordinacionem nove ∼e pro camera domini prioris *Ac. Durh.* 589 (cf. ib. 591: pro ligatura ∼e nove); **1386** j ∼am viridem cum armis meis et unam ∼am *bleu FormA* 427; **1390** Radulpho Steynour.. pro j nova ∼a *Ac. H. Derby* 18; **1403** unam ∼am rubeam et nigram palatam et poudratam cum albis turettis et costeras de opere tapecerie *Pat* 370 m. 29; **1430** lego..unam ∼am de rubeo worstede cum armis meis enbroditis pro ∼a Arundell cum alia ∼a..pro ∼a hospicii mei London' *Reg. Cant.* II 542.

8 (?) corner (cf. *Speculum* X 278 n. 2).

valvas sed nullus reserat nec limina pandit, / culmina ni fuerint aulis sublata quaternis Aldh. *Aen.* 55 (*Crismal*) 3.

2 aula [αὐλός], wind instrument, flute. **b** organ pipe.

lite graves aule, jocundula nabla querelis Hanv. IX 390. **b** *the pipes of organs*, cantes, ∼e *CathA.*

aulaeum, ∼a [CL < αὐλαία], halling, hanging, curtain. **b** (eccl.).

∼eum, curtina, ab aula *GlC* A 912; ∼ea, *streagl Ib.* 932; hic auro Parias onerant aulea columnas Hanv. IV 299; **c1450** accepi..dominacionem vestram..pro cubiculo nostro ornando alleis vel, ut †utricior [? l. triciori] vocabulo utar, sago viridi me donasse *Let. Ch. Ch.* 14; ∼um, A. *a doser* WW. **b** major relliquias quas tunc aulea tegebat Alcuin *SSEbor.* 366; ornatus ecclesie consistit in cortinis, ∼eis, pallis, sericis Beleth *RDO* 85. 89; ecclesiam..decenter ornatam, ∼eis historicis et pretiosis Grecorum palliis..vestitam Gir. *PI* III 30 p. 323.

2 hall (*cf. aula* 1a).

10.. aulaea, *heal* WW.

aulale v. aularis 2.

aulanus, belonging to the (king's) court.

amicis quos [Henricus I] ex plebeio genere inter ∼os juvenculos ad ministrandum assumptos..sibi..astrinxit *G. Steph.* I 12.

aularis, belonging to (the king's) court. **b** belonging to a hall of residence (eccl.). **c** (acad.). **d** (sb. m.) student attached to a hall.

s1455 dummodo ipse regis conciliarius fuerit, ..alearis pocius quam ∼is..erit nobis vita nostra *Reg. Whet.* I 166. **b** **1475** habent [vicarii] statuta ∼ia ad corrigendum defectus commissos infra aulam suam *Process. Sal.* 157. **c** **1412** quod principales aularum singuli..videant quod per eorum ∼es scolares eisdem..satisfiat *StatOx* 213; **1435** nisi sit scolaris ejus ∼is ad mensam in dicta aula *Cart. Osney* I 218; **1463** omnes coqui tam collegiati quam ∼es universitatis *MunAcOx* 701; **1514** ab illo statuto ∼i quo cavetur quod.. *Cant. Coll. Ox.* III 264. **d** **1556** ad regimen aularum assumantur viri etate matura..qui..∼es sue cure commissos possint..feliciter regere *StatOx* 371.

2 (sb. n.) halling, hanging, curtain.

1434 unum ∼e seu apparatum de rubeo worstede pro aula *Wills N. Country* 43 (= *Reg. Cant.* II 541); **1458** me recepisse..omnia..lectualia, aulalia, cameralia..michi legata *Cl* 308 m. 17*d*.

aularium, halling, hanging, curtain.

1431 duo banqueris de worstede cum toto ∼io de *le parlour Wills N. Country* 41.

auledus, aules v. auloedus. auleum v. aulaeum.

auleus [αὔλειος], belonging to the (king's) court.

1336 ad imperium regis domini sui terreni, cui, licet in quibusdam officiis ∼eis et negociis fiscalibus..strenue militasset, tota tamen animi intencione in Deum ferebatur *Lit. Cant.* II 116.

aulicus [αὐλικός], belonging to the (king's) court. **b** appropriate to a court, courtly, courteous. **c** (sb. m.) courtier.

Thomas aulam ingreditur et tribuente rege in aula ∼um officium suscipit quod vulgo nunc cancellaria dicitur H. Bos. *Thom.* II 8; a quatuor ∼is canibus, rabie plus quam canina furentibus Gir. *EH* I 20; **s1226** a primis annis ∼us et curialis regum satelles M. Par. *Maj.* III 112. **b** adeo quod post modicum non ceterorum coaulicorum ∼os quinimmo ipsos regios fastus assumeret H. Bos. *Thom.* II 7; hospitibus presto si te geris, aulicus esto Garl. *Mor. Scol.* 189. **c** natione Normannicus cum rege Willelmo priore quidam fuerat ∼us, Rannulfus..nomine Herm. Arch. 37; ego contempno que illi ∼i ambiunt J. Sal. *Pol.* 386c; adveniunt et plurimi ∼i, rege in vicino posito, ..gratia concertandi W. Fitzst. *Thom. prol.* 14.

†aulis, *s. dub.*

obviavit cuidam homunculo..cum ∼i et bidentili *NLA* (*Bertellinus*) I 166.

aulnetum v. alnetum.

aulo [αὐλών], strait.

Cyprus..ab oriente mari Syrie.., ab occidente mari Pamphylico, ..a septentrione ∼one Ciliciorum, a meridie.. Phenicie pelago cingitur Gerv. Tilb. II 12.

auloagium v. ollagium.

aulodium [cf. lodium], louver.

1306 allodium aule *MinAc* 866/16; **1447** pro factura unius ∼ii ibidem cum asseris *Comp. Custod. Convent. Pershore*; **1472** unum ∼ium defectivum et tectura coquine est defectiva (*Vis.*) *Fabr. York* 252.

auloedus [αὐλῳδός], piper, flute-player.

auledus, *reodpipere* Ælf. *Sup.*; *a pyper*, †aules [? l. auletes], auledus, fistulator *CathA.*

aumagium v. summagium. aumatium v. armarium. aumbrum v. 2 ambra. aumel- v. esmal-. aumenericum v. elemosynaria. aument- v. augment-, omentum. aumucia v. almucia. aumuntare v. amuntare. aunagium v. alnagium. auncella, auncera v. ancella. auncera v. haucera. auncinium v. antecenium. aundera v. andera. aunetum v. alnetum. aunsera v. ancella. aupex v. auceps. aupicium v. auspicium. auptumnus v. autumnus. auquilata v. aquiletta.

1 aura [CL], wind, weather, atmosphere. **b** breath. **c** (w. *popularis*) popular favour. **d** (fig.) effort.

molosos, / frustra qui superas implent latratibus auras Aldh. *VirgV* 575; si violentior ∼a insisteret.., obnixius orationi incumberet Bede *HE* IV 3; **801** has [litteras] in ∼as direxi, ut vento ferente in vestras pervenissent manus Alcuin *Ep.* 215; ∼a, *hwiða* vel *weder* Ælf. *Sup.*; si fieri potest et ∼a permiserit *RegulC* 36; animal..ventis pernicius, quod ∼as ipsas precurreret W. Malm. *GR* II 163; armis depositis ∼am captare satagit Map *NC* IV 7; occiduam temperiem..salubrior ∼a fecundat Gir. *TH* I 3; narrant medici quod in ∼a quadam epidimiali memoria hominum unius provincie..est corrupta Wycl. *Versut.* 102. **b** ∼as carpente sancto Confessore *Mir. J. Bev.* C 340. **c** ∼e popularis aucupator Gir. *EH* I 4; **c1197** popularis ∼e declinans extollentiam H. Reading (II) *Cel.* 31. **d** **1442** magnam sue vitalis ∼e porcionem..seculi rebus impendit *Pat* 453 m. 30.

2 aura v. avera.

auratio, gilding.

pro j saler argenteo..et pro ∼one ejusdem *Ac. H. Derby* 101.

auratus [CL], gilded. **b** (fig.). **c** wearing gilt spurs (epithet of knight).

Aldh. *VirgV* 207 (v. argentum 1a); bibli seriem..aurato grammate scriptam *Ib.* 1296; *Chr. Evesham* 280 (v. aurifrigiatus); **1345** [pro factura] j supertunice estivalis.. frounc[iate] de filo ∼o (*KRAc* 390/5) *Arch.* XXXI 7; Camd. *Br.* 139 (v. c infra). **b** illa..pudicitiae cultu splendescere et ∼is virtutum monilibus decorari desiderat Aldh. *VirgP* 17. **c** dominus Jacobus de Dumbar eques ∼us Ferr. *Kinloss* 34; equitem quendam ∼um Robertum Rochesterum Chauncy *Passio* 136; ad ornamentum [equitum] praeter gladium cingulum et calcaria ∼a accesserunt, unde milites et equites ∼i hodie vocantur Camd. *Br.* 139; **1591** ut..filii equitum ∼orum..gaudeant privilegiis filiorum nobilium *StatOx* 443.

2 (sb. f.) kind of fish, gilt-head (*cf. deaurata*). **b** tumour under eyelid, sty.

14.. hec ∼a, A. *a sedow* WW. **b** in palpebris ista vicia nascuntur, ∼a, scabies, grando. ..∼a est viscosum corpus cum pellicula Gilb. III 142 v. 1.

aurea v. aureus. aurealis v. aurialis.

aureolare, to crown.

to crowne, ∼are, coronare, laureare *CathA.*

aureolus, golden, brilliant. **b** (sb. m.) bird, golden oriole.

alter Olympus / ..aureolo populatur sidere noctem Hanv. I 245. **b** concinit auriolo nunc philomena L. Durh. *Dial.* I 20; auditur in silva propinqua sibilus avicule dulcisonus, quam alii picum, alii verius ∼um dixere. .. dicitur..∼us avicula aureo croceoque colore conspicua dulcemque suo in tempore pro cantu sibilum reddens Gir. *IK* II 6; ab ave ∼o Gilb. VI 257 v. 2; orioli aves sunt.. a sono vocis sic vulgariter appellate. coloris aurei sunt per totum, excepto quod in alis quasdam pennas cerulea varietate distinctas habent. ..orioli autem de picarum genere esse dicuntur, licet minores corpore sint aliisque coloribus nobilibus colorentur Upton 198.

2 (sb. f.) golden crown. **b** crown of glory, aureole, halo.

laurea, †cernane [l. crinale], sertum, diadema, corona, / addas aureolam †quo [? l. quod] paucis sic data dictam Garl. *Syn.* 1584b; **s1284** Alphonsus, regis primogenitus, veniens ad Westmonasterium quandam ∼am, que fuerat quondam principis Wallie Leolini, cum aliis jocalibus offerebat quibus B. regis Edwardi feretrum ornabatur *Flor. Hist.* III 61. **b** **1176** qui coronam auream creditur meruisse, gloriosi labore officii mereatur ∼am (*Lit. ad elect. Carnot.*) Diceto *YH* I 411; duplex corona, tam aurea sc. quam ∼a, pro communi commodo simul ac proprio feliciter acquiritur Gir. *Ad S. Langton* p. 402; cujus mors est nobis aureola J. Howd. *Phil.* 868; major erit merces doctorum qui sunt ∼am habituri, que intelligitur hic in splendore seculari Peckham *QA* 160; nec..∼am virginitati debitam consequetur Ockham *Pol.* II 455; in solitaria vita tres preeminencias adquisivit; privilegium predicatoris, meritum martiris, premium virginis. ista tria genera hominum habent in celo ∼am super auream [ME: *crune upe crune*] *AncrR* 52; ∼a est speciale mentis gaudium veniens ex opere precellenti et privilegiato *SB* 12.

3 (sb. f.) biblical compendium of Petrus Aureolus.

c1432 item liber vocatus Auriola Bibblie (Heete *Invent. Coll. Wint.*) *Arch. J.* XV 66.

aureus [CL], golden, of gold. **b** resembling gold. **c** (fig.). **d** woven w. gold. **e** or (her.). **f** (w. *pillula*) sort of pill (*cf. infra, 3b*). **g** (w. *numerus*) 'golden number' (w. ref. to lunar cycle). **h** (w. *malum*) quince.

aurea sternuntur fundo simulacra Minervae Aldh. *VirgV* 1331; vasa pretiosa..in quibus et crucem magnam ∼eam et calicem ∼eum Bede *HE* II 20; **735** ut hic opera tua..∼eis litteris fulgeant Bonif. *Ep.* 35; **s1219** in..filis ∼eis..et pannis pretiosis Wend. II 250; **1360** in folio ∼eo et argenteo *Ac. Durh.* 384; **1397** diversa ∼ea affixa feretro *Ib.* 445. **b** aurea devexi dum format sidera mundi Aldh. *VirgV* 743; cum sol ∼eum caelo demoverat ortum Felix *Guthl.* 41; **10..** ∼eus, *giolu* WW; aurea cesaries Gir. *Symb. metr.* II 11. **c** aurea tum propere penetrarat regna polorum / spiritus Aldh. *VirgV* 2160; **1012** (12c) ∼ea quondam secula..nullis territoriis usa noscuntur *CD* 1307; ∼ea tempora presagientes Gir. *TH* II 10; scribitur hic titulo tua laus, rex auree, tota / aurea, cum titulo conveniente nota *Itin. Ric.* VI 37 *postscr.* p. 450*n.* (cf. *EHR* V 321); aureus aurea dat et letus secula leta / Jupiter Neckam *DS* I 537; ad omnium generum causarum prosequendarum..disciplinam hanc presentem summam ∼eam compono. ..preoptati igitur operis cupidos..rudes et subtiles..ad mensam meam ∼eam invito W. Drogheda *SA prol.* (cf. *EHR* XII 646). **d** **1402** (v. auripictus); **1425** unum pannum ∼eum rubei coloris cum foliis ∼eis (*Pat*) *Foed.* X 346. **e** portat sex annulos ∼eos in campo rubeo; et G. sic: *il port de goules sex annulets dore* Bad. Aur. 132. **f** pill[ul]e ∼ee purgant caput Gad. 111. 2. **g** majus inconveniens accidit ex primatione designata per ∼eum numerum in kalendario Bacon *Tert.* 281; istud kalendarium..habet..duas tabulas ostendentes ∼eum numerum et litteram dominicalem pro omni tempore (Elveden *Cal.*) *SB* 5. **h** mala ∼ea, cochinum idem *Alph.* 108.

2 gold (of coin). **b** (sb. m.) gold coin, bezant.

modium plenum solidorum ∼eorum Eddi *Wilf.* 27; ∼eum nomisma Bede *HE* III 8; H. Cantor 20v. (v. byzantus); **c1220** lx solidi et obolus ∼eus *BBC* (*Frodsham*) 156; **1275** emit unum denarium ∼eum de Caterina.., quem denarium illa C. invenit *Hund.* I 280b; **1401** j nobile ∼eum cum j obulo ∼eo..; item j quadrans ∼eus ex dono domini H. de Percy *Ac. Durh.* 452. **b** mille tibi ∼eos offerebat dum illud efficeres J. Sal. *Pol.* 455B; **c1162** annuam duorum ∼eorum pensionem *Danelaw* 254; ∼eum [incidas] unum non prorsus ut argenteum set ducto directe incidentis cultello per medium talee non obliquando sicut fit in argenteo *Dial. Scac.* I 5 K; **s1191** jussit..denunciari ut milites singuli..ab ipso reciperent singulis mensibus quatuor ∼eos *Itin. Ric.* III 4; **c1220** solvent..j ∼eum vel ij solidos annuatim *Reg. Ant. Linc.* III no. 645; **1230** thesaurarius recepit..iiij ∼eos veteres..et iiij novos, quos liberavit..custodi cuneorum *LTRMem* 11 r. 5; Bracton 35 (v. argenteus 2b); **s1257** creavit rex monetam ∼eam denariorum ponderis ij sterlingorum de auro purissimo et voluit ut ille ∼eus curreret in pretio xx sterlingorum *Leg. Ant. Lond.* 29.

3 (sb. f.) crown of glory.

~ea est merces incorruptionis in eterna veritate et bonitate Hales *Qu.* 1131; *AncrR* 52 (v. aureolus 2b).

4 (sb. f.) **a** name of comet. **b** sort of medicament (*cf. supra, 1f*).

a [cometa] septima Maculia vel ~ea Gros. 37*n*. **b** post stupham detur ~ea †Elexendrina Gilb. III 151 v. 2 (cf. ib. 152. 1: ~ea Alexandrina vel Tyria); accipiatur mucillago fenugreci [etc.]..; et est optima medicina in omni dolore; et est de secretis meis; et voco eam ~eam Johannis Gad. 40. 1.

auriale [cf. auricularis 5], pillow, cushion.

1323 duo orrialia de serico vetera *IMisc* 94/24; ~e, *a cord or a pelowe* WW.

†**aurialis** [cf. 2 auriculus], earwig.

arwygyl, wyrme, aurealis *PP*; aurealis, A. *an erewygge* WW.

aurica v. amictus 2c. auricalc- v. orichalc-.

auricella, ear.

1290 predictus P. culpabilis est de latrocinio predicto. ..et, quia habuit ~am suam absissam, ideo.. *Gaol Del.* 36/1 r. 5*d*.

auricinctus, goldfinch.

~us, *goldfinc* Ælf. *Gl.*

auricolor, golden-coloured.

crisoletus, ~or, *goldbleoh* Ælf. *Gl.*; aves..pennis ~oribus, quas in capitibus ceu coronas aureas ferunt Turner *Av.* 83.

auricomus [CL], golden-haired. **b** (fig.).

10.. ~us, *gyldenfeaxa* WW. **b** ter caput auricoma contingit harundine Wulf. *Swith.* I 13.

auricula [CL], **~us,** ear: **a** (human); **b** (of animal).

a 799 uni ~ae suavia susurrare et alteri dura decantare Alcuin *Ep.* 175; **10..** auris, *inneweard eare*, ~a, *utweard eare* WW; **s1196** Eliensis episcopus ad ~am principis frequenter pro officio positus, nam cancellarius erat regis W. Newb. V 28; ejus [maurelle] / vim dolor auricule commoditate probat Neckam *DS* VII 272; **1242** capta..pro burgaria, ..amisit ~am per judicium curie *Assize R. Durh.* 71; **1265** amputavit partem capitis cum cerebro et ~am dextram *SelCCoron* 2; habebit j magnum ciphum plenum de meliore meg', qui in profunditate cooperiet ambas ~as prepositi *Cust. Bleadon* 209; due gutte tepide injiciantur in ~am Gad. 115 v. 1. **b** ~e talium animalium sunt in parte superiori capitis Bart. Angl. V 2; ad instar †~arium [? l. ~arum] asselli ambas manus..agitans *Hist. Meriadoci* 373.

2 ear-shaped object: **a** auricle (of heart); **b** plough-ear; **c** staple; **d** lug, projection, handle.

a cor membrum est..duas habens ~as, unam dextram, alteram sinistram Ric. Med. *Micr. Anat.* 219; ~e apparent extra quasi duo additamenta carnium, per quarum inferiora subintrat vena deportans sanguinem ab epate *Ps.-Ric. Anat.* 41; circa..~as cordis Gilb. IV 200v. 1; cor..cui et suae sunt utrinque ~ae D. Edw. *Anat.* B 4v. **b 1307** in hokis, capp', ~is et padul' ad carucas faciendis *MinAc Wint (Wroughton)*; **1319** in j cultro, ij potes, iiij annulis et j ~o ad caruc' faciendis de ij veteribus vomeribus cum j pecia ferri ad idem empta *MinAc Westm.* (*Pershore*) 22109; **1347** in iiij lynkes et j ~a carucali de ferro empt' *Ib.* 22123. **c 1345** in xv boltis ferreis cum xxij ~is pro dictis boltis ponendis (*KRAc* 492/24) *Building in Eng.* 300. **d a1350** in extremitatibus dyametri..sint due ~e rotunde..per quas ~as eadem tabula duobus foraminibus in pinnulis allidade circuli magni..perforatis immitatur *Turquet* 372; **1388** primus [calix] est magnus cum duabus ~is pro oblatis deputatus (*Invent. Westm.*) *Arch.* LII 231.

3 (w. *muris*) **a** mouse-ear hawkweed (*Hieracium pilosella*). **b** marjoram (*Origanum*). **c** mouse-ear chickweed (*Cerastium*).

a ~us muris, pilocella idem *SB* 12; murion, ~a muris idem *Ib.* 30; ~a muris, pilosella idem, parva habet folia et multa, aliquantulum pilosa; G. *pilousee*, A. *moushere* vel *langbeue Alph.* 17; ~a muris, A. *mushere* WW. **b** adde predictis majoranam, ~am muris, que habet proprietatem in paralesi Gad. 66 v. 1. **c** alsine..Latine ~a muris; sed non est nostra *mouseare*.., caeterum herba illa est quam nostrates mulieres vocant *chykwede* Turner *Herb.* A ii v.

auriculare, to deprive of an ear.

latro est de dicto porcello. et, quia modicum est latrocinium, ideo consideratum est quod ~etur *JustIt* 776 r. 33.

2 (p. ppl.) long-eared.

ex re nomen habens modo diceris auriculatus Nig. *SS* 153.

3 (dep.) to whisper.

s1328 inducebatur episcopus ad hoc per monachum aliquem ~antem sibi Graystanes 41; **s1377** cum non nominanda meretrix..secum ~ari voluisset, ..ipse..repente renuit oblectamenta sua *Chr. Angl.* 144; **s1381** capita velut ad ~andum, jam quasi ad osculandum, invicem super summitates lancearum..conjunxerunt Wals. *HA* II 3.

1 auricularis v. auricula 1b.

2 auricularis, auricular, confided to the ear.

cum ~is et ista sacramentalis confessio ex institucione hominum prosit multis, patet quod illa confessio est necessario facienda proprio sacerdoti Wycl. *Euch.* 333; quod ~is confessio..cum ficta potestate absolucionis exaltat superbiam sacerdotum (*Concl. Lollard.* 9) *Ziz.* 365; cur canonistae ~em confessionem de jure humano et positivo esse aiunt? Jewel *Apol.* 37.

2 (w. *digitus*) fitted to the ear. **b** (sb. m.) ear finger, little finger. **c** little toe.

brevi funiculo ~is fere digiti habente grossitudinem arrepto T. Mon. *Will.* I 5; **1271** repercussit..J. ..in parvo digito qui vocatur ~is *SelCCoron* 21; **1411** media pars digiti ~is sue manus dextre est gladio amputata *Reg. Heref.* 82. **b 10..** anularis, *hringfinger*, ~is, *earclæsnend*, ..~is, *earscrypel* WW; frons, oculi, naris, cervix, latus, auricularis, / os, guttur, mamme fiunt ibi pabula flamme (*Dissuasio concubitus*) *Sat. Poets* II 158; in summo [talee] ponunt m li. sic ut incisio ejus spissitudinis palme capax sit, c li. ut pollicis, xx li. ut ~is *Dial. Scac.* I 5 K; vena que est inter medicum et ~em, que salvatella appellatur *Ps.-Ric. Anat.* 44; hic ~is, A. *the lytylman* WW; *a litille finger*, ~is, ..auricularius *CathA*. **c** minue aliquem de ramis ejus qui sunt super dorsum pedis in medietate extrinseca, sc. in parte ~is Gilb. VII 325. 2.

3 (w. *herba* or as sb. f.) houseleek.

~is i. semperviva *SB* 12; semperviva, sticados citrinum, herba ~is idem, ..G. *jubarbe*, A. *syngrene Alph.* 167.

4 (sb. m.) confidant (*cf. auricularius*).

~em et consiliarium meum constitui *Hist. Meriadoci* 393; **s1387** rex Ricardus venit Londonias..comitantibus eum ~ibus suis reprobis Knighton II 241.

5 (sb. m. or n.) pillow, cushion (*cf. auricularium*).

pulvillulus, ..qui alio nomine dicitur ~is, sub sancto capite repertus est Herm. Arch. 20; **1208** pro pannis de serico ad faciendas teias ad ~ia nostra *Cl* 109a; **1249** venire faciat..quemdam lectum pulcrum..viz. quandam culcitram cum matracio..et quoddam coopertorium..et duo ~ia serica cum pulcro keverchevio *Cl* 247; ad officium hospitarii pertinet..ut habeat..culcitras, chalones et lintheamina.. munda.., ~ia honesta et..coopertoria ampla *Obs. Barnwell* 192; **1328** duo ~ia rubea, sindone coopert' *Reg. Exon.* 562; **1360** unum missale cum uno ~i et uno desco *Fabr. York* 278; **p1368** iij auricularia de taffeta viridi coloris *Invent. Norw.* 16.

auriculariter, by way of auricular confession.

quomodo confiteretur quis peccata commissa suo proprio sacerdoti nisi ~er et sibi abscondite ipsis solis noscentibus..? Wycl. *Euch.* 332.

auricularium, pillow, cushion (*cf. auricularis 5*).

1245 ~ium S. Edithe (*Invent. S. Paul.*) *Arch.* L 471; **1345** liberaverunt..unum corporale magnum.., unum ~ium consutum de serico, ut deserviant in magno altari *Sacr. Lichf.* 115; **1349** ad facienda coopertoria ~iorum et diversa paramenta pro balneis regis (*KRAc* 391/15) *Arch.* XXXI 13.

auricularius, confidant (*cf. auricularis 4*).

796 manualem nostrae familiaritatis ~ium vestrae direximus sanctitati Alcuin *Ep.* 93; solertes ~ii utile decretum palam dederunt Ord. Vit. X 9 p. 62; **c1200** vir Belial.. quem [Penda] sibi ~ium et consiliarium..constituerat (*Found. Pri. Stone*) *MonA* VI 227; **s1322** cum suis nefandis ~iis..rex ipse *Flor. Hist.* III 210; *a cownselour*, ..consultus, ..†anticularius, secretarius, ..*a secretary*, secretarius, ~ius *CathA*.

auriculatio, whispering.

1400 vocalis confessio seu privata penitencia est quedam ~o destruens evangelii libertatem (Purvey) *Ziz.* 402.

auriculator, whisperer, prompter.

s1455 illius projeccio vestra erit ereccio ad culmen honoris altius quam unquam antea habebatis dum ipse stabat ~or in auribus vestris *Reg. Whet.* I 170.

auriculatus v. auriculare 2.

auriculosus, auricular (*cf. auricularis 1*).

a1400 quod illud capitulum Penitenciis et Remissionibus 'omnis utriusque sexus', per quod ordinatur quedam nova ~a confessio, sc. vocalis, est plenum hypocrisi et heresi (Purvey) *Ziz.* 386.

†**auriculum,** (?) dross, lees (*cf. amurcalis*).

~um, †*dorsos GlC* A 889 (= *EE* 340. 7: *dros*); **10..** ~um, ..*dros* WW.

1 auriculus v. auricula 2b, 3a.

2 auriculus, ~um [cf. aurialis], earwig. **b** (?) glow-worm or silver fish.

~um, *earwicga GlC* A 891; **10..** ~um, *earwicga* WW. **b 14..** hic auriglus, A. *a sylverwurme* WW.

aurifaber, goldsmith.

Theodricus ~er tenet de rege *DB* I 63; Nicholaus ~er comitis Hugonis *Ib.* II 279; quidam~er, qui ei a secretis fuisset, scrinium sancti cum capite surripuit W. Malm. (*V. Aldh.*) *GP* V 263; veniente ~ro cum forcipe et infantilia ossa..a maternis visceribus extrahente *Chr. Evesham* 61; **1130** ~ris Londonie pro carbone *Pipe* 144; si fuerit aliquod opus aureum vel argenteum, unde venditor debeat dubitari, non ematur preter ~ros et monetarios (*Leg. Ed. Conf.*) *GAS* 668; **1167** Sotesbroch ~rorum [*Shottesbrook, Berks*] r.c. de dim. m. *Pipe* 10; ~er habeat caminum in summo perforatum Neckam *Ut.* 117; acersito clam ~ro laminas conjungi fecimus et feretro apponi Brakelond 152v.; **1221** faciatis habere Henrico de E. ~ro lx s. et xx d. pro iiij anulis aureis emptis ab eo *Cl* 446b; ~ri sedent ante fornaces suas et tabellas..et fabricant pateras de auro et argento, firmacula, monilia et spintera Garl. *Dict.* 128; **s1278** precepit rex quod omnes ~ri et custodes cuneorum..in civitatibus, burgis et villis mercatoriis caperentur *Chr. Peterb.* 26; ~ris.. commendamur nos [libri]..ut fiamus..repositoria bractearum R. Bury *Phil.* 4. 72; **1379** breve quod quilibet ~er habeat signum proprium in vasis que fecit (*LBLond. H*) *MGL* I 637; *Ziz.* 368 (v. armator); **1417** pro..apparatibus diversarum zonarum mali argenti..presentatis super eum ..per scrutatores ~rorum *Mem. York* I 247; hic ~er, A. *a goldesmythe* WW.

aurifabra, goldsmith (f.) or goldsmith's wife.

1317 tenementum Pady per Helenam ~ram *Cart. Osney* III 140.

aurifabria, ~ica, goldsmith's shop or quarter. **b** goldsmith's work.

addidit [Dunstanulum]..eodem tempore †aurifabre [? l. ~ie] assidere et..artis illius industriam experiri *Chr. Wallingf.* 42; **1235** duas sopas cum solariis..in ~ica in foro London' *ChartR* 28 m. 9; **1259** de illis tenementis..que sita sunt in ~ia..Oxonie *Cart. Osney* I 436; **1287** illud mesuagium..quod vocatur le Stonhalle juxta ~iam *Rec. Norw.* II 3; **c1290** illam seldam..in aurifabr' Bristoll'..quam E. aurifaber aliquando tenuit *Cart. Glam.* 891. **b 12..** vas sculptura magistrali aurifabrice (*sic*) decoratum *Chr. Rams.* liv *n.*; **1300** de..jocalibus diversis..et de ~ia diversa *Ac. Wardr.* p. 332.

aurifabricaria, goldsmiths' quarter.

1305 venit in ~ia London' ad vendendum quoddam salsarium argenti *Gaol Del.* 39/1 r. 4.

aurifabricatura, (right of doing) goldsmith's work (Norm.).

1173 dedisse..W. Cambiatori, aurifabro, ..totum cambium et totam ~am..totius Deppe *Act. Hen. II* I 475.

aurifabrilis, of a goldsmith.

Anketillus, monachus et aurifaber, quandoque in Daciam venerat, ubi..regiis preerat operibus ~ibus, monete custos et summus trapezita *G. S. Alb.* I 84; **s1314** per quendam monachum..qui et ipse peritus erat in opere ~i Wals. *HA* I 139; **14..** Alquinus et Anketillus velut Beseleel in ~i opere profecerunt Amund. II *app.* 304.

†**aurifabrum,** (?) erron. for *aurifrigium*.

1239 tres bonos baudekinos..consui et..circumquaque listari bono ~ro de competenti latitudine faciatis *Liberate* 13 m. 5.

aurifactorius, worked in gold thread.

ut..stolam sacerdotalem artificiosa operatione praepingeret, quam postea ad divinos cultus ~ia imitatione figuraret Osb. *V. Dunst.* 10.

1 aurifer [CL], gold-bearing. **b** gilded.

unde huic civitati..tanta omnium rerum facultas sit, quibus non dicam thesauris sed ~feris est feta Chaundler *Laud.* 113. **b** toracidas, tuentibus / retorquentes luminibus / imagines auriferis / Christi matris capitibus (Æthelwald) *Carm. Aldh.* 2. 175.

2 aurifer v. aurifex.

aurifex [CL], skilled in working gold. **b** (sb.) goldsmith.

manus pingendi..artificiose, digiti ~fices Gosc. *Edith* 68. **b** habeo fabros ferrarium, ~ficem [AS: *goldsmiþ*], argentarium Ælf. *Coll.* 99; Otho ~fex *DB* II 286 (cf. ib. I 190: Otho aurifaber); manus ~ficum vincebat expensarum pretium W. Malm. *GP* I 43; *a gold smythe*, aurifaber, †aurifer [? l. ~fex] *CathA*.

1 aurificium, goldsmith's work.

feminam..quam abbatissa ipsa ob fraudem ~ii damnaverat servitute Gosc. *Wulfh.* 14; **1196** in ~io [v.l. ~o], quo fraudes in seculo nonnumquam commisi, nunc atrocissime luo, dum frequenter in cumulum nummorum ardentium precipitatus..exuror (*Visio monachi Evesham.*) M. Par. *Maj.* II 431; **15..** solut' in ~io unius calicis pro mercurio *Ac. Durh.* 728.

2 aurificium v. aurifrigium.

aurificus, wrought in gold.

tertius aurifico resplendet in orbe topazon G. Amiens *Hast.* 765.

aurifilum, gold thread or wire.

a1100 cetere [cappe] sunt utcumque parate de ~o (*Invent.*) *Lib. Eli.* II 139; **1222** pallia pendentia xxxviij et pallium unum de ~o (*Invent.*) *Reg. S. Osm.* II 131; **1235** ij paria jectorum ad austurcos de serico et ~o *Chanc. Misc.* 3/4; **1295** offertoria..de rubeo serico listata ~o *Vis. S. Paul.* 324; ~um, A. *goldwyre* WW.

aurifis-, aurifix- v. aurifrig-.

aurifluus, golden.

regem..cujus pulchritudo ~o metallo comparari poterat *V. Osw.* 436.

aurifodina [CL], gold-mine.

~a, metallum *GlC* A 883; **10..** ~a, *gyldingwecg*, .. **14..** hec ~a, *a goldquarelle* WW; ~am habet in Craufurdiae tesquis Lesley *RGScot* 11.

aurifodium, ear-pick.

an erepyke, aurifricium, ~ium *CathA*.

aurifrag-, aurifras-, aurifrat-, aurifrax-, aurifres- v. aurifrig-. aurifricium v. aurifodium, aurifrigium.

aurifrigiaria, orphreyer (f.).

1183 Mabile ~frixarie regis ad pannos lxix s. *Pipe* 161; femina..operis texture scientia purpuraria nobilis extiterat et ~frixoria artificiose compositionis peroptima..enituerat R. COLD. *Cuthb.* 74; **s1235** retenta imperatrice cum una sua nutrice..et altera ancilla, ~frigiaria Londoniensi M. PAR. *Min.* II 380.

aurifrigiarium, orphrey-work.

1315 capam albam diasperatam cum ~frigerio de perulis *Invent. Ch. Ch.* 63; **1500** vestimentum..integrum..cum ~frigerio ante et retro *Ib.* 127; **1510** cum ~frigereo de panno aureo *Ib.* 158.

aurifrigiarius, orphreyer, worker in gold fringe.

1234 aurifaber, ~fraser, scriptor, carpentarius, wodiarius xxxiij s. vj d. *Cust. Glast.* 5; **1286** S. capellanus, R. ~frixa[rius], ..servientes de vestiario *MonA* III 158b; **1292** aurifabro xx s., ~frixario x s. *Sacr. Ely* II 6 (cf. ib. 69 [**1335**]: ~fixario; 168 [**1355**]: ~fixorio); **c1350** ipsa..per †~fusarium et lotricem ecclesie, sicut alia ecclesie vestimenta, corrigi faciat et lavari (*Ch.*) J. GLAST. 277; **1377** stipendia serviencium erga festum Natalis: ..~frigerio ij s. vj d. *DCCant DE* 127.

aurifrigiatrix, orphreyer (f.).

p1134 ij [albe] Liveve ~frixatricis *Lib. Eli.* III 50.

aurifrigiatura, orphrey-work.

1500 vestimentum..habet ~am ante et retro cum coronis inbrudatis *Invent. Ch. Ch.* 127.

aurifrigiatus, adorned w. orphreys, gold-fringed. **b** (of persons).

s1178 pretiose cappe et ~frigiate et vestimenta carissima ..ymbrium sustinebant infusiones M. PAR. *Min.* I 409; **1245** casula..ornata aurifrigio fino anterius ~frigiato *Invent. S. Paul.* 482; domicella A. ..legavit illi altari unam casulam de rubeo examito bene ~frigiatam *G. S. Alb.* I 284; iste abbas [T., ob. 1255] acquisivit..unam bonam albam et stolam cum manipulo de nigro serico †~frigerato cum tintinnabulis auratis *Chr. Evesham* 280 (cf. ib. 263*n.*); **1266** statuimus ut abbates..quibus mittre usus est..concessus.. in conciliis..mittris tantummodo aurefrigiatis non tamen aureas vel argenteas laminas aut gemmas habentibus uti possint (*Lit. Papae*) *Reg. Wint.* II 754; dedit idem abbas [R., ob. 1295] unam albam de rubeo samito cum ymaginibus stantibus †~fragiatis [? l. ~fragiatam] WHITTLESEY 148; **1373** summa..pannorum ~fricatorum *ExchScot* 440; **s1381** preter pannos sericos et ~friziatos in funeracione sua oblatos *Hist. Durh.* 3 p. 139; **1402** cape..~frisiate cum magnis ymaginibus auripictis *Invent. S. Paul.* 504; **a1413** duo paria [chirothecarum] cum *offrey*, †~friata cum capitibus AMUND. II *app.* 328; **1500** vestimentum album..cum foliis deliciarum ~frigiatum *Invent. Ch. Ch.* 127. **b** NECKAM *NR* I 58 (v. aurifrisius).

aurifrigium [CL aurum Phrygium *or* aurum fresum (*v. Zeitschr. f. rom. Phil.* XLIII 544), OF *orfreis*; cf. orfrasium], orphrey, (fringe of) gold-embroidered cloth.

hec Leviede fecit et facit ~frisium regis et regine *DB* I 74; Aluuid puella..habuit..dim. hidam quam G. vicecomes ei concessit..ut illa doceret filiam ejus ~frisium operari *Ib.* 149; **a1100** cappe..bene..parate ~friso et gemmis (*Invent.*) *Lib. Eli.* II 139 (cf. ib.: infule..parate..orfrisio); **a1100** xxxiiij cappas..quarum..ix sunt adornate usque ad pedes de ~fixo et xij cum tassallis et ~fixo *Process. Sal.* 184; casulam..~frigio..perornans EADMER *Mir. Dunst.* 23; albam ~frasio copiose ornatam ORD. VIT. VI 5 p. 30; **1155** pro ~frixo ad opus regis *Pipe* 3; E. archiepiscopus [ob. 1051]..dedit albam de purpura cum optimis ~frisiis paratam H. ALBUS 72; **c1160** cappas ~fisio bene paratas *Cart. Rams.* II 273; **1180** ad emendum ~frixium et sericum *Pipe* 150; opus plumarium est cum jam facto panno fila aurea aut argentea acu inseruntur ut fiat ~phrysium AD. SCOT. *TT* 645D; **s1191** rex..capellum ex scarlata gestabat in capite, docta manu artificum variarum avium formis seu bestiolarum acu operante ex ~fragio insutis *Itin. Ric.* II 37; utuntur [Cartusienses] alba et amictu, stola, fanone atque planeta planis et candidis, nec ornatis serico nec ~frisio seu gemmis AD. EYNS. *Hug.* IV 10; dalmati[c]e fines extremos limbus deauratus instar ~fraxii alicujus undique perambiendo circumluit R. COLD. *Cuthb.* 42; **1206** cintorium de ~frisio *Pat* 58b; **1218** apparatum..unius cape ad chorum.. cum..~frasio *Cl* 360a; capam holosericam..~frigio.. electo undique fimbriatam GIR. *JS* 7 p. 364; una [cappa] insignis operis..~friso in girum optimo pretiose purpure circumtecta *Lib. Eli.* II 3; **1240** in j casula..et almatica [cum] ~fratis *Cal. Liberate* 438; **1251** cappam cum lato ~fraxo *Cl* 498; **1289** mitram albam cum simplici ~fregio *Reg. Heref.* 214; **1388** [alba] cum paruris de ~fragiis aureis (*Invent. Westm.*) *Arch.* LII 242; magnum ~frisium ad ornandum altare J. GLAST. 167; *orfrey of vestment*, ~figium, ~frigium *PP*; **1445** casula antiqua de albo damasco cum ~ficiis rectis medio avibus et aliis operibus contextis *Invent. S. Paul.* 522; ~frigium, A. *goldwyre*, ..hoc ~figium, *a goldfre* WW; **1521** *a vestment* de nigro cum ~friciis panni rubii ad aurum *Fabr. York* 276.

aurifrisius [OF *orfrai* < ossifragus], osprey.

aves biformis nature quas ~ios vocant..quibus alterum pedem armatum..alterum vero clausum et pacificum.. nature ludentis opera contulit GIR. *TH* I 16; ~ius 'auram frigidam' sequens, altero pede predonem representat, altero mitissimam avem mentitur. ..~ius igitur potentum aurifrigiatorum typum gerit NECKAM *NR* I 58; aurifrisius in nostro sibi carmine partem / vendicat; huic frigens aura nocere nequit *Id. DS* II 683; ~ius, A. *an hospray* WW.

aurifrix-, aurifriz-, aurifus- v. aurifrig-.

auriga [CL], charioteer, driver, carter. **b** (fig.).

~a, *scridwisa* vel *wænere* ÆLF. *Gl.*; **1180** ij acato duarum quadrigarum ferratarum..et in conredio ~e *RScacNorm* I 84; a bigariis multorum domini effecti sunt ~arum MAP *NC* IV 16 p. 197; si agasonis..officium explere velit, ..lenta virga aurem regat, unde ~a nomen..sortitur, vel eo quod aurem equi regat NECKAM *Ut.* 108; **c1370** 'nobilis est natus' ..in isto dicto tollitur error aliquorum qui credebant eum fuisse filium ~e (J. BRIDL. *Gl.*) *Pol. Poems* I 133; hic ~a, *a carter* WW. **b** **s1389** sentina avaricie, ~a prodicionis, arca malicie..Michael atte Pole..concessit in fata WALS. *HA* II 187.

†aurigalis [? cf. 2 auricularis 3 *or* aurinaleucia], clary (*Salvia horminum*).

orminon sive, ut Latini, eminoda vel origalis sive rejectialis dicunt, tirsim habet cubitale[m].. *Alph.* 132.

aurigare, to drive (fig.), control.

binas eclesias, ut Christi bigas, et unam domum unica caritate ~abat GOSC. *Wulfh.* 4.

aurigenus, golden.

955 ob ejus amabile et ~um pretiolum, hoc est cxx solidos auri *CS* 903.

auriger, golden. **b** (fig.).

vestibus aurigeris in toto corpore plena / femina ÆTHELWULF *Abb.* 362. **b** vocibus aurigeris *Ib.* 687.

auriginosus v. auruginosus. auriglus v. 2 auriculus b.

aurilegium, acquisition of gold.

hec ars felicitat lato dominio, / ..argento copiat et aurilegio, / plusquam alkimie vana traditio (*Palpo* 23) *Ps.*-MAP *Poems* 107.

aurilegus, acquisitive of gold.

717 universi ~i ambrones..fragilia aranearum in cassum ..tetendisse retia dinoscuntur BONIF. *Ep.* 9.

aurimalliator, gold-beater.

1311 Johannes ~or *Cal. LB Lond.* B 20; **1396** *Ib.* H 429; **1374** *CalPat* 427.

†aurinaleucia [? cf. aurigalis], clary (*Salvia sclarea*).

~a, *orval, stedfast* secundum quendam laicum *Alph.* 17.

aurinus, woven w. gold.

1315 pannus unus rubeus ~us qui continet vij ulnas *Invent. Ch. Ch.* 75 (cf. ib. 66); **1339** quissinus..coopertus cum panno ~o (*Invent. Ch. Ch.*) *Arch. J.* LIII 283.

auriol- v. areola, aureolus, oriolum.

auripellis [cf. OF *orpel*], brass foil.

c1250 vexillum rubeum cum yconia B. Virginis de ~e *Vis. S. Paul.* 2; **1494** primus commissarius cardinalis offert duos panes magnos ~e crocei et duos ~e albi coloris coopertos..; secundus commissarius offert quatuor barillia vini, simili duntaxat ~e cooperta *Conc.* III 639a.

auripictus, gold-painted.

1402 cape preciose de panno aureo albi coloris ~e cum floribus de coronis aureis *Invent. S. Paul.* 500.

auripigmentum [CL; cf. orpimentum], orpiment (arsenic trisulphide); *v. et. arsenicum.*

sophisticantur metalla..mediantibus spiritibus quorum species sunt 4, sc. argentum vivum, sulphur, ~um et sal ammoniacum (M. SCOT *Part.*) *Med. Sci.* 295; in causa frigida valet unguentum de †auropigmento et oleo de amigdalis amaris GAD. 113 v. 1; adde modicum de colcotar, i. de atramento citrino vel de ~o citrino *Ib.* 118. 1; sandaraca, i. ~um rubeum; sed arsenicum est ~um citrinum *Alph.* 161.

aurippus v. Euripus. aurire v. haurire.

auris [CL], ear: **a** (human); **b** (of animal).

a crebrius hauriret si spurcas aure loquelas ALDH. *VirgV* 1939; pervenit ad ipsas principum ~es BEDE *HE* III 25; **10..** WW (v. auricula); Johannes frater regis, qui illo dudum ~es habuerat ut pro certo novit quod frater ad Angliam terga verterat DEVIZES 32v; ~is est instrumentum auditus et est dicta ~is a vocibus 'hauriendis' BART. ANGL. V 12; ~em adhibe et que tibi dixero mente retine *Arthur & Gorlagon* 152; **1265** habuit unam plagam in capite juxta ~em sinistram *SelCCoron* 30; ~is..accipitur dupliciter, uno modo pro illa cartilagine exteriori.., alio modo..pro illo nervo interiori veniente a cerebro per quod fit auditus GAD. 114. 2. **b** auribus ecce tuis si par tibi cauda fuisset NIG. *SS* 147; phocas..ad auditum ~es arrigere GIR. *TH* III 12.

2 ear-shaped object: **a** (w. ref. to auricle of heart); **b** plough-ear.

a sunt cordi duo orificia introitus duarum materierum, sanguinis sc. et aeris attracti, sicut due ~es *Ps.*-RIC. *Anat.* 23. **b** quoddam aratrum unica ~e vel ansa contentum est NECKAM *Ut.* 112; *Id. NR* II 169 (v. aratrum 1a); **c1280** due ~es (*Cart. Coton*) *Antiquity* XXVII 167.

3 (w. *leporis*) kind of plant, (?) dittany.

~is leporis, *halswyrt* ÆLF. *Gl.*; ~is leporis vel ~isfolia, †*half vyrt Gl. Durh.*

aurisecus, cutting gold.

devacuatrices sunt que devacuant fila, vel mulieres ~e [*gl.*: G. *trencheresses de or*] GARL. *Dict.* 13

aurisfolia v. auris 3. aurisia v. aorasia.

†auristragulatum, gold stripe.

[abbas T., ob. 1396] dedit..cortinas de rubeo panno serico cum ~o [? l. cum auro stragulato] *G. S. Alb.* II 399.

auritextura, weaving in gold thread.

[Ætheldreda] stolam..ex auro et lapidibus pretiosis.. docta ~e ingenio fecit *Lib. Eli.* I 9.

auritorium v. hauritorium.

aurivittis [*transl.* χρυσομίτρις (χρυσομῆτρις)], bird (identified w. goldfinch).

~is una est ex aviculis quae carduorum semine victitant. ..alii goldfincam..spinum, alii carduelem esse volunt. sed si quis praeter hanc aliam aurea vitta redimitam ostenderit, cui magis ~is nomen competat quam huic, opinionem meam facile patiar explodi TURNER *Av.* 16.

aurivomus, showering gold (fig.).

c798 ~os spiritualium sensuum gurgites gemmis scholasticae urbanitatis abundare ALCUIN *Ep.* 139.

aurkemonnus v. avermannus. aurocalcum v. orichalcum. auronum v. avronum.

aurora [CL], dawn, daybreak. **b** (fig.). **c** (title of book by Peter de Riga). **d** (?) a customary payment. **e** the East.

aurora in fulvis dum luxit lutea bigis ALDH. *VirgV* 1363; ipsa nocte, in cujus ultima parte, id est incipiente ~a, ..supernam migravit ad lucem BEDE *HE* III 8; ~a, *dægrima* ÆLF. *Gl.*; ~a..illius diei illucescente EADMER *Mir. Anselm.* 155; **1239** cum in ~a diei S. Thome Martiris venisset ad domum domini sui *SelPlForest* 71; [ballivus] prata pasturasque ambiat ne inde dampna fiant..in ~is *Fleta* 64; **1340** in ~a diei ante ortum solis *CBaron* 99; tercia [linea] ostendit quanta sit horarum planetarum nocturna et in pede habetur quanta sit ~a (ELVEDEN *Cal.*) *SB* 5. **b** virginitas dies, castitas ~a, jugalitas nox ALDH. *VirgP* 19; B. Maria, virgo perpetua, ..~a solis *Ib.* 40. **c** ut dicit auctor ~e BART. ANGL. XII 4. **d** **1543** dat' Georgio S. pro iiij diebus in festo Epiphanie circa sepulcram (*sic*) S. Cuthberti ij s. ij d., ~a j d.; item dat' eidem pro Johanne P., Johanne W., Johanne O., iiij diebus ad iij d. et pro ~a cuilibet j d. *Ac. Durh.* 743. **e** ultor ab aurora veniens GARL. *Tri. Eccl.* 108.

auroralis, of dawn.

s1130 duas..lineas quasi ~i luce plenas ab equinoctiali solis ortu usque ad equinoctialem ejus occasum porrectas aspexit J. WORC. 32.

aurorescere, to dawn. **b** (fig.).

10.. ~ere, *lihte* WW. **b** cum evangelii splendor ~eret ALDH. *VirgP* 60.

aurose, in gold.

imaginem domini Salvatoris formose atque ~e in tabula depictam GOSC. *Aug. Maj.* 61A.

aurosus, golden (of colour).

genus..herbe..~i coloris *Alph.* 9 (cf. ib. 69: flores ~os).

aurotextus [al. div.], woven w. gold thread.

pro ~a purpura induitur nigra..tunica GOSC. *Edith* 43; **1415** vestimentum de albo panno ~o *Reg. Cant.* II 59; unum tapetum cum panno serico ~o FLETE *Westm.* 85.

auruginosus, jaundiced.

dicitur morbus auriginosus et arcuatus ab yride.. vel ab ave aureolo, et tunc est color faciei croceus GILB. VI 257 v. 2; yeraruffini..curat..dissintericos, †aruginosos, artheticos *Ib.* VII 346 v. 1.

aurugo [CL], jaundice. **b** (bibl.) mildew, blight. **c** (fig.).

pe gulsoghte, ~o, hicterícia, ..mutacio coloris *CathA.* **b** **s1305** hoc anno fuit tanta uredo pariter et ~o et siccitas in estate quod in maxima parte deficeret fenum terre *Flor. Hist.* III 127; *the meldewe*, ~o, erugo, rubigo *CathA.* **c** **1169** aliqui jam venerunt qui veluti pestilens ventus adducti mendaciorum ~ine terram corrumpunt (*Lit. Archiep.*) *Becket Mat.* VII 15.

aurum [CL], gold. **b** (fig.). **c** gold leaf. **d** gold thread. **e** (w. *friscum*) orphrey (*cf. aurifrigium*). **f** counterfeit gold. **g** (*w. vivum*) quicksilver.

auri materiem fulvi obrizumque metallum ALDH. *VirgV* 157; **735** ut mihi cum ~o conscribas epistolas BONIF. *Ep.* 35; [adduco] pretiosas gemmas et aurum [AS: *gold*] ÆLF. *Coll.* 96; **c1128** omnem decimam de ~o quod mihi eveniet de Fif et Forthrif *EChScot* 65; **1211** pro iij m. ~i de Muscia et j m. de *paillole* iij obolis minus ad quandam coronam regis *Pipe* 107; Hispaniensium..~i pallentis copiam magnam GIR. *PI* III 29 p. 317; **1242** pro..ix firmaculis ~i de precio ..et ix firmaculis ~i de pondere *Pipe* 127; **1245** (v. baculus 4); **1253** mm marce ~i..tam in folio quam in moneta, cuneo et palea *Liberate* 29 m. 3; **1254** ~um tam in folio, cuneo, bisanciis, Augustalibus et aliis diversis monetis quam in palleola *RGasc* I 484 (cf. *CalPat* 314); dicitur.. ~um sol BACON *Tert. sup.* 83; ~um etiam aliquando designatur per lapidem vel corpus Hiberi fluminis vel Pactoli vel Tagi, vel alterius, quia in istis reperiuntur grana ~i. et, quia Hybernici dicuntur ab Hybero fluvio.., ideo ~um vocatur corpus Hybernicum vel lapis Hybernicus. .. et ~um minus rufum vocatur Anglia, quia ibi oritur. et ~um bonum dicitur Hispania, vel Apulia vel Polonia vel alia regio ubi bonum ~um habundat. rubificare est facere ~um *Ib.* 84; **1305** pro lx soldatis ~i venalis *EEC* 322; **1422** in incremento escambii diversorum nobilium..~i contrafacti et soldati et ~i bassi provenientis de lxv lib. viij unciis dim. ~i veteris cimentat' in ~um purum

KRAc 301/19 r. 1. **b** ALDH. *VirgP* 19 (v. aeramentum b). **c** ALCUIN *SSEbor* 279 (v. bratteola); hanc cocto solidavit sedulus auro HANV. IX 386; **s1257** ~um de folio quod semper solebat valere x m. nunc non valet nisi ix m. vel octo *Leg. Ant. Lond.* 30; **1366** (v. benevolus c); **1472** pro necessariis ad picturam magni campanilis, viz. pro xxxj c^{ma} lib. ~i malliati, c ad vj s. viij d. . . *Fabr. York* 77; ~um coctum vocatur ~um limatum, ~um malleatum, ~um laboratum, ~um bracteatum, ~um signatum, ~um coelatum, lamina solis, ~i folia *LC* 280. **d** **1240** pannos ad ~um *Cal. Liberate* 459; **1265** de uno bono et pulcro panno ad ~um ad cooperiendam inde tumbam Johanne *Cl* 70; **1288** iij panni de ~o *KRAc* 231/26 m. 2; **1303** pro cc libratis serici..et panni ~i *EEC* 272; **1333** pro ~o de Cipr', ~o in plata..et aliis rebus..emptis..ad opus Philippe regine *LTRMem* 105 r. 110; **1369** ~um de Cipro *CalPat* 279; **1412** j remenaunt ~i de Venicia *EEC* 688; **1415** una capa totaliter de ~o cum rosis rubeis et nigris florata (*Test.*) *Foed.* IX 273; **1435** duas †tunaklis [? l. tuniklas] de nigro arras pulverizatas cum ~o de Luke [*Lucca*] *Test. Ebor.* II 53; **1439** xij pannos aureos de ~o Cypri de campo rubeo..foliis viridibus..pulverizato AMUND. II 189; **1449** pro nonnullis pannis.., foderaturis, ~o de Veneciis et Cipree *ExchScot* 346 (cf. ib. 385). **e** **1204** mantellum de samitto rubeo fretatum de ~o frisco *RChart* 134a. **f** conjungunt stannum, cuprum et mercurium et inde faciunt ~um sophisticum *Correct. Alch.* 8; **1422** (v. 1a supra). **g** argentum vivum vocatur ~um vivum, sicut sepius abutitur Avicenna isto verbo BACON *Tert. Sup.* 83; ~um vivum est argentum vivum *LC* 225.

2 gold (as currency or medium of exchange). **b** (w. *novum*) reduced coinage of Edward IV. **c** (w. *reginae*), queen-gold, queen's share of fines or sim. paid to king.

955 (10c) pretiolum hoc est cxx solidos ~i *CS* 563; dedit.. markam ~i pro uno molino eorum *DB* I 2; [manerium reddit] ad opus reginae ii uncias auri *Ib.* 209; cc mancae ~i [AS: *mances goldes*] (*Quad.*) *GAS* 359; marcam ~i in medio talee sicut libram unam incidas *Dial. Scac.* I 5K; **a1180** (v. byzantus); **1338** cum ducentis florenis ~i vocatis *lambkyns Cl* 161 m. 18; **1422** in excambio ~i eo quod minus ponderabat novo pondere per statutum domini regis noviter editum *Ac. Durh.* 228. **b** **1464** in ponderibus pro novo ~o, ponderant' sc. x s. dim. nobil' et quadrant' ejusdem cunagii (*Comp. Mettingham*) *N. & Q. Ser.* 1, II 411. **c** **1156** telarii de Oxineford' r.c. de vj li. pro j m. ~i regine vj librarum *Pipe* 83; est..promisso compromissum ut, cum regi c vel cc m. promiserit, regine pariter teneatur pro c m. argenti regi promissis in j m. ~i *Dial. Scac.* II 26A; **1238** finem fecit cum rege pro xx m. pro habenda saisina terrarum que fuerunt patris sui, pro quo fine debet regine ij m. pro ~o suo *LTRMem* 12 r. 6; **1242** de xxj m. de ~o regine receptis..et allocatis Aaron Judeo Lond' in fine suo per breve regine directum Johanni Francisco custodi ~i regine in Scaccario *Pipe* 126–7; ad ~um regine solvit xl s. *State Tri. Ed. I* 33; **1352** ad opus domine P. regine Anglie de ~o suo de quodam fine facto xl m. *Rec. Leic.* II 81.

3 or (her.).

1384 arma..que sunt de ~o cum uno leone de azureo rampante *Pat* 317 m. 16; inter colores medios secundus est color aureus quia ~um ab aura est dictum.., eo quod repercussione aure plus refulget BAD. AUR. 97; portat de rubeo cum una stella de ~o; et sic G.: *il port de goules une estoil de ore Ib.* 133.

auscultare [CL], to listen. **b** (w. acc. or indir. qu.) to listen to, hear. **c** to heed. **d** to eavesdrop. **e** to give a (preliminary) hearing to. **f** to check (a copy) by hearing, collate.

ejus admonitionibus humiliter..in omnibus..~ans BEDE *HE* III 3; **14..** asculto, A. *to lystny* WW; **1573** abscondite sedebat ascultans et curam adhibens damis..in parco *Pat* 1105 m. 34. **b** acsi..Sirinarum concentus surdis auribus ~abat ALDH. *VirgP* 40; cum ~averitis [*ponne ge gehyran*] ecclesiae campanas ÆLF. *Coll.* 103; ut asscultaret..lectionem *Cust. Westm.* 258; **1335** bona nova..appetitis ascultare *Lit. Cant.* II 99; **s1399** asculta qualiter quosdam de suis coadjutoribus remuneravit *Dieul.* 145v. **c** sic Deus auscultat devota mente rogantes ALDH. *VirgV* 2049; ne ~etis..rumores tales quibus posset..scandalum generari *AncrR* 168; **1376** exemplum cujusdam litere..legisse..et illud..cum maturitate debita ascultasse *Reg. Aberd.* I 192. **d** **1391** assuetus est ascultare noctanter sub parietibus vicinorum *Leet Norw.* 70. **e** quicumque lecturus est in conventu aut aliquid cantaturus, si necesse habet, ab eo [sc. cantore] priusquam incipiat debet ascultari *Cust. Cant.* 90. **f** **1296** qui una mecum easdem litteras ad autenticas..diligenter et fideliter ascultarunt *Anglo-Scot. Rel.* 72; **1319** predictas literas..fideliter exemplavi et cum predicto registro una cum..clerico diligenter ascultavi *Reg. Roff. Ep.* f. 112.

auscultatio [CL], eavesdropping. **b** checking (of a copy).

exeunt..in auditionem vel ascultationem MAP *NC* II 23 p. 92. **b** **1440** post diligentem collacionem et ~onem *Reg. Dunferm.* no. 417.

auscultator [CL], listener. **b** eavesdropper. **c** scout.

attonitis auditoribus ignarisque ~oribus arcana mentis ipsorum recludentes ALDH. *VirgP* 27. **b** **1413** in nocte sub parietibus..et..communis ascultator et obauditor *Proc. J. P.* 97. **c** **1297** custodiam super costera maris..poni facias, viz. ascultatores, vigiles et signa..per quos..patria celeriter premuniri poterit de flota navium inimicorum nostrorum *Cl* 114 m. 24d.; **s1388** o stulti et insipientes, exploratores vel ascultatores extra exercitum non habentes, surgite nunc..! *Plusc.* X 9.

auscultus, a hearing.

1410 hujusmodi minus discrete cognita referentibus ascultum seu audienciam nolueritis impertiri *FormOx* 425.

ausculus v. musculus.

†ausibilis, audacious.

1188 quia Terram Sanctam prophanasti.., in tanti sceleris presumptuosam et plectibilem ~em audaciam debita animadversatione decernere..sollicitudo nos admonet (*Lit. Imp.*) R. HOWD. II 357.

ausili- v. auxili-. ausilla v. axilla. ausius v. audere 1c. ausliare v. auxiliari a. ausor v. haucera.

auspex [CL], diviner by observation of birds. **b** (fig.).

~ex, id est qui avium auguria intendit ALDH. *PR* 114; augur vel ~ex, *fugelweohlere* ÆLF. *Gl.*; *a divine* [v.l. *dyvynour*], ~ex, augur, auspicator, divinator *CathA*. **b** Agatho..aequi non marcidus auspex FRITH. 739.

auspicari [CL], to divine. **b** to inaugurate. **c** (?) to be auspicious.

7.. ~antur, *haelsadon GlC* A 948; *to divine*, ~ari, divinare *CathA*. **b** ~antes, initiantes *GlC* A 894. **c** rex..vix tandem effecta ~ante [v.l. aspirante] gratia Salvatoris *Enc. Emmae* II 16 (cf. aspirare 2a).

auspicate, auspiciously, successfully.

†auspicacissime [? l. ~atissime] munus suum peregit FERR. *Kinloss* 40.

auspicatio [CL], **~atus,** divination (by birds).

a dyv[in]ynge, auspicium in volatu avium, ..~atus, ~acio, divinacio *CathA*.

auspicator v. auspex.

auspicium [CL], auspice, (observation of) omen. **b** inauguration, beginning. **c** (w. *bonum*) prosperity, success.

THEOD. *Pen.* I xv 4 (v. augurium); cui regi, in ~ium suscipiendae fidei et regni caelestis, potestas etiam terreni creverat imperii BEDE *HE* II 9; consul Romanorum, dum nullius boni ominis sortiretur ~ium J. SAL. *Pol.* 409B; **s1113** quod in triste ~ium evenit M. PAR. *Min.* I 218; perterritus omine tristi et ~io infelici *Mir. J. Bev.* C 339. **b** ~ium, initium actionis *GlC* A 911; †aupicium, initium, *angin* ÆLF. *Gl.*; contigit ut in ipsis promotionis sue ~iis..visus sit offendisse regem AD. EYNS. *Hug.* III 9. **c** Ercombirchtus..meliori ~io principatu functus W. MALM. *GR* I 11.

austagium [OF *austage* < augustaticum], harvest due (cf. *Hund. & Hund. R.* 165).

1258 ~ium in eodem com. [*Dorset*]: de hundredo de Bruneshull' de ~io viij s.; de hundredo de Whyteweye de eodem xvj s. *LTRMiscR* 6/5 m. 3; **1301** de redditu ad festum S. Mich. quod vocatur *austage AncExt* 8 m. 8.

austat v. auferre 1a.

auster [CL], south wind. **b** south. **c** (pl.). **d** southern people or faction.

~er, *suðuuind GlC* A 951; **801** surgat aquilo vel ~er ALCUIN *Ep.* 215; ~er vel nothus, *suðen wind* ÆLF. *Gl.*; cavere ab haustro et borea GAD. 50 v. 1. **b** positus est in ecclesia..juxta altare ad ~rum BEDE *HE* V 19; ubi plus declinat ad austri / arcturique polos HANV. VIII 373; **c1253** [acra que jacet in longitudine versus] astrum et boream *Cart. Boxgrove* 120; **c1300** quod jacet in longitudine et latitudine juxta toftum predicte I. versus auxtrum *AncD* A 363. **c** lustro polos passim solos, non scando per austros ALDH. *Aen.* 5 (*Iris*) 4. **d** **s1461** austro tunc cesserat arctos, / et doluit casum *Reg. Whet.* I 413.

austercus v. asturcus.

austere, harshly, sternly.

[cervos] ~e praecipiens..de insula discedere exterminavit *V. Cuthb.* III 5; **1379** ~ius senteneiare deberet..contra quoscumque.. *Dip. Corr. Ric. II* 6; de Wilfridi..expulsione plures..chronicatores..nimis ~e, ..quasi hyperbolice, materiam dilatare noscuntur ELMH. *Cant.* 276.

austeritas [CL], harshness, rigour, cruelty. **b** (of weather). **c** austerity, hardship.

quaedam vetita et legis ~ate interdicta ALDH. *VirgP* 10; non putabat se..tantam paganorum umquam posse solum sufferre ~atem ASSER *Alf.* 42; **10..** ~ate, *reðnesse* WW; [musica] ~atem reponit, jocunditatem exponit GIR. *TH* III 12; **s1214** cum ~ate comminans quod, si voluntas eis non inesset, nihilominus..procederet G. COLD. *Durh.* 22; horum [abbatum] ~ati et pigricie imputatur quod cementum muri religionis monastice..dissipatur ELMH. *Cant.* 200. **b** aeris fugatur ~as KETEL *J. Bev.* 271; **1432** postquam robusta ventorum ~as et pluviarum copie..cessavissent (J. CARPENTER) *MGL* III 457. **c** philomela significat religiosos super duros ramos, id est ~ates religionis, habitantes O. CHERITON *Fab.* 42.

austerius v. asturcus, austere.

austerus [CL < αὐστηρός], sour, bitter. **b** harsh, stern. **c** powerful. **d** violent. **e** austere, ascetic.

folia buxi..immissa vinum molle faciunt vinum ~um GAD. 135. 1; in vino ~o *Alph.* 137. **b** ~ioris animi vir BEDE *HE* III 5; nobis tam ~us es et tam hispidum nobis dans supercilium MAP *NC* IV 16 p. 202; **s1399** [rex] dixit expresse vultu ~o et protervo quod leges sue erant in ore suo *V. Ric. II* 193; *felle*, acer, acerbus, asper, atrox, ~us, ~is *CathA*. **c** multus ~us homo [AS: *strec man*] vult..tueri suum hominem utro modo, sive pro libero sive pro servo (*Cons. Cnut.*) *GAS* 323 (= *Quad.*: multi *strecman*, id est potentes sive fortes). **d** sic prius austerus stat sub moderamine motus GOWER *VC* I 1897. **e** cum dicerent: 'mirum quod tam ~am tenere continentiam velis', respondebat: '~iora ego vidi' BEDE *HE* V 12; ad ~iorem vitam fratres invitabat audientes W. CANT. *Mir. Thom.* III 8.

austorium v. haustorium.

australis [CL], southern. **b** (n. pl.) southern parts, the south.

pontifex..ad ~ia regna tetendit EDDI *Wilf.* 64; provinciae..~es ad confinium usque Hymbrae BEDE *HE* V 23; ecclesiam villae quae ~is Burton dicitur FOLCARD *J. Bev.* 6; **c1270** una acra jacet..in ~issimo forlongo *Ch. R. de Bailol, Harwell* (*Berks R.O.*); **1372** ad scalarem †austrarem ecclesie *Arch. Bridgw.* 193; **1438** ex partibus boriali et ~i *FormA* 392; **1469** tam in latere ~i quam in latere boriali..cancelli *Ac. Durh.* 642; ~e, quod vocant Hispani, mare CAMD. *Br.* 163. **b** **s1215** si Stephanus Cantuariensis archiepiscopus in ~ibus et frater ejus Symon Eboracensis archiepiscopus factus in septentrionalibus dominarentur *Flor. Hist.* II 156.

2 (of persons) southern. **b** belonging to (or member of) the southern 'nation' (Oxford). **c** (fig.) mild as the south wind.

Aelli rex ~ium Saxonum BEDE *HE* II 5; ~es Picti *Ib.* III 4; **s1260** orta est discordia..in universitate Cantebrugie, facta..prius quadam..contumelia inter duos garciones, unum ~em et alterum aquilonarem *Flor. Hist.* II 458. **b** **1268** quatuor magistri..artium, duo sc. boriales et duo ~es *StatOx* 25; **1349** discordia..inter ~es et boriales, qui omnes in veritate unius et ejusdem nacionis sunt *Ib.* 151. **c** si male de domino fueris, de te bene dicet / vix pius australis socius, jocundus amicus D. BEC. 1259.

australiter, southerly, towards the south.

1423 per unum latus strate..secundum quod aldermanria sua jacet occidentaliter, orientaliter, borialiter, ~er, linialiter vel aliqualiter alio modo *BB Winchester* 59; **1441** (v. borealiter); **1539** jacet ~er ex parte orientali cancelle ecclesie (*MinAc* 7311) *Hist. Francisc. Eng.* 227.

austraris v. australis a.

Austrarius, Austrian.

s1193 a duce ~iorum captus est SILGRAVE 97.

Austrasiensis, Austrian.

s1193 Limpoldus dux ~is *Itin. Ric.* VI 37.

Austrasius, Austrasian.

s865 Lodowico Turingiam, ~ios Francos et Saxoniam dimisit W. MALM. *GR* II 110.

austratus v. 2 astratus. austriceria v. asturcaria.

Austricus, Austrian.

s1191 intrans / Austricus hanc [Tholomaida] princeps signa priora locat. / indignans victor sua posteriora locari, / Austrica vexilla jussit in antra jaci GARL. *Tri. Eccl.* 32–4.

austrinare [? < auster], to discolour or shrivel.

to defoule, attaminare, ..~are, coinquinare, ..*to make leyn*, ~are, ..macerare *CathA*.

austrinus [CL], southern. **b** (n. pl.) southern parts, the south. **c** (of people). **d** subject to prevailing south wind.

quando septentrionalis ventus post haustrinum venit GAD. 50. 2. **b** ~a Brettones occupaverant BEDE *HE* I 1. **c** apud Scottos ~os *Ib.* III 26; Angli, quamquam ab initio tripartitam sortirentur linguam, ~am scilicet, mediterraneam et borealem HIGD. I 59 p. 158. **d** si hyems ~a, pluviosa et tranquilla fiat et ver siccum boreale GAD. 37. 1.

Austrius, Austrasian.

s680 ~ii terga vertunt GERV. TILB. II 18.

Austrogothus v. Ostrogothus. austrum v. 2 astrum 2b. austucia v. astutia. austur- v. astur-. ausungia v. axungia. 1 ausus v. audere.

2 ausus [CL], audacity, presumption. **b** outrage. **c** enterprise, exploit.

ut ipsi Deo seipsum quodammodo proprie impietatis ~u preferret J. SAL. *Pol.* 465B; impunitas ~um prebebit delinquendi BRAKELOND 122; ~u prepropero seu temerario seque suosque tam..manifestis exponere periculis GIR. *RG* I 5; si quis ~u temerario machinatus sit in mortem regis BRACTON 118b; **1377** cum in conspectu dignitatis apostolice ..hausus humanus omnimodus conticescat *FormOx* 380; **s1382** ipsum ~u sacrilego papam nominare presumpserunt WALS. *HA* II 73. **b** **s1263** conjuratio ribaldorum qui.. majores..burgorum violentis ~ibus opprimebant WYKES 138. **c** nobiles..~us nihil eque impedit ut diffidentia GIR. *TH intr.* p. 5.

aut [CL], or. **b** (in indir. qu.). **c** (w. *nec*).

quis tantos casus aut quis tam plurima leti / suscipit.. vulnera? ALDH. *Aen.* 87. 5; quamvis Quintilis ardens / Sextilis aut etiam protelent tempora terris *Id. VirgV* 2782; ubicumque clericus aliquis aut monachus adveniret BEDE *HE* III 26; siquis fecerit sepem vel fossatum, ..aut arborem ..prostraverit *DB* I 1; ut..sensibus vulgi sententias sanctorum aut sapientum reponamus BACON *Maj.* I 17. **b** et cur non posset vinciri inquirit ab illo / an prius aut magicas didicisset forsitan artes ALCUIN *SSEbor* 810; **1226** ad assisam capiendam..utrum una acra terre..sit libera elemosina..aut laicum feodum *Pat* 80. **c** illum nec terrae nec possunt cingere caeli / nec mare..vallat / aut zonae mundi ALDH. *VirgV pref.* 32; quod eam [manum] nec producere aut contrahere..potuerit R. COLD. *Cuthb.* 108.

2 either..or (repeated). **b** (w. *vel* or *seu*).

680 aut veritatem ignorando aut falsitatem dissimulando obmutescunt ALDH. *Ep.* 4 p. 482; semper aut discere aut docere aut scribere dulce habui BEDE *HE* V 24; aut plus aut minus *DB* I 203; queritur de aliquo aut quid sit aut quale aut quantum aut qualiter se habeat ad aliquid aut quid agat aut quid patiatur aut quando sit aut ubi aut quomodo situm sit aut quid habeat BALSH. *AD* 130. **b** in carminibus Vergilii vel Lucani seu Persi Flacci aut Terenti ALDH. *Met.* 10 p. 90; actibus aut dictis seu solo noxia sensu *Id. VirgV* 2826 (cf. ib. 1461); **747** perpaucae sunt civitates in Longobardia vel in Francia aut in Gallia in qua non sit.. meretrix generis Anglorum BONIF. *Ep.* 78 p. 169; hoc exemplificatum est vel consuetum aut vulgatum, igitur tenendum BACON *Maj.* I 17; **1585** hiis quatuor vel tribus, quorum aut feodarius vel escaetor sit unus *Pat* 1303 m. 8*d*.

3 otherwise (= *sin minus*).

1254 oportet ut capella..de novo cooperietur; aut erit in brevi ruinosa *CalIMisc* I 205; **a1410** clamabit: "venias, fac finem de racione; / aut attachiatus eris et tua terra seisita" (*Vers. Exch.*) *EHR* XXXVI 60.

autelagium v. altaragium.

autem [CL], but, however, now, on the other hand. **b** (w. *quidem*). **c** (repeated) (?) on the one hand, ..on the other.

edictis sanctos crudelibus urgens, / ..ut Christum damnati voce negarent; / nolentes autem..tormenta luebant ALDH. *VirgV* 1872; at contra fuit quidam..cujus visiones, non ~em et conversatio, plurimis, sed non sibimet ipsi, profuit. fuit ~em..vir in officio militari positus, BEDE *HE* V 13; erat †autum monasterium amoenum *Ib.* III 19; siquis.. divadiatus fuerit, viii lib. regi emendabit; sin ~em, quietus erit erga regem *DB* I 1; Robertus vero apposuit eam [dim. virgam] huic manerio. hund[retum] ~em dicit quod nunquam ibi pertinuit *Ib.* 46b; **s1178** illis ~em..revertentibus, cum venirent ante portam ecclesie, ..ait sanctus Robertо: "progredere ad domum tuam in pace; ego ~em in meam.. regredior" M. PAR. *Min.* I 404; **s1178** ut hec omnia vera, non ~em fantastica credantur *Flor. Hist.* II 90; **s1398** unde .., cum duellare cepissent, rex ~em pacem statim proclamabat *Dieul.* 144; **1411** per priorem..si presens fuerit, ~em in ipsius absencia per suppriorem *Lit. Cant.* III 129. **b** pathos quidem Latina lingua passiones dicuntur; sunt autem numero sex ALDH. *Met.* 10 p. 94; similitudo.. apparens quidem specie, non existens ~em in re W. FITZST. *Thom.* 29. **c** protinus..ordinem judiciarium reciprocarunt: eos ~em dignos pena dimiserunt; aliorum ~em auferebant res FAVENT 4.

authenticare, to authenticate, stamp as genuine or authoritative.

laicis authenticat illum / pileus in capite VINSAUF *PN* 440; literas ipsius patentes super hoc facto ~ando et approbando postulavit GIR. *JS* 7 p. 356; **s1244** cornu spreto totius communitatis antiquo et a tempore quo non exstat memoria prius †auctentizato *Reg. Pinchbeck* I 53; cum doctrina magistri..~etur per concilium generale DUNS *Sent.* I v 1. 8; collegium cardinalium in questionibus fidei terminandis requirit aliorum concilium, ut magis autenticetur per consensum plurium determinacio eorum OCKHAM *Dial.* 480; antiquitas non auctenticat (KYN.) *Ziz.* 5; ex fide debemus credere quod quidquid humani actus ipse non autenticat est prophanum WYCL. *Civ. Dom.* I 439; **1400** quod eas [litteras]..transcribi..faceremus ac..transcripta..auctoritate nostra ordinaria auctenticare curaremus *FormOx* 186; **1406** ego..publicus apostolica auctoritate notarius..hoc presens publicum instrumentum confeci, publicavi, autenticavi et in hanc publicam formam redegi (*Instr.*) *Chr. S. Alb.* 8.

authenticatio, authentication.

s1216 de Veronica et ejus autenticatione M. PAR. *Maj.* III 7 *rub.*; **1369** per presentes, quibus sigillum nostrum ad fidele testimonium ac autenticacionem premissorum fecimus apponi *Melrose* II 459; multa sunt paris auctoritatis, dum tamen paritatem †autentificacionis eorum ex ignorancia divini judicii ignoramus WYCL. *Civ. Dom.* III 347; exponere autoritatem est veritatem ac autoritatem vel autenticacionem ejus supponere *Id. Ver.* I 270; **1435** graduaciones in eisdem [facultatibus] pro earum auctenticacione fiendas *EpAcOx* 130.

authentice, authentically, authoritatively.

1220 ut hec mea donatio..illibata permaneat, eam presenti scripto sigillo meo signat[am] autentice roboravi (*Ch.*) *Fabr. York app.* 144; **s1235** papa..eas [decretales] eleganter abbreviatas et collectas sollenniter et autentice per totius mundi latitudinem legi precepit et divulgari M. PAR. *Maj.* III 328; non quidem ~e et judicialiter definiendo, sed veridico dogmate et assercione simplici affirmando OCKHAM *Pol.* I 267; **1431** per litteras vestras patentes..autentice sigillatas *Lit. Cant.* III 157; **1549** ut registrentur ~e omnia testamenta *Conc. Scot.* II 110.

authenticus [LL < αὐθεντικός], (of documents) authentic, genuine. **b** (of seals) authentic or authoritative. **c** (of sources, pronouncements, or sim.) authoritative. **d** (of usages or sim.) approved by authority, authorized. **e** (of persons or institutions) having authority. **f** (w. *altare*) high altar (*cf.* 2 *altare* 1b).

1181 sicut in ~is eorum scriptis..continentur *BBC* (*Beverley, Ch. Papae*) 37; **s1181** pias bonorum collationes, quas sancti ejus predecessores..autentico scripto confirmaverant W. NEWB. III 5; **1289** litteris auctenticis *RGasc* II 377; **1344** litteras autenticas sigillo..predecessoris nostri..consignatas *Eng. Clergy* 279; summi pontifices in suis ~is privilegiis..ita dicunt ELMH. *Cant.* 82; **1423** presentes nostre litere obligatorie aut earum verum et aucteticum transumptum *RScot* 243b. **b** **s1192** litteras ..revocatorias..non vidimus.., nec earum transcriptum sigillis appositis et ~is consignatum *G. Ric. I* 242 (= R. HOWD. III 189: suppositis et auctenticis); cartam..cum ~o sigillo GIR. *RG* I 6 p. 35; **a1240** per sigilli nostri †attentici appositionem *Reg. Aberbr.* I 263 (cf. *Conc. Scot.* II 78 [**1420**]: sigillis †attenticis); **1263** quia sigillum predicti Nicholai episcopo Lincolniensi ignotum fuit, noluit ejus resignacionem admittere absque aliquo sigillo autentico (*Lit. Resign.*) *Ann. Durh.* 177; **1315** eidem fides plenaria adhibeatur sicut sigillo autentiquo *RGasc* IV 1626 (xvii); **1424** quia sigillum quod habeo minus est aucteticum, sigillum decani..procuravi hiis litteris apponi *Reg. Cant.* I 328. **c** verbi finalis sillaba ~is illustrium poetarum exemplis reperitur produci ALDH. *PR* 122 (cf. *Id. Met.* 10 p. 93: ~is versibus); nostra mediocritas, autentica veterum auctoritate subnixa *Id. VirgP* 30; quicquid ille protulit autenticum et sacrosanctum est J. SAL. *Pol.* 653D; potestatis ~e censura AD. MARSH *Ep.* 92 p. 218; legens ~as septem petitiones Dominice Orationis ECCLESTON *Adv. Min.* 65; non est auctenticum quod tot modis et non pluribus fiat absolutio nominativi BACON XV 104; diffinicionem. propriam dominii non legerunt in aliqua scriptura ~a OCKHAM *Pol.* I 308; quo [consilio] habito illud quod deliberatum est efficiatur magis autenticum *Id. Dial.* 885; sicut evidenter ostendunt libri ~i Novi et Veteris Testamenti BRADW. *CD* 29E; major antiquitas non facit majorem auctoritatem, quia tunc Vetus Testamentum esset magis ~um quam Evangelium (KYN.) *Ziz.* 5; primus modus [mortis Edmundi].. verior aliis et autenticior habetur BROMPTON 906; **1440** laudabili et ~o testimonio commendatus BEKYNTON I 136. **d** **1117** ut autentica ejus [ecclesie] privilegia juxta canonum sanctiones nullis perturbationibus violentur (*Lit. Papae*) W. MALM. *GP* I 69; respondit non eam [antiphonam Thome decantatam] ~am esse; nondum enim ex apostolica auctoritate catalogo martyrum martyr ascriptus erat W. CANT. *Mir. Thom.* I 11; **1288** in puplicam formam vel auctenticam redigere judicata *FormOx* 357; **s1406** omnia et singula supradicta..approbabit auctentico modo *Chr. S. Alb.* 6; **1488** promittentes..nos..literas nostras patentes ..approbatorias in forma debita et autentica..daturos *RScot* 482b. **e** si auctentice sunt persone, ..unum vel duos introducere poterunt in exteriorem domum Scaccarii *Dial. Scac.* I 7E; placuit viris autenticis carmina amatoria.. subducenda esse a manibus adolescentium (NECKAM *Sac.*) *Med. Sci.* 372; quid vilem in populo clerum et minus ~um reddit? GIR. *GE* II 34 p. 336; iiij ex vobis aut v ex potioribus et magis ~is *Id. Symb.* 31 p. 328; **s1078** hujus autentice ecclesie consuetudines claustrales prosequitur claustrum ecclesie B. Albani M. PAR. *Min.* I 25; **s1236** procurantibus rege et magnatibus, episcopis et aliis viris autenticis *Id. Maj.* III 372; **s1240** signis nostris et aliarum autenticarum personarum appensis *Reg. Malm.* I 393; auctentici abbates erunt in camera regis et alii in conventu et in dormitorio *Cust. Cant.* 254; **1425** coram vobis discretis viris, autentica persona [sc. notario] et testibus his presentibus *Reg. Cant.* I 183; **1449** coram notariis ~is *Reg. Whet.* I 154. **f** **1270** servicium..audire..in ecclesia parochiali et minime in auctentico altari chori..monachorum *Reg. Malm.* II 172; ducatur..abbas ad osculandum altare autenticum *Cust. Cant.* 70; **1441** volo..quod exequie mee solempniter fiant ad autenticum altare in magno choro..ecclesie *Test. Ebor.* II 186; **1555** sacerdos completurus officium indutus casula ad altare ~um assumpta..ad altare accedat *Process. Sal.* 85.

2 a (sb. n.) authentic or original document. **b** aphorism. **c** (sb. f.) 'authentic', 'novel' (constitution supplementary to Justinian's Code).

a **1072** reliqua reliquorum, tam autentica quam eorum exemplaria, in ea combustione..sunt absumpta (*Lit. Lanfranci*) W. MALM. *GP* I 29; **1196** sicut in auctentico inter ipsum et regem Francorum confecto continentur (*Lit. Archiep. Rotom.*) DICETO *YH* II 136; **s1213** cum hujus [v.l. hujusmodi] ~um a domino papa accepisset WEND. II 96; **1220** sicut continetur in autentico ipsius domini regis *Pat* 265; **c1230** in †attentico predictorum judicum *Dryburgh* 63; **c1236** requisitus utrum omnes articuli in illo exemplari contenti insererentur in autentico igne consumpto, dicit quod sic *MonA* II 419b; **s1236** per autenticum domini pape M. PAR. *Maj.* III 368; **s1246** cujus canonizationis auctenticum elegantissimum in libro de vita ipsius poterit qui curat reperire *Id. Min.* III 13; habes tu pro te aliquod autenticum sub sigillo ad hoc faciendum? *Proc. v. A. Kyteler* 5. **b** **s1294** Edwardus, cogitans..illud ~um: 'quicquid delirant reges, plectuntur Achivi' [HOR. *Epist.* I ii 14] *Ann. Ang. & Scot.* 327. **c** hodie oportet [editionem] in scriptis fieri, ut in ~a illa: 'offeratur ei libellus..' RIC. ANGL. *Summa* 1; institutiones Justiniani cum ~is et Infortiato SWAFHAM 99; **1277** renunciamus..privilegio fori..et..beneficio auctentice que loquitur 'de duobus reis' *Conc.* II 31; **1289** renunciantes auctentice 'presente'..et omni..beneficio juris.. *RGasc.* II 525; **1314** premissa..observabunt, renunciantes specialiter autentice †determinus posite in Codice sub titulo 'de arbitris' *CollectOx* II 268; ut habetur in ~a, 'ut ecclesia Romana c annorum gaudeat prescripcione' col. ii OCKHAM *Pol.* I 54.

authentificatio v. authenticatio. authentiquus v. authenticus 1b. authentizare v. authenticare.

authentus [cf. αὐθέντης], 'authent', a 'tone' in plain-song.

moderni..unumquemque modum in duos partiti sunt, ut videlicet ille canendi modus qui in acutis versaretur, ~us, id est auctoralis sive principalis vocaretur, qui vero magis in gravibus moram faceret plagis vel plagalis..seu subjugalis diceretur. distinguuntur autem sic: ~us protus apud Latinos cantores 'primus tonus' vocatur; plagis protus 'secundus'; ~us deuterus, 'tertius' [etc.]. ~us vero 'auctoralis', Grece αὐθέντης, sonat; auctoritatem namque ipsi αὐθεντίαν vocant J. COTTON 1404CD; quisquis modus acutus vocaretur auctentus, id est auctor vel princeps TUNSTEDE 229b.

author- v. auctor-. authumpnus v. autumnus.

Autisiodorensis, of Auxerre (Burgundy). **b** (w. *vinum*).

habens de..panno viridi ~i tunicam W. FITZST. *Thom.* 97. **b** **1186** pro ij tonellis vini ~is de modiatione *Pipe* 197; **1200** ad emendationem xx tonellorum vini Andegav' et v Aucerensis *Pipe* 89; **1212** pro ij tonellis ~is de prisa *Pipe* 45; **1242** vinum Aucer' *Cal. Liberate* 118

autompnus v. autumnus. autonom- v. antonom-. autor- v. auctor-.

autocephalus [αὐτοκέφαλος], autocephalous, having no head (or superior) but oneself.

autocefalus, per seipsos habent caput *Erf.* 2. 270. 7.

autrax v. anthrax.

autumare [CL], to affirm, declare. **b** to believe, suppose.

~ant, atfirmant *GlC* A 896; Pelagiani..se boni aliquid a seipsis absque gratia Dei habere stulta praesumptione ~ant BEDE *Tab.* I 3; **1337** super hac littera quid facere debemus nobis quidam periti in jure suum consilium ~abant, dicentes quod.. *Lit. Cant.* II 156. **b** **a690** neu..Scotticos sciolos..sugillare a quoquam ~er ALDH. *Ep.* 5 p. 493; autumat incassum.. / hoc sibi clasma tetrum sacras gessisse puellas *Id. VirgV* 2256; in domum comitis..quem..sibi amicissimum ~abat BEDE *HE* III 14; quem ~abat [*gl.*: putabat] esse defunctum *V. Osw.* 408; ad videndum, ut ~o, si jam fratres..propinquassent *V. Dunst.* B. 18; **10..** ~o, *ic wene* WW; dum deserta, quibus eos adesse ~averat,.. peteret G. MON. I 5; rex ~ans puerum esse qui plangitur MAP *NC* III 3 p. 128; quidam ~ant a Wandalis..nuncupationem Gaidelos traxisse GIR. *PI* I 18 p. 98; **s1303** si ~ent nos.. carnibus abundare, forte ab obsidione recedent *Flor. Hist.* III 310; ex equorum tumultu..bases terre fugam petere ~ant S. SIM. *Itin.* 52.

autumnalis (autumpnalis) [CL], autumnal, of autumn. **b** concerned w. harvest. **c** (w. *statutum*) harvest regulation, 'by-law'. **d** (w. *rex*) mock king at harvest festival (cf. *Med. Stage* I 143, 261*n.*). **e** (sb. n. pl.) harvest work.

†675 (12c) ~i torrido..caumate *CS* 37; tempore praepostero, id est vernali, non ~i ALDH. *VirgP* 38 p. 290; **c795** auctumnali frigore ALCUIN *Ep.* 86; ~is dies, *hærfestlic dæg* ÆLF. *Gl.*; **s1257** (v. aestivalis a); **1296** in instanti tempore ~i *Lit. Cant.* I 23. **b** **1209** in pane precariarum auptumnalium v quarteria [frumenti] *Crawley* 190 (= *Pipe Wint.* 51); **1242** in pratis falcandis et precariis ~ibus *Pipe* 137; de operibus estivalibus et ~ibus relaxatis *Ib.* 140; in custo ~i.., quia apud Eltham metunt ad decimam garbam *Ib.* 141; **c1260** pro..servicio carruum ~ium *Cart. Bilsington* 128; **1270** concedo..omnes fructus ~es dicti manerii una cum feno hujus anni *Cl* 286; **1325** expense ~es *Ac. Durh.* 165; **1345** pro opere uno ~i *Comp. Swith.* 145; **1423** pro festis ~ibus hoc anno c s. *Ac. Obed. Abingd.* 102. **c** **1329** conservatores statutorum ~ium presentant quod xv garbe frumenti abducte fuerunt de blado domini (*CourtR Halton*) *EHR* XLV 218; **1331** statuta ~ia: ..statutum fuit hic ne quis receptat..aliquos glanatores..qui possunt metere (*CourtR Newington*) *Ib.* 211. **d** **1488** recepcio denariorum: ..de x d. pro corona conducta regi †attumnali *Ac. Churchw. Bath* 88 (cf. ib. 91). **e** ista ultima lex vadiari potest ad salvandum ~ia HENGHAM *Magna* 5 (cf. ib. 11: in casu lucrandi ~ia aut redditum assisum).

autumnare, (autumpnare), to usher in autumn. **b** to do harvest work, reap.

autumnus ibi [in festo S. Bartholomei] incipit et terminatur ix Cal. Dec.; unde versus: dat Clemens hyemem, dat Petrus ver Cathedratus; / estuat Urbanus; autumnat Bartholomeus LYNDW. 194b. **b** **c1230** grossa animalia habere debent..cum animalibus domini postquam ~atum fuerit usque ad Natale *Doc. Bec* 59; **1277** in omnibus custis ~ancium cum *rypegos*, viij s. *Ac. Wellingb.* 17; **1295** in liberacione j garcionis custodientis oves dum bercarius ~avit *MinAc* 1070/8; **1296** in allec' et pane pro parte pro ~antibus *DL MinAc* 1/1 r. 4.

autumnarius, harvest worker, stacker.

a coker, autumpnarius *CathA*.

autumnatio, harvest work.

c1230 omnes homines manerii communiter post plenam ~onem debent percipere j s. vj d. de domino *Doc. Bec* 59.

autumnus (autumpnus) [CL], autumn. **b** harvest time, harvest. **c** harvest work.

arboribus..autumni quae fructum tempore perdunt ALDH. *CE* 4. 12. 19; ~us, illo [sc. sole] ad inferiora decidente, siccus [est] et frigidus BEDE *TR* 35; ver, autumpnus, hyems, estas dominantur in anno D. BEC. 2793; **1331** pro cana sua casei de authumpno ultimo preterito *ExchScot* 398; LYNDW. 194b (v. autumnare a). **b** **1185** in precariis ~i *Pipe* 125; facit j septimana j precem in autupno et in alia septimana ij *Rec. Templars* 64; **1209** in corredio..per v septimanas in auptumno *Crawley* 190 (= *Pipe Wint.* 50); **1220** salva..Roberto vestura sua de blado in auptumpno futuro *CurR* VIII 298; **c1244** faciunt..clerici..ludos quos vocant inductionem Maii sive ~i GROS. *Ep.* 107; **1294** custodes ~i presentant quod R. ..receptavit duas mulieres extraneas in campis dampnum faciend[o] per ~um *CourtR Rams.* 235 (cf. autumnalis c); **1345** de..custumariis pro eorum cariagio in ~o relaxato *Comp. Swith.* 146; **1374** habebit in ~o, viz. a festo S. Petri Advincla usque festum S. Michaelis per viij septimanas, j quarterium frumenti (*Cust. Stretham*) *Cust. Suss.* I 122; **1376** pro sociis in autompno xj d. *Ac. Obed. Abingd.* 38; **1423** si..homo.. miscuerit lollium inter fruges citra ~um *Reg. Whet.* II 390. **c** **1295** receperunt servientes maneriorum..pro ~o faciendo in siccis denariis liiij li. *Ac. Durh.* 494; **1323** eidem [garcioni] hac vice pro auctumpno suo ij s. *Ac. Obed. Abingd.* 3.

auvantagia v. avantagium 2b. auvus v. avus.

aux, augis [Ar. *awj*], 'auge', apogee. **b** (fig.).

non eris philosophie laribus educatus nisi scias..quid augis solis? NECKAM *NR* II 174; circulus est solis eccentricus, auge refulget / sol fervens, radiat abside dulce micans *Id. DS* I 489; punctus [in circulo solis] maxime elevatus a terra vocatur aux vel longitudo longior et punctus oppositus vocatur oppositio augis vel longitudo propior GROS. 22; motus..augium omnium stellarum *Id.* 27; centrum epicycli est in auge excentrica lune *Id.* 28; punctus in eccentrico qui maxime accedit ad firmamentum appellatur aux sive augis, quod interpretatur elevatio SACROB. *Sph.* 113; una pars eccentrici que vocatur oppositum augis descendit ad terram per v partes semidiametri eccentrici magis quam reliqua que dicitur aux BACON *Maj.* I 137; ecentricum epicicli Mercurii oportet alio modo depingere quia non habet augem deferentis fixam WALLINGF. *Albion* 354; epicyclos et eccentricos, auges atque geuzahar planetarum R. BURY *Phil.* 8. 127. **b** **c1430** ipse Johannis amor Whethamstede ubique proclamor, / ejus et alter honor hic lucis in †ange [l. auge] reponor (J. WHETHAMSTEDE) *MonA* II 200b.

auxatio v. axatio.

auxesis [αὔξησις], increase. **b** heightening of effect (rhet.).

auxessis, augmentum *Erf.* 2. 269. 55. **b** ad faciendam ~im potentiae caelestis 'ambos' dicit esse 'seniores' BEDE *Gen.* (xviii 11) 170; per rethoricam ~im..amplificari G. FOLIOT *Ep.* 128; genitivus..secundo positus ~im notat, ut sit sensus: 'homo est vanitas de numero vanitatum, immo est vanitas maxima vanitatum' NECKAM *Eccles.* (i 2) 74C; in ipsis nominibus dignitatum et locorum amplificatio quedam cum ~i notanda est *Ib.* 84D.

auxiatrix v. auctionator. auxiculatrix v. auxiliatrix.

auxiliabilis, helpful.

illius clementia celerius cunctis compatiendo ~is invocantibus exhibetur R. COLD. *Cuthb.* 52; ~iora erunt GILB. IV 177 v. 2.

auxilianter, as a helper or ally.

auxilianter obest et ab hoste meretur amari H. AVR. *Guthl.* 62. 9.

auxiliari [CL], **~iare,** to be helpful, give aid. **b** (trans.) to aid, care for. **c** to pay an 'aid' (to), contribute.

596 ut opus bonum, quod ~iante Domino coepistis, impleatis (*Lit. Papae*) BEDE *HE* I 23; nec [sacrificia haec] ~iari subjectis possunt *Ib.* I 7; **9..** fovere, i. alere, ~iari, *gehliwan* WW; **1215** quatinus eis sitis ~ientes (*sic*) et consulentes et intendentes ad..honorem nostrum *Cl* 228b; **1221** vulneravit..uxorem suam..sicut ipsa ei ~iari et succurrere voluit *SelPlCrown* 107; **1299** sperserunt et levaverunt fenum et †ausliaverunt *Doc. Bec* 178; **1316** socio suo auxsiliante..in foro *Rec. Leic.* I 298; **1321** requisiti si aliquis alius esset ~ians vel procurans ad illud factum, dicunt quod non *SelCCoron* 74; **1348** hominibus ~iantibus ad fugandum ..equicium ad faldam *Ac. Durh.* 546; **1350** intendant, consilient et ~ient *RScot* 736b. **b** et precibus rogitat se auxiliare piis ALCUIN *Carm.* 9. 178; auxiliare preces famulorum, virgo, tuorum *Ib.* 66. 2. 17; **1378** Rogero..~ianti eos pro aqua tractanda *Ac. Durh.* 586; **1381** †uno homini ~ianti unum equum..pro *le farssy Ib.* 590. **c** **c1202** auxilium mihi facient quando milites terre mee ~iabuntur *BBC (Egremont)* 91; **1221** habet tenentes in villa sua qui ad taillagia domini regis nolunt ~iari sicut solent et debent *SelPlCrown* 97; **1387** omnes custumarii debent talliari ad dominum suum abbatem in primo adventu suo..~iandum. preterea, si abbas..versus dominum regem graviter fuerit indebitatus, tunc debent ~iari dominum suum, si habuerit generale auxilium per abbatiam suam (*Cust. Rickinghall*) *Reg. Pri. Worc.* cxvi.

auxiliaris, helper.

infamatus abbas..,exilio..deportatus,..pro redemptione peccati ~aribus annumerata pecunia honori restitutus est W. MALM. *GP* II 91.

auxiliarius [CL], helpful. **b** (sb. m.) helper, ally.

†**868** (16c) necessarium nobis..arbitror..[Domini] gratiam in nostris necessitatibus ~iam implorare *CS* 521. **b** cum videret se..cum illo, qui plures habebat ~ios, non posse bello confligere BEDE *HE* III 14; **s1117** venit rex Francorum et ~ii sui cum exercitu suo in Normanniam DICETO *Chr.* 241; necesse est ad familiare subsidium evocari ~ios efficaces AD. MARSH *Ep.* 247 c. 4.

auxiliator [CL], helper.

Deus.., pius auxiliator egentum ALDH. *VirgV* 1910; **747** quia defensionis ~ores non habeat BONIF. *Ep.* 78 p. 165; omnipotens Dominus..in omnibus vestris negotiis promptus ~or assistat LANFR. *Ep.* 18. 525C; tuos Deus auxiliator / auget successus VINSAUF *PN* 2113; **p1381** cleri zelator fuit et pius auxiliator (ROB. SYRESTON *de T. Hatfeld*) *Hist. Durh.* p. 134; **1538** (v. assistator).

auxiliatrix, helpful, helping (f.). **b** helper (f.).

~ices Romanas..vexarunt legiones GIR. *DK* II 2; maximam manus ~icis in re tanta promissionem suscepit *Id. RG* III 13; **s1235** cum non manum porrigant egentibus ~icem, ut eis subveniant M. PAR. *Maj.* III 329; **1264** quod ad conservationem pacis..una mecum manum apponant ~icem (*AncC* IV 105) *RL* II 255. **b** mortis amara rapit †jocundus [? l. jocundis] auxiliatrix ELMH. *Metr. Hen. V* 1306; **c1430** sit illa vobis †auxiculatrix que in consiliis habitat [cf. *Prov.* viii 12] *Reg. Whet.* II 445.

auxilium [CL], help, aid. **b** (fig.). **c** abetment, complicity. **d** aid of court (esp. in voucher to warranty).

da pius auxilium clemens ALDH. *VirgV* 17; patronum rite rogabant / auxilium miseris ut ferret civibus ultro *Ib.* 820; Deus..servos suos..per bonorum ~ia adjuvabit EDDI *Wilf.* 4; confidens episcopus in divinum, ubi humanum deerat, ~ium BEDE *HE* II 7; ut..nature defectui artis succurrat [*gl.*: ausilium det] beneficium NECKAM *Ut.* 103; **1214** per ~ium Dei nullum malum ei faceret *SelPlCrown* 72; **1224** *Pat* 458 (v. avalagium b); **1322** abbas concessit.. Hugoni..quendam fratrem..conversum suum ad custodiendum blada..in ausilium dicti Hugonis *FormA* 91. **b** si forte ibi sol bissextile quaerat ~ium BEDE *TR* 46. **c** **1203** quod per ejus ~ium et consensum occisa fuit *SelPl Crown* 29; **1221** ipsi omnes fuerunt in ~io ad factum illud; et ideo custodiantur *PlCrGlouc* 64; **1296** appellavit..R... de precepto, vi et ~io *Eyre Kent* I 110; **1314** in ~io, consensu et forcia *Ib.* 122; **1475** (v. abettatio). **d** **1203** petiit ~ium curie; unde preceptum est quod habeat breve ad summonendum warantum suum *CurR* III 10; **1219** vocavit inde ad warantum Willelmum..per ~ium curie *Ib.* VIII 34; **1221** dat v m. pro habendo ~io *SelPlCrown* 101; **c1238** petit.. quod compellatur per ~ium curie ad respondendum eidem de exitibus bladi *RBExch* II 768; **1242** r.c. de x li. pro habendo ~io curie ad quandam terram recuperandam *Pipe* 136; **1275** pro ~io habendo versus R...ad debitum suum recuperandum *SelPlMan* 149; **1309** habuit ~ium; et in consimili casu *fuit graunte Year Bk. 2 Ed. II* 98; **1330** dicit quod ipse non potest..sine ipso domino rege inde respondere; et petit ~ium de ipso domino rege (*PlRCP*) *Ambrosden* II 12; nonne quam utiles sunt vocaciones ad warrantum? ~ia de his ad quos spectat reversio †tenementarum quo [? l. tenementorum que] in placitum deducant..; ~ia eciam de coperticipibus FORTESCUE *LLA* 53.

2 source or means of aid, resource. **b** (w. *domus*) housebote, right to take building material. **c** (w. *firmae*) income available towards payment of farm.

auctor ipse belli, perditis militibus sive ~iis, interemtus est BEDE *HE* III 24. **b** **a1242** si aliquis burgagium novum ceperit, ..~ium domus habebit in bosco meo *BBC 1042–1216 (Okehampton)* 55. **c** **1278** cepit nuces in dominico regis in ballia sua et cheminagium in ballia sua in ~ium firme sue *SelPlForest* 124.

3 'aid' (feudal) payable to landlord (*cf. Med. E. Anglia* 76). **b** (w. *nativorum* or sim.) tallage (v. *Cust. Rents* 90). **c** (w. *album*) rent payable in 'blanched' silver. **d** (w. *assisum*) a fixed rent (Norm.). **e** (w. *boum*) a cattle rent (Exeter diocese). **f** (w. *lini*) service or payment at flax harvest (Som.).

1184 per alia servicia que liberi homines mei mihi faciunt, sc. si opus fuerit juvabunt redimere corpus meum et facere militem primogenitum filium meum et ad maritandam primogenitam filiam meam, et, si liberi homines mei commune ~ium mihi dederint, dabunt mihi secundum suam tenuram (*Ch. Northampton*) *Eng. Feudalism* 276; postquam convenerit inter dominum et heredem tenentis sui de rationabili relevio.., poterit idem heres rationabilia ~ia de hominibus suis inde exigere...sunt preterea alii casus in quibus licet dominis similia ~ia..exigere ab hominibus suis, velut si filius et heres suus miles fiat vel si primogenitam filiam suam maritaverit GLANV. IX 8; **c1202** dabunt mihi ~ium ad faciendum militem unum de filiis meis *BBC (Egremont)* 91; post homagia suscepta petivit abbas ~ium a militibus, qui promiserunt ab unoquoque xx s. BRAKELOND 128; **1209** salvo generali ausilio abbatis [S. Edmundi] quantum pertinet ad tantum (*sic*) terram *Fines P. Norf & Suff* 522; **a1211** salvo ~io S. Ædmundi quando ponetur generaliter per viij hundredos et dim. *Kal. Samson* 94; **1227** concedimus..episcopo et successoribus suis quod pro necessitatibus suis et ecclesie sue tallagium vel rationabile ~ium capiant de..civibus suis *Ch. Sal.* 177; **1240** prior post primam creationem suam percipiat de singulis maneriis ad prioratum undique spectantibus speciale ~ium *Reg. Pri. Worc.* 138a; **c1240** dabunt ~ia quando generale ~ium ponitur per terram nostram *Feod. Durh.* 15n.; **c1250** excepto quod †quumcunque [? l. quandocumque] commune ~ium per totam terram nostram posu[er]imus dabunt nobis ~ium quantum ad j carucatam terre pertinet *Ib.* 16n.; sunt etiam quedam consuetudines que servitia non dicuntur nec concomitantia servitiorum, sicut sunt rationabilia ~ia ad filium primogenitum militem faciendum vel ad filiam primogenitam maritandam, que quidam ~ia fiunt de gratia et non de jure et pro necessitate et indigentia domini capitalis. ..et sunt hujusmodi ~ia personalia et non predialia; personas enim respiciunt et non feoda BRACTON 36b; **14..** racionabile ~ium de militibus et libere tenentibus *Reg. Brev.* 87. **b** **1208** in liberatis..decano.., tam de ~io quam gabulo et alio exitu, cxxiij li. *Pipe Wint.* 45; [abbas W., ob. 1222] quietum clamavit conventui totum ~ium de F. et A., sc. xx m. ad festum S. Mich., quod ipse et antecessores sui solebant capere SWAFHAM 111; **1267** omnes consuetudinarii dant ~ium in communi iiij librarum ad festum S. Mich. *Cart. Glouc.* III 97 (cf. ib. 188: dabit ~ium cum consuetudinariis secundum quantitatem terre et numerum animalium); idem r.c. de v li. de ~io nativorum sive de tallagio ad festum S. Mich. *FormMan* 14 (cf. ib. 28: summa valorum †aucoxorum xij s.); de certo ~io nativorum ad lardarium domini de consuetudine *Ib.* 29; **1326** de communi ~io nativorum ad festum Omnium Sanctorum *MinAc* 1141/1 (*Norw.*); **1370** cum ~io nativorum *Ib.* 1138/2 (*Exon.*). **c** *Cust. Rents* 109 (v. albus 6b). **d** **1203** r.c... de xl s. de ~io assiso in Goisbervill' *RScacNorm* II 507. **e** **1214** r.c...de xvj li...de ~io boum *Pipe* (*Exon. sede vacante*) 83. **f** **1285** item ~ium eorundem [custumariorum], lardarium eorundem, chirchettum eorundem et ~ium lini eorundem *Cl* 102 m. 8.

4 'aid' (mainly feudal in origin) payable to crown. **b** (Scot.). **c** (w. *munitionis*) burhbote. **d** (w. *vicecomitis*) sheriff's aid (v. *Cust. Rents* 124; *Med. Eng. Sheriff* 114). **e** (w. *hundredarii*) hundred aid (v. *Cust. Rents* 129). **f** (w. *militare* or *militum*) scutage. **g** (w. *novum*) customs duty first levied in 1266.

1103 volo ut omnia S. Edmundi sint quieti de omnimodis scottis et geldis et ~iis *Regesta* 644; hanc libertatem habuit sancta ecclesia usque ad tempus Willelmi junioris, qui de baronibus totius patrie ~ium petiit ad Normanniam retinendam de fratre suo Rodberto (*Leg. Ed. Conf.*) *GAS* 636; **1130** vic. debet vj li...de preterito ~io comitatus *Pipe* 20; **1168** vic. r.c. de dc et xvij li...de ~io civitatis ad maritandam filiam regis *Pipe* 3 (cf. ib. 160: de ~io filie regis); plurimum interest si donum vel ~ium civitatis per singula capita commorantium in ea a justitiis constituatur vel si cives summam aliquam que principe digna videatur justitiariis offerant *Dial. Scac.* II 13B; **1194** [de] ~iis datis ad redemptionem domini regis *CurR RC* I 69; **s1198** rex Anglie cepit de unaquaque carucata terre sive hyda totius Anglie v s. de ~io R. HOWD. IV 46; **1215** nullum..~ium ponatur in regno nostro nisi ad corpus nostrum redimendum et ad primogenitum filium nostrum militem faciendum et ad filiam nostram primogenitam semel maritandam, et ad hec non fit nisi rationabile ~ium *Magna Carta* 12; **1226** cum requisiti essent..barones nostri Londoniarum de competenti ~io nobis faciendo ad hereditatem nostram et jura nostra perquirenda in partibus transmarinis *MGL* II 36; **s1232** quibus [magnatibus] rex proposuit quod magnis esset debitis implicatus, unde necessitate compulsus ab omnibus generaliter ~ium postulavit M. PAR. *Maj.* III 212; **1235** utrum plenarie fuerit nobis responsum ad Scaccarium nostrum de ~io quod nobis nuper liberaliter concessistis ad maritandam sororem nostram *FormA* 5; **1260** de ~io dudum regi concesso ad primogenitum filium suum militem faciendum *Cl* 92; **1290** oneratus est versus regem de servicio ij militum in singulis scutagiis, ausiliis, releviis *RParl* I 48b; **s1339** [rex] remisit ~ia ad filium suum militem faciendum et filiam suam maritandam pro toto tempore suo *Eul. Hist.* III 204; **1472** ad quintam decimam vel aliquam aliam contribucionem seu imposicionem, ~ium vel subsidium..per viros seculares..faciendam (*Breve Regis*) *Reg. Whet.* II 137. **b** **c1163** concessi abbati de Scon colligere ~ia de pecuniis suis per suos proprios ministros; quare firmiter prohibeo ut non veniatis in terras ad predicta ~ia colligenda *Regesta Scot.* no. 252; **1234** excepto solummodo ~io domini regis quando sc. ipse..commune ~ium super totum regnum posuerit *Inchaffray* 45. **c** **940** (12c) pontis edificium munitionis castellique ~ium *CS* 761 (cf. ib. 931). **d** †**1100** *Regesta* 489; **1122** quieti..de omnibus ~iis vicecomitum et ministralium eorum *Ib.* 1316; **a1140** manerium..sit quietum..de..~iis justic' et vicecomitum *Regesta* III 278; **1156** quieti..de..~io vicecomitum et servientum (*Ch.*) *Ambrosden* I 157; **s1163** dabantur de hida bini solidi ministris regis qui vicecomitum loco comitatus servabant; quos voluit rex conscribere fisco...cui archiepiscopus in faciem restitit, dicens: "nec pro reditu dabimus eos...sed, si digne nobis deservierint vicecomites et servientes vel ministri provinciarum et homines nostros manu tenuerint, nequaquam eis deerimus in ~ium" GRIM *Thom.* 23; vic. habuit de dicta villa..de ~io vicecomitis lxx s. *RDomin* 3; **1199** quiete de.. ~io vicecomitum, sive capiatur per hidatas terre sive per carucatas *CalCh* I 216; **1279** *hundr' heyld*, sc. ~ium vicecomitis *Hund.* II 666; **1297** redditus hundredi: idem r.c. de xxj s. vj d. receptis de ~io vicecomitis per annum *Ac. Cornw.* I 57; **1311** est ibidem de redditu resoluto, viz. ad ~ium vicecomitis comitatus..per annum xij d. *IPM* 22/10. **e** **1240** G. Freman tenet j virgam terre pro v s. per annum.. et faciendo ~ium vicecomitis et hundredarii *Cart. Rams.* I 491 (cf. ib. 364: ~ium ..hundredi);†**1242** (1329) omnes denarios quos vicecomites nostri vel hundredarii aut eorum ballivi percipere consueverunt..pro ~iis vicecomitum, hundredariorum et ballivorum suorum *CalCh* V 151. **f** **s1204** convenerunt ad colloquium apud Oxoniam rex et magnates Anglie, ubi concessa sunt regi ~ia militaria, de quolibet scuto sc. ij m. et dim. WEND. I 320; ~ium militum *RBExch* II 768. **g** **1269** sciatis nos concessisse..civibus Londoniarum quod liberi et quieti sint..de novo ~io nostro quod habemus de dono domini regis patris nostri (*Pat*) *Leg. Ant. Lond.* 110.

5 (eccl.) **a** 'aid' payable to bishop (cf. *Becket to Langton* 151–2). **b** (Scot.; *cf. conevetum*). **c** (w. *secundum*) additional 'aid' imposed by archdeacon.

a **1196** de xxxij li...de ~iis ecclesiarum et personarum *Pipe* (*Durh. sede vacante*) 256; episcopus [Philippus, ob. 1208] a clericis eorum [monachorum] ~ia..exegit G. COLD. *Durh.* 12. **b** **1127** quatenus..omnes ecclesie vel capelle que ..ad ecclesiam S. Cuthberti pertinuerint libere..sint ab omni episcopali ~io, cana et conevethe *E. Ch. Scot.* 73; **c1250** quandam summam..pecunie..quam ipse idem pro porcione domini sui episcopi..decano de †Pete [? l. Perth] solvit ad ausilium domino episcopo Aberdene consu[e]te concessum *FormOx* 481. **c** **1156** cum in extremis agere videremur, Domino vovimus..quod consuetudinem de secundis ~iis, quam frater noster archidiaconus ecclesiis imposuit, destruemus et, ab ea relaxantes et liberantes ecclesias, sub anathemate prohibuimus ne ulterius ab aliquo exigantur (*Lit. Archiep.*) *Ep. J. Sal.* 49 (22); **1200** [capellanus] de senodalibus et ~iis archidiaconi respondebat et de omnibus aliis consuetudinibus que ad ecclesiam pertinent (*Cart. Lanthony*) *Becket to Langton* 192.

auxion- v. auction-. auxter v. auster. auxturus, auxurus v. asturcus. auxungia v. axungia. ava v. 1 avia. avadonia v. anadonia. avagium v. avalagium 2.

avalagium, toll on goods going downstream. **b** (Gasc.).

1174 debet iiij li. et xiij s. de ~io Tamise *Pipe* 115; **1206** sciatis nos dedisse..Jordano de Lond' ~ium Thamisie apud Bray cum omnibus pertinentiis et libertatibus.., reddendo inde singulis annis v m. argenti *RChart* 165a; **1207** concessimus Petronille comitisse Leircestr' quod habeat ~ium et karkiam batellorum et mercatum suum et pontem de Wara [*Herts*] *Pat* 69b; **1225** Jordanus de L. debet ij m. et dim. de firma avelagii Thamisie *LTRMem* 7 r. 10; **1242** r. c. de v m. de firma †avelagie Tamisye *Pipe* 62; **1248** namia capta apud Braye pro theloneo maereni nostri cariati per ~ium Tamisie apud Braye (*LTRMem*) *Hist. Exch.* 531; **1265** quia accepimus..quod T. de la Lok, qui.. habet..~ium Tamisie apud Braye, sustinuit dampnum racione inhibicionis nostre de ~io per Tamisiam.., ita quod naves transire nec descendere poterant versus London' sicut temporibus retroactis.., xxvj s...allocentur in firma sua de ~io predicto *Liberate* 42 m. 12. **b** **1224** sciatis nos, pro magnis expensis quas probi homines Burdegale posuerunt in firmatione..ville Burdegale,..concessisse eis in auxilium ville..firmande..totam consuetudinem de ~io vinorum suorum et aliorum *Pat* 458; **1267** magnam custumam

Burdegale de ~io vinorum et yssakum et custumam reyam ibidem *Pat* 85 m. 29.

2 (eels caught during) migration downstream (*cf. avalatio*).

solebant homines ville. .ire apud Laginghehe et reportare †avragium de anguillis de Sutreia BRAKELOND 150.v (cf. *MonA* III 164: †averagium).

3 letting down (*cf. avalare* b).

1504 unam postam in eadem [porta] pro cariagio et †avagio vasorum vini *Cl* 367 m. 23*d*. (cf. ib.: *a post. .for letyng downe of wyne*).

avalana v. abellana.

avalare [OF *avaler* < ad+vallis], to send downstream. **b** to let down, lower. **c** to cut down (from gallows).

1195 ad easdem naves adportandas et. .in eisdem. .ad mare advalandis *RScacNorm* I 185. **b 1198** pro iij estachiis ficandis ad avalandos tonellos regis in cellarium *Ib.* II 461; **1237** visores operis. .maremii et plumbi turris castri Hertf' ~andi et salvandi *LTRMem* 12 r. 2; **1297** in empcione xx petrarum cordarum de canabo ad aquam, terram, minam et lapides de minera extrahend' et minerarios et maeremium avaland' et ducend' *KRAc* 260/18 m. 2. **c 1318** per civitatem detrahatur. .usque ad furcas et ibidem vivus suspendatur et vivus avalletur; et postea decolletur. . et cor et viscera subtus furcas. .comburantur *SelCKB* IV p. 78.

avalaria [OF *avaleoire*], breeching (of harness).

1213 in. .cingulis et. .cordis ad carectam ligandam. .et iiij collariis et ij †analar' et ij bargiis et v capistris liberatis eidem [caretario] *Cl* 128b; in emptione facta de hernesio caretar' garderobe nostre, sc. pro ij paribus tractuum vij s., pro iij †alar' ij s., pro ij bridis x d. *Ib.* 153a; liberate R. Sellario. .pro duabus ~iis et duobus dossariis viij s. *Ib.* 153b; **1214** habere faciatis. .unam superdorsariam, j avellar', duas sellas *Ib.* 160b.

avalatio [cf. OF *avalaison*], (catching of eels during) migration downstream (*cf. avalagium* 2).

c1160 quamdiu. .episcopus nobis super. .molendino uno quod est ante portam castelli [*Sherborne, Dorset*] et super ~one anguillarum et super piscatura. .que nobis et episcopo est communis. .controversiam nullam movebit *Ch. Sal.* 33; **1231** concessimus. .abbatisse et sanctimonialibus de Godestowe. .quod. .percipiant decimam anguillarum vivariorum nostrorum de Wudestok' quotiens ebalatio anguillarum contigerit de eisdem vivariis *ChartR* 25 m. 11; **1261** est ibidem quidam lacus qui vocatur Wythornese Mar' de quo avallacio anguillarum valet per annum vj s. viij d. *Rent. & Surv.* (*Withernsea, Yorks*) 730 r. 5(2); **1306** de ~one gote ibidem nichil hoc anno, quia omnes anguilli ibidem capti fuerunt in mora regis apud Brustwyk [*Burstwick, Yorks*] in anno precedenti *MinAc* 1079/17 r. 14; **1308** cum parietibus domus avallacionis gote, pontibus et bayis. .reparandis *Ib.* 18 m. 9; **1308** piscaria in stagno valet per annum. .cum ~one anguillarum de gurgitibus xij d. (*Ext. Borley, Essex*) *Growth Eng. Indust.* 576.

2 letting down, lowering.

1323 in. .cariagio mine, saccorum, maeremii, perforacione et avallacione mortuorum operum *Pipe* 170 r. 53.

Avalterrae [OF *Avauterres*], Low Countries.

s1249 cum Bolonensibus et Flandrensibus et cum illis qui vulgariter de ~is dicuntur M. PAR. *Maj.* V 93 (cf. ib. VI 252: Flandrenses qui dicuntur de Avaltere).

avantagium [OF *avantage* < abante], advantage.

1236 quorum xv annorum spatio transacto, quilibet alii. . pannos poterunt deinde non requisita eorum licentia operari, ita quod idem B. et ejus socii nullum ~ium habebunt deinde in jam dictis (*Pat., Gasc.*) *RL* II 12; **s1333** Anglici, caute et prudenter divisis eorum turmis et ~iis preconsideratis, quod in hoc loco unus pugil contra tres sufficeret debellare *Plusc.* IX 28.

2 profit, perquisite, gain. **b** (in bargain) difference between long and short measure. **c** (w. *ponderis*). **d** difference between razed and heaped measure.

a1184 G. et J. tenent terram. .et R. S. tantum de alio cagio, unde reddit in anno iij d.; et istud socagium est de vantagio et non est de xv acris (*Cust. S. Edm.*) *Kal. Samson* 30; **c1200** tradidit. .ij bovatas terre. .cum ~iis et pertinentiis ad dictas bovatas pertinentibus *Couch. Furness* II 477; **1265** ita. .quod. .Adam singulis annis percipiat de ~io integram vesturam iiij acrarum *Cl* 97; **1319** ostendat. . racionem et modum per quos ~ium contentum in peticione accrescere posset regno (*RParl*) *Doc. Exch.* 37; **1348** concessimus insuper eidem R. omnia adventagia guerre que ibidem de bonis mobilibus per ipsum R. et suos adquiri contingent (*RGasc*) *Foed.* V 626; **1420** an ipsi piscenarii. . solverent annis singulis marinariis. .xij d. ad ~ium et sic piscenarii producerent terciam partem ludi pagine predicte *Mem. York* I 166; **1427** habeat. .uxor mea de bonis et catallis meis solomodo id quod ex lege habere poterit sine ~io vel incremento aliquali *Reg. Cant.* II 405; **1479** quousque. .promotus fuerit ad officium coronatoris. .cum omnibus avauntagiis dicto officio habitis *Reg. Whet.* II 204; **1488** officium marescalli. .Berwici. .unacum omnibus. .proficuis, commoditatibus, avauntagiis et emolumentis eidem officio . .usitatis *RScot* 483b; **1529** officium senescalli. .de Ewenny . ., cum proficuis, commoditatibus et advantagiis eidem officio. .debitis *Cart. Glam.* 1977. **b 1299** cetera [vellera] venduntur per universum ut infra, exceptis xij debilibus velleribus que mercator habuit de advantagio *DCCant Ac. Milton*; **1350** xxij vellera donantur mercatori ad †auvantagiam *Sacr. Ely* II 185; in avant[agio] mercatoris ad idem vij [vellera] viz. xxj vellera pro xx (*MinAc Maldon*, m. 3*d.*) *MFG*; **1398** cxv s. pro lx bidentibus et iij datis in advantagium mercatoris (*Stebbing*) *Ib.* **c 1346** in dclxv libris copr' alb' emptis pro eisdem [campanis] precio cent[ene] xvj s., unde de ~io ponderis ix li. copr', iiij li. viij s. *Sacr. Ely* II 138. **d 1297** onerat se recepisse. .cccc quarteria frumenti per mensuram Anglie rasam sine ~io (*KRAc* 6/9) *DocScot* II p. 127; **1297** in ~io dicti bladi pro mensura iiij bussell' *Ac. Cornw.* II 182; **1299** in ~io messure predictorum quarteriorum. ., viz. xxj quarteria pro xx *Pipe* 92 r. 28 (= *Chanc. R.* r. 7: aventagio); **1313** r.c. de cv quarteriis frumenti receptis superius de superempcione per mensuram rasam cum advantagio, viz. ad quelibet xx quarteria j quarterium de ~io secundum consuetudinem mercatorum *KRAc* 375/8 f. 21; **1321** in evantagio mercatorum in eadem vendicione ij quarteria *MinAc* 992/11; **1323** liberatum Simoni. .j quarterium ordei. .pro ~io suo de xx quarteriis ordei rasa mensura *Ac. Wellingb.* 130; **1335** de clxv quarteriis vj bussellis et dim. avene receptis. .per mensuram Angl' baleatam cum ~io, viz. ad quelibet viij quarteria avene j quarterium avene de ~io *KRAc* 19/3 m. 2 (cf. ib.: per mensuram Angl' rasam cum ~io, viz. ad quelibet xx quarteria j quarterium de ~io); **1374** in avant[agio] mercat[oris] ad idem v bussel' (*MinAc Maldon* m. 1*d.*) *MFG*.

avantia [OF *avence*], avens (*Geum*).

arnoglossa, lanceolata, †anancia, consolida. . GILB. II 86. 1; nasturcii ortol[ani] et avancie *Ib.* 98 v. 1; potio ex marrubio al[bo], ~ia. . *Ib.* V 232. 1; **12. .** avencia, i. *avence*, i. *harefot* WW; salsamenta debent esse de. .lavandula, piretro, aventia hortulana GAD. 66. 2; recipe plantaginis, aventie i. gariofilate, se[minis] canabi. . *Ib.* 123 v. 1; avencia, pes leporis, gariofilata, sanamunda, [o]zimus, G. et A. *avense Alph.* 17; avencia, A. *avance* WW.

avantiamentum [OF *avancement*], advancement, betterment.

1587 in consideracione melioris advanciamenti ipsius Edwardi *Pat* 1298 m. 10.

avantwarda [OF *avantwarde, avantguarde*; cf. antewarda], vanguard.

cum exercitus in hostem pergit. .faciunt avantwarde, et in reversione redrewarde *DB* I 179; illi domestici proditores de Morgannoch, qui vangardiam regere sperabantur, . . terga dederunt FORDUN *Cont.* XV 26; **s1415** nolebant permittere eorum architenentes. .accidere ad vangardiam ad honorem †consequendam *Plusc.* X 23; quod in omni bello regio ipse ac heredes sui vangardiam haberent *Extr. Chr. Scot.* 60.

avaragium v. averagium.

avare [CL], avariciously, parsimoniously.

quoties ~e aliquid aut parce nimis agi volebant GIR. *IK* I 12.

avarexia v. anorexia. avaria v. avenarius c.

avaricare, to covet.

nec. .delectationis alimonia animos ~antium pascit R. COLD. *Cuthb.* 32.

avaritia [CL], avarice, covetousness, greed.

delicta reorum / semper avaritiae nummi servire volentum ALDH. *VirgV* 2582; animum irae et ~iae victorem BEDE *HE* III 17; capitalia crimina secundum canones explicabo: prima superbia, invidia, fornicatio, inanis gloria, ira longo tempore, tristitia seculi, ~ia, ventris ingluvies EGB. *Pen.* 1; hoc nomen 'Roma' ex ~ia sueque diffinitionis formatur principiis; fit enim ex R et O et M et A et diffinitio cum ipsa, 'Radix Omnium Malorum Avaritia' MAP *NC* II 17; **1287** ~ia. .est amor immoderatus habendi bona temporalia et tunc est mortale peccatum *Conc. Syn.* 1067; **c1370** ~ia secundum peccatum mortale (J. BRIDL. *gl.*) *Pol. Poems* I 174.

avarities, avarice.

s1217 legatus. .tanquam tyrannus, ~ie persuadente, misit. .inquisitores perversos OXNEAD *Chr.* 143.

avarium v. averium.

1 avarus [CL], avaricious, covetous, greedy. **b** (sb. m.) miser.

Ebreae gentis regnator avarus [Achab] ALDH. *VirgV* 2595; si quis cupidus vel ~us, . .iii annos peniteat EGB. *Pen.* 4; ~us vel cupidus, *gitsere* ÆLF. *Gl.*; Walenses, . .vite prodigi, libertatis ~i MAP *NC* II 20. **b** minus ledunt ~os invisa suarum rerum detrimenta quam visa *Ib.* IV 16 p. 200; tristis avarus, / esuriens, sitiens, quid sit dare nescit egenus D. BEC. 2201.

2 (fig.) infertile. **b** scanty.

c1250 spineta condensa ad cultum redigentes ~am glebam [monachi] letis frugibus luxuriare cogebant *Couch. Kirkstall* 179 (= *MonA* V 531: †anarum globam). **b** si [hec aula, sc. mundus, facta est] ex abundanti [materia], non posset in luna deesse; si vero ex ~a et insufficiente, ut quid non potius ceteris deficit stellis quam lune? ADEL. *QN* 69.

2 Avarus, *Avar*.

s615 rex ~orum irrupit in fines Venetiarum R. NIGER I 56; ad regem ~orum Cacanum HIGD. V 16 p. 86.

3 avarus v. averus. avauntagium v. avantagium.

ave [CL; cf. avēre], hail! **b** (esp. w. *Maria* or equivalent) prayer or anthem. **c** bead.

have, salutatio *GlC* H 12; have, Hova altissime (ÆTHELWALD) *Carm. Aldh.* 5. 5; jam salvete, valete, vigete et avete ALCUIN *Carm.* 38. 8; lector, have! tibi caetera carpe tuapte FRITH. 1396; aveto, placidis praesul amabilis (WULFSTAN 143) *Anal. Hymn.* LI 1 165; 'pro merito de parte ducis, rex', inquit 'aveto!' G. AMIENS *Hast.* 289; hoc nomen 'ave', quod est pure Latinum, Grece exponunt, dicentes quod dicitur ab *a*, quod est 'sine', et *ve* BACON *Maj.* I 88; fine cibis facto, domino dicatur, "aveto" D. BEC. 1370. **b** licet dicat horas, paternoster et ave *AncrR* 36; **1416** qui legis hec pro me pater unum, supplico, prome; / adjungas et ave, Deus ut me liberet a ve (*Epitaph. J. Hemmingbrough*) *Hist. Durh.* p. 145; **s1449** extitit terremotus. .†que [? l. qui] duravit. . per spacium unius ave Maria *Chr. Hen. VI & Ed. IV* 150; **1472** precinendo. .ad magnam missam hanc antiphonam sive salutacionem vocatam 'ave gloriosa' in honore gloriose beatissimeque Virginis Marie *Reg. Brechin.* II 114; **1496** ad dicendum unum pater noster et unum ave Maria *ExchScot* 585. **c 1357** unum par de avees precii iij s. *Pat* 252 m. 6; **1422** de. .j parvo coffre viridi cum iij paribus paternosters de auro, unde ij paria de lx aves (*LTRAc. Wardr.*) *Arch.* LXX 98.

avehere [CL], to carry away.

~it, *onweg aferide GlC* A 908; avexerat, exportaverat *Ib.* 902.

avelacius v. alenatius. avelagium v. avalagium 1a. avelana, avellana v. abellana. avelenum v. elemosynarius. aveleon v. anethelaeon. avellaria v. avalaria.

avellere [CL], to tear away, pull out, pluck. **b** (fig.).

10. . avulsus, *aweg abroden* WW; munientes se per gyrum avulse terre aggere W. JUM. II 10; arbores. .stirpitus avulsas GIR. *TH* II 54; **1202** hec [monialis]. .sub feretrum. .se dedit in lamentum. .nec inde ~i poterat *Canon. G. Sempr.* 77; **1307** de pellibus lanutis avulsis *MinAc* 1079/18 m. 9 (cf. ib.: lana avulsa decimatur in pell'); **s1379** (v. alluvio 1a). **b** AD. MARSH *Ep.* 83 (v. avulsio).

avena [CL], oat, oats (often pl.). **b** (dist. acc. kind). **c** (w. *sterilis*) a wild grass. **d** (fig.) imperfect Christian.

~a, *atae GlC* A 917; bena, *atae Ib* B 85; xx acras frumenti et totidem ad ~as *DB* I 179b; innataque sibi virtute relaxat avena / duraque mollificat NECKAM *DS* VIII 13; sed domus infelix ubi cervisiatur avena P. BLOIS *Poems* 1155c; vinum vinee [restaurat humiditatem] scinceriorem quam vinum ~e et pomorum BACON IX 35; **1270** xiij quarteria advene *CartI Norm* 132; **1292** pro ij bussellis farine ~e *Sacr. Ely* II 5; **1297** dragetum: . .de iiij quar. j buss. ordei receptis ad semen et de ij quar. ~e receptis ad idem *Ac. Cornw.* I 22; **1298** xl quarteria brasii ~arum *Reg. Carl.* I 111; **1302** depastus fuit cum averiis suis. .awenas circumcrescentes *CourtR Hales* 457; **s1356** tanta fuit siccitas quod ordea, ~e, vesce, fabe et alia semina quadragesimalia. .modicum vel nihil crescebant AVESB. 136b; **1456** brasium ~e molit', iiij quart.; brasium ~e non molit', liiij quart.; ~e pro prebenda, cxx quart. *Ac. Durh.* 636. **b c1280** reddendo ad *foddercorn* domini abbatis xv quar. minute ~e *Suff. Hund.* 46; **1286** de xxvj quar. v. buss. grosse ~e de exitu. .xxij quar. vj buss. minute ~e de exitu *MinAc* 827/39 r. 3; **1329** de xl celdris. . de ~is nigris *ExchScot* 133; **1372** iij bussellos ~e cursalis *Arch. Bridgw.* 196; **1539** j buss. ~e vocate *swanehaver Feod. Durh.* 323. **c** phoenix, Romanis lolium murinum sive hordeum murinum dicitur; quibusdam ~a sterilis vocatur, . .quibusdam. .*waybent* TURNER *Herb.* B iv v. **d** inter ~as et lolia triticum rarum, multos nimirum vocatos invenies, paucos electos GIR. *TH* III 27.

2 oaten pipe (mus.).

pauper avena sono HANV. IX 390.

avenaceus [CL], **~aticus, ~icius,** oaten, made of oats. **b** sown w. oats.

1215 dabunt. .j celdram ~icie farine pacabilis *Reg. Dunferm.* 215; **1242** de firma farine †~iace *Pipe* (*Cumb*) 105; **1266** in x celdris farine ~atice *ExchScot* I 5; **1467** pro xiiij bollis. .farine ~atice liberatis ad leporarios regis. ., pro qualibet bolla allocantur due bolle avenarum *Ib.* VII 459; panis ~acius, A. *hafyrbred* WW; **1500** bladorum ~aceorum *Cart. Cockersand* 1164; semodiolus ~atie farine, . .*an hoope of oote mele* WHITTINGTON *Vulg.* 57; **1538** in sex celdris. . avenarum ex canis ~aticis. .de Keig *Rent. S. Andr.* 20. **b 1370** j d. de qualibet acra terre ~atice *Conc. Scot.* cxci *n.*

avenacius v. avenaceus a, adventicius 1c. 1 avenagium v. alnagium.

2 avenagium [OF *avenage*], a customary payment, (?) provision of oats (Norm.).

1180 vindicabat in illis [villis] sibi jus hospitandi, talliam, corvagium, ~ium J. SAL. *Ep.* 327. 377c; **1180** xl s. pro recognitione de ~io versus dominum suum *RScacNorm* I 87; **c1180** decimam foreste sue de Monte Roont in pasnagio et herbagio et brostagio et ~io et aliis pertinentiis *Act. Hen. II* II 154.

†avenalis, (?) *f.l.* for *vernalis*.

c1365 debent domino per annum ad semen yemale j diem . .et ad semen ~e j diem *Pipe Cloyne* 22.

avenama v. offnama. avenantum v. advenantum.

avenarius [CL], used for oats. **b** (sb. m.) avener, purveyor of oats (for fodder). **c** (sb. f.) office of avener.

11. . grangia ~ia in longitudine. .habet in directum iiij perticas et iij pedes *Dom. S. Paul.* 139. **b 1188** versus Nicholaum ~ium de Lond' *Pipe* 88; **1199** W. filius Herberti ~ii *Rec. Leic.* I 17; **1261** rex dedit Willelmo de H., ~io suo, . .catalla Rogeri G. *Cl* 342; **1304** quod cocus juratus, panetarius et ~ius fideliter computent de expensis *Ord. Ely* 26; stabularius, qui est eciam ~ius *Cust. Cant.* 64; **1335** ~iis regis, xj s. viij d. *Ac. Durh.* 530; **1379** Michaeli avynario *ExchScot* III 19 (cf. ib. II 574: M. ~io). **c 1290** servienti de ~ia. .facienti providencias de feno, avena et litera ad officium *Ac. Wardr.* (*Chanc. Misc.* 4/5) f. 6; **1332** operanti in ~ia regis et in stabulo juxta trahas *KRAc* 409/13 m. 3; **1334** [*sack for carrying oats. .sent back*] ad ~iam *Rec. Leic.*

II 14; **1389** ultra custagia cujusdam equi sui quem ipse in ~ia dicti hospicii nostri habet *Pat* 327 m. 21; **1443** uni clericorum nostrorum de aveneria nostra *Pat* 456 m. 37; **1460** commutate in avenas et liberate ad †avariam [? l. anariam] dominorum regis et regine, magistro †avarie testante receptum, xviij celdre *ExchScot* 69–70; **1461** clerico †averie [? l. anerie] nostre *Cl* 313 m. 27 (cf. *CalPat* 164); **1492** Ricardo Bright, provisori ~ie et liberate equorum nostrorum *Pat* 572 m. 22; **1496** ut patet in libris †averie domini regis *ExchScot* 595.

avenaticus, ~atius v. avenaceus.

avenator, avener (*cf. avenarius* b).

1209 Herbertus ~or *Rec. Leic.* I 21; **1275** ~ori archiepiscopi *Hund.* I 204; **1325** avene: ..in expensis ~oris domini comitis Wynton' comorantis ibidem per x dies, iij bussell' *Ac. Man. Wint.* (*Chilbolton*).

avenatum, porridge or gruel of oats.

cibus frigidus..qualis est portulaca, dactu[li], ~um.. GILB. III 134. 1; detur mica panis lota, ~um, colatura furfuris.. *Ib.* IV 193 v. 2; dietandi sunt..cum grossiori dieta.., cum ~o sc. et ordeato, sc. cum gruello facto de avenis vel de ordeo GAD. 10. 2.

avencia v. avantia. avendere v. arrentare a. aveniacus, ~icius v. avenaceus.

avenosus, made of oats.

1269 furniaverat panem ~um super craticulam, qui vocatur *cakes CalIMisc* (*Northumb*) I 2142.

aventagium v. avantagium.

aventailatus, fitted w. aventail.

1317 loricam bonam cum bacinetto umbrato et aventilato *PlRCP* 285 *irrot.* r. 1.

aventailum [OF *aventail, esventail*], aventail, neck armour or beaver of helmet.

1313 Johanni le Hauberjur..pro diversis hauberjonibus, gorgeriis et aventailiis..emptis..de diversis mercatoribus Paris' *KRAc* 275/8 f. 19d.; **1343** cum xxx paribus platarum, basinetorum et pisanorum cum eorundem aventailibus (*Cl*) *Foed.* V 384; **1368** unam loricam, quatuor adventall' *Cl* 206 m. 9; **1374** pro una pelle de roo pro aventaill' super bac[inett]' firmand' *KRAc* 397/10 r. 2; **1382** in asportacione loricarum, bacynettorum, aventallorum et aliarum armaturarum et artillarie regis (*KRAc* 400/10) *EHR* XXVI 696; **1386** basynettis cum ~is *IMisc* 237/3 r. 5.

aventatio v. arrentatio a. aventilatus v. aventailatus. 1 aventura v. adventura.

2 aventura [cf. OF *esventoire*], (?) winnowing-fan.

1211 expensa: ..in j ~a vj d. *Pipe Wint.* 105.

1 aventus, (?) pentice (OF *auvent*) or vent-pipe.

1388 quia quamplurima dampna..hominibus de Fletestret'..evenerunt per inundacionem aque conductus London', que pluries per fraccionem piparum ejusdem conductus domos..ac bona..sua..consumit in magnum dampnum eorundem.., quod quidem dampnum per unum ~um ibidem faciendum super dictum conductum..emendari posset, concessum est quod..faciant unum ~um *LBLond* H. f. 226b (cf. ib. in marg.: concessio ereccionis pinnaculi conductus).

2 aventus v. eventus.

1 avera [v. averus], draught-mare.

a1128 in dominio curie sunt ij carruce de xvj bobus et iiij vacce..et j aura [l. avra] *Chr. Peterb. app.* 159; ij aures et xj^{xx} oves *Ib.* 162; **1208** pasturam viij boum et x animalium ..et j aure *RChart* 155b; **1234** S. faber..debet..ferrare duas affras in duobus pedibus *Cust. Glast.* 42; in escambium pasture iiij averiorum et unius aure *FormA* 158; **1269** detentionis unius equi, bobi (*sic*), affre *CBaron* 80; **1284** habebit..pasturam ad sex boves et v vaccas..et unam affram in pastura *MonA* I 33; **1336** (v. averus).

2 avera, ~um, service of transport, (?) by horse.

de ~a id est servitium lx sol. *DB* I 9b; in servitio regis invenit j ~am et inwardum *Ib.* 132b; inveniebat vicecomiti iii ineuuard' et j ~am per annum *Ib.* 195 (cf. ib. 190: reddunt..unoquoque anno xii equos et xii inguardos); **c1120** invenit avras ad summagium *Cart. Burton* 26; inveniunt.. j equum apud Londoniam et avras ubicumque jubentur ad portandum cibum dominii *Ib.* 29; **c1300** isti cotarii nusquam capient avram nisi apud Icham vel Bramblinge *DCCant* J 46 (cf. *Gavelkind* 74).

1 averagium v. avalagium.

2 averagium, service of transporting goods (man.) or payment in lieu (*cf. Cust. Rents* 61–7). **b** (dist. acc. means of transport). **c** (Scot.) 'arriage'.

c1185 facient ~ium in omni Sabbato ad Maldune *Rec. Templars* 7; **11..** debet iiij ~ia et dim. de frumento *Reg. S. Ben. Holme* no. 234; **1204** faciendo ~ium secundum preceptum abbatis [S. Benedicti de Hulmo] de uno loco ad alium locum *CurR* III 97; **1214** de..feno vendito et herbagio et avragio *Pipe* 82; **1222** facit xij ~ia firmar' per annum et pro quolibet ~io quietus erit ab una operacione *Dom. S. Paul.* 34; **12..** operatur duobus diebus..et in tercio facit avaragium *Cart. Rams.* III 245; **c1253** debet afragium bis in anno ubicumque dominus voluerit, sc. inter portum de Pevenes' et de Sefford' *IMisc* 8/23; **1279** debet affragia que valent vj d. *Hund.* II 734; **1282** in liberacione domino abbati..de redditu de haveragio *Ac. Wellingb.* 27 (cf. ib. 48: de averagio); **c1283** quodlibet jugum [faciet] j ~ium de iij septimanis in iij septimanas et semper per diem Sabbati; ..et omnia ~ia fient a Wy usque ad Bellum; et ~ium est dim. summa vel frumenti vel ordei *Cust. Battle* 123 (cf. averagius); **1285** propter curta ~a infra v leucas habebit iiij scutell' ordei *Cust. Suss.* II 4; faciet ~ia quolibet altero die ubi requisitus fuerit infra x leucas vel solvet domino pro quolibet ~io ij d. *FormMan* 27 (cf. ib. 28: summa †areragiorum clx; cf. ib. 13: v s. de †averario); **c1300** averabit bis infra com. ..vel semel extra ad iiij parvos panes vel solvit pro ~io iij d. *Rent. Surv. R.* (*Ashill*) 465; **c1300** averland de Chistelet: Hamo..debet de tenemento suo apud Chistelet.. terciam partem unius ~ii *Reg. S. Aug.* 119; **1399** facere consueverunt inter quam plura alia diversa custumaria opera cariagia ~ia et servicia pro terris.. (*JustIt* 774) *Peasants' Rising* 21; **c1453** unum quodque ~ium estivale fieri debet inter Hokeday et gulam Augusti et per diem Sabbati, ut †sic [? l. sit] pro voluntate servientum facere cum ad hoc summoniti fuerint *Surv. Wye* 68. **b 12..** faciet ~ium quater per annum per aquam usque ad S. Ivonem.. et remotius *Cart. Rams.* I 432; **1251** ~ium pedile est portare ballivi aucas, ova et hujusmodi (*Cust. Ely*) *Cust. Rents* 66; **1269** r.c. ..de ij d. de ij ~iis cum equo, prec' ~ii j d.; et de xiij ~iis pedil', prec' ~ii j d. *MinAc* (*Cratfield, Suff*) 994/27; **1272** ~ia equina *Ib.* 28; **1277** faciet ~ium secundum turnum vicinorum per terram et aquam (*Inq. Ely*) *Eng. Corn Market* 7; **1279** faciet ~ium cum dorso *Hund.* II 602 (cf. ib. 603: cum corpore suo; 605: super dorsum suum); **c1300** nec averat cum equo set facit ~ium pedibus vel dat iij ob. *Rent. Surv. R.* (*Ashill*) 465; **1302** (v. bakaveragium); **1310** ~ium pedestre (*MinAc*) *MFG*. **c 1357** ne..~ia aut cariagia.. exigant *Melrose* II 435; **1365** quod dicta terra..libera sit.. de ~iis et cariagiis quibuscumque *RMSScot* 194; **1451** sine quocumque griswine pultri ~io aut cariagio *Reg. Brechin.* I 167; **1547** cum averragiis et carragiis *Reg. Aberd.* I 433; **1553** prebentes annuatim..hareagium, cariagium et debitum servicium *RMSScot* 745; **1555** extendens..in aragiis et caragiis ad summam ij d. *Melrose* II 604 (cf. ib. 605: in arreagiis et careagiis); **1566** cum ariagio, cariagio, devoriis et debito servicio usitato *Inchaffray* 165.

averagius, subject to transport service. **b** (sb. m.) tenant owing transport service.

c1283 virgata Trostel, que est quarta pars unius jugi averag', debet semper j averagium de xij septimanis in xij septimanas *Cust. Battle* 122; xxviij juga averag' pertinencia ad Wy *Ib.* 123 (cf. ib. 133 [**c1236**]: in villa de Wy sunt xxvj juga servilia et dim. averantia..et una virgata que dicitur Throstesierd). **b a1190** avaragii, quando redeunt de via, habebunt singuli j parvum panem de aula *Chr. Abingd.* II 243.

averalis, (?) used as a draught animal.

1295 de lacte xiiij vaccarum ~ium *MinAc* 1090/3 r. 1.

averare, ~iare [AS *aferan, aferian*; cf. averus], to perform transport service. **b** (trans.) to transport. **c** (? w. *opus* as obj.).

in quibusdam terris [villanus] debet..equitare et ~iare et summagium ducere [AS: *ridan and averian and lade lædan*] (*Quad., Rect.*) *GAS* 445; si ~iat [AS: *gif he aferað*], non cogitur operari quamdiu equus ejus foris moratur *Ib.* 446; **c1185** debent..in omni Sabbato ~are usque Maldone et bis ~are pedes usque Londoniam *Rec. Templars* 5–6 (cf. ib. 12: ~are cum equo ad xx leucas); **1222** qui non ~ant faciunt fotaver *Dom. S. Paul.* 3; debent..iij d. ob. de averselver eo quod non debeant longius ~are quam ad granarium S. Pauli *Ib.* 90; **1244** ~abit cum..participe suo, ita quod ambo simul ~abunt sicut dimidii virgatarii qui debent averagium *Cart. Rams.* I 442; **c1253** debet afrare pro cibo domini quotiens necesse fuerit *IMisc* 8/23; **1275** cepit de tenentibus de Bocton' injuste pro averagiis residui seminis, ubi ~are non tenebantur et ubi nichil fuit ad ~andum, xxv s. *Hund.* I 210; **1279** ~iabit ter in anno, ita quod possit redire ad prandium *Ib.* II 461; **1285** debet quelibet virgata ~are extra manerium semel in hieme et semel in estate..cum j equo; ..et vocatur *utaver*. ..et quelibet virgata debet ~are apud Suthm[allyng] bis in estate et bis in hieme, ..quod vocatur *inaver Cust. Suss.* II 36–7; **c1300** tenent quartam partem unius averland..et debent ~are quando preceptum sit usque ad Cantuariam et habebit tunc panem et cervisiam *Reg. S. Aug.* 119; quando debent averrare plenarie et communiter, tunc inveniet ipse equum suum ad everandum *Ib.* 199; **1316** averrabit cum sacco vel carecta sua *Terr. Fleet* 13; **1330** debet bis ~are ..et pro averagio habebit j panem de obolo *CourtR* (*Cuddington*) 204/44 r. 1; **1338** ~abit cum sacco et equo quo dominus voluerit *Cl* 161 m. 12. **b c1230** [quando] avrat bladum, portare debet dim. quarterium *Doc. Bec* 70; **1279** ~iabit cum sociis suis totum bladum domini sui quod vendiderit apud Cantebrugiam *Hund.* II 463; **c1300** debent ~are salem et bladum *Reg. S. Aug.* 101; **1306** debet ~are ad Bellum..dim. summam frumenti *Cust. Battle* 21. **c c1300** pro prenominatis operibus non relaxabitur quis de redditu suo †horsgabulum [? l. horsgabuli] nec non dimittitur aliquatenus pro aliquo opere nisi quando ~antur *Ib.* 78.

†averarium, transport service (*v. et. averagium* a).

c1236 lx juga et dim. sunt apud Wy, quorum xxx et una virgata averant et quodlibet ~iorum reddebat antiquitus xl d. *Cust. Battle* 133.

averarius v. avenarius b.

averata, transport service.

c1300 viij terre sullinge..debent invenire xij equos ad tres vices ad ~am, xij equos ad omnia; ista fient ad sitacionem domini..ad averandum bladum *Reg. S. Aug.* 206.

averclandus v. averlandum. 1 avēre v. ave.

2 avēre [CL], to desire or rejoice. **b** (pr. ppl.) desirous, longing.

avet, cupit, gaudet *GlC* A 933; *to desyre*, ..appetere, ..avere, captare *CathA*. **b** ipse jam prope †positum [l. positam] audiens et avens, ut †proprius [l. propius] accederet efflagitavit GIR. *GE* II 11 p. 225; rumpe jugo cor avens; res dabit ulta sonum ELMH. *Metr. Hen. V* 224.

3 avēre [OF *aveir* < habēre; cf. averium], possession, property.

1177 quantum rex Aldefonsus tenet de rege Navarre melioret cum suo proprio ~e quantum voluerit et potuerit (*Pactum*) *G. Hen. II* I 141.

avergere v. vergere. averia v. avenarius c, averium. averiare v. averare. averim v. aviro.

averinus, of a draught horse.

1344 de j corio affrino vendito, mortuo de morina *Ac. Trin. Dublin* 57.

averipondus, avoirdupois (*cf. averium* 1b).

c1314 navibus carcatis cum molis, lanis et ~dere *IMisc* 75/25.

averium, ~ia [OF *aveir* < habere; cf. 3 avere], resources, property, possession. **b** (w. *ponderis* or sim.) avoirdupois, goods sold by weight.

1220 sciatis me valde indigere auxilio vestro et avario vestro propter..castrum de Rupe Forti [*Rochefort, Gasc.*] firmandum (*AncC* IV 136) *RL* I 106; de avario vestro mihi succurrentes *Ib.* 107; **1267** quod nullus exponat mercimonia sua venditioni..quousque..custuma levetur, sub forisfactura totius ~ii de quo secus fieri contingeret (*Ch. Regis*) *Leg. Ant. Lond.* 104 (= *MGL* II 254); **s1205** cepit rex tertiam decimam partem omnium catallorum et ~iorum totius Anglie tam de viris religiosis quam de laicis *Ib. app.* 200; *havre or havyng of catel or oðer godis*, ~ium *PP*. **b 1267** quod nullus mercator..emat vel vendat.. †aliquid [v.l. aliquod] ~ium quod ponderari debeat vel tronari nisi per stateram vel tronam nostram (*Ch. Regis*) *Leg. Ant. Lond.* 104; **1267** cum..navi sua..cum ~io ponderis, rebus et aliis mercandisis suis carcata (*CurR*) *Law Merch.* II 10; **1289** de quolibet ~io de pondere, sc. de centena, ij d. *RGasc.* II 405; **1303** cum de prefatis mercatoribus nonnulli eorum alias exerceant mercandisas ut de ~io ponderis et de aliis rebus subtilibus..que ad certam custumam facile poni non poterunt (*Ord. Regis*) *MGL* II 209; **1303** custuma ~ii ponderis et aliarum mercium *EEC* 268; **1305** pro lxxiiij libratis ~ii ponderati *Ib.* 328; **1307** modus ponderandi ~ia ponderis ad civitatem Londonie veniencia..talis exstitit.. (*CoramR*) *Law Merch.* II 76; **1315** unum pondus de ~io ponderis in villa de Suthamton' extitit assignatum pro commodo mercatorum..in Angliam veniencium cum mercandisis suis de ~io ponderis *RParl* 332a; **1320** venditores vini et cervisie ac mercatores ~ii ponderis *MunCOx* 37; **c1410** merces vendibiles pretermittit vice nulla, / nec res subtiles nec āveria pondere tulla (*Vers. Exch.*) *EHR* XXXVI 59.

2 livestock, cattle (collect.). **b** farm animal, esp. head of cattle. **c** (payable as mortuary or sim.). **d** (w. *vivum*) head of livestock. **e** (w. *grossum*) head of cattle dist. from sheep etc. **f** (w. *otiosum*) beast not in use for ploughing etc. *Cf. averus*.

c1225 proprie ~ie clamant habere communam in terra vestra de Wateresfeld (*AncC* VI 84) *RL* I 272; **1256** debet custodire ix partem ~ii *Rent. & Surv. portf.* 10/33; **1345** pastura..depasta per ~iam domini *Comp. Swith.* 146 (cf. ib. 150). **b 1128** pasnagium ad porcos suos et ad alia ~ia sua (*Ch. Norm.*) ORD. VIT. *app.* V p. 203 (= *Regesta* 1553); si prepositus hundredi equos aut boves aut oves aut porcos vel cujuscumque generis ~ia [OF: *aveir*] vagantia restare fecerit (*Leis Will.*) *GAS* 497; ita oneraverunt eam [pasturam] ovibus et aliis ~iis quod non potest plus sustinere *RDomin.* 19; precipio tibi quod juste et sine dilatione facias habere G. ~ia sua per vadium et plegium, unde queritur quod R. ea cepit et detinet injuste GLANV. XII 12; **1196** de placito ~iorum detentorum contra vadium et plegium *CurR* I 25 (cf. ib. 125, 383); **c1200** pro singulis ~iis in..pastura agistatis..iij d. per annum *Rec. Leic.* I 5; **c1200** concessimus.. tria avaria sua que paschant in nostra dominica pastura *Cart. Osney* IV 211; abbas ~ia ejus cepit et vendidit BRAKELOND 139v; **1202** venit in prata..et illa per ~ia sua pavit *SelPlCrown* 14; **1214** capta fuerunt ~ia sua.., ita quod quedam pars illorum ~iorum adhuc est in parco, sc. iiij carucate boum et iij vacce *CurR* VII 183–4; **1228** abducere ~ia et catalla sua que habuit in manerio *Cl* 50; **c1230** debet..arare pro quolibet ~io bovino ad carucam ij acras *Doc. Bec* 37 (cf. ib. 41: pro quolibet ~io bovino maturo ad arandum); **1234** carucatores quando ponunt carucas in ~ia debent habere prandia sua *Cust. Glast.* 106; **1280** nec curia domini regis facit aliquam differenciam inter ~ia et catalla *SelCKB* I 64; **c1280** nec [potest] vendere bovem nec equum suum si ipsum bovem aut equum a vitulo aut a pullo nutrierit absque licencia domini; et dabit idem ~ium domino si ipsum voluerit, de precio vj d. (*Cust.*) *Crawley* 236; **a1300** habere in pastura duos greges multonum, v^{xx} ~ias juvenes *Kelso app.* p. 461; in estate..veniet ad operacionem suam quando ~ia pergunt de villa in campum *Cust. Bleadon* 202; **1327** quod uxores et pueros suos ac ~ia, bona et catalla sua quecumque elongent a partibus Marchie *RScot* 208b; propter ~ia, id est animalia muta, ne diu detineantur inclusa *RegiamM* IV 27; **1382** quod nullus..permittat aliqua ~ia sua intrare in le Frithfeld, nisi ~ia trahentia, ante festum S. Martini *Hal. Durh.* 174; **1533** injuste occupant et superonerant communiam ovibus et aliis ~iis suis *Banstead* II 102. **c** relevium villani: melius ~ium [OF: *le meillur aveir*], sive bos fuerit sive equus, sui domini erit (*Leis Will.*) *GAS* 507; **c1185** habebunt..ad obitum meliorem ~iam *Rec. Templars* 57; **c1217** iste sacrista primo obtinuit vivum ~ium secundo melius [v.l. bovem secundo meliorem] mortuorum cum corporibus eorum *Chr. Evesham* 267; **s1246** quod melius ~ium solvatur ecclesie pro domino domus defuncto et secundum melius ~ium pro domina domus defuncta, tam de equis quam de aliis animalibus *Ann. Dunstable* 170; habet ecclesia..de morte uxoris..de grege communi secundum melius ~ium [v.l. †avernum] *Fleta* 123; **1406** [lego] vicario..optimum ~ium meum *Test. Ebor.* III 42; **1583** reddendo..optimum ~ium nomine herietti sive farlevii *Pat* 1234 m. 12. **d** si clamaverit quis ~ium vivum [OF: *vif* *aveir*] quasi furto sibi surreptum (*Leis Will.*) *GAS* 507; **c1217** (v. 2c supra); **1289** si..aliquis..parochianorum.. viva ~ia habeat die mortis *Reg. Heref.* 213. **e a1200** si.. predictarum ovium non habuerint numerum in eadem pastura, de grossis ~iis suis habeant suplementum, sc. de cccc ovium numero lx grossorum animalium fiat mutacio *Reg. Newbattle* 97; **1370** pro quolibet grosso ~io..et quolibet bidenti..et quolibet equo *Hal. Durh.* 93. **f 1237** non debet habere communam nisi ad boves de caruca sua propria et non ad ~ia sua ociosa *CurR* XV 1936; poterit esse transgressio.. si fiat districcio per oves vel bestias carucarum cum sint alia ~ia ociosa *Fleta* 251; habebit iiij ~ia et j affrum in pastura ..cum ~iis domini ociosis *Cust. Bleadon* 208.

1 †averius, (?) for a draught horse or for transport service.

c1300 debet namiare..et habebit unum ~ium panem *Reg. S. Aug.* 123 (cf. *Cust. Battle* 5: debet xv averagia..et percipiet pro quolibet averagio..ij panes).

2 averius v. averus.

averlandum, ~us [ME; (?) *infl. by werkland*], land held by transport service.

c1182 (17c) Robertus..[tenet] ij averclandos pro iij s. et vadit pro corredio episcopi apud Glocestre vel alibi ubi opus fuerit *RBWorc* 351; **1299** (17c) avercklondi: ..[tenens] debet quolibet die in anno venire ad curiam domini episcopi summo mane cum equo suo et sacco et facere ei omnia que ei injuncta fuerint *Ib.* 99; **c1300** G. ..tenet j averland de Westbere..; et quando rex est in villa debet ducere apud Cantuariam j trussam straminis..; et debet ducere sal usque ad Sturee ad domum ubi allec ponitur.. *Reg. S. Aug.* 120; (cf. ib. 102: unumquodque ~um debet vij ova); **13..** idem habebit j acram stipularum..ad pascendum affrum suum; et vocatur *averlonde Cust. Bleadon* 204.

avermannus [ME: (?) *infl. by werkman*], tenant holding land by transport service.

c1182 in Ogginhale sunt ij avermeni..; et debent deferre corredium super dorsum quo fuerit opus *RBWorc* 170 (cf. ib. 17 [1299]: †arkmanni: J. ..tenet j averclandum); **12..** fuerunt viij aurkemonni, quorum quilibet operabatur singulis ebdomadis ij diebus.. *Reg. Pri. Worc.* 43b; **12..** sunt apud Menstre v ~i qui debent per totum quociens summonentur cum omnibus equis saccis averare ad Cantuariam..et summonere halimotum et namiare..et defferre bladum de curia ad batellum *Reg. S. Aug.* 28 (cf. ib. 27: debent namiare cum bedello et ceteris ~is); **1275** fecit dictos ~os ducere fimum..ad manerium suum *Hund.* (*Kent*) I 208 (cf. ib.: utrum ~i deberent servicium suum vel servicii redempciones).

avernum v. averium 2c.

Avernus [CL = *entry to Underworld*], Hell.

†1005 (13c) ~i cruciamenta sine fine luiturus *CD* 672*; hos quoque quos dudum male captivarat Avernus P. Blois *Euch.* 16. 1148A; querebant animam Dagoberti regis Averni / precones Garl. *Tri. Eccl.* 36; hec ~us, *helle* WW.

averocus v. haverocus.

averruncare [CL = *to ward off*; (?) *infl. by* eruncare], to uproot, abolish.

aberuncat, abstirpat *GlC* A 23 (cf. ib. 934); quas Christicolis pastor fundaverat edes / nisibus efferis averruncare [v.l. eradicare] parabant Frith. 1115.

averse, back to front.

s1001 Crescens..vili jumento ~e impositus circumducitur Diceto *Chr.* 160.

aversio [CL], turning away (*v. et. eversio*).

1197 (v. adversatio); futura maxima Christianorum ~o a fide erit tempore Antichristi Ockham *Dial.* 504; amor sui, ~o a Deo *Ib.* 592; peccatum.., quod est ~o voluntatis a bono incommutabili ad bonum commutabile Paul. Angl. *ASP* 1553.

aversor, denier.

799 dico te..confessorem Christi, non ~orem [v.l. adversorem] fidei Alcuin *Ep.* 166 p. 271.

1 avertere v. advertere 2.

2 avertere [CL], to turn away. **b** to avert, ward off, forfend.

ne forte..non sit qui reserat, averso illo qui claves tenere probatur Bede *HE* III 25 p. 189; si..loquerentur cum illo, ~erent illum a diis suis *Ib.* V 10; **a1190** caveas ne inde aliqua..suggestione ~aris *Canon. G. Sempr.* 98 v; [luna] decrescente et quasi vultum ~ente Gir. *TH* II 3; caput et humeros more sue [sc. Romane] gentis ~endo quasi sub indignatione respondit.. *Id. GE* II 36 p. 345; **1197** ut amici fortuiti fortune arridenti arrideant et cum eadem ab amicis vultum ~ant *Ep. Cant.* 415. **b** qua [admonitione] correcti per..fletus et preces iram a se..justi Judicis ~erent Bede *HE* IV 23; **1177** si alteruter nostrum in via decesserit, quod Deus ~at (*Tractatus*) Gir. *PI* II 5.

2 (dep.) to turn away from, reject.

S. Paule, tibi attuli [mortuum] eum: ne ~aris eum; ora pro eo Anselm (*Or.* 10) III 37.

avertibilis, able to be averted.

omnia illa evenient de voluntate divina, que respectu omnium volutorum est non impedibilis nec a quovis ~is Bradw. *CD* 704E.

averus, ~ius [(?) AS *eafor* (cf. *Archiv für neuere Sprachen* CIX 75–82); (?) *infl. by* averium 2; cf. averare], draught horse (esp. for ploughing).

848 (12c) ut sit liberatum..illud monasterium ab illis causis quas *cum feorme* et *eafor* vocitemus, ..a pastu equorum meorum omnium *CS* 454 (cf. ib.: *æfres* et *cum feorme*); ibi viii servi et unus afrus *DB* I 165; **1130** pro defectu boum et avrorum *Pipe* 2; **1167** pro ij affris x s. *Pipe* 16; **1177** cum instauramento octo boum et unius ~ii *Cart. Glouc.* I 207; xij bobus, iiij ~is, v vaccis, j tauro *RDomin.* 85; **c1185** ad instauramentum..honoris proficiendum..pro xlix bobus et ix affris *Cart. Glam.* 175; **c1190** pasturam sufficientem cccc ovibus, xvj animalibus, ij ~is et xij suibus *Kelso* 178; **1204** in roberia asportavit..x avros et xiij vaccas *CurR* III 93; **1209** ferrura iij carettariorum, vij avrorum *Pipe Wint.* 29; **1212** abduxerunt xiiij animalia, tam boves quam vaccas, et ij ~os *SelPlCrown* 60; **1212** de maneriis instaurandis, sc. E. de xxiiij bobus, duobus avar', xiij porcis, d et xxxiij ovibus et..C. de xxv bobus, j aver', xx porcis et m et l ovibus *Cl* 117b; **1227** de ix m. pro xviij awris carucariis *LTRMem* 10 m. 5; juravit abbas W. [ob. 1235] se c equos.. perdidisse, quorum alii erant manni, alii vero runcini, alii summarii, alii veredarii, alii vero ~ii *G. S. Alb.* I 259; **1247** pastura ad sex boves, duas vaccas, duos afferos *Cart. Osney* IV 161; **1252** xviij bestias, sive boves sive affros, ad carucas suas deputatas *Reg. Ant. Linc.* II 382; **1256** capere fecit xv averia sua..et iterum capere fecit tres haveros *G. S. Alb.* I 361; **1285** vic. liberet ei omnia catalla debitoris exceptis bobus et affris caruce (II *Westm.* c. 18) *StRealm* I 82; **1290** j affrus ad molendinum..et j pullus *Reg. Wint.* II 704; **1292** affra ij, precium xiij s. iiij d.; item boves xvj, precium bovis x s. *Reg. Malm.* II 378; *Cust. Bleadon* 208 (v. averium 2f); **c1300** pullani equorum primo compoto postquam nati sunt pullani vocantur, secundo compoto..superannales, tercio compoto..affri (*Regula Comp.*) *Seignorial Admin.* 173; **1305** quelibet carruca debet jungi de iiij bobus et iiij affris *Ext. Hadleigh* 230; **1308** carucas..cum bovibus et †apris et toto attilio *Conc.* II 301 (= *Foed.* III 120: affris); **1313** j palefridus, iij pullani et ij affri *Reg. Carl.* II 93; **1329** per vendicionem corii j affri mortui *ExchScot* 124; **1336** de j stalone xix affris femellis..et de ij affris mas (*sic*) *DL MinAc* 242/3886 m. 2d.; **1352** in j affro pro molendino v s. *Comp. Worc.* I 50; **s1435** herbam..cum quibusdam averiis, viz. equis, bobus, affris, vaccis, bidentibus et porcis, depasti fuerunt Amund. II 122; **1482** habere in communa..nisi xij averia et j affrum vel equum *CourtR Lygh* I f. 16.

avesagium [cf. AS *æfesne* = *pasturage*], (payment for) pasturage or pannage.

1222 debent..de singulis porcis j. d. pro *garsavese Dom. S. Paul.* 51; **1325** solvet pro quolibet porco obolum, quod vocatur *evese Banstead* 321 (cf. ib. 320: pro *grasavese* iiij d. ob.); **1336** est ibidem [*Baddow, Essex*] quedam consuetudo quod quilibet custumarius dabit ~ium pro porcis suis quos habuerit inter festum S. Mich. et S. Martini, viz. pro quolibet porco etatis j anni vel amplius ij d., et pro quolibet porco etatis dim. anni j d., et pro quolibet porcello unius quarterii anni ob., et pro iiij porcellis separatis, preter sues et porcellos lactantes pro quibus nichil dabit *IPM* 48/2 r. 10; **1358** est ibi [*Stoke Dabernon, Surrey*] ~ium de tenentibus ibidem ad festum S. Mich., quod valet per annum ij s. *Ib.* 139/21 r. 4; **1400** pasturabunt..in parco [*Rayleigh, Essex*]..xx porcos tempore avisagii *AncD* D300; **1451** terciam partem ~ii tocius dominii de Hertyng' [*Sussex*] *Cl* 301 m. 21d.; **1485** de pannagio porcorum..et..de avisagio vaccarum *MinAc* (*Somerset*) 974/6 r. 8; **1535** Framfeld [*Sussex*] valet..in ~io porcorum xx s. *Valor Eccl.* I 2a; **1587** ~ium porcorum infra forestam nostram [de Dyvynnock, *Brecon*] *Pat* 1301 m. 1 (cf. ib.: advisagium).

avesare, to pay pannage for.

a1300 ~abit porcos ut supra (*Inq. Barnes*) *Dom. S. Paul.* lxviii; **1336** cum semel dederunt avesagium pro sue, nunquam ~abunt eandem *IPM* 48/2 r. 15; **1431** pro uno porco non ~ato *MinAc Essex* (*Gt. Waltham*).

avete, ~o v. ave. avetileon v. anethelaeon.

1 avia [CL], **ava,** grandmother.

avia illorum, nomine Leonella *Hist. Abb. Jarrow* 36; **964** (12c) ego Eadgifu predicti regis ava *CS* 1191; avia, *ealdemoder* Ælf. *Sup.*; **c1180** quos R. ..avus meus eis dedit ..pro anima Roheisie uxoris ejus ave mee *AncD* A 2325; **1199** soror Alexandri fuit ava predicti S. *CurR RC* I 318; **1217** maritagium ave sue *Cl* 308a; istis [patruis etc.].. deficientibus, ad superiores fiet descensus [ab avo], sicut ad fratrem avi vel avie Bracton 68b; *beeldam, fadyris or moders* [*moder*], avia *PP*.

2 †avia, nightjar (bird).

hec nicticorax, A. *nyghtcrake*; hec avia, idem WW.

aviarium, haunt of birds (? infl. by *avius*).

~ia secreta nemora quae aves frequentant *GlC* A 916; ~ia, *weglæsa beara*, secreta nemora Ælf. *Gl.*

aviarius, poulterer.

ex adverso sunt constituti mercatores piscatorii, pullarii sive ~ii [A. *pulters*] Whittington *Vulg.* 66.

avicaptio, fowling place.

1328 decimas..molendinorum, piscariarum, ~onum *Lit. Cant.* I 266.

avicida, bird-slayer.

c1200 elevans oculos vidit ~am suum [sc. nisum] recentis adhuc cruoris in rostro signa preferentem *V. Bart. Farn.* 19.

avicipula, pitfall (? for birds).

pyttfal, decipula, ~a *PP*; ~a, A. *a putfalle* WW.

1 avicula [CL], little bird. **b** (fig.).

~e, paste frumento quod benedictione condierat, digredientem..secute, nunquam ab ejus divelli karitate potuerunt W. Malm. (*V. Aldh.*) *GP* V 247; **s1191** quidam remigantium, illius ~e que mergus dicitur tractus exemplo Diceto *YH* I 93; **s870** cum accipitre solus..naviculam ingressus, ut in insulis maris..anates et ~as alias aucuparet M. Par. *Maj.* I 393; **s1217** cecidit velum expansum super Francos ad instar retis super ~as irretitas *Ib.* III 29; [parvulus] gaudet..†~orum nidos explorare et ova vel pullos inventos..domum portare (Docking *Com.*) *Doc. Francisc.* 12. **b** retiacula quibus ~a Christi..videbatur intercepta Gosc. *Wulfh.* 2; **c1430** 'rara'..est hec 'avis..in terris'..que..nobis aurum accommodet; et propterea.. hanc vestre mentis ~am carioribus quibus poterimus graciarum..muneribus..depascimus *Reg. Whet.* II 450.

2 †avicula [? cf. avena], wild oat.

14.. hec ~a, A. *wyld hote* WW.

avicularius, fowler.

a fewler, auceps, aucupator, ~ius *CathA*.

avide [CL], greedily, eagerly.

[equus] partem feni tectorum ~e adprehendens traxit ad se *V. Cuthb.* I 6; nil ~ius quaesierim, nil libentius audierim, ..quam quod de universali omnium..fonte..dicitur Eriug. *Per.* 556A; quatinus..ad..explenda negotia..sese.. ~ius accingeret *G. Steph.* I 20; questui..~issime, ne dicam turpiter, inhiantes Neckam *NR* I 28.

aviditas [CL], greed, passionate desire.

957 (14c) tota mentis ~ate..scrutatus sum *CS* 997; iniquitas est insatiabilis falsorum honorum et falsarum divitiarum ~as Anselm (*Ep.* 117) III 253; antiquorum.. labores securiori ~ate cupivimus perscrutari R. Bury *Phil.* 9. 145; nimia sitis ~ate affligebatur S. Sim. *Itin.* 57.

†avidius, (?) grey, hoary (ME *grenew*).

9.. ~ius, *grionu*, aureus, *giolu* WW; nomina colorum: viridis, *grene*, ..~ius, *grinu* Ælf. *Gl.*

avidotus [? cf. aquaeductus c], drainage channel or tunnel, adit (in Devon lead-mines).

1301 in quo statu easdem mineras receperunt ac eciam in quo statu minere ille et avidodi tam subtus terram quam supra..extiterunt *Pat* 121 m. 26d. (= *CalPat* 625: †amdodi); **a1307** in cordis canib' emptis..ad aquam, terram et lapides de minera et veteribus ~is extrahend' *KRAc* 260/19 m. 1 (cf. ib.: de reparacione minere et factura avidodorum); **1323** in..mundacione avidodorum ad tascham *Pipe* 118 r. 53; **1439** fodere in eisdem mineris et auditis earundem *Pat* 444 m. 21 (cf. *FineR* 267 m. 17).

avidulus v. avidus.

avidus [CL], greedy, covetous, desirous.

~o Pharaonis exercitu..summerso Aldh. *VirgP* 12; velut [apes]..defruto..~a viscerum receptacula certatim implere contendunt *Ib.* 4; [Walenses] vindicte ~i, omnium rerum largissimi Map *NC* II 20; *covatus*, ambiciosus, avarus, ~us, avidulus *CathA*.

avigerulus, ~a, poulterer.

1393 est ibi pomilio, sic †anigĕrulus hic (R. Maidstone) *Pol. Poems* I 285; hic ~us, *a pulter*, ..hec ~a, que vendit aves WW; *a pulter*, ~us *CathA*.

avigilia v. aquileia. avilina v. abellana. Avincula v. Advincula. avinculus v. avunculus.

avinus, avian.

hirundines..~o forcipe flexuosi gutturis carmen canentes Felix *Guthl.* 39.

aviro, ~onus [OF *aviron*], oar.

1225 de quot navibus..confidere possimus de singulis portubus vestris [sc. de Quinque Portubus] cum xvj ~onis et ultra *Pat* 503; **1225** mandatum est..justiciario Hybernie ..quod fieri faciat cc ~ones de fraxino partim continentes longitudinem xij ulnarum, partim xiij, partim xiiij et eos.. venire faciat usque Winchelese *Cl* 14b; **1285** per servicium inveniendi j †averim [l. *averun*] et j hominem in j navi *Aids* III 6; **1462** [de qualibet centena] chevironum et ~onum *CalCh* VI 164.

avironatus, oar.

1147 debet homo..quo profundius potuerit intrare et, dum ultra ire nequiverit, avirunatum unum octo pedibus longum introrsus de diverso lanceando propellere; et a loco quo avirunatus ille transnatare deserit spacium xl pedum per cordam debet mensurari ibique signum in aqua infigi (*Ch. Sawtry*) *MonA* V 522b; **1279** ~um unum viij pedibus longum..lanceare *Hund.* II 664.

avis [CL], bird. **b** bird of prey (esp. falc.). **c** game bird. **d** royal bird (reserved for king's use).

aves minuriunt vel vernant vel vernicant Aldh. *PR* 131 p. 179; insula..avium ferax terra marique generis diversi Bede *HE* I 1; ut in quibusdam avium generibus in quibus femineus sexus semper major est et validior Anselm (*Mon.* 42) I 58; **11..** [12 Feb.] ~es incipiunt cantare (*Calend. Durh.*) *RHS Handbook of Dates* 44; cum potu recreentur aves, quare liquor absit / qui colamentum sanguinis esse solet? Neckam *DS* II 149. **b s1055** [Malgerius] venationibus et avium certaminibus sepius justo intendebat W. Malm. *GR* III 267; **1168** xl s. ad portandum aves regis ad mare *Pipe* 60; plurimi civium delectantur ludentes in avibus celi, nisis, accipitribus et hujusmodi W. Fitzst. *Thom. prol.* 18; falcones..propensiori diligentia quam cetere rapaces aves a bene instructis falconariis portantur Neckam *NR* I 28; notum est aves generosas mutari in casis *Ib.* 33; **1202** xxx s. ad perficiendam domum avium regis *Pipe* 280; aves prede Bart. Angl. XII 1; **1361** falcones silvestres et alias ~es de preda *Pat* 263 m. 3. **c** jus pulli, perdicis, avium campi Gilb. V 216. 2; **1334** pro decima de dxxxj avibus de ripa.. et de clvij heronibus et v egretz (*KRAc* 387/8) *NR Rec. Soc.* III 227; **1384** de phasianis, perdicibus, pluveris, quailis, alaudis et omnimodis aliis avibus de warenna (*Pat* 318) *SelPlForest* cxxx *n.*; **1485** pro empcione avium ferarum *Ac. Durh.* 649. **d** fit interdum ut aves regie regi..promittantur, accipitres sc. vel falcones *Dial. Scac.* II 25; **1309** debet habere omnes aves regales, sc. austrucium, falconum, cignum et hujusmodi aves *S. Jers.* XVIII 164; accipiter est avis regia que plus animo quam ungulis est armata UPTON 173.

2 (kinds of birds) **a** teal. **b** eider duck. **c** (?) egret. **d** puffin. **e** crane. **f** kind of wading bird (*cf.* Sp. *martinete*). **g** (*s. dub.*). **h** kingfisher. **i** hoopoe.

a est in Lagenia stagnum modicum aves S. Colemanni continens, anates sc. minores que vulgari vocabulo cercelle vocantur GIR. *TH* II 29. **b** aves ille B. Cuthberti specialiter nominantur: ab Anglis vero *lomes* vocantur, ab Saxonibus autem et qui Frisiam incolunt *eires* dicuntur R. COLD. *Cuthb.* 27; **1399** j dorsor' cum avibus S. Cuthberti *Ac. Durh.* 136. **c** insula.. / finibus Apulie dat Diomedis aves. / hec avis est fulice par forma, sed color albus NECKAM *DS* II 936 (cf. ib. III 396). **d** Lunday..cuniculos producit copiose, columbis eciam [et] strucionibus, quas vocat A. Neckam †Ganimedis [? l. Diomedis] aves, nidos habet pregnantes BAKER 104b. **e** gruem dicit [Martialis] avem Palamedis NECKAM *NR* I 46; et Palamedis aves cecini *Id. DS* III 31. **f** quedam avis dicitur S. Martini in Hispania, parvula ad modum reguli; hec graciles habet tibias ad modum †juncti [l. junci] et longas O. CHERITON *Fab.* 7. **g** BRINTON *Serm.* 12 (v. accitus); ~es paradisi volucres sunt sic vulgariter appellate..ob insignem pulchritudinem. ..super flumina Nili fluvii libenter habitat et raro alibi reperitur. sunt eciam alie aves que eciam aves paradisi appellate sunt, ex eo quod ignoratur unde veniant aut quo vadant; ..harum autem color est fuscus sive pallidus; minores tamen sunt quam monedule UPTON 176. **h** [incida] apud quosdam avis Petri piscatoris appellatur UPTON 197. **i** loquela avis †Socrate [? l. Socratis] habens v colores BACON IX 74.

3 a bird used in divination. **b** omen.

a (v. augurium). **b** bonis avibus iter peregrinationis arripiens W. CANT. *Mir. Thom.* VI 105.

4 (bot.) *v. lingua avis.*

avis- v. et. advis-. avisagium v. avesagium. aviseges v. amseges.

avitium [CL], birds (collect.).

~ium genus partim terrestre est, partim aquatile LINACRE *Emend. Lat.* 445.

avitus [CL], ancestral, traditional, old-established.

†a iutiis, antiquis *GlC* A 931 (cf. ib. 943; †avultis, regalibus); Nabal / qui..nomen avitum / ebrius exprobrat [cf. *1 Sam.* xxv] ALDH. *VirgV* 2526; ab errore ~o correctos BEDE *HE* V 15; ille ~us humani generis inimicus *V. Dunst.* B. 7; **s1164** archipresul victus..dicit se leges illas, quas rex ~as vocabat, suscepisse R. HOWD. I 222; **1254** omissis ~is et paternis sepulcris *Cart. Worc.* 464; **s1392** male creduli in Deum et tradiciones ~as WALS. *HA* II 208.

1 avius [CL], out of the way, pathless. **b** (sb. n. or f.) trackless waste.

oute of way, devius, ..avius, invius *CathA*. **b** latrones .. / abstrahunt qui exuvias / legentibus per avias (ÆTHELWALD) *Carm. Aldh.* II 58; avia plerosque aut viae difficiles in mortem subverterunt W. POIT. I 8; abiere per avia GARL. *Tri. Eccl.* 73.

2 avius v. avus. aviz- v. advis-. avoamentum, ~are, ~atio v. advoc-. 1 avocare v. advocare.

2 avocare [CL], to divert, distract, banish.

contigit..ut..dominus..placidum ab oculis somnum curis deditus ~aret *Chr. Rams.* 141; **s1099** nec..quisquam respectu prede ~avit animum quin ceptum persequerentur triumphum W. MALM. *GR* IV 370; canum cursibus ~ari *Id. GP* I 44; **s1171** quia longius ab urbe Romana maneret et ipse aliis regni sui negotiis ~aretur *Becket Mat.* IV 167.

avocatio v. advocatio. avoeria v. advocaria. avohare v. advocare.

avolare [CL], to fly away. **b** (fig.).

in vere dimitto eos [accipitres] ~are ad silvam [*ætwindan to wuda*] ÆLF. *Coll.* 99; nisus..consuetudinem oblitus ~andi et revolandi W. CANT. *Mir. Thom.* V 20; illa [apparitio] per fenestram ~avit MAP *NC* II 14; dum [bombyces] ~are parant GERV. TILB. III 56. **b** privilegium quo..supra nos ~are debent qui supra nos sunt H. BOS. *Thom.* IV 1.

avolatio, flying away, hasty departure. **b** ascent of soul to heaven.

iste inter sponsum et sponsam inquisitiones, ..allocutiones, ..discursus et recursus, ~ones, reversiones tot et elapsus, quid inter ipsos sunt nisi quedam suavia suavis.. amoris signa? H. BOS. *LM* 1369D; nec ullis illi [sc. Christo] ~onibus aut devolationibus ad hoc mysterium peragendum opus esse GARDINER *CC* 374. **b** **s1327** bene namque cum unoquoque agitur si talia cum contricione culpam in eo diluant aut penam debitam †immuniant [l. imminuant], quamvis immediatam †advelacionem [v.l. avolacionem] anime non efficiant HIGD. VII 44 p. 326.

avolatus, flying away, hasty departure.

auditum est, celebri pariter et leta fama velociori avium ~u..divulgatum, archiepiscopum..repatriasse (*Passio Thom.*) *Becket Mat.* IV 433; **s1242** rex Anglorum repentino ~u se contulit Blavium *Flor. Hist.* II 255.

avolta [cf. volta], vault.

capella [constructa per abbatem W., ob. 1235] in arduum surgens super suam crepidinem, que vulgariter ~a dicitur, dormitorii diminutionem supplet et defectum *G. S. Alb.* I 288.

avonculus v. avunculus. avou-, avow- v. advoc-. avr- v. et. aver-.

avronum [OF *avroigne* < habrotonum], 'averoyne', southernwood.

abrotonum Latini G[r]ecis debent. hanc herbam Galli auronum, ..Angli *sothernewod* nominant TURNER *Herb.* A ii.

avulsio [CL], tearing out, plucking. **b** (fig.).

1171 ut..misero..capulationem et oculorum ~ionem infligeret J. SAL. *Ep.* 305. 361A; **s1191** crebris petrariarum.. jactibus et lapidum ~onibus turri..prostrata *Itin. Ric.* III 14; **1307** in ~one ad vellera *MinAc* 1079/18 m. 9. **b** ecce disturbor, avellor, et concutior, sicut in cribro. ..etsi disturbationi, ~oni, concussioni..adversitatum accessus et ..temptationum insultus..immineant, certe mentem stabiliunt, erudiunt, emendant AD. MARSH *Ep.* 83.

avultus v. avitus.

avuncula, aunt.

1267 cum..ceperimus homagium Matillis..et Beatricis.., ~arum et heredum Johanne de Bello Campo *Cl* 367.

avunculus [CL], uncle (maternal or dub.). **b** paternal uncle (CL *patruus*). **c** cousin. **d** wife's uncle. **e** (courtesy title). **f** (w. *magnus*) great uncle.

famosus ille nepos patriarchae remeans ab ~o [sc. Laban] ALDH. *Met.* 2 p. 69; filius ~i [v.l. abunculi] sui BEDE *HE* V 19; **1219** Nicholaus †avinculus [v.l. ~us] suus *CurR* VIII 101; **1223** avonculus *KRMem* 6 r. 3; ex parte matris, si ~us et matertera..defecerint BRACTON 68b; de libero tenemento quod fuit C. de N. patris vel matris, fratris vel sororis, ~i vel amite..sue HENGHAM *Magna* 1. **b** defuncto Eliduro, suscepit Gorhboniani filius diadema regni et ~um..imitatus est G. MON. III 19; **1220** regem Ricardum ~um nostrum *Pat* 260; **1237** cartas R. regis advunculi nostri *LTRMem* 12 r. 2; **1262** P. Wyking petit gildam que fuit Stephani Wyking adwunculi sui *Gild Merch.* II 7; **1265** R. regis awnculi nostri *Cl* 91; **1269** Englecheria presentata per R. le W. awnculum ex parte patris *SelCCoron* 13; **s1377** [rex] dominum..Thomam Wodestoke, ~um suum [fecit] comitem Bokynghamie WALS. *HA* I 338; **1455** ~us noster Humfridus, nuper dux Gloucestrie (*Breve Regis*) *Reg. Whet.* I 181. **c** **s1300** obiit..dominus Ædmundus, comes Cornubie, ~us regis Edwardi *Ann. Ed. I* 448. **d** **1266** awunculo nostro Petro de Sabaudia *Cl* 225. **e** **1440** domino Henrico Anglie et Francie regi..domino et ~o nostro amantissimo (*Lit. Ducis Bavarie*) BEKYNTON I 180. **f** ~us meus magnus, *mines eames fæder* ÆLF. *Sup.*; tunc vocantur fratres et sorores avi vel avie ex parte matris et vocantur ~us magnus et matertera magna BRACTON 68b; **1445** magno ~o nostro Henrico cardinali Anglie *Cl* 295 m. 3.

avus [CL], grandfather. **b** ancestor.

~us, *aeldra faeder GlC* A 892; ~us, *ealdefæder* ÆLF. *Sup.*; **1198** W. ..petiit feodum iij militum..sicut terram illam que ei descendit ex parte G. ..avi sui, qui inde fuit saisitus.. tempore H. regis avi [i.e. Henrici I] *CurR* I 38; **1199** H. auvus patris sui *CurR RC* 358 (cf. ib. 317); **12..** unde placitum fuit inter dictos monachos et W. avium meum in curia domini regis J. *FormA* 55; cognatio parentum sive antecessorum..in linea recta ascendente..incipit a primo gradu, viz. a patre vel matre ascendente usque ad avum BRACTON 67. **b** quorum progenies et avi glomerantur avorum ALDH. *VirgV* 650; hic homines avos, atavos et tritavos longamque stirpis sue seriem..conspiciunt GIR. *TH* II 6.

avynarius v. avenarius b.

awaita, ~us [OF *agait, aguet*], wait, ambush. **b** (w. *maris*) coastguard service.

1414 jacuerunt in agayto pro Thoma M. et eum ceperunt *Proc. J. P.* 327; **1472** in via regia apud Pole [*Dorset*] jacuit in agaitu ad verberandum et interficiendum Johannem T. *CourtR Canford*. **b** **1203** debet ~am [v.l. waitam] maris *CurR* (*Cumb*) II 274.

award- v. esward-.

awarennare [OF < *a+warenne*], to put in status of warren.

1312 [piscaria] que est separalis et †agareunata [l. agarennata] (*Extent*) *Surv. Wye* xxii *n*.

awena v. avena. awnculus, awunculus v. avunculus. awoaria v. advocaria 1c. awrus v. averus.

1 axa, ~ia [ME; cf. ascia], axe.

1301 habuit..unam axiam precii j d. *CourtR Hales* 438; **1429** j axa pro focalibus *Ac. Obed. Abingd.* 110.

2 axa, ~um [ME (AS *eax*); cf. axis], axle.

1276 in †axione carectarum ij d.; in clutis ad axas xij d. *MinAc* 935/4 r. 1; **1281** in iiij exis ad longam caretam xij d.; ..in uno exo ad eandem iij d. (*Ac. Pri. Wint.*) *EHR* LXI 103; **1292** in una exa empta ad idem [par rotarum] *KRAc* 492/10 r. 2; **1341** in viij clutis emptis pro salvacione axorum *MinAc* 1120/11 r. 1; **1486** de..j axo cum viij clutis *Ac. Man. Coll. Wint.* (*Padbury*).

axare, ~ere, ~iare, ~ire [ME], to fit w. axles.

1209 in iij caretis axandis et multociens reparandis clutis ad easdem *Pipe Wint.* 35; **1276** in viij axibus emptis..; in stipendiis J. carpentarii ad carectas axandas et emendandas *MinAc* 751/5; **1280** in..rotis yaxandis cum scamellis faciendis *DCCant Ac. Ruckinge*; **1311** in carectis axendis et axibus ad idem emptis *MinAcWint* (*Silkstead*); **1314** in longa carecta axanda per v vices cum v axis ad idem emptis *Comp. Worc.* I 42; **1316** in..iij carectis axiandis *MinAc* 1132/13 r. B 2*d.*; **1324** in j axe empt' ad plaustrum, iiij d.; in eodem exando, ij d. *MinAcWestm.* 22114 (*Pershore*); **1325** in j carecta et j plaustro axiendis et frettandis *Ib.* 22115; **1345** in carectis per vices axandis cum maeremio domini *Comp. Swith.* 148

axasessus v. assassinus.

axatio, fitting w. axles.

1276 in †axione carectarum ij d. *MinAc* 935/4 r. 1; **1316** iij axes ad duos currus domicellarum et [? in] ~one eorundem *KRAc* 99/21 m. 1; **1330** in..ij axibus pro ~one carrectarum *Ac. Durh.* 518; **1391** pro factura..iij curruum cum auxacione *Ib.* 599; **1425** in solutis pro *fryttyng* v rotarum..et in uno axe empto cum ~one unius carete *Ambrosden* II 253.

axatus, belling (cry of stag).

equus hinnitum, cervus ~um..stridebant FELIX *Guthl.* 36.

†axe, (?) *f.l.* for *arte.*

s741 axe fletibus vultum suum perfundens THORNE 1772 (cf. ELMH. *Cant.* 317).

axedo [LL], axle-tree or linch-pin.

~o, *lynis GlC* A 963; †axredones, *lynisas Ib.* 962; **10..** de plaustris et de partibus ejus: ..~o, *lynis* WW.

axelare, ~iare [ME *axelen*], to fit w. axles.

1211 in bigis exulandis *Pipe Wint.* 18 (= *Crawley* 177); **1295** ad carectas axilandas et reparandas *MinAc* 1090/3 r. 5; **1300** in carettis axiliandis *Ib.* 935/14 r. 2.

axella v. axilla.

axellum [ME *axel*], axle.

1352 in ~is carete ad ij vices xiij d. cum emptis ~is *Comp. Worc.* I 50.

axere, axiare v. axare. axia v. 1 axa. axilare, ~iare v. axelare.

axilla [CL; cf. OF *aisselle*], armpit. **b** (part under) wing. **c** (fig.) action.

ascella, *ocusta GlC* A 837; usque ad ascellas..fluctuante [mari] tinctus est *V. Cuthb.* II 3; ascella vel subhircos, *oxn* vel *ruhoxn* ÆLF. *Gl.*; **10..** ascilla, *oxtan* WW; pallium.. furtim sibi praeripuit et sub ascella complicatum abscondit GOSC. *Mir. Aug.* 1 p. 536; sub acella apostema..excreverat W. CANT. *Mir. Thom.* IV 39; sumite nummos..sub ascella ejus sinistra MAP *NC* II 5; **s1190** modii tritici mensura modica, quam videlicet quis facile portaret sub ascella *Itin. Ric.* I 66; sunt..vene..sub asellis que dicuntur titillares RIC. MED. *Micr. Anat.* 228; pedes, poplites et asselle.. fomententur GILB. I 26 v. 1; apposita manu ad †oxellum *Mir. J. Bev.* C 334; **s1271** Edwardum..vulnerat..sub acella RISH. 70; **1280** vulnus in aissella recepit *IMisc* 20/11. **b** ausillae, alae minores *GlC* A 942; capite sub axellis inflexo NETTER *DAF* I 230; lava ei [falconi] alas et sub alas acellas ejus unge UPTON 190. **c** os ad acellam vertentes, ore et opere predicantes GIR. *GE* II 34 p. 337.

axillaris, axillary.

due partes ab eis [venis] separantur, una sc. ab ascelari, alia ab humerali *Ps.*-RIC. *Anat.* 44; basilica..ramificatur ad assellas, unde nuncupatur vena assellaris GILB. IV 93. 1.

aximel v. oxymel. axio v. axatio.

†axima [? cf. archonius], stack, stook.

10.. de frugibus: ..~a, *stoc* WW.

axioma [ἀξίωμα], axiom, proposition.

hec et his similia sunt quedam †anximata et ad artem propositam minus respicientia OCREATUS *Helceph* 135.

axire v. axare.

1 axis [CL], axle (of wheel). **b** axle, spindle (of mill-stone or bell).

axis, *aex GlC* A 964; qui carrum in tantum onerabat ut axis frangeretur *DB* I 268; **1276** (v. axare); **1333** in dicto axe carpentando et ad rotas aptando *LTRMem* 105 r. 194; **1425** (v. axatio); **1510** fines utriusque axidis (*sic*) in eisdem plaustris fixis (*sic*) *AncIndict* 455/22. **b** **1276** in j petra empta ad axem molendini *DCCant Ac. Agney*; **1282** pro quadam mola cum una axe ferrea empta ad fabricam castri (*Chanc. Misc.* 3/18) *Arch.* XVI 42; **s1396** in campanili..axis in quo una campana pendebat..in longum findebatur *Meaux* III 193.

2 axis (math. or astr.). **b** celestial pole. **c** sky. **d** visual axis. **e** orbit (fig.), career.

a polo arctico ad antarcticum axem ducunt J. SAL. *Pol.* 440B; quinta essentia circulariter mota est circa diametrum fixam. diameter fixa 'axis' vocatur Latine, Hebraica quidem *magual*; et extremitates axis 'poli' appellantur GROS. 13; cum moveatur octava spera..circa axem mundi SACROB. *Sph.* 92; nota quod differencia est inter diametrum et axem, quoniam diameter est circuli in plano..sed axis dicitur esse in corpore rotundo ut in spera ROB. ANGL. (II) *Sph.* 145. **b** in giro volvens jugiter non vergo deorsum, / .. quoniam sum proximus axi ALDH. *Aen.* 53 (*Arcturus*) 5; **a705** sub arctoo axe teneris confotum cunabulis *Id. Ep.* 7 (10) p. 499. **c** astra.. / lustrant axis ignifluam / molem (ÆTHELWALD) *Carm. Aldh.* 4. 20. **d** quoniam naturaliter duo oculi situm habent consimilem respectu nervi communis, tunc se habebunt axes oculorum uniformiter ad omnem punctum super quem cadunt BACON *Maj.* II 93; videndo diversas partes ejusdem materialis alius actus est confusior et alius distinccior, ut est propinquior puncto conjunccionis duorum axium piramidum radialium WYCL. *Act.* I 14. **e** quid..Macedoni Alexandro tam amplis.. titulis gloriam..accumulavit nisi quod in axis culmine.. constitutus..volubilem descensum maturata morte prevenit? GIR. *EH* II 31.

2 axis [CL], **~a,** board, plank. **b** (?) post.

solarium totum repente cum axibus et trabibus dissiluit et concidit W. MALM. *GR* II 161; [Wlstanus] qui nunquam pro fractura pontis equo descenderit, qui per summitatem fabricarum per angustissimos axes securus incesserit *Id. GP* IV 138. **b 1316** pro vj axsis emptis ad metas super forum bladorum *Rec. Leic.* I 298.

axsedula v. 1 acidula. axsis v. 2 axis. axum v. 2 axa.

axungia [CL], axle-grease, fat.

~ia, *tysel GlC* A 961; pinguior, en, multo scrofarum axungia glesco ALDH. *Aen.* 100. 48; [corvi] digna munera ferunt, dimidiam videlicet ~iam porcinam BEDE *Cuthb.* 20; **10..** ausungia, *rysle* WW; **c1190** †assugiam c porcorum meliorum habebit de celario ad sagimen (*Reg. Burton*) *MonA* III 43; illa unctuosa que habent majorem aquositatem.. minus bene nutriunt ignem, ut patet in †anxungia porcina, que minus nutrit ignem quam ovina BART. ANGL. XIX 41; ~ia porcina GILB. I 65. 1; inungatur cum assungia taxi vel taxonis vel gatti GAD. 17. 1; **1347** †axurgia porcina (*Ac. Pri. Lindisf.*) *Hist. N. Durh.* 90; auxungia *SB* 32 (v. abdomen); **1377** in exungia empta pro collis boum *Ac. Durh.* 386 (cf. ib. 387: auxungia); hic †afingea, pinguedo porci WW; **1531** pro cera, resina, visco, †anxagia *Fabr. York* 105.

axungiare, to grease (*cf. exungere*).

to grese, exungiare et secundum Hugonem auxungiare *CathA*.

ay- v. ai-.

†aza [cf. ascia *or* ME *adse*], (?) adze.

1291 in..securibus et azis, sarris et aliis utensilibus (*Ac. Sacr. Norw.*) *Arch. J.* XXXII 34.

azabar [? Ar. *az-zabarjad* (< Pers.) = chrysoprase, beryl or sim., conf. w. Ar. *az-zarāband* (< Pers.) = birthwort (*Aristolochia*)], a stone or herb that cures scorpion stings.

effigies scorpionis terrestris in ascensu Scorpionis celestis lapidi ~ar, qui et de genere onycharum videtur, insculptus contra venenum scorpii terrestris teste Haly valere probatur, sicut et herba que eodem nomine censetur juxta Avicennam contra hujusmodi venenum valet *Ps.*-GROS. 552.

azais v. azeisa.

†azananata [Ar. *az-zarnīkh* < ἀρσενικόν], orpiment.

~a, i. auripigmentum *Alph.* 18.

azarabaccara, azarum v. asara.

azarud [Ar. *'anzarūt* < Pers.], Persian gum.

sarcoas, sarcocolla, acarud, interpretatur gliconum, glutinum; guma est *Alph.* 162 (cf. ib. 2: acarus, sarcocolla idem est).

azeisa, ~ia [(?) OF; cf. assisa 11], flat stone, roofing slab.

1172 pro aszeisiis ad operiendas domos regis *Pipe* 98 (cf. ib. 99: pro c miliar' azesiarum); **1175** pro ~is *Pipe* 59; **1179** ad emendum cl milia azeziarum *Pipe* 10; **1187** pro lx milibus azesie emptis et pro eis ducendis a Dertemue usque Hantonam ad operiendas cameras regis *Pipe* 143; **1200** centum milia de azzeise mitti faciatis..ad opus domorum nostrarum de Nova Foresta *RNorm* 28; **1203** pro c [(?) m] adhesie empt' et miss' in Angliam ad opus domorum regis de Nova Foresta *RScacNorm* II 510; **1205** inveni..c milia de ~ia ad cooperiendum domos nostras Porstoch' *Cl* 52b; **1209** liberaverunt..iij m d azais..; in domibus et capella recooperiendis, iiij m. dim. *Pipe Wint.* 32; **1237** domum.. cooperiri facias de azeys *Liberate* 11 m. 11.

azephalus v. acephalus. azerum v. acerum.

Azige [Ar. *az-zīj* = *astronomical tables*], name of book attributed to Ptolemy.

de quibus omnibus [celestium corporum motibus etc.] a Ptolomeo in ~e compendiose scribitur ADEL. *Alch.* 17.

azilum v. asylum. Azimatus, ~ita v. Azymita. azimbia v. apsinthium. azimum v. ocimum. azimus v. azymus.

azimuth [Ar. *as-samt*], azimuth, celestial longitude.

1326 ~uth proprie est longitudo stelle a meridie; altitudo autem est proprie latitudo stelle ab orizonte WALLINGF. *Rect.* 345.

azoara [Ar. *as-sūra*], sura, chapter of Koran.

~a prima ROB. ANGL. *Koran* 8; unde in Alcorano dicitur sic, ~a lvi S. SIM. *Itin.* 71; in Alkorano suo azophara sua capitulo tercio Machometus ita scribit WYCL. *Ver.* I 254; **s1382** adeo ut..[Wyclyviani] pocius Machumeti suspicarentur discipuli, qui legem suam discutere prohibuit suis sequacibus sed cercius bellaci fortitudine eam defendere precepit.., Alcorani ~a quarta KNIGHTON *Cont.* 187.

azoc [Sp. Ar. *az-zūq*], mercury.

Maria dicit: nihil est quod a latone..suum possit auferre colorem. sed azoc est quasi ejus tegumentum ROB. ANGL. *Alch.* 514b; quum..nigredo..aufertur, ita quod album appareat laton quidem ~oc postea nominatur *Ib.* 515a; azoch est laton, est cuprum aureo colore tinctum. ..azoth est argentum vivum ex quovis corpore metallico tractum *LC*.

azophara v. azoara. azorius, ~ium v. azureus, azurum. azura v. azurum.

azurettus, azure, blue (of cloth).

1313 pro uno panno..de bluetto ~o *KRAc* 374/19 f. 13.

azureus, (w. *lapis*) lapis lazuli. **b** azure, blue. **c** (her.). **d** (w. *mina* or *minera*) (?) galena. *V. et. azurum.*

1208 pro iiij capsis ad iiij lapides asuurios *Cl* 103a. **b** gutte albe vel ~ee que inveniuntur in allumine de pluma M. SCOT *Lumen* 250; **1245** est littera prima partita de rubeo et azorio florata de viridi *Invent. S. Paul.* 498; **1314** in..lxx pannis de blueto asureo pro militibus (*DL MinAc*) *EHR* XLII 198; psalterium litteris aureis et †assuris scriptum WHITTLESEY 173; una cappa oloserica, sapphirei sive ~ei coloris ELMH. *Cant.* 99; caelici coloris, quem ~eum vocant BOECE 159. **c** premitto azoreum colorem aliis quia color ille ex commixtione coloris albi cum nigro resultat BAD. AUR. 96; armorum Anglie et Francie circumornatur tunica, in qua..trium florum aureorum in agro plantatorum ~eo splendor sydereus emicabat *Ps.*-ELMH. *Hen. V* 26 p. 61. **d 1301** (v. albus 5c); **1302** de j disco de mina azur' plumbi *MinAc* (*Chesh*) 771/1 r. 3.

azurum, ~a, ~ium [? Sp. Ar. *lazūrd*; cf. Ar. *lāzaward* < Pers.; cf. lazulum], lapis lazuli, azure (esp. as blue pigment). **b** blue silk. **c** azure (her.).

scriptor..habeat et fuscum pulverem vel ~am a Salamone repertam NECKAM *Ut.* 117; littere capitales nunc minio nunc viridi colore, ..nunc †atiro superbire videntur (*Id. Sac.*) *Med. Sci.* 361; de argento leviter fit ~um (M. SCOT *Part.*) *Ib.* 295; si ulterius [minium] calefacias, ..erit adzurium GILB. VII 351. 2; **1251** in capella B. Katerine..ejusdem historiam ultra altare absque auro et ~o honeste depingi.. faciatis (*AncC* II 116) *RL* II 67; dicunt aliqui quod color laçulus est color açuri, qui est vere medius BACON XIV 75; scientia que est..de ~io et minio et ceteris coloribus *Id. Tert.* 39; **1289** in..vermulone, ynde, asura..et aliis minutis emptis..ad emendaciones picture magne camere *KRAc* 467/6/2; locellum ligneum..interius undique depictum, medietas cum vermiculo, altera medietas cum azorio DOMERH. *Glast.* 336 (= J. GLAST. 181; asorio); **1342** in iij libris j quar. de asuro emptis, prec' libre iij s. *Sacr. Ely* II 121; **1346** omnes litere in principiis versuum erunt luminate de ~o et vermilione bonis *Fabr. York* 166; yris purpureum florem in modum ~i gerit *SB* 25; lapis agapis sive lazuli blavii est colore satis bonus; idem fit ~ium *Alph.* 90; **s1381** ista sufficere non valebat..populo quin quandam chartam antiquam reposcerent de libertatibus villanorum, cujus littere capitales fuerunt de auro una, altera de azorio WALS. *HA* I 475; *asure*, asura *PP*; ~a, A. *azure*, ..*asyre* WW. **b** *sylke*, ..sericum..: quadruplicis generis sunt serica dicta Latinis; / est album bissus velut est āsūra jacinctus *CathA*. **c 1384** arma..de auro cum uno leone de ~eo rampante *Pat* 317 m. 16; **1389** in quadam causa de et super armis de ~a cum una benda de auro (*Pat*) *Foed.* VII 621; portat de auro cum tribus tortellis rubeis cum una labella de azorio; *G. il port d'or troys torteux de gowles ove une labelle de asur* BAD. AUR. 184 (cf. ib. 185; de asorio).

Azymita [Ἀζυμίτης], Latin Christian, as using unleavened bread in eucharist. **b** (?) heretic in service of Saracens.

cum Graeci anathematizant Azimitas, sic enim nos vocant, anathematizant Christum ANSELM (*Azym.* 2) II 225. **b s1098** fama..percrebuit..Turcos, Agulanos, Azimitas et plurimas gentilium nationes adventare ORD. VIT. IX 9 p. 535; **s1099** principem militie soldani Persie et Turcos, Arabes, Saracenos, Publicanos, Azimatos, Persas, Agulanos et alias multas gentes in ore gladii fugantes FL. WORC. II 42.

azymus [ἄζυμος], unleavened. **b** (sb. m. or f.) unleavened bread, wafer. **c** (sb. m. or n. pl., usu. w. *tempus* or sim.) Passover. **d** Holy Week.

azimus, *ðeorf* ÆLF. *Gl.*; propter hoc solum videtur [Christus] se et carnem suam 'panem' vocasse et de pane corpus suum fecisse quia, sicut iste panis azimus sive fermentatus dat vitam transitoriam, ita corpus ejus aeternam, non quia fermentatus est vel azimus ANSELM (*Azym.* 1) II 224; [panis] debet esse ~us, quia Dominus in ~is consecravit GIR. *GE* I 8 p. 26; cocti pariter fuerant in clibano ..panes asimi et fermentati AD. EYNS. *Hug.* V 15 p. 179; reficiatur pane azimo GILB. III 173. 2; [Alexander I] ordinavit quod oblata fieret de ~o pane in modica quantitate HIGD. IV 13; **1382** confiteor..quod..post consecracionem non manet substancia panis..materialis in..sacramento, quia neque panis ~us neque fermentatus..'jam panis sed corpus Christi dicitur' (J. ASTON) *Ziz.* 332; *therf withowtyn sowre dowe*, azimus *PP*. **b 10..** azimos, *ðeorflingas* WW; **s1475** hoc modo, ut fertur, Judei ~um eorum cum sanguine Christiano faciunt annuatim *Eul. Hist. Cont.* I 294 (cf. ib.: ut sanguinem..traherent pro ~a eorum). **c** juxta legis scripturam, alia Paschae, alia solemnitas est ~orum BEDE *TR* 63; quia ipsa quoque dies Paschae a fermento castigari praecipitur, hanc Evangelii scriptura aliquando primam ~orum cognominant *Ib.*; **10..** azima, *andbita*, *beorma* WW; **s72** oportuit diebus azimorum Judeos interfici in quibus Salvatorem crucifixerunt DICETO *Chr.* 60; **s47** in Jerosolimis..seditio est exorta in diebus azimorum M. PAR. *Maj.* I 101; *pasche*, pascha (v.l. azima) *CathA*. **d s1106** cum..rex in Neustriam ante ~orum celebria transfretaret ORD. VIT. XI 12.

2 unleavened (fig.), uncontaminated. **b** (sb. pl.) unleavened bread (fig.), vital reality.

migret amor, qui licet azymam / fermentare non sinit animam J. HOWD. *Phil.* 473; contra famem audiendi verbum Dei..panes ~os de purissima simila sacre sophie confectos accuratissime paraverunt R. BURY *Phil.* 5. 76. **b** sic demum tota massa expurgabitur a veteri fermento, id est tota familia mundabitur ab inveterato furto et vasto consueto. tunc quidem fideles in singulis officiis fideliter ministrabunt et 'in azimis sinceritatis et veritatis' [cf. 1 *Cor.* v 8] *Obs. Barnwell* 190; dicta est Melsa quasi 'sapor mellis' vel *melsa* quod interpretatur 'rixa' vel 'in azimis'. ..dicitur 'in azimis' sinceritatis quidem, hoc est recte intencionis, perfecte veritatis et bone operacionis *Meaux* I 75.

3 (alch.) *s. dub.*

eam [sc. eudicam] reconde, neque quicquam cum ea facias donec acidum fiat: azim non existat, quoniam tua intentio penitus destitueretur ROB. ANGL. *Alch.* 517a.

B

B [CL], B (letter of alphabet).

B propinque est P litterae, qua saepe mutatur, ut 'supponit'.. BEDE *Orth.* 2775; "dicito B"; dixit ille et hoc *Id. HE* V 2; A ante B breviatur, ut..Barnabas..; excipitur Barabbas.., nam duplex B est BACON *Tert.* 258.

2 (♮), musical note: **a** natural; **b** flat.

a omne *ut* incipiens in C canitur per naturam cum suis sequentibus; ..in G per ♮ durum sive quadratam TUNST. 222b. **b** seu diatesseron seu diapente chorde concrepent, [Hibernici] semper tamen a B molli incipiunt et in idem redeunt GIR. *TH* III 154 (= BROMPTON 1075: a bemolli); B molle dicitur habere semitonium sub se et tonum supra se..et vocatur B rotunda TUNST. 222b.

Baal, pl. **~im** [Heb.], pagan deity (fig.).

non est ante Báālim timide curvatus *Poem S. Thom.* 74.

babatum [cf. DuC], horseshoe.

scho of hors, ferrus, babbatum *PP*.

babewinus [OF *babuin*], 'baboon', grotesque figure or gargoyle.

1295 imago..B. Marie..cum pede quadrato stante super quatuor parvos babewynos *Vis. S. Paul.* 338; **1303** vj babewyni in fundo †cuppi [? l. cuppe] aymellati (*KRAc* 363/6) *DocExch* 283; **1314** pro uno tapeto lanuto operato de diversis babwynis *KRAc* 375/9 f. 24; duo [tapeta] majora..cum †habeuuinis WHITTLESEY 169; omnino similes sunt babbewyno depicto et sculpto, qui collo, humeris et brachiis et facie prominens totam fabricam cum onerosa fatigatione se simulat supportare (HOLCOT *Wisdom*) *Eng. Friars* 167; **1345** [*silver salt-cellars enamelled with*] babbewinis et oisellettis *CalPat* 456; **13..** vestimentum..de blueto cum babewen' *Invent. Norw.* 24; **1388** alba brudata..cum babwinis pugnantibus (*Invent. Westm.*) *Arch.* LII 244; **c1405** ciphus deauratus coopertus..de aquilis, leonibus, coronis et aliis babonibus *Test. Ebor.* I 317; **c1443** palla..de serico cum babonis de auro *Cant. Coll. Ox.* I 2.

babicare [cf. OF *baver*], to slobber, drivel.

Herodes piceus in pice babicat *Ps.*-MAP (*Maria*) 198. 235.

babiger, fool, foolish.

~gera, stulta *GlC* B 30; *foole*, stultus, baburrus, ~ger, *PP*; *fonde*, ~ger, ..babilus, baburrus.. *CathA*.

babilus v. babiger. babo, babonus v. babewinus. babrilla v. librilla. babti- v. bapti-.

baburra, folly.

foltre, stoliditas, ..~a, *PP*; *fondnes*, ~a, demencia.. *CathA*; ~a, A. *sothede* WW.

baburrus, fool.

qui verum loquitur est hostis publicus, / baburrus stolidus, immo freneticus *Ps.*-MAP (*Palpo*) 108. 80; *PP*, *CathA*. (v. babiger).

babwynus v. babewinus.

baca (bacca), berry.

surculus.. / nigros bacarum portans in fronte corimbos ALDH. *Aen.* 94 (*Ebulus*) 3; **10..** bacce, *bergan* WW; laurus ~is nobilitatur NECKAM *NR* II 70 p. 170; planta quae dicitur ~a caprarum [(?) *ivy*] ALF. ANGL. *Plant.* 1; fructus lauri dicuntur ~e lauri BART. ANGL. XVII 48; ~e edere, carposcissi idem, fructus edere *Alph.* 19.

bacalar- v. bachelar-.

bacapulus [LL], bier.

flagitando..quatenus falerarent sonipedes eorum ac semet baccaulo imponerent LANTFR. *Mir. Swith.* 1. 331 F.

bacarium ~ina v. bicarium.

bacarius [etym. dub.], porpoise.

~ius, *meresuin GlC* B 166; bacharus, *mereswin ÆLF. Gl.*; delphin vel bocharius vel simones, *mereswin* ÆLF. *Sup.*

baccalaur- v. bachelar-.

baccara [cf. asara], hazelwort (*Asarum*).

marcelle, ~e, mali storac[is] GILB. II 112 v. 2; ~a herba est odorifera, folia habens aspera et lata *Alph.* 19.

baccaria v. 2 bercaria 2. baccaulus v. bacapulus.

bacchanal [CL], festival of Bacchus. **b** orgy, pagan life. **c** wine-press.

vaccanalia, patris Liberi †stupram [l. stupra] *GlC* V 30; in festis ~alibus, quum omnes homines..vino libidinibusque indulgent BOECE 312v. **b** barbari, qui adhuc veri Dei nescii bachanalia vivebant W. MALM. *GP* III 100 p. 215. **c** *a presse for wyne*, bachinal, ..torculare *CathA*.

bacchari, to rave, rage.

bachantes, *uuoedende GlC* B 48; vaccatur, insanit *Ib.* V 35; puer.. / bacchatur quoniam vagabundis passibus amens ALDH. *VirgV* 1482; †**995** (12c) cum gens pagana Cantiam bachando deleret *CD* 689; mors saeva furit, bacchatur et ensis G. AMIENS *Hast.* 499 (cf. 437); in monachos..furibunde bachatus W. MALM. *GP* I 17; currebant furentes atque ~antes GIR. *PI* I 20; **c1360** tunc ad quadrivium bachatur *Planct. Univ. Ox.* 81.

bacchia [cf. βακχεία], measure of wine.

bachia est mensura bachi BART. ANGL. XIX 125.

2 (?) frenzy.

de mechi bachia mechum deludere noli, / ne de te similis fieri delusio possit D. BEC. 2052.

bacchilatria, worship of Bacchus.

c1430 pro Deo ventrem in diebus colitis, immo..in noctibus..prohibitam ~am sompniatis *Reg. Whet.* II 389.

bacchilaur- v. bachelar-.

bacchīus [βακχεῖος], bacchic foot.

bachius unde appellatur? a Bacho, qui et Dionisius vocabatur ALDH. *PR* 123; ~ius ex brevi et duabus longis temporum quinque, ut 'pŏētāē' BEDE *AM* 2364.

Bacchus [CL < βάκχος], wine god. **b** wine.

†bachum [l. ~i] latex, vinum *GlC* B 22 (= *Erf.* 2. 270. 25: †bacillatex); ALDH. *PR* 123 (v. bacchius); ebrius initiat [? l. injiciat] vobis neu vincula Bachus ALCUIN *Carm.* 59. 22; en Bacchus, cetus Driadum dux, collis amator, / palmite pampineo tempora cinctus adest NECKAM *DS* VIII 23. **b 790** saluta fratres nostros in Bacho et berbice ALCUIN *Ep.* 8; D. BEC. 1717 (v. baratro); **13..** sidere, Virgo, tuo bachum September †opinat [l. opimat] (*Calendar*) *Miss. Westm.* I xiii.

baccile v. bacile. baccinare v. bacinare. baccinium v. bacinus, vaccinium. bacellum, ~us v. 1 & 2 bacillus. bacen- v. bacin-. bacerellus v. baterellus 1. baceum v. bassum. bachari v. bacchari.

bacha [Frk. *bah*], beck, stream.

te sed Igona suis jam piscibus atque Sigona / te pascant, satient, et tota Senonia bachis ALCUIN *Carm.* 8. 21; **a800** timeo ne Muslense ~a litterae submersae sint *Id. Ep.* 191.

bachabre v. cacabre. bacharus v. bacarius.

bachelaria [OF *bachelerie*], (?) gentry below the rank of knight (cf. *EHR* XVI 502, XVII 89; F. M. Powicke, *Henry III and Lord Edward* p. 407*n*.).

s1259 communitas bachelerie Anglie significavit domino E. filio regis..quod dominus rex..fecerat..omnia..que providerant barones *Ann. Burton* 471.

bachelariatus, degree or status of bachelor (acad.).

1311 debet habere statum ~us vel magisterii (*Digby Rolls* I) *Collect Ox* II 218; **1311** bacalariatum vel magistratum theologice facultatis *FormOx* 301; **1435** in singulis predictarum facultatum bifarius gradus, scilicet inferior, puta bacalariatus quasi semigradus et superior ut magistratus, in eadem universitate consueverunt haberi *EpAcOx* 130; te imploro..michi edicas, quare leges Anglie, ..in Universitatibus non docentur..et quare et in eisdem non dantur bacalariatus et doctoratus gradus FORTESCUE *LLA* 47; **1549** ad baccalaureatus seu magisterii lauream *Conc. Scot.* II 105; **c1592** bacchilaureatum in theologia *Stat Ox* 445.

bachelarius [OF *bacheler*; cf. 2 bacularis], 'bachelor' (young knight or feudal retainer inferior to knight). **b** (w. *miles*) knight bachelor (inferior to banneret etc.).

1200 Johannes..senescallo Pictavie..omnes feudos et terras quos dedimus bachellariis quos retinuimus de familia nostra in balliva vestra, qui homagium et fidelitates et ligentias nobis non fecerunt.. *RChart.* 59a; **1202** rex etc. omnibus bacheleriis Andegav' Turon' et Cenoman' *Pat.* 12b; **s1249** hastiludium commissum est..ubi multi de militibus universitatis regni, qui se volunt ~os appellari, sunt contriti M. PAR. *Maj.* V 83; **1262** vocari fecimus ~os nostros quod festinanter veniant ad succursum vobis prestandum contra Walenses *Cl* 270 (cf. ib. 161, 177); **1275** optulit se hoc deracionare per suum ~um *Hund.* I 66; **1292** dominus H. rex dedit predicta tenementa domino regi nunc dum fuit bachilarius *PQW* 679b (cf. 357a); **s1306** facti fuerunt milites Rogerus de Mortuomari..et Edmundus de Arundel una cum aliis bachilariis *Ann. Worc.* 558; **s1307** cuidam simplici bachilario de Gasconia, nomine Petro de Gavellestone *Ib.* 560; **s1339** quod cognatus noster arma gerit quadrata de armis Francie et Anglie compaginatis non nobis displicet, pro eo quod pauperiori nostre parentele bachulario partem armorum nostrorum regalium libenter concederemus deferendam BAKER 117; **1362** dilecto et fideli bachillario nostro David Flemyng *RMSScot* 175; **1385** bakelario [regis] *CalPat* 8; **s1404** cum sint armigeri et bachalarii, baronibus in divitiis equipollent *Eul. Hist. Cont.* III 400. **b 1360** militi dilecto bachilario nostro *Reg. Brechin.* I 15; **s1377** duo baronetti, duo ~i milites AD. MUR. *Cont. B* 229; **1388** militem bachilarium nostrum *RMSScot* 755.

2 title assumed by rebellious apprentices or journeymen (*cf. EHR* XXIV 316).

s1263 ex hac..protervia per universum regnum Anglie consuetudo detestabilis inolevit quod in omnibus pene civitatibus..fieret conjuratio ribaldorum qui se bachilarios publice proclamabant et majores urbium..violentis ausibus opprimebant WYKES 138; **p1264** memorandum quod ante bellum de Lewes quedam multitudo de villa S. Edmundi iij^{c} vel plus numero, qui se ~ii (*sic*) vocari fecerunt, per conspiracionem mutuam quandam gildam levaverunt quam gildam juvenum vocaverunt (*Reg. S. Edm.*) *Gild Merch.* II 31; **1279** venella per bachillarios London' tempore turbacionis fuit deobstructa (*Hund.*) *Lond. Ed. I & II* 152.

3 bachelor (acad.).

a1231 quilibet scolaris habeat magistrum proprium actu regentem, ..nisi fuerit bachillarius noviter incepturus *StatOx* 82; **1264** bachilarii in artibus quando responderint in vesperiis *Ib.* 36; **1268** magistris et bachilariis universitatis Oxonie *Ib.* 25; **1314** antequam hujusmodi bachalarii in facultate theologica magistrentur *Ib.* 116; **1350** scolares in artibus..nisi sint bachilarii cursorie legentes *Ib.* 24; assensurus gradum bachillarii *Ib.* 58; **c1250** convenerunt cancellarius et magistri et ~i quidam AD. MARSH *Ep.* 92; bacularius qui legit textum BACON *Min.* 328; **1305** per alios baccalaureos cursorie legere in eisdem (*New Coll. Misc. Deeds* 8) *Cart. Osney* I 111; **a1351** qui..contravenerit.., si bacallarius [fuerit] incepturus, ad incepcionem seu honorem magistralem numquam in posterum admittatur *Stat. Cantab.* 328; **1404** J. S. magistro in artibus et bacallario in decretis *Melrose* II 503; **1425** bacallarios facultatis arcium *Reg. Cant.* I 344; **1517** baccalaurei artium *Stat. Corp. Christ. Ox.* c. 24.

4 (?) senior pupil in grammar school (perh. a dist. word).

1309 ..statutum est quod, si aliquis ad culmen bacularioriorum ascendere voluerit, a magistro..proverbium accipiat et de eodem versus, litteras, rhythmum componant (*sic*) (*Stat. Sch. Gram. St. Alb.*) *Reg. Whet.* II 312; **1315** rector.. fecit per quosdam de bacularis et aliis in scolis existentibus inquisicionem (*Mun. Cath. Cant.*) *Educ. Ch.* 259; **1338** a bacularis de novo creandis in scolis gramaticalibus (*Mun. Beverley*) *Ib.* 294.

bachia v. bacchia, besca. bachifer v. bacifer. bachilar- v. bachelar-. bachillus v. 2 bacillus.

†bachio [cf. bacis], trowel.

a trowelle, ~o, trolla *CathA*.

†bachium [*for* bacrio], cruet.

crowett, ampulla, ~ium *CathA*.

1 bachus v. Bacchus.

2 †bachus, old (cf. Jerome, *Nom. Hebr.*: bacci, vetus).

bachi, antiqui *GlC* B 36.

3 bachus v. bacus. bacia v. bassum.

bacido [cf. baca], cluster of grapes. **b** (? misinterp. of *Prov. Graec.* 23: *pomarium fertile omne quod habet justus..; ~ones inferiores stultorum sermones*) counsel.

~o, botrus, *clyster ÆLF. Gl.* **b** ~ones, *raedinne GlC* B 3.

bacifer [CL; (?) *infl. by* Bacchus], bearing grapes.

vinea bachiferas trudit de palmite gemmas ALCUIN *Carm.* 59. 3.

bacile [cf. bacinus], basin.

fratres qui ad missam induendi sunt vadant ad locum constitutum ubi sit optimus ignis.., baccilia quoque et manutergia LANFR. *Const.* 93; **1125** in consecrationibus episcoporum..non manutergium, non baccilia [v.l. baccinia] et nihil omnino per violentiam..exigatur (*Conc. Lond.* 3) J. WORC. 20; aqua cum baccilibus argenteis *Cust. Westm.* 57; **c1400** dominus [abbas] Albanensis..habeat duo ~ia et unum pottum de argento ad aquam *MonA* II 236.

2 basin-shaped lamp. **b** lamp used for blinding (*cf. bacinare*).

a1250 fecit..in ecclesia coram altari tria ex argento baccilia cum unci[n]is suis argenteis..dependi, in quibus lumina..lucerent G. COLD. *Durh.* 7; **c1395** tria baccilia argentea ante summum altare pendencia *Invent. Ch. Ch.* 110. **b s1106** institit..quod..Robertus deberet exoculari et excecari cum †batili [l. bacili] ardenti KNIGHTON I 113.

1 bacillus, ~um, ~a, basin.

infirmitate ita gravatus est ut subito plenum majorem ~um sanguine excrearet H. ALBUS 93; quindecim ~as plenas sanguine *Ib.*; providere..ne de aqua calida..aut de †batellis [? l. bacellis] aut sapone defectus..habeatur *Cust. Westm.* 172; duo ~a argentea WHITTLESEY 173.

2 basin-shaped lamp.

altare holocausti cum vasis suis, ignium scilicet receptaculis..uncinis et basillis AD. SCOT *TT* 669.

2 bacillus, ~um [CL], staff, stick.

sustentans geminis sua languida membra bacillis WULF. *Swith.* II 1107; **1240** Walterum ictu cujusdam bachilli a manu sua evulsi..interfecit *Cl* 246; **s1295** ~is..fuscinulisque illusus..patibulo est affixus *Flor. Hist.* III 282; fragor ingens..tanquam bacello fracto..audientes stupidos reddidit admirantes *NLA* (*Edm.*) *app.* II 659; *staffe*, ~us *CathA*; **1624** cum quodam ~o vocato *a crickett bat*..quem..in manu sua..dextra..tenuit (*PRO*) *Assizes* 35/67/8.

3 bacillus v. 4 batellus.

bacinare [cf. bacile 2b; *also* abacinare (DuC)], to blind.

a1250 velud ursus ignito ere, sicut vulgo dicitur, baccinatur, dum ardenti desiderio aperit oculos in caduca J. GODARD *Ep.* 238.

bacinettus, 'basnet', (basin-shaped) helmet.

1292 in duobus ~is argenteis emptis apud Trapesend' [*Trebizond*] *KRAc* 308/14 m. 4; **1305** ~i: et pro v ~is emptis in grosso pro eadem garnistura *MinAcWWales* I 404; **1312** homines armatos cum aketonis, haubergettis et bacenettis *RScot.* 109a; **1318** habeat pro corpore suo in defensione regni unam sufficientem aketonam, unum bacinetum [v.l. basinetum] et chirothecas de guerra (*Stat. Rob.* I 27) *APScot* 113; **1325** de..vj ~is ferreis de visera, iij ~is cum umbr[aculo], iiij ~is ad modum Ispanie *LTRAc* 16 r. 38; **1326** aketonis, ~is [DuC s.v. aketonum: †borcinettis] et aliis hujusmodi armaturis (*Cl.*) *Foed.* IV 203; **1343** cum triginta paribus platarum, basinettorum [DuC: †basmettorum] et pisanorum (*Cl.*) *Ib.* V 384; **1390** pro panno albo et blodeo ..pro coopertura basenetti domini *Ac. H. Derby* 49.

bacinus, ~um, ~ium, ~a [OF *bacin*], basin. **b** (?) basin-shaped reliquary.

a1100 duo ~ia argentea (*Invent.*) *Process. Sal.* 183; **11..** ebullivit aqua..per totum baccinium (*Cod. Landav.*) *MonA* VI 1220; **1125** (v. bacile 1); **1130** in emptione..manutergiorum et ~orum *Pipe* 144; **1208** j par ~orum operatorum ad imagines et flores deauratorum (*Invent.*) *LTR Mem. PR* 122; **c1230** debet nuces ad mensuram unius ~i pleni colligere *Doc. Bec* 59; **1259** debet..habere..duos ~os plenos de avena..et..ij bascinos de ordeo *Cust. Glast.* 131; **s1251** dedit..duo paria ~arum SWAFHAM 119; **12..** per serjantiam †bastinorum [l. bascinorum] ad coronacionem domini regis *Fees* 345; **c1300** patelle auree ij, ..lavatorium et ~um *Reg. Malm.* II 378; **1310** coquina:..de j pari ~orum pro tartis *Ac. Exec. Ep. Exon.* 11; **s1404** in festo Cinerum.. cinerum bassinam sibi tenui AD. USK 95; **1434** unum bassinum seu pelvim cum aquario de argento *Reg. Cant.* II 540. **b s1391** fecit fieri ad corpora sanctorum tres bassinos argenteos cum cathenis argenteis THORNE 2196.

2 basin-shaped lamp. **b** basin-shaped helmet (*cf. bacinettus*).

a1241 ad luminare ~i ante altare B. Virginis *E. Ch. S. Paul* 114; **c1245** accendantur in choro tres ~i *Cust. Westm.* 269; **c1423** in cereis pro ~is emptis *Ac. Obed. Abingd.* 91; **1512** pro mundifactura candelabre et bacene *Ac. Churchw. Bath* 102. **b 1275** exoramus quatinus ij capellos ferreos, v ~os..tradatis *Reg. Heref.* 6; **1289** unum capellum ferreum cum quatuor ~iis *SelCKB* III p. cv; **1316** in linio panno et albo coreo pro..~is emendandis *Rec. Leic.* I 302; **c1350** j aketonem cum platis et ~o coloretto *Reg. S. Aug.* 302.

†bacis [cf. bachio], trowel.

14.. ~is, A. *a truel* WW.

acium v. bassum.

1 baco, baconus [OF *bacon* < Frk.], bacon, carcase of hog.

reddit c caseos et x bacons *DB* I 97; servo porcario.. pertinet habere..porcellum de sude..quando ~ones suos [AS: *spic*] bene corrediaverit (*Quad., Rect.*) *GAS* 449; pinguis bācō trabe pendens D. BEC. 2225; porcos..nutriunt, ~ones inde vendunt MAP *NC* I 24 p. 37; **1199** pro xv ~onibus et x carcosiis vaccarum *Pipe* 242; **1205** cariagium..xv ~onorum *Cl* 17a; **1207** dederunt regi tertiam decimam omnium que habebant..usque dimidium ~one[m] *Chr. Louth* 10 (cf. *Conc. Syn.* 7); ~ones quos pinguissimos emerat, trium quippe digitorum..in lardo solo pinguedinem preferentes, .. tenues jam reperit et exiles GIR. *Spec.* III 16 p. 231; **1234** porcarius..habebit quicquid cadit de uno porco preter~onem *Cust. Glast.* 114; **1288** vendunt ~onem superseminatam (*sic*) *Leet Norw.* 10; **1307** dimidia perna ~onis *Doc. Bec* 157; **1345** ad salandum viij ~ones *Comp. Swith.* 149.

2 baco v. basso.

baconare, to salt for bacon.

1214 porcos..bene salari et ~ari faciat *Cl* 177a.

bacropa [ME], back-rope of cart.

1364 in corio tannato empto pro pipis, bacropis et aliis necessariis ad carectas (*MinAc* 885/33) *Econ. Condit. app.* 78.

bactillus v. 4 batellus. bacuatus v. battuere c.

1 bacula, little berry (w. ref. to cochineal insect).

coccus infectivus frutex est sarmentosa habens in ipsis virgis ~as rotundas sicut lenticula *Alph.* 45.

2 bacula v. baculus 2h.

baculare, to cudgel.

canis a domino suo..virgis cesus aut etiam ~atus NECKAM *NR* II 157; GARL. *Epith.* VI 572 (v. baculus 1b); **s1248** tyro novellus..prostratus et egregie, ut introductiones militie initiales addisceret, ~atus [? *pun on bacularius*] M. PAR. *Maj.* V 18.

2 to fit with poles (Norf).

1290 in carettis..reparandis et ~andis hoc anno xij d. *MinAc* 935/12.

3 to invest with a pastoral staff or crozier.

p1465 pater electus qui bis fuit et baculatus, / bisque gregem rexit (*Vers.*) *Reg. Whet.* I 423.

1 bacularis, played w. a staff (*cf. baculus 1c*).

1363 idem populus ad jactus lapidum, lignorum et ferri et quidam ad pilam manualem, pedivam et ~arem et ad †canibucam [l. cambucam]..se indulgent (*Cl*) *Foed.* VI 417.

2 bacularis [cf. bachelarius], 'bachelor', young knight or retainer.

utitur solummodo quarundam vilium testimoniis personarum, etiam non legalium dictis ~ium HERM. ARCH. 25 p. 60; **s1100** Helie candidam jusserunt tunicam indui, pro qua Candidus ~is [*Blanc Bacheler*] solitus est..nuncupari ORD. VIT. X 17.

bacularius v. bachelarius.

baculator, cudgeller.

janitor ingressum nullus vetat; hostia nullus / percussor servat; hinc baculator abest GARL. *Epith.* VIII 676.

baculinus, fitted w. a staff (*cf. baculus 2g*).

1302 [cordas] pro fundis ~is inde faciendis *Ac. Chamb. Chesh.* 11.

baculus, ~um [CL], **~a,** stick, staff: **a** for walking (incl. pilgrimage); **b** for beating or striking (as in judicial combat); **c** for playing staff-ball, polo or sim.; **d** for keeping rings or keys; **e** for scraping coulter etc. (plough-staff); **f** for building or erecting hurdles.

a imbecilles artus ~o sustentans BEDE *HE* IV 29; in egressu monasterii sint famuli camerarii, habentes ibi ~os preparatos quos tribuant fratribus ad se sustentandos LANFR. *Const.* 122; **a1160** usque ad diem qua ~um peregrinationis S. Jacobi suscepi *Reg. Glasg.* 16; **s1190** rex Anglie recepit peram et ~um, signa peregrinationis sue *G. Ric. I* 111; quod..benedicciones facte super..~os peregrinorum sunt vera practica necromancie (*Concl. Lollard.*) *Ziz.* 362. **b** apto mihi baculum quo baculabo canem GARL. *Epith.* VI 572; **c1270** percussit cum quodam ~o de salice super humerum *SelCCoron* 2; **1282** cum ~o ferreo *IMisc* 41/15; **1315** cum uno ~o qui vocatur *Kentishstaf* de fraxino rotundo *CoramR* 220 r. 106; **a1130** petimus ut hoc scutum atque ~um istum..benedicere digneris ut sint arma invincibilia (*Duellum*) *GAS* 430; instat accusator et medio ~o flagellat adversarium W. CANT. *Mir. Thom.* III 40; **1230** et in armatura eorundem [probatorum] et conduccione scutorum et ~orum *Pipe* 293; qui sic convicti sunt et secum suum portant judicium, sicut sententialiter condemnati nullum habent appellum versus aliquem fidelem nec infidelem quia omnino frangitur eorum ~us BRACTON f. 152; **1476** vi et armis, sc. ~is et cultellis *March S. Wales* 89; **s1314** ~is ferratis Jedwardiae..decertant MAJOR V 3. **c 1277** ~is ad ipsam pilam aptatis *CalIMisc* I 2209; **1282** percuciendo in capud cum quodam ~o ad pilam *ICrim.* 22/10; prohibemus..currere cum pilis ad ~os vel ad manus *Cust. Cant.* 154; cujus [Soldani] solatii modus talis est.. qualis est pastorum in terra Christianorum cum pila et ~is curvis ludentium, hoc solum excepto quod..nobiles cum suo Soldano nunquam nisi in equis pilam percutiunt S. SIM. *Itin.* 52. **d 1205** recepimus..j ~um cum xx saphiris *Pat* 50a; **1267** duo ~i continentes xxij anulos *CalPat* 136; **1272** iiij ~os continentes cvi anulos cum rubetis (*Pat*) *Foed.* I 878; claves civitatis in ~o pendentes ELMH. *Hen. V* 62. **e 1236** eundo ad carucam suam jactavit ~um caruce ad unum bovem *Pat* 47 m. 13; **1267** in j ~o caruce ferrando *MinAc* 949/3; **1275** capere facit..viij boves junctos cum tota caruca cum ~o, stimulo et ferramento *Hund.* I 71a; **1355** in ij ~is pro carucis ferrandis *AcMan Wint.* (*Silkstead*). **f 1228** pro virgis et ~is ad cooperiendam domum *KRAc* 462/10; **1287** nec manum cum ~o ad faldam non percussit *Hund. Highworth* 305; **1293** in omnibus custis falde cum ~is, clatis et sagimine *Ac. Wellingb.* 62.

2 staff (stave), stock, etc. forming part of structure: **a** staff of cart or pack saddle; **b** staff of portable cross; **c** stretcher of net; **d** haft, handle; **e** barrel-stave; **f** bow-staff; **g** sling-staff; **h** stock of cross-bow or gun; **i** beam of balance or weigh-beam.

a 1248 in bacul' empt' ad carectam, j d. *AcMan Wint.* (*Little Hinton*); **1318** in j pari ~orum empto ad carect' *Ib.* (*Enford*); habebit..alterum ~um qui est ex altera parte equi portantis summam in occulo..arcis *Cust. Bleadon* 203 (cf. arcus 3b). **b 1404** j knoppe pro ~o qui ponitur super crucem *Ac. Durh.* 394; **1448** j crucem cupream portabilem cum ~o deaurato (*Invent. All Souls*) *ArchJ* LI 120. **c 1377** rete..habens unum ~um longitudinis x pedum hominis affixum in extremitatibus ipsius ~i duabus tabulis formatis ad modum unius *colerake IMisc.* 211/5. **d 1278** in una furca ferrea sine ~o *DCCant* (*Ac. Milton*). **e 1282** cuvario, pro..~is novis ponendis in doleis vini *KRAc* 4/3. **f 1420** quod nullus artis predicte diffindat, Anglice *clief*, aliquos ~os arcuales in shoppa sua *Mem. York* I 201. **g 1298** in.. ij coriis equinis ad cv fundas ad ~os *Pipe* 91 r. 23. **h 1247** attyliatori balistarum regis..inveniat ~as ad balistas *Cl* 6; **1266** (v. ballistarius b); **1284** provideat cccc ~os de taxo Yspanica pro balistis faciendis *Cl* 102 m. 11; **1385** in iiij ~is grossis et curtis ligatis cum ferro pro iiij canonibus parvis (*KRAc* 400/22) *EHR* XXVI 697. **i** sit regula seu ~us libre *AB* BACON *Maj.* I 170; **1352** in xij ~is de box emptis pro eisdem tronis..et pro virgis de ferro ad signandos predictos ~os *Pipe* 197 (*item Lond.*).

3 staff (fig.), support (*cf. Lev.* xxvi 26).

quod..vacuaretur omnis regio totius cibi ~o GILDAS *EB* 19; **793** ceteros ~o consolationis sustentate ALCUIN *Ep.* 17; sic factus est deinceps suspectus, qui credebatur ~us fortitudinis M. PAR. *Maj.* III 479; duplici remedio sive ~o HENGHAM *Magna* 9 p. 32.

4 metal bar, ingot.

1245 totum aurum quod habemus apud Novum Templum Lond' in bisant', bacul' et palliola *Pat* 56 m. 3.

5 baton (her.).

bende fiunt a dextero angulo scuti ad sinistram partem a differenciam fissurarum sive ~orum BAD. AUR. 190.

6 staff as token of seisin.

c1120 saisivit eum per quemdam ~um *Cart. Rams.* I 139; **c1120** per quemdam quem adhuc habemus ~um fecit..de terra..donationem super altare manuali *Ib.* II 262; **c1127** terram de S. per ~um Odonis Revelli qui in thesauro ecclesie reservatur..reddens, homo ejus efficitur (*Cart. Thorney*) *Eng. Justice* 140; **a1185** cum ~o reddidimus in manum.. abbatis in pleno capitulo terram illam [*York*] *CalPat 1429–36*, p. 363; **a1190** hanc donationem feci eis, presente et concedente Mauricio de C. et per ~um istam elemosinam meam confirmante *Danelaw* 105; **1227** ei seisinam fecit per fustum et ~um *BNB* III 638; fiet ei seisina secundum quod vulgariter dicitur per fustum et ~um BRACTON 40; **1290** jus.. per fustum et ~um reddidi *Kelso* I 44; **1430** in excambium pro terra sua..quam..ipse per ~um in manu prioris reddidit *Feod. Durh.* 20; **1496** per exhibicionem fustis et ~i *Melrose* II 590.

7 ward-staff or wake-staff (*cf. Cust. Rents* 135; H. M. Cam *Hundred & Hundred Rolls* 124); **b** (Scot.; *cf.* D. Murray *Early Burgh Organization in Scotland* I 23*n.*).

1195 villata de Bissopestru dicit quod non sunt in thethinga; set receperunt ~um ad ward' faciend' et deferunt ~um illum de domo ad domum quia de dominico domini regis sunt *CurR PR* 103; **c1236** ~us debet currere a festo S. Mich. usque ad Nativitatem et a Pascha usque ad festum S. Petri ad Vincula *Cust. Battle* 126; **1282** distringatur respondere ballivis de ~o pervigilato *Hund. Highworth* 195 (cf. ib. 100: theþingmannus..in misericordia quia non bene vigilavit cum *werstaf* cum tota theþinga); **1394** visus ~i vocatus *wardestaff* apud Cirencestr':..in quolibet hundredo est unus ~us vocatus *wakestaff* qui debet presentari et videri ad visum cujuslibet hundredi *Cart. Ciren.* II 741; **a1540** abbas de Cerne colore firme sue hundredi de Todcumbe..clamat unum annuum redditum de tenentibus predictis pro defectu custodie cujusdam ~i vocati *wakstaff* (*De Pidele Trenthyde*) *MSS. Coll. Wint.* **b c1270** cum ~us vigilie circumierit ostiatim, debet invenire aliquem..qui exibit quando ignitegium pulsaverit *Leg. IV Burg.* 81.

8 wand of office held by beadle or sim.

c1410 illis qui baculos portant ostendere debes / valde pios oculos et ludere 'prebeo prebes' (*Vers. Exchequer*) *EHR* XXXVI 61; **c1412** bedelli ~os suos in manus cancellarii et procuratorum in congregacione renunciant *StatOx* 217.

9 wand as emblem of kingship (= *virga*, dist. from sceptre).

hic datur ei ~us in manu sua (*Coronatio Regis*) EGB. *Pont.* 103 (*cf. Rec. Coronation* 7); **s1194** cum pervenissent sic ad gradum altaris, inclinavit rex super genua, habens ~um aureum in sinistra et sceptrum in dextra GERV. CANT. I 526.

10 crozier carried by bishop or abbot on analogy of shepherd's crook (*cf.* GIR. *Spec. infra*). **b** crozier of mock bishop in *Festum Stultorum*.

cum datur ~us, haec oratio dicitur: 'accipe ~um pastoralis officii et sis in corrigendis vitiis seviens' EGB. *Pont.* 3; regis..licentia ~um quendam a monasterio rapit usurpans HERM. ARCH. 25; **s1107** annuit rex et statuit ut..nunquam per dationem ~i pastoralis..quisquam de episcopatu..per regem..in Anglia investiretur FL. WORC. II 56; **s1101** episcopus..~um pastoralem secum sumens per funem descendit ORD. VIT. X 18; pene fractus est ~us ejus episcopalis nisi majus pretium dedisset H. HUNT. *HA* VI 21 (cf. 1b supra); Roffensis ecclesia, obeunte pastore suo, ~um pastoralem debet ad ecclesiam Cantuariensem portare A. TEWK. *Ep.* 3; ~os sanctorum in superiore parte recurvos, auro et argento vel ere contextos, in magna reverentia tam Hibernie et Scotie quam et Wallie populus et clerus habere solent GIR. *TH* III 33; oves gregis..lupinis morsibus atrociter laniari aperte conspiciunt, et nec ~is pastoralibus nec etiam vocibus clamosis occurrunt *Id. Spec.* IV 22 (cf. WALS. *HA* II 188); **c1330** [abbas] solemniter revestitus, scilicet in alba, capa, mitra, cirothecis et anulo, cum ~o pastorali *Cust. Cant.* 45; **1338** j ~us pastoralis de argento *Ac. Durh.* 376; **14..** ~i pastorales iij..unus..cum curvamine eburneo, ..unus cum curvamine corneo..unus cum transverso cristallino..duo absque curvamine (*Cart. Reading*) *EHR* III 117. **b 1245** ~us stultorum (*Invent. S. Paul*) *Arch.* L 472.

11 wand or staff carried in procession or in choir.

1235 electus..in processionibus supremus ex parte abbatis procedet..choralem ferens ~um *G. S. Alb.* I *app.* 521; in festis que celebrantur in cappis, aliquis fratrum monitu cantoris ~os festivos in chorum deferet et cantor concantoribus distribuet *Chr. Abingd.* II 370; in processionibus Rogationum duo ministri elemosinarii, hac et illac stantes ad ostium monasterii, cuilibet monacho ~um boxeum, vel alium magis idoneum, de manu in manum sunt assignaturi *Ib.* 406; **1388** ~i festivales sunt decem pro Nativitate Domini, quorum unus eburneus (*Invent. Westm.*) *Arch.* LII 277.

12 sealing-staff (*cf. Great Seal* 312).

1453 de..j ~o garnisato cum argento, ordinato ad deserviendum circa sigillum regis ad sigilland' litteras patentes et alia brevia, vocato *le selyngstaff Ac. Foreign* 87C.

2 baculus v. batulus.

bacus [OF *bac*], ferry-boat (*cf.* 2 *batus*).

†**1024** (**1417**) transitum †battorum [? l. baccorum]..sive navium per Sequanam ascendentium aut descendentium (*Ch. Duc. Norm.*) *MonA* VI 1108; **1198** pro bachis regis.. reparandis *RScacNorm* II 484; qui..ducebant iiij bacos apud Portum Gaudii priusquam pons factus esset *Ib.* 485; **1203** de..tribus doliis vini que sunt in †bato [MS.: baco] Roberti *RNorm* 78.

badellus, v. bedellus 2d. badia v. 2 baia. badiuola v. bajonula.

badius [CL], bay (horse).

10.. ~ius, *brun* WW; color iste probat, / bādius et roseus L. Durh. *Dial.* II 215; equos..~ios Balsh. *Ut.* 46; **1207** duos dextrarios baios crinitos *Cl* 79b; **1237** unum de equis regis.., videlicet Arabicum vel baium *Cl* 417; **1274** jumentum bayum *Hund.* I 169; **1313** pro uno cursorio claro ~io.., uno cursorio ~io obscuro.., uno cursorio bruno ~io *KRAc* 375/8 f. 13*d.*; pro equo..alio ~io bauzan *Ib.* f. 14; pro restauro unius equi sori ~ii *Ib.* f. 31; **1444** duorum veterum equorum chariett' domini, videlicet j albi et alterius baidii coloris *Comp. Dom. Buck.* 11; **c1452** j equi basii *Test. Ebor.* III 148 (cf. ib. II 34 [**1431**]: unam *felle* †brasii coloris); *an haknay*, ~ius, mannus *CathA*.

baeticius v. bateicius.

†**bafer**, fat, pot-bellied.

~er, grossus *GlC* B2; **14..** ~er, *gretwombed* WW.

†**baffa**, flitch.

14.. ~a, *a flycche of bacon* WW.

baga, ~us [OF *bague*; ME *bagge*], bag.

1277 sexaginta ~as vivi argenti (*JustIt*) *Law Merch.* III 139; **1284** pro reparacione baggorum in quibus dictum mel imponebatur et pro cordis emptis ad dictos baggos ligandos *KRAc* 351/9 m. 8; **1417** claves..in baggo sigillato contentas *DC Linc.* A. 2.30f. 65b.

2 bag or wallet for documents. **b** bag for King's Bench indictments concerning affairs of state (*baga de secretis*). **c** Petty Bag (department of Chancery).

1290 ~e et cofyne cum brevibus et aliis secretis domini regis..sigillate et posite in quibusdam cistis (*Pet. Parl.*) *Doc. Exch.* 60; **1300** emendacione..baggearum rotulorum *Ac. Wardr.* p. 359; **1326** baggos in quibus erant rotuli *Cart. Glam.* 1138; **1332** rotulos qui sunt in una ~a de canabo *LTRMem* 105, r. 16*d*; in ij baggis de coreo pro rotulis custodiendis *Sacr. Ely* II 117; **1357** per ~am coronatoris comitatus predicti (*KB ControlmtR*) *EHR* XXIII 513; **1400** per ~am custodum pacis *Ib.* 515. **b 1357** affilantur in ~a Bedeford de secretis *Ib.* 513; **1462** per ~am de secretis istius termini *Ib.* 523. **c 1389** omnes predicti clerici de secunda forma exceptis clericis de parva ~a *Chanc. Orders* p. 3; pertinent ad hanc curiam [sc. Cancellariam]..clerici parvae Bagiae tres Camd. *Br.* 143.

bagagium, baggage.

1418 cum duodecim personis et duodecim equis in comitiva sua ac ~iis et aliis rebus *RNorm* 243; **s1423** Gasconici..super baggacium [v.l. baggagium] ceperunt infundere post reregardiam *Plusc.* X 29; **1446** suscepit.. in salvum..conductum..clericum Scotum..cum..~iis, bogeis, fardellis, literis *RScot* 327a.

Bagatinus, Italian coin.

[in Ragusa] currunt ~i sicud Venetiis et tantum valent S. Sim. *Itin.* 16.

bagea v. baga, bagia.

bagepipa [ME *baggepipe*], bagpipe.

1288 cuidam garcioni cum una ~a pipanti coram rege *Ac. Wardr.* (*TRBk.* 201) p. 56; **s1400** excrescebat nimis insolencia indumentorum in regno et maxime togarum cum profundis et latis manicis vocatis vulgariter *pokys* ad modum bagpipe formatis *V. Ric. II* 172.

bageta, small badge.

1397 *tapiestre work* cum armis et baget' predicti comitis *IMisc* 266/11.

bagg- v. bag-.

bagia, ~ea [ME *bage*], badge (her.).

c1370 qui utitur tali colore in vestibus vel bagis suis (J. Bridl. *gl.*) *Pol. Poems* I 185; **c1421** pro ij sellis vapulatis de armis et ~eis regis *KRAc* 407/5 m. 3; ista signa..regia.. non sunt sua arma vel ~ia set solummodo liberate Upton 35; **s1485** consideratis signis et bagis hodierni victoris atque victi *Croyl. Cont. C* 575; **1542** qui de ipso recipere voluerit eadem †libertates [l. liberatas] signa vel ~ias ad ipsum serviendum (*Pat* 710) *Foed.* XIV 764.

bagnileuca v. banleuca a. bagpipa v. bagepipa.

†**bagula, ~um** [? cf. bajulus *or* pagulum], **a** bridle. **b** beetle (rammer).

a 7.. ~a, *bridels* WW; ~a, *bridel Ælf. Gl.* **b 10..** ~um, *biotul* WW.

bagus v. baga. bahardum v. baiardum. bahud-, bahurd-, bahurt- v. barhudum.

1 baia [OF *baie*], bay, inlet.

1427 quidam magnus cursus maritimus vocatus Montis Baia [*Mount's Bay, Cornw.*]..infra quam quidem baiam portus pacificus navibus portagii quaterviginti doliorum non existit *Pat* 422 m. 22.

2 baia, ~um [cf. bedum], bay of pond, mill-dam.

1175 in reparatione ~arum vivarii *Pipe* 126; **1180** de molendinis et baisio de Longolio *RScacNorm* I 59; **1206** quod ..facias bayas vivarii nostri *Cl* 66b; **1213** quod permittas magistrum militie Templi..aperire ~um molendini sui *Ib.* 159; **c1210** habebunt in baiis suis corbellas suas in *lavaleisun* [cf. avalatio] *FormA* 27; **1237** in maeremio prosternendo ad palas faciendas et in veteri ~a ponendas ad terram bene affirmandam *KRAc* 501/18 m. 3; **1293** non piscavit in fossicula bayarum [cf. ib. 236: in fossicula exclusarum] domini abbatis apud novum molendinum *CourtRHales* 240; **1333** in argillo fodiendo..et rammando circa dictas ~as [ad rotam molendini] *LTRMem* 105 r. 195; **1359** pro badiis vivarii nostri erigendis *AncD* C 4603.

3 baia, ~us [OF *baee* < badata], bay (compartment) of building.

1236 visores affidaverunt pro lx s. positis in j baya cooperienda plumbo *KRMem* 14 r. 13*d*; **1330** cepit..duas bayas de domo elemosinarie *CourtR* 195/2 m. 2; **1454** una domus videlicet aula et camera continent' duos bayos *AncD* C 3889; **1464** unum mesuagium.. continent' spacium trium ~arum in longitudine *Ib.* A 8449; **1470** habet j bayam orrei sui valde ruinosam *CourtR* 194/108 r. 1; **1518** unam domum de *postis and pannes* continentem tres bayas *Rec. Nott.* III 140.

baiardarius, ~or, baiardour, handbarrow man.

c1280 deferentibus cum cenovectoriis grossos lapides insculpandos ad asteleriam et extra, qui quidem nuncupantur bai[a]rdores *KRAc* 85/22 m. 6; de quibus operariis alii sunt ~ores *Ib.*; **1320** bayardarii.., hottarii.., falconarii *Ib.* 487/3; **1333** scaffatoribus et bayard'..operantibus super scaffot' *Ib.* 469/12 m. 2.

baiardum [OF *baiard*], handbarrow.

1198 minutis operariis, sc...mortereorum, chivereorum, ~eorum *RScacNorm* II 309; **1279** in..schotbord' emptis ad baiard' inde de novo faciend'..; in minutis clavis..ad.. falcones, baharda, civeria *KRAc* (*Tower*) 467/7/4; **1287** in iiij bayard' emptis ad dictam terram portandam ad wallam *MinAc* 1027/17 r. 5; **1325** portitoribus tractantibus petras cum baiard' de ponte usque astelriam *KRAc* 469/8 m. 4; **1371** [*smuggling*] quandam pipam..et unum lectum ad modum unius baiard' lanis plenos *CalCl* 258.

baiardus [OF *baiard*; cf. badius], bayard or bay. **b** (sb. m.) bay horse.

1290 in uno equo bayardo empto..c s. *Ac. Swinfield* 175; **1313** unus pullanus ~us *KRAc* 375/8 f. 16*d.*; **1427** lego.. servienti meo equum meum ~um in quo mecum equitare consuevit *Reg. Cant.* II 373. **b 1284** in j libra piperis empta..pro dentibus bayardi de Hop' et bauzani de Luda lavandis *KRAc* 97/3 m. 9; **1326** de xiij peciis cingulorum pro bayard' receptis *Pipe* 119 r. 38.

baicha v. barca. baidius v. badius. baihudum v. barhudum. baila v. 1 baillia. baillagium v. bailliagium.

1 baillia [OF *baillie*; cf. 1 bailliva, bajulia], baillie, bailiwick, authority or jurisdiction of official (esp. sheriff). **b** area of such jurisdiction. **c** ward, division of county (Northumb & Durh). **d** bailliery (Scot.).

c1072 omnes illos qui sub ballia et justitia tua sunt (*Breve Regis*) *EHR* VII 17; **1167** debet..de firma de Rotelande..dum R. G. tenuit balliam *Pipe* 12; celerarius..dixit se malle deponi de bailia sua quam aliquid facere contra conventum Brakelond 156; subrogatus..Radulpho..in ballia de Pembroch Gir. *JS* IV p. 227; **1265** rex cepit homagium Philippi..de ballia et omnibus..tenementis que..pater suus tenuit *Cl* 23. **b a1135** rex..omnibus vicecomitibus et ministris suis totius Anglie in quorum ~ia fugitivi abbatie de A. inventi fuerint (*Ch. Regis*) *Chr. Abingd.* II 81; **c1138** rex ..omnibus fidelibus suis..in quorum †baila et potestate abbas S. Augustini..terras habet *Regesta* III 154; **1166** est summonendus in ballia R. de H. *Pipe* 90; si..noveris in cujus ~ia vel comitatu [terram vel catalla] habuerit *Dial. Scac.* II 1 c; ubicumque inventus fuerit in ballia tua Glanv. XII 11; **1227** mandatum est vicecomiti..quod mercatum.. per ~iam suam clamari..faciat *Cl* 7. **c 1237** in ballia de Stoketon' *Cl* 568; **1293** ballia inter Tyn' et Coket (*JustIt* 651) *English Hundred Names* (O. S. Anderson) p. xxv. **d a1165** ballivi mei in quorum balliis ipsa bona sunt *Regesta Scot.* 222; **c1184** placita..que contingunt infra balliam alicujus vicecomitis (*Assisa Will.*) *APScot* 55; **1214** aliis burgis et burgensibus infra balliam de Aberden *BBC* 35; **1459** per castriwardas ballie compotancium *ExchScot* 537.

2 a office of *bailli* (Gasc.). **b** authority of *bailo* or sim. (It.).

a 1232 mandatum est..senescallo Wasconie quod ~iam quam F...prius habuit..ei committat *Cl* 116; **1279** balliam castellanie de Burgo *RGasc* II 51. **b 1370** per..commune Januensium transmissus fuit ambaxiator..cum plena potestate et baylia (*DipDocE* 259) *Foed.* VI 674; **1423** vexilliferi, magistri et sex cives officiales balie (*Act. Civ. Senarum*) Amund. I 140.

3 preceptory (of Templars).

1185 facta est ista inquisitio..per fratrem Galfridum.. quando ille suscepit baiiliam de Anglia *Rec. Templars* 1; **c1190** consilio fratris Willelmi..tunc procurantis ~iam de Londonia *Ib.* 169.

2 baillia v. 1 & 2 baillium.

bailliagium [OF *bailliage*], office of *bailli* (Fr.).

1378 de proficuis baillagii de Saunterre *Pat* 302 m. 14; **1408** ballivam et ~ium ville nostre de Polhon in senescalcia Landarum *RGasc* 112 m. 2.

2 office of bailiff (of honor or sim.).

1432 concessimus..~ium honoris Peverell' in comitatibus Norht' [etc.] *Pat* 431 m. 1; **1486** officia constabularii et janitoris castri nostri de Shirrefhoton' cum balliagio ville nostre ibidem *Pat* 563 m. 15(13); **1487** de ballagio [hundredi] *CalPat* 161.

bailliatus v. baillivata.

1 baillium, ~ia [OF *bail*], custody (Fr.): **a** (of person); **b** (of land).

a 1199 ut eis..puellas et viduas suas nuptui tradere..et ballia juvenum et puellarum sive viduarum habere..liceret (*Ch. Alienore*) J. Besly: *Hist. Poictou* 596. **b 1289** terra Pontivi..cujus ballium ad nos pertinet racione minoris etatis..filii..nostri *RGasc* III 585; terram de Pontivo.. habendam in ballium usque ad legitimam etatem..nati nostri *Ib.* 586.

2 grant of custody (of land or rent).

1196 nichil tenet in terra illa nisi ad firmam per balliam.. fratris sui *CurR* VII 332; **1203** utrum fuit seisitus..ut de feudo suo de illa dimidia bovata terre..an..ut de custodia de ballio..filii sui *Ib.* II 279; **1213** terra quam..tenet de ~io nostro *Cl* 144; **1218** occasione bailii quod consilium..regis.. mihi fecit de terris et serviciis *Pat* 174; **1219** habuit terram illam ex ballia Henrici *CurR* VIII 59; **1268** carucatam terre ..et j marcatam redditus quas Juliana..tenet †at [l. ad] vitam suam de ballio regis *Cl* 556.

3 custody of prisoner awaiting trial, bail.

1223 debet xx sol. pro A...ut tradatur in bailio *LTRMem* 6 r. 12*d*; **1238** traditus est in ballio Jacobo.., una cum aliis qui eum prius manuceperunt, ad habendum eum coram rege super corpora sua *Ib.* 12 r. 9*d*; **1239** recepit in ballium M. hominem suum ad habendum eum coram baronibus de Scaccario..tanquam prisonem *KRMem* 17 r. 8*d*; **1241** debeo distringere debitores burgensium unde habeant bailiam.. quod eis reddant debitum suum *BBC* (*Pembroke*) 228; **1256** B...detenta in prisona regis..habet breve vicecomiti ..quod ponatur per ballium *Cl* 9; **1417** morabitur in prisona ..absque tradicione in ballium vel alia deliberacione (*Chanc. Misc.*) *Law Merch.* II xcix; **1513** remansuri absque ballio vel manucaptione (*TreatyR*) *Foed.* XIII 369.

2 baillium, ~ia [OF *baile, balie*], bailey, courtyard of castle. **b** (dist. as outer, inner, or otherwise).

1142 in terris et turribus, in castellis et ~iis (*Ch. Mat. Imp.*) *Mandeville* 166; **1157** in una camera infra balium *Pipe* 152; **1172** in reparacione domorum regis in balia Turris de Lund' *Ib.* 144; **1246** ballium circa castrum nostrum Cestrie, ..amoto palo, ..claudi faciatis calce et petra (*AncC* II 67) *RL* II 45; **12..** inter terram predicti W. ..et fossam de balea castelli de Eya *Cart. Eye* f. 66; **s1263** castrum obsederunt et ballivam ceperunt *Leg. Ant. Lond.* 62. **b 1203** de cremento de Pikering'..cum ballia forinseca et warda castelli *Pipe* 200; **1236** breccam..in intrinseco ~io nostri castri Windesor' *Cal. Liberate* VI 2422; **1251** medium ballium castri nostri Noting' *Liberate* 28 m. 17; **1257** in superiori ballio castri *Cl* 70; **1261** eos [vigiles] tam in ballio forinseco quam alibi ubi opus fuerit commorari faciat *Ib.* 440; **1304** carpentario facienti unum pontem tractabilem inter interius et exterius ballium dicti castri *KRAc* 486/15 m. 2; **1313** diversas domos..de inferiori balliva Turris *Ib.* 468/20 f. 4; **1313** in intima balliva juxta magnam Turrim *Ib.* 496/16 f. 6; **1327** ballia exterior dicti castri est tota..ruinosa; ..ballia media indiget reparacione; ..ballia interior..videlicet magna turris cum turrell'..mur' circumquaque et camere sunt racionabiliter in bono statu *KR Ext. & Inq.* 10/2/22.

baillius [*var. of* baillivus], bailiff, agent.

c1155 Hugo comes Cestrie..baliis, ministris et famulis omnibusque suis hominibus *Danelaw* 99; **1172** per fidem balliorum suorum *Pipe* 86; constituere alium ballium suum vel senescallum de terris et rebus suis disponendis Glanv. XI 1; **1189** rex..vicecomitibus et omnibus bailiis suis totius Anglie *CalCh* IV 63; **1224** recepit sicut bailius domini sui xl li. de hydagiis *LTRMem* 6 r. 16*d*.

1 bailliva, ~ia [cf. 1 baillia], bailiwick, authority or jurisdiction of official (esp. sheriff). **b** area of such jurisdiction. **c** ward, division of county (*cf.* O. S. Anderson *English Hundred Names* pp. xxiv–xxvi; *Cumberland Place-names* III p. xiv).

qui pro balliva lunari se probat hostem / desipit D. Bec. 1652; **1186** xx li. remanent super vicecomites qui tenuerunt ballivam de xx annis preteritis de eodem lestagio *Pipe* 188; **1200** non amoveatur quamdiu se in illa balliva bene gesserit *BBC* (*Northampton*) 351; **c1236** contra constitutiones canonicas..faciunt ecclesiastice persone cum ballivas seculares tenent Gros. *Ep.* 72 p. 213; **c1250** inhibemus ne beneficiati sint vicecomites vel ballivas laicas teneant *Conc. Syn.* 648; **c1270** ballivus recipiens ~am jurabit sic: .."fideliter me geram in balliva mea" *CBaron* 77; **s1257** aldermanni, vicecomites et camerarius regis..degradati sunt et depositi de ballivis suis *Leg. Ant. Lond.* 36; **1329** ballivam marine [*Bristol*; cf. baillivus 3b] *CalPat* 443; **1471** officium aque ballive nostre Bristoll' *Pat* 528 m. 19. **b a1190** rex.. ministris suis..in quorum ~is..monachi de Bello habent terras *FormA* 296; **c1210** habent..aldermanni in civitatibus regni hujus in ballivis suis..eamdem dignitatem (*Leg. Ed.*) *GAS* 655; **1223** vicecomes Sussex' debet respondere..de exitibus terrarum..in balliva sua *LTRMem* 6 r. 1; **1242** vicecomiti Kantie..de bonis..in ballivia sua *RGasc* I 17; **1331** in proxima curia nostra tenenda in ballivia vestra *Lit. Cant* I 364. **c 1256** balliva inter Tynam et Coket (*JustIt* 642) *AssizeR Northumb* p. 103; **1278** balliva de Cumb' et Allerdal', que est de altera parte comitatus, venit per xij *JustIt* 132 r. 24*d*.

2 office of *bailli* (Gasc.).

1280 ballivi [per Vasconiam]..de omnibus balliviis..suis ..respondeant *RGasc* II 108; **1304** custumam seu balliviam vocatam de parvo issaco Burdegale *Ib.* III 424; **1305** bayliviam bastidarum *Ib.* 479.

2 bailliva, female bailiff.

1287 theþingmannus..in misericordia quia uxor sua fecit se ballivam et quesivit unam domum sine ballivo *Hund. Highworth* 304.

baillivata, ~us, bailiwick. **b** bailliery, baillieship (Scot.).

1276 duos homines qui custodient ballivatam prepositure Leycestrie *Rec. Leic.* I 174; **1357** [ballivus de Romene] habuit..ad expensas suas tempore ballivatus sui *Reg. Rough* 105; *baylyschyppe*, ballyatus *PP*; **1587** ballivattas *Pat* 1299 m. 11. **b** a**1430** litera balliviatus *Cop. Pri.S. Andr.* 45; **1468** officia balliatus et cameraríatus ecclesie *Reg. Brechin* II 109; **1559** virtute officii sui ballivatus *Scot. Grey Friars* II 203; **1579** in parochia de Myrtoun ballivata de Lauder *Dryburgh* 309.

2 office of *bailli* (Fr.).

1420 officia tam justitie parliamenti quam etiam balliviatus (*Treaty*) ELMH. *Hen. V Cont.* 141; regnum Anglie per comitatus ut regnum Francie per †balliovatus distinguitur FORTESCUE *LLA* 24.

†baillivicus, (?) bailiwick (C.I.).

1314 sequitur de misis [prioratus de Vallia]..item ballivo c libre, ..item ballivico xx libre *CartINorm.* 222.

baillivus [OF *baillif*, (?) < bajulīvus], bailiff (in general sense), agent or official: **a** (of king); **b** (of other person); **c** (fig.).

a**1116** Henricus rex Angl' omnibus ballivis suis et ministris totius Anglie *Regesta app.* cxii; (?) a**1130** rex..omnibus ~is meis de Anglia *Ib.* ccxxxiii; **1176** ~i domini regis respondeant ad Scaccarium..de omnibus perquisitionibus suis quas faciant in bailliis suis (*Ass. Clarendon* 10) *G. Hen. II* I 110; **1257** quod non sit coronator aut alius ballivus regis *Cl* 34; **1279** tunc custos regius seu ballivus *Reg. Ebor.* 37. **b** (?) c**1157** sine impedimento mei vel heredum meorum vel ballivorum nostrorum (*Ch. Com. Brit.*) *E Ch. Yorks* IV 31; **1185** bailivi episcopi *RDomin* 63; a**1200** versus R. Trussebut et ~os suos *CurR* I 3; **1267** ~i qui compotum dominis suis reddere tenentur (*Marlb.* 23) *StRealm* I 24; **1275** abbas.. habet duos ballivos equites ubi non solebat habere nisi unum *Hund.* II 7; in monachis..et in †baluis..et fere in omni genere hominum GAD. 32.2; hic ballivus, *a bayle* WW. **c** luna comparatur ballivo, qui habet terminare causas minores BACON IX 187; **1374** non sunt nisi ministri vel ballivi Domini WYCL. *Dom. Div.* 255.

2 bailiff, official subordinate to sheriff; **b** (attached to a hundred or sim.); **c** bailiff errant (unattached).

s**1170** rex..deposuit fere omnes vicecomites Anglie et ballivos eorum *G. Hen. II* I 5; **1327** dicit [vicecomes] quod fecit extractas de eisdem summonicionibus et fecit preceptum singulis ballivis suis ad levandum etc., et quod prefati ballivi sibi computare debuerant..de debitis exactis per summoniciones predictas *LTRMem* 99 r. 142; GOWER *VC* VI 463 (v. Acheron). **b 1200** interrogatus..si monstraverit illud factum vicecomiti vel ~o hundredi, dixit quod..vicecomiti vel preposito hundredi non monstravit *CurR* I 348; **1221** ballivus domini regis de hundredo hoc idem testatur *PlCrGlouc* 76; **1275** [ballivus sokne de Hornecastre] distri[n]xit ipsum per W. Bindewel tunc parvum ballivum *Hund.* I 300b; **1279** [boviculos] liberari fecit per ballivum juratum domini regis *Hund. Highworth* 130; **1542** in redditu resoluto ballivo wapentagii de Bridford *Rutland MSS.* (*Bailiffs' Ac. 31–4 Hen. VIII* r. 41d.). **c 1304** in vadiis.. ballivi itinerantis *MinAc* 997/15; **1307** ballivum nostrum errantem *CalPat* 80; **1461** officium ballivi itinerantis in com. Cornub' *Pat* 493 m. 19.

3 bailiff w. special sphere of authority. **b** water bailiff (*cf. aquaebaillivus*).

1227 ballivis de foresta de Chipeham [*Wilts*] *Cl* 3; **1259** ballivo honoris Bononie de Wyham *Cl* 367; **1278** ballivus curie baronum *CoramR* 37 r. 14d; **1285** vicecomites respondent quod preceperunt ballivis alicujus libertatis qui nichil inde fecerunt (*II Westm.* 39) *StRealm* I 90; **1298** lestus marisci de Romenal [*Romney, Kent*] tentus coram commun' ballivo et xxiiij juratoribus marisci *Reg. S. Aug.* 610 (cf. *Cart. Bilsington* 42); **1313** ballivus libertatis non potest recipere probationem de denariis inventis..infra libertatem suam nisi [etc.] *Eyre Kent* I 132. **b 1325** tanquam ballivum suum [sc. regine] de marina portus ibidem [*Sutton Vautort, Devon*] *CalPat* 145; **1398** ballivus aque maritime [*Dartmouth, Devon*] *Cl* 242 m. 7; **1439** officia scrutatoris et ballivi aque nostre de Severne *Pat* 444 m. 6; **1455** (cf. *Port Bk. Southampt. 1439–40*, pp. xlvii, l); **1485** officium aque ballivi ville nostre Bristoll' *Pat* 561 m. 27(9).

4 municipal official, sometimes identified w. reeve (*cf. praepositus*).

1205 rex ballivis de Suhamton' *Cl* 41a; **1203** ballivi de Thameworth' ceperunt toloneum de militibus comitatus Stafford' *SelPl Crown* 30; **1221** burgenses de Wich' [*Droitwich*] relaxaverunt demand' panis et cervisie, ita quod prepositi nec ~i habebunt aliud mercatum..quam alius vicinus *Ib.* 97; literas regis..~o de Pembroch..mitti procuravit GIR. *JS* IV 212; **1223** (cf. *Leet Norw.* pp. xviii *seqq.*); c**1250** rectores ..monopolios..et precipue ballivos et eorum uxores.. cibum et potum..detrahentes..investigent *Stat. Cantab.* 205; **1297** tunc capitali ballivo *Deeds Newcastle* 71; c**1299** tunc superiore ballivo ville Novi Castri *Ib.* 40; **1333** ballivis curie burgi de Elvet *Feod. Durh.* 75n.; **1336** major et ballivi ville predicte [Oxon'] qui pro tempore fuerint..assaiam panis et cerevisie in villa predicta..faciant (*Pat* 187) *Foed.* IV 693; **1419** vicecomites civitatis Londoniarum qui quondam ballivi dicebantur *MGL* I 42; **1537** sibi in singulos annos eligere binos suae civitatis gubernatores, ut consules, quos ballivos appellarunt P. VERG. XIV 243.

5 bailie (Scot.): **a** (of barony or sim.); **b** (of burgh).

a a**1165** M. rex Scotorum episcopis, comitibus, baronibus, vicecomitibus et ballivis suis *Regesta Scot.* 107 (cf. 222); ballivus qui habet potestatem ordinariam arbiter esse non potest *RegiamM* II 4; si ballivi faciant judicium et justiciam omni tempore *Iter Cam. Artic.* 1; c**1380** justiciariis, vicecomitibus, prepositis et eorum ballivis *Conc. Scot.* I ccxxxv. **b** juramentum ballivi burgi *APScot* 319; **1343** sigilla.. tunc temporis ballivorum burgi de Elgyn *Reg. Moray* 290.

6 *bailly* (C.I.), *bailli* (Fr.), or other official other than British.

1223 rex ~is insularum de Geres' et Gerner' *Cl* 534a; **1242** rex ~is suis de Olerone *RGasc* I 97; **1376** loco ~i et scabinorum et †cornemannorum..habeatis in eadem villa [*Calais*] unum majorem et duodecim aldermannos (*TreatyR*) *Foed.* VII 116; **1440** nobilibus viris ballivis, prioribus et proceribus conventus Rodi [*Rhodes*] BEKYNTON I 78; **1496** camerarius et superior ballivus Flandrie (*DipDoc E* 624) *Foed.* XII 578.

bainum [OF *bain* < balneum], bath (for falcons).

1275 empciones circa mutas: ..pro iiij li. de laton' ad claves baynorum *KRAc* 467/6/2 m. 11.

bainus v. vannus. Baioarius v. Bavarrus. baiolare, bairlare v. bajulare. baisium v. 2 baia.

1 †baissa, (?)lip.

animalium quedam habent in capite cornua, quedam nares, quedam ~as M. SCOT *Phys.* c. 20.

2 baissa [OF *baisse, baiasse*], maidservant.

1297 inveniet unum garcionem vel unam ~am..ad triturandum vel sarclandum (*Rent. Walton* m. 1) *MFG.*

baitagium [cf. ME *baiten*], baiting, provision for horse.

c**1472** quilibet equus percipit †bartagium [v.l. pro battagio; l. baitag', *as TRBk.* 230 f. 36v] j d. quad. *BBHouseh.* 104.

baitatio, baiting.

1444 cum expensis et †bartacionibus [l. baitacionibus] diversorum equorum ad hospicium predictum *Comp. Dom. Buck.* 20; **1454** in batac' unius equi; ..in batac' cum pabulo equorum *DCCant DE 16*.

baium v. 2 baia. baius v. badius, 3 baia. Baiuverus v. Bavarrus. bajol- v. bajul-.

bajonula [LL], litter.

bajanula, *ferbed* ÆLF. *Gl.*; s**1136** Normanniam..†badiuola [? l. badionola] jacens sua revectus visitat ORD. VIT. XIII 74; genera lectorum erant lectice, ..grabata que ~e dicuntur BALSH. *Ut.* 54; hec bojenila, i. lectus WW.

bajula v. bajulus.

bajulare [CL], to bear, carry. **b** to endure.

qui in sabanis..bajolabantur aegroti ALDH. *VirgP* 36 p. 284; adjuro te, creatura ferri..nec patiaris ab †illa [l. illo] inpune ~ari (*Jud. Dei*) *GAS* 412; fratrem bajolare volentes / ad Triadis nova tecta suum WULF. *Swith.* I 663; demissus ex humeris ~antium se egrotus OSB. *Mir. Dunst.* 5; amator sapiencie..ab omni pagina quam ~averit recedit doccior MAP *NC* III 3 p. 130; collum..caput bajolans et sustentans BART. ANGL. V 25; epistulam..juveni ~ans *Flor. Hist.* I 578; **1378** quas [cruces] tenetur quilibet factus ad Dei ymaginem ~are WYCL. *Ver.* III 170; **1456** paribus.. cerothecarum..pro falconibus †bairlandis [l. bajulandis] *ExchScot* 179. **b** quia..tanta laborum desolamina.. ~assent R. COLD. *Cuthb.* 21.

bajulatio, carrying (of cross): **a** (before archbishop); **b** (fig.).

a 1278 portionem agistamenti pasture..que cessit ~oni crucis archiepiscopatus [Cantuar'] *Cl* 95; **1302** ne archiepiscopi Cantuar' suspecta presencia in crucis †bavilacione.. exempcioni ecclesie S. Edmundi derogaret (*Chr. S. Edm.*) *EHR* LVIII 63; s**1353** Simon Cantuar' et Johannes Eborac' archiepiscopi †antequam [l. antiquam] contentionem super ~one crucis utriusque archiepiscopi..concordarunt BIRCHINGTON *Arch. Cant.* 43. **b** in utraque crucis ~one.. hanc..cotidie tollere..jubemur BEDE *Luke* 452.

2 bailing, giving security. **b** bailment, entrusting.

1355 ponitur in respectu secundum ~onem ipsius J. *Rec. Leic.* II 105. **b 1374** allocutus de ~one hujusmodi fraellorum falsorum ad vendendum *Pl. Mem. Lond.* A 19 m. 7.

bajulator, bearer, carrier.

s**1187** crucis ~ores episcopus Achonensis et cantor Sepulcri Dominici *Itin. Ric.* I 5 p. 15; **1252** hospicium ~oris sigilli regis apud Hensinton' *Cl* 44; s**1346** oriflamma..cum ~ore ipsius AD. MUR. *app.* 247; a**1440** brevicularum ~ori *Ac. Durh.* 234.

bajulatus, carrying. **b** (bearing) burden (fig.), office.

sanctum sentientes onus vestro dulci ~u HERM. ARCH. 47. **b 1281** quia [parochie]..sub nomine ~us ecclesie ad firmam laicis conceduntur *Conc. Syn.* 910; **1284** majestatem vestram, que a summo rege regni terreni optinet ~um (*LiberA*) *Foed.* II 278; **1284** nec de alio monasterii ~u se..intromittat PECKHAM *Ep.* 507.

bajulia [cf. baillia], jurisdiction of *bailli* (Gasc.).

1313 ad..limitacionem jurisdiccionis predicte et ~ie dicte ville de Romevo *RGasc.* II 1111.

2 commandery (of Hospitallers).

1313 facultatem..removendi eas [personas] a suis ~iis, domibus, officiis et administracionibus (*Lit. Procur.*) *Foed.* III 460; **1328** de arreragiis responsionum et firmarum tam ~iarum quam etiam camerarum Hospitalis et quondam Templi *Hosp. in Eng. app.* 217; **1375** *CalCl* 330.

bajulus [CL], (adj.) supporting. **b** portable, carried.

c**1170** patrem jam cadentem..~is manibus in cellam deferunt *Chr. Rams.* 156. **b** in ecclesia..est campana ~a virtuosissima GIR. *IK* I 1; cruce ~a..muniti *Ib.* 94; **1392** sicut ~a relacione quorumdam subditorum nostrorum accepimus *DipCorr. Ric. II* no. 165.

2 (sb. f.) holder, container, stoup.

1415 unam aque ~am pro aqua benedicta de argento (*Testam.*) *Foed.* IX 279.

3 (sb. m. or f.) bearer, carrier, supporter; **b** (of baby, *i.e.* nursemaid); **c** (of water, *i.e.*, holy water clerk; *cf. aquaebajulus*); **d** (of cross); **e** (of royal seal; *cf. custos*).

c**1112** bajula palmitis ulmus R. CANT. *S. Malch.* V 528; accipitres..~os exigunt diligentiores GIR. *TH* I 12 p. 38; a bajulo prioris [gladii] MAP *NC* III 2 p. 121. **b** mater ecclesia..circa ipsum nutricis et ~e officium executa M. PAR. *Maj.* III 601. **c** c**1430** aque ~i ecclesie S. Ebbe *MunCOx* 200. **d** archipresul..a crucis ~o ante ipsum crucem mox accipit H. Bos. *Thom.* III 37 p. 305; Gallia tota / est cum rege suo bajula facta crucis GARL. *Tri. Eccl.* 122. **e** s**1222** R. de Novilla, qui antea custos et ~us sigilli regii extiterat, regis fidelissimus cancellarius M. PAR. *Maj.* III 74; secreti sigilli regis ~us sive custos *V. Ric. II* 60; s**1401** cum ejus litteris ad privati sigilli ~um..directis *G. S. Alb.* III 491.

4 bearer (fig.), conferrer.

c**1090** reversus ~um medele invenit egrotum GOSC. *Mir. Iv.* lxi; Eadgarus, puer videlicet pacis ac justitiae ~us futurus OSB. *V. Dunst.* 19; bajula lethi J. EXON. *BT* II 253; **1237** non paruerunt pacis ~is discordie sectatores (*Lit. Cardinalis*) M. PAR. *Maj.* III 446.

5 bearer of letter or tidings, messenger.

c**750** per hunc ~um harum apicum (ÆTHELBERT) *Ep. Bonif.* 105; missa sum ad te boni nuntii ~a AILR. *Ed. Conf.* 764B; tradens epistulam ~o *Ib.* 753C; verborum ~i indigni GIR. *GE* I 54; clericum meum ~um litterarum *Id. Symb.* 31 p. 323; s**1260** ~o mandati *Chr. Melrose* 189; **1285** per presentium ~um PECKHAM *Ep.* 634; **1318** per harum [litterarum] ~um *FormOx* 42; **1546** ~us et nuncius *Reg. Glasg.* 560.

6 a royal minister, governor (*cf. baillivus*). **b** municipal official, *baile* (Gasc.). **c** abbot's agent (mon.).

a feliciter actis omnibus, totius pene regni ab ipso [Cnuto] constituitur [Godwinus] dux et ~us *V. Ed. Conf.* 38v; elegi te de populo, principemque constitui, prudentem et fidelem te sperans ~um fieri tocius regni MAP *NC* V 5 p. 224; veniunt latrones vel ~i principis..et totum consumunt O. CHERITON *Fab.* 42B; **1221** dixit Caliphus; ..oportet ut per terras conquisitas statuat ~os suos (*Lit. legati Damiette*) *Ann. Dunstable* 73; **1263** in regno Jerosolimitano ~us (*AncC* LV 2) *Foed.* I 395; electione amicorum et ~orum regis BACON V 28. **b 1281** scribaniam curie ~i S. Fidis *RGasc.* II 135; **1315** ~us..dicte ville, quocienscumque mutabitur, jurabit dictis juratis et burgensibus servare libertates *Ib.* IV 1626; **1438** prepositus, ~us, consules et universitas ville nostre S. Severi BEKYNTON I 23. **c 1255** ex tunc poterit electus [abbas] providere sibi de sociis qui secum commorentur quos ~os dicimus *G. S. Alb. app.* I 521; s**1257** archidiaconus S. Albani et dominus Johannes domini abbatis ~us et procurator M. PAR. *Maj.* V 615.

bakaveragium, carrying service on back (? of man or beast).

1302 custumarii debent per annum xlix averagia..et j ~ium (*Cust.*) *Suff. Hund.* 67 (cf. (*Cust. Ely*) *Cust. Rents* 66 [**1251**]: averagium super dorsum).

1 bala, ~us [OF *bale*], bale, package.

1242 pro una ~a piperis *RGasc.* I 31; **1252** ceperunt tres ballas avene *CurR* 146 r. 8; **1317** vacuata dicta ~a, ..fuit in ~a argillum et terra mixta cum allumine (*St. Ives*) *Law Merch.* I 106; **1328** in..j ~a gingiberis continente c iiij[xx] li. *ExchScot.* 117; **1371** tres ~os pellium lanutarum *Pat* 284 m. 22; **1387** mercandise..in ~is sub signis..mercatorum *IMisc* 237/14 r. 1; **1523** magnis balleis gadi (*PlRExch*) *Law Merch.* II 130.

2 bala v. 3 balea.

Balaamita, disciple of Balaam (*cf. Numbers* xxii).

~as videas plurimos qui, licet iniquam nolint ferre sententiam, ..justitiam partis unius in alteram transferre moliuntur J. SAL. *Pol.* 569A.

balaena [CL], **a** whale or other marine animal. **b** whale-meat. **c** whale-bone. **d** monster (fig.).

a ballena, *hran* GlC B 21; †palina, *hran Ib.* P 184; grandior in glaucis ballena fluctibus atra ALDH. *Aen.* 100. 65; capiuntur..delphines nec non et ~ae BEDE *HE* I 1; ire cum multis navibus in venatione ballene [AS: *on* *huntunge hranes*] ÆLF. *Coll.* 95; balena..*hwæl Id. Gl.*; **1199** in duabus baleinis in portu de Beiarid' *RChart* 17b; grossus piscis sicut balnea et sturgio et alii pisces regales BRACTON 14; **1296** quidam balignus inventus fuit ex parte Essex' *KRMisc* 2/2; **1305** balanus piscis qui pertinet ad coronam *Mem. Parl.* 110; **1309** balneam ad terram.. casualiter projectam *Pat* 132 m. 12*d.*; ad instar ~e que cum..pisciculis mare absorbuit FORTESCUE *LLA* 22; ~a, *porpeyse* WW; **1490** †baleria et alios pisces (*Tract.*) *Foed.* XII 382. **b** bālene carnes, phoce cetique secentur D. BEC. 940; **1265** xx pecie de ~a (*RHosp*) *Manners* 14; c**1324** centum ~e meliores de eodem anno salsat' pro xvi s., videlicet libra pro ij d. (*Lib. Cust.*) *MGL* II 119. **c** **1284** provideat..xx pecias de ~a..ad balistas *Cl* 102 m. 11; **1303** bracer de ~a (*KRAc* 363/18) *CalScot* II 1413; **1309** j mangna balista de balnea *MinAc* 997/18. **d** crudelissimam superbiae ~am, ceterarum virtutum devoratricem ALDH. *VirgP* 10.

balaenaria v. balingera.

balaenetta, ~us, small whale, *baleineau.*

1281 licenciam..piscandi et capiendi balenam, balenatum et cavelatum *RGasc* II 131; **1331** quedam balneta venit super terram domini W. de Kyme *IMisc.* 119/19.

balagius v. balasius. balaminus, ~ites v. balan-.

balancia, balanx [OF *balance* < *bilanx*], balance, weighing scale.

1196 v s. et vi d. ad balanc' et pondera ad cambium *Pipe* 19; **1204** balance per quas mercandie ponderantur *Pat* 42b; **1290** mercatores..petunt quod rex jubeat quod per balancias ponderetur *RParl* 47b; **1296** custos ~ie domini regis *MGL* II 107; **1300** pro duobus magnis balancis de corio emptis ad ponderandos lapides pro ingeniis *Ac. Wardr.* p. 73; **1329** pro tribus paribus ~earum *ExchScot* 221; **1340** in uno pari balancium *Ac. Durh* 36; **1404** j par de balandis *Ib.* 395.

2 weight (of hemp).

1211 pro mmm ~iarum fili de canno [v.l. canabo] secundum pondus de Bridiport ad funes navium faciendos *Pipe* 221; **1214** pro d ~iis canabi ad cordas faciendas *Pipe* 127.

balangera v. balingera.

balaninus [βαλάνινος], of behen.

oleum †balaminum conficitur sicut oleum amigdalinum *Alph.* 128.

balanites [βαλανίτης], kind of gem.

1338 unum scrinium auri..garnitum de saphiris..rubinis †balamitibus et aliis..petrariis (*TreatyR*) *Foed.* V 50.

1 balanus v. balaena.

2 balanus [βάλανος], behen or other nut.

balan' GILB. V 213. 2; balanon, i. glans; inde mirobalanus [etc.] *Alph.* 18–19; cornus, *a chestony tre*, ~us idem *CathA.*

balanx v. balancia.

balare [CL], to bleat; **b** (fig.).

†~atus [l. ~at], *bletid GlC* B 57; ~antes, oves *Ib.* B 20; haedi ~ant vel bebant, ..oves ~ant ALDH. *PR* 131; boves mugiebant ovesque ~abant R. COLD. *Cuthb.* 105; *G. S. Alb.* I 61 (v. blaterare). **b** rex brevis obsessus balat, rabiesque lupina / introitum querit GARL. *Tri. Eccl.* 14.

balasius [OF *balais*], balass, spinel ruby.

1205 baculum cum xlvj rub' bal' *Pat* 50a; **1215** annulos cum balesiis *Ib.* 149b; **1303** magna corona auri..cum preciosa petraria magnorum balesiorum, rubettorum et ameraldarum (*KRAc* 363/6) *DocExch* 277; **1409** lavacrum planum de auro cum perulis et balistis pulverizatum *Pat* 382 m. 16; **1420** unum *sharp* auri garnisatum de..grossis baleisiis (*Pat* 403) *Foed.* IX 908; **1424** firmaculum auri cum uno ~io in medio *Reg. Cant.* II 280; lapis qui dicitur balagius qui rubius est et perlucidus et hodie majoris utilitatis et precii est quam carbunculus UPTON 110; **1508** balagius..quem balasion vulgus nominat *Spons. Mariae* 30.

balastum v. ballastum.

1 balatio, bleating.

[diabolus] venit ad eum in ~one ovium *V. Osw.* 417.

2 & 3 balatio v. 1 & 2 ballatio.

balatola [It. *pallottola*], ballot, voting pebble (Genoa).

1370 absolventes se ad ~as albas et nigras (*DipDoc* E 259) *Foed.* VI 674.

†balatrare [cf. blaterare], to bawl.

c**1461** si scivissent Australes..perseverare.., fugassent ..istos boantes ~antesque Boreales *Reg. Whet.* I 391.

balatro [CL], buffoon or glutton (cf. *baratro*).

hinc mimi, ..~ones, emiliani..et tota joculatorum scena procedit J. SAL. *Pol.* 406A; bālātro voces, bălātro consumit inescas H. AVR. *CG* 103.

2 incendiary (AS *blæsere*).

a**1130** de ~onibus et de furtivis mortificatoribus (*Cons. Cnut.*) *GAS* 389 (*cf.Quad.* ib.: de blaseriis et murdritoribus).

balatus [CL], bleating, or lowing. **b** howling. *V. et. balare.*

aper grunnitum, ..bos ~um..stridebant FELIX *Guthl.* 36; **9..** *hlowung* WW; sicut agnus solo ~u matrem cognoscit BELETH *RDO* 48. 55; qui pastor ovile..ovi venienti ..non aperit antequam ~um audiat? MAP *NC* iv 6 p. 171. **b** canum caterva..qui latrando ~ibus in ipsum hyando fremebant R. COLD. *Cuthb.* 17.

balaustia [βαλαύστιον], pomegranate flower.

~ia est flos caducus maligranati BART. ANGL. XVII 21; accipe ~iam, psidiam GILB. II 79. 2; ~ie, i. flores granatorum GAD. 9. 1; *SB* 12.

balbere, ~escere, to stutter.

merula..canit estate, in hieme ~escit UPTON 198; *to stutte*, balbutire, ~ere, ~escere *CathA.*

balbicies v. balbuties.

balbus [CL], lisping, stuttering.

blessos ac balbos qui scaevis verba loquelis / fantes corrumpunt ALDH. *VirgV* 1087; ~us, qui dulcem linguam habet *GlC* B 16; ~us, *uulisp Ib.* 35; ~us, *stamer* ÆLF. *Gl.*; **9..** ~us..qui vult loqui et non potest, *wlips* vel *swetwyrda* WW; *stuttynge*, varcus, baurdus, blesus, ~us *CathA.*

balbushardus [cf. Fr. *balbuzard*], 'bald-buzzard', osprey.

omnia quae Aristoteles et Plinius percno hactenus tribuerunt Anglorum ~o conveniunt, si solam magnitudinem exceperis TURNER *Av.* 11.

balbuties, stuttering.

infantili ~e resonant impuberes et imberbes R. BURY *Phil.* 9. 154; *a stuttynge*, balbicies vel ~ies *CathA.*

balbutire, to stammer, stutter, slobber.

haec est ebriositas quando..lingua balbuttit EGB. *Pen.* xi 10; vidi pueros tam diu ~ientium vitia imitari ut postmodum nec cum vellent recte loqui potuerint J. SAL. *Pol.* 489B.; strepitu inarticulato et confuso ~iens W. CANT. *Mir. Thom.* VI 117; quod sequitur..titubans et ~iens nullatenus proferre potuit GIR. *GE* I 51 p. 153; [Witcleff] culpavit aliorum positiones.., dicens illos †balbutive [l. ~ire] loquentes NETTER *DAF* II 254 v; lingua brevis et ~iens *V. Ric. II* 169; *to slavyr*, ~ire *CathA.*

2 to ring false (with a tinny sound).

~ire dicitur [stannum] quia mixtura compositionis sue.. non in omnibus partibus suis mixtionis complete rationem attingit, sicut homo ~iens quedam verba attingit.., quedam non *Ps.*-GROS. 640.

balbutive v. balbutire.

balbutus, lisping, stammering.

~us, *stom, wlisp GlC* B 52.

balca v. balcus. balcan- v. balzan-. Balchus v. Blacus.

balco [? cf. It. *balcone*], (?) vestibule, entrance (to crypt).

illa, conspiciens quemdam clericum juvenem retro se stantem extra ~onem LANTFR. *Mir. Swith.* 2. 335 B; mulier juvenem cernens adsistere quendam / extra balconem WULF. *Swith.* II 166.

balcus, ~a [cf. AS *balca*, ON *balkr*; v. et. 1 bancus], balk, ridge (separating fields).

c**1150** terram meam de M. a ~o qui est inter vandelas demenii mei et vandelas hominum meorum *Cart. Whitby* II 525; c**1300** usque ad ~um qui ducitur ab eodem sico ultra H. *Melrose* II *app.* 17; c**1320** per ~am lapideam juxta terram arabilem del Morehuses sursum usque ad caput illius ~e ad quandam conjeriem lapidum *Kelso* 244; **1452** quandam peciam terre in suburbio [Leic', que]..extendit se a via regia usque ad communem ~um *Cl* 302 m. 4*d.*

2 balk, side-beam.

1141 grangia erat plena siligine usque ad ~um versus orientem. ..altitudo [grangie] sub ~o x pedes et super ~um usque ad festum viij pedes *Dom. S. Paul.* 136; **1335** quod quidem solar' continebit xxij pedes de ~o *DC Ebor* K.

baldekinus, ~um [OF *baudequin* < *Baldac*; cf. Ar. *Baghdādī*], baldachin (cloth of Bagdad), brocade. **b** canopy.

1218 pro uno ~o duplici liberato *Cl* 384b; **1232** quinque baudekinos cum auro et septem pannos de aresta *Cl* 71; **1244** viginti baudekina ad aurum *Cl* 261; **1245** capa..de balkeno rotato purpura (*Invent. S. Paul.*) *Arch.* L 480; s**1247** rex veste deaurata facta de preciosissimo ~o..sedens M. PAR. *Maj.* IV 644; abbas W. [ob. **1245**]..optulit duos pannos sericos ~os rubeos..unde..subsacrista fecit duas capas SWAFHAM 117; s**1300** stallo cum baudequinis et pannis sericis decentissime preparato *G. Durh.* 39; **1392** unam jupam longam de viridi baldequino *SelPlAdm.* I 15. **b** **1494** fit unum baldachinum pro papa album..latitudinis unius et altitudinis duarum cannarum, habens pendalia de carmusino *Conc.* III 638b.

baldemonia [etym. dub.], baldmoney (*Meum*) or (?) gentian.

valdemonia vel ~ia similis est silphio; ..radicibus utimur, G. et A. *baldemoyne Alph.* 189.

baldrea, ~eus [OF *baldrei*, *baudrei*], baldric, ornamental belt. **b** belt with hook for bending cross-bows. **c** belt for pulling bell.

1203 regalia nostra sc. ..tunicam, pallium, dalmaticam, baudream, sandalia *Pat* 35a; **1205** baldredum de..samitto cum kathmathis *Ib.* 55a. **b** **1212** pro duabus arbalastis.. et ij baldredis *Pipe Ir.* 46; **1221** fieri facias iiij bonos ~eos cum bonis crokis *Cl* 452; **1252** baudreos ad balistas nostras *Liberate* 28 m. 2; **1263** balistas..cum †bandereis [l. baudereis] *Reg. Heref.* 86; **1282** octo baliste cum quinque baudric' *TR Forest Proc.* 30 m. 36; bauderones pertinentes ad balistas *Ib.* 36*d*; c**1290** unam balistam cum baudrell' *IMisc* 49/40; **1306** iiij baldr' debiles..pro balistis..tentendis *KRAc* 486/20. **c** **1348** in iij bauderis novis emptis pro.. campanis *KRAc* 462/16 f. 5.

balducta v. balthuta.

baldus [cf. AS *bald*, OF *baud*], bold, spirited: **a** (of dogs); **b** (of men).

a **1210** iiij gupillerettos bonos et ~os *Pipe* 105; **1214** canes wulperettos et ~os *Ib.* 165. **b** s**1315** J. de Douglas, miles ~us et cautelosus *Lanercost* 231.

1 balea v. 2 baillium.

2 balea [Fr. *balai*], broom, besom.

1335 pro xl ~eis [*corr. from* besmes]..emptis..pro eisdem granariis mundandis, capiendo pro ~ea [*corr. from* besme] xx d. *KRAc* 19/3 m. 7.

3 balea [cf. Balearis], sling.

slynge, funda, bala, ..*staff slynge*, balia, fundibalista *PP.*

baleare [OF *balaier*], to sweep.

1260 terram subtus eum ~eari et aquam frigidam projici fecit *JustIt* 911 r. 8.

2 to raze, straik (in measuring grain).

1335 de cxxxviij quar. avene receptis..per mensuram Angl', videlicet iij bus. ~eatis et quarto cumulato sine avantagio *KRAc* 19/3 m. 1.

balearicus, discharged as from a sling.

balearica tela nefandi / hostis FRITH. 313.

Balearis, Balearic (stock epithet of sling or siege-engine). **b** (sb. n.) sling, siege-engine.

deiciuntur muri fundis ~ibus ingentia saxa rotantibus DEVIZES 34v; assint..funde ~es [*gl.*: a loco] NECKAM *Ut.* 104. **b** crates, ~e [*gl.*: *perers*] et cetere machine *Ib.*; *a staffe slynge*, baliare *CathA.*

baleina, balena, baleria v. balaena. balenaria v. balingera. balesium v. valisium. balesius v. balasius. balest- v. ballist-.

baletta, ~us [cf. bala], small bale.

1440 pro..iij balett' panni continentibus xxj pannos *Port Bk. Southampt.* 84; **1443** per liberacionem sex ballettorum walde *Cl* 293 m. 19*d*; **1461** habuerunt in dicta galea xxiiij balas et duas baletas carricatas in portu Scluse (*Chanc. Proc.*) *Prejudice & Promise* 185.

balia v. 2 baillium, 3 balea.

balidinus [? *infl. by* balzanus], dun or (?) piebald.

nomina colorum..~us, *hryte* ÆLF. *Gl.*; **1236** equum ~um *Cl* 384.

balidus, dun, dark brown.

~us, **9..** *dun*, ..**10..** *hrut* WW; **1390** pro j equo ballido *Ac. H. Derby* 5.

balignus v. balaena. balileatorium v. balneatorius.

balingera [? cf. balaena], balinger, (?) whale-boat.

1374 Francigenis per balangeram nostram captis *Reg. Rough* 189; **1379** due naves, due bargie et due ~e munite et arraiate pro guerra (*Pat*) *RParl* III 391a; s**1383** hostes armaverunt v vasa bellica que balingarie appellantur WALS. *YN* 338; **1403** cum..bargiis, balenariis et aliis navigiis (*DipDocE* 362) *Foed.* VIII 308; c**1435** in vj remis longis pro predicta ~a regis ordinata una cum uno velo vocato *mesansayll'* et uno velo vocato *fokesayll'* (*KRAc* 53/5 p. 17) *Sea Terms* II 79; **1444** capitaneus duarum balingarum (*sic*) *Pat* 458 m. 17*d.*

balist- v. balasius, ballist-. balkenus v. baldekinus. balla v. bala, ballote.

ballada [cf. Prov. *balada*], a form of dance music.

ab hoc [quinto]..modo proveniunt hoketi omnes, rondelli, ~e, coree, cantifractus HAUDLO 402.

ballardus v. 2 baselardus.

1 ballare [OF *baler*], to separate chaff and grain by shaking. **b** to tremble.

ipsius [androchie] etiam interest ventare, vannare vel ballare *Fleta* 173. **b** *to quake*, ~are, tremere *CathA.*

2 ballare [βάλλειν], to shoot.

librillis, telis, balistis undique ballant / Anglis obstare ELMH. *Metr. Hen. V* 271.

ballaria [βαλλάριον], campion (*Lychnis*).

lichitus, quam Latini genicularem i. bellariam vocant, florem habet similem viole *Alph.* 102.

ballastagium, ballast due.

1606 concedimus prefatis gardiano et assistentibus portus, Anglice *the harbor*, de Dovor' predict'..omnia et singula cranag', slusag', ballastag' harborag'..que antehac debita ..fuerunt *Pat* 1700 No. 1.

ballastum, ~rum [? ME], ballast.

1444 venit cum dicta navi in portum de Dersyngham et ibidem quiescens projecit ballastrum extra dictam navem videlicet zabulon' et arenam *BBAdm.* I 273; **1462** de firma pro licencia capiend' et abcariand' balast' pro navibus ibidem applicantibus *DLMinAc* 639/10376.

1 ballatio, dancing.

si quis balationes ante ecclesias sanctorum fecerit, .. tribus annis peniteat BART. EXON. *Pen.* 90.

2 †ballatio [? f.l. *for* bullatio], knob.

~io, *cnop GlC* B 51; **9..** balatio, *crop* WW.

ballebeta [Gael. *baile biataigh*], ballibetagh.

c1606 ~a continet 4 quartas sive villas; villa, Anglice *a balleboe*, 4 petias sive tatas et octo villatas; in petia communiter sunt 60 acre *Anal. Hib.* XII 85; terre numerantur per ~as, quartas et villatas *Ib.* 89.

ballena v. balaena.

†ballenrum, (?) genital organ or for *balzenum*, white patch.

equus ejus..ad dedecus suum dedecorabitur desuper †ballenro BRACTON 147b.

balleuca v. banleuca. ballia, ~ata, ~atus v. bailli-. ballidus v. balidus.

ballista (balista) [CL < βάλλειν], siege-catapult.

~a, *staefliðre GlC* B 8; ballistra, genus est machinae unde excutiuntur aste *Erf.* 2. 270. 21; ~is et petrariis capita interemptorum in castra Francorum emittentes W. MALM. *GR* IV 361; rex..~is et aliis machinis..oppidum expugnare aggressus est RIC. HEX. *Stand.* 40b; quod igitur a ~a tormentum majus exspectes? GIR. *IK* I 4.

2 crossbow (*cf. arcubalista, arbalista*).

balista, *gelocen boge* ÆLF. *Gl.*; **s1066** [dux Normannorum] pedites in fronte locavit sagittis armatos et ~is W. POIT. II 16 p. 184; **1205** notum facio..me recepisse..xxxij ~as cornatas ad j pedem et v ~as ad ij pedes et ij ~as ad tornum et j magnam ~am ad turnum (*Lit.*) *Pipe 8 John* p. xxvij; **1213** in quadam ~a de cornu ad stritum..cooperienda cordubano *Misae* 230; **s1215** capite spiculo ~e terebrato.. interiit WEND. II 116; **1224** (v. arcus 1d); **c1224** una balissa ad troil' [cf. trochlea] *Chanc. Misc.* 10/13/2; **1233** iij ~e ad troyel *KRMem.* 12 r. 8; **1246** iiij ~as ligneas et viij de cornu ad turnum.., xiiij de cornu sine telariis *Cl* 446; **1253** ~am Turonicam *Cl.* 173; **c1282** una ~a ad viz' [cf. vicia], due ~e ad duos pedes, quinque ~e ad unum pedem *TR Forest Proc.* 30 m. 36; **1284** provideat cccc baculos de taxo Yspanica pro ~is faciendis et cccc nuces et cccc claves et cccc stripodia et c baudreas et cc pecias de balena, j miliare de nervis, c milia de quarellis ad ~as duorum pedum et c milia de quarellis ad ~as unius pedis *Cl* 102 m. 11; **1298** unius ingenii facti pro ~is de vice tendendis *Pipe* 143 r. 23; caveant..a tensione balestrarum..et similibus GAD. 101 v. 2; **1306** una ~a de tour de cornu, j viz pro eadem tendenda.., ij ~e de ifo.., ij ~e de omello *KRAc* 486/20; **1337** xl telaria, xl nuces, xl clavos, duo milia nervorum, xxij strers, duo vicz, ..cornu, filum et carbones..pro factura ~arum *Cl* 158 m. 26; rex [Morwid]..~am suam tendens omnes suas sagittas emisit ad bestiam *Eul. Hist.* II 245 (cf. G. MON. III 15); **1429** pro reparacione balestarum regis *ExchScot* 511; ~a, *awblast, arowblaste* WW; **1535** Ligures sagittarios, qui arcubus utebantur quos ~as vocant P. VERG. XIX 375.

ballistare, ~ere, to shoot with a crossbow.

premisit pedites committere bella sagittis / et balistantes inserit in medio G. AMIENS *Hast.* 338 (cf. ib. 411); **s1303** viriliter se defendebant, ~endo circumquaque et lapides projiciendo *Ann. Ed. I* 484.

ballistaria (balist-), crossbow service.

1203 de xx s. pro serjanteria ~ie *Pipe* 227; **1219** Henricus Balistarius tenet..c acras terre per serjaunteriam ~ie [cf. ballistarius b] *Fees* 254; **12..** tenent totam Geveldale per balisteriam ad castrum Eboraci *Ib.* 350; **1235** de rege tenuit ..per servicium balistar' *ExcRFin* I 273.

ballistarius (balist-), crossbowman. **b** crossbow-maker. **c** man in charge of crossbows.

Walterus ~ius *DB* I 162; terre Gisleberti Balastarii *Ib.* II 444; trecenti loricati cum..~iis LANFR. *Ep.* 35. 534C; ~ii et sagittarii dirigebant spicula ORD. VIT. IX 13; **1212** in liberationibus ~iorum peditum *Pipe* 47; **s1235** exercitum de militibus et balastariis *Ann. Dunstable* 142; **c1250** nullus clericus ructuariis vel balestariis aut hujusmodi viris sanguinis preponatur *Conc. Syn.* 647 (cf. *Conc. Lateran.* IV 18: rottariis aut balistariis); **1261** secum ducat ~ios equites quotquot habere poterit de bono apparatu *Cl* 496; **1262** viginti ~ii pedites commorantes in municione castri Dovor' *Cl* 76; **1277** rotulus vadiorum ~iorum equitancium qui retenti fuerunt ad vadia regis *KRAc* 3/17; **s1192** rex..duos statuit ~ios quorum unius officium est tendendi, alterius jugiter pila jaciendi TREVET 144; **s1199** ~ius ..telum e castro dirigens regem..vulneravit *Meaux* I 335; **1386** galeas bene armatas..de uno patrono, ..xxx balastariis (*DipDoc* E 309) *Foed.* VII 521; **1490** vibrellarios et ~ios (*TreatyR*) *Ib.* XII 464. **b** **1229** mandatum est constabulario Dovr' quod omnes balistas regis lesas et deterioratas in Castro Dovr' que reparacione indigent liberari faciat Willelmo..~io regis ad ipsas reparandas *Cl* 181; **12..** Henricus ~ius tenet c acras terre..per servicium faciendi balistas *Fees* 386; **1266** in tribus duodenis baculorum de taxo emptorum ad officium ~ii *ExchScot* 5; hic ~ius, qui facit balistas WW. **c** **1222** pro domo reparanda in qua ~ius est qui servat balistas *Ac. Build. Hen. III* 44.

ballistere v. ballistare.

ballistrix, crossbowman's wife or (?) dancer (*cf.* OF *balerisse*).

1288 Johannette Balistrici de Vascon' redeunti ad partes suas de dono regis viij s. *Ac. Wardr. TRBk* 201 p. 63.

ballium, ~ius, balliv- v. baill-.

ballote [βαλλωτή], black horehound (*Ballota*) or (?) garlic (? by conf. of *prasion* and *prason*).

9.. †balla loca, †prasinum [l. prasium] WW; polloten, *craue lec Gl. Durh.*; multi dicunt ~e et multi marrubium nigrum *Alph.* 121.

1 ballum, ball.

9.. ~um, *poper* WW.

2 †ballum, (?) for **batallum,** clapper.

c1148 nec ad grangias campanas habeant, sed lignea ~a ad convocandos fratres (*Inst. Sempr.*) *MonA* VI 946 xxxix.

†balna, (?) bale.

1413 cum equis, harnesiis, ~is, manticis, bouges (*RScot* II 207b) *Foed.* IX 48.

balnea v. balaena, balneum.

balneare, to bathe (trans.); **b** (passive); **c** (reflexive).

[oves] balneat egrotas, exudat flumine lotas R. CANT. *Malch.* II 437; [Cordeilla] precipiens ut patrem..infirmum fingeret, ~aret, indueret, foveret G. MON. II 12; **1279** [debet] †balinare [l. balniare] dominum et aquam portare, et calefacere ad idem (*Inq.*) *Dom. S. Paul* lxxxiii; **1290** venatori regine exeunti curiam apud Tillebiri..cum canibus suis ad balneand' ipsos ibidem *Ac. Wardr.* (*Chanc. Misc.* 4/4) f. 59. **b** **1072** sic ~eentur qui volunt ~eari ut duobus diebus ante dominicam Nativitatem sint omnes ~eati LANFR. *Const.* 91; in jure ubi grus cocta fuit eum [accipitrem] ~eari facias et curabitur ADEL. *CA* 12; frequenter †bannearis H. LOS. *Ep.* 16; ~eari renui ob fetorem odoris sulphurei GREG. *Mir. Rom.* 12; senes sunt ~eandi in aqua dulci temperati caloris BACON IX 96; consueverunt..quater in anno..~eari *Cust. Westm.* 155; **s1426** rex suscepit ordinem militarem..cum triginta septem tironibus secum ~iatis AMUND. I 10 (cf. balneum 1b). **c** in Dominico.. panem non faciunt..nec ~eant se THEOD. *Pen.* II viii 1; ministri vel pueri se radant ac ~eent *RegulC* 47; **s1190** Fredericus..imperator..prosiliit in aquam ad ~eandum se *G. Ric. I* II 89; Fredericus..in quodam flumine Armenie.. se ~eans extinctus est HIGD. VII 24.

2 to bathe (intr.), take a bath, swim.

aquarius quando rex ~eat [capiat] iiii d. *Domus Reg.* 133; **s1190** quum [Fredericus]..~eando attigisset ulteriorem ripam R. NIGER 98; **1195** solet ~eare et piscari in aqua *CurR PR* 114; **c1330** poterunt..doceri..de modo balniandi *Cust. Cant.* 11; **1350** ne quis ~eat (*sic*) in aqua juxta fossatum Turris (*LBLond* F) *MGL* I 579.

balnearius [CL], concerned w. bathing. **b** (sb. m.) bath attendant. **c** (sb. n. or f.) bath-house.

in usu fratrum ~io camerarius conducet quendam ministrum, qui procuret administrationem balneatoriam cum ministro ablutorii *Chr. Abingd.* II 389. **b** **1376** tres lavendarii et ~ius..custodient..fratres in cameris *Lit. Cant.* III 4. **c** ~ium vel thermarium, *bæðhus* ÆLF. *Sup.*; duo lavatores in ~io *Cust. Westm.* 74; hostis antiquus.. in montis supercilio ~eum lapideum..construxit *NLA* (*Cuthb.*) I 217; **1483** in stipendio servientis in balneria *Comp. Swith.* 379.

balneaticum, bath-money.

captura, ..ubi sedet capturarius qui ~um exigit *GlC* C 181.

balneatio, bathing.

per medicinas extrinsecas sicut sunt inunctiones et ~ones BACON IX 12.

balneator [CL], bath attendant. **b** bather.

1460 balniator [recepit] ij d. *DCCant* DE 30. **b** **s1330** equus..se projecit in aquam ut -or *Ann. Paul.* 353.

balneatorius, concerned w. bathing. **b** (sb. n.) bath, bath-house.

Chr. Abingd. II 389 (v. balnearius a). **b** duobus servientibus ~ii *Cust. Cant.* I 63; licenciam..exeundi ut ad sartoriam aut balniatorium *Ib.* 84; capellam etiam..cum ~io ac aliis necessariis *Croyl.* 53; *bath*, balneum, balnearium, †balileatorium *PP*.

balneatrix, bath attendant (*f.*).

1302 [receptavit] in tercia domo unam balniatricem (*St. Ives*) *Law Merch.* I 84.

balneria v. balnearium. balneta v. balaenetta.

balneum [CL < βαλανεῖον], **~ea,** bath. **b** bath of knighthood (*cf. balneare 1b* s1426).

~eum, *stofa GlC* B 56; habet..fontes calidos..et ex eis fluvios ~earum calidarum omni aetati et sexui..accommodos BEDE *HE* I 1; **864** (11c) in illo famoso urbe qui nominatur et calidum ~eum, *þæt is æt þæm hatum baðum CS* 509; balnea Bathonie ferventia tempore quovis / egris festina sepe medentur ope NECKAM *DS* V 725; ut..ad ~eas veniamus BELETH *RDO* 114. 119; fiat ~eum in aqua marina vel in aquis sulfureis artificialibus GAD. 87 v. 2; encatisma est ~eum particulare sicut fit in dissinteria quando patiens sedet in decoctione aliquarum herbarum *SB* 20. **b** creantur et alio modo milites videlicet per ~eum, qui modus observatur in Anglia et aliis regnis ubi regnat pax UPTON 8; milites ~ei qui multis ~eorum et vigiliarum ceremoniis adhibitis..creati fuerunt solummodo in principum baptismo, nuptiis vel coronatione CAMD. *Br.* 140.

2 (w. *Marie*) *bain Marie* (alch.).

pone [Mercurium] in ~eo Marie et ibi dimittatur donec totum in aquam dissolvatur CUTCL. *LL* 6.

balsamare, to perfume. **b** to embalm.

virgo veris opes balsāmat oris odore GARL. *Epith.* VI 263. **b** mummia est quidam fructus qui invenitur in sepulcris corporum ~atorum *Alph.* 121.

balsamensis, balmy.

swete, armonicus, ~is, ..dulcis *CathA*.

balsamita, mint (*Mentha*).

abrotanum, ~a, salvia GILB. II 97. 2; ~a, ..sisimbrium, menta aquatica..A. *horsminte*, G. *mentastre Alph.* 19.

balsamiticus, balmy.

ossa..odorem spirabant suaviter fragrantem et ~um J. GLAST. 160.

†balsamitus (? ~icus), balmy.

donec totum corpus..~ito unguine inficeret W. MALM. *GP* I 66 p. 123; pretiosi et ~iti liquoris tres guttas *Eul. Hist. Annot.* III 22.

balsamum, ~us, balsam, balm (esp. as ingredient of chrism).

unctio que fit chrismate..propter abundantiam gratie duos liquores mixtos habet, oleum scilicet et ~um, oleum conscientie, ~um fame GIR. *GE* I 4; deinde misceatur [oleo] ~um ab episcopo *Offic. Sal.* 13 p. 178; **1323** ~o..indigemus pro ordinibus et aliis sacramentis..celebrandis *Lit. Cant.* I 109; illa famosissima vinea..de qua stillat ~us S. SIM. *Itin.* 57; **1377** ad custodiendum corpus regis a putrefaccione cum ~o et aliis unguentis et oleis *KRAc* 398/9 f. 23 v; nec pro crismate vel baptismo vel ~o..quicquam exigatur WYCL. *Sim.* 80; ~um gummi est *SB* 12.

balsamus, balsam tree.

balsamus eximii guttas desudat odoris NECKAM *DS* VIII 35; dicitur..~us arbor; ~um, destillans umor GERV. TILB. III 78; quidam..liquores de quibusdam arboribus..egrediuntur, ut ~us et therebitina BART. ANGL. XIX 49; balsamus est arbor, sunt balsama dicta liquores GARL. *Syn.* 1581D; xilobalsamum est lignum ~i *SB* 44.

1 †balsis, tetter (skin-disease).

~is, *teter GlC* B 6.

2 balsis v. 2 balus.

†balteo, (?) bench-cover.

14.. ~o, A. *a bancker* WW.

balteus, ~um [CL], belt, girdle, strap. **b** (fig.). **c** belt for bending crossbow. **d** belt as emblem of knighthood.

~eum, lorum *GlC* B 37; baltheus bullifer et diadema regni ac diversa ornamentorum gloria ALDH. *VirgP* 9; superhumerale strictum erat baltheo BEDE *Tab.* 474; vestes sacerdotis sint ibi..cingulum, sive tropheum, sive zona, sive ~eum NECKAM *Ut.* 119; **1384** pro uno baltheo serico vendito *Ac. Durh.* 424; in baltheo empto pro vexillo S. Cuthberti portando *Ib.* 425. **b** **a1150** totius jocunditatis ~eo desideramus accingi OSB. CLAR. *Ep.* 23 p. 97; **1171** carnalis insolentie motus..cilicio et jugis continentie ~eo cohibere P. BLOIS *Ep.* 27. 93D. **c** **1257** de x balistis ligneis viij balth'..et aliis appendiciis suis *MinAc* 1094/11 r. 4. **d** quem [Ethelstanum]..premature militem feceret, donatum chlamyde coccinea, gemmato baltheo W. MALM. *GR* II 133; **s1247** ipsum dominus rex cum aliis commilitonibus baltheo militari insignivit M. PAR. *Maj.* IV 644; **s1297** quidam comes..Willelmum [le Waleis] militari ~eo precinxit, faciens de predone militem, tanquam de corvo cygnum *Ann. Angl. & Scot.* 384; **s1323** degradatus est..: et sic vicissim discinctus est ~eo militari WALS. *HA* I 169.

balthuta, buttermilk, curds.

tenuclae..vel ~ae lactis sextario GILDAS *Pen.* 1; **10..** †baptua, *syring* WW; *posset*, balducta, effrotum *PP*; †bedulta, A. *possyt* WW; *a crudde*, balducta, coagillum, .. *a possett*, affrotrum, balducta *CathA*.

baltinus v. blatteus. 1 balus v. bala.

2 †balus [? cf. boia], iron fetter.

~us, *isernfestor GlC* B 38; **9..** †balsis, *isenfeter* WW.

baluus v. baillivus 1b. balva v. valva.

balzanifer, bearer of Templar standard (*cf. balzanus* 3).

s1237 cecidit..illustris miles Templarius..R. de Argentomio, ea die balcanifer M. PAR. *Maj.* III 405; **s1246** primicerius eorum et signifer, quem balcaniferum vocant *Ib.* IV 525.

balzanus [cf. OF *baucenc*; It. *balzano*], 'bausond', piebald (horse).

1207 reddidit j equum bauzanum *Cl* 92a; **1214** pro j [equo] baio baucano *Ib.* 168b; **a1220** legavit..runcinum baucennum *FormA* 423; **1242** pro pane et custodia cujusdam †bucstani commorantis apud Westm' *Liberate* 16 m. 6; **1265** equus balcanus (*RHosp.*) *Manners* 58; **1311** unius equi favii badii bausanni (*Muster Berw.*) *CalScot* III p. 394; **1313** equum nigrum bauceanum *KRAc* 14/15 r. 4; **1313** pro restauro..unius equi nigri baustandi *Cl* 130 m. 12; **1316** pro restauro..unius equi rubii liardi bauszandi..unius equi sori bauszanni..et unius equi badii bauszandi *RGasc* IV 1679; **1318** unius equi..sori bausianni *Cl* 135 m. 13.

2 'bauson', badger.

1322 possunt..fugare ad cervos, damas, †bauceum [? l. baucen', i.e. baucenos], cattas (*Ch. Haltemprice*) *MonA* VI 521; **1355** item ij bagges de pelle †bancini [l. baucini] *MunCOx* 132.

3 *beauséant*, black and white standard of Templars.

s1250 hinc dilacerabatur oloflamma, suppeditabatur balcanum M. Par. *Maj.* VI 195; bausanum vexillum assumpserunt Capgr. *Hen.* 158.

†bamba, bed.

14.. ∼a, lectus WW.

bambillus, horse-clog (Essex).

1498 pro factura pro duobus ∼is vocatis *horscloggs* (*MinAc Hen. VII* 691) *MonA* IV 564.

ban v. 1 bannum.

bana, ∼um [AS *bana*], bane, cause of death.

1195 pro stulta commendatione ∼e cujusdam occisi *Pipe* 6; **1224** recepit..x sol. de ∼is in comitatu de Norfulk *LTRMem* 6 r. 14*d*; **1230** vicecomes reddit compotum..de j. m. de precio unius ∼e *Pipe* 149: **1244** englescheria..presentatur de omnibus infortuniis unde ∼e non sunt presentes *JustIt* 201 r. 1; **c1320** [equus] qui fuit ∼um predicti garcionis *MGL* I 98.

banar- v. baner-.

banasteria, basket-bearer (f.) (Norm.).

a1190 queque banesteria [debet habere] vj d. *Act. Hen. II* II 329.

banastrum [OF *banastre*], basket for charcoal (Devon).

a1307 in iij baniastr' emptis pro carbonibus cariandis ad fornellos *KRAc* (*Mines*) 260/19 m. 6; in viij paribus banastr' *Ib.* m. 8; **1325** pro banastr', iiij d.; ..pro mina xx d. *LTR Mem* 95 r. 128.

banausus [βάναυσος], practising a handicraft.

dicuntur..bannausi qui naturaliter seu corporaliter operantes opere suo maculant corpus Ockham *Dial.* 794; **c1472** talis vocatur banna-usus, quasi in fornace bona sua consumens *BB Househ.* 86.

banca v. 1 & 2 bancus.

1 bancagium [cf. 1 bancus b], rent for dunes (C.I.).

1331 quiquidem denarii redduntur annuatim domino regi ..pro domibus suis bancam juxta (*sic*) maris edificatis, et vocatur iste redditus ∼ium *Ext. Guern.* 63.

2 bancagium [OF *banchage*; cf. 2 bancus 5a], stall-due (Gasc.).

1254 pro quolibet porco, si ibidem occidat et vendat, [debet] unum den. de ∼io; similiter pro vacca et bove duos den. *Pat* 66 m. 5*d* (*cf. RGasc* I 546).

bancale, ∼ium [OF *banqual*], banker, bench-cover.

†945 (13c) unam cortinam et unum ∼e concedo *CS* 812; **a1090** sedilia refectorii, capituli, claustri tegantur ∼ibus Lanfr. *Const.* 127; **c1170** dedit..ij cortinas, unum †baucale et sellam suam *Chr. Rams.* 85; **c1170** cum una cortina et uno banccalio *Reg. St. Benet Holme* 162; **c1330** cortinas, tapeta, bankalia ceteraque ornamenta *Cust. Cant.* I 101; **1398** duo paria ∼ium cum octo carrelibus ejusdem forme *Cl* 242 m. 10; **1466** ij ∼ia de Aras *Pat* 515 m. 13.

bancarium, ∼ius [cf. OF. *banquier*], banker, bench-cover.

1284 banquaria: item pro uno tapeto (*KRAc* 91/3) *Arch.* LXX 30; debet camerarius..disponere..ut camere tapetis et banqueriis ornentur *Fleta* 70; **1290** j bankerus in aula *Reg. Wint.* II 705; **1303** de uno bankario de wourstede *Ac. Exec. Ep. Lond.* 57; **1329** pro bancoriis aule comitis de Carric, ij pecias [panni radiati] *ExchScot* 229; **1443** j bankerium rubei et blodii coloris *Cant. Coll. Ox.* I 7; ∼ium, *a bankere* WW.

bancarius [cf. 2 bancus 5b], banker, money-changer.

1436 per solucionem factam Johanni de Pyno, ∼io de Bruges, pro negociis..domini regis in curia Romana perficiendis *ExchScot* 676; **c1516** aliis mercatoribus vel banchariis Romanam curiam sequentibus *Form. S. Andr.* I 115.

bancatum, bank, exchange.

1497 procuratorem..ad obligandum nos..in quibuscumque Curie Romane officiis aut quibuscunque mercatorum Flandrie aut Rome ubilibet aliis banchis seu banchatis, et specialiter..in bancho Nycholai Pagane quod dicitur Mostronense *Reg. Aberbr.* II 314.

banceus v. 2 bancus 1.

banchetum, banker, bench-cover.

a1100 xxxij dosseta lanea, lj ∼a *Lib. Eli.* II 139; scamnaque banchetis sunt nuda domusque tapetis R. Cant. *Malch.* III 63.

bancinus v. balzanus. bancorium v. bancarium.

1 bancus, ∼a [cf. AS *banca*, ON *banki*], bank, hill, mound. **b** dune (C.I.).

1246 ex quo..satisfecerint ei de †banco [(?) l. bauco; cf. balcus] et herbagio que ipsi consumpserunt in terra..que pertinet ad warectum instantis autumpni [*Herts*] *Cl* 446; **a1250** unam acram..terre super ∼um in villa..de Neuton.. et duas domos sub predicto ∼o *Reg. S. Bees* 157; **a1262** cujus [lande] una extremitas buttat usque ad bankam *Cart. Cockersand* 122; **1375** tenetur servare cursum aque de Wythem Streme infra ∼as ne aqua superabundet (*Anc. Indict.*) *Pub. Works* I 260; **1378** defendet dictos ∼os fossati ..a bestiis nocivis *MunCOx* 155. **b 1247** debent reddere.. de ∼a et hoga xx sol. Turonenses *Cl* 546 (= *Ext. Guern.* 26; cf. 1 bancagium); **1274** de incremento pro communa habenda in ∼o maris (*Chanc. Misc.* 10/5/2) *S. Jers.* II 32.

2 bancus, ∼um, ∼a [OF *banc* < Frk.], bench, seat.

1141 recepit ∼um et buffetum et ij mensas *Dom. S. Paul* 136; **c1160** unum †branchum tornatile *Ib.* 132; duo ∼a tornatilia *Ib.* 137; **1162** pro ∼o ad scaccarium tenendum *Pipe* 26; **1194** pro banceis emptis ad scaccarium baronum *Pipe* 177 (cf. 2 infra); forte sedens banco caveas pede tundere bancum D. Bec. 891; nondum a ∼o surrexerat Gir. *JS* 4 p. 256; sedit super ∼um et cepit garrulare cum astantibus Eccleston *Adv. Min.* 120; **c1280** quod nullus.. armarium sive banchum vel aliud cum serrura..habeat *Cust. Cant.* I 36; **1288** juxta quam parietem est superior ∼us aule predicte *Rec. Norw.* II 10; debet patiens jacere in ∼o..et ibidem debent brachia ligari ad ∼um Gad. 130. 2; **c1340** ∼as et descas *FormOx* 178.

2 bench in lawcourt, hence the court itself.

11.. defendent eam [terram] infra quatuor ∼os hundredi (*Cart. Colchester* 171) *EHR* X 732; inter quatuor ∼os regis (*Ib.* 227) *Ib.*; **1269** fuerunt infra quatuor ∼os et predicte loquele interfuerunt *AssizeR Northumb* 196; **a1291** personaliter infra ∼um vocata coram justiciario Cestrie concessit hanc donationem *Cart. Chester* 460; **1291** intravit infra ∼um et cepit rotulos de essoniis (*PlRCP*)*SelCKB* V cxviii; **1324** cum..securi fuerunt de itinere habendo..∼um cum sedilibus in aula..Turris..construxerunt *MGL* II 287; **14..** primo dicant ipsi sedentes per quatuor ∼os et postea omnes astantes *Cust. Fordwich* c. 2.

3 court of king's justices, normally held at Westminster, developing into Common Pleas. **b** Court of King's Bench, dealing with pleas nominally held *coram rege* (*cf. SelCKB* IV pp. xxvi *seqq.*, cxx; 1245 and 1252 *infra* may refer to 3a). **c** king's court in Ireland.

coram justitiis domini regis in ∼o residentibus Glanv. XI 1; **1194** dies fuit datus ei in ∼o apud Radinge in itinere justiciariorum *CurR RC* I 42; **1205** justiciarii de ∼o recordantur quod R. ..et R. ..venerunt in curiam domini regis coram justiciariis in ∼o *CurR* III 334; **1244** eligantur.. duo justitiarii in ∼o (*Provisio Magnatum*) M. Par. *Maj.* IV 367; **s1259** de placito de dote quod est coram bancho *Ann. Burton* 481; **1259** custodi brevium et rotulorum regis de ∼o *Cl* 450; [rex] habet etiam curiam et justitiarios in ∼o residentes qui cognoscunt de omnibus placitis de quibus auctoritatem habent cognoscendi Bracton 105b; habet eciam curiam suam et justiciarios suos residentes..in ∼o apud Westmonasterium *Fleta* 66; **s1265** placita de ∼o, que solebant deduci apud Westmonasterium *Leg. Ant. Lond.* 84; **1300** hoc esset contra formam Magne Carte, in qua continetur quod communia placita teneantur in certo loco, hoc est in ∼o (*CoramR* 124) *Abbr. Plac.* 283; **1291** in..bordis de quercu..emptis ad communem ∼um justiciariorum in magna aula predicti palacii [Westmonasterii] *Pipe* 136 r. 29*d*; **1327** coram W. de B. et sociis suis de communi ∼o *RParl. Ined.* 147; **1338** item in ∼o Communi, que (*sic*) est curia regis de placitis terrarum et tenementorum secundum leges Anglie placitatis *Hosp. in Eng.* 203; ∼us Communis quia communia placita inter subditos ex jure nostro quod commune vocant in hoc disceptantur nomen habet Camd. *Br.* 142. **b 1245** rex assignavit magistrum R. ..ad residendum in ∼o regis London' una cum aliis justiciariis ibidem residentibus *Cl* 302; **1252** constitutus est justiciarius ad sedendum ad ∼um regis London' et ad placitandum regi ibidem *Cl* 249; **1282** visum fuit justiciariis de ∼o r[egis] ..et similiter justiciariis de magno ∼o (*CoramR* 71) *Abbr. Plac.* 274; **1338** et in ∼o Regis; et est curia principalis Anglie, in qua curia omnia placita transgressionum et felonie et conspiracie placitantur *Hosp. in Eng.* 204; introducendo ∼um regis, ejus judicem vel placitum seculare in domum Domini Wycl. *Eccl.* 237; **c1402** in banco regis qui librat pondera legis Gower *CT* I 160; **s1393** ∼us regius et cancellaria translata fuerunt de Londoniis Eboracum Wals. *YN* 365; **1462** rex Edwardus..in propria persona in bancho suo regali Westmonasterii..proprium locum tenuit *Compilatio* 175; ∼us Regius, ita dictus quod rex ipse in eo praesidere solebat, Coronae placita tractat Camd. *Br.* 141. **c 1299** rex..justiciariis suis de ∼o Dublinie *BBC* 43.

4 free bench, widow's right of dower (*cf. francbancus*).

1217 quod uxores maritorum defunctorum habeant francum ∼um suum de terris sokemannorum *BNB* III 323 (*Kent*; cf. Bracton 309); **1241** Burga que fuit uxor Petri.. petit..medietatem manerii..sicut francum ∼um suum.. unde predictus Petrus..eam dotavit (*JustIt Kent*) *Gavelkind* 178; **1246** salvo..libero ∼o..matris sue *ChartR* 39 m. 14 (*London*); **1258** Innocenta in libera viduitate et ligia potestate sua concessit..liberum ∼um suum sive dotem *AncD* A 210 (*Kent*); **1260** [nomine dotis] vel liberi bangii *Cart. Osney* I 409; **1357** cum vir et uxor perquirunt tenementum aliquod in civitate predicta [Sar'] et vir moritur uxore superstite relicta, habeat ipsa uxor inde liberum quamdiu vixerit ∼um suum *Pat.* 251 m. 5; **1419** que habet francum ∼um suum et edificium receperit in bono statu, in eodem statu illud sustinebit *MGL* I 68.

5 a market stall (*cf.* 2 *bancagium*). **b** bank, money-changer's stall or office (*cf.* It. *banca, banco*).

a comes de Moritonio habet ibi [apud Eboracum]..ii ∼os in macello *DB* I 298. **b 1443** literas..per ∼um de Boromeis traditas Bekynton I 176; **s1402** in qua [sc. Roma].. quisque pecuniosus..ad sue promocionis effectum pecunias suas in mercatorum habuerat ∼o Ad. Usk 78; **1497** (v. bancatum); **1535** transmisi ad te per banchum A. de A. Hispani quicquid hactenus..corradere potui (T. Bedill) *Ep. Erasmi* XI 3058.

banda, ∼arius v. bend-. banderea v. baldrea. banditus v. bannire 2b.

bandum [*cf.* 1 bannum, banidum], small banner, pennon.

penone, lytyl baner, ∼um, pennum *PP*.

baneleuga v. banleuca.

banera, ∼ia, ∼ium [OF *banere*], banner, standard.

s1190 capta..civitate et ∼iis regis Anglie muris collocatis *Itin. Ric.* II 17; **1198** per servicium portandi ∼eram populi prosequentis per marinam *Fees* 11; **1212** per servicium ferendi banarium domini regis pedes infra iiij portus Anglie *Ib.* 104; **1208** pro auro ad ∼ias nostras..preparandas et.. pro ∼iis..illis depingendis *Cl* 109a; **1212** pro..xij penuncellis..et iiij ∼is platis ad opus [regis] *Pipe* 44; **c1215** homines de singulis parochiis cum penuncellis suis sequantur ∼iam aldermanni sui (*Collect. Lond.*) *EHR* XVII 728; **s1239** lxx milites capti sunt, quorum septem portabant ∼ia *Ann. Tewk.* 114; **1240** pro quadam ∼ia viridis coloris cum cruce aurea et gruibus aureis ex utraque parte.. oblata S. Edwardo *Liberate* 14 m. 2; **s1251** signa que vulgariter vexilla vel ∼e dicuntur M. Par *Min.* III 112; **s1315** Adam de Banastre.., quasi a rege jussus, ∼iam regis erexit *V. Ed. II* 214; **1496** eisdem..licentiam dedimus affigendi.. banneras nostras et insignia in quacumque..insula seu terra a se noviter inventis (*TreatyR* 176) *Foed.* XII 595; **1501** potestatem..navigandi..ad omnes partes..maris..sub banneris nostris *Pat.* 587 m. 20 (7).

baneretta, bannerette.

1466 pro serico pro baneretis pictis cum armis (*Invent. Fastolf*) *Paston Lett.* III 439.

banerettus, banneret, superior knight ranking next to baron; **b** (w. *miles*); **c** (*s. dub.*).

1264 cum ix ∼is cum xlviij militibus *KRAc* 3/2; **1288** receptus fuit dominus A. de Gavaston miles se altero tanquam ∼us ad feodum regis et robas sicut alii milites Vasconici *Ac. Wardr.* (*TRBk* 201) p. 70; **1293** ∼o Anglico pro vadiis suis..per diem iiij s. (*Pipe* 160) *RGasc* III p. cxli; **s1265** coadunatis..fere xx banerectis W. Guisb. 199 (= Knighton I 252; banarettis); **s1300** quod..irent de ∼is nostri exercitus cum sometariis..ut illos..salvarent *Ann. Ed. I* 441; **s1314** apud Bannokburne..ceciderunt..plures alii barones, ∼i et milites *G. Ed. II Bridl.* 46; **1339** ut statum et honorem teneat et continuet ∼i *Pat.* 201 m. 13; **s1345** multis..Francigenis interfectis, ..iij baronibus, xiij ∼is et multis militibus Avesb. 104b; ∼i, qui aliis baronetti, ..a baronibus secundi erant, quibus inditum nomen a vexillo Camd. *Br.* 138. **b 1260** faciant habere..duas robas sicut aliis militibus regis banericiis *Cl* 315; **1283** pro soldo xlj militum..de quibus erant septem banerici (*Liber B*) *Foed.* II 236; **1400** domini Radulfi Lumley militis ∼i *MunCOx* 278. **c 1386** vj lectos pro ∼is (*Testam.*) *FormA* p. 427.

baneria v. banera. banericus, ∼icius v. banerettus.

banerista, banneret.

s1380 numero integre armatorum mc, quorum d erant milites, xxvi banariste Fordun *GA* 189.

banerium v. banera. banesteria v. banasteria. bangius v. 2 bancus 4. baniastrum v. banastrum.

banidum [cf. bandum], badge (her.).

bage or bagge of armis, ∼um, bannudum *PP*.

banium v. 2 bannum. banker- v. bancarium.

banleuca [OF *banlieue*], banlieu, area of jurisdiction: **a** (Fr.); **b** (Eng.; *cf.* M. D. Lobel *Ecclesiastical Banleuca in England; Oxford Essays..to H. E. Salter* pp. 122–40).

a a1150 sergenteriam de bagnileuca Rothomagensi *Regesta* 381; **1153** Barbifluvium cum tali libertate quod per totam banleugam possit capere forisfactum suum *Ib.* 180; **1203** quod habeant communam in villa sua de Danfront et infra ∼am suam *Pat* 26; tam in villa de Faleis' quam extra villam infra benleucam *Ib.* 24b; **1236** de paduentiis..infra villam Burdegalie aut infra batleucam constitutis (*Pat*) *RL* II 11; **1313** infra terminos sue jurisdiccionis [sc. majoris Burdegale] que vulgo batleuca appellatur *RGasc* IV 1090; **1316** majores, jurati et communitas civitatis predicte [Burdegale] habere consueverunt batleugam civitatis ejusdem infra certos fines et limites circumquaque eandem civitatem tam per terram quam per aquam et infra eandem batleugam eisdem libertatibus..quas infra dictam civitatem habuerunt, uti et gaudere consueverunt *Ib.* 1603. **b 1171** infra burgum et extra usque ad terminos ∼arum ipsius burgi [*Maldon, Essex*] *BBC* 39; super omni eo quod infra leugam castro [de Tunebrige] circumjacentem est, que vulgo banleuga dicitur sive, ut dicatur Latinius, bannum leuge H. Bos. *Thom.* III 19; **1219** usque ad banleugam libertatis de Tunebrug' *Cl* 396a; quicquid est in villa S. Edmundi vel infra bannam leuccam de jure S. Edmundi est Brakelond 133; **1255** infra balleucam S. Edmundi *Cl* 103; **1233** infra baneleugam de Rames' nullatenus se intromittant *Cl* 287; **1286** abbas..clamat quamdam libertatem infra metas foreste, videlicet circa abbatiam suam de Ramеseye, quam vocat ∼am *Cart. Rams.* I 213; **a1300** assisa..capi debuit infra banleukam libertatis S. Johannis [Beverlacensis] *Meaux* II 154.

banna v. banleuca, 2 bannum.

bannagium [OF *banage*], a signorial impost (Norm.).

1202 Willelmum de Cortenay quietum esse faciatis de ∼o de hoc anno *RNorm* 67.

bannalis, jurisdictional (*cf. banleuca*).

a1190 molendina de Condeto [*Condé, Norm.*]..cum jure ∼is leuge molendinarie delationis *Act. Hen. II* II 362.

bannare v. bannire 2b. bannausus v. banausus. banneare v. balneare. banner- v. baner-. bannezare v. bannizare. bannialus v. bannitio. bannicus v. bannire 1b.

bannifer, banner-bearer (*v.* 1 *bannum*).

c**1360** clamant banniferi quod quisque clericus / tradatur carceri ut hostis publicus *Planct. Univ. Ox.* 83.

bannimentum, banishment (Fr.).

1279 cum..annullaverint ~um..quod in..Gombaldum ..fuerat promulgatum *RGasc* II 53; **1289** perdonamus.. banniamentum Arnaldi de A. ..banniti a toto ducatu *Ib.* 363; **1309** supplicavit nobis R.C. burgensis..Pontivi quod, cum ipse..minus juste bannitus existat, velimus sibi ~um predictum remittere *TreatyR* I 482.

bannire, ~are [cf. AS *bannan,* OF *banir*], to proclaim. **b** to levy (troops) by proclamation.

s**1233** eodem anno fuerunt itinerantes justiciarii in Cornubia; quorum metu omnes ad sylvas fugerunt: et ideo ~itum fuit ut omnes redirent ad pacem regis *Ann. Dunstable* 135. **b 1262** cum exercitu ~ito et multitudine armatorum tam Walensium quam aliorum qui non sunt ad fidem nec pacem regis *Pat* 77 m. 17*d*; **1270** Rex..Lewelino: ..intelleximus quod vos cum exercitu †bannico [l. ~ito] et multitudine armatorum..terras..in partibus vestris invadere proponitis *Cl* 235; **1271** Rex..Lewelino: ..intelleximus quod vos exercitum vestrum jam ~iri fecistis *Cart. Glam.* 760.

2 to lay (property) under ban, sequestrate (Gasc.). **b** to lay (persons) under ban, banish (*v. et. forisbannire*).

1252 cum comes in Vasconiam rediisset, ..terras quorundam ~ivit (*AncC* III 169) *RL* II 75; **1285** quod bajulus abbatis et sui servientes..~ire et pignorare possint..pro execucione officii sui *RGasc* II 271. **b 1186** Cremonensium, quos tanquam ~itos et publicos hostes imperii vestram decuit reverentiam evitare (*Lit. Teutonicorum*) DICETO *YH* II 45; **1266** inveniant fidejussionem..quod pacem..regni amodo servabunt..et..subeant..penitenciam secundum judicium ecclesie, exceptis ~itis quibus solus rex potest remittere (*Kenilworth* 14) *St. Realm* I 15; **1295** cum ~ire clericum extra regnum..idem sit in effectu quod et ipsum occidere, precipue cum taliter ~itus licite possit extra realem viam a quocumque occidi, petit..quod..nec bannetur clericus nec regnum abjurare cogatur *Conc. Syn.* 1146; **1303** sicut reus lese crimine majestatis perpetuo sit infamis et banditus *Reg. Carl.* II 50; **1313** major dictos B. et G. a villa predicta perpetuo ~ivit, licet..occasione..transgressionum predictarum ~iri nullatenus debuissent *RGasc* IV 1011; s**1326** rex Anglie exlegavit et ~ivit publice..uxorem suam HIGD. VII 42; ~iendo eum a civitate regia WYCL. *Ver.* III 231; s**1398** ducem..pro decem annis ~ivit a regno AD. USK 24; homines ~ati et (ut vocant) utlegati non possunt agere in aliquo foro *Praxis* 139.

bannitio, banishment.

1289 Arnaldum..occasione ~ionis..non molestent *RGasc* II 363; **1327** sub pena banniacionis et exilii *Lit. Cant.* I 220; c**1370** regina graviter sustinebat predictam ~ionem (J. BRIDL. *gl.*) *Pol. Poems* I 136; a**1350** in atrocibus delictis que ~ionem vel incarceracionem requirunt *Stat. Cantab.* 315; **1410** scolares..si hoc neglexerint ab universitate..per ~ionem ut membra putrida..abscidantur *StatOx.* 208; **1438** licet aliquis malefactor sic bannitus fuerit seu absque ~ione..captus extiterit *RScot* 308b.

bannizare, to banish.

1247 interfecimus..nostros etiam bannezatos (*Lit. Vicedom. Parmae*) M. PAR. *Maj.* VI 147 (=*Flor. Hist.* II 349: nostros quoque bannizatos).

bannoka [Gael. *bannach*], bannock.

panem sub cineribus vel prope cineres coctum, quem ~am (a vulgari Latinum fingendo) nostri appellitant MAJOR I 2.

bannonium [OF *banon*], open season for grazing (C.I.).

1300 averia diversorum tempore ~ii [*gl.*: i. tempore aperto] cepit et inparchavit *JustIt* 1158 r. 7.

bannudum v. banidum.

1 bannum [cf. bandum, baneria, bannifer], banner.

ban, *segn GlC* B 53; **1346** Scotorum banna surgunt, clamemus osanna (*Neville's Cross*) *Pol. Poems* I 42; c**1360** vexillo prodito ad domos properans / banno sic edito *ha wok* vociferans *Planct. Univ. Ox.* 87.

2 bannum, ~ium, ~a, ~us [cf. AS *gebann,* OF *ban* < Frk.], ban, proclamation (esp. of prohibition). **b** (breach of) regulation, restriction (Fr.). **c** exaction, imposition.

s**1074** papa synodo celebrata..~o interdixit clericis.. uxores habere S. DURH. *HR* 160; ad ~um regis [AS: *to cyniges gebanne*] (*Quad. Rect.*) *GAS* 444; ut omnis homo sit alii coadjutor..eorum qui ~um [AS: *gebodu*] hoc audiant (*Quad.*) *Ib.* 175; s**1229** ~um etiam in ecclesia publice proposuerunt quod nullus burgensium moleret ad molendina prioris *Ann. Dunstable* 121; **1231** rex..per ~um suum clamari fecit..quod..id fieri non permittat *Cl* 588; fiat ~us regis sub voce preconia..per hec verba quod nullus sit ita..audax quod..se moveat BRACTON 142; **1275** fuerunt ~i editi et puplicati ad ducendam lanam ad..partes transmarinas *Hund.* I 495; **1275** homines..cum gladiis et fustibus per plenum banium in eadem villa [de Sandwyco] levatum exierunt *SelCKB* I 13; **1279** contra proclamacionem et ~um interminacionis anathematis *Reg. Ebor.* 20; banna, *bane* [i.e. *proclamation*] *of a play PP.* **b** c**1160** recognovit quod nullum jus habebat..neque in terris, neque in vineis ..neque in incendio, neque in ~o, neque in furto (*Ch. Marmoutier*) *Act. Hen. II* I 322; **1315** cum nos in eadem villa [Marmande] ~um vinorum habeamus, videlicet quod in uno mense anni alia vina quam nostra vendi non debeant in eadem *RGasc* IV 1402. **c 1160** relaxavit eis abbas consuetudinem que vocatur ~um et consuetudinem.. allecium (*Ch. Fécamp*) *Act. Hen. II* I 227; **1203** salinas, quas habent in Oleronio..ut..possideant eas liberas et immunes ab omni ~o et consuetudine *RChart* 110; c**1218** ~um scotallorum per sacerdotes..prohibemus *Conc. Syn.* 64; **1239** sub excommunicationis pena et ~io decem milium marcarum (*Lit. Fred. Imp.*) M. PAR. *Maj.* III 633.

2 a ban on property, sequestration. **b** ban on person, exclusion, banishment.

a 1285 habeant..cogniciones feodorum suorum..et potestatem ponendi ~um in eis et pignorandi *RGasc* II 274; **1288** eidem..represaliarum seu ~i sentenciam et licenciam concedemus qua sibi licebit mercatores..de regno Anglie.. detinere quousque sibi..fuerit satisfactum (*Lit. Consulum etc. Bononiae*) *AncC* LV 10. **b 1273** habebit ~um per unum annum et unum diem secundum provisionem gilde *Rec. Leic.* I 113; **1289** cum A. ..pro raptu mulieris..bannitus existeret, ..remittimus dictum ~um *RGasc* II 417 (cf. bannimentum); **1309** eidem R. dictum ~ium..remittatis *TreatyR* I 482; **1415** rebelles, bannitos et proditores..quamcitius de rebellione, ~o aut proditione..constare poterit, ab imperio..et dominiis suis removebit *RParl* IV 97b.

3 marriage bann.

11.. interroget sacerdos ~a..sub hac forma (*Manuale Sal.*) *Mon. Rit.* I 52; c**1250** antequam fiat matrimonium per verba de presenti, in tribus diebus Dominicis aut festivis.. perquirat sacerdos..de legitimitate sponsi et sponse qui debent conjungi; ..sponsalia contrahentes abstineant sese a carnali copula ad invicem quousque matrimonium fuerit ~is precedentibus solemniter celebratum *Conc. Syn.* 643; cum ~um et trina denuntiatio in ecclesia fiat ante desponsationem BRACTON 307b; ~us et trina denunciatio *Fleta* 356; **1444** ~i inter eos tribus vicibus publice in ecclesia parochiali ..solempniter editi fuerunt et exacti *Pat.* 458 m. 15*d*; *sybreed* [i.e. *consanguinity*], banna *PP.*

banquerium v. bancarium. banum v. bana.

banus [Pers. *bān*], provincial governor.

si 'dolphinatus' sit nomen dignitatis, vel vocetur 'banus' sicut in Hungaria, certe in hoc non est vis UPTON 37.

†**bapis,** (?) tar, resin. **b** (?) banner, standard.

~is, *treuteru GlC* B 54; **9..** ~is, i. hortus vel *teru* WW. **b 9..** ~ys, *treuteru, bansegn* WW.

baptisma [βάπτισμα], baptism: **a** Christian; **b** non-Christian.

a nondum baptismate lotum ALDH. *VirgV* 679; cui.. tempore ~atis papa..Petri nomen imposuerat BEDE *HE* V 7; **735** homo quidam..alterius filium de sacri ~atis fonte elevans adoptavit sibi in filium BONIF. *Ep.* 33; sumeret ut sub eis sacram baptismatis undam ALCUIN *SS Ebor.* 195; unusquisque fidelium ~atis subit sacramentum ERIUG. *Per.* 611D; si irreprehensibiliter figurate baptizamus in aqua, licet illud ~a vetus, quod fuit hujus novi figura, in aqua fuerit ANSELM (*Praesc.* 4) II 228; nox..in qua et fides gentium et ~atis sacramentum et miraculorum Christi commendatur initium AILR. *Ed. Conf.* 787A; **1236** si..repugnat princeps..ecclesie, inobediens invenitur matri sue, que eum peperit de sacro fonte ~atis GROS. *Ep.* 23; qui nostrum ingressum sacro ~ate consecravit R. BURY *Phil.* 20. 248; postquam graciam ~atis susceperat BIRCHINGTON *Arch. Cant.* 1; ideo ~a illuminationis et regenerationis vocatus COLET *Sacr. Eccl.* 89. **b** Sarraceni..variis ~atibus et aliis cerimoniis sicut Judei utuntur BACON *Mor. Phil.* 194.

baptismalis, of baptism.

omnes fide Christi imbutos unda ~i lavit EADMER *Wilf.* 739B; terra..sancte ecclesie fundata est super aquas ~es NECKAM *DS* II 49; decimum lapidem ecclesie sue ~i..misit GIR. *RG* I 3; **1214** baptisterium habeatur in qualibet ecclesia ~i *Conc. Syn* 31 (= *EHR* XXX 290: ecclesia †baptizali); **1252** rogatus..quomodo hoc scivit quod dicta ecclesia constituta fuit ~is, dicit quod non aliter scit nisi quia in ea pueros baptizavit (*DC Lichf.*) *Arch. Soc. Derb.* V 152; c**1346** laus baptismalis violatur munere tristi *Pol. Poems* I 47; meretur ad minus tantam graciam quanta est gracia ~is BRADW. *CD* 387A; unitas ~is WYCL. *Chr. & Antichr.* 655; **1415** ecclesia..habet omnia signa parochialia, videlicet fontem ~em, campanile [etc.] *Reg. Bath* 207.

baptismaliter, with the grace conferred by baptism.

~er nullus credit nisi qui corporaliter per se suscipit sacramentum [sc. baptismi] NETTER *DAF* II 166v.

baptismatorium, font.

1446 pro rosyn et pyk cum aliis necessariis ad emendacionem ~ii *Fabr. York* 61.

baptismus, ~um [βαπτισμός], baptism.

purgatus maculis baptismi gurgite sacro ALDH. *VirgV* 1540; ~us..genere masculino et baptisma..neutro, ~um.. aeque neutro BEDE *Orth.* 2778; cum rex ipse cathecizatus fonte ~i cum sua gente ablueretur BEDE *HE* III 7; **735** de matrimonio commatrum, quarum filios in ~o suscepimus BONIF. *Ep.* 34; verus..~us constat non tam ablutione corporis quam fide cordis LANFR. *Corp. & Sang.* 424D; quibus datur gratia fidei Christianae, ..in ~o dimittitur originalis injustitia cum qua nascuntur ANSELM (*Praesc.* 8) II 274; ~i gratiam..adeptus est EADMER *HN* 113; Christianitatis et ~i petierunt..sibi contradendum sacramentum *Itin. Ric.* III 16; dicunt [Jacobite] quod parvulis non datur gracia in ~o S. SIM. *Itin.* 32; ~us, *a batym*; ..baptismum proprie fertur mundacio mentis; / exterior querit per aquam, baptisma vocatur; / hec vox baptismus signat utrumque simul WW; **1546** remissionem..peccatorum..fideique sacramentum ~um BEKINSAU I 743.

baptista [βαπτιστής], baptist, baptizer. **b** (as title of St. John).

cum aliter succurri non possit, ipse tuam sobolem baptizes aut ad ~am deferas PULL. *Sent.* 929B; Ninianus..doctor et ~a primus in Britannia *Eul. Hist.* II 178; s**644** obiit Paulinus ~a regis Edwini ELMH. *Cant.* 182; *a crystynar,* ~a *CathA.* **b** salutiferum mundus baptista Tonantem / diluit ALDH. *VirgV* 409; beatum praecursorem et ~am Domini viii Octobres in aequinoctio autumnali conceptum et in aestivo solstitio viii kal. Julias natum BEDE *TR* 30; sunt aliae tertiae dignitatis festivitates..Decollatio Johannis ~ae [29 *Aug.*] LANFR. *Const.* 134; per merita magni ~ae tui renova in me gratiam baptismi tui ANSELM (*Or.* 8) III 29; **1200** termino S. Johannis ~e *CurR I* 244; c**1225** ad Natale S.J.B. [24 *June*] *Ch. Sal.* 117; beatus Johannes.. factus est ~a Domini *AncrR* 52; juxta ~e sententiam OCKHAM *Dial.* 498; c**1370** Baptiste testis fiet quassatio pestis [*gl.*: scilicet in nativitate beati Johannis ~e] (J. BRIDL.) *Pol. Poems* I 147; c**1400** vigilia S. Johannis †Baptize *Miss. Rosslyn* 56; **1510** altare sanctorum Johannis ~e et Evangeliste *Invent. Ch. Ch.* 40.

2 (?) Knight or Hermit of St. John.

Baptiste [v.l. Babteni] Cruciferi atque Gillelmini / modo sunt in fieri, nunc merguntur fini PECKHAM *Def. Mend.* 298.

3 bestower of names.

1381 transubstantiatio..et impanatio, quibus utuntur ~e signorum in materia de eucharistia, non sunt fundabiles in Scriptura (WYCL. *Concl.*) *Ziz.* 105.

baptisterium [βαπτιστήριον], **a** baptistery, building for baptism. **b** font. **c** rite of baptism. **d** (indeterminate phrases).

a baptizabat in fluvio Sualua; ..nondum enim oratoria vel ~ia in ipso exordio nascentis ibi ecclesiae poterant aedificari BEDE *HE* II 14; hoc ~um caelesti visitatione dedicatum..sanctifica, ut quoscumque fons iste lavaturus est..indulgentiam omnium delictorum consequantur EGB. *Pont.* 53; **10..** ~io, *fulwiht stowe* WW; Constantinus fecit ~ium Romae M. PAR. *Maj.* I 160. **b** ut..parturientis gratiae vulva in ~io regeneratus..catholicorum coetibus adsisceretur ALDH. *VirgP* 43; ipsa aqua in ~io debet vergi EGB. *Pont.* 15; **1214** ~ium habeatur in qualibet ecclesia baptismali lapideum vel aliud competens, quod decenter operiatur et reverenter conservetur..; aqua vero ubi baptizatus fuerit puer ultra viij dies in ~io non servetur *Conc. Syn.* 31 (= *Reg. Aberd.* II 24: in †baptizaterio); **1220** ~ium ligneum et ecclesia discooperta (*Vis.*) *Reg. S. Osm.* I 279; c**1250** ~ium plumbeum *Vis. S. Paul* 9; **1342** ~ium non est coopertum nec seratum (*Vis. Totnes*) *EHR* XXVI 115; **1368** crismatorium et ~ium sub seruris *Invent. Norw.* 143; *a funte,* fons, ~ium *CathA.* **c** hanc ecclesiam eo respectu fabricavit ut et ~ia et examinationes judiciorum.. inibi celebrarentur EADMER *Breg.* 4; **12..** salvo..~io parvulorum matrici ecclesie *Reg. S. Thom. Dublin* no. 381; **1345** de xj s. v d. receptis de purificacionibus, ~iis, sponsalibus.. *Pri. Cold. app.* p. cv (*cf.* baptizarium). **d** nitido salutaris aque..abluti ~io S. DURH. II 5; s**1189** non habebit capella ~ium DICETO *YH* II 72; vas in quo lavantur [corporalia] sicut et ~ii nullis aliis usibus deputetur GIR. *GE* I 10; c**1236** determinant..utrum talis ecclesia vel capella habere debeat ~ium et sepulturam GROS. *Ep.* 72; homo..qui te facis appellari A per nomen ~ii BRACTON 141b; c**1250** plumbum est ibi rotundum pro baptistario *Vis. S. Paul.* 5; **1456** fontem ~ii *Test. Ebor.* III 154.

2 service-book for baptism.

ipsis sacerdotibus necessaria sunt ad discendum..liber sacramentorum, lectionarius, ~ium BART. EXON. *Pen.* xxiii f. 144 (*citing Gratian etc.*); **1362** in ligatura unius ~ii pro ecclesia *Ac. Durh.* 179.

baptisticus, baptismal (appl. to godson).

ipse et Cuthrid baptizat.., quem et ~um filium sumpsit ÆTHELW. II 6.

baptitura v. batitura. baptiza v. baptista 1b. baptizalis v. baptismalis.

baptizare [βαπτίζειν], to baptize, christen: **a** (person or absol.). **b** (thing). **c** (iron.) to immerse. **d** to sponsor as godparent. **e** (absol.) to accept baptism. **f** (p. ppl. as sb.) convert.

a diacones possunt ~are THEOD. *Pen.* II 2; **724** quod apud Christianos fidelium cotidie ~antur filii, quid aliud faciunt nisi a sorde et reatu gentilitatis..eos purgant? (DAN. WINT.) *Ep. Bonif.* 23; cum esset presbyter ordinatus, nullatenus..potuit cathecizandi vel ~andi ministerium discere BEDE *HE* V 6; cur ~ati..non statim fiunt incorruptibiles ANSELM (*Praesc.* 9) II 277; **1214** si [pueri] inveniantur expositi et utrum ~ati fuerint dubitetur, ~entur; ita tamen quod ante prolationem istorum verborum "ego ~o te in nomine Patris et Filii et Spiritus Sancti," que sola sunt de substantia baptismi.., hec a ~ante verba dicantur, nominante ~andum et dicente: "ego non intendo te rebaptizare; set, si ~atus non es, ego ~o te" *Conc. Syn.* 31; **1218** portatus fuit ad monasterium vivus et ~atus est et vixit..usque ad horam primam *Eyre Yorks* 7; **1233** non fuerunt manentes in villa illa nisi tantum tres homines..et apud Wockinges fuerunt..pueri ~ati *BNB* II 587; *to crysten,* ~are *CathA.* **b** in quibusdam locis ~atur campana ad designandum quod nulli licet predicare nisi ~ato NECKAM *NR* I 22; baptizatur aqua; set aquam baptizat eamque / dote renativa robur habere facit GARL. *Epith.* IX 497. **c** s**1265** fugerunt Wallenses..et in transeundo flumen Dee multi submersi sunt et reliqui denuo ~ati W. GUISB. 201. **d 1433** cuilibet ..puero per predictam Elizabet ~ato *Reg. Cant.* II 496. **e** de catechumenis exprimentibus se habere propositum ~andi OCKHAM *Dial.* 436. **f 1392** pro j lecto et j sclaveyn emptis pro Henrico ~ato *Ac. H. Derby* 230.

2 to christen (fig.), name.

s**1289** ex tunc..non est oblatus cervus; et, si recte ~aretur non deberet dici oblatio sed redditus GRAYSTANES 22;

politici..quasi in nomine suo communicarent talia baptisant terminos secundum consideracionem legis humane Wycl. *Dom. Div.* 256; *to name*, appellare, ∼are, nominare *CathA*.

†baptizarium [cf. baptisterium 1b and c], **a** font. **b** baptism.

a 1242 ∼ium..non sit ligneum sed lapideum *Conc. Scot.* II 54. **b 1353** de lxxix s. vj d. receptis de sponsalibus, ∼iis, purificacionibus et matrimoniis *Pri. Cold, app.* xxvi (cf. baptisterium 1c).

baptizaterium v. baptisterium 1b.

baptizatio, baptism, christening.

s1245 de ∼one cujusdam Judei *Meaux* II 70*n*; **1447** in ∼one filie comitis *Ac. Durh.* 630; **1559** de ∼one infantium *Conc. Scot.* II 174.

baptua v. balthuta.

baralipton, a logical mood.

Bacon XV 301 (v. barbara).

baratare [OF *barater*], to pick a quarrel with. **b** to foment (a suit) vexatiously or by way of barratry.

1305 T.D. indictatur..quod communiter vagat de nocte barettando homines, verberando et vulnerando *Gaol Del.* 39/1 r. 3*d*. **b 1622** se..paratos obligari..de respondendo cuicumque actioni contra dictam navem..deque re non barratanda *HCA Libel* 30/35.

baratator, barrator, trouble-maker.

Domine, ut a baratoribus de Norfolchia nos conservare digneris te rogamus Brakelond 124; **1239** iste rex pestilencie [Fretherícus] a tribus ∼oribus, scilicet Christo Jesu, Moyse et Machometo, totum mundum fuisse deceptum.. manifeste proponens (*Lit. Papae*) M. Par. *Maj.* III 607; tam Machometum quam Jesum vel Moysen, quod horribile est recitare, vocat baratorem *Ib.* 609; **1307** D. le J. indictatus.. quod est communis barettor *Gaol Del.* 39/2 r. 1*d*.; a pueritia ∼or existens tumultibus seculi intendebat Ockham *Pol.* II 596; **1516** contra hujusmodi malefactores, riotores, barrectatores, pacis perturbatores (*Supersedeas*) *EHR* XXVII 238; **1541** hospitat personas suspectuosas et barettores ac objurgatores *Augm. Bk.* 134 f. 40*d*.; **1588** communis barectator patrie *Gaol File Wales* 716/3.

barathralis, abysmal, hellish.

c1250 ∼is abyssi voraginem Ad. Marsh *Ep.* 189; Tartareos gladios baratralis fabricat hostis Garl. *Tri. Eccl.* 110; carcer est baratrale chaos *Ib.* 142.

barathrum [βάραθρον], pit. **b** Hell. **c** pit of darkness (fig.), *i.e.* obscurity or sin.

baratrum, sepulcrum *GlC* B 39; baratrum, *dael Ib.* 49; precipitium vaste patens.., quod quidem ∼um..Malfosse nuncupatur *Chr. Battle* 5. **b** alios..de latebroso leti ∼o.. reduxit ad superos Aldh. *VirgP* 26; 'baratrum' singulariter tantum effertur; sic autem vocabant gentiles locum apud inferos Bede *Orth.* 2779; maligni spiritus descenderunt in medium ∼i illius ardentis *Id. HE* V 12; baratrum, vorago profunda, *cwicsusl* vel *hellelic deopnes* Ælf. *Gl.*; **960** inextricabilem horendorum ∼orum voraginem incurrat *CS* 1055 (cf. ib. 935); **969** (13c) baraðri incendiis *CS* 1234; ne ruat in flammam baratri reus asperiorem R. Cant. *Poems* 262; imperium celi terre barathrique vorantis Garl. *Myst. Eccl.* 126. **c** qua tenus nullum..latebrosum confractae sinalephae ∼um lucem scandentis confundat Aldh. *Met.* 9 p. 81; in profundum superbiae ∼um *Id. VirgP* 11.

barator v. baratator, barrator. baratorium v. foratorium.

baratro [cf. balatro], wastrel.

studium non corrumpant baratrones, / Thaidis incudem, Bachum, luctas adamantes D. Bec. 1716.

baratum [OF *barat*], barter.

1437 causas et acciones..pro quibuscumque mutuis, barettis, escambiis et literis pagamenti (*Chanc. Misc.*) *Law Merch.* III 119.

1 barba, beard (human). **b** (of beast). **c** wattle of fowl.

∼am habebat prolixam Bede *HE* IV 14; sicut virum qui nondum debet habere ∼am non dedecet non habere Anselm (*Casus Diab.* 16) I 261; murilegus bene scit cui barbam lambere suescit Serlo Wilt. *Poems app.* III A 11. 1; si sit villosa, resecetur barba pilosa D. Bec. 1181; **s1422** ubicumque locorum perrexero, eos [sc. Scotos] in ∼am [i.e. *confronting me*] invenio *Plusc.* X 27. **b** ∼am hominis, ∼as pecudum dices Bede *Orth.* 2779. **c** palearia rubricata que vulgo dicuntur ∼e Neckam *NR* I 42.

2 (in plant names): **a** arum (*cf. arum*). **b** deadnettle. **c** burdock. **d** ribwort plantain. **e** hypocistis etc. **f** houseleek (or *s. dub.*). **g** withered rose.

a ∼a Aaron, iarus..A. *cokkowespitte Alph.* 21. **b** archangelica vel ∼a †anglia [? l. angelica], G. *archangle*, A. *ded[e]netle Ib.* 14. **c** ∼a elexis, ..lappa major, A. *clote*, cujus fructus vocatur A. *burre Ib.* 20. **d** ∼a filicana, id est centumnervia Gilb. II 112 v. 2. **e** medicine stiptice simplices frigide sunt..∼a hircina, virga pastoris Gad. 98 v. 1; ∼a yrsina..A. *buckstonge Alph.* 20; ∼a yrcina i. ypoquistidos *SB* 12. **f** constat quod alia herba est Jovis ∼a, alia ∼a Jovis Neckam *NR* II 166 (cf. *Id. DS* VII 136); ∼a Jovis vel Jovis ∼a..G. *jubarbe*, A. *syngrene, erewort, houslek Alph.* 20. **g** ∼a leporis, rosa passa idem *Alph.* 21.

3 barb (of arrow etc.).

si fit cum ∼is, tunc oportet elargare vulnus et intromittere cannulas circa ∼as illas Gad. 122 v. 1.

2 barba [CL barbus; cf. barbulus], ruff (fish).

14.. cornis, plagma, cum perca, gobio, barba [*gl.*: *ruff*] *Dieta* 56.

barbacana, ∼um, ∼us [OF *barbacane*, etym. dub.; (?) < Ar. *burj barrānī*], barbican, outwork.

1175 pro barbakana et porta una facienda *Pipe* 188; barbekena *Ib.* 165; **1180** in ∼a ante castrum et in porta et turella ejusdem ∼e reparanda *RScacNorm* I 90; **s1189** fontem..habentem ∼am novem turribus circumseptam Diceto *YH* II 66; **1221** pro nova barbakania xxxv s. viij d. *Ac. Build. Hen. III* 48; **1230** quantum maeremii opus fuerit ad barbicanas et palitia ipsius castri reparanda *Cl* 357; **1234** xl fusta ad quandam barbecanam inde faciendam *Cl* 31; **1243** †barbatariam ante portam castri *Liberate* 19 m. 8; **1255** ∼as que sunt extra muros ville *RGasc* I *suppl.* p. 50; **1255** quoddam ∼um factum fuit tempore gwerre *Hund.* II 80; **1260** janua barbecani debilis est *IMisc* 10/20; **1274** barbukana *Ib.* 33/36; **1275** quod barbakani et cetera aforciamenta contra dominum regem ibidem facta..prosternantur *SelCKB* I 14; **1323** quoddam barbicanum ante portam castri..muro lapideo et in eodem barbicano quandam portam cum ponte versatili..de novo facere *Cl* 141 m. 39; **c1380** tenementum..extendens..usque ad barbicanum castri *Mon. Exon.* 303.

barbacanagium, toll or due for building a barbican.

1336 [cives Winton'] quieti sint de barbicanagio sive barbican ac bretagio *ChartR* 123 m. 18; **1415** de..barbicanagio (*Ib.* 185) *MonA* VI 33; **1463** de..†barbicagio *ChartR* 193 m. 4.

barbalatus v. barbellatus. Barbanus v. Brabanus.

barbara, a logical mood.

barbara celarent darii ferio baralipton Bacon XV 301 (cf. *GLA* III 15).

barbaralixis v. barbarolexis. barbaratus v. barbellatus.

barbare, (p. ppl. *barbatus*) [CL] bearded. **b** 'bearded' tufted (bot.).

Hugo ∼us tenet de rege *DB* 49b; frater quidam laicus.. extra congregationem Fratrum sobrie, juste et pie intonsus et ∼us degebat Ailr. *SSHex.* 182; mulierem..umbilico tenus ∼am Gir. *TH* II 20; **1458** berbato brigatori *ExchScot* 418. **b** apium ∼um *Alph.* 13; tapsus ∼us *Ib.* 68 (*cf.* verbascum).

2 to barb, set (a fence) with thorns. **b** (p. ppl. *barbatus*) barbed (of arrow or sim.).

c1300 in haya parci supponenda et ∼anda per loca *MinAc* 863/8; **1322** in stipendio j hominis ∼antis de spinis palicium..per loca *Ib.* 1146/11 m. 2*d*.; **1384** unius operarii prosternentis spinas et cum eisdem ∼antis et emendantis veterem haiam *DL MinAc* 507/8228 r. 27. **b 1209** tulit arcum cum corda et una sagitta ∼a *SelPlForest* 2; **1228** tenuit..per servicium duarum sagittarum ∼arum quando rex venit usque Dertemore ad chaciandum *Cl* 62; **1315** cum sagitta ∼a que vocatur *clotharewe CoramR* 220 r. 105; **1437** reddendo..unam sagittam dupliciter ∼am Anglice vocatam *brodehokedarwe Cl* 287 m. 13*d*.

3 to barb, clip (wool).

1441 berdavit et ∼avit cxij pokas lane de crescencia de Cotyswold *Pat* 450 m. 11; **1472** saccos et clavos lane tam ∼ate et claccate quam non ∼ate et non claccate *Pat* 529 m. 8; **1532** nisi iidem [panni lanei] sint prius ∼ati, perpoliti Anglice *rowed* et tonsi *LTRMem* 306, *Rec. Trin.* r. 40.

barbaria, a barbering. **b** 'barbery', barber's shop.

a 1303 in ∼ia et lavandria comitis vj d. *KRAc* 11/6 m. 2. **b c1425** vitrationem fenestre ad ostium ∼ie *Mon. Francisc.* I 520.

barbarice, a savagely. **b** in the vernacular.

a s978 adest et rusticus cum suis ∼e frendens *Chr. Evesham* 41. **b** simbolum apostolorum..ab omnibus discatur, tam Latine quam ∼e Bart. Exon. *Pen.* 13 (*citing Conc. Chalon* [813]); liber ∼e [v.l. barbario] scriptus Ailr. *Nin. pref.* p. 140.

barbaricus [CL < βαρβαρικός], barbarous. **b** vernacular. **c** ornate, adorned w. gold.

respexit ille ad divinae auxilium pietatis, quo ab impietate ∼a posset eripi Bede *HE* III 24; vitam veraci quidem set nimis ∼o..exaratam stilo Ailr. *Nin. prol.* p. 138; [Carausius] Britonibus dixit quod, si ipsum regem facerent.. totam insulam a gente ∼a [i.e. *Saxon*] liberaret G. Mon. V 3. **b 949** ubi ruricole illius pagi ∼o nomine appellant Pendyfig [*Cornwall*] *CS* 877. **c** ∼a, auro ornata *GlC* B 29 (= *Erf.* 2. 270. 15: auro ornata vel subtilis in coloribus).

barbaries [CL], barbarity. **b** a barbarous practice. **c** a barbarous country. **d** barbarians (collect.). **e** vernacular language.

c745 quod ex operibus antiquorum excerpsi doctorum.. utiliter in tam perniciosa ∼ie ad memoriam debet reduci (Dan. Wint.) *Ep. Bonif.* 64 p. 135; nostrorum convictu et familiaritate limatus a puero, omnem rubiginem Scottice ∼iei deterserat W. Malm. *GR* V 400; Gir. *TH* III 10 (v. assuescere 1c); ∼iem gentis..informabat Elmh. *Cant.* 166. **b c1291** sedavit..rex Edwardus..belualem quandam gentis illius [Scotorum] ∼iem W. Newb. *Cont.* iv. **c** qua Scithica regna horrendam incolunt ∼iem Aldh. *Met.* 3; cum..ad tam longinquam..∼iem..transmigrarent Gosc. *Aug. Maj.* 53. **d s1138** ne a pessima ∼ie per ignaviam se omnes una die prosterni sinerent Ric. Hex. *Stand.* 42b; cum..loca sancta multis ∼ies fedaret spurcitiis H. Reading (II) *Cel.* 30; Europe paucos equites ferit Affrica tota, / barbaries Asie latius urget eos Garl. *Tri. Eccl.* 13. **e c1170** cyrographis que..Anglica ∼ie exarata invenimus..in Latinos apices transmutatis *Chr. Rams.* 176.

barbarismus [βαρβαρισμός], barbarism, in writing or conduct (*cf. barbarolexis*).

Vergilius..∼o tribrachum pro dactilo admisit Aldh. *Met.* 10 p. 95; inter Scillam soloecismi et ∼i barathrum *Id. VirgP* 59; **10..** ∼us, *miscweden word*, ∼i, *þa uncyste* WW; quid prodest vitare ∼um et solecismum in vocibus et incurrere ∼um et solecismum in rebus? Neckam *NR* II 175; si filios canonicorum suorum..ritu barbaro, ne ∼o dicamus, canonicare presumpserit Gir. *JS* 7 p. 366.

1 barbarius v. barbarice.

2 barbarius, barber, barber-surgeon.

heu! sunt que faciunt tria fastidire magistros: / barberius veteres et coquus atque canis Walt. Angl. *Fab.* 27 *app.* 2; vocavit suum barberium dicens ei, est modo tollere sanguinem? (M. Scot. *Intr.*) *Med. Sci.* 289; **1292** in uno ∼io, vj d. *KRAc* 308/15 m. 8 (cf. ib.: in uno barbirio).

barbarizare [βαρβαρίζειν], **a** to write or speak barbarously (or in the vernacular). **b** to utter barbarously. **c** to grow more barbarous (in language). **d** to act savagely.

a exaratura ∼antis lingua materiam..planare Nen. *Pref.* 127; apud Merleburgam, ubi fons est quem, si quis.. gustaverit, Gallice ∼at W. Map *NC* V 6 p. 246; [stylus] Hugonis..vel ∼ando triumphos explicet Ad. Eyns. *Hug.* V 17 p. 200. **b** [Judei] turbidas in Francos minas..∼abant Gerv. Cant. I 205. **c 1419** idem nomen *Portreve* pro nomine de *Portgreve* populus Anglicus, a Saxonica lingua processu temporis ∼ans, civitatum presidibus tribuebat *MGL* I 14. **d** *to be felle*: ∼are, crudere, .. *CathA*.

barbarizatio, translation (unwarrantable) into vernacular.

fundamentum istius protervie est litera Witcleff in ∼one cujusdam evangelii Netter *DAF* I 409.

barbarolexis [βαρβαρόλεξις], barbarism in speech. **b** misuse of language.

ne loquendo barbaralixim vel scribendo barbarismum incurrat Neckam *Ut.* 117. **b** barbarolexis adest quoniam trufator honorem / invenit, et rethor desipit arte sua Garl. *Tri. Eccl.* 116.

barbarus [CL < βάρβαρος], barbarous, uncivilized, or barbarian (sb.). **b** barbarous, cruel. **c** barbarous, vernacular (of language).

barbara convertens doctrinis agmina sacris Aldh. *VirgV* 502; unus ex ducibus paganus, alter quia ∼us erat pagano saevior Bede *HE* II 20; **9..** ∼us, i. truculentus, gentilis servus vel *ungereord* WW; **964** (13c) ego Ead[g]arus gentis Anglorum et ∼orum atque gentilium rex *CS* 1143; dum..in ∼a regione omnes pariter ut hostes metuerent Ord. Vit. II 26 p. 251; **c1150** in paludis antique ∼a cohabitatione proscriptus Osb. Clar. *Ep.* 30; gens ∼a et vere ∼a, quia non tantum ∼o vestium ritu verum etiam comis et barbis luxuriantibus..incultissima et omnes eorum mores ∼issimi sunt Gir. *TH* III 10; plerique ∼i, indignantes dominium, ..resistere decernebant G. Cold. *Durh.* 15. **b** homines.. durae ac ∼ae mentis Bede *HE* III 5. **c** pertaesus ∼ae loquellae, subintroduxit..alium suae linguae episcopum Bede *HE* III 7.

barbassus, -astus v. verbascum. barbataria v. barbacana.

barbatio, (?) setting (a fence) w. thorns (*cf. barbare 2a*).

1448 in ∼onem iiij perticarum (*MinAc Hatfield*) *MFG*.

barbator, barber, barber-surgeon.

regis..curiam sequuntur assidue..mimi, ∼ores.. P. Blois *Ep.* 14. 49; **1258** Thome ∼oris regis *Cl* 220; **s1290** episcopus..petiit ∼orem suum seu fleobotomatorem, ut ipsum sanguine minueret B. Cotton 174; **1327** servientes ..clericorum, percamenarii, ..∼ores et alii homines..de robis *MunCOx* 55.

barbatura, barbering.

c1300 Walterus le Barbour habuit..pelves pro officio ∼e *RParl* 257b.

barbatus v. barbare, barbiton. barbecan- v. barbacana.

barbelius [OF *barbele*], barbed.

1243 pro vj sagittis ∼iis *Fees* 1124.

barbellatus, barbed.

1204 reddendo..unam sagittam barbelatam *Fines RC* I 57; **1224** habeat..cc sagittas barbulatas *LTRMem* 6 r. 10 (= *KRMem* 7 r. 10: barbaratas); **c1244** tres sagittas barbillatas †sive [l. sine] fleche *CalIMisc* I 28; **1247** sagittas ∼as cum flechiis *LTRMem* 20 r. 1; **1247** sagittam barbalatam *CalCh* I 327; si telum barbulatum fuerit, summa cautela discoopertum trahi convenit Gilb. V 234. 1; **1286** sagitta barbeleta *IPM* 46/3 r. 2.

1 barbellus [OF *barbel*], barb (of arrow).

1542 pro reparacione *ly case* sagittarum et plumacione earum et barbillis *Ac. Coll. Wint.* (*Bursar*).

2 barbellus [OF *barbel*; cf. barbulus], barbel (fish).

1234 burrochie..ad capiendum tantummodo lamprones et ∼os et non majores pisces *E. Ch. S. Paul.* 260; **1415** pro.. rochys, barbell', flunderys (*KRAc* 321/32) *Analog. Cant. Pilgr.* 3; portat duos ∼os aureos terga adinvicem vertentes Bad. Aur. 201.

barberius v. 2 barbarius.

barbescere, to grow a beard.

quamobrem..ipsi [sc. viri] soli ~ant ADEL. *QN* 20; hec est cause quare vir et non mulier ~it BART. ANGL. V 15.

barbeton- v. barbiton-.

barbetta [cf. OF *barbete*], part of headdress, covering neck and breast. **b** barbette, platform.

1290 scut[ifero] domine Margarete filie regis pro..vj peciis coverch' et barbett' *Ac. Wardr.* (*Chanc. Misc.* 4/5) f. 2. **b 1359** pelum nostrum de Haywra vocatum Skirgill' una cum bretagio circa ~am ejusdem peli in statu competenti manuteneri [facias] *Cl* 197 m. 13.

barbeuta v. braveuta. barbibundium v. barbitondium. barbica v. berbica. barbican- v. barbacan-.

Barbifer, bearded friar.

itaque Barbiferi, Picati, Saccini / ..modo sunt in fieri, nunc merguntur fini PECKHAM *Def. Mend.* 297.

barbilla v. burbilia. barbillatus v. barbellatus. barbillus v. 1 barbellus. barbirius v. 2 barbarius.

barbiton, ~a [CL < βάρβιτος = *lyre*], (wind-chest of) organ. **b** wind instrument.

~um, genus organi *Erf.* 2. 270. 40; musica concisis et clamat barbita bombis ALDH. *VirgV* 2789 (cf. *Id. Aen.* 13); **10..** ~a bombis, organum WW; organa hydraulica, ubi.. per aque calefacte violentiam ventus emergens implet concavitatem ~i W. MALM. *GR* II 168 (= *Meaux* I 269: concavitatem †barbatus). **b 14..** ~a, *beme* [i.e. *trumpet*] WW; *schepherdys pype*, ~a *PP*.

barbitondium, a shaving. **b** barber's shop.

a *rasyr hows or schavynge*, †barbibundium *PP*; *a schavynge*, ~ium, tonsura *CathA*. **b** *barbowris schavynge hows*, ~ium *PP*; *a raster house*, ~ium, tonsorium *CathA*.

barbitonsio, shaving.

1474 pro barbetonsione *Ac. Coll. Wint.*

barbitonsor [barbae tonsor], barber, barber-surgeon.

1272 Waltero Barbytonsore *CalCh* II 180; **1294** omnes.. uno tempore radantur et ab uno ~ore (*Mem. S. Leon. York*) *MonA* VI 610; **1312** ~ores non ponant sanguinem in fenestris suis (*LBLond.* D 157) *MGL* I 250; **1352** Roberto Barber ~ori domini *Reg. Black Pr.* IV f. 44; **1413** quod ~ores non operent nec teneant shopas apertas diebus Dominicis *CalLBLond* I f. 125; **1490** barbetonsori *ExchScot* 203.

barbitonsorium, barber's shop.

1454 circa facturam muri inter cameram janitoris et ~ium *Ac. Coll. Reg.*) *Arch. Hist. Camb.* III 597*n*.

barbosus, bearded, unshaven.

s1053 Aed clericus ~us in Hibernia vir valde famosissimus et mirae religionis (MARIANUS SCOTUS) FL. WORC. I 211.

barbota [OF *barbote*], armoured boat.

s1219 galeias cum ~is et navibus aliis (OLIVERUS SCHOLASTICUS) M. PAR. *Maj.* III 46.

barbukana v. barbacana. barbulatus v. barbellatus.

barbulus [cf. barbellus], barbel (fish).

desunt..dulcis aque generosi pisces..lucii videlicet et.. ~i [v.l. barbili] GIR. *TH.* I 9; barbule, te parvi reputat Londonia, cum te / Parisius magni nominis esse sciat NECKAM *DS* III 639.

barca [LL], barque, boat. **b** (fig.).

~a, navis *GlC* B 13; donec barca rudi pulsabat litora rostro ALDH. *CE* 3. 23; nomina navium: ..~a, *flotscip* ÆLF. *Sup.*; enumeratis ~is [in Brachio S. Georgii]..inventa sunt ij milia dliij ~arum GIR. *Spec.* IV 9; **1317** posuit servientes suos ad portus Marempnie qui arestabant †baichas [l. barchas] sive naves sale oneratas (*RGasc* 32 m. 13) *Foed.* III 685; venimus..usque ad Babiloniam [i.e. *Cairo*]..ubi ~am ascendentes per fossatum sive cannale..navigamus S. SIM. *Itin.* 39; **1435** ~am sive batellam *Reg. Aberbr.* II 69; **1436** pro naulo ~e vocate *scowte ExchScot* 679; **1440** de ~a ejusdem carace intrante eodem die *Port Bk. Southampt.* 55; **1497** naves, carvellas, barquas et alia vasa *Pat* 579 m. 22 (2) *d*. **b** rimosa fragilis ingenii ~a..turbine quassata ALDH. *VirgP* 59; *Id. VirgV* 2809 (v. ancora b).

barcare v. barrare 1b, 1 & 2 bercare, 2 bercaria 3. barcaria v. 2 bercaria.

1 barcarius, shipwright.

a schyppe maker, ~ius, nauticus *CathA*.

2 & 3 barcarius v. 1 & 2 bercarius.

barcellus, small boat.

1242 habet litteras de conductu..pro se, filiis et hominibus suis in ~o suo contentis *RGasc* I 46 (cf. *CalPat.* 312).

barcius v. barsa. barda v. 1 & 2 berda.

bardana [OF *bardane*], burdock.

cum succo ~e GILB. II 81 v. 2; coquatur radix ~e, i. lappe inverse GAD. 97 v. 2; ~a, A. *clote, gert burr SB* 12; *a burre*, bardona, glis, lappa *CathA*.

bardare v. berdare.

bardigiosus, (?) stupid.

non ruricolarum ~os vagitus imitabatur FELIX *Guthl.* 12.

bardioriolus [? cf. bariulus, berbicariolus], bird, (?) tit.

~us, *colmase* ÆLF. *Gl.*

†bardisa, (?) barge.

1404 invenerunt unam ~am de Londoniis..et unam passingeram *Lit. Cant.* III 78.

bardona v. bardana.

1 bardus [CL], stupid.

~us, stultus *GlC* B 42; **9..** ~us, stultus, ineptus vel babiger WW.

2 bardus [CL < Gall.; cf. W. *bardd*], bard.

~i Kambrenses et cantores seu recitatores..genealogiam habent predictorum principum in libris eorum GIR. *DK* I 3; poetas quos ~os vocant..in hac natione multos invenies *Ib.* 12; mimos, histriones, ~os, parasitos..coegit.. manuaria arte victum quaerere BOECE IX 177v.

barectare v. warectare. barefella, barfella v. berefella.

barelborda, barrel-board.

1325 pro ~is (*Ac. Cust.*) *Bronnen* 327.

barele v. barile.

barellare, to pack in barrels.

1225 in xvij doliis vini nostri barelandis et cerclandis *Cl* 61a; **1440** officia..paccacionis..mercandisarum..paccatarum, doliatarum, pipatarum, ~atarum seu aliqualiter inclusarum *Pat* 448 m. 14.

barelletum [OF *barillet*], small barrel.

militi..cotidie liberetur a celario regis barillatum vini continens ad minus unum jalonem *Fleta* 70.

barellula, small barrel.

1480 de..quatuor barelulis tyriace, ..una barel cum ficubus (*KRAc* 129/2) *Bronnen* 1868.

1 barellus, ~um, ~a [OF *baril*; cf. barile], barrel, cask. **b** small ornamental barrel.

1170 pro xij barill' ferratis..pro conducendo vino regis *Pipe* 15; **1184** pro..xij ~is ferro ligatis *Pipe* 137; **1237** Willelmus le Butteler reddidit ad Scaccarium duos ~os cum vino *LTRMem* 12 r. 2*d* (= *KRMem* 16 r. 3*d*: duos barill'); **1253** uterque barillus continet l li. argenti *RGasc* I 353; **1290** ij barilla, ij cuve *Reg. Wint.* 704; **1290** in j barill' ad aquam benedictam capelle ducendam, ij d. *Ac. Swinfield* 180; **1485** de †varellis vacuis..venditis *Comp. Swith.* 382. **b 1300** duo barilli parvi de ligno †cavell' [l. canelle] argento ligati precii xl s. *Ac. Wardr.* 347; **1368** iiij phiole cum parvo ~o stanneo *Invent. Norw.* 32.

2 measure of volume, barrelful.

lagena vulgariter vocatur berillum sive costrillum BART. ANGL. XIX 125; **1265** pro j barillo sturjoni (*RHosp*) *Manners* 14; **1281** duos barillos arguille (*JustIt*) *Law Merch.* II 31; **1296** in xj barillis de ter *Ac. Galley Newcastle* 164; **1324** clamavit capere..duos barillos vini, videlicet duas lagenas (*Lib. Cust.*) *MGL* II 408; **1368** tria barella cinerum *RScot* 925a; **1390** pro vj barellis servisie continente la barella xxiiij galones *Ac. H.Derby* 10 (*cf. ib.*: le barellus continente xxiiij galones); **1532** quelibet ~a pro servicia Anglice vocata *a bere barell* contineat xxxvj lagenas Anglice vocatas *gallons* et..quelibet ~a pro servicia facta Anglice vocata *a ale barell* contineat xxxij lagenas *KRMem 311 Rec. Mich. r. 16* (cf. *Stat.* 23 *Hen. VIII* c. 4).

3 barrel for burnishing armour.

1274 unum barillum ad rollanda arma *IMisc* 33/36; **1305** in uno ~o empto pro armaturis..fraendis *MinAc W. Wales* I 406; **1388** unus ~us pro armatura *IMisc* 332 m. 55.

4 part of woodwork of windlass.

1333 pro j pecia meremii de quercu empta [pro] ~o dicte verne, longitudinis ix pedum, latitudinis quadratim j pedis et quartron' *KRAc* 469/12 m. 17.

2 barellus v. beryllus b. barelus v. carola. barettare, ~ator v. baratare, ~ator.

barettus, (?) small barrel.

1310 coquina: ..x d. de j ~o rotundo ferro legato [? l. ligato] et ij costrellis pro salsa *Ac. Exec. Ep. Exon.* 11.

barga v. 1 & 2 bargia.

bargagia, (?) big barge.

1335 duas ~ias et duas alias magnas naves *RScot* 392b; pro dupplici eskippamento earundem ~iarum et navium *Ib.*

barganare, ~iare [OF *bargaigner* (?) < Frk.], **a** to bargain, do business. **b** (trans.) to bargain (make an offer) for.

a nullus emat aliquid extra civitatem supra xx d.; sed in ea ~iet [AS *ceapige*] sub testimonio portireve (*Quad.*) *GAS* 157 (cf. ib. 234); **1353** respondit quod ipse personaliter cum prefatis nuper firmariis ~iare noluit propter distanciam inter eos initam *PlRExch.* 78 r. 116. **b 1206** bargeniavit ab eo pannum..et convenit inter eos de precio *CurR* IV 87; **1275** venit predictus R. et ~avit dictam pellem et S. predictus pellem eandem sibi concessit pro xx d. (*St. Ives*) *SelPlMan* 141; **1282** emptor..haberet rem quam barginaverat PECKHAM *Ep.* 344 p. 448; **1315** ~avit de quodam mercatore viij salmones pro xxiiij s. (*St. Ives*) *Law Merch.* I 97.

barganiator, trafficker.

c1300 quicunque voluerit se conqueri de conspiratoribus, falsarum querelarum sustentatoribus..et controversiarum †bargainatoribus (*Conspir.*) *StRealm* I 216.

barganium, ~ia [OF *bargain*], bargain, business agreement.

1315 venit dictus Henricus et dictum Rogerum de dicto ~io ejecit et dictos salmones pro xxviij s. emit (*St. Ives*) *Law Merch.* I 97; **1377** per..mediacionem..brocariorum et correctariorum ejusdem ~ei chevisavit et mutuatus fuit.. x li. *MGL* I 396; in accionibus personalibus de ~eis et contractibus *Ib.* 175 (= ib. 210: *des bargaynes et contractz*); **1383** habeant..potestatem postquam emptor racionabiliter monetam pro eisdem vinis semel vel bis venditori eorumdem vinorum optulerit, liberationem eorumdem vinorum in ~ia existentium dictis emptoribus faciendi *Cl* 222 m. 10*d*.; **1419** racione alicujus ~ii vendicionis vel donacionis *MunCOx* 188; **1507** pardonavimus..omnes et omnimodas usuras, contractus usurarum, ~ias corruptas (*Pat* 601) *Foed.* XIII 161; barganneas et convenciones facere et tractare *Ib.* 164.

2 undertaking.

1417 T. P. ..pro bargennia facta arte sua super turrim.. x m. *Stonor Pps.* I 30.

barganizare, a to bargain. **b** (trans.) to bargain (make an offer) for. **c** to bargain away.

a 14.. cum idem J. cum prefato B. ad quandam lastam halecis rubei ab eo emendam..~asset *Reg. Brev.* 96; **1507** emere, vendere, mercandizare, ..bargannizare et commutare (*Pat*) *Foed.* XIII 164. **b 1400** ad tot equos..pro denariis nostris..barganizand', emend' et providend' (*Pat.*) *Foed.* VIII 162. **c 1522** pro quadam pecunie summa.. ~averunt et vendiderunt iisdem medietatem predicti manerii *Cart. Glam.* 1826; **1543** dedi, concessi, ~avi, vendidi et hac presenti carta mea confirmavi..sex acras terre *FormA* 288.

barganizatio, bargain.

1392 omnes contractus seu vendiciones seu empciones seu ~ones seu excambia inter nos..et predictum J. *Cl* 234 m. 28*d*.; **1507** (*Pat*) *Foed.* XIII 164; **1522** juxta formam †burganizacionis et vendicionis *Cart. Glam.* 1826; **1539** in complementum execucionis et performacionis quarumdam ~onis et convencionis expressarum et specificatarum in.. indentura *FormA* 215.

bargemannus [ME], barge-man.

1362 pro bono servicio quod Alanus Prest de Lambhuth', ~us noster, nobis a longo tempore impendit *Pat* 265 m. 5; **1377** Alano Prest, bergemanno regis *IssueR* 460 m. 10.

bargetta, barget, small barge.

1403 per..magistrum cujusdam ~e de Colchestre *Cl* 252 m. 30.

1 bargia [OF *barge* < barca], barque, barge: **a** sea-going craft; **b** river craft; **c** (?) lighter.

a s1191 Alienor regina, inde regrediens per bargas venit Salernam *Itin. Ric.* II 26; **1217** navis..proficissitur..usque in insulam de Gerese et ~ia de Portmue similiter *Pat* 88; **1229** plures galie et ~ie..jam sunt per costeram maris de tota potestate regis Francorum parate ad..depredandum naves de potestate nostra *Cl* 245; **1257** de..uno ~ia ad xxviij remos *Cl* 155; **1257** duas galias quarum utraque sit ad l remos et duas ~ias quarum utraque sit ad xx remos *Liberate* 33 m. 1; **1341** omnes naves, ~eas et flunos hujusmodi de guerra parari et muniri faciant (*Cl*) *Foed.* V 232; **1378** *Mem. York* I 30 (v. arraiare 1c); **1377** parve ~ee vocate *balyngers Rec. Leic.* II 161; **1379** due naves, due ~ee et due balingere (*Pat*) *RParl* III 391a; **s1385** Calesienses..lucrati sunt xviij naves et quandam grandem ~iam WALS. *HA* II 135 (= *V. Ric. II* 64: †burgum); **c1578** ingens navis illa, episcopi ~ia vulgo nominata, ..naufragio periit LESLEY *RGScot* 304. **b 1276** quando magnus pons Cantebr' fractus fuit per diluvium aque, ..vicecomes fecit quandam ~iam et appropriavit sibi transitum *Hund.* I 55; **c1326** omnes.. servientes in ~ia qui dicuntur *kelers* (*Cart. Tynemouth*) *MonA* III 319; **1388** de aliquibus exitibus cujusdam ferie cum una ~ea appreciata ad x li. *LTR Ac. Esch.* 10 r. 13; **1421** super opere et broudatura unius coopertorii facti de panno rubeo pro ~ea regis *KRAc* 407/5 m. 3; **s1428** dux Norfolchie..fuit in periclo vite sue in ~ia sua juxta pontem Londonie, ubi multi fuerunt submersi W. WORC. *Ann.* 760; **s1471** corpus [regis Henrici]..in quadam..barga defertur humandum *Croyl. Cont.* C 556. **c 1296** in stipendiis unius garcionis deservientis homini ungenti ~iam *Ac. Galley Newcastle* 177.

2 bargia, ~ium [OF *barde* < Ar. *bardha'a*, vulg. *bardi'a*; cf. bassum], saddle-pad. **b** (?) collar-pad.

1208 in sella summariorum et in baric' et in alio minuto harnesio *Cl* 103b; **1213** pro..j ~ia ad sellam *Ib.* 128b; **1271** expense carectarum et carrorum: ..in ~ea emendanda cum panno laneo empto, iij d. *Pipe Wint.* (159299) r. 3*d*.; **1306** in ij paribus ~iorum ad carett', iij d. *MinAc* 935/19; **1316** pro coreo ad ~ias dictarum sellarum *KRAc* 99/21 m. 1; **1336** in j barga ad sellam carecte empta, iiij d, ob. *MinAc Wint.* (*Vernham Dean*). **b 1213** pro iiij collariis et ij avalariis et ij ~iis et v capistris *Cl* 128b; **1280** in..iij collariis, ij bargis, j pari traiciarum *Ac. Stratton* 111.

bargiata, barge-load.

1302 pro cariago unius ~e busce de bosco de Calystok' usque Chubbehole *KRAc* 260/22 m. 3.

bargina, foreign, foreigner or (?) parchment (? conf. w. *pergamena*).

nam rudis et priscae legis patefecit abyssum / septuaginta duos recludens bargina biblos, / quos nunc sacratis describit littera cartis ALDH. *VirgV* 1626; thesaurosque simul librorum forte Pelasgos / edidit in lucem, quos bargina texerat umbra *Ib.* 2151; ~a, *boccfel* ÆLF. *Gl.*; **10..** ~a, *þa elþeodigan oððe of elþeodiscre* WW.

barhudum, ~us, ~a [OF *bahut*], 'barehide', cart-cover.

1160 pro sellis et barhutis *Pipe* 13; **1172** pro bulgiis et ~is *Pipe* 145; **1176** pro..barhuziis *Pipe* 13; **1180** pro v barruzis et apparatu j carrete *Pipe* 150; **1180** pro bolgis et bahurd' et sella summarii *RScacNorm* I 70; pro..bocell' et bahurto et tractis et frenis *Ib.* 71; **1190** pro ij ~is ad eadem armamenta cooperienda *Pipe* 4; **1204** j bonam carectam ferratam..ad opus venationis nostre et unum barrutum longum ad opus ejusdem carecte *Cl* 5b; **1205** unam sellam sumarii et unum barid' *Ib.* 16b; **1205** sellas ad sumar' et barudos *Ib.* 54b; **1214** j barutum *Ib.* 140a; **1230** pro j barhud' ad cooperiendum papilionem xx s. *Pipe* 97; **1235** non fuit ausus clamare sed cooperuit capud suum quodam ~o *CurR* XV 1438 (cf. *EHR* X 296); **1242** pro xij bahudis magnis ad predictas xij carectas, videlicet pro quolibet bahudo ij m. *Liberate* 16 m. 6; **1285** in una bahuda longa et curta lxvj s. viij d. *KRAc* 351/18 m. 1; **1290** in bahur'..emendandis *Ac. Swinfield* 179; ejus [sc. servientis summariorum] est eciam carectas emere, saccos, bahuda et hujusmodi harnesium *Fleta* 80; **1299** in ix coriis boum emptis pro saccis et ~is *Ac. Durh.* 498; **1314** in j barura facienda *Ib.* 512; **1332** j carecta curta cum una bahuda longa (*KRAc* 386/7) *Arch.* LXXVII 121; **1342** in..reparacione baridorum *Sacr. Ely* II 107; **c1350** cum j †baihudo coriario ad eandem carrucam *Mon. Exon.* 344a; barusia, A. *a barhyde* WW.

†bariam [?], sinister omen.

auguria..in sinistro latere sunt confernova, confervetus, viviam, bariam, scassarnova, scassarvetus M. Scot. *Phys.* 56.

bariarius v. barrerarius. barica v. 2 bargia.

†baricus, fabulous Indian beast.

hec bestia vocatur ~us; ..idem est animal de quo Avicenna loquitur et Plinius [*NH* VIII 21: mantichora] Bart. Angl. XVIII 1.

baridum v. barhudum.

barile [OF *baril*; cf. 1 barellus], barrel (measure of fish).

1428 pro sex magnis ~ibus salmonum et sex parvis ~ibus salmonum *ExchScot* IV 446; **1460** in solucione octo ~ium birri *Ib.* VII 60; **1480** de custuma lxxvij lastarum barelium salmonum *Ib.* IX 63.

barillatum v. barellettum. barillus v. 1 barellus. barinettus v. baronettus a. bariqua v. barrica.

†barisellum, small barrel.

lagena..vocatur berillum..cujus diminutivum laguncula, quam nos dicimus ~um Bart. Angl. XIX 125.

baristarius v. barristarius.

†bariulus [? *for* variolus; *but* cf. bardioriolus], (?) kind of finch.

~us, *reagufinc*, *GlC* B 58; **9..** barrulus, *ragufinc* WW.

barius v. varius. bark- v. berc-. barmannus v. bermannus. barnagium v. baronagium. barneta v. bernaca.

1 baro [? CL baro = *lout*], slave.

680 diversas ob causas Petrum apostolum hunc [tonsurae] ritum sumpsisse asserimus: ..postremo, ut idem apostolus suique successores..ridiculosum gannaturae ludibrium in populo Romano portarent, quia et eorum ~ones et hostes exercitu superato sub corona vendere solebant Aldh. *Ep.* 4 p. 483.

2 baro [OF *ber*, *baron* (?) < Frk.], baron, royal vassal, or tenant in chief (*cf. Eng. Feudalism* 83–111): **a** (Eng.); **b** (Scot.); **c** (Ir.); **d** (Continent).

a **a1070** W. rex Anglorum..omnibus ~onibus Francis et Anglis *Regesta* p. 118 (cf. *EHR* XXV 388); judicio ~onum regis qui placitum tenuerunt *DB* I 2; coram episcopo Baiocensi et aliis ~onibus regis *Ib.* 175b; **1100** sciatis me..communi consilio ~onum regni Angliae..coronatum fuisse (*Ch. Hen. I*) *GAS* 521; si quis ~onum meorum, comitum sive aliorum qui de me tenent, mortuus fuerit *Ib.*; regis judices sint ~ones comitatus, qui liberas in eis terras habent (*Leg. Hen.*) *Ib.* 563 (*cf. Const. Clarendon* c. 11); [rex] nulli..episcoporum suorum concessum iri permittebat ut aliquem de ~onibus suis seu ministris..excommunicaret Eadmer *HN* 12 (cf. *GAS* 520); in debitis regiis requirendis.., baronum regis et ceterorum..par condicio non est *Dial. Scac.* II 19; hoc debet dominus rex de jure ~onibus suis, scilicet quod ob talem causam possint ~ones sui curias suas sic in curiam suam ponere Glanv. VIII 11; mortuo aliquo capitali ~one suo *Ib.* IX 6; miles quidam ex his qui dominici dicuntur in Francia, ~ones in Anglia Map *NC* IV 6 p. 159; **1209** quia est ~o domini regis et regem trahit ad warantum, dies datus est ei coram rege *SelPlForest* 9; pro libertate tenenda / bāronum Garl. *Tri. Eccl.* 54; **1256** rex ipsum pre aliis [justiciariis] vult honorari quia ~o regis est *Cl* 400; **1275** per quam portam borones (*sic*) in guerra habuerunt introitum..ad saltandum castrum *Hund.* I 397; **s1314** nobilis..barro Robertus de Clifforde cum multis aliis nobilibus Trokelowe 85. **b** **c1130** rex..~onibus, vicecomitibus, ministris et omnibus fidelibus suis totius Laudonie *E. Ch. Scot.* 91 (cf. ib. 30: tegnis et drengis de Lodenie); **s1138** rex..David duobus tegnionibus, id est ~onibus, suis Ric. Hex. *Stand.* 42; **1165** pro terris quas ego ~onibus et militibus meis dedi *Regesta Scot.* 265 (cf. ib. 183); placitum civile..aliud [pertinet] ad curiam ~onum, comitum, episcoporum *RegiamM* I 4; **1565** temporalium comitum et ~onum *Scot. Grey Friars* II 48. **c** **1200** salva assisa ~onum Hibernie de nativis suis *RChart* 97a; **1213** super sacramento fidelitatis nuper nobis prestito a ~onibus nostris Hybernie *Cl* 132b. **d** **s1040** juravit Theobaldus [comes Campaniensis] et xx ~ones castellenses cum eo et xl milites vavassores Diceto *Chr.* I 184; **1130** hunc [Papam] principes, capitanei et ~ones..frequentant (*Lit. Ep. Portuensis*) W. Malm. *HN* 454; **1346** ceciderunt..alii eciam barones et milites in numerum (*Lit. Confessoris Regis*) Ad. Mur. 216 (= Avesb. 109: *dez autrez countes et barons..et seignurs*).

2 applied to thane (*cf.* 1b) or other pre-Conquest dignitary.

omnes alii erant commendati aliis ~onibus T. R. E. *DB* II 287; omnis thainus [v.l. baro] meus [*ælc minra þegna*] (*Quad.*) *GAS* 182 (cf. ib. 567); **s905** occisus est..Adelwald ~o regis H. Hunt. *HA* V 153; omnes ~ones, scilicet teines et dreinges, ..conveniant (*Fest. S. Cuthb.*) *Hist. Durh. app.* cccxxxii (cf. G. T. Lapsley *County Palatine of Durham*, 24, 108); Saxones..jugulaverunt circiter ccccclx [Britonum] inter ~ones et consules G. Mon. VI 15.

3 tenant in chief of magnate.

1109 precatu..~onum nostrorum (*Ch. Comitis Northampt.*) *MonA* V 180 (cf. *Rec. Leic.* I 1); **c1120** concesserunt ante ~ones Ramesiensis ecclesie predictus abbas et..camerarius *Cart. Rams.* I 142; **a1121** residente in curia sua Bath' Johanne episcopo cum amicis et ~onibus *Cart. Bath* 49; **1148** communi consilio prioris de S. Pancratio et ~onum consulis [i.e. comitis] reddidi burgensibus Lewiensibus *BBC* (*Lewes*) I 203 (*cf. ib.* II 243 & 5 infra).

4 baron as hereditary title.

1387 volentes quod idem Johannes et heredes masculi de corpore suo exeuntes statum ~onis optineant ac domini de Beauchamp et ~ones de Kydemyster nuncupentur *Pat* 324 m. 12; **s1462** comes de Warwyk, comes de Kent, ..~o de Greystuk *Chr. Hen. VI & Ed. IV* 159.

5 title applied to free man (later restricted in sense): **a** (London); **b** (Cinque Ports); **c** (other city or town).

a habitatores aliarum urbium cives, hujus ~ones dicuntur W. Fitzst. *Thom. prol.* 8; **1190** testificatum fuit..a majoribus ~onibus civitatis (*Ch. Ep. Ely*) *Comm. Lond.* 253; **1215** ~onibus nostris de civitate nostra Londoniarum *RChart* 207; **s1248** et rex: "scio, scio..abundant enim illi rustici Londonienses, qui se ~ones appellant, usque ad nauseam" M. Par. *Maj.* V 22; a civibus Londoniensibus, quos propter civitatis dignitatem et civium antiquam libertatem ~ones consuevimus appellare *Ib.* 367; **1419** aldermanni tam nomine quam honore ~ones antiquitus dicebantur *MGL* I 33. **b** **a1158** ~ones mei de Hastingg[es] (*Cart. S. Benet Holm*) *Feudal Eng.* 561; **1200** ~onibus de Quinque Portubus *RChart* 60b; libertatem..quale[m] habent ~ones de Quinque Portubus Bracton 411b. **c** **1381** sunt tenentes ejusdem ville [de Corf] vocati ~ones *IMisc* 223/17.

6 baron (assessor) of the Exchequer: **a** (Westminster); **b** (Norm.); **c** (Ir.); **d** (Canterbury, mon.).

a **1120** rex..~onibus scaccarii salutem (*AncD* A 231) R. L. Poole *Exchequer in Twelfth Century* 39; **a1127** ~ones mei de scaccario (*Breve Hen. I*) *Ib.* 40; **1130** [cancellarius] non fuit ad scaccarium cum aliis ~onibus regis *Pipe* 140; ~ones qui ad scaccarium resident de victualibus sue domus..nichil solvunt *Dial. Scac.* I 8B; **1236** omnes ~ones residentes in scaccario nostro quieti sunt de sectis comitatuum *KRMem* 14 r. 8*d.*; justiciarii ibidem [in scaccario] commorantes ~ones esse dicimus, eo quod suis locis ~ones sedere solebant *Fleta* 28; **1317** eundem Walterum capitalem ~onem scaccarii nostri constituimus *Pat* 147 m. 11; **c1410** bāroni cui vis placeas, saltim capitali (*Vers. Exch.*) *EHR* XXXVI 59; apud praefectum Statarii, quem ~onem dicunt P. Verg. XIV 244; in hac [curia] judices sunt..capitalis ~o, ~ones alii tres Camd. *Br.* 142. **b** **a1123** per judicium ~onum de scaccario (*Ch. Bernardi Scriptoris* 9) *EHR* XIV 426. **c** **1207** rex justiciario Hibernie et ~onibus de scaccario Dublin' *Cl* 96b; **1419** secundario ~oni scaccarii Hibern' (*Pat. Hib.*) *RSelecti* 74. **d** **1473** petit allocari de denariis solutis ~onibus tempore scaccarii *DC Cant. Ac. Pri.* xvii 12 (cf. *Cant. Cath. Pri.* 20).

7 judge in market court (Ir.).

1223 quatuor homines dicte ville eligi debent ~ones ad tenenda placita nundinarum *Lib. Kilken.* 77.

8 man of note, worthy.

dentem..tanti ~onis [sc. S. Nicholai, archiepiscopi] nactus, Normanniam rediit Ord. Vit. VII 13; bāro bāronis gravis ac autenticus est vir Garl. *Syn.* 1581D (*cf. Id. Dict.* 128 *gl.*: ~ones dicuntur a *barim* quod est grave, quasi grave[s] persone).

9 husband (Anglo-Norm. *baron*).

12.. cum consensu boronum (*sic*) nostrorum *Ch. Derb.* 1788.

3 †baro [? misr. of Ar. *dūd*], worm infesting nose.

sunt aliquando vermes in naso et cum nasus comprimitur exeunt, qui vocantur ~ones vel nepones Gad. 131. 1.

baroco, baroko, a logical mood.

cesare, campestres, festino, barōco, darapti Bacon XV 301 (cf. *GLA* III 15).

baronagium, baronage, body or order of barons. **b** barony, feudal tenure.

1233 de communi consilio barnagii nostri *Cl* 317; **s1224** suscepit..sigilli custodiam totius barnagii Anglie assensu M. Par. *Min.* II 267; **s1239** dominus Papa scripsit regi Francorum significans eidem ut juberet epistolam coram ipso et toto ~io Francie..legi *Id. Maj.* III 624; quod universitas regni et ~ium hoc facere debeat Bracton 171b; **s1268** cum universum barnagium regni Anglie..venissent London' ad parlamentum *Leg. Ant. Lond.* 108; **s1328** comes Lancastrie gubernator regius per bernagium..constitutus *Meaux* II 358; nomine ~ii Anglie omnes quodammodo regni ordines continebantur Camd. *Br.* 137. **b** **1269** feodis que..de nobis tenuit in capite per ~ium *Cl* 81; **a1460** si ita sit quod tenent per ~ium de rege aut de aliqua dignitate ecclesie *BBAdm.* I 234.

baronalis, adherent of barons.

s1264 nec facere discerni poterat..qui dicerentur regales et qui ~es W. Guisb. 195.

baronatus, barony (Fr.).

1212 antiquus rex Henricus dedit..manerium de Mutford'..in aumentacione ~us de Baldemund' *Fees* 135.

baronessa v. baronissa.

baronettus [cf. banerettus], lesser baron. **b** baronet.

1318 occisis ~is de Scocia xxix Wals. *HA* I 154; **s1322** comes Lancastrie et cum eo barones, ~i et milites xc Baker 102; **s1340** [rex] precepit ut [W. de la Pole] pro barinetto haberetur *Meaux* III 48; **s1377** duo barones, duo ~i, duo bachilarii milites Ad. Mur. *Cont.* B 229; **1550** cum..ad ordinem statum gradum honorem et dignitatem ~i per nos erectus suscitatus et creatus extiterit (*Pat* 834) *EHR* XXXVI 227. **b** **1611** ordinavimus ereximus constituimus et creavimus quendam statum gradum dignitatem nomen et titulum ~i Anglice *of a Baronett* infra hoc regnum nostrum Anglie perpetuis temporibus duraturum *Pat* 1942 m. 4*d.*

baronia, barony, estate held in chief of the crown (*cf. EHR* xxxv 161–99): **a** (Eng.); **b** (Scot.); **c** (Ir.).

a **1142** concedo Roberto de Ver unam ~iam ad valentiam honoris Galfridi de Ver (*Carta M. Imp.*) *Mandeville* 182; **1164** episcopi et universe persone regni qui de rege tenent in capite habent possessiones suas de domino rege sicut ~iam *Const. Clar.* 11; quidam de rege tenent in capite, ~ias scilicet majores seu minores *Dial. Scac.* II 10D; nec episcopus nec abbas, quia eorum ~ie sunt de elemosina domini regis Glanv. VII 1; bailivi regis..saisiabunt abbatiam in manu sua, scilicet ~iam que pertinet ad abbatem Brakelond 144; **1205** quod terre et tenementa infra predictum burgum [*Shrewsbury*] et hundredum tractentur per legem Bretoll' et legem baronye et legem Anglescherie..*RChart* 142b (*cf. EHR* XV 307); ~ia sua tota, quam regalia reges appellant, ipsum [episcopum] ilico destitui jussit Gir. *Hug.* 8 p. 104; **s1244** rex..prohibuit ne novo electo..introitus in ~iam ecclesie sue pertinentem..concederetur M. Par. *Maj.* IV 402; **s1257** nominavit..rex et numeravit omnes Anglie, quarum ei occurrit memoria, ~ias inventque ccl *Ib.* V 617; **s1290** bona ~ie conventus a ~ia abbatis discreta sunt *G. S. Alb* II 4; **1276** tenuit de rege..in capite duas ~ias, scilicet lxxj feoda militum *Hund.* I 56; summoneri et venire debent omnes..illi qui habent terras et redditus ad valentiam..unius ~ie integre, sc. tresdecim feoda et terciam partem unius feodi militis *Mod. Ten. Parl.* 7. **b** **c1172** excepta assisa ~ie sue [*Annandale*] *Regesta Scot.* II 80; **1255** rex fecit inquisicionem fieri coram..justic' Scocie per plures ~ias *Reg. Dunferm.* 85; **a1321** sciatis nos dedisse..medietatem tocius ~ie de Wilton..infra vicecomitatum de Roxburghe *RMSScot* I 17; **1369** ministri regis non taxent..secundum numerum †davatarum [? l. davacarum] seu ~iarum (*Act. Dav. II*) *APScot* 174; **1469** per integras firmas ~ie de Ballincrefe *ExchScot* 615 (cf. ib. 23: dominii de B.). **c** **1282** compotus..receptoris ~iarum Veteris Ros et Insule *MinAc* 1239/11; **1540** extenta maneriorum..in ~ia de Moysenragh in comitatu Midie *Rent. & Surv. R* 934 r. 1*d.*

2 baronial tenure.

1185 ij bovatas quas tenet in ~ia de domino rege *RDomin.* 16; **1225** distringatur, quia tenet in barunia *LTRMem* 7 r. 18*d.* (cf. *Fees* I 75); quamvis hujusmodi terre dentur in liberam elemosinam, non solum dantur ecclesiis sed et personis tenendae in ~ia Bracton 286b; **a1321** sciatis nos dedisse..totam terram de Kymbrigham..tenendam..in liberam ~iam *RMS Scot* I no. 5; **1341** qui per ~iam nihil tenent de ipso [rege] nec ad parliamentum suum..venire sunt astricti (*Lit. Archiep. Cant.*) W. Guisb. *Cont.* II 373.

3 freehold in London or Cinque Ports.

1286 quesiti..qualiter ~ia in civitate London' que de domino rege tenetur possit legari *CoramR* 98 r. 31 (cf. *Gl. Arch.* 73); [custos V Portuum] eligi faciat de quolibet portu.., duos barones ad veniendum..ad parliamentum..et faciendum idem quod [v.l. quod facerent] ~ie sue, ac si ipsi de ~iis illis omnes..personaliter interessent ibidem *Mod. Ten. Parl.* 9.

4 lordship.

1242 salvis semper nobis..duobus cereis..reddendis in signum et testimonium ~ie nostre *Cart. Eye* f. 30.

5 nobility (collect.).

obsederunt Athelstanum cum ~ia sua in civitate [Wyntonie] Knighton I 21.

†baronicius, *f.l.* for *Baroncinus* (personal name).

(*AncC.* XI 61) *RL* II 308.

baronicus, baronial.

Reginaldus [de Mohun] qui bello ~ico honore excidit Camd. *Br.* 186.

baronissa, baroness, tenant in chief (f.) or wife of baron.

barones..et ~e et eorum superiores non affidabunt sed plegios invenient Bracton 351b; **1270** quia ipsa [M. Lungespee] ~a nostra est, cui..sicut nec aliis fidelibus regni nostri..deesse non possumus *Cl* 294; **s1344** fuerunt..ibidem..comitisse, ~e, necnon domine et domicelle Ad. Mur. *app.* 231; **1496** Eleanore Dowdale baronesse de Novan (*Comp. Subthes. Hib.*) *L. & P. Ric. III & Hen. VII* 309.

baronulus, lesser baron (*cf. baronettus*).

1513 universis vicecapitaneis, ..locatenentibus, baronibus

~is, dominis, nobilibus, militibus, ..in exercitu et armata nostra retentis (*Pat*) *Foed.* XIII 349 (*cf.* ib. 364).

barqua v. barca.

1 barra, ~us [OF *barre*], bar, rod. **b** bar blocking archway or road (*cf.* 4*c*). **c** door-bar. **d** window-bar.

1221 percussit eum cum quadam ~a, quod cecidit *Pl. Cr. Glouc.* 99; **1274** in xxj cleis de baris faciendis et xxiiij cleys de virgis faciendis *MinAc* 984/4 r. 4. **b 1238** quod archeam subtus privatam cameram regis versus aquam Tamisie bonis et fortibus ~is ferreis barrari faciat *Cl* 99; **1344** venellam cum duobus magnis lapidibus et duabus ~is ferreis obturavit *MGL* II 449. **c 1282** asportavit duas ~as euntes ex transverso portam *Rec. Leic.* I 198. **d 1304** pro fabricacione ~eorum ferri pro fenestris *MinAc* 771/4 m. 6; **1331** ~i ferrei fenestrarum magne aule *IMisc* 114/10; **1344** in..~is ferreis emptis pro dicta fenestra *Ac. Durh* 40; **s1404** Romani..hospicium invadunt, ..nihil penitus quantum fenestrarum ~as in eo relinquentes AD. USK 88.

2 transverse bar or wedge in barrel or sim.

1196 pro circulis et ~is et doliis reparandis *Pipe* 18; **1198** pro circulis et ~is ad tonellos vini servandos *Pipe* 183; **1324** ~a ferri ex transverso busselli domini regis *MGL* II 382.

3 band, stripe. **b** bar (her.).

1245 amictus est de aurifrigio puro cum ~is de margaritis (*Invent. S. Paul*) *Arch.* L 480; **1355** j chalonem cum ~is albis (*Invent.*) *MunCOx* 131; **1414** parvam zonam deauratam cum ~is rotundis *Reg. Cant.* III 319. **b** ~a est illa que ex transverso ducitur BAD. AUR. 138; non sunt vere ~e, quia non extenduntur totaliter per predicta arma UPTON 248–9.

4 (*cf. barrera*) **a** barrier against animals in woodland or fenland. **b** barricade (mil.). **c** town bar. **d** toll bar (Gasc.). **e** (pl.) lists (for jousting). **f** game of 'bars' (prisoner's base).

a 1260 quando wodewardi domini buscant.., tunc idem.. infirmabit ~as post decessum..wodewardorum *Cust. Glast.* 190; **1239** desicut..debent..tres battellos..ad cariandum lingna..per quandam ~am que firmata est in eadem lada, ..serviens..precludit ei ingressum per eandem ~am et serrat ~am illam cum clavi *CurR* 120 r. 7 (*Crowland*); **1374** ordinant quod †fecerunt [l. ~int] octo ~as super dictum fossatum ad impediendum cursus tam animalium extraneorum quam communariorum (*Inq. Ely*) *Terr. Fleet app.* 174 (cf. ib. pp. xlviii, xxxiv, xvi). **b** Gaufridus.. restitit eis et a ~is quas jam super nostros occupaverant.. repulit *Itin. Ric.* III 5. **c c1160** terram..extra portam Ebor'..juxta ~am occidentalem *Couch. Kirkstall* 145; **1265** in suburbio Eboraci juxta ~am de Mikelgate *Cl* 17; **1444** extra ~as boriales Beverlaci *Test. Ebor.* II 97; **a1188** extra ~am que est extra portam nostram que vocatur Bissupesgate *E. Ch. S. Paul* 47; **1204** extra ~am de Smedefeld' *CurR* III 189; **1204** extra ~am de Holeburne (*Fine*) *PN. Middx* 185; **1293** extra ~am Novi Templi London' *Pat* 112 m. 17; **1512** extra ~os Novi Templi (*Pat*) *Foed.* XIII 334. **d 1289** concedimus eis ~am ad pontem..ad relevacionem suorum sumptuum exitibus dicte ~e *RGasc* II 491 (cf. 211); **1314** (v. barragium 2). **e s1467** factis in Smythfeld, London, ~is et tentoriis *Compilatio* 181. **f** *bace-play*, ~i *PP*.

5 bar of lawcourt.

1288 inveniendo plegios legis recessit de ~a sine licencia (*St. Ives*) *Law Merch.* I 36 (*cf. Cal. CourtR Chester* 43); **a1290** (v. apprenticius 2); **1306** statim post pronunciacionem judicii predicti contemptabiliter ~am ascendit et ab ipso Rogero peciit..si judicium illud advocare vellet *Abbr. Plac.* 257a; **1324** precepit ut ad ~am, sc. ad illum locum duceretur ubi stare consueverunt latrones et rei *Proc. A. Kyteler* 14; **1345** tempore quo juratores dicte inquisicionis fuerunt ad ~am coram justiciariis..pro veredicto suo dicendo *SelCKB* VI 42; **1361** injuncto..hostiariis dicti scaccarii quod custodirent ~as et introitus ejusdem scaccarii *Ib.* V cxlii; **1389** clerici de secunda forma..sedeant extra ~am ejusdem Cancellarie tempore..placitorum tenendorum *Chanc. Orders* 3; **c1410** primitus intrabis ad barram corpore tristi / et tunc jurabis.. (*Vers. Exch.* 5) *EHR* XXXVI 59.

6 bar, objection (leg.).

1384 placitavit versus eum in ~am executionis finis predicti *RParl* III 192b; **1451** sufficienter materiam in ~am et exclusionem actionis..allegavit *Reg. Whet.* I 67; **1587** hujusmodi relaxacio [etc.] erit in ea parte sufficiens ~a, relaxacio, exoneracio et acquietancia versus nos..de et pro premissis *Pat* 1301 m. 40.

2 barra v. barsa. barrador v. barrator.

barragium, wedging of barrels.

1221 pro carcagio et ~io eorundem doliorum *Cl* 460b; **1230** pro ~io et sigillagio dictorum doliorum vini *Pipe* 201.

2 toll paid at toll bar (Gasc.).

1314 quod ipsi..barram pontis illius necnon et barras portarum et introituum ville Agenni predicte haberent..et ~ium perciperent..a transeuntibus *RGasc* IV 1207 (cf. ib. 1231).

barrans v. barrire.

barrare, ~eare, to bar, fit with bars. **b** to bar, wedge (a barrel).

1238 in fenestra ~ata ferro *Cl* 26; **1249** habeant duas fenestras versus gardinum..apertas, ita tamen quod..ferro ~entur *AncD* A 10849. **b 1205** quod..faciatis dolia bene ligari et ~ari *Cl* 41; **1225** in eisdem doliis †barcandis [l. bareandis], cerclandis et carcandis *Cl* 62 b (cf. ib. 118: barreandis); **1335** in..doleis ligandis, ~andis et †cartandis *Comp. Swith.* 228.

2 (p. ppl.) banded, striped. **b** barry (her.).

1215 zonam de rubeo corio ~atam *Pat* 145b; **1234** zonam bombicinam ~atam argento *CurR* XV 1108; **1245** panno.. ~ato minutis barris auri (*Invent. S. Paul*) *Arch.* L 488. **b** arma..vocantur ~ata quia aptantur ad modum barrarum BAD. AUR. 128; [arma] de coloribus invectis ~atis..sunt ~ata cum diversis coloribus in ipsis barris invectis *Ib.* 136; arma ~ata de coloribus rubio et albo invectis UPTON 231.

3 to bar, block.

1218 intraverunt domum illam et ~averunt hostia *Eyre Yorks.* 298; domum..nequiter et in felonia ~avit et fregit *Ib.* 224; **1275** contra..constabularium..dictam villam de Sandwyco..cathenis ~averunt et fossatis vallaverunt *SelCKB* I 13.

4 to subject to an imposition (Gasc.).

1254 non ~eabimus..villam vel bona hominum..ville aut per violenciam capiemus *RGasc* I 466 (*cf. CalPat* 303).

5 to bar, preclude (leg.).

1236 sed hoc falso dicit ad impediendum et ~andum †os [l. jus, *as CurR* XV 1882] ipsius *BNB* III 195; **1453** nec causa quacumque..de aliquo statum et hereditamentum sua infra regnum Scotie concernente..exhereditatus exclusus neque ~atus..existit (*RScot*) *Foed.* XI 339; **1471** ad excludendum et ~andum predictum R. ..ab actione sua predicta *Entries* 619b.

barrarius v. barrera 2 and 3.

barras [Ar. *baraṣ*; cf. albaras], leprosy.

quandoque provenit canicies ex infirmitate cutis ut in morphea et barras BACON IX 20.

barratare v. baratare.

barratim, barwise (her.).

de armis istis in quibus ponuntur tres corone ~im BAD. AUR. 142.

barratio, bar, exclusion (leg.).

1417 in plenam exclusionem et ~onem omnium et singularum condicionum *Cl* 267 m. 18*d*.

barrator [cf. barrare 2], fitter of bars.

1182 Rodberti Baratoris *Cart. Osney* II 6; **1237** cerclatoribus et ~toribus *Cal. Liberate* 277; **1254** emant..duas cavillas ad magnum ingenium regis..et tres barras ferreas et ea regi mittant et insuper omnes barradores quos habere poterunt *Cl* 259 (= *RGasc* I 417).

barreare v. barrare.

barrera, ~ia, ~ius [OF. *barrere, barriere*; cf. barra 5], **a** barrier, obstruction in water-course or street. **b** barricade (mil.). **c** town or toll bar. **d** (pl.) lists (for jousting).

a s1285 quod ~e et piles per abbatem S. Augustini in cursu aque erecte super calcetum..deponentur (*Compositio*) THORNE 1940; **1290** abbas S. Benedicti obstruxit quandam ripariam ~a et catena *RParl* I 56; **1288** levavit quandam ~am in via Norwici nocentem itinerantibus *Leet Norw.* 12. **b 1238** fieri facias..~as extra pontem castri *Liberate* 13 m. 26 (*sched.*); **1260** maeremium..ad ~as faciendas ante diversos pontes..castri [Wyndesor'] *Cl* 47; **1365** pro ~iis factis apud Edynburgh *ExchScot* 222. **c 1279** extra portam ~e de Burgo *RGasc* II 52; **1287** assignati fuerunt ad vigilandum ad pedem pontis S. Ivonis et ad custodiendum cathenam et ~am ibidem *Law Merch.* I 16. **d 1404** pro ~is factis pro duello apud Strivelin *ExchScot* 596.

2 bar in lawcourt. **b** bar or (?) official collecting dues at bar (Norm.).

1300 in scannis et ~is faciendis pro itinere..justiciariorum..apud Ely *MinAc* 1132/10 m. 15b; **1333** in maeremio, bordis et pilis emptis in villa Colcestr'..pro ~a ubi justiciarii consueti sunt sedere *LTRMem* 105 r. 194; ipse Thomas..per ereccionem corporis sui ultra ~am impetuose loquens *Ib.* r. 41; **c1460** ut..per assisam specialem..cogeret eum ad ~am accedere faterique..coram judicibus se errasse *Reg. Whet.* I 431. **b 1151** quod nullus eorum de terra sua intersignia a vicecomitatu accipiat ad ~um, sed ipse ~io affidet quod consuetudinem non debet, si ei aliter non crediderit; et nullus det aliquid ~io nisi sponte sua (*Ch. Rouen*) *Regesta* 729.

3 rail, railing (*cf.* ME *barrer*).

1291 pro cooperculo supra imaginem regine et ~iis circa eandem (*Lib. pro Regina*) *Manners* 121; **1386** volo quod cista corporis mei cooperiatur cum panno laneo de russeto et una cruce rubea et quod barrarii circa corpus meum die sepulture mee ordinentur de eadem †setta [l. secta] (*Test.*) *FormA* 429.

barrerarius, a bar-keeper (leg.). **b** barrister.

a 1292 rex..commisit..officium preconis, marescalli, hostiarii et ~ii..in itineribus *LTRMem* 63 r. 38; **1332** serjantiam hostiarii de scaccario..ad quam pertinent officia clamatoris et hostiarii in communi banco..necnon et officium marescalli, hostiarii, clamatoris et ~ii in omnibus itineribus justiciariorum *IPM* 31/33 r. 4; **1369** excepta tercia parte officiorum..proclamatorum et barriariorum in singulis itineribus *Pat* 280 m. 10; **1506** officium marescallorum, hostiariorum, proclamatorum et barriariorum tam in communi Banco..quam in singulis itineribus justiciariorum *Pat* 599 m. 6. **b 1455** duo de optimis barrer' (*Black. Bk. Lincoln's Inn*) *Hist. Eng. Bar* 522 n.

barrettator v. baratator. barreus v. barra. barriarius v. barrerarius.

barrica [cf. Sp. *barrica*], bareca, breaker, barrel.

1445 lxvi dolia et unam ~am vini de Vasconia *Cl* 295 m. 11; **1606** cum..unam bariquam malorum cidoniorum Anglice *quinces*..piratice ceperint *Pat* 1714 m. 28.

barridus [etym. dub.], oppressive, haughty.

barrida pravicolae qui stravi examina turbae FRITH. 1098; **c1370** pax erit in terra, rediet sed barrida guerra (J. BRIDL.) *Pol. Poems* I 176 (*gl.* ib. 177: i. forte bellum); barrida nam bella cancer parat ipse novella *Ib.* 194 (*gl.* ib. 196: unde est notandum quod est terminus 'barrida', vel descendit a 'barri' [βαρύ] quod est grave..vel..a 'barro -nis'..vel dicitur a 'barrus, barri' qui est elephans); **1440** ut ~us doctor et ampullosus didascolus te intitulas BEKYNTON I 116.

barrire [CL], to trumpet.

~it elefans cum vocem emittit *GlC* B 34; barrans, elefans *Erf.* 2. 270. 30; elefanti ~iunt vel strident ALDH. *PR* 132.

barristarius, (?) maker or fitter of wooden bars (*cf. barrator*).

1213 de bosco vendito..ad opus baristariorum c summis *DCCant. Rental* 38/1 m. 5.

1 †barritus, (?) set with bars, toothed.

plecte..ossa / formam barriti pectinis instar habent NECKAM *DS* III 436.

2 barritus [CL], roar (esp. trumpeting of elephant).

~us, *genung GlC* B 23; horrendos beluarum ~us ALDH. *VirgP* 28; **9..** ~us *geonung*, vel dissimilis, *gepota*, *rarung* WW; elephas..casum / barritu prodit NECKAM *DS* IX 50.

barrium [Sp. *barrio* < Ar. *barr*, Sp. Ar. *barrī*], suburb, extramural quarter (Gasc.).

1289 poterit habere..furnum in ..bastida et ~io.. bastide *RGasc* II 354; **1317** in eodem castro et ~io ejusdem castri *Ib.* IV 1807.

barro v. baro.

barrula, barrulet (her.).

sunt..~e que..depinguntur cum barra, ut hic patet et portat de argento cum una barra et duabus ~is de nigro BAD. AUR. 139; tales linee vocantur barule ad differenciam majorum barrarum UPTON 233.

barrulus v. bariulus.

barrura [cf. barrera, ME *barriour*], barrier, barricade. **b** (pl.) lists for jousting.

in stipendiis..faciencium ~as circa dictam domum..ne animalia prosternebant parietes ejusdem *DL MinAc* 242/3886 m. 3; **1469** super fossatum nostrum equitando, apertis ~is et cunctis remotis obstaculis *Croyl. Cont. B* 542. **b 1442** super factura quarundam listarum et ~arum de maeremio apud Westsmythfeld..pro certis punctis sive factis armorum (*Ac. Foreign 20 Hen. VI D*) *Analog. Cant. Pilg.* 23.

2 bar of a lawcourt.

1398 pro sedibus justiciariorum et clericorum necnon et formul' et barrur' infra domum predictam *KRAc* 575/28.

1 barrus v. barra.

2 barrus [CL], elephant.

~us, elefans *GlC* B 28; admissam tigrida barri / segnities inflexa fugat HANV. V 308; **c1370** (v. barridus); *an olyfaunte*, ..'signat idem barrus, elephans simul et elephantus' *CathA*.

barrutum, barruzum, v. barhudum.

barsa, ~us [AS *bærs*], barse, bass (fish).

a1200 dedit..de gersuma j aureum et duos ~os *AncD* A 2423; **1266** ~is marinis *CalIMisc* I 103; **1267** in j barcio de mari, xviij d. *Ac. Leyburn* 213; **1289** in vij hak', j barr' *Ac. Swinfield* 13; **1294** peciit..omnes caudas salmonum et ~arum..ad coquinam..conventus veniencium *Cart. Chester* II 353; **1324** barcium meliorem pro ij d. (*Lib. Cust.*) *MGL* II 118.

barselettus v. berselettus. barsus v. 2 burrus. bartagium, ~atio v. baitagium, ~atio.

bartona v. bertona. barudus v. barhudum.

†baruina, *s. dub.*

~a, *barriggæ GlC* B 56; †braugina, *barice Ib.* 196; **9..** †baruhina, *bericge*, ..†brugma, *barice* WW.

barula v. barrula.

barunculus, lesser baron (*cf. baronettus, baronulus*).

14.. hic ~us, *a baronet* WW.

barunia v. baronia. barura, barusia, barutum v. barhudum.

barytonare, to pronounce with a grave accent. **b** to shorten.

14.. baritonans, graviter accentuans WW. **b** *to schorte*, barritonare, corripere, breviare *CathA*.

barytonus [βαρύτονος], (?) slurring.

mos est barbarice locutionis et maxime Saxonum verba ac nomina..transformare apocopando ac sepius syncopando, ut pro Thoma *Tomme*; ..unde talis corruptio ~a vitium..inexcusabile comprimit ELMH. *Cant.* 338.

barzisa v. bersisa. basa v. 1 basis 2a, vasa. basalardus v. 1 baselardus.

basanarius, worker in basan.

1272 nec ~ius de opere alluti amodo se intromittat *MGL* III 441.

basanum, ~a [OF *basane* < Ar. *biṭānā*], basan, sheep's leather.

c1177 pro bazana viij d. (*Cust. Brissac*) *Act. Hen. II* II 55; abbas Willelmus [ob. 1235]..conventus calciamenta que de vili corio quod vulgariter *bazan* dicitur in alutam, id est *cordewan*, civiliter commutavit *G. S. Alb.* I 293 (cf. ib. *rub.* de sotularibus †basianis [? l. basani]); 1265 pro vj pellibus baszeni (*RHosp*) *Manners* 10; 1272 allutarius quisellos ad ocreas de †basanto..facere potest *MGL* III 442 (cf. basanarius); 1277 xxx balas de ~a (*JustIt*) *Law Merch.* III 139; 1275 de qualibet duodena bazanni *Pat* 94 m. 17; 1296 de qualibet duodena cordewani corves' et bazeni *Pat* 115 m. 8; 1329 duodena..bascenni *Pat* 172 m. 14; 1307 pro pellibus cuniculorum et basayna *EEC* 351; 1344 pro uno pari sotularium basene vendit' pro aluta *MGL* I 550 (= *CalLB Lond* F 98: de corio basene); 1349 visuras de bazano rubeo (*KRAc* 391/15) *Arch.* XXXI 39.

basari [< 1 basis], to be based.

1417 facultas eorum [studentium] septifera super qua non sine causis permaximis predicta mater nostra [sc. universitas] ~atur *Reg. Cant.* III 49 (cf. *Conc.* III 383).

bascatum v. baskettum.

bascauda [CL], basin.

†vescada, *mundleu GlC* V 83.

bascea v. bassum. bascennum v. basanum. bascin- v. bacin-.

Basclensis, Basque.

ipsos ex Hispania venisse et ~es vocatos esse..edoctus fuit G. Mon. III 12; classem invenit que ~es de Hispaniarum partibus illuc advectaverat Gir. *TH* III 8.

†basculum, (?) for *vasculum,* vessel.

1259 debet habere j ~um frumenti *Cust. Glast.* 131.

Basculus, Basque.

1179 de Brebantionibus et Arragonensibus, Navariis, ~is et Coterellis, qui tantam in Christianos immanitatem exercent (*Decr. Lateran.*) W. Newb. I 209 (*cf.* R. Howd. II 179; de..Basclis); 1284 vallecto..conducenti ~os *KRAc* 351/9 m. 9; 1314 majorem [etc.] civitatis nostre Baion'..ac..episcopum loci illius, ~os *RGasc* IV 1189.

1 baselardus, ~a [OF *baselard*; *cf.* OF *badelaire*], baselard, dagger carried in belt (? *cf. bastardus* 3d).

1349 coopertorium unius baselard' de *zatayn* (*KRAc*) *Arch.* XXXI 39; 1356 incidiando..vi et armis, scilicet gladiis et †blaselardis *SelCKB* VI 115 (cf. ib. 178; cum..baselardo); 1373 de..uno ~o et una zona *Pat* 288 m. 4; 1375 cum gladiis et bassellardis extractis *SessPLincs* 195; 1380 quod nullus dictorum scolarium..basilardum portet seu aliquem alium cultellum statui clericorum indecentem (*Pat*) *Foed.* VII 242; s1381 Johannes de Walworth..arrepto basillardo transfixit Jakke Straw in gutture Knighton *Cont.* II 137; 1393 duos baslardos hernesiatos cum argento *Pat* 338 m. 5; 1399 nullus presbyter..deferat †bastardum [l. baslardum] vel cultellum longum (*Pat*) *MonA* VI 1389; 1416 cum optimo basalardo meo *Reg. Cant.* II 103; 1431 basilardam meam parvam vocatam *hanger* cum argento harnesiatam *Ib.* 447; duos †basterdos [l. baslerdos] precii iiij s. *Reg. Brev. Jud.* 83b.

2 baselardus, 'baseling', base coin.

s1158 antiqua moneta [reprobatur], que *baselard* dicebatur; nova successit M. Par. *Min.* III 194 (cf. ib. I 358, *marginal note*: moneta tunc reprobata *baseling* dicebatur); s1180 nova moneta currit in Anglia post basileres circa festum S. Martini *Ann. Wav.* 242; s1298 monete nove, que vocabantur baslardi, pollardi, crocardi et rosarii..loco sterlingorum irrepserunt in Angliam *Meaux* II 272; anno MCCC moneta de ballardo prohibita fuit *Lib. Kilken.* 63; 1301 Agnes..legavit v s. ballardorum ad sustentacionem ecclesie..quos vicarius recepit et detinet *Reg. Exon.* 337; 1309 viginti denarii bellardi, quorum duo..currebant in Anglia pro sterlingo *Cl* 127 m. 18.

basena v. basanum. basenettus v. bacinettus. baseum v. bassum.

†basia, (?) for *vasum,* hive.

1331 basie apium (*Reg. Coventry*) *Antiq. Salop.* IX 308.

basianus v. basanum.

basiare [CL], to kiss.

coepit quasi limphaticus..caccabos complecti tetrasque sartagines ~iare Aldh. *VirgP* 50; 10.. bassiare, *cyssan* WW; *to kysse,* osculari, ~iare *CathA.*

basilardus, ~a v. 1 baselardus.

basilea [βασίλεια], queen.

basilla, regina *GlC* B 43; 1068 poscimus †et [l. ut] nostram salvet Christus basilēam (*Consecr. Reginae*) *Pont. Ebor.* 282.

basileïus [βασίλειος], kingly.

convenere duces necnon basileia pubes Frith. 464.

basileon v. basileus. basileris v. 2 baselardus.

†basileros, kind of palm-tree.

ramus ejus palme que Grece dicitur ~os avelli non potest si trahatur deorsum J. Sal. *Pol.* 552a.

basileus [βασιλεύς], **a** Roman emperor. **b** king (of the English). **c** heavenly ruler.

a s920 Romanus quidam humilis genere demum factus ~eus..imperialia indumenta..assumpsit R. Niger I 76. **b** basileon, rex *GlC* B 15; 935 (12c) ego Aeðelstanus nodante Dei gratia ~eus Anglorum *CS* 707; 940 ego Eadmundus..basyleos Anglorum *CS* 748; c1022 ego Cnut basileon Angelsaxonum *CD* 736; 1068 poscimus Anglorum nostrum salvet basilēum (*Consecr. Reginae*) *Pont. Ebor.* 282; 1069 Willelmus..victoriosus Anglorum ~eus (*Dipl.*) *Regesta* 28; *cf.* D. C. Douglas *William the Conqueror* 251 n. 4. **c** O theos agie, băsĭlĕū pie, quid loquar oro R. Cant. *Malch.* V 312.

2 (gen. pl. *~eon*) Books of Kings, incl. Samuel (bibl.).

~eon, liber Regum *GlC* B 1; in ~ion cautum est: 'quasi vermiculus ligni tenerrimus' Aldh. *PR* 134 (cf. 2 *Sam.* xxiii 8); in ~eon *Id. VirgP* 53; 10.. in ~eon, *in cyninga bocum* WW.

1 basilica [sc. domus], **a** palace. **b** church, esp. cathedral. **c** chapel or shrine.

a ~a, *cinges hof* vel *cyrce* Ælf. *Sup.*; Westmonasterium, ubi postea Rufus hujus Gilielmi filius ~am magnificentissime extruxit P. Verg. IX 154. **b** 685 dedicatio ~ae S. Pauli viii Kl. Mai (*Inscr., Jarrow*) P. Hunter Blair: *Introd. to Anglo-Saxon England* 156; plurima băsilicae sunt ornamenta recentis Aldh. *CE* 3. 69; 697 bassilicae B. Mariae..quae sita est in loco qui dicitur Limingae *CS* 97; curavit..majorem ipso in loco et augustiorem de lapide fabricare ~am Bede *HE* II 14; 933 ~as in honore De[i] sanctorumque ejus dedicatas *CS* 694; s1167 ~am cathedralem [*Béziers*] ingressus W. Newb. II 11; s1170 Thomas Cantuariensis..in ~a sedis sue martyrio coronatus est R. Niger II 166; s1183 in metropolitana ~a [*Rouen*] Trevet 101; 1189 huic ecclesie [*of St. John's Abbey, Colchester*]..concedimus..libertatem..ut nullus episcopus nec quicumque de judiciaria potestate in ipsam sanctam ~am vel manentes in ipsa..habeant potestatem *CalCh.* I 425; 1200 bis quoque officium..in matrici ~a [*parish church*] solutum est Ad. Eyns. *Hug.* V 17 p. 207; a1205 nata erat in vico cujus ~a in honore S. Clementis fuerat constructa *Canon. G. Sempr.* 159; 1237 ~arum dedicatio a veteri testamento initium dignoscitur habuisse..et in novo est a sanctis patribus observata *Conc. Syn.* 245; băsilicam simul ecclesiam conjungimus illis Garl. *Syn.* 1590a; s1296 mandavit archiepiscopus bullam apostolicam..per cathedrales ~as divulgari *Flor. Hist.* III 98; iste ~e appropriate..deficiunt in tectis Wycl. *Pol.* I 134; 1480 ~am et cemiterium in villa de Lamley de novo constructam *Fabr. York* 241. **c** Dionisii votive ~e summo fervore erat intenta Gosc. *Edith* 86; Hoelus..precepit edificare ~am super tumulum ipsius in monte quo jacebat G. Mon. X 3; s1269 fecit rex..super sanctum [Edwardum] novam ~am fieri totam auro..et gemmis coopertam *Leg. Ant. Lond.* 117.

2 [sc. tabula], part of turquet (astr.).

a1350 in cujus base est tabula quadrata..que tabula ~a dicitur; et hec tabula ~a tabule equinoctiali conjungitur..ita quod motus ~e super tabulam equinoctialem sit difficilis (*Turquet*) *Ox. Hist. Soc.* LXXVIII 370.

3 [sc. vena], basilic vein (med.).

sunt [vene] principales..cephalica [etc.] et ~a, id est epatica, que inferioribus partibus deservit et interpretatur fundamentalis Ric. Med. *Micr. Anat.* 227; ~a dirigitur a pelliculis velantibus costas et ramificatur ad assellas Gilb. IV 193. 1; nec est [vena spatularum] sub assellarum vena, quia tunc esset sub ~a interiori Gad. 9 v. 1.

2 basilica v. basilisca.

basilicon [βασιλικόν], a plaster.

~on est emplastrum de adipe, resina pini et oleo *Alph.* 19.

2 basil (*Ocimum*) or other herb.

ramusculus ~onis..sternutare facit Gilb. II 94 v. 2; digerentia melancoliam..semina sunt peonie, ..semen ~onis Gad. 15. 2; ~on, ozimum idem; ..i. semen brance ursine secundum quosdam *SB* 12; ~on, semen est majorane, ozimus idem *Alph.* 18.

basilides, atheling, prince.

qui autem archiepiscopi vel ~e [fidejussionem solverit, emendet] iii libris (*Cons. Cnuti*) *GAS* 351 (*cf Inst. Cnuti*, ib.: qui fregerit plegium archiepiscopi aut reguli, quem Angli vocant *æðeling*).

Basilidianus, Basilidian heretic.

pullulat..et [heresis] ~a, que passum Christum negat, sed alium similem sibi supposuisse [sc. dicit] R. Niger II 117.

basilisca, snakewort (*Dracunculus*), gentian or other herb.

est ~a herba que crescit ubi basiliscus nascitur Neckam *NR* II 65; basilica, i. serpentaria *SB* 12 (*Ib.* 16: cocodrilla); basilicus vel basilica, herba gentiana *Alph.* 18; ~a, A. *baldemonye* WW.

basiliscus [βασιλίσκος], basilisk, deadly serpent. **b** Satan.

~us, serpens quae flatu suo universa quae attigerit inurit *GlC* B 31; qui solo cetera necat aspectu, mors mustela ~o Gir. *TH* I 27; ~us Grece Latine dicitur regulus, eo quod sit..rex serpentum Bart. Angl. XVIII 15; *cocatryse PP*; rex serpencium WW. **b** exorcizo te, maledicte diabole et immundissime draco, ~e, serpens noxie (*Jud. Dei*) *GAS* 425

basilla v. basilea. basillus v. 1 bacillus. basin- v. bacin-.

1 basis [CL < βάσις], **~a,** base, foundation: **a** (of pillar, building, or sim.); **b** (of heart); **c** (of triangle, or surface of solid); **d** (fig.) support.

a lignum..longitudinis xij pedum ad faciendam domunculae ~im Bede *Cuthb.* 21; fundit quod remansit de ipsa aqua benedicta ad bassem altaris Egb. *Pont.* 39; ~is, *syl GlC* B 50; ~es, *tredelas* vel *stæpas*, ..~is, *post* Ælf. *Gl.*; pergens ad opus sancti martyris, cui ex lapidicina ~es extrahebat W. Cant. *Mir. Thom.* VI 13; unde statua Machometi ferrea in aere stet sine aliquo vinculo vel ~i Neckam *NR* II 98; ut nec ~es nec stylos columnarum illius efficerent firmitudinis ut sustinere sufficerent molem *Mir. J. Bev.* C 345; 1307 pro..virgis et petris ad basas emptis pro eadem [bercaria] *MinAc* 1079/18 m. 8; [J. abbas, ob. 1316] fecit..domum capituli..artificiose constructam cum volta optima absque ~e media *Chr. Evesham* 286; 1385 ad obstruend' ~es et platas..molendini aquatici *PlRCP* 497 r. 316; 1410 de j *crosseheved* de petra et j *crosseschaft* cum j †baso [l. base] *Test. Ebor.* III 49; 1445 columpna rotunda, cristalina continens reliquias..cum basa et coopertorio rotundis de argento deaurato (*Invent. S. Paul*) *Arch.* L 521; hec bassis, A. *growndwalle*, ..hec basys, *growndpelyr* WW. **b** cor..in medietate pectoris collocatum..~i insidens Alf. Angl. *Cor* iv. **c** quid ~is, quid catheta, ..contemplans Adel. *ED* 29; băsis opem tibi dat, cathetus et hypotenusa Neckam *DS* X 147; res visa est ~is et opponitur illi angulo J. Blund *An.* 93; omnia..habent angulos, puta et quod octo ~ium et quod duodecim ~ium et pyramis Bradw. *CD* 367e. **d** s1244 Anglie cancellarius, columpna veritatis et semper penes ipsum regnum ~is fidelitatis *Flor. Hist.* II 170; 1442 fidei orthodoxe ~es tutissime et columne..fiant Bekynton I 207.

2 foot (*cf. Acts* iii 7).

stetit supra pedes suos homo ac solidatis ~ibus ejus et plantis regi presentatur Ailr. *Ed. Conf.* 755b; potuit et ~es ejus et plantas ad plenum consolidare ut gressus rectos faceret Ben. Pet. *Mir. Thom. II* 8 (cf. ib. 40; *Lit. Cant.* III 191).

2 basis [cf. bassum; (?) *conf. w.* 1 basis], 'base', saddle-pad.

1337 in ij ~ibus emptis pro carectis, xviij d. *Comp. Swith.* 246; 1345 in j pari ~ium *Ib.* 148.

basium [CL], kiss.

bassia, oscula *GlC* B 26; dulcia compressis impendis basia buccis Aldh. *Aen.* 80. 8; blandis dans basia casta lacertis Frith. 170; 10.. bassia, *cossas* WW; W. Malm. *GP* II 78 (v. 1 artus 2d.); dum tenero dulcescunt basia fletu Hanv. IV 300; amplexus, basia dantur D. Bec. 2034.

basius v. badius.

baskettum [ME], basket.

1209 in j bascat, jd. *Pipe Wint.* 60; s1269 averia..solebant ponderari..per ~um suum *Leg. Ant. Lond.* 118; 1323 in uno ~o et iiij corbellis cum canevacio emptis pro predictis †clavibus [l. clavis] imponendis *Sacr. Ely* II 27; 1367 in j bascat' de virgis empto pro equis inde comessur' *MinAc* 840/28 m. 2; 1515 in iiij ~is emptis pro elemosina..querenda *Comp. Swith.* 461.

baslardus v. 1 & 2 baselardus. baso v. basso. Bassanus v. anser.

bassare, to weaken.

to make wayke, attenuare, ~are *CathA.*

bassaria [cf. bassus 1c], lower room.

bace chambyr, ~ia vel camera ~ia *PP.*

Bassaris [βασσαρίς], Bacchante.

bassarides, bachae *GlC* B 40.

bassatio, lowering.

1348 ob defectum prostracionis et ~onis molendini..quod ultra modum levatur et exaltatur (*CoramR*) *Pub. Works* II 242.

bassator v. ambasciator.

basse, a in a low position or on a lowly course (fig.). **b** in a low voice. **c** weakly. **d** (with *alte*) completely.

a respice homines celestes qui ascenderunt in altum et tunc videbis quam ~e [ME: *hu lowe*] tu stas *AncrR* 103; s1457 nec basse tendas, nec nimis alte petas (*Vers.*) *Reg. Whet.* I 288. **b** si obscure dicat vel ita ~e loquatur, dicat iterato et loquatur altius *Mod. Ten. Parl.* 33. **c** *waykly*, ~e, debiliter *CathA.* **d** c1170 (v. alte g); 1291 finali voto alte et ~e standi omnino se submiserunt (*PlRExch*) *Law Merch.* II 60; 1316 homines de Scocia qui ad voluntatem nostram venire voluerint alte et ~e *RScot* 168b.

bassellardus v. 1 baselardus.

bassetum, (?) a coarse cloth.

1290 in xvij ulnis de ~o grosso pro huciis ad equos xj s. vj d. *Ac. Swinfield* 113.

bassinus v. bacinus.

bassitudo, lowness.

que [arbores] propter suam summam ~inem et humilitatem minime umbre beneficium transeuntibus impendunt S. Sim. *Itin.* 82; 1361 'sub' et 'supra' in mundo sunt equivoca: nam aliquando dicunt altitudinem et ~inem..et aliquando dicunt absolute posicionem mundi Wycl. *Log.* III 9.

bassium v. basium, bassum.

basso [cf. bassum], saddle-pad or collar-pad.

1245 in sella ad carettam, j pari bason' *Pipe Wint.* (159287) r. 10d.; 1265 in j pare baconum de novo empt' et veteribus emendandis cum iiij colariis equorum emendandis *MinAc* 949/3.

bassum, ~ium, ~ia [cf. 2 basis, basso *and* (?) 2 bargia], 'base', saddle-pad. **b** (?) collar-pad.

1211 in..paronis, paronellis, baciis *Pipe Wint.* 95; **1248** in j sella cum baciis ad carectam, xij d. *Ac. Man. Wint.* (*Littleton*); **1273** in j sella cum baz'..; in veteribus bazis emendandis *MinAc* 935/4; **1299** in iij sellis ad carectam sine ~is *Ac. Man. Cant.* (*Milton, Essex*); **1299** in j pare baseorum *Ib. Wint.* (*Michelmersh*); **1307** in..j pari bac' de proprio corio faciend' cum canavac' et flockis ad idem emptis *Ib.* (*Chilbolton*); **1270** in una sella cum duobus paribus baciarum *MinAc* 1118/17 r. 3; **1301** carecte:..in j pari bascearum empto, j.d. ob. *Ib.* 991/25; **1290** in..†bastis [? l. bascis], tractibus et ferris equorum *Ac. Swinfield* 124; **1399** in j sella carectiva empta cum ~o ad dictam sellam (*Ac. Man. Wint. Harmondsworth*) *Arch.* LVIII 350; **1432** †basta *MFG.* **b** **1261** in ij paribus baceorum et ij paribus colar' emptis..; in veteribus colar' et baceis fractis reparandis et reimplendis *Ac. Man. Wint.* (*Alton Priors*); **1278** in uno collario cum ~o..ad equum carettarium *MinAc* 843/17; **1285** in j pari bazar' et j colar' *Ib.* 26.

bassus [LL], **a** low. **b** flat, shallow. **c** standing at a low level (? on ground floor). **d** low-lying (of land). **e** low (of tidal water). **f** (fig.) lowly, humble. **g** weak.

a **1205** ij ollas de ere bono..cum ~is pedibus et bonis *Cl* 22; **c1250** cum ex duobus parietibus construatur edificium ordinis, sc. moribus bonis et scientia,..parietem..morum permiserunt..~um esse ECCLESTON *Adv. Min.* 92; **a1350** sint sotulares erecti cum tribus vel quatuor nodulis circa tibias;..sotulares vero ~os cum uno nodulo et laqueatos.. interdicimus (*Artic. S. Juliani*) *G. S. Alb.* II 504; et sic de bassis succumbant alta GOWER *VC* I 523; **1415** corpus meum sepeliendum..absque aliqua tumba super me perficienda set super me stet una petra ~a *Reg. Cant.* II 59 (cf. ib. 455). **b** vas ut ~ius est liquoris capacius WYCL. *Mand. Div.* 145; **1464** unius ~e cratere argenti *Cl* 315 m. 6*d.*; unius ~e pecie argenti *Ib.* m. 7*d.*; *flatt,..flew,..schold,* ~us *PP.* **c** **1257** ~a garderoba thalami..filii nostri lambriscetur *RL* II 66; **14..** in ~a aula *Croyl. Cont.* B 536; **1453** scola philosophie naturalis alta prima:..scola philosophie moralis ~a secunda:..scola geometrie ~a tercia (*Rental*) *Cart. Osney* III 252–3; **1456** in camera †vassa [? l. bassa] sub ipsis [cameris] *Cant. Coll. Ox.* II 179; **1476** in quadam ~a camera..infra.. monasterium situata *Reg. Whet.* II 150; *bace chambyr..* camera ~a *PP.* **d** **1297** terra de dicta watergaynga ejecta super terram ~iorem dicti abbatis apponatur *Reg. S. Aug.* 611; **1392** terre..in terris ~is et inferioribus [*Lowlands*] regni *ExchScot* 287; **1470** pascua in ~is locis latentia *Reg. Whet.* I 385. **e** **1445** inter..regiam stratam..et ~am aquam Thamisie *Cl* 295 m. 18*d.* **f** **c1346** 'Anglia cor bassum teneas', dicit Deus, 'assum' (*Neville's Cross*) *Pol. Poems* I 51. **g** *wayke,* ~us, inpos *CathA.*

2 a low (in status), limited in scope: **a** of persons; **b** of jurisdiction (*cf. altus 7c*); **c** of tenure; **d** of the mass (spoken, not sung); **e** (w. *aurum*) base, of inferior quality.

a **c1375** [hominis] status est pauper[r]imus et ~us ex eo quod est terra BRINTON *Serm.* p. 45 (cf. ib. 103: servilis et ~e condicionis); **s1460** alicui alteri, alto vel ~o, parvo vel magno *Reg. Whet.* I 358. **b** **1279** jurisdiccionem et justiciam altam et ~am..ad ipsos pertinere..sicut francum.. allodium *RGasc* II 58; **1312** cum..in loco et repairio de Cambo ~am jurisdiccionem..explectare, viz. usque ad summam lx s. et infra, consueverint *Ib.* IV 1020. **c** **1321** tenuit dictum manerium..de domino rege in capite ut de antiquo dominico corone de ~a tenura, et nullum servicium facit..nisi tantummodo fidelitatem *IPM* 69/5 m. 5. **d** **1429** ~a vero missa per secundum capellanum..dicetur.. immediate post levacionem magne misse *Reg. Brechin* 48. **e** **1422** in diversis parcellis de auro ~o cimentat' in aurum purum *KRAc* 301/19 r. 1 (*cf.* aurum 1a, 1f).

3 (as sb. n.) foot, lower part (*cf. abaso*). **b** (in phr. w. *altum*) completely (*cf. basse*).

a **1392** totam aream..tam in declivo montis superius quam in ~o irriguo inferius *Reg. Aberd.* I 179; **1406** [episcopis] convenientibus in ~o sub domo capituli *Conc.* III 284; **1427** alio modo sumitur [anima] tantum secundum ~um ejus, quo corpus vivificat NETTER *DAF* I 112. **b** **1264** (v. altus 1d); **1293** supplicat quod possit..alto et ~o voluntati domini regis se submittere *RParl* I 104b; **1356** seisiti..ut de nativis suis, ad talliandum eos ad altum et ~um (*County Placita, Surrey*) *Enf. Stat. Lab.* 250; **1433** obedire in alto et ~o..promiserunt *Rec. Leic.* II 248.

basta v. bassum.

bastardia, bastardy, illegitimacy.

villenagium..probatum versus ipsum petentem assisam adimit; idem quoque effecit exceptio ~ie GLANV. XIII 11; **1199** prior dicit quod Thomas..est bastardus..; juratores eant sine die donec inquisitum fuerit de ~ia *CurR* I 80; **1228** ad eum non pertinet imponere ~iam tenenti suo *CurR* XIII 733; de hujusmodi objectione ~ie, utrum videlicet quis natus ante sponsalia vel matrimonium haberi posset pro legitimo BRACTON 416b; sunt..qui signum ~ie portant; et tales portant arma suorum parentum integra cum quadam benda ex transverso BAD. AUR. 138; **1406** allegavit ~iam sive illegitimacionem *Reg. Heref.* 31.

bastardire, to bastardize.

s1253 ob discordiam inter comitissam Flandrie et Johannem filium suum uterinum, quem ipsa nitebatur ~ire et exheredare *Ann. Burton* I 306.

bastardus, bastard (adj. or sb.).

s1139 comes Glaocestriae, Heinrici quondam regis Anglorum filius, sed ~us J. WORC. 55; numquid filio suo ~o potest quis filium et heredem habens de hereditate sua donare? GLANV. VII 1; Guillelmus Guillelmi regis ~i filius GIR. *IK* II 1; **1212** a tempore Willelmi ~i regis Anglie *Fees* 93; **a1218** diratonavit predictam terram contra R. fratrem suum ~um *Cart. Glam.* 220; **1210** ipsa ~a est et ipse legitimus *CurR* VI 63; **1227** bene potest esse quod sit filia sua, set est ~a *BNB* III 608; **1236** ad confirmandam hanc legem quod ~us sub pallio supra parentes nubentes extento positus surgit ~us GROS. *Ep.* 24; cum bastardia objecta fuerit alicui ex tali causa..quod ~us sit, et ideo ~us quia natus ante sponsalia sive matrimonium contractum inter patrem suum et matrem suam BRACTON 417; **1330** Beatrix null[i]us heres esse potest eo quod ~a est *Reg. Heref.* 42; **1438** [lego] residuum..Thomae filio meo ~o *Test. Ebor.* II 64; **s1471** prefecto ipsorum quodam Thoma ~o de Facombrege *Croyl. Cont.* C 556; filium..nothum sive ~um *Plusc.* VII 10; tritum..proverbium est: 'si bonus est ~us, hoc ei venit e casu' FORTESCUE *LLA* c. 40.

2 cross-bred (horse).

1397 de..j ~o stalone *IMisc* 266/7; **1411** de..ij equis ~is *Ac. Foreign* 45 r. 1; j dextrarius, ij ~i, xiij equi coursours *Ib.*

3 false, spurious, inferior (appl. to: **a** conger eel; **b** incense; **c** wild shoot or sucker; **d** sword (? *cf. 1 baselardus*); **e** saddle; **f** cloth; **g** sweet wine; **h** loaf).

a **1256** capere potest..unum gunger ~um vel unam rayam pro j d. *BBC* (*Newcastle*) 330. **b** **1324** pro incenso ~o viz. xxx li. empt' v s. *Sacr. Ely* II 42. **c** vitulamen.. dicitur illa planta ~a sive spuria et infructuosa que nascitur a radice vitis BART. ANGL. XVII 178. **d** **1410** pro morte cujusdam W. S...cum uno gladio ~o felonice interfecti *Pat* 383 m. 27 (cf. ib.: *bastardswerd*). **e** **1419** viij sellas ~as deauratas *Ac. Foreign* 52A. **f** **1410** unum pannum ~um de blanketto Londoniensi (*KRMem* 187) *Bronnen* I 875. **g** **1265** dimidii dolii de vino ~o (*RHosp*) *Manners* 81 (cf. ib.: dolium ~i); **1337** summa..recepcionis vinorum:..bastard', j pipa *KRAc* 78/18 m. 14; **1338** pro fretagio iiij doliorum vini ~i..captorum in quadam navi de Ispan' *Ib.* 20/27 r. 1*d.* **h** **1221** iiij panes de secundo pane, sc. de minore ~o *Cart. Osney* III 51.

bastaso [It. *bastaggio*], porter.

[pueri Veneti] fiunt mercatores et idem ~ones LIV. *Hen. V* 355.

bastellum v. bastilla. basterdus v. 1 baselardus.

basterna [CL], litter.

~a, *beer GlC* B 9; ~a, *scrid Ib.* 25; basternam linquit inanem / pergere cum pueris ALDH. *VirgV* 1896; bida vel ~a,..vel carpentum, *cræt ÆLF. Gl.*; ~am sine rotis BALSH. *Ut.* 50; *hors-bere,* lectica, ~a *PP.*

bastida [Prov.], fortified settlement (Gasc.).

1274 dedimus potestatem..senescallo..villas seu ~as.. construendi *RGasc* II 3; **1305** in bastita quadam *Ib.* III 451; **1315** dicta ~a et burgenses et habitatores ipsius comuniam habeant..sicut cetere ville et ~e ducatus Aquitanie, et.. sigillum comunie,..et..in dicta ~a et comunia sint sex jurati..; et bajulus cum juratis habebunt (*sic*) potestatem regendi..dictam villam *Ib.* IV 1626 (xvii); **1316** loca ~arum nostrarum de S. Gyno et Lieans.. claustura sufficienti indigent reparari pro majori salvacione locorum illorum et parcium adjacencium *Ib.* 1538; **1351** cum,..eo quod nullum fortalicium in ~a predicta extitit;..quoddam subsidium.. pro ~a predicta claudenda et fortificanda concessisset (*RGasc*) *Ann. Midi* LXVI 349.

bastile, wooden siege-tower.

s1386 cepit edificare unum ~e coram..villa de Brest.. cum vij turribus KNIGHTON *Cont.* 208.

bastilla, ~us, ~ia [Fr. *bastille*], siege-tower, fortification.

s1386 cum vidisset castellum de Brest..velut obsessum duobus castellis ligneis..jussit suos egredi et debellare ~as [v.l. batillas] illas *Chr. Angl.* 369; **s1418** municiones quedam, quas ~os appellant, ante sua menia..eriguntur *Ps.*-ELMH. *Hen. V* 59; **s1428** (v. bastilliatus); **s1435** dux Burgundie obsedit Calisiam;..dux..recessit per fugam, et suum bastellum cremabatur HERRISON *Abbr. Chr.* 5.

bastilliatus, fortified.

s1428 captis..ecclesiis monasterialibus..ex his alteratis et transmutatis fortalicia ~ata facta sunt ex omni parte civitatis..usque ad numerum vij bastilliarum fortissime munitarum *Plusc.* X 29.

bastinus v. bacinus. bastita v. bastida. bastlum v. bastum.

1 basto [OF *baston*], stick, staff (*cf. baculus*): **a** (for keeping rings); **b** (for making a sheepfold); **c** (forming stock of crossbow).

a **1303** annulus auri cum parvo saphiro per se in uno ~one (*KRAc* 363/6) *DocExch* 280. **b** **1312** xxiiij claios ad faldam cum iiij ~onibus ad eandem *AncD* A 11225. **c** **1298** ~ones de †hisse [? l. hiffe = Fr. *if*] pro †arblastris [MS. alblast'] (*KRAc* 7/1 m. 3) *DocScot* II 315; **1300** ~ones ad balistas *Ac. Wardr.* p. 151.

2 (?) long loaf shaped like a stick.

c1338 uterque senescallus habebit..de gustatoribus utroque die xij ~ones, duas tortatas *Gild. Merch.* II 335; fecerunt ~ones de furfure et non de longitudine sicut solent *Ib.* 331.

3 staff as token of seisin.

1201 predictus H. in prefata curia per fustum et ~onem reddidit abbati et monachis totum jus *Couch. Kirkstall* 104; **1227** simulata donatio..per fustum et ~onem *BNB* III 638 (*marg.*).

4 wand of office (Gasc.).

1285 servientes portent ~ones depictos signis tam regis.. quam abbatis *RGasc* II 271.

5 'baston', licence to leave gaol accompanied by official.

1504 salvo et secure in prisona predicta absque ballio, bast[one] seu manucapcione custodis *Cl* 364 m. 7*d.*

2 basto [cf. bastum], bast.

1292 in ij cordis de baston' *Ac. Man. Coll. Wint.* (*Durrington*).

bastonare, a to fit with poles. **b** to attach to a pole.

a **1266** in una careta et duobus carris ~andis, rilandis..et emendendis *MinAc* 1078/8 r. 4. **b** **1368** j tapetum ~atum *Invent. Norw.* 46.

bastonarius [cf. It. *bastoniere*], bearer of a wand or mace.

1290 hostiario et ~io camere principisse Salern' *Ac. Wardr.* (*Chanc. Misc.* 4/5) f. 46.

bastum [AS *bæst*], bast, bark fibre for rope-making.

1212 pro..xxj corda (*sic*) de canabo et xxxvij aliis cordis de ~o *Pipe* 47; **1265** in vij cordis de ~o ad affros ligandos in pastura, iij d. ob. *MinAc* 949/3; **1295** vij laste ~orum ad cordas navium *KRMisc* 2/1/3; **1297** in j corda de bastlo empta ad affros in pascuis tenend', j.d. *Ac. Cornw.* I 86.

baszenum v. basanum.

batagium [cf. 1 batus], boatage, boat-hire.

1325 in j molari empto apud London', una cum warfagio, ~io et cariagio (*Ac. Mersham*) *DCCant*; **1454** pro ~io de Gravesende usque London' (*Ac. Pri. DE* 16) *Ib.*; **1474** in botagio *Ac. Coll. Wint.*; **1547** pro botagio domini custodis et aliorum secum equitancium ad insulam Vectam *Ib.*

bataillamentum v. batillamentum. batallum, ~us v. batellum, 2 & 3 batellus.

batare [cf. bateiceum], to reclaim (land) by 'beat-burning' (Cornw).

1339 de vj s. viij d. receptis de xx acris terre ~ate anno precedenti et seminate hoc anno pro acra iiij d. *MinAc* 816/11 m. 8; de xx acris et dimidia terre de novo ~ate hoc anno ad seminandum anno futuro pro acra xij d. *Ib.* m. 8*d.*; **1347** de lvj acris vasti batant' (*sic*) et seminant' siligine (*MinAc Cornw*) *Arch. J.* V 121.

batatio v. baitatio.

bateiciare, to reclaim by 'beat-burning'.

1347 de..lxvj acris ad baticiand' et sabiland' et seminatis hoc anno (*MinAc Cornw*) *Arch. J.* V 121.

bateicium, ~ia [OF *bateiz*], denshiring, reclamation of land by 'beat-burning' (or land so reclaimed); *cf.* H. P. R. Finberg: *Tavistock Abbey* (Cambridge, 1951) 92.

1236 terra illa emendata est per baticium et alio modo *BNB* III 165 (*Devon*); **1246** non liceat..plus in bateyceum comburere de dicta terra de Legh' quam possint compostare (*Mun. Woburn* D 38/5) *Tavistock Abbey* 92; **1251** locaverunt terram illam hominibus ad excolendum et faciendum baticium *JustIt* 1178 (*Somerset*) r. 2; **12..** colere et appruare x acras..sive in baticio sive in alio wannagio (*Cart. Torre*) *Mon. Exon.* 180; **1286** in xiiij acris..batiscei houwandis et cremandis *MinAc* 827/39 (*Devon*) r. 2; **1293** debet..semel howare batit' *Fees* (*Devon*) 1313; **1207** de lxxxiij acris dim. baticii hoc anno assissis ad baticium *Ac. Cornw.* II 228; **1321** baticie in eodem vasto valent per annum xviij d. (*MinAc Cornw*) *Arch. J* V 121; **1332** [vastum] in baticio ad campipartem (*Wells MSS.*) *HMC Rep.* 12, I 351.

2 (?) beater or wicker hurdle.

1321 quoddam baticium precii xij d. et unum par spinarum pro lanis..asportavit *JustIt* 546 r. 45.

bateicius, (?) made of brushwood, wattled.

1213 fieri faciatis..tot cleias ~eas quot poteritis in bosco de W. ita quod quelibet contineat decem pedes in longitudine *Cl* 134; **1225** fieri facias..quingentas cleias bonas et bene ~ias *Ib.* 19 (cf. ib.: baeticias).

batella v. 2 batellus.

batellagium, boat-hire.

1282 pro..batillagio [vinorum] *KRAc* 4/3; **1286** in j novo molari empto..cum cariagio, batilagio, warwagio (*Ac. Meopham*) *DCCant*; **1293** cariagium, batillagium et portagium frumenti *RGasc* III cxliii; **1301** in batillagio dominorum J. [etc.]..de Novo Castro versus Tynemue (*KRAc* 308/30) *Poole Essays* 346; **1315** ~ium victualium *Mem. Ir.* 330; **1358** item in †botillagio..versus..S. Paulum (*Ac. Univ. Ox.*) *EHR* XXIV 737; **1390** Johanni Boteman pro batillagio *Ac.H. Derby* 7; **1464** in ~io..lx personarum de terra usque navem..de navi usque terram (*KRAc* 324/21) *EHR* XXI 737.

batellamentum v. batillamentum.

1 batellare [OF *bateler*], to carry by boat.

1401 in predictis iiij^{ml} sclatt' a Southampton'..~andis *Pipe Wint.* (159405) r. 19.

2 batellare [cf. batellum], to battel, receive battels (acad.).

1410 in aula vel collegio universitatis ubi commune

ponuntur, sive in aulis eisdem annexis ac cum eisdem communas ponentibus sive ~antibus *StatOx* 208.

3 batellare, ~iare v. batillare.

1 batellaria, boat-hire.

1299 in ~ia et portagio ad terram (*KRAc* 309/14) *DocScot* II 385*n*.

2 batellaria v. batillaria.

1 batellarius [OF *batelier*], boatman.

1289 vj ~iis assistentibus uni mar[inario], custodi bargie principis, pro navig[ando], per iiij tid' *KRAc* 486/1 m. 1; **1309** jurans se cicius non posse batellum adipisci. .quia ~ii fuerunt ad piscandum *PQW* 824a; **1317** de. .~io quia noluit cariare homines domini *CBaron* 124; **1318** Henrico le Shipman batillario pro locacione batelli sui *KRAc* 469/1*d*.; **1329** in solucione facta ~iis passagii domine regine *ExchScot* 217; **1350** quod. .~ii et quicumque alii artifices et operarii non capiant. .ultra id quod. .solvi consuevit (*Pat*) *Foed.* V 693.

2 batellarius, 'batteler', recipient of battels (acad.).

1488 de quisbusdam scolaribus ~iis *Cant. Coll. Ox.* II 218; **1507** placuit. .quod nulli ~ii sint ibi, eo quod injuriam publicam fecerunt scolaribus in refeccionibus suis *Reg. Merton* 356; **1562** batillariorum (v. batellum).

batellata, boat-load.

1221 pro remotione xl ~arum. .lapidum *Ac. Build. Hen. III* 30; **1225** tres ~as de minuta buscha *Cl* 24a; **1242** cum. .v ~is de sicca busca *Cl* 414; **1296** pro una ~a maeremii. .carianda usque ad placeam galee *Ac. Galley Newcastle* 165.

†batellia [? cf. 2 betella *or* 2 botellus], (?) bundle.

†a**1204** (c**1295**) de qualibet ~ia alliorum, nucium vel ceporum obolum *Reg. Wint.* II 743.

1 batellulus, fish-trap in form of little boat.

1286 batellus ille una cum ~o qui vocatur trunkus in quo circa x sol' pisc' *PQW* 309b.

2 batellulus, small clapper or striker (of clock).

1325 expense orologii: item in ~is ad cimbalas, vij d. (*Comp. Norw.*) *Arch.J.* XII 177.

1 batellum [(?)], battel, payment for board etc. (acad.).

1348 in communis ix d.; battellis j d. ob. (*Mun. Merton*) *Educ. Ch.* 302; **1394** in ~is domini W. . xiiij s.; . .summa ~orum xxxij s. *Cant. Coll. Ox.* II 133 (cf. ib. 138: in batallis); **1483** bursario. .~a ab alico socio petenti *Reg. Merton* 18; **1542** caucionem. .pro ~is et communiis. .collegio. .persolvendis *Deeds Balliol* 321; **1562** quemvis tam sociorum quam commensalium et battillariorum intra mensem. .quovis termino. .finito economo statum pro †battis omnibus satisfacturum *Reg. Coll. Exon.* 72.

2–4 batellum v. 2–3 batellus, 1 batillum. 1 batellus v. 1 bacillus.

2 batellus, ~a, ~um [OF *batel*], boat. **b** ferry-boat. **c** ship's boat, lighter. **d** fishing boat. **e** boat for use in ordeal pool.

1157 in duobus ~is emend' et iiii mersis *Pipe* 136; **1248** omne ~um dicte insule [*Guernsey*] *CallMisc* I p. 17; ~us cum onere et omni attillamento *Fleta* 37; **13..** quod nullus intret [navem] vel ~am cum victualibus *MGL* I 251 [= ib. 275: *es niefs ne en bateux*]; c**1341** batillus de mysyn' [*with mizen sail*] *IMisc* 146/5; c**1370** clamat quod. .habeant batalla sua. .per totam aquam suam apud Porthesgob *Rec. Caern.* 133; **1479** in batilda unde T. D. est magister *KRAc Cust.* 114/9 r. 4v. **b 1178** concessi ~um passagii mei de Munros *Reg. Aberbr.* I 5; **1505** Montros bettella assedatur Thome L. *Ib.* II 356; **1276** habuit unam ~am in aqua per quam gentes deberent transire pro argento *Hund.* I 49; **1285** C. at Bote. .tenet j ~um ad ducendum homines ultra aquam *Cust. Suss.* II 111. **c 1188** pro j ~o ad opus esnecce *Pipe* 180; **1228** quod ~um navis de S. Sebastiano. . liberari faciant *Cl* 106; c**1300** factura ~i qui dicitur *floyn* pertinentis ad galeam *KRAc* 501/23 m. 2; **1478** in una ~a ad navem *ExchScot* 149. **d** a**1200** duos ~os ad piscandum *Feod. Durh.* 138*n*.; **1204** habuit ~um suum errantem in piscaria illa *CurR* III 158; c**1225** cum per rete et per ~um piscaverint *Cart. Boarstall* 33; **1336** de qualibet ~a. . piscante ad piscariam de G. *CalScot* III 339; **1553** de qualibet nave vel batilda ibidem annuatim piscante *Pat* 848 m. 39 (*Ir.*). **e 1285** habet libertates, assisam panis et servicie, polum et batallum *Aids* II 17 (cf. ib.: batellum).

2 boat-load.

1443 pro batellagio iiij ~arum petrarum *Fabr. York* 57.

3 incense boat.

1315 vasa ad thus argentea: duo ~i. .cum ij cocliaribus *Invent. Ch. Ch.* 72.

3 batellus, ~um [OF *batel*; cf. baterellus], clapper of bell. **b** door-knocker.

plectri ~us, qui ferreus est, lingue eorum ministerii est effectus, qui predicationis dulcedine sonorus est; . .~um. . interius semicirculus corrio forato consociat R. Cold. *Cuthb.* 81; cum batallus ille decideret *Ib.* 92; artifices. .qui fundunt campanas de here sonoro, per quas in ecclesiis hore diei denunciantur motu batillorum et cordarum atractarum Garl. *Dict.* 125; **1420** pro uno batillo ad primam campanam *Ac. Churchw. Bath* 27 (cf. ib. 104; cum bactillo); **1439** in †bacillo [l. batillo] medie campane in turri defracto emendando cum eodem pendendo *Ac. Churchw. Glast.* 192; batillus, *a belle clapere* WW; **1523** campanis cordas inveniet et coria pro batillis (*Reg. Exon.*) *Mon. Exon.* 85. **b** at ille ~o exterius appendente iterum ferit R. Cold. *Godr.* 152.

2 clapper of mill.

molares qui molunt de faricapsia farinam, que batillo molendini descendit in alveum farinosum Garl. *Dict.* 130; lingua est quasi ~um [ME: *þe cleppe*] molendini *AncrR.* 17; *clappe or clatte of a mylle*, batillus *PP*; batillum, *clakke* WW.

baterare [ME *bateren* < OF *batre*], to 'batter', rework (iron tools). **b** to hew, dress (stone).

1325 fabro pro reparacione instrumentorum cementariorum . .videlicet. .pro vj martellis ~atis ij d. . .et pro xij ferris operabilibus. .~atis jd. *KRAc* 469/8 m. 1; **1335** pro securibus eorundem [cementariorum] ~andis *Sacr. Ely* II 68; **1388** ~antibus et acuentibus lxiiij secures *KRAc* 545/20. **b 1316** in xvj^{ml} petris traendis et baturendis *KRAc* 459/27 m. 2*d*.; **1317** batrantibus ad tascam de diversis quarrariis, videlicet mdxlviij pedes asshel[er] *Ib.* 486/29; **1354** Willelmo Sclatter pro petris batrandis *Ac. Durh.* 554.

baterarius, stone-hewer (*cf. Med. Mason* 83).

1317 batrarii ad tascam: . .batrantibus. .de diversis quarrariis *KRAc* 486/29.

bateratio, 'battering', reworking (of tools). **b** dressing (of stone).

1332 eidem [fabro] pro ~one xxij martellorum *KRAc* 469/11 m. 2; **1354** pro aceracione et ~one instrumentorum cementariorum *Ib.* 471/6 m. 4. **b 1401** pro ~one et apposicione cujuslibet mille [de sclat'] *Pipe Wint.* (159405) r. 17*d*.

baterellus, ~um [cf. 3 batellus], (?) part of pack harness.

1214 quatuor ~os et duo pectoralia et unum barutum et duo frena *Cl* 140a (cf. 153b, 160b); **1230** pro duobus paribus frenorum xvj d.; pro iiij baterell' [*Cal.*: †bacerell'] viij d. *Liberate* 9 m. 5.

2 a beetle of fulling-mill. **b** beetle for washing clothes.

a 1237 in iiij cariagiis ad flagella et baterell' facienda *KRAc* 501/18 m. 2. **b 1305** habentes in manibus eorum videlicet quilibet eorum unum *washbeetle*. .predicta Johanna cum ~o suo ipsum verberavit *PIRCP* 154 r. 92.

3 clapper of bell.

1243 occisa fuit per ~um cujusdam campane *JustIt* 756 r. 23; **1247** ~um cujusdam campane cecidit super E. *Ib.* 445 r. 10; **1268** furaverunt ~os cimbalarum ecclesie *Rec. Norw.* I 207; **1288** in correis emptis pro ~is magne campane pendendis *KRAc* 462/12 m. 1.

bateressa v. baterissa.

bateria, battery, violent attack.

1267 uxor W. . .appellavit J. . .de ~ia et roberia facta W. viro suo *SelCCoron* 11; s**1267** ne qui vindictam caperent de ~ia vel alia injuria *Leg. Ant. Lond.* 99; placitum de mahemio et ~ia *State Tri. Ed. I* 16; si queratur de ~ia, tunc affidat quod querimonia ejus sit vera *Fleta* 65; **1368** placita ~ie, sanguinis fusi, debiti, transgressionis. .possunt terminari. . coram majore ville Sandwici Thorne 2145; **14..** in placito ~ie et sanguinis fusi. .sunt tres essonie *Cust. Fordwich* 25.

2 wrought metal (? copper) ware.

1250 de qualibet duodena ~ie *Pat* 61 m. 4; **1284** de dimidia marcata cujuscumque mercerie vel ~ie venalis *Pat* 103 m. 7; **1286** de quolibet fraello †buterie [MS. baterie] (*JustIt* 346 r. 7*d*.) *PQW* 302b; **1299** emit quamdam ~iam, ut patella, olla enea et [? alia] mercimonia *Cal. Mayor's CourtR Lond.* p. 40 (MS. *reading*); **1303** ~ia nichil debet ad introitum *DocScot* 459; **1356** nullus de dicta mestera zonas garniri faceret. .de pejori metallo quam de auricalco, ~ia, ferro et assere (*Cl* 194) *RParl* II 456a; **1471** sive mechanico officio *baterie* vulgariter appellato insudent (*Pat*) *Foed.* XI 729.

3 a threshing. **b** threshing barn.

a 1211 in liberatione. .pro ~ia de Pund[lesforda] *Pipe Wint.* 171; **1232** in ~ia de ccxvij quar. dim. avene *Ib.* (159283) r. 9*d*.; **1257** bectaria: in viij quar. frumenti triturandis *Crawley* 217; **1277** ~ia: idem computat in tritur[acione] lxxv quar. . .frumenti. .; item in ~ia j quar. . .fabarum *MinAc* 843/12; **1297** de ~ia bladi *Ac. Cornw.* I 49. **b 1222** istas domos in dominico, sc. grangiam, boveriam et ~iam *Dom. S. Paul.* 43; **1247** quando nobis placuerit. .blada nostra triturare, . .capiet unum hominem ad grangiam, gernarium et ~iam custodiend' *Cl* 546 (*Guernsey*).

baterissa, threshing barn (*cf. bateria* 3).

1155 hec. .sunt instauramenta que recepit cum manerio aula scilicet, camera, horrea ij. ., bovaria, ~a, bracinum *Dom. S. Paul.* 134 (cf. ib.: bateressa).

batha v. botha a.

bathmum [*cf.* βαθμίς, βαθμός], thigh (*cf.* Birch: *An Ancient MS., Hants Rec. Soc.* 1889, 123).

9.. ~a, ~i, femora, *þeoh* WW.

batic- v. bateic-. batilda v. 2 batellus. batile v. bacile 2*b*. batilla v. vatillum. batillagium v. batellagium.

batillamentum [OF *batillement*], battlement, indented parapet.

1313 cementario. .operanti. .in turrello. .ad elarganda ~a pro springaldis. .situandis *KRAc* 469/1 f. 3; **1317** pro batellamento faciendo ad easdem [coquinas] *Ib.* 468/20 f. 10*d*.; **1352** pro iiij carect' petrarum de Reygate scapul[andis] per mold' empt' pro bataílliamento camerarum senescalli et marescalli regis *Ib.* 471/6 m. 23; **1492** latamos ad faciendum ~um [ecclesie] predictum retinuerunt *Rec. Nott.* III 20 **1512** N. Carpentario pro batilmentis *DCCant* C 11 f. 122a.

2 embattled (indented) rim of vessel.

1390 de. .uno aquario arg' deaur' cum batellamento super cooperculo ejusdem *Ac. Foreign* 25G.

batillare, to provide (ships) with defence works.

1213 pro. .bordis de sapa et quercu ad ~andas naves nostras *Cl* 152b; **1233** naves ~ari et. .eschypari faciant, ituras in servicio regis *Cl* 341; **1234** pro hechis [galearum] et eisdem ~andis *Pipe* 78 r. 16*d*.

2 to embattle (walls or buildings), provide with battlements.

1317 cementariis. .operantibus circa. .duas magnas coquinas ~andas *KRAc* 468/20 f. 11; pro iiij farcostatis petre rag'. .ad inde batelliand' parvam aulam *Ib.* f. 13; **1325** (v. 1 batillum); **1448** licenciam dedimus. .Thome Browne quod ipse maneria sua. .cum muris lapideis et cilicinis includere, kernellare et batellare. .possit *ChartR* 190 m. 47; **1491** muros et turres. .batellare, karnellare et machicollare *Pat* 572 m. 5.

3 to decorate with embattled (indented) rims.

1385 una pixis parva. .in quodam cooperculo batellat' *MonA* VI 1367; **1405** unum gobellum argenti deaurat' cum cooperculo batellat' *Test. Ebor.* I 318; **1440** unum discum ~atum *Pat* 446 m. 13; c**1500** duo candelabra argentea. . ~ata in summitate *Fabr. York* 217.

batillaria, battlement.

1286 eisdem. .pro batellar' v turrium predictarum. .; eisdem pro dealbacione earundem batellar[iarum]. .; eisdem pro batelliar' vj pannorum murorum predictorum *KRAc* 485/28 (*Conway*) m. 4.

batillatio, fitting with battlements.

1320 in stipendio. .cementarii operantis circa ~onem murorum ejusdem camere *KRAc* 482/1 (*Scarborough*) m 3.

1 batillum, battlement.

1325 in stipendiis iiij carpentariorum. .faciencium et batellancium cum predictis reyles et bord', postibus et solis, duo batella super summitate duarum turrium prius non batellatarum. .et in predictis duobus batellis dealbandis cum calce *MinAc* 1147/23 (*Skipton*) m. 3.

2 batillum v. vatillum. batillus v. 2–4 batellus, 2 batulus. batilmentum v. batillamentum. batisceum, ~itium v. bateicium.

batitura [cf. battuere, batura], pounded flesh. **b** metal filing.

martisia vel baptitura, *gebeaten flaesc* Ælf. *Gl.* **b** ~am ferri in mortario Gilb. V 231 v. 2; ponfiligos, i. ~a eris vel fuligo de fornace eris *SB* 34.

bativa v. batura *a*. batleuca, batleuga v. banleuca.

batrachium [βατράχιον; *cf.* botrax], ranunculus (bot.).

10.. nomina herbarum. .botracion, *clufðung*, . .batracion, *clufwyrt* WW; batrocum, *cluf vyrt*, . .botration, *cluf thunge* vel *thung Gl. Durh.*; herbis nimis calidis, ut porris, cepis, alleis et vastraciis Bart. Angl. IV 10; botracion, brutacia, herba scelerata, smirnon, apium risus idem *Alph.* 24.

batrare, ~arius v. baterare, ~arius.

battare [cf. βάττος], (?) to chatter.

~at, *geonath GlC* B 24.

battel-, battil- v. batel- batil-.

battuere [CL], **~are,** to beat, strike: **a** to practise buckler play; **b** to crush, pound; **c** to stamp with metal foil.

a dum inter ~endum minus caute se parma protegeret virga colludentis adversarii. .percussus Ben. Pet. *Mir. Thom.* IV 5. **b** batutus, percussus *GlC* B 33; batuitum, *gebeaten Ib.* 17; jus simul et pulpas battutas condo culinae Aldh. *Aen.* 40 (*Piper*) 4; **9..** batutas, *þa gebeatenan* WW. **c** banerias de armis nostris bene auro †bacuatas [MS. batuatas] *Cl* 193b.

1 battum v. batellum.

2 battum [ME *bat*], wad.

1351 lanas in velleribus et ~is *Sess. P. Essex* 131.

battus v. bacus, 2 batus.

1 batulus [cf. 1 batus], boat.

ejectis ancoris, ~is [v.l. †baculis] exploratores se dedunt littori *Enc. Emmae* II 5.

2 batulus [cf. 2 batus], bushel.

a buschelle, ~us liquidorum est, †bacus [l. batus], modius; batillus, modiolus *CathA*.

batum v. 3 batus.

batura [cf. bateria, batitura, battuere], beating: **a** battery, violent attack; **b** crushing, pounding; **c** beating of metal.

a 1256 fuerunt secum in auxilio ad dictam ~am et rescussionem *CourtR Rams.* 28; s**1229** Edwardus. .verberavit Aliciam. .et ipsam maletractavit, ita quod obiit de ~ura illa *MGL* I 91 (*cf.* ib. 98: de †bativa); c**1320** purgatio oritur de insultis, ~is, toltis *Ib.* 56. **b 1286** ~a pulverum ad coquinam (*KRAc* 91/7) *Arch.* LXX 52. **c 1286** pro coctura et ~a ponderis lx s. de auro *KRAc* 372/11 m. 3.

baturere v. baterare. 1 batus v. bacus.

2 batus [cf. AS *bát*], boat (*cf. bacus*).

qui ad pontem [London'] venisset cum uno ~o ubi piscis inesset (*Quad.*) *GAS* 232; **a1180** sciatis me concessisse.. unum ~um in piscatura Cestrie ubicumque voluerint, ad piscandum *MonA* VI 598; **1314** quoddam tolnetum de batto de Kairlion *IPM* 43/41; **1318** pons regis..cum lesione navium, scutarum, batellorum et grossorum ~orum fuit.. debilitatus *KRAc* 468/20 (*London*) f. 16 (20).

3 batus (Heb. *bath*), a measure of grain, variously identified.

nomina vasorum: ..~us, *amber* ÆLF. *Gl.*; dic pro vase bătum, proprio pro nomine Bātum SERLO WILT. 2. 16; de ~is vel amphoris sive metretis vulgo galones legitime jussit fieri mensure *Itin. Ric.* VI 37; ~us (*gl.*: *buscel*) NECKAM *Ut.* 106; ~us est mensura capiens sextaria l; et est ~us in liquidis sic [ut] in siccis chorus et ephi BART. ANGL. XIX 125; garcifer..in ~is profert avenam ad presepia GARL. *Dict.* 134; **a1280** bussellum sive ~um *AncD* A 796; *pek, mesure*, ~us, *PP*; ~us, A. *a bushell* vel secundum alios trium modiorum; ..~us, A. *a pecke* WW; *provande*, ~um *CathA*; **1528** una cum iij celdris v bollis una ferlota et uno ~o *Reg. Aberbr.* II 483; **1553** deducendo 5 bollas et 5½ ~os *lie peckis* frumenti *RMS Scot.* IV 817.

2 *a batis*, supposed title of official concerned with measuring grain etc.

abatis, *fætfellere* [*vat-filler*] ÆLF. *Gl.*; jure bătos ăbătis abbātis †curia [l. cura] reliquit H. AVR. *CG* 103; *avenere*, abatis *PP*; abatis, indeclinabile, hostiarius, pabularius *CathA*.

4 batus [βάτος], **a** blackberry. **b** elecampane (*Inula*).

a ~us, rubus ferens mora *SB* 12; ~us, i. morus rubi vel rubus *Alph.* 19. **b** ellenium multi simphitum vocant vel ~um..Latini autem ynulam dicunt *Alph.* 54.

batutus v. battuere.

baubare, ~ari, to bay.

~ant, latrant *GlC* B 41; canes ~antur vel latrant vel ganniunt ALDH. *PR* 131; [canis lunarius] insomnes noctes totas protrabit ~ando ad lunam CAIUS *Can.* 8.

baubellum [OF *baubel*], jewel, trinket.

s1199 [rex] tres partes thesauri sui et omnia ~a sua divisit Othoni nepoti suo R. HOWD. IV 83.

bauc- v. et. banc-.

baucalis [βαύκαλις], water-pot.

~em, gyllonem *GlC* B 27.

baucanus, ~eanus, ~ennus, ~eus v. balzanus.

baucia [? cf. daucus], parsnip.

~ie, rape, etc. GILB. V 212. 2; ~ia, pastinaca agrestis, sumitur quandoque pro domestica *SB* 12; ~ia, *pasnep or skyrwyt* WW (cf. skirewhittus).

baudekinus v. baldekinus. bauder- v. baldrea.

baudkinus [? cf. baldekinus], a copper coin.

p1280 secundum exemplum est baudkinorum [v.l. baukinorum], quorum quelibet libra continet de cupro pondus xiiij sterlingorum (*Tract. Novae Mon.*) *RBExch.* III 994.

baudr- v. baldrea. baurach v. borax. bausannus, bausiannus, baustandus v. balzanus.

†bausterium, (?) belt for bending crossbow (*cf. baldrea*).

c1350 legavit..j aketonem cum platis et..balista cum ~io et cornu *Reg. S. Aug.* 302.

bautaura [Turk. *bahādur*], an honorific title.

1291 iste litere nostre magno forti regi Haytoni ~a (*Lit. Soldani ad regem Armenie*) B. COTTON *Hist.* 218.

bauzanus v. balzanus.

bava [OF *bave*; *cf.* babicare], saliva.

propter ~as in ore M. SCOT *Phys.* 12.

Bavarrus, ~ius, ~iensis, Bavarian.

742 (v. Alamannus); a Neguio [orti sunt]..Boguarii NEN. *HB* 160; manus Francorum orientalis aderant ibi, Saxones quippe Baiuuerique ÆTHELW. IV 3; **s1138** Conradus dux Bawariorum FL. WORC. *Cont.* A II 101; **s891** rex Arnulfus cum Francis et Saxonibus et Baveriensibus H. HUNT. *HA* V 11; **s808** conflictus habitus est inter Avares et Bajoarios DICETO *Chr.* I 131; **s1338** rex..Coloniam adiit, ubi imperatorem ~um sibi conciliavit HIGD. VII 44.

bavenum [ME *bavein*], 'bavin', bundle of brushwood.

1319 *MFG* (*S. Ockendon*); **1371** reddit compotum de m^l^m^l^cc baven'..venditis *LTRAc* 4 r. D.

bavilatio v. bajulatio.

bavosus [< bava], drivelling, dull-witted.

c1190 ubi ~us et brutus nec suspicatur aliquid inquirendum LUCIAN *Chester* 54.

Bawarius v. Bavarrus.

baxea [CL], sort of sandal.

†~em [? l. ~eae], quas bacceas dicunt *GlC* B 47; ~ea, genus †caldei [l. calcei] muliebris *Erf.* 2. 270. 41; ~eae, *wifes sceos* ÆLF. *Gl.*

†baxus, sickle.

~us, **9..** *sicol*, **..10..** *sicel* WW.

bay- v. et. bai-.

bayrum v. varius. baza v. bassum. bazannum, bazenum v. basanum. Bazantius v. Byzantus.

bdella [βδέλλα], leech.

12.. bidella, i. *samsuns*, i. *lechis* WW.

bdellium [βδέλλιον], bdellium (bot.), sweet gum.

bidellium, arbor *GlC* B 98; mirra bidella storax cum thuris odore resinam / sponte dedere suam A. MEAUX *Susanna* 163; abdellum NECKAM *Ut.* 109; sicut galbanum, armoniacum, bdelium, storax GAD. 28. 1; ~ium gummi est *SB* 13; bedellium lacerinum [est] gumma cujusdam arboris que in Armenia nascitur *Alph.* 26; hoc bidellium, i. arbor dans bonum o[dorem] WW.

†beacita, starling.

~a, *stearn GlC* B 61; nomina avium: ..~a vel sturnus, *stearn* ÆLF. *Gl.*; **9..** beatica, *tearn* WW.

beare [CL], to bless.

Salvator clemens qui saecula cuncta beavit ALDH. *VirgV* 394; nostra quoque egregia jam tempora virgo beavit BEDE (*Hymn*) *HE* IV 20; quam fortuna beat, felix est illa senectus D. BEC. 2150; exteriorem hominem multiplici natura dote beaverat GIR. *EH* II 11.

2 (p. ppl. *beatus*) blest, blessed. **b** (of memory) revered. **c** (as personal title) blessed, saint. **d** (pl.) the saints, the blest (in heaven). **e** (compar. or superl.).

florebant sorte beata ALDH. *VirgV* 2745; quam [columbam] ille tunc vere ~us pia mentis aviditate contemplatus OSB. *V. Dunst.* 16; necesse est eam [summam essentiam] esse viventem, sapientem, ..justam, ~am, aeternam, et quidquid similiter absolute melius est quam non ipsum ANSELM (*Mon.* 15) I 29; ~orum spirituum visitatione EADMER *V. Osw.* 11; natus itaque ~us puer sacri baptismatis unda perfunditur AILR. *Ed. Conf.* 742B; **c1235** dedi..Deo..et S. Johanni Baptiste et ~is pauperibus sancte domus hospitalis S. Johannis Jerosolim.. *AncD* A 2316; illa ~a visione pacis superne Jerusalem BACON *Maj.* I 187; supplebitur imperfeccio visionis ~e..in animabus sanctis LUTTERELL *Vis. Beat.* I 104; **1343** quod per ~os apostolos legitur esse factum (*Lit. Regis*) AD. MUR 145; multe..creature volunt esse ~e WYCL. *Dom. Div.* 230. **b** ~ae memoriae Benedictum ALDH. *VirgP* 30; ~ae memoriae Vilfrid episcopus BEDE *HE* IV 19; vir ~ae recordationis Guthlac FELIX *Guthl.* 25. **c** ~us Augustinus in libro Civitatis Dei ALDH. *VirgP* 9; ~us Gregorius LANFR. *Ep.* 22. 527A; circa venerationem ~e Virginis Marie fervens erat OSB. *V. Dunst.* 86; **11..** in tempore ~i Wilfridi *Hexham* I 4; **1200** ~us Thomas archiepiscopus *CurR* I 320; **1262** canonici [sc. ecclesie] ~e Marie de Suthwerck' *Val. Norw.* 329; **1428** ~us Wyccliff, ut tuis [sc. heretici cujusdam] utamur verbis *Ziz.* 429. **d** ~orum gaudia BEDE *HE* III 19; ut evadam meritos dolores damnatorum et intrem in gaudia ~orum ANSELM (*Or.* 6) III 17; rex benedictus..inter ~os annumerabitur (*Proph. Merl.*) G. MON. VII 3. **e** o ~issime antistes ALDH. *Ep.* 1; ecclesia ~issimi apostolorum principis Petri BEDE *HE* IV 3 p. 212; ~issimum archiepiscopum.. Anselmum (*Quad.*) *GAS* 545; ad ecclesiam ~issime Virginis EADMER *V. Osw.* 36; necesse est..quemque fieri..in celis tanto meliorem quanto ~iorem PULL. *Sent.* 1008; de nobili prosapia ~issime Margarete Scotorum regine *Plusc.* VI 15.

beate [CL], blessedly, happily.

si quis ab iis [molestiis] liber vivit, ~e vivit ANSELM (*Mon.* 69) I 80.

beatificabilis, capable of beatitude.

anima.., in quantum est ~is et corpus ~e, nata est perficere corpus clarum et radiosum PECKHAM *QA* 159; utrum necesse sit ponere charitatem creatam formaliter inherentem nature ~i? DUNS *Sent.* I xvii 1. 1; ~is, id est potens habere beatificationem *Ps.*-OCKHAM *Princ. Theol.* 70; **1368** quod..homines damnati in inferno sunt reparabiles et ~es *Conc.* III 76.

beatificabilitas, capacity for beatitude.

idem est judicium de passione mortalitatis capta a causa materiali..et de ~ate secundum corpus et animam que competit sibi a causa finali WYCL. *Incarn.* 182.

beatificare, to beatify, bless. **b** (p. ppl. pl.) the blest.

qui..tantis laetitiis nostra tempora dignatus est ~are OSB. *Mir. Dunst.* 11; si ego non sum dignus qui sic debeam vestro amore ~ari ANSELM (*Or.* 7) III 24; [ipsius Dei, sicuti est, visio] plene ~at AD. SCOT. *Serm.* 123; **1331** caro et sanguis qui non ~ant michi revelarunt *Lit. Cant.* I 373 (cf. *Matth.* xvi 17); ibi Deus eos ~avit [ME: *gef ham bonen*] et se eis ostendit *AncrR* 50; **p1381** illa nomina 'reconciliatio', 'beatificatio' non significant principaliter animam sed medium vel modum quo anima ~atur vel reconciliatur Deo (WYNT.) *Ziz.* 203. **b** **1314** hec..~atis summe cedit ad gloriam *Mem. Ripon* 158.

beatificatio, beatification.

ad hoc quod dicit quod transmutatio plus tollit quam ~o PECKHAM *QA* 118; expectant post ultimum judicium..Dei visionem et suam ~onem OCKHAM *Dial.* 762; **p1381** cum dicitur 'visio Dei est ~o anime' (WYNT.) *Ziz.* 203.

beatificativus, beatific.

predicata connotativa..preter rem que Deus est..connotant extrinseca in obliquo, ut est creativum et ~um et hujusmodi *Ps.*-OCKHAM *Princ. Theol.* 52; quod sit Deus ~us creature racionalis WYCL. *Mand. Div.* 132.

beatificator, beatifier.

tunc complete sunt laudes..ipsi ~ori, qui beatificavit post hanc vitam que creavit septem diebus J. WALEYS *V. Relig.* I 16 f. 239; beneficio creatoris et recreatoris, ~oris et continui servatoris BRADW. *CD* 116C.

beatifice, beatifically.

tempus credendi et tempus ~e Deum videndi non compatiuntur se invicem OCKHAM *Dial.* 761; summe Deum diligere ~eve amare BRADW. *CD* 670D.

beatificus, beatific, conferring blessedness.

illam ~am vocem mereatur audire..: "venite, benedicti" EDDI *Wilf.* 32 (cf. *Matth.* xxv 34); benignitatis ~um patronum comminacionibus..provocare nitebatur (J. BRIDL.) *NLA* II 69; relicta opinione que perfeccionis finalis causam in actu visionis ~e solum ponit LUTTERELL *Vis. Beat.* I 103; si ~um premium hominis expectaretur in vita presenti, ..nullus beatitudinem non adeptus deberet ..exponere se morti BRADW. *CD* 107A; WYCL. *Act.* 43 (v. adhaesitio); a summa et ~a Trinitate ELMH. *Cant.* 213.

beatim, with a blessing.

c1190 ad sustentacionem trium scolarium..quos magister ~im eliget..et..ad elemosinarium..mittet, qui eis ~im in cibo et potu prospiciet (*Lib. Elem. Durh.*) *Educ. Ch.* 124.

beatitas [CL], happiness, blessedness.

prae ceteris feminis ~ate meruit excellere BEDE *Luke* 318; **c1040** futurae ~atis bravia perdat *CD* 769; bonos in celo ~ate donabit PULL. *Sent.* 802.

beatitudo [CL], **a** happiness. **b** blessedness (theol.).

a quis sic amet justitiam, veritatem, ~inem, incorruptibilitatem ut iis frui non appetat? ANSELM (*Mon.* 70) I 80; singularem sibi ~inem statuant in calamitate multorum J. SAL. *Pol.* 521A (cf. ib. 427C); si voluptas illis deesset, ~o minime plena esset (*Doctr. Mahom.*) S. SIM. *Itin.* 30. **b** aeternae ~inis coronam ALDH. *VirgP* 39; vitae, salutis et ~inis aeternae dona BEDE *HE* II 13; non aliam ~inem.. aestimamus esse promissam..quam ut omnes qui gloriam.. deificationis accepturi sunt, ultra locum et tempora ascendant ERIUG. *Per.* 482; quos attrahit suavitas Dei, eos satiat perpetua ~o ANSELM (*Ep.* 8) III 110; ante diem judicii vel post in ~ine WYCL. *Chr. & Antichr.* 673.

2 one of the Beatitudes (*Matth.* v).

hujus igitur ~inis prerogativis iste Dux [Ricardus].. floruit; quia quos audiebat discordes..reddebat concordes W. JUM. V 19; regum illorum..quibus octo ~inum jocunditas perennis..jocundatur H. HUNT. *HA* IV 21; de octo illis ~inibus quas Dominus in Evangelio ponit AD. SCOT. *Serm.* 316; in secunda ~ine BACON *Tert.* 253.

3 blessedness (title: **a** of pope; **b** of archbishop; **c** of other).

a meminisse debet ~o vestra LANFR. *Ep.* 17. 524B; interest ~inis vestre A. TEWK. *Addit. Thom.* 20; **1261** vestre ~ini grates referentes pro vestris apicibus *Cl.* 95; **1457** quos ..vestre ~ini facio recommendatos *Reg. Whet.* I 278. **b** **802** sicut in litteris vestrae ~inis lectum intellexi ALCUIN *Ep.* 255; **c1250** conservetur ~inis vestre..incolumitas in.. beatissima Virgine AD. MARSH *Ep.* 1. **c** **a690** illud.. almitati ~inis vestrae..promens ALDH. *Ep.* (*ad Ehfridum*) 5 p. 490.

beativus, beatific.

beatis / immo beativis indulge sumptibus HANV. IX 460.

beatrix, bestower (f.) of blessing.

meritorum dextra beatrix HANV. IX 391.

beatulus, minion.

noverca virtutis, prosperitas ~is suis sic applaudit ut noceat J. SAL. *Pol.* 389B.

beatus v. beare.

bebare, to bleat.

haedi balant vel ~ant ALDH. *PR* 131.

†bebella, *s. dub.*

~a, †sperta *GlC* B 89.

becagium [? cf. OF *becage* = *feeding of poultry*], payment for pasturage of cattle in forest (Macclesfield).

1330 reddit compotum de..xix s. vj d. de ~io boum tempore quadragesimali *MinAc* 802/1 r. 2; **1352** de iij s. x d. receptis de begagio quorundam averiorum infra forestam hoc anno *Ib.* 802/7 m. 1; **1352** de begagio nichil, quia dies solucionis non accidit ante festum Invencionis S. Crucis *Ib.* 802/6; **1362** perquisita hallemoti cum..pannagio, miner' carbonum et ~io *Ib.* 803/5 r. 1.

becassa [OF *becace*], woodcock.

faxianorum carnes valent eis, et ~e similiter bone sunt sive in pane sive in brodiis GAD. 55. 1; utatur volatilibus.. preterquam in aqua degentibus; ..bechasa tamen est bona *Ib.* 58 v. 2; **1344** iij perdric', ij s. j d.; ..vj bek', iij d.; xxx allaud', vj d. *KRAc* 390/11 r. 15d.

beccare [cf. OF *becher*], to hack (with a pick-axe or sim.).

1198 in costamento essartorum claudendorum et beccandorum in foresta de Bruis *RScac Norm* II 472.

beccus [OF *bec*], beak.

si habet accipitrem, perdat ~um et ungues BRACTON 147b.

becercium v. buticium. becha v. 6 beta. bechata v. bescata. bechea, ~ia, ~ium v. besca.

bechicon [βηχικόν], coltsfoot (*Tussilago*).

bichicon interpretatur ad tussym *Alph.* 23.

bechlatha [cf. hertlatha], beech-lath.

1333 pro c de ~is pro dict' mold' faciend' *KRAc* 469/12 m. 12.

†becnus, kind of fish.

c1324 turbonem meliorem pro vj d. . .; item brannum sardum et becnum meliorem pro iij d. (*Lib. Cust.*) *MGL* II 118.

beconagium, beacon.

1547 ~ia sive signa per mare littora et promontoria ejusdem pro direccione navium erecta *Pat* 804, m. 32.

†becta, (?) tail or (one-year-old) steer.

~a, †*staert GlC* B 91 (*cf.* WW: vecta, *enwintre*).

bectaria v. bateria 3a.

1 beda [ME *bede*], prayer. **b** bead.

1421 servicium. .solitum cum placebo et dirige et in crastino ~a cum missa pro defunctis consueta pro ipsorum animabus. .celebretur *Cop. Pri. S. Andr.* 102. **b 1386** ij paria de ~is de auro *FormA* 427.

2 beda v. bedum. Beddewinus v. Beduinus.

beddum [ME *bed*], lower framework (of cart).

1276 in reparacione ij ~orum karrorum de novo et lignum scapiliendum; . .in novo ~o ad carectam faciendo et axendo *Ac. Stratton* 189.

bedegar [Pers. *bādāvard*], bedeguar (rose-gall) or eglantine (wild rose).

succus macianorum cum succo ipsius ~ar pruritum tollit Gilb. III 143 v. 1; nomina silvestrium arborum: rannus et ~ar cum rumice Garl. *Dict.* 136; cum decoctione ~ar, i. eglentie, colluatur os Gad. 120. 2; ~ar est nodus rose albe silvestris vulgari nomine *eglenter SB* 12; ~ar est quedam tub[e]rositas crescens juxta radicem veperis qui vocatur *eglentier Alph.* 22; †bodarius, A. *heybrere* WW.

bedelinga [? ME], beadlery.

1234 G. Bedel tenet dimidiam virgatam terre pro ~a sua *Cust. Glast.* 115.

bedellanus, bedel (acad.).

1444 ego. .Sanctiandree dioscesis almeque universitatis ejusdem ~us *Midlothian* 303.

bedellaria [cf. bedellus 2], beadlery, office (or area of jurisdiction) of beadle (esp. of a hundred); **b** (W.); **c** (Ir.).

a1212 serjanciam de Westle que bedeleria appellatur, videlicet seminandum semina et in autumpno ad custodiand' messes *Kal. Samson* 113; **1238** terra quam Alanus Bedellus tenuit defendit se per ~iam ad voluntatem domini *BNB* III 245; **1285** infra bedelleriam de Manfeud *Cust. Suss.* II 35; **c1285** tenementum de La Hill tenetur de rege in capite in bedelleria, inveniendo unum bedellum in hundredo regis de Buddelegh [*Devon*] *Aids* I 325; **1329** seisitus. .de capitali balliva comitatus Dors' una cum bedelriis hundredorum de R. . .et S. *IPM* 36/21; **1347** concessionem. .de officio ~ie hundredi forinseci Bathon', cum omnibus emolumentis et proficuis que bedelli hundredi predicti. .percipere consueverant. .ac eciam cum omnibus execucionibus ad predictam ~iam pertinentibus *Pat* 221 m. 2; **1418** una cum bidellariis infra dicta hundreda *Cl* 268 m. 10; **1588** Bokested in bedelaria de Framfeild [*Sussex*] *Pat.* 1319 m. 2. **b 1340** ~iam de Stratwy in comitatu de Kermerdyn *Abbr. Orig.* II 131; **1348** Bergeveny. .budellus patrie. .reddet quolibet anno de budelaria sua xx s. *IPM* 91 r. 31. **c 1292** in ~iis predictis tales bedellos preficiant. .qui vicecomitibus nostris . .comitatuum predictorum intendentes sint *ChartR* 78 m. 8; **1298** cum officio bedelleriarum com. Waterford', Cork' et Kery *KRAc* 233/6.

bedellatus, office of bedel (acad.).

1456 superioris ~us officium in jure canonico et civili *EpAcOx.* 231; **c1456** contra Oxonienses regentes qui. .vendunt officium ~us Gascoigne *Loci* 49.

bedellium v. bdellium.

bedellus [cf. AS *bydel*, OF *bedel*], beadle, agent, servant. **b** beadle, manorial official, lord's agent (*cf. baillivus, praepositus*).

ut. .cesset invidere ~us magistro, minister domino Gir. *Symb.* 7 p. 223; **c1250** nec credatur dicto solius ministri vel ~i super alicujus diffamacione *Conc. Syn.* 650; **s1247** fratres Minores et Predicatores quos. .invitos jam suos fecit dominus papa thelonearios et ~os M. Par. *Maj.* IV 612. **b** modo habet rex in hoc manerio [*Leominster*]. .vi radmans et vii praepositos et vii ~os *DB* I 180 (cf. ib. 172); ~o pertinet ut pro servitio suo liberior sit ab operationibus quam alii homines (*Quad., Rect.* 18) *GAS* 451; **a1128** unus dat viij d., et hic est ~us aliorum *Chr. Peterb. app.* 166; **1229** in stipendiis prepositorum, bovariorum, herciatorum et ~orum *Pipe* 73 r. 1b; **c1253** si dominus voluerit habere prepositum de custumariis suis, quod ipse debet habere dim. virgatam quietam de operibus; item, si voluerit habere ~um de custumariis suis, ipse debet habere quartam partem j virgate quietam de redditu et de operibus *IMisc* 8/23; **1268** ita tamen quod tenentes predicti manerii teneantur ad faciendum sectam per quatuor homines et ~um ad magnam curiam nostram de Cantuar' *ChartR* 60 m. 12; **1270** dominus abbas elegit P. de W. budellum *CourtR Hales* 18; **1300** *bedillond*: . .una bovata terre quorum (*sic*) tenens debet esse bidellus domini et custodire blada domini in estate *IPM* 96/32; **1364** pro arreragiis redditus ~us domini [sc. abbatis Cant.] distringet (*Inq.*) Thorne 2140; **1535** Thome Harrys, ballivo sive bidello manerii de Ryall *Val. Eccl.* II 401.

2 beadle, official: **a** (of court); **b** (in hundred, wapentake, or sim.); **c** (in city or borough); **d** (in forest).

a mittit. .hec curia quos vocat justicias, vicecomites, . .~os, ut scrutentur argute Map *NC* I 10 p. 6; **1315** in. . stipendio unius bidelli colligentis redditus et perquisita curie et facientis attachiamenta *Cart. Boarstall* 573; **1331** ipsi ~i tempore domini Ranulphi comitis Cestrie. .omnes summoniciones faciendas in propria persona fecerunt *SelCKB* V 67; judex faciet partem appellantem per praeconem curiae, videlicet apparitorem vel ~um curiae. ., trina voce publice praeconizari *Praxis* 262. **b 1202** ~us testatus est quod vidit vulnus recens et sanguinem in wapentaco *SelPlCrown* 11; **1276** ballivi predicti castri. .tenuerunt turnos suos loco vicecomitis. .et habent quatuor ~os ubi non solent esse nisi duo *Hund.* I 113 (cf. ib. II 28: parvus ~us [? *under-beadle*]); **c1285, 1347** (v. bedellaria a); **1348** (v. bedellaria c). **c 11. .** ~us warde (*MSS. S. Paul's*) *HMC Rep.* 9 *app.* I, p. 62a; **1321** justiciarii fecerunt omnes ~os civitatis jurare quod ipsi eligerent duos homines meliores de tota garda sua *MGL* II 297 (cf. ib. I 37); **1201** (a1327) in dicto burgo [*Ipswich*] sint duo ~i jurati ad faciend' attachiamenta *Gild Merch.* II 119; **1248** ~um statuemus. . qui jurabit. .quod omnia attachiamenta. .presentabit *BBC* (*Poole*) 369; vocentur. .omnes ~i, id est servientes, qui ab ultima sessione camerarii in dicto burgo ministrarunt *Iter Cam.* 5; citatio facta burgensi in burgo. .sine ~o ejusdem burgi non est audienda *Leg. IV Burg.* 110. **d 1217** nullus forestarius vel ~us de cetero faciat scotal' (*Ch. Forest*) *St. Realm* I 20; **1273** in stipendiis prepositi, badelli et forestarii *Ch. & Rec. Heref.* 136.

3 beadle (eccl.).

1425 janitori clausi [ecclesie Sar.] et budello ibidem *Reg. Cant.* II 348; **1467** quod. .minister chori hujusmodi [ecclesie S. Egidii Edinb.] unum bidellum singula eidem officio incumbentia, que ministro. .ex honestate sacerdotali non congruunt, exercentem [teneret] *Mon. Hib. & Scot.* 456.

4 bedel (acad.).

c1250 duo tantum ~i seu apparitores juramento astricti habeantur, quorum alter scolarum theologie et decretorum alter autem aliarum onera. .subeat. . .intersint eciam virgam deferentes omnibus. .convocationibus *Stat. Cantab.* 207 (cf. ib. 321); **1338** ~us universitatis Cantebrigie *SelCKB* V 109; ~us proclamat quod quicumque veniat die assignato (Holcot *Wisdom*) *Eng. Friars* 144 *n.*; **1337** in ordinacione predicta sint ~i superiores singulis annis in reassumpcione virgarum suarum. .condempnati et ad ejus observacionem . .astricti *StatOx* 137; **1380** nullus in ~um elegetur nisi prius congregacioni regencium presentetur *Ib.* 68; **1511** bidellos singulas scolas universitatis visitantes *Ib.* 325; **1556** ~us superior facultatis artium et quilibet trium inferiorum ~orum *Ib.* 375; **1434** W. de B. S. Andree diocesis almeque universitatis ejusdem ~us *Reg. S. Andr.* 411.

bedelria v. bedellaria.

bedemannus [ME *bedeman*], beadsman: **a** crier; **b** almsman.

a 1275 a domo ~i extra Ludgate *Hund.* I 404; **1370** ~o dictum anniversarium in villa proclamanti *Little RB Bristol* I 199; **1423** lego duobus ~is [ecclesie Sar.] viij d. *Reg. Cant.* II 260; **1505** bedmanno qui obitum. .denunciabit *MonA* III 59. **b 1348** rusett pro ~is *Ac. Durh.* 545; **1379** xv bedmennis de Domo Dei pro pannis suis *Ib.* 587.

bederipa, ~ia, ~us, ~ium [ME *bed-rip*], (day's service of) boon reaping (*cf. benripa, precaria*).

a1185 per tres bedripas singulis annis faciendas cum tota familia domus *Cart. Osney* IV 141; debet serviens abbatis. . j die quando Magister voluerit ad suam ~am esse *Rec. Templars* 51; **1195** debet. .j bedripam cum j homine suo sine cibo, secundam cum omnibus famulis suis ad cibum domini sui *CurRPR* I 38; **1196** dabunt duos sol. annuatim. . pro tribus aratis et una bidripa que dicitur *hing' bidripe*, que ab eo exigebantur, salvis duabus bidripis quas. .faciet ad cibum abbatisse *Fines RC* (*Beds* 1/1/5) I 3; **1209** nativi domini regis de C. dum fuerunt. .ad manupastum patrum suorum et matrum, iidem parentes eos adquietant per ~as quas ipsi faciunt domino regi vel ejus firmario *Cart. Ciren.* I 266; **1234** facere debet j handaynam et iiij bedripos et habere garbas *Cust. Glast.* 35; debet triturare j stacam bladi contra ~am et aliam contra Natale *Ib.* 115; **12. .** ad quartum bedrippum. .habebunt j quar. et ij buss. siliginis ad *bedripmete Cust. Taunton* 20; **1268** facient. .unam bedrepam de predicto tenemento sicut liberi homines de manerio *ChartR* 57 m. 6; **1299** debet j hominem ad iij bydrippos *RB Worc.* 9; **1363** tres sunt cotrelli qui singuli reddunt per annum j d. et consuetudinem ad bedrepium *Ambrosden* II 138; **1375** idem et tota familia sua venient ad magnam ~am excepta uxore ejus; et ad parvam ~am invenient duos homines *IPM* 206/11; **1388** opera. .~ie valent per annum xxx s. *IMisc* 240/28; **1392** omnes tenentes sokemannorum simul cum tenentibus domini venient cum faucillis ad ~am domini (*Reg. Stoneleigh*) *Villainage in Eng.* 431; **1408** de Johanne O. . .j ~ium, j nederipium et *kyngesmede Reg. Ewell* 172.

bederna [? AS *bed-ærn* = *house of prayer*], bedern, common residence or refectory of canons or vicars choral (Yorks and Lincoln). **b** common fund of the same.

a1230 hiis testibus, magistro R. M. canonico Beverlacensi, . ., Thoma elemosinario de ~a *E. Ch. Yorks* III 1322; **1271** senescallus ~e Beverlaci *Cl* 426; **1275** ~a [Ebor'] est de terra B. Petri et data fuit. .vicariis Deo servientibus (*Inq.*) *MonA* VI 1193; **a1300** de ~a canonicorum Linc' *Reg. Ant. Linc.* II 336*n.*; **1304** ad emendos cibos ~e, sc. . .omnimodas escas de quibus ~a serviri debet *Mem. Beverley* I 25 (cf. ib. pp. xlix–liii); **1319** de quodam corrodio in ~a Beverlaci *Cl* 136 m. 2; **1345** unum messuagium. .juxta ~am in villa Ripon *Mem. Ripon* 155; **1391** a receptore, botellario et janitore ~e [Beverlaci] in eorum prefectione. .juramentum. . exigatur (*Ch. Archiep.*) *MonA* VI 1309; **s1393** archiepiscopus . .consecravit altare lapideum in capella ~e vicariorum ecclesie cathedralis *Chr. Pont. Ebor.* II 425; **1409** porta versus ~am est nimis. .aperta tempore prandii *Fabr. York* 244; **1549** domui ~e [*Howden*] *Cal. Pat* III 34. **b 1303** tam ~a quam portiones prebendarum suarum. .decrescere inceperunt *Mem. Beverley* I 4.

bedertha [ME *bed-erthe*], (day's service of) boon-ploughing (*cf. bederipa, benertha*).

1260 W. prepositus. .venit ad v †bedhurch' [l. bedhurthas] cum iiij bobus et valet vij d. *Cust. Glast.* 182.

bedewerus [*cf.* berroerius (DuC)], *native of Berry; hence light-armed soldier*], freebooter.

s1258 sicque facta est pax et tranquillitas liberrima dispersis predonibus quos ~os vocant. .tam in Roma quam vicinis partibus M. Par. *Maj.* V 709.

Bedewinus v. Beduinus. bedhurcha v. bedertha. bedmannus, bedmennus v. bedemannus. bedrep-bedrip- v. bederipa.

Beduinus [Ar. *badawī*], Bedouin.

1188 nobiscum habentur Bedewini, quos si opponeremus inimicis nostris sufficerent (*Lit. Saladini*) *Itin. Ric.* I 18; **s1187** ~i. .castellis et domibus non utuntur sed. .de rapinis. .vivunt *Expug. Terrae Sanctae* 9; **s1192** Beduwini qui se regi obligaverant Coggesh. 55; **1252** pro defensione. . terre [Babilonie, i.e. *Egypt*] contra Beddewinos et alios indigenas (*Lit. Thesaur. Hosp.*) M. Par. *Maj.* VI 206.

2 (?) Arabian (of a gem).

1215 unum lapidem bedewinum *Pat* 147b.

bedulta v. balthuta.

bedum, ~us, ~a [*cf.* baia], mill-dam.

c1160 in piscatione aque extra ~am molendini *Cart. Harrold* No. 3; **1212** ubi voluit curare beum molendini sui, per quem aqua deberet venire ad molendinum suum *CurR* (*Surrey*) VI 310; **c1215** inter. .pratum et vetus †benium de Oteri (*Cart. Otterton*) *Mon.Exon* 251 (cf. ib. 257: bedum); **a1296** que. .terra extendit se super ~um. .molendinorum *Reg. Malm.* II 95; **1298** ~um molendini *MinAc* 811/1 (*Cornw*) m. 1; **1337** beodum molendini *Capt. Seisine Cornub.* m. 2; **1538** de wera sive ~o *Fines* (*Devon*) 8/39/16; **1548** ex utraque parte ~e. .molendinorum *Cal. Pat.* 288.

Beemot v. Behemoth.

1 been [Pers. *bahman*], behen root, white (? *Silene*) or red (? *Limonium*).

~n alb' et rub' Gilb. V 228. 2; ~n est album et aliud rubeum *Alph.* 21.

2 been [? *cf.* Ar. *bān* = ben nut], white pepper.

oleum de ~n, i. de pipere albo et aliis piperibus Gad. 65 v. 2; ~n sunt grana que piper album dicimus *SB* 12.

beera v. 3 bera. begagium v. becagium.

Begardus [OF *begard*; *cf.* Begina], Beghard, member of lay brotherhood (banned in 1299).

unde et papa Clemens quintus damnat heresin ~orum Bradw. *CD* 326d.

Begina, ~us [OF *beguine*], Beguine, member of lay sisterhood, later also brotherhood (*cf. Begardus*).

s1243 quidam in Alemannia sub numerosa multitudine, mulieres precipue, habitum et mores religiosorum sibi assumentes, Beguinos sive Beguinas sese fecerunt appellari, ratione nominis incognita et auctore penitus ignoto M. Par. *Min.* II 476 (*cf. Flor. Hist.* II 267: Biguinas); **s1250** mulierum continentium, que se Beguinas volunt appellari, multitudo *Id. Maj.* V 194; dixit quod ~e sunt perfectissime. .religionis, quia vivunt propriis laboribus et non onerant exactionibus mundum Eccleston *Adv. Min.* 124; **1313** magistre et xxxvj sororibus de ordine ~arum ejusdem ville [*Montreuil*] (*KRAc* 375/8) *RGasc* IV p. xiv; **1332** ~e de Malyns j equum carectarium (*KRAc* 386/7) *Arch.* LXXVII 140; status mulierum que Beguyne vocantur reprobatur J. Burgh *PO* V 20.

2 (piece of) a sort of (? striped) cloth (? *cf.* Fr. *béguin*, sort of bonnet).

1310 de bonis. .mercatoris de Dikemuth' quatuor pannos ~os stragulatos ad lx s. appreciatos *Cl* 128 m. 25; **1325** pro una ~a [*n. marg.*: pannus] (*KRCustAc.* 93/22) *EEC* 378; **1329** panni: . .onerat se de iij ~is de radiato [etc.], de quibus in dorsario pro aula regis iij ~as *ExchScot* 255 (cf. ib. 173: per empcionem xix ~orum); **1337** in vj ulnis de begyno radiato pro roba. .xij s. *Ac. Durh.* 534; **1349** j pecia dim' begyna sindon[e] afforc[iata] (*KRAc* 391/15) *Arch.* XXXI 65; **1373** in empcione trium ~arum sindonis *ExchScot* 440.

Behemoth [cf. *Job* xl 10], serpent, hence Satan.

surrexit contra eum princeps Beemoth cum. .satellitibus suis *V. Osw.* 455 (cf. ib. 417); verbo tanquam verbere Beemot castigatus non ulterius conjugalem torum presumpsit infestare W. Cant. *Mir. Thom.* IV 2; nam corpus Behemoth ut scutum fusile fertur Elmh. *Metr. Hen. V* 93.

behemothicus, Satanic.

1026 (12c) si quis. .bohemotico instinctu. .hoc infringere conatus fuerit *CD* 743.

beja [Ar. *bayāḍ*], white lead (alch.).

est ergo solucio nostra ut tradas gabricum ~e in conjugium. . .conjunge servum nostrum rubeum sorori sue

odorifere Dastin *Ros.* 7; bejac est cerusa *LC* (*cf.* ib.: ~ae et garbilii conjugium).

bek' v. becassa.

bekerellus [OF *becquerolle*], beckerel, sort of derrick.

1325 pro xiiij bikerell' ferr' ad portand' spring[aldos], ad quemlibet bikerell' ij pixid' ferr' *KRAc* 165/1 m. 4; **1325** pro j *pyn* ferr' pro bokerello ad plumbum et lutum super diversos turellos wyndandum, v d.; ..pro quadam ligatura ferr' ad dictum bokerellum, vj d. *Ib.* 469/7 r. 8.

belbericus, belbricus v. belliricus. belecta v. beletta. belefreidum, belfreidum v. berefredum 2a.

belenum [βελένιον], **a** persea (bot.). **b** (identified as) henbane.

a ~um perniciosum natum in Persia transmutatur et transplantatum in Egyptum et in Syriam factum est comestibile Alf. Angl. *Plant.* I 17. **b** cum in libro De Veg. Aristotelis habetur '~um in Perside perniciosissimum..', ~um est Hispanicum et nullus..in Anglia potest per illam translationem scire quid est ~um; ..inveni quod est jusquiamus Bacon *Tert.* 91 (cf. Id. *Maj.* III 82; *CSPhil* 467).

beletta [OF *belete*], weasel.

1322 de exitibus ij columbar[ium] non respondet, quia fracta et vastata per belectas *MinAc* 1145/21 m. 23.

belidens [AS *behlidend*], closing naturally.

qui vulnus alicui faciet ac sanguinem, emendet hoc per uncias: ad singulas v den. in cooperto; in nudo pro singulis unciis x den.; et remaneat de cecis ictibus et belidentibus [v.l. belundintis] (*Leg. Hen.*) *GAS* 611.

bella [cf. ME *belle*], (?) bell-shaped vessel.

1290 ad coquinam: ..una olla, ij belles, xv patell' *Ac. Wardr.* (*Chanc. Misc.* 4/5) f. 3v.; **1420** invenimus..tres cupas..quatuor ~as argenti pedatas cum cooperculis (*Invent.*) *MonA* VI 935; **1485** factura iiij ollarum et iiij ~arum enearum ad coquinam *Comp. Swith.* 382.

bellardus v. 2 baselardus.

bellare [CL], **~ari,** to fight. **b** (trans.) to fight against. **c** to wage (war).

bellandi miseros stimulat quos vana cupido Aldh. *Aen.* 96. 2; ut multo plures aqua fugientes quam ~antes perderet ensis Bede *HE* III 24; ascendit montem rex bellaturus in hostem G. Amiens *Hast.* 373; Rodbertus..contra patriam ~abat W. Malm. *GR* III 283; litibus alternis quando bellantur amantes, / crescit in hoc bello linguarum pax animorum Vinsauf *PN* 880; **s1461** cum bonus est bellans et quem decet arma movere *Reg. Whet.* I 403. **b s1164** Henricus rex..ad ~andum Resum usque ad P. pervenit *Ann. Cambr.* 49; **s1212** ad ~andum regem Joannem Trevet 185; **s1191** de ~ando Sarracenos..promiserunt *Meaux* I 258. **c 1268** ut..nos..populum Christianum ad ~andum bellum suum exerceat ad salutem *Conc. Syn.* 782.

bellaria v. ballaria.

bellarium [CL], sweetmeat. **b** present.

significant ~ia omne genus mense secunde J. Sal. *Pol.* 734 D (cf. ib. 734 C); **1539** pro ~iis datis sociis cum ageretur comedia (*Ac. Coll. Magdalen*) *Med. Stage* II 249. **b** *presande*, exennium, ~ium *CathA*.

bellatim, in battle.

s1303 ut tanti per tantos tribus vicibus ~im in uno die.. turmatim sunt devicti *Plusc.* IX 1.

bellator [CL], warrior. **b** (as adj.).

bellator Christi Aldh. *VirgV* 2648; ~or spiritalis ~or cogitur esse carnalis Alcuin *Ep.* 2; **9..** ~or, *fihtling* WW; actus ~orum ex fabulis antiquorum..colligere *G. Herw.* 320; **s1224** cum a regis ~oribus due testudines.. subacte essent, invaserunt castellum M. Par. *Maj.* III 86. **b** Gedeon..cum ccc viris ~oribus Eddi *Wilf.* 13.

bellatorius [CL], military.

~ie artis industria.., dum docetur in otio, cautius exercetur in bello P. Blois *Ep.* 231. 527B.

bellatrix [CL], militant (f.).

Pallada Gorgoneam bellatricemque Medusam J. Exon. *BT* II 251; sperne tabernas / et bellatrices luctas D. Bec. 50.

belle [CL], finely (iron.).

~e scis actitare guerram qui hostibus prebes aque copiam W. Malm. *GR* IV 310.

bellectum v. 2 billettum 2a. bellericus v. belliricus.

belliator [ME *belleyetere*], bell-founder.

1475 de vendicione remanentis fusille enee tempore facture magne campane sic vendit' ~ori *Ac. Churchw. Sal.* 16.

bellicare, to fight.

s871 extendentes reges gladios vix sedaverunt populum ~antem S. Durh. *HR* 73.

bellice, conveniently for war.

anulus in quo clava..ad ipsius equitis..defensionem satis ~e ponitur S. Sim. *Itin.* 53.

bellicose, w. military skill. **b** in war.

in tres se terribiles turmas ordinate et ~e diviserunt *G. Steph.* I 9. **b s1321** contra regem..insurrexit ~e *G. Ed. II Bridl.* 67; **s1339** estimans se statim cum Anglicis congredi ~e *Meaux* III 41.

bellicosus [CL], warlike.

quidam ~us incentor..certaminis Aldh. *VirgP* 38 p. 289; in quo etiam bello..Osfrid juvenis ~us cecidit Bede *HE* II 20; **9..** ~us, pugnandi cupidus, *wigbære* WW; vir ~us et audax in gente sua Gir. *EH* I 6; acies..de ~is viris multum strenuis *Plusc.* IX 1.

bellicrepa [cf. CL Gl. ~a saltatio], **a** muster. **b** herald.

a *mustyr*, ~a *PP*; *a muster of men*, ~a *CathA*. **b** *an harott of harmes*, ~a *CathA*.

†belliculus [? for umbiliculus; cf. belliricus 2], (?) sea-snail; *cf. billerus*.

~i marini quasi umbilici circa litora maris reperiuntur *Alph.* 22.

bellicum [*cf.* OF *belece*], bullace, sloe.

~um, *slag GlC* B 75; **9..** brumela vel ~um, *sla* WW.

bellicus [CL], warlike.

gestantes bellica signa Aldh. *VirgV* 2462; se..satagunt magis..monasterialibus adscribere votis quam ~is exercere studiis Bede *HE* V 23; bellica jura tenentes G. Amiens *Hast.* 543; non in ~a classe sed sub pacis obtentu Gir. *TH* III 43; **1263** ne..~um faciat in barones..insultum (*Lit. Regis Rom.*) *Foed.* I 768.

bellificare, to fight.

to stryfe, ..bellare, ..~are, belligerare *CathA*.

bellificus, warlike.

c1280 quisquis videns hoc testatur / per signa bellifica (*De S. de Monte Forti*) *EHR* XI 318.

belliger [CL], warlike. **b** (sb.) warrior.

belliger impugnans elefantes vulnere sterno Aldh. *Aen.* 60 (*Monocerus*) 5; agmen belligerum G. Amiens *Hast.* 662; rixas belligeras..sperne D. Bec. 49. **b** qui propriis numquam confidit belliger armis Aldh. *VirgV* 2850; belliger iste Dei fortissima bella peregit (Wulfstan) *Anal. Hymn.* XLVIII 1. 3; **s1428** exutus servis, suis ~is denudatus *Plusc.* X 31.

belligerare, ~ari, to fight.

~at, pugnat *Erf.* 2. 271. 16; non facie ad faciem conflictu belligeramur Whaet. *Aen.* 15. 3; non minimam multitudinem ~antium secum ducens profectus est Ric. Hex. *Stand.* 42.

belligerosus, fit for battle.

c1403 multitudo imbecillorum..ad sua unusquisque revertebatur; valentes igitur et ~i coacti sunt longius ire *Dieul.* f. 146.

bellipotens, mighty in battle.

ubi bellipotens sumsit baptismatis undam / Edvin rex Alcuin *SS Ebor.* 1489 (cf. ib. 1326); **10..** ~ens, *wiga ōðe wigstrang* WW; princeps bellipotens Garl. *Tri. Eccl.* 67.

belliricus [Ar. *balīlaj*, Pers. *balīla*], belleric, bastard myrobalan (bot.).

emblici,..Indi, ~i Gilb. II 96. 2; olive marine, ~i marini *Ib.* 112 v. 2; ex mirabolanis nigris et emblicis et †belbricis Bacon IX 47; si sit de colera adusta.., tunc valent Indi, ~i, emblici infusi..in aqua plantaginis Gad. 6 v. 1; mirabolanorum species sunt quinque bonorum,/citrinus, ebulus, bellericus, emblicus, Indus *Alph.* 117.

2 (? conf. w. *umbilicus*; *cf. belliculus*).

~i marini lapides sunt parvi et albi; in rupibus marinis inveniuntur *SB* 12; †belberici marini sunt similes umbilicis; umbilicus, A. *navelwort* WW.

Bellona [CL], war goddess, valkyrie. **b** grandmother.

Bellona ferox infecit corda venenis Aldh. *VirgV* 1545; **9..** ~a, furia, dea belli, ..*wælcyrge* WW; bella fremunt, Bellona tuba, Mars intonat ense Hanv. VI 326; **s1387** hii.. milites plures erant Veneris quam ~e Wals. *HA* II 156. **b** *beeldam, moders modyr*, ~a *PP*.

2 [? by conf. w. *belua*], she-wolf, wild animal.

9.. ~a, *wylfen*, ..†ia, *wilde deor* WW.

bellu- v. et. belu-.

bellula, (?) daisy (*Bellis*).

illud..quod dicitur in ptesi de ~a et nasturcio valet ad idem Gilb. VI 240 v. 1.

bellum [CL], war, warfare, campaign. **b** (fig.) struggle.

qui occiderit hominem in puplico ~o, XL dies peniteat Theod. *Pen.* I iv 6; pacare students belli certamina saeva Aldh. *VirgV* 1552; justa pro salute gentis nostre ~a suscepimus Bede *HE* III 2; Mars, deus o belli, gladius qui sceptra coerces G. Amiens *Hast.* 345; alter in alterutrum plusquam civile peregit / bellum *Ib.* 136; *ferdwite* quod nos possumus dicere dimissionem ~i (*Inst. Cnuti*) *GAS* 317 (cf. ib. 319); iniquitas est cruenta ~orum confusio Anselm (*Ep.* 117) III 252; omnes eorum [Norwagiensium] expeditiones et ~a navali certamine fiunt Gir. *TH* II 11. **b** certamen stuprorum bella secundum / blanda cient caste Christo famulantibus Aldh. *VirgV* 2544; ut a Gallicanis antistitibus auxilium ~i spiritalis inquirant Bede *HE* I 17; bibendi ~a P. Blois *Ep.* 102. 319A (v. architriclinus).

2 battle, fight. **b** brawl. **c** pitched battle. **d** single combat, fight between champions.

ordine post pedites sperat stabilire quirites, / occursu belli sed sibi non licuit G. Amiens *Hast.* 342; qui fuit occisus in ~o Hastingensi *DB* II 409b; **s1066** commissum est.. ~um in festivitate S. Calixti; quo in loco rex Willelmus abbatiam nobilem postea..construxit et eam digne nomine Belli vocavit H. Hunt. *HA* VI 30; **s1337** mortuus est..in Scocia sine ~o Ad. Mur. 78; **1349** de ij annis post ~um Dunelm' *Ac. Durh.* 718; ad ~um veniunt manuale [*hand-to-hand*] Elmh. *Cant.* 252. **b** si, in curia vel domo sedicione orta, ~um etiam subsequatur et quivis alium fugientem in aliam domum infuget.., hamsocna reputetur (*Leg. Hen.*) *GAS* 597. **c** quicumque in obviacione hostili vel ~o campali fugerit (*Ib.*) *GAS* 569 (cf. ib. 558: in ~o campali vel navali); **s1187** rex Francie..disposuit acies suas ad ~um campestre R. Howd. II 317. **d** ut eum ad solitarium ~um invitaret *G. Herw.* 338; **s1355** personale ~um inter xxx Anglicos et xxx Francos *Plusc.* IX 41.

3 line of battle.

1217 ~is septem eleganter ordinatis densis agminibus processerunt in hostes (*Incid. de Terra Promissionis*) M. Par. *Maj.* III 17; **1322** rebelles nostri armati..se in ~a divisa more hostili contra nos direxerunt (*Cl*) *Parl. Writs* II ii *app.* 181b; **1366** concedimus..quod iidem reges..habeant primum ~um sive *delanterre* ante omnes mundi Christianos (*DipDocE* 237) *Foed.* VI 532; **s1415** ~um equestre posterius Elmh. *Hen. V* 55; **s1423** ad fugam compulserunt usque ad secundum ~um sive aciem ~i *Plusc.* X 29.

4 judicial combat (*cf. duellum*).

quidam homo comitis vult probare quod hundredum verum testatur vel juditio vel ~o *DB* II 146b; si quid ~o vel lege sacramentali..vel etiam judiciali repetatur (*Leg. Hen.*) *GAS* 555; qui ~um vadiaverit et per judicium defecerit, lx s. emendet *Ib.* 579; **a1133** nullus eorum [civium London'] faciat ~um (*Ch. Hen. I*) *Ib.* 525; **a1135** per legem se defendat burgensis, nisi sit de proditione, unde debeat se defendere ~o *BBC* (*Newcastle*) 132; **c1180** si ibi ~um sive judicium adjudicatum esset [*Norm.*] *Act. Hen. II* II 165; **1200** de quodam ~o inter eos concusso de terra quadam *CurR* I 222.

bellus [CL], beautiful, fine. **b** (in proper names).

surrexit bella puella Aldh. *VirgV* 604; nunc vestium velamina / bella produnt ornamina (Æthelwald) *Carm. Aldh.* 2. 118; ~us, ~issimus, comparativum non habet Bede *Orth.* 2778; **p732** ut..quod in bona juventute caepisti in senectute ~a ad gloriam Dei perficias Bonif. *Ep.* 94 (*ad Buggam*); **1232** unum ~um baudekinum cum auro *Liberate* 10 m. 6. **b** Ailwardus filius ~i *DB* II 391; Robertus ~us *Lib. Wint.* 548; **1220** de..Galfrido ~o *Fees* 297; R. de ~a Fago *DB* II 278b; **1145** de ~o Videre [*Belvoir, Leics*] *BM Cotton.* XI 6; rex..abbatiam †qui [? l. que] ~us Locus nomen accipit [*Beaulieu, Hants*] construere..disposuit Gir. *Hug.* II 1.

belmannus [ME *belleman*], bell-ringer.

1405 clerico parochiali..~o ibidem *Test. Ebor.* III 29; **1462** obitus: ..in campana vj d.; et ~o j d. *Ac. Churchw. Sal.* 9.

belone [βελόνη], (?) sword-fish.

belua marina quam alii delphinum, alii acum seu bolonem propter rostri acumen putavere André *Hen. VII* 115.

belongum [OF *beslonc*], lengthwise direction.

1246 vulneraverunt..forestarium..cum una sagitta sub mamilla sinistra ad profunditatem unius palme de ~o *SelPlForest* 80.

belota [Ar. *ballūṭ*], acorn.

fructuum quidam sunt..in cafta ut ~e [*gl.*: glandes] Alf. Angl. *Plant.* I 14.

†belsa, (?) bush.

9.. ~arum, *pyfela* vel *boxa* WW.

belta [ME], belt (for a bell).

1342 in vj stiropis et iiij bondis pro Baunse [*name of a bell*] x d.; in factura unius nove ~e de ferro domini, vj d. *Sacr. Ely* II 118.

belua [CL], wild beast, monster. **b** (fig.).

latebram qua horrens belva latebat Aldh. *VirgV* 2391; ut mare cum beluis sancto servire solebat Alcuin *SSEbor.* 711; bellua, *reðe deor* Ælf. *Gl.*; **10..** ~a, *egeslic nyten on sæ oððe on londe* WW; balenam vel aliam marinam belluam monstruosam Gir. *TH* II 12; capiuntur lupi et alie ~e aquatice et..presentatur ~a..adhuc cauda..palpitante J. Godard *Ep.* 223. **b** hanc belvam [sc. ebrietatem] studeat superare virago Aldh. *VirgV* 2534; belva maligna est Bonif. *Aen.* 3 (*Cupiditas*) 11.

belualis, bestial, monstrous.

sanguinem..sitire..belluale quidem est et crudele Gir. *PI* I 10; **s1291** sedavit..~em quandam gentis illius barbariem W. Newb. *Cont.* 575; **s1459** bellualis potius quam bestialis illa sevicia esse dicitur ubi nulla subsequitur misericordia *Reg. Whet.* I 354.

beluinus, a of a beast. **b** bestial, beast-like.

a a lupis immanibus circumseptum ~oque rictu devorandum W. Malm. *GP* I 44. **b s1190** quos..plusquam belluina illa confecit immanitas W. Newb. IV 10 p. 321; ~a voluptate J. Godard *Ep.* 224; belluine voracitatis virosa malignitas Ad. Marsh *Ep.* 13; bellum utpote rem ~am..abominantur More *Utopia* 243.

bema [βῆμα], step.

perfectorum est..altissima divinae theoriae bimata, hoc est gradus, superare Eriug. *Per.* 627B.

bemolle v. 2 B.

bemum [ME *bem*], plough-beam.

1276 in uno ~o ligando de ferro comitisse, j d. *Ac. Stratton* 189.

1 bena v. avena.

2 bena [ME *bene*], boon-work (*cf. precaria*).

c1182 queque virgata ~am suam proprio semine seminabit *RB Worc.* 110 (cf. ib. 408: cum ~am suam falcare debuerint); 1279 falcabit dim. acram prati pro j ~a *Hund.* II 632 (cf. ib. 657: arrabit dim. acram..que vocatur *bene*); 1342 non venit cum familia sua ad ~am *Rec. Elton* 312.

benda [ME *bend, band*; OF *bende*; cf. bondum], metal band or strip. **b** (w. *pedalis*) part of a cart ('foot-bend'). **c** neck-band.

1209 expensa [molendinorum]:..in ~is ferreis, vj d. *Pipe Wint.* 79; 1225 in viij ~is ferreis ad petrarias ligandas *Cl* 65a; 1237 in ~is ferreis ad trabem ligandam *KRAc* 501/18 m. 3; 1291 in ferro empto ad gumffos et ~as faciendas ad pontem *Ib.* 479/15 r. 1; 1294 fabro ad faciendum ~as ad ligandum gubernaculum *Ib.* 5/2 m. 2; 1295 custus carucarum:..in una nova ferrea ~a ad foramen cultri et reparacione aliarum ~arum *MinAc* 1090/3 r. 4; 1296 de qualibet ~a ferri venalis, j ob. *Pat* 115 m. 8 (cf. ib.: de uno pari ~arum ad rotas carette ligandas); 1333 quod ingenium [sc. vernum] continet duas bandas pendentes cum cavillis curtis *KRAc* 469/12 m. 18; 1373 in crukkis, bandis..et ceteris ferramentis emptis pro eisdem [domibus] *Ac. Durh.* 211. **b** 1307 in..carecta.. emendanda cum iij bend[is] pedal[ibus] ad idem faciendis *Ac. Man. Wint* (*Chilbolton*); cf. ib. (*Wonston*) [1386]: in emendatione veterirs carecte cum *fotbend*. **c** c1175 est etiam ibi quedam ~a, que in collo morientis fuit circumligata celerem patientibus..conferens sanitatem Ric. Ely *Etheldr.* 579.

2 ornamental band or stripe. **b** diagonal stripe, bend (her.).

1216 cyphos..cum pedibus et ~is deauratis *Pat* 170b; 1245 cape due rubee cum ~is transversoriis (*Invent. S. Paul.*) *Arch.* L 479 (cf. ib.: in ~is..sunt rose, in aliis.. pisciculi); arma quedam..vocantur bandaria quia sunt quasi de bandis facta Bad. Aur. 129. **b** s1321 armigeri.. indumenta ~as habuerunt Wals. *HA* I 161 (= Trokelowe 109: *bendes*); 1389 in quadam causa de et super armis de azura cum una ~a de auro (*Pat*) *Foed.* VII 621; tales [qui signum bastardie portant] portant arma suorum parentum integra cum quadam ~a ex transverso Bad. Aur. 138; illa vocatur ~a que ducitur a dextro cornu..scuti usque partem sinistram ejusdem ad differentiam fissurarum sive baculorum Upton 234.

3 measure of flax (*cf. binda*).

1285 ~e liny fuerunt invente ad domum Walteri *Hund. Highworth* 293.

bendare, to edge, border.

1216 tunicam albam de diaspr' ~atam de orfras' *Pat* 173a; 1252 faciat pannum..~ari in circuitu de aurifrigio *Cl* 287.

2 (p. ppl.) striped diagonally, bendy (her.).

1322 vestem ~atam *CalCl* 448 (cf. ib. 462); losenge fiunt in armis ~atis Bad. Aur. 200; in armis ~atis colores contenti equaliter dividuntur Upton 254.

bendarius, bendy (her.).

sunt etiam arma quedam que vocantur bandaria; ..et vocantur bandaria quia sunt quasi de bandis facta Bad. Aur. 129; portat arma ~ia de auro et azoreo *Ib.* 181.

bendatim, per bend (her.).

vocantur bendaria barrata quia sunt barrata et duo colores conjunguntur in singulis barris ~im Bad. Aur. 189 (cf. Upton 232).

bendula, bendlet (her.).

portat unam bendam et duas ~as aureas in campo rubeo Bad. Aur. 190; vocantur ~e ad differentiam magnarum bendarum Upton 234.

bene [CL; v. et. melius, optime], well (favourably, agreeably, rightly, etc.; *v. et benevenire*). **b** (ellipt.) it is well. **c** (w. *adeo* or *ita*) as well, as much.

quae in Galliis ~e disposita vidit Bede *HE* III 18; quamdiu ~e se haberet erga eum *DB* I 45b; quodcunque tempus ad ~e vivendum datur, eo quis debet esse contentus Gir. *PI* I 21; 1217 ~e placet nobis quod.. *Pat* 59 (cf. beneplacere); 1303 pro testamento isto ~e et legitime probato *Deeds Balliol* 167; 1378 juratores dicunt quod decenarii ~e et fideliter presentant (*CourtR*) *Banstead* 360. **b** at ille: "~e; ergo expectemus horam illam" Bede *HE* IV 22 p. 262. **c** multi..habent..maximum dampnum.., adeo ~e predicti H. et N. quam alii *State Tri. Ed. I* 44 (cf. 1 adeo 2); papa ita ~e potest decipi circa ea que sunt fidei sicut circa quecumque alia Ockham *Dial.* 687.

2 (in emphatic or concessive expressions) **a** fully (realize, believe, suppose). **b** positively (affirm or deny). **c** freely, readily (admit etc.). **d** (be) perfectly (willing, able, possible, permissible).

a 1220 ~e scivit quod fuerunt malefactores *SelPl Crown* 121; 1221 ~e credunt quod ipsi..eum occiderunt *SelPl Glouc.* 32; 1221 ~e intelligunt quod sit culpabilis *Ib.* p. 29; 1223 ~e putavit quod per libertatem illam illum levare potuit *CurR* XI 1034. **b** 1218 ~e dicunt quod ipsa nunquam dimisit se de terra *Eyre Yorks* 9; 1219 ~e defendit quod in nullo est contra finem illum *CurR* VIII 41; 1315 ~e defendit quod ipse nunquam fuit ballivus *Year Bk.* XVII 60. **c** 1218 ~e ponit se super juratam *Eyre Yorks* 121; 1220 cognoscit ~e quod..presentavit *CurR* VIII 342; 1228 vicecomes..mandavit ei quod ~e inde respondebit *KRMem* 9 r. 11; 1267 ~e concedit quod fecit..defaltam *Cl* 359. **d** 1217 ~e volumus quod saisinam..habeant *Pat* 59; 1297 rex..vult ~e quod..vadia eis solvantur *RGasc* III clxxxv; 1290 nunquam prohibuit narratores quin ~e possent fuisse de consilio..Rogeri *State Tri. Ed. I* 21; 1403 si contingat.. redditum..a retro esse.., ~e licebit..Johanni..distringere *FormA* 329.

3 (w. number) fully.

1214 misit quendam exercitum..~e circa xl homines *CurR* VII 243; c1250 decime..que ~e ix marcas valuerunt *FormOx* 479; 1289 fecit purpresturam..~e per octo pedes et amplius *Leet Norw.* 36; s1356 exploratores..~e ad ducentos homines *Eul. Hist.* III 222; et ~e alias quinque villas *V. Ric. II* 46.

4 (w. adj. or adv.) properly, very.

viri ~e religiosi Bede *HE* IV 17; ponemus..mollificativa donec reddatur [apostema] ~e molle Gilb. VII 320. 2; c1228 non est ~e certus *Feod. Durh.* 237; 1292 coram.. episcopo..~e tempestive venerunt *RParl* 70b; ~e mane.. apparuerunt *V. Ric. II* 45.

5 (w. *de..esse*) provisionally, w. moral rather than legal validity (*cf. Law Quarterly Rev.* LXII 130 *seq.*).

hoc fuit de ~e esse, non de necessitate Bacon *Tert.* 242; s1227 non sunt de substancia professionis, sunt tamen de ~e et honeste esse *Ann. Durh.* 23 (cf. Graystanes 10); 1384 preceptum fuit sepius per justiciarios de ~e esse quod iterum demandetur *JustIt* 1488 r. 62; 1419 consueverunt majores de ~e esse non de jure impetrare sibi tales commissiones regias *MGL* I 14.

6 (as subst.) well-being.

nil agis absque bene Serlo Wilt. 26. 6; a1550 idem J. remanebit cum catallis suis in ~e et in pace *Mem. Ripon* I 254.

benedicatio v. benedictio 2a.

benedicere [CL; al. div.], to speak in praise.

his rationibus..ad scribendum traductus, malebam aliene voluntati ~endo obtemperare quam proprie serviens voluntati a bene dicendo temperare Osb. *V. Dunst. prol.*

2 to praise, glorify (God). **b** (in interj. 'God be praised!')

trinus et unus Deus, ~tus in secula Anselm (*Prosl.* 26) I 122; plebs..viso hoc facto ~it Dominum Eadmer *V. Anselmi* II 43; omnibus admirantibus et ~entibus Deum in operibus suis Ailr. *Ed. Conf.* 779a; profert ista: "Deus sit benedictus, amen!" Garl. *Tri. Eccl.* 79; Deo operante qui solus est ~tus Rich *Edm.* 624. **b** 1227 recessi..sanus et incolumis, ~tus Deus (*AncC* VI 162) *RL* I 421; 1264 sedata ~tus Deus turbacione *Cl* 87; s1325 nec ille..aliquid mali inde habuit, ~tus Deus *Ann. Paul.* 310.

3 bless, bestow a blessing on.

rex benedicte, vale! G. Amiens *Hast.* 27; omnipotens Dominus vos ~at Lanfr. *Ep.* 18. 525c; Christus..apparuit, sacraque dextera super regem extensa signum sancte crucis eum ~endo depinxit Ailr. *Ed. Conf.* 760d; virginem et reginam theotocon ~tam R. Bury *Phil.* 20. 251; illum [secundum] diem Deus non ~xit *Eul. Hist.* I 8; sed Christi dextra prece matris eos benedixit Elmh. *Metr. Hen. V* 992.

4 bless, invoke a blessing on (a person); **b** (as a cure for sickness; *cf. Rois Thaumaturges* 94); **c** (as part of a ceremonial consecration to office or sim.).

~ens filium patriarcha Bede *HE* I 34; ore illius se ~i gaudebant *Ib.* III 26; †1082 (12c) ego W. episcopus.. cunctos istius ordinationis fautores perpetua Dei Omnipotentis..benedictione ~endo ~ens *Feod. Durh.* xlii; c1370 vanis Clementis volitat benedictio ventis [*gl.*: hic est notandum quod papa potest errare..et ~ere partem falsam] (J. Bridl.) *Pol. Poems* I 164, 165. **b** si ille ei manum imponere atque eum ~ere voluisset, statim melius haberet Bede *HE* V 5; venit ad infirmum.. / impositaque manu capiti benedixit eundem Alcuin *SS Ebor.* 1198; 1278 tribus egrotis ~tis de manu regis *Chanc. Misc.* 4/1 f. 20; 1289 pro infirmis quos rex ~xit *KRAc* 352/18; 1281 unum annulum aureum..talis virtutis ut quicunque percussus fuerit *del felun* et illo ~atur [? *by making the sign of the cross*]..recuperet sanitatem (*Test.*) *Cart. Osney* I 411. **c** Greci simul ~unt viduam et virginem et utramque abbatissam eligunt Theod. *Pen.* II iii 7; s967 Otto a Johanne in imperatorem ~itur R. Niger I 79; dum in reginam ipsa puella ~i debuisset Eadmer *HN* 343; ~itur puella in uxorem et in reginam coronatur Ailr. *Ed. Conf.* 784a; s1135 archiepiscopus Cantuariensis..eum..in regem benedixit H. Hunt. *HA* VIII 1; 1163 cum..fratres..monasterii..episcopum..requisissent ut R. electum suum ~eret in abbatem *Reg. Malm.* I 372; s1191 ~xit abbatem ante majus altare S. Pauli Diceto *YH* II 101; 1289 [pape] predecessor nondum ~tus et consecratus (*Lit. Papae*) *Foed.* II 427.

5 bless, consecrate (material objects).

diacones possunt..cibum et potum ~ere, non panem dare Theod. *Pen.* II ii 16; sportas.. / quas prius exorans palma benedixerat alma Aldh. *VirgV* 1612; manus ad panem ~endum missuri Bede *HE* III 6; miserat de aqua ~ta *Ib.* V 4; descendat abbas..ad fontes ~endos *RegulC* 48; est antiquus Anglorum mos ut omnis populus accedat ad episcopum et manibus in modum crucis expansis accipiat ~tum panem *V. Osw.* 455; eat ad panem ~tum quem Angli *corsnade* vocant (*Inst. Cnuti*) *GAS* 287; aspergens eos aqua ~ta dicat.. (*Jud. Dei*) *Ib.* 423; 1243 (v. aqua 2b); post hec benedicitur unda Garl. *Myst. Eccl.* 146; s1258 [abbas] novi presbyterii..propria manu primum lapidem ~xit Oxnead *S. Ben. Holme* 298; 1315 (v. benedictionalis); 1462 tres panes..per me ~tos et sanctificatos *Lit. Cant.* III 238.

6 (?) to swear profanely, curse.

s1302 videbatur sibi [sc. priori] quod sine reprehensione facere posset quicquid vellet, propter presentiam cardinalium non omittens ~ere nec..cum avibus ludere Graystanes *Hist. Durh.* c. 25; 1526 circa istud ~tum divortium (*Lit. Ep. Bath.*) *L. & P. Hen. VIII* IV 1109.

7 (imp. pl. as interj.) bless you! **b** (liturgical greeting) *benedicamus* [*Dominum*].

caritatis effectum dimidiatis ad advenas, "~ite" sine prebenda dantes hospitibus Devizes 25. **b** quod Benedicamus pueri cantare jubentur Garl. *Myst. Eccl.* 252.

8 (p. ppl.) **a** (as sb. n.) benediction. **b** (m. and f.) hymn or antiphon. **c** (f. *sc. aqua*) holy water. **d** (f. w. or without *herba*) herb bennet, valerian, hemlock or (?) avens; *v. et. carduus*.

a Christi persona reddit benedicta sacerdos Garl. *Myst. Eccl.* 211. **b** ~tus antiphona et collecta de Trinitate Lanfr. *Const.* 90; ad ~tus et ad Magnificat precipitur esse in albis *Ib.*; Ignatius martyr his apposuit Benedictus Garl. *Myst. Eccl. add.* p. 150; 1340 quando illam antiphonam ~ta ..cantari contigerit *Deeds Balliol* 297. **c** s1095 aspersa ~ta episcopus discessit *Eul. Hist.* III 48 (= W. Malm. *GR* IV 319: aqua ~ta). **d** trifera in quantitate majori et ~ta in minori mixtis Gilb. I 21. 2; (?) ~tam que in antidotario Latinorum invenitur Bacon IX 115; 12.. herba ~ta, i. *herbe beneit*, i. *hemeluc* WW; si de renibus in causa frigida, ponatur ~ta Gad. 6 v. 2; cicuta, ..conium, herba ~ta idem, G. *chenele*.., A. *hemelok* vel *hornwistel Alph.* 39; fu, valeriana, ..~ta idem *Ib.* 69; *an humlok*, cicuta, herba ~ta, intubus *CathA*.

benedicibilis, worthy of blessing.

preveniebat eum 'in benedictionibus dulcedinis' [*Psalm* xx 4] dulcem, amabilem et ~em illum exhibendo universis Ad. Eyns. *Hug.* I 3.

Benedictinus, Benedictine: **a** of St. Benedict. **b** (monk of the order) of St. Benedict.

a 1526 secundum declarationes ~as (*Vis. Thame*) *EHR* III 715 (cf. ib.: deffinitiones antiquae et novellae una cum ~is perlegantur); ~ae regulae Ferr. *Kinloss* 63. **b** mendicos..dispartiri jubeo in ~orum coenobia More *Ut.* 74; recentioris instituti monachos, scilicet ~os, induxit Camd. *Br.* 193.

benedictio, praise, glorification (of God).

1334 ut in Opificis ~onem et laudem tota machina mundialis assurgat *CollectOx* I 26; sancte meditaciones, benedixiones [ME: *blessunges*], genuflexiones..lavant venialia peccata *AncrR* 124.

2 benediction, blessing (of person); **b** (in epistolary salutation); **c** (as cure for sickness); **d** (in ceremonial consecration to office, or sim.).

inter ceteras..specialis ~onis glorias etiam maxima fuisse fertur humilitas Bede *HE* III 14; ~o Domini super capud B. Cuthberti descendisse dinoscitur R. Cold. *Cuthb.* 64; ut sic innocentium ei ~o vel extorta..refunderetur Gir. *IK* I 2; ecclesie nostre fundatrix cujus memoria in ~one est *Chr. Dale* 2 (cf. *V. Ed. II* 192); illa †benedicatio "crescite et multiplicamini" [*Gen.* i 22]..fuit data Ade extra Paradisum Ockham *Frat. Min.* 10; patres..~one perpetua recolendi R. Bury *Phil.* 5. 77; s1378 cujus memoria ~one est dormire Wals. *HA* I 372. **b** a1190 Gilebertus..dilectis filiis suis..salutem..cum Dei ~one et sua *Canon. G. Sempr.* 100v; c1236 R...Lincolniensis episcopus..domino H. de P. salutem gratiam et ~onem Gros. *Ep.* 25. **c** accepta ejus ~one convalui Bede *HE* V 6; [arbitratus] sibi ad recuperandam sanitatem utile fore si missa tanti viri ac ~one meruisset potiri Eadmer *V. Anselmi* II 41. **d** s762 Dorobernensium electus antistes ~onem et pallium a papa Paulo suscepit Diceto *Chr.* 124; 1125 in consecrationibus episcoporum vel abbatum ~onibus..nichil..exigatur (*Conc. Westm.* 3) J. Worc. 20; sic electo, sic in monasterio suscepto, sola restabat adhuc, ut sic consummarentur omnia, ~o ab episcopo percipienda *Chr. Battle* 160; c1236 abbates.. secundo in ~one vovent solenniter se observaturos regulam quam profitentur Gros. *Ep.* 72; s1452 movebatur..questio talis, an abbas..post resignationem reelectus debeat iterum benedici, aut sufficiat sibi primaria ~o *Reg. Whet.* I 19.

3 blessing, consecration (of material objects).

vir Deo deditus..fontium lymphas exorcizans et sacrae ~onis ubertate fecundans Aldh. *VirgP* 32 p. 271; quomodo in aqua ~onis pudicitiam et stuprum discrevisti (*Jud. Dei*) *GAS* 426; 1166 pro ~one fossarum apud S. Ædmundum *Pipe* 18; si ecclesiam..pontificali ~one in vita sua cerneret consummatam Ailr. *Ed. Conf.* 771a; 1325 circa ~onem decimarum *Ac. Durh.* 169; 1344 ~ones..et gracias ante prandium sive cenam et post dicendas (*Stat. Cotterstock*) *Eng. Clergy* 288; 1447 cum..vicarii..missam hanc ibidem cum ~one calicis celebrare..usitati fuissent (*Pat*) *MonA* VI 614.

4 gratuity, alms.

747 partem timiamatis..pro ~one et signo purae caritatis tibi direximus Bonif. *Ep.* 74; 'ut..praeparent repromissam ~onem hanc': dona pecuniae Lanfr. *Comment. Paul.* (2 *Cor.* ix 5) 243; pro quo eulogias ~onis, xxx sc. marcos argenti, ..erogavi Ord. Vit. V 14 p. 420; motus abbas ad clamorem pauperis, vocat fratrem qui panibus preerat ut petenti tribuat ~onem Serlo Gram. *Mon. Font.* 50; 1227 supplicans quatenus procurare velitis ad nos meum pinguem ~onem domini regis (*AncC* VI 162) *RL* I 422; 1337 quosdam..ad ~ones beneficiorum ecclesiasticorum.. promovere *FormOx* 89; quandocunque clericus..a populo ~onem receperit Wycl. *Sim.* 16.

benedictionalis, containing (written forms of) benedictions. **b** (sb. m. or n.) benedictional, service-book of benedictions.

c1290 ostendit eis librum ~em et omnia que agenda sunt in professione solempni *Ann. Durh.* 27; 1388 octavus et nonus liber ~es cum coronacione regum et aliis in eisdem contentis (*Invent. Westm.*) *Arch.* LII 234. **b** a1100 viij lectionales et ij ~es (*Invent.*) *Lib. Eli.* II 139; benedictione ..quam ille in ~i suo scribi fecerat Ad. Eyns. *Hug.* V 8; 1245 ~e Willelmi episcopi annuale, in quo continentur ~ones abbatum et consecrationes regum (*Invent. S. Paul*) *Arch.* L 498; ~e episcopale Domerh. *Glast.* 318; 1315 ~e pro pueris confirmandis et vestimentis benedicendis *Invent. Ch. Ch.* 75.

benedictionarius [sc. liber], benedictional.

hic casulam S. Dunstani et ~ium ejusdem..detulit Oxnead *S. Ben. Holme app.* 294; librum exorcismorum et quoscunque ~ios *Cust. Westm.* 49.

benedictorius, conferring a blessing.

ante ~iam manus impositionem egredi non presumant Gir. *GE* I 7.

benedilectus [al. div.], well-beloved.

s1355 se gratum et ~um semper regi adhibuit *Plusc.* I 42; 1438 ~um procuratorem Bekynton I 26.

benedispositus [al. div.], well-disposed.

1439 ~um principem pacifice regnare..decet Bekynton I 205.

beneducere [al. div.], to lead aright.

1346 fac, duc, dic et fer, benefac, beneduc, benedicas (*In Franciam*) *Pol. Poems* I 39.

benefacere [CL; al. div.], **a** to act rightly. **b** to confer a benefit (on).

a 1346 (v. beneducere); nec ideo dicitur liberum arbitrium quia libere potest ~facere et peccare Bradw. *CD* 448e. **b** qui eis pro Dei nomine aliquid ~fecerit (*Quad.*) *GAS* 79; [decanus] pluribus habebat ~facere quam simplex canonicus *Found. Waltham* 16; petit suppliciter ut preposito ~fiat Map *NC* V 5 p. 232; 1303 ut hec..†~ficiant [? l. ~fiant] dare velitis operam *Reg. Cant.* II 658.

2 (p. ppl. n.) benefit.

c795 aeternam sibi per temporalia ~facta promereri gloriam Alcuin *Ep.* 33; nonnumquam fractum collum datur ob benefactum Serlo Wilt. 71. 1; ob benefacta tibi nunquam malefacta rependas D. Bec. 776; nec ultor injurie nec ~facti retributor Map *NC* V 4 p. 211; 1272 in singulis ~factis et oracionibus que decetero fient in ecclesia sua *Fines* 204/11/314 (cf. beneficium 2); 1283 humana benivolencia multo magis ad ~ficiendum allicitur dum ~facta.. non leduntur *Reg. Heref.* 5; 1415 juris ~facto in omnibus semper salvo *Reg. Cant.* III 361.

benefactivus, beneficent (*cf.* εὐποιητικός).

honor est ~ae operationis signum: Aristotiles Skelton I 408.

benefactor, benefactor.

extremi decem [psalmi dicantur] pro familiaribus et ~oribus Lanfr. *Const.* 89; c1188 tradidimus carissimo amico et ~ori nostro H. Cantuariensi archidiacono terras.. *Ch. Sal.* 45; 1292 missa pro omnibus ~oribus domus *MunAcOx* 59; 1296 indulgencias ~oribus ecclesie concessas *Obs. Barnwell* 72; 1451 officium pro defunctis..~oribus *Mon. Francisc.* II 116.

benefactrix, benefactress.

1298 ~ices ecclesie *Reg. Cant.* II 816; 1412 Amabilia.. ~ix nostra *Invent. Ch. Ch.* 161*n*.

beneferre [al. div.], to bring benefits.

1346 Lucifer es, benefer (*In Franciam*) *Pol. Poems* I 39.

beneficentia v. beneficientia. beneficentissimus v. beneficus b. beneficere v. benefacere.

beneficialis, beneficial, conferring benefit.

liberam, benignam et ~em pardonationem *Entries* 599b.

2 concerning a benefice (eccl.); **b** (*sc. causa*) beneficial cause (eccl. law).

de natura titulorum ~ium Paul. Angl. *ASP* II 1528; 1522 in quadam causa ~i *Offic. S. Andr.* 121 (cf. *Praxis* 84). **b** 1549 ad evitandas lites in ~ibus *Conc. Scot.* II 114.

beneficialiter, beneficially, advantageously.

1486 commissarios..determinaturos..divisionem finium et terminorum hujusmodi adeo amicabiliter, benigne et ~er servand[am]..sicut..temporibus retroactis *RScot* 475b; 1552 [perdonatio] allocata et accepta..in omnibus..clausis ..majus ~er et valiabiliter *Entries* 600.

beneficiare, to invest w. a benefice (eccl.).

si quid..audisset sinistri de aliquo quem in ecclesia sua ~iare disponeret Ad. Eyns. *Hug.* V 5; ubi de re prorsus illicita, veluti..super electoribus suis ~iandis, pactio..premittitur Gir. *JS* 7 p. 347; quod provideret sibi sex..idoneos clericos..quos posset ~iare in ecclesia sua Eccleston *Adv. Min.* 114; 1341 pro pauperibus clericis ~iandis *Reg. Brev.* 52.

2 (p. ppl.) beneficed (eccl.). **b** (subst.) beneficed clerk.

1222 inhibemus ne quis clericus ~iatus vel in sacris ordinibus constitutus..ubi judicium sanguinis tractetur.. intersit *Conc. Syn.* 110; c1236 pro..nepote vestro in archidiaconatu predicto ~iato Gros. *Ep.* 36; c1240 scolaribus..universitatis non ~iatis et ~iatis *StatOx* 75; s1297 ejecti sunt omnes Angli de regno Scocie tam religiosi et clerici ~iati quam laici Fordun *GA* 100; persone ~iate a curis beneficiorum suorum pre timore mortis diverterant Birchington *Arch. Cant.* 42; c1400 presbiteri simplices non ~iati (*Concl. Lollard.*) *EHR* XXVI 747. **b** c1250 inhibemus ne ~iati sint vicecomites vel ballivas laicas teneant *Conc. Syn.* 648; s1246 papa..demandavit ut in Anglia omnes ~iati in suis beneficiis residentiam facientes tertiam partem bonorum suorum domino papa..conferrent M. Par. *Maj.* IV 580; s1324 religiosi et ~iati in hac terra de gente Francorum in maxima miseria degere cogebantur, cum eorum..beneficia..confiscabantur Wals. *HA* I 175.

beneficiarius, holder of benefice (eccl.). **b** holder of lay fief.

1299 Johannem..ecclesie nostre ~ium in pensione annua constituere..proponitis *Reg. Cant.* I 372; 1328 volumus.. quod magister..omnes ~ios jurisdiccionis nostre scolas suas exercere compellat (*Lit. Archid. S. Alb.*) *Reg. Whet. app.* II 308. **b** ~ius vulgo dicitur qui possessor est dominatus aut terrae cujus proprietas ad alterum pertinet P. Verg. XIII 224.

beneficiator, benefactor.

1322 [archiepiscopus] beneficiis acceptis ingratus timoris arrogantia ~orem persequitur (*Lit. Ed. II*) Birchington *Arch. Cant.* 26.

beneficientia [CL beneficentia], beneficence, bounty. **b** benefit, advantage.

c750 ut..hoc..munere a tua solita beneficentia ditarer (*Lit. Regis Cantiae*) *Ep. Bonif.* 105; in elemosinis et ~ie modis (*Leg. Hen.*) *GAS* 590; opera misericordie et ~ie Ockham *Dial.* 538. **b** Dominus noster justus judex tria ab eis subtraxit per que..plus nobis afficere potuerunt: primo autem ~iam portuum..principalium Elmh. *Hen. V* 74.

beneficiosus, beneficent.

c795 quominus ad me usque ~a munificentia pervolasset [caritas] Alcuin *Ep.* 79.

beneficium [CL], benefit: **a** boon, free gift; **b** advantage, profit; **c** benefit of clergy (right of trial in ecclesiastical court); **d** (w. abl.) by means (of), thanks to.

a caelestis ~ii munificentia Aldh. *PR* 142 p. 202; multi sunt qui ampliora a te ~ia quam ego et majores accipiunt dignitates Bede *HE* II 13; de ~iis et judiciis divinis *Ib.* IV 22; reor indignum beneficia tanta latere / aetatem Wulf. *Swith. prol.* 351; 9.. ~ium, i. donum, *freme, gife* WW; 1067 Willelmus Dei ~io rex Anglorum (*Ch. Peterb.*) *MonA* I 383; est autem assisa illa [sc. magna] regale quoddam ~ium clementia principis..populis indultum Glanv. II 7 (cf. 4 infra). **b** ~ium, *freomo GlC* B 68; hoc manerium dedit rex W. monachis pro ~io suo *DB* I 273 (*cf. VCH Derb* I 298); 1246 renunciantes ~io restitutionis in integrum super preteritis detencionibus *Reg. Paisley* 25; 1287 quod..aque benedicte ~ia solis scolaribus assignentur *Conc. Syn.* 1027; 1340 ejectis a domo..omne ~ium domus..denegetur *Deeds Balliol* 293; arbitror..illos in legis humane ~iis minorandos quos..postponit ecclesia in ~iis suis Fortescue *LLA* 41 (*pun on* 3). **c** 1363 dicunt quod ipsi clerici sunt et petunt quod ~ium clericale eis allocetur *Proc. J. P.* 284 (cf. ib. 264, *Entries* 55b); ut fures et parricidae convicti, qui ~io trium literarum, hoc est, quod legere sciant, servantur, stigmatiae fierent P. Verg. XXVI 612 (= *Id. Camd.* 130*n.*). **d** paulatim aliorum ~io ad subtiliora consurgunt J. Sal. *Pol.* 437a; multiplicate majestatis ~io magni fieri possumus Gir. *TH intr.* p. 5.

2 (spiritual) benefit conferred by religious house.

a1112 fratres Thornensis cenobii me..concesserunt collegam fieri et in cunctis ~iis suis simul secum eque perpetuo participari, unde..pro tanti ~ii adeptione ecclesiam de G. ..largitus sum *MonA* II 601; 1176 pro hac..donatione concesserunt mihi..monachi commune ~ium domus sue *BM Ch.* I 61; 1208 receperunt eum in singulis ~iis et oracionibus que fiunt in ecclesia sua *FormA* 220; 1259 abbas et conventus ipsum dominum R. et A. uxorem suam et liberos suos in ~iis spiritualibus que fiunt in ecclesia de Oseneya in perpetuum admiserunt participes *Cart. Osney* IV 297; 1336 ut animam..Johannis, qui..ab hac..luce..transivit, ..in communibus ~iis vestris recipiatis *Lit. Cant.* II 118.

3 benefice, salaried office or position (eccl.). **b** (dist. as involving cure of souls or 'simple', *i.e.* without cure). **c** yearly payment associated w. such office.

idem Robertus habet xlii domus hospitatas in Oxeneford' ..et pro j manerio tenet cum ~io S. Petri *DB* I 158 (cf. *VCH Ox* I 413); s1108 episcopi statuerunt..ut..presbyteri qui..preeligerent cum mulieribus habitare..omni ecclesiastico ~io privati extra chorum ponerentur Eadmer *HN* IV 231; 1182 abbas..ad vacans ~ium..archiepiscopo personam vel vicarium presentabit (*Ch. Hen. II*) Elmh. *Cant.* 451; 1200 dabit..Roberto..dim. m. ad se vestiendum quousque assignaverit ipsi R. in certo ecclesiastico ~io c s. redditus *CurR RC* II 174; 1222 clericos per subtractionem ~ii et officii volumus coherceri *Conc. Syn.* II 117; c1239 precipimus ut omnes rectores ecclesiarum et vicarii residenciam faciant in suis ~iis *Ib.* 273; s1265 legatus J. episcopum Wynton' ab officio et ~io suspendit *Leg. Ant. Lond.* 84; c1280 ecclesie parochiales seu ~ia prebendalia (*DipDoc.* E 1576) *DocExch.* 358; s1305 papa..~ia pinguia in Anglia ei [sc. nepoti suo] dedit Graystanes 27; 1342 omnes domus rectorie sunt pro statu ~ii competentes (*Vis. Arch. Totnes*) *EHR* XXVI 111; 1358 ~ium ecclesiasticum non potest licite sine institutione canonica obtineri *Reg. Glasg.* I 621; 1372 quorum [beneficiorum] quatuor sunt dignitates, viz. decanatus, cantoria, cancellaria et thezauraria, quintum vero, viz. archidiaconatus, officium est; ..et ista quinque ~ia tanquam incompassibilia cum aliis iis nuncupantur *Reg. Brechin.* 19; s1377 [J. Wiclif] juste privatus exstiterat per archiepiscopum Cant' quodam ~io..in universitate Oxon' situato *Chr. Angl.* 115; ut nos..possessiones ipsas modo sacerdotia modo ~ia vocemus P. Verg. XIV 257; 1585 pro primitiis spiritualium suorum ~iorum *DocCOx* 134. **b** 1242 quod..fratres [de Bello Loco]..decimas..infra parochiam de Abertarf..habeant..nomine simplicis ~ii in puram et perpetuam eleemosynam..sicut aliquod simplex ~ium in diocesi nostra (*Cart. Beauly*) *Trans. RHS* IV 36; c1260 nomine simplicis ~ii in ecclesia de H. *Melrose* I 327; a1300 de aliquo ~io ecclesiastico competenti cum cura vel sine cura *Chr. Peterb.* 47; c1357 si homicide..concederet [papa] facultatem plura ~ia curata retinendi Ric. Armagh. *Def. Cur.* II 1404; 1403 ~ium curatum et non curatum (*Pat*) *Foed.* VIII 293. **c** a1200 concessimus..ecclesie..de Gipeswic' et canonicis ibidem Deo servientibus..~ium vj marcarum argenti per annum in ecclesia de Gretingheham, salva nobis..presentacione et electione clerici qui..instituetur, qui securitatem prestabit quod jamdictum ~ium ..persolvet *AncD* A 3347; 1220 E. fuit inde persona.. reddendo..per annum eidem abbati dim. m. nomine ~ii *BNB* II 255 (cf. ib.: reddendo annuatim nomine pensionis dim. m.); 1222 dedimus..ecclesie..Malmesbyri et monachis ibidem Deo servientibus omnes decimas in parochia ecclesie de C. nomine perpetui ~ii possidendas *Ch. Sal.* 119; W. .. admissus est in ea [ecclesia] canonice persona institutus salvis lx s. annuis priori et canonicis [de Huntingdon] de eadem ecclesia nomine perpetui ~ii per manum dicti W. et successorum suorum percipiendis *Reg. Linc.* II 112.

4 royal grant of land etc., fief (not normal usage in England).

†858 (12c) ego Æðelbald..rex..concedo..ipsam terram.. episcopo..Wentanae aecclesiae; ..et nullus jam licentiam ulterius habeat..terram predictam alicui dandi..neque.. rogandi in ~ium *CS* 495; c1030 (1309) concedo..medietatem insule que dicitur Gener' [*Guernsey*]..et ex altera medietate quam..fidelis noster nomine Nigellus in ~io tenet omnia quecunque ex ipso ~io meis usibus proveniunt (*Ch. Duc. Norm.*) *PQW* 829a; a1087 (1247) in cujus regis W. carta continebantur hujusmodi libertates, viz. quod..abbas et monachi Fiscann' habeant terram de Staninges [*Steyning, Suss*]..cum omnibus..liberis consuetudinibus, quia hoc totum regale ~ium est *ChartR* 39 m. 6; precepit rex ut.. civitas Cantuaria, quam Lanfrancus..in ~io a rege tenebat, ..in alodium ecclesie Christi Cant'..transiret Eadmer *HN* 43.

beneficus [CL], beneficial, beneficent. **b** (superl. *beneficentissimus*).

9.. ~us, benefactor, *fremful* WW; utinam sentiant in se alumni tui quod sit..sibi..salubris et ~a quam ad te habent..devotio Eadmer *V. Osw.* 34; est et principi proprium ~um esse, quatinus cunctis beneficia prestet, nec tantum bonis et bene meritis Gir. *PI* I 19. **b** 1452 te in mortalibus mihi ~entissimum Bekynton I 273.

benefidus [al. div.], constant.

a1100 O benefida tuis adsis protectio servis! *Trop. Wint.* 4.

benemereri [CL; al. div.], **a** (pr. or p. ppl.) meritorious. **b** (p. ppl. as sb. n.) meritorious act, act of kindness.

a 1452 ~entibus honores virtutum premia largiuntur *EpAcOx* 308; 1426 [archidiaconatus] persone ~ite conferatur *Reg. Cant.* I 235; 1438 tantus tamque ~itus pater Bekynton I 28; regius secretarius ~itissimus André *Hen. VII* 56. **b** 1558 pro aliis ~itis et auxiliis nobis per..Johannem.. multipliciter factis *Scot. Grey Friars* II 110 (*cf.* ib. 44).

beneolens [< olere], camomile (bot.).

10.. ~entem, *magaðe* vel *camemelon* WW.

beneplacentia, good pleasure.

s1401 electione canonica et..regis ~ia est sublimatus Amund. I *app.* 417.

beneplacere [al. div.], **a** (pr. or p. ppl.) well-pleasing. **b** (p. ppl. n.) pleasure, good will.

a 1147 ut..~entem Deo religionem studeamus..propagare *EChScot* 180; O voluntas [Dei] bona, ~ens ac perfecta Ad. Scot. *Serm.* 115; 1174 ~itum ei [sc. creatori] servitium exhibere (*Lit. Papae*) Diceto *YH* I 390; s1367 relaturus domino pape non ~ita J. Reading *Chr.* 194b; c1430 jam vos Dominus ad portum deduxerat vestre ~ite voluntatis *Reg. Whet.* II *app.* 437. **b** Deus vitam vestram in ~ito suo conservet Lanfr. *Ep.* 32. 532a; a1159 ~ito Dei et assensu domini mei..concedo (*Ch.*) *EHR* XXXII 248; potentis est..pro ~ito suo punire..subjectos J. Sal. *Pol.* 514a; in voluntate justitiarum domini regis erit et in ~ito breviorem terminum dare Glanv. I 27; 1203 quamdiu ipsa erit ad ~itum et voluntatem nostram *Pat* 36b; 1308 vobis.. administracionem..commisimus usque ad nostre ~itum voluntatis *Lit. Cant.* III 385; 1334 ~itum vestrum super hiis significare velitis *Ib.* II 68; nisi voluerint de ~ito *Cust. Cant.* 184; ex ~ito regis Capgr. *Hen.* 165.

beneria v. benertha.

†beneroda [cf. *bena*], boon-ploughing of a rood of land, or (?) for *benerda* (*cf. benertha*).

c1252 quelibet virgata que non est ad censum arabit unam ~am ad hybernagium et aliam ad tramesiam *Cart. Rams.* I 366.

benertha [ME *bene-erthe*], boon ploughing (*cf. bedertha, benripa*).

c1182 semel in anno facient benhirdam et tunc debent arare jij quarterios *RBWorc* 408; c1230 in yeme..debet.. arare; †beneriam et herciare totam aruram †benerie cum cibo domini *Doc. Bec* 29; 1326 (v. bestia 2a).

beneta. ~um v. benta. benetus v. venetus.

benevalentia, good health.

c**1380** de mei status ~ia..gravis infirmitas..me vexavit *FormOx* 315.

benevenire [al. div.], to be welcome. **b** to welcome.

gratus mihi est multum adventus tuus et bene venisti Bede *HE* IV 9; **1182** centies milies bene veneris sicut.. socius imperii (*Lit. I. Angeli*) Diceto *YH* II 53; Anglice dixit "*wellecome to wike!*"..quod sonat in patria illa "bene veneris ad balliviam tuam!" *Latin Stories* 125; ~iat clericus meus, bonus et liberabilis abbas! *Ib.* 40. **b** s**1213** in terra nostra †benevenemini [? l. beneveniemini] in pace *Eul. Hist.* III 106; **1398** euntibus Londoniam..ad ~iendum archiepiscopum *Ac. Chamb. Cant.* 137.

benevole [CL], willingly.

c**1420** nec veniet, ..licet summonitus fuerit, nisi quando benivole venire potest *BB Winchester* f. 21 p. 50.

benevolens, benevolent.

a**1400** ad capescendam ejus benivolenciorem dominacionem *Meaux* III 222*n*.

benevolentia [CL], benevolence: **a** good will; **b** kind act; **c** (title); **d** imposition deemed to be a free gift.

a [patris] †benivoliam [v.l. benivolenciam] allicere volens G. Mon. II 11; est..omnium captanda benivolentia, que fons amicitie..est J. Sal. *Pol.* 484A; **1198** [de] xiij li. ..pro habendis terris suis cum ~ia regis *Pipe* 21; **1327** tunc saltem..tantam summam nobis mutuetis quod vestram possimus benivolenciam erga nos..experiri *RScot* I 219a. **b** **1483** bursa data fuit..Doctori Langton..propter suas multiplices ~ias erga civitatem *Lit. Cant.* III xxvii. **c** gratias ago ~iae tuae Bede *HE* II 12. **d** s**1473** nova et inaudita imposicio muneris ut per ~iam quilibet daret id quod vellet, imo verius quod nollet *Croyl. Cont.* C 558; **1475** collectoribus ~ie domino regi concesse (*Exch. Teller's Roll*) J. H. Ramsay: *Lancaster and York* II 402.

benevolus [CL], benevolent, favourable. **b** (subst.) well-wisher. **c** (w. *aurum*) a sort of gold-leaf (*cf. Building in Eng.* 166).

745 (12c) si quis benivola intentione praeditus hoc donativum ampliare voluerit *CS* 170; anima ~a talia non exquirit, 'in malevolam vero animam sapientia non introibit' [*Wisdom* i 4] Gir. *TH* I 13; s**1087** Normanniam Roberto..non tamen benivolo corde vel sereno vultu delegavit M. Par. *Min.* I 34; ventus ~us Elmh. *Hen. V* 104. **b** **798** benivolus Romanae consuetudinis Alcuin *Ep.* 145; **1265** ut de ipsis tanquam de ~is nostris..confidere possimus *Cl* 103; inquirentes..quis suus sit benivolus et specialis amicus Milemete *Nob.* 77. **c** **1366** empcio colorum..in iiij^c auri ~i empt'..pro predictis operibus, prec' centene vj s. *KRAc* 493/22 f. 5v.

bengi [Ar. *banj*], henbane (*Hyoscyamus*).

~i, i..jusquiamius albus *SB* 12.

benhirda v. benertha.

benigne [CL; cf. benigniter], kindly.

ab eo ~e susceptus Bede *HE* IV 1; ipsum..pie satis et e~ suscepit Gir. *EH* I 1; **1300** correcciones..~e exaudiant *Ord. Ely* 8.

benignitas, benignity, kindness. **b** (title).

~as omnipotentis Dei Egb. *Pont.* 1; [Jesus] praelargiens ..manifestam suam humanam ~atem Eriug. *Per.* 594D; **9..** ~as, *fremsumnes* WW; numquam tanta ~atis opus est exhibitione quanta in nova..ad probos mores conversione Anselm (*Ep.* 67) III 187; regis nostri larga ~as (*Quad.*) *GAS* 292; quos nature ~as elimaverit Gir. *TH* III 35. **b** †**615** ut vestra [sc. regis] ~as..monachorum habitationem statuat (*Lit. Papae*) W. Malm. *GP* I 30; si inveni gratiam in oculis sancte ~atis vestre [sc. episcopi] Ad. Marsh *Ep.* 32; c**1340** placeat regie vestre ~ati *Couch. Furness* II 698.

benigniter [cf. benigne], kindly.

10.. ~er, *medomlice* WW; **1443** pro modo innate benignitatis vestre ~er audire Bekynton I 232.

benignivolus, benevolent.

cumque benignivolo persolveret omnia corde Frith. 475; presul Adeluuoldus, corde benignivolus Wulf. *Swith. prol.* 70.

benignus [CL], kind, mild.

tum virgo Christum pulsabat corde benignum Aldh. *VirgV* 2038; pauperibus..semper humilis, ~us et largus fuit Bede *HE* III 6; ~ior et salubrior aura Gir. *TH* I 3; **1298** beningna pietate *Reg. Cant.* II 1318; optimi et ~issimi nominis..comes Elmh. *Hen. V* 31.

benium v. bedum. benivol- v. benevol-. benleuca v. banleuca. benn- v. venn-.

benripa [ME *benerip*], boon-reaping (*cf. bederipa, benhirda*).

12.. dabit..iij ~as *Reg. Pri. Worc.* 33b (cf. ib. 83b: ad messionem que vocatur *benrip*'); **1299** debet iij benrippas *RBWorc.* 44.

benta, ~um [ME *benet, bent*], bent-grass.

1220 cooperatorium de †bentta..ad domas suas *Dryburgh* 74 (cf. ib. 75: beneta); **1326** j mora pro turbis et beneto *BBSt.Davids* 170; **1372** pro ~is falcatis *CourtR. Meltham*; **1635** unam carucatam ~ee, Anglice *a load of heath Chanc. Forest Proc.* 49 r. 2.

beodum v. bedum.

1 bera [ME *bere*], bier.

1268 corpus..ubi jacuit super ~am combusserunt *Rec. Norw.* I 205.

2 bera [ME *bere*], bear barley.

1271 messerunt..xxvij acras ~e, ix acras ordei *Pipe Wint.* (159299) r. 11*d.*; **1296** in..iij quart' vij bus' ~e emptis *DLMinAc* 1/1, r. 7.

3 bera, ~ea, ~um [ME *ber*], beer (ale brewed with hops).

1397 vij barellis ~e *EEC* 439; **1413** cum..uno obolo de barello cervisie et beere *TreatyR* 96 m. 25; **1438** birra (*Lydd MSS.*) *HMC Rep.* V 518b; **1454** pro sex barilibus birre *Exch Scot* V 613; **1460** in solucione..duarum lastarum birri, octo parilium birri Hamburgh *Ib.* VII 60; **1554** pro 16 *ly tunne* duplicis birie *Ac. Burs. Coll. Wint.*; **1581** vendidit beream et serviciam suam post ratum de iiij d. *le gallon LTREnr. Estr.* 1/13; [hippelaphus] bibit..alam seu ~am avidissime Caius *Anim.* 11.

4 bera, [cf. MLLM], clearing (Touraine).

a**1180** dedimus..minagium..et nemus..cum fundo et ~a *Act. Hen. II* II 122.

berallus v. beryllus. berbagium v. berbiagium. berbatus v. barbare 1a.

berbeles (pl.) [ME *barbul* < barbula], pustules.

valet ad ~es que sunt pustule parve Gad. 49. 2; stercus murium..aufert..pustulas grossas que sunt ~es *Ib.*

berben- v. verben-.

berberis [Ar. *ambarbārīs*], barberry (bot.).

~is, scariola, portulaca Gilb. IV 197 v. 2; ~is, i. semen petrosilini Macedonis *SB* 12; ~ies sunt fructus cujusdam arboris A. *berberies Alph.* 22; †oriacantum [l. oxiacanthum] ..~is idem *Ib.* 131; oxiacantha..ab officinis et vulgo ~is dicitur Turner *Herb.* B iv.

berbex [CL vervex; *cf.* OF *brebiz*], wether.

790 (v. Bacchus b); **9..** ~ex, *rom* WW; habet..v animalia et cxxv ~ices *Dom. Exon.* 460; †**11..** (**1348**) pastura ad centum ~ices in Cutona [*Cowton, Yorks*] *ChartR* 135 m. 13; hec (*sic*) ~ex, A. *weder* WW.

berbiagium [OF *brebiage*], a rent paid in sheep (or commuted): **a** (Norm.); **b** (Devon and Cornw; *cf. Arch. J.* V 273–7).

a **1180** pro recognicione de ~io *RScacNorm.* I 17 (cf. ib. 10: pro berbagio difforciato). **b** **1284** valet ~ium in festo Invencionis S. Crucis annuatim x s. *IPM* 34/7/4; **1298** in decima ~ii iij s. vij d. *MinAc* 811/1 m. 1; **1301** de quodam certo redditu qui vocatur †berbragium tam liberorum quam custumariorum *Pipe* 146 r. 30 (2) *d.*; **1308** de ~io ad *la Hockeday* v oves matrices et v hogg' preter decimam *Mon. Exon.* 428; **1309** unusquisque dictorum tenencium dabit de ~io quartam partem j ovis et j agni ad terminum de Hokkeday vel dabit iij d. ob. quad. *IPM* 16/9 m. 5; **1337** ~ia levantur de aliquibus nativis racione personarum et non racione tenementorum *Capt. Seis. Cornub.* r 22*d.*

berbica, ewe.

14.. ~a, A *ewe* WW; *a yowe*, barbica *CathA*.

berbicariolus, bird, wren or (?) wagtail (Fr. *bergeronette*).

7.. birbicariolus, *werna GlC* B 136; **9..** de avibus, ..birbicariolus, *irpling*; **10..** berbigarulus vel tanticus, *yrðling* WW.

berbicarius [cf. 2 bercarius], shepherd.

1284 debent..esse brebicarii et haywordi *Reg. Wint.* II 672.

berbicio, sheep maggot.

intuetur sinum ejus [oves tondentis] et collum berbitionum examine scatere..; ac vermes edacissimos tollere cupiens talia..audivit Ad. Eyns. *Hug.* IV 12 p. 58.

berbicius, wether.

a**1350** pro quibuslibet v ~iis metet j rodam avene (*Cust. S. Edm.*) *Cust. Rents* 70.

berbragium v. berbiagium. berbrutus v. berebretus. berca v. brecca a.

1 bercare [ME *barken*], to tan.

1335 pro ij coriis..barkandis *Sacr. Ely* II 70; **1478** pro cij pellibus vitulinis barcatis *KRCustAc* 114/9 r. 2*d.*; **1486** officium..supervisoris omnium et singulorum coriorum tannatorum vel ~atorum aut tannandorum sive ~andorum ..ad scrutandum..infra domos, mansiones et tannarias sive bercarias omnium et singulorum alutariorum et tannariorum sive cordewannariorum et bercariorum hujus regni *Pat* 564 m. 16 (9).

2 bercare, (?) to fold sheep.

1426 cum libertate barcandi et pastura animalium *Melrose* II 547.

3 bercare v. 2 bercaria 3.

1 bercaria, tannery.

1486 (v. 1 bercare).

2 bercaria, ~ium [OF *bergerie*], (?) sheep-walk.

c**1090** donavit..in Spalding unam bercheriam et pascua pecorum *MonA* III 217; **1222** in marisco sunt iiij ~ie, quarum una vocatur Howich et potest sustinere novies xx capita promiscui sexus *Dom. S. Paul* 39; bercheriam nostram ducentarum ovium, sc. medietatem de Osmundeseye in terra et marisco (*Ch. Pri. Cant.*) *Gavelkind* 182; **1276** attraxit de via regia ad †berciam [? l. bercariam] suam de Eton' *Hund.* I 104.

2 sheep-fold, sheep-pen (*cf. Yorks. Arch. J.* XXXIX 447–50).

1144 medietatem decime..berchiariarum et porchariarum *E. Ch. Scot.* 162; **1160** dedimus eis iij acras terre..ad bercharium suam, claudendas sepi et fossato *E. Ch. Yorks* I 386; c**1190** dedi..de bosco meo summere ad sepes suas faciendas et faldas et bercharias super terram meam edificandas *Ib.* III 1652; **1182** concedo eis..barcariam suam in brueria facere *Ch. Gilb.* p. 82; **1191** in bergeria *Pipe* 33; **1209** pastura..ad cccc oves de berkeria sua *Couch. Kirkstall* p. 213; c**1240** capitulum habet berqueriam, videlicet quod quilibet residentium suorum habens sex..bidentes tenetur ibidem bidentium unam consignare *Cart. I Norm.* 397; c**1253** ad voluntatem domini est habendi ~ias vel..ammovendi illas et retinendi terras et pasturas in dominico *IMisc.* 8/23; c**1280** ducet fima de barcario *Crawley* 233; sunt.. quedam ad nocumentum levata de quibus non dabitur assisa, veluti de..furno, †baccaria, vaccaria *Fleta* 215; **1319** de..una †bericheria in pastura (*Pat*) *MonA* VI 557.

3 sheepcote, lambing shed.

1230 ad ~iam quandam sive domos alias in acris illis construendas *Cl* 324; berkeria lapide cooperta Domerh. *Glast.* 535; **1307** bercheria stramine cooperta *IPM* 127/33; **1366** unum cotagium quondam ~ia domini *Cart. Eynsham* II 136; **1372** in j sclattatore conducto ad lattandum et sclattandum de novo totam predictam ~iam *MinAc* 1156/13 m. 2; **1384** ~iam prioris..fregit et vij oves matrices cum vij agnis.. ibidem felonice furatus fuit *Proc. J. P.* 389; barcare, *schepecote PP*; barcaria, A. *schepehouse* WW.

1 bercarius, tanner.

1486 (v. 1 bercare).

2 bercarius [OF *bergier*; cf. berbicarius], shepherd. **b** pastor (eccl.).

ibi..vj servi et x berquarii *DB* I 26; a**1128** ibi sunt iiij bovarii..et j bercharius qui tenet bordellum *Chr. Peterb. app.* 162; c**1148** grangiarius.., major ~ius, custodes.. ovium monialium per priorem omnium in singulis domibus ponentur (*Inst. Sempr. 8*) *MonA* VI 946* xxi; c**1230** ~ius salvo custodire debet oves domini de latrone et omni periculo preter quam de subito morbo et per numerum et talliam eas recipere et eodem modo respondere *Doc. Bec* 49; **1271** in stipendio unius ~ii custodientis bidentes in falda *MinAc* 1128/1; **1274** quidam burgarius venit cum quadam grege ovium *Hund.* I 141; **1276** in..j domo ad ~ium facienda in qua juxta faldam jacebit *Ac. Stratton* 73; **1290** in expensis.. berkariorum conducencium oves et agnos emptos apud Montem Gomeri usque Ledebury *Ac. Swinfield* 176; **1375** quendam Adam quondam ~ium Johannis..extra servicium Johannis..pro salario excessivo, videlicet ij s. per annum.. plus quam cepit de Johanne, ..procuravit *Sess. P. Lincs.* 195; **1504** de acquietanciis redditus..j ~ii multonum, ..j barcarii ovium matricium *Crawley* 494. **b** **1408** presbiter et laicus non sunt bercarius unum / nec scelus in simili condicione gravat Gower *VC* III 1761.

bercator, (?) shepherd.

1275 inprisonavit Willelmum L. ~orem Willelmi de F. .. injuste *Hund.* I 438; c**1283** ~or..habebit lx garbas pro custodia bladi et vigilia *Cust. Battle* 82; ~or de villa alias oves matrices custodiet usque ad agnilationem *Cust. Bleadon* 207; **1316** *Cat.AncD* V A 10447.

bercel- v. bersel-. bercenarius v. bertonarius. bercher- v. bercar-.

bercia [OF *berz*], cradle.

1268 Alicia..etate dimidii anni sola jacendo in domo patris sui in ~ia sua *JustIt* 1051 (*Yorks*) r. 30; **1309** puer in ~ia jugulatus fuit per quendam porcum *S. Jers.* XVIII 160.

1 berciare [OF *bercier*], to rock in a cradle.

1212 Willelmus Baillebien tenet iij virgatas terre quas pater Johannis regis ei dedit in elemosinam quia ~iavit illum *Fees* 91.

2 berciare v. bersare.

1 †berda, a scold.

a scalde, ~a [v.l. mulier barda] *CathA*.

2 berda, a measure of cloth.

1307 in portagio..j bard' can[abi] *KRAc* 368/30 m. 6; **1325** pro v bard' canabi val. lxx li. *EEC* 384; **1340** de quolibet fardello, barda seu trussello panni canevacii et panni linei funibus ligatis *IMisc* 140/5.

berdare [ME *berden*; cf. barbare], to set (a fence) with thorns.

1374 in stipendio unius hominis emendantis defectus haiarum ejusdem parci et illas ~antis in locis quibus necesse fuerit *DLMinAc* 507/8227 m. 10.

2 to 'bard', clip (cloth).

1441 ~avit et barbavit cxij pokas lane *Pat* 450 m. 11; de quibusdam lanis..barbatis sive bardatis *Ib.*; **1460** summam ..saccorum lane bordate, forsate et claccate aut non bordate (*TreatyR* 143) *Foed.* XI 466; **1503** lanas illas claccare, ~are et mundare *Pat* 592 m. 5.

berea v. 3 bera.

berebarellus, beer-barrel.

1417 frettaverunt in diversis scafis lanam..et frumentum ..in diversis barellis vocatis ~is (*KRMem*) *Bronnen* 953.

berebretus [AS *bere-brytta*], granger, official in charge of granaries.

~o, id est horreario, pertinet habere crodinum ad ostium horrei in Augusto (*Quad. Rect.*) *GAS* 451; **1209** de Willelmo berebretto pro warranto *Pipe Wint.* p. 80; **1260** quicumque fuerit berebrutus erit quietus de ij s. de reddítu tantummodo et debet habere j acram frumenti *Cust. Glast.* 216; **1275** erunt prepositi vel berebructi si precipiuntur *Hund.* (*Wilts*) II 263; **1297** in stipendio unius †berebruccarii existentis ultra trituratores hoc anno per xij septimanas *Ac. Cornw* I 62; **1340** erit prepositus, messor, wodewardus et berbrutus si electus fuerit *Rent. & Surv.* 700 m. 1; **1401** in defectu forestarii, haiwardi et †berebeutt' *Pipe Wint.* (159405) r. 24*d*.

berefella, ~um [ME *bere-fel*], (?) bearskin collar; cf. *berefellarius*.

1290 ad reformacionem status..septem clericorum de Barefell' ejusdem ecclesie *Mem. Beverley* I 190; clericorum de Barfellis *Ib.* 191; **1306** vicarios et clericos de berfella *Ib.* 170; **1313** uni de septem clericis de ~o *Ib.* 304; **1422** capellanus habens personatum, officium seu beneficium unius clerici de berfell' in ecclesia collegiata B. Johannis Beverlaci *Pat* 407 m. 18.

berefellarius, a class of clerk, or (later) minor canon, (?) originally wearing bearskin collar (*cf. berefella*).

1305 clerici ~ii deservient in officiis suis sicut tenentur *Mem. Beverley* I 50 (cf. ib. lxvii); **1315** de juramento.. berfellariorum super continua residencia facienda *Ib.* 336; **1391** presentacio..personarum dudum vocatarum ~ii quos quidem ~ios..dominus J. de Thoresby dudum Ebor' archiepiscopus..ordinabat personis in ecclesia nostra.. Ebor' †officiando [? l. officiantibus]..in habitu conformari; sed, quia eorum turpe nomen ~iorum patens risui remanebat, dictos septem de cetero non ~ios sed personas volumus nuncupari (*Stat. Archiep.*) *MonA* VI 1309.

berefredum, ~a [OF *berfroi*], movable siege-tower. **b** (?) watch-tower.

ingentem machinam quam berfredum vocitant contra munitionem erexit et copiose bellicis apparatibus instruxit Ord. Vit. VIII 16 p. 362 (cf. ib. XII 36); machinam firmissimis compactam compagibus gradibus ad ascendendum dispositis, vulgo dictam ~um, ..coriis opertam et funibus et solidissimis ligneis tabulatis *Itin. Ric.* III 7; **1224** quod petrarias et mangonellos nostros et bereferrem.. disjungi facias *Cl* 617a; **1271** in cariagio maeremii..usque Kenill[ewurth'] in obsidione ejusdem castri ad quoddam berefridum inde faciendum *Liberate* 47 m. 4; **1300** unum berfrarium et alia ingenia..ad insultum faciendum castro de Karlaverok *Ac. Wardr.* p. 140. **b** magnum mesuagium ubi aula Ade de K...sita fuit cum berefrido ligneo vij^{xx} pedum in altitudine Brakelond 163v.

2 bell-tower, belfry; **b** the Belfry (a gaol at Berwick).

1234 habere faciat..xl quercus..ad quoddam ~um faciendum ad magnas campanas ecclesie Ebor' pendendas *Cl* 403; **1253** pro clavis ferri ad ecclesiam et berefridum *Ac. Build. Hen. III* 270; **1259** tegulam..que nunc est in berfrario ejusdem loci [*Westminster*] *Cl* 377; **s1272** prior [Norwici]..constituit homines suos..in belfreido campanarum *Flor. Hist.* III 25 (cf. ib.: in ostio belefreidi); **s1274** ascendentes super berefridam ubi campane dependebant *Leg. Ant. Lond.* 145; **1284** nullus regratarius emat..aliquod ..quod ad burgum differatur vendendum ante pulsationem campane in berefrido *Stat. Gild. Berwic.* 32; **1371** in campana pro *le clok* in berefrido pendenda *Fabr. York* 10. **b** **1331** allocantur eidem pro berfreta in manu communitatis vj li. *ExchScot* 361.

berellus v. beryllus. berem- v. berm-.

Berengarius, nickname of bear.

lupus defunctus est..~ius, sc. ursus, missam celebravit. O. Cheriton *Fab.* 43.

berennium v. brennum.

berewardus [ME], bearward.

1472 cum viij d. datis duobus ~is ducis Clarencie (*Ac. Coll. Wint.*) *Med. Stage* II 247.

berewica, ~um [AS *bere-wic*], 'berewick', outlying portion of manor.

a1082 manerium quod Feringes nominatur cum omnibus territoriis et beruwicis et appendiciis suis (*Dom. Westm.*) *Regesta* p. 123; de isto manerio dedit episcopus unam berewicham Herberto *DB* I 9b; huic manerio pertinuerunt ii bereuuicae *Ib.* 38b; ad hunc manerium adjacent hae bereuuitae *Ib.* 272; **1093** capellas quae sunt in ~is quae adjacent praedictis quatuor maneriis *MonA* VIII 1271 (cf. *VCH Derb* I 312); **c1107** ecclesiam..cum decimis et terris et redditibus et berwicis ad eam pertinentibus (*Ch. Battle*) *Regesta* p. 316; **11..** due grangie, una ad curiam, altera ad berwicam *Dom. S. Paul.* 136; **c1170** terram de Helingeye.. cum Snores ~o suo, quod foris insulam habetur *Chr. Rams.* 53; **c1174** nullus alius debet habere curiam vel †beriam in illa villa *Cart. Rams.* III 289 (cf. ib. I 245); **c1187** exceptis bervicis que †perpendebant illi manerio *MonA* VI 1027b (= *Act. Hen. II* II 293: †birvitis que appendebant).

berezisum v. bersisa. berf- v. berefredum.

berga [ME *bergh*], barrow, mound.

c1200 terram illam que vocatur crofta trium ~arum *Cart. Osney* II 195; **c1250** dimidiam acram..in berghis incipientem ad viam turbe *Cart. Sallay* 350.

bergemannus v. bargemannus. bergeria v. 2 bercaria.

bergueta [cf. Sp. *vergueta* = *rod*], 'verge', sort of candle.

1312 pro iij cereis et iiij ~is et aliis candelis cere factis pro luminari capelle castri Burdegale *RGasc.* IV *app.* p. 551.

beria v. berewica. bericheria v. 2 bercaria 2.

†berile [misr. of Ar. *narqā* < νάρκη], torpedo fish.

piscis qui vocatur †tarcon [l. narcon]; et dicitur piscis iste merguri; et secundum Avicennam..ca[pitul]o de stupore vocatur ~e Gad. 64 v. 2.

berillinus, berillus v. beryll-. berillum v. barellus.

berisia [cf. 3 bera; (?) *assimilated to* cervisia], beer or (?) wort (*cf. bersisa*).

1480 pro cervisia, pane et ~ia *Ac. Chamb. Cant.* 134 (cf. ib. 136: pro dimidio *le bunne* duplicis ~ie).

berivagium v. beveragium. berk- v. berc-. berlagius v. birelagius.

bermagister [German *bergmeister*], 'barmaster', manager of mine (*cf. VCH Derb* II 326).

1390 constituimus ipsum Willelmum [del Hokes] senescallum et bermaystrum nostrum de omnibus mineris nostris plumbi infra comitatum predictum [de Flynt] et ad curias nostras vocatas *bermotes* de mineris plumbi predictis tenendas *Recog. R. Chester* 62 r. 8 (2).

bermannagium, porterage.

1290 pro ~io, portagio, stillagio et aliis diversis expensis factis pro vinis..et alio..stauro ponendo in navi *Chanc. Misc.* 4/5 f. 9; **1300** in wyndagio, brimmagio, ~io vinorum et doliorum cum flore *Ac. Wardr.* p. 113; **1367** pro bermennagio, carcagio, shutagio, batillagio..celeragio, couperagio et aliis diversis custibus factis..circa vina predicta *KRAc* 396/2 f. 41.

bermannus [ME *berman*], porter.

1224 in barmannis locandis ad ccx dolia vini de prisa nostra ponenda in celariis nostris *Cl* 5b; **1287** una cum stipendiis ~orum adjuvancium eosdem [papillionarios] ad papillones..inportandas *Pipe* 136 r. 26; **c1300** de beremannis pro qualibet peisia salis portanda usque forum civitatis, iij d. *Chain Bk. Dublin* 235.

2 class of tenant charged with carrying service.

1285 ~i: M. de Aqua Kenet j curtilagium..; et debet cariare corredum domini archiepiscopi de mercato..ad curiam *Cust. Malling* (cf. *Cust. Suss* II 113–14).

bermayster v. bermagister. bermennagium v. bermannagium.

bermotum, 'barmoot', miners' court (*cf. bermagister*).

a1307 recepta den' de ~o: et de viij s. receptis de placitis et perquisitis beremoti in minera hoc anno *KRAc* (*Devon*) 260/19 m. 2 (cf. ib. 825/16 m. 7 [**1243**]: de bermannemot', viij d.).

1 †berna [? *for* verna], (?) bird (magpie or woodpecker).

~a, *higrae GlC* B 77; **9..** ~a, *higre* WW.

2 berna v. verna.

bernaca, barnacle goose.

aves..que ~e vocantur..aucis..palustribus similes Gir. *TH* I 15; bernekke non nascuntur nisi ex lignis salo obnoxiis Neckam *NR* 100; **1208** bernaces..aves sunt que..de uno ligno infinite procreantur in mari occidentali et per rostra dependent a ligno donec majores facte separantur a ligno et natare incipiunt P. Cornw. *Disp.* 150 n. 3; ad confinium abbacie de Faverethsam in littore maris arbuscule nascuntur ad quantitatem salicum; ex istis nodi pullulant..cumque.. excreverint formantur in aviculas, que post dies nature datos rostro dependent et vivificate.. in mare decidunt; ..quadragesimali tempore assate comeduntur considerata potius..nativa processione quam carnis sapiditate; avem vulgus †barnetam [v.l. barneclam] nominat Gerv. Tilb. III 133; **12..** avem que berneca dicitur particulatim dicerpserunt (*Ch. Haliwarfolc*) *Feod. Durh.* 203 *n.*; habet [Hibernia] aves quas bernaces vocant..quas de lignis abietinis quasi contra naturam natura producit Higd. I 32.

1 bernacula, ~us, barnacle goose.

prior anser a nostris hodie branta et bernicla vocatur... nidum berniclae..nemo vidit, nec mirum quum..berniclae ..spontaneam habeant generationem W. Turner *Av.* 7–8; [anserem brendinum] ornithopolae Londinenses bernaclum vocant, cum dicendum putem berndclacum.., quod antiqui Britanni anseres marinos..omnes *clakes* dicebant Caius *Anim.* 18; a nostris ~ae appellantur Stanihurst *Hib.* 231.

2 bernacula, ~us v. vernaculus. 1 bernagium v. baronagium.

2 bernagium [OF *brenage*], feudal payment for feeding dogs (Norm.).

a1100 clamo terram S. Marie de Surceio quietam de ~io *Regesta* 137; **a1160** alodium..quietum ab omni gravaria et ~io *Act. Hen. II* I 271; **1180** de ciiij^{xx} et iiij minis avene de ~io de Costentino *RScacNorm* I 39 (cf. ib. II 531).

bernardensus, labourer, (?) barrow-man (*cf. baiardarius*).

1221 duobus ~is pro nova dova perforanda *Ac. Build. Hen. III* 52; ~is pro remocione lapidum istorum a mari usque ad terram *Ib.* 54.

Bernardinus, of the order of St. Bernard.

1526 quotiens, quaeso, decebit claustralem ~um monachum cum mulierculis conversari? (*Lit. Ep. Linc*) *EHR* III 720 (cf. ib. 722: ex ~is monastice viventibus).

bernarius [OF *brenier*], 'berner', kennel-man.

c1136 ~ius [debet habere] iij d. in die *Domus Reg.* 135; **1176** in liberatione..unius ~ii et xviij canum *Pipe* 152; liberatio..falconariorum sive ~iorum ad ejus [constabularii] officium spectat *Dial. Scac.* I 5F; **1213** cum duobus venatoribus et xxviij canibus et ij berneriis *Cl* 134b; **1284** Gilberto ~io exeunti extra curiam cum canibus suis *KRAc* 351/11 m. 4; **1295** ~iis cerverettorum *Prests* 195; **1312** cum duobus ~iis haericiis et quatuor veutrariis haericiis et duobus ~iis daemericiis et duobus veutrariis daemericiis *Cl* 130 m. 31; **1340** venatori domini regis pro vadiis suis ad xij d., unius veutrarii ad ij d., unius ~ii ad j d. ob. et unius *caceken* ad j d. (*Ac. Wardr.*) *TRBk* 203 p. 186; **1399** ~ius canum nostrorum pro damis *Pat* 352 m. 12.

bernator, 'berner'.

1271 si contingat quod canes..in warenna predicta intrant, venatores seu ~ores..pro canibus cum cornu astracabunt et haulohabunt *AncD* A 306.

bernicla v. bernacula. berq- v. berc-. berruca v. verruca. berrus v. verres.

bersa, (?) area in forest reserved for shooting game. **b** (?) shooting.

1205 pasturam xl vaccarum..per totam ~am nostram in foresta nostra de Chipeham *RChart* 152b; **1209** interrogandi sunt qui visi fuerunt in foresta cum arcubus et sagittis in ~a *SelPlForest* 2 (cf. ib. 134); **1216** de boscis ubi dominicas chaceas et ~as nostras et defensam nostram habere consuevimus *Cl* 290a; **1255** serjantiam ad custodiend' ~am domini regis in forestam in partibus illis *Fees* 1290. **b** **1251** cepit unam damam cum leporariis suis et unum brokettum dami cum ~a in eadem foresta *SelPlForest* 98.

bersare [OF *berser*], to shoot (esp. game).

1200 ibi quendam canem ~avit *CurR RC* II 181; **1203** dampnum facientes in foresta..~ando et vastando *CurR* II 180; **1209** ~averunt unum cervum unde habuit mortem, ..et sagitta inventa fuit in dicto cervo unde fuit ~atus *SelPlForest* 65; **1209** malefactores..Matheum..fratrem forestarii ~averunt, ita quod..inde obiit *Ib.* 28; **1216** senescallus [remisit] petitionem de ~are in foresta mea ad tres arcus *Cart. Chester* 106; **1237** solitus fuit..berciare bestias.. et furari sicut malefactor *BNB* III 229; **1243** tractaverunt sagittis ad servientes comitisse ita quod equitur equi ~ati fuerunt *CurR* 126 r. 3; **1334** ~averunt unam bissam et illam occiderunt *DLForest Proc.* 3/16.

bersaria, shooting (of game), poaching.

1207 G. J. debet xx m. pro berseria *Pipe* 62; **1207** de R. de P. xxx m. pro berseria *Pat* 70b; **1211** R. de P. reddit compotum de viij m. ..pro ~ia *Pipe* 256.

bersator, shooter, poacher.

1207 debet dim. m. pro rescussione ~orum *Pipe* 185; **1209** recepit..canes et ~ores..qui venerunt ad currendum in Turrewode *SelPlForest* 10; **1330** si latro..vel ~or captus est in foresta per illum.., omnia catalla ejus illius sint *PQW* 637b.

berselettarius, man in charge of bercelets.

1310 duobus veutrariis, duobus berneriis et uno bercellettario cum xv leporariis, xxiiij heirett' et j bercelletto de canibus nostris *Cl* 128 m. 22; **1314** [cum uno] †percenettario *CalCl* 65.

berselettus [OF *berserez*], 'bercelet', hunting dog, lyam hound (*cf. King's Serjeants* 280).

1213 in expensis..xv valtrorum, ..xxxij bersereciorum *Misae* 231; **1213** cum..xxij canibus berserettis *Cl* 151a; **1229** mittit A. ..cum canibus suis berserettis ad currendum ad damum *Cl* 206; **1247** non intrabunt..forestam ad bersandum nisi cum ix arcubus et sex ~is *JustIt* 454 r. 12*d.*; **1253** dum fuit justiciarius de foresta cucurrit cum mota sua et leporariis suis et bercelettis *SelPlForest* 109; **c1271** custos ~orum domini regis percipit per diem iij d. pro corpore suo et pro iij ~is *Chanc. Misc.* 3/46/14; **1275** per servicium custodiendi unum canem †berteletum [l. bercelettum] *Hund.* I 159; **1293** clamabat habere..quinque arcus et unum ~um et wenlatores..ad fugandum in eadem chacia *JustIt* 807 r. 1*d.*; **1494** interfecit unum juvenculum..cum barselettis (*DLForestProc* 3/16) *Pickering* I 146.

bersella [? cf. bersa], (?) enclosure.

1352 [*near the*] bercellas [*of the Crutched Friars*] *CalLB Lond* F 248.

bersellus, hunting dog, (?) bercelet.

1309 per servicium custodiendi unum bercellum nostrum cum nos bercellum illum ibidem..mittere voluerimus *Cl* 127 m. 26.

bersisa, barley malt, wort (*cf. berisia*).

genus liquoris quod nostri ~am vocant in potum sumebat J. Ford *Wulf.* 3; **1261** inventus fuit submersus in quadam tina plena bersis'..precium tine et ~e iiij d. *JustIt* 82 r. 24; **1277** perpendentes doleum illud esse plenum berzillis et farina siliginis *SelCKB* I 34; **1282** berezisum ad cervisiam *KRAc* 4/3; hec barzisa, A. *wortte* WW.

bersorium, (?) shooting butt.

1280 metam in quodam ~io fixam tractarunt *IMisc* 38/23.

bertachia v. bretescha. bertelettus v. bercelettus.

bertha [? cf. AS *beorhþ = shelter*], city ward or ward-moot (*cf.* W. Somner *Antiquities of Canterbury* 52).

c1200 pro hac donatione. .facta et recordata in burgimoto civitatis Cant' pariter et in ~a de Burgate et etiam in curia prioris et conventus S. Gregorii *Cart. S. Greg. Cant.* 47 (cf. ib. 51); **a1223** recordata. .in burgimoto civitatis Cant' et in hundredo ~e de Northgate et de Westgate *Ib.* no. 74; **c1250** in burghimoto civitatis Cant' et in ~a de Newegate dedit michi. .xxv m. *Reg. S. Aug.* 588.

bertona, ~um [ME *berton*], barton, demesne farm or courtyard.

1209 in porta ad ~am, xij d. *Pipe Wint.* 21 (cf. ib. 66); **1217** viam que jacet. .inter ~am. .abbatis et conventus et curiam abbacie *Pat* 78; **1219** prior Bathonie tenet bartonam Bathonie. .et valet xx li. *Fees* 261; **1221** faciat habere G. comiti Glouc' plenam saisinam de ~a et de bosco de Furches extra Bristoll' *Cl* 448a; **1240** fieri faciatis apud Keninton' quandam novam grangiam cum quadam nova ~a subtus curiam nostram ibidem et ~am ipsam claudi faciatis muro versus prefatam curiam *Liberate* 14 m. 10; **c1250** ingressum et egressum a berthona mea *Reg. S. Aug.* 394; **1269** grangias, boverias et berkerias ~e nostre ibidem [*Marlborough*] *Liberate* 45 m. 2; **1281** in feno partim in ~am cariando *Ac. Stratton* 120; in hieme quando claudit circa berthonam vel ortum *Cust. Bleadon* 202; **13..** dedi . .totum ~um de porta orientali. .usque ad bruarium, sicut ~um plenarie continuit *AncD* A 7921; **1358** de bertouna *Reg. Rough* 129; **1388** bartona ibidem integra cum prato et campo gardinis et aliis pertinenciis valet per annum x li. *IMisc* 240/28; **1411** de pastura circa bartonam bercarie *Crawley* 305.

bertonarius, bartoner, steward or farmer of a barton.

1211 in quietanciis j ~ii, v s. *Pipe Wint.* 120; **1238** quia J. de B. monachus S. Swithuni, qui fuit custos bertone ejusdem domus juxta Winton', Romam adiit, . .ad nos pertinet. .alium ~ium. .ibidem substituere *Cl* 107; **1277–1428** berthonarius *DCCant Bartoner's Ac. Rolls* (passim); **1291** in stipendio ~ii qui fuit ultra messores (*Pipe Wint.*) *Econ. Hist. Rev., ser.* 2, XII 378; **1358** totum manerium. . cum. .bertona, terris et tenementis que ~ii modo tenent (*Pat*) *Mon. Exon.* 264; **1376** quod provideatur de officiis †bercenarii et garwentarii quod fraus antiqua mensurarum tollatur in eisdem *Conc.* III 111; **s1452** custos maneriorum et ~ius Stone *Chr.* 45b.

†bertrare [? cf. perjactare], (?) to plaster.

1376 in parietibus †bertrand' et doband' *MinAc* 900/12.

berugabulum v. brugabulum.

berula [LL], 'biller', (?) watercress (*Nasturtium*), water parsley (*Sium*), or brooklime (*Veronica beccabunga*); *cf. bibulta.*

extrahatur succus ~e Gilb. IV 194. 1; ~a, fabaria, idem levick *SB* 13; ~a similis est nasturcio aquatico sed acutiora habet folia; valet ad scrofulas maturandas; A. †*bilus* [v.l. *biller*] *Alph.* 21 (cf. ib. 69); *bellerne, water herbe*, burula *PP.*

berulus v. beryllus. beruuica, bervica, berwica, v. berewica.

beryllinus. of a beryl.

lux fulgens berillīna J. Howd. *Viola* 69; ut. .laminas chrystallinas ~asque. .in pulveres subtilissimos conteramus Dee *Monas* 22 p. 206.

beryllisticus, a (sb. m.) crystal-gazer. **b** (sb. f.) art of crystal-gazing.

a ~us hic in lamina crystallina omnia que sub caelo lunae . .versantur exactissime videre potest Dee *Monas pref.* p. 186. **b** ~a est ars in ejusmodi specillis visiones observandi *LC* 227.

beryllus [βήρυλλος], beryl: **a** gem; **b** burning-glass or eye-glass; **c** gazing crystal; **d** crystal reliquary; **e** gem (fig.), saint.

a berulus, gemmae genus *GlC* B 82; birillus, ut aqua splendet *Ib.* 97; tuque, berille, locum clarificas decimum G. Amiens *Hast.* 772; est oleo similis prestans virtute beryllus Neckam *DS* VI 185; **1404** plures lapides beralli et cristalli *Ac. Durh.* 394; liber. .qui habet exterius imaginem . .argenteam cum lapidibus crystallinis et ~is per circuitum positis Elmh. *Cant.* 99; hic berellus, A. *a berelleston* WW. **b** ignem celestem in subposita traicit per berillum J. Sal. *Pol.* 542D; ~us vitio oculorum medetur Neckam *NR* II 90; perquirere debet ignem de ~o exposito soli *Ord. Ebor.* II 275; **1305** pro ij barellis de cristallo deauratis. .domino pape. . presentatis *RGasc* III cc; **1419** lapis de birillo artificialiter in coreo nigro suspensus *Reg. Cant.* III 55. **c** berillus est speculum ex crystallo superstitiose consecratum ab auguristis *LC* 227. **d 1383** diversas reliquias. .in quodam berillo ad modum crucis facto inclusas *Ac. Durh* 440; **s1385** sanctas reliquias. .includi fecit in quodam feretro argenteo et deaurato cum nitidis birellis in utroque latere *Chr. Pont. Ebor.* C 426; **p1500** in magna berilla. .reliquie S. Thome apostoli (*MSS. DCCant*) *HMC Rep.* 9 *app.* I 126a. **e** protinus ammisso micuit sintagma berillo [v.l. benigno] Frith. 1159.

berzilla v. bersisa.

bes [CL; cf. bisse], two-thirds of an *as.*

bes sive bisse: viii unciae Bede *TR* 4 p. 184; qui exactionem et totius calumpniosi questus sibi ad minus bessem vendicant; nam aut solidum assem usurpant sibi aut. . trientem dumtaxat. .officialibus. .cedunt J. Sal. *Pol.* 580c; plus besses et centesimas usuras quam bonum et equum attendens W. Cant. *Thom.* II 8.

besac- v. bisac-. besagium, besandum v. bisaccium. besandis v. bezonis. besant- v. byzantus.

besasa [βησασᾶ], **a** wild rue (*Peganum harmala*). **b** autumn crocus (*Colchicum*).

a erimola. ., †bissona vel †bussaria, piganium, ruta agrestis idem *Alph.* 58; ruta, bissara, herba viola idem *Ib.* 157 (cf. ib. 26: brissaca, viola idem). **b** †bisala, hermodactilus idem *Ib.* 23.

besatium v. bisaccium.

besca [OF *besche*], spade.

c **1160** una ~a et ij secures *Dom. S. Paul* 132; **1172** pro ferris mm ~arum, c s. *Pipe* 122; **1212** civerias et beschas suas et trublas asportaverunt *CurR* VI 310; **1212** de centum fossatoribus cum ligonibus, beschiis et hoiis *Cl* 131; **1228** venire faciat ad regem. .de singulis duabus hidis comitatus sui unum hominem cum una trubla vel una bescha *Cl* 82; **1235** in j ~a ad fodiendum, ij d. *Pipe Wint.* (159284) r. 4; in j ~a ad fimum spargendum, iiij d. ob. *Ib.* r. 5d.; **1238** cum. .ipse foderet turbam. .contigit quendam [puerum]. .corruisse super beschiam quam idem R. tenebat in manu sua *Cl* 133; **1265** operarios cum bachiis, pikosiis et aliis utensilibus suis *Cl* 150; **1274** in. .novis bechiis ad eandem [vineam] (*Rental*) *Arch. Cant.* XLVI 144; **1286** becheam manualem *CalIMisc* I 2286.

2 right of cutting turves with a spade. **b** area of turbary cut with one spade in one season. **c** (?) turbary.

c1193 concessisse. .quatuor ~as fodientes in est maresco meo de Bullingbroc ad salinas suas sustinendas. *Danelaw* 381; **1211** in ~a ad †waterlecham [l. waterletham] de consuetudine *Pipe Wint.* 169; **a1216** dedisse. .sex beschas ad fodiendum glebas in marisco de B. . .[reddendo] pro qualibet bescha iij s. per annum *Ch. Gilb.* 53; **1282** licebit. . ibidem blestare. .usque ad medietatem totidem hominum et ~arum *Fine* (*Yorks*) 267/61/4. **b a1265** quod possint cariare. .xxx plaustratas turbarum de marisco meo de Toyntone quoque anno de duabus ~is quas habent de dono Philippi (*Ch.*) *Terr. Fleet, app.* 184; **1296** de xij s. de ij partibus j bechie in marisco venditis *DLMinAc* 1/1 r. 8; ut possit cariare terciam partem turbarum unius beschie ad salinam (*DLMinAc* 1/1) *Terr. Fleet, app.* 176; **13..** ~a est quod per unam vangam potest foderi a festo apostolorum Philippi et Jacobi [*1 May*] usque ad festum S. Petri ad Vincula [*1 Aug.*] (*DLMinAc* 242/3885) *Ib.* 184 (cf. ib. p. xiv). **c c1230** concedimus. .Adelildesholm cum †bechio et maresio sicut ipse Acelinus illud cinxit cum fossato suo *Cart. Rams.* I 79.

bescata, area of turbary (= *besca* 2b). **b** spit, spade's depth.

1193 duas †boscatas [l. bescatas] terre in insula de Aganas (*Ch. Tavistock*) *MonA* II 498 (cf. *EHR* LXII 374); **1208** duas acras Flandrenses in novo marisco de Iclesham et unam ~am terre inclusam (*Ch. Bayham*) *MonA* VI 914. **b c1230** reparabit xxxij pedes [fossati] in longitudine et unam bechatam in profunditate (*Cust. Hungerford*) *Doc. Bec* 67; **c1250** in fossato operato cum profunditate unius ~e et longitudine duarum perticarum *Cart. Rams.* I 461; **1285** fossabit xvj pedes in longitudine, iiij pedes in latitudine et ij beschatas de profundo pro j opere *Cust. Tangmere* (cf. *Cust. Suss.* II 12).

beschilla, little spade.

1171 pro mm picoisiis et m ~is, xv li. *Pipe* 84.

Beseleheliticus, of Bezaliel (*Exodus* xxxi).

arcam / Bēselehēlitīcā subtiliter arte politam Wulf. *Swith.* II 43.

besenta v. byzantus.

besilamentum [OF *besilement*], mutilation, defacement.

1397 rasuris sive ~is rotulorum (*Pat*) *Foed.* VIII 27.

besillare [OF *besiler*], to mutilate, deface (? or falsify).

1276 clericus. .vicecomitis Bark'. .besellavit breve domini regis *Hund.* I 13; **1294** communiter ~averunt brevia domini regis per falsas procuraciones *JustIt* 1095 r. 1.

bestia [CL], beast, animal. **b** (fig.).

bestia [sc. draco] delituit qui desaevire solebat Aldh. *VirgV* 554; ubi prius vel ~iae commorari vel homines bestialiter vivere consueverant Bede *HE* III 23 (cf. *Isaiah* xxxv 7); sicut ~iarum est nihil velle cum ratione Anselm (*Orig. Pecc.* 10) II 152; in hominem seu ~iam seviendo Gir. *TH* I 36; **c1250** anime. .exponende. .devorationi ~iarum agri Ad. Marsh *Ep.* 98 (cf. *Exodus* xxxiii 11 etc.); **1295** una cupa argentea. .cum opere levato de leunculis et aliis ~iis *Vis. S. Paul* 311; serpentes et scorpiones et alios latentes ~ias *Alph.* 177. **b** contra horrendam superbiae ~iam Aldh. *VirgP* 11; characterem ~ie. .in fronte [cf. *Rev.* xvi 2] W. Fitzst. *Thom.* 127; R. Bury *Phil.* 4. 61 (v. bipedalis); qui intellectum jubet principari, videtur jubere principari Deum et leges; qui autem hominem jubet, apponit et ~iam Burley *Comment. Pol.* 277.

2 farm animal: **a** (for ploughing); **b** (in pasture); **c** (for food).

a tunc xviii carucae hominum, modo vii; et hec perdicio fuit per mortem ~iarum *DB* II 1b; **1220** ~ias aratorias (*AncC* I 163) *RL* I 96; **1293** dicit se nullam ~iam propriam habere unde possit arare *SelPlMan* I 111; **1325** cum ~iis caruce (*CourtR*) *EHR* XLV 212; **1326** custumarii qui non habent ~ias carucatarias ad faciendum *le benerthe*. .facient alia opera *IPM* 97/1. **b 1251** clausus est parcus ille, ita quod ~ie damasce non possunt intrare *IMisc* 5/14; **c1280** habebit ~ias suas in herbagio domini (*Cust.*) *Crawley* 233; **1327** est. .in eisdem boscis quoddam escapium forinsecarum ~iarum *IPM* 3/7 r. 5; **13..** *hornegeld*. .de quadam consuetudine exacta. .de omni ~ia cornuta (*Explic. Vocum Veterum*) *Boldon Bk app.* lv; **1400** pasturabant xx ~ias stauri in parco *AncD* D 300. **c** ~ie ruminantis sc. ovis Gilb. VII 301 v. 2; **1328** in empcione. .martorum. .et. .pro expensis faciendis circa dictas ~ias *ExchScot* 118; **c1380** quod nullus carnifex. .grossas ~ias in Oxonia mactet *FormOx* I 254 (cf. *MGL* I 713).

3 beast of chase.

non debet venator formidolosus esse, quia varie ~ie morantur in silvis Ælf. *Coll.* 93; ibi. .parcus silvaticarum ~iarum *DB* I 8; parcus ~iis *Ib.* II 145; **1217** pro feonatione ~iarum nostrarum (*Ch. Forest.*) *StRealm* 20; **1229** boscum. . claudere bassa haya. .ita quod ~ie nostre possint libere. . intrare et exire *Cl* 181; **1232** ad capiendum in ea [foresta] xl ~ias, tam damos quam cervos *Cl* 57; **1251** ~ie silvestres *IMisc.* 5/14; **1288** currerunt. .ad quendam damum, qui non est ~ia de warenna (*CoramR* 128) *SelPlForest* cxxviii; **1292** tenet in defenso in eadem [chacia] cervos. .et cheverellos, cujusmodi ~ie ad warennam non pertinent *PQW* 787a; **1293** †gressas [l. grossas, *as* 208a etc.] ~ias cervos et bissas, damos et damas, et hujusmodi tenet in defenso *Ib.* 203b; **c1300** duas ~ias grossas vel duos capriolos *Form. Man.* 4; **1324** transgressiones factas in warenna de volucribus et aliis ~iis warenne *CBaron* 139; **1338** videtur. .consilio domini regis quod caprioli sunt ~ie de warenna et non de foresta, eo quod fugant alias feras de foresta (*CoramR* 315) *SelPlForest* xi.

4 skin, fur.

1403 septem millia. .~ias furure tam in mantellis quam in ~iis minime consutis, . .quatuor mantella de squyrell' continencia mille ~ias. . *Cl* 251 m. 8.

bestialis, a of a beast. **b** beastly, bestial.

a aut ~i more aut humano corpus comedere Lanfr. *Corp. & Sang.* 434B; quod. ., ~i exemplo admonitum, . .genus humanum sequitur Adel. *QN* 39; que sub ~i forma humana verba proferret Gir. *TH* II 19. **b** Deus fecit Adam. .ut. . non illa [propagandi potestate] uteretur ~i et irrationali voluptate sed humana et rationali voluntate Anselm (*Orig. Pecc* .10) II 152; "non cessatis. .eos verberare? et cum adulti sunt quales sunt?" "hebetes," inquit, "et ~es" Eadmer *V. Anselm.* I 22; quid eo ~ius, qui. .de media nocte surgit ut. .pugnet ad bestias J. Sal. *Pol.* 389D; homo sine literis. . in ~em dilabitur stoliditatem M. Par. *Min.* 1. 4; delectationibus ~ibus Bacon *CSPhil.* 411; **s1459** (v. belualis).

bestialitas, animal nature, bestiality.

pecus interfici jubetur non propter culpam, a qua ~as excusat Gir. *TH* II 24; dicitur. .'homo' ab humo et sonat in ~atem terrestrem Wycl. *Ente* 211; **1370** vocat eos porcos propter eorum immunditiam et ~atem (J. Bridl. *gl.*) *Pol. Poems* I 205.

bestialiter, like a beast, bestially.

ubi. .homines ~er vivere consueverant Bede *HE* III 23; gens ex bestiis solum et ~er vivens Gir. *TH* III 10; **1401** ~er desevire Bekynton I 153.

bestiarius, beast-like, savage.

felle, . .barbaricus, bestius, ~ius *CathA.*

2 (sb. m.) hunter of beasts.

~ius, venator bestiarum *GlC* B 84.

3 (sb. n.) cattle, animals (collect.). **b** dairy.

1289 licenciam. .pascendi. .in landis nostris ~ium seu animalia *RGasc* II 439 (cf. ib. 446). **b** *a derye*, androchiarium *CathA.*

4 (sb. n. or m.) book of beasts, bestiary.

c1396 ~ium, de naturis bestiarum *Meaux* III xcii; **c1432** cum. .libro. .cum moralisationibus volucrum et bestiarum vocato ~io Heete *Catal. Coll. Wint.* 68; **14..** in uno volumine ubi est etiam ~ius (*Cart. Reading*) *EHR* III 121.

bestiola [CL], small animal. **b** small horse.

canibus. .prepete cursu ~am insectantibus *G. Steph.* II 91; tantus erat numerus ~arum [sc. murium] W. Malm. *GR* III 290; hec ~a [sc. mustela] plus cordis habens quam corporis Gir. *TH* I 27; **s1191** (v. aurifrigium); oculis ejusdem ~e que ex instinctu sue nature cunniculos per domos. . subterraneas venatur S. Sim. *Itin.* 54. **b** *nagge or lytyl beeste*, bestula, equillus *PP.*

bestiuncula, tiny animal (louse).

c1180 inveniunt cilicium sic ~is obsitum ut. .quivis judicaret hostes majores minoribus minus nocuisse Grim *Thom.* 87.

bestius, beast-like, savage. **b** (sb. m., *sc. morbus*) murrain.

felle, . .barbaricus, ~ius, bestiarius *CathA.* **b** *muran' of bestis*, ~ius *Ib.*

bestula v. bestiola.

1 beta [CL], beet or orache.

10.. ~a, *bete* WW; nec tibi desunt olera si suppetit tibi facultas ~e. .et malve Neckam *NR* II 166; ~a. .est ortulana secundum Dyas [coridem] Bart. Angl. XVII 22; ~a major vel bleta. ., atriplex agrestis vel domestica idem, G. *arache blanc Alph.* 22.

2 beta [βῆτα], Greek letter.

alphabetum Grecum. .alpha, vita, gemma Bacon *Maj.* I 75.

3 beta, (?) second-grade bread (= *tortre*; *cf.* DuC).

14.. hec ~a est secundus panis WW.

4 †beta [? cf. βάτραχος], frog.

Grecia consuevit bēta[m] rana[m] vocitare / sicut in Isidoro scriptum reperitur Ibero GARL. *Syn.* 1582C.

5 beta [cf. betulus], birch.

∼a, *berc*, arbor dicitur *GlC* B 66; **9..** ∼a, *birce* WW.

6 beta [ME *bete*], 'beat', bundle (of flax).

c1250 dant linum ad molendinum, scilicet ad quamlibet garbam unam ∼am, per sic quod molendinarius linum conservet sine damno *Cart. Rams.* I 489; **1279** dabit j †becham [l. betham] lini de quolibet remell' *Hund.* (*Hunts*) II 657.

betaceus [CL = *of beet*], beet.

14.. betacius, A. *bete* WW.

betagium, betagh-tenure (Ir.).

1310 tenuit in ∼io in tenemento de Tassagard terciam partem xxvij acrarum terre per servicia inde debita *Mem. R. Ireland 3 Ed. II* (MS.) r. 7; **1365** tenet de domino in ∼io j messuagium ij acras terre, reddendo domino per annum xvj d. *Pipe Cloyne* 34.

betagius [Ir. *biatach*], betagh, serf (*cf.* G. J. Hand *English Law in Ireland*, 195, 216).

1212 xj cumbas ad relevandos pauperes betacos de Rathwer *Pipe Ir.* 32; **a1242** habebit..vicarius xij m. assignatas in decimis betasiorum meorum de Leuure *DL Deed* (D.L. 27) 296; **1252** non permittat quod aliquis subtrahat Olivero de Asprevill' betaldos suos Hybernienses vel alios de terra sua *Cl* 116; **1253** ∼ii ibidem tenentes de anno in annum j carrucatam terre pro iiij m. per annum *IPM* 15/1; **1260** de vaccis hominum meorum betaxorum domini comitis (*Ch. Regis Curcrie, Penshurst MSS.*) *HMC Rep.* 77. p. 31; **1261** si aliqui laici ascripti glebe, qui ∼ii vulgariter appellantur, aliqua de bonis suis ecclesiis..legant (*Lit. Papae*) *Doc. Ir.* 174 (cf. ib. 177); **1283** cum betachiis et omnibus aliis ad villatas illas spectantibus *Pat* 102 m. 11; **1288** opera dictorum ∼iorum nulla, eo quod onerantur de redditu *IPM* 52/5; **1290** supplicat..quod, cum..dominus rex ipsum feoffasset de quadam terra in montanis partibus Hibernie, eidem velit concedere quosdam petagios, qui in eadem terra manere solent, rehabere, et qui ob nimiam guerram in eisdem partibus habitam inde fugerunt *RParl. Exch.* 4 m. 2; **1331** quod una et eadem lex fiat tam Hibernicis quam Anglicis, excepta servitute ∼iorum penes dominos suos eodem modo quo usitatum est in Anglia de villanis *Stat. Ir.* I 324; **1334** sunt ibidem v villate terre quas diversi ∼ii tenent ad voluntatem domini *AncExt.* 52 m. 9; **c1350** terras..cum dominiis, ..serviciis, redditibus tam liberorum tenencium quam nativorum et ∼iorum (*Ch. Ards*) *MonA* VI 1123; **13..** quiquidem burgenses sunt ∼ii, quare non possunt ire ex villa nisi facere pasturam super terras dominicas domini *Pipe Cloyne* 18; predicti bitagii debent cariare bladum domini *Ib.* 8; **1404** maneria..episcopi..et ∼ii ejusdem a supportacione..onerum illicitorum..sint liberi *Ib.* 58.

beteicium v. buticium.

betella [cf. 6 beta; 3 batellus], 'beat', bundle (of flax).

1265 et de iij s. viij d. de cc ∼is lini venditis; ..item..de cc ∼is lini hoc anno preter decimam (*Pipe Wint.*) *Som. Arch. Soc.* CIV 94.

betemayum [ME], 'bitmay', (?) portion of river-bank often surrounded by water.

1375 iiij d. annui redditus quos ballivi domini regis solebant participere de quodam ∼o *Leet Norw.* 55; cf. ib. pp. 65 (*le bytemay*), 103.

beth, Hebrew letter.

in hoc principio *be resiz* sex littere sunt tantum apud Hebreos..videlicet *bez, rehs, alef, sin, joz, thave*; conjunge tertiam et primam..videlicet *aleph* et *beth* NECKAM *NR* I 1; alphabetum Hebreum.., aleph, beth, gimel BACON *Maj.* I 74.

Bethania, †Bethphania, commemoration of the miracle of Cana (6 Jan.).

BELETH *RDO* 73. 79 (v. apparitio 3d); Christus baptizatus est VI idus Jan. die Dominica et eadem die anno revoluto in Chana Galilee convertit aquam in vinum; ..que vocatur Epiphania tribus de causis: ..tercia facta est vel dicta Bethphania a *beth*, quod est domus, quasi apparitio facta in domo per conversionem aque in vinum *Eul. Hist.* I 74.

Bethleemita, Bethlehemite friar.

s1257 concessa est mansio fratribus ∼is in Cantebrugia.., quorum habitus similis est habitui Predicatorum; signatur autem capa eorum in pectore quadam stella rubra, v radiis crinita, in cujus medio quedam rotunditas est aerei coloris, propter stellam que apparuit in Bethleem nato Domino M. PAR. *Maj.* V 631.

†betica, weekly servant, hebdomadary.

9.. ∼a, *wicþegn* WW.

betonica v. vettonica. bettella v. 2 batellus 1b.

betuletum [cf. buletum], birch-holt.

betulentum, *byrchholt* ÆLF. *Gl.*; **10..** betuleum, *byrcholt* WW.

betulus [CL betulla < Gall.], birch; cf. 5 *beta*, *bulus*.

bitulus, *berc GlC* B 111; ∼us, *byrc* ÆLF. *Gl.*

betunus v. boto. beum v. bedum.

beus, blessed.

pia castra beorum / ingreditur felix ÆTHELWULF *Abb.* 18. 38.

beutificatio, beautification.

1582 unacum adornacione sive ∼one domus curie apud Hertford' *DL Ac. Var.* 10/5 f. 15.

bevarium v. 1 bruaria b.

bever, ∼erius [ME *bever*], beaver, beaver fur.

in..arctois regionibus, ubi abundant ∼eres, caudis hujusmodi..viri etiam..religiosi jejuniorum tempore pro pisce vescuntur GIR. *IK* II 3; fiber, idem castorque, biver GARL. *Syn.* 1583A; **1303** timbrum..∼eriorum seu hereminorum.. [debet] iiij d. (*Inq. Berwic.*) *DocScot* II 460; **1444** pro ij pellibus de ∼ero ad usum regis, v s. iij d. *ExchScot* 149.

beveragium [OF *bevrage*; cf. biber], **a** drink, beverage. **b** drink-money (to seal a bargain).

a 1206 habeat j navem cum cc modiis vini cum ∼io marinellorum quietam..ab omni consuetudine *Pat* 68a; **1421** nullus mercator extraneus..poterat..vendere in eadem villa [de Cadomo] ad detallium vel alias aleca seu bevragia quecumque (*RNorm* 15) *Foed.* X 48. **b 1199** emptor terre..dabit j d. burgensibus ad *beverage* (*Ch. Whitby*) *ChartR* 14b; **1277** Ricardo le Taylur pro preparacione carentiville ad boves iij s. et in suo ∼io iij d. *Rec. Leic.* I 178; **1281** burgensis..pro dolio removendo de uno sellario ad alterum dat ij d. ob., videlicet j d. ville et j d. ob. pro berivagio; et pro j dolio ad potum suum dabit denarium pro berivagio *Stat. Gild. Berw.* 42; **1291** super quam empcionem solvit ei j quad. in argento Dei et j potellum cervisie ad ∼ium precii j d. (*St. Ives*) *Law Merch.* I 52; **1367** pro diversis *nonschenches* et ∼iis *Arch. Bridgwater* 161; **1391** dati aurifabro..pro ∼io *Ac. H. Derby* 110.

beverinus, of beaver.

1138 prohibemus..sanctimoniales..marterinis, hereminis, ∼is pellibus..uti (*Conc. Lond.* 14) GERV. CANT. I 108; penula..∼a NECKAM *Ut.* 100; **1444** pro..x pellibus ∼is ad usus regis *ExchScot* 152.

bez v. beth. bezantius v. byzantus.

bezonis [? cf. Pers. *panj-nūsh*], sort of electuary.

digeratur materia..cum dyantos commune vel bezonis GILB. VI 237 v. 1; **1328** idem computat in..j lib. de drageto ..xlj lib. confeccionum de besandis et cedris *ExchScot* 119 (cf. ib. 235: xlj lib. de besaundes et cedria).

biannum [OF *bian*], biannual labour service, *corvée* (Fr.).

c1168 quieta ab omni consuetudine et talliata et cavalcata et ∼o *Act. Hen. II* I 426; **a1173** quieti de toto biennio *Ib.* 510; **c1182** dedisse..bianium meum quod etiam in terra illa habebam *Ib.* II 241; **1192** absque venda, telonio, ..tallia, navagio, monagio, biano (*Ch. Rotomag.*) *Thes. Nov. Anecdot.* I 649; **1289** de arreragiis redditus wiani in castellania de Blankefort *RGasc* II 393.

bianor [pers. name in Virgil *Ecl.* IX 60], brave, strong.

∼or, animo et corpore fortis *GlC* B 114.

bibacitas, drunkenness.

a dronkynnes, ∼as, ebrietas *CathA*.

bibalia, (pl.) drink-money.

1539 lathomis..in ∼ibus *Rent. S. Andr.* 71; **15..** octo denarios et ∼ia MYLN *Dunkeld* 96.

bibarium v. biber. bibarius v. bifarius b. bibatio v. bibitio. bibator v. bibitor.

bibax, drunken. **b** (sb.) drunkard.

due anicule, quibus nihil ∼acius W. MALM *GR* II 171; ego tamen utriusque [vini et cervisie] ∼ax sum J. SAL. *Ep.* 85 (33); gens penetranda tibi prelarga bibaxque loquaxque *Id. Enth. Pol.* 382A; qui ∼acior est alios..iniquitate transcendit *Id. Pol.* 725D. **b** *a drynker*, ∼ax *CathA*.

bibecium v. biber.

biber, ∼era, ∼erium, ∼arium, a drinking time. **b** drink-money (*cf. Building in Eng.* 79). **c** drink, beverage.

a c1148 junior serviat..ad ∼eres ante cenam; post ∼eres semel licet bibere (*Inst. Sempr.*) *MonA* VI 946* lxxx; **1509** post secundum ∼erium *Reg. Merton* 397. **b 1394** ad ∼eram j d. *Ac. Churchw. Bath* 15; **1470** pro ∼eriis ejus [sclatter'] et serviencium suorum xv d. *Cant. Coll. Ox.* II 191; **1509** pro †bibeciis datis carpentariis..ut diligencius insudarent operibus, iiij s. *Reg. Magdalen* (*NS*) I 66. **c 1420** cisare, cervisie, potus, ∼aria seu alie res et provisiones (*RNorm* 12) *Foed.* IX 850; ∼era, A. *a beverache* WW.

bibere [CL], to drink.

bibens nectar ALDH. *VirgV* 2505; misit ei calicem vini benedictum.., quem ut ∼it, surrexit BEDE *HE* V 5; nonne ∼is [AS: *drincst þu*] vinum? ÆLF. *Coll.* 102; **1102** ut presbiteri non eant ad potationes, nec ad pinnas ∼ant (*Conc. Lond.*) EADMER *HN* 164; vinum non aquatum ∼as, meros in janua Aquis GIR. *TH* I 35; **1220** libenter cum eo ∼eret *CurR* VIII 382; sedebit post prandium et ∼et quamdiu de die potest videre sine candelis accensis *Cust. Bleadon* 204.

biberium v. biber.

bibero [OF *biberon*], drinking cup, ladle.

1300 unum par pelvium cum ∼one *Ac. Wardr.* p. 341; **1340** due pelves argent'..quarum j cum ∼one cum j scuto quartellato de armis Anglie et Francie *Ac. Wardr.* (*TRBk* 203) p. 313; **1370** duas pelves argenti deauratas.., quarum una habet †bibonam [? l. biberonem] *Fabr. York* 185; **1390** de..uno calefactorio argenteo cum j ∼one..una pelve alba cum ∼one deaurat' in fundo *Ac. Foreign* 25 G *d*.

bibilus v. biblus.

bibio [LL], insect breeding in wine. **b** drunkard.

∼ones vel mustiones, *muscfleotan* vel *wurma smite* ÆLF. *Gl.*; reptilia..que [orta sunt] ex exhalationibus, ut ∼ones [v.l. bibrones] ex vino, papiliones ex aqua, sexto die facta sunt GERV. TILB. I 8 (cf. *Eul. Hist.* I 10); **a1250** ∼ones oriuntur ex vino sine motibus brutalibus J. GODARD *Ap.* 263; ∼iones, vermes, A. *myntys* WW. **b** *a drynker*, bibax, ∼io, bibo *CathA*.

bibitare, to drink heavily.

in omnem edendi et ∼andi superfluum ructum *G. Steph.* I 40.

bibitio, drinking, drink.

abbas..domos sacriste..funditus precepit erui, tanquam non essent digne stare super terram propter frequentes bibaciones et quedam tacenda que..viderat BRAKELOND 129; **a1220** de procuracione commestionis et ∼onis..illos quietos clamari *AncD* A 2554; iste ablativus 'usu' [rerum consumptibilium] accipitur pro comestione, induitione, ∼ione OCKHAM *Pol.* II 515.

bibitor, drinker.

bibulus, bibator *GlC* B 121; retinet..aquam Lethis, cujus non meminit ∼or MAP *NC* V 7 p. 251.

bibitorius, for drinking in (*cf.* R. Lennard: *Rural England* 405).

[domus] quales Anglici in singulis singulas habebant diocesibus ∼ias, *ghildhus* Anglice dictas MAP *NC* II 12.

biblia [cf. βιβλίον], bible. **b** Old Testament.

1095 habet ecclesia unum (*sic*) ∼iam in duobus voluminibus *Catalog. Durh.* 117; **1245** prima pars ∼ie veteris Anglice littere..; item alia ∼ia in duobus voluminibus nova.., cujus prima pars finit in Job.., secunda pars finit in epistula Jude (*Invent. S. Paul.*) *Arch.* L 496; interpretatio ∼ie per magistrum W. de Harundel .. correcta AD. MARSH *Ep.* 86; ∼iam versificatam BACON *Tert.* 54; **1268** volumus..quod ∼ia nostra glossata vendatur..; item dicto decano legamus ∼iam nostram simplicem *Test. Ep. Heref.* 4; **1303** respondent de una ∼ia in xiij voluminibus precii x li. ..et de xx s. de una parva ∼ia *Ac. Exec. Ep. Lond.* 50; **1338** habent in cavernis magnam copiam librorum legum aut medicine, et non est inter omnes una parva ∼ia quam possent in fine diei respicere RIC. ARMAGH *Serm.* 31; **1345** idem..de Hebraico pro textu sacre ∼ie..est censendum R. BURY *Phil.* 10. 166; **a1350** statutum est ut qui incipere in theologia proponit..aliquem librum de canone ∼ie legisse teneatur *StatOx* 50; **p1381** solum accipit Augustinum..cum aliis antiquis primitive ecclesie cum textu ∼ie et determinatione ecclesie (WYNT.) *Ziz.* 187; biblia que docuit, respice facta David GOWER *VC* VI 862. **b** hujus [Damasi] hortatu Jeronimus ∼iam transtulit de Hebreo in Latinum HIGD. IV 29.

biblice, with textual exposition.

1311 statutum est quod nullus legat bibliam ∼e nisi prius ..fuerit baccalaurius *Collect. Ox.* II 218; **1317** bibliam ∼e seu textualiter..legere *FormOx* 24; **a1350** statutum est ut qui incipere in theologia proponit..bibliam ∼e per triennium audisse..teneatur *StatOx* 50.

biblicus, biblical.

in eadem ecclesia [S. Pauli, Lond.] est capella B. Virginis ..∼is historiis vermiculata S. SIM. *Itin.* 4.

bibliographus [βιβλιογράφος], scribe.

∼us, *scryvener* WHITTINGTON *Vulg.* 67.

bibliopola [βιβλιοπώλης], bookseller (or scribe).

∼a, qui biblos vendit *GlC* B 120; librarius vel ∼a..vel scriba..*wrytere* ÆLF. *Gl.*; ex biblio, unde ∼e venditores librorum appellantur BELETH *RDO* 60. 66; *stacyoner, or he that sellyth bokys*, stacionarius, ∼a *PP*.

bibliotheca [βιβλιοθήκη], bookcase, library, collection of books. **b** book-cover. **c** bible.

itinerarium Petri x voluminibus digestum..elimavit, Rufino in Latinum ex Graecorum ∼is vertente ALDH. *VirgP* 25; historias..congregans, amplam ibi ac nobilissimam ∼am fecit BEDE *HE* V 20; ∼a vel armarium vel archivum, *boochord* ÆLF. *Sup.*; ∼a armarium significat et volumen aliquod magnum compactum ex omnibus libris Novi et Veteris Testamenti BELETH *RDO* 60. 66; congestis undique ∼e disperse thesauris ad studium redii GIR. *PI pref.* 1; **13..** dedit..maximam partem bibliotece *Cart. Bath* II no. 808. **b** quatuor evangelia de auro purissimo..scribere jussit necnon et ∼am librorum eorum, omnem de auro purissimo..fabrefactam, compaginare inclusores gemmarum praecepit EDDI *Wilf.* 17. **c a690** caelestis tetrica enodantes ∼ae problemata ALDH. *Ep.* 5 p. 492; spiritalis ∼ae formulas *Id. Met.* 3 p. 73; **754** tam praeclarum speculatorem caelestis ∼ae (*Lit. Arch. Cant.*) *Ep. Bonif.* 111 p. 239; nomine pandecten proprio vocitare memento / hoc corpus sacrum.., / quod nunc a multis constat bibliothēca dicta / nomine non proprio ALCUIN *Carm.* 65. 1. 3; **c960** (**11c**) janitor coelestis ∼ae et vas electionis predicator egregius apostolus Paulus *CS* 1007; Jeronymus..in primo ∼e prologo GIR. *TH* III 30; unam ∼am utriusque testamenti corpus integre continentem AD. EYNS. *Hug.* II 13; **1208** recepimus..sex libros ∼e in quibus continetur omne vetus testamentum *Cl* 108; fratres.. Minores..libros continue suos, videlicet ∼as, in forulis a collo dependentes bajulantes M. PAR. *Min.* II 110; **14..** ∼e iiij, prima in duobus voluminibus, secunda in tribus (*Cart. Reading*) *EHR* III 117; hec ∼a, *a bybulle*; biblioteca mea [? l. meam] servat meam [? mea] bibliotecam (*Vers.*) WW.

bibliothecarius, librarian.

†bibliothicatrix, qui codices †secat *GlC* B 122 (= *Erf.* 2. 271. 23: †bibliothecarum [? l. ~ius] qui codices †resecat [? recenset]); c1142 Gerardi..Romane ecclesie presbiteri cardinalis ac ~ii *Reg. Malm.* I 348.

bibliotista, librarian.

1464 Johanni..~e collegii *MunAcOx* 707.

biblus [βύβλος], papyrus, reed.

est juncus, scirpus, bibilus, papirus, arundo GARL. *Syn.* 1585D; *a seyfe*, juncus, ~us, cirpus *CathA.*

2 a book. **b** scripture, bible.

a Romuleis scribor biblis, sed voce Pelasga ALDH. *Aen.* 35 (*Nycticorax*) 6; 10.. ~um, *boc*, ..~os, *bec* WW. **b** pontificis.. / qui.. / imbutus fuerat conscripto dogmate bibli ALDH. *VirgV* 1037; quicquid neutericis confinxit apocripha biblis FRITH. 1210; 1337 deficiunt libri, viz. ~us Johannis de C... *Lit. Cant.* II 149.

bibo, drunkard.

c1157 potum quoque petens, quoniam non magis epulo quam ~o sum J. SAL. *Ep.* 76 (35); *a drynker*, bibax, bibio, ~o *CathA.*

bibona v. bibero. bibro v. bibio.

†bibulta [? cf. berula], 'biller' (*v. berula*) or wild turnip.

~a, *billeru GlC* B 141; diptamnus vel †bibulcos, *wilde næp* ÆLF. *Gl.*

bibulus [CL], thirsty, absorbent. **b** (fig.). **c** (subst.) drinker, drunkard.

bis binis bibulus potum de fontibus hausi ALDH. *Aen.* 83. (*Juvencus*) 2; [crapula] viribus aequalis bibulae perfecta sorori BONIF. *Aen.* (*Vit.* 5) 271; radices bibulas gaudet habere salix NECKAM *DS* VIII 52. **b** ingenium per florulenta scripturarum arva..~a curiositate decurrit ALDH. *VirgP* 4; rex..accusationibus prebens aures ~as *V. Waltheof* 251. **c** ~us, †bibator *GlC* B 121; *a drynker*, bibax, bibio, bibo, ~us *CathA.*

1 bica [? cf. βῖκος], cup, beaker (measure of ale).

a1256 quando aliquis ballivorum nostrorum prisam fecerit de cervisia.., non tenetur habere nisi primam bikam de uno obolo minus quam alibi vendita fuerit (*Ch. Launceston*) *Cal Pat 1381–5* p. 263; 1336 [*payment for*] bikas (*Ac. Launceston*) *Gild Merch.* II 85.

2 bica, ~us [ME *bike*; cf. bicarius], nest of wild bees. **b** swarm.

a1250 cum dimidio totius bosci de Hewode, cum niso et pannagio et byko (*Mun. Davenport*) *Chetham Soc.* Ser. 3, IX 86; a1260 in boscis et in planis, in nisis, in bikis *Cart. Cockersand* 691; 1277 non impedientes ipsos quo minus bicarius eorum ~as suas habere possit ubi antiquitus fieri consuevit [in foresta de Cestre] *Pat* 96 m. 22; 1286 furatus fuit ij bykos in bosco Edmundi Fiton *Eyre Chester* 12 r. 4. **b** 1397 R. D. invenit j bigam apum de extrahura *DL CourtR* (*Staffs*) 230/18 m. 2.

bicamera, double chamber.

13.. unam cameram magnam sc. solarium cum camino.., item unam ~am cum camino..ruinosam (*DC S. Paul.*) *HMC Rep.* I *app.* 37a.

bicameratus, two-chambered (of Noah's ark).

~am et tricameratam..arcam ALDH. *Met.* 2 p. 63; arca.. ~a est et tricamerata, quasi per cenacula et tristega GERV. TILB. I 24.

†bicarium [? cf. 1 bica], beaker, wine-jar.

a wyne potte, bacarium, bacarina, ..vas vinarium *CathA.*

bicarius [cf. 2 bica, OF *bigre*], bee-taker, bee-master.

†bochero [AS: *beoceorle*], id est apum custodi, pertinet, si *gafolheorde*..teneat, ut inde reddat (*Quad.*; *Rect.*) *GAS* 448; 1157 dedi eis..redditum omnium bigrorum quos ibi [in foresta] habebam (*Ch. Silli, Norm.*) *Act. Hen. II* I 131; 1277 (v. 2 bica).

bicaterassum v. bithalassum. bicellium v. biclinium.

biceps [CL], two-headed. **b** two-headed dragon.

~s, duo capita habens *GlC* B 104 (cf. ib. 107: ~s, qui duos dentes (*sic*) habet); 1245 volucres biscipites (*Invent. S. Paul.*) *Arch.* L 491. **b** hoc amphibim est serpens cum tribus (*sic*) capitibus, ..hic ~s, *a flyande eddyre* WW.

2 two-edged. **b** two-edged instrument, twibill.

romphea ~s ALDH. *Met.* 2 p. 66; habebat sicam bicipitem toxicatam BEDE *HE* II 9; ille biceps gladius non scindit forcius illis GOWER *VC* I 222 (cf. *Prov.* v 4). **b** *twybyl*, .., bisacuta, ~s *PP.*

3 two-edged (fig.). **b** in two parts.

facit illud decretum biceps ex utraque parte secans GIR. *GE* II 33 p. 327. **b** neutram mihi bicipitis petitionis partem..concedere *Id. Symb.* I 22 p. 266.

bichicon v. bechicon.

bicinium, duet.

~ium, *twegra sang* ÆLF. *Gl.*

bicirculus, pair of circles.

1388 alba..de viridi samite contexta cum leopardis in ~is (*Invent. Westm.*) *Arch.* LII 242.

bickaria v. bukinus.

biclinium [CL], couch seating two persons.

~ium, quasi †bicellium [? l. bisellium] *GlC* B 124.

bicoca, snipe (bird); cf. *becassa, 2 bugium.*

~a, *hæbreblete GlC* B 96; ~a, *hæferblæte* vel *pur* ÆLF. *Gl.*

bicolor, two-coloured; **b** (w. ref. to chequer board).

~or, *twihiwe* ÆLF. *Gl.*; urina ~or in idropisi est mortalis, sicut cum est ruffa inferius et livens superius GAD. 32. 2. **b** ludebat..in calculis ~oribus W. FITZST. *Thom.* 10; ad quadrangulam tabulam, que dicitur calculis ~oribus, vulgo scaccarium; potius autem est regis tabula nummis albicoloribus, ubi etiam placita corone regis tractantur *Ib.* 39.

bicorneus, two-horned (of crescent moon).

lunaris globi rotunditas..septenis figurarum speciebus variatur, hoc est ~ea et sectili ac reliquis ALDH. *Met.* 3 p. 72.

bicornis, two-horned. **b** two-pronged.

[vacca] altera Brunetta, fuit altera dicta Bicornis NIG. *SS* 207. **b** urgentur calibes furcos aptare bicornes FRITH. 888.

bicors, two-hearted, false.

femina queque bicors, linguam gerit ore bicoxam *Babio* 193.

bicoxus, two-legged (fig.), double.

Babio 193 (v. bicors).

bictonatus v. biothanatus.

bicubitus, two cubits long.

quoniam terminus corporis est ~us, dicitur et corpus ~um in longitudine NECKAM *NR* II 173; si lux multiplicatione sui infinita extendit materiam in dimensionem ~am GROS. 53; si queratur quomodo se habet So[crates], bene respondendum est '~us' BACON XV 203; adveniente corpore in loco continuo quod est †bicubicum *Id.* XIII 189.

Biculbitus v. Biturigiacus. bida v. 2 biga a. bidell- v. bdelli-, bedell-.

bidens [CL], two-toothed: **a** sheep (also fig.); **b** mattock or sim.

a luporum / qui lustrare solent mandras et saepta bidentum ALDH. *VirgV* 993; [oves] carent dentium efficacia, unde et ~tes appellantur ADEL. *QN* 24; quandoque ruminationis causa est instrumentorum penuria, ut in ~tibus NECKAM *NR* II 162; 1221 de latrocinio ~tium furatarum *PlCrGlouc* 229; c1360 ceduntur gladiis more bidencium *Planct. Univ. Ox.* 113; 1374 per vendicionem exituum multonum et aliorum ~cium *ExchScot* 453; hec †bidua, *a gymbyre* WW; 1475 pastor presentat ij ~tes matrices.. provenientes de extrahuris *CourtR Lygh* I f. 10. **b** 14.. hoc ~s, *a mattok*.., hic ~s, *a stybylle* WW.

bidentalis, two-pronged.

rusticus..furcam ferream..dejecit et verticem filiole sue ..nesciens trajecit..—erat enim furca ~is—altero dentalium verticem transfigens, altero scapulas perstringens W. CANT. *Mir. Thom.* VI 114.

bidentatus, two-toothed.

c1230 pannagiare debet..averium plene dentatum pro iij d. et ~um pro j d. ob. *Doc. Bec* 46; s905 hoc anno vermes ~i de aere ceciderunt, qui totam annonam Hibernie comederunt *Eul. Hist.* I 246.

†bidentilis (*s. dub.*).

obviavit cuidam homunculo..cum †auli et ~i [v.l. aulo et edentulo] *NLA* (*Bertellinus*) I 166.

bidentinus, of sheep, woollen.

maluit sponsare juvenculam..quam more monachorum ~is indui panniculis *V. Dunst.* B. 7.

bidictionalitas, composition of two words.

racio.., secundum quod attenditur circa sillabam, biliteralitas et triliteralitas; secundum quod attenditur [circa] dictionem, bisillabalitas et trisillabalitas; quod attenditur circa oracionem, ~as et tridictionalitas BACON XV 219.

bidrip- v. bederipa. bidua v. bidens a.

bidualis, lasting two days.

ut..jejunium in hebdomada ~e transigeret OSB. *V. Dunst.* 35.

biduanus, lasting two days.

~um vel triduanum sat est observare jejunium BEDE *HE* IV 23; ~is deinde cotidianis febribus..quatiebatur GOSC. *Wulsin* 22; post ~e quietis solatium quartane passionis timebatur accessus AILR. *Ed. Conf.* 788A; 1257 moram protraximus ~am (*Lit. Regis Rom.*) *Foed.* I 622 (cf. *Ann. Burton* 393).

2 (sb. f.) two-day fast.

lxxv psalmi cum totidem veniis..excusant ~am BART. EXON. *Pen.* 135.

biduum [CL], two-day period.

venit ad me ante ~um..nuntius BEDE *Pleg.* p. 307; se novam lunam..~o priusquam prima caneretur..vidisse *Id. TR* 43; emuli tui te ~o quesituri sunt R. COLD. *Cuthb.* 46; 1288 pastiliarii calefaciunt pastilios..per ~um et per triduum *Leet Norw.* 13 (cf. ib. 32).

biduvium [LL (?) < Gall.], tool, (?) bill-hook (*cf.* OF *vouge*).

acceptis securibus, asciis et †vidulis [v.l. guviis] aliisque multimodis ferramentis ad carecta et frutecta stirpanda ORD. VIT. IX 6 p. 500.

biennalis, lasting two years. **b** (subst.) two-year period.

historiam ~i lucubratione complevi GIR. *DK pref.* 1. 155; s1206 ~es inducias impetrarunt WEND. II 14; 1323 pro ij terminis decime ~is *Sacr. Ely* II 31; 1336 ~i languore corporis correptus *Lit. Cant.* II 118; 1407 numquid tunc incipiens tenetur ad lecturam ~em? *StatOx* 194. **b** s1382 postquam ~em fecisset in terra Sicilie, obiit peregrinus *Chr. Angl.* 349.

biennis, two years old or lasting two years.

9.. ~is, *twiwintre* WW; sedes morte patris spatio Romana bienni / muta silet GARL. *Tri. Eccl.* 18.

biennium [CL], two-year period.

coepta sunt haec ~io ante mortem regis BEDE *HE* III 21; in anno semel vel ~io GIR. *TH* II 13; 1271 per ~ium.. sequentem (*sic*) completum *Cl* 405; 1337 infra bihennium elapsum *Exch. Scot* 437.

biennum v. biannum.

bifacius, two-faced (of woven fabric).

1245 casula que dicitur bifatia, eo quod pannus est extra rubeus et intus niger (*Invent. S. Paul.*) *Arch.* L 483.

bifariam [CL], in two parts.

†~ia, duplici ratione *GlC* B 126; quod ~iam dividitur BEDE *Tab.* II 6; huic nos ~iam respondere possumus BELETH *RDO* 73. 79.

bifarie, in two parts, doubly.

[syllabae] longae..fiunt..natura quidem ~ie, aut productione videlicet singularum vocalium..aut duarum conjunctione BEDE *AM* 2351; ipsa auctoritate ~ie divisa *Id. TR* 2; hoc experimentum ~ie inveni NEN. *HB* 149; ~ie.. dividere aequali lance ASSER *Alf.* 99; ubi divididitur jus proprietatis..quandoque ~ie, trifarie, quadrifarie per subdivisiones BRACTON 68; 1433 tanti principis qui duorum regnorum regimini presidens ~ie coronatur (*Reg. S. Alb.*) *MonA* III 113.

1 bifarius [LL], two-fold. **b** equivocal. **c** (*s. dub.*).

†bisarius, bipertitus *GlC* B 127; civitas..nomine censetur ~io..Warlamecester [et]..Watlingcester M. PAR. *Maj.* I 156; [Caesar]..regibus..~ias et clementie simul et austeritatis direxit epistolas FORDUN *Chr.* II 14. **b** bilinguis, †bibarius *GlC* B 109; *dubylle-tonged*, ambiloquus, ~ius, bilinguis *CathA.* **c** †974 (12c) custodem..cenobii quod Angli biphario vocitant onomate Maldumesburg *CD* 584.

2 bifarius v. vivarium. bifatius v. bifacius.

bifidus [CL], divided (or dividing) in two.

dumque tremunt bifido corruptae scismate partes FRITH. 246; 9.. ~a, bis divisa, *twidæledu* WW.

bifinium, boundary stone or headland (in open field).

a meyre stane, ~ium [v.l. interfinium], ..*an hede-londe* †aviseges, ..~ium *CathA.*

bifoliatus, two-leaved.

1443 j cuntyr ~um *Cant. Coll. Ox.* I 7.

biforis, having two doors. **b** (pl.) double doors.

nidum molitur bifore valva NECKAM *DS* II 945. **b** valve vel ~es juxta porticum ponantur NECKAM *Ut.* 110; vibrat ~es *Latin Stories* 176; ~es..quemvis intromittunt MORE *Ut.* 48.

biformis, combining two shapes, hybrid, double.

sum mihi dissimilis, vultu membrisque biformis ALDH. *Aen.* 28 (*Minotaurus*) 1; 10.. ~is, *twihiowe, swa swa bið healf mon and healf fear* WW; catulos [canis et simie]..tam deformes ~is nature formas abhorrens GIR. *IK* II 11 (cf. *TH* I 16); graduum collatio, facta biformi / lege VINSAUF *PN* 241; biformem / reddit enim faciem dissona prosa metro GARL. *Tri. Eccl.* 3.

†bifultum, (*s. dub.*).

1232 totum molendinum..cum ~o quodam juxta idem molendinum (*Ch. Dore*) *ChartR* 27 m. 13 (= *MonA* V 555).

bifurcare, to bifurcate (trans.), cause to diverge. **b** (absol. or pass.) to fork.

ordo bifurcat iter: tum limite nititur artis, / tum sequitur stratam nature VINSAUF *PN* 87. **b** grave robur [aratri].. quod quasi ~ando in binas aures procedat NECKAM *Ut.* 112; c1220 inter duos rivulos qui ~antur a predicto ponte *Reg. Aberbr.* I 98; vena..~atur..circa poplitem GILB. VI 266. 1.

2 (p. ppl.) forked, two-pronged, divergent. **b** forked, *fourché* (her.). **c** consisting of two parts. **d** bipartite, written in duplicate. **e** wearing a two-peaked bonnet (? w. implication of duplicity).

cum setis ~atis GILB. II 82 v. 1; contractus a nativitate, qui gambas et pedes habuit..~atas *Mir. Montf.* 93; si [lapis] sit cornutus vel ~atus GAD. 130 v. 1; c**1307** ut inter ligna ~ata [*gallows*] promovear (*Passio Scotorum*) *Proc. Soc. Ant. Scot. NS* VII 168; in linea ~ata *NLA* (*Joseph*) II 82. **b** portat leonem..cum cauda ~ata BAD. AUR. 141; crux geminata sive duplicata, que..~ata notatur ELMH. *Cant.* 101. **c** [actiones competunt] quandoque versus duos vel plures cum sint disjuncte et ~ate BRACTON 102; **1423** de..hiis ~atis negotiationis..limitibus (*Lit. Abbatis*) AMUND. I *app.* 412. **d 1259** presenti scripto ~ato *Reg. Ant. Linc.* III 749; **1268** huic scripto bifurkato uterque predictorum sigillum suum apposuit *DL Cart. Misc.* 2/148 (*Lincoln*). **e 1396** quod sunt discipuli antichristi..monachi et canonici ~ati (*Concl. J. Wycliff*) *Conc.* III 230.

bifurcus, two-pronged.

municipium..in..oblonga rupis eminentia situm lingua marina..in capite ~o complectitur GIR. *IK* I 12.

1 biga v. 2 bica.

2 biga [CL], cart (not necessarily drawn by two horses). **b** chariot of the sun. **c** cart-load (*cf. bigata*).

~ae, sicut et trigae et quadrigae, pluraliter tantum [efferuntur]; sed in nostrorum literis scriptorum ~am invenimus et quadrigam BEDE *Orth.* 2779; †bida..vel carpentum, *cræt* ÆLF. *Gl.*; **9..** ~a, ubi ii equi currui junguntur, *horscræt* WW; s**1100** quem impositum ~a rudi et vili rusticus Wintoniam deferre voluit MAP *NC* V 6 p. 233; c**1200** liberum transitum..sibi et suis quadrigis et ~is et omnibus vecturis suis *Cart. Sallay* 256; **1208** unam ~am cum toto harnesio et tractu quatuor equorum *Cl* 110b; **1252** unam ~am cum unico equo semel in die in bosco suo ..errantem ad focale *MonA* VI 430; **1258** remanent in curia iiij ~e ferrate *Ac. Wellingb.* 3; **1264** cariabit..blada domini..cum..una ~a et duobus bobus *Reg. Whet. app.* II 326; **1329** pro coopertura ~e domine regine defuncte, j peciam [panni] *ExchScot* 255; **1431** octo boves cum quadam ~a vocata *wayn Reg. Cant.* II 451; ~a, *carte, cart, wayne* WW. **b** aurora in fulvis dum luxit lutea bigis ALDH. *VirgV* 1363. **c 1395** pro una ~a calcis *Cant. Coll. Ox.* II 141 (cf. ib. 242).

bigamia [cf. διγαμία], **a** bigamy. **b** remarriage.

a hic [Lamech] ~iam introduxit R. NIGER 2 (cf. HIGD. II 5). **b** Jeronimus..in questionum circa ~iam solutionibus..dormitasse..est visus GIR. *Spec.* II 23; c**1255** ne vir vel mulier ad ~iam transiens a presbytero benedicatur *Conc.* I 707; **1309** cum cognicio ~ie ad forum ecclesiasticum pertineat *Conc. Syn.* 1273; s**1344** si sibi [clerico] imponatur quod duas uxores duxerit sive unam viduam, quod super hoc justiciarii non habeant..potestatem ad triandum..~iam WALS. *YN* 283; *the secund weddynge*, ~ia, deuterogamia *CathA*.

bigamus [cf. δίγαμος], **a** (?) bigamous. **b** twice married or married to a widow.

a *weddyd to tweyne*, ~us *PP*. **b** si quis viduam accipit..non potest ordinari, sicut ~i THEOD. *Pen.* I ix 10; 'unius uxoris virum'..adjecit: si non virginem non tamen ~um LANFR. *Comment. Paul.* (1 *Tim.* iii 2) 352; **1214** qui ~i..vel alias corruptarum mariti fuerunt..non exequantur sacerdotis officium *Conc. Syn.* 25; **1276** de ~is quos dominus Papa in consilio Lugdunensi [**1274**] omni privilegio clericali privavit..constitutio illa intelligenda est quod..decetero non liberentur..prelatis *StRealm* I 43 (cf. *Fleta* 51); c**1300** vos amisistis privilegium clericale, eo quod estis ~us, quia matrimonium contraxistis cum vidua *Year Bk. 30–31 Ed. I app.* 530; **1368** desponsavit quandam Amabillam viduam..et sic..erat ~us *Pat* 278 m. 21; ~us est eo quod ipse ij uxores successive desponsarit *Entries* 106.

bigare, to drive a cart or carriage.

1451 attentis verbis D. Bonaventure, fratres non debere equitare neque ~are neque quadrigare nisi.. (*Abbr. Stat.*) *Mon. Francisc.* II 95.

bigarius, driver of a pair of horses, carter.

a collariis ~ii, a ~iis multorum domini effecti sunt aurigarum MAP *NC* IV 16; **1413** in dato ~iis vicarii..trahentibus lapides ad fundamenta cancelle *Rect. Adderbury* 8; **1415** assignavimus te ad lx ~ios..pro presenti passagio nostro versus partes transmarinas eligendum (*Pat*) *Foed.* IX 261; *cartere*, ~ius *PP*; **1537** ~iis..pro cariagio..salis *Ac. Durh.* 696.

bigata, ~us, cart-load.

s**1212** habuimus de feno vij ~as *Ann. Dunstable* 38; **1325** cariagium pro xx ~is turbarum pro focali *Pri. Cold.* 16; ~a, A. *a kartlode* WW; **1495** pro uno ~u de *ly lyme Arch. Hist. Camb.* II 15n.; **1507** pro uno ~o tegularum *Cant. Coll. Ox.* II 248; **1527** pro una †bigatura *ly evestone Ib.* 260.

bigator, carter.

1395 dat' ~ori..pro cariagio de bordis *Cant. Coll. Ox.* II 141; **1471** in solutis ~ori ad cariandum dictos *flyntes Ac. Chamb. Winchester.*

bigener, hybrid (? conf. w. *degener*).

†bigimen [? l. bigenerum], e duobus generibus conceptum *GlC* B 106; **9..** ~er, *aworden* vel *doe.* WW.

bigera, doublet.

dobelet, garment, ~a, ..baltheus, deplois *PP*.

bigermen, mixed grain, maslin.

mastilyon, ~en, mixtilio *CathA*.

†bigirdellus, (?) doublet.

1360 bona subscripta..arestavit, viz. ..duo paria botellorum et quatuor ~os *Cl* 197 m. 5.

bigrus v. bicarius. Biguina v. Begina.

†bigulis (?) *f.l.* for *bijugus* or dim. of *biga.*

~is, jugatis anima[li]bus *Erf.* 2. 271. 51.

†bigulus, (?) *f.l.* for *angulus.*

a**1310** viam a..calceta usque ~um de Bennerls *Meaux* II 213.

bihennium, v. biennium. bika, ~us, v. 1 & 2 bica. bikerellus v. bekerellus. bila v. 1 billa.

bilanx, bilancia [cf. balancia], balance, weighing scale. **b** (fig.) balanced judgement.

~ce, *tuiheolore*, *GlC* B 140; ~ces, *twa scale* ÆLF. *Gl.*; examen apis est, examen lingua bilancis GARL. *Syn.* 1588B; quod corpus..poneretur in lance bilanxis, et alia lanx impleretur pecuniis *NLA* (*Jurmin*) II 543; **13..** de ponderatione facta per ~cem *MGL* I 179 (= ib. 247: *par balaunce*); **1440** pro reparacione ~cie troni *ExchScot* 75; c**1500** unum par ~ciarum cum iiij stateris *Invent. Ch. Ch.* 129. **b** qui aequa discretionis ~ce singulorum facta trutinabit ALDH. *VirgP* 49.

bilare v. 1 billare.

bilbire [CL Gl.], to bubble, gurgle.

amfora profusa bilibit ALDH. *PR* 131; *swowyn or sowndyn as new alle or odyr lycour*, bylbio *PP*.

bilbus v. 1 & 2 bulbus. bilegium v. birelagia. bilet-bilect- v. billet-. bilho v. 1 billio. bilia v. 2 billa 1. bilibire v. bilbire.

bilibris [CL], **a** weight of two pounds.

a est..sextarius mensura ij librarum, quibus assumptis ~is nominatur BART. ANGL. XIX 125; quam..ad denarios pensari in ~i praecepit ASSER *Alf.* 104.

2 (?) weighing by a double standard (*cf. Deut.* xxv 13).

arguto fratres fratrum discrimine clades / pendite, ne rudibus pereant antiqua bilibris FRITH. 748.

bilinguis, double-tongued, equivocal, deceitful (person).

~is, †bibarius [? l. bifarius] *GlC* B 109; **8..** os ~e, *twispecne muð* WW; et centum linguas quisque bilinguis habet NECKAM *DS* III 198; sis stabilis, verbis, non sint tua verba bilinguis D. BEC. 94; damnant linguosi papam punguntque bilingues, / elingues lacerant GARL. *Tri. Eccl.* 15; **1327** quidam bilingwes..suggesserunt *Lit. Cant.* I 239.

biliosus [CL], bilious, choleric.

CS 1311 (v. algema); *angri*, iracundus, bilosus, fellitus *PP*; *angry*, †vilosus *CathA*.

bilis [CL], bile, gall, poison. **b** brine.

~e, *atr GlC* B 108; fel vel ~is, *gealla* ÆLF. *Gl.*; **9..** ~e, felle, *attr* WW; vessicula fellis..qua sanguis a ~e defecatus et purus evadit D. EDW. *Anat.* B IV. **b** [pontus] incestat aquas bilemque refundit / in vada blanda suam J. EXON. *BT* I 159.

2 bilious or melancholic humour. **b** envy, hostility.

nigra ~is stabilis [? l. stabiles], graves, compositos moribus dolososque facit BEDE *TR* 35 p. 247. **b** habeo quo utriusque ~em moveam ADEL. *QN* 24; commota ex his principis ~e W. MALM. *GP* I 49; casu bile tumens ad rixas ne movearis D. BEC. 705; species illius pulcritudinis ~em contuentibus dabat incentive cupiditatis R. COLD. *Cuthb.* 86.

bilitteralitas, composition of two letters.

BACON XV 219 (v. bidictionalitas).

bilium v. percurribilis.

bilix [CL], woven w. double thread, double. **b** (sb.) kersey.

bilices, duplices *GlC* B 105. **b** *carsay*, ~ix *CathA*.

1 billa, ~us [AS *bil*], bill, billhook, cutting tool or weapon. **b** bill, steel instrument for dressing millstones.

si quis in servum transeat, ..in signum..transitionis hujus ~um vel stumblum vel deinceps ad hunc modum servitutis arma suscipiat (*Leg. Hen.*) *GAS* 594; **1328** una ~a ad amputand' spinas precii ijd (*KRAc* 239/13) *Anal. Hib.* xxiv 194; **1413** percussit W. in capite cum uno ~o *SelC Coron.* 110; **1438** cum baculo et j ~a..verberaverunt et mutulaverunt *DL CourtR* 126/1875 m. 4*d.*; s**1314** ~is seu bipennibus decertant MAJOR V 3; **1588** vi et armis, viz. baculis, ~is et cultellis *Pat* 1320 m. 4. **b 1209** in ferro empto ad fusas, inkas et bilas faciendas ad novum molendinum *Pipe Wint.* 54; **1272** in acero empto ad bilos fabricandos ad dictam molam perforandam *Ib.* (159300) r. 9 (cf. ib. 9 *d.*: in byllis acuendis acerandis et elongandis); custus molendini..in ~a acuenda per annum xij d. *Form Man.* 33; **1314** in assero empto ad ~am molendini equini mundand' *Comp. Worc.* 42; **1383** in ij peciis ferri pro..ij ~is ac aliis instrumentis ferreis..molendini faciendis *MinAc* 1209 (15) m. 4*d.*; **1419** domos molendinorum..fregerunt et diversas ~as de ferro et acero factas..inter molares ibidem molantes posuerunt (*CoramR*) *Treat. J. P.* 71.

2 billa [? cf. OF *bille* = *piece of wood* (cf. 1 & 2 billettum); *possibly first applied to a wooden tab or tally*; *early evidence does not support connection with* bulla, *though some confusion occurred later* (v. 4 infra); libellus (cf. *Selden Soc.* XXX pp. xi–xiv, LX p. lxii, n. 2) *fits sense but not form*], tab, label, inventory, list, schedule.

1294 aliam [pocham] continentem xxvj li., .., prout patet in quadam ~a dicte poche appensa *Reg. Wint.* II 495; **1294** cccliiij li. ..de denariis domini H. ..in ix sacculis, prout patet per ~as eisdem sacculis consutas *Reg. S. Osm.* II 117; s**1294** aperuerunt cistas et numeraverunt pecuniam, si non fuerunt bilie invente de quantitate; si vero fuissent bilie, crediderunt biliis B. COTTON 238; **1299** memorandum quod..liberabantur ballivo..xxiiij disci [etc.]..in cujus rei testimonium presens ~a ad modum indenture confecta remanet penes Garderobam *KRAc* 356/24; **1343** tenor recordi et processus loquele de qua in ~a huic rotulo consuta fit mentio (*Breve*) THORNE 2072; **1383** una bursa..cum..diversis fragmentis reliquiarum sine ~is *Ac. Durh.* 427; **1453** ~a de diversis legatis.., diversis personis in eadem nominatis *Test. Ebor.* II 193.

2 note of receipt: **a** (of writ); **b** (of money in royal Wardrobe, Exchequer, etc.; *cf. Med. Admin. Hist.* I 50–1); **c** (by private person, sometimes serving as bond).

a 1302 quod vicecomites..~am de recepcione eorundem brevium..illis qui eam pecierint liberent *SelCKB* III 119; **1307** ~am diem et locum recepcionis istius brevis continentem eidem portitori liberetis (*Breve Ed. I*) *MGL* II 158; **1314** remedium contra vicecomites recusantes facere ~as et consignare super recepcione brevium regis *RParl* 322b. **b 1283** per ~am de Warderoba (*Lit. acquietancie Regis*) *Chr. Peterb.* 57 (cf. *Cal. ChancR Var.* 325); **1290** per ~am de Scaccario *KRMem.* 61 r. 3 (cf. ib. r. 7: per ~am de Garderoba); **1295** ~a pro magistro W. de Luda *Ib.* 68 r. 44; **1304** computet in Garderoba et habeat ~am (*Chanc. Misc.* 22/9) *CalScot* II 1555; **1320** cum ipsa mutuasset..x li. super quadam ~a de ccxx li. quas dominus rex ei debebat *RParl* 374b (cf. ib. 381: unam ~am signatam sigillo camerarii Scocie); **1327** per ~am thesaur[arii] *RScot* 215a; **1332** quandam ~am de Garderoba..continentem predictam summam *LTRMem* 105 r. 16*d.*; **1333** quod inde sibi fiat ~a de allocate de custubus predictis *Ib.* r. 154; c**1410** qui [baro Scaccarii] debet clare memoratori dare billam / ut breve cessare faciat cum viderit illam (*Vers. Exch.*) *EHR* XXXVI 59. **c 1318** per ~am de Recepta *Pat* 150 m. 12; **1356** in pane furniato pro expensis senescalli..iij busselli per ~am *Crawley* 274; **1400** debita clara..de domino T. de G. super compotum suum, ut patet per ~am liberatam executoribus, lxxij s. *Test. Ebor.* III 15; **1415** fatetur dominus comes..per ~am suam sub signeto suo signatam quod J. de L. ..recepit in custuma lane sue..iiij^{c} iiij^{xx}j li. *Exch Scot* IV 224; **1537** de diversis ~is obligatoriis in quibus predictus R. obligatus est *Sanct. Bev.* 461; **1595** super inde predictus R. W. apud Rochell' [in Gallia]..deliberavit prefato T. S.; tres ~as excambii *Entries* 338.

3 informal administrative document, serving as warrant etc. (*cf. Med. Admin. Hist.* V 113).

1301 [*letters of attorney warranted*] per ~am de Scaccario *Pat* 121 m. 31; **1302** per ~am missam sub privato sigillo *CalChart* III 24 (cf. *CalPat* 21); **14..** per ~am de privato sigillo *Reg. Brev.* 20; **1307** porrecta est quedam ~a sub magno sigillo de Cancellaria in hec verba: 'cum..rex..transgressionem..perdonavit..' *SelCKB* III 177; rex..commissarios constituit qui in regis obedientiam jurandos admitterent et eis ~as testimoniales de fide prestita liberarent *Ps.*-ELMH. *Hen. V* 47; **1448** per ~am signo manuali ipsius regis signatam, signeto aquile sigillatam *Cart. Glam.* 1614.

4 petition: **a** bill of complaint (informal petition of plaintiff) initiating proceedings in common law; **b** bill of exception in common law; **c** libel (Admiralty law); **d** bill of complaint in court of equity; **e** petition to king (or king and Council); **f** petition to king in Parliament, Parliamentary bill; **g** (various).

a c**1290** querela illa facta fuit..per ~am et non per breve *State Tri. Ed. I* 6; **1292** questus fuit per ~am..de detencione cujusdam debiti (*JustIt Salop*) *SelBEyre* 24; **1292** bene potuerunt ponere predictum W. ad legem vite et membrorum per vocem et per ~am quam N. ..porrexit versus W. ..de sedicione regem tangente, licet indictatus non esset per duodecim *SelCKB* II 133; s**1305** sedebant apud Gildhalam ad recipiendas ~as super articulis de trailbastone *Ann. Lond.* 137; **1319** alii in ~a originali nominati nondum convicti sunt nec placitaverunt (*CoramR*) *SelCWW* xlvii; **1320** justiciarii..querelas..audiant et terminent et..justiciam faciant per ~as sicut per brevia regis (*Pat*) *Parl. Writs* II ii *app.* 155; **1321** placitate et determinate fuerunt plures ~e inter querentes et defendentes..ubi justiciarii sedebant pro hujusmodi ~is per totum iter *MGL* II 368; **1336** pro stipendio domus sue ubi justiciarii ad ~as assiderunt *SelCKB* V 88; **1357** cum quidam justiciarii nostri Hibern' diversos homines Hibern'..per brevia, precepta, ~as et aliis modis voluntarie et absque indictamentis..arestaverint *StRealm* I 361; **1381** cum ballivi..per..carnifices..per diversas ~as suas..coram nobis in ..Scaccario implacitentur *Mem. York* I 120. **b** excipiens exceptionem in scriptis redactam petat quod justiciarius..sigillum apponat; et si querens prefatam ~am sigillatam..ostenderit.. *Fleta* 445; **1293** abbas super hoc petit ~am sibi consignari, ac si hoc quod dixit in forma excepcionis proposuisset *SelCKB* II 137. **c** c**1390** deliberata est ei copia ~e predicte et datus est ei dies ad respondendum *SelPlAdm* I 4. **d** c**1420** nullus..breve de subpena..conficiat..priusquam ~am cum manu unius Consiliariorum barram Cancellarie frequentancium recipiat et in filum Cancellarie imponat *Chanc. Orders* p. 7*d.*; s**1431** tenentes [abbatis] gravamina sua Cancellario regni..intimaverunt et ~as eidem porrexerunt AMUND. *S. Alb.* I 60; **1499** comparuit..ad respondendum ~e querele contra eum †propositum [? l. proposite] *SelCReq* 6. **e** s**1341** misit..archiepiscopus regi ac consilio suo schedulam sive ~am in Gallico W. GUISB. *Cont.* 369; **1381** que quidem peticio sive ~a in superiori parte intitulatur sic: *le roi a grantee ceste* *bille SelCExchCh 3*; **1382** responsio..patet in inquisicione huic brevi ac bulle consuta *Anc Pet* 15138 (cf. ib..quandam ~am nobis..exhibitam); **1388** talis consilii fuerunt cum predicto majore ac..Thoma Usk *skriveyn* ad scribendum ~as suas (*Coram R*) *Peasants' Rising 27*; s**1417** una ~a inter ceteras inventa est in qua supplicatur regi ut omnia bona temporalia ecclesiarum assumat in manu propria Capgr. *Hen.* 121. **f** s**1334** recuperavit..redditum. per ~am in pleno Parliamento et breve concessum *G. S. Alb.* II 266; **1372** [*restitution warranted*] per ~am de Parliamento *Pat* 287 m. 9; s**1376** porrecte fuerunt ~e et peticiones domino regi et suo consilio in sequenti Parliamento Thorne 2153; **1397** exhibuerat quandam ~am communibus regni nostri in..Parliamento existentibus (*Pat*) *RParl* III 407 (cf. ib. I 285a [**1312**]: *soient les billes terminez que liverez serront en Parlement*); s**1397** Henricus dux Herfordie proposuit unam bullam appellacionis de summa prodicione contra Thomam ducem Northfolchie *V. Ric. II* 144; s**1453** si ~a dicta transiret, sive evaderet domum illam [sc. Inferiorem Parliamenti] absque modificatione ulla *Reg. Whet.* I 93; **1587** vobis..auctoritatem..concedimus..cum dictis dominis [etc.] nostri regni Hibernie ad Parliamentum nostrum venire consuetis..de et super omnibus..articulis, materiis, ~is et provicionibus..per nos..mittendis..tractandi *Pat* 1302 m. 5 **g** s**1274** decanus Lincolniensis proposuit unam ~am excusatoriam [apud concilium Lugduni] quod terra Anglie in tantum fuerat depauperata..quod non possent levare aliquod subsidium Knighton I 270 (= Guisb. 214: cedulam excusatoriam); **1411** optulerunt majori et comparibus suis quandam bullam in Gallicis uerbis *BB Winchester* f. 13.

1 billare [cf. ME *billen*], (?) to chop or crush.

1302 in pomis bilandis ad ciseram *MinAc* 840/11 (*Essex*); **1305** in pomis ~andis et sisara facienda *Ib.* 840/12.

2 billare, to label.

1300 una bursa..que ~ata est in hunc modum: 'istam bursam dedit regi electus S. Augustini' *Ac. Wardr.* p. 351; **1302** diverse reliquie ~ate et non ~ate in uno feretro *KRAc* 357/13 m. 3; **1326** [in saccis] ~atis *CalPat* 339; **1343** in ij martellis pro dictis coffris firmandis et ~andis *KRAc* 290/23 m. 2.

billarius, (w. *ferrum*) billhook.

s**1314** ferrum in formam unci in extremo robusti ligni ~ium seu securim artifices componunt Major V 3.

billata v. 2 billettum 2b.

billerus, (?) kind of shellfish (*cf. belliculus, belliricus b*).

1339 in xij d. receptis de proficuo bilrorum sub Oldetrematon; et de iij d. ob. receptis de tolneto hostrearum ibidem hoc anno *MinAc* 816/11 (*Cornw*) r. 4; **1352** de xij d. de proficuo biller' in Veteri Trematon vend' *Ib.* 817/2 r. 5.

billettare [cf. 2 billare], to summarize in a bill or schedule.

1275 mandamus quod cartas predictas ab archa cyrographariorum extrahi et cum billitate [*Cal.* p. 180: †billicate] fuerint reponi et debita illa secundum legem.. Judaismi..levari faciatis *Cl* 92 m. 13.

1 billettum, ~a [OF *billete* = *peg*], billet block of wood: **a** (piece of) firewood; **b** curtain-rod; **c** rod of standard size; **d** swingle-bar (of harness).

a c**1300** habuit..bilettum et fagatt' pro focali *RParl* I 243a; **1327** lx^m busce de bilecto *KRMem* 103, r. 242*d.*; **1339** in centum de biletto empto ad ponendum in fornace de *lympett'*, x d. *KRAc* 462/15 m. 4; **1390** pro m bylettis *Ac. H. Derby* 12; **1455** ligneis fasciculis et billetis *Conc.* III 574. **b** **1290** in xxiiij anulis de ere, xij bilettis et cord' de canabo emptis ad curtinas mutarum *KRAc* 468/2, r. 8. **c** **1300** si que rethea in eadem piscaria inveniantur ultra assisam cujusdam billete per quam rethia predicta debent nodari et probari *IPM* 95/12. **d** **1311** in curbis et bilettis, iiij d. *DC Cant* (*Ac. Lydden*); **1340** in..iiij bilettis, ij *shidhames* et ij arcubus boum emptis *Ib.*

2 billettum, ~a [cf. 2 billa], schedule.

1317 que..acre mensurantur..et limitantur..secundum quod continetur in quadam ~a inter sigillum et scriptum ante consignacionem affixa *MonA* V 124.

2 note of receipt: **a** (of writ); **b** (of money).

a **1285** capiatur bilettum de vicecomite..in quo biletto contineantur nomina petentis et tenentis que nominantur in brevi, et..apponatur sigillum vicecomitis (*II Westm.* 39) *StRealm* I 90; apponat vicecomes ~o sigillum suum *Fleta* 151; **1292** profert quoddam bilettum brevis predicti sigillatum sigillis..militum..tunc ibidem presencium, eo quod.. vicecomes bilettum predictum sigillare contempsit *SelCKB* II 123 (cf. ib. V 120); **1293** profert quamdam ~am quodam sigillo pendente signatam, que testatur quod predictus vicecomes recepit predictum breve *RParl* I 94b (cf. *PQW* 227b); **14..** per inspectionem cujusdam bellecti sigillo.. vicecomitis consignati *Reg. Brev.* 13b (cf. ib. 31b: bilectum). **b** **1304** de iij s. de j quar' frumenti vendito ad opus comput' per j bilett' *MinAc* 997/15; **1329** per billetam Ade de B. testantem super compotum iiij li. *ExchScot* 162; **1428** custumarii et collectores billatas †sigillatatas scrutatoribus.. directas quantitates hujusmodi mercandisarum..continentes faciant *Cl* 279 m. 11; **1514** in expensis..ut patet per billat' inde confect' *Ac. Durh.* 664.

3 sealed note serving as warrant (for protection).

1417 dedimus vobis plenam..potestatem ad bilnetas sigillo vestro signatas..omnibus..qui sub proteccione et defensione nostris existunt et qui pro hujusmodi bilnetis habendis penes vos prosequi voluerint..dand' et concedend' (*RNorm*) *Foed* IX 504 (cf. *RNorm* 187: literas nostras de proteccione habent pro bilnetis suis).

4 petition, bill of complaint or sim.

1285 summoneatur respondere de concelemento, ut patet in ~a *Hund. Highworth* 297; **1287** clamat per bilettum suum habere visum franci plegii et wlt respondere sine brevi *PQW* 2a; **1288** nunquam hactenus usi sunt bylettas de libertatibus suis in itiner[acione] ista proponere (*Eyre R. Chester*) *EHR* XXXIX 86; **1290** eas [excepciones]..proponit in byletto et petit..quod sibi allocentur *SelCKB* II 7; tradidit predictis auditoribus quoddam bilettum de.. burgaria domus sue versus predictum Adam *Ib.* 18; per bilettum questus fuit *State Tri. Ed. I* 5; **1302** optulit se versus magistrum W. ..de placito transgressionis per duas bilettas *JustIt* (*Durh.*) 226 r. 5; **1306** justiciam faciemus cuilibet conquerenti per billetum nobis porrectum *BBC* (*Swansea*) 181.

billicare v. billettare.

1 billio [OF *billon*, (?) *infl. by* bullire 3], **a** base coin (containing excessive proportion of alloy). **b** bullion, precious metal (gold or silver) alloyed with copper etc., used for coining. **c** store or storehouse of bullion.

a p**1280** dicitur..bilho moneta defensa que videlicet cursu caret (*Tract. Nov. Mon.*) *RB Exch* III 997. **b** potest.. allaium monete Anglie fieri ex solo bilhone veteris monete Anglicane, que sola per se..sufficiens reddet allaium in argento *Ib.* 999; **1282** custodes reddunt compotum de cc li. de billone remanente de cambio Waterford' *Cl* 157 m. 3 (*sched.*); **1284** empciones argenti tam cismarini quam transmarini et billoni facti in cambio *Reg. Pinchbeck* II 10; **1289** inhibemus ne a..mercatoribus bilhonem aportantibus undecunque apud S. Macharium, ubi cuditur..moneta nostra, ad ipsam monetam exigatis..pedagia indebita *RGasc* II 390 (cf. ib. 469: ad custodiendum bilhonem ne extrahatur de terra); **1296** in monetagio nichil, quia dictus bilo non est fabricatus neque monetatus *KRAc* 288/25; **1304** pro monetagio..denariorum integrorum monetatorum ..de predicto argento tam de billone argento cismarino quam argento transmarino cum allayo eidem argento apposito *Ib.* 30 m. 9; **1367** x m. auri in billone (*DipDoc E* 231) *Foed.* VI 553; **1369** in ~one *CalPat* 279; **1422** in..xxij coronis veteribus et xvij coronis novis in bolion' *KRAc* 301/19 r. 4; **1465** ad reportandum..aliquam bullionem, massam sive platam auri vel argenti ad cambium sive minetam deliberandam *Cl* 317 m. 28; **1472** absque aliqua ~one seu aliqua uncia de ~one auri seu valore ejusdem de argento..magistro minete..portanda (*Pat*) *Foed.* XI 735. **c** **1335** quod..possint deferre ad cambia ad ~onem et non alibi argentum in plata *Cl* 156 m. 11; **1355** quod unicuique liceat hujusmodi novam monetam ad nostrum valorem ejusdem emere, ita quod eam ad bullionem nostram deferat ibidem fundendam (*Cl*) *Foed.* V 813; **1380** emolumentum omnium monetarum nostrarum et ~onum ibidem *RParl* III 74a; **1397** mercatores..unam unciam auri de cuneo extraneo pro quolibet sacco lane..ad bullionam nostram in Turri nostra London'..deferant *Ib.* 340a.

2 billio, metal rod kept in ampulla.

13.. finita benedictione fontium, mittat sacerdos oleum sanctum in aquam, crucem faciens de ipso oleo cum ipsa ~one que est in vase olei *Man. Ebor* 16 (cf. *Man. Sal.* 14*; *Lib. Evesham* 96).

billitare v. billettare. billo, ~onus v. billio.

billula [cf. 2 billa 4], brief petition.

1452 supplicamus tuam fraternitatem portitori presentis ~e credenciam adhibere *Cant. Coll. Ox.* III 103.

1 billus v. 1 billa.

2 billus [cf. OF *bille*], (?) ball.

c**1330** minuti irent..post prandium in gardinum, duntaxat nec luderent ad ~os nec aliquid aliud (*Const. Redburne*) *G. S. Alb.* II 205.

bilneta v. 2 billettum 3. bilo v. 1 billio, 3 bullio. bilosus v. biliosus. bilus v. 1 billa.

bilustris [CL], **†biluster,** lasting ten years.

silui..spatio ~ri temporis Gildas *EB* 1; decurso ~i temporis intervallo Aldh. *Met.* 2 p. 69; quinquies ~ris temporum circulis..theoricam..transegit vitam *Id. VirgP* 29.

bilustrum, decade.

~o..turbinis necdum..expleto Gildas *EB* 12; ~um, decem annis *GlC* B 99.

1 bima v. bema.

2 †bima [(?) cf. binna *or* bunnum], dung-basket.

1297 in ij ~is faciendis pro fima carianda cum virgis ad idem emptis *Ac. Cornw.* I 18.

bimalis [cf. bimus], two years old.

s**1274** quamdam ovem Hispanie morbidam, que totam gregem Anglie morbi traductione contaminavit, que erat de ~is boviculi quantitate Rish. 84.

bimare v. binare.

1 bimatus [CL], (child) two years old.

~us.., puer ij ..annorum *Erf.* 2. 271. 27.

2 bimatus [CL], age or period of two years.

10.. a ~u, ab e[t]ate duorum annorum WW; tertium a ~u aetatis agens annum W. Cant. *Mir. Thom.* II 41; inducias sibi .. ad ~um indultas Gerv. Cant. I 432; s**1252** quidam infans qui in festo Exaltationis S. Crucis ~um in etate expleverat M. Par. *Maj.* V 302.

bimembris, twofold.

multitudinem ~i divisione partitur J. Sal. *Pol.* 439c; divisio entis in decem genera est prima, nec alia ~is vel trimembris prior est Duns *Metaph.* V 6. 2 p. 50*d*.

bimenstris [CL adj.], period of two months.

798 traditaque est [Martis stella] Cancro per ~es Alcuin *Ep.* 149.

bimus, bimulus [CL], two winters (i.e. years) old.

bimus vel biennis vel bimulus, *twiwinter* Ælf. *Gl.*; tanquam ~us aut trimus prima rudimenta docendus infantie W. Cant. *Mir. Thom.* VI 116; terretur.. / ut puer †bunulus [l. bimulus] virgis vivacibus (*Palpo* 452) *Ps.*-Map 120.

binare, to double.

†bimatur [? l. ~atur], †duplicator [? l. duplicatur] *GlC* B 119; qui dolet amissis rebus dampnum sibi binat D. Bec. 555; *to dubylle*, †bimare, ~are, duplare.. *CathA*.

2 to replough (*cf. rebinare*).

1260 sumptus..quos fecit in seminando terras, arando, ~ando et warettando *Conc. Syn.* 648; **1413** in crofto warectato et ~ato *Ac. Obed. Abingd.* 76.

binarius, the number two.

c**798** est tertia pars [sexagenarii] vicenarius, sicut ~ius in senario Alcuin *Ep.* 133; an ternarius ~io major sit J. Sal. *Pol.* 649B; numerorum..quidam est punctalis, ut unitas, quidam linearis, ut ~ius Gilb. VI 243 v. 1; hic numerus qui ~ius dicitur ab aliquibus infamis dicitur, quia ab unitate per ~ium separamur Bart. Angl. XIX 113; cum duodecim leunculis aureis altrinsecus per singulos istorum sex graduum secundum ~ium †dispositos [l. dispositis] Ad. Marsh *Ep.* 77; ~ius erit numerus aureus Bacon *Maj.* I 206; ita quod una minor post numerum ~ium remaneat Hauboys 436. 2.

2 pair (esp. contrasted).

tres copulas aut tres ~ios..ad hanc posuerunt Gir. *Inv.* I 13 p. 125; primo..contrarietas..~io famosissimo continetur, id est corporeo et incorporeo *Ps.*-Gros. 310; c**1363** illum infamem ~ium amoris et timoris (*Concl. Lollard.*) *Ziz.* 489 (cf. Wycl. *Ver.* I 100).

binda, ~um [AS *binde*; cf. benda 3], bundle (as measure): **a** 250 eels; **b** 32 skins.

a c**1080** iij ~as anguillarum (*Cart. Ch. Ch.*) *Cant. Cath. Pri.* 129 n. 3; †lunda [l. binda] anguillarum constat ex x stikis et quelibet stika ex xxv anguillis *Fleta* 73 (cf. *Eng. Weights* 10). **b** **1275** capiunt..†ad [l. de] quolibet bind' pellium ovium ij s., quod quidem bind' continet triginta et duo pelles *Hund.* I 317; †lunda [l. binda] pellium continet xxxij timbria *Fleta* 73; **1303** ~a, scilicet xxxij pelles, [det] j d. *EEC.* 166.

2 'bind', withe used in wattling or thatching.

1299 in iij byndis cc dim. fessiculis virgarum emptis ad eadem [presepia] *MinAc* 1079/16 r. 2; **1362** in xviij summis virgarum emptis pro roddis et sprendlis et ~is inde faciendis ad cooperturam domorum *Ib.* 840/23 m. 2.

3 bandage.

extrema debent ligari cum institis vel ~is, quod idem est Gad. 10. 1; fascie et ligamenta et ~e sint munde, molles, leves et suaves *Ib.* 123. 1.

binghaia [ME *bingehaie*; cf. haia *or* haicia *and PN Elements* s.v. *bing*], enclosed portion of waste.

12.. exceptis bladis, prato, ..blestariis et pastura de Rostadec, quam solam mihi..a Kal. Maii usque ad festum Exaltacionis S. Crucis ad *bingeheys* reservavi *Mon. Exon.* 42; **12..** in prato, bosco, bladis vel rationabilibus binhaiis suis *Ib.* 180; excipiuntur..quedam..sicut rationabilia defensa.. qualia sunt blada, prata, *bingeheyes* sicut ad oves; item ad vaccas et vitulos suis temporibus Bracton 222b; **13..** terram..cum tota pastura..exceptis blado, prato et rationabilibus byngaiis (*Ch. Cornw*) *Arch. J.* VI 393 (cf. ib. V 123).

bini v. binus.

binna, ~um [ME *binne*], bin, grain-chest (*v. et. bima*).

c**1220** confirmo..primam multuram [post] illud quod sursum inventum fuerit in ~a in molendinis meis *MonA* VI 281; **1263** ad granarium dicti manerii..dictum bladum portabunt et extra ~am super eorundem tenentium proprium pannum mensurabunt (*Ch. Abb. Cant.*) Thorne 1912; **1294** in stipendio carpentarii pro ~a facienda et mangur' *Ac. Man. Cant.* (*Blean*); **1307** cum libertate molendi super molendinum aquaticum proximo post id quod in bynno constat *AncD* A 13198; **1313** pro..~is, nattis et lathis emptis pro diversis granariis *KRAc* 375/8 f. 21.

binomius, having two names. **b** playing a double role.

similiter et una persona plerumque seu res quevis ~ia vel trinomia ex causis variis variis sic nominibus censita H. Bos. *LM* 1364; alii..eundem fuisse asserunt sed ~ium, et quem nos Gurmundum, Hibernienses Turgesium vocare Gir. *TH* III 38; Merlinus.. / repertus est binomius / Silvestris Calidonius (*De Wallia* 297) Higd. I 38; s**1186** dicens ei.."Andrea Johannes"; erat enim ex fonte baptismatis et ex professione monachili ~ius Gerv. Cant. I 338. **b** c**1376** necesse est omnem curatum esse ~ium: nunc Jacob, supplantando secundum vitam activam triplicem inimicum, et nunc Israel..rectificando..appetitus..bestiales Wycl. *Civ. Dom.* I 176.

2 (sb. n.) double name or title.

precentor, qui eciam armarius dicitur, ~ium habet, unum quia habet custodiam librorum et aliud quia ad ipsum pertinet regere chorum; unum quidem nomen est officii, aliud vero dignitatis *Obs. Barnwell* 58; civitas..ab imperatore Kaerglou nuncupata est;..dicunt tamen quidam quod Cla[u]dius ibi filium genuerat, qui vocabatur Gloy, ..ob quam causam dicunt illum..civitatem nominasse Gloycestre; et sic de ~io cedit in ambiguum *Eul. Hist.* II 260.

binus [CL], (pl.) two each. **b** twice the usual number. **c** two. **d** (repeated w. *et*) two by two.

utuntur..jaculis ~is GIR. *TH* III 10. **b** in quo..pelago ~i aestus oceani..concurrunt BEDE *HE* IV 14. **c** extitit in Roma binarum forte sororum / fama ALDH. *VirgV* 2352; postquam bis binis fratres solidaveris annis FRITH. 1251; binis miratur equis privatus haberi G. AMIENS *Hast.* 509. **d** rectores chori ~i et ~i per xv dies *Offic. Sal.* 31; **s1296** per diversa Anglie castra ~i et ~i captivi fuerant consignati *Meaux* II 262; **1398** quolibet percipiente j repastum, sc. j ferculum carnis vel piscis, ~i et ~i *Ac. Man. Coll. Wint.* (*Harmondsworth*).

2 (sg.) each of two. **b** twofold, occurring twice. **c** (repeated w. *et*) each consisting of two units.

suras cum poplite bino / abstulit ALDH. *Aen.* 95. 5. **b 9..** ~o munere, *twifealdre gife* WW; de ~a apostolorum vocatione M. PAR. *Maj.* I 94; precepit ipsum duci coram eo ..per ~am vicem *State Tri. Ed. I* 7; **s1346** ~am Gallici patiebantur repulsam AD. MUR. *app.* 246; **1383** in qualibet septimana ~a vice fiant disputaciones *Lit. Cant.* II xxxii; **1407** nullus magister..legat..ultra ~am vicem aliquem librum.. *StatOx* 192; **1456** unica aut ~a appellacionis usitacio *Ib.* 278. **c** arsis et thesis..aequiperante temporum exagio pariter ponderabuntur, hoc est ~o et ~o ALDH. *PR* 125.

3 (w. *lex*, by misinterp. of *bilegium* or sim.) 'by-law' (*v. birelagia*).

1450 W. N. fregit ordinacionem et ~am legem inter se et R. B...factam, viz. de bataria et garul[itate] *CourtR Blunham* (*BedsRO* L 26/54) r. 10.

biothanatus [βιοθάνατος], one dying (deservedly) a violent death (esp. suicide).

extraneus ab ecclesiae societate inter ~os [MSS.: ~as] reputabitur ALDH. *VirgP* 31; ~as, *seolfbonan* GlC B 118; **9..** †bictonatus, *selfbona* WW; **c1100** cum reprobis et ~is ab aequissimo judice damnetur in die judicii (*Chirog.*) ORD. VIT. V 19; regem..venabulis confossum..veluti ~um absolutione indignum censuerunt Ib. X 14.

bioticus [βιωτικός], worldly.

canonicus qui mente biotticus atque / lubricus ante fuit WULF. *Swith.* I 181.

bipalmis, two spans long.

cameropa frutex est ~is *Alph.* 28 (cf. ib. 131: tirsim.. †~en).

†bipartio, 'jeopardy', gamble (*cf. bipartire* 1c; *jocus partitus*).

a1300 etiam si apparentibus partibus quereletur et respondeatur in loquela sive per non tenura[m] sive per quamcumque †bipertionem [vv. ll. biperteocum, bipertijocum, bipertiloquum, bipertitum] cavilletur lis illa.. HENGHAM *Magna* 4 p. 8.

bipartire (bipertire) [CL], to divide into two parts or groups. **b** (dep.). **c** (w. *ludum*) to play 'jeopardy' (*cf. bipartio*).

~itum, †*herbid* [? l. *helbid*] GlC B 128; hanc ~itam vitae qualitatem hoc modo..dirimit ALDH. *VirgP* 17; **c790** dedi illi xc tributaria terrae ~ita in duobus locis *CS* 265; inter episcopum et Eudonem soca ~ita *DB* 359b; hos [Papas] utrosque Romani ~iti elegerant H. HUNT. *HA* VII 41; insulam ~itam, cujus pars altera..spectabilis est..pars altera horribilis GIR. *TH* II 5; [bona] inter ipsum et liberos ~iri debent *Id. EH* I 35; **1195** terra..que ~ita fuit inter eos per finem *CurR PR* 33; ~itum..signum est in quo dum sol meat tempus..mixtum reddit D. MORLEY 38; **1508** sepientibus..et facientibus foveam in villa de O. ~iend[o] eandem *Ac. Durh.* 660. **b** hunc librum ~itus sum BEKINSAU I 735. **c** jam violat Violam Croceus, ludumque bipertit *Babio* 179.

2 (p. ppl.) **a** occurring in two stages. **b** (of land) worked on two-field system. **c** (of document) bipartite. **d** (of monk) (?) following a mixed rule. **e** (of colour) party. **f** (her.) party.

a ~itus lapidum casus *Mir. J. Bev.* C 347. **b** de terris vero ~itis debent ad carucam octies viginti acre computari, ut medietas pro warecto habeatur et medietas alia in hyeme et Quadragesima seminetur *Fleta* 159. **c** **c1286** parti hujus carte ~ite penes predictos H. et L. residenti sigilla nostra apposuimus *AncD* A 2653; **1296** huic scripto ~ito *Ib.* 3527; **c1315** per hoc presens instrumentum ~itum *Reg. Dunferm.* 347. **d** **c1380** secunda secta dicitur esse monachi ~iti, cujus patronus dicitur esse Benedictus et regula quam ex ejus sentencia B. Gregorius compilavit WYCL. *Chr. & Antichr.* 656. **e** **1371** j capucium ~itum cum una pars (*sic*) *motle Pl.MemLond.* A 16 m. 6; **1391** una gonella ~ita cum russeto furrato cum agnis *Ib.* A 33 m. 2b; *partye*, ~itus, ut toga ~ita *CathA*; **c1550** cum sex zonis †biperti coloris *Reg. Aberd.* II 192. **f** **c1315** capa..cum scutis bipartitibus (*sic*) *Invent. Ch. Ch.* 55; **1370** duas pelves argenti..cum armis Anglie et Francie in fundis ~itis *Fabr. York* 185.

bipartitor, *métayer* (tenant receiving half produce) (Gasc.).

1215 consuetudine..illa sublata qua dicunt se non debere decimare antequam messores vel ~ores vel terragitores partes suas non decimatas receperint (*Conc. Burdeg.*) *Pat* 140.

bipedalis [CL], two feet long. **b** two-footed. **c** of a two-footed animal. **d** composed of two metrical feet.

sume lineam ~em NECKAM *NR* II 173; satis est bipedalis asello / cauda NIG. *SS* 89. **b** bestia ~is [gl.: sc. mulier], cujus cohabitacio cum clericis vetabatur antiquitus R. BURY *Phil.* 4. 61. **c** quia quadrupedum prohibet sua regula carnes, / ..cupiunt carnem bipedalem NIG. *SS* 2131. **d** nunc bipedali / carmine laudes /../ care, canemus ALCUIN *Carm.* 54. 1.

bipennifer, carrying an axe.

s1251 carnifex ~fer ipsum percutiens in capite misit ad Tartara excerebratum M. PAR *Maj.* V 269.

bipennis [CL], two-edged. **b** (fig.).

9.. ~is securis, *twilafte æx* vel *twibile* WW; **1266** remanserunt..duodecim ~es †pyceys [l. pycoys'] *ExchScot* 30. **b** ut..quasi sub ~i dilemmate..concludam GIR. *TH* I 13 p. 45.

2 (sb. m. or f.) two-edged tool or weapon, twibill, battle-axe.

quamvis..crebri accolarum ~es [pinum]..succiderent ALDH. *VirgP* 26; arrepto limali ~e [v.l. ~i] tria virorum corpora..humo sternens mori coegit FELIX *Guthl.* 41; ~is, *twibille* vel *stanæx* ÆLF. *Gl.*; marmor mausolei ~i percussit W. MALM. *GP* IV 183; jam victe gladiis cessere bipennes [*Irish axes*] NECKAM *DS* V 909; Dacha bipennis GARL. *Tri. Eccl.* 28; **s1251** [pastores] gestabant..gladios, ~es, gaesa, sicas et anelacios M. PAR. *Maj.* V 248; **1281** de..homine interfecto..cum quodam ~i *Gaol Del.* 35B r. 41; halbardae Gallicanae ~is Lethensis haud multum dissimilis est, paulo tamen est longior MAJOR V 3; **1553** bypennis Anglice *twohande sworde Pat* 852 m. 29.

bipert- v. bipart-.

bipes [CL], biped.

animal erectum, risibile, ~es, ab humana proprietate quis separabit? GIR. *TH* II 21; qui monipes advenerat jam ~es effectus sine omni baculi adminiculo R. COLD. *Godr.* 606.

bipharius v. bifarius.

biplex, double.

dubylle, ..~ex, duplex *CathA*.

biplicitas, doubleness.

a dubylnes, ~as, duplicitas *CathA*.

bipondus, weight equal to two *asses*.

14.. ~us genus ponderis ex duabus assibus appositum WW.

bipunctalis, consisting of two points.

angulus mathematicus est situaliter in puncto mathematico et essencialiter terminative in base minima ~ WYCL. *Log.* III 50.

birbicariolus v. berbicariolus.

birchettum [cf. *PN Elements* s.v. *bircet*], birch-grove.

1321 in stipendiis iiij hominum prostrancium hayag'..in birchett' de Thunderl' [*Essex*] *MinAc* 843/9.

birelagia, ~ium [ME *birlaue*], 'by-law', village regulation about harvest, pasturage, etc. (*cf. EHR* XLV 208–31; *v. et. binus* 3).

a1230 si contingat..in predictis [bladis et pratis] dampnum fieri, emendabitur..secundum consuetudinem ~ie *Couch. Furness* II 455; **1277** si averia nostra deliquerint in bladis vel pratis dicti W...sive sua in nostris.., ex utraque parte fient emende secundum birelegia absque placito *Ib.* I 84; **1298** per consideracionem totius byrrelaghe *CourtR Wakefield* II 48; **1324** birelagh' *CourtR Lancs* 34; exceptis legibus de burlawis *RegiamM* IV 39. 8; **1401** ad istud halmotum *le Birlagh'men* de Halton [*Lancs*] presentant quod R. D. [et] W. G. fregerunt eorum birlagh' ab antiquo usitat' *DL CourtR* 3/42 r. 4; **1575** ordinatum est per juratores..omnia bilegia preantea per ipsos facta de cetero fore vacua [*Suffolk*] *Ib.* 118/1829 r. 6.

birelagius, enforcer of 'by-laws', burleyman (Lancs).

1501 ~ii ibidem [*Halton*] *DL CourtR* 6/83 r. 9; **1508** burelegii et *mossereves Ib.* 6/85 r. 11d.; **1577** halmotum primum dominii de Wydnes...officiarii infra dominium predictum hoc anno:..berlagii J. Herne, Hamfridus Lynaker ..jurati *Ib.* 133/12 r. 1; **1569** byrelegos *Rec. Prescot* (*Lancs & Chesh. R. S.*) 174 (cf. ib. 145).

birellus, birillus v. beryllus.

biremis [CL], w. double row of oars.

~is, ordo super alium GlC B 102.

birettum v. birretum. biria v. 3 bera. biriscus v. bitriscus.

biro [?], barley and bran loaf (Wilts).

1340 ad iij *alripes* percipiet iij panes, iij ~ones, potum sufficientem *RentSurv. R* 700 m. 2d.; percipiet die Nat' Domini ij panes frumenti..et ij biron' fact' de ordeo et furfure *Ib.* m. 1 (cf. ib. 699 m. 1: ij *byrons*).

birotum [LL], two-wheeled cart.

circiter octoginta viris, aliis trahentibus, aliis impellentibus, loco penitus ~um moveri non poterat W. CANT. *Mir. Thom.* VI 92.

birra v. 3 bera, birrus.

birratus [cf. birrus 3], pleated.

1281 precipimus ut clericus quilibet in sacris ordinibus constitutus vestem exteriorem gerat dissimilem militari, utpote anterius et posterius non ~am [v.l. burratam] *Conc. Syn.* 914; **s1281** Martinus Papa capas fratrum Carmelitarum mutavit in album, que prius erant stragulate et ~e RISH. 97; **1300** si quis monachus nimis curioso..apparatu uti presumat, videlicet..vestibus buratis aut varii coloris *Ord. Ely* 10; **1346** nec tunicas..fissas aut botonatas aut ~as seu curtatas vel etiam nimis strictas induant (*Const. Prov. Ben.*) *Conc.* II 730.

birretarius, cap-maker.

de ~iorum acubus transversatis NETTER *DAF* II 84v; birrhetarius, *capper* WHITTINGTON *Vulg.* 66 (cf. ib.: nectrix birrhetaria, *cappe knytter*).

birretum [cf. Pg. *birreto* etc. (?) < birrus], cap (esp. eccl. & acad., used as symbol of investiture).

1238 nec camiseis lineis nec ~is utantur *Cart. Worc.* 475; **1291** si [decedens] non habeat ~um [v.l. pirottum] vel culcitram, vij dentur denarii (*Const. Sodor.*) *Conc.* II 176; **s1294** Celestinus papa..piretum et pallium exuens *Flor. Hist.* III 276; **1298** illud [beneficium] eidem T. contulimus ac eum de ipso per nostrum birettum presentialiter investimus (*Lit. Archiep.*) THORNE 1969; **c1366** horas..canonicas dicturi.. ecclesias ingrediantur non capucia sed almucia vel ~a tenentes in capite *Reg. Abed.* II 62; **1388** v duodenas et dim. de cappis et birettis..ad usum archiepiscopi transmittere (*Cl*) *Foed.* VII 590; **1415** te canonicum et prebendarium in eadem ecclesia instituimus et per ~i nostri tradicionem investimus canonice de eisdem [canonicatu et prebenda] *Reg. Cant.* I 136; **1417** per nostri burreti tradicionem *Reg. Heref.* 3; **1425** nullus bachellarius..utatur tena vel ~o *StatOx* 229; in signum quod omnes justiciarii illi taliter extant graduati, quilibet eorum semper utitur, dum in curia regis sedet, ~o albo de serico FORTESCUE *LLA* 50; **1447** Agnes..notatur super nigromancia, incantacionibus et sortilegio, inspiciendo flammiola et ~a hominum et mulierum *Eng. Clergy* 221; **1469** pro..~is, pilleis et aliis minutis expensis ad usum domini regis *ExchScot* 590; **c1520** ~is cum cordulis ligatis *ConcScot* I cclxxvii (cf. ib. II 89: byrettis rotundis); **1523** de..birettis sive pilleis vulgariter vocatis *French bonettis or cappes* (*TreatyR*) *Foed.* XIV 3; **1530** pro factura..unius †biretr' [*for king's fool*] de panno rubro cum frengiis blodiis *KRAc* 421/3 f. 6v.

birricus, made of goat's hair.

~a vestis, ex lana caprarum valde delicata *GlC* B 110.

birrum v. 3 bera.

birrus, ~a [LL (?) < πυρρός; cf. burrus], cloak.

agmina pullatis coeunt vernacula birris FRITH. 1304; **9..** byrrum, *casul* WW; obtecta ~o mediocri..devenit ad tugurium Gosc. *Wulfh.* 2; quia interiorem hominem veste sacerdotali..induerat, nunc exteriorem indumento superficiario sub ~o secretius munivit GRIM *Thom.* (*ed.* Martène) 1739 (= ib. *ed.* Robertson 42: sub habitu exteriori); *faldyng, cloth*, falinga, ..~us *PP*; *a slavyn*, amphibalus, ~us *CathA*.

2 rag.

non fodeas dentes festucis..; / birro, si sit opus, illos conterge fricando D. BEC. 1018; gladiorum ~is exterguntur mucrones *Itin. Ric.* IV 35; *duddyd cloth*, ..~us *PP*.

3 pleat, fold, skirt.

tunicam..~is [*gl.: geruns*] munitam NECKAM *Ut.* 98; acus..grossas ad †byrritricas [(?) l. byrri tricas] [*gl. gerun*] poliendas *Ib.* 101; **1264** habens secum in ~o camisie sue signum quod fuit captum de ipso panno *Rec. Leic.* I 88; **1288** cidit ~um tabardi sui *CalIMisc* 2296; **1330** pro indumentis suis habeant..supertunicam talarem sine ~is (*Ord. Hosp. Strood*) *Reg. Roff.* 637; **1344** supertunicas..clausas desuper habeant sine ~o vel anteriori apertura quacunque (*Stat. Cotterstock*) *Eng. Clergy* 287; **1346** tunicas induunt.. quidam..birratas ante et retro; quidam quasi per circuitum habent ~as *Conc.* II 730; (?) **1425** (v. bissa 2); *a skyrte*, ~um, gremium *CathA*.

birsa v. bursa. birvita v. berewica.

birwa [? OF < birota; cf. OF *beroete* (*dim.*)], cart-load.

1275 ballivus cepit..j navem et iiij birwas [*sic* MS.] turbarum *Hund.* I 307.

bis [CL], twice. **b** twice as many. **c** (w. *per*).

alta bis clamat ab arce ALDH. *VirgV* 495; ut bis in anno uno Pascha celebraretur BEDE *HE* III 25; bis literis suis, ter ore proprio, dominum..petens MAP *NC* V p. 224; **1283** bis per annum *Cust. Battle* 54. **b** tertia stellarum rueret dum portio praeceps, / lucida bis tantum manserunt sidera sursum ALDH. *VirgV* 2747; bis sexies *Id. Met.* 3; temporum discrimine..bis quaterno *Id. PR* 126; bis binis vel amplius annorum spatiis *V. Osw.* 424; bis sex sibi milia centum / sunt pugnatorum G. AMIENS *Hast.* 223; diocesis bis quaternos continens archidiaconatus AD. EYNS. *Hug.* III 1. **c** **1232** in fusillo..molendini fract' per bis reparand' *Pipe Wint.* (159283) r. 11.

2 two.

a diluvio scilicet usque in tempore Abram nongenti anni migrantur et supra bis xl [= 942] ÆTHELW. I 1; **s836** imbuit contra bis populos arma *Ib.* III 3.

bisaccium [CL], **~ia,** saddlebag, wallet (*cf.* OF *besace*).

1190 pro harnesio ad..equos et liura ad bisaces *Pipe* 2; **1221** in duobus paribus besacarum ad denarios nostros imponendos *Cl* 450b; **1228** besatiorum *Cal. Liberate* 101; **1251** detulit in domum Henrici..duas besaceas cum cc libris *IMisc.* 5/25; **1290** in j pare besaciarum, vij capistris *Ac. Swinfield* 181; **1328** pro factura duorum parium de †besandis pro argento cariando *ExchScot* 118; **1372** super empcione besagiorum cum seruris pro dicta moneta imponenda *KRAc* 403/446 m. 4; *walet or poke*, †risaccia [l. bisaccia] *PP*.

bisacutus, two-edged, two-pointed. **b** (fig., w. ref. to spiritual and temporal power).

regem..cultello bis acuto percussit H. Hunt. *HA* VI 14; **1331** *mattok* ~us (*Invent. Ch. Ch.*) *Arch. J.* LIII 274; **s1340** Galli..gladiis ~is vulnerati Wals. *YN* 279; **s1415** ut Anglici palos ~os ante se in terra haberent defixos (*Latin Brut*) *Eng. Hist. Lit. 15c.* 317; *scharpe of bathe sydes*, anceps, ~us *CathA*. **b** cur non Petrus adest hic ubi Cesar abest? / ..O gladius Christi quid bisacutus agit? L. Durh. *Dial.* II 394; **1206** ex ore sedentis in throno procedit gladius ~us (*Lit. Papae*) *Chr. Evesham* 179.

2 (sb. f. or m.) two-edged axe, twibill.

unus bipennem vel ~am deferebat W. Cant. *V. Thom.* II 41; habeat etiam ~am [*gl.*: *bisagu*] ad radicandum vepres [etc.] Neckam *Ut.* 111; fecit..unam plagam mortalem.. quadam ~a Bracton 138; **1284** pro uno besacuto et j *royne* emptis ad municionem ejusdem castri *KRAc* 351/9 m. 5; **s1381** cartas..cum arcubus et sagittis, ~is, bipennibus, gladiis et fustibus extorserunt *G. S. Alb.* III 324; *twybyl*, ..~a, biceps *PP*.

bisala v. besasa **b**. bisant- v. byzant-. bisarius v. bifarius. bisceps v. biceps. biscinus v. bissinus.

biscoctus, twice cooked (of bread). **b** (sb. m.) biscuit.

victualia..exercitui apportanda, panem scilicet ~um et farinam *Itin. Ric.* IV 5; **a1250** panis..de siminello ponderabit minus de wastello de ij s., quia bis coctus est (*Assisa Panis*) *StRealm* I 199; **1292** vescimini..durissimo pane ~o *Reg. Wint.* I 52; panis ~us cum succo citoniorum..istis competit Gad. 23 v. 1. **b** *bysquyt, brede*, ~us *PP*.

bise- v. bisse-. bisellium v. biclinium.

bisia, bird, (?) greylag goose.

majores [auce], que vulgari vocabulo ~ie vel etiam grisie [v.l. trisie] vocantur, cum bruma statim in grege magno flante aquilone advercantur Gir. *TH* 1 23.

bismalva [OF *guimauve*], marsh mallow or hollyhock (*Althaea*).

emplastrum ex semine lini, malve, ~e Gilb. I 27. 2; semen..malvavisci i. ~e Gad. 60. 1; ~a, alta malva, altea idem, laciora habet folia quam alia malva et alcius crescit, A. *wymalve* vel *marshmalve Alph.* 22; altheam aliqui ibiscum nominant, officinae malvam ~am, nostrates *holy oke* Turner *Herb.* A ij.

bissa, ~ia [OF *bisse*], hind, female red deer (*cf.* 1 *bissus*).

1130 reddit compotum de c m. argenti pro placito ~e *Pipe* 14; **1147** decimas de..cervis, ~is et porcis *MonA* VI 867; **1170** inquiratur..de his qui in forestis suis forisfecerunt de cervis et ~is et aliis bestiis salvagiis (*Artic. Inq.*) Gerv. Cant. I 218; **1209** captus fuit sequendo cum canibus quatuor ~as *SelPl Forest* 2; **1221** inventus fuit seisitus de una ~ia integra *SelPl Crown* 85; **1241** admittat venatores regis ad capiend' xv byssas *Cl* 382; **1387** capiatis..de qualibet centena pellium..cervorum, ~arum, damorum et damarum j ob. *RScot* 87b.

bisse [cf. bes], two-thirds (of *as* or other quantity).

bes sive ~e: viii unciae Bede *TR* 4; si per tria quid dividere cupis, tertiam partem trien, duas residuas ~em nuncupabis *Ib.*; **798** addidit quoque duobus diebus et sex horis et ~e unius horae Alcuin *Ep.* 155 (cf. ib.: ~e, id est octo unciae unius horae); †astera [l. altera] pars assis semis, duo tertia bisse Garl. *Syn.* 1580d; aliam rationem hujusmodi nominis [sc. bisextus] quidam compotiste assignant, quia ex ~e momenti colligitur Bacon VI 18.

bissenus [al. div.], **a** (pl.) twelve. **b** twelfth.

a contra bis senos certantes arte magistros Aldh. *VirgV* 568; bis senis voluminibus Felix *Guthl.* 52; annis jam ~is Ad. Eyns. *Hug.* II (*proem.*). **b** dum ruber in caelo bisseno sidere scando Aldh. *Aen.* 37 (*Cancer*) 5; sol illustrarat bisseno Scorpion ortu (*Epitaph. Athelstani*) W. Malm. *GP* V p. 398; urbs.. / quondam bisseno Cesare tuta fuit Neckam *DS* V 184; Garl. *Tri. Eccl.* 88 (v. bissex).

1 bissettus (cf. OF *bisette*), 'bisset' (gold thread or sim.).

1332 una zona cum filo auri bysecta (*KRAc* 386/7) *Arch.* LXXVII 138; uno pari garteriorum de secta bisectorum *Ib.* 139.

2 bissettus [OF *biset*], brown bread.

12.. unam micham monacalem et unum bisettum *Cart. S. Neot.* f. 139.

bissex [al. div.], twelve (*cf. bis* 1b).

dictio bissena dat in ordine grammata bissex Garl. *Tri. Eccl.* 88.

bissextilis [CL], bissextile (of leap year).

si ~is annus est, etiam bissexti diem postquam transierit augmentare memento Bede *TR* 22; **797** nisi forte bisextilis immineat annus, qui unum adicere solet seu solari seu lunari anno, ut aestimo, diem Alcuin *Ep.* 126; huic [Julio] bissextilis auctori serviit annus Neckam *DS* V 201; huic dabitur quarto lux bissextilis in anno Garl. *Tri. Eccl.* 89; in anno ~i computetur unus dies scilicet plus in anno quam in aliis annis communibus Bacon *Tert.* 274; alius vero [annus Hebraicus] ~is seu embolismalis, qui per unum mensem lunarem xxix dierum et per unum diem non ~em.. excedit Bradw. *CD* 141d; J. Cesar..rationem ~em primus adinvenit *Eul. Hist.* I 63.

bissextus, bissextile, intercalary or (as sb. m.) leap year or extra day in leap year. **b** (fig.) misfortune.

[dies] quem..Romani sexto kalendarum Martiarum die, unde et ~um vocant, intercalare consuerunt Bede *TR* 38; **798** ~um..tarditas solaris cursus generat Alcuin *Ep.* 148; anno..proximo post ~um *Itin. Ric.* II 5; dies sic excrescens appellatur ~us Bracton 359b; **1282** ratione bisesti qui venire potuit infra annos predictos (*Decr. Papae*) *EHR* XXXII 53; *lepe yere*, ~us, bisextilis *CathA*. **b s1124** tunc bissextilis erat annus ac, sicut vulgo dici audivimus, super proditores revera corruit ~us Ord. Vit. XII 40 p. 464 (cf. ib. XIII 25).

bissia v. bissa.

†bissilla, (?) young hind (*cf. bissa*).

1261 rex mittit..venatores..ad capiend' sex bissas.. mandans..quod †~as illas [? l. bissas illas] capere permittant *Cl* 78 m. 19.

1 bissinus [cf. 2 bissus 2], made of hindskin or 'byse'.

1247 robam integram de bono..panno cum pulcra penula ~a et furrura competenti *Cl* 18; **1313** pro..corio biscino pro nodulis et laqueis pro eisdem [falconariis] faciendis *KRAc* 375/8 f. 44*d*.

2 bissinus v. byssinus.

bissona v. besasa.

1 †bissus, (?) *f.l.* for *bissa*, hind.

1293 cervum ~um damum damam *PQW* 223a (*sic* MS.; *but* cf. *ChartR* 30, m. 7: bissam); **1362** de..redditu xiij damorum vel cervorum tempore pinguedinis ferine et xiij damorum sive ~orum tempore fermisone *Pat* 266 m. 14 (*sic* MS.; *but* (?) l. damarum sive bissarum).

2 bissus [OF. *bis*], **a** brown (of bread). **b** bay (of horse).

a a1128 pistores qui cotidie habent ij panes albos et ij bisos cum cervisia *Chr. Peterb. app.* 167; **c1150** jejunans debet sedere in aere ante mensam et commedere bisum panem suum (*Reg. Reading*) *MonA* IV 44; pistores..faciant albos panes et bisos *Leg. IV Burg.* 60; **1259** [panem] bixum *Cart. Boxgrove* 172; **1303** panem ~um [*seized in bakehouse*] *Cal. Mayor's CourtR Lond.* (F) 152; **13..** emant tria quarteria frumenti..de quibus facient wastellum, panem levatum et panem ~um (*Assaium Panis*) *MGL* I 350. **b 1367** item.. unum equum ~um *Test. Karl.* 83.

2 (sb. m.) 'byse', fur of hind (*bissa*) or (?) squirrel (*cf. Horn Bk. Lond* 249*d*. [c. 1311]: *memorandum qe gris et bis est le dos en yver desquirel*); *v. et. byssus.*

1189 pro..ij penulis de *bisse* et xij ~is ad caputium *Pipe* 224; **1205** supertunicam de blou et ~o *Cl* 25; **1207** penulas de bysso *Cl.* 88; **1214** duas robas scarleti cum ~eis *Cl* 211; **1335** in j capucio de bysso empto *Comp. Swith.* 236; **1425** supertunica vel toga ampla sit et rotunda..sine ~is [? l. birris; cf. birrus 3] *MonA* VI 660.

3 bissus v. byssus.

bistarda, ~us [OF *bistarde* < avis tarda], bustard. **b** gannet.

1480 pro uno bustardo, ..pro ij caponibus *Ac. Chamb. Cant.* 136. **b** *gannte, bryde*, bisterda *PP*.

bisterni [al. div.], six.

a690 ~as..fisicae artis machinas Aldh. *Ep.* 5. p. 490 (cf. *Id. Aen.* 84. 2: oculi bis seni.. / bis ternumque caput).

bistinctus [al. div.], twice-dyed (δίβαφος).

curtinae..bistincto cocco sive vermiculo fulsisse describuntur Aldh. *VirgP* 15 (cf. *Exod.* xxvi 1); **9..** ~us coccus, *twegra bleo* WW 195 (cf. 212); non purpura utebatur aut cocco ~o J. Lond. *Commend. Ed. I* 5; sindonem et sericum et coccum bis tinctum R. Bury *Phil.* 4. 61.

bistinguium [AS *bystinge*], beestings, milk of newly calved cow.

vaccarii rectum est ut habeat lac vacce veteris..et primitivarum ~ium xiiii noctibus (*Quad., Rect.*) *GAS* 451.

bistorta, (?) bistort (*Polygonum*). **b** tormentil (*Potentilla*).

recipe nucis musca, gariof', ..~e ad pondus omnium Gilb. VII 301 v. 2; ~a virtutem habet constringendi, †consiliandi [v.l. consolidandi] et confortandi et valet ad concipiendum; G. *bistorte Alph.* 23. **b** heptaphillon, officinis ~a et tormentilla, nostratibus *tormentyll* et *tormeryke* Turner *Herb.* B i v.

bistucus [OF *bestik*], a disease of hawks.

~us dicitur cum pro fundamenti †obduratione[l. obturatione] bis simul egeritur Adel. *CA* 13.

bisulcus [CL], forked.

~um, †utrumque [l. utrimque] sulcatum *GlC* B 130.

bisus v. bissus, byssus.

bisyllabalitas, composition of two syllables.

Bacon XV 219 (v. bidictionalitas).

bitagius v. betagius. bitellum v. 1 buccula.

bitere [CL], **~i,** to go.

~ere, †irae [l. ire] *Erf.* 2. 271. 41; ~i, proficisci *GlC* B 123.

bithalassum, ~us [cf. διθάλασσος (*Acts* xxvii 41)], meeting-place of waters, spit of land.

†bythalasina, ubi duo maria conveniunt *GlC* B 231; cantus Sirenum et Tartarea bitalassa fallunt inscios H. Los. *Ep.* 42b; ibi mundi bitalassus (*Ruina Romae* 16) *Ps.*-Map 217; hic pelagus, pontum, freta, jungas †bicaterassum Garl. *Syn.* 1586c; insula [*Malta*]..ad quam difficilis est accessus propter †bitalissim, id est, litus in mare extensum *Eul. Hist.* II 92; *holme off a sonde in the see*, ..*roode of schyppys stondynge*, bitalassum *PP*.

bitirum v. butyrum.

bitorius, wren (or other small bird); cf. *berbicariolus, bitriscus*.

~ius, *erdling GlC* B 137; **9..** nomina avium..~ius vel pintorus, *wrenna Ælf. Gl.*; **10..** biturius, *wrænna* WW.

bitriscus [? Gall.], wren (or other bird).

9.. bitorius, *wrenna*, ~us WW; bitrisci volucris formam sequor et gero morem; / hec ut avis raucum meus edit sermo cricorem [*gl.*: *crie crie* vox est †bifrisci] R. Cant. *Poems* 260; regulus..qui et ~us dicitur J. Sal. *Pol.* 411d; biriscus, briscus, *a feyldefare* WW.

bittourus v. 1 butor. bitulus v. betulus.

bitumen [CL; cf. OF *beton*], mineral pitch, asphalt. **b** (fig.) cohesive force.

~en, *liim GlC* B 100; ~en, *anes cynnes lim Ælf. Gl.*; aspaltum dicitur quoddam genus gummi nigri quod a quibusdam dicitur ~en Judaicum *SB* 12. **b 705** omnes hii in Domino / ..erant juncti bitumine / germanitatis viscide (Æthelwold) *Carm. Aldh.* 2.75; fratres amoris ~ine in Christo constricti S. Sim. *Itin.* 1.

2 tar or pitch.

artifex subtilis expresserat sigillum regium ~ine formaveratque cuprium Map *NC* V 6 p. 246; **1288** ad vendendum ferrum, ..oleum, bytonum et hujusmodi (*St. Ives*) *Law Merch.* I 34; **1307** in j lagena butyminum, iiij d. (*MinAc*) *Econ. Condit. app.* 29; **1326** in flokkes emptis ad obstupand' cum dicto butumine defectus in baya molendini *Ac. Sheriffs* (*Yorks*) 49/13; **1375** in dim. lagena ~inis empta pro ovibus ungendis *Ac. Durh.* 46; hoc butumen, *terre* WW.

3 swamp.

1252 brokettus ibi transivit aquam et †resistit in quodam butimine *SelPlForest* 105; **1334** vastum quod vocatur Galgheved..non poterit appruari per acras propter remocionem ab omnibus villis et propter †bitumin *Surv. Denb.* 153.

bituminalis, (w. *lacus*) coal-pit.

in lacu ~i, que illi villule [*Chester-le-Street, Durh*] adjacet, se precipitem dedit, ubi dimersus occubuit R. Cold. *Godr.* 108.

bituminare, to caulk with pitch or sim.

ligna arcae levigata et ~ata Bede *Tab.* 444; cum [Alexander]..angusta viarum obstrueret molibus ~inatis *Flor. Hist.* I 65; fecit Noe arcam..intus et extra ~atam *Eul. Hist.* I 26; **1351** in salario j hominis †bitumantis parietes *Ac. Chamb. Chesh.* 197.

bituminarius, dauber.

dawber or cleyman, argillarius, butymarius *PP*.

bituminosus, of asphalt. **b** swampy.

in lacum ~um qui et Mare Mortuum et Sterile dicitur Gir. *TH* II 9. **b s1109** submerso palefrido in quodam luto ~o M. Par. *Min.* I 213; pastura †butinnosa *Surv. Denb.* 6.

Biturigiacus, sort of vine (Pliny *NH* xiv 4. 27).

[vites] †Biculbite..turbines..et calores optime sustinent Bart. Angl. XIX 180.

bivialis, a double-faced, false. **b** (?) approaching from two directions.

a si tibi suspectus sit iners bivialis amicus / qui te colloquiis absentem turpet amaris D. Bec. 823. **b** pro domino pugnes..; / ejus amore cadas biviali morte peremptus *Id.* 1325.

bivium [CL], road-fork. **b** (fig.) parting of the ways, choice of alternatives (*cf.* Isidore *Etym.* I 3. 7). **c** (fig.) dilemma, ambiguity.

iste pullus in ~io ligatus stabat Bede *Luke* 568; ~ium vel ~ia, *twiweg Ælf. Sup.*; **c1400** [canalis] ~ium pertransiens *Mon. Francisc.* I 510; ~ium, *a gaytschadyls*, ~ius, *a gateschedelle* WW. **b 799** tu vero, qui sedes in ~io, quare nihil demandasti illi qui habitat in Maresa? [cf. *Gen.* xxxviii 14] Alcuin *Ep.* 181; Gerbertus..cum Pytagoricum ~ium attigisset, ..profugit Hispaniam W. Malm. *GR* II 167; Y literam Pythagoras invenit ad exemplum humane vite, cujus prior virgula primam significat etatem incertam; ~ium, quod superest, ab adolescentia incipit, cujus dextera pars ardua, ..sinistra facilior.. Gerv. Tilb. I 20 p. 903;

figure Pythagorice ~ium R. Bury *Phil.* 4. 52; curritur in bivio; via namque vel ampla vel arta / . .erit Vinsauf *PN* 206. **c** in bivio ponor, binas amo; ducere conor / unam, vel neutram Serlo Wilt. 7. 1; ponitur in bivio qui lites cum pare format D. Bec. 513 (cf. ib. 1493).

bixus v. 2 bissus. bizant- v. byzantus. bizus v. 1 buteo. blacarius v. bladarius. blacta v. blatta.

Blacus, Wallachian, Vlach.

juxta terram Pascatyr sunt ~i [v.l. Balchi] de Blacia [v.l. Balchia] majore, a quo venerunt ~i in terram Assani inter Constantinopolim. .et Hungariam minorem Bacon *Maj.* I 367.

blada [? cf. bleda], lump (*cf.* Eng. 'blad').

1272 quatuor ~as cere *Liberate* 48 m. 11.

bladalis, a for carrying corn. **b** for grinding corn.

a 1344 in j carecta ~i et j carecta fimali *MinAc* 1082/5 r. 4 (2). **b** c1330 molendinum aquaticum ~e *AncD* B4859; 1574 *Pat* 1109 m. 25.

bladare, to sow with corn.

v acre terre. .cum frumento ~ate fuerunt *Entries* 561.

bladarius, for grinding corn.

†a1128 ecclesiam de Mousterol cum decimis bladi. .et molendinorum ~iorum (*Ch. S. Evroul*) Ord. Vit. *app.* xi p. 204 (= *Regesta* 1594); 1220 decimam theolonii molendini mei †blacarii [? l. blatarii] de Ewyas *MonA* VI 491; a1280 inter stagnum molendini ~ii et stagnum molendini fullonarii *Cart. Cockersand* 878.

2 (sb. m.) corn-dealer.

1303 cum Roberto Box ~io *Cal. L. B. Lond.* B 126; 1351 civis et ~ius Londonie *Reg. Roff. Ep.* I 85; 13. . quod nullus ~ius nec regratores aliorum victualium exeant civitatem ad emenda victualia *MGL* I 250 (= ib. 270: *mongere de blee*).

bladata v. imbladare.

bladatura, sowing or crop of corn.

1246 rex. .perdonavit ei xlviij s. qui ab eo exiguntur pro bladura cujusdam assarti *Cl* 384; 1292 clamant esse quieti de ~a tam de purpresturis quam de assartis in propriis dominicis terris suis *TRForestProc.* 14 m. 1; c1300 assignavimus. .terram. .cum domibus ibidem et tota ~a *Reg. Malm.* II 377; 1354 abbas. .perdonavit populo suo. . omnimodas transgressiones de foresta, tam de ~a quam de viridi et venatione (*CoramR*) *G. S. Alb.* III 49.

bladdus, bladeum v. bladum a.

bladifer, a for carrying corn. **b** for grinding corn.

a 1282 in corba ~fera empta *Ac. Man. Wint.* (*Michelmersh*); 1308 ad ij saccos ~feros *Crawley* 262; 1356 in j sporta ~fera *Ac. Obed. Abingd.* 8. **b** 1473 pro redditu capitis molendini ~feri *DCCant. Ac. Pri.* xvii 12; 1584 molendinum ~ferum *Pat* 1247 m. 8.

bladimentum, sowing of corn (*cf. imbladamentum*).

1215 in ~is et vastis boscorum *MonA* I 392.

bladium, (?) crop of wheat (C.I.); *cf. bladum.*

c1190 cum stramine unius ~ii, sc. frumenti, ad focum monachi ibi morantis *Cart. INorm.* 390 (cf. ib. 391).

bladonicus, for grinding corn.

1319 de iiij criblis farine avenarum de molendino ~o ejusdem W. de Ulverston [*Lancs*] *MonA* VI 556.

bladum [cf. OF *ble*], corn, grain (esp. wheat). **b** growing corn, crop. **c** (dist. as wheat, beans etc.). **d** wheat, w. ref. to use in bread. **e** corn paid as toll.

c1080 totam decimam de. .Elham, . .de bleio et de pasnagio et de molendinis (*Ch. Rochester*) *MonA* I 164; c1150 careta honerata ~o *Cart. Glam.* 96; c1185 molendinum . .de ~o et aliud *fulerez Rec. Templ.* 127; 1198 videnda sunt . .essarta. .imbladata. .et quo ~o vel legumine imbladata sint (*Regard. Forestae*) R. Howd. IV 65; c1200 omnes decimas ~i et leguminum *Chr. Battle* 190; 1222 debet. .j carrum . .ad portandum durum ~um et aliud ad portandum molle ~um *Dom. S. Paul.* 42; 1276 capiunt passagium. .de quolibet quarterio duri ~i j d. et de quarterio avene ob. *Hund.* I 105; 1236 visores empcionis instauri et ~i ad semen *KRMem* 14 r. 13*d.*; c1257 excepto ~o meo dominico *Reg. Brechin* I 5; 1279 nullus mercator extraneus emat infra burgum de homine extraneo bladea (*New Ross*) *BBC* 287; 1331 si caretta frangit eundo ad grangium, ita quod bladdus . .deterioratur *Ext. Guern.* 67; quisquiliae sunt purgamina ~orum *Alph.* 152; hoc ~um, *corne* WW. **b** iiii carrucatas de blato *DB* II 274; 1194 quod redderent. .~a sua que injuste asportaverunt *CurR RC* I 4; 1226 muros faciant ad includendum ~a vel prata *Melrose* I 227; c1250 taurus quidam ibat quotidie per prata et ~a ubicumque voluit Eccleston *Adv. Min.* 105; 1313 ~a crescentia que sunt de manuopere felonis non debent custodiri usque ad etatem heredis *Eyre Kent* I 87; 1319 tam in via quam in ~is crescentibus sanguis. .iter illorum patefecit *SelCKB* IV 90; 1352 secundum ~um [? *summer-sown corn*] *Comp. Worc.* I 67; c1370 blādo vastato, vineto non reparato [*gl.*: ~um dicitur seges dum est viridis in ~is et foliis existens] (J. Bridl.) *Pol. Poems* I 173, 175; ut blāda cardo nocens minuit, si non minuatur Gower *VC* V 601. **c** ~um. . valuit xxiiij li. . .in frumento et ordeo et fabis et avena et brasio *RDomin.* 5; 1221 xiiij quarteria ~i tam frumenti quam alteriusmodi *PlCrGlouc* 26; 1242 de xxxix quartariis . .frumenti et siliginis et ii quartariis. .ordei et lx quartariis . .v ene de blado anni xxv *Pipe* 118; 1296 de quolibet crannoco frumenti, fabarum, pisarum et cujuslibet alterius ~i *Pat* 115 m. 8; 1500 duas partes garbarum decimalium omnium ~orum avenaceorum, ordeaceorum, †piscareorum [? l. pisaceorum], †selateorum [? l. fabaceorum], et sigulaceorum *Cart. Cockersand* 1164. **d** 1190 mercator. .non potest emere in exercitu. .~um nisi similiter de illo panem fecerit (*Concord. Messan.*) R. Howd. III 60; a1190 panis de toto ~o debet esse bonus, ita quod nihil inde subtrahatur (*Assisa Panis*) *Growth Eng. Indust.* I 568; a1250 panis de deteriori ~o excedit wastellum de j d. (*Assisa Panis*) *StRealm* I 199; 13. . omnis panis de sordido frumento ut de ~o integro et de omni ~o (*Vellum Bk. Leic.*) *EHR* XIV 504. **e** 1288 michi tenebatur in ij quarteriis ~i tolneti. .de quodam molendino aquatico provenientis *AncD* C 6669; 1340 de xlv s. receptis de ~o S. Egidii de anno supradicto *Ac. Durh.* 202; 1523 ~um S. Egidii vel S. Marie Magdalene *Ib.* 255.

bladura v. bladatura.

blaëreticus, for grinding corn.

1237 pro palis. .ad aquam dividendam inter molendinum fulleric' et molendinum blaeric[ium] *KRAc* 501/18 m. 3; 1337 molendinum aquaticum blaer' *Capt. Seis. Cornub.* m. 21*d.*; 1377 molendinum ~um *Cl* 217 m. 38 (cf. *Cl* 268 m. 12).

blaëria [OF *blaerie*], corn due (Norm.).

1200 sciatis nos concessisse. .~iam de Cadomo habendam et tenendam. .reddendo inde annuatim x bisant' *RChart* 35.

blaese, with a lisp.

loqui. .blese ex proposito *AncrR* 69.

blaesus [CL < βλαισός], stammering, lisping. **b** (fig.) honeyed (of speech), fair-spoken.

blessus, *stom GlC* B 144; blessos ac balbos, qui scaevis verba loquelis / fantes corrumpunt Aldh. *VirgV* 1087; blesus, *†plips* [l. *wlips*], Ælf. *Gl.*; facit linguam cespitare et ~am vel traul' Gad. 121. 1. **b** lenibus et blesis sermonibus atque politis / . .loquuntur iniqui D.Bec. 767; ponere, nate, cave lites sub judice bleso *Id.* 1553; compositis ~i sermonis lenociniis utendo Neckam *NR* II 190; 1282 ~is Herefordensis episcopi labiis fidem adhibuisse vestra reverentia videbatur Peckham *Ep.* 306; c1370 seduus et blesus, hircus genitalia lesus [*gl.*: ~us est aliquis qui habet verba delectabilia et pulchra, falsa tamen] (J. Bridl.) *Pol. Poems* I 183, 185.

blanca v. blancus, blatta 2b.

blancare, to white-taw.

1309 in coreo unius porci mortui de morina ~ando ad sellam carectariam *Ac. Man. Wint.* (*Stockton*).

blanceus v. blancus.

blanchettus, ~a [OF *blanchet, blanket*], (piece of) 'blanket', white woollen cloth. **b** blanket (for bed).

c1180 pro. .vj alnis de ~o *FormA* xv; 1207 ad portandum burellos et bluettos et blankettos nostros *Cl* 82; 1212 pro cc. .ulnis de ~o tincto in grana ad sambucas *Pipe* 43; 1235 fieri faciatis tres bonas blaunchettas et tres bonos haubergettos et eos. .bene tingi faciatis in grana *Cl* 73; 1254 fecit unum blanketum et fuit in prima parte bona trama. .et alibi in locis pluribus debilis trama *Rec. Leic.* I 68; 1265 pro iij quarteriis blancetti pro camera ix d. (*RHosp*) *Manners* 74; 1296 unum par caligarum de blanketo et duo paria pedulorum similiter de blanketo *Obs. Barnwell* 196; 1303 de duobus pannis de blaunketo ad lectum *Ac. Exec. Ep. Lond.* 57; c1330 conversus. .habebit vestem clausam de blanketo denigrato *Cust. Cant.* I 278; 1371 octo peceas blanketti stricti de Gildeford *Pat* 284 m. 13; 1399 concessimus. .fratri J. S. ordinis Fratrum Minorum octo ulnas de russeto et octo ulnas de blanketo pro vestura sua *Pat* 352 m. 34. **b** 1303 de uno blaunketo, tribus *coverlys*, duobus chalone (*sic*) et uno *canevaz Ac. Exec. Ep. Lond.* 57; 1382 quinque paria linthiaminum et duos blanketos pro uno lecto (*Cl*) *Foed.* VII 356; 1405 c paria linthiaminum et blanketorum *Test. Ebor.* III 31; 1417 unum par blankettorum *Reg. Cant.* II 106.

2 white lead (*cf. abarath*).

blaunchet, cerusa idem *SB* 13.

blanchiatura, 'blanching' (testing by assay) or 'blanch-farm' (v. *blancus* 2).

1236 demandam viij li. quam faciunt. .vicecomiti Oxonie pro ~a comitatus Oxonie *Cl* 396; 1272 tenuit burgum [de Walingford]. .et valet per annum xl li. et x sol. pro blanchura *IPM* 42/1 r. 2; 1324 T. comes Lancastrie. .concessit x s. iiij d. redditus exeuntes de quibusdam tenementis in villa de Caldeyton [*Derb*]. .cum ~a redditus predicti, recipiend' per pondus, sic ut dictus comes eum recipere solebat *Pat* 160 m. 12.

blancum v. vinum.

blancus [OF *blanc*], white. **b** (in proper names).

1278 sicut ~um cheminum [(?) *chalk road*] ducit versus Tuewelgate. .et sic ad ~um cheminum de Warneford (*Compositio*) *Reg. Wint.* 1286–1304 652 (cf. ib. 718; *ChartR* II 367); 1418 lego. .unam tunicam †blancam [? l. blaveam] seu blodii coloris *Reg. Heref.* 44; 1442 j vestimentum *cheker* coloris albi et †blanci [l. blavei] *Test Ebor.* II 88. **b** Blancus [habet] vi domos *DB* II 104; Dimidius Blancus [habet] j domum *Ib.* 106; s1188 ad Blancham Guardam [*Palestine*] Diceto *YH* II 56; s1239 Blanchum Castrum [*Blane Castle*] in Wallia M. Par. *Maj.* III 619; 1242 Blanca Landa [*Northumb*] *CalPat* 270.

2 a 'blanched' (tested by assay). **b** 'blanch' (payable in 'blanched' silver or the equivalent). **c** (sb. n.) 'blanched' silver.

a reddit xii libras ~as de xx in ora *DB* I 39b; modo [valet] viii [li.] blanc' et xx sol. ad numerum *Ib.* II 131; [valet] lxxxx solidos blancas (*sic*) *Ib.* 135; 1130 vic. reddit compotum de xx m[arcis] arg[enti] bl[ancis] de firma de C. *Pipe* 40; 1156 debet xli li. bl[ancas] et xxx li. et viii s. numero *Pipe* 8; 1199 reddendo. .ccc libras sterlingorum ~orum (*Ch. London*) *MGL* II 250; 1199 reddendo per annum c octo li. sterlingorum blanceas de civitate Norwic' *RChart* 20b; 1204 terram de Brudeham de qua nobis reddi solebant per annum l solidi blanc' *Ib.* 141b; 1213 reddendo ad scaccarium nostrum xl libras ~as et x libras numero *BBC* (*Andover*) 229; 1222 computate vicecomiti Wiltes' in firma manerii de Mere ciiij^{xx} libras blanch' *Cl* 521a; s1270 cum [cives] temporibus transactis solvissent. .ccc libras sterlingorum ~orum, de cetero solvent cccc libras sterlingorum computatorum *Leg. Ant. Lond.* 124. **b** 1167 [debet] pro suo supplemento de firma bl[anca] lxxiiii s. et iiii d. numero *Pipe* 40; constat. .quid sit quasdam firmas solvi ~as, quasdam numero; firma quidem ~a solvitur cum ipsa, facto examine, dealbatur *DialScac* II 4E. **c** 1169 debet iiii li. et x s. pro ~o firme *Pipe* 69; 1205 in puram. .elemosinam. . solutam ab omni. .exactione seculari et de ~o quod ad scaccarium inde reddi deberet *RChart* 158b; 1242 rex perdonavit eidem N. blanc[um] tocius corporis comitatus Ebor' usque ad summam xl li., et de residuo predicti blanci dedit respectum *KRMem* 20 r. 12.

blande [CL], soothingly.

dum te ipsum forsan ~e decipiendo in propriam perniciem tibi male blandiendo mentiris Gir. *GE* II 8.

blandescere, to grow mild.

blandescit aspectus ut limes aurore J. Howd. *Cant.* 319.

†blandevus, (?) for *blandus* (*cf. grandaevus*).

1391 verbis mellifluis et ~is *FormOx* 412.

blandicellus, flatterer.

a fager, adulator, blanditor, ~us *CathA*.

blandienter, by flattery.

profanas pestes. .salvatoris sanctuarium. .et irrepentes fraudulenter et ~er invadentes Ad. Marsh *Ep.* 115.

blandificus, pleasant.

13. . ~aque libens perstrepe organa *Miss. Westm.* I 361.

blandifluus, conciliatory.

epistolam hortatoriam et ~am. .misit Gregorius Elmh. *Cant.* 102.

blandiloquium, fair words.

s1168 rex [legatis]. .responsis prudentibus et ~iis satisfaciens Gerv. Cant. I 205; s1196 ejus ~io populus placatus obtemperat Higd. VII 30 p. 148.

blandimentum [CL], blandishment, fawning.

non tormentorum supplicio sed ~orum lenocinio natum. . flectere nititur Aldh. *VirgP* 35 p. 278; 956 (12c) caducis prosperis vel ~is hujus seculi minime gaudent *CS* 938; [canis] venienti domino occurrens tam latratu quam caude ~o letitiam declarat Neckam *NR* II 157.

blandiri [CL], to fawn or smile upon, soothe. **b** (pr. ppl.) palliative.

illa que tunc carnalibus ~iebantur obtutibus Egb. *Pont.* 2; 9. . ~itur, *geswæslæcþ*, adolatur, *oleccaþ* WW; ecce quam manifeste convincuntur qui sibi tam inepte ~iuntur Gir. *GE* II 2; cura mendosa est cura que ~iendo sedat doloris vehementiam Gad. 119. 1; ~iente nobis aurora Elmh. *Hen. V* 104. **b** cura hujus morbi est duplex, vera et ~iens Gad. 53. 2.

blanditia [CL], flattery.

quid. .infidelius est quam eum cui fidem debeas circumvenire verborum ~iis J. Sal. *Pol.* 481c; vicerunt ~ie mulieris S. Sim. *Itin.* 37.

blandities, mildness, allurement.

venit en ista ~ies in hamo, quam si deglutiero, preda sum Map *NC* IV 6 p. 161; s1260 tanta fuit serenitas aeris et continua ~ies quod estivales. .iminere diceres amenitates *Flor. Hist.* II 461; 1415 quam nec allectiva ~ies nec consumptiva severitas potuit emollire Elmh. *Hen. V* 29.

blanditiosus, flattering.

fagynge, blandus, blandulus, ~us *CathA*.

blanditivus, flattering.

natura. .mentis verba medullis / blanditiva bibet Hanv. I 251.

blanditor, flatterer.

imbellium debellator, rebellium ~or Gir. *EH* II 15; presens blanditor, absens detractor Vinsauf *PN* 1297; ne robas suas hystrionibus, ~oribus. .vel menestrallis. .jubeat largiri *Fleta* 81.

blanditorius, flattering.

per ~iam adulationem J. Waleys *V. Relig.* 3. 246h.

blanditractare, to pet or tame.

to cherische or dawnte, ~are *CathA*.

blandius (? blandis), for *blandus*.

est res. .exitialis / qua sibi funestis preponere blandia cogit D. Bec. 482.

blandurellum [OF *blandurel*], 'blaundrel' (kind of apple).

1315 in vj^{c} blaundurell', vj s.; in ij^{c} aliorum pomorum xiiij d. *KRAc* 376/5; 1390 pro blaundellis *Ac. H. Derby* 11;

1393 in blaundrell' et vino emptis (*Ac. Dom. Episc.*) *Doc. Coll. Wint.*

blandus [CL], pleasing, flattering.

thalami luxus et gaudia blanda tororum ALDH. *VirgV* 2016; **9..** ~us, *lipe*..~is sermonibus, lenis verbis, *lipum* vel *swet-wyrdum* WW; temptans siquo modo curiam Romanam ~is vel dandis sibi inclinare potuisset *Becket Mat.* IV 166; vir dolosus, ~us, meticulosus GIR. *EH* II 15; ~is principum verbis allectus *Id. PI pref.* 1 p. 57.

blanius v. blavus. blas v. blax. blaselardus v. 1 baselardus.

blaserius [AS *blæsere*], incendiary.

diximus de ~iis et murdritoribus ut augeatur juramentum hujus abnegationis tripliciter (*Quad.*) *GAS* 389 (cf. ib. 155: *blasigeras* et qui furem vindicaverint sint ejusdem digni).

blasphemabilis, censurable.

ne religio Christiana privando imperatorem jure suo..~e redderet nomen Domini OCKHAM *Pol.* I 279.

blasphemare [bibl.], to blaspheme against (sacred person or thing). **b** (intr.) to blaspheme.

680 cum Judeis Christum ~antibus ALDH. *Ep.* 4 p. 484; gratiam Christi ~ando BEDE *HE* I 17; ex contristare consequitur quod ~atur Christianitas LANFR. *Comment. Paul.* (*Rom.* xiv 15) 150; **s1187** crucem tenent qui crucifixum ~ant WEND. I 142; ne infideles..occasionem haberent..doctrinam Domini ~andi OCKHAM *Pol.* I 47; **1463** cum..nomen Domini sanctum blasfemaverit *RScot* 409b. **b** que objurgaverat ~antem, miseratur..tormenta..patientem AILR. *Ed. Conf.* 784A; ~asse putabant legatum ECCLESTON *Adv. Min.* 112; cum..vidissent ymagines Crucifixi.., statim ~antes et super ipsas spuentes..insultabant S. SIM. *Itin.* 26; **c1363** ut..verum esse concedatur quod impii Judei dixerunt ~ando (KYN.) *Ziz.* 26.

2 to revile, insult. **b** (w. acc. and inf.) to accuse.

10.. blasvemiat, *tælep, yfelsap* WW; magum..apostolos ..~antem AILR. *Ed. Conf.* 783A; **s1263** intercepta est [regina] a Londoniensibus et ab eisdem enormiter ~ata et exclamata *Flor. Hist.* II 482; ~at omnia que ignorat BACON *CSPhil.* 408; **1318** bonorum..inimico, leges nostras.. ~ante *FormOx* 43; ab aliis ~amur, diffamamur et derisioni habemur OCKHAM *Err. Papae* 958; *to reprove*, arguere, .. accusare, ~are.., *to schame*, ..verecundari, ~are, scandalizare *CathA*. **b** Anselmum in hoc a rectitudine deviasse nonnulla pars hominum.. ~avit EADMER *HN* 138.

blasphemator, blasphemer, reviler.

s1198 nos [demones]..potestatem accepimus in ~ores tantum Virginis Marie R. HOWD. IV 68; **1239** cum idem ~or noster ausus alibi non fuisset in nostri nominis blasphemiam prorupisse (*Lit. Imp.*) M. PAR. *Maj.* III 547; **s1290** rex..proclamari fecit ut omnes Judei, utpota..~ores fidei Christiane, ..regni sui limina vacuarent *Ann. Osney* 326; **1447** est..~or nominis divini, jurando frequenter per singula ejus membra (*Court Bk. Linc.*) *Eng. Clergy* 229.

blaspheme, blasphemously.

c1363 auctor ejus †blaspheme [? l. blasphemie] culpabilis (*Concl. Lollard.*) *Ziz.* 487; **1412** quis excusare posset istas sectas fratrum, quin dimisso Christi ordine ~e eligant minus bonum? *Conc.* III 344.

blasphemia [bibl. < βλασφημία], blasphemy.

ut contemtor divum meritam ~ias suae poenam lueret BEDE *HE* I 7; in omnes sanctos ~ias dicere OSB. *Mir. Dunst.* 19 p. 149; ANSELM *Ep.* 136 (v. anathema b); dum sibi laus Satane placet et blasphemia Christi NIG. *Paul.* f. 48. 2; **1178** illis..opponebant quod ab ipsis audissent baptismum parvulis non prodesse et alias..~ias protulisse (*Ep. Chrysogoni*) *G. Hen. II* I 205; **1267** non solum est error, sed heresis, quia ~iam inducit BACON *Tert.* 121; **s1308** unam..heresim et ~iam in Deo irrogatam omnes [Templarii]..sunt confessi, videlicet quod magister ordinis..a culpa..debeat absolvere suos fratres *G. Ed. II Bridl.* 30; **c1363** donec..celata diu protervia in apertas ~ias prorupisset (*Intr.*) *Ziz.* 2; juxta reperti unius vel utriusque lese majestatis et ~ie criminis qualitatem ELMH. *Hen. V* 5.

2 reproach, blame, accusation.

9.. ~ia, vituperatio, *tæl* WW; si enim interrogares et postea sciens comederes, ~iam aspicientium incurreres LANFR. *Comment. Paul.* (1 *Cor.* x 27) 190; carmina famosa, blasphemia, scandala nulla / emergant a te D. BEC. 32; ad commendationem ecclesie primitive et ~iam moderne GIR. *GE* 32; **1322** honor nobis..exhibendus conversus est in opprobrium, devocio in ~iam et reverencia in contemptum (*Lit. J. Archiep.*) BIRCHINGTON *Arch. Cant.* 28; **a1400** ad.. emendas faciendas nos omnino, minis saltem et ~iis, compellere nitebantur *Meaux* III 181; blasphemeas.. patienter tolleravit BLAKMAN *Hen. VI* 19.

blasphemialis, blasphemous.

s1085 ceperunt pullulare in Anglia thelonea iniqua et consuetudines pessime et juramenta ~ia M. PAR. *Abbr.* 173.

blasphemium, for *blasphemia*, reproach.

alium vero, quem dixi ~ium fugientem, ..aperta occuluisse dicit *Enc. Emmae* 106.

blasphemosus, blasphemous.

ex opposito..predicte conclusionis sequuntur multa erronea et ~a CONWAY *Def. Mend.* 1422.

blasphemus [bibl. < βλάσφημος], blasphemous, blaspheming (of person, or organ of speech or thought). **b** (sb. m. or f.) blasphemer.

s1140 homo..in Deum etiam ~us W. MALM. *HN* 485; os ~um usque ad dexteram aurem retortum AILR. *Ed. Conf.* 783D; si blasphemus fuero, mox placebo Rome *Poem S. Thom.* 89; nemo desperet de se, si sit scelerosus, / si sit blasphemus D. BEC. 197; diffidentie vitium, quo mens ~a desperat AD. MARSH *Ep.* 173. **b** quasi diabolico preventam spiritu ~am durissimis sermonibus verberaret AILR. *Ed. Conf.* 783D; blasfemum juste percussum gratulantur *Id. SS Hex.* 10; ~us eadem hora spiritum moribundus exhalavit GIR. *GE* I 32; **1340** ut sic inter ~os Christiani nominis.. gladius catholicorum principum convertatur (*Lit. Regis*) AVESB. 88b; licet omnes ~os Christi impugnare OCKHAM *Dial.* 525; **s1417** [Oldcastelle] ut ~us et fautor hereticorum pessimus mortis ignominiam passus est CAPGR. *Hen.* 122.

2 blasphemous (of act, speech, or doctrine).

s1138 incredibile..est que scelesta et flagitiosa et ~a in Deum..exercitus ille Scotorum egerit J. HEX. *HR Cont.* 290; Nestoriana nequicia, que ~a rabie debacchari presumpsit in Virginem R. BURY *Phil.* 10. 164; quod est erroneum et ~um OCKHAM *Err. Papae* 960; **1378** [quod] lex Cristi, cum sit..seductissima et blasfemissima, est summe.. odibilis WYCL. *Ver.* II 3; **1382** nonnulla heretica, erronea, ~a, schismatica..docere (SWYND.) *Ziz.* 334; **1389** nonnulla heretica, erronea, †blasfemia [? l. blasfema] et alia diffamatoria..predicare presumpsit *Reg. Heref.* 234; plura loqui duxit; dux suspendi jubet illum, / ut blasphema trucis igne probanda forent ELMH. *Metr. Hen. V* 1274.

blast-, blastr- v. blest-. blastrum v. plastrum. blata v. blatta. blatarius v. bladarius. blateola v. bracteola.

blaterare [CL], to bleat or squeak.

arietes crissitant vel ~ant ALDH. *PR* 131; [Lyolf, c. 1090] multas [capras et oves] vendidit et emit unam campanam; quam cum audisset..sonare, jocose ait..: "eya, quam dulce ~ant capre mee et balant oves" *G. S. Alb.* I 61; GARL. *Syn.* 263 (v. 1 blatta b); *to cry*, ..vespertilionum [est] ~are *CathA*.

blatro v. blettro.

1 blatta [CL], moth, earwig, or other insect. **b** (? misinterp. of Virgil *Georg.* V 242: *lucifugis..blattis*), bat.

~is, *bitulum GlC* B 143; de nominibus insectorum..~a, *nihtbuttorfleoge*, ..*eorwicga* ÆLF. *Gl.*; **9..** blatis, *bitelum*; blatea, lucifuga, *wicga* WW; **10..** blata, *hræþbita* [? *beetle*] *Ib.* **b** res eadem blata vespertilioque vocata; / hinc declamare garritu sit blaterare GARL. *Syn.* 262; *a bakke*, blata, vespertilio *CathA*.

2 blatta [βλάττη], purple dye. **b** (w. *Byzantia*) a sort of medicament.

blata, genus purpurae *Erf.* 2. 271. 55; **14..** cespitat in phaleris yppus blattaque [*gl.* purpura] suppinus WW. **b** blacte bizantle GILB. IV 201. 1; †blace bizancie *Ib.* 200 v. 2; sicut attrahit..blanca byzantia..melancoliam *Ps.*-GROS. 614; suffumigetur cum blancha biçantia, quia excitabitur GAD. 63 v. 1; blacta est squama piscis et invenitur in fronte piscis degentis in conca rotunda tortuosa; sed nos utimur blacta bisantea i. Constantinopoli que sic solebat dici *Alph.* 26 (cf. *SB* 13: sed nos utimur blanca bisancia pro ea).

blatteus, purple (adj.).

s510 coronam auream cum geminis et tunicam †bracteam misit DICETO *Chr.* I 90 [l. blacteam, *as* Sig. Gembloux]; retibus que [Nero] †baltinis funibus extrahebat FORDUN *Chr.* II 24 (= Eutrop. VII 9: ~eis).

blatum v. bladum. blatus v. blax.

†blauharnum [AS *blæshorn*], horn for blowing.

pecoris tintinnum et canis hoppa et ~um [v.l. *blophorn*]: horum trium singulum est unum solidum valens (*Quad.*) *GAS* 194.

blaun- v. blan-. blavettus v. bluettus.

blavus, ~ius [cf. OF *bleu, blou* < Frk. *blao*; v. et. blodius, bludus], blue. **b** azure (her.). **c** (sb. m.) blue cloth. **d** (sb. n.) cornflower.

viridi, fulvo, floreo / fucata atque blaveo / ut peplorum per pallia / pulchra pandunt ornamina (ÆTHELWALD) *Carm. Aldh.* II 163; **9..** ~um, color est vestis, *bleo* WW; accipe pannum lineum ~um GILB. V 232 v. 1; saphiri et jacincti et consimiles lapides ~ei BART. ANGL. XVI 101; color indicus sive venetus est color ~ius *Ib.* XIX 21; color..~ius, qualis est saphiri vel..hiacynthi, causatur ex multo perspicuo cum multo terrestri subtili combusto *Ps.*-GROS. 631; burneta ~um habet florem ut edera terrestris *SB* 13; **1399** quod corpus nostrum in velveto vel sathanae †blanio, more regio, vestiatur (*Test. Regis*) *Foed.* VIII 76; **1429** in tunicis..de eodem colore, scilicet de persico vel ~io *Reg. Brechin* I 48; **c1540** induti togis talaribus ~iis *ly blew* coloris *Reg. Aberd.* II 114; cappas sericas..de blovio colore auro textas MYLN *Dunkeld* 45. **b** arma terribilia, ..serpentem ~ium hominem rubium..devorantem in campo albo AD. USK 75. **c** **1207** pro lxxviij ulnis de viridi et de blefo..ad opus venatorum nostrorum *Cl* 97; **1231** quod..emat..ad opus Isabelle sororis regis tunicam, supertunicam et pallium de blevio de Ipra *Cl* 5; **1245** robam integram de bono ~io *Cl* 375. **d** cyanus a Gallis teste Ruellio ~ium dicitur; hanc ego herbam arbitror esse quam Northumbria vocat *a blewblaw* aut *a blewbottell* TURNER *Herb.* A IV v.

blax [βλάξ], fool.

a folte, blas, baburrus, blatus *CathA*.

blecchiare [ME *blechen*], to bleach.

1365 in uno panno ~iato *Cal. Pl. Mem. Lond.* (A 10), II 39.

blectero, ~tro v. blettro.

bleda [? cf. blada], measure of salt.

1268 in xiiij ~is que faciunt j eskepp' v windell' salis emptis, v s. iij d. *MinAc* (*Cumb.*) 824/7 r. 1.

†bledstodius, (?) *f.l.*

de inventis et pauperibus et abjectis positum est..sicut de bledstodiis [v.l. blodstodiis, beldstodis; *ed.* 'bastardis'] (*Leg. Hen.* 78. 5) *GAS* 595.

blefus v. blavus c. bleium v. bladum a.

blemire [OF *blesmir, blemir*], to blemish (C.I.).

1324 atrociter verberavit quandam Aliciam Leeste cum plaga et sanguine et carne ~ita *JustIt* 1164, r. 18.

blemna v. problema. bleodus v. bludus. blese v. blaese.

blesshaga [? ME *blese* (= *flame*)+*hagh* (= *yard etc.*)], forge for iron smelting.

a1172 concessisse..ad predictum manerium de Newent [*Mon*] unam ~am et carbonem in nemus suum ad ~am sustinendam *Cart. Newent* f. 50 (= *MonA* VI 1077: blessagham).

blessus v. blaesus.

blesta, ~ia [Norm. Fr. *bleste, blette*], peat, turf. **b** (w. *mora*) peat moss.

c1250 herbagium bosci, turbe et ~e et bruera valent.. xl s. *IPM* (*Northumb*) 10/18 (= *Cal. Scot.* I 1967: †blesie); **c1250** dedi..pascua et fenum et ~ias in wasto meo *Reg. Exon.* 1602; **1290** racionabile estoverium suum de jawonibus et blest' *AncD* (*Cornw*) A 8639; **c1300** concessi..totum estowarium suum de blesturis meis, ubicumque ~a jacet in mora de Retyr *Ib.* 9955; **1297** in ~a et bruera [in Nova Foresta] hoc anno *MinAc* 981/19 r. 4; **1307** quod ipsi foderunt turbas et bletas in predicta foresta [de Knaresburgh] *RParl* I 200; **1324** fidit turbas sive ~as pro fumar[io] suo super communam *JustIt* (*C.I.*) 1165, r. 19; **1416** factura turbarum et ~arum (*Ac. Bromholm*) *Norf. Rec. Soc.* XVII 76. **b** **12..** secundum longitudinem fossati..usque ad angulum de bleta mora *AncD* (*Berks*) D 173.

blestare [OF *blester*], to cut turf. **b** (?) to clear of turf, or to break up clods (in or for).

1281 appropriavit sibi communam pasture..in mora de Castr' [*Lincs*]..et..fecit ~are in eadem sine warranto *PQW* 412a; **1282** quociescumque ipsos contigerit ~are vel turbas fodere, ..bene licebit eidem abbati..ibidem ~are..usque ad medietatem totidem hominum et bescarum *Fine* (*Yorks*) 267/61/4. **b** **1285** ~abit [*Cal.*: †blescabit] per j diem pro j opere *Cust. Suss.* II 25; ista opera expendit in triturando, terras ~ando, blad' sarclando *Ib.* 26; **1321** debet blastrare per totum [diem] pro j opere (*Ext. Goring*) *Cust. Suss.* III 49; debet blestrare [*Cal.*: †blestiare] ordeum domini per duos dies cum j homine *Ib.* 65; **1348** in terris domini hoc anno ~andis apud Wy [*Kent*] et Plumpton [*Sussex*] *MinAc* 899/7.

blestaria, ~ium, turbary.

c1150 de una dim. acra, molendino fuleratico et ~ia ad dictum molendinum pertinente *Mon. Exon.* 42; **c1200** [concessi] omnia necessaria sua ad ignem suum de blastario meo ubicumque voluerint *Ib.* 64; **12..** blestar' *AncD* (*Cornw*) A 8627; **1324** est ibidem bruer' et blether' que val' per annum x s. *IPM* (*Norf*) 83 r. 11; **1476** fodebat blester' in communa de Bokenham [*Norf*] *CourtR* 192/52 r. 3.

blestatio (?) clearing turf or breaking clods.

1370 blastracio, falcacio et sarculacio: in blastracione hoc anno vij s. ix d. *MinAc* (*Kent*) 899/24.

blestatura, turf-cutting, turbary.

1281 clamat habere communiam et ~am in eodem [sc. in mora] *PQW* (*Lincs*) 412a; **1300** abbas de Bello Loco cepit per viij annos blesturam in Nova Foresta, set quolibet anno valet blestura xx s. *Rent. Surv. P.* 14 (57) m. 2; **12..** dedi.. duas dietas blesture in mora de Trewelles *AncD* (*Cornw*) A 9263; *Ib.* 9955 (v. blesta); **1389** cum estaveriis suis de blestur', fuger', turbar' et javun' ad unum focum *Ib.* 8698.

blestatus, (?) turf-cutting.

1250 blestiatus et katia (*of the herbage*) (*Wells MSS.*) *HMC Rep.* 12 I 318.

blestrare v. blestare. blestro v. blettro. blestura v. blestatura. blesus v. blaesus. bleta v. blesta, blita.

†bletarius, (?) for *blecarius*, (bleacher) or *blatarius* (*cf. bladarius*).

12.. Gilbertus Lam ~ius [*of London*] *Cart. St. Thom. Hosp.* 691.

blethera v. blestaria.

blettro [OF *bleteron*], shoot or sapling.

1215 x quercus in parco nostro de Havering' et de blectronibus quantum voluerint (*Cl*) *LTR Mem. PR* 132; **1233** prosterni facit blecterones *CurR* XV 452; **1246** xl ~ones de fago ad reparand' exclusas vivarii *Cl* 465; **1248** debet invenire..ad reparacionem cujuslibet gurgitis duos ~ones per annum, qui vocantur *weltren Cl* 127; **12..** pro truncacione unius blestronis *SelPlForest* 64; **c1275** in xxviij fagis et v bletronibus..prosternendis *KRAc* 467/7/3; **1298** quia prostravit †blottron' *CourtR Wakefield* II 24; **1307** quidam parcus de blectronibus quercus ubi nullus subboscus *IPM* 3/5 r. 9; **1353** brettones [*worth* 12 d. *each*] *CalIMisc* III 145; **1377** xij quercus voc' blatrones..ad magnitudinem j pedis squar' *KRAc* 462/5.

blevettus, blewetus v. bluettus. blevius v. blavus c.

bliauta [OF *bliaut*], sort of tunic.

1204 pro bliaut' ejusdem [regine] furranda..; pro operacione cape et bliaut' *Cl* 14.

blictrire [cf. DuC], to froth.

sporgyn, spumo.., †blutrio *PP*.

blida [? ME *blithe* = *joyful* (*iron.*)], siege-engine.

1241 ingenium nostrum quod vocatur Blithe *Liberate* 15 m. 6; **1244** mandatum est..constabulario Dovor' quod duo ingenia regis, ..videlicet unum ingenium quod vocatur Blideh' et unum trubechettum, recipiat et quandam domum competentem ad predicta ingenia in castro Dovor' reparari ..faciat *Cl* 219; **1244** quod iij ingenia regis, ~am scilicet, trebuchet' et multonem, recipiat a magistro G. ingeniatore *Liberate* 20 m. 3; **1245** venire faciat..iiij virgas..ad ~am regis et magenellos suos..et iiij coria tannata et iiij alba.. ad fundas faciendas ad predictas machinas *Ib.* 21 m. 2; **1253** ~as et alia ingenia *Cl* 204 (= *RGasc* I 379); **1257** maeremium..ad tres ~as inde faciendas *Cl* 32; **s1266** levatis circumquaque [apud Kenylworthe] machinis novem, que vocantur blidis, lapides jacere non cessabant, confringentes ex his domos et turres ligneas; muros et opus lapideum prosternere volentes, in nullo dampnificare poterant *Ann. Dunstable* 242; **1302** idem reddit compotum de j blid' sine corda *MinAc W. Wales* I 474.

blita, ~um, ~is [βλίτον], beet or other herb.

~um, *clate GlC* B 142; ~um vel lappa, *clate* vel *clyfwyrt* ÆLF. *Gl.*; comedat ~as GILB. IV 204. 1; herbe..humide ut.. lactu[ca], blitis etc. *Ib.* II 104 v. 1; succus malve aut blete *Ib.* II 77 v. 1; cum succo herbe que dicitur bleta BACON IX 69 (cf. Id. V 97: que dicitur bletes); de oleribus utatur.. spinachiis, bletis, lactucis GAD. 47 v. 1; cum foliis blete bullite in vino *Ib.* 27 v. 1; beta major vel bleta vel bletis, atriplex agrestis vel domestica idem; G. *arache blanc Alph.* 22.

blocca [ME *blokke*], block of wood (used as fuel in smelting lead).

a1307 in vadiis carectariorum..cariancium maeremium, buscam, ~as et alia diversa necessaria *KRAc* 260/19 r. 4 (cf. ib. r. 3: in vadiis prostrancium et scindencium *blokkes* pro bolis).

bloccare, to stock (a lead furnace) w. fuel.

1302 Philippo de Yal facienti bolas et blockanti easdem per iij dies, vj d. *KRAc* 260/22 r. 4.

bloccarius, (?) maker of wooden blocks.

1302 ~iis quolibet capiente per diem iij d. ob. *KRAc* 482/20 (*Linlithgow*) r. 7 (cf. ib.: item..custodi ~iorum et supervisori cariagii in bosco).

blocwalterius [? cf. ME *walten* = *to turn*], stoker (in lead furnace).

1300 in vadiis..lotorum et lotricum mine, scissorum busce, sarrar[ior]um busce, ~iorum, fabrorum, carbonariorum *Pipe* 145 (*Devon*).

blodewita v. blodwita.

blodium [? cf. ME *bloding*], black pudding.

1519 fratres comedentes in refectorio per mensem preteritum non habuerunt ~ia Anglice *puddings Vis. Linc.* II 110.

blodius [cf. OF *bleu, blou*; v. et. blavus, bludus], blue cloth or colour. **b** (adj.) blue. **c** azure (her.). **d** purple.

1316 j *curtepy* de bludeo (*St. Ives*) *Law Merch.* I 101; **s1345** dedit..unum lectum de ~io *Hist. Durh.* 3; **1380** unam peciam de ~eo de *banquers Test. Karl.* 131; **1391** pro j ulna et dim. de ~eo de Lyra *Ac. H. Derby* 90; **1402** una toga duplicata de rubeo et ~io (*Inq.*) *DocCOx.* 238; **1503** cum aurifrigerio..cum ~io intexto *Invent. Ch. Ch.* 130. **b** **s1405** equitando..in ~io chimera et manicis chimere ejusdem coloris existentibus (*Martyrium R. Scrope*) *Misc. Scrope* 307; **1411** capa..de velveto ~io *Lit. Cant.* III 112; **1418** lego..unam tunicam †blancam [? l. blaveam] seu blodii coloris *Reg. Heref.* 44; **1425** duos pannos ~ei coloris (*Pat*) *Foed.* X 346; **1432** septem deifice virtutes in puellaribus effigiebus..solis indute jubaribus super femora ~ia celestina (*Reventus Hen. VI*) *MGL* III 459; *blew of colore*, ~ius *PP*; **1488** pro v li. de colore ~io Anglice *blew orch* et *blew yonde* (*Ac. Eton*) *Arch. Hist. Cambr.* I 412n. **c** **s1399** arma de rubio cum ligamine ~io AD. USK 38. **d** **1560** ij virg' velv[et] *purple* alias blod' pro *le facing Ac. L. Chamb.* 53 f. 27.

blodstodius v. bledstodius.

blodwita [AS *blodwite*], 'bloodwite', fine for bloodshed.

isti sochemanni dicunt se habuisse legrewitam et blodewitam et latrocinium suum *DB* (*Hunts*) I 204; in quibusdam locis qui ~am, id est forisfacturam sanguinis, fecerit solummodo reus est; in quibusdam etiam qui patitur (*Leg. Hen.*) *GAS* 567; **1194** quieti sint..de ~a *BBC* (*Portsmouth*) 151; **c1250** cum merchetis et blodwetis hominum suorum *Reg. Aberbr.* I 263; **1450** cum..bludewitis, heryheldis et marchetis mulierum *Reg. Glasg.* 376.

bloma, ~us [AS *bloma*], 'bloom', lump of iron.

reddunt xx ~as ferri *DB* (*Heref*) I 185b; una ~a ferri de unoquoque libero homine *Ib.* (*Som.*) 87b; ibi molinus reddens ii plumbas ferri *Ib.* 94; **1294** in j blom' de ferro iiij s. quad. *DCCant* (*Ac. W. Farleigh*) (*cf.* ib. *Meopham* **1284**: in ferro de *blomyren* empto ad carucas); **1327** in cariagio xxxij ~arum ferri..ad..castrum Dovor' *LTRMem* 99 r. 141; **1330** pro carbonibus faciendis ad dictos ~os conflandos (*KRAc* 890/22, *Kent*) *Arch.* LXIV 156; **1352** de xxvj ~is ferri de exitu dicte fabrice venditis, precium ~e iij s. iiij d. (*KRAc* 485/11) *Ib.* 160.

blomerius, for iron-smelting.

1314 una fabrica ~ia in predicto bosco [de Barleia, *Lincs*] et una fabrica operaria *ChartR* III 259.

blomforgium, 'bloom-forge', bloomery.

1357 idem respondet de lviij s. iiij d. receptis de uno ~io et j nailforgio existentibus infra forinsecum boscum apud Spofford [*Yorks*] *MinAc* 1121/10.

blondus v. blundus.

blottare [ME *blotten*], to blot.

1433 eundem numerum, ut in hoc magis videretur suspectum, cum novo incausto renovavit et ~avit *Cl* 283 m. 4*d*.

blottro v. blettro. blous v. bludus. blovettus v. bluettus. blovius v. blavus. bludeus v. blodius.

bludus [OF *bleu*; cf. blavus, blodius], blue cloth.

1237 pro..ulnis de viridi, burnetto, pounacio, bluo de ultra mare..et pro..ulnis de bluo et viridi et burnetto de Anglia *Pipe* 81 r. 13 (cf. ib.: pro..iij burnettis, v blois, j russetto); **1239** abstulit ei quandam supertunicam de bluto que vocatur gulum *CurR* 120 r. 18; **1242** pannos suos, scilicet blud', rusettum et burellum *CurR* 123 r. 2*d*.; (= *Law Merch.* II 4: †bludium); **1286** j pannus de bleodo (*KRAc* 91/7) *Arch.* LXX 50; pro duabus robis suis de bleodo et pers' furrandis *Ib.*

bluettus (sb.) blue cloth or colour. **b** (adj.) blue. **c** azure (her.).

1203 j capam de *bluet CurR* II 180; **1207** ad portandum burellos et ~os et blankettos nostros *Cl* 82; **1253** capam de bluveto *SelPlJews* 17; **1267** capam de blavetto *Rec. Norw.* I 210; **s1268** bloveti vel burneti amiciebatur indumento *Melrose* 208; **1269** utantur..vestibus humilibus et unius coloris, utpote de blueto, russeto..et consimili *Ch. Sal.* 348; **1279** [roba de] blevetto (*JustIt* 645) *CalScot* II p. 44; **1279** in xiiij ulnis panni de blueto ad opus nepotum domini scolarium Oxon' emptis, xxx s. *Ac. Stratton* 108; **1295** iij pecie panny de bleweto *KRMisc* 2/1 r. 5; **1310** unam tunicam de albo blueto..unam tunicam de nigro blueto *Arch. Bridgw.* 47; **1314** in..lxx pannis de blueto asureo pro militibus (*MinAc*) *EHR* XLII 198; **1351** cum capellis..de viridi vel blueto equitant *G. S. Alb.* II 452. **b** **1292** in tonsura unius pecii panni blevetti *KRAc* 308/13 m. 4; **1382** unam peciam panni blueti coloris (*Cl*) *Foed.* VII 356; **a1414** qui duo lapides..ponuntur in uno loculo de blueto serico (*Invent.*) AMUND. *app.* II 333; *blew of colore*, blodius, bluetus *PP*. **c** **1385** pro albis..gobonatis de armis et lozingis ~is *MonA* VI 1366.

blumbum v. plumbum.

blundus [OF *blond*], blond, fair (of hair). **b** (as proper name). **c** (?) light-coloured. **d** payable in 'blanched' silver (*cf. blancus* 2).

capilli ~i M. SCOT. *Phys.* 44. **b** terra Willelmi ~i *DB* I 337a; Rodbertus Blondus *DB* II 370; **a1155** sicut Rogerus de Guineio..tenuit tempore regis Willelmi ~i [i.e. *William Rufus*] avunculi mei *Cart. Stoke by Clare* f. 16; **1218** Willelmus ~us qui dicitur Whit *KRMem* 2 r. 4. **c** **1397** de..j panno de blod' carde, vj *cushens* de blond' [? l. bloud'] et nigr' *worsted IMisc* 266/11. **d** **1238** vicecomites..non fecerunt bursam de blund' firma, et ideo remanet extendenda ad xij d. *KRMem.* 17, r. 15.

blurus [(?) AS], bald.

9.. ~us, calvus, *blere* WW.

blutrire v. blictrire. blutus, bluus v. bludus bluvetus v. bluettus.

1 boa [CL], **boas,** serpent.

buas, serpens inormis, ab eo quod bovem glutiat *Erf.* 2. 272. 8; horrendum squamoso corpore draconem..quam boam vocant ab eo quoniam tantae inormitatis existat ut boves..voraciter gluttire soleat ALDH. *VirgP* 29; **11..** boas anguis Italie immensa mole prosequitur greges armentorum et..se uberibus innectit et suggens interimit, atque inde a boum depopulatione boas nomen accepit *Best. Leningrad* 31.

2 tumour, skin disease.

boas est..tumor in †cruore [l. crure] suffuso sanguine *Erf.* 2. 272. 7.

2 boa v. boia.

boare [CL], to boom, bellow. **b** (pr. ppl.) Thunderer (divine epithet).

rudibundi, id est rudentes et boantes ALDH. *PR* 131; more boat Marcus frendentis voce leonis ALCUIN *Carm.* 70. 8; ecce bootaurus.. / ..terribili voce boando venit NECKAM *DS* II 498; rauco murmure terra boat *Ib.* 500; *to rowt*, sicut bos, boare, mugire *CathA*. **b** †**934** ni satus alti subveniat Boantis *CS* 702 (*cf.* W. MALM. *GP* V 201, 250).

boaria v. bovaria.

boaticus, noisy, bombastic.

s1460 ceciderunt de Borealibus, suis ~is pompaticisque flatibus non obstantibus, ultra numerum xxv millium *Reg. Whet.* I 387.

boatus, bellowing, bragging. **b** peal, melodious sound.

a690 ceu tonitruali quodam ~u ALDH. *Ep.* 5 p. 490; clangisonis ~ibus FELIX *Guthl.* 31; Angli.., corrupta in multis patria lingua, peregrinos jam captant ~us et garritus HIGD. II 158; **1456** miles, qui cum urgenti fastu, flatu et ~u ad villam accesserat, recessit inde silentiose *Reg. Whet.* I 216; **1462** cessat nunc flatus grandis Boreeque boatus (J. WHET.) *Pol. Poems* II 264; *a rowtynge*, ~us, boema, mugitus *CathA*. **b** hinc resonando tubae varios dant mille boatus G. AMIENS *Hast.* 90; repetatur auctor / ille qui promsit lyricos boatus R. CANT. *Poems* 266.

bobellum v. bovellum. bobinare, ~ator v. bovin-.

bobinus [? *for* bovinus], (?) common fellow, yokel.

a ~o ilia Julianus conto perfossus moriens ait.. R. NIGER II 126; Chilpericus rex factus a ~o quem cedi ad stipitem jussit occiditur *Ib.* 144.

bobla v. bubla. bobon- v. bubonica. bobulcus v bubulcus.

bobulus [cf. boviculus, bubalus], bovine. **b** young ox.

~um, bovinum *GlC* B 170. **b** **1208** de suis catallis inventi fuerunt j juvenis bos..et ij ~i *CurR* V 248.

bocardo, a logical mood. **b** (humorous) name of a prison (Oxford and Cambridge).

felapton, disamis, datisi, bocardo, ferison BACON XV 301. **b** **s1318** per cancellarium et ballivos Oxonie captus et in Bokardo incarceratus fuit *Ann. Paul.* I 282; **1434** in ~o positus est *MunAcOx* 506; hic ~o A. *a prisoun* WW; **1495** pro mundacione bocardi (*Ac. Peterhouse*) *Building in Eng.* 282.

bocaseus [Turk. *boğasî*], bocassine (cotton fabric).

1436 unum *clocher* de blodio ~eo cum auro et argento bene operatum *Rec. Nott.* II 158.

bocattus v. bukettus.

1 †bocca [? cf. bassa], bass (fish).

~a marina [*gl.*: *barse de mer*] NECKAM *Ut.* 98.

2 bocca v. boëta. 3 bocca, bocea v. botium. boccus v. boscus. bocetum v. bucetum. bocharius v. bacarius. bocheius v. bucherius.

bochelanda [AS *bócland*], 'book-land', land granted by charter.

episcopus habet j mansionem quae vocatur Bovi..huic mansioni est addita terra xv tagnorum; una ex his ~is vocatur Wermehel et ibi mansit j tagnus. *DB Exon.* 135.

bocheria v. bucheria. bocherus v. bicarius. bochetus v. bukettus 1a.

bochor Mariae [Ar. *bakhūr Maryam*], cyclamen.

†bothor Marie, i. panis porcinus *SB* 13.

bochus v. boscus. bocium v. botium. boclear-, bocular- v. buccular-. bocramus v. bukaramus. boculus v. buccula 3. bod/a ~agium v. both/a, ~agium. bodarius v. bedegar.

bodekinus [ME *bodekin, boidekin*], dagger.

1345 vi et armis, scilicet gladiis, bokelariis, cultellis et bodekyno, in ipsum Thomam insultum fecit et ipsum.. bodekyno predicto vulneravit *SelCKB* VI 40.

bodellus v. 1 botellus. bodonicula v. bothonicula. boedum v. 1 borda 1a.

boëma [βόημα], hooting, hallooing, lowing.

howting..~ma..: *so ho, þe hare is fowndyn*, ~ma, lepus est inventus *PP*; *a halowynge of hundis*, ~ma, ..*a rowtynge*, boatus, ~ma, .. *CathA*.

Boem- v. Bohaem-. boeria v. bovaria.

boëta [*etym. dub.*], lantern.

1229 in ornatu chori..una lanterna vel ~a *Conc. Syn.* II 171 (= *Conc.* I 623: †bocca); **1287** in qualibet ecclesia..sit ..lucerna, ~a, campanelle *Ib.* 1006; **1330** ornamenta sunt sufficiencia, excepta una ~a, que defecit *Reg. Exon.* 572; **1342** lucerna et ~a deficiunt (*Vis. Totnes*) *EHR* XXVI 120; **c1350** diligentes sint..circa sconsas et boettas illuminandas *Mon. Exon.* 271.

Boetes v. Bootes. bofellum v. bovellum. boffettum v. 2 buffettum. bofor v. bosor. boga v. boia, 1 bugia, bulga. boget- v. bugettum, bulgetta.

†bogga, 'bodge', dry measure, (?) peck (Kent).

c1300 de ordeo ad turtas xij summe et dim., que continent secundum mensuram regis in foro xiij summas, ij bus[sellos], j bogg' *DCCant J.* p. 282; **1307** solverunt pro acra iij d. iij bog' salis et centum allec *Cart. Bilsington* 206 (cf. ib. 211: porcio cujuslibet acre per annum ij d. quad. de reddit, dim. busselus salis et j quarterium..).

bogia v. boia, 1 bugia, bulga. Boguarius v. Bavarrus.

bogula [(?) cf. buccula], bit, bridle.

~a, salivare, *brydel* ÆLF. *Gl.*

bogum [AS *boga*], ox-bow.

1185 Jordanus faber [tenet] dim. acram..pro xij d. pro operacione ij ~orum ferri *Rec. Templars* 66; **1235** in meremio empto ad carucas et ij carucis faciendis de novo et bugis et jugis, virgis, hartis per annum *Pipe Wint.* (159284) r. 4; **1248** in xij jugis et xviij ~is emptis *Ac. Man. Wint.* (*Wyke Regis*); **1276** in custu carucarum: ..in viij jugis x d. ob.; in viij bug', vj d. *Ac. Stratton* 189; **1309** in xij ~is boum emptis, viij d. *Ac. Man. Coll. Wint.* (*Sydling St. Nicholas*).

boha v. botha b.

Bohaemus, ~annus, ~icus, ~ius, Bohemian.

a850 Franci a Boemannis gravi proelio macerantur M. PAR. *Maj.* I 380; **1241** quod..gens Tartarorum..terras Boemiorum..invadet (*Lit. Com. Lotharing.*) *Ib.* IV 110; **1244** anathematizamus heresiarcham quem Boemi papam vocant (*Lit. Papae*) *Ann. Burton* 264; Boemia..abundat..bestiis, inter quas est quoddam animal cornibus et corpore bovi valde simile, quod lingua Boemica †*leoz* vocatur HIGD. I 36 p. 256; **1392** ixm ccclxv grossi Boemici, qui faciunt in *sterlynges* lxxj li. viij s. ix d. *Ac. H. Derby* 194; **1521** heresim ..Bohemicam (*Lit. T. Wolsey*) *EHR* XLI 419.

bohemoticus v. behemothicus.

boia (boja) [CL], shackle (esp. for neck). **b** yoke, (?) ox-bow (*cf. bogum*).

bogias, catenas *GlC* B 174; ~as in collo et compedes in cruribus nectunt ALDH. *VirgP* 33; **9..** ~as, catenas, *sweorcopsas* vel *handcopsas* WW; catenae diruptae sunt, ~ae in quatuor partes comminutae OSB. *Mir. Dunst.* 22; **1174** pro xl paribus ~arum et pro quater xx paribus anulorum ferreorum *Pipe* 133; sint in eis [oppidis]..tela / cum jaculis, funde, boie, gaiola, cathene D. BEC. 1863; cum ..tertio vectis que ~is immittitur exadverso altaris exsiliret, arreptas sacerdos ~as in ecclesia gratiosus appendit W. CANT. *Mir. Thom.* III 17; **1202** volumus quod [predictus Hugo] ponatur extra ~as et ponatur in †partibus [MS.: paribus] boiorum annulorum [? *ring chains*] *Pat* 17b (cf. ib. xi n. 3); **1251** in reparacione gaole Ebor' et ferro ad xj boyas et eisdem bois faciendis *Pipe* 95 r. 15; **1276** in ~is ferreis ad opus prisonum *Chanc. Misc.* 3/46/25; de bogis iiij li. vij s. *Sacr. Ely* II 20 (cf. ib. I *app.* 118); **1309** idem habuit ..cordas et boas precii vij s. *S. Jers.* XVIII 199 (cf. ib. 251: unum par anellorum sive ~arum); *soole, bestys tyyng*, ..~a; *wyhth, bonde*, ~a *PP*; *a fettyr*, ~a, compes..compes sit furis, sed equorum dico nomellam / boiaque colla ligat *CathA*. **b 9..** boia, arcus vel *geoc* WW.

boil- v. bull-.

boiria [cf. bovaria], (?) bovate or cow-pasture (Gasc.).

1308 quandam aliam terram seu ~iam que vocatur obarquet *RGasc* IV 48.

boisiare [OF *boisier*], to rebel, break faith.

1101 si aliquis comes Anglie vel alii homines illius terre regi ~iaverint, ita quod rex comitatum..amiserit *DipDoc* I 2 (= *Foed.* I. 2: bosiaverint).

boissellus v. bussellus.

boistagium [? cf. OF *boiste* = *box*], an impost levied from householders in Lincoln.

1275 adquisivit sibi duas carucatas terre..de pecunia murag' et boistag' *Hund.* I 322; **1325** *il y ad un torcionous prise q'il appelent †boyscage, que ascun homme de les mene gentz paieront j marc, ascun di' marc, soit il ia povre, qe meson tendre en la dite cite, il paiera vj d.* ..quoad duos primos articulos, de †buscag' [l. bustag'] videlicet et vigiliis, ..hujusmodi oppressiones et extorciones fiunt in dampnum regis et depauperacionem mediocr[i]um civitatis *RParl* I 433a.

boistarius [OF *boistier*], box-maker.

1220 Henrico Buistario pro tribus magnis bustis *Cl.* 440b.

bojenila v. bajonula. bokel- v. buccul-. bokerammus, bokeranda v. bukaramus. bokerellus v. bekerellus, buccularium. bokestall- v. bukestall-. bokett- v. bukettus. bokorammus v. bukaramus.

1 bola [? cf. bolla], 'bole', furnace with natural draught for smelting.

c**1295** lxxiiij pedes..plumbi de exitu nigre mine fuse per ~am cum nigro opere fuso per furnellum *KRAc* (*Devon*) 260/5 m. 2; **1300** liberavit fusoribus tam ~arum quam fornellorum ad fundendum pro plumbo fertili inde faciendo mmdvj †lade [l. ladas] tam albe quam nigre mine *Pipe* 145 (*Devon*); **1307** in sarratura bordorum pro ~is, fornellis et aliis diversis officinis et domibus regis..et in fundamentis et muris pro ~is et fornellis cum calce empta ad easdem *KRAc* 260/19 m. 4; **1323** in vadiis..carpentariorum reparancium.. ingenia, domum affinat', ~am, fornell' et alias diversas domus necessarias bolar[ii] et coadjut[orum] ejusdem *Pipe* 170 (*Devon*) r. 53; **1323** in..xvj lodis [mine]..cariandis.. usque ~as de Ladiclif [*Derb*] *Min Ac* 1147/11 m. 12; **1508** arbores..ad..edificandum et comburendum in domibus suis et ~is *AncD* (*Derb*) B 6490.

2 bola v. vola.

bolarius [cf. 1 bola], operating a 'bole'. **b** (sb.) smelter in charge of a 'bole'.

1300 tam a predictis ~iis quam fornellariis fusoribus *Pipe* 145 (*Devon*); **1323** lib[eravit] fusor[ibus] tam ~iis quam fornellariis ad fundendum pro plumbo fertili inde extrahendo predictas cccxxv ladas *Pipe* 170 r. 53. **b** a**1307** in vadiis ~iorum comburencium et fundencium minam per bolas et custodiencium easdem cum suis coadjutoribus *KRAc* 260/19 m. 3; **1325** Willelmo atte Hacche bollar[io] *LTRMem* 95 (*Devon*) r. 128; **1371** ad..mineatores, boliarios et meltarios..capiendos et eos in mineris nostris auri, argenti, stanni et plumbi in com. Glouc'..ponendos *Pat* 285 m. 31.

bolata, amount of ore smelted in one 'bole'.

1302 Ricardo Russel bolario pro conbustione unius ~e mine fuse per bolam ad taxam xiij s. ij d. *KRAc* (*Devon*) 260/22 m. 3.

bolcagium v. bulcagium.

bolendinus [It. *bolognino*], copper coin of Bologna, used as token or counter.

1389 fuit [monasterium] indebitatum in m v^c xxxij florenis et iiij bolon' (*Acquietantia*) THORNE 2194; **1466** recepta..a domino R. Billingham post adventum predicti domini R. ad urbem Romanam: ..item..solvi..xvij ducatos cum certis ~is *Pri. Cold.* 209.

bolengare [OF *bolengier*], to bake (Norm.).

c**1160** quod homines..infra Rothomagum et extra valeant ~are et omnia ministeria sua facere *Act. Hen. II* I 350.

1 bolengaria, bakery (of royal household).

1426 servientis nostri Johannis Threpland, clerici bolongerie nostre *Cl* 276 m. 10*d.*

2 bolengaria, bakeress.

c**1320** Philipota Greindaveyne ~ia *JustIt* (*C.I.*) 1168 r. 1.

bolengarius [OF *bolengier*], baker. **b** brewer.

1111 Willelmus Bulengarius (*Ch. S. Paul.*) *HMC Rep.* IX 68a; **1155** ~ii Lundon' debent ij marcas auri pro gilda sua *Pipe* 4; **1185** Rogerus Bulingarius ante hostium [tenet] j mesagium pro vj sol. *Rec. Templars* 15; **1309** assisa panis et vin ifracta est per subscriptos, viz. Colettam Goez..et Radulfum Naymes, ~ios *S. Jers.* XVIII 251; **1324** ~ii et pistores vendunt panem contra assisam *JustIt* (C.I.) 1164 r. 14*d.* **b 1332** de ~iis..dicunt quod R. C. [et al.] sunt ~ii cervisie..G. G., R. C. [et al.] sunt ~ii panis *Ib.* 1166 r. 17*d.*

bolet- v. et. bulet-, bullett-.

1 boletus [CL > βωλίτης], toadstool.

~us, fungus idem; crescit in terris; A. *tadestol* [v.l. padestol], G. *mussherums Alph.* 23; *a paddokstole*, ~us, fungus..; versus: 'boleti leti causa fuer[e] tui' *CathA*.

2 †boletus [? cf. buletellus], (?) frayed cloth.

14.. ~us, *tender old cloth* WW.

bolga v. bulga.

†bolhagium, *s. dub.*, (?) bull-paddock (ME *bole+hagh*).

1252 alnetum inter duo inferiora molendina sua et inter ~ium et aque ductum (*ChartR* 44) *MonA* (*Repton, Derb*) VI 430.

bolia v. bovile. boliarius v. bolarius. bolimides v. bulimodes. bolio v. 1 billio.

bolis, bolidium [βολίς; cf. *Acts* xxvii 28], plummet.

bolides, *sundgerd in scipe* vel *metrap GlC* B 178; **14..** hoc bolideum, *a plum of lede Ib.*; *plumbe of schypmen*, bolis, ~dis, vel boliolidis *PP*; *a plumme*, amissis, bolis, ciclus *CathA*.

bolism- v. bulim-.

1 bolla, ~us [cf. AS *bolla*, ON *boll*], bowl.

1316 item ij ~is pro morter' iij d. *Rec. Leic.* I 297; **1325** in xiij boll' pro pedibus fratrum lavandis *Ac. Durh.* 167; **1390** de una ~a argentea rotunda ad modum parve pelvis ponderante..xlviij s. ij d. *Ac. Foreign* 25G; **1393** quinque ~os argenti cum coopertoriis argenti *Pat* 338 m. 5; **1394** in ~is et boket pro coquina *Cant. Coll. Ox.* II 133; **1400** expense funerales: ..in viij ~is emptis, viij d. *Test. Ebor.* III 19.

2 bowl, liquid or dry measure: **a** of ale; **b** of honey (9½ gals.); **c** of salt; **d** (Scot. and N. Eng.) 'boll' of grain (6 bushels, later sometimes 2 bushels); **e** of ore (Devon and Cornw.).

a 11.. sex ~e cerevisie apte sufficientes in cena una x hominibus *Found. Waltham* 16; **12..** ad mensuram potus monachorum..constituit cifum quendam magnum, flasconem et dimidium sc. duas caritates et eo amplius in se continentem, quem cifum antiqui ~am Atheluuoldi vocabant (*Cart. Abingdon*) *MonA* I 517; c**1250** dedi..unam ~am de qualibet brascina cervisie in villa de Kenles [*Kells, Ir.*], viz. illam ~am cervisie quam ego nomine telonei..capere consuevi (*Ch. W. de Lacy*) *MonA* VI 1143; **1322** quatuor servientes ecclesie ad pulsandum..pro ignitegio habent de refector' j ~am cervisie, que continet terciam partem j juste *DCCant J.* 515 (cf. ib. 278); **13..** ~a debet continere sextarium, videlicet xij lagenas cervisie (*Assisa Mens.*) *APScot* 310. **b** a**1140** redderet..octo ringas fabarum..et octo ~as mellis *Cart. Rams.* III 163; **1255** quedam terra solebat reddere manerio de Brehull' unam ~am mellis..et mesura ~e quid contineat ignoramus *Hund.* I 21; **1276** unum ~um mellis continentem novem galonas et dim. [*Swanbourne, Bucks*] *Ib.* 47 (cf. ib. 37; *PQW* 94a); **1358** unam ~am mellis precii xiij s. iiij d. [*Swanbourne*] *IMisc* 177/9. **c 1202** ubi [*Winwick, Northants*] nullam consuetudinem capere debet..nisi de sale transeunte per terram suam, sc. de careta j ~am salis *SelPlCrown* I 21. **d 1228** monachi singulis annis xx ~as farine avene reddent capellano *Kelso* I 186; **1266** recepta..in farina avene x celdras, vj ~as et duas partes unius ~e *ExchScot* 1; c**1380** quilibet equorum debet habere dimidiam ~am bone avene (*Cart. Tynemouth*) *MonA* III 319; **1469** pro..quatuor ~is ordei, ..octo ~is frumenti *ExchScot* 631; **1528** cum quatuor ~is brasii *Scot. Grey Friars* II 314. **e 1451** de exitibus, ..~is, discis, ..et emolumentis quibuscumque de omnibus mineris nostris in com. predictis *Cl* 302 m. 32; **1453** solvendo nobis..quamlibet decimam ~am *del le ore*, videlicet cupri, stanni et plumbi *Pat* 477 m. 6; **1480** quintam decimam ~am de *ure Pat* 545 m. 14*d.*; **1563** octavam ~am sive vasum stanni *Pat* 995 m. 18.

2 bolla v. 1 bulla 3. bollagium v. bulcagium.

bollardus [? cf. OF *boleor*], derisive term applied to Benedictine, (?) trickster.

1291 excuciamus..vituperium Cantuariensis archiepiscopi, qui in contemptum personarum nostrarum consuevit nos in suis visitacionibus nominare musardos, brevitores, fatuos et ~os *Doc. Eng. Black Monks* I 133.

†bollare [? ME], (?) to poll, reduce to a bole.

1499 ~avit *le grete abell* super *le grene* (*MinAc Blackmore*) *MFG.*

bollarius v. bolarius.

bolletta, small bowl.

magnis vasis, que tancardi sive ~e dicebantur *Cust. Westm.* 99.

bolletum, bolnetum v. buletum bollio v. 4 bullio. bolon' v. bolendinus. bolone v. belone. bolongeria v. 1 bolengaria.

bolstera, ~um [ME *bolster*], **a** (?) bolster (for bed). **b** metal or wooden cushion or support.

a 1393 pro..xiij discis de electro et una ~a *Pat* 338 m. 18. **b 1270** in..ferro ad unum bolstrum sub axe [molendini] faciendum *MinAc* 1118/17 r. 3; c**1295** pro ij bolstris de cupero emptis *KRAc* (*Mines*) 260/7 m. 9*d.*; **1304** Rogero le Belgeter pro xxij lib. eris emptis..pro bolstris inde faciendis pro ponte dicti castri supportando *MinAc* 771/4 m. 7 (cf. *Ac. Chamb. Chesh.* 43); c**1385** pro vij peciis meremii de *fir* emptis et expensis pro bolstur' inde faciendis pro predictis machinis *KRAc* (*Tower of London*) 473/2 m. 6 (*cf. ib.* m. 11: pro..iiij bolstur' pro campanis..pendendis).

bolta, ~us [ME *bolt*], bolt: **a** blunt-headed arrow; **b** fastening of a door or sim.; **c** measure of cloth.

a 1363 quod quilibet..arcubus et sagittis vel pilettis aut ~is in jocis suis utatur artemque sagittandi discat et exerceat (*Cl*) *Foed.* VI 417. **b 1306** in coler', circulis, platis et ~is pro porta emptis *DCCant* (*Ac. Milton*); **1325** eidem [fabro] pro ij ~is et vj clapsis..pro dicto hostio garderobe *KRAc* 469/7 m. 8; **1354** magistro Andree Fabro pro ij paribus de *heng'* cum gumphis et cum ij ~is ferri ad dictam fenestram *Ib.* 471/6 m. 8; **1372** in iij quintallis ferri emptis pro diversis ferramentis ad v carucas, viz. pro annulis ferreis, ~is, clippis *MinAc* 900/5; **1398** duo paria de ~is ferreis cum tribus *shakeles Recog. R. Chester* 71 r. 7; **1478** pro ij ~is ferreis pro..camera *Cant. Coll. Ox.* II 202. **c 1328** in empcione..cxxx ulnarum de Karde pro xxv ~is *ExchScot* 117; **1329** onerat se de xviij ~is de card'..de quibus Rogero de I. xv; ..et sic debet iij ~as *Ib.* 232; **1393** concessimus mercatoribus..pannorum vocatorum *worstedes*.. quod ipsi ~os de *sengleworstedes*..extra regnum nostrum Anglie..ducere possint *Pat* 336 m. 3.

boltarius, (?) bolt-maker (but *cf. buletarius*).

c**1220** testibus..Hugone ~io *Cart. Osney* I 290.

bolterium v. buletarium.

1 bolus [βῶλος], mouthful, morsel.

parvus in ore bōlus ponatur, dente teratur / urbano D. BEC. 924; quod fratres inter seculares non comederent nisi tres ~os carnis ECCLESTON *Adv. Min.* 31; qui timet de veneno, ante comestionem comedat unum ~um BACON V 88; nomina pertinencia panatrie: ..hic ~us, hic murcellus, hec buccella, *a musselle* WW.

2 fine earth, silt. **b** (w. *Armenicus*) earth containing iron oxide.

est genus hic terre bōlus qui flumina stagnat / ventris inundantis diluviumque tenet GARL. *Epith.* IV 275; ~us dicitur lutum quod minerale nullum in se habet *LC* 227; ~us est coagulum specificum.., ut sit essentia quaedam liberata ab impuris [etc.] *Ib.* 226. **b** quibus coctis pulvis boli Ar[menici]..admisceatur GILB. V 218 v. 2 (cf. ib. I 72. 1: bolus Arme[nicus]); rabri qui et..dicitur ~us †Armenitus qui est lapis sive vena terre BART. ANGL. XVI 83; ~us Armenicus est quedam vena terre que in Armenia reperitur et per centum annos potest servari *Alph.* 24.

2 bolus v. bulus. bombac- v. bombyc-. bombarda v. bombardus.

bombardarius, bombardier, gunner.

1479 bumbardario *ExchScot* VIII 570; **1481** Johanni Bonnare, ~io *Ib.* IX 98.

bombardia, artillery.

1475 pro viij celdris carbonum..ad facturam bumbardorum necnon pro lignis et cariagio eorundem ad domum bumbardie in castro de Strivelin *ExchScot* 275.

bombardiaricus, for guns.

1567 pulveris ~i vocati *gunpowder SelPlAdm.* II 135.

bombardiator, bombardier.

1547 navium magistros, nautas, naucleros, vibrellatores sive ~ores, et marinarios, ac alias personas..pro navibus.. hujusmodi aptos (*Pat*) *Foed.* XV 161.

bombardicus, used for gunnery or guns.

s**1430** rex de Flandria fecit adduci machinam ~am voca tam *Lyoun Plusc.* XI 105.

bombardula, small cannon.

1561 ~arum confector (*SPDom Eliz.* 17/33) *Hug. Soc.* X 275.

bombardus, ~a [OF *bombarde*], bombard, cannon, fire-arm.

s**1413** mox bombardorum sonitu gentes fremuerunt ELMH. *Metr. Hen. V* 311; **1430** warantum..de deliberando.. ~os magnos et parvos, lapides ~orum [etc.] *Act. PC* IV 33; **1436** certis artificibus pro bumbardis, ingeniis et aliis instrumentis..bellicis *ExchScot* 677; s**1415** [Henricus] ~is.. muros quassat AD. USK 125; **1462** ad bumbardos, canones, *culverynes, fowlers, serpentynes* et alios canones quoscunque *Pat* 500 m. 18; **1473** pro cariagio sex parvorum bumbardorum dictorum *serpentynis* cum pulveribus in duobus curribus *ExchScot* 163; **1516** rerum novarum et artium ac machinarum curiosus, gestabat subinde ad cingulum suspensam ∼am (J. WATSON) *Ep. Erasmi* II 450; **s1430** ingentem ∼am, cui nomen erat Leo in Flandria, fabricari fecit MAJOR VI 13; **1562** atria bombardae nutant quassata fragore J. HERD *Hist. IV Regum* 20; **1568** vj ∼os, quorum tres sunt duplices alteri singulares, cum septem cameris eisdem pertinentibus *HCA Act Bk* 13 f. 72; **1573** cum..tormentis sive ∼is vulgariter vocatis *handgonnes* et *dagges Pat* 1104 m. 4.

bombarius, rowdy, full of empty sound.

omnia ista sunt ignorancium grammaticam sine fructu altercaciones ∼ie WYCL. *Log.* II 27.

bombator, bombardier.

1456 pro mensa quondam Johannis de Moravia, ∼oris regis *ExchScot* 116.

bombax, bombex, bombic- v. bombyx.

bombilare, to hum (*v. et. bombizare*).

inter pronunciandum observetur ne eodem vocis tono (apis in morem) ∼etur WHITTINGTON *Vulg.* 114.

1 bombinare, to rumble.

c1370 fercula fert fellis bombīnans femina bellis [*gl.*: requiescens in bombis et trullis suis] (J. BRIDL.) *Pol. Poems* I 183, 184.

2 bombinare v. bovinare.

bombire, to boom (of a bittern).

14.. hinc elephas barrit, onocrotulus hiccine bombit WW.

bombix v. bombyx.

bombizare, to buzz.

apes ambizant vel ∼ant ALDH. *PR* 131; bombizant vaspe, sonus est horrendus GOWER *VC* I 811; *to cry*, ..apum [est] ∼are vel bombilare *CathA*.

bomblastus, bombard, gun.

1443 bumblast', viz. *gunnes Rec. Norw.* I 340; **1460** vi et armis, viz..deploidibus defensivis, bumblastis ac aliis armis defensivis (*IMisc* 317) *EHR* XXXVII 255.

bombosus, booming, blaring.

∼a, *hlaegulendi GlC* B 171; dum stimulant Martem bombosa voce falanges ALDH. *VirgV* 1550; **9..** ∼a, *hlowende, putende* WW.

bombulus, rumbling, breaking wind (*cf. bombus c*).

1250 serjantia que quondam fuit Rollandi le Pettour.. pro qua debuit facere die Natali Domini singulis annis coram domino rege saltum et sifflettum et unum bumbulum *Fees* 1173.

bombus, ∼um, ∼a [βόμβος], bellow. **b** peal. **c** rumbling, breaking wind.

aurea hunc bombis nascentem bucula vatem / signavit ALDH. *VirgV* 285. **b** clamat barbita bombis *Ib.* 2789; omnia signa sonant feriunt atque aethera bombis WULF. *Swith.* I 1027. **c 1235** per servicium saltus, sibile et bunbi *Fees* 404; **c1370** (v. bombinare); *a farte*, bumbum, bumba, pedicio, trulla *CathA*.

bombycinus, ∼ius [CL; cf. OF *bombasin*], made of silk or (?) cotton. **b** (sb. m.) silkworm.

bombicinus, dirivatum nomen epitheton a bombicibus id est vermibus ALDH. *PR* 128; vestium nomina: ..bombicinum, *seolcen* ÆLF. *Gl.*; ∼i sericique velleris..copia GIR. *TH* I 37; **1234** unam zonam bombicinam barratam argento *CurR* XV 1110; bombicinium BART. ANGL. XVIII 17 (= Isidor. *Etym.* XIX 27); *I* ante *N* breviatur, ut adamantinus, ..bombichinus BACON *Tert.* 262; **s1274** civitas ipsa.. bombicinis et auro textis enituit indumentis WYKES 260. **b** bombicini, vermes qui texunt *GlC* B 151.

2 (sb. n.) **a** cotton (or other fabric). **b** doublet, haketon, jack, paltock.

a tela aranea, bombicinum, simphitum, gypsum.. GILB. IV 179 v. 2; bombicinium, *cotune PP*; bombacinum, *cotun' CathA*; bumbicinium, *Kotyn or pakclothe* WW. **b 1279** duo paria caligarum de ferro, duo †bombacima [l. bombacinia], unum †sambezionum [l. gambezionum]..tradatis *Reg. Heref.* 6; arma mea cum akedono et †lumbacinio [l. bumbacinio] meo *Form. Man.* 17; **1336** bombacia alia cum platis ferreis..que vix penetrari possint per sagittas *Illust. Scot.* 57; **1364** pro uno bombicinio ad opus regis..v li. *Exch Scot* 128; **14..** bombacilium, A. *cowrteby*; bombicinum, A. *a jakke*; bumbacinum, A. secundum quosdam *aketoun*; bombecina, *a acton*; †lombesina, *a paltoke* WW; *a jakke*, bombicinum *CathA*.

bombyx [βόμβυξ], silkworm.

serica purpureis praebens velamina peplis / quae moritura facit fetoso viscere bombix ALDH. *VirgV* 1147 (cf. Id. *Aen.* 7); bombyx, *sidwyrm* vel *seolcwyrm* ÆLF. *Gl.*; serica dum texit bombyx placidoque labori / sedulus insistit, est labor ipse cibus NECKAM *DS* IX 255; vermis qui bombex dicitur *Id. NR* II 164; bombex est vermis quidam nascens in frondibus..mori BART. ANGL. XVIII 17; caput ambit linea pepli / pro quo se bombix attenuare studet GARL. *Epith.* VI 370; bumbax, *selkeworme* WW.

2 cotton fibre.

arboribus bumbacem portantibus, que sunt parve et humiles, que per omnia emittunt bumbacem sicut rosa florem S. SIM. *Itin.* 40.

3 silk or cotton (fabric). **b** doublet (*cf. bombycinus* 2).

1208 pro v libris de bombace ad iij culcitras nostras *Cl* 103; **s1284** obturantes vulnus bombace *Ann. Worc.* 490; tente fiant de bombace vel panno lineo intincto in incausto GAD. 9. 2; **1342** in empcione iij librarum bombacis *ExchScot* 482. **b 1517** plures bumbices facti sunt et diverse lorice empte per inhabitatores ville ad ejus defencionem *Lib. Kilken.* 139.

bomolochus [βωμολόχος], jester.

dyssowre, þat cannot be sadde, †holomochus..Aristoteles in Ethicis, nugax *PP*.

bona v. 2 bunda.

1 bonagium [Ir. *buanachd*], 'bonaght', tribute paid to chiefs.

1525 illas terras liberas et immunes ab omni servitute laycali esse sententialiter decreverunt, tam in ∼io quam in ceteris aliis oneribus *Reg. Clogher* 247; **1557** promisit daturum se quolibet anno ∼ium centum Scoticis vulgariter nuncupatis *galloglasses* pro uno quarterio anni *Act. PC Ir.* 38.

2 †bonagium (? bovagium), a form of toll: **a** on ship; **b** at a fair (*cf. bothagium*).

a 1282 ad victualia j navis vij li. ij s. ij d. de Ros usque Rothelan cum lodmanagio et ∼io *KRAc* 4/3. **b 1298** magnum pondus, terragium, bovagium, seldagium (*Pipe Wint.*) *EEC* 28 n. 8.

bonare v. bundare.

bonasus [βόνασος], bison.

cum ∼i [costa] forsan esse possit, aut uri CAIUS *Anim.* 14.

†boncarium [? cf. bancarium], (*s. dub.*).

1205 pro ferro et incudibus..; pro x ∼iis lxiij s. et iiij d.; pro duabus carectis ferratis *Cl* 38a.

boncha v. buncha. bonda v. bondus, bunda.

bondacra, area held by bondage tenure.

c1300 dominus H. de H. ..arabit unam ∼am et herciabit *Pri. Cold. app.* cii.

bondagium, bondage: **a** tenure analogous to villeinage; **b** tenement held in such tenure; **c** (?) rent of bondage tenement; **d** status of bondage tenant; **e** (fig.) servitude.

a c1227 duas bovatas terre..que fuerunt de ∼io domini regis *Fees* (*Yorks*) 358; **1276** de iiij bovatis terre in Scalleby [*Yorks*], que solebant esse de dominico regis et tres sunt de ∼io et una de sokagio *Hund* I 131; **1279** tenuit predictas tres bovatas terre in ∼ium de domino rege..per servicium reddendi pro qualibet bovata terre per annum x d. *PQW* (*Yorks*) 190a; **1323** fecit finem..pro omnibus operibus suis.. provenientibus de j plena terra et de ij dim. terris que tenet de bond' domini, ita tamen quod ipse reddet omnem redditum suum assisum (*Cur. Ep. Ely*) *CBaron* 135; **1330** clamat tenere de domino in bundagio unum mesuagium *CourtR* 204/44 (*Cuddington, Surrey*) m. 1; **1380** sunt ibidem [*Tutbury, Staffs*] xxv tenentes qui tenent in ∼io et ad voluntatem xxxiij bovatas terre et reddunt pro qualibet bovata terre v s. ij d. ob. *MonA* III 396; **1381** quod nulla acra terre in com. predictis que in ∼io vel servicio tenetur altius quam ad iiij d. haberetur (*Pat*) *Foed.* VII 317; **1383** eedem octo acre bosci..fuerunt parcella..tenementorum que S. A. nuper nativus ipsius abbatis..tenuit in ∼io ut de jure illius ecclesie et ad voluntatem abbatis (*Assisa*) *G. S. Alb.* III 270; **1384** hameletta predicta tenetur de domino rege in bundagio et sic est dominicum ipsius domini regis *Rec. Caern.* 211; **1469** omnes virgate terre..ab antiquo tenebantur in ∼io; ..et postquam magna pestilencia fuit, viz. in tempore Edwardi tercii, alique tenure inde..permisse fuere in manus domini et postea dimisse per dominum pro certis redditibus; ..et sic alterata fuit tenura ∼ii et custum' oper' et servic'; et sic modo tenentur ad voluntatem domini (*Ext. Rustington, Sussex*) *Growth Eng. Indust.* 586. **b 1245** in Alwenton' [*Northumb.*] sunt ix bondi, quorum quilibet eorum tenet unum ∼ium *IPM* 3/9; **1296** F. relicta N. cepit ∼ium quod vir suus tenuit *Hal. Durh.* 1; **c1309** totam..terram..cum bondis, ∼iis, nativis et eorum sequelis, cum homagiis et serviciis *Melrose* II 422; **1310** si aliqui hujusmodi custumariorum fecerint alienationem ∼ii tenure sue alicui, solebant sursum reddere in curia..illam tenuram (*Cust. Sutton*) *Antiq. Warw.* 639; **1332** tenuit ibidem [in Novo castro super Tynam] sex ∼ia, quorum quodlibet continet unum toftum et xxviij acras terre *IPM* 31/32; **1336** de villa de E. cum.. serviciis ∼iorum.. non respondet (*Comp. Vic. Berw.*) *Cal Scot* III p. 323; **1380** terram..dedit..cum libere tenentibus, ∼iis et serviciis *Cart. Lindores* cxlix; **1409** cum..bondis, ∼iis, nativis *Reg. Brechin* 26. **c a1221** habendum et tenendum omnia prescripta cum homagiis, ..wardis, maritagiis, curiarum sectis, taylagiis, †bondagiis, auxiliis (*Ch. Hosp. Ludlow*) *MonA* VI 681 (cf. *Reg. Heref.* 1516–35 186). **d** si nativi domino suo negent nativitatem suam sive ∼ium, tunc attachientur..ad respondendum domino suo *Quon. Attach.* 56; diversus est modus nativitatis sive ∼ii; nam alii sunt nativi de avo et proavo..; similiter est alius modus ∼ii..ubi aliquis extraneus aliquam terram servilem..ceperit faciendo servicium servile..; tercius autem modus..∼ii est ubi aliquis liber homo..reddit seipsum..domino [ut] suum nativum seu bondum *Ib.*; **1381** licet nuper..certe littere nostre patentes..facte fuissent continentes quod nos universos ligeos et subditos nostros communes et alios certorum comitatuum regni nostri manumisimus et ipsos..ab omni ∼io et servicio exuimus et quietos fecimus, ..dictas litteras revocamus (*Pat*) *Foed.* VII 317; **s1381** rustici quidem fuistis et estis et in ∼io permanebitis non ut hactenus sed incomparabiliter viliori (RIC. II) WALS. *HA* II 18; **1396** ita quod nec ego..nec aliquis alius per nos..aliquam actionem ∼ii, villinagii seu nativitatis erga prefatos Willelmum [et al.]..vendicare poterimus *CalPat 1422–9* p. 336; **s1465** dominus abbas manumisit et ab omni jugo servitutis, villenagii seu ∼ii liberos fecit Thomam Crystmes..et..filias prefati Thome.. cum tota sequela earundem *Reg. Whet.* II 47. **e s1398** feceruntque quidam albas cartas per omnes comitatus regni sigillari tam per ecclesiasticos quam per seculares et omnes jurare fideliter observare que in eis scribenda forent, unde famam duri ∼ii futuri in tota communitate populi ventilabant *Dieul.* 144.

†bondagius, bondage tenant (*cf. bondagium* c).

1279 omnes bondag' predicti dabunt scutagium quando currit *Hund.* (*Oxon*) II 842b.

bondare v. bundare. bondarius v. 1 bordarius a. bondellus v. bundellus.

bondemannus [ME *bondeman*], bondage tenant.

1236 dicti homines de Alcmundebur' [*Hunts*] dicunt quod sunt villani et quod vocabantur bundemanni regum et pro voluntate ipsorum aliquando positi fuerunt ad denarios et aliquando ad servitia et dederunt herieta, merchetum et amerciamenta de placitis emergentia *CurR* XV 1981; **1324** de feodis domini regis et tenentibus suis de antiquo dominico corone, tam liberorum sokmannorum quam ∼orum, utrum ..alienata fuerint (*Artic. Corone*) *MGL* II 353.

bondenebedripa, (?) boon reaping by bondage tenant.

12.. inveniet j hominem ad ∼am proprio custu *Cart. Glouc.* III 129.

bondonare v. bundonare.

bondum [ME *bond* < ON *band*; cf. benda], band (for strengthening wheel). **b** hoop (hence girth) of barrel.

custus molendini: ..in duobus ∼is ad eandem rotam vj d. *FormMan.* 33; **1307** in ij ∼is ligni pro modiis j veteris carecte pro fimis, j d. ob. *Doc. Bec* 148. **b 1357** in j barello tarre de magn' bond' *Crawley* 281.

bondus, ∼a [ON *bonda, bondi*], freeholder, head of household.

ubi ∼a, id est paterfamilias, mansit sine compellatione et calumpnia, sint uxor et pueri in eodem sine querela (*Quad.*) *GAS* 359 (cf. ib. 559).

2 tenant in bondage (*cf. bondagium*): **a** (Scot.); **b** (Eng.).

a c1150 de hurdmannis et ∼is et gresmannis *EChScot* 182; **c1160** reddendo inde ∼is annuatim iiij s. *Reg. Newbattle* 163; **1266** item xij ∼is domini regis pro xxiij equis mortuis in servicio domini regis *ExchScot* 8; **c1309** (v. bondagium b); **1380** in attemptatis..concernentibus bundos comitis Marchie fiat requisitio *RScot* 30a; a probacione..ac testimonio repelluntur.. consanguinei, socii, nativi, ∼i (*Fragm. Collecta* 18) *APScot* I 380. **b 1245** (v. bondagium b); **c1250** unusquisque ∼us..dabit pro bovata xij d. (*Cart. Whitby*) *MonA* I 417; **a1290** si aliquis bundus ab antiquo vendiderit magnam partem terre sue.., inquirendum est ubi terre ille jacent; ..nec permittatur de cetero quod villani ita vendant terras suas (*Ord. Abbatis*) *G.S. Alb.* I 455; **1294** consuetudines quorundam ∼orum..qui vocantur *werkmen* ..et quorundam aliorum..∼orum qui vocantur *molemen* (*Lincs*) *Cl* 111 m. 5*d.*; **1303** servicia liberorum et ∼orum (*Lincs*) *MonA* VI 994; **1307** de liij s. iiij d. de ∼is de E. et S. pro pastura de S. per annum ad voluntatem episcopi *Boldon Bk, app.* xxxi; **1322** sunt ibidem xlj nativi qui tenent inter se diversas terras in bond[agio]; ..item est ibidem quidam redditus predictorum ∼orum custumariorum *IPM* (*Derb*) 76/6 r. 4; **1330** usi sunt eadem warenna tantum in dominicis terris suis..et non in aliis terris ∼orum suorum *PQW* (*Northants*) 564b; **s1381** rustici quos nativos vel ∼os vocamus, ..pro libertate tumultuare cepere et..nulli omnino alicujus de cetero astringi servicio meditati sunt WALS. *HA* I 454; **1386** omnibus tenentibus meis, viz. husbandis, *cotiers* et bond' *FormA* 428.

3 (?) land held in bondage.

1218 habet..iij carucatas in dominico et in ∼is vij bovatos *Eyre Yorks* 326.

bonettus [ME < OF *bonet*], bonnet sail (strip of canvas attached to foot of 'course').

1352 in j velo, j bonett'..emptis pro eadem navi *KRAc* 26/14; **a1365** pro emendacione duplicacionis veli de *la Godebyete*.., uno novo ∼o et uno novo velo *Ib.* 27/15 m. 5; **1371** in factura..iij ∼orum pro navi regis *Ib.* 31/7; **1432** item *le saylle* cum duobus ∼is (*KRMem*) *Bronnen* 1043; **1437** de vendicione unius veli parvi et debilis cum uno ∼o ejusdem *KRAc* 53/5 f. 2.

bonificare, ∼facere, to improve, make valuable. **b** to make virtuous. **c** to benefit, bless.

1291 expense que fient..pro terris ∼andis ut uberiores fructus producant (*Bulla*) B. COTTON 197 (cf. *Conc.* II 182). **b** ut patet ex circumstanciis ∼antibus actus moraliter WYCL. *Ente Praed.* 160 (cf. Id. *Ver.* II 42: per crementum circumstanciarum ∼faciencium). **c** cum Deus miseranter ∼at omnia opera sua WYCL. *Dom. Div.* 14.

bonificatio, benefit, blessing.

igitur ∼io Adam celestis excedit dampnificationem primi Adam WYCL. *Ver.* III 205; illa accidentalis existencia humanitatis Christi in hostia non equivalet ∼oni quam creatura haberet ex substancia desinente *Id. Euch.* 129.

bonificus, beneficent.

1497 haec ∼a, clarifica et vivifica vis vitae..vivificabit COLET *In 1 Cor.* (xv 22) 266.

bonitas, goodness: **a** (divine); **b** (human, esp. generosity).

a de summa divinae ~atis una essentia in tribus substantiis ERIUG. *Per.* 457D (v. et. bonus 1); summa Dei bonitas caeli quae saepta gubernas (WULFSTAN) *Anal. Hymn.* LI 142; quid summa ~as retribuet amanti..se, nisi se ipsam ANSELM (*Mon.* 70) I 80; sicut nec tua bonitas, / sic nec laudis immensitas / verbi claudetur modio J. HOWD. *Cyth.* 43. 4. **b** MAP *NC* III 1 (v. bonus 2a); tante fuit ~atis ut quos armis subegerat clementia magis vicerit GIR. *PI* I 14; sit tibi rara fides de feminea bonitate D. BEC. 2072; ex honesti finis intencione ~as moralis in opere sigillatur R. BURY *Phil.* 18. 231; s**1377** rex Edwardus inter omnes mundi magnificos gloriosus et ~atis immense AD. MUR. *Cont. A* 225.

2 act of generosity, bounty, tip.

11.. per servitia et ~ates quas faciebat pater ejus *Cart. Burton* 36; s**1322** hujus..viri [T. comitis Lanc'] copiose ~ates, elemosinarum largitiones et cetera pietatis opera.. tractatus exigunt speciales *Flor. Hist.* III 214; **1378** Ricardo F. pro ~ate xij d. *Ac. Durh.* 587; **1415** in j toga empta pro T. W. pro ~ate sua pro reparacione grangii *Ib.* 611.

bonum malanum (malagnum) v. malanum.

bonus [CL; v. et. melior, optimus], good (in absol. sense, w. ref. to deity).

Deus ergo non inconvenienter ~us dicitur et bonitas, quia omnia de nihilo in essentiam venire..clamat, ideoque Grece dicitur Deus καλός, id est ~us, διὰ τὸ πάντα καλεῖν εἰς οὐσίαν ERIUG. *Per.* 580CD; quod a summe justo summeque ~o creatore rerum nulla eo ~o ad quod facta est injuste privetur, certissime est tenendum ANSELM (*Mon.* 74) I 83; dii boni! GIR. *TH* III 53.

2 good (of persons): **a** virtuous; **b** (iron. or condescending) worthy; **c** of good standing, respectable; **d** admissible (leg.); **e** innocent, law-abiding (*cf.* 6b); **f** proficient, serviceable.

a rex erat vir ~us, et ~a ac sancta sobole felix BEDE *HE* III 7; ipso tuo opere testaris quia amabilis et laudabilis est omnis qui studet ~us esse ANSELM (*Ep.* 189) IV 75; sepe etiam ~i judices [AS: *þa godan deman*] habent malos vicarios (*Quad.*) *GAS* 475; non difficile..scribere quod ~is sua faciat utile bonitas, cum 'omnia ~is cooperentur in bonum' [*Rom.* viii 28] MAP *NC* III 1; absque labore bonis in ea bona cuncta fluentant D. BEC. 236; si bonus es morum, prudens, discretus honestus *Id.* 386; innata vir bonitate ~us GIR. *EH* I 43; ~orum arbitrio *Id. TH intr.* **b** "~e homo, semper fuit stultus et semper erit" W. FITZST. *Thom.* 47; vocate mihi ~um hominem illum GIR. *EH* I 40. **c** [virgunculam] de stirpe bona et claris natalibus ortam ALDH. *VirgV* 1784; c**1310** statum nostrum..apud ~os et graves apud quos non exstitimus diffamati (*Ch. Abbatis*) *Bury St. E.* 176; **1318** de communi consilio prelatorum, comitum, ~orum [? l. baronum] et procerum regni *Lit. Cant.* III 398. **d** si.. hoc coram ~is testibus [AS: *biforan godum witum*] non emerit (*Quad.*) *GAS* 101; si dominus tunc velit eum purgare cum duobus ~is tainis [*godum þegenum*] *Ib.* 228; a**1099** illos ..pone per ~os plegios *Regesta* p. 135; **1256** si dicta injuria.. per unum ~um hominem vel duos monstrari poterit *FormA* 86; **1291** (v. arbitratus). **e** **1275** ad ponendum se in inquisicione bona, si ~us fuerit an non *CourtR Wakefield* I 65; **1295** quod inde ~us est et fidelis, ponit se..in inquisicione *CourtR Hales* 323; **14..** esse volo ~us et fidelis domino nostro regi *Cust. Fordwich* 24. **f** o socii et ~i operarii [AS: *gode wyrhtan*] ÆLF. *Coll.* 100 (cf. ib. 99: probavi te habere ~os socios et valde necessarios); **1223** duos homines ~os et fortes ad..mangonellos nostros trahendos *Cl* 632a; **1261** cum ~is balistariis quot habere poterit *Cl* 496; **1293** ~us est et domino necessarius ad custodiendum oves *SelPlMan* 168.

3 good (of acts, opinions, faculties, events, institutions etc.): **a** virtuous (or implying virtue); **b** genuine, sound; **c** valid, adequate (leg.); **d** effective, beneficial, favourable, propitious.

a **680** quid enim prosunt ~orum operum emolumenta..? ALDH. *Ep.* 4 p. 481; animae eorum qui in operibus ~is de corpore exeunt BEDE *HE* V 12 (cf. ib. IV 23: peccata ~is operibus redimere); **1265** executores testamenti ~e memorie Philippe *FormA* 259. **b** **1199** ~a fide concessimus *RChart.* 30b; **1211** cum putasset quod eum portaret in ~a fide *SelPl Crown* 58; **1257** dum sane mentis extitit et ~e memorie *Cl* 63; s**1402** ipse resignavit cum ~a voluntate *Eul. Hist. Cont.* III 391. **c** **1212** homo legalis est et ~i testimonii *SelPl Crown* 66; **1274** ~am securitatem capiatis (*Lit. Regis*) *Leg. Ant. Lond.* 166; **1281** habuit inde ~am seisinam *Abbr. Plac.* 272; **1284** quamdiu ~am et sufficientem manucapcionem invenerint *BBC* 191; hec est ~a cautela HENGHAM *Magna* 2. **d** ~us cuntis videtur dolus MAP *NC* IV 16 p. 199; s**1219** reginam interficere nolite, timere ~um est M. PAR. *Maj.* III 51; **1251** vendant ad ~um forum hujusmodi robora *Cl* 428; **1258** (v. adventus 1b); s **1305** in die qui dicebatur ~us dies Veneris [*Good Friday*] *Ann. Lond.* 136; clara dies Pauli bona tempora denotat anni (ELVEDEN *Cal.*) *SB* 7; s**1377** statuta Parliamenti quod "Bonum" merito vocabatur WALS. *HA* I 324; **1384** nisi tantum de curialitate et ~a voluntate hominum ville predicte, quando ipsi ~um dominium et amiciciam invenerint (*Reg. Celler.*) *Bury St. E.* 177.

4 good, serviceable (of animals).

per aliud videtur dici ~us equus quia fortis est, et per aliud ~us equus quia velox est ANSELM (*Mon.* 1) I 14; equus x solid., si tam ~us [AS: *swa gód*] sit (*Quad.*) *GAS* 176; **1210** gupillerettos ~os et baldos *Pipe* 105; si [asini]essent ~i et juvenes, eos non venderemus *Latin Stories* 41.

5 good (of things): **a** useful, valuable, desirable; **b** well made, in good condition; **c** genuine; **d** full, complete.

a ibi..ii piscarie de x sol. et tercia piscaria valde ~a *DB* I 30b; s**1192** exitus omnium ~arum villarum..Anglie crescere..preter villam istam BRAKELOND 142v; potus sit vinum ~um subtile..delectabile GAD. 123 v. 2; fungus.. tam ~us quam malus *Alph.* 70. **b** **1205** ij ollas de ere ~o.. cum bassis pedibus et ~is *Cl* 22; **1225** j ~am et fortem carectam cum duobus ~is equis *Cl* 32b; a**1250** facient ea [molendinum et toralliam] adeo ~a sicut capiunt ea *Deeds Newcastle* 43; **1296** [lanam] ~am (v. bursare 1); **1346** (v. azurum a); **1454** item j mensa ~a, j mensa pro valectis *Ac. Durh.* 148; **1516** xij lodices, unde viij mediocriter ~i *Ib.* 253. **c** **1268** predicta carta non est ~a, immo falsa *SelPl Jews* 40; ecce bonus quadrans *Babio* 107; bonam..numerare monetam D. BEC. 1146; **1312** ad x s. Burdegalensium ~orum *RGasc* IV *app.* 564; **1374** ccc marcas sterlingorum in pecunia numerata ~orum et legalium *Reg. Paisley* 46. **d** **1216** assignetis ei..xx marcatas terre ~as *Cl* 248b.

6 (w. ref. to relig. movement or order) **a** Albigensian heretic. **b** Grandmontine. **c** Bonhomme (order of Austin Friars).

a s**1176** erant in provincia Tolosana quidam heretici qui se appellari faciebant Bonos Homines R. HOWD. II 105. **b** **1177** petitione ~orum Hominum de Grandi Monte motus *Act. Hen. II* II 64. **c** **1283** rectori Bonorum Virorum fratrum ecclesie in honore preciosi sanguinis Jesu Christi apud Esserugge [*Herts.*] fundate (*Carta Com. Cornub.*) *MonA* VI 515 (cf. ib. 517); **1383** rector et fratres de ordine S. Augustini Boni Homines vulgariter nuncupati [*Edington, Wilts.*] *Cl* 224 m. 40; **1508** duo religiosi ordinis Bonorum Hominum de Francia..hic appulerunt ANDRE *Hen. VII* 119; Guil. de Edington..collegium ~is, quod dixerunt, Hominibus erexit CAMD. *Br.* 213 (cf. ib. 344).

7 (sb. n.) **a** good deed. **b** something good or desirable, good condition, benefit. **c** acquittal (*cf.* 1e). **d** possession, (pl.) goods.

a s**912** eximie vir probitatis..post nonnulla que egerat ~a decessit FL. WORC. 121; **1265** quod dicti ballivi..nunquam fecerunt ~um ubi possent facere malum *IMisc* 27/41; s**1337** fecit ~um quod potuit AD. MUR. 78. **b** nec in comparatione hujuscemodi ~um [sc. legitimam jugalitatem] dehonestari video, sed quod melius est propensius laudari censeo ALDH. *VirgP* 9; justius multo est de incognitis ~um credere quam malum BEDE *HE* III 25; rationalem creaturam ad hoc esse factam ut summam essentiam amet super omnia ~a, sicut ipsa est summum ~um ANSELM (*Mon.* 68) I 79; ex quo ~i et mali discretionem habere potuit KETEL *J. Bev.* 276; ab Hibernia potestne aliquid ~i esse? GIR. *TH intr.* p. 6; **11..** monachi..fecerunt me et uxorem meam.. participes omnium ~orum ejusdem loci *Reg. Malm.* 449 (cf. *Scot. Grey Friars* II 263: ~orum spiritualium); **11..** volo ..quod omnes possessiones sue in ~o et in pace sint *FormA* 294; **1214** non credidit quod pro ~o suo illuc veniret *SelPl Crown* 72; s**1214** omnia quecunque ~a et honesta Gundulfus studuit ordinare, iste destruenda insistebat *Flor. Hist.* II 149; que tandem..pro ~o pacis unam marcam accepit BRAKELOND 133; **1222** ne archidiaconi..~um pacis impedire presumant si quando discordantes se sibi adinvicem voluerint concordare *Conc. Syn.* 116; a**1350** pro ~o pacis et tranquillitate universitatis *Stat. Cantab.* 318; **1353** pro ~o pacis et concordie *Lit. Cant.* III 219; pro ~o suo illi subtraxi ..illum [ciphum] *Latin Stories* 11; **1282** ipsum..monuimus ut ad ~um obediencie se converteret et mandata nostra.. adimpleret; ..abjecto ~o obediencie..rescripsit (*Reg. Cant.*) *Conc.* II 81 (cf. OCKHAM *Dial.* 816); **1365** causa ~i vicinitatis *Hal. Durh.* 44; tales qui in praxi cognoverunt quod non sunt facienda mala ut ~a eveniant (WYCL. *Ente*) *Wycl. & Ox.* 138*n.*; *Id. Quaest. Log.* 251 (v. acquisibilis); **1442** non tamen hujusmodi salutacionem in ~um [*in good part*] capientes, ipsum letaliter vulneraverunt (*DipDocE* 427) *Bronnen* 1251 (3). **c** **1220** quia ipsi ponunt se de ~o et de malo super veredictum et omnes villate idem dicunt quod sunt latrones, suspendantur *CurR* VIII 274 (cf. *SelPl Crown* 83); **1352** rectatus fuit..de feloniis et roberiis; ..de ~o et malo ponit se super patriam *Lib. Kilken.* 23. **d** ~a, *scaet GlC* B 150; duo castra ~is omnibus referta H. HUNT. *HA* VII 16; s**1165** [rex] presbyterorum ~a per diocesim Cant' decedentium..occupavit W. CANT. *V. Thom.* I 43; alienatoribus ~orum patrimonii Crucifixi NECKAM *NR* I 18; **1220** quia omnia ~a ei deficiunt, ..consideratum est quod suspendatur *CurR* VIII 396 (= *SelPlCrown* 134); **1254** estimatio ~orum ecclesiasticorum et temporalium abbatis *Val. Norw.* 520; **1269** nolumus quod ~a et catalla..virorum religiosorum..taxentur (*Breve*) *Conc.* II 22; **1277** licebit.. ~a sua mobilia et immobilia dare, legare et assignare *MGL* III 450; **1293** ~orum temporalium liberalissima ac spiritualium avida beneficiorum *StatOx* 101; **1343** subscripta ~a remanent in officio camerarii *Ac. Durh.* 171; **1380** vicarius.. in catallis suis seu ~is aliis distringat *Reg. Aberd.* I 134; **1460** cum propriis ~is domine regine *ExchScot* 24; **1510** sub obligatione omnium ~orum nostrorum patrimonialium et fiscalium (*DipDocE* 372) *Foed.* XIII 285; **1522** executorem et ~orum intromissorem *Offic. S. Andr.* 123.

bootaurus v. 1 butor.

Bootes [Βοώτης], Boötes (astr.).

Boetes, Septemtrio *GlC* B 157; miraturque citum Boreas ardere Boōten [v.l. Boetem] HANV. V 309.

borach/a, ~ia v. burrochius.

borago [(?) cf. Ar. *abū ḥuraysh*], borage (bot.).

mellificis apibus placidum bōrāginis usum / novit Aristeus NECKAM *DS* VII 241; ~o si cum aqua et zuccaro coquatur vel melle et detur in potu canales pulmonis emendat BACON IX 56; **12..** ~o, i. *burage* WW; [cordialia] temperata composita sunt diaboraginatum, quia 'dixit bōrāgo gau[dia] semper ago', diarodon.. GAD. 68. 2; buglossa..acuta habet folia ad modum ~inis *Alph.* 24; buglossum Grecis, Latinis est bovis lingua officinis ~o, vulgo *borrage* TURNER *Herb.* A iii v.

boratorium v. foratorium.

1 borax [Ar. *bawrāq, būraq* < Pers. *bura*], borax (or other chemical salt); **b** (form *baurach*).

Datin dicit: ..jam abstulimus nigredinem et cum sale anatron..et almizadir..fiximus albedinem, quare ei hoc nomen imponimus †borteza, quod Arabice tincar dicitur ROB. ANGL. *Alch.* 514b; cum isto [allumine] et pinguedine colcotar et melle sophisticatur ~ax M. SCOT *Lumen* 256 (cf. ib. 260: allumen Romanum †borbaci assimilatur); addatur ~ax et camphora GILB. III 156 v. 1; ~ax pulverizetur cum equali pondere piperis GAD. 49. 1; ~ax est quedam gumma unde consolidatur aurum, A. et G. *boreis Alph.* 23; ~ax est chrysocolla, batrachum et vocatur attinchar naturale..vel nitrum *LC* 227. **b** laxabimus cum..aqua mellis cum baurac GILB. VII 320. 1; sin eligeremus ex mediis mineralibus, ut sunt omnia genera magnesiarum, baurach.. *Spec. Alch.* 380; albaras liniatur cum nigella et baurach et aceto GAD 85. v. 2; baurath est quodlibet genus salsedinis et de quolibet sale potest intelligi, proprie autem de nitro *SB* 13; baurac est sal gemmae saphirium lithargyrum albificatum; est etiam sal †vitri [? l. nitri]..; etiam est attinchar, quodlibet genus salsuginis *LC* 226.

2 borax v. borith. borbax v. 1 borax a. borcellum v. bursellum. borcinettus v. bacinettus.

1 borda, ~um, ~us [AS *bord,* OF *bort* < Frk.], wooden board or plank. **b** (collect.) wood sawn into boards. **c** (?) planking (of mill-dam).

1169 in tingnis et ~is et pro eis ducendis apud Oreford' *Pipe* 31; **1212** faciatis habere..omnes ~os..ad domum nostram de Cantebr' *Cl* 128; **1242** de quolibet centum ~orum ad naves (*Pat*) *RGasc* I 128; **1248** de ~is quercinis que habet ad operaciones regis Westmonasterii faciat habere ..quingenta ~a *Cl* 70; **1248** cccc bordeas *Cal. Liberate* 198; **1266** cc ~as Estrenses ad operaciones castri..Windesor' *Cl* 185; **1282** fregit unam ~am super ostium Christiane B. *CourtR.Hales* 194; **1300** cum ~is ad fenestras emptis *MinAc* 1132/10 m. 15b; **1317** navem..~is de Dacia oneratam *Cl* 135 m. 20*d.*; **1336** tria milia ~arum de Estland *RScot* I 467a; **1355** in fissura cc ~orum thacgorum *KRAc* 544/36 m. 2 (cf. ib. m. 3: ~orum de *thak*'); **1359** instrumenta pro fabrina: ..vj bord' mensal' [? *for trestle table*] (*Pipe* 203 r. 33*d.*) *Sea Terms* II 66; **1406** (v. 2 bordare); **1410** de qualibet centena †boedorum [MS.: bordorum] venalium (*Pat*) *Foed.* VIII 634; **1506** pro sarracione ij rodarum et dim. burdarum *Ac. Durh.* 102. **b** **1167** pro ~o ad domos regis de Wudestoch *Pipe* 160; **1205** maremium et ~am et clavos ..ad reparandas domos *Cl* 56b; **1234** habere faciat..x quercus..ad ~um faciendum ad capellam..lambruscandam *Cl* 48; **1242** ~um de *sap* [cf. sappus]..ad faciendam cameram regine nostre in navi nostra *Liberate* 16 m. 7; **1291** xx quercus aptas ad ~am *Cl* 143 m. 5; **1435** maeremium, ~um, ferrum *Pat* 438 m. 21*d.*; **1573** centena ~i *Pat* 1106 m. 17. **c** de piscibus captis in burdis *Ac. Beaulieu* 75v.

2 (?) table. **b** table for display of goods, counter.

1356 j alg' pro pasto ad bord' pro vj bussellis pasti intus operandis *AncD* A 3779*d.* **b** **14..** nullus magister artificii predicti ~as shope sue exponat..neque mercimonia arti sue pertinencia in fenistris suis preponat *Mem. York* I 197.

3 side of ship.

1242 cc modios salis..cariari faciatis usque ~um navis *RGasc* I 45 (= *CalPat* 311); **12..** si quis emerit.., bladum, fabas aut pisas ad naves vel aliquod de consimilibus mercimoniis, ..solvat infra ~am cum optinuerit rem emptam *Stat. Gild. Berw.* 27; **1294** nullus emat aliquod genus bladi.. seu cetera venalia apud Berwicum venientia per mare nisi sit ante ~am navis videlicet *at þe Rade Bra* Ib. 49; a**1342** satisfaciendo dicto emptori precium partis sue quam emerit infra ~am navis (*Ch. Newcastle upon Tyne*) *Gild. Merch.* II 185.

2 borda [OF *borde*], cottage or small holding (Gasc.).

1285 habeant et retineant sibi domos suas, molendina, furnos, ~as, piscarias..et omnes alias proprietates quas tenent ad manus suas *RGasc* II 274.

bordagium [OF *bordage*], bordage tenure. **b** bordage tenement, small holding (Fr. & C.I.).

1309 iiij virgatas terre..quas J. C. hucusque tenuit in ~io per officium suspendendi felones *S. Jers.* XVIII 121; **1331** pro una boveta quam tenet hereditarie de ~io (*KRAc* 89/15) *Ib.* I 5. **b** c**1172** bordachium in quo manet Girardus *Act. Hen. II* I 574; c**1180** terram in qua fuit vinea et unum ~ium *Ib.* II 133; **1274** percipit rex annuatim de ~io Johannis H. j cabatellum frumenti (*Chanc. Misc.* 10/5/1) *S. Jers.* II 29; **1309** habet [rex] ibi aliud ~ium quod R. W. tenet continens iij virgatas terre *Ib.* XVIII 132; **1331** quatuor bordarii ejusdem parochie qui hereditarie tenent ~ia..debent racione ~ii hujusmodi facere districciones s[u]moniciones et alia minuta servicia *Ib.* I 9.

1 bordare v. berdare 2.

2 bordare, ~ire, to cover with boards, board up.

1235 in eisdem [cindulis] ponendis super aulam et aula ~anda *Pipe Wint.* (159284) r. 7; **1240** aperturas..duorum apenticiorum inter aulam nostram et cameram regine.. ~iri et duas fenestras..in eisdem borduris similiter facias *Liberate* 15 m. 23; **1240** cameram privatam capellanorum ~ari faciatis in modum navis *Cl* 178; **1323** in xxviij bordis emptis..ad ~andam stayram ejusdem camere *MinAc* 854/7; **1348** in ij carpentariis conductis pro gurgite molendini ~ando *Ac. Man. Wint.* (*Chilbolton*); **1382** carpentariis.. ~antibus muros inter..stabulum et domum feni *Comp. Swith.* 281; **1406** in burdis sarrandis pro una camera.. burdanda *MinAc* 916/6.

2 to border, edge

1245 baudekini..~ati rubeo (*Invent. S. Paul.*) *Arch.* L 491; c**1250** pallam altaris ~atam de panno serico *Vis. S. Paul.* 19.

bordaria, bordage tenant (f.).

c1120 Edeva est ~ia et operatur j die *Cart. Burton* 27.

1 bordarius [OF *bordier*], 'bordar', bordage tenant, small holder: **a** (Eng.); **b** (Norm. & C.I.).

a ad hanc aecclesiam adjacent xx masurae ~iorum *DB* I (*Hants*) 52; xxxvi ~i de iii hidis..et iiii ~ii de xl acris et x ~ii quisque de v acris et v cotarii quisque de iiii acris *Ib.* (*Midx*) 128; extra burgum c ~ii cum hortulis suis reddunt l sol. *Ib.* (*Warw*) 238; ibi xxii sochemanni et x ~ii sub ipsis habent ix car' de hac terra et xiii carucas *Ib.* (*Derb*) 273; cccclxxx ~ii qui propter pauperiem nullam reddunt consuetudinem *Ib.* II (*Norf*) 116b; et sunt x alii homines ~ii qui non habent suam propriam terram sed et manent in lxxxvi acris de supradicta terra *Ib.* (*Suff*) 290; †975 (13c) cum..xvj villanis et x bord' *CS* 1313; †1046 (a1100) iii mansas et quatuor hidas cum septem villanis et septem bord' *CD* 1335; 1091 terram unius ~ii in eadem villa [*Wanborough, Wilts*] (*Ch. Ep. Sal.*) *Reg. S. Osm.* I 199 (= *MGL* II 27); 1140 Netham [*Hants*] cum omnibus appendiciis suis in..essartis et molendinis et ~iis et aquis *Regesta* III 921; a1182 totum dominium meum de eadem villa [*Lawford, Warw*] in terris ~iorum et bovariorum *FormA* 244; 1183 quatuor ~ii [v.l. bondarii] reddunt pro iiij toftis et croftis iij sol. et faciunt iiij precaciones in autumpno *Boldon Bk.* 12; a1200 in unoquoque maneriorum istorum unum ~ium de duabus acris terre cum mansura solutum ab omni servitio *CalCh* (*Suff*) I 424; 1234 iij ~ii recipiunt conredum suum in aula abbatis die quo laborant *Cust. Glast.* 1. **b** 1137 dedit unum ~ium apud Oistreham, sc. Hugonem de Gardino, cum terra sua *Regesta* III 749; c1160 apud Hoistreham unum †fordarium, Hugonem sc. de Gardino, et unam acram terre *MonA* VI 1112 (*Act. Hen. II* I 299); 1274 prepositus, bedellus et bordaj [? l. bordarii] ij (*Chanc. Misc.* 10/5/3) *S. Jers.* II 44; 1331 debet idem prepositus namiare capitalem ~ium ejusdem parochie et ceteros (*KRAc* 89/15) *Ib.* I 9.

2 bordarius [cf. 1 borda], **a** (?) keeper of tables. **b** fitter of boards (in ship-building). **c** (*s. dub.*).

a nebularius [recipit] consuetudinarium cibum; ..~ius tantundem *Domus Reg.* 131. **b** pro vadiis x bordar'.. quorum †quelibet [l. quilibet] eorum capit per diem v d. *KRAc* 5/2 m. 1. **c** 1130 in perdonis..Waltero bordario ij s. *Pipe* 104.

bordcula [cf. ME *cule*], (?) keel.

1267 de uno batello empto sine ~a, j d. *MinAc* (*Winchelsea*) 1031/20 m. 3 (cf. ib. m. 6: sine bordchula).

bordea v. 1 borda. bordeare v. 2 burdare.

bordellum, ~us [OF *bordel*; cf. 2 borda], cottage, small holding.

c1100 tenet Morcarius i hidam et i virgatam et i bordell' de dominio; Levericus dim. hidam de dominio et ii bordell' terre libere [*Badby, Northants*] (*Terr. Evesham*) *EHR* XLVIII 198; a1115 Osbertus posuit ibi v bordell' partem in vico regis, et fecit eos pro amore Dei ad hospitandum pauperes *Lib. Wint.* 6b; a1128 et j bercharius qui tenet ~um *Chr. Peterb. app.* 162; 1199 intruserunt se in ~um quoddam *CurR RC* II 144; 1208 unum molendinum et tres ~os combussit (*Ch. Regis*) *BBExch.* I 382; 1211 in ij ~is de novo factis super terram vacuam *Pipe Wint.* 57; 1250 tenet unum ~um deputatum servicio B. Marie *Fees* 1249; 1267 de novis ~is sine licentia levatis, que de novo ponuntur ad annuum redditum *Cart. Glouc.* III 61.

2 bordel, brothel.

1397 Matilda T. tenet communem burdellum in domo sua, receptando adulteros et fornicatores in domo sua (*Vis. Heref.*) *EHR* XLIV 445; 1442 tenet commune ~um in tenemento suo *CourtR* (*Ashton, Wilts*) 208/5 m. 2d.; 1485 communiter et usualiter custodiunt..bordell' et enormitatem in domibus suis *Rec. Nott.* II 348.

borderare v. bordurare.

bordererus, used for fastening boards (*cf. bordnailum*).

1211 in mm clavis ~is et dc grossioribus clavis *Pipe Wint.* 131.

bordeura v. bordura.

bordeus, made of boards, wooden.

1245 fenestras ~eas integras *Cal. Liberate* 25.

bordile [cf. bordellum], cottage, small holding (Gasc.).

1292 murum..construxerat juxta ~e quod habet apud Boliac *RGasc* III 44; 1315 in perpetuam possessionem et seisinam de quodam ~i..in civitate Burdeg' *Ib.* IV 1371; 1347 (v. bordilerius).

bordilerius, tenant of *bordile*.

1347 burgenses vel habitatores ville Burdegale aut eorum familie, vel ~ii, etiamsi bordilia hujusmodi in feodo.. decani et capituli existere contingat, ..et omnes alii domicilia tenentes infra dictos limites (*Instr. Senesc. Aquit.*) *Arch. Mun. Bordeaux* I 353.

bordinarius v. burdinarius. bordire v. 2 bordare.

bordmannus [ME *bordman*], a class of tenant (used by a later clerk for the *bord'*, *i.e. bordarius*, of *DB*).

†1086 (c1330) in Coggeshal' [*Essex*]..tunc unus ~us. ..[in Bokkinge] tunc xxv bormanni *Reg. Ch. Ch.* (*Galba* E IV) f. 31b; 1286 in dicto manerio [*Wickham, Kent*] sunt quidam homines qui appellantur *bordmen*..qui debent tassare totum bladum domini [etc.] *CoramR* 98 r. 19.

bordnailum, board-nail.

1284 pro bordnaylis..emptis ad dictam porcheam *KRAc* 351/9 m. 5; 1510 pro iiij[xx] bordnalis pro *le pentesse Ac. Durh.* 105.

bordonus v. 2 burdo b.

bordtolla, a toll on shipping (Humber).

s1221–35 dedit nobis..totum theloneum suum et ~am ad mare..de Hornsebek; ..~a est de qualibet nave ad litus applicante iiij d. *Meaux* I 421.

bordula, little board.

1487 ad..maeremium, vitrum, ~as, tabulas, scindolas ac omnia alia pro operacionibus..necessaria *Pat* 567 m. 8.

bordum v. 1 borda.

bordura [OF *bordeure*, ME *bordure, border*], boarding, woodwork.

1236 quod ~am a tergo sedis regis in capella S. Stephani.. interius et exterius depingi faciat de viridi colore *Cl* 239; 1240 (v. 2 bordare); 1250 in braccino deest tota ~a, scilicet parietes, quia est de fusto *CalIMisc* I p. 30.

2 border: **a** (of cloth, esp. embroidered); **b** (of cup) rim; **c** (of shield, her.), bordure; **d** (of plot of land); **e** (of kingdom).

a 1238 in dimidio panno de aresta et tela cerata ad bordeuras *Cal. Liberate* 322; 1252 ~a de aurifrig' (*Liberate* 28) *CalScot* 1872; s1292 legavit..unum frontale de velveto rubeo, †brendato cum burdura [de] viridi velveto *Cart. Bath* II 158; 1321 duo [tapeta] magna..cum albis ~is et infra ~as cum vineis et rubeis rosis Whittlesey 169; 1395 unum dorsale de viridi..cum apris in ~a *Test. Ebor.* III 4; c1420 due cape de rubeo samite habentes ~as cum imaginibus de auro juxta *orfrays* (*Invent.*) Amund. II *app.* 343. **b** 1434 lego..ciphum meum argenteum coopertum in ~is deauratum *Reg. Cant.* II 507. **c** cum una ~a de nigro pulverizata cum talentis..; G. ..*un bordur de sable besaunt* Bad. Aur. 137; ~e sive fimbrie multe et diverse..portantur in armis; quarum quedam sunt plane, quedam ingradate, quedam talentate, quedam plane pulverizate, quedam scaccate, quedam gobonate et quedam invecte Upton 236. **d** 1392 succidi fecit ~am grossarum quercuum cujusdam bosci *IMisc* 252/12/1; 1433 licebit..dicte pasture borderam super ripam aque..plantare cum salicibus *Rec. Leic.* II 250. **e** 1434 qualiter villa predicta in frontera inimicorum nostrorum extra borderam terre nostre Anglie existit *RScot* 285b; 1485 suscepimus in salvum..conductum..centum personas ..etiam Scotos in regnum nostrum apud borderas versus Scociam..veniendo ibidem *Ib.* 467b.

bordurare, to border, edge (cloth). **b** (her.) to provide with a bordure.

1245 pro duobus cendaliis et opere ad ~andum quendam pannum *Liberate* 21 m. 12; 1349 ad eandem supertunicam ~andam cum rubanis de serico (*KRAc* 391/15) *Arch.* XXXI 19; 1388 [panni] ~ati de panno stragulato rubei et blodei sandelli unius secte (*Invent. Westm.*) *Ib.* LII 241; 1436 unus mantellus pro nostra domina borderatus cum *ly velvate Reg. Aberd.* II 142; 1489 cum coopertorio..borderato cum argento *Cart. Boarstall* p. 290. **b** illa arma dicuntur ~ata sive fimbriata si color ipsius bordure fuerit sequens per totum Bad. Aur. 186; in campo argenteo ~ato cum nigro talentatim; ..G. sic..*en argent bordure de sable talentée* Upton 237.

borduratio, bordering.

1580 pro ~one..iij *kirtles* rotund' *Ac. LChamb.* 71 f. 28v.

bordus v. borda.

borealis [LL], northern, lying towards the north. **b** †southern (!). **c** (sb. sg. or pl.) the north.

ad ~em Humbrae fluminis plagam Bede *HE* II 5; frigora bis ternis borealia depulit annis Alcuin *SSEbor.* 215; a ~i oceano ad Pyrenaeos usque montes H. Bos. *Thom.* II 8; ~ium insularum maxima Yslandia Gir. *TH* I 1; 1215 barones de partibus ~ibus *Pat* 129; 1272 mox borialis / turbo quatit puppes (*De Ed. Rege*) *Pol. Songs* 131; Normannia dicitur, quia in parte boriali Francie situatur *Eul. Hist.* I 373; 1469 pro emendacione..defectuum..tam in latere australi quam in latere boriali dicti cancelli *Ac. Durh.* 642. **b** *the sowthe wynde*: auster, australis, borialis *CathA*. **c** 786 rex longe in ~ibus commorabatur Alcuin *Ep.* 3; s1460 venit regina a boriali cum duce..de Somershed *Chr. Hen. VI & Ed. IV* 154.

2 (of persons) belonging to the north, (sb.) northerner. **b** belonging to (or member of) the northern 'nation' (Oxford).

s1214 iste [Gilbertus ep. Roff.] borialis de Northumbria oriundus satis manifestavit vera esse que de partibus illis dicuntur, quia 'ab Aquilone pandit omne malum' *Flor. Hist.* II 150; s1347 cum quibus [sc. Scotis] animose ~es congredi affectantes certatim properabant Ad. Mur. *app.* 252; s1415 Thomam Gray, militem borialem *Chr. S. Alb.* p. 87. **b** 1268, 1349 (v. australis 2b); 1407 procurator borialis universitatis *StatOx* 198.

3 subject to prevailing north wind.

Gad. 37. 1 (v. austrinus d).

borealiter, northerly, towards the north.

1423 (v. australiter); 1441 tres rode terre jacent australiter et borialiter *Cl* 291 m. 17*d.*; 1587 inter viam regiam borialiter et viam ducentem usque..Acle Comen australiter *Pat* 1299 m. 21.

boreare, to utter in windy language.

tolerandus amicus / qui boreat stolidas lingue levitate loquelas D. Bec. 674.

boreas [CL < βορέας], north wind. **b** the north (or north-east). **c** the south (!). **d** storm (fig.).

subito Boreas Austrum divertit G. Amiens *Hast.* 60; flante ~ia nimio frigore *NLA* (*Modwenna*) II 208. **b** ab ~ea, *eastannorþan GlC* B 152; ad ~eam Humbri fluminis Bede *HE* I 15; in ~eam se convertens Gir. *TH* I 2; nosti Hyperboreas Boree nomen dare partes Neckam *DS* II 93; 1316 in remotis partibus regni nostri versus ~iam existent' (*RomanR*) *Foed.* III 585; s1342 barones tam de ~ea quam de aliis partibus regni interfuerunt Ad. Mur. 123; 1446 ij acras terre..abuttantes super le Westmede versus ~iam *CourtR Carshalton* 62; a1529 vasta palus sed campestris borie memoratur / Branxton More Skelton I 190. **c** *the sowthe*, auster, ~ias, meridianum *CathA*. **d** sic mundi Boreis agitor Hanv. IX 382.

borecha v. burrochius. borellus v. burellus. boreshalder v. borgesalder. boreta v. brodetta.

boreus [CL < βόρειος] northern. **b** north (or north-east) wind.

Arcturus.., qui ~eo aquilonalis poli cardine volvitur Aldh. *Met.* 3; flatus durissimi ~ei *V. Osw.* 404. **b** 7.. ~eus, *eastnorðwind GlC* B 152.

borga, ~us [AS *borg, borh*; cf. bortreminga, friborga], frankpledge, tithing, group of households w. collective legal responsibility (in Kent & Sussex a territorial unit).

1177 de dimidia marca de Toki cum ~o, quia non habuit quem plegiavit *Pipe* (*Berks*) 49; 1199 H. de Rieis et ejus ~us reddunt compotum de xx s. pro fuga Radulfi *Pipe* (*Kent*) 67; 1230 ~a de Hatfeld' debet dim. m. pro quodam mortuo sepulto sine visu coronatoris *Pipe* (*Suss*) 11; 1236 sunt xiiij borgi, sc.: Bendrege [etc.] *Cust. Battle* 126 (v. et. borgesalder); c1250 si contingat wardas facere talagium aut donum abbati dare in †brog' de Litlemun[in]gham *Reg. S. Aug.* 431; 1275 ballivus..excaitoris cepit..de borgha de Brokesgate, que manu cepit Galfridum H. et non habuit coram justiciariis, iiij m. *Hund.* (*Kent*) I 201; comes Glovernie appropriavit sibi borgham de Heghardr', que est quarta pars hundredi *Ib.* 202; 1275 Johannes Peverel habet unam ~am de feodo Wincestr' pertinens (*sic*) ad dim. hundredum [de la Denne] et habet assisam panis et cervisie *Ib.* (*Suss*) II 207; 1275 in ~a de Wadeherst sunt xv virgate dim. et j ferling' terre native (*Ext. Tarring, Suss*) *Gavelkind* 22; 1286 si latro captus sit in villa domini, custodietur in molendino domini per custum borgh' de Wycham [*Kent*] *CoramR* 98 r. 19; 1313 manerium de Estwell [*Kent*] est infra precinctum hundredi regis de Estri in borgha de Soles *PQW* 318a (cf. ib. 339a); 1313 si cum eo non fuisset in servicio.. esset in borgha; et qui convictus est de felonia et sit in borgha, tota borgha in misericordia *Eyre Kent* 95; nulla habuerunt catalla nec fuerunt in burgo, quia extranei *Ib.* 61; 1315 alii in borwa predicta residentes *Year Bk.* XVII (*Kent*) 83; 1326 borghesalder et quatuor homines de qualibet borgha..tempore quo ipsi ad turnos vicecomitis..ad ea que visum franci plegii contingebant presentanda venerunt *Cl* 143 m. 15 (cf. *Reg. S. Aug.* 360); 1354 communitati burge de Recolvre *Lit. Cant.* II 322; 1372 debet sectam..ad hundredum domini regis de Brigge [*Bridge by Canterbury*] prout premunitus fuerit per borgham *IMisc* 201/5; 1535 de redditu custumariorum tenencium ibidem per annum vocato *warkeland*, viz. in burg' de Upperton [*in Eastbourne, Suss*] vj li..*Rutland MSS.* (*Visus Comp. Salop etc.* p. 45).

borgagium v. burgagium.

borgana, ~is [cf. *PN Elements* s.v. *burgæsn* (*burial place*)], (?) mound or ridge.

1170 dedi monachis ~es et marescum et vasta loca que sunt infra has xviij bovatas ad vertendum ad profectum et utilitatem suam *E. Ch. Yorks* XI 129; a1195 omnes ~es quas poterunt infra terram illam vertere sibi in terram cultam *Ib.* 143; a1200 cum ~is et marescis *Ib.* 130.

borgensis v. burgensis.

borgesalder [cf. borga; ME *borghesaldre, borgheshaldre*, (?) *borgh*+*alder* (= *elder*), *conf. w. halder* (= *holder*)], 'borsholder', headborough, tithingman.

1236 borgeshaldrus cum tota borga sua ducet..latronem ad hundredum *Cust. Battle* 136; potest quis alium recipere in franco plegio sicut borghyaldre quando voluerit Bracton 124b; 1279 tenentes..manerii solebant sequi hundreda predicta de tribus septimanis in tres septimanas per boreshaldr' et tres homines *PQW* (*Kent*) 341b (cf. ib. 345b: per borgesaldr' de Cherlton' et iiij homines); 1284 fuit submonitus per borgasaldrum et vocatus non venit *CourtR* (*Kent*) 182/1 m. 1; 1313 abbas [S. Aug. Cant.]..tenentes suos subtraxit de predicta secta facienda, de quibus modo venit nisi unus †borghealdir cum ij hominibus tantum (*Alloc. Libertatis*) Thorne 2021; 1313 equus et olla liberati fuerunt borghsaldro de Lenham ad respondendum de eisdem; ideo respondet W. de M. borghsalder *Eyre Kent* 80; 1315 omnes borwesaldres cum sua *borwe*, sc. decenarius cum sua decenna *Year Bk* (*Kent*) XVII 82; 1318 quilibet burghesalder cum quatuor hominibus de burgha sua *Ib.* XXII 297; 1326 fuit cum eodem borusaldro ubi cepit unam vaccam pro districcione *Reg. Roff. Ep.* I 195.

1 borgus v. borga.

2 †borgus, 'borsholder'.

1462 nec aliquis eorum..assignetur constabularius, decennarius, †borghus [? l. borghesaldrus]..aut alius officiarius.. extra fines..dicti marisci (*Ch. Romney*) *ChartR* 192 m. 3.

borialis, ~iter v. borealis, ~iter.

†boriarium [cf. foratorium], (?) borer.

1390 solut' pro j boriar' calibando *Ac. Bridge Masters* IX m. 9 (*London Guildhall R. O.*).

borias v. boreas. borica v. borith.

boriens [? boreas *conf. w.* oriens], north. **b** (adj.) northern.

1370 [versus] ~entem *CalCl* 190; **1417** et sic versus ~entem *Reg. Aberbr.* II 51. **b 1387** ex parte ~enti causeti (*CoramR*) *Pub. Works* 15.

borientalis, northern.

1251 wallam..ex parte ~i et aquam..ex parte australi *Reg. S. Aug.* 419; **1279** usque ad ~em costelam de Conygton Mere *Hund.* II 654; **1532** ex parte ~i *Reg. Aberbr.* II 507.

borientaliter, on the north.

1587 clausum..adjacens prope altam viam orientaliter et ~er *Pat* 1299 m. 19.

borith [Heb.], soapwort (*Saponaria*) or other herb.

10.. borith, erba fullonum, *leaðorwyrt* WW; herbam quandam [? *figwort*] que juxta rivulos et in aquosis locis nascitur, hanc poete †electrim vocant, phisici boricam Adel. *CA* 12; planta que dicitur boriza et est similis majorane Bacon IX 136; borith, herba saponaria seu herba fullonis.. i. nepta *SB* 13; borax vel borith, herba fullonum, saponaria idem, A. *crowesoppe*; ..†nonaclum [l. novaculum] cirurgie, lanceolata aquatica idem, A. *sperewort* [? *water-plantain*] *Alph.* 23.

borittus v. burrochius. borla v. burla. borna v. burna. boro v. baro. borreum v. burarium. borrum v. 2 burrus. borsa v. bursa. borteza v. borax a.

bortreminga [AS *borh-treming*; cf. tremura], view of frankpledge (Suff); *cf. EHR* XXXVIII 244.

1275 ~a de Gategrave solebat teneri per eosdem ballivos et subtracta est per homines de Oreford' *Hund.* II 188; **13..** item de †bortremio xij d. (*Cust. Bury St. E.*) *Cust. Rents* 172; p**1333** abbas S. Edmundi..habet in eadem villa [de Brethenham] homagium et liberum †bortermium *Reg. Pinchbeck* II 270.

borusalder v. borgesalder. borwa v. borga.

bos [CL], ox (esp. for ploughing). **b** cow. **c** (fig., type of clumsiness). *V. et. lingua bovis, oculus bovis.*

boves mugiunt vel reboant Aldh. *PR* 131; nomina ferarum: ..bos, *oxa* Ælf. *Gl.*; in dominio v boves arantes *DB* I 14; terra est dimidii bovis et ibi est semibos *Ib.* 218b; villani habent v boves in car[ruca] *Ib.* 275; habent vii boves ad carrucam *Dom. Exon.* 177; c**1100** dederunt terram ad octo boves *Cart. Chester* 19; c**1120** in Stratona..sunt ij [aratra] de xvj bobus *Cart. Burton* 25; quodsi bos [AS: *oxa*] cornu petierit virum aut mulierem (*Quad.*) *GAS* 33; **1194** inquiratur de quot bobus et averis singule caruce valeant instaurari..; erit autem pretium bovis iiij solidi (*Cap. Coronae* 23) R. Howd. III 265; **1227** de bobus de seisina [*seized for disseisins committed*] *CalCh* I 6 (cf. ib. II 192 [**1275**]: boves de disseisinis provenientes); **1232** quilibet bos et vacca juncti ad carucam arabunt j acram dim. episcopo; et ideo pariter respondent hoc anno de herbagio, quia multi boves erunt arabiles *Crawley* 201; **1260** una cum carucis et bobus carucarum *Cl.* 92; **1268** computat..de iij bovettis modo factis bobus *Ac. Wellingb.* 8; **1269** de placito injuste detencionis unius equi, †bobi, affre etc. *CBaron* 80; qualiter equus magis quam bos est sumptuosus videndum est: ..omnis bos vel vacca ad laborem caruce deputata a festo S. Luce usque ad festum Invencionis S. Crucis..ad presepe custoditur; ..bos de tribus et dim. mensuris avene, de quibus x faciunt bussellum, sufficienter poterit qualibet septimana sustentari *Fleta* 161; **1302** in duobus bobus emptis.. ad cariagium domini regis faciendum, xviij s. *KRAc* 482/20 r. 20; a**1330** licebit..imponere..viij boves carucales, ad pascendum *DLCourtR* 43/488; **1439** de ccliiij bobus, vaccis et bovettis *Ac. Durh.* 75. **b** vitulum bovis enixe W. Cant. *Mir. Thom.* VI 67; vitulum virilem bos edidit Gir. *TH* II 21; bobus lactantibus atque juvencis D. Bec. 2180. **c** mobilis esto, lepus levis, haud bos segnis in actus *Id.* 1206.

2 (w. *marinus*), seal.

accipe corium bovis marini; ..et est illud animal marinum pilosum, et vocatur Anglice *cele* Gad. 95 v. 2.

bosa v. botium.

bosagium [? cf. ME *bos, bose* = *stall*], a customary rent in East Anglia, (?) cow-penny or 'bosing-silver' (*cf. Cust. Rents* 77).

c**1230** debet ad busagium de quolibet bove iij annorum et ultra ob. et de qualibet vacca lactrice j d. singulis annis ad festum S. Crucis Invencionis (*Cust. Lessingham*) *Doc. Bec* 106; c**1250** singuli eorum in festo Invencionis S. Crucis, si habuerint vaccas, dant ad busagium j d. et pro juvenca pregnante j ob. et pro eo quod non jacebunt in falda abbatis [*Holme, Norf*] *Cart. Rams.* I 402; **1296** quedam consuetudo que vocatur busag' et valet per annum xij d. *IPM* (*Norf*) 77/3b, r. 22 (cf. ib. 76/5: redditus †boscag'); c**1300** solvit busagium viz. pro qualibet vacca lactante ob. et pro qualibet ove ob.; vel jacent in falda a vigilia Trinitatis usque Purificacionem B. Marie *Rent. Surv. R* (*Norf*) 465; **1302** busagium idem valet per annum vj s. viij d. solvendum ad festum Petri ad Vincula (*Ext. Coney Weston*) *Suff. Hund.* 68; **1314** de bosag' ad festum S. Mich. viij d. *IPM* (*Norf*) 43/32; c**1325** de consuetudinibus custumariorum videlicet faldagio, ~io, *hildersilver* et *hussilver* (*MinAc* 1141/1) *Cust. Rents* 57; **1388** quidam redditus vocatus ~ium, viz. pro capite cujuslibet vacce in certis hameletis ibidem j d. *IMisc* (*Norf*) 243/4; **1436** quieti de omnimodo passagio, pannagio, †boscagio *Entries* 674 b.

bosatus v. botiatus.

1 bosca [βοσκάς], duck, pochard.

illam [sc. pochardam] Aristotelis esse ~am judico Turner *Av.* 21.

2 bosca v. busca. 1 boscagium v. bosagium.

2 boscagium [OF *boschage*], woodland, weald (*cf. Cart. Bilsington* 35).

c**1160** feodum Ricardi de S. G. de ~io inter novum pontem et Lacneppe [*Suss*] *CalPat 1358–61* 535; **11..** do ecclesie [*Hurley, Berks*]..iiij solidatas terre in boschagio *FormA* 247 (cf. ib. 45); **1250** dedimus..terram nostram incultam..sicut est boschagium et essartum atque marescum *Mon. Exon.* 252; **1283** Bocholt', tenentes de ~io *Cust. Battle* 38; s**1209** predia [archiepiscopi] in manu sunt capta, ~ia combusta, prata diruta *Eul. Hist.* III 97; **1421** hospitale ..de Villaribus in ~io Baiocensis diocesis (*RNorm*) *Foed.* X 111.

boscalis, of wood. **b** wooded.

c**1300** de ~i venditione magnum habuit adjuvamen *G. S. Alb.* II 51. **b 1571** boscos et terras ~es *Entries* 397b; **1587** terra ~is *Pat* 1298 m. 2.

boscalium, ~ia [OF *boschal*], brushwood.

1397 boscus de buscalia vocatus Brochangre *IMisc* 267/13; **1421** de..xx acris de ~io in Somerby [*Lincs*]..x acris de ~io..in Bekforde [*Glos*] *Cl* 271 m. 8.

boscar- v. bostar.

boscaria, timber merchants' quarter (Timberhithe, London).

1275 quedam domus est in ~ia que solebat esse cellarium dominicum regis *Hund.* I 414.

boscata v. bescata.

boscatus, wooded.

1567 de novo redditu unius parcelle terre nuper bossate modo vastate vocate Oakecorne Parke *Rutland MSS., MinAc 4–9 Eliz.* p. 101 (cf. ib. *14–18 Eliz.* f. 108*d.*: una [parcella] vocatur Toodale Hagge, nuper ~a et modo vastata).

boscellus, ~um [cf. OF *boscel, boschel*], little wood.

c**1160** dedi..~um et sartum juxta campos de Salabi [*Lincs*] *Danelaw* 87; c**1200** a calceda que dividit moram et †bolkellum [? l. boskellum] *E. Ch. Yorks.* I 493 (cf. ib. 492: inter boscum et moram); **1220** servitia de quodam ~o quod de eo tenet in Selverleg' [*Cambs*] *CurR* IX 123; **1239** dedit ..quendam parvum ~um [*Suff*] *BNB* III 258; a**1310** boskellus [*Marton, Yorks*] *CalCh* III 156.

boscheronius [OF *boscheron*], woodcutter.

1198 boskeroniis qui prostrabant et escaplebant maremia *RScacNorm* II 309.

bosciculus, little wood.

1280 cum duobus ~is qui Personbuske vulgariter nuncupantur *Reg. Ebor.* 86.

bosculus, ~um, little wood or (?) low-growing wood.

1143 ~us de Personeswode prius vendebatur per abscisionem ramorum..et postea residuum dicti ~i vendebatur (*Cart. Pipewell*) *MonA* V 436; c**1189** rivulum descendentem de ~o *Cart. Glam.* 227; **1199** reddit comp. de c s. pro quodam ~o essartando *Pipe* 117; **1205** finem factum de quodam bosco et ~o *CurR* IV 8; c**1250** in omnibus boscis et ~is *Couch. Kirkstall* 82; c**1400** ~um quod vocatur le Frith *MonA* VI 376.

boscura, wood, grove.

1555 ~am in Crabtrefelde [*Staffs*] *CalPat* 137.

1 boscus, ~um [OF *bos, bois*], a wood, grove. **b** woodland.

1131 do..decimas de meis dominiis tam de planis quam de †bochis (*Ch. Hen. I, Conches*) *Gall. Christ.* XI *instr.* 129D; quin etiam de ~is et pratis..decima reddenda est (*Leg. Ed. Conf.*) *GAS* 632; **1184** defendit rex quod nullus agistet ~os suos antequam ~i regis agistentur (*Assisa Forestae*) R. Howd. II 246; **1199** quod ~um de Sumersham sit quietum ..de wastis *RChart* 12; c**1200** tres ~os leuga includit *Chr. Battle* 18; **1203** quod monachi..possint claudere omnes ~os suos qui non sunt in foresta et qui sunt extra forestam regis *Pipe* 132; **1203** furatus est iiij porcos domini sui in ~o de Bech' qui est clausus de haia et seratus *CurR* II 231; **1220** quod redderem G. de Clare barton' Bristollie, buscum de Furcis, chaciam de Keinesham (*AncC.* V 72) *RL* I 90; **1221** solebant trahere buscam suam de ~o *CurR* X 3; **1256** de bossis eorundem maneriorum *Cl* 20; c**1275** estoverium habebunt [in] omni communi ~o predicte ville..pertinente *Reg. S. Bees* 324; **1279** habet quoddam clausum ~um quod continet xl acras..ubi nullus communicare debet *PQW* 196a; c**1350** in bruscis et ~is *Melrose* II *app. no.* 22; s**1356** ad exitum unius magni ~i *Eul. Hist.* III 222; s**1420** eorum vexilla per ~os et nemora in insidiis clam veniencia perceperunt *Plusc.* X 25; **1539** quinque copecias ~i et ~a mea existencia in Morecrychell [*Dors*] *FormA* 215. **b** a**1071** manerium suum de Aldenham [*Herts*]..cum omnibus suis pertinentibus in ~o et plano (*Dom. Westm.*) *Regesta* p. 120; occupavit..i hidam inter ~um et planum *DB* (*Herts*) I 136b; silva quingent' porcorum; de ~o et pastura xiii sol. et iiii den. *Ib.* 138b: quantumcunque ex omni latere tam in ~o quam in plano prospicere posset Gir. *Spec.* II 1 p. 29; **1255** propter spissitudinem ~i..forestarii nescierunt quo devenerunt *SelPlForest* 77; **12..** †bocci et pasture.. penuriam *Ann. Durh.* 186; **1388** xl acre bossi *IMisc* 239/36.

2 wood (material) used as timber or firewood (*cf. busca*).

1106 sciatis me dedisse..ecclesie S. Marie Sar'..~um in foresta mea quantumcunque opus fuerit ad predictam ecclesiam tenendam et reficiendam *Regesta* 753; **1182** de xviij li. ..de boscho..vendito *Pipe* 62; **1221** de caretta honerata de ~o, ubi solebant capere j astelam, capiunt majus lignum *SelPlCrown* 90; **1236** Henewode unum jugum; et hoc jugum non habet ~um [? *right of collecting wood*] in Kingeswode set in wallis *Cust. Battle* 130; **1246** pro ~o domini furtive asportato *SelPlMan* 7; **1329** pro xxx ponderibus ~i ad comburendum *ExchScot* 125; **1329** ~um computabilem vocatum *talghwode CalCl* 449; **1359** ad maeremium et ~um pro sagittis inde faciendis apta..providenda et prosternenda *Pat* 258 m. 9*d.*; **1378** assendit super scalam et voluit querere ~um super unum solarium *SelCCoron* 91; **1493** in ~o xx d. *Comp. Swith.* 308.

3 wood dist. as: **a** full-grown or underwood; **b** living (green) or dead (dry).

a ~o nec subbosco nostro sine licentia..nemo manum apponat (*Ps.-Cnut Forest.*) *GAS* 625; **1216** custodito subbosco de Berchamsted', de grosso bosscho..vendi faciat *Cl* 248; **1219** sive de grosso ~o sive de riffleto *Pat* 211; **1243** dedit licentiam abbatisse..quod..possit vendere de claro ~o suo..ubi non sit subboscus, usque ad summam x li. *Cl.* 50; **1270** facta est magna destructio de grosso ~o et de exbrancatura in boscis supradictis *TR Forest Proc.* 229 m. 9*d.*; **1311** sunt ibidem in bosco qui vocatur le Chert cccv acre grossi ~i *Cust. Battle* 138; **1583** totum illud ~um et subboscum..vocatum Earles Wood *Pat* 1234 m. 6 (cf. ib.: eosdem ~os et subboscos..succident). **b** c**1108** ~um vivum ad edificandum et ardendum..; mortuum autem ~um cotidie ad vendendum ad iiij asinos (*Ch. St. Martin au Bos*) *Regesta* II p. 321; a**1128** reddunt per annum xxij sceppas avene pro mortuo ~o *Chr. Peterb. app.* 159; **1157** mortuum ~um ad ardendum et viride ad..edificia sua facienda (*Ch. Silli*) *Act. Hen. II* I 131; **1228** non licet monachis accipere in foresta meremium de quercu..; siccum autem, sc. mortuum ~um, ..capere possunt *Feod. Durh.* 236; **1253** vix posset aliquis transire per semitas illius foreste propter multitudinem mortui ~i *Rec. Leic.* I 43; **1255** habet..mortuum ~um quod cadit cum vento *Hund.* II 83; **1269** [salvo] mortuo et sicco ~o qui potest colligi sola manu sine utensili ferreo *SelPlForest* 46; **1281** in misericordia pro viridi ~o *SelPlMan* 30; s**1308** prefecto hujus solatii [sc. hastiludii] 'rex de viridi ~o' nomen dabatur; sed ~us viridis in mortuum vertebatur *Ann. Paul.* 264 (cf. *Ann. Lond.* 157: rex de Vertbois); **1336** de hominibus, mulieribus et pueris communam non habentibus portantibus siccum ~um super capita eorum *DL Coucher* 301b.

2 boscus v. botium.

†boscuus, woody, shrubby.

1412 ita quod spine, tribuli et alia germina ~a..viam supercrescerent *IMisc.* 290/8.

bosiare v. boisiare. boskellus v. boscellus. boskeronius v. boscheronius. boso v. 1 buzo. bosolum v. bossellum.

†bosor, flesh.

7.. †bofor, *lendislieg GlC* B 167; *beyst* [v.l. *byffe*] *flesch,* bossor *PP*; *befe,* ~or, carnes bovine *CathA.*

†bosretum [? cf. OF *borree*], birch-rod.

si acolitus phonastro vel correptorio [percutit], quod vulgus nostratum ~um nuncupat, non tenetur J. Sal. *Hist. Pont.* 3.

bossatus v. boscatus, botiatus.

bossellum [cf. OF *boce* < botium], (?) rounded moulding (arch.) or sim. (? *cf. boutellum*).

1253 pro iiij^{xx} pedibus et dim. de bosol' *Ac. Build. Hen. III* 226 (cf. ib. 250: pro..ix pedibus de *bosseus*); pro xlj buscellis, pretium buscelli iij d. *Ib.* 254.

bossellus v. bussellus. bossequus v. bubsequa. bossetum v. 2 buffettum. bossi, bossis v. boscus. bossor v. bosor.

bostar, ~arium, ~aria [LL], byre, cow-shed.

~are vel boviale, *scipen* Ælf. *Sup.*; s**1138** rex..unum [episcopum captum]..in ~ario in boum presepio..ponit Fl. Worc. *Cont.* A 108; cum [bos] tanquam cadaver protraheretur a ~are W. Cant. *Mir. Thom.* V 24; equo et mulo et asino stabulum paratur, ~ar bovi, ara porco, ovibus caula Neckam *NR* II 158; s**1234** terras..comitis Cornubie.. cum..bobus in ~aribus, caballis quoque in stabulis, ..incendio tradiderunt M. Par. *Maj.* III 264; est bostar statio bovis Garl. *Syn.* 1582B; **1266** cum grangiis et ~are *Pat* 84 m. 27; **1267** servientes prioris..litigabant in †boscare *SelCCoron* 10; abbas R. [ob. **1274**] levavit..unum †boscarium et unam bercariam Whittlesey 143; **1345** in ~aria sunt xxx boves pro carucis *Pri. Cold. app.* p. xvii; ubi sunt ..~aria sive presepia pro bobus et aliis animalibus Lyndw. 85k; *stal of beestys stondynge,* ~ar *PP*; **1502** in uno orrio et uno †boscare vocato *a shepyn Reg. Heref.* (*Mayew*) 11.

bostarius v. bustuarius.

†bostio, plough-boy.

~io, A. *a boye* WW; *a ploghe dryfer,* stigarius, ~io *CathA.*

bosunus v. 1 buzo.

1 bota [ME *bote*], repair (of fences), 'hayboot'.

1255 vj caretas de ramis pro ~a prostratis *Hund.* II 115.

2 bota, ~us [OF *bote*], boot.

a**1175** dabunt nobis annuatim..duo paria ~arum ad Pentecosten *E. Ch. Yorks* XI 242; c**1190** reddendo..nobis ..unas ~as ad festum S. Andree *Kelso* 250; **1200** precium.. iiij par ~arum ad feminas *Liberate* p. 9; [Grandimontani] sotularibus cum corrigiis utuntur itinerantes et domi ~is Gir. *Spec.* III 21 p. 257; **1225** paria †carrarum [MS.: botarum] (*AncC* IV 169) *RL* I 263; laxasque ferunt pede bōtas Garl. *Mor. Scol.* 426; c**1248** recipiet annuatim bis calciamenta, in yeme [sc. ~as] †fentratas [l. feutratas] et in estate ~as non †fentratas *Doc. Robertsbridge* (*HMC*) 103 (cf. ib. 96: unas ~as de alluto); **1313** Godewino allutar' London' pro..iiij paribus ~orum *KRAc* 374/19 f. 6; **1346** utuntur.. quidam siquidem ~is rostratis; quidam etiam nimis strictis

(*Const. Prov. Ben.*) *Conc.* II 730; **1367** in..redditu..unius paris ~arum †felcatarum [l. feltatarum] *RMS Scot* 91; **1423** loco ~arum..assignamus tibi ut uti valeas..calligis secularibus super casullas ascendentibus *Reg. Heref.* 33; **s1356** veni huc, ..decalciare..~as meas *Plusc.* IX 43.

3 bota v. 3 butta. botagium v. batagium, buttagium.

botam, botin, (?) **botina** [Ar. *buṭm*; cf. albotim], terebinth (bot.).

insitio..olivarum in botam Alf. Angl. *Plant.* I 16; aristologie..botine..dauci Gilb. VI 273 v. 2; †botra, i. terebentina *SB* 13; botin est terebenthina..collecta quum plus virium a coelestibus hausisse putatur; est etiam balsamus ex eadem tractatus artificiose, alias butimo *LC* 227.

botanare v. botonare.

botanicum [βοτανικόν], herb-garden.

~icum vel viridarium, *wyrttun* Ælf. *Gl.*

botaria v. 2 buttaria. boteicium v. buticium.

1 botellarius, maker of (leather) bottles.

1373 ordinacio ~iorum *CalLBLond* G 317.

2 botellarius, ~ia, boteler- v. butellar-.

1 botellus [CL], bowel, gut. **b** file (strung on gut) or (?) bundle (*cf. bundellus*).

pro stricto bodello quid faciendum esse judicas? Adel. *CA* 13 (cf. ib. 3: in budello). **b 1233** carta est in parvo bodello in deposito *KRMem* 13 r. 11.

2 botellus [OF *botel*; cf. batellia], 'bottle', bundle (of hay). **b** sheaf (of darts).

1327 quod extranei non hospitent fenum nec vendant per ~um (*LBLond* E f. 179) *MGL* I 721. **b c1335** vj botell' de darttis *IMisc* 128/19.

3 botellus, ~a [OF *boteille*], bottle, usu. of leather. **b** (?) drawing of a bottle.

1360 duo paria ~orum *Cl* 197 m. 5; **1390** de..ij ~is argent' deaur'..cum ij *baudrykes* de serico rubeo *Ac. Foreign* 25G; **1391** de..j botell' pro incausto *Ib.* 25D; **1391** pro..iij ~is pro croco *Ac. H. Derby* 74; **1393** duo paria de grappis, novem paria ~orum (*Cl*) *Foed.* VII 745; **1395** tres ~i de correo et unus vitrinus *Test. Ebor.* III 7; **1416** pro implecione ij ~orum de Romney *Ac. Durh.* 611; **1440** deliberaciones..vinorum, cervisiarum, beere ~orum, ciphorum ligneorum.. *Pat* 448 m. 33; **1534** pro emendacione unius ~e de corrio *Househ. Bk. Durh.* 293. **b 1349** unum lectum..poudratum cum ~is de argento habentibus zonas *taunes* (*KRAc* 391/15) *Arch.* XXXI 41.

botenare, ~arium v. boton-. boterac-, boterass-, boteric- v. butericius. boteria v. 2 buttaria.

botha, ~um [ON *buð*], booth, 'bothy', hut. **b** market stall. **c** (?) tolbooth.

1163 unam toftam in Perht cum ~a *Reg. S. Andr.* 54; **c1200** dedi..unum rete..et unum ~um et locum aptum ad rete siccandum (*Ch. Holme Cultram*) *MonA* V 607; **1240** angularem bodam *Cart. Fountains* I 258; **1241** in ~is nostris de Medio Vico [*Chesh*] reficiendis *Liberate* 15 m. 18; **1271** [dedit] locum suum in marisco de Dunston [*Lincs*], ubi †batha [MS.: botha] sua sita est (*ChartR*) *MonA* VI 342; **c1280** tres ~as in villa mea de Aynestrother *Dryburgh* 14; **1322** in plaustro..cariante meremium et turbas pro una nova ~a ad bolas de Ladyclif' [*Derb*] facienda *MinAc* 1146/11 m. 12; S. Brandanus in ea [insula] ~am, idiomate nostro *bothe*, id est cellam, construxit; unde et deinceps.. habetur binomia, quod aliquando Rothesay..sic et aliquando insula de Bothe..nuncupatur Fordun *Chr.* I 28; **1430** tenent..j domum et j ~am jacentes apud Neshend [*Hartlepool*]; ..sed illa ~a nunc jacet vasta *Feod. Durh.* 24. **b** faciunt in nundinis S. Cuthberti singuli ij villani j ~am *Boldon Bk.* 4; **c1190** (v. bothetarius); **a1240** unum toftum in Lancastre cum edificiis sc...in Markahastrete juxta bohas *Cart. Cockersand* 823; **c1260** de quadam ~a in vico fori *Deeds Newcastle* 78; **1288** non locabunt domos suas in ipsis nundinis..aliquibus mercatoribus..dummodo predicte selde seu ~e..non extiterint locate (*Plac. Chester*) *MonA* II 389; mercenarius qui habuerit ~am coopertam in foro die fori dabit obolum propter consuetudinem; ille vero qui non habet coopertam dabit quadrantem *Leg. IV Burg.* 37 (cf. ib. 65); habere faciatis..nomina fratrum gilde et tenentium ~as mercimonii *Iter Cam.* 1; **1552** ad edificandas v ~as sive oppellas (*Ch.*) *Scot. Grey Friars* II 231. **c 1244** in liberacione unius servientis custodientis ~am de Len [*Norf*] *Liberate* 21 m. 1 *sch.*

bothagium, payment for erecting stalls in a fair (*cf. bonagium*).

1232 salvo..dictis burgensibus [de Bernewell'] quod quieti sint in feria illa de toloneo, stallagio et bodagio [v.l. bothagio] *CurR* XIV 2136; **1441** concessimus ei picagium, stallagium, ~ium et tollagium..de novo mercato infra villam de Burcestre (*Pat*) *Ambrosden* II 410.

bothena [(?) Gael. *bothan*], lordship.

si quis manens in una ~a ceperit namos in alia ~a sine licencia domini vel ejus ballivi (*Assise David I* 21; cf. 22) *APScot* 9; **†1209** si aliquis emat bladum in aliqua ~a et transeat ad aliam ~am et ibi moram fecerit (*Assise Will.* 35) *Ib.* 60.

†bothetarius, (?) booth-keeper (but *cf. apothecarius*).

c1190 notum sit..me dedisse..Ricardo ~io..suam botham lapideam *E. Ch. Yorks* IV 82.

bothonia [? cf. 3 butta], (?) bucket.

~ia, *embrin GlC* B 146; **9..** ~ia, *æmbern* WW.

bothonicula, (?) small bucket, 'stoup'.

~a, *stoppa GlC* B 147; **9..** bodonicula, *amber*, †botholicula.., bothonicla, *stoppa* WW.

1 bothor v. bochor.

2 bothor [Ar. *buthūr* (pl.)], pimples, acne.

~or, i. pustule parve que fiunt in pueris *SB* 13; ~or aut cossi sunt apostemata parvula quaedam pustulosa faciei candida *LC* 227.

bothum v. botha.

botiatus, embossed.

1340 una cupa auri cum pede et cooperculo bossat' cum parvis aymell' de claro colore *Ac. Wardr.* (*TRBk* 203) p. 315; **1390** de..una pelve rotunda cum uno anulo et bosata circa bordur' *Ac. Foreign* 25G.

boticium v. buticium. boticularius v. buticularius. botillagium v. batellagium. botillarius v. butellarius. botin, botina v. botam.

botium, ~ia [OF *boce*], swelling, lump. **b** metal boss. **c** boss (arch.). **d** (?) bastion.

bocium fit in gula..ex amplitudine et dilatatione venarum Gilb. IV 153. 1; ~ium est apostema proveniens in gula, veluti struma *LC* 227. **b 1235** j cuppam argenteam deauratam et operatam de opere †Turcin' cum bocyys elev[atis] *ChancMisc* 3/4*d.*; **1419** lego..unum ciphum de masero cum uno bocio argenti infra *Reg. Cant.* II 173; **1477** Aula Ballioli habeat..unum ciphum, ..*chasset* de argento albo totaliter et cum boscis *Test. Ebor.* III 67. **c 1241** faciatis..dominicam cameram nostram in albo depingi de Veteri Testamento et Novo cum bocys deauratis *Liberate* 15 m. 17; **1289** vitrario pro reparacione unius bose ad tabernaculum lecti regis in sua magna camera *KRAc* 467/17 m. 8. **d 1291** in factura ij boccarum turrium gemellarum ad portam predictam a profundo rochee infra terram usque superficiem pontis de altitudine xxx pedum et spissitudine convenienti *KRAc* 486/7 (= *Building in England* 82: †boccarum); ab eisdem bociis versus castrum *Ib.*

botizella v. butisella. botlaria v. butellaria.

boto, ~onus [OF *boton*], hip (berry).

nomina herbarum: ..butunus, *heope* Ælf. *Gl.*; betunus, *heope Gl. Durh.*; **12..** butunus, i. *butuns*, i. *hoepe* WW.

2 stud or button.

1241 abstulit ei in roberia..unum butonem argenteum *JustIt* 695 r. 21; **1242** pro..~one auri *Pipe* 127; **1251** pro.. tribus duodenis butunorum de calcedon' et aliis butonis *Pipe* 95 r. 6; **1253** pro xxiiij butonibus de minutis perlis ad predictas lambellas *Liberate* 29 m. 10; **1272** in..empcione botunorum ad robas regine *Pipe* 116 r. 1*d.*; **1284** pro ij duodenis ~onum ad opus..filie regine *KRAc* 351/9 m. 14; **1290** pro liiij duodenis ~onorum emptorum pro capis trium filiarum *Ac. Wardr.* (*ChancMisc* 4/5) f. 10*d.*; **1303** unus lapis ad similitudinem jaspidis munitus argento cum ~one de curallo (*KRAc* 363/6) *DocExch* 279; **c1350** albe tunice butones abscidit *Offic. R. Rolle* xxv; **1352** ordinamus..quod vestes hujusmodi..sint clause desuper et inferius similiter, vel saltem absque ~onis scisse seu aperte *Conc.* III 30.

3 (?) pimple (*cf. bothor*).

1235 quidam parvus nuntius Willelmi Marescalli cum minutis butonibus venit cotidie ad inquirendum *CurR* XV 1438 (cf. *EHR* X 297).

botolaria v. butellaria.

botonare, to fit or fasten with buttons.

1345 pro factura ij corsettorum pro rege..~atorum cum laqueis serici et punctibus (*KRAc* 390/5) *Arch.* XXXI 7; **1349** ad fururandum dictum caban' et ~andum cum cristall' (*KRAc* 391/15) *Ib.* 21 (cf. 41); **1346** nec tunicas..fissas aut ~atas..vel etiam nimis strictas induant ipsi (*Const. Prov. Ben.*) *Conc.* II 730 (cf. ib. III 30); **a1350** tunica..habeat manicas..non consuticias nec aliqualiter ~atas (*Stat. S. Julian.*) *G. S. Alb.* II *app.* 485; **s1362** habent eciam capucia parva sub mento stricta modo mulierum ~ata *Eul. Hist.* III 230; **s1365** capuciis parvulis..laqueatis cum alis botenatis mento strictissime..uti ceperunt J. Reading 186; **1423** valeas..uti manicis tunice tue nigre habitui proximiori botanatis *Reg. Heref.* 33.

botonarium, stud, knob.

1344 quatuor botenaria de auro et aumelata, tria botenaria deaurata cum petris rubeis *Cl* 176 m. 11.

botonatio, fitting with buttons.

1345 pro qualibet tunica cum capucio, cum liniacione, fururacione et ~one (*KRAc* 390/5) *Arch.* XXXI 6.

botonettus, little stud or button.

1417 cum..margaretis de diversis sortibus, ~is, garnettis *Reg. Cant.* II 144.

botonus v. boto. botor v. 1 butor. botra v. botam. botracion v. batrachium. botracus, botras- v. butericius. botraria v. butellaria.

botrax [cf. βάτραχος], toad.

de nominibus insectorum: ..~ax vel botraca, *yce* Ælf. *Gl.*; sunt..reptilia..que in pedibus repunt, ut lacerte et botrace Bart. Angl. XVIII 1; ~ax que rubea dicitur genus est rane venenose *Id.* 16; portat tres ~aces nigros sive bufones Bad. Aur. 194; ~ax animal est quadripes, venenosum, in terra habitans et humore terreo nutritum; ..~ax sive bufo coloris est subnigri, subrufi vel pallidi Upton 154.

botria v. 2 buttaria.

botrus [βότρυς], cluster of grapes, grape or vine-flower. **b** (fig.) bud. **c** (fig.) nipple.

cum non sit ~us ad manducandum Gildas *EB* 86 (*cf. Micah* vii 1); pampinus immensos dum gignit palmite botros Aldh. *VirgV* 178; ~um, *clystri GlC* B 176; nomina arborum..bacido, botrus, *clyster* Ælf. *Gl.*; **9..** butros, *clystra* WW; Augusto mense declinante, quando et..~i in vineis et poma in viridariis copiam sui volentibus faciunt W. Malm. *GR* III 282; debet vinum prius exprimi; non enim ~us sacrificari integer debet Gir. *GE* I 8; vini peroptimi ex ~is Cypri *Itin. Ric.* II 31; est radix vitis, fructus sunt uva, racemus, / pampinus est folium, botrus flos, vinea totum (Docking *Com.*) *Doc. Francisc.* 106; amomum genus est herbe..cujus fructus similis est butruo *Alph.* 23; **s1380** de uno panno aureo..cum floribus et ~is *Hist. Durh.* 136. **b** nescio quid [Cistercienses]..in ~is promiserint; sed quicquid promiserint subsecutus est fructus, unde timemus arbores Map *NC* I 24; **1439** ne dicta vinea extrinsecis concuteretur turbinibus, quibus ~i scienciales..marcescere possent *EpAcOx* 193. **c** mamillula.. / castigata sedet, teneroque rotundula botro / pullulat Hanv. II 259.

botryo [βότρυον], cluster of grapes.

9.. corimbi, i. viti[s] racemi vel ~iones vel circuli, *wingeard hringas* vel *bergan* WW; **a1170** quid vitis gemmas, quid flores, quid botriones? (Steph. Rouen *De W. Com. Mellent.*) *Chr. Steph.* II 769; *tendron of a vyne*, †bratrio *PP.*

botsata [? ME *bōd*+*sæte*], right of abode granted to aliens.

c1324 de ~a Danorum..de ~a Norweygiorum (*Lib. Cust.*) *MGL* II 49 (cf. ib. 63: *ly Daneis ount botsate; ceo est a savoir, sojour tout lan*).

1 botta [OF *bote*], bundle.

celerarius solet accipere theloneum de lino tempore rotacionis, scilicet unam ~am de qualibet †cerna Brakelond 150v.

2 & 3 botta v. 1 & 3 butta. bottell- v. butell. botteras' v. butericius.

1 bottus, (?) wedge (? *cf.* OF *bot* = end); *cf.* 2 *butta.*

1326 in j securi pro torall' calcis, j martello, ij ~is pro calce frangendo..et in emendacione et acuacione securium, ~orum et aliorum utensilium *Pipe* 171 r. 38.

2 & 3 bottus v. 1 & 3 butta.

botula [cf. 2 bota], low boot.

botew, coturnus, ~a *PP.*

botularia v. buticularia. botularius v. butellarius. botur' v. 2 butor. botus v. 2 bota.

bouellarius [cf. OF *boel* < botellus], dealer in 'bowels' (sausages or haggis).

1333 quod carnifices..visceralia super stallis suis..non exponerent quodque ~ii et tripollarii in alto vico de Est Chep' et alibi in altis vicis constituti..ad laterales venellas transferentur *Cl* 153 m. 27.

boug-, boulg-, v. bulg-. bouiffatum v. 2 buffettum. boula, ~um, ~us v. builum, bulus. boulletus v. bulletta. bound- v. bund-.

boura [? cf. ME *bour*], form of tenement (? attached to 'bower', i.e. residence).

1567 dimittet ad opus proximi tenentis succedentis diversis stauros et stipitem, viz. pro una ~a integra xxj s. vj d. et [pro] tribus partibus de ~a xvj s. d. ob. et frumentum ad seminandum terram in campo estivali de terra ~e *Surv. Pembr.* (*Wilts*) 73 (cf. ib. pp. 77, xc).

bourdenagium, collectorship of a (?) ferry toll (Gasc.).

1415 concessimus..Hugoni Spenser officium ~ii civitatis nostre Burdegale (*Lit. Pat. Hen. V*) *Arch. Gironde* XVI 184.

boutagium v. buttagium.

boutellum [ME *boutel*], boss, moulding (arch.); *cf. bossellum.*

1291 una vousura inter predictas portas..de tribus ~is decenter ex lapidibus cementatis *KRAc* 486/7.

boutirum v. butyrum. bouvatus v. bovata.

bova [OF *bove*], vault. **b** cess-pit. **c** (*s. dub.*).

1198 minatoribus qui fecerunt ~as et scinderunt fossata de Roka et cellaria *RScacNorm* II 309; **1205** ut illos [minatores] ponatis apud Duvram et faciatis illos operari in ~is *Cl* 42; **1233** mandatum est vicecomiti Kancie quod..fieri faciat archias in introitu et exitu ~arum castri Dovr' *Liberate* 10 m. 9; **1240** quod motam turris castri nostri Noting', ubi nuper corruit, ..reparari facias, et similiter ~am que cecidit reparari facias cum arcubus et columpnis *Cl* 193. **b 1270** in una ~a juxta coquinam facienda ad sordes coquine recipiendas *MinAc* (*Carisbrooke, Hants*) 984/2 r. 2. **c 1296** in palis et cratibus portandis ad dictam exclusam et iterum reportandis ad ~am *Ac. Cornw.* I 134.

bovagium v. 2 bonagium.

bovaria, ~ium [OF *boverie*], measure of land (*cf. bovata*). **b** cattle pasture (*cf. boiria*).

1126 dedit..unam ~iam terre apud Brotebeiam [*Lincs*] *Regesta* p. 354 (cf. *MonA* VI 1080). **b** *an oxe pasture*, ~ium *CathA.*

2 cow-shed, byre.

1152 boveria habet xxxiij pedes in longitudine, xvj in latitudine, xiij in altitudine *Dom. S. Paul.* 129; **1167** in j grancia et j ~ia paranda *Pipe* 38; **1200** ~ium quoddam positum fuit in visu terre; ..et invenit ibi xvj vaccas et j taurum et j bovem..et bladum *CurR* I 218; **1205** ad faciendas ibidem ~ias suas et alias domos usibus suis necessarias *RChart* 152b; **1209** dat dim. m. ne boveria sua quam levavit super terram suam..removeatur *SelPlForest* 10; **1212** venerunt ad boveriam et fregerunt hostium et abduxerunt xiiij animalia *SelPlCrown* 60; **1245** boeria [hospitalis Burdegale] *CalCh* I 283; **1287** foragium portabit extra boveriam domini quando boves poni debent in stallis suis in boveria *Rec. Crondal* 87; quando ligant boves domini in boveriam in hieme *Cust. Bleadon* 206; **c1310** cooperiunt †bovoream super trabes *Reg. S. Aug.* 201; **1314** ingressu et egressu..ad eorum boariam *Reg. Heref.* 492; **1315** prosternendo unam boveriam precii xx m. *Year Bk.* XVII 120; **c1400** ..grangiam incomparabilem cum vaccaria sive boveria..noviter construxit *G. S. Alb.* III 445; **1404** in ~io sunt xiij boves *Ac. Durh.* 399; hoc boverium, A. *oxstalle* WW; **1547** unam domum sive mansionem et boveriam super edificatam *CalPat* 195.

bovarius [OF *bovier*], oxherd (*cf. VCH Worcs* I 274, *VCH Shropshire* I 302).

xxv villani et v bordarii et ii ~ii et iiii servi et iii coliberti *DB* I (*Heref*) 179b; in dominio sunt ii carucae et iii servi et unus liber ~ius *Ib.* (*Salop*) 255; **c1100** in Litleton' [*Worcs*] vi hide, iii caruce, vi ~ii (*Terr. Evesham*) *EHR* XLVIII 197; **c1120** quatuor ~ii in Straton'; ..quisque habet ij bovatas et iiij acras seminatas pro officio suo; ..acras autem debent reddere seminatas quando deferent boves *Cart. Burton* 25; **a1128** ibi sunt iiij ~ii, unusquisque eorum tenens v acras *Chr. Peterb. app.* 162 (cf. bubulcus); **1168** pro reficiendis domibus ~iorum qui custodiunt boves regis *Pipe* 208; **1260** iiij boverii, j carectarius, j bercarius, j porcarius et j daya erunt ad liberacionem *Cust. Glast.* 235; quilibet..carectarius simul cum affris jaceat sue carecte; et quod de carectariis dicitur, de ~iis cum suis bobus intelligatur *Fleta* 172; **c1345** in stipendio j ~ii et j custodis affrorum *Comp. Swith.* 148.

bovata, ~us, ~is, bovate, oxgang, area of land that can be ploughed in a season by one ox, *i.e.* by one-eighth of a plough-team (*cf. carrucata*); usu. *c.* 12–20 acres (esp. N. Eng. and Scot.; *cf. VCH Notts* I 208). **b** a smaller area (*bovata minor*), *c.* 5–10 acres. **c** (?) area of meadow or pasture appurtenant to a bovate.

tenet..v car[ucatas] terrae et dimidiam una ~a minus *DB* I (*Leics*) 232b; ii ~ae terrae geldantes *Ib.* (*Chesh*) 267; duo Anglici habent iii car[ucatas] terrae et v ~as *Ib.* (*Notts*) 283; **c1145** unam bovetam terre [*Lincs*] *Danelaw* 190; **11..** duos ~os terre et unum toftum in Legardeswude [*Berw*] *CalCh* III 90; **11..** in ea ~a sunt xxij acre vel amplius *Cart. Pontefr.* 290; **a1170** duas ~as terre xx acrarum de meo dominio in Keswic *E. Ch. Yorks* III 1866 (*cf. MonA* V 127); in Bliton' [*Lincs*]..iij magnas ~as et iiij tofta *Rec. Templars* 104 (cf. ib. p. clxxiii); **a1187** unam ~am terre lucrabilis de xx acris per perticam xviij pedum [*Lincs*] *Danelaw* 161; **a1189** duas ~as terre, sc. de domenio meo xx acras terre arabilis ex una parte ville et xx ex alia parte *Ib.* 41 (cf. ib. xxxiv n.: [j ~am] de nostro demenio parem aliis ~is nostre tenure totam simul jacentem ex orientali parte ville omnibus culturis terre nostre pertinentibus forinsecam, et totam simul jacentem ex occidentali parte ville in cultura proximiori Chilvingholm [*Lincs*]); **c1190** cum..ix ~is terre in quibus habentur c et viij acre terre *Ib.* (*Leics*) 258; **c1200** forinsecum servicium quantum pertinet ad unam bovatem terre unde sexdecim bovates faciunt tres quarteres feodi militis *E. Ch. Chesh.* 8 (2); **c1200** salvo..forinseco servicio..quantum pertinet ad xij ~as terre unde viij carucate faciunt feodum unius militis *MonA* (*Yorks*) VI 978; **1230** de duobus bouvatis terre in Swelington [*Yorks*] *Pipe* 268; **1240** sunt ibi iiij ~e terre, sc. due virgate *Reg. Pri. Worc.* 66a; **12..** dedi..unam carucatam terre..in Epplyngdone [*Durh*] cujus singule ~e sunt quindecim acrarum terre (*Pat*) *MonA* VI 732; **1280** ibidem sunt xxxiij bond' tenentes xxxiij ~as terre, quarum quelibet ~a continet xij acras per perticam [*Yorks*] *Reg. Richm. app.* 49; **1298** quoad unam ~am terre que continet sexdecim acras terre..et quoad aliam ~am de eisdem tenementis continentem decem et septem acras [*Huddersfield, Yorks*] *PlRCP* 124 r. 1; Danegelt, id est tallagium datum Danis, id est iij den. de qualibet ~a terre HIGD. II 96; **1321** j bovett' de terra dominic' et ij bovett' de terra husband' (*Rec. Coll. Merton*) *OED* (s.v. *husbandland*); **1352** ~a terre..que vocatur le Utterest Oxgang *PlRCP* 495 r. 312; **1353** requiritur..per legem Anglie..quod demanda in brevi fiat..per certum numerum carucatarum, ~arum, virgatarum seu acrarum terre (*PlRCP*) *Cart. Glam.* 1388; **1359** de duabus ~is terre in Tolyry *ExchScot* 580; *an oxgange of lande*, ~a *CathA*; **1535** de quodam redditu..vocato *oxgange pennys*, viz. de qualibet ~a terre ij d. *Rutland MSS.*(*MinAc 24–7 Hen. VIII Norf. etc.* p. 155). **b** **a1172** dimidiam carucatam terre..de minoribus bovetis [*Lincs*] *Ch. Gilb.* 84; **p1182** tres bovetas terre arabilis ex una parte ville et tres ex altera parte..unam videlicet bovetam decem acrarum [etc.] [*Lincs*] *Danelaw* 186; pro j bovata xxx d.; ..pro ij acris et dim. xv d. *Rec. Templars* (*Yorks*) 118; **a1189** octo acras terre que faciunt unam ~am in campis Danecastrie [*Yorks*] (*Breve Regis*) *CoramR* 137 r. 26; **a1200** que magna ~a et dimidia faciunt tres ~as parvas *Danelaw* (*Lincs*) p. xxviii n. 3; **1239** salvo forinseco servicio quantum pertinet ad dimidiam ~am terre..unde xiij carrucate terre faciunt feudum unius militis *MonA* (*Yorks*) V 137; **1280** ~e..quarum quelibet continet viij acras [*Aldeburgh, Suff*] *Reg. Richm. app.* 50; **1371** medietatem j ~e terre continentem quatuor acras terre in eadem ville [*Downham, Lancs*] *Cl* 208 m. 1. **c** **1184** adicimus..quinque ~as prati in le Westenge *Ch. Gilb.* 74 (cf. ib. p. xxii); **1469** mesuagium cum iiij ~is terre et prati *Test. Ebor.* III 170; **1583** duas ~as terre, prati et pasture [*Pembr*] *Pat* 1234 m. 18.

2 (Norm. & C.I.) *bouvée* (? smaller than oxgang).

1200 de tenemento Grosserii xxiiij s. pro iij ~is terre [*Jersey*] *RChart* 32b (cf. ib.; usque ad bovetam manerii); **1274** placita iij bovetarum terre (*Chanc. Misc* 10/5/1) *S. Jers.* II 27; **1331** nota quod xl perticate faciunt virgatam et iiij virgate acrum et v acra ~am et duodecim ~e faciunt carucatam *Ext. Guern.* 58; **1422** mansum unum et culturam in qua sunt v buveta terre (*Ch. Rouen*) *Foed.* X 237.

bovect- v. bovett-. boveculus v. boviculus.

†bovella, (?) for *bovetta*, heifer.

1379 lego..j vaccam et j ~am *Test. Karl.* 129.

bovellum, 'fold', byre.

bofellum, *falud GlC* B 148; **9..** ~um, *fald* WW; bobellum, *fald* ÆLF. *Gl.*

†bovellus, (?) for *bovettus*, steer.

1367 [lego] Ade famulo meo j ~um *Test. Karl.* 86.

bover- v. bovar-.

†bovestra, (?) bullock.

~a, *radre GlC* B 165.

1 bovetta, boveta v. bovata.

2 bovetta, heifer.

1253 due parve ~e femelle *SelPlForest* 107; **1307** habeant duas vaccas pascentes cum vaccis suis..et vij bovectas cum bovectis suis (*Compositio*) THORNE 2007; **1411** de j bovecta fe' [*ed.* fecunda; (?) l. femella] *Crawley* 306.

bovettarius, keeper of steers.

1269 in stipendio j ~ii *MinAc* (*Middx*) 915/3 (cf. ib. 10).

2 (?) tenant of bovate.

1375 quilibet tenens virgatam terre debet cariare..ij quadrigat' bladi..et ~ius j feni et aliud bladi *IMisc* (*Rutl*) 206/11.

bovettus [OF *bovet*], steer (usu. ox in third or fourth year).

1202 catalla ejus..ij vacce et j bovett' *SelPlCrown* 12; **1209** de ij ~is, iij geniculis remanentibus anno preterito; in adjunctis bobus ij, in adjunctis vaccis iij *Crawley* 191; **1233** de..~o trium annorum iij d., de boviculo duorum annorum ij d. et [de] ~o anniculo sive de dimidio anno j d. *Ib.* 207; **s1252** reliquid..xix bovectos et boviculos DOMERH. *Glast.* 522; **s1258** boveti et jenicie sunt de etate iij annorum et habent ij dentes latos et in anno quarto debent adjungi bobus et vaccis *FormMan Shorwell*; **1268** xxvj ~is, quorum vj fuerunt de ij annis..et ix alii de uno anno..et alii ix vituli *JustIt* 618 r. 9*d.*; **1268** computat de ij ~is modo factis bobus *Ac. Wellingb.* 8 (cf. ib. 87 [**1303**]: de v ~is iij annorum remanentibus, de quibus in adjuncto cum bobus iij); **1278** xi vacce, j bovett' mas, iiij bovicule fem', v vituli (*MinAc*) *Ambrosden* I 406; **1297** reddit compotum de v ~is de remanenti anno preterito; et adjunguntur cum bobus ij *Ac. Cornw.* I 39; de quatuor ~is venditis, precium cujuslibet x s.; et de iiij ~is vel boviculis venditis, precium cujuslibet iiij s. *FormMan* 13; **c1300** (v. boviculus); **1339** de j bovett' taurell' *MinAc* 1091/6; **1364** de j ~o de remanentibus et de ij de adjunccione boviculorum (*MinAc*) *Banstead* 346; **1371** item xvj ~i quatuor annorum *Pri. Coldingham app.* p. lxiii; **1372** item xiij †vovett' et vitulos *IMisc* 201/5; **1485** de pellibus ~orum *Comp. Swith.* 381; bovectus, A. *a stere* WW.

bovicida, ox-slaughterer.

bucida, qui boves mactat, *hryperheawere* ÆLF. *Gl.*; *oxe slaer, fleschour*..boviscida *CathA*.

bovicula, young heifer.

1222 recepit..de eisdem vaccis..lxxj vaccas, boves xxxvj, ~as xlij *LTRMem* 4 r. 3 (5); **1278** (v. bovettus); [Egyptus] boves nutrit mire magnitudinis..et oves velut ~as S. SIM. *Itin.* 43; **1434** lego..unam ~am *Test. Ebor.* II 39.

bovicularius, bullock-keeper.

c1310 stipend'..j vacar', j bovicular', j porcar' *LTR Ac.* 19 r. 43*d.* (cf. ib. r. 40: in stipend' custodis boviculorum).

boviculus, bullock (usu. ox in second or third year).

1220 orta..contencione inter eos de quodam ~o [v.l. bubulco] precii iiij s. quem idem R debuit dare cum filia sua *CurR* IX 60; **1233** (v. bovettus); **c1258** ~i sunt de etate ij annorum *Form. Man. Shorwell*; **1268** computat de viij ~is duorum annorum et amplius remanentibus, quorum v sunt masculi *Ac. Wellingb.* 8; **1270** ix ~is j anni *JustIt* 618 r. 23*d.*; **s1274** quamdam ovem Hispanie..que erat de bimalis ~i quantitate RISH. *Chr.* 84; **1278** xvj boves, j bovett', j juvencus, ij †bovitil' masculi (*MinAc*) *Ambrosden* I 406; **1279** reddit compotum de v ~is de rem[anentibus] et de iiij de adjunct[is]..de quibus in adjunct[is] cum bovettis v *Ac. Stratton* 105; **1297** de..uno ~o de etate unius anni et dimidii *Ac. Lenton* 6; **c1300** vituli primo compoto postquam nati sunt vituli vocantur, secundo compoto annales vocantur, tercio compoto ~i vocantur, quarto compoto bovecti vocantur (*Regula Comp. Belli Loci*) *Seignorial Admin.* 173; **1304** pro transgressione facta cum quatuor boveculis in erba domini *CourtR Hales* 485; **1305** ceperunt..boves et vaccas et †boviclos *Reg. Heref.* 410; **1338** item xiij ~i annales *Ac. Durh.* 200; **1364** respondet..de ij ~is de remanentibus et de ij de adjunccione vitulorum (*MinAc*) *Banstead* 346; **1416** restituant boves et †boviolos *Reg. Heref.* 91; hic ~us, A. *styrk*, ..A. *bullok* WW.

2 young hart, brocket.

1353 duos cervos, quatuor bissas, septem staggos et duos ~os cervorum cepit *Pat* 240 m. 9; **1366** ceperunt et occiderunt unum ~um cervi *TR Forest Proc.* 309 r. 10 (cf. ib. 310: ~us bisse).

bovigena [βουγενής], (unnatural) progeny of ox.

dicit Aristoteles [*Phys.* II 8] quod ~a et hujusmodi accidunt per corruptionem alicujus principii intrinseci BACON XIII 135.

bovile [CL], cow-shed, byre.

†bolia, stabula boum *GlC* B 160 (= *Erf.* 2. 272. 2: bobilia); ~e, stabulum, *scepensteal* vel *fald* ÆLF. *Gl.*; **9..** ~e, *scipen* WW (cf. bostar).

bovilla, a beef. **b** ox market.

a *beyst flesch*, ~a *PP*. **b** *an oxfayre*, ~a est locus ubi boves venduntur *CathA*.

bovinari [CL Gl.], **~are,** to revile, shout abuse.

s1461 dum isti bobinantes Boreales intendebant et immittebant suos arcus *Reg. Whet.* I 410; *to missay*, †bombinare, ..conviciari *CathA*.

bovinator [CL], waverer or (?) reviler.

bobinatores, inconstantes *GlC* B 158.

bovinus, belonging to an ox, or made of ox-hide. **b** bovine, of the nature of an ox.

x pelles caprinas et iiii coria ~a *DB* II 119; carnes et ovine / ventrem procurant; inflat caro queque bovina D. BEC. 2731; **1214** in..coriis bowin' tannatorum missis usque Dovr' *Cl* 143b; in Clen[t] sub spina jacet in convalle bovina [ME: *Cubeche*] (*Versus de S. Kenelmo*) M. PAR. *Maj.* I 373; duo paria sotular' bovin' *Obs. Barnwell* 226; **1329** per vendicionem xxij carcosiorum ~orum *ExchScot* 206; **s1330** tractus est ad caudas equorum super communi pelle ~a AD. MUR. 62*n.*; **1341** in ij arcubus ~is emptis *MinAc* 1120/11/r. 8; **1427** Aulam ~am [*Beef Hall*] *FormOx* 458; **1430** carnes ~as..dandas prisonariis *Test. Ebor.* II 8; **1433** in iiij paribus cathenarum cum anulis et stapulis ferreis emptis ad carucam ~am *Ac. Man. Wint.* (*Chilbolton*); **1454** juga ~a *Ac. Durh.* 150. **b** mulier..cleros..dans pocula lethes, / ordinis immemores †lethes facit esse bovinos D. BEC. 1978; semper iners virque bovinus eris *Babio* 256; habebat..totum corpus humanum preter extremitates que ~e fuerant GIR. *TH* II 21; **1430** pro xvj animalibus ~is *FormA* 286.

2 *lingua bovina* (bot.) *v. lingua*.

3 (sb. m.) oxgang (Scot.); *cf. bovata*.

12.. notum sit..me..dedisse duos ~os terre *Reg. S. Andr.* f. 119a.

boviolus, bovitilus v. boviculus. bovon v. 1 bubo b. bovorea v. bovaria. bowga v. bulga. bowinus v. bovinus.

bownculus, bullock (*cf. boviculus*).

1280 respondet de vj ~is de remanenti qui modo sunt bovetti; ..item..de vij vitulis masculis superannatis de remanenti qui modo sunt ~i *MinAc* 935/7*d.*

boxa [ME *box* < buxus; cf. buxis], box.

1517 in octo libris impositis in una ~a in communi cista pro thuribulariis empt' *Midlothian* 179; ~am tradidit mille ..mercas continentem MYLN *Dunkeld* 49; **1549** ~am tineam [*for holy oil*] *CalPat* 225.

boxare, to fit with axle boxes.

1299 in rotis ~andis, vj d. *Ac. Man. Cant.* (*Monkton*); **1310** in ij mediolis unius carecte ~andis *MinAc* 992/8; **1378** in stipendio j rotarii pro modiis carecte burs' et ~andis *Ac. Man. Wint.* (*Wootton St. Lawrence*).

boxeus v. buxeus.

boyare [Dutch *boeien*], to fit with extra planking so as to increase freeboard.

1327 in uno pari de *boȝinges* de quercu empto pro bargia boyȝanda; ..in ccc de magnis *spykynges* pro dicta bargia boyanda (*KRAc* 14/14) *Sea-Terms* I 38.

bozonus v. buzo.

1 braare [cf. OF *brai* = *pitch*], to 'bray', caulk.

1237 mandamus vobis quod duas galias nostras que sunt apud Winchelese sine dilatione ~are et reficere faciatis *Liberate* 11 m. 7; **1238** quod galias regis que sunt in custodia sua ~ari faciant *Cl* 108.

2 braare, to brace (? *cf.* OF *braier* = strap).

1316 pro..j *brayngrop* ad ~andam dictam carettam *KRAc* 99/21 m. 1.

Brabanicus, of Brabant.

c1302 ad partes tendens ~as *Chr. S. Edm.* 64.

Brabantianus, ~inus, ~ius, Brabanter; hence mercenary, routier, marauder. **b** coin of Brabant.

s1173 habuit secum [Henricus] viginti millia Brabancenorum, qui fideliter servierunt illi et non sine magna mercede quam eis dedit R. HOWD. II 47; **s1173** misit..Braibancenos suos, de quibus plus ceteris confidebat *G. Hen. II* I 56 (cf. ib.: Braibaceni); dum..Brabacenorum secta in pacis amatores seviret GERV. CANT. I 300 (cf. ib. 301: speciales pacis adversarios Braibacenos); **s1215** cum Flandrensibus et Brebanciis suis spurcissimis M. PAR. *Maj.* II 636; Brabantina manus cantando mortis ad horam / festinet GARL. *Tri. Eccl.* 43; **s1197** Brabantinorum vallatus catervis WALS. *YN* 120 (cf. ib. 101: a Brebantinis). **b** **1189** [Hospitalarii] plusquam octo milia Brabantinorum..expendidere (*Lit. Conradi de Monte Ferrario*) DICETO *YH* II 61; **s1299** mercatores alienigeni..introduxerant in Angliam..monetas..pessimi metalli pollardorum, .. scaldyngorum, †Brabancium, aquilarum W. GUISB. 333.

Brabantio, Brabanter etc. (as *Brabantianus*).

1174 unde hoc tibi quod Brebantionum factus es ductor gentique excommunicate et perditissime adhesisti? P. Blois *Ep.* 47. 138A; hec autem [secta] orta est in Brebanno, unde dicitur Brebeazonum; nam in primo latrunculi egressi legem sibi fecerunt omnino contra legem, et associati sunt eis.. fugitivi, clerici falsi, monachi evasi Map *NC* I 29; **s1174** rex ..cum..una Bribantionum turma in Angliam mature advehitur W. Newb. I 181; **1179** de Brebantionibus et.. Coterellis, qui tantam in Christianos immanitatem exercent ut..non cuilibet parcant etati aut sexui (*Decr. Lateran.*) *Ib.* 209 (= R. Howd. II 179: de Brabanconibus; *G. Hen. II* I 228: de Bribazonibus).

Brabanus, Brabanter.

s1338 ~os et Flandrenses sibi federavit Higd. VII 44; **c1370** frendent Barbani ambo nummis sine vani (J. Bridl.) *Pol. Poems* I 146.

brabasca v. verbascum

braca v. brecha.

bracae (braccae) [CL], breeches.

†tubroces [l. tribraces] vel ~e, *strapulas* Ælf. *Gl.*; laneis utuntur seu ~is caligatis seu caligis braccatis Gir. *TH* III 10; **1275** ipsum..de cubili suo nudum preter camisium et ~as ejecerunt *CourtR Wakefield* I 57; **1279** nudus et discalciatus, ~is dumtaxat retentis, ..incedat (*Lit. Papae*) *Reg. Ebor.* 38; **1306** invenit eundem Stephanum supratrahentem ~as suas *Mayor's CourtR Lond.* H m. 7b; **1310** dictum fuit ei quod, depositis bracciis verteret dorsum ad crucifixum (*Acta contra Templar.*) *Conc.* II 359; **s1365** inventa fuit una de suis capsellis plena..camisiis et ~is cilicinis *Hist. Durh.* 128; **1433** lego..unam camisiam cum uno pari ~arum *Reg. Cant.* II 470; ~e, *brechys* WW.

bracalis (braccalis), attached to breech-girdle.

1275 furatus fuit..unam bursam ~em cervinam *Hund.* I 275.

2 (sb. n. or m.; *cf. bracile*), breech-girdle, belt. **b** truss (med.).

1213 pro uno ~i ad opus domini regis unde tela venit de garderoba et argentum..ponderabat vj s. et aurum ad deaurandum constitit ij s. *Misae* 257; a †bracos bracale venit, lumbareque lumbis Garl.*Syn.* 1583A; **1282** mittimus vobis quandam schedulam..cujus transcriptum..inventum fuit in ~i L. quondam principis Wallie Peckham *Ep.* 373; **1300** unum ~e de laqueis de serico coopertum de samite rubeo munitum argento *Ac. Wardr.* p. 352; **1303** pro factura vj ~ium de corio et iiij ~ium de samit' provisorum pro corpore dicti domini [principis] *KRAc* 363/18 f. 10; **1330** in ij brakkalibus cum ligulis emptis pro priore *Ac. Durh.* 518; hoc ~e, A. *brygyrdylle*, ..*brekbelt* WW. **b** inter omnia remedia localia ~e vel colligar factum de bombace et bene aptatum magis eos juvat Gilb. VI 281. 2; pendeat ibi pila rotunda de panno lineo quod superponatur brachali..deinde emplastrum ponunt super eminentiam inter brachale et corpus Gad. 129 v. 2.

bracarii, breeches.

1222 gentes nostre in aqua erant usque ad braccarios et cinctoria (*Lit. P. de Albeneio*) Wend. II 263.

bracatare v. braciare 1a.

1 bracatus, a wearing breeches. **b** in the form of breeches.

a hujusmodi habitus ita notus est in nostris regionibus ut ex eo Gallia Braccata nominata sit Alcuin *Div. Off.* 38. 1240. **b** Gir. *TH* III 10 (v. bracae).

2 bracatus v. brachettus. bracca v. bracae, brecca d.

bracchialis (brachialis), adapted to the arm.

1234 debet..colligere viij acervos cooperture et in uno quoque acervo x garbas ~es, sc. quam grossas poterit trahere sub brachio suo dum tenet zonam per manum suam juxta latus suum *Cust. Glast.* 82.

2 (sb. n.) **a** sleeve. **b** arm-ring. **c** 'bracer' (arm-guard).

a manicae vel brachilia, *slyfa* Ælf. *Gl.*; **14..** deponat ~ia, i.e. manicas lineas, quas ponunt quidem super albam et tunicam ad conservanda munda brachia induta ab aqua *Pont. Sal.* 234. **b** armellae, brachialia *GlC* A 722; **9..** dextrocerium, i. ~e, armillum vel torium, *earmbeag* WW. **c** brachiale, A. *a wardebrace*, ..hec brachialia, *a brasere* WW.

bracchiata a armful. **b** arms' length, fathom.

a c1230 debet..stipulas colligere..et braciatam opere completo percipere *Doc. Bec* 56 (cf. ib.: braciatam faraginis). **b 1283** de quocunque solo de quatuor brassatis de lato et amplitudine et de duodecim de longitudine *RGasc* II 209; octo brachiatas terre..in longitudine *Ib.* 217; **1329** pro una corda longitudinis xvj teisarum seu brachiatarum *KRAc* 467/6/1.

bracchiolum (brachiolum), metal bar or strip (? brace) on a bell.

[tintinnabulum] inter ~a ansularum in regione superiori foramen gerit non modicum R. Cold. *Cuthb.* 81.

2 'bracer' (*cf. bracchialis 2c*).

vidi..cestus, clipeos, targia, ~a Garl. *Dict.* 130; hoc braciolum, A. *brasor* WW.

bracchitectum, 'bracer' (arm-guard).

14.. hoc brachitectum, *a braser* WW.

bracchium, ~ia, ~ius (brachium) [CL], arm. **b** fore-limb (of animal).

nectentes bracchia vinclis Aldh. *VirgV* 1837; ut ne ad os quidem adducere ipsum ~ium valeret Bede *HE* III 2; a juncturis quibus..manus a ~iis..porriguntur Gir. *TH* II 21; **1234** debet inde habere haverocum quantum potest sublevare inter †branchios super dorsum suum *Cust. Glast.* 160 (cf. ib. 163: inter brachios); ~ia a fortitudine sunt dicta; *bari* enim Grece 'forte' dicitur Latine Bart. Angl. V 27; †braebia [? l. brachia] presbyteri tendit prefatio facta Garl.*Myst. Eccl.* 601; **1268** tenui uxorem suam inter ~ia sua *JustIt* 618 r. 17d.; fractura ~ii, i. partis a cubito ad manum Gad. 124 v. 1; **s1342** comes in ~io ledebatur Ad. Mur. 124; **1551** de lxv virgatis panni linei vocat' *paynted clothes*..in quibus sunt flores et picta ~ia *Pat* 840 m. 14. **b** ursus.. validis ictibus ~ia commutans, verbera promittebat Felix *Guthl.* 36.

2 (fig.) power, support. **b** (w. *extendere*) to exert authority (*cf. Deut.* v 15 *etc.*). **c** (w. *saeculare*) 'secular arm', civil authority.

s1128 ut [regis] filia..in Christi ~io regnum Anglie sustineat J. Worc. 27; tanti regis validas manus et longa ~ia metuens Ord. Vit. IX 15 p. 598; **s1207** [Johannes rex] ponens spem et ~ium in pecunie thesauris *Flor. Hist.* II 133; **s1272** rogaverunt..regem..ut..vellet ad hoc ~ium et manum apponere ne.. *Leg. Ant. Lond.* 149; **s1355** in ~io potenti et manu valida *Plusc.* IX 41; cum tali pugnatorum potenti ~io quale sibi visum fuerit expediens adveniret Elmh. *Hen. V Cont.* 135; **s1461** noverat ipsos..advenisse.. cum ~io fortitudinis [cf. *Isaiah* lxii 8] ad partes istas *Reg. Whet.* I 393. **b** qui ei [daemoni] semper restiterat in ~io extento *V. Osw.* 464; **c1198** homo vanitatis / extendit brachium / in Christi sanctuarium (*Pol. Poems*) *EHR* V 318; ut papa eos in ~io extento domitos evincat M. Par. *Maj.* III 362; **c1350** non armis, non telis, non ~io extento, sed elacione, presumpcione (*Chr. Anon.*) *Illust. Scot.* 3; **a1400** si in hujusmodi cause patrocinio consuete benevolencie ~ium extenderitis *Pri. Cold.* 77. **c 1235** litteras impetravit domino regi directas quod ad hoc ~ium extenderet seculare *CurR* XV 1360; **s1240** papa seculare ~ium..in auxilium ejus advocavit *Flor. Hist.* II 241; ~io..seculari.. se suaque in manu forti tuebatur *G. S. Alb.* I 10; **1294** invocando..contra eos auxilium ~ii secularis *Reg. Carl.* I 91; **1340** rogamus quatinus..secularis vestre potestatis ~ium.. contra ipsos exercere velitis *FormOx* 145; **s1413** damnavit hereticum et ipsum ~io seculari tradidit Elmh. *Hen. V* 3.

3 arms' length, 'brace', fathom.

1254 quamlibet cathenam longitudinis unius bracie *RGasc* II 3171; **1332** pro una grossa cabla de canabo.. longitudinis xl teys' vel ~iorum *KRAc* 469/11 m. 7; **1384** j cheyne de ferro de iij ~iis et ultra *IMisc* 229/16 (cf. ib. 211/5 [1377]: rete..longitudinis trium tractuum ~iorum hominis vocatorum *fadmes*); **14..** duo ~ia tele de cortina *Mon. Rit.* II *app.* 257.

4 reliquary (containing an arm and shaped accordingly).

[abbas G., ob. **1146**] dedit..~ium unum argenteum in quo has reliquias recondidit *G. S. Alb.* I 94; custos..textis, ~iis, tabulis, aliisque reliquiarum philacteriis illud [altare].. decorabit *Cust. Westm.* 56 (cf. *Cust. Cant.* I 111: decorabitur magnum altare..philacteriis et ~iis argenteis sive aureis); **c1450** ~iis et aliis jocalibus Flete *Westm.* 73; **c1510** unum ~ium de argento deaurato cum manu et anulo continens brachium S. Wilfridi *Hist. Church York* III 384.

5 (?) 'brace', 'bracer', arm-guard.

1215 omnes galeas nostras et capellos ferr[eos] et medietatem bracearum (*Cl*) *LTR Mem. PR* 134; **1375** apprenticius ..furatus fuit..brasas, *brestplates* et similia ad valenciam xx s. *Leet Norw.* 64.

6 'brace', fastening, strap. **b** 'brace', leash (of hounds).

1186 pro coffris capelle regis et ~iis coffrarum *Pipe* 194; **1223** fieri faciatis bracios ad cofras capelle nostre portandas *Cl* 552; **1290** pro uno sacco ad pannos cum iij bratiis [? l. braciis] (*Chanc. Misc* 4/5) *Doc. Scot.* 138; **1325** in reparacione braciarum et phalerarum *Ac. Durh.* 167. **b 1402** reddendo nobis unum bras' leporariorum per annum *Pat* 1200 m. 8.

7 a arm (branch) of river. **b** arm (inlet or strait) of sea.

a c1102 ~ium..sicut egreditur de Taf et facit insulam quousque reingreditur in Taf *Cart. Glam.* 37; **1245** quod ipsi pontem fieri faciant ultra ~ium illud Thamis' quod currit inter insulam predictam et domos suas *Pat* 56 m. 6. **b 1189** unum molendinum ad pontem castelli de Penbrok' super ~ium maris *Rec. Templars* 142; mare illud strictum.. quod ~ium S. Georgii..nuncupatur Gir. *PI* III 20; ~ium S. Georgii quod apud antiquos vocatur Hellespontus Bacon *Maj.* I 355; **1378** usque Sevarne, quod est ~ium maris (*CoramR*) *Pub. Works* I 135; **1391** navem et bona predicta in quodam ~io maris in com. Ebor' infra admirallitatem predictam..capta *Cl* 232 m. 6d.; attingens ~ium marinum de Gravening..cum jam detinuisset salsus fluvius Elmh. *Hen. V* 100; **1430** in aqua de Trent, que est quoddam ~ium maris (*KRMem*) *Bronnen* 1026.

8 'brace', arch (of bridge). **b** (?) branch, subsidiary outlet (of sluice).

†c975 (12c) episcopus [Roffensis] incipit operari in orientali ~io [pontis] primam peram de terra *CS* 1321; **1343** tenentes episcopi Roffensis debent incipere facere pontem predictum in orientali ~io ejusdem pontis *IMisc* 149/24. **b 1331** debent..facere caput stanni, quod wlgaliter *escluse* nuncupatur, pro conservando aquam pro dicto molendino, excepto quod dominus rex debet facere circa excloturam in viciniori parte dicte excloture unam brachiam (*KRAc* 89/15) *S. Jers.* I 8.

9 arm of cross. **b** arm of transept. **c** branch of candlestick.

1295 crux..cum duobus camahutis in ~iis *Vis. S. Paul.* 312; **s1305** fecit deferri ante eum crucem argenteam..cum duabus brachiis [v.l. branchiis] ex transverso W. Guisb. 365. **b 1498** volo quod caro mea..sepeliatur in ~io boriali capelle S. Marie in ecclesia mea Eboracensi (*Test. Arch. Ebor.*) *BBExch.* 668. **c a1200** duo paria candelabrorum de argento et j magnum vij ~iarum *Chr. Abingd.* II 151; **12..** in precipalibus festis non illuminantur vij ~ia vel *gymes* ad primas vesperas *Cust. Westm. app.* 317; [candelabrum] in quinque dissectum ~ia sive ramos Ferr. *Kinloss* 74.

10 bar, beam or sim. resembling arm: **a** arm of balance (also fig.); **b** upright of ladder; **c** (?) curved handle of saw; **d** 'brace' (? tie-beam) of timber frame; **e** beam of siege-engine; **f** (?) axle (of windlass); **g** projection on mill-spindle.

a cum alterum ~iorum libre equalibus appensis nutum faciat per manum deprimentis Bacon *Maj.* I 170; **1303** statuimus quod..statera..vacua videatur, et quod ~ia sint equalia (*Stat. Nov. Cust.*) *MGL* II 208; **1307** ordinavit..quod ~ia ejusdem statere sint equalia (*CoramR*) *Law Merch.* II 76; ~ium equilibre qua nostra..merita pensabuntur R. Bury *Phil.* 20. 251. **b** vilitas et asperitas..sunt duo ~ia scale [ME: *leddre stalen*] sursum directe in celum, et inter ista duo ~ia fixi sunt gradus omnium virtutum *AncrR.* 137. **c** sica ad ligna majora sine ~iis, iij; sica ad ligna minora cum ~iis, ij (*Invent. Cant.*) *Arch. J.* LIII 274. **d 1233** xx copulas et lacertos et ~ia et alia pertinentia ad predictum maeremium *Cl* 347; **1327** in prostracione septem quercuum..pro sex postibus, duabus sullivis et decem ~iis inde faciendis pro quadam turri..inde emendanda *LTRMem* 99 r. 122d. **e 1303** pro iiij cheveronibus de quercu pro ~iis dicti ingenii *KRAc* 11/7. **f 1296** in duobus cheveronis emptis.. ad ~ia wyndagii *Ac. Galley Newcastle* 181; **1325** in stipendiis ij carpentariorum faciencium..j ~ium pro wyndas' pontis tract' magne turris *MinAc* 1147/23 m. 3. **g 1235** in bracis ad molendinum..; in brasis ad mol' *Pipe Wint.* (159284) r. 15; **1255** Gilbertus..molendinarius unxit fusillum cujusdam molendini ad ventum..; et, cum tetigisset fusillum illud, manus ipsius G. transiit inter fusillum et ~ia ipsius fusilli et volvebatur brachium suum circa fusillum illud *JustIt* 872 r. 29d.; **1284** in ferro empto pro brach' illius molendini ligand' *KRAc* 351/9 m. 4; **1286** in iiij libris eris ad..molendinum emptis, braso sub fusill' inde emendendo cum bend' ferr' ad trab' *MinAc* 827/39 r. 4; **1290** in stipendio j carpentarii pro ~iis et coggys dicte rote *DCCant* (*Ac. Meopham*); **1306** in j virga ad ~ium molendini empta et eadem in molendino imponenda *MinAc* 1079/17, r. 1; **1312** pro operacione rote interioris..molendini..et duorum ~iorum ejusdem fractorum de novo fac' *KRAc* 486/25; **1315** in..duobus ~iis pro exteriori [sc. rota] ejusdem molendini de novo facienda *Pipe* 170 r. 55d.; **1374** reparabunt rotam, axem ejusdem molendini [fulretici], tebias, pedes, ~ia et truncum *DLMinAc* 507/8227 r. 28.

bracci- v. braci-. bracea v. bracchium 5. braceare, ~eator v. braci-. bracen- v. bracin-.

bracera [OF *braciere*], 'bracer', arm-guard (*cf. bracchium* 5).

1284 cissori regis pro iiij[xx] ulnis tele emptis ad faciend' bracer' de armis S. Georgii pro peditibus regis..; eidem pro factura illarum bracer' *KRAc* 351/9 m. 2; **1303** armurario principis..pro uno pari bracer' de balen' *Ib.* 363/18 f. 10d.; **1327** j par platorum cum ~is *RR. K.'s Lynn* I 129.

braceria, 'brace', fathom (*cf. bracchium* 3).

1253 quatuor cabulas, quamlibet..de xxiiij ~iis *Cl* 182.

bracerissa [OF *braceresse*], ale-wife (*cf. braciatrix*).

1276 ballivus cepit de ~is iij sol. *Hund.*II. 176; **c1300** quod nulla ~a braciet cum stramine *Chain Bk. Dublin* 234.

1 bracha, ~ia [cf. brachetus], brach, bitch hound.

1276 in sustentacione unius ~ie cum v catulis *MinAc* 991/18; **1278** cum mittamus..xxiiij brachettos, duas ~as et xiiij leporarios, vobis mandamus quod canes illos.. transfretari..faciatis *ChancMisc* 35/8/18; aliquas ~as nostri, rachas Scoti..nominant..; sic enim canes foeminas in venatico genere vocare solent nostri Caius *Can.* 2b.

2 bracha v. 2 brecha, 2 broca. brachale v. bracale. brachanum v. brathanum. bracharius v. 1 braciarius.

brachetta [OF *brachete*], brachet bitch.

c1350 abbatiam de Forda..a se debere teneri per servicium..perhendinendi unam leporariam vel unam brachetam cum catulis suis quolibet anno *Mon. Exon.* 344; **1393** quandam brachetam Jolyf interfecerunt et in Maudeleynwell cum petris circa collum ejusdem brachete ligatis private projecerunt *IMisc* 254/17 (*cf. CalPat* p. 353).

brachettus [OF *brachet*], brachet, hound (*cf. King's Serjeants* 281–3).

c1157 habeat leporarios suos et brachetos suos ad lepores et vulpes capiendos *CalPat* 1377–81 p. 111; **†a1190 (1336)** quatuor bracatos ad leporem capiendum *MonA* IV 515 (*cf. CalCh* IV 379); **s1191** [Ricardus] misit Saladino..braschetos, id est odorisequos *G. Ric. I* 180; **1199** pro licentia habendi vj ~os et iij leporarios ad vulpem et leporem *Pipe* 20; **1209** requisiti..cujusmodi canes essent, R. ..dicit quod ~us et J. ..dicit quod mastinus fuit *SelPlForest* lxii *n.* 1; **1212** per j brachetum unius coloris *Fees* 228; **1213** mittimus..venatorem nostrum cum xl ~is vulpericiis et sex leporariis *Cl* 156; **1229** milites debent inquirere..quis habuerit..~os vel leporarios *Pat* 287; **1256** bragetti *CalIPM* no. 345; **1286** pro putura xxiiij ~orum regis per idem tempus [sc. iiij dies], iiij s. *KRAc* 351/20 m. 3; **1286** per serjanciam custodiendi unum ~um deymeretum *JustIt* 573 r. 74d.; **1340** per serjanciam..custodiendi unum ~um domini regis album habentem aures rubeas *IPM* 63/2.

brachi- v. et. bracchi-, brachy-, braci-. brachia v. 1 bracha, bracchium 3. brachile v. bracchialis, bracile. brachina v. brema.

†**brachinellum,** (?) malted loaf (*cf. bracinalis*).

secretarius..inveniet canestella et ~a †vini [? l. vinum] et claretum *Cust. Westm.* 68; eleemosinarius..inveniet siminella, gastella, canestella, ~a et wafras FLETE *Westm.* 96.

brachus v. brachys.

brachycatalectus, ~icus [βραχυκατάληκτος, βραχυκαταληκτικός], brachycatalectic.

Seneca..tetrametro brachicatalecto sic ait ALDH. *PR* 140 p. 194; ~o sive colopho *Id. VirgP* 4; qua ratione catalectici, brachicatalectici seu ipercatalectici versus sagaci argumentatione colligantur W. MALM. (*V. Aldh.*) *GP* V 195.

brachylexium [βραχύς + λέξις], brief utterance.

hujusce miscillo brachilexii contignabo innumeras Anglorum imperium sustinuisse..discordias O. CANT. *Pref. Frith.* 22.

brachylogia [βραχυλογία], brevity of speech.

14.. braciologia, A. *a shortspekynge* WW.

brachys [βραχύς], short.

brachus, brevis *GlC* B 184.

bracia v. bracchium 3, 6, 1 branchia, 2 broca.

braciagium [cf. bracinagium], (?) payment for right to brew (C.I.).

1309 ad brassagium iij s. vj d. (*JustIt*) *S. Jers.* XVIII 120; **1331** reddunt iidem tenentes ad festum S. Mich. vij s. vj d. Turon' de quodam redditu vocato brasagium, viz. pro qualibet bovata d. et ob. *Ext. Guern.* 88 (cf. ib. 26 [**1248**]: finem fecerunt..pro brasio faciendo et vocatur redditus ille *frocage*).

braciamentum, brewing.

1326 dabunt precium cervisie, viz. de quolibet ~o ij lagenas *BB St. Davids* 132.

bracianus, for grinding malt (*cf.* 2 *braciarius*).

1113 quoddam molendinum braissanum in Juliibona [*Lillebonne, Norm.*] *Regesta* II 326.

braciare [OF *bracier*], **a** to brew (intr.). **b** to brew (malt or grain, so as to make ale). **c** to brew (ale). **d** (?) to brew at or for (a tavern).

a cujuscunque uxor braziabat intus et extra civitatem [*Hereford*] dabat x den. per consuetudinem *DB* I 179; **a1147** quilibet burgensis potest ~iare et furniare sine licencia et sine tolneto *Cart. Glam.* 95; **1194** dixit ei quod non potuit in domo sua hospitari, quia fecit ~iare *CurR RC* I 60; **1212** quod nullus braciator †~iat [? l. ~iet] de nocte (*Consideratio contra incendium*) *MGL* II 86; **1236** averant set non brasiant *Cust. Battle* 132; **1255** quicunque de villa Oxonie ~iaverit ad vendendum exponat signum suum; alioquin amittat cervisiam *Arch. Ox.* I 20; **1281** habet quamdam liberam curiam ad quam summonet †bractatrices [MS: braciatrices]..contra assisam †bracatantes [MS: braceantes] (*JustIt* 498) *PQW* 395b; **1289** quia ~iant et non ponunt extra signum, ij s. *Leet Norw.* 28; **1366** ~iavit ad tabernam *Cart. Eynsham* II 19; brasio, A. *to brewe* WW. **b 1302** summa brasii ~iati *Sacr. Ely* II 21; **1330** iiij celdras avenarum braseatarum *ExchScot* 345; **1340** brasiavit iiij quarteria avene et vendidit contra assisam *CBaron* 100; **1472** volo quod..ij quarteria frumenti et quarteria brasei eisdem consonantia †frumentur [? l. furnientur] et brasientur *Test. Ebor.* III 200. **c 1221** quedam cervisia bratiata fuit in domo sua propria *PlCr Glouc* 100; quecunque femina brasiare voluerit cervisiam venalem, brasiet..per totum annum *Leg. IV Burg.* 63; **1266** per cervisiam brasiatam apud Kinros et missam ad servicium regis *ExchScot* 16; **1495** consideracione..servicie forcius braxate *Ib.* 514. **d c1300** quilibet dabit unam †matam cervisie si braceat †tabernam [? l. ad tabernam] *DCCant* J 46.

2 (?) to malt (bread).

1294 habebunt..furna ad furniand' panem suam propriam sine pane ~iato, qui de modo debet furniari ad furnam meam *BBC* (*Chesterfield*) 127.

3 (p. ppl. n.) a brew.

1251 si iste..~iaverit in villa, ..in primo ~iato erit quietus de *alemol* (*Cust. Ely*) *Cust. Rents* 37.

1 braciaria, ~ium [OF *bracerie*], brewery, brewhouse. **b** (?) brewing.

c1255 rivulus qui aquatico molendino nostro, quod juxta braseriam construitur, deservit *G. S. Alb.* I 323 (= *MonA* II 239); fecit ibi coquinam novam et braseriam [v.l. bracinam] SWAFHAM 120; **1284** de brasio ad breseriam *Reg. Malm.* I 202; **1322** in ostio granar' bracer' *DCCant* J 521; **1349** dominus contulit..serjanciam secundam in braxaria *Reg. Roff. Ep.* 241b; **13..** grangiam et †brixeriam *Couch. Kirkstall* 211; **1453** nihil..de granis in granario, nihilque..in brasaria *Reg. Whet.* I 103; brasiarium, ..brasorium, A. *brewhous* WW. **b** distrinxerunt B. A. pro quodam amerciamento braserie per ij urciolos eneos *Hund.* I 355.

2 braciaria, brewster, ale-wife.

brasiaria, A. *a brewstere* WW.

1 braciarius, brewer.

a1128 in bracino monachorum est j bracharius qui habet victum militis *Chr. Peterb. app.* 167; **1230** Osmerus bracerius debet dim. m. *Pipe* 209; brasiarius, A. *a brewer* WW.

2 braciarius, for grinding malt (*cf. bracianus*).

1114 do..in Julia Bona [*Lillebonne, Norm.*] unum molendinum brasarium de meo dominio *MonA* VI 1066; **1297** in meremio cariando..ad molendinum brasarium de novo faciendum *Ac. Cornw.* II 195.

braciata v. bracchiata.

braciatio, brewing.

1448 punicionem..pandoxatoribus pro eorum male brasiationibus..impositam *MunAcOx* 589 (cf. ib. 695); **1457** lego..omnia vasa pertinencia ad †brasionem *Test. Ebor.* II 212; **1531** vasa antedicta extendunt pro brasiacione sex quarteriorum brasii *AncD* A 1551.

1 braciator [cf. OF *braceor*], brewer.

a1150 terra que fuit Redmeri brachiatoris *Ch. Heref.* 18; **c1160** Haraldus braceator *Chr. Rams.* I 271; **1232** de prisa et consuetudine illa quam constabularii..capere consueverunt de ~oribus bertone de Merleberg', singulis bracinis cervisie venalis unum sextercium cervisie, quod dici consuevit *tolsester Cl.* 108; **1271** de pistoribus, bracciattoribus et cocis Judeorum ..statuimus quod nullus Christianus ..eis ministrare presumat in ministeriis predictis (*Pat*) *Leg. Ant. Lond. app.* 236; **1285** pistores et brasiatores *MunAcOx* 776; **1304** braseum..per visum brasiatoris..misceatur *Cant. Cath. Pri.* 211; quod quilibet brasiator vel brasiatrix faciens servisiam venalem reciperet de qualibet bolla boni brasei ordiacii nisi xij lagenas servisie taberne (*Assisa Panis*) *APScot* I 311; **1317** pro eo quod †~ores [? l. braciatrices *as* TROKELOWE 96] in diversis locis..cervisiam braciant et eam..nimis care vendunt (*Breve Regis*) *Ann. Lond.* 240; quod nunquam faciet mensurare bladum antequam a subcelerario et famulis suis, viz. pistore et brasiatore, sit visum *Cust. Cant.* 134; **1337** homines bracinas tenentes..qui mittunt ~ores suos cum vasis suis vocatis *tynes* ad dictum conductum *LB Lond.* D 99b; **1347** est ibidem [*Stamford, Lincs*] quedam consuetudo que vocatur *breustereyeld* levata per annum de omnibus ~oribus *IPM* 86 r. 4; *a maltster*, ..brasiator, ~trix *CathA*; **1539** est communis brassator et fugit assisam *Comp. Swith.* 142; **1583** braziatores servicie *DLCourtR* 131/2023 r. 3.

2 braciator [cf. imbraciator], 'embracer', briber of juries.

1390 communis brassator, manutentor et sustentator falsarum placitarum *Anc. Indict.* 168 r. 70.

braciatorium, ~ia, brew-house. **b** (?) *f.l.* for *brasium* (*v. bracium*).

ea que eis [sc. sacris tenementis] sunt adjuncta..sicut sunt ..coquine, pistoria et †bracitoria [v.l. braciatoria], sine quibus cultores religionis ecclesie deservire non possunt BRACTON 207b; **1466** lego..*les tubbes, troghes* et *standes* pertinencia pandoxatorie, brasiatorie et botellarie *Test. Ebor.* II 277. **b** de xx quarteriis frumenti, de quibus in †brasiatorio facto v quarteria *FormMan.* 15.

braciatricius, for brewing.

1303 totam illam domum ~iam, cum gardino, molis manualibus, plumbis et omnibus vasis et utensilibus ad officium ~ium..spectantibus *AncD* A 2700; **1573** domos brasiat' vocatas *malthowses and kilnes Pat* 1106 m. 25.

braciatrix, brewster, ale-wife.

1191 Agnes ~ix de Ovingham *Pipe* 66; **1269** ~ices summonite fuerunt pro assisa cervisie fracta *CBaron* 88; **s1275** mariscalli domini regis repererunt quod brasiatrices de villa assisam non servarunt; et villata fecit finem pro xl s. *Ann. Dunstable* 267; **1281** †bractatrices [MS: braciatrices] (*JustIt* 498) *PQW* 395b; **1287** nec fuit aliqua defalta..de puteis, fossatis vel braceatrecibus tempore ferie (*St. Ives*) *Law Merch.* I 18; quelibet brasiatrix ponat signum cervisie extra domum suam per fenestram vel ostium ut visibile sit omnibus et commune *Leg. IV Burg.* 63; **1317** (v. 1 braciator); **1359** de ~icibus de Clacmanane, quarum quelibet solebat dare per annum iiij d. *ExchScot* 573; hec brasiatrix, A. *brewster* WW.

braciatura, (payment for) brewing.

1228 reddit compotum de..releviis et forefactis et ~is et redditar' *Pipe* 72 (*Northumb*) r. 10 (2); **1261** item ~a in eadem villa [*Broughton, Cumb*] valet per annum xij d. *Rent. Surv. R.* 730 r. 7 (3*d.*); **1265** cervisia, i. ~a, v quart. ordei (*RHosp*) *Manners* 22; **1313** de x li. de quadam consuetudine que vocatur ~a *MinAc* (*Northumb*) 950/2 r. 1; **1326** dabunt precium servicie, viz. de qualibet brasiatura xiij lagenas *BB St. Davids* 152; **1353** focale pro ~a *Pat* 240 m. 27.

bracile [LL; cf. bracale], belt, girdle.

brahiale, *gyrdels GlC* B 181; zona vel zonarium vel brachile vel redimiculum, *gyrdel* ÆLF. *Gl.*; circumdedit collo ejus sacrista..martyris brachile cruentatum BEN. PET. *Mir. Thom.* II 38; **c1310** in serico empto pro bursa domini prioris et in factura braccilis, vj d. *Ac. Durh.* 511; ~e sive lumbare duplex de panno vel corio absque ferro *Cust. Cant.* 401 (cf. ib. 10).

bracina v. bracinum.

bracinagium [cf. braciagium], payment for right to brew (N. Eng.).

1245 in predictis villis sunt duo ~ia, que valent per annum xxv sol. *IPM* (*Northumb*) 3/9; **1270** de bracenagio ij s. iiij d. [*Yorks*] *Cl* 227; **1271** exceptis x d. ob. de redditu et ~io drengorum et villanorum de Seton' [*Northumb*] *Ib.* 346; **1297** de firma cotteriorum cum ~io selfodorum *Pipe* 143 (*Northumb*) r. 28*d.*; **c1380** solvunt pro ~io ville ibidem per annum..ij s. *Surv. Durh. Hatf.* 22; **1408** in viij bollis emptis ..pro brasinagio *Ac. Durh.* 606.

bracinalis, of brewing.

1448 artem brasinalem in domibus suis occupare intendunt *Lib. Cust. Northampt.* 102.

bracineus, for brewing.

1335 carta..de uno tenemento ~eo *Reg. Malm.* II lxxxv; **1354** cum..mesuagio ~eo..prope Paules Warf' in London' *IPM* 27/12 r. 12; **1370** habuit..unam domum ~eam, unam tabernam et quatuor shopas (*CoramR*) *Law Merch.* III 67; **1435** de tota domo mea ~ea vocata *le Crane on the Hoop Reg. Cant.* II 523; **1576** domum brasiniam sive tenementum vocatum..*le three Kinges Pat* 1147 m. 14.

†**braciniare,** to brew (ale).

1265 cervisia ~iata [? l. braciata], vij quart. ordei (*RHosp*) *Manners* 27.

†**braciniatura,** brewing.

1265 cervisia, i. ~a [? l. braciatura], ix quart. ordei (*RHosp*) *Manners* 38.

bracinum, ~ium, ~a [OF *bracin*], brewhouse, malt-house.

1141 in constantiis pistrini et ~i *Dom. S. Paul* 135; **c1160** ibi est..coquina et ~ium et domus una in qua faciunt braisium *Ib.* 132; **c1160** concessi..super burgagia sua furnum et ~um *BBC* (*Swansea*) 51; **a1183** quod ipsi cervisiam venalem in ~a sua vel aliena facere possent *Ib.* (*Tewkesbury*) 96; **1187** in reficiendo ~io ejusdem abbacie *Pipe* 28; **1221** rationabile estoverium..ad coquinam et brascinum suum *Cl* 470; **c1235** unam magnam domum in qua continentur coquina, ~um et pistrinum, tegula coopertam *E. Ch. S. Paul.* 241; **1250** in braccino deest tota bordura, sc. parietes, quia est de fusto *CalIMisc* I p. 30; **a1295** si..opportunum videatur conventui pistrinum et ~um habere separatim, bene liceat ei nova construere (*Ch. Abb.*) WHITTLESEY 146; **1300** in meremio ad..domos ~e empto *Reg. Carl.* I 179; **c1300** cum brasina ejusdem ville *Reg. Aberd.* I 25; **c1370** licitum fuit unicuique..emere et vendere et bracenas cervisie facere *Rec. Caern.* 137; **1450** item in brasina unum plumbum, unum calderium, unum *moldyng bord Test. Ebor.* II 144; **1457** cum terra et libertate brasine *Reg. Aberbr.* II 97; hoc brasinium, *a malthous* WW; ustrinam, brasinam et conficiendae cerevisiae domum FERR. *Kinloss* 26.

2 brew, brewing.

1221 solebant castellani capere cervisiam per villam primo die vendicionis et habere xxviij lagenas pro ij d. de uno ~o *PlCrGlouc* 108; **1230** [consuetudo] capienda de singulis brascinis cervisie ville Bristoll' *Cl* 295; **c1250** dedi..unam bollam de qualibet brascina cervisie in villa de Kenles [*Kells, Ir.*] (*Ch. W. de Lacy*) *MonA* VI 1143; tria..quarteria ordei et sex avene ad unumquodque ~um *Cust. Westm.* 103; **1322** de quolibet ~o integro iiij justas de *livreson DCCant.* J 509; **1398** de vij s. j d. ..de tolsystr' hoc anno, viz. de qualibet brasena j lagena precii j d. *Ac. Man. Coll. Wint.* (*Harmondsworth*).

3 (?) malt.

1317 tam frumentum quam ordeum..in †brasinam convertuntur (*Breve Regis*) *Ann. Lond.* 240 [? l. in braesium convertunt *as in* TROKELOWE 96].

braciologia v. brachylogia. braciolum v. bracchiolum.

bracionarium, malthouse.

brationarium, *mealthus* ÆLF. *Gl. Sup.*

†**bracista,** brewer.

11.. (14c) tenetur †properare [? l. preparare] ij cumbos brasii ad Natale..et tam bene tenetur facere quod ~a se teneat †precatum [? l. pacatum] (*Ext. Binham*) *Med. E. Anglia* 270.

bracitorium v. braciatorium.

bracium, ~ia [cf. braisis], malt (or grain for malting). **b** dist. acc. grain. **c** dist. as high-grade (*capitalis*) or ordinary.

bratium, *malt GlC* B 182; braisi iii modios *DB* I 162b; frumenti ii mod' et viii sextar' et tantundem brasii *Ib.* 69; **a1100** ad coquinam..unaquaque ebdomada vij treias frumenti et x treias braisii [v.l. braisis] *Lib. Eli.* II 136 (= *MonA* I 478); **c1160** domus una in qua faciunt braisium *Dom. S. Paul.* 132; **1224** [naves] carcate..breesio et blado *Cl* 604b; **a1250** molent..et portabunt de torallio ad molendinum et de molendino ad granarium totum brasium *Deeds Newcastle* 43; **c1250** faciet duas mittas braysie *Cart. Rams.* I 488; **1251** molendinum ad braesium (*AncC* II 116) *RL* II 67; **c1255** unum quarterium †braserii [l. brasii] (*Dom. Ipswich*) *Gild Merch.* II 125; abbas J. [ob. **1260**] cervisiam nostram, ..apponendo..circiter m summas bladi ad cervisiam apti, sc. hordei et avene commixtorum, quod bresia vulgariter appellatur, benigne emendavit *G. S. Alb.* I 323; **1265** c quarteria mixtilionis ad brasium *Cl* 53; de xl quart. ordei, de quibus in ~eo facto xxv quart. *FormMan* 15; **c1320** nullum braseum facient molare antequam braciator ..viderit si braseum bene ventetur et vannetur *Cant. Cath. Pri.* 218; **1324** tassum ordei..erat putrefactum et minus conveniens ad fundendum inde brasiam suam *CBaron* 137; **1361** breve ne blada seu bresana ducantur extra regnum (*LB Lond* G 87) *MGL* I 629; **1441** in brasio fuso *Ac. Obed. Abingd.* 157 (cf. ib. 161: brasio infuso); **1454** de custuma ~ii Anglicani *ExchScot* 626; Britanni..magno artificio suum potum conficiunt. primo hordeum..in aquam ponunt et, postquam in aqua tumuerit, ipsum..in domo in quadam planitie ponunt quousque quodammodo desiccetur. dehinc..juvenes ad ludendum super hordeum vocant..et.. quousque germinare et interiora quodammodo depromere videatur lusitant; post hoc totum hordeum in magnum cumulum colligunt et saporem circumquaque emtitunt. dein ipsum more avenae desiccant et calefaciunt novem vicibus interpolatis et ipsum superius verrunt; tunc ipsum non est plus hordeum sed quod braxium vocant MAJOR I 3; **1537** domum. .in qua brasseium paratur FERR. *Kinloss* 48. **b 1223** habere facias hominibus regis Norwag'. .l quarteria braesii ordeicei *Cl* 562; **1266** quarteria bresei tam ordei quam avenarum *Rec. Leic.* I 125; **1298** xx quar. brasii frumenti, xl quar. brasii avenarum *Reg. Carl.* I 111; **1329** computans . .de viij bollis brasei avene factis de ix bollis avene *Exch Scot* 132 (cf. ib. 147: summa recepte brasei ordei. ., de braseo avene. ., de braseo mixto); **1340** brasium drageti *Cl* 167 m. 48; **1378** in siccacione v *kilns* bras' aven' *Ac. Durh.* III 586 (cf. ib. 636). **c 1235** bladum de brasio cursario *Fees app.* 1363 (cf. ib. 274 [**1219**]: de j quar. de *chefbrais*); **1258** quarterium de communi brasio *Ann. Dunstable* 208; **1298** de iiij quar. . .capitalis brasei venditis. .precium quar. iiij s. viij d. . .; et de. .xlvij quar. . .cursalis brasei. ., precium quar. iiij s. *Ac. Cornw.* I 13; braseum capitale, . . braseum cursale *FormMan* 38–9; **1307** de j quar. brasii capitalis suprafusi de frumento et de iij quar. dim. brasii cursalis suprafusi de ordeo *Doc. Bec* 153; **1371** per. .iiij bussellos brassei cursalis *Arch. Bridgw.* 186.

bracius v. bracchium 6. braco v. brao.

braconaria, keepership of hounds.

1331 concessimus. .Galfrido le Brenynge officium serjancie et braconerie in foresta nostra de Cressy. .necnon vadia consueta pro sex canibus currentibus et uno l[i]mario *Pat* 177 m. 17.

braconarius [OF *braconier*], 'brackener', keeper of hounds.

~ii, unusquisque iij d. in die *DomusReg.* 135; **1284** pro vadiis j ~ii custodientis leporarios *KRAc* 351/11 r. 1; **1290** pro putura leporariorum. .et vadiis unius ~ii ipsos custodientis *Ac. Wardr.* (*ChancMisc.* 4/4) f. 55*d*.

bractatrix v. braciatrix. bractea, bracteola v. bratte-. bracteos v. brathy. bracteus v. blatteus, bratteus. bracus v. 1 broca.

brada [ME *brade*: cf. *PN Elements* 46] 'brade', broad field.

c1225 totam ~am Herewardi *Cart. Wardon* f. 82.

†bradigabo [? *for* bracii galio], hop (*Humulus*).

7. . ~o, *felduop GlC* B 183.

2 (? by conf. w. *wop* = *whoop*) shout.

9. . †bradigatio, ploratio campi, *felduop* WW.

bradiola v. bratteola.

bradyphonus [βραδύφωνος], slow of speech.

[dies quam] brădĭfōnus domino Moyses sacrarat amore ÆTHELW. IV 9 (cf. *Exod.* iv 10).

braebium v. bracchium 1. braellum v. braiellum. braemia v. brema. braesium v. bracium. bragator v. brigator. bragettus v. brachettus. bragma v. bregma.

1 Bragmannus [CL Bracmanus], Brahman.

magnus Alexander. .~orum insulam debellare parabat J. SAL. *Pol.* 534A; in Bragmani, in pagani regis est apicibus/ quod 'habemus, possidemus quecunque non cupimus' (*Oratio*) W. FITZST. *Thom.* 71; Bragmani. ., de quibus habetur in epistola Hieronymi Biblie preposita, sunt in India BACON *CS Theol.* 27.

2 Bragmannus [? cf. Provencal *braiman*; v. et. Brabantianus], mercenary, routier.

in ~orum morem conjuratas ad hoc catervas GIR. *EH* II 10; Normanni, Coterelli et ~i, quanquam suis in terris milites egregii sint *Id. DK* II 8 p. 220; nec jam ut monachus sed magis tanquam miles egregius sive ~us bene loricatus et armatus gladioque longo latere munitus et lancea manu concludens undique viriliter invasit *Id. Spec.* III 1 p. 132 (cf. ib. 243: ~i cruenti, quorum cedibus et incendiis vita repleta est).

brahena v. brao a. brahiale v. bracile.

braia [OF *braie*], 'braye', embankment.

1342 pro. .j braya ad portandum pontem *MinAc* 1091/6 m. 2.

braiare [OF *braire*], to cry.

si illa nocte qua nascitur filius vel filia simul moriantur mater et filius vel filia, adhuc vir gaudebit bonis illius terre in vita sua, ita tamen quod vir ille habeat testimonium duorum legalium virorum vel mulierum vicinarum qui audierunt infantem clamantem vel plorantem vel ~antem *Leg. IV Burg.* 41.

Braibacenus v. Brabantianus.

braiellum, ~a [OF *braiel* < bracale], belt, breech-girdle.

1207 pro zona et braello ad opus nostrum *Cl* 88b; **1275** ceperunt. .unum par novarum caligarum et unum novum braellum *Hund.* I 156; **1325** j ~um pro turniamento *LTRAc* 14 r. 6*d*.; **1327** combustio falsorum braellorum et bursarum (*LBLond.* E 180) *MGL* I 600.

braierium [OF *braier* < bracarium], breech-girdle.

1292 apud Neapolin. .in uno ~io pro capellano, j terin' x grana *KRAc* 308/15 m. 6.

braisis [OF *brais* < Gall. *bracis*] malt.

j molinus reddit xxiiij summas ~is *DB* I 146; **a1100** (v. bracium a).

braisium, ~ia v. bracium. braissanus v. bracianus. brakia v. 2 broca 2b. brakkale v. bracale. brama v. brema. 1 branca v. 1 branchia.

2 branca [cf. It. *branca* = *paw*], **a** (w. *ursina*) acanthus (bot.). **b** (w. *vulpina*) foxglove.

aqua decoctionis malve, brance ur[sine] et similium GILB. IV 182. 1; ~a ursina stipitem habet ut olus, folia magna et incisa, G. *branch[u]rsine*, A. *sedokke Alph.* 25; francursina, A. *berefot* WW; levem acanthum pederota et melamphillon eruditi nominant, officine ~am ursinam, vulgus *brank ursyne* appellat; porro foede hallucinantur qui putant ~am ursinam esse *bearefote*, quum illud potius sit helleborus niger TURNER *Herb.* A ii. **b** *fox glove*, apium, ~a vulpina *CathA*.

1 branchia [CL < βράγχια (pl.)], gill.

†braciae, *cian GlC* B 189 (= *EE* 348. 13: brancie); pisses respirant vaporem aque per brancos sive per brancias *Ps.-*RIC. *Anat.* 25; sicut pisces per brancas separant partem salsam. .ab aquosa insipida GAD. 135. 2; habebit dim. caput hujus piscis et de sequenti medietate sub brancia, quantum latitudinis tres digiti vel ala piscis amplectitur extendendo FLETE *Westm.* 66; brancia, A. *a gyle* WW.

2 branchia [OF *branche*], branch of a tree. **b** design of branch.

†a1178 calfagium. .de mortuo bosco et de ~is [v.l. ~iis] et de arboribus furcatis (*Ch. St. Evroul*) *Act. Hen. II* II 71; **1205** faciatis habere. .mairemium ad faciend' vaccariam unam. .de ~iis de bosco de Chippeham *Cl* 49b; **1228** dedit ~ias, plusquam centum ad faciendas porcarias, quas ipse [forestarius] et sui inciderunt *Feod. Durh.* 286; **1229** habere faciat. .xx carectatas busche. .de spinis, *arables* et ~iis *Cl.* 144; **1253** vij quercus cum ~iis *Cl* 182; **12. .** habet. .totas cablices et ~ia *IMisc* 20/14; **1287** pro hiis qui manent infra forestam cum capti fuerint. .amputantes bletrones, ~ias vel siccum de quercubus *SelPl Forest* 63. **b 1489** cornu harnisatum cum argento *pounced* cum litteris et braunchis *Cart. Boarstall app.* p. 289.

3 branchia v. bracchium 9a.

branchiare, to lop.

1325 carectas euntes ad viridem quercum ibidem. . branchiand' *Cl* 142 m. 16 (= *Cart. Tutbury* 97).

branchiatura [cf. OF *brancheure*], branches (collect.).

1222 neque de branchura per impulsionem venti prostrata aliquid amoveatur *Pat* 360; **1240** de brancuris. .quercuum *Cl* 211; **1242** de. .~a et quercubus venditis *Pipe* 337; **1251** habuerunt. .furcas et minutos cheverones de ~a et virgas ad wauluram *IMisc* 5/24; **1331** pro branchur', vj d. *KRAc* 131/25 m. 2*d*.

branchius v. bracchium 1.

branchos [βράγχος], hoarseness, sore throat.

si fluxus reumatis fluat. .ad radices lingue, vocatur branc', quod prefocatio faucium interpretatur GILB. III 151. 1; vitium in [uva]. .unde fiunt branci *Id.* IV 176. 2; ~us [est] quando [reuma] vadit ad fauces GAD. 50. 1; brancos est prefocacio faucium *SB* 13; brancos interpretatur faux: inde brancus apostema in fauce *Alph.* 26; *the pose*, brancus *CathA*.

branchum v. 2 bancus. branchura v. branchiatura. brancia v. 1 branchia. brancos, brancus v. 1 branchia, branchos. brandare v. broudare.

brandeum [? cf. πρανδιος = *fillet*], **a** corporal cloth. **b** 'buckram'.

a s441 Leo [I] papa. .~eum altaris quo consecratum corpus Domini involverat particulatim dividebat DICETO *Chr.* 84 (*from* Sig. Gembloux). **b 14. .** ~ium, A. *bokeram* WW.

Brandones (pl.) [OF *brandon* < Frk.], first Sunday in Lent (Fr.).

1262 data Paris' die Jovis post Brandon' (*Lit. Regis Francie*) *Foed.* I 742; **1268** coram vobis [sc. rege Francie] in curia vestra ad instantem diem ~onum *Pat* 86 m. 29.

branga v. pronga. branis v. brao. brannum v. brennum. brannus v. brema.

branta, brant or brent goose (*cf. brendinus*).

prior anser a nostris ~a et bernicla vocatur et fero ansere minor est TURNER *Av.* 7.

brao, ~onus [OF *braon* < Frk. *brado*], brawn: **a** fatted boar; **b** muscle of arm.

a 1225 pro tribus ~onis v s. et pro c carcosiis multonum xlv s. *Cl* 36; **1226** ~onem nostrum qui captus fuit in parco de Beckel' *Ib.* 145; **1240** emi faciatis. .xij braon' cum capitibus, que eciam capita integra amputari et cerebrum inde extrahi et ea coqui et bene susciri [faciatis] *Liberate* 15 m. 21; **1247** vij ~ones cum capitibus integris *Cl* 96; †braco vel caro callosa apri GAD. 76 v. 2 (cf. ib. 77. 2: †brahene apri); **1338** in dimidia scutella ~onis de stauro preempcionis rectoris de K. *Ac. Ep. Bath.* 124. **b s1284** cum. .sagitta per medium branem dextri brachii inter humerum et cubitum. .fecit et unam plagam *Ann. Dunstable* 310; **1320** repercussit dictum W. cum suo gladio et fecit ei plagam in dextro brachio sub vivo brauno *SelCKB* IV 93 (cf. *Thoresby Soc.* IV 132).

1 brasa v. bracchium 5.

2 †brasa, *s. dub.*

1297 in sepibus faciendis pro ~is ad taschiam ij s. *Ac. Cornw.* I 135.

brasarius v. 2 braciarius. braschetus v. brachettus. brasciare, braseare v. braciare. brascin-, brasen- v. bracin-. braseria v. 1 braciaria. braserium, braseum v. bracium. brasia- v. bracia-. brasica, ~icta v. brassica.

brasillarius, (?) dyer using brazil.

a1155 Hubertus ~ius (*DC St. Paul's*) *HMC Rep.* 9 *app.* I 62b.

brasillum, ~a, ~ium [OF *bresil*], brazil, brazil-wood (dye).

c1150 mercator. ., si piper. .vel alumen vel brasil' vel lacem. .attulerit, non minus quam xxv libr. simul vendat (*Lib. Lond.*) *GAS* 675; **†a1204** (**1295**) sciatis nos concessisse. . de carka alumi vel ~i vel incensi. .quadrantem (*Ch. Regis*) *Reg. Wint.* II 742; **1242** mercandisas contentas in nave que nuper applicuit apud Roianum. .sc. rys, amigdalas, alum' et brasill' *Cl* 504; distemperentur cum decoctione brasilii GILB. II 79 v. 2; **1285** pro ij unciis ~e emptis ad tingendas predictas ij uncias. .serici de colore crinium [serenarum] (*KRAC* 91/3) *Arch.* LXX 28; **1303** ~um ad introitum nichil dabit, ad exitum centum debet ij d. (*Cust. Berw.*) *EEC* 166; **1303** pro xv libratis bresilii (*Cust. Sandw.*) *Ib.* 271; **1318** unam balam brasilii ad valenciam xvij li. xiij s. vj d. *Cl* 136 m. 17.

brasin- v. et. bracin-.

brasinus, (?) brazen.

15. . de precio vasorum brasin' et lavacr' in claustro *Augm. Bk.* 442 f. 49.

brasio v. braciatio.

brasipurgium, brewer's draff.

draf, segisterium, acinacium, ~ium *CathA*.

brasium v. bracium. brasius v. badius. brasorium v. 1 braciaria. brassagium v. braciagium. brassata v. bracchiata. brassator v. 1 & 2 braciator. brasseium v. bracium.

brassica [CL], cabbage. **b** (w. *silvatica*) 'wood chervil'.

comprimit ardores febris artheticosque dolores / brassica NECKAM *DS* VII 212; brasica caulis nondum transplantatus; sed quandoque pro quolibet caule sumitur *SB* 13; brasicta, A. *jutes* WW. **b 10. .** ~a silvatica, *wuducerefille* WW.

brasurum [cf. braciatorium], brew-house.

1560 ecclesiam nostram nuper monasterii B. Petri Westmonasterii. .unacum omnibus capellis. .pistrinis, ~is, molendinis equinis. . *Pat* 858 m. 15.

brata, *s. dub.*

1337 quod ingenia vestra, viz. espringaldos et arcus cum brata bene. .parata. .transmitti faciatis *RScot* 484a.

brateola v. bratteola. brateschia v. bretescha.

brathanum [W. *brethyn*], tapestry, carpet.

super †brachanum, id est tapetum optimum MAP *NC* 25; panno. .qui vulgari vocabulo †*brachan* dicitur GIR. *IK* I 10.

bratheum v. brattea.

brathy [βράθυ], savin (*Juniperus sabina*).

savina, bracteos idem, G. et A. *saveyne Alph.* 158; sape, bracteos i[dem] GILB. V 225 v. 1 (*cf.* Id. II 119 v. 2: bracthei).

bratia v. 2 broca 1a. bratium v. bracium. bratrio v. botryo.

brattea [CL], gold leaf.

†brattanea lamina *GlC* B 193 (= *Erf.* 2. 272. 22; brattea, aurea lammina); bratea non auri fulvis pretiosa metallis ALDH. *Aen.* 96. 11; ~ea, *gylden læfr* ÆLF. *Gl.*; **9. .** bratea fila, torta aurea fila, *þa aprawenan goldþrædas* WW; bractea pertenuis faciem superenatat unde NECKAM *DS* IV 580; malleolum ad †britteas [*gl.*: *plates*] criseas formandas *Id. Ut.* 118; bractea interpretatur aurea lamina *Alph.* 26; aurifabris, proh dolor!, commendamur nos [libri]. .ut fiamus. . repositoria bractearum R. BURY *Phil.* 4. 72; *ful off golde* quod dicitur *golde-ful*, bratheum. .vel brathea *PP*.

bratteola, gold leaf.

serica parietibus tendens velamina sacris, auri blateolis pulchre distincta ALCUIN *SSEbor.* 279; **855** (11c) mihi perdonabat duas †bradiolas aureas †fabrefactos [v.l. fabrefactas] *CS* 487; **9. .** brateolis, laminis, *platungum* WW.

bratteus, made of gold leaf.

bratea flaventis depromit fila metalli ALDH. *VirgV* 173.

braud- v. broud-. braugina v. baruina. brauncha v. 2 branchia. braunus v. brao.

braveuta [βραβευτής], awarder or winner of prize.

†barbeuta, qui palmas dat *GlC* B 45; *a glayfe*, bravium (braveta qui dat vel qui accipit bravium); *a glayfe wynner*, braveta *CathA*.

bravialis, rewarded by a prize.

c1470 ut. .premiis. .haberet enumerari celestibus post expletum cursum stadii ~is *Reg. Whet.* I 429.

braviare, to compete for a prize.

1433 de diversis hominibus secum ~iantibus et ludentibus . .ad summam ix s. [lucratus fuit] *Rec. Nott.* II 134.

bravitor v. brevitor.

bravium [βραβεῖον], prize (in contest). **b** reward. **c** heavenly reward (*cf.* 1 *Cor.* ix 24; *Phil.* iii 14).

dum brăvium captat nec equum nec frena coaptat R. CANT. *Malch.* II 119; **c1239** precipimus ne quisquam levet arietes super rotas vel alios ludos statuat in quibus decertatur pro ~io GROS. *Ep.* 52 (= *Conc. Syn.* 274; cf. ib. 432); s1253 juvenes Londonienses, statuto pavone pro ~io, ad quintenam vires suas sunt experti M. PAR. *Abbr.* 325; mercedem cursus, brāvium victoria donat GARL. *Syn.* 1582C; in stadio currunt ambo, brāvium tamen unus / accipit GOWER *VC* IV 847; s1404 Romani..ad agonem.. ..conveniunt et juxta id B. Pauli dictum, 'omnes quidem currunt etc.', pro ~io fortiter certant AD. USK 94; *rennynge, game,* ~ium *PP*. **b** c1194 de familiaritate Ricardi.. ulteriore solus inter multos ~ium reportasti cancellarie nomen..nancissens DICETO (*Lit. ad W. Longchamp*) II *app.* 177; s1307 jugum abicere captivitatis et ~ium accipere libertatis W. GUISB. 372. **c** invictum Christi tropeum et ineluctabile ~ium licet paganus prudenter intellexit ALDH. *VirgP* 43; defunctusque puer conspexit brāvia vitae *Ib.* 245b; 799 ut curramus simul ad ~ium supernae vocationis ALCUIN *Ep.* 181; ut.. / reddat eis brāvium finita luce laborum WULF. *Swith.* I 180; c1040 ut..futurae beatitatis ~ia perdat *CD* 769; difficile est gravidum brāvia ferre virum H. HUNT. *HA* XI p. 166; licet fides ad scientie ~ium non perveniat J. SAL. *Pol.* 639A; munificus princeps prelarga stipendia nobis / conferet; en, brāvium, currite, Christus adest NECKAM *DS* III 760; multi mortalium in mundi stadio / certatim cursitant, sed casso studio, / nunquam videlicet potiti bravio (*Palpo*) *Ps.*-MAP *Poems* 106; 1305 quo ad salutis ~ium facilius pervenitur *Melrose* I 349; usque ad finem stadii..~iumque attingibile WYCL. *Dom. Div.* 228; nunc ad eterne beatitudinis ~ium cursus dirigit ELMH. *Hen. V Cont.* 160.

brax- v. braci-. braya v. braia. braydare v. broudare. braziare, ~iator v. braci-. Breban- v. Brabant-. brebicarius v. berbicarius.

brecca, ~ium [OF *breche* < Frk. *brecha*; cf. AS *bryce*], breach, break: **a** (in dam); **b** (in wall, accidental); **c** (in wall, made by attackers); **d** (in fence, used as gateway).

a 1202 prior levavit injuste duas breckas ad duo capita fossati et non fossatum *AssizeR Northants* 580; 1203 stagnum illud fractum fuit..per aquam et prior fecit obstrui brechas factas per aquam *Ib.* 827; 1212 non exaltavit stangnum..sed breckas que fracte fuerunt per inundacionem aque fecit [? sc. reparari] *CurR* VI 326; 1221 due †brecee [? l. brecce] aliquando fuerunt [in gurgite] juxta terram, set nesciunt..quando obstructe fuerunt *SelPlCrown* 113; 1234 omnes rupturas et ~as [per inundacionem aquarum].. obstruere et reparare *Cart. S. Neot.* 95v; a1250 ad faciendum unum parvum sepe..ad quoddam ~um stagni de B. ..ad salvandum pissem suam *AncD* C 5425; 1314 in obturacione berce ejusdem prioratus [de Bermundeseye] per inundacionem aque Tamisie facte *Cl* 132 m. 26 (cf. *Cal.* p. 130); 1324 in auxilium reparacionis..pontis nove ~e *Cl* 142 m. 22 (*Cal* p. 245: †brette); s1416 cepit includere ~am de Bermundeseye in parochia de Retherhithe *Ann. Berm.* 484 (cf. ib. 468: accidit magna ~a apud Retherhithe et planitiem de Bermundeseye..debriavit). **b** 1219 quod ~am illam muri castri nostri de Walingeford', que nuper cecidit per tempestatem, ..reparari facias *Cl* 390a; 1223 ~as muri castri nostri de Roffa, qui nuper cecidit, reparari facias *Cl* 577b; 1233 rex dedit burgensibus Stafford' lx quercus..ad claudend' tres brechias ville Salopie *Cl* 335; 1242 in reparacione..unius brecke in eodem castro *Liberate* 17 m. 5. **c** s1264 [S. de Monte Forti] asserens..morem fore Anglorum cum inducerent aliquem in ~am [quod] hunc dimittendo facerent caudam OXNEAD *Chr.* 225. **d** 1225 ad quandam ~am faciendam de palicio parci nostri de Havering' et ad stabiliam faciendam ad fugandas bestias de foresta per ~am illam usque in predictum parcum *Cl* 91b; 1232 quod permittat homines vicinarum villarum petra claudere..~as predicti parci ita quod averia sua non intrent in parcum illum *Cl* 63; 1258 salvo..libero introitu in dictam croftam et exitu per aliquam ~am juxta cimiterium *Cart. Osney* IV 487; 1461 nondum fecerunt diversas †briccas sive rupturas cujusdam haicis *CourtR Lygh* I f. 1; 1496 nondum fecerunt †braccas haic' suarum *Ib.* II f. 6v.

1 brecha v. brecca.

2 brecha, ~ia, ~is [cf. AS *bræc, brēc*; *PN Elements* 46, 47], assart, clearing.

a1135 monachi Gloucestrie..teneant suas duas ~es in manerio meo de Chelesworthe cum pratellis et grava que pertinent *Cart. Glouc.* I 239 (cf. ib.: concessisse..in manerio meo de Chelesworthe duas essartas et silvulam que est in medio eorum); c1150 bracam terre sub Flusrige *Reg. Malm.* I 454; c1180 illam terram que dicitur Bracha Presbiteri *Cart. Colne* f. 18; c1220 quod libere possint arare et excolere ~iam suam usque ad illud fossatum *Cart. Osney* IV 402; 1234 item *brechgavel* quod debet solvi ad festum S. Mich.: ..Sabina vidua pro quadam ~e xij d; ..Turkil pro Longo Frisco et Hundstichene, iiij d. *Cust. Glast.* 55 (cf. ib. 11: tenet j ~iam et reddit inde..ij sextarios mellis); 12.. de quadam domo in ~a de Radingate *Reg. S. Aug.* 156; 12.. pro vj virgatis et duabus brech', que equivalent unam virgatam *Reg. Pri. Worc.* 87a; c1300 concessimus..j dim. acram terre que jacet in ~ia..abbatis..et quod ipsi claudant et fossatum levent inter ~iam quondam Symonis ..et dictam ~iam *Reg. Malm.* II 352.

brechia v. brecca, brecha.

brechiare, to pierce.

1291 venit..persona de G. ..et Willelmum..cum puncto ..gladii ~iavit in capite, unde cerebrum exivit *Gaol Del.* 37/1 r. 1.

brechis v. brecha. brecka v. brecca. bredna v. brema. breesium v. bracium.

bregma [βρέγμα], top of head.

bragma est commissura duarum cellularum in supremo capite, sc. fantastice et racionalis *Alph.* 26.

brehonius [Ir. *breitheamhuin* (pl.)], 'brehon', lawgiver.

utuntur ad tales lites aestimandas quibusdam arbitris quos illi ~ios appellant; isti..retinent solummodo domestica quaedam psephismata, usu et diuturnitate corroborata, quorum animadversione artem aliquam ex rebus fictis.. conflatam pepererunt, quam..sibimet ipsis veluti abstrusa ..mysteria reservant STANIHURST *Hib.* 37.

breidare [ME *breiden*], to wattle.

1367 in dictis muris breydandis, cooperiendis et crestandis *MinAc* (*Essex*) 840/28; 1387 unius hominis [cooperientis] grangiam..et parietes ejus ~antis *Comp. Swith.* 414; 1401 in stipendiis ij hominum studancium et brudancium finem longi stabuli *Pipe Wint.* (159405) r. 13; 1449 pro stipendio j hominis brudantis..domum in circuitu *Crawley* 479; 1466 pro dicto tenemento studdando, breydando [etc.] *Ac. Churchw. Bath* 63; 1477 ad brudand' et dauband' muros *Comp. Swith.* 457.

breima, breisna v. brema.

breiserius [ME *brasier*], brazier (official of mint).

1359 cuidam breyserio..vj s. viij d. *ExchScot* 617.

brema, ~ia [OF *braisme* < Frk. *brahsima*], bream (fish). **b** (w. *marina*) sea bream (? *Pagellus* or *Sparus*).

1171 custamento capiendi et deferendi bresnias..ad vivarium regis *Pipe* 131; exsiliens de aqua grandis piscis projecit se..in gremium viri Dei, piscis, inquam, quam brennam vocant A. TEWK. *Add. Thom.* 17; c1200 concedo.. xxx breisnas singulis annis *MonA* III 618; brenna lupi fauces devitans sive senecis / ad cenosa fugit graraque turbat aquas NECKAM *DS* III 583; 1204 pro cariagio ~arum de vivario *Pipe* 146; 1228 habere faciat..xx bretnias vivas ..ad quendam vivarium..instaurandum *Cl* 18 (cf. ib. 73: brennias); 1231 de cc brednis vivis *Cl* 470; 1231 habere faciat..xx matrices bresnias..ponendas in vivario suo *Cl* 474; 1242 in xxx ~iis captis in vivario..et in pane positis et missis ad regem *Pipe* 176; 1256 in vivario regis..faciat habere Rogero..xx matrices braemias *Cl* 3; 1260 quatuor matrices bramas vivas capi..faciat *Cl* 122; 1273 lupos aquaticos et breymas *IPM* 2/3; vivaria..et hujusmodi piscarias suas quisque discretus bresmys et perchiis faciat instaurari *Fleta* 164; 1309 habebit..viij brem' pro j d. *IPM* 16/9 r. 6; c1324 item †brannum, sardum et becnum meliorem pro iij d. (*Lib. Cust.*) *MGL* II 118; pagri seu phagri [vocantur] bremmae P. VERG. I 1 p. 14. **b** pisces qui dicuntur *haddock* vel *gurnard* seu ~ia marina *Cust. Westm.* 76; marinis [piscibus] sicut merlongo..et †brachinis marinis et fluvialibus GAD. 55. 1; [chrysophryn, i.e. *dory*] vocant etiam bramam marinam CAIUS *Anim.* 27.

bremellus, (young) bream.

14.. nomina piscium..hic brimellus, *a breme* WW; hic brumillus, A. *brone Ib.*

bremetta, young bream.

1306 de viij lupis, c pikerellis et iiij^{xx} brem' et ~is venditis *MinAc* 1079/17 r. 5*d*. (cf. ib. 18 r. 9); 1415 pro.. playse.., bremett'.., mulett' (*KRAc* 321/32) *Analog. Cant. Pilgr.* 16 (cf. ib. 14: brement'); bremetica, *a breme* WW.

bremium [? cf. βρόμος], rush (bot.).

~ium, *earisc* ÆLF. *Gl.*

brena v. brennum.

brendinus, brant, brent (*cf. branta*).

anser ~us avis est marina, ..vulgus .. a coloris varietate *a brendgoose* nominat.. CAIUS *Anim.* 18.

brenna, ~ia v. brema.

brennum, ~ium, ~o [OF *bren, bran*], bran.

1190 si aliquis bladum emerit et de eo panem fecerit, tenetur lucrari in salma unum terrin tantum et bren' (*Concord. Messan.*) R. HOWD. III 60 (= *G. Ric. I* II 132: brennon'); a1190 pistor poterit..in quolibet quartinario frumenti lucrari tres d. et ~um (*Assisa Panis*) *Growth Eng. Indust.* I 568; 1202 pistor poterit..lucrari iij den. exceptis ~io et ij panibus ad furnarium (*Assisa Panis*) M. PAR. *Maj.* II 480; 1204 pistor [Winton'] habeat de lucro de unoquoque quarterio iiij d. vel tres et brenium *Pat* 41a; 1205 leporariis.. facias fieri ~um unde pascantur nisi die quo current *Cl* 26b; 1205 faciatis triturari c quarteros frumenti..et illos faciatis molere et farinam inde cum toto ~o poni faciatis salvo in tonellis *Cl* 31a; 1209 in ~io ad iij equos *Pipe Wint.* 60 (cf. ib. 159283 [1239] r. 11: in branno); 1277 pro †breun' [l. brenno] ad vitulos *Ac. Wellingb.* 17; 1288 in berennio empto ..ad arma domini regis freanda *KRAc* 462/12 m. 2; 1297 in cribris emptis..ad brenam cribrandam *Ac. Cornw.* I 135; 1329 de xvj celdris..branni pro canibus *ExchScot* 253; breno, *bran* WW.

brephotrophium [βρεφοτροφεῖον], foundling hospital, nursery.

loca necessitati humane deputata..quo se reciperent.. imbecilles: ..~ium BELETH *RDO* 2. 15; *norysry qwere yonge chyldyrne arn putte,* ~ium *PP*.

breseria v. 1 braciaria. breseum, ~ia v. bracium. bresilium v. brasillum.

†bresa, (?) malt loaf (*cf. braciare* 2).

c1240 capellani habebunt ~as [v.l. brosas] de pistrino sive de bracino cum necesse fuerit *Cart. Glouc.* III 280.

†bresion, (?) toadstool or species of plant; *cf. britia*.

9.. ~on, *bulut* WW.

bresma, bresnia v. brema.

brestclutum [ME], 'clout' (metal patch) on breast-board of plough (*i.e.* front of mould-board).

1299 in iiij ~is de veteribus clutis faciendis, j d. *MinAc Lopham, Norf*) 938/10; 13.. in iiij brestclut', iij underclut' et iiij clutis ponendis sub capitibus carucarum *Ib.* (*Wetheringsett, Suff*) 995/14 r. 2 (cf. ib. r. 3: in iij brestclout' emptis).

bresura v. presura. bretagium v. bretescha.

bretescha, ~ia, ~ium [OF *bretesche*], brattice (palisade, hoarding, or wooden guard-house) on castle, bridge, or sim. **b** obligation to maintain brattice. **c** brattice on ship.

c1135 usque ad la brutasca que est in capite australi pontis de Strete, ..de prenominata autem brutaschia totus mariscus versus occidentem W. MALM. *Glast.* 109; 1156 in operatione j bretesce super ipsum pontem [de castello] *Pipe* 107; 1173 in operatione castelli de Eya et reparatione veterum bretescarum *Pipe* 132 (cf. *EHR* XIX 230); 1190 in operatione vij ~iarum et emendatione pontis Novi Castelli super Limam *Pipe* 15; 1204 reparari facias fossata castelli Oxon' et domos et ~as *Cl* 2; 1215 unam levem bretascam fieri faciatis super pontem ad villam defendendam *Cl* 192b; 1218 combusserunt octo domos et duas britascas *Eyre Yorks* 416; 1220 una britaschia levata est super pontem, ita quod sexte partes aque de Tyna sunt infra britaschiam et villam de Novo Castro..et..sub britaschia illa est unus pons turnicius *Deeds Newcastle* 64; 1241 faciatis..bretachiam.. super novum pontem garitari et plumbo cooperiri *Liberate* 15 m. 17; bretaschiam quam nuper dedimus..episcopo cariari facias usque castrum ipsius episcopi *Ib.* m. 10 (*cf. Cl* 299); 1241 in cariagio ij bratteschiarum usque ad portum ..et in carpentaria ij britheschiarum in foresta *Pipe Chesh.* 68; 1245 quatuor alias brethachias fieri faciatis, ita quod octo bertachias habeatis promtas et paratas ad cariandum et levandum quando et ubi preceperimus *Cl* 289; 1253 totam breckam ballii Turris nostre Lond' firmari facias de palo cum quodam bretasch' *Liberate* 29 m. 1; 1255 duo millia bordorum ad faciendas brutachias et alia agenda *RGasc* I *suppl.* p. 27; 1261 fieri faciatis..ad utrumque pontem versatilem unam bretachiam levem ad defensionem pontis, ita quod pontes in elevacione sua conjungantur bretachiis *Cl* 502; 1266 britaschiam que erecta est ad capud magni vici de Aldredesgate *Cl* 184; 1300 in meremio empto ad bretachias circa idem castrum de novo faciendas *Reg. Carl.* I 179; c1300 pro uno britagio faciendo ultra posternum †velle [l. ville] de Carnarv'..; pro lx bordis..emptis pro eodem britachio *KRAc* 486/9 m. 3; 1313 in diversis locis.. ville [Bristoll'] bretagia et alia impedimenta fecerunt, non permittentes victualia..ad castrum nostrum..portari *Pat* 140 m. 5*d*.; 1331 defectus brutag' extra magnam portam ibidem ut in coopertura plumbi reparari potest cum xl s. *IMisc* 114/9; 1338 aula de Holmes cum bretasco..amoveatur *Cl* 161 m. 11; 1355 in..reparacione unius bretagii noviter facti super pontem versatilem, ut in novo maeremio, postibus, *bemes*, gistis, plaunchur', et de novo plumbo cooperti *KRAc* 544/36 m. 2; 1360 pro diversis instrumentis pro brutagio murorum civitatis *Ac. Mayor Winchester*; 1386 bretagia de meremio, que pro municione murorum castri..super muros..constructa fuerunt..asportata existunt *IMisc* 237/3 r. 4. **b** 1336 quod ipsi cives [Winton'].. sint quieti de barbicanagio sive barbican ac ~io et de omnibus aliis hujusmodi custumis *ChartR* 123 m. 19. **c** 1337 brettag' et alias defensiones pro municione ejusdem galeie *KRAc* 20/22.

2 movable siege-tower.

s1224 cum a regis bellatoribus ij testudines, quas Gallice *brutesches* appellant, ..subacte fuissent, invaserunt castellum WEND. II 280.

3 bell-tower.

1241 facias..gaiolam nostram ejusdem castri cum bretaschia in qua campane nostre dependent emendari *Liberate* 15. m. 16.

breteschiare, to fit with brattices.

1214 non invenit domum castellatam neque brittaschiatam set barratam *SelPl Crown* 70; 1272 quod castrum illud remaneret in eodem statu quo tunc fuit.., ita quod nichil rep[ar]aretur, exaltaretur, bretaschiaretur(*Pat*) *Cart. Glam.* 888; 1338 domum bretagiatam *CalPat* 172.

bretissementum, bratticing.

1401 supra ipsas fenestras superiores faciet in utroque muro *ailours* et ~a battellata de puro *achiler* (*Indent.*) *Hist. Durh. app.* clxxxviii.

bretnia v. brema. bretta v. brecca. Bretto v. Brito. bretto v. blettro. brettus v. 2 broccus. breud- v. broud-. breugabulum v. brugabulum. breunum v. brennum. brevarium v. breviarium.

brevarius, (?) clerk (Norm.).

a1100 Isembardo Brevario *Regesta* 425.

breve v. brevis 4–13.

brevettum, church brief, authority to collect alms.

1324 injungimus vobis..ne ad presens negocium exponendum aliquos admittatis questores preter eos qui nominatim in cedula annexa presentibus continentur; et ne ipsos..permittatis..aliud predicare seu exponere contra quod in ~o seu dicta cedula continetur (*Reg.*) *Fabr. York* 158*n.*; 1412 recepta de exitibus brevium: de cvj s. de manu ..commissarii domini episcopi per indenturam de ~is et legatis diversorum hominum *Ch. & Rec. Heref.* 268.

1 breviare [CL], to shorten, abridge: **a** (in space); **b** (in time); **c** (writing); **d** (metr. or mus.).

a cogitabant..corpus..in genibus inflectendo ~iare, donec ipso loculo caperetur BEDE *HE* IV 11. **b** multum ~iavit penitentiam ejus THEOD. *Pen.* I iii 3; ad opera ~ianda BEDE *TR* 7; 992 finem cum ense brevians (*Epitaph*) *V. Osw.* 473; dispendia noctis / producto breviasse mero HANV. II 263; c1410 hunc Deus emendet, breviet vel tempora vite (*Vers.*) *Couch. Furness* I 22. **c** Lucae moris est quae plene viderit ab aliis evangelistis exposita ~iare vel etiam..praeterire BEDE *Luke* 417. **d** ~iantur.. prĕhendo et quĕror BEDE *AM* 2357; quae caret his junctis brevitatur [v.l. breviatur] sillaba jure ALCUIN *Carm.* 118. 2 (cf. ib. 12: milĕs et alba segĕs crescens breviatur in ore); quorum..nominum, si penultimae natura longae sunt, nec etiam in metro ~iari possunt ABBO *QG* 3; est brevianda 'quŏque' conjunctio carmine quŏque SERLO WILT. *app.* IIA Q1; cum..visum sit prius quod omnes medie ~ientur, ista regula habet intelligi de semibrevibus ligatis HAUBOYS 444.

2 a to keep accounts of (expenses etc.). **b** to enter (names) on a writ, issue writs (for).

a Osbernus..Thomam..in ~iandis sumptibus reditibusque suis..occupabat GRIM *Thom.* 10; **1354** pro ij quart' papiri emptis pro expensis regis..inde ~iandis et scribendis *KRAc* 471/6 m. 17. **b 1198** per servicium ~iandi placita corone versus vicecomitem et faciendi summonitiones *Fees* 5 (cf. ib.: servicium ~iandi et faciendi districciones); **1211** aliud breve in qua [*sic*] juratores ~iati fuere non venit ad diem *CurR* VI 118.

2 breviare v. breviarium.

breviariolum, small breviary (eccl.).

tu psalteria, tu ~a..componis H. LOS. *Ep.* 43.

breviarium, ~e, ~ius, compendium, handbook. **b** breviary, compendium of psalter or daily office (eccl.).

c804 rogastis ut scriberemus vobis ~ium comatico ser mone qualiter homo laicus..Deo supplicare debeat ALCUIN *Ep.* 304; **13..** ~ium Sententiarum P. Lumbardi (*Invent.*) *Chr. Rams.* xc; rogatus quod de gestis antiquorum..modo chronico aliquid actitarem, istud ~ium..†ruda structura manu propria sculpavi *Eul. Hist.* I 2. **b a1100** xxii psalteria et vii ~ii (*Invent.*) *Lib. Eli.* II 139; sint ibi in ecclesia..missale, ~ium, antiphonarium NECKAM *Ut.* 119; **1220** ~ium vetus absque musica (*Invent.*) *Reg. S. Osm.* I 276; iste prior..post prioratum [i.e. p **1218**] fecit magnum ~ium, quod melius tunc fuit in monasterio *Chr. Evesham* 268; **1227** clerici faciant divinum officium secundum ordinem sancte Romane ecclesie, excepto psalterio, ex quo †poterint [l. poterunt] habere ~ia (*Regula Francisci*) M. PAR. *Maj.* III 138; **1236** libros et ornamenta ecclesie subscripta emi faciat..ponenda in capella regis..viz. unum psalterium..ympnarium, ~ium.. *Cl* 254; **1250** capella.. nullum breviare *CalIMisc.* p. 31; **1329** item [lego] ~ium secundum Stephanum de Langeton' (*DC Sal.*) *HMC Rep. Var. Coll.* I 376; insinuans quod fratres sui habituri essent usum ~iorum et librorum qui sunt ad divinum officium oportuni OCKHAM *Pol.* II 503; **1416** ~ium meum usus Sar' *Test. Ebor.* III 58; **14..** ~ia v, unum in duobus voluminibus (*Cart. Reading*) *EHR* III 122; hoc brevarium, *a brevyar* WW.

breviator, a bearer of mortuary roll (*cf. brevis* 6, *brevitor*). **b** collector of alms, limiter.

a 1244 commendatio T. Prioris in rotulo ~oris *ObitRDurh.* xxiv; **c1250** noveritis N. latorem presencium ~orem nostrum esse, quem ad universitatem vestram destinamus, humiliter exorantes quatenus defunctis nostris pia oracionum suffragia ..impendere..velitis *Ann. Durh.* 98; **1339** iiij ~oribus ordinum Predicatorum, Minorum [etc.], qui obitum suum per totam Angliam pronunciabunt *RR K's Lynn* I 147; **1450** Johannes Devell, ~or de Stodley *MonA* II 22. **b 1335** deputacio ~oris pro fabrica: ad pecunias colligend' et recipiend'..fidelium elemosinas nobis et fabrice ecclesie nostre..datas et dandas..exhibitorem presencium..constituimus *Fabr. York* 160.

brevicula v. breviculum.

brevicularius, bearer of mortuary roll (*cf. breviator*).

subelemosinario licitum est locutorium ingredi forinsecum, ut cum famulo de eodem et cum ~iis..loquatur *Cust. Westm.* 96; [elemosinarius] brevicula defunctorum ad locutorium recipiet ac succentori tradet et ut ~ii corredia consueta plenarie ac honorifice habeant..providebit *Cust. Cant.* 220.

breviculum, ~a, note, schedule, short letter. **b** mortuary roll (*cf. brevis* 6).

931 si..aliquis..hanc meae compositionis ac confirmationis ~am infringere..temptaverit *CS* 677; **934** hanc meae donationis ~am *Ib.* 704; illae res quae furatae sunt ibidem in uno ~o scriptae esse debent (*Jud. Dei*) *GAS* 425; **1127** in hoc ~o ostenditur quod..abbas..dedit Willelmo W. c sol. *Chr. Rams.* 256; **s1176** quid ei debeat Anglorum ecclesia.. sequentis ~e reserat continentia DICETO *YH* I 410; nunc nec unum extorqueblis..~um quod non redimas quatuor nummis MAP *NC* V 6 p. 248. **b** cum legitur ~um de aliquo fratre nostro defuncto *Cust. Westm.* 24; cura ~orum que pro fratribus de medio sublatis mitti solent *Cust. Cant.* I 99; **c1440** pro scriptura ~arum *Ac. Durh.* 234.

brevifactor, scribe, (?) writ-writer.

c1150 Drogone ~ore *E. Ch. Yorks* VII 60.

breviger, bearer of mortuary roll (*cf. breviator*).

~geri..comedent in refectorio iij diebus *Ord. York* III 376; **1493** nomina..in martilogio annotabuntur.., que quidem nomina in cedulis conscripta per ~gerum nostrum ad domos singulas religiosas nostri ordinis per totum Anglie circulum deferentur *Cl* 363 m. 3*d*.

brevigerulus, bearer of mortuary roll.

~o fratrum nostrorum defunctorum *Cust. Westm.* 177; **c1300** littera ~i *Lit. Cant.* I 13; **1488** ~us distortus in sua condicione facta (*sic*) *ObitRDurh.* 79; ~us, A. *a brevytour* WW.

†brevilator, bearer of mortuary roll.

brevia depositionis recipiet [elemosinarius].., si fuerint brevia conditionalia, †brevillator [? l. brevis lator] mandato consolabitur *Chr. Abingd.* II 405 (cf. ib.: brevium latores).

breviloquium, brevity of speech, short speech. **b** brief discourse (as book title).

s1205 quum dominus Papa adhuc ei diceret ut ~io uteretur, ..tandem completis allegationibus subticuit *Chr. Evesham* 152; **1282** hujusmodi mestuosam materiam sub ~io transeuntes (*Lit. Regis Rom.*) *Foed.* II 215; si quid eis necessarium fuerat, modeste signo aliquo aut ~io a famulis petebant *Cust. Cant.* 201; *a shorte speche*, ..~ium *CathA.* **b** ~ium vitae B. Wilfredi FRITH. (*title*); ~ium de Sapientia Sanctorum (*title*) J. WALEYS; **13..** ~ium Pauperis, sc. Summa Bonaventure in Scriptura (*Invent.*) *Chr. Rams.* 363.

breviloquus, laconic.

gentem hec [Yslandia] ~am et veridicam habet GIR. *TH* II 13; vir ~us et sermone perpauco sed ornato *Id. EH* I 43; bonum est ut audiatis eum quia ~us est ECCLESTON *Adv. Min.* 83.

†breviregium, king's writ.

quosdam per ~ia [? l. brevia regia], quosdam per incarceraciones..tribulatos FAVENT 4.

brevis [CL], short, small: **a** (in space); **b** (in time); **c** (in amount); **d** (of speech or writing).

a Hibernia..sicut contra Aquilonem..~ior BEDE *HE* I 1; brevis ales dimidiatur *Babio* 115 (cf. ib. 30); **a1220** quicquid / dextra brevis donat, longa sinistra rapit H. AVR. *Poems* 27. 172; **a1275** nova tumba [veteri]..unius pedis quantitate ~ior extitit *Lib. Eli.* II 147; [Turci] facies.. habent ~es et in parte superiori latas S. SIM. *Itin.* 54; **s1414** (v. brigantinus); **1465** iiij scale longiores, item ij scale ~iores *Ac. Durh.* 243. **b 671** ~i temporis intercapedine ALDH. *Ep.* 1 p. 477; cum..longissima dies..xv, ~issima viii compleat horas BEDE *HE* I 1; non enim ~em transitoriamque quaerit indagationem ERIUG. *Per.* 552B; quam ~is et fluxa sit vita GIR. *TH intr.* p. 3; **1260** quod ad curiam regis veniant ad ~em [i.e. *early*] diem inde responsuri *Cl* 147 (cf. *Reg. Malm.* I 43). **c s1324** constituens prelatis ..annonam..illorum statui nimis brevem *Flor. Hist.* III 226; vias strictas in quibus obsistentia ~issimi populi oppugnationi multorum millium suffecisset ELMH. *Hen. V* 15. **d** Testamenti Veteris ~is epitoma ALDH. *Met.* 2 p. 65; haec ..~ioribus strictisque comprehensa sermonibus nostris.. historiis indere placuit BEDE *HE* V 17; incipit quedam ~is relatio de Willelmo *BR Will.* I 1.

2 (sb. n., *sc. tempus*) a short time.

ut multos in ~i ab idolatria..converterent BEDE *HE* V 10; quorum doctrina Britonum fideles in Christo in ~i corroborati sunt G. MON. IV 20; **c1170** in ~i carinule tue compagines dissolvi..scias *Chr. Rams.* 100; **1218** rex..eis in ~i satisfaciet *Pat* 178; **1232** post ~e..Ranulphus..obiit *Meaux* I 436; in ~i postmodum..Saierum..disseisivimus *Ib.* II 6; **1254** reditum nostrum.., qui erit in ~i *Cl.* 308; **1334** rex Francorum..certos nuncios ad nos..infra ~e proponit destinare (*Cl*) *Foed.* IV 633; **s1335** magnates.. infra ~e..reducere promisit *Plusc.* IX 33; **1401** hoc unum et in ~i concludimus *FormOx* 201; **1473** rumor..erat..te velle in †~e..adventare *Lit. Cant.* III 260.

3 short (metr.). **b** (sb. f.) short syllable. **c** (sb. f., *sc.* (?) *nota*) breve (mus.).

tempora sunt duo, longa et ~e: ..~e est significatio correptae vocalis ALDH. *PR* 141 p. 200; omnis syllaba aut ~is est et tempus recipit unum..ut păter, aut longa est et duo recipit tempora, ut māter BEDE *AM* 2351; non solum metra sed rhythmi componuntur ex pedibus et longis et ~ibus BACON *Tert.* 257. **b** contra auctores posuit longam pro ~i *Ib.* **c** ~is..apud priores resoluta est in duas semibreves ODINGTON 235; quandocunque punctus quadratus invenitur qui caret omni tractu, ~is dicitur..; si tractum habeat a parte sinistra solummodo ascendentem, erecta ~is vocatur..; ~is vero duos tractus habens, quorum sinister longior est dextro, plicata ~is vocatur HAUDLO 384; ultima..~is valet duo tempora et vocatur altera ~is; que magis proprie potest dici ~is alterata *Id.* 385; que quidem notule alique vocantur longe et alique ~es TUNSTEDE 256b; sicut sunt octavi toni sive modi, sic sunt octave species figurarum, sc. larga, duplex longa, longa, ~is, semibrevis, minor, semiminor, minima HAUBOYS 405; ~ium alie recte, alie altere nominantur; recta ~is est prima que non valet nisi unum tempus, quod est minimum in plenitudine vocis *Id.* 419; ~is perfecta valet tres semibreves et tunc est de tempore perfecto; ~is imperfecta valet duas semibreves HOTHBY 330.

4 (sb. m. or n.) short letter or document, note. **b** (pl.) summary.

a1123 hoc idem testificati fuerunt per ~ia sua [*Norm.*] (*Cart. Merton*) *EHR* XIV 426; ut vix non dicam epistolam possim scribere sed ~e brevissimum P. BLOIS *Ep.* 142. 425B; nullus pro eo [sc. vicecomite] suscipietur, ..etiam si ~e suum direxerit se ratum habiturum quod ille vel ille pro se fecerit *Dial. Scac.* II 4B; rotulus qui exactorius dicitur, quem quidem nominant ~e de firmis *Ib.* I 14; **1198** ~e acquietationis quod idem B. mihi fecit *Pipe* 166; si breve portetur domino, post prandia detur D. BEC. 1330; **c1280** portabit ~ia domini sicut alii vicini sui *Crawley* 232; ecce aquila in cujus rostri acucie ~e pendulum..extendit *NLA* (*J. Bridl.*) II 72. **b 1453** demonstratio in ~ibus status porcionis abbacialis.. extracta ex rotulis *Reg. Whet.* I 105; **c1470** processus sub ~ibus super modo et forma quibus J. ..fuit..reelectus *Ib.* 5.

5 (sb. n.) amulet, charm.

demptis annulis et ~ibus que causa salutis collo morientis appenderant W. CANT. *Mir. Thom.* II 39; spiculum baliste vi maxima contortum..ad quoddam ~e, quod gestabat appensum collo et in pectus demissum, non solum restitit sed tanquam a ferrea lamina resiluit *Itin. Ric.* I 48.

6 (sb. m. or n.) death-bill, mortuary roll. **b** (?) church brief.

~es pro defunctis per manum illius..in capitulum deferri debent LANFR. *Const.* 154; **c1123** pro monachis S. Martini.. agimus iii^a^ officia in conventu cum ~is inde advenerit *Text. Roff.* 234; **c1148** si aliquid ~e pro defuncto legendum fuerit (*Inst. Sempr.*) *MonA* VI 946 xxix; [laicus] susceptus in morte..in habitu canonici..in~ibus mortuorum scribetur..; set non mittentur ~ia pro eo nisi habuerit cartam magistri *Ib.* lv; **c1180** ad ipsum pertinet..~ia mortuorum ad Glowecestriam mittere *Reg. Malm.* II 318; ~i depositionis ejus [defuncti] in capitulo perlecto, ab abbate..anima absolvetur *Chr. Abingd.* II 353; **c1290** presentium porrectori, quem pro defunctis nostris absolvendis ~ium nostrorum constituimus portitorem *Ann. Durh.* 99; **1423** (v. brevitor a); **c1470** idem nomen, quibusdam ~ibus inscriptum, ..ad universa monasteria..regni Anglie mittimus *Lit. Cant.* III xxxii. **b 1412** (v. brevettum).

7 (sb. n.) duty rota (mon.).

c1148 accipiens tabulam legat ~e; ..et dum ~e recitatur, qui nomen suum intellexerit inclinet; cui ebdomada aliqua ascripta fuerit, si intelliget se illam..non posse complere, potest misericordiam inde..querere (*Inst. Sempr.*) *MonA* VI 946 xxix.

8 (sb. m. or n.) schedule of lands etc., esp. return to Domesday inquest (*cf.* V. H. Galbraith *Making of Domesday Book*, 129 etc.).

rex W. concessit istas terras habendas..W. episcopo: sicut ipse recognovit audiente episcopo Dunelmensi, cui precepit ut hanc ipsam concessionem suam in ~ibus scriberet *DB* I 87b (*cf. Dom. Exon* 163); in E. jacent x hidae..et scriptae sunt in ~i de Hereford *Ib.* 178; geldant secundum hidas in ~i scriptas *Ib.* 203; has terras calumpniatur abbas de Ely secundum ~es regis *Ib.* II 125; de his xi hidis habet rex ix hidas et dim. ..in ~i suo *Inq. Cantab.* 77b; **a1100** ista terra inbreviata fuit in meis ~ibus ad opus ecclesie S. Benedicti, qui sunt in thesauro meo Wyntonie; et hoc testantur ~es mei de c acris terre (*Breve Regis*) *Regesta* lxxx (cf. *MonA* III 86); **1166** ut vobis per ~e nostrum pendens extra sigillum mandaremus quot milites..feodatos..haberemus *RBExch.* 275 (cf. ib. 248); **1172** unusquisque baronum fecit duos ~es, unum cum sigillo, alterum sine sigillo (*Ch. Mont. S. Mich., Norm.*) TORIGNI *app.* 349.

9 (sb. n.) papal brief (less formal than bull). **b** legatine brief.

s1183 injeci manum meam in peram..in qua scriptum domini pape continebatur et..extraxi scriptum illud cum ciffo, ita quod ~e tenui sub ciffo BRAKELOND 134; **1201** prior..trahit clericum suum..in curia Christianitatis per ~e domini pape *CurR* II 62; **1451** dominus noster Nicholaus quintus..per quoddam sue sanctitatis ~e in ultima nostra congregacione generali lectum et publicatum mandavit.. (*Stat. Gen.*) *Mon. Francisc.* II 82; **1515** dum legeremus copiosissimum vestre sanctitatis ~e (*Lit. Regis*) *Mon. Hib. & Scot.* 515b. **b 1220** ipsa protulit ~e domini legati patens quod testatur quod ipsa probavit sponsalia *CurR* IX 367.

10 (sb. m. or n.) executive writ issued under a seal of the king of England; **b** (dist. by opening formula); **c** (dist. by seal of issue); *cf. Royal Writs* (*Selden Soc.* 77).

1082 ut vobis sepe per ~es meos mandavi (*Lib. Eli.*) *Regesta* 153; neque..inde viderunt ~em regis et sigillum *DB* I 59; in ipsa aecclesia inventus est ~is cum sigillo regis E. praecipiens ut aecclesiae restituerentur [maneria ista] *Ib.* 78b; rex misit ei suum ~e et saisiret R. ..ex omnibus liberis hominibus.. *Ib.* II 377; **c1095** sciatis me recognovisse..per ~es meos quod pater meus concessit.. Legam ecclesie..de Wintonia (*Ch. Wint.*) *EHR* XXXV 388; **1111** precipio quod R. episcopus..habeat necessaria sua.. sicut precepi per aliud ~e meum ut ipse haberet (*Reg. Heref.*) *Regesta* 990; hec sunt jura que rex..habet: ..infractio pacis regie per manum vel ~e date (*Leg. Hen.*) *GAS* 556; **1167** per ~e regis de ultra mare *Pipe* 6; ad hunc pertinet ~ia regis de exitu scribere *Dial. Scac.* I 5v; illud [contrabreve] penes se reservabit clericus cancellarii in testimonium liberate facte per ~e regis originale *Ib.* 6A; mos curie nostre fuit ut gratis fierent et redderentur ~ia sigillata ministris curie que nomina sua vel negocia continerent MAP *NC* V 6 p. 242; **1198** debet xx s. pro habendo ~i de recognitione de vj carrucatis terre *Pipe* 42; miles quidam, nuncius regis, capitulo ~e regium palam porrexit, quo pro clerico quodam..rogavit quatinus ipsum in episcopum suum..eligere non postponerent GIR. *S. Hug.* II 3; **1226** ~e domini regis de c m. allocandis..est in forulo marescalli; et ~e illud venit clausum ad scaccarium *LTR Mem* 9 r. 2; **1281** per duo ~ia patencia in quibus continetur quod rex commisit eidem Bogoni..comitatus predictos (*Pipe* 125) *MinAc W. Wales* I 28; **1292** per inquisitionem.. per ~em nostrum factam *BBC* (*Limerick*) 37; **c1348** literas, quas ~ia nominant, plurimas in portubus diversis regni nostri acceperant ut me caperent RIC. ARMAGH *AP* 19; **1358** pro uno magno ~i recitanti cartam (*Ac. Univ. Ox.*) *EHR* XXIV 738; **1365** quoddam ~e nostrum vocatum *patent* felonice cepit *Pat* 272 m. 17; **1384** causa pluvie que.. descendebat per valvam ecclesie..super ~ia predicta, unde eadem ~ia sordidata et putrefacta devenerunt *Cl* 224 m. 15*d*.; *wryt of þe kyngis cowrt*, ~e *PP*. **b 1202** alias terras que continentur in ~i de cape *CurR* II 110; **1230** venit de domino rege ~e quod vocatur 'liberate' de liberando..l m. *LTRMem* 11 r. 9; **1242** habet ~e de liberate patens ejusdem date *RGasc* I 75; **1242** ~e nostrum de computate eis habere faciatis *Cl.* 503; **1266** nisi..sibi eas [marcas] allocari fecerimus per ~ia de computabitur et allocate *Ib.* 199; **1290** in cancellaria non sunt nisi tres forme ~ium de escaeta, 'quia utlagatus' vel 'suspensus' vel 'quia abjuravit regnum' *RParl* I 52b; **1292** fiat ~e de liberate, duplicatum sub testimonium baronum sine cera (*Ordinatio Scac. Hib.*) *EHR* XVIII 513; **a1350** per inquisitionem captam virtute ~is ad quod dampnum *Meaux* III 4; **1367** ut sic per ~ia de capias postmodum inde subsequencia diversas pecunie summas ab eis callide posset extorquere *Pat* 275 m. 2*d*. **c 1212** per ~e de parvo sigillo *Cl* 130b; **1294** per ~e de privato sigillo *Pat* 113 m. 20; **s1313** dominus rex mandavit hic ~e suum de magno sigillo *MGL* II 137; **1338** per ~e sub privato sigillo nostro mandavimus *RScot* I 523a; **1343** ~e de griffon' *KRAc* 290/23 m. 2; **1345** per aliud ~e regis de predicto sigillo griffonis (*Pipe* 198) *EHR* XXVI 688; **1388** ~e predictum, clausum et sigillatum magno sigillo domini regis Anglie cum cera alba more consueto Cancellarie ipsius domini regis, integrum et clausum in hujusmodi cera (*Cl* 229) *Great Seal* 303; **1400** ista littera fuit executa per ~ia sub magno sigillo absque ~i de privato sigillo eo quod clericus privati sigilli fuit absens (*Chanc. Warrant*) *Ib.* 87.

11 (sb. n.) king's writ initiating legal proceedings (*b. capitale, b. originale*) or furthering them (*b. judiciale*).

a**1130** prohibeo ne facias Hugoni O. pro aliquo ~i quicquam nisi rectum *Regesta* 1685a; a**1157** predictam terram calumpniaverunt euntes ad curiam regis et ab ipsa curia quoddam ~e recti H. priori attulerunt (*Cart. Spalding*) *Proc. Brit. Acad.* XIII 226; habebit..ad dominum suum, de quo idem clamat tenere, ~e de recto Glanv. XII 2 (cf. Bracton 328); precipe N. quod reddat R. unam hidam terre ..; et nisi fecerit summone eum..; et habeas ibi summonitores et hoc ~e *Ib.* I 6; **1200** dies datus est..quia non habuimus ~e capitale *CurR* I 259 (cf. ib. 432); **1201** vicecomes.. nullam vult facere summonitionem sine ~i originali *Ib.* II 79; **1215** nihil detur vel capiatur..pro ~i inquisitionis de vita et membris *Magna Carta* 36; ~e quidem, cum sit formatum ad similitudinem regule juris, ..rem que est breviter †enarrat [l. enarrat]: ..et sunt quedam ~ia formata super certis casibus et de cursu et de consilio totius regni..approbata; ..sunt etiam ~ia ex eis sequentia que dicuntur judicialia et sepius variantur secundum varietatem placitorum..; sunt etiam quedam que dicuntur magistralia et sepius variantur secundum varietatem casuum, factorum et querelarum, et quorum quedam sunt personalia, quedam realia, quedam mixta Bracton 413b; [brevium] originalium quedam aperta et quedam clausa *Ib*; **1259** dictus R. custo suo proprio debet perquirere omnia ~ia que huic negocio fuerint necessaria de cursu; si vero ex consensu utriusque partis ad placitum properandum voluerint ~e domini regis de perquisito habere.. *AncD* A 763; **1265** signabit..~ia illa que sunt de cursu..; ea tamen que sunt de precepto non nisi in presencia signantis signabit *Cl* 54; **1266** per parvum ~e nostrum clausum quo sokemanni nostri utuntur placitare *Ib.* 260; **1279** tenent ut villani et placitant per parvum ~e secundum consuetudinem manerii *Hund.* II 689; p**1285** in maneriis de antiquo dominico corone Anglie fit..pro tenentibus hujusmodi maneriorum parvum ~e de recto clausum *Mod. Comp. Brevia* 152; in ~i clauso adjudicentur dampna mulieribus, sed in patenti non *Fleta* 344; sunt..clerici juvenes et pedites, quibus..concessum est pro expeditione populi ~ia facere cursoria *Ib.* 78; **1290** omnia ~ia originalia et judicialia tangencia placita de eodem banco (*LTRMem*) *SelCKB* I clix; rotulos de assisis et juratis..una cum ~ibus inchoatis, ~ibus de preceptis et ~ibus finitis predictorum comitatuum (*Ib.*) *Ib.* clxiii; **1309** quodlibet [precipe] est ~e per se *Year Bk. 2 Ed. II* 52; **1313** in itinere justiciariorum non sunt nisi duo ~ia originalia de gracia, videlicet ~e de attincta et falso judicio, et aliquando ~e de attincta est de cursu *Eyre Kent* 51; **1315** de ~ibus judicialibus habeant [querentes] remedium de placeis unde ~ia illa exibunt *RParl* I 322b; **1343** in processu ~is de scire facias, quod est ~e originale *Cart. Ciren.* I no. 130; **1431** perquisivi ~e de forma donacionis in descendere..de tenementis predictis *Cl* 281 m. 13*d.*; 'per ~ia regia', i.e. literas sub quadam brevitate scriptas; et '~e' idem importat quod 'preceptum' vel 'citacio' Lyndw. 97z; **1445** cum quidam R. T. ..perquisisset de curia Cancellerie nostre duo ~ia de sub pena.., quorum unum cuidam Agneti M. ..directum et per T. G. et T. T. deliberatum .. predicta Agnes recepit et ad pedes suos projecit et surrexit quosdam .. qui predictos T. G. et T. T. ..~e nostrum predictum commedere compulsissent *Pat* 459 m. 2; episcopus..comitem Sarisburiae ea formula juris quod ~e de recto appellant juridici nostri in jus de hoc castro vocavit Camd. *Br.* 216.

12 writ of jurisdiction other than royal.

1229 prior..habebit..curiam suam..cum omnibus pertinentibus ad eam exceptis placitis corone et placitis terre motis per ~e episcopi *Feod. Durh.* 215; **1235** R. ..sequitur versus M. ..per ~e domini episcopi de quodam muro et fossato levatis *Assize R. Durh.* 76; **1306** cancellaria nostra.. aperta et presto sit omnibus et singulis ~ia petentibus (*Ch. W. de Braose*) *BBC* (*Swansea*) 182 (= *Cart. Glam.* 994).

13 brieve (Scots equivalent of writ).

c**1118** ego ipse vidi ~e et donum fratris mei Eadgari regis..et quicquid illud ~e eis testatur volo..ut libere.. habeant *E. Ch. Scot* 32; **1161** ne aliquis eos injuste detineat amodo super hoc ~e *Regesta Scot.* 195; **1290** habeat seisinam terre sue..per ~e de capella (*Tractatus*) *Foed.* II 483; **1318** si ita infeodatus impetraverit ~e de garentya de carta pendente assisa.. (*Stat. Rob. I* c. 13) *APScot* 110; quod nullus eiciatur extra liberum tenementum suum..sine ~i regis placitabili vel tali ~i quod adjacet (*Ib.* c. 25) *Ib.* 113; **1319** ~e perambulacionis..in forma capelle impetraverunt *Reg. Dunferm.* 352; ~e de proteccione domini regis infricta: rex vicecomiti tali: mandamus [etc.]..et habeatis ibidem summonicionis testimonium et hoc ~e *Quon. Attach.* 54.

brevitare v. breviare 1c.

brevitas, shortness, brevity: **a** (of space); **b** (of time); **c** (of diction).

a corporis ~atem animo recompensans Devizes 27v; a**1275** nova [tumba] a veteri prescripta ~ate [sc. uno pede] defecit *Lib. Eli.* II 147; serenissimus princeps..nec in molem titaniam indecenter elatus nec in pigmee ~atis paupertatem dejectus *Ps.*-Elmh. *Hen. V* 6. **b** plurimae ~atis noctes aestate Bede *HE* I 1; infra spacii ~atem, infra modici temporis angustiam, contigit. *Mir. J. Bev.* C 342. **c** insignia..succincta ~ate prelibavimus Gir. *IK* II 14; artis erit minus obscura res sub brevitate / stringere Neckam *DS* IV 834; **1202** hec vobis sub ~ate perstrinximus *Canon. G. Sempr.* 136v; ne sit curta nimis brevitas Vinsauf *PN* 559.

brevitator, bearer of mortuary roll (*cf. breviator, brevitor*).

1447 dat' ~ori S. Bertini xiij s. iiij d. (*Reg. Ch. Ch.*) *Arch. Cant.* LIII 15.

brevitellus, scroll used as phylactery.

philaterium..est..membrana vel ~us in quo Judei scribebant legem Bart. Angl. XIX 125.

breviter, a shortly, in a short time. **b** briefly, in a few words.

a 1359 destinetur..quambrevius poterit *Lit. Cant.* II 388; **1549** detur ei triduum ad respondendum; alioquin ~er arbitrio judicis *Conc. Scot.* II 125. **b 680** compendiose et ~er enucleabo Aldh. *Ep.* 4 p. 481; summatim, ~er vel commatice, *sceortlice* Ælf. *Sup.*; ut ~er multa comprehendam Bede *HE* III 17; ~er..respondere Eriug. *Per.* 552c; ut autem ~er complectar Gir. *TH* I 24.

brevitor, a bearer of mortuary roll (*cf. brevis* 6). **b** beggar seeking alms, 'limiter'. **c** writer (? of summary).

a 1296 ~oribus..elemosinarius providebit et ab eis recipiet brevia defunctorum *Obs. Barnwell* 176; **1307** ~ori cum domi moratur..[elemosinarius] provideat (*Const. Winchcombe*) *MonA* II 305; **13..** †brevitoris [l. brevitor] pro eo [sc. fratre defuncto] mittetur per Angliam ad suffragia a viris religiosis..pro eo petenda; camerarius autem stipendia ~oris persolvet *Cart. Bath.* II 152; **1423** ut ultima fratrum..dormicio..repositam habeat graciam, ..ordinatum est..ut preter illa brevia que cantor tenetur per proximiores internuncios ad cellas mittere, nova alia ac specialia cum nominibus eorum..ecclesie ~ori, quociens cum brevibus communibus exiturus fuerit, semper tradat (*Ordinacio Abbatis*) Amund. I 115; **1483** in denariis solutis †bravitori nichil hoc anno, quia nulli fratres decederunt *Comp. Swith.* 377 (cf. ib. 247: ~ori). **b 1291** (v. bollardus). **c 1492** Willelmo B., ~ori compotorum *ExchScot* 377.

breviusculus, very short.

s**1483** si Deus eum ab hoc seculo..infra tam ~um temporis spatium non vocasset *Croyl. Cont.* C 570; prandia ~a sunt, coenae largiores More *Ut.* 166; **1526** ut ex hac ~a consiliorum dilatione nolit quicquam..expectare (*Lit. Wolsey*) *Mon. Hib. & Scot.* 556.

brewgabulum v. brugabulum. brey- v. brei-.

bria [LL (?) *back formation* < ebrius etc.], measure, moderation.

alterius corio cindetur lingula larga; / de cute non propria sumitur absque bria Serlo Wilt. *app.* III B 28. 2; extra ~am..sobrietatis poni Gir. *GE* II 19 p. 260 (cf. ib. 27 p. 303); vino..ultra juste mensure ~am dato *Id. Spec.* III 12 p. 203 (cf. ib. 13 p. 209); a**1270** sobrius dicitur quasi sub ~a constitutus id est sub mensura (R. Bocking *V. Ric. Cicestr.*) *Acta SS Boll. Apr.* I 291; s**1455** sit tibi prandendi modus et bria parca bibendi (*Epigr.*) *Reg. Whet.* I 157; *a mawndrelle*, mensurale, ~a..*a mesure*, ~a, frugalitas *CathA*.

†**brianneus,** a form of service (? *cf. biannum*).

12.. domum cum tofto..quietam ab omni servicio et consuetudine preter ~eum servicium *Couch. Selby* II 8.

Briarēus, like Briareus, gigantic.

s**1461** gens est Cerberea, gens Spingia, gens Briarēa (*Vers.*) *Reg. Whet.* I 396.

briba [OF *bribe*], morsel (given as alms). **b** bribe.

14.. hec ~a, A. *lumpe* WW. **b 1376** *en tiel manere est le roy desceu par la dite fyn, bribez donez* [etc.]..dicunt quod verum est, tamen nesciunt de summis ~arum nec de summa finis (*Parl. & Council Proc.* 2) *Stud. 14 Cent.* 186.

brica v. 1 briga. bricca v. brecca. bricium v. britia.

bricius [cf. Ir. *breac*], kind of trout.

sunt et tertii [pisces] turtris, nisi quod maculis carent, per omnia similes; ..tertios vero ~ios vocant Gir. *TH* I 10.

brida [Fr. *bride* < Frk.], **a** bridle (*cf.* 1 *briga*). **b** (?) trapping (of horse).

a 1213 in..ij scingulis et iiij ~is et iiij capistris *Cl* 128b; **1305** Bernardus de Tarbe, carpentarius ~arum *RGasc* III 483 (*cf. CalCl 1318–23* p. 247). **b** ~a, A. *a trappe* WW.

bridguma [AS *brydguma*], bridegroom.

postea dicat ~a (id est sponsus) quid ei dare disponat (*Quad.*) *GAS* 443.

†**briensis,** (?) skin disease.

~is, i. *honduyrm GlC* B 179; surio vel ~is vel sirineus, *handwyrm* Ælf. *Gl.*; **9..** ~is, *teter* WW.

1 briga, bridle (*cf. brida*).

cum clerici S. Edmundi archiepiscopi peterent pro quodam consanguineo suo qui fuit veredarius, respondit sanctus: 'si ~a sua fracta est, ..faciam eam reparari; quod si reparari non possit, emam sibi novam; sed..statum suum nunquam mutabo' Eccleston *Adv. Min.* 115; **1405** lego.. sellam et ~am meam *Reg. Exon.* I 384; *brydyl*, brica *PP*.

2 briga [ME *brigge*], 'bridge', gang-plank.

1201 debet respondere..de quadam ~a navis de *wreg Pl.K. or J.* II 86.

3 briga [cf. OF *brigue*], strife, dispute, brawl.

1289 occisus in quadam ~a *RGasc* II 509; **1322** congregacio..in qua..predicta ~a totaliter sit sedata *StatOx* 124; **1327** dissencio seu ~e materia super decimis garbarum *Reg. S. Bees* 131; cum ~a, dubitacio vel casus difficilis pacis vel guerre emergat in regno vel extra, referatur et recitetur casus ille in scriptis in pleno Parliamento *Mod. Ten. Parl.* 17; s**1376** volunt quidam quod propter istam ~am rex per illos in Parliamento constitutos noluit gubernare Ad. Mur. *Cont.* A 221; **1381** brigis et rixis satiant / felle cunctos inebriant (*In Lollardos*) *Pol. Poems* I 234; **1382** de ~a et dissensione inter doctores religiosorum et magistrum N. H. (Herford) *Ziz.* 305; *brygge or debate*, ~a *PP*; **1473** pro ~a sedanda in exequiis ducis Glowcestrie *ArchOx* II 308.

†**brigacus,** share-beam (? of plough).

9.. ~us, *scearbeam* WW.

briganda, ~era, ~ina, ~inum, brigander, brigandine, light body armour.

1418 xxiiij brigantinas de panno lineo coopertas et sex brigantinas de velveto coopertas *RNorm* 237; **1451** modo guerrino arraiati..viz. baculis, arcubus, ..deploidibus defensivis, ..~eris..et aliis armis defensibilibus *Pat* 473 m. 16; **1459** Lygeyr Gallico pro factura ~inorum *ExchScot* VI 498; **1460** Ligiero Gallico factori briggandarum pro.. duobus paribus briggandarum *Ib.* VII 34; **1462** in duabus ulnis panni serici vocati *satynfigure* pro uno pari ~inarum cooperiendarum domino regi *Ib.* 145; **1466** in curassys, ~inis, jakkis (*Invent.*) *Paston Let.* III 441.

brigandarius, ~inarius, brigandine-maker, armourer.

1486 Radulfum de Pontieu ~inarium regis *CalPat* 126; **1526** ~ario domini regis *L. and P. Hen. VIII* IV 1939/9; **1537** officium brigendarii nostri (*Pat*) *Foed.* XIV 381; **1606** officium ~arii sive armorarii sui..infra Turrim Lond' *Pat* 1714 m. 21.

brigans [? cf. brigare], **a** armoured foot-soldier. **b** routier, brigand (*cf. EHR* XLVII 583–600).

a s**1423** apud Brosigner [*La Brossonière, Norm.*] ubi.. ducenti a ~antibus interfecti sunt *Extr. Chr. Scot.* 235. **b 1418** auctoritatem ad omnes et singulos ~antes per vos captos..per colla sua suspendi faciendi *RNorm* 238; **1458** ita quod..nec sint communes noctivagi seu ~antes (*Ch. Ep. S. Andr.*) *Mon. Hib. & Scot.* 410a.

brigantina v. briganda.

brigantinus, (lightly) armoured foot-soldier.

s**1346** Carolus de Bloys..cum..sexcentis hominibus armatis et duobus millibus balistariorum et sex millibus ~orum et triginta millibus peditum Britonum et aliorum Wals. *YN* 288; s**1414** reductus est [papa Johannes]..non indumentis religiositatis redimitus, sed ~orum more semivestitus, gestans ad latus sagittas breves qualiter utuntur equites illarum parcium qui *malendrini* dicuntur *Ib.* 453.

brigare, to dispute, quarrel.

c**1360** nulla briga ventilatur nisi..ex utraque parte sic ~ancium foret paritas vocum *StatOx* 127; **1377** nolentes.. vos adinvicem sic ~are set pocius inter vos amiciciam et vestram concordiam reformari *FormOx* 381.

brigator, brawler, disturber of the peace (Scot.).

[inquirendum] de ~oribus [v.l. †bragatoribus] omnibus in curia (*Iter Cam. Artic.*) *APScot* 317; **1458** per remissionem factam per regem D. H. berbato ~ori et nichil habenti in bonis *ExchScot* 418; **1504** communem ~orem noctivagum *Reg. Glasg.* 515.

brigbota [AS *brycgbot*], 'brigbote', obligation to repair bridge.

taini lex est..ut tria faciat pro terra sua, sc. expeditionem, burhbotam et brugbotam [v.l. brigbotam; AS *brycgeweorc*] (*Quad., Rect.*) *GAS* 444; qui burgbotam vel ~am vel *firdfare* supersederit cxx sol. forisfecerit (*Leg. Hen.*) *Ib.* 558.

brigendarius v. brigandarius.

Brigittinus, ~ensis, Brigittine (dedicated to St. Bridget).

s**1414** rex Henricus fundare cepit tria monasteria..juxta predium suum 'apud Shene' vulgariter appellatum: .. tercium ~inorum, qui S. Augustini profitentur regulam, que cum aliis adjectis ceremoniis vocatur ab eis Regula Salvatoris; hiis non licet..pecuniam tangere quovismodo Wals. *HA* II 301; **1570** Reginaldus professione..~ensis Chauncy *Passio* 80; Sion..quem Henricus V..Brigidianis virginibus construxit, totque virgines, sacerdotes et laicos fratres parietibus discretos constituit quot apostolorum et discipulorum Christi numerum aequarent Camd. *Br.* 367.

brigosus, contentious, quarrelsome. **b** (sb.) trouble-maker.

c**1378** opinionibus ~is et odiosis (*Excusat. contra J. Wycl.*) *EHR* XLIII 77; **1392** materiam litigiosam et ~am (Crompe) *Ziz* 344; **1424** nullus..sit..~us inter socios (*Ch. Hosp. Whittington*) *MonA* VI 747; **1435** hujusmodi abusionis malum, quod ~a et proterva elacio quorumdam..confovet *EpAcOx* 118; **1475** viri ~i, verbosi et incorrigibiles *Process. Sal.* 158. **b** *brygows or debate makere*, ~us *PP*.

brika [OF *briche, brique*], brick.

1440 circa facturam *le steyre*..et viam juxta *le dongeon*, ut in muris, petris et ~is (*Ac. Foreign*) *Windsor Castle n.* 27.

brimellus v. bremellus.

brimma [ME], 'brim', surface-sheet.

1369 vj brymmas sive superficies plumborum *CalIMisc* III 743.

brimmagium [?], a payment involved in the transport of casks.

1284 pro brymmagio x doleorum vini..usque Aberconeweye *KRAc* 351/9 m. 13; **1288** pro cariag' viij dol. vinorum ..usque Burdegalam, †brimmiag', carcag', discarcag' et aliis custibus *Ac.Wardr.* (*TRBk* 201) p. 9 (cf. ib. p. 20: pro ..brimmag'); **1300** ..wyndagio, ~io, bermannagio vinorum et doliorum cum flore veniencium ibidem [*Berwick*] *Ac. Wardr.* p. 113; **1313** pro brimmanag' iiij^xx doliorum..vini.. de celar' usque ad naves *KRAc* 375/8 (*Boston*) f. 19*d*. (cf. ib. f. 23: pro brummanagio doleorum vini et hospitacione eorundem in celar').

brimosus v. bromosus.

brinca [ME], 'brink', bluff of land.

a1250 octo *seilluns*..qui extenduntur usque brincham super heldam Turstani *Cart. Worc.* 296; **c1250** quandam brinccam [*Cal.*: †briuccam] terre juxta rivulum de Hope [*Salop*] *ChartR* 78 m. 8.

briocteris v. dryopteris. brionia v. bryonia.

†**brisa** [? *for* busa, cf. OF *bose*], privy.

a pryway, ~a, cloaca, cacabunda, †strica [? l. forica] *CathA*.

brisare v. brusare.

brisca [OF *bresche*], honeycomb.

an huny cambe, ~a, favus *CathA*.

briscellus v. bussellus 1b. briscus v. bitriscus, 2 bruscus. brissaca v. besasa. brisura v. brusura. britachium, ~agium v. bretescha.

Britannia [CL], Britain. **b** Brittany.

~ia insula in extremo ferme orbis limite.. GILDAS *EB* 3; Brittannia insula a quodam Bruto consule Romano dicta NEN. *HB* 147; ~ia igitur beatissima est insularum H. HUNT. *HA* I 1; Brutus de nomine suo insulam Brittanniam appellat, sociosque suos Brittones G. MON. I 16; ~ie majoris quatuor ab antiquo legimus partes fuisse GERV. TILB. II 10. **b s1075** rex in minorem Brytanniam suam movit expeditionem FL. WORC. II 12; sanctorum reliquias ex ~ia transmarina emptas W. MALM. *GP* II 85; in minorem ~iam que tunc Armorica sive Letavia dicebatur G. MON. VI 4; sileo de Namneto et toto minoris ~ie..comitatu J. SAL. *Pol.* 616B; in Gallico littore maris Britannici est minor ~ia, que Armorica dicitur GERV. TILB. II 10.

Britannica, cowslip (or other plant).

brittannica, *cusloppe* ÆLF. *Gl.*; **10..** brittanice, *hæwenydele* WW; brittannica, *viht meres vyrt* vel *heaven hindele Gl. Durh.*

Britannice, in Welsh.

Snotengaham..quod ~e Tigguocobauc interpretatur ASSER *Alf.* 30; civitatem que ~e..Kaerleur [v.l. Kaerleir], Saxonice vero Lerechestria nuncupatur G. MON. II 11; Rothericus Magnus qui ~e Rotheri Maur dicebatur GIR. *DK* I 2.

Britannicus, British (w. ref. to Britons or Welsh). **b** English (or incl. English).

propter vesanam Brettonici regis tyrannidem BEDE *HE* III 1; expulsi sunt..ab omnibus ~is regionibus NEN. *HB* 156; unde adhuc gens patrie lingua ~a sese Kambros appellat G. MON. II 1; *aber*..lingua ~a dicitur locus omnis ubi fluvius in fluvium cadit GIR. *IK* I 2; qua fronte genti nostre ~e gentem Anglicanam preferre ausus est *Id. Inv.* I 4; Gaufridus Monemutensis in suo ~o libro HIGD. I 47 p. 58. **b** avis..lingua ~a *jaia* TURNER *Av.* 77; [canes nostros] omnes ~os vocabo, ..quod una Insula Britannia ut Anglicos omnes sic quoque Scoticos omnes complectitur CAIUS *Can.* 3.

Britannigena, Briton (Welshman).

Cungarus apud Angligenas vocabatur; Doccuinus quasi 'doctor' apud ~as vocabatur *NLA* (*Cungarus*) I 249.

Britannus, Briton (Welshman, etc.). **b** Breton. **c** Englishman.

susceptam fidem Brittani..inviolatam..servabant BEDE *HE* I 4; contra Aquilonales ~os ÆTHELW. iii 3 (cf. ib. i 1; iv 3); Marius filius Arviragi regnavit apud ~os HIGD. IV 9 p. 416. **b s890** ad locum cujus situs inter ~os et Francos videtur ÆTHELW. iv 3; dux Normannorum cum Gallis atque Britannis / invasit terram G. AMIENS *Hast.* 159; Armoricos qui nunc ~i dicuntur H. HUNT. *HA* I 2. **c** venatibus..magis ~i sumus dediti quam..Scoti CAIUS *Can.* 4.

britasca, ~aschia v. bretescha.

britia, cress or (?) fenugreek (bot.); *cf.* *bresion*.

brittia, *cressa GlC* B 195; **9..** ~ia, *willecærse* WW; bricium, *cerse Gl. Durh.*

britnare [ME *britnen*], to 'britten', chop up (Notts).

1355 octo hominibus conductis ad prosternandum, brutnandum et modo debito diminuendum maeremium in Lyndehurst *KRAc* 544/36 m. 4; **1359** in duobus hominibus prosternantibus et ~antibus maeremium in Beskewod *Ib.* 478/5.

Brito, Briton (Welshman etc.). **b** Breton.

in primis haec insula Brettones solum, a quibus nomen accepit, incolas habuit BEDE *HE* I 1; [in Brittania insula] habitant quattuor gentes, Scotti, Picti, Saxones atque Brittones NEN. *HB* 147; **870** (10c) in monasterio quod lingua Brettonum [i.e. *Cornish*] †appellator [v.l. appellatur] Dinnurrin *CS* 527; Galli, pagani, ~ones et Scotti, Armorici.. ASSER *Alf.* 76; **s823** ~ones..a Domnaniensibus cesi sunt FL. WORC. I 65; ubi fuerit archiepiscopatus tempore ~onum cognitio labat W. MALM. *GP prol.*; Angli-Saxones ~onibus, qui nunc Gualli vocantur, imperium..abstulerunt ORD. VIT. IV 7 p. 230; G. MON. I 16 (v. Britannia a); **s1404** a quibus Grecis et habui quod Grecie proceres a dicto Constantino ejusque tribus avunculis..aliisque xxx milibus ~onibus cum eo de Britania illuc advectis..descenderunt AD. USK 97. **b** ~ones transmarinos W. MALM. *GR* V 402; indomitis ~onibus preerat, quorum perversitatem tolerare non poterat ORD. VIT. IX 18; paucos ex Armoricanis ~onibus G. MON. VIII 4; **s1189** ~ones..Richardo comiti adheserunt WEND. I 152.

Britonisare, to speak Welsh.

prima [lingua] meridiem versus est Vallica, qua Britones ~antes utuntur MAJOR I 4.

brittea v. brattea. brittia v. britia. briucca v. brinca. briwera v. 1 bruaria. brixeria v. 1 braciaria.

1 broca, ~us [AS *brōc*], water-meadow, marsh, 'brook' (esp. Kent & Sussex). **b** (?) brook, stream.

ibi ii acrae ~ae *DB* I (*Leics*) 237; silva pastilis..et parvum broc' *Ib.* (*Derb*) 273; habentes..xl acras prati et lxx acras ~e *Ib.* (*Lincs*) 347; **1142** brocham de Schotovere [*Oxon*] sicut semita extenditur a mora usque ad wodeweyam *Rec. Templars* 179; **c1200** Cnocke in Oxenelle cum brocco (*Doc. Robertsbridge*) *HMC Delisle and Dudley* I 52 (cf. ib. 69); **1240** quandam porcionem salis in ~o de Pevenesse *Cl* 246; **1240** factum est fossatum..inter moram et brochum *Reg. S. Aug.* 538 (cf. ib. 455); **1284** pro broka boriali *CalIPM* (*Suss*) I 533; **1285** R. C. tenet xxij acras terre, in ~o j acram *Cust. Suss* II 111; **1306** tenet j acram prati in ~o de Swynhame *Cust. Battle* 19; **1397** quidam ~us pro porcis sustinendis continent' (*sic*) xx acras terre *IMisc* (*Suss*) 269/6 (cf. ib.: cum quodam †braco); **1594** unius..parcelle terre ~i vocat' Brewers Brooke [*Suss*] *RecusantR* 2 r. 22*d*. **b a1220** et sic sequendo illum ~um qui vocatur Bradelebroc *Cart. Cochersand* 653.

2 broca, ~us [OF *broche*], pointed stick, skewer: **a** (for fastening sack); **b** (as thatching-pin); **c** (as stake).

a 1185 hoc servitium debet terra domino regi, sc. ..j gladium et j saccum cum brocca *RDomin* 59; **1219** debet invenire domino regi unum equum et unum saccum cum brocha in exercitu Wallie *Fees* 270; **1250** unum saccum et brochium ligneum *Ib.* 1172 (cf. *Hund.* I 157); si quis teneat per servitium inveniendi domino regi..saccum cum brochia pro aliqua necessitate vel utilitate exercitum suum contingente BRACTON 36; **1301** per servicium inveniendi domino regi in qualibet gwerra sua Wallie unum hominem, unum equum,..unum saccum et brokkam per xl dies *IPM* 101/1; **1290** in iij brach' ad saccos panetrie, viij d. *Ac. Swinfield* 131; **1290** pro..duobus frenis, uno sacco ad pannos cum iij braciis *Chanc. Misc.* 4/5 f. 8 (= *DocScot* I 138: †bratiis); *prik to pakkys*, broccus *PP*. **b 1297** in emendacione coperture domorum..; in brochiis ad idem colligendis, vj d. *Ac. Cornw.* I 61. **c 1306** palos pro brochiis in parco nostro Wyndesor' succidi..facias *Cl* 123 m. 15.

2 spit (for roasting). **b** 'stick' (measure of eels).

1265 sal et brochie, v d. (*RHosp*) *Manners* 48; **1313** [servicium inveniendi] brochias ad assandum carnem *CalIPM* V 391; **1383** duas patellas frix', tres brochias ferreas *Rec. Norw.* II 25. **b c1150** pro..x brochis anguillarum per annum *Cart. Rams.* I 150; **1199** quod debeant reddere de molendino suo..xij brochas anguillarum *CurR RC* II 118; **1200** x brakias anguillarum *CurR* I 178.

3 iron spike: **a** (for fastening); **b** (as tooth of harrow).

a 1245 ad duo capita feretri..apponuntur duo angeli argentei cum brochis ferreis (*Invent. S. Paul.*) *Arch.* L 469. **b 1293** in broch' ferr' ad herciam faciendam cum stipendio fabri, ix d. *Pipe Wint.* (*Taunton*).

4 brooch, pall-pin.

1207 pallium regale de purpura cum morsu et brocha auri *Pat* 77b; **1220** due broche auree ad pallium et dalmaticam, quarum in una est saphirus et in alia perla (*Receipt R* 3) *Rec. Coronation* 55.

5 tap, spigot; *ad brocam*, 'on the broach', retail.

c1148 nec..licet nobis vendere vinum ad tabernam sive ut vulgo dicitur ad broccam seu ut lingua Tautonica dicitur ad tappam (*Inst. Sempr.*) *MonA* VI 946 xl; **s1199** si.. vinatorem qui vinum vendat ad ~am contra hanc assisam invenerint R. HOWD. IV 99; **1224** de j tonello et dimidio vini regis venditi..ad brocham *LTRMem* 6 r. 16*d*.; **1229** quod nullus extraneus mercator..vendat vina ad brochum nisi in grosso *BBC* (*Drogheda*) 286; **1238** vinetarii ville vestre qui habent vina in celariis suis vendenda non vendunt ea ad brocham set in grosso *Cl* 44; **1289** vini quod..ad ~am vendetur *RGasc* III 581.

brocagium, 'brokage', brokerage, payment to agent for sale etc. **b** brokage (a local toll or export duty).

1285 mercatores..pro singulis doliis vini sui per abrocatores..venditis dare consueverunt vj d. pro ~io (*Breve Regis*) *MGL* I 401; **1299** Haukyno Flemyng pro brokagio xviij s. *Ac. Durh.* 496; **1305** xiij s. ix d. in lana reparanda et ~io lane *DL MinAc* 1/2 r. 9*d*.; **1360** in ~io summe muttuate ad usuram *ExchScot* 56; **1365** recepit summas predictas absque ~io aliquali *Cl* 203 m. 24; **1366** ~ia a diversis personis pro solucionibus den. nostrorum faciendis recepisse *Pat* 273 m. 16; **c1390** rex..pretextu brogagii recepti eorum affines diversimode ditavit FAVENT 3 (cf. ib. 4). **b 1342** custuma de brokagio diversarum navium frett' in dicto portu Sutht' versus partes exteras (*Ac. Cust.* 137/11) *Port Bks. Southampton 1469–71* p. xvi (cf. ib. xvii); **1429** de parvo theolonio mercandisarum exeuncium per terram extra Bargate seu alibi per terram cum brokagio bigarum *Steward's Bk. Southampton* I 8 (cf. ib. II 48); **1439** *Brokage Bk. Southampton 1439–40* p. 2.

brocali v. broccare.

brocalis [cf. 1 broca], marshy (Sussex).

c1270 terre ~is et..terre susan' (*Doc. Robertsbridge*) *HMC Delisle and Dudley* I 117 (cf. ib. 130); **12..** in duabus acris terre ~is que jacent..inter aquam decurrentem ad molendinum de Esburnham..et fossatum *AncD* C 3996; **1306** xv acre terre ~is *Cust. Battle* 18; **1325** de prato ~i ij acr' dim. *IPM* (*Sussex*) 98/2.

brocardicum, canon of Burkhard of Worms. **b** rule, formula.

imputabitur sibi qui talem advocatum sibi eligit, ut.. illud ~um [v.l.: illud generale..ut in Brocardo]: '..mala electio est in culpa' W. DROGHEDA *SA* 51. **b** hoc est unum brogardicum ad probandum omne impossibile WYCL. *Act.* 103.

brocare v. broccare.

brocaria, office of broker.

1300 abjuratio de officio ~ie carectarum *Cal. LB Lond.* C 67.

brocarius: **a** (*s. dub.*). **b** broker, agent. **c** toll-collector.

a 1211 de Edwardo ~io..de Alvrico ~io *Pipe Wint.* 114. **b a1280** statuimus quod ~ii sint electi per visum communitatis ville Berwici, qui dabunt singulis annis unum dolium vini communitati.., et nomina eorum per commune consilium inbrevientur *Stat. Gild. Berw.* 31; **1299** permisit ~ium et servientem suum apponere manus ad balancias in ponderando lanam *Rec. Leic.* I 225; **1375** si..fuere ~ii et correctarii ejusdem falsi barganei *MGL* I 399; **1444** ~io.. stapule Calesie *Cl* 294 m. 17*d*. **c 1477** ~ius bigarum et parvi thelonii *Brokage Bk. Southampton 1443–4* p. xii (cf. ib. xiii).

brocator, a broker, agent. **b** toll-collector.

a 1315 R. de L. ~or juratus..in ponderacione trium saccorum lane false ponderavit *Rec. Leic.* I 292; **1355** ne qui forstallatores, privati mercatores, broggatores, *braggers* sive *loders*, ..emant..pisces *StatIr.* I 400; **1356** pisces..ut brogatores vendunt et majorem partem de vendicione provenientem penes se retinent *Cl* 194 m. 6*d*.; **1357** si ipsi intercurrentes [de Hibernia] et ~ores falsa..suggesserint, pena debita puniantur *StRealm* I 361 (cf. ib. 362: cum ipsis justiciariis et eorum privatis consiliariis et ~oribus); **1395** broggator lanarum *CalPat* 626; **1575** cum..omnis negociacio et actio predicti cambii, escambii et recambii..precipue super quosdam homines communiter vocatos *brokers* dependeat.., sciatis..quod nos..officium et separale officium ~oris cambii, escambii et recambii facimus *Pat* 1068 m. 11. **b 1445** omnimodos ~ores mercandisarum, bigarum et batellarum *Brokage Bk. Southampton 1443–4* p. xiii.

broccare [It. *broccare*, OF *brochier*; cf. brochiare], to embroider, brocade.

1494 pro altari [in basilica S. Petri]..haberi debet frontale ~atum cum fazio de albo. ..fit unum baldachinum pro papa album, cum ricamis †brocali de auro *Conc.* III 638.

broccella [? cf. brusca], (?) little wood.

c1140 sciatis me dedisse..quandam ~am nomine Rahage [*Roehoe Wood*] *E. Ch. Yorks* IV 14.

1 broccus [AS *broc*], 'brock', badger.

1279 quibus canibus currit ad lupum, wlpem, catum, ~um, tessonem et leporem *Hund.* II 627.

2 broccus [? cf. It. *brocca* = *wine-jug*], (?) pannier (Gasc.).

1254 emat xl paria boum cum ~is mittenda regi..ad ingenia carianda *Cl* 297 (= *RGasc* I 444: †brettis); **1254** ad cariagia nostra..facienda..boves et ~os vestros [de Bersac] ad nos mittatis *RGasc* I 350 (cf. *CalPat* 298); **1255** in vendicione tede, brocorum et picheriorum *Ib. suppl.* 25; **1288** volens transire eques vel pedes seu cum carectis aut brocis *Ib.* II 289; **1289** in vehendo cum curribus seu brossis..res quascunque *Ib.* 378.

brocha, ~ea v. 1 & 2 broca.

brochettus [OF *brochete*; cf. 2 broca 1], skewer for fastening sack.

1309 per servicium inveniendi unum equum..cum quodam sacco et uno brocheto in gwerra domini regis Wallie *IPM* 7/22 (cf. *DocScot* 461).

brochia, ~ium v. 2 broca.

brochiare [OF *brochier*; cf. broccare], **a** to stretch (cloth) on tenterhooks. **b** to stake (a length of paling).

a 1255 contra consuetudinem gilde ~iavit super tentorium duo russeta *Rec. Leic.* I 72; **1262** emit pannum siccum ~iatum ab uno textore *Ib.* 96. **b 1257** [debet] ~iare xvj pedes *Cust. Suss.* I 34.

brocia v. brusca.

broculatrix [cf. 2 broca 5], (?) tapstress.

1256 quando quarterium frumenti venditur pro iij s., ..tunc debent..~ices vendere in civitatibus duas lagenas ad denarium *Ann. Burton* 376.

brocuragium [cf. brocagium], brokerage, office of broker. **b** brokage (toll or duty).

1443 officium ~ii de escambiis et securitatibus carracarum, navium et galearum in regnum nostrum Anglie exnunc veniencium *Pat* 456 m. 37. **b 1462** concessimus..prefatis majori et aldermannis [Cales']..assisam et ∼ium in portu ville predicte, prout ipsi antiquitus habere et percipere consueverunt *ChartR* 193 m. 30.

brocurator [cf. brocator; (?) *infl. by* procurator], wool-broker.

1313 deberet ponderasse lanam suam quasi communis ∼or inter dictum R. et quendam mercatorem extraneum *Rec. Leic.* I 279.

brocus v. 1 & 2 broca, 2 broccus. brodatus v. broudare.

broddum [ME *brod*], brad-nail.

1276 in iiij clutis cum ∼is ad axem caruce, iij d. *DCCant* (*Ac. Loose*); **1354** in c ∼is emptis pro clutis carucarum affirmandis *Ib.* (*Ac. Cliffe*); **1324** carecte: ..in c ∼is, j d. ob. (*MinAc*) *Econ. Condit. app.* 56; **1373** in..∼is et ceteris ferramentis *Ac. Durh.* 211.

broderaria v. brouderaria.

brodetta, (?) broth (*cf.* 1 *brodium, bruettum*).

si causa sit frigida, sint cibi vitelli ovorum et mica panis de ∼a, aqua pisorum vel cicerum et ordeatum GAD. 107 v. 2; sit cibus ejus aqua ciceris et †boreta [? l. broeta] pura pisorum subtilis et gruellum tenue *Id.* 110 v. 1.

brodiellum, broth.

browet, ∼um *PP.*

1 brodium [cf. OF *bro, breu*], broth.

que multiplicant lac..sunt multa, sicut potus aque frigide.., ∼ium epuli herbarum M. SCOT. *Phys.* 13; **s1238** familiares legati..∼ium calidum de calidariis bullientibus super vestimentum clericum projecerunt WYKES 84 (cf. M. PAR. *Min.* II 407; †broidum de fervente lebete super clericum quendam aspersit); ∼ium animalis habundantis in pinguedine non coagulatur BART. ANGL. V 63; si decoquantur in potagiis vel in ∼iis GAD. 5 v. 1; coquens..donec ∼ium fiant saginatum DASTIN *Ros.* 7; quando vadunt ad prandium, ..partem quoque ∼ii extra domum effundunt, ut sic dii isti recipiant partem suam BRADW. *CD* 14D; **1481** pro ∼io et speciebus *Ac. Chamb. Cant.* 144b; *a broth,* ∼ium *CathA.*

2 brodium, brodus [ME *brōd*], brood, fry, spawn (of fish etc.).

1377 capit ∼os ostriarum et dicta ostria nutriri facit in quadam fleta vocata le Siwardesflete [*Essex*] *IMisc* 211/5; trahunt ∼os hostriarum..cum rete vocato *dragge*..licet non sunt nisi latitudinis unius pollicis hominis *Ib.*; **1395** ∼ium quod vocatur *la frygh'* de murenis et salmonibus (*Anc. Indict.*) *Pub. Works* I 161.

broel, broeillus v. bruillus. broellarius v. bruillarius. broga v. borga. brogagium, brogardicum, brogator v. broc-.

brogus [cf. 1 bruaria], heath.

marica vel ∼us, *hæp* ÆLF. *Gl.*; ∼us, *head Gl. Durh.*

broidatus v. broudare. broidum v. 1 brodium. broidura v. broudatura. broiheria v. 1 bruaria b. broillus, ∼ius v. bruillus. broka, brokagium v. broc-.

brokettus [OF *broquet*], brocket, young buck (fallow deer).

1223 duos ∼os dammorum *Cl* 539b; **1237** capi faciat iiij damos, sc. ∼os, et vj damas et poni faciat in parco regis *Cl* 449; **1255** duo mastini..inventi fuerunt..dilacerantes unum ∼um *SelPlForest* xxv; **12..** si damum vel ∼um tempore firmationis ceperint *FormA* 304; **1276** xx damas et ∼os vivos ad parcum suum..inde instaurandum *Cl.* 93 m. 10.

brollius v. bruillus. brom v. 1 bromus.

bromius [? βρόμιος], rowdy fellow.

cum eum de dono suo..sollicitarent joculatores, ..dare consumptoriis et ∼iis non adquievit *Becket Mat.* IV 156.

bromosus [LL; cf. βρωμώδης], fetid; cf. 2 *brumosus.*

cum odore †brimoso [v.l. brumoso] et gustu amaro *Alph.* 136.

1 †bromus [? cf. βρῶμα *or* βρῶμος], marine worm (It. *bruma*). **b** (*s. dub.*). **c** seal (animal).

sunt..in fluvio del Far vermes graciles qui in lingua illa vocantur *brom,* quorum cibus est omne genus ligni R. HOWD. III 72. **b** ∼um, †sordum maris *Erf.* 2. 272. 25. **c** nomina ferarum: ..∼us marinus, *seolh* ÆLF. *Gl.*

2 bromus [ME *brōm*], broom, besom.

1313 pro vij ∼is..emptis ad inde mundand' combleas et gutterias in turri *KRAc* 469/16 f. 5 (cf. ib. 468/20 f. 8).

†broncus, *s. dub.*

c1200 qui palpat aulicos in aulam trahitur / et broncus Stephanus ab aula pellitur (*Palpo*) *Ps.-MAP Poems* 111.

brond- v. broud-. bronia v. bryonia. brosa v. bresa. brosca v. brusca. brossus v. 2 broccus. brostagium v. brustagium.

broudare [OF *broder, brosder* < Frk. *brusdan*; *infl. by* ME *breiden* (p. ppl. *brouden*), cf. breidare], to embroider.

c1080 viij casulas, una illarum brusdata (*Invent.*) *Lib. Eli* II 114; **s1114** [episcopus Roffensis] ecclesie..dedit duas casulas, ..sc. nigram ante et retro cum lista bruslatam et aliam *Flor. Hist.* II 44 (cf. ib. 67); hoc genus veli vulgo bustratum, quasi bis stratum, dicitur: primo enim fit tela, cui cum opere manuali supersuuntur multe picturationes AD. SCOT. *TT* 673 C; **1204** culcitram brusdatam cum papegallo *RChart* 134b; **1220** cum uno pari veterum sotularium brodatorum auro (*ReceiptR* 3) *Rec. Coronation* 55; **1235** j cervical' de samicto rubeo bruisdato *ChancMisc* 3/4; **1240** duas capas de samito breudatas *Cl* 255; **1241** qui melius sciant circa operationes brudatas *Ib.* 321; **1245** capa ..cum tassellis in quibus breudantur S. Petrus et S. Paulus *Invent. S. Paul.* 475; **s1267** iij albas brullatas THORNE 1915 (cf. *Cust. Cant.* 158); **1269** si..samitum..brudatum..non inveneritis, unum brudari..faciatis *Cl* 69; **1282** alba linea cum paratura brusdata *Reg. Wint.* II 382; **1292** †brendato (v. bordura 2a); **1303** due pecie panni de Tarso broidate cum ymaginibus B. Marie et Gabrielis archangeli (*KRAc* 363/6) *DocExch* 278; **1332** †alneriis [l. alveriis] de serico ad aurum braydato de perleis (*KRAc* 386/7) *Arch.* LXXVII 137; **1338** capam..†brandatam [l. braudatam] de ymaginibus (*TreatyR*) *Foed.* V 48; **1386** vestimentum rubeum de *velvet* cum *le veronike* in granis rosarum desuper †brondata [l. broudata] *FormA* 428; **1432** cum duobus pannis de imaginibus ∼atis *Reg. Glasg.* 325.

broudator, embroiderer.

1367 concessimus ei [sc. tapiciario nostro] talia vadia.. qualia broudeator noster a nobis percipit *Pat* 275 m. 6; **c1378** ∼ori domini nostri regis ad facturam m m garter'.. ordinat' et broudat' *KRAc* 400/4 m. 12; **1397** ipsum S...in mistera brouderie sub capitalibus broudiatoribus..nostris.. constituimus *Pat* 347 m. 30; **1514** †brusiatori pro reparacione ..caparum..et aliorum ornamentorum *Midlothian* 174.

broudatorius, of embroidery.

1467 in arte brudatoria artifex curiosissimus STONE *Chr.* 10b (cf. *Invent. Ch. Ch.* 119).

broudatura, embroidery.

1245 stola et manipulus ejusdem panni et breudure (*Invent. S. Paul.*) *Arch.* L 487; **1251** pro..purpretura, broidura et pro ix aurifr' *Liberate* 28 m. 19; **1253** pro uno samitto rubeo in quo brudata sunt arma nostra et pro broudura ejusdem samitti *Ib.* 29 m. 8; **1305** in facturam.. quarundam ∼arum ad opus..consortis nostre *Cl* 122 m. 13; **c1421** (v. brouderia); **1423** j roba..superoperata in broudura cum *garter* de serico et auro de Cipre cum isto dictamine *hony soit qi male y pense KRAc* 407/13 m. 22.

brouderare, to embroider.

1393 pro caligis..broideratis cum liberata dicti regis Hungarie *Ac. H. Derby* 285; **1402** unum lectum et unum tapetum de *rube worstede* ∼atum (*Cl*) *Foed.* VIII 277; **s1432** cives Londonie..ipsum [regem] honorifice recipientes in togis albis browderatis W. WORC. *Ann.* 760.

brouderaria, office of embroiderer.

1494 sibique ad palliandum facta sua litteras patentes de officio broderarie ad terminum vite sue concessit *DCCant* S 397b.

brouderarius, embroiderer.

1395 concessimus..W. S. ∼io officium rangeatoris foreste nostre de Pambere *Pat* 342 m. 13; **1400** (v. brouderia); **1452** officium ∼ii et linei armurarii nostri *Cl* 302 m. 21.

brouderator, embroiderer.

1461 [officium] †branderatoris [l. brauderatoris] et lenei armurarii *CalPat* 15.

brouderia, embroidery.

1398 cum Johanna D. *silkwoman*..nobis bene et fideliter ..pro expensis brauderie nostre..deservierit *Pat* 350 m. 6; **1400** brouderarios, scissores, pictores ac alios operarios ad misteram ∼ie pertinentes *Ib.* 362 m. 8; **c1421** super opere et broudatura unius coopertorii facti de panno rubeo pro bargea regis superoperati in ∼ia cum istis dictaminibus *une sanz pluis* et *humblement le requier KRAc* 407/5 m. 3.

broudura v. broudatura. brounbadius v. brunbadius. browderare v. brouderare.

1 bruaria, ∼ium [OF *bruiere*; cf. brogus], heather, heath (plant). **b** heath, heathland.

1150 habeant in Nova Foresta turbam et brueriam *CalCh* III 234; **c1160** liceat habere herbam et juncos et felgeram et bruieram *BBC* (*Gateshead*) 53; **1221** tres carectas itinerantes ..ad mortuum boscum vel ad brueriam *Cl* 452b; **1227** ita.. quod nihil assartent vel brueram succidant *Cl* 7; **c1240** turbam et briweram *CalCh* II 453; **c1250** licenciam..vellendi bruerium *Kelso* I 122; jus falcandi herbam vel brueram..ad rationabile estoverium BRACTON 222b; **1283** pro brueria trahenda ad furniandum et pandoxandum *MinAc* 1070/5 r. 2; **1296** quedam placea ubi bruera crescit, sc. *lyng,* que vendi potest ad finem..decem annorum pro xvj s. *IPM* (*Notts*) 76/8; **1333** in iiij carectis bruere emptis..ad stagnum et circa exclusas cum argillo miscend' *LTRMem* 105 r. 194; **1334** eradicare brueram et feugeram (*Plac. Forest.*) *Pat* 266 m. 38; **1358** in nova structura duorum cotagiorum..cum bruera empta ad coopertūram eorundem *Ac. Durh.* 124; **1367** ignem cuidam tasso bruere..imposuerunt *Pat* 276 m. 27d.; **s1385** quedam domus bruerio tecte *Extr. Chr. Scot.* 195; **1435** licenciam capiendi ∼ium in mora sua *Reg. Brechin.* I 84; *heth or lyng, fowaly,* ∼ium *PP*; hec pruera, *lingge* WW. **b †974** (13c) cum..segetibus, silvis, brueriis (*Ch. Ramsey*) *CD* 581; ∼ia ii leu' long' et lat' *DB* (*Dorset*) I 77b; **1107** duas virgatas terre et xx acras de brueria *Regesta* p. 318; **1139** brueriam et pasturam (*Cart. Haverholme*) *EHR* XXXIII 345; **c1175** in redditu broiherie de Mordona [*Dorset*] *CalCh* IV 131; **c1180** in petariis, in turbariis, in ∼iis *Melrose* I 60; **1200** in stagnis et vivariis et bruiariis *RChart* 69; **1205** inter brueriam et terram H. B. *CurR* III 328; **1243** vidende sunt purpresture..facte..in landis, in brueriis, in mariscis *Cl* 125; **c1250** dedi..v acras †bevarii [l. bruarii] super Burc (*Reg. Daventry*) *MonA* V 181; quare superonerat communem pasturam et brueram BRACTON 229b (cf. ib. 230b: rationabile estoverium suum in turbaria sua vel bruera); **1296** ∼ium quod vocatur Westling [*Norf*] *IPM* 77/3b, r. 22; **1314** juxta brueram que vocatur le Walkerisheth [*Worcs*] *AncD* C29; **1400** non fiat combustio †morum sive ∼ii nisi in mense Mercii (*Stat. Rob. III*) *APScot* 214; **s1461** evadentes usque ad brueram vocatam Barnet Heath *Reg. Whet.* I 391.

2 bruaria, ∼ium [ME], brewery.

1390 super clameo cujusdam parve domus que nuper fuit brueria..in vico del West de Dunstapl' *AncD* C 3018; **1439** utensilibus coquine et bruerii..exceptis *Test. Ebor.* II 74; **1580** a ruinosis parietibus pistrine et ∼ii ex occidente nostri monasterii *Dryburgh* 313.

†bruccus [cf. bracha], (?) hound.

10.. ∼us, *ræcc* WW.

brucetum v. bruscetum. bruceum, bruchya v. brusca.

bruchus [βροῦχος], locust, caterpillar, or other pest (esp. fig.); *v. et attelebus.*

∼us, genus locustae quod volat *GlC* B 190; ∼us, *cefer Ib.* 187; ∼us, *ceafor* [i.e. *chafer*] ÆLF. *Gl.*; tradunt phisiologi quod ex locusta nascitur brucus J. SAL. *Pol.* 590C; nec brucus †mor[ti]cinii sacrorum artuum illius flexuosa diriguit R. COLD. *Cuthb.* 2; **s1193** ut nulla vacaret occasio et.. residuum locuste ∼us..absumeret W. NEWB. IV 38 (cf. *Joel* i 4); hec est erugo sapientia qua vitiatur / et similis brūco nulla virere sinit GARL. *Epith.* VIII 720; **s1346** arcu, dente, brūco similes, pleni modo fuco / in Duram luco morbo cecidere caduco *Pol. Poems* I 44; **1458** si non venissent locusta et ∼us in nostras fruges *Reg. Whet.* I 321; brucus, A. *a taddepol,* ..*a breas* [i.e. *gadfly*] WW.

brucia, ∼ium v. brusca. bruciare v. brustare. 1 brucus v. bruchus.

2 †brucus, (?) for *buxus* (boxwood).

ciphos reparant de morinis et planis et ∼is GARL. *Dict.* 126.

brud- v. breidare, broud-. bruellus v. bruillus. bruera, ∼ia, ∼ium v. 1 & 2 bruaria.

†bruere, to brew.

a1300 ad panem coquendum et †carvinam bruendem [? l. cervisiam bruendam *or* braciandam] *Hist. Staffs* II 262 (cf. *BBC* 65).

bruettum [OF *broet*], broth (*cf.* 1 *brodium, brodetta*).

1266 parvis anguillis in bruecto *Cust. Westm.* 76; habebit ..gallinas cum fressang' in brueto et caseum *Cust. Bleadon* 204.

brugabulum [ME *breu-gavel*], payment for licence to brew.

c1110 liber de terris regis reddentibus langabulum et brug[abulum] in Wint[onia'] *Lib. Wint.* f. 1; **a1140** de langablo infra burgum Oxen'..cum brugablo et aliis omnibus rebus *Cart. Osney* IV 83 (cf. ib. 84, 85: cum burgabulo.., cum berugabulo); **1207** de vj s. j d. de burgabulo extra portam orientalem *Pipe Wint.* 77; **1211** de ∼o extra Kingate *Ib.* 161; **1297** exitus burgi [*Wilton*]: ..de breugabulo..et..de flesgabulo..et..de stocgabulo *Ac. Cornw.* I 75; de xlv s. vj d. de diversis brasiatoribus in civitate predicta [*Chichester*] de burgabulo hoc anno *Ib.* 100; **1300** placita [et] perquisita curie cum brewgabulo *IPM* (*Wilton*) 95/9; **1399** resolutio redditūum coquinario de burgabulo, langabulo.. *Reg. Malm.* II lxxxvii.

brugbota v. brigbota. brugma v. baruina. bruiaria, bruiera v. 1 bruaria.

bruillarius, park-keeper.

broellarius, *ediscueard GlC* B 186.

bruillettus, small covert.

1200 licenciam claudendi duos brulletos qui sunt extra reguard' foreste nostre *RChart* 45; **1235** carta regis Ricardi de licencia claudendi duos brulletos *CurR* XV 1472.

bruillus, ∼ius [OF *broil, bruil*], game-park, thicket, covert.

broel, *edisc, deortun GlC* B 185; **c1154** concedo..aisiamenta ..in foresta et boscis et ∼is meis (*Reg. Stoneleigh*) *MonA* V 447; **1157** xl s. de censu brolliorum de Andievra *Pipe* 174; **1204** assartum bruielli in Norwude *RChart* 131b; **1205** quod custodias..broillos nostros secundum viam que protenditur a Dorcestr' usque Bridiport *Cl* 50b; **1219** boscum..infra brullos Cicestr' *Cl* 385; **1220** quantum ibi habent brulii possint excolere *CurR* VIII 193; **1223** infra bailliam chacie ∼iorum de Keinesham *Pat* 419; **1225** totam venacionem quam capient in foresta et in bruiliis comitatus Norhant' *Cl* 31; **1228** bruilos nostros Cicestr', viz. bruilum qui vocatur Bruilus Regis et bruilum qui vocatur Depemers *Pipe* 72 r. 4 (2)*d.* (cf. *Cl* 272); **1261** cum..capi fecerit subboscum et virgas in broillio Notingh' ad..hurdicia..facienda *Cl* 4; **1273** [cum] broeillis *CalPat* 27; **1275** pro custodiendo dominicum boscum regis, sc. bruellum de Bedewind *Hund.* II 260; **1327** firmam ∼orum *LTRMem* 99 r. 140.

bruisdatus v. broudare. brukestus v. brusketus. brullatus v. broudare. brulletus v. bruillettus. brullus, ∼ius v. bruillus.

bruma [CL], midwinter.

prole virens aestate, tabescens tempore brumae ALDH. *Aen.* 1 (*Terra*) 4; longissimis in ∼a noctibus BEDE *TR* 24; **s1139** in articulo diei incipientis ∼e, hoc est VII idus Novembris J. WORC. 56; majores auce cum ∼a statim in grege magno..advectantur GIR. *TH* I 23; hec ∼a, *wynter* WW.

brumalis, wintry. **b** northern. **c** (n. pl. as sb.) (?) winter rains.

calor frigus brumale coquebat ALDH. *CE* 4.2.21; orto brumali turbine *Carm. Aldh.* 1. 20; aestivos necesse est dies longioribus, ~es vero brevioribus horis includi BEDE *TR* 3; **10..** ~ia, *þa winterlican* WW; tempore brumali sit victus deliciosus D. BEC. 2809. **b** factum est ut rex..~i populo ..relinqueretur *V. Dunst.* B 23. **c** ~ia, †rosina pluvia *GlC* B 191 (= *Erf.* 2. 272. 10: †brumaria).

1 brumare, to be wintry. **b** (?) to bite (like frosty wind).

noctibus..nivium densitate ~antibus R. COLD. *Godr.* 74; *to wyntyr*, ~are, brumescere, hybernare *CathA.* **b** quid scelus Eutrapeli brumet, nescit nisi Iesus D. BEC. 1232 (cf. HORACE *Ep.* I 18. 31).

2 brumare [ME], to bream, clean (a ship).

1303 conduxerunt duos homines de eadem villa ad navem suam ~andam *JustIt* 945.

brumaria [LL], **~ium,** lion's foot (*Leontice*).

leontopedion, quam Latini ~ium vocant, nascitur sepe cum tritico *Alph.* 96.

brumela v. prunella.

brumescere, to be wintry (cold). **b** (?) to experience winter (fig.), wither.

[Hibernia] ex omni..vento..quandoque ~it; ex omni quidem modico, ex nullo immoderate GIR. *TH* I 33; plura non ferunt tegmina, / quamvis brumescat borea (*Wallia* 84) HIGD. I 38. **b** hec rosa sub senio nondum brumescit HANV. I 255.

brumesta v. bumasta. brummanagium v. brimmagium. brumillus v. bremellus. 1 brumosus v. bromosus.

2 brumosus, wintry. **b** (?) wet (but *cf. bromosus*).

torribus ut pellat brumosis frigora nimbis ALDH. *CE* 4.1.25; **a690** ex Hiberniae ~is circionis insulae climatibus *Id. Ep.* 5 p. 489. **b** ~us annus, rosinosus *GlC* B 194.

brumula, winter (fig.), old age.

nondumque infundit aniles / brumula prima nives HANV. IX 385.

brunaticus v. bruneticus.

brunbadius [cf. brunus, badius], brown-bay.

1325 de xxij jumentis, quorum..v badia..et j brounbadium stellatum cum uno pede albo a retro *LTRAc* 16 r. 41.

1 bruncus [? cf. βρόγχος], snout.

~us, *wrot GlC* B 188.

2 bruncus [? cf. It. *gronco*], dodder (bot.).

~us, †rasta [l. rasca] lini idem *SB* 13; cuscute, podagra lini, †grinicus [v.l. gruncus], ~us idem, A. *doder Alph.* 46.

brunda [*supposed etym. of* Brundisium], antler.

~a, *heortes heafod* ÆLF. *Gl.*; **14..** hec ~a, *a harte horne* WW.; *an horne*, ~a cervi est *CathA.*

brunella v. prunella.

Brunellus, nickname of ass (used as type of the species).

"nomine Burnellus dicor", respondit asellus, / "notus ubique satis nomine reque simul" NIG. *SS* 791; Burnello calices confert, altaria porco GARL. *Tri. Eccl.* 36; ut homo predicatur de pluribus individuis et singularibus, ut de Socrate et Platone, et sic de aliis, asinus de Burnello et Balmino BACON XV 197; Socrates differt a ~o humanitate DUNS *Sent.* I iv 1. 2; ut vetus ipse suam curtam Burnellus inepte / caudam longari de novitate cupit GOWER *VC* I 201.

bruneta v. brunettus.

bruneticus, of burnet (brown cloth).

pannarii..vendunt pannos..burneticos, ..scarleticos et radiatos GARL. *Dict.* 128; **1300** vestes †brunatices [? l. bruneticas] et coopertoria ejusdem tincture a vestris usibus prohibemus *Reg. Cant.* II 854.

brunettus [OF *brunet*], brown (of cloth), burnet. **b** (sb. m., n., or f.) (piece of) burnet; *cf. brunus* 2.

1309 pannos burneti, persei et viridi coloris (*CoramR*) *Law Merch.* II 82; **c1335** in panno burnetto empto *DC Cant* D.E. 3 f. 2; **1349** ad faciendam sepulturam..j chariotam coopertam cum panno nigro ~o (*KRAc* 391/15) *Arch.* XXXI 50; **1344** quatenus, sicut nec rubii, nec burneti, nec blueti, sed dumtaxat Nigri Monachi nuncupamur, sic ad purum nigrum saltem in exterioribus vestimentis..nos aptemus (*Const. Prov. Ben.*) *Conc.* II 730; **1443** una chlamys burneti coloris *MunAcOx* 532; burnetus, A. *burnet*, color quidam est WW. **b** **1189** pro escarlatis et burnetis et viridibus pannis *Pipe* 223; **1194** pro..vij ulnis de burneta nigra *Pipe* 175; **1204** facias habere..valetto nostro unam.. robam de viridi vel burnetta *Cl* 3 (cf. ib. 61b: de burneto); **1213** pro ij ulnis et dim. de *hauberge* tinctis in nigra burnetta emptis..ad faciendum caligas (*Misae*) *DocExch* 235; **1222** nec ipse [moniales] vel monachi sive canonici regulares.. burnetto vel alio panno irregulari utantur *Conc. Syn.* 118; **1244** iiij burnettos bene tinctos *Cl* 175; **1274** de..ij capuciis de ~o novo *Hund.* I 137; **1288** iiij panni integri de burnetto pro militibus et clericis cum pellura *KRAc* 231/26 m. 12; **1342** supertunicas clausas de nigro ~o vel bluetto (*Ch. Hosp. Well*) *MonA* VI 702; cuilibet..fratri..ij virgatas burneti largi FLETE *Westm.* 133; brunus color potest fieri ex lana ipsa absque tinctura..; burnetum vero requirit tincturam et artificium hominum quo ad colorem LYNDW. 206d.

2 (sb. f., as name of dark cow; *cf. brunus* 1c).

altera Brunetta fuit, altera dicta Bicornis; / sed nigra Brunetta, flava Bicornis erat NIG. *SS* 207–8.

3 (sb. f.) bird (OF *brunete*), (?) hedge-sparrow.

aviculam quamdam que burneta vocatur adeo et hic in cellula sua mansuetam habebat..ut quotidie ad mensam suam..veniret GIR. *S. Hug.* I 1; ut ipse / attestantur aves, sicut burneta probavit H. AVR. *Hugh* 605; cucula quandoque ponit ovum in nido burnete O. CHERITON *Fab.* 4A.

4 (sb. f.) salad burnet (*Sanguisorba*) or (?) ground-pine (*Chamaepitys*).

12.. burneta, i. *sprungwurt* WW; fiat balneum in aqua decoctionis mercurialis, ..acedule, brunete.. GILB. VI 271; detur bruneta et comedatur cum sale sicut comeditur menta in estate GAD. 82. 2; burneta blavum habet florem ut edera terrestris, sed non adeo rotunda habet folia; et secundum quosdam campiteos dicitur *SB* 13; burneta blaveum habet florem ut edera terrestris..stipitem habet fissum in plures partes; G. et A. *burnete Alph.* 25.

brunicus [LL (Isidore)], stocky horse.

mannus vel brunnicus, *gepracen hors* ÆLF. *Gl.*

†bruntus, dark (? brown; but *cf. Clundus*).

nomina colorum: ..~us, *wann* ÆLF. *Gl.*

brunus [OF *brun* < Frk.], brown (of hair or complexion); **b** (as proper name); **c** (of horse or cow); **d** (of bread).

si..sit..patiens juvenis complexionis colerice, sc. macilentus, ~us, mobilis et levis GAD. 35 v. 2; plani sunt illi bruni densique capilli ELMH. *Metr. Hen. V* 74. **b** j liber homo ~us *DB* II 441b; **1130** Willelmo ~o *Pipe* 99. **c** **1214** pro j [equo] ~o falvo *Cl* 168b; **1300** equus ~us badius *Ac. Wardr.* p. 79 (cf. brunbadius); **1316** pro restauro..unius equi ~i badii cum stella in fronte *RGasc* IV 1679; **1427** una cum equo meo ~i coloris *Reg. Cant.* II 373; **1278** fugavit unam vaccam nigram ~am *Hund. Highworth* 86 (cf. brunettus 2). **d** **1345** habeat quilibet frater leprosus.. qualibet septimana septem panes, quorum..duo ~i colore, facti de frumento prout fuerit de garba excussum (*Const. Hosp. S. Juliani*) *G. S. Alb. app.* B II 489.

2 brown (of cloth), burnet or sim. **b** (sb. m.) brown cloth, burnet; (*cf. brunettus* 1).

dare toll' suum..duos grisengos pannos et unum ~um (*Quad.*) *GAS* 234; sex casulas optimas, unam sc. ~am de tenui †purpura [? l. purfilura] et opere subtili pretiosam SWAFHAM 100; **1291** j tabardum de ~o camelino (*St. Ives*) *Law Merch.* I 55; **1465** de *le chamlett* †brunio *ExchScot* 363; LYNDW. 206d (v. brunettus 1b). **b** **1432** duo *baudkynys* de ~o sine armis *Reg. Glasg.* 332.

brusa v. brusca.

1 brusare, ~iare [cf. OF *bruisier, brisier*, AS *brȳsan*], **a** to break, bruise. **b** to break into.

a **1198** S. ..appellat R. ..quod..verberavit eum et ~avit eum *CurR RC* I 203; **1221** ei fecerunt..j plagam in sinistro brachio, ita quod ei ~averunt parvum ossum ejusdem brachii *PlCrGlouc* 100. **b** **1204** male creditur de quadam †felda [l. selda]..brisata *CurR* III 144; **1212** appellat R. L. quod ipse fuit cum eo..ad ~andum quandam domum et ibi furati sunt plura *SelPlCrown* 65; **c1300** ipsa est latro, sed non ~iavit domum *Year Bk.* 30–31 *Ed. I, app.* II 537.

2 brusare v. bursare.

brusca, ~us, ~ia, ~ium [cf. OF *broce*], brushwood, scrub, thicket.

a1160 dedi eis unam culturam..et unam ~am *Danelaw* 192 (cf. ib. 348: brucium quod ibi habeo); **c1170** totam ~iam que ad Neubold pertinet *CalCh* III 319 (= *MonA* V 337: brusuam); **c1185** brociam dejuxta Laundam [*Norm.*] *MonA* VI 1081; **1189** haiam suam de Gerdelia et broscam suam de Bartona (*Ch. Ric. I*) *Foed.* (*ed.* 4) I 48; **1199** in.. boscis, alnetis, ~is, brueriis *CalCh* I 146; **1204** c acras tam de terra quam de ~ia in manerio de la Riveria *RChart* 131b; **1204** essartare quendam ~um *CurR* III 154; **1205** licentia essartandi brutias que sunt inter voletam de Langeclif et altum chiminum *Pipe* 34; **1222** Elyas [tenet] unam brusam ..pro xij d. *Dom. S. Paul.* 15; **1238** quod permittat abbatem de Keinesham habere fossatum suum circa brussam de Isingrave *Cl* 93; **1268** juxta bruchyam de Barton' *JustIt* 618 r. 14*d.*; **12..** sicut se habet in longum et latum, in brucis et planis *Reg. S. Thom. Dublin* 96 (cf. ib. 88: in bruscis); **1276** appropriavit sibi warennam..in ~o de Thorneton *Hund.* I 135; **1297** est ibi quidam ~us et valet per annum ut in herbagio ij s. *IPM* 78/7 r. 6; **c1318** in x acris brucei et vij acris pasture *Cart. Dublin* I 5; **c1350** in ~is et boscis *Melrose app.* 22.

2 brush (for painting).

1355 in filo empto pro brussis et pincellis pictorum inde ligandis *KRAc* 471/6 m. 9; **1422** pro ~is porcinis pro ~is faciendis ad dealbacionem *le severyse* in *le yle* ecclesie, xv d. *Fabr. York* 48; **1434** in ij brushis emptis *Ib.* 54.

bruscare v. brustare.

bruscetum, brushwood (growing), scrub. **b** brushwood (cut).

1203 de xvj acris de brusseto *Pipe* 180; **12..** jacet juxta brucetum Notingham' *Rec. Nott.* II 342; **12..** [dim. acra] ~i *Cart. Fountains* I 439; **1281** appropriavit in warenna quoddam brussetum quod est commune et ad eandem villam et ad villam de Crackeshale (*CoramR*) *SelCKB* I 92 (cf. *PQW* 186a); **1302** [ij acre] brusketti *CalIPM* p. 62; **a1328** [iiij acras de] brussato *CalCh* IV 72; **1331** [viij acras] brussetti *CalCl* 376. **b** **1269** ~um et escaet' bosci et stipula: idem reddit compotum de iij s. de ~o vendito apud Oldestrete *MinAc* 994/27.

bruscia v. brusca.

bruscosus, covered with brushwood, scrubby.

a1160 tam de terra ~a quam de terra arabili *CalCh* III 248.

1 bruscus v. brusca.

2 bruscus [cf. CL ruscum], butcher's broom, knee-holly (*Bruscus*).

holera..sparagus, ~us, mercurialis, blitus GILB. I 21 v. 2; ista est medicina mea specialissima ad omnem tumorem: ..accipe radicem ~i: fac bullire bene GAD. 28. 1; ~us, frutex est, †*licheholm SB* 13; ~us habet folia ad modum buxus, tantum spinosa, A. *keneholm Alph.* 27; de speciebus [valent ad fecunditatem] zinziber conditum, ..semen erice, semen mercurialis, semen brisci KYMER 19; humile [genus rusci] officinae vocant ~um, Angli *butcher's broome* et *petygrew*, TURNER *Herb.* C 1.

brusdatus v. broudare. brusea v. busca.

Bruselensis [sc. denarius], coin of Brussels.

a1275 ~es decidunt in libra iij s. communiter *RBExch* III 979.

brusiare v. brusare. brusiator v. broudator. bruskettum v. bruscetum.

brusketus [ME *brusket*], brisket, chest: **a** (of man); **b** (of animal).

a **1244** fregit ei ventrem suum et pectus suum et †brukestum suum *JustIt* (*Dorset*) 201 r. 5. **b** **1338** in spald' et brusket' emptis, xij d. *Ac. Durh* 35.

bruslatus v. broudare. brussa v. brusca. brussatum, brussettum v. bruscetum. brussura v. brusura.

brustagium, (payment for) right of browsing.

c1180 decimam forestarum..de Costantino.., cum decima pasnagii, ..brostagii et herbagii (*Ch. Montebourg*) *Act. Hen. II* II 151.

brustare [OF *broster* < Frk. *brustian*], to browse (on).

1233 [in bosco] fecit destructionem..et averia..immittit et bruciare facit totum subboscum, qui poni deberet in defenso *CurR* XV 452; **1237** placiam illam..ita bene.. claudi faciat ne fera vel aliqua bestia eam ingredi possit ad †bruscandum [l. brustandum] in ea *Cl* 416.

brustura, browsing.

12.. nec est ibi copia ferarum per quas boscus deterioratur per ~am dictarum ferarum *ChancMisc* 11/1/30.

brusua v. brusca.

†brusula, (?) patch of brushwood.

c1180 dedi eis vallem cum ~a in orientali parte (*Ch. Shap*) *MonA* VI 869.

brusura [OF *briseure*], **a** a bruise, bodily injury. **b** breaking into, breaking open. **c** breaking out of (gaol).

a **1198** brusavit eum ita quod noluit habuisse pejoramentum pro c sol. et ita quod maimatus est per illam ~am *CurR RC* I 203; si inveniantur plage aperte vel brussure per ictus orbos BRACTON 122; arma vero moluta plagam faciunt.., ligna vero et lapides faciunt ~as et orbes ictus, qui judicari non possunt ad plagam *Ib.* 145; **1572** cum pede illo scanni lignei..percussit..de quibus quidem plagis et brisura..obiit *Pat* 1089 m. 8. **b** **1212** appellati defendunt ~am domorum et hostiorum *SelPlCrown* 61 (cf. 66); **1277** R. C. captus pro suspicione unius forcelli, qui negat ~am et forcellum *Gaol Del.* 14/1 r. 13; **1286** R. ..et P. ..habuerunt custodiam porte cambii, ..sine quibus nullus potuit intrare vel exire vel strepitum vel ~am, introitum seu apertionem facere..quin suis constaret auditibus *Ib.* 36/1 r. 32; **c1300** quedem mulier..capta fuit pro ~a cujusdam domus et quia cepit ibidem tapetum *Year Bk.* 30–31 *Ed. I app.* II 537. **c** **1292** inculpati super fraccione, ~a et evasione gaole de Newegate *Gaol Del.* 87 r. 10*d*.

brutacia v. batrachium. brutachia, ~agium v. bretescha.

brutalis, brutish, bestial, animal (w. ref. to: **a** beasts; **b** men or their attributes or acts).

a bestia brutalis non impresepiat aula D. BEC. 2206; **a1250** bibiones oriuntur ex vino sine motibus ~ibus J. GODARD *Ap.* 263. **b** delectationes viles..et ~es BACON *Maj.* II 271; queritur..utrum †sunt [? l. sint] in homine due vires concupiscibiles, una humana sive intelligibilis, altera ~is sensibilis GROS. 269; **s1297** ut Scotis obviaret, ut ~em et presumptuosam eorum temeritatem attenuaret *Ann. Angl. & Scot.* 384; mores brutales Britonum / jam ex convictu Saxonum / commutantur in melius (*Wallia*) HIGD. I 38; crucem portare signat portantem non habere aliquam causam vel conditionem secundum quam possent sibi arma assignari, sed signat hominem ~em BAD. AUR. 127.

brutalitas, bestiality. **b** bestial act.

s1463 diversa..peccatorum genera, in que quorundam hominum inordinata ~as aliquoties incidere solet *Croyl. Cont.* B 539. **b** sicut..porci vilissimi comedunt, manus suas lingentes et barbas proprias fedantes atque alias ~ates inexplicabiles continue facientes S. SIM. *Itin.* 55.

brutaliter, like a beast.

Soldanus semper comedit..~er in terra S. SIM. *Itin.* 55; **s1440** cum nusquam in omni genere hominum conspexisset statum aliquem aut gradum quin ita corruperat viam suam super terram ut..~er potius quam rationabiliter victitaret AMUND. II 220.

brutasca v. bretescha. brutere v. brutescere.

brutescere [LL], to become (or be) brutish or bestial.

sic rationalis creatura ~it J. SAL. *Pol.* 389C; in bestiam ~it bestiarum dominator GIR. *TH* II 23; **c1426** hec plebs in specie, brutescens conditione (*Versus de Lollardis*) AMUND. I 230; *to be or wax or make fonde*, brutere, ~ere, dementare *CathA.*

bruteus, brutish.

nos, si fuerimus asini..aut aliqua inhumanitate ~ei, quo fidei..merito digni reperiemur? MAP *NC* IV 3 p. 156; *wylde*, acer, indomitus, ~eus, feralis *CathA.*

brutia v. brusca. brutnare v. britnare.

1 brutus [CL], brute (adj.), brutish, savage. **b** (compar.).

expertem sensus cum bruta mente vagando ALDH. *VirgV* 2429; nolumus esse sicut ~a animalia [AS: *stunte nytenu*], quae nihil sciunt nisi herbam et aquam ÆLF. *Coll.* 100; utrum ~a animalia animas habeant necne ADEL. *QN* 13; **s1160** per montanos Scotos, quos ~os vocant, et Galwalenses, qui nec locis nec personis parcere norunt FORDUN *GA* 10; **1406** que quidem victualia..J. W. ceperat de ~is Hibernicis rebellibus domini regis de villa de Dengell *LTR Mem.* 178 *rec.* r. 47. **b** est certe asello cui insidebat ~ior J. SAL. *Pol.* 749A.

2 (sb. n.) brute beast.

~a sensus habent ADEL. *QN* 13; numquid dicemus a ~is sumi sacramentaliter? GIR. *GE* IX 30; hec dantur ~is ad instructionem hominis BACON *Tert.* 44; **1314** [prisonum] corpora velut ~orum cadavera in preparatam foveam projecerunt (*Instr. de Predicatoribus*) *Flor. Hist.* III 164; fabule poetarum..fingentium ~a fuisse locuta OCKHAM *Dial.* 837; **c1400** necat pestilencia viros atque bruta (*Pestilentia*) *Pol. Poems* I 279.

2 Brutus, Brute, book of British history.

c1250 in quo etiam volumine continentur hystoria vetus Britonum que ~us appellatur..(*Lit. Pri. Ch. Ch.*) *N & Q* I i 21 (cf. ib. 22 [**a1443**]: ~us Latine); **1321** lego..librum meum qui dicitur ~us *Fabr. York* 158.

†bruuinus [? cf. bruchus *or* 1 bromus], (?) kind of insect.

10.. ~us, *lytel wycga* WW.

bryonia, white bryony (*cf. alphesora*). **b** hop.

brionia vel ampelos leuce.., *hwit wilde wingeard*, ..~ia, *wild cyrfet* vel *hwit wingeard* ÆLF. *Gl.*; [humiditas] naturaliter est mundificativa, ut patet..in radice brione BART. ANGL. IV 4; pocio de brionia cum vino vel cervisia est hic [contra fistulam] preciosa GAD. 126 v. 2; brionia, *wilde nepe* i. radix vitis albe secundum quosdam *SB* 13; brionia vel brion, scicida, cucurbita agrestis, alphesora idem; ejus folia assimulantur foliis vitis; G. *brione* vel *nave sauvage*, A. *wildenep Alph.* 26. **b** bronia, *hymelyc Gl. Durh.*

buas v. 1 boa.

bubalarius, oxherd (*cf. bubulcus*).

1172 in liberat' ~ii, xiii s. *Pipe* 140.

bubalinus, of wild ox or buffalo.

~a cornua fulvo metallo circa extremitates utrasque decorata ORD. VIT. IV 2 p. 168 (cf. W. POIT. II 44); carnibus bovinis ~is GILB. I 53. 2.

1 bubalus [CL < βούβαλος = *a species of antelope*], wild ox or buffalo. **b** bull. *V. et. lingua bubali.*

brutorum..bubulorum et tragelaforum ALDH. *PR* 114; lucror equo collum par forte pedesque bubalo WHÆTBERHT *Aen.* 45 (*Cameleo*) 2; ~is, *weosend GlC* B 213; urus, *wesend*, ~us, *wilde oxa* ÆLF. *Gl.*; animalia que, quanquam infra septa foreste vivunt, ..foreste tamen nequaquam censeri possunt, qualia sunt equi, ~i, vacce et similia (*Ps.-Cnut: Foresta*) *GAS* 625; aquis in cornu ~i haustis GIR. *TH* V 89; glutientes bubalum culicem colatis (*Ad Praelatos* 17) *Ps.-*MAP *Poems* 43; ~i cornu [*gl.*: major bove] NECKAM *Ut.* 102; habeat etiam..boves, ..buculas, ~os [*gl.*: *bugles*] *Ib.* 112; **s1252** de primis ~is in Angliam missis: missi sunt comiti Ricardo de partibus transmarinis ~i utriusque sexus, ut hujusmodi animalia in partibus nostris multiplicentur M. PAR. *Min.* III 119; **1317** unum cornu de ~o pro potu *PlRCP* 285 (*deeds*) r. 1; *bugulle, beeste*, buballus *PP*; hic ~us, A. *a bogelle* WW. **b 1547** j bubuli sive tauri *CalPat* I 259.

2 bubalus v. bubulcus. bubastus v. bumasta.

†bubla [? *for* bulla; *but* cf. bovellum], flood or (?) fold.

~a, *flod GlC* B 229; bobla, *flod* ÆLF. *Gl.*

1 bubo [CL], kind of owl. **b** (?) bittern (*cf.* 1 *buteo*).

~o, *uuf GlC* B 206; nomina avium: ..~o, *uf* ÆLF. *Gl.*; noctua, nictocorax, witur et bubo, quorum oculi 'tenebras amant, oderunt lucem' MAP *NC* I 10 p. 6 (cf. *John* iii 19); nocte clare videt ~o O. CHERITON *Fab.* 55; **12..** strix vel ~o, *ule* WW; [in Dalmatia] mulieres..portant in capite ornamentum cornutum velut ~ones S. SIM. *Itin.* 15; **s1457** bubo non pavo dicitur esse modo (*Vers. de R. Pecok*) *Reg. Whet.* I 288. **b** †bovon, †aves in palustris *GlC* B 163; ~o, avis vel nocturna †in [? l. vel] palustris *Erf.* 2. 272. 40; **9..** †buban, *raredumle* WW.

2 (?) 'night bird', prowler.

c1370 ducet bubones, piratas, vespiliones [*gl.*: i. aliquos homines qui raro veniunt ad bella vel qui ~onibus propter aliquam proprietatem assimilantur] (J. BRIDL.) *Pol. Poems* I 194, 196.

2 bubo [βουβών], tumour in groin or sim.

tumor..aliquando fit de ventositate et dicitur ~o BART. ANGL. VII 60; in ~onibus omnes febres male exceptis effimeris GILB. I 3 v. 2; inguina sunt partes..ubi conjunguntur coxe cum ancha, ubi eciam nascuntur ~ones inferiores GAD. 25 v. 2; ~o est apostema sive inflacio inguinis, vel est apostema ex ventositate *SB* 13; ibi [in inguinibus] nascuntur ~ones inferiores, que sunt emunctoria epatis *Ib.* 26; hic ~o..i. morbus sub ano WW.

bubonica [cf. CL bubonium], (?) yellow rattle (*Rhinanthus*).

10.. nomina herbarum: ..bobonica, *hratele* WW; bobonaca, *hrate Gl. Durh.*

buboscus v. buprestis.

bubsequa [LL], oxherd, neatherd.

a nowthyrde; ..bossequus, bubulcus etc. *CathA.*

bubula v. bubala.

bubulcus [CL], oxherd. **b** swineherd (*cf. subulcus*); *v. et boviculus* (1220).

†aubulcus, pastor boum *GlC* A 940; bobulcus, *hriðhiorde Ib.* B 164; agricolas quoque atque ~os et subulcos ALDH. *VirgP* 29; o ~e [AS: *oxanhyrde*], quid operaris tu? ..quando arator disjungit boves, ego duco eos ad pascua, et tota nocte sto super eos ÆLF. *Coll.* 91; **a1128** in ij hidis manent xiij villani et j presbiter et ij cotseti et iiij ~i, quorum iij manent in terra villanorum *Chr. Peterb. app.* 166 (cf. bovarius); **1130** villanis et bordariis et buris et ~is *Pipe* 2; **c1195** de terra ~orum *Carte Nativ.* 177; **c1224** decetero nullum recipiet..rusticum servientem, utpote daiam, carectarium, †bubulos et hujusmodi *Reg. S. Osm.* I 311; **1243** duobus ~is, qui fuerunt in insula de Lunday ad excolendas terras nostras *Liberate* 19 m. 6; **1275** venit †bubalus ejusdem domus extrahendo foragium ad bestias suas *Hund.* I 323; contra jura bovis bos spernit habere bubulcum GOWER *VC* I 243; hic ~us, A. *hoxhard* WW. **b 9..** de suibus: ..†bubullus, *swan* WW; **14..** hic ~us, *a swynherde Ib.*

1 bubulus, ox-like.

quantum pietatis, ut ita dicam ~ae mansuetudinis, intus in corde gestaret BEDE *Templ.* 793.

2 & 3 bubulus v. bubalus, bubulcus. bucata v. buccata. bucattus v. buketus.

1 bucca [CL], cheek.

a cheke, gena, ~a, buccella *CathA.*

2 mouth: **a** (human); **b** (animal).

a humanis horrent haec pabula buccis ALDH. *Aen.* 75. 5; **799** calidis ~is oscula in pavimento figere (?) ALCUIN *Ep.* 180; a ~is miserorum cibos abstrahentes W. MALM. *GR* IV 314; turgescentibus labris ~a clauditur T. MON. *Will.* VII 19; ligamen..per quod..~a clauditur et aperitur BART. ANGL. V 18. **b** [mus] avidis ~is momordit benedicti panis micas *V. Osw.* 455; predo vorax plus bucca bestie J. HOWD. *Phil.* 466.

3 mouth (of valley).

c1190 sicut Bothkil descendit usque ad ~am de Fulope *Kelso* I 249; **c1180** usque per ~am de Estfulhope *Melrose* I 143; **1236** per †buttam de Estfulhope *Ib.* 298.

2 †bucca, *s. dub.* (? *cf. butta*).

1208 vj marcas quas posuit in ~is ad opus nostrum *Cl* 103b; **1351** in j ~a cum sella empta xviij s. *Comp. Worc.* I 51.

3 bucca v. 2 buscia.

buccare, to blow.

14.. ~o, *to blowe* WW; hic aliquis ~at in cornu a retro post populum SKELTON I 295.

buccata, mouthful.

in balneo..duas ~as manducavi priusquam ungi inciperem J. SAL. *Pol.* 557D; **1232** cum commederet panem .., strangulatus fuit quadam bucata *JustIt* 62 r. 40.

buccea [cf. OF *bochiee* < buccata], mouthful.

detur statim unicuique panis ~ea priusquam recedant BELETH *RDO* 119. 122.

buccella, ~um [CL], mouthful, morsel. **b** cheek.

si comedi bucellam meam et non comedit pupillus meus BEDE *HE* II 1; **9..** buccilla, *geofola* WW; est melior panis mihi letificata bucella WALT. ANGL. *Fab.* 12 *add.* 1; Judas.. statim post ~am sumptam abiit GIR. *GE* I 54 (cf. *John* xiii 27); cum [rex] intinctam ~am ori applicuisset M. PAR. *Min.* I 166; **1409** si quis haberet unum panem et ipsum frangeret et..daret discipulis unum ~um *Conc.* III 327; *mussel*, bolus, morcellus, ~a *PP*. **b** *a cheke*, gena, bucca, ~a *CathA.*

buccellaris, condyloid.

investite fuerunt ossuum extremitates ~es et concave hoc corpore medio [sc. cartilagine] *Ps.-*RIC. *Anat.* 2 (cf. ib. 42: ut [cartilagines] sint vestimentum extremitatum ~ium ingredientium vacuitates alterius ossis).

buccellatim, by mouthfuls.

liquet quod..caro mea ~im sit..distribuenda PULL. *Sent.* 966; percipere..panem ~im UPTON 25.

buccellum v. buccella. buccetum v. bucetum. buccilla v. buccella. buccin- v. bucin-.

1 bucco [CL], dolt. **b** cadger, parasite.

~ones, stulti, rustici *GlC* B 219 **b** placere poteris hiis buccionibus / qui falsis epulas venantur laudibus (*Palpo* 241) *Ps.-*MAP *Poems* 113.

2 †bucco, (?) he-goat (ME *bukke*).

eo quod hujusmodi senescalli sint ductores..judiciorum comitatus, sicut ~o gregis *Fleta* 147.

1 buccula [CL], **~us,** cheek.

[immundi spiritus] macilenta facie, ..comis obustis, ~a crassa, pectore arduo FELIX *Guthl.* 31.

2 boss of shield.

buculus, *rondbeag GlC* B 208.

3 buckle (*cf.* OF *bocle*).

1204 unam zonam..cum una oniche in bucula et perlis *RChart* 134b; **1205** zonas cum buculis et membris aureis *Pat* 51b (cf. ib. 145b); **1235** j par cyngular' de serico de opere Saracen' cum buclis ferreis *ChancMisc* 3/4; **1254** octo cingulas ad dextrarios et palefridos sine buclis *Cl* 248; **1255** ~as et anulos de auro *Ch. & Rec. Heref.* 108; **1270** pro xiij cingulis cum bugul' emptis ad palefridos *ChancMisc* 3/7/24; **1295** morsus..cum duobus †bitellis (*Invent.*) *Hist. S. Paul. app.* 28 p. 310; **1297** pro..cingulis et supercingulis, †butallis et cribris (*Ac. Wardr*) *DocScot* II 147; accipe corium bovis marine et fac zonam; et buccolam ejus fac de balena; et ligamina ejus ~e fac de dente balene GAD. 95 v. 2; **1335** in ij bokelis emptis pro eisdem [surcinglis] *Sacr. Ely* II 69; **1439** pro..iiij buklis *Ac. Durh* 71; *a bukylle*, ~a, pluscula *CathA.*

4 curl, ringlet (Fr. *boucle*).

non facietis boculos ad dandum alicui *AncrR* 172.

2 buccula v. bucula.

buccularis, boss of shield.

9.. buculus vel bucularis, *randbeag* WW.

buccularium, ~ia, ~ius, shield-play, fencing.

1300 ad bucularium ludere *Cal. Mayor's CourtRLond.* C 86; **1340** j salar' de jaspide cum uno homine nudo ludente ad bokelar' *Ac. Wardr.* (*TRBk* 203) p. 321; **1340** nec artem nephariam boculariе discat vel exerceat *FormOx* 160 (cf. ib. 171); **c1350** de..utentibus arte bokelarie *StatOx* 88.

2 buckler.

1268 eidem [R.] invito j lanceam et j boclear' tradiderunt; et dictus R., cum habuerit targiam et lanceam, noluit cum eis procedere *JustIt* 618 r. 17; **1298** malefactores noctanter cum gladiis et bukelariis ac aliis armis..incedentes *Cl* 115 m. 8; **1311** j boclarium ad ludendum (*Ac. Wardr. BM*) *Sports & Pastimes* 164; **1320** perrexerunt ad ecclesiam ad audiendum vesperas portantes gladios et bokerellos cum eis *SelCKB* IV 92 (cf. *Thoresby Soc.* IV 131); percussit eum bis cum gladio suo, antequam dictus R. movebat se, recipiens ictus cum bokerello *Ib.* 93; **1339** cum hominibus armatis cum gladiis et bokelariis *Ib.* V 111; **1417** cum gladiis, daggariis et bucheleris *Reg. Cant.* IV 173 (cf. *Conc.* III 387).

bucculetta [OF *boclete*], little buckle.

1292 in xij bokelettis argenteis pro sotularibus domini *KRAc* 308/14 m. 3.

bucculus v. buccula, buculus.

†buccum [? cf. 1 bucco], folly.

10.. ~um, *dysig* WW.

buccus v. 1, 2, 3 butta. bucea v. 2 buscia. bucella v. buccella.

bucellus [OF *bucel*, (?) < butticellus; (?) *conf. w.* bussellus], small butt or leather bottle: **a** (for wine); **b** (for drawing water from mine).

a ut conveniamus semper ad unum mensem..sic cum ~orum impletione sic aliter [AS: *swa mid byttfyllinge swa elles*] (*Decretum sapientum London': Quad.*) *GAS* 178; **1158** pro *barilz* ferratis et non ferratis et buttis et ~is *Pipe* 112; **1160** pro..ii ~is et ii hosis ad vinum *Pipe* 13; **1171** pro buscellis et hosis *Pipe* 147; **1184** pro vi buszis et xii buszellis et xii barellis ferro ligatis *Pipe* 137; **1204** quod parari faciatis ad opus nostrum x ~os *Cl* 2a; **1214** xij buttas et ij †butellos [? l. bucellos] *Cl* 141b; **1248** serjantiam custodiendi buscellos domini regis cum vino suo *Fees* 1416; **1276** tenet duas hidas..per serjanciam ad portandum cum domino rege unum ~um vini *Hund.* I 12. **b 1294** in..corio bovino pro buscellis faciendis; ..ad ~os faciendos ad extrahendam aquam de mineris *KRAc* 260/4 m. 1.

bucerius [CL < βούκερας], horned (of cattle).

†buteriae, armenta *GlC* B 222 (= *Erf.* 2. 272. 37: ~iae, †armamenta); ~um pecus, bubalis *Ib.* 217; bubo, bubastus, bos, bostar, bucria, buris GARL. *Syn.* 1582B 246; sed cornuta sonat animalis †butria Grece *Ib.* 255.

bucetum [CL], cow-pasture or byre.

bucitum, *seotu GlC* B 226; buccetum, *hryðra fald* ÆLF. *Gl.*; **1381** buchettum (*granted for yearly rent of* 2d.) (*High Wycombe* MSS.) *HMC Rep.* V 557 a (cf. ib.: bugittum); *a buse for a noxe*, bocetum *CathA.*

buchelerum v. buccularium.

bucheria [OF *bocherie*], shambles, butchers' quarter.

1201 burgenses Lincolnie amoverunt ~iam a sede solita *CurR* II 20; **1275** prior de Hertford' capit..de heredibus R. le Macecrer ij s. de una selda in ~ia *Hund.* I 194; **1279** tota bocheria de Newegate ab uno capite ad aliud stat super terram domini regis (*Hund.*) *Lond. Ed. I & II* II 148; **1342** in bocheria Oxonie *Cart. Osney* I 417.

bucherius [OF *bochier*], butcher.

1180 admerciamenta de gildis adulterinis in civitate [Lond']: ..gilda bocheiorum..debet j m. *Pipe* 154; **1201** ponat bucheros per salvos plegios quod sint coram justiciariis..ostensuri quare amoverunt illam [bucheriam] *CurR* II 20.

buchetum v. bucetum. bucia v. 2 buscia. bucida v. bovicida.

bucina [CL], trumpet. **b** (fig.) summons.

~a pastoralis est et cornu recurvo fit BEDE *Orth.* 2778; **934** classica archangeli clangente †buecina *CS* 704 (cf. *CD* 1297); non ibidem buccinae sonitus audita est *V. Osw.* 438; buccina scabra modos HANV. IX 390; **c1245** si speculator viderit gladium venientem et non insonuerit buccina *Conc. Syn.* 438; **14..** hec tuba, A. *trumpe*; hec buccina, idem..; hec buccina, *a beme* WW. **b** nondum clangente evangelica ~a ALDH. *VirgP* 21; **680** hujuscemodi altercationis opprobrium apostolica compescit buccina *Id. Ep.* 4 p. 482.

bucinare [CL], to blow (a trumpet).

salpizo vel buccino, *ic byme* ÆLF. *Sup.*; GIR. *IK* I 6 (v. bucinator); tube buccinantes R. BURY *Phil.* 8. 136; **1509** ut valeremus aptissime buccinare *Reg. Merton* 380.

bucinator [CL], trumpeter.

tubicines et buccinatores quos *cornhiriez* vocant, ab *hir* quod est 'longum' et 'cornu', eo quod longis in cornubus flatum emittant, ..in ejusdem honore buccinare ceperunt GIR. *IK* I 6; **1209** septem busynatoribus Lewelini Walensis ad robas emendas *Misae* 124; **1373** pro bono servicio quod.. R. de B., *trompour*, nobis impendit..concessimus ei talia vadia qualia alii buccinatores nostri percipiunt *Pat* 289 m. 21; quarta fistula, distinctis locis perforata, quam buccinator..articulorum volubilitate, qua claudendo, qua aperiendo foramina, moderatur STANIHURST 38.

bucinus, trumpet-blast.

bucina est qua signum dat bucinator; ~us ipse canor ex hac editus BEDE *Orth.* 2778.

bucius v. dusius. buckettus v. bukettus. buckstallus v. bukestallus. bucla v. buccula.

bucleamen, midriff.

~en, *heorthama* ÆLF. *Gl.*

bucolicus [βουκολικός], pastoral (of verse).

definitio caesurae tetartitrochaici quam quidam tetarte ~on nuncupant ALDH. *Met.* 10 p. 96 (cf. ib.: regula ~i carminis); utinam ~a vel sticulcinia amatorum conquiescant in domo sapientis J. SAL. *Pol.* 729B.

bucor v. 2 butor 1. bucria v. bucerius. bucrum v. butrum. bucstalmum v. buphthalmon. bucstanus v. balzanus. 1 bucula v. buccula.

2 bucula [CL], heifer.

vacca vel buccula, *cu* ÆLF. *Gl.*; **9..** ~a, *cealf* WW; ~a, vacca *GlC* B 218; rusticus..habeat..juvencas, .. juvencos, buculos, onagros, ~as, bubalos NECKAM *Ut.* 112; ex Mauritaniae desertis locis advectum ad nos est animal..forma et aspectu inter cervam et juvencam, unde ..voco moschelaphum vel ~am cervinam CAIUS *Anim.* 9.

2 (? infl. by AS) he-goat.

buccula, *buuc GlC* B 223; **9..** buccula, *buc* WW; **9..** †bulbile, *bucce Ib.*

1 buculus v. buccula.

2 buculus [CL], bull-calf, bullock.

NECKAM *Ut.* (v. bucula); **1229** si iconomi ~os desideraverint habere ad suas efficiendas vaccas lac prebere [*I. of Man*] *MonA* V 253; **1442** [cuilibet] unum ~um et unam ovem *Reg. Linc.* f. 38; taurus, bos, vacca, bŭculus [*gl.*: *bulloke*] vitulusque, juvenca WW; **1533** de stauro domini iiij bucculi pro jugis *Househ. Bk. Durh.* 205.

buda [LL], rush-mat.

natte or matte, matta, ~a, storium *PP*.

budelaria v. bedellaria. budellus v. bedellus, 1 botellus. budgetum v. bugettum. buen' v. lineus.

†buere [? < imbuere], to pour.

butum, imbutum *GlC* B 207; *to spylle*, buere [v.l. luere], perfundere; *spyllt*, butus [v.l. lutus] *CathA*.

bufa [cf. It. *buffa*], trifle, jest.

1299 in parliamentis vestris..de vita, fide [etc.] .., non autem de truphis, ~is ac omnino inutilibus..collaciones inter vos decetero fieri precipimus *Reg. Cant.* 839.

buffare [OF *bofer*], to puff, blow.

tandem venit ventus ~ans et totum asportat O. CHERITON *Fab.* 15A.

1 buffettum [OF *buffet*], bellows.

1294 in v coreis equinis emptis pro buffectis reficiendis *KRAc* (*Mines*) 260/8 m. 1*d.*

2 buffettum [OF *buffet*], **a** (?) 'buffet', stool. **b** chest, sideboard.

a **1141** recepit..bancum et bufetum et ij mensas *Dom. S. Paul.* 136; **1323** (*chair and*) ~um (*worth 9d.*) *Cal. Coron. R. Lond.* 75; **1374** in camera: ..j parva catedra cum ij bouiffatis de Flandria (*Invent.*) *Pri. Cold.* lxxv. **b** **1328** unum boffettum cum serura pro denariis supra computandis, precii iiij s. *Reg. Exon.* 567; **1412** faciant indenturas suas.. irrotulari in quodam rotulo cum rotulis de cartis..et aliis munimentis jacens in communi boffetto stans in curia *BB Winchester* f. 14(= *Gild. Merch.* 259: †bosseto).

†bufficius, (?) curtain.

a1100 quatuor pallia altari ydonea et octo ~ios Ispanicos et tres pannos brusdatos de cerico ad opus altarium *Stat. Sal.* 36.

bufo [CL], toad (*v. et. fistula bufonis*).

limphas..potare, in quis atra ~onum turma..scatet ALDH. *Ep.* 3; de nominibus insectorum:..buffo, *tadige* ÆLF. *Gl.*; [Hibernia] caret ~onibus et ranis GIR. *TH* I 28; tu buffoni similis es, qui terre parcit et fame deperit MAP *NC* I 10 p. 9; pulverem rane commisce vel pulverem buffonis superpone GAD. 29 v. 1; **a1410** dic quod bufo crati, "maledicti tot dominati" (*Vers. Exch.*) *EHR* XXXVI 62.

2 'bufo' (alch.), 'black tincture'.

aquila ergo volans per aerem et ~o gradiens per terram est magisterium: idcirco separabis terram ab igne, subtile a spisso DASTYN *Ros.* 9.

buga v. 1 bugia. Bugarus, ~is v. Bulgarus. bugeramus v. bukaramus.

bugerescha, *s. dub.* (? *cf. bukaramus*).

1213 ad opus H. de Tracy pro j pari caligarum de Brug' x d. ..pro j ~a ad opus ejusdem..ix d. *Misae* 249; **1214** mittatis nobis tres duodenas de †lugereschiis..et..xij frusta laqueorum diversorum colorum *Cl* 167; **1214** pro iij duodenis de ~is *Pipe* 28.

bugerus v. Bulgarus 3.

bugettum [cf. 1 bugia], budge, sheep's fur.

12.. [capucium] de bugeto (*Reg. Winchcombe*) *EHR* VIII 553; **1277** quandam tunicam de †burgeto *GaolDel.* 35B r. 55*d.*; habeat in capite pileum foderatum de bogetto spisso GAD. 133 v. 2; **1327** quod forure de bujecto vel agnis sint unius ulne et quarterii unius ulne in longitudine *Cal Pat* 34; **1327** pro..duobus capuciis de nigro budgeto *Exch Scot* 76; **1337** furrura albi buggeti pro supertunicis *Ac. Durh.* 534; **1338** j balam de forura de bogetto grosso; j balam de bogetto pro capuciis *IMisc* 138/25.

1 bugia, ~ium [ME *bouge* ? < OF], budge, sheep's fur.

1285 furura de boga (*KRAc* 91/3) *Arch.* LXX 31; **1290** in iij capuciis de bug' *Ac. Swinfield* 184; **1305** pro xl libratis bogie *EEC* 316; **1346** iij furrur[a]s de buga alba et j capucium de buga alba (*KRAc*) *SelCKB* VI xxiii; **1426** capucia capparum..cum ~io furrata *Conc.* III 469.

2 bugia [cf. It. *bugia*], (?) lie, falsehood.

1323 ut..sagittent innocentes ~iis acutis *Lit. Cant.* I 110.

3 bugia v. bulga. bugittum v. bucetum. 1 bugium v. 1 bugia.

2 bugium, snipe, (?) conf. w. buzzard (*buteo*).

nomina avium: ..~ium, *hæfenblæte* ÆLF. *Gl.*; **10..** scorellus, *clodhamer and feldeware*, vel ~ium, ..~ium, *hæferblæte* WW.

bugla [OF *bugle*], bugle (*Ajuga*), conf. w. bugloss.

scabiose, ~e, pigle, sanigle GILB. II 85 v. 1; ~a, *bugle*, i. *wodebroun*, una maneries est habens florem rubeum, alia habens florem citrinum, et hec est melior *SB* 13; bugula, fistularia secundum Laur. *Alph.* 24; ~a folia habet aliquantulum rotunda et ad nigredinem vergencia, florem indum, G. et A. *bugle Ib.* 25.

bugleus v. buculus.

buglossa [βούγλωσσον], bugloss (*Anchusa*), conf. w. bugle.

fumiterre vel scabiose vel bugulosse GILB. III 142 v. 1; **12..** buglosa, i. *bugle*, i. *wudbrune* WW; aqua buglose cum lignoaloes accepta per os..valet in omni sincopi curabili GAD. 6. 2; ~a, lingua bovis idem; acuta habet folia ad modum boraginis, G. *lange de beof*, A. *oxtunge Alph.* 24.

buglum v. builum.

bugo [? cf. bunnum], log or tree-trunk.

1236 in foresta [de Windlesor']..faciat habere..carpentario regis..unum ~onem findendum ad iij pulinos faciendos ad discarcanda vina regis *Cl* 394.

bugula v. buccula, bugla. bugulossa v. buglossa.

bugulus [cf. bubalus, buculus], wild ox.

1212 pro xviij cornibus ~i parandis *Pipe* 49; **1275** nichil inventum fuit [in castro de Kilgarran] nisi tantum unum [? cornu] de bugleo et mortarium cum pestello *ChancMisc* 2/2/1; **1289** reddit compotum..de iiij cornubus ~i ad potandum (*Pipe* 134) *MinAc W. Wales* I 54.

bugum v. bogum. buhurd- v. burd-. buielum v. builum.

†builares [? l. bivillares *or* bundares; *or* cf. birelagia], (?) joint meetings of local courts.

c1340 Crukedebrugg', ubi ~es solebant teneri inter predicta maneria et ubi huthesia de roboria et latrocinio solet perduci et de libertate in libertatem recipi *RB Worc.* 242.

buillo, ~onus v. 4 bullio c.

builum [ME *buil*], 'boul' curved handle (of plough).

1235 in buglis et virgis emptis ad car[ucas] per annum xj d. ob. *Pipe Wint.* (159284) r. 4*d.*; **1264** in una nova caruca empta et in aliis reperendis (*sic*) quatuor jugis, xij boul' emptis *MinAc* (*Yorks*) 1078/8 r. 1; in..xj ~is emptis *Ib.*; in..ix buiel', tribus trabibus et alio meremio ad carucas empt' *Ib.* r. 5.

buinardus [OF *buisnart*], fool, dolt.

1169 episcopus Sarisberiensis respondit sic: "si ~us archiepiscopus meus [*gl.*: vel stultus archiepiscopus meus] precipit mihi aliquid facere quod facere non debeam, nunquid faciam?" (*Lit. W. Bonhart*) *Becket Mat.* VI 606.

buisellus v. bussellus. buistarius v. boistarius. bujectum v. bugettum.

bukaramus, ~a [cf. OF *boquerant*, It. *bucherame*], 'buckram', (piece of) fine linen or cotton cloth, originally from Bukhara.

1225 septem bokerandas..et j pannum de burello *Cl* 44b; **1235** camelotus niger, ..ij bugerami *ChancMisc* 3/4; **1238** pro uno ~o ad casulam cotidianam *Liberate* 12 m. 9; **1284** cissori regis pro iij bokerammis et j pecia cindonis de cursu emptis..ad penicell' inde faciend' *KRAc* 351/9 m. 5; **1292** pro tela de coton' pro pavilono cum duobus bocramis facto apud Trapesund' *Ib.* 308/13 m. 3; **1315** j albam de bokerammo *Invent. Ch. Ch.* 63; **c1400** habeat..equum solempnem coopertum bokorammo *MonA* II 236; **14..** capa de bysso, i.e. bokeram *Pont. Sal.* I 198.

bukelar- v. buccular-.

†bukellus, bucket (? for *bukettus*).

1239 duos bonos ~os ferro ligatos ad trahendam aquam ad puteum nostrum *Liberate* 13 m. 8.

bukestallare, to fit (palisade) with 'buckstalls'.

1379 in stipendiis iij hominum..raillancium et bokkestallancium palicium [parci] *MinAc* 1184/8 m. 1*d.*

bukestallus [ME], 'buck-stall', (service of making) hunting-net.

1195 in..haiis et bokestall' faciendis *RScacNorm* I 263; **1199** sint quieti..de misericordia foreste.., bukestall' et tristis (*Ch. Sempringham*) *RChart* 18b; **1240** warantum de retibus extendendis et ~is faciendis juxta marchiam foreste *CurR* 122 r. 6; **1279** plures habet buckstall' et *netgates* in eadem [chacia] quam habere debet *PQW* 752a; **1336** quoad hoc vocabulum quod dicitur 'bukstallis', dicit quod, ubi iidem homines tenentur ibidem convenire ad stabular' [v.l. stableiam] faciend' circa easdem feras et ad easdem congregandas, quod si non fecerint amercientur, ..ipse et homines sui..de hujusmodi consuetudinibus..quieti extiterunt (*DL Coucher* f. 298) *Pickering* III 105 (cf. ib. 109; quando dicti homines non veniunt ad tristas et bukstallos, amerciantur).

bukettus, ~a, ~um [cf. OF *buket*], bucket: **a** (for drawing water or brine from well); **b** (for milking); **c** (for other purposes).

a **1209** in j boketto et fune ad aquam extrahendam de puteo *Pipe Wint.* 82; **1211** in bucattis et tinis et ceteris paramentis *Ib.* II 18; **c1230** inveniet aquam bobus domini, sed dominus inveniet ei cordam et boketum ad trahendum *Doc. Bec* 35; **1236** hec inventa fuerunt in castro Norwic': ..j ~um ad fontem cum corda *KRMem* 14 r. 12*d.*; **1252** uti quodam communi ~o ad hauriendam salsam suam *Cl* 148 (cf. *CalIMisc* I p. 150; *Cart. Worc.* 477); **1253** pro bochetis.. emendandis *Ac. Build. Hen. III* 228; **1286** duabus bokettis ferro ligatis ad aquam hauriendam *IMisc* 46/3; **1320** in quodam homine locato ad petendum ~um de magno puteo infra donjonem *KRAc* 452/15 m. 3. **b** **1276** in custu daerie: ..in j bocatto, ij d. *Ac. Stratton* 191; **1297** in ollis, patellis, buckettis *Ac. Cornw.* I 19; in daerya..iiij ~e ad lactandum et unum magnum buketum ad aquam hauriendam *Form Man* 21; **1311** bokettus pro lacte *MinAc* 856/17 m. 3. **c** **1243** in..salsariis, ..ciphis et gatis et ~is emptis ad predictas naves muniendas *Liberate* 19 m. 4; **1290** in ~is ad elemosinam colligendam *Ac. Swinfield* 180; **1389** iij boketus (*sic*) pro piscaria *Ac. Obed. Abingd.* 57.

2 measure, bucketful: **a** (of butter); **b** (of quarrels).

a **1289** de quolibet boketo butiri, unum quadrantem *RGasc* II 406. **b** **1265** rex dedit E. filio suo ad tuitionem castri de Odyham v balistas.., de quibus due baliste sunt ad duos pedes et tres ad unum pedem, et tres bokettos quarellorum, de quibus unum bokettum est [sc. ad balistas] ad ij pedes et duo ad j pedem *Cl* 149; xij balistas ad duos pedes et quarellos usque ad quatuor ~os *Ib.* 159.

bukinus [cf. OF *boc*], of a he-goat. **b** (sb. f.) goat-skin.

1243 coria que fuerunt in navi mercatorum de Hyspania.. vendi faciant, retentis ~is *RGasc* I 179. **b** ~as quas emit apud Burdegalam *Ib.* 118 (= *CalPat* 368: †bickarias).

bukkum [? ME], 'plough-buck' (T-shaped end of plough-beam).

1352 in vj ~is pro carucis emptis, iij d. *Ac. Man. Wint.* (*Elton, Hunts*).

bukla v. buccula. bukstallus v. bukestallus.

bula [βουλή], counsel.

est pape bulla, Grece sententia bula H. AVR. *CG* f. 10. 19.

bulbile v. 2 bucula 2.

1 bulbus [CL < βολβός], bulb or bulbous plant.

semen ~i canini, id est cepule GILB. VII 286 v. 1; ~us, i. squilla vel cepa silvestris; ~us quando simpliciter pro radice narcisi ponitur, vel ~us est cepa canina; ~i, A. *chibollis SB* 13; ~us silicicus vel rufus, i. squilla; ..~us †scudius [l. studius], i. flos lupini *Alph.* 25; colcico vel ~us agrestis, que[m] dicunt effemeros, nascitur in fine autumpni *Ib.* 45; na[r]cisus, sive ~us ematicus sive ut Latini dicunt ~us vomificus, ..similis est porro in foliis *Ib.* 123; hic bilbus, *a lekes hed* WW.

2 †bulbus, marine animal, whelk (? conf. w. *polypus*, OF *polpe*).

sunt pisces bulbi, sumant armenta bubulci GARL. *Syn.* 1582B; **14..** bilbus, A. *a welke*, ..hic ~us, A. *a wylke* WW.

bulcagium, cargo due.

1343 de xvij s. ij d. receptis de consuetudine ancor[agii] liij navium ad portum [de Sandwico] applicancium, de bulcag' vij navium, de last[agio] ij navium et de consuetudine passagii xlj hominum deultra veniencium, viz. pro anc[oragio] navis ij d., pro bulcag' navis ij d., pro lastag' navis ij d., et pro homine ij d., *MinAc* 894/24; **1347** (v. bulcum); **1374** [*Winchelsea*] custumam..vocatam *ancorage* et *bulgage* navium *FineR* 175 m. 14; **14..** habebit..custumas..cum ankeragio, lastagio et bolcagio *Reg. S. Aug.* 154; **1452** concessimus..custumas navium [infra villam Berwici], viz. segeagium, mesuragium, bollagium *RScot* 355b (cf. *Cal. FineR* 216); **1506** cum..wharfagio, ~io, tronagio [de Nova Winchelsee] *Pat* 599 m. 21 (cf. *Cal* pp. 473, 345).

bulcum [ME *bulk*], cargo.

1347 de custuma proveniente de bulcag' xxiiij navium in dicto portu [de Sandwico] ~a sua..liberantium, viz. de qualibet navi ij d. *MinAc* 894/30.

bulducta v. balthuta. bulecta v. bulletta. bulengarius v. bolengarius. buleria v. 2 bullaria.

buletare, ~ire [OF *buleter, bureter*], to bolt, sift.

a1090 secretarius vas et locum quo farina [ad faciendum hostias] ~ari debet in circuitu cortina paret LANFR. *Const.* 150; **c1182** debent..bulletare ad molendinum *RB Worc.* 36; **1288** in uno dol[io] empto ad boletandum in bracinio *MinAc* 840/5; **1315** in stipendiis diversorum hominum predictam farinam bultancium *Doc. Ir.* 334; **1322** quod panis predicti Johannis erat nullius generis bladi sed collectio domus in qua bultavit quando domus erat mundata *MGL* III 415; **1327** frumentum ~ari.. faciat *KRMem* 103 r. 249; **1335** de frumento nostro..tantum quantum..moli poterit..moli et bultiri..faciatis *Cl* 156 m. 10; **1348** in vij bultellis emptis pro predicta flora bultanda *KRAc* 552/24.

buletarium [cf. buletellus], bolting-cloth.

a1190 pistor poterit..lucrari..in †buneter' obolum (*Assisa Panis*) *Growth Eng. Indust.* 568; **1290** in boletariis emptis *Doc. W. Abb. Westm.* 185; **1290** in buleteriis ad pistrinum ix d. *Ac. Swinfield* 177; **1292** pro bultario empto *Comp. Worc.* I 12; **1310** pistrinum: ..iiij d. de viij bolteriis venditis *Ac. Exec. Ep. Exon.* 10; **1335** in ~iis emptis *Comp. Swith.* 231.

buletarius, bolter (servant in bakehouse).

1322 [in pistrino] primus boletarius.., secundus boletarius *DCCant J* 512.

buletatio, bolting, sifting.

1243 in lxx doliis vacuis emptis ad farinam, gruellum et fabas imponendas, una cum ~one *Liberate* 19 m. 4; **1300** ~o farine frumenti *Ac. Wardr.* p. 110; **1348** in cariagio..frumenti..de molendino usque domum bultacionis, cum.. bultacione..pro quolibet quarterio j d. *KRAc* 552/24.

buletator [cf. OF *buleteor*], bolter.

c1268 in pistrino..duo buletores: unus eorum accipiet xiiij de panibus villarum, et alter xiiij in pistrino *Cart. Rams.* III 238 (cf. *MonA* II 549); **1338** duo molendinarii, unus *killeman*, unus bultator *Hosp. in Eng.* 98.

buletellare, to bolt, sift.

1284 pro xiij par' mucell'..emptis pro farina butell[anda] *KRAc* 351/9 m. 1; **1327** precipimus..medietatem frumenti predicti moli et bultellari et farinam inde in doliis poni *RScot* 220; **1344** habeat..in die Martis in Carnisprivio farinam bultellatam ponderis unius albi panis (*Stat. Hosp. S. Julian.*) *G. S. Alb.* II 490.

buletellus, ~a, [OF *buletel, buretel*], bolting-cloth.

s1202 pistor poterit..in quolibet quarterio lucrari iij d.. et in ~o obolum (*Assisa Panis*) M. PAR. *Maj.* II 481; **a1250** panis de *coket* de eodem blado et eodem bultello ponderabit plusquam wastellum ij solidos (*Assisa Panis*) *StRealm* I 199; **c1250** una ulna buretell' valet unum den. (*Comp. Faringdon, MS. Barlow* 49 [2]) *OED* (s.v. *treillis*); **1265** boletelle, ij s. (*RHosp*) *Manners* 16; **1283** in ~is cum filo *Dom. S. Paul.* 166; **1303** in lxxvj ulnis de bultell' *Ac. Durh.* 503; **1320** j bultellus pro j d. *Rec. Leic.* I 376; **13..** potest pistor lucrari..ad bultellum locandum obolum (*Vellum Bk. Leic.*) *EHR* XIV 504; **1390** *pur straynours* emptis..pro bultellis *Ac. H. Derby* 25; **1481** panes..bene bultatos cum bultello qui dicitur *coket Cart. Chich.* 735.

buletum [cf. betuletum, bulus], birch-wood, birch-tree.

1251 alnetum et bolnetum *CalPat* 115; **1261** vendi faciat de alneto et bolleto parci regis de Windesor' *Abbr. Orig.* I 18b (cf. *CalPat 1272–81* 390); **1315** [*waste in regard to..4 ash trees*] iiij bullect' et..tremell' *CourtR Wakefield* III 83.

buletura, bolting, sifting.

1290 pro boletura farine et furnitura iiij quart. *bisquyt Ac. Wardr.* (*Chanc. Misc.* 4/5) f. 9.

bulfinca, bullfinch.

1544 nominis etymologiam secutus, rubicillam Anglorum ~am et Germanorum bloudvincam esse conjicio TURNER *Av.* 86.

bulga, ~ia, ~ium [LL], 'bouge', leather bag or bottle.

casta cruentatum gestavit bulga tropeum ALDH. *VirgV* 2564 (*cf. Judith* xiii 11); ~ae, *lepercoddas*, ..~a, *hydig fæt* ÆLF. *Gl.*; **10..** ~a, *bælge oððe bylge* WW; **s1097** allate.. ante illum ~ie et mantice reserate sunt EADMER *HN* 101; **1170** pro ~iis et *barhuez* et sellis et apparatu summariorum regis *Pipe* 15; **1180** pro bolgis et bahurd' et sella summarii *RNorm* I 70; **1195** in xviij paribus ~iorum et xix sellis et trussis..et paneriis ad predictos summarios *Pipe* 175; **1213** pro bugiis ad arma domini regis *Misae* 243; **1290** pro ij paribus ~earum ad infra trussand' cacabos; ..pro uno pari ~earum ad aquam pro equo assignato ad portandas ipsas ~eas *Ac. Wardr.* (*Chanc. Misc.* 4/5) f. 3v; **a1307** in coriis bovinis emptis..pro ~eis inde faciendis ad aquam de minera extrahendam..cum factura dictorum ~eorum *KRAc* 260/19 m. 9; **1325** R. sutori facienti ~eas *LTRMem* 95 r. 128; **1355** pro operacionibus cofrorum, boulgearum, *clothsakkes* et *barhydes Pat* 246 m. 5; **1439** cum bogeis, manticis et aliis hernesiis *RScot* 315a (cf. ib. 325b: bugeis); *bale*, ~a, ..*bowge*, ~a *PP*; **1441** in quadam pixide in bougeis meis *Reg. Cant.* II 581; cum omnibus bonis et rebus quas secum cariare disposuit in bowgis vel manticis aut aliis quibuscumque cistis UPTON 85; **1455** cum..bogis et aliis hernesiis *Cl* 305 m. 4; **1458** pro uno pare buljearum *ExchScot* 383; **1475** T. B. *bogemaker*, ..assignavimus te ad coria et omnia alia pro bogeis, *berehides* et *clothsackes* fiendis necessaria..capienda *Pat* 535 m. 6d.

Bulgarus, ~is, Bulgarian.

s1095 ~orum fines ingrediens ad locum venit qui Belligravia nuncupatur M. PAR. *Maj.* II 49; **s1189** Huni et Alani, ~es et Pincenates *Itin. Ric.* I 21; **1223** ille..quem heretici Albigenses papam suum appellant, habitantem in finibus Bugarorum, Croatie et Dalmatie juxta Hungariorum nationem (*Lit. Ep. Portuensis*) WEND. II 272; **1237** innumerabilis plebs Rusie et regnum magne victorie Wlgarorum (*Lit. Archiep. Constantinop.*) M. PAR. *Maj.* III 460.

2 Bulgarian or Albigensian heretic.

s1236 invaluit heretica perversitas, eorum scilicet qui vulgariter dicuntur Paterini et Bugares, in partibus Transalpinis M. PAR. *Maj.* III 361 (cf. *Id. Min.* II 388: Bulgares); **s1238** ipsos..nomine vulgari Bugaros appellavit, sive essent Paterini sive Joviniani vel Albigenses vel aliis heresibus maculati *Ib.* 520; inquiri Būgăros permittit eosque peruri GARL. *Tri. Eccl.* 92.

3 usurer.

s1255 plenam habebant potestatem ipsi usurarii, quos Franci bugeros vulgariter appellant, insontes Dei famulos.. jacturis gravibus condemnare *G. S. Alb.* I 382.

bulgetta, 'budget', leather wallet.

1473 mercatores de regno Scocie..cum..caskett', fardellis, bougettis *RScot* 440a; **1484** cum comitiva sua, .. equis, salmis, valisiis, bogetis, rebus et bonis suis omnibus *Mon. Hib. & Scot.* 493b; **1499** quandam bogettam cum xx li. *Entries* 404b; **1515** ambassiatores Scotie cum..bonis, .. jocalibus, ~is, ferdellis *RScot* 582a.

bulgeum, bulgia v. bulga.

bulimalis, unnatural (of appetite).

fames est multiplex, canina et bolismalis GAD. 89 v. 2.

bulimaticus, afflicted w. unnatural appetite.

mulieri bolismatice GILB. V 207 v. 1.

bulimodes [βουλιμώδης], afflicted w. unnatural appetite.

†bolimides, qui ante cibum torquetur egrotus et post cibum cui sunt dolores indesinentes *GlC* B 161.

bulimus (βούλιμος), 'bulimy', unnatural appetite. **b** internal parasite.

si..dominum domus de quolibet excessu reprehenderit, ..a dapiferis dicitur pati bolismum, a pincernis hydropisim, a cocis febrem aut frenesim NIG. *Cur.* 158; nam canes bolismum continuum, i.e. appetitum immoderatum, patiuntur BART. ANGL. XVIII 26; bolismus, fastidium [etc.] GILB. V 206 v. 2; in canino appetitu et bolismo et fame sincopali GAD. 67. 2; bolismus est fames stomaci cum satietate membrorum..et dicitur bolismus quia a bolo satiatur *Id.* 89 v. 2; *a gredynes*, bolismus, edacitas *CathA*. **b** bulimus, vermis similis lacertae in stomacho hominis habitans *GlC* B 209.

bulingarius v. bolengarius. buljea v. bulga.

1 bulla [CL], bubble.

altius exurgens bulla resultat aquis NECKAM *DS* IV 487; aut in aqua motum lucida bulla facit GARL. *Tri. Eccl.* 31.

2 kind of plant, (?) mullein (*cf.* 2 *bullio*).

flecteria, ~a idem, G. *bayloun* [v.l. *beyllun*] *Alph.* 65.

3 stud, knob, boss.

pulchrior auratis, dum fulget fibula, bullis ALDH. *Aen.* 100. 25; †bollas, ornamenta cinguli *GlC* B 169; **9..** ~as, ornamenta cinguli, *forþgegyrdu* WW; stat super auratis virgae fabricatio bullis WULF. *Swith. prol.* 183 (cf. ib. I 1268); *a button*, fibula, nodulus, ~a; ..*a knoppe of a scho*, ~a, *CathA*.

4 round metal seal (esp. papal). **b** dist. as golden or leaden.

~a, *sigl GlC* B 197; sigillum vel ~a, *insegel* ÆLF. *Gl.*; Romani a tempore B. Gregorii ~as fuisse testati sunt et adhuc in Romana ecclesia aliqua ipsius privilegia bullata servari H. CANTOR 28; extrahens de scrinio suo septem scripta apostolica cum ~is pendentibus BRAKELOND 136; **s1229** ex una parte ~e imperialis imago regia, ..ex alia parte ~e insculpitur quedam civitas, sc. Roma; ..erat autem ~a aliquantulum major ~a pape M. PAR. *Maj.* III 176; **1247** juramentum secundum formam quam vobis sub ~a nostra mittimus interclusam *Mon. Hib. & Scot.* 47; in curiis prelatorum et principum una littera parvi valoris transit per plures manus antequam ~am recipiat aut sigillum BACON *Tert.* 57; predictorum errorum quamplurimi ..ad diversas mundi plagas sub ~a sunt transmissi OCKHAM *I. & P.* 3; istis firma datur Rome rota juris ibidem; / bullis signatur (*Vers.*) ELMH. *Cant.* 92. **b** **s1178** Willelmus rex Sicilie fieri fecit chartam Johanne regine uxori sue de dote sua sub ~a aurea TREVET 89; **1213** universitati vestre per hanc cartam aurea ~a nostra munitam volumus esse notum quod.. (*Ch. Regis*) *RChart* 195a; ex quibus patet ~am non incongrue plumbeam nostro apostolo competere Augustino ELMH. *Cant.* 122; **1445** veris ~is plumbeis more Romane curie impendentibus *Conc. Scot.* I civ (cf. *Reg. Aberd.* II 88).

5 bull, instrument under papal seal. **b** (w. *dimidia*) instrument under half-seal used by Pope before coronation. **c** instrument under imperial seal.

s1176 respondit R. Ebor. archiepiscopus quod episcopi Scotie subjectionem fecerant metropolitane ecclesie Eboraci ..et super hoc ostendit ~as *G. Hen. II* I 111 (cf. R. HOWD. II 92: super hoc privilegia Romanorum pontificum..premonstravit); notario meo, qui ~am cujus auctoritate litteras citationis..impetrare debuit amiserat GIR. *Symb.* I p. 213; **1232** instrumentum quod dominus episcopus Wigorn' ostendit contra nos, sc. ~am quandam per quam nos implacitavit *Ann. Tewk.* 89; **s1243** imperator..posuit..per mare galeas, ne ~arum portitores transmearent M. PAR. *Maj.* IV 256; **1260** si qui..cum ~is papalibus nobis aut regno nostro prejudicialibus applicuerint in portu vestro, ..ipsos cum litteris illis ibi arestari faciatis *Cl* 181; **1376** si caput ecclesie hodie concedit michi aliquid non cameraliter sed manifeste per ~as patulas WYCL. *Civ. Dom.* 387 (cf. *EHR* XXXV 566); tardantur bulle schismate stante diu ELMH. *Metr. Hen. V* 760; **1427** duos quaternos de copiis ~arum *MunAcOx* 285; **1534** episcopus Romanus qui in suis ~is pape nomen usurpat (*Ackn. of royal supremacy*) *Cart. Glam.* 1878. **b** **1294** [Papa Bonefacius] ordinavit quod xxij die ejusdem mensis deberet..coronari et sacrari, ante quod tempus nulla ~a per ipsum exivit a curia, quia statuit quod de cetero nulla ~a dimidia exeat a curia *Reg. Carl.* I 31 (cf. *Foed.* II 427 [**1289**]: cum sedes apostolica, ante consecrationem..electi in summum pontificem, cum defectiva ~a electi nomen nullatenus exprimente bullare litteras suas consuevit ab antiquo). **c** **s1193** a regis cancellario.., qui literas domini regis et ~am auream imperatoris secum detulit WEND. I 224.

2 bulla v. 2 billa 4.

bullaccus [ME], bullock.

1252 pro pastura j vacce et j ~i *DCCant H* f. 173a.

†bullainus, (?) bundle (*cf. bala*).

†a1204 de quolibet trousello pannorum..vel..pellium obolum; et, si per ~os vel per pondera advenerit, de quolibet bullinno et pondere quadrantem (*Ch.*) *Reg. Wint.* (*1282–1304*) II 742.

1 bullare, to seal with a *bulla*. **b** to provide (someone) with a bull. **c** to approve by a bull.

bullatas offert signato cortice cartas FRITH. 805 (cf. ib. 1220); **s1121** probatum est ~atas antiquitus cartas incendio..esse consumptas EADMER *HN* 347; privilegia illa perjurio..~are timuerunt H. CANTOR 28; **1164** litterarum domini pape..quas penes se ~atas esse..juraverunt J. SAL. *Ep.* 83. 70c; easdem litteras ~atas habemus bulla Eugenii pape GIR. *Inv.* II 2; **s1213** carta..regis, ..que prius cera signata fuerat nunc auro ~ata est WEND. II 95; **s1228** imperator..litteras auro ~atas Anglorum regi transmisit M. PAR. *Maj.* III 152; **s1239** asserebat..frater Helyas dominum papam..scripta..in camera sua ~are clam et sine fratrum assensu et etiam cedulas vacuas sed ~atas multas nuntiis suis tradere *Ib.* 628; **s1254** cartam domini regis Hispanie..auro ~atam *Ib.* V 450; **1248** copia.. litterarum apostolicarum in cordula canapis more Romane curie vera bulla domini nostri pape ~atarum (*Lit. Papae*) *Reg. Newbattle* 266; **s1294** invente fuerunt plures albe ~ate sine scriptura *Ann. Dunstable* 384; **1322** in ordinacione per bullam domini pape †~atam [? l. ~ata] *Reg. Aberbr.* I 203; quamvis [Papa] sermones suos nequaquam ~averit OCKHAM *Dial.* 451; **1394** quoddam previlegium..pape..filis de serico ~atum *Melrose* II 496; [littere] ad ~andum portantur PAUL. ANGL. *ASP* II 1552; *to sele*, ~are, sigillare *CathA*. **b** **s1313** veniunt legati et terram spoliant, veniunt ~ati et prebendas vendicant *V. Ed. II* 198; **1422** sit frater fratribus ipsis, / quos male dimisit, bullatus dum sibi vixit (*Vers. J. Abb. S. Alb.*) AMUND. I 88. **c** hodie quidem plus attendimus ad cartas, instrumenta vel bullas quam ad fructum operis sic ~ati WYCL. *Civ. Dom.* I 35.

2 bullare v. bullire 4.

1 bullaria, office for sealing of papal bulls.

c1423 pro bulla de jejunio: ..pro scriptore xxij flor.; item in ~ia xxij flor.; in registro viij flor. AMUND. II *app.* A 271; **c1484** quamdam porrexit supplicationem summo pontifici ipsamque..per Eugenium quartum signatam habuit; bullam tamen a ~ia non accepit, quia eam ad accipiendam nullum..opus fuit *Reg. Whet.* I *app.* D 465.

2 bullaria [< bullire], boilery, salt-house.

1285 dedimus..bulleriam [in Wychio]..salvo sale prioris Heref' quod appellatur *laghesalt Cart. Glouc.* III 223; **1298**

[salina de Wychio]cum boiller' *CalIPM* III p. 375; **1315** cum boylleria viij plumborum *Ib.* V p. 410; **1347** buleriam sex plumborum aque salse *CalPat* 336; **1397** unacum quadam salina et boilleriis quatuor plumborum aque salse in villa Wyche *Pat* 347 m. 20; **1441** Wyche: ..de firma ~ie ibidem, viz. xxix plumbariis aque salis, cum uno *saltehouse*, j *crybbe*, j *vyneyerd*, cum *lez seles* et *barowes* eidem pertinentibus *DL MinAc* 645/10461 r. 9; **1544** omnes illas xxix salinas sive plumbarias sive ~ias aque salse vocatas *fates*..alias *salthowses* alias *boylingleedes* sive *wychhowses* in Droytwiche *Pat* 738 m. 25.

bullaris, confirmed by a (papal) bull.

Deus non potest in alteracionem hujusmodi nisi conferendo graciam vel graciam subtrahendo, cui indubie ~is testificacio est inpertinens WYCL. *Civ. Dom.* I 255.

bullariter, in a (papal) bull.

si quis dicit vel ~er scribit quod sic solvit hominem vel ligat (WYCL. *Clav. Eccl.*) *Speculum* III 251.

bullarius, official affixing papal seal.

s1431 videns papa supplicacionem dictam honestam esse .., sibi signaturam imposuit, tradensque ea ~iis hanc.. bullam..scribi precepit AMUND. I 289.

bullatio v. ballatio.

bullator, official affixing papal seal.

1239 illum haberi..Christi vicarium..indigne fatemur.. quod dispensationes..[appendit] celatis fratrum consiliis, existens sibi ~or et scriptor et forsitan numerator (*Lit. Fred. Imp.*) M. PAR. *Maj.* III 586; **c1302** item in exenniis.. ~oribus xij floren. et ij Turon.; pro registro lx Turon.; pro bullis suarum litterarum supplicatoriarum j floren. *G. S. Alb.* II 57 (cf. *MonA* II 195).

bulletta, ~us [cf. OF *bullete*], leaden ball, bullet.

1550 omnia tormenta et omnes machine bellice cum omni suo apparatu, sc. pulverum, boulletorum, mortariorum.. (*DipDoc* E 1054) *Foed.* XV 213.

2 (sealed document serving as receipt for) toll etc.

1485 eum..per eadem regna [etc.] sine solutione alicujus dacii, pedagii, passagii, vectigalis, gabelle, bulectarum [etc.] ..ire..permittatis (*TreatyR*) *Foed.* XII 283.

bullettarius, official issuing *bullettae, i.e.* collecting toll etc.

1441 mandamus universis et singulis..theolonariis, tributariis, boletariis, ..quatinus..ambassatores..venire.. permittatis (*Lit. Imp.*) BEKYNTON II 102; **1471** rex..gabellatoribus, custumariis, scrutatoribus, bulletariis, theolonariis (*Pat*) *Foed.* XI 727; **1484** ancianis, gubernatoribus, presidibus, judicibus, theolonеariis, tributariis, boletariis, passuum custodibus.. (*Lit. Imp.*) *Ib.* XII 210.

bulliare v. bullire. bulliatio v. bullitio c. bulliator v. bullitor.

bullifer, adorned with studs.

baltheus ~er..ac diversa ornamentorum gloria ALDH. *VirgP* 9; **9..** ~fer, *bulberende*, ..*æstæned* WW.

bullinnus v. bullainus. 1 bullio, bulliona v. 1 billio.

2 bullio [cf. 2 bulla 2], kind of plant, (?) mullein (Fr. *bouillon-blanc*).

si consolide medie et ~onis manipulum teras et cum vino des succum bibere, si vomat, morietur, si non, vivet GILB. II 87.2.

3 bullio [cf. 2 bulla 3], stud, boss.

1475 in iiij paria claps' pro libris, ij s.; et in bilonibus ad idem, vj d. *Ac. Churchw. Sal.* 17; **1484** pro ~onibus de cupro ad imponendum super libros ecclesie *Ib.* 36.

4 bullio [cf. OF *boillon*], boiling (measure of **a** salt; **b** alum; **c** almonds).

a istae octo praedictae salinae regis et comitis in ipsa ebdomada qua bulliebant et exercebantur in die Veneris reddebant xvj ~ones, ex quibus xv faciebant unam summam salis *DB* I (*Chesh*) 268; **1216** de misericordia judicum de Wich [? de] triginta bullonibus salis *Cart. Chester* 106; **1280** in Northwico..iiij ~ones [salis] *CalIPM* II 360; **1297** tenuit..viij^{xx} boilones salis in Medio Wico *del hordurnesalt IPM* 79/7; **a1315** donationem..de iiij summis salis continentibus xl bullones pro dimidia salina sua (*Ch. Wombridge*) *MonA* VI 391. **b 1292** de quolibet ~one de alume iiij d. *CoramR* 129 r. 15*d*. **c 1224** unum buillonem amigdalarum *Cl* 587a; **1234** retineri faciat ad opus regis..viij ~ones amigdalarum *Cl* 381; **1237** vj boillones amigdalarum *Ib.* 424; **1242** pro xxviij buillonis amigdalarum xvj l. vij s. iij d. *RGasc* I 31; **1258** duos bolliones amigdalorum *Cl* 186; **1307** in..carectis cariantibus xij boillon' amigd'..*KRAc* 368/30 m. 7.

bullire [CL], **~iare,** to boil (intr.). **b** to foam. **c** to swarm (fig.). **d** (pr. ppl.) frothy (fig.).

bullantes, aquae cum exundant *GlC* B 221; cum Aetnaei montis incendia..~irent ALDH. *VirgP* 41; **716** igneum piceumque flumen ~iens et ardens BONIF. *Ep.* 10 p. 11; si aque ~ienti et calidissime aqua tepida..addatur ADEL. *QN* 34; **1189** pix ~iens super caput ejus effundatur (*Ch. Ric. I*) R. HOWD. III 36; sufficit ut..buliat quousque humiditas evaporet M. SCOT. *Lumen* 264; **s1237** brodium calidum de callidariis ~ientibus WYKES 84; **1363** per aquam ~iantem existentem in quadam olla enea *SelCCoron* 39; **1478** pro factura j thrye pro aqua bullente *Ac. Churchw. Bath* (XXV) 78 **b** cum bulliret brumalibus / undosus vortex fluctibus *Carm. Aldh.* I 105. **c** qua..forte cadaver / turpiter introrsum bulliret vermibus atris ALDH. *VirgV* 1400. **d** afferat [viator] inde [ab India] ~ientes nugas et impudentissima mendacia LUCIAN *Chester* 59.

2 to boil (trans.) **a** food; **b** salt (*v. et.* 4 *bullio* a); **c** wool; **d** leather (*v. et. corium*); **e** criminals.

a sal, piper, epar.. / sint contrita simul bullitaque D. BEC. 2655; decoctione herbarum ~itarum GILB. I 18. 1. **b 1252** habuerunt salsam suam in villa regis del Wych' et sal suum ~ire consueverunt *Cl* 148; **1316** si bondus domini ~iat [sc. sal] extra villam in aliquo marisco, dabit domino j modium salis *Terr. Fleet* 83. **c** warenciavit et ~ivit in aluma lanam *Rec. Leic.* I 102. **d 1303** pro uno coffino de corio ~ito *KRAc* 363/18 f. 11. **e 1308** R. H. post ultimas assisas convictus de falsa moneta ~itus fuit per judicium (*JustIt*) *S. Jers.* XVIII p. 255.

3 to melt (trans.).

aurum bullitum bibit illic Crassus GARL. *Tri. Eccl.* 141.

4 (?) to undergo secondary fermentation.

1305 de ij doleis vini de prisa capta anno quarto postea bullatis et venditis: ..et memorandum quod justiciarius et alii boni homines de patria habuerunt vina veniencia in eadem navi que singula fere bulliarunt et plura eorum..corrumpebantur *MinAc W. Wales* I 388; **1387** de quarto doleo vini rubei Vascon' nichil, quia rem[anens] bulliat' et nichil inde potuit habere *MinAc* 819/2, m. 6.

bullitio, a boiling. **b** measure of salt (= 4 *bullio a*). **c** melting down. **d** bubble, froth. **e** yeast.

a aqua..frigida permansit, nec..maximo igne supposito ad ~onem vel calefactionem movebatur *NLA* (*Bernac*) I 116. **b** salinae..non dabant has ~ones in die Veneris *DB* I (*Chesh*) 268 (cf. ib.: dabant omnes consuetudines ~onis). **c 1508** pro bulliacione unius cisterne *Ac. Durh.* 660. **d 1462** dum fuerit [cervisia]..plena ~onibus ventosis *MunAcOx* 695. **e** bullicio, A. *berme* WW.

bullitor, ~iator, boiler (of salt), 'weller'.

1316 si bondus domini bulliat infra villam bulliatorum ejus, ..dabit domino pro qualibet patella dimidium modium salis, et hujusmodi [? modii] vocantur *welleresmedes Terr. Fleet* 83.

bullitura, liquid (? bran-water) used in dyeing.

1259 ceperunt lanam tinctam in wayda et eam posuerunt ..in bultura ad colorem ejusdem lane faciendum nigriorem *Rec. Leic.* I 84 (cf. *Rec. Northampton* 229: *boyltur of wode*).

bullitus, boiling (sb.).

si aqua [v.l. aquae judicium] sit, calefiat donec excitetur ad ~um [AS: *to wylme*] (*Quad.*) *GAS* 386.

bullo v. 4 bullio. bullus v. bulus.

bulmago [cf. It. *bulimaca*], rest-harrow (*Ononis*).

~o, resta bovis, vel retinens boves idem, G. *restebeof*, A. *cammok* vel *ysenherde Alph.* 25.

bulso v. 1 buzo. bult- v. et. bulet-. bultellaria v. butellaria. bultura v. bullitura.

bulus, ~a [OF *boul* < betulla (Gall.)], birch. **b** (?) birchen (adj.).

1215 duo summagia..de ~o et alno et fraxino et salice et arabili *Cl* 220; **c1215** habeant in bosco suo..buul' ad domos suas ornandas in Nativitate B. J. Baptiste *BBC* (*Corbridge*) 57; **1245** hominibus regis de Pecco, quorum domus combuste sunt, faciat..succursum maeremii de alno et bull' *Cl* 310; **1271** distringantur..pro ~is quas ceperunt in..bosco *CourtR Hales* 25; **1289** cheverones de boul' ad scaffotas *KRAc* 479/15 r. 3; **1292** boulas *CalIMisc* I p. 445; **1305** illius sagitte sunt de boulo *PlRChester* 17 r. 13; **1326** cum ramis ~orum cindendis pro aula et cameris reparandis *ExchScot* 58; **1375** tres quercus et alias arbores quamplurimas, viz. corulos, bolos et spinas, ..succiderunt *IMisc* 205/15. **b 12..** habet ligna salic', alnea, ~a, salcea (*sic*) et totas cablices et branchia *Ib.* 20/14.

bulwarka [ME], bulwark.

unum forte fortalicium quod nos *barbican* seu *bulwerke* appellamus ELMH. *Hen. V* 17; **1573** officium custodis et capitanei..wallorum et ~arum nostrarum vocatarum Chatertons Bulwarke [etc., *Hants*] *Pat* 1099 m. 23.

bumasta, ~us [βούμαστος], kind of vine.

~e, uva in similitudinem mammae *GlC* B 214; est in Rhodano castrum Rocamaure; ..in hujus castri territorio sunt botri quos †brumestas vulgus nominat, grossiores acinos habentes; hi botri florent ut vinee, producunt racemos et spem sui cultoris eludunt; cum enim ad festum S. J. Baptiste perventum fuerit, ..nihil in illis quod ad fructum faciat reperitur GERV. TILB. III 102; *vyny that bryngyth forth grete grapys*, ~a *PP*; hic bubastus est vitis vel uva in agro WW.

bumb- v. bomb-. buna v. 2 bunda.

buncha [ME *bonche*], bunch (measure of garlic).

1421 pro dim. c bonchis allei *EEC.* 503; **1440** pro xc ~is allei *Port Bk. Southampton* 9.

1 bunda [cf. buncha], measure of garlic.

1393 de qualibet ~a allei venal' unum quadrantem *Pat* 337 m. 7.

2 bunda, ~us [OF *bodne, bone*], bound, boundary. **b** boundary-mark, landmark. **c** boundary-strip.

loca infra ~as duodecim hidarum contenta W. MALM. *Glast.* 110 (cf. *MonA* I 23); **1221** eis liberavit illam moram per ~as et per metas *PlCrGlouc* 81; **1229** inter predicta xxx feoda..et..xx feoda..certas metas et ~as fieri faciatis *Cl* 197; **1235** v carucatas terre..distincte, discrete et aperte et per..certas divisas, metas, terminos et ~os eis assignari facias *Cl* 74; si mete et bonde burgi bene et fideliter circumquaque custodiantur *Iter Cam.* 28; **c1300** predicte mete et bounde *Reg. Malm.* II 402; **1337** filum aque illius est buna inter Ruggeleye et Colton *JustIt* (*Staffs*) 1413 r. 7*d.*; **1428** prout per metas et ~as ibidem..ponendas plenius poterit apparere *Rec. Leic.* II 237; **1473** de warda de Tweda: ..de exitibus Curie Bondarum [*Bound Court*] *ExchScot* 140 (cf. ib. 211). **b** inde versus orientem usque ad *la brutasche*, quam posuimus primam ~am xij hidarum W. MALM. *Glast.* 108; **1275** (v. bundare); **1289** quia subtraxit quandam ~am positam inter ipsum et J. de F. *Leet Norw.* 22; **1353** a..~o ligneo fixo inter cimeterium..et clausum..usque ad alium ~um ligneum fixum super regiam stratam *Lit. Cant.* II 312–13. **c 12..** dimidiam acram super bonam que jacet inter terram que fuit Hugonis..et terram Simonis *Reg. Winchcombe* I 115; **1278** plantavit arbores injuste super unam ~am *SelPlMan* 92; **1301** male arravit unam ~am inter tenementum domini et suum tenementum *CourtR Hales* 411.

2 mark, target.

1282 tulit unum arcum in manu sua cum uno *pylat* et arcussit ad unam ~am juxta quemdam murum *IMisc* 41/19.

3 unit of width (of cloth).

1346 nulla draperia fiat nisi habeat sex ~as in latitudine *Little RB Bristol* II 2.

4 (*s. dub.*).

1300 nullus capiat plus pro labore mensurandi et cariandi quam ex antiqua consuetudine capi solebat et pro eisdem †~as (*Inq.*) *MGL* I 243.

bundagium v. bondagium.

bundare, ~iare, to bound, delimit.

c1250 ita quod..via ex utraque parte..~ata habeat.. latitudinem xxx pedum inter bundas *Cart. Wardon* 145; **1275** preceptum fuit..xij liberis hominibus ut bund[arent] quandam viam regalem..; et †tum [l. cum] ibi venerunt ad hoc faciendum, dictus B. abrad[icavit] dictos bundos per illos appositos *Hund.* I 511; **1278** est warenna sic ~ata.. (*Compositio*) *Reg. Wint. 1282–1304* 652; **1281** potest..dicta ecclesia..dictum nemus seu nemoris pechiam bonare seu limitare *Pat* 100 m. 22; senescallus Glastonie, qui predictam moram ~iare deberet et vexilla sua in bundis predictis apponeret in signum bunde DOMERH. *Glast.* 487; **1349** sicut terre et pasture ille..per certas metas ~antur et limitantur *IPM* 106/4; **1512** terre..boundate et limitate (*Reg. Glasg.*) *Scot. Grey Friars* II 246; **1586** acris..bondatis *Reg. Brechin app.* 353.

2 to border, edge; *cf.* 2 *bordare* 2 or (?) *broudare*.

1205 sandalia et sotulares de..samitto bondatos de orfreis *Pat* 55a.

bundatio, fixing the bounds, delimitation.

1324 carta regis Johannis de ~one foreste Essex' *TRForest Proc.* 16 r. 1; **c1400** pro ~one dicte terre..jurati..dicunt.. (*Reg. Wetheral*) *MonA* III 598; **1508** (v. bundator); **1599** bundavit unam peciam terre vaste legalibus ~onibus *Rec. Stan.* 68.

bundator, 'bounder', tenant of 'bound' (i.e. claim) in stannary.

1508 stannatoribus, ~oribus sive possessoribus operum stanni..qui non introduxerunt..nomina novorum possessorum..alicujus operis stanni de novo bundati..in proxima curia stannar' post bundacionem *Pat* 605 m. 29; **1613** dicti anguli debent esse renovati infra xij menses, aliter esse vacantes si sic fuerint capti per novum ~orem *Rec. Stan.* 59.

bundellus, ~a [ME], **a** bundle of documents, packet (*cf.* 1 *botellus b, bungellus*). **b** bundle (of arrows, twigs, or sim.).

a 1340 omnia..rotuli, ~e et memoranda..que..in.. Turri remanserunt, viz. in xviij bagis de canevace et uno saculo de corio (*Cl*) *Foed.* V 217; **1362** per Bagas de Secretis in ~o de Dynelay et alibi (*KB ControlmentR*) *EHR* XXIII 514; **1443** cum appareat..vos unum ~um in quo erant instrucciones regie..recepisse BEKYNTON I 186. **b 1300** xx bundill' scalon' *MinAc Essex* (*Birdbrook*); **1405** xl arcus, ciiij ~os de *bykeryngtakell* (*Pat*) *Foed.* VIII 384; **1421** pro ij bondellis sarrarum *EEC* 500; **1462** lxx ~os lini vocati *Holandflax* (*KRMem*) *Bronnen* 1522; **c1530** pro lx bundelis *osyers EEC* 195.

bundiare v. bundare.

bundonare [cf. OF *bondon*], to bung.

1228 pro predictis xxx et vij doleis vini cariandis et carcandis et..pro eisdem doleis barrandis et ~andis *Liberate* 7 m. 9; **1237** pro vinis cerclandis, barrandis, bondon[andis] et cariandis *Ib.* 11 m. 4.

bundura, boundary.

1282 forestarii capiunt coperones lignorum liberatorum mineariis ad bonduram minearum et faciunt inde comodum suum *TR Forest Proc.* 31 m. 17.

bundus v. 2 bunda. buneter' v. buletarium.

†bungellus, (?) bundle (*cf. bundellus, bungus*).

s1330 tandem invenerunt eum [sc. monachum] in ~o canapis medio †cautulose involutum THORNE 2056.

bungus [cf. OF *bonge*], (?) faggot.

in ~is faciendis iiij d. *Ac. Beaulieu* 75 v.

†**bunia** [? cf. 1 bunnum *or* bothonia], bushel or butt.

~ia, *byden GlC* B 228.

bunias [βουνίας], kind of turnip.

~ias, napicium, rapia idem, que elixa comeditur *Alph.* 24.

1 bunnum [ME *bune*], pipe, barrel.

1470 pro iij ~is de *beere* datis domino regi *Ac. Chamb. Cant.* 142.

2 bunnum [? cf. bugo], (?) tree-stump.

1452 tot robora et ~a quot pro vestura locum tenentis et forestariorum sufficere poterunt *Cart. Boarstall* 604.

buntinga [ME], bunting.

secundus passer magnus auctuario dicitur..: hunc Anglorum ~am..esse suspicor Turner *Av.* 71.

bunulus v. bimulus.

buphagon [βουφάγον], appetizer.

†butacon, corroborativum stomachi *Alph.* 25.

buphthalmon [βούφθαλμον], ox-eye (bot.).

10.. nomina herbarum:..bucstalmum, *hwit mægeðe* WW; butalmon vel butalmos, oculus bovis idem, A. *oxie Alph.* 24.

buprestis [βούπρηστις], kind of insect.

de nominibus insectorum:..~is, *twinwyrm* Ælf. *Gl.*; est, inquit [Plinius], animal parvulum simile scarabeo nomine †burestis Bart. Angl. XVIII 12; *byttyl, wyrme*, †buboscus *PP.*

buralis v. burralis. burallus v. burellus.

burarium [cf. butyrarium], (?) bowl of butter (Fr. *beurrier*).

1292 pro vivo argento et bureris [(?) *for use as sheep-salve*] *Sacr. Ely* II 7 (cf. ib. 18: pro ollis vivo argento et borreis emptis); **c1300** burar' v precii vij d. ob. *DCCant* J 27.

burata, (?) bowl of butter.

1200 pro d caseis et c et xx ~is, ix li. *Pipe* 243.

buratus v. birratus

burbilia (pl.), umbles (numbles), entrails (of deer).

nowmelys of a beest, ..burbalia..vel burbia *PP*; burbilium, A. *nombles*, ..hoc burburium, *owmlys*, ..hoc burbulum, A. *a umblye* WW; *þe nownbils of a dere*, ~ia, pepinum *CathA*; **1494** ambos humeros et barbillas cujusdam ferine.., que barbille proprie *nowmylles* vocantur *Pickering* I 150.

burbium v. suburbium.

burbutis [OF *borbote*], burbot (fish).

a1275 ad gurgites..innumerabiles anguille irretiuntur.., percide, rocee, ~es et †murenas *Lib. Eli.* II 105.

burcerus, ~ius v. bursarius. burcida v. bursicida. 1 burda v. borda.

2 burda [OF *borde*], jest.

index auctoris:..ridiculum vel ~a *Eul. Hist.* III 326 (cf. ib. I 235).

1 burdare v. 2 bordare 1.

2 burdare, ~iare [OF *behorder* < Frk.], to joust.

1234 inhibens..ne..buhurdare vel torneare presumant (*Pat*) *Foed.* I 332; **1242** clamari faciant..quod nulli conveniant ad turneandum vel ad ~iandum vel ad alias quascumque aventuras *Cl* 483 (cf. M. Par. *Maj.* VI 209: ad ~andum); **1299** ne quis miles armiger vel alius quicunque ..torneare, bordeare seu justas facere..presumat (*Cl*) *Foed.* (ed. 1816) I 916; **1341** turneare, ~eare, justas facere (*Cl*) *Foed.* V 223; **1353** quod nullus poterit turneare, ~are.. *Cal. LB Lond.* G 7 (= *MGL* I 629).

3 burdare [OF *border*], to jest.

s1342 erat [Benedictus XII] humillimus et affabilis ac cum omnibus ~ans *Meaux* III 39; **s1377** in tantum..erat [W. abbas Leicestrie] affabilis domino regi quod ~ando petebat a rege nundinas sibi concedi pro leporariis et canibus ..emendis Knighton II 127; **s1405** mihi ~ando dicere solebat: "ad fratres tuos vade habitumque tuum resume" Ad. Usk 100.

burdatio, jest.

parabole salvatoris erant narracio veridica rei geste, cum dominus veritatis non indiguit mendicare fabulas vel jocose mentiri ad populum edocendum; in exhortacionibus quidem debet ~o, sicut et falsitas, precipue semoveri Wycl. *Civ. Dom.* I 8.

Bardegalensis, coin of Bordeaux.

1242 xv solidos ~ium *RGasc* I 108; **1253** denarios regis.. tam sterlingorum quam ~ium *Ib.* 357; **1312** ad x s. Burd[egalensium] bonorum, quorum quinque valent unum sterling' *Ib.* IV *app.* p. 564; computato..pro v bonis Burd' per se et pro vj Burd' debilibus per se uno denario sterlingorum *Ib.* 573.

†**burdegalium** [? *for* bordelagium], small holding (*cf. bordellum*).

omnia bona, hereditates, terras, dominia, hospicia, ~ia (*sic* MS.), vineas.. (*RGasc* 121 m. 4) *Foed.* X 363.

burdeicium, ~ea [OF *behordeiz*], 'bourdis', joust, tournament.

1226 appellavit M. ..de placito pacis regis infracte in buhurdicio *CurR* XII 2247; **1234** quoddam buhurdicium captum est inter armigeros, qui pro buhurdicio illo..convenerint (*Pat*) *Foed.* I 332; **1280** congressum quendam..ad modum justarum et ~ii inter se facere proponunt *Cl* 97 m. 9; **s1288** condixerunt adinvicem quidam armigeri ut in habitu religiosorum quoddam hastiludium, quod *burdice* dicitur, ..celebrarent Guisb. 224; **1299** nolumus quod torneamenta, burdicie vel juste alique..fiant quamdiu guerra duraverit (*Cl*) *Foed.* (ed. 1816) I 916; **1306** ne quis torneamenta, justas seu ~eas facere seu alia hastiludia exercere presumat (*Cl*) *Foed.* II 981.

burdellum v. bordellum.

burdenum [ME], 'burden' (measure of: **a** steel; **b** fish; **c** moss).

a 1326 reddit compotum de ij barellis asceri, barello continente xx burth', quolibet continente xxx gadd' *Pipe* 171 r. 38. **b 1472** xiij burden' piscis salsi valent xliij s. iiij d. *KRCustAc.* 19/8 f. 5. **c 1536** de v d. pro burdinis masii *Ac. Churchw. Bath* 113.

burdicia, ~ium v. burdeicium, hurdicium.

burdinarius [? cf. 1 burdo], (?) castrated he-goat.

1340 liberarunt..lxiij agnos ultimi exitus, x bordinar', iiij haveros, lxv capras *MinAc* (*Brill, Bucks*) 1120/10 r. 6; **1341** de vj bordinar' receptis per indenturam et de iiij receptis de adjunccione haderell' anni precedentis remanent' *Ib.* 11 r. 6*d.*; **1343** [respondet] de j capro burdinar', lv capris, xviij haderell' et xxiij hadell' *Ib.* 12 r. 4 (4)*d.*

burdiwa [? cf. bordellum 1], tenement (Gasc.).

1253 vina pertinentia ad ~am Gaillardi de Solar' *Cl* 168 (= *RGasc* I 35).

1 burdo [LL], 'burdon', mule (offspring of stallion and she-ass).

prospectisque domum burdonibus ire cupivit Wulf. *Swith.* I 502; ~o, *hors of steden* vel *of asrenne* Ælf. *Gl.*; rusticus..habeat..multones, †ciciros [l. tityros] et ~ones Neckam *Ut.* 112; ~ones vel asini hunc liberius permeant callem Ad. Eyns. *Hug.* V 14 p. 164; nec mulus Yspanie nec destrarius Apulie nec †buredo Ethiopie..hoc asino nostro apcior Anglie..invenitur Ric. Armagh *Serm.* 79 p. 37; hic ~o, i. genitum inter equum et asinam WW; *a mule*, ~o, mulus, mula *CathA.*

2 burdo, ~onus [OF *bordon*], iron-shod staff. **b** ceremonial staff or rod of office.

Brianus..fecit sibi baculum ferreum et acutum; ..nec mora, cum aditum percutiendi habuisset, erexit ~onem, quem supra dixi, infixitque magum sub pectore atque eodem ictu interfecit G. Mon. XII 7. **b 1365** indulgemus ut tu et..successores tui [priores Wigornie] in episcopi Wigorniensis..absencia mitra..et chirothecis episcopalibus ac bordono argenteo botonum argenteum habente in capite ..uti..valeatis (*Lit. Papae*) *Conc.* III 201.

3 burdo [OF *bordon*], buzzing insect, (?) drone-fly.

atticus vel ~o, *dora* Ælf. *Gl.*; fucos, burdones, scarabeos, papiliones R. Cant. *Malch.* IV 111; **s1169** aperto mulieris sepulcro in Anglia, examen muscarum et ~onum fetidissimum est repertum R. Niger *Chr.* II 166; quando venit ~o vel vespa sonitum faciens, aranea in foramen suum fugit O. Cheriton *Fab.* 48B; qui quasi burdones [*gl.*: equi innaturales, *as if* 1 burdo] vivunt et gurguliones Garl. *Mor. Scol.* 404.

2 bourdon, drone, bass-stop of organ.

s1235 [abbas] presentetur Deo..ad majus altare pulsato classico, sonantibus chalamis, quos ~ones appellamus, cum horologio *G. S. Alb.* I *app.* D 520 (cf. *MonA* II 193).

burdura v. bordura 2.

burdus [cf. 1 burdo], baggage animal.

~us, *seamere* Ælf. *Gl.*

†**bureale,** *s. dub.* (? cf. burellus).

in festo S. Andree xv ~ia pro xv fratribus vel iiij s. *Cust. Cant.* I 196.

burelegius v. birelagius.

burellarius, maker of 'burel'.

1250..Pagano le Suwur et..sociis suis burelar' London' c et lv li. pro pannis ad elemosinam emptis *Liberate* 27 m. 17; **c1295** civi et burillario ipsius civitatis [London'] *AncD* A 1943; **1305** Ivoni de Wyttele, burlario *Cal. LB Lond.* B 154; **1321** si inveniatur defectus de filo vel textura, ..~ius qui fecit filum illud ibi debet amerciari ad dim. m. *MGL* II 420 (cf. *PQW* 466a); **1335** breve pro telariis Londoniarum..et contra ~ios *Ib.* I 724 (cf. *Cal. LB Lond.* E 291).

burellator, maker of 'burel'.

1298 custos et vicecomites venire fecerunt tinctores, ~ores, textores et fullones ad ordinandum..officium fullonum *MGL* II 128.

burellatus, *s. dub.* (N.B. Ref. to *pannus burillatus* in Strype's *London* (II v. 10) appears to be an error).

1235 j pannus de serico tenuissim[o] burellat' et scacciat' †tenuem de ij ulnis *Chanc. Misc.* 3/4; **1245** manipulus de panno serico nigro ~o (*Invent. S. Paul.*) *Arch.* L 488.

burellus [OF *burel*; cf. burra], 'burel', coarse woollen cloth.

1172 pro mm ulnis de burell' missis in Hiberniam *Pipe* 84; **c1177** pro trossello ~orum j d. (*Cust. Brissac*) *Act. Hen. II* II 56; **1198** abscissit ei tunicam et pallium de ~o *CurR* I 39; **1218** civibus nostris London' respectum dedimus de assisa ~orum suorum *Pat* 155; **1224** cum xiij peciis de ~o et una de viridi et xij de *bleu Cl* 625b; **1225** mercatores qui in ipsis [nundinis S. Ivonis] habuerint ~os ad vendendum secure.. eos vendant.., non obstante eo quod ~i illi non sunt de assisa *Cl* 25a; **1225** concessimus probis hominibus London' qui ~os fieri faciunt vel vendunt quod..non sint..vexati de ~is suis vendendis vel emendis, ita..quod minorem latitudinem non habeant quam ante constitutionem, [de russettis etc.] habuerunt *Pat* 523; **1236** pro cxxxiiij ulnis de ~o de ultra mare et c et iij ulnis de Toteneys et vili ~o *Pipe* 81 r. 13; "domina, ..date illi iiij ulnas [tele linee]..ad sudarium." at illa indignans ait: "sufficiunt ei tres ulne de borello" *Latin Stories* 10; **c1250** monachi dederunt michi tantum unde potui michi emere tunicam et mantellum de ~o *Cart. Glam.* 581; **s1269** ne..aliquod pannum adducerent in Angliam nisi essent de predicta longitudine et latitudine, exceptis ~is Normannie *Leg. Ant. Lond.* 125; **s1282** sacrista habuit capam ejus de ~o pal' *Ann. Worc.* 485; **p1272** antequam P. de Rupibus appropriavit sibi suburbium Winton', .. suburbanii qui operabantur ~os solebant reddere pro utensili suo v s. per annum (*Inq.*) *Arch. J.* VII 374; **c1292** de quibus..rex deberet habere de quolibet ministerio [i.e. *loom*] magno ~orum per annum v s. et de ministerio chalonum duplicium xij d. (*Inq.*) *Reg. Wint.* II 721. **1311** in iij ulnis et dim. de burallo empt' pro puero de botelar' *Ac. Durh.* 506; **1339** in iiij ulnis ~i scacciati *Ib.* 536; **a1380** faciet dominus N. de Bellocampo..pannum virgulatum sive ~um prosterni sub pedibus regis *Lib. Regal.* 3.

burestis v. buprestis. buretellus v. buletellus.

buretta [OF *buirete*], 'burette', cruet.

1435 legavit..unam crucem argenteam deauratam cum buretis *Reg. Cant.* II 586.

burga v. borga, burgus. burgabulum v. brugabulum.

burgagensis, burgage tenant (Ir.).

c1365 si essent ~es, deberent facere domino in omnibus ut ~es Kylmaclenyn *Pipe Cloyne* 26.

burgageria, area of burgage tenure or (?) burgage rent, (?) town land (Ir.); *cf.* 2 *burgaria b.*

1230 pro..animalibus..omnium in dicta villa et ~ia ejusdem habitancium *BBC* (*Cashel*) 71; **c1294** burgenses de Kynsales tenent in †burgaregiis suis tres carucatas terre et reddunt inde per annum viij li. xvij s. xj d. *IPM* 66/10; **1303** iiij burgagia..reddunt ~ie ij s. iiij d. per annum *RB Ormond* 50; **1333** est apud Dum [*Down*] quedam villa burg' cujus burg[enses] reddunt per annum..pro ~iis suis xl s. *IPM* 36/19; sunt apud Halywode iiij^{xx} acre terre in manibus burgensium, qui eas tenent in feodo tanquam ~iis suis †anexis [l. annexas] *Ib.* 20; **1496** habeant..jurisdiccionem.. infra villam predictam [*Youghal*] et suburbia ejusdem et infra ~iam dicte ville et libertates ejusdem *Pat* 579 m. 9.

1 burgagium, burglary.

1294 pro homicidiis, roberiis et ~iis domorum *RGasc* III 197; **1330** captus est..pro ~io shope ipsius Willelmi.. noctanter *Gaol Del.* 44 r. 3.

2 burgagium, ~ia [cf. OF *borgage*], burgage: **a** status of a burgess or right to hold land according to the custom of a borough (usu. freehold on payment of rent, w. right to alienate); **b** area within which borough custom applies; **c** tenement held according to borough custom.

a a1135 sciatis me concessisse..hominibus de Beverlaco liberum ~ium secundum liberas leges et consuetudines burgensium de Eboraco..cum omnibus liberis consuetudinibus et libertatibus suis *BBC* (*Beverley*) 23 (cf. ib. 24 [**c1154**]: liberale ~ium); **a1173** ita quod burgenses ejus in Heddune libere et quiete in libero ~io teneant sicut burgenses mei de Eboraco *Ib.* (*Hedon*) 38; **1171** concessisse..burgensibus de Maudon..tenementa sua que tenentur de me infra burgum et extra usque ad terminos banleucarum..per servitium liberi ~ii *Ib.* (*Maldon*) 39; **c1180** concessisse..Wytebyam in liberam ~iam et burgensibus ibidem manentibus libertatem ~ie et leges liberas liberaque jura *Ib.* (*Whitby*) 39; **1188** concessi..eis omnes tenuras suas infra muros et extra..tenendas in liberum ~ium, sc. per servicium landgabuli quod reddunt infra muros *Ib.* (*Bristol*) 40; **1194** ~ia..habenda et tenenda hereditarie in libero ~io de me (*Ch. Drogheda*) *EHR* XV 311; nos ab omni servitio..et aliis consuetudinibus ad dictam terram in [Ravenser] Odd..secundum consuetudinem ~ie pertinentibus..liberavit *Meaux* II 30; **s1394** quod possemus adquirere..tenementa [in Cantuaria]..tam ea que de ipso rege tenentur ut in libero ~io quam ea que sunt de feodo abbacie aut alieno, exceptis eis que de rege tenentur in capite per servicium militare Thorne 2197. **b a1135** si quis terram in ~io [v.l. in burgo] uno anno et una die juste et sine calumnia tenuerit, non respondeat calumnianti *BBC* (*Newcastle upon Tyne*) 71; **c1151** illud toftum quod fuit J. Capellani in ~io extra murum de Rogesburgh *E. Ch. Scot.* 241 (cf. *Reg. Dunferm.* 46); **1167** vicecomes reddit compotum..de exitu terre de ~io de Brug' [*Bridgnorth*] *Pipe* 63; habet..iij acras et dim. de ~io, unde solvit vj s. et dim. [*Wycombe, Bucks*] *RDomin* 37; **1242** de redditibus ~ii de Clune *Pipe* 8; **c1300** infra ~ium predictum [*Nether Weare, Som*] (*Pat*) *EHR* XV 309. **c a1147** addo.. viginti et unam acram terre..juxta villam de Kenefec [*Cynfig, Glam*] cum uno ~io in vico occidentali *Cart. Glouc.* II 135; **a1165** libertates quas episcopi Lincolnienses habuerunt in terra sua Lincolnie et in ~io suo tempore regis H.

avi mei *CalCh* IV 142; a1183 quod burgenses..tenerent ~ia sua..per liberum servicium, viz. quilibet eorum unum ~ium tenens illud per servicium xij d. per annum [teneret] *BBC* (*Tewkesbury*) 47 (cf. *CalCh* IV 425); a1184 si burgensis vult discedere et vendit ~ium suum et domum suam, det iij d. theolonario *Ib.* (*Swansea*) 65 (cf. ib. 67); 1198 omnes canonici [S. Thome, Dublin'] habeant unum ~ium liberum ..ab omnibus consuetudinibus et tallagiis et omnibus demandis preter langabulum *CalCh* II 387; 1201 David Tinctor dat domino regi j m. per sic quod masuagium suum quod habet in Carleolo sit ~ium et quod ipse habeat easdem libertates quas alii burgenses Carleoli habent *ROblat* 116; 1234 seisinam..de dimidio ~io *Cl* 470; 1242 de placito unius mesuagii et duorum borgagiorum *CurR* 123 r. 13; 1261 unum ~ium et unam seldam cum pertinenciis in burgo de Farham [*Hants*] *Cl* 395; 1263 si..contingat aliquod ~ium vacuum vel vastum esse (*Ch. Agardesley*) *EHR* XVI 335; quilibet dabit domino regi pro ~io suo quod defendit pro perticata terre v d. annuatim *Leg. IV Burg.* 1 (cf. ib. 41); 1275 habeant..decimas de ..~iis aratro cultis tocius parochie *Reg. Heref.* 44; 1291 non comparuerunt ad ~ia sua reedificanda (*Ch. Haverford*) *EHR* XV 518; 13.. burgensis non potest esse nisi habeat ~ium xij pedum in fronte (*Cust. Preston*) *Ib.* 497; 1372 concessi cuilibet burgensi ejusdem burgi unam rodam terre pro ~io suo (*Ch. Roby*) *Ib.* XVII 295; 1343 dicit quod illa que vocantur sic ~ia non sunt nisi mesuagia que tenebantur..ut de manerio predicto secundum consuetudinem manerii predicti *Cart. Ciren.* I 130 (cf. ib.: compertum est quod ibidem est burgus et per hoc bene liquet quod omnia tenementa in eodem burgo existencia sunt ~ia); 1344 omnia tenementa [in London'] ..tenentur de domino rege in capite ut liberum ~ium ad feodi firmam *MGL* I 191; 1430 R. H. burgensis de Hertilpole tenet ibidem ad firmam j ~ium..in Suthgate..et reddit inde ad scaccarium prioris Dunelm' per annum iij s. iiij d. *Feod. Durh.* 24.

burgagius, a held in burgage. **b** pertaining to a burgage (Scot.).

a 1396 redditum..de illa terra ~ia quam tenet ad feodofirmam..infra burgum de Aberden *Reg. Aberd.* II 293. **b** 1552 salvis..regibus..Scotie servitiis ~iis de dicta terra debitis (*Ch. Aberd.*) *Scot. Grey Friars* II 233.

burgalis, burghal (pertaining to: **a** a borough; **b** (Scot.) a burgh.)

a a1138 quicunque habet in villa S. Edmundi maisuras de ~i terra pro singulis maisuris dabit..singulos obolos *BBC* 46; a1155 solutas ab omni consuetudine ~i et alia *Ch. Heref.* 29; s1275 remanente villa [*Norwich*] quoad libertatum ~ium privationem in eo statu quo fuit Oxnead *Chr.* 247. **b** 1391 exitus dicti burgi..per firmam ~em et parvam custumam *ExchScot* 261; 1450 firmas ~es dicti burgi *Reg. Dunferm.* 432.

2 (sb. pl.) burghal farms (Scot.).

1468 deliberavit..de annuis ~ibus de hoc anno iij li. *ExchScot* 597.

burganizatio v. barganizatio.

burgare, ~iare [cf. OF *burgier*], to burgle, break into (a building). **b** (absol.). **c** to rob (a person) burglariously. **d** to steal (goods) burglariously.

c1200 pallium et napam que..dicit sibi furto fuisse sublata quando domus sua fuit fracta et ~ata *SelPlCrown* 79; 1242 ~averunt cameram Agnete *AssizeR. Durh.* 21; 1276 domus Ricardi..quadam nocte a latronibus ~ata fuit et bona sua asportata *Hund.* I 125; 1301 ivit ad domum predicti J. et ~avit ostium super eum *SelCCoron.* 69; 1309 rectatus quod ~iavit domum Radulfi (*JustIt*) *S. Jers.* XVIII 177; 1381 coegit homines de Maidenstane ~are edificia W. T. et N. H. (*Indict.*) *Peasants' Rising* 9. **b** 1266 invenit predictos A. et F. ~antes subtus hostia..domus, que uxor..Willelmi clauserat pre timore ipsorum *IMisc.* 13/21. **c** 1201 Walterus Wifin fuit ~atus, et de catallis suis de burgeria in domo sua facta invente fuerunt calige in domo Lefchildi *SelPlCrown* 4. **d** 1381 intravit domum T. H...et ~avit bona et catalla (*Indict.*) *Peasants' Rising* 9.

2 to break out of (prison).

1275 defendant..evasionem et quod..~averunt prisonam *Gaol Del.* 35A r. 7*d*.

burgaregia v. burgageria.

1 burgaria, burglary, house-breaking. **b** proceeds of burglary, swag. **c** gaol-breaking.

1191 debet xx m. ut replegiaretur de prisona regis, in qua positus fuit pro ~ia hospitalis *Pipe* 84; 1199 non habuit eum ad rectum de roberia et ~ia unde rettatus fuit *Pipe* 208; rettatus..de ~ia [v.l. burgeria] Bracton 154; 1285 captus fuit..pro †burglario [MS.: burgar'] domorum, roberiis etc. (*JustIt* 705) *DocCOx* 195; 1297 cognovit se latronem esse et maxime de burgeria cujusdam domus *Rec. Leic.* I 358; 1308 captus..pro ~ia molendini *Ib.* 372; 1303 ponebantur in inquisitione pro rege viz. pro ~ia et fractura thesaurarie sue *MGL* I 35 (cf. *Cal. LB Lond.* C 124). **b** 1201 xi ulne de linea tela de predicta burgeria vendite fuerunt..et alia burgeria tota *SelPlCrown* 4; 1221 burgatores qui burgaverunt domum Thome..in recessu suo dimiserunt quandam partem illius burgerie ad domum Edithe *Eyre Lincs & Worcs* 1166. **c** 1275 de concessione.. evasionis..et de ~ia gaole de Neweg[ate] *Gaol Del.* 35A r. 7*d*.; 1331 de ~ia gaole marescalcie *SelCKB* V 57; 1347 ~ia prisone *Ib.* cxxii.

2 burgaria [cf. OF *borgerie*], burgage, right to hold land by borough custom (Devon). **b** (?) area of burgage tenure (Ir.); *cf. burgageria.*

a1175 concessi burgensibus meis de Bradninch ~iam suam et placias suas sicut ille liberate sunt *BBC* 38. **b** 1282 rex commisit comitatum Typerar'..una cum placitis de ~ia Hibernicorum..custodiendum *Pat* 101 m. 5.

†burgarium, burgage tenement.

1487 burga de Combemartyn et Southmolton [*Devon*] et ~ia in eisdem *Pat* 565 m. 21.

burgarius v. 2 bercarius.

†burgasium, burgage tenement.

1261 si aliqui cives vel burgenses in aliqua civitate vel burgo aliquam domum vel fundum aut predium urbanum ad eos pertinentes, qui ~ia [? l. burgagia] vulgariter appellantur, alicui ecclesie..legant (*Lit. Papae*) *Doc. Ir.* 173 (cf. ib. 177).

burgatio, burglary.

1211 burgavit domum suam..et post illam ~onem.. venit ipse ad matrem suam *SelPlCrown* 58; 1275 nec de ~one domorum..nec insultacione domorum..nullum in talibus sciunt culpabilem *CourtR Wakefield* I 75; 1347 [pro] ~one [domus] *CalCl* 203.

burgator [cf. OF *burgeor*], burglar.

1195 occisus fuit de ~oribus *CurR PR* XIV 147; 1201 Lefchildus fuit receptator illorum ~orum *SelPlCrown* 4; 1227 ad respondendum..de capitulis subscriptis: ..de ~oribus et aliis malefactoribus..tempore pacis *Cl* 214; 1255 ipsum..interfecit fugientem tanquam latronem et ~orem domorum *Cl* 25; jurare debent quod utlagatos, robbatores et ~ores non receptabunt Bracton 115b; tempus..discernit predonem a fure et a ~ore, furemque diurnum a nocturno *Fleta* 15.

burgatrix, burglar (f.).

1242 Matilda..~ix est domorum et grangiarum *AssizeR Durh.* 47; 1277 ~ix domorum *CourtR Wakefield* I 173.

burgatura, burglary.

1309 ad standum recto..pro ~a domorum (*JustIt*) *S. Jers.* XVIII 171.

burgbota v. burhbota.

burgellus [OF *borgel*], little town.

1178 ecclesiam S. Michaelis de Lupis cum ~o (*Lit. Papae*) *Cart. INorm.* 20.

burgemotus v. burgimotus. burgenc- v. burgens-.

burgensia [OF *borgesie*], status of burgess. **b** area of burgage tenure.

1314 mandamus quatinus in renunciacione burgesie civium vel burgensium civitatis predicte [Burdegale] facienda decetero caveatis quod alicui sic renuncianti exempcio..custume vinorum..non solvende nullatenus concedatur *RGasc* IV 1262 (cf. ib. 1296); 1383 mandamus quod aliquos forinsecos in villa predicta [de Grymmesby] inhabitantes..qui ~iam ibidem acceptare et onera cum burgensibus supportare †voluerint [? l. noluerint] artificia aliqua..sicut burgenses exercere..minime permittatis *Cl* 224 m. 27; 1429 sub pena..forisfacture ~ie sue communitati ville *Doc. Beverley* 20; 1482 sub pena amissionis ~ie sue imperpetuum (*Ipswich*) *Gild. Merch.* II 127; 1484 nullus extraneus..extra..burgum [Pontisfracti]..commorans vigore seu colore ~ie aut pro eo quod exstat burgensis ibidem non sit nec eligatur major..burgi *ChartR* 198 m. 5. **b** a1160 concessisse burgensibus meis Damfronte omnibus infra muros castelli sive extra muros in burgesia manentibus quietanciam consuetudinum suarum *Act. Hen. II* I 203.

burgensialis, belonging to a burgess.

1263 forinsecus vel aliquis..non habens libertatem burgencialem *BBC* (*Oswestry*) 296 (cf. *Gild. Merch.* II 191); 1297 de redditu burgenciali de Walyngford' *Ac. Cornw.* I 111.

burgensis, resident in walled town on the Continent of Europe (Fr. *bourgeois* etc.).

ad hoc Robertus [dux] venerat ut in vicis illis [Rotomago etc.]..vagaretur, precarium victum a ~ibus nundinans W. Malm. *GR* IV 389; milites..et comprovinciales, tam rustici quam ~es Ord. Vit. XII 30 p. 425; c1157 unum ~em liberum ad Pontem Audomari (*Ch. Lire*) *Act. Hen.* II I 168; s1173 cum ~es de burgo [sc. Vernolio] vidissent quod ..necessaria eis defecissent *G. Hen. II* I 50; 1242 Bernardi ~is de Partenay *RGasc* I 10 (cf. not. ad loc.); 1315 omnes qui ~es dicte bastide fuerint et in dicta bastida domos construxerint *Ib.* IV 1626 (vi).

2 burgess, burgher, resident in borough or city: **a** (Eng.); **b** (W.); **c** (Ir.).

a viii ~es in Tamuuorde huic manerio [*Drayton, Staffs*] pertinent et ibi operantur sicut alii villani *DB* I 246b; dicunt Angligene ~es de Sciropesberie multum grave sibi esse quod ipsi reddunt totum geldum..quamvis..xliii Francigene ~es teneant masuras geldantes T.R.E. *Ib.* 252; in burgo Derby..erant ccxliii ~es manentes *Ib.* 280; modo..lxiii borg[enses] halle manentes *Ib.* II 286; 1103 volo..ut abbas et conventus et ~es S. Edmundi..habeant quitanciam de theloneis *CalCh* II 258; c1103 volo..ut omnes ~es et omnes illi qui in burgis morantur, tam Franci quam Angli, jurent.. servare monetam meam (*Breve Regis*) *GAS* 523; si intra burgum regis fiat infractio pacis, adeant ~es [AS: *seo buruhwaru*] et conquirant illum malefactorem (*Quad.*) *Ib.* 222; a 1135 ~is potest dare terram suam et vendere et ire quo voluerit *BBC* (*Newcastle upon Tyne*) 64; s1192 ~es.. responderunt se esse in assisa regis nec de tenementis que.. tenuerunt..in pace uno anno et uno die sine calumpnia se velle respondere contra libertatem ville et cartas suas Brakelond 143; homines ipsius ville [de Bello] ob ejusdem loci permaximam excellencie dignitatem ~es vocantur *Chr. Battle* 17; 1201 nullus ~ium..nisi residens fuerit in predicta villa de Helleston' has habebit libertates *RChart* 93; scolares [Oxonie] cum militibus, oppidanis et ~ibus multis Gir. *RG* II 16; 1228 de c li. concessis ~ibus: ..concessimus civibus nostris Eboraci..c li. *Cl* 43; 1293 in presencia..multorum..burgencium (*St. Ives*) *Law Merch.* I 63; ita..quod..†burgentes [l. burgences] habeant..mercaturas ad libertatem fori pertinentes *FormMan* 6; 13.. si quis ~is voluerit fieri, veniat in curia et reddet prefecto xij d. et capiet burgagium suum (*Cust. Preston*) *EHR* XV 496; togam..longam cum capucio rotulato ad modum ~is.. habuit Blakman *Hen. VI* 14; hic, hec ~is, *a burgys* WW. **b** ibi est novum burgum [*Rhyddlan*] et in eo xviii ~es inter comitem et Robertum..; ipsis ~ibus annuerunt leges et consuetudines que sunt in Hereford et in Bretuill *DB* I 269; a1184 notum sit..me concessisse..~ibus de Sweynesse has consuetudines.. *BBC* (*Swansea*) 19; s1257 villam Mungumbriam..combusserunt et Baldewinum et burg[ens]es alios multos..in eadem villa..occiderunt *Ann. Cambr.* 93. **c** a1176 sciatis me concessisse ~ibus meis de Dublin' quod habeant omnes libertates..suas plene et honorifice *Doc. Ir.* 2; 1194 dedisse..omnibus ~ibus meis de Drokedale.. burgagia sua eis attributa..legali..juramento legalium militum nostrorum et ~ium (*Drogheda*) *EHR* XV 311.

3 resident in burgh (Scot.).

a1150 concedo..eis [canonicis] herbergare quoddam burgum inter eandem ecclesiam et meum burgum et concedo ut ~es eorum habeant communionem vendendi res suas venales et emendi in foro meo libere..sicut mei proprii ~es (*Ch. Holyrood*) *E. Ch. Scot.* 153; quicunque factus fuerit novus ~is domini regis in primis jurabit fidelitatem domino regi et ballivis suis et communitati illius burgi in quo ~is factus est *Leg. IV Burg.* 2.

4 burgess dist. as: **a** greater or lesser; **b** having full or limited rights.

a nunc habet Ilbertus ibi [*Tanshelf, Yorks*] iiii car. et lx ~es minutos *DB* I 316b; modo sunt ibi [in burgo Derby] c ~es et alii xl minores *Ib.* 280; c1256 ~es de minori communia Oxonie conqueruntur..quod (*sic*) ~es magnates, quocienscumque dominus rex petit talliagium de eadem villa, per statuta et provisiones dictorum magnatum dicti minores ~es semper tallientur in duplum *IMisc* 10/7 (cf. ib.: magni ~es numquam pacant denarium). **b** in eodem burgo [*Ipswich*] habet Ricardus xiii ~es; ..unus eorum est servus, et super xii commendationem tenet *DB* II 393; 1156 sciatis me concessisse liberis ~ibus ville de Bureford.. omnes liberas consuetudines illas..quas habent liberi ~es de Oxenfordia in gilda mercatoria *BBC* 17; c1200 concessimus..quod predicti ~es sui de predicto burgo sint liberi ~es *Ib.* (*Bridgwater*) 101; 1275 sunt ibi [*Cardigan*] quidam qui vocantur ~es de vento et vico, qui reddunt per annum lxv s.; sed aliquando plus et aliquando minus, quia veniunt et recedunt pro eorum voluntate *IMisc* 33/31; sunt ibi [*Carmarthen*] quidam alii qui appellantur ~es de vento et vico *Ib.*; 1280 sunt ibi [*Cardigan*] lx et x chensarii qui dicuntur ~es de vento, quorum quilibet reddit per annum xij d. *AncExt* 51; 1304 de diversis hominibus [de Kaermerthin] dictis ~ibus de vento qui burgagia nec terras tenent sed ut gaudere possint eadem libertate qualem veri ~es possident [reddunt].. *MinAc W. Wales* I 238; a1313 dedi.. omnibus Anglicanis ~ibus et etiam chenceribus meis *BBC* (*Aberavon*) 29; 1307 sunt ibidem [*Tenbury, Worcs*] sex ~es adventicii, et reddunt per annum vj s. ..et sunt ibidem sensarii, et reddunt per annum vj s. viij d. *IPM* 4/1 r. 3.

5 burgess representing borough in Parliament.

debet mandari ballivis et probis hominibus burgorum quod ipsi ex se et pro se eligant duos idoneos, honestos et peritos ~es ad veniendum et interessendum ad Parliamentum *Mod. Ten. Parl.* 13; 1419 dicentes..quod ~es Parliamenti debent eligi per communitatem aperte in aula (*R. Guildh. King's Lynn*) *EHR* XLII 583; 1503 electi fuerunt ~es Parliamenti *Rec. Leic.* II 364.

burgent- v. burgens-. burgeria v. 1 burgaria. burgerith v. burhgerihtum.

burgesaticum, burgage tenement (Sicily).

1239 per antiquam constitutionem regni Sicilie revocata sunt feodalia et †bursesatica que habuerant per concessionem invasorum regni (*Lit. Nuncii Papae*) M. Par. *Maj.* III 555 (cf. ib. 556: si libere eis et perpetuo ~a liceret emere sive accipere).

burgeseria, burglary.

1284 dicit quod predictus E...predictam domum fregit. ..E...defendit omnem feloniam et burgeser' *Gaol Del.* 35B r. 33*d*.

burgesia v. burgensia

burgesor [OF *burgesor*], burglar (*cf. burgator*).

1292 se cognoverunt..esse latrones, depredatores, burgisores..in diversis locis *SelCCoron* 129.

burgetum v. bugettum. burgiare v. burgare.

burgimagister [cf. Germ. *Burgmeister*], burgomaster, chief magistrate (Germany etc.).

1315 ad blada et alia victualia capienda per ~tros, scabinos et consules et communitatem dicte ville de Bruges deputati fuerunt *RParl* I 358b; 1340 ad tractandum cum burgh'meistr' et scabinis villarum Gandavi et Brugges *Ac. Wardr.* (*TRBk* 203) p. 219; 1392 dilectis nobis burgomagistris civitatis Colonie *DipCorr. Ric. II* 114; 1395 magne prudencie viris burgomagistris..civitatis Basiliensis *Ib.* 162; 1404 ~er de Stralessound *Lit. Cant.* III 80; 1432 littere nostre ~is ville de Lubek deliberate fuerunt *Cl* 282 m. 13.

burgimotus, ~um, ~a [AS *burhgemot*], borough-moot, court held in borough.

habeatur in anno burgmotus [AS: *burhgemot*] ter et scyremotus bis (*Quad.*) *GAS* 203; pensandum erit omni domino..ut..suum hominem manuteneat, ..aliquando in hundreto.., aliquando in comitatu vel ~o vel hallimoto (*Leg. Hen.*) *Ib.* 577; c1200 pro hac donatione..facta et recordata in ~o civitatis Cant' *Cart. S. Greg. Cant.* 47; 1212 quod cives Wintonie essent ibi parati ad faciendum recordum et judicium desicut loquela illa fuit inter eos in ~o Wintonie *CurR* VI 291; c1230 [his testibus: ..toto] burghemoto de Portesmue *CalCh* I 119; c1250 in burmoto civitatis Cant' *Reg. S. Aug.* 576; **1252** seneschallus noster vel alius ballivus..in eadem villa burgemota teneant ad facienda omnibus jura *BBC* (*Weymouth*) 211; **1313** clamat.. habere..duas burghmotas per annum et wreccum maris in terris suis dominicis ibidem [*Erith, Kent*] *PQW* 321b; **1437** ad burghemotum tentum apud Wyntoniam..consideratum est.. *BB Winchester* 74; **1480** per majorem, aldermannos et plenum burgemotum civitatis Cantuarie *Ac. Chamb. Cant.* 135.

burgisor v. burgesor.

burgitentor [cf. borgesalder], 'borsholder'.

1388 quod..~ores et constabularii ac custodes pacis infra custodias suas habeant potestatem facere executionem statuti predicti *Cl* 228 m. 7 (*cf. Stat. Northampt.* 3 (*StRealm* 258): *burghaldres, conestables et gardeins de la pees*).

burglarium v. 1 burgaria. burgmotus v. burgimotus. burgomagister v. burgimagister.

burgravius [Germ. *Burggraf*], burgrave, hereditary castellan.

1441 mandamus..gubernatoribus, ..~iis, castellanis, ..ceterisque nostris et Imperii Sacri subditis (*Lit. Imp.*) BEKYNTON II 102.

burgularia [cf. burgaria], burglary.

1544 robberias, ~ias, insidiaciones *Pat* 738 m. 23; **1583** perdonamus omnes ~ias et burgulariter fracciones et intraciones domus mansionalis *Pat* 1236 m. 27.

burgulariter, burglariously.

1505 domum..~er et felonice fregit *Reg. Heref.* 69; **1551** †virgulariter *CalPat* IV 126; **1583** domum mansionalem..~er fregerunt et intraverunt *Pat* 1236 m. 27 (v. et. burgularia).

burgulator [cf. burgator], burglar.

1530 murdatorum, homicidarum, felonum, ~orum et quorumcumque suspectorum..murdri, homicidii, roberie et felonie (*Pat*) *Foed.* XIV 369.

Burgundio, Burgundian.

s**402** (v. 3 burgus 1); **747** sicut aliis gentibus Hispaniae et Provinciae et ~onum contingit BONIF. *Ep.* 73 p. 151; s**1273** commoventur..~ones in iram RISH. 80; s**1418** ~ones nocte Parisium intraverunt WALS. *YN* 486.

Burgundus, Burgundian.

ab Armenone [orti sunt]..~i NEN. *HB* 160; pauci Burgundi noviter baptismate loti GARL. *Tri. Eccl.* 107; post..Suevi et ~i..sedes sibi in ea [Gallia] fecerunt HIGD. I 27 p. 286.

1 burgus v. 1 bargia a. 2 burgus v. borga.

3 burgus, ~um, ~a [LL ?< πύργος; cf. AS *burh* etc.], fortified town in continental Europe (Fr. *bourg* etc.).

s**402** gens..supra Reni fluminis ripam resedit et, crebra habitacula que vulgo ~i vocantur condens, nomen ex opere assumpsit; a burgis enim Burgundiones appellari ceperunt DICETO *Chr.* I 80 (cf. HIGD. I 28 p. 296); s**1110** Henricus V.. ~um Pontis Tremuli [*Pontremoli, It.*] turribus et muris valde munitum..destruxit CAPGR. *Hen.* 37 (*from* G. DE VITERBO); s**1123** milites, turbis rusticorum et feminarum de circumjacentibus viculis ad forum properantium mixti, ~um [*Gisors*] libere intraverunt..et a burgensibus.. hospitio suscepti sunt ORD. VIT. XII 37; s**1173** erant infra Vernolium tres ~i preter castellum; ..unus illorum dicebatur magnus ~us *G. Hen. II* I 50; **1217** scribitur omnibus civitatibus, castris, ~is et villis Pictavie et Gasconie *Pat* 54; **1289** duobus ~is clausis adherentibus..castro *RGasc* II 435.

2 fortified town in pre-Conquest England (AS *burh*).

~os, castra *GlC* B 220; s**913** Edwardus..construxit ~um quendam Witham in Estsexe H. HUNT. *HA* V 15 (cf. M. PAR. *Maj.* I 440); instituimus ut omne ~um [AS: *burh*] refectum sit xiiii noctibus super Rogationes (*Quad.*) *GAS* 157; si quis ecclesiam requirat vel ~um meum [AS: *mine burh*] et ibi assalliatur vel affligatur *Ib.* 189; ut per..testimonium ejus..~i mensura [AS: *burhgemet*] et omne pondus sit *Ib.* 477; T.R.E. reddebat civitas de Glowcestre..xii sextaria mellis ad mensuram ejusdem ~i; ..in ~o civitatis sunt wastatae xiiii domus *DB* I 162; ~um de Grentebrige [*Cambridge*] pro uno hundret se defendebat T.R.E.; in hoc ~o fuerunt et sunt decem custodiae *Ib.* 189.

3 borough: **a** in post-Conquest England (*cf.* J. Tait: *The Medieval English Borough*, 1936); **b** in Wales; **c** in Ireland (*cf. burgageria*).

a in ipso manerio est novum ~um [? *Rye*] et ibi lxiiii burgenses reddentes viii li. ii s. minus *DB* I 17; tota hec terrarum burgensium [de Norwico] erat in dominio comitis Radulfi; et concessit eam regi in commune ad faciendum ~um inter se et regem *Ib.* II 118; **1130** ~um de Norhamtona: R.R. r.c. de firma ~i..; idem R. r.c. de auxilio ~i *Pipe* 133; a**1167** canonici..retinebant sibi et ~o suo.. omnes libertates ad liberum ~um spectantes *BBC* (*Launceston*) 379; edes petrine tibi sunt burgo residenti D. BEC. 1755; s**1192** conquesti sumus abbati.., dicentes redditus et exitus omnium bonarum villarum et ~orum Anglie crescere et augmentari in commodum possidencium..preter villam istam BRAKELOND 142v; **1198** burgenses de Gloecestr' r.c. de ij s. ut possint emere et vendere in gildhalla ad emendationem ~i *Pipe* 2; **1201** ut totum territorium subscriptum liberum sit ~um *BBC* (*Wells*) 2; **1200** cartam..per quam nullus eorum [hominum de Salopesb'] debet placitare extra ~um suum *CurR* I 224; **1235** dicit quod non tenetur ei respondere extra ~um 'Bedeford' *CurR* XV 1611; **1253** nullus..ut sutor..exerceat officium suum nisi sit in ~o [i.e. *a burgess*] (*Ch. Bolton*) *EHR* XVII 293; **1313** nulli sunt burgenses, quia nullus est ~us in comitatu Kancie (*Indors. brevis*) *Eyre Kent* I xxi; c**1360** villa de Ravenserodd, que villa quasi ~um videbatur, ..per inundationes maris.. deleta est *Meaux* III 16; **1398** cum villa de Oswaldestre..de omnimodis libertatibus ville et ~o mercatorio pertinentibus privilegiata existit (*Ch. Oswestry*; cf. *CalCh* V 373) *Firma Burgi* 250; villas, sub quarum appellatione continentur ~i atque civitates FORTESCUE *LLA* 24; *a burghe*, burgus *CathA*; **1498** rentale..de redditu in ~o ville Oxonie *Cart. Osney* III 275. **b** R. de Roelent [*Rhyddlan*] tenet de comite H. medietatem..castelli et ~i *DB* I 269; s**1106** confirmatio Henrici regis primi in qua confirmat..ecclesie de Theokesburia..decimas omnium reddituum dominicorum de ~o de Kairdif *Cart. Glam.* 39; a**1220** volumus..quod nullus mercator sit in terra nostra qui non sit residens in ~is nostris (*Ch. Haverfordwest*) *EHR* XV 520; **1395** quod predicta villa de Neweton' [*Carm*] decetero pro ~o libero habeatur et quod omnes Anglici..tenementa..tenentes in eadem villa..fiant decetero et habeantur liberi burgenses (*Pat*) *Gild. Merch.* II 385; s**1400** Oenus..†~as [MS. ~us] ubique per Anglicos inter eos inhabitatas..cremaverat AD. USK 47. **c** a**1210** nullus burgensis..respondeat de ullo placito quod perveniat infra metas ~i in castello nec alibi nisi in hundredo ville *BBC* (*Kilkenny*) 120; **1215** burgenses nostri de Dungarvan teneant predictas libertates ..infra ~um suum et extra *RChart* 211a; **1247** secundum consuetudinem ~i de Drogheda (*Ch. Regis*) *EHR* XV 312.

4 burgh (Scot.).

c**1120** in ~o de Rokesburge *E. Ch. Scot.* 35; c**1150** concessise huic Balduino clienti meo suum *toft* quod tenet..in Pert libere et quiete ab omni servitio ~i excepta vigilia infra ~um et claustura ~i secundum suam possessionem *Ib.* 248; c**1200** de firma ~i mei de Elgin *Reg. Moray* 9; c**1212** libertatem faciendi ~um et habendi portum *BBC* (*Arbroath*) 1; in omni ~o tocius regni Scocie superior illius ~i faciat xij legales burgenses sufficienciores et discreciores ~i sacramento suo asserere quod omnes leges..legitime conservabunt *Leg. IV Burg.* 112; **1316** ballivis..in eorum balliis seu ~is *Melrose* II 359; curavit..pagum suum a Finderne in baroniam ~um [*burgh of barony*] (sic vulgo loquuntur) cooptari FERR. *Kinloss* 40.

5 (w. ref. to tenure by 'borough English' *i.e.* ultimogeniture; *cf. VCH Notts* I 237).

1336 descendit jus..cuidam Thome ut filio juniori et heredi de tenemento in ~o Anglico secundum consuetudinem ville *Rec. Nott.* III 404 (cf. ib. I 58: [**1284**] congregatis burgensibus utriusque ~i ejusdem ville, ..eligant unum ballivum de uno ~o et alium de alio ~o pro diversitate consuetudinum in eisdem ~is habitarum).

burhbota [AS *burhbote*], obligation to repair fortification.

si quis ~am vel brigbotam (id est burgi vel pontis emendationem)..supersederit, emendet hoc erga regem cxx solidis (*Quad., Rect.*) *GAS* 353 (cf. ib. 444); (*Leg. Hen.*) *Ib.* 558 (v. brigbota).

burhgerihtum [AS *burhgeriht*], 'borough-right' (*s. dub.*). **b** a customary payment (Som.).

†**944** (12c) concedo ecclesiae S. Mariae Glastoniae..jura, consuetudines et forefacturas omnium terrarum suarum id est burhgerita et hundredsetena, athas et ordelas *CS* 794 (cf. W. MALM. *GR* II 143); iste consuetudines pertinent ad Tantone: *burgheristh*, latrones, pacis infractio *DB* (*Som*) I 87. **b** **1279** est ibidem [*Dunster*] quidam redditus vocatus *burgrith* proveniens de hundredo *IPM* 22/1 r. 2; **12..** idem [dabit] xv d. de *burgerith* et quietus erit de pannagio (*Cust. Taunton*) *Som. Rec. Soc.* LXVI 22 (cf. ib. pp. li–liii).

burhmannus [AS *burhman*], townsman.

non licebat eis aliquod forceapum facere ~is [sc. London'] (*Quad.*) *GAS* 234.

burill- v. burell-.

buris [CL], plough-beam (*cf. Antiquity* XVII 167).

~is, curbamentum aratri *GlC* B 210; ~is, *sulhbeam* ÆLF. *Gl.*; procedat robur curvando in ~im, que cauda bovis vel aratri interpretatur; ~is autem dicitur quasi *bos uros* NECKAM *Ut.* 112 (cf. *Id. NR* II 169); buris, trabs, †crapulus sunt neque restis eis GOWER *VC* I 280; *plowbeme*, ~is, ..temo *PP*.

burla [OF *borle*; cf. burellus, burra], wool flock (for stuffing mattress or saddle). **b** (?) candle-wick.

1238 pro *fusteyn, carde* et burl' ad predictam culcitram et matracium *Liberate* 13 m. 23; **1257** unum materacium de burl' *Cl* 33; **1270** cum..~a et sepo ad unam novam bargiam faciendam *MinAc* 1118/17 r. 4; **1321** [*saddles mended*] cum borla et *canevas* (*MinAc*) *MFG*; **1323** in emendacione iiij veterum sellarum et in octo libris ~e emptis pro eisdem *Ac. Wellingb.* 124. **b** **1306** in ij petris et dim. cepi empti pro candelis, xx d.; in borla empta, iij d., item ij d.; in stipendio unius hominis facientis candelas.., v d. *MinAc* 856/15 m. 2.

burlarius v. burellarius. burlawa v. birelagia.

burlura, 'burling', clearing (wool) of flaws.

1465 quod quilibet dictorum pannorum..sequatur.. ordinem faccionis..absque diversitate in textura, fullatura, nodulacione vel ~a *FineR* 274 m. 14 (*citing Stat* 4 Ed. IV c. 1; cf. *Pat* 1299 [**1586**] m. 1).

burmotus v. burgimotus.

burna [AS *burna*], (N. Eng. & Scot.) burn, stream. **b** (S. Eng.) (?) bourn, stream.

a**1165** sursum usque ad ~am de Fauhope que cadit in Ledre *Melrose* I 3 (cf. ib. 9); c**1205** inter ~am de Schotteschalef et viam per quam itur ad petariam *Reg. Glasg.* 85; a**1270** a Derwenta per ~am de Akedene contra montem (*Ch. Blanchland*) *MonA* VI 886; **1430** sicut Horsewelle oritur et descendit in ~am *Feod. Durh.* 55. **b** tendit..in rivulum..et ita ascendendo contra cursum aque usque ad domum Oswardi de la Burne..et sic sursum de illa ~a in viam W. MALM. *Glast.* 106 (cf. *MonA* I 23); **12..** concessi.. v acras terre..cum borna adversus austrum in parochia de Lamehith *Cart. Hosp. S. Thom.* no. 499 (cf. no. 558).

burneare v. burnire. Burnellus v. Brunellus. burnett- v. brunett-.

burnire, ~eare [OF *brunir, burnir*], to burnish.

1233 quod..arma regis..rotulari et quarellos regis ~iri [faciat] *Liberate* 10 m. 3; **1237** pro..cuppa ~eanda *Ib.* 11 m. 10; **1250** quod..vetera feretra bene ~iri..faciat *Cl* 320; **1282** ad burn[i]endum pelves episcopi *Rolls Merton* 134.

burnisare, to burnish.

1315 pro eodem [lavacro] ~ando *KRAc* 369/11 f. 45*d*.

burnissura, burnishing.

1287 pro ~a..[*lacuna in MS.*] argent' *KRAc* 351/28 m. 3.

burnitio, burnishing.

1282 vj d. pro ~one pelvium *Rolls Merton* 137.

burnitor, burnisher.

1305 Johannem ~orem auri *Gaol Del.* 1 r. 11.

burochius v. burrochius. burprestora v. purprestura.

burra, ~us [LL], coarse hair or flock (for stuffing mattresses etc.).

1206 pro duobus matracis de panno serico et fustanno cum ~o de scarletto *Pipe* 47; **1208** computate..xxv d. pro ~a et v d. pro nigra tela *Cl* 109a; **1290** in ~is ad sellas, vij d. *Ac. Swinfield* 181; **1316** in collariis reparandis cum corio, canevacio et ~a emptis ad idem *Ac. Man. Wint.* (*Houghton*); **1335** in..collaris..veteribus emendandis cum ~o et filo ad idem emptis *Comp. Swith.* 230.

burrachia v. burrochius.

burralis [? cf. burellus], (?) felty, matted.

exprimantur pulvilli illi intra manus et intra partes burales inferiores..collobii ipsius medici vel inter partes manutergii, et tunc erunt lati GAD. 122 v. 2.

burratus v. birratus. burretum v. birretum.

burrochius, ~ia [ME *burrok*, OF *bourroiche*], fish-trap.

c**1150** concedo monachis..liberam potestatem trahendi retia et jacendi borechas et piscandi *Cart. Glouc.* I 260; a**1200** de duobus ~iis in aqua de Saverne *CurR* I 13; **1209** in..burochio vivarii faciendo *Pipe Wint.* 67; **1221** molendinarius inventus fuit submersus in burroka sua *Eyre Lincs & Worcs* 1078; **1221** fuit cum ipso H. ad burricas domine sue et ipse rediit et idem H. non *PlCr Glouc.* 79; a**1226** utraque..pars habeat burrocas suas et alia ingenia sua..ad capiendum pisces *Cart. Boarstall* 33; **1234** tanta erit distancia inter ~ias ad lamprones capiendos *E. Ch. S. Paul.* 261; **1253** batellos vel retia vel †borittos [? l. boracos] ad nocumentum piscariarum regis in aqua Sabrine *Cl* 450; **1254** capciones lampredarum..et decimam quas custodes gurgitum et factores burrachiarum habere consueverunt tempore piscacionis lampredarum *Liberate* 30 m. 6; **1257** in v borachiis ad gurgitem emptis *MinAc* 1094/11; **1269** cubuerunt burochios *CalIMisc* I 375; **1263** captus fuit ad quendam burroccum..in aqua de Kingeston [*Surrey*] qui firmatus fuit quadam serura..et in eo furatus fuit piscem *JustIt* 874 r. 28*d.*; **1278** statutum est..quod omnes borachie ad omnia molendina..per totum comitatum [*Cumb*].. deponantur *Ib.* 132 r. 32*d.*; **1281** cum quidam, ..perpendentes quod..inhibuimus ne quis cum ingeniis que kidelli vocantur per aquas Tamisie..piscari presumat.., quedam alia ingenia que borache vocantur jam de novo ita densa fecerunt quod per ea fritum piscium aliquatenus transire non potest *Pat* 100 m. 14; **1282** in virgis emptis ad borrokos faciendos pro pisce capiendo *MinAc* (*Berks*) 1131/2 F 1; **1326** in v borachiis emptis pro piscibus cum eisdem capiendis in exclusis molendini *Pipe* 171 (*Worcs*) r. 36.

1 burrus v. burra.

2 burrus [CL < πυρρός; cf. birrus], red or brown.

†barsus, rufus, niger *GlC* B 48; †borrum, †rubum *Ib.* 173; ~um, *bruun Ib.* 211; **9..** ~us, rufus, niger, *burlis, brun* WW.

3 burrus [ME *burre*], burdock (bot.).

~us, *gertt clote SB* 13.

bursa [LL < βύρσα], **~um,** hide, skin.

byrsa, corium *GlC* B 234; exin tortores buculam deglobere byrsa / mandant ALDH. *VirgV* 1204 (cf. *Id. VirgP* 25 p. 279: birsae); consuunt lembum taurinis byrsis ÆTHELW. iv 3; **10..** byrse, *hyde* WW.

2 purse, money-bag; **b** (fig. and prov.).

crumenam..a zona dependentem..fur..incidit; qui mox ..nimio actus terrore..manum cum ~a nil dicendo tetendit in altum AD. EYNS. *Hug.* V 20 p. 231; **1199** appellat R. ..quod..abscidit ~am suam, et ostendit ~am assisam *CurR RC* I 315; **1221** rettatus de ~is scissis *PlCr Glouc.* 5; **1242** habuit in ~o suo x d. *AssizeR Durh.* 22; **1249** Johannes Milksop..furatus fuit xxxj d. a ~a Walteri *Ann. Tewk. app.* 515; marsupium, bursa, forulus loculusque, †tumetra [? l. crumena] GARL. *Syn.* 1583B; **1275** furatus fuit..unam ~am braccalem †cervinam *Hund.* I 275 (cf. ib.: in una ~a serica); de tributa recipientibus a latronibus et ~am cissoribus ne caperentur *Fleta* 24; **1304** aliquem malefactorem aut sectatorem burci *Gild. Merch.* II 239; **1313** unam markam in pecunia numerata in una ~a ad pectus pendente cepit *Leet Norw.* 67; **1313** furatus fuit de borsa dicte M. v d. ob. *Eyre Kent* I 70; ita quieti victitant / quod raro bursam bajulant (*Wallia* 162) HIGD. I 38 p. 408; **1370** judicium pillorii pro quodam burso cisso *MGL* I 602; hec~a, *a purs* WW. **b** Rogerius..cognomento Crumena, id est ~a ORD. VIT. VIII 7; **1168** precepit [rex] non timere minas aliquas, quia nunc dominum papam et omnes cardinales habet in ~a sua J. SAL. *Ep.* 239. 271C; nulla [causa] veniam consequitur nisi pro qua mater ore rugato loquitur ~a MAP *NC* V 7 p. 252; si bene noverint ~as pauperum emungere GIR. *GE* II 32; "heu morior", sibi bursa refert GARL. *Hon. Vit.* 245; **s1295** non sunt reversi [cardinales] vacui, immo ~as vacuantes W. GUISB. 258.

3 bag, pouch: **a** pack, (?) saddle-bag; **b** pouch for seal; **c** container for the host (eccl.).

a 1245 emi faciat..unum..pampilionem ad unum postum, quem ferre possit in ~a sua *Cl* 327. **b 1338** mandamus.. quod sigillum predictum..in quadam ~a sub sigillo vestro ..mittatis *RScot* 547a. **c 1220** non est ibi pixis continens eucharistiam, sed deponitur in quadam ~a serica *Reg. S. Osm.* I 312; **1287** sit corpus dominicum repositum in ~a mundissima et ipsa includatur sub cerura in pixide munda *Conc. Syn.* 991; **c1300** eukaristia in ~a contra constitutionem *Ch. Sal.* 370.

4 stock of money, fund, treasury.

a1128 de ~a abbatis xij d. *Chr. Peterb. app.* 161; **a1130** quod faciatis habere episcopo..de Norhtwic apud Lunam [*Bishop's Lynn*] omnes consuetudines suas et ~am et forum et portum et theloneum suum *CalCh* IV 439; solebat abbas ..dare vij s. ad wardam castelli de Norwico de sua ~a BRAKELOND 139v; **1206** [thesaurarii] redditus singularum obedientiarum in singulis ~is seorsum custodiant (*Vis. Ebor.*) *EHR* XLVI 450; **1211** si amplius voluerint potare, ement de ~a sua propria *SelPlCrown* 97; **1237** rex servientes ponat in partibus illis super ~as suas, qui pacem regis servent ibidem *Cl* 532; **1239** habemus in ~a de gilda sexaginta et xv s. *Rec. Leic.* I 61; **1279** nullus..ponderabit.. lanam donec ~a [? sc. gilde] veniat foras *Gild. Merch.* II 291; **1296** residuas d li. assignabit sibi percipiendas in ~a *Reg. Carl.* I 79; **c1350** emptor ipse dabit communi ~e illud precium *StatOx* 79; **1352** abbas non provideat per annum sub communi ~a ultra duos tonellos..vini pro camera sua *Cart. Ciren.* I 172; **1511** cum communi..~a, archa, sigillo, capitulo et aliis collegialibus insigniis *Midlothian* I 274.

5 burse (acad.), student's allowance.

1292 ut illi [abbates nostri ordinis] qui habent xx monachos et supra unum mittant ad studium cum ~a integra lx solidorum *FormOx* 300; **1349** donec communi ciste universitatis ebdomodalem exsolverit ~am suam *StatOx* 152; **1379** ~am suam..communitati..refundere debet *Ib.* 183; **1469** nec promoti sive promovendi pro tempore alibi quam in eodem collegio ~as solvere consuetas compellantur *Mon. Hib. & Scot.* 460.

6 a scrotum (human). **b** bladder (of pig).

a aperiunt ~am et dimittunt aquam fluere GILB. VI 255 v. 1; testiculi..indurantur aliquando in eorum ~a vel osseo GAD. 29 v. 2; osteum, i. ~a testiculorum *SB* 32. **b 1302** in..porcis necandis ad lardar'..in ollis terreis pro alba pinguedine et burs' imponend' *MinAc* 997/13.

7 (w. *pastoris*) shepherd's purse (*Capsella*). **b** (?) bluebell (*Hyacinthus*).

12.. ~a pastoris, i. *sanguinarie*, i. *blodwurt* WW; vade ad locum ubi crescit sanguinaria, i. ~a pastoris..et tunc suspende herbam circa collum patientis a quo fluit sanguis ..et stringet certissime GAD. 9 v. 1; capsellula, herba sanguinaria, ~a pastoris idem; florem facit album; G. *burse a pastur*, A. *pursewurt Alph.* 34; **14..** ~a pastoris, A. *shepardespurse* WW. **b 14..** hec ~a pastoris, *harebelle* WW.

bursalis, 'bursal', carrying a stipend.

1334 de sex prebendis ~ibus in dicta collegiata ecclesia *Reg. Exon.* II 753; **1523** prebendas ~es in dicta ecclesia obtinere et retinere licite valeant *Mon. Exon.* 83.

bursare, to pack (wool).

1291 ita quod lana que vocatur *tayller* dicte domus [*Pipewell*] brusetur inter communem lanam *Cl* 108 m. 9*d*. (cf. ib. lanas paratas, ~atas et ponderatas); **1296** tali condicione quod..mercatores lanam domus..reciperent in tres partes fideliter brusatam, videlicet in bonam, medianam et loccas electas *Couch. Kirkstall* 226.

2 to cover or protect (a cart-wheel).

1318 in ij rotis ~andis *Ac. Man. Wint.* (*Alton*); **1378** in stipendio j rotarii pro modiis carecte ~andis et boxandis *Ib.* (*Wootton*).

1 bursaria, bursary, treasury (mon.).

1278 computaverunt fratres R. et S. de bursar' domus Berncestr' coram auditor' *Ambrosden* I 408; **s1285** tradite sunt..omnes claves camere prioris et bursar' dicto domino Henrico [priori] *Ann. Durh.* 66; **1292** r.c. de pertinenciis ad ~iam *Comp. Worc.* I 9; **1422** due moniales..deputantur thesaurarie sive ~ie monasterii *Vis. Linc.* 49.

2 bursaria, bursaress, treasurer (mon.).

1397 objicitur contra priorissam quod..priorissa est ~ia (*Vis. Nun Monkton*) *MonA* IV 194; **1441** cellararia et subcelleraria et ~ie recipiunt omnes reventus domus et expendunt *Vis. Linc.* 120.

bursariatus, office of bursar (mon.).

1446 compotos suos de tempore quo occupavit officium ~us nobis tradidit *Pri. Cold.* 155.

bursarius, leather-worker.

9.. byrsarius vel byrseus, *leþerwyrhta* WW.

2 purser, purse-maker.

1166 Gaufridus ~ius debet cc m. de misericordia *Pipe* (*London*) 132; **1327** [de misterio] ~iorum *CalPlMemLond.* 33 (cf. *MGL* I 654); **1451** W. M. civis et ~ius Londonie *Cl* 301 m. 28*d*.

3 purse-keeper (w. implication of avarice).

ad noctis filium / Christi videlicet Judam bursarium (*Maria* 402) *Ps.*-MAP *Poems* 202; non illos dico ~ios quos elegit rex ut sint omnium summi, sed illos quos in rostra propria cupiditas..produxit MAP *NC* V 7 p. 253.

4 bursar, treasurer: **a** (mon.); **b** (acad.).

a s1285 prefectus..in priorem rimari fecit omnes compotos ~ii GRAYSTANES c. 21; **1292** rotulus ~ii *Comp. Worc.* I 11; **1329** abbati de Melros, ..per receptum Johannis de W. ~ii *ExchScot* 211; **a1395** querebantur..~ium in reparacione domorum..sui officii nimis fuisse remissum *G. S. Alb.* II 410; juxta tumulum tumulatur ejus dominus Adam Howton, domini Thome abbatis [ob. **1396**] ~ius, cujus laus et nomen spargitur "Boni ~ii" per totum dominium S. Albani AMUND. I *app.* D 437. **b 1311** procurator earum [scholarum]..qui et ~ius dicitur *MunAcOx* 89; **1496** in redditu soluto ~io collegii Ballioli *Cant. Coll. Ox.* II 225; **1535** stipendia..trium ~iorum vel dispensatorum ejusdem collegii [sc. Novi, Oxon.] singulis annis mutandorum et eligendorum..xl s. *Val. Eccl.* II 264.

5 scholar, student holding bursary.

ex stipendiis illorum [collegiorum] scholastici plurimi aluntur quos Parisii ~ios vocamus MAJOR I 5.

6 purser (naut.).

1450 receperunt..de J. M. .., ~io cujusdam bargie, .. diversa bona *Cl* 300 m. 18*d*.; **1474** quedam navis unde M. C. fuit magister, J. S. *quarter master*, J. G. burcerus et P. M. ..vitellarius *Pat* 534 m. 13*d*.; **1560** navis nuncupata *the Turteldove*, cujus..economus vero seu dispensator, scriba vel ~ius J. J. [extitit] *Act. PC Ir.* 103.

bursella v. bursula.

bursellum [OF *borsel*], 'bossel', medallion (of a mazer).

1458 murram cum stricto vinculo argenteo et deaurato ac uno borcello argenteo et deaurato in fundo ejusdem, habente ymaginem B. Marie *Cl* 309 m. 31*d*.

bursemagister, purser (naut.).

1412 quedam navis..cc portagii doliorum, unde J. P. magister, R. O. mercator et R. B. ~er extiterunt *Foed.* VIII 727.

bursesaticum v. burgesaticum.

burseus, leather-worker.

byrseus, *leðeruyrtha GlC* B 232; **9..** byrsarius vel byrseus, *leþerwyrhta* WW.

†**bursicida, a** purse-maker. **b** cutpurse.

a *purswerkere*, burcida fem. *PP*. **b** burcida, A. *a purskyttere* WW.

bursila v. bursula.

†**bursima** (pl.), (?) brushwood.

c1250 totum boskellum..cum omnibus ~is culture illorum [canonicorum] de Crossetwaith adherentibus *Cart. Healaugh* 155v.

bursiscissor, cutpurse.

1275 pro habendo quodam bursicissore capto in villa de Blida *Hund.* II 307.

bursista, (?) purse-maker.

c1393 hic cirothecarius bursistaque, caupo coquusque (R. MAIDSTONE) *Pol. Poems* I 285.

bursor, purser (naval).

a1460 admirallus faciet magistros et ~ores hujusmodi navium..venire *BB Adm.* I 238.

bursosus, pouchy, purse-like.

collum matricis ~um est, †multos [l. multas] habens pelliculas et involutiones ad modum burse..ut possit dilatari et constringi cum opus fuerit *Ps.*-RIC. *Anat.* 40.

bursula, little purse.

1224 vj ~as de serico de opere Saracenorum *Pat* 449; ex lino fiunt..sacculi et †bursile ad quodlibet necessarium BART. ANGL. XVII 96; *a purse*, bursa, bursella, ~a diminutivum *CathA*.

burthenum v. burdenum. burula v. berula.

burus [AS *gebur*; cf. geburus], (?) free peasant.

in dominio sunt..vi servi et xl villani et xvii ~i et xiii bordarii *DB* I (*Oxon*) 154b; in dominio sunt ii caruce et xviii villani et xi bordarii et ii ~i et presbyter *Ib.* (*Heref*) 182; **1130** villanis et bordariis et ~is et bubulcis *Pipe* (*Oxon*) 2.

†**busa**, *f.l.* for *Ousa* (River Ouse).

vel †busam [l. Ousam] vetitum corporibus fluere *V. Ed. Conf.* 53v.

busacia [cf. OF *bose*], dung.

quando venerunt [scrabones] ad ~ias vaccarum semper ibi moram fecerunt O. CHERITON *Fab.* 31.

busagium v. bosagium.

busardus, ~a [OF *busard*], buzzard.

~us in nido accipitris projecit unum ovum O. CHERITON *Fab.* 4; **1270** in *glu* empt' ad ~os in *wareine* capiendos *MinAc* (*Cambs*) 768/5 m. 2; **1272** qui quidem erius [sperva-riorum] fuit distructus per ~os *IMisc* 17/18; buteo, τριόρχης Graece dictus, Anglorum busharda est, nisi fallar TURNER *Av.* 2.

1 busca, ~ia, (?) **~us** [OF *busche*; (?) infl. by *boscus*], wood, esp. firewood.

c1180 dedi eis..in bosco meo..buschiam quantam unus equus potest portare *Melrose* I 135; **1189** concedimus..ij carretas errantes singulis diebus in bosco de S. ad deferendam ~am (*Ch. Godstow*) *MonA* IV 364; **1196** in custamento palorum et closture et busche *Pipe* 60; **1200** debent iiij s. de quadam flota ~ie *Pipe* 174; **1202** pistor poterit..in quolibet quarterio lucrari..in ~a iij d. (*Assisa Panis*) M. PAR. *Maj.* II 481; **1205** c carretatas de bona bosca fentecia *Cl* 56b; **1217** de illis qui..veniunt..ad ~am meremium, corticem vel carbonem emendum (*Ch. Forest*) *StRealm* I 21; **1225** xl carectatas de sicca buscha in foresta de Clarendon' ad ardendum in castro Sar' *Cl* 32b; **1234** wdewardus..habebit mortuam ~am, scilicet seckillones *Cust. Glast.* 57; **s1244** de qualibet scut[a] descendente in dicta Ripa [Regine] cum ~a sive blado capiendus est j d. *MGL* I 239; **1250** de providencia ~e et carbonis: ..quod.. carbonem et †boscam sufficientes venire faciant *Cl* 386; **1266** ~am..ad minam plumbi..comburendam *Cl* 204; **1276** villata de Eton' [*Berks*] solebat dare tolnetum †buste [? l. busce] navium *Hund.* I 18; **1283** [iij carectatas] †brusee [MS.: busce] *CalIPM* II 289; paratum sibi [sc. camerario] debet esse quicquid pro corpore suo fuerit necessarium, viz. cibus, potus, ~a [v.l. †busta] et candela *Fleta* 71; ad prosternendum et..asportandum buschiam DOMERH. *Glast.* 569; **1313** in carbone et †~o *Rec. Leic.* I 285; **1358** v centum de ~a vocata *kunchewode Pat* 284 m. 24; **1364** vendicio ~e: ..de *talwode*..et de..~a fracta (*MinAc*) *Banstead* 340.

2 †**busca,** (?) *f.l.* for *bussellus*.

1317 dum modo †~a ordei vendatur pro xv d. (*Gild R. Andover*) *Gild Merch.* II 312.

buscagium v. boistagium. buscalia v. boscalium. buscardus v. bussardus.

buscare [OF. *buschier*], to cut firewood.

1260 quando wodewardi domini ~ant.., tunc idem.. habebit cropp' *Cust. Glast.* 190; ~at per j diem cum dimidia carecta *Ib.* 197.

buscarius [cf. OF *buschier*], (?) woodmonger (but *cf. bucherius, boistarius*).

1294 per Baldewinum ~ium *Gaol Del.* 37/1 r. 1*d*.; **1311** Thomas de Hales, ~ius *Cal. LB Lond.* B 23; **1350** civi et ~io London' *AncD* B5994.

buscellum v. bossellum. buscellus v. bucellus, bussellus. 1 buscia, buschia, buscha v. busca.

2 buscia, ~ium [cf. OF *busse*], 'buss': **a** transport vessel; **b** fishing vessel (Dutch *buis*).

a s1189 applicuerunt ibi [ante Acram] naves et ~ie plusquam quingente, exceptis galeis et cursariis *G. Ric. I* II 95; **s1190** naves erant numero centum, et bucee xiiij, vasa magne capacitatis et mire agilitatis: ..una erat omnium navium dispositio; singule vero buciarum ordinatus et oneris duplum receperunt DEVIZES 28v.; **s1191** ascendit rex Ricardus navim cum exercitu suo cum cl navibus et vj et buceis xxiiij et galeis xxxix DICETO *YH* II 86; rex.. habens in comitatu suo xiij magnas naves quas †buccas [? l. buceas] vocant, triplici velorum †expassione dum equora sulcarent notabiles, ..se vento commisit *Ib.* 93 (= WEND. I 192: buccas triplici velorum expansione velificatas; M. PAR. *Min.* II 21: buzas cum velis triplicibus); **s1191** rex..prospexit..obviam venientem navem permaximam, quam buzam dicunt, a terra Jerosolimitana regressam *Itin. Ric.* II 28; **s1191** rex demersit magnam ~iam Sarracenorum FL. WORC. *Cont.* B 158; **1242** precipimus..quod xx ~ia que parata sunt ad opus nostrum contra transfretacionem nostram acquietari faciatis et kariari usque Portesmue *Cl* 416. **b 1417** Cornelius Jacobson magister busse vocate *Christofre* de Andewarp' *RNorm* 324 (cf. ib. 325: magister busshe); **1442** cum una buyssa velavit de Schiedam (*DipDocE* 427) *Bronnen* 1251 (5).

buscis v. 1 bussus. buscus v. busca. busellus, bushellus v. bussellus. busharda v. busardus.

busia [? cf. Fr. *bouse*], wisp (used as toilet paper).

binas / carpe tuis busias digitis, grossas, bene pressas, quas prestare pares patrono cum petit illas; / dentur e stando busie, non poplite curvo D. BEC. 1272–4.

†**busius** [(?)], fallow (colour).

nomina colorum: ..~ius, *fealu*, ÆLF. *Gl.*

busonus v. 1 buzo. bussa v. 2 buscia, bussus.

bussardus [? cf. buscia], transport ship.

1214 significavit..quod arestari fecistis quendam buzardum quem emerat pro xl s. ab hominibus..qui illum ceperant in partibus Britannie..; et ideo vobis mandamus quod ..buzardum illum ei deliberari..faciatis *Cl* 170b; **1230** habere faciant Emerico de Sacy unum buscardum ad transfretandum in nuntium regis *Cl* 311 (cf. ib. 315); **1309** devenit wreckum subter castrum..de ~o cum sale (*JustIt*) *S. Jers.* XVIII 123.

bussaria v. besasa.

bussellata, bushel.

1234 solent dare per scutellatas et postea per busselatas et nunquam consueverunt dare tantum avene quantum ipse petit *CurR* XV 1099.

†**bussellum** [cf. buccella], a sort of soft food.

licet de hujusmodi predictis..aliquando pitancia conceditur, admitti tamen de ~o vel de morterellis..aut de hujusmodi cibariis parvi precii penitus inhibetur *Cust. Westm.* 76.

bussellus, ~um, ~a [OF *boissel*; (?) *conf. w.* bucellus], large bowl with iron hoops, container (for grain etc.). **b** container of standard capacity, bushel measure.

in ij busellis cum ferro ligandis *FormMan* 33; **1390** unum buscellum ligatum cum ferro *PlRCP* 519 r. 499; **1410** utensilia: ..de..j ~o ferro ligato *Crawley* 303. **b 1221** mercatores salsarii qui vendunt salem cum ~is *SelPlCrown* 89; **1244** quilibet capitalis magister mensurator..inveniet quarterium, ~um, dimidiatum ~um et stricum *MGL* I 242; **s1273** quelibet mensura, sc. quarterium, dimidium et ~um, sigillata sit *Leg. Ant. Lond.* 168; **1276** J. R. in misericordia pro falso ~o *Hund. Highworth* 25; **a1280** item..~um sive batum *AncD* A796; **1321** thesaurarius domini regis.. misit per singulos comitatus singulas lagenas et ~os de ere, et..dicte mensure..assaiate fuerunt; ..et inventum est quod ~us civitatis continet equaliter octo lagenas; ..et probatus est regius ~us insufficiens..per cyathos circa decem *MGL* II 382; **1356** una cum standardo ~o, gallone, ulna et petra *MunAcOx* 186; **14..** faciet..cistam communem portari..una cum †briscello, communibus ponderibus, ulnis et mensuris *Cust. Fordwich* 5; **a1460** inquiratur de hiis utentibus falsis bushellis sive modiis.., ementes et vendentes cum ipsis bushellis grana, sal et carbones maritimos aut alia bona mensurabilia *BB Adm.* I 231.

2 dry measure, bushel (eight gallons).

a1128 reddunt..iij sceppas et iij buisellos frumenti *Chr. Peterb. app.* 160; **c1150** sex boissellos frumenti *Cart. I. Norm.* 285; **1186** pro j ~o seminis canabi *Pipe* 179; **c1200** emit †busseillam ordei (*DCCant*) *HMC Var. Coll.* I 238; **1207** concesserunt iij ~os de frumento et iij ~os de siligine; ..et quilibet ~us debet esse octava pars unius †quartor' *Fines RC* (*Beds*) I 73; **1233** fecit retinere..ad seminandum c et xx acras de frumento, sc. ad quamlibet acram tres ~os, et ad c acras seminandas de avena..ad..acram iiij ~os et ad xx acras seminandas de ordeo *Cl* (*Herts*) 190; **1247** debent molagium, sc. de qualibet boveta terre unum †bussollum et duas denaratas frumenti *Cl* 546; **c1248** duos bossellos farine de avena et duos bossellos fabarum *Doc. Robertsbr.* 103; mensuras tritici quas ~os dicimus M. PAR. *Maj.* V 594; **1260** quelibet acra potest seminari cum iij ~is frumenti vel iij ~is et dim. ordei vel v ~is avene vel iij ~is pisarum vel vescarum *Cust. Glast.* 235; **c1270** habebit..j ~am avene cumblatam *Reg. Wint.* II 662; **1274** xl bus [sellos] frumenti valentes vij quar[teria] secundum mensuram patrie (*Chanc. Misc.* 10/5/1) *S. Jers.* II 17; pondus octo librarum frumenti faciunt (*sic*) mensuram jalonis et octo jalonate frumenti faciunt ~um, de quibus octo consistit commune quarterium *Fleta* 73; **1297** in trituracione..xlv quart' j ~i London' siliginis *Ac. Lenton* 5; **c1300** qualibet (*sic*) firma de frumento continet xvj quarteria, sc. viij bussell' computatur (*sic*) pro quarterio si bene mensuratur vel parum plus *Dom. S. Paul.* 160 (cf. ib. 164*: quarterium vero bracini continet vij ~os); **1331** pro duobus buscellis farine..que constituunt octo bollas *ExchScot* 356; **s1369** (**1468**) hoc anno..cum..caristia bladi j buschellum frumenti pro iij s. vendebatur W. WORC. *Ann.* 749; **s1370** (**c1430**) hoc anno vendebatur busshellus frumenti Calisie pro iij s. iiij d. *Ann. Bermondsey* 478; **1533** pro..iiij ~is calcis *Comp. Swith.* 216.

bussha v. 2 buscia.

busso [OF *buisson*], bush.

1209 forestarii invenerunt in bosco..unam damam habentem gorgiam abscisam et prope inde invenerunt H... latentem sub quodam ~one *SelPlForest* 3.

bussollus v. bussellus.

bussulus [cf. It. *bossolo*], box.

recipiens semper solis radium per ~um magnum in culo totum perforatum ad instar sachi discusiti in ymaginem quam faciebamus ad valimentum cujusdam rei future et optate diu (M. SCOT. *Intr.* f. 114) *Med. Sci.* 289.

1 bussus, ~ius, ~a, ~is [OF *bus*; cf. 1 butta], wine-skin or (?) butt.

1184 pro vj buszis et xij buszellis *Pipe* 137; **1185** pro buzis et buszellis et barillis ferratis *Pipe* 217; **1205** quod faciatis fieri ad opus nostrum octo buzios bonos *Cl* 55; **1238** per serjantiam deferendi unam buzcam plenam vino ad dinerium domini regis (*JustIt* 37) *Fees* 1382; **1242** in vj ~is de vj sexteriis et vj de iij sexteriis de sexteriis de cute faciend' ad vina regis portanda *Pipe* 282; **1242** fieri faciatis xviij ~es de cute ad vina nostra portanda unde sex fiant de sex sextercis.. *Liberate* 16 m. 9; **1245** quod..xv busces de corio ad opus regis capi [faciant] et illis a quibus capti fuerint satisfaciant *Cl* 342.

2 bussus [LL], fat (adj.).

fatte, pinguis, arvinosus, ~us, crassus *CathA*.

3 bussus v. byssus. 1 busta v. busca.

2 †busta, lopped tree.

~a, incisa arbor ramis [truncatis] *GlC* B 203 (cf. *Gl. Leid.* xxxv 86).

3 busta [OF *buiste, boiste*; cf. boistarius], box.

a1170 una ~a aurea ad eucharistiam; una ~a argentea ad oblatas (*Invent.*) *Chr. Steph.* II 759; **1220** pro tribus magnis ~is ad brevia missa ad curiam Romanam, ij d. *Cl* 440b; **1390** j ~a pro eisdem [contours i.e. *counters*] imponendis *Ac. H. Derby* 5.

bustagium v. boistagium.

bustalis, monumental.

titulos bustali marmore scriptos NIG. *SS* 1247.

†bustallum [? cf. bostar], (?) cow-shed.

1385 tenent ~a et *hoggesties* in precinctu Summi Vici *CourtR Winchester*.

bustardus v. bistarda.

bustare, to bury.

~antes, sepelientes *GlC* B 215.

bustarinus v. bustuarius.

bustianus [OF *bustane*], 'bustian', a fine cotton cloth.

dedit [abbas Thomas, ob. **1396**] octo capas de albo ~o et octo tunicas de eodem pro juvenibus in minutis officiis ministraturis *G. S. Alb. Cont.* III 381; **1467** in j pari vestimentorum de ~o empto *Ac. Obed. Abingd.* 133.

busticetum, pyre or grave.

~a, locus ubi comburant corpora *GlC* B 201; ~a, sepulchra in agro *Ib.* 204.

bustratus v. broudare.

bustuarius [LL = *funeral attendant*], grave-digger.

hic bostarius, *a grafmakere* WW; *a grave maker*, †bustarinus *CathA*.

bustum [CL], **a** funeral pyre. **b** funeral mound, barrow, grave. **c** (?) corpse.

a omnia de nigris resurgent corpora bustis ALDH. *VirgV* 278; **747** super ~um illius [virginis] incensae et concrematae corruptorem ejus suspendunt BONIF. *Ep.* 73 p. 150; rogus, ~um, *forbærned* [*aad*] ÆLF. *Gl.* **b** mausoleum vel ~um, *kyninga byrgen* ÆLF. *Sup.*; **931** ~is sponte dehiscentibus *CS* 677; alterius [sc. Arturis nepotis] ~um..repertum est super oram maris, xiiij pedes longum W. MALM. *GR* III 287; cujus busta videns.. / flevit et inciso marmore scripsit ita NIG. *SS* 1099; celum sibi bustum / eligit NECKAM *DS* II 381; *a grave*, †bustulum; versus: 'est mausoleum, poliandrum, tumba, sepulcrum, / sarcofagus, bustum, tumulus', ..~um ubi cadavera sunt combusta *CathA*. **c** quo sancta jacent sua busta sepulchro WULF. *Swith. prol.* 377; didicit cujusdam homunculi..ibidem [sc. in tumulo] ~a contineri AD. EYNS. *Hug.* V 2 p. 79 (cf. IV 2 p. 8; V 11 p. 138); **c1381** versus metropolim Cantuaria que vocitatur / bustum portatur *Pol. Poems* I 228.

†bustus, shad (fish).

14.. butus, A. *shadde*, sed melius ~us WW.

busynator v. bucinator. busz- v. bucellus, bussardus, 1 bussus, 1 butta, 1 buzo. butacon v. buphagon. butalla v. buccula.

1 butare, to caw.

cornices ~ant ALDH. *PR* 131.

2 butare v. buttare. butaurus v. 1 butor. buteirum v. butyrum. butellare v. buletellare.

butellaria, ~ium [OF *boteillerie*; cf. buticularia], buttery, office of (royal) household concerned w. provision of wine etc.

de buteleria: magister pincerna [debet habere] sicut dapifer *Domus Reg.* 132; **1156** ad festum meum mihi serviant cum illis de bottellaria mea *BBC* (*Oxford*) 99 (= *SelCh* 199: butteillaria); **1204** pro una caretta ad ~iam regis *Pipe* 89; **1212** per serjanciam essendi marescallus buteilerie domini regis *Fees* 92; **1219** per servicium serviendi de cervisia in butillaria domini regis *Ib.* 255; **1225** duo dolia vini que liberaverunt in butelleria nostra *Cl* 35a; **1234** liberari faciat..valetto de buttelaria domini regis iiij dolia vini *Cl* 451; **1242** ad deserviendum in officio pannetarie et buttilarie *Cl* 451; **1242** caretario de butelario regis *Pipe* 281; **1332** vallettus botellarie nostre *Pat* 178 m. 20; **1366** in feodis servienclum tam in panetorio, ~ia et coquina quam in aliis domibus officialium *ExchScot* 253; **1495** de precio j dolii vini albi provenienti de officio butillerie domini regis infra portum Dublin' (*Comp. Subthes. Hib.*) *L. & P. Ric. III–Hen. VII* II 300.

2 buttery, store-room for bottles etc.

c1224 in butelleria (*Invent. Dublin*) *ChancMisc* 10/13/2; **1230** in custodia domorum ipsius episcopi..aut alicujus cellarii sui..Lincoln' vel butelleryе sue *Reg. Ant. Linc.* II no. 342; **1234** maeremium ad quandam novam coquinam faciendam infra castrum Wintonie et quandam butilleriam et dispensam faciendam ibidem *Cl* 37; **1295** utensilia..de botelaria (*Test. N. Longespee*) *EHR* XV 525; **1331** cooperculum..argenteum in botelria *Arch. J* LIII 270; **1336** super construccione..panterie et botelarie ad eandem aulam (*Ac. Stirling*) *CalScot* III 364; **1349** pro bultellaria..domine..j *tripe* pro ore domine (*KRAc* 391/15) *Arch* XXXI 80; **1390** spensam cum ~io *Reg. Aberbr.* II 39; **1400** in..ciphis emptis pro †butellia [? l. butelleria] *Test. Ebor.* III 19 (cf. ib. 45: butlaria); **1419** in..serruris..pro panetaria, botraria, porta orti *Rect. Adderbury* 22; **1450** pro factura solarii super promptuarium cum pariete dividente botlariam et pantleriam (*Ac. Peterhouse*) *Arch. Hist. Camb.* I 12n.; hec botelaria, A. *botelary*..hec botolaria, *a botry* WW.

butellarius [OF *boteillier*; cf. buticularius], butler, household official concerned w. provision of wine etc.: **a** (royal); **b** (other).

a 1290 Matheo de Columbariis, butillario regis (*Ac. Wardr.*) *DocScot* I 139; **1309** [teste] domino W. de S. butilario Scocie *Melrose* II 422; pro feodo ~ii x li. (*Leg. Malcolm.* 6) *APScot* 346; **1320** [constabularius Turris] clamavit capere de quolibet dolio vini quod ~ius domini regis caperet per prisam..duas lagenas (*Plac. Corone*) *MGL* II 408 (cf. ib. 296: nota quod botellarius domini regis et camerarius domini regis et coronator idem sunt); **1334** cuidam de botelariis domini regis *Ac. Durh.* 524; **1365** de quibus quidem doliis..vendidit maximam partem botellario regis *Cl* 203 m. 24; **1461** [officium] botellar' [in portu de Milford] *CalPat* 21. **b 1303** botelarius cetera spectantia ad boteleriam pro feodo suo vendicavit *Ac. Exec. Ep. Lond.* 58; **1309** paneterio, butilero et janitori *Rec. Leic.* I 265; **1322** panetarius qui est botellarius *DCCant* J 518; **1364** Godfrido Butiller, butillario domini episcopi S. Andree *ExchScot* 137; **1405** Jacobus quondam botillarius domini mei *Test. Ebor.* III 30; hic botularius, *a botelere* WW.

butelleragium, butlerage, duty levied by royal butler on imported wines.

1519 de eodem pro j *hogset* vini pro botteleragio *Ac. Havener Cornw.* (*PRO*) 1 f. 8; **1538** villa Suthampton': liber butleragii ibidem *TRBk* 184, f. 1.

butellus v. bucellus.

1 buteo [CL], **butius,** bird of prey (buzzard or kite) or (?) bittern (AS *frysca* = (?) 'froggar'); *cf.* 1 *bubo b.*

~io, *cyta GlC* B 199; ~io, *frysca Ib.* 227; **9..** butium, *cyta, frisca*, ..bizus, *tysca*, ..de avibus: ..butzus, *tysca* WW; nomina avium: ..~eo, *cyta* ÆLF. *Gl.*; TURNER *Av.* 2 (v. busardus).

2 buteo, beardless youth.

ephebus vel ~eo, *beardleas* ÆLF. *Sup.*; *yonge*, adolescens, .., †butro, impubis *CathA*.

buteracius, buterettus v. butericius. buteria v. bateria 2, bucerius, 1 & 2 buttaria.

butericius, ~ia [OF *boterez*], buttress. **b** (adj.) serving as a buttress.

1249 construet tres ~eos lapideos ad sustentandum murum predictum *AncD* A10849; **1275** [fecit purpresturam] de quodam buteretto lapideo longitudinis iij pedum et latitudinis ij pedum *Hund.* I 531; **1279** levaverunt tres ~ias lapideas ad murum suum supportandum (*Hund.*) *Lond. Ed. I & II* II 149; **1298** boteraciam juxta posternam (*KRAc* 7/6) *DocScot* II 320; **1301** botraci cancelli constabunt ij s. ad minus *Reg. Exon.* 397; **1327** oportet de novo facere unum boterac' petri (*sic*) ad sustinendum murum ejusdem castri *KRExt. & Inq.* 10/2/22; **1337** circa structuram novi buteracii ad corneram porte abbathie *Ac. Durh.* 534 (cf. ib. 377); **1368** usque ad quandam botteras' stantem ad ostium australe ecclesie *Pat* 277 m. 21; **c1412** boteracia seu suffoltaria ejusdem [claustri] *G. S. Alb. Cont.* III 496; **1424** pro muris dicti edificii de novo faciendis, cum vij botrasis ad idem *Rect. Adderbury* 78; **1447** infra corpus ejusdem [ecclesie]..altare..erigere et illud ibidem per spacium inter duas posituras sive butteracias in longitudine, et interiorem partem muri illius ac exteriorem partem positurarum sive butteraciarum predictarum in latitudine..cum quadam capella..includere *Lit. Cant.* III 194. **b 1249** pro ij piler' ~iis faciendis sub camera regis *LTRMem* 21 r. 3; **1271** ij columpnas botericias [*on the south side of the chapel*] *CalPat* 540.

butettus v. buttettus.

buticium [(?) OF *boteiz*; cf. 1 butta], small butt (of land).

1245 de vj d. de Samsone pro ~io sepis sue [*Ivingho, Bucks*] *Pipe Wint.* (159287) r. 6d.; **1276** tenet..unum boticium et reddit inde per annum..iiij d. [*Windsor*] *Hund.* I 18; **1277** dedimus vobis potestatem includendi et arentandi omnes placeas vacuas et beteicia [*Cal.*: †becercia] vacua extra coopertum in foresta nostra de Wyndesor'..et ideo vobis mandamus quod..cum placeas, boteicia et purpresturas predictas arentari feceritis arentacionem predictam.. mittatis *Pat* 96 m. 13; **1280** ad inquirendum de omnibus purpresturis et boteiciis per diversos constabularios castri nostri Wyndes'..factis *Ib.* 99 m. 8; **1316** cxxxv perticatas.. et ~ium apud Fifhyde [*Berks*] *Abbr. Orig.* I 232; **1324** boticium [terre arabilis] *CalIPM* (*Berks*) VI p. 361; **1358** unum messuagium cum curtillagio et uno botitio terre [*Artington, Surrey*] *Loseley MSS* (*Guildford*) 337/54.

buticularia [cf. butellaria], buttery (mon.).

1262 custodiam ~ie aule ostilar' [*S. Swith. Wint.*] *CalI Misc* I p. 95; **c1174** per servicium unius servientis ad serviendum hospitibus in aula de dispensa et ~ia *Reg. Malm.* II 396 (= *Chr. Ed. I & II* II cxix: in aula et dispensa et †botularia).

buticularius [cf. butellarius], butler: **a** (royal); **b** (other).

a c780 ille est sinscalcus, vero bŭticlarius ille ALCUIN *Carm.* 8. 3; **1179** signum Guidonis ~ii (*Ch. Regis Francie*) *Lit. Cant.* II 481; **1198** Willelmo..et Danieli ~iis regis *RScac Norm* II 311; **1257** Johanni filio regis Jerusalem', regni Francie ~io *Cl* 134; **1284** ~ius [Scocie] *CalScot* II no. 272; **1300** Guidonis de Castellione..boticularii Francie *TreatyR* I 140. **b** de ~io [v.l. pincerna] et Judeo WALT. ANGL. *Fab.* 59.

†butilla, (?) boat (*cf.* 1 *batellus*).

1215 cum navis.., que applicuit apud Ryam juxta ~am quam servientes Savarici..ceperunt et detinent, applicuerit in partibus vestris, illam retineatis *Pat* 161a.

butillar- v. butellar-. butimen v. bitumen. butinnosus v. bituminosus.

butinum [OF *butin*], booty, spoil.

1429 racione ~orum et lucrorum guerre proveniencium (*RNorm*) *Foed.* X 107.

butinus v. lutrinus. butio v. 1 buteo. butir- v. et. butyr-.

butire, (?) to push (with oar), row (*cf. buttare* 2).

"ut quid enim / aptarem dextras remis..?" / "hec ignota mihi virtus fuit estque butire" L. Durh. *Dial.* III 101.

butisella, ~us [cf. It. *botticella*], (?) jar, gourd, measure of ginger (*cf. curda*).

1234 retineri faciat ad opus regis..v vel sex ~os de gingibrat' *Cl* 381 (cf. *Cal. Liberate* 247); **1258** liberant..iij botizellas gingiberat *Cl* 186.

butiuncula, small plot of land.

9.. ~a, *tunyncel* WW.

butius v. 1 buteo. butlaria v. butellaria. butleragium v. butelleragium. buto v. boto.

1 butor, ~orus, ~orius, ~ora [OF *butor*], bittern (bird).

ecce bŏōtaurus, vulgaris sermo bŭtaurum / †dicitur, terribile [l. dicit, terribili] voce boando venit Neckam *DS* II 497 (cf. *Id. NR* I 54); **1241** emi facias..v duodenas ~orum *Liberate* 15 m. 11 (cf. ib. m. 21: *heiruns* sive *butors*); **1249** pro cignis, heyruncellis, ~oribus et gruibus *Cl* 222; **1318** consuete †coligant [l. colligunt] ova botorum et exportant extra mariscum *CBaron* (*Ely*) 126; butorius..avis est a sono vocis sic dicta, que crura habet longa, collum extentum, rostrum acutum et longum Upton 183; stellaris est quam Angli buttourum aut bittourum..nominant Turner *Av.* 15 (cf. ib. 64: grandisonam illam lacustrem avem, Anglis buttoram..vocatam).

2 butor, ~orium [OF *butoir*], butteris, tool for paring horse's hoof.

1241 in ~oriis, chivillis, sepo, uncto et in cista ad ferramenta reponenda *Liberate* 15 m. 5; **1310** mariscallia:..de j bicorn, iiij martellis, .., ij †bucoribus [l. butoribus] *Ac. Exec. Ep. Exon.* 12.

2 device for fishing, (?) 'butt'.

1247 quod..predicti fratres decetero possint piscari cum buttorio..in predicta aqua de Avene [*Warw*] *Fines* 243/21/48; **1255** liberam piscariam in veteri aqua cum sex burrochis et cum uno botur' *Ib.* 283/14/315; **a1329** de libera piscaria in aqua..de Avene..cum spurte et quolibet genere buttorii (*Ch. Thelsford*) *MonA* VI 1564.

†butra [(?) l. bruta], stupidity.

10.. ~a, *dysige* WW.

butria v. 2 buttaria.

†butrista [cf. butta], wine vessel.

bis septena tibi direxi carmina, Vasco, / tu quia misisti butristas ut quoque binas Alcuin *Carm.* 102. 16.

butrius v. bucerius. butro v. 2 buteo.

butrum [Ir. *bothar*], lane.

c1200 usque ad ~um inter Karkent et Dromenalewy (*Ch. Owney*) *Deeds Mon. & Ep. Ir.* p. 100 (= *MonA* VI 1137: †bucrum).

butruus v. botrus.

butsecarla [ON *buzukarl*], 'buscarl', sailor.

quando rex ibat in expeditione vel terra vel mari, habebat de hoc burgo [*Malmesbury*]..xx sol. ad pascendos suos buzecarl' *DB* I 64 b; **s1050** [Godwinus] omnes ~as de Heastinga et ubique circa ripas maris..in adjutorium sui allexit Fl. Worc. I 208 (= S. Durh. *HR* 139: buthsecarlas); **s1100** rex ..~is precepit mare custodire et observare ne quis de partibus Nortmannie fines adiret Anglie *Id.* II 48 (= R. Howd. I 158: buzsecarlis).

1 butta, ~is, ~us, ~um [? cf. OF *bot*], butt, small strip of land (? of irregular shape) in open field.

11.. ij bovatas terre in campis de Burdon..et preter hec ~as que jacent ad capud fossati *Feod. Durh.* 147*n.*; **1182** xx acras in Heilefurlung et ~es apud Y. ad complendum numerum xx acrarum *Ambrosden* I 188 (cf. ib. 261 [**1218**]: seilones terre que vocantur ~es); **c1200** dedi..quandam acram prati..cum v ~is predicte acre adjacentibus (*Cart. Westwood*) *MonA* VI 1009; **c1200** cum duobus ~is ex parte aquilonari illius sellionis *Reg. Ant. Linc.* VI 110; **c1210** cum crofto..quod continet xj seliones et v ~os *Reg. Linc.* I 37; **c1225** remanserunt..de predicta dimidia virgata iiij ~i terre que (*sic*) jacent in Fenmade *Cart. Dunstable* 73; **c1230** dat..iiij d...pro ij ~is existentibus in eadem crofta (*Cust. Atherstone*) *Doc. Bec* 103; **12..** unam ~am..que lanceat versus B. *Cart. Darley* I 307; **1266** sunt ibidem ~i selionum quos bondy tenent *IMisc* 13/6; **12..** ij bottas jacentes inter terram suam et terram Ricardi..ex transverso *Cart. Chester* 253; **a1300** unum bottum ultra sulcum *Reg. Malm.* II 273; **1325** iiij ~a que continent j acram *Ambrosden* I 577; **1399** aliquando iiij ~es, aliquando v, ..aliquando viij faciant unam acram secundum quantitatem earundem *Ib.* II 192; **1514** xij ~as terre arabilis continentes in se duas acras simul jacentes in campo ville Notingham *Rec. Nott.* III 124.

2 (?) saltern (Hants).

1167 idem reddit compotum de xxx s. de ~is *Pipe* 176; **1171** idem r.c. de xxx s. de ~is; ..idem r.c. de xxix s...de sale vendito *Pipe* 35–6; **1185** idem W. r.c. de xxx s. de buszis; ..idem W. r.c. de xiij s...de sale vendito reddendis quolibet anno nisi rex salliri fecerit *Pipe* 207; **1191** idem W. r.c. de j m. de sale ~orum vendito *Pipe* 85; **1199** de xxx s. ..de censu ~orum *Pipe* 2; **1221** de quolibet anno tres sol. quos ipsa Sarr' ecclesia percipere solet per annum de censu †buccorum Nove Foreste nostre *Cl* 447.

3 (?) *f.l.* for *bucca*.

1236 (v. 1 bucca 3).

4 end, tip (of a close) (C.I.).

1306 [clausum] butat ex uno buto super mariscum de C. *CartINorm.* 300.

2 butta, (*s. dub.*); (?) *cf. bottus*.

1424 de viij ~is et iiij vertivellis emptis pro domo bercarie *Rect. Adderbury* 78.

3 butta, ~us [cf. 1 bussus], butt, vessel for wine etc.

c840 (10c) de agro isto reddat xv modios de pura celia, hoc est ~am plenam, vasque plenum mellis (*Ch. Hereford*) *CS* 429; **1158** (v. bucellus); **c1160** ad curiam de Waletuna [sunt]..xij scutelle et ij †bucci [? l. butti] et parva tabella *Dom. S. Paul.* 132; **1164** pro ~is et bucellis *Pipe* 21; **1214** (v. bucellus); **12..** per servicium ij ~arum [v.l. buz] de vino dispensabili *Fees* 342; **1365** in empcione duarum botarum de *garneche ExchScot* 228; **1392** duas botas salmonum.. duas botas de Malvesey..pro vitellacione castri *Cl* 233 m. 13; **1404** xv parvas ~as vel urnas *Lit. Cant.* III 83; **1417** centum bottos de vino de Malvesyn *AncD* C6759; **1460** v botis et pipis *ExchScot* 657.

buttagium [OF *botage*], a duty on butts of wine (Norm.).

a1172 unam masuram in perreio Deppe, liberam et quietam ab omni consuetudine, teloneo, botagio, galonagio, tallia et omni exactione *Act. Hen. II* I 476 (cf. ib. 529: de boutagio).

buttare [(?) OF *boter*; cf. abuttare], to abut; **b** (refl.).

11.. iij seliones ~ant super curiam domini *Danelaw* lix; **11..** [selionem] qui butat super meum croftum *Ib.* 344; **c1220** concessi..dim. acram cujus unum caput ~at super magnam viam *Cart. Sallay* 580; **a1260** landam..cujus una extremitas ~at usque ad foveam *Cart. Cockersand* 86; **1306** (v. 1 butta 3); **1321** cum medietate unius acre terre ~antis super selionem Ricardi *Cl* 138 m. *2d.*; **1346** unam dim. acram capitalem..super quam v acre terre arabilis.. ~ant *AncD* C4222; **1374** cum domibus..~antibus super gabulum chori berefridi *Fabr. York* 185; **1399** xvij seliones ~ant totaliter in terram ipsius prioris vocat' Buttes *Ambrosden* II 191. **b** **c1400** [canalis] bivium pertransiens ~at se contra fenestram domus..ibique curvatur versus pontem *Mon. Francisc.* I 510.

2 to strike, whack.

12.. extraxit quendam gladium suum que vocatur *broche* et venit retro dictum R. et ipsum cum dicto *broche* ~avit in dorso *ICrim.* 34/15.

1 buttaria [cf. 1 butta], small strip of land.

1207 tres acre terre..cum buttera marisci que extendit usque ad ripam *RChart* (*Norf*) 170b; **1314** illa bovata terre in eadem villa [*Keddington, Lincs*] excepto tofto et excepta una buteria *ChartR* 101 m. 13.

2 buttaria [OF *boterie*; cf. 2 butta], buttery: **a** (royal); **b** (other); *cf. butellaria*.

a operarii ~ie [debent habere] consuetudinarium cibum tantum *Domus Reg.* 132; **1297** discis..pro buteria (*Ac. Wardr.*) *DocScot* II 147; **1300** valletti buterie regis *Ac. Wardr.* p. 318. **b** **1376** una aula de antiqua factura, cum pantria et butria *IMisc* 208/27; **1390** clerico buterie..pro ij potellis..vini Vasconie *Ac. H. Derby* 6; **1417** totum apparatum aule camere non legatum botarie *Reg. Cant.* IV 180; **1437** ut in celario, botria, lardario, coquina *Reg. Heref.* 226; **1478** in boteria septem sunt cocliaria *Reg. Whet.* II 181.

2 furnishings of buttery.

1415 lego..totam panetriam et boteriam excepto napreo *Reg. Cant.* II 78.

buttarius, butler, official in charge of wine-butts; *cf. butellarius*.

~ius [debet habere] consuetudinarium cibum et iij d. hominibus suis *Domus Reg.* 132.

butteil-, buttel-, buttil- v. butell-. buttera v. 1 buttaria. butteracia v. butericius. buttorium v. 2 butor 2.

buttettus, small butt (of wine).

1237 pro duobus butettis de *mure* et *franeboyse Liberate* 11 m. 13.

buttis v. 1 butta. buttourus v. 1 butor. buttus v. 1 & 3 butta. butumen v. bitumen. butunus v. boto. butur, ~urum v. butyrum. butus v. buere, bustus, 1 butta 3.

butyrarium [cf. burarium], butter-dish.

1254 butirarium argenti cum cooperculo deaurato *RGasc* I 485 (= *CalPat* 315).

butyratus, buttered.

cibi..viscosi ut anguille et pisces frixi butirati Gad. 60 v. 1.

butyrositas (butir-), butteriness.

substancias complentes vicem..electuariorum, sc. ~atem quam supplent vice electuarii restaurativi Gilb. I 72 v. 1; serositatis liquamen est a ~ate sequestrandum Bart. Angl. XIX 61.

butyrosus (butir-), buttery.

~a substancia extinguit acumen colere Gilb. V 221. 1; lac..nutrit et reparat racione ~e substancie Gad. 55 v. 2; substancia..opilativa, ~a, ..unctuosa Bart. Angl. XIX 59; roburque nostrum ut recentis in lacte, / visus noster ut butirosa suggentis J. Howd. *Cant* 255.

butyrum (butirum) [CL < βούτυρον], butter.

pane..et ferculo aliquatenus ~o imping[u]ato Gildas *Pen.* 1; tu ipse qui..nobis donasti hanc creaturam N. formatici casei vel ~i Egb. *Pont.* 132; mel compultimque bŭtūrque ministrat Alcuin *Carm.* 4. 9; mulgeo [oves meas] bis in die..et caseum et ~um [AS: *buteran*] facio Ælf. *Coll.* 91; de mensa:..vas buteri, *buterstoppa Id. Gl.*; unam ~i ruscam *DB* I 269; **a1160** omnem decimam domus mee in empcione..casei et ~i *E. Ch. Yorks* VI 153; additur agresti contractum lance bŭtȳrum [v.l. bŭtȳrum sub lance retractum] Hanv. II 272; caseolive / vel bŭtiri D. Bec. 1752; lac, bŭtirum, dactilus et zukarum Neckam *DS* IV 829; **1282** in buteiro empto ad colla boum *MinAc* 1237/1; **1290** habeat vicarius..decimam..casei, buturi, lactis *Cart. Sallay* 620; [pastor] habebit partem lactis quod est sub ~o quando perficitur ~um *Cust. Bleadon* 206; **1303** pro fabis et bitiro *EEC* 274; **1305** j pensa butire *Cant. Cath. Pri.* 160; **1308** xix petr' boutiri *Ac. Durh.* 2; **1313** emit caseum, buttyrium et ova veniencia versus forum..faciendo forstallum *Leet Norw.* 60; cooperuerunt eam [naviculam] coriis bovinis.., et linierunt omnes juncturas pellium ~o *NLA* (*Brendan*) I 140; ~um ovinum melius est quod in colore subrufum est et amplius pingue *Alph.* 25.

butzus v. 1 buteo. buulus v. bulus. buvetum v. bovata 2. buxa v. buxis.

†buxeria, [? cf. OF *buscherie*], (?) woodland (*Norm*).

c1160 dedit..feodum in predicto manerio [de Manul Gerolt] excepta ~ia..et precarias de ipsa ~ia et totum boscum suum de S. Maria Calida (*Ch. Ste. Barbe*) *MonA* VI 1112 (= *Act. Hen. II* I 299).

buxeus, of box-wood. **b** pale as box-wood.

10.. ~eus, *sio bixne* WW; baculum boxeum *Chr. Abingd.* II 406 (cf. baculus 11). **b** buxeus o quantos obtexit pallor inertes Aldh. *VirgV* 1013.

buxis, ~a [cf. boxa, pyxis], casket.

quod detraxerat cum pectine diligens reliquiarum more servabat in ~ide Herm. Arch. 4 p. 34; **a1100** ij ~ides argenteas deauratas *Stat. Sal.* 34; **1261** duo paria ~arum ferrar' *Cal. Liberate* 29; **1265** pro j ~a gingibrade (*RHosp*) *Manners* 20.

buxus, ~um [CL < πύξον], box-tree. **b** box-wood. **c** boxwood flute.

bux[um], *box GlC* B 198; ~us, *box* Ælf. *Gl.*; unus homo reddit inde fascem ~i in die Palmarum *DB* (*Salop*) I 252; cum..palmas non habemus, laurum vel ~um..deportamus Beleth *RDO* 94. 95; hic deficiunt..aralus et ~us, fructum non ferentes, scyphos tamen et manubria largientes Gir. *TH* III 10; tecta virore caput sed truncum pallida buxus Neckam *DS* VIII 55; semen ~i cum aqua rosata..summe valet in frenesi Gad. 6. 1. **b** ~us arbor erit, ~um materia ipsa Bede *Orth.* 2779; **1355** vj folia de ~o *MunCOx* 131. **c** ~us, tibiole *Erf.* 2. 272. 49; consonent tibie, tube, litui, ~us [*gl.*: *flegeles*] Neckam *Ut.* 104.

buyssa, buza v. 2 buscia. buzardus v. bussardus. buzca v. 1 bussus. buzecarla v. butsecarla. buzennus v. 1 buzo. buzius v. 1 bussus.

1 buzo, ~onus [OF *bouzon* < Frk. *bultjo*], bolt (for shooting birds etc.). **b** (as obligation in serjeanty).

1209 tulit arcum cum corda et una sagitta barbata et uno bulsone *SelPlForest* 2; **1218** abstulit ei unum buzon' *Eyre Yorks* 386; **1235** traxit intus duas sagittas et percussit.. W. quodam ~one super pectus (*JustIt* 865) *SelCWW* 64. **b** **1212** reddit j arcum sine corda..et xij sagittas et j buszonem *Fees* 223; **1236** per serjantiam unius arci v sagittarum et j †buzenn' *Ib.* 601; **1271** debuit invenire..unum hominem peditem ad servicium domini regis cum arcu et bosone per xl dies *Eyre Kent* I xxviii (cf. ib. [**1279**]: ad inveniendum..unum garcionem differentem unum arcum sine corda et unum ~onem sine pennis; cf. et. *CalIMisc* I 604); **1274** tenet quemdam redditum..pro j bozono ad *wytecokis*, qui valet ob. *IPM* 5/1 r. 3; **1348** per servicium inveniendi unum hominem peditem cum quodam arcu sine corda cum uno bosuno sine cappa *IPM* 91 r. 21.

2 bolt (for fastening).

1294 cum v ~onis ferri ad fundum galee jungendum *Ac. Galley Newcastle* 163 (cf. ib. 179: in viij petris ferri fabricandis ad ~ones); **1313** fabro operanti circa bosones, tenacula et alias clausturas ad almaria facta pro..libris in thesauraria *KRAc* 469/16 f. 3; **1318** in duobus busonis ferreis ad eadem hostia firmanda *Ib.* f. 19.

2 buzo, decisive member of bench of judges (*cf. EHR* XLVII 177–93, 545–67).

1212 milites de comitatu [Glouc'] qui consueti sunt interesse falsis judiciis et sunt ~ones judiciorum arestentur *CurR* VI 231; debent justitiarii se transferre in aliquem locum secretum et, vocatis ad se quatuor vel sex vel pluribus de majoribus de comitatu qui dicuntur ~ones comitatus et ad quorum nutum dependent vota aliorum, ..jurare debent quod utlagatos..non receptabunt Bracton 115b.

buzsecarla v. butsecarla. buzus v. 1 bussus.

bya [ME *bei*], 'bee' (necklet or bracelet).

1385 dedi..servienti nostro specierie nostre tres byas auri quas A. S...nuper in terra absconditas..invenit..et que ad x m. appreciantur *Cl* 226 m. 28.

byrettum v. birretum. byrritrica, byrrum v. birrus. byrs- v. burs-. bysectus v. 1 bissettus.

bysseus, silken.

1587 xxx unceas..cordule bissee et argentee mixte, Anglice vocatas *thirtie ounces..of silke and silver lace Pat* 1300 m. 12.

byssilineus, made of silk and linen.

vestes..~eas [*gl.*: de serico et lineo] BALSH. *Ut.* 52.

byssinus (bissinus) [*βύσσινος*], made of fine linen or other fabric. **b** made of satin. *Cf. bissinus.*

subucula bissina ALDH. *VirgP* 58; interior linea sive ~a, quod lini esse genus nobilissimum constat BEDE *Tab.* III 6; **10..** bysina, *hwit* WW; I ante N breviatur, ut ~us BACON *Tert.* 262; [angelus] casula ~a cum tunica coccinea.. illam ornans *NLA* (*Keyna*) II 103; **c1393** aurea coccinea bissīnaque tinctaque veste (R. MAIDSTONE) *Pol. Poems* I 284; duas [cappas]..villosas et ~as nigricantes FERR. *Kinloss* 76 (cf. ib. 31: duabus casulis, una †byssinia palmata). **b 1459** pro duabus ulnis..panni ~i dicti *satynfiguree Exch Scot* 500.

byssus (bissus) [*βύσσος*], fine linen or other fabric. **b** silk, satin, etc. *Cf. bissa.*

680 haec [tiara] bisso retorto rotunda erat ALDH. *Ep.* 4 p. 483 (cf. *Id. VirgP* 15; *Exod.* xxix 6); ~um, siricum retortum *GlC* B 113; ~um, *tuin Ib.* 230; legitur de divite [*Luke* xvi 19]..quod induebatur purpura et ~o BART. EXON. *Pen.* xxi; purpura martyrii cum bisso virginitatis NIG. *Laur.* 40b; camisia sindonis vel serici vel ~i [*gl.: cheysil*] materiam sorciatur vel saltem lini NECKAM *Ut.* 99; estque superposita byssus vice syndonis alba GARL. *Myst. Eccl.* 578; **s1306** confluentibus..ccc juvenibus..distribuebantur purpura, ~us, sindones et siclades *Flor. Hist.* III 131; papiliones plurimas purpura et ~o..et serico..confectas *NLA* (*Tundal*) II 310; **1380** v balas sinimi..et v balas bussi (*Cl*) *Foed.* VII 233; **c1393** purpura cum bisso tegit hos partita caballos (R. MAIDSTONE) *Pol. Poems* I 288; **1416** unum *jack* de nigro ~o *Reg. Cant.* II 93; **1500** pallium.. funerale ex nigro ~o *Invent. Ch. Ch.* 122; **1521** j frontell' de rubio ~o *Fabr. York* 278; **c1550** due cappe seu palle ex ~o villosa viridi *Reg. Aberd.* II 190. **b** *sylke*, ~us album..; versus: 'quadruplicis generis sunt serica dicta Latinis: / est album bissus' *CathA*; **1541** unam peciam ~i nigri vocatam *black saten Entries* 3b; **1574** unum galirum bisse, A. *a taffetye hat Pat* 1114 m. 34; unum pileum nocturnum bisse, A. *a velvett nyght cappe Ib.*; **1587** xiiij virgatas..nigri ~i, A. ..*white* (*sic*) *satten Pat* 1300 m. 12.

bythalasma v. bithalassum. bytonum v. bitumen.

byzantatus, bezanty, adorned with bezants.

1295 tunica..de panno indico tarsico besantato de auro *Vis. S. Paul.* 322; **1328** duo panni..besentati de auro *Reg. Exon.* 563; **1345** unus pannus de serico cum auro besentatus *Sacr. Lichf.* 112.

Byzantinus, gold coin of Byzantium, bezant.

Constantinopolis primum Bizantium dicta: formam antiqui vocabuli preferunt imperatorii nummi Bizantini vocati W. MALM. *GR* IV 354.

Byzantus, ~ius, ~a, ~ia, ~ium, gold coin of Byzantium, bezant.

archiepiscopus [Turstinus], sicut cardinales, bisancios aureos, quod presbyterium ab ipsis appellatur, a domino papa suscepit, quod cardinalibus et clericis suis apostolicus die coronationis sue distribuit H. CANTOR 20v; emit ensem ejusdem admiravisi lx ~eis ORD. VIT. IX 17 p. 622; **1159** r.c. de xx s. pro xii bizanciis *Pipe* 42; **1173** debet xl bazanc' *Pipe* 45; **c1175** sub annua unius bisantii vel ij s. sterlingorum pensione *E. Ch. S. Paul.* 124; **a1180** dedit..duos bisandos auri *AncD* A2178; peregrinus..servitii gratia ~eum acceperat W. CANT. *Mir. Thom.* VI 65; reddit bisancium vel ij s. *Boldon Bk.* 34; **1188** J. Barlibred debet xx ~ias *Pipe* 58; **s1188** convenit quod unusquisque homo qui posset solvere Saladino v ~ia et femina que posset solvere duo ~ia et dim. ..eruerentur a manibus Saracenorum DICETO *YH* II 56; **c1190** dedi..unum bisantem de talamo meo *Bk. Seals* no. 405; **a1200** dedit..unum bisantum *AncD* A1903; tantum auri in annulis et monilibus nec non et ~iis quod marcam argenteam equiparare valeret GIR. *Hug.* II 1; **1271** per finem xij besentarum quem..fecit nobiscum *Cl* 341; **1272** pro singula libra Turonensi tres bisantias auri †saracenatas et dim. tenemur..resortire (*AncC* VIII 28) *RL* II 348; **1292** summeteriis Saracenis..cij besaunt', qui valent dx asper' *KRAc* 308/15 m. 2; **c1324** pistor..dabit pro introitu suo unum besantum vel ij s. *MGL* II 105; in ea [sc. Alexandria] florentius valet tantum xxij Venetos grossos et besantium de auro xxvj S. SIM. *Itin.* 38.

2 gold ornament (roundel) resembling bezant.

1245 in circulo inferiori mitre sunt quasi bisantii triphuriati cum lapidibus peridotis *Invent. S. Paul.* 473 (cf. ib. 476: capa..pulverizatur tota bisantiis breudatis); dedit.. j casulam de thars' quasi cum bezancio extensellato WHITTLESEY 168; **1388** alba cum paruris crocei coloris cum ~iis (*Invent. Westm.*) *Arch.* LII 241; **a1413** una casula de sicladone pulverizato cum ~iis de auro AMUND. II *app.* 340.